The New Merriam-Webster Dictionary for LARGE PRINT Users

A Merriam-Webster®

G.K. HALL & CO.
Boston, Massachusetts
1989

Copyright © 1989 by Merriam-Webster Inc.

Philippines Copyright 1989 by Merriam-Webster Inc.

**Published in Large Print by arrangement with
Merriam-Webster Inc.**

Library of Congress Cataloging in Publication Data

The New Merriam-Webster dictionary for large print users
  1. English language—Dictionaries. 2. Large type books.
I. Merriam-Webster Inc.
[PE1625.N538 1989]   423   89-15437
ISBN 0-8161-4754-X (lg. print)

MADE IN THE UNITED STATES OF AMERICA

Contents

Preface

Long aware of the need for a dictionary for large print users, G. K. Hall & Co., pioneers in large print publishing, and Merriam-Webster Inc., foremost publishers of dictionaries for more than 140 years, combined resources in 1977 to make available *The Merriam-Webster Dictionary for Large Print Users*. G. K. Hall and Merriam-Webster have joined together once again to publish a newly revised edition of that important reference work.

The New Merriam-Webster Dictionary for Large Print Users reproduces in its entirety *The New Merriam-Webster Dictionary,* which is the fourth in the line of Merriam-Webster® paperback dictionaries that began in 1947. Firmly based on previous editions, it also draws much new information from *Webster's Ninth New Collegiate Dictionary.* Every entry and every section has been reexamined so that it offers much that is new while preserving the best aspects of preceding editions. The heart of *The New Merriam-Webster Dictionary for Large Print Users* is the A-Z vocabulary, which fills over 1000 pages. The core of the English vocabulary is to be found in the 60,000 entries included in those pages. Every definition is based on examples of actual use found among the more than 13,500,000 citations in the Merriam-Webster files.

As in the previous large print edition, the A-Z vocabulary features 18-point type guide words, 14-point type entries, and 12-point type definitions. The numerous supplementary sections appear in 16-point type. This unique publication has been approved by the Production Review Committee of the National Association of the visually Handicapped; it conforms to the accepted standards for reference books for large print users as established by NAVH.

The A-Z vocabulary is followed by several sections that dictionary users have long found helpful: a list of foreign words and phrases that often occur in English texts but that have not yet become part of the English vocabulary; a list of nations of the world and their populations; lists of American and Canadian places having populations greater than 16,500; a section devoted to widely used signs and symbols; and a collection of tables that give information about the books of the Bible, the metric system, weights and measures, money, and the planets. The A-Z vocabulary is preceded by a series of Explanatory Notes that should be read carefully by every user of the dictionary. An understanding of the information contained in these notes will add markedly to the satisfaction and pleasure that come from looking into the pages of a dictionary.

The New Merriam-Webster Dictionary for Large Print Users has been edited by an experienced staff of professional lexicographers and produced by the leading large print publisher in the United States. It reflects our joint belief that it will serve well those who are in need of a large print record of the English vocabulary of today.

Editorial Staff

Explanatory Notes

Entries

A boldface letter or a combination of such letters set flush with the left-hand margin of each column of type is a main entry. The main entry may consist of letters set solid, of letters joined by a hyphen, or of letters separated by one or more spaces:

> **hot** . . . *adj*
>
> **hot–blood•ed** . . . *adj*
>
> **hot dog** . . . *n*

The material in lightface type that follows each main entry on the same line and on succeeding indented lines presents information about the main entry.

The main entries follow one another in alphabetical order letter by letter: *bill of exchange* follows *billion; Day of Atonement* follows *daylight saving time.* Those containing an Arabic numeral are alphabetized as if the numeral were spelled out: *4-H* comes between *fourfold* and *Four Hundred; 3-D* comes between *three* and *three-dimensional.* Those derived from proper names beginning with abbreviated forms of *Mac-* are alphabetized as if spelled *mac-: McCoy* comes after *Maccabees* and before *mace.*

A pair of guide words is printed at the top of each page. These indicate that the entries falling alphabetically between the words at the top of the outer column of each page are found on that page.

The guide words are usually the alphabetically first and the alphabetically last entries on the page:

adjacent • adopt

Occasionally the last printed entry is not the alphabetically last entry. On page 229, for example, *dot matrix* is the last main entry, but *dotting,* an inflected form at *²dot,* is the alphabetically last entry and is therefore the second guide word. The alphabetically last entry is not used, however, if it follows alphabetically the first guide word on the succeeding page. Thus on page 287 *flatting* is not a guide word because it follows alphabetically the entry *flatboat* which is the first guide word on page 288.

Any boldface word—a main entry with definition, a variant, an inflected form, a defined or undefined run-on—may be used as a guide word.

When one main entry has exactly the same written form as another, the two are distinguished by superscript numerals preceding each word:

> **¹egg** . . . *vb*   **¹rash** . . . *adj*
>
> **²egg** *n*   **²rash** *n*

Words precede word elements made up of the same letters; solid compounds precede hyphenated compounds; hyphenated compounds precede open compounds; and lowercase entries precede those with an initial capital:

self . . . *n*   run·down . . . *n*   fed·er·al . . . *adj*

self- *comb form*   run–down . . . *adj*   Federal *n*

                        run down . . . *vb*

The centered dots within entry words indicate division points at which a hyphen may be put at the end of a line of print or writing. Thus the noun *res·er·va·tion* may be ended on one line and continued on the next in this manner:

                                      res-

ervation

                                      reser-

vation

                                      reserva-

tion

Centered dots are not shown after a single initial letter or before a single terminal letter because typesetters seldom cut off a single letter:

evict . . . *vb*

mighty . . . *adj*

oleo . . . *n*

Nor are they usually shown at the second and succeeding homographs of a word:

[1]**pi·lot** . . . *n*

[2]**pilot** *vb*

[3]**pilot** *adj*

There are acceptable alternative end-of-line divisions just as there are acceptable variant spellings and pronunciations, but no more than one division is shown for any entry in this dictionary.

A double hyphen at the end of a line in this dictionary (as in the definition at **dromedary**) stands for a hyphen that is retained when the word is written as a unit on one line. This kind of hyphen is represented in boldface words in this dictionary with an en dash, which appears whether or not it falls at the end of a line.

When a main entry is followed by the word *or* and another spelling, the two spellings are equal variants. Both are standard, and either one may be used according to personal inclination:

lou·ver *or* **lou·vre**

If two variants joined by *or* are out of alphabetical order, they remain equal variants. The one printed first is, however, slightly more common than the second:

coun·sel·or *or* **coun·sel·lor**

When another spelling is joined to the main entry by the word *also*, the spelling after *also* is a secondary variant and occurs less frequently than the first:

fo·gy *also* **fo·gey**

Secondary variants belong to standard usage and may be used according to personal inclination. If there are two secondary variants, the second is joined to the first by *or*. Once the word *also* is used to signal a secondary variant, all following variants are joined by *or*:

²**wool·ly** *also* **wool·ie** *or* **wooly**

Variants whose spelling puts them alphabetically more than a column away from the main entry are entered at their own alphabetical places and usually not at the main entry:

tsar . . . *var of* CZAR

Variants having a usage label appear only at their own alphabetical places:

la·bour *chiefly Brit var of* LABOR

To show all the stylings that are found for English compounds would require space that can be better used for other information. So this dictionary limits itself to a single styling for a compound:

book·sell·er

yes–man

home run

When a compound is widely used and one styling predominates, that styling is shown. When a compound is uncommon or when the evidence indicates that two or three stylings are approximately equal in frequency, the styling shown is based on the analogy of parallel compounds.

A main entry may be followed by one or more derivatives or by a homograph with a different functional label. These are run-on entries. Each is introduced by a lightface dash and each has a functional label. They are not defined, however, since their meanings are readily understood from the meaning of the root word:

healthy . . . *adj* . . . — **health·i·ly** . . . *adv* — **health·i·ness** . . . *n*

as·sent . . . *vb* . . . — **assent** *n*

A main entry may be followed by one or more phrases containing the entry word or an inflected form of it. These are also run-on entries. Each is introduced by a lightface dash but there is no functional label. They are, however, defined since their meanings are more than the sum of the meanings of their elements:

¹**go** . . . *vb* . . . — **go to bat for** : . . .

¹**hand** . . . *n* . . . — **at hand** : . . .

Defined phrases of this sort are run on at the entry constituting the first major element in the phrase. When there are variants, however, the run-on appears at the entry constituting the first major invariable element in the phrase:

¹**seed** . . . *n* . . . — **go to seed** *or* **run to seed 1:** . . .

Boldface words that appear within parentheses (as **co•ca** at **co•caine** and **jet engine** and **jet propulsion** at **jet–propelled**) are run-in entries.

Attention is called to the definition of *vocabulary entry* on page 814. The term *dictionary entry* includes all vocabulary entries as well as all boldface entries in the section headed "Foreign Words and Phrases."

Pronunciation

The matter between a pair of reversed virgules \   \ following the entry word indicates the pronunciation. The symbols used are explained in the chart printed inside the back cover.

A hyphen is used in the pronunciation to show syllabic division. These hyphens sometimes coincide with the centered dots in the entry word that indicate end-of-line division:

vol•ca•no \väl-ˈkā-nō\

Sometimes they do not:

grind•er \ˈgrīn-dər\

A high-set mark ˈ indicates major (primary) stress or accent; a low-set mark ˌ indicates minor (secondary) stress or accent:

cat•bird \ˈkat-ˌbərd\

The stress mark stands at the beginning of the syllable that receives the stress. A syllable with neither a high-set mark nor a low-set mark is unstressed:

The presence of variant pronunciations indicates that not all educated speakers pronounce words the same way. A second-place variant is not to be regarded as less acceptable than the pronunciation that is given first. It may, in fact, be used by as many educated speakers as the first variant, but the requirements of the printed page are such that one must precede the other:

eco·nom·ic \ˌek-ə-ˈnäm-ik, ˌē-kə-\

flac·cid \ˈflak-səd, ˈflas-əd\

Symbols enclosed by parentheses represent elements that are present in the pronunciation of some speakers but are absent from the pronunciation of other speakers, elements that are present in some but absent from other utterances of the same speaker, or elements whose presence or absence is uncertain:

fo·liage \ˈfō-l(ē-)ij\

duke \ˈd(y)ük\

Thus, the above parentheses indicate that some people say \ˈfō-lē-ij\ and others say \ˈfō-lij\; some \ˈdük\, others \ˈdyük\\\\\·

When a main entry has less than a full pronunciation, the missing part is to be supplied from a pronunciation in a preceding entry or within the same pair of reversed virgules:

out·er·most \-ˌmōst\

pa·la·ver \pə-ˈlav-ər, -ˈläv-\

The pronunciation of the first two syllables of *outermost* is found at the main entry *outer*. The hyphens before and after \ˈläv\ in the pronunciation of *palaver* indicate that both the first and the last parts of the pronunciation are to be taken from the immediately preceding pronunciation.

In general, no pronunciation is indicated for open compounds consisting of two or more English words that have own-place entry:

motor vehicle *n*

Only the first entry in a sequence of numbered homographs is given a pronunciation if their pronunciations are the same:

¹**mea·sure** \ˈmezh-ər, ˈmāzh-\ *n*

²**measure** *vb*

The pronunciation of unpronounced derivatives and compounds run on at a main entry is a combination of the pronunciation at the main entry and the pronunciation of the other element as given at its alphabetical place in the vocabulary:

— nar·row·ness *n*

— at last

Thus, the pronunciation of *narrowness* is the sum of the pronunciations given at *narrow* and *-ness;* that of *at last,* the sum of the pronunciations of the two elements that make up the phrase.

Functional Labels

An italic label indicating a part of speech or some other functional classification follows the pronunciation or, if no pronunciation is given, the main entry. The eight traditional parts of speech are indicated as follows:

fa·ce·tious . . . *adj*   **log·ger·head** . . . *n*

al·to·geth·er . . . *adv*   **in·to** . . . *prep*

if . . . *conj*   **we** . . . *pron*

amen . . . *interj*   **stul·ti·fy** . . . *vb*

Other italicized labels used to indicate functional classifications that are not traditional parts of speech include:

blvd *abbr*   **-hood** . . . *n suffix*

self- *comb form*   **-fy** . . . *vb suffix*

super- . . . *prefix*   **Na** *symbol*

-ous . . . *adj suffix*   **ought** . . . *verbal auxiliary*

-al·ly . . . *adv suffix*

Functional labels are sometimes combined:

can·ta·bi·le . . . *adv or adj*

Inflected Forms

Nouns

The plurals of nouns are shown in this dictionary when suffixation brings about a change of final *-y* to *-i-,* when the noun ends in a consonant plus *-o* or in *-ey,* when the noun ends in *-oo,* when the noun has an irregular plural or a zero plural or a foreign plural, when the noun is a compound that pluralizes any element but the last, when the noun has variant plurals, and when it is believed that the dictionary user might have reasonable doubts about the spelling of the plural or when the plural is spelled in a way contrary to what is expected:

dairy . . . *n, pl* **dair•ies**	**deer** . . . *n, pl* **deer**
po•ta•to . . . *n, pl* **-toes**	**al•ga** . . . *n, pl* **al•gae**
lack•ey . . . *n, pl* **lackeys**	**broth•er–in–law** . . . *n, pl* **brothers–in–law**
zoo . . . *n, pl* **zoos**	[1]**fish** . . . *n, pl* **fish** *or* **fish•es**
tooth . . . *n, pl* **teeth**	[2]**pi** . . . *n, pl* **pis**

Cutback inflected forms are used when the noun has three or more syllables:

atroc•i•ty . . . n, pl -ties

The plurals of nouns are usually not shown when the base word is unchanged by suffixation, when the noun is a compound whose second element is readily recognizable as a regular free form entered at its own place, or when the noun is unlikely to occur in the plural:

car•rot . . . n

horse•fly . . . n

po•lyg•a•my . . . n

Nouns that are plural in form and that regularly occur in plural construction are labeled *n pl*:

bifocals . . . n pl

Nouns that are plural in form but that are not always construed as plurals are appropriately labeled:

taps . . . n sing or pl

Verbs

The principal parts of verbs are shown in this dictionary when suffixation brings about a doubling of a final consonant or an elision of a final *-e* or a change of final *-y* to *-i-*, when final *-c* changes to *-ck-* in suffixation, when the verb ends in *-ey*, when the inflection is irregular, when there are variant inflected forms, and when it is believed that the dictionary user might have reasonable doubts about the spelling of an inflected form or when the inflected form is spelled in a way contrary to what is expected:

  beg . . . *vb* begged; beg•ging

  equate . . . *vb* equat•ed; equat•ing

  ¹fry . . . *vb* fried; fry•ing

  ²panic *vb* pan•icked . . .; pan•ick•ing

  obey . . . *vb* obeyed; obey•ing

  ¹break . . . *vb* broke . . .; bro•ken . . .; break•ing

  ¹trav•el . . . *vb* -eled *or* -elled; -el•ing *or* -el•ling

  ²visa *vb* vi•saed . . .; vi•sa•ing

  ²chagrin *vb* cha•grined . . .; cha•grin•ing

The principal parts of a regularly inflected verb are shown when it is desirable to indicate the pronunciation of one of the inflected forms:

  ²spell *vb* spelled \\'speld\\; spell•ing

  ²season *vb* sea•soned; sea•son•ing \\'sēz-(ə-)niŋ\\

Cutback inflected forms are usually used when the verb has three or more syllables, when it is a two-syllable word that ends in *-l* and has variant spellings, and when it is a compound whose second element is readily recognized as an irregular verb:

  mul•ti•ply . . . *vb* -plied; -ply•ing

  cav•il . . . *vb* -iled *or* -illed; -il•ing *or* -il•ling

  for•go *or* fore•go . . . *vb* -went . . .; -gone . . .; -go•ing

The principal parts of verbs are usually not shown when the base word is unchanged by suffixation or when the verb is a compound whose second element is readily recognizable as a regular free form entered at its own place:

  ²shield *vb*

  ¹out•reach . . . *vb*

Adjectives & Adverbs

The comparative and superlative forms of adjectives and adverbs are shown in this dictionary when suffixation brings about a doubling of a final consonant or an elision of a final *-e* or a change of final *-y* to *-i-*, when the word ends in *-ey*, when the inflection is irregular, and when there are variant inflected forms:

  ¹fat . . . *adj* fat•ter; fat•test

  ¹sure . . . *adj* sur•er; sur•est

¹**dry** . . . *adj* **dri•er** . . .; **dri•est**

hors•ey *or* **horsy** . . . *adj* **hors•i•er**; **-est**

bad . . . *adj* **worse** . . .; **worst**

sly . . . *adj* **sli•er** *also* **sly•er** . . .; **sli•est** *also* **sly•est**

The superlative forms of adjectives and adverbs of two or more syllables are usually cut back:

scanty . . . *adj* **scant•i•er**; **-est**

¹**ear•ly** . . . *adv* **ear•li•er**; **-est**

The comparative and superlative forms of regularly inflected adjectives and adverbs are shown when it is desirable to indicate the pronunciation of the inflected forms:

strong \\'stróŋ\ *adj* **stron•ger** \\'stróŋ-gər\; **stron•gest** \\'stróŋ-gəst\

The inclusion of inflected forms in *-er* and *-est* at adjective and adverb entries means nothing more about the use of *more* and *most* with these adjectives and adverbs than that their comparative and superlative degrees may be expressed in either way: *kindlier* or *more kindly; kindliest* or *most kindly.*

At a few adjective entries only the superlative form is shown:

²**mere** *adj* **mer•est**

The absence of the comparative form indicates that there is no evidence of its use.

The comparative and superlative forms of adjectives and adverbs are usually not shown when the base word is unchanged by suffixation or when the word is a compound whose second element is readily recognizable as a regular free form entered at its own place:

²**quiet** *adj*

un•hap•py . . . *adj*

Inflected forms are not shown at undefined run-ons.

Capitalization

Most entries in this dictionary begin with a lowercase letter. A few of these have an italicized label *often cap*, which indicates that the word is as likely to be capitalized as not and that it is as acceptable with an uppercase initial as it is with one in lowercase. Some entries begin with an uppercase letter, which indicates that the word is usually capitalized. The absence of an initial capital or of an *often cap* label indicates that the word is not ordinarily capitalized:

> **spice** . . . *n*
>
> **ba·bel** . . . *n, often cap*
>
> **Quak·er** . . . *n*

The capitalization of entries that are open or hyphenated compounds is similarly indicated by the form of the entry or by an italicized label:

> **living room** *n*
>
> **in·dia ink** . . . *n, often cap 1st I*
>
> **all–Amer·i·can** . . . *adj*
>
> **German shepherd** *n*
>
> **lazy Su·san** . . . *n*
>
> **Jack Frost** *n*

A word that is capitalized in some senses and lowercase in others shows variations from the form of the main entry by the use of italicized labels at the appropriate senses:

> **Apoc·ry·pha** . . . *n* **1** *not cap*
>
> ¹**Pres·by·te·ri·an** . . . *adj* **1** *often not cap*
>
> **cath·o·lic** . . . *adj* . . . **2** *cap*
>
> **east·ern** . . . *adj* **1** *often cap* . . . **2** *cap*

Etymology

This dictionary gives the etymologies for a number of the vocabulary entries. These etymologies are in boldface square brackets preceding the definition. Meanings given in roman type within these brackets are not definitions of the entry, but are meanings of the Middle English, Old English, or non-English words within the brackets.

The etymology gives the language from which words borrowed into English have come. It also gives the form of the word in that language or a representation of the word in our alphabet if the form in that language differs from that in English:

> **ae·gis** . . . [L, fr. Gk *aigis* goatskin]
>
> ¹**sav·age** . . . [ME *sauvage*, fr. MF, fr. ML *salvaticus*, fr. L *silvaticus* of the woods, wild . . .]

An etymology beginning with the name of a language (including ME or OE) and not giving the foreign (or Middle English or Old English) form indicates that this form is the same as the form of the entry word:

ibi•dem . . . [L]

na•dir . . . [ME, fr. MF . . .]

An etymology beginning with the name of a language (including ME or OE) and not giving the foreign (or Middle English or Old English) meaning indicates that this meaning is the same as the meaning expressed in the first definition in the entry:

tur•quoise . . . [ME *turkeis, turcas,* fr. MF *turquoyse* . . .]

Small superscript figures following words or syllables in an etymology refer to the tone of the word or syllable they follow. They are used only with forms cited for languages in which tonal variations distinguish words of different meaning that would otherwise sound alike.

kow•tow . . . [Chin $k'o^1$ $t'ou^2$, fr. $k'o^1$ to bump + $t'ou^2$ head]

Usage

Three types of status labels are used in this dictionary—temporal, regional, and stylistic—to signal that a word or a sense of a word is not part of the standard vocabulary of English.

The temporal label *obs* for "obsolete" means that there is no evidence of use since 1755:

^{3}**post** *n* **1** *obs*

The label *obs* is a comment on the word being defined. When a thing, as distinguished from the word used to designate it, is obsolete, appropriate orientation is usually given in the definition:

far•thin•gale . . . *n* . . . : a support (as of hoops) worn esp. in the 16th century to swell out a skirt

The temporal label *archaic* means that a word or sense once in common use is found today only sporadically or in special contexts:

com•mon•weal . . . *n* . . . **1** *archaic*

^{1}**thou** . . . *pron, archaic*

A word or sense limited in use to a specific region of the U.S. has an appropriate label. The adverb *chiefly* precedes a label when the word has some currency outside the specified region, and a double label is used to indicate considerable currency in each of two specific regions:

> ²**wash** *n* . . . **5** *West*
>
> **do·gie** . . . *n, chiefly West*
>
> **goo·ber** . . . *n, South & Midland*

Words current in all regions of the U.S. have no label.

A word or sense limited in use to one of the other countries of the English-speaking world has an appropriate regional label:

> **chem·ist** . . . *n* . . . **2** *Brit*
>
> **loch** . . . *n, Scot*
>
> ²**wireless** *n* . . . **2** *chiefly Brit*

The label *dial* for "dialect" indicates that the pattern of use of a word or sense is too complex for summary labeling: it usually includes several regional varieties of American English or of American and British English:

> ¹**boot** . . . *n, chiefly dial*
>
> **cal·a·boose** . . . *n* . . . *dial*

The stylistic label *slang* is used with words or senses that are especially appropriate in contexts of extreme informality:

> ¹**rap** . . . *n* . . . **3** *slang*
>
> **tick·er** . . . *n* . . . **3** *slang*

There is no satisfactory objective test for slang, especially with reference to a word out of context. No word, in fact, is invariably slang, and many standard words can be given slang applications.

Definitions are sometimes followed by verbal illustrations that show a typical use of the word in context. These illustrations are enclosed in angle brackets, and the word being illustrated is usually replaced by a lightface swung dash. The swung dash stands for the boldface entry word, and it may be followed by an italicized suffix:

> ¹**let·ter** . . . *n* . . . **4** . . . ⟨the ~ of the law⟩
>
> **deep–seated** . . . *adj* . . . **2** . . . ⟨~ convictions⟩

> **depth** . . . *n* . . . 2 . . . ⟨the ~*s* of the woods⟩
>
> ¹**fill** . . . *vb* . . . 6 . . . ⟨laughter ~*ed* the room⟩

The swung dash is not used when the form of the boldface entry word is changed in suffixation, and it is not used for open compounds:

> **en·gage** . . . *vb* . . . 3 . . . ⟨*engaged* his friend's attention⟩
>
> **drum up** *vb* 1 . . . ⟨*drum up* business⟩

Definitions are sometimes followed by usage notes that give supplementary information about such matters as idiom, syntax, and semantic relationship. A usage note is introduced by a lightface dash:

> **fro** . . . *adv* . . . — used in the phrase *to and fro*
>
> ²**gang** *vb* 1 . . . — usu. used with *up*
>
> ¹**jaw** . . . *n* . . . 2 . . . — usu. used in pl.
>
> ¹**ada·gio** . . . *adv or adj* . . . — used as a direction in music
>
> **blast off** . . . *vb* . . . — used esp. of rocket-propelled devices

Sometimes a usage note is used in place of a definition. Some function words (as conjunctions and prepositions) have chiefly grammatical meaning and little or no lexical meaning; most interjections express feelings but are otherwise untranslatable into lexical meaning; and some other words (as honorific titles) are more amenable to comment than to definition:

> **or** . . . *conj* — used as a function word to indicate an alternative
>
> ¹**in** . . . *prep* 1 — used to indicate physical surroundings
>
> **hal·le·lu·jah** . . . *interj* . . . — used to express praise, joy, or thanks
>
> **ex·cel·len·cy** . . . *n* . . . 2 — used as a title of honor

Sense Division

A boldface colon is used in this dictionary to introduce a definition:

> **found·ry** . . . *n* . . . : a building or works where metal is cast

It is also used to separate two or more definitions of a single sense:

> ²**yellow** *n* 1 : a color between green and orange in the spectrum : the color of ripe lemons or sunflowers

Boldface Arabic numerals separate the senses of a word that has more than one sense:

> **idol** . . . *n* **1** : an image worshiped as a god **2** : a false god **3** : an object of passionate devotion

A particular semantic relationship between senses is sometimes suggested by the use of one of the two italic sense dividers *esp* or *also*.

The sense divider *esp* (for *especially*) is used to introduce the most common meaning included in the more general preceding definition:

> **no•to•ri•ous** . . . *adj* : generally known and talked of; *esp* : widely and unfavorably known

The sense divider *also* is used to introduce a meaning related to the preceding sense by an easily understood extension of that sense:

> ¹**flour** . . . *n* : finely ground and sifted meal of a grain (as wheat); *also* : a fine soft powder

The order of senses is historical: the sense known to have been first used in English is entered first. This is not to be taken to mean, however, that each sense of a multisense word developed from the immediately preceding sense. It is altogether possible that sense 1 of a word has given rise to sense 2 and sense 2 to sense 3, but frequently sense 2 and sense 3 may have developed independently of one another from sense 1.

When an italicized label follows a boldface numeral, the label applies only to that specific numbered sense. It does not apply to any other boldface numbered senses:

> **craft** . . . *n* . . . **3** *pl usu* **craft**
>
> ¹**fa•ther** . . . *n* . . . **2** *cap* . . . **5** *often cap*
>
> ²**preview** *n* . . . **2** *also* **pre•vue** \-ˌvyü\
>
> **pub•li•can** . . . *n* . . . **2** *chiefly Brit*

At *craft* the *pl* label applies to sense **3** but to none of the other numbered senses. At *father* the *cap* label applies only to sense **2** and the *often cap* label only to sense **5**. At *preview* the variant spelling and pronunciation apply only to sense **2**, as does the *chiefly Brit* label at *publican*.

Cross-Reference

Four different kinds of cross-references are used in this dictionary: directional, synonymous, cognate, and inflectional. In each instance the cross-reference is readily recognized by the lightface small capitals in which it is printed.

A cross-reference following a lightface dash and beginning with *see* is a directional cross-reference. It directs the dictionary user to look elsewhere for further information:

¹yen . . . n . . . — see MONEY table

A cross-reference following a boldface colon is a synonymous cross-reference. It may stand alone as the only definition for an entry or for a sense of an entry; it may follow an analytical definition; it may be one of two or more synonymous cross-references separated by commas:

maize . . . n : INDIAN CORN

chap•let . . . n . . . 2 : a string of beads : NECKLACE

²dress n . . . 2 : FROCK, GOWN

cheek . . . n . . . 2 : IMPUDENCE, BOLDNESS, AUDACITY

A synonymous cross-reference indicates that a definition at the entry cross-referred to can be substituted as a definition for the entry or the sense in which the cross-reference appears.

A cross-reference following an italic *var of* ("variant of") is a cognate cross-reference:

Gipsy var of GYPSY

Occasionally a cognate cross-reference has a limiting label preceding *var of* as an indication that the variant is not standard English:

har•bour chiefly Brit var of HARBOR

A cross-reference following an italic label that identifies an entry as an inflected form (as of a noun or verb) is an inflectional cross-reference:

feet pl of FOOT

worn past part of WEAR

Inflectional cross-references appear only when the inflected form falls at least a column away from the entry cross-referred to.

Synonyms

A boldface **syn** near the end of an entry introduces words that are synonymous with the word being defined:

²**fear** . . . *n* . . . **syn** dread, fright, alarm, panic, terror, trepidation

Synonyms are not definitions although they may often be substituted for each other in context.

Combining Forms, Prefixes, & Suffixes

An entry that begins or ends with a hyphen is a word element that forms part of an English compound:

> **maxi-** *comb form* **1** . . . ⟨*maxi*-kilt⟩
>
> **ex-** . . . *prefix* . . . ⟨*ex*-president⟩
>
> **-ship** . . . *n suffix* **1** . . . ⟨friend*ship*⟩

Combining forms, prefixes, and suffixes are entered in this dictionary for two reasons: to make understandable the meaning of many undefined run-ons and to make recognizable the meaningful elements of words that are not entered in the dictionary.

Lists of Undefined Words

Lists of undefined words occur after the entries *anti-*, *in-*, *non-*, *over-*, *re-*, *self-*, *semi-*, *sub-*, *super-*, and *un-*. These words are undefined because they are self-explanatory: their meanings are simply the sum of a meaning of the prefix or combining form and a meaning of the second element.

Abbreviations & Symbols

Abbreviations and symbols for chemical elements are included as main entries in the vocabulary:

> **govt** *abbr* government
>
> **Fe** *symbol* . . . iron

Abbreviations have been normalized to one form. In practice, however, there is considerable variation in the use of periods and in capitalization (as *vhf, v.h.f., VHF,* and *V.H.F.*), and stylings other than those given in this dictionary are often acceptable.

Symbols that are not capable of being alphabetized are included in a separate section of the back matter headed "Signs and Symbols."

Abbreviations Used in This Work

ab	about	*esp*	especially
abbr	abbreviation	*F*	Fahrenheit, French
abl	ablative	*fem*	feminine
acc	accusative	*Flem*	Flemish
A.D.	anno Domini	*fr*	from
adj	adjective	*G*	German
adv	adverb	*Gael*	Gaelic
AF	Anglo-French	*Gk*	Greek
alter	alteration	*Gmc*	Germanic
Am	American	*Heb*	Hebrew
AmerF	American French	*Hung*	Hungarian
AmerInd	American Indian	*Icel*	Icelandic
AmerSp	American Spanish	*imit*	imitative
Ar	Arabic	*imper*	imperative
Arma	Aramaic	*interj*	interjection
B.C.	before Christ	*Ir*	Irish
Brit	British	*IrGael*	Irish Gaelic
C	centigrade	*irreg*	irregular
Calif	California	*It, Ital*	Italian
CanF	Canadian French	*Jp*	Japanese
cap	capital, capitalized	*K*	Kelvin
Celt	Celtic	*L*	Latin
cent	century	*LaF*	Louisiana French
Chin	Chinese	*LG*	Low German
comb	combining	*LGk*	Late Greek
compar	comparative	*LHeb*	Late Hebrew
conj	conjunction	*lit*	literally
Dan	Danish	*LL*	Late Latin
dat	dative	*masc*	masculine
deriv	derivative	*ME*	Middle English
dial	dialect	*MexSp*	Mexican Spanish
dim	diminutive	*MF*	Middle French
E	English	*MGk*	Middle Greek
Egypt	Egyptian	*ML*	Medieval Latin
Eng	English	*modif*	modification
Esk	Eskimo	*MS*	manuscript

n	noun	*Russ*	Russian
neut	neuter	*Sc*	Scotch, Scots
NGk	New Greek	*Scand*	Scandinavian
NHeb	New Hebrew	*ScGael*	Scottish Gaelic
NL	New Latin	*Scot*	Scottish
No	North	*Serb*	Serbian
Norw	Norwegian	*sing*	singular
n pl	noun plural	*Skt*	Sanskrit
obs	obsolete	*Slav*	Slavic
OE	Old English	*So*	South
OF	Old French	*Sp*	Spanish
OIt	Old Italian	*St*	Saint
ON	Old Norse	*superl*	superlative
OPer	Old Persian	*Sw*	Swedish
OProv	Old Provençal	*syn*	synonym, synonymy
orig	originally		
OW	Old Welsh	*trans*	translation
part	participle	*Turk*	Turkish
Per	Persian	*US*	United States
perh	perhaps	*USSR*	Union of Soviet Socialist Republics
Pg	Portuguese		
pl	plural		
Pol	Polish	*usu*	usually
pp	past participle	*var*	variant
prep	preposition	*vb*	verb
pres	present	*vi*	verb intransitive
prob	probably	*VL*	Vulgar Latin
pron	pronoun, pronunciation	*vt*	verb transitive
prp	present participle	*W*	Welsh

PRONUNCIATION SYMBOLS

ə.....**a**but, c**o**llect, s**u**ppose

ˈə,ˌə h**u**mdr**u**m

ᵊ.....(in ᵊl, ᵊn) batt**le**, cot-
t**on**; (in lᵊ, mᵊ, rᵊ)
French tab**le**, pris**me**,
tit**re**

ər....op**er**ation, f**ur**ther

a.....m**a**p, p**a**tch

ā.....d**ay**, f**a**te

ä.....b**o**ther, c**o**t, f**a**ther

ȧ.....a sound between \a\
and \ä\, as in an
Eastern New England
pronunciation of **au**nt,
ask

au̇....n**ow**, **ou**t

b.....**b**a**b**y, ri**b**

ch....**ch**in, ca**tch**

d.....**d**i**d**, a**dd**er

e.....s**e**t, r**e**d

ē.....b**ea**t, **ea**sy

f.....**f**i**f**ty, cu**ff**

g.....**g**o, bi**g**

h.....**h**at, a**h**ead

hw...**wh**ale

i.....t**i**p, ban**i**sh

ī.....s**i**te, b**uy**

j.....**j**ob, e**dge**

k.....**k**in, **c**ook

k̲.....German Ba**ch**, Scots
lo**ch**

l.....**l**i**l**y, coo**l**

m....**m**ur**m**ur, di**m**

n.....**n**i**n**e, ow**n**

ⁿ.....indicates that a preceding vowel is pro-
nounced through both
nose and mouth, as in
French bon \bōⁿ\

ŋ.....si**ng**, si**ng**er, fi**ng**er,
i**n**k

ō.....b**o**ne, holl**ow**

ȯ.....s**aw**

œ....French b**œu**f, German
H**ö**lle

œ̄....French f**eu**, German
H**öh**le

ȯi....t**oy**

p.....**p**e**pp**er, li**p**

r.....**r**a**r**ity

s.....**s**ource, le**ss**

sh....**sh**y, mi**ss**ion

t.....**t**ie, a**tt**ack

th....**th**in, e**th**er

t̲h̲....**th**en, ei**th**er

ü.....b**oo**t, few \ˈfyü\

u̇.....p**u**t, p**u**re \ˈpyu̇r\

ᵫ....German f**ü**llen

ᵫ̄....French r**ue**, German
f**üh**len

v.....**v**i**v**id, gi**v**e

w....**w**e, a**w**ay

y.....**y**ard, cue \ˈky**ü**\

ʸ.....indicates that a preceding \l\, \n\, or \w\
is modified by having
the tongue approximate
the position for \y\,
as in French di**gne**
\dēnʸ\

z.....**z**one, rai**s**e

zh....vi**s**ion, plea**s**ure

\.... slant line used in pairs
to mark the beginning
and end of a transcrip-
tion: \ˈpen\

ˈ.....mark at the beginning
of a syllable that has primary (strongest) stress:
\ˈshəf-əl-ˌbōrd\

ˌ.....mark at the beginning
of a syllable that has
secondary (next-stron-
gest) stress: \ˈshəf-əl-
ˌbōrd\

-.....mark of syllable division in pronunciations
(the mark of end-of-line
division in boldface en-
tries is a centered dot •)

( )....indicate that what is
symbolized between
sometimes occurs and
sometimes does not oc-
cur in the pronuncia-
tion of the word: **fac-
tory** \ˈfak-t(ə-)rē\ =
\ˈfak-tə-rē, ˈfak-trē\

A

¹**a** \'ā\ *n, pl* **a's** *or* **as** \'āz\ *often cap* **1** : the 1st letter of the English alphabet **2** : a grade rating a student's work as superior

²**a** \ə, (')ā\ *indefinite article* : ONE, SOME — used to indicate an unspecified or unidentified individual ⟨there's ∼ man outside⟩

³**a** *abbr, often cap* **1** absent **2** acre **3** alto **4** answer **5** area

AA *abbr* **1** Alcoholics Anonymous **2** antiaircraft **3** associate in arts

AAA *abbr* American Automobile Association

A and M *abbr* agricultural and mechanical

A and R *abbr* artists and repertory

aard·vark \'ärd-ˌvärk\ *n* [obs. Afrikaans, fr. Afrikaans *aard* earth + *vark* pig] : a large burrowing African mammal that feeds on ants and termites with its sticky tongue

ab *abbr* about

AB *abbr* **1** able-bodied seaman **2** airman basic **3** [NL *artium baccalaureus*] bachelor of arts

ABA *abbr* American Bar Association

aback \ə-'bak\ *adv* : by surprise ⟨taken ∼⟩

aba·cus \'ab-ə-kəs\ *n, pl* **aba·ci** \'ab-ə-ˌsī, -ˌkē\ *or* **aba·cus·es** : an instrument for making calculations by sliding counters along rods or grooves

¹**abaft** \ə-'baft\ *prep* : to the rear of

²**abaft** *adv* : toward or at the stern : AFT

ab·a·lo·ne \ˌab-ə-'lō-nē\ *n* : a large edible sea mollusk with a flattened slightly spiral shell with holes along the edge

¹**aban·don** \ə-'ban-dən\ *vb* [ME *abandounen*, fr. MF *abandoner*, fr. *abandon*, n., surrender, fr. *a bandon* in one's power] : to give up completely : FORSAKE, DESERT — **aban·don·ment** *n*

²**abandon** *n* : a thorough yielding to natural impulses; *esp* : ENTHUSIASM, EXUBERANCE

aban·doned \ə-'ban-dənd\ *adj* : morally unrestrained **syn** profligate, dissolute, reprobate

abase \ə-'bās\ *vb* **abased; abas·ing** : HUMBLE, DEGRADE — **abase·ment** *n*

abash \ə-'bash\ *vb* : to destroy the composure of : EMBARRASS — **abashment** *n*

abate \ə-'bāt\ *vb* **abat·ed; abat·ing 1** : to put an end to ⟨∼ a nuisance⟩ **2** : to decrease in amount, number, or degree

abate·ment \ə-'bāt-mənt\ *n* **1** : DECREASE **2** : an amount abated; *esp* : a deduction from the full amount of a tax

ab·at·toir \'ab-ə-ˌtwär\ *n* [F] : SLAUGHTERHOUSE

ab·ba·cy \'ab-ə-sē\ *n, pl* **-cies** : the office or term of office of an abbot or abbess

ab·bé \a-'bā, 'ab-ˌā\ *n* : a member of the French secular clergy — used as a title

ab·bess \'ab-əs\ *n* : the superior of a convent for nuns

ab·bey \'ab-ē\ *n, pl* **abbeys 1** : MONASTERY, CONVENT **2** : an abbey church

ab·bot \'ab-ət\ *n* [ME *abbod*, fr. OE, fr. LL *abbat-, abbas*, fr. LGk *abbas*, fr. Aramaic *abbā* father] : the superior of a monastery for men

abbr *abbr* abbreviation

ab·bre·vi·ate \ə-'brē-vē-ˌāt\ *vb* **-at·ed; -at·ing** : SHORTEN, CURTAIL; *esp* : to reduce to an abbreviation

ab·bre·vi·a·tion \ə-ˌbrē-vē-'ā-shən\ *n* **1** : the act or result of abbreviating **2** : a shortened form of a word or phrase used for brevity esp. in writing

¹**ABC** \ˌā-ˌbē-'sē\ *n, pl* **ABC's** *or* **ABCs** \-'sēz\ **1** : ALPHABET — usu. used in pl. **2** : RUDIMENTS

²**ABC** *abbr* American Broadcasting Company

Ab·di·as \ab-'dī-əs\ *n* — see BIBLE table

ab·di·cate \'ab-di-ˌkāt\ *vb* **-cat·ed; -cat·ing** : to give up (as a throne) formally — **ab·di·ca·tion** \ˌab-di-'kā-shən\ *n*

ab·do·men \'ab-də-mən, ab-'dō-mən\ *n* **1** : the cavity in or area of the body between the chest and the pelvis **2** : the part of the body posterior to the thorax in an arthropod — **ab·dom·i·nal**

\ab-'däm-ən-ᵊl\ *adj* — **ab·dom·i·nal·ly** \-ē\ *adv*

ab·duct \ab-'dəkt\ *vb* : to take away (a person) by force : KIDNAP — **ab·duc·tion** \-'dək-shən\ *n* — **ab·duc·tor** \-tər\ *n*

abeam \ə-'bēm\ *adv or adj* : on a line at right angles to a ship's keel

abed \ə-'bed\ *adv or adj* : in bed

ab·er·ra·tion \ˌab-ə-'rā-shən\ *n* **1** : deviation esp. from a moral standard or normal state **2** : unsoundness of mind : DERANGEMENT **3** : failure of a mirror or lens to produce exact point-to-point correspondence between an object and its image — **ab·er·rant** \a-'ber-ənt\ *adj*

abet \ə-'bet\ *vb* **abet·ted; abet·ting** [ME *abetten,* fr. MF *abeter,* fr. OF *beter* to bait] **1** : INCITE, ENCOURAGE **2** : to assist or support in the achievement of a purpose — **abet·tor** *or* **abet·ter** \-ər\ *n*

abey·ance \ə-'bā-əns\ *n* : a condition of suspended activity

ab·hor \əb-'hȯr, ab-\ *vb* **ab·horred; ab·hor·ring** [ME *abhorren,* fr. L *abhorrēre,* fr. *ab-* + *horrēre* to shudder] : LOATHE, DETEST — **ab·hor·rence** \-əns\ *n*

ab·hor·rent \-ənt\ *adj* : LOATHSOME, DETESTABLE

abide \ə-'bīd\ *vb* **abode** \-'bōd\ *or* **abid·ed; abid·ing** **1** : BEAR, ENDURE **2** : DWELL, REMAIN, LAST

abil·i·ty \ə-'bil-ət-ē\ *n, pl* **-ties** : the quality of being able : POWER, SKILL

ab·ject \'ab-ˌjekt, ab-'jekt\ *adj* : low in spirit or hope : CRINGING — **ab·jec·tion** \ab-'jek-shən\ *n* — **ab·ject·ly** \'ab-jekt-lē, ab-'jekt-\ *adv* — **ab·ject·ness** *n*

ab·jure \ab-'jur\ *vb* **ab·jured; ab·jur·ing** **1** : to renounce solemnly : RECANT **2** : to abstain from — **ab·ju·ra·tion** \ˌab-jə-'rā-shən\ *n*

abl *abbr* ablative

ab·late \a-'blāt\ *vb* **ab·lat·ed; ab·lat·ing** : to remove or become removed by cutting, eating or wearing away, evaporating, or vaporizing

ab·la·tion \a-'blā-shən\ *n* **1** : surgical cutting and removal **2** : removal of a part (as the outside of a nose cone) by melting or vaporization

ab·la·tive \'ab-lət-iv\ *adj* : of, relating to, or constituting a grammatical case (as in Latin) expressing typically the relation of separation and source — **ablative** *n*

ablaze \ə-'blāz\ *adj or adv* : being on fire : BLAZING

able \'ā-bəl\ *adj* **abler** \-b(ə-)lər\; **ablest** \-b(ə-)ləst\ **1** : having sufficient power, skill, or resources to accomplish an object **2** : marked by skill or efficiency — **ably** \-blē\ *adv*

-able *also* **-ible** \ə-bəl\ *adj suffix* **1** : capable of, fit for, or worthy of (being so acted upon or toward) 〈break*able*〉 〈collect*ible*〉 **2** : tending, given, or liable to 〈knowledge*able*〉 〈perish*able*〉

able–bod·ied \ˌā-bəl-'bäd-ēd\ *adj* : having a sound strong body

abloom \ə-'blüm\ *adj* : BLOOMING

ab·lu·tion \ə-'blü-shən, a-'blü-\ *n* : the washing of one's body or part of it

ABM \ˌā-(ˌ)bē-'em\ *n, pl* **ABM's** *or* **ABMs** : ANTIBALLISTIC MISSILE

Ab·na·ki \ab-'näk-ē\ *n, pl* **Abnaki** *or* **Abnakis** : a member of an American Indian people of Maine and southern Quebec

ab·ne·gate \'ab-ni-ˌgāt\ *vb* **-gat·ed; -gat·ing** **1** : SURRENDER, RELINQUISH **2** : DENY, RENOUNCE — **ab·ne·ga·tion** \ˌab-ni-'gā-shən\ *n*

ab·nor·mal \ab-'nȯr-məl\ *adj* : deviating from the normal or average — **ab·nor·mal·i·ty** \ˌab-nər-'mal-ət-ē, -(ˌ)nȯr-\ *n* — **ab·nor·mal·ly** \ab-'nȯr-mə-lē\ *adv*

¹**aboard** \ə-'bōrd\ *adv* **1** : ALONGSIDE **2** : on, onto, or within a car, ship, or aircraft **3** : in or into a group or association 〈welcome new workers ∼〉

²**aboard** *prep* : ON, ONTO, WITHIN

abode \ə-'bōd\ *n* **1** : STAY, SOJOURN **2** : HOME, RESIDENCE

abol·ish \ə-'bäl-ish\ *vb* : to do away with : ANNUL — **ab·o·li·tion** \ˌab-ə-'lish-ən\ *n*

ab·o·li·tion·ism \ˌab-ə-'lish-ə-ˌniz-əm\ *n* : advocacy of the abolition of slavery — **ab·o·li·tion·ist** \-'lish-(ə-)nəst\ *n or adj*

A–bomb \'ā-ˌbäm\ *n* : ATOM BOMB — **A–bomb** *vb*

abom·i·na·ble \ə-'bäm-(ə-)nə-bəl\ *adj* : ODIOUS, LOATHSOME, DETESTABLE

abominable snow·man \-'snō-mən, -ˌman\ *n, often cap A&S* : a mysterious animal reported as existing in the high Himalayas and usu. thought to be a bear

abom•i•nate \ə-'bäm-ə-ˌnāt\ *vb* **-nat•ed; -nat•ing** [L *abominari*, lit., to deprecate as an ill omen, fr. *ab-* away + *omen* omen] : LOATHE, DETEST

abom•i•na•tion \ə-ˌbäm-ə-'nā-shən\ *n* **1** : something abominable **2** : DISGUST, LOATHING

ab•orig•i•nal \ˌab-ə-'rij-(ə-)nəl\ *adj* : ORIGINAL, INDIGENOUS, PRIMITIVE

ab•orig•i•ne \ˌab-ə-'rij-ə-nē\ *n* : a member of the original race of inhabitants of a region : NATIVE

aborn•ing \ə-'bȯr-niŋ\ *adv* : while being born or produced

¹abort \ə-'bȯrt\ *vb* **1** : to cause or undergo abortion **2** : to terminate prematurely ⟨∼ a spaceflight⟩ — **abor•tive** \-'bȯrt-iv\ *adj*

²abort *n* : the premature termination of a mission of or a procedure relating to an aircraft or spacecraft

abor•tion \ə-'bȯr-shən\ *n* : a premature birth occurring before the fetus can survive; *also* : an induced expulsion of a fetus after, accompanied by, or followed by its death

abor•tion•ist \-sh(ə-)nəst\ *n* : one who induces abortions

abound \ə-'baünd\ *vb* **1** : to be plentiful : TEEM **2** : to be fully supplied

¹about \ə-'baüt\ *adv* **1** : on all sides **2** : AROUND **3** : NEARBY

²about *prep* **1** : on every side of **2** : near to **3** : on the verge of : GOING ⟨he was just ∼ to go⟩ **4** : CONCERNING

about–face \-'fās\ *n* : a reversal of direction or attitude — **about–face** *vb*

¹above \ə-'bəv\ *adv* **1** : in the sky; *also* : in or to heaven **2** : in or to a higher place; *also* : higher on the same page or on a preceding page

²above *prep* **1** : in or to a higher place than : OVER ⟨storm clouds ∼ the bay⟩ **2** : superior to ⟨he thought her far ∼ him⟩ **3** : more than : EXCEEDING

above•board \-ˌbȯrd\ *adv or adj* : without concealment or deception : OPENLY

abp *abbr* archbishop

abr *abbr* abridged; abridgment

ab•ra•ca•dab•ra \ˌab-rə-kə-'dab-rə\ *n* **1** : a magical charm or incantation against calamity **2** : GIBBERISH

abrade \ə-'brād\ *vb* **abrad•ed; abrad•ing**

1 : to wear away by rubbing **2** : to wear down in spirit : IRRITATE — **abrasion** \-'brā-zhən\ *n*

¹abra•sive \ə-'brā-siv\ *n* : a substance (as pumice) for grinding, smoothing, or polishing

²abrasive *adj* : tending to abrade : causing irritation ⟨∼ relationships⟩ — **abra•sive•ly** *adv* — **abra•sive•ness** *n*

abreast \ə-'brest\ *adv or adj* **1** : side by side **2** : up to a standard or level esp. of knowledge

abridge \ə-'brij\ *vb* **abridged; abridg•ing** [ME *abregen*, fr. MF *abregier*, fr. LL *abbreviare*, fr. L *ad* to + *brevis* short] : to lessen in length or extent : SHORTEN — **abridg•ment** *or* **abridge•ment** *n*

abroad \ə-'brȯd\ *adv or adj* **1** : over a wide area **2** : away from one's home **3** : outside one's country

ab•ro•gate \'ab-rə-ˌgāt\ *vb* **-gat•ed; -gat•ing** : ANNUL, REVOKE — **ab•ro•ga•tion** \ˌab-rə-'gā-shən\ *n*

abrupt \ə-'brəpt\ *adj* **1** : broken or as if broken off **2** : SUDDEN, HASTY **3** : so quick as to seem rude **4** : DISCONNECTED **5** : STEEP — **abrupt•ly** *adv*

abs *abbr* absolute

ab•scess \'ab-ˌses\ *n, pl* **ab•scess•es** [L *abscessus*, lit., act of going away, fr. *abscedere* to go away, fr. *abs-*, *ab-* away + *cedere* to go] : a collection of pus surrounded by inflamed tissue — **ab•scessed** \-ˌsest\ *adj*

ab•scis•sa \ab-'sis-ə\ *n, pl* **abscissas** *also* **ab•scis•sae** \-'sis-(ˌ)ē\ : the coordinate of a point in a plane coordinate system that is the distance of the point from the vertical axis found by measuring along the horizontal axis

ab•scis•sion \ab-'sizh-ən\ *n* **1** : the act or process of cutting off **2** : the natural separation of flowers, fruits, or leaves from plants — **ab•scise** \ab-'sīz\ *vb*

ab•scond \ab-'skänd\ *vb* : to depart secretly and hide oneself

ab•sence \'ab-səns\ *n* **1** : the state or time of being absent **2** : WANT, LACK **3** : INATTENTION

¹ab•sent \'ab-sənt\ *adj* **1** : not present **2** : LACKING **3** : INATTENTIVE

²ab•sent \ab-'sent\ *vb* : to keep (oneself) away

³ab•sent \'ab-sənt\ *prep* : in the absence of : WITHOUT

ab•sen•tee \,ab-sən-'tē\ *n* : one that is absent or absents himself

absentee ballot *n* : a ballot submitted (as by mail) in advance of an election by a voter who is unable to be present at the polls

ab•sen•tee•ism \,ab-sən-'tē-,iz-əm\ *n* : chronic absence (as from work or school)

ab•sent•mind•ed \,ab-sənt-'mīn-dəd\ *adj* : unaware of one's surroundings or action : INATTENTIVE — **ab•sent•mind•ed•ly** *adv* — **ab•sent•mind•ed•ness** *n*

ab•sinthe *also* **ab•sinth** \'ab-,sinth\ *n* [F] : a liqueur flavored esp. with wormwood and anise

ab•so•lute \'ab-sə-,lüt, ,ab-sə-'lüt\ *adj* **1** : free from imperfection or mixture **2** : free from control, restriction, or qualification **3** : lacking grammatical connection with any other word in a sentence ⟨∼ construction⟩ **4** : POSITIVE ⟨∼ proof⟩ **5** : relating to the fundamental units of length, mass, and time **6** : relating to a temperature scale on which the zero point (**absolute zero**) corresponds to complete absence of heat equal to −273.15°C **7** : FUNDAMENTAL, ULTIMATE — **ab•so•lute•ly** *adv*

absolute pitch *n* **1** : the position of a tone in a standard scale independently determined by its rate of vibration **2** : the ability to sing or name a note asked for or heard

absolute value *n* : the numerical value of a real number that for a positive number or zero is equal to the number itself and for a negative number is equal to the positive number which when added to it is equal to zero

ab•so•lu•tion \,ab-sə-'lü-shən\ *n* : the act of absolving; *esp* : a remission of sins pronounced by a priest in the sacrament of penance

ab•so•lut•ism \'ab-sə-,lüt-,iz-əm\ *n* **1** : the theory that a ruler or government should have unlimited power **2** : government by an absolute ruler or authority

ab•solve \əb-'zälv, -'sälv\ *vb* **ab•solved; ab•solv•ing** : to set free from an obligation or the consequences of guilt

ab•sorb \əb-'sòrb, -'zòrb\ *vb* **1** : ASSIMILATE, INCORPORATE **2** : to suck up or take in in the manner of a sponge **3** : to engage (one's attention) : ENGROSS **4** : to receive without recoil or echo ⟨a ceiling that ∼s sound⟩ **5** : to transform (radiant energy) into a different form usu. with a resulting rise in temperature — **ab•sorb•ing** *adj* — **ab•sorb•ing•ly** *adv*

ab•sor•bent *also* **ab•sor•bant** \əb-'sòr-bənt, -'zòr-\ *adj* : able to absorb ⟨∼ cotton⟩ — **ab•sor•ben•cy** \-bən-sē\ *n* — **absorbent** *also* **absorbant** *n*

ab•sorp•tion \əb-'sòrp-shən, -'zòrp-\ *n* **1** : a process of absorbing or being absorbed **2** : concentration of attention — **ab•sorp•tive** \-tiv\ *adj*

ab•stain \əb-'stān\ *vb* : to restrain oneself **syn** refrain, forbear — **ab•stain•er** *n* — **ab•sten•tion** \-'sten-chən\ *n*

ab•ste•mi•ous \ab-'stē-mē-əs\ *adj* [L *abstemius*, fr. *abs-* away + *temetum* mead] : sparing in use of food or drink : TEMPERATE — **ab•ste•mi•ous•ly** *adv*

ab•sti•nence \'ab-stə-nəns\ *n* : voluntary refraining esp. from eating certain foods or drinking liquor — **ab•sti•nent** \-nənt\ *adj*

abstr *abbr* abstract

¹**ab•stract** \ab-'strakt, 'ab-,strakt\ *adj* **1** : considered apart from a particular instance **2** : expressing a quality apart from an object ⟨*whiteness* is an ∼ word⟩ **3** : having only intrinsic form with little or no pictorial representation ⟨∼ painting⟩ — **ab•stract•ly** *adv* — **ab•stract•ness** \-'strak(t)-nəs, -,strak(t)-\ *n*

²**ab•stract** \'ab-,strakt; *2 also* ab-'strakt\ *n* **1** : SUMMARY, EPITOME **2** : an abstract thing or state

³**ab•stract** \ab-'strakt, 'ab-,strakt; *2 usu* 'ab-,strakt\ *vb* **1** : REMOVE, SEPARATE **2** : to make an abstract of : SUMMARIZE **3** : to draw away the attention of **4** : STEAL — **ab•stract•ed•ly** \ab-'strak-təd-lē, 'ab-,strak-\ *adv*

abstract expressionism *n* : art that expresses the artist's attitudes and emotions through abstract forms — **abstract expressionist** *n*

ab•strac•tion \ab-'strak-shən\ *n* **1** : the act of abstracting : the state of being abstracted **2** : an abstract idea **3** : an abstract work of art

ab•struse \əb-'strüs, ab-\ *adj* : hard to

understand : RECONDITE — **ab•struse•ly** *adv* — **ab•struse•ness** *n*

ab•surd \əb-'sərd, -'zərd\ *adj* [MF *absurde*, fr. L *absurdus*, fr. *ab-* from + *surdus* deaf, stupid] : RIDICULOUS, UNREASONABLE — **ab•sur•di•ty** \-ət-ē\ *n* — **ab•surd•ly** *adv*

abun•dant \ə-'bən-dənt\ *adj* [ME, fr. MF, fr. L *abundant-, abundans,* prp. of *abundare* to abound, fr. *ab-* from + *unda* wave] : more than enough : amply sufficient **syn** copious, plentiful, ample, bountiful — **abun•dance** \-dəns\ *n* — **abun•dant•ly** *adv*

¹**abuse** \ə-'byüs\ *n* **1** : a corrupt practice **2** : MISUSE **3** : coarse and insulting speech **4** : MISTREATMENT

²**abuse** \ə-'byüz\ *vb* **abused; abus•ing 1** : to attack in words : REVILE **2** : to put to a wrong use : MISUSE **3** : MISTREAT — **abus•er** *n* — **abu•sive** \-'byü-siv\ *adj* — **abu•sive•ly** *adv* — **abu•sive•ness** *n*

abut \ə-'bət\ *vb* **abut•ted; abut•ting** : to touch along a border : border on

abut•ment \ə-'bət-mənt\ *n* : a structure that supports weight or withstands lateral pressure (as at the end of a bridge)

abysm \ə-'biz-əm\ *n* : ABYSS

abys•mal \ə-'biz-məl\ *adj* **1** : immeasurably deep : BOTTOMLESS **2** : absolutely wretched ⟨~ living conditions of the poor⟩ — **abys•mal•ly** *adv*

abyss \ə-'bis\ *n* **1** : the bottomless pit in old accounts of the universe **2** : an immeasurable depth

abys•sal \ə-'bis-əl\ *adj* : of or relating to the bottom waters of the ocean depths

ac *abbr* account

Ac *symbol* actinium

AC *abbr* **1** air-conditioning **2** alternating current **3** [L *ante Christum*] before Christ **4** [L *ante cibum*] before meals **5** area code

aca•cia \ə-'kā-shə\ *n* : any of numerous leguminous trees or shrubs with round white or yellow flower clusters and often fernlike leaves

acad *abbr* academic; academy

ac•a•deme \'ak-ə-ˌdēm\ *n* : SCHOOL; *also* : academic environment

ac•a•dem•ic \ˌak-ə-'dem-ik\ *adj* **1** : of or relating to schools or colleges **2** : literary or general rather than technical **3** : theoretical rather than practical — **ac•a•dem•i•cal•ly** \-i-k(ə-)lē\ *adv*

ac•a•de•mi•cian \ˌak-əd-ə-'mish-ən, ə-ˌkad-ə-\ *n* : a member of a society of scholars or artists

ac•a•dem•i•cism \ˌak-ə-'dem-ə-ˌsiz-əm\ *also* **acad•e•mism** \ə-'kad-ə-ˌmiz-əm\ *n* : manner, style, or content conforming to the traditions or rules of an academy or movement

acad•e•my \ə-'kad-ə-mē\ *n, pl* **-mies** [Gk *Akadēmeia,* school of philosophy founded by Plato, fr. *Akadēmeia,* gymnasium where Plato taught, fr. *Akadēmos* Greek mythological hero] **1** : a school above the elementary level; *esp* : a private high school **2** : a society of scholars or artists

acan•thus \ə-'kan-thəs\ *n, pl* **acan•thus•es** *also* **acan•thi** \-'kan-ˌthī\ **1** : any of a genus of prickly herbs of the Mediterranean region **2** : an ornamentation (as on a column) representing the leaves of the acanthus

a cap•pel•la *also* **a ca•pel•la** \ˌäk-ə-'pel-ə\ *adv or adj* [It *a cappella* in chapel style] : without instrumental accompaniment ⟨the choir sang *a cappella*⟩

acc *abbr* accusative

ac•cede \ak-'sēd\ *vb* **ac•ced•ed; ac•ced•ing 1** : to become a party to an agreement **2** : to express approval **3** : to enter upon an office **syn** agree, acquiesce, assent, consent, subscribe

ac•ce•le•ran•do \ä-ˌchel-ə-'rän-dō\ *adv or adj* [It] : gradually faster — used as a direction in music

ac•cel•er•ate \ik-'sel-ə-ˌrāt, ak-\ *vb* **-at•ed; -at•ing 1** : to bring about earlier **2** : to speed up : QUICKEN — **ac•cel•er•a•tion** \-ˌsel-ə-'rā-shən\ *n*

ac•cel•er•a•tor \ik-'sel-ə-ˌrāt-ər, ak-\ *n* **1** : one that accelerates **2** : a pedal for controlling the speed of a motor-vehicle engine **3** : an apparatus for imparting high velocities to charged particles

ac•cel•er•om•e•ter \ik-ˌsel-ə-'räm-ət-ər, ak-\ *n* : an instrument for measuring acceleration or vibrations

¹**ac•cent** \'ak-ˌsent, ak-'sent\ *vb* : STRESS, EMPHASIZE

²**ac•cent** \'ak-ˌsent\ *n* **1** : a distinctive manner of pronunciation ⟨a foreign ~⟩ **2** : prominence given to one syllable of a word esp. by stress **3** : a mark (as ´, `, ^) over a vowel in writing or

printing used usu. to indicate a difference in pronunciation (as stress) from a vowel not so marked — **ac·cen·tu·al** \ak-'sench-(ə-)wəl\ *adj*

ac·cen·tu·ate \ak-'sen-chə-ˌwāt\ *vb* **-at·ed; -at·ing** : ACCENT — **ac·cen·tu·a·tion** \-ˌsen-chə-'wā-shən\ *n*

ac·cept \ik-'sept, ak-\ *vb* **1** : to receive willingly **2** : to agree to **3** : to assume an obligation to pay

ac·cept·able \ik-'sep-tə-bəl, ak-\ *adj* : capable or worthy of being accepted — **ac·cept·abil·i·ty** \ik-ˌsep-tə-'bil-ət-ē, ak-\ *n*

ac·cep·tance \ik-'sep-təns, ak-\ *n* **1** : the act of accepting **2** : the state of being accepted or acceptable **3** : an accepted bill of exchange

ac·cep·ta·tion \ˌak-ˌsep-'tā-shən\ *n* : the generally understood meaning of a word

¹ac·cess \'ak-ˌses\ *n* **1** : capacity to enter or approach **2** : a way of approach : ENTRANCE

²access *vb* : to get at : gain access to

ac·ces·si·ble \ik-'ses-ə-bəl, ak-, ek-\ *adj* **1** : capable of being reached ⟨~ by train⟩ **2** : capable of being used, seen, or known : OBTAINABLE ⟨~ information⟩ — **ac·ces·si·bil·i·ty** \-ˌses-ə-'bil-ət-ē\ *n*

ac·ces·sion \ik-'sesh-ən, ak-\ *n* **1** : something added **2** : increase by something added **3** : the act of acceding to an office or position

ac·ces·so·ry *also* **ac·ces·sa·ry** \ik-'ses-(ə-)rē, ak-\ *n, pl* **-ries 1** : something helpful but not essential **2** : a person who though not present abets or assists in the commission of an offense **syn** appurtenance, adjunct, appendage, appendix — **accessory** *adj*

ac·ci·dence \'ak-səd-əns\ *n* : a part of grammar that deals with inflections

ac·ci·dent \'ak-səd-ənt\ *n* **1** : an event occurring by chance or unintentionally **2** : CHANCE ⟨met by ~⟩ **3** : a nonessential property

ac·ci·den·tal \ˌak-sə-'dent-ᵊl\ *adj* **1** : happening unexpectedly or by chance **2** : happening without intent or through carelessness **syn** casual, fortuitous, incidental, chance — **ac·ci·den·tal·ly** \-'dent-(ᵊ-)lē\ *also* **ac·ci·dent·ly** \-'dent-lē\ *adv*

ac·claim \ə-'klām\ *vb* **1** : APPLAUD,

PRAISE **2** : to declare by acclamation **syn** extol, laud, commend, hail — **acclaim** *n*

ac·cla·ma·tion \ˌak-lə-'mā-shən\ *n* **1** : loud eager applause **2** : an overwhelming affirmative vote by shouting or applause rather than by ballot

ac·cli·mate \'ak-lə-ˌmāt, ə-'klī-mət\ *vb* **-mat·ed; -mat·ing** : to accustom to a new climate or situation — **ac·cli·ma·tion** \ˌak-lə-'mā-shən, ˌak-ˌlī-\ *n*

ac·cli·ma·tize \ə-'klī-mə-ˌtīz\ *vb* **-tized; -tiz·ing 1** : ACCLIMATE **2** : to become acclimated — **ac·cli·ma·ti·za·tion** \-ˌklī-mət-ə-'zā-shən\ *n*

ac·cliv·i·ty \ə-'kliv-ət-ē\ *n, pl* **-ties** : an ascending slope

ac·co·lade \'ak-ə-ˌlād\ *n* [F, fr. *accoler* to embrace, fr. L *ad-* to + *collum* neck] : a recognition of merit : AWARD

ac·com·mo·date \ə-'käm-ə-ˌdāt\ *vb* **-dat·ed; -dat·ing 1** : to make fit or suitable : ADAPT, ADJUST **2** : HARMONIZE, RECONCILE **3** : to provide with something needed **4** : to hold without crowding **5** : to undergo visual accommodation

ac·com·mo·dat·ing *adj* : OBLIGING

ac·com·mo·da·tion \ə-ˌkäm-ə-'dā-shən\ *n* **1** : something supplied to satisfy a need; *esp* : LODGINGS — usu. used in pl. **2** : the act of accommodating : ADJUSTMENT **3** : the automatic adjustment of the eye for seeing at different distances

ac·com·pa·ni·ment \ə-'kəmp-(ə-)nē-mənt\ *n* : something that accompanies another; *esp* : subordinate music to support a principal voice or instrument

ac·com·pa·ny \ə-'kəmp-(ə-)nē\ *vb* **-nied; -ny·ing 1** : to go or occur with : ATTEND **2** : to play an accompaniment for — **ac·com·pa·nist** \-(ə-)nəst\ *n*

ac·com·plice \ə-'käm-pləs, -'kəm-\ *n* : an associate in crime

ac·com·plish \ə-'käm-plish, -'kəm-\ *vb* : to bring to completion **syn** achieve, effect, execute, perform — **ac·com·plish·er** *n*

ac·com·plished \-plisht\ *adj* **1** : EXPERT, SKILLED **2** : established beyond doubt

ac·com·plish·ment \ə-'käm-plish-mənt, -'kəm-\ *n* **1** : COMPLETION **2** : something completed or effected **3** : an acquired excellence or skill

¹ac·cord \ə-'kȯrd\ *vb* [ME *accorden*, fr.

OF *acorder*, fr. L *ad*- to + *cord*-, *cor* heart] **1** : GRANT, CONCEDE **2** : AGREE, HARMONIZE — **ac·cor·dant** \-'kȯrd-ᵊnt\ *adj*

²**accord** *n* : AGREEMENT, HARMONY

ac·cor·dance \ə-'kȯrd-ᵊns\ *n* **1** : ACCORD **2** : the act of granting

ac·cord·ing·ly \ə-'kȯrd-iŋ-lē\ *adv* **1** : in accordance **2** : CONSEQUENTLY, SO

according to *prep* **1** : in conformity with ⟨paid *according to* ability⟩ **2** : as stated or attested by ⟨*according to* her he wasn't home⟩

¹**ac·cor·di·on** \ə-'kȯrd-ē-ən\ *n* [G *akkordion*, fr. *akkord* chord] : a portable keyboard instrument with a bellows and reeds

²**accordion** *adj* : folding like the bellows of an accordion ⟨∼ pleats⟩

ac·cost \ə-'kȯst\ *vb* [MF *accoster*, deriv. of L *ad*- to + *costa* rib, side] : to approach and speak to esp. aggressively

¹**ac·count** \ə-'kaȯnt\ *n* **1** : a statement of business transactions **2** : an arrangement with a vendor to supply credit **3** : a statement of reasons, causes, or motives **4** : VALUE, IMPORTANCE ⟨a person of no ∼⟩ **5** : a sum of money deposited in a bank and subject to withdrawal by the depositor — **on account of** : BECAUSE OF — **on no account** : under no circumstances — **on one's own account** : on one's own behalf

²**account** *vb* **1** : CONSIDER ⟨I ∼ him lucky⟩ **2** : to give an explanation — used with *for*

ac·count·able \ə-'kaȯnt-ə-bəl\ *adj* **1** : ANSWERABLE, RESPONSIBLE **2** : EXPLICABLE — **ac·count·abil·i·ty** \-ˌkaȯnt-ə-'bil-ət-ē\ *n*

ac·coun·tant \ə-'kaȯnt-ᵊnt\ *n* : a person skilled in accounting — **ac·coun·tan·cy** \-ᵊn-sē\ *n*

account executive *n* : a business executive (as in an advertising agency) in charge of a client's account

ac·count·ing \ə-'kaȯnt-iŋ\ *n* : the art or system of keeping and analyzing financial records

ac·cou·tre *or* **ac·cou·ter** \ə-'küt-ər\ *vb* -**cou·tred** *or* -**cou·tered**; -**cou·tring** *or* -**cou·ter·ing** \-'küt-ə-riŋ, 'kü-triŋ\ : EQUIP, OUTFIT

ac·cou·tre·ment *or* **ac·cou·ter·ment** \ə-'kü-trə-mənt, -'küt-ər-mənt\ *n* [F]

1 : the act of equipping **2** : an accessory item — usu. used in pl. **3** : an identifying characteristic

ac·cred·it \ə-'kred-ət\ *vb* **1** : to endorse or approve officially **2** : CREDIT — **ac·cred·i·ta·tion** \-ˌkred-ə-'tā-shən\ *n*

ac·cre·tion \ə-'krē-shən\ *n* **1** : growth or enlargement esp. by addition from without **2** : a product of accretion

ac·crue \ə-'krü\ *vb* **ac·crued; ac·cru·ing** **1** : to come by way of increase **2** : to be added by periodic growth — **ac·cru·al** \-əl\ *n*

acct *abbr* account; accountant

ac·cul·tur·a·tion \ə-ˌkəl-chə-'rā-shən\ *n* : cultural modification of an individual or group by borrowing and adapting traits from another culture

ac·cu·mu·late \ə-'kyü-myə-ˌlāt\ *vb* -**lat·ed; -lat·ing** [L *accumulare*, fr. *ad*- to + *cumulare* to heap up] : to heap or pile up **syn** amass, gather, collect, stockpile — **ac·cu·mu·la·tion** \-ˌkyü-myə-'lā-shən\ *n* — **ac·cu·mu·la·tor** \-'kyü-myə-ˌlāt-ər\ *n*

ac·cu·rate \'ak-yə-rət\ *adj* : free from error : EXACT, PRECISE — **ac·cu·ra·cy** \-rə-sē\ *n* — **ac·cu·rate·ly** *adv* — **ac·cu·rate·ness** *n*

ac·cursed \ə-'kərst, -'kər-səd\ *or* **ac·curst** \ə-'kərst\ *adj* **1** : being under a curse **2** : DAMNABLE, EXECRABLE

ac·cus·al \ə-'kyü-zəl\ *n* : ACCUSATION

ac·cu·sa·tive \ə-'kyü-zət-iv\ *adj* : of, relating to, or being a grammatical case marking the direct object of a verb or the object of a preposition — **accusative** *n*

ac·cuse \ə-'kyüz\ *vb* **ac·cused; ac·cus·ing** : to charge with an offense : BLAME — **ac·cu·sa·tion** \ˌak-yə-'zā-shən\ *n* — **ac·cus·er** *n*

ac·cused \ə-'kyüzd\ *n, pl* **accused** : the defendant in a criminal case

ac·cus·tom \ə-'kəs-təm\ *vb* : to make familiar through use or experience

ac·cus·tomed \ə-'kəs-təmd\ *adj* : USUAL, CUSTOMARY

¹**ace** \'ās\ *n* [ME *as* a die face marked with one spot, fr. OF, fr. L, unit, a copper coin] **1** : a playing card bearing a single large pip in its center **2** : a point (as in tennis) won by a single stroke **3** : a golf score of one stroke on a hole **4** : a combat pilot who has

brought down five or more enemy planes **5** : one that excels

²ace *vb* **aced; ac•ing 1** : to score an ace against (an opponent) **2** : to defeat decisively

³ace *adj* : of first rank or quality

ac•er•bate \'as-ər-ˌbāt\ *vb* -**bat•ed; -bat•ing** : IRRITATE, EXASPERATE

acer•bic \ə-'sər-bik, a-\ *adj* : acid in temper, mood, or tone

acer•bi•ty \ə-'sər-bət-ē\ *n, pl* -**ties** : SOURNESS, BITTERNESS

ac•e•tate \'as-ə-ˌtāt\ *n* **1** : a salt or ester of acetic acid **2** : a textile fiber made from cellulose and acetic acid; *also* : a fabric or plastic made of this fiber

ace•tic \ə-'sēt-ik\ *adj* : of, relating to, or producing acetic acid or vinegar

acetic acid *n* : a colorless pungent liquid acid that is the chief acid of vinegar and is used esp. in making chemical compounds

ac•e•tone \'as-ə-ˌtōn\ *n* : a volatile flammable fragrant liquid compound used in making other chemical compounds and as a solvent

ace•tyl•cho•line \ə-ˌsēt-ᵊl-'kō-ˌlēn\ *n* : a compound that is released at nerve endings of the autonomic nervous system and is active in the transmission of nerve impulses

acet•y•lene \ə-'set-ᵊl-ən, -ᵊl-ˌēn\ *n* : a colorless flammable gas used as a fuel (as in welding and soldering)

ace•tyl•sal•i•cyl•ic acid \ə-'sēt-ᵊl-ˌsal-ə-ˌsil-ik-\ *n* : ASPIRIN 1

ache \'āk\ *vb* **ached; ach•ing 1** : to suffer a usu. dull persistent pain **2** : LONG, YEARN — **ache** *n*

achieve \ə-'chēv\ *vb* **achieved; achiev•ing** [ME *acheven,* fr. MF *achever* to finish, fr. *a-* to (fr. L *ad-*) + *chief* end, head, fr. L *caput*] : to gain by work or effort **syn** accomplish, attain, realize — **achieve•ment** *n* — **achiev•er** *n*

Achil•les' heel \ə-ˌkil-ēz-\ *n* [fr. the story that the Gk. warrior Achilles was vulnerable only in the heel] : a vulnerable point

Achilles tendon \ə-ˌkil-ēz-\ *n* : the strong tendon joining the muscles in the calf of the leg to the bone of the heel

ach•ro•mat•ic \ˌak-rə-'mat-ik\ *adj* : giving an image almost free from extraneous colors ⟨∼ lens⟩

achy \'ā-kē\ *adj* **ach•i•er; ach•i•est** : afflicted with aches — **ach•i•ness** *n*

¹ac•id \'as-əd\ *adj* **1** : sour or biting to the taste; *also* : sharp or sour in manner **2** : of or relating to an acid — **acid•i•ty** \ə-'sid-ət-ē\ *n*

²acid *n* **1** : a sour substance **2** : a usu. water-soluble chemical compound that has a sour taste, reacts with a base to form a salt, and reddens litmus **3** : LSD — **acid•ic** \ə-'sid-ik\ *adj*

acid•i•fy \ə-'sid-ə-ˌfī\ *vb* -**fied; -fy•ing 1** : to make or become acid **2** : to change into an acid — **acid•i•fi•ca•tion** \-ˌsid-ə-fə-'kā-shən\ *n*

ac•i•do•sis \ˌas-ə-'dō-səs\ *n, pl* -**do•ses** \-'dō-ˌsēz\ : an abnormal state of reduced alkalinity of the blood and body tissues

acid precipitation *n* : precipitation with above normal acidity that is caused esp. by atmospheric pollutants

acid rain *n* : acid precipitation in the form of rain

acid test *n* : a severe or crucial test

acid•u•lous \ə-'sij-ə-ləs\ *adj* : somewhat acid in taste or manner

ack *abbr* acknowledge; acknowledgment

ack–ack \'ak-ˌak\ *n* [Brit. signalmen's telephone pron. of *AA,* abbr. of *antiaircraft*] : an antiaircraft gun; *also* : antiaircraft fire

ac•knowl•edge \ik-'näl-ij, ak-\ *vb* -**edged; -edg•ing 1** : to recognize the rights or authority of **2** : to admit as true **3** : to express thanks for; *also* : to report receipt of **4** : to recognize as valid — **ac•knowl•edg•ment** *also* **ac•knowl•edge•ment** *n*

ACLU *abbr* American Civil Liberties Union

ac•me \'ak-mē\ *n* [Gk *akmē*] : the highest point

ac•ne \'ak-nē\ *n* [Gk *aknē,* MS var. of *akmē,* lit., point] : a skin disorder marked by inflammation of skin glands and hair follicles and by pimple formation esp. on the face

ac•o•lyte \'ak-ə-ˌlīt\ *n* **1** : one who assists the clergyman in a liturgical service **2** : FOLLOWER

ac•o•nite \'ak-ə-ˌnīt\ *n* **1** : MONKSHOOD **2** : a drug obtained from a common Old World monkshood

acorn \'ā-ˌkȯrn, -kərn\ *n* : the nut of the oak

acorn squash *n* : an acorn-shaped dark green winter squash with a ridged surface and sweet yellow to orange flesh

acous·tic \ə-'kü-stik\ *or* **acous·ti·cal** \-sti-kəl\ *adj* **1** : of or relating to the sense or organs of hearing, to sound, or to the science of sounds **2** : deadening sound ⟨∼ tile⟩ **3** : operated by or utilizing sound waves — **acous·ti·cal·ly** \-k(ə-)lē\ *adv*

acous·tics \ə-'kü-stiks\ *n sing or pl* **1** : the science of sound **2** : the qualities in a room that make it easy or hard for a person in it to hear distinctly

ac·quaint \ə-'kwānt\ *vb* [ME *acquainten*, deriv. of L *ad-* + *cognoscere* to know] **1** : to cause to know personally **2** : INFORM

ac·quain·tance \ə-'kwānt-ᵊns\ *n* **1** : personal knowledge **2** : a person with whom one is acquainted — **ac·quain·tance·ship** *n*

ac·qui·esce \ˌak-wē-'es\ *vb* **-esced; -escing** : to accept or comply without open opposition **syn** consent, agree, assent, accede — **ac·qui·es·cence** \-'es-ᵊns\ *n* — **ac·qui·es·cent** \-ᵊnt\ *adj* — **ac·qui·es·cent·ly** *adv*

ac·quire \ə-'kwī(ə)r\ *vb* **ac·quired; ac·quir·ing** : to come into possession of : GET

ac·quired \ə-'kwī(ə)rd\ *adj* **1** : gained by or as a result of effort or experience **2** : caused by environmental forces and not passed from parent to offspring in the genes ⟨∼ characteristics⟩

acquired immune deficiency syndrome *n* : AIDS

acquired immunodeficiency syndrome *n* : AIDS

ac·quire·ment \-mənt\ *n* **1** : ATTAINMENT, ACCOMPLISHMENT **2** : the act of acquiring

ac·qui·si·tion \ˌak-wə-'zish-ən\ *n* **1** : ACQUIREMENT **2** : something acquired

ac·quis·i·tive \ə-'kwiz-ət-iv\ *adj* : eager to acquire : GREEDY — **ac·quis·i·tive·ly** *adv* — **ac·quis·i·tive·ness** *n*

ac·quit \ə-'kwit\ *vb* **ac·quit·ted; ac·quit·ting** **1** : to pronounce not guilty **2** : to conduct (oneself) usu. satisfactorily — **ac·quit·tal** \-ᵊl\ *n*

acre \'ā-kər\ *n* **1** *pl* : LANDS, ESTATE **2** — see WEIGHT table

acre·age \'ā-k(ə-)rij\ *n* : area in acres

ac·rid \'ak-rəd\ *adj* **1** : sharp and biting in taste or odor **2** : bitterly irritating : CAUSTIC — **acrid·i·ty** \a-'krid-ət-ē, ə-\ *n* — **ac·rid·ness** *n*

ac·ri·mo·ny \'ak-rə-ˌmō-nē\ *n, pl* **-nies** : harsh or biting sharpness of language or feeling — **ac·ri·mo·ni·ous** \ˌak-rə-'mō-nē-əs\ *adj*

ac·ro·bat \'ak-rə-ˌbat\ *n* [F *acrobate*, fr. Gk *akrobatēs*, fr. *akrobatos* walking up high, fr. *akros* topmost + *bainein* to go] : a performer of gymnastic feats — **ac·ro·bat·ic** \ˌak-rə-'bat-ik\ *adj*

ac·ro·bat·ics \ˌak-rə-'bat-iks\ *n sing or pl* : the performance of an acrobat

ac·ro·nym \'ak-rə-ˌnim\ *n* : a word (as *radar*) formed from the initial letter or letters of each of the successive parts or major parts of a compound term

ac·ro·pho·bia \ˌak-rə-'fō-bē-ə\ *n* : abnormal dread of being at a great height

acrop·o·lis \ə-'kräp-ə-ləs\ *n* [Gk *akropolis*, fr. *akros* topmost + *polis* city] : the upper fortified part of an ancient Greek city

¹across \ə-'krȯs\ *adv* **1** : to or on the opposite side **2** : so as to be understandable or acceptable : OVER ⟨get the point ∼⟩

²across *prep* **1** : to or on the opposite side of ⟨ran ∼ the street⟩ ⟨standing ∼ the street⟩ **2** : on at an angle ⟨slapped him ∼ the face⟩; *esp* : on so as to cross ⟨a log ∼ the road⟩

across–the–board *adj* **1** : placed to win if a competitor wins, places, or shows ⟨an ∼ bet⟩ **2** : including all classes or categories ⟨an ∼ wage increase⟩

acros·tic \ə-'krȯs-tik\ *n* **1** : a composition usu. in verse in which the initial or final letters of the lines taken in order form a word or phrase **2** : a series of words of equal length arranged to read the same horizontally or vertically — **acrostic** *adj*

acryl·ic \ə-'kril-ik\ *n* **1** : ACRYLIC RESIN **2** : a paint in which the vehicle is acrylic resin **3** : a quick-drying synthetic fiber used for woven and knitted cloth

acrylic resin *n* : a glassy thermoplastic used for cast and molded parts or as coatings and adhesives

¹act \'akt\ *n* **1** : a thing done : DEED **2**

: STATUTE, DECREE **3** : a main division of a play; *also* : an item on a variety program **4** : an instance of insincere behavior : PRETENSE

²**act** *vb* **1** : to perform by action esp. on the stage; *also* : FEIGN, SIMULATE, PRETEND **2** : to conduct oneself : BEHAVE **3** : to perform a specified function **4** : to produce an effect

³**act** *abbr* **1** active **2** actual

ACT *abbr* Australian Capital Territory

actg *abbr* acting

ACTH \ˌā-ˌsē-(ˌ)tē-ˈach\ *n* : a protein hormone of the pituitary gland that stimulates the adrenal cortex

act·ing \ˈak-tiŋ\ *adj* : doing duty temporarily or for another ⟨∼ president⟩

ac·tin·i·um \ak-ˈtin-ē-əm\ *n* : a radioactive metallic chemical element

ac·tion \ˈak-shən\ *n* **1** : a legal proceeding **2** : the manner or method of performing **3** : ACTIVITY **4** : ACT, DEED **5** : the accomplishment of a thing usu. over a period of time, in stages, or with the possibility of repetition **6** *pl* : CONDUCT **7** : COMBAT, BATTLE **8** : the events of a literary plot **9** : an operating mechanism ⟨the ∼ of a gun⟩; *also* : the way it operates ⟨stiff ∼⟩

ac·tion·able \ˈak-sh(ə-)nə-bəl\ *adj* : affording ground for an action or suit at law

ac·ti·vate \ˈak-tə-ˌvāt\ *vb* **-vat·ed; -vat·ing** **1** : to spur into action; *also* : to make active, reactive, or radioactive **2** : to treat (as carbon) so as to improve adsorptive properties **3** : to aerate (sewage) to favor the growth of organisms that cause decomposition **4** : to set up (a military unit) formally; *also* : to call to active duty — **ac·ti·va·tion** \ˌak-tə-ˈvā-shən\ *n*

ac·tive \ˈak-tiv\ *adj* **1** : causing action or change **2** : asserting that the grammatical subject performs the action represented by the verb ⟨∼ voice⟩ **3** : BRISK, LIVELY **4** : presently in operation or use **5** : tending to progress or to cause degeneration ⟨∼ tuberculosis⟩ — **active** *n* — **ac·tive·ly** *adv*

ac·tiv·ism \ˈak-ti-ˌviz-əm\ *n* : a doctrine or practice that emphasizes vigorous action for political ends — **ac·tiv·ist** \-vəst\ *n or adj*

ac·tiv·i·ty \ak-ˈtiv-ət-ē\ *n, pl* **-ties** **1** : the quality or state of being active **2** : an

occupation in which one is engaged

ac·tor \ˈak-tər\ *n* : one that acts in a play or motion picture

ac·tress \ˈak-trəs\ *n* : a woman who is an actor

Acts \ˈak(t)s\ *or* **Acts of the Apostles** — see BIBLE table

ac·tu·al \ˈak-ch(ə-w)əl\ *adj* : really existing : REAL — **ac·tu·al·i·ty** \ˌak-chə-ˈwal-ət-ē\ *n* — **ac·tu·al·iza·tion** \ˌak-ch(ə-w)ə-lə-ˈzā-shən\ *n* — **ac·tu·al·ize** \ˈak-ch(ə-w)ə-ˌlīz\ *vb*

ac·tu·al·ly \ˈak-ch(ə-w)ə-lē\ *adv* : in fact or in truth : REALLY

ac·tu·ary \ˈak-chə-ˌwer-ē\ *n, pl* **-ar·ies** : one who calculates insurance risks and premiums — **ac·tu·ar·i·al** \ˌak-chə-ˈwer-ē-əl\ *adj*

ac·tu·ate \ˈak-chə-ˌwāt\ *vb* **-at·ed; -at·ing** **1** : to put into action **2** : to move to action — **ac·tu·a·tor** \-ˌwāt-ər\ *n*

act up *vb* **1** : MISBEHAVE **2** : to function improperly

acu·ity \ə-ˈkyü-ət-ē\ *n, pl* **-ities** : keenness of perception

acu·men \ə-ˈkyü-mən\ *n* : mental keenness and penetration **syn** discernment, insight, percipience, perspicacity

acu·pres·sure \ˈak-yu̇-ˌpresh-ər\ *n* : SHIATSU

acu·punc·ture \ˈak-yu̇-ˌpəŋk-chər\ *n* : an orig. Chinese practice of puncturing the body (as with needles) at specific points to cure disease or relieve pain — **acu·punc·tur·ist** \ˌak-yu̇-ˈpəŋk-chə-rəst\ *n*

acute \ə-ˈkyüt\ *adj* **acut·er; acut·est** [L *acutus*, pp. of *acuere* to sharpen, fr. *acus* needle] **1** : SHARP, POINTED **2** : containing less than 90 degrees ⟨an ∼ angle⟩ **3** : sharply perceptive; *esp* : mentally keen **4** : SEVERE ⟨∼ distress⟩; *also* : having a sudden onset, sharp rise, and short duration ⟨∼ inflammation⟩ **5** : of, marked by, or being an accent mark having the form ´ — **acute·ly** *adv* — **acute·ness** *n*

ad \ˈad\ *n* : ADVERTISEMENT

AD *abbr* **1** after date **2** [L *anno Domini*] in the year of our Lord — often printed in small capitals

ad·age \ˈad-ij\ *n* : an old familiar saying : PROVERB, MAXIM

¹**ada·gio** \ə-ˈdäj-(ē-ˌ)ō, -ˈdäzh-\ *adv or*

adj [It] : in slow time — used as a direction in music

²adagio *n, pl* **-gios 1** : an adagio movement **2** : a ballet duet or trio displaying feats of lifting and balancing

¹ad•a•mant \'ad-ə-mənt, -ˌmant\ *n* [ME, fr. OF, fr. L *adamant-, adamas* hardest metal, diamond, fr. Gk] : a stone believed to be impenetrably hard — **ad•a•man•tine** \ˌad-ə-'man-ˌtēn, -ˌtīn\ *adj*

²adamant *adj* : INFLEXIBLE, UNYIELDING — **ad•a•mant•ly** *adv*

Ad•am's apple \'ad-əmz-\ *n* : the projection in front of the neck formed by the largest cartilage of the larynx

adapt \ə-'dapt\ *vb* : to make suitable or fit (as for a new use or for different conditions) **syn** adjust, accommodate, conform — **adapt•abil•i•ty** \ə-ˌdap-tə-'bil-ət-ē\ *n* — **adapt•able** *adj* — **ad•ap•ta•tion** \ˌad-ˌap-'tā-shən, -əp-\ *n* — **adap•tive** \ə-'dap-tiv\ *adj*

adapt•er *also* **adap•tor** \ə-'dap-tər\ *n* **1** : one that adapts **2** : a device for connecting two dissimilar parts of an apparatus **3** : an attachment for adapting apparatus for uses not orig. intended

ADC *abbr* **1** aide-de-camp **2** Aid to Dependent Children

add \'ad\ *vb* **1** : to join to something else so as to increase in number or amount **2** : to combine (numbers) into one sum

ad•dend \'ad-ˌend\ *n* : a number to be added to another

ad•den•dum \ə-'den-dəm\ *n, pl* **-da** \-də\ [L] : something added; *esp* : a supplement to a book

¹ad•der \'ad-ər\ *n* **1** : a poisonous European viper or a related snake **2** : any of various harmless No. American snakes (as the hognose snake)

²add•er \'ad-ər\ *n* : one that adds; *esp* : a device that performs addition

¹ad•dict \ə-'dikt\ *vb* **1** : to devote or surrender (oneself) to something habitually or excessively **2** : to cause (a person) to become physiologically dependent upon a drug — **ad•dic•tive** \-'dik-tiv\ *adj*

²ad•dict \'ad-(ˌ)ikt\ *n* : one who is addicted (as to a drug)

ad•dic•tion \ə-'dik-shən\ *n* : the quality or state of being addicted; *esp* : compulsive need for habit-forming drugs

ad•di•tion \ə-'dish-ən\ *n* **1** : the act or process of adding; *also* : something added **2** : the operation of combining numbers to obtain their sum **syn** accretion, increment, accession, augmentation

ad•di•tion•al \ə-'dish-(ə-)nəl\ *adj* : coming by way of addition : ADDED, EXTRA — **ad•di•tion•al•ly** \-ē\ *adv*

¹ad•di•tive \'ad-ət-iv\ *adj* **1** : of, relating to, or characterized by addition **2** : produced by addition — **ad•di•tiv•i•ty** \ˌad-ə-'tiv-ət-ē\ *n*

²additive *n* : a substance added to another in small quantities to effect a desired change in properties ⟨food ∼s⟩

ad•dle \'ad-ᵊl\ *vb* **ad•dled; ad•dling** \'ad-(ə-)liŋ\ **1** : to throw into confusion : MUDDLE **2** : to become rotten ⟨*addled* eggs⟩

addn *abbr* addition

addnl *abbr* additional

add–on \'ad-ˌȯn, -ˌän\ *n* : something added as a supplement; *esp* : a component (as of a computer system) that increases capability

¹ad•dress \ə-'dres\ *vb* **1** : to direct the attention of (oneself) **2** : to direct one's remarks to : deliver an address to **3** : to mark directions for delivery on **4** : to identify (as a memory location) by an address

²ad•dress \ə-'dres, 'ad-ˌres\ *n* **1** : skillful management **2** : a formal speech : LECTURE **3** : the place where a person or organization may be communicated with **4** : the directions for delivery placed on mail **5** : a location (as in a computer's memory) where particular data is stored

ad•dress•ee \ˌad-ˌres-'ē, ə-ˌdres-'ē\ *n* : one to whom something is addressed

ad•duce \ə-'d(y)üs\ *vb* **ad•duced; ad•duc•ing** : to offer as argument, reason, or proof **syn** advance, allege, cite, submit

-ade \'ād\ *n suffix* **1** : act : action ⟨block*ade*⟩ **2** : product; *esp* : sweet drink ⟨lime*ade*⟩

ad•e•nine \'ad-ᵊn-ˌēn\ *n* : one of the purine bases that make up the genetic code of DNA and RNA

ad•e•noid \'ad-(ᵊ-)ˌnȯid\ *n* : an enlarged mass of tissue near the opening of the nose into the throat — usu. used in pl.

— **adenoid** *or* **ad·e·noi·dal** \ˌad-(ə-)ˈnȯid-əl\ *adj*

aden·o·sine tri·phos·phate \ə-ˈden-ə-ˌsēn-trī-ˈfäs-ˌfāt\ *n* : ATP

¹**ad·ept** \ˈad-ˌept\ *n* : EXPERT

²**adept** \ə-ˈdept\ *adj* : highly skilled : EXPERT — **adept·ly** *adv* — **adept·ness** *n*

ad·e·quate \ˈad-i-kwət\ *adj* : equal to or sufficient for a specific requirement — **ad·e·qua·cy** \-kwə-sē\ *n* — **ad·e·quate·ly** *adv*

ad·here \ad-ˈhiər, əd-\ *vb* **ad·hered; ad·her·ing 1** : to give support : maintain loyalty **2** : to stick fast : CLING — **ad·her·ence** \-ˈhir-əns\ *n* — **ad·her·ent** \-ənt\ *adj or n*

ad·he·sion \ad-ˈhē-zhən, əd-\ *n* **1** : the act or state of adhering **2** : the union of bodily tissues abnormally grown together after inflammation; *also* : the newly formed uniting tissue **3** : the molecular attraction between the surfaces of bodies in contact

¹**ad·he·sive** \-ˈhē-siv, -ziv\ *adj* **1** : tending to adhere : STICKY **2** : prepared for adhering

²**adhesive** *n* : an adhesive substance

adhesive tape *n* : tape coated on one side with an adhesive mixture; *esp* : one used to secure bandages and cover wounds

¹**ad hoc** \ˈad-ˈhäk, -ˈhōk\ *adv* [L, for this] : for the case at hand apart from other applications

²**ad hoc** *adj* : concerned with or formed for a particular purpose ⟨an *ad hoc* committee⟩ ⟨*ad hoc* solutions⟩

adi·a·bat·ic \ˌad-ē-ə-ˈbat-ik\ *adj* : occurring without loss or gain of heat — **adi·a·bat·i·cal·ly** \-i-k(ə-)lē\ *adv*

adieu \ə-ˈd(y)ü\ *n, pl* **adieus** *or* **adieux** \ə-ˈd(y)üz\ : FAREWELL — often used interjectionally

ad in·fi·ni·tum \ˌad-ˌin-fə-ˈnīt-əm\ *adv or adj* : without end or limit

ad in·ter·im \ad-ˈin-tə-rəm, -ˌrim\ *adv* : for the intervening time — **ad interim** *adj*

adi·os \ˌad-ē-ˈōs, ˌäd-\ *interj* [Sp *adiós,* lit., to God] — used to express farewell

ad·i·pose \ˈad-ə-ˌpōs\ *adj* : of or relating to animal fat : FATTY

adj *abbr* **1** adjective **2** adjutant

ad·ja·cent \ə-ˈjās-ᵊnt\ *adj* : situated near or next **syn** adjoining, contigu-

ous, abutting, juxtaposed, conterminous

ad·jec·tive \ˈaj-ik-tiv\ *n* : a word that typically serves as a modifier of a noun — **ad·jec·ti·val** \ˌaj-ik-ˈtī-vəl\ *adj* — **ad·jec·ti·val·ly** \-ē\ *adv*

ad·join \ə-ˈjȯin\ *vb* : to be situated next to

ad·join·ing *adj* : touching or bounding at a point or line

ad·journ \ə-ˈjərn\ *vb* **1** : to suspend indefinitely or until a stated time **2** : to transfer to another place — **ad·journ·ment** *n*

ad·judge \ə-ˈjəj\ *vb* **ad·judged; ad·judg·ing 1** : JUDGE, ADJUDICATE **2** : to hold or pronounce to be : DEEM **3** : to award by judicial decision

ad·ju·di·cate \ə-ˈjüd-i-ˌkāt\ *vb* **-cat·ed; -cat·ing** : to settle judicially — **ad·ju·di·ca·tion** \ə-ˌjüd-i-ˈkā-shən\ *n*

ad·junct \ˈaj-ˌəŋkt\ *n* : something joined or added to another but not essentially a part of it **syn** appendage, appurtenance, accessory, appendix

ad·jure \ə-ˈjür\ *vb* **ad·jured; ad·jur·ing** : to command solemnly : urge earnestly **syn** beg, beseech, implore — **ad·ju·ra·tion** \ˌaj-ə-ˈrā-shən\ *n*

ad·just \ə-ˈjəst\ *vb* **1** : to bring to agreement : SETTLE **2** : to cause to conform : ADAPT, FIT **3** : REGULATE ⟨∼ a watch⟩ — **ad·just·able** *adj* — **ad·just·er** *also* **ad·jus·tor** \ə-ˈjəs-tər\ *n* — **ad·just·ment** \ə-ˈjəs(t)-mənt\ *n*

ad·ju·tant \ˈaj-ət-ənt\ *n* : one who assists; *esp* : an officer who assists a commanding officer by handling correspondence and keeping records

ad·ju·vant \ˈaj-ə-vənt\ *n* : one that helps or facilitates; *esp* : something that enhances the effectiveness of medical treatment — **adjuvant** *adj*

¹**ad–lib** \ˈad-ˈlib\ *vb* **ad–libbed; ad–lib·bing** : IMPROVISE — **ad–lib** *n*

²**ad–lib** *adj* : spoken, composed, or performed without preparation

ad lib \ˈad-ˈlib\ *adv* [NL *ad libitum*] **1** : at one's pleasure **2** : without limit

ad li·bi·tum \ad-ˈlib-ət-əm\ *adj* [NL, in accordance with desire] : omissible according to a performer's wishes — used as a direction in music

adm *abbr* administration; administrative

ADM *abbr* admiral

ad•man \\'ad-,man\ *n* : one who writes, solicits, or places advertisements

admin *abbr* administration

ad•min•is•ter \əd-'min-ə-stər\ *vb* **-tered; -ter•ing** \-st(ə-)riŋ\ **1** : MANAGE, SUPERINTEND **2** : to mete out : DISPENSE **3** : to give ritually or remedially ⟨~ quinine for malaria⟩ **4** : to perform the office of administrator — **ad•min•is•tra•ble** \-strə-bəl\ *adj* — **ad•min•is•trant** \-strənt\ *n*

ad•min•is•tra•tion \əd-,min-ə-'strā-shən, (,)ad-\ *n* **1** : the act or process of administering **2** : MANAGEMENT **3** : the body of persons directing the government of a country **4** : the term of office of an administrative officer or body — **ad•min•is•tra•tive** \əd-'min-ə-,strāt-iv\ *adj* — **ad•min•is•tra•tive•ly** *adv*

ad•min•is•tra•tor \əd-'min-ə-,strāt-ər\ *n* : one that administers; *esp* : one who settles an intestate estate

ad•mi•ra•ble \\'ad-m(ə-)rə-bəl\ *adj* : worthy of admiration : EXCELLENT — **ad•mi•ra•bly** \-blē\ *adv*

ad•mi•ral \\'ad-m(ə-)rəl\ *n* [ME, fr. MF *amiral* admiral & ML *admiralis* emir, *admirallus* admiral, deriv. of Ar *amīr* commander] : a commissioned officer in the navy ranking next below a fleet admiral

ad•mi•ral•ty \\'ad-m(ə-)rəl-tē\ *n* **1** *cap* : a British government department formerly having authority over naval affairs **2** : the court having jurisdiction over maritime questions

ad•mire \əd-'mī(ə)r\ *vb* **ad•mired; ad•mir•ing** [MF *admirer*, fr. L *admirari*, fr. *ad-* to + *mirari* to wonder] : to regard with high esteem — **ad•mi•ra•tion** \,ad-mə-'rā-shən\ *n* — **ad•mir•er** *n* — **ad•mir•ing•ly** \-'mī-riŋ-lē\ *adv*

ad•mis•si•ble \əd-'mis-ə-bəl\ *adj* : that can be or is worthy to be admitted or allowed : ALLOWABLE ⟨~ evidence⟩ — **ad•mis•si•bil•i•ty** \-,mis-ə-'bil-ət-ē\ *n*

ad•mis•sion \əd-'mish-ən\ *n* **1** : the granting of an argument **2** : the acknowledgment of a fact **3** : the act of admitting **4** : the privilege of being admitted **5** : a fee paid for admission

ad•mit \əd-'mit\ *vb* **ad•mit•ted; ad•mit•ting 1** : PERMIT, ALLOW **2** : to allow to enter **3** : to recognize as genuine or valid — **ad•mit•ted•ly** *adv*

ad•mit•tance \əd-'mit-ᵊns\ *n* : permission to enter

ad•mix \ad-'miks\ *vb* : MINGLE, MIX

ad•mix•ture \ad-'miks-chər\ *n* **1** : something added in mixing **2** : MIXTURE

ad•mon•ish \ad-'män-ish\ *vb* : to warn gently : reprove with a warning **syn** chide, reproach, rebuke, reprimand, reprove — **ad•mo•ni•tion** \,ad-mə-'nish-ən\ *n* — **ad•mon•i•to•ry** \ad-'män-ə-,tōr-ē\ *adj*

ad nau•se•am \ad-'nò-zē-əm\ *adv* [L] : to a sickening degree

ado \ə-'dü\ *n* **1** : bustling excitement : FUSS **2** : TROUBLE

ado•be \ə-'dō-bē\ *n* [Sp, fr. Ar *aṭ-ṭūb*, fr. Coptic *tōbe*] **1** : sun-dried brick; *also* : clay for making such bricks **2** : a structure made of adobe bricks — **adobe** *adj*

ad•o•les•cence \,ad-ᵊl-'es-ᵊns\ *n* : the process or period of growth between childhood and maturity — **ad•o•les•cent** \-ᵊnt\ *adj or n*

adopt \ə-'däpt\ *vb* **1** : to take (a child of other parents) as one's own child **2** : to take up and practice as one's own **3** : to accept formally and put into effect — **adop•tion** \-'däp-shən\ *n*

adop•tive \ə-'däp-tiv\ *adj* : made or acquired by adoption ⟨~ father⟩ — **adop•tive•ly** *adv*

ador•able \ə-'dōr-ə-bəl\ *adj* **1** : worthy of adoration **2** : extremely charming — **ador•ably** \-blē\ *adv*

adore \ə-'dòr\ *vb* **adored; ador•ing** [MF *adorer*, fr. L *adorare*, fr. *ad-* to + *orare* to speak, pray] **1** : WORSHIP **2** : to regard with reverent admiration **3** : to be extremely fond of — **ad•o•ra•tion** \,ad-ə-'rā-shən\ *n*

adorn \ə-'dòrn\ *vb* : to decorate with ornaments — **adorn•ment** *n*

ad•re•nal \ə-'drēn-ᵊl\ *adj* : of, relating to, or being a pair of endocrine organs (**adrenal glands**) that are located near the kidneys and produce several hormones and esp. epinephrine

adren•a•line \ə-'dren-ᵊl-ən\ *n* : EPINEPHRINE

adrift \ə-'drift\ *adv or adj* **1** : afloat without motive power or moorings **2** : without guidance or purpose

adroit \ə-'dròit\ *adj* [F, fr. OF, fr. *a-* to + *droit* right] **1** : dexterous with one's hands **2** : SHREWD, RESOURCEFUL

syn canny, clever, cunning, ingenious — **adroit•ly** *adv* — **adroit•ness** *n*

ad•sorb \ad-'sȯrb, -'zȯrb\ *vb* : to take up (as molecules of gases) and hold on the surface of a solid or liquid — **ad•sorp•tion** \-'sȯrp-shən, -'zȯrp-\ *n* — **ad•sorp•tive** \-'sȯrp-tiv, -'zȯrp-\ *adj*

ad•u•late \'aj-ə-ˌlāt\ *vb* **-lat•ed; -lat•ing** : to flatter or admire excessively — **ad•u•la•tion** \ˌaj-ə-'lā-shən\ *n*

¹**adult** \ə-'dəlt, 'ad-ˌəlt\ *adj* [L *adultus,* pp. of *adolescere* to grow up, fr. *ad-* to + *-olescere* (fr. *alescere* to grow)] : fully developed and mature — **adult•hood** *n*

²**adult** *n* : one that is adult; *esp* : a human being after an age (as 18) specified by law

adul•ter•ant \ə-'dəl-tə-rənt\ *n* : something used to adulterate another

adul•ter•ate \ə-'dəl-tə-ˌrāt\ *vb* **-at•ed; -at•ing** [L *adulterare,* fr. *ad-* to + *alter* other] : to make impure by mixing in a foreign or inferior substance — **adul•ter•a•tion** \-ˌdəl-tə-'rā-shən\ *n*

adul•tery \ə-'dəl-t(ə-)rē\ *n, pl* **-ter•ies** : sexual unfaithfulness of a married person — **adul•ter•er** \-tər-ər\ *n* — **adul•ter•ess** \-t(ə-)rəs\ *n* — **adul•ter•ous** \-t(ə-)rəs\ *adj*

ad•um•brate \'ad-əm-ˌbrāt\ *vb* **-brat•ed; -brat•ing** 1 : to foreshadow vaguely : INTIMATE 2 : to suggest or disclose partially 3 : SHADE, OBSCURE — **ad•um•bra•tion** \ˌad-əm-'brā-shən\ *n*

adv *abbr* 1 adverb 2 advertisement

ad va•lor•em \ˌad-və-'lōr-əm\ *adj* [L, according to the value] : imposed at a percentage of the value ⟨an *ad valorem* tax⟩

¹**ad•vance** \əd-'vans\ *vb* **ad•vanced; ad•vanc•ing** 1 : to bring or move forward 2 : to assist the progress of 3 : to promote in rank 4 : to make earlier in time 5 : LEND 6 : PROPOSE 7 : to raise in rate : INCREASE — **ad•vance•ment** *n*

²**advance** *n* 1 : a forward movement 2 : IMPROVEMENT 3 : a rise esp. in price or value 4 : OFFER — **in advance** : BEFOREHAND

³**advance** *adj* : made, sent, or furnished ahead of time

ad•van•tage \əd-'vant-ij\ *n* 1 : superiority of position 2 : BENEFIT, GAIN 3 : the 1st point won in tennis after deuce —

ad•van•ta•geous \ˌad-ˌvan-'tā-jəs, -vən-\ *adj* — **ad•van•ta•geous•ly** *adv*

ad•vent \'ad-ˌvent\ *n* 1 *cap* : a penitential period beginning four Sundays before Christmas 2 : ARRIVAL; *esp, cap* : the coming of Christ

ad•ven•ti•tious \ˌad-vən-'tish-əs\ *adj* 1 : ACCIDENTAL, INCIDENTAL 2 : arising or occurring sporadically or in other than the usual location ⟨∼ buds⟩ — **ad•ven•ti•tious•ly** *adv*

¹**ad•ven•ture** \əd-'ven-chər\ *n* 1 : a risky undertaking 2 : a remarkable and exciting experience — **ad•ven•tur•ous** \-'vench-(ə-)rəs\ *adj*

²**adventure** *vb* **-ven•tured; -ven•tur•ing** \-'vench-(ə-)riŋ\ : RISK, HAZARD

ad•ven•tur•er \əd-'vench-(ə-)rər\ *n* 1 : a person who engages in new and risky undertakings 2 : a person who follows a military career for adventure or profit 3 : a person who tries to gain wealth by questionable means

ad•ven•ture•some \əd-'ven-chər-səm\ *adj* : inclined to take risks

ad•ven•tur•ess \əd-'vench-(ə-)rəs\ *n* : a female adventurer

ad•verb \'ad-ˌvərb\ *n* : a word that typically serves as a modifier of a verb, an adjective, or another adverb — **ad•ver•bi•al** \ad-'vər-bē-əl\ *adj* — **ad•ver•bi•al•ly** \-ē\ *adv*

¹**ad•ver•sary** \'ad-və(r)-ˌser-ē\ *n, pl* **-sar•ies** : FOE

²**adversary** *adj* : involving antagonistic parties or interests

ad•verse \ad-'vərs, 'ad-ˌvərs\ *adj* 1 : acting against or in a contrary direction 2 : UNFAVORABLE — **ad•verse•ly** *adv*

ad•ver•si•ty \ad-'vər-sət-ē\ *n, pl* **-ties** : hard times : MISFORTUNE

ad•vert \ad-'vərt\ *vb* : REFER

ad•ver•tise \'ad-vər-ˌtīz\ *vb* **-tised; -tis•ing** 1 : INFORM, NOTIFY 2 : to call public attention to esp. in order to sell — **ad•ver•tis•er** *n*

ad•ver•tise•ment \ˌad-vər-'tīz-mənt; əd-'vərt-əs-mənt\ *n* 1 : the act of advertising 2 : a public notice intended to advertise something

ad•ver•tis•ing \'ad-vər-ˌtī-ziŋ\ *n* : the business of preparing advertisements

ad•vice \əd-'vīs\ *n* 1 : recommendation with regard to a course of action : COUNSEL 2 : INFORMATION, REPORT

ad·vis·able \əd-'vī-zə-bəl\ *adj* : proper to be done : EXPEDIENT — **ad·vis·abil·i·ty** \-ˌvī-zə-'bil-ət-ē\ *n*

ad·vise \əd-'vīz\ *vb* **ad·vised; ad·vis·ing** **1** : to give advice to : COUNSEL **2** : INFORM, NOTIFY **3** : CONSULT, CONFER — **ad·vis·er** *or* **ad·vi·sor** \-'vī-zər\ *n*

ad·vised \əd-'vīzd\ *adj* : thought out : CONSIDERED ⟨well-*advised*⟩ — **ad·vis·ed·ly** \-'vī-zəd-lē\ *adv*

ad·vise·ment \əd-'vīz-mənt\ *n* : careful consideration

ad·vi·so·ry \əd-'vīz-(ə-)rē\ *adj* **1** : having or exercising power to advise **2** : containing advice

¹ad·vo·cate \'ad-və-kət, -ˌkāt\ *n* [deriv. of L *advocare* to summon, fr. *ad*- to + *vocare* to call] **1** : one who pleads another's cause **2** : one who argues or pleads for a cause or proposal — **ad·vo·ca·cy** \-və-kə-sē\ *n*

²ad·vo·cate \-ˌkāt\ *vb* **-cat·ed; -cat·ing** : to plead in favor of — **ad·vo·ca·tion** \ˌad-və-'kā-shən\ *n*

advt *abbr* advertisement

adz *or* **adze** \'adz\ *n* : a cutting tool that has a curved blade set at right angles to the handle and is used in shaping wood

AEC *abbr* Atomic Energy Commission

ae·gis \'ē-jəs\ *n* [L, fr. Gk *aigis* goatskin] **1** : SHIELD, PROTECTION **2** : PATRONAGE, SPONSORSHIP

ae·o·li·an harp \ē-ˌō-lē-ən-\ *n* : a box with strings that produce musical sounds when wind blows on them

ae·on \'ē-ən,'ē-ˌän\ *n* : an indefinitely long time : AGE

aer·ate \'a(-ə)r-ˌāt\ *vb* **aer·at·ed; aer·at·ing** **1** : to supply (blood) with oxygen by respiration **2** : to supply or impregnate with air **3** : to combine or charge with gas — **aer·a·tion** \ˌa(-ə)r-'ā-shən\ *n* — **aer·a·tor** \'a(-ə)r-ˌāt-ər\ *n*

¹ae·ri·al \'ar-ē-əl, ā-'ir-ē-əl\ *adj* **1** : inhabiting, occurring in, or done in the air **2** : AIRY **3** : of or relating to aircraft

²aer·i·al \'ar-ē-əl\ *n* : ANTENNA 2

ae·ri·al·ist \'ar-ē-ə-ləst, ā-'ir-\ *n* : a performer of feats above the ground esp. on a flying trapeze

ae·rie \'a(ə)r-ē, 'i(ə)r-ē\ *n* : a highly placed nest (as of an eagle)

aer·o·bat·ics \ˌar-ə-'bat-iks\ *n sing or pl* : spectacular flying feats and maneuvers

aer·o·bic \ˌa(-ə)r-'rō-bik\ *adj* : living or active only in the presence of oxygen ⟨~ bacteria⟩ — **aer·obe** \'a(-ə)r-ˌōb\ *n* — **aer·o·bi·cal·ly** \-bi-k(ə-)lē\ *adv*

aer·o·bics \-biks\ *n sing or pl* : a system of exercises designed to improve the body's ability to take in and use oxygen

aero·drome \'ar-ə-ˌdrōm\ *n, chiefly Brit* : AIRFIELD, AIRPORT

aero·dy·nam·ics \ˌar-ō-dī-'nam-iks\ *n* : the science dealing with the forces acting on bodies in motion in a gas (as air) — **aero·dy·nam·ic** \-ik\ *or* **aero·dy·nam·i·cal** \-i-kəl\ *adj* — **aero·dy·nam·i·cal·ly** \-i-k(ə-)lē\ *adv*

aero·naut \'ar-ə-ˌnȯt\ *n* : one who operates or travels in an airship or balloon

aero·nau·tics \ˌar-ə-'nȯt-iks\ *n* : the science of aircraft operation — **aero·nau·ti·cal** \-i-kəl\ *or* **aero·nau·tic** \-ik\ *adj*

aero·plane \'ar-ə-ˌplān\ *chiefly Brit var of* AIRPLANE

aero·sol \'ar-ə-ˌsäl, -ˌsȯl\ *n* **1** : a suspension of fine solid or liquid particles in a gas **2** : a substance (as an insecticide or cosmetic) dispensed from a pressurized container as an aerosol

aero·space \'ar-ō-ˌspās\ *n* : the earth's atmosphere and the space beyond — **aerospace** *adj*

aery \'a(ə)r-ē\ *adj* **aer·i·er; -est** : having an aerial quality : ETHEREAL

aes·thete \'es-ˌthēt\ *n* : a person having or affecting sensitivity to beauty esp. in art

aes·thet·ic \es-'thet-ik\ *adj* **1** : of or relating to aesthetics : ARTISTIC **2** : appreciative of the beautiful — **aes·thet·i·cal·ly** \-i-k(ə-)lē\ *adv*

aes·thet·ics \-'thet-iks\ *n* : a branch of philosophy dealing with the nature, creation, and appreciation of beauty

aes·ti·vate *var of* ESTIVATE

AF *abbr* **1** air force **2** audio frequency

¹afar \ə-'fär\ *adv* : from, at, or to a great distance

²afar *n* : a great distance

AFB *abbr* air force base

AFC *abbr* **1** American Football Conference **2** automatic frequency control

AFDC *abbr* Aid to Families with Dependent Children

af·fa·ble \'af-ə-bəl\ *adj* : courteous and agreeable in conversation — **af·fa·bil-**

i·ty \ˌaf-ə-'bil-ət-ē\ *n* — **af·fa·bly** \'af-ə-blē\ *adv*

af·fair \ə-'faər\ *n* [ME *affaire,* fr. MF, fr. *a faire* to do] **1** : something that relates to or involves one : CONCERN **2** : a romantic or sexual attachment of limited duration

¹af·fect \ə-'fekt, a-\ *vb* **1** : to be fond of using or wearing **2** : SIMULATE, ASSUME, PRETEND

²affect *vb* : to produce an effect on : INFLUENCE, IMPRESS

af·fec·ta·tion \ˌaf-ˌek-'tā-shən\ *n* : an attitude or mode of behavior assumed by a person in an effort to impress others

af·fect·ed \ə-'fek-təd, a-\ *adj* **1** : pretending to some trait which is not natural **2** : artificially assumed to impress others — **af·fect·ed·ly** *adv*

af·fect·ing \ə-'fek-tiŋ, a-\ *adj* : arousing pity, sympathy, or sorrow ⟨an ∼ story⟩ — **af·fect·ing·ly** *adv*

¹af·fec·tion \ə-'fek-shən\ *n* : tender attachment : LOVE — **af·fec·tion·ate** \-sh(ə-)nət\ *adj* — **af·fec·tion·ate·ly** *adv*

²affection *n* : DISEASE, DISORDER ⟨an ∼ of the brain⟩

af·fer·ent \'af-ə-rənt, -ˌer-ənt\ *adj* : bearing or conducting inward toward a more central part and esp. a nerve center (as the brain or spinal cord) ⟨∼ nerves⟩

af·fi·ance \ə-'fī-əns\ *vb* **-anced; -anc·ing** : BETROTH, ENGAGE

af·fi·da·vit \ˌaf-ə-'dā-vət\ *n* [ML, he has made an oath] : a sworn statement in writing

¹af·fil·i·ate \ə-'fil-ē-ˌāt\ *vb* **-at·ed; -at·ing** : to associate as a member or branch — **af·fil·i·a·tion** \-ˌfil-ē-'ā-shən\ *n*

²af·fil·i·ate \ə-'fil-ē-ət\ *n* : an affiliated person or organization

af·fin·i·ty \ə-'fin-ət-ē\ *n, pl* **-ties 1** : KINSHIP, RELATIONSHIP **2** : attractive force : ATTRACTION, SYMPATHY

af·firm \ə-'fərm\ *vb* **1** : CONFIRM, RATIFY **2** : to assert positively **syn** aver, avow, avouch, declare, assert — **af·fir·ma·tion** \ˌaf-ər-'mā-shən\ *n*

¹af·fir·ma·tive \ə-'fər-mət-iv\ *adj* : asserting that the fact is so : POSITIVE

²affirmative *n* **1** : an expression of affirmation or assent **2** : the side that upholds the proposition stated in a debate

affirmative action *n* : an active effort to improve the employment or educational opportunities of members of minority groups and women

¹af·fix \ə-'fiks\ *vb* : ATTACH, ADD

²af·fix \'af-ˌiks\ *n* : one or more sounds or letters attached to the beginning or end of a word and serving to produce a derivative word or an inflectional form

af·fla·tus \ə-'flāt-əs\ *n* : divine inspiration

af·flict \ə-'flikt\ *vb* : to cause pain and distress to **syn** rack, try, torment, torture — **af·flic·tion** \-'flik-shən\ *n*

af·flic·tive \ə-'flik-tiv\ *adj* : causing affliction : DISTRESSING — **af·flic·tive·ly** *adv*

af·flu·ence \'af-ˌlü-ən(t)s; a-'flü-, ə-\ *n* : abundant supply; *also* : WEALTH, RICHES — **af·flu·ent** \-ənt\ *adj*

af·ford \ə-'fōrd\ *vb* **1** : to manage to bear or bear the cost of without serious harm or loss **2** : PROVIDE, FURNISH

af·for·es·ta·tion \a-ˌför-ə-'stā-shən\ *n* : the act or process of establishing forest cover — **af·for·est** \a-'för-əst, -'fär-\ *vb*

af·fray \ə-'frā\ *n* : FIGHT, FRAY

af·fright \ə-'frīt\ *vb* : FRIGHTEN, ALARM — **affright** *n*

af·front \ə-'frənt\ *vb* **1** : INSULT **2** : CONFRONT — **affront** *n*

af·ghan \'af-ˌgan\ *n* : a blanket or shawl of colored wool knitted or crocheted in sections

Af·ghan \'af-ˌgan\ *n* : a native or inhabitant of Afghanistan — **Afghan** *adj*

Afghan hound *n* : any of a breed of tall slim swift hunting dogs with a coat of silky thick hair and a long silky top knot

af·ghani \af-'gan-ē\ *n* — see MONEY table

afi·cio·na·do \ə-ˌfish(-ē)-ə-'näd-ō, -ˌfis-ē-\ *n, pl* **-dos** [Sp, deriv. of *afición* affection] : DEVOTEE, FAN

afield \ə-'fēld\ *adv or adj* **1** : to, in, or on the field **2** : away from home **3** : out of the way : ASTRAY

afire \ə-'fī(ə)r\ *adj or adv* : being on fire : BURNING

AFL *abbr* American Football League

aflame \ə-'flām\ *adj or adv* : FLAMING

AFL-CIO *abbr* American Federation of

Labor and Congress of Industrial Organizations

afloat \ə-'flōt\ *adj or adv* **1** : borne on or as if on the water **2** : being on board ship **3** : ADRIFT

aflut•ter \ə-'flət-ər\ *adj* **1** : FLUTTERING **2** : nervously excited

afoot \ə-'fût\ *adv or adj* **1** : on foot **2** : in action : in progress

afore•men•tioned \ə-'fōr-'men-chənd\ *adj* : mentioned previously

afore•said \-ˌsed\ *adj* : said or named before

afore•thought \-ˌthot\ *adj* : PREMEDITATED ⟨with malice ∼⟩

a for•ti•o•ri \ˌä-ˌfört-ē-'ōr-ē\ *adv* [NL, lit., from the stronger (argument)] : with even greater reason

afoul of \ə-'faùl-əv\ *prep* **1** : in or into collision or entanglement with **2** : in or into conflict with

Afr *abbr* Africa; African

afraid \ə-'frād, *South also* ə-'fre(ə)d\ *adj* : FRIGHTENED, FEARFUL

A–frame \'ā-ˌfrām\ *n* : a building having triangular front and rear walls with the roof reaching to the ground

afresh \ə-'fresh\ *adv* : ANEW, AGAIN

Af•ri•can \'af-ri-kən\ *n* **1** : a native or inhabitant of Africa **2** : NEGRO — **African** *adj*

African violet *n* : a tropical African plant widely grown indoors for its velvety fleshy leaves and showy purple, pink, or white flowers

Af•ri•kaans \ˌaf-ri-'käns\ *n* : a language developed from 17th century Dutch that is one of the official languages of the Republic of So. Africa

¹**Af•ro** \'af-rō\ *adj* : having the hair shaped into a round bushy mass

²**Afro** *n, pl* **Afros** : an Afro hairstyle

Af•ro–Amer•i•can \ˌaf-rō-ə-'mer-ə-kən\ *n* : an American of African and esp. of Negroid descent — **Afro–American** *adj*

aft \'aft\ *adv* : near, toward, or in the stern of a ship or the tail of an aircraft

AFT *abbr* American Federation of Teachers

¹**af•ter** \'af-tər\ *adv* : AFTERWARD, SUBSEQUENTLY

²**after** *prep* **1** : behind in place **2** : later than **3** : intent on the seizure, mastery, or achievement of ⟨he's ∼ your job⟩

³**after** *conj* : following the time when

⁴**after** *adj* **1** : LATER **2** : located toward the rear

af•ter•birth \'af-tər-ˌbərth\ *n* : the placenta and membranes of the fetus that are expelled after childbirth

af•ter•burn•er \-ˌbər-nər\ *n* : a device incorporated in the tail pipe of a turbojet engine for injecting fuel into the hot exhaust gases and burning it to provide extra thrust

af•ter•care \-ˌkeər\ *n* : the care, nursing, or treatment of a convalescent patient

af•ter•deck \-ˌdek\ *n* : the rear half of the deck of a ship

af•ter•ef•fect \'af-tə-rə-ˌfekt\ *n* : an effect that follows its cause after an interval

af•ter•glow \'af-tər-ˌglō\ *n* : a glow remaining where a light has disappeared

af•ter•im•age \'af-tə-ˌrim-ij\ *n* : a usu. visual sensation continuing after the stimulus causing it has ended

af•ter•life \'af-tər-ˌlīf\ *n* : an existence after death

af•ter•math \-ˌmath\ *n* **1** : a second growth crop esp. of hay **2** : CONSEQUENCES, EFFECTS **syn** aftereffect, upshot, result, outcome

af•ter•noon \ˌaf-tər-'nün\ *n* : the time between noon and evening

af•ter–shave \'af-tər-ˌshāv\ *n* : a usu. scented lotion for the face after shaving

af•ter•taste \-ˌtāst\ *n* : a sensation (as of flavor) continuing after the stimulus causing it has ended

af•ter–tax \'af-tər-ˌtaks\ *adj* : remaining after payment of taxes and esp. of income tax ⟨an ∼ profit⟩

af•ter•thought \-ˌthot\ *n* : a later thought; *also* : something thought of later

af•ter•ward \'af-tə(r)-wərd\ *or* **af•ter•wards** \-wərdz\ *adv* : at a later time

Ag *symbol* [L *argentum*] silver

AG *abbr* **1** adjutant general **2** attorney general

again \ə-'gen, -'gin\ *adv* **1** : once more : ANEW **2** : on the other hand **3** : in addition : BESIDES

against \ə-'genst\ *prep* **1** : directly opposite to : FACING **2** : in opposition to **3** : as defense from **4** : so as to touch

or strike ⟨threw him ~ the wall⟩; *also*
: TOUCHING

¹agape \ə-ˈgāp\ *adj or adv* : having the
mouth open in wonder or surprise
: GAPING

²aga·pe \ä-ˈgä-pā, ˈäg-ə-ˌpā\ *n* [Gk, lit.,
love] : self-giving loyal concern that
freely accepts another and seeks his
or her good

agar \ˈäg-ˌär\ *n* **1** : a jellylike substance
extracted from a red alga and used
esp. as a gelling and stabilizing agent
in foods **2** : a culture medium containing agar

agar–agar \ˌäg-ˌär-ˈäg-ˌär\ *n* : AGAR

ag·ate \ˈag-ət\ *n* **1** : a striped or clouded
quartz **2** : a playing marble of agate or
of glass

aga·ve \ə-ˈgäv-ē\ *n* : any of a genus of
spiny-leaved plants (as a century
plant) related to the amaryllis

agcy *abbr* agency

¹age \ˈāj\ *n* **1** : the length of time during
which a being or thing has lived or
existed **2** : the time of life at which
some particular qualification is
achieved; *esp* : MAJORITY **3** : the latter
part of life **4** : a long time **5** : a period
in history

²age *vb* **aged; ag·ing** *or* **age·ing 1** : to
grow old or cause to grow old **2** : to
become or cause to become mature or
mellow

-age \ij\ *n suffix* **1** : aggregate : collection ⟨track*age*⟩ **2** : action : process
⟨haul*age*⟩ **3** : cumulative result of
⟨break*age*⟩ **4** : rate of ⟨dos*age*⟩ **5**
: house or place of ⟨orphan*age*⟩ **6**
: state : rank ⟨vassal*age*⟩ **7** : fee
: charge ⟨post*age*⟩

aged \ˈā-jəd *for 1;* ˈājd *for 2*\ *adj* **1** : of
advanced age **2** : having attained a
specified age ⟨a man ~ 40 years⟩

age·less \ˈāj-ləs\ *adj* **1** : not growing old
or showing the effects of age **2** : TIME-
LESS, ETERNAL ⟨an ~ story⟩

agen·cy \ˈā-jən-sē\ *n, pl* **-cies 1** : one
through which something is accom-
plished : INSTRUMENTALITY **2** : the office or function of an agent **3** : an establishment doing business for
another **4** : an administrative division
(as of a government) **syn** means, medium, vehicle

agen·da \ə-ˈjən-də\ *n* : a list of things to
be done : PROGRAM

agent \ˈā-jənt\ *n* **1** : one that acts **2**
: MEANS, INSTRUMENT **3** : a person acting or doing business for another **syn**
attorney, deputy, proxy, delegate

Agent Orange *n* : an herbicide widely
used in the Vietnam War that is composed of 2,4-D and 2,4,5-T and contains a toxic contaminant

agent pro·vo·ca·teur \ˈäzh-ˌäⁿ-prō-
ˌväk-ə-ˈtər, ˈā-jənt-\ *n, pl* **agents
provocateurs** \ˈäzh-ˌäⁿ-prō-ˌväk-ə-
ˈtər, ˈā-jənts-prō-\ [F] : a person hired
to infiltrate a group and incite its
members to illegal action

age of consent : the age at which one is
legally competent to give consent (as
to marriage)

age–old \ˈāj-ˈōld\ *adj* : having existed
for ages : ANCIENT

ag·er·a·tum \ˌaj-ə-ˈrāt-əm\ *n, pl* **-tums**
: any of a large genus of tropical
American plants that are related to the
daisies and have small showy heads of
blue or white flowers

Ag·ge·us \a-ˈgē-əs\ *n* — see BIBLE table

¹ag·glom·er·ate \ə-ˈgläm-ə-ˌrāt\ *vb* **-at-
ed; -at·ing** [L *agglomerare* to heap up,
join, fr. *ad-* to + *glomer-, glomus*
ball] : to gather into a mass : CLUSTER
— **ag·glom·er·a·tion** \-ˌgläm-ə-
ˈrā-shən\ *n*

²ag·glom·er·ate \-rət\ *n* : rock composed
of volcanic fragments

ag·glu·ti·nate \ə-ˈglüt-ᵊn-ˌāt\ *vb* **-nat·ed;
-nat·ing 1** : to cause to adhere : gather
into a group or mass **2** : to cause (as
red blood cells or bacteria) to collect
into clumps — **ag·glu·ti·na·tion** \-ˌglüt-
ᵊn-ˈā-shən\ *n*

ag·gran·dize \ə-ˈgran-ˌdīz, ˈag-rən-\ *vb*
-dized; -diz·ing : to make great or
greater — **ag·gran·dize·ment** \ə-ˈgran-
dəz-mənt, -ˌdīz-; ˌag-rən-ˈdīz-\ *n*

ag·gra·vate \ˈag-rə-ˌvāt\ *vb* **-vat·ed;
-vat·ing 1** : to make more severe : IN-
TENSIFY **2** : IRRITATE — **ag·gra·va·tion**
\ˌag-rə-ˈvā-shən\ *n*

¹ag·gre·gate \ˈag-ri-gət\ *adj* : formed by
the gathering of units into one mass

²ag·gre·gate \-ˌgāt\ *vb* **-gat·ed; -gat·ing**
: to collect into one mass

³ag·gre·gate \-gət\ *n* : a mass or body of
units or parts somewhat loosely associated with one another; *also* : the
whole amount

ag·gre·ga·tion \ˌag-ri-ˈgā-shən\ *n* **1** : a

group, body, or mass composed of many distinct parts **2** : the collecting of units or parts into a mass or whole

ag·gres·sion \ə-'gresh-ən\ *n* **1** : an unprovoked attack **2** : the practice of making attacks **3** : hostile, injurious, or destructive behavior or outlook esp. when caused by frustration — **ag·gres·sor** \-'gres-ər\ *n*

ag·gres·sive \ə-'gres-iv\ *adj* **1** : tending toward or exhibiting aggression; *esp* : marked by combative readiness **2** : marked by driving energy or initiative : ENTERPRISING — **ag·gres·sive·ly** *adv* — **ag·gres·sive·ness** *n*

ag·grieve \ə-'grēv\ *vb* **ag·grieved; ag·griev·ing 1** : to cause grief to **2** : to inflict injury on : WRONG

aghast \ə-'gast\ *adj* : struck with amazement or horror

ag·ile \'aj-əl\ *adj* : able to move quickly and easily — **agil·i·ty** \ə-'jil-ət-ē\ *n*

ag·i·tate \'aj-ə-ˌtāt\ *vb* **-tat·ed; -tat·ing 1** : to move with an irregular rapid motion **2** : to stir up : EXCITE **3** : to discuss earnestly **4** : to attempt to arouse public feeling — **ag·i·ta·tion** \ˌaj-ə-'tā-shən\ *n* — **ag·i·ta·tor** \'aj-ə-ˌtāt-ər\ *n*

ag·it·prop \'aj-ət-ˌpräp\ *n* [Russ] : political propaganda promulgated esp. through the arts

agleam \ə-'glēm\ *adj* : GLEAMING

aglit·ter \ə-'glit-ər\ *adj* : GLITTERING

aglow \ə-'glō\ *adj* : GLOWING

ag·nos·tic \ag-'näs-tik, əg-\ *adj* [Gk *agnōstos* unknown, unknowable, fr. *a-* un- + *gnōstos* known] : of or relating to the belief that the existence of any ultimate reality (as God) is unknown and prob. unknowable — **agnostic** *n* — **ag·nos·ti·cism** \-'näs-tə-ˌsiz-əm\ *n*

ago \ə-'gō\ *adj or adv* : earlier than the present time

agog \ə-'gäg\ *adj* [MF *en gogues* in mirth] : full of excitement : EAGER

¹**a–go–go** \ä-'gō-ˌgō\ *n* [*Whisky à Gogo,* café and discotheque in Paris, France, fr. F *à gogo* galore] : a nightclub for dancing to pop music : DISCOTHEQUE

²**a–go–go** *adj* : GO-GO

ag·o·nize \'ag-ə-ˌnīz\ *vb* **-nized; -niz·ing** : to suffer or cause to suffer agony — **ag·o·niz·ing·ly** *adv*

ag·o·ny \'ag-ə-nē\ *n, pl* **-nies** [ME *ago-*

nie, fr. L *agonia,* fr. Gk *agōnia* struggle, anguish, fr. *agōn* gathering, contest for a prize] : extreme pain of mind or body **syn** suffering, distress, misery

agony column *n* : a newspaper column of personal advertisements relating esp. to missing relatives or friends

ago·ra \ˌäg-ə-'rä\ *n, pl* **ago·rot** \-'rōt\ — see *shekel* at MONEY table

ag·o·ra·pho·bia \ˌag-ə-rə-'fō-bē-ə\ *n* : abnormal fear of being in open spaces — **ag·o·ra·pho·bic** \-'fō-bik, -'fäb-ik\ *adj or n*

agr *abbr* agricultural; agriculture

agrar·i·an \ə-'grer-ē-ən\ *adj* **1** : of or relating to land or its ownership ⟨∼ reforms⟩ **2** : of or relating to farmers or farming interests — **agrarian** *n* — **agrar·i·an·ism** *n*

agree \ə-'grē\ *vb* **agreed; agree·ing 1** : ADMIT, CONCEDE **2** : to be similar : CORRESPOND **3** : to express agreement or approval **4** : to be in harmony **5** : to settle by common consent **6** : to be fitting or healthful : SUIT

agree·able \ə-'grē-ə-bəl\ *adj* **1** : PLEASING, PLEASANT **2** : ready to consent **3** : being in harmony : CONSONANT — **agree·able·ness** *n* — **agree·ably** \-blē\ *adv*

agree·ment \ə-'grē-mənt\ *n* **1** : harmony of opinion or action **2** : mutual understanding or arrangement; *also* : a document containing such an arrangement

agric *abbr* agricultural; agriculture

ag·ri·cul·ture \'ag-ri-ˌkəl-chər\ *n* : FARMING, HUSBANDRY — **ag·ri·cul·tur·al** \ˌag-ri-'kəlch-(ə-)rəl\ *adj* — **ag·ri·cul·tur·ist** \-rəst\ *or* **ag·ri·cul·tur·al·ist** \-(ə-)rə-ləst\ *n*

agron·o·my \ə-'grän-ə-mē\ *n* : a branch of agriculture that deals with the raising of crops and the care of the soil — **ag·ro·nom·ic** \ˌag-rə-'näm-ik\ *adj* — **agron·o·mist** \ə-'grän-ə-məst\ *n*

aground \ə-'graund\ *adv or adj* : on or onto the bottom or shore ⟨ran ∼⟩

agt *abbr* agent

ague \'ā-gyü\ *n* : a fever (as malaria) with recurrent chills and sweating

ahead \ə-'hed\ *adv or adj* **1** : in or toward the front **2** : into or for the future ⟨plan ∼⟩ **3** : in or toward a more advantageous position

ahead of *prep* **1** : in front or advance of **2** : in excess of : ABOVE

AHL *abbr* American Hockey League

ahoy \ə-'hȯi\ *interj* — used in hailing ⟨ship ∼⟩

AI *abbr* artificial intelligence

¹**aid** \'ād\ *vb* : to provide with what is useful in achieving an end : ASSIST

²**aid** *n* **1** : ASSISTANCE **2** : ASSISTANT

AID *abbr* Agency for International Development

aide \'ād\ *n* : a person who acts as an assistant; *esp* : a military officer assisting a superior

aide–de–camp \ˌād-di-'kamp, -'käᵐ\ *n, pl* **aides–de–camp** \ˌādz-di-\ [F] : AIDE

aid·man \'ād-ˌman\ *n* : an army medical corpsman attached to a field unit

AIDS \'ādz\ *n* [*a*cquired *i*mmuno*d*eficiency *s*yndrome] : a serious disease associated with infection of the cells of the immune system by a retrovirus, occurring esp. in homosexual and bisexual men and in intravenous drug abusers, and recognized clinically usu. by a life-threatening infection (as pneumonia) or Kaposi's sarcoma or both in addition to marked depression of the immune system

AIDS–related complex *n* : a collection of symptoms (as fever, weight loss, and lymphadenopathy) that is associated with the presence of antibodies to the AIDS virus and is followed by the development of AIDS in a certain proportion of cases

AIDS virus *n* : the retrovirus associated with AIDS and the AIDS-related complex

ai·grette \ā-'gret, 'ā-ˌgret\ *n* [F, plume, egret] : a plume or decorative tuft for the head

ail \'āl\ *vb* **1** : to be the matter with : TROUBLE **2** : to be unwell

ai·lan·thus \ā-'lan-thəs\ *n* : any of a genus of Asian trees or shrubs with pinnate leaves and ill-scented greenish flowers

ai·le·ron \'ā-lə-ˌrän\ *n* : a movable part of an airplane wing used in banking

ail·ment \'āl-mənt\ *n* : a bodily disorder

¹**aim** \'ām\ *vb* [ME *aimen*, fr. MF *aesmer* & *esmer*; MF *aesmer*, fr. OF, fr. *a-* to (fr. L *ad-*) + *esmer* to estimate, fr. L *aestimare*] **1** : to point a weapon at an object **2** : to direct one's efforts : ASPIRE **3** : to direct to or toward a specified object or goal

²**aim** *n* **1** : the direction of a weapon **2** : OBJECT, PURPOSE — **aim·less** \-ləs\ *adj* — **aim·less·ly** *adv* — **aim·less·ness** *n*

AIM *abbr* American Indian Movement

ain't \'ānt\ **1** : are not **2** : is not **3** : am not — though disapproved by many and more common in less educated speech, used orally in most parts of the U.S. by many educated speakers esp. in the phrase *ain't I*

Ai·nu \'ī-nü\ *n, pl* **Ainu** *or* **Ainus** **1** : a member of an indigenous Caucasoid people of Japan **2** : the language of the Ainu people

¹**air** \'aər\ *n* **1** : the gaseous mixture surrounding the earth **2** : a light breeze **3** : COMPRESSED AIR ⟨∼ sprayer⟩ **4** : AIRCRAFT ⟨∼ patrol⟩ **5** : AVIATION ⟨∼ safety⟩ **6** : the medium of transmission of radio waves; *also* : RADIO, TELEVISION **7** : the outward appearance of a person or thing : MANNER **8** : an artificial manner **9** : MELODY, TUNE

²**air** *vb* **1** : to expose to the air **2** : to expose to public view

air bag *n* : a bag designed to fill automatically with gas to protect automobile passengers in case of accident

air·boat *n* : a shallow-draft boat driven by an airplane propeller

air·borne \'aər-ˌbȯrn\ *adj* : supported or transported by air

air brake *n* **1** : a brake operated by a piston driven by compressed air **2** : a surface for lowering an airplane's speed

air·brush \-ˌbrəsh\ *n* : a device for applying a fine spray (as of paint) by compressed air — **airbrush** *vb*

air–con·di·tion \ˌaər-kən-'dish-ən\ *vb* : to equip with an apparatus for filtering air and controlling its humidity and temperature — **air con·di·tion·er** \-'dish-(ə-)nər\ *n*

air·craft \'aər-ˌkraft\ *n, pl* **aircraft** : a vehicle for traveling through the air

aircraft carrier *n* : a warship with a deck on which airplanes can be launched and landed

air·drome \-ˌdrōm\ *n* : AIRPORT

air·drop \-ˌdräp\ *n* : delivery of cargo or personnel by parachute from an airplane in flight — **air–drop** *vb*

Aire·dale terrier \'aər-ˌdāl-\ *n* : any of a

breed of large terriers with a hard wiry coat

air·fare \-ˌfaər\ *n* : fare for travel by airplane

air·field \ˈaər-ˌfēld\ *n* **1** : the landing field of an airport **2** : AIRPORT

air·flow \-ˌflō\ *n* : the motion of air relative to a body in it

air·foil \-ˌfȯil\ *n* : an airplane surface (as a wing or rudder) designed to produce reaction from the air

air force *n* : the military organization of a nation for air warfare

air·frame \-ˌfrām\ *n* : the structure of an airplane or rocket without the power plant

air·freight \-ˈfrāt\ *n* : freight transport by air in volume; *also* : the charge for this service

air gun *n* **1** : a gun operated by compressed air **2** : a hand tool that works by compressed air; *esp* : AIRBRUSH

air lane *n* : AIRWAY 1

air·lift \ˈaər-ˌlift\ *n* : transportation (as of supplies or passengers) by aircraft — **airlift** *vb*

air·line \-ˌlīn\ *n* : a transportation system using airplanes

air·lin·er \ˈaər-ˌlī-nər\ *n* : a large passenger airplane operated by an airline

air lock *n* : an airtight chamber separating areas of different pressure

air·mail \ˈaər-ˈmāl, -ˌmāl\ *n* : the system of transporting mail by airplane; *also* : mail so transported — **airmail** *vb*

air·man \-mən\ *n* **1** : an enlisted man in the air force in one of the three ranks below sergeant **2** : AVIATOR, PILOT

airman basic *n* : an enlisted man of the lowest rank in the air force

airman first class *n* : an enlisted person in the air force with a rank just below that of sergeant

air mass *n* : a large horizontally homogeneous body of air

air·mo·bile \ˈaər-ˌmō-bəl, -ˌbēl\ *adj* : of, relating to, or being a military unit whose members are transported to combat areas usu. by helicopter

air·plane \-ˌplān\ *n* : a fixed-wing aircraft heavier than air that is driven by a propeller or jet engine and supported by the reaction of the air against its wings

air·play \-ˌplā\ *n* : the playing of recorded material on the air by a radio station

air pocket *n* : a condition of the atmosphere that causes an airplane to drop suddenly

air police *n* : the military police of an air force

air·port \ˈaər-ˌpȯrt\ *n* : a place maintained for the landing and takeoff of aircraft and for receiving and discharging passengers and cargo

air raid *n* : an attack by armed airplanes on a surface target

air·ship \ˈaər-ˌship\ *n* : a lighter-than-air aircraft having propulsion and steering systems

air·sick \-ˌsik\ *adj* : affected with motion sickness associated with flying — **air·sick·ness** *n*

air·space \-ˌspās\ *n* : the space above a nation and under its jurisdiction

air·speed \-ˌspēd\ *n* : the speed (as of an airplane) with relation to the air as distinguished from its speed relative to the earth

air·strip \-ˌstrip\ *n* : a runway without normal airport facilities

air·tight \ˈaər-ˈtīt\ *adj* **1** : so tightly sealed that no air can enter or escape **2** : leaving no opening for attack

air–to–air *adj* : launched from one airplane in flight at another; *also* : involving aircraft in flight

air·wave \ˈaər-ˌwāv\ *n* : AIR 6 — usu. used in pl.

air·way \-ˌwā\ *n* **1** : a regular route for airplanes **2** : AIRLINE

air·wor·thy \-ˌwər-ˌthē\ *adj* : fit or safe for operation in the air ⟨an ∼ plane⟩ — **air·wor·thi·ness** *n*

airy \ˈa(ə)r-ē\ *adj* **air·i·er; -est 1** : LOFTY **2** : lacking in reality : EMPTY **3** : DELICATE **4** : BREEZY

aisle \ˈīl\ *n* [ME *ile,* fr. MF *aile* wing, fr. L *ala*] **1** : the side of a church nave separated by piers from the nave proper **2** : a passage between sections of seats

ajar \ə-ˈjär\ *adj or adv* : partly open

AK *abbr* Alaska

aka *abbr* also known as

AKC *abbr* American Kennel Club

akim·bo \ə-ˈkim-bō\ *adj or adv* : having the hand on the hip and the elbow turned outward

akin \ə-'kin\ *adj* **1** : related by blood **2** : similar in kind

Al *symbol* aluminum

AL *abbr* **1** Alabama **2** American League **3** American Legion

¹-al \əl\ *adj suffix* : of, relating to, or characterized by ⟨direction*al*⟩

²-al *n suffix* : action : process ⟨rehears*al*⟩

Ala *abbr* Alabama

ALA *abbr* Automobile Legal Association

al·a·bas·ter \'al-ə-ˌbas-tər\ *n* **1** : a compact fine-textured usu. white and translucent gypsum mineral often carved into objects (as vases) **2** : a hard translucent calcite

à la carte \ˌal-ə-'kärt, ˌäl-\ *adv or adj* [F] : with a separate price for each item on the menu

alac·ri·ty \ə-'lak-rət-ē\ *n* : cheerful readiness : BRISKNESS

à la mode \ˌal-ə-'mōd, ˌäl-\ *adj* [F, according to the fashion] **1** : FASHIONABLE, STYLISH **2** : topped with ice cream

¹alarm \ə-'lärm\ *also* **ala·rum** \ə-'lär-əm, -'lar-\ *n* [ME *alarme*, fr. MF, fr. It *all'arme*, lit., to the weapon] **1** : a warning signal **2** : the terror caused by sudden danger

²alarm *also* **alarum** *vb* **1** : to warn of danger **2** : to arouse to a sense of danger : FRIGHTEN

alarm·ist \ə-'lär-məst\ *n* : a person who alarms others esp. needlessly

alas \ə-'las\ *interj* — used to express unhappiness, pity, or concern

al·ba·core \'al-bə-ˌkȯr\ *n, pl* **-core** *or* **-cores** : any of several tunas

Al·ba·nian \al-'bā-nē-ən\ *n* : a native or inhabitant of Albania

al·ba·tross \'al-bə-ˌtrȯs, -ˌträs\ *n, pl* **-tross** *or* **-tross·es** : a large web-footed seabird related to the petrels

al·be·it \ȯl-'bē-ət, al-\ *conj* : even though : ALTHOUGH

al·bi·no \al-'bī-nō\ *n, pl* **-nos** : a person or lower animal lacking coloring matter in the skin, hair, and eyes — **al·bi·nism** \'al-bə-ˌniz-əm\ *n*

al·bum \'al-bəm\ *n* **1** : a book with blank pages used for making a collection (as of stamps) **2** : one or more phonograph records or tape recordings produced as a single unit

al·bu·men \al-'byü-mən\ *n* **1** : the white of an egg **2** : ALBUMIN

al·bu·min \al-'byü-mən\ *n* : any of numerous water-soluble proteins of blood, milk, egg white, and plant and animal tissues

al·bu·min·ous \al-'byü-mə-nəs\ *adj* : containing or resembling albumen or albumin

alc *abbr* alcohol

al·cal·de \al-'käl-dē\ *n* : the chief administrative and judicial officer of a Spanish or Spanish-American town

al·ca·zar \al-'käz-ər, -'kaz-\ *n* [Sp *alcázar*, fr. Ar *al-qaṣr* the castle] : a Spanish fortress or palace

al·che·my \'al-kə-mē\ *n* : medieval chemistry chiefly concerned with efforts to turn base metals into gold — **al·che·mist** \'al-kə-məst\ *n*

al·co·hol \'al-kə-ˌhȯl\ *n* [NL, fr. ML, powdered antimony, fr. Sp, fr. Ar *al-kuḥul* the powdered antimony] **1** : a colorless flammable liquid that is the intoxicating element in fermented and distilled liquors **2** : any of various carbon compounds similar to alcohol **3** : beverages containing alcohol

¹al·co·hol·ic \ˌal-kə-'hȯl-ik, -'häl-\ *adj* **1** : of, relating to, caused by, or containing alcohol **2** : affected with alcoholism — **al·co·hol·i·cal·ly** \-i-k(ə-)lē\ *adv*

²alcoholic *n* : a person affected with alcoholism

al·co·hol·ism \'al-kə-ˌhȯl-ˌiz-əm\ *n* : continued excessive and usu. uncontrollable use of alcoholic drinks; *also* : the abnormal state associated with such use

al·cove \'al-ˌkōv\ *n* **1** : a nook or small recess opening off a larger room **2** : a niche or arched opening (as in a wall)

ald *abbr* alderman

al·der \'ȯl-dər\ *n* : a tree or shrub related to the birches and growing in wet areas

al·der·man \'ȯl-dər-mən\ *n* : a member of a city legislative body

ale \'āl\ *n* : an alcoholic beverage brewed from malt and hops that is usu. more bitter than beer

ale·a·tor·ic \ˌā-lē-ə-'tȯr-ik\ *adj* : improvised or random in character ⟨∼ music⟩

ale·a·to·ry \'ā-lē-ə-ˌtōr-ē\ *adj* : ALEATORIC

alee \ə-ˈlē\ *adv* : on or toward the lee

ale·house \ˈāl-ˌhaùs\ *n* : a place where ale is sold to be drunk on the premises

¹**alert** \ə-ˈlərt\ *adj* [It *all' erta*, lit., on the ascent] **1** : watchful against danger **2** : quick to perceive and act — **alert·ly** *adv* — **alert·ness** *n*

²**alert** *n* **1** : a signal given to warn of danger **2** : the period during which an alert is in effect

³**alert** *vb* **1** : WARN **2** : to make aware of

Aleut \ˌal-ē-ˈüt, ə-ˈlüt\ *n* **1** : a member of a people of the Aleutian and Shumagin islands and the western part of Alaska peninsula **2** : the language of the Aleuts

ale·wife \ˈāl-ˌwīf\ *n* : a food fish of the herring family abundant esp. on the Atlantic coast

Al·ex·an·dri·an \ˌal-ig-ˈzan-drē-ən\ *adj* **1** : of or relating to Alexander the Great **2** : HELLENISTIC

al·ex·an·drine \-ˈzan-drən\ *n, often cap* : a line of six iambic feet

al·fal·fa \al-ˈfal-fə\ *n* : a leguminous plant widely grown for hay and forage

al·fres·co \al-ˈfres-kō\ *adj or adv* [It] : taking place in the open air

alg *abbr* algebra

al·ga \ˈal-gə\ *n, pl* **al·gae** \ˈal-(ˌ)jē\ : any of a group of lower plants having chlorophyll but no vascular system and including seaweeds and related freshwater plants — **al·gal** \-gəl\ *adj*

al·ge·bra \ˈal-jə-brə\ *n* [ML, fr. Ar *al-jabr*] : a branch of mathematics using symbols (as letters) to explore the relationships between numbers and the operations used to work with them — **al·ge·bra·ic** \ˌal-jə-ˈbrā-ik\ *adj* — **al·ge·bra·ical·ly** \-ˈbrā-ə-k(ə-)lē\ *adv*

Al·ge·ri·an \al-ˈjir-ē-ən\ *n* : a native or inhabitant of Algeria — **Algerian** *adj*

AL·GOL *or* **Al·gol** \ˈal-ˌgäl, -ˌgòl\ *n* [*algo*rithmic *l*anguage] : a language for programming a computer esp. to work scientific problems

Al·gon·qui·an \al-ˈgän-kwē-ən, -ˈgäŋ-\ *n* : a member of an American Indian people of the Ottawa river valley

al·go·rithm \ˈal-gə-ˌrith-əm\ *n* : a procedure for solving a problem (as in mathematics)

¹**alias** \ˈā-lē-əs, ˈāl-yəs\ *adv* [L, otherwise, fr. *alius* other] : otherwise called

²**alias** *n* : an assumed or additional name

¹**al·i·bi** \ˈal-ə-ˌbī\ *n* [L, elsewhere, fr. *alius* other] **1** : a plea offered by an accused person of not having been at the scene of commission of an offense **2** : an excuse (as for failure)

²**alibi** *vb* **-bied; -bi·ing 1** : to make an excuse for **2** : to offer an excuse

¹**alien** \ˈā-lē-ən, ˈāl-yən\ *adj* : FOREIGN

²**alien** *n* : a foreign-born resident who has not been naturalized

alien·able \ˈāl-yə-nə-bəl, ˈā-lē-ə-nə-\ *adj* : transferable to the ownership of another ⟨∼ property⟩

alien·ate \ˈā-lē-ə-ˌnāt, ˈāl-yə-\ *vb* **-at·ed; -at·ing 1** : to transfer (property) to another **2** : to make hostile where previously friendship had existed : ESTRANGE — **alien·ation** \ˌā-lē-ə-ˈnā-shən, ˌāl-yə-\ *n*

alien·ist \-nəst\ *n* : PSYCHIATRIST; *esp* : one specializing in the legal aspects of psychology

¹**alight** \ə-ˈlīt\ *vb* **alight·ed** *also* **alit** \ə-ˈlit\ **alight·ing 1** : to get down (as from a vehicle) **2** : to come to rest from the air **syn** settle, land, perch

²**alight** *adj* : lighted up

align *also* **aline** \ə-ˈlīn\ *vb* **1** : to bring into line **2** : to array on the side of or against a cause — **align·ment** *also* **aline·ment** *n*

¹**alike** \ə-ˈlīk\ *adj* : LIKE **syn** akin, analogous, similar, comparable

²**alike** *adv* : EQUALLY

al·i·ment \ˈal-ə-mənt\ *n* : FOOD, NUTRIMENT

al·i·men·ta·ry \ˌal-ə-ˈmen-t(ə-)rē\ *adj* : of, relating to, or functioning in nourishment or nutrition

alimentary canal *n* : a tube that extends from the mouth to the anus and functions in the digestion and absorption of food and the elimination of residues

al·i·mo·ny \ˈal-ə-ˌmō-nē\ *n, pl* **-nies** [L *alimonia* sustenance, fr. *alere* to nourish] : an allowance made to one spouse by the other for support pending or after legal separation or divorce

A–line \ˈā-ˌlīn\ *adj* : having a flared bottom and a close-fitting top ⟨an ∼ skirt⟩

alive \ə-ˈlīv\ *adj* **1** : having life : LIVING **2** : being in force or operation **3** : SENSITIVE ⟨∼ to the danger⟩ **4** : ANIMATED ⟨streets ∼ with traffic⟩

aliz·a·rin \ə-'liz-ə-rən\ *n* : an orange or red crystalline compound made synthetically and used as a red dye

alk *abbr* alkaline

al·ka·li \'al-kə-ˌlī\ *n, pl* **-lies** *or* **-lis 1** : a substance (as a hydroxide) that has a bitter taste and neutralizes acids **2** : a mixture of salts in the soil of some dry regions in such amount as to make ordinary farming impossible — **al·ka·line** \-kə-lən, -ˌlīn\ *adj* — **al·ka·lin·i·ty** \ˌal-kə-'lin-ət-ē\ *n*

al·ka·loid \'al-kə-ˌlȯid\ *n* : any of various usu. basic and bitter organic compounds found esp. in seed plants

al·kane \'al-ˌkān\ *n* : a hydrocarbon in which each carbon atom is bonded to 4 other atoms

al·kyd \'al-kəd\ *n* : any of numerous thermoplastic synthetic resins used esp. for protective coatings

¹**all** \'ȯl\ *adj* **1** : the whole of **2** : the greatest possible **3** : every one of

²**all** *adv* **1** : WHOLLY **2** : so much ⟨∼ the better for it⟩ **3** : for each side ⟨the score is two ∼⟩

³**all** *pron* **1** : every one : the whole number, quantity, or amount ⟨∼ of you are welcome⟩ ⟨∼ of the money is gone⟩ **2** : EVERYTHING

Al·lah \'al-ə, ä-'lä\ *n* [Ar] : the supreme being of Islam

all–Amer·i·can \ˌȯl-ə-'mer-ə-kən\ *adj* **1** : composed wholly of American elements **2** : representative of the U.S. as a whole; *esp* : selected as the best in the U.S. — **all–American** *n*

all–around \ˌȯl-ə-'raund\ *adj* : having ability in many fields : VERSATILE

al·lay \ə-'lā\ *vb* **1** : to reduce in severity **2** : to put at rest **syn** alleviate, lighten, relieve, ease, assuage

all clear *n* : a signal that a danger has passed

al·lege \ə-'lej\ *vb* **al·leged; al·leg·ing 1** : to state as a fact without proof **2** : to bring forward as a reason or excuse — **al·le·ga·tion** \ˌal-i-'gā-shən\ *n* — **al·leg·ed·ly** \ə-'lej-əd-lē\ *adv*

al·le·giance \ə-'lē-jəns\ *n* **1** : loyalty owed by a citizen to his government **2** : loyalty to a person or cause

al·le·go·ry \'al-ə-ˌgȯr-ē\ *n, pl* **-ries** : the expression through symbolic figures and actions of truths or generalizations about human conduct or experi-

ence — **al·le·gor·i·cal** \ˌal-ə-'gȯr-i-kəl\ *adj*

¹**al·le·gro** \ə-'leg-rō, -'lā-grō\ *adv or adj* [It, merry] : in a brisk lively tempo — used as a direction in music

²**allegro** *n, pl* **-gros** : an allegro movement

al·le·lu·ia \ˌal-ə-'lü-yə\ *interj* : HALLELUJAH

al·ler·gen \'al-ər-jən\ *n* : something that causes allergy — **al·ler·gen·ic** \ˌal-ər-'jen-ik\ *adj*

al·ler·gist \'al-ər-jəst\ *n* : a specialist in allergies

al·ler·gy \'al-ər-jē\ *n, pl* **-gies** [G *allergie,* fr. Gk *allos* other + *ergon* work] : exaggerated or abnormal reaction (as by sneezing, itching, or rashes) to substances, situations, or physical states harmless to most people — **al·ler·gic** \ə-'lər-jik\ *adj*

al·le·vi·ate \ə-'lē-vē-ˌāt\ *vb* **-at·ed; -at·ing** : to make easier to be endured **syn** lighten, mitigate, relieve, allay — **al·le·vi·a·tion** \ə-ˌlē-vē-'ā-shən\ *n*

al·ley \'al-ē\ *n, pl* **alleys 1** : a place for bowling; *esp* : a hardwood lane **2** : a narrow street or passageway esp. between buildings

al·ley·way \'al-ē-ˌwā\ *n* : ALLEY 2

All·hal·lows \ȯl-'hal-ōz\ *n, pl* **Allhallows** : ALL SAINTS' DAY

al·li·ance \ə-'lī-əns\ *n* : a union to promote common interests **syn** league, coalition, confederacy, federation

al·lied \ə-'līd, 'al-ˌīd\ *adj* : joined in alliance

al·li·ga·tor \'al-ə-ˌgāt-ər\ *n* [Sp *el lagarto* the lizard, fr. L *lacertus* lizard] : either of two large short-legged reptiles resembling crocodiles but having a shorter and broader snout

alligator pear *n* : AVOCADO

al·lit·er·ate \ə-'lit-ə-ˌrāt\ *vb* **-at·ed; -at·ing 1** : to form an alliteration **2** : to arrange so as to make alliteration

al·lit·er·a·tion \ə-ˌlit-ə-'rā-shən\ *n* : the repetition of initial sounds in adjacent words or syllables — **al·lit·er·a·tive** \-'lit-ə-ˌrāt-iv\ *adj*

al·lo·cate \'al-ə-ˌkāt\ *vb* **-cat·ed; -cat·ing** : ALLOT, ASSIGN — **al·lo·ca·tion** \ˌal-ə-'kā-shən\ *n*

al·lot \ə-'lät\ *vb* **al·lot·ted; al·lot·ting** : to distribute as a share or portion **syn**

assign, apportion, allocate — **al·lot·ment** *n*

all–out \'òl-'aùt\ *adj* : using maximum energy or resources ⟨an ∼ offensive⟩

all over *adv* : EVERYWHERE

al·low \ə-'laù\ *vb* 1 : to assign as a share ⟨∼ time for rest⟩ 2 : to reckon as a deduction 3 : ADMIT, CONCEDE 4 : PERMIT 5 : to make allowance ⟨∼ for expansion⟩ — **al·low·able** *adj*

al·low·ance \-əns\ *n* 1 : an allotted share 2 : money given regularly for expenses 3 : the taking into account of mitigating circumstances

al·loy \'al-ˌòi, ə-'lòi\ *n* 1 : a substance composed of metals fused together 2 : an admixture of something that debases — **al·loy** \ə-'lòi, 'al-ˌòi\ *vb*

all right *adv* 1 : beyond doubt : CERTAINLY 2 : SATISFACTORILY 3 : YES — **all right** *adj*

All Saints' Day *n* : a church feast observed November 1 in honor of all the saints

All Souls' Day *n* : a day of prayer observed November 2 for the souls of the faithful departed

all·spice \'òl-ˌspīs\ *n* : the berry of a West Indian tree of the myrtle family; *also* : the mildly pungent and aromatic spice made from it

¹**all–star** \ˌòl-ˌstär\ *adj* : composed wholly or chiefly of star performers

²**all–star** \'òl-ˌstär\ *n* : a member of an all-star team

all told *adv* : with everything counted

al·lude \ə-'lüd\ *vb* **al·lud·ed; al·lud·ing** [L *alludere*, lit., to play with] : to refer indirectly or by suggestion — **al·lu·sion** \-'lü-zhən\ *n* — **al·lu·sive** \-'lü-siv\ *adj* — **al·lu·sive·ly** *adv* — **al·lu·sive·ness** *n*

al·lure \ə-'lùr\ *vb* **al·lured; al·lur·ing** : to entice by charm or attraction — **allure** *n* — **al·lure·ment** *n*

al·lu·vi·um \ə-'lü-vē-əm\ *n, pl* **-vi·ums** *or* **-via** \-vē-ə\ : soil material (as clay or gravel) deposited by running water — **al·lu·vi·al** \-vē-əl\ *adj or n*

¹**al·ly** \ə-'lī, 'al-ˌī\ *vb* **al·lied; al·ly·ing** : to unite in alliance

²**al·ly** \'al-ˌī, ə-'lī\ *n, pl* **allies** : one united with another in an alliance

-al·ly \(ə-)lē\ *adv suffix* : ²-LY ⟨terrif*ically*⟩

al·ma ma·ter \ˌal-mə-'mät-ər\ *n* [L, fostering mother] 1 : a school, college, or university that one has attended 2 : the song or hymn of a school, college, or university

al·ma·nac \'òl-mə-ˌnak, 'al-\ *n* : a publication containing astronomical and meteorological data and often a miscellany of other information

al·man·dite \'al-mən-ˌdīt\ *n* : a deep red garnet containing iron and aluminum

al·mighty \òl-'mīt-ē\ *adj* 1 *often cap* : having absolute power over all ⟨*Almighty* God⟩ 2 : relatively unlimited in power

Almighty *n* : GOD 1

al·mond \'äm-ənd, 'am-; 'al-mənd\ *n* : a small tree related to the peach; *also* : the edible nutlike kernel of its fruit

al·mo·ner \'al-mə-nər, 'äm-ə-\ *n* : a person who distributes alms

al·most \'òl-ˌmōst, òl-'mōst\ *adv* : only a little less than : NEARLY

alms \'ämz, 'älmz\ *n, pl* **alms** [ME *almesse, almes,* fr. OE *ælmesse, ælms,* fr. L *eleemosyna* alms, fr. Gk *eleēmosynē* pity, alms, fr. *eleēmōn* merciful] : something given freely to relieve the poor

alms·house \-ˌhaùs\ *n, Brit* : a privately financed home for the poor

al·oe \'al-ō\ *n* 1 : any of a large genus of succulent chiefly southern African plants related to the lilies 2 *pl* : the dried juice of the leaves of an aloe used as a strong laxative and tonic

aloft \ə-'lòft\ *adv* 1 : high in the air 2 : on or to the higher rigging of a ship

alo·ha \ə-'lō-ə, ä-'lō-hä\ *interj* [Hawaiian] — used to express greeting or farewell

alone \ə-'lōn\ *adj* 1 : separated from others 2 : not including anyone or anything else : ONLY **syn** lonely, lonesome, lone, solitary — **alone** *adv*

¹**along** \ə-'lòŋ\ *prep* 1 : on or near in a lengthwise direction ⟨walk ∼ the street⟩ ⟨sail ∼ the coast⟩ 2 : at a point on or during ⟨stopped ∼ the way⟩

²**along** *adv* 1 : FORWARD, ON 2 : as a companion or associate ⟨bring her ∼⟩ 3 : all the time ⟨knew it all ∼⟩

along·shore \ə-'lòŋ-'shōr\ *adv or adj* : along the shore or coast

¹**along·side** \-ˌsīd\ *adv* : along or by the side

²**alongside** *prep* : side by side with; *specif* : parallel to

alongside of *prep* : ALONGSIDE

aloof \ə-'lüf\ *adj* : removed or distant in interest or feeling : reserved — **aloofness** *n*

al·o·pe·cia \ˌal-ə-pē-sh(ē-)ə\ *n* : BALDNESS

aloud \ə-'laud\ *adv* : using the voice so as to be clearly heard

alp \'alp\ *n* : a high rugged mountain

al·paca \al-'pak-ə\ *n* : a So. American mammal related to the llama; *also* : its fine long woolly hair or cloth made from this

al·pha·bet \'al-fə-ˌbet, -bət\ *n* : the set of letters used in writing a language arranged in a conventional order

al·pha·bet·i·cal \ˌal-fə-'bet-i-kəl\ *or* **al·pha·bet·ic** \-'bet-ik\ *adj* 1 : arranged in the order of the letters of the alphabet 2 : of or employing an alphabet — **al·pha·bet·i·cal·ly** \-i-k(ə-)lē\ *adv*

al·pha·bet·ize \'al-fə-bə-ˌtīz\ *vb* **-ized; -iz·ing** : to arrange in alphabetical order — **al·pha·bet·iz·er** *n*

al·pha·nu·mer·ic \ˌal-fə-n(y)u-'mer-ik\ *adj* : consisting of letters and numbers and often other symbols ⟨an ~ code⟩ *also* : being a character in an alphanumeric system

alpha particle \ˌal-fə-\ *n* : a positively charged particle identical with the nucleus of a helium atom that is ejected at high speed in certain radioactive transformations

alpha ray *n* : a stream of alpha particles

alpha rhythm *n* : ALPHA WAVE

alpha wave *n* : an electrical rhythm of the brain often associated with a state of wakeful relaxation

Al·pine \'al-ˌpīn\ *adj* 1 : relating to, located in, or resembling the Alps mountains of south central Europe 2 *often not cap* : of, relating to, or growing on upland slopes above the highest elevation where trees grow

al·ready \ol-'red-ē\ *adv* : prior to a specified or implied time : PREVIOUSLY

al·right \ol-'rīt\ *adv* : ALL RIGHT

al·so \'ol-sō\ *adv* : in addition : TOO

al·so–ran \-ˌran\ *n* 1 : a horse or dog that finishes out of the money in a race 2 : a contestant that does not win

alt *abbr* 1 alternate 2 altitude

Alta *abbr* Alberta

al·tar \'ol-tər\ *n* 1 : a structure on which sacrifices are offered or incense is burned in worship 2 : a table used as a center of ritual

al·tar·piece \'ol-tər-ˌpēs\ *n* : a work of art that decorates the space above and behind the altar

¹**al·ter** \'ol-tər\ *vb* **al·tered; al·ter·ing** \-t(ə-)riŋ\ 1 : to make or become different 2 : CASTRATE, SPAY — **al·ter·a·tion** \ˌol-tə-'rā-shən\ *n*

²**alter** *abbr* alteration

al·ter·ca·tion \ˌol-tər-'kā-shən\ *n* : a noisy or angry dispute

al·ter ego \ˌol-tər-'ē-gō\ *n* [L, lit., second I] : a second self; *esp* : a trusted friend

¹**al·ter·nate** \'ol-tər-ˌnāt, 'al-\ *vb* **-nat·ed; -nat·ing** : to occur or cause to occur by turns — **al·ter·na·tion** \ˌol-tər-'nā-shən, ˌal-\ *n*

²**al·ter·nate** \-nət\ *adj* 1 : arranged or succeeding by turns 2 : every other 3 : being an alternative ⟨an ~ route⟩ — **al·ter·nate·ly** *adv*

³**alternate** *n* : SUBSTITUTE

alternating current *n* : an electric current that reverses its direction at regular intervals

al·ter·na·tive \ol-'tər-nət-iv, al-\ *adj* : that may be chosen in place of something else — **alternative** *n*

al·ter·na·tor \'ol-tər-ˌnāt-ər, 'al-\ *n* : an electric generator for producing alternating current

al·though *also* **al·tho** \ol-'thō\ *conj* : in spite of the fact that : even though

al·tim·e·ter \al-'tim-ət-ər, 'al-tə-ˌmēt-ər\ *n* : an instrument for measuring altitude

al·ti·tude \'al-tə-ˌt(y)üd\ *n* 1 : angular distance above the horizon 2 : vertical distance : HEIGHT 3 : the perpendicular distance in a geometric figure from the vertex to the base, from the vertex of an angle to the side opposite, or from the base to a parallel side or face

al·to \'al-tō\ *n, pl* **altos** [It, lit., high, fr. L *altus*] : the lowest female voice; *also* : a singer or instrument having the range of such a voice

al·to·geth·er \ˌol-tə-'geth-ər\ *adv* 1 : WHOLLY 2 : on the whole

al·tru·ism \'al-trü-ˌiz-əm\ *n* : unselfish interest in the welfare of others — **al-**

tru·ist \-əst\ *n* — **al·tru·is·tic** \ˌal-trü-ˈis-tik\ *adj* — **al·tru·is·ti·cal·ly** \-ti-k(ə-)lē\ *adv*

al·um \ˈal-əm\ *n* **1** : either of two colorless crystalline aluminum-containing compounds having a sweetish-sour taste and used esp. as an emetic or as an astringent and styptic **2** : a colorless aluminum salt used in purifying water and in tanning and dyeing

alu·mi·na \ə-ˈlü-mə-nə\ *n* : the oxide of aluminum occurring in nature as corundum and in bauxite

al·u·min·i·um \ˌal-yə-ˈmin-ē-əm\ *n, chiefly Brit* : ALUMINUM

alu·mi·nize \ə-ˈlü-mə-ˌnīz\ *vb* **-nized; -niz·ing** : to treat or coat with aluminum

alu·mi·num \ə-ˈlü-mə-nəm\ *n* : a silver-white malleable ductile light metallic element that is the most abundant metal in the earth's crust

alum·na \ə-ˈləm-nə\ *n, pl* **-nae** \-(ˌ)nē\ : a woman graduate or former student of a college or school

alum·nus \ə-ˈləm-nəs\ *n, pl* **-ni** \-ˌnī\ [L, foster son, pupil, fr. *alere* to nourish] : a graduate or former student of a college or school

al·ways \ˈȯl-wēz, -wəz, -(ˌ)wāz\ *adv* **1** : at all times : INVARIABLY **2** : FOREVER

Alz·hei·mer's disease \ˈälts-ˌhī-mərz-, ˈalz-\ *n* : a degenerative disease of the central nervous system characterized esp. by premature senile mental deterioration

am *pres 1st sing of* BE

¹Am *abbr* America; American

²Am *symbol* americium

¹AM \ˈā-ˌem\ *n* : a broadcasting system using amplitude modulation; *also* : a radio receiver for broadcasts made by such a system — **AM** *adj*

²AM *abbr* **1** ante meridiem — often not cap. **2** [NL *artium magister*] master of arts

AMA *abbr* American Medical Association

amah \ˈäm-(ˌ)ä\ *n* : an Oriental female servant; *esp* : a Chinese nurse

amain \ə-ˈmān\ *adv, archaic* : with full force or speed

amal·gam \ə-ˈmal-gəm\ *n* **1** : an alloy of mercury with another metal used in making dental cements **2** : a mixture of different elements

amal·gam·ate \ə-ˈmal-gə-ˌmāt\ *vb* **-at·ed; -at·ing** : to unite into one body or organization — **amal·ga·ma·tion** \-ˌmal-gə-ˈmā-shən\ *n*

aman·u·en·sis \ə-ˌman-yə-ˈwen-səs\ *n, pl* **-en·ses** \-ˌsēz\ : one employed to write from dictation or to copy what another has written : SECRETARY

am·a·ranth \ˈam-ə-ˌranth\ *n* **1** : any of a large genus of coarse herbs sometimes grown for their showy flowers **2** : a flower that never fades

am·a·ran·thine \ˌam-ə-ˈran-thən, -ˌthīn\ *adj* : relating to or resembling an amaranth : UNFADING, UNDYING

am·a·ryl·lis \ˌam-ə-ˈril-əs\ *n* : any of various plants of a group related to the lilies; *esp* : any of several African herbs having bulbs and grown for their clusters of large showy flowers

amass \ə-ˈmas\ *vb* : ACCUMULATE

am·a·teur \ˈam-ə-ˌtər, -ət-ər, -ə-ˌt(y)u̇r, -ə-ˌchu̇r, -ə-chər\ *n* [F, fr. L *amator* lover, fr. *amare* to love] **1** : a person who engages in a pursuit for pleasure and not as a profession **2** : a person who is not expert — **amateur** *adj* — **am·a·teur·ish** \ˌam-ə-ˈtər-ish, -ˈt(y)u̇r-\ *adj* — **am·a·teur·ism** \ˈam-ə-ˌtər-ˌiz-əm, -ət-ə-ˌriz-, -ə-ˌt(y)u̇r-ˌiz-, -ˌchu̇r-ˌiz-, -chə-ˌriz-\ *n*

am·a·tive \ˈam-ət-iv\ *adj* : disposed or disposing to love : AMOROUS — **am·a·tive·ly** *adv* — **am·a·tive·ness** *n*

am·a·to·ry \ˈam-ə-ˌtōr-ē\ *adj* : of or expressing sexual love

amaze \ə-ˈmāz\ *vb* **amazed; amaz·ing** : to overwhelm with wonder : ASTOUND **syn** astonish, surprise, dumbfound — **amaze·ment** *n* — **amaz·ing·ly** *adv*

am·a·zon \ˈam-ə-ˌzän, -ə-zən\ *n* **1** *cap* : a member of a race of female warriors repeatedly warring with the ancient Greeks of mythology **2** : a tall strong masculine woman — **am·a·zo·ni·an** \ˌam-ə-ˈzō-nē-ən\ *adj, often cap*

amb *abbr* ambassador

am·bas·sa·dor \am-ˈbas-əd-ər\ *n* : a country's representative in a foreign land — **am·bas·sa·do·ri·al** \-ˌbas-ə-ˈdōr-ē-əl\ *adj* — **am·bas·sa·dor·ship** *n*

am·ber \ˈam-bər\ *n* : a yellowish or brownish fossil resin used esp. for ornamental objects; *also* : the color of this resin

am•ber•gris \'am-bər-ˌgris, -ˌgrēs\ *n* : a waxy substance from the sperm whale used in making perfumes

am•bi•dex•trous \ˌam-bi-'dek-strəs\ *adj* : using both hands with equal ease — **am•bi•dex•trous•ly** *adv*

am•bi•ence *or* **am•bi•ance** \'am-bē-əns, äⁿ-byäⁿs\ *n* : a surrounding or pervading atmosphere

am•bi•ent \'am-bē-ənt\ *adj* : SURROUNDING

am•big•u•ous \am-'big-yə-wəs\ *adj* : capable of being understood in more than one way — **am•bi•gu•i•ty** \ˌam-bə-'gyü-ət-ē\ *n*

am•bi•tion \am-'bish-ən\ *n* [ME, fr. MF or L; MF, fr. L *ambition- ambitio,* lit., going around, fr. *ambitus,* pp. of *ambire,* fr. *ambi-* around + *ire* to go] : eager desire for success or power

am•bi•tious \am-'bish-əs\ *adj* : characterized by ambition — **am•bi•tious•ly** *adv*

am•biv•a•lence \am-'biv-ə-ləns\ *n* : simultaneous attraction toward and repulsion from a person, object, or action — **am•biv•a•lent** \-lənt\ *adj*

¹**am•ble** \'am-bəl\ *vb* **am•bled; am•bling** \-b(ə-)liŋ\ : to go at an amble

²**amble** *n* : an easy gait esp. of a horse

am•bro•sia \am-'brō-zh(ē-)ə\ *n* : the food of the Greek and Roman gods — **am•bro•sial** \-zh(ē-)əl\ *adj*

am•bu•lance \'am-byə-ləns\ *n* : a vehicle equipped for carrying the injured or sick

am•bu•lant \'am-byə-lənt\ *adj* : moving about : AMBULATORY

¹**am•bu•la•to•ry** \'am-byə-lə-ˌtōr-ē\ *adj* **1** : of, relating to, or adapted to walking **2** : able to walk about

²**ambulatory** *n, pl* **-ries** : a sheltered place (as in a cloister) for walking

am•bus•cade \'am-bə-ˌskād\ *n* : AMBUSH

am•bush \'am-ˌbush\ *n* : a trap by which concealed persons attack an enemy by surprise — **ambush** *vb*

amdt *abbr* amendment

ame•ba, ame•bic, ame•boid var of AMOEBA, AMOEBIC, AMOEBOID

ame•lio•rate \ə-'mēl-yə-ˌrāt\ *vb* **-rat•ed; -rat•ing** : to make or grow better : IMPROVE — **ame•lio•ra•tion** \-ˌmēl-yə-'rā-shən\ *n*

amen \(')ā-'men, (')ä-\ *interj* — used esp. at the end of prayers to express solemn ratification or approval

ame•na•ble \ə-'mē-nə-bəl, -'men-ə-\ *adj* **1** : ANSWERABLE **2** : easily managed : TRACTABLE

amend \ə-'mend\ *vb* **1** : to change for the better : IMPROVE **2** : to alter formally in phraseology

amend•ment \ə-'men(d)-mənt\ *n* **1** : correction of faults **2** : the process of amending a parliamentary motion or a constitution; *also* : the alteration so proposed or made

amends \ə-'men(d)z\ *n sing or pl* : compensation for injury or loss

ame•ni•ty \ə-'men-ət-ē, -'mē-nət-\ *n, pl* **-ties 1** : AGREEABLENESS **2** : something serving to comfort or convenience **3** : a gesture observed in social relationships

Amer *abbr* America; American

amerce \ə-'mərs\ *vb* **amerced; amercing 1** : to penalize by a fine determined by the court **2** : PUNISH — **amerce•ment** *n*

Amer•i•can \ə-'mer-ə-kən\ *n* **1** : a native or inhabitant of No. or So. America **2** : a citizen of the U.S. — **American** *adj* — **Amer•i•can•ism** \-ə-kə-ˌniz-əm\ *n* — **Amer•i•can•iza•tion** \ə-ˌmer-ə-kə-nə-'zā-shən\ *n* — **Amer•i•can•ize** \ə-'mer-ə-kə-ˌnīz\ *vb*

Amer•i•ca•na \ə-ˌmer-ə-'kan-ə, -'kän-\ *n pl* : materials concerning or characteristic of America, its civilization, or its culture; *also* : a collection of these

American Indian *n* : a member of any of the aboriginal peoples of No. and So. America except the Eskimos

American plan *n* : a hotel plan whereby the daily rates cover the cost of room and meals

American Sign Language *n* : a sign language for the deaf in which meaning is conveyed by a system of hand gestures and placement

am•er•i•ci•um \ˌam-ə-'ris(h)-ē-əm\ *n* : a radioactive metallic chemical element produced artificially from plutonium

AmerInd *abbr* American Indian

Am•er•in•di•an \ˌam-ə-'rin-dē-ən\ *adj* : of or relating to American Indians or their culture — **Amerindian** *n*

am•e•thyst \'am-ə-thəst\ *n* [ME *amatiste,* fr. OF & L; OF, fr. L *amethys-*

tus, fr. Gk *amethystos,* lit., remedy against drunkenness, fr. *a-* not + *methyein* to be drunk, fr. *methy* wine] : a gemstone consisting of clear purple or bluish violet quartz

ami·a·ble \'ā-mē-ə-bəl\ *adj* **1** : AGREE-ABLE **2** : having a friendly and sociable disposition — **ami·a·bil·i·ty** \ˌā-mē-ə-'bil-ət-ē\ *n* — **ami·a·bly** \'ā-mē-ə-blē\ *adv*

am·i·ca·ble \'am-i-kə-bəl\ *adj* : FRIEND-LY, PEACEABLE — **am·i·ca·bly** \-blē\ *adv*

amid \ə-'mid\ *or* **amidst** \-'midst\ *prep* : in or into the middle of : AMONG

amid·ships \ə-'mid-ˌships\ *adv* : in or near the middle of a ship

ami·no acid \ə-ˌmē-nō-\ *n* : any of numerous nitrogen-containing acids that include some which are used by cells to build proteins

¹amiss \ə-'mis\ *adv* **1** : WRONGLY **2** : ASTRAY **3** : IMPERFECTLY

²amiss *adj* **1** : WRONG **2** : out of place

am·i·ty \'am-ət-ē\ *n, pl* **-ties** : FRIEND-SHIP; *esp* : friendly relations between nations

am·me·ter \'am-ˌet-ər\ *n* : an instrument for measuring electric current in amperes

am·mo \'am-ō\ *n* : AMMUNITION

am·mo·nia \ə-'mō-nyə\ *n* [NL, fr. L *sal ammoniacus* sal ammoniac (ammonium chloride), lit., salt of Ammon, fr. Gk *ammōniakos* of Ammon, fr. *Ammōn* Ammon, Amen, an Egyptian god near one of whose temples it was prepared] **1** : a colorless gaseous compound of nitrogen and hydrogen used in refrigeration and in the making of fertilizers and explosives **2** : a solution (**ammonia water**) of ammonia in water

am·mo·ni·um \ə-'mō-nē-əm\ *n* : an ion or chemical group derived from ammonia by combination with hydrogen

ammonium chloride *n* : a white crystalline volatile salt used in batteries and as an expectorant

am·mu·ni·tion \ˌam-yə-'nish-ən\ *n* **1** : projectiles fired from guns **2** : explosive items used in war **3** : material for use in attack or defense

Amn *abbr* airman

am·ne·sia \am-'nē-zhə\ *n* : abnormal loss of memory — **am·ne·si·ac** \-z(h)ē-

ˌak\ *or* **am·ne·sic** \-zik, -sik\ *adj or n*

am·nes·ty \'am-nə-stē\ *n, pl* **-ties** : an act granting a pardon to a group of individuals — **amnesty** *vb*

am·nio·cen·te·sis \ˌam-nē-ō-ˌsen-'tē-səs\ *n, pl* **-te·ses** \-'tē-ˌsēz\ : the surgical insertion of a hollow needle through the abdominal wall and uterus of a pregnant female esp. to obtain fluid used to check for chromosomal abnormality and to determine sex

amoe·ba \ə-'mē-bə\ *n, pl* **-bas** *or* **-bae** \-(ˌ)bē\ : any of various tiny one-celled protozoans that lack permanent cell organs and occur esp. in water and soil — **amoe·bic** \-bik\ *adj*

amoe·boid \-ˌbȯid\ *adj* : resembling an amoeba esp. in moving or readily changing shape

amok \ə-'mək, -'mäk\ *or* **amuck** \-'mək\ *adv* : in a violently excited state ⟨run ∼⟩

among \ə-'məŋ\ *also* **amongst** \-'məŋst\ *prep* **1** : in or through the midst of **2** : in the number or class of **3** : in shares to each of **4** : by common action of

amon·til·la·do \ə-ˌmän-tə-'läd-ō\ *n, pl* **-dos** [Sp] : a medium dry sherry

amor·al \ā-'mȯr-əl\ *adj* : neither moral nor immoral; *esp* : being outside the sphere to which moral judgments apply — **amor·al·ly** *adv*

am·o·rous \'am-(ə-)rəs\ *adj* **1** : inclined to love **2** : being in love — **am·o·rous·ly** *adv* — **am·o·rous·ness** *n*

amor·phous \ə-'mȯr-fəs\ *adj* **1** : SHAPE-LESS, FORMLESS **2** : not crystallized

am·or·tize \'am-ər-ˌtīz, ə-'mȯr-\ *vb* **-tized; -tiz·ing** : to extinguish (as a mortgage) usu. by payment on the principal at the time of each periodic interest payment — **amor·ti·za·tion** \ˌam-ərt-ə-'zā-shən, ə-ˌmȯrt-\ *n*

Amos \'ā-məs\ — see BIBLE table

¹amount \ə-'maůnt\ *vb* **1** : to reach as a total **2** : to be equivalent

²amount *n* **1** : the total number or quantity **2** : a principal sum plus the interest on it

amour \ə-'můr, ä-, a-\ *n* : a love affair esp. when illicit

amour pro·pre \ˌam-ˌůr-'prōpr³, ˌäm-ˌůr-'prōpr³\ *n* [F] : SELF-ESTEEM

¹amp \'amp\ *n* : AMPLIFIER; *also* : a unit

consisting of an electronic amplifier and a loudspeaker

²amp *abbr* ampere

am·per·age \\'am-p(ə-)rij\\ *n* : the strength of a current of electricity expressed in amperes

am·pere \\'am-₁piər\\ *n* : a unit of electric current equivalent to a steady current produced by one volt applied across a resistance of one ohm

am·per·sand \\'am-pər-₁sand\\ *n* [fr. *and per se and,* spoken form of the phrase *& per se and,* lit., (the character) & by itself (stands for the word) *and*] : a character & used for the word *and*

am·phet·amine \\am-'fet-ə-₁mēn, -mən\\ *n* : a compound or one of its derivatives used esp. as a stimulant of the nervous system

am·phib·i·an \\am-'fib-ē-ən\\ *n* 1 : an amphibious organism; *esp* : any of a class of animals (as frogs and newts) intermediate between fishes and reptiles 2 : a vehicle designed to operate on both land and water

am·phib·i·ous \\am-'fib-ē-əs\\ *adj* [Gk *amphibios,* lit., living a double life, fr. *amphi-* on both sides + *bios* mode of *life*] 1 : able to live both on land and in water 2 : adapted for both land and water 3 : made by joint action of land, sea, and air forces invading from the sea; *also* : trained for such action

am·phi·bole \\'am-fə-₁bōl\\ *n* : any of a group of rock-forming minerals containing calcium, magnesium, iron, aluminum, and sodium combined with silica

am·phi·the·ater \\'am-fə-₁thē-ət-ər\\ *n* : an oval or circular structure with rising tiers of seats around an arena

am·pho·ra \\'am-fə-rə\\ *n, pl* **-rae** \\-₁rē\\ *or* **-ras** : an ancient Greek jar or vase with two handles that rise almost to the level of the mouth

am·ple \\'am-pəl\\ *adj* **am·pler** \\-plər\\ **am·plest** \\-pləst\\ 1 : LARGE, CAPACIOUS 2 : enough to satisfy : ABUNDANT — **am·ply** \\-plē\\ *adv*

am·pli·fy \\'am-plə-₁fī\\ *vb* **-fied; -fy·ing** 1 : to expand by extended treatment 2 : to increase (voltage, current, or power) in magnitude or strength 3 : to make louder — **am·pli·fi·ca·tion** \\₁am-plə-fə-'kā-shən\\ *n* — **am·pli·fi·er** \\'am-plə-₁fī(-ə)r\\ *n*

am·pli·tude \\-₁t(y)üd\\ *n* 1 : ample extent : FULLNESS 2 : the extent of a vibratory movement (as of a pendulum) or of an oscillation (as of an alternating current or a radio wave)

amplitude modulation *n* 1 : modulation of the amplitude of a radio carrier wave in accordance with the strength of the signal 2 : a broadcasting system using amplitude modulation

am·poule *or* **am·pule** *also* **am·pul** \\'am-₁pyül, -pül\\ *n* : a small sealed bulbous glass vessel used to hold a solution for hypodermic injection

am·pu·tate \\'am-pyə-₁tāt\\ *vb* **-tat·ed; -tat·ing** : to cut off ⟨∼ a leg⟩ — **am·pu·ta·tion** \\₁am-pyə-'tā-shən\\ *n*

am·pu·tee \\₁am-pyə-'tē\\ *n* : one who has had a limb amputated

amt *abbr* amount

amuck \\ə-'mək\\ var of AMOK

am·u·let \\'am-yə-lət\\ *n* : an ornament worn as a charm against evil

amuse \\ə-'myüz\\ *vb* **amused; amus·ing** : to entertain in a light or playful manner : DIVERT — **amuse·ment** *n*

AMVETS \\'am-₁vets\\ *abbr* American Veterans (of World War II)

am·y·lase \\'am-ə-₁lās, -₁lāz\\ *n* : any of several enzymes that accelerate the breakdown of starch and glycogen

an \\ən, (')an\\ *indefinite article* : A — used before words beginning with a vowel sound

¹-an \\ən\\ *or* **-ian** \\(ē-)ən\\ *also* **-ean** \\(ē-)ən, 'ē-ən\\ *n suffix* 1 : one that belongs to ⟨American⟩ ⟨Bostonian⟩ ⟨crustacean⟩ 2 : one skilled in or specializing in ⟨phonetician⟩

²-an *or* **-ian** *also* **-ean** *adj suffix* 1 : of or belonging to ⟨American⟩ ⟨Floridian⟩ 2 : characteristic of : resembling ⟨Mozartean⟩

AN *abbr* airman (Navy)

an·a·bol·ic steroid \\₁an-ə-₁bäl-ik-\\ *n* : any of a group of synthetic hormones sometimes taken by athletes in training to increase temporarily the size of their muscles

anach·ro·nism \\ə-'nak-rə-₁niz-əm\\ *n* 1 : the error of placing a person or thing in the wrong period 2 : one that is chronologically out of place — **anach·ro·nis·tic** \\ə-₁nak-rə-'nis-tik\\ *adj*

an·a·con·da \\₁an-ə-'kän-də\\ *n* : a large

So. American snake that suffocates and kills its prey by constriction

an•a•dem \\'an-ə-ˌdem\ *n, archaic* : GARLAND, CHAPLET

anae•mia, anae•mic var of ANEMIA, ANEMIC

an•aer•obe \\'an-ə-ˌrōb\ *n* : an anaerobic organism

an•aer•o•bic \ˌan-ə-'rō-bik\ *adj* : living, active, or occurring in the absence of free oxygen

an•aes•the•sia, an•aes•thet•ic var of ANESTHESIA, ANESTHETIC

ana•gram \\'an-ə-ˌgram\ *n* : a word or phrase made by transposing the letters of another word or phrase

¹anal \\'ān-ᵊl\ *adj* **1** : of, relating to, or situated near the anus **2** : of, relating to, or characterized by the stage of psychosexual development in psychoanalytic theory during which one is concerned esp. with feces **3** : of, relating to, or characterized by personality traits (as parsimony and ill humor) considered typical of fixation at the anal stage of development

²anal *abbr* **1** analogy **2** analysis; analytic

an•al•ge•sia \ˌan-ᵊl-'jē-zhə\ *n* : insensibility to pain — **an•al•ge•sic** \-'jē-zik, -sik\ *adj*

an•al•ge•sic \-'jē-zik, -sik\ *n* : an agent for producing analgesia

analog computer \ˌan-ᵊl-ˌȯg-, -ˌäg-\ *n* : a computer that operates with numbers represented by directly measurable quantities (as voltages)

anal•o•gous \ə-'nal-ə-gəs\ *adj* : similar in one or more respects but not homologous

an•a•logue *or* **an•a•log** \\'an-ᵊl-ˌȯg, -ˌag\ *n* **1** : something that is analogous or similar to something else **2** : an organ similar in function to one of another animal or plant but different in structure or origin

anal•o•gy \ə-'nal-ə-jē\ *n, pl* **-gies** **1** : inference that if two or more things agree in some respects they will probably agree in others **2** : a likeness in one or more ways between things otherwise unlike — **an•a•log•i•cal** \ˌan-ᵊl-'äj-i-kəl\ *adj* — **an•a•log•i•cal•ly** \-i-k(ə-)lē\ *adv*

anal•y•sis \ə-'nal-ə-səs\ *n, pl* **-y•ses** \-ˌsēz\ [NL, fr. Gk, fr. *analyein* to break up, fr. *ana-* up + *lyein* to loos-

en] **1** : separation of a thing into the parts or elements of which it is composed **2** : an examination of a thing to determine its parts or elements; *also* : a statement showing the results of such an examination **3** : PSYCHOANALYSIS — **an•a•lyst** \\'an-ᵊl-əst\ *n* — **an•a•lyt•ic** \ˌan-ᵊl-'it-ik\ *or* **an•a•lyt•i•cal** \-i-kəl\ *adj*

an•a•lyze \\'an-ᵊl-ˌīz\ *vb* **-lyzed; -lyz•ing** : to make an analysis of

an•a•pest \\'an-ə-ˌpest\ *n* : a metrical foot of two unaccented syllables followed by one accented syllable — **an•a•pes•tic** \ˌan-ə-'pes-tik\ *adj or n*

an•ar•chism \\'an-ər-ˌkiz-əm\ *n* : the theory that all government is undesirable — **an•ar•chist** \-kəst\ *n or adj* — **an•ar•chis•tic** \ˌan-ər-'kis-tik\ *adj*

an•ar•chy \\'an-ər-kē\ *n* **1** : a social structure without government or law and order **2** : utter confusion — **an•ar•chic** \a-'när-kik\ *adj*

anas•to•mo•sis \ə-ˌnas-tə-'mō-səs\ *n, pl* **-mo•ses** \-ˌsēz\ **1** : the union of parts or branches (as of blood vessels) **2** : NETWORK

anat *abbr* anatomical; anatomy

anath•e•ma \ə-'nath-ə-mə\ *n* **1** : a solemn curse **2** : a person or thing accursed; *also* : one intensely disliked

anath•e•ma•tize \-ˌtīz\ *vb* **-tized; -tiz•ing** : to pronounce an anathema against : CURSE

anat•o•mize \ə-'nat-ə-ˌmīz\ *vb* **-mized; -miz•ing** : to dissect so as to examine the structure and parts; *also* : ANALYZE

anat•o•my \ə-'nat-ə-mē\ *n, pl* **-mies** [LL *anatomia* dissection, fr. Gk *anatomē,* fr. *anatemnein* to dissect, fr. *ana-* up + *temnein* to cut] **1** : a branch of science dealing with the structure of organisms **2** : structural makeup esp. of an organism or any of its parts **3** : a separating into parts for detailed study : ANALYSIS, ANATOMIZING — **an•a•tom•ic** \ˌan-ə-'täm-ik\ *or* **an•a•tom•i•cal** \-i-kəl\ *adj* — **an•a•tom•i•cal•ly** \-i-k(ə-)lē\ *adv* — **anat•o•mist** \ə-'nat-ə-məst\ *n*

anc *abbr* ancient

-ance \əns\ *n suffix* **1** : action or process ⟨further*ance*⟩ : instance of an action or process ⟨perform*ance*⟩ **2** : quality or state : instance of a quality or state ⟨protuber*ance*⟩ **3** : amount or degree ⟨conduct*ance*⟩

an•ces•tor \ˈan-ˌses-tər\ *n* [ME *ancestre,* fr. OF, fr. L *antecessor* one that goes before, fr. *antecedere* to go before, fr. *ante-* before + *cedere* to go] : one from whom an individual is descended

an•ces•tress \ˈan-ˌses-trəs\ *n* : a female ancestor

an•ces•try \ˈan-ˌses-trē\ *n* **1** : line of descent : LINEAGE **2** : ANCESTORS — **an•ces•tral** \an-ˈses-trəl\ *adj*

¹an•chor \ˈaŋ-kər\ *n* **1** : a heavy metal device attached to a ship that catches hold of the bottom and holds the ship in place **2** : ANCHORPERSON

²anchor *vb* **an•chored; an•chor•ing** \-k(ə-)riŋ\ : to hold or become held in place by or as if by an anchor

an•chor•age \ˈaŋ-k(ə-)rij\ *n* : a place suitable for ships to anchor

an•cho•rite \ˈaŋ-kə-ˌrīt\ *n* : HERMIT

an•chor•man \ˈaŋ-kər-ˌman\ *n* **1** : the member of a team who competes last **2** : an anchorperson who is a man

an•chor•per•son \-ˌpər-sən\ *n* : a broadcaster who reads the news and introduces the reports of other broadcasters

an•chor•wom•an \-ˌwu̇m-ən\ *n* **1** : a woman who competes last **2** : an anchorperson who is a woman

an•cho•vy \ˈan-ˌchō-vē, an-ˈchō-\ *n, pl* **-vies** *or* **-vy** : a small herringlike fish used esp. for sauces and relishes

an•cien ré•gime \ˌäⁿs-yaⁿ-rā-zhēm\ *n* **1** : the political and social system of France before the Revolution of 1789 **2** : a system no longer prevailing

¹an•cient \ˈān-shənt\ *adj* **1** : having existed for many years **2** : belonging to times long past; *esp* : belonging to the period before the Middle Ages

²ancient *n* **1** : an aged person **2** *pl* : the peoples of ancient Greece and Rome

an•cil•lary \ˈan-sə-ˌler-ē\ *adj* **1** : SUBORDINATE, SUBSIDIARY **2** : AUXILIARY, SUPPLEMENTARY

-ancy \ən-sē\ *n suffix* : quality or state ⟨flamboy*ancy*⟩

and \ən(d), (ˈ)and\ *conj* — used to indicate connection or addition esp. of items within the same class or type or to join words or phrases of the same grammatical rank or function

¹an•dan•te \än-ˈdän-ˌtā, -ˈdänt-ē\ *adv or adj* [It, lit., going, prp. of *andare* to go] : moderately slow — used as a direction in music

²andante *n* : an andante movement

and•iron \ˈan-ˌdī(-ə)rn\ *n* : one of a pair of metal supports for firewood in a fireplace

and/or \ˈan-ˈdȯr\ *conj* — used to indicate that either *and* or *or* may apply ⟨men ∼ women means men *and* women or men *or* women⟩

an•dro•gen \ˈan-drə-jən\ *n* : a male sex hormone

an•droid \ˈan-ˌdrȯid\ *n* : an automaton with human form

an•ec•dote \ˈan-ik-ˌdōt\ *n* [F, fr. Gk *anekdota* unpublished items, fr. *a-* not + *ekdidonai* to publish] : a brief story of an interesting usu. biographical incident — **an•ec•dot•al** \ˌan-ik-ˈdōt-ᵊl\ *adj*

ane•mia \ə-ˈnē-mē-ə\ *n* **1** : a condition in which blood is deficient in quantity, in red blood cells, or in hemoglobin and which is marked by pallor, weakness, and irregular heart action **2** : lack of vitality — **ane•mic** \ə-ˈnē-mik\ *adj*

an•e•mom•e•ter \ˌan-ə-ˈmäm-ət-ər\ *n* : an instrument for measuring the force or speed of the wind

anem•o•ne \ə-ˈnem-ə-nē\ *n* : any of a large genus of herbs related to the buttercups that have showy flowers without petals but with conspicuous often colored sepals

anent \ə-ˈnent\ *prep* : ABOUT, CONCERNING

an•es•the•sia \ˌan-əs-ˈthē-zhə\ *n* : loss of bodily sensation

an•es•the•si•ol•o•gy \-ˌthē-zē-ˈäl-ə-jē\ *n* : a branch of medical science dealing with anesthesia and anesthetics — **an•es•the•si•ol•o•gist** \-jəst\ *n*

¹an•es•thet•ic \ˌan-əs-ˈthet-ik\ *adj* : of, relating to, or capable of producing anesthesia

²anesthetic *n* : an agent that produces anesthesia — **anes•the•tist** \ə-ˈnes-thət-əst\ *n* — **anes•the•tize** \-thə-ˌtīz\ *vb*

anew \ə-ˈn(y)ü\ *adv* : over again : from a new start

an•gel \ˈān-jəl\ *n* [ME, fr. OF *angele,* fr. L *angelus,* fr. Gk *angelos,* lit., messenger] **1** : a spiritual being superior to man **2** : an attendant spirit ⟨guardian ∼⟩ **3** : a winged figure of human form in art **4** : MESSENGER, HARBINGER **5** : a person held to resemble an angel **6** : a financial backer — **an·gel·ic** \an-'jel-ik\ *or* **an·gel·i·cal** \-i-kəl\ *adj* — **an·gel·i·cal·ly** \-i-k(ə-)lē\ *adv*

an·gel·fish \'ān-jəl-ˌfish\ *n* : any of several bright-colored tropical fishes that are flattened from side to side

an·gel·i·ca \an-'jel-i-kə\ *n* : a biennial herb related to the carrot whose roots and fruit furnish a flavoring oil

¹an·ger \'aŋ-gər\ *n* [ME, affliction, anger, fr. ON *angr* grief] : a strong feeling of displeasure **syn** wrath, ire, rage, fury, indignation

²anger *vb* **an·gered; an·ger·ing** \-g(ə-)riŋ\ : to make angry

an·gi·na \an-'jī-nə\ *n* [L, quinsy] : a disorder (as of the heart) marked by attacks of intense pain; *esp* : ANGINA PECTORIS — **an·gi·nal** \an-'jīn-ᵊl\ *adj*

angina pec·to·ris \-'pek-t(ə-)rəs\ *n* : a heart disease marked by brief attacks of sharp chest pain caused by deficient oxygenation of heart muscles

an·gio·sperm \'an-jē-ə-ˌspərm\ *n* : any of a class of vascular plants (as orchids or roses) having the seeds in a closed ovary

¹an·gle \'aŋ-gəl\ *n* **1** : a sharp projecting corner **2** : the figure formed by the meeting of two lines in a point **3** : a point of view **4** : a special technique or plan : GIMMICK

²angle *vb* **an·gled; an·gling** \-g(ə-)liŋ\ : to turn, move, or direct at an angle

³angle *vb* **an·gled; an·gling** \-g(ə-)liŋ\ : to fish with a hook and line — **an·gler** \-glər\ *n* — **an·gling** \-gliŋ\ *n*

an·gle·worm \'aŋ-gəl-ˌwərm\ *n* : EARTHWORM

An·gli·can \'aŋ-gli-kən\ *adj* **1** : of or relating to the established episcopal Church of England **2** : of or relating to England or the English nation — **Anglican** *n* — **An·gli·can·ism** \-kə-ˌniz-əm\ *n*

an·gli·cize \'aŋ-glə-ˌsīz\ *vb* **-cized; -ciz·ing** *often cap* **1** : to make English (as in habits, speech, character, or outlook) **2** : to borrow (a foreign word or phrase) into English without changing form or spelling and sometimes without changing pronunciation — **an·gli·ci·za·tion** \ˌaŋ-glə-sə-'zā-shən\ *n, often cap*

An·glo \'aŋ-glō\ *n, pl* **Anglos** : a non-Latin Caucasian inhabitant of the U.S.

An·glo–French \ˌaŋ-glō-'french\ *n* : the French language used in medieval England

An·glo·phile \'aŋ-glə-ˌfīl\ *also* **An·glo·phil** \-ˌfil\ *n* : one who greatly admires England and things English

An·glo·phobe \'aŋ-glə-ˌfōb\ *n* : one who is averse to England and things English

An·glo–Sax·on \ˌaŋ-glō-'sak-sən\ *n* **1** : a member of any of the Germanic peoples who invaded England in the 5th century A.D. **2** : a member of the English people **3** : Old English — **Anglo–Saxon** *adj*

an·go·ra \aŋ-'gōr-ə, an-\ *n* **1** : yarn or cloth made from the hair of an Angora goat or rabbit **2** *cap* : any of a breed of cats, goats, or rabbits with a long silky coat

an·gry \'aŋ-grē\ *adj* **an·gri·er; -est** : feeling or showing anger **syn** enraged, wrathful, irate, indignant, mad — **an·gri·ly** \-grə-lē\ *adv*

angst \'äŋst\ *n* [G] : a feeling of anxiety

ang·strom \'aŋ-strəm\ *n* : a unit of length equal to one ten-billionth of a meter

an·guish \'aŋ-gwish\ *n* : extreme pain or distress esp. of mind — **an·guished** \-gwisht\ *adj*

an·gu·lar \'aŋ-gyə-lər\ *adj* **1** : having one or more angles **2** : sharp-cornered **3** : being thin and bony — **an·gu·lar·i·ty** \ˌaŋ-gyə-'lar-ət-ē\ *n*

An·gus \'aŋ-gəs\ *n* : any of a breed of usu. black hornless beef cattle originating in Scotland

an·hy·drous \an-'hī-drəs\ *adj* : free from water

an·i·line \'an-ᵊl-ən\ *n* : an oily poisonous liquid used in making dyes, medicines, and explosives

an·i·mad·vert \ˌan-ə-ˌmad-'vərt\ *vb* : to remark critically : express censure — **an·i·mad·ver·sion** \-'vər-zhən\ *n*

¹an·i·mal \'an-ə-məl\ *n* **1** : any of a kingdom of living things typically differing from plants in capacity for active movement, in rapid response to stimulation, and in lack of cellulose cell walls **2** : a lower animal as distinguished from man; *also* : MAMMAL

²animal *adj* **1** : of, relating to, or derived from animals **2** : of or relating to the physical as distinguished from the mental or spiritual **syn** carnal, fleshly, sensual

an·i·mal·cule \ˌan-ə-ˈmal-kyül\ *n* : a tiny animal usu. invisible to the naked eye

¹an·i·mate \ˈan-ə-mət\ *adj* : having life

²an·i·mate \-ˌmāt\ *vb* **-mat·ed; -mat·ing 1** : to impart life to **2** : to give spirit and vigor to **3** : to make appear to move ⟨∼ a cartoon for motion pictures⟩ — **an·i·mat·ed** *adj*

an·i·ma·tion \ˌan-ə-ˈmā-shən\ *n* **1** : LIVELINESS, VIVACITY **2** : a motion picture made from a series of drawings simulating motions by means of slight progressive changes

an·i·mism \ˈan-ə-ˌmiz-əm\ *n* : attribution of conscious life to nature as a whole or to inanimate objects — **an·i·mist** \-məst\ *n* — **an·i·mis·tic** \ˌan-ə-ˈmis-tik\ *adj*

an·i·mos·i·ty \ˌan-ə-ˈmäs-ət-ē\ *n, pl* **-ties** : ILL WILL, RESENTMENT

an·i·mus \ˈan-ə-məs\ *n* : deep-seated resentment and hostility

an·ion \ˈan-ˌī-ən, -ˌī-ˌän\ *n* : a negatively charged ion

an·ise \ˈan-əs\ *n* : an herb related to the carrot with aromatic seeds (**aniseed** \-ə(s)-ˌsēd\) used in flavoring

an·is·ette \ˌan-ə-ˈset, -ˈzet\ *n* [F] : a usu. colorless sweet liqueur flavored with aniseed

ankh \ˈaŋk\ *n* : a cross having a loop for its upper vertical arm and serving esp. in ancient Egypt as an emblem of life

an·kle \ˈaŋ-kəl\ *n* : the joint or region between the foot and the leg

an·kle·bone \ˌan-kəl-ˈbōn, ˈaŋ-kəl-ˌbōn\ *n* : the bone that in human beings bears the weight of the body and with the tibia and fibula forms the ankle joint

an·klet \ˈaŋ-klət\ *n* **1** : something (as an ornament) worn around the ankle **2** : a short sock reaching slightly above the ankle

ann *abbr* **1** annals **2** annual

an·nals \ˈan-ᵊlz\ *n pl* **1** : a record of events in chronological order **2** : his-

torical records — **an·nal·ist** \-ᵊl-əst\ *n*

an·neal \ə-ˈnēl\ *vb* : to make (as glass or steel) less brittle by heating and then cooling

¹an·nex \ə-ˈneks, ˈan-ˌeks\ *vb* **1** : to attach as an addition **2** : to incorporate (as a territory) within a political domain — **an·nex·a·tion** \ˌan-ˌek-ˈsā-shən\ *n*

²an·nex \ˈan-ˌeks, -iks\ *n* : a subsidiary or supplementary structure

an·ni·hi·late \ə-ˈnī-ə-ˌlāt\ *vb* **-lat·ed; -lat·ing** : to destroy completely — **an·ni·hi·la·tion** \-ˌnī-ə-ˈlā-shən\ *n*

an·ni·ver·sa·ry \ˌan-ə-ˈvərs-(ə-)rē\ *n, pl* **-ries** : the annual return of the date of some notable event and esp. a wedding

an·no Do·mi·ni \ˌan-ō-ˈdäm-ə-nē, -ˈdō-mə-, -ˌnī\ *adv, often cap A* [ML, in the year of the Lord] — used to indicate that a time division falls within the Christian era

an·no·tate \ˈan-ə-ˌtāt\ *vb* **-tat·ed; -tat·ing** : to furnish with notes — **an·no·ta·tion** \ˌan-ə-ˈtā-shən\ *n* — **an·no·ta·tor** \ˈan-ə-ˌtāt-ər\ *n*

an·nounce \ə-ˈnaúns\ *vb* **-nounced; -nounc·ing 1** : to make known publicly **2** : to give notice of the arrival or presence of — **an·nounce·ment** *n*

an·nounc·er \ə-ˈnaún-sər\ *n* : a person who introduces radio or television programs, reads commercials and news summaries, and gives station identification

an·noy \ə-ˈnói\ *vb* : to disturb or irritate esp. by repeated acts : VEX **syn** irk, bother, pester, tease, harass — **an·noy·ing·ly** \-ˈnói-iŋ-lē\ *adv*

an·noy·ance \ə-ˈnói-əns\ *n* **1** : the act of annoying **2** : the state of being annoyed **3** : NUISANCE

¹an·nu·al \ˈan-yə(-wə)l\ *adj* **1** : covering the period of a year **2** : occurring once a year : YEARLY **3** : completing the life cycle in one growing season ⟨∼ plants⟩ — **an·nu·al·ly** \-ē\ *adv*

²annual *n* **1** : a publication appearing once a year **2** : an annual plant

annual ring *n* : the layer of wood produced by a single year's growth of a woody plant

an·nu·i·tant \ə-ˈn(y)ü-ət-ənt\ *n* : a beneficiary of an annuity

an·nu·i·ty \ə-ˈn(y)ü-ət-ē\ *n, pl* **-i·ties** : an

amount payable annually; *also* : the right to receive such a payment

an•nul \ə-'nəl\ *vb* **an•nulled; an•nul•ling** : to make legally void — **an•nul•ment** *n*

an•nu•lar \'an-yə-lər\ *adj* : ring-shaped

annular eclipse *n* : an eclipse in which a thin outer ring of the sun's disk is not covered by the moon's disk

an•nun•ci•ate \ə-'nən-sē-,āt\ *vb* **-at•ed; -at•ing** : ANNOUNCE

an•nun•ci•a•tion \ə-,nən-sē-'ā-shən\ *n* **1** : ANNOUNCEMENT **2** *cap* : March 25 observed as a church festival commemorating the announcement of the Incarnation

an•nun•ci•a•tor \ə-'nən-sē-,āt-ər\ *n* : one that annunciates; *specif* : a usu. electrically controlled signal board or indicator

an•ode \'an-,ōd\ *n* **1** : the positive electrode of an electrolytic cell **2** : the negative terminal of a battery **3** : the electron-collecting electrode of an electron tube — **an•od•ic** \a-'näd-ik\ *or* **an•od•al** \-'nōd-əl\ *adj*

an•od•ize \'an-ə-,dīz\ *vb* **-ized; -iz•ing** : to subject (a metal) to electrolytic action as the anode of a cell in order to coat with a protective or decorative film

an•o•dyne \'an-ə-,dīn\ *n* : something that relieves pain : a soothing agent

anoint \ə-'nȯint\ *vb* **1** : to apply oil to esp. as a sacred rite **2** : CONSECRATE — **anoint•ment** *n*

anom•a•lous \ə 'näm-ə-ləs\ *adj* : deviating from a general rule : ABNORMAL

anom•a•ly \ə-'näm-ə-lē\ *n, pl* **-lies** : something anomalous : IRREGULARITY

¹anon \ə-'nän\ *adv, archaic* : SOON

²anon *abbr* anonymous; anonymously

anon•y•mous \ə-'nän-ə-məs\ *adj* : of unknown or undeclared origin or authorship — **an•o•nym•i•ty** \,an-ə-'nim-ət-ē\ *n* — **anon•y•mous•ly** \ə-'nän-ə-məs-lē\ *adv*

anoph•e•les \ə-'näf-ə-,lēz\ *n* [NL, genus name, fr. Gk *anōphelēs* useless, fr. *a-* not + *ophelos* advantage, help] : any of a genus of mosquitoes that includes all mosquitoes which transmit malaria to human beings

an•o•rec•tic \,an-ə-'rek-tik\ *also* **an•o•ret•ic** \-'ret-ik\ *adj* : ANOREXIC — **anorectic** *n*

an•orex•ia \,an-ə-'rek-sē-ə\ *n* : loss of appetite esp. when prolonged

anorexia ner•vo•sa \-nər-'vō-sə\ *n* : a psychological and endocrine disorder primarily of young women marked esp. by faulty eating patterns, malnutrition, and usu. excessive weight loss

an•orex•ic \,an-ə-'rek-sik\ *adj* **1** : lacking or causing loss of appetite **2** : affected with or as if with anorexia nervosa — **anorexic** *n*

¹an•oth•er \ə-'nəth-ər\ *adj* **1** : some other **2** : being one in addition : one more

²another *pron* **1** : an additional one : one more **2** : one that is different from the first or present one

ans *abbr* answer

¹an•swer \'an-sər\ *n* **1** : something spoken or written in reply to a question **2** : a solution of a problem

²answer *vb* **an•swered; an•swer•ing** \'ans-(ə-)riŋ\ **1** : to speak or write in reply to **2** : to be responsible **3** : to be adequate — **an•swer•er** *n*

an•swer•able \'ans-(ə-)rə-bəl\ *adj* **1** : subject to taking blame or responsibility **2** : capable of being refuted

answering service *n* : a commercial service that answers telephone calls for its clients

¹ant \'ant\ *n* : any of a family of small social insects related to the bees and living in communities usu. in earth or wood

²ant *abbr* antonym

Ant *abbr* Antarctica

ant- — see ANTI-

¹-ant \ənt\ *n suffix* **1** : one that performs or promotes (a specified action) ⟨cool*ant*⟩ **2** : thing that is acted upon (in a specified manner) ⟨inhal*ant*⟩

²-ant *adj suffix* **1** : performing (a specified action) or being (in a specified condition) ⟨propell*ant*⟩ **2** : promoting (a specified action or process) ⟨expector*ant*⟩

ant•ac•id \ant-'as-əd\ *n* : an agent that counteracts acidity — **antacid** *adj*

an•tag•o•nism \an-'tag-ə-,niz-əm\ *n* **1** : active opposition or hostility **2** : opposition in physiological action — **an•tag•o•nis•tic** \-,tag-ə-'nis-tik\ *adj*

an•tag•o•nist \-nəst\ *n* : ADVERSARY, OPPONENT

an•tag•o•nize \an-'tag-ə-,nīz\ *vb* **-nized; -niz•ing** : to provoke the hostility of

ant·arc·tic \ant-'ärk-tik, -'ärt-ik\ *adj, often cap* : of or relating to the south pole or the region near it

antarctic circle *n, often cap A&C* : the parallel of latitude that is approximately 66½ degrees south of the equator

¹an·te \'ant-ē\ *n* : a poker stake put up by each player before he sees his hand; *also* : an amount paid : PRICE

²ante *vb* **an·ted; an·te·ing 1** : to put up (an ante) **2** : PAY

ant·eat·er \'ant-,ēt-ər\ *n* : any of several mammals (as an aardvark) that feed on ants

an·te·bel·lum \,ant-i-'bel-əm\ *adj* : existing before a war; *esp* : existing before the U.S. Civil War of 1861-65

an·te·ced·ent \,ant-ə-'sēd-ᵊnt\ *n* **1** : a noun, pronoun, phrase, or clause referred to by a personal or relative pronoun **2** : a preceding event or cause **3** *pl* : the significant conditions of one's earlier life **4** *pl* : ANCESTORS — **antecedent** *adj*

an·te·cham·ber \'ant-i-,chām-bər\ *n* : ANTEROOM

an·te·date \'ant-i-,dāt\ *vb* **1** : to date (a paper) as of an earlier day than that on which the actual writing or signing is done **2** : to precede in time

an·te·di·lu·vi·an \,ant-i-də-'lü-vē-ən, -dī-\ *adj* **1** : of the period before the biblical flood **2** : ANTIQUATED, OBSOLETE

an·te·lope \'ant-ᵊl-,ōp\ *n, pl* **-lope** *or* **-lopes** [ME, fabulous heraldic beast, prob. fr. MF *antelop* savage animal with sawlike horns, fr. ML *anthalopus*, fr. LGk *antholops*] **1** : any of various Old World cud-chewing mammals related to the oxen but with smaller lighter bodies and horns that extend upward and backward **2** : PRONGHORN

an·te me·ri·di·em \'ant-i-mə-'rid-ē-əm\ *adj* [L] : being before noon

an·ten·na \an-'ten-ə\ *n, pl* **-nae** \-(,)ē\ *or* **-nas** [ML, fr. L, sail yard] **1** : one of the long slender paired segmented sensory organs on the head of an arthropod (as an insect or crab) **2** *pl usu* **-nas** : a metallic device (as a rod or wire) for sending out or receiving radio waves

an·te·pe·nult \,ant-i-'pē-,nəlt\ *also* **an-**

te·pen·ul·ti·ma \-pi-'nəl-tə-mə\ *n* : the 3d syllable of a word counting from the end — **an·te·pen·ul·ti·mate** \-pi-'nəl-tə-mət\ *adj or n*

an·te·ri·or \an-'tir-ē-ər\ *adj* **1** : situated before or toward the front **2** : situated near or nearer to the head **3** : coming before in time **syn** preceding, previous, prior, antecedent

an·te·room \'ant-i-,rüm, -,rum\ *n* : a room forming the entrance to another and often used as a waiting room

an·them \'an-thəm\ *n* **1** : a sacred vocal composition **2** : a song or hymn of praise or gladness

an·ther \'an-thər\ *n* : the part of a stamen of a seed plant that contains pollen

ant·hill \'ant-,hil\ *n* : a mound thrown up by ants or termites in digging their nest

an·thol·o·gy \an-'thäl-ə-jē\ *n, pl* **-gies** [NL *anthologia* collection of epigrams, fr. MGk, fr. Gk, flower gathering, fr. *anthos* flower + *logia* collecting, fr. *legein* to gather] : a collection of literary selections — **an·thol·o·gist** \-jəst\ *n* — **an·thol·o·gize** \-,jīz\ *vb*

an·thra·cite \'an-thrə-,sīt\ *n* : a hard glossy coal that burns without much smoke

an·thrax \'an-,thraks\ *n* : an infectious and usu. fatal bacterial disease of warm-blooded animals (as cattle and sheep); *also* : a bacterium causing anthrax

an·thro·po·cen·tric \,an-thrə-pə-'sen-trik\ *adj* : interpreting or regarding the world in terms of human values and experiences

¹an·thro·poid \'an-thrə-,pȯid\ *n* : any of several large tailless apes (as a gorilla)

²anthropoid *adj* **1** : resembling a human being esp. in shape **2** : resembling an ape esp. in action

an·thro·pol·o·gy \,an-thrə-'päl-ə-jē\ *n* : the science of human beings and esp. of their physical characteristics, their origin and the distribution of races, their environment and social relations, and their culture — **an·thro·po·log·i·cal** \-pə-'läj-i-kəl\ *adj* — **an·thro·pol·o·gist** \-'päl-ə-jəst\ *n*

an·thro·po·mor·phism \,an-thrə-pə-'mȯr-,fiz-əm\ *n* : an interpretation of what is not human or personal in terms of human or personal characteristics : HUMANIZATION — **an•thro•po•mor•phic** \-fik\ *adj*

an•ti \'an-ˌtī, 'ant-ē\ *n, pl* **antis** : one who is opposed

anti- \ˌant-i, -ē; ˌan-ˌtī\ *or* **ant-** *or* **anth-** *prefix* **1** : opposite in kind, position, or action **2** : opposing : hostile toward **3** : counteractive **4** : preventive of : curative of

antiaircraft	anti–imperialism
anti–American	anti–imperialist
antibacterial	antilabor
anticapitalist	antimalarial
anti–Catholic	antimicrobial
anticlerical	antislavery
anticolonial	antispasmodic
anticommunism	antistatic
anticommunist	antisubmarine
antidemocractic	antitank
antiestablishment	antitrust
antifascist	antiviral

an•ti•abor•tion \ˌant-ē-ə-'bȯr-shən, ˌan-ˌtī-\ *adj* : opposed to abortion

an•ti•bal•lis•tic missile \ˌant-i-bə-ˌlis-tik-, ˌan-ˌtī-\ *n* : a missile for intercepting and destroying ballistic missiles

an•ti•bi•ot•ic \-bī-'ät-ik, -bē-\ *n* : a substance produced by or derived by chemical alteration of a substance produced by a microorganism (as a fungus or bacterium) that in dilute solution inhibits or kills another microorganism — **antibiotic** *adj*

an•ti•body \'ant-i-ˌbäd-ē\ *n* : any of the bodily substances produced in response to specific foreign substances or organisms (as a disease-producing microorganism) and counteracting their effects

¹**an•tic** \'ant-ik\ *n* : an often wildly playful or funny act or action

²**antic** *adj* [It *antico* ancient, fr. L *antiquus*] **1** *archaic* : GROTESQUE **2** : PLAYFUL

an•ti•can•cer \ˌant-i-'kan-sər, ˌan-ˌtī-\ *adj* : used or effective against cancer ⟨~ drugs⟩

An•ti•christ \'ant-i-ˌkrīst\ *n* **1** : one who denies or opposes Christ **2** : a false Christ

an•tic•i•pate \an-'tis-ə-ˌpāt\ *vb* **-pat•ed; -pat•ing 1** : to foresee and provide for beforehand **2** : to look forward to — **an•tic•i•pa•tion** \-ˌtis-ə-'pā-shən\ *n* — **an•tic•i•pa•to•ry** \-'tis-ə-pə-ˌtȯr-ē\ *adj*

an•ti•cli•max \ˌant-i-'klī-ˌmaks\ *n* : something closing a series that is strikingly less important than what has preceded it — **an•ti•cli•mac•tic** \-klī-'mak-tik\ *adj*

an•ti•cline \'ant-i-ˌklīn\ *n* : an arch of layers of rock in the earth's crust

an•ti•co•ag•u•lant \ˌant-i-kō-'ag-yə-lənt\ *n* : a substance that hinders the clotting of blood — **anticoagulant** *adj*

an•ti•cy•clone \ˌant-i-'sī-ˌklōn\ *n* : a system of winds that rotates about a center of high atmospheric pressure — **an•ti•cy•clon•ic** \-sī-'klän-ik\ *adj*

¹**an•ti•de•pres•sant** \ˌant-i-di-'pres-ᵊnt, ˌan-ˌtī-\ *adj* : used or tending to relieve psychic depression ⟨~ drugs⟩

²**antidepressant** *n* : an antidepressant drug

an•ti•dote \'ant-i-ˌdōt\ *n* : a remedy to counteract the effects of poison

an•ti•fer•til•i•ty \-fər-'til-ət-ē\ *adj* : tending to control excess or unwanted fertility : CONTRACEPTIVE ⟨~ agents⟩

an•ti•freeze \'ant-i-ˌfrēz\ *n* : a substance that prevents a liquid from freezing

an•ti•gen \'ant-i-jən\ *n* : a usu. protein or carbohydrate substance (as a toxin or an enzyme) capable of stimulating an immune response — **an•ti•gen•ic** \ˌant-i-'jen-ik\ *adj* — **an•ti•ge•nic•i•ty** \-jə-'nis-ət-ē\ *n*

an•ti•grav•i•ty \ˌant-i-'grav-ət-ē, ˌan-ˌtī-\ *adj* : reducing or canceling the effect of gravity

an•ti•he•ro \'ant-i-ˌhē-rō, 'an-ˌtī-\ *n* : a protagonist who is notably lacking in heroic qualities (as courage)

an•ti•his•ta•mine \ˌant-i-'his-tə-ˌmēn, ˌan-ˌtī-, -mən\ *n* : any of various drugs used in treating allergies and colds

an•ti•hy•per•ten•sive \-ˌhī-pər-'ten-siv\ *n* : a substance that is effective against high blood pressure — **antihypertensive** *adj*

an•ti–in•flam•ma•to•ry \-in-'flam-ə-ˌtōrē\ *adj* : counteracting inflammation — **anti–inflammatory** *n*

an•ti–in•tel•lec•tu•al \-ˌint-ᵊl-'ek-chəwəl\ *adj* : opposing or hostile to intellectuals or to an intellectual view or approach

an•ti•knock \ˌant-i-'näk\ *n* : a fuel additive to prevent knocking in an internal-combustion engine

an·ti·log·a·rithm \ˌant-i-'lȯg-ə-ˌrith-əm, ˌan-ˌtī-, -'läg-\ *n* : the number corresponding to a given logarithm

an·ti·ma·cas·sar \ˌant-i-mə-'kas-ər\ *n* : a cover to protect the back or arms of furniture

an·ti·mag·net·ic \ˌant-i-mag-'net-ik, ˌan-ˌtī-\ *adj* : having a balance unit composed of alloys that will not remain magnetized ⟨an ∼ watch⟩

an·ti·mat·ter \'ant-i-ˌmat-ər\ *n* : matter composed of the counterparts of ordinary matter

an·ti·mo·ny \'ant-ə-ˌmō-nē\ *n* : a brittle silvery white metallic chemical element used in alloys

an·ti·neu·tron \-'n(y)ü-ˌträn\ *n* : the uncharged antiparticle of the neutron

an·ti·no·mi·an \ˌant-i-'nō-mē-ən\ *n* : one who denies the validity of moral laws

an·tin·o·my \an-'tin-ə-mē\ *n, pl* **-mies** : a contradiction between two seemingly true statements

an·ti·nov·el \'ant-i-ˌnäv-əl, 'an-ˌtī-\ *n* : a work of fiction that lacks all or most of the traditional features of the novel

an·ti·nu·cle·ar \ˌant-i-'n(y)ü-klē-ər\ *adj* : opposing the use or production of nuclear power plants

an·ti·ox·i·dant \ˌant-ē-'äk-səd-ənt, ˌan-ˌtī-\ *n* : a substance that inhibits oxidation — **antioxidant** *adj*

an·ti·par·ti·cle \'ant-i-ˌpärt-i-kəl, 'an-ˌtī-\ *n* : an elementary particle identical to another elementary particle in mass but opposite to it in electric and magnetic properties

an·ti·pas·to \ˌant-i-'pas-tō, ˌänt-i-'päs-\ *n, pl* **-ti** : any of various typically Italian hors d'oeuvres

an·tip·a·thy \an-'tip-ə-thē\ *n, pl* **-thies 1** : settled aversion or dislike **2** : an object of aversion — **an·ti·pa·thet·ic** \ˌant-i-pə-'thet-ik\ *adj*

an·ti·per·son·nel \ˌant-i-ˌpərs-ᵊn-'el, ˌan-ˌtī-\ *adj* : designed for use against military personnel ⟨∼ mine⟩

an·ti·per·spi·rant \-'pər-spə-rənt\ *n* : a cosmetic preparation used to check excessive perspiration

an·tiph·o·nal \an-'tif-ən-ᵊl\ *adj* : per-

formed by two alternating groups — **an·tiph·o·nal·ly** \-ē\ *adv*

an·ti·pode \'ant-ə-ˌpōd\ *n, pl* **an·tip·o·des** \an-'tip-ə-ˌdēz\ [ME *antipodes*, pl., persons dwelling at opposite points on the globe, fr. L, fr. Gk, fr. pl. of *antipod-, antipous* with feet opposite, fr. *anti-* against + *pod-, pous* foot] : the parts of the earth diametrically opposite — usu. used in pl. — **an·tip·o·dal** \an-'tip-əd-ᵊl\ *adj* — **an·tip·o·de·an** \(ˌ)an-ˌtip-ə-'dē-ən\ *adj*

an·ti·pol·lu·tion \ˌant-i-pə-'lü-shən\ *adj* : designed to prevent, reduce, or eliminate pollution ⟨∼ laws⟩

an·ti·pope \'ant-i-ˌpōp\ *n* : one elected or claiming to be pope in opposition to the pope canonically chosen

an·ti·pov·er·ty \ˌant-i-'päv-ərt-ē, ˌan-ˌtī-\ *adj* : of or relating to legislation designed to relieve poverty

an·ti·pro·ton \-'prō-ˌtän\ *n* : the antiparticle of the proton

an·ti·quar·i·an \ˌant-ə-'kwer-ē-ən\ *adj* **1** : of or relating to antiquities **2** : dealing in old books — **antiquarian** *n* — **an·ti·quar·i·an·ism** *n*

an·ti·quary \'ant-ə-ˌkwer-ē\ *n, pl* **-quaries** : a person who collects or studies antiquities

an·ti·quat·ed \'ant-ə-ˌkwāt-əd\ *adj* : OUT-OF-DATE, OLD-FASHIONED

¹an·tique \an-'tēk\ *n* : an object made in a bygone period

²antique *adj* **1** : belonging to antiquity **2** : OLD-FASHIONED **3** : of a bygone style or period

³antique *vb* **-tiqued; -tiqu·ing** : to finish or refinish in antique style : give an appearance of age to

an·tiq·ui·ty \an-'tik-wət-ē\ *n, pl* **-ties 1** : ancient times **2** : great age **3** *pl* : relics of ancient times **4** *pl* : matters relating to ancient culture

an·ti–Sem·i·tism \ˌant-i-'sem-ə-ˌtiz-əm, ˌan-ˌtī-\ *n* : hostility toward Jews as a religious or social minority — **an·ti–Se·mit·ic** \-sə-'mit-ik\ *adj*

an·ti·sep·tic \ˌant-ə-'sep-tik\ *adj* **1** : killing or checking the growth of germs that cause decay or infection **2** : scrupulously clean : ASEPTIC — **antiseptic** *n* — **an·ti·sep·ti·cal·ly** \-ti-k(ə-)lē\ *adv*

an·ti·se·rum \'ant-i-ˌsir-əm, 'an-ˌtī-\ *n* : a serum containing antibodies

an·ti·so·cial \-'sō-shəl\ *adj* **1** : disliking the society of others **2** : contrary or hostile to the well-being of society ⟨crime is ∼⟩

an·tith·e·sis \an-'tith-ə-səs\ *n, pl* **-e·ses** \-ˌsēz\ **1** : the opposition or contrast of ideas **2** : the direct opposite

an·ti·thet·i·cal \ˌant-ə-'thet-i-kəl\ *also* **an·ti·thet·ic** \-ik\ *adj* : constituting or marked by antithesis — **an·ti·thet·i·cal·ly** \-i-k(ə-)lē\ *adv*

an·ti·tox·in \ˌant-i-'täk-sən\ *n* : an antibody that is able to neutralize a particular toxin, is formed when the toxin is introduced into the body, and is produced in lower animals for use in treating human diseases (as diphtheria); *also* : a serum containing antitoxin

an·ti·tu·mor \ˌant-i-'t(y)ü-mər, ˌan-ˌtī-\ *adj* : ANTICANCER

an·ti·ven·in \-'ven-ən\ *n* : an antitoxin to a venom; *also* : a serum containing such antitoxin

ant·ler \'ant-lər\ *n* [ME *aunteler*, fr. MF *antoillier*, fr. L *anteocularis* located before the eye, fr. *ante-* before + *oculus* eye] : the solid usu. branched horn of a deer; *also* : a branch of this horn — **ant·lered** \-lərd\ *adj*

ant lion *n* : any of various insects having a long-jawed larva that digs a conical pit in which it lies in wait for insects (as ants) on which it feeds

ant·onym \'ant-ə-ˌnim\ *n* : a word of opposite meaning

anus \'ā-nəs\ *n* [L] : the lower or posterior opening of the alimentary canal

an·vil \'an-vəl\ *n* **1** : a heavy iron block on which metal is shaped **2** : INCUS

anx·i·ety \aŋ-'zī-ət-ē\ *n, pl* **-et·ies** **1** : painful uneasiness of mind usu. over an anticipated ill **2** : abnormal apprehension and fear often accompanied by physiological signs (as sweating and increased pulse), by doubt about the nature and reality of the threat itself, and by self-doubt

anx·ious \'aŋk-shəs\ *adj* **1** : uneasy in mind : WORRIED **2** : earnestly wishing : EAGER — **anx·ious·ly** *adv*

¹any \'en-ē\ *adj* **1** : one chosen at random **2** : of whatever number or quantity

²any *pron* **1** : any one or ones ⟨take ∼ of the books you like⟩ **2** : any amount ⟨∼ of the money not used is to be returned⟩

³any *adv* : to any extent or degree : AT ALL ⟨could not walk ∼ farther⟩

any·body \-ˌbäd-ē, -bəd-\ *pron* : ANYONE

any·how \-ˌhau̇\ *adv* **1** : in any way **2** : NEVERTHELESS; *also* : in any case

any·more \ˌen-ē-'mōr\ *adv* **1** : any longer **2** : at the present time

any·one \-(ˌ)wən\ *pron* : any person

any·place \-ˌplās\ *adv* : ANYWHERE

any·thing \-ˌthiŋ\ *pron* : any thing whatever

any·time \'en-ē-ˌtīm\ *adv* : at any time whatever

any·way \-ˌwā\ *adv* : ANYHOW

any·where \-ˌhweər\ *adv* : in or to any place

any·wise \-ˌwīz\ *adv* : in any way whatever

A–OK \ˌā-ō-'kā\ *adv or adj* : very definitely OK

A1 \'ā-'wən\ *adj* : of the finest quality

A/1C *abbr* airman first class

aor·ta \ā-'ȯrt-ə\ *n, pl* **-tas** *or* **-tae** \-ē\ : the main artery that carries blood from the heart — **aor·tic** \-'ȯrt-ik\ *adj*

ap *abbr* **1** apostle **2** apothecaries'

AP *abbr* **1** American plan **2** Associated Press

apace \ə-'pās\ *adv* : SWIFTLY

Apache \ə-'pach-ē *for 1;* ə-'pash *for 2*\ *n, pl* **Apache** *or* **Apach·es** \-'pach-ēz, -'pash(-əz)\ **1** : a member of an American Indian people of the southwestern U.S.; *also* : any of the languages of the Apache people **2** *not cap* : a member of a gang of criminals esp. in Paris

ap·a·nage var of APPANAGE

apart \ə-'pärt\ *adv* **1** : separately in place or time **2** : ASIDE **3** : in two or more parts : to pieces

apart·heid \ə-'pär-ˌtāt, -ˌtīt\ *n* [Afrikaans] : a policy of racial segregation practiced in the Republic of So. Africa

apart·ment \ə-'pärt-mənt\ *n* : a room or set of rooms occupied as a dwelling; *also* : a building divided into individual dwelling units

ap·a·thy \'ap-ə-thē\ *n* **1** : lack of emotion **2** : lack of interest : INDIFFERENCE — **ap·a·thet·ic** \ˌap-ə-'thet-ik\ *adj* — **ap·a·thet·i·cal·ly** \-i-k(ə-)lē\ *adv*

ap·a·tite \\'ap-ə-ˌtīt\ *n* : any of a group of minerals that are phosphates of calcium and are used as a source of phosphorus

APB *abbr* all points bulletin

¹**ape** \\'āp\ *n* 1 : any of the larger tailless primates (as a baboon or gorilla); *also* : MONKEY 2 : MIMIC, IMITATOR; *also* : a large uncouth person

²**ape** *vb* **aped; ap·ing** : IMITATE, MIMIC

ape–man \\'āp-ˌman\ *n* : a primate intermediate in character between true man and the higher apes

aper·çu \ä-per-sᵫ̄, ˌap-ər-'sü\ *n, pl* **aperçus** \-sᵫ̄(z), -'süz\ : an immediate impression; *esp* : INSIGHT

aper·i·tif \ˌäp-ˌer-ə-'tēf\ *n* : an alcoholic drink taken as an appetizer

ap·er·ture \\'ap-ə(r)-ˌchùr, -chər\ *n* : OPENING, HOLE

apex \\'ā-ˌpeks\ *n, pl* **apex·es** *or* **api·ces** \\'ā-pə-ˌsēz, 'ap-ə-\ : the highest point : PEAK

apha·sia \ə-'fā-zh(ē-)ə\ *n* : loss or impairment of the power to use or comprehend words — **apha·sic** \-zik\ *adj or n*

aph·elion \a-'fēl-yən\ *n, pl* **-elia** \-yə\ [NL, fr. *apo-* away from + Gk *hēlios* sun] : the point in an object's orbit most distant from the sun

aphid \\'ā-fəd, 'af-əd\ *n* : a small insect that sucks the juices of plants

aphis \\'ā-fəs, 'af-əs\ *n, pl* **aphi·des** \\'ā-fə-ˌdēz, 'af-ə-\ : APHID

aph·o·rism \\'af-ə-ˌriz-əm\ *n* : a short saying stating a general truth : MAXIM — **aph·o·ris·tic** \ˌaf-ə-'ris-tik\ *adj*

aph·ro·di·si·ac \ˌaf-rə-'diz-ē-ˌak, -'dē-zē-\ *adj* : exciting sexual desire — **aphrodisiac** *n*

api·ary \\'ā-pē-ˌer-ē\ *n, pl* **-ar·ies** : a place where bees are kept — **api·a·rist** \-pē-ə-rəst\ *n*

api·cal \\'ā-pi-kəl, 'ap-i-\ *adj* : of, relating to, or situated at an apex — **api·cal·ly** \-k(ə-)lē\ *adv*

apiece \ə-'pēs\ *adv* : for each one

aplomb \ə-'pläm, -'pləm\ *n* [F, lit., perpendicularity, fr. MF, fr. *a plomb*, lit., according to the plummet] : complete composure or self-assurance

APO *abbr* army post office

Apoc *abbr* 1 Apocalypse 2 Apocrypha

apoc·a·lypse \ə-'päk-ə-ˌlips\ *n* 1 : a writing prophesying a cataclysm in which evil forces are destroyed 2 *cap* — see BIBLE table — **apoc·a·lyp·tic** \-ˌpäk-ə-'lip-tik\ *also* **apoc·a·lyp·ti·cal** \-ti-kəl\ *adj*

Apoc·ry·pha \ə-'päk-rə-fə\ *n* 1 *not cap* : writings of dubious authenticity 2 : books included in the Septuagint and Vulgate but excluded from the Jewish and Protestant canons of the Old Testament — see BIBLE table 3 : early Christian writings not included in the New Testament

apoc·ry·phal \-fəl\ *adj* 1 *often cap* : of or resembling the Apocrypha 2 : not canonical : SPURIOUS — **apoc·ry·phal·ly** \-ē\ *adv*

apo·gee \\'ap-ə-(ˌ)jē\ *n* [F *apogée*, fr. NL *apogaeum*, fr. Gk *apogaion*, fr. *apo* away from + *gē* earth] : the point at which an orbiting object is farthest from the body being orbited

apo·lit·i·cal \ˌā-pə-'lit-i-kəl\ *adj* 1 : having an aversion for or no interest in political affairs 2 : having no political significance — **apo·lit·i·cal·ly** \-k(ə-)lē\ *adv*

apol·o·get·ic \ə-ˌpäl-ə-'jet-ik\ *adj* : expressing apology — **apol·o·get·i·cal·ly** \-i-k(ə-)lē\ *adv*

ap·o·lo·gia \ˌap-ə-'lō-j(ē-)ə\ *n* : APOLOGY; *esp* : an argument in support or justification

apol·o·gize \ə-'päl-ə-ˌjīz\ *vb* **-gized; -gizing** : to make an apology : express regret — **apol·o·gist** \-jəst\ *n*

apol·o·gy \ə-'päl-ə-jē\ *n, pl* **-gies** 1 : a formal justification : DEFENSE 2 : an expression of regret for a wrong

apo·lune \\'ap-ə-ˌlün\ *n* : the point in a lunar orbit farthest from the moon's surface

ap·o·plexy \\'ap-ə-ˌplek-sē\ *n* : STROKE 3 — **ap·o·plec·tic** \ˌap-ə-'plek-tik\ *adj*

aport \ə-'pōrt\ *adv* : on or toward the left side of a ship

apos·ta·sy \ə-'päs-tə-sē\ *n, pl* **-sies** : a renunciation or abandonment of a former loyalty (as to a religion) — **apostate** \ə-'päs-ˌtāt, -tət\ *adj or n*

a pos·te·ri·o·ri \ˌä-pō-ˌstir-ē-'ōr-ē\ *adj* [L, lit., from the latter] : relating to or derived by reasoning from observed facts — **a posteriori** *adv*

apos·tle \ə-'päs-əl\ *n* 1 : one of the group composed of Jesus' 12 original disciples and Paul 2 : the first prominent missionary to a region or group **3** : one who initiates or first advocates a great reform — **apos·tle·ship** n

ap·os·tol·ic \ˌap-ə-'stäl-ik\ adj **1** : of or relating to an apostle or to the New Testament apostles **2** : of or relating to a succession of spiritual authority from the apostles **3** : PAPAL

¹**apos·tro·phe** \ə-'päs-trə-(ˌ)fē\ n : the rhetorical addressing of a usu. absent person or a usu. personified thing (as in "O grave, where is thy victory?")

²**apostrophe** n : a punctuation mark ' used esp. to indicate the possessive case or the omission of a letter or figure

apos·tro·phize \ə-'päs-trə-ˌfīz\ vb **-phized; -phiz·ing** : to address as if present or capable of understanding

apothecaries' weight n : a system of weights based on the troy pound and ounce and used chiefly by pharmacists — see WEIGHT table

apoth·e·cary \ə-'päth-ə-ˌker-ē\ n, pl **-car·ies** [ME apothecarie, fr. ML apothecarius, fr. LL, shopkeeper, fr. L apotheca storehouse, fr. Gk apothēkē, fr. apotithenai to put away] : DRUGGIST

ap·o·thegm \'ap-ə-ˌthem\ n : APHORISM, MAXIM

apo·the·o·sis \ə-ˌpäth-ē-'ō-səs, ˌap-ə-'thē-ə-səs\ n, pl **-o·ses** \-ˌsēz\ **1** : DEIFICATION **2** : the perfect example

app abbr **1** apparatus **2** appendix

ap·pall also **ap·pal** \ə-'pol\ vb **ap·palled; ap·pall·ing** : to overcome with horror : DISMAY

Ap·pa·loo·sa \ˌap-ə-'lü-sə\ n : any of a breed of saddle horses developed in northwestern No. America that have small dark spots or blotches on a white coat

ap·pa·nage \'ap-ə-nij\ n **1** : provision (as a grant of land) made by a sovereign or legislative body for dependent members of the royal family **2** : a rightful adjunct

ap·pa·ra·tus \ˌap-ə-'rat-əs, -'rāt-\ n, pl **-tus·es** or **-tus** [L] **1** : a set of materials or equipment for a particular use **2** : a complex machine or device : MECHANISM **3** : the organization of a political party or underground movement

¹**ap·par·el** \ə-'par-əl\ vb **-eled** or **-elled;** **-el·ing** or **-el·ling** **1** : CLOTHE, DRESS **2** : ADORN

²**apparel** n : CLOTHING, DRESS

ap·par·ent \ə-'par-ənt\ adj **1** : open to view : VISIBLE **2** : EVIDENT, OBVIOUS **3** : appearing as real or true : SEEMING — **ap·par·ent·ly** adv

ap·pa·ri·tion \ˌap-ə-'rish-ən\ n : a supernatural appearance : GHOST

ap·peal \ə-'pēl\ vb **1** : to take steps to have (a case) reheard in a higher court **2** : to plead for help, corroboration, or decision **3** : to arouse a sympathetic response — **appeal** n

ap·pear \ə-'piər\ vb **1** : to become visible **2** : to come formally before an authority **3** : SEEM **4** : to become evident **5** : to come before the public

ap·pear·ance \ə-'pir-əns\ n **1** : the act of appearing **2** : outward aspect : LOOK **3** : PHENOMENON

ap·pease \ə-'pēz\ vb **ap·peased; ap·peas·ing** **1** : to cause to subside : ALLAY **2** : PACIFY, CONCILIATE; esp : to buy off by concessions — **ap·pease·ment** n

ap·pel·lant \ə-'pel-ənt\ n : one who appeals esp. from a judicial decision

ap·pel·late \ə-'pel-ət\ adj : having power to review decisions of a lower court

ap·pel·la·tion \ˌap-ə-'lā-shən\ n : NAME, DESIGNATION

ap·pel·lee \ˌap-ə-'lē\ n : one against whom an appeal is taken

ap·pend \ə-'pend\ vb : to attach esp. as something additional : AFFIX

ap·pend·age \ə-'pen-dij\ n **1** : something appended to a principal or greater thing **2** : a projecting part of the body (as an antenna) esp. when paired with one on each side **syn** accessory, adjunct, appendix, appurtenance

ap·pen·dec·to·my \ˌap-ən-'dek-tə-mē\ n, pl **-mies** : surgical removal of the intestinal appendix

ap·pen·di·ci·tis \ə-ˌpen-də-'sīt-əs\ n : inflammation of the intestinal appendix

ap·pen·dix \ə-'pen-diks\ n, pl **-dix·es** or **-di·ces** \-də-ˌsēz\ [L] **1** : supplementary matter added at the end of a book **2** : a narrow blind tube usu. about three or four inches long that extends from the cecum in the lower right-hand part of the abdomen

ap·per·tain \ˌap-ər-'tān\ vb : to belong as a rightful part or privilege

ap·pe·tite \'ap-ə-‚tīt\ *n* [ME *apetit*, fr. MF, fr. L *appetitus*, fr. *appetere* to strive after, fr. *ad-* to + *petere* to go to] **1** : natural desire for satisfying some want or need esp. for food **2** : TASTE, PREFERENCE

ap·pe·tiz·er \'ap-ə-‚tī-zər\ *n* : a food or drink taken just before a meal to stimulate the appetite

ap·pe·tiz·ing \-ziŋ\ *adj* : tempting to the appetite — **ap·pe·tiz·ing·ly** *adv*

appl *abbr* applied

ap·plaud \ə-'plȯd\ *vb* : to show approval esp. by clapping

ap·plause \ə-'plȯz\ *n* : approval publicly expressed (as by clapping)

ap·ple \'ap-əl\ *n* : a rounded fruit with firm white flesh and a seedy core; *also* : a tree that bears this fruit

ap·ple·jack \-‚jak\ *n* : a liquor distilled from fermented cider

ap·pli·ance \ə-'plī-əns\ *n* **1** : INSTRUMENT, DEVICE **2** : a piece of household equipment (as a stove or toaster) operated by gas or electricity

ap·pli·ca·ble \'ap-li-kə-bəl, ə-'plik-ə-\ *adj* : capable of being applied : RELEVANT — **ap·pli·ca·bil·i·ty** \‚ap-li-kə-'bil-ət-ē, ə-‚plik-ə-\ *n*

ap·pli·cant \'ap-li-kənt\ *n* : one who applies

ap·pli·ca·tion \‚ap-lə-'kā-shən\ *n* **1** : the act of applying **2** : assiduous attention **3** : REQUEST; *also* : a form used in making a request **4** : something placed or spread on a surface **5** : capacity for use

ap·pli·ca·tor \'ap-lə-‚kāt-ər\ *n* : one that applies; *esp* : a device for applying a substance (as medicine or polish)

ap·plied \ə-'plīd\ *adj* : put to practical use

ap·pli·qué \‚ap-lə-'kā\ *n* [F] : a fabric decoration cut out and fastened to a larger piece of material — **appliqué** *vb*

ap·ply \ə-'plī\ *vb* **ap·plied; ap·ply·ing 1** : to put to practical use **2** : to place in contact : put or spread on a surface **3** : to employ with close attention **4** : to submit a request **5** : to have reference or connection

ap·point \ə-'pȯint\ *vb* **1** : to fix or set officially ⟨~ a day for trial⟩ **2** : to name officially **3** : to fit out : EQUIP

ap·poin·tee \ə-‚pȯin-'tē, ‚a-\ *n* : a person appointed

ap·point·ive \ə-'pȯint-iv\ *adj* : subject to appointment

ap·point·ment \ə-'pȯint-mənt\ *n* **1** : the act of appointing **2** : a nonelective office or position **3** : an arrangement for a meeting **4** *pl* : FURNISHINGS, EQUIPMENT

ap·por·tion \ə-'pōr-shən\ *vb* **-tioned; -tion·ing** \-sh(ə-)niŋ\ : to distribute proportionately : ALLOT — **ap·por·tion·ment** *n*

ap·po·site \'ap-ə-zət\ *adj* : APPROPRIATE, RELEVANT — **ap·po·site·ly** *adv* — **ap·po·site·ness** *n*

ap·po·si·tion \‚ap-ə-'zish-ən\ *n* : a grammatical construction in which a noun or pronoun is followed by another that explains it (as *the poet* and *Burns* in ''a biography of the poet Burns'')

ap·pos·i·tive \ə-'päz-ət-iv, a-\ *adj* : of, relating to, or standing in grammatical apposition — **appositive** *n*

ap·praise \ə-'prāz\ *vb* **ap·praised; ap·prais·ing** : to set a value on — **ap·prais·al** \-'prā-zəl\ *n* — **ap·prais·er** *n*

ap·pre·cia·ble \ə-'prē-shə-bəl\ *adj* : large enough to be recognized and measured — **ap·pre·cia·bly** \-blē\ *adv*

ap·pre·ci·ate \ə-'prē-shē-‚āt\ *vb* **-at·ed; -at·ing 1** : to value justly **2** : to be aware of **3** : to be grateful for **4** : to increase in value — **ap·pre·ci·a·tion** \-‚prē-shē-'ā-shən\ *n*

ap·pre·cia·tive \ə-'prē-shət-iv, -shē-‚āt-\ *adj* : having or showing appreciation

ap·pre·hend \‚ap-ri-'hend\ *vb* **1** : ARREST **2** : to become aware of **3** : to look forward to with dread **4** : UNDERSTAND — **ap·pre·hen·sion** \-'hen-chən\ *n*

ap·pre·hen·sive \-'hen-siv\ *adj* : viewing the future with anxiety — **ap·pre·hen·sive·ly** *adv* — **ap·pre·hen·sive·ness** *n*

¹ap·pren·tice \ə-'prent-əs\ *n* **1** : a person learning a craft under a skilled worker **2** : BEGINNER — **ap·pren·tice·ship** *n*

²apprentice *vb* **-ticed; -tic·ing** : to bind or set at work as an apprentice

ap·prise \ə-'prīz\ *vb* **ap·prised; ap·pris·ing** : INFORM

ap·proach \ə-'prōch\ *vb* **1** : to move nearer to **2** : to be almost the same as **3** : to make advances to esp. for the purpose of creating a desired result **4** : to take preliminary steps toward — **approach** *n* — **ap•proach•able** *adj*

ap•pro•ba•tion \ˌap-rə-ˈbā-shən\ *n* : APPROVAL

¹**ap•pro•pri•ate** \ə-ˈprō-prē-ˌāt\ *vb* **-at•ed; -at•ing 1** : to take possession of **2** : to set apart for a particular use

²**ap•pro•pri•ate** \ə-ˈprō-prē-ət\ *adj* : fitted to a purpose or use : SUITABLE **syn** proper, fit, apt, befitting — **ap•pro•pri•ate•ly** *adv* — **ap•pro•pri•ate•ness** *n*

ap•pro•pri•a•tion \ə-ˌprō-prē-ˈā-shən\ *n* : money set aside by formal action for a specific use

ap•prov•al \ə-ˈprü-vəl\ *n* : an act of approving — **on approval** : subject to a prospective buyer's acceptance or refusal

ap•prove \ə-ˈprüv\ *vb* **ap•proved; ap•prov•ing 1** : to have or express a favorable opinion of **2** : to accept as satisfactory : RATIFY

approx *abbr* approximate; approximately

¹**ap•prox•i•mate** \ə-ˈpräk-sə-mət\ *adj* : nearly correct or exact — **ap•prox•i•mate•ly** *adv*

²**ap•prox•i•mate** \-ˌmāt\ *vb* **-mat•ed; -mat•ing** : to come near : APPROACH — **ap•prox•i•ma•tion** \ə-ˌpräk-sə-ˈmā-shən\ *n*

appt *abbr* appoint; appointed; appointment

ap•pur•te•nance \ə-ˈpərt-(ə)nəns\ *n* : something that belongs to or goes with another thing **syn** accessory, adjunct, appendage, appendix — **ap•pur•te•nant** \-(ə)nənt\ *adj*

Apr *abbr* April

APR *abbr* annual percentage rate

apri•cot \ˈap-rə-ˌkät, ˈā-prə-\ *n* [deriv. of Ar *al-birqûq*] : an oval orange-colored fruit resembling the related peach and plum in flavor; *also* : a tree bearing apricots

April \ˈā-prəl\ *n* [ME, fr. OF & L; OF *avrill*, fr. L *Aprilis*] : the 4th month of the year having 30 days

a pri•o•ri \ˌä-prē-ˈōr-ē\ *adj* [L, from the former] **1** : characterized by or derived by reasoning from self-evident propositions **2** : independent of experience — **a priori** *adv*

apron \ˈā-prən, -pərn\ *n* [ME, alter. (resulting fr. incorrect division of *a na-*

pron) of *napron*, fr. MF *naperon*, dim. of *nape* cloth, modif. of L *mappa* napkin] **1** : a garment tied over the front of the body to protect the clothes **2** : a paved area for parking or handling airplanes

¹**ap•ro•pos** \ˌap-rə-ˈpō, ˈap-rə-ˌpō\ *adv* [F *à propos*, lit., to the purpose] **1** : OPPORTUNELY **2** : BY THE WAY

²**apropos** *adj* : being to the point

apropos of *prep* : with regard to

apse \ˈaps\ *n* : a projecting usu. semi–circular and vaulted part of a building (as a church)

¹**apt** \ˈapt\ *adj* **1** : well adapted : SUITABLE **2** : having an habitual tendency : LIKELY **3** : quick to learn — **apt•ly** *adv* — **apt•ness** \ˈap(t)-nəs\ *n*

²**apt** *abbr* **1** apartment **2** aptitude

ap•ti•tude \ˈap-tə-ˌt(y)üd\ *n* **1** : natural ability : TALENT **2** : capacity for learning **3** : APPROPRIATENESS

aqua \ˈak-wə, ˈäk-\ *n* : a light greenish blue color

aqua•cul•ture *also* **aqui•cul•ture** \ˈak-wə-ˌkəl-chər, ˈäk-\ *n* : the cultivation of aquatic plants or animals (as fish or shellfish) for human use

aqua•ma•rine \ˌak-wə-mə-ˈrēn, ˌäk-\ *n* **1** : a bluish green gem **2** : a pale blue to light greenish blue

aqua•naut \ˈak-wə-ˌnȯt, ˈäk-\ *n* : a person who lives in an underwater shelter for an extended period

aqua•plane \-ˌplān\ *n* : a board towed behind a motorboat and ridden by a person standing on it — **aquaplane** *vb*

aqua re•gia \ˌak-wə-ˈrē-j(ē-)ə\ *n* [NL, lit., royal water] : a mixture of nitric and hydrochloric acids that dissolves gold or platinum

aquar•i•um \ə-ˈkwar-ē-əm\ *n, pl* **-i•ums** *or* **-ia** \-ē-ə\ **1** : a container (as a glass tank) in which living aquatic animals and plants are kept **2** : a place where aquatic animals and plants are kept and shown

Aquar•i•us \ə-ˈkwar-ē-əs\ *n* [L, lit., water carrier] **1** : a zodiacal constellation between Capricorn and Pisces usu. pictured as a man pouring water **2** : the 11th sign of the zodiac in astrology; *also* : one born under this sign

¹**aquat•ic** \ə-ˈkwät-ik, -ˈkwat-\ *adj* **1** : growing or living in or frequenting water **2** : performed in or on water

²**aquatic** *n* : an aquatic animal or plant

aqua·vit \'äk-wə-ˌvēt\ *n* : a clear liquor flavored with caraway seeds

aqua vi·tae \ˌak-wə-'vīt-ē, ˌäk-\ *n* [ME, fr. ML, lit., water of life] : a strong alcoholic liquor (as brandy)

aq·ue·duct \'ak-wə-ˌdəkt\ *n* **1** : a conduit for carrying running water **2** : a structure carrying a canal over a river or hollow **3** : a passage in a bodily part

aque·ous \'ā-kwē-əs, 'ak-wē-\ *adj* **1** : WATERY **2** : made of, by, or with water

aqueous humor *n* : a clear fluid occupying the space between the lens and the cornea of the eye

aqui·fer \'ak-wə-fər, 'äk-\ *n* : a water-bearing stratum of permeable rock, sand, or gravel

aq·ui·line \'ak-wə-ˌlīn, -lən\ *adj* **1** : of or resembling an eagle **2** : hooked like an eagle's beak ⟨an ~ nose⟩

ar *abbr* arrival; arrive

Ar *symbol* argon

AR *abbr* Arkansas

-ar \ər\ *adj suffix* : of or relating to ⟨molecul*ar*⟩ : being ⟨spectacul*ar*⟩ : resembling ⟨oracul*ar*⟩

Ar·ab \'ar-əb\ *n* **1** : a member of a Semitic people of the Arabian peninsula in southwestern Asia **2** : a member of an Arabic-speaking people — **Arab** *adj* — **Ara·bi·an** \ə-'rā-bē-ən\ *adj or n*

ar·a·besque \ˌar-ə-'besk\ *n* : a design of interlacing lines forming figures of flowers, foliage, and sometimes animals

¹**Ar·a·bic** \'ar-ə-bik\ *n* : a Semitic language of southwestern Asia and north Africa

²**Arabic** *adj* **1** : of or relating to the Arabs, Arabic, or the Arabian peninsula in southwestern Asia **2** : expressed in or making use of Arabic numerals

Arabic numeral *n* : one of the number symbols 1, 2, 3, 4, 5, 6, 7, 8, 9, and 0

ar·a·ble \'ar-ə-bəl\ *adj* : fit for or cultivated by plowing : suitable for crops

arach·nid \ə-'rak-nəd\ *n* : any of a class of usu. 8-legged arthropods comprising the spiders, scorpions, mites, and ticks — **arachnid** *adj*

Ar·a·ma·ic \ˌar-ə-'mā-ik\ *n* : an ancient Semitic language

Arap·a·ho *or* **Arap·a·hoe** \ə-'rap-ə-ˌhō\ *n, pl* **Arapaho** *or* **Arapahos** *or* **Arapahoe** *or* **Arapahoes** : a member of an American Indian people of the western U.S.

ar·bi·ter \'är-bət-ər\ *n* : one having power to decide : JUDGE

ar·bi·trage \'är-bə-ˌträzh\ *n* [F, fr. MF, arbitration] : the purchase and sale of the same or equivalent security in different markets in order to profit from price discrepancies

ar·bi·tra·geur \ˌär-bə-(ˌ)trä-'zhər\ *or* **ar·bi·trag·er** \'är-bə-ˌträzh-ər\ *n* : one who practices arbitrage

ar·bit·ra·ment \är-'bit-rə-mənt\ *n* **1** : the act of deciding a dispute **2** : the judgment given by an arbitrator

ar·bi·trary \'är-bə-ˌtrer-ē\ *adj* **1** : AUTOCRATIC, DESPOTIC **2** : determined by will or caprice : selected at random — **ar·bi·trari·ly** \ˌär-bə-'trer-ə-lē\ *adv* — **ar·bi·trari·ness** \'är-bə-ˌtrer-ē-nəs\ *n*

ar·bi·trate \'är-bə-ˌtrāt\ *vb* **-trat·ed; -trat·ing 1** : to act as arbitrator **2** : to act on as arbitrator **3** : to submit for decision to an arbitrator — **ar·bi·tra·tion** \ˌär-bə-'trā-shən\ *n*

ar·bi·tra·tor \'är-bə-ˌtrāt-ər\ *n* : one chosen to settle differences between two parties in a controversy

ar·bor \'är-bər\ *n* [ME *erber* plot of grass, arbor, fr. OF *herbier* plot of grass, fr. *herbe* herb, grass] : a shelter formed of or covered with vines or branches

ar·bo·re·al \är-'bōr-ē-əl\ *adj* **1** : of, relating to, or resembling a tree **2** : living in trees ⟨~ monkeys⟩

ar·bo·re·tum \ˌär-bə-'rēt-əm\ *n, pl* **-retums** *or* **-re·ta** \-'rēt-ə\ [L, place grown with trees, fr. *arbor* tree] : a place where trees and plants are grown for scientific and educational purposes

ar·bor·vi·tae \ˌär-bər-'vīt-ē\ *n* : any of various evergreen trees with scalelike leaves that are related to the pines

ar·bu·tus \är-'byüt-əs\ *n* : TRAILING ARBUTUS

¹**arc** \'ärk\ *n* **1** : a sustained luminous discharge of electricity (as between two electrodes) **2** : a continuous portion of a curved line (as part of the circumference of a circle)

²**arc** *vb* : to form an electric arc

ARC *abbr* **1** American Red Cross **2** AIDS-related complex

ar·cade \är-'kād\ *n* **1** : an arched or covered passageway; *esp* : one lined with shops **2** : a row of arches with their supporting columns

ar·cane \är-'kān\ *adj* : SECRET, MYSTERIOUS

¹**arch** \'ärch\ *n* **1** : a curved structure spanning an opening (as a door or window) **2** : something resembling an arch **3** : ARCHWAY

²**arch** *vb* **1** : to cover with an arch **2** : to form or bend into an arch

³**arch** *adj* **1** : CHIEF, EMINENT **2** : ROGUISH, MISCHIEVOUS — **arch·ly** *adv* — **arch·ness** *n*

⁴**arch** *abbr* architect; architectural; architecture

ar·chae·ol·o·gy *or* **ar·che·ol·o·gy** \,är-kē-'äl-ə-jē\ *n* : the study of past human life as revealed by relics left by ancient peoples — **ar·chae·o·log·i·cal** \-kē-ə-'läj-i-kəl\ *adj* — **ar·chae·ol·o·gist** \-kē-'äl-ə-jəst\ *n*

ar·cha·ic \är-'kā-ik\ *adj* **1** : belonging to an earlier time : ANTIQUATED **2** : having the characteristics of the language of the past and surviving chiefly in specialized uses ⟨~ words⟩ — **ar·cha·i·cal·ly** \-i-k(ə-)lē\ *adv*

arch·an·gel \'ärk-,ān-jəl\ *n* : an angel of high rank

arch·bish·op \ärch-'bish-əp\ *n* : a bishop of high rank — **arch·bish·op·ric** \-ə-(,)prik\ *n*

arch·dea·con \-'dē-kən\ *n* : a clergyman who assists a diocesan bishop in ceremonial or administrative functions

arch·di·o·cese \-'dī-ə-səs, -,sēz, -,sēs\ *n* : the diocese of an archbishop

arch·duke \-'d(y)ük\ *n* **1** : a sovereign prince **2** : a prince of the imperial family of Austria

arch·en·e·my \'ärch-'en-ə-mē\ *n, pl* **-mies** : a principal enemy

Ar·cheo·zo·ic \,är-kē-ə-'zō-ik\ *adj* : of, relating to, or being the earliest era of geologic history extending from the formation of the earth almost 4 billion years ago to about 1.4 billion years ago — **Archeozoic** *n*

ar·chery \'ärch-(ə-)rē\ *n* : the art or practice of shooting with bow and arrows — **ar·cher** \'är-chər\ *n*

ar·che·type \'är-ki-,tīp\ *n* : the original pattern or model of all things of the same type

arch·fiend \'ärch-'fēnd\ *n* : a chief fiend; *esp* : SATAN

ar·chi·epis·co·pal \,är-kē-ə-'pis-kə-pəl\ *adj* : of or relating to an archbishop

ar·chi·man·drite \,är-kə-'man-,drīt\ *n* : a dignitary in an Eastern church ranking below a bishop

ar·chi·pel·a·go \,är-kə-'pel-ə-,gō, ,är-chə-\ *n, pl* **-goes** *or* **-gos 1** : a sea dotted with islands **2** : a group of islands

ar·chi·tect \'är-kə-,tekt\ *n* : a person who plans buildings and oversees their construction

ar·chi·tec·ture \'är-kə-,tek-chər\ *n* **1** : the art or science of planning and building structures **2** : method or style of building — **ar·chi·tec·tur·al** \,är-kə-'tek-chə-rəl, -'tek-shrəl\ *adj* — **ar·chi·tec·tur·al·ly** \-ē\ *adv*

ar·chi·trave \'är-kə-,trāv\ *n* : the supporting horizontal member just above the columns in a building in the classical style of architecture

ar·chive \'är-,kīv\ *n* : a place for keeping public records; *also* : public records — often used in pl.

ar·chi·vist \'är-kə-vəst, -,kī-\ *n* : a person in charge of archives

ar·chon \'är-,kän, -kən\ *n* : a chief magistrate of ancient Athens

arch·way \'ärch-,wā\ *n* : a passageway under an arch; *also* : an arch over a passage

arc lamp *n* : a gas-filled electric lamp that produces light when a current arcs between incandescent electrodes

¹**arc·tic** \'ärk-tik, 'ärt-ik\ *adj* [ME *artik,* fr. L *articus,* fr. Gk *arktikos,* fr. *arktos* bear, Ursa Major, north] **1** *often cap* : of or relating to the north pole or the region near it **2** : FRIGID

²**arc·tic** \'ärt-ik, 'ärk-tik\ *n* : a rubber overshoe that reaches to the ankle or above

arctic circle *n, often cap A &C* : the parallel of latitude that is approximately 66½ degrees north of the equator

-ard \ərd\ *also* **-art** \ərt\ *n suffix* : one that is characterized by performing some action, possessing some quality, or being associated with some thing esp. conspicuously or excessively ⟨bragg*art*⟩ ⟨dull*ard*⟩

ar·dent \'ärd-ᵊnt\ *adj* **1** : characterized

by warmth of feeling : PASSIONATE **2** : FIERY, HOT **3** : GLOWING — **ar·dent·ly** *adv*

ar·dor \'ärd-ər\ *n* **1** : warmth of feeling : ZEAL **2** : burning heat

ar·du·ous \'ärj-(ə-)wəs\ *adj* : DIFFICULT, LABORIOUS — **ar·du·ous·ly** *adv* — **ar·du·ous·ness** *n*

¹**are** *pres 2d sing or pres pl of* BE

²**are** \'a(ə)r\ *n* — see METRIC SYSTEM table

ar·ea \'ar-ē-ə\ *n* **1** : a flat surface or space **2** : the amount of surface included (as within the lines of a geometric figure) **3** : REGION **4** : range or extent of some thing or concept : FIELD

area code *n* : a 3-digit number that identifies each telephone service area in a country (as the U.S. or Canada)

area·way \-,wā\ *n* : a sunken space for giving access, air, and light to a basement

are·na \ə-'rē-nə\ *n* [L *harena, arena* sand, sandy place] **1** : an enclosed area used for public entertainment **2** : a sphere of activity or competition

ar·gent \'är-jənt\ *adj* : of or resembling silver : SILVERY

Ar·gen·tine \'är-jən-,tēn, -,tīn\ *or* **Ar·gen·tin·ean** *or* **Ar·gen·tin·i·an** \,är-jən-'tin-ē-ən\ *n* : a native or inhabitant of Argentina — **Argentine** *or* **Argentinean** *or* **Argentinian** *adj*

ar·gen·tite \'är-jən-,tīt\ *n* : a dark gray mineral that is an important ore of silver

ar·gil·la·ceous \,är-jə-'lā-shəs\ *adj* : CLAYEY

ar·gon \'är-,gän\ *n* [Gk, neut. of *argos* idle, lazy, fr. *a-* not + *ergon* work; fr. its relative inertness] : a colorless odorless gaseous chemical element found in the air and used for filling electric bulbs

ar·go·sy \'är-gə-sē\ *n, pl* **-sies 1** : a large merchant ship **2** : FLEET

ar·got \'är-gət, -,gō\ *n* : the language of a particular group or class esp. of the underworld

argu·able \'är-gyə-wə-bəl\ *adj* : open to argument, dispute, or question

ar·gue \'är-gyü\ *vb* **ar·gued; ar·gu·ing 1** : to give reasons for or against something **2** : to contend in words : DISPUTE **3** : DEBATE **4** : to persuade by giving reasons

ar·gu·ment \'är-gyə-mənt\ *n* **1** : a reason offered in proof **2** : discourse intended to persuade **3** : QUARREL

ar·gu·men·ta·tion \,är-gyə-mən-'tā-shən\ *n* : the art of formal discussion

ar·gu·men·ta·tive \,är-gyə-'ment-ət-iv\ *adj* : inclined to argue

ar·gyle *also* **ar·gyll** \'är-,gīl\ *n, often cap* : a geometric knitting pattern of varicolored diamonds on a single background color; *also* : a sock knit in this pattern

aria \'är-ē-ə\ *n* : an accompanied elaborate vocal solo forming part of a larger work

ar·id \'ar-əd\ *adj* **1** : DRY, BARREN **2** : having insufficient rainfall to support agriculture — **arid·i·ty** \ə-'rid-ət-ē\ *n*

Ar·i·es \'ar-(ē-),ēz\ *n* [L, lit., ram] **1** : a zodiacal constellation between Pisces and Taurus usu. pictured as a ram **2** : the 1st sign of the zodiac in astrology; *also* : one born under this sign

aright \ə-'rīt\ *adv* : RIGHTLY, CORRECTLY

arise \ə-'rīz\ *vb* **arose** \-'rōz\; **aris·en** \-'riz-ᵊn\; **aris·ing** \-'rī-ziŋ\ **1** : to get up **2** : ORIGINATE **3** : ASCEND **syn** rise, derive, spring, issue

ar·is·toc·ra·cy \,ar-ə-'stäk-rə-sē\ *n, pl* **-cies 1** : government by a noble or privileged class; *also* : a state so governed **2** : the governing class of an aristocracy **3** : UPPER CLASS — **aris·to·crat** \ə-'ris-tə-,krat\ *n* — **aris·to·crat·ic** \ə-,ris-tə-'krat-ik\ *adj*

arith *abbr* arithmetic; arithmetical

arith·me·tic \ə-'rith-mə-,tik\ *n* **1** : a branch of mathematics that deals with computations with numbers **2** : COMPUTATION, CALCULATION — **ar·ith·met·ic** \,ar-ith-'met-ik\ *or* **ar·ith·met·i·cal** \-i-kəl\ *adj* — **ar·ith·met·i·cal·ly** \-i-k(ə-)lē\ *adv* — **arith·me·ti·cian** \ə-,rith-mə-'tish-ən\ *n*

arithmetic mean *n* : the sum of a set of numbers divided by the number of numbers in the set

Ariz *abbr* Arizona

ark \'ärk\ *n* **1** : a boat held to resemble that of Noah at the time of the Deluge **2** : the sacred chest in which the ancient Hebrews kept the tablets of the Law

Ark *abbr* Arkansas

¹**arm** \'ärm\ *n* **1** : a human upper limb;

also : a corresponding limb of a lower animal with a backbone **2** : something resembling an arm in shape or position ⟨an ∼ of a chair⟩ **3** : POWER, MIGHT ⟨the ∼ of the law⟩ — **armed** \'ärmd\ *adj* — **arm·less** *adj*

²arm *vb* : to furnish with weapons

³arm *n* **1** : WEAPON **2** : a branch of the military forces **3** *pl* : the hereditary heraldic devices of a family

ar·ma·da \är-'mäd-ə, -'mād-\ *n* : a fleet of armed ships

ar·ma·dil·lo \ˌär-mə-'dil-ō\ *n*, *pl* **-los** : any of several small burrowing mammals with the head and body protected by an armor of bony plates

Ar·ma·ged·don \ˌär-mə-'ged-ᵊn\ *n* : a final conclusive battle between the forces of good and evil; *also* : the site or time of this

ar·ma·ment \'är-mə-mənt\ *n* **1** : military strength **2** : arms and equipment (as of a tank or combat unit) **3** : the process of preparing for war

ar·ma·ture \'är-mə-ˌchùr, -chər\ *n* **1** : a protective covering or structure (as the spines of a cactus) **2** : the part including the conductors in an electric generator or motor in which the current is induced; *also* : the movable part in an electromagnetic device (as an electric bell or a loudspeaker)

arm·chair \'ärm-ˌcheər\ *n* : a chair with supports for the arms

armed forces *n pl* : the combined military, naval, and air forces of a nation

arm·ful \'ärm-ˌfùl\ *n*, *pl* **armfuls** *or* **arms·ful** \'ärmz-ˌfùl\ : as much as the arm can hold

arm·hole \'ärm-ˌhōl\ *n* : an opening for the arm in a garment

ar·mi·stice \'är-mə-stəs\ *n* : temporary suspension of hostilities by mutual agreement : TRUCE

arm·let \'ärm-lət\ *n* : a band worn around the upper arm

ar·mor \'är-mər\ *n* **1** : protective covering **2** : armored forces and vehicles — **ar·mored** \-mərd\ *adj*

ar·mor·er \'är-mər-ər\ *n* **1** : one that makes arms and armor **2** : one that services firearms

ar·mo·ri·al \är-'mōr-ē-əl\ *adj* : of or bearing heraldic arms

ar·mory \'ärm-(ə-)rē\ *n*, *pl* **ar·mor·ies** **1** : a place where arms are stored **2** : a factory where arms are made

arm·pit \'ärm-ˌpit\ *n* : the hollow under the junction of the arm and shoulder

arm·rest \-ˌrest\ *n* : a support for the arm

ar·my \'är-mē\ *n*, *pl* **armies** **1** : a body of men organized for war **2** *often cap* : the complete military organization of a country for land warfare **3** : a great number **4** : a body of persons organized to advance a cause

army ant *n* : any of various nomadic social ants

ar·my·worm \'är-mē-ˌwərm\ *n* : any of numerous moths whose larvae move about destroying crops

ar·ni·ca \'är-ni-kə\ *n* **1** : any of several herbs related to the daisies **2** : a soothing preparation of dried arnica flowers used on bruises and sprains; *also* : dried arnica flowers

aro·ma \ə-'rō-mə\ *n* : a usu. pleasing odor : FRAGRANCE — **ar·o·mat·ic** \ˌar-ə-'mat-ik\ *adj*

arose past of ARISE

¹around \ə-'raùnd\ *adv* **1** : in or along a circuit **2** : on all sides **3** : NEARBY **4** : from one place to another **5** : in an opposite direction ⟨turn ∼⟩

²around *prep* **1** : SURROUNDING ⟨trees ∼ the house⟩ **2** : to or on the other side of ⟨∼ the corner⟩ **3** : NEAR ⟨stayed right ∼ home⟩ **4** : along the circuit of ⟨go ∼ the world⟩

arouse \ə-'raùz\ *vb* **aroused; arous·ing** **1** : to awaken from sleep **2** : to stir up — **arous·al** \-'raù-zəl\ *n*

ar·peg·gio \är-'pej-(ē-ˌ)ō\ *n*, *pl* **-gios** [It fr. *arpeggiare* to play on the harp, fr. *arpa* harp] : a chord whose notes are performed in succession and not simultaneously

arr *abbr* **1** arranged **2** arrival; arrive

ar·raign \ə-'rān\ *vb* **1** : to call before a court to answer to an indictment **2** : to accuse of wrong or imperfection — **ar·raign·ment** *n*

ar·range \ə-'rānj\ *vb* **ar·ranged; ar·rang·ing** **1** : to put in order **2** : to come to an agreement about : SETTLE **3** : to adapt (a musical composition) to voices or instruments other than those for which it was orig. written — **ar·range·ment** *n* — **ar·rang·er** *n*

ar·rant \'ar-ənt\ *adj* : being notoriously without moderation : EXTREME

ar·ras \'ar-əs\ *n, pl* **arras 1** : TAPESTRY **2** : a wall hanging or screen of tapestry

¹ar·ray \ə-'rā\ *vb* **1** : to arrange in order **2** : to dress esp. splendidly

²array *n* **1** : a regular arrangement **2** : rich apparel **3** : an imposing group

ar·rears \ə-'riərz\ *n pl* **1** : a state of being behind in the discharge of obligations ⟨in ∼ with the payments⟩ **2** : overdue debts

¹ar·rest \ə-'rest\ *vb* **1** : STOP, CHECK **2** : to take into legal custody

²arrest *n* **1** : the act of stopping; *also* : the state of being stopped **2** : the act of taking into custody by legal authority

ar·riv·al \ə-'rī-vəl\ *n* **1** : the act of arriving **2** : one that arrives

ar·rive \ə-'rīv\ *vb* **ar·rived; ar·riv·ing 1** : to reach a destination **2** : to be near or at hand ⟨the time to go finally *arrived*⟩ **3** : to attain success

ar·ro·gant \'ar-ə-gənt\ *adj* : offensively exaggerating one's own importance — **ar·ro·gance** \-gəns\ *n* — **ar·ro·gant·ly** *adv*

ar·ro·gate \-ˌgāt\ *vb* **-gat·ed; -gat·ing** : to claim or seize without justification as one's right

ar·row \'ar-ō\ *n* **1** : a missile shot from a bow and usu. having a slender shaft, a pointed head, and feathers at the butt **2** : a pointed mark used to indicate direction

ar·row·head \'ar-ō-ˌhed\ *n* : the pointed end of an arrow

ar·row·root \-ˌrüt, -ˌru̇t\ *n* : an edible starch from the roots of any of several tropical American plants; *also* : a plant yielding arrowroot

ar·royo \ə-'rȯi-ə, -ō\ *n, pl* **-royos** [Sp] **1** : a watercourse in a dry region **2** : a water-carved gully or channel

ar·se·nal \'ärs-nəl, -ᵊn-əl\ *n* [deriv. of Ar *dār ṣinā'ah* house of manufacture] **1** : a place for making and storing arms and military equipment **2** : STORE, REPERTORY

ar·se·nic \'ärs-nik, -ᵊn-ik\ *n* **1** : a solid brittle poisonous chemical element of grayish color and metallic luster **2** : a very poisonous oxygen compound of arsenic used in making glass and insecticides

ar·son \'ärs-ᵊn\ *n* : the malicious burning of property

¹art \'ärt\ *n* **1** : skill acquired by experience or study **2** : a branch of learning; *esp* : one of the humanities **3** : an occupation requiring knowledge or skill **4** : the use of skill and imagination in the production of things of beauty; *also* : works so produced **5** : ARTFULNESS

²art *abbr* **1** article **2** artificial **3** artillery

-art — see -ARD

ar·te·ri·al \är-'tir-ē-əl\ *adj* **1** : of or relating to an artery; *also* : relating to or being the bright red oxygenated blood found in most arteries **2** : of, relating to, or being a route for through traffic

ar·te·ri·ole \är-'tir-ē-ˌōl\ *n* : one of the small terminal twigs of an artery that ends in capillaries — **ar·te·ri·o·lar** \-ˌtir-ē-'ō-lər\ *adj*

ar·te·rio·scle·ro·sis \är-ˌtir-ē-ō-sklə-'rō-səs\ *n* : a chronic disease in which arterial walls are abnormally thickened and hardened — **ar·te·rio·scle·rot·ic** \-'rät-ik\ *adj or n*

ar·tery \'ärt-ə-rē\ *n, pl* **-ter·ies 1** : one of the tubular vessels that carry the blood from the heart **2** : a main channel of transportation or communication; *esp* : a principal channel in a branching system

ar·te·sian well \är-ˌtē-zhən-\ *n* **1** : a bored well gushing water like a fountain **2** : a relatively deep-bored well

art·ful \'ärt-fəl\ *adj* **1** : INGENIOUS **2** : CRAFTY — **art·ful·ly** \-ē\ *adv* — **art·ful·ness** *n*

ar·thri·tis \är-'thrīt-əs\ *n, pl* **-thri·ti·des** \-'thrit-ə-ˌdēz\ : inflammation of the joints — **ar·thrit·ic** \-'thrit-ik\ *adj or n*

ar·thro·pod \'är-thrə-ˌpäd\ *n* : any of a phylum of invertebrate animals comprising those (as insects, spiders, or crabs) with segmented bodies and jointed limbs — **arthropod** *adj*

ar·thros·co·py \är-'thräs-kə-pē\ *n, pl* **-pies** : visual examination of the interior of a joint (as the knee) with a special surgical instrument — **ar·thro·scope** \'är-thrə-ˌskōp\ *n* — **ar·thro·scop·ic** \ˌär-thrə-'skäp-ik\ *adj*

ar·ti·choke \'ärt-ə-ˌchōk\ *n* [It dial. *articiocco*, fr. Ar *al-khurshūf*] : a tall herb related to the daisies; *also* : its edible flower head

ar·ti·cle \'ärt-i-kəl\ *n* [ME, fr. OF, fr. L *articulus* joint, division, dim. of *artus* joint] **1** : a distinct part of a written document **2** : a nonfictional prose composition forming an independent part of a publication **3** : a word (as *an, the*) used with a noun to limit or give definiteness to its application **4** : a member of a class of things; *esp* : COMMODITY

ar·tic·u·lar \är-'tik-yə-lər\ *adj* : of or relating to a joint

¹**ar·tic·u·late** \är-'tik-yə-lət\ *adj* **1** : divided into meaningful parts : INTELLIGIBLE **2** : able to speak; *also* : expressing oneself readily and effectively **3** : JOINTED — **ar·tic·u·late·ly** *adv* — **ar·tic·u·late·ness** *n*

²**ar·tic·u·late** \-ˌlāt\ *vb* **-lat·ed; -lat·ing 1** : to utter distinctly **2** : to unite by or as if by joints — **ar·tic·u·la·tion** \-ˌtik-yə-'lā-shən\ *n*

ar·ti·fact \'ärt-ə-ˌfakt\ *n* : a usu. simple object (as a tool) showing human workmanship or modification

ar·ti·fice \'ärt-ə-fəs\ *n* **1** : TRICK; *also* : TRICKERY **2** : an ingenious device; *also* : INGENUITY

ar·ti·fi·cer \är-'tif-ə-sər, 'ärt-ə-fə-sər\ *n* : a skilled workman

ar·ti·fi·cial \ˌärt-ə-'fish-əl\ *adj* **1** : produced by art rather than nature; *also* : made by man to imitate nature **2** : not genuine : FEIGNED — **ar·ti·fi·ci·al·i·ty** \-ˌfish-ē-'al-ət-ē\ *n* — **ar·ti·fi·cial·ly** \-'fish(ə-)lē\ *adv* — **ar·ti·fi·cial·ness** \-'fish-əl-nəs\ *n*

artificial insemination *n* : introduction of semen into the uterus or oviduct by other than natural means

artificial intelligence *n* : the capability of a machine to imitate intelligent human behavior

artificial respiration *n* : the rhythmic forcing of air into and out of the lungs of a person whose breathing has stopped

ar·til·lery \är-'til-(ə-)rē\ *n, pl* **-ler·ies 1** : large-bore mounted firearms usu. operated by crews **2** : a branch of the army armed with artillery — **ar·til·ler·ist** \-'til-ə-rəst\ *n*

ar·ti·san \'ärt-ə-zən, -sən\ *n* : a skilled manual worker

art·ist \'ärt-əst\ *n* **1** : one who practices an art; *esp* : one who creates objects of beauty **2** : ARTISTE

ar·tiste \är-'tēst\ *n* : a skilled public performer

ar·tis·tic \är-'tis-tik\ *adj* : showing taste and skill — **ar·tis·ti·cal·ly** \-ti-k(ə-)lē\ *adv*

art·ist·ry \'ärt-ə-strē\ *n* : artistic quality or ability

art·less \'ärt-ləs\ *adj* **1** : lacking art or skill **2** : free from artificiality : NATURAL **3** : free from guile : SINCERE — **art·less·ly** *adv* — **art·less·ness** *n*

art nou·veau \ˌär(t)-nü-'vō\ *n, often cap A & N* [F, lit., new art] : a late 19th century decorative style characterized by sinuous lines and leaf-shaped forms

arty \'ärt-ē\ *adj* **art·i·er; -est** : showily or pretentiously artistic — **art·i·ly** \'ärt-ᵊl-ē\ *adv* — **art·i·ness** \-ē-nəs\ *n*

ar·um \'ar-əm\ *n* : any of a genus of plants (as the jack-in-the-pulpit or a skunk cabbage) with flowers in a fleshy enclosed spike

ARV *abbr* American Revised Version

¹**-ary** \ˌer-ē\ *n suffix* : thing or person belonging to or connected with ⟨functionary⟩

²**-ary** *adj suffix* : of, relating to, or connected with ⟨budgetary⟩

Ary·an \'ar-ē-ən, 'er-; 'är-yən\ *adj* **1** : INDO-EUROPEAN **2** : NORDIC — **Aryan** *n*

¹**as** \əz, (ˌ)az\ *adv* **1** : to the same degree or amount : EQUALLY ⟨∼ green as grass⟩ **2** : for instance ⟨various trees, ∼ oak or pine⟩ **3** : when considered in a specified relation ⟨my opinion ∼ distinguished from his⟩

²**as** *conj* **1** : in the same amount or degree in which ⟨green ∼ grass⟩ **2** : in the same way that ⟨farmed ∼ his father before him had farmed⟩ **3** : WHILE, WHEN ⟨spoke to me ∼ I was leaving⟩ **4** : THOUGH ⟨improbable ∼ it seems⟩ **5** : SINCE, BECAUSE ⟨∼ I'm not wanted, I'll go⟩ **6** : that the result is ⟨so guilty ∼ to leave no doubt⟩

³**as** *pron* **1** : THAT — used after *same* or *such* ⟨it's the same price ∼ before⟩ **2** : a fact that ⟨he's rich, ∼ you know⟩

⁴**as** *prep* : in the capacity or character of ⟨this will serve ∼ a substitute⟩

As *symbol* arsenic

AS *abbr* **1** American Samoa **2** Anglo=Saxon

asa•fet•i•da *or* **asa•foe•ti•da** \ˌas-ə-ˈfit-əd-ē, -ˈfet-əd-ə\ *n* : an ill-smelling plant gum formerly used in medicine

ASAP *abbr* as soon as possible

as•bes•tos \as-ˈbes-təs, az-\ *n* : a noncombustible grayish mineral that occurs in fibrous form and is used as a fireproof material

as•cend \ə-ˈsend\ *vb* **1** : to move upward : MOUNT, CLIMB **2** : to succeed to : OCCUPY ⟨he ∼ed the throne⟩

as•cen•dan•cy *also* **as•cen•den•cy** \ə-ˈsen-dən-sē\ *n* : controlling influence : DOMINATION

¹as•cen•dant *also* **as•cen•dent** \ə-ˈsen-dənt\ *n* : a dominant position

²ascendant *also* **ascendent** *adj* **1** : moving upward **2** : DOMINANT

as•cen•sion \ə-ˈsen-chən\ *n* : the act or process of ascending

Ascension Day *n* : the Thursday 40 days after Easter observed in commemoration of Christ's ascension into heaven

as•cent \ə-ˈsent\ *n* **1** : the act of mounting upward : CLIMB **2** : degree of upward slope

as•cer•tain \ˌas-ər-ˈtān\ *vb* : to learn by inquiry — **as•cer•tain•able** *adj*

as•cet•ic \ə-ˈset-ik\ *adj* : practicing self-denial esp. for religious reasons : AUSTERE — **ascetic** *n* — **as•cet•i•cism** \-ˈset-ə-ˌsiz-əm\ *n*

ASCII \ˈas-kē\ *n* [*American Standard Code for Information Interchange*] : a computer code for representing alphanumeric information

ascor•bic acid \ə-ˌskȯr-bik-\ *n* : VITAMIN C

as•cot \ˈas-kət, -ˌkät\ *n* [*Ascot* Heath, racetrack near Ascot, England] : a broad neck scarf that is looped under the chin

as•cribe \ə-ˈskrīb\ *vb* **as•cribed; as•crib•ing** : to refer to a supposed cause, source, or author : ATTRIBUTE — **as•crib•able** *adj* — **as•crip•tion** \-ˈskrip-shən\ *n*

asep•tic \ā-ˈsep-tik\ *adj* : free or freed from disease-causing germs

asex•u•al \ā-ˈsek-sh(ə-w)əl\ *adj* **1** : lacking sex or functional sex organs **2** : occurring or formed without the production and union of two kinds of germ cells ⟨∼ reproduction⟩ — **asex•u•al•ly** \(ˈ)ā-ˈseksh-(ə-)wə-lē\ *adv*

as for *prep* : with regard to : CONCERNING ⟨*as for* the others, they were late⟩

¹ash \ˈash\ *n* **1** : any of a genus of trees related to the olive and having winged seeds and bark with grooves and ridges **2** : the tough elastic wood of an ash

²ash *n* **1** : the solid matter left when material is burned **2** : fine mineral particles from a volcano **3** *pl* : the remains of the dead human body

ashamed \ə-ˈshāmd\ *adj* **1** : feeling shame **2** : restrained by anticipation of shame ⟨∼ to say anything⟩ — **asham•ed•ly** \-ˈshā-məd-lē\ *adv*

ash•en \ˈash-ən\ *adj* : resembling ashes (as in color); *esp* : deadly pale

ash•lar \ˈash-lər\ *n* : hewn or squared stone; *also* : masonry of such stone

ashore \ə-ˈshōr\ *adv* : on or to the shore

as how *conj* : THAT ⟨allowed *as how* she was glad to be here⟩

ash•ram \ˈäsh-rəm\ *n* : a religious retreat esp. of a Hindu sage

ash•tray \ˈash-ˌtrā\ *n* : a receptacle for tobacco ashes

Ash Wednesday *n* : the 1st day of Lent

ashy \ˈash-ē\ *adj* **ash•i•er; -est** : ASHEN

Asian \ˈā-zhən, -shən\ *adj* : of, relating to, or characteristic of the continent of Asia or its people — **Asian** *n*

Asi•at•ic \ˌā-z(h)ē-ˈat-ik\ *adj* : ASIAN — sometimes taken to be offensive — **Asiatic** *n*

¹aside \ə-ˈsīd\ *adv* **1** : to or toward the side **2** : out of the way : AWAY

²aside *n* : an actor's words heard by the audience but supposedly not by other characters on stage

aside from *prep* **1** : BESIDES ⟨*aside from* being pretty, she's intelligent⟩ **2** : with the exception of ⟨*aside from* one D his grades are excellent⟩

as if *conj* **1** : as it would be if ⟨it's *as if* nothing had changed⟩ **2** : as one would if ⟨he acts *as if* he'd never been away⟩ **3** : THAT ⟨it seems *as if* nothing ever happens around here⟩

as•i•nine \ˈas-ᵊn-ˌīn\ *adj* [L *asininus,* fr. *asinus* ass] : STUPID, FOOLISH — **as•i•nin•i•ty** \ˌas-ᵊn-ˈin-ət-ē\ *n*

ask \ˈask\ *vb* **asked** \ˈas(k)t\ **ask•ing 1** : to call on for an answer **2** : UTTER ⟨∼ a question⟩ **3** : to make a request of

⟨~ him for help⟩ **4** : to make a request for ⟨~ help of her⟩ **5** : to set as a price ⟨~ed $800 for the car⟩ **6** : INVITE

askance \ə-'skans\ *adv* **1** : with a side glance **2** : with distrust

askew \ə-'skyü\ *adv or adj* : out of line : AWRY

ASL *abbr* American Sign Language

¹aslant \ə-'slant\ *adv or adj* : in a slanting direction

²aslant *prep* : over or across in a slanting direction

asleep \ə-'slēp\ *adv or adj* **1** : in or into a state of sleep **2** : DEAD **3** : NUMB **4** : INACTIVE

as long as *conj* **1** : provided that ⟨do as you like *as long as* you get home on time⟩ **2** : INASMUCH AS, SINCE ⟨*as long as* you're up, turn on the light⟩

as of *prep* : AT, DURING, FROM, ON ⟨takes effect *as of* July 1⟩

asp \'asp\ *n* : a small poisonous African snake

as•par•a•gus \ə-'spar-ə-gəs\ *n* : a tall branching perennial herb related to the lilies; *also* : its edible young stalks

as•par•tame \as-'pär-₁tām\ *n* : a crystalline low-calorie sweetener

as•pect \'as-₁pekt\ *n* **1** : a position facing a particular direction **2** : APPEARANCE, LOOK **3** : PHASE

as•pen \'as-pən\ *n* : any of several poplars with leaves that flutter in the slightest breeze

as•per•i•ty \a-'sper-ət-ē, ə-\ *n, pl* **-ties 1** : ROUGHNESS **2** : harshness of temper

as•per•sion \ə-'spər-zhən\ *n* : the act of calumniating; *also* : a calumnious remark

as•phalt \'as-₁fȯlt\ *or* **as•phal•tum** \as-'fȯl-təm\ *n* : a dark solid or somewhat plastic substance that is found in natural beds or obtained as a residue in petroleum refining and is used in paving streets, in roofing houses, and in paints

asphalt jungle *n* : a big city or a specified part of a big city

as•pho•del \'as-fə-₁del\ *n* : any of several Old World herbs related to the lilies and bearing flowers in long erect spikes

as•phyx•ia \as-'fik-sē-ə\ *n* : a lack of oxygen or excess of carbon dioxide in the body usu. caused by interruption of breathing and causing unconsciousness

as•phyx•i•ate \-sē-₁āt\ *vb* **-at•ed; -at•ing** : SUFFOCATE — **as•phyx•i•a•tion** \-₁fik-sē-'ā-shən\ *n*

as•pic \'as-pik\ *n* [F, lit., asp] : a savory meat jelly

as•pi•rant \'as-p(ə-)rənt, ə-'spī-rənt\ *n* : one who aspires **syn** candidate, applicant, seeker

as•pi•rate \'as-p(ə-)rət\ *n* **1** : an independent sound \h\ or a character (as the letter *h*) representing it **2** : a consonant having aspiration as its final component

as•pi•ra•tion \₁as-pə-'rā-shən\ *n* **1** : the pronunciation or addition of an aspirate; *also* : the aspirate or its symbol **2** : a drawing of something in, out, up, or through by or as if by suction **3** : a strong desire to achieve something noble; *also* : an object of this desire

as•pire \ə-'spī(ə)r\ *vb* **as•pired; as•pir•ing 1** : to have a noble desire or ambition **2** : to rise aloft

as•pi•rin \'as-p(ə-)rən\ *n, pl* **aspirin** *or* **aspirins 1** : a white crystalline drug used to relieve pain and fever **2** : a tablet of aspirin

as regards *or* **as respects** *prep* : in regard to : with respect to

ass \'as\ *n* **1** : any of several long-eared animals smaller than the related horses; *esp* : DONKEY **2** : a stupid person

as•sail \ə-'sāl\ *vb* : to attack violently — **as•sail•able** *adj* — **as•sail•ant** *n*

as•sas•sin \ə-'sas-ⁿn\ *n* [deriv. of Ar *ḥashshāshīn*, pl. of *ḥashshāsh* hashish-user, fr. *hashīsh* hashish] : a murderer esp. for hire or fanatical reasons

as•sas•si•nate \ə-'as-ⁿn-₁āt\ *vb* **-nat•ed; -nat•ing** : to murder by sudden or secret attack — **as•sas•si•na•tion** \-₁sas-ⁿn-'ā-shən\ *n*

as•sault \ə-'sȯlt\ *n* **1** : a violent attack **2** : an unlawful attempt or threat to do harm to another — **assault** *vb*

¹as•say \'as-₁ā, a-'sā\ *n* : analysis to determine the quantity of one or more components present in a sample (as of an ore or drug)

²as•say \a-'sā, 'as-₁ā\ *vb* **1** : TRY, ATTEMPT **2** : to subject (as an ore or drug) to an assay **3** : to make a critical estimate of

as·sem·blage \ə-'sem-blij, *3 & 4 also* ˌas-ˌäm-'bläzh\ *n* **1** : a collection of persons or things : GATHERING **2** : the act of assembling **3** : an artistic composition made from scraps, junk, and odds and ends **4** : the art of making assemblages

as·sem·ble \ə-'sem-bəl\ *vb* **-bled; -bling** \-b(ə-)liŋ\ **1** : to collect into one place : CONGREGATE **2** : to fit together the parts of **3** : to meet together : CONVENE

as·sem·bly \ə-'sem-blē\ *n, pl* **-blies 1** : a gathering of persons : MEETING **2** *cap* : a legislative body; *esp* : the lower house of a legislature **3** : a signal for troops to assemble **4** : the fitting together of parts (as of a machine)

assembly language *n* : a symbolic language for programming a computer that is a close approximation of machine language

assembly line *n* : an arrangement of machines, equipment, and workers in which work passes from operation to operation in a direct line

as·sem·bly·man \ə-'sem-blē-mən\ *n* : a member of a legislative assembly

as·sem·bly·wom·an \-ˌwùm-ən\ *n* : a woman who is a member of an assembly

as·sent \ə-'sent\ *vb* : AGREE, CONCUR — **assent** *n*

as·sert \ə-'sərt\ *vb* **1** : to state positively **2** : to demonstrate the existence of **syn** declare, affirm, protest, avow, claim — **as·ser·tive** \-'sərt-iv\ *adj* — **as·ser·tive·ness** *n*

as·ser·tion \ə-'sər-shən\ *n* : a positive statement

as·sess \ə-'ses\ *vb* **1** : to fix the rate or amount of **2** : to impose (as a tax) at a specified rate **3** : to evaluate for taxation — **as·sess·ment** *n* — **as·ses·sor** \-ər\ *n*

as·set \'as-ˌet\ *n* **1** *pl* : the entire property of a person or company that may be used to pay debts **2** : ADVANTAGE, RESOURCE

as·sev·er·ate \ə-'sev-ə-ˌrāt\ *vb* **-at·ed; -at·ing** : to assert earnestly — **as·sev·er·a·tion** \-ˌsev-ə-'rā-shən\ *n*

as·sid·u·ous \ə-'sij-(ə-)wəs\ *adj* : steadily attentive : DILIGENT — **as·si·du·i·ty** \ˌas-ə-'d(y)ü-ət-ē\ *n* — **as·sid·u·ous·ly** *adv* — **as·sid·u·ous·ness** *n*

as·sign \ə-'sīn\ *vb* **1** : to transfer (property) to another **2** : to appoint to a duty **3** : PRESCRIBE ⟨∼ a lesson⟩ **4** : FIX, SPECIFY ⟨∼ a limit⟩ **5** : ASCRIBE ⟨∼ a reason⟩ — **as·sign·able** *adj*

as·sig·na·tion \ˌas-ig-'nā-shən\ *n* : an appointment for a lovers' meeting; *also* : the resulting meeting

assigned risk *n* : a poor risk (as an accident-prone motorist) that an insurance company is forced to insure by state law

as·sign·ment \ə-'sīn-mənt\ *n* **1** : the act of assigning **2** : something assigned

as·sim·i·late \ə-'sim-ə-ˌlāt\ *vb* **-lat·ed; -lat·ing 1** : to take up and absorb as nourishment; *also* : to absorb into a cultural tradition **2** : COMPREHEND **3** : to make or become similar — **as·sim·i·la·tion** \-ˌsim-ə-'lā-shən\ *n*

¹as·sist \ə-'sist\ *vb* : HELP, AID — **as·sis·tance** \-'sis-təns\ *n*

²assist *n* **1** : an act of assistance **2** : the act of a player who enables a teammate to make a putout (as in baseball) or score a goal (as in hockey)

as·sis·tant \ə-'sis-tənt\ *n* : one who assists : HELPER

as·size \ə-'sīz\ *n* **1** : a judicial inquest **2** *pl* : the former regular sessions of the superior courts in English counties

assn *abbr* association

assoc *abbr* associate; associated; association

¹as·so·ci·ate \ə-'sō-s(h)ē-ˌāt\ *vb* **-at·ed; -at·ing 1** : to join in companionship or partnership **2** : to connect in thought

²as·so·ci·ate \-s(h)ē-ət, -shət\ *n* **1** : a fellow worker : PARTNER **2** : COMPANION **3** *often cap* : a degree conferred esp. by a junior college ⟨∼ in arts⟩ — **associate** *adj*

as·so·ci·a·tion \ə-ˌsō-s(h)ē-'ā-shən\ *n* **1** : the act of associating **2** : an organization of persons : SOCIETY

as·so·cia·tive \ə-'sō-s(h)ē-ˌāt-iv, -shət-iv\ *adj* : of, relating to, or involved in association and esp. mental association

as·so·nance \'as-ə-nəns\ *n* : repetition of vowels esp. as an alternative to rhyme in verse

as soon as *conj* : immediately at or just after the time that ⟨we'll start *as soon as* he comes⟩

as•sort \ə-'sȯrt\ *vb* **1** : to distribute into like groups **2** : HARMONIZE

as•sort•ed \-'sȯrt-əd\ *adj* : consisting of various kinds

as•sort•ment \-'sȯrt-mənt\ *n* : a collection of assorted things or persons

asst *abbr* assistant

as•suage \ə-'swāj\ *vb* **as•suaged; as•suag•ing** **1** : to make (as pain or grief) less : EASE **2** : SATISFY **syn** alleviate, relieve, lighten, mitigate

as•sume \ə-'süm\ *vb* **as•sumed; as•sum•ing** **1** : to take upon oneself **2** : to pretend to have **3** : to take as granted though not proved

as•sump•tion \ə-'səmp-shən\ *n* **1** : the taking up of a person into heaven **2** *cap* : a church festival commemorating the Assumption of Mary and celebrated on August 15 **3** : a taking upon oneself **4** : PRETENSION **5** : SUPPOSITION

as•sur•ance \ə-'shu̇r-əns\ *n* **1** : PLEDGE **2** *chiefly Brit* : INSURANCE **3** : SECURITY **4** : SELF-CONFIDENCE; *also* : AUDACITY

as•sure \ə-'shu̇r\ *vb* **as•sured; as•sur•ing** **1** : INSURE **2** : to give confidence to **3** : to state confidently to **4** : to make certain the attainment of

as•sured \ə-'shu̇rd\ *n, pl* **assured** *or* **assureds** : the beneficiary of an insurance policy

as•ta•tine \'as-tə-ˌtēn\ *n* : an unstable radioactive chemical element

as•ter \'as-tər\ *n* : any of various mostly fall-blooming leafy-stemmed herbs with daisylike purple, white, pink, or yellow flower heads

as•ter•isk \'as-tə-ˌrisk\ *n* [L *asteriscus,* fr. Gk *asteriskos,* lit., little star, dim. of *astēr*] : a character * used as a reference mark or as an indication of the omission of letters or words

astern \ə-'stərn\ *adv or adj* **1** : in, at, or toward the stern **2** : BACKWARD

as•ter•oid \'as-tə-ˌrȯid\ *n* : one of thousands of small planets between Mars and Jupiter with diameters under 500 miles (800 kilometers)

asth•ma \'az-mə\ *n* : an often allergic disorder marked by difficulty in breathing and a cough — **asth•mat•ic** \az-'mat-ik\ *adj or n*

as though *conj* : AS IF

astig•ma•tism \ə-'stig-mə-ˌtiz-əm\ *n* : a defect in a lens or an eye causing im-

proper focusing — **as•tig•mat•ic** \ˌas-tig-'mat-ik\ *adj*

astir \ə-'stər\ *adj* : being in action : MOVING

as to *prep* **1** : ABOUT, CONCERNING ⟨uncertain *as to* what went on⟩ **2** : ACCORDING TO ⟨graded *as to* size⟩

as•ton•ish \ə-'stän-ish\ *vb* : to strike with sudden and usu. great wonder : AMAZE — **as•ton•ish•ing•ly** *adv* — **as•ton•ish•ment** *n*

as•tound \ə-'staund\ *vb* : to fill with bewilderment or wonder — **as•tound•ing•ly** *adv*

¹astrad•dle \ə-'strad-ᵊl\ *adv* : on or above and extending onto both sides

²astraddle *prep* : ASTRIDE

as•tra•khan \'as-trə-kən, -ˌkan\ *n, often cap* **1** : karakul of Russian origin **2** : a cloth with a usu. wool, curled, and looped pile resembling karakul

as•tral \'as-trəl\ *adj* : of or relating to the stars

astray \ə-'strā\ *adv or adj* **1** : off the right way or route **2** : into error

¹astride \ə-'strīd\ *adv* **1** : with one leg on each side **2** : with legs apart

²astride *prep* : with one leg on each side of

¹as•trin•gent \ə-'strin-jənt\ *adj* : able or tending to shrink body tissues — **as•trin•gen•cy** \-jən-sē\ *n*

²astringent *n* : an astringent agent or substance

astrol *abbr* astrologer; astrology

as•tro•labe \'as-trə-ˌlāb\ *n* : an instrument for observing the positions of celestial bodies

as•trol•o•gy \ə-'sträl-ə-jē\ *n* : divination based on the supposed influence of the stars upon human events — **as•trol•o•ger** \-ə-jər\ *n* — **as•tro•log•i•cal** \ˌas-trə-'läj-i-kəl\ *adj*

astron *abbr* astronomer; astronomy

as•tro•naut \'as-trə-ˌnȯt\ *n* : a traveler in a spacecraft

as•tro•nau•tics \ˌas-trə-'nȯt-iks\ *n* : the science of the construction and operation of spacecraft — **as•tro•nau•tic** \-ik\ *or* **as•tro•nau•ti•cal** \-i-kəl\ *adj*

as•tro•nom•i•cal \ˌas-trə-'näm-i-kəl\ *also* **as•tro•nom•ic** \-ik\ *adj* **1** : of or relating to astronomy **2** : extremely large ⟨an ∼ amount of money⟩

astronomical unit *n* : a unit of length used in astronomy equal to the mean distance of the earth from the sun or about 93 million miles (150 million kilometers)

as·tron·o·my \ə-'strän-ə-mē\ *n, pl* **-mies** : the science of the celestial bodies and of their magnitudes, motions, and constitution — **as·tron·o·mer** \-ə-mər\ *n*

as·tro·phys·ics \ˌas-trə-'fiz-iks\ *n* : astronomy dealing esp. with the physical properties and dynamic processes of celestial objects — **as·tro·phys·i·cal** \-i-kəl\ *adj* — **as·tro·phys·i·cist** \-'fiz-(ə-)səst\ *n*

as·tute \ə-'st(y)üt, a-\ *adj* [L *astutus,* fr. *astus* craft] : shrewdly discerning; *also* : WILY — **as·tute·ly** *adv* — **as·tute·ness** *n*

asun·der \ə-'sən-dər\ *adv or adj* 1 : into separate pieces ⟨torn ∼⟩ 2 : separated in position

ASV *abbr* American Standard Version

¹**as well as** *conj* : and in addition : and moreover ⟨brave *as well as* loyal⟩

²**as well as** *prep* : in addition to : BESIDES ⟨the coach, *as well as* the team, is ready⟩

asy·lum \ə-'sī-ləm\ *n* [ME, fr. L, fr. Gk *asylon,* neut. of *asylos* inviolable, fr. *a-* not + *sylon* right of seizure] 1 : a place of refuge 2 : protection given to esp. political fugitives 3 : an institution for the care of the needy or afflicted and esp. of the insane

asym·met·ri·cal \ˌā-sə-'me-tri-kəl\ *or* **asym·met·ric** \-trik\ *adj* : not symmetrical — **asym·me·try** \(')ā-'sim-ə-trē\ *n*

as·ymp·tote \'as-əm(p)-ˌtōt\ *n* : a straight line that is associated with a curve and tends to approximate it along an infinite branch — **as·ymp·tot·ic** \ˌas-əm(p)-'tät-ik\ *adj* — **as·ymp·tot·i·cal·ly** \-i-k(ə-)lē\ *adv*

¹**at** \ət, (')at\ *prep* 1 — used to indicate a point in time or space ⟨be here ∼ 3 o'clock⟩ ⟨he is ∼ the hotel⟩ 2 — used to indicate a goal ⟨swung ∼ the ball⟩ ⟨laugh ∼ him⟩ 3 — used to indicate position or condition ⟨∼ rest⟩ 4 — used to indicate means, cause, or manner ⟨sold ∼ auction⟩

²**at** \'ät\ *n, pl* **at** — see *kip* at MONEY table

At *symbol* astatine

AT *abbr* automatic transmission

at all \ət-'ol, ə-'tol, at-'ol\ *adv* : in any

way : in any circumstances ⟨not *at all* likely⟩

at·a·vism \'at-ə-ˌviz-əm\ *n* : appearance in an individual of a character typical of ancestors more remote than its parents; *also* : such an individual or character — **at·a·vis·tic** \ˌat-ə-'vis-tik\ *adj*

ate past of EAT

¹**-ate** \ət, ˌāt\ *n suffix* 1 : one acted upon (in a specified way) ⟨distill*ate*⟩ 2 : chemical compound or complex derived from a (specified) compound or element ⟨acet*ate*⟩

²**-ate** *n suffix* 1 : office : function : rank : group of persons holding a (specified) office or rank ⟨episcop*ate*⟩ 2 : state : dominion : jurisdiction ⟨emir*ate*⟩

³**-ate** *adj suffix* 1 : acted on (in a specified way) : being in a (specified) state ⟨temper*ate*⟩ ⟨degener*ate*⟩ 2 : marked by having ⟨vertebr*ate*⟩

⁴**-ate** \ˌāt\ *vb suffix* : cause to be modified or affected by ⟨pollin*ate*⟩ : cause to become ⟨activ*ate*⟩ : furnish with ⟨aer*ate*⟩

ate·lier \ˌat-ᵊl-'yā\ *n* 1 : an artist's studio 2 : WORKSHOP

athe·ist \'ā-thē-əst\ *n* : one who denies the existence of God — **athe·ism** \-ˌiz-əm\ *n* — **athe·is·tic** \ˌā-thē-'is-tik\ *adj*

ath·e·nae·um *or* **ath·e·ne·um** \ˌath-ə-'nē-əm\ *n* : LIBRARY 1

ath·ero·scle·ro·sis \ˌath-ə-rō-sklə-'rō-səs\ *n* : arteriosclerosis characterized by the deposition of fatty substances in and the hardening of the inner layer of the arteries — **ath·ero·scle·rot·ic** \-'rät-ik\ *adj*

athirst \ə-'thərst\ *adj* 1 *archaic* : THIRSTY 2 : EAGER, LONGING

ath·lete \'ath-ˌlēt\ *n* [ME, fr. L *athleta,* fr. Gk *athlētēs,* fr. *athlein* to contend for a prize, fr. *athlon* prize, contest] : one trained to compete in athletics

athlete's foot *n* : ringworm of the feet

ath·let·ic \ath-'let-ik\ *adj* 1 : of or relating to athletes or athletics 2 : VIGOROUS, ACTIVE 3 : STURDY, MUSCULAR

ath·let·ics \ath-'let-iks\ *n sing or pl* : exercises and games requiring physical skill, strength, and endurance

athletic supporter *n* : an elastic pouch used to support the male genitals and worn esp. during athletic activity

¹**athwart** \ə-'thwȯrt\ *prep* **1** : ACROSS **2** : in opposition to

²**athwart** *adv* : obliquely across

atilt \ə-'tilt\ *adv or adj* **1** : in a tilted position **2** : with lance in hand

Atl *abbr* Atlantic

at·las \'at-ləs\ *n* : a book of maps

atm *abbr* atmosphere; atmospheric

at·mo·sphere \'at-mə-ˌsfiər\ *n* **1** : the mass of air surrounding the earth **2** : a surrounding influence **3** : a unit of pressure equal to the pressure of air at sea level or about 14.7 pounds per square inch (10 newtons per square centimeter) **4** : a dominant effect — **at·mo·spher·ic** \ˌat-mə-'sfir-ik, -'sfer-\ *adj* — **at·mo·spher·i·cal·ly** \-i-k(ə-)lē\ *adv*

at·mo·spher·ics \ˌat-mə-'sfir-iks, -'sfer-\ *n pl* : disturbances produced in a radio receiver by atmospheric electrical phenomena

atoll \'a-ˌtȯl, -ˌtäl, 'ā-\ *n* : a coral island consisting of a reef surrounding a lagoon

at·om \'at-əm\ *n* [ME, fr. L *atomus*, fr. Gk *atomos*, fr. *atomos* indivisible, fr. *a-* not + *temnein* to cut] **1** : a tiny particle : BIT **2** : the smallest particle of a chemical element that can exist alone or in combination

atom bomb *n* : a very destructive bomb utilizing the energy released by splitting the atom

atom·ic \ə-'täm-ik\ *adj* **1** : of or relating to atoms, atomic energy, or atom bombs **2** : extremely small

atomic clock *n* : a precision clock regulated by the natural vibration of atoms or molecules (as of cesium or ammonia)

atomic energy *n* : energy that can be liberated by changes (as by fission or fusion) in the nucleus of an atom

atomic number *n* : the number of protons in the nucleus of an element

at·om·ize \'at-ə-ˌmīz\ *vb* **-ized; -iz·ing** : to reduce to minute particles

at·om·iz·er \'at-ə-ˌmī-zər\ *n* : a device for reducing a liquid to a very fine spray (as for spraying the throat)

atom smasher *n* : ACCELERATOR 3

aton·al \ā-'tōn-ᵊl\ *adj* : marked by avoidance of traditional musical tonality — **ato·nal·i·ty** \ˌā-tō-'nal-ət-ē\ *n* — **aton·al·ly** \ā-'tōn-ᵊl-ē\ *adv*

atone \ə-'tōn\ *vb* **atoned; aton·ing** **1** : to make amends **2** : EXPIATE

atone·ment \ə-'tōn-mənt\ *n* **1** : the reconciliation of God and man through the death of Jesus Christ **2** : reparation for an offense

atop \ə-'täp\ *prep* : on top of

ATP \ˌā-ˌtē-'pē\ *n* [*adenosine tri*phosphate] : a compound that occurs widely in living tissue and supplies energy for many cellular processes by undergoing enzymatic hydrolysis

atri·um \'ā-trē-əm\ *n, pl* **atria** \-trē-ə\ *also* **atri·ums** **1** : the central hall of a Roman house **2** : an anatomical cavity or passage; *esp* : one of the chambers of the heart that receives blood from the veins — **atri·al** \-trē-əl\ *adj*

atro·cious \ə-'trō-shəs\ *adj* **1** : savagely brutal, cruel, or wicked **2** : very bad : ABOMINABLE — **atro·cious·ly** *adv* — **atro·cious·ness** *n*

atroc·i·ty \ə-'träs-ət-ē\ *n, pl* **-ties** **1** : ATROCIOUSNESS **2** : an atrocious act or object

¹**at·ro·phy** \'a-trə-fē\ *n, pl* **-phies** : decrease in size or wasting away of a bodily part or tissue

²**atrophy** *vb* **-phied; -phy·ing** : to cause or undergo atrophy

at·ro·pine \'a-trə-ˌpēn\ *n* : a drug from belladonna and related plants used esp. to relieve spasms and to dilate the pupil of the eye

att *abbr* **1** attached **2** attention **3** attorney

at·tach \ə-'tach\ *vb* **1** : to seize legally in order to force payment of a debt **2** : to bind by personal ties **3** : FASTEN, CONNECT **4** : to be fastened or connected

at·ta·ché \ˌat-ə-'shā, ˌa-ˌta-, ə-ˌta-\ *n* [F] : a technical expert on the diplomatic staff of an ambassador

at·ta·ché case \ə-'tash-ā-, ˌat-ə-'shā-\ *n* : a small thin suitcase used esp. for carrying papers and documents

at·tach·ment \ə-'tach-mənt\ *n* **1** : legal seizure of property **2** : connection by ties of affection and regard **3** : a device attached to a machine or implement **4** : a connection by which one thing is attached to another

¹**at·tack** \ə-'tak\ *vb* **1** : to set upon with

force or words : ASSAIL, ASSAULT **2** : to set to work on

²**attack** *n* **1** : an offensive action **2** : a fit of sickness

at·tain \ə-ˈtān\ *vb* **1** : ACHIEVE, ACCOMPLISH **2** : to arrive at : REACH — **at·tain·abil·i·ty** \ə-ˈtā-nə-ˈbil-ət-ē\ *n* — **at·tain·able** *adj*

at·tain·der \ə-ˈtān-dər\ *n* : extinction of the civil rights of a person upon sentence of death or outlawry

at·tain·ment \ə-ˈtān-mənt\ *n* **1** : the act of attaining **2** : ACCOMPLISHMENT

at·taint \ə-ˈtānt\ *vb* : to condemn to loss of civil rights

at·tar \ˈat-ər\ *n* [Per ʿatir perfumed, fr. Ar, fr. ʿitr perfume] : a fragrant floral oil

at·tempt \ə-ˈtempt\ *vb* : to make an effort toward : TRY — **attempt** *n*

at·tend \ə-ˈtend\ *vb* **1** : to look after : TEND **2** : to be present with : ACCOMPANY **3** : to be present at **4** : to apply oneself **5** : to pay attention **6** : to take charge ⟨I'll ∼ to that⟩

at·ten·dance \ə-ˈten-dəns\ *n* **1** : the act or fact of attending **2** : the number of persons present

¹**at·ten·dant** \ə-ˈten-dənt\ *n* : one that attends another to render a service

²**attendant** *adj* : ACCOMPANYING ⟨∼ circumstances⟩

at·ten·tion \ə-ˈten-chən\ *n* **1** : the act or state of applying the mind to an object **2** : CONSIDERATION **3** : an act of courtesy **4** : a position of readiness for further orders assumed on command by a soldier — **at·ten·tive** \-ˈtent-iv\ *adj* — **at·ten·tive·ly** *adv* — **at·ten·tive·ness** *n*

at·ten·u·ate \ə-ˈten-yə-ˌwāt\ *vb* **-at·ed; -at·ing 1** : to make or become thin **2** : WEAKEN — **at·ten·u·a·tion** \-ˌten-yə-ˈwā-shən\ *n*

at·test \ə-ˈtest\ *vb* **1** : to certify as genuine by signing as a witness **2** : MANIFEST **3** : TESTIFY — **at·tes·ta·tion** \ˌa-ˌtes-ˈtā-shən\ *n*

at·tic \ˈat-ik\ *n* : the space or room in a building immediately below the roof

¹**at·tire** \ə-ˈtī(ə)r\ *vb* **at·tired; at·tir·ing** : DRESS, ARRAY

²**attire** *n* : DRESS, CLOTHES

at·ti·tude \ˈat-ə-ˌt(y)üd\ *n* **1** : the arrangement of the parts of a body : POSTURE **2** : a mental position or feeling with regard to a fact or state **3** : the position of something in relation to something else

at·ti·tu·di·nize \ˌat-ə-ˈt(y)üd-ᵊn-ˌīz\ *vb* **-nized; -niz·ing** : to assume an affected mental attitude : POSE

attn *abbr* attention

at·tor·ney \ə-ˈtər-nē\ *n, pl* **-neys** : a legal agent qualified to act for persons in legal proceedings

attorney general *n, pl* **attorneys general** *or* **attorney generals** : the chief legal representative and adviser of a nation or state

at·tract \ə-ˈtrakt\ *vb* **1** : to draw to or toward oneself : cause to approach **2** : to draw by emotional or aesthetic appeal **syn** charm, fascinate, allure, captivate, enchant — **at·trac·tive** \-ˈtrak-tiv\ *adj* — **at·trac·tive·ly** *adv* — **at·trac·tive·ness** *n*

at·trac·tant \ə-ˈtrak-tənt\ *n* : a substance used to attract insects or other animals

at·trac·tion \ə-ˈtrak-shən\ *n* **1** : the act or power of attracting; *esp* : personal charm **2** : an attractive quality, object, or feature **3** : a force tending to draw particles together

attrib *abbr* attributive; attributively

¹**at·tri·bute** \ˈa-trə-ˌbyüt\ *n* **1** : an inherent characteristic **2** : a word ascribing a quality; *esp* : ADJECTIVE

²**at·trib·ute** \ə-ˈtrib-yət\ *vb* **-ut·ed; -ut·ing 1** : to explain as to cause or origin ⟨∼ the illness to fatigue⟩ **2** : to regard as a characteristic **syn** ascribe, credit, charge, impute — **at·trib·ut·able** *adj* — **at·tri·bu·tion** \ˌa-trə-ˈbyü-shən\ *n*

at·trib·u·tive \ə-ˈtrib-yət-iv\ *adj* : joined directly to a modified noun without a linking verb ⟨*red* in *red hair* is an ∼ adjective⟩ — **attributive** *n*

at·tri·tion \ə-ˈtrish-ən\ *n* **1** : the act of wearing away by or as if by rubbing **2** : a reduction (as in personnel) as a result of resignation, retirement, or death

at·tune \ə-ˈt(y)ün\ *vb* : to bring into harmony : TUNE

atty *abbr* attorney

atyp·i·cal \ā-ˈtip-i-kəl\ *adj* : not typical : IRREGULAR

Au *symbol* [L *aurum*] gold

au·burn \ˈȯ-bərn\ *adj* : reddish brown — **auburn** *n*

au cou·rant \ˌō-ků-ˈräᵐ\ *adj* [F, lit., in the current] : UP-TO-DATE

¹**auc·tion** \ˈȯk-shən\ *n* [L *auction-, auctio,* lit., increase, fr. *auctus,* pp. of *augēre* to increase] : public sale of property to the highest bidder

²**auction** *vb* **auc·tioned; auc·tion·ing** \-sh(ə-)niŋ\ : to sell at auction

auction bridge *n* : a bridge game in which tricks made in excess of the contract are scored toward game

auc·tion·eer \ˌȯk-shə-ˈniər\ *n* : an agent who conducts an auction

auc·to·ri·al \ȯk-ˈtȯr-ē-əl\ *adj* : of or relating to an author

aud *abbr* audit; auditor

au·da·cious \ȯ-ˈdā-shəs\ *adj* 1 : DARING, BOLD 2 : INSOLENT — **au·da·cious·ly** *adv* — **au·da·cious·ness** *n* — **au·dac·i·ty** \ȯ-ˈdas-ət-ē\ *n*

¹**au·di·ble** \ˈȯd-ə-bəl\ *adj* : capable of being heard — **au·di·bil·i·ty** \ˌȯd-ə-ˈbil-ət-ē\ *n* — **au·di·bly** \ˈȯd-ə-blē\ *adv*

²**audible** *n* : AUTOMATIC 2

au·di·ence \ˈȯd-ē-əns\ *n* 1 : a formal interview 2 : an opportunity of being heard 3 : an assembly of listeners or spectators

¹**au·dio** \ˈȯd-ē-ˌō\ *adj* 1 : of or relating to frequencies (as of radio waves) corresponding to those of audible sound waves 2 : of or relating to sound or its reproduction and esp. high-fidelity reproduction 3 : relating to or used in the transmission or reception of sound

²**audio** *n* 1 : the transmission, reception, or reproduction of sound 2 : the section of television or motion-picture equipment that deals with sound

au·di·ol·o·gy \ˌȯd-ē-ˈäl-ə-jē\ *n* : a branch of science dealing with hearing and esp. with the treatment of individuals having trouble with hearing — **au·di·o·log·i·cal** \-ē-ə-ˈläj-i-kəl\ *adj* — **au·di·ol·o·gist** \-ē-ˈäl-ə-jəst\ *n*

au·dio·phile \ˈȯd-ē-ō-ˌfīl\ *n* : one who is enthusiastic about high-fidelity sound reproduction

au·dio·vi·su·al \ˌȯd-ē-ō-ˈvizh-(ə-w)əl\ *adj* : of, relating to, or making use of both hearing and sight

au·dio·vi·su·als \-wəlz\ *n pl* : audiovisual materials (as filmstrips)

¹**au·dit** \ˈȯd-ət\ *n* : a formal examination and verification of financial accounts

²**audit** *vb* 1 : to perform an audit on or for 2 : to attend (a course) without expecting formal credit

¹**au·di·tion** \ȯ-ˈdish-ən\ *n* : HEARING; *esp* : a trial performance to appraise an entertainer's merits

²**audition** *vb* **-tioned; -tion·ing** \-ˈdish-(ə-)niŋ\ : to give an audition to; *also* : to give a trial performance

au·di·tor \ˈȯd-ət-ər\ *n* 1 : LISTENER 2 : a person who audits

au·di·to·ri·um \ˌȯd-ə-ˈtȯr-ē-əm\ *n* 1 : the part of a public building where an audience sits 2 : a hall or building used for public gatherings

au·di·to·ry \ˈȯd-ə-ˌtȯr-ē\ *adj* : of or relating to hearing or to the sense or organs of hearing

auf Wie·der·seh·en \aůf-ˈvēd-ər-ˌzān\ *interj* [G] — used to express farewell

Aug *abbr* August

au·ger \ˈȯ-gər\ *n* : a boring tool

aught \ˈȯt, ˈät\ *n* : ZERO, CIPHER

aug·ment \ȯg-ˈment\ *vb* : ENLARGE, INCREASE — **aug·men·ta·tion** \ˌȯg-mən-ˈtā-shən\ *n*

au gra·tin \ō-ˈgrat-ᵊn, ȯ-, -ˈgrät-\ *adj* [F, lit., with the burnt scrapings from the pan] : covered with bread crumbs or grated cheese and browned

¹**au·gur** \ˈȯ-gər\ *n* : DIVINER, SOOTHSAYER

²**augur** *vb* 1 : to foretell esp. from omens 2 : to give promise of : PRESAGE

au·gu·ry \ˈȯ-g(y)ə-rē\ *n, pl* **-ries** 1 : divination from omens 2 : OMEN, PORTENT

au·gust \ȯ-ˈgəst\ *adj* : marked by majestic dignity or grandeur — **au·gust·ly** *adv* — **au·gust·ness** *n*

Au·gust \ˈȯ-gəst\ *n* [ME, fr. OE, fr. L *Augustus,* fr. *Augustus* Caesar] : the eighth month of the year having 31 days

au jus \ō-ˈzhü(s), -ˈjüs; ō-zhu̇̄\ *adj* [F] : served in the juice obtained from roasting

auk \ˈȯk\ *n* : any of several stocky black-and-white diving seabirds that breed in colder parts of the northern hemisphere

auld \ˈȯl(d), ˈäl(d)\ *adj, chiefly Scot* : OLD

aunt \ˈant, ˈȧnt\ *n* 1 : the sister of one's father or mother 2 : the wife of one's uncle

au pair \ˈō-ˈpaər\ *n* [F, on even terms] : a foreign girl who does domestic work for a family in return for room and board and the opportunity to learn the family's language

au·ra \'ȯr-ə\ *n* **1** : a distinctive atmosphere surrounding a given source **2** : a luminous radiation

au·ral \'ȯr-əl\ *adj* : of or relating to the ear or to the sense of hearing

aurar *pl of* EYRIR

au·re·ate \'ȯr-ē-ət\ *adj* **1** : of a golden color or brilliance **2** : RESPLENDENT, ORNATE

au·re·ole \'ȯr-ē-ˌōl\ *or* **au·re·o·la** \ȯ-'rē-ə-lə\ *n* : HALO, NIMBUS

au re·voir \ˌōr-əv-'wär\ *n* [F, lit., till seeing again] : GOOD-BYE

au·ri·cle \'ȯr-i-kəl\ *n* : an atrium of the heart

au·ric·u·lar \ȯ-'rik-yə-lər\ *adj* **1** : told privately ⟨∼ confession⟩ **2** : known by the sense of hearing

au·ro·ra \ə-'rōr-ə\ *n, pl* **auroras** *or* **au·ro·rae** \-(ˌ)ē\ : a luminous phenomenon of streamers or arches of light appearing in the upper atmosphere esp. of a planet's polar regions — **au·ro·ral** \-əl\ *adj*

aurora aus·tra·lis \-ȯ-'strā-ləs\ *n* : an aurora that occurs in earth's southern hemisphere

aurora bo·re·al·is \-ˌbōr-ē-'al-əs\ *n* : an aurora that occurs in earth's northern hemisphere

AUS *abbr* Army of the United States

aus·pice \'ȯ-spəs\ *n, pl* **aus·pic·es** \-spə-səz, -ˌsēz\ [L *auspicium*, fr. *auspic-*, *auspex* diviner by birds, fr. *avis* bird + *specere* to look, look at] **1** : observation in augury **2** : a prophetic sign or omen **3** *pl* : kindly patronage and protection

aus·pi·cious \ȯ-'spish-əs\ *adj* **1** : promising success : FAVORABLE **2** : FORTUNATE, PROSPEROUS — **aus·pi·cious·ly** *adv*

aus·tere \ȯ-'stiər\ *adj* **1** : STERN, SEVERE, STRICT **2** : ABSTEMIOUS **3** : UNADORNED ⟨∼ style⟩ — **aus·tere·ly** *adv* — **aus·ter·i·ty** \ȯ-'ster-ət-ē\ *n*

¹aus·tral \'ȯs-trəl\ *adj* : SOUTHERN

²aus·tral \aů-'sträl\ *n, pl* **aus·tral·es** \-'sträl-ās\ *also* **australs** — see MONEY table

Aus·tra·lian \ȯ-'strāl-yən\ *n* : a native or inhabitant of Australia — **Australian** *adj*

Aus·tri·an \'ȯ-strē-ən\ *n* : a native or inhabitant of Austria — **Austrian** *adj*

Aus·tro·ne·sian \ˌȯs-trə-'nē-zhən\ *adj* : of, relating to, or constituting a family of languages spoken in the area extending from Madagascar eastward through the Malay peninsula to Hawaii and Easter Island

auth *abbr* **1** authentic **2** author **3** authorized

au·then·tic \ə-'thent-ik, ȯ-\ *adj* : GENUINE, REAL — **au·then·ti·cal·ly** \-i-k(ə-)lē\ *adv* — **au·then·tic·i·ty** \ˌȯ-ˌthen-'tis-ət-ē\ *n*

au·then·ti·cate \ə-'thent-i-ˌkāt, ȯ-\ *vb* **-cat·ed; -cat·ing** : to prove genuine — **au·then·ti·ca·tion** \-ˌthent-i-'kā-shən\ *n*

au·thor \'ȯ-thər\ *n* [ME *auctour*, deriv. of L *auctor* originator, author, fr. *auctus*, pp. of *augēre* to increase] **1** : one that writes or composes a literary work **2** : one that originates or creates

au·thor·ess \'ȯ-th(ə-)rəs\ *n* : a woman author

au·thor·i·tar·i·an \ȯ-ˌthär-ə-'ter-ē-ən, ə-, -ˌthȯr-\ *adj* **1** : characterized by or favoring the principle of blind obedience to authority **2** : characterized by or favoring concentration of political power in an authority not responsible to the people

au·thor·i·ta·tive \ə-'thär-ə-ˌtāt-iv, ȯ-, -'thȯr-\ *adj* : supported by, proceeding from, or being an authority : TRUSTWORTHY — **au·thor·i·ta·tive·ly** *adv*

au·thor·i·ty \ə-'thär-ət-ē, ȯ-, -'thȯr-\ *n, pl* **-ties** **1** : a citation used in support of a statement or in defense of an action; *also* : the source of such a citation **2** : one appealed to as an expert **3** : power to influence thought or behavior **4** : freedom granted : RIGHT **5** : persons in command; *esp* : GOVERNMENT

au·tho·rize \'ȯ-thə-ˌrīz\ *vb* **-rized; -riz·ing** **1** : SANCTION **2** : to give legal power to — **au·tho·ri·za·tion** \ˌȯ-th(ə-)rə-'zā-shən\ *n*

au·thor·ship \'ȯ-thər-ˌship\ *n* **1** : the state of being an author **2** : the source of a piece of writing, music, or art

au·tism \'ȯ-ˌtiz-əm\ *n* : absorption in self-centered subjective mental activity (as daydreaming, fantasies, delusions, and hallucinations) esp. when accompanied by marked withdrawal from reality — **au·tis·tic** \ȯ-'tis-tik\ *adj*

au·to \'ȯt-ō\ *n, pl* **autos** : AUTOMOBILE

au·to·bahn \'ȯt-ō-ˌbän, 'aut-\ *n* : a German expressway

au·to·bi·og·ra·phy \ˌȯt-ə-bī-'äg-rə-fē, -bē-\ *n* : the biography of a person narrated by himself — **au·to·bi·og·ra·pher** \-fər\ *n* — **au·to·bi·o·graph·i·cal** \-ˌbī-ə-'graf-i-kəl\ *adj*

au·toch·tho·nous \ȯ-'täk-thə-nəs\ *adj* : INDIGENOUS, NATIVE

au·toc·ra·cy \ȯ-'täk-rə-sē\ *n, pl* **-cies** : government by one person having unlimited power — **au·to·crat** \'ȯt-ə-ˌkrat\ *n* — **au·to·crat·ic** \ˌȯt-ə-'krat-ik\ *adj* — **au·to·crat·i·cal·ly** \-i-k(ə-)lē\ *adv*

[1]**au·to·graph** \'ȯt-ə-ˌgraf\ *n* **1** : an original manuscript **2** : a person's signature written by hand

[2]**autograph** *vb* : to write one's signature on

au·to·im·mune \ˌȯt-ō-im-'yün\ *adj* : of, relating to, or caused by antibodies or lymphocytes that attack molecules, cells, or tissues of the organism producing them 〈∼ diseases〉 — **au·to·im·mu·ni·ty** \-im-'yün-ət-ē\ *n*

au·to·mate \'ȯt-ə-ˌmāt\ *vb* **-mat·ed; -mat·ing 1** : to operate by automation **2** : to convert to automatic operation

[1]**au·to·mat·ic** \ˌȯt-ə-'mat-ik\ *adj* **1** : INVOLUNTARY **2** : made so that certain parts act in a desired manner at the proper time : SELF-ACTING — **au·to·mat·i·cal·ly** \-i-k(ə-)lē\ *adv*

[2]**automatic** *n* **1** : an automatic device; *esp* : an automatic firearm **2** : a substitute play called by a football quarterback at the line of scrimmage

au·to·ma·tion \ˌȯt-ə-'mā-shən\ *n* **1** : the technique of making an apparatus, a process, or a system operate automatically **2** : the state of being operated automatically **3** : automatic operation of an apparatus, process, or system by mechanical or electronic devices that replace human operators

au·tom·a·tize \ȯ-'täm-ə-ˌtīz\ *vb* **-tized; -tiz·ing** : to make automatic — **au·tom·a·ti·za·tion** \-ˌtäm-ət-ə-'zā-shən\ *n*

au·tom·a·ton \ȯ-'täm-ət-ən, -ə-ˌtän\ *n, pl* **-atons** *or* **-a·ta** \-ət-ə, -ə-ˌtä\ **1** : an

automatic machine; *esp* : ROBOT **2** : an individual who acts mechanically

au·to·mo·bile \'ȯt-ə-mō-ˌbēl, ˌȯt-ə-mə-'bēl\ *n* : a usu. 4-wheeled automotive vehicle for passenger transportation on streets and roadways — **au·to·mo·bil·ist** \-ˌbē-ləst, -'bē-\ *n*

au·to·mo·tive \ˌȯt-ə-'mōt-iv\ *adj* **1** : of or relating to automobiles, trucks, or buses **2** : SELF-PROPELLED

au·to·nom·ic nervous system \ˌȯt-ə-'näm-ik-\ *n* : a part of the vertebrate nervous system that governs involuntary actions and that consists of the sympathetic nervous system and the parasympathetic nervous system

au·ton·o·mous \ȯ-'tän-ə-məs\ *adj* : having the right or power of self-government — **au·ton·o·mous·ly** *adv* — **au·ton·o·my** \-mē\ *n*

au·top·sy \'ȯ-ˌtäp-sē, 'ȯt-əp-\ *n, pl* **-sies** [Gk *autopsia* act of seeing with one's own eyes, fr. *autos* self + *opsis* sight] : examination of a dead body usu. with dissection sufficient to determine the cause of death or extent of change produced by disease — **autopsy** *vb*

au·tumn \'ȯt-əm\ *n* : the season between summer and winter — **au·tum·nal** \ȯ-'təm-nəl\ *adj*

aux *or* **auxil** *abbr* auxiliary

[1]**aux·il·ia·ry** \ȯg-'zil-yə-rē, -'zil-(ə-)rē\ *adj* **1** : providing help **2** : functioning in a subsidiary capacity **3** : accompanying a verb form to express person, number, mood, or tense 〈∼ verbs〉

[2]**auxiliary** *n, pl* **-ries 1** : an auxiliary person, group, or device **2** : an auxiliary verb

aux·in \'ȯk-sən\ *n* : a plant hormone that stimulates growth in length

av *abbr* **1** avenue **2** average **3** avoirdupois

AV *abbr* **1** ad valorem **2** audiovisual **3** Authorized Version

[1]**avail** \ə-'vāl\ *vb* : to be of use or advantage : HELP, BENEFIT

[2]**avail** *n* : USE 〈effort was of no ∼〉

avail·able \ə-'vā-lə-bəl\ *adj* **1** : USABLE **2** : ACCESSIBLE — **avail·abil·i·ty** \-ˌvā-lə-'bil-ət-ē\ *n*

av·a·lanche \'av-ə-ˌlanch\ *n* : a mass of snow, ice, earth, or rock sliding down a mountainside

avant–garde \ˌäv-ˌän(t)-'gärd\ *n* [F,

vanguard] : those esp. in the arts who create or apply new or experimental ideas and techniques — **avant–garde** *adj*

av·a·rice \\'av-(ə-)rəs\ *n* : excessive desire for wealth : GREED — **av·a·ri·cious** \\,av-ə-'rish-əs\ *adj*

avast \ə-'vast\ *vb imper* — a nautical command to stop or cease

av·a·tar \\'av-ə-,tär\ *n* [Skt *avatāra* descent] : INCARNATION

avaunt \ə-'vȯnt\ *adv* : AWAY, HENCE

avdp *abbr* avoirdupois

ave *abbr* avenue

Ave Ma·ria \\,äv-,ā-mə-'rē-ə\ *n* : HAIL MARY

avenge \ə-'venj\ *vb* **avenged; aveng·ing** : to take vengeance for — **aveng·er** *n*

av·e·nue \\'av-ə-,n(y)ü\ *n* **1** : a way or route to a place or goal : PATH **2** : a broad street esp. when bordered by trees

aver \ə-'vər\ *vb* **averred; aver·ring** : to declare positively

¹av·er·age \\'av-(ə-)rij\ *n* [modif. of MF *avarie* damage to ship or cargo, fr. It *avaria,* fr. Ar *'awārīyah* damaged merchandise] **1** : ARITHMETIC MEAN **2** : a ratio (as a rate per thousand) of successful tries to total tries ⟨batting ∼ of .303⟩

²average *adj* **1** : equaling or approximating an arithmetic mean **2** : being about midway between extremes **3** : not out of the ordinary : COMMON

³average *vb* **av·er·aged; av·er·ag·ing 1** : to be at or come to an average **2** : to be usually **3** : to find the average of

averse \ə-'vərs\ *adj* : having an active feeling of dislike or reluctance ⟨∼ to exercise⟩

aver·sion \ə-'vər-zhən\ *n* **1** : a feeling of repugnance for something with a desire to avoid it **2** : something decidedly disliked

avert \ə-'vərt\ *vb* **1** : to turn aside or away ⟨∼ the eyes⟩ **2** : to ward off

avg *abbr* average

avi·an \\'ā-vē-ən\ *adj* [L *avis* bird] : of, relating to, or derived from birds

avi·ary \\'ā-vē-,er-ē\ *n, pl* **-ar·ies** : a place where live birds are kept usu. for exhibition

avi·a·tion \\,ā-vē-'ā-shən, ,av-ē-\ *n* **1** : the operation of heavier-than-air aircraft **2** : aircraft manufacture, devel-

opment, and design — **avi·a·tor** \\'ā-vē-,āt-ər, 'av-ē-\ *n*

avi·a·trix \\,ā-vē-'ā-triks, ,av-ē-\ *n, pl* **-trix·es** \-trik-səz\ *or* **-tri·ces** \-trə-,sēz\ : a woman airplane pilot

av·id \\'av-əd\ *adj* **1** : craving eagerly : GREEDY **2** : enthusiastic in pursuit of an interest — **avid·i·ty** \ə-'vid-ət-ē, a-\ *n* — **av·id·ly** *adv*

avi·on·ics \\,ā-vē-'än-iks, ,av-ē-\ *n pl* : electronics designed for use in aerospace vehicles — **avi·on·ic** \-ik\ *adj*

avi·ta·min·osis \\,ā-,vīt-ə-mə-'nō-səs\ *n, pl* **-o·ses** \-,sēz\ : disease resulting from vitamin deficiency

avo \\'av-(,)ü\ *n, pl* **avos** — see *pataca* at MONEY table

av·o·ca·do \\,av-ə-'käd-ō, ,äv-\ *n, pl* **-dos** *also* **-does** [modif. of Sp *aguacate,* fr. Nahuatl *ahuacatl,* lit., testicle] : a usu. green pear-shaped fruit with rich oily flesh that is produced by a tropical American tree; *also* : this tree

av·o·ca·tion \\,av-ə-'kā-shən\ *n* : a subordinate occupation pursued esp. for pleasure : HOBBY

av·o·cet \\'av-ə-,set\ *n* : any of several long-legged shorebirds with webbed feet and slender upward-curving bills

avoid \ə-'vȯid\ *vb* **1** : to keep away from : SHUN **2** : to prevent the occurrence of **3** : to refrain from — **avoid·able** *adj* — **avoid·ance** \-ᵊns\ *n*

av·oir·du·pois \\,av-ərd-ə-'pȯiz\ *n* [ME *avoir de pois* goods sold by weight, fr. OF, lit., goods of weight] **1** : AVOIRDUPOIS WEIGHT **2** : WEIGHT, HEAVINESS; *esp* : personal weight

avoirdupois weight *n* : a system of weights based on a pound of 16 ounces and an ounce of 16 drams — see WEIGHT table

avouch \ə-'vaúch\ *vb* **1** : to declare positively : AVER **2** : GUARANTEE

avow \ə-'vaú\ *vb* : to declare openly — **avow·al** \-'vaú(-ə)l\ *n*

avun·cu·lar \ə-'vəŋ-kyə-lər\ *adj* : of, relating to, or resembling an uncle

await \ə-'wāt\ *vb* : to wait for : EXPECT

¹awake \ə-'wāk\ *vb* **awoke** \-'wōk\ *also* **awaked** \-'wākt\; **awaked** *or* **awo·ken** \-'wō-kən\ *also* **awoke; awak·ing** : to bring back to consciousness after sleep : wake up

²awake *adj* : not asleep; *also* : ALERT

awak·en \ə-'wā-kən\ *vb* **awak·ened; awak·en·ing** \-'wāk-(ə-)niŋ\ : AWAKE

¹award \ə-'word\ *vb* **1** : to give by judicial decision ⟨~ damages⟩ **2** : to give in recognition of merit or achievement ⟨~ a prize⟩

²award *n* **1** : a final decision : JUDGMENT **2** : something awarded : PRIZE

aware \ə-'waər\ *adj* : having perception or knowledge : CONSCIOUS, INFORMED — **aware·ness** *n*

awash \ə-'wosh, -'wäsh\ *adj* **1** : washed by waves or tide **2** : AFLOAT **3** : FLOODED

¹away \ə-'wā\ *adv* **1** : from this or that place ⟨go ~⟩ **2** : out of the way **3** : in another direction ⟨turn ~⟩ **4** : out of existence ⟨fade ~⟩ **5** : from one's possession ⟨give ~⟩ **6** : without interruption ⟨chatter ~⟩ **7** : at a distance in space or time ⟨far ~⟩ ⟨~ back in 1910⟩

²away *adj* **1** : ABSENT **2** : distant in space or time ⟨a lake 10 miles ~⟩

¹awe \'o\ *n* **1** : profound and reverent dread of the supernatural **2** : respectful fear inspired by authority

²awe *vb* **awed; aw·ing** : to inspire with awe

aweigh \ə-'wā\ *adj* : just clear of the bottom and hanging perpendicularly ⟨anchors ~⟩

awe·some \'o-səm\ *adj* **1** : expressive of awe **2** : inspiring awe

awe·struck \-,strək\ *also* **awe·strick·en** \-,strik-ən\ *adj* : filled with awe

aw·ful \'o-fəl\ *adj* **1** : inspiring awe **2** : extremely disagreeable **3** : very great — **aw·ful·ly** \-ē\ *adv*

awhile \ə-'hwīl\ *adv* : for a while

awhirl \ə-'hwərl\ *adj* : in a whirl : WHIRLING

awk·ward \'o-kwərd\ *adj* **1** : CLUMSY **2** : UNGRACEFUL **3** : difficult to explain : EMBARRASSING **4** : difficult to deal with — **awk·ward·ly** *adv* — **awk·ward·ness** *n*

awl \'ol\ *n* : a pointed instrument for making small holes

aw·ning \'on-iŋ\ *n* : a rooflike cover (as of canvas) extended over or in front of a place as a shelter

AWOL \'ā-,wol, ,ā-,dəb-əl-yü-,ō-'el\ *n* : a person who is absent without leave — **AWOL** *adj or adv*

awry \ə-'rī\ *adv or adj* **1** : ASKEW **2** : out of the right course : AMISS

ax *or* **axe** \'aks\ *n* : a chopping or cutting tool with an edged head fitted parallel to a handle

ax·i·al \'ak-sē-əl\ *adj* **1** : of, relating to, or functioning as an axis **2** : situated around, in the direction of, on, or along an axis — **ax·i·al·ly** \'ak-sē-ə-lē\ *adv*

ax·i·om \'ak-sē-əm\ *n* [L *axioma*, fr. Gk *axioma*, lit., honor, fr. *axioun* to think worthy, fr. *axios* worth, worthy] **1** : a statement generally accepted as true : MAXIM **2** : a proposition regarded as a self-evident truth — **ax·i·om·at·ic** \,ak-sē-ə-'mat-ik\ *adj* — **ax·i·om·at·i·cal·ly** \-i-k(ə-)lē\ *adv*

ax·is \'ak-səs\ *n, pl* **ax·es** \-,sēz\ **1** : a real or imaginary straight line passing through a body that actually or supposedly revolves upon it ⟨the earth's ~⟩ **2** : one of the reference lines of a system of coordinates **3** : a straight line with respect to which a body or figure is symmetrical **4** : a bodily structure around which parts are arranged in a symmetrical way; *esp* : the main stem of a plant from which leaves and branches arise **5** : an alliance between major powers

ax·le \'ak-səl\ *n* : a shaft on which a wheel revolves

ayah \'ī-ə\ *n* [Hindi *āyā*, fr. Pg *aia*, fr. L *avia* grandmother] : a native nurse or maid in India

aya·tol·lah \,ī-ə-'tō-lə, -'täl-ə, -'təl-ə, 'ī-ə-,; ,ī-ə-tə-'lä\ *n* [Per, lit., sign of God, fr. Ar *ayat* sign, miracle + *allāh* God] : an Islamic religious leader — used as a title of respect

¹aye *also* **ay** \'ā\ *adv* : ALWAYS, EVER

²aye *also* **ay** \'ī\ *adv* : YES

³aye *also* **ay** \'ī\ *n, pl* **ayes** : an affirmative vote

AZ *abbr* Arizona

aza·lea \ə-'zāl-yə\ *n* : any of numerous rhododendrons with funnel-shaped blossoms and usu. deciduous leaves

az·i·muth \'az-(ə-)məth\ *n* : horizontal direction expressed as an angular distance

Az·tec \'az-,tek\ *n* : a member of an American Indian people that founded the Mexican empire and were conquered by Hernan Cortes in 1519 — **Az·tec·an** *adj*

azure \\'azh-ər\\ *n* : the blue of the clear sky — **azure** *adj*

B

[1]b \\'bē\\ *n, pl* **b's** *or* **bs** \\'bēz\\ *often cap* **1** : the 2d letter of the English alphabet **2** : a grade rating a student's work as good

[2]b *abbr, often cap* **1** bachelor **2** bass **3** bishop **4** book **5** born

B *symbol* boron

Ba *symbol* barium

BA *abbr* **1** bachelor of arts **2** batting average

bab•bitt metal \\'bab-ət-\\ *n* : an alloy used for lining bearings; *esp* : one containing tin, copper, and antimony

bab•ble \\'bab-əl\\ *vb* **bab•bled; bab•bling** \\-(ə-)liŋ\\ **1** : to utter meaningless sounds **2** : to talk foolishly or excessively — **babble** *n* — **bab•bler** \\-(ə-)lər\\ *n*

babe \\'bāb\\ *n* **1** : BABY **2** *slang* : GIRL, WOMAN

ba•bel \\'bā-bəl, 'bab-əl\\ *n, often cap* [fr. the Tower of *Babel,* Gen 11:4–9] : a place or scene of noise and confusion; *also* : a confused sound **syn** hubbub, racket, din, uproar, clamor

ba•boon \\ba-'bün\\ *n* [ME *babewin,* fr. MF *babouin,* fr. *baboue* grimace] : any of several large apes of Asia and Africa with doglike muzzles

ba•bush•ka \\bə-'büsh-kə, -'bush-\\ *n* [Russ, grandmother, dim. of *baba* old woman] : a kerchief for the head

[1]ba•by \\'bā-bē\\ *n, pl* **babies** **1** : a very young child : INFANT **2** : the youngest or smallest of a group **3** : a childish person — **baby** *adj* — **ba•by•hood** *n* — **ba•by•ish** *adj*

[2]baby *vb* **ba•bied; ba•by•ing** : to tend or treat often with excessive care

baby's breath *n* : any of a genus of herbs that are related to the pinks and have small delicate flowers

ba•by–sit \\'bā-bē-ˌsit\\ *vb* **-sat** \\-ˌsat\\; **-sit•ting** : to care for children usu. during a short absence of the parents — **ba•by–sit•ter** *n*

bac•ca•lau•re•ate \\ˌbak-ə-'lȯr-ē-ət\\ *n* **1** : the degree of bachelor conferred by colleges and universities **2** : a sermon delivered to a graduating class

bac•ca•rat \\ˌbäk-ə-'rä, ˌbak-\\ *n* : a card game played esp. in European casinos

bac•cha•nal \\'bak-ən-ᵊl, ˌbak-ə-'nal, ˌbäk-ə-'näl\\ *n* **1** : REVELER **2** : drunken revelry : BACCHANALIA

bac•cha•na•lia \\ˌbak-ə-'nāl-yə\\ *n, pl* **bacchanalia** : a drunken orgy — **bac•cha•na•lian** \\-'nāl-yən\\ *adj or n*

bach•e•lor \\'bach-(ə-)lər\\ *n* **1** : a person who has received the usu. lowest degree conferred by a 4-year college **2** : a man who has not married — **bach•e•lor•hood** *n*

bach•e•lor•ette \\ˌbach(-ə)-lə-'ret\\ *n* : a young unmarried woman

bachelor's button *n* : a European plant related to the daisies and having blue, pink, or white flower heads

ba•cil•lus \\bə-'sil-əs\\ *n, pl* **-li** \\-ˌī\\ [NL, fr. ML, small staff, dim. of L *baculus* staff] : any of numerous rod-shaped bacteria; *also* : a disease-producing bacterium — **bac•il•lary** \\'bas-ə-ˌler-ē\\ *adj*

[1]back \\'bak\\ *n* **1** : the rear or dorsal part of the human body; *also* : the corresponding part of a lower animal **2** : the part or surface opposite the front **3** : a player in the backfield in football — **back•less** \\-ləs\\ *adj*

[2]back *adv* **1** : to, toward, or at the rear **2** : AGO **3** : so as to be restrained or retarded **4** : to, toward, or in a former place or state **5** : in return or reply

[3]back *adj* **1** : located at or in the back; *also* : REMOTE **2** : OVERDUE **3** : moving or operating backward **4** : not current **syn** posterior, hind, rear

[4]back *vb* **1** : SUPPORT, UPHOLD **2** : to go or cause to go backward or in reverse **3** : to furnish with a back : form the back of

back•ache \\'bak-ˌāk\\ *n* : pain in the back; *esp* : a dull persistent pain in the lower back

back–bench•er \\-'ben-chər\\ *n* : a rank=

and-file member of a British legislature

back·bite \-₁bīt\ *vb* **-bit** \-₁bit\; **-bit·ten** \-₁bit-ᵊn\; **-bit·ing** \-₁bīt-iŋ\ : to say mean or spiteful things about someone who is absent — **back·bit·er** *n*

back·board \-₁bōrd\ *n* : a board or construction placed at the back or serving as a back

back·bone \-'bōn, -₁bōn\ *n* **1** : the bony column in the back of a vertebrate that is the chief support of the trunk and consists of a jointed series of vertebrae enclosing and protecting the spinal cord **2** : firm resolute character

back·drop \'bak-₁dräp\ *n* : a painted cloth hung across the rear of a stage

back·er \'bak-ər\ *n* : one that supports **syn** upholder, guarantor, sponsor, patron

back·field \-₁fēld\ *n* : the football players whose positions are behind the line

¹back·fire \-₁fī(ə)r\ *n* : a loud noise caused by the improperly timed explosion of fuel in the cylinder of an internal-combustion engine

²backfire *vb* **1** : to make or undergo a backfire **2** : to have a result opposite to what was intended

back·gam·mon \'bak-₁gam-ən\ *n* : a game played with pieces on a double board in which the moves are determined by throwing dice

back·ground \'bak-₁graund\ *n* **1** : the scenery behind something **2** : the setting within which something takes place; *also* : the sum of a person's experience, training, and understanding

back·hand \'bak-₁hand\ *n* : a stroke (as in tennis) made with the back of the hand turned in the direction in which the hand is moving; *also* : the side on which such a stroke is made — **backhand** *vb*

back·hand·ed \'bak-'han-dəd\ *adj* **1** : using or made with a backhand **2** : INDIRECT, DEVIOUS; *esp* : SARCASTIC

back·hoe \'bak-₁hō\ *n* : an excavating machine having a bucket that is drawn toward the machine in operation

back·ing \'bak-iŋ\ *n* **1** : something forming a back **2** : SUPPORT, AID; *also* : a body of supporters

back·lash \'bak-₁lash\ *n* **1** : a sudden violent backward movement or reaction **2** : a strong adverse reaction

¹back·log \-₁lȯg, -₁läg\ *n* **1** : a large log at the back of a hearth fire **2** : an accumulation of tasks unperformed or materials not processed

²backlog *vb* : to accumulate in reserve

back of *prep* : BEHIND

back out *vb* : to withdraw esp. from a commitment or contest

¹back·pack \'bak-₁pak\ *n* : a camping pack supported by an aluminum frame and carried on the back

²backpack *vb* : to hike with a backpack — **back·pack·er** *n*

back·ped·al \'bak-₁ped-ᵊl\ *vb* : RETREAT

back·rest \-₁rest\ *n* : a rest for the back

back·side \-'sīd\ *n* : BUTTOCKS

back·slap \-₁slap\ *vb* : to display excessive cordiality — **back·slap·per** *n*

back·slide \-₁slīd\ *vb* **-slid** \-₁slid\; **-slid** *or* **-slid·den** \-₁slid-ᵊn\; **-slid·ing** \-₁slīd-iŋ\ : to lapse morally or in religious practice — **back·slid·er** *n*

back·spin \-₁spin\ *n* : a backward rotary motion of a ball

¹back·stage \'bak-₁stāj\ *adj* **1** : relating to or occurring in the area behind a stage **2** : of or relating to the private lives of theater people **3** : of or relating to the inner working or operation

²back·stage \'bak-'stāj\ *adv* **1** : in or to a backstage area **2** : SECRETLY

back·stairs \-₁staərz\ *adj* : SECRET, FURTIVE; *also* : SORDID, SCANDALOUS

¹back·stop \-₁stap\ *n* : something serving as a stop behind something else; *esp* : a screen or fence to keep a ball from leaving the field of play

²backstop *vb* **1** : to serve as a backstop to **2** : SUPPORT

back·stretch \'bak-'strech\ *n* : the side opposite the homestretch on a racecourse

back·stroke \-₁strōk\ *n* : a swimming stroke executed on the back

back talk *n* : an impudent, insolent, or argumentative reply

back·track \'bak-₁trak\ *vb* **1** : to retrace one's course **2** : to reverse a position or stand

back·up \-₁əp\ *n* : one that serves as a substitute or alternative

¹back·ward \'bak-wərd\ *or* **back·wards** \-wərdz\ *adv* **1** : toward the back **2** : with the back foremost **3** : in a reverse or contrary direction or way **4** : toward the past; *also* : toward a worse state

²backward *adj* **1** : directed, turned, or done backward **2** : DIFFIDENT, SHY **3** : retarded in development — **backward·ness** *n*

back·wash \'bak-ˌwȯsh, -ˌwäsh\ *n* : backward movement (as of water or air) produced by a propelling force (as the motion of oars)

back·wa·ter \-ˌwȯt-ər, -ˌwät-\ *n* **1** : water held or turned back in its course **2** : an isolated or backward place or condition

back·woods \-ˈwu̇dz\ *n pl* **1** : wooded or partly cleared areas far from cities **2** : a remote or isolated place

ba·con \'bā-kən\ *n* : salted and smoked meat from the sides or back of a pig

bacteria pl of BACTERIUM

bac·te·ri·cid·al \bak-ˌtir-ə-ˈsīd-ᵊl\ *adj* : destroying bacteria — **bac·te·ri·cide** \-ˈtir-ə-ˌsīd\ *n*

bac·te·ri·ol·o·gy \bak-ˌtir-ē-ˈäl-ə-jē\ *n* **1** : a science dealing with bacteria **2** : bacterial life and phenomena — **bac·te·ri·o·log·ic** \bak-ˌtir-ē-ə-ˈläj-ik\ *or* **bac·te·ri·o·log·i·cal** \-ˈläj-i-kəl\ *adj* — **bac·te·ri·ol·o·gist** \bak-ˌtir-ē-ˈäl-ə-jəst\ *n*

bac·te·rio·phage \bak-ˈtir-ē-ə-ˌfāj\ *n* : any of various viruses that attack specific bacteria

bac·te·ri·um \bak-ˈtir-ē-əm\ *n, pl* **-ria** \-ē-ə\ [NL, fr. Gk *baktērion* staff] : any of a class of microscopic plants including some that are disease producers and others that are valued esp. for their chemical effects (as fermentation) — **bac·te·ri·al** \-ē-əl\ *adj*

bad \'bad\ *adj* **worse** \'wərs\; **worst** \'wərst\ **1** : below standard : POOR; *also* : UNFAVORABLE ⟨a ∼ report⟩ **2** : SPOILED, DECAYED **3** : WICKED; *also* : not well-behaved : NAUGHTY **4** : DISAGREEABLE ⟨a ∼ taste⟩; *also* : HARMFUL **5** : DEFECTIVE, FAULTY ⟨∼ wiring⟩; *also* : not valid ⟨a ∼ check⟩ **6** : UNWELL, ILL **7** : SORRY, REGRETFUL **syn** evil, wrong, immoral, iniquitous, wicked — **bad·ly** *adv* — **bad·ness** *n*

bade past and past part of BID

badge \'baj\ *n* : a device or token usu. worn as a sign of status

¹bad·ger \'baj-ər\ *n* : any of several stur-dy burrowing mammals with long claws on their forefeet

²badger *vb* **bad·gered; bad·ger·ing** \'baj-(ə-)riŋ\ : to harass or annoy persistently

ba·di·nage \ˌbad-ᵊn-ˈäzh\ *n* [F] : playful talk back and forth : BANTER

bad·land \'bad-ˌland\ *n* : a region marked by intricate erosional sculpturing and scanty vegetation — usu. used in pl.

bad·min·ton \'bad-ˌmint-ᵊn\ *n* : a court game played with light rackets and a shuttlecock volleyed over a net

Bae·de·ker \'bād-i-kər, 'bed-\ *n* : GUIDEBOOK

¹baf·fle \'baf-əl\ *vb* **baf·fled; baf·fling** \-(ə-)liŋ\ : FRUSTRATE, THWART, FOIL; *also* : PERPLEX

²baffle *n* : a device (as a wall or screen) to deflect, check, or regulate flow (as of liquid or sound)

¹bag \'bag\ *n* : a flexible usu. closable container (as for storing or carrying)

²bag *vb* **bagged; bag·ging 1** : DISTEND, BULGE **2** : to put in a bag **3** : to get possession of; *esp* : to take in hunting **syn** trap, snare, catch, capture, collar

ba·gasse \bə-ˈgas\ *n* [F] : plant residue (as of sugarcane) left after a product (as juice) has been extracted

bag·a·telle \ˌbag-ə-ˈtel\ *n* [F] : TRIFLE

ba·gel \'bā-gəl\ *n* [Yiddish *beygel*, deriv. of Old High German *boug* ring] : a hard glazed doughnut-shaped roll

bag·gage \'bag-ij\ *n* **1** : the traveling bags and personal belongings of a traveler : LUGGAGE **2** : a worthless or contemptible woman

bag·gy \'bag-ē\ *adj* **bag·gi·er; -est** : puffed out or hanging like a bag — **bag·gi·ly** \'bag-ə-lē\ *adv* — **bag·gi·ness** \-ē-nəs\ *n*

bag·man \-mən\ *n* : a person who collects or distributes illicitly gained money on behalf of another

ba·gnio \'ban-yō\ *n, pl* **bagnios** [It *bagno*, lit., public baths] : BROTHEL

bag of waters : a double-walled fluid-filled sac that encloses and protects the fetus in the womb and that breaks releasing its fluid during the process of birth

bag·pipe \'bag-ˌpīp\ *n* : a musical wind instrument consisting of a bag, a tube with valves, and sounding pipes — often used in pl.

ba·guette \ba-'get\ *n* [F, lit., rod] : a gem having the shape of a long narrow rectangle; *also* : the shape itself

baht \'bät\ *n, pl* **baht** *also* **bahts** — see MONEY table

¹bail \'bāl\ *n* : a container for ladling water out of a boat

²bail *vb* : to dip and throw out water from a boat

³bail *n* : security given to guarantee a prisoner's appearance when legally required; *also* : one giving such security or the release secured

⁴bail *vb* : to release under bail; *also* : to procure the release of by giving bail — **bail·able** \'bā-lə-bəl\ *adj*

⁵bail *n* : the arched handle of a pail or kettle

bai·liff \'bā-ləf\ *n* **1** : an aide of a British sheriff who serves writs and makes arrests; *also* : a minor officer of a U.S. court **2** : an estate or farm manager esp. in Britain : STEWARD

bai·li·wick \'bā-li-ˌwik\ *n* : one's special province or domain **syn** territory, field, sphere, domain, province

bails·man \'bālz-mən\ *n* : one who gives bail for another

bairn \'baərn\ *n, chiefly Scot* : CHILD

¹bait \'bāt\ *vb* **1** : to persecute by continued attacks **2** : to harass with dogs usu. for sport ⟨~ a bear⟩ **3** : to furnish (as a hook) with bait **4** : ALLURE, ENTICE **5** : to give food and drink to (as an animal) **syn** badger, heckle, hound

²bait *n* **1** : a lure for catching animals (as fish) **2** : LURE, TEMPTATION **syn** snare, trap, decoy, come-on, enticement

bai·za \'bī-(ˌ)zä\ *n* — see *rial* at MONEY table

baize \'bāz\ *n* : a coarse feltlike fabric

¹bake \'bāk\ *vb* **baked; bak·ing** **1** : to cook or become cooked in dry heat esp. in an oven **2** : to dry and harden by heat ⟨~ bricks⟩ — **bak·er** *n*

²bake *n* : a social gathering featuring baked food

baker's dozen *n* : THIRTEEN

bak·ery \'bā-k(ə-)rē\ *n, pl* **-er·ies** : a place for baking or selling baked goods

bake·shop \'bāk-ˌshäp\ *n* : BAKERY

baking powder *n* : a powder that consists of a carbonate, an acid, and a starch and that makes the dough rise in baking cakes and biscuits

baking soda *n* : SODIUM BICARBONATE

bak·sheesh \'bak-ˌshēsh\ *n* : payment (as a tip or bribe) to expedite service

bal *abbr* balance

bal·a·lai·ka \ˌbal-ə-'lī-kə\ *n* : a triangular wooden instrument related to the guitar and used esp. in the U.S.S.R.

¹bal·ance \'bal-əns\ *n* [ME, fr. OF, fr. LL *bilanc-, bilanx* having two scalepans, fr. L *bi* two + *lanc-, lanx* plate] **1** : a weighing device : SCALE **2** : a weight, force, or influence counteracting the effect of another **3** : an oscillating wheel used to regulate a watch or clock **4** : a state of equilibrium **5** : REMAINDER, REST; *esp* : an amount in excess esp. on the credit side of an account — **bal·anced** \-ənst\ *adj*

²balance *vb* **bal·anced; bal·anc·ing** **1** : to compute the balance of an account **2** : to arrange so that one set of elements equals another; *also* : to equal or equalize in weight, number, or proportions **3** : WEIGH **4** : to bring or come to a state or position of equipoise; *also* : to bring into harmony or proportion

balance wheel *n* : a wheel that regulates or stabilizes the motion of a mechanism

bal·boa \bal-'bō-ə\ *n* — see MONEY table

bal·brig·gan \bal-'brig-ən\ *n* : a knitted cotton fabric used esp. for underwear

bal·co·ny \'bal-kə-nē\ *n, pl* **-nies** **1** : a platform projecting from the side of a building and enclosed by a railing **2** : a gallery inside a building

¹bald \'bȯld\ *adj* **1** : lacking a natural or usual covering (as of hair) **2** : UNADORNED, PLAIN **syn** bare, barren, naked, nude — **bald·ness** *n*

²bald *vb* : to become bald

bal·da·chin \'bȯl-də-kən, 'bal-\ *or* **bal·da·chi·no** \ˌbal-də-'kē-nō\ *n, pl* **baldachins** *or* **baldachinos** : a canopylike structure over an altar

bald eagle *n* : an eagle of No. America that when mature has white head and neck feathers and a white tail

bal·der·dash \'bȯl-dər-ˌdash\ *n* : NONSENSE

bal·dric \'bȯl-drik\ *n* : a belt worn over the shoulder to carry a sword or bugle

¹bale \'bāl\ *n* : a large bundle or closely packed package

²bale *vb* **baled; bal•ing** : to pack in a bale — **bal•er** *n*

ba•leen \bə-'lēn\ *n* : WHALEBONE

bale•ful \'bāl-fəl\ *adj* : DEADLY, HARMFUL; *also* : OMINOUS **syn** sinister, malefic, maleficent, malign

¹balk \'bȯk\ *n* **1** : HINDRANCE, CHECK, SETBACK **2** : an illegal motion of the pitcher in baseball while in position

²balk *vb* **1** : BLOCK, THWART **2** : to stop short and refuse to go on **3** : to commit a balk in sports **syn** frustrate, baffle, foil, thwart

balky \'bȯ-kē\ *adj* **balk•i•er; -est** : likely to balk

¹ball \'bȯl\ *n* **1** : a rounded body or mass (as at the base of the thumb or for use as a missile or in a game) **2** : a game played with a ball **3** : a pitched baseball that misses the strike zone and is not swung at by the batter **4** : a hit or thrown ball in various games ⟨foul ∼⟩

²ball *vb* : to form into a ball

³ball *n* : a large formal dance

bal•lad \'bal-əd\ *n* **1** : a simple song : AIR **2** : a narrative poem of strongly marked rhythm suitable for singing **3** : a slow romantic dance song

bal•lad•eer \ˌbal-ə-'diər\ *n* : a singer of ballads

¹bal•last \'bal-əst\ *n* **1** : heavy material used to stabilize a ship or control a balloon's ascent **2** : crushed stone laid in a railroad bed or used in making concrete

²ballast *vb* : to provide with ballast **syn** balance, stabilize, steady

ball bearing *n* : a bearing in which the revolving part turns upon steel balls that roll easily in a groove; *also* : one of the balls in such a bearing

ball•car•ri•er \'bȯl-ˌkar-ē-ər\ *n* : the football player carrying the ball in an offensive play

bal•le•ri•na \ˌbal-ə-'rē-nə\ *n* : a female ballet dancer

bal•let \'ba-ˌlā, ba-'lā\ *n* **1** : dancing in which fixed poses and steps are combined with light flowing movements often to convey a story; *also* : a theatrical art form using ballet dancing **2** : a company of ballet dancers

bal•let•o•mane \ba-'let-ə-ˌmān\ *n* : a devotee of ballet

bal•lis•tic missile \bə-'lis-tik-\ *n* : a self-propelled missile that is guided during ascent and that falls freely during descent

bal•lis•tics \-tiks\ *n sing or pl* **1** : the science of the motion of projectiles (as bullets) in flight **2** : the flight characteristics of a projectile — **ballistic** *adj*

ball of fire : an unusually energetic person

¹bal•loon \bə-'lün\ *n* **1** : a bag filled with gas or heated air so as to rise and float in the atmosphere **2** : a toy consisting of an inflatable rubber bag — **bal•loon•ist** *n*

²balloon *vb* **1** : to travel in a balloon **2** : to swell or puff out **3** : to increase rapidly

¹bal•lot \'bal-ət\ *n* [It *ballotta* small ball used in secret voting, fr. It dial., dim. of *balla* ball] **1** : a piece of paper used to cast a vote **2** : the action or a system of voting; *also* : the right to vote

²ballot *vb* : to decide by ballot : VOTE

¹ball•park \'bȯl-ˌpark\ *n* : a park in which ball games are played

²ballpark *adj* : approximately correct ⟨∼ estimate⟩

ball•point \'bȯl-ˌpȯint\ *n* : a pen whose writing point is a small rotating metal ball that inks itself from an inner container

ball•room \'bȯl-ˌrüm, -ˌrum\ *n* : a large room for dances

bal•ly•hoo \'bal-ē-ˌhü\ *n, pl* **-hoos** : extravagant statements and claims made for publicity — **ballyhoo** *vb*

balm \'bäm, 'bälm\ *n* **1** : a fragrant healing or soothing lotion or ointment **2** : any of several spicy fragrant herbs **3** : something that comforts or soothes

balmy \'bäm-ē, 'bäl-mē\ *adj* **balm•i•er; -est** **1** : gently soothing : MILD **2** : FOOLISH, ABSURD **syn** soft, bland, mild, gentle — **balm•i•ness** *n*

ba•lo•ney \bə-'lō-nē\ *n* : NONSENSE

bal•sa \'bȯl-sə\ *n* : the extremely light strong wood of a tropical American tree; *also* : the tree

bal•sam \'bȯl-səm\ *n* **1** : a fragrant aromatic and usu. resinous substance oozing from various plants; *also* : a preparation containing or smelling like balsam **2** : a balsam-yielding tree (as balsam fir) **3** : a common garden ornamental plant

balsam fir *n* : a resinous American evergreen tree that is widely used for pulpwood and as a Christmas tree

Bal·ti·more oriole \ˌbȯl-tə-ˌmȯr-\ *n* : a common American oriole in which the male is brightly colored with orange, black, and white

bal·us·ter \ˈbal-ə-stər\ *n* [F *balustre*, fr. It *balaustro*, fr. *balaustra* wild pomegranate flower, fr. L *balaustium*; fr. its shape] : an upright support of a rail (as of a staircase)

bal·us·trade \-ə-ˌstrād\ *n* : a row of balusters topped by a rail

bam·boo \bam-ˈbü\ *n, pl* **bamboos** : any of various woody mostly tall tropical grasses including some with strong hollow stems used for building, furniture, or utensils

bamboo curtain *n, often cap B&C* : a political, military, and ideological barrier in the Orient

bam·boo·zle \bam-ˈbü-zəl\ *vb* **-boo·zled; -boo·zling** \-ˈbüz-(ə-)liŋ\ : TRICK, HOODWINK

¹ban \ˈban\ *vb* **banned; ban·ning** : PROHIBIT, FORBID

²ban *n* **1** : CURSE **2** : a legal or formal prohibiting

³ban \ˈbän\ *n, pl* **ba·ni** \ˈbän-ē\ — see *leu* at MONEY table

ba·nal \bə-ˈnäl, -ˈnal; ˈbān-ᵊl\ *adj* [F] : COMMONPLACE, TRITE — **ba·nal·i·ty** \bā-ˈnal-ət-ē\ *n*

ba·nana \bə-ˈnan-ə\ *n* : a treelike tropical plant bearing thick clusters of yellow or reddish finger-shaped fruit; *also* : this fruit

¹band \ˈband\ *n* **1** : something that binds, ties, or goes around **2** : a strip or stripe that can be distinguished (as by color or texture) from nearby matter **3** : a range of wavelengths (as in radio) **4** : a group of grooves on a phonograph record containing recorded sound

²band *vb* **1** : to tie up, finish, or enclose with a band **2** : to gather or unite in a company or for some common end — **band·er** *n*

³band *n* : a group of persons, animals, or things; *esp* : a group of musicians organized for playing together

¹ban·dage \ˈban-dij\ *n* : a strip of material used esp. in dressing wounds

²bandage *vb* **ban·daged; ban·dag·ing** : to dress or cover with a bandage

ban·dan·na *or* **ban·dana** \ban-ˈdan-ə\ *n* : a large colored figured handkerchief

B and B *abbr* bed-and-breakfast

band·box \ˈban(d)-ˌbäks\ *n* : a usu. cylindrical box for carrying clothing

band·ed \ˈban-dəd\ *adj* : having or marked with bands

ban·de·role *or* **ban·de·rol** \ˈban-də-ˌrōl\ *n* : a long narrow forked flag or streamer

ban·dit \ˈban-dət\ *n* [It *bandito*, fr. *bandire* to banish] **1** *pl also* **ban·dit·ti** \ban-ˈdit-ē\ : an outlaw who lives by plunder; *esp* : a member of a band of marauders **2** : ROBBER — **ban·dit·ry** \ˈban-də-trē\ *n*

ban·do·lier *or* **ban·do·leer** \ˌban-də-ˈlir\ *n* : a belt slung over the shoulder esp. to carry ammunition

band saw *n* : a saw in the form of an endless steel belt running over pulleys

band·stand \ˈban(d)-ˌstand\ *n* : a usu. roofed platform on which a band or orchestra performs outdoors

b and w *abbr* black and white

band·wag·on \ˈband-ˌwag-ən\ *n* **1** : a wagon carrying musicians in a parade **2** : a movement that attracts support because it seems to be gaining popularity

¹ban·dy \ˈban-dē\ *vb* **ban·died; ban·dy·ing 1** : to exchange (as blows or quips) esp. in rapid succession **2** : to use in a glib or offhand way

²bandy *adj* : curved outward ⟨~ legs⟩

bane \ˈbān\ *n* **1** : POISON **2** : WOE, HARM; *also* : a source of this — **bane·ful** *adj*

¹bang \ˈbaŋ\ *vb* **1** : BUMP ⟨fell and ~ed his knee⟩ **2** : to strike, thrust, or move usu. with a loud noise

²bang *n* **1** : a resounding blow **2** : a sudden loud noise

³bang *adv* : DIRECTLY, RIGHT

⁴bang *n* : a fringe of hair cut short (as across the forehead) — usu. used in pl.

⁵bang *vb* : to cut a bang in

Ban·gla·deshi \ˌbäŋ-glə-ˈdesh-ē\ *n* : a native or inhabitant of Bangladesh — **Bangladeshi** *adj*

ban·gle \ˈbaŋ-gəl\ *n* : BRACELET; *also* : a loose-hanging ornament

bang–up \'baŋ-ˌəp\ *adj* : FIRST-RATE, EXCELLENT ⟨a ∼ job⟩

bani pl of ³BAN

ban·ish \'ban-ish\ *vb* **1** : to require by authority to leave a country **2** : to drive out : EXPEL **syn** exile, ostracize, deport, expel, relegate — **ban·ish·ment** *n*

ban·is·ter \'ban-ə-stər\ *n* **1** : one of the upright supports of a handrail along a staircase **2** : the handrail of a staircase

ban·jo \'ban-ˌjō\ *n, pl* **banjos** *also* **banjoes** : a musical instrument with a long neck, a drumlike body, and usu. five strings — **ban·jo·ist** *n*

¹bank \'baŋk\ *n* **1** : a piled-up mass (as of cloud or earth) **2** : an undersea elevation **3** : rising ground bordering a lake, river, or sea **4** : the sideways slope of a surface along a curve or of a vehicle as it rounds a curve

²bank *vb* **1** : to form a bank about **2** : to cover (as a fire) with fuel to keep inactive **3** : to build (a curve) with the roadbed or track inclined laterally upward from the inside edge **4** : to pile or heap in a bank; *also* : to arrange in a tier **5** : to incline (an airplane) laterally

³bank *n* [ME, fr. MF or It; MF *banque,* fr. It *banca,* lit., bench] **1** : an establishment concerned esp. with the custody, loan, exchange, or issue of money, the extension of credit, and the transmission of funds **2** : a stock of or a place for holding something in reserve ⟨a blood ∼⟩

⁴bank *vb* **1** : to conduct the business of a bank **2** : to deposit money or have an account in a bank — **bank·er** *n* — **bank·ing** *n*

⁵bank *n* : a group of objects arranged close together (as in a row or tier) ⟨a ∼ of file drawers⟩

bank·book \'baŋk-ˌbůk\ *n* : the depositor's book in which a bank records deposits and withdrawals

bank·card \-ˌkärd\ *n* : a credit card issued by a bank

bank note *n* : a promissory note issued by a bank and circulating as money

bank·roll \'baŋk-ˌrōl\ *n* : supply of money : FUNDS

¹bank·rupt \'baŋk-(ˌ)rəpt\ *n* : an insolvent person; *esp* : one whose proper-

ty is turned over by court action to a trustee to be handled for the benefit of his creditors — **bankrupt** *vb*

²bankrupt *adj* **1** : reduced to financial ruin; *esp* : legally declared a bankrupt **2** : wholly lacking in or deprived of some essential ⟨∼ soils⟩ — **bank·rupt·cy** \'baŋk-(ˌ)rəp-(t)sē\ *n*

¹ban·ner \'ban-ər\ *n* **1** : a piece of cloth attached to a staff and used by a leader as his standard **2** : FLAG

²banner *adj* : distinguished from all others esp. in excellence ⟨a ∼ year⟩

ban·nock \'ban-ək\ *n* : a flat oatmeal or barley cake usu. cooked on a griddle

banns \'banz\ *n pl* : public announcement esp. in church of a proposed marriage

ban·quet \'baŋ-kwət\ *n* [MF, fr. It *banchetto,* fr. dim. of *banca* bench, bank] : a ceremonial dinner — **banquet** *vb*

ban·quette \baŋ-'ket\ *n* : a long upholstered bench esp. along a wall

ban·shee \'ban-shē\ *n* [ScGael *bean≠sīth,* fr. or akin to Old Irish *ben sīde* woman of fairyland] : a female spirit in Gaelic folklore whose wailing warns a family that one of them will soon die

ban·tam \'bant-əm\ *n* **1** : any of numerous small domestic fowls that are often miniatures of standard breeds **2** : a small but pugnacious person

¹ban·ter \'bant-ər\ *vb* : to speak to in a witty and teasing manner

²banter *n* : good-natured witty joking

bant·ling \'bant-liŋ\ *n* : a young child

Ban·tu \'ban-ˌtü\ *n, pl* **Bantu** *or* **Bantus** **1** : a member of a family of Negroid peoples occupying equatorial and southern Africa **2** : a group of African languages spoken generally in equatorial and southern Africa

Ban·tu·stan \ˌban-tů-'stan, ˌbän-tů-'stän\ *n* : an all-black enclave in the Republic of So. Africa with a limited degree of self-government

ban·yan \'ban-yən\ *n* [earlier *banyan* Hindu merchant, fr. Hindi *baniyā;* fr. a merchant's pagoda erected under a tree of the species in Iran] : a large East Indian tree whose aerial roots grow downward to the ground and form new trunks

ban·zai \bän-'zī\ *n* : a Japanese cheer or cry of triumph

bao·bab \'bau̇-,bab, 'bā-ə-\ *n* : an Old World tropical tree with short swollen trunk and sour edible gourdlike fruits

bap·tism \'bap-,tiz-əm\ *n* **1** : a Christian sacrament signifying spiritual rebirth and symbolized by the ritual use of water **2** : an act of baptizing — **bap·tis·mal** \bap-'tiz-məl\ *adj*

baptismal name *n* : GIVEN NAME

Bap·tist \'bap-təst\ *n* : a member of any of several Protestant denominations emphasizing baptism by immersion

bap·tis·tery *or* **bap·tis·try** \'bap-tə-strē\ *n, pl* **-ter·ies** *or* **-tries** : a place esp. in a church used for baptism

bap·tize \bap-'tīz, 'bap-,tīz\ *vb* **bap·tized; bap·tiz·ing** [ME *baptizen,* fr. OF *baptiser,* fr. L *baptizare,* fr. Gk *baptizein* to dip, baptize, fr. *baptos* dipped, fr. *baptein* to dip] **1** : to administer baptism to; *also* : CHRISTEN **2** : to purify esp. by an ordeal

¹bar \'bär\ *n* **1** : a long narrow piece of material (as wood or metal) used esp. for a lever, fastening, or support **2** : BARRIER, OBSTACLE **3** : the railing in a law court at which prisoners are stationed; *also* : the legal profession or the whole body of lawyers **4** : a stripe, band, or line much longer than wide **5** : a counter at which food or esp. drink is served; *also* : BARROOM **6** : a vertical line across the musical staff

²bar *vb* **barred; bar·ring** **1** : to fasten, confine, or obstruct with or as if with a bar or bars **2** : to mark with bars : STRIPE **3** : to shut or keep out : EXCLUDE **4** : FORBID, PREVENT

³bar *prep* : EXCEPT

⁴bar *abbr* barometer; barometric

Bar *abbr* Baruch

barb \'bärb\ *n* **1** : a sharp projection extending backward (as from the point of an arrow) **2** : a biting critical remark — **barbed** \'bärbd\ *adj*

bar·bar·ian \bär-'ber-ē-ən\ *adj* **1** : of, relating to, or being a land, culture, or people alien to and usu. believed to be inferior to one's own **2** : lacking refinement, learning, or artistic or literary culture — **barbarian** *n*

bar·bar·ic \bär-'bar-ik\ *adj* **1** : BARBARIAN **2** : marked by a lack of restraint : WILD **3** : PRIMITIVE, UNSOPHISTICATED

bar·ba·rism \'bär-bə-,riz-əm\ *n* **1** : the social condition of barbarians; *also*

: the use or display of barbarian or barbarous acts, attitudes, or ideas **2** : a word or expression that offends standards of correctness or purity

bar·ba·rous \'bär-b(ə-)rəs\ *adj* **1** : lacking culture or refinement **2** : using linguistic barbarisms **3** : mercilessly harsh or cruel — **bar·bar·i·ty** \bär-'bar-ət-ē\ *n* — **bar·ba·rous·ly** *adv*

¹bar·be·cue \'bär-bi-,kyü\ *n* : a social gathering at which barbecued food is served

²barbecue *vb* **-cued; -cu·ing** **1** : to cook over hot coals or on a revolving spit **2** : to cook in a highly seasoned vinegar sauce

bar·bell \'bär-,bel\ *n* : a bar with adjustable weights attached to each end used for exercise and in weight-lifting competition

bar·ber \'bär-bər\ *n* [ME, fr. MF *barbeor,* fr. *barbe* beard, fr. L *barba*] : one whose business is cutting and dressing hair and shaving and trimming beards

bar·ber·ry \'bär-,ber-ē\ *n* : any of a genus of spiny shrubs bearing yellow flowers followed by oblong red berries

bar·bi·tal \'bär-bə-,tȯl\ *n* : a white crystalline addictive hypnotic often administered in the form of its soluble sodium salt

bar·bi·tu·rate \bär-'bich-ə-rət\ *n* : any of various compounds (as a salt or ester) formed from an organic acid (**bar·bi·tu·ric acid** \,bär-bə-,t(y)ùr-ik-\); *esp* : one used as a sedative or hypnotic

bar·ca·role *or* **bar·ca·rolle** \'bär-kə-,rōl\ *n* : a Venetian boat song characterized by a beat suggesting a rowing rhythm; *also* : a piece of music imitating this

bar chart *n* : BAR GRAPH

bar code *n* : a set of printed and variously spaced bars and sometimes numerals that is designed to be scanned to identify the object it labels

bard \'bärd\ *n* : POET

¹bare \'baər\ *adj* **bar·er; bar·est** **1** : NAKED **2** : UNCONCEALED, EXPOSED **3** : EMPTY **4** : leaving nothing to spare : MERE **5** : PLAIN, UNADORNED **syn** nude, bald, naked — **bare·ness** *n*

²**bare** *vb* **bared; bar·ing** : to make or lay bare : UNCOVER

bare·back \-ˌbak\ *or* **bare·backed** \-ˈbakt\ *adv or adj* : without a saddle

bare·faced \-ˈfāst\ *adj* 1 : having the face uncovered; *esp* : BEARDLESS 2 : not concealed : OPEN

bare·foot \-ˌfut\ *or* **bare·foot·ed** \-ˈfut-əd\ *adv or adj* : with bare feet

bare–hand·ed \-ˈhan-dəd\ *adv or adj* 1 : without gloves 2 : without tools or weapons

bare·head·ed \-ˈhed-əd\ *adv or adj* : without a hat

bare·ly \ˈbaər-lē\ *adv* 1 : PLAINLY, MEAGERLY 2 : by a narrow margin : only just ⟨∼ enough money⟩ **syn** hardly, scarcely

bar·fly \ˈbär-ˌflī\ *n* : a drinker who frequents bars

¹**bar·gain** \ˈbär-gən\ *n* 1 : AGREEMENT 2 : an advantageous purchase 3 : a transaction, situation, or event regarded in the light of its results

²**bargain** *vb* 1 : to negotiate over the terms of an agreement; *also* : to come to terms 2 : BARTER

¹**barge** \ˈbärj\ *n* 1 : a broad flat-bottomed boat usu. moved by towing 2 : a motorboat supplied to a flagship (as for an admiral) 3 : a ceremonial boat elegantly furnished — **barge·man** \-mən\ *n*

²**barge** *vb* **barged; barg·ing** 1 : to carry by barge 2 : to move or thrust oneself clumsily or rudely

bari·tone \ˈbar-ə-ˌtōn\ *n* [F *baryton* or It *baritono,* fr. Gk *barytonos* deep sounding, fr. *barys* heavy + *tonos* tone] : a male voice between bass and tenor; *also* : a man with such a voice

bar·i·um \ˈbar-ē-əm\ *n* : a silver-white metallic chemical element that occurs only in combination

¹**bark** \ˈbärk\ *vb* 1 : to make the short loud cry of a dog 2 : to speak or utter in a curt loud tone : SNAP

²**bark** *n* : the sound made by a barking dog

³**bark** *n* : the tough corky outer covering of a woody stem or root

⁴**bark** *vb* 1 : to strip the bark from 2 : to rub the skin from : ABRADE

⁵**bark** *n* : a 3-masted ship with foremast and mainmast square-rigged and mizzenmast fore-and-aft rigged

bar·keep \ˈbär-ˌkēp\ *or* **bar·keep·er** \-ˌkē-pər\ *n* : BARTENDER

bark·er \ˈbär-kər\ *n* : a person who stands at the entrance esp. to a show and tries to attract customers to it

bar·ley \ˈbär-lē\ *n* : a cereal grass with seeds used as food and in making malt liquors; *also* : its seed

bar mitz·vah \bär-ˈmits-və\ *n, often cap B&M* [Heb *bar miṣwāh,* lit., son of the (divine) law] 1 : a Jewish boy who at about 13 years of age assumes religious responsibilities 2 : the ceremony recognizing a boy as a bar mitzvah

barn \ˈbärn\ *n* [ME *bern,* fr. OE *bereærn,* fr. *bere* barley + *ærn* place] : a building used esp. for storing hay and grain and for housing livestock or farm equipment

bar·na·cle \ˈbär-ni-kəl\ *n* : any of numerous small marine crustaceans free-swimming when young but fixed (as to rocks, whales, or ships) when adult

barn·storm \ˈbärn-ˌstorm\ *vb* : to travel through the country making brief stops to entertain (as with shows or flying stunts) or to campaign for political office

barn·yard \-ˌyärd\ *n* : a usu. fenced area adjoining a barn

baro·graph \ˈbar-ə-ˌgraf\ *n* : a recording barometer

ba·rom·e·ter \bə-ˈräm-ət-ər\ *n* : an instrument for measuring atmospheric pressure — **baro·met·ric** \ˌbar-ə-ˈme-trik\ *adj*

bar·on \ˈbar-ən\ *n* : a member of the lowest grade of the British peerage — **ba·ro·ni·al** \bə-ˈrō-nē-əl\ *adj* — **bar·ony** \ˈbar-ə-nē\ *n*

bar·on·age \-ə-nij\ *n* : PEERAGE

bar·on·ess \-ə-nəs\ *n* 1 : the wife or widow of a baron 2 : a woman holding a baronial title in her own right

bar·on·et \ˈbar-ə-nət\ *n* : a man holding a rank of honor below a baron but above a knight — **bar·on·et·cy** \-sē\ *n*

ba·roque \bə-ˈrōk, -ˈräk\ *adj* : marked by elaborate and sometimes grotesque ornamentation and esp. by curved and plastic figures

ba·rouche \bə-ˈrüsh\ *n* [G *barutsche,* fr. It *biroccio,* deriv. of LL *birotus* two-wheeled, fr. L *bi* two + *rota* wheel] : a 4-wheeled carriage with a high driver's seat in front and a folding top

bar·racks \'bar-əks\ *n sing or pl* : a building or group of buildings for lodging soldiers

bar·ra·cu·da \ˌbar-ə-'küd-ə\ *n, pl* **-da** *or* **-das** : any of several large predaceous sea fishes including some used for food

bar·rage \bə-'räzh, -'räj\ *n* : a heavy concentration of fire (as of artillery)

bar·ra·try \'bar-ə-trē\ *n, pl* **-tries 1** : the purchase or sale of office or preferment in church or state **2** : a fraudulent breach of duty by the master or crew of a ship intended to harm the owner or cargo **3** : the practice of inciting lawsuits or quarrels

barred \'bärd\ *adj* : STRIPED

¹bar·rel \'bar-əl\ *n* **1** : a round bulging cask with flat ends of equal diameter **2** : the amount contained in a barrel **3** : a cylindrical or tubular part ⟨gun ∼⟩

²barrel *vb* **-reled** *or* **-relled; -rel·ing** *or* **-rel·ling 1** : to pack in a barrel **2** : to travel at high speed

barrel roll *n* : an airplane maneuver in which a complete revolution about the longitudinal axis is made

¹bar·ren \'bar-ən\ *adj* **1** : STERILE, UNFRUITFUL **2** : unproductive of results ⟨a ∼ scheme⟩ **3** : lacking interest or charm **4** : DULL, STUPID — **bar·ren·ness** \-ən-nəs\ *n*

²barren *n* : a tract of barren land

bar·rette \bä-'ret, bə-\ *n* : a clasp or bar for holding the hair in place

¹bar·ri·cade \'bar-ə-ˌkād, ˌbar-ə-'kād\ *vb* **-cad·ed; -cad·ing** : to block, obstruct, or fortify with a barricade

²barricade *n* [F, fr. MF, fr. *barriquer* to barricade, fr. *barrique* barrel] **1** : a hastily thrown-up obstruction or fortification **2** : BARRIER, OBSTACLE

bar·ri·er \'bar-ē-ər\ *n* : something that separates, demarcates, or serves as a barricade ⟨racial ∼s⟩

barrier reef *n* : a coral reef roughly parallel to a shore and separated from it by a lagoon

bar·ring \'bär-iŋ\ *prep* : excluding by exception : EXCEPTING

bar·rio \'bär-ē-ˌō, 'bar-\ *n, pl* **-ri·os 1** : a district of a city or town in a Spanish-speaking country **2** : a Spanish-speaking quarter in a U.S. city

bar·ris·ter \'bar-ə-stər\ *n* : a British counselor admitted to plead in the higher courts

bar·room \'bär-ˌrüm, -ˌrum\ *n* : a room or establishment whose main feature is a bar for the sale of liquor

¹bar·row \'bar-ō\ *n* : a large burial mound of earth and stones

²barrow *n* : a male hog castrated while young

³barrow *n* **1** : HANDBARROW **2** : WHEELBARROW **3** : a cart with a boxlike body and two shafts for pushing it

Bart *abbr* baronet

bar·tend·er \'bär-ˌten-dər\ *n* : one that serves liquor at a bar

bar·ter \'bärt-ər\ *vb* : to trade by exchange of goods — **barter** *n*

Ba·ruch \'bär-ˌük, bə-'rük\ *n* — see BIBLE table

bas·al \'bā-səl\ *adj* **1** : situated at or forming the base **2** : BASIC

basal metabolism *n* : the turnover of energy in a fasting and resting organism using energy solely to maintain vital cellular activity, respiration, and circulation as measured by the rate at which heat is given off

ba·salt \bə-'sȯlt, 'bā-ˌsȯlt\ *n* : a dark fine-grained igneous rock — **ba·sal·tic** \bə-'sȯl-tik\ *adj*

¹base \'bās\ *n, pl* **bas·es** \'bā-səz\ **1** : BOTTOM, FOUNDATION **2** : a side or face on which a geometrical figure stands; *also* : the length of a base **3** : a main ingredient or fundamental part **4** : the point of beginning an act or operation **5** : a place on which a force depends for supplies **6** : the number of units in a given digit's place of a number system that is required to give the numeral 1 in the next higher place ⟨the decimal system uses a ∼ of 10⟩; *also* : such a system using an indicated base ⟨convert from ∼ 10 to ∼ 2⟩ **7** : any of the four stations at the corners of a baseball diamond **8** : a chemical compound (as lime or ammonia) that reacts with an acid to form a salt, has a salty taste, and turns litmus blue **syn** basis, ground, groundwork, footing, foundation

²base *vb* **based; bas·ing 1** : to form or serve as a base for **2** : ESTABLISH

³base *adj* **1** : of inferior quality : DEBASED, ALLOYED **2** : CONTEMPTIBLE,

IGNOBLE **3** : MENIAL, DEGRADING **4** : of little value **syn** low, vile, despicable, wretched — **base·ly** adv — **base·ness** n

base·ball \'bās-ˌbȯl\ n : a game played with a bat and ball by two teams on a field with four bases arranged in a diamond; also : the ball used in this game

base·board \-ˌbōrd\ n : a line of boards or molding covering the joint of a wall and the adjoining floor

base·born \-'bȯrn\ adj **1** : of humble birth **2** : of illegitimate birth **3** : MEAN, IGNOBLE

base exchange n : a post exchange at a naval or air force base

base hit n : a hit in baseball that enables the batter to reach base safely with no error made and no base runner forced out

base·less \-ləs\ adj : having no base or basis : GROUNDLESS

base·line \'bās-ˌlīn\ n **1** : a line serving as a basis esp. to calculate or locate something **2** : the area within which a baseball player must keep when running between bases

base·ment \-mənt\ n **1** : the part of a building that is wholly or partly below ground level **2** : the lowest or fundamental part of something

base on balls : an advance to first base given to a baseball player who receives four balls

base runner n : a baseball player who is on base or is attempting to reach a base

¹bash \'bash\ vb **1** : to strike violently : BEAT **2** : to smash by a blow

²bash n **1** : a heavy blow **2** : a festive social gathering : PARTY

bash·ful \'bash-fəl\ adj : inclined to shrink from public attention — **bash·ful·ness** n

ba·sic \'bā-sik\ adj **1** : of, relating to, or forming the base or essence : FUNDAMENTAL **2** : of, relating to, or having the character of a chemical base ⟨a ∼ substance⟩ **syn** underlying, basal, fundamental, primary — **ba·si·cal·ly** \-sik(ə-)lē\ adv — **ba·sic·i·ty** \bā-'sis-ət-ē\ n

ba·sil \'baz-əl, 'bās-\ n : either of two mints with fragrant leaves used in cooking

ba·sil·i·ca \bə-'sil-i-kə, -'zil-\ n [L, fr. Gk basilikē, fr. fem. of basilikos royal, fr. basileus king] **1** : an early Christian church building consisting of nave and aisles with clerestory and apse **2** : a Roman Catholic church given ceremonial privileges

bas·i·lisk \'bas-ə-ˌlisk, 'baz-\ n [ME, fr. L basiliscus, fr. Gk basiliskos, fr. dim. of basileus king] : a legendary reptile with fatal breath and glance

ba·sin \'bās-ᵊn\ n **1** : an open usu. circular vessel with sloping sides for holding liquid (as water) **2** : a hollow or enclosed place containing water; also : the region drained by a river

ba·sis \'bā-səs\ n, pl **ba·ses** \-ˌsēz\ **1** : FOUNDATION, BASE **2** : a fundamental principle

bask \'bask\ vb **1** : to expose oneself to comfortable heat **2** : to enjoy something warmly comforting ⟨∼ing in his friends' admiration⟩

bas·ket \'bas-kət\ n : a container made of woven material (as twigs or grasses); also : any of various lightweight usu. wood containers — **bas·ket·ful** n

bas·ket·ball \-ˌbȯl\ n : a game played on a court by two teams who try to throw an inflated ball through a raised goal; also : the ball used in this game

basket case n **1** : one who has all four limbs amputated **2** : one that is totally incapacitated or inoperative

basket weave n : a textile weave resembling the checkered pattern of a plaited basket

bas mitz·vah \bäs-'mits-və\ n, often cap B&M [Heb bath miṣwāh, lit., daughter of the (divine) law] **1** : a Jewish girl who at about 13 years of age assumes religious responsibilities **2** : the ceremony recognizing a girl as a bas mitzvah

Basque \'bask\ n **1** : a member of a people inhabiting a region bordering on the Bay of Biscay in northern Spain and southwestern France **2** : the language of the Basque people — **Basque** adj

bas—re·lief \ˌbä-ri-'lēf\ n [F] : a sculpture in relief with the design raised very slightly from the background

¹bass \'bas\ n, pl **bass** or **bass·es** : any of numerous sport and food fishes (as a striped bass)

²bass \'bās\ adj : of low pitch

³**bass** \'bās\ *n* **1** : a deep sound or tone **2** : the lower half of the musical pitch range **3** : the lowest male singing voice **4** : a singer or instrument having a bass voice or part

bas•set hound \'bas-ət-\ *n* : any of an old French breed of short-legged dogs with long ears and crooked front legs

bas•si•net \ˌbas-ə-'net\ *n* : a baby's bed that resembles a basket and often has a hood over one end

bas•so \'bas-ō\ *n, pl* **bassos** *or* **bas•si** \'bäs-ˌē\ [It] : a bass singer

bas•soon \bə-'sün\ *n* : a musical wind instrument lower in pitch than the oboe

bass•wood \'bas-ˌwùd\ *n* : any of several New World lindens or their wood

bast \'bast\ *n* : BAST FIBER

¹**bas•tard** \'bas-tərd\ *n* **1** : an illegitimate child **2** : an offensive or disagreeable person

²**bastard** *adj* **1** : ILLEGITIMATE **2** : of an inferior or nontypical kind, size, or form; *also* : SPURIOUS — **bas•tardy** *n*

bas•tard•ize \'bas-tər-ˌdīz\ *vb* **-ized; -iz•ing** : to reduce from a higher to a lower state : DEBASE

¹**baste** \'bāst\ *vb* **bast•ed; bast•ing** : to sew with long stitches so as to keep temporarily in place

²**baste** *vb* **bast•ed; bast•ing** : to moisten (as meat) at intervals with liquid while cooking

bast fiber *n* : a strong woody plant fiber obtained chiefly from phloem and used esp. in making ropes

bas•ti•na•do \ˌbas-tə-'nād-ō, -'näd-\ *or* **bas•ti•nade** \ˌbas-tə-'nād, -'näd\ *n, pl* **-na•does** *or* **-nades** **1** : a blow or beating esp. with a stick **2** : a punishment consisting of beating the soles of the feet

bas•tion \'bas-chən\ *n* : a projecting part of a fortification; *also* : a fortified position — **bas•tioned** \-chənd\ *adj*

¹**bat** \'bat\ *n* **1** : a stout stick : CLUB **2** : a sharp blow **3** : an implement (as of wood) used to hit a ball (as in baseball) **4** : a turn at batting — usu. used with *at*

²**bat** *vb* **bat•ted; bat•ting** : to hit with or as if with a bat

³**bat** *n* : any of an order of night-flying mammals with forelimbs modified to form wings

⁴**bat** *vb* **bat•ted; bat•ting** : WINK, BLINK

batch \'bach\ *n* **1** : a quantity (as of bread) baked at one time **2** : a quantity of material for use at one time or produced at one operation

bate \'bāt\ *vb* **bat•ed; bat•ing** : MODERATE, REDUCE

bath \'bath, 'båth\ *n, pl* **baths** \'bathz, 'baths, 'båthz, 'båths\ **1** : a washing of the body **2** : water for washing the body **3** : a liquid in which objects are immersed so that it can act on them **4** : BATHROOM

bathe \'bāth\ *vb* **bathed; bath•ing** **1** : to wash in liquid and esp. water; *also* : to apply water or a medicated liquid to ⟨*bathed* her eyes⟩ **2** : to take a bath; *also* : to take a swim **3** : to wash along, over, or against so as to wet **4** : to suffuse with or as if with light — **bath•er** *n*

bath•house \'bath-ˌhaùs, 'båth-\ *n* **1** : a building equipped for bathing **2** : a building containing dressing rooms for bathers

bathing suit *n* : SWIMSUIT

batho•lith \'bath-ə-ˌlith\ *n* : a great mass of igneous rock that forced its way into or between other rocks and that stopped in its rise a considerable distance below the surface

ba•thos \'bā-ˌthäs\ *n* [Gk, lit., depth] **1** : the sudden appearance of the commonplace in otherwise elevated matter or style **2** : insincere or overdone pathos — **ba•thet•ic** \bə-'thet-ik\ *adj*

bath•robe \'bath-ˌrōb, 'båth-\ *n* : a loose usu. absorbent robe worn before and after bathing or as a dressing gown

bath•room \-ˌrüm, -ˌrùm\ *n* : a room containing a bathtub or shower and usu. a washbowl and toilet

bath•tub \-ˌtəb\ *n* : a usu. fixed tub for bathing

bathy•scaphe \'bath-i-ˌskaf, -ˌskäf\ *also* **bathy•scaph** \-ˌskaf\ *n* : a navigable undersea craft for deep-sea exploration

bathy•sphere \-ˌsfiər\ *n* : a steel diving sphere for deep-sea observation

bathy•ther•mo•graph \ˌbath-i-'thər-mə-ˌgraf\ *n* : an instrument that records water temperature as a function of depth

ba•tik \bə-'tēk, 'bat-ik\ *n* [Malay] **1** : an

Indonesian method of hand-printing textiles by coating with wax the parts not to be dyed; *also* : a design so executed **2** : a fabric printed by batik

ba·tiste \bə-'tēst\ *n* : a fine sheer fabric of plain weave

bat·man \'bat-mən\ *n* : an orderly of a British military officer

ba·ton \bə-'tän\ *n* : STAFF, ROD; *esp* : a stick with which the leader directs an orchestra or band

bats·man \'bats-mən\ *n* : a batter esp. in cricket

bat·tal·ion \bə-'tal-yən\ *n* **1** : a large body of troops organized to act together : ARMY **2** : a military unit composed of a headquarters and two or more units (as companies)

¹bat·ten \'bat-ᵊn\ *vb* **bat·tened; bat·ten·ing** \'bat-(ᵊ-)niŋ\ **1** : to grow or make fat **2** : THRIVE

²batten *n* : a strip of wood used esp. to seal or strengthen a joint

³batten *vb* **bat·tened; bat·ten·ing** \'bat-(ᵊ-)niŋ\ : to fasten with battens

¹bat·ter \'bat-ər\ *vb* : to beat or damage with repeated blows

²batter *n* : a soft mixture (as for cake) basically of flour and liquid

³batter *n* : one that bats; *esp* : the player whose turn it is to bat

battering ram *n* : an ancient military machine for battering down walls

bat·tery \'bat-(ə-)rē\ *n, pl* **-ter·ies 1** : BEATING; *esp* : unlawful beating or use of force on a person **2** : a grouping of artillery pieces for tactical purposes; *also* : the guns of a warship **3** : a group of electric cells for furnishing electric current; *also* : a single electric cell ⟨a flashlight ∼⟩ **4** : a number of similar items grouped or used as a unit ⟨a ∼ of tests⟩ **5** : the pitcher and catcher of a baseball team

bat·ting \'bat-iŋ\ *n* : layers or sheets of cotton or wool (as for lining quilts)

¹bat·tle \'bat-ᵊl\ *n* [ME *batel,* fr. OF *bataille* battle, fortifying tower, battalion, fr. LL *battalia* combat, alter. of *battualia* fencing exercises, fr. L *battuere* to beat] : a general military engagement; *also* : an extended contest or controversy

²battle *vb* **bat·tled; bat·tling** \'bat-(ᵊ-)liŋ\ : to engage in battle : CONTEND, FIGHT

bat·tle–ax \'bat-ᵊl-,aks\ *n* **1** : a long-handled ax formerly used as a weapon **2** : a quarrelsome domineering woman

battle fatigue *n* : COMBAT FATIGUE

bat·tle·field \'bat-ᵊl-,fēld\ *n* : a place where a battle is fought

bat·tle·ment \-mənt\ *n* : a decorative or defensive parapet on top of a wall

bat·tle·ship \-,ship\ *n* : a warship of the most heavily armed and armored class

bat·tle·wag·on \-,wag-ən\ *n* : BATTLE-SHIP

bat·ty \'bat-ē\ *adj* **bat·ti·er; -est** : CRAZY, FOOLISH

bau·ble \'bȯ-bəl\ *n* : TRINKET

baux·ite \'bȯk-,sīt\ *n* : a clayey substance that is the chief ore of aluminum

bawd \'bȯd\ *n* **1** : MADAM 2 **2** : PROSTITUTE

bawdy \'bȯd-ē\ *adj* **bawd·i·er; -est** : OBSCENE, LEWD — **bawd·i·ly** \'bȯd-ᵊl-ē\ *adv* — **bawd·i·ness** \-ē-nəs\ *n*

¹bawl \'bȯl\ *vb* : to cry or cry out loudly; *also* : to scold harshly

²bawl *n* : a long loud cry : BELLOW

¹bay \'bā\ *adj* : reddish brown

²bay *n* **1** : a bay-colored animal **2** : a reddish brown

³bay *n* : the European laurel; *also* : a shrub or tree resembling this

⁴bay *n* **1** : a section or compartment of a building or vehicle **2** : a compartment projecting outward from the wall of a building and containing a window **(bay window)**

⁵bay *vb* : to bark with deep long tones

⁶bay *n* **1** : the position of one unable to escape and forced to face danger **2** : a baying of dogs

⁷bay *n* : an inlet of a body of water (as the sea) usu. smaller than a gulf

bay·ber·ry \'bā-,ber-ē\ *n* : a hardy deciduous shrub of coastal eastern No. America bearing small hard berries coated with a white wax used for candles; *also* : its fruit

bay leaf *n* : the dried leaf of the European laurel used in cooking

¹bay·o·net \'bā-ə-nət, ,bā-ə-'net\ *n* : a daggerlike weapon made to fit on the muzzle end of a rifle

²bayonet *vb* **-net·ed** *also* **-net·ted; -net·ing** *also* **-net·ting** : to use or stab with a bayonet

bay•ou \'bī-ō, -ü\ *n* [Louisiana French, fr. Choctaw *bayuk*] : a marshy or sluggish body of water

bay rum *n* : a fragrant liquid used esp. as a cologne or after-shave lotion

ba•zaar \bə-'zär\ *n* **1** : a group of shops : MARKETPLACE **2** : a fair for the sale of articles usu. for charity

ba•zoo•ka \bə-'zü-kə\ *n* [*bazooka* (a crude musical instrument made of pipes and a funnel)] : a weapon consisting of a tube and launching an explosive rocket able to pierce armor

¹BB \'bē-(,)bē\ *n* : a small round shot pellet

²BB *abbr* base on balls

BBB *abbr* Better Business Bureau

BBC *abbr* British Broadcasting Corporation

bbl *abbr* barrel; barrels

BC *abbr* **1** before Christ — often printed in small capitals **2** British Columbia

BCD \,bē-,sē-'dē\ *n* [*binary coded decimal*] : a computer code for representing alphanumeric information

B cell *n* [*bone-marrow-derived cell*] : any of the lymphocytes that secrete antibodies when mature

B complex *n* : VITAMIN B COMPLEX

bd *abbr* **1** board **2** bound

bdl *or* **bdle** *abbr* bundle

bdrm *abbr* bedroom

be \(')bē\ *vb, past 1st & 3d sing* **was** \(')wəz, 'wäz\; *2d sing* **were** \(')wər\; *pl* **were**; *past subjunctive* **were**; *past part* **been** \(')bin\; *pres part* **be•ing** \'bē-iŋ\; *pres 1st sing* **am** \əm, (')am\; *2d sing* **are** \ər, (')är\; *3d sing* **is** \(')iz, əz\; *pl* **are**; *pres subjunctive* **be 1** : to equal in meaning or symbolically ⟨God *is* love⟩; *also* : to have a specified qualification or relationship ⟨leaves *are* green⟩ ⟨this fish *is* a trout⟩ **2** : to have objective existence ⟨there *was* once an old woman⟩; *also* : to have or occupy a particular place ⟨here *is* your pen⟩ **3** : to take place : OCCUR ⟨the meeting *is* tonight⟩ **4** — used with the past participle of transitive verbs as a passive voice auxiliary ⟨the door *was* opened⟩ **5** — used as the auxiliary of the present participle in expressing continuous action ⟨he *is* sleeping⟩ **6** — used as an auxiliary with the past participle of some in-

transitive verbs to form archaic perfect tenses **7** — used as an auxiliary with *to* and the infinitive to express futurity, prearrangement, or obligation ⟨he *is* to come when called⟩

Be *symbol* beryllium

¹beach \'bēch\ *n* : a sandy or gravelly part of the shore of an ocean or lake

²beach *vb* : to run or drive ashore

beach buggy *n* : DUNE BUGGY

beach•comb•er \'bēch-,kō-mər\ *n* : one who searches along a shore for useful or salable flotsam and refuse

beach•head \'bēch-,hed\ *n* : an area on an enemy-held shore occupied by an advance attacking force to protect the later landing of troops or supplies

bea•con \'bē-kən\ *n* **1** : a signal fire **2** : a guiding or warning signal (as a lighthouse) **3** : a radio transmitter emitting signals for guidance of aircraft

¹bead \'bēd\ *n* [ME *bede* prayer, prayer bead, fr. OE *bed, gebed* prayer] **1** *pl* : a series of prayers and meditations made with a rosary **2** : a small piece of material pierced for threading on a line (as in a rosary) **3** : a small globular body **4** : a narrow projecting rim or band — **bead•ing** *n* — **beady** *adj*

²bead *vb* : to form into a bead

bea•dle \'bēd-ᵊl\ *n* : a usu. English parish officer whose duties include keeping order in church

bea•gle \'bē-gəl\ *n* : a small short-legged smooth-coated hound

beak \'bēk\ *n* : the bill of a bird and esp. of a bird of prey; *also* : a pointed projecting part — **beaked** \'bēkt\ *adj*

bea•ker \'bē-kər\ *n* **1** : a large drinking cup with a wide mouth **2** : a thin-walled laboratory vessel with a wide mouth

¹beam \'bēm\ *n* **1** : a large long piece of timber or metal **2** : the bar of a balance from which the scales hang **3** : the breadth of a ship at its widest part **4** : a ray or shaft of light **5** : a collection of nearly parallel rays (as X rays) or particles (as electrons) **6** : a constant radio signal transmitted for the guidance of pilots; *also* : the course indicated by this signal

²beam *vb* **1** : to send out light **2** : to aim (a broadcast) by directional antennas **3** : to smile with joy

¹bean \'bēn\ *n* : the edible seed borne in

pods by some leguminous plants; *also* : a plant or a pod bearing these

²**bean** *vb* : to strike on the head with an object

bean·bag \'bēn-ˌbag\ *n* : a cloth bag partially filled typically with dried beans and used as a toy

bean·ball \'bēn-ˌbȯl\ *n* : a pitched baseball thrown at a batter's head

bean curd *n* : a food like soft cheese made from soybeans

bean·ie \'bē-nē\ *n* : a small round tight-fitting skullcap

beano \'bē-nō\ *n, pl* **beanos** : BINGO

¹**bear** \'baər\ *n, pl* **bears** 1 *or pl* **bear** : any of a family of large heavy mammals with shaggy hair and small tails 2 : a gruff or sullen person 3 : one who sells (as securities) in expectation of a price decline — **bear·ish** *adj*

²**bear** *vb* **bore** \'bōr\; **borne** \'bōrn\ *also* **born** \'bȯrn\; **bear·ing** 1 : CARRY 2 : to be equipped with 3 : to give as testimony ⟨∼ witness to the facts of the case⟩ 4 : to give birth to; *also* : PRODUCE, YIELD ⟨a tree that ∼s regularly⟩ 5 : ENDURE, SUSTAIN ⟨∼ pain⟩ ⟨*bore* the weight on piles⟩; *also* : to exert pressure or influence 6 : to be or become directed ⟨∼ to the right⟩ — **bear·able** *adj* — **bear·er** *n*

¹**beard** \'biərd\ *n* 1 : the hair that grows on the face of a man 2 : a growth of bristly hairs (as on rye or the chin of a goat) — **beard·ed** \-əd\ *adj* — **beard·less** *adj*

²**beard** *vb* : to confront boldly

bear·ing \'ba(ə)r-iŋ\ *n* 1 : manner of carrying oneself : COMPORTMENT 2 : a supporting object, purpose, or point 3 : a machine part in which another part (as an axle or pin) turns 4 : an emblem in a coat of arms 5 : the position or direction of one point with respect to another or to the compass; *also* : a determination of position 6 *pl* : comprehension of one's situation 7 : connection with or influence on something; *also* : SIGNIFICANCE

bear·skin \'baər-ˌskin\ *n* : an article made of the skin of a bear

beast \'bēst\ *n* 1 : ANIMAL 1; *esp* : a 4-footed mammal 2 : a contemptible person **syn** brute, animal, creature

¹**beast·ly** \'bēst-lē\ *adj* **beast·li·er; -est** 1 : of, relating to, or resembling a beast

2 : ABOMINABLE, DISAGREEABLE — **beast·li·ness** \-lē-nəs\ *n*

²**beastly** *adv* : VERY

¹**beat** \'bēt\ *vb* **beat; beat·en** \'bēt-ᵊn\ *or* **beat; beat·ing** 1 : to strike repeatedly 2 : TREAD 3 : to affect or alter by beating ⟨∼ metal into sheets⟩ 4 : to sound (as an alarm) on a drum 5 : OVERCOME; *also* : SURPASS 6 : to act or arrive before ⟨∼ his brother home⟩ 7 : THROB — **beat·er** *n*

²**beat** *n* 1 : a single stroke or blow esp. of a series; *also* : PULSATION 2 : a rhythmic stress in poetry or music or the rhythmic effect of these 3 : a regularly traversed course

³**beat** *adj* 1 : EXHAUSTED 2 : of or relating to beatniks

⁴**beat** *n* : BEATNIK

be·atif·ic \ˌbē-ə-'tif-ik\ *adj* : giving or indicative of great joy or bliss

be·at·i·fy \bē-'at-ə-ˌfī\ *vb* **-fied; -fy·ing** 1 : to make supremely happy 2 : to declare to have attained the blessedness of heaven and authorize the title "Blessed" for — **be·at·i·fi·ca·tion** \-ˌat-ə-fə-'kā-shən\ *n*

be·at·i·tude \bē-'at-ə-ˌt(y)üd\ *n* 1 : a state of utmost bliss 2 : any of the declarations made in the Sermon on the Mount (Mt 5:3–12) beginning "Blessed are"

beat·nik \'bēt-nik\ *n* : a person who behaves and dresses unconventionally and is inclined to exotic philosophizing and extreme self-expression

beau \'bō\ *n, pl* **beaux** \'bōz\ *or* **beaus** [F, fr. *beau* beautiful, fr. L *bellus* pretty] 1 : a man of fashion : DANDY 2 : SUITOR, LOVER

beau geste \bō-'zhest\ *n, pl* **beaux gestes** *or* **beau gestes** \bō-'zhest\ : a graceful or magnanimous gesture

beau ide·al \ˌbō-ī-'dē(-ə)l\ *n, pl* **beau ideals** : the perfect type or model

Beau·jo·lais \ˌbō-zhō-'lā\ *n* : a French red table wine

beau monde \bō-'mänd, -mōⁿd\ *n, pl* **beau mondes** \-'män(d)z\ *or* **beaux mondes** \bō-mōⁿd\ : the world of high society and fashion

beau·te·ous \'byüt-ē-əs\ *adj* : BEAUTIFUL — **beau·te·ous·ly** *adv*

beau·ti·cian \byü-'tish-ən\ *n* : COSMETOLOGIST

beau·ti·ful \'byüt-i-fəl\ *adj* : characterized by beauty : LOVELY **syn** pretty, fair, comely, lovely — **beau·ti·ful·ly** \-f(ə-)lē\ *adv*

beautiful people *n pl, often cap B&P* : people who are identified with international society

beau·ti·fy \'byüt-ə-ˌfī\ *vb* **-fied; -fy·ing** : to make more beautiful — **beau·ti·fi·ca·tion** \ˌbyüt-ə-fə-'kā-shən\ *n* — **beau·ti·fi·er** *n*

beau·ty \'byüt-ē\ *n, pl* **beauties** : qualities that give pleasure to the senses or exalt the mind : LOVELINESS; *also* : something having such qualities

beauty shop *n* : an establishment where hairdressing, facials, and manicures are done

beaux arts \bō-'zär\ *n pl* [F] : FINE ARTS

bea·ver \'bē-vər\ *n, pl* **beavers** : a large fur-bearing rodent that builds dams and underwater houses of mud and sticks; *also* : its fur

be·calm \bi-'käm, -'kälm\ *vb* : to keep (as a ship) motionless by lack of wind

be·cause \bi-'kȯz, -'kəz\ *conj* : for the reason that

because of *prep* : by reason of

beck \'bek\ *n* : a beckoning gesture; *also* : SUMMONS

beck·on \'bek-ən\ *vb* **beck·oned; beck·on·ing** \'bek-(ə-)niŋ\ : to summon or signal esp. by a nod or gesture; *also* : ATTRACT

be·cloud \bi-'klau̇d\ *vb* : OBSCURE

be·come \bi-'kəm\ *vb* **-came** \-'kām\; **-come; -com·ing** 1 : to come to be ⟨∼ tired⟩ 2 : to suit or be suitable to ⟨her dress ∼s her⟩

be·com·ing \-'kəm-iŋ\ *adj* : SUITABLE, FIT; *also* : ATTRACTIVE — **be·com·ing·ly** *adv*

¹**bed** \'bed\ *n* 1 : an article of furniture to sleep on 2 : a plot of ground prepared for plants 3 : FOUNDATION, BOTTOM ⟨river ∼⟩ 4 : LAYER, STRATUM

²**bed** *vb* **bed·ded; bed·ding** 1 : to put or go to bed 2 : to fix in a foundation : EMBED 3 : to plant in beds 4 : to lay or lie flat or in layers

bed–and–breakfast *adj* : offering lodging and breakfast ⟨a ∼ place⟩ — **bed–and–breakfast** *n*

be·daub \bi-'dȯb\ *vb* : SMEAR

be·daz·zle \bi-'daz-əl\ *vb* : to confuse by or as if by a strong light — **be·daz·zle·ment** *n*

bed·bug \'bed-ˌbəg\ *n* : a wingless bloodsucking bug infesting houses and esp. beds

bed·clothes \'bed-ˌklō(th)z\ *n pl* : BEDDING 1

bed·ding \'bed-iŋ\ *n* 1 : materials for making up a bed 2 : FOUNDATION

be·deck \bi-'dek\ *vb* : ADORN

be·dev·il \bi-'dev-əl\ *vb* 1 : HARASS, TORMENT 2 : CONFUSE, MUDDLE

be·dew \bi-'d(y)ü\ *vb* : to wet with or as if with dew

bed·fast \'bed-ˌfast\ *adj* : BEDRIDDEN

bed·fel·low \'bed-ˌfel-ō\ *n* 1 : one sharing the bed of another 2 : a close associate : ALLY

be·di·zen \bi-'dīz-ᵊn, -'diz-\ *vb* [*be-* + *dizen*, fr. earlier *disen* to dress a distaff with flax, fr. Dutch] : to dress or adorn with showy or vulgar finery

bed·lam \'bed-ləm\ *n* [*Bedlam*, popular name for the Hospital of St. Mary of Bethlehem, London, an insane asylum, fr. ME *Bedlem* Bethlehem] 1 : an insane asylum 2 : a scene of uproar and confusion

bed·ou·in *or* **bed·u·in** \'bed(-ə)-wən\ *n, pl* **bedouin** *or* **bedouins** *or* **beduin** *or* **beduins** *often cap* : a nomadic Arab of the Arabian, Syrian, or No. African deserts

bed·pan \'bed-ˌpan\ *n* : a shallow vessel used by a person in bed for urination or defecation

bed·post \-ˌpōst\ *n* : the post of a bed

be·drag·gled \bi-'drag-əld\ *adj* : soiled and disordered as if by being drenched

bed·rid·den \'bed-ˌrid-ᵊn\ *adj* : kept in bed by illness or weakness

bed·rock \-'räk\ *n* : the solid rock underlying surface materials (as soil) — **bedrock** *adj*

bed·roll \-ˌrōl\ *n* : bedding rolled up for carrying

bed·room \-ˌrüm, -ˌru̇m\ *n* : a room containing a bed and used esp. for sleeping

bed·side \'bed-ˌsīd\ *n* : the place beside a bed esp. of a sick or dying person

bed·sore \'bed-ˌsōr\ *n* : an ulceration of tissue deprived of nutrition by prolonged pressure

bed·spread \-ˌspred\ *n* : a usu. ornamental outer cover for a bed

bed·stead \-ˌsted, -ˌstid\ *n* : the framework of a bed

bed·time \-ˌtīm\ *n* : time for going to bed

bed–wet·ting \-ˌwet-iŋ\ *n* : involuntary discharge of urine esp. in bed during sleep — **bed–wet·ter** *n*

¹bee \ˈbē\ *n* : a social and colonial 4-winged insect often kept in hives for the honey it produces; *also* : any of various related insects

²bee *n* : a gathering of people for a specific purpose

beech \ˈbēch\ *n, pl* **beech·es** *or* **beech** : any of a genus of deciduous hardwood trees with smooth gray bark and small sweet triangular nuts; *also* : the wood of a beech — **beech·en** \ˈbē-chən\ *adj*

beech·nut \ˈbēch-ˌnət\ *n* : the nut of a beech

¹beef \ˈbēf\ *n, pl* **beefs** \ˈbēfs\ *or* **beeves** \ˈbēvz\ **1** : the flesh of a steer, cow, or bull; *also* : the dressed carcass of a beef animal **2** : a steer, cow, or bull esp. when fattened for food **3** : MUSCLE, BRAWN **4** *pl* **beefs** : COMPLAINT

²beef *vb* **1** : STRENGTHEN — usu. used with *up* **2** : COMPLAIN

beef·eat·er \-ˌēt-ər\ *n* : a yeoman of the guard of an English monarch

beef·steak \ˈbēf-ˌstāk\ *n* : a slice of beef suitable for broiling or frying

beefy \ˈbē-fē\ *adj* **beef·i·er; -est** : THICKSET, BRAWNY

bee·hive \ˈbē-ˌhīv\ *n* : HIVE 1, 3

bee·keep·er \-ˌkē-pər\ *n* : a raiser of bees — **bee·keep·ing** *n*

bee·line \-ˌlīn\ *n* : a straight direct course

been past part of BE

beep·er \ˈbē-pər\ *n* : a portable electronic device that alerts the person carrying it when it receives a special radio signal

beer \ˈbiər\ *n* : an alcoholic beverage brewed from malt and hops — **beery** *adj*

bees·wax \ˈbēz-ˌwaks\ *n* : WAX 1

beet \ˈbēt\ *n* : a garden plant with edible leaves and a thick sweet root used as a vegetable, as a source of sugar, or as forage; *also* : its root

¹bee·tle \ˈbēt-ᵊl\ *n* : any of an order of insects having four wings of which the stiff outer pair covers the membranous inner pair when not in flight

²beetle *vb* **bee·tled; bee·tling** : to jut out : PROJECT

be·fall \bi-ˈfȯl\ *vb* **-fell** \-ˈfel\; **-fall·en** \-ˈfȯ-lən\ : to happen to : OCCUR

be·fit \bi-ˈfit\ *vb* : to be suitable to

be·fog \bi-ˈfȯg, -ˈfäg\ *vb* : OBSCURE; *also* : CONFUSE

¹be·fore \bi-ˈfōr\ *adv or adj* **1** : in front **2** : EARLIER

²before *prep* **1** : in front of ⟨stood ∼ him⟩ **2** : earlier than ⟨got there ∼ me⟩ **3** : in a more important category than ⟨put quality ∼ quantity⟩

³before *conj* **1** : earlier than the time when ⟨he got here ∼ I did⟩ **2** : more willingly than ⟨he'd starve ∼ he'd steal⟩

be·fore·hand \bi-ˈfōr-ˌhand\ *adv or adj* : in advance

be·foul \bi-ˈfau̇l\ *vb* : SOIL

be·friend \bi-ˈfrend\ *vb* : to act as friend to

be·fud·dle \bi-ˈfəd-ᵊl\ *vb* : MUDDLE, CONFUSE

beg \ˈbeg\ *vb* **begged; beg·ging** **1** : to ask as a charity; *also* : ENTREAT **2** : EVADE; *also* : assume as established ⟨∼ the question⟩

be·get \bi-ˈget\ *vb* **-got** \-ˈgät\; **-got·ten** \-ˈgät-ᵊn\ *or* **-got; -get·ting** : to become the father of : SIRE

¹beg·gar \ˈbeg-ər\ *n* : one that begs esp. as a way of life

²beggar *vb* **beg·gared; beg·gar·ing** \ˈbeg-(ə-)riŋ\ : IMPOVERISH

beg·gar·ly \ˈbeg-ər-lē\ *adj* **1** : marked by unrelieved poverty ⟨a ∼ life⟩ **2** : contemptibly mean or inadequate

beg·gary \ˈbeg-ə-rē\ *n* : extreme poverty

be·gin \bi-ˈgin\ *vb* **be·gan** \-ˈgan\; **be·gun** \-ˈgən\; **be·gin·ning** **1** : to do the first part of an action; *also* : to undertake or undergo initial steps : COMMENCE **2** : to come into being : ARISE; *also* : FOUND **3** : ORIGINATE, INVENT — **be·gin·ner** *n*

be·gone \bi-ˈgȯn\ *vb* : to go away : DEPART — used esp. in the imperative

be·go·nia \bi-ˈgōn-yə\ *n* : any of a genus of tropical herbs widely grown for their showy leaves and waxy flowers

be·grime \bi-ˈgrīm\ *vb* **be·grimed; be·grim·ing** : to make dirty

be•grudge \bi-'grəj\ *vb* **1** : to give or concede reluctantly **2** : to take little pleasure in : be annoyed by **3** : to envy the pleasure or enjoyment of

be•guile \-'gīl\ *vb* **be•guiled; be•guil•ing 1** : DECEIVE, CHEAT **2** : to while away **3** : to coax by wiles

be•guine \bi-'gēn\ *n* [AmerF *béguine,* fr. F *béguin* flirtation] : a vigorous popular dance of the islands of Saint Lucia and Martinique

be•gum \'bā-gəm, 'bē-\ *n* : a Muslim woman of high rank

be•half \bi-'haf, -'hȧf\ *n* : BENEFIT, SUPPORT, DEFENSE

be•have \bi-'hāv\ *vb* **be•haved; be•having 1** : to bear, comport, or conduct oneself in a particular and esp. a proper way **2** : to act, function, or react in a particular way

be•hav•ior \bi-'hā-vyər\ *n* : way of behaving; *esp* : personal conduct — **be•hav•ior•al** \-vyə-rəl\ *adj*

be•hav•ior•ism \bi-'hā-vyə-ˌriz-əm\ *n* : a school of psychology concerned with the objective evidence of behavior without reference to conscious experience

be•head \bi-'hed\ *vb* : to cut off the head of

be•he•moth \bi-'hē-məth, 'bē-ə-ˌmäth\ *n* : a huge powerful animal described in Job 40:15–24 that is probably the hippopotamus; *also* : something of monstrous size or power

be•hest \bi-'hest\ *n* **1** : COMMAND **2** : an urgent prompting

¹**be•hind** \bi-'hīnd\ *adv or adj* **1** : BACK, BACKWARD **2** : LATE, SLOW

²**behind** *prep* **1** : in or to a place or situation in back of or to the rear of ⟨look ∼ you⟩ ⟨the staff stayed ∼ the troops⟩ **2** : inferior to (as in rank) : BELOW ⟨three games ∼ the first-place team⟩ **3** : in support of : SUPPORTING ⟨we're ∼ you all the way⟩

be•hind•hand \bi-'hīnd-ˌhand\ *adj* **1** : being in arrears **2** : lagging behind the times **syn** tardy, late, overdue, belated

be•hold \bi-'hōld\ *vb* **-held** \-'held\; **-hold•ing 1** : to have in sight : SEE **2** — used imperatively to direct the attention **syn** view, observe, notice, espy — **be•hold•er** *n*

be•hold•en \bi-'hōl-dən\ *adj* : OBLIGATED, INDEBTED

be•hoof \bi-'hüf\ *n* : ADVANTAGE, PROFIT

be•hoove \bi-'hüv\ *or* **be•hove** \-'hōv\ *vb* **be•hooved** *or* **be•hoved; be•hoov•ing** *or* **be•hov•ing** : to be necessary, proper, or advantageous for

beige \'bāzh\ *n* : a pale dull yellowish brown — **beige** *adj*

be•ing \'bē-iŋ\ *n* **1** : EXISTENCE; *also* : LIFE **2** : the qualities or constitution of an existent thing **3** : a living thing; *esp* : PERSON

be•la•bor \bi-'lā-bər\ *vb* **1** : to assail (as with words) tiresomely or at length **2** : to beat soundly

be•lat•ed \bi-'lāt-əd\ *adj* : DELAYED, LATE

be•lay \bi-'lā\ *vb* **1** : to wind (a rope) around a pin or cleat in order to hold secure **2** : QUIT, STOP — used in the imperative

belch \'belch\ *vb* **1** : to expel (gas) from the stomach through the mouth **2** : to gush forth ⟨a volcano ∼*ing* lava⟩ — **belch** *n*

bel•dam *or* **bel•dame** \'bel-dəm\ *n* [ME *beldam* grandmother, fr. MF *bel* beautiful + ME *dam* lady, mother] : an old woman; *esp* : HAG

be•lea•guer \bi-'lē-gər\ *vb* **1** : BESIEGE **2** : HARASS ⟨∼*ed* parents⟩

bel•fry \'bel-frē\ *n, pl* **belfries** [ME *belfrey,* alter. of *berfrey,* fr. MF *berfrei,* deriv. of Gk *pyrgos phorētos* movable war tower] : a tower for a bell (as on a church); *also* : the part of the tower in which the bell hangs

Belg *abbr* Belgian; Belgium

Bel•gian \'bel-jən\ *n* : a native or inhabitant of Belgium — **Belgian** *adj*

be•lie \bi-'lī\ *vb* **-lied; -ly•ing 1** : MISREPRESENT **2** : to prove (something) false **3** : to run counter to

be•lief \bə-'lēf\ *n* **1** : CONFIDENCE, TRUST **2** : something (as a tenet or creed) believed **syn** conviction, opinion, persuasion, sentiment

be•lieve \bə-'lēv\ *vb* **be•lieved; be•lieving 1** : to have religious convictions **2** : to have a firm conviction about something : accept as true **3** : to hold as an opinion : SUPPOSE — **be•liev•able** *adj* — **be•liev•er** *n*

be•like \bi-'līk\ *adv, archaic* : PROBABLY

be•lit•tle \bi-'lit-ᵊl\ *vb* **-lit•tled; -lit•tling**

\-ˈlit-(ᵊ-)liŋ\ : to make seem little or less; *also* : DISPARAGE

¹**bell** \ˈbel\ *n* **1** : a hollow metallic device that makes a ringing sound when struck **2** : the sounding or stroke of a bell (as on shipboard to tell the time); *also* : time so indicated **3** : something with the flared form of a typical bell

²**bell** *vb* : to provide with a bell

bel·la·don·na \ˌbel-ə-ˈdän-ə\ *n* [It, lit., beautiful lady; fr. its cosmetic use] : a drug or extract used esp. to relieve spasms and pain or to dilate the eye and obtained from a poisonous European herb related to the potato; *also* : this herb

bell–bot·toms \ˈbel-ˈbät-əmz\ *n pl* : pants with wide flaring bottoms — **bell–bottom** *adj*

bell·boy \ˈbel-ˌbȯi\ *n* : BELLHOP

belle \ˈbel\ *n* : an attractive and popular girl or woman

belles let·tres \bel-letrᵊ\ *n pl* [F] : literature that is an end in itself and not practical or purely informative — **bel·le·tris·tic** \ˌbel-ə-ˈtris-tik\ *adj*

bell·hop \ˈbel-ˌhäp\ *n* : a hotel or club employee who takes guests to rooms, carries luggage, and runs errands

bel·li·cose \ˈbel-i-ˌkōs\ *adj* : WARLIKE, PUGNACIOUS **syn** belligerent, quarrelsome, combative, contentious, pugnacious — **bel·li·cos·i·ty** \ˌbel-i-ˈkäs-ət-ē\ *n*

bel·lig·er·en·cy \bə-ˈlij(-ə)-rən-sē\ *n* **1** : the status of a nation engaged in war **2** : BELLIGERENCE, TRUCULENCE

bel·lig·er·ent \-rənt\ *adj* **1** : waging war **2** : TRUCULENT **syn** bellicose, pugnacious, combative, contentious, warlike — **bel·lig·er·ence** \-rᵊns\ *n* — **belligerent** *n*

bel·low \ˈbel-ō\ *vb* **1** : to make the deep hollow sound characteristic of a bull **2** : to call or utter in a loud deep voice — **bellow** *n*

bel·lows \-ōz, -əz\ *n sing or pl* : a closed boxlike device with sides that can be spread apart and then pressed together to draw in air and expel it through a tube

bells \ˈbelz\ *n pl* : BELL-BOTTOMS

bell·weth·er \ˈbel-ˈweth-ər, -ˌweth-\ *n* : one that takes the lead or initiative

¹**bel·ly** \ˈbel-ē\ *n, pl* **bellies** [ME *bely* bellows, belly, fr. OE *belg* bag, skin] **1** : ABDOMEN; *also* : STOMACH **2** : the underpart of an animal's body

²**belly** *vb* **bel·lied; bel·ly·ing** : BULGE

¹**bel·ly·ache** \ˈbel-ē-ˌāk\ *n* : pain in the abdomen

²**bellyache** *vb* : COMPLAIN

belly button *n* : NAVEL

belly dance *n* : a usu. solo dance emphasizing movement of the belly — **belly dance** *vb* — **belly dancer** *n*

belly laugh *n* : a deep hearty laugh

be·long \bi-ˈlȯŋ\ *vb* **1** : to be suitable or appropriate; *also* : to be properly situated ⟨shoes ∼ in the closet⟩ **2** : to be the property ⟨this ∼s to me⟩; *also* : to be attached (as through birth or membership) ⟨∼ to a club⟩ **3** : to form an attribute or part ⟨this wheel ∼s to the cart⟩ **4** : to be classified ⟨whales ∼ among the mammals⟩

be·long·ings \-ˈlȯŋ-iŋz\ *n pl* : GOODS, EFFECTS, POSSESSIONS

be·loved \bi-ˈləv(-ə)d\ *adj* : dearly loved — **beloved** *n*

¹**be·low** \bi-ˈlō\ *adv* **1** : in or to a lower place or rank **2** : on earth **3** : in hell **syn** under, beneath, underneath

²**below** *prep* **1** : in or to a lower place than **2** : inferior to (as in rank)

¹**belt** \ˈbelt\ *n* **1** : a strip (as of leather) worn about the waist **2** : an endless band passing around pulleys or cylinders to communicate motion or convey material **3** : a region marked by some distinctive feature; *esp* : one suited to a particular crop

²**belt** *vb* **1** : to encircle or secure with a belt **2** : to beat with or as if with a belt **3** : to mark with an encircling band

³**belt** *n* **1** : a jarring blow : WHACK **2** : DRINK ⟨a ∼ of whiskey⟩

belt–tightening *n* : a reduction in spending

belt·way \ˈbelt-ˌwā\ *n* : a highway skirting an urban area

be·lu·ga \bə-ˈlü-gə\ *n* : a white sturgeon of the Black sea, Caspian sea, and their tributaries that is a source of caviar

bel·ve·dere \ˈbel-və-ˌdiər\ *n* [It, lit., beautiful view] : a structure (as a summerhouse) designed to command a view

be·mire \bi-ˈmī(ə)r\ *vb* : to cover or soil with or sink in mire

be·moan \bi-ˈmōn\ *vb* : LAMENT, DE-

PLORE syn bewail, grieve, moan, weep

be•muse \bi-ˈmyüz\ vb : BEWILDER, CONFUSE

¹bench \ˈbench\ n **1** : a long seat for two or more persons **2** : the seat of a judge in court; *also* : the office or dignity of a judge **3** : COURT; *also* : JUDGES **4** : a table for holding work and tools ⟨a carpenter's ∼⟩

²bench \ˈbench\ vb **1** : to furnish with benches **2** : to seat on a bench **3** : to remove from or keep out of a game

bench mark n **1** : a mark on a permanent object serving as an elevation reference in topographical surveys **2** *usu* **bench•mark** : a point of reference for measurement; *also* : STANDARD

bench warrant n : a warrant issued by a presiding judge or by a court against a person guilty of contempt or indicted for a crime

¹bend \ˈbend\ vb **bent** \ˈbent\; **bend•ing** **1** : to draw (as a bow) taut **2** : to curve or cause a change of shape in ⟨∼ a bar⟩ **3** : to turn in a certain direction ⟨*bent* his steps toward town⟩ **4** : to make fast : SECURE **5** : SUBDUE **6** : RESOLVE, DETERMINE ⟨*bent* on self-destruction⟩; *also* : APPLY ⟨*bent* themselves to the task⟩ **7** : DEFLECT **8** : to curve downward **9** : YIELD, SUBMIT

²bend n : a knot by which a rope is fastened (as to another rope)

³bend n **1** : an act or process of bending **2** : something bent; *esp* : CURVE **3** *pl* : a painful and dangerous disorder caused by release of gas bubbles in the tissues upon too rapid decrease in air pressure after a stay in a compressed atmosphere

bend•er \ˈben-dər\ n : SPREE

¹be•neath \bi-ˈnēth\ adv : BELOW, UNDERNEATH syn under, underneath, below

²beneath prep **1** : BELOW, UNDER ⟨stood ∼ a tree⟩ **2** : unworthy of ⟨considered such behavior ∼ her⟩

bene•dic•tion \ˌben-ə-ˈdik-shən\ n : the invocation of a blessing esp. at the close of a public worship service

bene•fac•tion \-ˈfak-shən\ n : a charitable donation syn contribution, alms, beneficence, offering

bene•fac•tor \ˈben-ə-ˌfak-tər\ n : one that confers a benefit and esp. a benefaction

bene•fac•tress \-ˌfak-trəs\ n : a woman who is a benefactor

ben•e•fice \ˈben-ə-fəs\ n : an ecclesiastical office to which the revenue from an endowment is attached

be•nef•i•cence \bə-ˈnef-ə-səns\ n **1** : beneficent quality **2** : BENEFACTION

be•nef•i•cent \-sənt\ adj : doing or producing good (as by acts of kindness or charity); *also* : productive of benefit

ben•e•fi•cial \ˌben-ə-ˈfish-əl\ adj : being of benefit or help : HELPFUL syn advantageous, profitable, favorable, propitious — **ben•e•fi•cial•ly** \-ē\ adv

ben•e•fi•cia•ry \ˌben-ə-ˈfish-ē-ˌer-ē, -ˈfish-(ə-)rē\ n, pl **-ries** : one that receives a benefit (as the income of a trust or the proceeds of an insurance)

¹ben•e•fit \ˈben-ə-ˌfit\ n **1** : ADVANTAGE ⟨the ∼s of exercise⟩ **2** : useful aid : HELP; *also* : material aid provided or due (as in sickness or unemployment) as a right **3** : a performance or event to raise funds for some person or cause

²benefit vb **-fit•ed** \-ˌfit-əd\ *also* **-fit•ted**; **-fit•ing** *also* **-fit•ting** **1** : to be useful or profitable to **2** : to receive benefit

be•nev•o•lence \bə-ˈnev(-ə)-ləns\ n **1** : charitable nature **2** : an act of kindness : CHARITY — **be•nev•o•lent** \-lənt\ adj

be•night•ed \bi-ˈnīt-əd\ adj **1** : overtaken by darkness or night **2** : living in ignorance

be•nign \bi-ˈnīn\ adj **1** : of a gentle disposition; *also* : showing kindness **2** : of a mild kind; *esp* : not malignant ⟨∼ tumors⟩ syn benignant, kind, kindly, good-hearted — **be•nig•ni•ty** \-ˈnig-nət-ē\ n

be•nig•nant \-ˈnig-nənt\ adj : BENIGN 1 syn kind, kindly, good-hearted

ben•i•son \ˈben-ə-sən, -zən\ n : BLESSING, BENEDICTION

bent \ˈbent\ n **1** : strong inclination or interest; *also* : TALENT **2** : power of endurance syn talent, aptitude, gift, flair, knack, genius

ben•thic \ˈben-thik\ adj : of, relating to, or occurring at the bottom of a body of water

ben•thos \ˈben-ˌthäs\ n : organisms that live on or in the bottom of bodies of water

ben•ton•ite \ˈbent-ᵊn-ˌīt\ n : an absorptive clay used esp. as a filler (as in paper)

bent·wood \'bent-ˌwu̇d\ *adj* : made of wood bent into shape ⟨a ~ rocker⟩

be·numb \bi-'nəm\ *vb* **1** : DULL, DEADEN **2** : to make numb esp. by cold

ben·zene \'ben-ˌzēn\ *n* : a colorless volatile flammable liquid hydrocarbon used in organic synthesis and as a solvent

ben·zine \'ben-ˌzēn\ *n* : any of various flammable petroleum distillates used as solvents for fats or as motor fuels

ben·zo·ate \'ben-zə-ˌwāt\ *n* : a salt or ester of benzoic acid

ben·zo·ic acid \ben-ˌzō-ik-\ *n* : a white crystalline acid used as a preservative and antiseptic and in synthesizing chemicals

ben·zo·in \'ben-zə-wən, -ˌzȯin\ *n* : a balsamlike resin from trees of southern Asia used esp. in medicine and perfumes

be·queath \bi-'kwēth, -'kwēth\ *vb* [ME *bequethen*, fr. OE *becwethan*, fr. *be-* + *cwethan* to say] **1** : to leave by will **2** : to hand down

be·quest \bi-'kwest\ *n* **1** : the action of bequeathing **2** : something bequeathed : LEGACY

be·rate \-'rāt\ *vb* : to scold harshly

Ber·ber \'bər-bər\ *n* : a member of a Caucasoid people of northwestern Africa

ber·ceuse \ber-'sə(r)z\ *n, pl* **berceuses** \-'sə(r)z(-əz)\ [F, fr. *bercer* to rock] **1** : LULLABY **2** : a musical composition that resembles a lullaby

¹be·reaved \bi-'rēvd\ *adj* : suffering the death of a loved one — **be·reave·ment** *n*

²bereaved *n, pl* **bereaved** : one who is bereaved

be·reft \-'reft\ *adj* **1** : deprived of or lacking something — usu. used with *of* **2** : BEREAVED

be·ret \bə-'rā\ *n* : a round soft cap with no visor

berg \'bərg\ *n* : ICEBERG

beri·beri \ˌber-ē-'ber-ē\ *n* : a deficiency disease marked by weakness, wasting, and nerve damage and caused by lack of thiamine

berke·li·um \'bər-klē-əm\ *n* : an artificially prepared radioactive chemical element

Ber·mu·das \bər-'myüd-əz\ *n pl* : BERMUDA SHORTS

Bermuda shorts *n pl* : knee-length walking shorts

ber·ry \'ber-ē\ *n, pl* **berries 1** : a small pulpy fruit (as a strawberry) **2** : a simple fruit (as a grape, tomato, or banana) with the wall of the ripened ovary thick and pulpy **3** : the dry seed of some plants (as coffee)

ber·serk \bə(r)-'sərk, -'zərk\ *adj* [ON *berserkr* warrior frenzied in battle, fr. *björn* bear + *serkr* shirt] : FRENZIED, CRAZED — **berserk** *adv*

¹berth \'bərth\ *n* **1** : room enough for a ship to maneuver **2** : the place where a ship lies at anchor **3** : a place to sit or sleep esp. on a ship or vehicle **4** : JOB, POSITION **syn** post, situation, office, appointment

²berth *vb* **1** : to bring or come into a berth **2** : to allot a berth to

ber·yl \'ber-əl\ *n* : a hard silicate mineral occurring as green, yellow, pink, or white crystals

be·ryl·li·um \bə-'ril-ē-əm\ *n* : a light strong metallic chemical element used as a hardener in alloys

be·seech \bi-'sēch\ *vb* **-sought** \-'sȯt\ *or* **-seeched; -seech·ing** : to ask earnestly : ENTREAT **syn** implore, beg, plead, supplicate, importune

be·seem \bi-'sēm\ *vb, archaic* : to be seemly or fitting : BEFIT

be·set \-'set\ *vb* **1** : TROUBLE, HARASS **2** : ASSAIL; *also* : to hem in : SURROUND

be·set·ting *adj* : persistently present or assailing

¹be·side \bi-'sīd\ *adv, archaic* : BESIDES

²beside *prep* **1** : by the side of ⟨sit ~ me⟩ **2** : BESIDES **3** : not relevant to

¹be·sides \bi-'sīdz\ *prep* **1** : other than ⟨there's nobody here ~ me⟩ **2** : together with ⟨~ being pretty, she's intelligent⟩

²besides *adv* **1** : in addition : ALSO **2** : MOREOVER

be·siege \bi-'sēj\ *vb* : to lay siege to; *also* : IMPORTUNE — **be·sieg·er** *n*

be·smear \-'smiər\ *vb* : SMEAR

be·smirch \-'smərch\ *vb* : SMIRCH, SOIL

be·som \'bē-zəm\ *n* : BROOM

be·sot \bi-'sät\ *vb* **be·sot·ted; be·sot·ting** : to make dull or stupid; *esp* : to muddle with drunkenness

be·spat·ter \-'spat-ər\ *vb* : SPATTER

be·speak \bi-'spēk\ *vb* **-spoke** \-'spōk\; **-spo·ken** \-'spō-kən\; **-speak·ing 1** : to hire or arrange for beforehand **2** : IN-DICATE, SIGNIFY **3** : FORETELL

be·sprin·kle \-'sprin-kəl\ *vb* : SPRINKLE

¹**best** \'best\ *adj,* superlative of GOOD **1** : excelling all others **2** : most productive (as of good or satisfaction) **3** : LARGEST, MOST

²**best** *adv,* superlative of WELL **1** : in the best way **2** : MOST

³**best** *n* : something that is best

⁴**best** *vb* : to get the better of : OUTDO

bes·tial \'bes-chəl\ *adj* **1** : of or relating to beasts **2** : resembling a beast esp. in lack of intelligence or reason

bes·ti·al·i·ty \,bes-chē-'al-ət-ē\ *n, pl* **-ties 1** : the condition or status of a lower animal **2** : display or gratification of bestial traits or impulses

bes·ti·ary \'bes-chē-,er-ē\ *n, pl* **-ar·ies** : a medieval allegorical or moralizing work on the appearance and habits of animals

be·stir \bi-'stər\ *vb* : to rouse to action

best man *n* : the principal groomsman at a wedding

be·stow \bi-'stō\ *vb* **1** : PUT, PLACE, STOW **2** : to present as a gift : CONFER — **be·stow·al** *n*

be·stride \bi-'strīd\ *vb* **-strode** \-'strōd\; **-strid·den** \-'strid-ᵊn\; **-strid·ing** \-'strīd-in\ : to ride, sit, or stand astride

¹**bet** \'bet\ *n* **1** : something that is risked or pledged on the outcome of a contest **2** : an agreement requiring the person whose guess about a result proves wrong to give something to a person whose guess proves right; *also* : the making of such an agreement

²**bet** *vb* **bet** *also* **bet·ted; bet·ting 1** : to stake on the outcome of an issue ⟨*bet* $2 on the race⟩ **2** : to make a bet with **3** : to lay a bet

³**bet** *abbr* between

be·take \bi-'tāk\ *vb* **-took** \-'tùk\; **-tak·en** \-'tā-kən\; **-tak·ing** : to cause (oneself) to go

be·ta particle \'bāt-ə-\ *n* : an electron or positron ejected from an atomic nucleus during radioactive transformation; *also* : a high-speed electron or positron

beta ray *n* **1** : BETA PARTICLE **2** : a stream of beta particles

be·ta·tron \'bāt-ə-,trän\ *n* : an electron accelerator

be·tel \'bēt-ᵊl\ *n* : a climbing pepper whose leaves are chewed together with lime and betel nut as a stimulant esp. by southern Asians

betel nut *n* : the astringent seed of an Asian palm that is chewed with betel leaves

bête noire \,bet-nə-'wär, ,bāt-\ *n, pl* **bêtes noires** \,bet-nə-'wär(z), ,bāt-\ [F, lit., black beast] : a person or thing strongly disliked or feared

beth·el \'beth-əl\ *n* [Heb *bēth'ēl* house of God] : a place of worship esp. for seamen

be·think \bi-'think\ *vb* **-thought** \-'thòt\; **-think·ing** : to cause (oneself) to call to mind or consider

be·tide \bi-'tīd\ *vb* : to happen to

be·times \bi-'tīmz\ *adv* : in good time : EARLY **syn** soon, seasonably, timely

be·to·ken \bi-'tō-kən\ *vb* **-to·kened; -to·ken·ing** \-'tōk-(ə-)nin\ **1** : to give evidence of **2** : PRESAGE **syn** indicate, attest, bespeak, testify

be·tray \bi-'trā\ *vb* **1** : to lead astray; *esp* : SEDUCE **2** : to deliver to an enemy by treachery **3** : to prove unfaithful to **4** : to reveal unintentionally; *also* : SHOW, INDICATE **syn** mislead, delude, deceive, beguile — **be·tray·al** *n* — **be·tray·er** *n*

be·troth \bi-'träth, -'tròth, -'trōth, *or with* th\ *vb* : to promise to marry : AF-FIANCE — **be·troth·al** *n*

be·trothed *n* : the person to whom one is betrothed

¹**bet·ter** \'bet-ər\ *adj,* comparative of GOOD **1** : more than half **2** : improved in health **3** : more attractive, favorable, or commendable **4** : more advantageous or effective **5** : improved in accuracy or performance

²**better** *vb* **1** : to make or become better **2** : SURPASS, EXCEL

³**better** *adv,* comparative of WELL **1** : in a superior manner **2** : to a higher or greater degree; *also* : MORE

⁴**better** *n* **1** : something better; *also* : a superior esp. in merit or rank **2** : AD-VANTAGE

bet·ter·ment \'bet-ər-mənt\ *n* : IM-PROVEMENT

bet·tor *or* **bet·ter** \'bet-ər\ *n* : one that bets

¹**be·tween** \bi-ˈtwēn\ *prep* **1** : by the common action of ⟨earned $10,000 ∼ the two of them⟩ **2** : in the interval separating ⟨an alley ∼ two buildings⟩ **3** : marking or constituting the interrelation or interaction of ⟨hostility ∼ nations⟩ **4** : in point of comparison of ⟨choose ∼ two cars⟩

²**between** *adv* : in an intervening space or interval

be·twixt \bi-ˈtwikst\ *adv or prep* : BETWEEN

¹**bev·el** \ˈbev-əl\ *n* **1** : a device for adjusting the slant of the surfaces of a piece of work **2** : the angle or slant that one surface or line makes with another when not at right angles

²**bevel** *vb* **-eled** *or* **-elled; -el·ing** *or* **-el·ling** \ˈbev-(ə-)liŋ\ **1** : to cut or shape (as an edge or surface) to a bevel **2** : INCLINE, SLANT

bev·er·age \ˈbev-(ə-)rij\ *n* : a drinkable liquid

bevy \ˈbev-ē\ *n, pl* **bev·ies 1** : a large group or collection **2** : a group of animals and esp. quail together

be·wail \bi-ˈwāl\ *vb* : LAMENT **syn** deplore, bemoan, grieve, moan, weep

be·ware \-ˈwaər\ *vb* : to be on one's guard : be wary of

be·wil·der \bi-ˈwil-dər\ *vb* **-wil·dered; -wil·der·ing** \-d(ə-)riŋ\ : PERPLEX, CONFUSE **syn** mystify, distract, puzzle — **be·wil·der·ment** *n*

be·witch \-ˈwich\ *vb* **1** : to affect by witchcraft **2** : CHARM, FASCINATE **syn** enchant, attract, captivate — **be·witch·ment** *n*

bey \ˈbā\ *n* **1** : a former Turkish provincial governor **2** : the former native ruler of Tunis or Tunisia

¹**be·yond** \bē-ˈänd\ *adv* **1** : FARTHER **2** : BESIDES

²**beyond** *prep* **1** : on or to the farther side of **2** : out of the reach or sphere of **3** : BESIDES

be·zel \ˈbē-zəl, ˈbez-əl\ *n* **1** : a sloping edge on a cutting tool **2** : the faceted part of a cut gem that rises above the setting **3** : a usu. grooved rim holding a transparent covering (as on a watch)

bf *abbr* boldface

BG *or* **B Gen** *abbr* brigadier general

bhang \ˈbaŋ\ *n* : a narcotic and intoxicant product of the hemp plant

Bi *symbol* bismuth

BIA *abbr* Bureau of Indian Affairs

bi·an·nu·al \(ˈ)bī-ˈan-yə(-wə)l\ *adj* : occurring twice a year — **bi·an·nu·al·ly** \-ē\ *adv*

¹**bi·as** \ˈbī-əs\ *n* **1** : a line diagonal to the grain of a fabric **2** : PREJUDICE, BENT

²**bias** *adv* : on the bias : DIAGONALLY

³**bias** *vb* **bi·ased** *or* **bi·assed; bi·as·ing** *or* **bi·as·sing** : PREJUDICE

bi·as–ply tire \ˈbī-əs-ˌplī-\ *n* : a pneumatic tire having crossed layers of ply cord set diagonally to the center line of the tread

bi·ath·lon \bī-ˈath-lən, -ˌlän\ *n* : a composite athletic contest consisting of cross-country skiing and target shooting with a rifle

¹**bib** \ˈbib\ *n* : a protective cover tied under a child's chin to protect the clothes

²**bib** *abbr* Bible; biblical

bi·be·lot \ˈbē-bə-ˌlō\ *n, pl* **bibelots** \-ˌlō(z)\ : a small household ornament or decorative object

Bi·ble \ˈbī-bəl\ *n* [ME, fr. OF, fr. ML *biblia*, fr. Gk, pl. of *biblion* book, fr. *byblos* papyrus, book, fr. *Byblos*, ancient Phoenician city from which papyrus was exported] **1** : the sacred scriptures of Christians comprising the Old and New Testaments **2** : the sacred scriptures of Judaism or of some other religion — **bib·li·cal** \ˈbib-li-kəl\ *adj*

bib·li·og·ra·phy \ˌbib-lē-ˈäg-rə-fē\ *n, pl* **-phies 1** : the history or description of writings or publications **2** : a list of writings (as on a subject or of an author) — **bib·li·og·ra·pher** \-fər\ *n* — **bib·li·o·graph·ic** \-lē-ə-ˈgraf-ik\ *also* **bib·li·o·graph·i·cal** \-i-kəl\ *adj*

bib·lio·phile \ˈbib-lē-ə-ˌfīl\ *n* : a lover of books

bib·u·lous \ˈbib-yə-ləs\ *adj* **1** : highly absorbent **2** : fond of alcoholic beverages

bi·cam·er·al \ˈbī-ˈkam-(ə-)rəl\ *adj* : having or consisting of two legislative branches

bi·car·bon·ate \ˈbī-ˈkär-bə-ˌnāt, -nət\ *n* : an acid carbonate

bicarbonate of soda : SODIUM BICARBONATE

bi·cen·te·na·ry \ˌbī-sen-ˈten-ə-rē, bī-ˈsent-ᵊn-ˌer-ē\ *n* : BICENTENNIAL — **bicentenary** *adj*

bi·cen·ten·ni·al \ˌbī-sen-'ten-ē-əl\ *n* : a 200th anniversary or its celebration — **bicentennial** *adj*

bi·ceps \'bī-ˌseps\ *n, pl* **biceps** *also* **bicepses** [NL, fr. L, two-headed, fr. *bi-* two + *caput* head] : a muscle (as in the front of the upper arm) having two points of origin

bi·chlo·ride of mercury \bī-'klȯr-ˌīd-\ : MERCURIC CHLORIDE

¹**bick·er** \'bik-ər\ *n* : QUARRELING, ALTERCATION

²**bicker** *vb* **bick·ered; bick·er·ing** \-(ə-)riŋ\ : to contend in petty altercation : SQUABBLE

bi·con·cave \ˌbī-(ˌ)kän-'kāv, bī-'kän-ˌkāv\ *adj* : concave on both sides ⟨red blood cells are ∼⟩

bi·con·vex \ˌbī-(ˌ)kän-'veks, 'bī-'kän-ˌveks\ *adj* : convex on both sides

bi·cus·pid \bī-'kəs-pəd\ *n* : PREMOLAR

¹**bi·cy·cle** \'bī-ˌsik-əl\ *n* : a light 2-wheeled vehicle with a steering handle, saddle, and pedals

²**bicycle** *vb* **-cy·cled; -cy·cling** \-ˌsik-(ə-)liŋ, -ˌsīk-\ : to ride a bicycle — **bi·cy·cler** \-lər\ *n* — **bi·cy·clist** \-ləst\ *n*

¹**bid** \'bid\ *vb* **bade** \'bad, 'bād\ *or* **bid; bid·den** \'bid-ᵊn\ *or* **bid** *also* **bade; bid·ding** 1 : COMMAND, ORDER 2 : INVITE 3 : to give expression to 4 : to make a bid : OFFER — **bid·der** *n*

²**bid** *n* 1 : an act of bidding; *also* : a chance or turn to bid 2 : an offer (as at an auction) of what one will give for something; *also* : the thing or sum offered 3 : INVITATION 4 : an announcement by a player in a card game of what he or she proposes to accomplish; *also* : an attempt to win or gain

bid·da·ble \'bid-ə-bəl\ *adj* 1 : OBEDIENT, DOCILE 2 : capable of being bid

bid·dy \'bid-ē\ *n, pl* **biddies** : a hen or young chicken

bide \'bīd\ *vb* **bode** \'bōd\ *or* **bid·ed; bided; bid·ing** 1 : WAIT, TARRY 2 : DWELL 3 : to wait for

bi·det \bi-'dā\ *n* : a fixture about the height of a chair seat used esp. for bathing the external genitals and the posterior parts of the body

bi·di·rec·tion·al \ˌbī-də-'rek-sh(ə-)nəl\ *adj* : involving, moving, or taking place in two usu. opposite directions — **bi·di·rec·tion·al·ly** *adv*

bi·en·ni·al \bī-'en-ē-əl\ *adj* 1 : taking place once in two years 2 : lasting two years 3 : producing leaves the first year and fruiting and dying the second year — **biennial** *n* — **bi·en·ni·al·ly** \-ē\ *adv*

bi·en·ni·um \bī-'en-ē-əm\ *n, pl* **-niums** *or* **-nia** \-ē-ə\ [L, fr. *bi-* two + *annus* year] : a period of two years

bier \'biər\ *n* : a stand bearing a coffin or corpse

bi·fo·cal \bī-'fō-kəl\ *adj* : having two focal lengths

bifocals \bī-'fō-kəlz\ *n pl* : eyeglasses with lenses that have one part that corrects for near vision and one for distant vision

bi·fur·cate \'bī-fər-ˌkāt, bī-'fər-\ *vb* **-cat·ed; -cat·ing** : to divide into two branches or parts — **bi·fur·ca·tion** \ˌbī-fər-'kā-shən\ *n*

big \'big\ *adj* **big·ger; big·gest** 1 : large in size, amount, or scope 2 : PREGNANT; *also* : SWELLING 3 : IMPORTANT, IMPOSING **syn** great, large, oversize — **big·ness** *n*

big·a·my \'big-ə-mē\ *n* : the act of marrying one person while still legally married to another — **big·a·mist** \-məst\ *n* — **big·a·mous** \-məs\ *adj*

big bang theory *n* : a theory in astronomy: the universe originated from the explosion of a single mass of material so that the pieces are still flying apart

big brother *n* 1 : an older brother 2 : a man who befriends a delinquent or friendless boy 3 *cap both Bs* : the leader of an authoritarian state or movement

Big Dipper *n* : DIPPER 3

big·foot \'big-ˌfut\ *n* : SASQUATCH

big·horn \'big-ˌhȯrn\ *n, pl* **bighorn** *or* **bighorns** : a wild sheep of mountainous western No. America

bight \'bīt\ *n* 1 : a curve in a coast; *also* : the bay formed by such a curve 2 : a slack part in a rope

big–name \'big-'nām\ *adj* : widely popular ⟨a ∼ performer⟩ — **big name** *n*

big·ot \'big-ət\ *n* : one intolerantly devoted to his or her own church, party, or opinion **syn** fanatic, enthusiast, zealot — **big·ot·ed** \-ət-əd\ *adj* — **big·ot·ry** \-ə-trē\ *n*

big shot \'big-ˌshät\ *n* : an important person

big time \-ˌtīm\ *n* 1 : a high-paying

vaudeville circuit requiring only two performances a day **2** : the top rank of an activity or enterprise — **big–tim・er** \-ˌtī-mər\ *n*

big top *n* **1** : the main tent of a circus **2** : CIRCUS

big・wig \ˈbig-ˌwig\ *n* : BIG SHOT

bike \ˈbīk\ *n* **1** : BICYCLE **2** : MOTORCY-CLE

bik・er *n* : MOTORCYCLIST; *esp* : one who is a member of an organized gang

bike・way \ˈbīk-ˌwā\ *n* : a thoroughfare for bicycles

bi・ki・ni \bə-ˈkē-nē\ *n* : a woman's brief 2-piece bathing suit

bi・lat・er・al \bī-ˈlat-(ə-)rəl\ *adj* **1** : having or involving two sides **2** : affecting reciprocally two sides or parties — **bi・lat・er・al・ly** \-ē\ *adv*

bile \ˈbīl\ *n* **1** : a bitter greenish fluid secreted by the liver that aids in the digestion of fats **2** : an ill-humored mood

bilge \ˈbilj\ *n* **1** : the part of a ship that lies between the bottom and the point where the sides go straight up **2** : stale or worthless remarks or ideas

bi・lin・gual \bī-ˈliŋ-gwəl\ *adj* : expressed in, knowing, or using two languages

bil・ious \ˈbil-yəs\ *adj* **1** : marked by or suffering from disordered liver function **2** : IRRITABLE, CHOLERIC — **bil・ious・ness** *n*

bilk \ˈbilk\ *vb* : CHEAT, SWINDLE

¹bill \ˈbil\ *n* : the jaws of a bird together with their horny covering; *also* : a mouth structure (as of a turtle) resembling these

²bill *vb* : to caress fondly

³bill *n* **1** : a written document or note; *esp* : a draft of a law presented to a legislature for enactment **2** : a written statement of a legal wrong suffered or of some breach of law **3** : an itemized statement of particulars **4** : an itemized account of the separate cost of goods sold, services performed, or work done **5** : an advertisement (as a poster or handbill) displayed or distributed **6** : a piece of paper money

⁴bill *vb* **1** : to enter in or prepare a bill; *also* : to submit a bill or account to **2** : to advertise by bills or posters

bill・board \-ˌbōrd\ *n* : a flat surface on which advertising bills are posted

¹bil・let \ˈbil-ət\ *n* **1** : an order requiring a person to provide lodging for a soldier; *also* : quarters assigned by or as if by such an order **2** : POSITION, APPOINTMENT

²billet *vb* : to assign lodging to by billet

bil・let–doux \ˌbil-ā-ˈdü\ *n, pl* **billets–doux** \-ā-ˈdü(z)\ [F *billet doux,* lit., sweet letter] : a love letter

bill・fold \ˈbil-ˌfōld\ *n* : WALLET

bil・liards \ˈbil-yərdz\ *n* : any of several games played on a rectangular table by driving balls against each other or into pockets with a cue

bil・lings・gate \ˈbil-iŋz-ˌgāt, *Brit usu* -git\ *n* [*Billingsgate,* old gate and fish market, London, England] : coarsely abusive language

bil・lion \ˈbil-yən\ *n* **1** : a thousand millions **2** *Brit* : a million millions — **billion** *adj* — **bil・lionth** \-yənth\ *adj or n*

bill of exchange : a written order from one party to another to pay to a person named in the bill a specified sum of money

¹bil・low \ˈbil-ō\ *n* **1** : WAVE; *esp* : a great wave **2** : a rolling mass (as of fog or flame) like a great wave — **bil・lowy** \ˈbil-ə-wē\ *adj*

²billow *vb* : to rise and roll in waves; *also* : to swell out ⟨~*ing* sails⟩

bil・ly \ˈbil-ē\ *n, pl* **billies** : BILLY CLUB

billy club *n* : a heavy usu. wooden club; *esp* : a policeman's club

bil・ly goat \ˈbil-ē-\ *n* : a male goat

bi・met・al \ˈbī-ˌmet-ᵊl\ *adj* : BIMETALLIC — **bimetal** *n*

bi・me・tal・lic \ˌbī-mə-ˈtal-ik\ *adj* : made of two different metals — often used of devices having a bonded expansive part — **bimetallic** *n*

bi・met・al・lism \bī-ˈmet-ᵊl-ˌiz-əm\ *n* : the policy of using two metals at fixed ratios to form a standard of value for a monetary system

¹bi・month・ly \bī-ˈmənth-lē\ *adj* **1** : occurring every two months **2** : occurring twice a month : SEMIMONTHLY — **bimonthly** *adv*

²bimonthly *n* : a bimonthly publication

bin \ˈbin\ *n* : a box, crib, or enclosure used for storage

bi・na・ry \ˈbī-nə-rē\ *adj* **1** : consisting of two things or parts : DOUBLE **2** : relating to, being, or belonging to a system of numbers having 2 as its base ⟨the ∼ digits 0 and 1⟩ **3** : involving a choice between or condition of two alternatives only (as on-off, yes-no) — **binary** *n*

binary star *n* : a system of two stars revolving around each other

bin·au·ral \bī-'nȯr-əl\ *adj* : of or relating to sound reproduction involving the use of two separated microphones and two transmission channels to achieve a stereophonic effect

bind \'bīnd\ *vb* **bound** \'baȯnd\; **bind·ing 1** : TIE; *also* : to restrain as if by tying **2** : to put under an obligation; *also* : to constrain with legal authority **3** : BANDAGE **4** : to unite into a mass **5** : to compel as if by a pledge **6** : to strengthen or decorate with a band **7** : to fasten together and enclose in a cover ⟨∼ books⟩ **8** : to exert a tying, restraining, or compelling effect — **bind·er** *n*

bind·ing \'bīn-diŋ\ *n* : something (as a ski fastening, a cover, or an edging fabric) used to bind

binge \'binj\ *n* : SPREE

bin·go \'biŋ-gō\ *n, pl* **bingos** : a game of chance played with cards having numbered squares corresponding to numbered balls drawn at random and won by covering five squares in a row

bin·na·cle \'bin-i-kəl\ *n* [alter. of ME *bitakle*, fr. Pg or Sp; Pg *bitácola* & Sp *bitácula*, fr. L *habitaculum* dwelling place, fr. *habitare* to inhabit] : a container holding a ship's compass

¹bin·oc·u·lar \bī-'näk-yə-lər, bə-\ *adj* : of, relating to, or adapted to the use of both eyes — **bin·oc·u·lar·ly** *adv*

²bin·oc·u·lar \bə-'näk-yə-lər, bī-\ *n* **1** : a binocular optical instrument (as a microscope) **2** : a hand-held optical instrument composed of two telescopes and a focusing device — usu. used in pl.

bi·no·mi·al \bī-'nō-mē-əl\ *n* **1** : a mathematical expression consisting of two terms connected by the sign plus (+) or minus (−) **2** : a biological species name consisting of two terms — **binomial** *adj*

bio·chem·is·try \ˌbī-ō-'kem-ə-strē\ *n* : chemistry that deals with the chemical compounds and processes occurring in living things — **bio·chem·i·cal**

\-i-kəl\ *adj or n* — **bio·chem·ist** \-əst\ *n*

bio·de·grad·able \-di-'grād-ə-bəl\ *adj* : capable of being broken down esp. into innocuous products by the actions of living things (as microorganisms) ⟨a ∼ detergent⟩ — **bio·de·grad·abil·i·ty** \-ˌgrād-ə-'bil-ət-ē\ *n* — **bio·deg·ra·da·tion** \-ˌdeg-rə-'dā-shən\ *n* — **bio·de·grade** \-di-'grād\ *vb*

bio·feed·back \-'fēd-ˌbak\ *n* : the technique of making unconscious or involuntary bodily processes (as heartbeat or brain waves) objectively perceptible to the senses (as by use of an oscilloscope) in order to manipulate them by conscious mental control

biog *abbr* biographer; biographical; biography

bio·ge·og·ra·phy \ˌbī-ō-jē-'äg-rə-fē\ *n* : a branch of biology that deals with the distribution of plants and animals — **bio·ge·og·ra·pher** \-fər\ *n*

bi·og·ra·phy \bī-'äg-rə-fē, bē-\ *n, pl* **-phies** : a written history of a person's life; *also* : such writings in general — **bi·og·ra·pher** \-fər\ *n* — **bi·o·graph·i·cal** \ˌbī-ə-'graf-i-kəl\ *also* **bi·o·graph·ic** \-ik\ *adj*

biol *abbr* biologic; biological; biologist; biology

biological clock *n* : an inherent timing mechanism inferred to exist in some living systems (as a cell) in order to explain various cyclical physiological and behavioral responses

biological warfare *n* : warfare in which living organisms (as bacteria) are used to harm the enemy or his livestock and crops

bi·ol·o·gy \bī-'äl-ə-jē\ *n* [G *biologie*, fr. Gk *bios* mode of life + *logos* word] **1** : a science that deals with living beings and life processes **2** : the life processes of an organism or group — **bi·o·log·i·cal** \ˌbī-ə-'läj-i-kəl\ *also* **bi·o·log·ic** \-ik\ *adj* — **bi·ol·o·gist** \bī-'äl-ə-jəst\ *n*

bio·med·i·cal \ˌbī-ō-'med-i-kəl\ *adj* : of, relating to, or involving biological, medical, and physical science

bi·on·ic \bī-'än-ik\ *adj* : having normal biological capability or performance enhanced by or as if by electronic or mechanical devices

bio·phys·ics \ˌbī-ō-'fiz-iks\ *n* : a branch of science concerned with the application of physical principles and methods to biological problems — **bio·phys·i·cal** \-i-kəl\ *adj* — **bio·phys·i·cist** \-'fiz-ə-səst\ *n*

bi·op·sy \'bī-ˌäp-sē\ *n, pl* **-sies** : the removal of tissue, cells, or fluids from the living body for examination

bio·rhythm \'bī-ō-ˌri̱th-əm\ *n* : an inherent rhythm that appears to control or initiate various biological processes

bio·sphere \'bī-ə-ˌsfiər\ *n* **1** : the part of the world in which life can exist **2** : living beings together with their environment

bi·ot·ic \bī-'ät-ik\ *adj* : of or relating to life; *esp* : caused by living beings

bi·o·tin \'bī-ə-tən\ *n* : a member of the vitamin B complex found esp. in yeast, liver, and egg yolk and active in growth promotion

bi·o·tite \'bī-ə-ˌtīt\ *n* : a dark mica containing iron, magnesium, potassium, and aluminum

bi·par·ti·san \bī-'pärt-ə-zən\ *adj* : representing or composed of members of two parties

bi·par·tite \-'pär-ˌtīt\ *adj* **1** : being in two parts **2** : shared by two ⟨~ treaty⟩

bi·ped \'bī-ˌped\ *n* : a 2-footed animal

bi·plane \'bī-ˌplān\ *n* : an airplane with two wings placed one above the other

bi·po·lar \bī-'pō-lər\ *adj* : having or involving the use of two poles — **bi·po·lar·i·ty** \ˌbī-pō-'lar-ət-ē\ *n*

bi·ra·cial \bī-'rā-shəl\ *adj* : of, relating to, or involving members of two races

¹**birch** \'bərch\ *n* **1** : any of a genus of mostly short-lived deciduous shrubs and trees with membranous outer bark and pale close-grained wood; *also* : this wood **2** : a birch rod or bundle of twigs for flogging — **birch** *or* **birch·en** \'bər-chən\ *adj*

²**birch** *vb* : WHIP, FLOG

Birch·er \'bər-chər\ *n* : a member or adherent of the John Birch Society — **Birch·ism** \'bər-ˌchiz-əm\ *n* — **Birch·ist** \-chəst\ *or* **Birch·ite** \-ˌchīt\ *n*

bird \'bərd\ *n* : any of a class of warm-blooded egg-laying vertebrates having the body feathered and the forelimbs modified to form wings

bird·bath \'bərd-ˌbath, -ˌbȧth\ *n* : a usu. ornamental basin set up for birds to bathe in

bird·house \-ˌhaůs\ *n* : an artificial nesting place for birds; *also* : AVIARY

bird·ie \'bərd-ē\ *n* : a score of one under par on a hole in golf

bird·lime \-ˌlīm\ *n* : a sticky substance smeared on twigs to snare small birds

bird of paradise : any of numerous brilliantly colored plumed birds of the New Guinea area

bird of prey : a carnivorous bird that feeds wholly or chiefly on carrion or on meat taken by hunting

bird·seed \'bərd-ˌsēd\ *n* : a mixture of small seeds (as of hemp or millet) used for feeding birds

bird's—eye \'bərd-ˌzī\ *adj* **1** : seen from above as if by a flying bird ⟨~ view⟩; *also* : CURSORY **2** : marked with spots resembling birds' eyes ⟨~ maple⟩; *also* : made of bird's-eye wood

bi·ret·ta \bə-'ret-ə\ *n* : a square cap with three ridges on top worn esp. by Roman Catholic clergymen

birr \'bir, 'bər\ *n* — see MONEY table

birth \'bərth\ *n* **1** : the act or fact of being born or of bringing forth young **2** : LINEAGE, DESCENT **3** : ORIGIN, BEGINNING

birth control *n* : control of the number of children born esp. by preventing or lessening the frequency of conception

birth·day \'bərth-ˌdā\ *n* : the day or anniversary of one's birth

birth defect *n* : a physical or biochemical defect present at birth and inherited or environmentally induced

birth·mark \'bərth-ˌmärk\ *n* : an unusual mark or blemish on the skin at birth

birth·place \-ˌplās\ *n* : place of birth or origin

birth·rate \-ˌrāt\ *n* : the number of births for every 100 or every 1000 persons in a given area or group during a given time

birth·right \-ˌrīt\ *n* : a right, privilege, or possession to which one is entitled by birth **syn** legacy, patrimony, heritage, inheritance

birth·stone \-ˌstōn\ *n* : a gemstone associated symbolically with the month of one's birth

bis·cuit \'bis-kət\ *n* [ME *bisquite*, fr. MF *bescuit*, fr. (*pain*) *bescuit* twice-cooked bread] **1** : a crisp flat cake; *esp, Brit* : CRACKER **2** 2 : a small quick bread made from dough that has been rolled and cut or dropped from a spoon

bi·sect \'bī-ˌsekt\ *vb* : to divide into two usu. equal parts; *also* : CROSS, INTERSECT — **bi·sec·tion** \'bī-ˌsek-shən\ *n* — **bi·sec·tor** \-tər\ *n*

bi·sex·u·al \bī-'sek-sh(ə-w)əl\ *adj* 1 : possessing characters of or having sexual desire for both sexes 2 : of, relating to, or involving two sexes — **bisexual** *n* — **bi·sex·u·al·i·ty** \ˌbī-ˌsek-shə-'wal-ət-ē\ *n*

bish·op \'bish-əp\ *n* [ME *bisshop,* fr. OE *bisceop,* fr. L *episcopus,* fr. Gk *episkopos,* lit., overseer, fr. *epi-* on, over + *skeptesthai* to look] 1 : a clergyman ranking above a priest and typically governing a diocese 2 : any of various Protestant church officials who superintend other clergy 3 : a chess piece that can move diagonally across any number of adjoining unoccupied squares

bish·op·ric \'bish-ə-prik\ *n* 1 : DIOCESE 2 : the office of bishop

bis·muth \'biz-məth\ *n* : a heavy brittle grayish white metallic chemical element used in alloys and medicine

bi·son \'bīs-ᵊn, 'bīz-\ *n, pl* **bison** : BUFFALO 2

bisque \'bisk\ *n* : a thick cream soup

bis·tro \'bēs-trō, 'bis-\ *n, pl* **bistros** [F] 1 : a small or unpretentious European restaurant 2 : BAR; *also* : NIGHTCLUB

¹**bit** \'bit\ *n* 1 : the part of a bridle that is placed in a horse's mouth 2 : the biting or cutting edge or part of a tool

²**bit** *n* 1 : a morsel of food; *also* : a small piece or quantity of something 2 : a small coin; *also* : a unit of value equal to 12½ cents 3 : something small or trivial; *also* : an indefinite usu. small degree or extent ⟨a ∼ tired⟩

³**bit** *n* [*bi*nary digi*t*] : a unit of computer information equivalent to the result of a choice between two alternatives; *also* : its physical representation

¹**bitch** \'bich\ *n* 1 : a female canine; *esp* : a female dog 2 : a malicious, spiteful, and domineering woman

²**bitch** *vb* : COMPLAIN

¹**bite** \'bīt\ *vb* **bit** \'bit\; **bit·ten** \'bit-ᵊn\ *also* **bit**; **bit·ing** \'bīt-iŋ\ 1 : to grip with teeth or jaws; *also* : to wound or sting with or as if with fangs 2 : to cut or pierce with or as if with a sharp-edged instrument 3 : to cause to smart or sting 4 : CORRODE 5 : to take bait

²**bite** *n* 1 : the act or manner of biting 2 : MORSEL, SNACK 3 : a wound made by biting; *also* : a biting sensation

bit·ing \'bīt-iŋ\ *adj* : SHARP, CUTTING

bit·ter \'bit-ər\ *adj* 1 : being or inducing the one of the basic taste sensations that is acrid, astringent, or disagreeable and is suggestive of hops 2 : marked by intensity or severity (as of distress or hatred) 3 : extremely harsh or cruel — **bit·ter·ly** *adv* — **bit·ter·ness** *n*

bit·tern \'bit-ərn\ *n* : any of various small or medium-sized herons with a booming cry

bit·ters \'bit-ərz\ *n sing or pl* : a usu. alcoholic solution of bitter and often aromatic plant products used in mixing drinks and as a mild tonic

¹**bit·ter·sweet** \'bit-ər-ˌswēt\ *n* 1 : a poisonous nightshade with purple flowers and orange-red berries 2 : a woody vine with yellow capsules that open when ripe and disclose scarlet seed coverings

²**bittersweet** *adj* : being at once both bitter and sweet

bi·tu·mi·nous coal \bə-'t(y)ü-mə-nəs-, bī-\ *n* : a coal that when heated yields considerable volatile waste matter

bi·valve \'bī-ˌvalv\ *n* : an animal (as a clam) with a shell composed of two separate parts that open and shut — **bivalve** *adj*

¹**biv·ouac** \'biv(-ə)-ˌwak\ *n* [F, fr. LG *biwake,* fr. *bi* at + *wake* guard] : a temporary encampment or shelter

²**bivouac** *vb* **-ouacked; -ouack·ing** : to form a bivouac : CAMP

¹**bi·week·ly** \'bī-'wē-klē\ *adj* 1 : occurring every two weeks : FORTNIGHTLY 2 : occurring twice a week — **biweekly** *adv*

²**biweekly** *n* : a biweekly publication

bi·year·ly \-'yiər-lē\ *adj* 1 : BIENNIAL 2 : BIANNUAL

bi·zarre \bə-'zär\ *adj* : ODD, ECCENTRIC, FANTASTIC — **bi·zarre·ly** *adv*

bk *abbr* 1 bank 2 book

Bk *symbol* berkelium

bkg *abbr* banking

bkgd *abbr* background

bks *abbr* barracks

bkt *abbr* **1** basket **2** bracket

bl *abbr* **1** bale **2** barrel **3** blue

blab \'blab\ *vb* **blabbed; blab·bing** : TATTLE, GOSSIP

¹black \'blak\ *adj* **1** : of the color black; *also* : very dark **2** : SWARTHY **3** : of or relating to a group of dark-haired dark-skinned people **4** : NEGRO; *also* : AFRO-AMERICAN **5** : SOILED, DIRTY **6** : lacking light ⟨a ∼ night⟩ **7** : WICKED, EVIL ⟨∼ deeds⟩ ⟨∼ magic⟩ **8** : DISMAL, GLOOMY ⟨a ∼ outlook⟩ **9** : SULLEN ⟨a ∼ mood⟩ — **black·ish** *adj* — **black·ly** *adv* — **black·ness** *n*

²black *n* **1** : a black pigment or dye; *also* : something (as clothing) that is black **2** : the color characteristic of soot or coal **3** : a person of a dark-skinned race; *esp* : NEGRO

³black *vb* : BLACKEN

black·a·moor \'blak-ə-ˌmur\ *n* : NEGRO

black–and–blue \ˌblak-ən-'blü\ *adj* : darkly discolored from blood effused by bruising

black art *n* : MAGIC, WITCHCRAFT

black·ball \'blak-ˌbol\ *n* : a black object used to cast a negative vote; *also* : such a vote — **black·ball** *vb*

black bass *n* : any of several freshwater sunfishes native to eastern and central No. America

¹black belt \'blak-ˌbelt\ *n, often cap both Bs* : an area densely populated by blacks

²black belt \-'belt\ *n* **1** : a rating of expert (as in judo or karate) **2** : one who holds a black belt

black·ber·ry \'blak-ˌber-ē\ *n* : the usu. black or purple juicy but seedy edible fruit of various brambles; *also* : a plant bearing this fruit

black·bird \'blak-ˌbərd\ *n* : any of various birds (as the red-winged blackbird) of which the male is largely or wholly black

black·board \-ˌbord\ *n* : a dark smooth surface (as of slate) used for writing or drawing on usu. with chalk

black·body \'blak-'bäd-ē\ *n* : a body or surface that completely absorbs incident radiation

black box *n* : a usu. complicated electronic device whose components and workings are unknown or mysterious to the user

black death *n* : a form of bacterial plague that spread rapidly in Europe and Asia in the 14th century

black·en \'blak-ən\ *vb* **black·ened; black·en·ing** \-(ə-)niŋ\ **1** : to make or become black **2** : DEFAME, SULLY

black eye *n* : a discoloration of the skin around the eye from bruising

black–eyed Su·san \ˌblak-ˌīd-'süz-ᵊn\ *n* : either of two No. American plants that are related to the daisies and have deep yellow to orange flower heads with dark conical centers

Black·foot \'blak-ˌfut\ *n, pl* **Black·feet** *or* **Blackfoot** : a member of an American Indian people of Montana, Alberta, and Saskatchewan

black·guard \'blag-ərd, -ˌärd\ *n* : SCOUNDREL, RASCAL

black·head \'blak-ˌhed\ *n* : a small oily mass plugging the outlet of a skin gland

black·ing \'blak-iŋ\ *n* : a substance applied to something to make it black

¹black·jack \-ˌjak\ *n* **1** : a leather-covered club with a flexible handle **2** : a card game in which the object is to be dealt cards having a higher count than the dealer but not exceeding 21

²blackjack *vb* : to hit with or as if with a blackjack

black light *n* : invisible ultraviolet or infrared radiation

black·list \'blak-ˌlist\ *n* : a list of persons who are disapproved of and are to be punished (as by refusal of jobs or a boycott) — **blacklist** *vb*

black·mail \'blak-ˌmāl\ *n* : extortion by threats esp. of public exposure; *also* : something so extorted — **blackmail** *vb* — **black·mail·er** *n*

black market *n* : illicit trade in goods; *also* : a place where such trade is carried on

Black Mass *n* : a travesty of the Christian mass ascribed to worshipers of Satan

Black Muslim *n* : a member of a chiefly black group that professes Islamic religious belief

black nationalist *n, often cap B&N* : a member of a group of militant blacks who advocate separatism from whites and the formation of self-governing black communities — **black nationalism** *n, often cap B&N*

black·out \'blak-ˌau̇t\ *n* **1** : a period of darkness due to electrical power failure **2** : a transitory loss or dulling of vision or consciousness **3** : the prohibition or restriction of the telecasting of sports events to ensure ticket sales — **black out** \-ˈau̇t\ *vb*

Black Panther *n* : a member of an organization of militant black Americans

black power *n* : the mobilization of the political and economic power of black Americans esp. to further racial equality

black sheep *n* : a discreditable member of an otherwise respectable group

black·smith \'blak-ˌsmith\ *n* : a worker who shapes heated iron by hammering it

black·thorn \-ˌthȯrn\ *n* : a European thorny plum

black·top \'blak-ˌtäp\ *n* : a very dark material containing mixtures of hydrocarbons (as asphalt) used esp. for surfacing roads — **blacktop** *vb*

black widow *n* : a venomous New World spider having the female black with an hourglass-shaped red mark on the underside of the abdomen

blad·der \'blad-ər\ *n* : a sac in which liquid or gas is stored; *esp* : one in a vertebrate into which urine passes from the kidneys

blade \'blād\ *n* **1** : a leaf of a plant and esp. of a grass; *also* : the flat part of a leaf as distinguished from its stalk **2** : something (as the flat part of an oar or an arm of a propeller) resembling the blade of a leaf **3** : the cutting part of an instrument or tool **4** : SWORD; *also* : SWORDSMAN **5** : a dashing fellow ⟨a gay ∼⟩ **6** : the runner of an ice skate

blain \'blān\ *n* : an inflammatory swelling or sore

¹blame \'blām\ *vb* **blamed; blam·ing** [ME *blamen,* fr. OF *blamer,* fr. L *blasphemare* to blaspheme, fr. Gk *blasphēmein*] **1** : to find fault with **2** : to hold responsible or responsible for **syn** censure, denounce, condemn, criticize — **blam·able** *adj*

²blame *n* **1** : CENSURE, REPROOF **2** : responsibility for fault or error **syn** guilt, fault, culpability, onus — **blame·less** *adj* — **blame·less·ly** *adv*

blame·wor·thy \-ˌwər-thē\ *adj* : deserving blame — **blame·wor·thi·ness** *n*

blanch \'blanch\ *vb* **1** : BLEACH **2** : to make or become white or pale

blanc·mange \blə-ˈmänj, -ˈmäⁿzh\ *n* [ME *blancmanger,* fr. MF *blanc manger,* lit., white food] : a dessert made from gelatin or a starchy substance and milk usu. sweetened and flavored

bland \'bland\ *adj* **1** : smooth in manner : SUAVE **2** : gently soothing ⟨a ∼ diet⟩; *also* : INSIPID **syn** gentle, mild, soft, balmy — **bland·ly** *adv* — **bland·ness** *n*

blan·dish·ment \'blan-dish-mənt\ *n* : flattering or coaxing speech or action : CAJOLERY

¹blank \'blaŋk\ *adj* **1** : showing or causing an appearance of dazed dismay; *also* : EXPRESSIONLESS **2** : DULL, EMPTY ⟨∼ moments⟩ **3** : free from writing or marks; *also* : having spaces to be filled in **4** : ABSOLUTE, DOWNRIGHT ⟨a ∼ refusal⟩ **5** : not shaped in final form — **blank·ly** *adv* — **blank·ness** *n*

²blank *n* **1** : an empty space **2** : a form with spaces for the entry of data **3** : the center of a target **4** : an unfinished form (as of a key) **5** : a cartridge with propellant and a wad but no projectile

³blank *vb* **1** : to cover or close up : OBSCURE **2** : to keep from scoring

blank check *n* **1** : a signed check with the amount unspecified **2** : complete freedom of action

¹blan·ket \'blaŋ-kət\ *n* **1** : a heavy woven often woolen covering **2** : a covering layer ⟨a ∼ of snow⟩

²blanket *vb* : to cover with a blanket

³blanket *adj* : covering a group or class ⟨∼ insurance⟩; *also* : applicable in all instances ⟨∼ rules⟩

blank verse *n* : unrhymed iambic pentameter

blare \'blaər\ *vb* **blared; blar·ing** : to sound loud and harsh; *also* : to proclaim loudly — **blare** *n*

blar·ney \'blär-nē\ *n* [*Blarney stone,* a stone in Blarney Castle, near Cork, Ireland, held to bestow skill in flattery on those who kiss it] : skillful flattery : BLANDISHMENT

bla·sé \blä-ˈzā\ *adj* [F] : not responsive to pleasure or excitement as a result of excessive indulgence; *also* : SOPHISTICATED

blas·pheme \blas-'fēm\ *vb* **blas·phemed; blas·phem·ing 1** : to speak of or address with irreverence **2** : to utter blasphemy

blas·phe·my \'blas-fə-mē\ *n, pl* **-mies 1** : the act of expressing lack of reverence for God **2** : irreverence toward something considered sacred — **blas·phe·mous** \-məs\ *adj*

¹blast \'blast\ *n* **1** : a violent gust of wind; *also* : its effect **2** : sound made by a wind instrument **3** : a current of air forced at high pressure through a hole in a furnace (**blast furnace**) **4** : a sudden withering esp. of plants : BLIGHT **5** : EXPLOSION; *also* : the often destructive wave of increased air pressure that moves outward from an explosion

²blast *vb* **1** : BLIGHT **2** : to shatter by or as if by an explosive

blast off \(')blast-'öf\ *vb* : TAKE OFF 4 — used esp. of rocket-propelled devices — **blast–off** \'blast-ˌöf\ *n*

bla·tant \'blāt-ᵊnt\ *adj* : offensively obtrusive : vulgarly showy **syn** vociferous, boisterous, clamorous, obstreperous — **bla·tan·cy** \-ᵊn-sē\ *n* — **bla·tant·ly** *adv*

blath·er \'blath-ər\ *vb* **blath·ered; blath·er·ing** \-(ə-)riŋ\ : to talk foolishly — **blather** *n*

blath·er·skite \'blath-ər-ˌskīt\ *n* : a blustering talkative person

¹blaze \'blāz\ *n* **1** : FIRE **2** : intense direct light accompanied by heat **3** : something (as a dazzling display or sudden outburst) suggesting fire ⟨a ∼ of autumn leaves⟩ **syn** glare, glow, flame

²blaze *vb* **blazed; blaz·ing 1** : to burn brightly; *also* : to flare up **2** : to be conspicuously bright : GLITTER

³blaze *vb* **blazed; blaz·ing** : to make public

⁴blaze *n* **1** : a white mark on the face of an animal **2** : a mark made on a tree or other fixed object usu. to leave a trail

⁵blaze *vb* **blazed; blaz·ing** : to mark (as a tree or trail) with blazes

blaz·er \'blā-zər\ *n* : a sports jacket often with notched collar and pockets that are stitched on

¹bla·zon \'blāz-ᵊn\ *n* **1** : COAT OF ARMS **2** : ostentatious display

²blazon *vb* **bla·zoned; bla·zon·ing** \'blāz-(ə-)niŋ\ **1** : to publish widely : PROCLAIM **2** : DECK, ADORN

bldg *abbr* building

bldr *abbr* builder

¹bleach \'blēch\ *vb* : WHITEN, BLANCH

²bleach *n* : a preparation used in bleaching

bleach·ers \'blē-chərz\ *n sing or pl* : a usu. uncovered stand containing lower-priced tiered seats for spectators

bleak \'blēk\ *adj* **1** : desolately barren and windswept **2** : lacking warm or cheering qualities — **bleak·ish** *adj* — **bleak·ly** *adv* — **bleak·ness** *n*

blear \'bliər\ *adj* : dim with water or tears ⟨∼ eyes⟩

bleary \'bli(ə)r-ē\ *adj* **1** : dull or dimmed esp. from fatigue or sleep **2** : poorly outlined or defined

bleat \'blēt\ *n* : the cry of a sheep or goat or a sound like it — **bleat** *vb*

bleed \'blēd\ *vb* **bled** \'bled\; **bleed·ing 1** : to lose or shed blood **2** : to be wounded; *also* : to feel pain or distress **3** : to flow or ooze from a wounded surface; *also* : to draw fluid from ⟨∼ a tire⟩ **4** : to extort money from

bleed·er \'blēd-ər\ *n* : one that bleeds; *esp* : HEMOPHILIAC

bleeding heart *n* **1** : a garden plant related to the poppies that has deep pink drooping heart-shaped flowers **2** : one who shows extreme sympathy esp. for an object of alleged persecution

¹blem·ish \'blem-ish\ *vb* : to spoil by a flaw : MAR

²blemish *n* : a noticeable flaw

¹blench \'blench\ *vb* [ME *blenchen* to deceive, blench, fr. OE *blencan* to deceive] : FLINCH, QUAIL **syn** shrink, recoil, wince, start

²blench *vb* : to grow or make pale

¹blend \'blend\ *vb* **blend·ed; blend·ing 1** : to mix thoroughly **2** : to prepare (as coffee) by mixing different varieties **3** : to combine into an integrated whole **4** : HARMONIZE **syn** fuse, merge, mingle, coalesce — **blend·er** *n*

²blend *n* : a product of blending **syn** compound, composite, alloy, mixture

bless \'bles\ *vb* **blessed** \'blest\ *also* **blest** \'blest\; **bless·ing** [ME *blessen*, fr. OE *blētsian*, fr. *blōd* blood; fr. the use of blood in consecration] **1** : to hallow or consecrate by religious rite or word **2** : to make the sign of the cross over **3** : to invoke divine care for **4** : PRAISE, GLORIFY **5** : to confer happiness upon

bless·ed \'bles-əd\ *also* **blest** \'blest\ *adj* **1** : HOLY **2** : BEATIFIED **3** : DELIGHTFUL — **bless·ed·ness** *n*

bless·ing \'bles-iŋ\ *n* **1** : the act or words of one who blesses **2** : a thing conducive to happiness **3** : grace said at a meal

blew past of BLOW

¹**blight** \'blīt\ *n* **1** : a plant disease or injury marked by withering; *also* : an organism causing a blight **2** : an impairing or frustrating influence; *also* : an impaired or damaged condition

²**blight** *vb* : to affect with or suffer from blight

blimp \'blimp\ *n* : a nonrigid airship

¹**blind** \'blīnd\ *adj* **1** : lacking or grossly deficient in ability to see; *also* : intended for blind persons **2** : not based on reason, evidence, or knowledge ⟨∼ faith⟩ **3** : not intelligently controlled or directed ⟨∼ chance⟩ **4** : performed solely by the aid of instruments within an airplane ⟨a ∼ landing⟩ **5** : hard to discern or make out : HIDDEN ⟨a ∼ seam⟩ **6** : lacking an opening or outlet ⟨a ∼ alley⟩ — **blind·ly** *adv* — **blind·ness** \'blīn(d)-nəs\ *n*

²**blind** *vb* **1** : to make blind **2** : DAZZLE **3** : DARKEN; *also* : HIDE

³**blind** *n* **1** : something (as a shutter) to hinder vision or keep out light **2** : a place of concealment **3** : SUBTERFUGE

blind date *n* : a date between persons who have not previously met; *also* : either of these persons

blind·er \'blīn-dər\ *n* : either of two flaps on a horse's bridle to prevent it from seeing to the side

blind·fold \'blīn(d)-ˌfōld\ *vb* : to cover the eyes of with or as if with a bandage — **blindfold** *n*

¹**blink** \'bliŋk\ *vb* **1** : WINK **2** : TWINKLE **3** : EVADE, IGNORE

²**blink** *n* **1** : GLIMMER, SPARKLE **2** : a usu. involuntary shutting and opening of the eye

blink·er \'bliŋ-kər\ *n* : a blinking light used as a signal

blin·tze \'blint-sə\ *or* **blintz** \'blints\ *n*

[Yiddish *blintse*] : a thin rolled pancake with a filling usu. of cream cheese

blip \'blip\ *n* **1** : an image on a radar screen **2** : ABERRATION 1

bliss \'blis\ *n* : complete happiness : JOY **syn** beatitude, blessedness — **bliss·ful** \-fəl\ *adj* — **bliss·ful·ly** \-fə-lē\ *adv*

¹**blis·ter** \'blis-tər\ *n* **1** : a raised area of skin containing watery fluid; *also* : an agent that causes blisters **2** : something (as a raised spot in paint) suggesting a blister **3** : a disease of plants marked by large swollen patches on the leaves

²**blister** *vb* **blis·tered**; **blis·ter·ing** \-t(ə-)riŋ\ : to develop a blister; *also* : to cause blisters

blithe \'blīth, 'blīth\ *adj* **blith·er**; **blith·est** : happily lighthearted **syn** merry, jovial, jolly, jocund — **blithe·ly** *adv* — **blithe·some** \-səm\ *adj*

blitz \'blits\ *n* **1** : an intensive series of air raids **2** : a fast intensive campaign **3** : a rush of the passer by the defensive linebackers in football — **blitz** *vb*

blitz·krieg \-ˌkrēg\ *n* [G, lit., lightning war, fr. *blitz* lightning + *krieg* war] : a sudden violent enemy attack

bliz·zard \'bliz-ərd\ *n* : a long severe snowstorm

blk *abbr* **1** black **2** block

bloat \'blōt\ *vb* : to swell by or as if by filling with water or air

bloat·er \'blōt-ər\ *n* : a fat herring or mackerel lightly salted and smoked

blob \'bläb\ *n* : a small lump or drop of a thick consistency

bloc \'bläk\ *n* [F, lit., block] : a combination of individuals or groups (as nations) working for a common purpose

¹**block** \'bläk\ *n* **1** : a solid piece of substantial material (as wood or stone) **2** : HINDRANCE, OBSTRUCTION; *also* : interruption of normal function of body or mind ⟨heart ∼⟩ **3** : a frame enclosing one or more pulleys and having a hook or strap by which it may be attached to objects **4** : a quantity of things considered as a unit ⟨a ∼ of seats⟩ **5** : a large building divided into separate units (as apartments or offices) **6** : a row of houses or shops **7** : a city square; *also* : the distance along one of the sides of such a square

8 : a piece of material with a hand-cut design on its surface from which copies are to be made

²block *vb* **1** : OBSTRUCT, CHECK **2** : to outline roughly ⟨~ out a statue⟩ **3** : to provide or support with a block ⟨~ up a wheel⟩ **syn** bar, impede, hinder, obstruct

¹block·ade \blä-'kād\ *vb* **block·ad·ed; block·ad·ing** : to subject to a blockade

²blockade *n* : the shutting off of a place usu. by troops or ships to prevent entrance or exit

block·bust·er \'bläk-,bəs-tər\ *n* : one that is very large, successful, or violent ⟨a ~ of a movie⟩

block·head \'bläk-,hed\ *n* : DOLT, DUNCE

block·house \-,haüs\ *n* : a small strong building used as a shelter (as from enemy fire) or observation post

¹blond *or* **blonde** \'bländ\ *adj* : fair in complexion; *also* : of a light or bleached color ⟨~ mahogany⟩ — **blond·ish** \-ish\ *adj*

²blond *or* **blonde** *n* : a person having blond hair

blood \'bləd\ *n* **1** : the red liquid that circulates in the heart, arteries, and veins of animals **2** : LIFEBLOOD; *also* : LIFE **3** : LINEAGE, STOCK **4** : KINSHIP; *also* : KINDRED **5** : the taking of life **6** : TEMPER, PASSION **7** : DANDY 1 — **blood·less** *adj* — **blood·stained** \-,stānd\ *adj* — **bloody** *adj*

blood bank *n* : a place where blood or plasma is stored

blood·bath \'bləd-,bath, -,bȧth\ *n* : MASSACRE

blood count *n* : the determination of the number of blood cells in a specific volume of blood; *also* : the number of cells so determined

blood·cur·dling \-,kərd-(ə-)liŋ\ *adj* : causing great horror or fear : TERRIFYING

blood·ed \'bləd-əd\ *adj* **1** : entirely or largely purebred ⟨~ horses⟩ **2** : having blood of a specified kind ⟨warm= *blooded* animals⟩

blood group *n* : one of the classes into which human beings can be separated by the presence or absence in their blood of specific antigens

blood·hound \'bləd-,haünd\ *n* : a large powerful hound with long drooping

ears, a wrinkled face, and keen sense of smell

blood·let·ting \-,let-iŋ\ *n* **1** : PHLEBOTOMY **2** : BLOODSHED

blood·line \-,līn\ *n* : a sequence of direct ancestors esp. in a pedigree

blood·mo·bile \-mō-,bēl\ *n* : a motor vehicle equipped for collecting blood from donors

blood poisoning *n* : invasion of the bloodstream by virulent microorganisms from a focus of infection accompanied esp. by chills, fever, and prostration

blood pressure *n* : pressure of the blood on the walls of blood vessels and esp. arteries

blood·root \'bləd-,rüt, -,rüt\ *n* : a plant related to the poppy that has a red root and sap, a solitary leaf, and a white flower in early spring

blood·shed \-,shed\ *n* : wounding or taking of life : CARNAGE, SLAUGHTER

blood·shot \-,shät\ *adj* : inflamed to redness ⟨~ eyes⟩

blood·stain \-,stān\ *n* : a discoloration caused by blood — **blood·stained** \-,stānd\ *adj*

blood·stone \-,stōn\ *n* : a green quartz sprinkled with red spots

blood·stream \-,strēm\ *n* : the flowing blood in a circulatory system

blood·suck·er \-,sək-ər\ *n* : an animal that sucks blood; *esp* : LEECH — **blood·suck·ing** \-iŋ\ *adj*

blood test *n* : a test of the blood; *esp* : one for syphilis

blood·thirsty \'bləd-,thər-stē\ *adj* : eager to shed blood — **blood·thirst·i·ly** \-,thər-stə-lē\ *adv* — **blood·thirst·i·ness** \-stē-nəs\ *n*

blood type *n* : BLOOD GROUP — **blood– typ·ing** \-,tī-piŋ\ *n*

blood vessel *n* : a vessel (as a vein or artery) in which blood circulates in an animal

Bloody Mary \-'me(ə)r-ē\ *n, pl* **Bloody Marys** : a drink made essentially of vodka and tomato juice

¹bloom \'blüm\ *n* **1** : FLOWER 1; *also* : flowers or amount of flowers (as of a plant) **2** : the period or state of flowering **3** : a state or time of beauty and vigor **4** : a powdery coating esp. on fruits and leaves **5** : rosy color; *also*

: an appearance of freshness or health — **bloomy** *adj*

²bloom *vb* **1** : to produce or yield flowers **2** : to glow esp. with healthy color **syn** flower, blossom

bloo·mers \\'blü-mərz\ *n pl* [Amelia *Bloomer* †1894 Am. pioneer in feminism] : a woman's garment of short loose trousers gathered at the knee

bloop·er \\'blü-pər\ *n* **1** : an embarrassing blunder made in public **2** : a fly ball hit barely beyond a baseball infield

¹blos·som \\'bläs-əm\ *n* : the flower of a plant : BLOOM

²blossom *vb* : FLOWER, BLOOM

¹blot \\'blät\ *n* **1** : SPOT, STAIN ⟨ink ∼s⟩ **2** : BLEMISH **syn** stigma, brand, slur

²blot *vb* **blot·ted; blot·ting 1** : SPOT, STAIN **2** : OBSCURE, ECLIPSE ⟨∼ out the sun⟩ **3** *obs* : MAR; *esp* : DISGRACE **4** : to dry or remove with or as if with blotting paper **5** : to make a blot

blotch \\'bläch\ *n* : a usu. large and irregular spot or mark (as of ink or color) — **blotch** *vb* — **blotchy** *adj*

blot·ter \\'blät-ər\ *n* **1** : a piece of blotting paper **2** : a book for preliminary records (as of sales or arrests)

blot·ting paper *n* : a soft spongy paper used to absorb ink

blouse \\'blaus, 'blauz\ *n* **1** : a loose outer garment like a smock **2** : a usu. loose garment reaching from the neck to about the waist level

¹blow \\'blō\ *vb* **blew** \\'blü\; **blown** \\'blōn\; **blow·ing 1** : to move forcibly ⟨the wind *blew*⟩ **2** : to send forth a current of gas (as air) **3** : to act on with a current of gas or vapor; *esp* : to drive with such a current **4** : to sound or cause to sound ⟨∼ a horn⟩ **5** : PANT, GASP; *also* : to expel moist air in breathing ⟨the whale *blew*⟩ **6** : BOAST; *also* : BLUSTER **7** : MELT — used of an electrical fuse **8** : to shape or form by blown or injected air ⟨∼ glass⟩ **9** : to shatter or destroy by or as if by explosion **10** : to make breathless by exertion **11** : to spend recklessly — **blower** *n*

²blow *n* **1** : a usu. strong blowing of air : GALE **2** : BOASTING, BRAG **3** : a blowing from the mouth or nose or through or from an instrument

³blow *vb* **blew** \\'blü\; **blown** \\'blōn\; **blow·ing** : FLOWER, BLOOM

⁴blow *n* **1** : a forcible stroke **2** : COMBAT ⟨come to ∼s⟩ **3** : a severe and usu. unexpected calamity

blow–by–blow \-bī-, -bə-\ *adj* : minutely detailed ⟨∼ account⟩

blow·fly \\'blō-ˌflī\ *n* : any of various two-winged flies (as a bluebottle) that deposit their eggs or maggots on meat or in wounds

blow·gun \-ˌgən\ *n* : a tube from which an arrow or a dart may be shot by the force of the breath

blow·out \\'blō-ˌaut\ *n* : a bursting of something (as a tire) because of pressure of the contents (as air)

blow·pipe \\'blō-ˌpīp\ *n* : a small tube for blowing gas (as air) into a flame so as to concentrate and increase the heat

blow·sy *also* **blow·zy** \\'blau-zē\ *adj* : DISHEVELED, SLOVENLY

blow·torch \\'blō-ˌtorch\ *n* : a small portable burner whose flame is made hotter by a blast of air or oxygen

blow·up \\'blō-ˌəp\ *n* **1** : EXPLOSION **2** : an outburst of temper **3** : a photographic enlargement

blowy \\'blō-ē\ *adj* : WINDY

BLT \ˌbē-ˌel-'tē\ *n* : a bacon, lettuce, and tomato sandwich

¹blub·ber \\'bləb-ər\ *vb* **blub·bered; blub·ber·ing** \\'bləb-(ə-)riŋ\ : to cry noisily

²blubber *n* **1** : the fat of large sea mammals (as whales) **2** : a noisy crying

¹blud·geon \\'bləj-ən\ *n* : a short often loaded club

²bludgeon *vb* : to strike with or as if with a bludgeon

¹blue \\'blü\ *adj* **blu·er; blu·est 1** : of the color blue; *also* : BLUISH **2** : MELANCHOLY; *also* : DEPRESSING **3** : PURITANICAL **4** : INDECENT

²blue *n* **1** : a color between green and violet in the spectrum : the color of the clear daytime sky **2** : something (as clothing or the sky) that is blue

blue baby *n* : a baby with bluish skin due to faulty circulation caused by a heart defect

blue·bell \-ˌbel\ *n* : any of various plants with blue bell-shaped flowers

blue·ber·ry \\'blü-ˌber-ē, -b(ə-)rē\ *n* : the edible blue or blackish berry of various shrubs of the heath family; *also* : one of these shrubs

blue•bird \-ˌbərd\ *n* : any of several small songbirds related to the robin but with blue above esp. in the male

blue–black \-ˈblak\ *adj* : being of a dark bluish hue

blue•bon•net \ˈblü-ˌbän-ət\ *n* : a low= growing annual lupine of Texas with silky foliage and blue flowers

blue•bot•tle \ˈblü-ˌbät-ᵊl\ *n* : any of several blowflies with iridescent blue bodies or abdomens

blue cheese *n* : cheese marked with veins of greenish blue mold

blue–col•lar \ˈblü-ˈkäl-ər\ *adj* : of, relating to, or being the class of workers whose duties call for work clothes

blue•fish \-ˌfish\ *n* : a marine sport and food fish bluish above and silvery below

blue•grass \-ˌgras\ *n* : KENTUCKY BLUEGRASS

blue jay \-ˌjā\ *n* : an American crested jay with upper parts bright blue that occurs east of the Rocky mountains

blue jeans *n pl* : pants usu. made of blue denim

blue•nose \ˈblü-ˌnōz\ *n* : one who advocates a rigorous moral code

blue•point \ˈblü-ˌpȯint\ *n* : a small delicate oyster orig. from Long Island, New York

blue•print \-ˌprint\ *n* **1** : a photographic print in white on a blue ground used esp. for copying mechanical drawings and architects' plans **2** : a detailed plan of action — **blueprint** *vb*

blues \ˈblüz\ *n pl* **1** : MELANCHOLY **2** : music in a style marked by recurrent minor intervals and melancholy lyrics

blue•stock•ing \ˈblü-ˌstäk-iŋ\ *n* : a woman having intellectual interests

blu•et \ˈblü-ət\ *n* : a low American herb with dainty solitary bluish flowers

blue whale *n* : a very large whalebone whale that may reach a weight of 100 tons (90 metric tons) and a length of 100 feet (30 meters)

¹bluff \ˈbləf\ *adj* **1** : having a broad flattened front **2** : rising steeply with a broad flat front **3** : OUTSPOKEN, FRANK **syn** abrupt, blunt, brusque, curt, gruff

²bluff *n* : a high steep bank : CLIFF

³bluff *vb* : to frighten or deceive by pretense or a mere show of strength

⁴bluff *n* : an act or instance of bluffing; *also* : one who bluffs

blu•ing *or* **blue•ing** \ˈblü-iŋ\ *n* : a preparation of blue or violet dyes used in laundering to counteract yellowing of white fabrics

blu•ish \ˈblü-ish\ *adj* : somewhat blue

¹blun•der \ˈblən-dər\ *vb* **blun•dered; blun•der•ing** \-d(ə-)riŋ\ **1** : to move clumsily or unsteadily **2** : to make a stupid or needless mistake

²blunder *n* : an avoidable and usu. serious mistake

blun•der•buss \ˈblən-dər-ˌbəs\ *n* [fr. obs. Dutch *donderbus,* fr. Dutch *donder* thunder + obs. Dutch *bus* gun] : an obsolete short-barreled firearm with a flaring muzzle

¹blunt \ˈblənt\ *adj* **1** : not sharp : DULL **2** : lacking in tact : BLUFF **syn** brusque, curt, gruff, abrupt, crusty — **blunt•ly** *adv* — **blunt•ness** *n*

²blunt *vb* : to make or become dull

¹blur \ˈblər\ *n* **1** : a smear or stain that obscures **2** : something vaguely seen or perceived — **blur•ry** \-ē\ *adj*

²blur *vb* **blurred; blur•ring** : DIM, CLOUD, OBSCURE

blurb \ˈblərb\ *n* : a short publicity notice (as on a book jacket)

blurt \ˈblərt\ *vb* : to utter suddenly and impulsively

blush \ˈbləsh\ *n* : a reddening of the face (as from modesty or confusion) : FLUSH — **blush** *vb* — **blush•ful** *adj*

blus•ter \ˈbləs-tər\ *vb* **blus•tered; blus•ter•ing** \-t(ə-)riŋ\ **1** : to blow in stormy noisy gusts **2** : to talk or act with noisy swaggering threats — **bluster** *n* — **blus•tery** \-t(ə-)rē\ *adj*

blvd *abbr* boulevard

B lymphocyte *n* : B CELL

BM *abbr* **1** basal metabolism **2** bowel movement

BMR *abbr* basal metabolic rate

BO *abbr* **1** body odor **2** box office **3** branch office

boa \ˈbō-ə\ *n* **1** : a large snake (as the **boa con•stric•tor** \ˌbō-ə-kən-ˈstrik-tər\ or the related anaconda) that suffocates and kills its prey by constriction **2** : a fluffy scarf usu. of fur or feathers fur or feathers

boar \ˈbōr\ *n* : a male swine; *also* : WILD BOAR

¹board \ˈbōrd\ *n* **1** : the side of a ship **2**

: a thin flat length of sawed lumber; *also* : material (as cardboard) or a piece of material formed as a thin flat firm sheet **3** *pl* : STAGE **1 4** : a table spread with a meal; *also* : daily meals esp. when furnished for pay **5** : a table at which a council or magistrates sit **6** : a group or association of persons organized for a special responsibility (as the management of a business or institution); *also* : an organized commercial exchange

²**board** *vb* **1** : to go aboard ⟨~ a boat⟩ **2** : to cover with boards **3** : to provide or be provided with meals and often lodging — **board•er** *n*

board•ing•house \'bōrd-iŋ-ˌhaùs\ *n* : a house at which persons are boarded

board•walk \'bōrd-ˌwòk\ *n* : a promenade (as of planking) along a beach

boast \'bōst\ *vb* **1** : to praise oneself **2** : to mention or assert with excessive pride **3** : to prize as a possession; *also* : HAVE ⟨the house ~s a fireplace⟩ — **boast** *n* — **boast•ful** \-fəl\ *adj* — **boast•ful•ly** \-ē\ *adv*

boat \'bōt\ *n* : a vessel (as a canoe or ship) for traveling through water

boat•er \'bōt-ər\ *n* **1** : one that travels in a boat **2** : a stiff straw hat

boat•man \'bōt-mən\ *n* : a man who manages, works on, or deals in boats

boat•swain \'bōs-ᵊn\ *n* : a subordinate officer of a ship in charge of the hull and related equipment

¹**bob** \'bäb\ *vb* **bobbed; bob•bing 1** : to move up and down jerkily or repeatedly **2** : to emerge, arise, or appear suddenly or unexpectedly

²**bob** *n* : a bobbing movement

³**bob** *n* **1** : a knob, knot, twist, or curl esp. of ribbons, yarn, or hair **2** : a short haircut of a woman or child **3** : FLOAT 2 **4** : a weight hanging from a line

⁴**bob** *vb* **bobbed; bob•bing** : to cut hair in a bob

⁵**bob** *n, pl* **bob** *slang Brit* : SHILLING

bob•bin \'bäb-ən\ *n* : a cylinder or spindle for holding or dispensing thread (as in a sewing machine)

bob•ble \'bäb-əl\ *vb* **bob•bled; bob•bling** \-(ə-)liŋ\ : FUMBLE — **bobble** *n*

bob•by \'bäb-ē\ *n, pl* **bobbies** [*Bobby,* nickname for *Robert,* after Sir *Robert* Peel, who organized the London police force] *Brit* : POLICEMAN

bob•by pin \'bäb-ē-\ *n* : a flat wire hairpin with prongs that press close together

bob•cat \'bäb-ˌkat\ *n* : a small usu. rusty-colored No. American lynx

bob•o•link \'bäb-ə-ˌliŋk\ *n* : an American migratory songbird related to the meadowlarks

bob•sled \'bäb-ˌsled\ *n* **1** : a short sled usu. used as one of a joined pair **2** : a racing sled with two pairs of runners, a steering wheel, and a hand brake — **bobsled** *vb*

bob•white \(ˈ)bäb-ˈhwīt\ *n* : any of a genus of quail; *esp* : one of the eastern and central U.S.

boc•cie *or* **boc•ci** *or* **boc•ce** \'bäch-ē\ *n* : Italian lawn bowling played on a long narrow court

bock \'bäk\ *n* : a dark heavy beer usu. sold in early spring

bod \'bäd\ *n* : BODY

¹**bode** \'bōd\ *vb* **bod•ed; bod•ing** : to indicate by signs : PRESAGE

²**bode** past of BIDE

bo•de•ga \bō-'dā-gə\ *n* [Sp, fr. L *apotheca* storehouse] : a store specializing in Hispanic groceries

bod•ice \'bäd-əs\ *n* [alter. of *bodies,* pl. of *body*] : the usu. close-fitting part of a dress above the waist

bod•i•less \'bäd-i-ləs, 'bäd-ᵊl-əs\ *adj* : lacking a body or material form

¹**bod•i•ly** \'bäd-ᵊl-ē\ *adj* : of or relating to the body ⟨~ welfare⟩

²**bodily** *adv* **1** : in the flesh **2** : as a whole ⟨lifted the crate up ~⟩

bod•kin \'bäd-kən\ *n* **1** : DAGGER **2** : a pointed implement for punching holes in cloth **3** : a blunt needle for drawing tape or ribbon through a loop or hem

body \'bäd-ē\ *n, pl* **bod•ies 1** : the physical whole of a living or dead organism; *also* : the trunk or main mass of an organism as distinguished from its appendages **2** : a human being : PERSON **3** : the main part of something **4** : a mass of matter distinct from other masses **5** : GROUP **6** : VISCOSITY, FIRMNESS **7** : richness of flavor — used esp. of wines — **bod•ied** \'bäd-ēd\ *adj*

body English *n* : bodily motions made in a usu. unconscious effort to influence the movement of a propelled object (as a ball)

body·guard \'bäd-ē-ˌgärd\ *n* : a personal guard; *also* : RETINUE

body stocking *n* : a sheer close-fitting one-piece garment for the torso that often has sleeves and legs

body·work \'bäd-ē-ˌwərk\ *n* : the making or repairing of vehicle bodies

Boer \'bōr, 'bu̇r\ *n* [Dutch, lit., farmer] : a South African of Dutch or Huguenot descent

¹**bog** \'bäg, 'bȯg\ *n* : wet, spongy, poorly drained, and usu. acid ground — **bog·gy** *adj*

²**bog** *vb* **bogged; bog·ging** : to sink into or as if into a bog

bo·gey *also* **bo·gie** *or* **bo·gy** \'bu̇g-ē, 'bō-gē *for 1*; 'bō-gē *for 2*\ *n, pl* **bogeys** *also* **bogies 1** : SPECTER, HOBGOBLIN; *also* : a source of fear or annoyance **2** : a score of one over par on a hole in golf

bo·gey·man \'bu̇g-ē-ˌman, 'bō-gē-, 'bü-gē-\ *n* : an imaginary monster used in threatening children

bog·gle \'bäg-əl\ *vb* **bog·gled; bog·gling** \-(ə-)liŋ\ : to overwhelm or be overwhelmed with fright or amazement

bo·gus \'bō-gəs\ *adj* : SPURIOUS, SHAM

Bo·he·mi·an \bō-'hē-mē-ən\ *n* **1** : a native or inhabitant of Bohemia **2** *often not cap* : VAGABOND, WANDERER **3** *often not cap* : a person (as a writer or artist) living an unconventional life — **bohemian** *adj, often cap*

¹**boil** \'bȯil\ *n* : an inflamed swelling on the skin containing pus

²**boil** *vb* **1** : to heat or become heated to a temperature (**boiling point**) at which vapor is formed and rises in bubbles ⟨water ∼s and changes to steam⟩; *also* : to act on or be acted on by a boiling liquid ⟨∼ eggs⟩ **2** : to be in a state of seething agitation

³**boil** *n* : the act or state of boiling

boil·er \'bȯi-lər\ *n* **1** : a container in which something is boiled **2** : a strong vessel used in making steam **3** : a tank holding hot water

boil·er·mak·er \'bȯi-lər-ˌmā-kər\ *n* : whiskey with a beer chaser

bois·ter·ous \'bȯi-st(ə-)rəs\ *adj* : noisily turbulent or exuberant — **bois·ter·ous·ly** *adv*

bok choy \'bäk-'chȯi\ *n* : a Chinese vegetable related to the mustards that forms a loose head of green leaves with long thick white stalks

bo·la \'bō-lə\ *or* **bo·las** \-ləs\ *n, pl* **bolas** \-ləz\ *also* **bo·las·es** [AmerSp *bolas*, fr. Sp *bola* ball] : a cord with weights attached to the ends for hurling at and entangling an animal

bold \'bōld\ *adj* **1** : COURAGEOUS, INTREPID **2** : IMPUDENT **3** : STEEP **4** : ADVENTUROUS, FREE ⟨a ∼ thinker⟩ **syn** dauntless, brave, valiant — **bold·ly** *adv* — **bold·ness** \'bōl(d)-nəs\ *n*

bold·face \'bōl(d)-ˌfās\ *n* : a heavy-faced type; *also* : printing in boldface — **bold–faced** \-'fāst\ *adj*

bole \'bōl\ *n* : the trunk of a tree

bo·le·ro \bə-'le(ə)r-ō\ *n, pl* **-ros 1** : a Spanish dance or its music **2** : a short loose jacket open at the front

bo·li·var \bə-'lē-ˌvär, 'bäl-ə-vər\ *n, pl* **-vars** *or* **-va·res** \ˌbäl-ə-'vär-ˌās, ˌbō-li-\ — see MONEY table

boll \'bōl\ *n* : a seed pod (as of cotton)

boll weevil *n* : a small grayish weevil that infests the cotton plant both as a larva and as an adult

boll·worm \'bōl-ˌwərm\ *n* : any of several moths and esp. the corn earworm whose larvae feed on cotton bolls

bo·lo \'bō-lō\ *n, pl* **bolos** : a long heavy single-edged knife of Philippine origin

bo·lo·gna \bə-'lō-nē\ *n* [short for *Bologna sausage*, fr. *Bologna*, Italy] : a large smoked sausage of beef, veal, and pork

Bol·she·vik \'bōl-shə-ˌvik\ *n, pl* **Bolsheviks** *also* **Bol·she·vi·ki** \ˌbōl-shə-'vik-ē\ [Russ *bol'shevik*, fr. *bol'she* larger] **1** : a member of the party that seized power in Russia in the revolution of November 1917 **2** : COMMUNIST — **Bolshevik** *adj*

bol·she·vism \'bōl-shə-ˌviz-əm\ *n, often cap* : the doctrine or program of the Bolsheviks advocating violent overthrow of capitalism

¹**bol·ster** \'bōl-stər\ *n* : a long pillow or cushion extending from side to side of a bed

²**bolster** *vb* **bol·stered; bol·ster·ing** \-st(ə-)riŋ\ : to support with or as if with a bolster; *also* : REINFORCE

¹**bolt** \'bōlt\ *n* **1** : a missile (as an arrow) for a crossbow or catapult **2** : a flash of lightning : THUNDERBOLT **3** : a sliding bar used to fasten a door **4** : a roll

of cloth or wallpaper of specified length **5** : a rod with a head at one end and a screw thread at the other used to hold objects in place **6** : a metal cylinder that drives the cartridge into the chamber of a firearm

²**bolt** *vb* **1** : to move suddenly (as in fright or hurry) : START, DASH **2** : to break away (as from association) ⟨~ a political convention⟩ **3** : to secure or fasten with a bolt **4** : to swallow hastily or without chewing

³**bolt** *n* : an act of bolting

⁴**bolt** *vb* : SIFT ⟨~ flour⟩

bo·lus \'bō-ləs\ *n* **1** : a large pill **2** : a soft mass of chewed food

¹**bomb** \'bäm\ *n* **1** : a fused explosive device designed to detonate under specified conditions (as impact) **2** : a container of material (as insecticide) under pressure for release in a fine spray **3** : a long pass in football

²**bomb** *vb* : to attack with bombs

bom·bard \bäm-'bärd, bəm-\ *vb* **1** : to attack esp. with artillery or bombers **2** : to assail persistently **3** : to subject to the impact of rapidly moving particles (as electrons) — **bom·bard·ment** *n*

bom·bar·dier \,bäm-bə(r)-'diər\ *n* : a bomber-crew member who releases the bombs

bom·bast \'bäm-,bast\ *n* [fr. *bombast* cotton padding, fr. MF *bombace*, fr. ML *bombax* cotton, alter. of L *bombyx* silkworm, silk, fr. Gk] : pretentious wordy speech or writing — **bom·bas·tic** \bäm-'bas-tik\ *adj*

bom·ba·zine \,bäm-bə-'zēn\ *n* **1** : a silk fabric in twill weave dyed black **2** : a twilled fabric with silk warp and worsted filling

bomb·er \'bäm-ər\ *n* : one that bombs; *esp* : an airplane for dropping bombs

bomb·proof \'bäm-,prüf\ *adj* : safe against the explosive force of bombs

bomb·shell \'bäm-,shel\ *n* **1** : BOMB 1 **2** : one that stuns, amazes, or completely upsets

bona fide \'bō-nə-,fīd, 'bän-ə-; ,bō-nə-'fīd-ē, -'fīd-ə\ *adj* [L, in good faith] **1** : made in good faith ⟨a *bona fide* agreement⟩ **2** : GENUINE, REAL ⟨a *bona fide* bargain⟩ **syn** authentic

bo·nan·za \bə-'nan-zə\ *n* [Sp, lit., fair weather, fr. ML *bonacia*, alter. of L *malacia* calm at sea, fr. Gk *malakia*,

lit., softness, fr. *malakos* soft] : something yielding a rich return

bon·bon \'bän-,bän\ *n* : a candy with a creamy center and a soft covering (as of chocolate)

¹**bond** \'bänd\ *n* **1** : FETTER **2** : a binding or uniting force or tie ⟨~s of friendship⟩ **3** : an agreement or obligation often made binding by a pledge of money or goods **4** : a person who acts as surety for another **5** : an interest≈bearing certificate of public or private indebtedness **6** : the state of goods subject to supervision pending payment of taxes or duties due ⟨imports held in ~⟩

²**bond** *vb* **1** : to assure payment of duties or taxes on (goods) by giving a bond **2** : to insure against losses caused by the acts of ⟨~ a bank teller⟩ **3** : to make or become firmly united as if by bonds ⟨~ iron to copper⟩

bond·age \'bän-dij\ *n* : SLAVERY, SERVITUDE

bond·hold·er \'bänd-,hōl-dər\ *n* : one that owns a government or corporation bond

bond·ing *n* : the formation of a close personal relationship esp. through frequent or constant association ⟨~ of mother and child⟩

bond·man \'bän(d)-mən\ *n* : SLAVE, SERF

¹**bonds·man** \'bän(d)z-mən\ *n* : BONDMAN

²**bondsman** *n* : SURETY 3

bond·wom·an \'bänd-,wum-ən\ *n* : a female slave or serf

¹**bone** \'bōn\ *n* **1** : a hard largely calcareous tissue forming most of the skeleton of a vertebrate animal; *also* : one of the pieces of bone making up a vertebrate skeleton **2** : a hard animal substance (as ivory or whalebone) similar to true bone **3** : something made of bone — **bone·less** *adj* — **bony** *also* **bon·ey** \'bō-nē\ *adj*

²**bone** *vb* **boned; bon·ing** : to free from bones ⟨~ a chicken⟩

bone black *n* : the black carbon residue from calcined bones used esp. as a pigment

bone meal *n* : fertilizer or feed made of crushed or ground bone

bon·er \'bō-nər\ *n* : a stupid and ridiculous blunder

bone up *vb* **1** : CRAM 3 **2** : to refresh

one's memory ⟨*boned up* on the speech before giving it⟩

bon·fire \\'bän-ˌfī(ə)r\\ *n* [ME *bonefire* a fire of bones, fr. *bon* bone + *fire*] : a large fire built in the open air

bon·go \\'bäŋ-gō\\ *n, pl* **bongos** *also* **bongoes** [AmerSp *bongó*] : one of a pair of small tuned drums played with the hands

bon·ho·mie \\ˌbän-ə-'mē\\ *n* [F *bonhomie,* fr. *bonhomme* good-natured man, fr. *bon* good + *homme* man] : good-natured easy friendliness

bo·ni·to \\bə-'nēt-ō\\ *n, pl* **-tos** *or* **-to** : any of several medium-sized tunas

bon mot \\bōⁿ-'mō\\ *n, pl* **bons mots** \\bōⁿ-'mō(z)\\ *or* **bon mots** \\-'mō(z)\\ [F, lit., good word] : a clever remark

bon·net \\'bän-ət\\ *n* : a covering (as a cap) for the head; *esp* : a hat for a woman or infant tied under the chin

bon·ny \\'bän-ē\\ *adj* **bon·ni·er; -est** *chiefly Brit* : ATTRACTIVE, FAIR; *also* : FINE, EXCELLENT

bon·sai \\bōn-'sī\\ *n, pl* **bonsai** [Jp] : a potted plant (as a tree) dwarfed by special methods of culture; *also* : the art of growing such a plant

bo·nus \\'bō-nəs\\ *n* : something in addition to what is expected

bon vi·vant \\ˌbän-vē-'vänt, ˌbōⁿ-vē-'väⁿ\\ *n, pl* **bons vivants** \\ˌbän-vē-'vänts, ˌbōⁿ-vē-'väⁿ(z)\\ *or* **bon vivants** *same*\\ [F, lit., good liver] : a person having cultivated, refined, and sociable tastes esp. in food and drink

bon voy·age \\ˌbōⁿv-ˌwī-'äzh, -ˌwä-'yäzh; ˌbän-\\ *n* : FAREWELL — often used as an interjection

bonze \\'bänz\\ *n* : a Buddhist monk

boo \\'bü\\ *n, pl* **boos** : a shout of disapproval or contempt — **boo** *vb*

boo·by \\'bü-bē\\ *n, pl* **boobies** : an awkward ineffective person : DOPE

booby hatch *n* : an insane asylum

booby prize *n* : an award for the poorest performance in a contest

booby trap *n* : a trap for the unwary; *esp* : a concealed explosive device set to go off when some harmless-looking object is touched

boo·dle \\'büd-ᵊl\\ *n* **1** : bribe money **2** : a large amount of money

¹book \\'bùk\\ *n* **1** : a set of sheets bound into a volume **2** : a long written or printed narrative or record **3** : a major

division of a long literary work **4** *cap* : BIBLE

²book *vb* **1** : to engage, reserve, or schedule by or as if by writing in a book ⟨~ seats on a plane⟩ **2** : to enter charges against in a police register

book·case \\-ˌkās\\ *n* : a piece of furniture consisting of shelves to hold books

book·end \\-ˌend\\ *n* : a support to hold up a row of books

book·ie \\'bùk-ē\\ *n* : BOOKMAKER

book·ish \\'bùk-ish\\ *adj* **1** : fond of books and reading **2** : inclined to rely unduly on book knowledge

book·keep·er \\'bùk-ˌkē-pər\\ *n* : one who records the accounts or transactions of a business — **book·keep·ing** \\-piŋ\\ *n*

book·let \\'bùk-lət\\ *n* : PAMPHLET

book·mak·er \\'bùk-ˌmā-kər\\ *n* : one who determines odds and receives and pays off bets — **book·mak·ing** \\-kiŋ\\ *n*

book·mark \\-ˌmärk\\ *or* **book·mark·er** \\-ˌmär-kər\\ *n* : a marker for finding a place in a book

book·mo·bile \\'bùk-mō-ˌbēl\\ *n* : a truck that serves as a traveling library

book·plate \\'bùk-ˌplāt\\ *n* : a label pasted in a book to show who owns it

book·sell·er \\'bùk-ˌsel-ər\\ *n* : one who sells books; *esp* : the proprietor of a bookstore

book·shelf \\-ˌshelf\\ *n* : a shelf for books

book·worm \\'bùk-ˌwərm\\ *n* **1** : a person unusually devoted to reading and study **2** : an insect larva (as of a beetle) that feeds on the binding and paste of a book

¹boom \\'büm\\ *n* **1** : a long spar used to extend the bottom of a sail **2** : a beam projecting from the upright pole of a derrick to support or guide the object lifted **3** : a line of floating timbers used to obstruct passage or catch floating objects

²boom *vb* **1** : to make a deep hollow sound : RESOUND **2** : to grow or cause to grow rapidly esp. in value, esteem, or importance

³boom *n* **1** : a booming sound or cry **2** : a rapid expansion or increase esp. of economic activity

boo·mer·ang \\'bü-mə-ˌraŋ\\ *n* [native name in Australia] : a bent or angular club that can be so thrown as to return near the starting point

¹boon \'bün\ *n* [ME, fr. ON *bōn* petition] : BENEFIT, BLESSING **syn** favor, gift, largess, present

²boon *adj* [ME *bon*, fr. MF, good] : INTIMATE, CONGENIAL

boon·docks \'bün-ˌdäks\ *n pl* [Tagalog (language of the Philippines) *bundok* mountain] **1** : rough country filled with dense brush **2** : a rural area

boon·dog·gle \'bün-ˌdäg-əl, -ˌdȯg-\ *n* : a useless or wasteful project or activity

boor \'bu̇r\ *n* **1** : YOKEL **2** : a rude or insensitive person **syn** churl, lout, clown, clodhopper — **boor·ish** *adj*

boost \'büst\ *vb* **1** : to push up from below **2** : INCREASE, RAISE ⟨∼ prices⟩ **3** : AID, PROMOTE ⟨voted a bonus to ∼ morale⟩ — **boost** *n* — **boost·er** *n*

¹boot \'büt\ *n, chiefly dial* : something to equalize a trade — **to boot** : BESIDES

²boot *vb, archaic* : AVAIL, PROFIT

³boot *n* **1** : a covering for the foot and leg **2** : a protective sheath (as of a flower) **3** *Brit* : an automobile trunk **4** : KICK; *also* : a discharge from employment **5** : a navy or marine corps trainee

⁴boot *vb* **1** : KICK **2** : to eject or discharge summarily

boot·black \'büt-ˌblak\ *n* : a person who shines shoes

boo·tee *or* **boo·tie** \'büt-ē\ *n* : an infant's knitted or crocheted sock

booth \'büth\ *n, pl* **booths** \'bü*th*z, 'büths\ **1** : a small enclosed stall (as at a fair) **2** : a small enclosure giving privacy for a person ⟨voting ∼⟩ ⟨telephone ∼⟩ **3** : a restaurant accommodation having a table between backed benches

boot·leg \'büt-ˌleg\ *vb* : to make, transport, or sell (as liquor) illegally — **boot·leg** *adj or n* — **boot·leg·ger** *n*

boot·less \'büt-ləs\ *adj* : USELESS **syn** futile, vain, abortive, fruitless — **boot·less·ly** *adv*

boo·ty \'büt-ē\ *n, pl* **booties** : PLUNDER, SPOIL

¹booze \'büz\ *vb* **boozed; booz·ing** : to drink liquor to excess — **booz·er** *n*

²booze *n* : intoxicating liquor — **boozy** *adj*

bop \'bäp\ *vb* **bopped; bop·ping** : HIT, SOCK — **bop** *n*

BOQ *abbr* bachelor officers' quarters

bor *abbr* borough

bo·rate \'bōr-ˌāt\ *n* : a salt or ester of boric acid

bo·rax \'bōr-ˌaks\ *n* : a crystalline borate of sodium that occurs as a mineral and is used as a flux and cleanser

bor·del·lo \bȯr-'del-ō\ *n, pl* **-los** [It] : BROTHEL

¹bor·der \'bȯrd-ər\ *n* **1** : EDGE, MARGIN **2** : BOUNDARY, FRONTIER **syn** rim, brim, brink, fringe, perimeter

²border *vb* **bor·dered; bor·der·ing** \'bȯrd-(ə-)riŋ\ **1** : to put a border on **2** : ADJOIN **3** : VERGE

bor·der·land \'bȯrd-ər-ˌland\ *n* **1** : territory at or near a border **2** : an outlying or intermediate region often not clearly defined

bor·der·line \-ˌlīn\ *adj* : being in an intermediate position or state; *esp* : not quite up to what is standard or expected ⟨∼ intelligence⟩

¹bore \'bōr\ *vb* **bored; bor·ing 1** : to make a hole in with or as if with a drill **2** : to make (as a well) by boring or digging away material **syn** perforate, drill, prick, puncture — **bor·er** *n*

²bore *n* **1** : a hole made by or as if by boring **2** : a cylindrical cavity **3** : the diameter of a hole or tube; *esp* : the interior diameter of a gun barrel or engine cylinder

³bore past of BEAR

⁴bore *n* : a tidal flood with a high abrupt front

⁵bore *n* : one that causes boredom

⁶bore *vb* **bored; bor·ing** : to weary with tedious dullness

bo·re·al \'bōr-ē-əl\ *adj* : of, relating to, or located in northern regions

bore·dom \'bōrd-əm\ *n* : the condition of being bored

bo·ric acid \ˌbōr-ik-\ *n* : a white crystalline weak acid that contains boron and is used as an antiseptic

born \'bȯrn\ *adj* **1** : brought into life by birth **2** : NATIVE ⟨American-*born*⟩ **3** : having special natural abilities or character from birth ⟨a ∼ leader⟩

born–again *adj* : having experienced a revival of a personal faith or conviction ⟨∼ believer⟩ ⟨∼ liberal⟩

borne past part of BEAR

bo·ron \'bōr-ˌän\ *n* : a chemical element that occurs in nature only in combination (as in borax)

bor·ough \'bər-ō\ *n* **1** : a British town that sends one or more members to Parliament; *also* : an incorporated British urban area **2** : an incorporated town or village in some U.S. states; *also* : any of the five political divisions of New York City **3** : a civil division of the state of Alaska corresponding to a county in most other states

bor·row \'bär-ō\ *vb* **1** : to take or receive (something) temporarily and with intent to return **2** : to take into possession or use from another source : DERIVE, APPROPRIATE ⟨∼ a metaphor⟩

borscht *or* **borsch** \'bórsh(t)\ *n* [Russ *borshch*] : a soup made mainly from beets

bosh \'bäsh\ *n* [Turk *boş* empty] : foolish talk or action : NONSENSE

bosky \'bäs-kē\ *adj* : covered with trees or shrubs

¹bo·som \'búz-əm, 'búz-\ *n* **1** : the front of the human chest; *esp* : the female breasts **2** : the part of a garment covering the breast **3** : the seat of secret thoughts and feelings — **bo·somed** \-əmd\ *adj*

²bosom *adj* : CLOSE, INTIMATE

¹boss \'bäs, 'bós\ *n* : a knoblike ornament : STUD

²boss *vb* : to ornament with bosses

³boss \'bós\ *n* **1** : one (as a foreman or manager) exercising control or supervision **2** : a politician who controls votes or dictates policies — **bossy** *adj*

⁴boss \'bós\ *vb* : to act as a boss : SUPERVISE

bo·sun \'bōs-ᵊn\ *var of* BOATSWAIN

bot *abbr* botanical; botanist; botany

bot·a·ny \'bät-(ᵊ-)nē\ *n, pl* **-nies** **1** : a branch of biology dealing with plants and plant life **2** : plant life (as of a given region); *also* : the biology of a plant or plant group — **bo·tan·i·cal** \bə-'tan-i-kəl\ *adj* — **bot·a·nist** \'bät-(ᵊ-)nəst\ *n* — **bot·a·nize** \-ᵊn-ˌīz\ *vb*

botch \'bäch\ *vb* : to foul up hopelessly : BUNGLE — **botch** *n*

¹both \'bōth\ *adj* : being the two : affecting the one and the other

²both *pron* : both ones : the one as well as the other

³both *conj* — used as a function word to indicate and stress the inclusion of each of two or more things specified by coordinated words, phrases, or clauses ⟨∼ New York and London⟩

both·er \'bä<u>th</u>-ər\ *vb* **-ered; -er·ing** \-(ə-)riŋ\ : WORRY, PESTER, TROUBLE **syn** vex, annoy, irk, provoke — **bother** *n* — **both·er·some** \-səm\ *adj*

¹bot·tle \'bät-ᵊl\ *n* **1** : a container (as of glass) with a narrow neck and usu. no handles **2** : the quantity held by a bottle **3** : intoxicating liquor

²bottle *vb* **bot·tled; bot·tling** \'bät-(ᵊ-)liŋ\ **1** : to confine as if in a bottle : RESTRAIN **2** : to put into a bottle

bot·tle·neck \'bät-ᵊl-ˌnek\ *n* **1** : a narrow passage or point of congestion **2** : something that obstructs or impedes

bot·tom \'bät-əm\ *n* **1** : an under or supporting surface; *also* : BUTTOCKS **2** : the surface on which a body of water lies **3** : the lowest part or place; *also* : an inferior position ⟨start at the ∼⟩ **4** : low land along a river — **bottom** *adj* — **bot·tom·less** *adj*

bot·tom·land \'bät-əm-ˌland\ *n* : BOTTOM 4

bottom line *n* **1** : the essential point : CRUX **2** : the final result : OUTCOME

bottom out *vb* : to reach a low point before rebounding ⟨a security market that *bottoms out*⟩

bot·u·lism \'bäch-ə-ˌliz-əm\ *n* : acute food poisoning caused by a bacterial toxin in food

bou·doir \'büd-ˌwär, 'búd-\ *n* [F, fr. *bouder* to pout] : a woman's private room

bouf·fant \bü-'fänt, 'bü-ˌfänt\ *adj* [F] : puffed out ⟨∼ hairdos⟩

bough \'baú\ *n* : a usu. large or main branch of a tree

bought past and past part of BUY

bouil·la·baisse \ˌbü-yə-'bäs\ *n* [F] : a highly seasoned fish stew made with at least two kinds of fish

bouil·lon \'bü-ˌyän; 'búl-ˌyän, -yən\ *n* : a clear soup made usu. from beef

boul·der \'bōl-dər\ *n* : a large detached rounded or worn mass of rock — **bouldered** \-dərd\ *adj*

bou·le·vard \'búl-ə-ˌvärd, 'bül-\ *n* [F, modif. of Middle Dutch *bolwerc* bulwark; so called because the first boulevards were laid out on the sites of razed city fortifications] : a broad often landscaped thoroughfare

bounce \'baúns\ *vb* **bounced; bounc·ing**
1 : to cause to rebound ⟨∼ a ball⟩ **2**
: to rebound after striking — **bounce** *n*

bounc·er \'baún-sər\ *n* : someone employed in a public place to remove disorderly persons

¹bound \'baúnd\ *adj* : intending to go

²bound *n* : LIMIT, BOUNDARY — **bound·less** *adj* — **bound·less·ness** *n*

³bound *vb* **1** : to set limits to **2** : to form the boundary of **3** : to name the boundaries of

⁴bound past and past part of BIND

⁵bound *adj* **1** : constrained by or as if by bonds : CONFINED, OBLIGED **2** : enclosed in a binding or cover **3** : RESOLVED, DETERMINED; *also* : SURE

⁶bound *n* **1** : LEAP, JUMP **2** : REBOUND, BOUNCE

⁷bound *vb* : SPRING, BOUNCE

bound·ary \'baún-d(ə-)rē\ *n, pl* **-aries**
: something that marks or fixes a limit (as of territory) **syn** border, frontier, march

bound·en \'baún-dən\ *adj* : BINDING

boun·te·ous \'baúnt-ē-əs\ *adj* **1** : GENEROUS **2** : ABUNDANT — **boun·te·ous·ly** *adv*

boun·ti·ful \'baúnt-i-fəl\ *adj* **1** : giving freely **2** : PLENTIFUL — **boun·ti·ful·ly** *adv*

boun·ty \'baúnt-ē\ *n, pl* **bounties** [ME *bounte* goodness, fr. OF *bonté*, fr. L *bonitas*, fr. *bonus* good] **1** : GENEROSITY **2** : something given liberally **3** : a reward, premium, or subsidy given usu. for doing something

bou·quet \bō-'kā, bü-\ *n* [F, fr. MF, thicket, fr. OF *bosc* forest] **1** : flowers picked and fastened together in a bunch **2** : a distinctive aroma (as of wine) **syn** scent, fragrance, perfume, redolence

bour·bon \'bər-bən\ *n* : a whiskey distilled from a corn mash

bour·geois \'búrzh-ˌwä, búrzh-'wä\ *n, pl* **bourgeois** \-ˌwä(z), -'wä(z)\ [MF, lit., citizen of a town, fr. *borc* town, borough, fr. L *burgus* fortified place, of Gmc origin] : a middle-class person — **bourgeois** *adj*

bour·geoi·sie \ˌbúrzh-ˌwä-'zē\ *n* : a social order dominated by bourgeois

bourn *or* **bourne** \'bōrn, 'búrn\ *n, archaic* : BOUNDARY; *also* : DESTINATION

bourse \'búrs\ *n* : a European stock exchange

bout \'baút\ *n* **1** : CONTEST, MATCH **2** : OUTBREAK, ATTACK ⟨a ∼ of measles⟩ **3** : SESSION

bou·tique \bü-'tēk\ *n* : a fashionable specialty shop

bou·ton·niere \ˌbüt-ᵊn-'iər\ *n* : a flower or bouquet worn in a buttonhole

bo·vine \'bō-ˌvīn, -ˌvēn\ *adj* : of, relating to, or resembling the ox or cow — **bovine** *n*

¹bow \'baú\ *vb* **1** : SUBMIT, YIELD **2** : to bend the head or body (as in submission, courtesy, or assent)

²bow *n* : an act or posture of bowing

³bow \'bō\ *n* **1** : BEND, ARCH; *esp* : RAINBOW **2** : a weapon for shooting arrows; *also* : ARCHER **3** : a knot formed by doubling a line into two or more loops **4** : a wooden rod strung with horsehairs for playing an instrument of the violin family

⁴bow \'bō\ *vb* **1** : BEND, CURVE **2** : to play (an instrument) with a bow

⁵bow \'baú\ *n* : the forward part of a ship — **bow** *adj*

bowd·ler·ize \'bōd-lə-ˌrīz, 'baúd-\ *vb* **-ized; -iz·ing** : to expurgate by omitting parts considered vulgar

bow·el \'baú(-ə)l\ *n* **1** : INTESTINE — usu. used in pl. **2** : one of the divisions of the intestine **3** *pl* : the inmost parts ⟨the ∼s of the earth⟩

bow·er \'baú(-ə)r\ *n* : a shelter of boughs or vines : ARBOR

¹bowl \'bōl\ *n* **1** : a concave vessel used to hold liquids **2** : a drinking vessel **3** : a bowl-shaped part or structure — **bowl·ful** \-ˌfúl\ *n*

²bowl *n* **1** : a ball for rolling on a level surface in bowling **2** : a cast of the ball in bowling

³bowl *vb* **1** : to play a game of bowling; *also* : to roll a ball in bowling **2** : to travel (as in a vehicle) rapidly and smoothly **3** : to strike or knock down with a moving object; *also* : to overwhelm with surprise

bowlder var of BOULDER

bow·legged \'bō-ˌleg-əd\ *adj* : having legs that bow outward at or below the knee — **bow·leg** \'bō-ˌleg\ *n*

¹bowl·er \'bō-lər\ *n* : one that bowls

²bow·ler \'bō-lər\ *n* : DERBY 3

bow·line \'bō-lən, -ˌlīn\ *n* : a knot used

to form a loop that neither slips nor jams

bowl·ing \\'bō-liŋ\ *n* : any of various games in which balls are rolled on a green or alley at an object or a group of objects; *esp* : TENPINS

bow·man \\'bō-mən\ *n* : ARCHER

bow·sprit \\'baủ-ˌsprit\ *n* : a spar projecting forward from the prow of a ship

bow·string \\'bō-ˌstriŋ\ *n* : the cord connecting the two ends of a bow

¹**box** \\'bäks\ *n, pl* **box** *or* **box·es** : an evergreen shrub or small tree used esp. for hedges

²**box** *n* **1** : a rigid typically rectangular receptacle often with a cover; *also* : the quantity held by a box **2** : a small compartment (as for a group of theater patrons); *also* : a boxlike receptacle or division **3** : any of six spaces on a baseball diamond where the batter, pitcher, coaches, and catcher stand **4** : PREDICAMENT

³**box** *vb* : to furnish with or enclose in or as if in a box

⁴**box** *n* : a punch or slap esp. on the ear

⁵**box** *vb* **1** : to strike with the hand **2** : to engage in boxing with : fight with the fists **syn** smack, cuff, strike, slap

box·car \\'bäks-ˌkär\ *n* : a roofed freight car usu. with sliding doors in the sides

¹**box·er** \\'bäk-sər\ *n* : one that engages in boxing

²**boxer** *n* : a compact short-haired usu. fawn or brindled dog of a breed of German origin

box·ing \\'bäk-siŋ\ *n* : the sport of fighting with the fists

box office *n* : an office (as in a theater) where admission tickets are sold

box·wood \\'bäks-ˌwủd\ *n* : the tough hard wood of the box; *also* : a box tree or shrub

boy \\'bói\ *n* **1** : a male child : YOUTH **2** : SON — **boy·hood** \-ˌhủd\ *n* — **boy·ish** *adj* — **boy·ish·ly** *adv* — **boy·ish·ness** *n*

boy·cott \\'bói-ˌkät\ *vb* [Charles C. *Boycott* †1897 E land agent in Ireland who was ostracized for refusing to reduce rents] : to refrain from having any dealings with — **boycott** *n*

Boy Scout *n* : a member of the Boy Scouts of America

boy·sen·ber·ry \\'bóiz-ᵊn-ˌber-ē, 'bóis-\ *n* : a large bramble fruit with a raspber-

ry flavor; *also* : the hybrid plant bearing it developed by crossing blackberries and raspberries

bp *abbr* bishop

BP *abbr* **1** blood pressure **2** boiling point

bpl *abbr* birthplace

BPOE *abbr* Benevolent and Protective Order of Elks

br *abbr* **1** branch **2** brass **3** brown

¹**Br** *abbr* Britain; British

²**Br** *symbol* bromine

BR *abbr* bedroom

bra \\'brä\ *n* : BRASSIERE

¹**brace** \\'brās\ *vb* **braced; brac·ing 1** *archaic* : to make fast : BIND **2** : to tighten preparatory to use; *also* : to get ready for : prepare oneself **3** : INVIGORATE **4** : to furnish or support with a brace; *also* : STRENGTHEN **5** : to set firmly; *also* : to gain courage or confidence

²**brace** *n, pl* **brac·es 1** *or pl* **brace** : two of a kind ⟨∼ of dogs⟩ **2** : a crank-shaped device for turning a bit **3** : something (as a tie, prop, or clamp) that distributes, directs, or resists pressure or weight **4** *pl* : SUSPENDERS **5** : an appliance for supporting a body part (as the shoulders) **6** *pl* : dental appliances used to exert pressure to straighten misaligned teeth **7** : a mark { or } or ∼ used to connect words or items to be considered together

brace·let \\'brā-slət\ *n* [ME, fr. MF, dim. of *bras* arm, fr. L *bracchium,* fr. Gk *brachiōn*] : an ornamental band or chain worn around the wrist

bra·ce·ro \brä-'ser-ō\ *n, pl* **-ros** : a Mexican laborer admitted to the U.S. esp. for seasonal farm work

brack·en \\'brak-ən\ *n* : a large coarse fern; *also* : a growth of such ferns

¹**brack·et** \\'brak-ət\ *n* **1** : a projecting framework or arm designed to support weight; *also* : a shelf on such framework **2** : one of a pair of punctuation marks [ ] used esp. to enclose interpolated matter **3** : a continuous section of a series; *esp* : one of a graded series of income groups

²**bracket** *vb* **1** : to furnish or fasten with brackets **2** : to place within brackets; *also* : to separate or group with or as if with brackets

brack·ish \'brak-ish\ *adj* : somewhat salty — **brack·ish·ness** *n*

bract \'brakt\ *n* : an often modified leaf on or at the base of a flower stalk

brad \'brad\ *n* : a slender nail with a small head

brae \'brā\ *n, chiefly Scot* : a hillside esp. along a river

brag \'brag\ *vb* **bragged; brag·ging** : to talk or assert boastfully — **brag** *n*

brag·ga·do·cio \ˌbrag-ə-'dō-s(h)ē-ˌō, -(ˌ)shō\ *n, pl* **-cios 1** : BRAGGART, BOASTER **2** : empty boasting **3** : arrogant pretension : COCKINESS

brag·gart \'brag-ərt\ *n* : one who brags

Brah·man *or* **Brah·min** \'bräm-ən *for 1;* 'bräm-, 'bram-, 'bram- *for 2*\ *n* **1** : a Hindu of the highest caste traditionally assigned to the priesthood **2** : any of a breed of large vigorous humped cattle developed in the southern U.S. from Indian stock **3** *usu* **Brahmin** : a person of high social standing and cultivated intellect and taste

Brah·man·ism \'bräm-ə-ˌniz-əm\ *n* : orthodox Hinduism

¹braid \'brād\ *vb* **1** : to form (strands) into a braid : PLAIT; *also* : to make by braiding **2** : to ornament with braid

²braid *n* **1** : a cord or ribbon of three or more interwoven strands; *also* : a length of braided hair **2** : a narrow ornamental fabric of intertwined threads

braille \'brāl\ *n, often cap* : a system of writing for the blind that uses characters made up of raised dots

¹brain \'brān\ *n* **1** : the part of the vertebrate nervous system that is the organ of thought and nervous coordination, is made up of nerve cells and their fibers, and is enclosed in the skull; *also* : a centralized mass of nerve tissue in an invertebrate **2** : INTELLECT, INTELLIGENCE — often used in pl. — **brained** \'brānd\ *adj* — **brain·less** *adj* — **brainy** *adj*

²brain *vb* **1** : to kill by smashing the skull **2** : to hit on the head

brain·child \-ˌchīld\ *n* : a product of one's creative imagination

brain death *n* : final cessation of activity in the central nervous system esp. as indicated by a flat electroencephalogram

brain drain *n* : a migration of professional people (as scientists) from one country to another usu. for higher pay

brain·storm \-ˌstorm\ *n* : a sudden burst of inspiration

brain·wash·ing \'brān-ˌwȯsh-iŋ, -ˌwäsh-\ *n* **1** : a forcible attempt by indoctrination to induce someone to give up his basic political, social, or religious beliefs and attitudes and to accept contrasting regimented ideas **2** : persuasion by propaganda or salesmanship — **brain·wash** *vb*

brain wave *n* : rhythmic fluctuation of voltage between parts of the brain; *also* : a current produced by brain waves

braise \'brāz\ *vb* **braised; brais·ing** : to cook (meat) slowly in fat and little moisture in a closed pot

¹brake \'brāk\ *n* : any of a genus of tall coarse ferns with compound fronds

²brake *n* : a device for slowing or stopping motion esp. by friction — **brake·less** *adj*

³brake *vb* **braked; brak·ing 1** : to slow or stop by or as if by a brake **2** : to apply a brake

⁴brake *n* : rough or wet land heavily overgrown (as with thickets or reeds)

brake·man \'brāk-mən\ *n* : a train crew member who inspects the train and assists the conductor

bram·ble \'bram-bəl\ *n* : any of a large genus of prickly shrubs (as a blackberry) related to the roses; *also* : any rough prickly shrub or vine

bran \'bran\ *n* : broken husks of cereal grain sifted from flour or meal

¹branch \'branch\ *n* [ME, fr. OF *branche,* fr. L *branca* paw] **1** : a natural subdivision (as a bough or twig) of a plant stem **2** : a division (as of an antler or a river) related to a whole like a plant branch to its stem **3** : a discrete unit or element of a complex system (as of knowledge, people, or business); *esp* : a division of a family descended from one ancestor — **branched** \'brancht\ *adj*

²branch *vb* **1** : to develop branches **2** : DIVERGE

¹brand \'brand\ *n* **1** : a piece of charred or burning wood **2** : a mark made (as by burning) usu. to identify; *also* : a mark of disgrace : STIGMA **3** : a class of goods identified as the product of a particular firm or producer **4** : a distinctive kind ⟨his own ∼ of humor⟩

²brand *vb* **1** : to mark with a brand **2** : STIGMATIZE

bran·dish \'bran-dish\ *vb* : to shake or wave menacingly **syn** flourish, flash, flaunt

brand–new \'bran-'n(y)ü\ *adj* : conspicuously new and unused

bran·dy \'bran-dē\ *n, pl* **brandies** [short for *brandywine*, fr. Dutch *brandewijn*, fr. Middle Dutch *brantwijn*, fr. *brant* distilled + *wijn* wine] : a liquor distilled from wine or fermented fruit juice — **brandy** *vb*

brash \'brash\ *adj* **1** : IMPETUOUS **2** : aggressively self-assertive

brass \'bras\ *n* **1** : an alloy of copper and zinc; *also* : an object of brass **2** : brazen self-assurance — **brassy** *adj*

bras·se·rie \ˌbras-(ə-)'rē\ *n* : an informal usu. French restaurant serving simple hearty food

brass hat *n* : a high-ranking military officer

bras·siere \brə-'ziər\ *n* : a woman's close-fitting undergarment designed to support the breasts

brat \'brat\ *n* : an ill-behaved child — **brat·ty** *adj*

bra·va·do \brə-'väd-ō\ *n, pl* **-does** *or* **-dos** **1** : blustering swaggering conduct **2** : a show of bravery

¹brave \'brāv\ *adj* **brav·er; brav·est** [MF, fr. It & Sp *bravo* courageous, wild, fr. L *barbarus* barbarous] **1** : showing courage **2** : EXCELLENT, SPLENDID **syn** bold, intrepid, courageous, valiant — **brave·ly** *adv*

²brave *vb* **braved; brav·ing** : to face or endure bravely

³brave *n* : an American Indian warrior

brav·ery \'brāv-(ə-)rē\ *n, pl* **-er·ies** : COURAGE

bra·vo \'bräv-ō\ *n, pl* **bravos** : a shout of approval — often used as an interjection in applauding

bra·vu·ra \brə-'v(y)ùr-ə\ *n* **1** : a florid brilliant musical style **2** : self-assured brilliant performance

brawl \'brȯl\ *n* : a noisy quarrel **syn** fracas, row, rumpus, scrap, fray, melee — **brawl** *vb* — **brawl·er** *n*

brawn \'brȯn\ *n* : strong muscles; *also* : muscular strength — **brawny** *adj*

bray \'brā\ *n* : the characteristic harsh cry of a donkey — **bray** *vb*

braze \'brāz\ *vb* **brazed; braz·ing** : to solder with an alloy (as brass) that melts at a lower temperature than that of the metals being joined — **braz·er** *n*

bra·zen \'brāz-ᵊn\ *adj* **1** : made of brass **2** : sounding harsh and loud **3** : of the color of brass **4** : marked by contemptuous boldness — **bra·zen·ly** *adv* — **bra·zen·ness** \'brāz-ᵊn-(n)əs\ *n*

¹bra·zier \'brā-zhər\ *n* : a worker in brass

²brazier *n* **1** : a vessel holding burning coals (as for heating) **2** : a device on which food is grilled

Bra·zil·ian \brə-'zil-yən\ *n* : a native or inhabitant of Brazil — **Brazilian** *adj*

Bra·zil nut \brə-'zil-\ *n* : a triangular oily edible nut borne in large capsules by a tall So. American tree; *also* : the tree

¹breach \'brēch\ *n* **1** : a breaking of a law, obligation, tie (as of friendship), or standard (as of conduct) **2** : an interruption or opening made by or as if by breaking through **syn** violation, transgression, infringement, trespass

²breach *vb* : to make a breach in

¹bread \'bred\ *n* **1** : baked food made basically of flour or meal **2** : FOOD

²bread *vb* : to cover with bread crumbs before cooking

bread·bas·ket \'bred-ˌbas-kət\ *n* : a major cereal-producing region

bread·fruit \-ˌfrüt\ *n* : a round usu. seedless fruit resembling bread in color and texture when baked; *also* : a tall tropical tree related to the mulberry and bearing breadfruit

bread·stuff \-ˌstəf\ *n* : GRAIN, FLOUR

breadth \'bredth, 'bretth\ *n* **1** : WIDTH **2** : SPACIOUSNESS; *also* : liberality of taste or views

bread·win·ner \'bred-ˌwin-ər\ *n* : a member of a family whose wages supply its livelihood

¹break \'brāk\ *vb* **broke** \'brōk\; **bro·ken** \'brō-kən\; **break·ing** **1** : to separate into parts usu. suddenly or violently : come or force apart **2** : TRANSGRESS ⟨∼ a law⟩ **3** : to force a way into, out of, or through **4** : to disrupt the order or unity of ⟨∼ ranks⟩ ⟨∼ up a gang⟩; *also* : to bring to submission or helplessness **5** : EXCEED, SURPASS ⟨∼ a record⟩ **6** : RUIN **7** : to make known **8** : HALT, INTERRUPT; *also* : to act or change abruptly (as a course or activity) **9** : to come esp. suddenly into being or notice ⟨as day ∼s⟩ **10** : to fail under stress **11** : HAPPEN, DEVELOP — **break•able** *adj or n*

²**break** *n* **1** : an act of breaking **2** : a result of breaking; *esp* : an interruption of continuity ⟨coffee ∼⟩ ⟨a ∼ for the commercial⟩ **3** : a stroke of good luck

break•age \'brā-kij\ *n* **1** : the action of breaking **2** : articles or amount broken **3** : loss due to things broken

break•down \'brāk-ˌdaùn\ *n* **1** : functional failure; *esp* : a physical, mental, or nervous collapse **2** : DISINTEGRATION **3** : DECOMPOSITION **4** : ANALYSIS, CLASSIFICATION — **break down** \(ˈ)brāk-ˈdaùn\ *vb*

break•er \'brā-kər\ *n* **1** : one that breaks **2** : a wave that breaks into foam (as against the shore)

break•fast \'brek-fəst\ *n* : the first meal of the day — **breakfast** *vb*

break•front \'brāk-ˌfrənt\ *n* : a large cabinet whose center section projects beyond the flanking end sections

break in \(ˈ)brāk-ˈin\ *vb* **1** : to enter a building by force **2** : INTERRUPT; *also* : INTRUDE **3** : TRAIN

break out \(ˈ)brāk-ˈaùt\ *vb* **1** : to develop or erupt suddenly and with force **2** : to develop a skin rash

break•through \'brāk-ˌthrü\ *n* **1** : an act or instance of breaking through an obstruction or defensive line **2** : a sudden advance in knowledge or technique

break•up \'brāk-ˌəp\ *n* **1** : DISSOLUTION **2** : a division into smaller units — **break up** *vb*

break•wa•ter \'brāk-ˌwȯt-ər, -ˌwät-\ *n* : a structure built to protect a harbor or beach from the force of waves

bream \'brim, brēm\ *n, pl* **bream** *or* **breams** : any of various small freshwater sunfishes

breast \'brest\ *n* **1** : either of two milk-producing glandular organs situated on the front of the chest esp. in the human female **2** : the front part of the body between the neck and the abdomen **3** : the seat of emotion and thought

breast•bone \'bres(t)-ˈbōn, -ˌbōn\ *n* : STERNUM

breast–feed \'brest-ˌfēd\ *vb* : to feed (a baby) from a mother's breast rather than from a bottle

breast•plate \'bres(t)-ˌplāt\ *n* : a metal plate of armor for protecting the breast

breast•stroke \-ˌstrōk\ *n* : a swimming stroke executed by extending the arms in front of the head while drawing the knees forward and outward and then sweeping the arms back with palms out while kicking backward and outward

breast•work \'brest-ˌwərk\ *n* : a temporary fortification

breath \'breth\ *n* **1** : the act or power of breathing **2** : a slight breeze **3** : air inhaled or exhaled in breathing **4** : spoken sound **5** : SPIRIT — **breathless** *adj* — **breath•less•ly** *adv*

breathe \'brēth\ *vb* **breathed; breath•ing** **1** : to inhale and exhale **2** : LIVE **3** : to halt for rest **4** : to utter softly or secretly

breath•tak•ing \'breth-ˌtā-kiŋ\ *adj* **1** : making one out of breath **2** : EXCITING, THRILLING ⟨∼ beauty⟩

brec•cia \'brech-(ē-)ə\ *n* : a rock consisting of sharp fragments held in fine-grained material

breech \'brēch\ *n* **1** *pl* \usu 'brich-əz\ : trousers ending near the knee; *also* : PANTS **2** : BUTTOCKS, RUMP **3** : the part of a firearm at the rear of the barrel

¹**breed** \'brēd\ *vb* **bred** \'bred\; **breed•ing** **1** : BEGET; *also* : ORIGINATE **2** : to propagate sexually; *also* : MATE **3** : BRING UP, NURTURE **4** : to produce (fissionable material) from material that is not fissionable **syn** generate, reproduce, procreate, propagate — **breed•er** *n*

²**breed** *n* **1** : a strain of similar and presumably related plants or animals usu. developed under the influence of man **2** : KIND, SORT, CLASS

breed•ing *n* **1** : ANCESTRY **2** : training in polite social interaction **3** : sexual propagation of plants or animals

¹**breeze** \'brēz\ *n* : a light wind — **breezy** *adj*

²**breeze** *vb* **breezed; breez•ing** : to progress quickly and easily

breeze•way \'brēz-ˌwā\ *n* : a roofed open passage connecting two buildings (as a house and garage)

breth•ren \'breth-(ə-)rən, -ˌərn\ *pl of* BROTHER — used esp. in formal or solemn address

Brethren *n pl* : members of one of several Protestant denominations originating chiefly in a German religious movement and stressing personal religious experience

bre•vet \bri-'vet\ *n* : a commission giving a military officer higher nominal rank than that for which he receives pay — **brevet** *vb*

bre•via•ry \'brē-vyə-rē, -vē-ˌer-ē\ *n, pl* **-ries** : a book of prayers, hymns, psalms, and readings used by Roman Catholic priests

brev•i•ty \'brev-ət-ē\ *n, pl* **-ties** : shortness of duration; *esp* : shortness or conciseness of expression

brew \'brü\ *vb* **1** : to prepare (as beer) by steeping, boiling, and fermenting **2** : to prepare (as tea) by soaking in hot water — **brew** *n* — **brew•er** *n* — **brew•ery** \'brü-ə-rē, 'brù(-ə)r-ē\ *n*

bri•ar \'brī(-ə)r\ *n* : a tobacco pipe made from the root of a brier

¹bribe \'brīb\ *n* [ME, something stolen, fr. MF, bread given to a beggar] : something (as money or a favor) given or promised to a person to influence conduct

²bribe *vb* **bribed; brib•ing** : to corrupt or influence by offering a bribe — **brib•ery** \'brī-b(ə-)rē\ *n*

bric–a–brac \'brik-ə-ˌbrak\ *n pl* [F] : small ornamental articles

¹brick \'brik\ *n* : a block molded from moist clay and hardened by heat used esp. for building

²brick *vb* : to close, cover, or pave with bricks

brick•bat \'brik-ˌbat\ *n* **1** : a piece of a broken brick esp. when thrown as a missile **2** : an uncomplimentary remark

brick•lay•er \'brik-ˌlā-ər\ *n* : a person who builds or paves with bricks — **brick•lay•ing** \-ˌlā-iŋ\ *n*

¹brid•al \'brīd-ᵊl\ *n* [ME *bridale*, fr. OE *brȳdealu*, fr. *brȳd* bride + *ealu* ale] : MARRIAGE, WEDDING

²bridal *adj* : of or relating to a bride or a wedding

bride \'brīd\ *n* : a woman just married or about to be married

bride•groom \'brīd-ˌgrüm, -ˌgrùm\ *n* : a man just married or about to be married

brides•maid \'brīdz-ˌmād\ *n* : a woman who attends a bride at her wedding

¹bridge \'brij\ *n* **1** : a structure built over a depression or obstacle for use as a passageway **2** : something (as the upper part of the nose) resembling a bridge in form or function; *esp* : a platform over the deck of a ship **3** : an artificial replacement for missing teeth

²bridge *vb* **bridged; bridg•ing** : to build a bridge over — **bridge•able** *adj*

³bridge *n* : a card game for four players developed from whist

bridge•head \-ˌhed\ *n* : an advanced position seized in enemy territory as a foothold

bridge•work \-ˌwərk\ *n* : dental bridges

¹bri•dle \'brīd-ᵊl\ *n* **1** : headgear with which a horse is controlled **2** : CURB, RESTRAINT

²bridle *vb* **bri•dled; bri•dling** \'brīd-(ᵊ-)liŋ\ **1** : to put a bridle on; *also* : to restrain with or as if with a bridle **2** : to show hostility or scorn usu. by tossing the head

¹brief \'brēf\ *adj* **1** : short in duration or extent **2** : CONCISE; *also* : CURT — **brief•ly** *adv* — **brief•ness** *n*

²brief *n* **1** : a concise statement or document; *esp* : one summarizing a law client's case or a legal argument **2** *pl* : short snug underpants

³brief *vb* : to give final instructions or essential information to

brief•case \'brēf-ˌkās\ *n* : a flat flexible case for carrying papers

¹bri•er *or* **bri•ar** \'brī(-ə)r\ *n* : a plant (as a bramble or rose) with a thorny or prickly woody stem; *also* : a group or mass of brier bushes — **bri•ery** \'brī(-ə)r-ē\ *adj*

²brier *or* **briar** *n* : a heath of southern Europe with a root used for making pipes

¹brig \'brig\ *n* : a 2-masted square= rigged sailing ship

²brig *n* : the place of confinement for offenders on a naval ship

³brig *abbr* **1** brigade **2** brigadier

bri•gade \brig-'ād\ *n* **1** : a military unit

composed of a headquarters, one or more units of infantry or armored forces, and supporting units **2** : a group organized for a particular purpose (as fire-fighting)

brig·a·dier general \ˌbrig-ə-ˌdiər-\ *n* : a commissioned officer (as in the army) ranking next below a major general

brig·and \ˈbrig-ənd\ *n* : BANDIT — **brig·and·age** \-ən-dij\ *n*

brig·an·tine \ˈbrig-ən-ˌtēn\ *n* : a 2-masted square-rigged ship not carrying a square mainsail

Brig Gen *abbr* brigadier general

bright \ˈbrīt\ *adj* **1** : SHINING, RADIANT **2** : ILLUSTRIOUS, GLORIOUS **3** : INTELLIGENT, CLEVER; *also* : LIVELY, CHEERFUL **syn** brilliant, lustrous, beaming, radiant — **bright·ly** *adv* — **bright·ness** *n*

bright·en \ˈbrīt-ᵊn\ *vb* **bright·ened**; **bright·en·ing** \ˈbrīt-(ᵊ-)niŋ\ : to make or become bright or brighter — **bright·en·er** \-(ᵊ-)nər\ *n*

¹**bril·liant** \ˈbril-yənt\ *adj* [F *brillant*, prp. of *briller* to shine, fr. It *brillare*, fr. *brillo* beryl, fr. L *beryllus*] **1** : very bright **2** : STRIKING, DISTINCTIVE **3** : very intelligent **syn** radiant, lustrous, beaming, lucid, bright, lambent — **bril·liance** \-yəns\ *or* **bril·lian·cy** \-yən-sē\ *n* — **bril·liant·ly** *adv*

²**brilliant** *n* : a gem cut in a particular form with many facets

bril·lian·tine \ˈbril-yən-ˌtēn\ *n* : a usu. oily dressing for the hair

brim \ˈbrim\ *n* : EDGE, RIM **syn** brink, border, verge, fringe — **brim·less** *adj*

brim·ful \-ˈfůl\ *adj* : full to the brim

brim·stone \ˈbrim-ˌstōn\ *n* : SULFUR

brin·dled \ˈbrin-dᵊld\ *adj* : having dark streaks or flecks on a gray or tawny ground ⟨a ∼ Great Dane⟩

brine \ˈbrīn\ *n* **1** : water saturated with salt **2** : OCEAN — **brin·i·ness** \ˈbrī-nē-nəs\ *n* — **briny** \ˈbrī-nē\ *adj*

bring \ˈbriŋ\ *vb* **brought** \ˈbrȯt\; **bring·ing** \ˈbriŋ-iŋ\ **1** : to cause to come with one **2** : INDUCE, PERSUADE, LEAD **3** : PRODUCE, EFFECT **4** : to sell for — **bring·er** *n*

bring about *vb* : to cause to take place : EFFECT

bring up *vb* **1** : to give a parent's fostering care to **2** : to come or bring to a sudden halt **3** : to call to notice **4** : VOMIT

brink \ˈbriŋk\ *n* **1** : an edge at the top of a steep place **2** : the point of onset

brio \ˈbrē-ō\ *n* : VIVACITY, SPIRIT

bri·oche \brē-ˈōsh, -ˈȯsh\ *n* [F] : a roll baked from light yeast dough rich with eggs and butter

bri·quette *or* **bri·quet** \brik-ˈet\ *n* : a compacted often brick-shaped mass of fine material ⟨a charcoal ∼⟩

brisk \ˈbrisk\ *adj* **1** : ALERT, LIVELY **2** : INVIGORATING **syn** agile, spry, nimble — **brisk·ly** *adv* — **brisk·ness** *n*

bris·ket \ˈbris-kət\ *n* : the breast or lower chest of a quadruped

bris·ling *or* **bris·tling** \ˈbriz-liŋ, ˈbris-\ *n* : a small sardinelike herring

¹**bris·tle** \ˈbris-əl\ *n* : a short stiff coarse hair — **bris·tly** \-(ə-)lē\ *adj*

²**bristle** *vb* **bris·tled**; **bris·tling** \ˈbris-(ə-)liŋ\ **1** : to stand stiffly erect **2** : to show angry defiance **3** : to appear as if covered with bristles

Brit *abbr* Britain; British

Bri·tan·nia metal \bri-ˌtan-yə-, -ˌtan-ē-ə-\ *n* : a silver-white alloy of tin, antimony, and copper similar to pewter

Bri·tan·nic \bri-ˈtan-ik\ *adj* : BRITISH

britch·es \ˈbrich-əz\ *n pl* : BREECHES, TROUSERS

Brit·ish \ˈbrit-ish\ *n pl* : the people of Great Britain or the Commonwealth — **British** *adj*

British thermal unit *n* : the quantity of heat needed to raise the temperature of one pound of water one degree Fahrenheit

Brit·on \ˈbrit-ᵊn\ *n* **1** : a member of a people inhabiting Britain before the Anglo-Saxon invasion **2** : a native or inhabitant of Great Britain

brit·tle \ˈbrit-ᵊl\ *adj* **brit·tler** \ˈbrit-(ᵊ-)lər\; **brit·tlest** \-ləst, -ᵊl-əst\ : easily broken or snapped : FRAGILE **syn** crisp, crumbly, friable

bro *abbr* brother

¹**broach** \ˈbrōch\ *n* : a pointed tool

²**broach** *vb* **1** : to pierce (as a cask) in order to draw the contents **2** : to introduce as a topic of conversation

¹**broad** \ˈbrȯd\ *adj* **1** : WIDE **2** : SPACIOUS **3** : CLEAR, OPEN **4** : OBVIOUS **5** : COARSE, CRUDE ⟨∼ stories⟩ **6** : liberal in outlook **7** : GENERAL **8** : dealing with essential points — **broad·ly** *adv* — **broad·ness** *n*

²**broad** *n*, *slang* : WOMAN

¹broad·cast \\'bród-ˌkast\ *vb* **broadcast** *also* **broad·cast·ed; broad·cast·ing 1** : to scatter or sow broadcast **2** : to make widely known **3** : to transmit a broadcast — **broad·cast·er** *n*

²broadcast *adv* : to or over a wide area

³broadcast *n* **1** : the transmission of sound or images by radio or television **2** : a single radio or television program

broad·cloth \-ˌklóth\ *n* **1** : a smooth dense woolen cloth **2** : a fine soft cloth of cotton, silk, or synthetic fiber

broad·en \\'bród-ᵊn\ *vb* **broad·ened; broad·en·ing** \\'bród-(ᵊ-)niŋ\ : WIDEN

broad·loom \-ˌlüm\ *adj* : woven on a wide loom esp. in a solid color ⟨a ∼ carpet⟩

broad–mind·ed \-'mīn-dəd\ *adj* : free from prejudice — **broad–mind·ed·ly** *adv* — **broad–mind·ed·ness** *n*

broad·side \-ˌsīd\ *n* **1** : a sheet of paper printed usu. on one side (as an advertisement) **2** : the part of a ship's side above the waterline **3** : all of the guns on one side of a ship; *also* : their simultaneous firing **4** : a volley of abuse or denunciation

broad–spectrum *adj* : having a wide range esp. of effectiveness ⟨∼ antibiotics⟩

broad·sword \\'bród-ˌsórd\ *n* : a broad≠bladed sword

broad·tail \-ˌtāl\ *n* : a flat and wavy fur or skin of a very young or premature karakul lamb

bro·cade \brō-'kād\ *n* : a usu. silk fabric with a raised design

broc·co·li \\'bräk-(ə-)lē\ *n* [It, pl. of *broccolo* flowering top of a cabbage, dim. of *brocco* small nail, sprout, fr. L *broccus* projecting] : an open branching cauliflower whose young flowering shoots are used as a vegetable

bro·chette \brō-'shet\ *n* : SKEWER

bro·chure \brō-'shür\ *n* [F, fr. *brocher* to sew, fr. MF, to prick, fr. OF *brochier,* fr. *broche* pointed tool] : PAMPHLET, BOOKLET

bro·gan \\'brō-gən, brō-'gan\ *n* : a heavy shoe; *esp* : a work shoe reaching to the ankle

brogue \\'brōg\ *n* : a dialect or regional pronunciation; *esp* : an Irish accent

broi·der \\'bróid-ər\ *vb* : EMBROIDER — **broi·dery** \\'bróid-(ə-)rē\ *n*

broil \\'bróil\ *vb* : to cook by exposure to radiant heat : GRILL — **broil** *n*

broil·er \\'brói-lər\ *n* **1** : a utensil for broiling **2** : a young chicken fit for broiling

¹broke \\'brōk\ past of BREAK

²broke *adj* : PENNILESS

bro·ken \\'brō-kən\ *adj* **1** : SHATTERED **2** : having gaps or breaks : INTERRUPTED, DISRUPTED **3** : SUBDUED, CRUSHED **4** : BANKRUPT **5** : imperfectly spoken — **bro·ken·ly** *adv*

bro·ken·heart·ed \ˌbrō-kən-'härt-əd\ *adj* : overcome by grief or despair

bro·ker \\'brō-kər\ *n* : an agent who negotiates contracts of purchase and sale

bro·ker·age \\'brō-k(ə-)rij\ *n* **1** : the business of a broker **2** : the fee or commission charged by a broker

bro·mide \\'brō-ˌmīd\ *n* **1** : a compound of bromine and another element or chemical group including some (as potassium bromide) used as sedatives **2** : a trite remark or notion

bro·mid·ic \brō-'mid-ik\ *adj* : DULL, TIRESOME ⟨∼ remarks⟩

bro·mine \\'brō-ˌmēn\ *n* [F *brome* bromine, fr. Gk *brōmos* stink] : a deep red liquid corrosive chemical element that gives off an irritating vapor

bronc \\'bräŋk\ *n* : BRONCO

bron·chi·al \\'bräŋ-kē-əl\ *adj* : of, relating to, or affecting the bronchi or their branches

bron·chi·tis \brän-'kīt-əs, bräŋ-\ *n* : inflammation of the bronchi and their branches — **bron·chit·ic** \-'kit-ik\ *adj*

bron·chus \\'bräŋ-kəs\ *n, pl* **bron·chi** \\'bräŋ-ˌkī, -ˌkē\ : either of the main divisions of the windpipe each leading to a lung

bron·co \\'bräŋ-kō\ *n, pl* **broncos** [MexSp, fr. Sp, rough, wild] : an unbroken or partly broken range horse of western No. America; *also* : MUSTANG

bron·to·sau·rus \ˌbränt-ə-'sór-əs\ *or* **bron·to·saur** \\'bränt-ə-ˌsór\ *n* [deriv. of Gk *brontē* thunder + *sauros* lizard] : any of various large 4-footed and probably herbivorous dinosaurs

Bronx cheer \\'bräŋks-\ *n* : RASPBERRY 2

¹bronze \\'bränz\ *vb* **bronzed; bronz·ing** : to give the appearance of bronze to

²bronze *n* **1** : an alloy of copper and tin

and sometimes other elements; *also* : something made of bronze **2** : a yellowish brown color — **bronzy** \\'brän-zē\ *adj*

brooch \\'brōch, 'brüch\ *n* : an ornamental clasp or pin

¹brood \\'brüd\ *n* : a family of young animals or children and esp. of birds

²brood *vb* **1** : to sit on eggs to hatch them; *also* : to shelter (hatched young) with the wings **2** : to think anxiously or gloomily about something : PONDER

³brood *adj* : kept for breeding ⟨a ~ mare⟩

brood·er \\'brüd-ər\ *n* **1** : one that broods **2** : a heated structure for raising young birds

¹brook \\'brúk\ *vb* : TOLERATE, BEAR

²brook *n* : a small natural stream of water

brook·let \-lət\ *n* : a small brook

brook trout *n* : a common speckled cold-water char of eastern No. America

broom \\'brüm, 'brùm\ *n* **1** : any of several shrubs of the legume family with long slender branches and usu. yellow flowers **2** : an implement for sweeping orig. made from twigs — **broom·stick** \-ˌstik\ *n*

bros *abbr* brothers

broth \\'bròth\ *n, pl* **broths** \\'bròths, 'bròthz\ **1** : liquid in which meat or sometimes vegetable food has been cooked **2** : a fluid culture medium

broth·el \\'bräth-əl, 'bròth-\ *n* : an establishment where prostitutes are available

broth·er \\'brəth-ər\ *n, pl* **brothers** *also* **breth·ren** \\'breth-(ə-)rən, 'breth-ərn\ **1** : a male having one or both parents in common with another individual; *also* : KINSMAN **2** : a kindred human being **3** : a man who is a religious but not a priest — **broth·er·li·ness** \-lē-nəs\ *n* — **broth·er·ly** \-lē\ *adj*

broth·er·hood \\'brəth-ər-ˌhùd\ *n* **1** : the state of being brothers or a brother **2** : ASSOCIATION, FRATERNITY **3** : the whole body of persons in a business or profession

broth·er–in–law \\'brəth-(ə-)rən-ˌlò, 'brəth-ərn-ˌlò\ *n, pl* **brothers–in–law** \\'brəth-ərz-ən-\ : the brother of one's

spouse; *also* : the husband of one's sister or of one's spouse's sister

brougham \\'brü-(ə)m, 'brō-(ə)m\ *n* **1** : a light closed horse-drawn carriage with the driver outside in front **2** : COUPÉ 2 **3** : a sedan having no roof over the driver's seat

brought past and past part of BRING

brou·ha·ha \\'brü-ˌhä-ˌhä\ *n* : HUBBUB, UPROAR

brow \\'braú\ *n* **1** : the eyebrow or the ridge on which it grows; *also* : FOREHEAD **2** : the projecting upper part of a steep place

brow·beat \\'braú-ˌbēt\ *vb* **-beat;** **-beat·en** \-'bēt-³n\ *or* **-beat;** **-beat·ing** : to intimidate by sternness or arrogance : BULLY **syn** intimidate, hector

¹brown \\'braún\ *adj* : of the color brown; *also* : of dark or tanned complexion

²brown *n* : a color like that of coffee or chocolate that is a blend of red and yellow darkened by black — **brown·ish** *adj*

³brown *vb* : to make or become brown

brown bag·ging \-'bag-iŋ\ *n* : the practice of carrying one's lunch usu. in a brown bag — **brown bag·ger** \-'bag-ər\ *n*

brown·ie \\'braú-nē\ *n* **1** : a legendary cheerful elf who performs good deeds at night **2** *cap* : a member of the Girl Scouts from 6 through 8 years of age

brown·out \\'braún-ˌaút\ *n* : a curtailment in electrical power; *also* : a period of reduced illumination due to such curtailment

brown rice *n* : hulled but unpolished rice that retains most of the bran layers

brown·stone \\'braún-ˌstōn\ *n* : a dwelling faced with reddish brown sandstone

¹browse \\'braúz\ *vb* **browsed; brows·ing** **1** : to feed on browse; *also* : GRAZE **2** : to read bits at random in a book or collection of books

²browse *n* : tender shoots, twigs, and leaves fit for food for cattle

bru·in \\'brü-ən\ *n* : BEAR

¹bruise \\'brüz\ *vb* **bruised; bruis·ing** **1** : to inflict a bruise on; *also* : to become bruised **2** : to break down by pounding ⟨~ garlic for a salad⟩

²bruise *n* : a surface injury to flesh : CONTUSION

bruis·er \'brü-zər\ *n* : a big husky man

bruit \'brüt\ *vb* : to noise abroad

brunch \'brənch\ *n* : a meal that combines a late breakfast and an early lunch

bru·net *or* **bru·nette** \brü-'net\ *adj* [F *brunet,* masc., *brunette,* fem., brownish, fr. OF, fr. *brun* brown] : of dark or relatively dark pigmentation; *esp* : having brown or black hair and eyes — **brunet** *or* **brunette** *n*

brunt \'brənt\ *n* : the main shock, force, or stress esp. of an attack

¹brush \'brəsh\ *n* **1** : BRUSHWOOD **2** : scrub vegetation or land covered with it

²brush *n* **1** : a device composed of bristles set in a handle and used esp. for cleaning or painting **2** : a bushy tail (as of a fox) **3** : an electrical conductor that makes contact between a stationary and a moving part of a generator or motor **4** : a light rubbing or touching

³brush *vb* **1** : to treat (as in cleaning or painting) with a brush **2** : to remove with or as if with a brush; *also* : to dispose of in an offhand manner **3** : to touch gently in passing

⁴brush *n* : SKIRMISH **syn** encounter, run= in

brush–off \'brəsh-ˌȯf\ *n* : an abrupt or offhand dismissal

brush up *vb* : to renew one's skill

brush·wood \'brəsh-ˌwùd\ *n* **1** : small branches lopped from trees or shrubs **2** : a thicket of shrubs and small trees

brusque \'brəsk\ *adj* [F *brusque,* fr. It *brusco,* fr. ML *bruscus* a plant with stiff twigs used for brooms] : CURT, BLUNT, ABRUPT **syn** gruff, bluff, crusty, short — **brusque·ly** *adv*

brus·sels sprout \ˌbrəs-əl(z)-\ *n, often cap B* : one of the edible small heads borne on the stalk of a cabbagelike plant; *also, pl* : this plant

bru·tal \'brüt-ᵊl\ *adj* **1** : resembling or befitting a brute (as in coarseness or cruelty) **2** : HARSH, SEVERE ⟨~ weather⟩ — **bru·tal·i·ty** \brü-'tal-ət-ē\ *n* — **bru·tal·ly** \'brüt-ᵊl-ē\ *adv*

bru·tal·ize \'brüt-ᵊl-ˌīz\ *vb* **-ized; -iz·ing** **1** : to make brutal **2** : to treat brutally

¹brute \'brüt\ *adj* [ME, fr. MF *brut* rough, fr. L *brutus* stupid, lit., heavy] **1** : of, relating to, or typical of beasts **2** : BRUTAL **3** : UNREASONING; *also* : purely physical

²brute *n* **1** : BEAST 1 **2** : a brutal person **syn** animal, creature

brut·ish \'brüt-ish\ *adj* **1** : BRUTE 1 **2** : stupidly cruel or sensual; *also* : UNREASONING

BS *abbr* bachelor of science

BSA *abbr* Boy Scouts of America

BSc *abbr* bachelor of science

bskt *abbr* basket

Bt *abbr* baronet

btry *abbr* battery

Btu *abbr* British thermal unit

bu *abbr* bushel

¹bub·ble \'bəb-əl\ *n* **1** : a globule of gas in a liquid **2** : a thin film of liquid filled with gas **3** : something lacking firmness or solidity — **bub·bly** \-(ə-)lē\ *adj*

²bubble *vb* **bub·bled; bub·bling** \'bəb-(ə-)liŋ\ : to form, rise in, or give off bubbles

bu·bo \'b(y)ü-bō\ *n, pl* **buboes** : an inflammatory swelling of a lymph gland

bu·bon·ic plague \b(y)ü-ˌbän-ik-\ *n* : a plague caused by a bacterium transmitted to human beings by flea bites and marked esp. by chills and fever and by buboes usu. in the groin

buc·ca·neer \ˌbək-ə-'niər\ *n* : PIRATE

¹buck \'bək\ *n, pl* **bucks 1** *or pl* **buck** : a male animal (as a deer or antelope) **2** : DANDY **3** : DOLLAR

²buck *vb* **1** : to spring with a quick plunging leap ⟨a ~ing horse⟩ **2** : to charge against something; *also* : to strive for advancement sometimes without regard to ethical behavior

buck·board \-ˌbōrd\ *n* : a 4-wheeled vehicle with a floor of long springy boards

buck·et \'bək-ət\ *n* **1** : PAIL **2** : an object resembling a bucket in collecting, scooping, or carrying something — **buck·et·ful** *n*

bucket seat *n* : a low separate seat for one person (as in an automobile)

buck·eye \'bək-ˌī\ *n* : a tree related to the horse chestnut that occurs chiefly in the central U.S.; *also* : its large nutlike seed

buck fever *n* : nervous excitement of an inexperienced hunter at the sight of game

¹**buck·le** \'bək-əl\ *n* : a clasp (as on a belt) for two loose ends

²**buckle** *vb* **buck·led; buck·ling** \'bək-(ə-)liŋ\ **1** : to fasten with a buckle **2** : to apply oneself with vigor **3** : to crumple up : BEND, COLLAPSE

³**buckle** *n* : BEND, FOLD, KINK

buck·ler \'bək-lər\ *n* : SHIELD

buck·ram \'bək-rəm\ *n* : a coarse stiff cloth used esp. for binding books

buck·saw \'bək-ˌsȯ\ *n* : a saw set in a usu. H-shaped frame and used for sawing wood

buck·shot \'bək-ˌshät\ *n* : lead shot that is from .24 to .33 inch (about 6.1 to 8.4 millimeters) in diameter

buck·skin \-ˌskin\ *n* **1** : the skin of a buck **2** : a soft usu. suede-finished leather — **buckskin** *adj*

buck·tooth \-'tüth\ *n* : a large projecting front tooth — **buck–toothed** \-'tütht\ *adj*

buck·wheat \-ˌhwēt\ *n* : either of two plants grown for their triangular seeds which are used as a cereal grain; *also* : these seeds

bu·col·ic \byü-'käl-ik\ *adj* [L *bucolicus,* fr. Gk *boukolikos,* fr. *boukolos* one who tends cattle, fr. *bous* head of cattle + *-kolos* (akin to L *colere* to cultivate)] : RURAL, RUSTIC

¹**bud** \'bəd\ *n* **1** : an undeveloped plant shoot (as of a leaf or a flower); *also* : a partly opened flower **2** : an asexual reproductive structure **3** : something not yet mature

²**bud** *vb* **bud·ded; bud·ding 1** : to form or put forth buds; *also* : to reproduce by asexual buds **2** : to be or develop like a bud **3** : to propagate a desired variety (as of peach) by inserting a bud in a plant of a different variety

Bud·dhism \'bü-ˌdiz-əm, 'bùd-ˌiz-\ *n* : a religion of eastern and central Asia growing out of the teachings of Gautama Buddha — **Bud·dhist** \'büd-əst, 'bùd-\ *n or adj*

bud·dy \'bəd-ē\ *n, pl* **buddies** : COMPANION; *esp* : a fellow soldier

budge \'bəj\ *vb* **budged; budg·ing** : MOVE, STIR, SHIFT

bud·ger·i·gar \'bəj-(ə-)rē-ˌgär, ˌbəj-ə-'rē-\ *n* : a small brightly colored Australian parrot often kept as a pet

¹**bud·get** \'bəj-ət\ *n* [ME *bowgette,* fr. MF *bougette,* dim. of *bouge* leather bag, fr. L *bulga*] **1** : STOCK, SUPPLY **2** : a financial report containing estimates of income and expenses; *also* : a plan for coordinating income and expenses

²**budget** *vb* **1** : to allow for in a budget **2** : to draw up a budget

³**budget** *adj* : INEXPENSIVE

bud·gie \'bəj-ē\ *n* : BUDGERIGAR

¹**buff** \'bəf\ *n* **1** : a dull yellow-orange color **2** : FAN, ENTHUSIAST

²**buff** *adj* : of the color buff

³**buff** *vb* : POLISH, SHINE

buf·fa·lo \'bəf-ə-ˌlō\ *n, pl* **-lo** *or* **-loes** *also* **-los 1** : WATER BUFFALO **2** : a large shaggy-maned No. American wild bovine mammal with short horns and heavy forequarters with a large muscular hump

¹**buf·fer** \'bəf-ər\ *n* : something that lessens shock (as from a physical or financial blow)

²**buffer** *n* : one that buffs

¹**buf·fet** \'bəf-ət\ *n* : BLOW, SLAP

²**buffet** *vb* **1** : to strike with the hand; *also* : to pound repeatedly **2** : to struggle against or on **syn** beat, batter, drub, pummel, thrash

³**buf·fet** \(ˌ)bə-'fā, bü-\ *n* **1** : SIDEBOARD **2** : a counter for refreshments; *also* : a meal at which people serve themselves (as from a buffet)

buff leather *n* : a strong supple oil= tanned leather

buf·foon \(ˌ)bə-'fün\ *n* [MF *bouffon,* fr. It *buffone,* fr. ML *bufon-, bufo,* fr. L, toad] : CLOWN **2 syn** fool, jester — **buf·foon·ery** \-(ə-)rē\ *n*

¹**bug** \'bəg\ *n* **1** : an insect or other creeping or crawling invertebrate animal; *esp* : an insect pest (as a bedbug) **2** : any of an order of insects with sucking mouthparts and incomplete metamorphosis that includes many plant pests **3** : an unexpected mistake or imperfection ⟨a ~ in a computer program⟩ **4** : a disease-producing germ; *also* : a disease caused by it **5** : a concealed listening device

²**bug** *vb* **bugged; bug·ging 1** : BOTHER, ANNOY **2** : to plant a concealed microphone in

bug·a·boo \'bəg-ə-ˌbü\ *n, pl* **-boos** : BOGEY 1

bug·bear \'bəg-ˌbaər\ *n* : BOGEY 1; *also* : a source of dread

bug·gy \\'bəg-ē\ *n, pl* **buggies** : a light carriage

bu·gle \\'byü-gəl\ *n* [ME, buffalo, instrument made of buffalo horn, bugle, fr. OF, fr. L *buculus*, dim. of *bos* head of cattle] : a valveless brass wind instrument resembling a trumpet and used esp. for military calls — **bu·gler** \-glər\ *n*

¹**build** \\'bild\ *vb* **built** \\'bilt\; **build·ing** 1 : to form or have formed by ordering and uniting materials ⟨∼ a house⟩; *also* : to bring into being or develop 2 : to produce or create gradually ⟨∼ an argument on facts⟩ 3 : INCREASE, ENLARGE; *also* : ENHANCE 4 : to engage in building — **build·er** *n*

²**build** *n* : form or mode of structure; *esp* : PHYSIQUE

build·ing \\'bil-diŋ\ *n* 1 : a usu. roofed and walled structure (as a house) for permanent use 2 : the art or business of constructing buildings

build·up \\'bild-,əp\ *n* : the act or process of building up; *also* : something produced by this

built–in \\'bil-'tin\ *adj* 1 : forming an integral part of a structure 2 : INHERENT

bulb \\'bəlb\ *n* 1 : an underground resting stage of a plant (as a lily or an onion) consisting of a short stem base bearing one or more buds enclosed in overlapping leaves; *also* : a fleshy plant structure (as a tuber) resembling a bulb 2 : a plant having or growing from a bulb 3 : a rounded more or less bulb-shaped object or part (as for an electric lamp) — **bul·bous** \\'bəl-bəs\ *adj*

Bul·gar·i·an \,bəl-'gar-ē-ən, bül-\ *n* : a native or inhabitant of Bulgaria — **Bulgarian** *adj*

¹**bulge** \\'bəlj\ *vb* **bulged; bulg·ing** : to become or cause to become protuberant

²**bulge** *n* : a swelling projecting part

bu·li·mia \b(y)ü-'lim-ē-ə, -'lēm-\ *n* : an abnormal and constant craving for food — **bu·lim·ic** \-'lim-ik\ *adj or n*

¹**bulk** \\'bəlk\ *n* 1 : MAGNITUDE, VOLUME 2 : material (as indigestible fibrous residues of food) that forms a mass in the intestine 3 : a large mass 4 : the major portion

²**bulk** *vb* 1 : to have a bulky appearance 2 : to appear as a factor : LOOM

bulk·head \\'bəlk-,hed\ *n* 1 : a partition separating compartments 2 : a structure built to cover a shaft or a cellar stairway

bulky \\'bəl-kē\ *adj* **bulk·i·er; -est** : having bulk; *esp* : being large and unwieldy

¹**bull** \\'bül\ *n* 1 : the adult male of a bovine animal; *also* : a usu. adult male of various other large animals (as the elephant or walrus) 2 : one who buys securities or commodities in expectation of a price increase — **bull·ish** *adj*

²**bull** *adj* 1 : MALE 2 : large of its kind 3 : RISING ⟨a ∼ market⟩

³**bull** *n* [ME *bulle*, fr. ML *bulla*, fr. L, bubble, amulet] : a papal letter

⁴**bull** *n, slang* : NONSENSE

⁵**bull** *abbr* bulletin

¹**bull·dog** \\'bül-,dóg\ *n* : any of a breed of compact muscular short-haired dogs of English origin

²**bulldog** *vb* : to throw (a steer) by seizing the horns and twisting the neck

bull·doze \-,dōz\ *vb* 1 : to move, clear, or level with a tractor-driven machine (**bull·doz·er**) having a broad blade for pushing 2 : to force as if by using a bulldozer

bul·let \\'bül-ət\ *n* [MF *boulette* small ball & *boulet* missile, dims. of *boule* ball] : a missile to be shot from a firearm — **bul·let·proof** \,bül-ət-'prüf\ *adj*

bul·le·tin \\'bül-ət-ᵊn\ *n* 1 : a brief public report intended for immediate release on a matter of public interest 2 : a periodical publication (as of a college) — **bulletin** *vb*

bull·fight \\'bül-,fīt\ *n* : a spectacle in which people ceremonially fight with and usu. kill bulls in an arena — **bull·fight·er** *n*

bull·frog \-,fróg, -,fräg\ *n* : FROG; *esp* : a large deep-voiced frog

bull·head \-,hed\ *n* : any of several common freshwater catfishes of the U.S.

bull·head·ed \-'hed-əd\ *adj* : stupidly stubborn : HEADSTRONG

bul·lion \\'bül-yən\ *n* : gold or silver esp. in bars or ingots

bull·ock \\'bül-ək\ *n* : a young bull; *also* : STEER

bull pen *n* : a place on a baseball field where relief pitchers warm up; *also*

: the relief pitchers of a baseball team

bull session *n* : an informal discussion

bull's–eye \'bùl-ˌzī\ *n, pl* **bull's–eyes** : the center of a target; *also* : a shot that hits the bull's-eye

¹**bul·ly** \'bùl-ē\ *n, pl* **bullies** : a person habitually cruel to others who are weaker

²**bully** *adj* : EXCELLENT, FIRST-RATE — often used interjectionally

³**bully** *vb* **bul·lied; bul·ly·ing** : to behave as a bully toward : DOMINEER **syn** browbeat, intimidate, hector

bul·rush \'bùl-ˌrəsh\ *n* : any of several large rushes or sedges of wetlands

bul·wark \'bùl-(ˌ)wərk, -ˌwòrk; 'bəl-(ˌ)wərk\ *n* **1** : a wall-like defensive structure **2** : a strong support or protection in danger

¹**bum** \'bəm\ *adj* **1** : WORTHLESS ⟨∼ advice⟩ **2** : DISABLED ⟨a ∼ knee⟩

²**bum** *vb* **bummed; bum·ming 1** : to wander as a tramp; *also* : LOAF **2** : to seek or gain by begging

³**bum** *n* : an idle worthless fellow : LOAFER

bum·ble·bee \'bəm-bəl-ˌbē\ *n* : any of numerous large hairy social bees

bum·mer \'bəm-ər\ *n* : an unpleasant experience

¹**bump** \'bəmp\ *n* **1** : a local bulge; *esp* : a swelling of tissue **2** : a sudden forceful blow or impact — **bumpy** *adj*

²**bump** *vb* **1** : to strike or knock forcibly; *also* : to move or alter by bumping **2** : to collide with

¹**bum·per** \'bəm-pər\ *n* **1** : a cup or glass filled to the brim **2** : something unusually large — **bumper** *adj*

²**bump·er** \'bəm-pər\ *n* : a device for absorbing shock or preventing damage; *esp* : a metal bar at either end of an automobile

bump·kin \'bəmp-kən\ *n* : an awkward and unsophisticated country person

bump·tious \'bəmp-shəs\ *adj* : obtusely and often noisily self-assertive

bun \'bən\ *n* : a sweet biscuit or roll

¹**bunch** \'bənch\ *n* **1** : SWELLING **2** : CLUSTER, GROUP — **bunchy** *adj*

²**bunch** *vb* : to form into a group or bunch

bun·co *or* **bun·ko** \'bəŋ-kō\ *n, pl* **buncos** *or* **bunkos** : a swindling scheme — **bunco** *vb*

¹**bun·dle** \'bən-dᵊl\ *n* **1** : several items

bunched and fastened together; *also* : something wrapped for carrying **2** : a considerable amount : LOT **3** : a small group esp. of mostly parallel nerve or muscle fibers

²**bundle** *vb* **bun·dled; bun·dling** \'bənd-(ᵊ-)liŋ\ : to gather or tie in a bundle

bun·dling \'bənd-(ᵊ-)liŋ\ *n* : a former custom of a courting couple's occupying the same bed without undressing

bung \'bəŋ\ *n* : the stopper in the bunghole of a cask

bun·ga·low \'bəŋ-gə-ˌlō\ *n* : a one-storied house with a low-pitched roof

bung·hole \'bəŋ-ˌhōl\ *n* : a hole for emptying or filling a cask

bun·gle \'bəŋ-gəl\ *vb* **bun·gled; bun·gling** \-g(ə-)liŋ\ : to do badly : BOTCH — **bungle** *n* — **bun·gler** \-g(ə-)lər\ *n*

bun·ion \'bən-yən\ *n* : an inflamed swelling of the first joint of the big toe

¹**bunk** \'bəŋk\ *n* : BED; *esp* : a built-in bed that is often one of a tier

²**bunk** *n* : BUNKUM, NONSENSE

bun·ker \'bəŋ-kər\ *n* **1** : a bin or compartment for storage (as for coal on a ship) **2** : a protective embankment or dugout **3** : a sand trap or embankment constituting a hazard on a golf course

bun·kum *or* **bun·combe** \'bəŋ-kəm\ *n* [*Buncombe* County, N.C.; fr. the defense of a seemingly irrelevant speech made by its congressional representative that he was speaking to Buncombe] : insincere or foolish talk

bun·ny \'bən ē\ *n, pl* **-nies** : RABBIT

Bun·sen burner \ˌbən-sən-\ *n* : a gas burner usu. consisting of a straight tube with air holes at the bottom

¹**bunt** \'bənt\ *vb* **1** : BUTT **2** : to push or tap a baseball lightly without swinging the bat

²**bunt** *n* : an act or instance of bunting; *also* : a bunted ball

¹**bun·ting** \'bənt-iŋ\ *n* : any of numerous small stout-billed finches

²**bunting** *n* : a thin fabric used esp. for flags; *also* : FLAGS

¹**buoy** \'bü-ē, 'bòi\ *n* **1** : a floating object anchored in water to mark something (as a channel, shoal, or rock) **2** : a float consisting of a ring of buoyant material to support a person who has fallen into the water

²**buoy** *vb* **1** : to mark by a buoy **2** : to keep afloat **3** : to raise the spirits of

buoy·an·cy \'bȯi-ən-sē, 'bü-yən-\ *n* **1** : the tendency of a body to float or rise when submerged in a fluid **2** : the power of a fluid to exert an upward force on a body placed in it **3** : resilience of spirit — **buoy·ant** \-ənt, -yənt\ *adj*

¹bur \'bər\ var of BURR

²bur *abbr* bureau

¹bur·den \'bərd-ᵊn\ *n* **1** : LOAD; *also* : CARE, RESPONSIBILITY **2** : something oppressive : ENCUMBRANCE **3** : CARGO; *also* : capacity for cargo

²burden *vb* **bur·dened; bur·den·ing** \'bərd-(ᵊ)niŋ\ : LOAD, OPPRESS — **bur·den·some** \-səm\ *adj*

³burden *n* **1** : REFRAIN, CHORUS **2** : a main theme or idea : GIST

bur·dock \'bər-ˌdäk\ *n* : any of a genus of coarse composite herbs with globe-shaped flower heads surrounded by prickly bracts

bu·reau \'byur-ō\ *n, pl* **bureaus** *also* **bu·reaux** \-ōz\ [F, desk, cloth covering for desks, fr. OF *burel* woolen cloth, fr. L *burra* shaggy cloth] **1** : a chest of drawers for bedroom use **2** : an administrative unit (as of a government department) **3** : a branch of a publication or wire service in an important news center

bu·reau·cra·cy \byu-'räk-rə-sē\ *n, pl* **-cies 1** : a body of appointive government officials **2** : administration characterized by specialization of functions under fixed rules and a hierarchy of authority; *also* : an unwieldy administrative system deficient in initiative and flexibility — **bu·reau·crat** \'byur-ə-ˌkrat\ *n* — **bu·reau·crat·ic** \ˌbyur-ə-'krat-ik\ *adj*

bur·geon \'bər-jən\ *vb* : to put forth fresh growth (as from buds) : grow vigorously : FLOURISH

bur·gess \'bər-jəs\ *n* **1** : a citizen of a borough **2** : an official or representative usu. of a borough

burgh \'bər-ō\ *n* : a Scottish town

bur·gher \'bər-gər\ *n* **1** : TOWNSMAN **2** : a prosperous solid citizen

bur·glary \'bər-glə-rē\ *n, pl* **-glar·ies** : forcible entry into a building and esp. a dwelling with intent to steal — **bur·glar** \-glər\ *n* — **bur·glar·ize** \'bər-glə-ˌrīz\ *vb*

bur·gle \'bər-gəl\ *vb* **bur·gled; bur·gling** \-g(ə-)liŋ\ : to commit burglary on

bur·go·mas·ter \'bər-gə-ˌmas-tər\ *n* : the chief magistrate of a town in some European countries

Bur·gun·dy \'bər-gən-dē\ *n, pl* **-dies** : a red or white table wine

buri·al \'ber-ē-əl\ *n* : the act or process of burying

burl \'bərl\ *n* : a hard woody often flattened hemispherical outgrowth on a tree

bur·lap \'bər-ˌlap\ *n* : a coarse fabric usu. of jute or hemp used esp. for bags

¹bur·lesque \(ˌ)bər-'lesk\ *n* [*burlesque,* adj. (comic, droll), fr. F, fr. It *burlesco,* fr. *burla* joke, fr. Sp] **1** : a witty or derisive literary or dramatic imitation **2** : broadly humorous theatrical entertainment consisting of several items (as songs, skits, or dances)

²burlesque *vb* **bur·lesqued; bur·lesqu·ing** : to make ludicrous by burlesque : MOCK **syn** caricature, parody, travesty

bur·ly \'bər-lē\ *adj* **bur·li·er; -est** : strongly and heavily built : HUSKY **syn** muscular, brawny, beefy, hefty

Bur·mese \ˌbər-'mēz, -'mēs\ *n, pl* **Burmese** : a native or inhabitant of Burma — **Burmese** *adj*

¹burn \'bərn\ *vb* **burned** \'bərnd, 'bərnt\ *or* **burnt** \'bərnt\; **burn·ing 1** : to be on fire **2** : to feel or look as if on fire **3** : to alter or become altered by or as if by the action of fire or heat **4** : to use as fuel ⟨∼ coal⟩; *also* : to destroy by fire ⟨∼ trash⟩ **5** : to cause or make by fire ⟨∼ a hole⟩; *also* : to affect as if by heat

²burn *n* : an injury or effect produced by or as if by burning

burn·er \'bər-nər\ *n* : the part of a fuel-burning or heat-producing device where the flame or heat is produced

bur·nish \'bər-nish\ *vb* : to make shiny esp. by rubbing : POLISH — **bur·nish·er** *n* — **bur·nish·ing** *adj or n*

bur·noose *or* **bur·nous** \(ˌ)bər-'nüs\ *n* : a hooded cloak worn esp. by Arabs

burn·out \'bər-ˌnaut\ *n* **1** : the cessation of operation of a jet or rocket engine **2** : exhaustion of one's physical or emotional strength

burp \'bərp\ *n* : an act of belching — **burp** *vb*

burp gun *n* : a small submachine gun

burr \\'bər\ *n* **1** *usu* **bur** : a rough or prickly envelope of a fruit; *also* : a plant that bears burs **2** : roughness left in cutting or shaping metal **3** : WHIR — **bur·ry** *adj*

bur·ri·to \bə-'rēt-ō\ *n* [AmerSp, fr. Sp, lit., little donkey, dim. of *burro*] : a flour tortilla rolled around a filling and baked

bur·ro \\'bər-ō, 'bùr-\ *n, pl* **burros** [Sp] : a usu. small donkey

¹**bur·row** \\'bər-ō\ *n* : a hole in the ground made by an animal (as a rabbit)

²**burrow** *vb* **1** : to form by tunneling ⟨∼ a way through the snow⟩; *also* : to make a burrow **2** : to progress by or as if by digging — **bur·row·er** *n*

bur·sar \\'bər-sər\ *n* : a treasurer esp. of a college

bur·si·tis \(ˌ)bər-'sīt-əs\ *n* : inflammation of the serous sac (**bur·sa** \\'bər-sə\) of a joint (as the elbow or shoulder)

¹**burst** \\'bərst\ *vb* **burst** *or* **burst·ed; burst·ing 1** : to fly apart or into pieces **2** : to show one's feelings suddenly; *also* : PLUNGE ⟨∼ into song⟩ **3** : to enter or emerge suddenly : SPRING **4** : to be filled to the breaking point

²**burst** *n* **1** : a sudden outbreak or effort : SPURT **2** : EXPLOSION **3** : an act or result of bursting

Bu·run·di·an \bù-'rün-dē-ən\ *n* : a native or inhabitant of Burundi

bury \\'ber-ē\ *vb* **bur·ied; bury·ing 1** : to deposit in the earth; *also* : to inter with funeral ceremonies **2** : CONCEAL, HIDE

¹**bus** \\'bəs\ *n, pl* **bus·es** *or* **bus·ses** [short for *omnibus*, fr. F, fr. L, for all, dat. pl. of *omnis* all] : a large motor-driven passenger vehicle

²**bus** *vb* **bused** *or* **bussed; bus·ing** *or* **bus·sing 1** : to travel or transport by bus **2** : to work as a busboy

³**bus** *abbr* business

bus·boy \\'bəs-ˌbȯi\ *n* : a waiter's helper

bus·by \\'bəz-bē\ *n, pl* **busbies** : a military full-dress fur hat

bush \\'bùsh\ *n* **1** : SHRUB **2** : rough uncleared country **3** : a thick tuft or mat — **bushy** *adj*

bushed \\'bùsht\ *adj* : TIRED, EXHAUSTED

bush·el \\'bùsh-əl\ *n* — see WEIGHT table

bush·ing \\'bùsh-iŋ\ *n* : a usu. removable cylindrical lining in an opening of a mechanical part to limit the size of the opening, resist wear (as in a bearing for an axle), or serve as a guide

bush·mas·ter \\'bùsh-ˌmas-tər\ *n* : a large venomous tropical American snake

bush·whack \-ˌhwak\ *vb* **1** : to live or hide out in the woods **2** : AMBUSH — **bush·whack·er** *n*

busi·ly \\'biz-ə-lē\ *adv* : in a busy manner

busi·ness \\'biz-nəs, -nəz\ *n* **1** : OCCUPATION, CALLING; *also* : TASK, MISSION **2** : a commercial or industrial enterprise; *also* : TRADE ⟨∼ is good⟩ **3** : AFFAIR, MATTER **4** : personal concerns **syn** commerce, industry, trade, traffic

busi·ness·man \-ˌman\ *n* : a man engaged in business esp. as an executive

busi·ness·per·son \-ˌpərs-ᵊn\ *n* : a businessman or businesswoman

busi·ness·wom·an \-ˌwùm-ən\ *n* : a woman engaged in business esp. as an executive

bus·kin \\'bəs-kən\ *n* **1** : a laced boot reaching halfway to the knee **2** : tragic drama

buss \\'bəs\ *n* : KISS — **buss** *vb*

¹**bust** \\'bəst\ *n* [F *buste*, fr. It *busto*, fr. L *bustum* tomb] **1** : sculpture representing the upper part of the human figure **2** : the part of the human torso between the neck and the waist; *esp* : the breasts of a woman

²**bust** *vb* **bust·ed** *also* **bust; bust·ing 1** : BREAK, SMASH; *also* : BURST **2** : to ruin financially **3** : DEMOTE **4** : TAME **5** *slang* : ARREST

³**bust** *n* **1** : a drinking session **2** : a complete failure : FLOP **3** : a business depression **4** : PUNCH, SOCK **5** *slang* : a police raid

¹**bus·tle** \\'bəs-əl\ *vb* **bus·tled; bus·tling** \\'bəs-(ə-)liŋ\ : to move or work in a brisk fussy way

²**bustle** *n* : briskly energetic activity

³**bustle** *n* : a pad or frame formerly worn to swell out the fullness at the back of a woman's skirt

¹**busy** \\'biz-ē\ *adj* **busi·er; -est 1** : engaged in action : not idle **2** : being in use ⟨∼ telephones⟩ **3** : full of activity ⟨∼ streets⟩ **4** : OFFICIOUS **syn** employed, engaged, occupied

²**busy** *vb* **bus·ied; busy·ing** : to make or keep busy : OCCUPY

busy·body \ˈbiz-ē-ˌbäd-ē\ *n* : MEDDLER

busy·work \-ˌwərk\ *n* : work that appears productive but only keeps one occupied

¹**but** \(ˈ)bət\ *conj* **1** : except for the fact ⟨would have protested ∼ that he was afraid⟩ **2** : as to the following, namely ⟨there's no doubt ∼ he's the guilty one⟩ **3** : without the concomitant that ⟨never rains ∼ it pours⟩ **4** : on the contrary ⟨not one, ∼ two job offers⟩ **5** : yet nevertheless ⟨would like to go, ∼ I can't⟩; *also* : while on the contrary ⟨would like to go ∼ he is busy⟩ **6** : yet also ⟨came home sadder ∼ wiser⟩ ⟨poor ∼ proud⟩

²**but** *prep* : other than : EXCEPT ⟨there's no one here ∼ me⟩

bu·tane \ˈbyü-ˌtān\ *n* : either of two gaseous hydrocarbons used as a fuel

¹**butch·er** \ˈbuch-ər\ *n* [ME *bocher*, fr. OF *bouchier*, fr. *bouc* he-goat] **1** : one who slaughters animals or dresses their flesh; *also* : a dealer in meat **2** : one that kills brutally or needlessly — **butch·ery** \-(ə-)rē\ *n*

²**butcher** *vb* **butch·ered; butch·er·ing** \-(ə-)riŋ\ **1** : to slaughter and dress for meat ⟨∼ hogs⟩ **2** : to kill barbarously

but·ler \ˈbət-lər\ *n* [ME *buteler*, fr. OF *bouteillier* bottle bearer, fr. *bouteille* bottle] : the chief male servant of a household

¹**butt** \ˈbət\ *vb* : to strike with the head or horns

²**butt** *n* : a blow or thrust with the head or horns

³**butt** *n* : a large cask

⁴**butt** *n* **1** : TARGET **2** : an object of abuse or ridicule

⁵**butt** *n* : a large, thicker, or bottom end of something

⁶**butt** *vb* **1** : ABUT **2** : to place or join edge to edge without overlapping

butte \ˈbyüt\ *n* : an isolated steep-sided hill

¹**but·ter** \ˈbət-ər\ *n* [ME, fr. OE *butere*, fr. L *butyrum* butter, fr. Gk *boutyron*, fr. *bous* cow + *tyros* cheese] **1** : a solid edible emulsion of fat obtained from cream by churning **2** : a substance resembling butter — **but·tery** *adj*

²**butter** *vb* : to spread with butter

but·ter–and–eggs \ˌbət-ə-rə-ˈnegz\ *n sing or pl* : a common perennial herb related to the snapdragon that has showy yellow and orange flowers

but·ter·cup \ˈbət-ər-ˌkəp\ *n* : any of a genus of herbs usu. having yellow flowers with five petals and sepals

but·ter·fat \-ˌfat\ *n* : the natural fat of milk and chief constituent of butter

but·ter·fin·gered \-ˌfiŋ-gərd\ *adj* : likely to let things fall or slip through the fingers — **but·ter·fin·gers** \-gərz\ *n sing or pl*

but·ter·fly \-ˌflī\ *n* : any of a group of slender day-flying insects with four broad wings covered with bright-colored scales

but·ter·milk \-ˌmilk\ *n* : the liquid remaining after butter is churned

but·ter·nut \-ˌnət\ *n* : the edible oily nut of an American tree related to the walnut; *also* : this tree

but·ter·scotch \-ˌskäch\ *n* : a candy made from brown sugar, corn syrup, and water; *also* : the flavor of such candy

but·tock \ˈbət-ək\ *n* **1** : the back of a hip that forms one of the fleshy parts on which a person sits **2** *pl* : the seat of the body : RUMP

¹**but·ton** \ˈbət-ᵊn\ *n* **1** : a small knob secured to an article (as of clothing) and used as a fastener by passing it through a buttonhole or loop **2** : something that resembles a button **3** : PUSH BUTTON

²**button** *vb* **but·toned; but·ton·ing** \ˈbət-(ᵊ-)niŋ\ : to close or fasten with buttons

¹**but·ton·hole** \ˈbət-ᵊn-ˌhōl\ *n* : a slit or loop for a button to pass through

²**buttonhole** *vb* : to detain in conversation by or as if by holding on to the outer garments of

¹**but·tress** \ˈbət-rəs\ *n* **1** : a projecting structure to support a wall **2** : PROP, SUPPORT

²**buttress** *vb* : PROP, SUPPORT

bu·tut \bu-ˈtüt\ *n* — see *dalasi* at MONEY table

bux·om \ˈbək-səm\ *adj* : healthily plump; *esp* : full-bosomed

¹**buy** \ˈbī\ *vb* **bought** \ˈbȯt\; **buy·ing** : to obtain for a price : PURCHASE; *also* : BRIBE — **buy·er** *n*

²**buy** *n* **1** : PURCHASE 1, 2 **2** : an exceptional value

¹**buzz** \'bəz\ *vb* **1** : to make a buzz **2** : to fly low over in an airplane

²**buzz** *n* : a low humming sound (as of bees in flight)

buz•zard \'bəz-ərd\ *n* : any of various usu. large birds of prey and esp. the turkey vulture

buzz•er \'bəz-ər\ *n* : a device that signals with a buzzing sound

buzz saw *n* : CIRCULAR SAW

BV *abbr* Blessed Virgin

BWI *abbr* British West Indies

bx *abbr* box

BX *abbr* base exchange

¹**by** \(')bī, bə\ *prep* **1** : NEAR ⟨stood ∼ the window⟩ **2** : through or through the medium of : VIA ⟨left ∼ the door⟩ **3** : PAST ⟨drove ∼ the house⟩ **4** : DURING, AT ⟨studied ∼ night⟩ **5** : no later than ⟨get here ∼ 3 p.m.⟩ **6** : through the means or direct agency of ⟨got it ∼ fraud⟩ ⟨was seen ∼ the others⟩ **7** : in conformity with : ACCORDING TO ⟨did it ∼ the book⟩ **8** : with respect to ⟨an electrician ∼ trade⟩ **9** : to the amount or extent of ⟨won ∼ a nose⟩ ⟨overpaid ∼ $3⟩ **10** — used to express relationship in multiplication, in division, and in measurements ⟨divide *a* ∼ *b*⟩ ⟨multiply ∼ 6⟩ ⟨15 feet ∼ 20 feet⟩

²**by** \'bī\ *adv* **1** : near at hand; *also* : IN ⟨stopped ∼ to chat⟩ **2** : PAST **3** : ASIDE, APART

bye \'bī\ *n* : a position of a participant in a tournament who has no opponent after pairs are drawn and advances to the next round without playing

by–elec•tion *also* **bye–election** \'bī-ə-ˌlek-shən\ *n* : a special election held between regular elections in order to fill a vacancy

by•gone \'bī-ˌgȯn\ *adj* : gone by : PAST — **bygone** *n*

by•law *or* **bye•law** \'bī-ˌlȯ\ *n* : a rule adopted by an organization for managing its internal affairs

by–line \'bī-ˌlīn\ *n* : a line at the beginning of a newspaper story or magazine article giving the writer's name

BYO *abbr* bring your own

BYOB *abbr* bring your own booze; bring your own bottle

¹**by•pass** \'bī-ˌpas\ *n* : a passage to one side or around a blocked or congested area

²**bypass** *vb* : to avoid by means of a bypass

by•path \-ˌpath, -ˌpath\ *n* : BYWAY

by•play \'bī-ˌplā\ *n* : action engaged in at the side of a stage while the main action proceeds

by–prod•uct \-ˌpräd-(ˌ)əkt\ *n* : a product or result produced in addition to the main product or result

by•stand•er \-ˌstan-dər\ *n* : one present but not participating **syn** onlooker, witness, spectator, eyewitness

byte \'bīt\ *n* : a group of bits that a computer processes as a unit ⟨an 8-bit ∼⟩

by the way *adv* : in passing : INCIDENTALLY

by•way \'bī-ˌwā\ *n* **1** : a little-traveled side road **2** : a secondary aspect

by•word \-ˌwərd\ *n* **1** : PROVERB **2** : an object of scorn

C

¹**c** \'sē\ *n, pl* **c's** *or* **cs** \'sēz\ *often cap* **1** : the 3d letter of the English alphabet **2** : a grade rating a student's work as fair

²**c** *abbr, often cap* **1** calorie **2** carat **3** Celsius **4** cent **5** centigrade **6** centimeter **7** century **8** chapter **9** circa **10** cocaine **11** copyright

C *symbol* carbon

ca *abbr* circa

Ca *symbol* calcium

CA *abbr* **1** California **2** chartered accountant **3** chief accountant **4** chronological age

cab \'kab\ *n* **1** : a light closed horse-drawn carriage **2** : TAXICAB **3** : the covered compartment for the engineer and controls of a locomotive; *also* : a similar compartment (as on a truck)

CAB *abbr* Civil Aeronautics Board

ca•bal \kə-'bal\ *n* [F *cabale*, fr. ML *cabbala* cabala, fr. Heb *quabbālāh*, lit., received (lore)] : a secret group of plotters or political conspirators

ca·ba·la \\'kab-ə-lə, kə-'bäl-ə\ *n, often cap* **1** : a medieval Jewish mysticism marked by belief in creation through emanation and a cipher method of interpreting scriptures **2** : esoteric doctrine or beliefs

ca·bana \kə-'ban-(y)ə\ *n* : a shelter at a beach or swimming pool

cab·a·ret \\,kab-ə-'rā\ *n* : NIGHTCLUB

cab·bage \\'kab-ij\ *n* [ME *caboche,* fr. OF head] : a vegetable related to the turnip with a dense head of leaves

cab·bie *or* **cab·by** \\'kab-ē\ *n, pl* **cabbies** : a driver of a cab

cab·in \\'kab-ən\ *n* **1** : a private room on a ship; *also* : a compartment below deck on a small boat for passengers or crew **2** : an aircraft or spacecraft compartment for passengers, crew, or cargo **3** : a small simple one-story house

cabin boy *n* : a boy acting as servant on a ship

cabin class *n* : a class of accommodations on a passenger ship superior to tourist class and inferior to first class

cabin cruiser *n* : CRUISER 3

cab·i·net \\'kab-(ə-)nət\ *n* **1** : a case or cupboard for holding or displaying articles (as jewels, specimens, or documents) **2** : an upright case housing a radio or television receiver **3** : the advisory council of a head of state (as a president or sovereign)

cab·i·net·mak·er \-,mā-kər\ *n* : a woodworker who makes fine furniture — **cab·i·net·mak·ing** \-,mā-kiŋ\ *n*

cab·i·net·work \-,wərk\ *n* : the finished work of a cabinetmaker

¹ca·ble \\'kā-bəl\ *n* **1** : a very strong rope, wire, or chain **2** : a bundle of insulated wires usu. twisted around a central core **3** : CABLEGRAM **4** : CABLE TELEVISION

²cable *vb* **ca·bled; ca·bling** \\'kā-b(ə-)liŋ\ : to telegraph by cable

cable car *n* : a vehicle moved by an endless cable

ca·ble·gram \\'kā-bəl-,gram\ *n* : a message sent by a submarine telegraph cable

cable television *n* : a system of television reception in which signals from distant stations are sent by cable to the receivers of paying subscribers

cab·o·chon \\'kab-ə-,shän\ *n* : a gem or bead cut in convex form and highly polished but not given facets; *also* : this style of cutting — **cabochon** *adv*

ca·boose \kə-'büs\ *n* : a car usu. at the rear of a freight train for the use of the train crew and railroad workers

cab·ri·o·let \\,kab-rē-ə-'lā\ *n* [F] **1** : a light 2-wheeled one-horse carriage **2** : a convertible coupe

cab·stand \\'kab-,stand\ *n* : a place for cabs to park while waiting for passengers

ca·cao \kə-'kaủ, -'kā-ō\ *n, pl* **cacaos** [Sp] : a So. American tree whose seeds (**cacao beans**) are the source of cocoa and chocolate; *also* : its dried fatty seeds

cac·cia·to·re \\,käch-ə-'tōr-ē\ *adj* [It] : cooked with tomatoes and herbs ⟨veal ∼⟩

¹cache \\'kash\ *n* [F] : a hiding place esp. for preserving provisions; *also* : something hidden or stored in a cache

²cache *vb* **cached; cach·ing** : to place or store in a cache

ca·chet \ka-'shā\ *n* [F] **1** : a seal used esp. as a mark of official approval **2** : a feature or quality conferring prestige; *also* : PRESTIGE **3** : a usu. flour paste capsule containing medicine **4** : a design, inscription, or advertisement printed or stamped on mail

cack·le \\'kak-əl\ *vb* **cack·led; cack·ling** \-(ə-)liŋ\ **1** : to make the sharp broken cry characteristic of a hen **2** : to laugh or chatter noisily — **cackle** *n* — **cack·ler** \-(ə-)lər\ *n*

ca·coph·o·ny \ka-'käf-ə-nē\ *n, pl* **-nies** : harsh or discordant sound — **ca·coph·o·nous** \-nəs\ *adj*

cac·tus \\'kak-təs\ *n, pl* **cac·ti** \-,tī\ *also* **cac·tus·es** *or* **cactus** : any of a large family of drought-resistant flowering plants with fleshy usu. jointed stems and with leaves replaced by scales or prickles

cad \\'kad\ *n* : a man who does not behave like a gentleman esp. toward women — **cad·dish** \-ish\ *adj* — **cad·dish·ly** *adv* — **cad·dish·ness** *n*

ca·dav·er \kə-'dav-ər\ *n* : a dead body : CORPSE

ca·dav·er·ous \kə-'dav-(ə-)rəs\ *adj* : suggesting a corpse esp. in gauntness or pallor **syn** wasted, emaciated, gaunt — **ca·dav·er·ous·ly** *adv*

cad·die *or* **cad·dy** \'kad-ē\ *n, pl* **caddies** [F *cadet* military cadet] : one that assists a golfer esp. by carrying his clubs — **caddie** *or* **caddy** *vb*

cad·dy \'kad-ē\ *n, pl* **caddies** [Malay *kati* a unit of weight] : a small box, can, or chest; *esp* : one to keep tea in

ca·dence \'kād-ᵊns\ *n* : the measure or beat of a rhythmical flow : RHYTHM — **ca·denced** \-ᵊnst\ *adj*

ca·den·za \kə-'den-zə\ *n* [It] : a brilliant sometimes improvised passage usu. toward the close of a musical composition

ca·det \kə-'det\ *n* [F, fr. F dial. *capdet* chief, fr. L *capitellum*, fr. L *caput* head] **1** : a younger son or brother **2** : a student in a service academy

Ca·dette scout \kə-,det-\ *n* : a Girl Scout between the ages of 12 and 14

cadge \'kaj\ *vb* **cadged; cadg·ing** : SPONGE, BEG — **cadg·er** *n*

cad·mi·um \'kad-mē-əm\ *n* : a bluish white metallic chemical element used in protective platings

cad·re \'kad-rē\ *n* [F] **1** : FRAMEWORK **2** : a nucleus esp. of trained personnel capable of assuming control and training others **3** : a group of indoctrinated leaders active in promoting the interests of a revolutionary party

ca·du·ceus \kə-'d(y)ü-sē-əs, -shəs\ *n, pl* **-cei** \-sē-,ī\ [L] **1** : the staff of a herald; *esp* : a representation of a staff with two entwined snakes and two wings at the top **2** : an insignia bearing a caduceus and symbolizing a physician

cae·cum var of CECUM

Cae·sar \'sē-zər\ *n* **1** : any of the Roman emperors succeeding Augustus Caesar — used as a title **2** *often not cap* : a powerful ruler : AUTOCRAT, DICTATOR; *also* : the civil or temporal power

caesarean *or* **caesarian** var of CESAREAN

cae·su·ra \si-'z(h)ùr-ə\ *n, pl* **-suras** *or* **-su·rae** \-'z(h)ùr-(,)ē\ : a break in the flow of sound usu. in the middle of a line of verse

ca·fé \ka-'fā, kə-\ *n* [F, lit., coffee] **1** : RESTAURANT **2** : BARROOM **3** : NIGHTCLUB

ca·fé au lait \(,)ka-,fā-ō-'lā\ *n* : coffee with hot milk in about equal parts

caf·e·te·ria \,kaf-ə-'tir-ē-ə\ *n* [AmerSp *cafetería* retail coffee store, fr. Sp *café* coffee] : a restaurant in which the customers serve themselves or are served at a counter

caf·feine \ka-'fēn, 'ka-,fēn\ *n* : a stimulating alkaloid found esp. in coffee and tea

caf·tan \kaf-'tan, 'kaf-,tan\ *n* [Russ *kaftan*, fr. Turk, fr. Per *qaftān*] : an ankle-length garment with long sleeves worn in countries of the eastern Mediterranean

¹cage \'kāj\ *n* **1** : an openwork enclosure for confining an animal **2** : something resembling a cage

²cage *vb* **caged; cag·ing** : to put or keep in or as if in a cage

ca·gey *also* **ca·gy** \'kā-jē\ *adj* **ca·gi·er; -est** : wary of being trapped or deceived : SHREWD — **ca·gi·ly** \'kā-jə-lē\ *adv* — **ca·gi·ness** \-jē-nəs\ *n*

CAGS *abbr* Certificate of Advanced Graduate Study

ca·hoot \kə-'hüt\ *n* : PARTNERSHIP, LEAGUE — usu. used in pl. ⟨officials in ∼s with the underworld⟩

cai·man \kā-'man, kī-; 'kā-mən\ *n* : any of several Central and So. American relatives of the crocodiles

cairn \'kaərn\ *n* : a heap of stones serving as a memorial or a landmark

cais·son \'kā-,sän, 'kās-ᵊn\ *n* **1** : a usu. 2-wheeled vehicle for artillery ammunition **2** : a watertight chamber used in underwater construction work or as a foundation

caisson disease *n* : ³BEND 3

cai·tiff \'kāt-əf\ *adj* [ME *caitif*, fr. OF, captive, vile, fr. L *captivus* captive] : being base, cowardly, or despicable — **caitiff** *n*

ca·jole \kə-'jōl\ *vb* **ca·joled; ca·jol·ing** [F *cajoler*] : to persuade or coax esp. with flattery or false promises : WHEEDLE — **ca·jole·ment** *n* — **ca·jol·ery** \-'jōl-(ə-)rē\ *n*

Ca·jun \'kā-jən\ *n* : a Louisianian descended from French-speaking immigrants from Acadia (Nova Scotia)

¹cake \'kāk\ *n* **1** : a food made from batter that may be fried or baked into a usu. small flat shape **2** : a sweet baked food made from batter or dough usu. containing a leaven (as baking powder) **3** : a substance hardened or molded into a solid mass ⟨a ~ of soap⟩

²**cake** *vb* **caked; cak·ing 1** : ENCRUST **2** : to form or harden into a cake

cake·walk \ˈkāk-ˌwȯk\ *n* **1** : a stage dance typically involving a high prance with backward tilt **2** : a one‑sided contest

cal *abbr* **1** calendar **2** caliber

Cal *abbr* **1** California **2** calorie

cal·a·bash \ˈkal-ə-ˌbash\ *n* : the fruit of a gourd; *also* : a utensil made from its shell

cal·a·boose \ˈkal-ə-ˌbüs\ *n* [Sp *calabozo* dungeon] *dial* : JAIL

ca·la·di·um \kə-ˈlād-ē-əm\ *n* : any of a genus of tropical American ornamental plants related to the arums

cal·a·mari \ˌkäl-ə-ˈmär-ē\ *n* [It] : squid used as food

cal·a·mine \ˈkal-ə-ˌmīn\ *n* : a lotion of oxides of zinc and iron

ca·lam·i·ty \kə-ˈlam-ət-ē\ *n, pl* **-ties 1** : great distress or misfortune **2** : an event causing great harm or loss and affliction : DISASTER — **ca·lam·i·tous** \-ət-əs\ *adj* — **ca·lam·i·tous·ly** *adv* — **ca·lam·i·tous·ness** *n*

calc *abbr* calculate; calculated

cal·car·e·ous \kal-ˈkar-ē-əs\ *adj* : containing calcium or calcium carbonate; *also* : resembling calcium carbonate in hardness

cal·cif·er·ous \kal-ˈsif-(ə-)rəs\ *adj* : producing or containing calcium carbonate

cal·ci·fy \ˈkal-sə-ˌfī\ *vb* **-fied; -fy·ing** : to make or become calcareous — **cal·ci·fi·ca·tion** \ˌkal-sə-fə-ˈkā-shən\ *n*

cal·ci·mine \ˈkal-sə-ˌmīn\ *n* : a thin water paint used esp. on plastered surfaces — **calcimine** *vb*

cal·cine \kal-ˈsīn\ *vb* **cal·cined; cal·cin·ing** : to heat to a high temperature but without fusing to drive off volatile matter and often to reduce to powder — **cal·ci·na·tion** \ˌkal-sə-ˈnā-shən\ *n*

cal·cite \ˈkal-ˌsīt\ *n* : a crystalline mineral consisting of calcium carbonate — **cal·cit·ic** \kal-ˈsit-ik\ *adj*

cal·ci·um \ˈkal-sē-əm\ *n* : a silver-white soft metallic chemical element occurring only in combination

calcium carbonate *n* : a substance found in nature as limestone and marble and in plant ashes, bones, and shells

cal·cu·late \ˈkal-kyə-ˌlāt\ *vb* **-lat·ed; -lat·ing** [L *calculare*, fr. *calculus* small stone, pebble used in reckoning] **1** : to determine by mathematical processes : COMPUTE **2** : to reckon by exercise of practical judgment : ESTIMATE **3** : to design or adapt for a purpose **4** : COUNT, RELY — **cal·cu·la·ble** \-lə-bəl\ *adj* — **cal·cu·la·tor** \-ˌlāt-ər\ *n*

cal·cu·lat·ed \-ˌlāt-əd\ *adj* : undertaken after estimating the probability of success or failure ⟨a ~ risk⟩

cal·cu·lat·ing \-ˌlāt-iŋ\ *adj* : marked by shrewd consideration esp. of self-interest — **cal·cu·lat·ing·ly** *adv*

cal·cu·la·tion \ˌkal-kyə-ˈlā-shən\ *n* **1** : the process or an act of calculating **2** : the result of an act of calculating **3** : studied care : CAUTION

cal·cu·lus \ˈkal-kyə-ləs\ *n, pl* **-li** \-ˌlī\ *also* **-lus·es** [L, pebble (used in reckoning)] **1** : a method of computation or calculation in a special notation (as of logic) **2** : a branch of higher mathematics concerned esp. with rates of change and the finding of lengths, areas, and volumes **3** : a concretion usu. of mineral salts esp. in hollow organs or ducts

cal·de·ra \kal-ˈder-ə, kȯl-, -ˈdir-\ *n* [Sp, lit., caldron] : a large crater usu. formed by the collapse of a volcanic cone

cal·dron \ˈkȯl-drən\ *n* : a large kettle

¹**cal·en·dar** \ˈkal-ən-dər\ *n* **1** : an arrangement of time into days, weeks, months, and years; *also* : a sheet or folder containing such an arrangement for a period **2** : an orderly list

²**calendar** *vb* **-dared; -dar·ing** \-d(ə-)riŋ\ : to enter in a calendar

¹**cal·en·der** \ˈkal-ən-dər\ *vb* : to press (as cloth or paper) between rollers or plates so as to make smooth or glossy or to thin into sheets

²**calender** *n* : a machine for calendering

ca·lends \ˈkal-əndz, ˈkāl-\ *n sing or pl* : the first day of the ancient Roman month

ca·len·du·la \kə-ˈlen-jə-lə\ *n* : any of a

genus of yellow-flowered herbs related to the daisies

¹calf \\'kaf, 'kȧf\\ *n, pl* **calves** \\'kavz, 'kȧvz\\ **1** : the young of the domestic cow; *also* : the young of various other large mammals (as the elephant or whale) **2** : CALFSKIN

²calf *n, pl* **calves** \\'kavz, 'kȧvz\\ : the fleshy back of the leg below the knee

calf·skin \\'kaf-ˌskin, 'kȧf-\\ *n* : leather made of the skin of a calf

cal·i·ber *or* **cal·i·bre** \\'kal-ə-bər\\ *n* [MF *calibre,* fr. It *calibro,* fr. Ar *qālib* shoemaker's last] **1** : the diameter of a projectile **2** : the diameter of the bore of a gun **3** : degree of excellence or importance

cal·i·brate \\'kal-ə-ˌbrāt\\ *vb* **-brat·ed; -brat·ing 1** : to measure the caliber of **2** : to determine, correct, or put the measuring marks on ⟨∼ a thermometer⟩ — **cal·i·bra·tion** \\ˌkal-ə-'brā-shən\\ *n*

cal·i·co \\'kal-i-ˌkō\\ *n, pl* **-coes** *or* **-cos** : cotton cloth; *esp* : a cheap cotton printed fabric — **calico** *adj*

Calif *abbr* California

Cal·i·for·nia poppy \\ˌkal-ə-'fȯr-nyə-\\ *n* : a widely cultivated herb with pale yellow to red flowers that is related to the poppies

cal·i·for·ni·um \\ˌkal-ə-'fȯr-nē-əm\\ *n* : an artificially prepared radioactive chemical element

cal·i·per *or* **cal·li·per** \\'kal-ə-pər\\ *n* **1** : an instrument with two adjustable legs used to measure the thickness of objects or distances between surfaces — usu. used in pl. ⟨a pair of ∼s⟩ **2** : a device consisting of two plates lined with a frictional material that press against the sides of a rotating wheel or disk in certain brake systems

ca·liph *or* **ca·lif** \\'kā-ləf, 'kal-əf\\ *n* : a successor of Muhammad as head of Islam — used as a title — **ca·liph·ate** \\-ˌāt, -ət\\ *n*

cal·is·then·ics \\ˌkal-əs-'then-iks\\ *n sing or pl* [Gk *kalos* beautiful + *sthenos* strength] : bodily exercises without apparatus or with light hand apparatus — **cal·is·then·ic** *adj*

calk \\'kȯk\\ var of CAULK

¹call \\'kȯl\\ *vb* **1** : SHOUT, CRY; *also* : to utter a characteristic cry **2** : to utter in a loud clear voice **3** : to announce au-

thoritatively **4** : SUMMON **5** : to make a request or demand ⟨∼ for an investigation⟩ **6** : to get or try to get in communication by telephone **7** : to demand payment of (a loan); *also* : to demand surrender of (as a bond issue) for redemption **8** : to make a brief visit **9** : to speak of or address by name : give a name to **10** : to estimate or consider for practical purposes ⟨∼ it ten miles⟩ **11** : to halt because of unsuitable conditions **12** : to temporarily transfer control of computer processing to (as a section of a computer program) — **call·er** *n*

²call *n* **1** : SHOUT **2** : the cry of an animal (as a bird) **3** : a request or a command to come or assemble : INVITATION, SUMMONS **4** : DEMAND, CLAIM; *also* : REQUEST **5** : a brief usu. formal visit **6** : an act of calling on the telephone **7** : a temporary transfer of control of computer processing to a particular set of instructions

cal·la lily \\'kal-ə-\\ *n* : a plant whose flowers form a fleshy yellow spike surrounded by a lilylike usu. white leaf

call·back \\'kȯl-ˌbak\\ *n* : a recall by a manufacturer of a product to correct a defect

call–board \\-ˌbord\\ *n* : a board for posting notices (as of rehearsal calls)

call down *vb* : REPRIMAND

call girl *n* : a prostitute with whom appointments are made by phone

cal·lig·ra·phy \\kə-'lig-rə-fē\\ *n* : beautiful or elegant handwriting; *also* : the art of producing such writing — **cal·lig·ra·pher** \\-fər\\ *n*

call in *vb* **1** : to order to return or be returned **2** : to summon to one's aid **3** : to report by telephone

call·ing \\'kȯ-liŋ\\ *n* **1** : a strong inner impulse toward a particular course of action **2** : the activity in which one customarily engages as an occupation

cal·li·ope \\kə-'lī-ə-(ˌ)pē, 'kal-ē-ˌōp\\ *n* [fr. *Calliope,* chief of the Muses, fr. L, fr. Gk *Kalliopē*] : a musical instrument consisting of a series of whistles played by keys arranged as in an organ

call number *n* : a combination of characters assigned to a library book to indicate its place on a shelf

call off *vb* : CANCEL

cal·los·i·ty \ka-ˈläs-ət-ē, kə-\ *n, pl* **-ties 1** : the quality or state of being callous **2** : CALLUS 1

¹**cal·lous** \ˈkal-əs\ *adj* **1** : being thickened and usu. hardened ⟨∼ skin⟩ **2** : hardened in feeling — **cal·lous·ly** *adv* — **cal·lous·ness** *n*

²**callous** *vb* : to make callous

cal·low \ˈkal-ō\ *adj* [ME *calu* bald, fr. OE] : lacking adult sophistication : IMMATURE — **cal·low·ness** *n*

call–up \ˈkȯl-ˌəp\ *n* : an order to report for active military service

call up \(ˈ)kȯl-ˈəp\ *vb* : to summon for active military duty

¹**cal·lus** \ˈkal-əs\ *n* **1** : a callous area on skin or bark **2** : tissue that is converted into bone in the healing of a bone fracture

²**callus** *vb* : to form a callus

¹**calm** \ˈkäm, ˈkalm\ *adj* : marked by calm : STILL, PLACID, SERENE — **calm·ly** *adv* — **calm·ness** *n*

²**calm** *vb* : to make or become calm

³**calm** *n* **1** : a period or a condition of freedom from storms, high winds, or rough water **2** : complete or almost complete absence of wind **3** : a state of tranquility

cal·o·mel \ˈkal-ə-məl, -ˌmel\ *n* : a chloride of mercury used esp. as a purgative and fungicide

ca·lor·ic \kə-ˈlȯr-ik\ *adj* **1** : of or relating to heat **2** : of or relating to calories

cal·o·rie *also* **cal·o·ry** \ˈkal-(ə-)rē\ *n, pl* **-ries** : a unit for measuring heat; *esp* : one for measuring the value of foods for producing heat and energy in the human body equivalent to the amount of heat required to raise the temperature of one kilogram of water one degree Celsius

cal·o·rif·ic \ˌkal-ə-ˈrif-ik\ *adj* : CALORIC

cal·o·rim·e·ter \ˌkal-ə-ˈrim-ət-ər\ *n* : an apparatus for measuring quantities of heat — **cal·o·rim·e·try** \ˌkal-ə-ˈrim-ə-trē\ *n*

cal·u·met \ˈkal-yə-ˌmet, -mət\ *n* : an American Indian ceremonial pipe

ca·lum·ni·ate \kə-ˈləm-nē-ˌāt\ *vb* **-at·ed; -at·ing** : to accuse falsely and maliciously : SLANDER **syn** defame, malign, libel, slander, traduce — **ca·lum·ni·a·tion** \-ˌləm-nē-ˈā-shən\ *n* — **ca·lum·ni·a·tor** \-ˈləm-nē-ˌāt-ər\ *n*

cal·um·ny \ˈkal-əm-nē\ *n, pl* **-nies** : false and malicious accusation — **ca·lum·ni·ous** \kə-ˈləm-nē-əs\ *adj*

calve \ˈkav, ˈkàv\ *vb* **calved; calv·ing** : to give birth to a calf

calves pl of CALF

Cal·vin·ism \ˈkal-və-ˌniz-əm\ *n* : the theological system of John Calvin and his followers — **Cal·vin·ist** \-və-nəst\ *n or adj* — **Cal·vin·is·tic** \ˌkal-və-ˈnis-tik\ *adj*

ca·lyp·so \kə-ˈlip-sō\ *n, pl* **-sos** : a style of music originating in the British West Indies and having lyrics that usu. satirize local personalities and events

ca·lyx \ˈkā-liks, ˈkal-iks\ *n, pl* **ca·lyx·es** *or* **ca·ly·ces** \ˈkā-lə-ˌsēz, ˈkal-ə-\ : the outside usu. green or leaflike part of a flower consisting of sepals

cam \ˈkam\ *n* : a rotating or sliding projection (as on a wheel) in a mechanical linkage by which rotary motion is transformed into linear motion or vice versa

ca·ma·ra·de·rie \ˌkam-(ə-)ˈrad-ə-rē, ˌkäm-(ə-)ˈräd-\ *n* [F] : friendly feeling and goodwill among comrades

cam·bi·um \ˈkam-bē-əm\ *n, pl* **-bi·ums** *or* **-bia** \-bē-ə\ : a thin cellular layer between xylem and phloem of most higher plants from which new tissues develop — **cam·bi·al** \-bē-əl\ *adj*

Cam·bri·an *adj* : of, relating to, or being the earliest period of the Paleozoic era — **Cambrian** *n*

cam·bric \ˈkām-brik\ *n* : a fine thin white linen or cotton fabric

came past of COME

cam·el \ˈkam-əl\ *n* : either of two large hoofed cud-chewing mammals used esp. in desert regions of Asia and Africa for carrying burdens and for riding

camel hair *also* **camel's hair** *n* **1** : the hair of a camel or a substitute for it **2** : cloth made of camel hair or of camel hair and wool

ca·mel·lia \kə-ˈmēl-yə\ *n* : any of several shrubs or trees related to the tea plant and grown in warm regions and greenhouses for their showy roselike flowers

Cam·em·bert \ˈkam-əm-ˌbeər\ *n* : a soft surface-ripened cheese with a grayish rind and yellow interior

cam•eo \ˈkam-ē-ˌō\ *n, pl* **-eos 1** : a gem carved in relief; *also* : a small medallion with a profiled head in relief **2** : a brief appearance by a well-known actor in a play or movie

cam•era \ˈkam-(ə-)rə\ *n* : a closed light-proof box with a lens through which the image of an object is recorded on a light-sensitive material; *also* : an electronic device that forms an image and converts it into an electrical signal (as for television broadcast) — **cam•era•man** \ˈkam-(ə-)rə-ˌman, -mən\ *n*

Cam•er•oo•ni•an \ˌkam-ə-ˈrü-nē-ən\ *n* : a native or inhabitant of the Republic of Cameroon or the Cameroons region — **Cameroonian** *adj*

cam•i•sole \ˈkam-ə-ˌsōl\ *n* : a short sleeveless undergarment for women

camomile *var of* CHAMOMILE

cam•ou•flage \ˈkam-ə-ˌfläzh, -ˌfläj\ *n* [F] **1** : the disguising of military equipment with paint, nets, or foliage; *also* : the disguise itself **2** : a deceptive expedient — **camouflage** *vb*

¹**camp** \ˈkamp\ *n* **1** : a place where tents or buildings are erected for usu. temporary shelter **2** : a collection of tents or other shelters **3** : a body of persons encamped — **camp•ground** \-ˌgraund\ *n* — **camp•site** \-ˌsīt\ *n*

²**camp** *vb* **1** : to make or occupy a camp **2** : to live in a camp or outdoors

³**camp** *n* **1** : exaggerated effeminate mannerisms **2** : something so outrageous or in such bad taste as to be considered amusing — **camp** *adj* — **camp•i•ly** \ˈkam-pə-lē\ *adv* — **camp•i•ness** \-pē-nəs\ *n* — **campy** \ˈkam-pē\ *adj*

⁴**camp** *vb* : to engage in camp : exhibit the qualities of camp

cam•paign \kam-ˈpān\ *n* **1** : a series of military operations forming one distinct stage in a war **2** : a series of activities designed to bring about a particular result ⟨advertising ∼⟩ — **campaign** *vb* — **cam•paign•er** *n*

cam•pa•ni•le \ˌkam-pə-ˈnē-lē\ *n, pl* **-ni•les** *or* **-ni•li** \-ˈnē-lē\ : a usu. freestanding bell tower

cam•pa•nol•o•gy \ˌkam-pə-ˈnäl-ə-jē\ *n* : the art of bell ringing — **cam•pa•nol•o•gist** \-jəst\ *n*

camp•er \ˈkam-pər\ *n* **1** : one that camps **2** : a portable dwelling (as a specially equipped vehicle) for use during casual travel and camping

Camp Fire Girl *n* : a member of a national organization of girls from 7 to 18

camp follower *n* **1** : a civilian (as a prostitute) who follows a military unit to attend or exploit its personnel **2** : a follower of a group who is not an adherent; *esp* : a politician who joins a movement solely for personal gain

cam•phor \ˈkam(p)-fər\ *n* : a gummy volatile fragrant compound obtained from an evergreen Asian tree (**camphor tree**) and used esp. in medicine

camp meeting *n* : a series of evangelistic meetings usu. held outdoors

camp•o•ree \ˌkam-pə-ˈrē\ *n* : a gathering of Boy Scouts or Girl Scouts from a given geographic area

cam•pus \ˈkam-pəs\ *n* [L, plain] : the grounds and buildings of a college or school; *also* : a central grassy part of the grounds

cam•shaft \ˈkam-ˌshaft\ *n* : a shaft to which a cam is fastened

¹**can** \kən, (ˈ)kan\ *vb, past* **could** \kəd, (ˈ)kud\; *pres sing & pl* **can 1** : be able to **2** : may perhaps ⟨∼ he still be alive⟩ **3** : be permitted by conscience or feeling to ⟨you ∼ hardly blame him⟩ **4** : have permission or liberty to ⟨you ∼ go now⟩

²**can** \ˈkan\ *n* **1** : a typically cylindrical metal container or receptacle ⟨garbage ∼⟩ ⟨coffee ∼⟩ **2** : JAIL

³**can** \ˈkan\ *vb* **canned; can•ning 1** : to put in a can : preserve by sealing in airtight cans or jars **2** *slang* : to discharge from employment **3** *slang* : to put a stop or an end to **4** : to record on discs or tape — **can•ner** *n*

Can *or* **Canad** *abbr* Canada; Canadian

Can•a•da goose \ˈkan-əd-ə-\ *n* : a common wild goose of No. America

Ca•na•di•an \kə-ˈnād-ē-ən\ *n* : a native or inhabitant of Canada — **Canadian** *adj*

ca•naille \kə-ˈnī, -ˈnäl\ *n* [F, fr. It *canaglia*, fr. *cane* dog] : RABBLE, RIFFRAFF

ca•nal \kə-ˈnal\ *n* **1** : a tubular passage in the body : DUCT **2** : an artificial waterway (as for boats or irrigation)

can•a•lize \ˈkan-ᵊl-ˌīz\ *vb* **-lized; -liz•ing 1** : to provide with a canal or make into or like a channel **2** : to provide with an outlet; *esp* : to direct into preferred channels — **ca·nal·iza·tion** \ˌkan-ᵊl-ə-ˈzā-shən\ *n*

can·a·pé \ˈkan-ə-pē, -ˌpā\ *n* [F, lit., sofa, fr. ML *canopeum, canapeum* mosquito net] : a piece of bread or toast or a cracker topped with a savory food

ca·nard \kə-ˈnärd\ *n* : a false or unfounded report or story

ca·nary \kə-ˈner-ē\ *n, pl* **ca·nar·ies** [fr. the *Canary* islands] **1** : a usu. sweet wine similar to Madeira **2** : a usu. yellow or greenish finch often kept in a cage **3** : a bright yellow

ca·nas·ta \kə-ˈnas-tə\ *n* [Sp, lit., basket] : rummy played with two full decks of cards plus four jokers

canc *abbr* canceled

can·can \ˈkan-ˌkan\ *n* : a woman's dance of French origin characterized by high kicking

¹can·cel \ˈkan-səl\ *vb* **-celed** *or* **-celled; -cel·ing** *or* **-cel·ling** \-s(ə-)liŋ\ [ME *cancellen*, fr. MF *canceller*, fr. L *cancellare* to make like a lattice, fr. *cancer* lattice] **1** : to destroy the force or validity of : ANNUL **2** : to match in force or effect : OFFSET **3** : to cross out : DELETE **4** : to remove (a common divisor) from a numerator and denominator; *also* : to remove (equivalents) on opposite sides of an equation or account **5** : to mark (a postage stamp or check) so that it cannot be reused **6** : to neutralize each other's strength or effect — **can·cel·la·tion** \ˌkan-sə-ˈlā-shən\ *n* — **can·cel·er** *or* **can·cel·ler** \ˈkan(t)-s(ə-)lər\ *n*

²cancel *n* **1** : CANCELLATION **2** : a deleted part

can·cer \ˈkan-sər\ *n* [L, lit., crab] **1** *cap* : a zodiacal constellation between Gemini and Leo usu. pictured as a crab **2** *cap* : the 4th sign of the zodiac in astrology; *also* : one born under this sign **3** : a malignant tumor that tends to spread in the body **4** : a malignant evil that corrodes slowly and fatally — **can·cer·ous** \ˈkans-(ə-)rəs\ *adj* — **can·cer·ous·ly** *adv*

can·de·la·bra \ˌkan-də-ˈläb-rə, -ˈlab-\ *n* : an ornamental branched candlestick or lamp with several lights

can·de·la·brum \-rəm\ *n, pl* **-bra** \-rə\ *also* **-brums** : CANDELABRA

can·des·cent \kan-ˈdes-ᵊnt\ *adj* : glowing or dazzling esp. from great heat — **can·des·cence** \-ᵊns\ *n*

can·did \ˈkan-dəd\ *adj* **1** : FRANK, STRAIGHTFORWARD **2** : relating to photography of subjects acting naturally or spontaneously without being posed — **can·did·ly** *adv* — **can·did·ness** *n*

can·di·da·cy \ˈkan-(d)əd-ə-sē\ *n, pl* **-cies** : the state of being a candidate

can·di·date \ˈkan-(d)ə-ˌdāt, -(d)əd-ət\ *n* [L *candidatus*, fr. *candidatus* clothed in white, fr. *candidus* white; fr. the white toga worn by candidates in ancient Rome] : one who seeks or is proposed for an office, honor, or membership

can·di·da·ture \ˈkan-(d)əd-ə-ˌchủr\ *n, chiefly Brit* : CANDIDACY

can·died \ˈkan-dēd\ *adj* : preserved in or encrusted with sugar

¹can·dle \ˈkan-dᵊl\ *n* : a usu. slender mass of tallow or wax molded around a wick and burned to give light

²candle *vb* **can·dled; can·dling** \ˈkan-(d)liŋ, -dᵊl-iŋ\ : to examine (as eggs) by holding between the eye and a light — **can·dler** \-d(ə-)lər\ *n*

can·dle·light \ˈkan-dᵊl-(l)īt\ *n* **1** : the light of a candle; *also* : any soft artificial light **2** : the time when candles are lit : TWILIGHT

Can·dle·mas \ˈkan-dᵊl-məs\ *n* : February 2 observed as a church festival in commemoration of the presentation of Christ in the temple

can·dle·pin \-ˌpin\ *n* : a slender bowling pin tapering toward top and bottom used in a bowling game (**candlepins**) with a smaller ball than that used in tenpins

can·dle·stick \-ˌstik\ *n* : a holder with a socket for a candle

can·dle·wick \-ˌwik\ *n* : a soft cotton yarn; *also* : embroidery made with this yarn usu. in tufts

can·dor \ˈkan-dər\ *n* : FRANKNESS, OUTSPOKENNESS

C and W *abbr* country and western

¹can·dy \ˈkan-dē\ *n, pl* **candies** : a confection made from sugar often with flavoring and filling

²candy *vb* **can·died; can·dy·ing 1** : to encrust in sugar often by cooking in a syrup **2** : to make attractive : SWEET-EN **3** : to crystallize or become crystallized into sugar

candy strip•er \-ˌstrī-pər\ *n* : a teenage volunteer nurse's aide

¹cane \ˈkān\ *n* **1** : a slender hollow or pithy stem (as of a reed or bramble) **2** : a tall woody grass or reed (as sugarcane) **3** : a walking stick; *also* : a rod for flogging

²cane *vb* **caned; can•ing 1** : to beat with a cane **2** : to weave or make with cane — **can•er** *n*

cane•brake \ˈkān-ˌbrāk\ *n* : a thicket of cane

¹ca•nine \ˈkā-ˌnīn\ *n* [L *caninus*, fr. *canis* dog] **1** : a pointed tooth between the outer incisor and the first premolar **2** : DOG

²canine *adj* : of or relating to dogs or to the family to which they belong

can•is•ter \ˈkan-ə-stər\ *n* **1** : a small box for holding a dry product (as tea) **2** : a perforated box containing material to absorb or filter a harmful substance in the air

can•ker \ˈkaŋ-kər\ *n* : a spreading sore that eats into tissue — **can•ker•ous** \ˈkaŋ-k(ə-)rəs\ *adj*

can•ker•worm \-ˌwərm\ *n* : either of two moths and esp. their larvae that are pests of forest and shade trees

can•na \ˈkan-ə\ *n* : any of a genus of tropical herbs with large leaves and racemes of bright-colored flowers

can•na•bis \ˈkan-ə-bəs\ *n* : any of the psychoactive preparations (as marijuana) or chemicals (as THC) derived from hemp; *also* : HEMP

canned \ˈkand\ *adj* : prepared in standardized form for general use or wide distribution

can•nery \ˈkan-(ə-)rē\ *n, pl* **-ner•ies** : a factory for the canning of foods

can•ni•bal \ˈkan-ə-bəl\ *n* [NL *Canibalis* a member of a Caribbean Indian people, fr. Sp *Caníbal*, fr. a native word *Caniba* or *Carib*] : one that eats the flesh of its own kind — **can•ni•bal•ism** \ˈkan-ə-bə-ˌliz-əm\ *n* — **can•ni•bal•is•tic** \ˌkan-ə-bə-ˈlis-tik\ *adj*

can•ni•bal•ize \ˈkan-ə-bə-ˌlīz\ *vb* **-ized; -iz•ing 1** : to take usable parts from (as an inoperative machine) to construct or repair another machine **2** : to practice cannibalism

can•non \ˈkan-ən\ *n, pl* **cannons** *or* **cannon** [MF *canon*, fr. It *cannone*, lit., large tube, fr. *canna* reed, tube, fr. L, cane, reed] **1** : an artillery piece supported on a carriage or mount **2** : a large-caliber automatic gun on an aircraft

can•non•ade \ˌkan-ə-ˈnād\ *n* : a heavy fire of artillery — **cannonade** *vb*

can•non•ball \ˈkan-ən-ˌbȯl\ *n* : a usu. round solid missile for firing from a cannon

can•non•eer \ˌkan-ə-ˈniər\ *n* : an artillery gunner

can•not \ˈkan-ˌät; kə-ˈnät\ : can not — **cannot but** : to be unable to do otherwise than

can•nu•la \ˈkan-yə-lə\ *n, pl* **-las** *or* **-lae** \-ˌlē\ : a small tube for insertion into a body cavity or into a duct or vessel

can•ny \ˈkan-ē\ *adj* **can•ni•er; -est** : PRUDENT, SHREWD — **can•ni•ly** \ˈkan-ᵊl-ē\ *adv* — **can•ni•ness** \ˈkan-ē-nəs\ *n*

ca•noe \kə-ˈnü\ *n* : a light narrow boat with sharp ends and curved sides that is usu. propelled by paddles — **canoe** *vb* — **ca•noe•ist** *n*

¹can•on \ˈkan-ən\ *n* **1** : a regulation decreed by a church council; *also* : a provision of canon law **2** : an official or authoritative list (as of the saints or the books of the Bible) **3** : an accepted principle ⟨the ~s of good taste⟩

²canon *n* : a clergyman on the staff of a cathedral

ca•ñon \ˈkan-yən\ var of CANYON

ca•non•i•cal \kə-ˈnän-i-kəl\ *adj* **1** : of, relating to, or forming a canon **2** : conforming to a general rule or acceptable procedure : ORTHODOX **3** : of or relating to a clergyman who is a canon — **ca•non•i•cal•ly** \-k(ə-)lē\ *adv*

ca•non•i•cals \-kəlz\ *n pl* : the vestments prescribed by canon for an officiating clergyman

can•on•ize \ˈkan-ə-ˌnīz\ *vb* **can•on•ized** \-ˌnīzd\; **can•on•iz•ing 1** : to declare an officially recognized saint **2** : GLORIFY, EXALT — **can•on•iza•tion** \ˌkan-ə-nə-ˈzā-shən\ *n*

canon law *n* : the law governing a church

canon regular *n, pl* **canons regular** : a member of one of several Roman

Catholic religious institutes of regular priests living in community

can•o•py \\'kan-ə-pē\ *n, pl* **-pies** [ME *canope*, fr. ML *canopeum* mosquito net, fr. L *conopeum*, fr. Gk *kōnōpion*, fr. *kōnōps* mosquito] : an overhanging cover, shelter, or shade — **canopy** *vb*

¹cant \\'kant\ *n* **1** : an oblique or slanting surface **2** : TILT, SLANT

²cant *vb* : to give a slant to

³cant *vb* **1** : to beg in a whining manner **2** : to talk hypocritically

⁴cant *n* **1** : the special idiom of a profession or trade : JARGON **2** : insincere speech; *esp* : insincerely pious words or statements

Cant *abbr* Canticle of Canticles

can•ta•bi•le \kän-'täb-ə-ˌlā\ *adv or adj* [It] : in a singing manner — used as a direction in music

can•ta•loupe *also* **can•te•loupe** \\'kant-ᵊl-ˌōp\ *n* : MUSKMELON; *esp* : one with orange flesh and rough skin

can•tan•ker•ous \kan-'taŋ-k(ə-)rəs\ *adj* : ILL-NATURED, QUARRELSOME — **can•tan•ker•ous•ly** *adv* — **can•tan•ker•ous•ness** *n*

can•ta•ta \kən-'tät-ə\ *n* [It] : a choral composition usu. accompanied by organ, piano, or orchestra

can•teen \kan-'tēn\ *n* [F *cantine* bottle case, canteen (store), fr. It *cantina* wine cellar, fr. *canto* corner] **1** : a flask for carrying liquids **2** : a place of recreation and entertainment for military personnel **3** : a small cafeteria or counter at which snacks are served

can•ter \\'kant-ər\ *n* : a horse's 3-beat gait resembling but smoother and slower than a gallop — **canter** *vb*

Can•ter•bury bell \ˌkant-ə(r)-ˌber-ē-\ *n* : any of several plants related to the bluebell that are cultivated for their showy flowers

can•ti•cle \\'kant-i-kəl\ *n* : SONG; *esp* : any of several liturgical songs taken from the Bible

Canticle of Canticles *n* — see BIBLE table

¹can•ti•le•ver \\'kant-ᵊl-ˌē-vər\ *n* : a projecting beam or structure supported only at one end; *also* : either of a pair of such structures projecting toward each other so that when joined they form a bridge

²cantilever *vb* **1** : to project as a can-

tilever **2** : to build as a cantilever **3** : to support by a cantilever ⟨a ∼ed shelf⟩

can•tle \\'kant-ᵊl\ *n* : the upwardly projecting rear part of a saddle

can•to \\'kan-ˌtō\ *n, pl* **cantos** [It, fr. L *cantus* song] : one of the major divisions of a long poem

can•ton \\'kant-ᵊn, 'kan-ˌtän\ *n* : a small territorial division of a country; *esp* : one of the political divisions of Switzerland — **can•ton•al** \\'kant-ᵊn-əl, kan-'tän-ᵊl\ *adj*

can•ton•ment \kan-'tōn-mənt, -'tän-\ *n* : usu. temporary quarters for troops

can•tor \\'kant-ər\ *n* : a synagogue official who sings liturgical music and leads the congregation in prayer

can•vas *also* **can•vass** \\'kan-vəs\ *n* **1** : a strong cloth formerly much used for making tents and sails **2** : a set of sails **3** : a group of tents **4** : a piece of cloth prepared as a surface to receive oil paint; *also* : an oil painting **5** : the canvas-covered floor of a boxing or wrestling ring

can•vas•back \\'kan-vəs-ˌbak\ *n* : a No. American wild duck with red head and gray back

¹can•vass *also* **can•vas** \\'kan-vəs\ *vb* : to go through (a district) or to go to (persons) to solicit votes or orders for goods or to determine public opinion or sentiment — **can•vass•er** *n*

²canvass *n* : an act of canvassing (as the solicitation of votes or survey of public opinion)

can•yon \\'kan-yən\ *n* : a deep narrow valley with high steep sides

caou•tchouc \\'kaů-ˌchůk, -ˌchük\ *n* : RUBBER 3

¹cap \\'kap\ *n* **1** : a covering for the head esp. with a visor and no brim; *also* : something resembling such a covering **2** : a container holding an explosive charge **3** : an upper limit (as on expenditures)

²cap *vb* **capped; cap•ping** **1** : to provide or protect with a cap **2** : to form a cap over : CROWN **3** : OUTDO, SURPASS **4** : CLIMAX

³cap *abbr* **1** capacity **2** capital **3** capitalize; capitalized

CAP *abbr* Civil Air Patrol

ca•pa•ble \\'kā-pə-bəl\ *adj* : having ability, capacity, or power to do something : ABLE, COMPETENT — **ca·pa·bil·i·ty** \ˌkā-pə-ˈbil-ət-ē\ *n* — **ca·pa·bly** \ˈkā-pə-blē\ *adv*

ca·pa·cious \kə-ˈpā-shəs\ *adj* : able to contain much — **ca·pa·cious·ly** *adv* — **ca·pa·cious·ness** *n*

ca·pac·i·tance \kə-ˈpas-ət-əns\ *n* : the property of an electric nonconductor that permits the storage of energy

ca·pac·i·tor \kə-ˈpas-ət-ər\ *n* : an electronic circuit device for temporary storage of electrical energy

¹**ca·pac·i·ty** \kə-ˈpas-ət-ē\ *n, pl* **-ties 1** : legal qualification or fitness **2** : the ability to contain, receive, or accommodate **3** : extent of space : VOLUME **4** : ABILITY **5** : position or character assigned or assumed

²**capacity** *adj* : equaling maximum capacity ⟨a ~ crowd⟩

cap–a–pie *or* **cap–à–pie** \ˌkap-ə-ˈpē\ *adv* [MF] : from head to foot : at all points

ca·par·i·son \kə-ˈpar-ə-sən\ *n* **1** : an ornamental covering for a horse **2** : TRAPPINGS, ADORNMENT — **caparison** *vb*

¹**cape** \ˈkāp\ *n* **1** : a point of land jutting out into water **2** *usu cap* : CAPE COD COTTAGE

²**cape** *n* : a sleeveless garment hanging from the neck over the shoulders

Cape Cod cottage \ˌkāp-ˌkäd-\ *n* : a compact rectangular dwelling of one or one-and-a-half stories usu. with a steep gable roof

¹**ca·per** \ˈkā-pər\ *n* : the flower bud or young berry of a Mediterranean shrub pickled for use as a relish; *also* : this shrub

²**caper** *vb* **ca·pered; ca·per·ing** \-p(ə-)riŋ\ : to leap about in a playful manner : PRANCE

³**caper** *n* **1** : a froliscome leap **2** : a capricious escapade **3** : an illegal or questionable act

cape·skin \ˈkāp-ˌskin\ *n* : a light flexible leather made from sheepskins

Cape Verd·ian \-ˈvərd-ē-ən\ *n* : a native or inhabitant of the Republic of Cape Verde

cap·ful \ˈkap-ˌfùl\ *n* : as much as a cap will hold

cap·il·lar·i·ty \ˌkap-ə-ˈlar-ət-ē\ *n, pl* **-ties** : the action by which the surface of a liquid where it is in contact with a solid (as in a slender tube) is raised or lowered depending on the relative attraction of the molecules of the liquid for each other and for those of the solid

¹**cap·il·lary** \ˈkap-ə-ˌler-ē\ *adj* **1** : resembling a hair **2** : having a very small bore ⟨~ tube⟩ **3** : of or relating to capillaries or to capillarity

²**capillary** *n, pl* **-lar·ies** : any of the tiny thin-walled blood vessels that carry blood between the smallest arteries and their corresponding veins

¹**cap·i·tal** \ˈkap-ət-ᵊl\ *adj* **1** : conforming to the series A, B, C rather than a, b, c ⟨~ letters⟩ ⟨~ G⟩ **2** : punishable by death ⟨a ~ crime⟩ **3** : most serious ⟨a ~ error⟩ **4** : first in importance or position : CHIEF; *also* : being the seat of government ⟨the ~ city⟩ **5** : of or relating to capital ⟨~ expenditures⟩; *esp* : relating to or being assets that add to the long-term net worth of a corporation **6** : FIRST-RATE, EXCELLENT

²**capital** *n* **1** : accumulated wealth esp. as used to produce more wealth **2** : the total face value of shares of stock issued by a company **3** : capitalists considered as a group **4** : ADVANTAGE, GAIN **5** : a letter larger than the ordinary small letter and often different in form **6** : the capital city of a state or country; *also* : a city preeminent in some activity ⟨the fashion ~ of the world⟩

³**capital** *n* : the top part or piece of an architectural column

capital gain *n* : the increase in value of an asset (as stock or real estate) between the time it is bought and the time it is sold

capital goods *n pl* : machinery, tools, factories, and commodities used in the production of goods

cap·i·tal·ism \ˈkap-ət-ᵊl-ˌiz-əm\ *n* : an economic system characterized by private or corporate ownership of capital goods and by prices, production, and distribution of goods that are determined mainly in a free market

¹**cap·i·tal·ist** \-əst\ *n* **1** : a person who has capital esp. invested in business **2** : a person of great wealth : PLUTOCRAT **3** : a believer in capitalism

²**capitalist** *or* **cap·i·tal·is·tic** \ˌkap-ət-ᵊl-ˈis-tik\ *adj* **1** : owning capital **2**

: practicing or advocating capitalism **3** : marked by capitalism — **cap·i·tal·is·ti·cal·ly** \-ti-k(ə-)lē\ *adv*

cap·i·tal·iza·tion \ˌkap-ət-ᵊl-ə-'zā-shən\ *n* **1** : the act or process of capitalizing **2** : the total amount of money used as capital in a business

cap·i·tal·ize \'kap-ət-ᵊl-ˌīz\ *vb* **-ized; -iz·ing 1** : to write or print with an initial capital or in capitals **2** : to convert into or use as capital **3** : to supply capital for **4** : to gain by turning something to advantage : PROFIT

cap·i·tal·ly \'kap-ət-ᵊl-ē\ *adv* : ADMIRABLY, EXCELLENTLY

cap·i·ta·tion \ˌkap-ə-'tā-shən\ *n* : a direct uniform tax levied on each person

cap·i·tol \'kap-ət-ᵊl\ *n* : the building in which a legislature holds its sessions

ca·pit·u·late \kə-'pich-ə-ˌlāt\ *vb* **-lat·ed; -lat·ing 1** : to surrender esp. on conditions agreed upon **2** : to cease resisting : ACQUIESCE **syn** submit, yield, succumb, cave, defer — **ca·pit·u·la·tion** \-ˌpich-ə-'lā-shən\ *n*

ca·pon \'kā-ˌpän, -pən\ *n* : a castrated male chicken

cap·puc·ci·no \ˌkap-ə-'chē-nō, ˌkäp-\ *n* [It, lit., Capuchin; fr. the likeness of its color to that of a Capuchin's habit] : espresso mixed with foamy hot milk or cream and often flavored with cinnamon

ca·pric·cio \kə-'prē-ch(ē-ˌ)ō\ *n, pl* **-cios** : an instrumental piece in free form usu. lively in tempo and brilliant in style

ca·price \kə-'prēs\ *n* [F, fr. It *capriccio*, lit., head with hair standing on end, shudder, fr. *capo* head + *riccio* hedgehog] **1** : a sudden whim or fancy **2** : an inclination to change one's mind impulsively **3** : CAPRICCIO — **ca·pri·cious** \kə-'prish-əs\ *adj* — **ca·pri·cious·ly** *adv* — **ca·pri·cious·ness** *n*

Cap·ri·corn \'kap-ri-ˌkȯrn\ *n* **1** : a zodiacal constellation between Sagittarius and Aquarius usu. pictured as a goat **2** : the 10th sign of the zodiac in astrology; *also* : one born under this sign

cap·ri·ole \'kap-rē-ˌōl\ *n* : ³CAPER 1; *esp* : an upward leap of a horse with a backward kick at the height of the leap — **capriole** *vb*

caps *abbr* **1** capitals **2** capsule

cap·si·cum \'kap-si-kəm\ *n* : PEPPER 2

cap·size \'kap-ˌsīz, kap-'sīz\ *vb* **cap·sized; cap·siz·ing** : UPSET, OVERTURN

cap·stan \'kap-stən, -ˌstan\ *n* **1** : a machine for moving or raising heavy weights that consists of a vertical drum which can be rotated and around which cable is turned **2** : a rotating shaft that drives recorder tape

cap·su·lar \'kap-sə-lər\ *adj* : of, relating to, or resembling a capsule

cap·su·lat·ed \-ˌlāt-əd\ *adj* : enclosed in a capsule

¹cap·sule \'kap-səl, -sül\ *n* **1** : an enveloping cover (as of a bodily joint) ⟨a spore ∼⟩; *esp* : an edible shell enclosing medicine or vitamins to be swallowed **2** : a dry fruit made of two or more united carpels that splits open when ripe **3** : a small pressurized compartment for a pilot or astronaut

²capsule *adj* **1** : very brief **2** : very compact

Capt *abbr* captain

¹cap·tain \'kap-tən\ *n* **1** : a commander of a body of troops **2** : a commissioned officer in the army, air force, or marine corps ranking next below a major **3** : an officer in charge of a ship; *esp* : a commissioned officer in the navy ranking next below a rear admiral or a commodore **4** : a leader of a side or team **5** : a dominant figure — **cap·tain·cy** *n*

²captain *vb* : to be captain of : LEAD

cap·tion \'kap-shən\ *n* **1** : a heading esp. of an article or document : TITLE **2** : the explanatory matter accompanying an illustration **3** : a motion-picture subtitle — **cap·tion** *vb*

cap·tious \'kap-shəs\ *adj* : marked by an inclination to find fault — **cap·tious·ly** *adv* — **cap·tious·ness** *n*

cap·ti·vate \'kap-tə-ˌvāt\ *vb* **-vat·ed; -vat·ing** : to attract and hold irresistibly by some special charm or art — **cap·ti·va·tion** \ˌkap-tə-'vā-shən\ *n* — **cap·ti·va·tor** \'kap-tə-ˌvāt-ər\ *n*

cap·tive \'kap-tiv\ *adj* **1** : made prisoner esp. in war **2** : kept within bounds : CONFINED **3** : held under control — **captive** *n* — **cap·tiv·i·ty** \kap-'tiv-ət-ē\ *n*

cap·tor \'kap-tər\ *n* : one that captures

¹cap·ture \'kap-chər\ *n* **1** : the act of

capturing **2** : one that has been captured

²**capture** *vb* **cap·tured; cap·tur·ing 1** : to take captive : WIN, GAIN **2** : to preserve in a relatively permanent form

Ca·pu·chin \\'kap-yə-shən\ *n* : a member of an austere branch of the order of St. Francis of Assisi engaged in missionary work and preaching

car \\'kär\ *n* **1** : a vehicle moving on wheels **2** : the compartment of an elevator **3** : the part of a balloon or airship that carries passengers or equipment

ca·ra·bao \,kar-ə-'baủ\ *n, pl* **-bao** *or* **-baos** : a water buffalo esp. in the Philippines

car·a·bi·neer *or* **car·a·bi·nier** \,kar-ə-bə-'niər\ *n* : a soldier armed with a carbine

car·a·cole \\'kar-ə-,kōl\ *n* : a half turn to right or left executed by a mounted horse — **caracole** *vb*

ca·rafe \kə-'raf, -'räf\ *n* : a bottle with a flaring lip used esp. to hold wine

car·a·mel \\'kar-ə-məl, 'kär-məl\ *n* **1** : an amorphous substance obtained by heating sugar and used for flavoring and coloring **2** : a firm chewy candy

car·a·pace \\'kar-ə-,pās\ *n* : a protective case or shell on the back of some animals (as turtles or crabs)

¹**carat** *var of* KARAT

²**car·at** \\'kar-ət\ *n* : a unit of weight for precious stones equal to 200 milligrams

car·a·van \\'kar-ə-,van\ *n* **1** : a group of travelers journeying together through desert or hostile regions **2** : a group of vehicles traveling in a file

car·a·van·sa·ry \,kar-ə-'van-sə-rē\ *or* **car·a·van·se·rai** \-sə-,rī\ *n, pl* **-ries** *or* **-rais** *or* **-rai** [Per *kārwānsarāī,* fr. *kārwān* caravan + *sarāī* palace, inn] **1** : an inn in eastern countries where caravans rest at night **2** : HOTEL, INN

car·a·vel \\'kar-ə-,vel\ *n* : a small 15th and 16th century ship with a broad bow, high narrow poop, and usu. three masts

car·a·way \\'kar-ə-,wā\ *n* : an aromatic herb related to the carrot with fruits (**caraway seed**) used in seasoning and medicine; *also* : its fruit

car·bide \\'kär-,bīd\ *n* : a compound of carbon with another element

car·bine \\'kär-,bēn, -,bīn\ *n* : a short= barreled lightweight rifle

car·bo·hy·drate \,kär-bō-'hī-,drāt, -drət\ *n* : any of various compounds composed of carbon, hydrogen, and oxygen (as sugars and starches)

car·bol·ic acid \,kär-,bäl-ik-\ *n* : PHENOL

car·bon \\'kär-bən\ *n* **1** : a nonmetallic chemical element occurring in nature as diamond and graphite and as a constituent of coal, petroleum, and limestone **2** : a sheet of carbon paper; *also* : CARBON COPY **1**

car·bo·na·ceous \,kär-bə-'nā-shəs\ *adj* : relating to, containing, or composed of carbon

¹**car·bon·ate** \\'kär-bə-,nāt, -nət\ *n* : a salt or ester of carbonic acid

²**car·bon·ate** \-,nāt\ *vb* **-at·ed; -at·ing** : to impregnate with carbon dioxide ⟨a *carbonated* beverage⟩ — **car·bon·ation** \,kär-bə-'nā-shən\ *n*

carbon black *n* : any of various black substances consisting chiefly of carbon used esp. as pigments

carbon copy *n* **1** : a copy made by carbon paper **2** : DUPLICATE

carbon dating *n* : the determination of the age of old material (as an archaeological specimen) by means of the content of carbon 14

carbon dioxide *n* : a heavy colorless gas that does not support combustion and is formed in animal respiration and in the combustion and decomposition of organic substances

carbon 14 *n* : a heavy radioactive form of carbon used in dating archaeological and geological materials

car·bon·ic acid \kär-,bän-ik-\ *n* : a weak acid that decomposes readily into water and carbon dioxide

car·bon·if·er·ous \,kär-bə-'nif-(ə-)rəs\ *adj* **1** : producing or containing carbon or coal **2** *cap* : of, relating to, or being the period of the Paleozoic era between the Devonian and the Permian — **Carboniferous** *n*

carbon monoxide *n* : a colorless odorless very poisonous gas formed by the incomplete burning of carbon

carbon paper *n* : a thin paper coated

with a pigment and used for making copies

carbon tet·ra·chlo·ride \-,te-trə-'klōr-,īd\ *n* : a colorless nonflammable toxic liquid used esp. as a solvent

carbon 12 *n* : the most abundant isotope of carbon having a nucleus of 6 protons and 6 neutrons and used as a reference in the determination of other atomic masses

car·boy \'kär-,bȯi\ *n* [Per *qarāba,* fr. Ar *qarrābah* demijohn] : a large container for liquids

car·bun·cle \'kär-,bəŋ-kəl\ *n* : a painful inflammation of the skin and underlying tissue that discharges pus from several openings — **car·bun·cu·lar** \kär-'bəŋ-kyə-lər\ *adj*

car·bu·re·tor \'kär-b(y)ə-,rāt-ər\ *n* : an apparatus for supplying an internal‑combustion engine with an explosive mixture of vaporized fuel and air

car·cass \'kär-kəs\ *n* : a dead body; *esp* : one of an animal dressed for food

car·cin·o·gen \kär-'sin-ə-jən\ *n* : an agent causing or inciting cancer — **car·ci·no·gen·ic** \,kärs-ᵊn-ō-'jen-ik\ *adj* — **car·ci·no·ge·nic·i·ty** \-jə-'nis-ət-ē\ *n*

car·ci·no·ma \,kärs-ᵊn-'ō-mə\ *n, pl* **-mas** *or* **-ma·ta** \-mət-ə\ : a malignant tumor of epithelial origin — **car·ci·no·ma·tous** \-'ō-mət-əs\ *adj*

¹card \'kärd\ *vb* : to comb with a card : cleanse and untangle before spinning — **card·er** *n*

²card *n* : an instrument for combing fibers (as wool or cotton)

³card *n* **1** : PLAYING CARD **2** *pl* : a game played with playing cards; *also* : card playing **3** : a usu. clownishly amusing person : WAG **4** : a flat stiff usu. small piece of paper, cardboard, or plastic **5** : PROGRAM; *esp* : a sports program

⁴card *vb* **1** : to list or schedule on a card **2** : SCORE

⁵card *abbr* cardinal

car·da·mom \'kärd-ə-məm\ *n* : the aromatic capsular fruit of an East Indian herb related to the ginger whose seeds are used as a condiment and in medicine; *also* : this plant

card·board \'kärd-,bōrd\ *n* : PAPERBOARD

card–car·ry·ing \'kärd-,kar-ē-iŋ\ *adv* : being a regularly enrolled member of an organized group and esp. of the Communist party and not merely a sympathizer with its ideals and programs

card catalog *n* : a catalog (as of books) in which the entries are arranged systematically on cards

car·di·ac \'kärd-ē-,ak\ *adj* **1** : of, relating to, or located near the heart **2** : of, relating to, or affected with heart disease

car·di·gan \'kärd-i-gən\ *n* : a sweater or jacket usu. without a collar and with a full-length opening in the front

¹car·di·nal \'kärd-(ᵊ-)nəl\ *n* [ME, fr. OF, fr. LL *cardinalis,* fr. L *cardo* hinge] **1** : an ecclesiastical official of the Roman Catholic Church ranking next below the pope **2** : a crested No. American finch that is nearly completely red in the male

²cardinal *adj* : of basic importance : CHIEF, MAIN, PRIMARY — **car·di·nal·ly** \-ē\ *adv*

car·di·nal·ate \-ət, -,āt\ *n* : the office, rank, or dignity of a cardinal

cardinal flower *n* : a No. American plant that bears a spike of brilliant red flowers

cardinal number *n* : a number (as 1, 5, 82, 357) that is used in simple counting and answers the question "how many?"

cardinal point *n* : one of the four principal compass points north, south, east, and west

car·di·ol·o·gy \,kärd-ē-'äl-ə-jē\ *n* : the study of the heart and its action and diseases — **car·di·ol·o·gist** \-'äl-ə-jəst\ *n*

car·dio·pul·mo·nary resuscitation \'kärd-ē-ō-'pùl-mə-,ner-ē-\ *n* : a procedure to restore normal breathing after cardiac arrest that includes the clearance of air passages to the lungs, heart massage by the exertion of pressure on the chest, and the use of drugs

car·dio·vas·cu·lar \,kärd-ē-ō-'vas-kyə-lər\ *adj* : of or relating to the heart and blood vessels

card·sharp·er \'kärd-,shär-pər\ *or* **card·sharp** \-,shärp\ *n* : a cheater at cards

¹care \'keər\ *n* **1** : a heavy sense of responsibility : WORRY, ANXIETY **2** : watchful attention : HEED **3** : CHARGE, SUPERVISION **4** : a person or thing that is an object of anxiety or solicitude

²**care** *vb* **cared; car•ing 1** : to feel anxiety **2** : to feel interest **3** : to give care **4** : to have a liking, fondness, taste, or inclination **5** : to be concerned about ⟨~ what happens⟩

CARE *abbr* Cooperative for American Relief to Everywhere

ca•reen \kə-'rēn\ *vb* **1** : to cause (a boat) to lean over on one side **2** : to sway from side to side

¹**ca•reer** \kə-'riər\ *n* [MF *carrière,* fr. Old Provençal *carriera* street, fr. ML *carraria* road for vehicles, fr. L *carrus* car] **1** : a course of action or events; *esp* : a person's progress in his or her chosen occupation **2** : an occupation or profession followed as a life's work

²**career** *vb* : to go at top speed esp. in a headlong manner

care•free \'keər-,frē\ *adj* : free from care or worry

care•ful \-fəl\ *adj* **care•ful•ler; care•ful•lest 1** : using or taking care : VIGILANT **2** : marked by solicitude, caution, or prudence — **care•ful•ly** \-ē\ *adv* — **care•ful•ness** *n*

care•less \-ləs\ *adj* **1** : free from care : UNTROUBLED **2** : UNCONCERNED, IN-DIFFERENT **3** : not taking care **4** : not showing or receiving care — **care•less•ly** *adv* — **care•less•ness** *n*

¹**ca•ress** \kə-'res\ *n* : a tender or loving touch or embrace

²**caress** *vb* : to touch or stroke tenderly or lovingly — **ca•ress•er** *n*

car•et \'kar-ət\ *n* [L, is missing, fr. *carēre* to be lacking] : a mark ∧ used to indicate the place where something is to be inserted

care•tak•er \'keər-,tā-kər\ *n* **1** : one in charge usu. as occupant in place of an absent owner **2** : one temporarily ful-filling the functions of an office

care•worn \-,wōərn\ *adj* : showing the effects of grief or anxiety

car•fare \'kär-,faər\ *n* : passenger fare (as on a streetcar or bus)

car•go \'kär-gō\ *n, pl* **cargoes** *or* **cargos** : the goods carried in a ship, airplane, or vehicle : FREIGHT

car•hop \'kär-,häp\ *n* : one who serves customers at a drive-in restaurant

Ca•rib•be•an \,kar-ə-'bē-ən, kə-'rib-ē-ən\ *adj* : of or relating to the eastern and southern West Indies or the Caribbean sea

car•i•bou \'kar-ə-,bü\ *n, pl* **caribou** *or* **caribous** : any of several large deer of northern No. America and Siberia with palmate antlers in both sexes that are grouped with the reindeer in one species

car•i•ca•ture \'kar-i-kə-,chùr\ *n* **1** : dis-torted representation to produce a ridiculous effect **2** : a representation esp. in literature or art having the qualities of caricature — **caricature** *vb* — **car•i•ca•tur•ist** \-,chùr-əst\ *n*

car•ies \'kar-ēz\ *n, pl* **caries** : tooth de-cay

car•il•lon \'kar-ə-,län\ *n* : a set of tuned bells sounded by hammers controlled by a keyboard

car•il•lon•neur \,kar-ə-lə-'nər\ *n* [F] : a carillon player

car•i•ous \'kar-ē-əs\ *adj* : affected with caries

car•load \'kär-'lōd, -,lōd\ *n* : a load that fills a car

car•mi•na•tive \kär-'min-ət-iv\ *adj* : ex-pelling gas from the alimentary canal — **carminative** *n*

car•mine \'kär-mən, -,mīn\ *n* : a vivid red

car•nage \'kär-nij\ *n* : great destruction of life : SLAUGHTER

car•nal \'kärn-ᵊl\ *adj* **1** : of or relating to the body **2** : SENSUAL — **car•nal•i•ty** \kär-'nal-ət-ē\ *n* — **car•nal•ly** \'kärn-ᵊl-ē\ *adv*

car•na•tion \kär-'nā-shən\ *n* : a cultivat-ed pink of any of numerous usu. dou-ble-flowered varieties derived from an Old World species

car•nau•ba wax \kär-'nȯ-bə-, ,kär-nə-'ü-bə-\ *n* : a brittle yellowish wax from a Brazilian palm that is used esp. in polishes

car•ne•lian \kär-'nēl-yən\ *n* : a hard tough reddish quartz used as a gem

car•ni•val \'kär-nə-vəl\ *n* [It *carnevale,* fr. *carnelevare,* lit., removal of meat] **1** : a season of merrymaking just be-fore Lent **2** : a boisterous merrymak-ing **3** : a traveling enterprise offering amusements **4** : an organized pro-gram of entertainment

car•niv•o•ra \kär-'niv-ə-rə\ *n pl* : car-nivorous mammals

car•ni•vore \'kär-nə-,vōr\ *n* : a flesh=

eating animal; *esp* : any of an order of mammals (as dogs, cats, bears, minks, and seals) feeding mostly on animal flesh

car·niv·o·rous \kär-'niv-(ə-)rəs\ *adj* **1** : feeding on animal tissues **2** : of or relating to the carnivores — **car·niv·o·rous·ly** *adv* — **car·niv·o·rous·ness** *n*

car·ny *or* **car·ney** *or* **car·nie** \'kär-nē\ *n, pl* **carnies** *or* **carneys** **1** : CARNIVAL 3 **2** : one who works with a carnival

car·ol \'kar-əl\ *n* : a song of joy, praise, or devotion — **carol** *vb* — **car·ol·er** *or* **car·ol·ler** \-ə-lər\ *n*

car·om \'kar-əm\ *n* **1** : a shot in billiards in which the cue ball strikes two other balls **2** : a rebounding esp. at an angle — **carom** *vb*

car·o·tene \'kar-ə-,tēn\ *n* : any of several orange to red pigments formed esp. in plants and used as a source of vitamin A

ca·rot·id \kə-'rät-əd\ *adj* : of, relating to, or being the chief artery or pair of arteries that pass up the neck and supply the head — **carotid** *n*

ca·rous·al \kə-'rau̇-zəl\ *n* : CAROUSE

ca·rouse \kə-'rau̇z\ *n* [MF *carrousse,* fr. *carous,* adv., all out (in *boire carous* to empty the cup), fr. G *garaus*] : a drunken revel — **carouse** *vb* — **ca·rous·er** *n*

car·ou·sel \,kar-ə-'sel, 'kar-ə-,sel\ *n* : MERRY-GO-ROUND

¹**carp** \'kärp\ *vb* : to find fault : CAVIL, COMPLAIN — **carp·er** *n*

²**carp** *n, pl* **carp** *or* **carps** : a long-lived freshwater fish of sluggish waters often raised for food

¹**car·pal** \'kär-pəl\ *adj* : relating to the wrist or the bones of the wrist

²**carpal** *n* : a carpal element or bone

car·pe di·em \,kär-pē-'dē-,em, -'dī-\ *n* [L, enjoy the day] : enjoyment of the present without concern for the future

car·pel \'kär-pəl\ *n* : one of the highly modified leaves that together form the ovary of a flower of a seed plant

car·pen·ter \'kär-pən-tər\ *n* : one who builds or repairs wooden structures — **carpenter** *vb* — **car·pen·try** \-trē\ *n*

car·pet \'kär-pət\ *n* : a heavy fabric used esp. as a floor covering — **carpet** *vb*

car·pet·bag \-,bag\ *n* : a traveling bag common in the 19th century

car·pet·bag·ger \-,bag-ər\ *n* : a Northerner in the South after the American Civil War usu. seeking private gain under the reconstruction governments

car·pet·ing \,kär-pət-iŋ\ *n* : material for carpets; *also* : CARPETS

car pool *n* : an arrangement by a group of automobile drivers who take turns driving their own cars and carrying the others as passengers — **car·pool** \-,pül\ *vb*

car·port \'kär-,pōrt\ *n* : an open-sided automobile shelter

car·pus \'kär-pəs\ *n* : the wrist or its bones

car·ra·geen·an *or* **car·ra·geen·in** \,kar-ə-'gē-nən\ *n* : a colloid extracted esp. from a dark purple branching seaweed and used in foods esp. to stabilize and thicken them

car·rel \'kar-əl\ *n* : a table with bookshelves often partitioned or enclosed for individual study in a library

car·riage \'kar-ij\ *n* **1** : the act of carrying **2** : manner of holding the body **3** : a wheeled vehicle **4** *Brit* : a railway passenger coach **5** : a movable part of a machine for supporting some other moving part

carriage trade *n* : trade from well-to-do or upper-class people

car·ri·er \'kar-ē-ər\ *n* **1** : one that carries **2** : a person or organization in the transportation business **3** : one who carries germs of a disease in his or her system but is immune to the disease **4** : one who has a gene for a trait or condition that is not expressed in his or her system **5** : an electromagnetic wave whose amplitude or frequency is varied in order to convey a radio or television signal

carrier pigeon *n* : a pigeon used esp. to carry messages

car·ri·on \'kar-ē-ən\ *n* : dead and decaying flesh

car·rot \'kar-ət\ *n* : the elongated orange-red root of a common garden plant that is eaten as a vegetable; *also* : this plant

car·rou·sel var of CAROUSEL

¹**car·ry** \'kar-ē\ *vb* **car·ried; car·ry·ing 1** : to move while supporting : TRANSPORT, CONVEY, TAKE **2** : to influence by mental or emotional appeal **3** : to get

possession or control of : CAPTURE, WIN **4** : to transfer from one place (as a column) to another ⟨~ a number in addition⟩ **5** : to have or wear on one's person; *also* : to bear within one **6** : INVOLVE, IMPLY **7** : to hold or bear (oneself) in a specified way **8** : to keep in stock for sale **9** : to sustain the weight or burden of : SUPPORT **10** : to prolong in space, time, or degree **11** : to keep on one's books as a debtor **12** : to succeed in (an election) **13** : to win adoption (as in a legislature) **14** : PUBLISH, PRINT **15** : to reach or penetrate to a distance

²carry *n* **1** : an act or method of carrying ⟨fireman's ~⟩ **2** : PORTAGE **3** : the range of a gun or projectile or of a struck or thrown ball

car·ry·all \\ˈkar-ē-ˌȯl\\ *n* **1** : a light covered carriage for four or more persons **2** : a capacious bag or case

carry away *vb* : to arouse to a high and often excessive degree of emotion

carrying charge *n* : a charge added to the price of merchandise sold on the installment plan

car·ry·on \\ˈkar-ē-ˌȯn, -ˌän\\ *n* : a piece of luggage suitable for being carried aboard an airplane by a passenger — **car·ry–on** \\ˈkar-ē-ˌȯn, -ˌän\\ *adj*

carry on \\ˌkar-ē-ˈȯn, -ˈän\\ *vb* **1** : CONDUCT, MANAGE **2** : to behave in a foolish, excited, or improper manner **3** : to continue in spite of hindrance or discouragement

carry out *vb* **1** : to put into execution **2** : to bring to a successful conclusion

car·sick \\ˈkär-ˌsik\\ *adj* : affected with motion sickness esp. in an automobile — **car sickness** *n*

¹cart \\ˈkärt\\ *n* **1** : a heavy 2-wheeled wagon **2** : a small wheeled vehicle

²cart *vb* : to convey in or as if in a cart — **cart·er** *n*

cart·age \\ˈkärt-ij\\ *n* : the act of or rate charged for carting

carte blanche \\ˈkärt-ˈblänsh\\ *n, pl* **cartes blanches** \\ˈkärt-ˈblänsh(-əz)\\ [F, lit., blank document] : full discretionary power

car·tel \\kär-ˈtel\\ *n* : a combination of independent business enterprises designed to limit competition **syn** pool, syndicate, monopoly, trust

car·ti·lage \\ˈkärt-ᵊl-ij\\ *n* : an elastic tissue composing most of the skeleton of embryonic and very young vertebrates and later mostly turning into bone in higher vertebrates — **car·ti·lag·i·nous** \\ˌkärt-ᵊl-ˈaj-ə-nəs\\ *adj*

car·tog·ra·phy \\kär-ˈtäg-rə-fē\\ *n* : the making of maps — **car·tog·ra·pher** \\-fər\\ *n*

car·ton \\ˈkärt-ᵊn\\ *n* : a cardboard box or container

car·toon \\kär-ˈtün\\ *n* **1** : a preparatory sketch (as for a painting) **2** : a drawing intended as humor, caricature, or satire **3** : COMIC STRIP — **cartoon** *vb* — **car·toon·ist** *n*

car·tridge \\ˈkär-trij\\ *n* **1** : a tube containing a complete charge for a firearm **2** : a container of material for insertion into an apparatus **3** : a case containing photographic film **4** : a small case containing a needle and transducer that attaches to the tone arm of a phonograph **5** : a case containing a magnetic tape or disk **6** : a case for holding integrated circuits containing a computer program ⟨a video-game ~⟩

cart·wheel \\ˈkärt-ˌhwēl\\ *n* **1** : a large coin (as a silver dollar) **2** : a lateral handspring with arms and legs extended

carve \\kärv\\ *vb* **carved; carv·ing** **1** : to cut with care or precision : shape by cutting **2** : to cut into pieces or slices **3** : to slice and serve meat at table — **carv·er** *n*

cary·at·id \\ˌkar-ē-ˈat-əd\\ *n, pl* **-ids** *or* **-i·des** \\-ə-ˌdēz\\ : a sculptured draped female figure used as an architectural column

ca·sa·ba \\kə-ˈsäb-ə\\ *n* : any of several muskmelons with a yellow rind and sweet flesh

¹cas·cade \\kas-ˈkād\\ *n* **1** : a steep usu. small waterfall **2** : something arranged in a series or succession of stages so that each stage derives from or acts upon the product of the preceding

²cas·cade *vb* **cas·cad·ed; cas·cad·ing** : to fall, pass, or connect in or as if in a cascade

cas·cara \\kas-ˈkar-ə\\ *n* : the dried bark of a small Pacific coastal tree of the U.S. and southern Canada used as a laxative; *also* : this tree

¹case \ˈkās\ *n* **1** : a particular instance or situation **2** : an inflectional form of a noun, pronoun, or adjective indicating its grammatical relation to other words; *also* : such a relation whether indicated by inflection or not **3** : what actually exists or happens : FACT **4** : a suit or action in law : CAUSE **5** : a convincing argument **6** : an instance of disease or injury; *also* : PATIENT **7** : INSTANCE, EXAMPLE — **in case 1** : IF **2** : as a precaution **3** : as a precaution against the event that — **in case of** : in the event of

²case *n* **1** : a box or container for holding something; *also* : a box with its contents **2** : an outer covering **3** : a divided tray for holding printing type **4** : CASING 2

³case *vb* **cased; cas·ing 1** : to enclose in or cover with a case **2** : to inspect esp. with intent to rob

ca·sein \kā-ˈsēn, ˈkā-sē-ən\ *n* : any of several phosphorus-containing proteins occurring in or produced from milk

case·ment \ˈkās-mənt\ *n* : a window sash that opens like a door; *also* : a window having such a sash

case·work \-ˌwərk\ *n* : social work that involves the individual person or family — **case·work·er** *n*

¹cash \ˈkash\ *n* [MF or It; MF *casse* money box, fr. It *cassa,* fr. L *capsa* chest] **1** : ready money **2** : money or its equivalent paid at the time of purchase or delivery

²cash *vb* : to pay or obtain cash for

ca·shew \ˈkash-ü, kə-ˈshü\ *n* : an edible kidney-shaped nut of a tropical American tree related to the sumacs; *also* : the tree

¹ca·shier \ka-ˈshiər\ *vb* : to dismiss from service; *esp* : to dismiss in disgrace

²cash·ier \ka-ˈshiər\ *n* **1** : a bank official responsible for moneys received and paid out **2** : one who receives and records payments

cashier's check *n* : a check drawn by a bank upon its own funds and signed by its cashier

cash in *vb* **1** : to convert into cash ⟨*cash in* bonds⟩ **2** : to settle accounts and withdraw from a gambling game or business deal **3** : to obtain financial profit or advantage

cash·mere \ˈkazh-ˌmiər, ˈkash-\ *n* : fine wool from the undercoat of an Indian goat (**cashmere goat**) or a yarn spun of this; *also* : a soft twilled fabric orig. woven from this yarn

cash register *n* : a business machine that indicates each sale and often records the money received

cas·ing \ˈkā-siŋ\ *n* **1** : something that encases **2** : the frame of a door or window

ca·si·no \kə-ˈsē-nō\ *n, pl* **-nos** [It, fr. *casa* house] **1** : a building or room for social amusements; *esp* : one used for gambling **2** *also* **cas·si·no** : a card game in which players win cards by matching those on the table

cask \ˈkask\ *n* [MF *casque* helmet, fr. Sp *casco* potsherd, skull, helmet, fr. *cascar* to break] : a barrel-shaped container usu. for liquids; *also* : the quantity held by such a container

cas·ket \ˈkas-kət\ *n* **1** : a small box (as for jewels) **2** : COFFIN

casque \ˈkask\ *n* : HELMET

cas·sa·va \kə-ˈsäv-ə\ *n* : any of several tropical spurges with rootstocks yielding a nutritious starch from which tapioca is prepared; *also* : the rootstock or its starch

cas·se·role \ˈkas-ə-ˌrōl, ˈkaz-\ *n* **1** : a dish in which food may be baked and served **2** : a dish cooked and served in a casserole

cas·sette *also* **ca·sette** \kə-ˈset\ *n* **1** : a lightproof container for photographic plates or film **2** : a plastic case containing magnetic tape

cas·sia \ˈkash-ə\ *n* **1** : a coarse cinnamon bark **2** : any of various East Indian leguminous herbs, shrubs, and trees of which several yield senna

cas·sit·er·ite \kə-ˈsit-ə-ˌrīt\ *n* : a dark mineral that is the chief tin ore

cas·sock \ˈkas-ək\ *n* : an ankle-length garment worn esp. by Roman Catholic and Anglican clergy

cas·so·wary \ˈkas-ə-ˌwer-ē\ *n, pl* **-war·ies** : any of several large birds closely related to the emu

¹cast \ˈkast\ *vb* **cast; cast·ing 1** : THROW, FLING **2** : DIRECT ⟨~ a glance⟩ **3** : to deposit (a ballot) formally **4** : to throw off, out, or away : DISCARD, SHED **5** : COMPUTE; *esp* : to add up **6** : to assign the parts of (a play) to actors;

also : to assign to a role or part **7** : to shape (a substance) by pouring in liquid or plastic form into a mold and letting harden without pressure **8** : to make (as a knot or stitch) by looping or catching up

²**cast** *n* **1** : THROW, FLING **2** : a throw of dice **3** : the group of actors to whom parts in a play are assigned **4** : something formed in or as if in a mold; *also* : a rigid surgical dressing (as for protecting and supporting a fractured bone) **5** : TINGE, HUE **6** : APPEARANCE, LOOK **7** : something thrown out or off, shed, or expelled ⟨worm ∼s⟩

cas·ta·net \ˌkas-tə-ˈnet\ *n* [Sp *castañeta*, fr. *castaña* chestnut, fr. L *castanea*] : a rhythm instrument consisting of two small wooden, ivory, or plastic shells held in the hand and clicked together

cast·away \ˈkas-tə-ˌwā\ *adj* **1** : thrown away : REJECTED **2** : cast adrift or ashore as a survivor of a shipwreck — **castaway** *n*

caste \ˈkast\ *n* [Port *casta*, lit., race, lineage, fr. fem. of *casto* pure, chaste, fr. L *castus*] **1** : one of the hereditary social classes in Hinduism **2** : a division of a society based on wealth, inherited rank, or occupation **3** : social position : PRESTIGE **4** : a system of rigid social stratification

cas·tel·lat·ed \ˈkas-tə-ˌlāt-əd\ *adj* : having battlements like a castle

cast·er \ˈkas-tər\ *n* **1** *or* **cas·tor** : a small container to hold salt or pepper at the table **2** : a small wheel that turns freely and is used to support and move furniture, trucks, and machines

cas·ti·gate \ˈkas-tə-ˌgāt\ *vb* **-gat·ed; -gat·ing** : to punish or criticize severely — **cas·ti·ga·tion** \ˌkas-tə-ˈgā-shən\ *n* — **cas·ti·ga·tor** \ˈkas-tə-ˌgāt-ər\ *n*

cast·ing \ˈkas-tiŋ\ *n* **1** : CAST 7 **2** : something cast in a mold

casting vote *n* : a deciding vote cast by a presiding officer to break a tie

cast iron *n* : a hard brittle alloy of iron, carbon, and silicon cast in a mold

cas·tle \ˈkas-əl\ *n* **1** : a large fortified building or set of buildings **2** : a large or imposing house **3** : ³ROOK

castle in the air : an impracticable project

cast–off \ˈkas-ˌtȯf\ *adj* : thrown away or aside : DISCARDED — **cast·off** *n*

cas·tor oil \ˌkas-tər-\ *n* : a thick yellowish oil extracted from the poisonous seeds of an herb (**castor–oil plant**) and used as a lubricant and cathartic

cas·trate \ˈkas-ˌtrāt\ *vb* **cas·trat·ed; cas·trat·ing** : to deprive of sex glands and esp. testes — **cas·trat·er** *or* **cas·tra·tor** \-ər\ *n* — **cas·tra·tion** \ka-ˈstrā-shən\ *n*

ca·su·al \ˈkazh-(ə-w)əl\ *adj* **1** : resulting from or occurring by chance **2** : OCCASIONAL, INCIDENTAL **3** : OFFHAND, NONCHALANT **4** : designed for informal use ⟨∼ clothing⟩ — **ca·su·al·ly** \-ē\ *adv* — **ca·su·al·ness** *n*

ca·su·al·ty \ˈkazh-(ə-w)əl-tē\ *n, pl* **-ties** **1** : serious or fatal accident **2** : a military person lost through death, injury, sickness, or capture or through being missing in action **3** : a person or thing injured, lost, or destroyed

ca·su·ist·ry \ˈkazh-ə-wə-strē\ *n, pl* **-ries** : adroit and esp. false or misleading argument or reasoning usu. about morals — **ca·su·ist** \-wəst\ *n* — **ca·su·is·tic** \ˌkazh-ə-ˈwis-tik\ *or* **ca·su·is·ti·cal** \-ti-kəl\ *adj*

ca·sus bel·li \ˌkäs-əs-ˈbel-ē, ˌkā-səs-ˈbel-ˌī\ *n, pl* **ca·sus belli** \ˌkäs-ˌüs-, ˌkā-ˌsüs-\ [NL, occasion of war] : a cause or pretext for a declaration of war

¹**cat** \ˈkat\ *n* **1** : a common domestic mammal long kept by human beings as a pet or for catching rats and mice **2** : any of various animals (as the lion, lynx, or leopard) of the same family as the domestic cat **3** : a spiteful woman **4** : CAT-O'-NINE-TAILS **5** *slang* : GUY

²**cat** *abbr* catalog

CAT *abbr* computerized axial tomography

ca·tab·o·lism \kə-ˈtab-ə-ˌliz-əm\ *n* : destructive metabolism involving the release of energy and resulting in the breakdown of complex materials — **cat·a·bol·ic** \ˌkat-ə-ˈbäl-ik\ *adj*

cat·a·clysm \ˈkat-ə-ˌkliz-əm\ *n* : a violent change or upheaval — **cat·a·clys·mal** \ˌkat-ə-ˈkliz-məl\ *or* **cat·a·clys·mic** \-ˈkliz-mik\ *adj*

cat·a·comb \ˈkat-ə-ˌkōm\ *n* : an underground burial place with galleries and recesses for tombs

cat·a·falque \ˈkat-ə-ˌfalk, -ˌfȯ(l)k\ *n* : an

ornamental structure sometimes used in solemn funerals to hold the body

cat·a·lep·sy \\'kat-ᵊl-ˌep-sē\ *n, pl* **-sies** : a trancelike nervous condition characterized esp. by loss of voluntary motion — **cat·a·lep·tic** \ˌkat-ᵊl-'ep-tik\ *adj or n*

¹cat·a·log *or* **cat·a·logue** \\'kat-ᵊl-ˌȯg\ *n* **1** : LIST, REGISTER **2** : a systematic list of items with descriptive details; *also* : a book containing such a list

²catalog *or* **catalogue** *vb* **-loged** *or* **-logued; -log·ing** *or* **-logu·ing 1** : to make a catalog of **2** : to enter in a catalog — **cat·a·log·er** *or* **cat·a·logu·er** *n*

ca·tal·pa \kə-'tal-pə\ *n* : a broad-leaved tree with showy flowers and long slim pods

ca·tal·y·sis \kə-'tal-ə-səs\ *n, pl* **-y·ses** \-ˌsēz\ : the change and esp. increase in the rate of a chemical reaction brought· about by a substance (**cat·a·lyst** \\'kat-ᵊl-əst\) that is itself unchanged at the end of the reaction — **cat·a·lyt·ic** \ˌkat-ᵊl-'it-ik\ *adj* — **cat·a·lyt·i·cal·ly** \-i-k(ə-)lē\ *adv*

catalytic converter *n* : an automobile exhaust-system component in which a catalyst changes harmful gases into mostly harmless products

cat·a·lyze \\'kat-ᵊl-ˌīz\ *vb* **-lyzed; -lyz·ing** : to bring about the catalysis of (a chemical reaction)

cat·a·ma·ran \ˌkat-ə-mə-'ran\ *n* [Tamil (a language of southern India) *kaṭṭumaram,* fr. *kaṭṭu* to tie + *maram* tree] : a boat with twin hulls

cat·a·mount \\'kat-ə-ˌmau̇nt\ *n* : COUGAR; *also* : LYNX

cat·a·pult \\'kat-ə-ˌpəlt, -ˌpu̇lt\ *n* **1** : an ancient military machine for hurling missiles (as stones and arrows) **2** : a device for launching an airplane (as from an aircraft carrier) — **catapult** *vb*

cat·a·ract \\'kat-ə-ˌrakt\ *n* **1** : a cloudiness of the lens of the eye obstructing vision **2** : a large waterfall; *also* : steep rapids in a river

ca·tarrh \kə-'tär\ *n* : inflammation of a mucous membrane esp. of the nose and throat — **ca·tarrh·al** \-əl\ *adj*

ca·tas·tro·phe \kə-'tas-trə(ˌ)fē\ *n* [Gk *katastrophē,* fr. *katastrephein* to overturn, fr. *kata-* down + *strephein* to turn] **1** : a great disaster or misfor-

tune **2** : utter failure — **cat·a·stroph·ic** \ˌkat-ə-'sträf-ik\ *adj* — **cat·a·stroph·i·cal·ly** \-i-k(ə-)lē\ *adv*

cata·ton·ic \ˌkat-ə-'tän-ik\ *adj* : of, relating to, or marked by schizophrenia characterized esp. by stupor, negativism, rigidity, purposeless excitement, and abnormal posturing — **catatonic** *n*

cat·bird \\'kat-ˌbərd\ *n* : an American songbird with a catlike mewing call

cat·boat \\'kat-ˌbōt\ *n* : a single-masted sailboat with a single large sail extended by a long boom

cat·call \-ˌkȯl\ *n* : a sound like the cry of a cat; *also* : a noise made to express disapproval — **catcall** *vb*

¹catch \\'kach, 'kech\ *vb* **caught** \\'kȯt\; **catch·ing 1** : to capture esp. after pursuit **2** : TRAP **3** : to discover esp. unexpectedly : SURPRISE, DETECT **4** : to become suddenly aware of **5** : to take hold of : SNATCH ⟨∼ at a straw⟩ **6** : INTERCEPT **7** : to get entangled **8** : to become affected with or by ⟨∼ fire⟩ ⟨∼ cold⟩ **9** : to seize and hold firmly; *also* : FASTEN **10** : OVERTAKE **11** : to be in time for ⟨∼ a train⟩ **12** : to take in and retain **13** : to look at or listen to

²catch *n* **1** : something caught **2** : the act of catching; *also* : a game consisting of throwing and catching a ball **3** : something that catches or checks or holds immovable ⟨a door ∼⟩ **4** : one worth catching esp. as a mate **5** : FRAGMENT, SNATCH **6** : a concealed difficulty or complication

catch·all \-ˌȯl\ *n* : something to hold a variety of odds and ends

catch–as–catch–can \ˌkach-əz-ˌkach-'kan, ˌkech-əz-ˌkech-\ *adj* : using any means available

catch·er \\'kach-ər, 'kech-\ *n* : one that catches; *esp* : a player stationed behind home plate in baseball

catch·ing \-iŋ\ *adj* **1** : INFECTIOUS, CONTAGIOUS **2** : ALLURING, CATCHY

catch·ment \\'kach-mənt, 'kech-\ *n* **1** : the action of catching water **2** : something that catches water

catch on *vb* **1** : UNDERSTAND **2** : to become popular

catch·pen·ny \-ˌpen-ē\ *adj* : designed esp. to get small sums of money from the ignorant ⟨a ∼ plan⟩

catch–22 \-ˌtwent-ē-'tü\ *n, pl* **catch–22's** *or* **catch–22s** *often cap* C [fr.

Catch-22, a paradoxical rule found in the novel *Catch-22* (1961) by Joseph Heller] : a problematic situation for which the only solution is denied by a circumstance inherent in the problem or by a rule; *also* : the circumstance or rule that denies a solution

catch•up \\'kech-əp, 'kach-\\ var of CATSUP

catch up *vb* : to travel or work fast enough to overtake or complete

catch•word \\'kach-ˌwərd, 'kech-\\ *n* **1** : GUIDE WORD **2** : a word or expression representative of a party, school, or point of view

catchy \\'kach-ē, 'kech-\\ *adj* **catch•i•er; -est 1** : likely to attract attention **2** : easily remembered ⟨∼ music⟩ **3** : TRICKY

cat•e•chism \\'kat-ə-ˌkiz-əm\\ *n* : a summary or test (as of religious doctrine) usu. in the form of questions and answers — **cat•e•chist** \\-ˌkist\\ *n* — **cat•e•chize** \\ˌkīz\\ *vb*

cat•e•chu•men \\ˌkat-ə-'kyü-mən\\ *n* : a religious convert receiving training before baptism

cat•e•gor•i•cal \\ˌkat-ə-'gȯr-i-kəl\\ *adj* **1** : ABSOLUTE, UNQUALIFIED **2** : of, relating to, or constituting a category — **cat•e•gor•i•cal•ly** \\-i-k(ə-)lē\\ *adv*

cat•e•go•rize \\'kat-i-gə-ˌrīz\\ *vb* **-rized; riz•ing** : to put into a category : CLASSIFY — **cat•e•go•ri•za•tion** \\ˌkat-i-gə-rə-'zā-shən\\ *n*

cat•e•go•ry \\'kat-ə-ˌgȯr-ē\\ *n, pl* **-ries** : a division used in classification; *also* : CLASS, GROUP, KIND

ca•ter \\'kāt-ər\\ *vb* **1** : to provide a supply of food **2** : to supply what is wanted — **ca•ter•er** *n*

cat•er•cor•ner \\ˌkat-ē-'kȯr-nər, ˌkat-ə-, ˌkit-ē-\\ *or* **cat•er–cor•nered** *adv or adj* [obs. *cater* (four-spot of cards or dice) + E *corner*] : in a diagonal or oblique position

cat•er•pil•lar \\'kat-ə(r)-ˌpil-ər\\ *n* [ME *catyrpel*, fr. OF *catepelose*, lit., hairy cat] : a wormlike often hairy insect larva esp. of a butterfly or moth

cat•er•waul \\'kat-ər-ˌwȯl\\ *vb* : to make a harsh cry — **caterwaul** *n*

cat•fish \\'kat-ˌfish\\ *n* : any of several big-headed stout-bodied fishes with slender tactile processes around the mouth

cat•gut \\-ˌgət\\ *n* : a tough cord made usu. from sheep intestines

ca•thar•sis \\kə-'thär-səs\\ *n, pl* **ca•tharses** \\-ˌsēz\\ **1** : an act of purging or purification **2** : elimination of a psychological problem by bringing it to consciousness and affording it expression

ca•thar•tic \\kə-'thärt-ik\\ *adj or n* : PURGATIVE

ca•the•dral \\kə-'thē-drəl\\ *n* : the principal church of a diocese

cath•e•ter \\'kath-ət-ər\\ *n* : a tube for insertion into a bodily passage or cavity esp. for injecting or drawing off material

cath•ode \\'kath-ˌōd\\ *n* **1** : the negative electrode of an electrolytic cell **2** : the positive terminal of a battery **3** : the electron-emitting electrode of an electron tube — **ca•thod•ic** \\ka-'thäd-ik\\ *or* **cath•od•al** \\'kath-ˌōd-ᵊl\\

cathode–ray tube *n* : a vacuum tube in which a beam of electrons is projected on a fluorescent screen and produces a luminous spot

cath•o•lic \\'kath-(ə-)lik\\ *adj* **1** : GENERAL, UNIVERSAL **2** *cap* : of or relating to Catholics and esp. Roman Catholics

Cath•o•lic \\'kath-(ə-)lik\\ *n* : a member of a church claiming historical continuity from the ancient undivided Christian church; *esp* : a member of the Roman Catholic Church — **Ca•thol•i•cism** \\kə-'thäl-ə-ˌsiz-əm\\ *n*

cath•o•lic•i•ty \\ˌkath-ə-'lis-ət-ē\\ *n, pl* **-ties 1** *cap* : the character of being in conformity with a Catholic church **2** : liberality of sentiments or views **3** : comprehensive range

cat•ion \\'kat-ˌī-ən\\ *n* : the ion in an electrolyte that migrates to the cathode; *also* : a positively charged ion

cat•kin \\'kat-kən\\ *n* : a long flower cluster (as of a willow) bearing crowded flowers and prominent bracts

cat•like \\-ˌlīk\\ *adj* : resembling a cat or its behavior; *esp* : STEALTHY

cat•nap \\-ˌnap\\ *n* : a very short light nap — **catnap** *vb*

cat•nip \\-ˌnip\\ *n* : an aromatic mint that is esp. attractive to cats

cat–o'–nine–tails \\ˌkat-ə-'nīn-ˌtālz\\ *n, pl* **cat–o'–nine–tails** : a whip made of usu. nine knotted cords with a handle

CAT scan \\'kat-, 'sē-'ā-'tē-\\ *n* [computerized *axial tomography*] : an image made by computed tomography

CAT scanner *n* : a medical instrument consisting of integrated X-ray and computing equipment that is used to make CAT scans

cat's cradle *n* : a game played with a string looped on the fingers in such a way as to resemble a small cradle

cat's–eye \\'kats-,ī\\ *n, pl* **cat's–eyes** : any of various iridescent gems

cat's–paw \\-,po\\ *n, pl* **cat's–paws** : a person used by another as a tool

cat·sup \\'kech-əp, 'kach-; 'kat-səp\\ *n* [Malay *kĕchap* spiced fish sauce] : a seasoned tomato puree

cat·tail \\'kat-,tāl\\ *n* : a tall reedlike marsh plant with furry brown spikes of tiny flowers

cat·tle \\'kat-ᵊl\\ *n pl* : LIVESTOCK; *esp* : domestic bovines (as cows, bulls, or calves) — **cat·tle·man** \\-mən, -,man\\ *n*

cat·ty \\'kat-ē\\ *adj* **cat·ti·er, -est** : slyly spiteful — **cat·ti·ly** \\'kat-ᵊl-e\\ *adv* — **cat·ti·ness** \\-ē-nəs\\ *n*

cat·ty–cor·ner *or* **cat·ty–cor·nered** var of CATERCORNER

CATV *abbr* community antenna television

cat·walk \\'kat-,wok\\ *n* : a narrow walk (as along a bridge)

Cau·ca·sian \\ko-'kā-zhən, -'kazh-ən\\ *adj* : of or relating to the white race of mankind — **Caucasian** *n* — **Cau·ca·soid** \\'ko-kə-,soid\\ *adj or n*

cau·cus \\'ko-kəs\\ *n* : a meeting of a group of persons belonging to the same political party or faction usu. to decide upon policies and candidates — **cau·cus** *vb*

cau·dal \\'kod-ᵊl\\ *adj* : of, relating to, or located near the tail or the hind end of the body — **cau·dal·ly** \\-ē\\ *adv*

cau·di·llo \\kau-'thē-(y)ō, -'thēl-yō\\ *n, pl* **-llos** : a Spanish or Latin-American military dictator

caught \\'kot\\ past and past part of CATCH

caul \\'kol\\ *n* : the inner fetal membrane of higher vertebrates esp. when covering the head at birth

cauldron var of CALDRON

cau·li·flow·er \\'ko-li-,flau(-ə)r\\ *n* [It *cavolfiore*, fr. *cavolo* cabbage (fr. L *caulis* stem, cabbage) + *fiore* flower] : a garden plant closely related to cab-

bage and grown for its compact edible head of undeveloped flowers; *also* : this head

cauliflower ear *n* : an ear deformed from injury and excessive growth of scar tissue

¹caulk \\'kok\\ *vb* [ME *caulken*, fr. OF *cauquer* to trample, fr. L *calcare*, fr. *calx* heel] : to make the seams of (a boat) watertight by filling with waterproofing material; *also* : to make tight against leakage ⟨~ a pipe joint⟩ — **caulk·er** *n*

²caulk *also* **caulk·ing** \\'ko-kiŋ\\ *n* : material used to caulk

cau·ri \\'kau-rē\\ *n, pl* **cauris** — see *syli* at MONEY table

caus·al \\'ko-zəl\\ *adj* 1 : expressing or indicating cause 2 : relating to or acting as a cause — **cau·sal·i·ty** \\ko-'zal-ət-ē\\ *n* — **caus·al·ly** \\'ko-zə-lē\\ *adv*

cau·sa·tion \\ko-'zā-shən\\ *n* 1 : the act or process of causing 2 : the means by which an effect is produced

¹cause \\'koz\\ *n* 1 : REASON, MOTIVE 2 : something that brings about a result; *esp* : a person or thing that is the agent of bringing something about 3 : a suit or action in court : CASE 4 : a question or matter to be decided 5 : a principle or movement earnestly supported — **cause·less** *adj*

²cause *vb* **caused; caus·ing** : to be the cause or occasion of — **caus·ative** \\'ko-zət-iv\\ *adj* — **caus·er** *n*

cause cé·lè·bre \\,koz-sā-'lebrᵊ, ,koz-\\ *n, pl* **causes célèbres** \\same\\ [F, lit., celebrated case] 1 : a legal case that excites widespread interest 2 : a notorious incident or episode

cau·se·rie \\,koz-(ə-)'rē\\ *n* [F] 1 : an informal conversation : CHAT 2 : a short informal composition

cause·way \\'koz-,wā\\ *n* : a raised way or road across wet ground or water

¹caus·tic \\'ko-stik\\ *adj* 1 : CORROSIVE 2 : SHARP, INCISIVE ⟨~ wit⟩

²caustic *n* 1 : a substance that burns or destroys organic tissue by chemical action 2 : SODIUM HYDROXIDE

cau·ter·ize \\'kot-ə-,rīz\\ *vb* **-ized; iz·ing** : to burn or sear usu. to prevent infection or bleeding — **cau·ter·iza·tion** \\,kot-ə-rə-'zā-shən\\ *n*

¹cau·tion \\'ko-shən\\ *n* 1 : ADMONITION, WARNING 2 : prudent forethought to minimize risk : WARINESS **3** : one that arouses astonishment — **cau·tion·ary** \-shə-ˌner-ē\ adj

²caution vb **cau·tioned; cau·tion·ing** \ˈkȯsh(ə-)niŋ\ : to advise caution to : WARN

cau·tious \ˈkȯ-shəs\ adj : marked by or given to caution : CAREFUL — **cau·tious·ly** adv — **cau·tious·ness** n

cav abbr **1** cavalry **2** cavity

cav·al·cade \ˌkav-əl-ˈkād\ n **1** : a procession of riders or carriages; also : a procession of vehicles **2** : a dramatic sequence or procession

¹cav·a·lier \ˌkav-ə-ˈliər\ n [MF, fr. It cavaliere, fr. Old Provençal cavalier, fr. LL caballarius groom, fr. L caballus horse] **1** : a mounted soldier : KNIGHT **2** cap : an adherent of Charles 1 of England **3** : a debonair person

²cavalier adj **1** : gay and easy in manner : DEBONAIR **2** : DISDAINFUL, HAUGHTY — **cav·a·lier·ly** adv

cav·al·ry \ˈkav-əl-rē\ n, pl **-ries** : troops mounted on horseback or moving in motor vehicles — **cav·al·ry·man** \-mən, -ˌman\ n

¹cave \ˈkāv\ n : a natural underground chamber with an opening to the surface

²cave vb **caved; cav·ing 1** : to collapse or cause to collapse **2** : to cease to resist : SUBMIT — usu. used with in

ca·ve·at \ˈkav-ē-ˌat, -ˌät; ˈkäv-ē-ˌät\ n [L, let him beware] : WARNING

caveat emp·tor \-ˈemp-tər, -ˌtȯr\ n [NL, let the buyer beware] : a warning principle in trading that buyers should be alert to see that they get the quantity and quality paid for

cave–in \ˈkā-ˌvin\ n **1** : the action of caving in **2** : a place where earth has caved in

cave·man \ˈkāv-ˌman\ n **1** : a cave dweller esp. of the Stone Age **2** : one who acts with rough or violent directness esp. toward women

cav·ern \ˈkav-ərn\ n : a cave often of large or unknown size — **cav·ern·ous** adj — **cav·ern·ous·ly** adv

cav·i·ar or **cav·i·are** \ˈkav-ē-ˌär, ˈkäv-\ n : the salted roe of a large fish (as sturgeon) used as an appetizer

cav·il \ˈkav-əl\ vb **-iled** or **-illed; il·ing** or **il·ling** \-(ə-)liŋ\ : to find fault without

good reason : make frivolous objections — **cavil** n — **cav·il·er** or **cav·il·ler** n

cav·ing \ˈkā-viŋ\ n : the sport of exploring caves : SPELUNKING

cav·i·ta·tion \ˌkav-ə-ˈtā-shən\ n : the formation of partial vacuums in a liquid by a swiftly moving solid body (as a propeller) or by high-frequency sound waves; also : a cavity so formed

cav·i·ty \ˈkav-ət-ē\ n, pl **-ties 1** : an unfilled space within a mass : a hollow place **2** : an area of decay in a tooth

ca·vort \kə-ˈvȯrt\ vb : PRANCE, CAPER

ca·vy \ˈkā-vē\ n, pl **cavies** : GUINEA PIG

caw \ˈkȯ\ vb : to utter the harsh call of the crow or a similar cry — **caw** n

cay \ˈkē, ˈkā\ n : ⁴KEY

cay·enne pepper \ˌkī-ˌen-, ˌkā-\ n : a condiment consisting of ground dried fruits or seeds of a hot pepper

cay·man var of CAIMAN

Ca·yu·ga \kā-ˈü-gə, kī-\ n, pl **Cayuga** or **Cayugas** : a member of an American Indian people of New York

Cay·use \ˈkī-ˌ(y)üs, kī-ˈ(y)üs\ n **1** pl **Cayuse** or **Cayuses** : a member of an American Indian people of Oregon and Washington **2** pl **cayuses,** not cap, West : a native range horse of the western U.S.

Cb symbol columbium

CB \ˈsē-ˈbē\ n : CITIZENS BAND

CBC abbr Canadian Broadcasting Corporation

CBD abbr cash before delivery

CBS abbr Columbia Broadcasting System

CBW abbr chemical and biological warfare

cc abbr cubic centimeter

CC abbr **1** carbon copy **2** community college **3** country club

CCC abbr Civilian Conservation Corps

CCD \ˈsē-ˈsē-ˈdē\ n : CHARGE-COUPLED DEVICE

CCTV abbr closed-circuit television

CCU abbr **1** cardiac care unit **2** coronary care unit **3** critical care unit

ccw abbr counterclockwise

cd abbr cord

Cd symbol cadmium

CD abbr **1** certificate of deposit **2** Civil Defense

CDR abbr commander

CDT *abbr* central daylight (saving) time

Ce *symbol* cerium

CE *abbr* **1** chemical engineer **2** civil engineer **3** Corps of Engineers

cease \'sēs\ *vb* **ceased; ceas·ing** : to come or bring to an end : STOP

cease–fire \'sēs-'fī(ə)r\ *n* : a suspension of active hostilities

cease·less \'sēs-ləs\ *adj* : being without pause or stop : CONTINUOUS — **cease·less·ly** *adv* — **cease·less·ness** *n*

ce·cum \'sē-kəm\ *n, pl* **ce·ca** \-kə\ : the blind pouch at the beginning of the large intestine into which the small intestine opens — **ce·cal** \-kəl\ *adj*

ce·dar \'sēd-ər\ *n* : any of a genus of trees related to the pines that are noted for their fragrant durable wood; *also* : this wood

cede \'sēd\ *vb* **ced·ed; ced·ing 1** : to yield or give up esp. by treaty **2** : AS-SIGN, TRANSFER — **ced·er** *n*

ce·di \'sād-ē\ *n* — see MONEY table

ce·dil·la \si-'dil-ə\ *n* : a mark placed under the letter *c* (as ç) to show that the *c* is to be pronounced like *s*

ceil·ing \'sē-liŋ\ *n* **1** : the overhead inside lining of a room **2** : the height above the ground of the base of the lowest layer of clouds when over half of the sky is obscured **3** : the greatest height at which an airplane can operate efficiently **4** : a prescribed upper limit ⟨price ∼⟩

cel·an·dine \'sel-ən-ˌdīn, -ˌdēn\ *n* : a yellow-flowered herb related to the poppies

cel·e·brate \'sel-ə-ˌbrāt\ *vb* **-brat·ed; -brat·ing 1** : to perform (as a sacrament) with appropriate rites **2** : to honor (as a holiday) by solemn ceremonies or by refraining from ordinary business **3** : to observe a notable occasion with festivities **4** : EXTOL — **cel·e·brant** \-brənt\ *n* — **cel·e·bra·tion** \ˌsel-ə-'brā-shən\ *n* — **cel·e·bra·tor** \'sel-ə-brāt-ər\ *n*

cel·e·brat·ed \-əd\ *adj* : widely known and often referred to **syn** distinguished, renowned, noted, famous, illustrious, notorious

ce·leb·ri·ty \sə-'leb-rət-ē\ *n, pl* **-ties 1** : the state of being celebrated : RE-NOWN **2** : a celebrated person

ce·ler·i·ty \sə-'ler-ət-ē\ *n* : SPEED, RAPID-ITY

cel·ery \'sel-(ə-)rē\ *n, pl* **-er·ies** : a European herb related to the carrot and widely grown for the crisp edible stems of its leaves

celery cabbage *n* : CHINESE CABBAGE

ce·les·ta \sə-'les-tə\ *or* **ce·leste** \sə-'lest\ *n* : a keyboard instrument with hammers that strike steel plates

ce·les·tial \sə-'les-chəl\ *adj* **1** : HEAVEN-LY, DIVINE **2** : of or relating to the sky — **ce·les·tial·ly** \-ē\ *adv*

celestial navigation *n* : navigation by observation of the positions of celestial bodies

celestial sphere *n* : an imaginary sphere of infinite radius against which the celestial bodies appear to be projected

cel·i·ba·cy \'sel-ə-bə-sē\ *n* **1** : the state of being unmarried; *esp* : abstention by vow from marriage **2** : CHASTITY

cel·i·bate \'sel-ə-bət\ *n* : one who lives in celibacy — **celibate** *adj*

cell \'sel\ *n* **1** : a small room (as in a convent or prison) usu. for one person; *also* : a small compartment, cavity, or bounded space **2** : a tiny mass of protoplasm that contains a nucleus, is enclosed by a membrane, and forms the fundamental unit of living matter **3** : a container holding an electrolyte either for generating electricity or for use in electrolysis **4** : a single unit in a device for converting radiant energy into electrical energy

cel·lar \'sel-ər\ *n* **1** : BASEMENT 1 **2** : the lowest position (as in an athletic league) **3** : a stock of wines

cel·lar·age \'sel-ə-rij\ *n* : cellar space esp. for storage

cel·lar·ette *or* **cel·lar·et** \ˌsel-ə-'ret\ *n* : a case or cabinet for a few bottles of wine or liquor

cel·lo \'chel-ō\ *n, pl* **cellos** : a bass member of the violin family tuned an octave below the viola — **cel·list** \-əst\ *n*

cel·lo·phane \'sel-ə-ˌfān\ *n* : a thin transparent material made from cellulose and used as a wrapping

cel·lu·lar \'sel-yə-lər\ *adj* : of, relating to, or consisting of cells

cel·lu·lite \'sel-yə-ˌlīt\ *n* : lumpy fat in the thighs, hips, and buttocks of some women

cel·lu·lose \-ˌlōs\ *n* : a complex carbohydrate of the cell walls of plants used esp. in making paper or rayon — **cel·lu·los·ic** \ˌsel-yə-ˈlō-sik\ *adj or n*

Cel·sius \ˈsel-sē-əs\ *adj* : relating to or having a scale for measuring temperature on which the interval between the triple point and the boiling point of water is divided into 99.99 degrees with 0.01° being the triple point and 100.00° the boiling point

Celt \ˈselt, ˈkelt\ *n* : a member of any of a group of peoples (as the Irish or Welsh) of western Europe — **Celt·ic** *adj*

cem·ba·lo \ˈchem-bə-ˌlō\ *n, pl* **-ba·li** \-ˌlē\ *or* **-balos** [It] : HARPSICHORD

¹**ce·ment** \si-ˈment\ *n* **1** : a powder that is produced from a burned mixture chiefly of clay and limestone and that is used in mortar and concrete; *also* : CONCRETE **2** : a binding element or agency **3** : CEMENTUM; *also* : a substance for filling cavities in teeth

²**cement** *vb* **1** : to unite by or as if by cement **2** : to cover with concrete — **ce·ment·er** *n*

ce·men·tum \si-ˈment-əm\ *n* : a specialized external bony layer of the part of a tooth normally within the gum

cem·e·tery \ˈsem-ə-ˌter-ē\ *n, pl* **-ter·ies** [ME *cimitery*, fr. MF *cimitere*, fr. LL *coemeterium*, fr. Gk *koimētērion* sleeping chamber, burial place, fr. *koiman* to put to sleep] : a burial ground : GRAVEYARD

cen·o·bite \ˈsen-ə-ˌbīt\ *n* : a member of a religious group living together in a monastic community — **cen·o·bit·ic** \ˌsen-ə-ˈbit-ik\ *adj*

ceno·taph \ˈsen-ə-ˌtaf\ *n* [F *cénotaphe*, fr. L *cenotaphium*, fr. Gk *kenotaphion*, fr. *kenos* empty + *taphos* tomb] : a tomb or a monument erected in honor of a person whose body is elsewhere

Ce·no·zo·ic \ˌsē-nə-ˈzō-ik, ˌsen-ə-\ *adj* [deriv. of Gk *kainos* new, recent] : of, relating to, or being the most recent of the five eras of geologic history extending from about 70 million years ago to the present — **Cenozoic** *n*

cen·ser \ˈsen-sər\ *n* : a vessel for burning incense (as in a religious ritual)

¹**cen·sor** \ˈsen-sər\ *n* **1** : one of two early Roman magistrates whose duties included taking the census **2** : an official who inspects printed matter or sometimes motion pictures with power to suppress anything objectionable — **cen·so·ri·al** \sen-ˈsōr-ē-əl\ *adj*

²**censor** *vb* : to subject to censorship

cen·so·ri·ous \sen-ˈsōr-ē-əs\ *adj* : marked by or given to censure : CRITICAL — **cen·so·ri·ous·ly** *adv* — **cen·so·ri·ous·ness** *n*

cen·sor·ship \ˈsen-sər-ˌship\ *n* **1** : the action of a censor esp. in stopping the transmission or publication of matter considered objectionable **2** : the office of a Roman censor

¹**cen·sure** \ˈsen-chər\ *n* **1** : the act of blaming or condemning sternly **2** : an official reprimand

²**censure** *vb* **cen·sured; cen·sur·ing** \ˈsench-(ə-)riŋ\ : to find fault with and criticize as blameworthy — **cen·sur·able** *adj*

cen·sus \ˈsen-səs\ *n* **1** : a periodic governmental count of population **2** : COUNT, TALLY

¹**cent** \ˈsent\ *n* [MF, hundred, fr. L *centum*] **1** : a monetary unit equal to ¹⁄₁₀₀ of a basic unit of value — see *birr, dollar, gulden, leone, lilangeni, rand, rupee, shilling* at MONEY table **2** : a coin, token, or note representing one cent

²**cent** *abbr* **1** centigrade **2** central **3** century

cen·taur \ˈsen-ˌtȯr\ *n* : any of a race of creatures in Greek mythology half man and half horse

¹**cen·ta·vo** \sen-ˈtäv-(ˌ)ō\ *n, pl* **-vos** — see *colon, cordoba, lempira, peso, quetzal, sucre* at MONEY table

²**cen·ta·vo** \-ˈtäv-(ˌ)ü, -(ˌ)ō\ *n, pl* **-vos** — see *dobra, escudo, metical* at MONEY table

cen·te·nar·i·an \ˌsent-ᵊn-ˈer-ē-ən\ *n* : a person who is 100 or more years old

cen·te·na·ry \sen-ˈten-ə-rē, ˈsent-ᵊn-ˌer-ē\ *n, pl* **-ries** : CENTENNIAL — **centenary** *adj*

cen·ten·ni·al \sen-ˈten-ē-əl\ *n* : a 100th anniversary or its celebration — **centennial** *adj*

¹**cen·ter** \ˈsent-ər\ *n* **1** : the point that is equally distant from all points on the circumference of a circle or surface of a sphere; *also* : MIDDLE 1 **2** : the point about which an activity concentrates or from which something originates **3**

: a region of concentrated population **4** : a middle part **5** *often cap* : political figures holding moderate views esp. between those of conservatives and liberals **6** : a player occupying a middle position (as in football or basketball)

²**center** *vb* **1** : to place or fix at or around a center or central area **2** : to gather to a center : CONCENTRATE **3** : to have a center : FOCUS

cen·ter·board \'sent-ər-ˌbōrd\ *n* : a retractable keel used esp. in sailboats

cen·ter·piece \'sent-ər-ˌpēs\ *n* **1** : an object in a central position; *esp* : an adornment in the center of a table **2** : one that is of central importance or interest

cen·tes·i·mal \sen-'tes-ə-məl\ *adj* : marked by or relating to division into hundredths

¹**cen·tes·i·mo** \chen-'tez-ə-ˌmō\ *n, pl* **-mi** \-(ˌ)mē\ — see *lira* at MONEY table

²**cen·tes·i·mo** \sen-'tes-ə-ˌmō\ *n, pl* **-mos** — see *balboa, peso* at MONEY table

cen·ti·grade \'sent-ə-ˌgrād, 'sänt-\ *adj* : relating to, conforming to, or having a thermometer scale on which the interval between the freezing and boiling points of water is divided into 100 degrees with 0° representing the freezing point and 100° the boiling point ⟨10° ∼⟩

cen·ti·gram \-ˌgram\ *n* — see METRIC SYSTEM table

cen·ti·li·ter \'sent-i-ˌlēt-ər\ *n* — see METRIC SYSTEM table

cen·time \'sän-ˌtēm\ *n* — see *dinar, dirham, franc, gourde* at MONEY table

cen·ti·me·ter \'sent-ə-ˌmēt-ər, 'sänt-\ *n* — see METRIC SYSTEM table

centimeter–gram–second *adj* : CGS

cen·ti·mo \'sent-ə-ˌmō\ *n, pl* **-mos** — see *bolivar, colon, ekuele, guarani, peseta* at MONEY table

cen·ti·pede \'sent-ə-ˌpēd\ *n* [L *centipeda,* fr. *centi-* hundred + *pes* foot] : any of a class of long flattened segmented arthropods with one pair of legs on each segment except the first which has a pair of poison fangs

¹**cen·tral** \'sen-trəl\ *adj* **1** : constituting a center **2** : ESSENTIAL, PRINCIPAL **3** : situated at, in, or near the center **4** : centrally placed and superseding separate units ⟨∼ heating⟩ — **cen·tral·ly** \-ē\ *adv*

²**central** *n* **1** : a telephone exchange or an operator handling calls there **2** : a central controlling office

cen·tral·ize \'sen-trə-ˌlīz\ *vb* **-ized; -izing** : to bring to a central point or under central control — **cen·tral·iza·tion** \ˌsen-trə-lə-'zā-shən\ *n* — **cen·tral·iz·er** \'sen-trə-ˌlī-zər\ *n*

central nervous system *n* : the part of the nervous system which integrates nervous function and activity and which in vertebrates consists of the brain and spinal cord

cen·tre *chiefly Brit var of* CENTER

cen·trif·u·gal \sen-'trif-yə-gəl, -'trif-i-gəl\ *adj* [NL *centrifugus,* fr. *centr-* center + *fugere* to flee] **1** : proceeding or acting in a direction away from a center or axis **2** : using or acting by centrifugal force

centrifugal force *n* : the force that tends to impel a thing or parts of a thing outward from a center of rotation

cen·tri·fuge \'sen-trə-ˌfyüj\ *n* : a machine using centrifugal force (as for separating substances of different densities or for removing moisture)

cen·trip·e·tal \sen-'trip-ət-ᵊl\ *adj* [NL *centripetus,* fr. *centr-* center + L *petere* seek] : proceeding or acting in a direction toward a center or axis

centripetal force *n* : the force needed to keep an object revolving about a point moving in a circular path

cen·trist \'sen-trəst\ *n* **1** *often cap* : a member of a center party **2** : one who holds moderate views

cen·tu·ri·on \sen-'t(y)ùr-ē-ən\ *n* : an officer commanding a Roman century

cen·tu·ry \'sench-(ə-)rē\ *n, pl* **-ries 1** : a subdivision of a Roman legion **2** : a group or sequence of 100 like things **3** : a period of 100 years

century plant *n* : a Mexican agave maturing and flowering only once in many years and then dying

CEO *abbr* chief executive officer

ce·phal·ic \sə-'fal-ik\ *adj* **1** : of or relating to the head **2** : directed toward or situated on or in or near the head

ce·ram·ic \sə-'ram-ik\ *n* **1** *pl* : the art or process of making articles from a nonmetallic mineral (as clay) by firing **2**

: a product produced by ceramics — **ceramic** *adj*

ce·ra·mist \sə-'ram-əst\ *or* **ce·ram·i·cist** \sə-'ram-ə-səst\ *n* : one who engages in ceramics

¹**ce·re·al** \'sir-ē-əl\ *adj* [L *cerealis*, fr. *Ceres*, the Roman goddess of agriculture] : relating to grain or to the plants that produce it; *also* : made of grain

²**cereal** *n* **1** : a grass (as wheat) yielding grain suitable for food; *also* : its grain **2** : grain of a cereal prepared for use as a breakfast food

cer·e·bel·lum \,ser-ə-'bel-əm\ *n, pl* **-bellums** *or* **-bel·la** \-'bel-ə\ [ML, fr. L, dim. of *cerebrum*] : a part of the brain that projects over the medulla and is concerned esp. with coordination of muscular action and with bodily balance — **cer·e·bel·lar** \-'bel-ər\ *adj*

ce·re·bral cortex \sə-,rē-brəl-, ,ser-ə-\ *n* : the surface layer of gray matter of the cerebrum that functions chiefly in coordination of higher nervous activity

cerebral palsy *n* : a disorder caused by brain damage usu. before or during birth and marked esp. by defective muscle control

cer·e·brate \'ser-ə-,brāt\ *vb* **-brat·ed; -brat·ing** : THINK — **cer·e·bra·tion** \,ser-ə-'brā-shən\ *n*

ce·re·brum \sə-'rē-brəm, 'ser-ə-\ *n, pl* **-brums** *or* **-bra** \-brə\ [L] : the enlarged front and upper part of the brain that contains the higher nervous centers — **ce·re·bral** \sə-'rē-brəl, 'ser-ə-\ *adj* — **ce·re·bral·ly** \-ē\ *adv*

cere·cloth \'siər-,klòth\ *n* : cloth treated with melted wax or gummy matter and formerly used esp. for wrapping a dead body

cere·ment \'ser-ə-mənt, 'siər-mənt\ *n* : a shroud for the dead

¹**cer·e·mo·ni·al** \,ser-ə-'mō-nē-əl\ *adj* : of, relating to, or forming a ceremony — **cer·e·mo·ni·al·ly** \-ē\ *adv*

²**ceremonial** *n* : a ceremonial act or system : RITUAL, FORM

cer·e·mo·ni·ous \,ser-ə-'mō-nē-əs\ *adj* **1** : devoted to forms and ceremony **2** : CEREMONIAL **3** : according to formal usage or procedure **4** : marked by ceremony — **cer·e·mo·ni·ous·ly** *adv* — **cer·e·mo·ni·ous·ness** *n*

cer·e·mo·ny \'ser-ə-,mō-nē\ *n, pl* **-nies 1**

: a formal act or series of acts prescribed by law, ritual, or convention **2** : a conventional act of politeness **3** : a mere outward form **4** : FORMALITY

ce·re·us \'sir-ē-əs\ *n* : any of various cacti of the western U.S. and tropical America

ce·rise \sə-'rēs\ *n* [F, lit., cherry] : a moderate red

ce·ri·um \'sir-ē-əm\ *n* : a malleable metallic chemical element used esp. in alloys

cer·met \'sər-,met\ *n* : a strong alloy of a heat-resistant compound and a metal used esp. for turbine blades

cert *abbr* certificate; certification; certified; certify

¹**cer·tain** \'sərt-ᵊn\ *adj* **1** : FIXED, SETTLED **2** : proved to be true **3** : of a specific but unspecified character ⟨∼ people in authority⟩ **4** : DEPENDABLE, RELIABLE **5** : INDISPUTABLE, UNDENIABLE **6** : assured in mind or action — **cer·tain·ly** *adv*

²**certain** *pron* : certain ones

cer·tain·ty \-tē\ *n, pl* **-ties 1** : something that is certain **2** : the quality or state of being certain

cer·tif·i·cate \sər-'tif-i-kət\ *n* **1** : a document testifying to the truth of a fact **2** : a document testifying that one has fulfilled certain requirements (as of a course or school) **3** : a document evidencing ownership or debt

cer·ti·fi·ca·tion \,sərt-ə-fə-'kā-shən\ *n* **1** : the act of certifying : the state of being certified **2** : a certified statement

certified milk *n* : milk produced in dairies that operate under the rules and regulations of an authorized medical milk commission

certified public accountant *n* : an accountant who has met the requirements of a state law and has been granted a state certificate

cer·ti·fy \'sərt-ə-,fī\ *vb* **-fied; -fy·ing 1** : VERIFY, CONFIRM **2** : to endorse officially **3** : to guarantee (a bank check) as good by a statement to that effect stamped on its face **4** : to provide with a usu. professional certificate or license **syn** accredit, approve, sanction, endorse — **cer·ti·fi·able** \-,fī-ə-bəl\ *adj* — **cer·ti·fi·ably** \-blē\ *adv* — **cer·ti·fi·er** *n*

cer·ti·tude \\'sərt-ə-ˌt(y)üd\ *n* : the state of being or feeling certain

ce·ru·le·an \sə-'rü-lē-ən\ *adj* : AZURE

ce·ru·men \sə-'rü-mən\ *n* : EARWAX

cer·vi·cal \\'sər-vi-kəl\ *adj* : of or relating to a neck or cervix

cer·vix \\'sər-viks\ *n, pl* **cer·vi·ces** \-və-ˌsēz\ *or* **cer·vix·es** 1 : NECK; *esp* : the back part of the neck 2 : a constricted portion of an organ or part; *esp* : the narrow outer end of the uterus

ce·sar·e·an *also* **ce·sar·i·an** \si-'zar-ē-ən, -'zer-\ *n* : CESAREAN SECTION — **cesarean** *also* **cesarian** *adj*

cesarean section *also* **cesarian section** *n* [fr. the legend that Julius Caesar was born this way] : surgical incision of the walls of the abdomen and uterus for delivery of offspring

ce·si·um \\'sē-zē-əm\ *n* : a silver-white soft ductile chemical element

ces·sa·tion \se-'sā-shən\ *n* : a temporary or final ceasing (as of action)

ces·sion \\'sesh-ən\ *n* : a yielding (as of rights) to another

cess·pool \\'ses-ˌpül\ *n* : an underground pit or tank for receiving household sewage

cf *abbr* [L *confer*] compare

Cf *symbol* californium

CF *abbr* cystic fibrosis

cg *or* **cgm** *abbr* centigram

CG *abbr* 1 coast guard 2 commanding general

cgs \\'sē-ˌjē-'es\ *adj, often cap C&G&S* : of, relating to, or being a system of units based on the centimeter as the unit of length, the gram as the unit of weight, and the second as the unit of time

ch *abbr* 1 chain 2 champion 3 chapter 4 church

CH *abbr* 1 clearinghouse 2 courthouse 3 customhouse

Cha·blis \\'shab-ˌlē; sha-'blē\ *n, pl* **Chablis** \-ˌlēz, -'blēz\ 1 : a dry sharp white Burgundy wine 2 : a white California wine that is a blend of several grapes

cha–cha \\'chä-ˌchä\ *n* : a fast rhythmic ballroom dance of Latin American origin

Chad·ian \\'chad-ē-ən\ *n* : a native or inhabitant of Chad — **Chadian** *adj*

chafe \\'chāf\ *vb* **chafed; chaf·ing** 1 : IR-RITATE, VEX 2 : FRET 3 : to warm by rubbing 4 : to rub so as to wear away; *also* : to make sore by rubbing

cha·fer \\'chā-fər\ *n* : any of various large beetles

¹chaff \\'chaf\ *n* 1 : debris (as husks) separated from grain in threshing 2 : something comparatively worthless — **chaffy** \-ē\ *adj*

²chaff *n* : light jesting talk : BANTER

³chaff *vb* : to tease in a good-natured manner

chaf·fer \\'chaf-ər\ *vb* : BARGAIN, HAGGLE — **chaf·fer·er** *n*

chaf·finch \\'chaf-ˌinch\ *n* : a European finch with a cheerful song

chaf·ing dish \\'chā-fiŋ-\ *n* : a utensil for cooking food at the table

¹cha·grin \shə-'grin\ *n* : mental uneasiness or annoyance caused by failure, disappointment, or humiliation

²chagrin *vb* **cha·grined** \-'grind\; **cha·grin·ing** \-'grin-iŋ\ : to cause to feel chagrin

¹chain \\'chān\ *n* 1 : a flexible series of connected links 2 : a chainlike surveying instrument; *also* : a unit of length equal to 66 feet (about 20 meters) 3 : a series of things linked together **syn** train, string, sequence, succession, series

²chain *vb* : to fasten, bind, or connect with a chain; *also* : FETTER

chain gang *n* : a gang of convicts chained together

chain letter *n* : a letter sent to several persons with a request that each send copies to an equal number of persons

chain mail *n* : flexible armor of interlocking metal rings

chain reaction *n* 1 : a series of events in which each event initiates the succeeding one 2 : a chemical or nuclear reaction yielding products that cause further reactions of the same kind

chain saw *n* : a portable power saw that has teeth linked together to form an endless chain

chain–smoke \\'chān-'smōk\ *vb* : to smoke esp. cigarettes continuously

chain store *n* : any of numerous stores under the same ownership that sell the same lines of goods

¹chair \\'cheər\ *n* 1 : a seat with a back for one person 2 : ELECTRIC CHAIR 3 : an official seat; *also* : an office or

position of authority or dignity **4**
: CHAIRMAN
²**chair** *vb* : to act as chairman of
chair lift *n* : a motor-driven conveyor
for skiers consisting of seats hung
from a moving cable
chair·man \\'cheər-mən\ *n* : the presiding officer of a meeting or of a committee — **chair·man·ship** *n*
chair·wom·an \-ˌwum-ən\ *n* : a woman
who acts as chairman
chaise \\'shāz\ *n* **1** : a 2-wheeled carriage with a folding top **2** : a light carriage or pleasure cart
chaise longue \\'shāz-'lóŋ\ *n, pl* **chaise
longues** \-'lóŋ(z)\ [F *chaise longue,*
lit., long chair] : a long couch-like
chair
chaise lounge \-'launj\ *n* : CHAISE
LONGUE
chal·ced·o·ny \kal-'sed-ᵊn-ē\ *n, pl* **-nies**
: a translucent pale blue or gray
quartz
chal·co·py·rite \ˌkal-kə-'pī-ˌrīt\ *n* : a
yellow mineral constituting an important ore of copper
cha·let \sha-'lā\ *n* **1** : a herdsman's cabin in the Swiss mountains **2** : a building in the style of a Swiss cottage with
a wide roof overhang
chal·ice \\'chal-əs\ *n* : a drinking cup;
esp : the eucharistic cup
¹**chalk** \\'chók\ *n* **1** : a soft limestone **2**
: chalk or chalky material esp. when
used as a crayon — **chalky** *adj*
²**chalk** *vb* **1** : to rub or mark with chalk
2 : to record with or as if with chalk —
usu. used with *up*
chalk·board \\'chók-ˌbōrd\ *n* : BLACK-
BOARD
chalk up *vb* **1** : ASCRIBE, CREDIT **2** : AT-
TAIN, ACHIEVE
¹**chal·lenge** \\'chal-ənj\ *vb* **chal·lenged;
chal·leng·ing** [ME *chalengen* to accuse, fr. OF *chalengier,* fr. L *calum-
niari* to accuse falsely, fr. *calumnia*
calumny] **1** : to order to halt and
prove identity **2** : to take exception to
: DISPUTE **3** : to issue an invitation to
compete against one esp. in single
combat : DARE, DEFY — **chal·leng·er** *n*
²**challenge** *n* **1** : a summons to a duel **2**
: an invitation to compete in a sport **3**
: a calling into question **4** : an exception taken to a juror **5** : a sentry's
command to halt and prove identity **6**

: a stimulating or interesting task or
problem
chal·lis \\'shal-ē\ *n, pl* **chal·lises** \-ēz\ : a
lightweight clothing fabric of wool,
cotton, or synthetic yarns
cham \\'kam\ *var of* KHAN
cham·ber \\'chām-bər\ *n* **1** : ROOM; *esp*
: BEDROOM **2** : an enclosed space or
compartment **3** : a hall for meetings of
a legislative body **4** : a judge's consultation room — usu. used in pl. **5** : a
legislative or judicial body; *also* : a
council for a business purpose **6** : the
part of a firearm that holds the cartridge or powder charge during firing
— **cham·bered** \-bərd\ *adj*
cham·ber·lain \\'chām-bər-lən\ *n* **1** : a
chief officer in the household of a king
or nobleman **2** : TREASURER
cham·ber·maid \-ˌmād\ *n* : a maid who
takes care of bedrooms
chamber music *n* : music intended for
performance by a few musicians before a small audience
chamber of commerce : an association
of businesspeople for promoting commercial and industrial interests in the
community
cham·bray \\'sham-ˌbrā\ *n* : a lightweight clothing fabric of white and
colored threads
cha·me·leon \kə-'mēl-yən\ *n* [ME
camelion, fr. MF, fr. L *chamaeleon,*
fr. Gk *chamaileōn,* fr. *chamai* on the
ground + *leōn* lion] : a small lizard
whose skin changes color esp. according to its surroundings
¹**cham·fer** \\'cham-fər\ *n* : a beveled edge
²**chamfer** *vb* **1** : to cut a furrow in (as a
column) : GROOVE **2** : to make a
chamfer on : BEVEL
cham·ois \\'sham-ē\ *n, pl* **cham·ois**
\-ē(z)\ **1** : a small goatlike antelope of
Europe and the Caucasus region of
the U.S.S.R. **2** *also* **cham·my** \-ē\ : a
soft leather made esp. from the skin of
the sheep or goat **3** : a cotton fabric
made in imitation of chamois leather
cham·o·mile \\'kam-ə-ˌmīl, -ˌmēl\ *n*
: any of a genus of strong-scented
herbs related to the daisies and having
flower heads that yield a bitter medicinal substance
¹**champ** \\'champ, 'chämp\ *vb* **1** : to
chew noisily **2** : to show impatience
of delay or restraint

²champ \'champ\ *n* : CHAMPION

cham·pagne \sham-'pān\ *n* : a white effervescent wine

cham·paign \sham-'pān\ *n* : a stretch of flat open country

¹cham·pi·on \'cham-pē-ən\ *n* **1** : a militant advocate or defender **2** : one that wins first prize or place in a contest **3** : one that is acknowledged to be better than all others

²champion *vb* : to protect or fight for as a champion **syn** back, advocate, uphold, support

cham·pi·on·ship \-ˌship\ *n* **1** : the position or title of a champion **2** : the act of championing : DEFENSE **3** : a contest held to determine a champion

¹chance \'chans\ *n* **1** : something that happens without apparent cause **2** : the unpredictable element in existence : LUCK, FORTUNE **3** : OPPORTUNITY **4** : the likelihood of a particular outcome in an uncertain situation : PROBABILITY **5** : RISK **6** : a raffle ticket — **chance** *adj* — **by chance** : in the haphazard course of events

²chance *vb* **chanced; chanc·ing 1** : to take place by chance : HAPPEN **2** : to come casually and unexpectedly — used with *upon* **3** : to leave to chance **4** : to accept the risk of

chan·cel \'chan-səl\ *n* : the part of a church including the altar and choir

chan·cel·lery *or* **chan·cel·lory** \'chan-s(ə-)lə-rē\ *n, pl* **-ler·ies** *or* **-lor·ies 1** : the position or office of a chancellor **2** : the building or room where a chancellor works **3** : the office or staff of an embassy or consulate

chan·cel·lor \'chan-s(ə-)lər\ *n* **1** : a high state official in various countries **2** : the head of a university **3** : a judge in the equity court in various states of the U.S. **4** : the chief minister of state in some European countries — **chan·cel·lor·ship** *n*

chan·cery \'chans-(ə-)rē\ *n, pl* **-cer·ies 1** : any of various courts of equity in the U.S. and Britain **2** : a record office for public or diplomatic archives **3** : a chancellor's court or office **4** : the office of an embassy

chan·cre \'shaŋ-kər\ *n* [F, fr. L *cancer*] : a primary sore or ulcer at the site of entry of an infective agent (as of syphilis)

chan·croid \'chaŋ-ˌkroid\ *n* : a sexually transmitted disease caused by a bacterium and characterized by chancres that differ from those of syphilis in lacking hardened margins

chancy \'chan-sē\ *adj* **chanc·i·er; -est 1** *Scot* : AUSPICIOUS **2** : RISKY

chan·de·lier \ˌshan-də-'liər\ *n* : a branched lighting fixture suspended from a ceiling

chan·dler \'chan-dlər\ *n* [ME *chandeler* a maker or seller of candles, fr. MF *chandelier*, fr. OF, fr. *chandelle* candle, fr. L *candela*] : a dealer in provisions and supplies of a specified kind ⟨ship's ∼⟩ — **chan·dlery** *n*

¹change \'chānj\ *vb* **changed; chang·ing 1** : to make or become different : ALTER **2** : to replace with another **3** : EXCHANGE **4** : to give or receive an equivalent sum in notes or coins of usu. smaller denominations or of another currency **5** : to put fresh clothes or covering on ⟨∼ a bed⟩ **6** : to put on different clothes — **change·able** *adj* — **chang·er** *n*

²change *n* **1** : the act, process, or result of changing **2** : a fresh set of clothes to replace those being worn **3** : money given in exchange for other money of higher denomination **4** : surplus money returned to a person who offers payment exceeding the sum due **5** : coins esp. of small denominations — **change·ful** *adj* — **change·less** *adj*

change·ling \'chānj-liŋ\ *n* : a child secretly exchanged for another in infancy

change of life : MENOPAUSE

change·over \'chānj-ˌō-vər\ *n* : CONVERSION, TRANSITION

change ringing *n* : the art or practice of ringing a set of tuned bells in continually varying order

¹chan·nel \'chan-ᵊl\ *n* **1** : the bed of a stream **2** : the deeper part of a waterway **3** : STRAIT **4** : a means of passage or transmission **5** : a range of frequencies of sufficient width for a single radio or television transmission **6** : a usu. tubular enclosed passage : CONDUIT **7** : a long gutter, groove, or furrow

²channel *vb* **-neled** *or* **-nelled; -neling** *or* **-nel·ling 1** : to make a channel in **2** : to direct into or through a channel

chan·nel·ize \'chan-ᵊl-ˌīz\ *vb* **-ized; -iz-ing** : CHANNEL — **chan·nel·iza·tion** \ˌchan-ᵊl-ə-'zā-shən\ *n*

chan·son \shäⁿ-sõᵐ\ *n, pl* **chan·sons** \-sõⁿ(z)\ : SONG; *esp* : a cabaret song

¹**chant** \'chant\ *vb* **1** : SING; *esp* : to sing a chant **2** : to sing or speak in the manner of a chant **3** : to celebrate or praise in song — **chant·er** *n*

²**chant** *n* **1** : a repetitive melody in which several words are sung to one tone : SONG; *esp* : a liturgical melody **2** : a manner of singing or speaking in musical monotones

chan·teuse \shäⁿ-'tə(r)z, shan-'tüz\ *n, pl* **chan·teuses** \-'tə(r)z(-əz), -'tüz(-əz)\ [F] : a female concert or nightclub singer

chan·tey *or* **chan·ty** \'shant-ē, 'chant-\ *n, pl* **chanteys** *or* **chanties** : a song sung by sailors in rhythm with their work

chan·ti·cleer \ˌchant-ə-'kliər, ˌshant-\ *n* : ROOSTER

Cha·nu·kah \'ḵän-ə-kə, 'hän-\ *var of* HANUKKAH

cha·os \'kā-ˌäs\ *n* **1** *often cap* : the confused unorganized state existing before the creation of distinct forms **2** : complete disorder **syn** confusion, jumble, snarl, muddle, disarray — **cha·ot·ic** \kā-'ät-ik\ *adj* — **cha·ot·i·cal·ly** \-i-k(ə-)lē\ *adv*

¹**chap** \'chap\ *vb* **chapped; chap·ping** : to dry and crack open usu. from wind and cold ⟨*chapped* lips⟩

²**chap** *n* : a jaw with its fleshy covering — usu. used in pl.

³**chap** *n* : FELLOW

⁴**chap** *abbr* chapter

chap·ar·ral \ˌshap-ə-'ral\ *n* **1** : a dense impenetrable thicket of shrubs or dwarf trees **2** : an ecological community of southern California comprised of shrubby plants

chap·book \'chap-ˌbu̇k\ *n* : a small book of ballads, tales, or tracts

cha·peau \sha-'pō\ *n, pl* **cha·peaus** \-'pōz\ *or* **cha·peaux** \-'pō(z)\ [MF] : HAT

cha·pel \'chap-əl\ *n* [ME, fr. OF *chapele*, fr. ML *cappella*, fr. LL *cappa* cloak; fr. the cloak of St. Martin of Tours preserved as a sacred relic in a chapel built for that purpose] **1** : a private or subordinate place of worship **2** : an assembly at an educational institution usu. including devotional exercises **3** : a place of worship used by a Christian group other than the established church

¹**chap·er·on** *or* **chap·er·one** \'shap-ə-ˌrōn\ *n* [F *chaperon*, lit., hood, fr. MF, head covering, fr. *chape*] **1** : a person (as a matron) who accompanies young unmarried women in public for propriety **2** : an older person who accompanies young people at a social gathering to ensure proper behavior

²**chaperon** *or* **chaperone** *vb* **-oned; -on·ing** **1** : ESCORT, GUIDE **2** : to act as a chaperon to or for — **chap·er·on·age** \-ˌrō-nij\ *n*

chap·fall·en \'chap-ˌfȯ-lən, 'chäp-\ *adj* **1** : having the lower jaw hanging loosely **2** : DEJECTED, DEPRESSED

chap·lain \'chap-lən\ *n* **1** : a clergyman officially attached to a special group (as the army) **2** : a person chosen to conduct religious exercises (as for a club) — **chap·lain·cy** \-sē\ *n*

chap·let \'chap-lət\ *n* **1** : a wreath for the head **2** : a string of beads : NECKLACE

chap·man \'chap-mən\ *n, Brit* : an itinerant dealer : PEDDLER

chaps \'shaps, 'chaps\ *n pl* [fr. MexSp *chaparreras*] : leather leggings resembling trousers without a seat that are worn esp. by western ranch hands

chap·ter \'chap-tər\ *n* **1** : a main division of a book **2** : a body of canons (as of a cathedral) **3** : a local branch of a society or fraternity

¹**char** \'chär\ *n, pl* **char** *or* **chars** : any of a genus of trouts (as the common brook trout) with small scales

²**char** *vb* **charred; char·ring** **1** : to burn to charcoal **2** : SCORCH **3** : to burn to a cinder

³**char** *vb* **charred; char·ring** : to work as a cleaning woman

char·a·banc \'shar-ə-baŋ\ *n, Brit* : a sight-seeing motor coach

char·ac·ter \'kar-ik-tər\ *n* [ME *caracter*, fr. MF *caractère*, fr. L *character* mark, distinctive quality, fr. Gk *charaktēr*, fr. *charassein* to scratch, engrave] **1** : a graphic symbol (as a letter) used in writing or printing **2** : a symbol that represents information; *also* : a representation of such a character that may be accepted by a computer **3** : a distinguishing feature : ATTRIBUTE **4** : the complex of mental and ethical traits marking a person or a group **5** : a person marked by conspicuous often peculiar traits **6** : one of the persons in a novel or play **7** : REPUTATION **8** : moral excellence

¹**char·ac·ter·is·tic** \ˌkar-ik-tə-ˈris-tik\ *n* : a distinguishing trait, quality, or property

²**characteristic** *adj* : serving to mark individual character **syn** individual, peculiar, distinctive — **char·ac·ter·is·ti·cal·ly** \-ti-k(ə-)lē\ *adv*

char·ac·ter·ize \ˈkar-ik-tə-ˌrīz\ *vb* **-ized; -iz·ing 1** : to describe the character of **2** : to be a characteristic of — **char·ac·ter·iza·tion** \ˌkar-ik-t(ə-)rə-ˈzā-shən\ *n*

cha·rades \shə-ˈrādz\ *n sing or pl* : a guessing game in which contestants act out the syllables of a word to be guessed

char·coal \ˈchär-ˌkōl\ *n* **1** : a porous carbon prepared from vegetable or animal substances **2** : a piece of fine charcoal used in drawing; *also* : a drawing made with charcoal

chard \ˈchärd\ *n* : a beet lacking the enlarged root but having leaves and stalks often cooked as a vegetable

char·don·nay \ˌshard-ᵊn-ˈā\ *n, often cap* [F] : a dry white wine of Chablis type

¹**charge** \ˈchärj\ *vb* **charged; charg·ing 1** : to load or fill to capacity **2** : to give an electric charge to; *also* : to restore the activity of (a storage battery) by means of an electric current **3** : to impose a task or responsibility on **4** : COMMAND, ORDER **5** : ACCUSE **6** : to rush against : rush forward in assault **7** : to make liable for payment; *also* : to record a debt or liability against **8** : to fix as a price — **charge·able** *adj*

²**charge** *n* **1** : a quantity (as of fuel or ammunition) required to fill something to capacity **2** : a store or accumulation of force **3** : an excess or deficiency of electrons in a body **4** : THRILL, KICK **5** : a task or duty imposed **6** : CARE, RESPONSIBILITY **7** : one given into another's care **8** : instructions from a judge to a jury **9** : COST, EXPENSE, PRICE; *also* : a debit to an account **10** : ACCUSATION, INDICTMENT **11** : ATTACK, ASSAULT

charge–coupled device *n* : a semiconductor device used esp. as an optical sensor

char·gé d'af·faires \shär-ˌzhäd-ə-ˈfaer\ *n, pl* **chargés d'affaires** \-ˌzhä(z)d-ə-\ [F] : a diplomat who substitutes for an ambassador or minister

¹**char·ger** \ˈchär-jər\ *n* : a large platter

²**charg·er** *n* **1** : a device or a workman that charges something **2** : WAR-HORSE

char·i·ot \ˈchar-ē-ət\ *n* : a 2-wheeled vehicle of ancient times used in war and in races and processions — **char·i·o·teer** \ˌchar-ē-ə-ˈtiər\ *n*

cha·ris·ma \kə-ˈriz-mə\ *also* **char·ism** \ˈkar-ˌiz-əm\ *n, pl* **cha·ris·ma·ta** \kə-ˈriz-mət-ə\ *also* **charisms** : a personal quality of leadership arousing popular loyalty or enthusiasm — **char·is·mat·ic** \ˌkar-əz-ˈmat-ik\ *adj*

char·i·ta·ble \ˈchar-ət-ə-bəl\ *adj* **1** : liberal in giving to needy people **2** : merciful or lenient in judging others **syn** benevolent, philanthropic, altruistic, humanitarian — **char·i·ta·ble·ness** *n* — **char·i·ta·bly** \-blē\ *adv*

char·i·ty \ˈchar-ət-ē\ *n, pl* **-ties 1** : goodwill toward or love of humanity **2** : an act or feeling of generosity **3** : the giving of aid to the poor; *also* : ALMS **4** : an institution engaged in relief of the poor **5** : leniency in judging others **syn** mercy, clemency, lenity

char·la·tan \ˈshär-lə-tən\ *n* : a person pretending to knowledge or ability that he lacks : QUACK

Charles·ton \ˈchärl-stən\ *n* : a lively ballroom dance in which the knees are twisted in and out and the heels are swung sharply outward on each step

char·ley horse \ˈchär-lē-ˌhörs\ *n* : pain and stiffness from muscular strain in an arm or leg

¹**charm** \ˈchärm\ *n* [ME *charme*, fr. OF, fr. L *carmen* song, fr. *canere* to sing] **1** : an act or expression believed to have magic power **2** : something worn about the person to ward off evil or bring good fortune : AMULET **3** : a trait that fascinates or allures **4** : physical grace or attraction **5** : a small ornament worn on a bracelet or chain

²**charm** *vb* **1** : to affect by or as if by a magic spell **2** : to protect by or as if by

charms **3** : FASCINATE, ENCHANT **syn** allure, captivate, bewitch, attract —
charm·er \ˈchär-mər\ n
charm·ing \ˈchär-miŋ\ adj : extremely pleasing or delightful — **charm·ing·ly** adv
char·nel house \ˈchärn-ᵊl-\ n : a building or chamber in which bodies or bones are deposited
¹chart \ˈchärt\ n **1** : MAP **2** : a sheet giving information in the form of a table, list, or diagram; also : GRAPH
²chart vb **1** : to make a chart of **2** : PLAN
¹char·ter \ˈchärt-ər\ n **1** : an official document granting rights or privileges (as to a colony, town, or college) from a sovereign or a governing body **2** : CONSTITUTION **3** : a written instrument from a society creating a branch **4** : a mercantile lease of a ship
²charter vb **1** : to grant a charter to **2** Brit : CERTIFY ⟨∼ed engineer⟩ **3** : to hire, rent, or lease for temporary use —
char·ter·er n
charter member n : an original member of an organization
char·treuse \shär-ˈtrüz, -ˈtrüs\ n : a variable color averaging a brilliant yellow green
char·wom·an \ˈchär-ˌwùm-ən\ n : a cleaning woman esp. in large buildings
chary \ˈchar-ē\ adj **chari·er; -est** [ME, sorrowful, dear, fr. OE cearig sorrowful, fr. caru sorrow] **1** : CAUTIOUS, CIRCUMSPECT **2** : SPARING — **char·i·ly** \ˈchar-ə-lē\ adv
¹chase \ˈchās\ n **1** : PURSUIT; also : HUNTING **2** : QUARRY **3** : a tract of unenclosed land used as a game preserve
²chase vb **chased; chas·ing 1** : to follow rapidly : PURSUE **2** : HUNT **3** : to seek out ⟨chasing down clues⟩ **4** : to cause to depart or flee : drive away **5** : RUSH, HASTEN
³chase vb **chased; chas·ing** : to decorate (a metal surface) by embossing or engraving
⁴chase n : FURROW, GROOVE
chas·er \ˈchā-sər\ n **1** : one that chases **2** : a mild drink (as beer) taken after hard liquor
chasm \ˈkaz-əm\ n : GORGE 2
chas·sis \ˈshas-ē, ˈchas-ē\ n, pl **chas·sis** \-ēz\ : a supporting framework (as for the body of an automobile or the parts of a radio set)
chaste \ˈchāst\ adj **chast·er; chast·est 1** : innocent of unlawful sexual intercourse : VIRTUOUS, PURE **2** : CELIBATE **3** : pure in thought : MODEST **4** : severe or simple in design — **chaste·ly** adv — **chaste·ness** n
chas·ten \ˈchās-ᵊn\ vb **chas·tened; chas·ten·ing** \ˈchās-(ᵊ-)niŋ\ : to correct through punishment or suffering : DISCIPLINE; also : PURIFY — **chas·ten·er** n
chas·tise \chas-ˈtīz\ vb **chas·tised; chas·tis·ing** [ME chastisen, alter. of chasten] **1** : to punish esp. bodily **2** : to censure severely : CASTIGATE — **chas·tise·ment** \-mənt, ˈchas-təz-\ n
chas·ti·ty \ˈchas-tət-ē\ n : the quality or state of being chaste; esp : sexual purity
cha·su·ble \ˈchaz-ə-bəl, ˈchas-\ n : the outer vestment of the celebrant at the Eucharist
chat \ˈchat\ n : light familiar informal talk — **chat** vb
châ·teau \sha-ˈtō\ n, pl **châ·teaus** \-ˈtōz\ or **châ·teaux** \-ˈtō(z)\ [F, fr. L castellum castle, dim. of castra camp] **1** : a feudal castle in France **2** : a large country house **3** : a French vineyard estate
chat·e·laine \ˈshat-ᵊl-ˌān\ n **1** : the mistress of a chateau **2** : a clasp or hook for a watch, purse, or keys
chat·tel \ˈchat-ᵊl\ n **1** : an item of tangible property other than real estate **2** : SLAVE, BONDMAN
chat·ter \ˈchat-ər\ vb **1** : to utter speechlike but meaningless sounds **2** : to talk idly, incessantly, or fast **3** : to click repeatedly or uncontrollably — **chatter** n — **chat·ter·er** n
chat·ter·box \ˈchat-ər-ˌbäks\ n : one who talks incessantly
chat·ty \ˈchat-ē\ adj **chat·ti·er; -est** : TALKATIVE — **chat·ti·ly** \ˈchat-ᵊl-ē\ adv — **chat·ti·ness** \-ē-nəs\ n
¹chauf·feur \ˈshō-fər, shō-ˈfər\ n [F, lit., stoker, fr. chauffer to heat] : a person employed to drive an automobile
²chauffeur vb **chauf·feured; chauf·feur·ing** \ˈshō-f(ə-)riŋ, shō-ˈfər-iŋ\ **1** : to do the work of a chauffeur **2** : to transport in the manner of a chauffeur
chaunt \ˈchȯnt, ˈchänt\ var of CHANT
chau·vin·ism \ˈshō-və-ˌniz-əm\ n [F

chauvinisme, fr. Nicolas *Chauvin,* soldier of excessive patriotism and devotion to Napoleon] **1** : excessive or blind patriotism **2** : an attitude of superiority toward members of the opposite sex — **chau·vin·ist** \-və-nəst\ *n or adj* — **chau·vin·is·tic** \ˌshō-və-ˈnis-tik\ *adj* — **chau·vin·is·ti·cal·ly** \-ti-k(ə-)lē\ *adv*

cheap \ˈchēp\ *adj* **1** : INEXPENSIVE **2** : costing little effort to obtain **3** : worth little : SHODDY, TAWDRY **4** : worthy of scorn **5** : STINGY — **cheap** *adv* — **cheap·ly** *adv* — **cheap·ness** *n*

cheap·en \ˈchē-pən\ *vb* **cheap·ened; cheap·en·ing** \ˈchēp-(ə-)niŋ\ **1** : to make or become cheap or cheaper in price or value **2** : to make tawdry

cheap·skate \ˈchēp-ˌskāt\ *n* : a niggardly person; *esp* : one seeking to avoid his or her share of costs

¹cheat \ˈchēt\ *vb* **1** : to deprive of something through fraud or deceit **2** : to practice fraud or trickery **3** : to violate rules (as of a game) dishonestly — **cheat·er** *n*

²cheat *n* **1** : the act of deceiving : FRAUD, DECEPTION **2** : one that cheats : a dishonest person

¹check \ˈchek\ *n* **1** : a sudden stoppage of progress **2** : a sudden pause or break **3** : something that stops or restrains **4** : a standard for testing or evaluation **5** : EXAMINATION, INVESTIGATION **6** : the act of testing or verifying **7** : a written order to a bank to pay money **8** : a ticket or token showing ownership or identity **9** : a slip indicating an amount due **10** : a pattern in squares; *also* : a fabric in such a pattern **11** : a mark typically ✔ placed beside an item to show that it has been noted **12** : CRACK, SPLIT

²check *vb* **1** : to slow down or stop : BRAKE **2** : to restrain the action or force of : CURB **3** : to compare with a source, original, or authority : VERIFY **4** : to inspect or test for satisfactory condition **5** : to mark with a check as examined **6** : to consign for shipment for one holding a passenger ticket **7** : to mark into squares **8** : to leave or accept for safekeeping in a checkroom **9** : to correspond point by point : TALLY **10** : CRACK, SPLIT

check·book \ˈchek-ˌbuk\ *n* : a book containing blank checks

¹check·er \ˈchek-ər\ *n* : a piece in the game of checkers

²checker *vb* **check·ered; check·er·ing** \ˈchek-(ə-)riŋ\ **1** : to variegate with different colors or shades **2** : to vary with contrasting elements ⟨a ∼ed career⟩ **3** : to mark into squares

³checker *n* : one that checks; *esp* : one who checks out purchases in a supermarket

check·er·ber·ry \ˈchek-ə(r)-ˌber-ē\ *n* : WINTERGREEN 1; *also* : the spicy red fruit of this plant

check·er·board \-ə(r)-ˌbōrd\ *n* : a board of 64 squares of alternate colors used in various games

check·ers \ˈchek-ərz\ *n* : a game for two played on a checkerboard with each player having 12 pieces

check in *vb* : to report one's presence or arrival (as at a hotel)

check·list \ˈchek-ˌlist\ *n* : a list of items that may easily be referred to

check·mate \ˈchek-ˌmāt\ *vb* [ME *chekmaten,* fr. *chekmate,* interj. used to announce checkmate, fr. MF *eschec mat,* fr. Ar *shāh māt,* fr. Per, lit., the king is left unable to escape] **1** : to thwart completely : DEFEAT, FRUSTRATE **2** : to attack (an opponent's king) in chess so that escape is impossible — **checkmate** *n*

check·off \ˈchek-ˌȯf\ *n* : the deduction of union dues from a worker's paycheck by the employer

check·out \ˈchek-ˌaut\ *n* **1** : the action or an instance of checking out **2** : a counter at which checking out is done **3** : the process of examining and testing something as to readiness for intended use **4** : the process of familiarizing oneself with the operation of a mechanical thing (as an airplane)

check out \-ˈaut\ *vb* **1** : to settle one's account (as at a hotel) and leave **2** : to total or have totaled the cost of purchases in a store and to make or receive payment for them

check·point \ˈchek-ˌpȯint\ *n* : a point at which a check is performed

check·room \-ˌrüm, -ˌrum\ *n* : a room at which baggage, parcels, or clothing is checked

check•up \-ˌəp\ *n* : EXAMINATION; *esp* : a general physical examination

ched•dar \ˈched-ər\ *n, often cap* : a hard mild to sharp white or yellow cheese of smooth texture

cheek \ˈchēk\ *n* 1 : the fleshy side part of the face 2 : IMPUDENCE, BOLDNESS, AUDACITY 3 : BUTTOCK 1

cheek•bone \ˈchēk-ˈbōn, -ˌbōn\ *n* : the bone or bony ridge below the eye

cheeky \ˈchē-kē\ *adj* **cheek•i•er; -est** : IMPUDENT, SAUCY — **cheek•i•ly** \ˈchē-kə-lē\ *adv* — **cheek•i•ness** \-kē-nəs\ *n*

cheep \ˈchēp\ *vb* : to utter faint shrill sounds : PEEP — **cheep** *n*

¹**cheer** \ˈchiər\ *n* [ME *chere* face, cheer, fr. OF, face] 1 : state of mind or heart : SPIRIT 2 : ANIMATION, GAIETY 3 : hospitable entertainment : WELCOME 4 : food and drink for a feast 5 : something that gladdens 6 : a shout of applause or encouragement

²**cheer** *vb* 1 : to give hope or courage to : COMFORT 2 : to make glad 3 : to urge on esp. by shouts 4 : to applaud with shouts 5 : to grow or be cheerful — usu. used with *up* — **cheer•er** *n*

cheer•ful \ˈchiər-fəl\ *adj* 1 : having or showing good spirits 2 : conducive to good spirits : pleasant and bright — **cheer•ful•ly** \-ē\ *adv* — **cheer•ful•ness** *n*

cheer•lead•er \ˈchiər-ˌlēd-ər\ *n* : a person who directs organized cheering esp. at a sports event

cheer•less \ˈchiər-ləs\ *adj* : BLEAK, DISPIRITING — **cheer•less•ly** *adv* — **cheer•less•ness** *n*

cheery \ˈchi(ə)r-ē\ *adj* **cheer•i•er; -est** : LIVELY, BRIGHT, GAY — **cheer•i•ly** \ˈchir-ə-lē\ *adv* — **cheer•i•ness** \-ē-nəs\ *n*

cheese \ˈchēz\ *n* : the curd of milk usu. pressed into cakes and cured for use as food

cheese•burg•er \ˈchēz-ˌbər-gər\ *n* : a hamburger containing a slice of cheese

cheese•cake \-ˌkāk\ *n* 1 : a dessert consisting of a creamy filling usu. containing cheese baked in a shell 2 : photographs of attractive usu. scantily clad women

cheese•cloth \-ˌklȯth\ *n* : a lightweight coarse cotton gauze

cheese•par•ing \-ˌpa(ə)r-iŋ\ *n* : miserly or petty economizing — **cheeseparing** *adj*

cheesy \ˈchē-zē\ *adj* **chees•i•er; -est** 1 : resembling, suggesting, or containing cheese 2 *slang* : CHEAP 3

chee•tah \ˈchēt-ə\ *n* [Hindu *cītā*, fr. Skt *citrakāya* tiger, fr. *citra* bright + *kāya* body] : a large long-legged spotted swift-moving African and formerly Asian cat

chef \ˈshef\ *n* 1 : a cook who manages the kitchen (as of a restaurant) 2 : COOK

chef d'oeu•vre \shā-dœvrᵊ\ *n, pl* **chefs d'oeuvre** \-dœvrᵊ\ : MASTERPIECE

chem *abbr* chemical; chemist; chemistry

¹**chem•i•cal** \ˈkem-i-kəl\ *adj* 1 : of, relating to, used in, or produced by chemistry 2 : acting or operated or produced by chemicals — **chem•i•cal•ly** \-i-k(ə-)lē\ *adv*

²**chemical** *n* : a substance obtained by a chemical process or used for producing a chemical effect

chemical engineering *n* : engineering dealing with the industrial application of chemistry

chemical warfare *n* : warfare using incendiary mixtures, smokes, or irritant, burning, or asphyxiating gases

che•mise \shə-ˈmēz\ *n* 1 : a woman's one-piece undergarment 2 : a loose straight-hanging dress

chem•ist \ˈkem-əst\ *n* 1 : one trained in chemistry 2 *Brit* : PHARMACIST

chem•is•try \ˈkem-ə-strē\ *n, pl* **-tries** 1 : the science that deals with the composition, structure, and properties of substances and of the changes they undergo 2 : chemical composition or properties ⟨the ~ of gasoline⟩ 3 : a strong mutual attraction

che•mo•ther•a•py \ˌkē-mō-ˈther-ə-pē\ *n* : the use of chemicals in the treatment or control of disease — **che•mo•ther•a•peu•tic** \-ˌther-ə-ˈpyüt-ik\ *adj*

che•nille \shə-ˈnēl\ *n* [F, lit., caterpillar, fr. L *canicula*, dim. of *canis* dog] : a fabric with a deep fuzzy pile often used for bedspreads and rugs

cheque \ˈchek\ *chiefly Brit* var of ¹CHECK 7

cher•ish \ˈcher-ish\ *vb* 1 : to hold dear : treat with care and affection 2 : to keep deeply in mind

Cher•o•kee \\'cher-ə-(ˌ)kē\\ *n, pl* **Cherokee** *or* **Cherokees** : a member of an American Indian people orig. of Tennessee and No. Carolina; *also* : their language

che•root \\shə-'rüt\\ *n* : a cigar cut square at both ends

cher•ry \\'cher-ē\\ *n, pl* **cherries** [ME *chery,* fr. OF *cherise* (taken as a plural), fr. LL *ceresia,* fr. L *cerasus* cherry tree, fr. Gk *kerasos*] **1** : the small fleshy pale yellow to deep blackish red fruit of a tree related to the roses; *also* : the tree or its wood **2** : a variable color averaging a moderate red

chert \\'chərt, 'chat\\ *n* : a rock resembling flint and consisting essentially of fine crystalline quartz or fibrous chalcedony — **cherty** \\-ē\\ *adj*

cher•ub \\'cher-əb\\ *n* **1** *pl* **cher•u•bim** \\'cher-(y)ə-ˌbim\\ : an angel of the 2d highest rank **2** *pl* **cherubs** : a chubby rosy person — **che•ru•bic** \\chə-'rü-bik\\ *adj*

chess \\'ches\\ *n* : a game for two played on a board of 64 squares of alternate colors with each player having 16 pieces — **chess•board** \\-ˌbōrd\\ *n* — **chess•man** \\-ˌman, -mən\\ *n*

chest \\'chest\\ *n* **1** : a box, case, or boxlike receptacle for storage or shipping **2** : the part of the body enclosed by the ribs and sternum

ches•ter•field \\'ches-tər-ˌfēld\\ *n* : an overcoat with a velvet collar

chest•nut \\'ches-(ˌ)nət\\ *n* **1** : the edible nut of any of a genus of trees related to the beech and oaks; *also* : this tree **2** : a grayish to reddish brown **3** : an old joke or story

chet•rum \\'chet-rəm\\ *n, pl* **chetrums** *or* **chetrum** — see *ngultrum* at MONEY table

che•val glass \\shə-'val-\\ *n* : a full-length mirror that may be tilted in a frame

che•va•lier \\ˌshev-ə-'liər, shə-'val-ˌyā\\ *n* : a member of one of various orders of knighthood or of merit

chev•i•ot \\'shev-ē-ət\\ *n, often cap* **1** : a twilled fabric with a rough nap **2** : a sturdy soft-finished cotton fabric

chev•ron \\'shev-rən\\ *n* : a sleeve badge of one or more V-shaped or inverted V-shaped stripes worn to indicate rank or service (as in the armed forces)

¹chew \\'chü\\ *vb* : to crush or grind with the teeth — **chew•able** *adj* — **chew•er** *n*

²chew *n* **1** : an act of chewing **2** : something for chewing

chewy \\'chü-ē\\ *adj* : requiring chewing ⟨∼ candy⟩

Chey•enne \\shī-'an, -'en\\ *n, pl* **Cheyenne** *or* **Cheyennes** [CanF, fr. Dakota *Shaiyena,* fr. *shaia* to speak unintelligibly] : a member of an American Indian people of the western plains of the U.S.; *also* : their language

chg *abbr* **1** change **2** charge

Chi•an•ti \\kē-'änt-ē, -'ant-\\ *n* : a dry usu. red wine

chiao \\'tyaù\\ *n, pl* **chiao** : a monetary unit of the People's Republic of China equal to ¹⁄₁₀ yuan

chiar•oscu•ro \\kē-ˌär-ə-'sk(y)ùr-ō\\ *n, pl* **-ros** [It, fr. *chiaro* clear, light + *oscuro* obscure, dark] **1** : pictorial representation in terms of light and shade without regard to color **2** : the arrangement or treatment of light and dark parts in a pictorial work of art

¹chic \\'shēk\\ *n* : STYLISHNESS

²chic *adj* : cleverly stylish : SMART; *also* : currently fashionable

chi•cane \\shik-'ān\\ *n* : CHICANERY

chi•ca•nery \\-'ān-(ə-)rē\\ *n, pl* **-ner•ies** : TRICKERY, DECEPTION

Chi•ca•no \\chi-'kän-ō\\ *n, pl* **-nos** : an American of Mexican descent — **Chicano** *adj*

chi•chi \\'shē-(ˌ)shē, 'chē-(ˌ)chē\\ *adj* [F] **1** : SHOWY, FRILLY **2** : ARTY, PRECIOUS **3** : CHIC — **chichi** *n*

chick \\'chik\\ *n* **1** : a young chicken; *also* : a young bird **2** : a young woman

chick•a•dee \\'chik-ə-(ˌ)dē\\ *n* : any of several small grayish American birds with black or brown caps

Chick•a•saw \\'chik-ə-ˌsò\\ *n, pl* **Chickasaw** *or* **Chickasaws** : a member of an American Indian people of Mississippi and Alabama

¹chick•en \\'chik-ən\\ *n* **1** : a common domestic fowl esp. when young; *also* : its flesh used as food **2** : COWARD

²chicken *adj* **1** *slang* : COWARDLY **2** *slang* : insistent on petty esp. military discipline

chicken feed *n, slang* : an insignificant sum of money

chick·en·heart·ed \ˌchik-ən-ˈhärt-əd\ *adj* : TIMID, COWARDLY

chicken out *vb* : to lose one's courage

chicken pox *n* : an acute contagious virus disease esp. of children characterized by a low fever and vesicles

chick–pea \ˈchik-ˌpē\ *n* : an Asian leguminous herb cultivated for its short pods with one or two edible seeds; *also* : its seed

chick·weed \ˈchik-ˌwēd\ *n* : any of several low-growing small-leaved weeds related to the pinks

chi·cle \ˈchik-əl\ *n* : a gum from the latex of a tropical evergreen tree used as the chief ingredient of chewing gum

chic·o·ry \ˈchik-(ə-)rē\ *n, pl* **-ries** : a usu. blue-flowered herb related to the daisies and grown for its root and for use in salads; *also* : its dried ground root used for flavoring or adulterating coffee

chide \ˈchīd\ *vb* **chid** \ˈchid\ *or* **chid·ed** \ˈchīd-əd\; **chid** *or* **chid·den** \ˈchid-ᵊn\ *or* **chided**; **chid·ing** \ˈchīd-iŋ\ : to speak disapprovingly to **syn** reproach, reprove, reprimand, admonish, scold, rebuke

¹**chief** \ˈchēf\ *adj* **1** : highest in rank **2** : most eminent or important **syn** principal, main, leading, major — **chief·ly** *adv*

²**chief** *n* **1** : the leader of a body or organization : HEAD **2** : the principal or most valuable part — **chief·dom** *n*

chief master sergeant *n* : a noncommissioned officer of the highest rank in the air force

chief of staff 1 : the ranking officer of a staff in the armed forces **2** : the ranking office of the army or air force

chief of state : the formal head of a national state as distinguished from the head of the government

chief petty officer *n* : an enlisted man in the navy ranking next below a senior chief petty officer

chief·tain \ˈchēf-tən\ *n* : a chief esp. of a band, tribe, or clan — **chief·tain·cy** \-sē\ *n* — **chief·tain·ship** *n*

chief warrant officer *n* : a warrant officer of senior rank

chif·fon \shif-ˈän, ˈshif-ˌ\ *n* [F, lit., rag,

fr. *chiffe* old rag] : a sheer fabric esp. of silk

chif·fo·nier \ˌshif-ə-ˈniər\ *n* : a high narrow chest of drawers

chig·ger \ˈchig-ər\ *n* : a bloodsucking larval mite that irritates the skin

chi·gnon \ˈshēn-ˌyän\ *n* [F] : a knot of hair worn at the back of the head

Chi·hua·hua \chə-ˈwä-ˌwä\ *n* : a very small large-eared dog of a breed that originated in Mexico

chil·blain \ˈchil-ˌblān\ *n* : a sore or inflamed swelling (as on the feet or hands) caused by exposure to cold

child \ˈchīld\ *n, pl* **chil·dren** \ˈchil-drən\ **1** : an unborn or recently born person **2** : a young person between the periods of infancy and youth **3** : a male or female offspring : SON, DAUGHTER **4** : one strongly influenced by another or by a place or state of affairs — **child·ish** *adj* — **child·ish·ly** *adv* — **child·ish·ness** *n* — **child·less** *adj* — **child·less·ness** *n* — **child·like** *adj*

child·bear·ing \ˈchīld-ˌbar-iŋ\ *n* : CHILDBIRTH — **childbearing** *adj*

child·birth \-ˌbərth\ *n* : the act or process of giving birth to offspring

child·hood \-ˌhüd\ *n* : the state or time of being a child

child·proof \-ˌprüf\ *adj* : made to prevent tampering by children

child's play *n* : a simple task or act

Chil·ean \ˈchil-ē-ən, chə-ˈlā-ən\ *n* : a native or inhabitant of Chile — **Chilean** *adj*

chili *or* **chile** *or* **chil·li** \ˈchil-ē\ *n, pl* **chilies** *or* **chil·es** *or* **chil·lies** **1** : a pungent pepper related to the tomato **2** : a thick sauce of meat and chilies **3** : CHILI CON CARNE

chili con car·ne \ˌchil-ē-ˌkän-ˈkär-nē, -kən-\ *n* [Sp *chile con carne* chili with meat] : a spiced stew of ground beef and chilies or chili powder usu. with beans

chili powder *n* : a seasoning made of ground hot peppers and other spices

¹**chill** \ˈchil\ *n* **1** : a feeling of coldness accompanied by shivering **2** : moderate coldness **3** : a check to enthusiasm or warmth of feeling

²**chill** *adj* **1** : moderately cold **2** : COLD, RAW **3** : DISTANT, FORMAL ⟨a ∼ reception⟩ **4** : DEPRESSING, DISPIRITING

³**chill** *vb* **1** : to make or become cold or

chilly **2** : to make cool esp. without freezing **3** : to harden the surface of (as metal) by sudden cooling — **chiller** *n*

chilly \\'chil-ē\ *adj* **chill·i·er; -est 1** : noticeably cold **2** : unpleasantly affected by cold **3** : lacking warmth of feeling — **chill·i·ness** *n*

¹**chime** \\'chīm\ *n* **1** : a set of bells musically tuned **2** : the sound of a set of bells — usu. used in pl. **3** : a musical sound suggesting bells

²**chime** *vb* **chimed; chim·ing 1** : to make bell-like sounds **2** : to indicate (as the time of day) by chiming **3** : to be or act in accord : be in harmony

chime in *vb* : to break into or join in a conversation

chi·me·ra *or* **chi·mae·ra** \kī-'mir-ə, kə-\ *n* [L *chimaera,* fr. Gk *chimaira* she-goat, chimera] **1** : an imaginary monster made up of incongruous parts **2** : a frightful or foolish fancy

chi·me·ri·cal \-'mer-i-kəl\ *also* **chi·me·ric** \-ik\ *adj* **1** : FANTASTIC, IMAGINARY **2** : inclined to fantastic schemes

chim·ney \\'chim-nē\ *n, pl* **chimneys 1** : a vertical structure extending above the roof of a building for carrying off smoke **2** : a glass tube around a lamp flame

chimp \\'chimp, 'shimp\ *n* : CHIMPANZEE

chim·pan·zee \ˌchim-ˌpan-'zē, ˌshim-, -pən-; chim-'pan-zē, shim-\ *n* : an African manlike ape

¹**chin** \\'chin\ *n* : the part of the face below the lower lip including the prominence of the lower jaw — **chin·less** *adj*

²**chin** *vb* **chinned; chin·ning** : to raise (oneself) while hanging by the hands until the chin is level with the support

chi·na \\'chī-nə\ *n* : porcelain ware; *also* : domestic pottery in general

Chi·na·town \-ˌtaun\ *n* : the Chinese quarter of a city

chinch bug \\'chinch-\ *n* : a small black and white bug destructive to cereal grasses

chin·chil·la \chin-'chil-ə\ *n* **1** : a small So. American rodent with soft pearl-gray fur; *also* : its fur **2** : a heavy long-napped woolen cloth

chine \\'chīn\ *n* **1** : BACKBONE, SPINE; *also* : a cut of meat including the backbone or part of it **2** : RIDGE, CREST

Chi·nese \chī-'nēz, -'nēs\ *n, pl* **Chinese 1** : a native or inhabitant of China **2** : any of a group of related languages of China — **Chinese** *adj*

Chinese cabbage *n* **1** : BOK CHOY **2** : a Chinese vegetable related to the cabbage that forms tight elongate cylindrical heads of pale green to cream-colored leaves

Chinese checkers *n* : a game in which each player in turn transfers a set of marbles from a home point to the opposite point of a pitted 6-pointed star

Chinese gooseberry *n* : a subtropical vine that bears kiwifruit; *also* : KIWIFRUIT

Chinese lantern *n* : a collapsible translucent cover for a light

¹**chink** \\'chiŋk\ *n* : a small crack or fissure

²**chink** *vb* : to fill the chinks of : stop up

³**chink** *n* : a slight sharp metallic sound

⁴**chink** *vb* : to make a slight sharp metallic sound

chi·no \\'chē-nō\ *n, pl* **chinos 1** : a usu. khaki cotton twill **2** *pl* : an article of clothing made of chino

Chi·nook \shə-'nuk, chə-, -'nuk\ *n, pl* **Chinook** *or* **Chinooks** : a member of an American Indian people of Oregon

chintz \\'chints\ *n* : a usu. glazed printed cotton cloth

chintzy \\'chint-sē\ *adj* **chintz·i·er; -est 1** : decorated with or as if with chintz **2** : GAUDY, CHEAP

chin–up \\'chin-ˌəp\ *n* : the act of chinning oneself

¹**chip** \\'chip\ *n* **1** : a small usu. thin and flat piece (as of wood) cut or broken off **2** : a thin crisp morsel of food **3** : a counter used in games (as poker) **4** *pl, slang* : MONEY **5** : a flaw left after a chip is removed **6** : a very small slice of silicon containing electronic circuits

²**chip** *vb* **chipped; chip·ping 1** : to cut or break chips from **2** : to break off in small pieces at the edges **3** : to play a chip shot

chip in *vb* : CONTRIBUTE

chip·munk \\'chip-ˌməŋk\ *n* : any of various ground-dwelling squirrels found in No. America into Mexico and in Asia

chipped beef \\'chip(t)-\ *n* : smoked dried beef sliced thin

¹**chip·per** \\'chip-ər\ *n* : one that chips

²**chipper** *adj* : LIVELY, CHEERFUL

Chip·pe·wa \'chip-ə-ˌwȯ, -ˌwä, -ˌwā, -wə\ *n, pl* **Chippewa** *or* **Chippewas** : OJIBWA

chip shot *n* : a short usu. low shot to the green in golf

chi·rog·ra·phy \kī-'räg-rə-fē\ *n* : HANDWRITING, PENMANSHIP — **chi·ro·graph·ic** \ˌkī-rə-'graf-ik\ *adj*

chi·rop·o·dy \kə-'räp-əd-ē, shə-\ *n* : PODIATRY — **chi·rop·o·dist** \-əd-əst\ *n*

chi·ro·prac·tic \'kī-rə-ˌprak-tik\ *n* : a system of therapy based esp. on manipulation of body structures — **chi·ro·prac·tor** \-tər\ *n*

chirp \'chərp\ *n* : a short sharp sound characteristic of a small bird or cricket — **chirp** *vb*

¹**chis·el** \'chiz-əl\ *n* : a metal tool with a cutting edge at the end of a blade used in chipping away and shaping wood, stone, or metal

²**chisel** *vb* **-eled** *or* **-elled; -el·ing** *or* **-el·ling** \'chiz-(ə-)liŋ\ **1** : to work with or as if with a chisel **2** : to obtain by shrewd often unfair methods; *also* : CHEAT — **chis·el·er** \-(ə-)lər\ *n*

¹**chit** \'chit\ *n* [ME *chitte* kitten, cub] **1** : CHILD **2** : a pert young woman

²**chit** *n* [Hindi *ciṭṭhī* letter, note] : a signed voucher for a small debt

chit·chat \'chit-ˌchat\ *n* : casual or trifling conversation

chi·tin \'kīt-ᵊn\ *n* : a sugar polymer that forms part of the hard outer integument esp. of insects — **chi·tin·ous** *adj*

chit·ter·lings *or* **chit·lins** \'chit-lənz\ *n pl* : the intestines of hogs esp. prepared as food

chi·val·ric \shə-'val-rik\ *adj* : relating to chivalry : CHIVALROUS

chiv·al·rous \'shiv-əl-rəs\ *adj* **1** : of or relating to chivalry **2** : marked by honor, courtesy, and generosity **3** : marked by especial courtesy to women — **chiv·al·rous·ly** *adv* — **chiv·al·rous·ness** *n*

chiv·al·ry \'shiv-əl-rē\ *n, pl* **-ries 1** : a body of knights **2** : the system or practices of knighthood **3** : the spirit or character of the ideal knight

chive \'chīv\ *n* : an herb related to the onion that has leaves used for flavoring

chlo·ral hydrate \ˌklȯr-əl-\ *n* : a white crystalline compound used as a hypnotic and sedative

chlor·dane \'klȯr-ˌdān\ *also* **chlor·dan** \-ˌdan\ *n* : a viscous liquid insecticide

chlo·ride \'klȯr-ˌīd\ *n* : a compound of chlorine with another element or group

chlo·ri·nate \'klȯr-ə-ˌnāt\ *vb* **-nat·ed; -nat·ing** : to treat or cause to combine with chlorine or a chlorine-containing compound — **chlo·ri·na·tion** \ˌklȯr-ə-'nā-shən\ *n* — **chlo·ri·na·tor** \'klȯr-ə-ˌnāt-ər\ *n*

chlo·rine \'klȯr-ˌēn\ *n* : a nonmetallic chemical element that is found alone as a heavy strong-smelling greenish yellow irritating gas and is used as a bleach, oxidizing agent, and disinfectant

chlo·rite \'klȯr-ˌīt\ *n* : a usu. green mineral found with and resembling mica

chlo·ro·flu·o·ro·car·bon \ˌklȯr-ə-'flȯr-ə-ˌkär-bən, -'flu̇r-\ *n* : a gaseous compound that contains carbon, chlorine, fluorine, and sometimes hydrogen and is used esp. as a solvent, a refrigerant, and an aerosol propellant

¹**chlo·ro·form** \'klȯr-ə-ˌfȯrm\ *n* : a colorless heavy fluid with etherlike odor used as a solvent and anesthetic

²**chloroform** *vb* : to treat with chloroform to produce anesthesia or death

chlo·ro·phyll \-ˌfil\ *n* : the green coloring matter of plants that functions in photosynthesis

chm *abbr* chairman

chock \'chäk\ *n* : a wedge for steadying something or for blocking the movement of a wheel — **chock** *vb*

chock·a·block \'chäk-ə-ˌbläk\ *adj* : very full : CROWDED

chock–full \'chək-'fu̇l, 'chäk-\ *adj* : full to the limit : CRAMMED

choc·o·late \'chäk-(ə-)lət, 'chȯk-\ *n* [Sp, fr. Nahuatl (an Indian language of southern Mexico) *xocoatl*] **1** : a food prepared from ground roasted cacao beans; *also* : a drink prepared from this **2** : a candy made of or with a coating of chocolate **3** : a dark brown color

Choc·taw \'chäk-ˌtȯ\ *n, pl* **Choctaw** *or* **Choctaws** : a member of an American Indian people of Mississippi, Alabama, and Louisiana; *also* : their language

¹choice \\'chȯis\ *n* **1** : the act of choosing : SELECTION **2** : the power or opportunity of choosing : OPTION **3** : the best part **4** : a person or thing selected **5** : a variety offered for selection

²choice *adj* **choic·er; choic·est 1** : worthy of being chosen **2** : selected with care **3** : of high quality

choir \\'kwī(-ə)r\ *n* **1** : an organized company of singers esp. in a church **2** : the part of a church occupied by the singers

choir·boy \\'kwī(-ə)r-ˌbȯi\ *n* : a boy member of a church choir

choir·mas·ter \-ˌmas-tər\ *n* : the director of a choir (as in a church)

¹choke \\'chōk\ *vb* **choked; chok·ing 1** : to hinder breathing (as by obstructing the windpipe) : STRANGLE **2** : to check the growth or action of **3** : CLOG, OBSTRUCT **4** : to decrease or shut off the air intake of the carburetor of a gasoline engine to make the fuel mixture richer **5** : to perform badly in a critical situation

²choke *n* **1** : the act of choking **2** : a narrowing in size toward the muzzle in the bore of a gun **3** : a valve for choking a gasoline engine

chok·er \\'chō-kər\ *n* : something (as a necklace) worn tightly around the neck

cho·ler \\'käl-ər, 'kō-lər\ *n* : a tendency toward anger : IRASCIBILITY

chol·era \\'käl-ə-rə\ *n* : a disease marked by severe vomiting and dysentery; *esp* : an often fatal epidemic disease (**Asiatic cholera**) chiefly of southeastern Asia caused by a bacillus

cho·ler·ic \\'käl-ə-rik, kə-'ler-ik\ *adj* **1** : IRASCIBLE **2** : ANGRY, IRATE

cho·les·ter·ol \kə-'les-tə-ˌrȯl\ *n* : a physiologically important waxy substance found in animal tissues and implicated experimentally in arteriosclerosis

chomp \\'chämp, 'chȯmp\ *vb* : to chew or bite on something heavily

choose \\'chüz\ *vb* **chose** \chōz\; **cho·sen** \\'chōz-ᵊn\; **choos·ing** \chü-ziŋ\ **1** : to select esp. after consideration **2** : DECIDE **3** : to think proper : see fit : PLEASE — **choos·er** *n*

choosy *or* **choos·ey** \\'chü-zē\ *adj* **choos·i-**er; **-est** : very particular in making choices

¹chop \\'chäp\ *vb* **chopped; chop·ping 1** : to cut by repeated blows **2** : to cut into small pieces : MINCE **3** : to strike (a ball) with a short quick downward stroke

²chop *n* **1** : a sharp downward blow or stroke **2** : a small cut of meat often including part of a rib **3** : a short abrupt motion (as of a wave)

³chop *n* **1** : an official seal or stamp **2** : a mark on goods to indicate quality or kind; *also* : QUALITY, GRADE

chop·house \\'chäp-ˌhaůs\ *n* : RESTAURANT

chop·per \\'chäp-ər\ *n* **1** : one that chops **2** : HELICOPTER

chop·pi·ness \\'chäp-ē-nəs\ *n* : the quality or state of being choppy

¹chop·py \\'chäp-ē\ *adj* **chop·pi·er; -est** : CHANGEABLE, VARIABLE ⟨a ∼ wind⟩

²choppy *adj* **chop·pi·er; -est 1** : rough with small waves **2** : JERKY, DISCONNECTED — **chop·pi·ly** \\'chäp-ə-lē\ *adv*

chops \\'chäps\ *n pl* : the fleshy covering of the jaws

chop·stick \\'chäp-ˌstik\ *n* : one of a pair of sticks used chiefly in oriental countries for lifting food to the mouth

chop su·ey \chäp-'sü-ē\ *n, pl* **chop sueys** : a dish made typically of bean sprouts, bamboo shoots, celery, onions, mushrooms, and meat or fish and served with rice

cho·ral \\'kōr-əl\ *adj* : of, relating to, or sung by a choir or chorus or in chorus — **cho·ral·ly** \-ē\ *adv*

cho·rale \kə-'ral, -'räl\ *n* **1** : a hymn or psalm sung in church; *also* : a hymn tune or a harmonization of a traditional melody **2** : CHORUS, CHOIR

¹chord \\'kȯrd\ *n* [alter. of ME *cord*, short for *accord*] : three or more musical tones sounded simultaneously

²chord *n* **1** : CORD, STRING; *esp* : a cord-like anatomical structure **2** : a straight line joining two points on a curve

chore \\'chōr\ *n* **1** *pl* : the daily light work of a household or farm **2** : a routine task or job **3** : a difficult or disagreeable task

cho·rea \kə-'rē-ə\ *n* : a nervous disorder marked by spasmodic uncontrolled movements

cho·re·og·ra·phy \ˌkōr-ē-'äg-rə-fē\ *n, pl*

-phies : the art of dancing or of arranging dances and esp. ballets — **cho·re·o·graph** \'kōr-ē-ə-ˌgraf\ vb — **cho·re·og·ra·pher** \ˌkōr-ē-'äg-rə-fər\ n — **cho·reo·graph·ic** \ˌkōr-ē-ə-'graf-ik\ adj — **cho·reo·graph·i·cal·ly** \-i-k(ə-)1ē\ adv

cho·ris·ter \'kōr-ə-stər\ n : a singer in a choir

chor·tle \'chȯrt-ᵊl\ vb **chor·tled; chor·tling** \'chȯrt-(ᵊ-)liŋ\ : to laugh or chuckle esp. in satisfaction or exultation — **chortle** n

¹**chorus** \'kōr-əs\ n 1 : an organized company of singers : CHOIR 2 : a group of dancers and usu. singers (as in a musical comedy) 3 : a part of a song repeated at intervals 4 : a composition to be sung by a chorus; also : group singing 5 : sounds uttered by a number of persons or animals together

²**chorus** vb : to sing or utter in chorus

chose past of CHOOSE

cho·sen \'chōz-ᵊn\ adj : selected or marked for special favor or privilege

¹**chow** \'chaū\ n : FOOD

²**chow** n : CHOW CHOW

chow·chow \'chaū-ˌchaū\ n : chopped mixed pickles in mustard sauce

chow chow \'chaū-ˌchaū\ n : any of a breed of thick-coated straight-legged muscular dogs with a blue-black tongue and a short tail curled close to the back

chow·der \'chaūd-ər\ n : a soup or stew made from seafood or vegetables and containing milk or tomatoes

chow mein \'chaū-'mān\ n : a seasoned stew of shredded or diced meat, mushrooms, and vegetables that is usu. served with fried noodles

chrism \'kriz-əm\ n : consecrated oil used esp. in baptism and confirmation

Christ \'krīst\ n [L Christus, fr. Gk Christos, lit., anointed, trans. of Heb māshīah] : Jesus esp. as the Messiah — **Christ·like** adj — **Christ·ly** adj

chris·ten \'kris-ᵊn\ vb **chris·tened; chris·ten·ing** \'kris-(ᵊ-)niŋ\ 1 : BAPTIZE 2 : to name at baptism 3 : to name or dedicate (as a ship) by a ceremony suggestive of baptism — **chris·ten·ing** n

Chris·ten·dom \'kris-ᵊn-dəm\ n 1 : the entire body of Christians 2 : the part of the world in which Christianity prevails

¹**Chris·tian** \'kris-chən\ n : an adherent of Christianity

²**Christian** adj 1 : of or relating to Christianity 2 : based on or conforming with Christianity 3 : of or relating to a Christian 4 : professing Christianity

chris·ti·an·ia \ˌkris-chē-'an-ē-ə, ˌkris-tē-\ n : CHRISTIE

Chris·ti·an·i·ty \ˌkris-chē-'an-ət-ē\ n : the religion derived from Jesus Christ, based on the Bible as sacred scripture, and professed by Christians

Chris·tian·ize \'kris-chə-ˌnīz\ vb **-ized; -iz·ing** : to make Christian

Christian name n : GIVEN NAME

Christian Science n : a religion and system of healing founded by Mary Baker Eddy and taught by the Church of Christ, Scientist — **Christian Scientist** n

chris·tie or **chris·ty** \'kris-tē\ n, pl **christies** : a skiing turn made by shifting body weight forward and skidding into a turn with parallel skis

Christ·mas \'kris-məs\ n : December 25 celebrated as a church festival in commemoration of the birth of Christ and observed as a legal holiday

Christmas club n : a savings account in which regular deposits are made to provide money for Christmas shopping

Christ·mas·tide \'kris-mə-ˌstīd\ n : the season of Christmas

chro·mat·ic \krō-'mat-ik\ adj 1 : of or relating to color 2 : proceeding by half steps of the musical scale — **chro·mat·i·cism** \-'mat-ə-ˌsiz-əm\ n

chro·mato·graph \krō-'mat-ə-ˌgraf\ n : an instrument used in chromatography

chro·ma·tog·ra·phy \ˌkrō-mə-'täg-rə-fē\ n : the separation of a complex mixture into its component compounds as a result of the different rates at which the compounds travel through or over a stationary substance due to differing affinities for the substance — **chro·mato·graph·ic** \krō-ˌmat-ə-'graf-ik\ adj — **chro·mato·graph·i·cal·ly** \-i-k(ə-)lē\ adv

chrome \'krōm\ n 1 : CHROMIUM 2 : a chromium pigment 3 : something plated with an alloy of chromium

chro·mi·um \'krō-mē-əm\ *n* : a bluish white metallic element used esp. in alloys and chrome plating

chro·mo·some \'krō-mə-ˌsōm, -ˌzōm\ *n* : one of the usu. elongated bodies in a cell nucleus that contains most or all of the DNA or RNA comprising the genes — **chro·mo·som·al** \ˌkrō-mə-'sō-məl, -'zō-\ *adj*

chro·mo·sphere \'krō-mə-ˌsfiər\ *n* : the lower atmosphere of a star (as the sun)

chron *abbr* **1** chronicle **2** chronological; chronology

Chron *abbr* Chronicles

chron·ic \'krän-ik\ *adj* : marked by long duration or frequent recurrence ⟨a ∼ disease⟩; *also* : HABITUAL ⟨a ∼ grumbler⟩ — **chron·i·cal·ly** \-i-k(ə-)lē\ *adv*

¹chron·i·cle \'krän-i-kəl\ *n* : HISTORY, NARRATIVE

²chronicle *vb* **-cled; -cling** \-k(ə-)liŋ\ : to record in or as if in a chronicle — **chron·i·cler** \-k(ə-)lər\ *n*

Chronicles *n* — see BIBLE table

chro·no·graph \'krän-ə-ˌgraf\ *n* : an instrument for measuring and recording time intervals with accuracy — **chro·no·graph·ic** \ˌkrän-ə-'graf-ik\ *adj* — **chro·nog·ra·phy** \krə-'näg-rə-fē\ *n*

chro·nol·o·gy \krə-'näl-ə-jē\ *n, pl* **-gies** **1** : the science that deals with measuring time and dating events **2** : a chronological list or table **3** : arrangement of events in the order of their occurrence — **chron·o·log·i·cal** \ˌkrän-ᵊl-'äj-i-kəl\ *adj* — **chron·o·log·i·cal·ly** \-i-k(ə-)lē\ *adv* — **chro·nol·o·gist** \krə-'näl-ə-jəst\ *n*

chro·nom·e·ter \krə-'näm-ət-ər\ *n* : a very accurate timepiece

chrys·a·lid \'kris-ə-ləd\ *n* : CHRYSALIS

chrys·a·lis \'kris-ə-ləs\ *n, pl* **chry·sal·i·des** \kris-'al-ə-ˌdēz\ *or* **chrys·a·lis·es** : an insect pupa in a firm case without a cocoon

chry·san·the·mum \kris-'an-thə-məm\ *n* [L, fr. Gk *chrysanthemon*, fr. *chrysos* gold + *anthemon* flower] : any of a genus of plants related to the daisies including some grown for their showy flowers or for medicinal products or insecticides; *also* : a flower of a chrysanthemum

chrys·o·lite \'kris-ə-ˌlīt\ *n* : OLIVINE

chub \'chəb\ *n, pl* **chub** *or* **chubs** : any of various small freshwater fishes related to the carp

chub·by \'chəb-ē\ *adj* **chub·bi·er; -est** : PLUMP — **chub·bi·ness** *n*

¹chuck \'chək\ *vb* **1** : to give a pat or tap **2** : to toss or throw with a short motion of the arms **3** : DISCARD; *also* : EJECT **4** : to have done with

²chuck *n* **1** : a light pat under the chin **2** : TOSS

³chuck *n* **1** : a cut of beef including most of the neck and the parts around the shoulder blade and the first three ribs **2** : a device for holding work or a tool in a machine (as a lathe)

chuck·hole \'chək-ˌhōl\ *n* : POTHOLE

chuck·le \'chək-əl\ *vb* **chuck·led; chuck·ling** \-(ə-)liŋ\ : to laugh in a quiet hardly audible manner — **chuckle** *n*

chuck wagon *n* : a wagon equipped with a stove and food supplies

¹chug \'chəg\ *n* : a dull explosive sound made by or as if by a laboring engine

²chug *vb* **chugged; chug·ging** : to move or go with chugs

chuk·ka \'chək-ə\ *n* : a short usu. ankle-length leather boot with two pairs of eyelets

chuk·ker *or* **chuk·kar** \'chək-ər\ *or* **chuk·ka** \-ə\ *n* : a playing period of a polo game

¹chum \'chəm\ *n* : an intimate friend

²chum *vb* **chummed; chum·ming** **1** : to room together **2** : to be a close friend

chum·my \'chəm-ē\ *adj* **chum·mi·er; -est** : INTIMATE, SOCIABLE — **chum·mi·ly** \'chəm-ə-lē\ *adv* — **chum·mi·ness** \-ē-nəs\ *n*

chump \'chəmp\ *n* : FOOL, BLOCKHEAD

chunk \'chəŋk\ *n* **1** : a short thick piece **2** : a sizable amount

chunky \'chəŋ-kē\ *adj* **chunk·i·er; -est** **1** : STOCKY **2** : containing chunks

church \'chərch\ *n* [OE *cirice*, fr. LGk *kyriakon*, short for *kyriakon dōma*, lit., the Lord's house, fr. Gk *Kyrios* Lord + *dōma* house] **1** : a building esp. for Christian public worship **2** : the whole body of Christians **3** : DENOMINATION **4** : CONGREGATION **5** : public divine worship

church·go·er \'chərch-ˌgō(-ə)r\ *n* : one who habitually attends church — **church·go·ing** \-ˌgō-iŋ\ *adj or n*

church·less \'chərch-ləs\ *adj* : not affiliated with a church

church•man \\'chərch-mən\\ *n* **1** : CLER-
GYMAN **2** : a member of a church

church•war•den \\'chərch-ˌwȯrd-ᵊn\\ *n*
: WARDEN 5

church•yard \\-ˌyärd\\ *n* : a yard that belongs to a church and is often used as
a burial ground

churl \\'chərl\\ *n* **1** : a medieval peasant
2 : RUSTIC **3** : a rude ill-bred person —
churl•ish *adj* — **churl•ish•ly** *adv* —
churl•ish•ness *n*

¹churn \\'chərn\\ *n* : a container in which
milk or cream is violently stirred in
making butter

²churn *vb* **1** : to stir in a churn; *also* : to
make (butter) by such stirring **2** : to
shake around violently

churn out *vb* : to produce mechanically
and in large quantity

chute \\'shüt\\ *n* **1** : an inclined surface,
trough, or passage down or through
which something may pass ⟨a coal ∼⟩
⟨a mail ∼⟩ **2** : PARACHUTE

chut•ney \\'chət-nē\\ *n, pl* **chutneys** : a
condiment of acid fruits with raisins,
dates, and onions

chutz•pah \\'hut-spə, 'k̲ut-, -(ˌ)spä\\ *n*
: supreme self-confidence

CIA *abbr* Central Intelligence Agency

cía *abbr* [Sp *compañía*] company

ciao \\'chau̇\\ *interj* [It, fr. It dial., alter.
of *schiavo* (I am your) slave, fr. ML
sclavus] — used to express greeting or
farewell

ci•ca•da \\sə-'kād-ə\\ *n* : any of a family
of stout-bodied insects related to the
aphids and having wide blunt heads
and large transparent wings

ci•ca•trix \\'sik-ə-ˌtriks\\ *n, pl* **ci•ca•tri•ces**
\\ˌsik-ə-'trī-ˌsēz\\ [L] : a scar resulting
from formation and contraction of fibrous tissue in a flesh wound

ci•ce•ro•ne \\ˌsis-ə-'rō-nē, ˌchē-chə-\\ *n,*
pl **-ni** \\-(ˌ)nē\\ : a guide who conducts
sightseers

CID *abbr* Criminal Investigation Department

ci•der \\'sīd-ər\\ *n* : juice pressed from
fruit (as apples) and used as a beverage, vinegar, or flavoring

cie *abbr* [F *compagnie*] company

ci•gar \\sig-'är\\ *n* : a roll of tobacco for
smoking

cig•a•rette \\ˌsig-ə-'ret, 'sig-ə-ˌret\\ *n* [F,
dim. of *cigare* cigar] : a slender roll of

cut tobacco enclosed in paper for
smoking

cig•a•ril•lo \\ˌsig-ə-'ril-ō, -'rē-ō\\ *n, pl* **-los**
[Sp] **1** : a very small cigar **2** : a cigarette wrapped in tobacco rather than
paper

ci•lan•tro \\si-'län-trō, -'lan-\\ *n* : leaves
of coriander used as a flavoring or garnish

cil•i•ate \\'sil-ē-ˌāt\\ *n* : any of a group of
protozoans characterized by cilia

cil•i•um \\'sil-ē-əm\\ *n, pl* **-ia** \\-ē-ə\\ **1** : a
minute short hairlike process; *esp*
: one of a cell **2** : EYELASH

C in C *abbr* commander in chief

cinch \\'sinch\\ *n* **1** : a girth for holding a
saddle or a pack in place **2** : a sure or
an easy thing — **cinch** *vb*

cin•cho•na \\siŋ-'kō-nə\\ *n* : any of a
genus of So. American trees; *also*
: the bitter quinine-containing bark of
a cinchona

cinc•ture \\'siŋk-chər\\ *n* : BELT, GIRDLE

cin•der \\'sin-dər\\ *n* **1** : SLAG **2** *pl* : ASHES
3 : a hot piece of partly burned wood
or coal **4** : a fragment of lava from an
erupting volcano — **cinder** *vb* — **cin•**
dery *adj*

cinder block *n* : a building block made
of cement and coal cinders

cin•e•ma \\'sin-ə-mə\\ *n* **1** : a motion-picture theater **2** : MOVIES — **cin•e•mat•ic**
\\ˌsin-ə-'mat-ik\\ *adj*

cin•e•ma•theque \\ˌsin-ə-mə-'tek\\ *n* : a
small movie house specializing in
avant-garde films

cin•e•ma•tog•ra•phy \\ˌsin-ə-mə-'täg-
rə-fē\\ *n* : motion-picture photography
— **cin•e•ma•tog•ra•pher** \\-fər\\ *n* — **cin•**
e•mat•o•graph•ic \\-ˌmat-ə-'graf-ik\\ *adj*

cin•er•ar•i•um \\ˌsin-ə-'rer-ē-əm\\ *n, pl* **-ia**
\\-ē-ə\\ : a place to receive the ashes of
the cremated dead — **cin•er•ary** \\'sin-
ə-ˌrer-ē\\ *adj*

cin•na•bar \\'sin-ə-ˌbär\\ *n* : a red mineral that is the only important ore of
mercury

cin•na•mon \\'sin-ə-mən\\ *n* : a spice consisting of the highly aromatic bark of
any of several trees related to the true
laurel; *also* : a tree that yields cinnamon

cinque•foil \\'siŋk-ˌfȯil, 'saŋk-\\ *n* : any
of a genus of plants related to the
roses with leaves having five lobes

¹ci•pher \\'sī-fər\\ *n* [ME, fr. MF *cifre*, fr.

ML *cifra,* fr. Ar *ṣifr* empty, zero] **1** : ZERO, NAUGHT **2** : a method of secret writing

²**cipher** *vb* **ci·phered; ci·pher·ing** \-f(ə-)riŋ\ : to compute arithmetically

cir *or* **circ** *abbr* circular

cir·ca \'sər-kə\ *prep* : ABOUT ⟨~ 1600⟩

cir·ca·di·an \ˌsər-'kad-ē-ən, ˌsər-kə-'dī-ən\ *adj* : being, having, characterized by, or occurring in approximately 24-hour intervals (as of biological activity)

¹**cir·cle** \'sər-kəl\ *n* **1** : a closed curve every point of which is equally distant from a fixcd point within it **2** : something in the form of a circle **3** : an area of action or influence **4** : CYCLE **5** : a group bound by a common tie

²**circle** *vb* **cir·cled; cir·cling** \-k(ə-)liŋ\ **1** : to enclose in a circle **2** : to move or revolve around; *also* : to move in a circle

cir·clet \'sər-klət\ *n* : a small circle; *esp* : a circular ornament

cir·cuit \'sər-kət\ *n* **1** : a boundary around an enclosed space **2** : a moving or revolving around (as in an orbit) **3** : a regular tour (as by a judge) around an assigned territory **4** : the complete path of an electric current **5** : LEAGUE; *also* : a chain of theaters — **cir·cuit·al** \-kət-ᵊl\ *adj*

circuit breaker *n* : a switch that automatically interrupts an electric circuit under an abnormal condition

circuit court *n* : a court that sits at two or more places within one judicial district

cir·cu·itous \ˌsər-'kyü-ət-əs\ *adj* **1** : not being forthright or direct in language or action **2** : having a circular or winding course

cir·cuit·ry \'sər-kə-trē\ *n, pl* **-ries** : the plan or the components of an electric circuit

cir·cu·ity \ˌsər-'kyü-ət-ē\ *n, pl* **-ities** : INDIRECTION

¹**cir·cu·lar** \'sər-kyə-lər\ *adj* **1** : having the form of a circle : ROUND **2** : moving in or around a circle **3** : CIRCUITOUS **4** : sent around to a number of persons ⟨a ~ letter⟩ — **cir·cu·lar·i·ty** \'sər-kyə-'lar-ət-ē\ *n*

²**circular** *n* : a paper (as an advertising leaflet) intended for wide distribution

cir·cu·lar·ize \'sər-kyə-lə-ˌrīz\ *vb* **-ized;** **-iz·ing 1** : to send circulars to **2** : to poll by questionnaire

circular saw *n* : a power saw with a round cutting blade

cir·cu·late \'sər-kyə-ˌlāt\ *vb* **-lat·ed; -lat·ing 1** : to move or cause to move in a circle, circuit, or orbit **2** : to pass from place to place or from person to person — **cir·cu·la·tion** \ˌsər-kyə-'lā-shən\ *n*

cir·cu·la·to·ry \'sər-kyə-lə-ˌtōr-ē\ *adj* : of or relating to circulation or the circulatory system

circulatory system *n* : the system of blood, blood vessels, lymphatic vessels, and heart concerned with the circulation of the blood and lymph

cir·cum·am·bu·late \ˌsər-kəm-'am-byə-ˌlāt\ *vb* **-lat·ed; -lat·ing** : to circle on foot esp. ritualistically

cir·cum·cise \'sər-kəm-ˌsīz\ *vb* **-cised;** **-cis·ing** : to cut off the foreskin of — **cir·cum·ci·sion** \ˌsər-kəm-'sizh-ən\ *n*

cir·cum·fer·ence \sər-'kəm-f(ə-)rəns\ *n* **1** : the perimeter of a circle **2** : the external boundary or surface of a figure or object

cir·cum·flex \'sər-kəm-ˌfleks\ *n* : the mark ^ over a vowel

cir·cum·lo·cu·tion \ˌsər-kəm-lō-'kyü-shən\ *n* : the use of unnecessary words in expressing an idea

cir·cum·lu·nar \-'lü-nər\ *adj* : revolving about or surrounding the moon

cir·cum·nav·i·gate \-'nav-ə-ˌgāt\ *vb* : to go completely around esp. by water — **cir·cum·nav·i·ga·tion** \-ˌnav-ə-'gā-shən\ *n*

cir·cum·po·lar \-'pō-lər\ *adj* **1** : continually visible above the horizon ⟨a ~ star⟩ **2** : surrounding or found near a terrestrial pole

cir·cum·scribe \'sər-kəm-ˌskrīb\ *vb* **1** : to limit narrowly the range or activity of **2** : to draw a line around — **cir·cum·scrip·tion** \ˌsər-kəm-'skrip-shən\ *n*

cir·cum·spect \'sər-kəm-ˌspekt\ *adj* : careful to consider all circumstances and consequences : PRUDENT — **cir·cum·spec·tion** \ˌsər-kəm-'spek-shən\ *n*

cir·cum·stance \'sər-kəm-ˌstans\ *n* **1** : a fact or event that must be considered along with another fact or event **2** : surrounding conditions **3** *pl* : situation with regard to wealth **4** : CEREMONY **5** : CHANCE, FATE

cir·cum·stan·tial \ˌsər-kəm-ˈstan-chəl\ *adj* **1** : consisting of or depending on circumstances **2** : INCIDENTAL **3** : containing full details — **cir·cum·stan·tial·ly** \-ē\ *adv*

cir·cum·vent \ˌsər-kəm-ˈvent\ *vb* : to check or defeat esp. by stratagem

cir·cus \ˈsər-kəs\ *n* **1** : a usu. traveling show that features feats of physical skill and daring, wild animal acts, and performances by clowns **2** : a circus performance; *also* : the equipment, livestock, and personnel of a circus

cirque \ˈsərk\ *n* : a deep steep-walled mountain basin shaped like half a bowl

cir·rho·sis \sə-ˈrō-səs\ *n, pl* **-rho·ses** \-ˌsēz\ [NL, fr. Gk *kirrhos* orange colored] : fibrosis esp. of the liver — **cir·rhot·ic** \-ˈrät-ik\ *adj or n*

cir·rus \ˈsir-əs\ *n, pl* **cir·ri** \ˈsir-ˌī\ : a wispy white cloud usu. of minute ice crystals at high altitudes

cis·lu·nar \(ˈ)sis-ˈlü-nər\ *adj* : lying between the earth and the moon or the moon's orbit

cis·tern \ˈsis-tərn\ *n* : an often underground tank for storing water

cit *abbr* **1** citation; cited **2** citizen

cit·a·del \ˈsit-əd-ᵊl, -ə-ˌdel\ *n* **1** : a fortress commanding a city **2** : STRONGHOLD

ci·ta·tion \sī-ˈtā-shən\ *n* **1** : an official summons to appear (as before a court) **2** : QUOTATION **3** : a formal statement of the achievements of a person; *also* : a specific reference in a military dispatch to meritorious performance of duty

cite \ˈsīt\ *vb* **cit·ed; cit·ing** **1** : to summon to appear before a court **2** : QUOTE **3** : to refer to esp. in commendation or praise

citi·fied \ˈsit-i-ˌfīd\ *adj* : of, relating to, or characterized by an urban style of living

cit·i·zen \ˈsit-ə-zən\ *n* **1** : an inhabitant of a city or town **2** : a person who owes allegiance to a government and is entitled to government protection — **cit·i·zen·ship** *n*

cit·i·zen·ry \-rē\ *n, pl* **-ries** : a whole body of citizens

citizens band *n* : a range of radio frequencies set aside for private radio communications

cit·ric acid \ˌsit-rik-\ *n* : a sour organic acid obtained from lemon and lime juices or by fermentation of sugars and used as a flavoring

cit·ron \ˈsit-rən\ *n* **1** : the oval lemonlike fruit of an Asian citrus tree **2** : a small hard-fleshed watermelon used esp. in pickles and preserves

cit·ro·nel·la \ˌsit-rə-ˈnel-ə\ *n* : an oil obtained from a grass of southern Asia and used in perfumes and as an insect repellent

cit·rus \ˈsit-rəs\ *n, pl* **citrus** *or* **cit·rus·es** : any of a genus of often thorny evergreen trees or shrubs grown in warm regions for their fruits (as the orange, lemon, lime, and grapefruit)

city \ˈsit-ē\ *n, pl* **cit·ies** [ME *citie* large or small town, fr. OF *cité* capital city, fr. ML *civitas*, fr. L, citizenship, state, city of Rome, fr. *civis* citizen] **1** : an inhabited place larger or more important than a town **2** : a municipality in the U.S. governed under a charter granted by the state; *also* : an incorporated municipal unit of the highest class in Canada

city manager *n* : an official employed by an elected council to direct the administration of a city government

city–state \ˈsit-ē-ˈstāt, -ˌstāt\ *n* : an autonomous state consisting of a city and surrounding territory

civ *abbr* civil; civilian

civ·et \ˈsiv-ət\ *n* : a yellowish strong smelling substance obtained from a catlike mammal (**civet cat**) of Africa or Asia and used in making perfumes

civic \ˈsiv-ik\ *adj* : of or relating to a city, citizenship, or civil affairs

civ·ics \-iks\ *n* : a social science dealing with the rights and duties of citizens

civ·il \ˈsiv-əl\ *adj* **1** : of or relating to citizens or to the state as a political body **2** : COURTEOUS, POLITE **3** : of or relating to legal proceedings in connection with private rights and obligations ⟨the ∼ code⟩ **4** : of or relating to the general population : not military or ecclesiastical

civil defense *n* : the protective measures and emergency relief activities conducted by civilians in case of hostile attack, sabotage, or natural disaster

civil disobedience *n* : refusal to obey governmental commands esp. as a nonviolent means of protest

civil engineer *n* : an engineer whose training or occupation is in the designing and construction chiefly of public works (as roads or harbors) — **civil engineering** *n*

ci·vil·ian \sə-'vil-yən\ *n* : a person not on active duty in a military, police, or fire-fighting force

ci·vil·i·ty \sə-'vil-ət-ē\ *n, pl* **-ties 1** : POLITENESS, COURTESY **2** : a polite act or expression

civ·i·li·za·tion \ˌsiv-ə-lə-'zā-shən\ *n* **1** : a relatively high level of cultural and technological development **2** : the culture characteristic of a time or place

civ·i·lize \'siv-ə-ˌlīz\ *vb* **-lized; -liz·ing 1** : to raise from a primitive state to an advanced and ordered stage of cultural development **2** : REFINE — **civ·i·lized** *adj*

civil liberty *n* : freedom from arbitrary governmental interference specifically by denial of governmental power — usu. used in pl.

civ·il·ly \'siv-ə(l)-lē\ *adv* **1** : in terms of civil rights, matters, or law ⟨∼ dead⟩ **2** : in a civil manner : POLITELY

civil rights *n pl* : the nonpolitical rights of a citizen; *esp* : those guaranteed by the 13th and 14th amendments to the Constitution and by acts of Congress

civil servant *n* : a member of a civil service

civil service *n* : the administrative service of a government

civil war *n* : a war between opposing groups of citizens of the same country

civ·vies \'siv-ēz\ *n pl* : civilian clothes as distinguished from a military uniform

CJ *abbr* chief justice

ck *abbr* **1** cask **2** check

cl *abbr* class

Cl *symbol* chlorine

¹clack \'klak\ *vb* **1** : CHATTER, PRATTLE **2** : to make or cause to make a clatter

²clack *n* **1** : rapid continuous talk : CHATTER **2** : a sound of clacking ⟨the ∼ of a typewriter⟩

clad \'klad\ *adj* **1** : CLOTHED, COVERED **2** : being or consisting of coins made of outer layers of one metal bonded to a core of a different metal ⟨∼ coinage⟩

¹claim \'klām\ *vb* **1** : to ask for as one's own; *also* : to take as the rightful owner **2** : to call for : REQUIRE **3** : to state as a fact : MAINTAIN

²claim *n* **1** : a demand for something due **2** : a right to something usu. in another's possession **3** : an assertion open to challenge **4** : something claimed

claim·ant \'klā-mənt\ *n* : a person making a claim

clair·voy·ant \klar-'vȯi-ənt\ *adj* [F, fr. *clair* clear + *voyant* seeing] **1** : unusually perceptive **2** : having the power of discerning objects not present to the senses — **clair·voy·ance** \-əns\ *n* — **clairvoyant** *n*

clam \'klam\ *n* **1** : any of numerous bivalve mollusks including many that are edible **2** : DOLLAR

clam·bake \-ˌbāk\ *n* : a party or gathering (as at the seashore) at which food is cooked usu. on heated rocks covered by seaweed

clam·ber \'klam-bər\ *vb* **clam·bered; clam·ber·ing** \'klam-b(ə-)riŋ, 'klam-(ə-)riŋ\ : to climb awkwardly (as by scrambling)

clam·my \'klam-ē\ *adj* **clam·mi·er; -est** : being damp, soft, sticky, and usu. cool — **clam·mi·ness** *n*

¹clam·or \'klam-ər\ *n* **1** : a noisy shouting **2** : a loud continuous noise **3** : vigorous protest or demand — **clam·or·ous** *adj*

²clamor *vb* **clam·ored; clam·or·ing** \'klam-(ə-)riŋ\ : to make a clamor

¹clamp \'klamp\ *n* : a device that holds or presses parts together firmly

²clamp *vb* : to fasten with or as if with a clamp

clamp down \(')klamp-'daủn\ *vb* : to impose restrictions : become repressive — **clamp·down** \'klamp-ˌdaủn\ *n*

clam·shell \'klam-ˌshel\ *n* : a bucket or grapple (as on a dredge) having two hinged jaws

clam up *vb* : to become silent

clan \'klan\ *n* [ME, fr. ScGael *clann* offspring, clan, fr. Old Irish *cland* plant, offspring, fr. L *planta* plant] : a group (as in the Scottish Highlands) made up of households whose heads claim descent from a common ancestor — **clan·nish** *adj* — **clan·nish·ness** *n*

clan·des·tine \klan-'des-tən\ *adj* : held in or conducted with secrecy

clang \'klaŋ\ *n* : a loud metallic ringing sound — **clang** *vb*

clan·gor \'klaŋ-(g)ər\ *n* : a resounding clang or medley of clangs

clank \'klaŋk\ *n* : a sharp brief metallic ringing sound — **clank** *vb*

¹**clap** \'klap\ *vb* **clapped; clap·ping** 1 : to strike noisily 2 : APPLAUD

²**clap** *n* 1 : a loud noisy crash 2 : the noise made by clapping the hands

³**clap** *n* : GONORRHEA

clap·board \'klab-ərd; 'kla(p)-,bōrd\ *n* : a narrow board thicker at one edge than the other used for siding — **clap·board** *vb*

clap·per \'klap-ər\ *n* : one that makes a clapping sound; *esp* : the tongue of a bell

clap·trap \'klap-,trap\ *n* : pretentious nonsense

claque \'klak\ *n* [F, fr. *claquer* to clap] 1 : a group hired to applaud at a performance 2 : a group of self-seeking flatterers

clar·et \'klar-ət\ *n* [ME, fr. MF (*vin*) *claret* clear wine] : a dry red wine

clar·i·fy \'klar-ə-,fī\ *vb* **-fied; -fy·ing** : to make or become clear — **clar·i·fi·ca·tion** \,klar-ə-fə-'kā-shən\ *n*

clar·i·net \,klar-ə-'net\ *n* : a single-reed woodwind instrument in the form of a cylindrical tube with moderately flaring end — **clar·i·net·ist** *or* **clar·i·net·tist** \-əst\ *n*

clar·i·on \'klar-ē-ən\ *adj* : brilliantly clear ⟨a ∼ call to action⟩

clar·i·ty \'klar-ət-ē\ *n* : CLEARNESS

¹**clash** \'klash\ *vb* 1 : to make or cause to make a clash 2 : CONFLICT, COLLIDE

²**clash** *n* 1 : a noisy usu. metallic sound of collision 2 : a hostile encounter; *also* : a conflict of opinion

¹**clasp** \'klasp\ *n* 1 : a device (as a hook) for holding objects or parts together 2 : EMBRACE, GRASP

²**clasp** *vb* 1 : to fasten with a clasp 2 : EMBRACE 3 : GRASP

¹**class** \'klas\ *n* 1 : a group of students meeting regularly in a course; *also* : a group graduating together 2 : a course of instruction; *also* : the period when such a course is taught 3 : social rank; *also* : high quality 4 : a group of the same general status or nature; *esp* : a major category in biological classification that is above the order and below the phylum 5 : a division or rating based on grade or quality — **class·less** *adj*

²**class** *vb* : CLASSIFY

class action *n* : a legal action undertaken in behalf of the plaintiffs and all others having an identical interest in the alleged wrong

¹**clas·sic** \'klas-ik\ *adj* 1 : serving as a standard of excellence; *also* : TRADITIONAL 2 : CLASSICAL 2 3 : notable esp. as the best example 4 : AUTHENTIC

²**classic** *n* 1 : a work of enduring excellence and esp. of ancient Greece or Rome; *also* : its author 2 : a traditional event

clas·si·cal \'klas-i-kəl\ *adj* 1 : CLASSIC 2 : of or relating to the ancient Greek and Roman classics 3 : of or relating to a form or system of primary significance before modern times ⟨∼ economics⟩ 4 : concerned with a general study of the arts and sciences — **clas·si·cal·ly** \-k(ə-)lē\ *adv*

clas·si·cism \'klas-ə-,siz-əm\ *n* 1 : the principles or style of the literature or art of ancient Greece and Rome 2 : adherence to traditional standards believed to be universally valid — **clas·si·cist** \-səst\ *n*

clas·si·fied \'klas-ə-,fīd\ *adj* : withheld from general circulation for reasons of national security

clas·si·fy \'klas-ə-,fī\ *vb* **-fied; -fy·ing** : to arrange in or assign to classes — **clas·si·fi·able** *adj* — **clas·si·fi·ca·tion** \,klas-ə-fə-'kā-shən\ *n*

class·mate \'klas-,māt\ *n* : a member of the same class (as in a college)

class·room \-,rüm-, -,rùm\ *n* : a room (as in a school) in which classes meet

classy \'klas-ē\ *adj* **class·i·er; -est** : ELEGANT, STYLISH

clat·ter \'klat-ər\ *n* : a rattling sound ⟨the ∼ of dishes⟩ — **clatter** *vb*

clause \'klȯz\ *n* 1 : a group of words having its own subject and predicate but forming only part of a compound or complex sentence 2 : a separate part of an article or document

claus·tro·pho·bia \,klȯ-strə-'fō-bē-ə\ *n* : abnormal dread of being in closed or narrow spaces — **claus·tro·pho·bic** \-bik\ *adj*

clav·i·chord \'klav-ə-ˌkȯrd\ *n* : an early keyboard instrument in use before the piano

clav·i·cle \'klav-i-kəl\ *n* [F *clavicule*, fr. NL *clavicula*, fr. L, dim. of L *clavis* key] : COLLARBONE

cla·vier \klə-'viər; 'klā-vē-ər\ *n* 1 : the keyboard of a musical instrument 2 : an early keyboard instrument

¹**claw** \'klȯ\ *n* 1 : a sharp usu. curved nail on the toe of an animal 2 : a sharp curved process (as on the foot of an insect); *also* : a pincerlike organ at the end of a limb of some arthropods (as a lobster) — **clawed** \'klȯd\ *adj*

²**claw** *vb* : to rake, seize, or dig with or as if with claws

clay \'klā\ *n* 1 : an earthy material that is plastic when moist but hard when fired and is used in making pottery; *also* : finely divided soil consisting largely of such clay 2 : EARTH, MUD 3 : a plastic substance used for modeling 4 : the mortal human body — **clay·ey** \'klā-ē\ *adj*

clay·more \'klā-ˌmōr\ *n* : a large 2-edged sword formerly used by Scottish Highlanders

clay pigeon *n* : a saucer-shaped target thrown from a trap in trapshooting

¹**clean** \'klēn\ *adj* 1 : free from dirt or disease 2 : PURE; *also* : HONORABLE 3 : THOROUGH ⟨made a ~ sweep⟩ 4 : TRIM ⟨a ship with ~ lines⟩; *also* : EVEN 5 : habitually neat — **clean** *adv* — **clean·ly** \'klēn-lē\ *adv* — **clean·ness** \'klēn-nəs\ *n*

²**clean** *vb* : to make or become clean — **clean·er** *n*

clean–cut \'klēn-'kət\ *adj* 1 : cut so that the surface or edge is smooth and even 2 : sharply defined or outlined 3 : giving an effect of wholesomeness

clean·ly \'klen-lē\ *adj* **clean·li·er; -est** 1 : careful to keep clean 2 : habitually kept clean — **clean·li·ness** *n*

clean room \'klēn-ˌrüm, -ˌrum\ *n* : an uncontaminated room maintained for the manufacture or assembly of objects (as precision parts)

cleanse \'klenz\ *vb* **cleansed; cleans·ing** : to make clean — **cleans·er** *n*

¹**clean·up** \'klēn-ˌəp\ *n* 1 : an act or instance of cleaning 2 : a very large profit

²**cleanup** *adj* : being 4th in the batting order of a baseball team

clean up \(')klēn-'əp\ *vb* : to make a spectacular business profit

¹**clear** \'kliər\ *adj* 1 : BRIGHT, LUMINOUS; *also* : UNTROUBLED, SERENE 2 : CLOUDLESS 3 : CLEAN, PURE; *also* : TRANSPARENT 4 : easily heard, seen, or understood 5 : capable of sharp discernment; *also* : free from doubt 6 : INNOCENT 7 : free from restriction, obstruction, or entanglement — **clear** *adv* — **clear·ly** *adv* — **clear·ness** *n*

²**clear** *vb* 1 : to make or become clear 2 : to go away : DISPERSE 3 : to free from accusation or blame; *also* : to certify as trustworthy 4 : EXPLAIN 5 : to get free from obstruction 6 : SETTLE 7 : NET 8 : to get rid of : REMOVE 9 : to jump or go by without touching; *also* : PASS

³**clear** *n* : a clear space or part

clear·ance \'klir-əns\ *n* 1 : an act or process of clearing 2 : the distance by which one object clears another

clear–cut \'kliər-'kət\ *adj* 1 : sharply outlined 2 : DEFINITE, UNEQUIVOCAL

clear·head·ed \-'hed-əd\ *adj* : having a clear understanding : PERCEPTIVE

clear·ing \'kli(ə)r-iŋ\ *n* 1 : a tract of land cleared of wood and brush 2 : the passage of checks and claims through a clearinghouse

clear·ing·house \-ˌhaüs\ *n* : an institution maintained by banks for making an exchange of checks and claims held by each bank against other banks

cleat \'klēt\ *n* : a piece of wood or metal fastened on or projecting from something to give strength, provide a grip, or prevent slipping

cleav·age \'klē-vij\ *n* 1 : a splitting apart : SPLIT 2 : the depression between a woman's breasts esp. when exposed by a low-cut dress

¹**cleave** \'klēv\ *vb* **cleaved** \'klēvd\ *or* **clove** \'klōv\; **cleaved; cleav·ing** : ADHERE, CLING

²**cleave** *vb* **cleaved** \'klēvd\ *also* **cleft** \'kleft\ *or* **clove** \'klōv\; **cleaved** *also* **cleft** *or* **clo·ven** \'klō-vən\; **cleav·ing** 1 : to divide by force : split asunder 2 : DIVIDE

cleav•er \'klē-vər\ *n* : a heavy chopping knife for cutting meat

clef \'klef\ *n* : a sign placed on the staff in music to show what pitch is represented by each line and space

cleft \'kleft\ *n* : FISSURE, CRACK

cleft palate *n* : a split in the roof of the mouth that appears as a birth defect

clem•a•tis \'klem-ət-əs; kli-'mat-əs\ *n* : a vine related to the buttercups that has showy usu. white or purple flowers

clem•en•cy \'klem-ən-sē\ *n, pl* **-cies** **1** : disposition to be merciful **2** : mildness of weather

clem•ent \-ənt\ *adj* **1** : MERCIFUL, LENIENT **2** : TEMPERATE, MILD

clench \'klench\ *vb* **1** : CLINCH 1 **2** : to hold fast **3** : to set or close tightly

clere•sto•ry \'kliər-ˌstōr-ē\ *n* : an outside wall of a room or building that rises above an adjoining roof and contains windows

cler•gy \'klər-jē\ *n* : a body of religious officials authorized to conduct services

cler•gy•man \-ji-mən\ *n* : a member of the clergy

cler•ic \'kler-ik\ *n* : CLERGYMAN

cler•i•cal \'kler-i-kəl\ *adj* **1** : of or relating to the clergy or a clergyman **2** : of or relating to a clerk

cler•i•cal•ism \'kler-i-kə-ˌliz-əm\ *n* : a policy of maintaining or increasing the power of a religious hierarchy

clerk \'klərk, *Brit* 'klärk\ *n* **1** : CLERIC **2** : an official responsible for correspondence, records, and accounts; *also* : a person employed to perform general office work **3** : a store salesman — **clerk** *vb* — **clerk•ship** *n*

clev•er \'klev-ər\ *adj* **1** : showing skill or resourcefulness **2** : marked by wit or ingenuity — **clev•er•ly** *adv* — **clev•er•ness** *n*

clev•is \'klev-əs\ *n* : a U-shaped shackle used for attaching or suspending parts

¹clew \'klü\ *n* **1** : CLUE **2** : a metal loop on a lower corner of a sail for holding ropes

²clew *vb* : to haul (a sail) up or down by ropes through the clews

cli•ché \kli-'shā\ *n* [F] : a trite phrase or expression — **cli•chéd** \-'shād\ *adj*

¹click \'klik\ *vb* **1** : to make or cause to make a click **2** : to fit or work together smoothly

²click *n* : a slight sharp noise

cli•ent \'klī-ənt\ *n* **1** : DEPENDENT **2** : a person who engages the professional services of another; *also* : PATRON, CUSTOMER

cli•en•tele \ˌklī-ən-'tel, ˌklē-ən-\ *n* : a body of clients and esp. customers

cliff \'klif\ *n* : a high steep face of rock

cliff–hang•er \-ˌhaŋ-ər\ *n* **1** : an adventure serial or melodrama usu. presented in installments each of which ends in suspense **2** : a contest whose outcome is in doubt up to the very end

cli•mac•ter•ic \klī-'mak-t(ə-)rik\ *n* **1** : a major turning point or critical stage **2** : MENOPAUSE; *also* : a corresponding period in the male

cli•mate \'klī-mət\ *n* [ME *climat*, fr. MF, fr. LL *clima*, fr. Gk *klima* inclination, latitude, climate, fr. *klinein* to lean] **1** : a region having specific climatic conditions **2** : the average weather conditions at a place over a period of years **3** : the prevailing set of conditions (as temperature and humidity) indoors **4** : a prevailing atmosphere or environment ⟨the ∼ of opinion⟩ — **cli•mat•ic** \klī-'mat-ik\ *adj* — **cli•mat•i•cal•ly** \-i-k(ə-)lē\ *adv*

cli•ma•tol•o•gy \ˌklī-mə-'täl-ə-jē\ *n* : the science that deals with climates — **cli•ma•to•log•i•cal** \ˌklī-mət-ᵊl-'äj-i-kəl\ *adj* — **cli•ma•to•log•i•cal•ly** \-k(ə-)lē\ *adv* — **cli•ma•tol•o•gist** \-mə-'täl-ə-jəst\ *n*

¹cli•max \'klī-ˌmaks\ *n* [L, fr. Gk *klimax* ladder, fr. *klinein* to lean] **1** : a series of ideas or statements so arranged that they increase in force and power from the first to the last; *also* : the last member of such a series **2** : the highest point **3** : ORGASM — **cli•mac•tic** \klī-'mak-tik\ *adj*

²climax *vb* : to come or bring to a climax

¹climb \'klīm\ *vb* **1** : to rise to a higher point **2** : to go up or down esp. by use of hands and feet; *also* : to ascend in growing — **climb•er** *n*

²climb *n* **1** : a place where climbing is necessary **2** : the act of climbing : ascent by climbing

clime \'klīm\ *n* : CLIMATE

¹clinch \'klinch\ *vb* **1** : to turn over or flatten the end of something sticking out ⟨∼ a nail⟩; *also* : to fasten by clinching **2** : to make final : SETTLE **3** : to hold fast or firmly

²clinch *n* **1** : a fastening by means of a clinched nail, rivet, or bolt **2** : an act or instance of clinching in boxing

clinch·er \'klin-chər\ *n* : one that clinches; *esp* : a decisive fact, argument, act, or remark

cling \'kliŋ\ *vb* **clung** \'kleŋ\; **cling·ing** **1** : to adhere as if glued; *also* : to hold or hold on tightly **2** : to have a strong emotional attachment

cling·stone \'kliŋ-ˌstōn\ *n* : any of various fruits (as some peaches) whose flesh adheres strongly to the pit

clin·ic \'klin-ik\ *n* **1** : medical instruction featuring the examination and discussion of actual cases **2** : a group meeting for teaching a certain skill and working on individual problems ⟨a reading ∼⟩ **3** : a facility (as of a hospital) for diagnosis and treatment of outpatients

clin·i·cal \'klin-i-kəl\ *adj* **1** : of, relating to, or typical of a clinic; *esp* : involving direct observation of the patient **2** : scientifically dispassionate — **clin·i·cal·ly** \-k(ə-)lē\ *adv*

cli·ni·cian \klin-'ish-ən\ *n* : one qualified in the clinical practice of medicine, psychiatry, or psychology as distinguished from one specializing in laboratory or research techniques

¹clink \'kliŋk\ *vb* : to make or cause to make a sharp short metallic sound

²clink *n* : a clinking sound

clin·ker \'kliŋ-kər\ *n* : stony matter fused by fire (as in a furnace from impurities in coal) : SLAG

¹clip \'klip\ *vb* **clipped; clip·ping** : to fasten with a clip

²clip *n* **1** : a device that grips, clasps, or hooks **2** : a cartridge holder for a rifle

³clip *vb* **clipped; clip·ping** **1** : to cut or cut off with shears **2** : CURTAIL, DIMINISH **3** : HIT, PUNCH **4** : to illegally block (an opponent) in football

⁴clip *n* **1** : a 2-bladed instrument for cutting esp. the nails **2** : a sharp blow **3** : a rapid pace

clip·board \'klip-ˌbōrd\ *n* : a small writing board with a spring clip at the top for holding papers

clip joint *n, slang* : an establishment (as a nightclub) that makes a practice of defrauding its customers

clip·per \'klip-ər\ *n* **1** : an implement for clipping esp. the hair or nails — usu. used in pl. **2** : a fast sailing ship

clip·ping \'klip-iŋ\ *n* : a piece clipped from something (as a newspaper)

clique \'klēk, 'klik\ *n* [F] : a small exclusive group of people : COTERIE — **cliqu·ey** \'klēk-ē, 'klik-\ *adj* — **cliqu·ish** \-ish\ *adj*

cli·to·ris \'klit-ə-rəs\ *n, pl* **cli·to·ri·des** \kli-'tōr-ə-ˌdēz\ : a small organ at the anterior or ventral part of the vulva homologous to the penis — **cli·to·ral** \-rəl\ *adj*

clk *abbr* clerk

clo *abbr* clothing

¹cloak \'klōk\ *n* **1** : a loose outer garment **2** : something that conceals

²cloak *vb* : to cover or hide with a cloak

cloak–and–dag·ger *adj* : involving or suggestive of espionage

clob·ber \'kläb-ər\ *vb* **clob·bered; clob·ber·ing** \-(ə-)riŋ\ **1** : to pound mercilessly; *also* : to hit with force : SMASH **2** : to defeat overwhelmingly

cloche \'klōsh\ *n* [F, lit., bell] : a woman's small hat that somewhat resembles a helmet

¹clock \'kläk\ *n* : a timepiece not intended to be carried on the person

²clock *vb* **1** : to time (a person or a performance) by a timing device **2** : to register (as speed) on a mechanical recording device — **clock·er** *n*

³clock *n* : an ornamental figure on a stocking or sock

clock·wise \'kläk-ˌwīz\ *adv* : in the direction in which the hands of a clock move — **clockwise** *adj*

clock·work \-ˌwərk\ *n* : machinery containing a set of small cogwheels

clod \'kläd\ *n* **1** : a lump esp. of earth or clay **2** : a dull or insensitive person

clod·hop·per \-ˌhäp-ər\ *n* **1** : an uncouth rustic **2** : a large heavy shoe

¹clog \'kläg\ *n* **1** : a weight so attached as to impede motion **2** : a thick-soled shoe

²clog *vb* **clogged; clog·ging** **1** : to impede with a clog : HINDER **2** : to obstruct passage through **3** : to become filled with extraneous matter

cloi·son·né \ˌklȯiz-ᵊn-'ā\ *adj* : a colored decoration made of enamels poured into the divided areas in a design outlined with wire or metal strips

¹**clois•ter** \'klȯi-stər\ *n* [ME *cloistre,* fr. OF, fr. ML *claustrum,* fr. L, bar, bolt, fr. *claudere* to close] **1** : a monastic establishment **2** : a covered usu. colonnaded passage on the side of a court — **clois•tral** \-strəl\ *adj*

²**cloister** *vb* : to shut away from the world

clone \'klōn\ *n* [Gk *klōn* twig] **1** : the offspring produced asexually from an individual (as a plant increased by grafting) **2** : an individual grown from a single body cell of its parent and genetically identical to the parent **3** : one that appears to be a copy of an original form — **clon•al** \'klōn-ᵊl\ *adj* — **clone** *vb*

clop \'kläp\ *n* : a sound made by or as if by a hoof or wooden shoe against pavement — **clop** *vb*

¹**close** \'klōz\ *vb* **closed; clos•ing 1** : to bar passage through : SHUT **2** : to suspend the operations (as of a school) **3** : END, TERMINATE **4** : to bring together the parts or edges of; *also* : to fill up **5** : GRAPPLE ⟨∼ with the enemy⟩ **6** : to enter into an agreement — **clos•able** *or* **close•able** *adj*

²**close** \'klōz\ *n* : CONCLUSION, END

³**close** \'klōs\ *adj* **clos•er; clos•est 1** : having no openings **2** : narrowly restricting or restricted **3** : limited to a privileged class **4** : SECLUDED; *also* : SECRETIVE **5** : RIGOROUS **6** : SULTRY, STUFFY **7** : STINGY **8** : having little space between items or units **9** : fitting tightly; *also* : SHORT ⟨∼ haircut⟩ **10** : NEAR **11** : INTIMATE ⟨∼ friends⟩ **12** : ACCURATE **13** : decided by a narrow margin ⟨a ∼ game⟩ — **close** *adv* — **close•ly** *adv* — **close•ness** *n*

closed circuit *n* : television installation in which the signal is transmitted by wire to a limited number of receivers

closed shop *n* : an establishment having only members of a labor union on the payroll

close•fist•ed \'klōs-'fis-təd\ *adj* : STINGY

close–knit \-'nit\ *adj* : closely bound together by social, cultural, economic, or political ties

close•mouthed \-'mau̇thd, -'mau̇tht\ *adj* : cautious in speaking

close•out \'klōz-ˌau̇t\ *n* : a sale of a business's entire stock at low prices

close out \'klōz-'au̇t\ *vb* **1** : to dispose of by a closeout **2** : to dispose of a business : sell out

¹**clos•et** \'kläz-ət, 'klȯz-\ *n* **1** : a small room for privacy **2** : a small compartment for household utensils or clothing **3** : WATER CLOSET

²**closet** *vb* : to take into a private room for an interview

close–up \'klōs-ˌəp\ *n* **1** : a photograph or movie shot taken at close range **2** : an intimate view or examination of something

clo•sure \'klō-zhər\ *n* **1** : an act of closing : the condition of being closed **2** : something that closes **3** : CLOTURE

clot \'klät\ *n* : a mass formed by a portion of liquid (as blood or cream) thickening and sticking together — **clot** *vb*

cloth \'klȯth\ *n, pl* **cloths** \'klȯthz, 'klȯths\ **1** : a pliable fabric made usu. by weaving or knitting natural or synthetic fibers and filaments **2** : TABLECLOTH **3** : distinctive dress of the clergy; *also* : CLERGY

clothe \'klōth\ *vb* **clothed** *or* **clad** \'klad\; **cloth•ing 1** : DRESS **2** : to express by suitably significant language

clothes \'klō(th)z\ *n pl* **1** : CLOTHING **2** : BEDCLOTHES

clothes•horse \-ˌhȯrs\ *n* **1** : a frame on which to hang clothes **2** : a conspicuously dressy person

clothes moth *n* : a small pale insect whose larvae eat wool, fur, and feathers

clothes•pin \'klō(th)z-ˌpin\ *n* : a device for fastening clothes on a line

clothes•press \-ˌpres\ *n* : a receptacle for clothes

cloth•ier \'klōth-yər, 'klō-thē-ər\ *n* : a maker or seller of clothing

cloth•ing \'klō-thiŋ\ *n* : garments in general

clo•ture \'klō-chər\ *n* : the closing or limitation (as by calling for a vote) of debate in a legislative body

¹**cloud** \'klau̇d\ *n* [ME, rock, cloud, fr. OE *clūd* rock, hill] **1** : a visible mass of water or ice particles usu. high in the air **2** : a usu. visible mass of minute airborne particles; *also* : a mass of obscuring matter in interstellar space **3** : CROWD, SWARM ⟨a ∼ of

mosquitoes⟩ **4** : something having a dark or threatening aspect — **cloud·i·ness** \-ē-nəs\ *n* — **cloud·less** *adj* — **cloudy** *adj*

²cloud *vb* **1** : to darken or hide with or as if with a cloud **2** : OBSCURE **3** : TAINT, SULLY

cloud·burst \-,bərst\ *n* : a sudden heavy rainfall

cloud·let \-lət\ *n* : a small cloud

cloud nine *n* : a feeling of extreme well-being or elation — usu. used with *on*

¹clout \'klaut\ *n* **1** : a blow esp. with the hand **2** : PULL, INFLUENCE

²clout *vb* : to hit forcefully

¹clove \'klōv\ *n* : one of the small bulbs that grows at the base of the scales of a large bulb ⟨a ∼ of garlic⟩

²clove past of CLEAVE

³clove *n* [ME *clowe,* fr. OF *clou (de giro-fle),* lit., nail of clove, fr. L *clavus* nail] : the dried flower bud of an East Indian tree used esp. as a spice

clo·ven \'klō-vən\ past part of CLEAVE

cloven foot *n* : a foot (as of a sheep) with the front part divided into two parts — **cloven–foot·ed** \-'fut-əd\ *adj*

cloven hoof *n* : CLOVEN FOOT — **cloven–hoofed** \-'huft, -'huvd\ *adj*

clo·ver \'klō-vər\ *n* : any of a genus of leguminous herbs with usu. 3-parted leaves and dense flower heads

clo·ver·leaf \-,lēf\ *n, pl* **cloverleafs** \-,lēfs\ *or* **clo·ver·leaves** \-,lēvz\ : a road plan passing one highway over another and routing turning traffic without left turns or direct crossings

¹clown \'klaun\ *n* **1** : BOOR **2** : a fool or comedian in an entertainment (as a circus) — **clown·ish** *adj* — **clown·ish·ly** *adv* — **clown·ish·ness** *n*

²clown *vb* : to act like a clown

cloy \'kloi\ *vb* : to disgust or nauseate with excess of something orig. pleasing — **cloy·ing·ly** \-iŋ-lē\ *adv*

clr *abbr* clear

¹club \'kləb\ *n* **1** : a heavy wooden stick or staff used as a weapon; *also* : BAT **2** : any of a suit of playing cards marked with a black figure resembling a clover leaf **3** : a group of persons associated for a common purpose; *also* : the meeting place of such a group

²club *vb* **clubbed; club·bing** **1** : to strike with a club **2** : to unite or combine for a common cause

club·foot \'kləb-'fut\ *n* : a misshapen foot twisted out of position from birth — **club·foot·ed** \-'fut-əd\ *adj*

club·house \'kləb-,haus\ *n* **1** : a house occupied by a club **2** : locker rooms used by an athletic team

club sandwich *n* : a sandwich of three slices of bread with two layers of meat and lettuce, tomato, and mayonnaise

club soda *n* : SODA WATER 1

club steak *n* : a small steak cut from the end of the short loin

cluck \'klək\ *n* : the call of a hen esp. to her chicks — **cluck** *vb*

¹clue \'klü\ *n* : something that guides through an intricate procedure or maze; *esp* : a piece of evidence leading to the solution of a problem

²clue *vb* **clued; clue·ing** *or* **clu·ing** : to provide with a clue; *also* : to give information to ⟨∼ me in⟩

¹clump \'kləmp\ *n* **1** : a group of things clustered together **2** : a heavy tramping sound

²clump *vb* : to tread clumsily and noisily

clum·sy \'kləm-zē\ *adj* **clum·si·er; -est** **1** : lacking dexterity, nimbleness, or grace **2** : not tactful or subtle — **clum·si·ly** \'kləm-zə-lē\ *adv* — **clum·si·ness** \-zē-nəs\ *n*

clung past and past part of CLING

¹clus·ter \'kləs-tər\ *n* : GROUP, BUNCH

²cluster *vb* **clus·tered; clus·ter·ing** \-t(ə-)riŋ\ : to grow or gather in a cluster

¹clutch \'kləch\ *vb* : to grasp with or as if with the hand

²clutch *n* **1** : the claws or a hand in the act of grasping; *also* : CONTROL, POWER **2** : a device for gripping an object **3** : a coupling used to connect and disconnect a driving and a driven part of a mechanism; *also* : a lever or pedal operating such a coupling **4** : a crucial situation

³clutch *adj* : made, done, or successful in a crucial situation

⁴clutch *n* **1** : a nest or batch of eggs; *also* : a brood of chicks **2** : GROUP, BUNCH

¹clut·ter \'klət-ər\ *vb* : to fill or cover with a disorderly scattering of things

²clutter *n* : a crowded mass

cm *abbr* centimeter

Cm *symbol* curium

CM *abbr* [Commonwealth of the Northern Mariana Islands] Northern Mariana Islands

cmdr *abbr* commander

cml *abbr* commercial

CMSgt *abbr* chief master sergeant

CNO *abbr* chief of naval operations

CNS *abbr* central nervous system

co *abbr* **1** company **2** county

Co *symbol* cobalt

CO *abbr* **1** Colorado **2** commanding officer **3** conscientious objector

c/o *abbr* care of

¹coach \ˈkōch\ *n* **1** : a large closed 4-wheeled carriage with an elevated outside front seat for the driver **2** : a railroad passenger car esp. for day travel **3** : BUS **4** : a private tutor; *also* : one who instructs or trains a team of performers

²coach *vb* **1** : to go in a horse-drawn coach **2** : to instruct, direct, or prompt as a coach — **coach·er** *n*

coach·man \-mən\ *n* : a man whose business is driving a coach or carriage

co·ad·ju·tor \ˌkō-ə-ˈjüt-ər, kō-ˈaj-ət-ər\ *n* : ASSISTANT; *esp* : an assistant bishop having the right of succession

co·ag·u·lant \kō-ˈag-yə-lənt\ *n* : something that produces coagulation

co·ag·u·late \kō-ˈag-yə-ˌlāt\ *vb* **-lat·ed; -lat·ing** : CLOT — **co·ag·u·la·tion** \kō-ˌag-yə-ˈlā-shən\ *n*

¹coal \ˈkōl\ *n* **1** : EMBER **2** : a black solid combustible mineral used as fuel

²coal *vb* **1** : to supply with coal **2** : to take in coal

co·alesce \ˌkō-ə-ˈles\ *vb* **co·alesced; co·alesc·ing** : to grow together; *also* : FUSE **syn** merge, blend, mingle, mix — **co·ales·cence** \-ˈles-ᵊns\ *n*

coal·field \ˈkōl-ˌfēld\ *n* : a region where deposits of coal occur

coal gas *n* : gas from coal; *esp* : gas distilled from bituminous coal and used for heating

co·ali·tion \ˌkō-ə-ˈlish-ən\ *n* : UNION; *esp* : a temporary union for a common purpose — **co·ali·tion·ist** *n*

coal oil *n* : KEROSENE

coal tar *n* : tar distilled from bituminous coal and used in dyes and drugs

co–an·chor \ˈkō-ˈaŋ-kər\ *n* : a newscaster who shares the duties of head broadcaster

coarse \ˈkōrs\ *adj* **coars·er; coars·est 1**

: of ordinary or inferior quality **2** : composed of large parts or particles ⟨∼ sand⟩ **3** : CRUDE ⟨∼ manners⟩ **4** : ROUGH, HARSH — **coarse·ly** *adv* — **coarse·ness** *n*

coars·en \ˈkōrs-ᵊn\ *vb* **coars·ened; coars·en·ing** \ˈkōrs-(ᵊ-)niŋ\ : to make or become coarse

¹coast \ˈkōst\ *n* [ME *cost*, fr. MF *coste*, fr. L *costa* rib, side] **1** : SEASHORE **2** : a slide down a slope — **coast·al** *adj*

²coast *vb* **1** : to sail along the shore **2** : to move (as downhill on a sled or as on a bicycle while not pedaling) without effort

coast·er *n* **1** : one that coasts **2** : a shallow container or a plate or mat to protect a surface

coaster brake *n* : a brake in the hub of the rear wheel of a bicycle

coast guard *n* : a military force employed in guarding or patrolling a coast — **coast·guards·man** \ˈkōst-ˌgärdz-mən\ *n*

coast·line \ˈkōst-ˌlīn\ *n* : the outline or shape of a coast

¹coat \ˈkōt\ *n* **1** : an outer garment for the upper part of the body **2** : an external growth (as of fur or feathers) on an animal **3** : a covering layer

²coat *vb* : to cover usu. with a finishing or protective coat

coat·ing \ˈkōt-iŋ\ *n* : COAT, COVERING

coat of arms : the heraldic bearings (as of a person) usu. depicted on an escutcheon

coat of mail : a garment of metal scales or rings worn as armor

co·au·thor \ˈkō-ˈȯ-thər\ *n* : a joint or associate author — **coauthor** *vb*

coax \ˈkōks\ *vb* : WHEEDLE; *also* : to gain by gentle urging or flattery

co·ax·i·al \ˈkō-ˈak-sē-əl\ *adj* : having coincident axes — **co·ax·i·al·ly** \-ē\ *adv*

coaxial cable *n* : a cable that consists of a tube of electrically conducting material surrounding a central conductor

cob \ˈkäb\ *n* **1** : a male swan **2** : CORN-COB **3** : a short-legged stocky horse

co·balt \ˈkō-ˌbȯlt\ *n* [G *kobalt*, alter. of *kobold*, lit., goblin, fr. its occurrence in silver ore, believed to be due to goblins] : a tough shiny silver-white magnetic metallic chemical element found with iron and nickel

cobalt chloride *n* : a chloride of cobalt; *esp* : one that is blue when dry, turns deep pink in the presence of moisture, and is used to indicate humidity

cob•ble \\'käb-əl\ *vb* **cob•bled; cob•bling** \\-(ə-)liŋ\ : to make or put together roughly or hastily

cob•bler \\'käb-lər\ *n* **1** : a mender or maker of shoes **2** : a deep-dish fruit pie with a thick crust

cob•ble•stone \\'käb-əl-ˌstōn\ *n* : a naturally rounded stone larger than a pebble and smaller than a boulder

co•bra \\'kō-brə\ *n* : any of several venomous snakes of Asia and Africa that when excited expand the skin of the neck into a broad hood

cob•web \\'käb-ˌweb\ *n* [ME *coppeweb,* fr. *coppe* spider, fr. OE ātor*coppe*] **1** : SPIDERWEB; *also* : a thread spun by a spider or insect larva **2** : something flimsy or entangling

co•caine \kō-'kān, 'kō-ˌkān\ *n* : a drug that is obtained from the leaves of a So. American shrub (**co•ca** \\'kō-kə\), can result in severe psychological dependence, and is sometimes used as a local anesthetic

coc•cus \\'käk-əs\ *n, pl* **coc•ci** \\'käk-ˌ(s)ī\ : a spherical bacterium

coc•cyx \\'käk-siks\ *n, pl* **coc•cy•ges** \\'käk-sə-ˌjēz\ *also* **coc•cyx•es** \\'käk-sik-səz\ : the end of the spinal column beyond the sacrum esp. in man

co•chi•neal \\'käch-ə-ˌnēl\ *n* : a red dye made from the dried bodies of females of a tropical American insect (**cochineal insect**)

co•chlea \\'kō-klē-ə, 'käk-lē-\ *n, pl* **co•chle•as** *or* **co•chle•ae** \\-(k)lē-ˌē, -ˌī\ : the usu. spiral part of the inner ear containing nerve endings which carry information about sound to the brain — **co•chle•ar** \\-lē-ər\ *adj*

¹cock \\'käk\ *n* **1** : the adult male of a bird and esp. of the common domestic chicken **2** : VALVE, FAUCET **3** : LEADER **4** : the hammer of a firearm; *also* : the position of the hammer when ready for firing

²cock *vb* **1** : to draw back the hammer of a firearm **2** : to set or draw back in readiness for some action ⟨~ your

arm to throw⟩ **3** : to turn or tilt usu. to one side

³cock *n* : a small pile (as of hay)

cock•ade \kä-'kād\ *n* : an ornament worn on the hat as a badge

cock•a•tiel \ˌkäk-ə-'tēl\ *n* : a small crested parrot often kept as a cage bird

cock•a•too \\'käk-ə-ˌtü\ *n, pl* **-toos** [D *kaketoe,* fr. Malay *kakatua*] : a large crested brilliantly colored Australian parrot

cock•a•trice \\'käk-ə-trəs, -ˌtrīs\ *n* : a legendary serpent with a deadly glance

cock•crow \\'käk-ˌkrō\ *n* : DAWN

cocked hat \\'käkt-\ *n* : a hat with the brim turned up on two or three sides

cock•er•el \\'käk-(ə-)rəl\ *n* : a young male domestic chicken

cock•er spaniel \ˌkäk-ər-\ *n* [*cocking* (woodcock hunting)] : any of a breed of small spaniels with long ears, square muzzle, and silky coat

cockeyed \\'käk-'īd\ *adj* **1** : turned or tilted to one side **2** : slightly crazy : FOOLISH

cock•fight \\-ˌfīt\ *n* : a contest of gamecocks usu. fitted with metal spurs

¹cock•le \\'käk-əl\ *n* : any of several weedy plants related to the pinks

²cockle *n* : a bivalve mollusk with a heart-shaped shell

cock•le•shell \\-ˌshel\ *n* **1** : the shell of a cockle **2** : a light flimsy boat

cock•ney \\'käk-nē\ *n, pl* **cockneys** [ME *cokeney,* lit., cocks' egg, fr. *cok* cock + *ey* egg, fr. OE ǣg] : a native of London and esp. of the East End of London; *also* : the dialect of a cockney

cock•pit \\'käk-ˌpit\ *n* **1** : a pit for cockfights **2** : an open space in the deck from which a small boat is steered **3** : a space in an aircraft fuselage for the pilot

cock•roach \\'käk-ˌrōch\ *n* : any of an order of active nocturnal insects including some which infest houses and ships

cock•sure \\'käk-'shu̇r\ *adj* **1** : perfectly sure : CERTAIN **2** : COCKY

cock•tail \\'käk-ˌtāl\ *n* **1** : an iced drink made of liquor and flavoring ingredients **2** : an appetizer (as tomato juice) served as a first course of a meal

cocky \'käk-ē\ *adj* **cock·i·er; -est** : marked by overconfidence : PERT, CONCEITED — **cock·i·ly** \'käk-ə-lē\ *adv* — **cock·i·ness** \-ē-nəs\ *n*

co·coa \'kō-kō\ *n* **1** : CACAO **2** : chocolate deprived of some of its fat and powdered; *also* : a drink made of this heated with water or milk

co·co·nut \'kō-kə-(ˌ)nət\ *n* : a large edible nut produced by a tall tropical palm (**coconut palm**)

co·coon \kə-'kün\ *n* : a case usu. of silk which an insect larva forms and in which it passes the pupal stage

cod \'käd\ *n, pl* **cod** *also* **cods** : a soft=finned large-mouthed food fish of the No. Atlantic

COD *abbr* **1** cash on delivery **2** collect on delivery

co·da \'kōd-ə\ *n* : a closing section in a musical composition that is formally distinct from the main structure

cod·dle \'käd-ᵊl\ *vb* **cod·dled; cod·dling** \'käd-(ə-)liŋ\ **1** : to cook slowly in water below the boiling point **2** : PAMPER

¹code \'kōd\ *n* **1** : a systematic statement of a body of law **2** : a system of principles or rules ⟨moral ∼⟩ **3** : a system of signals **4** : a system of symbols (as in secret communication) with special meanings **5** : GENETIC CODE

²code *vb* **cod·ed; cod·ing** : to put into the form or symbols of a code

co·deine \'kō-ˌdēn, 'kōd-ē-ən\ *n* : a narcotic drug obtained from opium and used esp. in cough remedies

co·dex \'kō-ˌdeks\ *n, pl* **co·di·ces** \'kōd-ə-ˌsēz, 'käd-\ : a manuscript book (as of the Scriptures or classics)

cod·fish \'käd-ˌfish\ *n* : COD

cod·ger \'käj-ər\ *n* : an odd or cranky fellow

cod·i·cil \'käd-ə-səl, -ˌsil\ *n* : a legal instrument modifying an earlier will

cod·i·fy \'käd-ə-ˌfī, 'kōd-\ *vb* **-fied; -fy·ing** : to arrange in a systematic form — **cod·i·fi·ca·tion** \ˌkäd-ə-fə-'kā-shən, ˌkōd-\ *n*

cod·ling \'käd-liŋ\ *n* **1** : a young cod **2** : HAKE

co·ed \'kō-ˌed\ *n* : a female student in a coeducational institution — **coed** *adj*

co·ed·u·ca·tion \ˌkō-ˌej-ə-'kā-shən\ *n* : the education of male and female students at the same institution —

co·ed·u·ca·tion·al \-sh(ə-)nəl\ *adj* — **co·ed·u·ca·tion·al·ly** \-ē\ *adv*

co·ef·fi·cient \ˌkō-ə-'fish-ənt\ *n* **1** : a constant factor as distinguished from a variable in a mathematical term **2** : a number that serves as a measure of some property (as of a substance or device)

coel·en·ter·ate \si-'lent-ə-ˌrāt, -rət\ *n* : any of a phylum of radially symmetrical invertebrate animals including the corals, sea anemones, and jellyfishes

co·equal \kō-'ē-kwəl\ *adj* : equal with another — **coequal** *n* — **co·equal·i·ty** \ˌkō-ē-'kwäl-ət-ē\ *n* — **co·equal·ly** \kō-'ē-kwə-lē\ *adv*

co·erce \kō-'ərs\ *vb* **co·erced; co·erc·ing** **1** : RESTRAIN, REPRESS **2** : COMPEL **3** : ENFORCE — **co·er·cion** \-'ər-zhən, -shən\ *n* — **co·er·cive** \-'ər-siv\ *adj*

co·eval \kō-'ē-vəl\ *adj* : of the same age — **coeval** *n*

co·ex·ist \ˌkō-ig-'zist\ *vb* **1** : to exist together or at the same time **2** : to live in peace with each other — **co·ex·is·tence** \-'zis-təns\ *n*

co·ex·ten·sive \ˌkō-ik-'sten-siv\ *adj* : having the same scope or extent in space or time

C of C *abbr* Chamber of Commerce

cof·fee \'kȯ-fē\ *n* [It & Turk; It *caffè*, fr. Turk *kahve*, fr. Ar *qaḥwa*] : a drink made from the roasted and ground seeds of a fruit of a tropical shrub or tree; *also* : these seeds (**coffee beans**) or a plant producing them

cof·fee·house \-ˌhau̇s\ *n* : a place where refreshments (as coffee) are sold

coffee klatch \-ˌklach\ *n* : KAFFEE=KLATSCH

cof·fee·pot \-ˌpät\ *n* : a pot for brewing or serving coffee

coffee shop *n* : a small restaurant

coffee table *n* : a low table customarily placed in front of a sofa

cof·fer \'kȯ-fər\ *n* : a chest or box used esp. for valuables

cof·fer·dam \-ˌdam\ *n* : a watertight enclosure from which water is pumped to expose the bottom of a body of water and permit construction

cof·fin \'kȯ-fən\ *n* : a box or chest for a corpse to be buried in

C of S *abbr* chief of staff

¹cog \'käg\ *n* : a tooth on the rim of a

wheel or gear — **cogged** \'kägd\ *adj*

²**cog** *abbr* cognate

co•gen•e•ra•tion \ˌkō-ˌjen-ə-'rā-shən\ *n* : the simultaneous generation of electricity and heat from the same fuel

co•gent \'kō-jənt\ *adj* : having power to compel or constrain : CONVINCING — **co•gen•cy** \-jən-sē\ *n*

cog•i•tate \'käj-ə-ˌtāt\ *vb* **-tat•ed; -tat•ing** : THINK, PONDER — **cog•i•ta•tion** \ˌkäj-ə-'tā-shən\ *n* — **cog•i•ta•tive** \'käj-ə-ˌtāt-iv\ *adj*

co•gnac \'kōn-ˌyak\ *n* : a French brandy

cog•nate \'käg-ˌnāt\ *adj* **1** : of the same or similar nature **2** : RELATED; *esp* : related by descent from the same ancestral language — **cognate** *n*

cog•ni•tive \'käg-nət-iv\ *adj* : of, relating to, or being conscious mental activity (as thinking, remembering, or learning) — **cog•ni•tion** \käg-'ni-shən\ *n*

cog•ni•zance \'käg-nə-zəns\ *n* **1** : apprehension by the mind : AWARENESS **2** : NOTICE, HEED — **cog•ni•zant** \'käg-nə-zənt\ *adj*

cog•no•men \käg-'nō-mən, 'käg-nə-\ *n, pl* **cognomens** *or* **cog•no•mi•na** \käg-'näm-ə-nə, -'nō-mə-\ : NAME; *esp* : NICKNAME

co•gno•scen•te \ˌkän-yə-'shent-ē\ *n, pl* **-scen•ti** \-ē\ [obs. It] : CONNOISSEUR

cog•wheel \'käg-ˌhwēl\ *n* : a wheel with cogs or teeth

co•hab•it \kō-'hab-ət\ *vb* : to live together as husband and wife — **co•hab•i•ta•tion** \-ˌhab-ə-'tā-shən\ *n*

co•here \kō-'hiər\ *vb* **co•hered; co•her•ing** : to stick together

co•her•ent \kō-'hir-ənt\ *adj* **1** : having the quality of cohering **2** : logically consistent — **co•her•ence** \-əns\ *n* — **co•her•ent•ly** *adv*

co•he•sion \kō-'hē-zhən\ *n* **1** : a sticking together **2** : molecular attraction by which the particles of a body are united — **co•he•sive** \-siv\ *adj* — **co•he•sive•ly** *adv* — **co•he•sive•ness** *n*

co•ho \'kō-ˌhō\ *n, pl* **cohos** *or* **coho** : a rather small salmon with light-colored flesh

co•hort \'kō-ˌhort\ *n* **1** : a group of warriors or followers **2** : COMPANION, ACCOMPLICE

coif \'kȯif; *2 usu* 'kwäf\ *n* **1** : a close-fitting hat **2** : COIFFURE

coif•feur \kwä-'fər\ *n* [F] : HAIRDRESSER

coif•feuse \kwä-'fə(r)z, -'f(y)üz\ *n* : a female hairdresser

coif•fure \kwä-'fyùr\ *n* : a manner of arranging the hair

¹**coil** \'kȯil\ *vb* : to wind in a spiral shape

²**coil** *n* : a series of rings or loops (as of coiled rope, wire, or pipe) : RING, LOOP

¹**coin** \'kȯin\ *n* [ME, fr. MF, wedge, corner, fr. L *cuneus* wedge] : a piece of metal issued by government authority as money

²**coin** *vb* **1** : to make (a coin) esp. by stamping : MINT **2** : CREATE, INVENT ⟨~ a phrase⟩ — **coin•er** *n*

coin•age \'kȯi-nij\ *n* **1** : the act or process of coining **2** : COINS

co•in•cide \ˌkō-ən-'sīd, 'kō-ən-ˌsīd\ *vb* **-cid•ed; -cid•ing** **1** : to occupy the same place in space or time **2** : to correspond or agree exactly

co•in•ci•dence \kō-'in-səd-əns\ *n* **1** : exact agreement **2** : occurrence together apparently without reason; *also* : an event that so occurs

co•in•ci•dent \-səd-ənt\ *adj* **1** : of similar nature **2** : occupying the same space or time — **co•in•ci•den•tal** \kō-ˌin-sə-'dent-ᵊl\ *adj*

co•itus \'kō-ət-əs\ *n* [L, fr. pp. of *coire* to come together] : SEXUAL INTERCOURSE — **co•ital** \-ət-ᵊl\ *adj*

¹**coke** \'kōk\ *n* : a hard gray porous fuel made by heating soft coal to drive off most of its volatile material

²**coke** *n* : COCAINE

col *abbr* **1** colonial; colony **2** column

Col *abbr* **1** colonel **2** Colorado **3** Colossians

COL *abbr* **1** colonel **2** cost of living

co•la \'kō-lə\ *n* : a carbonated soft drink usu. containing sugar, caffeine, caramel, and special flavoring

col•an•der \'kəl-ən-dər, 'käl-\ *n* : a perforated utensil for draining food

¹**cold** \'kōld\ *adj* **1** : having a low or decidedly subnormal temperature **2** : lacking warmth of feeling **3** : suffering or uncomfortable from lack of warmth — **cold•ly** *adv* — **cold•ness** \'kōl(d)-nəs\ *n* — **in cold blood** : with premeditation : DELIBERATELY

²**cold** *n* **1** : a condition marked by low

temperature; *also* : cold weather **2** : a chilly feeling **3** : a bodily disorder popularly associated with chilling; *esp* : COMMON COLD

³**cold** *adv* : TOTALLY, FINALLY

cold–blood·ed \'kōld-'bləd-əd\ *adj* **1** : lacking normal human feelings **2** : having a body temperature not internally regulated but close to that of the environment **3** : sensitive to cold

cold duck *n* : a blend of sparkling burgundy and champagne

cold feet *n pl* : doubt or fear that prevents action

cold shoulder *n* : cold or unsympathetic behavior — **cold–shoul·der** *vb*

cold sore *n* : a group of blisters appearing in or about the mouth in the oral form of herpes simplex

cold sweat *n* : concurrent perspiration and chill usu. associated with fear, pain, or shock

cold turkey *n* : abrupt complete cessation of the use of an addictive drug

cold war *n* : a conflict characterized by the use of means short of sustained overt military action

cole·slaw \'kōl-,slò\ *n* [D *koolsla,* fr. *kool* cabbage + *sla* salad] : a salad made of raw cabbage

col·ic \'käl-ik\ *n* : sharp sudden abdominal pain — **col·icky** \'käl-i-kē\ *adj*

col·i·se·um \,käl-ə-sē-əm\ *n* : a large structure esp. for athletic contests

coll *abbr* college

col·lab·o·rate \kə-'lab-ə-,rāt\ *vb* **-rat·ed; -rat·ing 1** : to work jointly with others (as in writing a book) **2** : to cooperate with an enemy force occupying one's country — **col·lab·o·ra·tion** \-,lab-ə-'rā-shən\ *n* — **col·lab·o·ra·tor** \-'lab-ə-,rāt-ər\ *n*

col·lage \kə-'läzh\ *n* [F, gluing] : an artistic composition of fragments (as of printed matter) pasted on a picture surface

¹**col·lapse** \kə-'laps\ *vb* **col·lapsed; col·laps·ing 1** : to shink together abruptly **2** : DISINTEGRATE; *also* : to fall in : give way **3** : to break down physically or mentally; *esp* : to fall helpless or unconscious **4** : to fold down compactly — **col·laps·ible** *adj*

²**collapse** *n* : BREAKDOWN

¹**col·lar** \'käl-ər\ *n* **1** : a band, strip, or chain worn around the neck or the

neckline of a garment **2** : something resembling a collar — **col·lar·less** *adj*

²**collar** *vb* : to seize by the collar; *also* : CAPTURE, GRAB

col·lar·bone \-,bōn\ *n* : the bone of the shoulder that joins the breastbone and the shoulder blade

col·lard \'käl-ərd\ *n* : a stalked smooth-leaved kale — usu. used in pl.

col·late \kə-'lāt; 'käl-,āt, 'kōl-\ *vb* **col·lat·ed; col·lat·ing 1** : to compare (as two texts) carefully and critically **2** : to assemble in proper order

¹**col·lat·er·al** \kə-'lat-(ə-)rəl\ *adj* **1** : associated but of secondary importance **2** : descended from the same ancestors but not in the same line **3** : PARALLEL **4** : of, relating to, or being collateral used as security; *also* : secured by collateral

²**collateral** *n* : property (as stocks) used as security for the repayment of a loan

col·la·tion \kə-'lā-shən, kä-, kō-\ *n* **1** : a light meal **2** : the act, process, or result of collating

col·league \'käl-,ēg\ *n* : an associate esp. in a profession

¹**col·lect** \'käl-ikt, -,ekt\ *n* : a short prayer comprising an invocation, petition, and conclusion

²**col·lect** \kə-'lekt\ *vb* **1** : to bring or come together into one body or place : ASSEMBLE **2** : to gather from numerous sources ⟨~ stamps⟩ **3** : to gain control of ⟨~ his thoughts⟩ **4** : to receive payment of — **col·lect·ible** *or* **col·lect·able** *adj or n* — **col·lec·tion** \-'lek-shən\ *n* — **col·lec·tor** \-'lek-tər\ *n*

³**col·lect** \kə-'lekt\ *adv or adj* : to be paid for by the receiver

col·lect·ed \kə-'lek-təd\ *adj* : SELF-POSSESSED, CALM

¹**col·lec·tive** \kə-'lek-tiv\ *adj* **1** : of, relating to, or denoting a group of individuals considered as a whole **2** : formed by collecting **3** : involving all members of a group as distinct from its individuals **4** : shared or assumed by all members of the group — **col·lec·tive·ly** *adv*

²**collective** *n* **1** : GROUP **2** : a cooperative unit or organization

collective bargaining *n* : negotiation between an employer and union representatives

col·lec·tiv·ism \kə-'lek-ti-,viz-əm\ *n* : a

political or economic theory advocating collective control esp. over production and distribution

col·lec·tiv·ize \-ˌvīz\ *vb* **-ized; -iz·ing** : to organize under collective control

col·leen \kä-ˈlēn, ˈkäl-ˌēn\ *n* : an Irish girl

col·lege \ˈkäl-ij\ *n* [ME, fr. MF, fr. L *collegium* society, fr. *collega* colleague, fr. *com-* with + *legare* to appoint] **1** : a building used for an educational or religious purpose **2** : an institution of higher learning granting a bachelor's degree; *also* : an institution offering instruction esp. in a vocational or technical field ⟨barber ∼⟩ **3** : an organized body of persons having common interests or duties ⟨∼ of cardinals⟩ — **col·le·giate** \kə-ˈlē-jət\ *adj*

col·le·gi·al·i·ty \kə-ˌlē-jē-ˈal-ət-ē\ *n* : the relationship of colleagues

col·le·gian \kə-ˈlē-jən\ *n* : a college student

col·le·gi·um \kə-ˈleg-ē-əm, -ˈläg-\ *n, pl* **-gia** \-ē-ə\ *or* **-giums** : a governing group in which each member has approximately equal power

col·lide \kə-ˈlīd\ *vb* **col·lid·ed; col·lid·ing** **1** : to come together with solid impact **2** : to come into conflict : CLASH — **col·li·sion** \-ˈlizh-ən\ *n*

col·lie \ˈkäl-ē\ *n* : a large dog of a breed with rough-coated and smooth-coated varieties developed in Scotland for herding sheep

col·lier \ˈkäl-yər\ *n* **1** : a coal miner **2** : a ship for carrying coal

col·liery \ˈkäl-yə-rē\ *n, pl* **-lier·ies** : a coal mine and its associated buildings

col·li·mate \ˈkäl-ə-ˌmāt\ *vb* **-mat·ed; -mat·ing** : to make (as rays of light) parallel

col·lo·ca·tion \ˌkäl-ə-ˈkā-shən\ *n* **1** : a placing together or side by side; *also* : the result of such placing **2** : a noticeable arrangement or conjoining of linguistic elements (as words)

col·lo·di·on \kə-ˈlōd-ē-ən\ *n* : a sticky substance that hardens in the air and is used to cover wounds and coat photographic films

col·loid \ˈkäl-ˌȯid\ *n* : a substance in the form of submicroscopic particles that when in solution or suspension do not settle out; *also* : such a substance together with the medium in which it is dispersed — **col·loi·dal** \kə-ˈlȯid-ᵊl\ *adj*

colloq *abbr* colloquial

col·lo·qui·al \kə-ˈlō-kwē-əl\ *adj* : of, relating to, or characteristic of conversation and esp. of familiar and informal conversation

col·lo·qui·al·ism \-ˈlō-kwē-ə-ˌliz-əm\ *n* : a colloquial expression

col·lo·qui·um \kə-ˈlō-kwē-əm\ *n, pl* **-qui·ums** *or* **-quia** \-kwē-ə\ : CONFERENCE, SEMINAR

col·lo·quy \ˈkäl-ə-kwē\ *n, pl* **-quies** : a usu. formal conversation or conference

col·lu·sion \kə-ˈlü-zhən\ *n* : secret agreement or cooperation for an illegal or deceitful purpose — **col·lu·sive** \-ˈlü-siv\ *adj*

Colo *abbr* Colorado

co·logne \kə-ˈlōn\ *n* [*Cologne*, Germany] : a perfumed liquid consisting of alcohol and aromatic oils — **co·logned** \-ˈlōnd\ *adj*

¹co·lon \ˈkō-lən\ *n, pl* **colons** *or* **co·la** \-lə\ : the part of the large intestine extending from the cecum to the rectum — **co·lon·ic** \kō-ˈlän-ik\ *adj*

²colon *n, pl* **colons** : a punctuation mark : used esp. to direct attention to following matter

³co·lon \kə-ˈlōn\ *n, pl* **co·lo·nes** \-ˈlō-ˌnäs\ — see MONEY table

col·o·nel \ˈkərn-ᵊl\ *n* [alter. of *coronel*, fr. MF, fr. It *colonnello* column of soldiers, colonel, fr. L *columna*] : a commissioned officer (as in the army) ranking next below a brigadier general

¹co·lo·nial \kə-ˈlō-nē-əl, -nyəl\ *adj* **1** : of, relating to, or characteristic of a colony; *also* : possessing or composed of colonies **2** *often cap* : of or relating to the original 13 colonies forming the U.S.

²colonial *n* : a member or inhabitant of a colony

co·lo·nial·ism \-ˌiz-əm\ *n* : control by one power over a dependent area or people; *also* : a policy advocating or based on such control — **co·lo·nial·ist** \-əst\ *n or adj*

col·o·nist \ˈkäl-ə-nəst\ *n* **1** : COLONIAL **2** : one who takes part in founding a colony

col·o·nize \ˈkäl-ə-ˌnīz\ *vb* **-nized; -niz·ing** **1** : to establish a colony in or on **2**

: to settle in a colony — **col·o·ni·za·tion** \ˌkäl-ə-nə-ˈzā-shən\ *n* — **col·o·niz·er** *n*

col·on·nade \ˌkäl-ə-ˈnād\ *n* : an evenly spaced row of columns usu. supporting the base of the roof structure

col·o·ny \ˈkäl-ə-nē\ *n, pl* **-nies** **1** : a body of people living in a new territory; *also* : the territory inhabited by these people **2** : a localized population of organisms ⟨a ∼ of bees⟩ **3** : a group with common interests situated in close association ⟨a writers' ∼⟩; *also* : the area occupied by such a group

col·o·phon \ˈkäl-ə-fən, -ˌfän\ *n* **1** : an inscription placed at the end of a book with facts relative to its production **2** : a distinctive symbol used by a printer or publisher

¹col·or \ˈkəl-ər\ *n* **1** : a phenomenon of light (as red or blue) or visual perception that enables one to differentiate otherwise identical objects; *also* : a hue as contrasted with black, white, or gray **2** : APPEARANCE **3** : complexion tint **4** *pl* : FLAG; *also* : military service ⟨a call to the ∼s⟩ **5** : VIVIDNESS, INTEREST — **col·or·ful** *adj* — **col·or·less** *adj*

²color *vb* **col·ored; col·or·ing** \ˈkəl-(ə-)riŋ\ **1** : to give color to; *also* : to change the color of **2** : BLUSH

Col·o·ra·do potato beetle \ˌkäl-ə-ˈrad-ō-, -ˈräd-\ *n* : a black-and-yellow striped beetle that feeds on the leaves of the potato

col·or·ation \ˌkəl-ə-ˈrā-shən\ *n* : use or arrangement of colors

col·or·a·tu·ra \ˌkəl-ə-rə-ˈt(y)ùr-ə\ *n* **1** : elaborate ornamentation in vocal music **2** : a soprano specializing in coloratura

col·or–blind \ˈkəl-ər-ˌblīnd\ *adj* : partially or totally unable to distinguish one or more chromatic colors — **color blindness** *n*

¹col·ored \ˈkəl-ərd\ *adj* **1** : having color **2** : SLANTED, BIASED **3** : of a race other than the white; *esp* : NEGRO

²colored *n, pl* **colored** *or* **coloreds** *often cap* : a colored person

col·or·fast \ˈkəl-ər-ˌfast\ *adj* : having color that does not fade or run — **col·or·fast·ness** *n*

co·los·sal \kə-ˈläs-əl\ *adj* : of very great size or degree

Co·los·sians \kə-ˈläsh-ənz\ *n* — see BIBLE table

co·los·sus \kə-ˈläs-əs\ *n, pl* **co·los·sus·es** \-ˈläs-ə-səz\ *or* **co·los·si** \-ˈläs-ˌī\ [L] : a gigantic statue; *also* : something of great size or scope

col·por·teur \ˈkäl-ˌpōrt-ər\ *n* [F] : a peddler of religious books

colt \ˈkōlt\ *n* : FOAL; *also* : a young male horse, ass, or zebra — **colt·ish** *adj*

col·um·bine \ˈkäl-əm-ˌbīn\ *n* [ME, fr. ML *columbina*, fr. L, fem. of *columbinus* dovelike, fr. *columba* dove] : any of a genus of plants with showy spurred flowers that are related to the buttercups

co·lum·bi·um \kə-ˈləm-bē-əm\ *n* : NIOBIUM

Columbus Day \kə-ˈləm-bəs-\ *n* : the 2d Monday in October or formerly October 12 observed as a legal holiday in many states in commemoration of the landing of Columbus

col·umn \ˈkäl-əm\ *n* **1** : one of two or more vertical sections of a printed page; *also* : a special department (as in a newspaper) **2** : a supporting pillar; *also* : something resembling such a column ⟨a ∼ of water⟩ **3** : a long row (as of soldiers) — **co·lum·nar** \kə-ˈləm-nər\ *adj*

col·um·nist \ˈkäl-əm-(n)əst\ *n* : one who writes a newspaper or magazine column

com *or* **comm** *abbr* **1** command; commander **2** commerce; commercial **3** commission; commissioner **4** committee **5** common **6** commonwealth

co·ma \ˈkō-mə\ *n* : a state of deep unconsciousness caused by disease, injury, or poison — **co·ma·tose** \ˈkō-mə-ˌtōs, ˈkäm-ə-\ *adj*

Co·man·che \kə-ˈman-chē\ *n, pl* **Comanche** *or* **Comanches** : a member of an American Indian people ranging from Wyoming and Nebraska south into New Mexico and Texas

¹comb \ˈkōm\ *n* **1** : a toothed instrument for arranging the hair or for separating and cleaning textile fibers **2** : a fleshy crest on the head of a fowl **3** : HONEYCOMB — **comb** *vb* — **combed** \ˈkōmd\ *adj*

²comb *abbr* combination; combining

com·bat \kəm-ˈbat, ˈkäm-ˌbat\ *vb* **-bat-**

ed or **-bat·ted; -bat·ing** or **-bat·ting 1** : FIGHT, CONTEND **2** : to struggle or work against : OPPOSE — **com·bat** \'käm-ˌbat\ n — **com·bat·ant** \kəm-'bat-ᵊnt, 'käm-bət-ənt\ n — **com·bat·ive** \kəm-'bat-iv\ adj

combat fatigue n : a traumatic neurotic or psychotic reaction occurring under conditions (as wartime combat) that cause intense stress

comb·er \'kō-mər\ n **1** : one that combs **2** : a long curling wave of the sea

com·bi·na·tion \ˌkäm-bə-'nā-shən\ n **1** : a result or product of combining **2** : a sequence of letters or numbers chosen in setting a lock **3** : the act or process of combining; also : the quality or state of being combined

¹**com·bine** \kəm-'bīn\ vb **com·bined; com·bin·ing** : to become one : UNITE

²**com·bine** \'käm-ˌbīn\ n **1** : COMBINATION; esp : one made to secure business or political advantage **2** : a machine that harvests and threshes grain while moving over the field

comb·ings \'kō-miŋz\ n pl : loose hairs or fibers removed by a comb

combining form n : a linguistic form that occurs only in compounds or derivatives

com·bo \'käm-bō\ n, pl **combos** : a small jazz or dance band

com·bus·ti·ble \kəm-'bəs-tə-bəl\ adj : capable of being burned — **com·bus·ti·bil·i·ty** \-ˌbəs-tə-'bil-ət-ē\ n — **combustible** n

com·bus·tion \kəm-'bəs-chən\ n **1** : an act or instance of burning **2** : slow oxidation (as in thc animal body)

comdg abbr commanding

comdr abbr commander

comdt abbr commandant

come \(')kəm\ vb **came** \'kām\; **come; com·ing** \'kəm-iŋ\ **1** : APPROACH **2** : ARRIVE **3** : to reach the point of being or becoming ⟨~ to a boil⟩ **4** : AMOUNT ⟨the bill came to $10⟩ **5** : to take place **6** : ORIGINATE, ARISE **7** : to be available **8** : REACH, EXTEND **9** : to experience orgasm — **come across** : to meet or find by chance — **come to pass** : HAPPEN — **come upon** : to come across

come·back \'kəm-ˌbak\ n **1** : RETORT **2** : RECOVERY — **come back** \(ˌ)kəm-'bak\ vb

co·me·di·an \kə-'mēd-ē-ən\ n **1** : an ac-

tor in comedy **2** : an amusing person **3** : an entertainer specializing in comedy

co·me·di·enne \-ˌmēd-ē-'en\ n : a woman who is a comedian

come·down \'kəm-ˌdaùn\ n : a descent in rank or dignity

com·e·dy \'käm-əd-ē\ n, pl **-dies** [ME, fr. MF comedie, fr. L comoedia, fr. Gk kōmōidia, fr. kōmos revel + aeidein to sing] **1** : a light amusing play with a happy ending **2** : a literary work treating a comic theme or written in a comic style **3** : humorous entertainment

come·ly \'kəm-lē\ adj **come·li·er; -est** : good-looking : HANDSOME — **come·li·ness** n

come off vb : SUCCEED

come–on \'kəm-ˌȯn, -ˌän\ n : INDUCEMENT, LURE

come out vb **1** : to come into public view **2** : to declare oneself **3** : TURN OUT **5** ⟨everything came out all right⟩ — **come out with** : SAY 1

com·er \'kəm-ər\ n : a promising beginner

¹**co·mes·ti·ble** \kə-'mes-tə-bəl\ adj : EDIBLE

²**comestible** n : FOOD — usu. used in pl.

com·et \'käm-ət\ n [ME comete, fr. OE cometa, fr. L, fr. Gk komētēs, lit., long-haired, fr. komē hair] : a small bright celestial body that develops a cloudy tail when near the sun

come to vb : to regain consciousness

come·up·pance \kə-'məp-əns\ n : a deserved rebuke or penalty

com·fit \'kəm-fət\ n : a candied fruit or nut

¹**com·fort** \'kəm-fərt\ n **1** : CONSOLATION **2** : freedom from pain, trouble, or anxiety; also : something that gives such freedom — **com·fort·less** adj

²**comfort** vb **1** : to give strength and hope to **2** : CONSOLE

com·fort·able \'kəm(f)t-ə-bəl, 'kəm-fərt-\ adj **1** : providing comfort **2** : more than adequate **3** : feeling at ease — **com·fort·ably** \-blē\ adv

com·fort·er \'kəm-fə(r)t-ər\ n **1** : one that comforts **2** : QUILT

com·fy \'kəm-fē\ adj : COMFORTABLE

¹**com·ic** \'käm-ik\ adj **1** : relating to comedy or comic strips **2** : provoking

laughter or amusement **syn** laughable, funny, farcical — **com·i·cal** *adj*

²**comic** *n* **1** : COMEDIAN **2** : COMIC BOOK

comic book *n* : a magazine containing sequences of comic strips

comic strip *n* : a group of cartoons in narrative sequence

coming \\'kəm-iŋ\\ *adj* **1** : APPROACHING, NEXT **2** : gaining importance

co·mi·ty \\'käm-ət-ē, 'kō-mət-\\ *n, pl* **-ties** : friendly civility : COURTESY

coml *abbr* commercial

comm *abbr* — see COM

com·ma \\'käm-ə\\ *n* : a punctuation mark , used esp. as a mark of separation within the sentence

¹**com·mand** \\kə-'mand\\ *vb* **1** : to direct authoritatively : ORDER **2** : DOMINATE, CONTROL, GOVERN **3** : to overlook from a strategic position

²**command** *n* **1** : the act of commanding **2** : ability to control : MASTERY **3** : an order given **4** : an electrical signal that actuates a device (as a computer); *also* : the activation of a device by means of such a signal **5** : a body of troops under a commander; *also* : an area or position that one commands **6** : a position of highest authority

com·man·dant \\'käm-ən-,dant, -,dänt\\ *n* : an officer in command

com·man·deer \\,käm-ən-'diər\\ *vb* : to take possession of by force

com·mand·er \\kə-'man-dər\\ *n* **1** : LEADER, CHIEF; *esp* : an officer commanding an army or subdivision of an army **2** : a commissioned officer in the navy ranking next below a captain

commander in chief : one who holds supreme command of the armed forces

com·mand·ment \\kə-'man(d)-mənt\\ *n* : COMMAND, ORDER; *esp* : any of the Ten Commandments

command module *n* : a space vehicle module designed to carry the crew and reentry equipment

com·man·do \\kə-'man-dō\\ *n, pl* **-dos** *or* **-does** [Afrikaans *kommando*, fr. Dutch *commando* command] : a member of a military unit trained for surprise raids

command sergeant major *n* : a noncommissioned officer in the army ranking above a first sergeant

com·mem·o·rate \\kə-'mem-ə-,rāt\\ *vb* **-rat·ed; -rat·ing** **1** : to call or recall to mind **2** : to serve as a memorial of — **com·mem·o·ra·tion** \\-,mem-ə-'rā-shən\\ *n*

com·mem·o·ra·tive \\kə-'mem-(ə-)rət-iv, -'mem-ə-,rāt-iv\\ *adj* : intended to commemorate an event

com·mence \\kə-'mens\\ *vb* **com·menced; com·menc·ing** : BEGIN, START

com·mence·ment \\-mənt\\ *n* **1** : the act or time of a beginning **2** : the graduation exercises of a school or college

com·mend \\kə-'mend\\ *vb* **1** : to commit to one's care **2** : RECOMMEND **3** : PRAISE — **com·mend·able** \\-'men-də-bəl\\ *adj* — **com·mend·ably** \\-blē\\ *adv* — **com·men·da·tion** \\,käm-ən-'dā-shən, -,en-\\ *n*

com·men·su·ra·ble \\kə-'mens-(ə-)rə-bəl\\ *adj* : having a common measure; *esp* : divisible by a common unit an integral number of times

com·men·su·rate \\kə-'mens(-ə)-rət, -'mench(-ə)-\\ *adj* : equal in measure or extent; *also* : PROPORTIONAL, CORRESPONDING ⟨a job ∼ with her abilities⟩

com·ment \\'käm-,ent\\ *n* **1** : an expression of opinion **2** : an explanatory, illustrative, or critical note or observation : REMARK — **comment** *vb*

com·men·tary \\'käm-ən-,ter-ē\\ *n, pl* **-tar·ies** : a systematic series of comments

com·men·ta·tor \\-,tāt-ər\\ *n* : one who comments; *esp* : one who gives talks on news events on radio or television

com·merce \\'käm-(,)ərs\\ *n* : the buying and selling of commodities : TRADE

¹**com·mer·cial** \\kə-'mər-shəl\\ *adj* : having to do with commerce; *also* : designed for profit or for mass appeal — **com·mer·cial·ly** \\-ē\\ *adv*

²**commercial** *n* : an advertisement broadcast on radio or television

com·mer·cial·ism \\kə-'mər-shə-,liz-əm\\ *n* **1** : a spirit, method, or practice characteristic of business **2** : excessive emphasis on profit

com·mer·cial·ize \\-,līz\\ *vb* **-ized; -iz·ing** **1** : to manage on a business basis for profit **2** : to exploit for profit

com·mi·na·tion \\,käm-ə-'nā-shən\\ *n* : DENUNCIATION — **com·mi·na·to·ry** \\'käm-ə-nə-,tōr-ē\\ *adj*

com·min·gle \\kə-'miŋ-gəl\\ *vb* : MINGLE, BLEND

com·mis·er·ate \\kə-'miz-ə-,rāt\\ *vb* **-at-**

ed; -at·ing : to feel or express pity
: SYMPATHIZE — **com·mis·er·a·tion**
\-ˌmiz-ə-ˈrā-shən\ n

com·mis·sar \ˈkäm-ə-ˌsär\ n [Russ] : a
Communist party official assigned to
a military unit to teach and enforce
party principles and policy

com·mis·sar·i·at \ˌkäm-ə-ˈser-ē-ət\ n 1
: a system for supplying troops with
food 2 : a department headed by a
commissar

com·mis·sary \ˈkäm-ə-ˌser-ē\ n, pl **-sar·ies** : a store for equipment and provisions esp. for military personnel

¹**com·mis·sion** \kə-ˈmish-ən\ n 1 : a warrant granting certain powers and imposing certain duties 2 : a certificate
conferring military rank and authority
3 : authority to act as agent for another; also : something to be done by an
agent 4 : a body of persons charged
with performing a duty 5 : the doing
of some act; also : the thing done 6
: the allowance made to an agent for
transacting business for another

²**commission** vb **-mis·sioned; -mis·sion-
ing** \-ˈmish-(ə-)niŋ\ 1 : to give a commission to 2 : to order to be made 3
: to put (a ship) into a state of readiness for service

commissioned officer n : an officer of
the armed forces holding rank by virtue of a commission from the president

com·mis·sion·er \kə-ˈmish-(ə-)nər\ n 1
: a member of a commission 2 : an
official in charge of a department of
public service 3 : the administrative
head of a professional sport — **com-
mis·sion·er·ship** n

com·mit \kə-ˈmit\ vb **com·mit·ted; com-
mit·ting** 1 : to put into charge or trust
: ENTRUST 2 : to put in a prison or
mental institution 3 : TRANSFER, CON-
SIGN 4 : PERPETRATE ⟨∼ a crime⟩ 5 : to
pledge or assign to some particular
course or use — **com·mit·ment** n —
com·mit·tal n

com·mit·tee \kə-ˈmit-ē\ n : a body of
persons selected to consider and act
or report on some matter — **com·mit-
tee·man** \-mən\ n — **com·mit·tee·wom-
an** \-ˌwu̇m-ən\ n

commo abbr commodore

com·mode \kə-ˈmōd\ n [F, fr. com-
mode, adj., suitable, convenient, fr. L

commodus, fr. com- with + modus
measure] 1 : a movable washstand
with cupboard underneath 2 : TOILET
3

com·mo·di·ous \kə-ˈmōd-ē-əs\ adj
: comfortably spacious : ROOMY

com·mod·i·ty \kə-ˈmäd-ət-ē\ n, pl **-ties** 1
: a product of agriculture or mining 2
: an article of commerce ⟨wheat and
soybeans are traded as commodities⟩

com·mo·dore \ˈkäm-ə-ˌdōr\ n 1 : a
commissioned officer in the navy
ranking next below a rear admiral 2
: an officer commanding a group of
merchant ships; also : the chief officer of a yacht club

¹**com·mon** \ˈkäm-ən\ adj 1 : belonging to
or serving the community : PUBLIC 2
: shared by a number in a group 3
: widely or generally known, found,
or observed : FAMILIAR ⟨∼ knowl-
edge⟩ 4 : VERNACULAR 3 ⟨∼ names⟩ 5
: not above the average esp. in social
status **syn** universal, general, generic
— **com·mon·ly** adv

²**common** n 1 pl : the common people 2
pl : a dining hall 3 pl, cap : the lower
house of the British and Canadian par-
liaments 4 : a piece of land held in
common by a community — **in
common** : shared together

com·mon·al·ty \ˈkäm-ən-ᵊl-tē\ n, pl **-ties**
: the common people

common cold n : a contagious respiratory disease caused by a virus and
characterized by a sore, swollen, and
inflamed nose and throat, usu. by
much mucus, and by coughing and
sneezing

common denominator n 1 : a common
multiple of the denominators of a
number of fractions 2 : a common
trait or theme

common divisor n : a number or expression that divides two or more numbers
or expressions without remainder

com·mon·er \ˈkäm-ə-nər\ n : one of the
common people : one having no rank
of nobility

common fraction n : a fraction in which
the numerator and denominator are
both integers and are separated by a
horizontal or slanted line

common law n : a group of legal practices and traditions based on judges'
decisions and social customs and usu.

having the same force as laws passed by legislative bodies

common logarithm *n* : a logarithm whose base is 10

common market *n* : an economic unit formed to remove trade barriers among members

common multiple *n* : a multiple of each of two or more numbers or expressions

¹**com·mon·place** \'käm-ən-ˌplās\ *n* : something that is ordinary or trite

²**commonplace** *adj* : ORDINARY

common sense *n* : ordinary good sense and judgment

com·mon·weal \'käm-ən-ˌwēl\ *n* **1** *archaic* : COMMONWEALTH **2** : the general welfare

com·mon·wealth \-ˌwelth\ *n* **1** : the body of people politically organized into a state **2** : STATE; *also* : an association or federation of autonomous states

com·mo·tion \kə-'mō-shən\ *n* **1** : DISTURBANCE, UPRISING **2** : AGITATION

com·mu·nal \kə-'myün-ᵊl, 'käm-yən-ᵊl\ *adj* **1** : of or relating to a commune or community **2** : marked by collective ownership and use of property **3** : shared or used in common

¹**com·mune** \kə-'myün\ *vb* **communed; com·mun·ing** : to communicate intimately

²**com·mune** \'käm-ˌyün; kə-'myün\ *n* **1** : the smallest administrative district in some European countries **2** : a community organized on a communal basis

com·mu·ni·ca·ble \kə-'myü-ni-kə-bəl\ *adj* : capable of being communicated ⟨~ diseases⟩ — **com·mu·ni·ca·bil·i·ty** \-ˌmyü-ni-kə-'bil-ət-ē\ *n*

com·mu·ni·cant \-'myü-ni-kənt\ *n* **1** : a church member entitled to receive Communion **2** : one that communicates; *esp* : INFORMANT

com·mu·ni·cate \kə-'myü-nə-ˌkāt\ *vb* **-cat·ed; -cat·ing 1** : to make known **2** : TRANSMIT, IMPART **3** : to receive Communion **4** : to be in communication **5** : JOIN, CONNECT

com·mu·ni·ca·tion \kə-ˌmyü-nə-'kā-shən\ *n* **1** : an act of transmitting **2** : MESSAGE **3** : exchange of information or opinions **4** : a means of com-

municating — **com·mu·ni·ca·tive** \kə-'myü-nə-ˌkāt-iv, -ni-kət-iv\ *adj*

com·mu·nion \kə-'myü-nyən\ *n* **1** : a sharing of something with others **2** *cap* : a Christian sacrament in which bread and wine are partaken of as a commemoration of the death of Christ; *also* : the act of receiving the sacrament **3** : intimate fellowship or rapport **4** : a body of Christians having a common faith and discipline

com·mu·ni·qué \kə-'myü-nə-ˌkā, -ˌmyü-nə-'kā\ *n* : BULLETIN 1

com·mu·nism \'käm-yə-ˌniz-əm\ *n* **1** : social organization in which goods are held in common **2** : a theory of social organization advocating common ownership of means of production and a distribution of products of industry based on need **3** *cap* : a political doctrine based on revolutionary Marxian socialism that is the official ideology of the U.S.S.R. and some other countries; *also* : a system of government in which one party controls state-owned means of production — **com·mu·nist** \-nəst\ *n or adj,* often *cap* — **com·mu·nis·tic** \ˌkäm-yə-'nis-tik\ *adj,* often *cap*

com·mu·ni·ty \kə-'myü-nət-ē\ *n, pl* **-ties 1** : a body of people living in the same place under the same laws; *also* : a natural population of plants and animals that interact ecologically and live in one place (as a pond) **2** : society at large **3** : joint ownership **4** : SIMILARITY, LIKENESS

community college *n* : a nonresidential 2-year college that is usu. government-supported

community property *n* : property held jointly by husband and wife

com·mu·ta·tion \ˌkäm-yə-'tā-shən\ *n* : substitution of one form of payment or penalty for another

com·mu·ta·tive \'käm-yə-ˌtāt-iv, kə-'myüt- ət-\ *adj* : of, relating to, having, or being the property that a given mathematical operation and set have when the result obtained using any two numbers of the set with the operation does not differ with the order in which the numbers are used ⟨addition of the real numbers is ~⟩ — **com·mu·ta·tiv·i·ty** \kə-ˌmyüt-ə-'tiv-ət-ē, ˌkäm-yə-tə-\ *n*

com·mu·ta·tor \\'käm-yə-ˌtāt-ər\ *n* : a device (as on a generator or motor) for changing the direction of electric current

¹com·mute \kə-'myüt\ *vb* **com·mut·ed; com·mut·ing 1** : EXCHANGE **2** : to substitute a less severe penalty for (one more severe) **3** : to travel back and forth regularly — **com·mut·er** *n*

²commute *n* : a trip made in commuting

comp *abbr* **1** comparative **2** compiled; compiler **3** composition **4** compound

¹com·pact \kəm-'pakt, (')käm-\ *adj* **1** : SOLID, DENSE **2** : BRIEF, SUCCINCT **3** : occupying a small volume by efficient use of space ⟨~ camera⟩ — **com·pact·ly** *adv* — **com·pact·ness** *n*

²compact *vb* : to pack together

³com·pact \'käm-ˌpakt\ *n* **1** : a small case for cosmetics **2** : a small automobile

⁴com·pact \'käm-ˌpakt\ *n* : AGREEMENT, COVENANT

compact disc *n* : a small plastic optical disc usu. containing recorded music

¹com·pan·ion \kəm-'pan-yən\ *n* [OF *compagnon*, fr. LL *companion-, companio,* lit., one who shares bread, fr. L *com-* together + *panis* bread] **1** : an intimate friend or associate : COMRADE **2** : one that is closely connected with something similar — **com·pan·ion·able** *adj* — **com·pan·ion·ship** *n*

²companion *n* : COMPANIONWAY

com·pan·ion·way \-ˌwā\ *n* : a ship's stairway from one deck to another

com·pa·ny \'kəmp-(ə-)nē\ *n, pl* **-nies 1** : association with others : FELLOWSHIP; *also* : COMPANIONS **2** : GUESTS **3** : a group of persons or things **4** : an infantry unit consisting of two or more platoons and normally commanded by a captain **5** : a group of musical or dramatic performers **6** : the officers and crew of a ship **7** : an association of persons for carrying on a business **syn** party, band, troop, troupe, corps, outfit

com·pa·ra·ble \'käm-p(ə-)rə-bəl\ *adj* : capable of being compared **syn** parallel, similar, like, alike, corresponding — **com·pa·ra·bil·i·ty** \ˌkäm-p(ə-)rə-'bil-ət-ē\ *n*

¹com·par·a·tive \kəm-'par-ət-iv\ *adj* **1** : of, relating to, or constituting the degree of grammatical comparison that denotes increase in quality, quantity, or relation **2** : RELATIVE ⟨a ~ stranger⟩ — **com·par·a·tive·ly** *adv*

²comparative *n* : the comparative degree or a comparative form in a language

¹com·pare \kəm-'paər\ *vb* **com·pared; com·par·ing 1** : to represent as like something : LIKEN **2** : to examine for likenesses and differences **3** : to inflect or modify (an adjective or adverb) according to the degrees of comparison

²compare *n* : the possibility of comparing ⟨beauty beyond ~⟩

com·par·i·son \-'par-ə-sən\ *n* **1** : the act of comparing : relative estimate **2** : change in the form of an adjective or adverb to show different levels of quality, quantity, or relation

com·part·ment \kəm-'pärt-mənt\ *n* **1** : a separate division **2** : a section of an enclosed space : ROOM

com·part·men·tal·ize \kəm-ˌpärt-'ment-ᵊl-ˌīz\ *vb* **-ized; -iz·ing** : to separate into compartments

¹com·pass \'kəm-pəs, 'käm-\ *vb* [ME *compassen,* fr. OF *compasser* to measure, fr. (assumed) VL *compassare* to pace off, fr. L *com-* + *passus* pace] **1** : CONTRIVE, PLOT **2** : to make a circuit of; *also* : SURROUND **3** : BRING ABOUT, ACHIEVE

²compass *n* **1** : BOUNDARY, CIRCUMFERENCE **2** : an enclosed space **3** : RANGE, SCOPE **4** : a device for determining direction by means of a magnetic needle swinging freely and pointing to the magnetic north; *also* : a nonmagnetic device that indicates direction **5** : an instrument for drawing circles or transferring measurements consisting of two legs joined by a pivot

com·pas·sion \kəm-'pash-ən\ *n* : sympathetic feeling : PITY, MERCY — **com·pas·sion·ate** \-(ə-)nət\ *adj*

com·pat·i·ble \kəm-'pat-ə-bəl\ *adj* : able to exist or act together harmoniously ⟨~ colors⟩ ⟨~ drugs⟩ **syn** consonant, congenial, sympathetic — **com·pat·i·bil·i·ty** \-ˌpat-ə-'bil-ət-ē\ *n*

com·pa·tri·ot \kəm-'pā-trē-ət, -trē-ˌät\ *n* : a fellow countryman

com·peer \'käm-ˌpiər\ *n* : EQUAL, PEER

com·pel \kəm-'pel\ *vb* **com·pelled; com-**

pel·ling : to drive or urge with force : CONSTRAIN

com·pen·di·um \kəm-'pen-dē-əm\ *n, pl* **-di·ums** *or* **-dia** \-dē-ə\ **1** : a brief summary of a larger work or of a field of knowledge **2** : COLLECTION

com·pen·sate \'käm-pən-ˌsāt\ *vb* **-sat·ed; -sat·ing 1** : to be equivalent to in value or effect : make up for **2** : PAY, REMUNERATE **syn** balance, offset, counterbalance, counterpoise — **com·pen·sa·tion** \ˌkäm-pən-'sā-shən\ *n* — **com·pen·sa·to·ry** \kəm-'pen-sə-ˌtōr-ē\ *adj*

com·pete \kəm-'pēt\ *vb* **com·pet·ed; com·pet·ing** : CONTEND, VIE

com·pe·tence \'käm-pət-əns\ *n* **1** : adequate means for subsistence **2** : FITNESS, ABILITY

com·pe·ten·cy \-pət-ən-sē\ *n, pl* **-cies** : COMPETENCE

com·pe·tent \-pət-ənt\ *adj* : CAPABLE, FIT, QUALIFIED

com·pe·ti·tion \ˌkäm-pə-'tish-ən\ *n* **1** : the act of competing : RIVALRY **2** : CONTEST, MATCH; *also* : one's competitors — **com·pet·i·tive** \kəm-'pet-ət-iv\ *adj* — **com·pet·i·tive·ly** *adv* — **com·pet·i·tive·ness** *n*

com·pet·i·tor \kəm-'pet-ət-ər\ *n* : one that competes : RIVAL

com·pile \kəm-'pīl\ *vb* **com·piled; com·pil·ing** [ME *compilen,* fr. MF *compiler,* fr. L *compilare* to plunder] **1** : to collect and edit into a volume **2** : to compose out of materials from other documents **3** : to translate (a computer program) with a compiler **4** : to build up gradually ⟨∼ a record of four wins and two losses⟩ — **com·pi·la·tion** \ˌkäm-pə-'lā-shən\ *n*

com·pil·er \kəm-'pī-lər\ *n* **1** : one that compiles **2** : a computer program that translates another program written in a programming language into machine language

com·pla·cence \kəm-'plās-ᵊns\ *n* : SATISFACTION; *esp* : SELF-SATISFACTION — **com·pla·cent** \-ᵊnt\ *adj* — **com·pla·cent·ly** *adv*

com·pla·cen·cy \-ᵊn-sē\ *n, pl* **-cies** : COMPLACENCE

com·plain \kəm-'plān\ *vb* **1** : to express grief, pain, or discontent **2** : to make a formal accusation — **com·plain·ant** *n* — **com·plain·er** *n*

com·plaint \kəm-'plānt\ *n* **1** : expression of grief, pain, or dissatisfaction **2** : a bodily ailment or disease **3** : a formal accusation against a person

com·plai·sance \kəm-'plās-ᵊns, ˌkäm-plā-'zans\ *n* [F] : disposition to please — **com·plai·sant** \-ᵊnt, -'zant\ *adj*

com·pleat \kəm-'plēt\ *adj* : PROFICIENT

com·plect·ed \kəm-'plek-təd\ *adj* : having a specified facial complexion ⟨dark-*complected*⟩

¹com·ple·ment \'käm-plə-mənt\ *n* **1** : a quantity needed to make a thing complete **2** : full quantity, number, or amount **3** : an added word by which a predicate is made complete **4** : a substance in blood that combines with antibodies to destroy antigens — **com·ple·men·ta·ry** \ˌkäm-plə-'men-t(ə-)rē\ *adj*

²com·ple·ment \-ˌment\ *vb* : to be complementary to : fill out

¹com·plete \kəm-'plēt\ *adj* **com·plet·er; -est 1** : having no part lacking **2** : brought to an end **3** : fully realized : THOROUGH — **com·plete·ly** *adv* — **com·plete·ness** *n* — **com·ple·tion** \-'plē-shən\ *n*

²complete *vb* **com·plet·ed; com·plet·ing 1** : FINISH, CONCLUDE **2** : to make whole or perfect

¹com·plex \'käm-ˌpleks\ *n* : something made up of or involving an often intricate combination of elements; *esp* : a system of repressed desires, memories, and ideas that exert a dominant influence on the personality and behavior ⟨a guilt ∼⟩

²com·plex \käm-'pleks, kəm-'pleks, 'käm-ˌpleks\ *adj* **1** : composed of two or more parts **2** : consisting of a main clause and one or more subordinate clauses ⟨∼ sentence⟩ **3** : COMPLICATED, INTRICATE — **com·plex·i·ty** \kəm-'plek-sət-ē, käm-\ *n*

complex fraction *n* : a fraction with a fraction or mixed number in the numerator or denominator or both

com·plex·ion \kəm-'plek-shən\ *n* **1** : the hue or appearance of the skin esp. of the face **2** : general appearance — **com·plex·ioned** \-shənd\ *adj*

complex number *n* : a number (as $3 + 4\sqrt{-1}$) formed by adding a real number to the product of a real number and the square root of minus one

com·pli·ance \kəm-'plī-əns\ *n* **1** : the act of complying to a demand or proposal **2** : a disposition to yield — **com·pli·ant** \-ənt\ *adj*

com·pli·cate \'käm-plə-ˌkāt\ *vb* **-cat·ed; -cat·ing** : to make or become complex or intricate — **com·pli·ca·tion** \ˌkäm-plə-'kā-shən\ *n*

com·pli·cat·ed \'käm-plə-ˌkāt-əd\ *adj* **1** : consisting of parts intricately combined **2** : difficult to analyze, understand, or explain — **com·pli·cat·ed·ly** *adv*

com·plic·i·ty \kəm-'plis-ət-ē\ *n, pl* **-ties** : the state of being an accomplice

¹com·pli·ment \'käm-plə-ment\ *n* **1** : an expression of approval or courtesy; *esp* : a flattering remark **2** *pl* : best wishes : REGARDS

²com·pli·ment \-ˌment\ *vb* : to pay a compliment to

com·pli·men·ta·ry \ˌkäm-plə-'men-t(ə-)rē\ *adj* **1** : containing or expressing a compliment **2** : given free as a courtesy ⟨∼ ticket⟩

com·ply \kəm-'plī\ *vb* **com·plied; com·ply·ing** : ACQUIESCE, YIELD

¹com·po·nent \kəm-'pō-nənt, 'käm-ˌpō-\ *n* : a component part **syn** ingredient, element, factor, constituent

²component *adj* : serving to form a part of : CONSTITUENT

com·port \kəm-'pōrt\ *vb* **1** : AGREE, ACCORD **2** : CONDUCT **syn** behave, acquit, deport

com·port·ment \-mənt\ *n* : BEHAVIOR, BEARING

com·pose \kəm-'pōz\ *vb* **com·posed; com·pos·ing** **1** : to form by putting together : FASHION **2** : to produce (as pages of type) by composition **3** : ADJUST, ARRANGE **4** : CALM, QUIET **5** : to practice composition ⟨∼ music⟩ — **com·posed** \-'pōzd\ *adj* — **com·pos·er** *n*

composing stick *n* : a hand-held compositor's tray with an adjustable slide for setting type

¹com·pos·ite \käm-'päz-ət, kəm-\ *adj* **1** : made up of distinct parts or elements **2** : of, relating to, or being a large family of flowering plants (as the daisy) that bear many small flowers united into compact heads resembling single flowers

²composite *n* **1** : something composite **2** : a plant of the composite family **syn** blend, compound, mixture, amalgamation

com·po·si·tion \ˌkäm-pə-'zish-ən\ *n* **1** : the act or process of composing; *esp* : arrangement of elements in artistic form **2** : the arrangement or production of type for printing **3** : MAKEUP, CONSTITUTION **4** : a product of mixing various elements or ingredients **5** : a literary, musical, or artistic product; *esp* : ESSAY

com·pos·i·tor \kəm-'päz-ət-ər\ *n* : one who sets type

com·post \'käm-ˌpōst\ *n* : a fertilizing material consisting largely of decayed organic matter

com·po·sure \kəm-'pō-zhər\ *n* : CALMNESS, SELF-POSSESSION

com·pote \'käm-ˌpōt\ *n* **1** : fruits cooked in syrup **2** : a bowl (as of glass) usu. with a base and stem from which compotes, fruits, nuts, or sweets are served

¹com·pound \(')käm-'paund, kəm-\ *vb* [ME *compounen,* fr. MF *compondre,* fr. L *componere,* fr. *com-* together + *ponere* to put] **1** : COMBINE **2** : to form by combining parts ⟨∼ a medicine⟩ **3** : SETTLE ⟨∼ a dispute⟩ **4** : to increase (as interest) by an amount that itself increases; *also* : to add to **5** : to forbear prosecution of (an offense) in return for some reward

²com·pound \'käm-ˌpaund\ *adj* **1** : made up of two or more parts **2** : composed of united similar parts esp. of a kind usu. separate ⟨a ∼ plant ovary⟩ **3** : formed by the combination of two or more otherwise independent elements ⟨∼ sentence⟩

³com·pound \'käm-ˌpaund\ *n* **1** : a word consisting of parts that are words **2** : something formed from a union of elements or parts; *esp* : a distinct substance formed by the union of two or more chemical elements **syn** mixture, composite, blend, admixture, alloy

⁴com·pound \'käm-ˌpaund\ *n* [by folk etymology fr. Malay *kampong* group of buildings, village] : an enclosure containing buildings

compound interest *n* : interest computed on the sum of an original principal and accrued interest

com·pre·hend \ˌkäm-pri-'hend\ *vb* **1**

: UNDERSTAND **2** : INCLUDE — **com•pre•hen•si•ble** \-'hen-sə-bəl\ *adj* — **com•pre•hen•sion** \-'hen-chən\ *n* — **com•pre•hen•sive** \-siv\ *adj*

¹com•press \kəm-'pres\ *vb* : to squeeze together : CONDENSE **syn** constrict, contract, shrink — **com•pressed** *adj* — **com•pres•sion** \-'presh-ən\ *n* — **com•pres•sor** \-'pres-ər\ *n*

²com•press \'käm-,pres\ *n* : a soft often wet or medicated pad used to press upon an injured bodily part

compressed air *n* : air under pressure greater than that of the atmosphere

com•prise \kəm-'prīz\ *vb* **com•prised; com•pris•ing** **1** : INCLUDE, CONTAIN **2** : to be made up of **3** : COMPOSE, CONSTITUTE

¹com•pro•mise \'käm-prə-,mīz\ *n* : a settlement of differences reached by mutual concessions; *also* : the agreement thus made

²compromise *vb* **-mised; -mis•ing** **1** : to settle by compromise **2** : to endanger the reputation of

comp•trol•ler \kən-'trō-lər, 'kämp-,trō-\ *n* : an official who audits and supervises expenditures and accounts

com•pul•sion \kəm-'pəl-shən\ *n* **1** : COERCION **2** : an irresistible impulse **syn** constraint, force, violence, duress — **com•pul•sive** \-siv\ *adj* — **com•pul•so•ry** \-'pəls-(ə-)rē\ *adj*

com•punc•tion \kəm-'pəŋk-shən\ *n* : anxiety arising from guilt : REMORSE

com•pute \kəm-'pyüt\ *vb* **com•put•ed; com•put•ing** : CALCULATE, RECKON — **com•pu•ta•tion** \,käm-pyù-'tā-shən\ *n* — **com•pu•ta•tion•al** *adj*

computed tomography *n* : radiography in which a three-dimensional image of a body structure is constructed by computer from a series of plane cross-sectional images made along an axis

com•put•er \kəm-'pyüt-ər\ *n* : a programmable electronic device that can store, retrieve, and process data

com•put•er•ize \kəm-'pyüt-ə-,rīz\ *vb* **-ized; -iz•ing** **1** : to carry out, control, or produce by means of a computer **2** : to provide with computers **3** : to store in a computer; *also* : put into a form that a computer can use — **com•put•er•iza•tion** \-,pyüt-ə-rə-'zā-shən\ *n*

computerized axial tomography *n* : COMPUTED TOMOGRAPHY

com•rade \'käm-,rad, -rəd\ *n* [MF *comarade* group sleeping in one room, roommate, companion, fr. Sp *comarada*, fr. *cámara* room, fr. LL *camera*] : COMPANION, ASSOCIATE — **com•rade•ly** *adj* — **com•rade•ship** *n*

¹con \'kän\ *vb* **conned; con•ning** **1** : MEMORIZE **2** : STUDY

²con *adv* : in opposition : AGAINST

³con *n* : an opposing argument, person, or position

⁴con *vb* **conned; con•ning** **1** : SWINDLE **2** : PERSUADE, CAJOLE

⁵con *n* : CONVICT

con brio \kän-'brē-ō, kōn-\ *adv* : with spirit : VIGOROUSLY — used as a direction in music

conc *abbr* concentrated

con•cat•e•na•tion \(,)kän-,kat-ə-'nā-shən\ *n* : a series connected like links in a chain — **con•cat•e•nate** \kän-'kat-ə-,nāt\ *vb*

con•cave \(')kän-'kāv\ *adj* : curved or rounded inward like the inside of a bowl — **con•cav•i•ty** \kän-'kav-ət-ē\ *n*

con•ceal \kən-'sēl\ *vb* : to place out of sight : HIDE — **con•ceal•ment** *n*

con•cede \kən-'sēd\ *vb* **con•ced•ed; con•ced•ing** **1** : to admit to be true **2** : GRANT, YIELD **syn** allow, acknowledge, admit, avow, confess

con•ceit \kən-'sēt\ *n* **1** : excessively high opinion of oneself, one's appearance, or ability : VANITY **2** : an elaborate or strained metaphor — **con•ceit•ed** \-əd\ *adj*

con•ceive \kən-'sēv\ *vb* **con•ceived; con•ceiv•ing** **1** : to become pregnant **2** : to form an idea of : THINK, IMAGINE — **con•ceiv•able** \-'sē-və-bəl\ *adj* — **con•ceiv•ably** \-blē\ *adv*

con•cel•e•brant \kən-'sel-ə-brənt\ *n* : one of two or more members of the clergy celebrating the Eucharist or Mass together

¹con•cen•trate \'kän-sən-,trāt\ *vb* **-trat•ed; -trat•ing** **1** : to gather into one body, mass, or force **2** : to make less dilute **3** : to fix one's powers, efforts, or attentions on one thing

²concentrate *n* : something concentrated

con•cen•tra•tion \,kän-sən-'trā-shən\ *n* **1** : the act or process of concentrating : the state of being concentrated; *esp*

: direction of attention on a single object **2** : the relative content of a component : STRENGTH

concentration camp *n* : a camp where persons (as prisoners of war or political prisoners) are confined

con·cen·tric \kən-'sen-trik\ *adj* **1** : having a common center ⟨∼ circles⟩ **2** : COAXIAL

con·cept \'kän-ˌsept\ *n* : THOUGHT, NOTION, IDEA — **con·cep·tu·al** \kən-'sep-chə(-wə)l\ *adj*

con·cep·tion \kən-'sep-shən\ *n* **1** : the act of conceiving or being conceived **2** : the power to form ideas or concepts **3** : IDEA, CONCEPT **4** : the originating of something

con·cep·tu·al·ize \-'sep-chə(-wə)-ˌlīz\ *vb* **-ized; -iz·ing** : to form a conception of

¹con·cern \kən-'sərn\ *vb* **1** : to relate to **2** : to be the business of : INVOLVE **3** : ENGAGE, OCCUPY

²concern *n* **1** : INTEREST, ANXIETY **2** : AFFAIR, MATTER **3** : a business organization **syn** care, worry, anxiety, disquiet, unease

con·cerned \-'sərnd\ *adj* : ANXIOUS, TROUBLED

con·cern·ing \-'sər-niŋ\ *prep* : relating to : REGARDING

con·cern·ment \kən-'sərn-mənt\ *n* **1** : something in which one is concerned **2** : IMPORTANCE, CONSEQUENCE

¹con·cert \'kän-(ˌ)sərt\ *n* **1** : agreement in a plan or design **2** : a concerted action **3** : a public performance of several musical compositions

²con·cert \kən-'sərt\ *vb* : to plan together

con·cert·ed \kən-'sərt-əd\ *adj* : mutually agreed on; *also* : performed in unison

con·cer·ti·na \ˌkän-sər-'tē-nə\ *n* : an instrument of the accordion family

con·cert·mas·ter \'kän-sərt-ˌmas-tər\ *or* **con·cert·meis·ter** \-ˌmī-stər\ *n* : the leader of the first violins of an orchestra and assistant to the conductor

con·cer·to \kən-'chert-ō\ *n, pl* **-ti** \-(ˌ)ē\ *or* **-tos** [It] : a piece for one or more solo instruments and orchestra in three movements

con·ces·sion \kən-'sesh-ən\ *n* **1** : an act of conceding or yielding **2** : something yielded **3** : a grant by a government of land or of a right to use it **4** : a

grant of a portion of premises for some specific purpose — **con·ces·sion·ary** \-'sesh-ə-ˌner-ē\ *adj*

con·ces·sion·aire \kən-ˌsesh-ə-'na(ə)r, -'ne(ə)r\ *n* : one that owns or operates a concession

conch \'käŋk, 'känch\ *n, pl* **conchs** \'käŋks\ *or* **conch·es** \'kän-chəz\ : a large spiral-shelled marine gastropod mollusk; *also* : its shell

con·cierge \kōⁿ-'syerzh\ *n, pl* **cierges** \-'syerzh(-əz)\ [F, fr. L *conservus* fellow slave, fr. *com-* with + *servus* slave] **1** : a resident in an apartment building who performs services for the tenants **2** : a usu. multilingual hotel staff member

con·cil·i·ate \kən-'sil-ē-ˌāt\ *vb* **-at·ed; -at·ing 1** : to bring into agreement : RECONCILE **2** : to gain the goodwill of — **con·cil·i·a·tion** \-ˌsil-ē-'ā-shən\ *n* — **con·cil·ia·to·ry** \-'sil-yə-ˌtōr-ē, -'sil-ē-ə-\ *adj*

con·cise \kən-'sīs\ *adj* : expressing much in few words : TERSE, SUCCINCT — **con·cise·ly** *adv* — **con·cise·ness** *n*

con·clave \'kän-ˌklāv\ *n* [ML, fr. L, room that can be locked, fr. *com-* together + *clavis* key] : a private gathering; *also* : CONVENTION

con·clude \kən-'klüd\ *vb* **con·clud·ed; con·clud·ing 1** : to bring to a close : END **2** : DECIDE, JUDGE **3** : to bring about as a result **syn** close, finish, terminate, complete, halt, end

con·clu·sion \kən-'klü-zhən\ *n* **1** : the logical consequence of a reasoning process **2** : TERMINATION, END **3** : OUTCOME, RESULT — **con·clu·sive** \-siv\ *adj* — **con·clu·sive·ly** *adv*

con·coct \kən-'käkt, kän-\ *vb* **1** : to prepare by combining diverse ingredients **2** : DEVISE ⟨∼ a scheme⟩ — **con·coc·tion** \-'käk-shən\ *n*

con·com·i·tant \-'käm-ət-ənt\ *adj* : ACCOMPANYING, ATTENDING — **concomitant** *n*

con·cord \'kän-ˌkȯrd, 'käŋ-\ *n* : AGREEMENT, HARMONY

con·cor·dance \kən-'kȯrd-ᵊns\ *n* **1** : an alphabetical index of words in a book or in an author's works with the passages in which they occur **2** : AGREEMENT

con·cor·dant \-ᵊnt\ *adj* : HARMONIOUS, AGREEING

con·cor·dat \kən-'kȯr-ˌdat\ *n* : AGREE-MENT, COVENANT

con·course \'kän-ˌkōrs\ *n* **1** : a flocking together of people : GATHERING **2** : an open space or hall (as in a bus terminal) where crowds gather

con·cres·cence \kən-'kres-ᵊns\ *n* : a growing together — **con·cres·cent** \-ᵊnt\ *adj*

¹con·crete \kän-'krēt, 'kän-ˌkrēt\ *adj* **1** : naming a real thing or class of things : not abstract **2** : not theoretical : ACTUAL **3** : made of or relating to concrete

²con·crete \'kän-ˌkrēt, kän-'krēt\ *vb* **con·cret·ed; con·cret·ing 1** : SOLIDIFY **2** : to cover with concrete

³con·crete \'kän-ˌkrēt, kän-'krēt\ *n* : a hard building material made by mixing cement, sand, and gravel with water

con·cre·tion \kän-'krē-shən\ *n* : a hard mass esp. when formed abnormally in the body

con·cu·bine \'käŋ-kyu̇-ˌbīn\ *n* [ME, fr. MF, fr. L *concubina*, fr. *com-* with + *cubare* to lie] : a woman who is not legally a wife but lives with a man and has a recognized position in his household — **con·cu·bi·nage** \kän-'kyü-bə-nij\ *n*

con·cu·pis·cence \kän-'kyü-pə-səns\ *n* : ardent sexual desire : LUST

con·cur \kən-'kər\ *vb* **con·curred; con·cur·ring 1** : to act together **2** : AGREE **3** : COINCIDE **syn** unite, combine, cooperate, band, join

con·cur·rence \-'kər-əns\ *n* **1** : agreement in action or opinion **2** : CONJUNCTION, COINCIDENCE

con·cur·rent \-'kər-ənt\ *adj* **1** : happening or operating at the same time **2** : joint and equal in authority

con·cus·sion \kən-'kəsh-ən\ *n* **1** : AGITATION, SHAKING **2** : a sharp sudden blow or collision; *also* : bodily injury (as to the brain) resulting from a sudden jar

con·demn \kən-'dem\ *vb* **1** : to declare to be wrong **2** : to convict of guilt **3** : to sentence judically **4** : to pronounce unfit for use ⟨∼ a building⟩ **5** : to declare forfeited or taken for public use **syn** denounce, censure, blame, criticize, reprehend — **con·dem·na·tion** \ˌkän-ˌdem-'nā-shən\ *n* — **con·dem·na·to·ry** \kən-'dem-nə-ˌtōr-ē\ *adj*

con·den·sate \'kän-dən-ˌsāt, kən-'den-\ *n* : a product of condensation

con·dense \kən-'dens\ *vb* **con·densed; con·dens·ing 1** : to make or become more compact or dense : CONCENTRATE **2** : to change from vapor to liquid **syn** contract, shrink, compress, constrict — **con·den·sa·tion** \ˌkän-ˌden-'sā-shən, -dən-\ *n*

con·dens·er \kən-'den-sər\ *n* **1** : one that condenses **2** : CAPACITOR

con·de·scend \ˌkän-di-'send\ *vb* : to assume an air of superiority **syn** stoop, deign — **con·de·scend·ing·ly** \-'sen-diŋ-lē\ *adv* — **con·de·scen·sion** \-'sen-chən\ *n*

con·dign \kən-'dīn, 'kän-ˌdīn\ *adj* : DESERVED, APPROPRIATE ⟨∼ punishment⟩

con·di·ment \'kän-də-mənt\ *n* : something used to make food savory; *esp* : a pungent seasoning (as pepper)

¹con·di·tion \kən-'dish-ən\ *n* **1** : something essential to the occurrence of some other thing **2** : state of being **3** : station in life : social rank **4** : state in respect to fitness (as for action or use); *esp* : state of health **5** *pl* : state of affairs : CIRCUMSTANCES

²condition *vb* **-di·tioned; -di·tion·ing 1** : to put into proper condition for action or use **2** : to adapt, modify, or mold to respond in a particular way **3** : to modify so that an act or response previously associated with one stimulus becomes associated with another

con·di·tion·al \kən-'dish-(ə-)nəl\ *adj* : containing, implying, or depending on a condition — **con·di·tion·al·ly** \-ē\ *adv*

con·di·tioned *adj* : determined or established by conditioning

con·dole \kən-'dōl\ *vb* **con·doled; con·dol·ing** : to express sympathetic sorrow — **con·do·lence** \kən-'dō-ləns, 'kän-də-\ *n*

con·dom \'kän-dəm, 'kən-\ *n* : a usu. membranous or rubber sheath worn over the penis to prevent pregnancy or the transmission of sexually transmitted disease during sexual intercourse

con·do·min·i·um \ˌkän-də-'min-ē-əm\ *n, pl* **-ums 1** : joint sovereignty (as by two or more nations) **2** : a politically dependent territory under condominium **3** : individual ownership of a unit (as an apartment) in a multiunit structure; *also* : a unit so owned

con•done \kən-'dōn\ *vb* **con•doned; con•don•ing** : to overlook or forgive (an offense) by treating the offender as if he had done nothing wrong **syn** excuse, pardon, forgive, remit — **con•do•na•tion** \ˌkän-də-'nā-shən\ *n*

con•dor \'kän-dər, -ˌdȯr\ *n* [Sp *cóndor*, fr. Quechua (a So. American Indian language) *kúntur*] : a very large American vulture of the high Andes; *also* : a related nearly extinct vulture of southern California now resident only in captivity

con•duce \kən-'d(y)üs\ *vb* **con•duced; con•duc•ing** : to lead or contribute to a result — **con•du•cive** *adj*

¹con•duct \'kän-(ˌ)dəkt\ *n* **1** : MANAGEMENT, DIRECTION **2** : BEHAVIOR

²con•duct \kən-'dəkt\ *vb* **1** : GUIDE, ESCORT **2** : MANAGE, DIRECT **3** : to act as a medium for conveying **4** : BEHAVE, BEAR — **con•duc•tion** \-'dək-shən\ *n*

con•duc•tance \kən-'dək-təns\ *n* : the readiness with which a conductor transmits an electric current

con•duc•tive \kən-'dək-tiv\ *adj* : having the power to conduct (as heat or electricity) — **con•duc•tiv•i•ty** \ˌkän-ˌdək-'tiv-ət-ē\ *n*

con•duc•tor \kən-'dək-tər\ *n* **1** : one that conducts **2** : a collector of fares in a public conveyance **3** : the leader of a musical ensemble

con•duit \'kän-ˌd(y)ü-ət, -d(w)ət\ *n* **1** : a channel for conveying fluid **2** : a tube or trough for protecting electric wires or cables **3** : a means of transmitting or distributing

con•dyle \'kän-ˌdīl, -dᵊl\ *n* : an articular prominence of a bone — **con•dy•lar** \-də-lər\ *adj*

cone \'kōn\ *n* **1** : the scaly fruit of trees of the pine family **2** : a solid figure formed by rotating a right triangle about one of its legs **3** : a solid figure that slopes evenly to a point from a usu. circular base **4** : something shaped like a cone

Con•es•to•ga \ˌkän-ə-'stō-gə\ *n* : a broad-wheeled covered wagon formerly used for transporting freight across the prairies

co•ney \'kō-nē\ *n, pl* **coneys** **1** : a rabbit or its fur **2** : PIKA

conf *abbr* conference

con•fab \'kän-ˌfab, kən-'fab\ *n* : CONFABULATION

con•fab•u•la•tion \kən-ˌfab-yə-'lā-shən\ *n* : CHAT; *also* : CONFERENCE

con•fec•tion \kən-'fek-shən\ *n* : a fancy dish or sweet; *also* : CANDY

con•fec•tion•er \-sh(ə-)nər\ *n* : a maker of or dealer in confections (as candies)

con•fec•tion•ery \-shə-ˌner-ē\ *n, pl* **-er•ies** **1** : sweet foods **2** : a confectioner's place of business

Confed *abbr* Confederate

con•fed•er•a•cy \kən-'fed-(ə-)rə-sē\ *n, pl* **-cies** **1** : LEAGUE, ALLIANCE **2** *cap* : the 11 southern states that seceded from the U.S. in 1860 and 1861

¹con•fed•er•ate \kən-'fed-(ə-)rət\ *adj* **1** : united in a league : ALLIED **2** *cap* : of or relating to the Confederacy

²confederate *n* **1** : ALLY, ACCOMPLICE **2** *cap* : an adherent of the Confederacy

³con•fed•er•ate \-'fed-ə-ˌrāt\ *vb* **-at•ed; -at•ing** : to unite in a confederacy or a conspiracy

con•fed•er•a•tion \kən-ˌfed-ə-'rā-shən\ *n* **1** : an act of confederating : ALLIANCE **2** : LEAGUE

con•fer \kən-'fər\ *vb* **con•ferred; con•fer•ring** **1** : GRANT, BESTOW **2** : to exchange views : CONSULT — **con•fer•ee** \ˌkän-fə-'rē\ *n*

con•fer•ence \'kän-f(ə-)rəns\ *n* : an interchange of views; *also* : a meeting for this purpose

con•fess \kən-'fes\ *vb* **1** : to acknowledge or disclose one's misdeed, fault, or sin **2** : to acknowledge one's sins to God or to a priest **3** : to receive the confession of (a penitent) **syn** admit, own, avow, concede, grant

con•fess•ed•ly \-'fes-əd-lē\ *adv* : by confession : ADMITTEDLY

con•fes•sion \-'fesh-ən\ *n* **1** : an act of confessing (as in the sacrament of penance) **2** : an acknowledgment of guilt **3** : a formal statement of religious beliefs **4** : a religious body having a common creed — **con•fes•sion•al** *adj*

con•fes•sion•al \-'fesh-(ə-)nəl\ *n* : a place where a priest hears confessions

con•fes•sor \kən-'fes-ər, 2 *also* 'kän-ˌfes-\ *n* **1** : one that confesses **2** : a priest who hears confessions

con•fet•ti \kən-'fet-ē\ *n* [It, pl. of *confet-*

to sweetmeat, fr. ML *confectum,* fr. L *conficere* to prepare] : bits of colored paper or ribbon for throwing about in celebration

con·fi·dant \'kän-fə-ˌdant, -ˌdänt\ *n* : one to whom secrets are confided

con·fide \kən-'fīd\ *vb* **con·fid·ed; con·fid·ing** **1** : to have or show faith : TRUST ⟨∼ in a friend⟩ **2** : to tell confidentially ⟨∼ a secret⟩ **3** : ENTRUST

¹con·fi·dence \'kän-fəd-əns\ *n* **1** : TRUST, RELIANCE **2** : SELF-ASSURANCE, BOLDNESS **3** : a state of trust or intimacy — **con·fi·dent** \-fəd-ənt\ *adj* — **con·fi·dent·ly** *adv*

²confidence *adj* : of or relating to swindling by false promises

con·fi·den·tial \ˌkän-fə-'den-chəl\ *adj* **1** : SECRET, PRIVATE **2** : enjoying or treated with confidence ⟨∼ clerk⟩ — **con·fi·den·tial·ly** \-ē\ *adv*

con·fig·u·ra·tion \kən-ˌfig-yə-'rā-shən\ *n* : structural arrangement of parts : SHAPE

con·fine \kən-'fīn\ *vb* **con·fined; con·fin·ing** **1** : to restrict to a particular place or situation **2** : IMPRISON **3** : to keep within limits : RESTRAIN — **con·fine·ment** *n* — **con·fin·er** *n*

con·fines \'kän-ˌfīnz\ *n pl* : BOUNDS, BORDERS

con·firm \kən-'fərm\ *vb* **1** : to make firm or firmer **2** : RATIFY **3** : to administer the rite of confirmation to **4** : VERIFY, CORROBORATE — **con·fir·ma·to·ry** \-'fər-mə-ˌtōr-ē\ *adj* — **con·firmed** *adj*

con·fir·ma·tion \ˌkän-fər-'mā-shən\ *n* **1** : a religious ceremony admitting a person to full membership in a church or synagogue **2** : an act of ratifying or corroborating; *also* : PROOF

con·fis·cate \'kän-fə-ˌskāt\ *vb* **-cat·ed; -cat·ing** [L *confiscare,* fr. *com-* with + *fiscus* treasury] : to take possession of by or as if by public authority — **con·fis·ca·tion** \ˌkän-fə-'skā-shən\ *n* — **con·fis·ca·to·ry** \kən-'fis-kə-ˌtōr-ē\ *adj*

con·fla·gra·tion \ˌkän-flə-'grā-shən\ *n* : FIRE; *esp* : a large disastrous fire

¹con·flict \'kän-ˌflikt\ *n* **1** : WAR **2** : a clash between hostile or opposing elements or ideas

²con·flict \kən-'flikt\ *vb* : to show antagonism or irreconcilability : CLASH

con·flu·ence \'kän-ˌflü-əns, kən-'flü-\ *n* **1** : a coming together at one point **2** : the meeting or place of meeting of two or more streams — **con·flu·ent** \-ənt\ *adj*

con·flux \'kän-ˌfləks\ *n* : CONFLUENCE

con·fo·cal \kän-'fō-kəl\ *adj* : having the same foci — **con·fo·cal·ly** \-ē\ *adv*

con·form \kən-'förm\ *vb* **1** : to make or be like : AGREE **2** : to obey customs or standards — **con·form·able** *adj*

con·for·mance \kən-'för-məns\ *n* : CONFORMITY

con·for·ma·tion \ˌkän-för-'mā-shən\ *n* : arrangement and congruity of parts

con·for·mi·ty \kən-'för-mət-ē\ *n, pl* **-ties** **1** : HARMONY, AGREEMENT **2** : COMPLIANCE, OBEDIENCE

con·found \kən-'faùnd, kän-\ *vb* **1** : to throw into disorder or confusion : DISMAY **2** : to mix up : CONFUSE **syn** bewilder, puzzle, perplex, befog

con·fra·ter·ni·ty \ˌkän-frə-'tər-nət-ē\ *n* : a society devoted to a religious or charitable cause

con·frere \'kän-ˌfreər, 'kōⁿ-\ *n* : COLLEAGUE, COMRADE

con·front \kən-'frənt\ *vb* **1** : to face esp. in challenge : OPPOSE **2** : to cause to face or meet — **con·fron·ta·tion** \ˌkän-frən-'tā-shən\ *n*

Con·fu·cian·ism \kən-'fyü-shən-ˌiz-əm\ *n* : a religion growing out of the teachings of the Chinese philosopher Confucius — **Con·fu·cian** *n or adj*

con·fuse \kən-'fyüz\ *vb* **con·fused; con·fus·ing** **1** : to make mentally unclear or uncertain; *also* : to disturb the composure of **2** : to mix up : JUMBLE **syn** muddle, befuddle, addle, fluster — **con·fus·ed·ly** \-'fyü-zəd-lē\ *adv*

con·fu·sion \-'fyü-zhən\ *n* **1** : DISORDER, JUMBLE **2** : turmoil or uncertainty of mind

con·fute \kən-'fyüt\ *vb* **con·fut·ed; con·fut·ing** : to overwhelm by argument : REFUTE — **con·fu·ta·tion** \ˌkän-fyü-'tā-shən\ *n*

cong *abbr* congress; congressional

con·ga \'käŋ-gə\ *n* : a Cuban dance of African origin performed by a group usu. in single file

con·geal \kən-'jēl\ *vb* **1** : FREEZE **2** : to make or become hard or thick

con·ge·ner \'kän-jə-nər\ *n* : one related to another; *esp* : one of the same taxonomic genus as another plant or animal — **con·ge·ner·ic** \ˌkän-jə-'ner-ik\ *adj*

con·ge·nial \kən-'jē-nyəl\ *adj* 1 : KIN-DRED, SYMPATHETIC 2 : suited to one's taste or nature : AGREEABLE — **con·ge·ni·al·i·ty** \-ˌjē-nē-'al-ət-ē\ *n* — **con·ge·nial·ly** \-'jē-nyə-lē\ *adv*

con·gen·i·tal \kən-'jen-ə-t³l\ *adj* : existing at or dating from birth but usu. not hereditary **syn** inborn, innate, natural

con·ger eel \ˌkän-gər-\ *n* : a large edible marine eel

con·ge·ries \'kän-jə-(ˌ)rēz\ *n, pl* **congeries** *same*\ : AGGREGATION, COLLECTION

con·gest \kən-'jest\ *vb* 1 : to cause excessive fullness of the blood vessels of (as a lung) 2 : to obstruct by overcrowding — **con·ges·tion** \-'jes-chən\ *n* — **con·ges·tive** \-'jes-tiv\ *adj*

¹**con·glom·er·ate** \kən-'gläm-(ə-)rət\ *adj* [L *conglomerare* to roll together, fr. *com-* together + *glomerare* to wind into a ball, fr. *glomer-, glomus* ball] : made up of parts from various sources

²**con·glom·er·ate** \-ə-ˌrāt\ *vb* **-at·ed; -at·ing** : to form into a ball or mass — **con·glom·er·a·tion** \-ˌgläm-ə-'rā-shən\ *n*

³**con·glom·er·ate** \-(ə-)rət\ *n* 1 : a mass formed of fragments from various sources; *esp* : a rock composed of fragments varying from pebbles to boulders held together by a cementing material 2 : a widely diversified corporation

con·grat·u·late \kən-'grach-ə-ˌlāt\ *vb* **-lat·ed; -lat·ing** : to express sympathetic pleasure to on account of success or good fortune : FELICITATE — **con·grat·u·la·tion** \-ˌgrach-ə-'lā-shən\ *n* — **con·grat·u·la·to·ry** \-'grach-ə-lə-ˌtōr-ē\ *adj*

con·gre·gate \'käŋ-gri-ˌgāt\ *vb* **-gat·ed; -gat·ing** [ME *congregaten*, fr. L *congregare*, fr. *com-* together + *greg-, grex* flock] : ASSEMBLE

con·gre·ga·tion \ˌkäŋ-gri-'gā-shən\ *n* 1 : an assembly of persons met esp. for worship; *also* : a group that habitually so meets 2 : a company or order of religious persons under a common rule 3 : the act or an instance of congregating

con·gre·ga·tion·al \-sh(ə-)nəl\ *adj* 1 : of or relating to a congregation 2 *cap* : observing the faith and practice of certain Protestant churches which recognize the independence of each congregation in church matters — **con·gre·ga·tion·al·ism** \-ˌiz-əm\ *n, often cap* — **con·gre·ga·tion·al·ist** \-əst\ *n, often cap*

con·gress \'käŋ-grəs\ *n* 1 : an assembly esp. of delegates for discussion and usu. action on some question 2 : the body of senators and representatives constituting a nation's legislature — **con·gres·sio·nal** \kən-'gresh-(ə-)nəl\ *adj*

con·gress·man \'käŋ-grəs-mən\ *n* : a member of a congress

con·gress·wom·an \-ˌwùm-ən\ *n* : a female member of a congress

con·gru·ence \kən-'grü-əns, 'käŋ-grə-wəns\ *n* : the quality of according or coinciding : CONGRUITY — **con·gru·ent** \kən-'grü-ənt, 'käŋ-grə-wənt\ *adj*

con·gru·en·cy \-ən-sē, -wən-\ *n, pl* **-cies** : CONGRUENCE

con·gru·ity \kən-'grü-ət-ē, kän-\ *n, pl* **-ities** : correspondence between things — **con·gru·ous** \'käŋ-grə-wəs\ *adj*

con·ic \'kän-ik\ *adj* 1 : of or relating to a cone 2 : CONICAL

con·i·cal \'kän-i-kəl\ *adj* : resembling a cone esp. in shape

co·ni·fer \'kän-ə-fər, 'kōn-\ *n* : any of an order of shrubs or trees (as the pines) that usu. are evergreen and bear cones — **co·nif·er·ous** \kō-'nif-(ə-)rəs\ *adj*

conj *abbr* conjunction

con·jec·ture \kən-'jek-chər\ *n* : GUESS, SURMISE — **con·jec·tur·al** \-chə-rəl\ *adj* — **conjecture** *vb*

con·join \kən-'jöin\ *vb* : to join together — **con·joint** \-'jöint\ *adj*

con·ju·gal \'kän-ji-gəl, kən-'jü-\ *adj* : of or relating to marriage : MATRIMONIAL

¹**con·ju·gate** \'kän-ji-gət, -jə-ˌgāt\ *adj* 1 : united esp. in pairs : COUPLED 2 : of kindred origin and meaning ⟨*sing* and *song* are ∼⟩

²**con·ju·gate** \-jə-ˌgāt\ *vb* **-gat·ed; -gat·ing** 1 : INFLECT ⟨∼ a verb⟩ 2 : to join together : COUPLE

con·ju·ga·tion \ˌkän-jə-'gā-shən\ *n* 1 : a schematic arrangement of the inflectional forms of a verb 2 : the act of conjugating : the state of being conjugated

con·junct \kən-'jəŋkt, kän-\ *adj* : JOINED, UNITED

con·junc·tion \kən-'jəŋk-shən\ *n* **1** : UNION, COMBINATION **2** : occurrence at the same time **3** : a word that joins together sentences, clauses, phrases, or words

con·junc·ti·va \ˌkän-ˌjəŋk-'tī-və\ *n, pl* **-vas** *or* **-vae** \-(ˌ)vē\ : the mucous membrane lining the inner surface of the eyelids and continuing over the forepart of the eyeball

con·junc·tive \kən-'jəŋk-tiv\ *adj* **1** : CONNECTIVE **2** : CONJUNCT **3** : being or functioning like a conjunction

con·junc·ti·vi·tis \kən-ˌjəŋk-ti-'vīt-əs\ *n* : inflammation of the conjunctiva

con·junc·ture \kən-'jəŋk-chər\ *n* **1** : CONJUNCTION, UNION **2** : a combination of circumstances or events esp. producing a crisis

con·jure \'kän-jər, 'kən- *for 1, 2;* kən-'jůr *for 3*\ *vb* **con·jured; con·jur·ing** \'känj-(ə-)riŋ, 'kənj-; kən-'jů(ə)r-iŋ\ **1** : to implore earnestly or solemnly **2** : to practice magic; *esp* : to summon (as a devil) by sorcery **3** : to practice sleight of hand — **con·ju·ra·tion** \ˌkän-jů-'rā-shən, ˌkən-\ *n* — **con·jur·er** *or* **con·ju·ror** \'kän-jər-ər, 'kən-\ *n*

conk \'käŋk\ *vb* : BREAK DOWN; *esp* : STALL ⟨the motor ~ed out⟩

Conn *abbr* Connecticut

con·nect \kə-'nekt\ *vb* **1** : JOIN, LINK **2** : to associate in one's mind — **con·nec·tor** *n*

con·nec·tion \kə-'nek-shən\ *n* **1** : JUNCTION, UNION **2** : logical relationship : COHERENCE; *esp* : relation of a word to other words in a sentence **3** : family relationship **4** : BOND, LINK **5** : a person related by blood or marriage **6** : relationship in social affairs or in business **7** : an association of persons; *esp* : a religious denomination

¹con·nec·tive \kə-'nek-tiv\ *adj* : connecting or functioning in connecting — **con·nec·tiv·i·ty** \ˌkä-ˌnek-'tiv-ət-ē\ *n*

²connective *n* : a word (as a conjunction) that connects words or word groups

con·nip·tion \kə-'nip-shən\ *n* : a fit of rage, hysteria, or alarm

con·nive \kə-'nīv\ *vb* **con·nived; con·niv·ing** [F or L; F *conniver*, fr. L *conivēre*

to close the eyes, connive] **1** : to pretend ignorance of something one ought to oppose as wrong **2** : to cooperate secretly : give secret aid — **con·niv·ance** *n*

con·nois·seur \ˌkän-ə-'sər\ *n* : a critical judge in matters of art or taste

con·no·ta·tion \ˌkän-ə-'tā-shən\ *n* : a meaning in addition to or apart from the thing explicitly named or described by a word

con·no·ta·tive \'kän-ə-ˌtāt-iv, kə-'nōt-ət-\ *adj* **1** : connoting or tending to connote **2** : relating to connotation

con·note \kə-'nōt\ *vb* **con·not·ed; con·not·ing** : to suggest or mean along with or in addition to the explicit meaning

con·nu·bi·al \kə-'n(y)ü-bē-əl\ *adj* : of or relating to marriage : CONJUGAL

con·quer \'käŋ-kər\ *vb* **con·quered; conquer·ing** \-k(ə-)riŋ\ **1** : to gain by force of arms : WIN **2** : to get the better of : OVERCOME **syn** defeat, subjugate, subdue, overthrow, vanquish — **conquer·or** \-kər-ər\ *n*

con·quest \'kän-ˌkwest, 'käŋ-\ *n* **1** : an act of conquering : VICTORY **2** : something conquered

con·quis·ta·dor \kȯn-'kēs-tə-ˌdȯr, kän-'k(w)is-\ *n, pl* **con·quis·ta·do·res** \-ˌkēs-tə-'dȯr-ēz, -ˌk(w)is-\ *or* **con·quis·ta·dors** : CONQUEROR; *esp* : a leader in the Spanish conquest of America and esp. of Mexico and Peru in the 16th century

cons *abbr* consonant

con·san·guin·i·ty \ˌkän-ˌsan-'gwin-ət-ē, -ˌsaŋ-\ *n, pl* **-ties** : blood relationship — **con·san·guin·e·ous** \-'gwin-ē-əs\ *adj*

con·science \'kän-chəns\ *n* : consciousness of the moral right and wrong of one's own acts or motives — **conscience·less** *adj*

con·sci·en·tious \ˌkän-chē-'en-chəs\ *adj* : guided by one's own sense of right and wrong **syn** scrupulous, honorable, honest, upright, just — **con·sci·en·tious·ly** *adv*

conscientious objector *n* : one who refuses to serve in the armed forces or to bear arms on moral or religious grounds

con·scious \'kän-chəs\ *adj* **1** : AWARE **2** : known or felt by one's inner self **3** : mentally awake or alert : not asleep

or unconscious **4** : INTENTIONAL —
con•scious•ly *adv* — **con•scious•ness** *n*
con•script \kən-'skript\ *vb* : to enroll by
compulsion for military or naval service — **con•script** \'kän-ˌskript\ *n* —
con•scrip•tion \kən-'skrip-shən\ *n*
con•se•crate \'kän-sə-ˌkrāt\ *vb* **-crat•ed;**
-crat•ing 1 : to induct (as a bishop)
into an office with a religious rite **2**
: to make or declare sacred ⟨∼ a
church⟩ **3** : to devote solemnly to a
purpose — **con•se•cra•tion** \ˌkän-sə-
'krā-shən\ *n*
con•sec•u•tive \kən-'sek-(y)ət-iv\ *adj*
: following in regular order : SUCCES-
SIVE — **con•sec•u•tive•ly** *adv*
con•sen•su•al \kən-'sench-(ə-)wel,
-'sen-shəl\ *adj* : involving or based on
mutual consent
con•sen•sus \kən-'sen-səs\ *n* **1** : agreement in opinion, testimony, or belief **2**
: collective opinion
¹con•sent \kən-'sent\ *vb* : to give assent
or approval
²consent *n* : approval or acceptance of
something done or proposed by another
con•se•quence \'kän-sə-ˌkwens\ *n* **1**
: RESULT **2** : IMPORTANCE **syn** effect,
outcome, aftermath, upshot
con•se•quent \-kwənt, -ˌkwent\ *adj*
: following as a result or effect
con•se•quen•tial \ˌkän-sə-'kwen-chəl\
adj **1** : having significant consequences **2** : showing self-importance
con•se•quent•ly \'kän-sə-ˌkwent-lē,
-kwənt-\ *adv* : as a result : ACCORD-
INGLY
con•ser•van•cy \kən-'sər-vən-sē,\ *n, pl*
-cies : an organization or area designated to conserve and protect natural
resources
con•ser•va•tion \ˌkän-sər-'vā-shən\ *n*
: PRESERVATION; *esp* : planned management of natural resources
con•ser•va•tion•ist \-sh(ə-)nəst\ *n* : a
person who advocates conservation
esp. of natural resources
con•ser•va•tism \kən-'sər-və-ˌtiz-əm\ *n*
: disposition to keep to established
ways : opposition to change
¹con•ser•va•tive \kən-'sər-vət-iv\ *adj* **1**
: PRESERVATIVE **2** : disposed to maintain existing views, conditions, or institutions **3** : MODERATE, CAUTIOUS —
con•ser•va•tive•ly *adv*

²conservative *n* : a person who is conservative esp. in politics
con•ser•va•tor \kən-'sər-vət-ər, 'kän-
sər-ˌvāt-\ *n* **1** : PROTECTOR, GUARDIAN
2 : one named by a court to protect
the interests of an incompetent (as a
child)
con•ser•va•to•ry \kən-'sər-və-ˌtōr-ē\ *n,
pl* **-ries 1** : GREENHOUSE **2** : a place of
instruction in one of the fine arts (as
music)
¹con•serve \kən-'sərv\ *vb* **con•served;**
con•serv•ing : to keep from losing or
wasting : PRESERVE
²con•serve \'kän-ˌsərv\ *n* **1** : CONFEC-
TION; *esp* : a candied fruit **2** : PRE-
SERVE; *esp* : one prepared from a mixture of fruits
con•sid•er \kən-'sid-ər\ *vb* **-ered; -er•ing**
\-(ə-)riŋ\ [ME *consideren,* fr. MF *con-
siderer,* fr. L *considerare,* lit., to observe the stars, fr. *sider-, sidus* star] **1**
: THINK, PONDER **2** : HEED, REGARD **3**
: JUDGE, BELIEVE — **con•sid•ered** *adj*
con•sid•er•able \-'sid-ər(-ə)-bəl, -'sid-rə-
bəl\ *adj* **1** : IMPORTANT **2** : large in extent, amount, or degree — **con•sid•er•
ably** \-blē\ *adv*
con•sid•er•ate \kən-'sid-(ə-)rət\ *adj* : observant of the rights and feelings of
others **syn** thoughtful, attentive
con•sid•er•ation \kən-ˌsid-ə-'rā-shən\ *n*
1 : careful thought : DELIBERATION **2**
: a matter taken into account **3**
: thoughtful attention **4** : JUDGMENT,
OPINION **5** : RECOMPENSE
con•sid•er•ing \-(ə-)riŋ\ *prep* : in view of
: taking into account
con•sign \kən-'sīn\ *vb* **1** : ENTRUST, COM-
MIT **2** : to deliver formally **3** : to send
(goods) to an agent for sale — **con•
sign•ee** \ˌkän-sə-'nē, -ˌsī-; kən-ˌsī-\ *n*
— **con•sign•or** \ˌkän-sə-'nor, -ˌsī-;
kən-ˌsī-\ *n*
con•sign•ment \kən-'sīn-mənt\ *n*
: something consigned esp. in a single
shipment
con•sist \kən-'sist\ *vb* **1** : to be inherent
: LIE — used with *in* **2** : to be composed or made up
con•sis•tence \kən-'sis-təns\ *n* : CONSIS-
TENCY
con•sis•ten•cy \-tən-sē\ *n, pl* **-cies 1**
: COHESIVENESS, FIRMNESS **2** : agreement or harmony in parts or of different things **3** : UNIFORMITY ⟨∼ of be-

havior⟩ — **con·sis·tent** \-tənt\ *adj* — **con·sis·tent·ly** *adv*

con·sis·to·ry \kən-'sis-t(ə-)rē\ *n, pl* **-ries** : a solemn assembly (as of Roman Catholic cardinals)

consol *abbr* consolidated

¹**con·sole** \'kän-ˌsōl\ *n* **1** : the desk-like part of an organ at which the organist sits **2** : a panel or cabinet for the controls of an electronic or mechanical device **3** : a cabinet for a radio or television set resting directly on the floor **4** : a small storage cabinet between bucket seats in an automobile

²**con·sole** \kən-'sōl\ *vb* **con·soled; con·sol·ing** : to soothe the grief of : COMFORT, SOLACE — **con·so·la·tion** \ˌkän-sə-'lā-shən\ *n* — **con·so·la·to·ry** \kən-'sōl-ə-ˌtōr-ē, -'säl-\ *adj*

con·sol·i·date \kən-'säl-ə-ˌdāt\ *vb* **-dat·ed; -dat·ing** **1** : to unite or become united into one whole : COMBINE **2** : to make firm or secure **3** : to form into a compact mass — **con·sol·i·da·tion** \-ˌsäl-ə-'dā-shən\ *n*

con·som·mé \ˌkän-sə-'mā\ *n* [F] : a clear soup made from well-seasoned meat broth

con·so·nance \'kän-s(ə-)nəns\ *n* **1** : AGREEMENT, HARMONY **2** : repetition of consonants esp. as an alternative to rhyme in verse

¹**con·so·nant** \-s(ə-)nənt\ *adj* : having consonance, harmony, or agreement **syn** consistent, compatible, congruous, congenial, sympathetic, agreeable

²**consonant** *n* **1** : a speech sound (as \p\, \g\, \n\, \l\, \s\, \r\) characterized by constriction or closure at one or more points in the breath channel **2** : a letter other than *a, e, i, o,* and *u* — **con·so·nan·tal** \ˌkän-sə-'nant-ᵊl\ *adj*

¹**con·sort** \'kän-ˌsȯrt\ *n* **1** : a ship accompanying another **2** : SPOUSE, MATE

²**con·sort** \kən-'sȯrt\ *vb* **1** : to keep company **2** : ACCORD, HARMONIZE

con·sor·tium \kən-'sȯrt-ē-əm, -'sȯr-sh(ē-)əm\ *n, pl* **-sor·tia** \-'sȯrt-ē-ə, -'sȯr-sh(ē-)ə\ [L, fellowship] : an international business or banking agreement or combination

con·spec·tus \kən-'spek-təs\ *n* **1** : a brief survey or summary **2** : OUTLINE, SYNOPSIS

con·spic·u·ous \kən-'spik-yə-wəs\ *adj*

: attracting attention : PROMINENT, STRIKING **syn** noticeable, remarkable, outstanding — **con·spic·u·ous·ly** *adv*

con·spir·a·cy \kən-'spir-ə-sē\ *n, pl* **-cies** : an agreement among conspirators : PLOT

con·spire \kən-'spī(ə)r\ *vb* **conspired; con·spir·ing** : to plan secretly an unlawful act : PLOT — **con·spir·a·tor** \-'spir-ət-ər\ *n*

const *abbr* **1** constant **2** constitution; constitutional

con·sta·ble \'kän-stə-bəl, 'kən-\ *n* [ME *conestable,* fr. OF, fr. LL *comes stabuli,* lit., officer of the stable] : a public officer responsible for keeping the peace

con·stab·u·lary \kən-'stab-yə-, ˌler-ē\ *n, pl* **-lar·ies** **1** : the police of a particular district or country **2** : a police force organized like the military

con·stan·cy \'kän-stən-sē\ *n, pl* **-cies** **1** : firmness of mind **2** : STABILITY

¹**con·stant** \-stənt\ *adj* **1** : STEADFAST, FAITHFUL **2** : FIXED, UNCHANGING **3** : continually recurring : REGULAR — **con·stant·ly** *adv*

²**constant** *n* : something unchanging

con·stel·la·tion \ˌkän-stə-'lā-shən\ *n* : any of 88 groups of stars forming patterns

con·ster·na·tion \ˌkän-stər-'nā-shən\ *n* : amazed dismay and confusion

con·sti·pa·tion \ˌkän-stə-'pā-shən\ *n* : abnormally difficult or infrequent bowel movements — **con·sti·pate** \'kän-stə-ˌpāt\ *vb*

con·stit·u·en·cy \kən-'stich-ə-wən-sē\ *n, pl* **-cies** : a body of constituents; *also* : an electoral district

¹**con·stit·u·ent** \-wənt\ *n* **1** : one entitled to vote for a representative for a district **2** : a component part

²**constituent** *adj* **1** : COMPONENT **2** : having power to create a government or frame or revise a constitution

con·sti·tute \'kän-stə-ˌt(y)üt\ *vb* **-tut·ed; -tut·ing** **1** : to appoint to an office or duty **2** : SET UP, ESTABLISH ⟨~ a law⟩ **3** : MAKE UP, COMPOSE

con·sti·tu·tion \ˌkän-stə-'t(y)ü-shən\ *n* **1** : an established law or custom **2** : the physical makeup of the individual **3** : the structure, composition, or makeup of something ⟨~ of the sun⟩ **4** : the basic law in a politically organized body; *also* : a document containing such law

¹con·sti·tu·tion·al \-sh(ə-)nəl\ *adj* **1** : of or relating to the constitution of body or mind **2** : of or relating to the constitution of a state or society — **con·sti·tu·tion·al·ly** \-ē\ *adv*

²constitutional *n* : an exercise (as a walk) taken for one's health

con·sti·tu·tion·al·i·ty \-ˌt(y)ü-shə-ˈnal-ət-ē\ *n* : the condition of being in accordance with the constitution of a state or society

con·sti·tu·tive \ˈkän-stə-ˌt(y)üt-iv, kən-ˈstich-ət-iv\ *adj* : CONSTITUENT, ESSENTIAL

constr *abbr* construction

con·strain \kən-ˈstrān\ *vb* **1** : COMPEL, FORCE **2** : CONFINE **3** : RESTRAIN

con·straint \-ˈstrānt\ *n* **1** : COMPULSION; *also* : RESTRAINT **2** : unnaturalness of manner produced by a repression of one's natural feelings

con·strict \kən-ˈstrikt\ *vb* : to draw together : SQUEEZE — **con·stric·tion** \-ˈstrik-shən\ *n* — **con·stric·tive** \-ˈstrik-tiv\ *adj*

con·stric·tor \kən-ˈstrikt-ər\ *n* : a snake that suffocates its prey by crushing in its coils

con·struct \kən-ˈstrəkt\ *vb* : BUILD, MAKE — **con·struc·tor** \-ˈstrək-tər\ *n*

con·struc·tion \kən-ˈstrək-shən\ *n* **1** : INTERPRETATION **2** : the art, process, or manner of building; *also* : something built : STRUCTURE **3** : syntactical arrangement of words in a sentence — **con·struc·tive** \-tiv\ *adj*

con·struc·tion·ist \-sh(ə-)nəst\ *n* : one who construes a legal document (as the U.S. Constitution) in a specific way ⟨a strict ∼⟩

con·strue \kən-ˈstrü\ *vb* **con·strued; con·stru·ing** **1** : to explain the mutual relations of words in a sentence; *also* : TRANSLATE **2** : EXPLAIN, INTERPRET — **con·stru·able** *adj*

con·sub·stan·ti·a·tion \ˌkän-səb-ˌstan-chē-ˈā-shən\ *n* : the actual substantial presence and combination of the body of Christ with the eucharistic bread and wine

con·sul \ˈkän-səl\ *n* **1** : a chief magistrate of the Roman republic **2** : an official appointed by a government to reside in a foreign country to care for

the commercial interests of that government's citizens — **con·sul·ar** \-sə-lər\ *adj* — **con·sul·ate** \-lət\ *n* — **con·sul·ship** *n*

con·sult \kən-ˈsəlt\ *vb* **1** : to ask the advice or opinion of **2** : CONFER — **con·sul·tant** \-ᵊnt\ *n* — **con·sul·ta·tion** \ˌkän-səl-ˈtā-shən\ *n*

con·sume \kən-ˈsüm\ *vb* **con·sumed; con·sum·ing** **1** : DESTROY ⟨*consumed* by fire⟩ **2** : to spend wastefully **3** : to eat up : DEVOUR **4** : to absorb the attention of : ENGROSS — **con·sum·able** *adj* — **con·sum·er** *n*

con·sum·er·ism \kən-ˈsü-mə-ˌriz-əm\ *n* : the promotion of consumers' interests (as against false advertising)

¹con·sum·mate \kən-ˈsəm-ət\ *adj* : COMPLETE, PERFECT **syn** finished, accomplished

²con·sum·mate \ˈkän-sə-ˌmāt\ *vb* **-mat·ed; -mat·ing** : to make complete : FINISH, ACHIEVE — **con·sum·ma·tion** \ˌkän-sə-ˈmā-shən\ *n*

con·sump·tion \kən-ˈsəmp-shən\ *n* **1** : progressive bodily wasting away; *also* : TUBERCULOSIS **2** : the act of consuming or using up **3** : the use of economic goods

¹con·sump·tive \-ˈsəmp-tiv\ *adj* **1** : tending to consume **2** : relating to or affected with consumption

²consumptive *n* : a person who has consumption

cont *abbr* **1** containing **2** contents **3** continent; continental **4** continued **5** control

¹con·tact \ˈkän-ˌtakt\ *n* **1** : a touching or meeting of bodies **2** : ASSOCIATION, RELATIONSHIP; *also* : CONNECTION, COMMUNICATION **3** : CONTACT LENS

²contact *vb* **1** : to come or bring into contact : TOUCH **2** : to get in communication with

contact lens *n* : a thin lens fitting over the cornea

con·ta·gion \kən-ˈtā-jən\ *n* **1** : the passing of disease by contact **2** : a contagious disease; *also* : its causative agent **3** : transmission of an influence on the mind or emotions

con·ta·gious \-jəs\ *adj* **1** : communicable by contact; *also* : relating to contagion or to contagious diseases **2** : exciting similar emotion or conduct in others

con·tain \kən-'tān\ *vb* **1** : RESTRAIN **2** : to have within : HOLD **3** : COMPRISE, INCLUDE — **con·tain·ment** *n*

con·tain·er \kən-'tā-nər\ *n* : RECEPTACLE; *esp* : one for shipment of goods

con·tain·er·ship \-nər-,ship\ *n* : a ship esp. designed or equipped for carrying very large containers of cargo

con·tam·i·nant \kən-'tam-ə-nənt\ *n* : something that contaminates

con·tam·i·nate \kən-'tam-ə-,nāt\ *vb* **-nat·ed; -nat·ing** : to soil, stain, or infect by contact or association — **con·tam·i·na·tion** \-,tam-ə-'nā-shən\ *n*

contd *abbr* continued

con·temn \kən-'tem\ *vb* : to view or treat with contempt

con·tem·plate \'känt-əm-,plāt\ *vb* **-plat·ed; -plat·ing** [L *contemplari,* fr. *templum* space marked out for observation of auguries] **1** : to view or consider with continued attention **2** : INTEND — **con·tem·pla·tion** \,känt-əm-'plā-shən\ *n* — **con·tem·pla·tive** \kən-'tem-plət-iv; 'känt-əm-,plāt-\ *adj*

con·tem·po·ra·ne·ous \kən-,tem-pə-'rā-nē-əs\ *adj* : CONTEMPORARY

con·tem·po·rary \kən-'tem-pə-,rer-ē\ *adj* **1** : occurring or existing at the same time **2** : marked by characteristics of the present period — **contemporary** *n*

con·tempt \kən-'tempt\ *n* **1** : the act of despising : the state of mind of one who despises : DISDAIN **2** : the state of being despised **3** : disobedience to or open disrespect of a court or legislature

con·tempt·ible \kən-'temp-tə-bəl\ *adj* : deserving contempt : DESPICABLE — **con·tempt·ibly** \-blē\ *adv*

con·temp·tu·ous \-'temp-chə(-wə)s\ *adj* : feeling or expressing contempt — **con·temp·tu·ous·ly** *adv*

con·tend \kən-'tend\ *vb* **1** : to strive against rivals or difficulties; *also* : ARGUE, DEBATE **2** : MAINTAIN, ASSERT — **con·tend·er** *n*

¹**con·tent** \kən-'tent\ *adj* : SATISFIED

²**content** *vb* : SATISFY; *esp* : to limit (oneself) in requirements or actions

³**content** *n* : CONTENTMENT

⁴**con·tent** \'kän-,tent\ *n* **1** : something contained ⟨~s of a room⟩ ⟨~s of a bottle⟩ **2** : subject matter or topics treated (as in a book) **3** : MEANING, SIGNIFICANCE **4** : the amount of material contained

con·tent·ed \kən-'tent-əd\ *adj* : SATISFIED — **con·tent·ed·ly** *adv* — **con·tent·ed·ness** *n*

con·ten·tion \kən-'ten-chən\ *n* **1** : CONTEST, STRIFE **2** : an idea or point for which a person argues — **con·ten·tious** \-chəs\ *adj*

con·tent·ment \kən-'tent-mənt\ *n* : ease of mind : SATISFACTION

con·ter·mi·nous \kən-'tər-mə-nəs, kän-\ *adj* : having the same or a common boundary — **con·ter·mi·nous·ly** *adv*

¹**con·test** \kən-'test\ *vb* **1** : to engage in strife : FIGHT **2** : CHALLENGE, DISPUTE — **con·tes·tant** \-'tes-tənt\ *n*

²**con·test** \'kän-,test\ *n* : STRUGGLE, COMPETITION

con·text \'kän-,tekst\ *n* [ME, weaving together of words, fr. L *contextus* coherence, fr. *contexere* to weave together] : the part of a discourse surrounding a word or group of words that helps to explain the meaning of the word or word group; *also* : the circumstances surrounding an act or event

con·tig·u·ous \kən-'tig-yə-wəs\ *adj* : being in contact : TOUCHING; *also* : NEXT, ADJOINING — **con·ti·gu·i·ty** \,känt-ə-'gyü-ət-ē\ *n*

con·ti·nence \'känt-ᵊn-əns\ *n* **1** : SELF-RESTRAINT; *esp* : voluntary refraining from sexual intercourse **2** : the ability to retain urine or feces voluntarily within the body — **con·ti·nent** \-ᵊn-ənt\ *adj*

con·ti·nent \'känt-(ə-)nənt\ *n* **1** : one of the great divisions of land on the globe **2** *cap* : the continent of Europe

¹**con·ti·nen·tal** \,känt-ᵊn-'ent-ᵊl\ *adj* **1** : of or relating to a continent; *esp, often cap* : of or relating to the continent of Europe **2** *often cap* : of or relating to the colonies later forming the U.S.

²**continental** *n* **1** *often cap* : a soldier in the Continental army **2** : EUROPEAN

continental shelf *n* : a shallow submarine plain forming a border to a continent

continental slope *n* : a usu. steep slope from a continental shelf to the ocean floor

con·tin·gen·cy \kən-'tin-jən-sē\ *n, pl* **-cies** : a chance or possible event

¹**con·tin·gent** \-jənt\ *adj* **1** : liable but not certain to happen : POSSIBLE **2** : happening by chance : not planned **3** : dependent on something that may or may not occur **4** : CONDITIONAL **syn** accidental, casual, incidental, odd

²**contingent** *n* : a quota (as of troops) supplied from an area or group

con·tin·u·al \kən-'tin-yə(-wə)l\ *adj* **1** : CONTINUOUS, UNBROKEN **2** : steadily recurring — **con·tin·u·al·ly** \-ē\ *adv*

con·tin·u·ance \-yə-wəns\ *n* **1** : unbroken succession **2** : a continuing in a state or course of action : DURATION **3** : adjournment of legal proceedings

con·tin·u·a·tion \kən-ˌtin-yə-'wā-shən\ *n* **1** : extension or prolongation of a state or activity **2** : resumption after an interruption; *also* : something that carries on after a pause or break

con·tin·ue \kən-'tin-yü\ *vb* **-tin·ued; -tinu·ing** **1** : PERSEVERE **2** : ENDURE, LAST **3** : to remain in a place or condition : ABIDE, STAY **4** : to resume (as a story) after an intermission **5** : EXTEND; *also* : to persist in **6** : to allow to remain **7** : to keep (a legal case) on the calendar or undecided

con·ti·nu·ity \ˌkänt-ᵊn-'(y)ü-ət-ē\ *n, pl* **-ities** **1** : the condition of being continuous **2** : something that has or provides continuity

con·tin·u·ous \kən-'tin-yə-wəs\ *adj* : continuing without interruption : UNBROKEN — **con·tin·u·ous·ly** *adv*

con·tin·u·um \-yə-wəm\ *n, pl* **-ua** \-yə-wə\ *also* **-u·ums** : something that is the same throughout or consists of a series of variations or of a sequence of things in regular order

con·tort \kən-'tȯrt\ *vb* : to twist out of shape — **con·tor·tion** \-'tȯr-shən\ *n*

con·tor·tion·ist \-'tȯr-sh(ə-)nəst\ *n* : an acrobat able to twist the body into unusual postures

con·tour \'kän-ˌtu̇r\ *n* [F, fr. It *contorno* fr. *contornare* to round off, sketch in outline, fr. L *com-* together + *tornare* to turn in a lathe, fr. *tornus* lathe] **1** : OUTLINE **2** : SHAPE, FORM — often used in pl. ⟨the ~s of a statue⟩

contr *abbr* contract; contraction

con·tra·band \'kän-trə-ˌband\ *n* : goods legally prohibited in trade; *also* : smuggled goods

con·tra·cep·tion \ˌkän-trə-'sep-shən\ *n* : intentional prevention of conception and pregnancy — **con·tra·cep·tive** \-'sep-tive\ *adj or n*

¹**con·tract** \'kän-ˌtrakt\ *n* **1** : a binding agreement : COVENANT **2** : an undertaking to win a specified number of tricks in contract bridge — **con·trac·tu·al** \kən-'trak-chə(-wə)l\ *adj* — **con·trac·tu·al·ly** \-ē\ *adv*

²**con·tract** \kən-'trakt, *1 usu* 'kän-ˌtrakt\ *vb* **1** : to become affected with ⟨~ a disease⟩ **2** : to establish or undertake by contract **3** : SHRINK, LESSEN; *esp* : to draw together esp. so as to shorten ⟨~ a muscle⟩ **4** : to shorten (a word) by omitting letters or sounds in the middle — **con·trac·tion** \kən-'trak-shən\ *n* — **con·trac·tor** \'kän-ˌtrak-tər, kən-'trak-\ *n*

con·trac·tile \kən-'trak-tᵊl\ *adj* : able to contract — **con·trac·til·i·ty** \ˌkän-ˌtrak-'til-ət-ē\ *n*

con·tra·dict \ˌkän-trə-'dikt\ *vb* : to state the contrary of : deny the truth of — **con·tra·dic·tion** \-'dik-shən\ *n* — **con·tra·dic·to·ry** \-'dik-t(ə-)rē\ *adj*

con·tra·dis·tinc·tion \ˌkän-trə-dis-'tiŋk-shən\ *n* : distinction by contrast

con·trail \'kän-ˌtrāl\ *n* : streaks of condensed water vapor created in the air by an airplane or rocket at high altitudes

con·tral·to \kən-'tral-tō\ *n, pl* **-tos** : the lowest female voice; *also* : a singer having such a voice

con·trap·tion \kən-'trap-shən\ *n* : CONTRIVANCE, DEVICE

con·tra·pun·tal \ˌkän-trə-'pənt-ᵊl\ *adj* : of or relating to counterpoint

con·tra·ri·ety \ˌkän-trə-'rī-ət-ē\ *n, pl* **-eties** : the state of being contrary : DISAGREEMENT, INCONSISTENCY

con·trari·wise \'kän-ˌtrer-ē-ˌwīz, kən-'trer-\ *adv* **1** : on the contrary **2** : VICE VERSA

con·trary \'kän-ˌtrer-ē; *4 often* kən-'tre(ə)r-ē\ *adj* **1** : opposite in nature or position **2** : COUNTER, OPPOSED **3** : UNFAVORABLE **4** : unwilling to accept control or advice — **con·trari·ly** \-ˌtrer-ə-lē, -'trer-\ *adv* — **con·trary** \n 'kän-ˌtrer-ē, *adv like adj*\ *n or adv*

¹**con·trast** \kən-'trast\ *vb* [F *contraster*,

fr. MF, to oppose, resist, fr. (assumed) VL *contrastare,* fr. L *contra-* against + *stare* to stand] **1** : to show differences when compared **2** : to compare in such a way as to show differences

²**con·trast** \'kän-ˌtrast\ *n* **1** : diversity of adjacent parts in color, emotion, tone, or brightness ⟨the ∼ of a photograph⟩ **2** : unlikeness as shown when things are compared : DIFFERENCE

con·tra·vene \ˌkän-trə-'vēn\ *vb* **-vened; -ven·ing 1** : to go or act contrary to ⟨∼ a law⟩ **2** : CONTRADICT

con·tre·temps \'kän-trə-ˌtäⁿ, kōⁿ-trə-täⁿ\ *n, pl* **con·tre·temps** \-ˌtäⁿ(z)\ : an inopportune embarrassing occurrence

contrib *abbr* contribution; contributor

con·trib·ute \kən-'trib-yət\ *vb* **-ut·ed; -ut·ing** : to give along with others (as to a fund) : supply or furnish a share to : HELP, ASSIST — **con·tri·bu·tion** \ˌkän-trə-'byü-shən\ *n* — **con·trib·u·tor** \kən-'trib-yət-ər\ *n* — **con·trib·u·to·ry** \-yə-ˌtōr-ē\ *adj*

con·trite \'kän-ˌtrīt, kən-'trīt\ *adj* : PENITENT, REPENTANT — **con·tri·tion** \kən-'trish-ən\ *n*

con·triv·ance \kən-'trī-vəns\ *n* **1** : a mechanical device : APPLIANCE **2** : SCHEME, PLAN

con·trive \kən-'trīv\ *vb* **con·trived; con·triv·ing 1** : PLAN, DEVISE **2** : FRAME, MAKE **3** : to bring about with difficulty — **con·triv·er** *n*

¹**con·trol** \kən-'trōl\ *vb* **con·trolled; con·trol·ling 1** : to exercise restraining or directing influence over : REGULATE **2** : DOMINATE, RULE

²**control** *n* **1** : power to direct or regulate **2** : RESERVE, RESTRAINT **3** : a device for regulating a mechanism

con·trol·ler \kən-'trō-lər, 'kän-ˌtrō-lər\ *n* **1** : COMPTROLLER **2** : one that controls

con·tro·ver·sy \'kän-trə-ˌvər-sē\ *n, pl* **-sies** : a clash of opposing views : DISPUTE — **con·tro·ver·sial** \ˌkän-trə-ˌvər-shəl, -sē-əl\ *adj*

con·tro·vert \'kän-trə-ˌvərt, ˌkän-trə-'vərt\ *vb* : DENY, CONTRADICT — **con·tro·vert·ible** *adj*

con·tu·ma·cious \ˌkän-t(y)ə-'mā-shəs\ *adj* : stubbornly resisting or disobeying authority **syn** rebellious, insubor-

dinate, seditious — **con·tu·ma·cy** \kən-'t(y)ü-mə-sē, 'kän-t(y)ə-\ *n* — **con·tu·ma·cious·ly** *adv*

con·tu·me·ly \kən-'t(y)ü-mə-lē, 'kän-t(y)ə-ˌmē-lē\ *n, pl* **-lies** : contemptuous treatment : INSULT

con·tu·sion \kən-'t(y)ü-zhən\ *n* : BRUISE — **con·tuse** \-'t(y)üz\ *vb*

co·nun·drum \kə-'nən-drəm\ *n* : RIDDLE

con·ur·ba·tion \ˌkän-(ˌ)ər-'bā-shən\ *n* : a continuous network of urban communities

conv *abbr* **1** convention **2** convertible

con·va·lesce \ˌkän-və-'les\ *vb* **-lesced; -lesc·ing** : to recover health gradually — **con·va·les·cence** \-'les-ᵊns\ *n* — **con·va·les·cent** \-ᵊnt\ *adj or n*

con·vec·tion \kən-'vek-shən\ *n* : circulatory motion in a fluid due to warmer portions rising and cooler denser portions sinking; *also* : the transfer of heat by such motion — **con·vec·tion·al** \-'vek-sh(ə-)nəl\ *adj* — **con·vec·tive** \-'vek-tiv\ *adj*

convection oven *n* : an oven with a fan that circulates hot air uniformly and continuously around the food

con·vene \kən-'vēn\ *vb* **con·vened; con·ven·ing** : ASSEMBLE, MEET

con·ve·nience \kən-'vē-nyəns\ *n* **1** : SUITABLENESS **2** : a laborsaving device **3** : a suitable time **4** : personal comfort : EASE

con·ve·nient \-nyənt\ *adj* **1** : suited to one's comfort or ease **2** : placed near at hand — **con·ve·nient·ly** *adv*

con·vent \'kän-vənt, -ˌvent\ *n* [ME *covent,* fr. OF, fr. ML *conventus,* fr. L, assembly, fr. *convenire* come together] : a local community or house of a religious order esp. of nuns — **con·ven·tu·al** \kən-'ven-chə-wəl, kän-\ *adj*

con·ven·ti·cle \kən-'vent-i-kəl\ *n* : MEETING; *esp* : a secret meeting for worship

con·ven·tion \kən-'ven-chən\ *n* **1** : an agreement esp. between states on a matter of common concern **2** : MEETING, ASSEMBLY **3** : an assembly of delegates convened for some purpose **4** : generally accepted custom, practice, or belief

con·ven·tion·al \-'vench-(ə-)nəl\ *adj* **1** : sanctioned by general custom **2** : COMMONPLACE, ORDINARY **syn** formal, ceremonial, solemn — **con·ven·tion·al-**

i•ty \-₁ven-chə-¹nal-ət-ē\ *n* — **con•ven•tion•al•ize** \-¹vench-(ə-)nə-₁līz\ *vb* — **con•ven•tion•al•ly** \-¹vench-(ə-)nəl-ē\ *adv*

con•verge \kən-¹vərj\ *vb* **con•verged; con•verg•ing** : to approach one common center or single point — **con•ver•gence** \kən-¹vər-jəns\ *or* **con•ver•gen•cy** \-jən-sē\ *n* — **con•ver•gent** \-jənt\ *adj*

con•ver•sant \kən-¹vərs-³nt\ *adj* : having knowledge and experience

con•ver•sa•tion \₁kän-vər-¹sā-shən\ *n* : an informal talking together — **con•ver•sa•tion•al** \-sh(ə-)nəl\ *adj*

¹con•verse \¹kän-₁vərs\ *n* : CONVERSATION

²con•verse \kən-¹vərs\ *vb* **con•versed; con•vers•ing** : to engage in conversation

³con•verse \¹kän-₁vərs\ *n* : a statement related to another statement by having its hypothesis and conclusion or its subject and predicate reversed or interchanged

⁴con•verse \kən-¹vərs, ¹kän-₁vərs\ *adj* : reversed in order or relation — **con•verse•ly** *adv*

con•ver•sion \kən-¹vər-zhən\ *n* **1** : a change in nature or form **2** : an experience associated with a decisive adoption of religion

¹con•vert \kən-¹vərt\ *vb* **1** : to turn from one belief or party to another **2** : TRANSFORM, CHANGE **3** : MISAPPROPRIATE **4** : EXCHANGE — **con•vert•er** *or* **con•ver•tor** \-ər\ *n* — **con•vert•ible** *adj*

²con•vert \¹kän-₁vərt\ *n* : one who has undergone religious conversion

con•vert•ible \kən-¹vərt-ə-bəl\ *n* : an automobile with a top that may be lowered or removed

con•vex \kän-¹veks, ¹kän-₁veks\ *adj* : curved or rounded like the exterior of a sphere or circle — **con•vex•i•ty** \kən-¹vek-sət-ē, kän-\ *n*

con•vey \kən-¹vā\ *vb* **1** : CARRY, TRANSPORT **2** : TRANSMIT, TRANSFER — **con•vey•er** *or* **con•vey•or** \-ər\ *n*

con•vey•ance \-¹vā-əns\ *n* **1** : the act of conveying **2** : a legal paper transferring ownership of property **3** : VEHICLE

¹con•vict \kən-¹vikt\ *vb* : to prove or find guilty

²con•vict \¹kän-₁vikt\ *n* : a person serving a prison sentence

con•vic•tion \kən-¹vik-shən\ *n* **1** : the act of convicting esp. in a court **2** : the state of being convinced : strong belief

con•vince \kən-¹vins\ *vb* **con•vinced; con•vinc•ing** : to bring by demonstration or argument to a sure belief — **con•vinc•ing** *adj* — **con•vinc•ing•ly** *adv*

con•viv•ial \kən-¹viv-yəl, -¹viv-ē-əl\ *adj* [LL *convivialis*, fr. L *convivium* banquet, fr. *com-* together + *vivere* to live] : enjoying companionship and the pleasures of feasting and drinking : JOVIAL, FESTIVE — **con•viv•i•al•i•ty** \-₁viv-ē-¹al-ət-ē\ *n* — **con•viv•ial•ly** \-¹viv-yə-lē, -¹viv-ē-ə-lē\ *adv*

con•vo•ca•tion \₁kän-və-¹kā-shən\ *n* **1** : a ceremonial assembly (as of clergymen) **2** : the act of convoking

con•voke \kən-¹vōk\ *vb* **con•voked; con•vok•ing** : to call together to a meeting

con•vo•lut•ed \¹kän-və-₁lüt-əd\ *adj* **1** : folded in curved or tortuous windings **2** : INVOLVED, INTRICATE

con•vo•lu•tion \₁kän-və-¹lü-shən\ *n* : a tortuous or sinuous structure; *esp* : one of the ridges of the brain

¹con•voy \¹kän-₁vöi, kən-¹vöi\ *vb* : to accompany for protection

²con•voy \¹kän-₁vöi\ *n* **1** : one that convoys; *esp* : a protective escort for ships, persons, or goods **2** : the act of convoying **3** : a group of moving vehicles

con•vulse \kən-¹vəls\ *vb* **con•vulsed; con•vuls•ing** : to agitate violently

con•vul•sion \kən-¹vəl-shən\ *n* **1** : an abnormal and violent involuntary contraction or series of contractions of muscle **2** : a violent disturbance — **con•vul•sive** \-¹vəl-siv\ *adj* — **con•vul•sive•ly** *adv*

cony var of CONEY

coo \¹kü\ *n* : a soft low sound made by doves or pigeons; *also* : a sound like this — **coo** *vb*

¹cook \¹kük\ *n* : one who prepares food for eating

²cook *vb* **1** : to prepare food for eating **2** : to subject to heat or fire — **cook•er** *n* — **cook•ware** \-₁waər\ *n*

cook•book \-₁bük\ *n* : a book of cooking directions and recipes

cook·ery \'kùk-(ə-)rē\ *n, pl* **-er·ies** : the art or practice of cooking

cook·ie *or* **cooky** \'kùk-ē\ *n, pl* **cook·ies** : a small sweet flat cake

cook·out \'kùk-ˌaùt\ *n* : an outing at which a meal is cooked and served in the open

¹cool \'kül\ *adj* **1** : moderately cold **2** : not excited : CALM **3** : not ardent **4** : IMPUDENT **5** : protecting from heat **6** *slang* : very good **7** : employing understatement **syn** unflappable, composed, collected, unruffled, nonchalant — **cool·ly** \'kül-(l)ē\ *adv* — **cool·ness** *n*

²cool *vb* : to make or become cool

³cool *n* **1** : a cool time or place **2** : INDIFFERENCE; *also* : SELF-ASSURANCE, COMPOSURE ⟨kept his ∼⟩

cool·ant \'kü-lənt\ *n* : a usu. fluid cooling agent

cool·er \'kü-lər\ *n* **1** : a container for keeping food or drink cool **2** : JAIL, PRISON **3** : a tall iced drink

coo·lie \'kü-lē\ *n* [Hindi *kulī*] : an unskilled laborer usu. in or from the Far East

coon \'kün\ *n* : RACCOON

coon·hound \-ˌhaùnd\ *n* : a sporting dog trained to hunt raccoons

coon·skin \-ˌskin\ *n* : the pelt of a raccoon; *also* : something (as a cap) made of this

¹coop \'küp, 'kùp\ *n* : a small enclosure or building usu. for poultry

²coop *vb* : to confine in or as if in a coop

co—op \'kō-ˌäp\ *n* : COOPERATIVE

coo·per \'kü-pər, 'kùp-ər\ *n* : one who makes or repairs barrels or casks — **cooper** *vb* — **coo·per·age** \'kü-p(ə-)rij, 'kùp-(ə-)\ *n*

co·op·er·ate \kō-'äp-ə-ˌrāt\ *vb* : to act jointly with another or others — **co·op·er·a·tion** \-ˌäp-ə-'rā-shən\ *n* — **co·op·er·a·tor** \-'äp-ə-ˌrāt-ər\ *n*

¹co·op·er·a·tive \kō-'äp-(ə-)rət-iv, -'äp-ə-ˌrāt-\ *adj* **1** : willing to work with others **2** : of or relating to an association formed to enable its members to buy or sell to better advantage by eliminating middlemen's profits

²cooperative *n* : a cooperative association

co—opt \kō-'äpt\ *vb* **1** : to choose or elect as a colleague **2** : ABSORB, ASSIMILATE; *also* : TAKE OVER

¹co·or·di·nate \kō-'órd-(ə-)nət\ *adj* **1** : equal in rank or order **2** : of equal rank in a compound sentence ⟨∼ clause⟩ **3** : joining words or word groups of the same rank

²coordinate *n* **1** : one of a set of numbers used in specifying the location of a point on a surface or in space **2** *pl* : articles (as of clothing) designed to be used together and to attain their effect through pleasing contrast

³co·or·di·nate \kō-'órd-ᵊn-ˌāt\ *vb* **-nat·ed; -nat·ing** **1** : to make or become coordinate **2** : to work or act together harmoniously — **co·or·di·na·tion** \-ˌórd-ᵊn-'ā-shən\ *n* — **co·or·di·na·tor** \-'órd-ᵊn-ˌāt-ər\ *n*

coot \'küt\ *n* **1** : a dark-colored ducklike bird related to the rails **2** : any of several No. American sea ducks **3** : a harmless simple person

coo·tie \'küt-ē\ *n* : a body louse

cop \'käp\ *n* : POLICEMAN

co·part·ner \'kō-'pärt-nər\ *n* : PARTNER

¹cope \'kōp\ *n* : a long cloaklike ecclesiastical vestment

²cope *vb* **coped; cop·ing** : to struggle to overcome problems or difficulties

copi·er \'käp-ē-ər\ *n* : one that copies; *esp* : a machine for making copies

co·pi·lot \'kō-ˌpī-lət\ *n* : an assistant pilot of an aircraft or spacecraft

cop·ing \'kō-piŋ\ *n* : the top layer of a wall

co·pi·ous \'kō-pē-əs\ *adj* : LAVISH, ABUNDANT — **co·pi·ous·ly** *adv* — **co·pi·ous·ness** *n*

cop—out \'käp-ˌaùt\ *n* : an excuse for copping out; *also* : an act of copping out

cop out \(')käp-'aùt\ *vb* : to back out (as of an unwanted responsibility)

cop·per \'käp-ər\ *n* **1** : a malleable reddish metallic chemical element that is one of the best conductors of heat and electricity **2** : a coin or token made of copper — **cop·pery** *adj*

cop·per·head \'käp-ər-ˌhed\ *n* : a largely coppery brown venomous snake esp. of the eastern and central U.S.

cop·pice \'käp-əs\ *n* : THICKET

co·pra \'kō-prə\ *n* : dried coconut meat yielding coconut oil

copse \'käps\ *n* : THICKET

cop·ter \'käp-tər\ *n* : HELICOPTER

cop·u·la \\'käp-yə-lə\ *n* : LINKING VERB
— **cop·u·la·tive** \-ˌlāt-iv\ *adj*

cop·u·late \\'käp-yə-ˌlāt\ *vb* **-lat·ed; -lat·ing** : to engage in sexual intercourse
— **cop·u·la·tion** \ˌkäp-yə-'lā-shən\ *n*
— **cop·u·la·to·ry** \\'käp-yə-lə-ˌtōr-ē\ *adj*

¹**copy** \\'käp-ē\ *n, pl* **cop·ies 1** : an imitation or reproduction of an original work **2** : material to be set in type **syn** duplicate, reproduction, facsimile, replica

²**copy** *vb* **cop·ied; copy·ing 1** : to make a copy of **2** : IMITATE — **copy·ist** *n*

copy·book \\'käp-ē-ˌbùk\ *n* : a book containing copies esp. of penmanship for learners to imitate

copy·boy \-ˌbȯi\ *n* : one who carries copy and runs errands (as in a newspaper office)

copy·cat \-ˌkat\ *n* : a slavish imitator

copy·desk \-ˌdesk\ *n* : the desk at which newspaper copy is edited

copy editor *n* : one who edits newspaper copy and writes headlines; *also* : one who reads and corrects manuscript copy in a publishing house

copy·read·er \-ˌrēd-ər\ *n* : COPY EDITOR

¹**copy·right** \-ˌrīt\ *n* : the sole right to reproduce, publish, and sell a literary or artistic work

²**copyright** *vb* : to secure a copyright on

copy·writ·er \\'käp-ē-ˌrīt-ər\ *n* : a writer of advertising copy

co·quet *or* **co·quette** \kō-'ket\ *vb* **co·quet·ted; co·quet·ting** : FLIRT — **co·quet·ry** \\'kō-kə-trē, kō-'ke-trē\ *n*

co·quette \kō-'ket\ *n* [F, fem. of *coquet,* dim. of *coq* cock] : FLIRT — **co·quett·ish** *adj*

cor *abbr* corner

Cor *abbr* Corinthians

cor·a·cle \\'kȯr-ə-kəl\ *n* [W *corwgl*] : a boat made of hoops covered with horsehide or canvas

cor·al \\'kȯr-əl\ *n* **1** : a stony or horny material that forms the skeleton of colonies of tiny sea polyps and includes a red form used in jewelry; *also* : a coral-forming polyp or polyp colony **2** : a deep pink color — **coral** *adj*

coral snake *n* : any of several venomous chiefly tropical New World snakes brilliantly banded in red, black, and yellow or white

cor·bel \\'kȯr-bəl\ *n* : a bracket-shaped architectural member that projects from a wall and supports a weight

¹**cord** \\'kȯrd\ *n* **1** : a usu. heavy string consisting of several strands woven or twisted together **2** : a long slender anatomical structure (as a tendon or nerve) **3** : a small flexible insulated electrical cable used to connect an appliance with a receptacle **4** : a cubic measure used esp. for firewood and equal to a stack 4×4×8 feet (about 3.6 cubic meters) **5** : a rib or ridge on cloth

²**cord** *vb* **1** : to tie or furnish with a cord **2** : to pile (wood) in cords

cord·age \\'kȯrd-ij\ *n* : ROPES, CORDS; *esp* : ropes in the rigging of a ship

¹**cor·dial** \\'kȯr-jəl\ *n* **1** : a stimulating medicine or drink **2** : LIQUEUR

²**cordial** *adj* [ME, fr. ML *cordialis,* fr. L *cord-, cor* heart] : warmly receptive or welcoming : HEARTFELT, HEARTY — **cor·di·al·i·ty** \ˌkȯr-jē-'al-ət-ē, kȯr-'jal-; kȯrd-'yal-\ *n* — **cor·dial·ly** \\'kȯr-jə-lē\ *adv*

cor·dil·le·ra \ˌkȯrd-ᵊl-'(y)er-ə\ *n* [Sp] : a group of mountain ranges — **cor·dil·le·ran** *adj*

cord·less \\'kȯrd-ləs\ *adj* : having no cord; *esp* : powered by a battery ⟨~ tools⟩

cor·do·ba \\'kȯrd-ə-bə, -ə-və\ *n* — see MONEY table

cor·don \\'kȯrd-ᵊn\ *n* **1** : an ornamental cord or ribbon **2** : an encircling line composed of individual units — **cordon** *vb*

cor·do·van \\'kȯrd-ə-vən\ *n* : a soft fine-grained leather

cor·du·roy \\'kȯrd-ə-ˌrȯi\ *n, pl* **-roys** : a heavy ribbed fabric; *also, pl* : trousers of this material

cord·wain·er \\'kȯrd-ˌwā-nər\ *n* : SHOEMAKER

¹**core** \\'kōr\ *n* **1** : the central usu. inedible part of some fruits (as the apple); *also* : an inmost part of something **2** : GIST, ESSENCE

²**core** *vb* **cored; cor·ing** : to take out the core of — **cor·er** *n*

CORE \\'kōr\ *abbr* Congress of Racial Equality

co·re·spon·dent \ˌkō-ri-'spän-dənt\ *n* : a person named as guilty of adultery with the defendant in a divorce suit

co·ri·an·der \\'kōr-ē-ˌan-dər\ *n* : an herb

related to the carrot; *also* : its aromatic dried fruit used as a flavoring

Cor·in·thi·ans \kə-'rin-thē-ənz\ *n* — see BIBLE table

¹**cork** \'kȯrk\ *n* **1** : the tough elastic bark of a European oak (**cork oak**) used esp. for stoppers and insulation; *also* : a stopper of this **2** : a tissue of a woody plant making up most of the bark — **corky** *adj*

²**cork** *vb* : to furnish with or stop up with cork or a cork

cork·screw \'kȯrk-ˌskrü\ *n* : a device for drawing corks from bottles

corm \'kȯrm\ *n* : a solid bulblike underground part of a stem (as of the crocus or gladiolus)

cor·mo·rant \'kȯrm-(ə-)rənt, 'kȯr-mə-ˌrant\ *n* [ME *cormeraunt,* fr. MF *cormorant,* fr. OF *cormareng,* fr. *corp* raven + *marenc* of the sea, fr. L *marinus*] : a dark seabird used in the Orient to catch fish

¹**corn** \'kȯrn\ *n* **1** : the seeds of a cereal grass and esp. of the chief cereal crop of a region (as wheat in Britain and Indian corn in the U.S.); *also* : a cereal grass **2** : sweet corn served as a vegetable

²**corn** *vb* : to salt (as beef) in brine and preservatives

³**corn** *n* : a local hardening and thickening of skin (as on a toe)

corn bread *n* : bread made with cornmeal

corn·cob \-ˌkäb\ *n* : the woody core on which the kernels of Indian corn are arranged

corn·crib \-ˌkrib\ *n* : a crib for storing ears of Indian corn

cor·nea \'kȯr-nē-ə\ *n* : the transparent part of the coat of the eyeball covering the iris and the pupil — **cor·ne·al** *adj*

corn earworm *n* : a moth whose larva is esp. destructive to Indian corn

¹**cor·ner** \'kȯ-nər\ *n* [ME, fr. OF *cornere,* fr. *corne* horn, corner, fr. L *cornu* horn, point] **1** : the point or angle formed by the meeting of lines, edges, or sides **2** : the place where two streets come together **3** : a quiet secluded place **4** : a position from which retreat or escape is impossible **5** : control of enough of the available supply (as of a commodity) to permit manipulation of the price

²**cor·ner** *vb* **cor·nered; cor·ner·ing** \'kȯrn-(ə-)riŋ\ **1** : to drive into a corner **2** : to get a corner on ⟨~ the wheat market⟩ **3** : to turn a corner

cor·ner·stone \'kȯr-nər-ˌstōn\ *n* **1** : a stone forming part of a corner in a wall; *esp* : such a stone laid with special ceremonies **2** : something of basic importance

cor·net \kȯr-'net\ *n* : a brass band instrument resembling the trumpet

corn flour *n, Brit* : CORNSTARCH

corn·flow·er \'kȯrn-ˌflau̇(-ə)r\ *n* : BACHELOR'S BUTTON

cor·nice \'kȯr-nəs\ *n* : the horizontal projecting part crowning the wall of a building

corn·meal \'kȯrn-'mēl, -ˌmēl\ *n* : meal ground from corn

corn·row \'kȯrn-ˌrō\ *vb* : to braid (sections of hair) flat to the scalp in rows — **cornrow** *n*

corn·stalk \'kȯrn-ˌstȯk\ *n* : a stalk of Indian corn

corn·starch \-ˌstärch\ *n* : a starch made from corn and used in cookery as a thickening agent

corn syrup *n* : a syrup obtained by partial hydrolysis of cornstarch

cor·nu·co·pia \ˌkȯr-n(y)ə-'kō-pē-ə\ *n* [LL, fr. L *cornu copiae* horn of plenty] : a horn-shaped container filled with fruits and grain emblematic of abundance

corny \'kȯr-nē\ *adj* **corn·i·er; -est** : tiresomely simple or sentimental

co·rol·la \kə-'räl-ə, -'rōl-\ *n* : the petals of a flower

cor·ol·lary \'kȯr-ə-ˌler-ē\ *n, pl* **-lar·ies 1** : a deduction from a proposition already proved true **2** : CONSEQUENCE, RESULT

co·ro·na \kə-'rō-nə\ *n* **1** : a colored ring surrounding the sun or moon; *esp* : a shining ring around the sun seen during eclipses **2** : a faint glow adjacent to the surface of a conductor at high voltage — **co·ro·nal** \'kȯr-ən-ᵊl, kə-'rōn-ᵊl\ *adj*

cor·o·nal \'kȯr-ən-ᵊl\ *n* : a circlet for the head

¹**cor·o·nary** \'kȯr-ə-ˌner-ē\ *adj* : of or relating to the heart or its blood vessels

²**coronary** *n, pl* **-nar·ies 1** : a coronary blood vessel **2** : CORONARY THROMBOSIS

coronary thrombosis *n* : the blocking by

a thrombus of one of the arteries supplying the heart tissues

cor·o·na·tion \ˌkȯr-ə-'nā-shən\ *n* : the act or ceremony of crowning a monarch

cor·o·ner \'kȯr-ə-nər\ *n* : a public official whose chief duty is to investigate the causes of deaths possibly not due to natural causes

cor·o·net \ˌkȯr-ə-'net\ *n* **1** : a small crown indicating rank lower than sovereignty **2** : an ornamental band worn around the temples

corp *abbr* **1** corporal **2** corporation

¹cor·po·ral \'kȯr-p(ə-)rəl\ *adj* : of or relating to the body ⟨∼ punishment⟩

²corporal *n* : a noncommissioned officer (as in the army) ranking next below a sergeant

cor·po·rate \'kȯr-p(ə-)rət\ *adj* **1** : INCORPORATED; *also* : belonging to an incorporated body **2** : combined into one body

cor·po·ra·tion \ˌkȯr-pə-'rā-shən\ *n* **1** : the municipal authorities of a town or city **2** : a legal creation authorized to act with the rights and liabilities of a person ⟨a business ∼⟩

cor·po·re·al \kȯr-'pōr-ē-əl\ *adj* **1** : PHYSICAL, MATERIAL **2** *archaic* : BODILY — **cor·po·re·al·i·ty** \(ˌ)kȯr-ˌpōr-ē-'al-ət-ē\ *n* — **cor·po·re·al·ly** \-ē-ə-lē\ *adv*

corps \'kōr\ *n, pl* **corps** \'kōrz\ [F, fr. L *corpus* body] **1** : an organized subdivision of a country's military forces **2** : a group acting under common direction

corpse \'kȯrps\ *n* : a dead body

corps·man \'kōr(z)-mən\ *n* : an enlisted man trained to give first aid

cor·pu·lence \'kȯr-pyə-ləns\ *or* **cor·pu·len·cy** \-lən-sē\ *n* : excessive fatness — **cor·pu·lent** \-lənt\ *adj*

cor·pus \'kȯr-pəs\ *n, pl* **cor·po·ra** \-pə-rə\ [ME, fr. L] **1** : BODY; *esp* : CORPSE **2** : a body of writings or works

cor·pus·cle \'kȯr-(ˌ)pəs-əl\ *n* **1** : a minute particle **2** : a living cell (as in blood or cartilage) not aggregated into continuous tissues — **cor·pus·cu·lar** \kȯr-'pəs-kyə-lər\ *adj*

cor·pus de·lic·ti \ˌkȯr-pəs-di-'lik-ˌtī, -tē\ *n, pl* **corpora delicti** [NL, lit., body of the crime] : the substantial fact establishing that a crime has been committed; *also* : the body of a victim of murder

corr *abbr* **1** correct; corrected; correction **2** correspondence; correspondent; corresponding

cor·ral \kə-'ral\ *n* [Sp] : an enclosure for confining or capturing animals; *also* : an enclosure for defense — **corral** *vb*

¹cor·rect \kə-'rekt\ *vb* **1** : to make right **2** : REPROVE, CHASTISE — **cor·rect·able** \-'rek-tə-bəl\ *adj* — **cor·rec·tion** \-'rek-shən\ *n* — **cor·rec·tion·al** \-'rek-sh(ə-)nəl\ *adj* — **cor·rec·tive** \-'rek-tiv\ *adj*

²correct *adj* **1** : conforming to a conventional standard **2** : agreeing with fact or truth — **cor·rect·ly** \kə-'rek-(t)lē\ *adv* — **cor·rect·ness** \-'rek(t)-nəs\ *n*

cor·re·late \'kȯr-ə-ˌlāt\ *vb* **-lat·ed; -lat·ing** : to connect in a systematic way : establish the mutual relations of — **cor·re·late** \-lət, -ˌlāt\ *n* — **cor·re·la·tion** \ˌkȯr-ə-'lā-shən\ *n*

cor·rel·a·tive \kə-'rel-ət-iv\ *adj* **1** : reciprocally related **2** : regularly used together (as *either* and *or*) — **correlative** *n*

cor·re·spond \ˌkȯr-ə-'spänd\ *vb* **1** : to be in agreement : SUIT, MATCH **2** : to communicate by letter — **cor·re·spond·ing·ly** \-'spän-diŋ-lē\ *adv*

cor·re·spon·dence \-'spän-dəns\ *n* **1** : agreement between particular things **2** : communication by letters; *also* : the letters exchanged

¹cor·re·spon·dent \-'spän-dənt\ *adj* **1** : SIMILAR **2** : FITTING, CONFORMING

²correspondent *n* **1** : something that corresponds **2** : a person with whom one communicates by letter **3** : a person employed to contribute news regularly from a place

cor·ri·dor \'kȯr-əd-ər, -ə-ˌdȯr\ *n* **1** : a passageway into which compartments or rooms open (as in a hotel or school) **2** : a narrow strip of land esp. through foreign-held territory **3** : a densely populated strip of land including two or more major cities

cor·ri·gen·dum \ˌkȯr-ə-'jen-dəm\ *n, pl* **-da** \-də\ [L] : an error in a printed work discovered after printing and shown with its correction on a separate sheet

cor·ri·gi·ble \ˈkȯr-ə-jə-bəl\ *adj* : CORRECTABLE

cor·rob·o·rate \kə-ˈräb-ə-ˌrāt\ *vb* **-rat·ed; -rat·ing** [L *corroborare,* fr. *robur* strength] : to support with evidence : CONFIRM — **cor·rob·o·ra·tion** \-ˌräb-ə-ˈrā-shən\ *n* — **cor·rob·o·ra·tive** \-ˈräb-ə-ˌrāt-iv, -ˈräb-(ə-)rət-\ *adj* — **cor·rob·o·ra·to·ry** \-ˈräb-(ə-)rə-ˌtōr-ē\ *adj*

cor·rode \kə-ˈrōd\ *vb* **cor·rod·ed; cor·rod·ing** : to eat or be eaten away gradually (as by chemical action) — **cor·ro·sion** \-ˈrō-zhən\ *n* — **cor·ro·sive** \-ˈrō-siv\ *adj or n*

cor·ru·gate \ˈkȯr-ə-ˌgāt\ *vb* **-gat·ed; -gat·ing** : to form into wrinkles or ridges and grooves — **cor·ru·gat·ed** *adj* — **cor·ru·ga·tion** \ˌkȯr-ə-ˈgā-shən\ *n*

¹cor·rupt \kə-ˈrəpt\ *vb* **1** : to make evil : DEPRAVE; *esp* : BRIBE **2** : ROT, SPOIL — **cor·rupt·ible** *adj* — **cor·rup·tion** \-ˈrəp-shən\ *n*

²corrupt *adj* : DEPRAVED, DEBASED

cor·sage \kȯr-ˈsäzh, -ˈsäj\ *n* [F, bust, bodice, fr. OF, bust, fr. *cors* body, fr. L *corpus*] **1** : the waist or bodice of a dress **2** : a bouquet to be worn or carried

cor·sair \ˈkȯr-ˌsaər\ *n* : PIRATE

cor·set \ˈkȯr-sət\ *n* : a stiffened undergarment worn for support or to give shape to the waist and hips

cor·tege *also* **cor·tège** \kȯr-ˈtezh, ˈkȯr-ˌtezh\ *n* [F] : PROCESSION; *esp* : a funeral procession

cor·tex \ˈkȯr-ˌteks\ *n, pl* **cor·ti·ces** \ˈkȯrt-ə-ˌsēz\ *or* **cor·tex·es** : an outer or covering layer of an organism or one of its parts ⟨the adrenal ∼⟩ ⟨∼ of a plant stem⟩; *esp* : the outer layer of gray matter of the brain — **cor·ti·cal** \ˈkȯrt-i-kəl\ *adj*

cor·ti·sone \ˈkȯrt-ə-ˌsōn, -ˌzōn\ *n* : an adrenal hormone used in treating rheumatoid arthritis

co·run·dum \kə-ˈrən-dəm\ *n* : a very hard aluminum-containing mineral used as an abrasive or in some crystalline forms as a gem

cor·us·cate \ˈkȯr-ə-ˌskāt\ *vb* **-cat·ed; -cat·ing** : FLASH, SPARKLE — **cor·us·ca·tion** \ˌkȯr-ə-ˈskā-shən\ *n*

cor·vette \kȯr-ˈvet\ *n* **1** : a naval sailing ship smaller than a frigate **2** : an armed escort ship smaller than a destroyer

co·ry·za \kə-ˈrī-zə\ *n* : an inflammatory disorder of the upper respiratory tract; *esp* : COMMON COLD

COS *abbr* **1** cash on shipment **2** chief of staff

co·sig·na·to·ry \kō-ˈsig-nə-ˌtōr-ē\ *n* : a joint signer

co·sign·er \ˈkō-ˌsī-nər\ *n* : COSIGNATORY; *esp* : a joint signer of a promissory note

¹cos·met·ic \käz-ˈmet-ik\ *n* : a cosmetic preparation

²cosmetic *adj* [Gk *kosmētikos* skilled in adornment, fr. *kosmein* to arrange, adorn, fr. *kosmos* order, ornament, universe] **1** : intended to beautify the hair or complexion **2** : SUPERFICIAL

cos·me·tol·o·gist \ˌkäz-mə-ˈtäl-ə-jəst\ *n* : one who gives beauty treatments — **cos·me·tol·o·gy** \-jē\ *n*

cos·mic \ˈkäz-mik\ *also* **cos·mi·cal** \-mi-kəl\ *adj* **1** : of or relating to the cosmos **2** : VAST, GRAND — **cos·mi·cal·ly** \-mi-k(ə-)lē\ *adv*

cosmic ray *n* : a stream of very penetrating atomic nuclei that enter the earth's atmosphere from outer space

cos·mog·o·ny \käz-ˈmäg-ə-nē\ *n, pl* **-nies** : the origin or creation of the world or universe

cos·mol·o·gy \käz-ˈmäl-ə-jē\ *n, pl* **-gies** : a branch of astronomy dealing with the origin and structure of the universe — **cos·mo·log·i·cal** \ˌkäz-mə-ˈläj-i-kəl\ *adj* — **cos·mol·o·gist** \käz-ˈmäl-ə-jəst\ *n*

cos·mo·naut \ˈkäz-mə-ˌnȯt\ *n* : a Soviet astronaut

cos·mo·pol·i·tan \ˌkäz-mə-ˈpäl-ət-ᵊn\ *adj* : belonging to all the world : not local **syn** universal, global, catholic — **cosmopolitan** *n*

cos·mos \ˈkäz-məs, 1 *also* -ˌmōs, -ˌmäs\ *n* **1** : UNIVERSE **2** : a tall garden herb related to the daisies

co·spon·sor \ˈkō-ˌspän-sər, -ˈspän-\ *n* : a joint sponsor — **cosponsor** *vb*

cos·sack \ˈkäs-ˌak, -ək\ *n* [Russ *kazak* & Ukrainian *kozak,* fr. Turk *kazak* free person] : a member of a group of frontiersmen of southern Russia organized as cavalry in the czarist army

¹cost \ˈkȯst\ *n* **1** : the amount paid or charged for something : PRICE **2** : the loss or penalty incurred in gaining something **3** *pl* : expenses incurred in a law suit

²cost *vb* **cost; cost•ing 1** : to require a specified amount in payment **2** : to cause to pay, suffer, or lose

co–star \'kō-₁stär\ *n* : one of two leading players in a motion picture or play — **co–star** *vb*

cos•tive \'käs-tiv\ *adj* : affected with or causing constipation

cost•ly \'kȯst-lē\ *adj* **cost•li•er; -est** : of great cost or value : not cheap **syn** dear, valuable, expensive — **cost•li•ness** *n*

cos•tume \'käs-₁t(y)üm\ *n* : CLOTHES, ATTIRE; *also* : a suit or dress characteristic of a period or country — **cos•tum•er** \'käs-₁t(y)ü-mər\ *n* — **cos•tu•mi•er** \käs-'t(y)ü-mē-ər\ *n, chiefly Brit*

costume jewelry *n* : inexpensive jewelry

co•sy \'kō-zē\ var of COZY

¹cot \'kät\ *n* : a small house : COTTAGE

²cot *n* : a small often collapsible bed

cote \'kōt, 'kät\ *n* : a small shed or coop (as for sheep or doves)

co•te•rie \'kōt-ə-₁rē, ₁kōt-ə-'rē\ *n* [F] : an intimate often exclusive group of persons with a common interest

co•ter•mi•nous \-mə-nəs\ *adj* : having the same scope or duration

co•til•lion \kō-'til-yən, kə-\ *n* **1** : a complicated formal dance with frequent changing of partners **2** : a formal ball

cot•tage \'kät-ij\ *n* : a small house — **cot•tag•er** *n*

cottage cheese *n* : a soft uncured cheese made from soured skim milk

cot•ter *or* **cot•tar** \'kät-ər\ *n* : a farm laborer occupying a cottage and often a small holding

cotter pin *n* : a metal strip bent into a pin whose ends can be spread apart after insertion through a hole or slot

cot•ton \'kät-ᵊn\ *n* [ME *coton*, fr. MF, fr. Ar *quṭn*] **1** : a soft fibrous usu. white substance composed of hairs attached to the seeds of a plant related to the mallow; *also* : this plant **2** : thread or cloth made of cotton — **cot•tony** *adj*

cot•ton•mouth \'kät-ᵊn-₁maủth\ *n* : WATER MOCCASIN

cot•ton•seed \-₁sēd\ *n* : the seed of the cotton plant yielding a protein-rich meal and a fixed oil (**cottonseed oil**) used esp. in cooking

cot•ton•tail \-₁tāl\ *n* : an American rabbit with a white-tufted tail

cot•ton•wood \-₁wủd\ *n* : a poplar with cottony hair on its seed

cot•y•le•don \₁kät-ᵊl-'ēd-ᵊn\ *n* : the first leaf or one of the first pair or whorl of leaves developed by a seed plant

¹couch \'kaủch\ *vb* **1** : to lie or place on a couch **2** : to phrase in a certain manner

²couch *n* : a piece of furniture (as a bed or sofa) that one can sit or lie on

couch•ant \'kaủ-chənt\ *adj* : lying down with the head raised ⟨coat of arms with lion ~⟩

cou•gar \'kü-gər, -₁gär\ *n, pl* **cougars** *also* **cougar** [F *couguar*, fr. NL *cuguacuarana*, modif. of Tupi (a Brazilian Indian language) *suasuarana*, lit., false deer, fr. *suasú* deer + *rana* false] : a large tawny wild American cat

cough \'kȯf\ *vb* : to force air from the lungs with short sharp noises; *also* : to expel by coughing — **cough** *n*

could \kəd, (')kủd\ past of CAN — used as an auxiliary in the past or as a polite or less forceful alternative to *can* in the present

cou•lee \'kü-lē\ *n* **1** : a small stream **2** : a dry streambed **3** : GULLY

cou•lomb \'kü-₁läm, -₁lōm\ *n* : a unit of electric charge equal to the electricity transferred by a current of one ampere in one second

coun•cil \'kaủn-səl\ *n* **1** : ASSEMBLY, MEETING **2** : an official body of lawmakers ⟨a city ~⟩ — **coun•cil•or** *or* **coun•cil•or** \-s(ə-)lər\ *n* — **coun•cil•man** \-səl-mən\ *n* — **coun•cil•wom•an** \-₁wủm-ən\ *n*

¹coun•sel \'kaủn-səl\ *n* **1** : ADVICE **2** : a plan of action **3** : deliberation together **4** *pl* **counsel** : LAWYER

²counsel *vb* **-seled** *or* **-selled; -sel•ing** *or* **-sel•ling** \-s(ə-)liŋ\ **1** : ADVISE, RECOMMEND **2** : CONSULT

coun•sel•or *or* **coun•sel•lor** \'kaủn-s(ə-)lər\ *n* **1** : ADVISER **2** : LAWYER

¹count \'kaủnt\ *vb* [ME *counten*, fr. MF *compter*, fr. L *computare*, fr. *com-* with + *putare* to consider] **1** : to name or indicate one by one in order to find the total number **2** : to recite numbers in order **3** : CONSIDER, ACCOUNT **4** : RELY ⟨you can ∼ on him⟩ **5** : to be of value or account — **countable** *adj*

²**count** *n* **1** : the act of counting; *also* : the total obtained by counting **2** : a particular charge in an indictment or legal declaration

³**count** *n* [MF *comte,* fr. LL *comes,* fr. L, companion, one of the imperial court, fr. *com-* with + *ire* to go] : a European nobleman whose rank corresponds to that of a British earl

count•down \'kau̇nt-ˌdau̇n\ *n* : a backward counting in fixed units (as seconds) to indicate the time remaining before an event (as the launching of a rocket) — **count down** \-'dau̇n\ *vb*

¹**coun•te•nance** \'kau̇nt-(ə-)nəns\ *n* **1** : the human face esp. as an indicator of mood or character **2** : FAVOR, APPROVAL

²**countenance** *vb* **-nanced; -nanc•ing** : SANCTION, TOLERATE

¹**count•er** \'kau̇nt-ər\ *n* **1** : a piece (as of metal or ivory) used in reckoning or in games **2** : a level surface over which business is transacted, food is served, or work is conducted

²**coun•ter** *vb* : to act in opposition to

³**count•er** *n* : a device for recording a number or amount

⁴**coun•ter** *adv* : in an opposite direction : CONTRARY

⁵**coun•ter** *n* **1** : OPPOSITE, CONTRARY **2** : an answering or offsetting force or blow

⁶**coun•ter** *adj* : CONTRARY, OPPOSITE

coun•ter•act \ˌkau̇nt-ər-'akt\ *vb* : to lessen the force of : OFFSET — **coun•ter•ac•tive** \-'ak-tiv\ *adj*

coun•ter•at•tack \'kau̇nt-ər-ə-ˌtak\ *n* : an attack made to oppose an enemy's attack — **counterattack** *vb*

¹**coun•ter•bal•ance** \'kau̇nt-ər-ˌbal-əns\ *n* : a weight or influence that balances another

²**counterbalance** \ˌkau̇nt-ər-'bal-əns\ *vb* : to oppose with equal weight or influence

coun•ter•claim \'kau̇nt-ər-ˌklām\ *n* : an opposing claim esp. in law

coun•ter•clock•wise \ˌkau̇nt-ər-'kläk-ˌwīz\ *adv* : in a direction opposite to that in which the hands of a clock rotate — **counterclockwise** *adj*

coun•ter•cul•ture \'kau̇nt-ər-ˌkəl-chər\ *n* : a culture esp. of the young with values and mores that run counter to those of established society

coun•ter•es•pi•o•nage \ˌkau̇nt-ər-'es-pē-ə-ˌnäzh, -nij\ *n* : activities intended to discover and defeat enemy espionage

¹**coun•ter•feit** \'kau̇nt-ər-ˌfit\ *vb* **1** : to copy or imitate in order to deceive **2** : PRETEND, FEIGN — **coun•ter•feit•er** *n*

²**counterfeit** *adj* : SHAM, SPURIOUS; *also* : FORGED

³**counterfeit** *n* : something counterfeit : FORGERY **syn** fraud, sham, fake, imposture, deceit, deception

coun•ter•in•sur•gen•cy \ˌkau̇nt-ər-in-'sər-jən-sē\ *n* : military activity designed to deal with insurgents

coun•ter•in•tel•li•gence \ˌkau̇nt-ər-in-'tel-ə-jəns\ *n* : organized activities of an intelligence service designed to counter the activities of an enemy's intelligence service

count•er•man \'kau̇nt-ər-ˌman, -mən\ *n* : one who tends a counter

coun•ter•mand \'kau̇nt-ər-ˌmand\ *vb* : to withdraw (an order already given) by a contrary order

coun•ter•mea•sure \-ˌmezh-ər\ *n* : an action undertaken to counter another

coun•ter•of•fen•sive \-ə-ˌfen-siv\ *n* : a large-scale counterattack

coun•ter•pane \'kau̇nt-ər-ˌpān\ *n* : BEDSPREAD

coun•ter•part \-ˌpärt\ *n* : a person or thing very closely like or corresponding to another person or thing

coun•ter•point \-ˌpȯint\ *n* : music in which one melody is accompanied by one or more other melodies all woven into a harmonious whole

coun•ter•poise \-ˌpȯiz\ *n* : COUNTERBALANCE

coun•ter•rev•o•lu•tion \ˌkau̇nt-ə(r)-ˌrev-ə-'lü-shən\ *n* : a revolution opposed to a current or earlier one — **coun•ter•rev•o•lu•tion•ary** \-shə-ˌner-ē\ *adj or n*

coun•ter•sign \'kau̇nt-ər-ˌsīn\ *n* **1** : a confirmatory signature added to a writing already signed by another person **2** : a secret signal that must be given by a person who wishes to pass a guard — **countersign** *vb*

coun•ter•sink \'kau̇nt-ər-ˌsiŋk\ *vb* **-sunk**

\-ˌsəŋk\; **-sink·ing 1** : to form a funnel-shaped enlargement at the outer end of a drilled hole **2** : to set the head of (as a screw) at or below the surface — **countersink** *n*

coun·ter·spy \-ˌspī\ *n* : a spy engaged in counterespionage

coun·ter·ten·or \-ˌten-ər\ *n* : a tenor with an unusually high range

coun·ter·vail \ˌkaůnt-ər-ˈvāl\ *vb* : COUNTERACT

coun·ter·weight \ˈkaůnt-ər-ˌwāt\ *n* : COUNTERBALANCE

count·ess \ˈkaůnt-əs\ *n* **1** : the wife or widow of a count or an earl **2** : a woman holding the rank of a count or an earl in her own right

count·ing·house \ˈkaůnt-iŋ-ˌhaůs\ *n* : a building or office for keeping books and conducting business

count·less \ˈkaůnt-ləs\ *adj* : INNUMERABLE

coun·tri·fied *also* **coun·try·fied** \ˈkən-tri-ˌfīd\ *adj* **1** : RURAL, RUSTIC **2** : UNSOPHISTICATED **3** : played or sung in the manner of country music

¹**coun·try** \ˈkən-trē\ *n, pl* **countries** [ME *contree*, fr. OF *contrée*, fr. ML *contrata*, fr. L *contra* against, on the opposite side] **1** : REGION, DISTRICT **2** : FATHERLAND **3** : a nation or its territory **4** : rural regions as opposed to towns and cities

²**country** *adj* **1** : RURAL **2** : of or relating to country music ⟨a ∼ singer⟩

country and western *n* : COUNTRY MUSIC

country club *n* : a suburban club for social life and recreation; *esp* : one having a golf course

coun·try–dance \ˈkən-trē-ˌdans\ *n* : an English dance in which partners face each other esp. in rows

coun·try·man \ˈkən-trē-mən, *2 often* -ˌman\ *n* **1** : an inhabitant of a certain country **2** : COMPATRIOT **3** : one raised in the country : RUSTIC

country music *n* : music derived from or imitating the folk style of the southern U.S. or of the Western cowboy

coun·try·side \ˈkən-trē-ˌsīd\ *n* : a rural area or its people

coun·ty \ˈkaůnt-ē\ *n, pl* **counties 1** : the domain of a count **2** : a territorial division of a country or state for purposes of local government

coup \ˈkü\ *n, pl* **coups** \ˈküz\ [F, blow, stroke] **1** : a brilliant sudden stroke or stratagem **2** : COUP D'ÉTAT

coup de grace \ˌküd-ə-ˈgräs\ *n, pl* **coups de grace** \ˌküd-ə-\ [F *coup de grâce,* lit., stroke of mercy] : a deathblow or final decisive stroke or event

coup d'état \ˌküd-ə-ˈtä\ *n, pl* **coups d'état** \ˌküd-ə-ˈtä(z)\ [F, lit., stroke of state] : a sudden violent overthrow of a government by a small group

cou·pé *or* **coupe** \kü-ˈpā, *2 often* ˈküp\ *n* [F *coupé,* fr. *couper* to cut] **1** : a closed carriage for two persons inside with an outside seat for the driver in front **2** *usu* **coupe** : a 2-door automobile with an enclosed body

¹**cou·ple** \ˈkəp-əl\ *vb* **cou·pled; cou·pling** \-(ə-)liŋ\ : to link together

²**couple** *n* **1** : two persons closely associated; *esp* : a man and a woman married or otherwise paired **2** : PAIR **3** : BOND, TIE **4** : an indefinite small number : FEW ⟨a ∼ of days ago⟩

cou·plet \ˈkəp-lət\ *n* : two successive rhyming lines of verse

cou·pling \ˈkəp-liŋ (*usual for 2*), -ə-liŋ\ *n* **1** : CONNECTION **2** : a device for connecting two parts or things

cou·pon \ˈk(y)ü-ˌpän\ *n* **1** : a statement attached to a bond showing interest due and designed to be cut off and presented for payment **2** : a certificate given to a purchaser of goods and redeemable in merchandise, cash, or services; *also* : a similar ticket or form surrendered for other purposes ⟨a ration ∼⟩ **3** : a part of an advertisement to be cut off to use as an order blank or inquiry form or to obtain a discount on merchandise

cour·age \ˈkər-ij\ *n* : ability to conquer fear or depair : BRAVERY, VALOR — **cou·ra·geous** \kə-ˈrā-jəs\ *adj* — **cou·ra·geous·ly** *adv*

cou·ri·er \ˈkůr-ē-ər, ˈkər-ē-\ *n* : one who bears messages or information esp. for the diplomatic or military services

¹**course** \ˈkōrs\ *n* **1** : PROGRESS, PASSAGE; *also* : direction of progress **2** : the ground or path over which something moves **3** : method of procedure : CONDUCT, BEHAVIOR **4** : an ordered series of acts or proceedings : sequence of events **5** : a series of instruction periods dealing with a subject **6** : the se-

ries of studies leading to graduation from a school or college **7** : the part of a meal served at one time — **of course** : as might be expected

²course *vb* **coursed; cours•ing 1** : to hunt with dogs ⟨∼ a rabbit⟩ **2** : to run or go speedily

cours•er \\'kōr-sər\ *n* : a swift or spirited horse

¹court \\'kōrt\ *n* **1** : the residence of a sovereign or similar dignitary **2** : a sovereign and his officials and advisers as a governing power **3** : an assembly of the retinue of a sovereign **4** : an open space enclosed by a building or buildings **5** : a space walled or marked off for playing a game (as tennis or basketball) **6** : the place where justice is administered; *also* : a judicial body or a meeting of a judicial body **7** : HOMAGE, COURTSHIP

²court *vb* **1** : to try to gain the favor of **2** : WOO **3** : ATTRACT, TEMPT

cour•te•ous \\'kərt-ē-əs\ *adj* : marked by respect for others : CIVIL, POLITE — **cour•te•ous•ly** *adv*

cour•te•san \\'kōrt-ə-zən, 'kərt-\ *n* : PROSTITUTE

cour•te•sy \\'kərt-ə-sē\ *n, pl* **-sies 1** : courteous behavior : POLITENESS **2** : a favor courteously performed

court•house \\'kōrt-₁haús\ *n* : a building in which courts of law are held or county offices are located

court•ier \\'kōrt-ē-ər, 'kōrt-yər\ *n* : a person in attendance at a royal court

court•ly \\'kōrt-lē\ *adj* **court•li•er; -est** : REFINED, ELEGANT, POLITE **syn** gallant, gracious — **court•li•ness** *n*

court–mar•tial \\'kōrt-₁mär-shəl\ *n, pl* **courts–martial** : a military or naval court for trial of offenses against military or naval law; *also* : a trial by this court — **court–martial** *vb*

court•room \-₁rüm, -₁rùm\ *n* : a room in which a court of law is held

court•ship \-₁ship\ *n* : the act of courting : WOOING

court•yard \-₁yärd\ *n* : an enclosure next to a building

cous•in \\'kəz-ᵊn\ *n* [ME *cosin*, fr. OF, fr. L *consobrinus*, fr. *com-* with + *sobrinus* cousin on the mother's side, fr. *soror* sister] : a child of one's uncle or aunt

cou•ture \kü-'tùr, -'tüᵉr\ *n* [F] : the busi-

ness of designing fashionable custom-made women's clothing; *also* : the designers and establishments engaged in this business

cou•tu•ri•er \kü-'tùr-ē-ər, -ē-₁ā\ *n* [F, dressmaker] : the owner of an establishment engaged in couture

cove \\'kōv\ *n* **1** : a trough for lights at the upper part of a wall **2** : a small sheltered inlet or bay

co•ven \\'kəv-ən\ *n* : an assembly or band of witches

cov•e•nant \\'kəv-(ə-)nənt\ *n* : a formal binding agreement : COMPACT — **cov•e•nant** \\'kəv-(ə-)nənt, -ə-₁nant\ *vb*

¹cov•er \\'kəv-ər\ *vb* **cov•ered; cov•er•ing** \\'kəv-(ə-)riŋ\ **1** : to bring or hold within range of a firearm **2** : PROTECT, SHIELD **3** : HIDE, CONCEAL **4** : to place something over or upon **5** : INCLUDE, COMPRISE **6** : to have as one's field of activity ⟨one salesman ∼s the state⟩ **7** : to buy (stocks) in order to have them for delivery on a previous short sale

²cover *n* **1** : something that protects or shelters **2** : LID, TOP **3** : CASE, BINDING **4** : TABLECLOTH **5** : a cloth used on a bed **6** : SCREEN, DISGUISE **7** : an envelope or wrapper for mail

cov•er•age \\'kəv-(ə-)rij\ *n* **1** : the act or fact of covering **2** : the total group covered : SCOPE

cov•er•all \\'kəv-ər-₁ól\ *n* : a one-piece outer garment worn to protect one's clothes — usu. used in pl.

cover charge *n* : a charge made by a restaurant or nightclub in addition to the charge for food and drink

cover crop *n* : a crop planted to prevent soil erosion and to provide humus

cov•er•let \\'kəv-ər-lət\ *n* : BEDSPREAD

¹co•vert \\'kō-(₁)vərt, 'kəv-ərt\ *adj* **1** : HIDDEN, SECRET **2** : SHELTERED — **co•vert•ly** *adv*

²co•vert \\'kəv-ərt, 'kō-vərt\ *n* **1** : a secret or sheltered place; *esp* : a thicket sheltering game **2** : a feather covering the bases of the quills of the wings and tail of a bird **3** : a firm durable twilled cloth usu. of mixed-color yarns

cov•er–up \\'kəv-ər-₁əp\ *n* **1** : a device for masking or concealing **2** : a usu. concerted effort to keep an illegal or unethical act or situation from being made public

cov•et \\'kəv-ət\ *vb* : to desire enviously

(what belongs to another) — **cov•et•ous** *adj* — **cov•et•ous•ness** *n*

cov•ey \ˈkəv-ē\ *n, pl* **coveys** [ME, fr. MF *covee*, fr. OF, fr. *cover* to sit on, brood over, fr. L *cubare* to lie] **1** : a bird with her brood of young **2** : a small flock (as of quail)

¹cow \ˈkaů\ *n* **1** : the mature female of cattle or of an animal (as the moose) of which the male is called *bull* **2** : any domestic bovine animal irrespective of sex or age

²cow *vb* : INTIMIDATE, DAUNT, OVERAWE

cow•ard \ˈkaů(-ə)rd\ *n* [ME, fr. OF *coart*, fr. *coe* tail, fr. L *cauda*] : one who lacks courage or shows shameful fear or timidity — **coward** *adj* — **cow•ard•ice** \-əs\ *n* — **cow•ard•ly** *adv or adj*

cow•bird \ˈkaů-ˌbərd\ *n* : a small No. American bird that lays its eggs in the nests of other birds

cow•boy \-ˌbȯi\ *n* : one (as a mounted ranch hand) who tends cattle or horses

cow•er \ˈkaů(-ə)r\ *vb* : to shrink or crouch down from fear or cold : QUAIL

cow•girl \ˈkaů-ˌgərl\ *n* : a girl or woman who tends cattle or horses

cow•hand \ˈkaů-ˌhand\ *n* : COWBOY

cow•hide \-ˌhīd\ *n* **1** : the hide of a cow; *also* : leather made from it **2** : a coarse whip of braided rawhide

cowl \ˈkaůl\ *n* **1** : a monk's hood **2** : the top part of the front of the body of an automobile to which the windshield is attached

cow•lick \ˈkaů-ˌlik\ *n* : a turned-up tuft of hair that resists control

cowl•ing \ˈkaů-liŋ\ *n* : a usu. metal covering for the engine or another part of an airplane

cow•man \ˈkaů-mən, -ˌman\ *n* : COWBOY; *also* : a cattle owner or rancher

co•work•er \ˈkō-ˌwər-kər\ *n* : a fellow worker

cow•poke \ˈkaů-ˌpōk\ *n* : COWBOY

cow pony *n* : a strong and agile horse trained for herding cattle

cow•pox \ˈkaů-ˌpäks\ *n* : a mild disease of the cow that when communicated to man protects against smallpox

cow•punch•er \-ˌpən-chər\ *n* : COWBOY

cow•slip \ˈkaů-ˌslip\ *n* **1** : a yellow-flowered European primrose **2** : MARSH MARIGOLD

cox•comb \ˈkäks-ˌkōm\ *n* : a conceited foolish person : FOP

cox•swain \ˈkäk-sən, -ˌswān\ *n* : the steersman of a ship's boat or a racing shell

coy \ˈkȯi\ *adj* [ME, quiet, shy, fr. MF *coi* calm, fr. L *quietus* quiet] : BASHFUL, SHY; *esp* : pretending shyness — **coy•ly** *adv* — **coy•ness** *n*

coy•ote \ˈkī-ˌōt, kī-ˈōt-ē\ *n, pl* **coyotes** *or* **coyote** : a mammal of No. America related to the domestic dog and the wolves

coy•pu \ˈkȯi-pü\ *n* : NUTRIA 2

coz•en \ˈkəz-ᵊn\ *vb* [obs. It *cozzonare*, fr. It *cozzone* horse trader, fr. L *cocio* trader] : CHEAT, DEFRAUD — **coz•en•age** \-ij\ *n*

¹co•zy \ˈkō-zē\ *adj* **co•zi•er; -est** : SNUG, COMFORTABLE — **co•zi•ly** \ˈkō-zə-lē\ *adv* — **co•zi•ness** \-zē-nəs\ *n*

²cozy *n, pl* **cozies** : a padded covering for a vessel (as a teapot) to keep the contents hot

cp *abbr* **1** compare **2** coupon

CP *abbr* **1** chemically pure **2** command post **3** communist party

CPA *abbr* certified public accountant

cpd *abbr* compound

CPI *abbr* consumer price index

Cpl *abbr* corporal

CPO *abbr* chief petty officer

CPOM *abbr* master chief petty officer

CPOS *abbr* senior chief petty officer

CPR *abbr* cardiopulmonary resuscitation

CPT *abbr* captain

CQ *abbr* charge of quarters

cr *abbr* credit; creditor

Cr *symbol* chromium

¹crab \ˈkrab\ *n* : any of various crustaceans with a short broad shell and small abdomen

²crab *n* : an ill-natured person

crab apple *n* : a small often highly colored sour apple; *also* : a tree that produces crab apples

crab•bed \ˈkrab-əd\ *adj* **1** : MOROSE, PEEVISH **2** : CRAMPED, IRREGULAR

crab•by \ˈkrab-ē\ *adj* **crab•bi•er; -est** : CROSS, ILL-NATURED

crab•grass \ˈkrab-ˌgras\ *n* : a weedy grass with creeping or sprawling stems that root freely at the nodes

crab louse *n* : a louse infesting the pubic region in man

¹**crack** \ˈkrak\ vb **1** : to break with a sharp sudden sound **2** : to break with or without completely separating into parts **3** : to fail in tone or become harsh ⟨her voice ∼ed⟩ **4** : to subject (as a petroleum oil) to heat for breaking down into lighter products (as gasoline)

²**crack** n **1** : a sudden sharp noise **2** : a witty or sharp remark **3** : a narrow break or opening : FISSURE **4** : a sharp blow **5** : ATTEMPT, TRY **6** : highly purified cocaine in the form of small chips used for smoking

³**crack** adj : extremely proficient

crack•down \ˈkrak-ˌdaùn\ n : an act or instance of taking positive disciplinary action ⟨a ∼ on gambling⟩ — **crack down** \-ˈdaùn\ vb

crack•er \ˈkrak-ər\ n **1** : FIRECRACKER **2** : a dry thin crispy baked bread product made of flour and water

crack•er•jack \-ˌjak\ n : something very excellent — **crackerjack** adj

crack•le \ˈkrak-əl\ vb **crack•led**; **crack•ling** \-(ə-)liŋ\ **1** : to make small sharp snapping noises **2** : to develop fine cracks in a surface — **crackle** n — **crack•ly** \-(ə-)lē\ adj

crack•pot \ˈkrak-ˌpät\ n : an eccentric person

crack–up \ˈkrak-ˌəp\ n : CRASH, WRECK; also : BREAKDOWN

¹**cra•dle** \ˈkrād-ᵊl\ n **1** : a baby's bed or cot **2** : INFANCY ⟨from ∼ to the grave⟩ **3** : a place of origin **4** : a framework or support (as for a telephone receiver)

²**cradle** vb **cra•dled**; **cra•dling** \ˈkrād-(ᵊ-)liŋ\ **1** : to place in or as if in a cradle **2** : NURSE, REAR

cra•dle•song \ˈkrād-ᵊl-ˌsòŋ\ n : LULLABY

craft \ˈkraft\ n **1** : ART, SKILL; also : an occupation requiring special skill **2** : CUNNING, GUILE **3** pl usu **craft** : a boat esp. of small size; also : AIRCRAFT, SPACECRAFT

crafts•man \ˈkrafts-mən\ n : a skilled artisan — **crafts•man•ship** n

crafty \ˈkraf-tē\ adj **craft•i•er**; **-est** : CUNNING, DECEITFUL, SUBTLE — **craft•i•ly** \ˈkraf-tə-lē\ adv — **craft•i•ness** \-tē-nəs\ n

crag \ˈkrag\ n : a steep rugged cliff or rock — **crag•gy** \-ē\ adj

cram \ˈkram\ vb **crammed**; **cram•ming** **1** : to pack in tight : JAM **2** : to eat greedily **3** : to study rapidly under pressure for an examination

¹**cramp** \ˈkramp\ n **1** : a sudden painful contraction of muscle **2** : sharp abdominal pain — usu. used in pl.

²**cramp** vb **1** : to affect with a cramp or cramps **2** : to restrain from free action : HAMPER **3** : to turn (the front wheels) sharply to the side

cran•ber•ry \ˈkran-ˌber-ē, -b(ə-)rē\ n : the red acid berry of any of several trailing plants related to the heaths; also : one of these plants

¹**crane** \ˈkrān\ n **1** : any of a family of tall wading birds related to the rails; also : any of several herons **2** : a machine for lifting and carrying heavy objects

²**crane** vb **craned**; **cran•ing** : to stretch one's neck to see better

crane fly n : any of numerous long-legged slender two-winged flies that resemble large mosquitoes but do not bite

cranial nerve n : any of the nerves that arise in pairs from the lower surface of the brain and pass through openings in the skull to the periphery of the body

cra•ni•um \ˈkrā-nē-əm\ n, pl **-ni•ums** or **-nia** \-nē-ə\ : SKULL; esp : the part enclosing the brain — **cra•ni•al** \-əl\ adj

¹**crank** \ˈkraŋk\ n **1** : a bent part of an axle or shaft or an arm at right angles to the end of a shaft by which circular motion is imparted to or received from it **2** : an eccentric person **3** : a bad-tempered person : GROUCH

²**crank** vb : to start or operate by turning a crank

crank•case \ˈkraŋk-ˌkās\ n : the housing of a crankshaft

crank out vb : to produce in a mechanical manner

crank•shaft \ˈkraŋk-ˌshaft\ n : a shaft turning or driven by a crank

cranky \ˈkraŋ-kē\ adj **crank•i•er**; **-est** **1** : IRRITABLE **2** : operating uncertainly or imperfectly

cran•ny \ˈkran-ē\ n, pl **crannies** : CREVICE, CHINK

crape \ˈkrāp\ n : CREPE; esp : black crepe used in mourning

craps \ˈkraps\ n : a gambling game played with two dice

crap•shoot•er \ˈkrap-ˌshüt-ər\ n : a person who plays craps

¹**crash** \ˈkrash\ vb **1** : to break noisily

: SMASH **2** : to damage an airplane in landing **3** : to enter or attend without invitation or without paying ⟨∼ a party⟩

²crash *n* **1** : a loud sound (as of things smashing) **2** : an instance of crashing ⟨a plane ∼⟩; *also* : COLLISION **3** : a sudden failure (as of a business)

³crash *adj* : marked by concerted effort over the shortest possible time

⁴crash *n* : coarse linen fabric used for towels and draperies

crash–land \\'krash-'land\\ *vb* : to land an aircraft or spacecraft under emergency conditions usu. with damage to the craft — **crash landing** *n*

crass \\'kras\\ *adj* : STUPID, GROSS — **crass•ly** *adv*

crate \\'krāt\\ *n* : a container often of wooden slats — **crate** *vb*

cra•ter \\'krāt-ər\\ *n* [L, mixing bowl, crater, fr. Gk *kratēr,* fr. *kerannynai* to mix] **1** : the depression around the opening of a volcano **2** : a depression formed by the impact of a meteorite or by the explosion of a bomb or shell

cra•vat \\krə-'vat\\ *n* : NECKTIE

crave \\'krāv\\ *vb* **craved; crav•ing 1** : to ask for earnestly : BEG **2** : to long for : DESIRE

cra•ven \\'krā-vən\\ *adj* : COWARDLY — **craven** *n*

crav•ing \\'krā-viŋ\\ *n* : an urgent or abnormal desire

craw•fish \\'krȯ-ˌfish\\ *n* **1** : CRAYFISH 1 **2** : SPINY LOBSTER

¹crawl \\'krȯl\\ *vb* **1** : to move slowly by drawing the body along the ground **2** : to advance feebly, cautiously, or slowly **3** : to be swarming with or feel as if swarming with creeping things ⟨a place ∼*ing* with ants⟩ ⟨her flesh ∼*ed*⟩

²crawl *n* **1** : a very slow pace **2** : a prone speed swimming stroke

cray•fish \\'krā-ˌfish\\ *n* **1** : any of numerous freshwater crustaceans usu. much smaller than the related lobsters **2** : SPINY LOBSTER

cray•on \\'krā-ˌän, -ən\\ *n* : a stick of chalk or wax used for writing, drawing, or coloring; *also* : a drawing made with such material — **crayon** *vb*

¹craze \\'krāz\\ *vb* **crazed; craz•ing** [ME *crasen* to crush, craze] : to make or become insane

²craze *n* : FAD, MANIA

cra•zy \\'krā-zē\\ *adj* **cra•zi•er; -est 1** : mentally disordered : INSANE **2** : wildly impractical; *also* : ERRATIC — **cra•zi•ly** \\'krā-zə-lē\\ *adv* — **cra•zi•ness** \\-zē-nəs\\ *n*

CRC *abbr* Civil Rights Commission

creak \\'krēk\\ *vb* : to make a prolonged squeaking or grating sound — **creak** *n* — **creaky** *adj*

¹cream \\'krēm\\ *n* **1** : the yellowish fat-rich part of milk **2** : a thick smooth sauce, confection, or cosmetic **3** : the choicest part **4** : a pale yellow color — **creamy** *adj*

²cream *vb* **1** : to prepare with a cream sauce **2** : to beat or blend into creamy consistency **3** : to defeat decisively

cream cheese *n* : a cheese made from whole milk enriched with cream

cream•ery \\'krēm-(ə-)rē\\ *n, pl* **-er•ies** : an establishment where butter and cheese are made or milk and cream are prepared for sale

crease \\'krēs\\ *n* : a mark or line made by or as if by folding — **crease** *vb*

cre•ate \\krē-'āt\\ *vb* **cre•at•ed; cre•at•ing** : to bring into being : cause to exist : MAKE, PRODUCE — **cre•ative** \\-'āt-iv\\ *adj* — **cre•ativ•i•ty** \\ˌkre-(ˌ)ā-'tiv-ət-ē, ˌkrē-ə-\\ *n*

cre•ation \\krē-'ā-shən\\ *n* **1** : the act of creating or producing ⟨∼ of the world⟩ **2** : something that is created **3** : all created things : WORLD

cre•ation•ism \\krē-'ā-shə-ˌniz-əm\\ *n* : a doctrine or theory holding that matter, the various forms of life, and the world were created by God out of nothing — **cre•ation•ist** \\-shə-nəst\\ *n or adj*

cre•ator \\krē-'āt-ər\\ *n* **1** : one that creates : MAKER, AUTHOR **2** *cap* : GOD 1

crea•ture \\'krē-chər\\ *n* : a lower animal; *also* : a human being

crèche \\'kresh\\ *n* [F, manger, crib] : a representation of the Nativity scene

cre•dence \\'krēd-³ns\\ *n* : BELIEF

cre•den•tial \\kri-'den-chəl\\ *n* : something that gives a basis for credit or confidence

cre•den•za \\kri-'den-zə\\ *n* [It, lit., belief, confidence] : a sideboard, buffet, or bookcase usu. without legs

cred•i•ble \\'kred-ə-bəl\\ *adj* : TRUSTWORTHY, BELIEVABLE — **cred•i•bil•i•ty** \\ˌkred-ə-'bil-ət-ē\\ *n*

¹cred·it \\'kred-ət\ *vb* **1** : BELIEVE **2** : to give credit to

²credit *n* [MF, fr. It *credito*, fr. L *creditum* something entrusted to another, loan, fr. *credere* to believe, entrust] **1** : the balance (as in a bank) in a person's favor **2** : time given for payment for goods sold on trust **3** : an accounting entry of payment received **4** : BELIEF, FAITH **5** : financial trustworthiness **6** : ESTEEM **7** : a source of honor or distinction **8** : a unit of academic work

cred·it·able \\'kred-ət-ə-bəl\ *adj* : worthy of esteem or praise — **cred·it·ably** \-blē\ *adv*

credit card *n* : a card authorizing purchases on credit

cred·i·tor \\'kred-ət-ər\ *n* : a person to whom money is owed

cre·do \\'krēd-ō, 'krād-\ *n, pl* **credos** [ME, fr. L, I believe] : CREED

cred·u·lous \\'krej-ə-ləs\ *adj* : inclined to believe esp. on slight evidence — **cre·du·li·ty** \kri-'d(y)ü-lət-ē\ *n*

Cree \\'krē\ *n, pl* **Cree** *or* **Crees** : a member of an American Indian people of Manitoba and Saskatchewan

creed \\'krēd\ *n* [ME *crede*, fr. OE *crēda*, fr. L *credo* I believe, first word of the Apostles' and Nicene Creeds] : a statement of the essential beliefs of a religious faith

creek \\'krēk, 'krik\ *n* **1** *chiefly Brit* : a small inlet **2** : a stream smaller than a river and larger than a brook

Creek \\'krēk\ *n* : a member of an American Indian people of Alabama, Georgia, and Florida

creel \\'krēl\ *n* : a wicker basket esp. for carrying fish

creep \\'krēp\ *vb* **crept** \\'krept\; **creeping 1** : CRAWL **2** : to grow over a surface like ivy **3** : to feel as though insects were crawling on the skin — **creep** *n* — **creep·er** *n*

creep·ing \\'krē-piŋ\ *adj* : developing or advancing by imperceptible degrees

creepy \\'krē-pē\ *adj* **creep·i·er; -est** : having or producing a nervous shivery fear

cre·mate \\'krē-,māt\ *vb* **cre·mat·ed; cre·mat·ing** : to reduce (a dead body) to ashes with fire — **cre·ma·tion** \kri-'mā-shən\ *n*

cre·ma·to·ry \\'krē-mə-,tōr-ē, 'krem-ə-\ *n, pl* **-ries** : a furnace for cremating; *also* : a structure containing such a furnace

crème \\'krem, 'krēm\ *n, pl* **crèmes** \\'krem(z), 'krēmz\ [F, lit., cream] : a sweet liqueur

cren·el·at·ed *or* **cren·el·at·ed** \\'kren-əl-,āt-əd\ *adj* : having battlements ⟨a ~ tower⟩ — **cren·el·la·tion** \,kren-əl-'ā-shən\ *n*

Cre·ole \\'krē-,ōl\ *n* : a descendant of early French or Spanish settlers of the U.S. Gulf states preserving their speech and culture; *also* : a person of mixed French or Spanish and Negro descent speaking a dialect of French or Spanish

cre·o·sote \\'krē-ə-,sōt\ *n* : an oily liquid obtained by distillation of coal tar and used in preserving wood

crepe *or* **crêpe** \\'krāp\ *n* : a light crinkled fabric of any of various fibers

crepe su·zette \,krāp-sù-'zet\ *n, pl* **crepes suzette** \,krāp(s)-sù-'zet\ *or* **crepe suzettes** \,krāp-sù-'zets\ : a thin folded or rolled pancake in a hot orange-butter sauce that is sprinkled with a liqueur and set ablaze for serving

cre·pus·cu·lar \kri-'pəs-kyə-lər\ *adj* **1** : of, relating to, or resembling twilight **2** : active in the twilight ⟨~ insects⟩

cre·scen·do \krə-'shen-dō\ *adv or adj* [It] : increasing in loudness — used as a direction in music — **crescendo** *n*

cres·cent \\'kres-ᵊnt\ *n* [ME *cressant*, fr. MF *creissant*, fr. *creistre* to grow, increase, fr. L *crescere*] : the moon at any stage between new moon and first quarter and between last quarter and new moon; *also* : something shaped like the figure of the crescent moon with a convex and a concave edge — **cres·cen·tic** \kre-'sent-ik, krə-\ *adj*

cress \\'kres\ *n* : any of several salad plants related to the mustards

¹crest \\'krest\ *n* **1** : a tuft or process on the head of an animal (as a bird) **2** : a heraldic device **3** : an upper part, edge, or limit ⟨the ~ of a hill⟩ — **crest·ed** \\'kres-təd\ *adj* — **crest·less** *adj*

²crest *vb* **1** : CROWN **2** : to reach the crest of **3** : to rise to a crest

crest·fall·en \\'krest-,fò-lən\ *adj* : DISPIRITED, DEJECTED

Cre·ta·ceous \kri-'tā-shəs\ *adj* : of, relating to, or being the latest period of the Mesozoic era — **Cretaceous** *n*

cre·tin \\'krēt-ᵊn\\ *n* [F *crétin*, fr. F dial. *cretin* Christian, human being, kind of idiot found in the Alps, fr. L *christianus* Christian] **1** : one affected with cretinism **2** : a stupid person

cre·tin·ism \\-ᵢiz-əm\\ *n* : a usu. congenital abnormal condition characterized by physical stunting and mental deficiency

cre·tonne \\'krē-ᵢtän\\ *n* : a strong unglazed cotton cloth for curtains and upholstery

cre·vasse \\kri-'vas\\ *n* : a deep fissure esp. in a glacier

crev·ice \\'krev-əs\\ *n* : a narrow fissure

¹crew \\'krü\\ *chiefly Brit* past of CROW

²crew \\'krü\\ *n* [ME *crue*, lit., reinforcement, fr. MF *creue* increase, fr. *creistre* to grow, fr. L *crescere*] **1** : a body of people trained to work together for certain purposes **2** : a group of people who operate a ship, train, aircraft, or spacecraft **3** : the rowers and coxswain of a racing shell; *also* : the sport of rowing engaged in by a crew — **crew·man** \\-mən\\ *n*

crew cut *n* : a very short bristly haircut

crew·el \\'krü-əl\\ *n* : slackly twisted worsted yarn used for embroidery — **crew·el·work** \\-ᵢwərk\\ *n*

¹crib \\'krib\\ *n* **1** : a manger for feeding animals **2** : a small bedstead for a child **3** : a building or bin for storage (as of grain) **4** : a translation prepared to aid a student in preparing a lesson

²crib *vb* **cribbed**; **crib·bing 1** : to put in a crib **2** : STEAL, PLAGIARIZE — **crib·ber** *n*

crib·bage \\'krib-ij\\ *n* : a card game usu. played by two players and scored on a board (**cribbage board**)

crib death *n* : SUDDEN INFANT DEATH SYNDROME

crick \\'krik\\ *n* : a painful spasm of muscles (as of the neck)

¹crick·et \\'krik-ət\\ *n* : any of various leaping insects related to the grasshoppers and noted for the chirping noises of the male

²cricket *n* : a game played with a bat and ball by two teams on a field centering upon two wickets each defended by a batsman

cri·er \\'krī-(-ə)r\\ *n* : one who calls out proclamations and announcements

crime \\'krīm\\ *n* : a serious offense against the public law

¹crim·i·nal \\'krim-ən-ᵊl\\ *adj* **1** : involving or being a crime **2** : relating to crime or its punishment — **crim·i·nal·i·ty** \\ᵢkrim-ə-'nal-ət-ē\\ *n* — **crim·i·nal·ly** \\'krim-ən-ᵊl-ē\\ *adv*

²criminal *n* : one who has committed a crime

crim·i·nol·o·gy \\ᵢkrim-ə-'näl-ə-jē\\ *n* : the scientific study of crime and criminals — **crim·i·nol·o·gist** \\ᵢkrim-ə-'näl-ə-jəst\\ *n*

¹crimp \\'krimp\\ *vb* : to cause to become crinkled, wavy, or bent

²crimp *n* : something (as a curl in hair) produced by or as if by crimping

¹crim·son \\'krim-zən\\ *n* : a deep purplish red — **crimson** *adj*

²crimson *vb* : to make or become crimson

cringe \\'krinj\\ *vb* **cringed**; **cring·ing** : to shrink in fear : WINCE, COWER

crin·kle \\'kriŋ-kəl\\ *vb* **crin·kled**; **crin·kling** \\-k(ə-)liŋ\\ : to turn or wind in many short bends or curves; *also* : WRINKLE, RIPPLE — **crinkle** *n* — **crin·kly** \\-k(ə-)lē\\ *adj*

crin·o·line \\'krin-ᵊl-ən\\ *n* **1** : an open= weave cloth used for stiffening and lining **2** : a full stiff skirt or underskirt made of crinoline

¹crip·ple \\'krip-əl\\ *n* : a lame or disabled person

²cripple *vb* **crip·pled**; **crip·pling** \\-(ə-)liŋ\\ **1** : to make lame **2** : to make useless or imperfect

cri·sis \\'krī-səs\\ *n, pl* **cri·ses** \\'krī-ᵢsēz\\ [L, fr. Gk *krisis*, lit., decision, fr. *krinein* to decide] **1** : the turning point for better or worse in an acute disease or fever **2** : a decisive or critical moment

crisp \\'krisp\\ *adj* **1** : CURLY, WAVY **2** : BRITTLE **3** : FIRM, FRESH ⟨~ lettuce⟩ **4** : being sharp and clear **5** : LIVELY, SPARKLING **6** : FROSTY, SNAPPY; *also* : BRACING — **crisp** *vb* — **crisp·ly** *adv* — **crisp·ness** *n* — **crispy** *adj*

¹criss·cross \\'kris-ᵢkros\\ *vb* **1** : to mark with crossed lines **2** : to go or pass back and forth

²crisscross *adj* : marked or characterized by crisscrossing — **crisscross** *adv*

³crisscross *n* : a pattern formed by crossed lines

crit *abbr* critical; criticism

cri·te·ri·on \krī-'tir-ē-ən\ *n, pl* **-ria** \-ē-ə\ : a standard on which a judgment may be based

crit·ic \'krit-ik\ *n* **1** : a person who judges literary or artistic works **2** : one inclined to find fault

crit·i·cal \'krit-i-kəl\ *adj* **1** : inclined to criticize **2** : relating to criticism or critics **3** : requiring careful judgment **4** : being or relating to a condition or disease involving danger of death **5** : being a crisis **6** : UNCERTAIN — **crit·i·cal·ly** \-i-k(ə-)lē\ *adv*

crit·i·cism \'krit-ə-ˌsiz-əm\ *n* **1** : the act of criticizing; *esp* : CENSURE **2** : a judgment or review **3** : the art of judging works of literature or art

crit·i·cize \'krit-ə-ˌsīz\ *vb* **-cized; -ciz·ing** **1** : to judge as a critic : EVALUATE **2** : to find fault : express criticism **syn** blame, censure, condemn

cri·tique \krə-'tēk\ *n* : a critical estimate or discussion

crit·ter \'krit-ər\ *n* : CREATURE

croak \'krōk\ *n* : a hoarse harsh cry (as of a frog) — **croak** *vb*

cro·chet \krō-'shā\ *n* [F, hook, crochet, fr. MF, dim. of *croche* hook] : needlework done with a single thread and hooked needle — **crochet** *vb*

crock \'kräk\ *n* : a thick earthenware pot or jar

crock·ery \'kräk-(ə-)rē\ *n* : EARTHENWARE

croc·o·dile \'kräk-ə-ˌdīl\ *n* [ME & L; ME *cocodrille,* fr. OF, fr. ML *cocodrillus,* alter. of L *crocodilus,* fr. Gk *krokodilos* lizard, crocodile, fr. *krokē* pebble + *drillos* worm] : any of several thick-skinned long-bodied reptiles of tropical and subtropical waters

cro·cus \'krō-kəs\ *n, pl* **cro·cus·es** *also* **crocus** *or* **cro·ci** \-ˌkī\ : any of a large genus of low herbs related to the irises and having brightly colored flowers borne singly in early spring

crois·sant \k(rə-ˌ)wä-'säⁿ\ *n, pl* **croissants** \-'säⁿ(z)\ : a rich crescent-shaped roll

crone \'krōn\ *n* : WITCH 2

cro·ny \'krō-nē\ *n, pl* **cronies** : a close friend esp. of long standing

¹crook \'krúk\ *vb* : to curve or bend sharply

²crook *n* **1** : a bent or curved implement **2** : SWINDLER, THIEF **3** : a bent or curved part; *also* : BEND, CURVE

crook·ed \'krúk-əd\ *adj* **1** : having a crook : BENT, CURVED **2** : DISHONEST — **crook·ed·ly** *adv* — **crook·ed·ness** *n*

croon \'krün\ *vb* : to sing or hum in a gentle murmuring voice — **croon·er** *n*

¹crop \'kräp\ *n* **1** : the handle of a whip; *also* : a short riding whip **2** : a pouch in the throat of many birds and insects where food is received **3** : something that can be harvested; *also* : the yield at harvest

²crop *vb* **cropped; crop·ping** **1** : to remove the tips of : cut off short; *also* : TRIM **2** : to feed on by cropping **3** : to devote (land) to crops **4** : to appear unexpectedly

crop·land \-ˌland\ *n* : land devoted to the production of plant crops

crop·per \'kräp-ər\ *n* : a raiser of crops; *esp* : SHARECROPPER

cro·quet \krō-'kā\ *n* : a game in which mallets are used to drive wooden balls through a series of wickets set out on a lawn

cro·quette \krō-'ket\ *n* [F] : a small often rounded mass of minced meat, fish, or vegetables fried in deep fat

cro·sier \'krō-zhər\ *n* : a staff carried by bishops and abbots

¹cross \'krós\ *n* **1** : a structure consisting of an upright beam and a crossbar used esp. by the ancient Romans for execution **2** : a figure of the cross on which Christ was crucified used as a Christian symbol **3** : a hybridizing of unlike individuals or strains; *also* : a product of this **4** : a punch delivered with a circular motion over an opponent's lead

²cross *vb* **1** : to lie or place across; *also* : INTERSECT **2** : to cancel by marking a cross on or by lining through **3** : THWART, OBSTRUCT **4** : to go or extend across : TRAVERSE **5** : HYBRIDIZE **6** : to meet and pass on the way

³cross *adj* **1** : lying across **2** : CONTRARY, OPPOSED **3** : marked by bad temper **4** : HYBRID — **cross·ly** *adv*

cross·bar \'krós-ˌbär\ *n* : a transverse bar or piece

cross·bones \-ˌbōnz\ *n pl* : two leg or

arm bones placed or depicted cross-wise

cross·bow \-ˌbō\ *n* : a short bow mounted crosswise at the end of a wooden stock that shoots short arrows

cross·breed \ˈkrȯs-ˌbrēd, -ˈbrēd\ *vb* -**bred** \-ˈbred\; -**breed·ing** : HYBRIDIZE

cross–coun·try \-ˈkən-trē\ *adj* 1 : extending or moving across a country 2 : proceeding over the countryside (as fields and woods) rather than by roads 3 : of or relating to racing or skiing over the countryside instead of over a track or run — **cross–country** *adv*

cross·cur·rent \-ˈkər-ənt\ *n* 1 : a current running counter to another 2 : a conflicting tendency — usu. used in pl.

¹**cross·cut** \-ˌkət\ *vb* : to cut or saw crosswise esp. of the grain of wood

²**crosscut** *adj* 1 : made or used for cross-cutting ⟨a ~ saw⟩ 2 : cut across the grain

³**crosscut** *n* : something that cuts through transversely

cross–ex·am·ine \ˌkrȯs-ig-ˈzam-ən\ *vb* : to examine with questions to check the answers to previous questions — **cross–ex·am·i·na·tion** \-ˌzam-ə-ˈnā-shən\ *n*

cross–eyed \ˈkrȯs-ˌīd\ *adj* : having one or both eyes turned inward toward the nose

cross–fer·til·iza·tion \-ˌfərt-ᵊl-ə-ˈzā-shən\ *n* 1 : fertilization between sex cells produced by separate individuals or sometimes by individuals of different kinds; *also* : CROSS-POLLINATION 2 : a broadening or productive interchange (as between cultures) — **cross–fer·til·ize** \-ˈfərt-ᵊl-ˌīz\ *vb*

cross fire *n* 1 : crossing lines of fire in combat 2 : rapid or angry interchange

cross hair *n* : one of the fine wires or threads in the eyepiece of an optical instrument used as a reference line

cross·hatch \ˈkrȯs-ˌhach\ *vb* : to mark with a series of parallel lines that cross esp. obliquely — **cross–hatch·ing** *n*

cross·ing \ˈkrȯ-siŋ\ *n* 1 : a place or structure for crossing something (as a street or river) 2 : a point of intersection (as of a street and a railroad track)

cross·over \ˈkrȯs-ˌō-vər\ *n* 1 : CROSSING 2 : a member of one political party who votes in the primary of the other party

cross·piece \ˈkrȯs-ˌpēs\ *n* : a crosswise member

cross–pol·li·na·tion \ˌkrȯs-ˌpäl-ə-ˈnā-shən\ *n* : transfer of pollen from one flower to the stigma of another — **cross–pol·li·nate** \ˈkrȯs-ˈpäl-ə-ˌnāt\ *vb*

cross–pur·pose \ˈkrȯs-ˈpər-pəs\ *n* : a purpose contrary to another purpose ⟨working at ~s⟩

cross–ques·tion \-ˈkwes-chən\ *vb* : CROSS-EXAMINE

cross–re·fer \ˌkrȯs-ri-ˈfər\ *vb* : to refer by a notation or direction from one place to another (as in a book or list) — **cross–ref·er·ence** \ˈkrȯs-ˈref-(ə-)rəns\ *n*

cross·road \ˈkrȯs-ˌrōd\ *n* 1 : a road that crosses a main road or runs between main roads 2 : a place where roads meet — usu. used in pl. 3 : a crucial point where a decision must be made

cross section *n* 1 : a section cut across something; *also* : a representation made by or as if by such cutting 2 : a number of persons or things selected from a group that show the general nature of the whole group — **cross–sec·tion·al** *adj*

cross·walk \ˈkrȯs-ˌwȯk\ *n* : a specially marked path for pedestrians crossing a street

cross·ways \-ˌwāz\ *adv* : CROSSWISE

cross·wise \-ˌwīz\ *adv* : so as to cross something : ACROSS — **crosswise** *adj*

cross·word \ˌkrȯs-ˌwərd\ *n* : a puzzle in which words are fitted into a pattern of numbered squares in answer to clues

crotch \ˈkräch\ *n* : an angle formed by the parting of two legs, branches, or members

crotch·et \ˈkräch-ət\ *n* : an odd notion : WHIM — **crotch·ety** *adj*

crouch \ˈkraůch\ *vb* 1 : to stoop or bend low 2 : CRINGE, COWER — **crouch** *n*

croup \ˈkrüp\ *n* : laryngitis esp. of infants marked by a hoarse ringing cough and difficult breathing — **croupy** *adj*

crou·pi·er \ˈkrü-pē-ər, -pē-ˌā\ *n* [F, lit., rider on the rump of a horse, fr. *croupe* rump] : an employee of a gambling casino who collects and pays bets at a gaming table

crou•ton \'krü-ˌtän\ *n* [F *croûton,* dim. of *croûte* crust] : a small cube of bread toasted or fried crisp

¹crow \'krō\ *n* **1** : any of various large glossy black birds related to the jays **2** *cap* : a member of an American Indian people of the region between the Platte and Yellowstone rivers; *also* : the language of the Crow people

²crow *vb* **1** : to make the loud shrill sound characteristic of the cock **2** : to utter a sound expressive of pleasure **3** : EXULT, GLOAT; *also* : BRAG, BOAST

³crow *n* : the cry of the cock

crow•bar \'krō-ˌbär\ *n* : a metal bar usu. wedge-shaped at the end for use as a pry or lever

¹crowd \'kraud\ *vb* **1** : to press close **2** : to collect in numbers : THRONG **3** : CRAM, STUFF

²crowd *n* : a large number of people gathered together at random : THRONG

¹crown \'kraun\ *n* **1** : a mark of victory or honor; *esp* : the title of a champion in a sport **2** : a royal headdress **3** : the top of the head **4** : the highest part (as of a tree or tooth) **5** *often cap* : sovereign power; *also* : MONARCH **6** : a formerly used British silver coin — **crowned** \'kraund\ *adj*

²crown *vb* **1** : to place a crown on **2** : HONOR **3** : TOP, SURMOUNT **4** : to fit (a tooth) with an artificial crown

crown vetch *n* : a European leguminous herb with umbels of pink-and-white flowers and sharp-angled pods

crow's–foot \'krōz-ˌfut\ *n, pl* **crow's–feet** \-ˌfēt\ : any of the wrinkles around the outer corners of the eyes — usu. used in pl.

crow's nest *n* : a partly enclosed platform high on a ship's mast for use as a lookout

CRT *abbr* cathode-ray tube

cru•cial \'krü-shəl\ *adj* : DECISIVE; *also* : IMPORTANT, SIGNIFICANT

cru•ci•ble \'krü-sə-bəl\ *n* : a heat-resistant container in which material can be subjected to great heat

cru•ci•fix \'krü-sə-ˌfiks\ *n* : a representation of Christ on the cross

cru•ci•fix•ion \ˌkrü-sə-'fik-shən\ *n* : the act of crucifying; *esp, cap* : the crucifying of Christ

cru•ci•form \'krü-sə-ˌförm\ *adj* : cross‑shaped

cru•ci•fy \'krü-sə-ˌfī\ *vb* **-fied; -fy•ing 1** : to put to death by nailing or binding the hands and feet to a cross **2** : MORTIFY 1 **3** : TORTURE, PERSECUTE

¹crude \'krüd\ *adj* **crud•er; crud•est 1** : not refined : RAW ⟨∼ oil⟩ ⟨∼ statistics⟩ **2** : lacking grace, taste, tact, or polish : RUDE — **crude•ly** *adv* — **cru•di•ty** \'krüd-ət-ē\ *n*

²crude *n* : unrefined petroleum

cru•el \'krü-əl\ *adj* **cru•el•er** *or* **cru•el•ler; cru•el•est** *or* **cru•el•lest** : causing pain and suffering to others : MERCILESS — **cru•el•ly** \-ē\ *adv* — **cru•el•ty** \-tē\ *n*

cru•et \'krü-ət\ *n* : a small usu. glass bottle for vinegar, oil, or sauce

cruise \'krüz\ *vb* **cruised; cruis•ing** [D *kruisen* to make a cross, cruise, fr. L *crux* cross] **1** : to sail about touching at a series of ports **2** : to travel for enjoyment **3** : to travel about the streets at random **4** : to travel at the most efficient operating speed ⟨the *cruising* speed of an airplane⟩ — **cruise** *n*

cruis•er \'krü-zər\ *n* **1** : SQUAD CAR **2** : a large fast moderately armored and gunned warship **3** : a motorboat equipped for living aboard

crul•ler \'krəl-ər\ *n* **1** : a small sweet cake in the form of a twisted strip fried in deep fat **2** *North & Midland* : an unraised doughnut

¹crumb \'krəm\ *n* : a small fragment

²crumb *vb* **1** : to break into crumbs **2** : to cover with crumbs

crum•ble \'krəm-bəl\ *vb* **crum•bled; crum•bling** \-b(ə-)liŋ\ : to break into small pieces : DISINTEGRATE — **crum•bly** \-b(ə-)lē\ *adj*

crum•my *or* **crumby** \'krəm-ē\ *adj* **crum•mi•er** *or* **crumb•i•er; -est 1** : MISERABLE, FILTHY **2** : CHEAP, WORTHLESS

crum•pet \'krəm-pət\ *n* : a small round unsweetened bread cooked on a griddle

crum•ple \'krəm-pəl\ *vb* **crum•pled; crum•pling** \-p(ə-)liŋ\ **1** : to crush together : RUMPLE **2** : COLLAPSE

¹crunch \'krənch\ *vb* : to chew with a grinding noise; *also* : to grind or press with a crushing noise

²crunch *n* **1** : an act of or a sound made

by crunching **2** : a tight or critical situation — **crunchy** *adj*

cru·sade \krü-'sād\ *n* **1** *cap* : any of the expeditions in the 11th, 12th, and 13th centuries undertaken by Christian countries to take the Holy Land from the Muslims **2** : a reforming enterprise undertaken with zeal — **crusade** *vb* — **cru·sad·er** *n*

cruse \'krüz, 'krüs\ *n* : a jar for water or oil

¹crush \'krəsh\ *vb* **1** : to squeeze out of shape **2** : HUG, EMBRACE **3** : to grind or pound to small bits **4** : OVERWHELM, SUPPRESS

²crush *n* **1** : an act of crushing **2** : a violent crowding **3** : INFATUATION

crust \'krəst\ *n* **1** : the outside part of bread; *also* : a piece of old dry bread **2** : the cover of a pie **3** : a hard surface layer — **crust·al** *adj*

crus·ta·cean \ˌkrəs-'tā-shən\ *n* : any of a large class of mostly aquatic arthropods (as lobsters or crabs) having a firm crustlike shell

crusty *adj* **crust·i·er; -est 1** : having or being a crust **2** : CROSS, GRUMPY

crutch \'krəch\ *n* : a supporting device; *esp* : a support fitting under the armpit for use by the disabled in walking

crux \'krəks, 'krüks\ *n, pl* **crux·es 1** : a puzzling or difficult problem **2** : a crucial point

cru·za·do \krü-'zäd-ō\ *n* — see MONEY table

¹cry \'krī\ *vb* **cried; cry·ing 1** : to call out : SHOUT **2** : WEEP **3** : to proclaim publicly; *also* : to advertise wares by calling out

²cry *n, pl* **cries 1** : a loud outcry **2** : APPEAL, ENTREATY **3** : a fit of weeping **4** : the characteristic sound uttered by an animal

cry·ba·by \'krī-ˌbā-bē\ *n* : one who cries easily or often

cryo·gen·ic \ˌkrī-ə-'jen-ik\ *adj* : of or relating to the production of very low temperatures; *also* : involving the use of a very low temperature — **cryo·gen·i·cal·ly** \-i-k(ə-)lē\ *adv*

cryo·gen·ics \-iks\ *n* : a branch of physics that relates to the production and effects of very low temperatures

cryo·lite \'krī-ə-ˌlīt\ *n* : a usu. white mineral used in making aluminum

crypt \'kript\ *n* : a chamber wholly or partly underground

cryp·tic \'krip-tik\ *adj* : meant to be puzzling or mysterious

cryp·to·gram \'krip-tə-ˌgram\ *n* : a communication in cipher or code

cryp·tog·ra·phy \krip-'täg-rə-fē\ *n* : the coding and decoding of secret messages — **cryp·tog·ra·pher** \-fər\ *n*

crys·tal \'kris-t³l\ *n* [ME *cristal*, fr. OF, fr. L *crystallum*, fr. Gk *krystallos* ice, crystal] **1** : transparent quartz **2** : something resembling crystal (as in transparency); *esp* : a clear glass used for table articles **3** : a body that is formed by solidification of a substance and has a regular repeating arrangement of atoms and often of external plane faces ⟨a snow ∼⟩ ⟨a salt ∼⟩ **4** : the transparent cover of a watch dial — **crys·tal·line** \-tə-lən\ *adj*

crys·tal·lize \'kris-tə-ˌlīz\ *vb* **-lized; -liz·ing 1** : to assume or cause to assume a crystalline form **2** : to take or cause to take a fixed and definite form — **crys·tal·li·za·tion** \ˌkris-tə-lə-'zā-shən\ *n*

crys·tal·log·ra·phy \ˌkris-tə-'läg-rə-fē\ *n* : the science dealing with the forms and structures of crystals — **crys·tal·log·ra·pher** \-fər\ *n*

cs *abbr* case; cases

Cs *symbol* cesium

CS *abbr* **1** civil service **2** county seat

C/S *abbr* cycles per second

CSA *abbr* Confederate States of America

CSM *abbr* command sergeant major

CST *abbr* central standard time

ct *abbr* **1** carat **2** cent **3** count **4** county **5** court

CT *abbr* **1** central time **2** Connecticut

ctg *or* **ctge** *abbr* cartage

ctn *abbr* carton

ctr *abbr* **1** center **2** counter

cu *abbr* cubic

Cu *symbol* [L *cuprum*] copper

cub \'kəb\ *n* : a young individual of some animals (as a fox, bear, or lion)

Cu·ban \'kyü-bən\ *n* : a native or inhabitant of Cuba — **Cuban** *adj*

cub·by·hole \'kəb-ē-ˌhōl\ *n* : a snug place (as for storing things)

¹cube \'kyüb\ *n* **1** : a solid having 6 equal square sides **2** : the product obtained by taking a number 3 times as a factor ⟨27 is the ~ of 3⟩

²**cube** *vb* **cubed; cub·ing 1** : to raise to the third power **2** : to form into a cube **3** : to cut into cubes

cube root *n* : a number whose cube is a given number

cu·bic \ˈkyü-bik\ *also* **cu·bi·cal** *adj* **1** : having the form of a cube **2** : having length, width, and height **3** : being the volume of a cube whose edge is a specified unit

cu·bi·cle \ˈkyü-bi-kəl\ *n* : a small separate space (as for sleeping or studying)

cubic measure *n* : a unit (as cubic inch) for measuring volume — see METRIC SYSTEM table, WEIGHT table

cub·ism \ˈkyü-ˌbiz-əm\ *n* : a style of art characterized by the abstraction of natural forms into fragmented geometric shapes

cu·bit \ˈkyü-bət\ *n* : an ancient unit of length equal to about 18 inches (46 centimeters)

Cub Scout *n* : a member of the program of the Boy Scouts of America for boys 8–10 years of age

cuck·old \ˈkək-əld, ˈkük-\ *n* : a man whose wife is unfaithful

¹**cuck·oo** \ˈkük-ü, ˈkük-\ *n, pl* **cuckoos** : a largely grayish brown European bird that lays its eggs in the nests of other birds for them to hatch

²**cuckoo** *adj* : SILLY, FOOLISH

cu·cum·ber \ˈkyü-(ˌ)kəm-bər\ *n* : the long fleshy many-seeded fruit of a vine of the gourd family that is grown as a garden vegetable; *also* : this vine

cud \ˈkəd\ *n* : food brought up into the mouth by ruminating animals (as cows) from the first stomach to be chewed again

cud·dle \ˈkəd-ᵊl\ *vb* **cud·dled; cud·dling** \ˈkəd-(ᵊ-)liŋ\ : to lie close

cud·gel \ˈkəj-əl\ *n* : a short heavy club — **cudgel** *vb*

¹**cue** \ˈkyü\ *n* **1** : a word, phrase, or action in a play serving as a signal for the next actor to speak or act **2** : HINT — **cue** *vb*

²**cue** *n* : a tapered rod for striking the balls in billiards or pool

cue ball *n* : the ball a player strikes with a cue in billiards or pool

¹**cuff** \ˈkəf\ *n* **1** : a part (as of a sleeve or glove) encircling the wrist **2** : the folded hem of a trouser leg

²**cuff** *vb* : to strike esp. with the open hand : SLAP

³**cuff** *n* : a blow with the hand esp. when open

cui·sine \kwi-ˈzēn\ *n* : manner of cooking; *also* : the food so prepared

cuke \ˈkyük\ *n* : CUCUMBER

cul–de–sac \ˌkəl-di-ˈsak, ˌkül-\ *n, pl* **culs–de–sac** \ˌkəl(z)-, ˌkül(z)-\ *also* **cul–de–sacs** \ˌkəl-də-ˈsaks, ˌkül-\ [F, lit., bottom of the bag] : a street or passage closed at one end

cu·li·nary \ˈkəl-ə-ˌner-ē, ˈkyü-lə-\ *adj* : of or relating to cookery

¹**cull** \ˈkəl\ *vb* : to pick out from a group : CHOOSE

²**cull** *n* : something rejected from a group or lot as worthless or inferior

cul·mi·nate \ˈkəl-mə-ˌnāt\ *vb* **-nat·ed; -nat·ing** : to reach the highest point — **cul·mi·na·tion** \ˌkəl-mə-ˈnā-shən\ *n*

cu·lotte \ˈk(y)ü-ˌlät, k(y)ù-ˈlät\ *n* [F, breeches, fr. dim. of *cul* backside] : a divided skirt; *also* : a garment having a divided skirt — often used in pl.

cul·pa·ble \ˈkəl-pə-bəl\ *adj* : deserving blame — **cul·pa·bil·i·ty** \ˌkəl-pə-ˈbil-ət-ē\ *n*

cul·prit \ˈkəl-prət\ *n* [Anglo-French (the French of medieval England) *cul.* (abbr. of *culpable* guilty) + *prest, prit* ready (i.e. to prove it), fr. L *praestus*] : one accused or guilty of a crime

cult \ˈkəlt\ *n* **1** : formal religious veneration **2** : a religious system; *also* : its adherents **3** : faddish devotion; *also* : a group of persons showing such devotion — **cult·ist** *n*

cul·ti·vate \ˈkəl-tə-ˌvāt\ *vb* **-vat·ed; -vating 1** : to prepare for the raising of crops **2** : to foster the growth of ⟨~ vegetables⟩ **3** : REFINE, IMPROVE **4** : ENCOURAGE, FURTHER — **cul·ti·va·ble** \-və-bəl\ *adj* — **cul·ti·vat·able** \-ˌvāt-ə-bəl\ *adj* — **cul·ti·va·tion** \ˌkəl-tə-ˈvā-shən\ *n* — **cul·ti·va·tor** \ˈkəl-tə-ˌvāt-ər\ *n*

cul·ture \ˈkəl-chər\ *n* **1** : TILLAGE, CULTIVATION; *also* : the growing of a particular crop ⟨grape ~⟩ **2** : the act of developing by education and training **3** : refinement of intellectual and artistic taste **4** : a particular form or stage of civilization; *also* : a society characterized by such a culture — **cul·tur·al** \ˈkəlch-(-ə)-rəl\ *adj* — **cul·tur·al·ly** \-ē\ *adv* — **cul·tured** \ˈkəl-chərd\ *adj*

cul·vert \ˈkəl-vərt\ *n* : a drain crossing under a road or railroad

cum *abbr* cumulative

cum·ber \ˈkəm-bər\ *vb* **cum·bered; cum·ber·ing** \-b(ə-)riŋ\ : to weigh down : BURDEN

cum·ber·some \ˈkəm-bər-səm\ *adj* : hard to handle or manage because of size or weight

cum·brous \ˈkəm-brəs\ *adj* : CUMBER-SOME

cum·mer·bund \ˈkəm-ər-ˌbənd\ *n* [Hindi *kamarband,* fr. Per, fr. *kamar* waist + *band*] : a broad sash worn as a waistband

cu·mu·la·tive \ˈkyü-myə-lət-iv, -ˌlāt-\ *adj* : increasing in force or value by successive additions

cu·mu·lo·nim·bus \ˌkyü-myə-lō-ˈnim-bəs\ *n* : an anvil-shaped cumulus cloud extending to great heights

cu·mu·lus \ˈkyü-myə-ləs\ *n, pl* **-li** \-ˌlī, -ˌlē\ : a massive cloud having a flat base and rounded outlines

cu·ne·i·form \kyü-ˈnē-ə-ˌfórm\ *adj* **1** : wedge-shaped **2** : composed of wedge-shaped characters ⟨∼ alphabet⟩

cun·ner \ˈkən-ər\ *n* : a small American food fish of the New England coast

cun·ni·lin·gus \ˌkən-i-ˈliŋ-gəs\ *also* **cun·ni·linc·tus** \-ˈliŋk-təs\ *n* : oral stimulation of the vulva or clitoris

¹cun·ning \ˈkən-iŋ\ *adj* **1** : SKILLFUL, DEXTEROUS **2** : marked by wiliness and trickery **3** : CUTE — **cun·ning·ly** *adv*

²cunning *n* **1** : SKILL **2** : CRAFTINESS, SLYNESS

¹cup \ˈkəp\ *n* **1** : a small bowl-shaped drinking vessel **2** : the contents of a cup **3** : communion wine **4** : something resembling a cup : a small bowl or hollow — **cup·ful** *n*

²cup *vb* **cupped; cup·ping** : to curve into the shape of a cup

cup·bear·er \ˈkəp-ˌbar-ər\ *n* : one who has the duty of filling and serving cups of wine

cup·board \ˈkəb-ərd\ *n* : a small storage closet

cup·cake \ˈkəp-ˌkāk\ *n* : a small cake baked in a cuplike mold

Cu·pid \ˈkyü-pəd\ *n* : a winged naked figure of an infant often with a bow and arrow that represents the god Cupid

cu·pid·i·ty \kyù-ˈpid-ət-ē\ *n, pl* **-ties** : excessive desire for money : AVARICE

cu·po·la \ˈkyü-pə-lə, -ˌlō\ *n* : a small structure on top of a roof or building

cu·prite \ˈk(y)ü-ˌprīt\ *n* : a mineral that is an ore of copper

¹cur \ˈkər\ *n* : a mongrel dog

²cur *abbr* **1** currency **2** current

cu·rate \ˈkyur-ət\ *n* **1** : a clergyman in charge of a parish **2** : a clergyman who assists a rector or vicar — **cu·ra·cy** \-ə-sē\ *n*

cu·ra·tive \ˈkyur-ət-iv\ *adj* : relating to or used in the cure of diseases — **curative** *n*

cu·ra·tor \kyù-ˈrāt-ər\ *n* : CUSTODIAN; *esp* : one in charge of a place of exhibit (as a museum or zoo)

¹curb \ˈkərb\ *n* **1** : a bit that exerts pressure on a horse's jaws **2** : CHECK, RESTRAINT **3** : a raised edging (as of stone or concrete) along a paved street

²curb *vb* : to hold in or back : RESTRAIN

curb·ing \ˈkər-biŋ\ *n* **1** : the material for a curb **2** : CURB

curd \ˈkərd\ *n* : the thick protein-rich part of coagulated milk

cur·dle \ˈkərd-ᵊl\ *vb* **cur·dled; cur·dling** \ˈkərd-(ᵊ-)liŋ\ : to form curds; *also* : SPOIL, SOUR

¹cure \ˈkyur\ *n* **1** : spiritual care **2** : recovery or relief from disease **3** : a curative agent : REMEDY **4** : a course or period of treatment

²cure *vb* **cured; cur·ing** **1** : to restore to health : HEAL, REMEDY **2** : to process for storage or use ⟨∼ bacon⟩; *also* : to become cured — **cur·able** *adj*

cu·ré \kyù-ˈrā\ *n* [F] : a parish priest

cure–all \ˈkyur-ˌól\ *n* : a remedy for all ills : PANACEA

cu·ret·tage \ˌkyur-ə-ˈtäzh\ *n* : a surgical scraping and cleaning by means of a scoop, loop, or ring

cur·few \ˈkər-ˌfyü\ *n* [ME, fr. MF *covrefeu,* signal given to bank the hearth fire, curfew, fr. *covrir* to cover + *feu* fire, fr. L *focus* hearth] : a regulation that specified persons (as children) be off the streets at a set hour of the evening; *also* : the sounding of a signal (as a bell) at this hour

cu·ria \'k(y)ùr-ē-ə\ *n, pl* **cu·ri·ae** \'kyùr-ē-ˌē, 'kùr-ē-ˌī\ *often cap* : the body of congregations, tribunals, and offices through which the pope governs the Roman Catholic Church

cu·rie \'kyùr-ē\ *n* : a unit of radioactivity equal to 37 billion disintegrations per second

cu·rio \'kyùr-ē-ˌō\ *n, pl* **cu·ri·os** : an object or article valued because it is strange or rare

cu·ri·ous \'kyùr-ē-əs\ *adj* 1 : having a desire to investigate and learn 2 : STRANGE, UNUSUAL, ODD — **cu·ri·os·i·ty** \ˌkyùr-ē-'äs-ət-ē\ *n* — **cu·ri·ous·ly** *adv*

cu·ri·um \'kyùr-ē-əm\ *n* : a metallic radioactive element produced artificially

¹**curl** \'kərl\ *vb* 1 : to form into ringlets 2 : CURVE, COIL — **curl·er** *n*

²**curl** *n* 1 : a lock of hair that coils : RINGLET 2 : something having a spiral or twisted form — **curly** *adj*

cur·lew \'kərl-(y)ü\ *n, pl* **curlews** *or* **curlew** : any of various long-legged brownish birds that have a down-curved bill and are related to the woodcocks

curli·cue \'kər-li-ˌkyü\ *n* : a fancifully curved or spiral figure

cur·rant \'kər-ənt\ *n* 1 : a small seedless raisin 2 : the acid berry of a shrub related to the gooseberry; *also* : this plant

cur·ren·cy \'kər-ən-sē\ *n, pl* **-cies** 1 : general use or acceptance 2 : something that is in circulation as a medium of exchange : MONEY

¹**cur·rent** \'kər-ənt\ *adj* 1 : occurring in or belonging to the present 2 : used as a medium of exchange 3 : generally accepted or practiced

²**current** *n* 1 : the part of a body of fluid moving continuously in a certain direction; *also* : the swiftest part of a stream 2 : a flow of electric charge; *also* : the rate of such flow

cur·ric·u·lum \kə-'rik-yə-ləm\ *n, pl* **-la** \-lə\ *also* **-lums** [L, racecourse, fr. *currere* to run] : a course of study offered by a school or one of its divisions

¹**cur·ry** \'kər-ē\ *vb* **cur·ried; cur·ry·ing** 1 : to clean the coat of (a horse) with a currycomb 2 : to treat (tanned leath-

er) esp. by incorporating oil or grease — **curry fa·vor** \-'fā-vər\ : to seek to gain favor by flattery or attention

²**cur·ry** \'kər-ē\ *n, pl* **curries** : a powder of blended spices used in cooking; *also* : a food seasoned with curry

cur·ry·comb \-ˌkōm\ *n* : a comb used esp. to curry horses — **currycomb** *vb*

¹**curse** \'kərs\ *n* 1 : a prayer for harm to come upon one 2 : something that is cursed 3 : something that comes as if in response to a curse : SCOURGE

²**curse** *vb* **cursed; curs·ing** 1 : to call on divine power to send injury upon 2 : BLASPHEME 3 : AFFLICT **syn** execrate, damn, anathematize, objurgate

cur·sive \'kər-siv\ *adj* : written or formed with the strokes of the letters joined together and the angles rounded

cur·sor \'kər-sər\ *n* : a bright figure (as a pointer) on a computer screen to indicate a character to be revised or a position where data is to be entered

cur·so·ry \'kərs-(ə)-rē\ *adj* : hastily and often superficially done : HASTY — **cur·so·ri·ly** \-rə-lē\ *adj*

curt \'kərt\ *adj* : rudely short or abrupt — **curt·ly** *adv*

cur·tail \(ˌ)kər-'tāl\ *vb* : to cut off the end of : SHORTEN — **cur·tail·ment** *n*

cur·tain \'kərt-ᵊn\ *n* 1 : a hanging screen that can be drawn back esp. at a window 2 : the screen between the stage and auditorium of a theater — **curtain** *vb*

curt·sy *or* **curt·sey** \'kərt-sē\ *n, pl* **curtsies** *or* **curtseys** : a courteous bow made by women chiefly by bending the knees — **curtsy** *or* **curtsey** *vb*

cur·va·ceous *also* **cur·va·cious** \ˌkər-'vā-shəs\ *adj* : having a well-proportioned feminine figure marked by pronounced curves

cur·va·ture \'kər-və-ˌchùr\ *n* : a measure or amount of curving : BEND

¹**curve** \'kərv\ *vb* **curved; curv·ing** : to bend from a straight line or course

²**curve** *n* 1 : a line esp. when curved 2 : something that bends or curves without angles ⟨a ∼ in the road⟩ 3 : a ball thrown so that it swerves from a normal course

cur·vet \(ˌ)kər-'vet\ *n* : a prancing leap of a horse — **curvet** *vb*

¹**cush·ion** \'kùsh-ən\ *n* 1 : a soft pillow or

pad to rest on or against **2** : the springy pad inside the rim of a billiard table **3** : something soft that prevents discomfort or protects against injury

²**cushion** *vb* **cush·ioned; cush·ion·ing** \-(ə-)niŋ\ **1** : to provide (as a seat) with a cushion **2** : to soften or lessen the force or shock of

cusp \ˈkəsp\ *n* : a pointed end or part (as of a tooth)

cus·pid \ˈkəs-pəd\ *n* : a canine tooth

cus·pi·dor \ˈkəs-pə-ˌdȯr\ *n* : SPITTOON

cus·tard \ˈkəs-tərd\ *n* : a sweetened mixture of milk and eggs baked, boiled, or frozen

cus·to·di·al \ˌkəs-ˈtōd-ē-əl\ *adj* : marked by watching and protecting rather than seeking to cure ⟨∼ care⟩

cus·to·di·an \ˌkəs-ˈtōd-ē-ən\ *n* : one who has custody (as of a building)

cus·to·dy \ˈkəs-təd-ē\ *n, pl* **-dies** : immediate care or charge

¹**cus·tom** \ˈkəs-təm\ *n* **1** : habitual course of action : recognized usage **2** *pl* : taxes levied on imports **3** : business patronage

²**custom** *adj* **1** : made to personal order **2** : doing work only on order

cus·tom·ary \ˈkəs-tə-ˌmer-ē\ *adj* **1** : based on or established by custom ⟨∼ rent⟩ **2** : commonly practiced or observed : HABITUAL — **cus·tom·ar·i·ly** \ˌkəs-tə-ˈmer-ə-lē\ *adv*

cus·tom–built \ˌkəs-təm-ˈbilt\ *adj* : built to individual order

cus·tom·er \ˈkəs-tə-mər\ *n* : BUYER, PURCHASER; *esp* : a regular or frequent buyer

cus·tom·house \ˈkəs-təm-ˌhaůs\ *n* : the building where customs are paid

cus·tom·ize \ˈkəs-tə-ˌmīz\ *vb* **-ized; -iz·ing** : to build, fit, or alter according to individual specifications

cus·tom–made \ˌkəs-təm-ˈ(m)ād\ *adj* : made to individual order

¹**cut** \ˈkət\ *vb* **cut; cut·ting** **1** : to penetrate or divide with a sharp edge : CLEAVE, GASH; *also* : to experience the growth of (a tooth) through the gum **2** : to hurt the feelings of **3** : to strike sharply **4** : SHORTEN, REDUCE **5** : to remove by severing or paring **6** : INTERSECT, CROSS **7** : to divide into parts **8** : to go quickly or change direction abruptly **9** : to cause to stop

²**cut** *n* **1** : a customary segment of a meat

carcass **2** : SHARE **3** : something made by cutting : GASH, CLEFT **4** : an excavated channel or roadway **5** : BAND **4** **6** : a sharp stroke or blow **7** : REDUCTION ⟨∼ in wages⟩ **8** : the shape or manner in which a thing is cut

cut–and–dried \ˌkət-ᵊn-ˈdrīd\ *also* **cut–and–dry** \-ˈdrī\ *adj* : according to a plan, set procedure, or formula

cu·ta·ne·ous \kyů-ˈtā-nē-əs\ *adj* : of, relating to, or affecting the skin

cut·back \ˈkət-ˌbak\ *n* **1** : something cut back **2** : REDUCTION

cute \ˈkyüt\ *adj* **cut·er; cut·est** [short for *acute*] **1** : CLEVER, SHREWD **2** : daintily attractive : PRETTY

cu·ti·cle \ˈkyüt-i-kəl\ *n* **1** : an outer layer (as of skin) **2** : dead or horny epidermis esp. around a fingernail — **cu·tic·u·lar** \kyů-ˈtik-yə-lər\ *adj*

cut in \ˌkət-ˈin\ *vb* **1** : to thrust oneself between others **2** : to interrupt a dancing couple and take one as one's partner

cut·lass \ˈkət-ləs\ *n* : a short heavy curved sword

cut·ler \ˈkət-lər\ *n* : one who makes, deals in, or repairs cutlery

cut·lery \ˈkət-lə-rē\ *n* : edged or cutting tools; *esp* : implements for cutting and eating food

cut·let \ˈkət-lət\ *n* : a slice of meat (as veal) for broiling or frying

cut·off \ˈkət-ˌȯf\ *n* **1** : the channel formed when a stream cuts through the neck of an oxbow; *also* : SHORTCUT **2** : a device for cutting off **3** *pl* : shorts orig. made from jeans with the legs cut off at the knees or higher

cut·out \ˈkət-ˌaůt\ *n* : something cut out or prepared for cutting out from something else ⟨a page of animal ∼s⟩

cut out \ˌkət-ˈaůt\ *vb* **1** : to be all that one can handle ⟨had her work *cut out* for her⟩ **2** : DISCONNECT **3** : to cease operating ⟨the engine *cut out*⟩ **4** : ELIMINATE ⟨*cut out* unnecessary expense⟩

cut–rate \ˈkət-ˈrāt\ *adj* : relating to or dealing in goods sold at reduced rates

cut·ter \ˈkət-ər\ *n* **1** : a tool or a machine for cutting **2** : a ship's boat for carrying stores and passengers **3** : a small armed boat in government service **4** : a light sleigh

¹**cut·throat** \ˈkət-ˌthrōt\ *n* : MURDERER

²**cutthroat** *adj* **1** : MURDEROUS, CRUEL **2** : MERCILESS, RUTHLESS ⟨∼ competition⟩

cutthroat trout *n* : a large American trout with a red mark under the jaw

¹**cut·ting** \'kət-iŋ\ *n* : a piece of a plant able to grow into a new plant

²**cutting** *adj* **1** : SHARP, EDGED **2** : marked by piercing cold **3** : likely to hurt the feelings : SARCASTIC

cut·tle·fish \'kət-ᵊl-ˌfish\ *n* : a 10-armed mollusk related to the squid with an internal shell (**cut·tle·bone** \-ˌbōn\) composed of calcium compounds

cut·up \'kət-ˌəp\ *n* : one that clowns or acts boisterously — **cut up** \ˌkət-'əp\ *vb*

cut·worm \-ˌwərm\ *n* : any of various smooth-bodied moth larvae that feed on plants at night

cw *abbr* clockwise

CWO *abbr* **1** cash with order **2** chief warrant officer

cwt *abbr* hundredweight

-cy \sē\ *n suffix* **1** : action : practice ⟨mendican*cy*⟩ **2** : rank : office ⟨chaplain*cy*⟩ **3** : body : class ⟨magistra*cy*⟩ **4** : state : quality ⟨accura*cy*⟩

cy·an \'sī-ˌan, -ən\ *n* : a greenish blue color

cy·a·nide \'sī-ə-ˌnīd, -nəd\ *n* : a poisonous compound of carbon and nitrogen with either sodium or potassium

cy·ber·net·ics \ˌsī-bər-'net-iks\ *n* : the science of communication and control theory that is concerned esp. with the comparative study of automatic control systems — **cy·ber·net·ic** *adj*

cyc *or* **cycl** *abbr* cyclopedia

cy·cla·men \'sī-klə-mən\ *n* : any of a genus of plants related to the primroses and grown for their showy nodding flowers

¹**cy·cle** \'sī-kəl\ *n* **1** : a period of time occupied by a series of events that repeat themselves regularly and in the same order **2** : a recurring round of operations or events **3** : one complete occurrence of a periodic process (as a vibration or current alternation) **4** : a circular or spiral arrangement **5** : a long period of time : AGE **6** : BICYCLE **7** : MOTORCYCLE — **cy·clic** \'sī-klik, 'sik-lik\ *or* **cy·cli·cal** \'sī-kli-kəl, 'sik-li-\ *adj* — **cy·cli·cal·ly** \-k(ə-)lē\ *also* **cy·clic·ly** \'sī-kli-klē, 'sik-li-\ *adv*

²**cy·cle** \'sī-kəl\ *vb* **cy·cled; cy·cling** \'sī-k(ə-)liŋ, 'sik(-ə)-\ : to ride a cycle

cy·clist \'sī-k(ə-)ləst\ *n* : one who rides a cycle

cy·clone \'sī-ˌklōn\ *n* **1** : a storm or system of winds that rotates about a center of low atmospheric pressure and advances at 20 to 30 miles an hour (about 30 to 50 kilometers per hour) **2** : TORNADO — **cy·clon·ic** \sī-'klän-ik\ *adj*

cy·clo·pe·dia *or* **cy·clo·pae·dia** \ˌsī-klə-'pēd-ē-ə\ *n* : ENCYCLOPEDIA

cy·clo·tron \'sī-klə-ˌträn\ *n* : a device for giving high speed to charged particles by magnetic and electric fields

cyg·net \'sig-nət\ *n* : a young swan

cyl *abbr* cylinder

cyl·in·der \'sil-ən-dər\ *n* : the solid figure formed by turning a rectangle about one side as an axis; *also* : a body or space of this form ⟨an engine ∼⟩ ⟨a bullet in the ∼ of a revolver⟩ — **cy·lin·dri·cal** \sə-'lin-dri-kəl\ *adj*

cym·bal \'sim-bəl\ *n* : one of a pair of concave brass plates clashed together

cyme \'sīm\ *n* : an inflorescence of several flowers each on a stem with the first-opening central flower on the main stem and later-opening flowers developing from lateral buds

cyn·ic \'sin-ik\ *n* [MF or L, MF *cynique*, fr. L *cynicus*, fr. Gk *kynikos*, lit., like a dog, fr. *kyōn* dog] : one who attributes all actions to selfish motives — **cyn·i·cal** \-i-kəl\ *adj* — **cyn·i·cal·ly** \-k(ə-)lē\ *adv* — **cyn·i·cism** \'sin-ə-ˌsiz-əm\ *n*

cy·no·sure \'sī-nə-ˌshur, 'sin-ə-\ *n* [MF & L; MF, Ursa Minor, guide, fr. L *cynosura* Ursa Minor, fr. Gk *kynosoura*, fr. *kynos oura* dog's tail] : a center of attraction

CYO *abbr* Catholic Youth Organization

cy·press \'sī-prəs\ *n* **1** : any of a genus of scaly-leaved evergreen trees related to the pines **2** : either of two large swamp trees of the southern U.S. with hard red wood **3** : the wood of a cypress

cyst \'sist\ *n* : an abnormal closed bodily sac usu. containing liquid — **cys·tic** \'sis-tik\ *adj*

cystic fibrosis *n* : a common hereditary disease marked esp. by deficiency of pancreatic enzymes and by respiratory symptoms

cy•tol•o•gy \sī-'täl-ə-jē\ *n* : a branch of biology dealing with cells — **cy•to•log•i•cal** \ˌsīt-ᵊl-'äj-i-kəl\ *or* **cy•to•log•ic** \-'äj-ik\ *adj* — **cy•tol•o•gist** \sī-'täl-ə-jəst\ *n*

cy•to•plasm \'sīt-ə-ˌplaz-əm\ *n* : the protoplasm of a cell that lies external to the nucleus — **cy•to•plas•mic** \ˌsīt-ə-'plaz-mik\ *adj*

cy•to•sine \'sīt-ə-ˌsēn\ *n* : a chemical base that is a pyrimidine coding genetic information in DNA and RNA

CZ *abbr* Canal Zone

czar \'zär\ *n* : the ruler of Russia until 1917; *also* : one having great authority — **czar•ist** *n or adj*

cza•ri•na \zä-'rē-nə\ *n* : the wife of a czar

Czech \'chek\ *n* **1** : a native or inhabitant of Czechoslovakia **2** : the language of the Czechs — **Czech** *adj*

Czecho•slo•vak \ˌchek-ə-'slō-ˌväk, -ˌvak\ *or* **Czecho•slo•va•ki•an** \-slō-'väk- ē-ən, -'vak-\ *adj* : of, relating to, or characteristic of Czechoslovakia or its people — **Czechoslovak** *or* **Czechoslovakian** *n*

D

¹d \'dē\ *n, pl* **d's** *or* **ds** \'dēz\ *often cap* **1** : the 4th letter of the English alphabet **2** : a grade rating a student's work as poor

²d *abbr, often cap* **1** date **2** daughter **3** day **4** dead **5** deceased **6** degree **7** [L *denarius*] penny; pence **8** depart; departure **9** diameter

D *symbol* deuterium

DA *abbr* **1** deposit account **2** district attorney **3** don't answer

¹dab \'dab\ *n* **1** : a sudden blow or thrust : POKE; *also* : PECK **2** : a gentle touch or stroke : PAT

²dab *vb* **dabbed; dab•bing 1** : to strike or touch gently : PAT **2** : to apply lightly or irregularly : DAUB

³dab *n* **1** : DAUB **2** : a small amount

dab•ble \'dab-əl\ *vb* **dab•bled; dab•bling** \-(ə-)liŋ\ **1** : to wet by splashing : SPATTER **2** : to paddle or play in or as if in water **3** : to work or concern oneself without serious effort

dace \'dās\ *n, pl* **dace** : any of various small No. American freshwater fishes related to the carp

da•cha \'däch-ə\ *n* [Russ, lit., gift; fr. its frequently being the gift of a ruler] : a Russian country house

dachs•hund \'däks-ˌhunt\ *n, pl* **dachshunds** [G, fr. *dachs* badger + *hund* dog] : a small dog of a breed of German origin with a long body, short legs, and long drooping ears

dac•tyl \'dak-tᵊl\ *n* [ME *dactile*, fr. L

dactylus, fr. Gk *daktylos*, lit., finger; fr. the fact that the three syllables have the first one longest like the joints of the finger] : a metrical foot of one accented syllable followed by two unaccented syllables — **dac•tyl•ic** \dak-'til-ik\ *adj or n*

dad \'dad\ *n* : FATHER

Da•da \'däd-(ˌ)ä\ *n* : a movement in art and literature based on deliberate irrationality and negation of traditional artistic values — **da•da•ism** \-ˌiz-əm\ *n, often cap* — **da•da•ist** \-ˌist\ *n or adj, often cap*

dad•dy \'dad-ē\ *n, pl* **daddies** : FATHER

dad•dy long•legs \ˌdad-ē-'lȯŋ-ˌlegz\ *n, pl* **daddy longlegs** : any of various arachnids resembling the true spiders but having small rounded bodies and long slender legs

dae•mon *var of* DEMON

daf•fo•dil \'daf-ə-ˌdil\ *n* : any of a genus of bulbous herbs with usu. large flowers having a trumpetlike center

daf•fy \'daf-ē\ *adj* **daf•fi•er; -est** : DAFT

daft \'daft\ *adj* : FOOLISH; *also* : INSANE — **daft•ness** *n*

dag•ger \'dag-ər\ *n* **1** : a sharp pointed knife for stabbing **2** : a character † used as a reference mark or to indicate a death date

da•guerre•o•type \də-'ger-(ē-)ə-ˌtīp\ *n* : an early photograph produced on a silver or a silver-covered copper plate

dahl•ia \'dal-yə, 'däl-\ *n* : any of a

genus of tuberous herbs related to the daisies and having showy flowers

¹dai•ly \'dā-lē\ *adj* **1** : occurring, done, or used every day or every weekday **2** : of or relating to every day ⟨∼ visitors⟩ **3** : computed in terms of one day ⟨∼ wages⟩ — **daily** *adv*

²daily *n, pl* **dailies** : a newspaper published every weekday

daily double *n* : a system of betting on races in which the bettor must pick the winners of two stipulated races in order to win

¹dain•ty \'dānt-ē\ *n, pl* **dainties** [ME *deinte,* fr. OF *deintié,* fr. L *dignitas* dignity, worth] : something delicious or pleasing to the taste : DELICACY

²dainty *adj* **dain•ti•er; -est 1** : pleasing to the taste **2** : delicately pretty **3** : having or showing delicate taste; *also* : FASTIDIOUS — **dain•ti•ly** \'dānt-ᵊl-ē\ *adv* — **dain•ti•ness** \-ē-nəs\ *n*

dai•qui•ri \'dī-kə-rē, 'dak-ə-rē\ *n* [*Daiquirí,* Cuba] : a cocktail made of rum, lime juice, and sugar

dairy \'de(ə)r-ē\ *n, pl* **dair•ies** [ME *deyerie,* fr. *deye* dairymaid, fr. OE *dǣge* kneader of bread] **1** : CREAMERY **2** : a farm specializing in milk production

dairy•ing \'der-ē-iŋ\ *n* : the business of operating a dairy

dairy•maid \-ˌmād\ *n* : a woman employed in a dairy

dairy•man \-mən, -ˌman\ *n* : a person who operates a dairy farm or works in a dairy

da•is \'dā-əs\ *n* : a raised platform usu. above the floor of a hall or large room

dai•sy \'dā-zē\ *n, pl* **daisies** [ME *dayeseye,* fr. OE *dǣgesēage,* fr. *dǣg* day + *ēage* eye] : any of numerous composite plants having flower heads in which the marginal flowers resemble petals

daisy wheel *n* : a printing element for an electric typewriter or computer printer that consists of a disk having spokes with type on the end

Da•ko•ta \də-'kōt-ə\ *n, pl* **Dakotas** *also* **Dakota** : a member of an American Indian people of the northern Mississippi valley; *also* : their language

da•la•si \dä-'läs-ē\ *n, pl* **dalasi** *or* **dalasis** — see MONEY table

dale \'dāl\ *n* : VALLEY

dal•ly \'dal-ē\ *vb* **dal•lied; dal•ly•ing 1** : to act playfully; *esp* : to play amorously **2** : to waste time **3** : LINGER, DAWDLE — **dal•li•ance** \-əns\ *n*

dal•ma•tian \dal-'mā-shən\ *n, often cap* : any of a breed of medium-sized dogs having a white short-haired coat with black or brown spots

¹dam \'dam\ *n* : a female parent — used esp. of a domestic animal

²dam *n* : a barrier (as across a stream) to prevent the flow of water — **dam** *vb*

¹dam•age \'dam-ij\ *n* **1** : loss or harm due to injury to persons, property, or reputation **2** *pl* : compensation in money imposed by law for loss or injury ⟨bring a suit for ∼s⟩

²damage *vb* **dam•aged; dam•ag•ing** : to cause damage to

dam•a•scene \'dam-ə-ˌsēn\ *vb* **-scened; -scen•ing** : to ornament (as iron or steel) with wavy patterns or with inlaid work of precious metals

dam•ask \'dam-əsk\ *n* **1** : a firm lustrous reversible figured fabric used for household linen **2** : a tough steel having decorative wavy lines

dame \'dām\ *n* **1** : a woman of rank, station, or authority **2** : an elderly woman **3** : WOMAN

damn \'dam\ *vb* **damned; damn•ing** \'dam-iŋ\ [ME *dampnen,* fr. OF *dampner,* fr. L *damnare,* fr. *damnum* damage, loss, fine] **1** : to condemn esp. to hell **2** : CURSE — **damned** *adj*

dam•na•ble \'dam-nə-bəl\ *adj* **1** : liable to or deserving punishment **2** : DETESTABLE ⟨∼ weather⟩ — **dam•na•bly** \-blē\ *adv*

dam•na•tion \dam-'nā-shən\ *n* **1** : the act of damning **2** : the state of being damned

¹damp \'damp\ *n* **1** : a noxious gas **2** : MOISTURE

²damp *vb* : DAMPEN

³damp *adj* : MOIST — **damp•ness** *n*

damp•en \'dam-pən\ *vb* **damp•ened; damp•en•ing** \'damp-(ə-)niŋ\ **1** : to check or diminish in activity or vigor **2** : to make or become damp

damp•er \'dam-pər\ *n* : one that damps; *esp* : a valve or movable plate (as in the flue of a stove, furnace, or fireplace) to regulate the draft

dam•sel \'dam-zəl\ *n* : GIRL, MAIDEN

dam•sel•fly \-ˌflī\ *n* : any of a group of insects that are closely related to the dragonflies but fold their wings above the body when at rest

dam·son \\'dam-zən\\ *n* : a plum with acid purple fruit; *also* : its fruit

Dan *abbr* Daniel

¹dance \\'dans\\ *vb* **danced; danc·ing 1** : to glide, step, or move through a set series of movements usu. to music **2** : to move quickly up and down or about **3** : to perform or take part in as a dancer — **danc·er** *n*

²dance *n* **1** : an act or instance of dancing **2** : a social gathering for dancing **3** : a piece of music (as a waltz) by which dancing may bc guided **4** : the art of dancing

D & C *abbr* dilation and curettage

dan·de·li·on \\'dan-dᵊl-ˌī-ən\\ *n* [MF *dent de lion,* lit., lion's tooth] : any of a genus of common yellow-flowered composite herbs

dan·der \\'dan-dər\\ *n* : ANGER, TEMPER

dan·di·fy \\'dan-di-ˌfī\\ *vb* **-fied; -fy·ing** : to cause to resemble a dandy

dan·dle \\'dan-dᵊl\\ *vb* **dan·dled; dan·dling** : to move up and down in one's arms or on one's knee in affectionate play

dan·druff \\'dan-drəf\\ *n* : a whitish scurf on the scalp that comes off in small scales

¹dan·dy \\'dan-dē\\ *n, pl* **dandies 1** : a man unduly attentive to dress **2** : something excellent in its class

²dandy *adj* **dan·di·er; -est** : very good : FIRST-RATE

Dane \\'dān\\ *n* : a native or inhabitant of Denmark

dan·ger \\'dān-jər\\ *n* **1** : exposure or liability to injury, harm, or evil **2** : something that may cause injury or harm **syn** peril, hazard, risk, jeopardy

dan·ger·ous \\'dānj-(ə-)rəs\\ *adj* **1** : HAZARDOUS, PERILOUS **2** : able or likely to inflict injury — **dan·ger·ous·ly** *adv*

dan·gle \\'daŋ-gəl\\ *vb* **dan·gled; dan·gling** \\-g(ə-)liŋ\\ **1** : to hang loosely esp. with a swinging motion : SWING **2** : to be a hanger-on or dependent **3** : to be left without proper grammatical connection in a sentence **4** : to keep hanging uncertainly

Dan·iel \\'dan-yəl\\ *n* — see BIBLE table

Dan·ish \\'dā-nish\\ *n* : the language of the Danes — **Danish** *adj*

Danish pastry *n* : a pastry made of a rich yeast-raised dough

dank \\'daŋk\\ *adj* : disagreeably wet or moist : DAMP

dan·seuse \\dänⁿ-'sə(r)z, dän-'süz\\ *n* [F] : a female ballet dancer

dap·per \\'dap-ər\\ *adj* **1** : SPRUCE, TRIM **2** : being alert and lively in movement and manners : JAUNTY

dap·ple \\'dap-əl\\ *vb* **dap·pled; dap·pling** : to mark with different-colored spots

DAR *abbr* Daughters of the American Revolution

¹dare \\'daər\\ *vb* **dared; dar·ing 1** : to have sufficient courage : be bold enough to **2** : CHALLENGE **3** : to confront boldly

²dare *n* : an act or instance of daring : CHALLENGE

dare·dev·il \\-ˌdev-əl\\ *n* : a recklessly bold person

dar·ing \\'da(ə)r-iŋ\\ *n* : venturesome boldness — **daring** *adj* — **dar·ing·ly** *adv*

¹dark \\'därk\\ *adj* **1** : being without light or without much light **2** : not light in color ⟨a ~ suit⟩ **3** : GLOOMY **4** : being without knowledge and culture ⟨the *Dark* Ages⟩ **5** : SECRETIVE — **dark·ly** *adv* — **dark·ness** *n*

²dark *n* **1** : absence of light : DARKNESS; *esp* : NIGHT **2** : a dark or deep color — **in the dark 1** : in secrecy **2** : in ignorance

dark adaptation *n* : the process by which the eye adapts to seeing in weak light — **dark–adapt·ed** \\ˌdär-kə-'dap-təd\\ *adj*

dark·en \\'där-kən\\ *vb* **dark·ened; dark·en·ing** \\'därk-(ə-)niŋ\\ **1** : to make or grow dark or darker **2** : DIM **3** : BESMIRCH, TARNISH **4** : to make or become gloomy or forbidding

dark horse *n* : a contestant or a political figure whose abilities and chances as a contender are not known

dark·ling \\'där-kliŋ\\ *adj* **1** : DARK ⟨a ~ plain⟩ **2** : MYSTERIOUS

dark·room \\'därk-ˌrüm, -ˌrum\\ *n* : a room which is protected from light and in which photographic plates and film are developed

dark·some \\'därk-səm\\ *adj* : DARK

¹dar·ling \\'där-liŋ\\ *n* **1** : a dearly loved person **2** : FAVORITE

²**darling** *adj* **1** : dearly loved : FAVORITE **2** : very pleasing : CHARMING

darn \\'därn\\ *vb* : to mend with interlacing stitches — **darn•er** *n*

darning needle *n* **1** : a needle for darning **2** : DRAGONFLY

¹**dart** \\'därt\\ *n* **1** : a small missile with a point on one end and feathers on the other; *also, pl* : a game in which darts are thrown at a target **2** : something causing a sudden pain **3** : a stitched tapering fold in a garment **4** : a quick movement

²**dart** *vb* **1** : to throw with a sudden movement **2** : to thrust or move suddenly or rapidly

dart•er \\'därt-ər\\ *n* : any of numerous small American freshwater fishes related to the perches

Dar•win•ism \\'där-wə-ˌniz-əm\\ *n* : a theory of the origin and perpetuation of new species of plants and animals through the action of natural selection on chance variations — **Dar•win•ist** \\-nəst\\ *n or adj*

¹**dash** \\'dash\\ *vb* **1** : to knock, hurl, or thrust violently **2** : SMASH **3** : SPLASH, SPATTER **4** : RUIN **5** : DEPRESS, SADDEN **6** : to perform or finish hastily **7** : to move with sudden speed

²**dash** *n* **1** : a sudden burst or splash **2** : a stroke of a pen **3** : a punctuation mark — that is used esp. to indicate a break in the thought or structure of a sentence **4** : a small addition ⟨add a ∼ of salt⟩ **5** : flashy showiness **6** : animation in style and action **7** : a sudden rush or attempt ⟨made a ∼ for the door⟩ **8** : a short foot race

dash•board \\-ˌbōrd\\ *n* : an instrument panel below the windshield in an automobile or aircraft

dash•er \\'dash-ər\\ *n* : a device (as in a churn) that agitates or stirs up something

da•shi•ki \\də-'shē-kē\\ *or* **dai•shi•ki** \\dī-\\ *n* [modif. of Yoruba (an African language) *danshiki*] : a usu. brightly colored loose-fitting pullover garment

dash•ing \\'dash-iŋ\\ *adj* **1** : marked by vigorous action **2** : marked by smartness esp. in dress and manners

das•tard \\'das-tərd\\ *n* : COWARD; *esp* : one who sneakingly commits malicious acts — **das•tard•ly** *adj*

dat *abbr* dative

da•ta \\'dāt-ə, 'dat-\\ *n sing or pl* : factual information (as measurements or statistics) used as a basis for reasoning, discussion, or calculation

data processing *n* : the action or process of supplying a computer with information and having the computer use it to produce a desired result

¹**date** \\'dāt\\ *n* [ME, fr. OF, deriv. of L *dactylus*, fr. Gk *daktylos*, lit., finger] : the edible fruit of a tall Old World palm; *also* : this palm

²**date** *n* [ME, fr. MF, fr. LL *data*, fr. *data* (as in *data Romae* given at Rome), fr. L *dare* to give] **1** : the day, month, or year of an event **2** : a statement giving the time of execution or making (as of a coin or check) **3** : the period to which something belongs **4** : APPOINTMENT; *esp* : a social engagement between two persons of opposite sex **5** : a person of the opposite sex with whom one has a social engagement — **to date** : up to the present moment

³**date** *vb* **dat•ed; dat•ing** **1** : to record the date of or on **2** : to determine, mark, or reveal the date, age, or period of **3** : to make or have a date with **4** : ORIGINATE ⟨∼s from ancient times⟩ **5** : EXTEND ⟨*dating* back to childhood⟩ **6** : to show qualities typical of a past period

dat•ed \\'dāt-əd\\ *adj* **1** : provided with a date **2** : OLD-FASHIONED

date•less \\'dāt-ləs\\ *adj* **1** : ENDLESS **2** : having no date **3** : too ancient to be dated **4** : TIMELESS

date•line \\'dāt-ˌlīn\\ *n* : a line in a publication giving the date and place of composition or issue — **dateline** *vb*

da•tive \\'dāt-iv\\ *adj* : of, relating to, or constituting a grammatical case marking typically the indirect object of a verb — **dative** *n*

da•tum \\'dāt-əm, 'dat-, 'dät-\\ *n, pl* **da•ta** \\-ə\\ *or* **datums** : a single piece of data : FACT

dau *abbr* daughter

¹**daub** \\'dȯb\\ *vb* **1** : to cover with soft adhesive matter **2** : SMEAR, SMUDGE **3** : to paint crudely — **daub•er** *n*

²**daub** *n* **1** : something daubed on : SMEAR **2** : a crude picture

daugh•ter \\'dȯt-ər\\ *n* **1** : a female offspring esp. of human beings **2** : a human female having a specified ancestor or belonging to a group of common ancestry

daugh·ter–in–law \'dȯt-ə-rən-ˌlȯ, -ərn-ˌlȯ\ *n, pl* **daugh·ters–in–law** \-ər-zən-\ : the wife of one's son

daunt \'dȯnt\ *vb* [ME *daunten*, fr. OF *danter*, alter. of *donter*, fr. L *domitare* to tame] : to lessen the courage of : INTIMIDATE, OVERWHELM

daunt·less \-ləs\ *adj* : FEARLESS, UN-DAUNTED

dau·phin \'dȯ-fən\ *n, often cap* : the eldest son of a king of France

DAV *abbr* Disabled American Veterans

dav·en·port \'dav-ən-ˌpōrt\ *n* : a large upholstered sofa

da·vit \'dā-vət, 'dav-ət\ *n* : either of a pair of small cranes used esp. on ships for raising and lowering small boats

daw·dle \'dȯd-ᵊl\ *vb* **daw·dled; daw·dling** \'dȯd-(ᵊ-)liŋ\ **1** : to spend time wastefully or idly **2** : LOITER — **daw·dler** \'dȯd-(ᵊ-)lər\ *n*

¹dawn \'dȯn\ *vb* **1** : to begin to grow light as the sun rises **2** : to begin to appear or develop **3** : to begin to be understood ⟨the solution ∼*ed* on him⟩

²dawn *n* **1** : the first appearance of light in the morning **2** : a first appearance : BEGINNING ⟨the ∼ of a new era⟩

day \'dā\ *n* **1** : the period of light between one night and the next; *also* : DAYLIGHT **2** : the period of the earth's rotation on its axis **3** : a period of 24 hours beginning at midnight **4** : a specified day or date ⟨wedding ∼⟩ **5** : a specified time or period : AGE ⟨in olden ∼*s*⟩ **6** : the conflict or contention of the day **7** : the time set apart by usage or law for work ⟨the 8-hour ∼⟩

day·bed \'dā-ˌbed\ *n* : a couch that can be converted into a bed

day·book \-ˌbu̇k\ *n* : DIARY, JOURNAL

day·break \-ˌbrāk\ *n* : DAWN

day–care \'dā-ˌkeər\ *adj* : relating to or providing supervision and facilities for preschool children during the day

day·dream \'dā-ˌdrēm\ *n* : a pleasant reverie — **daydream** *vb*

day·light \'dā-ˌlīt\ *n* **1** : the light of day **2** : DAYTIME **3** : DAWN **4** : understanding of something that has been obscure **5** *pl* : CONSCIOUSNESS; *also* : WITS

daylight saving time *n* : time usu. one hour ahead of standard time

Day of Atonement : YOM KIPPUR

day school *n* : a private school without boarding facilities

day student *n* : a student who attends regular classes at a college or preparatory school but does not live there

day·time \'dā-ˌtīm\ *n* : the period of daylight

daze \'dāz\ *vb* **dazed; daz·ing** **1** : to stupefy esp. by a blow **2** : DAZZLE — **daze** *n*

daz·zle \'daz-əl\ *vb* **daz·zled; daz·zling** \-(ə-)liŋ\ **1** : to overpower with light **2** : to impress greatly or confound with brilliance — **dazzle** *n*

db *or* **dB** *abbr* decibel

d/b/a *abbr* doing business as

dbl *abbr* double

DC *abbr* **1** [It *da capo*] from the beginning **2** direct current **3** District of Columbia **4** doctor of chiropractic

DD *abbr* **1** days after date **2** demand draft **3** dishonorable discharge **4** doctor of divinity

D day *n* [*D*, abbr. for *day*] : a day set for launching an operation (as an invasion)

DDS *abbr* **1** doctor of dental science **2** doctor of dental surgery

DDT \ˌdē-(ˌ)dē-'tē\ *n* : a persistent insecticide poisonous to many higher animals

DE *abbr* Delaware

dea·con \'dē-kən\ *n* [ME *dekene*, fr. OE *dēacon*, fr. LL *diaconus*, fr. Gk *diakonos*, lit., servant] : a subordinate officer in a Christian church

dea·con·ess \'dē-kə-nəs\ *n* : a woman chosen to assist in the church ministry

de·ac·ti·vate \dē-'ak-tə-ˌvāt\ *vb* : to make inactive or ineffective

¹dead \'ded\ *adj* **1** : LIFELESS **2** : DEATH-LIKE, DEADLY ⟨in a ∼ faint⟩ **3** : NUMB **4** : very tired **5** : UNRESPONSIVE **6** : EX-TINGUISHED ⟨∼ coals⟩ **7** : INANIMATE, INERT **8** : no longer active or functioning : EXHAUSTED, EXTINCT ⟨a ∼ battery⟩ ⟨a ∼ volcano⟩ **9** : lacking power, significance, or effect ⟨a ∼ custom⟩ **10** : OBSOLETE ⟨a ∼ language⟩ **11** : lacking in gaiety or animation ⟨a ∼ party⟩ **12** : QUIET, IDLE, UNPRODUCTIVE ⟨∼ capital⟩ **13** : lacking elasticity ⟨a ∼ tennis ball⟩ **14** : not circulating : STAG-

NANT ⟨∼ air⟩ **15** : lacking warmth, vigor, or taste ⟨∼ wine⟩ **16** : absolutely uniform ⟨∼ level⟩ **17** : UNERRING, EXACT ⟨a ∼ shot⟩ **18** : ABRUPT ⟨a ∼ stop⟩ **19** : COMPLETE ⟨a ∼ loss⟩

²dead *n, pl* **dead 1** : one that is dead — usu. used collectively ⟨the living and the ∼⟩ **2** : the time of greatest quiet ⟨the ∼ of the night⟩

³dead *adv* **1** : UTTERLY ⟨∼ right⟩ **2** : in a sudden and complete manner ⟨stopped ∼⟩ **3** : DIRECTLY ⟨∼ ahead⟩

dead·beat \-ˌbēt\ *n* : one who persistently fails to pay his debts or his way

dead·en \ˈded-ᵊn\ *vb* **dead·ened; dead·en·ing** \ˈded-(ᵊ-)niŋ\ **1** : to impair in force, activity, or sensation : BLUNT ⟨∼ pain⟩ **2** : to lessen the luster or spirit of **3** : to make (as a wall) soundproof

dead end *n* **1** : an end (as of a street) without an exit **2** : a position, situation, or course of action that leads to nothing further — **dead–end** \ˌded-ˌend\ *adj*

dead heat *n* : a contest in which two or more contestants tie (as by crossing the finish line simultaneously)

dead letter *n* **1** : something that has lost its force or authority without being formally abolished **2** : a letter that cannot be delivered or returned

dead·line \ˈded-ˌlīn\ *n* : a date or time before which something must be done

dead·lock \ˈded-ˌläk\ *n* : a stoppage of action because neither faction in a struggle will give in — **deadlock** *vb*

¹dead·ly \ˈded-lē\ *adj* **dead·li·er; -est 1** : likely to cause or capable of causing death **2** : HOSTILE, IMPLACABLE **3** : very accurate : UNERRING **4** : tending to deprive of force or vitality ⟨a ∼ habit⟩ **5** : suggestive of death **6** : very great : EXTREME — **dead·li·ness** *n*

²deadly *adv* **1** : suggesting death ⟨∼ pale⟩ **2** : EXTREMELY ⟨∼ dull⟩

deadly sin *n* : one of seven sins of pride, covetousness, lust, anger, gluttony, envy, and sloth held to be fatal to spiritual progress

dead·pan \ˈded-ˌpan\ *adj* : marked by an impassive manner or expression — **deadpan** *vb*

dead reckoning *n* : the determination of the position of a ship or aircraft solely from the record of the direction and distance of its course

dead·weight \ˈded-ˈwāt\ *n* **1** : the unrelieved weight of an inert mass **2** : a ship's load including the weight of cargo, fuel, crew, and passengers

dead·wood \-ˌwu̇d\ *n* **1** : wood dead on the tree **2** : useless personnel or material

deaf \ˈdef\ *adj* **1** : unable to hear **2** : unwilling to hear or listen ⟨∼ to all suggestions⟩ — **deaf·ness** *n*

deaf·en \ˈdef-ən\ *vb* **deaf·ened; deaf·en·ing** \-(ə-)niŋ\ : to make deaf

deaf–mute \ˈdef-ˌmyüt\ *n* : a deaf person who cannot speak

¹deal \ˈdēl\ *n* **1** : a usu. large or indefinite quantity or degree ⟨a great ∼ of support⟩ **2** : the act or right of distributing cards to players in a card game; *also* : HAND

²deal *vb* **dealt** \ˈdelt\; **deal·ing** \ˈdē-liŋ\ **1** : DISTRIBUTE; *esp* : to distribute playing cards to players in a game **2** : ADMINISTER, DELIVER ⟨*dealt* him a blow⟩ **3** : to concern itself : TREAT ⟨the book ∼s with crime⟩ **4** : to take action in regard to something ⟨∼ with offenders⟩ **5** : TRADE; *also* : to sell or distribute something as a business ⟨∼ in used cars⟩ — **deal·er** *n*

³deal *n* **1** : BARGAINING, NEGOTIATION; *also* : TRANSACTION **2** : treatment received ⟨a raw ∼⟩

⁴deal *n* : wood or a board of fir or pine

deal·er·ship \ˈdē-lər-ˌship\ *n* : an authorized sales agency

deal·ing \ˈdē-liŋ\ *n* **1** *pl* : friendly or business transactions **2** : a way of acting or of doing business

dean \ˈdēn\ *n* [ME *deen,* fr. MF *deien,* fr. LL *decanus,* lit., chief of ten, fr. L *decem* ten] **1** : a clergyman who is head of a group of canons or of joint pastors of a church **2** : the head of a division, faculty, college, or school of a university **3** : a college or secondary school administrator in charge of counseling and disciplining students **4** : the senior member of a group ⟨the ∼ of a diplomatic corps⟩ — **dean·ship** *n*

dean·ery \ˈdēn-(ə-)rē\ *n, pl* **-er·ies** : the office, jurisdiction, or official residence of a clerical dean

¹dear \ˈdiər\ *adj* **1** : highly valued : PRECIOUS **2** : AFFECTIONATE, FOND **3** : EX-

PENSIVE **4** : HEARTFELT — **dear·ly** *adv* — **dear·ness** *n*

²dear *n* : a loved one : DARLING

Dear John \-'jän\ *n* : a letter (as to a soldier) in which a woman breaks off a marital or romantic relationship

dearth \'dərth\ *n* : SCARCITY, FAMINE

death \'deth\ *n* **1** : the end of life **2** : the cause of loss of life **3** : the state of being dead **4** : DESTRUCTION, EXTINCTION **5** : SLAUGHTER — **death·like** *adj*

death·bed \'deth-'bed\ *n* **1** : the bed in which a person dies **2** : the last hours of life

death·blow \'deth-'blō\ *n* : a destructive or killing stroke or event

death·less \'deth-ləs\ *adj* : IMMORTAL, IMPERISHABLE ⟨~ fame⟩

death·ly \'deth-lē\ *adj* **1** : FATAL **2** : of, relating to, or suggestive of death ⟨a ~ pallor⟩ — **deathly** *adv*

death rattle *n* : a sound produced by air passing through mucus in the lungs and air passages of a dying person

death's–head \'deths-,hed\ *n* : a human skull emblematic of death

death·watch \'deth-,wäch\ *n* : a vigil kept over the dead or dying

deb \'deb\ *n* : DEBUTANTE

de·ba·cle \di-'bäk-əl, -'bak-əl\ *n* [F *débâcle*] : DISASTER, FAILURE, ROUT ⟨stock market ~⟩

de·bar \di-'bär\ *vb* : to bar from having or doing something : PRECLUDE

de·bark \di-'bärk\ *vb* : DISEMBARK — **de·bar·ka·tion** \,dē-,bär-'kā-shən\ *n*

de·base \di-'bās\ *vb* : to lower in character, quality, or value **syn** degrade, corrupt, deprave — **de·base·ment** *n*

de·bate \di-'bāt\ *vb* **de·bat·ed; de·bat·ing** **1** : to discuss or examine a question by presenting and considering arguments on both sides **2** : to take part in a debate — **de·bat·able** *adj* — **debate** *n* — **de·bat·er** *n*

de·bauch \di-'bòch\ *vb* : SEDUCE, CORRUPT — **de·bauch·ery** \-(ə-)rē\ *n*

de·ben·ture \di-'ben-chər\ *n* : a certificate of indebtedness; *esp* : a bond secured only by the general assets of the issuing government or company

de·bil·i·tate \di-'bil-ə-,tāt\ *vb* **-tat·ed; -tat·ing** : to impair the health or strength of

de·bil·i·ty \di-'bil-ət-ē\ *n, pl* **-ties** : an infirm or weakened state

¹deb·it \'deb-ət\ *vb* : to enter as a debit : charge with or as a debit

²debit *n* **1** : an entry in an account showing money paid out or owed **2** : a disadvantageous or unfavorable quality or character

deb·o·nair \,deb-ə-'naər\ *adj* [ME *debonere*, fr. OF *debonaire*, fr. *de bon aire* of good family or nature] : gaily and gracefully charming : LIGHTHEARTED

de·bouch \di-'baùch, -'büsh\ *vb* [F *déboucher*, fr. *dé-* out of + *bouche* mouth] : to come out into an open area

de·brief \di-'brēf\ *vb* : to question (as a pilot back from a mission) in order to obtain useful information

de·bris \də-'brē, dā-; 'dā-,brē\ *n, pl* **debris** \-'brēz, -,brēz\ **1** : the remains of something broken down or destroyed : RUINS **2** : an accumulation of fragments of rock

debt \'det\ *n* **1** : SIN, TRESPASS **2** : a condition of owing; *esp* : the state of owing money in amounts greater than one can pay **3** : something owed : OBLIGATION

debt·or \'det-ər\ *n* **1** : one guilty of neglect or violation of duty **2** : one that owes a debt

de·bunk \dē-'bəŋk\ *vb* : to expose the sham or falseness of ⟨~ a rumor⟩

de·but \'dā-,byü, dā-'byü\ *n* **1** : a first appearance **2** : a formal entrance into society

deb·u·tante \'deb-yù-,tänt\ *n* : a young woman making her formal entrance into society

dec *abbr* **1** deceased **2** decrease

Dec *abbr* December

de·cade \'dek-,ād, -əd; de-'kād\ *n* : a period of 10 years

dec·a·dence \'dek-əd-əns, di-'kād-³ns\ *n* : DETERIORATION, DECLINE — **dec·a·dent** \'dek-əd-ənt, di-'kād-³nt\ *adj or n*

deca·gon \'dek-ə-,gän\ *n* : a plane polygon of 10 angles and 10 sides

de·cal \'dē-,kal\ *n* : a picture, design, or label made to be transferred (as to glass) from specially prepared paper

de·cal·co·ma·nia \di-,kal-kə-'mā-nē-ə\ *n* [F *décalcomanie*, fr. *décalquer* to copy by tracing (fr. *calquer* to trace, fr. It *calcare*, lit., to trample, fr. L) + *manie* mania, fr. LL *mania*] : DECAL

Deca·logue \\'dek-ə-ˌlȯg\ *n* : the ten commandments of God given to Moses on Mount Sinai

de·camp \di-'kamp\ *vb* **1** : to break up a camp **2** : to depart suddenly

de·cant \di-'kant\ *vb* : to pour (liquor) gently

de·cant·er \di-'kant-ər\ *n* : an ornamental glass bottle for serving wine

de·cap·i·tate \di-'kap-ə-ˌtāt\ *vb* **-tat·ed; -tat·ing** : BEHEAD — **de·cap·i·ta·tion** \-ˌkap-ə-'tā-shən\ *n*

deca·syl·lab·ic \ˌdek-ə-sə-'lab-ik\ *adj* : having or composed of verses having 10 syllables — **decasyllabic** *n*

de·cath·lon \di-'kath-lən, -ˌlän\ *n* : an athletic contest in which each competitor participates in each of a series of 10 track-and-field events

de·cay \di-'kā\ *vb* **1** : to decline from a sound or prosperous condition **2** : to cause or undergo decomposition ⟨radium ∼s slowly⟩; *esp* : to break down while spoiling : ROT — **decay** *n*

decd *abbr* deceased

de·cease \di-'sēs\ *n* : DEATH

¹**de·ceased** \-'sēst\ *adj* : no longer living; *esp* : recently dead

²**deceased** *n, pl* **deceased** : a dead person

de·ce·dent \di-'sēd-ᵊnt\ *n* : a deceased person

de·ceit \di-'sēt\ *n* **1** : DECEPTION **2** : TRICK **3** : DECEITFULNESS

de·ceit·ful \-fəl\ *adj* **1** : practicing or tending to practice deceit **2** : MISLEADING, DECEPTIVE ⟨a ∼ answer⟩ — **de·ceit·ful·ly** *adv* — **de·ceit·ful·ness** *n*

de·ceive \di-'sēv\ *vb* **de·ceived; de·ceiv·ing** **1** : to cause to believe an untruth **2** : to use or practice deceit — **de·ceiv·er** *n*

de·cel·er·ate \dē-'sel-ə-ˌrāt\ *vb* **-at·ed; -at·ing** : to slow down

De·cem·ber \di-'sem-bər\ *n* [ME *Decembre,* fr. OF, fr. L *December* (tenth month), fr. *decem* ten] : the 12th month of the year having 31 days

de·cen·cy \'dēs-ᵊn-sē\ *n, pl* **-cies 1** : PROPRIETY **2** : conformity to standards of taste, propriety, or quality **3** : standard of propriety — usu. used in pl.

de·cen·ni·al \di-'sen-ē-əl\ *adj* **1** : consisting of 10 years **2** : happening every 10 years ⟨∼ census⟩

de·cent \'dēs-ᵊnt\ *adj* **1** : conforming to standards of propriety, good taste, or morality **2** : modestly clothed **3** : free from immodesty or obscenity **4** : ADEQUATE ⟨∼ housing⟩ — **de·cent·ly** *adv*

de·cen·tral·iza·tion \dē-ˌsen-trə-lə-'zā-shən\ *n* **1** : the distribution of powers from a central authority to regional and local authorities **2** : the redistribution of population and industry from urban centers to outlying areas — **de·cen·tral·ize** \-'sen-trə-ˌlīz\ *vb*

de·cep·tion \di-'sep-shən\ *n* **1** : the act of deceiving **2** : the fact or condition of being deceived **3** : FRAUD, TRICK — **de·cep·tive** \-'sep-tiv\ *adj* — **de·cep·tive·ly** *adv*

deci·bel \'des-ə-ˌbel, -bəl\ *n* : a unit for measuring the relative loudness of sounds

de·cide \di-'sīd\ *vb* **de·cid·ed; de·cid·ing** [ME *deciden,* fr. MF *decider,* fr. L *decidere,* lit., to cut off, fr. *caedere* to cut] **1** : to arrive at a solution that ends uncertainty or dispute about **2** : to bring to a definitive end ⟨one blow *decided* the fight⟩ **3** : to induce to come to a choice **4** : to make a choice or judgment

de·cid·ed \di-'sīd-əd\ *adj* **1** : CLEAR, UNMISTAKABLE **2** : FIRM, DETERMINED — **de·cid·ed·ly** *adv*

de·cid·u·ous \di-'sij-ə-wəs\ *adj* **1** : falling off usu. at the end of a period of growth or function ⟨∼ leaves⟩ ⟨a ∼ tooth⟩ **2** : having deciduous parts ⟨∼ trees⟩

deci·gram \'des-ə-ˌgram\ *n* — see METRIC SYSTEM table

deci·li·ter \'des-ə-ˌlēt-ər\ *n* — see METRIC SYSTEM table

¹**dec·i·mal** \'des-ə-məl\ *adj* : based on the number 10 : reckoning by tens

²**decimal** *n* : any number expressed in base 10; *esp* : DECIMAL FRACTION

decimal fraction *n* : a fraction (as .25 = $25/100$ or .025 = $25/1000$) or mixed number (as 3.025 = 3 $25/1000$) in which the denominator is a power of 10 usu. expressed by use of the decimal point

decimal point *n* : the dot at the left of a decimal fraction (as .678) less than one or between the parts of a mixed number (as 3.678) composed of a whole number and a decimal fraction

dec·i·mate \'des-ə-ˌmāt\ *vb* **-mat·ed; -mat·ing 1** : to take or destroy the 10th part of **2** : to destroy a large part of

dec·i·me·ter \'des-ə-ˌmēt-ər\ *n* — see METRIC SYSTEM table

de·ci·pher \di-'sī-fər\ *vb* **1** : to translate from secret writing (as code) **2** : to make out the meaning of despite indistinctness — **de·ci·pher·able** *adj*

de·ci·sion \di-'sizh-ən\ *n* **1** : the act or result of deciding **2** : promptness and firmness in deciding : DETERMINATION

de·ci·sive \-'sī-siv\ *adj* **1** : having the power to decide ⟨the ∼ vote⟩ **2** : RESOLUTE, DETERMINED **3** : CONCLUSIVE ⟨a ∼ victory⟩ — **de·ci·sive·ly** *adv* — **de·ci·sive·ness** *n*

¹deck \'dek\ *n* **1** : a floorlike platform of a ship; *also* : something resembling the deck of a ship **2** : a pack of playing cards

²deck *vb* **1** : ARRAY **2** : DECORATE **3** : to furnish with a deck **4** : KNOCK DOWN, FLOOR

deck·hand \'dek-ˌhand\ *n* : a sailor who performs manual duties

deck·le edge \ˌdek-əl-\ *n* : the rough untrimmed edge of paper — **deck·le-edged** \ˌdek-ə-'lejd\ *adj*

de·claim \di-'klām\ *vb* : to speak or deliver in the manner of a formal speech — **dec·la·ma·tion** \ˌdek-lə-'mā-shən\ *n* — **de·clam·a·to·ry** \di-'klam-ə-ˌtōr-ē\ *adj*

de·clar·a·tive \di-'klar-ət-iv\ *adj* : making a declaration ⟨∼ sentence⟩

de·clare \di-'klaer\ *vb* **de·clared; de·clar·ing** **1** : to make known formally or explicitly : ANNOUNCE ⟨∼ war⟩ **2** : to state emphatically : AFFIRM **3** : to make a full statement of — **dec·la·ra·tion** \ˌdek-lə-'rā-shən\ *n* — **de·clar·a·to·ry** \di-'klar-ə-ˌtōr-ē\ *adj* — **de·clar·er** *n*

de·clas·si·fy \dē-'klas-ə-ˌfī\ *vb* : to remove or reduce the security classification of

de·clen·sion \di-'klen-chən\ *n* **1** : the inflectional forms of a noun, pronoun, or adjective **2** : DECLINE, DETERIORATION **3** : DESCENT, SLOPE

¹de·cline \di-'klīn\ *vb* **de·clined; de·clin·ing** **1** : to slope downward : DESCEND **2** : DROOP **3** : RECEDE **4** : WANE **5** : to withhold consent; *also* : REFUSE, REJECT **6** : INFLECT 2 ⟨∼ a noun⟩ — **de·clin·able** *adj* — **dec·li·na·tion** \ˌdek-lə-'nā-shən\ *n*

²decline *n* **1** : a gradual sinking and wasting away **2** : a change to a lower state or level **3** : the time when something is approaching its end **4** : a descending slope **5** : a wasting disease; *esp* : pulmonary tuberculosis

de·cliv·i·ty \di-'kliv-ət-ē\ *n, pl* **-ties** : a steep downward slope

de·code \dē-'kōd\ *vb* : to convert (a coded message) into ordinary language — **de·cod·er** *n*

dé·col·le·té \dā-ˌkäl-ə-'tā\ *adj* [F] **1** : wearing a strapless or low-necked gown **2** : having a low-cut neckline

de·com·mis·sion \ˌdē-kə-'mish-ən\ *vb* : to take out of commission

de·com·pose \ˌdē-kəm-'pōz\ *vb* **1** : to separate into constituent parts **2** : to break down in decay : ROT — **de·com·po·si·tion** \dē-ˌkäm-pə-'zish-ən\ *n*

de·com·press \ˌdē-kəm-'pres\ *vb* : to release (as a diver) from pressure or compression — **de·com·pres·sion** \-'presh-ən\ *n*

de·con·ges·tant \ˌdē-kən-'jes-tənt\ *n* : an agent that relieves congestion (as of mucous membranes)

de·con·tam·i·nate \ˌdē-kən-'tam-ə-ˌnāt\ *vb* : to rid of contamination (as radioactive material) — **de·con·tam·i·na·tion** \-ˌtam-ə-'nā-shən\ *n*

de·con·trol \ˌdē-kən-'trōl\ *vb* : to end control of ⟨∼ prices⟩

de·cor *or* **dé·cor** \dā-'kȯr, 'dā-ˌkȯr\ *n* : DECORATION; *esp* : the arrangement of accessories in interior decoration

dec·o·rate \'dek-ə-ˌrāt\ *vb* **-rat·ed; -rat·ing** **1** : to make more attractive by adding something beautiful or becoming : ADORN, EMBELLISH **2** : to award a mark of honor (as a medal) to

dec·o·ra·tion \ˌdek-ə-'rā-shən\ *n* **1** : the act or process of decorating **2** : ORNAMENT **3** : a badge of honor

dec·o·ra·tive \'dek-(ə-)rət-iv\ *adj* : ORNAMENTAL

dec·o·ra·tor \'dek-ə-ˌrāt-ər\ *n* : one that decorates; *esp* : a person who designs or executes the interiors of buildings and their furnishings

dec·o·rous \'dek-ə-rəs, di-'kōr-əs\ *adj* : PROPER, SEEMLY, CORRECT

de·co·rum \di-'kōr-əm\ *n* [L] **1** : conformity to accepted standards of conduct **2** : ORDERLINESS, PROPRIETY

¹de·coy \'dē-ˌkȯi, di-'kȯi\ *n* : something that lures or entices; *esp* : an artificial bird used to attract live birds within shot

²de·coy \di-'kȯi, 'dē-,kȯi\ *vb* : to lure by or as if by a decoy : ENTICE

¹de·crease \di-'krēs\ *vb* **de·creased; de·creas·ing** : to grow or cause to grow less : DIMINISH

²de·crease \'dē-,krēs\ *n* **1** : the process of decreasing **2** : REDUCTION

¹de·cree \di-'krē\ *n* **1** : ORDER, EDICT **2** : a judicial decision

²decree *vb* **de·creed; de·cree·ing 1** : COMMAND **2** : to determine or order judicially

dec·re·ment \'dek-rə-mənt\ *n* **1** : gradual decrease **2** : the quantity lost by diminution or waste

de·crep·it \di-'krep-ət\ *adj* : broken down with age : WORN-OUT — **de·crep·i·tude** \-ə-,t(y)üd\ *n*

de·cre·scen·do \,dā-krə-'shen-dō\ *adv or adj* : with a decrease in volume — used as a direction in music

de·crim·i·nal·ize \dē-'krim-ən-ᵊl-,īz\ *vb* : to remove or reduce the criminal status of

de·cry \di-'krī\ *vb* **1** : to belittle publicly **2** : to find fault with : CONDEMN

ded·i·cate \'ded-i-,kāt\ *vb* **-cat·ed; -cat·ing 1** : to devote to the worship of a divine being esp. with sacred rites **2** : to set apart for a definite purpose **3** : to inscribe or address as a compliment — **ded·i·ca·tion** \,ded-i-'kā-shən\ *n* — **ded·i·ca·to·ry** \'ded-i-kə-,tōr-ē\ *adj*

de·duce \di-'d(y)üs\ *vb* **de·duced; de·duc·ing 1** : to derive by reasoning : INFER **2** : to trace the course of ⟨∼ their lineage⟩ — **de·duc·ible** *adj*

de·duct \di-'dəkt\ *vb* : SUBTRACT — **de·duct·ible** *adj*

de·duc·tion \di-'dək-shən\ *n* **1** : SUBTRACTION **2** : something that is or may be subtracted : ABATEMENT **3** : the deriving of a conclusion by reasoning : the conclusion so reached — **de·duc·tive** \-'dək-tiv\ *adj*

¹deed \'dēd\ *n* **1** : something done **2** : FEAT, EXPLOIT **3** : a document containing some legal transfer, bargain, or contract

²deed *vb* : to convey or transfer by deed

dee·jay \'dē-'jā\ *n* : DISC JOCKEY

deem \'dēm\ *vb* : THINK, JUDGE

de·em·pha·size \dē-'em-fə-,sīz\ *vb* : to refrain from emphasizing — **de·em·pha·sis** \-fə-səs\ *n*

¹deep \'dēp\ *adj* **1** : extending far down, back, within, or outward **2** : having a specified extension downward or backward **3** : difficult to understand; *also* : MYSTERIOUS, OBSCURE ⟨a ∼ dark secret⟩ **4** : WISE **5** : ENGROSSED, INVOLVED ⟨∼ in thought⟩ **6** : INTENSE, PROFOUND ⟨∼ sleep⟩ **7** : dark and rich in color ⟨a ∼ red⟩ **8** : having a low musical pitch or range ⟨a ∼ voice⟩ **9** : situated well within **10** : covered, enclosed, or filled often to a specified degree — **deep·ly** *adv*

²deep *adv* **1** : DEEPLY **2** : far on : LATE ⟨∼ in the night⟩

³deep *n* **1** : an extremely deep place or part; *esp* : OCEAN **2** : the middle or most intense part ⟨the ∼ of winter⟩

deep·en \'dē-pən\ *vb* **deep·ened; deep·en·ing** \'dēp-(ə-)niŋ\ : to make or become deep or deeper

deep–freeze \'dēp-'frēz\ *vb* **-froze** \-'frōz\; **-fro·zen** \-'frōz-ᵊn\ : QUICK=FREEZE

deep–root·ed \-'rüt-əd, -'rut-\ *adj* : deeply implanted or established

deep–sea \,dēp-'sē\ *adj* : of, relating to, or occurring in the deeper parts of the sea ⟨∼ fishing⟩

deep–seat·ed \'dēp-'sēt-əd\ *adj* **1** : situated far below the surface **2** : firmly established ⟨∼ convictions⟩

deer \'diər\ *n, pl* **deer** [ME, deer, animal, fr. OE *dēor* beast] : any of a family of ruminant mammals with cloven hoofs and usu. antlers esp. in the males

deer·fly \-,flī\ *n* : any of numerous small horseflies

deer·skin \-,skin\ *n* : leather made from the skin of a deer; *also* : a garment of such leather

de·es·ca·late \dē-'es-kə-,lāt\ *vb* : to decrease in extent, volume, or scope : REDUCE ⟨∼ the war⟩ — **de·es·ca·la·tion** \dē-,es-kə-'lā-shən\ *n*

def *abbr* **1** defendant **2** definite **3** definition

de·face \di-'fās\ *vb* : to destroy or mar the face or surface of — **de·face·ment** *n*

de fac·to \di-'fak-tō, dā-\ *adj or adv* **1** : actually existing ⟨*de facto* segregation⟩ **2** : actually exercising power ⟨*de facto* government⟩

de·fal·ca·tion \ˌdē-ˌfal-'kā-shən, ˌdē-ˌfȯl-; ˌdef-əl-\ *n* : EMBEZZLEMENT

de·fame \di-'fām\ *vb* **de·famed; de·fam·ing** : to injure or destroy the reputation of by libel or slander — **def·a·ma·tion** \ˌdef-ə-'mā-shən\ *n* — **de·fam·a·to·ry** \di-'fam-ə-ˌtōr-ē\ *adj*

de·fault \di-'fȯlt\ *n* **1** : failure to do something required by duty or law ⟨the defendant failed to appear and was held in ∼⟩ **2** : failure to compete in or to finish an appointed contest ⟨lose a race by ∼⟩ — **default** *vb* — **de·fault·er** *n*

¹de·feat \di-'fēt\ *vb* **1** : FRUSTRATE, NULLIFY **2** : to win victory over : BEAT

²defeat *n* **1** : FRUSTRATION **2** : an overthrow of an army in battle **3** : loss of a contest

de·feat·ism \-ˌiz-əm,\ *n* : acceptance of or resignation to defeat — **de·feat·ist** \-əst\ *n or adj*

def·e·cate \'def-i-ˌkāt\ *vb* **-cat·ed; -cat·ing** **1** : to free from impurity or corruption : REFINE **2** : to discharge feces from the bowels — **def·e·ca·tion** \ˌdef-i-'kā-shən\ *n*

¹de·fect \'dē-ˌfekt, di-'fekt\ *n* : BLEMISH, FAULT, IMPERFECTION

²de·fect \di-'fekt\ *vb* : to desert a cause or party esp. in order to espouse another — **de·fec·tion** \-'fek-shən\ *n* — **de·fec·tor** \-'fek-tər\ *n*

de·fec·tive \di-'fek-tiv\ *adj* : FAULTY, DEFICIENT — **defective** *n*

de·fend \di-'fend\ *vb* [ME *defenden*, fr. OF *defendre*, fr. L *defendere*, fr. *de-* from + *-fendere* to strike] **1** : to repel danger or attack from **2** : to act as attorney for **3** : to oppose the claim of another in a lawsuit : CONTEST **4** : to maintain against opposition ⟨∼ an idea⟩ — **de·fend·er** *n*

de·fen·dant \di-'fen-dənt\ *n* : a person required to make answer in a legal action or suit

de·fense *or* **de·fence** \di-'fens\ *n* **1** : the act of defending : resistance against attack **2** : means, method, or capability of defending **3** : an argument in support **4** : the answer made by the defendant in a legal action **5** : a defending party, group, or team — **de·fense·less** *adj* — **de·fen·si·ble** *adj*

defense mechanism *n* : an often unconscious mental process (as repression or sublimation) that assists in reaching compromise solutions to personal problems

¹de·fen·sive \di-'fen-siv\ *adj* **1** : serving or intended to defend or protect **2** : of or relating to the attempt to keep an opponent from scoring (as in a game) — **de·fen·sive·ly** *adv* — **de·fen·sive·ness** *n*

²defensive *n* : a defensive position

¹de·fer \di-'fər\ *vb* **de·ferred; de·fer·ring** [ME *deferren, differren,* fr. MF *differer,* fr. L *differre* to postpone, be different] : POSTPONE, PUT OFF

²defer *vb* **deferred; deferring** [ME *deferren, differren,* fr. MF *deferer, defferer,* fr. LL *deferre,* fr. L, to bring down, bring, fr. *ferre* to carry] : to submit or yield to the opinion or wishes of another

def·er·ence \'def-(ə-)rəns\ *n* : courteous, respectful, or ingratiating regard for another's wishes — **def·er·en·tial** \ˌdef-ə-'ren-chəl\ *adj*

de·fer·ment \di-'fər-mənt\ *n* : the act of delaying; *esp* : official postponement of military service

de·fi·ance \di-'fī-əns\ *n* **1** : CHALLENGE **2** : a tendency to resist : contempt of opposition

de·fi·ant \-ənt\ *adj* : full of defiance ⟨a ∼ gesture⟩ — **de·fi·ant·ly** *adv*

de·fi·bril·la·tor \dē-'fib-rə-ˌlāt-ər, -'fīb-\ *n* : an electronic device used to restore the rhythm of a fibrillating heart by applying an electric shock to it — **de·fi·bril·late** \-ˌlāt\ *vb* — **de·fi·bril·la·tion** \dē-ˌfib-rə-'lā-shən, -ˌfīb-\ *n*

deficiency disease *n* : a disease (as scurvy or beriberi) caused by a lack of essential dietary elements and esp. a vitamin or mineral

de·fi·cient \di-'fish-ənt\ *adj* : lacking in something necessary (as for completeness or health) : DEFECTIVE — **de·fi·cien·cy** \-'fish-ən-sē\ *n*

def·i·cit \'def-ə-sət\ *n* : a deficiency in amount; *esp* : an excess of expenditures over revenue

¹de·file \di-'fīl\ *vb* **de·filed; de·fil·ing** **1** : to make filthy **2** : CORRUPT **3** : to violate the chastity of **4** : to violate the sanctity of : DESECRATE **5** : DISHONOR — **de·file·ment** *n*

²de·file \di-ˈfīl, ˈdē-ˌfīl\ *n* : a narrow passage or gorge

de·fine \di-ˈfīn\ *vb* **de·fined; de·fin·ing 1** : to set forth the meaning of ⟨∼ a word⟩ **2** : to fix or mark the limits of **3** : to clarify in outline or character — **de·fin·able** *adj* — **de·fin·er** *n*

def·i·nite \ˈdef-(ə-)nət\ *adj* **1** : having distinct limits : FIXED **2** : clear in meaning **3** : typically designating an identified or immediately identifiable person or thing — **def·i·nite·ly** *adv* — **def·i·nite·ness** *n*

def·i·ni·tion \ˌdef-ə-ˈnish-ən\ *n* **1** : an act of determining or settling **2** : a statement of the meaning of a word or word group; *also* : the action or process of stating such a meaning **3** : the action or the power of making definite and clear : CLARITY, DISTINCTNESS

de·fin·i·tive \di-ˈfin-ət-iv\ *adj* **1** : DECISIVE, CONCLUSIVE **2** : being authoritative and apparently exhaustive **3** : serving to define or specify precisely

de·flate \di-ˈflāt\ *vb* **de·flat·ed; de·flat·ing 1** : to release air or gas from **2** : to cause to contract from an abnormally high level : reduce from a state of inflation **3** : to become deflated

de·fla·tion \-ˈflā-shən\ *n* **1** : an act or instance of deflating : the state of being deflated **2** : reduction in the volume of available money or credit resulting in a decline of the general price level

de·flect \di-ˈflekt\ *vb* : to turn aside — **de·flec·tion** \-ˈflek-shən\ *n*

de·flo·ra·tion \ˌdef-lə-ˈrā-shən\ *n* : rupture of the hymen

de·flow·er \dē-ˈflau̇(-ə)r\ *vb* : to deprive of virginity : RAVISH

de·fog \dē-ˈfȯg, -ˈfäg\ *vb* : to remove fog or condensed moisture from — **de·fog·ger** *n*

de·fo·li·ant \dē-ˈfō-lē-ənt\ *n* : a chemical spray or dust applied to plants to cause the leaves to drop off prematurely

de·fo·li·ate \-lē-ˌāt\ *vb* : to deprive of leaves esp. prematurely — **de·fo·li·a·tion** \dē-ˌfō-lē-ˈā-shən\ *n* — **de·fo·li·a·tor** \dē-ˈfō-lē-ˌāt-ər\ *n*

de·for·es·ta·tion \dē-ˌfȯr-ə-ˈstā-shən\ *n* : the action or process of clearing an area of forests; *also* : the state of having been cleared of forests — **de·for·est** \(ˈ)dē-ˈfȯr-əst, -ˈfär-\ *vb*

de·form \di-ˈfȯrm\ *vb* **1** : DISFIGURE, DEFACE **2** : to make or become misshapen or changed in shape — **de·for·ma·tion** \ˌdē-ˌfȯr-ˈmā-shən, ˌdef-ər-\ *n*

de·for·mi·ty \di-ˈfȯr-mət-ē\ *n, pl* **-ties 1** : the state of being deformed **2** : a physical blemish or distortion

de·fraud \di-ˈfrȯd\ *vb* : CHEAT

de·fray \di-ˈfrā\ *vb* : to provide for the payment of : PAY — **de·fray·al** *n*

de·frost \di-ˈfrȯst\ *vb* **1** : to thaw out **2** : to free from ice — **de·frost·er** *n*

deft \ˈdeft\ *adj* : quick and neat in action — **deft·ly** *adv* — **deft·ness** *n*

de·funct \di-ˈfəŋkt\ *adj* : DEAD, EXTINCT ⟨a ∼ organization⟩

de·fuse \dē-ˈfyüz\ *vb* **1** : to remove the fuse from (as a bomb) **2** : to make less harmful, potent, or tense

de·fy \di-ˈfī\ *vb* **de·fied; de·fy·ing** [ME *defyen* to renounce faith in, challenge, fr. OF *defier*, fr. *de-* from + *fier* to entrust, fr. L *fidere* to trust] **1** : CHALLENGE, DARE **2** : to refuse boldly to obey or to yield to : DISREGARD ⟨∼ the law⟩ **3** : WITHSTAND, BAFFLE ⟨a scene that *defies* description⟩

deg *abbr* degree

de·gas \dē-ˈgas\ *vb* : to remove gas from

de·gen·er·a·cy \di-ˈjen-(ə-)rə-sē\ *n, pl* **-cies 1** : the state of being degenerate **2** : the process of becoming degenerate

¹de·gen·er·ate \di-ˈjen-(ə-)rət\ *adj* : fallen or deteriorated from a former, higher, or normal condition — **de·gen·er·a·cy** \-rə-sē\ *n* — **de·gen·er·a·tion** \-ˌjen-ə-ˈrā-shən\ *n* — **de·gen·er·a·tive** \-ˈjen-ə-ˌrāt-iv\ *adj*

²de·gen·er·ate \di-ˈjen-ə-ˌrāt\ *vb* : to undergo deterioration (as in morality, intelligence, structure, or function)

³de·gen·er·ate \-(ə-)rət\ *n* : a degenerate person; *esp* : a sexual pervert

de·grad·able \di-ˈgrād-ə-bəl\ *adj* : capable of being chemically degraded ⟨∼ detergents⟩

de·grade \di-ˈgrād\ *vb* **1** : to reduce from a higher to a lower rank or degree **2** : DEBASE, CORRUPT — **deg·ra·da·tion** \ˌdeg-rə-ˈdā-shən\ *n*

de·gree \di-ˈgrē\ *n* [ME, fr. OF *degré*, fr. (assumed) VL *degradus*, fr. L *gradus* step, grade] **1** : a step in a series **2** : the extent, intensity, or scope of something esp. as measured by a graded series **3** : one of the forms or sets of forms used in the comparison of an adjective or adverb **4** : a rank or grade of official, ecclesiastical, or social position; *also* : the civil condition of a person **5** : a title conferred upon students by a college, university, or professional school upon completion of a unified program of study **6** : a unit of measure for angles and arcs that for angles is equal to an angle with its vertex at the center of a circle and its sides cutting off 1/360 of the circumference and that for an arc of a circle is equal to 1/360 of the circumference **7** : a line or space of the musical staff; *also* : a note or tone of a musical scale

de·horn \dē-'horn\ *vb* : to deprive of horns

de·hu·man·ize \dē-'hyü-mə-ˌnīz\ *vb* : to divest of human qualities or personality — **de·hu·man·iza·tion** \ˌdē-ˌhyü-mə-nə-'zā-shən\ *n*

de·hu·mid·i·fy \ˌdē-hyü-'mid-ə-ˌfī\ *vb* : to remove moisture from (as the air) — **de·hu·mid·i·fi·er** \-'mid-ə-ˌfī(-ə)r\ *n*

de·hy·drate \dē-'hī-ˌdrāt\ *vb* : to remove water from ⟨*dehydrated* by fever⟩ ⟨~ fruits⟩; *also* : to lose liquid — **de·hy·dra·tion** \ˌdē-hī-'drā-shən\ *n*

de·hy·dro·ge·nate \ˌdē-hī-'dräj-ə-ˌnāt\ *vb* : to remove hydrogen from — **de·hy·dro·ge·na·tion** \ˌdē-hī-ˌdräj-ə-'nā-shən\ *n*

de·ice \dē-'īs\ *vb* : to keep free or rid of ice — **de·ic·er** *n*

de·i·fy \'dē-ə-ˌfī\ *vb* **-fied; -fy·ing 1** : to make a god of **2** : WORSHIP, GLORIFY — **de·i·fi·ca·tion** \ˌdē-ə-fə-'kā-shən\ *n*

deign \'dān\ *vb* [ME *deignen*, fr. OF *deignier*, fr. L *dignare, dignari*, fr. *dignus* worthy] : CONDESCEND

de·ion·ize \dē-'ī-ə-ˌnīz\ *vb* : to remove ions from

de·ism \'dē-ˌiz-əm\ *n, often cap* : a system of thought advocating natural religion based on human reason rather than revelation — **de·ist** \'dē-əst\ *n, often cap* — **de·is·tic** \dē-'is-tik\ *adj*

de·i·ty \'dē-ət-ē\ *n, pl* **-ties 1** : DIVINITY **2** **2** *cap* : GOD 1 **3** : a god or goddess

de·ject·ed \di-'jek-təd\ *adj* : low in spirits : SAD — **de·ject·ed·ly** *adv*

de·jec·tion \di-'jek-shən\ *n* : lowness of spirits : DEPRESSION

de ju·re \dē-'jur-ē\ *adv or adj* : existing or exercising power by legal right ⟨*de jure* government⟩

deka·gram \'dek-ə-ˌgram\ *n* — see METRIC SYSTEM table

deka·li·ter \-ˌlēt-ər\ *n* — see METRIC SYSTEM table

deka·me·ter \-ˌmēt-ər\ *n* — see METRIC SYSTEM table

del *abbr* delegate; delegation

Del *abbr* Delaware

Del·a·ware \'del-ə-ˌwaər\ *n, pl* **Delaware** *or* **Delawares** : a member of an American Indian people orig. of the Delaware valley; *also* : their language

¹de·lay \di-'lā\ *n* **1** : the act of delaying : the state of being delayed **2** : the time for which something is delayed

²delay *vb* **1** : POSTPONE, PUT OFF **2** : to stop, detain, or hinder for a time **3** : to move or act slowly

de·lec·ta·ble \di-'lek-tə-bəl\ *adj* **1** : highly pleasing : DELIGHTFUL **2** : DELICIOUS

de·lec·ta·tion \ˌdē-ˌlek-'tā-shən\ *n* : DELIGHT, PLEASURE, DIVERSION

¹del·e·gate \'del-i-gət, -ˌgāt\ *n* **1** : DEPUTY, REPRESENTATIVE **2** : a member of the lower house of the legislature of Maryland, Virginia, or West Virginia

²del·e·gate \-ˌgāt\ *vb* **-gat·ed; -gat·ing 1** : to entrust to another ⟨*delegated* his authority⟩ **2** : to appoint as one's delegate

del·e·ga·tion \ˌdel-i-'gā-shən\ *n* **1** : the act of delegating **2** : one or more persons chosen to represent others

de·lete \di-'lēt\ *vb* **de·let·ed; de·let·ing** [L *delēre* to wipe out, destroy] : to eliminate esp. by blotting out, cutting out, or erasing — **de·le·tion** \-'lē-shən\ *n*

del·e·te·ri·ous \ˌdel-ə-'tir-ē-əs\ *adj* : HARMFUL, NOXIOUS

delft \'delft\ *n* **1** : a Dutch pottery with an opaque white glaze and predominantly blue decoration **2** : glazed pottery esp. when blue and white

delft·ware \-ˌwaər\ *n* : DELFT

deli \'del-ē\ *n, pl* **del·is** : DELICATESSEN

¹de·lib·er·ate \di-'lib-ə-ˌrāt\ *vb* **-at·ed; -at·ing** : to consider carefully — **de·lib·er·a·tion** \-ˌlib-ə-'rā-shən\ *n*

²de·lib·er·ate \di-'lib-(ə-)rət\ *adj* [L

deliberare to weigh in mind, ponder, fr. *libra* scale, pound] **1** : determined after careful thought **2** : done or said intentionally **3** : UNHURRIED, SLOW — **de·lib·er·ate·ly** *adv* — **de·lib·er·ate·ness** *n*

de·lib·er·a·tive \-ˈlib-ə-ˌrāt-iv, -ˈlib(-ə)-rət-\ *adj* : of, relating to, or marked by deliberation ⟨∼ assembly⟩ — **de·lib·er·a·tive·ly** *adv*

del·i·ca·cy \ˈdel-i-kə-sē\ *n, pl* **-cies 1** : something pleasing to eat because it is rare or luxurious **2** : FINENESS, DAINTINESS; *also* : FRAILTY **3** : nicety or expressiveness of touch **4** : precise perception and discrimination : SENSITIVITY **5** : sensibility in feeling or conduct; *also* : SQUEAMISHNESS **6** : the quality or state of requiring delicate handling

del·i·cate \ˈdel-i-kət\ *adj* **1** : pleasing to the senses of taste or smell esp. in a mild or subtle way **2** : marked by daintiness or charm : EXQUISITE **3** : FASTIDIOUS, SQUEAMISH, SCRUPULOUS **4** : easily damaged : FRAGILE; *also* : SICKLY **5** : requiring skill or tact **6** : marked by care, skill, or tact **7** : marked by minute precision : very sensitive — **del·i·cate·ly** *adv*

del·i·ca·tes·sen \ˌdel-i-kə-ˈtes-ᵊn\ *n pl* [G, pl. of *delicatesse* delicacy, fr. F *délicatesse*] **1** : ready-to-eat food products (as cooked meats and prepared salads) **2** *sing, pl* **delicatessens** : a store where delicatessen are sold

de·li·cious \di-ˈlish-əs\ *adj* : affording great pleasure : DELIGHTFUL; *esp* : very pleasing to the taste or smell — **de·li·cious·ly** *adv*

¹de·light \di-ˈlīt\ *n* **1** : great pleasure or satisfaction : JOY **2** : something that gives great pleasure — **de·light·ful** \-fəl\ *adj* — **de·light·ful·ly** \-ē\ *adv*

²delight *vb* **1** : to take great pleasure **2** : to satisfy greatly : PLEASE

de·light·ed \-əd\ *adj* : highly pleased : GRATIFIED — **de·light·ed·ly** *adv*

de·lim·it \di-ˈlim-ət\ *vb* : to fix the limits of : BOUND

de·lin·eate \di-ˈlin-ē-ˌāt\ *vb* **-eat·ed; -eat·ing 1** : SKETCH, PORTRAY **2** : to picture in words : DESCRIBE — **de·lin·ea·tion** \-ˌlin-ē-ˈā-shən\ *n*

de·lin·quen·cy \di-ˈliŋ-kwən-sē\ *n, pl* **-cies** : the quality or state of being delinquent

¹de·lin·quent \-kwənt\ *n* : a delinquent person

²delinquent *adj* **1** : offending by neglect or violation of duty or of law **2** : being overdue in payment

del·i·quesce \ˌdel-i-ˈkwes\ *vb* **-quesced; -quesc·ing** : MELT, DISSOLVE; *esp* : to become liquid by absorbing moisture from the air — **del·i·ques·cent** \-ˈkwes-ᵊnt\ *adj*

de·lir·i·um \di-ˈlir-ē-əm\ *n* [L, fr. *delirare* to be crazy, fr. *de-* from + *lira* furrow] : mental disturbance marked by confusion, disordered speech, and hallucinations; *also* : violent excitement — **de·lir·i·ous** \-ē-əs\ *adj* — **de·lir·i·ous·ly** *adv*

delirium tre·mens \-ˈtrē-mənz, -ˈtrem-ənz\ *n* : a violent delirium with tremors that is induced by excessive and prolonged use of alcoholic liquors

de·liv·er \di-ˈliv-ər\ *vb* **-ered; -er·ing** \-(ə-)riŋ\ **1** : to set free : SAVE **2** : CONVEY, TRANSFER ⟨∼ a letter⟩ **3** : to assist in giving birth or at the birth of **4** : UTTER, COMMUNICATE **5** : to send to an intended target or destination — **de·liv·er·ance** *n* — **de·liv·er·er** *n*

de·liv·ery \di-ˈliv-(ə-)rē\ *n, pl* **-er·ies** : the act of delivering something; *also* : something delivered

dell \ˈdel\ *n* : a small secluded valley

de·louse \dē-ˈlaůs\ *vb* : to remove lice from

del·phin·i·um \del-ˈfin-ē-əm\ *n* : any of a genus of mostly perennial herbs related to the buttercups with tall branching spikes of irregular flowers

del·ta \ˈdel-tə\ *n* [Gk, fr. *delta,* fourth letter of the Gk alphabet, Δ, which an alluvial delta resembles in shape] : triangular silt-formed land at the mouth of a river — **del·ta·ic** \del-ˈtā-ik\ *adj*

de·lude \di-ˈlüd\ *vb* **de·lud·ed; de·lud·ing** : MISLEAD, DECEIVE, TRICK

¹del·uge \ˈdel-yüj\ *n* **1** : a flooding of land by water **2** : a drenching rain **3** : a great amount or number ⟨a ∼ of Christmas mail⟩

²deluge *vb* **del·uged; del·ug·ing 1** : INUNDATE, FLOOD **2** : to overwhelm as if with a deluge

de·lu·sion \di-ˈlü-zhən\ *n* : a deluding or

being deluded; *esp* : a persistent belief in something false typical of some mental disorders — **de·lu·sion·al** \-'lüzh-(ə-)nəl\ *adj* — **de·lu·sive** \-'lü-siv\ *adj*

de·luxe \di-'lùks, -'ləks, -'lüks\ *adj* : notably luxurious or elegant

delve \'delv\ *vb* **delved; delv·ing 1** : DIG **2** : to seek laboriously for information

dely *abbr* delivery

Dem *abbr* Democrat; Democratic

de·mag·ne·tize \dē-'mag-nə-,tīz\ *vb* : to cause to lose magnetic properties — **de·mag·ne·ti·za·tion** \dē-,mag-nət-ə-'zā-shən\ *n*

dem·a·gogue *or* **dem·a·gog** \'dem-ə-,gäg\ *n* [Gk *dēmagōgos*, fr. *dēmos* people + *agōgos* leading, fr. *agein* to lead] : a person who appeals to the emotions and prejudices of people esp. in order to gain political power — **dem·a·gogu·ery** \-,gäg-(ə-)rē\ *n* — **dem·a·gogy** \-,gäg-ē, -,gäj-ē\ *n*

¹de·mand \di-'mand\ *n* **1** : an act of demanding or asking esp. with authority; *also* : something claimed as due **2** : the ability and desire to buy goods or services; *also* : the quantity of goods wanted at a stated price **3** : a seeking or being sought after : urgent need **4** : a pressing need or requirement

²demand *vb* **1** : to ask for with authority : claim as due **2** : to ask earnestly or in the manner of a command **3** : REQUIRE, NEED ⟨an illness that ∼s care⟩

de·mar·cate \di-'mär-,kāt, 'dē-,mär-\ *vb* **-cat·ed; -cat·ing 1** : to mark the limits of **2** : SEPARATE — **de·mar·ca·tion** \,dē-,mär-'kā-shən\ *n*

de·marche \dā-'märsh\ *n* : a course of action : MANEUVER

¹de·mean \di-'mēn\ *vb* **de·meaned; de·mean·ing** : to behave or conduct (oneself) usu. in a proper manner

²demean *vb* **de·meaned; de·mean·ing** : DEGRADE, DEBASE

de·mean·or \di-'mē-nər\ *n* : CONDUCT, BEARING

de·ment·ed \di-'ment-əd\ *adj* : MAD, INSANE — **de·ment·ed·ly** *adv*

de·men·tia \di-'men-chə\ *n* **1** : mental deterioration **2** : INSANITY

de·mer·it \di-'mer-ət\ *n* **1** : FAULT **2** : a mark placed against a person's record for some fault or offense

de·mesne \di-'mān, -'mēn\ *n* **1** : REALM

2 : manorial land actually possessed by the lord and not held by free tenants **3** : ESTATE **4** : REGION

demi·god \'dem-i-,gäd\ *n* : a mythological being with more power than a mortal but less than a god

demi·john \'dem-i-,jän\ *n* [F *damejeanne*, lit., Lady Jane] : a large glass or pottery bottle enclosed in wickerwork

de·mil·i·ta·rize \dē-'mil-ə-tə-,rīz\ *vb* : to strip of military forces, weapons, or fortifications — **de·mil·i·tar·iza·tion** \dē-,mil-ə-t(ə-)rə-'zā-shən\ *n*

demi·mon·daine \,dem-i-,män-'dān\ *n* : a woman of the demimonde

demi·monde \'dem-i-,mänd\ *n* [F *demi-monde*, fr. *demi-* half + *monde* world] **1** : a class of women on the fringes of respectable society supported by wealthy lovers **2** : a group engaged in activity of doubtful legality or propriety

de·min·er·al·ize \dē-'min-(ə-)rə-,līz\ *vb* : to remove the mineral matter from

de·mise \di-'mīz\ *n* **1** : LEASE **2** : transfer of sovereignty to a successor ⟨∼ of the crown⟩ **3** : DEATH **4** : loss of status

demi·tasse \'dem-i-,tas\ *n* [F *demitasse*, fr. *demi-* half + *tasse* cup, fr. MF, fr. Ar *ṭass*, fr. Per *tast*] : a small cup of black coffee; *also* : the cup used to serve it

de·mo·bi·lize \di-'mō-bə-,līz, dē-\ *vb* **1** : to discharge from military service **2** : to change from a state of war to a state of peace — **de·mo·bi·li·za·tion** \di-,mō-bə-lə-'zā-shən, dē-\ *n*

de·moc·ra·cy \di-'mäk-rə-sē\ *n, pl* **-cies 1** : government by the people; *esp* : rule of the majority **2** : a government in which the supreme power is held by the people **3** : a political unit that has a democratic government **4** *cap* : the principles and policies of the Democratic party in the U.S. **5** : the common people esp. when constituting the source of political authority **6** : the absence of hereditary or arbitrary class distinctions or privileges

dem·o·crat \'dem-ə-,krat\ *n* **1** : one who believes in or practices democracy **2** *cap* : a member of the Democratic party of the U.S.

dem·o·crat·ic \,dem-ə-'krat-ik\ *adj* **1** : of, relating to, or favoring democracy **2** *often cap* : of or relating to one of the two major political parties in the U.S. associated in modern times with policies of broad social reform and internationalism **3** : relating to or appealing to the common people ⟨∼ art⟩ **4** : not snobbish

de•moc•ra•tize \di-ˈmäk-rə-ˌtīz\ *vb* **-tized; -tiz•ing** : to make democratic

dé•mo•dé \ˌdā-mō-ˈdā\ *adj* [F] : no longer fashionable : OUT-OF-DATE

de•mo•graph•ics \ˌdem-ə-ˈgraf-iks, ˌdēm-\ *n pl* : the statistical characteristics of human populations

de•mog•ra•phy \di-ˈmäg-rə-fē\ *n* : the statistical study of human populations and esp. their size and distribution and the number of births and deaths — **de•mog•ra•pher** \-fər\ *n* — **de•mo•graph•ic** \ˌdem-ə-ˈgraf-ik, ˌdēm-\ *adj* — **de•mo•graph•i•cal•ly** \-i-k(ə-)lē\ *adv*

dem•oi•selle \ˌdem-(w)ə-ˈzel\ *n* [F] : a young woman

de•mol•ish \di-ˈmäl-ish\ *vb* **1** : to destroy by breaking apart : RAZE **2** : SMASH **3** : to put an end to

de•mo•li•tion \ˌdem-ə-ˈlish-ən, ˌdē-mə-\ *n* : the act of demolishing; *esp* : destruction by means of explosives

de•mon *or* **dae•mon** \ˈdē-mən\ *n* **1** : an evil spirit : DEVIL **2** *usu daemon* : an attendant power or spirit **3** : one that has unusual drive or effectiveness

de•mon•e•tize \dē-ˈmän-ə-ˌtīz, -ˈmən-\ *vb* : to stop using as money or as a monetary standard ⟨∼ silver⟩ — **de•mon•e•ti•za•tion** \dē-ˌmän-ət-ə-ˈzā-shən, -ˌmən-\ *n*

de•mo•ni•ac \di-ˈmō-nē-ˌak\ *also* **de•mo•ni•a•cal** \ˌdē-mə-ˈnī-ə-kəl\ *adj* **1** : possessed or influenced by a demon **2** : DEVILISH, FIENDISH

de•mon•ic \di-ˈmän-ik\ *also* **de•mon•i•cal** \-i-kəl\ *adj* : DEMONIAC 2

de•mon•ol•o•gy \ˌdē-mə-ˈnäl-ə-jē\ *n* **1** : the study of demons **2** : belief in demons

de•mon•stra•ble \di-ˈmän-strə-bəl\ *adj* **1** : capable of being demonstrated or proved **2** : APPARENT, EVIDENT

dem•on•strate \ˈdem-ən-ˌstrāt\ *vb* **-strat•ed; -strat•ing 1** : to show clearly **2** : to prove or make clear by reasoning or evidence **3** : to explain esp. with many examples **4** : to show publicly ⟨∼ a new car⟩ **5** : to make a pub-

lic display (as of feelings or military force) ⟨∼ in protest⟩ — **dem•on•stra•tion** \ˌdem-ən-ˈstrā-shən\ *n* — **dem•on•stra•tor** \ˈdem-ən-ˌstrāt-ər\ *n*

¹de•mon•stra•tive \di-ˈmän-strət-iv\ *adj* **1** : domonstrating as real or true **2** : characterized by demonstration **3** : pointing out the one referred to and distinguishing it from others of the same class ⟨∼ pronoun⟩ ⟨∼ adjective⟩ **4** : marked by display of feeling : EFFUSIVE — **de•mon•stra•tive•ly** *adv* — **de•mon•stra•tive•ness** *n*

²demonstrative *n* : a demonstrative word and esp. a pronoun

de•mor•al•ize \di-ˈmȯr-ə-ˌlīz\ *vb* **1** : to corrupt in morals **2** : to weaken in discipline or spirit : DISORGANIZE — **de•mor•al•iza•tion** \di-ˌmȯr-ə-lə-ˈzā-shən\ *n*

de•mote \di-ˈmōt\ *vb* **de•mot•ed; de•mot•ing** : to reduce to a lower gradc or rank — **de•mo•tion** \-ˈmō-shən\ *n*

de•mot•ic \di-ˈmät-ik\ *adj* : of or relating to the people ⟨∼ Greek⟩

¹de•mul•cent \di-ˈməl-sənt\ *adj* : SOOTHING

²demulcent *n* : a usu. mucilaginous or oily substance used to soothe or protect an irritated mucous mcmbrane

de•mur \di-ˈmər\ *vb* **de•murred; de•mur•ring** [ME *demeoren* to linger, fr. OF *demorer*, fr. L *demorari*, fr. *morari* to linger, fr. *mora* delay] : to take exception : OBJECT — **de•mur** *n*

de•mure \di-ˈmyu̇r\ *adj* **1** : quietly modest : DECOROUS **2** : affectedly modest, reserved, or serious : PRIM — **de•mure•ly** *adv*

de•mur•rage \di-ˈmər-ij\ *n* : the detention of a ship by the shipper or receiver beyond the time allowed for loading, unloading, or sailing; *also* : a charge for detaining a ship, freight car, or truck for such a delay

de•mur•rer \di-ˈmər-ər\ *n* : a claim by the defendant in a legal action that the plaintiff does not have sufficient grounds to proceed

den \ˈden\ *n* **1** : a shelter or resting place of a wild animal **2** : a hiding place (as for thieves) **3** : a dirty wretched place in which people live or gather ⟨∼s of misery⟩ **4** : a cozy private little room

Den *abbr* Denmark

de·na·ture \dē-'nā-chər\ *vb* **de·na·tured; de·na·tur·ing** \-'nāch-(ə-)riŋ\ : to remove the natural qualities of; *esp* : to makc (alcohol) unfit for drinking

den·drol·o·gy \den-'dräl-ə-jē\ *n* : the study of trees — **den·drol·o·gist** \-ə-jəst\ *n*

den·gue \'deŋ-gē, -ˌgā\ *n* [Sp] : an acute infectious disease characterized by headache, severe joint pain, and rash

de·ni·al \di-'nī(-ə)l\ *n* 1 : rejection of a request 2 : refusal to admit the truth of a statement or charge; *also* : assertion that something alleged is false 3 : DISAVOWAL 4 : restriction on one's own activity or desires

de·nier \'den-yər\ *n* : a unit of fineness for silk, rayon, or nylon yarn

den·i·grate \'den-i-ˌgrāt\ *vb* **-grat·ed; -grat·ing** [L *denigrare,* fr. *nigrare* to blacken, fr. *niger* black] : to cast aspersions on : DEFAME

den·im \'den-əm\ *n* [F *(serge) de Nîmes* serge of Nîmes, France] 1 : a firm durable twilled usu. cotton fabric woven with colored warp and white filling threads 2 *pl* : overalls or trousers of usu. blue denim

den·i·zen \'den-ə-zən\ *n* : INHABITANT

de·nom·i·nate \di-'näm-ə-ˌnāt\ *vb* : to give a name to : DESIGNATE

de·nom·i·nate number \di-ˌnäm-ə-nət-\ *n* : a number (as 7 in *7 feet*) that specifies a quantity in terms of a unit of measurement

de·nom·i·na·tion \di-ˌnäm-ə-'nā-shən\ *n* 1 : an act of denominating 2 : a value or size of a series of related values (as of money) 3 : NAME, DESIGNATION; *esp* : a general name for a class of things 4 : a religious body comprising a number of local congregations having similar beliefs — **de·nom·i·na·tion·al** \-sh(ə-)nəl\ *adj*

de·nom·i·na·tor \di-'näm-ə-ˌnāt-ər\ *n* : the part of a fraction that is below the line

de·no·ta·tive \'dē-nō-ˌtāt-iv, di-'nōt-ət-iv\ *adj* 1 : denoting or tending to denote 2 : relating to denotation

de·note \di-'nōt\ *vb* 1 : to mark out plainly : INDICATE 2 : to make known 3 : MEAN, NAME — **de·no·ta·tion** \ˌdē-nō-'tā-shən\ *n*

de·noue·ment \ˌdā-ˌnü-'mäⁿ\ *n* [F *dénouement,* lit., untying, fr. MF *des-*

nouement, fr. *desnouer* to untie, fr. OF *desnoer,* fr. *noer* to tie, fr. L *nodare,* fr. *nodus* knot] : the final outcome of the dramatic complications in a literary work

de·nounce \di-'naůns\ *vb* **de·nounced; de·nounc·ing** 1 : to point out as deserving blame or punishment 2 : to inform against : ACCUSE 3 : to announce formally the termination of (as a treaty) — **de·nounce·ment** *n*

de no·vo \di-'nō-vō\ *adv* [L] : ANEW, AGAIN

dense \'dens\ *adj* **dens·er; dens·est** 1 : marked by compactness or crowding together of parts : THICK ⟨a ∼ forest⟩ ⟨a ∼ fog⟩ 2 : DULL, STUPID — **dense·ly** *adv* — **dense·ness** *n*

den·si·ty \'den-sət-ē\ *n, pl* **-ties** 1 : the quality or state of being dense 2 : the quantity of something per unit volume, unit area, or unit length

dent \'dent\ *n* 1 : a small depressed place made by a blow or by pressure 2 : an impression or effect made usu. against resistance 3 : initial progress — **dent** *vb*

den·tal \'dent-ᵊl\ *adj* : of or relating to the teeth or dentistry — **den·tal·ly** \-ē\ *adv*

dental floss *n* : a thread used to clean between the teeth

dental hygienist *n* : one who is licensed in the cleaning and examining of teeth

den·tate \'den-ˌtāt\ *adj* : having pointed projections : NOTCHED

den·ti·frice \'dent-ə-frəs\ *n* [MF, fr. L *dentifricium,* fr. *dent-, dens* tooth + *fricare* to rub] : a powder, paste, or liquid for cleaning the teeth

den·tin \'dent-ᵊn\ *or* **den·tine** \'den-ˌtēn, den-'tēn\ *n* : a calcareous material like bone but harder and denser that composes the principal mass of a tooth — **den·tin·al** \den-'tēn-ᵊl, 'dent-ᵊn-əl\ *adj*

den·tist \'dent-əst\ *n* : one who is licensed in the care, treatment, and replacement of teeth — **den·tist·ry** *n*

den·ti·tion \den-'tish-ən\ *n* : the character of a set of teeth esp. with regard to number, kind, and arrangement; *also* : TEETH

den·ture \'den-chər\ *n* : an artificial replacement for teeth

de·nude \di-'n(y)üd\ *vb* **de·nud·ed; de-**

nud·ing : to strip the covering from —
de·nu·da·tion \dē-(ˌ)n(y)ü-ˈdā-shən\ *n*

de·nun·ci·a·tion \di-ˌnən-sē-ˈā-shən\ *n*
: the act of denouncing; *esp* : a public accusation

de·ny \di-ˈnī\ *vb* **de·nied; de·ny·ing 1** : to declare untrue **2** : to refuse to recognize or acknowledge : DISAVOW **3** : to refuse to grant ⟨∼ a request⟩ **4** : to reject as false ⟨∼ a theory⟩

de·o·dar \ˈdē-ə-ˌdär\ *also* **de·o·da·ra** \ˌdē-ə-ˈdär-ə\ *n* [Hindi *deodār*, fr. Skt *devadāru*, lit., timber of the gods, fr. *deva* god + *dāru* wood] : an East Indian cedar

de·odor·ant \dē-ˈōd-ə-rənt\ *n* : a preparation that destroys or masks unpleasant odors

de·odor·ize \dē-ˈōd-ə-ˌrīz\ *vb* : to eliminate the offensive odor of

de·ox·i·dize \dē-ˈäk-sə-ˌdīz\ *vb* : to remove oxygen from

de·oxy·ri·bo·nu·cle·ic acid \dē-ˈäk-si-ˌrī-bō-n(y)ü-ˌklē-ik-\ *n* : DNA

de·oxy·ri·bose \dē-ˌäk-si-ˈrī-ˌbōs\ *n* : a sugar with five carbon and four oxygen atoms in each molecule that is part of DNA

dep *abbr* **1** depart; departure **2** deposit **3** deputy

de·part \di-ˈpärt\ *vb* **1** : to go away : go away from : LEAVE **2** : DIE **3** : to turn aside : DEVIATE

de·part·ment \di-ˈpärt-mənt\ *n* **1** : a distinct sphere : PROVINCE **2** : a functional or territorial division (as of a government, business, or college) — **de·part·men·tal** \di-ˌpärt-ˈment-ᵊl, ˌdē-\ *adj*

department store *n* : a store selling a wide variety of goods arranged in several departments

de·par·ture \di-ˈpär-chər\ *n* **1** : the act of going away **2** : a starting out (as on a journey) **3** : DIVERGENCE

de·pend \di-ˈpend\ *vb* **1** : to be determined by or based on some action or condition ⟨our success ∼s on his cooperation⟩ **2** : TRUST, RELY ⟨you can ∼ on me⟩ **3** : to be dependent esp. for financial support **4** : to hang down ⟨a vine ∼ing from a tree⟩

de·pend·able \di-ˈpen-də-bəl\ *adj* : TRUSTWORTHY, RELIABLE — **de·pend·abil·i·ty** \-ˌpen-də-ˈbil-ət-ē\ *n*

de·pen·dence *also* **de·pen·dance** \di-ˈpen-dəns\ *n* **1** : the quality or state of being dependent; *esp* : the quality or state of being influenced by or subject to another **2** : RELIANCE, TRUST **3** : something on which one relies **4** : drug addiction; *also* : HABITUATION 2

de·pen·den·cy \-dən-sē\ *n, pl* **-cies 1** : DEPENDENCE **2** : a territory under the jurisdiction of a nation but not formally annexed by it

¹**de·pen·dent** \di-ˈpen-dənt\ *adj* **1** : hanging down **2** : determined or conditioned by another; *also* : affected with drug dependence **3** : relying on another for support **4** : subject to another's jurisdiction **5** : SUBORDINATE 4

²**dependent** *also* **de·pen·dant** \-dənt\ *n* : one that is dependent; *esp* : a person who relies on another for support

de·pict \di-ˈpikt\ *vb* **1** : to represent by a picture **2** : to describe in words — **de·pic·tion** \-ˈpik-shən\ *n*

de·pil·a·to·ry \di-ˈpil-ə-ˌtōr-ē\ *n, pl* **-ries** : an agent for removing hair, wool, or bristles

de·plane \dē-ˈplān\ *vb* : to get out of an airplane

de·plete \di-ˈplēt\ *vb* **de·plet·ed; de·plet·ing** : to exhaust esp. of strength or resources — **de·ple·tion** \-ˈplē-shən\ *n*

de·plor·able \di-ˈplōr-ə-bəl\ *adj* **1** : LAMENTABLE **2** : WRETCHED — **de·plor·ably** \-blē\ *adv*

de·plore \-ˈplōr\ *vb* **de·plored; de·plor·ing 1** : to feel or express grief for **2** : to regret strongly **3** : to consider unfortunate or deserving of disapproval

de·ploy \di-ˈploi\ *vb* : to spread out (as troops or ships) in order for battle — **de·ploy·ment** \-mənt\ *n*

de·po·nent \di-ˈpō-nənt\ *n* : one who gives evidence esp. in writing

de·pop·u·late \dē-ˈpäp-yə-ˌlāt\ *vb* : to reduce greatly the population of by destroying or driving away the inhabitants — **de·pop·u·la·tion** \dē-ˌpäp-yə-ˈlā-shən\ *n*

de·port \di-ˈpōrt\ *vb* **1** : CONDUCT, BEHAVE **2** : BANISH, EXILE — **de·por·ta·tion** \ˌdē-ˌpōr-ˈtā-shən\ *n*

de·port·ment \di-ˈpōrt-mənt\ *n* : BEHAVIOR, BEARING

de·pose \di-ˈpōz\ *vb* **de·posed; de·pos·ing 1** : to remove from high office (as of king) **2** : to testify under oath or by affidavit

¹**de·pos·it** \di-'päz-ət\ *vb* **de·pos·it·ed** \-'päz-ət-əd\; **de·pos·it·ing** 1 : to place for safekeeping or as a pledge; *esp* : to put money in a bank 2 : to lay down : PUT 3 : to let fall or sink ⟨sand and silt ∼*ed* by a flood⟩ — **de·pos·i·tor** \-'päz-ət-ər\ *n*

²**deposit** *n* 1 : the state of being deposited ⟨money on ∼⟩ 2 : something placed for safekeeping; *esp* : money deposited in a bank 3 : money given as a pledge 4 : an act of depositing 5 : something laid or thrown down ⟨a ∼ of silt by a river⟩ 6 : an accumulation of mineral matter (as ore, oil, or gas) in nature

de·po·si·tion \ˌdep-ə-'zish-ən, ˌdē-pə-\ *n* 1 : an act of removing from a position of authority 2 : TESTIMONY 3 : the process of depositing 4 : DEPOSIT

de·pos·i·to·ry \di-'päz-ə-ˌtōr-ē\ *n, pl* **-ries** : a place where something is deposited esp. for safekeeping

de·pot *1, 2 usu* 'dep-ō, *3 usu* 'dēp-\ *n* 1 : STOREHOUSE 2 : a place where military supplies are kept or where troops are assembled and trained 3 : a building for railroad or bus passengers : STATION

depr *abbr* depreciation

de·prave \di-'prāv\ *vb* **de·praved**; **de·prav·ing** [ME *depraven*, fr. MF *depraver*, fr. L *depravare* to pervert, fr. *pravus* crooked, bad] : CORRUPT, PERVERT — **de·praved** *adj* — **de·prav·i·ty** \-'prav-ət-ē\ *n*

dep·re·cate \'dep-ri-ˌkāt\ *vb* **-cat·ed**; **-cat·ing** [L *deprecari* to avert by prayer, fr. *precari* to pray] 1 : to express disapproval of 2 : DEPRECIATE — **dep·re·ca·tion** \ˌdep-ri-'kā-shən\ *n*

dep·re·ca·to·ry \'dep-ri-kə-ˌtōr-ē\ *adj* 1 : expressing deprecation : APOLOGETIC 2 : serving to deprecate

de·pre·ci·ate \di-'prē-shē-ˌāt\ *vb* **-at·ed**; **-at·ing** [LL *depretiare*, fr. L *pretium* price] 1 : to lessen in price or value 2 : UNDERVALUE, BELITTLE, DISPARAGE — **de·pre·ci·a·tion** \-ˌprē-shē-'ā-shən\ *n*

dep·re·da·tion \ˌdep-rə-'dā-shən\ *n* : a laying waste or plundering — **dep·re·date** \'dep-rə-ˌdāt\ *vb*

de·press \di-'pres\ *vb* 1 : to press down : cause to sink to a lower position 2 : to lessen the activity or force of 3 : SADDEN, DISCOURAGE 4 : to lessen in price or value — **de·pres·sor** \di-'pres-ər\ *n*

de·pres·sant \di-'pres-ᵊnt\ *n* : one that depresses; *esp* : an agent that reduces bodily functional activity — **depressant** *adj*

de·pressed \di-'prest\ *adj* 1 : low in spirits; *also* : affected with emotional depression 2 : suffering from economic depression

de·pres·sion \di-'presh-ən\ *n* 1 : an act of depressing : a state of being depressed 2 : a pressing down : LOWERING 3 : a state of feeling sad 4 : an emotional disorder marked esp. by sadness, inactivity, difficulty in thinking and concentration, and feelings of dejection 5 : a depressed area or part 6 : a period of low general economic activity with widespread unemployment

¹**de·pres·sive** \di-'pres-iv\ *adj* 1 : tending to depress 2 : characterized or affected by psychological depression

²**depressive** *n* : one who is psychologically depressed

de·pri·va·tion \ˌdep-rə-'vā-shən\ *n* : an act or instance of depriving : LOSS; *also* : PRIVATION

de·prive \di-'prīv\ *vb* **de·prived**; **de·priv·ing** 1 : to take something away from ⟨∼ a king of his power⟩ 2 : to stop from having something

dept *abbr* department

depth \'depth\ *n, pl* **depths** \'dep(th)s\ 1 : something that is deep; *esp* : the deep part of a body of water 2 : a part that is far from the outside or surface ⟨the ∼s of the woods⟩ 3 : ABYSS 4 : the middle or innermost part ⟨the ∼ of winter⟩ 5 : an extreme state (as of misery); *also* : the worst part ⟨the ∼s of despair⟩ 6 : the perpendicular distance downward from a surface; *also* : the distance from front to back 7 : the quality of being deep 8 : the degree of intensity

depth charge *n* : an explosive device for use underwater esp. against submarines

dep·u·ta·tion \ˌdep-yə-'tā-shən\ *n* 1 : the act of appointing a deputy 2 : DELEGATION

de·pute \di-'pyüt\ *vb* **de·put·ed**; **de·put·ing** : DELEGATE

dep·u·tize \'dep-yə-ˌtīz\ *vb* **-tized; -tiz-ing** : to appoint as deputy

dep·u·ty \'dep-yət-ē\ *n, pl* **-ties 1** : a person appointed to act for or in place of another **2** : an assistant empowered to act as a substitute in the absence of his superior **3** : a member of a lower house of a legislative assembly

der *or* **deriv** *abbr* derivation; derivative

de·rail \di-'rāl\ *vb* : to cause to run off the rails — **de·rail·ment** *n*

de·rail·leur \di-'rā-lər\ *n* [F *dérailleur*] : a device for shifting gears on a bicycle by moving the chain from one set of exposed gears to another

de·range \di-'rānj\ *vb* **de·ranged; de·rang·ing 1** : DISARRANGE, UPSET **2** : to make insane — **de·range·ment** *n*

der·by \'dər-bē, *Brit* 'där-\ *n, pl* **derbies 1** : a horse race usu. for three-year-olds held annually **2** : a race or contest open to all **3** : a man's stiff felt hat with dome-shaped crown and narrow brim

¹**der·e·lict** \'der-ə-ˌlikt\ *adj* **1** : abandoned by the owner or occupant ⟨a ∼ ship⟩ **2** : NEGLIGENT ⟨∼ in his duty⟩

²**derelict** *n* **1** : something voluntarily abandoned; *esp* : a ship abandoned on the high seas **2** : a destitute homeless social misfit : VAGRANT, BUM

der·e·lic·tion \ˌder-ə-'lik-shən\ *n* **1** : the act of abandoning : the state of being abandoned **2** : a failure in duty

de·ride \di-'rīd\ *vb* **de·rid·ed; de·rid·ing** [L *deridēre*, fr. *ridēre* to laugh] : to laugh at scornfully : make fun of : RID-ICULE — **de·ri·sion** \-'rizh-ən\ *n* — **de·ri·sive** \-'rī-siv\ *adj* — **de·ri·sive·ly** *adv* — **de·ri·so·ry** \-'rī-sə-rē\ *adj*

de ri·gueur \də-rē-'gər\ *adj* [F] : prescribed or required by fashion, etiquette, or custom

der·i·va·tion \ˌder-ə-'vā-shən\ *n* **1** : the formation of a word from an earlier word or root; *also* : an act of ascertaining or stating the derivation of a word **2** : ETYMOLOGY **3** : SOURCE, ORIGIN; *also* : DESCENT **4** : an act or process of deriving

¹**de·riv·a·tive** \di-'riv-ət-iv\ *n* **1** : a word formed by derivation **2** : something derived

²**derivative** *adj* : derived from something else

de·rive \di-'rīv\ *vb* **de·rived; de·riv·ing**

[ME *deriven*, fr. MF *deriver*, fr. L *derivare*, fr. *de-* from + *rivus* stream] **1** : to receive or obtain from a source **2** : to obtain from a parent substance **3** : INFER, DEDUCE **4** : to trace the origin, descent, or derivation of **5** : to come from a certain source

der·mal \'dər-məl\ *adj* : of or relating to the skin

der·ma·ti·tis \ˌdər-mə-'tīt-əs\ *n* : skin inflammation

der·ma·tol·o·gy \-'täl-ə-jē\ *n* : a branch of science dealing with the skin and its disorders — **der·ma·tol·o·gist** \-jəst\ *n*

der·mis \'dər-məs\ *n* : the sensitive vascular inner layer of the skin

der·o·gate \'der-ə-ˌgāt\ *vb* **-gat·ed; -gat-ing 1** : to cause to seem inferior : DIS-PARAGE **2** : DETRACT — **der·o·ga·tion** \ˌder-ə-'gā-shən\ *n*

de·rog·a·to·ry \di-'räg-ə-ˌtōr-ē\ *adj* : intended to lower the reputation of a person or thing : DISPARAGING

der·rick \'der-ik\ *n* [obs. *derrick* hangman, gallows, fr. *Derick*, name of 17th cent. E hangman] **1** : a hoisting apparatus : CRANE **2** : a framework over a drill hole (as for oil) supporting machinery

der·ri·ere *or* **der·ri·ère** \ˌder-ē-'eər\ *n* : BUTTOCKS

der·ring–do \ˌder-iŋ-'dü\ *n* : daring action : DARING

der·rin·ger \'der-ən-jər\ *n* : a short-barreled pocket pistol

der·vish \'dər-vish\ *n* [Turk *derviş*, lit., beggar, fr. Per *darvēsh*] : a member of a Muslim religious order noted for devotional exercises (as bodily movements leading to a trance)

de·sal·i·nate \dē-'sal-ə-ˌnāt\ *vb* **-nat·ed; -nat·ing** : DESALT — **de·sal·i·na·tion** \-ˌsal-ə-'nā-shən\ *n*

de·sal·i·nize \dē-'sal-ə-ˌnīz\ *vb* **-nized; -niz·ing** : DESALT — **de·sal·i·ni·za·tion** \-ˌsal-ə-nə-'zā-shən\ *n*

de·salt \dē-'sȯlt\ *vb* : to remove salt from ⟨∼ seawater⟩ — **de·salt·er** *n*

des·cant \'des-ˌkant\ *vb* **1** : to sing or play part music : SING **2** : to discourse or write at length

de·scend \di-'send\ *vb* **1** : to pass from a higher to a lower place or level : pass, move, or climb down or down along **2** : DERIVE ⟨∼ed from royalty⟩ **3** : to pass by inheritance or transmission **4** : to incline, lead, or extend downward **5** : to swoop down in a sudden attack

¹de·scen·dant *or* **de·scen·dent** \di-ˈsen-dənt\ *adj* **1** : DESCENDING **2** : proceeding from an ancestor or source

²descendant *or* **descendent** *n* **1** : one descended from another or from a common stock **2** : one deriving directly from a precursor or prototype

de·scent \di-ˈsent\ *n* **1** : ANCESTRY, BIRTH, LINEAGE **2** : the act or process of descending **3** : SLOPE **4** : a descending way (as a downgrade) **5** : a sudden hostile raid or assault **6** : a downward step (as in station or value) : DECLINE

de·scribe \di-ˈskrīb\ *vb* **de·scribed; de·scrib·ing 1** : to represent or give an account of in words **2** : to trace the outline of — **de·scrib·able** *adj*

de·scrip·tion \di-ˈskrip-shən\ *n* **1** : an account of something; *esp* : an account that presents a picture to a person who reads or hears it **2** : KIND, SORT — **de·scrip·tive** \-ˈskrip-tiv\ *adj*

de·scry \di-ˈskrī\ *vb* **de·scried; de·scry·ing 1** : to catch sight of **2** : to discover by observation or investigation

des·e·crate \ˈdes-i-ˌkrāt\ *vb* **-crat·ed; -crat·ing** : PROFANE — **des·e·cra·tion** \ˌdes-i-ˈkrā-shən\ *n*

de·seg·re·gate \dē-ˈseg-ri-ˌgāt\ *vb* : to eliminate segregation in; *esp* : to free of any law, provision, or practice requiring isolation of the members of a particular race in separate units — **de·seg·re·ga·tion** \dē-ˌseg-ri-ˈgā-shən\ *n*

de·sen·si·tize \dē-ˈsen-sə-ˌtīz\ *vb* : to make (a sensitized or hypersensitive individual) insensitive or nonreactive to a sensitizing agent — **de·sen·si·ti·za·tion** \dē-ˌsen-sət-ə-ˈzā-shən\ *n*

¹des·ert \ˈdez-ərt\ *n* : a dry barren region incapable of supporting a population without an artificial water supply

²des·ert \ˈdez-ərt\ *adj* : of, relating to, or resembling a desert; *esp* : being barren and without life ⟨a ~ island⟩

³de·sert \di-ˈzərt\ *n* **1** : worthiness of reward or punishment **2** : a just reward or punishment

⁴de·sert \di-ˈzərt\ *vb* **1** : to withdraw from **2** : FORSAKE — **de·sert·er** *n* — **de·ser·tion** \-ˈzər-shən\ *n*

de·serve \di-ˈzərv\ *vb* **de·served; de·serv·ing** : to be worthy of : MERIT — **de·serv·ing** *adj*

de·served·ly \-ˈzər-vəd-lē\ *adv* : according to merit : JUSTLY

des·ic·cate \ˈdes-i-ˌkāt\ *vb* **-cat·ed; -cat·ing** : DRY, DEHYDRATE — **des·ic·ca·tor** \ˈdes-i-ˌkāt-ər\ *n*

de·sid·er·a·tum \di-ˌsid-ə-ˈrät-əm, -ˌzid-, -ˈrāt-\ *n, pl* **-ta** \-ə\ [L] : something desired as essential or needed

¹de·sign \di-ˈzīn\ *vb* **1** : to conceive and plan out in the mind **2** : INTEND **3** : to devise for a specific function or end **4** : to make a pattern or sketch of **5** : to conceive and draw the plans for ⟨~ an airplane⟩

²design *n* **1** : a particular purpose : deliberate planning **2** : a mental project or scheme : PLAN **3** : a secret project or scheme : PLOT **4** *pl* : aggressive or evil intent — used with *on* or *against* **5** : a preliminary sketch or plan : DELINEATION **6** : an underlying scheme that governs functioning, developing, or unfolding : MOTIF **7** : the arrangement of elements or details in a product or a work of art **8** : a decorative pattern **9** : the art of executing designs

¹des·ig·nate \ˈdez-ig-ˌnāt, -nət\ *adj* : chosen for an office but not yet installed ⟨ambassador ~⟩

²des·ig·nate \-ˌnāt\ *vb* **-nat·ed; -nat·ing 1** : to appoint or choose by name for a special purpose **2** : to mark or point out : INDICATE; *also* : SPECIFY, STIPULATE **3** : to call by a name or title — **des·ig·na·tion** \ˌdez-ig-ˈnā-shən\ *n*

designated hitter *n* : a baseball player designated at the start of the game to bat in place of the pitcher without causing the pitcher to be removed from the game

de·sign·er \di-ˈzī-nər\ *n* **1** : one who creates plans for a project or structure **2** : one who designs and manufactures high-fashion clothing — **designer** *adj*

de·sign·ing \di-ˈzī-niŋ\ *adj* : CRAFTY, SCHEMING

de·sir·able \di-ˈzī-rə-bəl\ *adj* **1** : PLEASING, ATTRACTIVE ⟨a ~ woman⟩ **2** : ADVISABLE ⟨~ legislation⟩ — **de·sir·abil·i·ty** \-ˌzī-rə-ˈbil-ət-ē\ *n*

¹de·sire \di-ˈzī(ə)r\ *vb* **de·sired; de·sir·ing** [ME *desiren*, fr. OF *desirer*, fr. L *desiderare*, fr. *sider-, sidus* star] **1** : to long, hope, or wish for : COVET 2 : REQUEST

²desire *n* 1 : a strong wish : LONGING, CRAVING 2 : an expressed wish : REQUEST 3 : something desired

de·sir·ous \di-ˈzīr-əs\ *adj* : eagerly wishing : DESIRING

de·sist \di-ˈzist, -ˈsist\ *vb* : to cease to proceed or act

desk \ˈdesk\ *n* [ME *deske*, fr. ML *desca*, fr. It *desco* table, fr. L *discus* dish, disc] 1 : a table, frame, or case esp. for writing and reading 2 : a counter, stand, or booth at which a person performs duties 3 : a specialized division of an organization (as a newspaper) ⟨city ∼⟩

¹des·o·late \ˈdes-ə-lət, ˈdez-\ *adj* 1 : DESERTED, ABANDONED 2 : FORSAKEN, LONELY 3 : DILAPIDATED 4 : BARREN, LIFELESS 5 : CHEERLESS, GLOOMY — **des·o·late·ly** *adv*

²des·o·late \-ˌlāt\ *vb* **-lat·ed; -lat·ing** : to make desolate : lay waste : make wretched

des·o·la·tion \ˌdes-ə-ˈlā-shən, ˌdez-\ *n* 1 : the action of desolating 2 : GRIEF, SADNESS 3 : LONELINESS 4 : DEVASTATION, RUIN 5 : barren wasteland

des·oxy·ri·bo·nu·cle·ic acid \de-ˌzäk-sē-ˈrī-bō-n(y)ü-ˌklē-ik-\ *n* : DNA

¹de·spair \di-ˈspaər\ *vb* : to lose all hope or confidence — **de·spair·ing** *adj* — **de·spair·ing·ly** *adv*

²despair *n* 1 : utter loss of hope 2 : a cause of hopelessness

des·patch \dis-ˈpach\ var of DISPATCH

des·per·a·do \ˌdes-pə-ˈräd-ō, -ˈrad-\ *n*, *pl* **-does** *or* **-dos** : a bold or reckless criminal

des·per·ate \ˈdes-p(ə-)rət\ *adj* 1 : being beyond or almost beyond hope : causing despair 2 : RASH 3 : extremely intense — **des·per·ate·ly** *adv*

des·per·a·tion \ˌdes-pə-ˈrā-shən\ *n* 1 : a loss of hope and surrender to despair 2 : a state of hopelessness leading to rashness

des·pi·ca·ble \di-ˈspik-ə-bəl, ˈdes-pik-\ *adj* : deserving to be despised — **de·spi·ca·bly** \-blē\ *adv*

de·spise \di-ˈspīz\ *vb* **de·spised; de·spising** 1 : to look down on with contempt or aversion : DISDAIN, DETEST 2 : to regard as negligible, worthless, or distasteful

de·spite \di-ˈspīt\ *prep* : in spite of

de·spoil \di-ˈspȯil\ *vb* : to strip of belongings, possessions, or value — **de·spoil·er** *n* — **de·spoil·ment** *n*

de·spo·li·a·tion \di-ˌspō-lē-ˈā-shən\ *n* : the act of plundering : the state of being despoiled

¹de·spond \di-ˈspänd\ *vb* : to become discouraged or disheartened

²despond *n* : DESPONDENCY

de·spon·den·cy \-ˈspän-dən-sē\ *n* : DEJECTION, HOPELESSNESS — **de·spon·dent** \-dənt\ *adj*

des·pot \ˈdes-pət, -ˌpät\ *n* [MF *despote*, fr. Gk *despotēs* master] 1 : a ruler with absolute power and authority : AUTOCRAT, TYRANT 2 : a person exercising power abusively, oppressively, or tyrannously — **des·pot·ic** \des-ˈpätik\ *adj* — **des·po·tism** \ˈdes-pə-ˌtiz-əm\ *n*

des·sert \di-ˈzərt\ *n* : a course of sweet food, fruit, or cheese served at the close of a meal

des·ti·na·tion \ˌdes-tə-ˈnā-shən\ *n* 1 : a purpose for which something is destined 2 : an act of appointing, setting aside for a purpose, or predetermining 3 : a place to which one is journeying or to which something is sent

des·tine \ˈdes-tən\ *vb* **des·tined; des·tining** 1 : to settle in advance 2 : to designate, assign, or dedicate in advance 3 : to be bound or directed ⟨freight *destined* for English ports⟩

des·ti·ny \ˈdes-tə-nē\ *n*, *pl* **-nies** 1 : something to which a person or thing is destined : FATE, FORTUNE 2 : a predetermined course of events

des·ti·tute \ˈdes-tə-ˌt(y)üt\ *adj* 1 : lacking something needed or desirable 2 : extremely poor — **des·ti·tu·tion** \ˌdes-tə-ˈt(y)ü-shən\ *n*

de·stroy \di-ˈstrȯi\ *vb* 1 : to put an end to : RUIN 2 : KILL

de·stroy·er \di-ˈstrȯi(-ə)r\ *n* 1 : one that destroys 2 : a small speedy warship

¹de·struct \di-ˈstrəkt\ *vb* : DESTROY

²destruct *n* : the deliberate destruction of a rocket after launching

de·struc·ti·ble \di-ˈstrək-tə-bəl\ *adj* : capable of being destroyed — **de·struc·ti·bil·i·ty** \di-ˌstrək-tə-ˈbil-ət-ē\ *n*

de·struc·tion \di-ˈstrək-shən\ *n* 1 : RUIN 2 : the action or process of destroying something 3 : a destroying agency

de·struc·tive \di-'strək-tiv\ *adj* **1** : causing destruction : RUINOUS **2** : designed or tending to destroy — **de·struc·tive·ly** *adv* — **de·struc·tive·ness** *n*

de·struc·tor \di-'strək-tər\ *n* : a furnace for burning refuse : INCINERATOR

de·sue·tude \'des-wi-ˌt(y)üd\ *n* : DISUSE

des·ul·to·ry \'des-əl-ˌtōr-ē\ *adj* : passing aimlessly from one thing or subject to another : DISCONNECTED

det *abbr* **1** detached; detachment **2** detail

de·tach \di-'tach\ *vb* **1** : to separate esp. from a larger mass **2** : DISENGAGE, WITHDRAW — **de·tach·able** *adj*

de·tached \di-'tacht\ *adj* **1** : not joined or connected : SEPARATE **2** : ALOOF, IMPARTIAL ⟨a ∼ attitude⟩

de·tach·ment \di-'tach-mənt\ *n* **1** : SEPARATION **2** : the dispatching of a body of troops or part of a fleet from the main body for special service; *also* : the portion so dispatched **3** : a small permanent military unit different in composition from normal units **4** : indifference to worldly concerns : ALOOFNESS, UNWORLDLINESS **5** : IMPARTIALITY

¹de·tail \di-'tāl, 'dē-ˌtāl\ *n* [F *détail*, fr. OF *detail* slice, piece, fr. *detaillier* to cut in pieces, fr. *taillier* to cut] **1** : a dealing with something item by item ⟨go into ∼⟩; *also* : ITEM, PARTICULAR ⟨the ∼s of a story⟩ **2** : selection (as of soldiers) for special duty; *also* : the persons thus selected

²detail *vb* **1** : to report in detail **2** : ENUMERATE, SPECIFY **3** : to select for some special duty

de·tain \di-'tān\ *vb* **1** : to hold in or as if in custody **2** : STOP, DELAY

de·tect \di-'tekt\ *vb* : to discover the nature, existence, presence, or fact of — **de·tect·able** *adj* — **de·tec·tion** \-'tek-shən\ *n* — **de·tec·tor** \-tər\ *n*

¹de·tec·tive \di-'tek-tiv\ *adj* **1** : fitted or used for detection ⟨a ∼ device for coal gas⟩ **2** : of or relating to detectives

²detective *n* : a person employed or engaged in detecting lawbreakers or getting information that is not readily accessible

dé·tente \dā-'tänt\ *n* [F] : a relaxation of strained relations or tensions (as between nations)

de·ten·tion \di-'ten-chən\ *n* **1** : the act or fact of detaining : CONFINEMENT; *esp* : a period of temporary custody prior to disposition by a court **2** : a forced delay

de·ter \di-'tər\ *vb* **de·terred; de·ter·ring** [L *deterrēre*, fr. *terrēre* to frighten] **1** : to turn aside, discourage, or prevent from acting (as by fear) **2** : INHIBIT

de·ter·gent \di-'tər-jənt\ *n* : a cleansing agent; *esp* : a chemical product similar to soap in its cleaning ability

de·te·ri·o·rate \di-'tir-ē-ə-ˌrāt\ *vb* **-rat·ed; -rat·ing** : to make or grow worse : DEGENERATE — **de·te·ri·o·ra·tion** \-ˌtir-ē-ə-'rā-shən\ *n*

de·ter·min·able \-'tər-mə-nə-bəl\ *adj* : capable of being determined; *esp* : ASCERTAINABLE

de·ter·mi·nant \-mə-nənt\ *n* **1** : something that determines or conditions **2** : a hereditary factor : GENE

de·ter·mi·nate \di-'tər-mə-nət\ *adj* **1** : having fixed limits : DEFINITE **2** : definitely settled — **de·ter·mi·na·cy** \-nə-sē\ *n* — **de·ter·mi·nate·ness** *n*

de·ter·mi·na·tion \di-ˌtər-mə-'nā-shən\ *n* **1** : the act of coming to a decision; *also* : the decision or conclusion reached **2** : the act of fixing the extent, position, or character of something **3** : accurate measurement (as of length or volume) **4** : firm or fixed purpose

de·ter·mine \di-'tər-mən\ *vb* **-mined; -min·ing** \-'tərm-(ə-)niŋ\ **1** : to fix conclusively or authoritatively **2** : to come to a decision : SETTLE, RESOLVE **3** : to fix the form or character of beforehand : ORDAIN; *also* : REGULATE **4** : to find out the limits, nature, dimensions, or scope of ⟨∼ a position at sea⟩ **5** : to be the cause of or reason for : DECIDE

de·ter·mined \-'tər-mənd\ *adj* **1** : DECIDED, RESOLVED **2** : FIRM, RESOLUTE — **de·ter·mined·ly** \-mən-dlē, -mə-nəd-lē\ *adv* — **de·ter·mined·ness** \-mən(d)-nəs\ *n*

de·ter·min·ism \di-'tər-mə-ˌniz-əm\ *n* : a doctrine that acts of the will, natural events, or social changes are determined by preceding events or natural causes — **de·ter·min·ist** \-nəst\ *n or adj*

de·ter·rence \di-'tər-əns\ *n* : the act, process, or capacity of deterring

de·ter·rent \-ənt\ *adj* **1** : serving to deter **2** : relating to deterrence — **deterrent** *n*

de·test \di-'test\ *vb* [ME *detesten*, fr. L *detestari*, lit., to curse while calling a deity to witness, fr. *de-* from + *testari* to call to witness] : LOATHE, HATE — **de·test·able** *adj* — **de·tes·ta·tion** \ˌdē-ˌtes-'tā-shən\ *n*

de·throne \di-'thrōn\ *vb* : to remove from a throne : DEPOSE — **de·throne·ment** *n*

det·o·nate \'det-ᵊn-ˌāt, 'det-ə-ˌnāt\ *vb* **-nat·ed; -nat·ing** : to explode or cause to explode with violence — **det·o·na·tion** \ˌdet-ᵊn-'ā-shən, ˌdet-ə-'nā-\ *n*

det·o·na·tor \'det-ᵊn-ˌāt-ər, -ə-ˌnāt-\ *n* : a device for detonating a high explosive

¹de·tour \'dē-ˌtůr\ *n* : a roundabout way temporarily replacing part of a route

²detour *vb* : to go by detour

de·tox·i·fy \dē-'täk-sə-ˌfī\ *vb* **-fied; -fy·ing 1** : to remove a poison or toxin or the effect of such from **2** : to free (as a drug user or alcoholic) from an intoxicating or addictive substance or from dependence on it — **de·tox·i·fi·ca·tion** \dē-ˌtäk-sə-fə-'kā-shən\ *n*

de·tract \di-'trakt\ *vb* **1** : to take away : WITHDRAW, SUBTRACT **2** : DISTRACT — **de·trac·tion** \-'trak-shən\ *n* — **de·trac·tor** \-'trak-tər\ *n*

de·train \dē-'trān\ *vb* : to leave or cause to leave a railroad train

det·ri·ment \'de-trə-mənt\ *n* : injury or damage or its cause : HURT — **det·ri·men·tal** \ˌde-trə-'ment-ᵊl\ *adj* — **det·ri·men·tal·ly** \-ē\ *adv*

de·tri·tus \di-'trīt-əs\ *n, pl* **de·tri·tus** : fragments resulting from disintegration (as of rocks) : DEBRIS

deuce \'d(y)üs\ *n* **1** : a two in cards or dice **2** : a tie in tennis with both sides at 40 **3** : DEVIL — used chiefly as a mild oath

Deut *abbr* Deuteronomy

deu·te·ri·um \d(y)ü-'tir-ē-əm\ *n* : the isotope of hydrogen that is of twice the mass of ordinary hydrogen

Deu·ter·on·o·my \ˌd(y)üt-ə-'rän-ə-mē\ *n* — see BIBLE table

deut·sche mark \ˌdȯi-chə-'märk\ *n* — see MONEY table

dev *abbr* deviation

de·val·ue \dē-'val-yü\ *vb* : to reduce the international exchange value of ⟨~ a currency⟩ — **de·val·u·a·tion** \dē-ˌval-yə-'wā-shən\ *n*

dev·as·tate \'dev-ə-ˌstāt\ *vb* **-tat·ed; -tat·ing 1** : to bring to ruin : lay waste **2** : to reduce to chaos, disorder, or helplessness — **dev·as·ta·tion** \ˌdev-ə-'stā-shən\ *n*

de·vel·op \di-'vel-əp\ *vb* **1** : to unfold gradually or in detail **2** : to place (exposed photographic material) in chemicals in order to make the image visible **3** : to bring out the possibilities of **4** : to make more available or usable ⟨~ natural resources⟩ **5** : to acquire gradually ⟨~ a taste for olives⟩ **6** : to go through a natural process of growth and differentiation : EVOLVE **7** : to become apparent — **de·vel·op·er** *n* — **de·vel·op·ment** *n* — **de·vel·op·men·tal** \-ˌvel-əp-'ment-ᵊl\ *adj*

de·vi·ant \'dē-vē-ənt\ *adj* : deviating esp. from some accepted norm (as of behavior) — **de·vi·ance** \-əns\ *n* — **de·vi·an·cy** \-ən-sē\ *n* — **deviant** *n*

de·vi·ate \'dē-vē-ˌāt\ *vb* **-at·ed; -at·ing** [LL *deviare*, fr. L *de-* from + *via* way] : to turn aside from a course, standard, principle, or topic — **de·vi·ate** \-vē-ət, -vē-ˌāt\ *n* — **de·vi·a·tion** \ˌdē-vē-'ā-shən\ *n*

de·vice \di-'vīs\ *n* **1** : SCHEME, STRATAGEM **2** : a piece of equipment or a mechanism for a special purpose **3** : DESIRE, INCLINATION ⟨left to his own ~s⟩ **4** : an emblematic design

¹dev·il \'dev-əl\ *n* [ME *devel*, fr. OE *dēofol*, fr. LL *diabolus*, fr. Gk *diabolos*, lit., slanderer, fr. *diaballein* to throw across, slander, fr. *dia-* across + *ballein* to throw] **1** *often cap* : the personal supreme spirit of evil **2** : DEMON **3** : a wicked person **4** : a reckless or dashing person **5** : FELLOW ⟨poor ~⟩ ⟨lucky ~⟩

²devil *vb* **-iled** *or* **-illed; -il·ing** *or* **-il·ling** \'dev-(ə-)liŋ\ **1** : to chop fine and season highly ⟨~ed eggs⟩ **2** : TEASE, ANNOY

dev·il·ish \'dev-(ə-)lish\ *adj* **1** : resembling or befitting a devil **2** : EXTREME, EXCESSIVE — **dev·il·ish·ly** *adv* — **dev·il·ish·ness** *n*

dev·il·ment \'dev-əl-mənt, -ˌment\ *n* : MISCHIEF

dev·il·ry \-rē\ *or* **dev·il·try** \-trē\ *n, pl*

-il·ries *or* **-il·tries 1** : action performed with the help of the devil **2** : reckless mischievousness

de·vi·ous \'dē-vē-əs\ *adj* **1** : deviating from a straight line : ROUNDABOUT **2** : ERRING **3** : TRICKY

¹de·vise \di-'vīz\ *vb* **de·vised; de·vis·ing 1** : INVENT **2** : PLOT **3** : to give (real estate) by will

²devise *n* **1** : a disposing of real property by will **2** : a will or clause of a will disposing of real property **3** : property given by will

de·vi·tal·ize \dē-'vīt-ᵊl-ˌīz\ *vb* : to deprive of life or vitality

de·void \di-'vȯid\ *adj* : entirely lacking : DESTITUTE ⟨a book ~ of interest⟩

de·voir \dəv-'wär\ *n* **1** : DUTY **2** : a formal act of civility or respect

de·volve \di-'välv\ *vb* **de·volved; de·volv·ing** : to pass from one person to another by succession or transmission — **dev·o·lu·tion** \ˌdev-ə-'lü-shən, ˌdē-və-\ *n*

De·vo·ni·an \di-'vō-nē-ən\ *adj* : of, relating to, or being the period of the Paleozoic era between the Silurian and the Mississippian — **Devonian** *n*

de·vote \di-'vōt\ *vb* **de·vot·ed; de·vot·ing 1** : to set apart for a special purpose : DEDICATE **2** : to give up to wholly or chiefly

de·vot·ed \-'vōt-əd\ *adj* : characterized by loyalty and devotion

dev·o·tee \ˌdev-ə-'tē, -'tā\ *n* : an ardent follower, supporter, or enthusiast (as of a religion, art form, or sport)

de·vo·tion \di-'vō-shən\ *n* **1** : religious fervor **2** : an act of prayer or private worship — usu. used in pl. **3** : a religious exercise for private use **4** : the act of devoting or quality of being devoted ⟨~ to music⟩ **5** : strong love or affection — **de·vo·tion·al** \-sh(ə-)nəl\ *adj*

de·vour \di-'vau̇(ə)r\ *vb* **1** : to eat up greedily or ravenously **2** : WASTE, ANNIHILATE **3** : to take in eagerly by the senses or mind ⟨~ a book⟩ — **de·vour·er** *n*

de·vout \di-'vau̇t\ *adj* **1** : devoted to religion : PIOUS **2** : expressing devotion or piety **3** : EARNEST, SINCERE — **de·vout·ly** *adv* — **de·vout·ness** *n*

dew \'d(y)ü\ *n* : moisture that con-

denses on the surfaces of cool bodies at night — **dewy** *adj*

DEW *abbr* distant early warning

dew·ber·ry \'d(y)ü-ˌber-ē\ *n* : any of several sweet edible berries related to and resembling blackberries

dew·claw \-ˌklȯ\ *n* : a digit on the foot of a mammal that does not reach the ground; *also* : its claw or hoof

dew·drop \-ˌdräp\ *n* : a drop of dew

dew·lap \-ˌlap\ *n* : loose skin hanging under the neck of various animals (as a bovine)

dew point *n* : the temperature at which the moisture in the air begins to condense

dex·ter·i·ty \dek-'ster-ət-ē\ *n, pl* **-ties 1** : mental skill or quickness **2** : readiness and grace in physical activity; *esp* : skill and ease in using the hands

dex·ter·ous *or* **dex·trous** \'dek-strəs\ *adj* **1** : CLEVER **2** : done with skillfulness **3** : skillful and competent with the hands — **dex·ter·ous·ly** *adv*

dex·trose \'dek-ˌstrōs\ *n* : the naturally occurring form of glucose found in plants and blood

DFC *abbr* Distinguished Flying Cross

DFM *abbr* Distinguished Flying Medal

DG *abbr* **1** [LL *Dei gratia*] by the grace of God **2** director general

DH *abbr* designated hitter

dhow \'dau̇\ *n* : an Arab sailing ship usu. having a long overhang forward and a high poop

DI *abbr* drill instructor

dia *abbr* diameter

di·a·be·tes \ˌdī-ə-'bēt-ēz, -'bēt-əs\ *n* : an abnormal state marked by passage of excessive amounts of urine; *esp* : one (**diabetes mel·li·tus** \-'mel-ət-əs\) in which insulin is deficient and the urine and blood contain excess sugar — **di·a·bet·ic** \-'bet-ik\ *adj or n*

di·a·bol·ic \ˌdī-ə-'bäl-ik\ *or* **di·a·bol·i·cal** \-i-kəl\ *adj* : DEVILISH, FIENDISH — **di·a·bol·i·cal·ly** \-k(ə-)lē\ *adv*

di·a·crit·ic \ˌdī-ə-'krit-ik\ *n* : a mark accompanying a letter and indicating a sound value different from that of the same letter when unmarked — **di·a·crit·i·cal** \-'krit-i-kəl\ *adj*

di·a·dem \'dī-ə-ˌdem\ *n* : CROWN; *esp* : a band worn on or around the head as a badge of royalty

di·aer·e·sis \dī-'er-ə-səs\ *n, pl* **-e·ses**

\-ˌsēz\ : a mark¨ placed over a vowel to show that it is pronounced in a separate syllable (as in *naïve*)

diag *abbr* **1** diagonal **2** diagram

di·ag·no·sis \ˌdī-ig-ˈnō-səs, -əg-\ *n, pl* **-no·ses** \-ˌsēz\ : the art or act of identifying a disease from its signs and symptoms; *also* : the decision reached by diagnosis — **di·ag·nose** \ˈdī-ig-ˌnōs, -əg-\ *vb* — **di·ag·nos·tic** \ˌdī-ig-ˈnäs-tik, -əg-\ *adj* — **di·ag·nos·ti·cian** \-ˌnäs-ˈtish-ən\ *n*

¹**di·ag·o·nal** \dī-ˈag-(ə-)nəl\ *adj* **1** : extending from one corner to the opposite corner in a 4-sided figure **2** : running in a slanting direction ⟨∼ stripes⟩ **3** : having slanting markings or parts ⟨a ∼ weave⟩ — **di·ag·o·nal·ly** \-ē\ *adv*

²**diagonal** *n* **1** : a diagonal line **2** : a diagonal direction **3** : a diagonal row, arrangement, or pattern

¹**di·a·gram** \ˈdī-ə-ˌgram\ *n* : a drawing, sketch, plan, or chart that makes something easier to understand — **di·a·gram·mat·ic** \ˌdī-ə-grə-ˈmat-ik\ *adj* — **di·a·gram·mat·i·cal·ly** \-i-k(ə-)lē\ *adv*

²**diagram** *vb* **-gramed** \-ˌgramd\ *or* **-grammed; -gram·ing** \-ˌgram-iŋ\ *or* **-gram·ming** : to represent by a diagram

¹**di·al** \ˈdī(-ə)l\ *n* [ME, fr. L *dies* day] **1** : the face of a sundial **2** : the face of a timepiece **3** : a plate or face with a pointer and numbers that indicate something ⟨the ∼ of a gauge⟩ **4** : a disk with a knob or slots that is turned for making connections (as on a telephone) or for regulating operation (as of a radio)

²**dial** *vb* **di·aled** *or* **di·alled; di·al·ing** *or* **di·al·ling** **1** : to manipulate a dial so as to operate or select **2** : to make a telephone call or connection

³**dial** *abbr* dialect

di·a·lect \ˈdī-ə-ˌlekt\ *n* : a regional variety of a language

di·a·lec·tic \ˌdī-ə-ˈlek-tik\ *n* : the process or art of reasoning correctly

di·a·logue *also* **di·a·log** \ˈdī-ə-ˌlog\ *n* **1** : a conversation between two or more persons **2** : the parts of a literary or dramatic composition that represent conversation

di·al·y·sis \dī-ˈal-ə-səs\ *n, pl* **-y·ses** \-ˌsēz\ : the separation of substances from solution by means of their unequal diffusion through semipermeable membranes

diam *abbr* diameter

di·am·e·ter \dī-ˈam-ət-ər\ *n* [ME *diametre*, fr. MF, fr. L *diametros*, fr. Gk, fr. *dia-* through + *metron* measure] **1** : a straight line passing through the center of a figure or body; *esp* : a straight line that passes through the center of a circle and divides it in half **2** : the length of a diameter

di·a·met·ric \ˌdī-ə-ˈme-trik\ *or* **di·a·met·ri·cal** \-tri-kəl\ *adj* **1** : of, relating to, or constituting a diameter **2** : completely opposed or opposite — **di·a·met·ri·cal·ly** \-tri-k(ə-)lē\ *adv*

di·a·mond \ˈdī-(ə-)mənd\ *n* **1** : a hard brilliant mineral that consists of crystalline carbon and is used as a gem **2** : a flat figure having four equal sides, two acute angles, and two obtuse angles **3** : any of a suit of playing cards marked with a red diamond **4** : IN-FIELD; *also* : the entire playing field in baseball

di·a·mond·back rattlesnake \ˈdī-(ə-)mən(d)-ˌbak-\ *n* : a large and very deadly rattlesnake

di·an·thus \dī-ˈan-thəs\ *n* : ¹PINK 1

di·a·pa·son \ˌdī-ə-ˈpāz-ᵊn, -ˈpās-\ *n* **1** : an organ stop covering the range of the organ **2** : the range of notes sounded by a voice or instrument

¹**di·a·per** \ˈdī(-ə)-pər\ *n* **1** : a cotton or linen fabric woven in a simple geometric pattern **2** : a piece of folded cloth drawn up between the legs of a baby and fastened about the waist

²**diaper** *vb* **di·a·pered; di·a·per·ing** \-p(ə-)riŋ\ **1** : to ornament with diaper designs **2** : to put a diaper on

di·aph·a·nous \dī-ˈaf-ə-nəs\ *adj* : so fine of texture as to be transparent

di·a·pho·ret·ic \ˌdī-ə-fə-ˈret-ik\ *adj* : having the power to increase perspiration — **diaphoretic** *n*

di·a·phragm \ˈdī-ə-ˌfram\ *n* **1** : a sheet of muscle between the chest and abdominal cavities of a mammal **2** : a vibrating disk (as in a telephone receiver) **3** : a cup-shaped device usu. of thin rubber fitted over the uterine cervix to act as a mechanical contraceptive barrier — **di·a·phrag·mat·ic** \ˌdī-ə-frə(g)-'mat-ik, -ˌfrag-\ *adj*

di·a·rist \'dī-ə-rəst\ *n* : one who keeps a diary

di·ar·rhea *or* **di·ar·rhoea** \ˌdī-ə-'rē-ə\ *n* : abnormally frequent and watery bowel movements

di·a·ry \'dī-(ə-)rē\ *n, pl* **-ries** : a daily record esp. of personal experiences and observations; *also* : a book for keeping such private notes and records

di·as·to·le \dī-'as-tə-(ˌ)lē\ *n* : the stretching of the cavities of the heart during which they fill with blood — **di·a·stol·ic** \ˌdī-ə-'stäl-ik\ *adj*

di·as·tro·phism \dī-'as-trə-ˌfiz-əm\ *n* : the process of deformation of the earth's crust by which major relief features are formed — **di·a·stroph·ic** \ˌdī-ə-'sträf-ik\ *adj*

dia·ther·my \'dī-ə-ˌthər-mē\ *n* : the generation of heat in tissue by electric currents for medical or surgical purposes

di·a·tom \'dī-ə-ˌtäm\ *n* : any of a class of planktonic one-celled or colonial algae with skeletons of silica

di·atom·ic \ˌdī-ə-'täm-ik\ *adj* : having two atoms in the molecule

di·at·o·mite \dī-'at-ə-ˌmīt\ *n* : a light crumbly siliceous material derived chiefly from diatom remains and used esp. as a filter

di·a·tribe \'dī-ə-ˌtrīb\ *n* : a bitter or violent attack in speech or writing

dib·ble \'dib-əl\ *n* : a pointed hand tool for making holes (as for planting bulbs) in the ground — **dibble** *vb*

¹**dice** \'dīs\ *n, pl* **dice** : DIE 1

²**dice** *vb* **diced; dic·ing 1** : to cut into small cubes ⟨∼ carrots⟩ **2** : to play games with dice

di·chot·o·my \dī-'kät-ə-mē\ *n, pl* **-mies** : a division or the process of dividing into two esp. mutually exclusive or contradictory groups — **di·chot·o·mous** \-məs\ *adj*

dick·er \'dik-ər\ *vb* **dick·ered; dick·er·ing** \'dik-(ə-)riŋ\ : BARGAIN, HAGGLE

dick·ey *or* **dicky** \'dik-ē\ *n, pl* **dickeys** *or* **dick·ies** : a small fabric insert worn to fill in the neckline

di·cot·y·le·don \ˌdī-ˌkät-ᵊl-'ēd-ᵊn\ *n* : any of a group of seed plants having

an embryo with two cotyledons — **di·cot·y·le·don·ous** *adj*

dict *abbr* dictionary

¹**dic·tate** \'dik-ˌtāt\ *vb* **dic·tat·ed; dic·tat·ing 1** : to speak or read for a person to transcribe or for a machine to record **2** : COMMAND, ORDER — **dic·ta·tion** \dik-'tā-shən\ *n*

²**dic·tate** \'dik-ˌtāt\ *n* : an authoritative rule, prescription, or injunction : COMMAND ⟨the ∼s of conscience⟩

dic·ta·tor \'dik-ˌtāt-ər\ *n* **1** : a person ruling absolutely and often brutally and oppressively **2** : one that dictates

dic·ta·to·ri·al \ˌdik-tə-'tōr-ē-əl\ *adj* : of, relating to, or characteristic of a dictator or a dictatorship

dic·ta·tor·ship \dik-'tāt-ər-ˌship, 'dik-ˌtāt-\ *n* **1** : the office or term of office of a dictator **2** : autocratic rule, control, or leadership **3** : a government or country in which absolute power is held by a dictator or a small clique

dic·tion \'dik-shən\ *n* **1** : choice of words esp. with regard to correctness, clearness, or effectiveness : WORDING **2** : ENUNCIATION

dic·tio·nary \'dik-shə-ˌner-ē\ *n, pl* **-nar·ies** : a reference book containing words usu. alphabetically arranged along with information about their forms, pronunciations, functions, etymologies, meanings, and syntactical and idiomatic uses

dic·tum \'dik-təm\ *n, pl* **dic·ta** \-tə\ *also* **dictums** : a formal authoritative statement : PRONOUNCEMENT

did past of DO

di·dac·tic \dī-'dak-tik\ *adj* **1** : intended primarily to instruct; *esp* : intended to teach a moral lesson **2** : making moral observations

di·do \'dīd-ō\ *n, pl* **didoes** *or* **didos** : a foolish or mischievous act

¹**die** \'dī\ *vb* **died; dy·ing** \'dī-iŋ\ **1** : to stop living : EXPIRE **2** : to pass out of existence ⟨a *dying* race⟩ **3** : to disappear or subside gradually ⟨the wind *died* down⟩ **4** : to long keenly ⟨*dying* to go⟩ **5** : STOP ⟨the motor *died*⟩

²**die** \'dī\ *n, pl* **dice** \'dīs\ *or* **dies** \'dīz\ **1** *pl* **dice** : a small cube marked on each face with one to six spots and used usu. in pairs in various games and gambling **2** *pl* **dies** : a device used in

shaping or stamping an object or material

die·hard \'dī-ˌhärd\ *n* : one who resists against hopeless odds

diel·drin \'dē(ə)l-drən\ *n* : a persistent chlorinated hydrocarbon insecticide

die·sel \'dē-zəl, -səl\ *n* **1** : DIESEL ENGINE **2** : a vehicle driven by a diesel engine

diesel engine *n* : an internal-combustion engine in whose cylinders air is compressed to a temperature sufficiently high to ignite the fuel

die·sel·ing \'dēz-(ə-)liŋ\ *n* : an instance of an internal-combustion engine continuing to operate after the ignition has been turned off

¹di·et \'dī-ət\ *n* [ME *diete,* fr. OF, fr. L *diaeta* prescribed diet, fr. Gk *diaita,* lit., manner of living] **1** : the food and drink regularly consumed (as by a person or group) : FARE **2** : an allowance of food prescribed with reference to a particular state (as ill health) — **di·etary** \'dī-ə-ˌter-ē\ *adj or n*

²diet *vb* : to eat or cause to eat less or according to a prescribed rule — **di·et·er** *n*

di·etet·ics \ˌdī-ə-'tet-iks\ *n sing or pl* : the science or art of applying the principles of nutrition to diet — **di·etet·ic** *adj*

di·eti·tian *or* **di·eti·cian** \ˌdī-ə-'tish-ən\ *n* : a specialist in dietetics

dif *or* **diff** *abbr* difference

dif·fer \'dif-ər\ *vb* **dif·fered; dif·fer·ing** \-(ə-)riŋ\ **1** : to be unlike **2** : DISAGREE

dif·fer·ence \'dif-(ə-)rəns, 'dif-ərns\ *n* **1** : UNLIKENESS ⟨~ in their looks⟩ **2** : distinction or discrimination in preference **3** : DISAGREEMENT, DISSENSION; *also* : an instance or cause of disagreement ⟨unable to settle their ~s⟩ **4** : the amount by which one number or quantity differs from another

dif·fer·ent \'dif-(ə-)rənt, 'dif-ərnt\ *adj* **1** : UNLIKE, DISSIMILAR **2** : not the same ⟨~ age groups⟩ ⟨seen at ~ times⟩ ⟨try a ~ book⟩ **3** : UNUSUAL, SPECIAL — **dif·fer·ent·ly** *adv*

¹dif·fer·en·tial \ˌdif-ə-'ren-chəl\ *adj* : showing, creating, or relating to a difference

²differential *n* **1** : the amount or degree by which things differ **2** : DIFFERENTIAL GEAR

differential gear *n* : an arrangement of gears in an automobile that allows one wheel to go faster than another (as in rounding curves)

dif·fer·en·ti·ate \ˌdif-ə-'ren-chē-ˌāt\ *vb* **-at·ed; -at·ing** **1** : to make or become different **2** : to recognize or state the difference ⟨~ between two plants⟩ — **dif·fer·en·ti·a·tion** \-ˌren-chē-'ā-shən\ *n*

dif·fi·cult \'dif-i-(ˌ)kəlt\ *adj* **1** : hard to do or make **2** : hard to understand or deal with ⟨~ reading⟩ ⟨a ~ child⟩

dif·fi·cul·ty \-(ˌ)kəl-tē\ *n, pl* **-ties** **1** : difficult nature ⟨the ~ of a task⟩ **2** : DISAGREEMENT ⟨settled their *difficulties*⟩ **3** : OBSTACLE ⟨overcome *difficulties*⟩ **4** : TROUBLE ⟨in financial *difficulties*⟩ **syn** hardship, rigor, vicissitude

dif·fi·dent \'dif-əd-ənt\ *adj* **1** : lacking confidence : TIMID **2** : RESERVED, UNASSERTIVE — **dif·fi·dence** \-əns\ *n* — **dif·fi·dent·ly** *adv*

dif·frac·tion \dif-'rak-shən\ *n* : the bending or spreading of a light beam esp. when passing through narrow slits or when reflecting from a ruled surface

¹dif·fuse \dif-'yüs\ *adj* **1** : VERBOSE, WORDY ⟨~ writing⟩ **2** : not concentrated : SCATTERED ⟨~ light⟩

²dif·fuse \dif-'yüz\ *vb* **dif·fused; dif·fus·ing** : to pour out or spread widely — **dif·fu·sion** \-'yü-zhən\ *n*

¹dig \'dig\ *vb* **dug** \'dəg\; **dig·ging** **1** : to turn up the soil (as with a spade) **2** : to hollow out or form by removing earth ⟨~ a hole⟩ **3** : to uncover or seek by turning up earth ⟨~ potatoes⟩ **4** : DISCOVER ⟨~ up information⟩ **5** : POKE, THRUST ⟨~ a person in the ribs⟩ **6** : to work hard **7** : NOTICE, APPRECIATE; *also* : LIKE, ADMIRE

²dig *n* **1** : THRUST, POKE **2** : a cutting remark : GIBE

³dig *abbr* digest

¹di·gest \'dī-ˌjest\ *n* : a summation or condensation of a body of information or of a literary work

²di·gest \dī-'jest, də-\ *vb* **1** : to think over and arrange in the mind **2** : to convert (food) into simpler forms that can be absorbed by the body **3** : to compress into a short summary — **di·gest·ibil·i·ty** \-ˌjes-tə-'bil-ət-ē\ *n* — **di·gest·ible** *adj* — **di·ges·tion** \-'jes-chən\ *n* — **di·ges·tive** \-'jes-tiv\ *adj*

dig in *vb* **1** : to dig defensive trenches **2** : to go resolutely to work **3** : to begin eating

dig·it \'dij-ət\ *n* [ME, fr. L *digitus* finger, toe] **1** : any of the Arabic numerals 1 to 9 and usu. the symbol 0 **2** : FINGER, TOE

dig·i·tal \'dij-ət-ᵊl\ *adj* **1** : of, relating to, or done with a finger or toe **2** : of, relating to, or using calculation directly with digits rather than through measurable physical quantities ⟨a ~ computer⟩ **3** : providing a readout in numerical digits ⟨a ~ watch⟩ — **dig·i·tal·ly** \-ē\ *adv*

dig·i·tal·is \ˌdij-ə-'tal-əs\ *n* : a drug from the common foxglove that is a powerful heart stimulant; *also* : FOXGLOVE

dig·ni·fied \'dig-nə-ˌfīd\ *adj* : showing or expressing dignity

dig·ni·fy \-ˌfī\ *vb* **-fied; -fy·ing** : to give dignity or distinction to : HONOR

dig·ni·tary \'dig-nə-ˌter-ē\ *n, pl* **-tar·ies** : a person of high position or honor

dig·ni·ty \'dig-nət-ē\ *n, pl* **-ties** **1** : the quality or state of being worthy, honored, or esteemed : true worth : EXCELLENCE **2** : high rank, office, or position **3** : formal reserve of manner or language

di·graph \'dī-ˌgraf\ *n* : a group of two successive letters whose phonetic value is a single sound (as *ea* in *bread*)

di·gress \dī-'gres, də-\ *vb* : to turn aside esp. from the main subject in writing or speaking — **di·gres·sion** \-'gresh-ən\ *n* — **di·gres·sive** \-'gres-iv\ *adj*

dike \'dīk\ *n* : a bank of earth to control water : LEVEE

dil *abbr* dilute

di·lap·i·dat·ed \də-'lap-ə-ˌdāt-əd\ *adj* : fallen into partial ruin or decay — **di·lap·i·da·tion** \-ˌlap-ə-'dā-shən\ *n*

di·late \dī-'lāt, 'dī-ˌlāt\ *vb* **di·lat·ed; di·lat·ing** : SWELL, DISTEND, EXPAND — **dil·a·ta·tion** \ˌdil-ə-'tā-shən\ *n* — **di·la·tion** \dī-'lā-shən\ *n*

dil·a·to·ry \'dil-ə-ˌtōr-ē\ *adj* **1** : DELAYING **2** : TARDY, SLOW

di·lem·ma \də-'lem-ə\ *n* : a choice between equally unsatisfactory alternatives

dil·et·tante \ˌdil-ə-'tänt(-ē), -'tant(-ē)\ *n, pl* **-tantes** *or* **-tan·ti** \-'tänt-ē, -'tant-ē\ [It, fr. *dilettare* to delight, fr. L *dilectare*] : a person having a superficial interest in an art or a branch of knowledge

dil·i·gent \'dil-ə-jənt\ *adj* : characterized by steady, earnest, and energetic application and effort : PAINSTAKING — **dil·i·gence** \-jəns\ *n* — **dil·i·gent·ly** *adv*

dill \'dil\ *n* : an herb related to the carrot with aromatic leaves and seeds used in pickles

dil·ly \'dil-ē\ *n, pl* **dil·lies** : one that is remarkable or outstanding

dil·ly·dal·ly \'dil-ē-ˌdal-ē\ *vb* : to waste time by loitering or delay

¹di·lute \dī-'lüt, də-\ *vb* **di·lut·ed; di·lut·ing** : to lessen the consistency or strength of by mixing with something else — **di·lu·tion** \-'lü-shən\ *n*

²dilute *adj* : DILUTED, WEAK

¹dim \'dim\ *adj* **dim·mer; dim·mest** **1** : LUSTERLESS, DULL **2** : not bright or distinct : OBSCURE, FAINT **3** : not seeing or understanding clearly — **dim·ly** *adv* — **dim·ness** *n*

²dim *vb* **dimmed; dim·ming** **1** : to make or become dim or lusterless **2** : to reduce the light from (headlights) by switching to the low beam

³dim *abbr* **1** dimension **2** diminished **3** diminutive

dime \'dīm\ *n* [ME, tenth part, tithe, fr. MF, fr. L *decima*, fr. fem. of *decimus* tenth, fr. *decem* ten] : a U.S. coin worth ¹⁄₁₀ dollar

di·men·sion \də-'men-chən, dī-\ *n* **1** : measurement of extension (as in length, height, or breadth) **2** : EXTENT, SCOPE, PROPORTIONS — usu. used in pl. — **di·men·sion·al** \-'mench-(ə-)nəl\ *adj* — **di·men·sion·al·i·ty** \-ˌmen-chə-'nal-ət-ē\ *n*

di·min·ish \də-'min-ish\ *vb* **1** : to make less or cause to appear less **2** : BELITTLE **3** : DWINDLE **4** : TAPER — **dim·i·nu·tion** \ˌdim-ə-'n(y)ü-shən\ *n*

di·min·u·en·do \də-ˌmin-(y)ə-'wen-dō\ *adv or adj* : DECRESCENDO

¹di·min·u·tive \də-'min-yət-iv\ *n* **1** : a diminutive word or affix **2** : a diminutive individual

²diminutive *adj* **1** : indicating small size and sometimes the state or quality of being lovable, pitiable, or contemptible ⟨the ~ suffixes *-ette* and *-ling*⟩ **2** : extremely small : TINY

dim·i·ty \ˈdim-ət-ē\ *n, pl* **-ties** : a thin usu. corded cotton fabric

dim·mer \ˈdim-ər\ *n* : a device for controlling the amount of light from an electric lighting unit

di·mor·phic \(ˈ)dī-ˈmȯr-fik\ *adj* : occurring in two distinct forms — **di·mor·phism** \-ˌfiz-əm\ *n*

¹**dim·ple** \ˈdim-pəl\ *n* : a small depression esp. in the cheek or chin

²**dimple** *vb* **dim·pled; dim·pling** : to form dimples (as in smiling)

din \ˈdin\ *n* : a loud confused mixture of noises

di·nar \di-ˈnär\ *n* **1** — see MONEY table **2** — see *rial* at MONEY table

dine \ˈdīn\ *vb* **dined; din·ing** [ME *dinen,* fr. OF *diner,* fr. (assumed) VL *disjejunare* to break one's fast, deriv. of L *jejunus* fasting] **1** : to eat dinner **2** : to give a dinner to : FEED

din·er \ˈdī-nər\ *n* **1** : one that dines **2** : a railroad dining car **3** : a restaurant usu. resembling a dining car

di·nette \dī-ˈnet\ *n* : an alcove or small room used for dining

din·ghy \ˈdiŋ-ē\ *n, pl* **dinghies** **1** : a small rowboat **2** : LIFE RAFT

din·gle \ˈdiŋ-gəl\ *n* : a small wooded valley

din·go \ˈdiŋ-gō\ *n, pl* **dingoes** : a reddish brown wild dog of Australia

din·gus \ˈdiŋ-(g)əs\ *n* : DOODAD

din·gy \ˈdin-jē\ *adj* **din·gi·er; -est** **1** : DARK, DULL **2** : not fresh or clean : GRIMY — **din·gi·ness** *n*

din·ky \ˈdiŋ-kē\ *adj* **din·ki·er; -est** : SMALL, INSIGNIFICANT

din·ner \ˈdin-ər\ *n* : the main meal of the day; *also* : a formal banquet

din·ner·ware \ˈdin-ər-ˌwaər\ *n* : china, glassware, or tableware used in table service

di·no·fla·gel·late \ˌdī-nō-ˈflaj-ə-lət, -ˌlāt\ *n* : any of an order of planktonic plantlike flagellates of which some cause red tide

di·no·saur \ˈdī-nə-ˌsȯr\ *n* [fr. Gk *deinos* terrible + *sauros* lizard] : any of a group of extinct long-tailed reptiles often of huge size

dint \ˈdint\ *n* **1** : FORCE ⟨reached the top by ∼ of sheer grit⟩ **2** : DENT

di·o·cese \ˈdī-ə-səs, -ˌsēz, -ˌsēs\ *n, pl* **-ces·es** \-sə-səz, -ˌsē-zəz, -ˌsē-səz, -ə-ˌsēz\ : the territorial jurisdiction of a bishop — **di·oc·e·san** \dī-ˈäs-ə-sən, ˌdī-ə-ˈsēz-ᵊn\ *adj or n*

di·ode \ˈdī-ˌōd\ *n* **1** : an electron tube having a cathode and anode **2** : a semiconductor device that functions as a rectifier

di·ox·in \dī-ˈäk-sən\ *n* : a hydrocarbon that occurs esp. as a persistent toxic impurity in herbicides (as Agent Orange)

¹**dip** \ˈdip\ *vb* **dipped; dip·ping** **1** : to plunge temporarily or partially under the surface (as of a liquid) **2** : to thrust in a way to suggest immersion **3** : to scoop up or out : LADLE **4** : to lower and then raise quickly ⟨∼ a flag in salute⟩ **5** : to drop or slope down esp. suddenly ⟨the moon *dipped* below the crest⟩ **6** : to decrease moderately and usu. temporarily ⟨prices *dipped*⟩ **7** : to reach inside or as if inside or below a surface ⟨*dipped* into their savings⟩ **8** : to delve casually into something; *esp* : to read superficially ⟨∼ into a book⟩

²**dip** *n* **1** : an act of dipping; *esp* : a short swim **2** : inclination downward : DROP **3** : something obtained by or used in dipping **4** : a sauce or soft mixture into which food may be dipped **5** : a liquid into which something may be dipped (as for cleansing or coloring)

diph·the·ria \dif-ˈthir-ē-ə, dip-\ *n* : an acute contagious bacterial disease marked by fever and by coating of the air passages with a membrane that interferes with breathing

diph·thong \ˈdif-ˌthȯŋ, ˈdip-\ *n* : two vowel sounds joined in one syllable to form one speech sound (as *ou* in *out*)

dip·loid \ˈdip-ˌlȯid\ *adj* : having the basic chromosome number doubled — **diploid** *n*

di·plo·ma \də-ˈplō-mə\ *n, pl* **diplomas** : an official record of graduation from or of a degree conferred by a school

di·plo·ma·cy \də-ˈplō-mə-sē\ *n* **1** : the art and practice of conducting negotiations between nations **2** : TACT

dip·lo·mat \ˈdip-lə-ˌmat\ *n* : one employed or skilled in diplomacy — **dip·lo·mat·ic** \ˌdip-lə-ˈmat-ik\ *adj*

di·plo·ma·tist \də-ˈplō-mət-əst\ *n* : DIPLOMAT

dip·per \ˈdip-ər\ *n* **1** : any of a genus of birds that are related to the thrushes and are skilled in diving **2** : something (as a ladle or scoop) that dips or is used for dipping **3** *cap* : the seven bright stars of Ursa Major arranged in a form resembling a dipper **4** *cap* : the seven bright stars of Ursa Minor arranged in a form resembling a dipper with the North Star forming the outer end of the handle

dip·so·ma·nia \ˌdip-sə-ˈmā-nē-ə\ *n* : an uncontrollable craving for alcoholic liquors — **dip·so·ma·ni·ac** \-nē-ˌak\ *n*

dip·stick \ˈdip-ˌstik\ *n* : a graduated rod for indicating depth

dip·ter·ous \ˈdip-tə-rəs\ *adj* : of, relating to, or being a two-winged fly — **dip·ter·an** \-rən\ *adj or n*

dir *abbr* director

dire \ˈdī(ə)r\ *adj* **dir·er; dir·est 1** : very horrible : DREADFUL **2** : warning of disaster **3** : EXTREME

¹**di·rect** \də-ˈrekt, dī-\ *vb* **1** : ADDRESS ⟨~ a letter⟩; *also* : to impart orally : AIM ⟨~ a remark to the gallery⟩ **2** : to regulate the activities or course of : guide the supervision, organizing, or performance of **3** : to cause to turn, move, or point or to follow a certain course **4** : to point, extend, or project in a specified line or course **5** : to request or instruct with authority **6** : to show or point out the way

²**direct** *adj* **1** : stemming immediately from a source, cause, or reason ⟨~ result⟩ **2** : being or passing in a straight line of descent : LINEAL ⟨~ ancestor⟩ **3** : leading from one point to another in time or space without turn or stop : STRAIGHT **4** : NATURAL, STRAIGHTFORWARD ⟨a ~ manner⟩ **5** : operating without an intervening agency or step ⟨~ action⟩ **6** : effected by the action of the people or the electorate and not by representatives ⟨~ legislation⟩ **7** : consisting of or reproducing the exact words of a speaker ⟨~ discourse⟩ — **direct** *adv* — **di·rect·ly** \də-ˈrek-(t)lē, dī-\ *adv* — **di·rect·ness** \-ˈrek(t)-nəs\ *n*

direct current *n* : an electric current flowing in one direction only

di·rec·tion \də-ˈrek-shən, dī-\ *n* **1** : MANAGEMENT, GUIDANCE **2** : COMMAND, ORDER, INSTRUCTION **3** : the course or line along which something moves, lies, or points **4** : TENDENCY, TREND — **di·rec·tion·al** \-sh(ə-)nəl\ *adj*

di·rec·tive \də-ˈrek-tiv, dī-\ *n* : a general instruction as to procedure

di·rec·tor \də-ˈrek-tər, dī-\ *n* **1** : one that directs : MANAGER, SUPERVISOR, CONDUCTOR **2** : one of a group of persons who direct the affairs of an organized body — **di·rec·tor·ship** *n*

di·rec·tor·ate \də-ˈrek-t(ə-)rət, dī-\ *n* **1** : the office or position of director **2** : a board of directors; *also* : membership on such a board **3** : an executive staff

di·rec·to·ry \-t(ə-)rē\ *n, pl* **-ries** : an alphabetical or classified list of names and addresses

dire·ful \ˈdī(ə)r-fəl\ *adj* : producing dire effects

dirge \ˈdərj\ *n* : a song of lamentation; *also* : a slow mournful piece of music

dir·ham \ˈdir-həm\ *n* **1** — see MONEY table **2** — see *dinar, riyal* at MONEY table

di·ri·gi·ble \ˈdir-ə-jə-bəl, də-ˈrij-ə-\ *n* : AIRSHIP

dirk \ˈdərk\ *n* : DAGGER 1

dirndl \ˈdərn-dᵊl\ *n* [short for G *dirndlkleid,* fr. G dial. *dirndl* girl + G *kleid* dress] : a full skirt with a tight waistband

dirt \ˈdərt\ *n* **1** : a filthy or soiling substance (as mud, dust, or grime) **2** : loose or packed earth : SOIL **3** : moral uncleanness **4** : scandalous gossip **5** : embarrassing or incriminating information

¹**dirty** \ˈdərt-ē\ *adj* **dirt·i·er; -est 1** : SOILED, FILTHY **2** : INDECENT, SMUTTY ⟨~ talk⟩ **3** : BASE, UNFAIR ⟨a ~ trick⟩ **4** : STORMY, FOGGY ⟨~ weather⟩ **5** : not clear in color : DULL ⟨a ~ red⟩ — **dirt·i·ness** \ˈdərt-ē-nəs\ *n* — **dirty** *adv*

²**dirty** *vb* **dirt·ied; dirty·ing** : to make or become dirty

dis·able \dis-ˈā-bəl\ *vb* **dis·abled; dis·abling** \-b(ə-)liŋ\ **1** : to disqualify legally **2** : to make unable to perform by or as if by illness, injury, or malfunction — **dis·abil·i·ty** \ˌdis-ə-ˈbil-ət-ē\ *n*

dis·abuse \ˌdis-ə-ˈbyüz\ *vb* : to free from error or fallacy

di·sac·cha·ride \dī-ˈsak-ə-ˌrīd\ *n* : a sugar that yields two molecules of simple sugar upon hydrolysis

dis·ad·van·tage \ˌdis-əd-ˈvant-ij\ *n* **1** : loss or damage esp. to reputation or finances **2** : an unfavorable, inferior, or prejudicial condition; *also* : HANDICAP — **dis·ad·van·ta·geous** \dis-,ad-,van-'tā-jəs, -vən-\ *adj*

dis·af·fect \,dis-ə-'fekt\ *vb* : to alienate the affection or loyalty of : cause discontent in ⟨the troops were ∼ed⟩ — **dis·af·fec·tion** \-'fek-shən\ *n*

dis·agree \,dis-ə-'grē\ *vb* **1** : to fail to agree **2** : to differ in opinion **3** : to have an unpleasant effect ⟨fried foods ∼ with her⟩ — **dis·agree·ment** *n*

dis·agree·able \-ə-bəl\ *adj* **1** : causing discomfort : UNPLEASANT, OFFENSIVE **2** : ILL-TEMPERED, PEEVISH — **dis·agree·able·ness** *n* — **dis·agree·ably** \-blē\ *adv*

dis·al·low \,dis-ə-'laủ\ *vb* : to refuse to admit or recognize : REJECT ⟨∼ a claim⟩ — **dis·al·low·ance** *n*

dis·ap·pear \,dis-ə-'piər\ *vb* **1** : to pass out of sight **2** : to cease to be : become lost — **dis·ap·pear·ance** *n*

dis·ap·point \,dis-ə-'pòint\ *vb* : to fail to fulfill the expectation or hope of — **dis·ap·point·ment** *n*

dis·ap·pro·ba·tion \dis-,ap-rə-'bā-shən\ *n* : DISAPPROVAL

dis·ap·prov·al \,dis-ə-'prü-vəl\ *n* : adverse judgment : CENSURE

dis·ap·prove \-'prüv\ *vb* **1** : CONDEMN **2** : to feel or express disapproval ⟨∼s of smoking⟩ **3** : REJECT

dis·arm \dis-'ärm\ *vb* **1** : to take arms or weapons from **2** : to reduce the size and strength of the armed forces of a country **3** : to make harmless, peaceable, or friendly : win over ⟨a ∼ing smile⟩ — **dis·ar·ma·ment** \-'är-mə-mənt\ *n*

dis·ar·range \,dis-ə-'rānj\ *vb* : to disturb the arrangement or order of — **dis·ar·range·ment** *n*

dis·ar·ray \-'rā\ *n* **1** : DISORDER, CONFUSION **2** : disorderly or careless dress

dis·as·sem·ble \,dis-ə-'sem-bəl\ *vb* : to take apart

dis·as·so·ci·ate \-'sō-s(h)ē-,āt\ *vb* : to detach from association

di·sas·ter \diz-'as-tər, dis-\ *n* [MF *desastre,* fr. It *disastro,* fr. *astro* star, fr. L *astrum*] : a sudden or great misfortune — **di·sas·trous** \-'as-trəs\ *adj* — **di·sas·trous·ly** *adv*

dis·avow \,dis-ə-'vaủ\ *vb* : to deny responsibility for : REPUDIATE — **dis·avow·al** \-'vaủ(-ə)l\ *n*

dis·band \dis-'band\ *vb* : to break up the organization of : DISPERSE

dis·bar \dis-'bär\ *vb* : to expel from the legal profession — **dis·bar·ment** *n*

dis·be·lieve \,dis-bə-'lēv\ *vb* **1** : to hold not to be true or real ⟨*disbelieved* his testimony⟩ **2** : to withhold or reject belief — **dis·be·lief** \-'lēf\ *n* — **dis·be·liev·er** *n*

dis·bur·den \dis-'bərd-ᵊn\ *vb* : to rid of a burden

dis·burse \dis-'bərs\ *vb* **dis·bursed; dis·burs·ing** : to pay out : EXPEND — **dis·burse·ment** *n*

¹**disc** var of DISK

²**disc** *abbr* discount

dis·card \dis-'kärd, 'dis-,kärd\ *vb* **1** : to let go a playing card from one's hand; *also* : to play (a card) from a suit other than a trump but different from the one led **2** : to get rid of as unwanted — **dis·card** \'dis-,kärd\ *n*

disc brake *n* : a brake that operates by the friction of a pair of plates pressing against the sides of a rotating disc

dis·cern \dis-'ərn, diz-\ *vb* **1** : to detect with the eyes : DISTINGUISH **2** : DISCRIMINATE **3** : to come to know or recognize mentally — **dis·cern·ible** *adj* — **dis·cern·ment** *n*

dis·cern·ing \-iŋ\ *adj* : revealing insight and understanding

¹**dis·charge** \dis-'chärj, 'dis-,chärj\ *vb* **1** : to relieve of a charge, load, or burden : UNLOAD; *esp* : to remove the electrical energy from ⟨∼ a storage battery⟩ **2** : SHOOT ⟨∼ a gun⟩ ⟨∼ an arrow⟩ **3** : to set free ⟨∼ a prisoner⟩ **4** : to dismiss from service or employment ⟨∼ a soldier⟩ **5** : to let go or let off ⟨∼ passengers⟩ **6** : to give forth fluid ⟨the river ∼s into the ocean⟩ **7** : to get rid of by paying or doing ⟨∼ a debt⟩

²**dis·charge** \'dis-,chärj, dis-'chärj\ *n* **1** : the act of discharging, unloading, or releasing **2** : something that discharges; *esp* : a certification of release or payment **3** : a firing off (as of a gun) **4** : a flowing out (as of blood from a wound); *also* : something that is emitted ⟨a purulent ∼⟩ **5** : release or dismissal esp. from an office or employment; *also* : complete separation from military service **6** : a flow of electricity (as through a gas)

dis·ci·ple \dis-'ī-pəl\ *n* **1** : one who accepts and helps to spread the teachings of another; *also* : a convinced adherent **2** *cap* : a member of the Disciples of Christ

dis·ci·pli·nar·i·an \ˌdis-ə-plə-'ner-ē-ən\ *n* : one who enforces order

dis·ci·plin·ary \'dis-ə-plə-ˌner-ē\ *adj* : of or relating to discipline; *also* : CORRECTIVE ⟨take ∼ action⟩

¹dis·ci·pline \'dis-ə-plən\ *n* **1** : PUNISHMENT **2** : a field of study : SUBJECT **3** : training that corrects, molds, or perfects **4** : control gained by obedience or training : orderly conduct **5** : a system of rules governing conduct

²discipline *vb* **-plined; -plin·ing** **1** : PUNISH **2** : to train or develop by instruction and exercise esp. in self-control **3** : to bring under control ⟨∼ troops⟩; *also* : to impose order upon

disc jockey *n* : a person who conducts a radio show of popular recorded music

dis·claim \dis-'klām\ *vb* : to deny having a connection with or responsibility for : DISAVOW — **dis·claim·er** *n*

dis·close \dis-'klōz\ *vb* : to expose to view — **dis·clo·sure** \-'klō-zhər\ *n*

dis·co \'dis-kō\ *n, pl* **discos** **1** : DISCOTHEQUE **2** : popular dance music characterized by hypnotic rhythm, repetitive lyrics, and electronically produced sounds

dis·col·or \dis-'kəl-ər\ *vb* : to alter or change in hue or color : STAIN — **dis·col·or·ation** \dis-ˌkəl-ə-'rā-shən\ *n*

dis·com·bob·u·late \ˌdis-kəm-'bäb-(y)ə-ˌlāt\ *vb* **-lat·ed; -lat·ing** : UPSET, CONFUSE

dis·com·fit \dis-'kəm-fət, *esp South* ˌdis-kəm-'fit\ *vb* : UPSET, FRUSTRATE — **dis·com·fi·ture** \dis-'kəm-fə-ˌchùr\ *n*

¹dis·com·fort \dis-'kəm-fərt\ *vb* : to make uncomfortable or uneasy

²discomfort *n* : lack of comfort : uneasiness of mind or body : DISTRESS

dis·com·mode \ˌdis-kə-'mōd\ *vb* **-mod·ed; -mod·ing** : INCONVENIENCE, TROUBLE

dis·com·pose \-kəm-'pōz\ *vb* **1** : AGITATE **2** : DISARRANGE — **dis·com·po·sure** \-'pō-zhər\ *n*

dis·con·cert \ˌdis-kən-'sərt\ *vb* : CONFUSE, UPSET

dis·con·nect \ˌdis-kə-'nekt\ *vb* : to undo the connection of — **dis·con·nec·tion** \-'nek-shən\ *n*

dis·con·nect·ed \-əd\ *adj* : not connected : RAMBLING, INCOHERENT — **dis·con·nect·ed·ly** *adv*

dis·con·so·late \dis-'kän-sə-lət\ *adj* **1** : CHEERLESS **2** : hopelessly sad — **dis·con·so·late·ly** *adv*

dis·con·tent \ˌdis-kən-'tent\ *n* : uneasiness of mind : DISSATISFACTION — **dis·con·tent·ed** *adj*

dis·con·tin·ue \ˌdis-kən-'tin-yü\ *vb* **1** : to break the continuity of : cease to operate, use, or take **2** : END — **dis·con·tin·u·ance** \-yə-wəns\ *n* — **dis·con·ti·nu·i·ty** \dis-ˌkänt-ən-'(y)ü-ət-ē\ *n* — **dis·con·tin·u·ous** \ˌdis-kən-'tin-yə-wəs\ *adj*

dis·cord \'dis-ˌkȯrd\ *n* **1** : lack of agreement or harmony : DISSENSION, CONFLICT **2** : a harsh combination of musical sounds **3** : a harsh or unpleasant sound — **dis·cor·dant** \dis-'kȯrd-ᵊnt\ *adj* — **dis·cor·dant·ly** *adv*

dis·co·theque \'dis-kə-ˌtek\ *n* : a nightclub for dancing to live or recorded music

¹dis·count \'dis-ˌkaùnt\ *n* **1** : a reduction made from a regular or list price **2** : a deduction of interest in advance when lending money

²dis·count \'dis-ˌkaùnt, dis-'kaùnt\ *vb* **1** : to deduct from the amount of a bill, debt, or charge usu. for cash or prompt payment; *also* : to sell or offer for sale at a discount **2** : to lend money after deducting the discount ⟨∼ a note⟩ **3** : DISREGARD; *also* : MINIMIZE **4** : to make allowance for bias or exaggeration; *also* : DISBELIEVE **5** : to take into account (as a future event) in present calculations — **dis·count·able** *adj* — **dis·count·er** *n*

dis·coun·te·nance \dis-'kaùnt-(ᵊ-)nəns\ *vb* **1** : EMBARRASS, DISCONCERT **2** : to look with disfavor on

dis·cour·age \dis-'kər-ij\ *vb* **-aged; -ag·ing** **1** : to deprive of courage or confidence : DISHEARTEN **2** : to hinder by inspiring fear of consequences : DETER **3** : to attempt to dissuade — **dis·cour·age·ment** *n* — **dis·cour·ag·ing·ly** \-ij-iŋ-lē\ *adv*

¹dis·course \'dis-ˌkōrs\ *n* [ME *discours,* fr. ML & LL *discursus;* ML, argument, fr. LL, conversation, fr. L, act of running about, fr. *discurrere* to run about, fr. *currere* to run] **1** : CONVERSATION **2** : formal and usu. extended expression of thought on a subject

²**dis·course** \dis-ˈkōrs\ *vb* **dis·coursed; dis·cours·ing 1** : to express oneself in esp. oral discourse **2** : TALK, CONVERSE

dis·cour·te·ous \dis-ˈkərt-ē-əs\ *adj* : lacking courtesy : UNCIVIL, RUDE — **dis·cour·te·ous·ly** *adv*

dis·cour·te·sy \-ˈkərt-ə-sē\ *n* : RUDENESS; *also* : a rude act

dis·cov·er \dis-ˈkəv-ər\ *vb* **1** : to make known or visible **2** : to obtain sight or knowledge of for the first time : FIND — **dis·cov·er·er** *n*

dis·cov·ery \dis-ˈkəv-(e-)rē\ *n, pl* **-er·ies 1** : the act or process of discovering **2** : something discovered **3** : the disclosure usu. before a civil trial of pertinent facts or documents

¹**dis·cred·it** \dis-ˈkred-ət\ *vb* **1** : DISBELIEVE **2** : to cause disbelief in the accuracy or authority of **3** : DISGRACE — **dis·cred·it·able** *adj*

²**discredit** *n* **1** : loss of reputation **2** : lack or loss of belief or confidence

dis·creet \dis-ˈkrēt\ *adj* : showing good judgment; *esp* : capable of observing prudent silence — **dis·creet·ly** *adv*

dis·crep·an·cy \dis-ˈkrep-ən-sē\ *n, pl* **-cies 1** : DIFFERENCE, DISAGREEMENT **2** : an instance of being discrepant

dis·crep·ant \-ənt\ *adj* [L *discrepans*, prp. of *discrepare* to sound discordantly, fr. *crepare* to rattle, creak] : being at variance : DISAGREEING

dis·crete \dis-ˈkrēt, ˈdis-ˌkrēt\ *adj* **1** : individually distinct **2** : NONCONTINUOUS

dis·cre·tion \dis-ˈkresh-ən\ *n* **1** : the quality of being discreet : PRUDENCE **2** : individual choice or judgment **3** : power of free decision or latitude of choice — **dis·cre·tion·ary** *adj*

dis·crim·i·nate \dis-ˈkrim-ə-ˌnāt\ *vb* **-nat·ed; -nat·ing 1** : DISTINGUISH, DIFFERENTIATE **2** : to make a distinction in favor of or against one person or thing as compared with others — **dis·crim·i·na·tion** \-ˌkrim-ə-ˈnā-shən\ *n*

dis·crim·i·nat·ing \-ˌnāt-iŋ\ *adj* : marked by discrimination; *esp* : DISCERNING, JUDICIOUS

dis·crim·i·na·to·ry \dis-ˈkrim-ə-

nə-ˌtōr-ē\ *adj* : marked by esp. unjust discrimination ⟨∼ treatment⟩

dis·cur·sive \dis-ˈkər-siv\ *adj* : passing from one topic to another : RAMBLING — **dis·cur·sive·ly** *adv* — **dis·cur·sive·ness** *n*

dis·cus \ˈdis-kəs\ *n, pl* **dis·cus·es** : a disk that is hurled for distance in a track-and-field contest

dis·cuss \dis-ˈkəs\ *vb* [ME *discussen*, fr. L *discutere*, fr. *dis-* apart + *quatere* to shake] **1** : to argue or consider carefully by presenting the various sides **2** : to talk about — **dis·cus·sion** \-ˈkəsh-ən\ *n*

dis·cus·sant \dis-ˈkəs-ᵊnt\ *n* : one who takes part in a formal discussion

¹**dis·dain** \dis-ˈdān\ *n* : CONTEMPT, SCORN — **dis·dain·ful** \-fəl\ *adj* — **dis·dain·ful·ly** \-ē\ *adv*

²**disdain** *vb* **1** : to look upon with scorn **2** : to reject or refrain from because of disdain

dis·ease \diz-ˈēz\ *n* : an abnormal bodily condition that impairs functioning and can usu. be recognized by signs and symptoms : SICKNESS — **dis·eased** \-ˈēzd\ *adj*

dis·em·bark \ˌdis-əm-ˈbärk\ *vb* : to go or put ashore from a ship — **dis·em·bar·ka·tion** \dis-ˌem-ˌbär-ˈkā-shən\ *n*

dis·em·body \ˌdis-əm-ˈbäd-ē\ *vb* : to deprive of bodily existence

dis·em·bow·el \-ˈbau̇(-ə)l\ *vb* : EVISCERATE 1 — **dis·em·bow·el·ment** *n*

dis·en·chant \ˌdis-ᵊn-ˈchant\ *vb* : DISILLUSION — **dis·en·chant·ment** *n*

dis·en·cum·ber \ˌdis-ᵊn-ˈkəm-bər\ *vb* : to free from something that burdens

dis·en·fran·chise \ˌdis-ᵊn-ˈfran-ˌchīz\ *vb* : DISFRANCHISE — **dis·en·fran·chise·ment** *n*

dis·en·gage \ˌdis-ᵊn-ˈgāj\ *vb* : RELEASE, EXTRICATE, DISENTANGLE — **dis·en·gage·ment** *n*

dis·en·tan·gle \ˌdis-ᵊn-ˈtaŋ-gəl\ *vb* : to free from entanglement : UNRAVEL

dis·equi·lib·ri·um \dis-ˌē-kwə-ˈlib-rē-əm\ *n* : loss or lack of equilibrium

dis·es·tab·lish \ˌdis-ə-ˈstab-lish\ *vb* : to end the establishment of; *esp* : to deprive of the status of an established church — **dis·es·tab·lish·ment** *n*

dis·es·teem \ˌdis-ə-ˈstēm\ *n* : lack of esteem : DISFAVOR, DISREPUTE

di·seuse \dē-'zə(r)z, -'züz\ *n, pl* **diseuses** \-'zə(r)z(-əz), -'züz(-əz)\ [F] : a skilled and usu. professional woman reciter

dis·fa·vor \dis-'fā-vər\ *n* 1 : DISAPPROVAL, DISLIKE 2 : the state or fact of being no longer favored

dis·fig·ure \dis-'fig-yər\ *vb* : to spoil the appearance of ⟨*disfigured* by a scar⟩ — **dis·fig·ure·ment** *n*

dis·fran·chise \dis-'fran-ˌchīz\ *vb* : to deprive of a franchise, a legal right, or a privilege; *esp* : to deprive of the right to vote — **dis·fran·chise·ment** *n*

dis·gorge \-'gȯrj\ *vb* : VOMIT; *also* : to discharge forcefully or confusedly

¹**dis·grace** \dis-'grās\ *vb* : to bring reproach or shame to

²**disgrace** *n* 1 : SHAME, DISHONOR; *also* : a cause of shame 2 : the condition of being out of favor : loss of respect — **dis·grace·ful** \-fəl\ *adj* — **dis·grace·ful·ly** \-ē\ *adv*

dis·grun·tle \dis-'grənt-ᵊl\ *vb* **dis·grun·tled; dis·grun·tling** : to put in bad humor

¹**dis·guise** \dis-'gīz\ *vb* **dis·guised; dis·guis·ing** 1 : to change the appearance of to conceal the identity or to resemble another 2 : HIDE, CONCEAL

²**disguise** *n* 1 : clothing put on to conceal one's identity or counterfeit another's 2 : an outward appearance that hides what something really is

¹**dis·gust** \dis-'gəst\ *n* : AVERSION, REPUGNANCE

²**disgust** *vb* : to provoke to loathing, repugnance, or aversion : be offensive to — **dis·gust·ed·ly** *adv* — **dis·gust·ing·ly** \-'gəs-tiŋ-lē\ *adv*

¹**dish** \'dish\ *n* [ME, fr. OE *disc* plate, fr. L *discus* quoit, disk, dish, fr. Gk *diskos,* fr. *dikein* to throw] 1 : a vessel used for serving food 2 : the food served in a dish ⟨a ~ of berries⟩ 3 : food prepared in a particular way 4 : something resembling a dish esp. in being shallow and concave

²**dish** *vb* 1 : to put into a dish 2 : to make concave like a dish

dis·ha·bille \ˌdis-ə-'bēl\ *n* [F *déshabillé*] : the state of being dressed in a casual or careless manner

dis·har·mo·ny \dis-'här-mə-nē\ *n* : lack of harmony — **dis·har·mo·ni·ous** \ˌdis-(ˌ)här-'mō-nē-əs\ *adj*

dish·cloth \'dish-ˌklȯth\ *n* : a cloth for washing dishes

dis·heart·en \dis-'härt-ᵊn\ *vb* : DISCOURAGE, DEJECT

dished \'disht\ *adj* : CONCAVE

di·shev·el \dish-'ev-əl\ *vb* **-shev·eled** *or* **-shev·elled; -shev·el·ing** *or* **-shev·el·ling** [ME *discheveled,* fr. MF *deschevelé,* fr. *descheveler* to disarrange the hair, fr. *chevel* hair, fr. L *capillus*] : to let hang or fall loosely in disorder : DISARRAY — **di·shev·eled** *or* **di·shev·elled** *adj*

dis·hon·est \dis-'än-əst\ *adj* : not honest : UNTRUSTWORTHY, DECEITFUL — **dis·hon·est·ly** *adv* — **dis·hon·es·ty** \-ə-stē\ *n*

¹**dis·hon·or** \dis-'än-ər\ *vb* 1 : DISGRACE 2 : to refuse to accept or pay ⟨~ a check⟩

²**dishonor** *n* 1 : lack or loss of honor 2 : SHAME, DISGRACE 3 : something dishonorable : a cause of disgrace 4 : the act of dishonoring a negotiable instrument when presented for payment — **dis·hon·or·able** \-'än-(ə-)rə-bəl, -'än-ər-bəl\ *adj* — **dis·hon·or·ably** \-blē\ *adv*

dish out *vb* : to give freely

dish·rag \'dish-ˌrag\ *n* : DISHCLOTH

dish·wash·er \-ˌwȯsh-ər, -ˌwäsh-\ *n* : a person or machine that washes dishes

dish·wa·ter \-ˌwȯt-ər, -ˌwät-\ *n* : water in which dishes have been or are to be washed

dis·il·lu·sion \ˌdis-ə-'lü-zhən\ *vb* **-sioned; -sion·ing** \-'lüzh-(ə-)niŋ\ : to free from mistaken beliefs or foolish hopes — **dis·il·lu·sion·ment** *n*

dis·in·cli·na·tion \dis-ˌin-klə-'nā-shən\ *n* : a feeling of unwillingness or aversion : DISTASTE

dis·in·cline \ˌdis-ᵊn-'klīn\ *vb* : to make or be unwilling

dis·in·fect \ˌdis-ᵊn-'fekt\ *vb* : to cleanse of infection-causing germs — **dis·in·fec·tant** \-'fek-tənt\ *n* — **dis·in·fec·tion** \-'fek-shən\ *n*

dis·in·gen·u·ous \-'jen-yə-wəs\ *adj* : lacking in candor : not frank or naive

dis·in·her·it \ˌdis-ᵊn-'her-ət\ *vb* : to deprive of the right to inherit

dis·in·te·grate \dis-'int-ə-ˌgrāt\ *vb* 1 : to break or decompose into constituent parts or small particles 2 : to destroy the unity or integrity of — **dis·in·te·gra·tion** \dis-ˌint-ə-'grā-shən\ *n*

dis·in·ter \ˌdis-ᵊn-ᵗtər\ *vb* **1** : to take from the grave or tomb **2** : UNEARTH

dis·in·ter·est·ed \dis-ᵗin-t(ə-)rəs-təd, -tə-ˌres-\ *adj* **1** : not interested **2** : free from selfish motive or interest : UNBIASED — **dis·in·ter·est·ed·ness** *n*

dis·join \dis-ᵗjȯin\ *vb* : SEPARATE

dis·joint \dis-ᵗjȯint\ *vb* : to separate the parts of : DISCONNECT; *also* : to separate at the joints

dis·joint·ed \-əd\ *adj* **1** : DISCONNECTED; *esp* : INCOHERENT **2** : separated at or as if at the joint

disk *or* **disc** \ᵗdisk\ *n* **1** : something round and flat; *esp* : a flat rounded anatomical structure (as the central part of the flower head of a composite plant or a pad of cartilage between vertebrae) **2** *usu* **disc** : a phonograph record **3** : a round flat plate coated with a magnetic substance on which data for a computer is stored

¹**dis·like** \dis-ᵗlīk\ *n* : a feeling of distaste or disapproval

²**dislike** *vb* : to regard with dislike : DISAPPROVE

dis·lo·cate \ᵗdis-lō-ˌkāt, dis-ᵗlō-\ *vb* **1** : to put out of place; *esp* : to displace (a bone or joint) from normal connections 〈∼ a shoulder〉 **2** : DISRUPT — **dis·lo·ca·tion** \ˌdis-(ˌ)lō-ᵗkā-shən\ *n*

dis·lodge \dis-ᵗläj\ *vb* : to force out of a place esp. of rest, hiding, or defense

dis·loy·al \dis-ᵗlȯi(-ə)l\ *adj* : lacking in loyalty — **dis·loy·al·ty** *n*

dis·mal \ᵗdiz-məl\ *adj* [ME, fr. *dismal*, n., days marked as unlucky in medieval calendars, fr. ML *dies mali*, lit., evil days] **1** : showing or causing gloom or depression **2** : lacking interest or merit — **dis·mal·ly** \-ē\ *adv*

dis·man·tle \dis-ᵗmant-ᵊl\ *vb* **-tled; -tling** \-ᵗmant-(ə-)liŋ\ **1** : to take apart **2** : to strip of furniture and equipment — **dis·man·tle·ment** *n*

dis·may \dis-ᵗmā\ *vb* : to cause to lose courage or resolution from alarm or fear : DAUNT — **dismay** *n* — **dis·may·ing·ly** \-iŋ-lē\ *adv*

dis·mem·ber \dis-ᵗmem-bər\ *vb* **-bered; -ber·ing** \-b(ə-)riŋ\ **1** : to cut off or separate the limbs or parts of **2** : to break up or tear into pieces — **dis·mem·ber·ment** *n*

dis·miss \dis-ᵗmis\ *vb* **1** : to send away **2** : to send or remove from office, ser-vice, or employment **3** : to put aside or out of mind **4** : to refuse further judicial hearing or consideration to 〈the judge ∼ed the charge〉 — **dis·miss·al** *n*

dis·mount \dis-ᵗmaʉnt\ *vb* **1** : to get down from something (as a horse or bicycle) **2** : UNHORSE **3** : DISASSEMBLE

dis·obe·di·ence \ˌdis-ə-ᵗbēd-ē-əns\ *n* : neglect or refusal to obey — **dis·obe·di·ent** \-ənt\ *adj*

dis·obey \ˌdis-ə-ᵗbā\ *vb* : to fail to obey : be disobedient

dis·oblige \ˌdis-ə-ᵗblīj\ *vb* **1** : to go counter to the wishes of **2** : INCONVEN-IENCE

¹**dis·or·der** \dis-ᵗȯrd-ər\ *vb* **1** : to disturb the order of **2** : to cause disorder in 〈a ∼ed digestion〉

²**disorder** *n* **1** : lack of order : CONFUSION **2** : breach of the peace or public order : TUMULT **3** : an abnormal state of body or mind : AILMENT

dis·or·der·ly \-lē\ *adj* **1** : offensive to public order or decency; *also* : guilty of disorderly conduct **2** : marked by disorder : DISARRANGED 〈a ∼ desk〉 — **dis·or·der·li·ness** *n*

dis·or·ga·nize \dis-ᵗȯr-gə-ˌnīz\ *vb* : to break up the regular system of : throw into disorder — **dis·or·ga·ni·za·tion** \dis-ˌȯrg-(ə-)nə-ᵗzā-shən\ *n*

dis·ori·ent \dis-ᵗōr-ē-ˌent\ *vb* : to cause to be confused or lost — **dis·ori·en·ta·tion** \dis-ˌōr-ē-ən-ᵗtā-shən\ *n*

dis·own \dis-ᵗōn\ *vb* : REPUDIATE, RE-NOUNCE, DISCLAIM

dis·par·age \dis-ᵗpar-ij\ *vb* **-aged; -ag·ing** [ME *disparagen* to degrade by marriage below one's class, disparage, fr. MF *desparagier* to marry below one's class, fr. OF, fr. *parage* extraction, lineage, fr. *per* peer] **1** : to lower in rank or reputation : DEGRADE **2** : BE-LITTLE — **dis·par·age·ment** *n* — **dis·par·ag·ing·ly** \-ij-iŋ-lē\ *adv*

dis·pa·rate \ᵗdis-p(ə-)rət, dis-ᵗpar-ət\ *adj* : distinct in quality or character — **dis·par·i·ty** \dis-ᵗpar-ət-ē\ *n*

dis·pas·sion·ate \dis-ᵗpash-(ə-)nət\ *adj* : not influenced by strong feeling : CALM, IMPARTIAL — **dis·pas·sion** \-ən\ *n* — **dis·pas·sion·ate·ly** *adv*

¹**dis·patch** \dis-ᵗpach\ *vb* **1** : to send off or away with promptness or speed esp. on official business **2** : to put to

death **3** : to attend to rapidly or efficiently — **dis·patch·er** n

²dispatch n **1** : the act of dispatching; *esp* : SHIPMENT **2** : the act of putting to death **3** : MESSAGE **4** : a news item sent in by a correspondent to a newspaper **5** : promptness and efficiency in performing a task

dis·pel \dis-ˈpel\ vb **dis·pelled; dis·pel·ling** : to drive away by scattering : DISSIPATE

dis·pens·able \dis-ˈpen-sə-bəl\ adj : capable of being dispensed with

dis·pen·sa·ry \dis-ˈpens-(ə-)rē\ n, pl **-ries** : a place where medicine or medical or dental aid is dispensed

dis·pen·sa·tion \ˌdis-pən-ˈsā-shən\ n **1** : a system of rules for ordering affairs **2** : a particular arrangement or provision esp. of nature **3** : an exemption from a rule or from a vow or oath **4** : the act of dispensing **5** : something dispensed or distributed

dis·pense \dis-ˈpens\ vb **dis·pensed; dis·pens·ing 1** : to portion out **2** : ADMINISTER ⟨~ justice⟩ **3** : EXEMPT **4** : to make up and give out (remedies) — **dis·pens·er** n — **dispense with 1** : SUSPEND **2** : to do without

dis·perse \dis-ˈpərs\ vb **dis·persed; dis·pers·ing** : to break up and scatter about : SPREAD — **dis·per·sal** \-ˈpər-səl\ n — **dis·per·sion** \-ˈpər-zhən\ n

dis·pir·it \dis-ˈpir-ət\ vb : DEPRESS, DISCOURAGE, DISHEARTEN

dis·place \dis-ˈplās\ vb **1** : to remove from the usual or proper place; esp : to expel or force to flee from home or native land ⟨displaced persons⟩ **2** : to move out of position ⟨water displaced by a floating object⟩ **3** : to take the place of : REPLACE

dis·place·ment \dis-ˈplās-mənt\ n **1** : the act of displacing : the state of being displaced **2** : the volume or weight of a fluid displaced by a floating body (as a ship) **3** : the difference between the initial position of an object and a later position

¹dis·play \dis-ˈplā\ vb : to present to view

²display n **1** : a displaying of something **2** : an electronic device (as a cathode-ray tube) that gives information in visual form; also : the visual information

dis·please \dis-ˈplēz\ vb **1** : to arouse the disapproval and dislike of **2** : to be offensive to : give displeasure

dis·plea·sure \dis-ˈplezh-ər\ n : a feeling of dislike and irritation

dis·port \dis-ˈpōrt\ vb **1** : DIVERT, AMUSE **2** : FROLIC **3** : DISPLAY

dis·pos·able \dis-ˈpō-zə-bəl\ adj **1** : remaining after deduction of taxes ⟨~ income⟩ **2** : designed to be used once and then thrown away ⟨~ diapers⟩ — **disposable** n

dis·pos·al \dis-ˈpō-zəl\ n **1** : CONTROL, COMMAND **2** : an orderly arrangement **3** : a getting rid of **4** : MANAGEMENT, ADMINISTRATION **5** : the transfer of something into new hands

dis·pose \dis-ˈpōz\ vb **dis·posed; dis·pos·ing 1** : to give a tendency to : INCLINE ⟨disposed to accept⟩ **2** : to put in place : ARRANGE ⟨troops disposed for withdrawal⟩ **3** : SETTLE — **dis·pos·er** n — **dispose of 1** : to transfer to the control of another **2** : to get rid of **3** : to deal with conclusively

dis·po·si·tion \ˌdis-pə-ˈzish-ən\ n **1** : the act or power of disposing : DISPOSAL ⟨funds at their ~⟩ **2** : RELINQUISHMENT **3** : ARRANGEMENT **4** : TENDENCY, INCLINATION **5** : natural attitude toward things ⟨a cheerful ~⟩

dis·pos·sess \ˌdis-pə-ˈzes\ vb : to put out of possession or occupancy — **dis·pos·ses·sion** \-ˈzesh-ən\ n

dis·praise \dis-ˈprāz\ vb : DISPARAGE — **dispraise** n

dis·pro·por·tion \ˌdis-prə-ˈpōr-shən\ n : lack of proportion, symmetry, or proper relation — **dis·pro·por·tion·ate** \-sh(ə-)nət\ adj

dis·prove \dis-ˈprüv\ vb : to prove to be false — **dis·proof** \-ˈprüf\ n

dis·pu·tant \dis-ˈpyüt-ᵊnt, ˈdis-pyət-ənt\ n : one that is engaged in a dispute

dis·pu·ta·tion \ˌdis-pyə-ˈtā-shən\ n **1** : DEBATE **2** : an oral defense of an academic thesis

dis·pu·ta·tious \-shəs\ adj : inclined to dispute : ARGUMENTATIVE

¹dis·pute \dis-ˈpyüt\ vb **dis·put·ed; dis·put·ing 1** : ARGUE, DEBATE **2** : WRANGLE **3** : to deny the truth or rightness of **4** : to struggle against or over : CONTEST — **dis·put·able** \dis-ˈpyüt-ə-

bəl, **'dis-pyət-ə-bəl**\ *adj* — **dis·put·er**
\dis-**'**pyüt-ər\ *n*

²**dis·pute** *n* **1** : DEBATE **2** : QUARREL

dis·qual·i·fy \dis-**'**kwäl-ə-₁fī\ *vb* : to
make or declare unfit or not qualified
— **dis·qual·i·fi·ca·tion** \-₁kwäl-ə-fə-
'kā-shən\ *n*

¹**dis·qui·et** \dis-**'**kwī-ət\ *vb* : to make uneasy or restless : DISTURB

²**disquiet** *n* : lack of peace or tranquillity
: ANXIETY

dis·qui·etude \dis-**'**kwī-ə-₁t(y)üd\ *n*
: AGITATION, ANXIETY

dis·qui·si·tion \₁dis-kwə-**'**zish-ən\ *n* : a
formal inquiry or discussion

¹**dis·re·gard** \₁dis-ri-**'**gärd\ *vb* : to pay no
attention to : treat as unworthy of no-
tice or regard

²**disregard** *n* : the act of disregarding
: the state of being disregarded : NE-
GLECT — **dis·re·gard·ful** *adj*

dis·re·pair \₁dis-ri-**'**paər\ *n* : the state of
being in need of repair

dis·rep·u·ta·ble \dis-**'**rep-yət-ə-bəl\ *adj*
: not reputable : DISCREDITABLE; *esp*
: having a bad reputation

dis·re·pute \₁dis-ri-**'**pyüt\ *n* : loss or
lack of reputation : low esteem

dis·re·spect \₁dis-ri-**'**spekt\ *n* : DIS-
COURTESY — **dis·re·spect·ful** *adj*

dis·robe \dis-**'**rōb\ *vb* : UNDRESS

dis·rupt \dis-**'**rəpt\ *vb* **1** : to break apart
2 : to throw into disorder — **dis·rup·
tion** \-**'**rəp-shən\ *n* — **dis·rup·tive**
\-**'**rəp-tiv\ *adj*

dis·sat·is·fac·tion \dis-₁at-əs-**'**fak-shən\
n : DISCONTENT

dis·sat·is·fy \dis-**'**at-əs-₁fī\ *vb* : to fail to
satisfy : DISPLEASE — **dis·sat·is·fied** *adj*

dis·sect \dis-**'**ekt\ *vb* **1** : to divide into
parts esp. for examination and study **2**
: ANALYZE — **dis·sec·tion** \-**'**ek-shən\ *n*

dis·sect·ed *adj* : cut deeply into narrow
lobes ⟨a ∼ leaf⟩

dis·sem·ble \dis-**'**em-bəl\ *vb* **-bled;**
-bling \-b(ə-)liŋ\ **1** : to hide under or
put on a false appearance : conceal
facts, intentions, or feelings under
some pretense **2** : SIMULATE — **dis·
sem·bler** \-b(ə-)lər\ *n*

dis·sem·i·nate \dis-**'**em-ə-₁nāt\ *vb* **-nat-
ed; -nat·ing** : to spread abroad as if
sowing seed ⟨∼ ideas⟩ — **dis·sem·i·na·
tion** \-₁em-ə-**'**nā-shən\ *n*

dis·sen·sion \dis-**'**en-chən\ *n* : disagreement in opinion : DISCORD

¹**dis·sent** \dis-**'**ent\ *vb* **1** : to withhold assent **2** : to differ in opinion

²**dissent** *n* **1** : difference of opinion; *esp*
: religious nonconformity **2** : a written statement in which a justice dis-
agrees with the opinion of the majori-
ty — **dis·sen·tient** \-**'**en-chənt\ *adj or n*

dis·sent·er \dis-**'**ent-ər\ *n* **1** : one that
dissents **2** *cap* : an English Nonconformist

dis·ser·ta·tion \₁dis-ər-**'**tā-shən\ *n* : an
extended usu. written treatment of a
subject; *esp* : one submitted for a doc-
torate

dis·ser·vice \dis-**'**ər-vəs\ *n* : INJURY,
HARM, MISCHIEF

dis·sev·er \dis-**'**ev-ər\ *vb* : SEPARATE,
DISUNITE

dis·si·dent **'**dis-əd-ənt\ *adj* [L *dissid-
ens,* prp. of *dissidēre* to sit apart,
disagree, fr. *dis-* apart + *sedēre* to sit]
: disagreeing with an opinion or a
group — **dis·si·dence** \-əns\ *n* —
dissident *n*

dis·sim·i·lar \dis-**'**im-ə-lər\ *adj* : UNLIKE
— **dis·sim·i·lar·i·ty** \dis-₁im-ə-**'**lar-
ət-ē\ *n*

dis·sim·u·late \dis-**'**im-yə-₁lāt\ *vb* : to
hide under a false appearance : DIS-
SEMBLE — **dis·sim·u·la·tion** \dis-₁im-
yə-**'**lā-shən\ *n*

dis·si·pate **'**dis-ə-₁pāt\ *vb* **-pat·ed; -pat-
ing 1** : to break up and drive off : DIS-
PERSE, SCATTER ⟨∼ a crowd⟩ **2** : DISPEL,
DISSOLVE ⟨the breeze *dissipated* the
fog⟩ **3** : SQUANDER **4** : to break up and
vanish **5** : to be dissolute; *esp* : to
drink alcoholic beverages to excess —
dis·si·pat·ed *adj* — **dis·si·pa·tion** \dis-ə-
'pā-shən\ *n*

dis·so·ci·ate \dis-**'**ō-s(h)ē-₁āt\ *vb* **-at·ed;
-at·ing** : DISCONNECT, DISUNITE — **dis·
so·ci·a·tion** \dis-₁ō-s(h)ē-**'**ā-shən\ *n*

dis·so·lute **'**dis-ə-₁lüt\ *adj* : loose in
morals or conduct — **dis·so·lute·ly** *adv*
— **dis·so·lute·ness** *n*

dis·so·lu·tion \₁dis-ə-**'**lü-shən\ *n* **1** : the
action or process of dissolving **2**
: separation of a thing into its parts **3**
: DECAY; *also* : DEATH **4** : the termination or breaking up of an assembly or
a partnership

dis·solve \diz-**'**älv\ *vb* **1** : to separate
into component parts **2** : to pass or
cause to pass into solution ⟨sugar ∼s
in water⟩ **3** : TERMINATE, DISPERSE ⟨∼

parliament⟩ **4** : to waste or fade away ⟨his courage *dissolved*⟩ **5** : to be overcome emotionally ⟨~ in tears⟩ **6** : to resolve itself as if by dissolution

dis·so·nance \ˈdis-ə-nəns\ *n* : DISCORD — **dis·so·nant** \-nənt\ *adj*

dis·suade \dis-ˈwād\ *vb* **dis·suad·ed; dis·suad·ing** : to advise against a course of action : persuade or try to persuade not to do something — **dis·sua·sion** \-ˈwā-zhən\ *n* — **dis·sua·sive** \-ˈwā-siv\ *adj*

dist *abbr* **1** distance **2** district

¹**dis·taff** \ˈdis-ˌtaf\ *n, pl* **distaffs** \-ˌtafs, -ˌtavz\ **1** : a staff for holding the flax, tow, or wool in spinning **2** : a woman's work or domain **3** : the female branch or side of a family

²**distaff** *adj* : MATERNAL, FEMALE

dis·tal \ˈdis-tᵊl\ *adj* **1** : away from the point of attachment or origin **2** : of, relating to, or being the surface of a tooth that faces the back of the mouth — **dis·tal·ly** \-ē\ *adv*

¹**dis·tance** \ˈdis-təns\ *n* **1** : measure of separation in space or time **2** : EXPANSE **3** : the full length ⟨go the ~⟩ **4** : spatial remoteness **5** : COLDNESS, RESERVE **6** : DIFFERENCE, DISPARITY **7** : a distant point

²**distance** *vb* **dis·tanced; dis·tanc·ing** : to leave far behind : OUTSTRIP

dis·tant \ˈdis-tənt\ *adj* **1** : separate in space : AWAY **2** : FAR-OFF **3** : far apart **4** : not close in relationship ⟨a ~ cousin⟩ **5** : different in kind **6** : RESERVED, ALOOF, COLD ⟨~ politeness⟩ **7** : coming from or going to a distance — **dis·tant·ly** *adv* — **dis·tant·ness** *n*

dis·taste \dis-ˈtāst\ *n* : DISINCLINATION, DISLIKE — **dis·taste·ful** *adj*

dis·tem·per \dis-ˈtem-pər\ *n* : a bodily disorder usu. of a domestic animal; *esp* : a contagious often fatal virus disease of dogs

dis·tend \dis-ˈtend\ *vb* : EXPAND, SWELL — **dis·ten·si·ble** \-ˈten-sə-bəl\ *adj* — **dis·ten·sion** *or* **dis·ten·tion** \-chən\ *n*

dis·tich \ˈdis-(ˌ)tik\ *n* : a strophic unit of two lines

dis·till *also* **dis·til** \dis-ˈtil\ *vb* **dis·tilled; dis·till·ing** **1** : to fall or let fall drop by drop **2** : to obtain or purify by distillation — **dis·till·er** *n* — **dis·till·ery** \-(ə-)rē\ *n*

dis·til·late \ˈdis-tə-ˌlāt, -lət\ *n* : a liquid product condensed from vapor during distillation

dis·til·la·tion \ˌdis-tə-ˈlā-shən\ *n* : the driving off of gas or vapor from liquids or solids by heat and then condensing to a liquid product

dis·tinct \dis-ˈtiŋkt\ *adj* **1** : SEPARATE, INDIVIDUAL **2** : presenting a clear unmistakable impression — **dis·tinct·ly** *adv* — **dis·tinct·ness** *n*

dis·tinc·tion \dis-ˈtiŋk-shən\ *n* **1** : the act of distinguishing a difference **2** : DIFFERENCE **3** : a distinguishing quality or mark **4** : special honor or recognition

dis·tinc·tive \dis-ˈtiŋk-tiv\ *adj* **1** : clearly marking a person or a thing as different from others **2** : having or giving style or distinction — **dis·tinc·tive·ly** *adv* — **dis·tinc·tive·ness** *n*

dis·tin·guish \dis-ˈtiŋ-gwish\ *vb* [MF *distinguer*, fr. L *distinguere*, lit., to separate by pricking] **1** : to recognize by some mark or characteristic **2** : to hear or see clearly : DISCERN **3** : to make distinctions ⟨~ between right and wrong⟩ **4** : to set apart : mark as different — **dis·tin·guish·able** *adj*

dis·tin·guished \-gwisht\ *adj* **1** : marked by eminence or excellence **2** : befitting an eminent person

dis·tort \dis-ˈtȯrt\ *vb* **1** : to twist out of the true meaning **2** : to twist out of a natural, normal, or original shape or condition — **dis·tor·tion** \-ˈtȯr-shən\ *n*

distr *abbr* distribute; distribution

dis·tract \dis-ˈtrakt\ *vb* **1** : to draw (the attention or mind) to a different object : DIVERT **2** : to stir up or confuse with conflicting emotions or motives : HARASS — **dis·trac·tion** \-ˈtrak-shən\ *n*

dis·trait \di-ˈstrā\ *adj* [F, fr. L *distractus*] : ABSENTMINDED, DISTRAUGHT

dis·traught \dis-ˈtrȯt\ *adj* : PERPLEXED, CONFUSED; *also* : CRAZED

¹**dis·tress** \dis-ˈtres\ *n* **1** : suffering of body or mind : PAIN, ANGUISH **2** : TROUBLE, MISFORTUNE **3** : a condition of danger or desperate need — **dis·tress·ful** *adj*

²**distress** *vb* **1** : to subject to great strain or difficulties **2** : UPSET

dis·trib·ute \dis-ˈtrib-yət\ *vb* **-ut·ed; -ut·ing** **1** : to divide among several or many : APPORTION **2** : to spread out : SCATTER; *also* : DELIVER **3** : CLASSIFY

— **dis·tri·bu·tion** \ˌdis-trə-ˈbyü-shən\ *n*

dis·trib·u·tive \dis-ˈtrib-yət-iv\ *adj* **1** : of or relating to distribution **2** : being or concerned with a mathematical operation (as multiplication in $a(b + c) = ab + ac$) that produces the same result when operating on a whole mathematical expression as when operating on each part and collecting the results — **dis·trib·u·tive·ly** *adv*

dis·trib·u·tor \dis-ˈtrib-yət-ər\ *n* **1** : one that distributes **2** : an agent or agency for marketing goods **3** : a device for directing current to the spark plugs of an engine

dis·trict \ˈdis-(ˌ)trikt\ *n* **1** : a fixed territorial division (as for administrative or electoral purposes) **2** : an area, region, or section with a distinguishing character

district attorney *n* : the prosecuting attorney of a judicial district

¹**dis·trust** \dis-ˈtrəst\ *vb* : to feel no confidence in : SUSPECT

²**distrust** *n* : a lack of trust or confidence : SUSPICION, WARINESS — **dis·trust·ful** \-fəl\ *adj* — **dis·trust·ful·ly** \-ē\ *adv*

dis·turb \dis-ˈtərb\ *vb* **1** : to interfere with : INTERRUPT **2** : to alter the position or arrangement of **3** : to destroy the tranquillity or composure of **4** : make uneasy **4** : to throw into disorder **5** : INCONVENIENCE — **dis·tur·bance** \-ˈtər-bəns\ *n* — **dis·turb·er** *n*

dis·turbed \-ˈtərbd\ *adj* : showing symptoms of mental or emotional illness

dis·unite \ˌdis-yü-ˈnīt\ *vb* : DIVIDE, SEPARATE

dis·uni·ty \dis-ˈyü-nət-ē\ *n* : lack of unity; *esp* : DISSENSION

dis·use \-ˈyüs\ *n* : a cessation of use or practice

¹**ditch** \ˈdich\ *n* : a long narrow channel or trench dug in the earth

²**ditch** *vb* **1** : to enclose with a ditch; *also* : to dig a ditch in **2** : to get rid of : DISCARD **3** : to make a forced landing of an airplane on water

dith·er \ˈdith-ər\ *n* : a highly nervous, excited, or agitated state

dit·to \ˈdit-ō\ *n, pl* **dittos** [It dial., pp. of It *dire* to say, fr. L *dicere*] **1** : the same or more of the same : ANOTHER — used to avoid repeating a word ⟨lost: one book (new); ∼ (old)⟩ **2** : a mark composed of a pair of inverted commas or apostrophes used as a symbol for the word *ditto*

dit·ty \ˈdit-ē\ *n, pl* **ditties** : a short simple song

di·uret·ic \ˌdī-(y)ə-ˈret-ik\ *adj* : tending to increase urine flow — **diuretic** *n*

di·ur·nal \dī-ˈərn-ᵊl\ *adj* **1** : DAILY **2** : of, relating to, or occurring in the daytime

div *abbr* **1** divided **2** dividend **3** division **4** divorced

di·va \ˈdē-və\ *n, pl* **divas** *or* **di·ve** \-ˌvä\ [It, lit., goddess, fr. L, fem. of *divus* divine, god] : PRIMA DONNA

di·va·gate \ˈdī-və-ˌgāt\ *vb* **-gat·ed; -gat·ing** : to wander about or stray from a course or subject : DIVERGE — **di·va·ga·tion** \ˌdī-və-ˈgā-shən\ *n*

di·van \ˈdī-ˌvan, di-ˈvan\ *n* : COUCH, SOFA

¹**dive** \ˈdīv\ *vb* **dived** \ˈdīvd\ *or* **dove** \ˈdōv\; **dived; div·ing** **1** : to plunge into water headfirst **2** : SUBMERGE **3** : to descend or fall precipitously **4** : to descend in an airplane at a steep angle **5** : to plunge into some matter or activity **6** : DART, LUNGE — **div·er** *n*

²**dive** *n* **1** : the act or an instance of diving **2** : a sharp decline **3** : a disreputable bar or place of amusement

di·verge \də-ˈvərj, dī-\ *vb* **di·verged; di·verg·ing** **1** : to move or extend in different directions from a common point : draw apart **2** : to differ in character, form, or opinion **3** : DEVIATE **4** : DEFLECT — **di·ver·gence** \-ˈvər-jəns\ *n* — **di·ver·gent** \-jənt\ *adj*

di·vers \ˈdī-vərz\ *adj* : VARIOUS

di·verse \dī-ˈvərs, də-, ˈdī-ˌvərs\ *adj* **1** : UNLIKE **2** : composed of distinct forms or qualities ⟨the ∼ nature of man⟩ — **di·verse·ly** *adv*

di·ver·si·fy \də-ˈvər-sə-ˌfī, dī-\ *vb* **-fied; -fy·ing** : to make different or various in form or quality — **di·ver·si·fi·ca·tion** \-ˌvər-sə-fə-ˈkā-shən\ *n*

di·ver·sion \də-ˈvər-zhən, dī-\ *n* **1** : a turning aside from a course, activity, or use : DEVIATION **2** : something that diverts or amuses : PASTIME

di·ver·si·ty \də-ˈvər-sət-ē, dī-\ *n, pl* **-ties** **1** : the condition of being different : VARIETY **2** : an instance or a point of difference

di·vert \də-ˈvərt, dī-\ *vb* **1** : to turn from a course or purpose : DEFLECT **2** : DISTRACT **3** : ENTERTAIN, AMUSE

di·vest \dī-ˈvest, də-\ *vb* **1** : to strip esp. of clothing, ornament, or equipment **2** : to deprive or dispossess esp. of property, authority, or rights

¹**di·vide** \də-ˈvīd\ *vb* **di·vid·ed; di·vid·ing** **1** : SEPARATE; *also* : CLASSIFY **2** : CLEAVE, PART **3** : DISTRIBUTE, APPORTION **4** : to possess or make use of in common : share in **5** : to cause to be separate, distinct, or apart from one another **6** : to separate into opposing sides or parties **7** : to mark divisions on **8** : to subject to or use in mathematical division **9** : to branch out

²**divide** *n* : WATERSHED 1

div·i·dend \ˈdiv-ə-ˌdend\ *n* **1** : an individual share of something distributed **2** : BONUS **3** : a number to be divided by another **4** : a sum or fund to be divided or distributed

di·vid·er \də-ˈvīd-ər\ *n* **1** : one that divides (as a partition) ⟨room ∼⟩ **2** *pl* : COMPASS 5

div·i·na·tion \ˌdiv-ə-ˈnā-shən\ *n* **1** : the art or practice of using omens or magic powers to foretell the future **2** : unusual insight or intuitive perception

¹**di·vine** \də-ˈvīn\ *adj* **di·vin·er; -est** **1** : of, relating to, or being God or a god **2** : supremely good : SUPERB; *also* : HEAVENLY — **di·vine·ly** *adv*

²**divine** *n* **1** : CLERGYMAN **2** : THEOLOGIAN

³**divine** *vb* **di·vined; di·vin·ing** **1** : INFER, CONJECTURE **2** : PROPHESY **3** : DOWSE — **di·vin·er** *n*

di·vin·ing rod \də-ˈvī-niŋ-\ *n* : a forked rod believed to reveal the presence of water or minerals by dipping downward when held over a vein

di·vin·i·ty \də-ˈvin-ət-ē\ *n, pl* **-ties** **1** : THEOLOGY **2** : the quality or state of being divine **3** : a divine being; *esp* : GOD 1

di·vis·i·ble \də-ˈviz-ə-bəl\ *adj* : capable of being divided — **di·vis·i·bil·i·ty** \-ˌbil-ət-ē\ *n*

di·vi·sion \də-ˈvizh-ən\ *n* **1** : DISTRIBUTION, SEPARATION **2** : one of the parts or groupings into which a whole is divided **3** : DISAGREEMENT, DISUNITY **4** : something that divides or separates **5** : the mathematical operation of finding how many times one number or quantity is contained in another **6** : a large self-contained military unit **7** : an administrative or operating unit of a governmental, business, or educational organization — **di·vi·sion·al** \-ˈvizh-(ə-)nəl\ *adj*

di·vi·sive \də-ˈvī-siv, -ˈviz-iv\ *adj* : creating disunity or dissension — **di·vi·sive·ly** *adv* — **di·vi·sive·ness** *n*

di·vi·sor \də-ˈvī-zər\ *n* : the number by which a dividend is divided

di·vorce \də-ˈvōrs\ *n* **1** : a complete legal breaking up of a marriage **2** : SEPARATION, SEVERANCE — **divorce** *vb* — **di·vorce·ment** *n*

di·vor·cé \də-ˌvōr-ˈsā\ *n* [F] : a divorced man

di·vor·cée \də-ˌvōr-ˈsā, -ˈsē\ *n* : a divorced woman

div·ot \ˈdiv-ət\ *n* : a piece of turf dug from a golf fairway in making a stroke

di·vulge \də-ˈvəlj, dī-\ *vb* **di·vulged; di·vulg·ing** : REVEAL, DISCLOSE

Dix·ie·land \ˈdik-sē-ˌland\ *n* : lively jazz music in a style developed in New Orleans

diz·zy \ˈdiz-ē\ *adj* **diz·zi·er; -est** [ME *disy*, fr. OE *dysig* stupid] **1** : having a sensation of whirling : GIDDY **2** : causing or caused by giddiness — **diz·zi·ly** \ˈdiz-ə-lē\ *adv* — **diz·zi·ness** \-ē-nəs\ *n*

DJ *abbr* disc jockey

dk *abbr* **1** dark **2** deck **3** dock

dl *abbr* deciliter

DLitt *or* **DLit** *abbr* [L *doctor litterarum*] doctor of letters; doctor of literature

DLO *abbr* dead letter office

dm *abbr* decimeter

DMD *abbr* [NL *dentariae medicinae doctor*] doctor of dental medicine

DMZ *abbr* demilitarized zone

dn *abbr* down

DNA \ˌdē-ˌen-ˈā\ *n* : any of various nucleic acids usu. of cell nuclei that are the molecular basis of heredity in many organisms

¹**do** \(ˈ)dü\ *vb* **did** \(ˈ)did\; **done** \ˈdən\; **do·ing** \ˈdü-iŋ\; **does** \(ˈ)dəz\ **1** : to bring to pass : ACCOMPLISH **2** : ACT, BEHAVE ⟨∼ as I say⟩ **3** : to be active or busy ⟨up and ∼ing⟩ **4** : HAPPEN ⟨what's ∼ing?⟩ **5** : to work at ⟨he *does* tailoring⟩ **6** : PREPARE ⟨*did* his homework⟩ **7** : to put in order (as by cleaning or arranging) ⟨∼ the dishes⟩ **8**

: DECORATE ⟨*did* the hall in blue⟩ **9** : GET ALONG ⟨he *does* well⟩ **10** : CARRY ON, MANAGE **11** : to feel or function better ⟨could ∼ with some food⟩ **12** : RENDER ⟨sleep will ∼ you good⟩ **13** : FINISH ⟨when he had *done*⟩ **14** : EXERT ⟨*did* my best⟩ **15** : PRODUCE ⟨*did* a poem⟩ **16** : to play the part of **17** : CHEAT ⟨*did* him out of his share⟩ **18** : TRAVERSE, TOUR **19** : TRAVEL **20** : to serve out in prison **21** : to serve the needs or purpose of : SUIT **22** : to be fitting or proper **23** — used as an auxiliary verb (1) before the subject in an interrogative sentence ⟨*does* he work?⟩ and after some adverbs ⟨never *did* he say so⟩ , (2) in a negative statement ⟨I *don't* know⟩ , (3) for emphasis ⟨he *does* know⟩ , and (4) as a substitute for a preceding predicate ⟨he works harder than I ∼⟩ — **do away with 1** : to put an end to **2** : DESTROY, KILL — **do by** : to act toward in a specified way : TREAT ⟨*did* right *by* her⟩ — **do for** : to bring about the death or ruin of — **do one's thing** : to do what is personally satisfying

²do *abbr* ditto

DOA *abbr* dead on arrival

DOB *abbr* date of birth

dob·bin \'däb-ən\ *n* [*Dobbin*, nickname for *Robert*] **1** : a farm horse **2** : a quiet plodding horse

Do·ber·man pin·scher \ˌdō-bər-mən-'pin-chər\ *n* : a short-haired medium-sized dog of a breed of German origin

do·bra \'dō-brə\ *n* — see MONEY table

dob·son·fly \'däb-sən-ˌflī\ *n* : a large-eyed winged insect with long slender mandibles in the male and a large carnivorous aquatic larva

¹doc \'däk\ *n* : DOCTOR

²doc *abbr* document

do·cent \'dōs-³nt, dō(t)-'sent\ *n* [obs. G (now *dozent*), deriv. of L *docēre* to teach] : TEACHER, LECTURER

doc·ile \'däs-əl\ *adj* [L *docilis*, fr. *docēre* to teach] : easily taught, led, or managed : TRACTABLE — **do·cil·i·ty** \dä-'sil-ət-ē\ *n*

¹dock \'däk\ *n* : any of a genus of coarse weedy herbs related to buckwheat

²dock *vb* **1** : to cut off the end of : cut short **2** : to take away a part of : deduct from ⟨∼ a man's wages⟩

³dock *n* **1** : an artificial basin to receive ships **2** : a slip between two piers to receive ships **3** : a wharf or platform for loading or unloading materials

⁴dock *vb* **1** : to bring or come into dock **2** : to join (as two spacecraft) mechanically in space

⁵dock *n* : the place in a court where a prisoner stands or sits during trial

dock·age \'däk-ij\ *n* : the provision or use of a dock; *also* : the charge for using a dock

dock·et \'däk-ət\ *n* **1** : a formal abridged record of the proceedings in a legal action; *also* : a register of such records **2** : a list of legal causes to be tried **3** : a calendar of matters to be acted on : AGENDA **4** : a label attached to a document containing identification or directions — **docket** *vb*

dock·hand \'däk-ˌhand\ *n* : LONGSHOREMAN

dock·work·er \-ˌwər-kər\ *n* : LONGSHOREMAN

dock·yard \-ˌyärd\ *n* : SHIPYARD

¹doc·tor \'däk-tər\ *n* [ME *doctour* teacher, doctor, fr. MF & ML; MF, fr. ML *doctor*, fr. L, teacher, fr. *docēre* to teach] **1** : a person holding one of the highest academic degrees (as a PhD) conferred by a university **2** : one skilled in healing arts; *esp* : an academically and legally qualified physician, surgeon, dentist, or veterinarian **3** : a person who restores or repairs things — **doc·tor·al** \-t(ə-)rəl\ *adj*

²doctor *vb* **doc·tored; doc·tor·ing** \-t(ə-)riŋ\ **1** : to give medical treatment to **2** : to practice medicine **3** : REPAIR **4** : to adapt or modify for a desired end **5** : to alter deceptively

doc·tor·ate \'däk-t(ə-)rət\ *n* : the degree, title, or rank of a doctor

doc·tri·naire \ˌdäk-trə-'naər\ *n* [F] : one who attempts to put an abstract theory into effect without regard to practical difficulties — **doctrinaire** *adj*

doc·trine \'däk-trən\ *n* **1** : something that is taught **2** : DOGMA, TENET — **doc·tri·nal** \-trən-³l\ *adj*

docu·dra·ma \'däk-yə-ˌdräm-ə, -ˌdram-ə\ *n* : a television or motion-picture drama that deals with historical events

doc·u·ment \'däk-yə-mənt\ *n* : a paper

that furnishes information, proof, or support of something else — **doc·u·ment** \-ˌment\ *vb* — **doc·u·men·ta·tion** \ˌdäk-yə-mən-'tā-shən\ *n*

doc·u·men·ta·ry \ˌdäk-yə-'men-t(ə-)rē\ *adj* **1** : consisting of documents; *also* : being in writing ⟨∼ proof⟩ **2** : giving a factual presentation in artistic form ⟨a ∼ movie⟩ — **documentary** *n*

DOD *abbr* Department of Defense

¹dod·der \'däd-ər\ *n* : any of a genus of leafless elongated wiry parasitic herbs deficient in chlorophyll

²dodder *vb* **dod·dered; dod·der·ing** \'däd-(ə-)riŋ\ **1** : to tremble or shake usu. from age **2** : to progress feebly and unsteadily

¹dodge \'däj\ *vb* **dodged; dodg·ing 1** : to move suddenly aside; *also* : to avoid or evade by so doing **2** : to avoid by trickery or evasion

²dodge *n* **1** : an act of evading by sudden bodily movement **2** : an artful device to evade, deceive, or trick **3** : EXPEDIENT

do·do \'dōd-ō\ *n, pl* **dodoes** *or* **dodos** [Port *doudo,* fr. *doudo* silly, stupid] **1** : a heavy flightless extinct bird related to the pigeons but larger than a turkey and formerly found on the island of Mauritius **2** : one hopelessly behind the times; *also* : a stupid person

doe \'dō\ *n, pl* **does** *or* **doe** : an adult female deer; *also* : the female of a mammal of which the male is called buck — **doe·skin** \-ˌskin\ *n*

DOE *abbr* Department of Energy

do·er \'dü-ər\ *n* : one that does

does pres 3d sing of DO, pl of DOE

doff \'däf\ *vb* [ME *doffen,* fr. *don* to do + *of* off] **1** : to take off (the hat) in greeting or as a sign of respect **2** : to rid oneself of

¹dog \'dȯg\ *n* **1** : a flesh-eating domestic mammal related to the wolves; *esp* : a male of this animal **2** : a worthless person **3** : FELLOW, CHAP ⟨you lucky ∼⟩ **4** : a mechanical device for holding something **5** : uncharacteristic or affected stylishness or dignity ⟨put on the ∼⟩ **6** *pl* : RUIN ⟨gone to the ∼s⟩

²dog *vb* **dogged; dog·ging 1** : to hunt or track like a hound **2** : to worry as if by pursuit with dogs : HOUND

dog·bane \'dȯg-ˌbān\ *n* : any of a genus

of mostly poisonous herbs with milky juice and often showy flowers

dog·cart \-ˌkärt\ *n* : a light one-horse carriage with two seats back to back

dog·catch·er \-ˌkach-ər, -ˌkech-\ *n* : a community official assigned to catch and dispose of stray dogs

dog·ear \'dȯg-ˌiər\ *n* : the turned-down corner of a leaf of a book — **dog–eared** \-ˌiərd\ *adj*

dog·fight \'dȯg-ˌfīt\ *n* : a fight between two or more fighter planes usu. at close quarters

dog·fish \-ˌfish\ *n* : any of various small sharks

dog·ged \'dȯg-əd\ *adj* : stubbornly determined : TENACIOUS — **dog·ged·ly** *adv* — **dog·ged·ness** *n*

dog·ger·el \'dȯg-(ə-)rəl\ *n* : verse that is loosely styled and irregular in measure esp. for comic effect

dog·gie bag *or* **doggy bag** \'dȯg-ē-\ *n* : a bag provided by a restaurant to a customer for carrying home leftover food

¹dog·gy *or* **dog·gie** \'dȯg-ē\ *n, pl* **doggies** : a small dog

²dog·gy *adj* **dog·gi·er; -est** : of or resembling a dog ⟨a ∼ odor⟩

dog·house \'dȯg-ˌhaůs\ *n* : a shelter for a dog — **in the doghouse** : in a state of disfavor

do·gie \'dō-gē\ *n, chiefly West* : a motherless calf in a range herd

dog·leg \'dȯg-ˌleg\ *n* : a sharp bend or angle (as in a road) — **dogleg** *vb*

dog·ma \'dȯg-mə\ *n* **1** : a tenet or code of tenets **2** : a doctrine or body of doctrines formally proclaimed by a church

dog·ma·tism \'dȯg-mə-ˌtiz-əm\ *n* : positiveness in stating matters of opinion esp. when unwarranted or arrogant — **dog·mat·ic** \dȯg-'mat-ik\ *adj* — **dog·mat·i·cal·ly** \-i-k(ə-)lē\ *adv*

dog·tooth violet \'dȯg-ˌtüth-\ *n* : any of a genus of wild spring-flowering bulbous herbs related to the lilies

dog·trot \'dȯg-ˌträt\ *n* : a gentle trot — **dogtrot** *vb*

dog·wood \'dȯg-ˌwůd\ *n* : any of a genus of trees and shrubs having heads of small flowers often with showy bracts

doi·ly \'dȯi-lē\ *n, pl* **doilies** : a small often decorative mat

do in *vb* **1** : RUIN **2** : KILL **3** : TIRE, EXHAUST **4** : CHEAT

do·ings \'dü-iŋz\ *n pl* : ACTS, DEEDS, EVENTS

do–it–your·self \ˌdü-ə-chər-'self\ *adj* : of, relating to, or designed for use by or as if by an amateur or hobbyist — **do–it–your·self·er** \-'sel-fər\ *n*

dol *abbr* dollar

dol·drums \'dōl-drəmz, 'däl-\ *n pl* **1** : a spell of listlessness or despondency **2** : a part of the ocean near the equator abounding in calms **3** : a state of inactivity, stagnation, or slump ⟨business is in the ∼⟩

¹**dole** \'dōl\ *n* **1** : a distribution esp. of food, money, or clothing to the needy; *also* : something so distributed **2** : a grant of government funds to the unemployed

²**dole** *vb* **doled; dol·ing** **1** : to give or distribute as a charity **2** : to give in small portions : PARCEL ⟨∼ out food⟩

dole·ful \'dōl-fəl\ *adj* : full of grief : SAD — **dole·ful·ly** \-ē\ *adv*

doll \'däl, 'dȯl\ *n* **1** : a small figure of a human being used esp. as a child's plaything **2** : a pretty woman **3** : an attractive person

dol·lar \'däl-ər\ *n* [Dutch or LG *daler,* fr. G *taler,* short for *joachimstaler,* fr. Sankt *Joachimsthal,* Bohemia, where talers were first made] **1** : any of various basic monetary units (as in the U.S. and Canada) — see MONEY table **2** : a coin, note, or token representing one dollar

dol·lop \'däl-əp\ *n* : LUMP, BLOB

doll up *vb* **1** : to dress elegantly or extravagantly **2** : to make more attractive

dol·ly \'däl-ē\ *n, pl* **dollies** : a small wheeled truck used in moving heavy loads; *esp* : a wheeled platform for a television or movie camera

dol·men \'dōl-mən, 'däl-\ *n* : a prehistoric monument consisting of two or more upright stones supporting a horizontal stone slab

do·lo·mite \'dō-lə-ˌmīt, 'däl-ə-\ *n* : a mineral found in broad layers as a compact limestone

do·lor \'dō-lər, 'däl-ər\ *n* : mental suffering or anguish : SORROW — **do·lor·ous** *adj* — **do·lor·ous·ly** *adv* — **do·lor·ous·ness** *n*

dol·phin \'däl-fən\ *n* **1** : any of various small toothed whales with the snout more or less elongated into a beak **2** : either of two active food fishes of tropical and temperate seas

dolt \'dōlt\ *n* : a stupid fellow — **dolt·ish** *adj*

dom *abbr* **1** domestic **2** dominant **3** dominion

-dom \dəm\ *n suffix* **1** : dignity : office ⟨duke*dom*⟩ **2** : realm : jurisdiction ⟨king*dom*⟩ **3** : state or fact of being ⟨free*dom*⟩ **4** : those having a (specified) office, occupation, interest, or character ⟨official*dom*⟩

do·main \dō-'mān, də-\ *n* **1** : complete and absolute ownership of land **2** : land completely owned **3** : a territory over which dominion is exercised **4** : a sphere of influence or action ⟨the ∼ of science⟩

dome \'dōm\ *n* **1** : a large hemispherical roof or ceiling **2** : a structure or natural formation that resembles the dome of a building

¹**do·mes·tic** \də-'mes-tik\ *adj* **1** : living near or about the habitations of humans **2** : TAME, DOMESTICATED **3** : relating and limited to one's own country or the country under consideration **4** : of or relating to the household or the family **5** : devoted to home duties and pleasures **6** : INDIGENOUS — **do·mes·ti·cal·ly** \-ti-k(ə-)lē\ *adv*

²**domestic** *n* : a household servant

do·mes·ti·cate \də-'mes-ti-ˌkāt\ *vb* **-cat·ed; -cat·ing** : to adapt to life in association with and to the use of human beings — **do·mes·ti·ca·tion** \-ˌmes-ti-'kā-shən\ *n*

do·mes·tic·i·ty \ˌdō-ˌmes-'tis-ət-ē, də-\ *n, pl* **-ties** **1** : the quality or state of being domestic or domesticated **2** : domestic activities or life

do·mi·cile \'däm-ə-ˌsīl, 'dō-mə-; 'däm-ə-səl\ *n* : a dwelling place : HOME — **domicile** *vb* — **dom·i·cil·i·ary** \ˌdäm-ə-'sil-ē-ˌer-ē, ˌdō-mə-\ *adj*

dom·i·nance \'däm-ə-nəns\ *n* **1** : AUTHORITY, CONTROL **2** : the property of a genetic dominant that prevents expression of a genetic recessive

¹**dom·i·nant** \'däm-ə-nənt\ *adj* **1** : controlling or prevailing over all others **2** : overlooking from a high elevation **3** : producing or being a bodily char-

acteristic that is expressed when a contrasting recessive gene or trait is present

²dominant n : a dominant gene or a character which it controls

dom·i·nate \'däm-ə-ˌnāt\ vb **-nat·ed; -nat·ing 1** : RULE, CONTROL **2** : to have a commanding position or controlling power over **3** : to rise high above in a position suggesting power to dominate

dom·i·na·tion \ˌdäm-ə-'nā-shən\ n **1** : supremacy or preeminence over another **2** : exercise of mastery or preponderant influence

dom·i·neer \ˌdäm-ə-'niər\ vb **1** : to rule in an arrogant manner **2** : to be overbearing

do·mi·nie \1 oftenest 'däm-ə-nē, 2 oftenest 'dō-mə-\ n **1** chiefly Scot : SCHOOLMASTER **2** : CLERGYMAN

do·min·ion \də-'min-yən\ n **1** : DOMAIN **2** : supreme authority : SOVEREIGNTY **3** often cap : a self-governing nation of the Commonwealth

dom·i·no \'däm-ə-ˌnō\ n, pl **-noes** or **-nos 1** : a long loose hooded cloak usu. worn with a half mask as a masquerade costume **2** : a flat rectangular block used as a piece in a game (**dominoes**)

¹don \'dän\ vb **donned; don·ning** [do + on] : to put on (as clothes)

²don n [Sp, fr. L dominus lord, master] **1** : a Spanish nobleman or gentleman — used as a title prefixed to the Christian name **2** : a head, tutor, or fellow in an English university

do·ña \'dō-nyə\ n : a Spanish woman of rank — used as a title prefixed to the Christian name

do·nate \'dō-ˌnāt\ vb **do·nat·ed; do·nat·ing 1** : to make a gift of : CONTRIBUTE **2** : to make a donation

do·na·tion \dō-'nā-shən\ n **1** : the action of making a gift esp. to a charity **2** : a free contribution : GIFT

¹done \'dən\ past part of DO

²done adj **1** : doomed to failure, defeat, or death **2** : gone by : OVER ⟨when day is ∼⟩ **3** : cooked sufficiently **4** : conformable to social convention

dong \'dȯŋ, 'däŋ\ n — see MONEY table

don·key \'däŋ-kē, 'dəŋ-\ n, pl **donkeys 1** : a domestic mammal classified with

the asses **2** : a stupid or obstinate person

don·ny·brook \'dän-ē-ˌbrùk\ n, often cap [Donnybrook Fair, annual Irish event once known for its brawls] : an uproarious brawl

do·nor \'dō-nər\ n : one that gives, donates, or presents

donut var of DOUGHNUT

doo·dad \'dü-ˌdad\ n : a small article whose common name is unknown or forgotten

doo·dle \'düd-ᵊl\ vb **doo·dled; doo·dling** \'düd-(ᵊ-)liŋ\ : to draw or scribble aimlessly while occupied with something else — **doodle** n — **doo·dler** \'düd-(ᵊ-)lər\ n

doom \'düm\ n **1** : JUDGMENT, SENTENCE; esp : a judicial condemnation or sentence **2** : DESTINY, FATE **3** : RUIN, DEATH — **doom** vb

dooms·day \'dümz-ˌdā\ n : JUDGMENT DAY

door \'dōr\ n **1** : a barrier by which an entry is closed and opened; also : a similar part of a piece of furniture **2** : DOORWAY **3** : a means of access

door·jamb \-ˌjam\ n : an upright piece forming the side of a door opening

door·keep·er \-ˌkē-pər\ n : one who tends a door

door·knob \-ˌnäb\ n : a knob that when turned releases a door latch

door·man \-ˌman, -mən\ n : one who tends a door and assists people by calling taxis and helping them in and out of cars

door·mat \-ˌmat\ n : a mat placed before or inside a door for wiping dirt from the shoes

door·plate \-ˌplāt\ n : a nameplate on a door

door·step \-ˌstep\ n : a step or series of steps before an outer door

door·way \-ˌwā\ n **1** : the opening that a door closes **2** : a means of gaining access

door·yard \-ˌyärd\ n : a yard outside the door of a house

do·pa \'dō-pə\ n : a form of an amino acid that is used esp. in the treatment of Parkinson's disease

¹dope \'dōp\ n **1** : a preparation for giving a desired quality **2** : a drug preparation esp. when narcotic or addictive

and used illegally **3** : a stupid person **4**
: INFORMATION
²dope *vb* **doped; dop•ing 1** : to treat with
dope; *esp* : to give a narcotic to **2**
: FIGURE OUT — usu. used with *out*
dop•ey *also* **dopy** \'dō-pē\ *adj* **dop•i•er;
-est 1** : dulled by alcohol or a narcotic
2 : SLUGGISH **3** : STUPID
dorm \'dȯrm\ *n* : DORMITORY
dor•mant \'dȯr-mənt\ *adj* : INACTIVE;
esp : not actively growing or functioning ⟨∼ buds⟩ — **dor•man•cy** \-mən-sē\
n
dor•mer \'dȯr-mər\ *n* [MF *dormeor* dormitory, fr. L *dormitorium,* fr. *dormire*
to sleep] : a window built upright in a
sloping roof
dor•mi•to•ry \'dȯr-mə-ˌtōr-ē\ *n, pl* **-ries
1** : a room for sleeping; *esp* : a large
room containing a number of beds **2**
: a residence hall providing sleeping
rooms
dor•mouse \'dȯr-ˌmaus\ *n* : any of numerous Old World squirrellike rodents
dor•sal \'dȯr-səl\ *adj* : of, relating to, or
located near or on the surface of the
body that in man is the back but in
most other animals is the upper surface — **dor•sal•ly** \-ē\ *adv*
do•ry \'dōr-ē\ *n, pl* **dories** : a flat-bottomed boat with high flaring sides and
a sharp bow
DOS *abbr* disk operating system
¹dose \'dōs\ *n* [F, fr. LL *dosis,* fr. Gk,
lit., act of giving, fr. *didonai* to give] **1**
: a measured quantity (as of medicine)
to be taken or administered at one
time **2** : the quantity of radiation administered or absorbed — **dos•age**
\'dō-sij\ *n*
²dose *vb* **dosed; dos•ing 1** : to give in
doses **2** : to give medicine to
do•sim•e•ter \dō-'sim-ət-ər\ *n* : a device
for measuring doses of X rays or of
radioactivity — **do•sim•e•try** \-ə-trē\ *n*
dos•sier \'dȯs-ˌyā, 'dȯs-ē-ˌā\ *n* [F, bundle of documents labeled on the back,
dossier, fr. *dos* back, fr. L *dorsum*] : a
file of papers containing a detailed report or detailed information
¹dot \'dät\ *n* **1** : a small spot : SPECK **2** : a
small round mark **3** : a precise point
esp. in time ⟨be here on the ∼⟩
²dot *vb* **dot•ted; dot•ting 1** : to mark with

a dot ⟨∼ an *i*⟩ **2** : to cover with or as
if with dots
DOT *abbr* Department of Transportation
dot•age \'dōt-ij\ *n* : feebleness of mind
esp. in old age : SENILITY
dot•ard \-ərd\ *n* : a person in dotage
dote \'dōt\ *vb* **dot•ed; dot•ing 1** : to be
feebleminded esp. from old age **2** : to
be lavish or excessive in one's attention, affection, or fondness ⟨*doted* on
her niece⟩
dot matrix *n* : a rectangular arrangement of dots from which alphanumeric characters can be formed (as by a
computer printer)
Dou•ay Version \dü-'ā-\ *n* : an English
translation of the Vulgate used by Roman Catholics
¹dou•ble \'dəb-əl\ *adj* **1** : TWOFOLD, DUAL
2 : consisting of two members or parts
3 : being twice as great or as many **4**
: folded in two **5** : having more than
one whorl of petals ⟨∼ roses⟩
²double *vb* **dou•bled; dou•bling** \'dəb-
(ə-)liŋ\ **1** : to make, be, or become
twice as great or as many **2** : to make
a call in bridge that increases the trick
values and penalties of (an opponent's
bid) **3** : FOLD **4** : CLENCH **5** : to be or
cause to be bent over **6** : to take the
place of another **7** : to hit a double **8**
: to turn sharply and suddenly; *esp*
: to turn back on one's course
³double *adv* **1** : DOUBLY **2** : two together
⟨sleep ∼⟩
⁴double *n* **1** : something twice another in
size, strength, speed, quantity, or value **2** : a hit in baseball that enables the
batter to reach second base **3** : COUN-
TERPART, DUPLICATE; *esp* : a person
who closely resembles another **4**
: UNDERSTUDY, SUBSTITUTE **5** : a sharp
turn : REVERSAL **6** : FOLD **7** : a combined bet placed on two different contests **8** *pl* : a game between two pairs
of players **9** : an act of doubling in a
card game
double bond *n* : a chemical bond in
which two atoms in a molecule share
two pairs of electrons
double cross *n* : an act of betraying or
cheating esp. an associate — **dou•ble–
cross** \ˌdəb-əl-'krȯs\ *vb* — **dou•ble–
cross•er** *n*
dou•ble–deal•ing \-'dē-liŋ\ *n* : DUPLICITY

— **dou·ble–deal·er** \-'dē-lər\ *n* — **double–dealing** *adj*

dou·ble–deck·er \-'dek-ər\ *n* : something having two decks, levels, or layers

dou·ble–dig·it \‚dəb-əl-'dij-ət\ *adj* : amounting to 10 percent or more

dou·ble en·ten·dre \‚düb(-ə)-‚län-'tä^{n}dr^ə, ‚dəb-ə-\ *n, pl* **double entendres** \-'tä^{n}dr^ə, -'tä^{n}d-rəz\ [obs. F, lit., double meaning] : a word or expression capable of two interpretations one of which is usu. risqué

dou·ble·head·er \‚dəb-əl-'hed-ər\ *n* : two games played consecutively on the same day

double helix *n* : a helix or spiral consisting of two strands (as of DNA) in the surface of a cylinder which coil around its axis

dou·ble–joint·ed \-'jöint-əd\ *adj* : having a joint that permits an exceptional degree of freedom of motion of the parts joined

double play *n* : a play in baseball by which two players are put out

double pneumonia *n* : pneumonia involving both lungs

dou·blet \'dəb-lət\ *n* 1 : a man's close-fitting jacket worn in Europe esp. in the 16th century 2 : one of two similar or identical things

dou·ble take \'dəb-əl-‚tāk\ *n* : a delayed reaction to a surprising or significant situation after an initial failure to notice anything unusual

dou·ble–talk \-‚tök\ *n* : language that appears to be meaningful but in fact is a mixture of sense and nonsense

double up *vb* : to share accommodations designed for one

dou·bloon \‚dəb-'lün\ *n* : a former gold coin of Spain and Spanish America

dou·bly \'dəb-lē\ *adv* 1 : in a twofold manner 2 : to twice the degree

¹**doubt** \'daùt\ *vb* 1 : to be uncertain about 2 : to lack confidence in : DISTRUST, FEAR 3 : to consider unlikely — **doubt·able** *adj* — **doubt·er** *n*

²**doubt** *n* 1 : uncertainty of belief or opinion 2 : a condition causing uncertainty, hesitation, or suspense ⟨the outcome was in ∼⟩ 3 : DISTRUST 4 : an inclination not to believe or accept

doubt·ful \'daùt-fəl\ *adj* 1 : QUESTION-ABLE 2 : UNDECIDED — **doubt·ful·ly** \-ē\ *adv*

¹**doubt·less** \'daùt-ləs\ *adv* 1 : without doubt 2 : PROBABLY

²**doubtless** *adj* : free from doubt

douche \'düsh\ *n* [F] 1 : a jet of fluid (as water) directed against a part or into a cavity of the body; *also* : a cleansing with a douche 2 : a device for giving douches — **douche** *vb*

dough \'dō\ *n* 1 : a mixture that consists of flour or meal and a liquid (as milk or water) and is stiff enough to knead or roll 2 : something resembling dough esp. in consistency 3 : MONEY — **doughy** \'dō-ē\ *adj*

dough·boy \-‚bói\ *n* : an American infantryman esp. in World War I

dough·nut \-(‚)nət\ *n* : a small usu. ring-shaped cake fried in fat

dough·ty \'daùt-ē\ *adj* **dough·ti·er; -est** : ABLE, STRONG, VALIANT

Doug·las fir \‚dəg-ləs-\ *n* : a tall evergreen timber tree of the western U.S.

do up *vb* 1 : to prepare (as by cleaning) for use 2 : to wrap up

dour \'daù(ə)r, 'dùr\ *adj* [ME, fr. L *durus* hard] 1 : STERN, HARSH 2 : GLOOMY, SULLEN

douse \'daùs, 'daùz\ *vb* **doused; dousing** 1 : to plunge into water 2 : DRENCH 3 : EXTINGUISH

¹**dove** \'dəv\ *n* 1 : any of numerous pigeons; *esp* : a small wild pigeon 2 : an advocate of peace or of a peaceful policy — **dove·cote** \-‚kōt, -‚kät\ *also* **dove·cot** \-‚kät\ *n* — **dov·ish** \'dəv-ish\ *adj*

²**dove** \'dōv\ past of DIVE

¹**dove·tail** \'dəv-‚tāl\ *n* : something that resembles a dove's tail; *esp* : a flaring tenon and a mortise into which it fits tightly

²**dovetail** *vb* 1 : to join (as timbers) by means of dovetails 2 : to fit skillfully together to form a whole ⟨our plans ∼ perfectly⟩

dow·a·ger \'daù-i-jər\ *n* 1 : a widow owning property or a title from her deceased husband 2 : a dignified elderly woman

dowdy \'daùd-ē\ *adj* **dowd·i·er; -est** : lacking neatness and charm : SHABBY, UNTIDY; *also* : lacking smartness

dow·el \'daù(-ə)l\ *n* : a pin used for fastening together two pieces (as of board) — **dowel** *vb*

¹**dow·er** \ˈdau̇(-ə)r\ *n* **1** : the part of a deceased husband's real estate which the law gives for life to his widow **2** : DOWRY

²**dower** *vb* : to supply with a dower or dowry : ENDOW

dow·itch·er \ˈdau̇-i-chər\ *n, pl* **dowitchers** : any of several long-billed wading birds related to the sandpipers

¹**down** \ˈdau̇n\ *n* : a rolling usu. treeless upland with sparse soil — usu. used in pl.

²**down** *adv* **1** : toward or in a lower physical position **2** : to a lying or sitting position **3** : toward or to the ground, floor, or bottom **4** : as a down payment ⟨paid $5 ∼⟩ **5** : on paper ⟨put ∼ what he says⟩ **6** : in a direction that is the opposite of up **7** : SOUTH **8** : to or in a lower or worse condition or status **9** : from a past time **10** : to or in a state of less activity **11** : into defeat ⟨voted the motion ∼⟩

³**down** *prep* : down in, on, along, or through : toward the bottom of

⁴**down** *vb* **1** : to go or cause to go or come down **2** : DEFEAT **3** : to cause (a football) to be out of play

⁵**down** *adj* **1** : occupying a low position; *esp* : lying on the ground **2** : directed or going downward **3** : being in a state of reduced or low activity **4** : DEPRESSED, DEJECTED **5** : SICK ⟨∼ with a cold⟩ **6** : FINISHED, DONE

⁶**down** *n* **1** : a low or falling period (as in activity, emotional life, or fortunes) **2** : one of a series of attempts to advance a football

⁷**down** *n* **1** : a covering of soft fluffy feathers; *also* : such feathers **2** : a downlike covering or material

down·beat \ˈdau̇n-ˌbēt\ *n* : the downward stroke of a conductor indicating the principally accented note of a measure of music

down·cast \-ˌkast\ *adj* **1** : DEJECTED **2** : directed down ⟨a ∼ glance⟩

down·draft \-ˌdraft\ *n* : a downward current of gas (as air in a chimney)

down·er \ˈdau̇-nər\ *n* **1** : a depressant drug; *esp* : BARBITURATE **2** : a depressing experience or situation

down·fall \ˈdau̇n-ˌfȯl\ *n* **1** : a sudden fall (as from high rank) **2** : a fall (as of rain) esp. when sudden or heavy **3** : something that causes a downfall — **down·fall·en** \-ˌfȯ-lən\ *adj*

¹**down·grade** \ˈdau̇n-ˌgrād\ *n* **1** : a downward grade or slope (as of a road) **2** : a decline toward a worse condition

²**downgrade** *vb* : to lower in grade, rank, position, or status

down·heart·ed \-ˈhärt-əd\ *adj* : DEJECTED

down·hill \ˈdau̇n-ˈhil\ *adv* : toward the bottom of a hill — **downhill** \-ˌhil\ *adj*

down·load \ˈdau̇n-ˌlōd\ *vb* : to transfer (as data) from one computer to another device

down payment *n* : a part of the full price paid at the time of purchase or delivery with the balance to be paid later

down·pour \ˈdau̇n-ˌpōr\ *n* : a heavy rain

down·range \-ˈrānj\ *adv or adj* : toward the target area of a firing range

¹**down·right** \-ˌrīt\ *adv* : THOROUGHLY

²**downright** *adj* **1** : ABSOLUTE, UTTER ⟨a ∼ lie⟩ **2** : PLAIN, BLUNT ⟨a ∼ man⟩

down·shift \-ˌshift\ *vb* : to shift an automotive vehicle into a lower gear

down·size \-ˌsīz\ *vb* : to design or produce in smaller size

Down's syndrome *or* **Down syndrome** \ˈdau̇n(z)-\ *n* : a birth defect characterized by mental deficiency, slanting eyes, a broad short skull, broad hands with short fingers, and the presence of an extra chromosome

down·stage \ˈdau̇n-ˈstāj\ *adv or adj* : toward or at the front of a theatrical stage

down·stairs \ˈdau̇n-ˈstaərz\ *adv* : on or to a lower floor and esp. the main or ground floor — **downstairs** *adj or n*

down·stream \ˈdau̇n-ˈstrēm\ *adv or adj* : in the direction of flow of a stream

down·stroke \-ˌstrōk\ *n* : a stroke made in a downward direction

down·swing \-ˌswiŋ\ *n* **1** : a swing downward **2** : DOWNTURN

down–to–earth \ˌdau̇n-tə-ˈ(w)ərth\ *adj* : PRACTICAL, REALISTIC

down·town \ˈdau̇n-ˌtau̇n\ *n* : the main business district of a town or city — **downtown** \ˌdau̇n-ˌtau̇n\ *adj or adv*

down·trod·den \ˈdau̇n-ˈträd-ᵊn\ *adj* : suffering oppression

down·turn \-ˌtərn\ *n* : a turning downward esp. in business activity

¹down·ward \'daún-wərd\ *or* **down-wards** \-wərdz\ *adv* **1** : from a higher to a lower place or condition **2** : from an earlier time **3** : from an ancestor or predecessor

²downward *adj* : directed toward or situated in a lower place or condition

down·wind \'daún-'wind\ *adv or adj* : in the direction toward which the wind is blowing

downy \'daú-nē\ *adj* **down·i·er; -est** : resembling or covered with down

downy mildew *n* : any of various parasitic fungi producing whitish masses esp. on the underside of plant leaves; *also* : a plant disease caused by downy mildew

downy woodpecker *n* : a small black-and-white woodpecker of No. America

dow·ry \'daú(ə)r-ē\ *n, pl* **dowries** : the property that a woman brings to her husband in marriage

dowse \'daúz\ *vb* **dowsed; dows·ing** : to use a divining rod esp. to find water — **dows·er** *n*

dox·ol·o·gy \däk-'säl-ə-jē\ *n, pl* **-gies** : a usu. short hymn of praise to God

doy·en \'dói-ən, 'dwä-ˌyaⁿ(n)\ *n* : the senior or most experienced person in a group

doy·enne \dói-'(y)en, dwä-'yen\ *n* : a woman who is a doyen

doz *abbr* dozen

doze \'dōz\ *vb* **dozed; doz·ing** : to sleep lightly — **doze** *n*

doz·en \'dəz-ᵊn\ *n, pl* **dozens** *or* **dozen** [ME *dozeine,* fr. OF *dozaine,* fr. *doze* twelve, fr. L *duodecim,* fr. *duo* two + *decem* ten] : a group of twelve — **doz-enth** \-ᵊnth\ *adj*

¹DP \'dē-'pē\ *n, pl* **DP's** *or* **DPs** : a displaced person

²DP *abbr* **1** data processing **2** double play

dpt *abbr* department

DPT *abbr* diphtheria-pertussis-tetanus (vaccines)

dr *abbr* **1** debtor **2** dram **3** drive **4** drum

Dr *abbr* doctor

DR *abbr* **1** dead reckoning **2** dining room

drab \'drab\ *adj* **drab·ber; drab·best** **1** : being of a light olive-brown color **2** : DULL, MONOTONOUS, CHEERLESS — **drab·ness** *n*

drach·ma \'drak-mə\ *n, pl* **drach·mas** *or* **drach·mai** \-ˌmī\ *or* **drach·mae** \-(ˌ)mē\ — see MONEY table

dra·co·ni·an \drā-'kō-nē-ən, drə-\ *adj, often cap* : HARSH, CRUEL

¹draft \'draft, 'dráft\ *n* **1** : the act of drawing or hauling **2** : the act or an instance of drinking or inhaling; *also* : the portion drunk or inhaled in one such act **3** : DOSE, POTION **4** : the force required to pull an implement **5** : DELINEATION, PLAN, DESIGN; *also* : a preliminary sketch, outline, or version ⟨a rough ∼ of a speech⟩ **6** : the act of drawing (as from a cask); *also* : a portion of liquid so drawn **7** : the depth of water a ship draws esp. when loaded **8** : the selection of a person esp. for compulsory military service; *also* : the persons so selected **9** : an order for the payment of money drawn by one person or bank on another **10** : a heavy demand : STRAIN **11** : a current of air; *also* : a device to regulate air supply (as to a fire) — **on draft** : ready to be drawn from a receptacle ⟨beer *on draft*⟩

²draft *adj* **1** : used or adapted for drawing loads ⟨∼ animals⟩ **2** : being or having been on draft ⟨∼ beer⟩ **3** : constituting a preliminary sketch, outline, or version

³draft *vb* **1** : to select usu. on a compulsory basis; *esp* : to conscript for military service **2** : to draw the preliminary sketch, version, or plan of **3** : COMPOSE, PREPARE **4** : to draw off or away — **draft·ee** \draf-'tē, dráf-\ *n*

drafts·man \'draft-smən, 'dráft-\ *n* : one who draws plans (as for buildings or machinery)

drafty \'draf-tē, 'dráf-\ *adj* **draft·i·er; -est** : exposed to a draft

¹drag \'drag\ *n* **1** : something (as a harrow, grapnel, sledge, or clog) that is dragged along over a surface **2** : the act or an instance of dragging **3** : something that hinders progress **4** : STREET ⟨the main ∼⟩ **5** : woman's dress worn by a man **6** : something boring ⟨the party was a ∼⟩

²drag *vb* **dragged; drag·ging** **1** : HAUL **2** : to move with painful slowness or difficulty **3** : to force into or out of some situation, condition, or course of action **4** : to pass (time) in pain or tedium **5** : PROTRACT ⟨∼ a story out⟩ **6** : to hang or lag behind **7** : to trail along on the ground **8** : to explore, search, or fish with a drag **9** : DRAW, PUFF ⟨∼ on a cigarette⟩ — **drag•ger** n

drag•net \-ˌnet\ n **1** : NET, TRAWL **2** : a network of planned actions for pursuing and catching ⟨a police ∼⟩

drag•o•man \'drag-ə-mən\ n, pl **-mans** or **-men** \-mən\ : an interpreter employed esp. in the Near East

drag•on \'drag-ən\ n [ME, fr. OF, fr. L dracon-, draco serpent, dragon, fr. Gk drakōn serpent] : a fabulous animal usu. represented as a huge winged scaly serpent with a crested head and large claws

drag•on•fly \-ˌflī\ n : any of a group of large harmless 4-winged insects

¹dra•goon \drə-'gün, dra-\ n [F dragon dragon, dragoon, fr. MF] : a heavily armed mounted soldier

²dragoon vb : to force or attempt to force into submission by violent measures

drag race n : an acceleration contest between vehicles

drag strip n : a site for drag races

¹drain \'drān\ vb **1** : to draw off or flow off gradually or completely **2** : to exhaust physically or emotionally **3** : to make or become gradually dry or empty **4** : to carry away the surface water of : discharge surface or surplus water **5** : EMPTY, EXHAUST — **drain•er** n

²drain n **1** : a means (as a channel or sewer) of draining **2** : the act of draining **3** : DEPLETION **4** : BURDEN, STRAIN ⟨a ∼ on his savings⟩

drain•age \-ij\ n **1** : the act or process of draining; also : something that is drained off **2** : a means for draining : DRAIN, SEWER **3** : an area drained

drain•pipe \'drān-ˌpīp\ n : a pipe for drainage

drake \'drāk\ n : a male duck

dram \'dram\ n **1** — see WEIGHT table **2** : FLUIDRAM **3** : a small drink

dra•ma \'dräm-ə, 'dram-\ n [LL, fr. Gk, deed, drama, fr. dran to do, act] **1** : a literary composition designed for theatrical presentation **2** : dramatic art, literature, or affairs **3** : a series of events involving conflicting forces — **dra•mat•ic** \drə-'mat-ik\ adj — **dra-**

mat•i•cal•ly \-i-k(ə-)lē\ adv — **dram•a•tist** \'dram-ət-əst, 'dräm-\ n

dra•ma•tize \'dram-ə-ˌtīz, 'dräm-\ vb **-tized; -tiz•ing 1** : to adapt for or be suitable for theatrical presentation **2** : to present or represent in a dramatic manner — **dram•a•ti•za•tion** \ˌdram-ət-ə-'zā-shən, ˌdräm-\ n

drank past and past part of DRINK

¹drape \'drāp\ n **1** : CURTAIN **2** : arrangement in or of folds **3** : the cut or hang of clothing

²drape vb **draped; drap•ing 1** : to cover or adorn with or as if with folds of cloth **2** : to cause to hang or stretch out loosely or carelessly **3** : to arrange or become arranged in flowing lines or folds

drap•er \'drā-pər\ n, chiefly Brit : a dealer in cloth and sometimes in clothing and dry goods

drap•ery \'drā-p(ə-)rē\ n, pl **-er•ies 1** Brit : DRY GOODS **2** : a decorative fabric esp. when hung loosely and in folds : HANGINGS **3** : the draping or arranging of materials

dras•tic \'dras-tik\ adj : HARSH, RIGOROUS, SEVERE ⟨∼ punishment⟩ — **dras•ti•cal•ly** \-ti-k(ə-)lē\ adv

draught \'draft\ , **draughty** \'draf-tē\ chiefly Brit var of DRAFT, DRAFTY

draughts \'drafts\ n, Brit : CHECKERS

¹draw \'drȯ\ vb **drew** \'drü\; **drawn** \'drȯn\; **draw•ing 1** : HAUL, DRAG **2** : to cause to go in a certain direction ⟨drew him aside⟩ **3** : to move or go steadily or gradually ⟨night ∼s near⟩ **4** : ATTRACT, ENTICE **5** : PROVOKE, ROUSE ⟨drew enemy fire⟩ **6** : INHALE ⟨∼ a deep breath⟩ **7** : to bring or pull out **8** : to force out from cover or possession ⟨∼ trumps⟩ **9** : to extract the essence from ⟨∼ tea⟩ **10** : EVISCERATE **11** : to require (a specified depth) to float in **12** : ACCUMULATE, GAIN ⟨∼ing interest⟩ **13** : to take money from a place of deposit : WITHDRAW **14** : to receive regularly from a source ⟨∼ a salary⟩ **15** : to take (cards) from a stack or the dealer **16** : to receive or take at random ⟨∼ a winning number⟩ **17** : to bend (a bow) by pulling back the string **18** : WRINKLE, SHRINK **19** : to change shape by or as if by pulling or stretching ⟨a face drawn with sorrow⟩ **20** : to leave (a contest) undecided

: TIE **21** : DELINEATE, SKETCH **22** : to write out in due form : DRAFT ⟨∼ up a will⟩ **23** : FORMULATE ⟨∼ comparisons⟩ **24** : DEDUCE **25** : to spread or elongate (metal) by hammering or by pulling through dies **26** : to produce or allow a draft or current of air ⟨the furnace ∼s well⟩ **27** : to swell out in a wind ⟨all sails ∼ing⟩

²draw *n* **1** : the act, process, or result of drawing **2** : a lot or chance drawn at random **3** : a contest left undecided or deadlocked : TIE **4** : ATTRACTION

draw·back \'drȯ-ˌbak\ *n* : HINDRANCE, HANDICAP

draw·bridge \-ˌbrij\ *n* : a bridge made to be drawn up, down, or aside

draw·er \'drȯ(-ə)r\ *n* **1** : one that draws **2** *pl* : an undergarment for the lower part of the body **3** : a sliding boxlike compartment (as in a table or desk)

draw·ing \'drȯ(-)iŋ\ *n* **1** : an act or instance of drawing; *esp* : an occasion when something is decided by drawing lots **2** : the act or art of making a figure, plan, or sketch by means of lines **3** : a representation made by drawing : SKETCH

drawing card *n* : one that attracts attention or patronage

drawing room *n* : a formal reception room

drawl \'drȯl\ *vb* : to speak or utter slowly with vowels greatly prolonged — **drawl** *n*

draw on *vb* : APPROACH ⟨night *draws on*⟩

draw out *vb* **1** : PROLONG **2** : to cause to speak freely

draw·string \'drȯ-ˌstriŋ\ *n* : a string, cord, or tape for use in closing a bag or controlling fullness in garments or curtains

draw up *vb* **1** : to prepare a draft or version of **2** : to pull oneself erect **3** : to bring or come to a stop

dray \'drā\ *n* : a strong low cart for carrying heavy loads

¹dread \'dred\ *vb* **1** : to fear greatly **2** : to feel extreme reluctance to meet or face

²dread *n* : great fear esp. of some harm to come

³dread *adj* **1** : causing great fear or anxiety **2** : inspiring awe

dread·ful \'dred-fəl\ *adj* **1** : inspiring dread or awe : FRIGHTENING **2** : ex-

tremely distasteful, unpleasant, or shocking — **dread·ful·ly** \-ē\ *adv*

dread·locks \'dred-ˌläks\ *n pl* : long braids of hair over the entire head

dread·nought \'dred-ˌnȯt\ *n* : a battleship armed with big guns of the same caliber

¹dream \'drēm\ *n* [ME *dreem,* fr. OE *drēam* noise, joy] **1** : a series of thoughts, images, or emotions occurring during sleep **2** : a dreamlike vision : DAYDREAM, REVERIE **3** : something notable for its beauty, excellence, or enjoyable quality **4** : IDEAL — **dream·like** *adj* — **dreamy** *adj*

²dream \'drēm\ *vb* **dreamed** \'dremt, 'drēmd\ *or* **dreamt** \'dremt\; **dreaming 1** : to have a dream of **2** : to indulge in daydreams or fantasies : pass (time) in reverie or inaction **3** : IMAGINE — **dream·er** *n*

dream·land \'drēm-ˌland\ *n* : an unreal delightful country that exists in imagination or in dreams

dream up *vb* : INVENT, CONCOCT

dream·world \-ˌwərld\ *n* : a world of illusion or fantasy

drear \'driər\ *adj* : DREARY

drea·ry \'dri(ə)r-ē\ *adj* **drea·ri·er; -est** [ME *drery,* fr. OE *drēorig* sad, bloody, fr. *drēor* gore] **1** : DOLEFUL, SAD **2** : DISMAL, GLOOMY — **drea·ri·ly** \'drir-ə-lē\ *adv*

¹dredge \'drej\ *vb* **dredged; dredg·ing** : to gather or search with or as if with a dredge — **dredg·er** *n*

²dredge *n* : a machine or barge for removing earth or silt

³dredge *vb* **dredged; dredg·ing** : to coat (food) by sprinkling (as with flour)

dregs \'dregz\ *n pl* **1** : SEDIMENT 1 **2** : the most undesirable part ⟨the ∼ of humanity⟩

drench \'drench\ *vb* : to wet through

¹dress \'dres\ *vb* **1** : to make or set straight : ALIGN **2** : to prepare for use; *esp* : BUTCHER **3** : TRIM, EMBELLISH ⟨∼ a store window⟩ **4** : to put clothes on : CLOTHE; *also* : to put on or wear formal or fancy clothes **5** : to apply dressings or medicine to **6** : to arrange (the hair) by combing, brushing, or curling **7** : to apply fertilizer to **8** : SMOOTH, FINISH ⟨∼ leather⟩

²dress *n* **1** : APPAREL, CLOTHING **2**

: FROCK, GOWN — **dress·mak·er** \-₁mā-kər\ *n* — **dress·mak·ing** \-₁mā-kiŋ\ *n*

³dress *adj* : suitable for a formal occasion; *also* : requiring formal dress

dres·sage \drə-'säzh\ *n* [F] : the execution by a trained horse of complex movements in response to barely perceptible signals from its rider

dress down *vb* : to scold severely

¹dress·er \'dres-ər\ *n* : a chest of drawers or bureau with a mirror

²dresser *n* : one that dresses

dress·ing \-iŋ\ *n* **1** : the act or process of one who dresses **2** : a sauce for adding to a dish (as a salad) **3** : a seasoned mixture usu. used as a stuffing (as for poultry) **4** : material used to cover an injury

dressing gown *n* : a loose robe worn esp. while dressing or resting

dressy \'dres-ē\ *adj* **dress·i·er; -est** **1** : showy in dress **2** : STYLISH, SMART

drew past of DRAW

¹drib·ble \'drib-əl\ *vb* **drib·bled; drib·bling** \-(ə-)liŋ\ **1** : to fall or flow in drops : TRICKLE **2** : DROOL **3** : to propel by successive slight taps or bounces

²dribble *n* **1** : a small trickling stream or flow **2** : a drizzling shower **3** : the dribbling of a ball or puck

drib·let \'drib-lət\ *n* **1** : a trifling amount **2** : a drop of liquid

dri·er *also* **dry·er** \'drī(-ə)r\ *n* **1** : a substance dissolved in paints, varnishes, or inks to speed drying **2** *usu dryer* : a device for drying

¹drift \'drift\ *n* **1** : the motion or course of something drifting **2** : a mass of matter (as snow or sand) blown up by wind **3** : earth, gravel, and rock deposited by a glacier or by running water **4** : a general underlying design or tendency : MEANING

²drift *vb* **1** : to float or be driven along by or as if by a current of water or air **2** : to pile up under the force of the wind or water

drift·er \'drif-tər\ *n* : a person without aim, ambition, or initiative

drift·wood \'drift-₁wùd\ *n* : wood drifted or floated by water

¹drill \'dril\ *n* **1** : a boring tool **2** : the training of soldiers in marching and the manual of arms **3** : strict training and instruction in a subject

²drill *vb* **1** : to instruct and exercise by repetition **2** : to train in or practice military drill **3** : to bore with a drill — **drill·er** *n*

³drill *n* **1** : a shallow furrow or trench in which seed is sown **2** : an agricultural implement for making furrows and dropping seed into them

⁴drill *n* : a firm cotton fabric in twill weave

drill·mas·ter \'dril-₁mas-tər\ *n* : one who drills; *esp* : an instructor in military drill

drill press *n* : an upright drilling machine in which the drill is pressed to the work usu. by a hand lever

drily *var of* DRYLY

¹drink \'driŋk\ *vb* **drank** \'draŋk\; **drunk** \'drəŋk\ *or* **drank; drink·ing** **1** : to swallow liquid : IMBIBE **2** : ABSORB **3** : to take in through the senses ⟨∼ in the beautiful scenery⟩ **4** : to give or join in a toast **5** : to drink alcoholic beverages esp. to excess — **drink·able** *adj* — **drink·er** *n*

²drink *n* **1** : BEVERAGE **2** : alcoholic liquor **3** : a draft or portion of liquid **4** : excessive consumption of alcoholic beverages

¹drip \'drip\ *vb* **dripped; drip·ping** **1** : to fall or let fall in drops **2** : to let fall drops of moisture or liquid ⟨a *dripping* faucet⟩ **3** : to overflow with or as if with moisture

²drip *n* **1** : a falling in drops **2** : liquid that falls, overflows, or is extruded in drops **3** : the sound made by or as if by falling drops

¹drive \'drīv\ *vb* **drove** \'drōv\; **driv·en** \'driv-ən\; **driv·ing** **1** : to urge, push, or force onward **2** : to direct the movement or course of **3** : to convey in a vehicle **4** : to set or keep in motion or operation **5** : to carry through strongly ⟨∼ a bargain⟩ **6** : FORCE, COMPEL ⟨*driven* by hunger to steal⟩ **7** : to project, inject, or impress forcefully ⟨*drove* the lesson home⟩ **8** : to bring into a specified condition ⟨the noise ∼s me crazy⟩ **9** : to produce by opening a way ⟨∼ a well⟩ **10** : to rush and press with violence ⟨a *driving* rain⟩ **11** : to propel an object of play (as a golf ball) by a hard blow — **driv·er** *n*

²drive *n* **1** : a trip in a carriage or automobile **2** : a driving together of animals (as for capture or slaughter) **3** : the guiding of logs downstream to a mill **4** : the act of driving a ball; *also* : the flight of a ball **5** : DRIVEWAY **6** : a public road for driving (as in a park) **7** : an offensive or aggressive move : a military attack **8** : an intensive campaign ⟨membership ∼⟩ **9** : the state of being hurried and under pressure **10** : NEED, LONGING **11** : dynamic quality **12** : the apparatus by which motion is imparted to a machine **13** : a device for reading and writing on magnetic media (as magnetic tape or disks)

drive–in \ˈdrī-ˌvin\ *adj* : accommodating patrons while they remain in their automobiles — **drive–in** *n*

¹**driv·el** \ˈdriv-əl\ *vb* -eled *or* -elled; -el·ing *or* -el·ling \-(ə-)liŋ\ **1** : DROOL, SLAVER **2** : to talk or utter stupidly, carelessly, or in an infantile way — **driv·el·er** \-(ə-)lər\ *n*

²**drivel** *n* : NONSENSE

drive shaft *n* : a shaft that transmits mechanical power

drive·way \ˈdrīv-ˌwā\ *n* : a short private road leading from the street to a house, garage, or parking lot

¹**driz·zle** \ˈdriz-əl\ *n* : a fine misty rain

²**drizzle** *vb* **driz·zled; driz·zling** \-(ə-)liŋ\ : to rain in very small drops

drogue \ˈdrōg\ *n* : a small parachute for slowing down or stabilizing something (as an astronaut's capsule)

droll \ˈdrōl\ *adj* [F *drôle*, fr. *drôle* scamp, fr. MF *drolle*, fr. Middle Dutch, imp] : having a humorous, whimsical, or odd quality ⟨a ∼ expression⟩ — **droll·ery** \-(ə-)rē\ *n* — **drol·ly** \ˈdrō(l)-lē\ *adv*

drom·e·dary \ˈdräm-ə-ˌder-ē\ *n, pl* **-dar·ies** [ME *dromedarie*, fr. MF *dromedaire*, fr. LL *dromedarius*, fr. L *dromad-, dromas*, fr. Gk, running] : CAMEL; *esp* : a domesticated one≈ humped camel of western Asia and northern Africa

¹**drone** \ˈdrōn\ *n* **1** : a male honeybee **2** : one that lives on the labors of others : PARASITE **3** : a pilotless aircraft or ship controlled by radio

²**drone** *vb* **droned; dron·ing** : to sound with a low dull monotonous murmuring sound : speak monotonously

³**drone** *n* : a deep monotonous sound

drool \ˈdrül\ *vb* **1** : to let liquid flow from the mouth **2** : to talk foolishly

droop \ˈdrüp\ *vb* **1** : to hang or incline downward **2** : to sink gradually **3** : LANGUISH — **droop** *n*

¹**drop** \ˈdräp\ *n* **1** : the quantity of fluid that falls in one spherical mass **2** *pl* : a dose of medicine measured by drops **3** : a small quantity of drink **4** : the smallest practical unit of liquid measure **5** : something (as a pendant or a small round candy) that resembles a liquid drop **6** : FALL **7** : a decline in quantity or quality **8** : a descent by parachute **9** : the distance through which something drops **10** : a slot into which something is to be dropped **11** : something that drops or has dropped

²**drop** *vb* **dropped; drop·ping** **1** : to fall or let fall in drops **2** : to let fall : LOWER ⟨∼ a glove⟩ ⟨*dropped* his voice⟩ **3** : SEND ⟨∼ me a note⟩ **4** : to let go : DISMISS ⟨∼ the subject⟩ **5** : to knock down : cause to fall **6** : to go lower : become less ⟨prices *dropped*⟩ **7** : to come or go unexpectedly or informally ⟨∼ in to call⟩ **8** : to pass from one state into a less active one ⟨∼ off to sleep⟩ **9** : to move downward or with a current **10** : QUIT ⟨*dropped* out of the race⟩ — **drop back** : to move toward the rear — **drop behind** : to fail to keep up

drop·kick \-ˈkik\ *n* : a kick made by dropping a ball to the ground and kicking it at the moment it starts to rebound — **drop–kick** *vb*

drop·let \ˈdräp-lət\ *n* : a tiny drop

drop–off \ˈdräp-ˌof\ *n* **1** : a steep or perpendicular descent **2** : a marked decline ⟨a ∼ in attendance⟩

drop off \dräp-ˈof\ *vb* : to fall asleep

drop out \dräp-ˈaut\ *vb* : to withdraw from participation or membership; *esp* : to leave school before graduation — **drop·out** \ˈdräp-ˌaut\ *n*

drop·per \ˈdräp-ər\ *n* **1** : one that drops **2** : a short glass tube with a rubber bulb used to measure out liquids by drops

drop·pings *n pl* : DUNG

drop·sy \ˈdräp-sē\ *n* [ME *dropesie*, short for *ydropesie*, fr. OF, fr. L *hydropisis*, fr. Gk *hydrōps*, fr. *hydōr* water] : EDEMA — **drop·si·cal** \-si-kəl\ *adj*

dross \ˈdräs\ *n* **1** : the scum that forms

on the surface of a molten metal **2** : waste matter : REFUSE

drought *also* **drouth** \'draut(h)\ *n* : a long spell of dry weather

¹drove \'drōv\ *n* **1** : a group of animals driven or moving in a body **2** : a crowd of people moving or acting together

²drove past of DRIVE

drov·er \'drō-vər\ *n* : one that drives domestic animals usu. to market

drown \'draun\ *vb* **drowned** \'draund\; **drown·ing** **1** : to suffocate by submersion esp. in water **2** : to become drowned **3** : to cover with water **4** : OVERCOME, OVERPOWER

drowse \'drauz\ *vb* **drowsed**; **drows·ing** : DOZE — **drowse** *n*

drowsy \'drau-zē\ *adj* **drows·i·er**; **-est** **1** : ready to fall asleep **2** : making one sleepy — **drows·i·ly** \'drau-zə-lē\ *adv* — **drows·i·ness** \-zē-nəs\ *n*

drub \'drəb\ *vb* **drubbed**; **drub·bing** **1** : to beat severely : PUMMEL, THRASH **2** : to defeat decisively

drudge \'drəj\ *vb* **drudged**; **drudg·ing** : to do hard, menial, or monotonous work — **drudge** *n* — **drudg·ery** \-(ə-)rē\ *n*

¹drug \'drəg\ *n* **1** : a substance used as or in medicine **2** : a substance (as heroin or marijuana) affecting bodily activities often in a harmful way and taken for other than medical reasons

²drug *vb* **drugged**; **drug·ging** : to affect with drugs; *esp* : to stupefy with a narcotic

drug·gist \'drəg-əst\ *n* : a dealer in drugs and medicines; *also* : PHARMACIST

drug·store \'drəg-ˌstōr\ *n* : a retail shop where medicines and miscellaneous articles are sold

dru·id \'drü-əd\ *n, often cap* : one of an ancient Celtic priesthood of Gaul, Britain, and Ireland appearing in legends as magicians and wizards

¹drum \'drəm\ *n* **1** : a percussion instrument usu. consisting of a hollow cylinder with a skin or plastic head stretched over one or both ends that is beaten with the hands or with a stick **2** : the sound of a drum; *also* : a similar sound **3** : a drum-shaped object

²drum *vb* **drummed**; **drum·ming** **1** : to beat a drum **2** : to sound rhythmically

: THROB, BEAT **3** : to summon or assemble by or as if by beating a drum **4** : EXPEL ⟨*drummed* out of camp⟩ **5** : to drive or force by steady effort ⟨~ a lesson into his head⟩ **6** : to strike or tap repeatedly so as to produce rhythmic sounds

drum·beat \'drəm-ˌbēt\ *n* : a stroke on a drum or its sound

drum·lin \'drəm-lən\ *n* : an oval hill of glacial drift

drum major *n* : the leader of a marching band

drum ma·jor·ette \ˌdrəm-ˌmā-jə-'ret\ *n* : a girl or woman who leads a marching band; *also* : a baton twirler who accompanies a marching band

drum·mer \'drəm-ər\ *n* **1** : one that plays a drum **2** : a traveling salesman

drum·stick \-ˌstik\ *n* **1** : a stick for beating a drum **2** : the lower segment of a fowl's leg

drum up *vb* **1** : to bring about by persistent effort ⟨*drum up* business⟩ **2** : INVENT, ORIGINATE

¹drunk past part of DRINK

²drunk \'drəŋk\ *adj* **1** : having the faculties impaired by alcohol **2** : dominated by an intense feeling ⟨~ with power⟩ **3** : of, relating to, or caused by intoxication

³drunk *n* **1** : a period of excessive drinking **2** : a drunken person : DRUNKARD

drunk·ard \'drəŋ-kərd\ *n* : one who is habitually drunk

drunk·en \'drəŋ-kən\ *adj* **1** : DRUNK **2** : given to habitual excessive use of alcohol **3** : of, relating to, or resulting from intoxication **4** : unsteady or lurching as if from intoxication — **drunk·en·ly** *adv* — **drunk·en·ness** \-kən-nəs\ *n*

drupe \'drüp\ *n* : a partly fleshy one-seeded fruit (as a plum or cherry) that remains closed at maturity

¹dry \'drī\ *adj* **dri·er** \'drī(-ə)r\; **dri·est** \'drī-əst\ **1** : free or freed from water or liquid **2** : characterized by loss or lack of water or moisture **3** : lacking freshness : WITHERED; *also* : low in or deprived of succulence ⟨~ fruits⟩ **4** : not being in or under water ⟨~ land⟩ **5** : THIRSTY **6** : marked by the absence of alcoholic beverages **7** : no longer liquid or sticky ⟨the ink is ~⟩ **8** : containing or employing no liquid **9** : not giving milk ⟨a ∼ cow⟩ **10** : lacking natural lubrication ⟨a ∼ cough⟩ **11** : solid as opposed to liquid ⟨∼ groceries⟩ **12** : SEVERE **13** : not productive : BARREN **14** : marked by a matter-of-fact, ironic, or terse manner of expression ⟨∼ humor⟩ **15** : UNINTERESTING, WEARISOME **16** : not sweet ⟨∼ wine⟩ **17** : relating to, favoring, or practicing prohibition of alcoholic beverages — **dry•ly** adv — **dry•ness** n

²**dry** vb **dried; dry•ing** : to make or become dry

³**dry** n, pl **drys** : PROHIBITIONIST

dry•ad \'drī-əd, -ˌad\ n : WOOD NYMPH

dry cell n : a battery whose contents are not spillable

dry–clean \'drī-ˌklēn\ vb : to clean (fabrics) chiefly with solvents (as naphtha) other than water — **dry cleaning** n

dry dock \'drī-ˌdäk\ n : a dock that can be kept dry during ship construction or repair

dry•er var of DRIER

dry farm•ing n : farming without irrigation in areas of limited rainfall — **dry–farm** vb — **dry farm•er** n

dry goods \'drī-ˌgu̇dz\ n pl : cloth goods (as fabrics, ribbon, and ready-to-wear clothing)

dry ice n : solid carbon dioxide used chiefly as a refrigerant

dry measure n : a series of units of capacity for dry commodities — see METRIC SYSTEM table, WEIGHT table

dry run n : REHEARSAL, TRIAL

dry•wall \'drī-ˌwȯl\ n : PLASTERBOARD

DSC abbr **1** Distinguished Service Cross **2** doctor of surgical chiropody

DSM abbr Distinguished Service Medal

DSO abbr Distinguished Service Order

DST abbr daylight saving time

DTP abbr diphtheria, tetanus, pertussis (vaccines)

d.t.'s \(')dē-'tēz\ n pl, often cap D&T : DELIRIUM TREMENS

du•al \'d(y)ü-əl\ adj **1** : TWOFOLD, DOUBLE **2** : having a double character or nature — **du•al•ism** \-ə-ˌliz-əm\ n — **du•al•i•ty** \d(y)ü-'al-ət-ē\ n

¹**dub** \'dəb\ vb **dubbed; dub•bing 1** : to confer knighthood upon **2** : NAME, NICKNAME

²**dub** n : a clumsy person : DUFFER

³**dub** vb **dubbed; dub•bing** : to add (sound effects) to a motion picture or to a radio or television production

du•bi•ety \d(y)u̇-'bī-ət-ē\ n, pl **-eties 1** : UNCERTAINTY **2** : a matter of doubt

du•bi•ous \'d(y)ü-bē-əs\ adj **1** : occasioning doubt : UNCERTAIN **2** : feeling doubt : UNDECIDED **3** : QUESTIONABLE — **du•bi•ous•ly** adv — **du•bi•ous•ness** n

du•cal \'d(y)ü-kəl\ adj : of or relating to a duke or dukedom

duc•at \'dək-ət\ n : a gold coin formerly used in various European countries

duch•ess \'dəch-əs\ n **1** : the wife or widow of a duke **2** : a woman holding the rank of duke in her own right

duchy \'dəch-ē\ n, pl **duch•ies** : the territory of a duke or duchess : DUKEDOM

¹**duck** \'dək\ n, pl **ducks** : any of various swimming birds related to but smaller than geese and swans

²**duck** vb **1** : to thrust or plunge under water **2** : to lower the head or body suddenly **3** : BOW, BOB **4** : DODGE **5** : to evade a duty, question, or responsibility ⟨∼ the issue⟩

³**duck** n **1** : a durable closely woven usu. cotton fabric **2** pl : clothes made of duck

duck•bill \'dək-ˌbil\ n : PLATYPUS

duck•ling \'dək-liŋ\ n : a young duck

duck•pin \-ˌpin\ n **1** : a small bowling pin shorter and wider in the middle than a tenpin **2** pl but sing in constr : a bowling game using duckpins

duct \'dəkt\ n : a tube or canal for conveying a bodily fluid; also : a pipe or tube for electrical conductors — **duct•less** \'dək-tləs\ adj

duc•tile \'dək-t³l\ adj **1** : capable of being drawn out (as into wire) or hammered thin **2** : DOCILE — **duc•til•i•ty** \ˌdək-'til-ət-ē\ n

ductless gland n : an endocrine gland

dud \'dəd\ n **1** : one that fails completely **2** : a missile that fails to explode

dude \'d(y)üd\ n **1** : FOP, DANDY **2** : a city person; esp : an Easterner in the West

dude ranch n : a vacation resort offering activities (as horseback riding) typical of western ranches

dud•geon \'dəj-ən\ n : ill humor : RESENTMENT ⟨in high ∼⟩

duds \'dədz\ n pl : CLOTHES

¹**due** \'d(y)ü\ adj [ME, fr. MF deu, pp. of devoir to owe, fr. L debēre] **1**

: owed or owing as a debt **2** : owed or owing as a right **3** : APPROPRIATE, FITTING **4** : SUFFICIENT, ADEQUATE **5** : REGULAR, LAWFUL ⟨∼ process of law⟩ **6** : ATTRIBUTABLE, ASCRIBABLE ⟨∼ to negligence⟩ **7** : PAYABLE ⟨a bill ∼ today⟩ **8** : required or expected to happen ⟨∼ to arrive soon⟩

²due *n* **1** : something that rightfully belongs to one ⟨give to each his ∼⟩ **2** : something owed : DEBT **3** *pl* : FEES, CHARGES

³due *adv* : DIRECTLY, EXACTLY ⟨∼ north⟩

du•el \\'d(y)ü-əl\\ *n* : a combat between two persons; *esp* : one fought with weapons in the presence of witnesses — **duel** *vb* — **du•el•ist** *n*

du•en•de \\dü-'en-dā\\ *n* [Sp dial., charm, fr. Sp, ghost, goblin, fr. *duen de casa,* prob. fr. *dueño de casa* owner of a house] : the power to attract through personal magnetism and charm

du•en•na \\d(y)ü-'en-ə\\ *n* **1** : an elderly woman in charge of the younger ladies in a Spanish or Portuguese family **2** : CHAPERON

du•et \\d(y)ü-'et\\ *n* : a musical composition for two performers

due to *prep* : BECAUSE OF

duf•fel bag \\'dəf-əl-\\ *n* : a large cylindrical bag for personal belongings

duf•fer \\'dəf-ər\\ *n* : an incompetent or clumsy person

dug past and past part of DIG

dug•out \\'dəg-ˌau̇t\\ *n* **1** : a boat made by hollowing out a log **2** : a shelter dug in the ground **3** : a low shelter facing a baseball diamond that contains the players' bench

DUI *abbr* driving under the influence

duke \\'d(y)ük\\ *n* **1** : a sovereign ruler of a continental European duchy **2** : a nobleman of the highest rank; *esp* : a member of the highest grade of the British peerage **3** *slang* : FIST 1 — usu. used in pl. — **duke•dom** *n*

dul•cet \\'dəl-sət\\ *adj* **1** : sweet to the ear **2** : AGREEABLE, SOOTHING

dul•ci•mer \\'dəl-sə-mər\\ *n* **1** : a wire≠stringed instrument of trapezoidal shape played with light hammers held in the hands **2** *or* **dul•ci•more** \\-ˌmōr, -ˌmȯr\\ : an American folk instrument with three or four strings held on the lap and played by plucking or strumming

¹dull \\'dəl\\ *adj* **1** : mentally slow : STUPID **2** : slow in perception or sensibility **3** : LISTLESS **4** : slow in action : SLUGGISH ⟨a ∼ market⟩ **5** : BLUNT **6** : lacking brilliance or luster **7** : DIM, INDISTINCT **8** : not resonant or ringing **9** : low in saturation and lightness ⟨∼ color⟩ **10** : TEDIOUS, UNINTERESTING **11** : CLOUDY, OVERCAST — **dull•ness** *or* **dulness** *n* — **dul•ly** \\'dəl-(l)ē\\ *adv*

²dull *vb* : to make or become dull

dull•ard \\'dəl-ərd\\ *n* : a stupid person

du•ly \\'d(y)ü-lē\\ *adv* : in a due manner, time, or degree

du•ma \\'dü-mə\\ *n* : the principal legislative assembly in czarist Russia

dumb \\'dəm\\ *adj* **1** : lacking the power of speech **2** : SILENT **3** : STUPID — **dumb•ly** *adv*

dumb•bell \\'dəm-ˌbel\\ *n* **1** : a bar with weights at the end used for gymnastic exercises **2** : one who is stupid

dumb•found *or* **dum•found** \\ˌdəm-'fau̇nd\\ *vb* : ASTONISH, AMAZE

dumb•wait•er \\'dəm-'wāt-ər\\ *n* : a small elevator for conveying food and dishes or small goods from one story of a building to another

dum•dum \\'dəm-ˌdəm\\ *n* : a bullet (as one with a hollow point) that expands more than usual upon hitting an object

dum•my \\'dəm-ē\\ *n, pl* **dummies 1** : a dumb person **2** : the exposed hand in bridge played by the declarer in addition to his own hand; *also* : a bridge player whose hand is a dummy **3** : an imitation of something used as a substitute **4** : one seeming to act for itself but really acting for another **5** : a pattern arrangement of matter to be reproduced esp. by printing

¹dump \\'dəmp\\ *vb* : to let fall in a mass : UNLOAD ⟨∼ coal⟩

²dump *n* **1** : a place for dumping something (as refuse) **2** : a reserve supply; *esp* : one of military materials ⟨an ammunition ∼⟩ **3** : a slovenly or dilapidated place

dump•ing \\-iŋ\\ *n* : the selling of goods in quantity at below market price esp. in international trade

dump•ling \\'dəm-pliŋ\\ *n* **1** : a small mass of boiled or steamed dough **2** : a dessert of fruit baked in biscuit dough

dumps \\'dəmps\\ *n pl* : a dull gloomy state of mind : low spirits ⟨in the ∼⟩

dump truck *n* : a truck for transporting and dumping loose materials

dumpy \'dəm-pē\ *adj* **dump·i·er; -est** : short and thick in build

¹**dun** \'dən\ *n* : a slightly brownish dark gray

²**dun** *vb* **dunned; dun·ning 1** : to make persistent demands for payment **2** : PLAGUE, PESTER — **dun** *n*

dunce \'dəns\ *n* [John *Duns* Scotus, whose once accepted writings were ridiculed in the 16th cent.] : a dull-witted and stupid person

dun·der·head \'dən-dər-,hed\ *n* : DUNCE, BLOCKHEAD

dune \'d(y)ün\ *n* : a hill or ridge of sand piled up by the wind

dune buggy *n* : a motor vehicle with oversize tires for use on sand

¹**dung** \'dəŋ\ *n* : MANURE

²**dung** *vb* : to dress (land) with dung

dun·ga·ree \,dəŋ-gə-'rē\ *n* **1** : a heavy coarse cotton twill; *esp* : blue denim **2** *pl* : clothes made of blue denim

dun·geon \'dən-jən\ *n* [ME *donjon*, fr. MF, fr. (assumed) ML *dominion-, dominio*, fr. L *dominus* lord] : a dark prison commonly underground

dung·hill \'dəŋ-,hil\ *n* : a manure pile

dunk \'dəŋk\ *vb* **1** : to dip or submerge temporarily in liquid **2** : to submerge oneself in water

duo \'d(y)ü-(,)ō\ *n, pl* **du·os 1** : DUET **2** : PAIR

duo·dec·i·mal \,d(y)ü-ə-'des-ə-məl\ *adj* : of, relating to, or being a system of numbers with a base of 12

du·o·de·num \,d(y)ü-ə-'dē-nəm, d(y)ù-'äd-ᵊn-əm\ *n, pl* **-de·na** \-'dē-nə, -ᵊn-ə\ *or* **-denums** : the part of the small intestine extending from the stomach to the jejunum — **du·o·de·nal** \-'dēn-ᵊl, -ᵊn-əl\ *adj*

dup *abbr* **1** duplex **2** duplicate

¹**dupe** \'d(y)üp\ *n* : one who is easily deceived or cheated : FOOL

²**dupe** *vb* **duped; dup·ing** : to make a dupe of : DECEIVE, FOOL

du·ple \'d(y)ü-pəl\ *adj* : having two beats or a multiple of two beats to the measure ⟨∼ time⟩

¹**du·plex** \'d(y)ü-,pleks\ *adj* : DOUBLE

²**duplex** *n* : something duplex; *esp* : a 2-family house

¹**du·pli·cate** \'d(y)ü-pli-kət\ *adj* **1** : consisting of or existing in two corre-

sponding or identical parts or examples **2** : being the same as another

²**du·pli·cate** \'d(y)ü-pli-,kāt\ *vb* **-cat·ed; -cat·ing 1** : to make double or twofold **2** : to make an exact copy of — **du·pli·ca·tion** \,d(y)ü-pli-'kā-shən\ *n*

³**du·pli·cate** \-kət\ *n* : a thing that exactly resembles another in appearance, pattern, or content : COPY

du·pli·ca·tor \'d(y)ü-pli-,kāt-ər\ *n* : COPIER

du·plic·i·ty \d(y)ù-'plis-ət-ē\ *n, pl* **-ties** : deception by pretending to feel and act one way while acting another

du·ra·ble \'d(y)ur-ə-bəl\ *adj* : able to exist for a long time without significant deterioration ⟨∼ clothing⟩ — **du·ra·bil·i·ty** \,d(y)ur-ə-'bil-ət-ē\ *n*

durable press *n* : PERMANENT PRESS

du·rance \'d(y)ur-əns\ *n* : IMPRISONMENT

du·ra·tion \d(y)ù-'rā-shən\ *n* : the time during which something exists or lasts

du·ress \d(y)ù-'res\ *n* : compulsion by threat ⟨confession made under ∼⟩

dur·ing \,d(y)ur-iŋ\ *prep* **1** : THROUGHOUT ⟨swims every day ∼ the summer⟩ **2** : at some point in ⟨broke in ∼ the night⟩

dusk \'dəsk\ *n* **1** : the darker part of twilight esp. at night **2** : partial darkness

dusky \'dəs-kē\ *adj* **dusk·i·er; -est 1** : somewhat dark in color **2** : SHADOWY — **dusk·i·ness** *n*

¹**dust** \'dəst\ *n* **1** : particles of powdery matter **2** : the particles into which something disintegrates **3** : something worthless **4** : the surface of the ground — **dust·less** *adj* — **dusty** *adj*

²**dust** *vb* **1** : to make free of or remove dust **2** : to sprinkle with fine particles **3** : to sprinkle in the form of dust

dust bowl *n* : a region suffering from long droughts and dust storms

dust devil *n* : a small whirlwind containing sand or dust

dust·er \'dəs-tər\ *n* **1** : one that removes dust **2** : a dress-length housecoat **3** : one that scatters fine particles; *esp* : a device for applying insecticides to crops

dust·pan \'dəst-,pan\ *n* : a shovel-shaped pan for sweepings

dust storm *n* : a violent wind carrying dust across a dry region

dutch \'dəch\ *adv, often cap* : with each person paying his or her own way ⟨go ∼⟩

Dutch \'dəch\ *n* 1 **Dutch** *pl* : the people of the Netherlands 2 : the language of the Netherlands — **Dutch** *adj* — **Dutch·man** \-mən\ *n*

Dutch elm disease *n* : a fungous disease of elms characterized by yellowing of the foliage, defoliation, and death

Dutch treat *n* : an entertainment (as a meal) for which each person pays his or her own way

du·te·ous \'d(y)üt-ē-əs\ *adj* : DUTIFUL, OBEDIENT

du·ti·able \'d(y)üt-ē-ə-bəl\ *adj* : subject to a duty ⟨∼ imports⟩

du·ti·ful \'d(y)üt-i-fəl\ *adj* 1 : motivated by a sense of duty ⟨a ∼ son⟩ 2 : coming from or showing a sense of duty ⟨∼ affection⟩ — **du·ti·ful·ly** \-f(ə-)lē\ *adv* — **du·ti·ful·ness** *n*

du·ty \'d(y)üt-ē\ *n, pl* **duties** 1 : conduct or action required by one's occupation or position 2 : assigned service or business; *esp* : active military service 3 : a moral or legal obligation 4 : TAX 5 : the service required (as of a machine) : USE ⟨a heavy-*duty* tire⟩

DV *abbr* 1 [L *Deo volente*] God willing 2 Douay Version

DVM *abbr* doctor of veterinary medicine

¹**dwarf** \'dworf\ *n, pl* **dwarfs** \'dwȯ(ə)rfs\ *or* **dwarves** \'dworvz\ : one that is much below normal size — **dwarf·ish** *adj*

²**dwarf** *vb* 1 : to restrict the growth or development of : STUNT 2 : to cause to appear smaller ⟨people *dwarfed* by tall trees⟩

dwell \'dwel\ *vb* **dwelt** \'dwelt\ *or* **dwelled** \'dweld, 'dwelt\; **dwell·ing** [ME *dwellen*, fr. OE *dwellan* to go astray, hinder] 1 : ABIDE, REMAIN 2 : RESIDE, EXIST 3 : to keep the attention directed 4 : to write or speak at length or insistently — **dwell·er** *n*

dwell·ing \'dwel-iŋ\ *n* : RESIDENCE

DWI *abbr* driving while intoxicated

dwin·dle \'dwin-dᵊl\ *vb* **dwin·dled**; **dwin·dling** \'dwin-d(ə-)liŋ\ : to make or become steadily less : DIMINISH

dwt *abbr* pennyweight

Dy *symbol* dysprosium

dyb·buk \'dib-ək\ *n, pl* **dyb·bu·kim** \ˌdib- u̇-'kēm\ *also* **dybbuks** : a wandering soul believed in Jewish folklore to enter and possess a person

¹**dye** \'dī\ *n* 1 : color produced by dyeing 2 : material used for coloring or staining

²**dye** *vb* **dyed; dye·ing** 1 : to impart a new color to esp. by impregnating with a dye 2 : to take up or impart color in dyeing

dye·stuff \'dī-ˌstəf\ *n* : DYE 2

dying *pres part of* DIE

dyke *var of* DIKE

dy·nam·ic \dī-'nam-ik\ *also* **dy·nam·i·cal** \-i-kəl\ *adj* : of or relating to physical force producing motion : ENERGETIC, FORCEFUL

¹**dy·na·mite** \'dī-nə-ˌmīt\ *n* : an explosive made of nitroglycerin absorbed in a porous material; *also* : a blasting explosive made without nitroglycerin

²**dynamite** *vb* **-mit·ed; -mit·ing** : to blow up with dynamite

dy·na·mo \'dī-nə-ˌmō\ *n, pl* **-mos** : an electrical generator

dy·na·mom·e·ter \ˌdī-nə-'mäm-ət-ər\ *n* : an instrument for measuring mechanical power (as of an engine)

dy·nas·ty \'dī-nəs-tē, -ˌnas-\ *n, pl* **-ties** 1 : a succession of rulers of the same family 2 : a powerful group or family that maintains its position for a long time — **dy·nas·tic** \dī-'nas-tik\ *adj*

dys·en·tery \'dis-ᵊn-ˌter-ē\ *n, pl* **-ter·ies** : a disorder marked by diarrhea with blood and mucus in the feces

dys·lex·ia \dis-'lek-sē-ə\ *n* : a disturbance of the ability to read — **dys·lex·ic** \-sik\ *adj or n*

dys·pep·sia \dis-'pep-shə, -sē-ə\ *n* : INDIGESTION — **dys·pep·tic** \-'pep-tik\ *adj or n*

dys·pro·si·um \dis-'prō-zē-əm\ *n* : a metallic chemical element that forms highly magnetic compounds

dys·tro·phy \'dis-trə-fē\ *n, pl* **-phies** : any of several disorders involving atrophy of muscular tissue; *esp* : MUSCULAR DYSTROPHY

dz *abbr* dozen

E

¹e \ˈē\ n, pl e's or es \ˈēz\ often cap 1 : the 5th letter of the English alphabet 2 : the base of the system of natural logarithms having the approximate value 2.71828 3 : a grade rating a student's work as poor or failing

²e abbr, often cap 1 east; eastern 2 error 3 excellent

E symbol einsteinium

ea abbr each

¹each \ˈēch\ adj : being one of the class named ⟨∼ man⟩

²each pron : every individual one

³each adv : APIECE ⟨cost five cents ∼⟩

each other pron : each of two or more in reciprocal action or relation ⟨looked at each other⟩

ea·ger \ˈē-gər\ adj : marked by urgent or enthusiastic desire or interest ⟨∼ to learn⟩ syn avid, anxious, ardent, keen — ea·ger·ly adv — ea·ger·ness n

ea·gle \ˈē-gəl\ n 1 : a large bird of prey related to the hawks 2 : a score of two under par on a hole in golf

ea·glet \ˈē-glət\ n : a young eagle

-ean — see -AN

E and OE abbr errors and omissions excepted

¹ear \ˈiər\ n 1 : the organ of hearing; also : the outer part of this in a vertebrate 2 : something resembling a mammal's ear in shape, position, or function 3 : an ability to understand and appreciate something heard ⟨a good ∼ for music⟩ 4 : sympathetic attention

²ear n : the fruiting spike of a cereal (as wheat)

ear·ache \-ˌāk\ n : an ache or pain in the ear

ear·drum \-ˌdrəm\ n : a thin membrane that receives and transmits sound waves in the ear

eared \ˈiərd\ adj : having ears — used esp. in combination ⟨a long-eared dog⟩

earl \ˈərl\ n [ME erl, fr. OE eorl warrior, nobleman] : a member of the British peerage ranking below a marquess and above a viscount — earl·dom \-dəm\ n

ear·lobe \ˈiər-ˌlōb\ n : the pendent part of the ear

¹ear·ly \ˈər-lē\ adv ear·li·er; -est : at an early time (as in a period or series)

²early adj ear·li·er; -est 1 : of, relating to, or occurring near the beginning 2 : ANCIENT, PRIMITIVE 3 : occurring before the usual time ⟨an ∼ breakfast⟩; also : occurring in the near future

¹ear·mark \ˈiər-ˌmärk\ n : an identification mark (as on the ear of an animal)

²earmark vb : to designate for a specific purpose

ear·muff \-ˌməf\ n : one of a pair of ear coverings worn as protection against cold

earn \ˈərn\ vb 1 : to receive as a return for service 2 : DESERVE, MERIT syn gain, secure, get, obtain, acquire, win

¹ear·nest \ˈər-nəst\ n : an intensely serious state of mind ⟨spoke in ∼⟩

²earnest adj 1 : seriously intent and sober ⟨an ∼ face⟩ ⟨an ∼ attempt⟩ 2 : GRAVE, IMPORTANT syn solemn, sedate, staid, sober — ear·nest·ly adv — ear·nest·ness \-nəs(t)-nəs\ n

³earnest n 1 : something of value given by a buyer to a seller to bind a bargain 2 : PLEDGE

earn·ings \ˈər-ninz\ n pl 1 : something (as wages) earned 2 : the balance of revenue after deduction of costs and expenses

ear·phone \ˈiər-ˌfōn\ n : a device that reproduces sound and is worn over or in the ear

ear·plug \-ˌpləg\ n : a protective device for insertion into the opening of the ear

ear·ring \-ˌrin\ n : an ornament for the earlobe

ear·shot \-ˌshät\ n : range of hearing

ear·split·ting \-ˌsplit-in\ adj : intolerably loud or shrill

earth \ˈərth\ n 1 : SOIL, DIRT 2 : LAND, GROUND 3 : the planet inhabited by man : WORLD

earth·en \ˈər-thən\ adj : made of earth or baked clay

earth·en·ware \-ˌwaər\ n : slightly porous opaque pottery fired at low heat

earth·ling \'ərth-liŋ\ *n* : an inhabitant of the earth

earth·ly \'ərth-lē\ *adj* : having to do with the earth esp. as distinguished from heaven — **earth·li·ness** *n*

earth·quake \-ˌkwāk\ *n* : a shaking or trembling of a portion of the earth

earth science *n* : any of the sciences (as geology or meteorology) that deal with the earth or one of its parts

earth·shak·ing \'ərth-ˌshā-kiŋ\ *adj* : of fundamental importance

earth·ward \-wərd\ *or* **earth·wards** \-wərdz\ *adv* : toward the earth

earth·work \'ərth-ˌwərk\ *n* : an embankment or fortification of earth

earth·worm \-ˌwərm\ *n* : a long segmented worm found in damp soil

earthy \'ər-thē\ *adj* **earth·i·er; -est 1** : consisting of or resembling soil **2** : PRACTICAL **3** : COARSE, GROSS — **earth·i·ness** \'ər-thē-nəs\ *n*

ear·wax \'ier-ˌwaks\ *n* : the yellow waxy secretion from the ear

ear·wig \-ˌwig\ *n* : any of numerous insects with slender many-jointed antennae and a pair of appendages resembling forceps at the end of the body

¹ease \'ēz\ *n* **1** : comfort of body or mind **2** : naturalness of manner **3** : freedom from difficulty or effort **syn** relaxation, rest, repose, comfort, leisure

²ease *vb* **eased; eas·ing 1** : to relieve from distress **2** : to lessen the pressure or tension of **3** : to make or become less difficult ⟨~ credit⟩

ea·sel \'ē-zəl\ *n* [Dutch, lit., ass] : a frame to hold a painter's canvas or a picture

¹east \'ēst\ *adv* : to or toward the east

²east *adj* **1** : situated toward or at the east **2** : coming from the east

³east *n* **1** : the general direction of sunrise **2** : the compass point directly opposite to west **3** *cap* : regions or countries east of a specified or implied point — **east·er·ly** \'ē-stər-lē\ *adv or adj* — **east·ward** *adv or adj* — **east·wards** *adv*

Eas·ter \'ē-stər\ *n* : a church feast observed on a Sunday in March or April in commemoration of Christ's resurrection

east·ern \'ē-stərn\ *adj* **1** *often cap* : of, relating to, or characteristic of a region designated East **2** *cap* : of, relating to, or being the Christian churches originating in the Church of the Eastern Roman Empire **3** : lying toward or coming from the east — **East·ern·er** *n*

easy \'ē-zē\ *adj* **eas·i·er; -est 1** : marked by ease ⟨an ~ life⟩; *esp* : not causing distress or difficulty ⟨~ tasks⟩ **2** : MILD, LENIENT ⟨be ~ on him⟩ **3** : GRADUAL ⟨an ~ slope⟩ **4** : free from pain, trouble, or worry ⟨rest ~⟩ **5** : LEISURELY ⟨an ~ pace⟩ **6** : NATURAL ⟨an ~ manner⟩ **7** : COMFORTABLE ⟨an ~ chair⟩ **syn** facile, simple, effortless — **eas·i·ly** \'ēz-(ə-)lē\ *adv* — **eas·i·ness** \-ē-nəs\ *n*

easy·go·ing \ˌē-zē-'gō-iŋ\ *adj* : taking life easy : CAREFREE

eat \'ēt\ *vb* **ate** \'āt\; **eat·en** \'ēt-ᵊn\; **eat·ing 1** : to take in as food : take food **2** : to use up : DEVOUR **3** : CORRODE — **eat·able** *adj or n* — **eat·er** *n*

eat·ery \'ēt-ə-rē\ *n, pl* **-er·ies** : LUNCHEONETTE, RESTAURANT

eaves \'ēvz\ *n pl* : the overhanging lower edge of a roof

eaves·drop \'ēvz-ˌdräp\ *vb* : to listen secretly — **eaves·drop·per** *n*

¹ebb \'eb\ *n* **1** : the flowing back of water brought in by the tide **2** : a point or state of decline

²ebb *vb* **1** : to recede from the flood state **2** : DECLINE ⟨as his fortunes ~ed⟩

EBCDIC \'ep-sə-ˌdik\ *n* [extended binary coded decimal interchange code] : a computer code for representing alphanumeric information

¹eb·o·ny \'eb-ə-nē\ *n, pl* **-nies** : a hard heavy wood of Old World tropical trees (**ebony trees**) related to the persimmon

²ebony *adj* **1** : made of or resembling ebony **2** : BLACK, DARK

ebul·lient \i-'bùl-yənt, -'bəl-\ *adj* **1** : BOILING, AGITATED **2** : EXUBERANT — **ebul·lience** \-yəns\ *n*

ec·cen·tric \ik-'sen-trik\ *adj* **1** : deviating from a usual or accepted pattern **2** : deviating from a circular path ⟨~ orbits⟩ **3** : set with axis or support off center ⟨an ~ cam⟩; *also* : being off center **syn** erratic, queer, singular, curious, odd — **eccentric** *n* — **ec·cen·tri·cal·ly** \-tri-k(ə-)lē\ *adv* — **ec·cen·tric·i·ty** \ˌek-ˌsen-'tris-ət-ē\ *n*

Eccles *abbr* Ecclesiastes

Ec·cle·si·as·tes \ik-ˌlē-zē-ˈas-tēz\ — see BIBLE table

ec·cle·si·as·tic \ik-ˌlē-zē-ˈas-tik\ *n* : CLERGYMAN

ec·cle·si·as·ti·cal \-ti-kəl\ *or* **ec·cle·si·as·tic** \-tik\ *adj* : of or relating to a church esp. as an institution ⟨∼ art⟩ — **ec·cle·si·as·ti·cal·ly** \-ti-k(ə-)lē\ *adv*

Ec·cle·si·as·ti·cus \ik-ˌlē-zē-ˈas-ti-kəs\ *n* — see BIBLE table

Ecclus *abbr* Ecclesiasticus

ECG *abbr* electrocardiogram

ech·e·lon \ˈesh-ə-ˌlän\ *n* [F *échelon,* lit., rung of a ladder] **1** : a steplike arrangement (as of troops or airplanes) **2** : a level (as of authority or responsibility) within an organization

echi·no·derm \i-ˈkī-nə-ˌdərm\ *n* : any of a phylum of marine animals (as starfishes and sea urchins) having similar body parts (as the arms of a starfish) arranged around a central axis and often having a calcium-containing outer skeleton

echo \ˈek-ō\ *n, pl* **ech·oes** : repetition of a sound caused by a reflection of the sound waves; *also* : the reflection of a radar signal by an object — **echo** *vb*

echo·lo·ca·tion \ˌek-o-lō-ˈkā-shən\ *n* : a process for locating distant or invisible objects by means of sound waves reflected back to the sender (as a bat or submarine) by the objects

éclair \ā-ˈklaər\ *n* [F, lit., lightning] : an oblong shell of light pastry with whipped cream or custard filling

éclat \ā-ˈklä\ *n* [F] **1** : a dazzling effect or success **2** : ACCLAIM

eclec·tic \e-ˈklek-tik, i-\ *adj* : selecting or made up of what seems best of varied sources — **eclectic** *n*

¹eclipse \i-ˈklips\ *n* **1** : the total or partial obscuring of one heavenly body by another; *also* : a passing into the shadow of a heavenly body **2** : a falling into obscurity, decline, or disgrace

²eclipse *vb* **eclipsed; eclips·ing** : to cause an eclipse of

eclip·tic \i-ˈklip-tik\ *n* : the great circle of the celestial sphere that is the apparent path of the sun

ec·logue \ˈek-ˌlȯg, -ˌläg\ *n* : a pastoral poem

ECM *abbr* European Common Market

ecol *abbr* ecological; ecology

ecol·o·gy \i-ˈkäl-ə-jē, e-\ *n, pl* **-gies** [G *ökologie,* fr. Gk *oikos* house] **1** : a branch of science concerned with the relationships between organisms and their environment **2** : the pattern of relations between organisms and their environment — **eco·log·i·cal** \ˌē-kə-ˈläj-i-kəl, ˌek-ə-\ *also* **eco·log·ic** \-ik\ *adj* — **eco·log·i·cal·ly** \-i-k(ə-)lē\ *adv* — **ecol·o·gist** \i-ˈkäl-ə-jəst, e-\ *n*

econ *abbr* economics; economist; economy

eco·nom·ic \ˌek-ə-ˈnäm-ik, ˌē-kə-\ *adj* : of or relating to the satisfaction of material needs of humans

eco·nom·i·cal \-ˈnäm-i-kəl\ *adj* **1** : THRIFTY **2** : operating with little waste or at a saving **syn** frugal, sparing, provident, thrifty — **ec·o·nom·i·cal·ly** \-k(ə-)lē\ *adv*

eco·nom·ics \ˌek-ə-ˈnäm-iks, ˌē-kə-\ *n* : a branch of knowledge dealing with the production, distribution, and consumption of goods and services — **econ·o·mist** \i-ˈkän-ə-məst\ *n*

econ·o·mize \i-ˈkän-ə-ˌmīz\ *vb* **-mized; -miz·ing** : to practice economy : be frugal

¹econ·o·my \i-ˈkän-ə-mē\ *n, pl* **-mies** [MF *yconomie,* fr. ML *oeconomia,* fr. Gk *oikonomia,* fr. *oikonomos* household manager, fr. *oikos* house + *nemein* to manage] **1** : thrifty management or use of resources; *also* : an instance of this **2** : manner of arrangement or functioning : ORGANIZATION **3** : an economic system ⟨a money ∼⟩

²economy *adj* : ECONOMICAL ⟨∼ cars⟩

eco·sys·tem \ˈē-kō-ˌsis-təm, ˈek-ō-\ *n* : the complex of an ecological community and its environment functioning as a unit in nature

ecru \ˈek-rü, ˈā-krü\ *n* [F *écru* unbleached] : BEIGE

ec·sta·sy \ˈek-stə-sē\ *n, pl* **-sies** : extreme and usu. rapturous emotional excitement — **ec·stat·ic** \ek-ˈstat-ik, ik-ˈstat-\ *adj* — **ec·stat·i·cal·ly** \-i-k(ə-)lē\ *adv*

Ecua *abbr* Ecuador

ec·u·men·i·cal \ˌek-yə-ˈmen-i-kəl\ *adj* : general in extent or influence; *esp* : promoting or tending toward worldwide Christian unity — **ec·u·men·i·cal·ly** \-k(ə-)lē\ *adv*

ec·ze·ma \ig-ˈzē-mə, ˈeg-zə-mə, ˈek-sə-\

n : an itching skin inflammation with crusted lesions — **ec·zem·a·tous** \ig-ˈzem-ət-əs\ *adj*

ed *abbr* **1** edited; edition; editor **2** education

¹**-ed** \d *after a vowel or* b, g, j, l, m, n, ŋ, r, <u>th</u>, v, z, zh; əd, id *after* d, t; t *after other sounds*\ *vb suffix or adj suffix* **1** — used to form the past participle of regular weak verbs ⟨end*ed*⟩ ⟨fad*ed*⟩ ⟨tri*ed*⟩ ⟨patt*ed*⟩ **2** — used to form adjectives of identical meaning from Latin-derived adjectives ending in *-ate* ⟨pinnat*ed*⟩ **3** : having : characterized by ⟨cultur*ed*⟩ ⟨two-legg*ed*⟩; *also* : having the characteristics of ⟨big-ot*ed*⟩

²**-ed** *vb suffix* — used to form the past tense of regular weak verbs ⟨judg*ed*⟩ ⟨deni*ed*⟩ ⟨dropp*ed*⟩

Edam \ˈēd-əm, ˈē-ˌdam\ *n* : a yellow Dutch pressed cheese made in balls

ed·dy \ˈed-ē\ *n, pl* **eddies** : WHIRLPOOL — **eddy** *vb*

edel·weiss \ˈād-ᵊl-ˌwīs, -ˌvīs\ *n* [G, fr. *edel* noble + *weiss* white] : a small perennial woolly herb that is related to the thistles and grows high in the Alps

ede·ma \i-ˈdē-mə\ *n* : abnormal accumulation of watery fluid in connective tissue or in a serous cavity; *also* : a condition marked by such accumulation — **edem·a·tous** \-ˈdem-ət-əs\ *adj*

Eden \ˈēd-ᵊn\ *n* : PARADISE 2

¹**edge** \ˈej\ *n* **1** : the cutting side of a blade **2** : power to cut or penetrate : SHARPNESS **3** : the line where something begins or ends; *also* : the area adjoining such an edge **4** : ADVANTAGE — **edged** \ˈejd\ *adj*

²**edge** *vb* **edged; edg·ing 1** : to give or form an edge **2** : to move or force gradually ⟨∼ into a crowd⟩ — **edg·er** *n*

edge·ways \ˈej-ˌwāz\ *adv* : SIDEWAYS

edg·ing \ˈej-iŋ\ *n* : something that forms an edge or border ⟨a lace ∼⟩

edgy \ˈej-ē\ *adj* **edg·i·er; -est 1** : SHARP ⟨an ∼ tone⟩ **2** : TENSE, NERVOUS — **edg·i·ness** \ˈej-ē-nəs\ *n*

ed·i·ble \ˈed-ə-bəl\ *adj* : fit or safe to be eaten — **ed·i·bil·i·ty** \ˌed-ə-ˈbil-ət-ē\ *n* — **edible** *n*

edict \ˈē-ˌdikt\ *n* : DECREE

ed·i·fi·ca·tion \ˌed-ə-fə-ˈkā-shən\ *n* : in-struction and improvement esp. in morality — **ed·i·fy** \ˈed-ə-ˌfī\ *vb*

ed·i·fice \ˈed-ə-fəs\ *n* : a usu. large building

ed·it \ˈed-ət\ *vb* **1** : to revise and prepare for publication **2** : to direct the publication and policies of (as a newspaper) — **ed·i·tor** \ˈed-ət-ər\ *n* — **ed·i·tor·ship** *n*

edi·tion \i-ˈdish-ən\ *n* **1** : the form in which a text is published **2** : the total number of copies (as of a book) published at one time **3** : VERSION

¹**ed·i·to·ri·al** \ˌed-ə-ˈtōr-ē-əl\ *adj* **1** : of, relating to, or functioning as an editor **2** : being an editorial; *also* : expressing opinion — **ed·i·to·ri·al·ly** \-ē\ *adv*

²**editorial** *n* : an article (as in a newspaper) giving the views of a publisher; *also* : an expression of opinion resembling an editorial ⟨a television ∼⟩

ed·i·to·ri·al·ize \ˌed-ə-ˈtōr-ē-ə-ˌlīz\ *vb* **-ized; -iz·ing 1** : to express an opinion in an editorial **2** : to introduce opinions into factual reporting **3** : to express an opinion — **ed·i·to·ri·al·iza·tion** \-ˌtōr-ē-ə-lə-ˈzā-shən\ *n* — **ed·i·to·ri·al·iz·er** *n*

EDP *abbr* electronic data processing

EDT *abbr* Eastern daylight (saving) time

educ *abbr* education; educational

ed·u·ca·ble \ˈej-ə-kə-bəl\ *adj* : capable of being educated

ed·u·cate \ˈej-ə-ˌkāt\ *vb* **-cat·ed; -cat·ing 1** : to provide with schooling **2** : to develop mentally and morally **syn** train, discipline, school, instruct, teach — **ed·u·ca·tor** \-ˌkāt-ər\ *n*

ed·u·ca·tion \ˌej-ə-ˈkā-shən\ *n* **1** : the action or process of educating or being educated **2** : a field of knowledge dealing with technical aspects of teaching — **ed·u·ca·tion·al** \-sh(ə-)nəl\ *adj*

educational television *n* : PUBLIC TELEVISION

educe \i-ˈd(y)üs\ *vb* **educed; educ·ing 1** : ELICIT, EVOKE **2** : DEDUCE **syn** extract, evince, extort

EE *abbr* electrical engineer

EEC *abbr* European Economic Community

EEG *abbr* **1** electroencephalogram **2** electroencephalograph

eel \\'ēl\\ *n* : any of numerous snakelike fishes with a smooth slimy skin

EEO *abbr* equal employment opportunity

ee•rie *also* **ee•ry** \\'i(ə)r-ē\\ *adj* **ee•ri•er; -est** : WEIRD, UNCANNY — **ee•ri•ly** \\'ir-ə-lē\\ *adv*

eff *abbr* efficiency

ef•face \\i-'fās, e-\\ *vb* **ef•faced; ef•fac•ing** : to obliterate or obscure by or as if by rubbing out **syn** erase, delete, annul, cancel, expunge — **ef•face•able** *adj* — **ef•face•ment** *n*

¹ef•fect \\i-'fekt\\ *n* **1** : RESULT **2** : MEANING, INTENT **3** : APPEARANCE **4** : FULFILLMENT **5** : INFLUENCE **6** *pl* : GOODS, POSSESSIONS **7** : the quality or state of being operative : OPERATION **syn** consequence, outcome, upshot, aftermath, result, issue

²effect *vb* **1** : ACCOMPLISH ⟨∼ repairs⟩ **2** : to put into effect ⟨∼ changes⟩

ef•fec•tive \\i-'fek-tiv\\ *adj* **1** : producing a decisive or desired effect **2** : IMPRESSIVE, STRIKING **3** : ready for service or action **4** : being in effect — **ef•fec•tive•ly** *adv* — **ef•fec•tive•ness** *n*

ef•fec•tu•al \\i-'fek-chə(-wə)l\\ *adj* : producing an intended effect : ADEQUATE — **ef•fec•tu•al•ly** \\-ē\\ *adv*

ef•fec•tu•ate \\i-'fek-chə-ˌwāt\\ *vb* **-at•ed; -at•ing** : BRING ABOUT, EFFECT

ef•fem•i•nate \\ə-'fem-ə-nət\\ *adj* : marked by qualities more typical of and suitable to women than men; : UNMANLY — **ef•fem•i•na•cy** \\-nə-sē\\ *n*

ef•fen•di \\e-'fen-dē\\ *n* [Turk *efendi* master, fr. NGk *aphentēs,* alter. of Gk *authentēs*] : a man of property, authority, or education in an eastern Mediterranean country

ef•fer•ent \\'ef-ə-rənt\\ *adj* : bearing or conducting outward from a more central part ⟨∼ nerves⟩

ef•fer•vesce \\ˌef-ər-'ves\\ *vb* **-vesced; -vesc•ing** : to bubble and hiss as gas escapes; *also* : to be exhilarated — **ef•fer•ves•cence** \\-'ves-ᵊns\\ *n* — **ef•fer•ves•cent** \\-ᵊnt\\ *adj* — **ef•fer•ves•cent•ly** *adv*

ef•fete \\e-'fēt\\ *adj* : worn out : EXHAUSTED; *also* : DECADENT

ef•fi•ca•cious \\ˌef-ə-'kā-shəs\\ *adj* : producing an intended effect ⟨∼ remedies⟩ **syn** effectual, effective, efficient — **ef•fi•ca•cy** \\'ef-i-kə-sē\\ *n*

ef•fi•cient \\i-'fish-ənt\\ *adj* : productive of desired effects esp. without loss or waste : COMPETENT — **ef•fi•cien•cy** \\-ən-sē\\ *n* — **ef•fi•cient•ly** *adv*

ef•fi•gy \\'ef-ə-jē\\ *n, pl* **-gies** : IMAGE; *esp* : a crude figure of a hated person

ef•flo•resce \\ˌef-lə-'res\\ *vb* **-resced; -resc•ing** : to burst forth : BLOOM

ef•flo•res•cence \\-'res-ᵊns\\ *n* **1** : the period or state of flowering **2** : the action or process of developing **3** : fullness of manifestation : CULMINATION — **ef•flo•res•cent** \\-ᵊnt\\ *adj*

ef•flu•ence \\'ef-ˌlü-əns\\ *n* **1** : something that flows out **2** : an action or process of flowing out — **ef•flu•ent** \\-ənt\\ *adj or n*

ef•flu•vi•um \\e-'flü-vē-əm\\ *n, pl* **-via** \\-vē-ə\\ *or* **-vi•ums** [L outflow] **1** : a usu. unpleasant emanation **2** : a by-product usu. in the form of waste

ef•fort \\'ef-ərt\\ *n* **1** : EXERTION, ENDEAVOR; *also* : a product of effort **2** : active or applied force — **ef•fort•less** *adj* — **ef•fort•less•ly** *adv*

ef•fron•tery \\i-'frənt-ə-rē\\ *n, pl* **-ter•ies** : shameless boldness : IMPUDENCE **syn** temerity, audacity, brass, gall, nerve

ef•ful•gence \\i-'fùl-jəns, -'fəl-\\ *n* : radiant splendor : BRILLIANCE — **ef•ful•gent** \\-jənt\\ *adj*

ef•fu•sion \\i-'fyü-zhən, e-\\ *n* : a gushing forth; *also* : unrestrained utterance — **ef•fuse** \\-'fyüz, e-\\ *vb* — **ef•fu•sive** \\i-'fyü-siv, e-\\ *adj*

eft \\'eft\\ *n* : NEWT

EFT *or* **EFTS** *abbr* electronic funds transfer (system)

e.g. \\f(ə-)rig-'zam-pəl, (')ē-'jē\\ *abbr* [L *exempli gratia*] for example

Eg *abbr* Egypt; Egyptian

egal•i•tar•i•an•ism \\i-ˌgal-ə-'ter-ē-ə-ˌniz-əm\\ *n* : a belief in human equality esp. in social, political, and economic affairs — **egal•i•tar•i•an** *adj or n*

¹egg \\'eg\\ *vb* [ME *eggen,* fr. ON *eggja;* akin to OE *ecg* edge] : to urge to action

²egg *n* [ME *egge,* fr. ON *egg;* akin to OE *æg* egg, L *ovum*] **1** : a rounded usu. hard-shelled reproductive body esp. of birds and reptiles from which the young hatches; *also* : the egg of domestic poultry as an article of food ⟨allergic to ∼s⟩ **2** : a germ cell produced by a female

egg·beat·er \'eg-ˌbēt-ər\ *n* : a hand-operated kitchen utensil for beating, stirring, or whipping

egg cell *n* : EGG 2

egg·head \-ˌhed\ *n* : INTELLECTUAL, HIGHBROW

egg·nog \-ˌnäg\ *n* : a drink consisting of eggs beaten up with sugar, milk or cream, and often alcoholic liquor

egg·plant \-ˌplant\ *n* : the edible usu. large and purplish fruit of a plant related to the potato; *also* : the plant

egg roll *n* : a thin egg-dough casing filled with minced vegetables and often bits of meat and usu. fried in deep fat

egg·shell \'eg-ˌshel\ *n* : the hard exterior covering of an egg

egis \'ē-jəs\ var of AEGIS

eg·lan·tine \'eg-lən-ˌtīn, -ˌtēn\ *n* : SWEETBRIER

ego \'ē-gō\ *n, pl* **egos** [L, I] **1** : the self as distinguished from others **2** : the one of the three divisions of the psyche in psychoanalytic theory that serves as the organized conscious mediator between the person and reality

ego·cen·tric \ˌē-gō-'sen-trik\ *adj* : concerned or overly concerned with the self; *esp* : SELF-CENTERED

ego·ism \'ē-gə-ˌwiz-əm\ *n* **1** : a doctrine holding self-interest to be the motive or the valid end of action **2** : excessive concern for oneself usu. without exaggerated feelings of self-importance — **ego·ist** \-wəst\ *n* — **ego·is·tic** \ˌē-gə-'wis-tik\ *adj* — **ego·is·ti·cal·ly** \-ē\ *adv*

ego·tism \'ē-gə-ˌtiz-əm\ *n* **1** : the practice of talking about oneself too much **2** : an exaggerated sense of self-importance : CONCEIT — **ego·tist** \-təst\ *n* — **ego·tis·tic** \ˌē-gə-'tis-tik\ *or* **ego·tis·ti·cal** \-ti-kəl\ *adj* — **ego·tis·ti·cal·ly** \-ē\ *adv*

ego trip *n* : an act that enhances and satisfies one's ego

egre·gious \i-'grē-jəs\ *adj* [L *egregius* outstanding from the herd, fr. *ex, e* out of + *greg-, grex* flock, herd] : notably bad : FLAGRANT — **egre·gious·ly** *adv* — **egre·gious·ness** *n*

egress \'ē-ˌgres\ *n* : a way out : EXIT

egret \'ē-grət, i-'gret\ *n* : any of various herons that bear long plumes during the breeding season

Egyp·tian \i-'jip-shən\ *n* **1** : a native or inhabitant of Egypt **2** : the language of the ancient Egyptians from earliest times to about the 3d century A.D. — **Egyptian** *adj*

EHF *abbr* extremely high frequency

ei·der \'īd-ər\ *n* : any of several northern sea ducks that yield a soft down

ei·der·down \-ˌdaùn\ *n* : the down of the eider **2** : a quilt filled with eiderdown

ei·do·lon \ī-'dō-lən\ *n, pl* **-lons** *or* **-la** \-lə\ **1** : an insubstantial image : PHANTOM **2** : IDEAL

eight \'āt\ *n* **1** : one more than seven **2** : the 8th in a set or series **3** : something having eight units; *esp* : an 8-cylinder engine or automobile — **eight** *adj or pron* — **eighth** \'ātth\ *adj or adv or n*

eight ball *n* : a black pool ball numbered 8 — **behind the eight ball** : in a highly disadvantageous position or baffling situation

eigh·teen \'ā(t)-'tēn\ *n* : one more than 17 — **eighteen** *adj or pron* — **eigh·teenth** \-'tēnth\ *adj or n*

eighty \'āt-ē\ *n, pl* **eight·ies** : eight times 10 — **eight·i·eth** \'āt-ē-əth\ *adj or n* — **eighty** *adj or pron*

ein·stei·ni·um \īn-'stī-nē-əm\ *n* : an artificially produced radioactive element

¹**ei·ther** \'ē-thər, 'ī-\ *adj* **1** : being the one and the other of two : EACH ⟨trees on ∼ side⟩ **2** : being the one or the other of two ⟨take ∼ road⟩

²**either** *pron* : the one or the other

³**either** *conj* — used as a function word before the first of two or more words or word groups of which the last is preceded by *or* to indicate that they represent alternatives ⟨a statement is ∼ true or false⟩

ejac·u·late \i-'jak-yə-ˌlāt\ *vb* **-lat·ed; -lat·ing 1** : to eject a fluid (as semen) **2** : to utter suddenly : EXCLAIM — **ejac·u·la·tion** \-ˌjak-yə-'lā-shən\ *n* — **ejac·u·la·to·ry** \-'jak-yə-lə-ˌtōr-ē\ *adj*

eject \i-'jekt\ *vb* : to drive or throw out or off **syn** expel, oust, evict, dismiss — **ejec·tion** \-'jek-shən\ *n*

ejection seat *n* : an emergency escape seat for propelling an occupant out of an airplane

eke \'ēk\ *vb* **eked; ek·ing** : to gain, supplement, or extend usu. with effort —

usu. used with *out* ⟨~ out a living⟩

EKG *abbr* [G *elektrokardiogramm*] **1** : electrocardiogram **2** : electrocardiograph

ekue·le \ā-ˈkwā-(ˌ)lā\ *n, pl* **ekuele** — see MONEY table

el *abbr* elevation

¹**elab·o·rate** \i-ˈlab-(ə-)rət\ *adj* **1** : planned or carried out with care and in detail **2** : being complex and usu. ornate — **elab·o·rate·ly** *adv* — **elab·o·rate·ness** *n*

²**elab·o·rate** \i-ˈlab-ə-ˌrāt\ *vb* **-rat·ed; -rat·ing 1** : to build up from simpler ingredients **2** : to work out in detail : develop fully — **elab·o·ra·tion** \-ˌlab-ə-ˈrā-shən\ *n*

élan \ā-läⁿ\ *n* [F] : ARDOR, SPIRIT

eland \ˈē-lənd, -ˌland\ *n, pl* **eland** *also* **elands** [Afrikaans, elk] : either of two large African antelopes with spirally twisted horns

elapse \i-ˈlaps\ *vb* **elapsed; elaps·ing** : to slip by : PASS

¹**elas·tic** \i-ˈlas-tik\ *adj* **1** : SPRINGY **2** : FLEXIBLE, PLIABLE **3** : ADAPTABLE **syn** resilient, supple, stretch — **elas·tic·i·ty** \-ˌlas-ˈtis-ət-ē, ˌē-ˌlas-\ *n*

²**elastic** *n* **1** : elastic material **2** : a rubber band

elate \i-ˈlāt\ *vb* **elat·ed; elat·ing** : to fill with joy — **ela·tion** \-ˈlā-shən\ *n*

¹**el·bow** \ˈel-ˌbō\ *n* **1** : the joint of the arm; *also* : the outer curve of the bent arm **2** : a bend or joint resembling an elbow in shape

²**elbow** *vb* : to push aside with the elbow; *also* : to make one's way by elbowing

el·bow·room \ˈel-ˌbō-ˌrüm, -ˌrùm\ *n* **1** : room for moving the elbows freely **2** : enough space for work or operation

¹**el·der** \ˈel-dər\ *n* : ELDERBERRY 2

²**elder** *adj* **1** : OLDER **2** : EARLIER, FORMER **3** : of higher rank : SENIOR

³**elder** *n* **1** : an older individual : SENIOR **2** : one having authority by reason of age and experience **3** : a church officer

el·der·ber·ry \ˈel-də(r)-ˌber-ē\ *n* **1** : the edible black or red fruit of a shrub or tree related to the honeysuckle and bearing flat clusters of small white or pink flowers **2** : a tree or shrub bearing elderberries

el·der·ly \ˈel-dər-lē\ *adj* **1** : rather old;

esp : past middle age **2** : of, relating to, or characteristic of later life

el·dest \ˈel-dəst\ *adj* : of the greatest age

El Do·ra·do \ˌel-də-ˈräd-ō, -ˈrād-\ *n* [Sp, lit., the gilded one] : a place of vast riches or abundance

elec *abbr* electric; electrical; electricity

¹**elect** \i-ˈlekt\ *adj* **1** : CHOSEN, SELECT **2** : elected but not yet installed in office ⟨the president-*elect*⟩

²**elect** *n, pl* **elect 1** : a selected person **2** *pl* : a select or exclusive group

³**elect** *vb* **1** : to select by vote (as for office or membership) **2** : CHOOSE, PICK **syn** prefer, select

elec·tion \i-ˈlek-shən\ *n* **1** : an act or process of electing **2** : the fact of being elected

elec·tion·eer \i-ˌlek-shə-ˈniər\ *vb* : to work for the election of a candidate or party

¹**elec·tive** \i-ˈlek-tiv\ *adj* **1** : chosen or filled by election **2** : permitting a choice : OPTIONAL

²**elective** *n* : an elective course or subject of study

elec·tor \i-ˈlek-tər\ *n* **1** : one qualified to vote in an election **2** : one elected to an electoral college — **elec·tor·al** \i-ˈlek-t(ə-)rəl\ *adj*

electoral college *n* : a body of electors who elect the president and vice president of the U.S.

elec·tor·ate \i-ˈlek-t(ə-)rət\ *n* : a body of persons entitled to vote

elec·tric \i-ˈlek-trik\ *or* **elec·tri·cal** \-tri-kəl\ *adj* [NL *electricus* produced from amber by friction, electric, fr. ML, of amber, fr. L *electrum* amber, fr. Gk *ēlektron*] **1** : of, relating to, operated by, or produced by electricity **2** : ELECTRIFYING, THRILLING — **elec·tri·cal·ly** \-k(ə-)lē\ *adv*

electrical storm *n* : THUNDERSTORM

electric chair *n* : a chair used in legal electrocution

electric eye *n* : PHOTOELECTRIC CELL

elec·tri·cian \i-ˌlek-ˈtrish-ən\ *n* : one who installs, operates, or repairs electrical equipment

elec·tric·i·ty \i-ˌlek-ˈtris-(ə-)tē\ *n, pl* **-ties 1** : a form of energy that occurs in nature and is observable in natural phenomena (as lightning) and that can be produced by friction, chemical reaction, or mechanical effort **2** : electric current

elec·tri·fy \i-'lek-trə-ˌfī\ *vb* **-fied; -fy·ing 1** : to charge with electricity **2** : to equip for use of electric power **3** : THRILL — **elec·tri·fi·ca·tion** \-ˌlek-trə-fə-'kā-shən\ *n*

elec·tro·car·dio·gram \i-ˌlek-trō-'kärd-ē-ə-ˌgram\ *n* : the tracing made by an electrocardiograph

elec·tro·car·dio·graph \-ˌgraf\ *n* : an instrument for recording the changes of electrical potential occurring during the heartbeat — **elec·tro·car·dio·graph·ic** \-ˌkärd-ē-ə-'graf-ik\ *adj* — **elec·tro·car·di·og·ra·phy** \-ē-'äg-rə-fē\ *n*

elec·tro·chem·is·try \-'kem-ə-strē\ *n* : a branch of chemistry that deals with the relation of electricity to chemical changes — **elec·tro·chem·i·cal** \-'kem-i-kəl\ *adj*

elec·tro·cute \i-'lek-trə-ˌkyüt\ *vb* **-cut·ed; -cut·ing** : to kill by an electric shock; *esp* : to kill (a criminal) in this way — **elec·tro·cu·tion** \-ˌlek-trə-'kyü-shən\ *n*

elec·trode \i-'lek-ˌtrōd\ *n* : a conductor used to establish electrical contact with a nonmetallic part of a circuit

elec·tro·en·ceph·a·lo·gram \-in-'sef-ə-lə-ˌgram\ *n* : the tracing of the electrical activity of the brain that is made by an electroencephalograph

elec·tro·en·ceph·a·lo·graph \-ˌgraf\ *n* : an apparatus for detecting and recording the electrical activity of the brain — **elec·tro·en·ceph·a·lo·graph·ic** \-ˌsef-ə-lə-'graf-ik\ *adj* — **elec·tro·en·ceph·a·log·ra·phy** \-'läg-rə-fē\ *n*

elec·trol·o·gist \i-ˌlek-'träl-ə-jəst\ *n* : one that uses electrical means to remove hair, warts, moles, and birthmarks from the body

elec·trol·y·sis \i-ˌlek-'träl-ə-səs\ *n* **1** : the production of chemical changes by passage of an electric current through an electrolyte **2** : the destruction of hair roots with an electric current — **elec·tro·lyt·ic** \-trə-'lit-ik\ *adj*

elec·tro·lyte \i-'lek-trə-ˌlīt\ *n* : a nonmetallic electric conductor in which current is carried by the movement of ions; *also* : a substance whose solution or molten form is such a conductor

elec·tro·mag·net \i-ˌlek-trō-'mag-nət\ *n* : a core of magnetic material surrounded by a coil of wire through which an electric current is passed to magnetize the core

elec·tro·mag·net·ic \-mag-'net-ik\ *adj* : of, relating to, or produced by electromagnetism

electromagnetic radiation *n* : a series of electromagnetic waves

electromagnetic wave *n* : a wave (as a radio wave, an X ray, or a wave of visible light) that consists of associated electric and magnetic effects and that travels at the speed of light

elec·tro·mag·ne·tism \i-ˌlek-trō-'mag-nə-ˌtiz-əm\ *n* **1** : magnetism developed by a current of electricity **2** : physics dealing with the relations between electricity and magnetism

elec·tro·mo·tive force \i-ˌlek-trə-ˌmōt-iv-\ *n* : the work per unit charge required to carry a positive charge around a closed path in an electric field

elec·tron \i-'lek-ˌträn\ *n* : a negatively charged elementary particle that forms the part of an atom outside the nucleus

elec·tron·ic \i-ˌlek-'trän-ik\ *adj* : of or relating to electrons or electronics — **elec·tron·i·cal·ly** \-i-k(ə-)lē\ *adv*

electronic mail *n* : messages sent and received electronically

elec·tron·ics \i-ˌlek-'trän-iks\ *n* **1** : the physics of electrons and their utilization **2** : electronic devices or equipment

electron microscope *n* : an instrument in which a focused beam of electrons is used to produce an enlarged image of a minute object on a fluorescent screen or photographic plate

electron tube *n* : a device in which electrical conduction by electrons takes place within a container and which is used for the controlled flow of electrons

elec·tro·pho·re·sis \i-ˌlek-trə-fə-'rē-səs\ *n* : the movement of suspended particles through a fluid by an electromotive force — **elec·tro·pho·ret·ic** \-'rēt-ik\ *adj*

elec·tro·plate \i-'lek-trə-ˌplāt\ *vb* : to coat (as with metal) by electrolysis

elec·tro·pos·i·tive \i-ˌlek-trō-'päz-ət-iv\

adj : having a tendency to give up electrons

elec·tro·shock therapy \-trō-ˌshäk-\ *n* : the treatment of mental disorder by the induction of coma with an electric current

elec·tro·stat·ics \i-ˌlek-trə-ˈstat-iks\ *n* : physics dealing with the interactions of stationary electric charges

el·ee·mos·y·nary \ˌel-i-ˈmäs-ᵊn-ˌer-ē\ *adj* : CHARITABLE

el·e·gance \ˈel-i-gəns\ *n* **1** : refined gracefulness; *also* : tasteful richness (as of design) **2** : something marked by elegance — **el·e·gant** \-gənt\ *adj.* — **el·e·gant·ly** *adv*

el·e·gy \ˈel-ə-jē\ *n, pl* **-gies** : a poem expressing grief for one who is dead; *also* : a reflective poem usu. melancholy in tone — **ele·gi·ac** \ˌel-ə-ˈjī-ək, -ˌak\ *adj*

elem *abbr* elementary

el·e·ment \ˈel-ə-mənt\ *n* **1** *pl* : weather conditions; *esp* : severe weather ⟨boards exposed to the ∼s⟩ **2** : natural environment ⟨in her ∼⟩ **3** : a constituent part **4** *pl* : the simplest principles (as of an art or science) : RUDIMENTS **5** : a basic member of a mathematical set **6** : a substance not separable by ordinary chemical means into substances different from itself **syn** component, ingredient, factor, constituent — **el·e·men·tal** \ˌel-ə-ˈment-ᵊl\ *adj*

el·e·men·ta·ry \ˌel-ə-ˈmen-t(ə-)rē\ *adj* : SIMPLE, RUDIMENTARY; *also* : of, relating to, or teaching the basic subjects of education

elementary particle *n* : a subatomic particle (as the electron or photon) of matter and energy that does not appear to be made up of other smaller particles

elementary school *n* : a school usu. including the first six or the first eight grades

el·e·phant \ˈel-ə-fənt\ *n* : any of a family of huge thickset nearly hairless mammals that have the snout lengthened into a trunk and two long curving pointed tusks which furnish ivory

el·e·phan·ti·a·sis \ˌel-ə-fən-ˈtī-ə-səs\ *n, pl* **-a·ses** \-ˌsēz\ : enlargement and thickening of tissues in response esp. to infection by minute parasitic worms

el·e·phan·tine \ˌel-ə-ˈfan-ˌtēn, -ˌtīn, ˈel-ə-fən-\ *adj* **1** : of great size or strength **2** : CLUMSY, PONDEROUS

elev *abbr* elevation

el·e·vate \ˈel-ə-ˌvāt\ *vb* **-vat·ed; -vat·ing** **1** : to lift up : RAISE **2** : EXALT, ENNOBLE **3** : ELATE

el·e·va·tion \ˌel-ə-ˈvā-shən\ *n* **1** : the height to which something is raised (as above sea level) **2** : a lifting up **3** : something (as a hill or swelling) that is elevated **syn** altitude, height

el·e·va·tor \ˈel-ə-ˌvāt-ər\ *n* **1** : a cage or platform for conveying something from one level to another **2** : a building for storing and discharging grain **3** : a movable surface on an airplane to produce motion up or down

elev·en \i-ˈlev-ən\ *n* **1** : one more than 10 **2** : the 11th in a set or series **3** : something having 11 units; *esp* : a football team — **eleven** *adj or pron* — **elev·enth** \-ənth\ *adj or n*

elf \ˈelf\ *n, pl* **elves** \ˈelvz\ : a mischievous fairy — **elf·in** \ˈel-fən\ *adj* — **elf·ish** \ˈel-fish\ *adj*

ELF *abbr* extremely low frequency

elic·it \i-ˈlis-ət\ *vb* : to draw out or forth **syn** evoke, educe, extract, extort

elide \i-ˈlīd\ *vb* **elid·ed; elid·ing** : to suppress or alter by elision

el·i·gi·ble \ˈel-ə-jə-bəl\ *adj* : qualified to participate or to be chosen — **el·i·gi·bil·i·ty** \ˌel-ə-jə-ˈbil-ət-ē\ *n* — **eligible** *n*

elim·i·nate \i-ˈlim-ə-ˌnāt\ *vb* **-nat·ed; -nat·ing** [L *eliminatus,* pp. of *eliminare,* fr. *limen* threshold] **1** : EXCLUDE, EXPEL; *esp* : to pass (wastes) from the body **2** : to leave out : IGNORE — **elim·i·na·tion** \-ˌlim-ə-ˈnā-shən\ *n*

eli·sion \i-ˈlizh-ən\ *n* : the omission of a final or initial sound or a word; *esp* : the omission of an unstressed vowel or syllable in a verse to achieve a uniform rhythm

elite \ā-ˈlēt\ *n* [F *élite*] **1** : the choice part; *also* : a superior group **2** : a typewriter type providing 12 characters to the inch

elit·ism \-ˈlēt-ˌiz-əm\ *n* : leadership or rule by an elite; *also* : advocacy of such elitism

elix·ir \i-ˈlik-sər\ *n* [ME, fr. ML, fr. Ar

al-iksīr the elixir, fr. al the + iksīr elixir] **1** : a substance held capable of prolonging life indefinitely; also : PANACEA **2** : a sweetened alcoholic medicinal solution

Eliz·a·be·than \i-ˌliz-ə-ˈbē-thən\ adj : of, relating to, or characteristic of Elizabeth I of England or her times

elk \ˈelk\ n, pl **elks** **1** : the largest existing deer of Europe and Asia related to the American moose and having broad spreading antlers **2** : a large North American deer with curved antlers having many branches

¹**ell** \ˈel\ n : a unit of length; esp : a former English cloth measure of 45 inches (1.1 meters)

²**ell** n : an extension at right angles to a building **syn** wing, annex, arm

el·lipse \i-ˈlips, e-\ n : a closed curve of oval shape

el·lip·sis \i-ˈlip-səs, e-\ n, pl **el·lip·ses** \-ˌsēz\ **1** : omission from an expression of a word clearly implied **2** : marks (as . . . or ***) to show omission

el·lip·soid \i-ˈlip-ˌsȯid, e-\ n : a surface all plane sections of which are circles or ellipses — **ellipsoid** or **el·lip·soi·dal** \-ˌlip-ˈsȯid-ᵊl\ adj

el·lip·tic \i-ˈlip-tik, e-\ or **el·lip·ti·cal** \-ti-kəl\ adj **1** : of, relating to, or shaped like an ellipse **2** : of, relating to, or marked by ellipsis — **el·lip·ti·cal·ly** \-ti-k(ə-)lē\ adv

elm \ˈelm\ n : any of a genus of large graceful trees that have toothed leaves and nearly circular one-seeded winged fruits and are often grown as shade trees; also : the wood of an elm

el·o·cu·tion \ˌel-ə-ˈkyü-shən\ n : the art of effective public speaking — **el·o·cu·tion·ist** \-sh(ə-)nəst\ n

elon·gate \i-ˈlȯŋ-ˌgāt\ vb **-gat·ed; -gat·ing** : to make or grow longer **syn** extend, lengthen, prolong, protract — **elon·ga·tion** \(ˌ)ē-ˌlȯŋ-ˈgā-shən\ n

elope \i-ˈlōp\ vb **eloped; elop·ing** : to run away esp. to be married — **elope·ment** n

el·o·quent \ˈel-ə-kwənt\ adj **1** : having or showing clear and forceful expression **2** : clearly showing some feeling or meaning — **el·o·quence** \-kwəns\ n — **el·o·quent·ly** adv

¹**else** \ˈels\ adv **1** : in a different manner or place or at a different time ⟨where ~ can we meet⟩ **2** : OTHERWISE ⟨obey or ~ you'll be sorry⟩

²**else** adj : OTHER; esp : being in addition ⟨what ~ do you want⟩

else·where \-ˌhweər\ adv : in or to another place

elu·ci·date \i-ˈlü-sə-ˌdāt\ vb **-dat·ed; -dat·ing** : to make clear usu. by explanation **syn** clarify, explain, illuminate — **elu·ci·da·tion** \-ˌlü-sə-ˈdā-shən\ n

elude \ē-ˈlüd\ vb **elud·ed; elud·ing** **1** : EVADE **2** : to escape the notice of

elu·sive \ē-ˈlü-siv\ adj : tending to elude : EVASIVE — **elu·sive·ly** adv — **elu·sive·ness** n

el·ver \ˈel-vər\ n [alter. of eelfare (migration of eels)] : a young eel

elves pl of ELF

Ely·si·um \i-ˈliz(h)-ē-əm\ n, pl **-si·ums** or **-sia** \-ē-ə\ : PARADISE **2** — **Ely·sian** \-ˈlizh-ən\ adj

em \ˈem\ n : a length approximately the width of the letter M

EM abbr **1** electromagnetic **2** electron microscope **3** enlisted man

ema·ci·ate \i-ˈmā-shē-ˌāt\ vb **-at·ed; -at·ing** : to become or cause to become very thin — **ema·ci·a·tion** \-ˌmās(h)ē-ˈā-shən\ n

emalangeni pl of LILANGENI

em·a·nate \ˈem-ə-ˌnāt\ vb **-nat·ed; -nat·ing** : to come out from a source **syn** proceed, spring, rise, arise, originate — **em·a·na·tion** \ˌem-ə-ˈnā-shən\ n

eman·ci·pate \i-ˈman-sə-ˌpāt\ vb **-pat·ed; -pat·ing** : to set free **syn** liberate, release, deliver, discharge — **eman·ci·pa·tion** \-ˌman-sə-ˈpā-shən\ n — **eman·ci·pa·tor** \-ˈman-sə-ˌpāt-ər\ n

emas·cu·late \i-ˈmas-kyə-ˌlāt\ vb **-lat·ed; -lat·ing** : CASTRATE, GELD; also : WEAKEN — **emas·cu·la·tion** \-ˌmas-kyə-ˈlā-shən\ n

em·balm \im-ˈbäm, -ˈbälm\ vb : to treat (a corpse) with preservative preparations — **em·balm·er** n

em·bank \im-ˈbaŋk\ vb : to enclose or confine by an embankment

em·bank·ment \-mənt\ n : a raised structure (as of earth) to hold back water or carry a roadway

em·bar·go \im-ˈbär-gō\ n, pl **-goes** [Sp, fr. embargar to bar] : a prohibition on commerce — **embargo** vb

em·bark \im-ˈbärk\ vb **1** : to put or go

on board a ship or airplane **2** : to make a start — **em·bar·ka·tion** \ˌem-ˌbär-ˈkā-shən\ *n*

em·bar·rass \im-ˈbar-əs\ *vb* **1** : CONFUSE, DISCONCERT **2** : to involve in financial difficulties **3** : HINDER, IMPEDE — **em·bar·rass·ing·ly** *adv* — **em·bar·rass·ment** *n*

em·bas·sy \ˈem-bə-sē\ *n, pl* **-sies 1** : the function, position, or mission of an ambassador **2** : a group of representatives headed by an ambassador **3** : the official residence and offices of an ambassador

em·bat·tle \im-ˈbat-ᵊl\ *vb* **-tled; -tling** \-ˈbat-(ᵊ-)liŋ\ : to arrange in order for battle

em·bat·tled *adj* **1** : engaged in battle, conflict, or controversy **2** : being a site of battle, conflict, or controversy **3** : characterized by conflict or controversy

em·bed \im-ˈbed\ *vb* **em·bed·ded; em·bed·ding** : to enclose closely in a surrounding mass

em·bel·lish \im-ˈbel-ish\ *vb* **1** : ADORN, DECORATE **2** : to add ornamental details to **syn** beautify, deck, bedeck, garnish, ornament, dress — **em·bel·lish·ment** *n*

em·ber \ˈem-bər\ *n* **1** : a glowing or smoldering fragment from a fire **2** *pl* : smoldering remains of a fire

em·bez·zle \im-ˈbez-əl\ *vb* **-zled; -zling** \-(ə-)liŋ\ : to steal (as money) by falsifying records — **em·bez·zle·ment** *n* — **em·bez·zler** \-(ə-)lər\ *n*

em·bit·ter \im-ˈbit-ər\ *vb* **1** : to make bitter **2** : to arouse bitter feelings in

em·bla·zon \-ˈblāz-ᵊn\ *vb* **1** : to adorn with heraldic devices **2** : to display conspicuously

em·blem \ˈem-bləm\ *n* : something (as an object or picture) suggesting another object or an idea : SYMBOL — **em·blem·at·ic** \ˌem-blə-ˈmat-ik\ *also* **em·blem·at·i·cal** \-i-kəl\ *adj*

em·body \im-ˈbäd-ē\ *vb* **em·bod·ied; em·body·ing 1** : INCARNATE **2** : to express in definite form **3** : to incorporate into a system or body **syn** combine, incorporate, integrate — **em·bodi·ment** \-ˈbäd-i-mənt\ *n*

em·bold·en \im-ˈbōl-dən\ *vb* : to inspire with courage

em·bo·lism \ˈem-bə-ˌliz-əm\ *n* : the ob-

struction of a blood vessel by a foreign or abnormal particle

em·bon·point \äⁿ-bōⁿ-pwaⁿ\ *n* [F] : plumpness of person : STOUTNESS

em·boss \im-ˈbäs, -ˈbòs\ *vb* : to ornament with raised work

em·bou·chure \ˌäm-bù-ˈshùr\ *n* [F, deriv. of *bouche* mouth] : the position and use of the lips in producing a musical tone on a wind instrument

em·bow·er \im-ˈbaù-(-ə)r\ *vb* : to shelter or enclose in a bower

¹**em·brace** \im-ˈbrās\ *vb* **em·braced; em·brac·ing 1** : to clasp in the arms; *also* : CHERISH, LOVE **2** : ENCIRCLE **3** : TAKE UP, ADOPT; *also* : WELCOME **4** : INCLUDE **5** : to participate in an embrace **syn** comprehend, involve, encompass, embody

²**embrace** *n* : an encircling with the arms

em·bra·sure \im-ˈbrā-zhər\ *n* **1** : a recess of a door or window **2** : an opening in a wall through which a cannon is fired

em·bro·ca·tion \ˌem-brə-ˈkā-shən\ *n* : LINIMENT

em·broi·der \im-ˈbròid-ər\ *vb* **-dered; -der·ing** \-(ə-)riŋ\ **1** : to ornament with or do needlework **2** : to elaborate with exaggerated detail

em·broi·dery \im-ˈbròid-(ə-)rē\ *n, pl* **-der·ies 1** : the forming of decorative designs with needlework **2** : something embroidered

em·broil \im-ˈbròil\ *vb* **1** : to throw into confusion or strife **2** : to involve in conflict or difficulties — **em·broil·ment** *n*

em·bryo \ˈem-brē-ˌō\ *n, pl* **embryos** : a living thing in its earliest stages of development — **em·bry·on·ic** \ˌem-brē-ˈän-ik\ *adj*

em·bry·ol·o·gy \ˌem-brē-ˈäl-ə-jē\ *n* : a branch of biology dealing with embryos and their development — **em·bry·o·log·i·cal** \-i-kəl\ *adj* — **em·bry·ol·o·gist** \-brē-ˈäl-ə-jəst\ *n*

em·cee \ˈem-ˈsē\ *n* : MASTER OF CEREMONIES — **emcee** *vb*

emend \ē-ˈmend\ *vb* : to correct usu. by altering the text of **syn** rectify, revise, amend — **emen·da·tion** \ˌē-ˌmen-ˈdā-shən\ *n*

emer *abbr* emeritus

¹**em·er·ald** \ˈem-(ə-)rəld\ *n* : a green beryl prized as a gem

²**emerald** *adj* : brightly or richly green

emerge \i-ˈmərj\ *vb* **emerged; emerg·ing** : to rise, come forth, or come out into view **syn** appear, loom, show — **emer·gence** \-ˈmər-jəns\ *n* — **emer·gent** \-jənt\ *adj*

emer·gen·cy \i-ˈmər-jən-sē\ *n, pl* **-cies** : an unforeseen event or condition requiring prompt action **syn** exigency, contingency, crisis, juncture

emer·i·ta \i-ˈmer-ət-ə\ *adj* : EMERITUS — used of a woman

emer·i·tus \i-ˈmer-ət-əs\ *adj* [L] : retired from active duty ⟨professor ~⟩

em·ery \ˈem-(ə-)rē\ *n, pl* **em·er·ies** : a dark granular corundum used esp. for grinding and polishing

emet·ic \i-ˈmet-ik\ *n* : an agent that induces vomiting — **emetic** *adj*

emf *abbr* electromotive force

em·i·grate \ˈem-ə-ˌgrāt\ *vb* **-grat·ed; -grat·ing** : to leave a place (as a country) to settle elsewhere — **em·i·grant** \-i-grənt\ *n* — **em·i·gra·tion** \ˌem-ə-ˈgrā-shən\ *n*

émi·gré *also* **emi·gré** \ˈem-i-ˌgrā, ˌem-i-ˈgrā\ *n* [F] : a person who emigrates esp. because of political conditions

em·i·nence \ˈem-ə-nəns\ *n* **1** : high rank or position; *also* : a person of high rank or attainments **2** : a lofty place

em·i·nent \ˈem-ə-nənt\ *adj* **1** : CONSPICUOUS, EVIDENT **2** : DISTINGUISHED, PROMINENT ⟨~ men⟩ — **em·i·nent·ly** *adv*

eminent domain *n* : a right of a government to take private property for public use

emir \i-ˈmiər, ā-\ *n* [Ar *amīr* commander] : a native ruler in parts of Africa and Asia — **emir·ate** \ˈem-ər-ət\ *n*

em·is·sary \ˈem-ə-ˌser-ē\ *n, pl* **-sar·ies** : AGENT; *esp* : a secret agent

emit \ē-ˈmit\ *vb* **emit·ted; emit·ting 1** : to give off or out ⟨~ light⟩; *also* : EJECT **2** : EXPRESS, UTTER — **emis·sion** \-ˈmish-ən\ *n* — **emit·ter** *n*

emol·lient \i-ˈmäl-yənt\ *adj* : making soft or supple; *also* : soothing esp. to the skin or mucous membrane — **emol·lient** *n*

emol·u·ment \i-ˈmäl-yə-mənt\ *n* [ME, fr. L *emolumentum*, lit., miller's fee, fr. *emolere* to grind up] : the product (as salary or fees) of an employment

emote \i-ˈmōt\ *vb* **emot·ed; emot·ing** : to give expression to emotion in or as if in a play

emo·tion \i-ˈmō-shən\ *n* : a usu. intense feeling (as of love, hate, or despair) — **emo·tion·al** \-sh(ə-)nəl\ *adj* — **emo·tion·al·ly** \-ē\ *adv*

emp *abbr* emperor; empress

em·pa·thy \ˈem-pə-thē\ *n* : the capacity for experiencing as one's own the feelings of another — **em·path·ic** \em-ˈpath-ik\ *adj*

em·pen·nage \ˌäm-pə-ˈnäzh, ˌem-\ *n* [F] : the tail assembly of an airplane

em·per·or \ˈem-pər-ər\ *n* : the sovereign ruler of an empire

em·pha·sis \ˈem-fə-səs\ *n, pl* **-pha·ses** \-ˌsēz\ : particular stress or prominence given (as to a phrase in speaking or to a phase of action)

em·pha·size \-ˌsīz\ *vb* **-sized; -siz·ing** : to place emphasis on : STRESS

em·phat·ic \im-ˈfat-ik, em-\ *adj* : uttered with emphasis : STRESSED — **em·phat·i·cal·ly** \-ˈfat-i-k(ə-)lē\ *adv*

em·phy·se·ma \ˌem-fə-ˈzē-mə, -ˈsē-\ *n* : a condition marked esp. by abnormal expansion of the air spaces of the lungs and often by impairment of heart action

em·pire \ˈem-ˌpī(ə)r\ *n* **1** : a large state or a group of states under a single sovereign who is usu. an emperor **2** : imperial sovereignty or dominion

em·pir·i·cal \im-ˈpir-i-kəl\ *also* **em·pir·ic** \-ik\ *adj* : based on observation; *also* : subject to verification by observation or experiment ⟨~ laws⟩ — **em·pir·i·cal·ly** \-i-k(ə-)lē\ *adv*

em·pir·i·cism \im-ˈpir-ə-ˌsiz-əm, em-\ *n* : the practice of relying on observation and experiment esp. in the natural sciences — **em·pir·i·cist** \-səst\ *n*

em·place·ment \im-ˈplās-mənt\ *n* **1** : a prepared position for weapons or military equipment **2** : PLACEMENT

¹**em·ploy** \im-ˈplȯi\ *vb* **1** : to make use of **2** : to use the services of **3** : OCCUPY, DEVOTE — **em·ploy·er** *n*

²**employ** *n* : EMPLOYMENT

em·ploy·ee *or* **em·ploye** \im-ˌplȯi-ˈē, ˌem-; im-ˈplȯi-ˌē, em-\ *n* : a person who works for another

em·ploy·ment \im-ˈplȯi-mənt\ *n* **1** : OCCUPATION, ACTIVITY **2** : the act of employing : the condition of being employed

em·po·ri·um \im-'pōr-ē-əm, em-\ *n, pl* **-ri·ums** *also* **-ria** \-ē-ə\ [L, fr. Gk *emporion,* fr. *emporos* traveler, trader] : a commercial center; *esp* : a store carrying varied articles

em·pow·er \im-'pau̇(-ə)r\ *vb* : AUTHORIZE

em·press \'em-prəs\ *n* **1** : the wife or widow of an emperor **2** : a woman holding an imperial title

¹emp·ty \'emp-tē\ *adj* **emp·ti·er; -est 1** : containing nothing **2** : UNOCCUPIED, UNINHABITED **3** : lacking value, force, sense, or purpose **syn** vacant, blank, void, stark, vacuous — **emp·ti·ness** \-tē-nəs\ *n*

²empty *vb* **emp·tied; emp·ty·ing 1** : to make or become empty **2** : to discharge contents; *also* : to transfer by emptying

³empty *n, pl* **empties** : an empty container or vehicle

emp·ty–hand·ed \,emp-tē-'han-dəd\ *adj* **1** : having nothing in the hands **2** : having acquired or gained nothing

em·py·re·an \,em-pī-'rē-ən, -pə-\ *n* : the highest heaven; *also* : FIRMAMENT

EMT \'ē-'em-'tē\ *n* [*e*mergency *m*edical *t*echnician] : a person trained and certified to provide basic medical services before and during transportation to a hospital

¹emu \'ē-myü\ *n* : a swift-running flightless Australian bird smaller than the related ostrich

²emu *abbr* electromagnetic unit

em·u·late \'em-yə-,lāt\ *vb* **-lat·ed; -lat·ing** : to strive to equal or excel — **em·u·la·tion** \,em-yə-'lā-shən\ *n* — **em·u·lous** \'em-yə-ləs\ *adj*

emul·si·fi·er \i-'məl-sə-,fī(-ə)r\ *n* : something promoting the formation and stabilizing of an emulsion

emul·si·fy \-,fī\ *vb* **-fied; -fy·ing** : to convert (as an oil) into an emulsion — **emul·si·fi·ca·tion** \i-,məl-sə-fə-'kā-shən\ *n*

emul·sion \i-'məl-shən\ *n* **1** : a mixture of mutually insoluble liquids in which one is dispersed in droplets throughout the other ⟨an ∼ of oil in water⟩ **2** : a light-sensitive coating on photographic film or paper

en \'en\ *n* : a length approximately half the width of the letter *M*

¹-en \ən, ᵊn\ *also* **-n** \n\ *adj suffix* : made of : consisting of ⟨earth*en*⟩

²-en *vb suffix* **1** : become or cause to be ⟨sharp*en*⟩ **2** : cause or come to have ⟨length*en*⟩

en·able \in-'ā-bəl\ *vb* **en·abled; en·abling** \-b(ə-)liŋ\ **1** : to make able or feasible **2** : to give legal power, capacity, or sanction to

en·act \in-'akt\ *vb* **1** : to make into law **2** : to act out — **en·act·ment** *n*

enam·el \in-'am-əl\ *n* **1** : a glasslike substance used for coating the surface of metal or pottery **2** : the hard outer layer of a tooth **3** : a usu. glossy paint that forms a hard coat — **enamel** *vb*

enam·el·ware \-,waər\ *n* : metal utensils coated with enamel

en·am·or \in-'am-ər\ *vb* **-ored; -or·ing** \-(ə-)riŋ\ : to inflame with love

en·am·our *chiefly Brit* var of ENAMOR

en bloc \än-'bläk\ *adv or adj* : as a whole : in a mass

enc *or* **encl** *abbr* enclosure

en·camp \in-'kamp\ *vb* : to make camp — **en·camp·ment** *n*

en·cap·su·late \in-'kap-sə-,lāt\ *vb* **-lat·ed; -lat·ing 1** : to encase or become encased in a capsule **2** : to condense (as a report) into a few words — **en·cap·su·la·tion** \-,kap-sə-'lā-shən\ *n*

en·case \in-'kās\ *vb* : to enclose in or as if in a case

-ence \əns, ᵊns\ *n suffix* **1** : action or process ⟨emerg*ence*⟩ : instance of an action or process ⟨refer*ence*⟩ **2** : quality or state ⟨depend*ence*⟩

en·ceinte \än-'sant\ *adj* : PREGNANT

en·ceph·a·li·tis \in-,sef-ə-'līt-əs\ *n, pl* **-lit·i·des** \-'lit-ə-,dēz\ : inflammation of the brain — **en·ceph·a·lit·ic** \-'lit-ik\ *adj*

en·ceph·a·lo·my·eli·tis \in-,sef-ə-lō-,mī-ə-'līt-əs\ *n* : concurrent inflammation of the brain and spinal cord

en·chain \in-'chān\ *vb* : FETTER, CHAIN

en·chant \in-'chant\ *vb* **1** : BEWITCH **2** : ENRAPTURE, FASCINATE — **en·chant·er** *n* — **en·chant·ing·ly** *adv* — **en·chant·ment** *n* — **en·chant·ress** \-'chan-trəs\ *n*

en·chi·la·da \,en-chə-'läd-ə\ *n* : a tortilla rolled with meat filling and served with chili-seasoned sauce

en·ci·pher \in-'sī-fər, en-\ *vb* : ENCODE

en•cir•cle \in-ˈsər-kəl\ *vb* : to pass completely around : SURROUND — **en•cir•cle•ment** *n*

en•clave \ˈen-ˌklāv; ˈän-ˌklāv\ *n* : a territorial or culturally distinct unit enclosed within foreign territory

en•close \in-ˈklōz\ *vb* 1 : to shut up or in; *esp* : to surround with a fence 2 : to include along with something else in a parcel or envelope ⟨∼ a check⟩ — **en•clo•sure** \in-ˈklō-zhər\ *n*

en•code \in-ˈkōd, en-\ *vb* : to convert (a message) into code

en•co•mi•um \en-ˈkō-mē-əm\ *n, pl* **-mi•ums** *or* **-mia** \-mē-ə\ [L] : high or glowing praise

en•com•pass \in-ˈkəm-pəs\ *vb* 1 : ENCIRCLE 2 : ENVELOP, INCLUDE

¹**en•core** \ˈän-ˌkōr\ *n* : a demand for repetition or reappearance; *also* : a further performance (as of a singer) in response to such a demand

²**encore** *vb* **en•cored; en•cor•ing** : to request an encore from

¹**en•coun•ter** \in-ˈkaȯnt-ər\ *n* 1 : a hostile meeting; *esp* : COMBAT 2 : a chance meeting

²**encounter** *vb* 1 : to meet as an enemy : FIGHT 2 : to meet usu. unexpectedly

en•cour•age \in-ˈkər-ij\ *vb* **-aged; -ag•ing** 1 : to inspire with courage and hope 2 : STIMULATE, INCITE 3 : FOSTER — **en•cour•age•ment** *n* — **en•cour•ag•ing•ly** *adv*

en•croach \in-ˈkrōch\ *vb* [ME *encrochen* to seize, fr. MF *encrochier*, fr. OF, fr. *croche* hook] : to enter or force oneself gradually upon another's property or rights — **en•croach•ment** *n*

en•crust \in-ˈkrəst\ *vb* : to provide with or form a crust

encrustation var of INCRUSTATION

en•cum•ber \in-ˈkəm-bər\ *vb* **-bered; -ber•ing** \-b(ə-)riŋ\ 1 : to weigh down : BURDEN 2 : to hinder the function or activity of — **en•cum•brance** \-brəns\ *n*

ency *or* **encyc** *abbr* encyclopedia

-en•cy \ən-sē, ᵊn-\ *n suffix* : quality or state ⟨despond*ency*⟩

¹**en•cyc•li•cal** \in-ˈsik-li-kəl, en-\ *adj* : addressed to all the individuals of a group

²**encyclical** *n* : an encyclical letter; *esp* : a papal letter to the bishops of the church

en•cy•clo•pe•dia *also* **en•cy•clo•pae•dia** \in-ˌsī-klə-ˈpēd-ē-ə\ *n* [ML *encyclopaedia* course of general education, fr. Gk *enkyklios paideia* general education] : a work treating the various branches of learning — **en•cy•clo•pe•dic** \-ˈpēd-ik\ *adj*

en•cyst \in-ˈsist, en-\ *vb* : to form or become enclosed in a cyst — **en•cyst•ment** *n*

¹**end** \ˈend\ *n* 1 : the part of an area that lies at the boundary; *also* : a point which marks the extent or limit of something or at which something ceases to exist 2 : a ceasing of a course (as of action or activity); *also* : DEATH 3 : the ultimate state; *also* : RESULT, ISSUE 4 : REMNANT 5 : PURPOSE, OBJECTIVE 6 : a player stationed at the extremity of a line (as in football) 7 : a share, operation, or aspect of an undertaking

²**end** *vb* 1 : to bring or come to an end 2 : DESTROY; *also* : DIE 3 : to form or be at the end of **syn** close, conclude, terminate, finish, complete

en•dan•ger \in-ˈdān-jər\ *vb* **-gered; -ger•ing** \-ˈdānj-(ə-)riŋ\ : to bring into danger

en•dan•gered \-jərd\ *adj* : threatened with extinction ⟨∼ species⟩

en•dear \in-ˈdiər\ *vb* : to cause to become an object of affection

en•dear•ment \-mənt\ *n* : a sign of affection : CARESS

en•deav•or \in-ˈdev-ər\ *vb* **-ored; -or•ing** \-(ə-)riŋ\ : TRY, ATTEMPT — **endeavor** *n*

en•dem•ic \en-ˈdem-ik, in-\ *adj* : restricted or peculiar to a particular place ⟨∼ plants⟩ ⟨an ∼ disease⟩ — **endemic** *n*

end•ing \ˈen-diŋ\ *n* : something that forms an end; *esp* : SUFFIX

en•dive \ˈen-ˌdīv\ *n* 1 : an herb related to chicory and grown as a salad plant 2 : the blanched shoot of chicory

end•less \ˈend-ləs\ *adj* 1 : having no end : ETERNAL 2 : united at the ends : CONTINUOUS ⟨an ∼ belt⟩ **syn** interminable, everlasting, unceasing, ceaseless, unending — **end•less•ly** *adv*

end•most \ˈend-ˌmōst\ *adj* : situated at the very end

end•note \-ˌnōt\ *n* : a note placed at the end of the text (as of an article, chapter, or book)

en·do·crine \\'en-də-krən, -ˌkrīn, -ˌkrēn\\ *adj* : producing secretions that are distributed by way of the bloodstream ⟨∼ glands⟩ — **endocrine** *n* — **en·do·cri·nol·o·gist** \\ˌen-də-kri-'näl-ə-jəst\\ *n* — **en·do·cri·nol·o·gy** \\-jē\\ *n*

en·dog·e·nous \\en-'däj-ə-nəs\\ *adj* : caused or produced by factors inside the organism or system ⟨∼ psychic depression⟩ — **en·dog·e·nous·ly** *adv*

en·dorse \\in-'dȯrs\\ *vb* **en·dorsed; en·dors·ing** 1 : to sign one's name on the back of (as a check) for some purpose 2 : APPROVE, SANCTION **syn** accredit, certify — **en·dorse·ment** *n*

en·do·scope \\'en-də-ˌskōp\\ *n* : an instrument with which the interior of a hollow organ (as the rectum) may be visualized — **en·do·scop·ic** \\ˌen-də-'skäp-ik\\ *adj* — **en·dos·co·py** \\en-'däs-kə-pē\\ *n*

en·do·ther·mic \\ˌen-də-'thər-mik\\ *also* **en·do·ther·mal** \\-məl\\ *adj* : characterized by or formed with absorption of heat

en·dow \\in-'daů\\ *vb* 1 : to furnish with funds for support ⟨∼ a school⟩ 2 : to furnish with something freely or naturally — **en·dow·ment** *n*

end run *n* : a football play in which the ballcarrier attempts to run wide around the end

en·due \\in-'d(y)ü\\ *vb* **en·dued; en·du·ing** : to provide with some quality or power

en·dur·ance \\in-'d(y)ùr-əns\\ *n* 1 : DURATION 2 : the ability to withstand hardship or stress : FORTITUDE

en·dure \\in-'d(y)ùr\\ *vb* **en·dured; en·dur·ing** 1 : LAST, PERSIST 2 : to suffer firmly or patiently : BEAR 3 : TOLERATE **syn** continue, abide, persist — **en·dur·able** *adj*

end·ways \\'end-ˌwāz\\ *adv or adj* 1 : with the end forward 2 : LENGTHWISE 3 : on end

end·wise \\-ˌwīz\\ *adv or adj* : ENDWAYS

ENE *abbr* east-northeast

en·e·ma \\'en-ə-mə\\ *n, pl* **enemas** *also* **ene·ma·ta** \\ˌen-ə-'mät-ə, 'en-ə-mə-tə\\ : injection of liquid into the rectum; *also* : material so injected

en·e·my \\'en-ə-mē\\ *n, pl* **-mies** : one that attacks or tries to harm another : FOE; *esp* : a military opponent

en·er·get·ic \\ˌen-ər-'jet-ik\\ *adj* : marked by energy : ACTIVE, VIGOROUS **syn** strenuous, lusty, dynamic, vital — **en·er·get·i·cal·ly** \\-i-k(ə-)lē\\ *adv*

en·er·gize \\'en-ər-ˌjīz\\ *vb* **-gized; -giz·ing** : to give energy to

en·er·giz·er \\-ˌjī-zər\\ *n* : ANTIDEPRESSANT

en·er·gy \\'en-ər-jē\\ *n, pl* **-gies** 1 : vigorous action : EFFORT 2 : capacity for action 3 : capacity for performing work 4 : usable power (as heat or electricity); *also* : the resources for producing such power **syn** strength, might, vigor

energy level *n* : one of the stable states of constant energy that may be assumed by a physical system (as the electrons in an atom)

en·er·vate \\'en-ər-ˌvāt\\ *vb* **-vat·ed; -vat·ing** : to lessen the strength or vigor of : weaken in mind or body — **en·er·va·tion** \\ˌen-ər-'vā-shən\\ *n*

en·fee·ble \\in-'fē-bəl\\ *vb* **-bled; -bling** \\-b(ə-)liŋ\\ : to make feeble **syn** weaken, debilitate, sap, undermine, cripple — **en·fee·ble·ment** *n*

en·fi·lade \\'en-fə-ˌlād, -ˌläd\\ *n* : gunfire directed along the length of an enemy battle line

en·fold \\in-'fōld\\ *vb* 1 : ENVELOP 2 : EMBRACE

en·force \\in-'fōrs\\ *vb* 1 : COMPEL ⟨∼ obedience by threats⟩ 2 : to execute effectively ⟨∼ the law⟩ — **en·force·able** *adj* — **en·force·ment** *n*

en·fran·chise \\in-'fran-ˌchīz\\ *vb* **-chised; -chis·ing** 1 : to set free (as from slavery) 2 : to admit to citizenship; *also* : to grant the vote to — **en·fran·chise·ment** \\-ˌchīz-mənt, -chəz-\\ *n*

eng *abbr* engine; engineer; engineering

Eng *abbr* England; English

en·gage \\in-'gāj\\ *vb* **en·gaged; en·gag·ing** 1 : PLEDGE; *esp* : to bind by a pledge to marry 2 : EMPLOY, HIRE 3 : to attract and hold esp. by interesting ⟨*engaged* his friend's attention⟩; *also* : to cause to participate 4 : to commence or take part in a venture 5 : to bring or enter into conflict 6 : to connect or interlock with : MESH; *also* : to cause to mesh

en·gage·ment \\in-'gāj-mənt\\ *n* 1 : APPOINTMENT 2 : EMPLOYMENT 3 : a mutual promise to marry 4 : a hostile encounter

en·gag·ing *adj* : ATTRACTIVE — **en·gag·ing·ly** *adv*

en·gen·der \in-'jen-dər\ *vb* **-dered; -der·ing** \-d(ə-)riŋ\ **1** : BEGET **2** : BRING ABOUT, CREATE **syn** generate, breed, occasion, produce

en·gine \'en-jən\ *n* [ME *engin,* fr. OF, fr. L *ingenium* natural disposition, talent] **1** : a mechanical device **2** : a machine for converting energy into mechanical motion **3** : LOCOMOTIVE

¹**en·gi·neer** \,en-jə-'niər\ *n* **1** : a member of a military group devoted to engineering work **2** : a designer or builder of engines **3** : one trained in engineering **4** : one that operates an engine

²**engineer** *vb* : to lay out or manage as an engineer **syn** guide, pilot, lead, steer

en·gi·neer·ing \-iŋ\ *n* : the practical applications of scientific and mathematical principles

En·glish \'iŋ-glish\ *n* **1** : the language of England, the U.S., and many areas now or formerly under British rule **2** **English** *pl* : the people of England — **English** *adj* — **En·glish·man** \-mən\ *n* — **En·glish·wom·an** \-,wum-ən\ *n*

English horn *n* : a woodwind instrument longer than and having a range lower than the oboe

English setter *n* : any of a breed of bird dogs with a flat silky coat of white with flecks or patches of black or brown

English sparrow *n* : HOUSE SPARROW

English system *n* : a system of weights and measures in which the foot is the principal unit of length and the pound is the principal unit of weight

engr *abbr* **1** engineer **2** engraved

en·gram \'en-,gram\ *n* : a hypothetical change in neural tissue postulated in order to account for persistence of memory

en·grave \in-'grāv\ *vb* **en·graved; en·grav·ing** **1** : to produce (as letters or lines) by incising a surface **2** : to incise (as stone or metal) to produce a representation (as of letters or figures) esp. that may be printed from **3** : PHOTOENGRAVE — **en·grav·er** *n*

en·grav·ing \in-'grā-viŋ\ *n* **1** : the art of one who engraves **2** : an engraved plate; *also* : a print made from it

en·gross \in-'grōs\ *vb* : to take up the whole interest or attention of **syn** monopolize, absorb, consume

en·gulf \in-'gəlf\ *vb* : to flow over and enclose

en·hance \in-'hans\ *vb* **en·hanced; en·hanc·ing** : to make greater (as in value or desirability) **syn** heighten, intensify, magnify — **en·hance·ment** *n*

enig·ma \i-'nig-mə\ *n* [L *aenigma,* fr. Gk *ainigma,* fr. *ainissesthai* to speak in riddles, fr. *ainos* fable] : something obscure or hard to understand : PUZZLE

enig·mat·ic \,en-ig-'mat-ik\ *adj* : resembling an enigma **syn** obscure, cryptic, mystifying — **en·ig·mat·i·cal·ly** \-i-k(ə-)lē\ *adv*

en·isle \in-'īl\ *vb* : ISOLATE

en·jamb·ment \in-'jam-mənt\ *or* **en·jambe·ment** *same,* or än-zhänb-(ə-)mäm\ *n* [F *enjambement*] : the running over of a sentence from one verse or couplet into another so that closely related words fall in different lines

en·join \in-'jȯin\ *vb* **1** : COMMAND, ORDER **2** : FORBID **syn** direct, bid, charge, command, instruct

en·joy \in-'jȯi\ *vb* **1** : to have for one's benefit or use ⟨~ good health⟩ **2** : to take pleasure or satisfaction in ⟨~ed the concert⟩ **syn** like, love, relish, fancy — **en·joy·able** *adj* — **en·joy·ment** *n*

enl *abbr* **1** enlarged **2** enlisted

en·large \in-'lärj\ *vb* **en·larged; en·larg·ing** **1** : to make or grow larger **2** : ELABORATE **syn** increase, augment, multiply, expand — **en·large·ment** *n*

en·light·en \in-'līt-ᵊn\ *vb* **-ened; -en·ing** \-'līt-(ᵊ-)niŋ\ **1** : INSTRUCT, INFORM **2** : to give spiritual insight to **syn** illuminate, edify — **en·light·en·ment** *n*

en·list \in-'list\ *vb* **1** : to engage for service in the armed forces **2** : to secure the aid or support of — **en·list·ee** \-,lis-'tē\ *n* — **en·list·ment** \-'lis(t)-mənt\ *n*

en·list·ed \in-'lis-təd\ *adj* : of, relating to, or forming the part of a military force below commissioned or warrant officers

en·liv·en \in-'lī-vən\ *vb* : to give life, action, or spirit to : ANIMATE

en masse \än-'mas\ *adv* [F] : in a body : as a whole

en·mesh \in-'mesh\ *vb* : to catch or entangle in or as if in meshes

en·mi·ty \'en-mət-ē\ *n, pl* **-ties** : ILL WILL; *esp* : mutual hatred **syn** hostility, antipathy, animosity, rancor, antagonism

en·no·ble \in-'ō-bəl\ *vb* **-bled; -bling** \-b(ə-)liŋ\ : ELEVATE, EXALT; *esp* : to raise to noble rank — **en·no·ble·ment** *n*

en·nui \'än-'wē\ *n* [F] : BOREDOM

enor·mi·ty \i-'nȯr-mət-ē\ *n, pl* **-ties** 1 : a grave offense against order, right, or decency 2 : great wickedness 3 : IMMENSITY

enor·mous \i-'nȯr-məs\ *adj* [L *enormis,* fr. *e, ex* out of + *norma* rule] 1 : exceedingly wicked 2 : great in size, number, or degree : HUGE **syn** immense, vast, gigantic, colossal, mammoth, elephantine

¹**enough** \i-'nəf\ *adj* : SUFFICIENT **syn** adequate, satisfactory, sufficing

²**enough** *adv* 1 : SUFFICIENTLY 2 : FULLY, QUITE 3 : TOLERABLY

³**enough** *pron* : a sufficient number, quantity, or amount

en·plane \in-'plān\ *vb* : to board an airplane

en·quire \in-'kwī(ə)r\ , **en·qui·ry** \'in-ˌkwī(ə)r-ē, in-'kwī(ə)r-; 'in-kwə-rē, 'iŋ-\ var of INQUIRE, INQUIRY

en·rage \in-'rāj\ *vb* : to fill with rage

en·rap·ture \in-'rap-chər\ *vb* **en·raptured; en·rap·tur·ing** : DELIGHT

en·rich \in-'rich\ *vb* 1 : to make rich or richer 2 : ORNAMENT, ADORN — **en·rich·ment** *n*

en·roll *or* **en·rol** \in-'rōl\ *vb* **en·rolled; en·roll·ing** 1 : to enter or register on a roll or list 2 : to offer (oneself) for enrolling — **en·roll·ment** *n*

en route \än-'rüt, en-\ *adv or adj* : on or along the way

ENS *abbr* ensign

en·sconce \in-'skäns\ *vb* **en·sconced; en·sconc·ing** 1 : SHELTER, CONCEAL 2 : to settle snugly or securely **syn** secrete, hide, cache, stash

en·sem·ble \än-'säm-bəl\ *n* [F, fr. *ensemble* together, fr. L *insimul* at the same time] 1 : SET, WHOLE 2 : integrated music of two or more parts 3 : a complete costume of harmonizing garments 4 : a group of persons (as musicians) acting together to produce a particular effect or end

en·sheathe \in-'shēth\ *vb* : to cover with or as if with a sheath

en·shrine \in-'shrīn\ *vb* 1 : to enclose in or as if in a shrine 2 : to cherish as sacred

en·shroud \in-'shraud\ *vb* : SHROUD, OBSCURE

en·sign \'en-sən, *1 also* 'en-ˌsīn\ *n* 1 : FLAG; *also* : BADGE, EMBLEM 2 : a commissioned officer in the navy ranking next below a lieutenant junior grade

en·si·lage \'en-sə-lij\ *n* : the process of converting feed crops into silage; *also* : SILAGE

en·sile \en-'sīl\ *vb* **en·siled; en·sil·ing** : to prepare and store (fodder) for silage

en·slave \in-'slāv\ *vb* : to make a slave of — **en·slave·ment** *n*

en·snare \in-'snaər\ *vb* : SNARE, TRAP **syn** entrap, bag, catch, capture

en·sue \in-'sü\ *vb* **en·sued; en·su·ing** : to follow as a consequence or in time : RESULT

en·sure \in-'shùr\ *vb* **en·sured; en·sur·ing** : INSURE, GUARANTEE **syn** assure, secure

en·tail \in-'tāl\ *vb* 1 : to limit the inheritance of (property) to the owner's lineal descendants or to a class thereof 2 : to include or involve as a necessary step or result — **en·tail·ment** *n*

en·tan·gle \in-'taŋ-gəl\ *vb* : TANGLE, CONFUSE — **en·tan·gle·ment** *n*

en·tente \än-'tänt\ *n* [F agreement, understanding] : an understanding providing for joint action; *also* : parties linked by such an entente

en·ter \'ent-ər\ *vb* **en·tered; en·ter·ing** \'ent-ə-riŋ, 'en-triŋ\ 1 : to go or come in or into 2 : to become a member of : JOIN ⟨∼ the ministry⟩ 3 : BEGIN 4 : to take part in : CONTRIBUTE 5 : to go into or upon and take possession 6 : to set down (as in a list) : REGISTER 7 : to place (a complaint) before a court; *also* : to put on record ⟨∼ed his objections⟩

en·ter·i·tis \ˌent-ə-'rīt-əs\ *n* : intestinal inflammation; *also* : a disease marked by this

en·ter·prise \'ent-ər-ˌprīz\ *n* 1 : UNDERTAKING, PROJECT 2 : readiness for daring action : INITIATIVE 3 : a business organization

en·ter·pris·ing \-ˌprī-ziŋ\ *adj* : bold and vigorous in action : ENERGETIC

en·ter·tain \ˌent-ər-'tān\ *vb* **1** : to treat or receive as a guest **2** : AMUSE, DIVERT **3** : to hold in mind **syn** harbor, shelter, lodge, house, billet — **en·ter·tain·er** *n* — **en·ter·tain·ment** *n*

en·thrall *or* **en·thral** \in-'throl\ *vb* **en·thralled; en·thrall·ing** **1** : to hold spellbound **2** : ENSLAVE

en·throne \in-'thrōn\ *vb* **1** : to seat on or as if on a throne **2** : EXALT

en·thuse \in-'th(y)üz\ *vb* **en·thused; en·thus·ing** **1** : to make enthusiastic **2** : to show enthusiasm

en·thu·si·asm \in-'th(y)ü-zē-ˌaz-əm\ *n* [Gk *enthousiasmos,* fr. *enthousiazein* to be inspired, fr. *entheos* inspired, fr. *theos* god] **1** : strong warmth of feeling : keen interest : FERVOR **2** : a cause of fervor — **en·thu·si·ast** \-ˌast, -əst\ *n* — **en·thu·si·as·tic** \in-ˌth(y)ü-zē-'as-tik\ *adj* — **en·thu·si·as·ti·cal·ly** \-ti-k(ə-)lē\ *adv*

en·tice \in-'tīs\ *vb* **en·ticed; en·tic·ing** : ALLURE, TEMPT — **en·tice·ment** *n*

en·tire \in-'tī(ə)r\ *adj* : COMPLETE, WHOLE **syn** sound, perfect, intact, undamaged — **en·tire·ly** *adv*

en·tire·ty \in-'tī-rət-ē, -'tī-(ə)rt-ē\ *n, pl* **-ties** **1** : COMPLETENESS **2** : WHOLE, TOTALITY

en·ti·tle \in-'tīt-ᵊl\ *vb* **en·ti·tled; en·ti·tling** \-'tīt-(ᵊ-)liŋ\ **1** : NAME, DESIGNATE **2** : to give a right or claim to

en·ti·tle·ment \in-'tīt-ᵊl-mənt\ *n* : a government program providing benefits to members of a specified group

en·ti·ty \'ent-ət-ē\ *n, pl* **-ties** **1** : EXISTENCE, BEING **2** : something with separate and real existence

en·tomb \in-'tüm\ *vb* : to place in a tomb : BURY — **en·tomb·ment** \-'tüm-mənt\ *n*

en·to·mol·o·gy \ˌent-ə-'mäl-ə-jē\ *n* : a branch of zoology that deals with insects — **en·to·mo·log·i·cal** \-mə-'läj-i-kəl\ *adj* — **en·to·mol·o·gist** \ˌent-ə-'mäl-ə-jəst\ *n*

en·tou·rage \ˌän-tù-'räzh\ *n* [F] : RETINUE

en·tr'acte \'äⁿn-ˌtrakt\ *n* [F] **1** : something (as a dance) performed between two acts of a play **2** : the interval between two acts of a play

en·trails \'en-ˌtrālz\ *n pl* : VISCERA; *esp* : INTESTINES

en·train \in-'trān\ *vb* : to put or go aboard a railroad train

¹**en·trance** \'en-trəns\ *n* **1** : a means or place of entry **2** : the act of entering **3** : permission or right to enter

²**en·trance** \in-'trans\ *vb* **en·tranced; en·tranc·ing** : CHARM, DELIGHT

en·trant \'en-trənt\ *n* : one that enters esp. as a competitor

en·trap \in-'trap\ *vb* : ENSNARE, TRAP — **en·trap·ment** *n*

en·treat \in-'trēt\ *vb* : to ask earnestly or urgently : BESEECH **syn** beg, implore, plead, supplicate — **en·treaty** \-'trēt-ē\ *n*

en·trée *or* **en·tree** \'än-ˌtrā\ *n* [F *entrée*] **1** : the principal dish of the meal in the U.S. **2** : ENTRANCE **syn** entry, access, admission, admittance

en·trench \in-'trench\ *vb* **1** : to surround with a trench; *also* : to establish in a strong defensive position ⟨~ed customs⟩ **2** : ENCROACH, TRESPASS — **en·trench·ment** *n*

en·tre·pre·neur \ˌän-trə-prə-'nər\ *n* [F, fr. OF, fr. *entreprendre* to undertake] : one who organizes and assumes the risk of a business or enterprise

en·tro·py \'en-trə-pē\ *n, pl* **-pies** **1** : a measure of the unavailable energy of a closed thermodynamic system **2** : an ultimate state of inert uniformity

en·trust \in-'trəst\ *vb* **1** : to commit something to as a trust **2** : to commit to another with confidence **syn** confide, consign, relegate, commend

en·try \'en-trē\ *n, pl* **entries** **1** : ENTRANCE 1, 2; *also* : VESTIBULE 2 **2** : an entering in a record; *also* : an item so entered **3** : a headword with its definition or identification; *also* : VOCABULARY ENTRY **4** : one entered in a contest

en·twine \in-'twīn\ *vb* : to twine together or around

enu·mer·ate \i-'n(y)ü-mə-ˌrāt\ *vb* **-at·ed; -at·ing** **1** : to determine the number of : COUNT **2** : LIST — **enu·mer·a·tion** \-ˌn(y)ü-mə-'rā-shən\ *n*

enun·ci·ate \ē-'nən-sē-ˌāt\ *vb* **-at·ed; -at·ing** **1** : to state definitely; *also* : ANNOUNCE, PROCLAIM **2** : PRONOUNCE, ARTICULATE — **enun·ci·a·tion** \-ˌnən-sē-'ā-shən\ *n*

en•ure•sis \,en-yu̇-'rē-səs\ *n* : involuntary discharge of urine : BED-WETTING

env *abbr* envelope

en•vel•op \in-'vel-əp\ *vb* : to enclose completely with or as if with a covering — **en•vel•op•ment** *n*

en•ve•lope \'en-və-,lōp, 'än-\ *n* 1 : a usu. paper container for a letter 2 : WRAPPER, COVERING 3 : the bag containing the gas in a balloon or airship

en•ven•om \in-'ven-əm\ *vb* 1 : to poison with venom 2 : EMBITTER

en•vi•able \'en-vē-ə-bəl\ *adj* : highly desirable — **en•vi•ably** \-blē\ *adv*

en•vi•ous \'en-vē-əs\ *adj* : feeling or showing envy — **en•vi•ous•ly** *adv* — **en•vi•ous•ness** *n*

en•vi•ron•ment \in-'vī-rən-mənt\ *n* 1 : SURROUNDINGS 2 : the whole complex of factors (as soil, climate, and living things) that influence the form and the ability to survive of a plant or animal or ecological community — **en•vi•ron•men•tal** \-,vī-rən-'ment-ᵊl\ *adj*

en•vi•ron•men•tal•ist \-ᵊl-əst\ *n* : a person concerned about the quality of the human environment

en•vi•rons \in-'vī-rənz\ *n pl* 1 : SUBURBS 2 : SURROUNDINGS; *also* : VICINITY

en•vis•age \in-'viz-ij\ *vb* **-aged; -ag•ing** : to have a mental picture of

en•voy \'en-,vȯi, 'än-\ *n* 1 : a diplomatic agent 2 : REPRESENTATIVE, MESSENGER

¹**en•vy** \'en-vē\ *n, pl* **envies** [ME *envie,* fr. OF, fr. L *invidia,* fr. *invidus* envious, fr. *invidēre* to look askance at, envy, fr. *vidēre* to see] : grudging desire for or discontent at the sight of another's excellence or advantages; *also* : an object of envy

²**envy** *vb* **en•vied; en•vy•ing** : to feel envy toward or on account of

en•zyme \'en-,zīm\ *n* : any of various complex proteins produced by living cells that induce or accelerate chemical reactions (as in the digestion of food) at body temperatures without being permanently altered — **en•zy•mat•ic** \,en-zə-'mat-ik\ *adj*

Eo•cene \'ē-ə-,sēn\ *adj* : of, relating to, or being the epoch of the Tertiary between the Paleocene and the Oligocene — **Eocene** *n*

eo•lian \ē-'ō-lē-ən\ *adj* : borne, deposited, or produced by the wind

EOM *abbr* end of month

eon \'ē-ən, 'ē-,än\ *var of* AEON

EP *abbr* European plan

EPA *abbr* Environmental Protection Agency

ep•au•let *also* **ep•au•lette** \,ep-ə-'let\ *n* [F *épaulette,* dim. of *épaule* shoulder] : a shoulder ornament esp. on a uniform

épée \'ep-,ā, ā-'pā\ *n* [F] : a fencing or dueling sword

Eph *or* **Ephes** *abbr* Ephesians

ephed•rine \i-'fed-rən\ *n* : a drug used in relieving hay fever, asthma, and nasal congestion

ephem•er•al \i-'fem(-ə)-rəl\ *adj* [Gk *ephēmeros* lasting a day, daily, fr. *hēmera* day] : SHORT-LIVED, TRANSITORY **syn** passing, fleeting, transient, evanescent

Ephe•sians \i-'fē-zhənz\ *n* — see BIBLE table

ep•ic \'ep-ik\ *n* : a long poem in elevated style narrating the deeds of a hero — **epic** *adj*

epi•cen•ter \'ep-i-,sent-ər\ *n* : the point on the earth's surface directly above the point of origin of an earthquake

ep•i•cure \'ep-i-,kyu̇r\ *n* : a person with sensitive and discriminating tastes esp. in food and wine

ep•i•cu•re•an \,ep-i-kyu̇-'rē-ən, -'kyu̇r-ē-\ *n* : EPICURE — **epicurean** *adj*

¹**ep•i•dem•ic** \,ep-ə-'dem-ik\ *adj* : affecting many persons at one time ⟨∼ disease⟩; *also* : excessively prevalent

²**epidemic** *n* : an epidemic outbreak esp. of disease

epi•der•mis \,ep-ə-'dər-məs\ *n* : an outer layer esp. of skin — **epi•der•mal** \-məl\ *adj*

epi•glot•tis \-'glät-əs\ *n* : a thin plate of flexible tissue protecting the tracheal opening during swallowing

ep•i•gram \'ep-ə-,gram\ *n* : a short witty poem or saying — **ep•i•gram•mat•ic** \,ep-ə-grə-'mat-ik\ *adj*

ep•i•lep•sy \'ep-ə-,lep-sē\ *n, pl* **-sies** : a disorder typically marked by disturbed electrical rhythms of the central nervous system, by attacks of convulsions, and by loss of consciousness — **ep•i•lep•tic** \,ep-ə-'lep-tik\ *adj or n*

ep•i•logue *or* **ep•i•log** \'ep-ə-,lȯg, -,läg\ *n*

: a speech addressed to the spectators by an actor at the end of a play

epi·neph·rine also **epi·neph·rin** \ˌep-ə-ˈnef-rən\ n : an adrenal hormone used medicinally esp. as a heart stimulant, a muscle relaxant, and a vasoconstrictor

Epiph·a·ny \i-ˈpif-ə-nē\ n, pl **-nies** : January 6 observed as a church festival in commemoration of the coming of the Magi to Jesus at Bethlehem

epis·co·pa·cy \i-ˈpis-kə-pə-sē\ n, pl **-cies** 1 : government of a church by bishops 2 : EPISCOPATE

epis·co·pal \i-ˈpis-kə-pəl\ adj 1 : of or relating to a bishop or episcopacy 2 cap : or or relating to the Protestant Episcopal Church

Epis·co·pa·lian \i-ˌpis-kə-ˈpāl-yən\ n : a member of the Protestant Episcopal Church

epis·co·pate \i-ˈpis-kə-pət, -ˌpāt\ n 1 : the rank, office, or term of a bishop 2 : a body of bishops

ep·i·sode \ˈep-ə-ˌsōd, -ˌzōd\ n [Gk epeisodion, fr. epeisodios coming in besides, fr. eisodios coming in, fr. eis into + hodos road, journey] 1 : a unit of action in a dramatic or literary work 2 : an incident in a course of events : OCCURRENCE ⟨a feverish ∼⟩ — **ep·i·sod·ic** \ˌep-ə-ˈsäd-ik, -ˈzäd-\ adj

epis·tle \i-ˈpis-əl\ n 1 cap : one of the letters of the New Testament 2 : LETTER — **epis·to·lary** \i-ˈpis-tə-ˌler-ē\ adj

ep·i·taph \ˈep-ə-ˌtaf\ n : an inscription in memory of a dead person

ep·i·tha·la·mi·um \ˌep-ə-thə-ˈlā-mē-əm\ or **ep·i·tha·la·mi·on** \-mē-ən\ n pl **-mi·ums** or **-mia** \-mē-ə\ : a song or poem in honor of a bride and bridegroom

ep·i·the·li·um \ˌep-ə-ˈthē-lē-əm\ n, pl **-lia** \-lē-ə\ : a cellular membrane covering a bodily surface or lining a cavity — **ep·i·the·li·al** \-lē-əl\ adj

ep·i·thet \ˈep-ə-ˌthet, -thət\ n : a characterizing and often abusive word or phrase

epit·o·me \i-ˈpit-ə-mē\ n 1 : ABSTRACT, SUMMARY 2 : EMBODIMENT — **epit·o·mize** \-ˌmīz\ vb

ep·och \ˈep-ək, ˈep-ˌäk\ n : a usu. extended period : ERA, AGE — **ep·och·al** \ˈep-ə-kəl, ˈep-ˌäk-əl\ adj

ep·oxy \i-ˈpäk-sē\ vb **ep·ox·ied** or **ep-** oxyed; **ep·oxy·ing** : to glue with epoxy resin

epoxy resin n : a synthetic resin used in coatings and adhesives

Ep·som salts \ˈep-səm-\ n : a bitter colorless or white magnesium salt with cathartic properties

eq abbr 1 equal 2 equation

equa·ble \ˈek-wə-bəl, ˈē-kwə-\ adj : UNIFORM, EVEN; esp : free from unpleasant extremes — **eq·ua·bil·i·ty** \ˌek-wə-ˈbil-ət-ē, ˌē-kwə-\ n — **eq·ua·bly** \ˈek-wə-blē, ˈē-kwə-\ adv

¹**equal** \ˈē-kwəl\ adj 1 : of the same measure, quantity, value, quality, number, or degree as another 2 : IMPARTIAL 3 : free from extremes 4 : able to cope with a situation or task syn same, identical, equivalent, tantamount — **equal·i·ty** \i-ˈkwäl-ət-ē\ n — **equal·ly** \ˈē-kwə-lē\ adv

²**equal** vb **equaled** or **equalled**; **equal·ing** or **equal·ling** : to be or become equal to : MATCH

³**equal** n : one that is equal; esp : a person of like rank, abilities, or age

equal·ize \ˈē-kwə-ˌlīz\ vb **-ized**; **-iz·ing** : to make equal, uniform, or constant — **equal·iza·tion** \ˌē-kwə-lə-ˈzā-shən\ n — **equal·iz·er** \ˈē-kwə-ˌlī-zər\ n

equa·nim·i·ty \ˌē-kwə-ˈnim-ət-ē, ˌek-wə-\ n, pl **-ties** : COMPOSURE

equate \i-ˈkwāt\ vb **equat·ed**; **equat·ing** : to make, treat, or regard as equal or comparable

equa·tion \i-ˈkwā-zhən, -shən\ n 1 : an act of equating : the state of being equated 2 : a usu. formal statement of equivalence (as between mathematical or logical expressions) with the relation typically symbolized by the sign =

equa·tor \i-ˈkwāt-ər\ n : an imaginary circle around the earth that is everywhere equally distant from the two poles — **equa·to·ri·al** \ˌē-kwə-ˈtōr-ē-əl, ˌek-wə-\ adj

equer·ry \ˈek-wə-rē, i-ˈkwer-ē\ n, pl **-ries** 1 : an officer in charge of the horses of a prince or nobleman 2 : a personal attendant of a member of the British royal family

¹**eques·tri·an** \i-ˈkwes-trē-ən\ adj 1 : of or relating to horses, horsemen, or horsemanship 2 : representing a person on horseback

²**equestrian** *n* : one that rides on horseback

eques·tri·enne \i-ˌkwes-trē-ˈen\ *n* : a female rider on horseback

equi·dis·tant \ˌē-kwə-ˈdis-tənt\ *adj* : equally distant

equi·lat·er·al \ˌē-kwə-ˈlat-(ə-)rəl\ *adj* : having all sides or faces equal ⟨∼ triangles⟩

equi·lib·ri·um \ˌē-kwə-ˈlib-rē-əm, ˌek-wə-\ *n, pl* **-ri·ums** *or* **-ria** \-rē-ə\ : a state of balance between opposing forces or actions **syn** poise, balance, equipoise

equine \ˈē-ˌkwīn, ˈek-ˌwīn\ *adj* [L *equinus,* fr. *equus* horse] : of or relating to the horse — **equine** *n*

equi·nox \ˈē-kwə-ˌnäks, ˈek-wə-\ *n* : either of the two times each year when the sun appears directly overhead at the equator and day and night are everywhere of equal length that occur about March 21 and September 23 — **equi·noc·tial** \ˌē-kwə-ˈnäk-shəl, ˌek-wə-\ *adj*

equip \i-ˈkwip\ *vb* **equipped; equip·ping** : to supply with needed resources

eq·ui·page \ˈek-wə-pij\ *n* : a horse=drawn carriage usu. with its attendant servants

equip·ment \i-ˈkwip-mənt\ *n* **1** : things used in equipping : SUPPLIES, OUTFIT **2** : the equipping of a person or thing : the state of being equipped

equi·poise \ˈek-wə-ˌpȯiz, ˈē-kwə-\ *n* **1** : BALANCE, EQUILIBRIUM **2** : COUNTERBALANCE

eq·ui·ta·ble \ˈek-wət-ə-bəl\ *adj* : JUST, FAIR — **eq·ui·ta·bly** \-blē\ *adv*

eq·ui·ta·tion \ˌek-wə-ˈtā-shən\ *n* : the act or art of riding on horseback

eq·ui·ty \ˈek-wət-ē\ *n, pl* **-ties** **1** : JUSTNESS, IMPARTIALITY **2** : value of a property or of an interest in it in excess of claims against it

equiv *abbr* equivalent

equiv·a·lent \i-ˈkwiv(-ə)-lənt\ *adj* : EQUAL; *also* : virtually identical **syn** same, tantamount — **equiv·a·lence** \-ləns\ *n* — **equivalent** *n*

equiv·o·cal \i-ˈkwiv-ə-kəl\ *adj* **1** : AMBIGUOUS **2** : UNCERTAIN **3** : SUSPICIOUS, DUBIOUS ⟨∼ behavior⟩ **syn** obscure, dark, vague, enigmatic — **equiv·o·cal·ly** \-ē\ *adv*

equiv·o·cate \i-ˈkwiv-ə-ˌkāt\ *vb* **-cat·ed;**

-cat·ing **1** : to use misleading language **2** : to avoid giving a definite answer — **equiv·o·ca·tion** \-ˌkwiv-ə-ˈkā-shən\ *n*

¹**-er** \ər\ *adj suffix or adv suffix* — used to form the comparative degree of adjectives and adverbs of one syllable ⟨hott*er*⟩ ⟨dri*er*⟩ and of some adjectives and adverbs of two syllables ⟨complet*er*⟩ and sometimes of longer ones

²**-er** \ər\ *also* **-ier** \ē-ər, yər\ *or* **-yer** \yər\ *n suffix* **1** : a person occupationally connected with ⟨hatt*er*⟩ ⟨law*yer*⟩ **2** : a person or thing belonging to or associated with ⟨old-tim*er*⟩ **3** : a native of : resident of ⟨New York*er*⟩ **4** : one that has ⟨double-deck*er*⟩ **5** : one that produces or yields ⟨pork*er*⟩ **6** : one that does or performs (a specified action) ⟨report*er*⟩ **7** : one that is a suitable object of (a specified action) ⟨broil*er*⟩ **8** : one that is ⟨foreign*er*⟩

Er *symbol* erbium

ER *abbr* emergency room

era \ˈir-ə, ˈer-ə, ˈē-rə\ *n* [LL *aera,* fr. L, counters, pl. of *aes* copper, money] **1** : a chronological order or system of notation reckoned from a given date as basis **2** : a period typified by some special feature **3** : any of the five major divisions of geologic time **syn** age, epoch, period, time

ERA *abbr* Equal Rights Amendment

erad·i·cate \i-ˈrad-ə-ˌkāt\ *vb* **-cat·ed; -cat·ing** [L *eradicatus,* pp. of *eradicare,* fr. *e-* out + *radix* root] : UPROOT, ELIMINATE **syn** exterminate, annihilate, abolish, extinguish — **erad·i·ca·ble** \-ˈrad-i-kə-bəl\ *adj*

erase \i-ˈrās\ *vb* **erased; eras·ing** : to rub or scratch out (as written words); *also* : OBLITERATE **syn** cancel, efface, delete, expunge — **eras·er** \i-ˈrā-sər\ *n* — **era·sure** \-shər\ *n*

er·bi·um \ˈər-bē-əm\ *n* : a rare metallic element

¹**ere** \(ˌ)eər\ *prep* : BEFORE

²**ere** *conj* : BEFORE

¹**erect** \i-ˈrekt\ *adj* **1** : not leaning or lying down : UPRIGHT **2** : being in a state of physiological erection

²**erect** *vb* **1** : BUILD **2** : to fix or set in an upright position **3** : SET UP; *also* : ESTABLISH, DEVELOP

erec·tile \i-ˈrek-təl, -ˌtīl\ *adj* : capable of becoming erect ⟨∼ tissue⟩ ⟨∼ feathers of a bird⟩

erec·tion \i-'rek-shən\ *n* **1** : the turgid state of a previously flaccid bodily part when it becomes dilated with blood **2** : CONSTRUCTION

ere·long \eər-'lȯŋ\ *adv* : before long

er·e·mite \'er-ə-ˌmīt\ *n* : HERMIT

er·go \'er-gō, 'ər-\ *adv* [L] : THEREFORE

er·got \'ər-gət, -ˌgät\ *n* **1** : a disease of rye and other cereals caused by a fungus; *also* : this fungus **2** : a medicinal compound or preparation derived from an ergot fungus

Erie \'i(ə)r-ē\ *n* : a member of an American Indian people of the Lake Erie region; *also* : their language

er·mine \'ər-mən\ *n, pl* **ermines 1** : any of several weasels with winter fur mostly white; *also* : the white fur of an ermine **2** : a rank or office whose official robe is ornamented with ermine

erode \i-'rōd\ *vb* **erod·ed; erod·ing** : to diminish or destroy by degrees; *esp* : to gradually eat into or wear away ⟨soil *eroded* by wind and water⟩ — **erod·ible** \-'rōd-ə-bəl\ *adj*

erog·e·nous \i-'räj-ə-nəs\ *adj* **1** : sexually sensitive ⟨∼ zones⟩ **2** : of, relating to, or arousing sexual feelings

ero·sion \i-'rō-zhən\ *n* : the process or state of being eroded — **ero·sion·al** \-'rōzh-(ə-)nəl\ *adj* — **ero·sion·al·ly** \-ē\ *adv*

ero·sive \i-'rō-siv\ *adj* : tending to erode — **ero·sive·ness** *n*

erot·ic \i-'rät-ik\ *adj* : relating to or dealing with sexual love : AMATORY — **erot·i·cal·ly** \-i-k(ə-)lē\ *adv* — **erot·i·cism** \i-'rät-ə-ˌsiz-əm\ *n*

err \'ər, 'er\ *vb* : to be or do wrong

er·rand \'er-ənd\ *n* : a short trip taken to do something; *also* : the object or purpose of such a trip

er·rant \'er-ənt\ *adj* **1** : WANDERING **2** : straying outside proper bounds **3** : deviating from an accepted pattern or standard

er·ra·ta \e-'rät-ə\ *n* : a list of corrigenda

er·rat·ic \ir-'at-ik\ *adj* **1** : IRREGULAR, CAPRICIOUS **2** : ECCENTRIC, UNUSUAL — **er·rat·i·cal·ly** \-i-k(ə-)lē\ *adv*

er·ra·tum \e-'rät-əm\ *n, pl* **-ta** \-ə\ : CORRIGENDUM

er·ro·ne·ous \ir-'ō-nē-əs, e-'rō-\ *adj* : INCORRECT — **er·ro·ne·ous·ly** *adv*

er·ror \'er-ər\ *n* **1** : a usu. ignorant or unintentional deviating from accuracy or truth ⟨made an ∼ in adding⟩ **2** : a defensive misplay in baseball **3** : the state of one that errs ⟨to be in ∼⟩ **4** : a product of mistake ⟨a typographical ∼⟩ — **er·ror·less** *adj*

er·satz \'er-ˌzäts\ *adj* [G] : SUBSTITUTE, SYNTHETIC ⟨∼ flour⟩

erst \'ərst\ *adv, archaic* : ERSTWHILE

¹erst·while \-ˌhwīl\ *adv* : in the past : FORMERLY

²erstwhile *adj* : FORMER, PREVIOUS

er·u·di·tion \ˌer-(y)ə-'dish-ən\ *n* : LEARNING, SCHOLARSHIP — **er·u·dite** \'er-(y)ə-ˌdīt\ *adj*

erupt \i-'rəpt\ *vb* **1** : to burst forth or cause to burst forth : EXPLODE **2** : to break through a surface ⟨teeth ∼ing through the gum⟩ **3** : to break out with or as if with a skin rash — **erup·tion** \-'rəp-shən\ *n* — **erup·tive** \-tiv\ *adj*

-ery \(ə-)rē\ *n suffix* **1** : qualities collectively : character : -NESS ⟨snobb*ery*⟩ **2** : art : practice ⟨cook*ery*⟩ **3** : place of doing, keeping, producing, or selling (the thing specified) ⟨fish*ery*⟩ ⟨bak*ery*⟩ **4** : collection : aggregate ⟨fin*ery*⟩

ery·sip·e·las \ˌer-ə-'sip-(ə-)ləs, ˌir-\ *n* : an acute bacterial disease marked by fever and severe skin inflammation

er·y·the·ma \ˌer-ə-'thē-mə\ *n* : abnormal redness of the skin due to capillary congestion (as in inflammation)

eryth·ro·cyte \i-'rith-rə-ˌsīt\ *n* : RED BLOOD CELL

Es *symbol* einsteinium

¹-es \əz, iz *after* s, z, sh, ch; z *after* v *or a vowel*\ *n pl suffix* — used to form the plural of most nouns that end in s ⟨glass*es*⟩, z ⟨fuzz*es*⟩, sh ⟨bush*es*⟩, ch ⟨peach*es*⟩, or a final y that changes to i ⟨lad*ies*⟩ and of some nouns ending in f that changes to v ⟨loav*es*⟩

²-es *adv suffix* : ²-s

³-es *vb suffix* — used to form the third person singular present of most verbs that end in s ⟨bless*es*⟩, z ⟨fizz*es*⟩, sh ⟨hush*es*⟩, ch ⟨catch*es*⟩, or a final y that changes to i ⟨defi*es*⟩

es·ca·late \'es-kə-ˌlāt\ *vb* **-lat·ed; -lat·ing** : to increase in extent, volume, number, intensity, or scope — **es·ca·la·tion** \ˌes-kə-'lā-shən\ *n*

es·ca·la·tor \'es-kə-ˌlāt-ər\ *n* : a power-driven set of stairs

es·cal·lop \is-'käl-əp, -'kal-\ var of SCAL-LOP

es·ca·pade \'es-kə-ˌpād\ *n* [F, action of escaping] : a mischievous adventure : PRANK

¹es·cape \is-'kāp\ *vb* **es·caped; es·cap·ing** [ME *escapen,* fr. OF *escaper,* fr. (assumed) VL *excappare,* fr. L *ex-* out + LL *cappa* head covering, cloak] **1** : to get free or away **2** : to avoid a threatening evil **3** : to miss or succeed in averting ⟨∼ injury⟩ **4** : ELUDE ⟨his name ∼s me⟩ **5** : to be produced or uttered involuntarily by ⟨let a sob ∼ him⟩

²escape *n* **1** : flight from or avoidance of something unpleasant **2** : LEAKAGE **3** : a means of escape

³escape *adj* : providing a means or way of escape

es·cap·ee \is-ˌkā-'pē, ˌes-(ˌ)kā-\ *n* : one that has escaped esp. from prison

escape velocity *n* : the minimum velocity needed by a body (as a rocket) to escape from the gravitational field of a celestial body (as the earth)

es·cap·ism \is-'kā-ˌpiz-əm\ *n* : diversion of the mind to imaginative activity as an escape from routine — **es·cap·ist** \-pəst\ *adj or n*

es·ca·role \'es-kə-ˌrōl\ *n* : ENDIVE 1

es·carp·ment \is-'kärp-mənt\ *n* **1** : a steep slope in front of a fortification **2** : a long cliff

es·chew \is-'chü\ *vb* : SHUN, AVOID

¹es·cort \'es-ˌkȯrt\ *n* : one (as a person or warship) accompanying another esp. as a protection or courtesy

²es·cort \is-'kȯrt, es-\ *vb* : to accompany as an escort

es·crow \'es-ˌkrō\ *n* : something (as a deed or a sum of money) delivered by one person to another to be delivered to a third party only upon the fulfillment of a condition; *also* : a fund or deposit serving as an escrow

es·cu·do \is-'küd-ō\ *n, pl* **-dos** — see MONEY table

es·cutch·eon \is-'kəch-ən\ *n* : the usu. shield-shaped surface on which a coat of arms is shown

Esd *abbr* Esdras

Es·dras \'ez-drəs\ *n* — see BIBLE table

ESE *abbr* east-southeast

Es·ki·mo \'es-kə-ˌmō\ *n* **1** : a member of a group of peoples of northern Can-ada, Greenland, Alaska, and eastern Siberia **2** : the language of the Eskimo people

Eskimo dog *n* : a sled dog of American origin

ESL *abbr* English as a second language

esoph·a·gus \i-'säf-ə-gəs\ *n, pl* **-gi** \-ˌgī, -ˌjī\ : a muscular tube that leads from the cavity behind the mouth to the stomach — **esoph·a·geal** \-ˌsäf-ə-'jē-əl\ *adj*

es·o·ter·ic \ˌes-ə-'ter-ik\ *adj* **1** : designed for or understood only by the specially initiated **2** : PRIVATE, SECRET

esp *abbr* especially

ESP \ˌē-ˌes-'pē\ *n* : extrasensory perception

es·pa·drille \'es-pə-ˌdril\ *n* [F] : a flat sandal usu. having a fabric upper and a flexible sole

es·pal·ier \is-'pal-yər, -ˌyā\ *n* : a plant (as a fruit tree) trained to grow flat against a support — **espalier** *vb*

es·pe·cial \is-'pesh-əl\ *adj* : SPECIAL, PARTICULAR — **es·pe·cial·ly** \-'pesh-(ə-)lē\ *adv*

Es·pe·ran·to \ˌes-pə-'rant-ō, -'rän-tō\ *n* : an artificial international language based as far as possible on words common to the chief European languages

es·pi·o·nage \'es-pē-ə-ˌnäzh, -nij\ *n* [F *espionnage*] : the practice of spying

es·pla·nade \'es-plə-ˌnäd\ *n* : a level open stretch or area; *esp* : one for walking or driving along a shore

es·pous·al \is-'paů-zəl\ *n* **1** : BETROTHAL; *also* : WEDDING **2** : a taking up (as of a cause) as a supporter — **es·pouse** \-'paůz\ *vb*

espres·so \e-'spres-ō\ *n, pl* **-sos** [It (*caffè*) *espresso,* lit., pressed out coffee] : coffee brewed by forcing steam through finely ground darkly roasted coffee beans

es·prit \is-'prē\ *n* : sprightly wit

es·prit de corps \is-ˌprēd-ə-'kȯr\ *n* [F] : the common spirit existing in the members of a group

es·py \is-'pī\ *vb* **es·pied; es·py·ing** : to catch sight of **syn** behold, see, view, descry

Esq *or* **Esqr** *abbr* esquire

es·quire \'es-ˌkwī(ə)r\ *n* [ME, fr. MF *esquier* squire, fr. LL *scutarius,* fr. L *scutum* shield] **1** : a man of the English gentry ranking next below a knight **2** : a candidate for knighthood serving as attendant to a knight **3** — used as a title of courtesy

-ess \əs, ₁es\ *n suffix* : female ⟨author*ess*⟩

¹**es•say** \e-ˈsā, ˈes-ˌā\ *vb* : ATTEMPT, TRY

²**es•say** *n* **1** \ˈes-ˌā, e-ˈsā\ : ATTEMPT **2** \ˈes-ˌā\ : a literary composition usu. dealing with a subject from a limited or personal point of view — **es•say•ist** \ˈes-ˌā-əst\ *n*

es•sence \ˈes-ᵊns\ *n* **1** : fundamental nature or quality **2** : a substance distilled or extracted from another substance (as a plant or drug) and having the special qualities of the original substance ⟨∼ of peppermint⟩ **3** : PERFUME

¹**es•sen•tial** \i-ˈsen-chəl\ *adj* **1** : containing or constituting an essence ⟨free speech is an ∼ right of citizenship⟩ ⟨∼ oils⟩ **2** : of the utmost importance : INDISPENSABLE **syn** imperative, necessary, necessitous — **es•sen•tial•ly** \-ē\ *adv*

²**essential** *n* : something essential

est *abbr* **1** established **2** estimate; estimated

EST *abbr* eastern standard time

¹**-est** \əst, ist\ *adj suffix or adv suffix* — used to form the superlative degree of adjectives and adverbs of one syllable ⟨fatt*est*⟩ ⟨lat*est*⟩ , of some adjectives and adverbs of two syllables ⟨lucki*est*⟩ ⟨often*est*⟩ , and less often of longer ones ⟨beggarli*est*⟩

²**-est** \əst, ist\ *or* **-st** \st\ *vb suffix* — used to form the archaic second person singular of English verbs (with *thou*) ⟨gett*est*⟩ ⟨did*st*⟩

es•tab•lish \is-ˈtab-lish\ *vb* **1** : to make firm or stable **2** : ORDAIN **3** : FOUND ⟨∼ a settlement⟩; *also* : EFFECT **4** : to put on a firm basis : SET UP ⟨∼ a son in business⟩ **5** : to gain acceptance or recognition of (as a claim or fact) ⟨∼*ed* his right to help⟩; *also* : PROVE

es•tab•lish•ment \-mənt\ *n* **1** : something established **2** : a place of residence or business with its furnishings and staff **3** : an established ruling or controlling group ⟨the literary ∼⟩ **4** : the act or state of establishing or being established

es•tate \is-ˈtāt\ *n* **1** : STATE, CONDITION; *also* : social standing : STATUS **2** : a social or political class ⟨the three ∼s of nobility, clergy, and commons⟩ **3** : a person's possessions : FORTUNE **4** : a landed property

¹**es•teem** \is-ˈtēm\ *n* : high regard

²**esteem** *vb* **1** : REGARD **2** : to set a high value on **syn** respect, admire, revere

es•ter \ˈes-tər\ *n* : an often fragrant organic compound formed by the reaction of an acid and an alcohol

Esth *abbr* Esther

Es•ther \ˈes-tər\ *n* — see BIBLE table

esthete, esthetic, esthetics var of AESTHETE, AESTHETIC, AESTHETICS

es•ti•ma•ble \ˈes-tə-mə-bəl\ *adj* : worthy of esteem

¹**es•ti•mate** \ˈes-tə-ˌmāt\ *vb* **-mat•ed; -mat•ing 1** : to give or form an approximation (as of value, size, or cost) **2** : JUDGE, CONCLUDE **syn** evaluate, value, rate, appraise, assay, assess — **es•ti•ma•tor** \-ˌmā-tər\ *n*

²**es•ti•mate** \ˈes-tə-mət\ *n* **1** : OPINION, JUDGMENT **2** : a rough or approximate calculation **3** : a statement of the cost of work to be done

es•ti•ma•tion \ˌes-tə-ˈmā-shən\ *n* **1** : JUDGMENT, OPINION **2** : ESTIMATE **3** : ESTEEM, HONOR

es•ti•vate \ˈes-tə-ˌvāt\ *vb* **-vat•ed; -vat•ing** : to pass the summer in an inactive or resting state — **es•ti•va•tion** \ˌes-tə-ˈvā-shən\ *n*

Es•to•nian \e-ˈstō-nē-ən\ *n* : a native or inhabitant of Estonia

es•trange \is-ˈtrānj\ *vb* **es•tranged; es•trang•ing** : to alienate the affections or confidence of — **es•trange•ment** *n*

es•tro•gen \ˈes-trə-jən\ *n* : a substance (as a sex hormone) that tends to cause estrus and the development of secondary sex characteristics in the female — **es•tro•gen•ic** \ˌes-trə-ˈjen-ik\ *adj*

estrous cycle *n* : the cycle of changes in the endocrine and reproductive systems of a female mammal from the beginning of one period of estrus to the beginning of the next

es•trus \ˈes-trəs\ *n* : a periodic state of sexual excitability during which the female of most mammals is willing to mate with the male and is capable of becoming pregnant : HEAT — **es•trous** \-trəs\ *adj*

es•tu•ary \'es-chə-ˌwer-ē\ *n, pl* **-ar•ies** : an arm of the sea at the mouth of a river

ET *abbr* eastern time

ETA *abbr* estimated time of arrival

et al \et-'al\ *abbr* [L *et alii* (masc.), *et aliae* (fem.), or *et alia* (neut.)] and others

etc \ən-'sō-ˌfōrth, et-'set-ə-rə, -'se-trə\ *abbr* et cetera

et cet•era \et-'set-ə-rə, -'se-trə\ [L] and others esp. of the same kind

etch \'ech\ *vb* [Dutch *etsen*, fr G *ätzen*, lit., to feed] **1** : to make lines on (as metal) usu. by the action of acid; *also* : to produce (as a design) by etching **2** : to delineate clearly — **etch•er** *n*

etch•ing \-iŋ\ *n* **1** : the act, process, or art of etching **2** : a design produced on or print made from an etched plate

ETD *abbr* estimated time of departure

eter•nal \i-'tərn-ᵊl\ *adj* : EVERLASTING, PERPETUAL — **eter•nal•ly** \-ē\ *adv*

eter•ni•ty \i-'tər-nət-ē\ *n, pl* **-ties 1** : infinite duration **2** : IMMORTALITY

¹-eth \əth, ith\ *or* **-th** \th\ *vb suffix* — used to form the archaic third person singular present of verbs ⟨go*eth*⟩ ⟨do*th*⟩

²-eth — see ²-TH

eth•ane \'eth-ˌān\ *n* : a colorless odorless gaseous hydrocarbon found in natural gas and used esp. as a fuel

eth•a•nol \'eth-ə-ˌnȯl\ *n* : ALCOHOL 1

ether \'ē-thər\ *n* **1** : the upper regions of space; *also* : the gaseous element formerly held to fill these regions **2** : a light flammable liquid used as an anesthetic and solvent

ethe•re•al \i-'thir-ē-əl\ *adj* **1** : CELESTIAL, HEAVENLY **2** : exceptionally delicate AIRY, DAINTY — **ethe•re•al•ly** \-ē\ *adv* — **ethe•re•al•ness** *n*

eth•i•cal \'eth-i-kəl\ *adj* **1** : of or relating to ethics **2** : conforming to accepted and esp. professional standards of conduct **syn** virtuous, moral, principled — **eth•i•cal•ly** \-i-k(ə-)lē\ *adv*

eth•ics \'eth-iks\ *n sing or pl* **1** : a discipline dealing with good and evil and with moral duty **2** : moral principles or practice

Ethi•o•pi•an \ˌē-thē-'ō-pē-ən\ *n* : a native or inhabitant of Ethiopia — **Ethiopian** *adj*

¹eth•nic \'eth-nik\ *n* : a member of a minority ethnic group who retains its customs, language, or social views

²ethnic *adj* : of or relating to races or large groups of people classed according to common traits and customs — **eth•ni•cal•ly** \-ni-k(ə-)lē\ *adv*

eth•nol•o•gy \eth-'näl-ə-jē\ *n* : a science dealing with the races of man, their origin, distribution, characteristics, and relations — **eth•no•log•i•cal** \ˌeth-nə-'läj-i-kəl\ *adj* — **eth•nol•o•gist** \eth-'näl-ə-jəst\ *n*

etho•l•o•gy \ē-'thäl-ə-jē\ *n* : the scientific and objective study of animal behavior — **etho•log•i•cal** \ˌē-thə-'läj-i-kəl, ˌeth-ə-\ *adj* — **ethol•o•gist** \ē-'thäl-ə-jəst\ *n*

ethos \'ē-ˌthäs\ *n* : the distinguishing character, sentiment, moral nature, or guiding beliefs of a person, group, or institution

ethyl alcohol *n* : ALCOHOL 1

eth•yl•ene \'eth-ə-ˌlēn\ *n* : a colorless flammable gas found in coal gas or obtained from petroleum

eti•ol•o•gy \ˌēt-ē-'äl-ə-jē\ *n* **1** : CAUSE, ORIGIN; *esp* : the causes of a disease or abnormal condition **2** : a branch of medicine concerned with the causes and origins of diseases — **eti•o•log•ic** \ˌēt-ē-ə-'läj-ik\ *or* **eti•o•log•i•cal** \-i-kəl\ *adj*

et•i•quette \'et-i-kət, -ˌket\ *n* [F *étiquette*, lit., ticket] : the forms prescribed by custom or authority to be observed in social, official, or professional life **syn** propriety, decorum, decency, dignity

Etrus•can \i-'trəs-kən\ *n* **1** : the language of the Etruscans **2** : an inhabitant of ancient Etruria — **Etruscan** *adj*

et seq *abbr* [L *et sequens*] and the following one; [L *et sequentes* (masc. & fem. pl.) or *et sequentia* (neut. pl.)] and the following ones

-ette \'et, ˌet, ət, it\ *n suffix* **1** : little one ⟨din*ette*⟩ **2** : female ⟨major*ette*⟩

étude \'ā-ˌt(y)üd\ *n* [F, lit., study] : a musical composition for practice to develop technical skill

ety *abbr* etymology

et•y•mol•o•gy \ˌet-ə-'mäl-ə-jē\ *n, pl* **-gies 1** : the history of a linguistic form (as a word) shown by tracing its development and relationships **2** : a branch of linguistics dealing with etymologies

— **et•y•mo•log•i•cal** \-mə-'läj-i-kəl\ *adj*
— **et•y•mol•o•gist** \-'mäl-ə-jəst\ *n*
Eu *symbol* europium
eu•ca•lyp•tus \,yü-kə-'lip-təs\ *n, pl* **-ti** \-,tī\ *or* **-tus•es** : any of a genus of mostly Australian evergreen trees widely grown for shade or their wood, oils, resins, and gums
Eu•cha•rist \'yü-k(ə-)rəst\ *n* : COMMUNION 2 — **eu•cha•ris•tic** \,yü-kə-'ris-tik\ *adj, often cap*
¹**eu•chre** \'yü-kər\ *n* : a card game in which the side naming the trump must take three of five tricks to win
²**euchre** *vb* **eu•chred; eu•chring** \-k(ə-)riŋ\ : CHEAT, TRICK
eu•clid•e•an *also* **eu•clid•i•an** \yü-'klid-ē-ən\ *adj, often cap* : of or relating to the geometry of Euclid or a geometry based on similar axioms
eu•gen•ics \yü-'jen-iks\ *n* : a science dealing with the improvement (as by selective breeding) of hereditary qualities esp. of human beings — **eu•gen•ic** \-ik\ *adj*
eu•lo•gy \'yü-lə-jē\ *n, pl* **-gies** **1** : a speech in praise of some person or thing **2** : high praise — **eu•lo•gis•tic** \,yü-lə-'jis-tik\ *adj* — **eu•lo•gize** \'yü-lə-,jīz\ *vb*
eu•nuch \'yü-nək\ *n* : a castrated man
eu•phe•mism \'yü-fə-,miz-əm\ *n* [Gk *euphēmismos,* fr. *euphēmos* auspicious, sounding good, fr. *eu-* good + *phēmē* speech] : the substitution of a mild or pleasant expression for one offensive or unpleasant; *also* : the expression substituted — **eu•phe•mis•tic** \,yü-fə-'mis-tik\ *adj*
eu•pho•ni•ous \yü-'fō-nē-əs\ *adj* : pleasing to the ear
eu•pho•ny \'yü-fə-nē\ *n, pl* **-nies** : the effect produced by words so combined as to please the ear
eu•pho•ria \yü-'fōr-ē-ə\ *n* : a marked feeling of well-being or elation — **eu•phor•ic** \-'fȯr-ik\ *adj*
Eur *abbr* Europe; European
Eur•asian \yü-'rā-zhən, -shən\ *adj* **1** : of mixed European and Asian origin **2** : of or relating to Europe and Asia — **Eurasian** *n*
eu•re•ka \yü-'rē-kə\ *interj* [Gk *heurēka* I have found, fr. *heuriskein* to find; fr. the exclamation attributed to Ar-

chimedes on discovering a method for determining the purity of gold] — used to express triumph on a discovery
Eu•ro•bond \'yur-ō-,bänd\ *n* : a bond of a U.S. corporation that is sold outside the U.S. but that is valued and paid for in dollars and yields interest in dollars
Eu•ro•cur•ren•cy \,yur-ō-'kər-ən-sē, -'kə-rən-\ *n* : moneys (as of the U.S. and Japan) held outside their countries of origin and used in the money markets of Europe
Eu•ro•dol•lar \'yur-ō-,däl-ər\ *n* : a U.S. dollar held (as by a bank) outside the U.S. and esp. in Europe
Eu•ro•pe•an \,yur-ə-'pē-ən\ *n* : a native or inhabitant of Europe — **European** *adj*
European plan *n* : a hotel plan whereby the daily rates cover only the cost of the room
eu•ro•pi•um \yu-'rō-pē-əm\ *n* : a metallic chemical element
eu•sta•chian tube \yu-'stā-shən-\ *n, often cap E* : a tube connecting the inner cavity of the ear with the throat and equalizing air pressure on both sides of the eardrum
eu•tha•na•sia \,yü-thə-'nā-zh(ē-)ə\ *n* [Gk, easy death, fr. *eu-* good + *thanatos* death] : MERCY KILLING
eu•tro•phi•ca•tion \yu-,trō-fə-'kā-shən\ *n* : the process by which a body of water becomes rich in dissolved nutrients (as phosphates) and often shallow with a seasonal deficiency in dissolved oxygen — **eu•tro•phic** \yu-'trō-fik\ *adj*
EVA *abbr* extravehicular activity
evac•u•ate \i-'vak-yə-,wāt\ *vb* **-at•ed; -at•ing** **1** : EMPTY **2** : to discharge wastes from the body **3** : to remove or withdraw from : VACATE — **evac•u•a•tion** \-,vak-yə-'wā-shən\ *n*
evac•u•ee \i-,vak-yə-'wē\ *n* : an evacuated person
evade \i-'vād\ *vb* **evad•ed; evad•ing** : to manage to avoid esp. by dexterity or slyness : ELUDE, ESCAPE
eval•u•ate \i-'val-yə-,wāt\ *vb* **-at•ed; -at•ing** : APPRAISE, VALUE — **eval•u•a•tion** \-,val-yə-'wā-shən\ *n*
ev•a•nes•cent \,ev-ə-'nes-ᵊnt\ *adj* : tending to vanish like vapor **syn** passing,

transient, transitory, momentary —
ev·a·nes·cence \-ᵊns\ *n*

evan·gel·i·cal \ˌē-ˌvan-ˈjel-i-kəl, ˌev-ən-\ *adj* [LL *evangelium* gospel, fr. Gk *evangelion,* fr. *eu-* good + *angelos* messenger] **1** : of or relating to the Christian gospel esp. as presented in the four Gospels **2** : of or relating to certain Protestant churches emphasizing the authority of Scripture and the importance of preaching as contrasted with ritual **3** : ZEALOUS ⟨∼ fervor⟩ — **Evangelical** *n* — **Evan·gel·i·cal·ism** \-kə-ˌliz-əm\ *n* — **evan·gel·i·cal·ly** \-k(ə-)lē\ *adv*

evan·ge·lism \i-ˈvan-jə-ˌliz-əm\ *n* **1** : the winning or revival of personal commitments to Christ **2** : militant or crusading zeal — **evan·ge·lis·tic** \-ˌvan-jə-ˈlis-tik\ *adj* — **evan·ge·lis·ti·cal·ly** \-ti-k(ə-)lē\ *adv*

evan·ge·list \i-ˈvan-jə-ləst\ *n* **1** *often cap* : the writer of any of the four Gospels **2** : one who evangelizes; *esp* : a preacher who conducts revival services

evan·ge·lize \i-ˈvan-jə-ˌlīz\ *vb* **-lized; -liz·ing** **1** : to preach the gospel **2** : to convert to Christianity

evap *abbr* evaporate

evap·o·rate \i-ˈvap-ə-ˌrāt\ *vb* **-rat·ed; -rat·ing** **1** : to pass off or cause to pass off in vapor **2** : to disappear quickly **3** : to drive out the moisture from (as by heat) — **evap·o·ra·tion** \-ˌvap-ə-ˈrā-shən\ *n* — **evap·o·ra·tor** \-ˌrāt-ər\ *n*

evap·o·rite \i-ˈvap-ə-ˌrīt\ *n* : a sedimentary rock that originates by the evaporation of seawater in an enclosed basin

eva·sion \i-ˈvā-zhən\ *n* **1** : an act or instance of evading **2** : a means of evading; *esp* : an equivocal statement used in evading — **eva·sive** \i-ˈvā-siv\ *adj* — **eva·sive·ness** *n*

eve \ˈēv\ *n* **1** : EVENING **2** : the period just before some important event

¹even \ˈē-vən\ *adj* **1** : LEVEL, FLAT **2** : REGULAR, SMOOTH **3** : EQUAL, FAIR **4** : BALANCED; *also* : fully revenged **5** : divisible by two **6** : EXACT **syn** stable, uniform, steady, constant — **even·ly** *adv* — **even·ness** \-vən-nəs\ *n*

²even *adv* **1** : EXACTLY, PRECISELY **2** : FULLY, QUITE **3** : at the very time **4** — used as an intensive to stress identity

⟨∼ we know that⟩ **5** — used as an intensive to stress the comparative degree ⟨did ∼ better⟩

³even *vb* **evened; even·ing** \ˈēv-(ə-)niŋ\ : to make or become even

even·hand·ed \ˌē-vən-ˈhan-dəd\ *adj* : FAIR, IMPARTIAL

eve·ning \ˈēv-niŋ\ *n* : the end of the day and early part of the night

evening primrose *n* : a coarse biennial herb with yellow flowers that open in the evening

evening star *n* : a bright planet seen esp. in the western sky at or after sunset

even·song \ˈē-vən-ˌsȯŋ\ *n, often cap* **1** : VESPERS **2** : evening prayer esp. when sung

event \i-ˈvent\ *n* [MF or L; MF, fr. L *eventus,* fr. *evenire* to happen, fr. *venire* to come] **1** : OCCURRENCE **2** : a noteworthy happening **3** : CONTINGENCY ⟨in the ∼ of rain⟩ **4** : a contest in a program of sports — **event·ful** *adj*

even·tide \ˈē-vən-ˌtīd\ *n* : EVENING

even·tu·al \i-ˈvench-(ə-w)əl\ *adj* : coming at some later time : ULTIMATE — **even·tu·al·ly** \-ē\ *adv*

even·tu·al·i·ty \i-ˌven-chə-ˈwal-ət-ē\ *n, pl* **-ties** : a possible event or outcome

even·tu·ate \i-ˈven-chə-ˌwāt\ *vb* **-at·ed; -at·ing** : to result finally

ev·er \ˈev-ər\ *adv* **1** : ALWAYS **2** : at any time **3** : in any way : AT ALL

ev·er·bloom·ing \ˌev-ər-ˈblü-miŋ\ *adj* : blooming more or less continuously throughout the growing season

ev·er·glade \ˈev-ər-ˌglād\ *n* : a low-lying tract of swampy or marshy land

ev·er·green \-ˌgrēn\ *adj* : having foliage that remains green ⟨coniferous trees are mostly ∼⟩ — **evergreen** *n*

¹ev·er·last·ing \ˌev-ər-ˈlas-tiŋ\ *adj* **1** : enduring forever : ETERNAL **2** : keeping form or color for a long time when dried ⟨∼ flowers⟩ — **ev·er·last·ing·ly** *adv*

²everlasting *n* **1** : ETERNITY ⟨from ∼⟩ **2** : a plant with everlasting flowers; *also* : its flower

ev·er·more \ˌev-ər-ˈmōr\ *adv* : FOREVER

ev·ery \ˈev-rē\ *adj* **1** : being each one of a group **2** : all possible ⟨given ∼ chance⟩; *also* : COMPLETE ⟨have ∼ confidence⟩

ev•ery•body \\'ev-ri-ˌbäd-ē, -bəd-\\ *pron* : every person

ev•ery•day \\'ev-rē-ˌdā\\ *adj* : used or fit for daily use : ORDINARY

ev•ery•one \\-(ˌ)wən\\ *pron* : EVERYBODY

ev•ery•thing \\'ev-rē-ˌthiŋ\\ *pron* : all that exists; *also* : all that is relevant

ev•ery•where \\'ev-rē-ˌhweər\\ *adv* : in every place or part

evg *abbr* evening

evict \\i-'vikt\\ *vb* : to put (a person) out from a property by legal process; *also* : EXPEL **syn** eject, oust, dismiss — **evic•tion** \\-'vik-shən\\ *n*

ev•i•dence \\'ev-əd-əns\\ *n* 1 : an outward sign 2 : PROOF, TESTIMONY; *esp* : matter submitted in court to determine the truth of alleged facts

ev•i•dent \\'ev-əd-ənt\\ *adj* : clear to the vision and understanding **syn** manifest, distinct, obvious, apparent, plain — **ev•i•dent•ly** \\'ev-əd-ənt-lē, -ə-ˌdent-\\ *adv*

¹**evil** \\'ē-vəl\\ *adj* **evil•er** *or* **evil•ler; evil•est** *or* **evil•lest** 1 : WICKED 2 : causing or threatening distress or harm : PERNICIOUS — **evil•ly** *adv*

²**evil** *n* 1 : a source of sorrow or distress : CALAMITY 2 : the fact of suffering, misfortune, and wrongdoing — **evil-do•er** \\ˌē-vəl-'dü-ər\\ *n*

evil–mind•ed \\ˌē-vəl-'mīn-dəd\\ *adj* : having an evil disposition or evil thoughts

evince \\i-'vins\\ *vb* **evinced; evinc•ing** : SHOW, REVEAL

evis•cer•ate \\i-'vis-ə-ˌrāt\\ *vb* **-at•ed; -at•ing** 1 : to remove the entrails of 2 : to deprive of vital content or force — **evis•cer•a•tion** \\-ˌvis-ə-'rā-shən\\ *n*

evoke \\i-'vōk\\ *vb* **evoked; evok•ing** : to call forth or up — **evo•ca•tion** \\ˌē-vō-'kā-shən, ˌev-ə-\\ *n* — **evoc•a•tive** \\i-'väk-ət-iv\\ *adj*

evo•lu•tion \\ˌev-ə-'lü-shən\\ *n* 1 : a process of change in a particular direction 2 : one of a series of prescribed movements (as in a dance or military exercise) 3 : a theory that the various kinds of plants and animals are descended from other kinds that lived in earlier times and that the differences are due to inherited changes that took place over many generations — **evo•lu•tion•ary** \\-shə-ˌner-ē\\ *adj* — **evo•lu•tion•ist** \\-sh(ə-)nəst\\ *n*

evolve \\i-'välv\\ *vb* **evolved; evolv•ing** [L *evolvere* to unroll] : to develop by or as if by evolution

EW *abbr* enlisted woman

ewe \\'yü\\ *n* : a female sheep

ew•er \\'yü-ər\\ *n* : a vase-shaped jug

¹**ex** \\(ˌ)eks\\ *prep* [L] : out of : FROM

²**ex** \\'eks\\ *n* : a former spouse

³**ex** *abbr* 1 example 2 express 3 extra

Ex *abbr* Exodus

ex- \\e *also occurs in this prefix where only* i *is shown below (as in* "express") *and* ks *sometimes occurs where only* gz *is shown (as in* "exact")\\ *prefix* 1 : out of : outside 2 : former ⟨*ex*-president⟩

ex•ac•er•bate \\ig-'zas-ər-ˌbāt\\ *vb* **-bat•ed; -bat•ing** : to make more violent, bitter, or severe — **ex•ac•er•ba•tion** \\-ˌzas-ər-'bā-shən\\ *n*

¹**ex•act** \\ig-'zakt\\ *vb* 1 : to compel to furnish 2 : to call for as suitable or necessary — **ex•ac•tion** \\-'zak-shən\\ *n*

²**exact** *adj* : precisely accurate or correct **syn** right, precise, proper, nice — **ex•act•ly** \\-zak-(t)lē\\ *adv* — **ex•act•ness** \\-'zak(t)-nəs\\ *n*

ex•act•ing \\ig-'zak-tiŋ\\ *adj* 1 : greatly demanding ⟨an ∼ taskmaster⟩ 2 : requiring close attention and precision

ex•ac•ti•tude \\ig-'zak-tə-ˌt(y)üd\\ *n* : the quality or state of being exact

ex•ag•ger•ate \\ig-'zaj-ə-ˌrāt\\ *vb* **-at•ed; -at•ing** [L *exaggeratus*, pp. of *exaggerare*, lit., to heap up, fr. *agger* heap] : to enlarge (as a statement) beyond bounds : OVERSTATE — **ex•ag•ger•at•ed•ly** *adv* — **ex•ag•ger•a•tion** \\-ˌzaj-ə-'rā-shən\\ *n* — **ex•ag•ger•a•tor** \\-'zaj-ə-rāt-ər\\ *n*

ex•alt \\ig-'zolt\\ *vb* 1 : to raise up esp. in rank, power, or dignity 2 : GLORIFY 3 : to elate the mind or spirits — **ex•al•ta•tion** \\ˌeg-ˌzol-'tā-shən, ˌek-ˌsol-\\ *n*

ex•am \\ig-'zam\\ *n* : EXAMINATION

ex•am•ine \\ig-'zam-ən\\ *vb* **ex•am•ined; ex•am•in•ing** \\-(ə-)niŋ\\ 1 : to inspect closely 2 : QUESTION; *esp* : to test by questioning **syn** interrogate, query, quiz, catechize — **ex•am•i•na•tion** \\-ˌzam-ə-'nā-shən\\ *n*

ex•am•ple \\ig-'zam-pəl\\ *n* 1 : something forming a model to be followed or avoided 2 : a representative sample 3 : a problem to be solved in order to show the application of some rule

ex·as·per·ate \ig-'zas-pə-ˌrāt\ *vb* **-at·ed; -at·ing** : VEX, IRRITATE — **ex·as·per·a·tion** \ig-ˌzas-pə-'rā-shən\ *n*

exc *abbr* **1** excellent **2** except

ex·ca·vate \'ek-skə-ˌvāt\ *vb* **-vat·ed; -vat·ing 1** : to hollow out; *also* : to form by hollowing out **2** : to dig out and remove (as earth) **3** : to reveal to view by digging away a covering — **ex·ca·va·tion** \ˌek-skə-'vā-shən\ *n* — **ex·ca·va·tor** \'ek-skə-ˌvāt-ər\ *n*

ex·ceed \ik-'sēd\ *vb* **1** : to go or be beyond the limit of **2** : SURPASS

ex·ceed·ing·ly \-iŋ-lē\ *or* **ex·ceed·ing** *adv* : EXTREMELY, VERY

ex·cel \ik-'sel\ *vb* **ex·celled; ex·cel·ling** : SURPASS, OUTDO

ex·cel·lence \'ek-s(ə-)ləns\ *n* **1** : the quality of being excellent **2** : an excellent or valuable quality : VIRTUE **3** : EXCELLENCY 2

ex·cel·len·cy \-s(ə-)lən-sē\ *n, pl* **-cies 1** : EXCELLENCE **2** — used as a title of honor

ex·cel·lent \'ek-s(ə-)lənt\ *adj* : very good of its kind : FIRST-CLASS — **ex·cel·lent·ly** *adv*

ex·cel·si·or \ik-'sel-sē-ər\ *n* : fine curled wood shavings used esp. for packing fragile items

¹ex·cept \ik-'sept\ *also* **ex·cept·ing** \-'sep-tiŋ\ *prep* **1** : not including ⟨daily ~ Sundays⟩ **2** : other than : BUT ⟨saw no one ~ him⟩

²except *vb* **1** : to take or leave out **2** : OBJECT

³except *also* **excepting** *conj* : ONLY ⟨I'd go, ~ it's too far⟩

ex·cep·tion \ik-'sep-shən\ *n* **1** : the act of excepting **2** : something excepted **3** : OBJECTION

ex·cep·tion·able \ik-'sep-sh(ə-)nə-bəl\ *adj* : OBJECTIONABLE

ex·cep·tion·al \ik-'sep-sh(ə-)nəl\ *adj* **1** : UNUSUAL **2** : SUPERIOR — **ex·cep·tion·al·ly** \-'sep-sh(ə-)nə-lē\ *adv*

ex·cerpt \'ek-ˌsərpt, 'eg-ˌzərpt\ *n* : a passage selected or copied : EXTRACT — **excerpt** \ek-'sərpt, eg-'zərpt; 'ek-ˌsərpt, 'eg-ˌzərpt\ *vb*

ex·cess \ik-'ses, 'ek-ˌses\ *n* **1** : SUPERFLUITY, SURPLUS **2** : the amount by which one quantity exceeds another **3** : INTEMPERANCE — **excess** *adj* — **ex·ces·sive** \ik-'ses-iv\ *adj* — **ex·ces·sive·ly** *adv*

exch *abbr* exchange; exchanged

¹ex·change \iks-'chānj, 'eks-ˌchānj\ *n* **1** : the giving or taking of one thing in return for another : TRADE **2** : a substituting of one thing for another **3** : interchange of valuables and esp. of bills of exchange or money of different countries **4** : a place where things and services are exchanged; *esp* : a marketplace for securities **5** : a central office in which telephone lines are connected for communication

²exchange *vb* **ex·changed; ex·chang·ing** : to transfer in return for some equivalent : BARTER, SWAP — **ex·change·able** \iks-'chān-jə-bəl\ *adj*

ex·che·quer \'eks-ˌchek-ər\ *n* [ME *escheker*, fr. OF *eschequier* chessboard, counting table] : TREASURY; *esp* : a national treasury

ex·cise \'ek-ˌsīz, -ˌsīs\ *n* : a tax on the manufacture, sale, or consumption of goods within a country

ex·ci·sion \-'sizh-ən\ *n* : removal by or as if by cutting out esp. by surgical means — **ex·cise** \ik-'sīz\ *vb*

ex·cit·able \ik-'sīt-ə-bəl\ *adj* : easily excited — **ex·cit·abil·i·ty** \-ˌsīt-ə-'bil-ət-ē\ *n*

ex·cite \ik-'sīt\ *vb* **ex·cit·ed; ex·cit·ing 1** : to stir up the emotions of : ROUSE **2** : to increase the activity of : STIMULATE **syn** provoke, stimulate, pique, quicken — **ex·ci·ta·tion** \ˌek-ˌsī-'tā-shən, ˌek-sə-\ *n* — **ex·cit·ed·ly** *adv*

ex·cite·ment \ik-'sīt-mənt\ *n* : AGITATION, STIR

ex·claim \iks-'klām\ *vb* : to cry out, speak, or utter sharply or vehemently — **ex·cla·ma·tion** \ˌeks-klə-'mā-shən\ *n* — **ex·clam·a·to·ry** \iks-'klam-ə-ˌtōr-ē\ *adj*

exclamation point *n* : a punctuation mark ! used esp. after an interjection or exclamation

ex·clude \iks-'klüd\ *vb* **ex·clud·ed; ex·clud·ing 1** : to shut out (as from using or participating) : BAR **2** : to put out : EXPEL — **ex·clu·sion** \-'klü-zhən\ *n*

ex·clu·sive \iks-'klü-siv\ *adj* **1** : reserved for particular persons **2** : snobbishly aloof; *also* : STYLISH **3** : SOLE ⟨~ rights⟩; *also* : UNDIVIDED **syn** chic, modish, smart, swank, fashionable — **ex•clu•sive•ly** *adv* — **ex•clu•sive•ness** *n*

exclusive of *prep* : not taking into account

ex•cog•i•tate \ek-'skäj-ə-ˌtāt\ *vb* : to think out : DEVISE

ex•com•mu•ni•cate \ˌek-skə-'myü-nə-ˌkāt\ *vb* : to cut off officially from communion with the church — **ex•com•mu•ni•ca•tion** \-ˌmyü-nə-'kā-shən\ *n*

ex•co•ri•ate \ek-'skōr-ē-ˌāt\ *vb* **-at•ed; -at•ing** : to criticize severely — **ex•co•ri•a•tion** \(ˌ)ek-ˌskōr-ē-'ā-shən\ *n*

ex•cre•ment \'ek-skrə-mənt\ *n* : waste discharged from the body and esp. from the alimentary canal — **ex•cre•men•tal** \ˌek-skrə-'ment-ᵊl\ *adj*

ex•cres•cence \ik-'skres-ᵊns\ *n* : OUTGROWTH; *esp* : an abnormal outgrowth (as a wart) — **ex•cres•cent** \-ᵊnt\ *adj*

ex•cre•ta \ik-'skrēt-ə\ *n pl* : waste matter separated or eliminated from an organism

ex•crete \ik-'skrēt\ *vb* **ex•cret•ed; ex•cret•ing** : to separate and eliminate wastes from the body esp. in urine — **ex•cre•tion** \-'skrē-shən\ *n* — **ex•cre•to•ry** \'ek-skrə-ˌtōr-ē\ *adj*

ex•cru•ci•at•ing \ik-'skrü-shē-ˌāt-iŋ\ *adj* [L *excruciare,* fr. *cruciare* to crucify, fr. *crux* cross] : intensely painful or distressing **syn** agonizing, harrowing, torturous — **ex•cru•ci•at•ing•ly** *adv*

ex•cul•pate \'ek-(ˌ)skəl-ˌpāt\ *vb* **-pat•ed; -pat•ing** : to clear from alleged fault or guilt **syn** absolve, exonerate, acquit, vindicate, clear

ex•cur•sion \ik-'skər-zhən\ *n* **1** : EXPEDITION; *esp* : a pleasure trip **2** : DIGRESSION — **ex•cur•sion•ist** \-'skərzh-(ə-)nəst\ *n*

ex•cur•sive \-'skər-siv\ *adj* : constituting or characterized by digression

¹ex•cuse \ik-'skyüz\ *vb* **ex•cused; ex•cus•ing** [ME *excusen,* fr. OF *excuser,* fr. L *excusare,* fr. *causa* cause, explanation] **1** : to offer excuse for **2** : PARDON **3** : to release from an obligation **4** : JUSTIFY — **ex•cus•able** *adj*

²excuse \ik-'skyüs\ *n* **1** : an act of excusing **2** : grounds for being excused : JUSTIFICATION **3** : something that excuses or is a reason for excusing

exec *abbr* executive

ex•e•cra•ble \'ek-si-krə-bəl\ *adj* **1** : DETESTABLE **2** : very bad ⟨∼ spelling⟩

ex•e•crate \'ek-sə-ˌkrāt\ *vb* **-crat•ed; -crat•ing** [L *exsecratus,* pp. of *exsecrari* to put under a curse, fr. *ex-* out of + *sacer* sacred] : to denounce as evil or detestable; *also* : DETEST — **ex•e•cra•tion** \ˌek-sə-'krā-shən\ *n*

ex•e•cute \'ek-si-ˌkyüt\ *vb* **-cut•ed; -cut•ing** **1** : to carry to completion : PERFORM **2** : to do what is called for by (as a law) **3** : to put to death in accordance with a legal sentence **4** : to produce in accordance with a plan or design **5** : to do what is needed to give legal force to (as a deed) — **ex•e•cu•tion** \ˌek-si-'kyü-shən\ *n* — **ex•e•cu•tion•er** \-sh(ə-)nər\ *n*

¹ex•ec•u•tive \ig-'zek-(y)ət-iv\ *adj* **1** : designed for or related to carrying out plans or purposes **2** : of or relating to the enforcement of laws and the conduct of affairs

²executive *n* **1** : the branch of government with executive duties **2** : one having administrative or managerial responsibility

ex•ec•u•tor \ig-'zek-(y)ət-ər\ *n* : the person named in a will to carry out its provisions

ex•ec•u•trix \ig-'zek-(y)ə-ˌtriks\ *n, pl* **ex•ec•u•tri•ces** \-ˌzek-(y)ə-'trī-ˌsēz\ *or* **ex•ec•u•trix•es** \-'zek-(y)ə-ˌtrik-səz\ : a woman who is an executor

ex•e•ge•sis \ˌek-sə-'jē-səs\ *n, pl* **-ge•ses** \-'jē-ˌsēz\ : explanation or critical interpretation of a text

ex•e•gete \'ek-sə-ˌjēt\ *n* : one who practices exegesis

ex•em•plar \ig-'zem-ˌplär, -plər\ *n* **1** : one that serves as a model or pattern; *esp* : an ideal model **2** : a typical instance or example

ex•em•pla•ry \ig-'zem-plə-rē\ *adj* : serving as a pattern; *also* : COMMENDABLE

ex•em•pli•fy \ig-'zem-plə-ˌfī\ *vb* **-fied; -fy•ing** : to illustrate by example : serve as an example of — **ex•em•pli•fi•ca•tion** \-ˌzem-plə-fə-'kā-shən\ *n*

¹ex•empt \ig-'zempt\ *adj* : free from some liability to which others are subject

²exempt *vb* : to make exempt : EXCUSE — **ex•emp•tion** \ig-'zemp-shən\ *n*

¹ex•er•cise \'ek-sər-ˌsīz\ *n* **1** : EMPLOYMENT, USE ⟨∼ of authority⟩ **2** : exertion made for the sake of training **3** : a task or problem done to develop skill **4** *pl* : a public exhibition or ceremony

²**exercise** *vb* **-cised; -cis•ing 1** : EXERT ⟨∼ control⟩ **2** : to train by or engage in exercise **3** : WORRY, DISTRESS — **ex•er•cis•er** *n*

ex•ert \ig-'zərt\ *vb* : to bring or put into action ⟨∼ influence⟩ ⟨∼ed himself⟩ — **ex•er•tion** \-'zər-shən\ *n*

ex•hale \eks-'hāl\ *vb* **ex•haled; ex•hal•ing 1** : to breathe out **2** : to give or pass off in the form of vapor — **ex•ha•la•tion** \ˌeks-(h)ə-'lā-shən\ *n*

¹**ex•haust** \ig-'zȯst\ *vb* **1** : to use up wholly **2** : to tire or wear out **3** : to draw out completely (as air from a jar); *also* : EMPTY **4** : to develop (a subject) completely

²**exhaust** *n* **1** : the escape of used vapor or gas from an engine; *also* : the gas that escapes **2** : a system of pipes through which exhaust escapes

ex•haus•tion \ig-'zȯs-chən\ *n* : extreme weariness : FATIGUE

ex•haus•tive \ig-'zȯ-stiv\ *adj* : covering all possibilities : THOROUGH

¹**ex•hib•it** \ig-'zib-ət\ *vb* **1** : to display esp. publicly **2** : to present to a court in legal form **syn** display, show, parade, flaunt — **ex•hi•bi•tion** \ek-sə-'bish-ən\ *n* — **ex•hib•i•tor** \ig-'zib-ət-ər\ *n*

²**exhibit** *n* **1** : an act or instance of exhibiting; *also* : something exhibited **2** : something produced and identified in court for use as evidence

ex•hi•bi•tion•ism \ˌek-sə-'bish-ə-ˌniz-əm\ *n* : the act or practice of so behaving as to attract undue attention sometimes by indecent exposure — **ex•hi•bi•tion•ist** \-'bish-(ə-)nəst\ *n or adj*

ex•hil•a•rate \ig-'zil-ə-ˌrāt\ *vb* **-rat•ed; -rat•ing** : ENLIVEN, STIMULATE — **ex•hil•a•ra•tion** \-ˌzil-ə-'rā-shən\ *n*

ex•hort \ig-'zȯrt\ *vb* : to urge, advise, or warn earnestly — **ex•hor•ta•tion** \ˌeks-ˌȯr-tā-shən, ˌegz-, -ər-\ *n*

ex•hume \igz-'(y)üm, iks-'(h)yüm\ *vb* **ex•humed; ex•hum•ing** [F or ML; F *exhumer*, fr. ML *exhumare*, fr. L *ex* out of + *humus* earth] : DISINTER — **ex•hu•ma•tion** \ˌeks-(h)yü-'mā-shən, ˌegz-(y)ü-\ *n*

ex•i•gen•cy \'ek-sə-jən-sē, ig-'zij-ən-\ *n*, *pl* **-cies 1** : urgent need **2** *pl* : REQUIRE-MENTS — **ex•i•gent** \'ek-sə-jənt\ *adj*

ex•ig•u•ous \ig-'zig-yə-wəs\ *adj* : scanty in amount — **ex•i•gu•i•ty** \ˌeg-zi-'gyü-ət-ē\ *n*

¹**ex•ile** \'eg-ˌzīl, 'ek-ˌsīl\ *n* **1** : BANISH-MENT **2** : a person driven from his native place

²**exile** *vb* **ex•iled; ex•il•ing** : BANISH, EXPEL **syn** expatriate, deport, ostracize

ex•ist \ig-'zist\ *vb* **1** : to have being **2** : to continue to be : LIVE

ex•is•tence \ig-'zis-təns\ *n* **1** : continuance in living **2** : actual occurrence **3** : something existing — **ex•is•tent** \-tənt\ *adj*

ex•is•ten•tial \ˌeg-zis-'ten-chəl, ˌek-sis-\ *adj* **1** : of or relating to existence **2** : EMPIRICAL **3** : having being in time and space **4** : of or relating to existentialism or existentialists

ex•is•ten•tial•ism \ˌeg-zis-'ten-chə-ˌliz-əm\ *n* : a philosophy centered upon the analysis of existence and stressing the freedom, responsibility, and usu. the isolation of the individual — **ex•is•ten•tial•ist** \-ləst\ *adj or n*

ex•it \'eg-zət, 'ek-sət\ *n* **1** : a departure from a stage **2** : a going out or away; *also* : DEATH **3** : a way out of an enclosed space **4** : a point of departure from an expressway — **exit** *vb*

exo•bi•ol•o•gy \ˌek-sō-bī-'äl-ə-jē\ *n* : biology concerned with life originating or existing outside the earth or its atmosphere — **exo•bi•ol•o•gist** \-bī-'äl-ə-jəst\ *n*

exo•crine gland \'ek-sə-krən-, -ˌkrīn-, -ˌkrēn-\ *n* : a gland (as a sweat gland or a kidney) that releases a secretion externally by means of a canal or duct

Exod *abbr* Exodus

ex•o•dus \'ek-səd-əs\ *n* : a mass departure : EMIGRATION

Ex•o•dus *n* — see BIBLE table

ex of•fi•cio \ˌek-sə-'fish-ē-ˌō\ *adv or adj* : by virtue of or because of an office ⟨*ex officio* chairman⟩

ex•og•e•nous \ek-'säj-ə-nəs\ *adj* : caused or produced by factors outside the organism or system — **ex•og•e•nous•ly** *adv*

ex•on•er•ate \ig-'zän-ə-ˌrāt\ *vb* **-at•ed; -at•ing** [ME *exoneraten*, fr. L *ex-onerare* to unburden, fr. *ex-* out + *onus* load] : to free from blame **syn**

acquit, absolve, exculpate, vindicate — **ex·on·er·a·tion** \-ˌzän-ə-'rā-shən\ *n*

ex·or·bi·tant \ig-'zȯr-bət-ənt\ *adj* : exceeding what is usual or proper

ex·or·cise \'ek-ˌsȯr-ˌsīz, -sər-\ *vb* **-cised; -cis·ing 1** : to get rid of by or as if by solemn command **2** : to free of an evil spirit — **ex·or·cism** \-ˌsiz-əm\ *n* — **ex·or·cist** \-ˌsist\ *n*

exo·sphere \'ek-sō-ˌsfiər\ *n* : the outermost region of the atmosphere

exo·ther·mic \ˌek-sō-'thər-mik\ *adj* : characterized by or formed with evolution of heat

ex·ot·ic \ig-'zät-ik\ *adj* : FOREIGN, STRANGE — **exotic** *n* — **ex·ot·i·cal·ly** \-i-k(ə-)lē\ *adv* — **ex·ot·i·cism** \-'zät-ə-ˌsiz-əm\ *n*

exp *abbr* **1** expense **2** experiment **3** export **4** express

ex·pand \ik-'spand\ *vb* **1** : to open up : UNFOLD **2** : ENLARGE **3** : to develop in detail **syn** amplify, swell, distend, inflate, dilate — **ex·pand·er** *n*

ex·panse \ik-'spans\ *n* : a broad extent (as of land or sea)

ex·pan·sion \ik-'span-chən\ *n* **1** : the act or process of expanding **2** : the quality or state of being expanded **3** : an expanded part or thing

ex·pan·sive \ik-'span-siv\ *adj* **1** : tending to expand or to cause expansion **2** : warmly benevolent or emotional **3** : of large extent or scope — **ex·pan·sive·ly** *adv* — **ex·pan·sive·ness** *n*

ex par·te \eks-'pärt-ē\ *adv or adj* [ML] : from a one-sided point of view

ex·pa·ti·ate \ek-'spā-shē-ˌāt\ *vb* **-at·ed; -at·ing** : to talk or write at length — **ex·pa·ti·a·tion** \ek-ˌspā-shē-'ā-shən\ *n*

¹**ex·pa·tri·ate** \ek-'spā-trē-ˌāt\ *vb* **-at·ed; -at·ing** : EXILE — **ex·pa·tri·a·tion** \ek-ˌspā-trē-'ā-shən\ *n*

²**ex·pa·tri·ate** \ek-'spā-trē-ˌāt, -trē-ət\ *adj* : living in a foreign country — **expatriate** *n*

ex·pect \ik-'spekt\ *vb* **1** : SUPPOSE, THINK **2** : to look forward to : ANTICIPATE **3** : to consider reasonable, due, or necessary **4** : to consider to be obliged

ex·pec·tan·cy \-'spek-tən-sē\ *n, pl* **-cies 1** : EXPECTATION **2** : the expected amount (as of years of life)

ex·pec·tant \-tənt\ *adj* : EXPECTING; *esp*

: expecting the birth of a child — **ex·pec·tant·ly** *adv*

ex·pec·ta·tion \ˌek-ˌspek-'tā-shən\ *n* **1** : the act or state of expecting **2** : prospect of good or bad fortune — usu. used in pl. **3** : something expected

ex·pec·to·rant \ik-'spek-t(ə-)rənt\ *n* : an agent that promotes the discharge or expulsion of mucus from the respiratory tract — **expectorant** *adj*

ex·pec·to·rate \-tə-ˌrāt\ *vb* **-rat·ed; -rat·ing** : SPIT — **ex·pec·to·ra·tion** \-ˌspek-tə-'rā-shən\ *n*

ex·pe·di·ence \ik-'spēd-ē-əns\ *n* : EXPEDIENCY

ex·pe·di·en·cy \-ən-sē\ *n, pl* **-cies 1** : fitness to some end **2** : use of expedient means and methods; *also* : something expedient

¹**ex·pe·di·ent** \ik-'spēd-ē-ənt\ *adj* [ME, fr. MF or L; MF, fr. L *expediens* prp. of *expedire* to extricate, arrange, be advantageous, fr. *ex-* out + *ped-, pes* foot] **1** : adapted for achieving a particular end **2** : marked by concern with what is advantageous; *esp* : governed by self-interest

²**expedient** *n* : something expedient; *esp* : a temporary means to an end

ex·pe·dite \'ek-spə-ˌdīt\ *vb* **-dit·ed; -dit·ing** : to carry out promptly; *also* : to speed up

ex·pe·dit·er \-ˌdīt-ər\ *n* : one that expedites; *esp* : one employed to ensure efficient movement of goods or supplies in a business

ex·pe·di·tion \ˌek-spə-'dish-ən\ *n* **1** : a journey for a particular purpose; *also* : the persons making it **2** : efficient promptness

ex·pe·di·tion·ary \-'dish-ə-ˌner-ē\ *adj* : of, relating to, or constituting an expedition; *also* : sent on military service abroad

ex·pe·di·tious \ˌek-spə-'dish-əs\ *adj* : marked by or acting with prompt efficiency **syn** swift, fast, rapid, speedy

ex·pel \ik-'spel\ *vb* **ex·pelled; ex·pel·ling** : to drive or force out : EJECT

ex·pend \ik-'spend\ *vb* **1** : to pay out : SPEND **2** : UTILIZE; *also* : USE UP — **ex·pend·able** *adj*

ex·pen·di·ture \ik-'spen-di-chər, -də-ˌchùr\ *n* **1** : the act or process of expending **2** : something expended

ex·pense \ik-'spens\ *n* **1** : EXPENDITURE

2 : COST 3 : a cause of expenditure 4 : SACRIFICE

ex·pen·sive \ik-'spen-siv\ *adj* : COSTLY, DEAR — **ex·pen·sive·ly** *adv*

¹**ex·pe·ri·ence** \ik-'spir-ē-əns\ *n* 1 : observation or practice resulting in or tending toward knowledge; *also* : the resulting state of enhanced comprehension and efficiency 2 : a state of being affected from without (as by events); *also* : an affecting event ⟨a startling ∼⟩ 3 : something or the totality experienced (as by a person or community)

²**experience** *vb* **-enced; -enc·ing** 1 : FIND OUT, DISCOVER 2 : to know as an experience : SUFFER, UNDERGO

ex·pe·ri·enced \-ənst\ *adj* : made capable by repeated experience

¹**ex·per·i·ment** \ik-'sper-ə-mənt\ *n* : a controlled procedure carried out to discover, test, or demonstrate something; *also* : the process of testing — **ex·per·i·men·tal** \-ˌsper-ə-'ment-ᵊl\ *adj*

²**ex·per·i·ment** \-ˌment\ *vb* : to make experiments — **ex·per·i·men·ta·tion** \ik-ˌsper-ə-mən-'tā-shən\ *n* — **ex·per·i·men·ter** \-'sper-ə-ˌment-ər\ *n*

¹**ex·pert** \'ek-ˌspərt\ *adj* : showing special skill or knowledge — **ex·pert·ly** *adv* — **ex·pert·ness** *n*

²**ex·pert** \'ek-ˌspərt\ *n* : an expert person : SPECIALIST

ex·per·tise \ˌek-(ˌ)spər-'tēz\ *n* : the skill of an expert

ex·pi·ate \'ek-spē-ˌāt\ *vb* **-at·ed; -at·ing** : to make amends : ATONE — **ex·pi·a·tion** \ˌek-spē-'ā-shən\ *n*

ex·pi·a·to·ry \'ek-spē-ə-ˌtōr-ē\ *adj* : serving to expiate

ex·pire \ik-'spī(ə)r, ek-\ *vb* **ex·pired; ex·pir·ing** 1 : to breathe one's last breath : DIE 2 : to come to an end 3 : to breathe out from or as if from the lungs — **ex·pi·ra·tion** \ˌek-spə-'rā-shən\ *n*

ex·plain \ik-'splān\ *vb* [ME *explanen,* fr. L *explanare,* lit., to make level, fr. *planus* level, flat] 1 : to make clear 2 : to give the reason for — **ex·pla·na·tion** \ˌek-splə-'nā-shən\ *n* — **ex·plan·a·to·ry** \ik-'splan-ə-ˌtōr-ē\ *adj*

ex·ple·tive \'ek-splət-iv\ *n* : a usu. profane exclamation

ex·pli·ca·ble \ek-'splik-ə-bəl, 'ek-(ˌ)splik-\ *adj* : capable of being explained

ex·pli·cate \'ek-splə-ˌkāt\ *vb* **-cat·ed; -cat·ing** : to give a detailed explanation of

ex·plic·it \ik-'splis-ət\ *adj* : clearly and precisely expressed — **ex·plic·it·ly** *adv* — **ex·plic·it·ness** *n*

ex·plode \ik-'splōd\ *vb* **ex·plod·ed; ex·plod·ing** [L *explodere* to drive off the stage by clapping, fr. *ex-* out + *plaudere* to clap] 1 : DISCREDIT ⟨∼ a belief⟩ 2 : to burst or cause to burst violently and noisily ⟨∼ a bomb⟩ ⟨the boiler *exploded*⟩ 3 : to undergo a rapid chemical or nuclear reaction with production of heat and violent expansion of gas ⟨∼ dynamite⟩ 4 : to give forth a sudden strong and noisy outburst of emotion ⟨∼ with rage⟩

ex·plod·ed \-əd\ *adj* : showing the parts separated but in correct relationship to each other ⟨an ∼ view of a carburetor⟩

¹**ex·ploit** \'ek-ˌsplȯit\ *n* : DEED; *esp* : a notable or heroic act

²**ex·ploit** \ik-'splȯit\ *vb* 1 : to put to productive use ⟨∼ resources⟩; *also* : UTILIZE 2 : to use unfairly for one's own advantage — **ex·ploi·ta·tion** \ˌek-ˌsplȯi-'tā-shən\ *n*

ex·plore \ik-'splōr\ *vb* **ex·plored; ex·plor·ing** 1 : to look into or travel over thoroughly 2 : to examine carefully ⟨∼ a wound⟩ — **ex·plo·ra·tion** \ˌek-splə-'rā-shən\ *n* — **ex·plor·a·to·ry** \ik-'splōr-ə-ˌtōr-ē\ *adj* — **ex·plor·er** *n*

ex·plo·sion \ik-'splō-zhən\ *n* : the act or an instance of exploding

ex·plo·sive \ik-'splō-siv\ *adj* 1 : relating to or able to cause explosion 2 : tending to explode — **explosive** *n* — **ex·plo·sive·ly** *adv*

ex·po \'ek-ˌspō\ *n, pl* **expos** : EXPOSITION 2

ex·po·nent \ik-'spō-nənt, 'ek-ˌspō-\ *n* 1 : a symbol written above and to the right of a mathematical expression to signify how many times it is to be used as a factor ⟨in a^3 the ∼ 3 indicates that a is to be used three times in the product $a·a·a$⟩ 2 : INTERPRETER, EXPOUNDER 3 : ADVOCATE, CHAMPION — **ex·po·nen·tial** \ˌek-spə-'nen-chəl\ *adj* — **ex·po·nen·tial·ly** \-ē\ *adv*

ex·po·nen·ti·a·tion \ˌek-spə-ˌnen-chē-

ˈā-shen\ *n* : the mathematical operation of raising a quantity to a power

¹ex·port \ek-ˈspōrt, ˈek-ˌspōrt\ *vb* : to send (as merchandise) to foreign countries — **ex·por·ta·tion** \ˌek-ˌspōr-ˈtā-shən, -spər-\ *n* — **ex·port·er** \ek-ˈspōrt-ər, ˈek-ˌspōrt-\ *n*

²ex·port \ˈek-ˌspōrt\ *n* **1** : something exported esp. for trade **2** : an act or the business of exporting

ex·pose \ik-ˈspōz\ *vb* **ex·posed; ex·pos·ing** **1** : to deprive of shelter or protection **2** : to submit or subject to an action or influence; *esp* : to subject (as photographic film) to radiant energy (as light) **3** : to display esp. for sale **4** : to bring to light : DISCLOSE

ex·po·sé *or* **ex·po·se** \ˌek-spō-ˈzā\ *n* : an exposure of something discreditable

ex·po·si·tion \ˌek-spə-ˈzish-ən\ *n* **1** : a setting forth of the meaning or purpose (as of a writing); *also* : discourse designed to convey information **2** : a public exhibition

ex·pos·i·tor \ik-ˈspäz-ət-ər\ *n* : one who explains : COMMENTATOR

ex·pos·tu·late \ik-ˈspäs-chə-ˌlāt\ *vb* : to reason earnestly with a person esp. in dissuading : REMONSTRATE — **ex·pos·tu·la·tion** \-ˌspäs-chə-ˈlā-shən\ *n*

ex·po·sure \ik-ˈspō-zhər\ *n* **1** : the fact or condition of being exposed **2** : the act or an instance of exposing **3** : the length of time for which a film is exposed **4** : a section of a photographic film for one picture

ex·pound \ik-ˈspaund\ *vb* **1** : STATE **2** : INTERPRET, EXPLAIN — **ex·pound·er** *n*

¹ex·press \ik-ˈspres\ *adj* **1** : EXPLICIT; *also* : EXACT, PRECISE **2** : SPECIFIC ⟨his ~ purpose⟩ **3** : traveling at high speed and esp. with few stops ⟨~ train⟩; *also* : adapted to high speed use ⟨~ roads⟩ — **ex·press·ly** *adv*

²express *adv* : by express ⟨ship it ~⟩

³express *n* **1** : a system for the prompt transportation of goods; *also* : a company operating such a service or the shipments so transported **2** : an express vehicle

⁴express *vb* **1** : to make known : SHOW, STATE ⟨~ regret⟩; *also* : SYMBOLIZE **2** : to squeeze out : extract by pressing **3** : to send by express

ex·pres·sion \ik-ˈspresh-ən\ *n* **1** : UTTERANCE **2** : something that represents or symbolizes : SIGN; *esp* : a mathematical symbol or combination of signs and symbols representing a quantity or operation **3** : a significant word or phrase; *also* : manner of expressing (as in writing or music) **4** : facial aspect or vocal intonation indicative of feeling — **ex·pres·sion·less** *adj*

ex·pres·sion·ism \ik-ˈspresh-ə-ˌniz-əm\ *n* : a theory or practice in art of seeking to depict the artist's subjective responses to objects and events — **ex·pres·sion·ist** \-ˈspresh-(ə-)nəst\ *n or adj* — **ex·pres·sion·is·tic** \-ˌspresh-ə-ˈnis-tik\ *adj*

ex·pres·sive \ik-ˈspres-iv\ *adj* **1** : of or relating to expression **2** : serving to express — **ex·pres·sive·ly** *adv* — **ex·pres·sive·ness** *n*

ex·press·way \ik-ˈspres-ˌwā\ *n* : a divided superhighway with limited access

ex·pro·pri·ate \ek-ˈsprō-prē-ˌāt\ *vb* **-at·ed; -at·ing** : to deprive of possession or the right to own — **ex·pro·pri·a·tion** \(ˌ)ek-ˌsprō-prē-ˈā-shən\ *n*

expt *abbr* experiment

ex·pul·sion \ik-ˈspəl-shən\ *n* : an expelling or being expelled : EJECTION

ex·punge \ik-ˈspənj\ *vb* **ex·punged; ex·pung·ing** [L *expungere* to mark for deletion by dots, fr. *ex-* out + *pungere* to prick] : OBLITERATE, ERASE

ex·pur·gate \ˈek-spər-ˌgāt\ *vb* **-gat·ed; -gat·ing** : to clear (as a book) of objectionable passages — **ex·pur·ga·tion** \ˌek-spər-ˈgā-shən\ *n*

ex·qui·site \ek-ˈskwiz-ət, ˈek-(ˌ)skwiz-\ *adj* [ME *exquisit,* fr. L *exquisitus,* fr. pp. of *exquirere* to search out, fr. *quaerere* to seek] **1** : excellent in form or workmanship **2** : keenly appreciative **3** : pleasingly beautiful or delicate **4** : INTENSE

ext *abbr* **1** extension **2** exterior **3** external **4** extra **5** extract

ex·tant \ˈek-stənt; ek-ˈstant\ *adj* : EXISTENT; *esp* : not lost or destroyed

ex·tem·po·ra·ne·ous \ek-ˌstem-pə-ˈrā-nē-əs\ *adj* : not planned beforehand : IMPROMPTU — **ex·tem·po·ra·ne·ous·ly** *adv*

ex·tem·po·rary \ik-ˈstem-pə-ˌrer-ē\ *adj* : EXTEMPORANEOUS

ex·tem·po·re \ik-ˈstem-pə-(ˌ)rē\ *adv* : EXTEMPORANEOUSLY

ex·tem·po·rize \ik-ˈstem-pə-ˌrīz\ *vb*

-rized; -riz·ing : to do something extemporaneously

ex·tend \ik-ˈstend\ *vb* **1** : to spread or stretch forth or out (as in reaching or straightening) **2** : to exert or cause to exert to full capacity **3** : PROFFER ⟨∼ credit⟩ **4** : PROLONG ⟨∼ a note⟩ **5** : to make greater or broader ⟨∼ knowledge⟩ ⟨∼ a business⟩ **6** : to stretch out or reach across a distance, space, or time **syn** lengthen, elongate, protract — **ex·tend·able** *or* **ex·tend·ible** \-ˈsten-də-bəl\ *adj*

ex·ten·sion \ik-ˈsten-chən\ *n* **1** : an extending or being extended **2** : educational programs (as correspondence courses) that reach beyond the campus of a school **3** : an additional part ⟨∼ on a house⟩

ex·ten·sive \ik-ˈsten-siv\ *adj* : of considerable extent : FAR-REACHING, BROAD — **ex·ten·sive·ly** *adv*

ex·tent \ik-ˈstent\ *n* **1** : the size, length, or bulk of something ⟨a property of large ∼⟩ **2** : the degree or measure of something ⟨the ∼ of his guilt⟩

ex·ten·u·ate \ik-ˈsten-yə-ˌwāt\ *vb* **-at·ed; -at·ing** : to lessen the seriousness of — **ex·ten·u·a·tion** \-ˌsten-yə-ˈwā-shən\ *n*

¹ex·te·ri·or \ek-ˈstir-ē-ər\ *adj* **1** : EXTERNAL **2** : suitable for use on an outside surface ⟨∼ paint⟩

²exterior *n* : an exterior part or surface

ex·ter·mi·nate \ik-ˈstər-mə-ˌnāt\ *vb* **-nat·ed; -nat·ing** : to get rid of completely **syn** extirpate, eradicate, abolish, annihilate — **ex·ter·mi·na·tion** \-ˈstər-mə-ˈnā-shən\ *n*

ex·ter·mi·na·tor \ik-ˈstər-mə-ˌnāt-ər\ *n* : one that exterminates; *esp* : a person whose occupation is destroying household vermin with chemicals

¹ex·ter·nal \ek-ˈstərn-ᵊl\ *adj* **1** : outwardly perceivable; *also* : SUPERFICIAL **2** : of, relating to, or located on the outside or an outer part **3** : arising or acting from without; *also* : FOREIGN ⟨∼ affairs⟩ — **ex·ter·nal·ly** \-ē\ *adv*

²external *n* : an external feature

ex·tinct \ik-ˈstiŋkt\ *adj* **1** : EXTINGUISHED ⟨with hope ∼⟩; *also* : no longer active (as a volcano) **2** : no longer existing (as a kind of plant or animal) or in use (as a language) — **ex·tinc·tion** \ik-ˈstiŋk-shən\ *n*

ex·tin·guish \ik-ˈstiŋ-gwish\ *vb* : to put out (as a fire); *also* : to bring to an end (as by destroying) — **ex·tin·guish·able** *adj* — **ex·tin·guish·er** *n*

ex·tir·pate \ˈek-stər-ˌpāt\ *vb* **-pat·ed; -pat·ing** [L *exstirpatus,* pp. *exstirpare,* fr. *ex-* out + *stirps* trunk, root] **1** : UPROOT **2** : to destroy completely **syn** exterminate, eradicate, abolish, annihilate — **ex·tir·pa·tion** \ˌek-stər-ˈpā-shən\ *n*

ex·tol *also* ex·toll \ik-ˈstōl\ *vb* **ex·tolled; ex·tol·ling** : to praise highly : GLORIFY **syn** laud, eulogize

ex·tort \ik-ˈstȯrt\ *vb* [L *extortus,* pp. of *extorquēre* to wrench out, extort, fr. *ex-* out + *torquēre* to twist] : to obtain by force or improper pressure ⟨∼ a bribe⟩ — **ex·tor·tion** \-ˈstȯr-shən\ *n* — **ex·tor·tion·er** *n* — **ex·tor·tion·ist** *n*

ex·tor·tion·ate \ik-ˈstȯr-sh(ə-)nət\ *adj* : EXCESSIVE, EXORBITANT — **ex·tor·tion·ate·ly** *adv*

¹ex·tra \ˈek-strə\ *adj* **1** : ADDITIONAL **2** : SUPERIOR **syn** spare, surplus, superfluous

²extra *n* **1** : something (as a charge) added **2** : a special edition of a newspaper **3** : an additional worker or performer (as in a group scene)

³extra *adv* : beyond what is usual

¹ex·tract \ik-ˈstrakt, *esp for 3* ˈek-ˌstrakt\ *vb* **1** : to draw out; *esp* : to pull out forcibly ⟨∼ a tooth⟩ **2** : to withdraw (as a juice or a constituent) by a physical or chemical process **3** : to select for citation : QUOTE — **ex·tract·able** *adj* — **ex·trac·tion** \-ˈstrak-shən\ *n* — **ex·trac·tor** \-tər\ *n*

²ex·tract \ˈek-ˌstrakt\ *n* **1** : EXCERPT, CITATION **2** : a product (as a juice or concentrate) obtained by extracting

ex·tra·cur·ric·u·lar \ˌek-strə-kə-ˈrik-yə-lər\ *adj* : lying outside the regular curriculum; *esp* : of or relating to school-connected activities (as sports) carrying no academic credit

ex·tra·dite \ˈek-strə-ˌdīt\ *vb* **-dit·ed; -dit·ing** : to obtain by or deliver up to extradition

ex·tra·di·tion \ˌek-strə-ˈdish-ən\ *n* : surrendering an alleged criminal to a different jurisdiction for trial

ex·tra·mar·i·tal \ˌek-strə-ˈmar-ət-ᵊl\ *adj* : of or relating to sexual intercourse by a married person with someone other than his or her spouse

ex·tra·mu·ral \-ˈmyur-əl\ *adj* : existing or functioning beyond the bounds of an organized unit

ex·tra·ne·ous \ek-ˈstrā-nē-əs\ *adj* 1 : coming from without ⟨∼ moisture⟩ 2 : not intrinsic ⟨∼ incidents in a story⟩; *also* : IRRELEVANT ⟨∼ digressions⟩ — **ex·tra·ne·ous·ly** *adv*

ex·traor·di·nary \ik-ˈstrȯrd-ᵊn-ˌer-ē, ˌek-strə-ˈȯrd-\ *adj* 1 : notably unusual or exceptional 2 : employed on special service — **ex·traor·di·nari·ly** \ik-ˌstrȯrd-ᵊn-ˈer-ə-lē, ˌek-strə-ˌȯrd-\ *adv*

ex·trap·o·late \ik-ˈstrap-ə-ˌlāt\ *vb* **-lat·ed; -lat·ing** : to infer (unknown data) from known data — **ex·trap·o·la·tion** \-ˌstrap-ə-ˈlā-shən\ *n*

ex·tra·sen·so·ry \ˌek-strə-ˈsens-(ə-)rē\ *adj* : not acting or occurring through the known senses ⟨∼ perception⟩

ex·tra·ter·res·tri·al \-tə-ˈres-trē-əl\ *adj* : originating or existing outside the earth or its atmosphere ⟨∼ life⟩ — **extraterrestrial** *n*

ex·tra·ter·ri·to·ri·al \-ˌter-ə-ˈtōr-ē-əl\ *adj* : existing or taking place outside the territorial limits of a jurisdiction

ex·tra·ter·ri·to·ri·al·i·ty \-ˌtōr-ē-ˈal-ət-ē\ *n* : exemption from the application or jurisdiction of local law or tribunals ⟨diplomats enjoy ∼⟩

ex·trav·a·gant \ik-ˈstrav-i-gənt\ *adj* 1 : EXCESSIVE ⟨∼ claims⟩ 2 : unduly lavish : WASTEFUL 3 : too costly **syn** immoderate, exorbitant, extreme, inordinate, undue — **ex·trav·a·gance** \-gəns\ *n* — **ex·trav·a·gant·ly** *adv*

ex·trav·a·gan·za \ik-ˌstrav-ə-ˈgan-zə\ *n* 1 : a literary or musical work marked by extreme freedom of style and structure 2 : a spectacular show

ex·tra·ve·hic·u·lar \ˌek-strə-vē-ˈhik-yə-lər\ *adj* : taking place outside a vehicle (as a spacecraft) ⟨∼ activity⟩

¹**ex·treme** \ik-ˈstrēm\ *adj* 1 : very great or intense ⟨∼ cold⟩ 2 : very severe or drastic ⟨∼ measures⟩ 3 : going to great lengths or beyond normal limits ⟨politically ∼⟩ 4 : most remote ⟨the ∼ end⟩ 5 : UTMOST; *also* : MAXIMUM ⟨an ∼ effort⟩ — **ex·treme·ly** *adv*

²**extreme** *n* 1 : something located at one end or the other of a range or series 2 : EXTREMITY 4

extremely high frequency *n* : a radio frequency in the highest range of the radio frequency spectrum

ex·trem·ism \ik-ˈstrē-ˌmiz-əm\ *n* : the quality or state of being extreme; *esp* : advocacy of extreme political measures : RADICALISM — **ex·trem·ist** \-məst\ *n or adj*

ex·trem·i·ty \ik-ˈstrem-ət-ē\ *n, pl* **-ties** 1 : the most remote part or point 2 : a limb of the body; *esp* : a human hand or foot 3 : the greatest need or danger 4 : the utmost degree; *also* : a drastic or desperate measure

ex·tri·cate \ˈek-strə-ˌkāt\ *vb* **-cat·ed; -cat·ing** [L *extricatus*, pp. of *extricare*, fr. *ex-* out + *tricae* trifles, perplexities] : to free from an entanglement or difficulty **syn** disentangle, untangle, disencumber — **ex·tri·ca·ble** \ik-ˈstrik-ə-bəl, ek-; ˈek-(ˌ)strik-\ *adj* — **ex·tri·ca·tion** \ˌek-strə-ˈkā-shən\ *n*

ex·trin·sic \ek-ˈstrin-zik, -sik\ *adj* 1 : not forming part of or belonging to a thing 2 : EXTERNAL — **ex·trin·si·cal·ly** \-zi-k(ə-)lē, -si-\ *adv*

ex·tro·vert *or* **ex·tra·vert** \ˈek-strə-ˌvərt\ *n* : a person who is interested only or mostly in things outside the self — **ex·tro·ver·sion** *or* **ex·tra·ver·sion** \ˌek-strə-ˈvər-zhən\ *n* — **ex·tro·vert·ed** *or* **ex·tra·vert·ed** *adj*

ex·trude \ik-ˈstrüd\ *vb* **ex·trud·ed; ex·trud·ing** 1 : to force, press, or push out 2 : to shape (as plastic) by forcing through a die — **ex·tru·sion** \-ˈstrü-zhən\ *n* — **ex·trud·er** *n*

ex·tru·sive \ik-ˈstrü-siv\ *adj* : relating to or formed by geological extrusion from the earth in a molten state or as volcanic ash

ex·u·ber·ant \ig-ˈzü-b(ə-)rənt\ *adj* 1 : joyously unrestrained 2 : PROFUSE — **ex·u·ber·ance** \-b(ə-)rəns\ *n* — **ex·u·ber·ant·ly** *adv*

ex·ude \ig-ˈzüd\ *vb* **ex·ud·ed; ex·ud·ing** [L *exsudare*, fr. *ex-* out + *sudare* to sweat] 1 : to discharge slowly through pores or cuts : OOZE 2 : to give off or out conspicuously or abundantly ⟨∼s charm⟩ — **ex·u·date** \ˈek-s(y)ù-ˌdāt\ *n* — **ex·u·da·tion** \ˌek-s(y)ù-ˈdā-shən\ *n*

ex·ult \ig-ˈzəlt\ *vb* : to rejoice in triumph : GLORY — **ex·ul·tant** \-ˈzəlt-ᵊnt\ *adj* — **ex·ul·tant·ly** *adv* — **ex·ul·ta·tion** \ˌek-(ˌ)səl-ˈtā-shən, ˌeg-(ˌ)zəl-\ *n*

ex·urb \'ek-ˌsərb, 'eg-ˌzərb\ *n* : a region outside a city and its suburbs inhabited chiefly by well-to-do families — **ex·ur·bia** \ek-'sər-bē-ə, eg-'zer-\ *n*

ex·ur·ban·ite \ek-'sər-bə-ˌnīt; eg-'zər-\ *n* : one who lives in an exurb

-ey — see -Y

¹eye \'ī\ *n* **1** : an organ of sight typically consisting of a globular structure in a socket of the skull with thin movable covers bordered with hairs **2** : VISION, PERCEPTION; *also* : faculty of discrimination ⟨a good ∼ for bargains⟩ **3** : POINT OF VIEW, JUDGMENT — often used in pl. ⟨an offender in the ∼s of the law⟩ **4** : something suggesting an eye ⟨the ∼ of a needle⟩; *esp* : an undeveloped bud (as on a potato) — **eyed** \'īd\ *adj*

²eye *vb* **eyed; eye·ing** *or* **ey·ing** : to look at : WATCH

eye·ball \'ī-ˌbȯl\ *n* : the globular capsule of the vertebrate eye

eye·brow \'ī-ˌbraů\ *n* : the bony arch forming the upper edge of the eye socket; *also* : the hair growing on this

eye·drop·per \'ī-ˌdräp-ər\ *n* : DROPPER 2

eye·glass \'ī-ˌglas\ *n* **1** : a lens variously mounted for personal use as an aid to vision **2** *pl* : GLASSES, SPECTACLES

eye·lash \'ī-ˌlash\ *n* **1** : the fringe of hair edging the eyelid — usu. used in pl. **2** : a single hair of the eyelashes

eye·let \'ī-lət\ *n* **1** : a small reinforced hole in material intended for ornament or for passage of something (as a cord or lace) **2** : a typically metal ring for reinforcing an eyelet : GROMMET

eye·lid \'ī-ˌlid\ *n* : either of the movable lids of skin and muscle that can be closed over the eyeball

eye·lin·er \'ī-ˌlī-nər\ *n* : makeup used to emphasize the contour of the eyes

eye–open·er \'ī-ˌōp(-ə)-nər\ *n* : something startling or surprising — **eye–open·ing** \-niŋ\ *adj*

eye·piece \'ī-ˌpēs\ *n* : the lens or combination of lenses at the eye end of an optical instrument

eye shadow *n* : a colored cosmetic applied to the eyelids to accent the eyes

eye·sight \'ī-ˌsīt\ *n* : SIGHT, VISION

eye·sore \'ī-ˌsōr\ *n* : something offensive to view

eye·strain \'ī-ˌstrān\ *n* : weariness or a strained state of the eye

eye·tooth \'ī-'tüth\ *n* : a canine tooth of the upper jaw

eye·wash \'ī-ˌwȯsh, -ˌwäsh\ *n* **1** : an eye lotion **2** : misleading or deceptive statements, actions, or procedures

eye·wit·ness \'ī-'wit-nəs\ *n* : a person who actually sees something happen

ey·rie \'ī(ə)r-ē, *or like* AERIE\ var of AERIE

ey·rir \'ā-ˌriər\ *n, pl* **au·rar** \'aů-ˌrär\ — see *krona* at MONEY table

Ez *or* **Ezr** *abbr* Ezra

Ezech *abbr* Ezechiel

Eze·chiel \i-'zē-kyəl\ *n* — see BIBLE table

Ezek *abbr* Ezekiel

Eze·kiel \i-'zē-kyəl\ *n* — see BIBLE table

Ez·ra \'ez-rə\ *n* — see BIBLE table

F

¹f \'ef\ *n, pl* **f's** *or* **fs** \'efs\ *often cap* **1** : the 6th letter of the English alphabet **2** : a grade rating a student's work as failing

²f *abbr, often cap* **1** Fahrenheit **2** false **3** family **4** farad **5** female **6** feminine **7** forte **8** French **9** frequency

³f *symbol* **1** focal length **2** the relative aperture of a photographic lens — often written *f/* **3** function

F *symbol* fluorine

FAA *abbr* Federal Aviation Agency

Fa·bi·an \'fā-bē-ən\ *adj* : of, relating to, or being a society of socialists organized in England in 1884 to spread socialist principles gradually — **Fabian** *n* — **Fa·bi·an·ism** *n*

fa·ble \'fā-bəl\ *n* **1** : a legendary story of supernatural happenings **2** : a narration intended to teach a lesson; *esp* : one in which animals speak and act like people **3** : FALSEHOOD

fa·bled \'fā-bəld\ *adj* **1** : FICTITIOUS **2** : told or celebrated in fable

fab·ric \'fab-rik\ *n* [MF *fabrique*, fr. L *fabrica* workshop, structure] **1**

: STRUCTURE, FRAMEWORK ⟨the ~ of society⟩ 2 : CLOTH; *also* : a material that resembles cloth

fab•ri•cate \\'fab-ri-ˌkāt\ *vb* **-cat•ed; -cat•ing 1** : CONSTRUCT, MANUFACTURE **2** : INVENT, CREATE **3** : to make up for the sake of deception — **fab•ri•ca•tion** \\ˌfab-ri-'kā-shən\ *n*

fab•u•lous \\'fab-yə-ləs\ *adj* **1** : resembling a fable : LEGENDARY **2** : told in or based on fable **3** : INCREDIBLE, MARVELOUS — **fab•u•lous•ly** *adv*

fac *abbr* **1** facsimile **2** faculty

fa•cade *also* **fa•çade** \fə-'säd\ *n* [F *façade*, fr. It *facciata*, fr. *faccia* face] **1** : the principal face or front of a building **2** : a false, superficial, or artificial appearance ⟨a ~ of composure⟩

¹face \\'fās\ *n* **1** : the front part of the head **2** : PRESENCE ⟨in the ~ of danger⟩ **3** : facial expression : LOOK ⟨put a sad ~ on⟩ **4** : GRIMACE ⟨made a ~⟩ **5** : outward appearance ⟨looks easy on the ~ of it⟩ **6** : BOLDNESS **7** : DIGNITY, PRESTIGE ⟨afraid to lose ~⟩ **8** : the surface of something; *esp* : the front or principal surface — **faced** \\'fāst\ *adj* — **face•less** *adj* — **face•less•ness** *n*

²face *vb* **faced; fac•ing 1** : to confront brazenly **2** : to line near the edge esp. with a different material; *also* : to cover the front or surface of ⟨~ a building with marble⟩ **3** : to bring face to face ⟨*faced* him with proof⟩ **4** : to stand or sit with the face toward ⟨~ the sun⟩ **5** : to front on ⟨a house *facing* the park⟩ **6** : to oppose firmly ⟨*faced* up to his foe⟩ **7** : to turn the face or body in a specified direction

face•down \\'fās-'daún\ *adv* : with the face downward

face–lift•ing \-ˌlif-tiŋ\ *n* **1** : a plastic operation for removal of facial defects (as wrinkles or sagging) usu. associated with aging **2** : MODERNIZATION

face–off \\'fās-ˌȯf\ *n* **1** : a method of putting a puck in play in ice hockey by dropping it between two opposing players each of whom attempts to control it **2** : CONFRONTATION

fac•et \\'fas-ət\ *n* [F *facette*, dim. of *face*] **1** : one of the small plane surfaces of a cut gem **2** : ASPECT, PHASE

fa•ce•tious \fə-'sē-shəs\ *adj* **1** : FLIPPANT

2 : JOCULAR, JOCOSE — **fa•ce•tious•ly** *adv* — **fa•ce•tious•ness** *n*

¹fa•cial \\'fā-shəl\ *adj* : of or relating to the face

²facial *n* : a facial treatment

fac•ile \\'fas-əl\ *adj* **1** : easily accomplished, handled, or attained **2** : SUPERFICIAL **3** : readily manifested and often insincere ⟨~ prose⟩ **4** : READY, FLUENT ⟨a ~ writer⟩

fa•cil•i•tate \fə-'sil-ə-ˌtāt\ *vb* **-tat•ed; -tat•ing** : to make easier

fa•cil•i•ty \fə-'sil-ət-ē\ *n, pl* **-ties 1** : the quality of being easily performed **2** : ease in performance : APTITUDE **3** : PLIANCY **4** : something that makes easier an action, operation, or course of conduct **5** : something (as a hospital) built or installed for a particular purpose

fac•ing \\'fā-siŋ\ *n* **1** : a lining at the edge esp. of a garment **2** *pl* : the collar, cuffs, and trimmings of a uniform coat **3** : an ornamental or protective layer **4** : material for facing

fac•sim•i•le \fak-'sim-ə-lē\ *n* [L *fac simile* make similar] **1** : an exact copy **2** : the transmitting of printed matter or pictures by wire or radio for reproduction

fact \\'fakt\ *n* **1** : DEED; *esp* : CRIME ⟨accessory after the ~⟩ **2** : the quality of being actual **3** : something that exists or occurs : EVENT; *also* : a piece of information about such a fact

fac•tion \\'fak-shən\ *n* : a group or combination (as in a government) acting together within and usu. against a larger body : CLIQUE — **fac•tion•al•ism** \-sh(ə-)nə-ˌliz-əm\ *n*

fac•tious \\'fak-shəs\ *adj* **1** : of, relating to, or caused by faction **2** : inclined to faction or the formation of factions : causing dissension

fac•ti•tious \fak-'tish-əs\ *adj* : ARTIFICIAL, SHAM ⟨a ~ display of grief⟩

¹fac•tor \\'fak-tər\ *n* **1** : AGENT **2** : something that actively contributes to a result **3** : GENE **4** : any of the numbers or symbols in mathematics that when multiplied together form a product; *esp* : any of the integers that divide a given integer without a remainder

²factor *vb* **fac•tored; fac•tor•ing** \-t(ə-)riŋ\ **1** : to work as a factor **2** : to find the mathematical factors of and esp. the prime mathematical factors of

¹fac·to·ri·al \fak-'tōr-ē-əl\ *adj* : of, relating to, or being a factor

²factorial *n* : the product of all the positive integers from one to a given integer

fac·to·ry \'fak-t(ə-)rē\ *n, pl* **-ries 1** : a trading post where resident factors trade **2** : a building or group of buildings used for manufacturing

fac·to·tum \fak-'tōt-əm\ *n* [NL, lit., do everything, fr. L *fac* do + *totum* everything] : an employee with numerous varied duties

facts of life : the physiological processes and behavior involved in sex and reproduction

fac·tu·al \'fak-chə(-wə)l\ *adj* : of or relating to facts; *also* : based on fact — **fac·tu·al·ly** \-ē\ *adv*

fac·ul·ty \'fak-əl-tē\ *n, pl* **-ties 1** : ability to act or do : POWER; *also* : natural aptitude **2** : one of the powers of the mind or body ⟨the ～ of hearing⟩ **3** : the teachers in a school or college or one of its divisions

fad \'fad\ *n* : a practice or interest followed for a time with exaggerated zeal : CRAZE — **fad·dish** *adj* — **fad·dist** *n*

fade \'fād\ *vb* **fad·ed; fad·ing 1** : WITHER **2** : to lose or cause to lose freshness or brilliance of color **3** : VANISH **4** : to grow dim or faint

FADM *abbr* fleet admiral

fae·cal, fae·ces var of FECAL, FECES

fa·er·ie *also* **fa·ery** \'fā-rē, 'fa(ə)r-ē\ *n, pl* **fa·er·ies 1** : FAIRYLAND **2** : FAIRY

¹fag \'fag\ *vb* **fagged; fag·ging 1** : DRUDGE **2** : to act as a fag **3** : TIRE, EXHAUST

²fag *n* **1** : an English public-school boy who acts as servant to another **2** : MENIAL, DRUDGE

³fag *n* : CIGARETTE

fag end *n* **1** : the last part or coarser end of a web of cloth **2** : the untwisted end of a rope **3** : REMNANT **4** : the extreme end

fag·ot *or* **fag·got** \'fag-ət\ *n* : a bundle of sticks or twigs esp. as used for fuel

fag·ot·ing *or* **fag·got·ing** *n* : an embroidery produced by tying threads in hourglass-shaped clusters

Fah *or* **Fahr** *abbr* Fahrenheit

Fahr·en·heit \'far-ən-ˌhīt\ *adj* : relating to, conforming to, or having a ther-

mometer scale with the boiling point of water at 212 degrees and the freezing point at 32 degrees above zero

fa·ience *or* **fa·ïence** \fā-'äns\ *n* [F] : earthenware decorated with opaque colored glazes

¹fail \'fāl\ *vb* **1** : to become feeble; *esp* : to decline in health **2** : to die away **3** : to stop functioning **4** : to fall short ⟨～ed in his duty⟩ **5** : to be or become absent or inadequate **6** : to be unsuccessful **7** : to become bankrupt **8** : DISAPPOINT, DESERT **9** : NEGLECT

²fail *n* : FAILURE ⟨without ～⟩

¹fail·ing \'fā-liŋ\ *n* : WEAKNESS, SHORTCOMING

²failing *prep* : in the absence or lack of

faille \'fīl\ *n* : a somewhat shiny closely woven ribbed silk, rayon, or cotton fabric

fail–safe \'fāl-ˌsāf\ *adj* **1** : incorporating a counteractive feature for a possible source of failure **2** : having no chance of failure

fail·ure \'fāl-yər\ *n* **1** : a failing to do or perform **2** : a state of inability to perform a normal function adequately ⟨heart ～⟩ **3** : a fracturing under or yielding to stress **4** : a lack of success **5** : BANKRUPTCY **6** : DEFICIENCY **7** : DETERIORATION, BREAKDOWN **8** : one that has failed

¹fain \'fān\ *adj, archaic* **1** : GLAD **2** : INCLINED **3** : OBLIGED

²fain *adv, archaic* **1** : WILLINGLY **2** : RATHER

¹faint \'fānt\ *adj* [ME *faint, feint,* fr. OF, fr. *faindre, feindre* to feign, shirk] **1** : COWARDLY, SPIRITLESS **2** : weak, dizzy, and likely to faint **3** : lacking vigor or strength : FEEBLE ⟨～ praise⟩ **4** : INDISTINCT, DIM — **faint·ly** *adv* — **faint·ness** *n*

²faint *vb* : to lose consciousness

³faint *n* : the action of fainting; *also* : the resulting condition

faint·heart·ed \'fānt-'härt-əd\ *adj* : lacking courage : TIMID

¹fair \'faər\ *adj* **1** : attractive in appearance : BEAUTIFUL **2** : superficially pleasing : SPECIOUS **3** : CLEAN, PURE **4** : CLEAR, LEGIBLE **5** : not stormy or cloudy ⟨～ weather⟩ **6** : JUST **7** : conforming with the rules : ALLOWED; *also* : being within the foul lines ⟨～ ball⟩ **8** : open to legitimate pursuit or attack ⟨∼ game⟩ **9** : PROMISING, LIKELY ⟨a ∼ chance of winning⟩ **10** : favorable to a ship's course ⟨a ∼ wind⟩ **11** : light in coloring : BLOND **12** : ADEQUATE — **fair·ness** *n*

²fair *adv* : FAIRLY

³fair *n* **1** : a gathering of buyers and sellers at a stated time and place for trade **2** : a competitive exhibition (as of farm products) **3** : a sale of assorted articles usu. for a charitable purpose

fair·ground \-ₗgrau̇nd\ *n* : an area where outdoor fairs, circuses, or exhibitions are held

fair·ing \ˈfa(ə)r-iŋ\ *n* : a structure for producing a smooth outline and reducing drag (as on an airplane)

fair·ly \ˈfa(ə)r-lē\ *adv* **1** : HANDSOMELY, FAVORABLY ⟨∼ situated⟩ **2** : QUITE, COMPLETELY **3** : in a fair manner : JUSTLY **4** : MODERATELY, TOLERABLY ⟨a ∼ easy job⟩

fair–spo·ken \ˈfaər-ˈspō-kən\ *adj* : pleasant and courteous in speech

fair–trade \-ˈtrād\ *adj* : of, relating to, or being an agreement between a producer and a seller that branded merchandise will be sold at or above a specified price ⟨∼ items⟩ — **fair–trade** *vb*

fair·way \-ₗwā\ *n* : the mowed part of a golf course between tee and green

fairy \ˈfa(ə)r-ē\ *n, pl* **fai·ries** [ME *fairie* fairyland, fairy people, fr. OF *faerie*, fr. *feie, fee* fairy, fr. L *Fata*, goddess of fate, fr. *fatum* fate] : an imaginary being of folklore and romance usu. having diminutive human form and magic powers

fairy·land \-ₗland\ *n* **1** : the land of fairies **2** : a beautiful or charming place

fairy tale *n* **1** : a simple children's story about fairies **2** : FIB

fait ac·com·pli \ˈfät-ₗak-ₗōⁿ-ˈplē\ *n, pl* **faits accomplis** *same, or* -ˈplēz\ [F, accomplished fact] : a thing accomplished and presumably irreversible

faith \ˈfāth\ *n, pl* **faiths** \ˈfāths, ˈfāthz\ [deriv. of L *fides*] **1** : allegiance to duty or a person : LOYALTY **2** : belief and trust in God **3** : complete trust **4** : a system of religious beliefs — **faith·ful** \-fəl\ *adj* — **faith·ful·ly** \-ē\ *adv* — **faith·ful·ness** *n*

faith·less \ˈfāth-ləs\ *adj* **1** : DISLOYAL **2** : not to be relied on : UNTRUSTWORTHY

— **faith·less·ly** *adv* — **faith·less·ness** *n*

¹fake \ˈfāk\ *adj* : COUNTERFEIT, SHAM

²fake *vb* **faked; fak·ing** **1** : to treat so as to falsify **2** : COUNTERFEIT **3** : PRETEND, SIMULATE — **fak·er** *n*

³fake *n* **1** : IMITATION, FRAUD, COUNTERFEIT **2** : IMPOSTOR

fa·kir \fə-ˈkiər\ *n* [Ar *faqīr*, lit., poor man] **1** : a Muslim mendicant : DERVISH **2** : a wandering Hindu holy man who performs tricks

fal·chion \ˈfȯl-chən\ *n* : a broad-bladed slightly curved medieval sword

fal·con \ˈfal-kən, ˈfȯ(l)-\ *n* **1** : a hawk trained for use in falconry **2** : any of various swift long-winged dark-eyed hawks having a beak adapted to snapping the spine of prey

fal·con·ry \ˈfal-kən-rē, ˈfȯl-, ˈfō-\ *n* **1** : the art of training hawks to hunt in cooperation with a person **2** : the sport of hunting with hawks — **fal·con·er** \-ər\ *n*

¹fall \ˈfȯl\ *vb* **fell** \ˈfel\; **fall·en** \ˈfȯ-lən\; **fall·ing** **1** : to descend freely by the force of gravity **2** : to hang freely **3** : to come as if by descending ⟨darkness *fell*⟩ **4** : to become uttered **5** : to lower or become lowered : DROP ⟨her eyes *fell*⟩ **6** : to leave an erect position suddenly and involuntarily **7** : STUMBLE, STRAY **8** : to drop down wounded or dead : die in battle **9** : to become captured or defeated **10** : to suffer ruin or failure **11** : to commit an immoral act **12** : to move or extend in a downward direction **13** : SUBSIDE, ABATE **14** : to decline in quality, activity, quantity, or value **15** : to assume a look of shame or dejection ⟨her face *fell*⟩ **16** : to occur at a certain time **17** : to come by chance **18** : DEVOLVE **19** : to have the proper place or station ⟨the accent ∼s on the first syllable⟩ **20** : to come within the scope of something **21** : to pass from one condition to another ⟨*fell* ill⟩ **22** : to set about heartily or actively ⟨∼ to work⟩ — **fall flat** : to produce no response or result — **fall for** **1** : to fall in love with **2** : to become a victim of — **fall foul** **1** : to have a collision **2** : to have a quarrel : CLASH — **fall from grace** : BACKSLIDE — **fall into line** : to comply with a certain course of action — **fall over oneself** *or* **fall over backward** : to dis-

play excessive eagerness — **fall short**
1 : to be deficient **2** : to fail to attain

²**fall** *n* **1** : the act of falling **2** : a falling
out, off, or away : DROPPING **3** : AU-
TUMN **4** : a thing or quantity that falls
⟨a light ∼ of snow⟩ **5** : COLLAPSE,
DOWNFALL **6** : the surrender or capture of a besieged place **7** : departure
from virtue or goodness **8** : SLOPE **9**
: WATERFALL — usu. used in pl. **10** : a
decrease in size, quantity, degree, or
value ⟨a ∼ in price⟩ **11** : the distance
which something falls **12** : an act of
forcing a wrestler's shoulders to the
mat; *also* : a bout of wrestling

fal·la·cious \fə-'lā-shəs\ *adj* **1** : embodying a fallacy ⟨a ∼ argument⟩ **2**
: MISLEADING, DECEPTIVE

fal·la·cy \'fal-ə-sē\ *n, pl* **-cies 1** : a false
or mistaken idea **2** : an often plausible
argument using false or illogical reasoning

fall back \'fȯl-'bak\ *vb* : RETREAT, RE-
CEDE

fall guy *n* **1** : one that is easily duped **2**
: SCAPEGOAT

fal·li·ble \'fal-ə-bəl\ *adj* **1** : liable to be
erroneous **2** : capable of making a
mistake

fall·ing–out \ˌfȯ-liŋ-'aut\ *n, pl* **fallings–
out** *or* **falling–outs** : QUARREL

falling star *n* : METEOR

fal·lo·pi·an tube \fə-ˌlō-pē-ən-\ *n, often
cap F* : either of the pair of anatomical
tubes that carry the egg from the
ovary to the uterus

fall·out \'fȯl-ˌaut\ *n* **1** : the often radioactive particles that result from a nuclear explosion and descend through
the air **2** : an incidental result : BY≠
PRODUCT

fall out \(')fȯl-'aut\ *vb* : QUARREL

fal·low \'fal-ō\ *n* **1** : land for crops allowed to lie idle during the growing
season **2** : the tilling of land without
sowing it for a season — **fal·low** *vb* —
fallow *adj*

false \'fȯls\ *adj* **fals·er; fals·est 1** : not
genuine : ARTIFICIAL **2** : intentionally
untrue **3** : adjusted or made so as to
deceive ⟨∼ scales⟩ **4** : tending to mislead : DECEPTIVE ⟨∼ promises⟩ **5** : not
true ⟨∼ concepts⟩ **6** : not faithful or
loyal : TREACHEROUS **7** : not essential
or permanent ⟨∼ front⟩ **8** : inaccurate
in pitch **9** : based on mistaken ideas

— **false·ly** *adv* — **false·ness** *n* — **fal·si-
ty** \'fȯl-sət-ē\ *n*

false·hood \'fȯls-ˌhud\ *n* **1** : LIE **2** : absence of truth or accuracy **3** : the
practice of lying

fal·set·to \fȯl-'set-ō\ *n, pl* **-tos** [It, fr.
dim. of *falso* false] : an artificially
high voice; *esp* : an artificial singing
voice that overlaps and extends above
the range of the full voice esp. of a
tenor

fal·si·fy \'fȯl-sə-ˌfī\ *vb* **-fied; -fy·ing 1**
: to make false : change so as to de-
ceive **2** : LIE **3** : MISREPRESENT **4** : to
prove to be false — **fal·si·fi·ca·tion**
\ˌfȯl-sə-fə-'kā-shən\ *n*

fal·ter \'fȯl-tər\ *vb* **fal·tered; fal·ter·ing**
\-t(ə-)riŋ\ **1** : to move unsteadily
: STUMBLE, TOTTER **2** : to hesitate in
speech : STAMMER **3** : to hesitate in
purpose or action : WAVER, FLINCH —
fal·ter·ing·ly \-t(ə-)riŋ-lē\ *adv*

fam *abbr* **1** familiar **2** family

fame \'fām\ *n* : public reputation : RE-
NOWN — **famed** \'fāmd\ *adj*

fa·mil·ial \fə-'mil-yəl\ *adj* **1** : of, relating to, or characteristic of a family **2**
: tending to occur in more members of
a family than expected by chance
alone ⟨a ∼ disorder⟩

¹**fa·mil·iar** \fə-'mil-yər\ *n* **1** : COMPANION
2 : a spirit held to attend and serve or
guard a person **3** : one who frequents
a place

²**familiar** *adj* **1** : closely acquainted : IN-
TIMATE **2** : of or relating to a family **3**
: INFORMAL **4** : FORWARD, PRESUMPTU-
OUS **5** : frequently seen or experi-
enced **6** : of everyday occurrence —
fa·mil·iar·ly *adv*

fa·mil·iar·i·ty \fə-ˌmil-'yar-ət-ē, -ˌmil-ē-
'(y)ar-\ *n, pl* **-ties 1** : close friendship
: INTIMACY **2** : INFORMALITY **3** : an unduly bold or forward act or expression
: IMPROPRIETY **4** : close acquaintance
with something

fa·mil·iar·ize \fə-'mil-yə-ˌrīz\ *vb* **-ized;
-iz·ing 1** : to make known or familiar **2**
: to make thoroughly acquainted : AC-
CUSTOM

fam·i·ly \'fam-(ə-)lē\ *n, pl* **-lies** [ME
familie, fr. L *familia* household] **1** : a
group of persons of common ancestry
: CLAN **2** : a group of individuals living
under one roof and under one head
: HOUSEHOLD **3** : a group of things hav-

ing common characteristics; *esp* : a group of related plants or animals ranking in biological classification above a genus and below an order **4** : a social group composed of parents and their children

family planning *n* : planning intended to determine the number and spacing of one's children through effective methods of birth control

family tree *n* : GENEALOGY; *also* : a genealogical diagram

fam·ine \\'fam-ən\\ *n* **1** : an extreme scarcity of food **2** : a great shortage

fam·ish \\'fam-ish\\ *vb* **1** : STARVE **2** : to suffer for lack of something necessary

fa·mous \\'fā-məs\\ *adj* **1** : widely known **2** : honored for achievement **3** : EXCELLENT, FIRST-RATE **syn** renowned, celebrated, noted, notorious, distinguished, eminent, illustrious

fa·mous·ly *adv* : SPLENDIDLY, EXCELLENTLY

¹fan \\'fan\\ *n* : a device (as a hand-waved triangular piece or a mechanism with blades) for producing a current of air

²fan *vb* **fanned; fan·ning 1** : to drive away the chaff from grain by winnowing **2** : to move (air) with or as if with a fan **3** : to direct a current of air upon ⟨~ a fire⟩ **4** : to stir up to activity : STIMULATE **5** : to spread like a fan **6** : to strike out in baseball

³fan *n* : an enthusiastic follower or admirer

fa·nat·ic \\fə-'nat-ik\\ *or* **fa·nat·i·cal** \\-i-kəl\\ *adj* [L *fanaticus* inspired by a deity, frenzied, fr. *fanum* temple] : marked by excessive enthusiasm and often intense uncritical devotion — **fanatic** *n* — **fa·nat·i·cism** \\fə-'nat-ə-ˌsiz-əm\\ *n*

fan·ci·er \\'fan-sē-ər\\ *n* : a person who breeds or grows some kind of animal or plant for points of excellence

fan·ci·ful \\'fan-si-fəl\\ *adj* **1** : full of fancy : guided by fancy : WHIMSICAL **2** : coming from the fancy rather than from the reason **3** : curiously made or shaped — **fan·ci·ful·ly** \\-f(ə-)lē\\ *adv*

¹fan·cy \\'fan-sē\\ *n, pl* **fancies** [ME *fantasie, fantsy* fantasy, fancy, fr. MF *fantasie,* fr. L *phantasia,* fr. Gk, appearance, imagination] **1** : LIKING, INCLINATION; *also* : LOVE **2** : NOTION,

IDEA, WHIM ⟨a passing ~⟩ **3** : IMAGINATION **4** : TASTE, JUDGMENT

²fancy *vb* **fan·cied; fan·cy·ing 1** : LIKE **2** : IMAGINE **3** : to believe without evidence **4** : to believe without being certain

³fancy *adj* **fan·ci·er; -est 1** : WHIMSICAL **2** : not plain : ORNAMENTAL **3** : of particular excellence **4** : bred esp. for a showy appearance **5** : above the usual price or the real value : EXTRAVAGANT **6** : executed with technical skill and superior grace — **fan·ci·ly** \\'fan-sə-lē\\ *adv*

fancy dress *n* : a costume (as for a masquerade) chosen to suit a fancy

fan·cy–free \\'fan-sē-ˌfrē\\ *adj* : not centering the attention on any one person or thing; *esp* : not in love

fan·cy·work \\'fan-sē-ˌwərk\\ *n* : ornamental needlework (as embroidery)

fan·dan·go \\fan-'daŋ-gō\\ *n, pl* **-gos** : a lively Spanish or Spanish-American dance

fane \\'fān\\ *n* : TEMPLE

fan·fare \\'fan-ˌfaər\\ *n* **1** : a flourish of trumpets **2** : a showy display

fang \\'faŋ\\ *n* : a long sharp tooth; *esp* : a grooved or hollow tooth of a venomous snake

fan–jet \\'fan-ˌjet\\ *n* **1** : a jet engine having a fan in its forward end that draws in extra air whose compression and expulsion provide extra thrust **2** : an airplane powered by a fan-jet

fan·light \\'fan-ˌlīt\\ *n* : a semicircular window with radiating bars like the ribs of a fan set over a door or window

fan·tail \\'fan-ˌtāl\\ *n* **1** : a fan-shaped tail or end **2** : an overhang at the stern of a ship

fan·ta·sia \\fan-'tā-zhə, -z(h)ē-ə; ˌfant-ə-'zē-ə\\ *also* **fan·ta·sie** \\ˌfant-ə-'zē ˌfänt-\\ *n* : a musical composition free and fanciful in form

fan·ta·size \\'fant-ə-ˌsīz\\ *vb* **-sized; -siz·ing** : IMAGINE, DAYDREAM

fan·tas·tic \\fan-'tas-tik\\ *also* **fan·tas·ti·cal** \\-ti-kəl\\ *adj* **1** : IMAGINARY, UNREAL, UNREALISTIC **2** : conceived by unrestrained fancy : GROTESQUE **3** : exceedingly or unbelievably great **4** : ECCENTRIC — **fan·tas·ti·cal·ly** \\-ti-k(ə-)lē\\ *adv*

fan·ta·sy \\'fant-ə-sē\\ *n, pl* **-sies 1** : IMAGINATION, FANCY **2** : a product of the

imagination : ILLUSION **3** : FANTASIA —
fantasy *vb*

¹far \'fär\ *adv* **far·ther** \-thər\ *or* **fur·ther**
\'fər-\; **far·thest** *or* **fur·thest** \-thəst\ **1**
: at or to a considerable distance in
space or time ⟨∼ from home⟩ **2** : by a
broad interval : WIDELY, MUCH ⟨∼ bet-
ter⟩ **3** : to or at a definite distance,
point, or degree ⟨as ∼ as I know⟩ **4**
: to an advanced point or extent ⟨go ∼
in his field⟩ — **by far** : GREATLY — **far
and away** : DECIDEDLY — **so far** : until
now

²far *adj* **farther** *or* **further; farthest** *or*
furthest 1 : remote in space or time
: DISTANT **2** : DIFFERENT ⟨a ∼ cry from
former methods⟩ **3** : LONG ⟨a ∼ jour-
ney⟩ **4** : being the more distant of two
⟨on the ∼ side of the lake⟩

far·ad \'far-,ad, -əd\ *n* : a unit of
capacitance equal to the capacitance
of a capacitor having a potential difference of one volt between its plates
when it is charged with one coulomb
of electricity

far·away \,fär-ə-,wā\ *adj* **1** : DISTANT,
REMOTE **2** : DREAMY

farce \'färs\ *n* **1** : a broadly satirical
comedy with an improbable plot **2**
: the humor characteristic of farce or
pretense **3** : a ridiculous action, display, or pretense — **far·ci·cal** \'fär-si-
kəl\ *adj*

¹fare \'faər\ *vb* **fared; far·ing 1** : GO,
TRAVEL **2** : GET ALONG, SUCCEED **3**
: EAT, DINE

²fare *n* **1** : the price charged to transport
a person **2** : a person paying a fare
: PASSENGER **3** : range of food : DIET;
also : material provided for use, consumption, or enjoyment

¹fare·well \faər-'wel\ *vb imper* : get
along well — used interjectionally to
or by one departing

²farewell *n* **1** : a wish of well-being at
parting : GOOD-BYE **2** : LEAVE-TAKING

³fare·well \,faər-,wel\ *adj* : PARTING, FI-
NAL ⟨a ∼ concert⟩

far·fetched \'fär-'fecht\ *adj* : not easily
or naturally deduced or introduced
: IMPROBABLE

far–flung \-'fləŋ\ *adj* : widely spread or
distributed

fa·ri·na \fə-'rē-nə\ *n* [L, meal, flour] : a
fine meal (as of wheat) used in puddings or as a breakfast cereal

far·i·na·ceous \,far-ə-'nā-shəs\ *adj* **1**
: containing or rich in starch **2** : having a mealy texture or surface

¹farm \'färm\ *n* [ME *ferme* rent, lease,
fr. OF, lease, fr. *fermer* to fix, make a
contract, fr. L *firmare* to make firm,
fr. *firmus* firm] **1** : a tract of land used
for raising crops or livestock **2** : a mi-
nor-league subsidiary of a major=
league baseball team

²farm *vb* : to use (land) as a farm ⟨∼ed
200 acres⟩; *also* : to raise crops or
livestock esp. as a business — **farm·er**
n

farm·hand \'färm-,hand\ *n* : a farm laborer

farm·house \-,haus\ *n* : a dwelling on a
farm

farm·ing \'fär-miŋ\ *n* : the practice of
agriculture

farm·land \'färm-,land\ *n* : land used or
suitable for farming

farm out *vb* : to turn over (as a task) to
another

farm·stead \'färm-,sted\ *also* **farm-
stead·ing** \-iŋ\ *n* : the buildings and adjacent service areas of a farm

farm·yard \-,yärd\ *n* : space around or
enclosed by farm buildings

far–off \'fär-'òf\ *adj* : remote in time or
space : DISTANT

fa·rouche \fə-'rüsh\ *adj* [F] **1** : marked
by shyness and lack of polish **2** : WILD

far–out \'fär-'aut\ *adj* : very unconventional : EXTREME ⟨∼ clothes⟩

far·ra·go \fə-'räg-ō, -'rā-gō\ *n, pl* **-goes**
[L, mixed fodder] : a confused collec-
tion : MIXTURE

far–reach·ing \'fär-'rē-chiŋ\ *adj* : having a wide range or effect

far·ri·er \'far-ē-ər\ *n* : one that shoes
horses

¹far·row \'far-ō\ *vb* : to give birth to a
farrow

²farrow *n* : a litter of pigs

far·see·ing \'fär-'sē-iŋ\ *adj* : FARSIGHTED

far·sight·ed \'fär-'sīt-əd\ *adj* **1** : seeing
or able to see to a great distance **2**
: JUDICIOUS, WISE, SHREWD **3** : affected
with an eye condition in which the
image comes into focus behind the
retina — **far·sight·ed·ness** *n*

¹far·ther \'fär-thər\ *adv* **1** : at or to a
greater distance or more advanced
point **2** : more completely

²**farther** *adj* **1** : more distant **2** : ADDI-
TIONAL

far·ther·most \-ˌmōst\ *adj* : most distant

¹**far·thest** \ˈfär-thəst\ *adj* : most distant

²**farthest** *adv* **1** : to or at the greatest
distance : REMOTEST **2** : to the most
advanced point **3** : by the greatest degree or extent : MOST

far·thing \ˈfär-thiŋ\ *n* : a former British
monetary unit equal to ¼ of a penny;
also : a coin representing this unit

far·thin·gale \ˈfär-thən-ˌgāl, -thiŋ-\ *n*
[modif. of MF *verdugale*, fr. Sp *ver-*
dugado, fr. *verdugo* young shoot of a
tree, fr. *verde* green, fr. L *viridis*] : a
support (as of hoops) worn esp. in the
16th century to swell out a skirt

fas·ci·cle \ˈfas-i-kəl\ *n* **1** : a small bundle
or cluster (as of flowers or roots) **2**
: one of the divisions of a book published in parts — **fas·ci·cled** \-kəld\ *adj*

fas·ci·nate \ˈfas-ᵊn-ˌāt\ *vb* -nat·ed; -nat-
ing [L *fascinare*, fr. *fascinum* witch-
craft] **1** : to transfix and hold spellbound by an irresistible power **2**
: ALLURE **3** : to be irresistibly attractive — **fas·ci·na·tion** \ˌfas-ᵊn-ˈā-shən\
n

fas·cism \ˈfash-ˌiz-əm\ *n, often cap* : a
political philosophy, movement, or
regime that exalts nation and often
race and stands for a centralized autocratic government headed by a dic-
tatorial leader, severe economic and
social regimentation, and forcible
suppression of opposition — **fas·cist**
\-əst\ *n or adj, often cap* — **fas·cis·tic**
\fa-ˈshis-tik\ *adj, often cap*

¹**fash·ion** \ˈfash-ən\ *n* **1** : the make or
form of something **2** : MANNER, WAY **3**
: a prevailing custom, usage, or style
4 : the prevailing style (as in dress)
syn mode, vogue, rage, trend

²**fashion** *vb* **fash·ioned; fash·ion·ing**
\ˈfash-(ə-)niŋ\ **1** : MOLD, CONSTRUCT **2**
: FIT, ADAPT

fash·ion·able \ˈfash-(ə-)nə-bəl\ *adj* **1**
: dressing or behaving according to
fashion : STYLISH **2** : of or relating to
the world of fashion ⟨~ resorts⟩ —
fash·ion·ably \-blē\ *adv*

¹**fast** \ˈfast\ *adj* **1** : firmly fixed **2** : tightly shut **3** : adhering firmly **4** : STUCK **5**
: STAUNCH ⟨~ friends⟩ **6** : characterized by quick motion, operation, or

effect ⟨a ~ trip⟩ ⟨a ~ track⟩ **7** : indicating ahead of the correct time ⟨the
clock is ~⟩ **8** : not easily disturbed
: SOUND ⟨a ~ sleep⟩ **9** : permanently
dyed; *also* : being proof against fading
⟨colors ~ to sunlight⟩ **10** : DISSIPATED,
WILD **11** : sexually promiscuous **syn**
rapid, swift, fleet, quick, speedy,
hasty

²**fast** *adv* **1** : in a firm or fixed manner
⟨stuck ~ in the mud⟩ **2** : SOUNDLY,
DEEPLY ⟨~ asleep⟩ **3** : SWIFTLY **4**
: RECKLESSLY

³**fast** *vb* **1** : to abstain from food **2** : to
eat sparingly or abstain from some
foods

⁴**fast** *n* **1** : the act or practice of fasting **2**
: a time of fasting

fast·back \ˈfas(t)-ˌbak\ *n* : an automobile having a roof with a long slope to
the rear

fast·ball \ˈfas(t)-ˌból\ *n* : a baseball
pitch thrown at full speed

fas·ten \ˈfas-ᵊn\ *vb* **fas·tened; fas·ten·ing**
\ˈfas-(ᵊ-)niŋ\ **1** : to attach or join by or
as if by pinning, tying, or nailing **2** : to
make fast : fix securely **3** : to fix or
set steadily ⟨~ed his eyes on her⟩ **4**
: to become fixed or joined — **fas·ten-**
er \ˈfas-(ə-)nər\ *n*

fas·ten·ing \ˈfas-(ᵊ-)niŋ\ *n* : something
that fastens : FASTENER

fast–food \ˌfas(t)-ˈfüd\ *adj* : specializing in food that is prepared and
served quickly ⟨a ~ restaurant⟩

fas·tid·i·ous \fas-ˈtid-ē-əs\ *adj* **1** : overly difficult to please **2** : showing or
demanding excessive delicacy or care
— **fas·tid·i·ous·ly** *adv* — **fas·tid·i·ous-**
ness *n*

fast·ness \ˈfas(t)-nəs\ *n* **1** : the quality
or state of being fast **2** : a fortified or
secure place : STRONGHOLD

fast–talk \ˈfas(t)-ˈtók\ *vb* : to influence
by persuasive and usu. deceptive talk

¹**fat** \ˈfat\ *adj* **fat·ter; fat·test** **1** : FLESHY,
PLUMP **2** : OILY, GREASY **3** : well filled
out : BIG **4** : well stocked : ABUNDANT
5 : PROFITABLE — **fat·ness** *n*

²**fat** *n* **1** : animal tissue rich in greasy or
oily matter **2** : any of numerous ener-
gy-rich esters that occur naturally in
animal fats and in plants and are soluble in organic solvents (as ether) but
not in water **3** : the best or richest

portion ⟨lived on the ∼ of the land⟩ 4 : OBESITY 5 : excess matter

fa·tal \\'fāt-ᵊl\\ *adj* 1 : FATEFUL 2 : MORTAL, DEADLY, DISASTROUS — **fa·tal·ly** \\-ē\\ *adv*

fa·tal·ism \\-ˌiz-əm\\ *n* : the belief that events are determined by fate — **fa·tal·ist** \\-əst\\ *n* — **fa·tal·is·tic** \\ˌfāt-ᵊl-'is-tik\\ *adj*

fa·tal·i·ty \\fā-'tal-ət-ē, fə-\\ *n, pl* -ties 1 : DEADLINESS 2 : the quality or state of being destined for disaster 3 : FATE 4 : death resulting from a disaster or accident

fat·back \\'fat-ˌbak\\ *n* : a fatty strip from the back of the hog usu. cured by salting and drying

fat cat *n* 1 : a wealthy contributor to a political campaign 2 : a wealthy privileged person

fate \\'fāt\\ *n* [ME, fr. MF or L; fr. L *fatum*, lit., what has been spoken, fr. *fari* to speak] 1 : the cause beyond man's control that is held to determine events : DESTINY 2 : LOT, FORTUNE 3 : DISASTER; *esp* : DEATH 4 : END, OUTCOME 5 *cap, pl* : the three goddesses of classical mythology who determine the course of human life

fat·ed \\'fā-təd\\ *adj* : decreed, controlled, or marked by fate

fate·ful \\'fāt-fəl\\ *adj* 1 : OMINOUS, PROPHETIC 2 : IMPORTANT, DECISIVE 3 : DEADLY, DESTRUCTIVE 4 : determined by fate — **fate·ful·ly** \\-ē\\ *adv*

fath *abbr* fathom

fat·head \\'fat-ˌhed\\ *n* : a stupid person — **fat·head·ed** \\-'hed-əd\\ *adj*

fa·ther \\'fä<u>th</u>-ər\\ *n* 1 : a male parent 2 *cap* : God esp. as the first person of the Trinity 3 : FOREFATHER 4 : one deserving the respect and love given to a father 5 *often cap* : an early Christian writer accepted by the church as an authoritative witness to its teaching and practice 6 : ORIGINATOR ⟨the ∼ of modern radio⟩; *also* : SOURCE 7 : PRIEST — used esp. as a title 8 : one of the leading men ⟨city ∼s⟩ — **fa·ther·hood** \\-ˌhùd\\ *n* — **fa·ther·less** *adj* — **fa·ther·ly** *adj*

²**father** *vb* 1 : BEGET 2 : to be the founder, producer, or author of 3 : to treat or care for as a father

father–in–law \\'fä<u>th</u>-(ə-)rən-ˌlò\\ *n, pl*

fa·thers–in–law \\-ər-zən-\\ : the father of one's husband or wife

fa·ther·land \\'fä<u>th</u>-ər-ˌland\\ *n* 1 : one's native land 2 : the native land of one's ancestors

¹**fath·om** \\'fa<u>th</u>-əm\\ *n* [ME *fadme*, fr. OE *fæthm* outstretched arms, fathom] : a unit of length equal to 6 feet (about 1.8 meters) used esp. for measuring the depth of water

²**fathom** *vb* 1 : to measure by a sounding line 2 : PROBE 3 : to penetrate and come to understand — **fath·om·able** \\'fa<u>th</u>-ə-mə-bəl\\ *adj*

fath·om·less \\'fa<u>th</u>-əm-ləs\\ *adj* : incapable of being fathomed

¹**fa·tigue** \\fə-'tēg\\ *n* [F] 1 : manual or menial work performed by military personnel 2 *pl* : the uniform or work clothing worn on fatigue and in the field 3 : weariness from labor or use 4 : the tendency of a material to break under repeated stress

²**fatigue** *vb* **fa·tigued; fa·tigu·ing** : WEARY, TIRE

fat·ten \\'fat-ᵊn\\ *vb* : to make or grow fat

¹**fat·ty** \\'fat-ē\\ *adj* **fat·ti·er; -est** 1 : containing fat esp. in unusual amounts 2 : GREASY

²**fatty** *n, pl* **fatties** : a fat person

fatty acid *n* : any of numerous acids that contain only carbon, hydrogen, and oxygen and that occur naturally in fats and various oils

fa·tu·i·ty \\fə-'t(y)ü-ət-ē\\ *n, pl* -ities : FOOLISHNESS, STUPIDITY

fat·u·ous \\'fach-(ə-)wəs\\ *adj* : FOOLISH, INANE, SILLY — **fat·u·ous·ly** *adv*

fau·bourg \\fō-'bùr\\ *n* 1 : SUBURB; *esp* : a suburb of a French city 2 : a city quarter

fau·ces \\'fò-ˌsēz\\ *n pl* [L, throat] : the narrow passage located between the soft palate and the base of the tongue that joins the mouth to the pharynx

fau·cet \\'fòs-ət, 'fäs-\\ *n* : a fixture for drawing off a liquid (as from a pipe)

¹**fault** \\'fòlt\\ *n* 1 : a weakness in character : FAILING 2 : IMPERFECTION, IMPAIRMENT 3 : an error esp. in service in a net or racket game 4 : MISDEMEANOR; *also* : MISTAKE 5 : responsibility for something wrong 6 : a fracture in the earth's crust accompanied by a displacement of one side relative to the other — **fault·i·ly** \\'fòl-tə-lē\\ *adv* —

fault·less adj — **fault·less·ly** adv — **faulty** adj

²**fault** vb 1 : to commit a fault : ERR 2 : to fracture so as to produce a geologic fault 3 : to find a fault in

fault·find·er \'fȯlt-ˌfīn-dər\ n : a person who tends to find fault or complain — **fault·find·ing** \-diŋ\ n or adj

faun \'fȯn\ n : a Roman god of fields and herds represented as part goat and part man

fau·na \'fȯn-ə\ n, pl **faunas** also **fau·nae** \-ˌē, -ˌī\ [LL Fauna, sister of Faunus (the Roman god of animals)] : animals or animal life esp. of a region, period, or environment — **fau·nal** \-ᵊl\ adj

fau·vism \'fō-ˌviz-əm\ n, often cap : a movement in painting characterized by vivid colors, free treatment of form, and a vibrant and decorative effect — **fau·vist** \-vəst\ n, often cap

faux pas \'fō-ˌpä\ n, pl **faux pas** \-ˌpä(z)\ [F, lit., false step] : BLUNDER; esp : a social blunder

¹**fa·vor** \'fā-vər\ n 1 : friendly regard shown toward another esp. by a superior 2 : APPROVAL 3 : PARTIALITY 4 : POPULARITY 5 : gracious kindness; also : an act of such kindness 6 pl : effort in one's behalf : ATTENTION 7 : a token of love (as a ribbon) usu. worn conspicuously 8 : a small gift or decorative item given out at a party 9 : a special privilege 10 archaic : LETTER 11 : BEHALF, INTEREST

²**favor** vb **fa·vored**; **fa·vor·ing** \'fāv-(ə-)riŋ\ 1 : to regard or treat with favor 2 : OBLIGE 3 : ENDOW ⟨~ed by nature⟩ 4 : to treat gently or carefully : SPARE ⟨~ a lame leg⟩ 5 : PREFER 6 : SUPPORT, SUSTAIN 7 : FACILITATE ⟨darkness ~s attack⟩ 8 : RESEMBLE ⟨he ~s his father⟩

fa·vor·able \'fāv-(ə-)rə-bəl\ adj 1 : APPROVING 2 : HELPFUL, PROMISING, ADVANTAGEOUS ⟨~ weather⟩ — **fa·vor·ably** \-blē\ adv

fa·vor·ite \'fāv-(ə-)rət\ n 1 : a person or a thing that is favored above others 2 : a competitor regarded as most likely to win — **favorite** adj

favorite son n : a candidate supported by the delegates of his state at a presidential nominating convention

fa·vor·it·ism \'fāv-(ə-)rət-ˌiz-əm\ n : PARTIALITY, BIAS

fa·vour chiefly Brit var of FAVOR

¹**fawn** \'fȯn, 'fän\ n 1 : a young deer 2 : a variable color averaging a light grayish brown

²**fawn** vb 1 : to show affection ⟨a dog ~ing on its master⟩ 2 : to court favor by a cringing or flattering manner

fax \'faks\ n : FACSIMILE 2

fay \'fā\ n : FAIRY, ELF — **fay** adj

faze \'fāz\ vb **fazed**; **faz·ing** : to disturb the composure or courage of : DAUNT

FBI abbr Federal Bureau of Investigation

FCC abbr Federal Communications Commission

FD abbr fire department

FDA abbr Food and Drug Administration

FDIC abbr Federal Deposit Insurance Corporation

Fe symbol [L ferrum] iron

fe·al·ty \'fē(-ə)l-tē\ n, pl **-ties** : LOYALTY, ALLEGIANCE

¹**fear** \'fi(ə)r\ vb 1 : to have a reverent awe of ⟨~ God⟩ 2 : to be afraid of : have fear 3 : to be apprehensive

²**fear** n 1 : an unpleasant often strong emotion caused by expectation or awareness of danger; also : an instance of or a state marked by this emotion 2 : anxious concern : SOLICITUDE 3 : profound reverence esp. toward God **syn** dread, fright, alarm, panic, terror, trepidation

fear·ful \-fəl\ adj 1 : causing fear 2 : filled with fear 3 : showing or caused by fear 4 : extremely bad, intense, or large — **fear·ful·ly** \-ē\ adv

fear·less \-ləs\ adj : free from fear : BRAVE — **fear·less·ly** adv — **fear·less·ness** n

fear·some \-səm\ adj 1 : causing fear 2 : TIMID

fea·si·ble \'fē-zə-bəl\ adj 1 : capable of being done or carried out ⟨a ~ plan⟩ 2 : SUITABLE 3 : REASONABLE, LIKELY — **fea·si·bil·i·ty** \ˌfē-zə-'bil-ət-ē\ n — **fea·si·bly** \'fē-zə-blē\ adv

¹**feast** \'fēst\ n 1 : an elaborate meal : BANQUET 2 : FESTIVAL 1

²**feast** vb 1 : to take part in a feast; also : to give a feast for 2 : to enjoy some unusual pleasure or delight 3 : DELIGHT, GRATIFY

feat \'fēt\ n : DEED, EXPLOIT, ACHIEVE-

MENT; *esp* : an act notable for courage, skill, endurance, or ingenuity

¹**feath·er** \'feth̷-ər\ *n* 1 : one of the light horny outgrowths that form the external covering of the body of a bird 2 : PLUME 3 : PLUMAGE 4 : KIND, NATURE ⟨birds of a ∼⟩ 5 : ATTIRE, DRESS ⟨in full ∼⟩ 6 : CONDITION, MOOD ⟨in fine ∼⟩ — **feath·ered** \-ərd\ *adj* — **feath·er·less** *adj* — **feath·ery** *adj* — **a feather in one's cap** : a mark of distinction : HONOR

²**feather** *vb* 1 : to furnish with a feather ⟨∼ an arrow⟩ 2 : to cover, clothe, line, or adorn with feathers — **feather one's nest** : to provide for oneself esp. while in a position of trust

feath·er·bed·ding \'feth̷-ər-ˌbed-iŋ\ *n* : the requiring of an employer usu. under a union rule or safety statute to employ more workers than are needed

feath·er·edge \-ˌej\ *n* : a very thin sharp edge; *esp* : one that is easily broken or bent over

feath·er·weight \-ˌwāt\ *n* : one that is very light in weight; *esp* : a boxer weighing more than 118 but not over 126 pounds

¹**fea·ture** \'fē-chər\ *n* 1 : the shape or appearance of the face or its parts 2 : a part of the face : LINEAMENT 3 : a prominent part or characteristic 4 : a special attraction (as in a motion picture or newspaper) 5 : something offered to the public or advertised as particularly attractive — **fea·ture·less** *adj*

²**feature** *vb* 1 : to picture in the mind : IMAGINE 2 : to give special prominence to ⟨∼ a story in a newspaper⟩ 3 : to play an important part

feaze \'fēz, 'fāz\ var of FAZE

Feb *abbr* February

feb·ri·fuge \'feb-rə-ˌfyüj\ *n* : a medicine for relieving fever — **febrifuge** *adj*

fe·brile \'feb-rəl, -ˌrīl; 'fēb-\ *adj* : FEVERISH

Feb·ru·ary \'feb-(y)ə-ˌwer-ē, 'feb-rə-\ *n* [ME *Februarie*, fr. L *Februarius*, fr. *Februa*, pl., feast of purification] : the second month of the year having 28 and in leap years 29 days

fe·ces \'fē-ˌsēz\ *n pl* : bodily waste discharged from the intestine — **fe·cal** \-kəl\ *adj*

feck·less \'fek-ləs\ *adj* 1 : WEAK, INEFFECTIVE 2 : WORTHLESS, IRRESPONSIBLE

fe·cund \'fek-ənd, 'fēk-\ *adj* : FRUITFUL, PROLIFIC — **fe·cun·di·ty** \fi-'kən-dət-ē, fe-\ *n*

fe·cun·date \'fek-ən-ˌdāt, 'fē-kən-\ *vb* **-dat·ed; -dat·ing** 1 : to make fecund 2 : IMPREGNATE — **fe·cun·da·tion** \ˌfek-ən-'dā-shən, ˌfē-kən-\ *n*

fed *abbr* federal; federation

fed·er·al \'fed(-ə)-rəl\ *adj* 1 : formed by a compact between political units that surrender individual sovereignty to a central authority but retain certain limited powers 2 : of or constituting a form of government in which power is distributed between a central authority and constituent territorial units 3 : of or relating to the central government of a federation 4 *cap* : FEDERALIST 5 *often cap* : of, relating to, or loyal to the federal government or the Union armies of the U.S. in the American Civil War — **fed·er·al·ly** \-ē\ *adv*

Federal *n* : a supporter of the U.S. government in the Civil War; *esp* : a soldier in the federal armies

federal district *n* : a district (as the District of Columbia) set apart as the seat of the central government of a federation

fed·er·al·ism \'fed(-ə)-rə-ˌliz-əm\ *n* 1 *often cap* : the distribution of power in an organization (as a government) between a central authority and the constituent units 2 : support or advocacy of federalism 3 *cap* : the principles of the Federalists

fed·er·al·ist \-ləst\ *n* 1 : an advocate of federalism 2 *often cap* : an advocate of a federal union between the American colonies after the Revolution and of adoption of the U.S. Constitution 3 *cap* : a member of a major political party in the early years of the U.S. favoring a strong centralized national government — **federalist** *adj, often cap*

fed·er·al·ize \'fed(-ə)-rə-ˌlīz\ *vb* **-ized; -iz·ing** 1 : to unite in or under a federal system 2 : to bring under the jurisdiction of a federal government

fed·er·ate \'fed-ə-ˌrāt\ *vb* **-at·ed; -at·ing** : to join in a federation

fed·er·a·tion \ˌfed-ə-'rā-shən\ *n* 1 : the

act of federating; *esp* : the forming of a federal union **2** : a federal government **3** : a union of organizations

fedn *abbr* federation

fe·do·ra \fi-'dōr-ə\ *n* : a low soft felt hat with the crown creased lengthwise

fed up *adj* : satiated, tired, or disgusted beyond endurance

fee \'fē\ *n* **1** : an estate in land held from a feudal lord **2** : an inherited or heritable estate in land **3** : a fixed charge; *also* : a charge for a professional service **4** : TIP

fee·ble \'fē-bəl\ *adj* **fee·bler** \-b(ə-)lər\; **fee·blest** \-b(ə-)ləst\ [ME *feble*, fr. OF, fr. L *flebilis* lamentable, wretched, fr. *flēre* to weep] **1** : DECREPIT, FRAIL **2** : INEFFECTIVE, INADEQUATE ⟨a ∼ protest⟩ — **fee·ble·ness** *n* — **fee·bly** \-blē\ *adv*

fee·ble·mind·ed \ˌfē-bəl-'mīn-dəd\ *adj* : lacking normal intelligence — **fee·ble·mind·ed·ness** *n*

¹feed \'fēd\ *vb* **fed** \'fed\; **feed·ing 1** : to give food to; *also* : to give as food **2** : EAT 1; *also* : PREY **3** : to furnish what is necessary to the growth or function of — **feed·er** *n*

²feed *n* **1** : a usu. large meal **2** : food for livestock **3** : material supplied (as to a furnace) **4** : a mechanism for feeding material to a machine

feed·back \'fēd-ˌbak\ *n* **1** : the return to the input of a part of the output of a machine, system, or process **2** : response esp. to one in authority about an activity or policy

feed·lot \'fēd-ˌlät\ *n* : land on which cattle are fattened for market

feed·stuff \-ˌstəf\ *n* : ²FEED 2

¹feel \'fēl\ *vb* **felt** \'felt\; **feel·ing 1** : to perceive or examine through physical contact : TOUCH, HANDLE **2** : EXPERIENCE; *also* : to suffer from **3** : to ascertain by cautious trial ⟨∼ out public sentiment⟩ **4** : to be aware of **5** : to be conscious of an inward impression, state of mind, or physical condition **6** : BELIEVE, THINK **7** : to search for something with the fingers : GROPE **8** : to seem esp. to the touch **9** : to have sympathy or pity

²feel *n* **1** : the sense of touch **2** : SENSATION, FEELING **3** : the quality of a thing as imparted through touch

feel·er \'fē-lər\ *n* **1** : one that feels; *esp*

: a tactile organ (as on the head of an insect) **2** : a proposal or remark made to find out the views of other people

¹feel·ing \'fē-liŋ\ *n* **1** : the sense of touch; *also* : a sensation perceived by this **2** : a state of mind ⟨a ∼ of loneliness⟩ **3** *pl* : general emotional condition : SENSIBILITIES ⟨hurt their ∼s⟩ **4** : OPINION, BELIEF, SENTIMENT **5** : capacity to respond emotionally

²feeling *adj* **1** : SENSITIVE; *esp* : easily moved emotionally **2** : expressing emotion or sensitivity — **feel·ing·ly** *adv*

feet *pl of* FOOT

feign \'fān\ *vb* **1** : to give a false appearance of : SHAM ⟨∼ illness⟩ **2** : to assert as if true : PRETEND

feint \'fānt\ *n* : something feigned; *esp* : a mock blow or attack intended to distract attention from the real point of attack — **feint** *vb*

feld·spar \'fel(d)-ˌspär\ *n* : any of a group of crystalline minerals consisting of silicates of aluminum with either potassium, sodium, calcium, or barium

fe·lic·i·tate \fi-'lis-ə-ˌtāt\ *vb* **-tat·ed; -tat·ing** : CONGRATULATE — **fe·lic·i·ta·tion** \-ˌlis-ə-'tā-shən\ *n*

fe·lic·i·tous \fi-'lis-ət-əs\ *adj* **1** : suitably expressed ; APT **2** : PLEASANT, DELIGHTFUL — **fe·lic·i·tous·ly** *adv*

fe·lic·i·ty \fi-'lis-ət-ē\ *n, pl* **-ties 1** : the quality or state of being happy; *esp* : great happiness **2** : something that causes happiness **3** : a pleasing manner or quality esp. in art or language : APTNESS **4** : an apt expression

fe·line \'fē-ˌlīn\ *adj* [L *felinus*, fr. *felis* cat] **1** : of or relating to cats or their kin **2** : SLY, TREACHEROUS **3** : STEALTHY — **feline** *n*

¹fell \'fel\ *n* : SKIN, HIDE, PELT

²fell *vb* **1** : to cut, beat, or knock down ⟨∼ trees⟩; *also* : KILL **2** : to sew (a seam) by folding one raw edge under the other

³fell past of FALL

⁴fell *adj* : CRUEL, FIERCE; *also* : DEADLY

fel·lah \'fel-ə, fə-'lä\ *n, pl* **fel·la·hin** or **fel·la·heen** \ˌfel-ə-'hēn\ : a peasant or agricultural laborer in Arab countries (as Egypt or Syria)

fel·la·tio \fə-'lā-shē-ˌō\ *also* **fel·la·tion** \-'lā-shən\ *n* [deriv. of L *fellare* to suck] : oral stimulation of the penis

fel·low \'fel-ō\ n [ME felawe, fr. OE fēolaga, fr. ON fēlagi, fr. fēlag partnership, fr. fē cattle, money + lag act of laying] 1 : COMRADE, ASSOCIATE 2 : EQUAL, PEER 3 : one of a pair : MATE 4 : a member of an incorporated literary or scientific society 5 : MAN, BOY 6 : BOYFRIEND 7 : a person granted a stipend for advanced study

fel·low·man \,fel-ō-'man\ n : a kindred human being

fel·low·ship \'fel-ō-,ship\ n 1 : the condition of friendly relationship existing among persons : COMRADESHIP 2 : a community of interest or feeling 3 : a group with similar interests 4 : the position of a fellow (as of a university) 5 : the stipend granted a fellow

fellow traveler n : a person who sympathizes with and often furthers the ideals and program of an organized group (as the Communist party) without joining it or regularly participating in its activities

fel·on \'fel-ən\ n 1 : one who has committed a felony 2 : WHITLOW

fel·o·ny \'fel-ə-nē\ n, pl -nies : a serious crime punishable by a heavy sentence — **fe·lo·ni·ous** \fə-'lō-nē-əs\ adj

¹felt \'felt\ n 1 : a cloth made of wool and fur often mixed with natural or synthetic fibers 2 : a material resembling felt

²felt past and past part of FEEL

fem abbr 1 female 2 feminine

fe·male \'fē-,māl\ adj [ME, alter. of femel, deriv. of ML femella, fr. L, girl, dim. of femina woman] : of, relating to, or being the sex that bears young; also : PISTILLATE syn feminine, womanly, womanlike, womanish, effeminate — **female** n

¹fem·i·nine \'fem-ə-nən\ adj 1 : of the female sex; also : characteristic of or appropriate or peculiar to women 2 : of, relating to, or constituting the gender that includes most words or grammatical forms referring to females — **fem·i·nin·i·ty** \,fem-ə-'nin-ət-ē\ n

²feminine n : a noun, pronoun, adjective, or inflectional form or class of the feminine gender; also : the feminine gender

fem·i·nism \'fem-ə-,niz-əm\ n 1 : the theory of the political, economic, and social equality of the sexes 2 : organized activity on behalf of women's rights and interests — **fem·i·nist** \-nəst\ n or adj

femme fa·tale \,fem-fə-'tal\ n, pl **femmes fa·tales** \-'tal(z)\ [F, lit., disastrous woman] : a seductive woman : SIREN

fe·mur \'fē-mər\ n, pl **fe·murs** or **fem·o·ra** \'fem-(ə-)rə\ : the long bone of the thigh — **fem·o·ral** \'fem-(ə-)rəl\ adj

¹fen \'fen\ n : low swampy land

²fen \'fən\ n, pl **fen** — see yuan at MONEY table

¹fence \'fens\ n [ME fens, short for defens defense] 1 : a barrier (as of wood or wire) to prevent escape or entry or to mark a boundary 2 : a person who receives stolen goods; also : a place where stolen goods are disposed of — **on the fence** : in a position of neutrality or indecision

²fence vb **fenced; fenc·ing** 1 : to enclose with a fence 2 : to keep in or out with a fence 3 : to practice fencing 4 : to use tactics of attack and defense esp. in debate — **fenc·er** n

fenc·ing \'fen-siŋ\ n 1 : the art or practice of attack and defense with the foil, épée, or saber 2 : the fences of a property or region 3 : material used for building fences

fend \'fend\ vb 1 : to keep or ward off : REPEL 2 : SHIFT ⟨~ for himself⟩

fend·er \'fen-dər\ n : a protective device (as a guard over the wheel of an automobile or as a screen before a fire)

fen·es·tra·tion \,fen-ə-'strā-shən\ n : the arrangement and design of windows and doors in a building

Fe·ni·an \'fē-nē-ən\ n : a member of a secret 19th century Irish and Irish–American organization dedicated to the overthrow of British rule in Ireland

fen·nel \'fen-ᵊl\ n : a garden plant related to the carrot and grown for its aromatic foliage and seeds

FEPC abbr Fair Employment Practices Commission

fe·ral \'fir-əl, 'fer-\ adj 1 : SAVAGE 2 : WILD 1 3 : having escaped from domestication and become wild

fer–de–lance \'ferd-ᵊl-'ans\ n, pl **fer–de–**

lance [F, lit., lance iron, spearhead] : a large venomous pit viper of Central and So. America

¹**fer·ment** \fər-'ment\ vb **1** : to cause or undergo fermentation **2** : to be or cause to be in a state of agitation or intense activity

²**fer·ment** \'fər-ˌment\ n **1** : a living organism (as a yeast) causing fermentation by its enzymes; also : ENZYME **2** : AGITATION, TUMULT

fer·men·ta·tion \ˌfər-mən-'tā-shən, -ˌmen-\ n **1** : chemical decomposition of an organic substance (as in the souring of milk or the formation of alcohol from sugar) in the absence of oxygen by enzymatic action often with formation of gas **2** : AGITATION, UNREST

fer·mi·um \'fer-mē-əm, 'fər-\ n : an artificially produced radioactive metallic chemical element

fern \'fərn\ n : any of an order of vascular plants resembling seed plants in having root, stem, and leaflike fronds but reproducing by spores instead of by flowers and seeds

fern·ery \'fərn-(ə-)rē\ n, pl **-er·ies** **1** : a place for growing ferns **2** : a collection of growing ferns

fe·ro·cious \fə-'rō-shəs\ adj **1** : FIERCE, SAVAGE **2** : extremely intense ⟨~ heat⟩ — **fe·ro·cious·ly** adv — **fe·ro·cious·ness** n

fe·roc·i·ty \fə-'räs-ət-ē\ n : the quality or state of being ferocious

¹**fer·ret** \'fer-ət\ n : a partially domesticated usu. white European mammal related to the weasels and used esp. for hunting rodents

²**ferret** vb **1** : to hunt game with ferrets **2** : to drive out of a hiding place **3** : to find and bring to light by searching ⟨~ out the truth⟩

fer·ric \'fer-ik\ adj : of, relating to, or containing iron

ferric oxide n : an oxide of iron that is found in nature as hematite and as rust and that is used as a pigment and for polishing

Fer·ris wheel \'fer-əs-\ n : an amusement device consisting of a large upright power-driven wheel carrying seats that remain horizontal around its rim

fer·ro·mag·net·ic \ˌfer-ō-mag-'net-ik\ adj : of or relating to substances that are easily magnetized

fer·rous \'fer-əs\ adj : of, relating to, or containing iron

fer·rule \'fer-əl\ n : a metal ring or cap around a slender wooden shaft to prevent splitting

¹**fer·ry** \'fer-ē\ vb **fer·ried; fer·ry·ing** [ME ferien, fr. OE ferian to carry, convey] **1** : to carry by boat over a body of water **2** : to cross by a ferry **3** : to convey from one place to another

²**ferry** n, pl **ferries** **1** : a place where persons or things are ferried **2** : FERRYBOAT

fer·ry·boat \'fer-ē-ˌbōt\ n : a boat used in ferrying

fer·tile \'fərt-ᵊl\ adj **1** : producing plentifully : PRODUCTIVE ⟨~ soils⟩ **2** : capable of developing or reproducing ⟨~ eggs⟩ ⟨a ~ family⟩ **syn** fruitful, prolific, fecund, productive — **fer·til·i·ty** \(ˌ)fər-'til-ət-ē\ n

fer·til·ize \'fərt-ᵊl-ˌīz\ vb **-ized; -iz·ing** **1** : to unite with in the process of fertilization ⟨one sperm ~s each egg⟩ **2** : to apply fertilizer to — **fer·til·iza·tion** \ˌfərt-ᵊl-ə-'zā-shən\ n

fer·til·iz·er \-ˌī-zər\ n : material (as manure or a chemical mixture) for enriching land

fer·ule \'fer-əl\ also **fer·u·la** \'fer-(y)ə-lə\ n : a rod or ruler used to punish children

fer·ven·cy \'fər-vən-sē\ n, pl **-cies** : FERVOR

fer·vent \'fər-vənt\ adj **1** : very hot : GLOWING **2** : marked by great intensity of feeling — **fer·vent·ly** adv

fer·vid \-vəd\ adj **1** : very hot **2** : ARDENT, ZEALOUS — **fer·vid·ly** adv

fer·vor \'fər-vər\ n **1** : intense heat **2** : intensity of feeling or expression

fes·tal \'fest-ᵊl\ adj : FESTIVE

¹**fes·ter** \'fes-tər\ n : a pus-filled sore

²**fester** vb **fes·tered; fes·ter·ing** \-t(ə-)riŋ\ **1** : to form pus **2** : PUTREFY, ROT **3** : RANKLE

fes·ti·val \'fes-tə-vəl\ n **1** : a time of celebration marked by special observances; esp : an occasion marked with religious ceremonies **2** : a periodic season or program of cultural events or entertainment ⟨a dance ~⟩

fes·tive \'fes-tiv\ adj **1** : of, relating to,

or suitable for a feast or festival **2** : JOYFUL, GAY — **fes•tive•ly** *adv*

fes•tiv•i•ty \fes-'tiv-ət-ē\ *n, pl* **-ties 1** : FESTIVAL 1 **2** : the quality or state of being festive **3** : festive activity

¹fes•toon \fes-'tün\ *n* [F *feston,* fr. It *festone,* fr. *festa* festival] **1** : a decorative chain or strip hanging between two points **2** : a carved, molded, or painted ornament representing a decorative chain

²festoon *vb* **1** : to hang or form festoons on **2** : to shape into festoons

fe•tal \'fēt-ᵊl\ *adj* : of, relating to, or being a fetus

fetal position *n* : a resting position with body curved, legs bent and drawn toward the chest, head bowed forward, and arms tucked in in the manner of the fetus in the womb that is assumed in some forms of psychic disorder

fetch \'fech\ *vb* **1** : to go or come after and bring or take back ⟨teach a dog to ~ a stick⟩ **2** : to cause to come : bring out ⟨~*ed* tears from the eyes⟩ **3** : to sell for **4** : to give by striking ⟨~ him a blow⟩

fetch•ing \'fech-iŋ\ *adj* : ATTRACTIVE, PLEASING — **fetch•ing•ly** *adv*

¹fete *or* **fête** \'fāt, 'fet\ *n* [F *fête,* fr. OF *feste*] **1** : FESTIVAL **2** : a large elaborate entertainment or party

²fete *or* **fête** *vb* **fet•ed** *or* **fêt•ed; fet•ing** *or* **fêt•ing 1** : to honor or commemorate with a fete **2** : to pay high honor to

fet•id \'fet-əd\ *adj* : having an offensive smell : STINKING

fe•tish *also* **fe•tich** \'fet-ish, 'fēt-\ *n* [F & Pg; F *fétiche,* fr. Pg *feitiço,* fr. *feitiço* artificial, false, fr. L *facticius* factitious] **1** : an object (as an idol or image) believed to have magical powers (as in curing disease) **2** : an object of unreasoning devotion or concern **3** : an object whose real or fantasied presence is psychologically necessary for sexual gratification

fe•tish•ism \-ish-ˌiz-əm\ *n* : belief in, devotion to, or pathological attachment to fetishes — **fe•tish•ist** \-ish-əst\ *n* — **fe•tish•is•tic** \ˌfet-ish-'is-tik, ˌfēt-\ *adj*

fet•lock \'fet-ˌläk\ *n* : a projection on the back of a horse's leg above the hoof; *also* : a tuft of hair on this

fet•ter \'fet-ər\ *n* **1** : a chain or shackle for the feet **2** : something that confines : RESTRAINT — **fetter** *vb*

fet•tle \'fet-ᵊl\ *n* : a state of fitness or order : CONDITION ⟨in fine ~⟩

fe•tus \'fēt-əs\ *n* : an unborn or unhatched vertebrate esp. after its basic structure is laid down; *esp* : a developing human being in the uterus from usu. three months after pregnancy occurs to birth

feud \'fyüd\ *n* : a prolonged quarrel; *esp* : a lasting conflict between families or clans marked by violent attacks undertaken for revenge — **feud** *vb*

feu•dal \'fyüd-ᵊl\ *adj* **1** : of, relating to, or having the characteristics of a medieval fee **2** : of, relating to, or characteristic of feudalism

feu•dal•ism \'fyüd-ᵊl-ˌiz-əm\ *n* : a system of political organization prevailing in medieval Europe in which a vassal renders service to a lord and receives protection and land in return; *also* : a similar political or social system — **feu•dal•is•tic** \ˌfyüd-ᵊl-'is-tik\ *adj*

¹feu•da•to•ry \'fyüd-ə-ˌtōr-ē\ *adj* : owing feudal allegiance

²feudatory *n, pl* **-ries 1** : a person who holds lands by feudal law or usage **2** : FIEF

fe•ver \'fē-vər\ *n* **1** : a rise in body temperature above the normal; *also* : a disease of which this is a chief symptom **2** : a state of heightened emotion or activity **3** : CRAZE — **fe•ver•ish** *adj* — **fe•ver•ish•ly** *adv*

¹few \'fyü\ *pron* : not many : a small number

²few *adj* **1** : consisting of or amounting to a small number **2** : not many but some ⟨caught a ~ fish⟩ — **few•ness** *n*

³few *n* **1** : a small number of units or individuals ⟨a ~ of them⟩ **2** : a special limited number ⟨among the ~⟩

few•er \'fyü-ər\ *pron* : a smaller number of persons or things

fey \'fā\ *adj* **1** *chiefly Scot* : fated to die; *also* : marked by a foreboding of death or calamity **2** : able to see into the future : VISIONARY **3** : marked by an otherworldly air or attitude **4** : CRAZY, TOUCHED

fez \'fez\ *n, pl* **fez•zes** *also* **fez•es** : a round red felt hat that has a flat top and a tassel but no brim

ff *abbr* **1** folios **2** [*following*] and the following ones **3** fortissimo

FHA *abbr* Federal Housing Administration

fi·an·cé \ˌfē-ˌän-ˈsā\ *n* [F, fr. MF, fr. *fiancer* to promise, betroth, fr. OF *fiancier*, fr. *fiance* promise, trust, fr. *fier* to trust, fr. L *fidere*] : a man engaged to be married

fi·an·cée \ˌfē-ˌän-ˈsā\ *n* : a woman engaged to be married

fi·as·co \fē-ˈas-kō\ *n, pl* **-coes** [F] : a complete failure

fi·at \ˈfē-ət, -ˌat, -ˌät; ˈfī-ət, -ˌat\ *n* [L, let it be done] : an authoritative and often arbitrary order or decree

fiat money *n* : paper currency backed only by the authority of the government and not by metal

¹**fib** \ˈfib\ *n* : a trivial or childish lie

²**fib** *vb* **fibbed; fib·bing** : to tell a fib — **fib·ber** *n*

fi·ber *or* **fi·bre** \ˈfī-bər\ *n* **1** : a threadlike substance or structure (as a muscle cell or fine root); *esp* : a natural (as wool or flax) or artificial (as rayon) filament capable of being spun or woven **2** : ROUGHAGE **3** : an element that gives texture or substance **4** : basic toughness : STRENGTH — **fi·brous** \-brəs\ *adj*

fi·ber·board \-ˌbōrd\ *n* : a material made by compressing fibers (as of wood) into stiff sheets

fi·ber·fill \-ˌfil\ *n* : man-made fibers used as a filling material (as for cushions)

fi·ber·glass \-ˌglas\ *n* : glass in fibrous form used in making various products (as yarn and insulation)

fiber optics *n* **1** *pl* : thin transparent fibers of glass or plastic that are enclosed by a less refractive material and that transmit light by internal reflection; *also* : a bundle of such fibers used in an instrument **2** : the technique of the use of fiber optics — **fiber–optic** *adj*

fi·bril \ˈfīb-rəl, ˈfib-\ *n* : a small fiber

fi·bril·la·tion \ˌfib-rə-ˈlā-shən, ˌfīb-\ *n* : rapid irregular contractions of muscle fibers (as of the heart) — **fib·ril·late** \ˈfib-rə-ˌlāt, ˈfīb-\ *vb*

fi·brin \ˈfī-brən\ *n* : a white insoluble fibrous protein formed from fibrinogen in the clotting of blood

fi·brin·o·gen \fī-ˈbrin-ə-jən\ *n* : a globulin produced in the liver, present esp. in blood plasma, and converted into fibrin during clotting of blood

fi·broid \ˈfīb-ˌrȯid, ˈfib-\ *adj* : resembling, forming, or consisting of fibrous tissue ⟨∼ tumors⟩

fi·bro·sis \fī-ˈbrō-səs\ *n* : a condition marked by abnormal increase of fiber-containing tissue

fib·u·la \ˈfib-yə-lə\ *n, pl* **-lae** \-lē, -lī\ *or* **-las** : the outer and usu. the smaller of the two bones of the hind limb below the knee — **fib·u·lar** \-lər\ *adj*

FICA *abbr* Federal Insurance Contributions Act

fiche \ˈfēsh, ˈfish\ *n, pl* **fiche** : MICROFICHE

fi·chu \ˈfish-ü\ *n* [F] : a woman's light triangular scarf draped over the shoulders and fastened in front

fick·le \ˈfik-əl\ *adj* : not firm or steadfast in disposition or character : INCONSTANT — **fick·le·ness** *n*

fic·tion \ˈfik-shən\ *n* **1** : something (as a story) invented by the imagination **2** : fictitious literature (as novels) — **fic·tion·al** \-sh(ə-)nəl\ *adj* — **fic·tion·al·ly** \-ē\ *adv*

fic·ti·tious \fik-ˈtish-əs\ *adj* **1** : of, relating to, or characteristic of fiction : IMAGINARY **2** : FEIGNED **syn** chimerical, fanciful, fantastic, unreal

¹**fid·dle** \ˈfid-ᵊl\ *n* : VIOLIN

²**fiddle** *vb* **fid·dled; fid·dling** \ˈfid-(ᵊ-)liŋ\ **1** : to play on a fiddle **2** : to move the hands or fingers restlessly **3** : PUTTER **4** : MEDDLE, TAMPER — **fid·dler** \ˈfid-(ᵊ-)lər\ *n*

fiddler crab *n* : a burrowing crab with one claw much enlarged in the male

fid·dle·stick \ˈfid-ᵊl-ˌstik\ *n* **1** *archaic* : a violin bow **2** *pl* : NONSENSE — used as an interjection

fi·del·i·ty \fə-ˈdel-ət-ē, fī-\ *n, pl* **-ties** **1** : the quality or state of being faithful **2** : ACCURACY ⟨∼ of a news report⟩ ⟨∼ in sound reproduction⟩ **syn** allegiance, loyalty, devotion, fealty

¹**fidg·et** \ˈfij-ət\ *n* **1** *pl* : uneasiness or restlessness as shown by nervous movements **2** : one that fidgets — **fidg·ety** *adj*

²**fidget** *vb* : to move or cause to move or act restlessly or nervously

fi·du·cia·ry \fə-ˈd(y)ü-shē-ˌer-ē, -shə-rē\ *adj* **1** : involving a confidence or trust **2** : held or holding in trust for another ⟨∼ accounts⟩ — **fiduciary** *n*

fie \'fī\ *interj* — used to express disgust or disapproval

fief \'fēf\ *n* : a feudal estate : FEE

¹**field** \'fēld\ *n* **1** : open country **2** : a piece of cleared land for cultivation or pasture **3** : a piece of land yielding some special product **4** : the place where a battle is fought; *also* : BATTLE **5** : an area, division, or sphere of activity ⟨the ∼ of science⟩ ⟨salesmen in the ∼⟩ **6** : an area for military exercises **7** : an area for sports **8** : a background on which something is drawn or projected ⟨a flag with white stars on a ∼ of blue⟩ **9** : a region or space in which a given effect (as magnetism) exists — **field** *adj*

²**field** *vb* **1** : to handle a batted or thrown baseball while on defense **2** : to put into the field **3** : to answer satisfactorily ⟨∼ a tough question⟩ — **field•er** *n*

field day *n* **1** : a day devoted to outdoor sports and athletic competition **2** : a time of extraordinary pleasure or opportunity

field event *n* : a track-and-field event (as weight-throwing) other than a race

field glass *n* : a hand-held binocular telescope — usu. used in pl.

field hockey *n* : a field game played between two teams of 11 players each whose object is to knock a ball into the opponent's goal with a curved stick

field marshal *n* : an officer (as in the British army) of the highest rank

field–test \-ˌtest\ *vb* : to test (as a new product) in a natural environment — **field test** *n*

fiend \'fēnd\ *n* **1** : DEVIL 1 **2** : DEMON **3** : an extemely wicked or cruel person **4** : a person excessively devoted to a pursuit **5** : ADDICT ⟨dope ∼⟩ — **fiend•ish** *adj* — **fiend•ish•ly** *adv*

fierce \'fiərs\ *adj* **fierc•er; fierc•est 1** : violently hostile or aggressive in temperament **2** : PUGNACIOUS **3** : INTENSE **4** : furiously active or determined **5** : wild or menacing in appearance **syn** ferocious, barbarous, savage, cruel — **fierce•ly** *adv* — **fierce•ness** *n*

fi•ery \'fī(-ə)-rē\ *adj* **fi•er•i•er; -est 1** : consisting of fire **2** : BURNING, BLAZING **3** : FLAMMABLE **4** : hot like a fire : INFLAMED, FEVERISH **5** : RED **6** : full of emotion or spirit **7** : IRRITABLE — **fi•eri•ness** \'fī(-ə)-rē-nəs\ *n*

fi•es•ta \fē-'es-tə\ *n* [Sp] : FESTIVAL

fife \'fīf\ *n* [G *pfeife* pipe, fife] : a small shrill flutelike musical instrument

FIFO *abbr* first in, first out

fif•teen \fif-'tēn\ *n* : one more than 14 — **fifteen** *adj or pron* — **fif•teenth** \-'tēnth\ *adj or n*

fifth \'fifth\ *n* **1** : one that is number five in a countable series **2** : one of five equal parts of something **3** : a unit of measure for liquor equal to ⅕ U.S. gallon (about 0.75 liter) — **fifth** *adj or adv*

fifth column *n* : a group of secret supporters of a nation's enemy that engage in espionage or sabotage within the country — **fifth col•um•nist** \-'käl-əm-(n)əst\ *n*

fifth wheel *n* : one that is unnecessary and often burdensome

fif•ty \'fif-tē\ *n, pl* **fifties** : five times 10 — **fif•ti•eth** \-tē-əth\ *adj or n* — **fifty** *adj or pron*

fif•ty–fif•ty \ˌfif-tē-'fif-tē\ *adj* **1** : shared equally ⟨a ∼ proposition⟩ **2** : half favorable and half unfavorable

¹**fig** \'fig\ *n* : a usu. pear-shaped edible fruit of warm regions; *also* : a tree related to the mulberry that bears this fruit

²**fig** *abbr* **1** figurative; figuratively **2** figure

¹**fight** \'fīt\ *vb* **fought** \'fȯt\; **fight•ing 1** : to contend against another in battle or physical combat **2** : BOX **3** : to put forth a determined effort **4** : STRUGGLE, CONTEND **5** : to attempt to prevent the success or effectiveness of **6** : WAGE **7** : to gain by struggle

²**fight** *n* **1** : a hostile encounter : BATTLE **2** : a boxing match **3** : a verbal disagreement **4** : a struggle for a goal or an objective **5** : strength or disposition for fighting ⟨full of ∼⟩

fight•er \-ər\ *n* **1** : one that fights; *esp* : WARRIOR **2** : BOXER **3** : a fast maneuverable airplane armed for destroying enemy aircraft

fig•ment \'fig-mənt\ *n* : something imagined or made up

fig·u·ra·tion \ˌfig-(y)ə-'rā-shən\ *n* **1** : FORM, OUTLINE **2** : an act or instance of representation in figures and shapes

fig·u·ra·tive \'fig-(y)ə-rət-iv\ *adj* **1** : EMBLEMATIC **2** : SYMBOLIC, METAPHORICAL ⟨∼ language⟩ **3** : characterized by figures of speech — **fig·u·ra·tive·ly** *adv*

¹**fig·ure** \'fig-yər\ *n* **1** : NUMERAL **2** *pl* : arithmetical calculations **3** : a written or printed character **4** : PRICE, AMOUNT **5** : SHAPE, FORM, OUTLINE **6** : the graphic representation of a form and esp. of a person **7** : a diagram or pictorial illustration of textual matter **8** : a combination of points, lines, or surfaces in geometry ⟨a circle is a closed plane ∼⟩ **9** : PATTERN, DESIGN **10** : appearance made or impression produced ⟨they cut quite a ∼⟩ **11** : a series of movements (as in a dance) **12** : PERSONAGE

²**figure** *vb* **fig·ured; fig·ur·ing** \'fig-yə-riŋ\ **1** : to represent by or as if by a figure or outline : PORTRAY **2** : to decorate with a pattern **3** : to indicate or represent by numerals **4** : REGARD, CONSIDER **5** : to be or appear important or conspicuous **6** : COMPUTE, CALCULATE

fig·ure·head \'fig-(y)ər-ˌhed\ *n* **1** : a figure on the bow of a ship **2** : a head or chief in name only

figure of speech : a form of expression (as a simile or metaphor) that uses words in other than a plain or literal way

figure out *vb* **1** : FIND OUT, DISCOVER **2** : SOLVE

fig·u·rine \ˌfig-(y)ə-'rēn\ *n* : a small carved or molded figure

Fi·ji·an \'fē-ˌjē-ən, fi-'jē-ən\ *n* : a native or inhabitant of the Pacific island country of Fiji — **Fijian** *adj*

fil·a·ment \'fil-ə-mənt\ *n* : a fine thread or threadlike object, part, or process — **fil·a·men·tous** \ˌfil-ə-'ment-əs\ *adj*

fil·bert \'fil-bərt\ *n* : the sweet thick‿shelled nut of either of two European hazels; *also* : a shrub or small tree bearing filberts

filch \'filch\ *vb* : to steal furtively

¹**file** \'fīl\ *n* : a usu. steel tool with a ridged or toothed surface used esp. for smoothing a hard substance

²**file** *vb* **filed; fil·ing** : to rub, smooth, or cut away with a file

³**file** *vb* **filed; fil·ing** [ME *filen*, fr. MF *filer* to string documents on a string or wire, fr. *fil* thread, fr. L *filum*] **1** : to arrange in order **2** : to enter or record officially or as prescribed by law ⟨∼ a lawsuit⟩ **3** : to send (copy) to a newspaper

⁴**file** *n* **1** : a device (as a folder or cabinet) by means of which papers may be kept in order **2** : a collection of papers or publications usu. arranged or classified

⁵**file** *n* : a row of persons, animals, or things arranged one behind the other

⁶**file** *vb* **filed; fil·ing** : to march or proceed in file

fi·let mi·gnon \ˌfil-(ˌ)ā-mēn-'yōⁿ, fi-ˌlā-\ *n, pl* **filets mignons** \-(ˌ)ā-mēn-'yōⁿz, -ˌlā-\ [F, lit., dainty fillet] : a fillet of beef cut from the thick end of a beef tenderloin

fil·ial \'fil-ē-əl, 'fil-yəl\ *adj* : of, relating to, or befitting a son or daughter

fil·i·bus·ter \'fil-ə-ˌbəs-tər\ *n* [Sp *filibustero*, lit., freebooter] **1** : a military adventurer; *esp* : an American engaged in fomenting 19th century Latin American uprisings **2** : the use of delaying tactics (as extremely long speeches) esp. in a legislative assembly; *also* : an instance of this practice — **filibuster** *vb* — **fil·i·bus·ter·er** *n*

fil·i·gree \'fil-ə-ˌgrē\ *n* [F *filigrane*] : ornamental openwork (as of fine wire)

fil·ing \'fī-liŋ\ *n* **1** : the act of one who files **2** : a small piece scraped off by a file ⟨iron ∼s⟩

Fil·i·pi·no \ˌfil-ə-'pē-nō\ *n, pl* **Filipinos** : a native or inhabitant of the Philippines — **Filipino** *adj*

¹**fill** \'fil\ *vb* **1** : to make or become full **2** : to stop up : PLUG ⟨∼ a cavity⟩ **3** : FEED, SATIATE **4** : SATISFY, FULFILL ⟨∼ all requirements⟩ **5** : to occupy fully **6** : to spread through ⟨laughter ∼ed the room⟩ **7** : OCCUPY ⟨∼ the office of president⟩ **8** : to put a person in ⟨∼ a vacancy⟩ **9** : to supply as directed ⟨∼ a prescription⟩

²**fill** *n* **1** : a full supply; *esp* : a quantity that satisfies or satiates **2** : material used esp. for filling a low place

¹**fill·er** \'fil-ər\ *n* **1** : one that fills **2** : a substance added to another substance

(as to increase bulk or weight) **3** : a material used for filling cracks and pores in wood before painting

²**fil·ler** \'fil-ˌeər\ n, pl **fillers** or **filler** — see *forint* at MONEY table

¹**fil·let** \'fil-ət, *in sense 2* fi-'lā, 'fil-(ˌ)ā\ *also* **fi·let** \fi-'lā, 'fil-(ˌ)ā\ n [ME *filet*, fr. MF, dim. of *fil* thread] **1** : a narrow band, strip, or ribbon **2** : a piece or slice of boneless meat or fish; *esp* : the tenderloin of beef

²**fil·let** \'fil-ət, *in sense 2 also* fi-'lā, 'fil-(ˌ)ā\ vb **1** : to bind or adorn with or as if with a fillet **2** : to cut into fillets

fill in \(')fil-'in\ vb **1** : to provide necessary or recent information **2** : to serve as a temporary substitute

fill·ing \'fil-iŋ\ n **1** : material used to fill something 〈a ∼ for a tooth〉 **2** : the yarn interlacing the warp in a fabric **3** : a food mixture used to fill pastry or sandwiches

filling station n : SERVICE STATION

fil·lip \'fil-əp\ n **1** : a blow or gesture made by a flick or snap of the finger across the thumb **2** : something that serves to arouse or stimulate — **fillip** vb

fil·ly \'fil-ē\ n, pl **fillies** : a young female horse usu. less than four years old

¹**film** \'film\ n **1** : a thin skin or membrane **2** : a thin coating or layer **3** : a flexible strip of chemically treated material used in taking pictures **4** : MOTION PICTURE — **filmy** adj

²**film** vb **1** : to cover with a film **2** : to make a motion picture of

film·dom \'film-dəm\ n : the motion-picture industry

film·og·ra·phy \fil-'mäg-rə-fē\ n, pl **-phies** : a list or catalog of motion pictures relating usu. to a particular actor or director

film·strip \'film-ˌstrip\ n : a strip of film bearing images to be projected on a screen as still pictures

fils \'fils\ n, pl **fils** — see *dinar, dirham, rial* at MONEY table

¹**fil·ter** \'fil-tər\ n **1** : a porous material through which a fluid is passed to separate out matter in suspension; *also* : a device containing such material **2** : a device for suppressing waves of certain frequencies; *esp* : one (as for a camera) that absorbs light of certain colors

²**filter** vb **fil·tered; fil·ter·ing** \-t(ə-)riŋ\ **1** : to remove by means of a filter **2** : to pass through a filter — **fil·ter·able** *also* **fil·tra·ble** \-t(ə-)rə-bəl\ adj — **fil·tra·tion** \fil-'trā-shən\ n

filter bed n : a bed of sand or gravel for filtering water or sewage

filth \'filth\ n [ME, fr. OE *fylth*, fr. *fūl* foul] **1** : foul matter; *esp* : loathsome dirt or refuse **2** : moral corruption **3** : OBSCENITY — **filth·i·ness** \'fil-thē-nəs\ n — **filthy** \'fil-thē\ adj

fil·trate \'fil-ˌtrāt\ n : material that has passed through a filter

¹**fin** \'fin\ n **1** : one of the thin external processes by which an aquatic animal (as a fish) moves through water **2** : a fin-shaped part (as on an airplane) **3** : FLIPPER 2 — **finned** \'find\ adj

²**fin** abbr **1** finance; financial **2** finish

fi·na·gle \fə-'nā-gəl\ vb **-gled; -gling** \-g(ə-)liŋ\ **1** : to obtain by indirect or dishonest means : WANGLE **2** : to use devious dishonest methods to achieve one's ends — **fi·na·gler** \-g(ə-)lər\ n

¹**fi·nal** \'fīn-ᵊl\ adj **1** : not to be altered or undone **2** : ULTIMATE **3** : relating to or occurring at the end or conclusion — **fi·nal·i·ty** \fī-'nal-ət-ē, fə-\ n — **fi·nal·ly** \'fīn-(ᵊ-)lē\ adv

²**final** n **1** : a deciding match, game, or trial — usu. used in pl. **2** : the last examination in a course — usu. used in pl.

fi·na·le \fə-'nal-ē, fi-'näl-\ n : the close or end of something; *esp* : the last section of a musical composition

fi·nal·ist \'fīn-ᵊl-əst\ n : a contestant in the finals of a competition

fi·nal·ize \'fīn-ᵊl-ˌīz\ vb **-ized; -iz·ing** : to put in final or finished form

¹**fi·nance** \fə-'nans, 'fī-ˌnans\ n [ME, payment, ransom, fr. MF, fr. *finer* to end, pay, fr. *fin* end, fr. L *finis* boundary, end] **1** pl : money resources available esp. to a government or business **2** : management of money affairs

²**finance** vb **fi·nanced; fi·nanc·ing** **1** : to raise or provide funds for **2** : to furnish with necessary funds **3** : to sell or supply on credit

finance company n : a company that makes usu. small short-term loans usu. to individuals

fi·nan·cial \fə-'nan-chəl, fī-\ adj : having to do with finance or financiers ⟨in ~ circles⟩ — **fi·nan·cial·ly** \-ˈnanch-(ə-)lē\ *adv*

fi·nan·cier \ˌfin-ən-ˈsiər, ˌfī-ˌnan-\ *n* 1 : a person skilled in managing public moneys 2 : a person who invests large sums of money

finch \ˈfinch\ *n* : any of numerous songbirds (as sparrows, linnets, or buntings) with strong conical bills

¹**find** \ˈfīnd\ *vb* **found** \ˈfaund\; **find·ing** 1 : to meet with either by chance or by searching or study : ENCOUNTER, DISCOVER 2 : to obtain by effort or management ⟨~ time to read⟩ 3 : to arrive at : REACH ⟨the bullet *found* its mark⟩ 4 : EXPERIENCE, DETECT, PERCEIVE, FEEL 5 : to gain or regain the use of ⟨*found* his voice again⟩ 6 : PROVIDE, SUPPLY 7 : to settle upon and make a statement about ⟨~ a verdict⟩

²**find** *n* 1 : an act or instance of finding 2 : something found; *esp* : a valuable item of discovery

find·er \ˈfīn-dər\ *n* : one that finds; *esp* : a device on a camera showing the view being photographed

fin de siè·cle \ˌfaⁿ-də-sē-ˈeklᵊ\ *adj* [F, end of century] : of, relating to, or characteristic of the close of the 19th century

find·ing \ˈfīn-diŋ\ *n* 1 : the act of finding 2 : FIND 2 3 : the result of a judicial proceeding or inquiry

find out *vb* : to learn by study, observation, or search : DISCOVER

¹**fine** \ˈfīn\ *n* : money exacted as a penalty for an offense

²**fine** *vb* **fined; fin·ing** : to impose a fine on : punish by a fine

³**fine** *adj* **fin·er; fin·est** 1 : free from impurity 2 : very thin in gauge or texture 3 : not coarse 4 : SUBTLE, SENSITIVE ⟨a ~ distinction⟩ 5 : superior in quality, conception, or appearance 6 : ELEGANT, REFINED — **fine·ly** *adv* — **fine·ness** \ˈfīn-nəs\ *n*

⁴**fine** *adv* : FINELY

fine art *n* : art (as painting, sculpture, or music) concerned primarily with the creation of beautiful objects — usu. used in pl.

fin·ery \ˈfīn-(ə-)rē\ *n, pl* **-er·ies** : ORNAMENT, DECORATION; *esp* : showy clothing and jewels

fine·spun \ˈfīn-ˈspən\ *adj* : developed with extremely or excessively fine delicacy or detail

fi·nesse \fə-ˈnes\ *n* 1 : refinement or delicacy of workmanship, structure, or texture 2 : CUNNING, SUBTLETY — **finesse** *vb*

fine–tune \ˈfīn-ˈtün\ *vb* : to adjust so as to bring to the highest level of performance or effectiveness

fin·fish \ˈfin-ˌfish\ *n* : FISH 2

¹**fin·ger** \ˈfiŋ-gər\ *n* 1 : any of the five divisions at the end of the hand; *esp* : one other than the thumb 2 : something that resembles or does the work of a finger 3 : a part of a glove into which a finger is inserted

²**finger** *vb* **fin·gered; fin·ger·ing** \-g(ə-)riŋ\ 1 : to perform with the fingers or with a certain fingering 2 : to mark the notes of a piece of music as a guide in playing 3 : to touch or feel with the fingers : HANDLE 4 : to point out

fin·ger·board \ˈfiŋ-gər-ˌbōrd\ *n* : the part of a stringed instrument against which the fingers press the strings to vary the pitch

finger bowl *n* : a basin to hold water for rinsing the fingers at table

fin·ger·ing \ˈfiŋ-g(ə-)riŋ\ *n* 1 : handling or touching with the fingers 2 : the act or method of using the fingers in playing an instrument 3 : the marking of the method of fingering

fin·ger·ling \ˈfiŋ-gər-liŋ\ *n* : a small fish

fin·ger·nail \ˈfiŋ-gər-ˌnāl\ *n* : the nail of a finger

fin·ger·print \-ˌprint\ *n* : the pattern of marks made by pressing the tip of a finger or thumb on a surface; *esp* : an ink impression of such a pattern taken for the purpose of identification — **fingerprint** *vb*

fin·ger·tip \-ˌtip\ *n* : the tip of a finger

fin·i·al \ˈfin-ē-əl\ *n* : an ornamental projection or end (as on a spire)

fin·ick·ing \ˈfin-i-kiŋ\ *adj* : FINICKY

fin·icky \ˈfin-i-kē\ *adj* : excessively particular in taste or standards

fi·nis \ˈfin-əs\ *n* : END, CONCLUSION

¹**fin·ish** \ˈfin-ish\ *vb* 1 : TERMINATE 2 : to use or dispose of entirely 3 : to bring to completion : ACCOMPLISH; *also* : PERFECT 4 : to put a final coat or surface on 5 : to come to the end of a course or undertaking — **fin·ish·er** *n*

²finish n 1 : END, CONCLUSION 2 : something that completes or perfects 3 : the final treatment or coating of a surface

fi·nite \'fī-ₙnīt\ adj 1 : having definite or definable limits 2 : having a limited nature or existence 3 : being neither infinite nor infinitesimal

fink \'fiŋk\ n 1 : a contemptible person 2 : STRIKEBREAKER 3 : INFORMER

Finn \'fin\ n : a native or inhabitant of Finland

fin·nan had·die \ₙfin-ən-'had-ē\ n : smoked haddock

¹Finn·ish \'fin-ish\ adj : of or relating to Finland, the Finns, or Finnish

²Finnish n : the language of Finland

fin·ny \'fin-ē\ adj 1 : having or characterized by fins 2 : relating to or being fish

fiord var of FJORD

fir \'fər\ n : an erect evergreen tree related to the pines; also : its light soft wood

¹fire \'fī(ə)r\ n 1 : the light or heat and esp. the flame of something burning 2 : ENTHUSIASM, ZEAL 3 : fuel that is burning (as in a stove or fireplace) 4 : destructive burning of something (as a house) 5 : the discharge of firearms — **fire·less** adj

²fire vb **fired; fir·ing** 1 : KINDLE, IGNITE ⟨∼ a house⟩ 2 : STIR, ENLIVEN ⟨∼ the imagination⟩ 3 : to dismiss from employment 4 : SHOOT ⟨∼ a gun⟩ ⟨∼ an arrow⟩ 5 : BAKE ⟨firing pottery in a kiln⟩ 6 : to apply fire or fuel to something ⟨∼ a furnace⟩

fire ant n : either of two small fiercely stinging South American ants that are pests in the southeastern U.S. esp. in fields used to grow crops

fire·arm \'fī(ə)r-ₙärm\ n : a weapon (as a rifle or pistol) from which a shot is discharged by an explosion of gunpowder

fire·ball \'fī(ə)r-ₙbȯl\ n 1 : a ball of fire 2 : a very bright meteor 3 : the highly luminous cloud of vapor and dust created by a nuclear explosion 4 : a highly energetic person

fire·boat \'fī(ə)r-ₙbōt\ n : a boat equipped for fighting fires

fire·bomb \-ₙbäm\ n : an incendiary bomb — **firebomb** vb

fire·box \-ₙbäks\ n 1 : a chamber (as of a furnace) that contains a fire 2 : a box containing a fire alarm

fire·brand \-ₙbrand\ n 1 : a piece of burning wood 2 : a person who creates unrest or strife : AGITATOR

fire·break \-ₙbrāk\ n : a barrier of cleared or plowed land intended to check a forest or grass fire

fire·brick \-ₙbrik\ n : a brick capable of withstanding great heat and used for lining furnaces or fireplaces

fire·bug \'fī(ə)r-ₙbəg\ n : a person who deliberately sets destructive fires

fire·clay \-ₙklā\ n : clay capable of withstanding high temperatures and used esp. for firebrick and crucibles

fire·crack·er \'fī(ə)r-ₙkrak-ər\ n : a paper tube containing an explosive and a fuse and usu. set off for amusement

fire·damp \-ₙdamp\ n : a combustible mine gas that consists chiefly of methane

fire engine n : a motor vehicle with equipment for extinguishing fires

fire escape n : a stairway or ladder for escape from a burning building

fire·fly \'fī(ə)r-ₙflī\ n : any of various small night-flying beetles that produce flashes of light for courtship purposes

fire·house \'fī(ə)r-ₙhau̇s\ n : FIRE STATION

fire irons n pl : tools for tending a fire esp. in a fireplace

fire·man \-mən\ n 1 : a member of a company organized to put out fires 2 : STOKER

fire·place \'fī(ə)r-ₙplās\ n 1 : a framed opening made in a chimney to hold an open fire : HEARTH 2 : an outdoor structure of brick or stone for an open fire

fire·plug \-ₙpləg\ n : HYDRANT

fire·pow·er \-ₙpau̇(-ə)r\ n : the ability to deliver gunfire or warheads on a target

¹fire·proof \-'prüf\ adj : proof against or resistant to fire

²fireproof vb : to make fireproof

fire screen n : a protecting wire screen before a fireplace

¹fire·side \'fī(ə)r-ₙsīd\ n 1 : a place near the fire or hearth 2 : HOME

²fireside adj : having an informal or intimate quality

fire station *n* : a building housing fire engines and usu. firemen

fire tower *n* : a tower (as in a forest) from which a watch for fires is kept

fire·trap \'fī(ə)r-ˌtrap\ *n* : a building or place apt to catch on fire or difficult to escape from in case of fire

fire truck *n* : FIRE ENGINE

fire·wa·ter \'fī(ə)r-ˌwȯt-ər, -ˌwät-\ *n* : intoxicating liquor

fire·wood \-ˌwu̇d\ *n* : wood cut for fuel

fire·work \-ˌwərk\ *n* : a device designed to produce a display of light, noise, and smoke by the burning of explosive or flammable materials

firing line *n* **1** : a line from which fire is delivered against a target **2** : the forefront of an activity

¹firm \'fərm\ *adj* **1** : securely fixed in place **2** : SOLID, VIGOROUS ⟨a ∼ handshake⟩ **3** : having a solid or compact texture ⟨∼ flesh⟩ **4** : not subject to change of fluctuation : STEADY ⟨∼ prices⟩ **5** : STEADFAST **6** : indicating firmness or resolution ⟨a ∼ mouth⟩ — **firm·ly** *adv* — **firm·ness** *n*

²firm *vb* : to make or become firm

³firm *n* [G *firma*, fr. It, signature, deriv. of L *firmare* to make firm, confirm] **1** : the name under which a company transacts business **2** : a business partnership of two or more persons **3** : a business enterprise

fir·ma·ment \'fər-mə-mənt\ *n* : the arch of the sky : HEAVENS

firm·ware \'firm-ˌwaər\ *n* : computer programs contained permanently in a hardware device (as read-only memory)

¹first \'fərst\ *adj* : preceding all others as in time, order, or importance

²first *adv* **1** : before any other **2** : for the first time **3** : in preference to something else

³first *n* **1** : number one in a countable series **2** : something that is first **3** : the lowest forward gear in an automotive vehicle

first aid *n* : emergency care or treatment given an injured or ill person

first·born \'fərs(t)-ˌbȯrn\ *adj* : ELDEST — **firstborn** *n*

first class *n* : the best or highest group in a classification — **first–class** *adj or adv*

first·hand \'fərst-ˌhand\ *adj* : coming directly from the original source ⟨∼ knowledge⟩ — **firsthand** *adv*

first lady *n, often cap F&L* : the wife or hostess of the chief executive of a political unit (as a country)

first lieutenant *n* : a commissioned officer (as in the army) ranking next below a captain

first·ling \'fərst-liŋ\ *n* : one that comes or is produced first

first·ly \-lē\ *adv* : in the first place : FIRST

first–rate \-'rāt\ *adj* : of the first order of size, importance, or quality — **first–rate** *adv*

first sergeant *n* **1** : a noncommissioned officer serving as the chief assistant to the commander of a military unit (as a company) **2** : a rank in the army below a command sergeant major and in the marine corps below a sergeant major

first–string \'fərs(t)-'striŋ\ *adj* : being a regular as distinguished from a substitute

firth \'fərth\ *n* [ME, fr. ON *fjörthr*] : a narrow arm of the sea

fis·cal \'fis-kəl\ *adj* [L *fiscalis*, fr. *fiscus* basket, treasury] **1** : of or relating to taxation, public revenues, or public debt **2** : of or relating to financial matters

¹fish \'fish\ *n, pl* **fish** *or* **fish·es** **1** : a water-dwelling animal — usu. used in combination ⟨star*fish*⟩ ⟨shell*fish*⟩ **2** : any of numerous cold-blooded water-breathing vertebrates with fins, gills, and usu. scales **3** : the flesh of fish used as food

²fish *vb* **1** : to attempt to catch fish **2** : to seek something by roundabout means ⟨∼ for praise⟩ **3** : to search for something underwater **4** : to engage in a search by groping **5** : to draw forth

fish–and–chips \ˌfish-ən-'chips\ *n pl* : fried fish and french fried potatoes

fish·bowl \'fish-ˌbōl\ *n* **1** : a bowl for the keeping of live fish **2** : a place or condition that affords no privacy

fish·er \'fish-ər\ *n* **1** : one that fishes **2** : a large dark brown No. American arboreal carnivorous mammal related to the weasels

fish·er·man \-mən\ *n* : a person engaged in fishing; *also* : a fishing boat

fish·ery \'fish-(ə-)rē\ *n, pl* **-er·ies** : the

business of catching fish; *also* : a place for catching fish

fish•hook \'fish-ˌhu̇k\ *n* : a usu. barbed hook for catching fish

fish•ing \'fish-iŋ\ *n* : the business or sport of catching fish

fish ladder *n* : an arrangement of pools by which fish can pass around a dam

fish protein concentrate *n* : flour made of pulverized dried fish

fish•wife \'fish-ˌwīf\ *n* **1** : a woman who sells fish **2** : a vulgar abusive woman

fishy \'fish-ē\ *adj* **fish•i•er; -est 1** : of or resembling fish **2** : QUESTIONABLE

fis•sion \'fish-ən, 'fizh-\ *n* [L *fissio,* fr. *fissus,* pp. of *findere* to split] **1** : a cleaving into parts **2** : a method of reproduction in which a living cell or body divides into two or more parts each of which grows into a whole new individual **3** : the splitting of an atomic nucleus resulting in the release of large amounts of energy — **fis•sion•able** \'fish-(ə-)nə-bəl, 'fizh-\ *adj*

fis•sure \'fish-ər\ *n* : a narrow opening or crack

fist \'fist\ *n* **1** : the hand with fingers doubled into the palm **2** : INDEX 6

fist•ful \-ˌfu̇l\ *n* : HANDFUL

fist•i•cuffs \'fis-ti-ˌkəfs\ *n pl* : a fight with usu. bare fists

fis•tu•la \'fis-chə-lə\ *n, pl* **-las** *or* **-lae** : an abnormal passage leading from an abscess or hollow organ — **fis•tu•lous** \-ləs\ *adj*

¹fit \'fit\ *adj* **fit•ter; fit•test 1** : adapted to a purpose : APPROPRIATE **2** : PROPER, RIGHT, BECOMING **3** : PREPARED, READY **4** : physically and mentally sound — **fit•ly** *adv* — **fit•ness** *n*

²fit *n* **1** : a sudden violent attack (as of bodily disorder) **2** : a sudden outburst (as of laughter)

³fit *vb* **fit•ted** *also* **fit; fit•ting 1** : to be suitable for or to : BEFIT **2** : to be correctly adjusted to or shaped for **3** : to insert or adjust until correctly in place **4** : to make a place or room for **5** : to be in agreement or accord with **6** : PREPARE **7** : ADJUST **8** : SUPPLY, EQUIP **9** : BELONG — **fit•ter** *n*

⁴fit *n* : the fact, condition, or manner of fitting or being fitted

fit•ful \'fit-fəl\ *adj* : not regular : INTERMITTENT ⟨∼ sleep⟩ — **fit•ful•ly** \-ē\ *adv*

¹fit•ting \'fit-iŋ\ *adj* : APPROPRIATE, SUITABLE — **fit•ting•ly** *adv*

²fitting *n* **1** : the action or act of one that fits; *esp* : a trying on of clothes being made or altered **2** : a small often standardized part ⟨a plumbing ∼⟩

five \'fīv\ *n* **1** : one more that four **2** : the 5th in a set or series **3** : something having five units; *esp* : a basketball team — **five** *adj or pron*

¹fix \'fiks\ *vb* **1** : to make firm, stable, or fast **2** : to give a permanent or final form to ⟨∼ a photographic film⟩ **3** : AFFIX, ATTACH **4** : to hold or direct steadily ⟨∼es his eyes on the horizon⟩ **5** : ESTABLISH ⟨∼ a date⟩ **6** : ASSIGN ⟨∼ blame⟩ **7** : to set in order : ADJUST **8** : PREPARE **9** : to make whole or sound again **10** : to get even with **11** : to influence by improper or illegal methods ⟨∼ a horse race⟩ — **fix•er** *n*

²fix *n* **1** : PREDICAMENT **2** : a determination of position (as of a ship) **3** : an accurate determination or understanding **4** : an act of improper influence (as bribery) **5** : a shot of a narcotic **6** : something that fixes or restores

fix•a•tion \fik-'sā-shən\ *n* : an obsessive or unhealthy preoccupation or attachment — **fix•ate** \'fik-ˌsāt\ *vb*

fix•a•tive \'fik-sət-iv\ *n* : something (as a varnish for crayon drawings) that stabilizes or sets

fixed \'fikst\ *adj* **1** : securely placed or fastened : STATIONARY **2** : not volatile **3** : SETTLED, FINAL **4** : INTENT, CONCENTRATED ⟨a ∼ stare⟩ **5** : supplied with a dcfinite amount of something needed (as money) — **fixed•ly** \'fik-səd-lē\ *adv* — **fixed•ness** \-nəs\ *n*

fixed star *n* : a star so distant that its motion can be measured only by very precise observations over long periods

fix•i•ty \'fik-sət-ē\ *n, pl* **-ties** : the quality or state of being fixed or stable

fix•ture \'fiks-chər\ *n* : something firmly attached as a permanent part of some other thing ⟨an electrical ∼⟩

¹fizz \'fiz\ *vb* : to make a hissing or sputtering sound

²fizz *n* : an effervescent beverage

¹fiz•zle \'fiz-əl\ *vb* **fiz•zled; fiz•zling** \-(ə-)liŋ\ **1** : FIZZ **2** : to fail after a good start

²fizzle *n* : FAILURE
fjord \fē-'órd\ *n* : a narrow inlet of the sea between cliffs or steep slopes
fl *abbr* 1 [L *floruit*] flourished 2 fluid
FL *or* **Fla** *abbr* Florida
flab \'flab\ *n* : soft flabby body tissue
flab·ber·gast \'flab-ər-,gast\ *vb* : ASTOUND
flab·by \'flab-ē\ *adj* **flab·bi·er; -est** : lacking firmness and substance : FLACCID ⟨∼ muscles⟩ — **flab·bi·ness** \'flab-ē-nəs\ *n*
flac·cid \'flak-səd, 'flas-əd\ *adj* : deficient in firmness ⟨∼ plant stems⟩
fla·con \'flak-ən\ *n* : a small usu. ornamental bottle with a tight cap
¹flag \'flag\ *n* : any of various irises; *esp* : a wild iris
²flag *n* 1 : a usu. rectangular piece of fabric of distinctive design that is used as a symbol (as of a nation) or as a signaling device 2 : something used like a flag to signal or attract attention 3 : one of the cross strokes of a musical note less that a quarter note in value
³flag *vb* **flagged; flag·ging** 1 : to signal with or as if with a flag; *esp* : to signal to stop ⟨∼ a taxi⟩ 2 : to put a flag on
⁴flag *vb* **flagged; flag·ging** 1 : to be loose, yielding, or limp : DROOP 2 : to become unsteady, feeble, or spiritless ⟨his interest *flagged*⟩ 3 : to decline in interest or attraction ⟨the topic *flagged*⟩
⁵flag *n* : a hard flat stone suitable for paving
flag·el·late \'flaj-ə-,lāt\ *vb* **-lat·ed; -lat·ing** : to punish by whipping — **flag·el·la·tion** \,flaj-ə-'lā-shən\ *n*
fla·gel·lum \flə-'jel-əm\ *n, pl* **-la** \-ə\ *also* **-lums** : a tapering process that projects singly or in groups from a cell and is the primary organ of motion of many microorganisms — **fla·gel·lar** \-'jel-ər\ *adj*
fla·geo·let \,flaj-ə-'let, -'lā\ *n* [F] : a small woodwind instrument belonging to the flute class
fla·gi·tious \flə-'jish-əs\ *adj* : grossly wicked : VILLAINOUS
flag·on \'flag-ən\ *n* : a container for liquids usu. with a handle, spout, and lid
flag·pole \'flag-,pōl\ *n* : a pole to raise a flag on
fla·grant \'flā-grənt\ *adj* [L *flagrans*,

prp. of *flagrare* to burn] : conspicuously bad — **fla·grant·ly** *adv*
fla·gran·te de·lic·to \flə-,grant-ē-di-'lik-tō\ *adv* [ML, lit., while the crime is blazing] : in the very act of committing a misdeed
flag·ship \'flag-,ship\ *n* 1 : the ship that carries the commander of a fleet or subdivision thereof and flies his flag 2 : the most important one of a group ⟨a ∼ store⟩
flag·staff \-,staf\ *n* : FLAGPOLE
flag·stone \-,stōn\ *n* : ⁵FLAG
¹flail \'flāl\ *n* : a tool for threshing grain by hand
²flail *vb* 1 : to beat with or as if with a flail 2 : to move as if swinging a flail
flair \'flaər\ *n* [F, lit., sense of smell, fr. OF, odor, fr. *flairier* to give off an odor, fr. LL *flagrare*, fr. L *fragrare*] 1 : discriminating sense 2 : natural aptitude : BENT ⟨a ∼ for acting⟩
flak \'flak\ *n, pl* **flak** [G, fr. *flieger-abwehrkanonen*, fr. *flieger* flyer + *abwehr* defense + *kanonen* cannons] : antiaircraft guns or bursting shells fired from them
¹flake \'flāk\ *n* 1 : a small loose mass or bit 2 : a thin flattened piece or layer : CHIP — **flaky** *adj*
²flake *vb* **flaked; flak·ing** : to form or separate into flakes
flam·beau \'flam-,bō\ *n, pl* **flambeaux** \-,bōz\ *or* **flambeaus** [F, fr. MF, fr. *flambe* flame] : a flaming torch
flam·boy·ant \flam-'bói-ənt\ *adj* : FLORID, SHOWY — **flam·boy·ance** \-əns\ *n* — **flam·boy·an·cy** \-ən-sē\ *n* — **flam·boy·ant·ly** *adv*
flame \'flām\ *n* 1 : the glowing gaseous part of a fire 2 : a state of blazing combustion 3 : a flamelike condition 4 : burning zeal or passion 5 : BRILLIANCE 6 : SWEETHEART — **flame** *vb* — **flam·ing** \'flā-miŋ\ *adj*
fla·men·co \flə-'meŋ-kō\ *n, pl* **-cos** [Sp, Flemish, like a Gypsy, fr. Dutch *Vlaminc* Fleming] : a vigorous rhythmic dance style of the Spanish Gypsies
flame·throw·er \'flām-,thrō(-ə)r\ *n* : a device that expels from a nozzle a burning stream of liquid or semiliquid fuel under pressure
fla·min·go \flə-'miŋ-gō\ *n, pl* **-gos** *also* **-goes** : any of several long-legged long-necked tropical water birds with

scarlet wings and a broad bill bent downward

flam·ma·ble \'flam-ə-bəl\ *adj* : easily ignited and quick-burning — **flam·ma·bil·i·ty** *n* — **flammable** *n*

flange \'flanj\ *n* : a rim used for strengthening or guiding something or for attachment to another object

¹flank \'flaŋk\ *n* **1** : the fleshy part of the side between the ribs and the hip; *also* : the side of a quadruped **2** : SIDE **3** : the right or left of a formation

²flank *vb* **1** : to attack or threaten the flank of **2** : to be situated on the side of : BORDER

flank·er \'flaŋ-kər\ *n* : a football player stationed wide of the formation slightly behind the line of scrimmage as a pass receiver

flan·nel \'flan-ᵊl\ *n* **1** : a soft twilled wool or worsted fabric with a napped surface **2** : a stout cotton fabric napped on one side **3** *pl* : flannel underwear or trousers

flan·nel·ette \ˌflan-ᵊl-'et\ *n* : a lightweight cotton flannel

¹flap \'flap\ *n* **1** : a stroke with something broad : SLAP **2** : something broad, limber, or flat and usu. thin that hangs loose ⟨the ~ of a pocket⟩ **3** : the motion or sound of something broad and limber as it swings to and fro **4** : a state of excitement or confusion

²flap *vb* **flapped; flap·ping 1** : to beat with something broad and flat **2** : FLING **3** : to move (as wings) with a beating motion **4** : to sway loosely usu. with a noise of striking

flap·jack \-ˌjak\ *n* : PANCAKE

flap·per \'flap-ər\ *n* **1** : one that flaps **2** : a young woman of the 1920s who showed freedom from conventions (as in conduct)

¹flare \'flaər\ *vb* **flared; flar·ing 1** : to flame with a sudden unsteady light **2** : to become suddenly excited or angry ⟨~ up⟩ **3** : to spread outward

²flare *n* **1** : an unsteady glaring light **2** : a blaze of light used to signal or illuminate; *also* : a device for producing such a blaze

flare–up \-ˌəp\ *n* : a sudden outburst or intensification

¹flash \'flash\ *vb* **1** : to break forth in or like a sudden flame **2** : to appear or pass suddenly or with great speed **3** : to send out in or as if in flashes ⟨~ a message⟩ **4** : to make a sudden display (as of brilliance or feeling) **5** : to gleam or glow intermittently **6** : to fill by a sudden rush of water **7** : to expose to view very briefly ⟨~ a badge⟩ **syn** glance, glint, sparkle, twinkle — **flash·er** *n*

²flash *n* **1** : a sudden burst of light **2** : a movement of a flag or light in signaling **3** : a sudden and brilliant burst (as of wit) **4** : a brief time **5** : SHOW, DISPLAY; *esp* : ostentatious display **6** : one that attracts notice; *esp* : an outstanding athlete **7** : GLIMPSE, LOOK **8** : a first brief news report **9** : a device for producing a brief and very bright flash of light for taking photographs **10** : a quick-spreading flame or momentary intense outburst of radiant heat

³flash *adj* **1** : of sudden origin and short duration ⟨a ~ fire⟩ **2** : involving brief exposure to an intense agent (as heat or cold) ⟨~ freezing of food⟩

flash·back \'flash-ˌbak\ *n* : introduction into the chronological sequence of events (as in a literary or theatrical work) of an event of earlier occurrence

flash·bulb \-ˌbəlb\ *n* : an electric light bulb in which metal foil or wire is burned to produce a brief and very bright flash of light for taking photographs

flash card *n* : a card bearing words, numbers, or pictures briefly displayed usu. by a teacher as a learning aid

flash·cube \'flash-ˌkyüb\ *n* : a cubical device incorporating four flashbulbs

flash·gun \-ˌgən\ *n* : a device for holding and operating a flashbulb

flash·ing \'flash-iŋ\ *n* : sheet metal used in waterproofing roof valleys or the angle between a chimney and a roof

flash·light \'flash-ˌlīt\ *n* : a small battery-operated portable electric light

flash point *n* : the lowest temperature at which vapors above a volatile combustible substance ignite in air when exposed to flame

flashy \'flash-ē\ *adj* **flash·i·er; -est 1** : momentarily dazzling **2** : BRIGHT **3** : SHOWY — **flash·i·ly** \'flash-ə-lē\ *adv* — **flash·i·ness** \-ē-nəs\ *n*

flask \'flask\ *n* : a flattened bottle= shaped container ⟨a whiskey ∼⟩

¹**flat** \'flat\ *n* **1** : a level surface of land : PLAIN **2** : a flat part or surface **3** : a musical tone one half step lower than a specified tone; *also* : a character b on the musical staff indicating a flat **4** : something flat **5** : an apartment on one floor **6** : a deflated tire

²**flat** *adj* **flat·ter; flat·test 1** : having a smooth, level, or even surface **2** : spread out along a surface; *also* : be- ing or characterized by a horizontal line **3** : having a broad smooth surface and little thickness **4** : DOWNRIGHT, POSITIVE ⟨a ∼ refusal⟩ **5** : FIXED, UN- CHANGING ⟨charge a ∼ rate⟩ **6** : EXACT, PRECISE ⟨in four minutes ∼⟩ **7** : DULL, UNINTERESTING ⟨a ∼ story⟩; *also* : IN- SIPID ⟨a ∼ taste⟩ **8** : DEFLATED **9** : low- er that the true pitch; *also* : lower by a half step ⟨a ∼ note⟩ **10** : free from gloss — **flat·ly** *adv* — **flat·ness** *n*

³**flat** *adv* **1** : FLATLY **2** : COMPLETELY ⟨∼ broke⟩ **3** : below the true musical pitch

⁴**flat** *vb* **flat·ted; flat·ting 1** : FLATTEN **2** : to lower in pitch esp. by a half step **3** : to sing or play below the true pitch

flat·bed \'flat-ˌbed\ *n* : a truck or trailer with a body in the form of a platform or shallow box

flat·boat \-ˌbōt\ *n* : a flat-bottomed boat used esp. for carrying bulky freight

flat·car \-ˌkär\ *n* : a railroad freight car without sides or roof

flat·fish \-ˌfish\ *n* : any of a group of flattened bony sea fishes with both eyes on the upper side

flat·foot \-ˌfut, -ˈfut\ *n, pl* **flat·feet** \-ˌfēt, -ˈfēt\ : a condition in which the arch of the foot is flattened so that the en- tire sole rests upon the ground — **flat‐ foot·ed** \-ˈfut-əd\ *adj*

Flat·head \-ˌhed\ *n, pl* **Flatheads** *or* **Flathead** : a member of an American Indian people of Montana

flat·iron \-ˌī(-ə)rn\ *n* : IRON 3

flat·land \-ˌland\ *n* : land lacking sig- nificant variation in elevation

flat out \-ˈaut\ *adv* **1** : BLUNTLY, DIRECT- LY **2** : at top speed

flat·ten \'flat-ᵊn\ *vb* **flat·tened; flat·ten- ing** \'flat-(ᵊ-)niŋ\ : to make or become flat

flat·ter \'flat-ər\ *vb* [ME *flateren*, fr. OF *flater* to lick, flatter] **1** : to praise too much or without sincerity **2** : to represent too favorably ⟨the picture ∼s her⟩ **3** : to judge (oneself) favor- ably or too favorably — **flat·ter·er** *n*

flat·tery \'flat-ə-rē\ *n, pl* **-ter·ies** : flat- tering speech or attentions : insincere or excessive praise

flat·top \'flat-ˌtäp\ *n* **1** : AIRCRAFT CARRI- ER **2** : CREW CUT

flat·u·lent \'flach-ə-lənt\ *adj* **1** : full of gas ⟨a ∼ stomach⟩ **2** : TURGID ⟨∼ ora- tory⟩ — **flat·u·lence** \-ləns\ *n*

fla·tus \'flāt-əs\ *n* : gas formed in the intestine or stomach

flat·ware \'flat-ˌwaər\ *n* : eating and serving utensils (as forks, spoons, and knives)

flat·worm \-ˌwürm\ *n* : any of a phylum of flattened mostly parasitic segment- ed worms (as trematodes and tape- worms)

flaunt \'flont\ *vb* **1** : to display oneself to public notice **2** : to wave or flutter showily **3** : to display ostentatiously or impudently : PARADE — **flaunt** *n*

flau·tist \'flot-əst, 'flaut-\ *n* [It *flautista*] : FLUTIST

¹**fla·vor** \'flā-vər\ *n* **1** : the quality of something that affects the sense of taste or of taste and smell; *also* : the resulting sensation **2** : a substance that adds flavor **3** : characteristic or predominant quality — **fla·vor·ful** *adj* — **fla·vor·less** *adj* — **fla·vor·some** *adj*

²**flavor** *vb* **fla·vored; fla·vor·ing** \'flāv- (ə-)riŋ\ : to give or add flavor to

fla·vor·ing *n* : FLAVOR 2

fla·vour *chiefly Brit var of* FLAVOR

flaw \'flo\ *n* : a small often hidden de- fect — **flaw·less** *adj*

flax \'flaks\ *n* : a fiber that is the source of linen; *also* : a blue-flowered plant grown for this fiber and its oily seeds

flax·en \'flak-sən\ *adj* **1** : made of flax **2** : resembling flax esp. in pale soft straw color

flay \'flā\ *vb* **1** : to strip off the skin or surface of **2** : to criticize harshly

flea \'flē\ *n* : any of an order of small wingless leaping bloodsucking insects

flea·bane \-ˌbān\ *n* : any of various plants of the daisy family once be- lieved to drive away fleas

flea–bit·ten \-ˌbit-ᵊn\ *adj* : bitten by or infested with fleas

flea market *n* : a usu. open-air market for secondhand articles and antiques

¹fleck \ˈflek\ *vb* : STREAK, SPOT

²fleck *n* **1** : SPOT, MARK **2** : FLAKE, PARTICLE

fledg·ling \ˈflej-liŋ\ *n* **1** : a young bird with flight feathers newly developed **2** : an immature or inexperienced person

flee \ˈflē\ *vb* **fled** \ˈfled\; **flee·ing 1** : to run away often from danger or evil **2** : to run away from **3** : VANISH

¹fleece \ˈflēs\ *n* **1** : the woolly coat of an animal and esp. a sheep **2** : a soft or woolly covering — **fleecy** *adj*

²fleece *vb* **fleeced; fleec·ing 1** : to strip of money or property by fraud or extortion **2** : SHEAR

fleer \ˈfliər\ *vb* : to laugh or grimace in a coarse manner : SNEER

¹fleet \ˈflēt\ *vb* : to pass rapidly

²fleet *n* [ME *flete*, fr. OE *flēot* ship, fr. *flēotan* to float] **1** : a group of warships under one command **2** : a group of ships or vehicles (as trucks or airplanes) under one management

³fleet *adj* **1** : SWIFT, NIMBLE **2** : not enduring : FLEETING — **fleet·ness** *n*

fleet admiral *n* : a commissioned officer of the highest rank in the navy

fleet·ing \ˈflēt-iŋ\ *adj* : passing swiftly

Flem·ing \ˈflem-iŋ\ *n* : a member of a Germanic people inhabiting chiefly northern Belgium

Flem·ish \ˈflem-ish\ *n* **1** : the Germanic language of the Flemings **2** **Flemish** *pl* : FLEMINGS — **Flemish** *adj*

flesh \ˈflesh\ *n* **1** : the soft parts of an animal's body; *esp* : muscular tissue **2** : MEAT **3** : the physical being of man as distinguished from the soul **4** : human beings; *also* : living beings **5** : STOCK, KINDRED **6** : fleshy plant tissue (as fruit pulp) — **fleshed** \ˈflesht\ *adj*

flesh fly *n* : a two-winged fly whose maggots feed on flesh

flesh·ly \ˈflesh-lē\ *adj* **1** : CORPOREAL, BODILY **2** : CARNAL, SENSUAL **3** : not spiritual : WORLDLY

flesh·pot \ˈflesh-ˌpät\ *n* **1** *pl* : bodily comfort : LUXURY **2** : a place of lascivious entertainment — usu. used in pl.

fleshy \ˈflesh-ē\ *adj* **flesh·i·er; -est 1** : consisting of or resembling animal flesh **2** : PLUMP, FAT

flew past of FLY

flex \ˈfleks\ *vb* : to bend esp. repeatedly

flex·i·ble \ˈflek-sə-bəl\ *adj* **1** : capable of being flexed : PLIANT **2** : yielding to influence : TRACTABLE **3** : readily changed or changing : ADAPTABLE **syn** elastic, supple, resilient, springy — **flex·i·bil·i·ty** \ˌflek-sə-ˈbil-ət-ē\ *n*

flex·ure \ˈflek-shər\ *n* : TURN, FOLD, BEND

flib·ber·ti·gib·bet \ˌflib-ərt-ē-ˈjib-ət\ *n* : a silly flighty person

¹flick \ˈflik\ *n* **1** : a light sharp jerky stroke or movement **2** : a sound produced by a flick **3** : FLICKER

²flick *vb* **1** : to strike lightly with a quick sharp motion **2** : FLUTTER, DART, FLIT

¹flick·er \ˈflik-ər\ *vb* **flick·ered; flick·er·ing** \-(ə-)riŋ\ **1** : to move irregularly or unsteadily : FLUTTER **2** : to burn fitfully or with a fluctuating light ⟨a ~ing candle⟩

²flicker *n* **1** : an act of flickering **2** : a sudden brief movement ⟨a ~ of an eyelid⟩ **3** : a momentary stirring ⟨a ~ of interest⟩ **4** : a slight indication : HINT **5** : a wavering light

³flicker *n* : a large insect-eating North American woodpecker with yellow or red on the underside of the wings and tail

flied past of FLY

fli·er \ˈflī(-ə)r\ *n* **1** : one that flies; *esp* : PILOT **2** : a reckless or speculative undertaking **3** : an advertising circular for mass distribution

¹flight \ˈflīt\ *n* **1** : an act or instance of flying **2** : the ability to fly **3** : a passing through the air or through space **4** : the distance covered in a flight **5** : swift movement **6** : a trip made by or in an airplane or spacecraft **7** : a group of similar individuals (as birds or airplanes) flying as a unit **8** : a passing (as of the imagination) beyond ordinary limits **9** : a series of stairs from one landing to another — **flight·less** *adj*

²flight *n* : an act or instance of running away

flight bag *n* **1** : a lightweight traveling

bag with zippered outside pockets **2** : a small canvas satchel

flight line *n* : a parking and servicing area for airplanes

flighty \'flīt-ē\ *adj* **flight·i·er; -est 1** : easily upset : VOLATILE **2** : easily excited : SKITTISH **3** : IRRESPONSIBLE, SILLY

flim·flam \'flim-ˌflam\ *n* : DECEPTION, FRAUD

flim·sy \'flim-zē\ *adj* **flim·si·er; -est 1** : lacking strength or substance **2** : of inferior materials and workmanship **3** : having little worth or plausibility ⟨a ∼ excuse⟩ — **flim·si·ly** \'flim-zə-lē\ *adv* — **flim·si·ness** \-zē-nəs\ *n*

flinch \'flinch\ *vb* [MF *flenchir* to bend] : to shrink from or as if from physical pain : WINCE

¹fling \'fliŋ\ *vb* **flung** \'fləŋ\; **fling·ing** \'fliŋ-iŋ\ **1** : to move hastily, brusquely, or violently ⟨*flung* out of the room⟩ **2** : to kick or plunge vigorously **3** : to throw with force or recklessness : HURL; *also* : to cast as if by throwing **4** : to put suddenly into a state or condition

²fling *n* **1** : an act or instance of flinging **2** : a casual try : ATTEMPT **3** : a period of self-indulgence

flint \'flint\ *n* **1** : a hard quartz that produces a spark when struck by steel **2** : an alloy used for producing a spark in lighters — **flinty** *adj*

flint glass *n* : heavy glass containing an oxide of lead that is used for optical structures (as lenses)

flint·lock \'flint-ˌläk\ *n* **1** : a lock for a firearm using a flint to ignite the charge **2** : a firearm fitted with a flintlock

¹flip \'flip\ *vb* **flipped; flip·ping 1** : to turn by tossing ⟨∼ a coin⟩ **2** : to turn over; *also* : to leaf through **3** : FLICK, JERK ⟨∼ a light switch⟩ **4** : to lose self-control — **flip** *n*

²flip *adj* : FLIPPANT, IMPERTINENT

flip·pant \'flip-ənt\ *adj* : lacking proper respect or seriousness — **flip·pan·cy** \'flip-ən-sē\ *n*

flip·per \'flip-ər\ *n* **1** : a broad flat limb (as of a seal) adapted for swimming **2** : a paddlelike shoe used in skin diving

flip side *n* : the reverse and usu. less popular side of a phonograph record

¹flirt \'flərt\ *vb* **1** : to move erratically : FLIT **2** : to behave amorously without serious intent **3** : to show casual interest ⟨∼ed with the idea of quitting⟩ — **flir·ta·tion** \ˌflər-'tā-shən\ *n* — **flir·ta·tious** \-shəs\ *adj*

²flirt *n* **1** : an act or instance of flirting **2** : a person who flirts

flit \'flit\ *vb* **flit·ted; flit·ting** : to pass or move quickly or abruptly from place to place : DART

flitch \'flich\ *n* : a side of pork cured and smoked as bacon

fliv·ver \'fliv-ər\ *n* : a small cheap usu. old automobile

¹float \'flōt\ *n* **1** : something (as a raft) that floats **2** : a cork buoying up the baited end of a fishing line **3** : a hollow ball that floats at the end of a lever in a cistern or tank and regulates the level of the liquid **4** : a vehicle with a platform to carry an exhibit **5** : a soft drink with ice cream floating in it

²float *vb* **1** : to rest on the surface of or be suspended in a fluid **2** : to move gently on or through a fluid **3** : to cause to float **4** : to wander esp. without a permanent home ⟨the ∼ing population⟩ **5** : FLOOD **6** : to offer (securities) in order to finance an enterprise **7** : to finance by floating an issue of stocks or bonds **8** : to arrange for ⟨∼ a loan⟩ — **float·er** *n*

¹flock \'fläk\ *n* **1** : a group of birds or mammals assembled or herded together **2** : a group of people under the guidance of a leader; *esp* : CONGREGATION **3** : a large number

²flock *vb* : to gather or move in a flock

floe \'flō\ *n* : a flat mass of floating ice

flog \'fläg\ *vb* **flogged; flog·ging** : to beat severely with a rod or whip : LASH — **flog·ger** *n*

¹flood \'fləd\ *n* **1** : a great flow of water over the land **2** : the flowing in of the tide **3** : an overwhelming volume

²flood *vb* **1** : to cover or become filled with a flood **2** : to fill abundantly or excessively; *esp* : to supply (a carburetor) with too much fuel **3** : to pour forth in a flood

flood·gate \'fləd-ˌgāt\ *n* : a gate for controlling a body of water : SLUICE

flood·light \-ˌlīt\ *n* : a lamp that throws a broad beam of light; *also* : the beam itself — **floodlight** *vb*

flood·plain \-ˌplān\ *n* : a plain that may be submerged by floodwaters

flood tide *n* **1** : a rising tide **2** : an overwhelming quantity **3** : a high point : PEAK

flood·wa·ter \ˈfləd-ˌwȯt-ər, -ˌwät-\ *n* : the water of a flood

¹**floor** \ˈflōr\ *n* **1** : the bottom of a room on which one stands **2** : a ground surface **3** : a story of a building **4** : a main level space (as in a legislative chamber) distinguished from a platform or gallery **5** : AUDIENCE **6** : the right to speak from one's place in an assembly **7** : a lower limit ⟨put a ∼ under wheat prices⟩ — **floor·ing** \-iŋ\ *n*

²**floor** *vb* **1** : to furnish with a floor **2** : to knock down **3** : SHOCK, OVERWHELM **4** : DEFEAT

floor·board \-ˌbōrd\ *n* **1** : a board in a floor **2** : the floor of an automobile

floor leader *n* : a member of a legislative body who has charge of a party's organization and strategy on the floor

floor show *n* : a series of acts presented in a nightclub

floor·walk·er \ˈflōr-ˌwȯ-kər\ *n* : a person employed in a retail store to oversee the sales force and aid customers

floo·zy *or* **floo·zie** \ˈflü-zē\ *n, pl* **floozies** : a tawdry or immoral woman

flop \ˈfläp\ *vb* **flopped; flop·ping 1** : FLAP **2** : to throw oneself down heavily, clumsily, or in a relaxed manner ⟨*flopped* into a chair⟩ **3** : FAIL — **flop** *n*

flop·house \ˈfläp-ˌhaủs\ *n* : a cheap hotel

flop·py \ˈfläp-ē\ *adj* **flop·pi·er; -est** : tending to flop; *esp* : soft and flexible

floppy disk *n* : a small flexible disk with a magnetic coating on which computer data can be stored

flo·ra \ˈflōr-ə\ *n, pl* **floras** *also* **flo·rae** \-ˌē, -ˌī\ [L *Flora*, Roman goddess of flowers] : plants or plant life esp. of a region or period

flo·ral \ˈflōr-əl\ *adj* : of or relating to flowers or a flora

flo·res·cence \flȯ-ˈres-ᵊns, flə-\ *n* : a state or period of being in bloom or flourishing — **flo·res·cent** \-ᵊnt\ *adj*

flor·id \ˈflȯr-əd\ *adj* **1** : excessively flowery in style : ORNATE ⟨∼ writing⟩ **2** : tinged with red : RUDDY

flo·rin \ˈflȯr-ən\ *n* **1** : an old gold coin first struck at Florence in 1252 **2** : a gold coin of a European country patterned after the Florentine florin **3** : a modern silver coin in the Netherlands and in Great Britain **4** : GULDEN

flo·rist \ˈflōr-əst\ *n* : one who deals in flowers

¹**floss** \ˈfläs\ *n* **1** : waste or short silk fibers that cannot be reeled **2** : soft thread of silk or mercerized cotton used for embroidery; *also* : DENTAL FLOSS **3** : a lightweight wool knitting yarn **4** : a fluffy filamentous mass esp. of plant fiber ⟨milkweed ∼⟩

²**floss** *vb* : to use dental floss on (one's teeth)

flossy \ˈfläs-ē\ *adj* **floss·i·er; -est 1** : of, relating to, or having the characteristics of floss; *also* : DOWNY **2** : STYLISH, GLAMOROUS

flo·ta·tion \flō-ˈtā-shən\ *n* : the process or an instance of floating

flo·til·la \flō-ˈtil-ə\ *n* [Sp, dim. of *flota* fleet] : FLEET 1; *esp* : a fleet of small ships

flot·sam \ˈflät-səm\ *n* : floating wreckage of a ship or its cargo

¹**flounce** \ˈflaủns\ *vb* **flounced; flounc·ing 1** : to move with exaggerated jerky motions **2** : to go with sudden determination

²**flounce** *n* : an act or instance of flouncing

³**flounce** *n* : a strip of fabric attached by one edge (as to a skirt)

¹**floun·der** \ˈflaủn-dər\ *n, pl* **flounder** *or* **flounders** : FLATFISH; *esp* : one important as food

²**flounder** *vb* **floun·dered; floun·der·ing** \-d(ə-)riŋ\ **1** : to struggle to move or obtain footing **2** : to proceed clumsily ⟨∼ed through his speech⟩

¹**flour** \ˈflaủ(ə)r\ *n* : finely ground and sifted meal of a grain (as wheat); *also* : a fine soft powder — **floury** *adj*

²**flour** *vb* : to coat with or as if with flour

¹**flour·ish** \ˈflər-ish\ *vb* **1** : THRIVE, PROSPER **2** : to be in a state of activity or production ⟨∼ed about 1850⟩ **3** : to reach a height of development or influence **4** : to make bold and sweeping gestures **5** : BRANDISH

²**flourish** *n* **1** : a florid embellishment or passage ⟨a ∼ of drums⟩ **2** : WAVE ⟨with

a ∼ of his cane⟩ **3** : a dramatic action ⟨introduced her with a ∼⟩

¹flout \'flaůt\ *vb* **1** : SCORN **2** : to indulge in scornful behavior : MOCK

²flout *n* : INSULT, MOCKERY

¹flow \'flō\ *vb* **1** : to issue or move in a stream **2** : RISE ⟨the tide ebbs and ∼s⟩ **3** : ABOUND **4** : to proceed smoothly and readily **5** : to have a smooth continuity **6** : to hang loose and billowing **7** : COME, ARISE **8** : MENSTRUATE

²flow *n* **1** : an act of flowing **2** : FLOOD 1, 2 **3** : a smooth uninterrupted movement **4** : STREAM; *also* : a mass of material that has flowed when molten **5** : the quantity that flows in a certain time **6** : MENSTRUATION **7** : YIELD, PRODUCTION **8** : a continuous flow of energy

flow•chart \'flō-ˌchärt\ *n* : a symbolic diagram showing step-by-step progression through a procedure

flow diagram *n* : FLOWCHART

¹flow•er \'flaů(-ə)r\ *n* **1** : a plant branch modified for seed production and bearing leaves specialized into floral organs (as petals) **2** : a plant cultivated or outstanding for its blossoms **3** : the best part or example **4** : the finest most vigorous period **5** : a state of blooming or flourishing — **flow•ered** \'flaů(-ə)rd\ *adj* — **flow•er•less** *adj*

²flower *vb* **1** : to produce flowers : BLOOM **2** : DEVELOP; *also* : FLOURISH

flower girl *n* : a little girl who carries flowers at a wedding

flower head *n* : a very short compact flower cluster suggesting a single flower

flow•er•pot \'flaů(-ə)r-ˌpät\ *n* : a pot in which to grow plants

flow•ery \'flaů(-ə)r-ē\ *adj* **1** : full of or covered with flowers **2** : full of fine words or phrases — **flow•er•i•ness** *n*

flown \'flōn\ past part of FLY

fl oz *abbr* fluidounce

flu \'flü\ *n* **1** : INFLUENZA **2** : any of several minor virus ailments usu. with respiratory symptoms

flub \'fləb\ *vb* **flubbed; flub•bing** : BOTCH, BLUNDER — **flub** *n*

fluc•tu•ate \'flək-chə-ˌwāt\ *vb* **-at•ed; -at•ing** **1** : to move up and down or back and forth **2** : WAVER, VACILLATE

— **fluc•tu•a•tion** \ˌflək-chə-'wā-shən\ *n*

flue \'flü\ *n* : a passage (as in a chimney) for directing a current (as of smoke or gases)

flu•ent \'flü-ənt\ *adj* **1** : capable of flowing : FLUID **2** : ready or facile in speech ⟨∼ in French⟩ **3** : effortlessly smooth and rapid ⟨∼ speech⟩ — **flu•en•cy** \-ən-sē\ *n* — **flu•ent•ly** *adv*

¹fluff \'fləf\ *n* **1** : NAP, DOWN ⟨∼ from a pillow⟩ **2** : something fluffy **3** : something inconsequential **4** : BLUNDER; *esp* : an actor's lapse of memory

²fluff *vb* **1** : to make or become fluffy ⟨∼ up a pillow⟩ **2** : to make a mistake

fluffy \'fləf-ē\ *adj* **fluff•i•er; -est** **1** : having, covered with, or resembling fluff or down **2** : being light and soft or airy ⟨a ∼ omelet⟩ **3** : FATUOUS, SILLY

¹flu•id \'flü-əd\ *adj* **1** : capable of flowing like a liquid or gas **2** : likely to change or move **3** : showing a smooth easy style ⟨∼ movements⟩ **4** : available for a different use; *esp* : easily converted into cash ⟨∼ assets⟩ — **flu•id•i•ty** \flü-'id-ət-ē\ *n*

²fluid *n* : a substance tending to flow or take the shape of its container ⟨liquids and gases are ∼s⟩

flu•id•ounce \ˌflü-əd-'aůns\ *n* — see WEIGHT table

flu•idram \ˌflü-ə(d)-'dram\ *n* — see WEIGHT table

¹fluke \'flük\ *n* : any of various trematode flatworms

²fluke *n* **1** : the part of an anchor that fastens in the ground **2** : a barbed head (as of a harpoon) **3** : a lobe of a whale's tail

³fluke *n* : a stroke of luck ⟨won by a ∼⟩

flume \'flüm\ *n* **1** : an inclined channel for carrying water (as for power) **2** : a ravine or gorge with a stream running through it

flung past and past part of FLING

flunk \'fləŋk\ *vb* : to fail esp. in an examination or course

flun•ky *or* **flun•key** \'fləŋ-kē\ *n, pl* **flunkies** *or* **flunkeys** **1** : a liveried servant; *also* : one performing menial duties **2** : YES-MAN

flu•o•res•cence \ˌflü(-ə)r-'es-ᵊns\ *n* : emission of radiation usu. as visible light during exposure to radiation from some other source; *also* : the emitted radiation — **flu·o·resce** \-'es\ *vb* — **flu·o·res·cent** \-'es-ᵊnt\ *adj*

fluorescent lamp *n* : a tubular electric lamp in which light is produced by the action of ultraviolet light on a fluorescent material that coats the inner surface of the lamp

flu·o·ri·date \'flùr-ə-ˌdāt\ *vb* **-dat·ed; -dat·ing** : to add a fluoride to (as drinking water) to reduce tooth decay — **flu·o·ri·da·tion** \ˌflùr-ə-'dā-shən\ *n*

flu·o·ride \'flù(-ə)r-ˌīd\ *n* : a compound of fluorine with another chemical element or group

flu·o·ri·nate \'flùr-ə-ˌnāt\ *vb* **-nat·ed; -nat·ing** : to treat or cause to combine with fluorine or a compound of fluorine — **flu·o·ri·na·tion** \ˌflùr-ə-'nā-shən\ *n*

flu·o·rine \'flù(-ə)r-ˌēn, -ən\ *n* : a pale yellowish flammable irritating toxic gaseous chemical element

flu·o·rite \'flù(-ə)r-ˌīt\ *n* : a mineral that consists of a fluoride of calcium used as a flux and in making glass

flu·o·ro·car·bon \ˌflù(-ə)r-ō-'kär-bən\ *n* : a compound containing fluorine and carbon used chiefly as a lubricant, refrigerant, or nonstick-coating material

flu·o·ro·scope \'flùr-ə-ˌskōp\ *n* : an instrument for observing the internal structure of an opaque object (as the living body) by means of X rays — **flu·o·ro·scop·ic** \ˌflùr-ə-'skäp-ik\ *adj* — **flu·o·ros·co·py** \-pē\ *n*

flu·o·ro·sis \ˌflùr-'ō-səs\ *n* : an abnormal condition (as spotting of the tooth enamel) caused by fluorine or its compounds

flur·ry \'flər-ē\ *n, pl* **flurries 1** : a gust of wind **2** : a brief light snowfall **3** : COMMOTION, BUSTLE **4** : a brief outburst of activity ⟨a ∼ of trading⟩ — **flurry** *vb*

¹flush \'fləsh\ *vb* : to cause (a bird) to take wing suddenly

²flush *n* : a hand of cards all of the same suit

³flush *n* **1** : a sudden flow (as of water) **2** : a surge esp. of emotion ⟨a ∼ of triumph⟩ **3** : a tinge of red : BLUSH **4** : a fresh and vigorous state ⟨in the ∼ of youth⟩ **5** : a passing sensation of extreme heat

⁴flush *vb* **1** : to flow and spread suddenly and freely **2** : to glow brightly **3**

: BLUSH **4** : to wash out with a rush of fluid **5** : INFLAME, EXCITE **6** : to cause to blush

⁵flush *adj* **1** : full of life and vigor **2** : of a ruddy healthy color **3** : filled to overflowing **4** : AFFLUENT **5** : readily available : ABUNDANT **6** : having an unbroken or even surface **7** : directly abutting : immediately adjacent **8** : set even with the left edge of the type page or column

⁶flush *adv* **1** : in a flush manner **2** : SQUARELY ⟨a blow ∼ on the chin⟩

⁷flush *vb* : to make flush

flus·ter \'fləs-tər\ *vb* : to put into a state of agitated confusion : UPSET — **fluster** *n*

flute \'flüt\ *n* **1** : a hollow pipelike musical instrument **2** : a grooved pleat **3** : CHANNEL, GROOVE — **flute** *vb* — **fluted** *adj*

flut·ing \'flüt-iŋ\ *n* : fluted decoration

flut·ist \'flüt-əst\ *n* : a flute player

¹flut·ter \'flət-ər\ *vb* [ME *floteren* to float, flutter, fr. OE *floterian*, fr. *flotian* to float] **1** : to flap the wings rapidly **2** : to move with quick wavering or flapping motions **3** : to vibrate in irregular spasms **4** : to move about or behave in an agitated aimless manner — **flut·tery** \-ə-rē\ *adj*

²flutter *n* **1** : an act of fluttering **2** : a state of nervous confusion **3** : FLURRY, COMMOTION

¹flux \'fləks\ *n* **1** : an act of flowing **2** : a state of continuous change **3** : a substance used to aid in fusing metals

²flux *vb* : FUSE

¹fly \'flī\ *vb* **flew** \'flü\; **flown** \'flōn\; **flying 1** : to move in or pass through the air with wings **2** : to move through the air or before the wind **3** : to float or cause to float, wave, or soar in the air **4** : FLEE **5** : to fade and disappear : VANISH **6** : to move or pass swiftly **7** : to become expended or dissipated rapidly **8** : to pursue or attack in flight **9** : to operate or travel in an aircraft or spacecraft **10** : to journey over by flying **11** : AVOID, SHUN **12** : to transport by flying

²fly *n, pl* **flies 1** : the action or process of flying : FLIGHT **2** *pl* : the space over a theater stage **3** : a garment closing concealed by a fold of cloth extending over the fastener **4** : the outer canvas of a tent with a double top **5** : the length of an extended flag from its staff or support **6** : a baseball hit high into the air — **on the fly** : while still in the air

³**fly** *vi* **flied; fly•ing** : to hit a fly in baseball

⁴**fly** *n, pl* **flies 1** : a winged insect — usu. used in combination ⟨butter*fly*⟩ **2** : TWO-WINGED FLY; *esp* : one (as a housefly) that is large and stout-bodied **3** : a fishhook dressed to suggest an insect

fly•able \'flī-ə-bəl\ *adj* : suitable for flying or being flown

fly ball *n* : ²FLY 6

fly•blown \'flī-ˌblōn\ *adj* : not pure : TAINTED, CORRUPT

fly•by \'flī-ˌbī\ *n, pl* **flybys 1** : a usu. low-altitude flight past a designated point by an aircraft **2** : a flight of a spacecraft past a heavenly body (as Jupiter) close enough to obtain scientific data; *also* : a spacecraft that makes a flyby

fly–by–night \'flī-bə-ˌnīt\ *adj* **1** : seeking a quick profit usu. by shady acts **2** : TRANSITORY, PASSING

fly casting *n* : the act or practice of throwing the lure in angling with artificial flies

fly•catch•er \'flī-ˌkach-ər, -ˌkech-\ *n* : a small bird that feeds on insects caught in flight

fly•er var of FLIER

flying boat *n* : a seaplane with a hull designed for floating

flying buttress *n* : a projecting arched structure to support a wall or building

flying fish *n* : any of numerous fishes with long fins suggesting wings that enable them to glide some distance through the air

flying saucer *n* : an unidentified flying object reported to be saucer-shaped or disk-shaped

flying squirrel *n* : any of several No. American squirrels with folds of skin connecting the forelegs and hind legs that enable them to make long gliding leaps

fly•leaf \'flī-ˌlēf\ *n* : a blank leaf at the beginning or end of a book

fly•pa•per \-ˌpā-pər\ *n* : paper poisoned or coated with a sticky substance for killing or catching flies

fly•speck \-ˌspek\ *n* **1** : a speck of fly dung **2** : something small and insignificant — **flyspeck** *vb*

fly•way \-ˌwā\ *n* : an established air route of migratory birds

fly•wheel \-ˌhwēl\ *n* : a heavy wheel for regulating the speed of machinery

fm *abbr* fathom

Fm *symbol* fermium

FM \'ef-'em\ *n* : a broadcasting system using frequency modulation; *also* : a radio receiver of such a system — **FM** *adj*

fn *abbr* footnote

fo *or* **fol** *abbr* folio

FO *abbr* foreign office

foal \'fōl\ *n* : the young of a horse or related animal; *esp* : one under one year — **foal** *vb*

¹**foam** \'fōm\ *n* **1** : a mass of bubbles formed on the surface of a liquid : FROTH, SPUME **2** : material (as rubber) in a lightweight cellular form — **foamy** *adj*

²**foam** *vb* : to form foam : FROTH

fob \'fäb\ *n* **1** : a short strap, ribbon, or chain attached esp. to a pocket watch **2** : a small ornament worn on a fob

FOB *abbr* free on board

fob off *vb* **1** : to put off with a trick, excuse, or inferior substitute **2** : to pass or offer as genuine **3** : to put aside

FOC *abbr* free of charge

focal length *n* : the distance of a focus from a lens or concave mirror

fo'•c'sle var of FORECASTLE

¹**fo•cus** \'fō-kəs\ *n, pl* **fo•ci** \-ˌsī\ *also* **fo•cus•es** [L, *hearth*] **1** : a point at which rays (as of light, heat, or sound) meet or diverge or appear to diverge; *esp* : the point at which an image is formed by a mirror, lens, or optical system **2** : FOCAL LENGTH **3** : adjustment (as of eyes or eyeglasses) that gives clear vision **4** : central point : CENTER — **fo•cal** \'fō-kəl\ *adj* — **fo•cal•ly** \-ē\ *adv*

²**focus** *vb* **-cused** *also* **-cussed; -cus•ing** *also* **cus•sing 1** : to bring or come to a focus ⟨~ rays of light⟩ **2** : CENTER ⟨~ attention on a problem⟩ **3** : to adjust the focus of

fod•der \'fäd-ər\ *n* : coarse dry food (as cornstalks) for livestock

foe \'fō\ *n* [ME *fo*, fr. OE *fāh*, fr. *fāh* hostile] : ENEMY

FOE *abbr* Fraternal Order of Eagles

foehn *or* **föhn** \'fə(r)n, 'fœn, 'fān\ *n* [G föhn] : a warm dry wind blowing down a mountainside

foe·man \'fō-mən\ *n* : FOE

foe·tal, foe·tus *chiefly Brit* var of FETAL, FETUS

¹fog \'fȯg, 'fäg\ *n* **1** : fine particles of water suspended in the lower atmosphere **2** : mental confusion — **fog·gy** *adj*

²fog *vb* **fogged; fog·ging** : to obscure or become obscured with or as if with fog

fog·horn \-ˌhȯrn\ *n* : a horn sounded in a fog to give warning

fo·gy *also* **fo·gey** \'fō-gē\ *n, pl* **fogies** *also* **fogeys** : a person with old-fashioned ideas ⟨he's an old ∼⟩

foi·ble \'fȯi-bəl\ *n* : a minor failing or weakness in character or behavior

¹foil \'fȯil\ *vb* [ME *foilen* to trample, full cloth, fr. MF *fouler*] **1** : to prevent from attaining an end : DEFEAT **2** : to bring to naught : THWART

²foil *n* : a fencing weapon with a light flexible blade tapering to a blunt point

³foil *n* [ME, leaf, fr. MF *foille, foil*, fr. L *folium*] **1** : a very thin sheet of metal **2** : one that serves as a contrast to another

foist \'fȯist\ *vb* : to pass off (something false or worthless) as genuine

¹fold \'fōld\ *n* **1** : an enclosure for sheep **2** : a group of people with a common faith, belief, or interest

²fold *vb* : to house (sheep) in a fold

³fold *vb* **1** : to lay one part over or against another part **2** : to clasp together **3** : EMBRACE **4** : to bend (as a layer of rock) into folds **5** : to incorporate into a mixture by overturning repeatedly without stirring or beating **6** : to become doubled or pleated **7** : FAIL, COLLAPSE

⁴fold *n* **1** : a doubling or folding over **2** : a part doubled or laid over another part

fold·away \ˌfōl-də-ˌwā\ *adj* : designed to fold out of the way or out of sight

fold·er \'fōl-dər\ *n* **1** : one that folds **2** : a folded printed circular **3** : a folded cover or large envelope for loose papers

fol·de·rol \'fäl-də-ˌräl\ *n* **1** : a useless trifle **2** : NONSENSE

fold·out \'fōld-ˌaut\ *n* : a folded leaf (as in a magazine) larger in some dimensions than the page

fo·liage \'fō-l(ē-)ij\ *n* : a mass of leaves (as of a plant or forest)

fo·li·at·ed \'fō-lē-ˌāt-əd\ *adj* : separable into layers

fo·lio \'fō-lē-ˌō\ *n, pl* **fo·li·os** **1** : a leaf of a book; *also* : a page number **2** : the size of a piece of paper cut two from a sheet **3** : a book printed on folio pages

¹folk \'fōk\ *n, pl* **folk** *or* **folks** **1** : a group of people forming a tribe or nation; *also* : the largest number or most characteristic part of such a group **2** *pl* : PEOPLE, PERSONS ⟨country ∼⟩ ⟨old ∼s⟩ **3** *folks pl* : the persons of one's own family

²folk *adj* : of, relating to, or originating among the common people ⟨∼ music⟩

folk·lore \-ˌlōr\ *n* : customs, beliefs, stories, and sayings of a people handed down from generation to generation — **folk·lor·ist** \-əst\ *n*

folk mass *n* : a mass in which traditional liturgical music is replaced by folk music

folk·sing·er \'fōk-ˌsiŋ-ər\ *n* : a singer of folk songs — **folk·sing·ing** \-ˌsiŋ-iŋ\ *n*

folksy \'fōk-sē\ *adj* **folks·i·er; -est** **1** : SOCIABLE, FRIENDLY **2** : informal, casual, or familiar in manner or style

folk·way \'fōk-ˌwā\ *n* : a way of thinking, feeling, or acting common to a given group of people; *esp* : a traditional social custom

fol·li·cle \'fäl-i-kəl\ *n* **1** : a small anatomical cavity or gland ⟨a hair ∼⟩ **2** : a small fluid-filled cavity in the ovary of a mammal enclosing a developing egg

fol·low \'fäl-ō\ *vb* **1** : to go or come after **2** : PURSUE **3** : OBEY **4** : to proceed along **5** : to engage in as a way of life ⟨∼ the sea⟩ ⟨∼ a profession⟩ **6** : to come after in order or rank or natural sequence **7** : to keep one's attention fixed on **8** : to result from **syn** succeed, ensue, supervene — **fol·low·er** *n* — **follow suit** **1** : to play a card of the same suit as the card led **2** : to follow an example set

¹fol·low·ing \'fäl-ə-wiŋ\ *adj* **1** : next after

: SUCCEEDING **2** : that immediately follows

²following *n* : a group of followers, adherents, or partisans

³following *prep* : subsequent to : AFTER

follow–up \'fäl-ə-ˌwəp\ *n* : a system or instance of pursuing an initial effort by supplementary action

fol·ly \'fäl-ē\ *n, pl* **follies** [ME *folie,* fr. OF, fr. *fol* fool] **1** : lack of good sense **2** : a foolish act or idea : FOOLISHNESS **3** : an excessively costly or unprofitable undertaking

fo·ment \fō-'ment\ *vb* : to stir up : INSTIGATE

fo·men·ta·tion \ˌfō-mən-'tā-shən, -ˌmen-\ *n* **1** : a hot moist material (as a damp cloth) applied to the body to ease pain **2** : the act of fomenting : INSTIGATION

fond \'fänd\ *adj* [ME, fr. *fonne* fool] **1** : FOOLISH, SILLY ⟨∼ pride⟩ **2** : prizing highly : DESIROUS ⟨∼ of praise⟩ **3** : strongly attracted or predisposed ⟨∼ of music⟩ **4** : foolishly tender : INDULGENT; *also* : LOVING, AFFECTIONATE **5** : CHERISHED, DEAR ⟨his ∼*est* hopes⟩ — **fond·ly** \'fän-(d)lē\ *adv* — **fond·ness** \'fän(d)-nəs\ *n*

fon·dant \'fän-dənt\ *n* : a creamy preparation of sugar used as a basis for candies or icings

fon·dle \'fän-dᵊl\ *vb* **fon·dled; fon·dling** \-(d)liŋ, -dᵊl-iŋ\ : to touch or handle lovingly : CARESS, PET

fon·due *also* **fon·du** \fän-'d(y)ü\ *n* [F] : a preparation of melted cheese usu. flavored with wine or brandy

¹font \'fänt\ *n* **1** : a receptacle for baptismal or holy water **2** : FOUNTAIN, SOURCE

²font *n* : an assortment of printing type of one size and style

food \'füd\ *n* **1** : material taken into an organism and used for growth, repair, and vital processes and as a source of energy; *also* : organic material produced by green plants and used by them as food **2** : solid nutritive material as distinguished from drink **3** : something that nourishes, sustains, or supplies ⟨∼ for thought⟩

food chain *n* : a hierarchical arrangement of organisms in an ecological community such that each uses the next usu. lower member as a food source

food poisoning *n* : a digestive illness caused by bacteria or by chemicals in food

food·stuff \'füd-ˌstəf\ *n* : something with food value; *esp* : a specific nutrient (as fat or protein)

food web *n* : the interacting food chains of an ecological community

¹fool \'fül\ *n* [ME, fr. OF *fol,* fr. LL *follis,* fr. L, bellows, bag] **1** : a person who lacks sense or judgment **2** : JESTER **3** : DUPE **4** : IDIOT

²fool *vb* **1** : to spend time idly or aimlessly **2** : to meddle or tamper thoughtlessly or ignorantly **3** : JOKE **4** : DECEIVE **5** : FRITTER ⟨∼ed away his time⟩

fool·ery \'fül-(ə-)rē\ *n, pl* **-er·ies 1** : the habit of fooling : the behavior of a fool **2** : a foolish act : HORSEPLAY

fool·har·dy \'fül-ˌhärd-ē\ *adj* : foolishly daring : RASH — **fool·har·di·ness** \-ˌhärd-ē-nəs\ *n*

fool·ish \'fü-lish\ *adj* **1** : showing or arising from folly or lack of judgment **2** : ABSURD, RIDICULOUS **3** : ABASHED — **fool·ish·ly** *adv* — **fool·ish·ness** *n*

fool·proof \'fül-ˌprüf\ *adj* : so simple or reliable as to leave no opportunity for error, misuse, or failure

fools·cap \'fül-ˌskap\ *n* [fr. the watermark of a fool's cap formerly applied to such paper] : a size of paper typically 16×13 inches

¹foot \'fut\ *n, pl* **feet** \'fēt\ *also* **foot 1** : the terminal part of a leg on which one stands **2** — see WEIGHT table **3** : a group of syllables forming the basic unit of verse meter **4** : something resembling an animal's foot in position or use **5** *foot pl, chiefly Brit* : INFANTRY **6** : the lowest part : BOTTOM **7** : the part at the opposite end from the head **8** : the part (as of a stocking) that covers the foot

²foot *vb* **1** : DANCE **2** : to go on foot **3** : to add up **4** : to pay or provide for paying

foot·age \'fut-ij\ *n* : length expressed in feet

foot·ball \'fut-ˌbȯl\ *n* **1** : any of several games played by two teams on a rectangular field with goalposts at each end; *esp* : one in which the ball is in possession of one team at a time and is advanced by running or passing **2** : the ball used in football

foot·board \-ˌbōrd\ *n* **1** : a narrow platform on which to stand or brace the feet **2** : a board forming the foot of a bed

foot·bridge \-ˌbrij\ *n* : a bridge for pedestrians

foot·ed \ˈfu̇t-əd\ *adj* : having a foot or feet of a specified kind or number ⟨flat-*footed*⟩ ⟨four-*footed*⟩

-foot·er \ˈfu̇t-ər\ *comb form* : one that is a specified number of feet in height, length, or breadth ⟨a six-*footer*⟩

foot·fall \ˈfu̇t-ˌfȯl\ *n* : the sound of a footstep

foot·hill \-ˌhil\ *n* : a hill at the foot of higher hills or mountains

foot·hold \-ˌhōld\ *n* **1** : a hold for the feet : FOOTING **2** : a position usable as a base for further advance

foot·ing \ˈfu̇t-iŋ\ *n* **1** : the placing of one's feet in a stable position **2** : the act of moving on foot **3** : a place or space for standing : FOOTHOLD **4** : position with respect to one another : STATUS **5** : BASIS **6** : the sum of a column of figures

foot·less \ˈfu̇t-ləs\ *adj* **1** : having no feet **2** : INEPT

foot·lights \-ˌlīts\ *n pl* **1** : a row of lights along the front of a stage floor **2** : the stage as a profession

foo·tling \ˈfu̇t-liŋ\ *adj* **1** : INEPT **2** : TRIVIAL

foot·lock·er \ˈfu̇t-ˌläk-ər\ *n* : a small trunk designed to be placed at the foot of a bed (as in a barracks)

foot·loose \-ˌlüs\ *adj* : having no ties : FREE, UNTRAMMELED

foot·man \-mən\ *n* : a male servant who attends a carriage, waits on table, admits visitors, and runs errands

foot·note \-ˌnōt\ *n* **1** : a note of reference, explanation, or comment placed usu. at the bottom of a page **2** : COMMENTARY

foot·pad \-ˌpad\ *n* : a round somewhat flat foot on the leg of a spacecraft for distributing weight to minimize sinking into a surface

foot·path \ˈfu̇t-ˌpath, -ˌpȧth\ *n* : a narrow path for pedestrians

foot·print \-ˌprint\ *n* : an impression of the foot

foot·race \-ˌrās\ *n* : a race run on foot

foot·rest \-ˌrest\ *n* : a support for the feet

foot·sore \-ˌsōr\ *adj* : having sore or tender feet (as from much walking)

foot·step \-ˌstep\ *n* **1** : the mark of the foot : TRACK **2** : TREAD **3** : distance covered by a step : PACE **4** : a step on which to ascend or descend **5** : a way of life, conduct, or action

foot·stool \-ˌstül\ *n* : a low stool to support the feet

foot·wear \-ˌwaər\ *n* : apparel (as shoes or boots) for the feet

foot·work \-ˌwərk\ *n* : the management of the feet (as in boxing)

fop \ˈfäp\ *n* : DANDY **1** — **fop·pery** \-(ə-)rē\ *n* — **fop·pish** *adj*

¹for \fər, (ˈ)fȯr\ *prep* **1** : as a preparation toward ⟨dress ∼ dinner⟩ **2** : toward the purpose or goal of ⟨need time ∼ study⟩ ⟨money ∼ a trip⟩ **3** : so as to reach or attain ⟨run ∼ cover⟩ **4** : as being ⟨took him ∼ a fool⟩ **5** : because of ⟨cry ∼ joy⟩ **6** — used to indicate a recipient ⟨a letter ∼ you⟩ **7** : in support of ⟨fought ∼ his country⟩ **8** : directed at : AFFECTING ⟨a cure ∼ what ails you⟩ **9** — used with a noun or pronoun followed by an infinitive to form the equivalent of a noun clause ⟨∼ you to go would be silly⟩ **10** : in exchange as equal to : so as to return the value of ⟨a lot of trouble ∼ nothing⟩ ⟨pay $10 ∼ a hat⟩ **11** : CONCERNING ⟨a stickler ∼ detail⟩ **12** : CONSIDERING ⟨tall ∼ his age⟩ **13** : through the period of ⟨served ∼ three years⟩ **14** : in honor of

²for *conj* : BECAUSE

³for *abbr* **1** foreign **2** forestry

fora *pl of* FORUM

¹for·age \ˈfȯr-ij\ *n* **1** : food for animals esp. when taken by browsing or grazing **2** : a search for provisions

²forage *vb* **for·aged; for·ag·ing** **1** : to collect forage from **2** : to wander in search of provisions **3** : to get by foraging **4** : to make a search : RUMMAGE

for·ay \ˈfȯr-ˌā\ *vb* : to raid esp. in search of plunder : PILLAGE — **foray** *n*

¹for·bear \fȯr-ˈbaər\ *vb* **-bore** \-ˈbōr\; **-borne** \-ˈbōrn\; **-bear·ing** **1** : to refrain from : ABSTAIN **2** : to be patient — **for·bear·ance** \-ˈbar-əns\ *n*

²forbear *var of* FOREBEAR

for·bid \fər-ˈbid\ *vb* **-bade** \-ˈbad, -ˈbād\

or **-bad** \-ˈbad\; **-bid·den** \-ˈbid-ᵊn\; **-bid·ding 1** : to command against : PROHIBIT **2** : HINDER, PREVENT **syn** enjoin, interdict, inhibit, ban

for·bid·ding \-iŋ\ *adj* : DISAGREEABLE, REPELLENT

forbode var of FOREBODE

¹force \ˈfōrs\ *n* **1** : strength or energy esp. of an exceptional degree : active power **2** : capacity to persuade or convince **3** : military strength; *also,* *pl* : the whole military strength (as of a nation) **4** : a body (as of persons or ships) available for a particular purpose **5** : VIOLENCE, COMPULSION **6** : an influence (as a push or pull) that causes motion or a change of motion — **force·ful** \-fəl\ *adj* — **force·ful·ly** \-ē\ *adv* — **in force 1** : in great numbers **2** : VALID, OPERATIVE

²force *vb* **forced; forc·ing 1** : COMPEL, COERCE **2** : to cause through necessity ⟨*forced* to admit defeat⟩ **3** : to press, attain to, or effect against resistance or inertia ⟨~ your way through⟩ **4** : to raise or accelerate to the utmost ⟨~ the pace⟩ **5** : to produce with unnatural or unwilling effort ⟨*forced* laughter⟩ **6** : to hasten (as in growth) by artificial means

for·ceps \ˈfor-səps\ *n, pl* **forceps** [L] : a hand-held instrument for grasping, holding, or pulling objects esp. for delicate operations (as by a surgeon)

forc·ible \ˈfor-sə-bəl\ *adj* **1** : obtained or done by force **2** : showing force or energy : POWERFUL — **forc·i·bly** \-blē\ *adv*

¹ford \ˈfōrd\ *n* : a place where a stream may be crossed by wading

²ford *vb* : to cross (a body of water) by wading

¹fore \ˈfōr\ *adv* : in, toward, or adjacent to the front : FORWARD

²fore *adj* : being or coming before in time, order, or space

³fore *n* : something that occupies a front position

⁴fore *interj* — used by a golfer to warn anyone within range of the probable line of flight of his ball

fore–and–aft \ˌfōr-ə-ˈnaft\ *adj* : lying, running, or acting along the length of a structure (as a ship)

¹fore·arm \ˈfōr-ˈärm\ *vb* : to arm in advance : PREPARE

²fore·arm \ˈfōr-ˌärm\ *n* : the part of the arm between the elbow and the wrist

fore·bear *or* **for·bear** \-ˌbaər\ *n* : ANCESTOR, FOREFATHER

fore·bode *also* **for·bode** \fōr-ˈbōd, fȯr-\ *vb* **1** : to have a premonition esp. of misfortune **2** : FORETELL, PREDICT **syn** augur, bode, foreshadow, portend, promise — **fore·bod·ing** *n*

fore·cast \ˈfōr-ˌkast\ *vb* **-cast** *also* **-cast·ed; -cast·ing 1** : PREDICT, CALCULATE ⟨~ weather conditions⟩ **2** : to indicate as likely to occur — **forecast** *n* — **fore·cast·er** *n*

fore·cas·tle \ˈfōk-səl\ *n* **1** : the forward part of the upper deck of a ship **2** : the living area for the crew in the forward part of a ship

fore·close \fōr-ˈklōz\ *vb* **1** : to shut out : PRECLUDE **2** : to take legal measures to terminate a mortgage and take possession of the mortgaged property

fore·clo·sure \-ˈklō-zhər\ *n* : the act of foreclosing; *esp* : the legal procedure of foreclosing a mortgage

fore·doom \fōr-ˈdüm\ *vb* : to doom beforehand

fore·fa·ther \ˈfōr-ˌfäth-ər\ *n* **1** : ANCESTOR **2** : a person of an earlier period and common heritage

forefend var of FORFEND

fore·fin·ger \-ˌfiŋ-gər\ *n* : the finger next to the thumb

fore·foot \-ˌfut\ *n* : either of the front feet of a quadruped

fore·front \-ˌfrənt\ *n* : the foremost part or place : VANGUARD

fore·gath·er var of FORGATHER

¹fore·go \fōr-ˈgō\ *vb* **-went** \-ˈwent\; **-gone** \-ˈgȯn\; **-go·ing** \-ˈgō-iŋ\ : PRECEDE

²forego var of FORGO

fore·go·ing \-ˈgō-iŋ\ *adj* : PRECEDING

fore·gone \ˌfōr-ˌgȯn\ *adj* : determined in advance ⟨a ~ conclusion⟩

fore·ground \ˈfōr-ˌgraund\ *n* **1** : the part of a scene or representation that appears nearest to and in front of the spectator **2** : a position of prominence

fore·hand \-ˌhand\ *n* : a stroke (as in tennis) made with the palm of the hand turned in the direction in which the hand is moving; *also* : the side on which such a stroke is made — **forehand** *adj*

fore·hand·ed \-ˈhan-dəd\ *adj* : mindful of the future : THRIFTY, PRUDENT

fore·head \ˈfȯr-əd, ˈfōr-ˌhed\ *n* : the part of the face above the eyes

for·eign \ˈfȯr-ən\ *adj* [ME *forein*, fr. OF, fr. LL *foranus* on the outside, fr. L *foris* outside] **1** : situated outside a place or country and esp. one's own country **2** : born in, belonging to, or characteristic of some place or country other than the one under consideration ⟨~ language⟩ **3** : not connected or pertinent **4** : related to or dealing with other nations ⟨~ affairs⟩ **5** : occurring in an abnormal situation in the living body ⟨a ~ body in the eye⟩

for·eign·er \ˈfȯr-ə-nər\ *n* : a person belonging to or owing allegiance to a foreign country

foreign minister *n* : a governmental minister for foreign affairs

fore·know \fōr-ˈnō\ *vb* **-knew** \-ˈn(y)ü\; **-known** \-ˈnōn\; **-know·ing** : to have previous knowledge of — **fore·knowl·edge** \-ˈnäl-ij\ *n*

fore·la·dy \ˈfōr-ˌlād-ē\ *n* : a woman who acts as a foreman

fore·leg \-ˌleg\ *n* : a front leg

fore·limb \-ˌlim\ *n* : either of an anterior pair of limbs (as wings, arms, or fins)

fore·lock \-ˌläk\ *n* : a lock of hair growing from the front part of the head

fore·man \ˈfōr-mən\ *n* **1** : a spokesperson of a jury **2** : a person in charge of a group of workers

fore·mast \-ˌmast\ *n* : the mast nearest the bow of a ship

fore·most \-ˌmōst\ *adj* : first in time, place, or order : most important : PREEMINENT — **foremost** *adv*

fore·name \-ˌnām\ *n* : a first name

fore·named \-ˌnāmd\ *adj* : previously named : AFORESAID

fore·noon \-ˌnün\ *n* : MORNING

¹fo·ren·sic \fə-ˈren-sik\ *adj* [L *forensis* public, forensic, fr. *forum* forum] : belonging to, used in, or suitable to courts of law or to public speaking or debate

²forensic *n* **1** : an argumentative exercise **2** *pl* : the art or study of argumentative discourse

fore·or·dain \ˌfōr-ȯr-ˈdān\ *vb* : to ordain or decree beforehand : PREDESTINE

fore·part \ˈfōr-ˌpärt\ *n* **1** : the anterior part of something **2** : the earlier part of a period of time

fore·quar·ter \-ˌkwȯrt-ər\ *n* : the front half of a lateral half of the body or carcass of a quadruped ⟨a ~ of beef⟩

fore·run·ner \ˈfōr-ˌrən-ər\ *n* **1** : one that goes before to give notice of the approach of others : HARBINGER **2** : PREDECESSOR, ANCESTOR **syn** precursor, herald

fore·sail \ˈfōr-ˌsāl, -səl\ *n* : the largest sail on the foremast of a square-rigged ship or schooner

fore·see \fōr-ˈsē\ *vb* **-saw** \-ˈsȯ\; **-seen** \-ˈsēn\; **-see·ing** : to see or realize beforehand : EXPECT **syn** foreknow, divine, apprehend, anticipate — **fore·see·able** *adj*

fore·shad·ow \-ˈshad-ō\ *vb* : to give a hint or suggestion of beforehand

fore·short·en \fōr-ˈshȯrt-ᵊn\ *vb* : to shorten (a detail) in a drawing or painting so that it appears to have depth

fore·sight \ˈfōr-ˌsīt\ *n* **1** : the act or power of foreseeing **2** : an act of looking forward; *also* : a view forward **3** : care or provision for the future : PRUDENCE — **fore·sight·ed** \-əd\ *adj* — **fore·sight·ed·ness** *n*

fore·skin \-ˌskin\ *n* : a fold of skin enclosing the end of the penis

for·est \ˈfȯr-əst\ *n* [ME, fr. OF, fr. ML *forestis*, fr. L *foris* outside] : a large thick growth of trees and underbrush — **for·est·ed** \ˈfȯr-ə-stəd\ *adj* — **for·est·land** \ˈfȯr-əst-ˌland\ *n*

fore·stall \fōr-ˈstȯl, fȯr-\ *vb* **1** : to keep out, hinder, or prevent by measures taken in advance **2** : ANTICIPATE

forest ranger *n* : a person in charge of the management and protection of a portion of a forest

for·est·ry \ˈfȯr-ə-strē\ *n* : the science of growing and caring for forests — **for·est·er** \ˈfȯr-ə-stər\ *n*

foreswear var of FORSWEAR

¹fore·taste \ˈfōr-ˌtāst\ *n* : an advance indication, warning, or notion

²fore·taste \fōr-ˈtāst\ *vb* : to taste beforehand : ANTICIPATE

fore·tell \fōr-ˈtel\ *vb* **-told** \-ˈtōld\; **-tell·ing** : to tell of beforehand : PREDICT **syn** forecast, prophesy, prognosticate

fore·thought \ˈfōr-ˌthȯt\ *n* **1** : PREMEDI-

TATION **2** : consideration for the future

fore·to·ken \fōr-'tō-kən\ vb **-kened; -ken·ing** \-'tōk-(ə-)niŋ\ : to indicate in advance

fore·top \'fōr-ˌtäp\ n : a platform near the top of a ship's foremast

for·ev·er \fȯr-'ev-ər\ adv **1** : for a limitless time **2** : at all times : ALWAYS

for·ev·er·more \-ˌev-ər-'mōr\ adv : FOREVER

fore·warn \fōr-'wȯrn\ vb : to warn beforehand

forewent past of FOREGO

fore·wing \'fōr-ˌwiŋ\ n : either of the anterior wings of a 4-winged insect

fore·wom·an \'fōr-ˌwüm-ən\ n : FORELADY

fore·word \-ˌwərd\ n : PREFACE

¹for·feit \'fȯr-fət\ n **1** : something forfeited : PENALTY, FINE **2** : FORFEITURE **3** : something deposited and then redeemed on payment of a fine **4** pl : a game in which forfeits are exacted

²forfeit vb : to lose or lose the right to by some error, offense, or crime

for·fei·ture \'fȯr-fə-ˌchùr\ n **1** : the act of forfeiting **2** : something forfeited : PENALTY

for·fend \fȯr-'fend\ vb **1** : PREVENT **2** : PROTECT, PRESERVE

for·gath·er or **fore·gath·er** \fȯr-'gath-ər, fōr-, -'geth-\ vb **1** : to come together : ASSEMBLE **2** : to meet someone usu. by chance

¹forge \'fōrj\ n [ME, fr. OF, fr. L fabrica, fr. faber smith] : a furnace or shop with its furnace where metal is heated and worked

²forge vb **forged; forg·ing 1** : to form (metal) by heating and hammering **2** : FASHION, SHAPE ⟨~ an agreement⟩ **3** : to make or imitate falsely esp. with intent to defraud ⟨~ a signature⟩ — **forg·er** n — **forg·ery** \'fōrj-(ə-)rē\ n

³forge vb **forged; forg·ing** : to move ahead steadily but gradually

for·get \fər-'get\ vb **-got** \-'gät\; **-got·ten** \-'gät-ᵊn\ or **-got; -get·ting 1** : to be unable to think of or recall **2** : to fail to become mindful of at the proper time **3** : NEGLECT, DISREGARD — **for·get·ful** \-'get-fəl\ adj — **for·get·ful·ly** \-ē\ adv

for·get–me–not \fər-'get-mē-ˌnät\ n : any of a genus of small herbs having bright-blue or white flowers usu. arranged in a curving spike

forg·ing \'fōr-jiŋ\ n : a piece of forged work

for·give \fər-'giv\ vb **-gave** \-'gāv\; **-giv·en** \-'giv-ən\; **-giv·ing 1** : PARDON, ABSOLVE **2** : to give up resentment of **3** : to grant relief from payment of — **for·giv·able** adj — **for·give·ness** n

for·giv·ing \-iŋ\ adj **1** : showing forgiveness : inclined or ready to forgive **2** : allowing room for error or weakness

for·go or **fore·go** \fȯr-'gō, fōr-\ vb **-went** \-'went\; **-gone** \-'gȯn\; **-go·ing** \-'gō-iŋ\ : to abstain from : GIVE UP, RENOUNCE

fo·rint \'fȯr-int\ n, pl **forints** also **forint** — see MONEY table

¹fork \'fȯrk\ n **1** : an implement with two or more prongs for taking up (as in eating), piercing, pitching, or digging **2** : a forked part, tool, or piece of equipment **3** : a dividing into branches or a place where something branches; also : a branch of such a fork

²fork vb **1** : to divide into two or more branches **2** : to give the form of a fork to ⟨~ing her fingers⟩ **3** : to raise or pitch with a fork ⟨~ hay⟩

forked \'fȯrkt, 'fȯr-kəd\ adj : having a fork : shaped like a fork ⟨~ lightning⟩

fork·lift \'fȯrk-ˌlift\ n : a machine for hoisting heavy objects by means of steel fingers inserted under the load

for·lorn \fər-'lȯrn\ adj **1** : sad and lonely because of isolation or desertion **2** : WRETCHED **3** : nearly hopeless — **for·lorn·ly** adv

forlorn hope n [modif. of Dutch verloren hoop, lit., lost band] **1** : a body of men selected to perform a perilous service **2** : a desperate or extremely difficult enterprise

¹form \'fȯrm\ n **1** : SHAPE, STRUCTURE **2** : a body esp. of a person : FIGURE **3** : the essential nature of a thing **4** : established manner of doing or saying something **5** : FORMULA **6** : a document with blank spaces for insertion of information ⟨tax ~⟩ **7** : CEREMONY, CONVENTIONALITY **8** : manner of performing according to recognized standards **9** : a long seat : BENCH **10** : a model of the human figure used for displaying clothes **11** : MOLD ⟨a ~ for concrete⟩ **12** : type or plates in a frame ready for printing **13** : MODE,

KIND, VARIETY ⟨coal is a ∼ of carbon⟩ **14** : orderly method of arrangement; *also* : a particular kind or instance of such arrangement ⟨the sonnet ∼ in poetry⟩ **15** : the structural element, plan, or design of a work of art **16** : a bounded surface or volume **17** : a grade in a British secondary school or in some American private schools **18** : RACING FORM **19** : known ability to perform; *also* : condition (as of an athlete) suitable for performing **20** : one of the ways in which a word is changed to show difference in use ⟨the plural ∼ of a noun⟩

²**form** *vb* **1** : to give form or shape to : FASHION, MAKE **2** : TRAIN, INSTRUCT **3** : DEVELOP, ACQUIRE ⟨∼ a habit⟩ **4** : CONSTITUTE, COMPOSE **5** : to arrange in order ⟨∼ a battle line⟩ **6** : to take form : ARISE ⟨clouds are ∼ing⟩ **7** : to take a definite form, shape, or arrangement

¹**for•mal** \'för-məl\ *adj* **1** : based on conventional forms and rules; *also* : being or requiring elegant dress and manners ⟨a ∼ reception⟩ **2** : done in due or lawful form ⟨a ∼ contract⟩ **3** : CEREMONIOUS, PRIM ⟨a ∼ manner⟩ **4** : NOMINAL — **for•mal•ly** \-ē\ *adv*

²**formal** *n* : something (as a social event) formal in character

form•al•de•hyde \för-'mal-də-ˌhīd\ *n* : a colorless pungent gas used in water solution as a preservative and disinfectant

for•mal•ism \'för-mə-ˌliz-əm\ *n* : strict adherence to set forms

for•mal•i•ty \för-'mal-ət-ē\ *n, pl* **-ties** **1** : the quality or state of being formal **2** : compliance with formal or conventional rules **3** : an established form that is required or conventional

for•mal•ize \'för-mə-ˌlīz\ *vb* **-ized; -iz•ing** **1** : to give a certain or definite form to **2** : to make formal; *also* : to give formal status or approval to

¹**for•mat** \'för-ˌmat\ *n* **1** : the general composition or style of a publication **2** : the general plan or arrangement of something

²**format** *vb* **for•mat•ted; for•mat•ting** : to produce (as a book, printed matter, or data) in a particular form

for•ma•tion \för-'mā-shən\ *n* **1** : a giving form to something : DEVELOPMENT **2**

: something that is formed **3** : STRUCTURE, SHAPE **4** : an arrangement of persons, ships, or airplanes

for•ma•tive \'för-mət-iv\ *adj* **1** : giving or capable of giving form : CONSTRUCTIVE **2** : of, relating to, or characterized by important growth or formation ⟨a child's ∼ years⟩

for•mer \'för-mər\ *adj* **1** : PREVIOUS, EARLIER **2** : FOREGOING **3** : being first mentioned or in order of two things

for•mer•ly \-lē\ *adv* : in time past : HERETOFORE, PREVIOUSLY

form•fit•ting \'förm-ˌfit-iŋ\ *adj* : conforming to the outline of the body

for•mi•da•ble \'för-məd-ə-bəl, för-'mid-\ *adj* **1** : exciting fear, dread, or awe **2** : imposing serious difficulties — **for•mi•da•bly** \-blē\ *adv*

form•less \'förm-ləs\ *adj* : having no definite shape or form

form letter *n* **1** : a letter on a frequently recurring topic that can be sent to different people at different times **2** : a letter sent out in many printed copies to a large number of people

for•mu•la \'för-myə-lə\ *n, pl* **-las** *or* **-lae** \-ˌlē, -ˌlī\ **1** : a set form of words for ceremonial use **2** : RECIPE, PRESCRIPTION **3** : a milk mixture or substitute for a baby **4** : a group of symbols or figures joined to express information concisely **5** : a prescribed or set form or method

for•mu•late \-ˌlāt\ *vb* **-lat•ed; -lat•ing** **1** : to express in a formula **2** : to state definitely and clearly **3** : to prepare according to a formula — **for•mu•la•tion** \ˌför-myə-'lā-shən\ *n*

for•ni•ca•tion \ˌför-nə-'kā-shən\ *n* : human sexual intercourse other than between a man and his wife — **for•ni•cate** \'för-nə-ˌkāt\ *vb* — **for•ni•ca•tor** \-ˌkāt-ər\ *n*

for•sake \fər-'sāk\ *vb* **for•sook** \-'su̇k\; **for•sak•en** \-'sā-kən\; **for•sak•ing** [ME *forsaken,* fr. OE *forsacan,* fr. *sacan* to dispute] **1** : GIVE UP, RENOUNCE **2** : to quit or leave entirely : ABANDON

for•sooth \fər-'süth\ *adv* : in truth : INDEED

for•swear *or* **fore•swear** \för-'swaər\ *vb* **-swore** \-'swōr\; **-sworn** \-'swōrn\; **-swear•ing** **1** : to renounce earnestly or under oath **2** : to deny under oath **3** : to swear falsely : commit perjury

for·syth·ia \fər-'sith-ē-ə\ *n* : any of a genus of shrubs related to the olive and having yellow bell-shaped flowers appearing before the leaves in early spring

fort \'fōrt\ *n* [ME *forte*, fr. MF *fort*, fr. *fort* strong, fr. L *fortis*] 1 : a fortified place 2 : a permanent army post

¹**forte** \'fōrt, 'fōr-ˌtā\ *n* [F *fort*, fr. *fort*, adj., strong] : something in which a person excels

²**for·te** \'fōr-ˌtā\ *adv or adj* [It, fr. *forte* strong] : LOUDLY, POWERFULLY — used as a direction in music

forth \'fōrth\ *adv* 1 : FORWARD, ONWARD ⟨from that day ∼⟩ 2 : out into view ⟨put ∼ leaves⟩

forth·com·ing \fōrth-'kəm-iŋ\ *adj* : coming or available soon ⟨the ∼ holidays⟩ ⟨the funds will be ∼⟩

forth·right \'fōrth-ˌrīt\ *adj* : free from ambiguity or evasiveness : going straight to the point ⟨a ∼ anwser⟩ — **forth·right·ly** *adv* — **forth·right·ness** *n*

forth·with \fōrth-'with, -'with\ *adv* : IMMEDIATELY

for·ti·fy \'fōrt-ə-ˌfī\ *vb* **-fied; -fy·ing** 1 : to strengthen by military defenses 2 : to give physical strength or endurance to 3 : ENCOURAGE 4 : ENRICH ⟨∼ bread with vitamins⟩ — **for·ti·fi·ca·tion** \ˌfōrt-ə-fə-'kā-shən\ *n*

for·tis·si·mo \fōr-'tis-ə-ˌmō\ *adv or adj* : very loud — used as a direction in music

for·ti·tude \'fōrt-ə-ˌt(y)üd\ *n* : strength of mind that enables a person to meet danger or bear pain or adversity with courage **syn** grit, backbone, pluck, guts

fort·night \'fōrt-ˌnīt\ *n* [ME *fourtenight*, fr. *fourtene night* fourteen nights] : two weeks — **fort·night·ly** \-lē\ *adj or adv*

for·tress \'fōr-trəs\ *n* : FORT 1

for·tu·itous \fōr-'t(y)ü-ət-əs\ *adj* 1 : happening by chance 2 : FORTUNATE

for·tu·ity \-ət-ē\ *n, pl* **-ities** 1 : the quality or state of being fortuitous 2 : a chance event or occurrence

for·tu·nate \'fōrch-(ə-)nət\ *adj* 1 : coming by good luck 2 : LUCKY — **for·tu·nate·ly** *adv*

for·tune \'fōr-chən\ *n* 1 : an apparent cause of something that happens to one suddenly and unexpectedly : CHANCE, LUCK 2 : what happens to a person : good or bad luck 3 : FATE, DESTINY 4 : RICHES, WEALTH

fortune hunter *n* : a person who seeks wealth esp. by marriage

for·tune–tell·er \-ˌtel-ər\ *n* : a person who professes to tell future events — **for·tune–tell·ing** \-iŋ\ *n or adj*

for·ty \'fōrt-ē\ *n, pl* **forties** : four times 10 — **for·ti·eth** \'fōrt-ē-əth\ *adj or n* — **forty** *adj or pron*

for·ty–five \ˌfōrt-ē-'fīv\ *n* 1 : a .45 caliber handgun — usu. written .45 2 : a phonograph record designed to be played at 45 revolutions per minute

for·ty–nin·er \ˌfōrt-ē-'nī-nər\ *n* : a person in the rush to California for gold in 1849

forty winks *n sing or pl* : a short sleep

fo·rum \'fōr-əm\ *n, pl* **forums** *also* **fo·ra** \-ə\ [L] 1 : the marketplace or central meeting place of an ancient Roman city 2 : a medium (as a publication) of open discussion 3 : COURT 4 : a public assembly, lecture, or program involving audience or panel discussion

¹**for·ward** \'fōr-wərd\ *adj* 1 : being near or at or belonging to the front 2 : EAGER, READY 3 : BRASH, BOLD 4 : notably advanced or developed : PRECOCIOUS 5 : moving, tending, or leading toward a position in front ⟨a ∼ movement⟩ 6 : EXTREME, RADICAL 7 : of, relating to, or getting ready for the future — **for·ward·ness** *n*

²**forward** *adv* : to or toward what is before or in front

³**forward** *n* : a player stationed near the front of his team (as in hockey) or in the corner (as in basketball)

⁴**forward** *vb* 1 : to help onward : ADVANCE 2 : to send forward : TRANSMIT 3 : to send or ship onward

for·ward·er \-wərd-ər\ *n* : one that forwards; *esp* : an agent who forwards goods — **for·ward·ing** \-iŋ\ *n*

for·wards \'fōr-wərdz\ *adv* : FORWARD

¹**fos·sil** \'fäs-əl\ *adj* [L *fossilis* dug up, fr. *fossus*, pp. of *fodere* to dig] 1 : being or resembling a fossil ⟨∼ plants⟩ 2 : of or relating to fossil feuls

²**fossil** *n* 1 : a trace or impression or the remains of a plant or animal preserved in the earth's crust from past ages 2 : a person whose ideas are out-of-date — **fos·sil·ize** *vb*

fossil fuel *n* : a fuel (as coal or oil) that is formed in the earth from plant or animal remains

¹fos·ter \'fös-tər\ *adj* [ME, fr. OE *fōstor-*, fr. *fōstor* food, feeding] : affording, receiving, or sharing nourishment or parental care though not related by blood or legal ties ⟨~ parent⟩ ⟨~ child⟩

²foster *vb* **fos·tered; fos·ter·ing** \-t(ə-)riŋ\ **1** : to give parental care to : NURTURE **2** : to promote the growth or development of : ENCOURAGE

fos·ter·ling \-tər-liŋ\ *n* : a foster child

Fou·cault pendulum \ˌfü-'kō-\ *n* : a device that consists of a heavy weight hung by a long wire and that swings in a constant direction which appears to change showing that the earth rotates

fought past and past part of FIGHT

¹foul \'faul\ *adj* **1** : offensive to the senses : LOATHSOME; *also* : clogged with dirt **2** : ODIOUS, DETESTABLE **3** : OBSCENE, ABUSIVE **4** : DISAGREEABLE, STORMY ⟨~ weather⟩ **5** : TREACHEROUS, DISHONORABLE, UNFAIR **6** : marking the bounds of a playing field ⟨~ lines⟩; *also* : being outside the foul line ⟨~ ball⟩ ⟨~ territory⟩ **7** : containing marked-up corrections **8** : ENTANGLED — **foul·ly** \-ē\ *adv* — **foul·ness** *n*

²foul *n* **1** : an entanglement or collision in fishing or sailing **2** : an infraction of the rules in a game or sport; *also* : a baseball hit outside the foul line

³foul *vb* **1** : to make or become foul or filthy **2** : to make or hit a foul **3** : to entangle or become entangled **4** : OBSTRUCT, BLOCK : **5** : to collide with

⁴foul *adv* : in a foul manner

fou·lard \fu-'lärd\ *n* : a lightweight silk of plain or twill weave usu. decorated with a printed pattern

foul·mouthed \'faul-'mauthd, -'mautht\ *adj* : given to the use of obscene, profane, or abusive language

foul play *n* : VIOLENCE; *esp* : MURDER

foul–up \'faul-ˌəp\ *n* **1** : a state of being fouled up **2** : a mechanical difficulty

foul up \(')faul-'əp\ *vb* **1** : to spoil by mistakes or poor judgment **2** : to make a mistake : BUNGLE

¹found \'faund\ past and past part of FIND

²found *vb* **1** : to take the first steps in building ⟨~ a colony⟩ **2** : to set or ground on something solid : BASE **3** : to establish and often to provide for the future maintenance of ⟨~ a college⟩ — **found·er** *n*

³found *vb* : to melt (metal) and pour into a mold — **found·er** *n*

foun·da·tion \faun-'dā-shən\ *n* **1** : the act of founding **2** : a basis upon which something stands or is supported ⟨suspicions without ~⟩ **3** : funds given for the permanent support of an institution : ENDOWMENT; *also* : an institution so endowed **4** : supporting structure : BASE **5** : CORSET — **foun·da·tion·al** \-sh(ə-)nəl\ *adj*

foun·der \'faun-dər\ *vb* **foun·dered; foun·der·ing** \-d(ə-)riŋ\ **1** : to make or become lame ⟨~ a horse⟩ **2** : COLLAPSE **3** : SINK ⟨a ~ing ship⟩ **4** : FAIL

found·ling \'faun-(d)liŋ\ *n* : an infant found after its unknown parents have abandoned it

found·ry \'faun-drē\ *n, pl* **foundries** : a building or works where metal is cast

fount \'faunt\ *n* : SOURCE, FOUNTAIN

foun·tain \'faunt-ᵊn\ *n* **1** : a spring of water **2** : SOURCE **3** : an artificial jet of water **4** : a container for liquid that can be drawn off as needed

foun·tain·head \-ˌhed\ *n* : SOURCE

fountain pen *n* : a pen with a reservoir that feeds the writing point with ink

four \'fōr\ *n* **1** : one more than three **2** : the 4th in a set or series **3** : something having four units — **four** *adj or pron*

four·flush \-ˌfləsh\ *vb* : to make a false claim : BLUFF — **four–flush·er** \-ər\ *n*

four·fold \-ˌfōld, -'fōld\ *adj* **1** : being four times as great or as many **2** : having four units or members — **four·fold** \-'fōld\ *adv*

4–H \'fōr-'āch\ *adj* : of or relating to a program set up by the U.S. Department of Agriculture to help young people become productive citizens — **4–H'·er** \-ər\ *n*

Four Hundred *or* **400** *n* : the exclusive social set of a community — used with *the*

four–in–hand \'fōr-ən-ˌhand\ *n* **1** : a necktie tied in a slipknot with long ends overlapping vertically in front **2** : a team of four horses driven by one person; *also* : a vehicle drawn by such a team

four–o'clock \'fōr-ə-ˌkläk\ *n* : a garden plant with fragrant yellow, red, or white flowers without petals that open late in the afternoon

four–post·er \'fōr-'pō-stər\ *n* : a bed with tall corner posts orig. designed to support curtains or a canopy

four·score \'fōr-'skōr\ *adj* : being four times twenty : EIGHTY

four·some \'fōr-səm\ *n* 1 : a group of four persons or things 2 : a golf match between two pairs of partners

four·square \-'skwaər\ *adj* 1 : SQUARE 2 : marked by boldness and conviction; *also* : FORTHRIGHT — **foursquare** *adv*

four·teen \'fōr-'tēn\ *n* : one more than 13 — **fourteen** *adj or pron* — **four·teenth** \-'tēnth\ *adj or n*

fourth \'fōrth\ *n* 1 : one that is number four in a countable series 2 : one of four equal parts of something — **fourth** *adj or adv*

fourth estate *n, often cap F&E* : the public press

4WD *abbr* four-wheel drive

four–wheel \ˌfōr-ˌhwēl\ *or* **four·wheeled** \-ˌhwēld\ *adj* : acting on or by means of four wheels of an automotive vehicle

¹**fowl** \'faul\ *n, pl* **fowl** *or* **fowls** 1 : BIRD 2 : a cock or hen of the domestic chicken; *also* : the flesh of these used as food

²**fowl** *vb* : to hunt wildfowl

¹**fox** \'fäks\ *n, pl* **fox·es** *also* **fox** 1 : any of various flesh-eating mammals related to the wolves but smaller and with shorter legs and a more pointed muzzle; *also* : the fur of a fox 2 : a clever crafty person 3 *cap* : a member of an American Indian people formerly living in Wisconsin

²**fox** *vb* : TRICK, OUTWIT

foxed \'fäkst\ *adj* : discolored with yellowish brown stains

fox·glove \'fäks-ˌgləv\ *n* : a plant related to the snapdragons and grown for its showy spikes of dotted white or purple tubular flowers and as a source of digitalis

fox·hole \-ˌhōl\ *n* : a pit dug for protection against enemy fire

fox·hound \-ˌhaund\ *n* : any of various large swift powerful hounds used in hunting foxes

fox terrier *n* : a small lively terrier that

occurs in varieties with smooth dense coats or with harsh wiry coats

fox–trot \'fäks-ˌträt\ *n* 1 : a short broken slow trotting gait 2 : a ballroom dance in duple time

foxy \'fäk-sē\ *adj* **fox·i·er; -est** 1 : resembling or suggestive of a fox 2 : WILY; *also* : CLEVER

foy·er \'föi-ər, 'föi-ˌ(y)ā\ *n* [F, lit., fireplace, fr. ML *focarius,* fr. L *focus* hearth] : LOBBY; *also* : an entrance hallway

FPC *abbr* fish protein concentrate

fpm *abbr* feet per minute

FPO *abbr* fleet post office

fps *abbr* feet per second

fr *abbr* 1 father 2 franc 3 friar 4 from

¹**Fr** *abbr* French

²**Fr** *symbol* francium

fra·cas \'frāk-əs, 'frak-\ *n, pl* **fra·cas·es** \-ə-səz\ [F, din, row, fr. It *fracasso,* fr. *fracassare* to shatter] : BRAWL

frac·tion \'frak-shən\ *n* 1 : a number (as ½ or ¾) indicating one or more equal parts or the division of one number by another; *also* : a number (as 3.323) consisting of a whole number and a decimal 2 : FRAGMENT 3 : PORTION — **frac·tion·al** \-sh(ə-)nəl\ *adj* — **frac·tion·al·ly** \-ē\ *adv*

frac·tious \'frak-shəs\ *adj* 1 : tending to be troublesome : hard to handle or control 2 : QUARRELSOME, IRRITABLE

frac·ture \'frak-chər\ *n* 1 : a breaking of something and esp. a bone 2 : CRACK, CLEFT — **fracture** *vb*

frag·ile \'fraj-əl, -ˌīl\ *adj* : easily broken : DELICATE — **fra·gil·i·ty** \frə-'jil-ət-ē\ *n*

¹**frag·ment** \'frag-mənt\ *n* : a part broken off, detached, or incomplete

²**frag·ment** \-ˌment\ *vb* : to break into fragments — **frag·men·ta·tion** \ˌfrag-mən-'tā-shən, -ˌmən-\ *n*

frag·men·tary \'frag-mən-ˌter-ē\ *adj* : made up of fragments : INCOMPLETE

fra·grant \'frā-grənt\ *adj* : sweet or agreeable in smell — **fra·grance** \-grəns\ *n* — **fra·grant·ly** *adv*

frail \'frāl\ *adj* 1 : morally or physically weak 2 : FRAGILE, DELICATE

frail·ty \'frā(-ə)l-tē\ *n, pl* **frailties** 1 : the quality or state of being frail 2 : a fault due to weakness

¹**frame** \'frām\ *vb* **framed; fram·ing** 1 : PLAN, CONTRIVE 2 : FORMULATE 3 : SHAPE, CONSTRUCT 4 : DRAW UP ⟨~ a

constitution⟩ **5** : to fit or adjust for a purpose : ARRANGE **6** : to provide with or enclose in a frame **7** : to make appear guilty — **fram·er** *n*

²frame *n* **1** : something made of parts fitted and joined together **2** : the physical makeup of the body **3** : an arrangement of structural parts that gives form or support **4** : a supporting or enclosing border or open case (as for a window or picture) **5** : a particular state or disposition (as of mind) : MOOD **6** : one picture of a series (as on a length of motion-picture film or of television images) **7** : FRAME-UP

³frame *adj* : having a wood frame

frame–up \'frām-ˌəp\ *n* : a scheme to cause an innocent person to be accused of a crime; *also* : the action resulting from such a scheme

frame·work \-ˌwərk\ *n* : a basic supporting part or structure

franc \'fraŋk\ *n* — see MONEY table

fran·chise \'fran-ˌchīz\ *n* [ME, fr. OF, fr. *franchir* to free, fr. *franc* free] **1** : a special privilege granted to an individual or group ⟨a ~ to operate a ferry⟩ **2** : a constitutional or statutory right or privilege; *esp* : the right to vote

fran·chi·see \ˌfran-ˌchī-'zē, -chə-\ *n* : one who is granted a marketing franchise

fran·chis·er \'fran-ˌchī-zər\ *n* **1** : FRANCHISEE **2** : FRANCHISOR

fran·chi·sor \ˌfran-ˌchī-'zȯr, -chə-\ *n* : one that grants a marketing franchise

fran·ci·um \'fran-sē-əm\ *n* : a radioactive metallic chemical element

Fran·co–Amer·i·can \ˌfraŋ-kō-ə-'mer-ə-kən\ *n* : an American of French or esp. French-Canadian descent — **Franco–American** *adj*

fran·gi·ble \'fran-jə-bəl\ *adj* : BREAKABLE — **fran·gi·bil·i·ty** \ˌfran-jə-'bil-ət-ē\ *n*

¹frank \'fraŋk\ *adj* : marked by free, forthright, and sincere expression — **frank·ly** *adv* — **frank·ness** *n*

²frank *vb* : to mark (a piece of mail) with an official signature or sign indicating that it can be mailed free; *also* : to mail in this manner

³frank *n* **1** : a signature, mark, or stamp on a piece of mail indicating that it can be mailed free **2** : the privilege of sending mail free of charge

Fran·ken·stein \'fraŋ-kən-ˌstīn\ *n* **1** : a creation that ruins its originator **2** : a monster in the shape of a man

frank·furt·er *or* **frank·fort·er** \'fraŋk-fə(r)t-ər, -ˌfərt-\ *or* **frank·furt** *or* **frank·fort** \-fərt\ *n* : a seasoned sausage (as of beef or beef and pork)

frank·in·cense \'fraŋ-kən-ˌsens\ *n* : a fragrant resin burned as incense

fran·tic \'frant-ik\ *adj* : wildly excited — **fran·ti·cal·ly** \-i-k(ə-)lē\ *adv* — **fran·tic·ly** \-i-klē\ *adv*

frap·pé \fra-'pā\ *or* **frappe** \'frap, fra-'pā\ [F *frappé*, fr. pp. of *frapper* to strike, chill] *n* **1** : an iced or frozen mixture or drink **2** : a thick milk shake — **frap·pé** *or* **frap·pe** \fra-'pā\ *adj*

fra·ter·nal \frə-'tərn-ᵊl\ *adj* **1** : of, relating to, or involving brothers **2** : of, relating to, or being a fraternity or society **3** : FRIENDLY, BROTHERLY — **fra·ter·nal·ly** \-ē\ *adv*

fra·ter·ni·ty \frə-'tər-nət-ē\ *n, pl* **-ties 1** : a social, honorary, or professional organization; *esp* : a social club of male college students **2** : BROTHERLINESS, BROTHERHOOD **3** : men of the same class, profession, or tastes

frat·er·nize \'frat-ər-ˌnīz\ *vb* **-nized; -niz·ing 1** : to mingle as friends **2** : to associate on intimate terms with citizens or troops of a hostile nation — **frat·er·ni·za·tion** \ˌfrat-ər-nə-'zā-shən\ *n*

frat·ri·cide \'fra-trə-ˌsīd\ *n* **1** : one that kills his brother or sister **2** : the act of a fratricide — **frat·ri·cid·al** \ˌfra-trə-'sīd-ᵊl\ *adj*

fraud \'frȯd\ *n* **1** : DECEIT, TRICKERY **2** : TRICK **3** : IMPOSTOR, CHEAT

fraud·u·lent \'frȯ-jə-lənt\ *adj* : characterized by, based on, or done by fraud : DECEITFUL — **fraud·u·lent·ly** *adv*

fraught \'frȯt\ *adj* : full of or accompanied by something specified ⟨~ with danger⟩

¹fray \'frā\ *n* : BRAWL, FIGHT; *also* : DISPUTE

²fray *vb* **1** : to wear (as an edge of cloth) by rubbing **2** : to separate the threads at the edge of **3** : STRAIN, IRRITATE ⟨~ed nerves⟩

fraz·zle \'fraz-əl\ *vb* **fraz·zled; fraz·zling** \'fraz-(ə-)liŋ\ **1** : FRAY **2** : to put in a state of extreme physical or nervous fatigue — **frazzle** *n*

¹**freak** \'frēk\ *n* **1** : WHIM, CAPRICE **2** : a strange, abnormal, or unusual person or thing **3** : a person who uses an illicit drug **4** : an ardent enthusiast — **freakish** *adj*

²**freak** *vb* **1** : to experience or appear to experience the effects (as hallucinations) of taking illicit drugs — often used with *out* **2** : to disturb one's calmness of mind : UPSET — often used with *out* — **freak–out** \'frēk-ˌaut\ *n*

freck·le \'frek-əl\ *n* : a brownish spot on the skin — **freckle** *vb*

¹**free** \'frē\ *adj* **fre·er; fre·est 1** : having liberty **2** : not controlled by others : INDEPENDENT; *also* : not allowing slavery **3** : made or done voluntarily : SPONTANEOUS **4** : released or not suffering from something unpleasant **5** : not subject to a duty, tax, or other charge **6** : not obstructed : CLEAR **7** : not being used or occupied **8** : not fastened **9** : LAVISH **10** : OPEN, FRANK **11** : given without charge **12** : not literal or exact **13** : not restricted by conventional forms — **free·ly** *adv*

²**free** *vb* **freed; free·ing 1** : to set free **2** : RELIEVE, RID **3** : DISENTANGLE, CLEAR **syn** release, liberate, discharge, emancipate, loose

³**free** *adv* **1** : FREELY **2** : without charge

free·bie *or* **free·bee** \'frē-bē\ *n* : something given without charge

free·board \'frē-ˌbōrd\ *n* : the vertical distance between the waterline and the upper edge of the side of a boat

free·boo·ter \'frē-ˌbüt-ər\ *n* [D *vrijbuiter*, fr. *vrijbuit* plunder, fr. *vrij* free + *buit* booty] : PLUNDERER, PIRATE

free·born \-ˈbȯrn\ *adj* **1** : not born in vassalage or slavery **2** : of, relating to, or befitting one that is freeborn

freed·man \'frēd-mən, -ˌman\ *n* : a man freed from slavery

free·dom \'frēd-əm\ *n* **1** : the quality or state of being free : INDEPENDENCE **2** : EXEMPTION, RELEASE **3** : EASE, FACILITY **4** : FRANKNESS **5** : unrestricted use **6** : a political right; *also* : FRANCHISE, PRIVILEGE

free–for–all \'frē-fə-ˌrȯl\ *n* : a competition or fight open to all comers and usu. with no rules : BRAWL — **free–for–all** *adj*

free·hand \'frē-ˌhand\ *adj* : done without mechanical aids or devices

free·hold \ˌfrē-ˌhōld\ *n* : ownership of an estate for life usu. with the right to bequeath it to one's heirs; *also* : an estate thus owned — **free·hold·er** *n*

free lance *n* : one who pursues a profession (as writing) without long-term contractual commitments to any one employer — **free–lance** *adj or vb*

free–living \'frē-ˈliv-iŋ\ *adj* : being neither parasitic nor symbiotic ⟨∼ organisms⟩

free·load \'frē-ˌlōd\ *vb* : to impose upon another's generosity or hospitality — **free·load·er** *n*

free love *n* : the practice of living openly with one of the opposite sex without marriage

free·man \'frē-mən, -ˌman\ *n* **1** : one who has civil or political liberty **2** : one having the full rights of a citizen

Free·ma·son \-ˌmās-ᵊn\ *n* : a member of a secret fraternal society called Free and Accepted Masons — **Free·ma·son·ry** \-rē\ *n*

free·stand·ing \'frē-ˈstan-diŋ\ *adj* : standing alone or on its own foundation

free·stone \'frē-ˌstōn\ *n* **1** : a stone that may be cut freely without splitting **2** : a fruit stone to which the flesh does not cling; *also* : a fruit (as a peach or cherry) having such a stone

free·think·er \-ˈthiŋ-kər\ *n* : one who forms opinions on the basis of reason independently of authority; *esp* : one who doubts or denies religious dogma — **free·think·ing** *n or adj*

free trade *n* : trade between nations without restrictions (as high taxes on imports)

free verse *n* : verse whose meter is irregular or whose rhythm is not metrical

free·way \'frē-ˌwā\ *n* : an expressway with fully controlled access

free·wheel \-ˈhwēl\ *vb* : to move, live, or drift along freely or irresponsibly

free·will \ˌfrē-ˌwil\ *adj* : VOLUNTARY

free will *n* : voluntary choice or decision

¹**freeze** \'frēz\ *vb* **froze** \'frōz\; **fro·zen** \'frōz-ᵊn\; **freez·ing 1** : to harden or cause to harden into a solid (as ice) by loss of heat **2** : to chill or become

chilled with cold **3** : to become coldly formal in manner; *also* : to act toward in a stiff and formal way **4** : to damage by frost **5** : to adhere solidly by freezing **6** : to cause to grip tightly or remain in immovable contact **7** : to become clogged with ice **8** : to become fixed or motionless **9** : to fix at a certain stage or level

²freeze *n* **1** : a state of weather marked by low temperature **2** : an act or instance of freezing ⟨a price ~⟩ **3** : the state of being frozen

freeze–dry \\'frēz-ˌdrī\\ *vb* : to dry in a frozen state under vacuum esp. for preservation — **freeze–dried** *adj*

freez•er \\'frē-zər\\ *n* : a compartment, device, or room for freezing food or keeping it frozen

¹freight \\'frāt\\ *n* **1** : payment for carrying goods **2** : CARGO **3** : BURDEN **4** : the carrying of goods by a common carrier **5** : a train that carries freight

²freight *vb* **1** : to load with goods for transportation **2** : BURDEN, CHARGE **3** : to ship or transport by freight

freight•er \\'frāt-ər\\ *n* : a ship or airplane used chiefly to carry freight

French \\'french\\ *n* **1** : the language of France **2 French** *pl* : the people of France — **French** *adj* — **French•man** \\-mən\\ *n* — **French•wom•an** \\-ˌwùm-ən\\ *n*

french fry *vb, often cap 1st F* : to fry (as strips of potato) in deep fat until brown — **french fry** *n, often cap 1st F*

French horn *n* : a curved brass instrument with a funnel-shaped mouthpiece and a flaring bell

fre•net•ic \\fri-'net-ik\\ *adj* : FRENZIED, FRANTIC — **fre•net•i•cal•ly** \\-i-k(ə-)lē\\ *adv*

fren•zy \\'fren-zē\\ *n, pl* **frenzies** : temporary madness or a violently agitated state — **fren•zied** \\-zēd\\ *adj*

freq *abbr* frequency, frequent, frequently

fre•quen•cy \\'frē-kwən-sē\\ *n, pl* **-cies** **1** : the fact or condition of occurring frequently **2** : rate of occurrence **3** : the number of cycles per second of an alternating current **4** : the number of waves (as of sound or electromagnetic energy) that pass a fixed point each second

frequency modulation *n* : variation of the frequency of a carrier wave according to another signal; *also* : a broadcasting system using such modulation

¹fre•quent \\'frē-kwənt\\ *adj* **1** : happening often or at short intervals **2** : HABITUAL — **fre•quent•ly** *adv*

²fre•quent \\frē-'kwent, 'frē-kwənt\\ *vb* : to associate with, be in, or resort to habitually — **fre•quent•er** *n*

fres•co \\'fres-kō\\ *n, pl* **frescoes** [It, fr. *fresco* fresh] : the art of painting on fresh plaster; *also* : a painting done by this method

fresh \\'fresh\\ *adj* **1** : not salt ⟨~ water⟩ **2** : PURE, INVIGORATING **3** : fairly strong : BRISK ⟨~ breeze⟩ **4** : not altered by processing (as freezing or canning) **5** : VIGOROUS, REFRESHED **6** : not stale, sour, or decayed ⟨~ bread⟩ **7** : not faded **8** : not worn or rumpled **9** : experienced, made, or received newly or anew **10** : ADDITIONAL, ANOTHER ⟨made a ~ start⟩ **11** : ORIGINAL, VIVID **12** : INEXPERIENCED **13** : newly come or arrived ⟨~ from school⟩ **14** : IMPUDENT — **fresh•ly** *adv* — **fresh•ness** *n*

fresh•en \\'fresh-ən\\ *vb* **fresh•ened; fresh•en•ing** \\-(ə-)niŋ\\ : to make, grow, or become fresh

fresh•et \\'fresh-ət\\ *n* : an overflowing of a stream (as by heavy rains)

fresh•man \\'fresh-mən\\ *n* **1** : BEGINNER, NEWCOMER **2** : a 1st-year student

fresh•wa•ter \\'fresh-ˌwȯt-ər, -ˌwät-\\ *adj* : of, relating to, or living in fresh water

¹fret \\'fret\\ *vb* **fret•ted; fret•ting** [ME *freten* to devour, fret, fr. OE *fretan* to devour] **1** : to become irritated : WORRY, VEX **2** : WEAR, CORRODE; *also* : FRAY **3** : RUB, CHAFE **4** : to make by wearing away **5** : GRATE ⟨the siren *fretted* at their nerves⟩ **6** : AGITATE, RIPPLE

²fret *n* : an irritated or worried state ⟨in a ~⟩

³fret *n* : ornamental work esp. of straight lines in symmetrical patterns

⁴fret *n* : one of a series of ridges across the fingerboard of a stringed musical instrument — **fret•ted** *adj*

fret•ful \\'fret-fəl\\ *adj* : IRRITABLE — **fret•ful•ly** \\-ē\\ *adv* — **fret•ful•ness** *n*

fret·saw \-ˌsȯ\ *n* : a narrow-bladed saw used for cutting curved outlines

fret·work \-ˌwərk\ *n* **1** : decoration consisting of frets **2** : ornamental openwork or work in relief

Fri *abbr* Friday

fri·a·ble \ˈfrī-ə-bəl\ *adj* : easily pulverized ⟨∼ soil⟩

fri·ar \ˈfrī(-ə)r\ *n* [ME *frere, fryer,* fr. OF *frere,* lit., brother, fr. L *frater*] : a member of a mendicant religious order

fri·ary \ˈfrī(-ə)r-ē\ *n, pl* **-ar·ies** : a monastery of friars

¹fric·as·see \ˈfrik-ə-ˌsē, ˌfrik-ə-ˈsē\ *n* : a dish made of meat (as chicken or veal) cut into pieces and stewed in a gravy

²fricassee *vb* **-seed; -see·ing** : to cook as a fricassee

fric·tion \ˈfrik-shən\ *n* **1** : the rubbing of one body against another **2** : the force that resists motion between bodies in contact **3** : clash in opinions between persons or groups : DISAGREEMENT — **fric·tion·al** *adj*

friction tape *n* : a usu. cloth tape impregnated with insulating material and an adhesive and used esp. to protect and insulate electrical conductors

Fri·day \ˈfrīd-ē\ *n* : the sixth day of the week

fried·cake \ˈfrīd-ˌkāk\ *n* : DOUGHNUT, CRULLER

friend \ˈfrend\ *n* **1** : a person attached to another by respect or affection **2** : ACQUAINTANCE **3** : one who is not hostile **4** : one who supports or favors something ⟨a ∼ of art⟩ **5** *cap* : a member of the Society of Friends : QUAKER — **friend·less** \ˈfren-(d)ləs\ *adj* — **friend·li·ness** \ˈfren-(d)lē-nəs\ *n* — **friend·ly** *adj* — **friend·ship** \ˈfren(d)-ˌship\ *n*

frieze \ˈfrēz\ *n* : an ornamental often sculptured band extending around something (as a building or room)

frig·ate \ˈfrig-ət\ *n* **1** : a square-rigged warship **2** : a warship smaller than a destroyer used for escort and patrol duties

fright \ˈfrīt\ *n* **1** : sudden terror : ALARM **2** : something that is ugly or shocking

fright·en \ˈfrīt-ᵊn\ *vb* **fright·ened; fright·en·ing** \ˈfrīt-(ᵊ-)niŋ\ **1** : to make afraid **2** : to drive away or out by frightening

3 : to become frightened — **fright·en·ing·ly** *adv*

fright·ful \ˈfrīt-fəl\ *adj* **1** : TERRIFYING **2** : STARTLING **3** : EXTREME ⟨∼ thirst⟩ — **fright·ful·ly** \-ē\ *adv* — **fright·ful·ness** *n*

frig·id \ˈfrij-əd\ *adj* **1** : intensely cold **2** : lacking warmth or ardor : INDIFFERENT **3** : abnormally averse to or unable to achieve orgasm during sexual intercourse — used esp. of women — **fri·gid·i·ty** \frij-ˈid-ət-ē\ *n*

frigid zone *n* : the area or region between the arctic circle and the north pole or between the antarctic circle and the south pole

frill \ˈfril\ *n* **1** : a gathered, pleated, or ruffled edging **2** : an ornamental addition : something unessential — **frilly** \-ē\ *adj*

fringe \ˈfrinj\ *n* **1** : an ornamental border consisting of short threads or strips hanging from an edge or band **2** : something that resembles a fringe : BORDER **3** : something on the margin of an activity, process, or subject matter — **fringe** *vb*

fringe benefit *n* **1** : an employment benefit paid for by an employer without affecting basic wage rates **2** : any additional benefit

frip·pery \ˈfrip-(ə-)rē\ *n, pl* **-per·ies** [MF *friperie*] **1** : cheap showy finery **2** : pretentious display

frisk \ˈfrisk\ *vb* **1** : to leap, skip, or dance in a lively or playfuly way : GAMBOL **2** : to search (a person) esp. for concealed weapons by running the hand rapidly over the clothing

frisky \ˈfris-kē\ *adj* **frisk·i·er; -est** : FROLICSOME — **frisk·i·ly** \ˈfris-kə-lē\ *adv* — **frisk·i·ness** \-kē-nəs\ *n*

¹frit·ter \ˈfrit-ər\ *n* : a small lump of fried batter often containing fruit or meat

²fritter *vb* **1** : to reduce or waste piecemeal **2** : to break into small fragments

fritz \ˈfrits\ *n* : a state of disorder or disrepair — used in the phrase *on the fritz*

friv·o·lous \ˈfriv-(ə-)ləs\ *adj* **1** : of little importance : TRIVIAL **2** : lacking in seriousness — **fri·vol·i·ty** \friv-ˈäl-ət-ē\ *n* — **friv·o·lous·ly** *adv*

frizz \ˈfriz\ *vb* : to curl in small tight curls — **frizz** *n* — **frizzy** *adj*

¹friz·zle \ˈfriz-əl\ *vb* **friz·zled; friz·zling** \-(ə-)liŋ\ : FRIZZ, CURL — **frizzle** *n*

²**frizzle** *vb* **friz·zled; friz·zling 1** : to fry until crisp and curled **2** : to cook with a sizzling noise

fro \'frō\ *adv* : BACK, AWAY — used in the phrase *to and fro*

frock \'fräk\ *n* **1** : an outer garment worn by monks and friars **2** : an outer garment worn esp. by men **3** : a woman's or girl's dress

frock coat *n* : a man's usu. double= breasted coat with knee-length skirts

frog \'frȯg, 'fräg\ *n* **1** : any of various largely aquatic smooth-skinned tail-less leaping amphibians **2** : an ornamental braiding for fastening the front of a garment by a loop through which a button passes **3** : a condition in the throat causing hoarseness **4** : a small holder (as of metal, glass, or plastic) with perforations or spikes that is placed in a bowl or vase to keep cut flowers in position

frog·man \'frȯg-ˌman, 'fräg-, -mən\ *n* : a swimmer equipped to work underwater for long periods of time

¹**frol·ic** \'fräl-ik\ *vb* **frol·icked; frol·ick-ing 1** : to make merry **2** : to play about happily : ROMP

²**frolic** *n* **1** : a playful or mischievous action **2** : FUN, MERRIMENT — **frol·ic-some** \-səm\ *adj*

from \(')frəm, 'främ\ *prep* **1** — used to show a starting point ⟨a letter ∼ home⟩ **2** — used to show removal or separation ⟨subtract 3 ∼ 9⟩ **3** — used to show a material, source, or cause ⟨suffering ∼ a cold⟩

frond \'fränd\ *n* : a usu. large divided leaf esp. of a fern or palm tree

¹**front** \'frənt\ *n* **1** : FOREHEAD; *also* : the whole face **2** : external and often feigned appearance **3** : a region of active fighting; *also* : a sphere of activity **4** : a political coalition **5** : the side of a building containing the main entrance **6** : the forward part or surface **7** : FRONTAGE **8** : a boundary between two dissimilar air masses **9** : a position directly before or ahead of something else **10** : a person, group, or thing used to mask the identity or true character or activity of the actual controlling agent

²**front** *vb* **1** : FACE **2** : to serve as a front **3** : CONFRONT

front·age \'frənt-ij\ *n* **1** : a piece of land that fronts something (as on a river or road) **2** : the front side of a building **3** : the extent or measure of a frontage

front·al \'frənt-ᵊl\ *adj* **1** : of, relating to, or next to the forehead **2** : of, relating to, or directed at the front ⟨a ∼ attack⟩ — **fron·tal·ly** \-ᵊl-ē\ *adv*

fron·tier \ˌfrən-'tiər\ *n* **1** : a border between two countries **2** : a region that forms the margin of settled territory **3** : the outer limits of knowledge or achievement ⟨the ∼s of science⟩ — **fron·tiers·man** \-'tiərz-mən\ *n*

fron·tis·piece \'frənt-ə-ˌspēs\ *n* : an illustration preceding and usu. facing the title page of a book

front man *n* : a person serving as a front or figurehead

front·ward \'frənt-wərd\ *or* **front·wards** \-wərdz\ *adv or adj* : toward the front

¹**frost** \'frȯst\ *n* **1** : freezing temperature **2** : a covering of tiny ice crystals on a cold surface — **frosty** *adj*

²**frost** *vb* **1** : to cover with frost **2** : to put icing on (as a cake) **3** : to produce a slightly roughened surface on (as glass) **4** : to injure or kill by frost

¹**frost·bite** \'frȯs(t)-ˌbīt\ *vb* **-bit** \-ˌbit\; **-bit·ten** \-ˌbit-ᵊn\; **-bit·ing** \-ˌbīt-iŋ\ : to injure by frost or frostbite

²**frostbite** *n* : the freezing or the local effect of a partial freezing of some part of the body

frost heave *n* : an upthrust of pavement caused by freezing of moist soil

frost·ing \'frȯ-stiŋ\ *n* **1** : ICING **2** : dull finish on metal or glass

froth \'frȯth\ *n, pl* **froths** \'frȯths, 'frȯthz\ **1** : bubbles formed in or on a liquid **2** : something light or frivolous — **frothy** *adj*

frou-frou \'frü-frü\ *n* [F] **1** : a rustling esp. of a woman's skirts **2** : frilly ornamentation esp. in women's clothing

fro·ward \'frō-(w)ərd\ *adj* : DISOBEDI-ENT, WILLFUL

frown \'fraun\ *vb* **1** : to wrinkle the forehead (as in anger, displeasure, or thought) : SCOWL **2** : to look with disapproval **3** : to express with a frown — **frown** *n*

frow·sy *or* **frow·zy** \'frau-zē\ *adj* **frow·si-er** *or* **frow·zi·er; -est** : having a slovenly or uncared-for appearance

froze past of FREEZE

fro·zen \'frōz-ᵊn\ *adj* **1** : treated, affected, or crusted over by freezing **2** : subject to long and severe cold **3** : expressing or characterized by cold unfriendliness **4** : incapable of being changed, moved, or undone : FIXED ⟨~ wages⟩ **5** : not available for present use ⟨~ capital⟩

FRS *abbr* Federal Reserve System

frt *abbr* freight

fruc•ti•fy \'frək-tə-ˌfī, 'frùk-\ *vb* **-fied; -fy•ing 1** : to bear fruit **2** : to make fruitful or productive

fru•gal \'frü-gəl\ *adj* : ECONOMICAL, THRIFTY — **fru•gal•i•ty** \frü-'gal-ət-ē\ *n* — **fru•gal•ly** \'frü-gə-lē\ *adv*

¹fruit \'früt\ *n* [ME, fr. OF, fr. L *fructus* fruit, use, fr. *frui* to enjoy, have the use of] **1** : a usu. useful product of plant growth; *esp* : a usu. edible and sweet reproductive body (as a strawberry or apple) of a seed plant **2** : a product of fertilization in a plant; *esp* : the ripe ovary of a seed plant with its contents and appendages **3** : CONSEQUENCE, RESULT — **fruit•ed** \-əd\ *adj*

²fruit *vb* : to bear or cause to bear fruit

fruit•cake \'früt-ˌkāk\ *n* : a rich cake containing nuts, dried or candied fruits, and spices

fruit fly *n* : any of various small two-winged flies whose larvae feed on fruit or decaying vegetable matter

fruit•ful \'früt-fəl\ *adj* **1** : yielding or producing fruit **2** : very productive ⟨a ~ soil⟩; *also* : bringing results ⟨a ~ idea⟩ — **fruit•ful•ly** \-fə-lē\ *adv* — **fruit•ful•ness** *n*

fru•ition \frü-'ish-ən\ *n* **1** : ENJOYMENT **2** : the state of bearing fruit **3** : REALIZATION, ACCOMPLISHMENT

fruit•less \'früt-ləs\ *adj* **1** : not bearing fruit **2** : producing no good results : UNSUCCESSFUL ⟨a ~ attempt⟩ — **fruit•less•ly** *adv*

fruity \'früt-ē\ *adj* **fruit•i•er; -est** : resembling a fruit esp. in flavor

frumpy \'frəm-pē\ *adj* **frump•i•er; -est** : DRAB, DOWDY

frus•trate \'frəs-ˌtrāt\ *vb* **frus•trat•ed; frus•trat•ing 1** : to balk in an endeavor : BLOCK **2** : to bring to nothing **3** : to fill with dissatisfaction due to unresolved problems or unfulfilled needs — **frus•trat•ing•ly** \-iŋ-lē\ *adv* — **frus•tra•tion** \ˌfrəs-'trā-shən\ *n*

frus•tum \'frəs-təm\ *n, pl* **frustums** *or*

frus•ta \-tə\ : the part of a cone or pyramid formed by cutting off the top by a plane parallel to the base

frwy *abbr* freeway

¹fry \'frī\ *vb* **fried; fry•ing 1** : to cook in a pan or on a griddle over a fire esp. with the use of fat **2** : to undergo frying

²fry *n, pl* **fries 1** : a dish of something fried **2** : a social gathering where fried food is eaten

³fry *n, pl* **fry 1** : recently hatched fishes; *also* : very small adult fishes **2** : members of a group or class ⟨small ~⟩

fry•er \'frī(-ə)r\ *n* **1** : something (as a young chicken) suitable for frying **2** : a deep utensil for frying foods

FSLIC *abbr* Federal Savings and Loan Insurance Corporation

ft *abbr* **1** feet; foot **2** fort

FTC *abbr* Federal Trade Commission

fuch•sia \'fyü-shə\ *n* **1** : any of a genus of shrubs related to the evening primrose and grown for their showy nodding often red or purple flowers **2** : a vivid reddish purple

fud•dle \'fəd-ᵊl\ *vb* **fud•dled; fud•dling** : MUDDLE, CONFUSE

fud•dy–dud•dy \'fəd-ē-ˌdəd-ē\ *n, pl* **-dies** : a person who is old-fashioned, pompous, unimaginative, or fussy

¹fudge \'fəj\ *vb* **fudged; fudg•ing 1** : to cheat or exaggerate by blurring or overstepping a boundary **2** : to avoid coming to grips with something

²fudge *n* **1** : NONSENSE **2** : a soft creamy candy of milk, sugar, butter, and flavoring

¹fu•el \'fyü-əl\ *n* : a substance (as coal) used to produce heat or power by combustion; *also* : a substance from which nuclear energy can be liberated

²fuel *vb* **-eled** *or* **-elled; -el•ing** *or* **-el•ling** : to provide with or take in fuel

fuel cell *n* : a device that continuously changes the chemical energy of a fuel directly into electrical energy

¹fu•gi•tive \'fyü-jət-iv\ *n* **1** : one who flees or tries to escape **2** : something elusive or hard to find

²fugitive *adj* **1** : running away or trying to escape **2** : likely to vanish suddenly : not fixed or lasting

fugue \'fyüg\ *n* **1** : a musical composition in which different parts successively repeat the theme **2** : a disturbed state of consciousness characterized by acts that are not recalled upon recovery

füh·rer *or* **fueh·rer** \\ˈfyu̇r-ər, ˈfir-\ *n* : LEADER — used chiefly of the leader of the German Nazis

¹**-ful** \fəl\ *adj suffix, sometimes* **-ful·ler;** *sometimes* **-ful·lest** **1** : full of ⟨event*ful*⟩ **2** : characterized by ⟨peace*ful*⟩ **3** : having the qualities of ⟨master*ful*⟩ **4** : tending, given, or liable to ⟨mourn*ful*⟩

²**-ful** \ˌfu̇l\ *n suffix* : number or quantity that fills or would fill ⟨room*ful*⟩

ful·crum \ˈfu̇l-krəm, ˈfəl-\ *n, pl* **ful·crums** *or* **ful·cra** \-krə\ [LL, fr. L, bedpost] : the support on which a lever turns

ful·fill *or* **ful·fil** \fu̇l-ˈfil\ *vb* **ful·filled; ful·fill·ing** **1** : to put into effect **2** : to bring to an end **3** : SATISFY — **ful·fill·ment** *n*

¹**full** \ˈfu̇l\ *adj* **1** : FILLED **2** : complete esp. in detail, number, or duration **3** : having all the distinguishing characteristics ⟨a ∼ member⟩ **4** : MAXIMUM **5** : rounded in outline ⟨a ∼ figure⟩ **6** : possessing or containing an abundance ⟨∼ of wrinkles⟩ **7** : having an abundance of material ⟨a ∼ skirt⟩ **8** : satisfied esp. with food or drink **9** : having volume or depth of sound **10** : completely occupied with a thought or plan — **full·ness** *also* **ful·ness** \ˈfu̇l-nəs\ *n*

²**full** *adv* **1** : VERY, EXTREMELY **2** : ENTIRELY **3** : STRAIGHT, SQUARELY ⟨hit him ∼ in the face⟩

³**full** *n* **1** : the utmost extent **2** : the highest or fullest state or degree **3** : the requisite or complete amount

⁴**full** *vb* : to shrink and thicken (woolen cloth) by moistening, heating, and pressing — **full·er** *n*

full·back \ˈfu̇l-ˌbak\ *n* : a football back stationed between the halfbacks

full–blood·ed \ˈfu̇l-ˈbləd-əd\ *adj* : of unmixed ancestry : PUREBRED

full–blown \-ˈblōn\ *adj* **1** : being at the height of bloom **2** : fully mature or developed

full–bod·ied \-ˈbäd-ēd\ *adj* : marked by richness and fullness

full dress *n* : the style of dress worn for ceremonial or formal occasions

full–fledged \ˈfu̇l-ˈflejd\ *adj* **1** : fully developed **2** : having full plumage

full moon *n* : the moon with its whole disk illuminated

full–scale \ˈfu̇l-ˈskāl\ *adj* **1** : identical to an original in proportion and size ⟨∼ drawing⟩ **2** : involving full use of available resources ⟨a ∼ revolt⟩

full tilt *adv* : at high speed

full–time \ˈfu̇l-ˈtīm\ *adj or adv* : involving or working a full or regular schedule

ful·ly \ˈfu̇l-ē\ *adv* **1** : in a full manner or degree : COMPLETELY **2** : at least

ful·mi·nate \ˈfu̇l-mə-ˌnāt, ˈfəl-\ *vb* **-nat·ed; -nat·ing** [ME *fulminaten*, fr. ML *fulminare*, fr. L, to flash with lightning, strike with lightning, fr. *fulmen* lightning] **1** : to utter or send out censure or invective : condemn severely **2** : EXPLODE — **ful·mi·na·tion** \ˌfu̇l-mə-ˈnā-shən, ˌfəl-\ *n*

ful·some \ˈfu̇l-səm\ *adj* **1** : COPIOUS, ABUNDANT ⟨∼ detail⟩ **2** : OFFENSIVE, DISGUSTING **3** : excessively flattering ⟨∼ praise⟩

fu·ma·role \ˈfyü-mə-ˌrōl\ *n* : a hole in a volcanic region from which hot gases issue

fum·ble \ˈfəm-bəl\ *vb* **fum·bled; fum·bling** \-b(ə-)liŋ\ **1** : to grope about clumsily **2** : to fail to hold, catch, or handle properly — **fumble** *n*

¹**fume** \ˈfyüm\ *n* : a usu. irritating smoke, vapor, or gas

²**fume** *vb* **fumed; fum·ing** **1** : to treat with fumes **2** : to give off fumes **3** : to express anger or annoyance

fu·mi·gant \ˈfyü-mi-gənt\ *n* : a substance used for fumigation

fu·mi·gate \ˈfyü-mə-ˌgāt\ *vb* **-gat·ed; -gat·ing** : to treat with fumes to disinfect or destroy pests — **fu·mi·ga·tion** \ˌfyü-mə-ˈgā-shən\ *n* — **fu·mi·ga·tor** \ˈfyü-mə-ˌgāt-ər\ *n*

fun \ˈfən\ *n* [E dial. *fun* to hoax] **1** : something that provides amusement or enjoyment **2** : ENJOYMENT

¹**func·tion** \ˈfəŋk-shən\ *n* **1** : OCCUPATION **2** : special purpose **3** : the particular purpose for which a person or thing is specially fitted or used or for which a thing exists ⟨the ∼ of a knife is cutting⟩; *also* : the natural or proper action of a bodily part in a living thing ⟨the ∼ of the heart⟩ **4** : a formal cere-

mony or social affair **5** : the mathematical relationship that assigns to each element of a set one and only one element of the same or another set **6** : a variable (as a quality, trait, or measurement) that depends on and varies with another ⟨height is a ∼ of age in children⟩ — **func·tion·al** \-sh(ə-)nəl\ *adj* — **func·tion·al·ly** \-ē\ *adv* — **func·tion·less** *adj*

²function *vb* **func·tioned; func·tion·ing** \-sh(ə-)niŋ\ **1** : SERVE **2** : OPERATE, WORK

func·tion·ary \'fəŋk-shə-ˌner-ē\ *n, pl* **-ar·ies** : one who performs a certain function; *esp* : OFFICIAL

function word *n* : a word (as a preposition, auxiliary verb, or conjunction) expressing the grammatical relationship between other words

¹fund \'fənd\ *n* [L *fundus* bottom, piece of landed property] **1** : STORE, SUPPLY **2** : a sum of money or resources intended for a special purpose **3** *pl* : available money **4** : an organization administering a special fund

²fund *vb* **1** : to provide funds for **2** : to convert (a short-term obligation) into a long-term interest-bearing debt

fun·da·men·tal \ˌfən-də-'ment-ᵊl\ *adj* **1** : serving as an origin : PRIMARY **2** : BASIC, ESSENTIAL **3** : RADICAL ⟨∼ change⟩ **4** : of central importance : PRINCIPAL — **fundamental** *n* — **fun·da·men·tal·ly** \-ē\ *adv*

fun·da·men·tal·ism \-ˌiz-əm\ *n, often cap* : a Protestant religious movement emphasizing the literal infallibility of the Bible — **fun·da·men·tal·ist** \-əst\ *adj or n*

¹fu·ner·al \'fyün-(ə-)rəl\ *adj* **1** : of, relating to, or constituting a funeral **2** : FUNEREAL **2**

²funeral *n* : the ceremonies held for a dead person usu. before burial

fu·ner·ary \'fyü-nə-ˌrer-ē\ *adj* : of, used for, or associated with burial

fu·ne·re·al \fyù-'nir-ē-əl\ *adj* **1** : of or relating to a funeral **2** : suggesting a funeral

fun·gi·cide \'fən-jə-ˌsīd, 'fəŋ-gə-\ *n* : an agent that kills or checks the growth of fungi — **fun·gi·cid·al** \ˌfən-jə-'sīd-ᵊl, ˌfən-gə-\ *adj*

fun·gus \'fəŋ-gəs\ *n, pl* **fun·gi** \'fən-ˌjī, 'fəŋ-ˌgī\ *also* **fun·gus·es** \'fəŋ-gə-səz\ : any of a large group of lower plants that lack chlorophyll and include molds, mildews, mushrooms, and yeasts — **fun·gal** \-gəl\ *adj* — **fun·gous** \-gəs\ *adj*

fu·nic·u·lar \fyù-'nik-yə-lər, fə-\ *n* : a cable railway ascending a mountain

funk \'fəŋk\ *n* : a depressed state of mind

funky \'fəŋ-kē\ *adj* **funk·i·er; -est 1** : having an earthy, unsophisticated style and feeling; *esp* : having the style and feeling of blues **2** : odd or quaint in appearance or style

¹fun·nel \'fən-ᵊl\ *n* **1** : a cone-shaped utensil with a tube used for catching and directing a downward flow (as of liquid) **2** : FLUE, SMOKESTACK

²funnel *vb* **-neled** *also* **-nelled; -nel·ing** *also* **-nel·ling 1** : to pass through or as if through a funnel **2** : to move to a central point or into a central channel

¹fun·ny \'fən-ē\ *adj* **fun·ni·er; -est 1** : AMUSING **2** : FACETIOUS **3** : QUEER, ODD **4** : UNDERHANDED

²funny *n, pl* **funnies** : a comic strip or a comic section (as of a newspaper)

funny bone *n* : a place at the back of the elbow where a blow compresses a nerve and causes a painful tingling sensation

¹fur \'fər\ *n* **1** : an article of clothing made of or with fur **2** : the hairy coat of a mammal esp. when fine, soft, and thick; *also* : this coat dressed for human use — **fur** *adj* — **furred** \'fərd\ *adj*

²fur *abbr* furlong

fur·be·low \'fər-bə-ˌlō\ *n* **1** : FLOUNCE, RUFFLE **2** : showy trimming

fur·bish \'fər-bish\ *vb* **1** : to make lustrous : POLISH **2** : to give a new look to : RENOVATE

fu·ri·ous \'fyùr-ē-əs\ *adj* **1** : FIERCE, ANGRY, VIOLENT **2** : BOISTEROUS **3** : INTENSE — **fu·ri·ous·ly** *adv*

furl \'fərl\ *vb* **1** : to wrap or roll (as a sail or a flag) close to or around something **2** : to curl in furls — **furl** *n*

fur·long \'fər-ˌlȯŋ\ *n* [ME, fr. OE *furlang*, fr. *furh* furrow + *lang* long] : a unit of length equal to 220 yards (about 201 meters)

fur·lough \'fər-lō\ *n* [Dutch *verlof*, lit., permission] : a leave of absence from duty granted esp. to a soldier — **furlough** *vb*

fur·nace \\'fər-nəs\\ *n* : an enclosed structure in which heat is produced

fur·nish \\'fər-nish\\ *vb* **1** : to provide with what is needed : EQUIP **2** : SUPPLY, GIVE

fur·nish·ings \\-iŋs\\ *n pl* **1** : articles or accessories of dress **2** : FURNITURE

fur·ni·ture \\'fər-ni-chər\\ *n* : equipment that is necessary, useful, or desirable; *esp* : movable articles (as chairs, tables, or beds) for a room

fu·ror \\'fyůr-ˌór\\ *n* **1** : ANGER, RAGE **2** : a contagious excitement; *esp* : a fashionable craze **3** : UPROAR

fu·rore \\-ˌōr\\ *n* [It] : FUROR 2, 3

fur·ri·er \\'fər-ē-ər\\ *n* : one who prepares or deals in fur

fur·ring \\'fər-iŋ\\ *n* : wood or metal strips applied to a wall or ceiling to form a level surface or an air space

fur·row \\'fər-ō\\ *n* **1** : a trench in the earth made by or as if by a plow **2** : a narrow groove or wrinkle — **furrow** *vb*

fur·ry \\'fər-ē\\ *adj* **fur·ri·er; -est 1** : resembling or consisting of fur **2** : covered with fur

¹fur·ther \\'fər-thər\\ *adv* **1** : ¹FARTHER 1 **2** : in addition : MOREOVER **3** : to a greater extent or degree

²further *vb* **fur·thered; fur·ther·ing** \\'fərth-(ə-)riŋ\\ : to help forward — **fur·ther·ance** \\'fərth-(ə-)rəns\\ *n*

³further *adj* **1** : ²FARTHER 1 **2** : ADDITIONAL

fur·ther·more \\'fər-thə(r)-ˌmōr\\ *adv* : in addition to what precedes : BESIDES

fur·ther·most \\-thər-ˌmōst\\ *adj* : most distant : FARTHEST

fur·thest \\'fər-thəst\\ *adv or adj* : FARTHEST

fur·tive \\'fərt-iv\\ *adj* [F or L; F *furtif*, fr. L *furtivus*, fr. *furtum* theft, fr. *fur* thief] : done by stealth : SLY — **fur·tive·ly** *adv* — **fur·tive·ness** *n*

fu·ry \\'fyůr-ē\\ *n, pl* **furies 1** : violent anger : RAGE **2** : extreme fierceness or violence **3** : FRENZY

furze \\'fərz\\ *n* : GORSE

¹fuse \\'fyüz\\ *n* **1** : a cord or cable that is set afire to ignite an explosive charge **2** *usu* **fuze** : a mechanical or electrical device for setting off the explosive

charge of a projectile, bomb, or torpedo

²fuse *or* **fuze** \\'fyüz\\ *vb* **fused** *or* **fuzed; fus·ing** *or* **fuz·ing** : to equip with a fuse

³fuse *vb* **fused; fus·ing 1** : MELT **2** : to unite by or as if by melting together — **fus·ible** *adj*

⁴fuse *n* : an electrical safety device having a metal wire or strip that melts and interrupts the circuit when the current becomes too strong

fu·se·lage \\'fyü-sə-ˌläzh, -zə-\\ *n* : the central body portion of an airplane that holds the crew, passengers, and cargo

fu·sil·lade \\'fyü-sə-ˌläd, -ˌlād\\ *n* : a number of shots fired simultaneously or in rapid succession

fu·sion \\'fyü-zhən\\ *n* **1** : the act or process of melting or making plastic by heat **2** : union by or as if by melting **3** : the union of light atomic nuclei to form heavier nuclei with the release of huge quantities of energy

¹fuss \\'fəs\\ *n* **1** : needless bustle or excitement : COMMOTION **2** : effusive praise **3** : a state of agitation **4** : OBJECTION, PROTEST **5** : DISPUTE

²fuss *vb* : to make a fuss

fuss·bud·get \\'fəs-ˌbəj-ət\\ *n* : one who fusses about trifles

fussy \\'fəs-ē\\ *adj* **fuss·i·er; -est 1** : IRRITABLE **2** : requiring or giving close attention to details **3** : revealing a sometimes extreme concern for niceties : FASTIDIOUS ⟨not ∼ about food⟩ — **fuss·i·ly** \\'fəs-ə-lē\\ *adv* — **fuss·i·ness** \\-ē-nəs\\ *n*

fus·tian \\'fəs-chən\\ *n* **1** : a strong cotton and linen cloth **2** : pretentious writing or speech

fus·ty \\'fəs-tē\\ *adj* **fus·ti·er; -est** [ME, fr. *fust* wine cask, fr. MF, club, cask, fr. L *fustis*] **1** : MUSTY **2** : OLD-FASHIONED

fut *abbr* future

fu·tile \\'fyüt-ᵊl, 'fyü-ˌtīl\\ *adj* **1** : USELESS, VAIN **2** : FRIVOLOUS, TRIVIAL — **fu·til·i·ty** \\fyü-'til-ət-ē\\ *n*

¹fu·ture \\'fyü-chər\\ *adj* **1** : of, relating to, or constituting a verb tense that expresses time yet to come **2** : coming after the present

²future *n* **1** : time that is to come **2** : what is going to happen **3** : an expectation of advancement or progressive development **4** : the future tense; *also* : a verb form in it

fu·tur·ism \\'fyü-chə-ˌriz-əm\ *n* : a modern movement in art, music, and literature that tries esp. to express the energy and activity of mechanical processes — **fu·tur·ist** \\'fyüch-(ə-)rəst\ *n*

fu·tur·is·tic \ˌfyü-chə-'ris-tik\ *adj* : of or relating to the future or to futurism; *also* : very modern

fu·tu·ri·ty \fyù-'t(y)ùr-ət-ē\ *n, pl* **-ties 1** : FUTURE **2** : the quality or state of be-

ing future **3** *pl* : future events or prospects

fuze var of FUSE

fuzz \\'fəz\ *n* : fine light particles or fibers (as of down or fluff)

fuzzy \\'fəz-ē\ *adj* **fuzz·i·er; -est 1** : having or resembling fuzz **2** : INDISTINCT — **fuzz·i·ness** \\'fəz-ē-nəs\ *n*

fwd *abbr* forward

FWD *abbr* front-wheel drive

FY *abbr* fiscal year

-fy \ˌfī\ *vb suffix* : make : form into ⟨dandi*fy*⟩

FYI *abbr* for your information

G

¹g \\'jē\ *n, pl* **g's** *or* **gs** \\'jēz\ *often cap* **1** : the 7th letter of the English alphabet **2** : a unit of force equal to the force exerted by gravity on a body at rest and used to indicate the force to which a body is subjected when accelerated **3** *slang* : a sum of $1000

²g *abbr, often cap* **1** game **2** gauge **3** good **4** gram **5** gravity

ga *abbr* gauge

¹Ga *abbr* Georgia

²Ga *symbol* gallium

GA *abbr* **1** general assembly **2** general average **3** general of the army **4** Georgia

gab \\'gab\ *vb* **gabbed; gab·bing** : to talk in a rapid or thoughtless manner : CHATTER — **gab** *n*

gab·ar·dine \\'gab-ər-ˌdēn\ *n* **1** : GABERDINE 1, 2 **2** : a firm durable twilled fabric having diagonal ribs and made of various fibers; *also* : a garment of gabardine

gab·ble \\'gab-əl\ *vb* **gab·bled; gab·bling** \-(ə-)liŋ\ : JABBER, BABBLE

gab·by \\'gab-ē\ *adj* **gab·bi·er; -est** : TALKATIVE, GARRULOUS

gab·er·dine \\'gab-ər-ˌdēn\ *n* **1** : a long coat or smock worn chiefly by Jews in medieval times **2** : an English laborer's smock **3** : GABARDINE

gab·fest \\'gab-ˌfest\ *n* **1** : an informal gathering for general talk **2** : an extended conversation

ga·ble \\'gā-bəl\ *n* : the triangular part of the end of a building formed by the

sides of the roof sloping from the ridgepole down to the eaves — **ga·bled** \-bəld\ *adj*

gad \\'gad\ *vb* **gad·ded; gad·ding** : to be on the go to little purpose — usu. used with *about* — **gad·der** *n*

gad·about \\'gad-ə-ˌbaùt\ *n* : a person who flits about in social activity

gad·fly \\'gad-ˌflī\ *n* **1** : a fly that bites or harasses livestock **2** : a usu. intentionally annoying and persistently critical person

gad·get \\'gaj-ət\ *n* : DEVICE, CONTRIVANCE — **gad·ge·teer** \ˌgaj-ə-'tiər\ *n* — **gad·get·ry** \\'gaj-ə-trē\ *n*

gad·o·lin·i·um \ˌgad-ᵊl-'in-ē-əm\ *n* : a magnetic metallic chemical element

¹Gael \\'gāl\ *n* : a Celtic inhabitant of Ireland or Scotland

²Gael *abbr* Gaelic

Gael·ic \\'gā-lik\ *adj* : of or relating to the Gaels or their languages — **Gaelic** *n*

gaff \\'gaf\ *n* **1** : a spear used in taking fish or turtles; *also* : a metal hook for holding or lifting heavy fish **2** : the spar supporting the top of a fore-and-aft sail **3** : rough treatment : ABUSE — **gaff** *vb*

gaffe \\'gaf\ *n* : a social blunder

gaf·fer \\'gaf-ər\ *n* : an old man

¹gag \\'gag\ *vb* **gagged; gag·ging 1** : to prevent from speaking or crying out by stopping up the mouth **2** : to prevent from speaking freely **3** : to retch or cause to retch **4** : OBSTRUCT, CHOKE **5** : BALK **6** : to make quips

²gag *n* **1** : something thrust into the mouth esp. to prevent speech or outcry **2** : an official check or restraint on free speech **3** : a laugh-provoking remark or act **4** : PRANK, TRICK

¹gage \'gāj\ *n* **1** : a token of defiance; *esp* : a glove or cap cast on the ground as a pledge of combat **2** : SECURITY

²gage var of GAUGE

gag·gle \'gag-əl\ *n* [ME *gagyll*, fr. *gagelen* to cackle] **1** : a flock of geese **2** : GROUP, CLUSTER

gai·ety \'gā-ət-ē\ *n, pl* **-eties 1** : MERRYMAKING **2** : MERRIMENT **3** : FINERY

gai·ly \'gā-lē\ *adv* : in a gay manner

¹gain \'gān\ *n* **1** : PROFIT **2** : ACQUISITION, ACCUMULATION **3** : INCREASE

²gain *vb* **1** : to get possession of : EARN **2** : WIN ⟨∼ a victory⟩ **3** : ACHIEVE ⟨∼ strength⟩ **4** : to arrive at **5** : PERSUADE **6** : to increase in ⟨∼ momentum⟩ **7** : to run fast ⟨the watch ∼s a minute a day⟩ **8** : PROFIT **9** : INCREASE **10** : to improve in health — **gain·er** *n*

gain·ful \'gān-fəl\ *adj* : PROFITABLE — **gain·ful·ly** \-ē\ *adv*

gain·say \gān-'sā\ *vb* **-said** \-'sād, -'sed\; **-say·ing** \-'sā-iŋ\; **-says** \-'sāz, -'sez\ [ME *gainsayen*, fr. *gain-* against + *-sayen* to say] **1** : DENY, DISPUTE **2** : to speak against — **gain·say·er** *n*

gait \'gāt\ *n* : manner of moving on foot; *also* : a particular pattern or style of such moving — **gait·ed** \-əd\ *adj*

gai·ter \'gāt-ər\ *n* **1** : a leg covering reaching from the instep to ankle, mid-calf, or knee **2** : an ankle-high shoe with elastic gores in the sides **3** : an overshoe with a fabric upper

¹gal \'gal\ *n* : GIRL

²gal *abbr* gallon

Gal *abbr* Galatians

ga·la \'gā-lə, 'gal-ə, 'gäl-ə\ *n* : a gay celebration : FESTIVITY — **gala** *adj*

ga·lac·tose \gə-'lak-ˌtōs\ *n* : a sugar less soluble and less sweet than glucose

Ga·la·tians \gə-'lā-shənz\ *n* — see BIBLE table

gal·axy \'gal-ək-sē\ *n, pl* **-ax·ies** [ME *galaxie, galaxias*, fr. LL *galaxias*, fr. Gk, fr. *galakt-, gala* milk] **1** *often cap* : MILKY WAY GALAXY — used with *the*

2 : a very large group of stars **3** : an assemblage of brilliant or famous persons or things — **ga·lac·tic** \gə-'lak-tik\ *adj*

gale \'gāl\ *n* **1** : a strong wind **2** : an emotional outburst (as of laughter)

ga·le·na \gə-'lē-nə\ *n* : a lustrous bluish gray mineral that consists of the sulfide of lead and is the chief ore of lead

¹gall \'gȯl\ *n* **1** : BILE **2** : something bitter to endure **3** : RANCOR **4** : IMPUDENCE

²gall *n* : a sore on the skin caused by chafing

³gall *vb* **1** : CHAFE; *esp* : to become sore or worn by rubbing **2** : VEX, HARASS

⁴gall *n* : a swelling of plant tissue caused by parasites (as fungi or mites)

¹gal·lant \gə-'lant, gə-'länt, 'gal-ənt\ *n* **1** : a young man of fashion **2** : a man who shows a marked fondness for the company of women and who is esp. attentive to them **3** : SUITOR

²gal·lant \'gal-ənt (*usual for 2, 3, 4*); gə-'lant, gə-'länt (*usual for 5*)\ *adj* **1** : showy in dress or bearing : SMART **2** : SPLENDID, STATELY **3** : SPIRITED, BRAVE **4** : CHIVALROUS, NOBLE **5** : polite and attentive to women — **gallant·ly** *adv*

gal·lant·ry \'gal-ən-trē\ *n, pl* **-ries 1** *archaic* : gallant appearance **2** : an act of marked courtesy **3** : courteous attention to a woman **4** : conspicuous bravery

gall·blad·der \'gȯl-ˌblad-ər\ *n* : a membranous muscular sac attached to the liver in which bile is stored

gal·le·on \'gal-ē-ən\ *n* : a large square‑rigged sailing ship formerly used esp. by the Spanish

gal·le·ria \ˌgal-ə-'rē-ə\ *n* [It] : a roofed and usu. glass-enclosed promenade or court

gal·lery \'gal(-ə)-rē\ *n, pl* **-ler·ies 1** : an outdoor balcony; *also* : PORCH, VERANDA **2** : a long narrow room or hall; *esp* : one with windows along one side **3** : a narrow passage (as one made underground by a miner or through wood by an insect) **4** : a room where works of art are exhibited; *also* : an organization dealing in works of art **5** : a balcony in a theater, auditorium, or church; *esp* : the highest one in a theater **6** : a body of spectators (as at a tennis match) **7** : a photographer's studio — **gal·ler·ied** \-rēd\ *adj*

gal·ley \'gal-ē\ *n, pl* **galleys** **1** : a long low ship propelled esp. by oars and formerly used esp. in the Mediterranean sea **2** : the kitchen esp. of a boat or airplane **3** : a tray to hold printer's type that has been set; *also* : proof from type in such a tray

Gal·lic \'gal-ik\ *adj* : of or relating to Gaul or France

gal·li·mau·fry \ˌgal-ə-'mȯ-frē\ *n, pl* **-fries** [MF *galimafree* hash] : HODGE-PODGE

gal·li·nule \'gal-ə-ˌn(y)ü(ə)l\ *n* : any of several aquatic birds related to the rails

gal·li·um \'gal-ē-əm\ *n* : a rare bluish white metallic chemical element

gal·li·vant \'gal-ə-ˌvant\ *vb* : to go roaming about for pleasure

gal·lon \'gal-ən\ *n* — see WEIGHT table

¹gal·lop \gal-əp\ *vb* **1** : to go or cause to go at a gallop **2** : to run fast — **gal·lop·er** *n*

²gallop *n* **1** : a springing gait of a quadruped; *esp* : a fast 3-beat gait of a horse **2** : a ride or run at a gallop

gal·lows \'gal-ōz\ *n, pl* **gallows** *or* **gallows·es** : a frame usu. of two upright posts and a crosspiece from which criminals are hanged

gall·stone \'gȯl-ˌstōn\ *n* : an abnormal concretion occurring in the gallbladder or bile passages

gal·lus·es \'gal-ə-səz\ *n pl, chiefly dial* : SUSPENDERS

ga·lore \gə-'lōr\ *adj* [IrGael *go leor* enough] : ABUNDANT, PLENTIFUL

ga·losh \gə-'läsh\ *n* : a high overshoe

galv *abbr* galvanized

gal·va·nize \'gal-və-ˌnīz\ *vb* **-nized; -nizing** **1** : to stimulate as if by an electric shock **2** : to coat (iron or steel) with zinc — **gal·va·ni·za·tion** \ˌgal-və-nə-'zā-shən\ *n* — **gal·va·niz·er** \'gal-və-ˌnī-zər\ *n*

gal·va·nom·e·ter \ˌgal-və-'näm-ət-ər\ *n* : an instrument for detecting or measuring a small electric current

Gam·bi·an \'gam-bē-ən\ *n* : a native or inhabitant of Gambia — **Gambian** *adj*

gam·bit \'gam-bət\ *n* [It *gambetto*, lit., act of tripping someone, fr. *gamba* leg] **1** : a chess opening in which a player risks one or more minor pieces to gain an advantage in position **2** : a calculated move : STRATAGEM

¹gam·ble \'gam-bəl\ *vb* **gam·bled; gambling** \-b(ə-)liŋ\ **1** : to play a game for money or other stakes **2** : SPECULATE, BET, WAGER **3** : VENTURE, HAZARD — **gam·bler** \-blər\ *n*

²gamble *n* : a risky undertaking

gam·bol \'gam-bəl\ *vb* **-boled** *or* **-bolled; -bol·ing** *or* **-bol·ling** \-b(ə-)liŋ\ : to skip about in play : FRISK — **gambol** *n*

gam·brel roof \ˌgam-brəl-\ *n* : a roof with a lower steeper slope and an upper flatter one on each side

¹game \'gām\ *n* **1** : AMUSEMENT, DIVERSION **2** : SPORT, FUN **3** : SCHEME, PROJECT **4** : a line of work : PROFESSION **5** : CONTEST **6** : animals hunted for sport or food; *also* : the flesh of a game animal

²game *vb* **gamed; gam·ing** : to play for a stake : GAMBLE

³game *adj* : PLUCKY — **game·ly** *adv* — **game·ness** *n*

⁴game *adj* : LAME ⟨a ~ leg⟩

game·cock \'gām-ˌkäk\ *n* : a rooster trained for fighting

game fish *n* : SPORT FISH

game·keep·er \'gām-ˌkē-pər\ *n* : a person in charge of the breeding and protection of game animals or birds on a private preserve

game·some \'gām-səm\ *adj* : MERRY

game·ster \'gām-stər\ *n* : GAMBLER

gam·ete \'gam-ˌēt\ *n* : a matured germ cell — **ga·met·ic** \gə-'met-ik\ *adj*

game theory *n* : the analysis of a situation involving conflicting interests (as in business) in terms of gains and losses among opposing players

gam·in \'gam-ən\ *n* [F] **1** : a boy who hangs out on the streets **2** : GAMINE 2

ga·mine \ga-'mēn\ *n* **1** : a girl who hangs out on the streets **2** : a small playfully mischievous girl

gam·ma globulin \'gam-ə-\ *n* : a blood protein fraction rich in antibodies; *also* : a solution of this from human blood donors that is given to provide immunity against some infectious diseases (as measles)

gamma rays *n pl* : very penetrating radiation similar to X rays but of shorter wavelength

gam·mer \'gam-ər\ *n, archaic* : an old woman

gam·mon \\'gam-ən\\ *n, chiefly Brit* : a cured ham or side of bacon

gam·ut \\'gam-ət\\ *n* [ML *gamma,* lowest note of a medieval scale (fr. LL, 3d letter of the Greek alphabet) + *ut,* lowest of each series of six tones in the scale] : an entire range or series

gamy *or* **gam·ey** \\'gā-mē\\ *adj* **gam·i·er; -est 1** : GAME, PLUCKY **2** : having the flavor of game esp. when slightly tainted ⟨∼ meat⟩ **3** : SCANDALOUS; *also* : DISREPUTABLE — **gam·i·ness** \\-mē-nəs\\ *n*

¹**gan·der** \\'gan-dər\\ *n* : a male goose

²**gander** *n* : LOOK, GLANCE

¹**gang** \\'gaŋ\\ *n* **1** : a set of implements or devices arranged to operate together **2** : a group of persons working or associated together; *esp* : a group of criminals or young delinquents

²**gang** *vb* **1** : to attack in a gang — usu. used with *up* **2** : to form into or move or act as a gang

gang·land \\'gaŋ-ˌland\\ *n* : the world of organized crime

gan·gling \\'gaŋ-gliŋ\\ *adj* : LANKY, SPINDLING

gan·gli·on \\'gaŋ-glē-ən\\ *n, pl* **-glia** \\-glē-ə\\ *also* **-gli·ons** : a mass of nerve cells outside the central nervous system; *also* : NUCLEUS **3** — **gan·gli·on·ic** \\ˌgaŋ-glē-'än-ik\\ *adj*

gang·plank \\'gaŋ-ˌplaŋk\\ *n* : a movable bridge from a ship to the shore

gang·plow \\-ˌplau̇\\ *n* : a plow that turns two or more furrows at one time

gan·grene \\'gaŋ-ˌgrēn, gaŋ-'grēn\\ *n* : the death of soft tissues in a local area of the body due to loss of the blood supply — **gangrene** *vb* — **gan·gre·nous** \\'gaŋ-grə-nəs\\ *adj*

gang·ster \\'gaŋ-stər\\ *n* : a member of a gang of criminals : RACKETEER

gang·way \\'gaŋ-ˌwā\\ *n* **1** : a passage into, through, or out of an enclosed place **2** : GANGPLANK

gan·net \\'gan-ət\\ *n, pl* **gannets** *also* **gannet** : any of several large fish-eating usu. white and black marine birds that breed on offshore islands

gant·let \\'gȯnt-lət\\ var of GAUNTLET

gan·try \\'gan-trē\\ *n, pl* **gantries** : a frame structure on side supports over or around something

GAO *abbr* General Accounting Office

gaol \\'jāl\\ , **gaol·er** \\'jā-lər\\ *chiefly Brit* var of JAIL, JAILER

gap \\'gap\\ *n* **1** : BREACH, CLEFT **2** : a mountain pass **3** : a blank space **4** : a wide difference in character or attitude

gape \\'gāp, 'gap\\ *vb* **gaped; gap·ing 1** : to open the mouth wide **2** : to open or part widely **3** : to stare with mouth open **4** : YAWN — **gape** *n*

¹**gar** \\'gär\\ *n* : any of several fishes that have a long body resembling that of a pike and long narrow jaws

²**gar** *abbr* garage

GAR *abbr* Grand Army of the Republic

¹**ga·rage** \\gə-'räzh, -'räj\\ *n* [F] : a building for housing or repairing automobiles

²**garage** *vb* **ga·raged; ga·rag·ing** : to keep or put in a garage

garage sale *n* : a sale of used household articles held on one's own premises

garb \\'gärb\\ *n* **1** : style of dress **2** : outward form : APPEARANCE — **garb** *vb*

gar·bage \\'gär-bij\\ *n* **1** : food waste **2** : unwanted or useless material

gar·ble \\'gär-bəl\\ *vb* **gar·bled; gar·bling** \\-b(ə-)liŋ\\ [ME *garbelen,* fr. It *garbellare* to sift, fr. Ar *ghirbāl* sieve] : to distort the meaning or sound of ⟨∼ a story⟩ ⟨∼ words⟩

gar·çon \\gär-'sōᵐ\\ *n, pl* **garçons** \\-'sōⁿ(z)\\ [F, boy, waiter] : WAITER

¹**gar·den** \\'gärd-ᵊn\\ *n* **1** : a plot for growing fruits, flowers, or vegetables **2** : a public recreation area; *esp* : one for displaying plants or animals

²**garden** *vb* **gar·dened; gar·den·ing** \\'gärd-(ᵊ-)niŋ\\ : to develop or work in a garden — **gar·den·er** \\'gärd-(ᵊ-)nər\\ *n*

gar·de·nia \\gär-'dē-nyə\\ *n* [NL, genus name, fr. Alexander *Garden* †1791 Scot. naturalist] : the fragrant white or yellow flower of any of a genus of trees or shrubs of the madder family; *also* : one of these trees

garden–variety *adj* : COMMONPLACE, ORDINARY

gar·fish \\'gär-ˌfish\\ *n* : GAR

gar·gan·tuan \\gär-'ganch-(ə-)wən\\ *adj, often cap* : of tremendous size or volume

gar·gle \\'gär-gəl\\ *vb* **gar·gled; gar·gling** \\-g(ə-)liŋ\\ : to rinse the throat with liquid agitated by air forced through it from the lungs — **gargle** *n*

gar·goyle \\'gär-ˌgȯil\ *n* **1** : a waterspout in the form of a grotesque human or animal figure projecting from the roof or eaves of a building **2** : a grotesquely carved figure

gar·ish \\'ga(ə)r-ish\ *adj* : FLASHY, GLARING, SHOWY, GAUDY

¹gar·land \\'gär-lənd\ *n* : a wreath or rope of leaves or flowers

²garland *vb* : to form into or deck with a garland

gar·lic \\'gär-lik\ *n* [ME *garlek,* fr. OE *gārlēac,* fr. *gār* spear + *lēac* leek] : an herb related to the lilies and grown for its pungent bulbs used in cooking; *also* : its bulb — **gar·licky** \-li-kē\ *adj*

gar·ment \\'gär-mənt\ *n* : an article of clothing

gar·ner \\'gär-nər\ *vb* **gar·nered; gar·ner·ing** \\'gärn-(ə-)riŋ\ **1** : to gather into storage **2** : to acquire by effort **3** : ACCUMULATE, COLLECT

gar·net \\'gär-nət\ *n* [ME *grenat,* fr. MF, fr. *grenat,* adj., red like a pomegranate, fr. *(pomme) grenate* pomegranate] : a transparent deep red mineral sometimes used as a gem

gar·nish \\'gär-nish\ *vb* **1** : DECORATE, EMBELLISH **2** : to add decorative or savory touches to (food) — **garnish** *n*

gar·nish·ee \ˌgär-nə-'shē\ *vb* **-eed; -ce·ing** **1** : to serve with a garnishment **2** : to take (as a debtor's wages) by legal authority

gar·nish·ment \\'gär-nish-mənt\ *n* **1** : GARNISH **2** : a legal warning to the holder of property of a debtor to give it to a creditor; *also* : the attachment of such property to satisfy a creditor

gar·ni·ture \-ni-chər, -nə-ˌchù(ə)r\ *n* : EMBELLISHMENT, TRIMMING

gar·ret \\'gar-ət\ *n* [ME *garette* watchtower, fr. MF *garite*] : the part of a house just under the roof : ATTIC

gar·ri·son \\'gar-ə-sən\ *n* **1** : a military post; *esp* : a permanent military installation **2** : the troops stationed at a garrison — **garrison** *vb*

garrison state *n* : a state organized on a primarily military basis

gar·rote *or* **ga·rotte** \gə-'rät, -'rōt\ *n* [Sp *garrote*] **1** : a method of execution by strangling with an iron collar; *also* : the iron collar used **2** : strangulation esp. for the purpose of robbery; *also*

: an implement for this purpose — **garrote** *or* **garotte** *vb*

gar·ru·lous \\'gar-ə-ləs\ *adj* : CHATTERING, TALKATIVE, WORDY — **gar·ru·li·ty** \gə-'rü-lət-ē\ *n* — **gar·ru·lous·ly** \\'gar-ə-ləs-lē\ *adv* — **gar·ru·lous·ness** *n*

gar·ter \\'gärt-ər\ *n* : a band or strap worn to hold up a stocking or sock

garter snake *n* : any of numerous harmless American snakes with longitudinal stripes on the back

¹gas \\'gas\ *n, pl* **gas·es** *also* **gas·ses** [NL, alter. of L *chaos* space, chaos] **1** : a fluid (as hydrogen or air) that tends to expand indefinitely **2** : a gas or mixture of gases used as a fuel or anesthetic **3** : a substance that can be used to produce a poisonous, asphyxiating, or irritant atmosphere **4** : GASOLINE — **gas·eous** \-ē-əs, 'gash-əs\ *adj*

²gas *vb* **gassed; gas·sing** **1** : to treat with gas; *also* : to poison with gas **2** : to fill with gasoline

gash \\'gash\ *n* : a deep long cut — **gash** *vb*

gas·ket \\'gas-kət\ *n* : material (as rubber or metal) used to prevent a joint from leaking

gas·light \\'gas-ˌlīt\ *n* **1** : light made by burning illuminating gas **2** : a gas flame; *also* : a gas lighting fixture

gas mask *n* : a mask connected to a chemical air filter and used to protect the face and lungs against poison gases

gas·o·line *also* **gas·o·lene** \\'gas ə ˌlēn, ˌgas-ə-'lēn\ *n* : a flammable liquid made esp. by blending products from natural gas and petroleum and used as a motor fuel

gasp \\'gasp\ *vb* **1** : to catch the breath with emotion (as shock) **2** : to breathe laboriously : PANT **3** : to utter in a gasping manner — **gasp** *n*

gas·tric \\'gas-trik\ *adj* : of, relating to, or located near the stomach

gastric juice *n* : the acid digestive secretion of the stomach

gas·tri·tis \gas-'trīt-əs\ *n* : inflammatory disorder of the stomach

gas·tro·en·ter·ol·o·gy \ˌgas-trō-ˌent-ə-'räl-ə-jē\ *n* : a branch of medicine dealing with the alimentary canal — **gas·tro·en·ter·ol·o·gist** \-jəst\ *n*

gas·tro·in·tes·ti·nal \ˌgas-trō-in-'tes-tən-ᵊl\ *adj* : of, relating to, affecting, or including both stomach and intestine

gas•tron•o•my \gas-'trän-ə-mē\ n [F *gastronomie,* fr. Gk *Gastronomia,* title of a 4th cent. B.C. poem, fr. *gastēr* belly] : the art of good eating — **gas•tro•nom•ic** \ˌgas-trə-'näm-ik\ *also* **gas•tro•nom•i•cal** \-i-kəl\ *adj*

gas•tro•pod \'gas-trə-ˌpäd\ n : any of a large class of mollusks (as snails, whelks, and slugs) with a muscular foot and a spiral shell or none

gas•works \'gas-ˌwərks\ n pl : a plant for manufacturing gas

gate \'gāt\ n 1 : an opening for passage in a wall or fence 2 : a city or castle entrance often with defensive structures 3 : the frame or door that closes a gate 4 : a device (as a valve) for controlling the passage of a fluid or signal 5 : the total admission receipts or the number of people at an event

gate–crash•er \'gāt-ˌkrash-ər\ n : one who enters without paying admission or attends without invitation

gate•keep•er \-ˌkē-pər\ n : a person who tends or guards a gate

gate•post \'gāt-ˌpōst\ n : the post to which a gate is hung or the one against which it closes

gate•way \-ˌwā\ n 1 : an opening for a gate 2 : a means of entrance or exit

¹**gath•er** \'gath-ər\ vb **gath•ered; gath•er•ing** \-(ə-)riŋ\ 1 : to bring together : COLLECT 2 : PICK, HARVEST 3 : to pick up little by little 4 : to gain or win by gradual increase : ACCUMULATE ⟨∼ speed⟩ 5 : to summon up ⟨∼ courage to dive⟩ 6 : to draw about or close to something 7 : to pull (fabric) along a line of stitching into puckers 8 : GUESS, DEDUCE, INFER 9 : ASSEMBLE 10 : to swell out and fill with pus 11 : GROW, INCREASE — **gath•er•er** n — **gath•er•ing** n

²**gather** n : a puckering in cloth made by gathering

GATT *abbr* General Agreement on Tariffs and Trade

gauche \'gōsh\ *adj* [F, lit., left] : lacking social experience or grace

gau•che•rie \ˌgōsh-(ə-)'rē\ n : a tactless or awkward action

gau•cho \'gaù-chō\ n, pl **gauchos** : a cowboy of the So. American pampas

gaud \'gòd\ n : ORNAMENT, TRINKET

gaudy \'gòd-ē\ *adj* **gaud•i•er; -est** : ostentatiously or tastelessly ornamented **syn** garish, flashy, glaring, tawdry — **gaud•i•ly** \'gòd-ᵊl-ē\ *adv* — **gaud•i•ness** \-ē-nəs\ n

¹**gauge** *or* **gage** \'gāj\ n 1 : measurement according to some standard or system 2 : DIMENSIONS, SIZE 3 *usu gage* : an instrument for measuring, testing, or registering

²**gauge** *or* **gage** vb **gauged** *or* **gaged; gauging** *or* **gag•ing** 1 : MEASURE 2 : to determine the capacity or contents of 3 : ESTIMATE, JUDGE

gaunt \'gònt\ *adj* 1 : being thin and angular (as from hunger or suffering) 2 : BARREN, DESOLATE — **gaunt•ness** n

¹**gaunt•let** \'gònt-lət\ n 1 : a protective glove 2 : a challenge to combat 3 : a dress glove extending above the wrist

²**gauntlet** n 1 : a double file of men armed with weapons (as clubs) with which to strike at an individual who is made to run between them 2 : ORDEAL

gauze \'gòz\ n : a very thin often transparent fabric used esp. for draperies and surgical dressings — **gauzy** *adj*

gave past of GIVE

gav•el \'gav-əl\ n : the mallet of a presiding officer or auctioneer

ga•votte \gə-'vät\ n : a dance of French peasant origin marked by the raising rather than sliding of the feet

gawk \'gòk\ vb : to gape or stare stupidly

gawky \'gò-kē\ *adj* **gawk•i•er; -est** : AWKWARD, CLUMSY

gay \'gā\ *adj* 1 : MERRY 2 : BRIGHT, LIVELY 3 : brilliant in color 4 : given to social pleasures; *also* : LICENTIOUS 5 : HOMOSEXUAL

gay•ety, gay•ly var of GAIETY, GAILY

gaz *abbr* gazette

gaze \'gāz\ vb **gazed; gaz•ing** : to fix the eyes in a steady intent look — **gaze** n — **gaz•er** n

ga•ze•bo \gə-'zā-bō, -'zē-\ n, pl **-bos** 1 : BELVEDERE 2 : a freestanding roofed structure usu. open on the sides

ga•zelle \gə-'zel\ n, pl **gazelles** *also* **gazelle** : any of several small swift graceful antelopes

¹**ga•zette** \gə-'zet\ n 1 : NEWSPAPER 2 : an official journal

²**gazette** vb **ga•zett•ed; ga•zett•ing** *chiefly*

Brit : to announce or publish in a gazette

gaz•et•teer \ˌgaz-ə-ˈtiər\ *n* : a geographical dictionary

GB *abbr* Great Britain

GCA *abbr* ground-controlled approach

gd *abbr* good

Gd *symbol* gadolinium

GDR *abbr* German Democratic Republic

Ge *symbol* germanium

gear \ˈgiər\ *n* **1** : CLOTHING **2** : movable property : GOODS **3** : EQUIPMENT ⟨fishing ∼⟩ ⟨photographic ∼⟩ **4** : a mechanism that performs a specific function ⟨steering ∼⟩ **5** : a toothed wheel that interlocks with another toothed wheel or shaft for transmitting motion **6** : working adjustment of gears ⟨in ∼⟩ **7** : an adjustment of transmission gears (as of an automobile or bicycle) that determines speed and direction of travel — **gear** *vb* — **gear•ing** \-iŋ\ *n*

gear•box \ˈgiər-ˌbäks\ *n* : TRANSMISSION 3

gear•shift \-ˌshift\ *n* : a mechanism by which transmission gears are shifted

gear wheel *n* : COGWHEEL

GED *abbr* general equivalency diploma

geese *pl of* GOOSE

gee•zer \ˈgē-zər\ *n* : an odd or eccentric man

Gei•ger counter \ˈgī-gər-\ *or* **Gei•ger– Mül•ler counter** \-ˈmyül-ər-, -ˈmil-, -ˈməl-\ *n* : an electronic instrument for detecting the presence of cosmic rays or radioactive substances

gei•sha \ˈgā-shə, ˈgē-\ *n, pl* **geisha** *or* **geishas** [Jp, fr. *gei* art + *-sha* person] : a Japanese girl who is trained to provide entertaining company for men

gel \ˈjel\ *n* : a solid jellylike colloid (as gelatin dessert) — **gel** *vb*

gel•a•tin *also* **gel•a•tine** \ˈjel-ət-ᵊn\ *n* : glutinous material and esp. protein obtained from animal tissues by boiling and used as a food, in dyeing, and in photography; *also* : an edible jelly formed with gelatin — **ge•lat•i•nous** \jə-ˈlat-(ᵊ-)nəs\ *adj*

geld \ˈgeld\ *vb* : CASTRATE

geld•ing \ˈgel-diŋ\ *n* : a gelded individual; *esp* : a castrated male horse

gel•id \ˈjel-əd\ *adj* : extremely cold

gem \ˈjem\ *n* **1** : JEWEL **2** : a usu. valuable stone cut and polished for ornament **3** : something valued for beauty or perfection

Gem•i•ni \ˈjem-ə-(ˌ)nē, -ˌnī; ˈgem-ə-ˌnē\ *n* **1** : a zodiacal constellation between Taurus and Cancer usu. pictured as twins sitting together **2** : the 3d sign of the zodiac in astrology; *also* : one born under this sign

gem•ol•o•gy *or* **gem•mol•o•gy** \je-ˈmäl-ə-jē, jə-\ *n* : the science of gems — **gem•olog•i•cal** *or* **gem•mo•log•i•cal** \ˌjem-ə-ˈläj-i-kəl\ *adj* — **gem•ol•o•gist** *or* **gem•mol•o•gist** \-jəst\ *n*

gem•stone \ˈjem-ˌstōn\ *n* : a mineral or petrified material that when cut and polished can be used in jewelry

gen *abbr* **1** general **2** genitive

Gen *abbr* Genesis

Gen AF *abbr* general of the air force

gen•darme \ˈzhän-ˌdärm, ˈjän-\ *n* [F, intended as sing. of *gensdarmes,* pl. of *gent d'armes,* lit., armed people] : one of a body of soldiers esp. in France serving as an armed police force

gen•dar•mer•ie *or* **gen•dar•mery** \jän-ˈdärm-ə-rē, zhän-\ *n, pl* **-mer•ies** : a body of gendarmes

gen•der \ˈjen-dər\ *n* **1** : SEX 1 **2** : any of two or more divisions within a grammatical class that determine agreement with and selection of other words or grammatical forms

gene \ˈjēn\ *n* : a part of DNA or sometimes RNA that contains chemical information needed to make a particular protein (as an enzyme) controlling or influencing an inherited bodily trait or activity (as eye color) or that influences or controls the activity of another gene or genes — **gen•ic** \ˈjē-nik, ˈjen-\ *adj*

ge•ne•al•o•gy \ˌjē-nē-ˈäl-ə-jē, -ˈal-\ *n, pl* **-gies** : PEDIGREE, LINEAGE; *also* : the study of family pedigrees — **ge•ne•a•log•i•cal** \ˌjē-nē-ə-ˈläj-i-kəl, ˌjen-ē-\ *adj* — **ge•ne•a•log•i•cal•ly** \-k(ə-)lē\ *adv* — **ge•ne•al•o•gist** \ˌjē-nē-ˈäl-ə-jəst, ˌjen-ē-; -ˈal-\ *n*

genera *pl of* GENUS

¹gen•er•al \ˈjen-(ə-)rəl\ *adj* **1** : of or relating to the whole : not local **2** : taken as a whole **3** : relating to or covering all instances ⟨a ∼ conclusion⟩ **4** : not limited in meaning : not specific ⟨a ∼ outline⟩ **5** : common to many ⟨a ∼

custom⟩ **6** : not special or specialized **7** : holding superior rank ⟨inspector ∼⟩ — **gen•er•al•ly** \-ē\ adv

²**general** n **1** : something that involves or is applicable to the whole **2** : a commissioned officer ranking next below a general of the army or a general of the air force **3** : a commissioned officer of the highest rank in the marine corps — **in general** : for the most part

general assembly n **1** : a legislative assembly; esp : a U.S. state legislature **2** cap G&A : the supreme deliberative body of the United Nations

gen•er•a•lis•si•mo \ˌjen-(ə-)rə-ˈlis-ə-ˌmō\ n, pl **-mos** [It, fr. generale general] : COMMANDER IN CHIEF

gen•er•al•i•ty \ˌjen-ə-ˈral-ət-ē\ n, pl **-ties 1** : the quality or state of being general **2** : GENERALIZATION 2 **3** : a vague or inadequate statement **4** : the greatest part : BULK

gen•er•al•iza•tion \ˌjen-(ə-)rə-lə-ˈzā-shən\ n **1** : the act or process of generalizing **2** : a general statement, law, principle, or proposition

gen•er•al•ize \ˈjen-(ə-)rə-ˌlīz\ vb **-ized; -iz•ing 1** : to make general **2** : to draw general conclusions from **3** : to reach a general conclusion esp. on the basis of particular instances **4** : to extend throughout the body

general of the air force : a commissioned officer of the highest rank in the air force

general of the army : a commissioned officer of the highest rank in the army

general practitioner n : a physician or veterinarian who does not limit his practice to a specialty

gen•er•al•ship \ˈjen-(ə-)rəl-ˌship\ n **1** : office or tenure of office of a general **2** : military skill as a high commander **3** : LEADERSHIP

general store n : a retail store that carries a wide variety of goods but is not divided into departments

gen•er•ate \ˈjen-ə-ˌrāt\ vb **-at•ed; -at•ing** : to bring into existence : PRODUCE

gen•er•a•tion \ˌjen-ə-ˈrā-shən\ n **1** : a body of living beings constituting a single step in the line of descent from an ancestor; also : the average period between generations **2** : PRODUCTION ⟨∼ of electric current⟩

gen•er•a•tive \ˈjen-(ə-)rət-iv, ˈjen-ə-ˌrāt-

iv\ adj : having the power or function of generating, originating, producing, or reproducing ⟨∼ organs⟩

gen•er•a•tor \ˈjen-ə-ˌrāt-ər\ n : one that generates; esp : a machine by which mechanical energy is changed into electrical energy

ge•ner•ic \jə-ˈner-ik\ adj **1** : not specific : GENERAL **2** : not protected by a trademark ⟨a ∼ drug⟩ **3** : of or relating to a genus — **generic** n

gen•er•ous \ˈjen-(ə-)rəs\ adj **1** : free in giving or sharing **2** : HIGH-MINDED, NOBLE **3** : ABUNDANT, AMPLE, COPIOUS — **gen•er•os•i•ty** \ˌjen-ə-ˈräs-ət-ē\ n — **gen•er•ous•ly** \ˈjen-(ə-)rəs-lē\ adv — **gen•er•ous•ness** n

gen•e•sis \ˈjen-ə-səs\ n, pl **-e•ses** \-ˌsēz\ : the origin or coming into existence of something

Gen•e•sis \ˈjen-ə-səs\ n — see BIBLE table

gene—splic•ing \-ˌsplī-siŋ\ n : the technique by which recombinant DNA is produced and made to function in an organism

ge•net•ic \jə-ˈnet-ik\ adj : of or relating to the origin, development, or causes of something; also : of or relating to genetics — **ge•net•i•cal•ly** \-i-k(ə-)lē\ adv

genetic code n : the chemical code that is the basis of genetic inheritance and consists of triplets of three linked chemical groups which specify particular kinds of amino acids used to make proteins or which start or stop the process of making proteins

genetic engineering n : the directed alteration of genetic material by intervention in genetic processes; esp : GENE-SPLICING

ge•net•ics \jə-ˈnet-iks\ n : a branch of biology dealing with heredity and variation — **ge•net•i•cist** \-ˈnet-ə-səst\ n

ge•nial \ˈjē-nyəl\ adj **1** : favorable to growth or comfort ⟨∼ sunshine⟩ **2** : CHEERFUL, KINDLY ⟨a ∼ host⟩ — **ge•nial•i•ty** \ˌjē-nē-ˈal-ət-ē, jēn-ˈyal-\ n — **ge•nial•ly** \ˈjē-nyə-lē\ adv

-gen•ic \ˈjen-ik\ adj comb form **1** : producing : forming **2** : produced by : formed from **3** : suitable for production or reproduction by (such) a medium

ge·nie \ˈjē-nē\ *n, pl* **ge·nies** *also* **ge·nii** \ˈjē-nē-ˌī\ [F *génie*, fr. Ar *jinnīy*] : a supernatural spirit that often takes human form

gen·i·tal \ˈjen-ə-tᵊl\ *adj* **1** : concerned with reproduction ⟨~ organs⟩ **2** : of, relating to, or characterized by the stage of psychosexual development in which oral and anal impulses are subordinated to adaptive interpersonal mechanisms — **gen·i·tal·ly** \-tə-lē\ *adv*

gen·i·ta·lia \ˌjen-ə-ˈtāl-yə\ *n pl* : reproductive organs; *esp* : the external genital organs — **gen·i·ta·lic** \-ˈtal-ik, -ˈtāl-\ *adj*

gen·i·tals \ˈjen-ə-tᵊlz\ *n pl* : GENITALIA

gen·i·tive \ˈjen-ət-iv\ *adj* : of, relating to, or constituting a grammatical case marking typically a relationship of possessor or source — **genitive** *n*

gen·i·to·uri·nary \ˌjen-ə-tō-ˈyur-ə-ˌner-ē\ *adj* : of or relating to the genital and urinary organs or functions

ge·nius \ˈjē-nyəs\ *n, pl* **ge·nius·es** *or* **ge·nii** \-nē-ˌī\ [L, tutelary spirit, fondness for social enjoyment, fr. *gignere* to beget] **1** *pl* **genii** : an attendant spirit of a person or place; *also* : a person who influences another for good or evil **2** : a strong leaning or inclination **3** : a peculiar or distinctive character or spirit (as of a nation or a language) **4** *pl usu* **genii** : SPIRIT, GENIE **5** : a single strongly marked capacity or aptitude **6** : extraordinary intellectual power; *also* : a person having such power

genl *abbr* general

geno·cide \ˈjen-ə-ˌsīd\ *n* : the deliberate and systematic destruction of a racial, political, or cultural group

-g·e·nous \j-ə-nəs\ *adj comb form* **1** : producing : yielding **2** : having (such) an origin

genre \ˈzhän-rə, ˈzhäⁿ-; ˈzhäⁿ(-ə)r\ *n* **1** : a distinctive type or category esp. of literary composition **2** : a style of painting in which everyday subjects are treated realistically

gens \ˈjenz, ˈgens\ *n, pl* **gen·tes** \ˈjen-ˌtēz, ˈgen-ˌtās\ : a Roman clan embracing the families of the same stock in the male line

gent *n* : GENTLEMAN

gen·teel \jen-ˈtēl\ *adj* **1** : ARISTOCRATIC **2** : ELEGANT, STYLISH **3** : POLITE, REFINED **4** : maintaining the appearance of superior or middle-class social status **5** : marked by false delicacy, prudery, or affectation

gen·tian \ˈjen-chən\ *n* : any of numerous herbs with opposite leaves and showy usu. blue flowers in the fall

gen·tile \ˈjen-ˌtīl\ *n* [LL *gentilis* heathen, pagan, lit., belonging to the nations, fr. L *gent-, gens* family, clan, nation] **1** *often cap* : a person who is not Jewish **2** : HEATHEN, PAGAN — **gentile** *adj, often cap*

gen·til·i·ty \jen-ˈtil-ət-ē\ *n, pl* **-ties** **1** : good birth and family **2** : the qualities characteristic of a well-bred person **3** : good manners **4** : maintenance of the appearance of superior or middle-class social status

¹**gen·tle** \ˈjent-ᵊl\ *adj* **gen·tler** \ˈjent-(ə-)lər\; **gen·tlest** \ˈjent-(ə-)ləst\ **1** : belonging to a family of high social station **2** : of, relating to, or characteristic of a gentleman **3** : KIND, AMIABLE **4** : TRACTABLE, DOCILE **5** : not harsh, stern, or violent **6** : SOFT, DELICATE **7** : MODERATE — **gen·tly** \ˈjent-lē\ *adv*

²**gentle** *vb* **gen·tled; gen·tling** \ˈjent-(ə-)liŋ\ **1** : to make mild, docile, soft, or moderate **2** : MOLLIFY, PLACATE

gen·tle·folk \ˈjent-ᵊl-ˌfōk\ *also* **gen·tle·folks** \-ˌfōks\ *n* : persons of good family and breeding

gen·tle·man \ˈjent-ᵊl-mən\ *n* **1** : a man of good family **2** : a well-bred man **3** : MAN — used in pl. as a form of address — **gen·tle·man·ly** *adj*

gen·tle·wom·an \ˈjent-ᵊl-ˌwum-ən\ *n* **1** : a woman of good family **2** : a woman attending a lady of rank **3** : a woman with very good manners : LADY

gen·tri·fi·ca·tion \ˌjen-trə-fə-ˈkā-shən\ *n* : the immigration of middle-class people into a run-down or recently renewed city area — **gen·tri·fy** \ˈjen-trə-ˌfī\ *vb*

gen·try \ˈjen-trē\ *n, pl* **gentries** **1** : people of good birth, breeding, and education : ARISTOCRACY **2** : the class of English people between the nobility and the yeomanry **3** : PEOPLE; *esp* : persons of a designated class

gen·u·flect \ˈjen-yə-ˌflekt\ *vb* : to bend

the knee esp. in worship — **gen·u·flec·tion** \ˌjen-yə-ˈflek-shən\ n

gen·u·ine \ˈjen-yə-wən\ adj 1 : AUTHENTIC, REAL 2 : SINCERE, HONEST — **gen·u·ine·ly** adv — **gen·u·ine·ness** \-wən-(n)əs\ n

ge·nus \ˈjē-nəs\ n, pl **gen·era** \ˈjen-ə-rə\ [L, birth, race, kind] : a category of biological classification that ranks between the family and the species and contains related species

geo·cen·tric \ˌjē-ō-ˈsen-trik\ adj 1 : relating to or measured from the earth's center 2 : having or relating to the carth as a center

geo·chem·is·try \-ˈkem-ə-strē\ n : a branch of geology that deals with the chemical composition of and chemical changes in the earth — **geo·chem·i·cal** \-ˈkem-i-kəl\ adj — **geo·chem·ist** \-ˈkem-əst\ n

ge·ode \ˈjē-ˌōd\ n : a nodule of stone having a cavity lined with mineral matter

¹**geo·de·sic** \ˌjē-ə-ˈdes-ik\ adj : made of a framework of light straight-sided polygons in tension ⟨a ∼ dome⟩

²**geodesic** n : the shortest line between two points on a surface

ge·od·e·sy \jē-ˈäd-ə-sē\ n : a branch of applied mathematics that determines the exact positions of points and the figures and areas of large portions of the earth's surface, the shape and size of the earth, and the variations of terrestrial gravity and magnetism — **geo·det·ic** \ˌjē-ə-ˈdet-ik\ adj

geodetic survey n : a survey of a large land area in which corrections are made for the curving of the earth's surface

geog abbr geographic; geographical; geography

ge·og·ra·phy \jē-ˈäg-rə-fē\ n, pl **-phies** 1 : a science that deals with the natural features of the earth and the climate, products, and inhabitants 2 : the natural features of a region — **ge·og·ra·pher** \-fər\ n — **geo·graph·ic** \ˌjē-ə-ˈgraf-ik\ or **geo·graph·i·cal** \-i-kəl\ adj — **geo·graph·i·cal·ly** \-i-k(ə-)lē\ adv

geol abbr geologic; geological; geology

ge·ol·o·gy \jē-ˈäl-ə-jē\ n, pl **-gies** 1 : a science that deals with the history of the earth and its life esp. as recorded

in rocks; also : a study of the solid matter of a celestial body (as the moon) 2 : the geologic features of an area — **ge·o·log·ic** \ˌjē-ə-ˈläj-ik\ or **ge·o·log·i·cal** \-i-kəl\ adj — **geo·log·i·cal·ly** \-i-k(ə-)lē\ adv — **ge·ol·o·gist** \jē-ˈäl-ə-jəst\ n

geom abbr geometric; geometrical; geometry

geo·mag·net·ic \ˌjē-ō-mag-ˈnet-ik\ adj : of or relating to the magnetism of the earth — **geo·mag·ne·tism** \-ˈmag-nə-ˌtiz-əm\ n

geometric mean n : the nth root of the product of n numbers; esp : a number that is the second term of three consecutive terms of a geometric progression ⟨the geometric mean of 9 and 4 is 6⟩

geometric progression n : a progression (as 1, ½, ¼) in which the ratio of a term to its predecessor is always the same

ge·om·e·try \jē-ˈäm-ə-trē\ n, pl **-tries** : a branch of mathematics dealing with the relations, properties, and measurements of solids, surfaces, lines, points, and angles — **ge·om·e·ter** \ˈäm-ət-ər\ n — **ge·o·met·ric** \ˌjē-ə-ˈme-trik\ or **ge·o·met·ri·cal** \-tri-kəl\ adj

geo·phys·ics \ˌjē-ə-ˈfiz-iks\ n : the physics of the earth — **geo·phys·i·cal** \-i-kəl\ adj — **geo·phys·i·cist** \-ˈfiz-ə-səst\ n

geo·pol·i·tics \-ˈpäl-ə-ˌtiks\ n : a combination of political and geographic factors relating to a state

geo·ther·mal \-ˈthər-məl\ also **geo·ther·mic** \-mik\ adj : of, relating to, or using the heat of the earth's interior

ger abbr gerund

Ger abbr German; Germany

ge·ra·ni·um \jə-ˈrā-nē-əm\ n [L, fr. Gk geranion, fr. geranos crane] 1 : any of a genus of herbs with usu. deeply cut leaves and pink, purple, or white flowers followed by long slender dry fruits 2 : any of a genus of herbs of the same family as the geraniums that have clusters of scarlet, pink, or white flowers with the sepals joined at the base into a hollow tube closed at one end

ger·bil also **ger·bile** \ˈjər-bəl\ n : any of numerous Old World burrowing desert rodents with long hind legs

ge·ri·at·ric \ˌjer-ē-ˈa-trik\ *adj* : of or relating to aging, the aged, or geriatrics

ge·ri·at·rics \-triks\ *n* : a branch of medicine dealing with the problems and diseases of old age and aging

germ \ˈjərm\ *n* **1** : a bit of living matter capable of growth and development (as into an organism) **2** : SOURCE, RUDIMENTS **3** : MICROORGANISM; *esp* : one causing disease

Ger·man \ˈjər-mən\ *n* **1** : a native or inhabitant of Germany **2** : the language of Germany, Austria, and parts of Switzerland — **German** *adj* — **German·ic** \jər-ˈman-ik\ *adj*

ger·mane \jər-ˈmān\ *adj* [ME *germain*, lit., having the same parents, fr. MF] : RELEVANT, PERTINENT

ger·ma·ni·um \jər-ˈmā-nē-əm\ *n* : a grayish white hard chemical element used as a semiconductor

German measles *n sing or pl* : an acute contagious virus disease milder than typical measles but damaging to the fetus when occurring early in pregnancy

German shepherd *n* : an intelligent responsive working dog often used in police work and as a guide dog for the blind

germ cell *n* : an egg or sperm or one of their antecedent cells

ger·mi·cide \ˈjər-mə-ˌsīd\ *n* : an agent that destroys germs — **ger·mi·cid·al** \ˌjər-mə-ˈsīd-əl\ *adj*

ger·mi·nal \ˈjərm-(ə-)nəl\ *adj* : of or relating to a germ or germ cell; *also* : EMBRYONIC

ger·mi·nate \ˈjər-mə-ˌnāt\ *vb* **-nat·ed; -nat·ing 1** : to begin to develop : SPROUT **2** : to come into being : EVOLVE — **ger·mi·na·tion** \ˌjər-mə-ˈnā-shən\ *n*

ger·on·tol·o·gy \ˌjer-ən-ˈtäl-ə-jē\ *n* : a scientific study of aging and the problems of the aged — **ger·on·to·log·i·cal** \jə-ˌränt-əl-ˈäj-i-kəl\ *adj* — **ger·on·tol·o·gist** \ˌjer-ən-ˈtäl-ə-jəst\ *n*

ger·ry·man·der \ˈjer-ē-ˌman-dər\ *vb* **-man·dered; -man·der·ing** \-d(ə-)riŋ\ : to divide into election districts so as to give one political party an advantage — **gerrymander** *n*

ger·und \ˈjer-ənd\ *n* : a word having the characteristics of both verb and noun

ge·sta·po \gə-ˈstäp-ō\ *n, pl* **-pos** [G, fr. *G*eheime *Sta*atspolizei, lit., secret state police] : a secret-police organization operating esp. against suspected political criminals

ges·ta·tion \je-ˈstā-shən\ *n* : PREGNANCY, INCUBATION — **ges·tate** \ˈjes-ˌtāt\ *vb*

ges·tic·u·late \je-ˈstik-yə-ˌlāt\ *vb* **-lat·ed; -lat·ing** : to make gestures esp. when speaking — **ges·tic·u·la·tion** \-ˌstik-yə-ˈlā-shən\ *n*

ges·ture \ˈjes-chər\ *n* **1** : a movement usu. of the body or limbs that expresses or emphasizes an idea, sentiment, or attitude **2** : something said or done by way of formality or courtesy, as a symbol or token, or for its effect on the attitudes of others — **ges·tur·al** \-chə-rəl\ *adj* — **gesture** *vb*

ge·sund·heit \gə-ˈzùnt-ˌhīt\ *interj* [G, lit., health] — used to wish good health esp. to one who has just sneezed

¹get \ˈget\ *vb* **got** \ˈgät\; **got** *or* **got·ten** \ˈgät-ᵊn\; **get·ting 1** : to gain possession of (as by receiving, acquiring, earning, buying, or winning) : PROCURE, OBTAIN, FETCH **2** : to succeed in coming or going ⟨*got* home early⟩ **3** : to cause to come or go ⟨*got* the car to the station⟩ **4** : BEGET **5** : to cause to be in a certain condition or position ⟨don't ~ wet⟩ **6** : BECOME ⟨~ sick⟩ **7** : PREPARE **8** : SEIZE **9** : to move emotionally; *also* : IRRITATE **10** : BAFFLE, PUZZLE **11** : HIT **12** : KILL **13** : to be subjected to ⟨~ the measles⟩ **14** : to receive as punishment **15** : to find out by calculation **16** : HEAR; *also* : UNDERSTAND **17** : PERSUADE, INDUCE **18** : HAVE ⟨he's *got* no money⟩ **19** : to have as an obligation or necessity ⟨he has *got* to come⟩ **20** : to establish communication with **21** : to be able : CONTRIVE, MANAGE **22** : to leave at once

²get \ˈget\ *n* : OFFSPRING, PROGENY

get along *vb* **1** : GET BY **2** : to be on friendly terms

get·away \ˈget-ə-ˌwā\ *n* **1** : START **2** : ESCAPE

get by *vb* : to meet one's needs

get–to·geth·er \ˈget-tə-ˌgeth-ər\ *n* : an informal social gathering

get·up \ˈget-ˌəp\ *n* **1** : general composition or structure **2** : OUTFIT, COSTUME

gew·gaw \'g(y)ü-ˌgȯ\ *n* : a showy trifle : BAUBLE, TRINKET

gey·ser \'gī-zər\ *n* [Icelandic *geysir* gusher] : a spring that intermittently shoots up hot water and steam

Gha·na·ian \gä-'nä-(y)ən\ *n* : a native or inhabitant of Ghana — **Ghanaian** *adj*

ghast·ly \'gast-lē\ *adj* **ghast·li·er; -est 1** : HORRIBLE, SHOCKING **2** : resembling a ghost : DEATHLIKE, PALE **syn** gruesome, grim, lurid, grisly, macabre

ghat \'gȯt\ *n* [Hindi] : a broad flight of steps that is situated on an Indian riverbank and provides access to the water

gher·kin \'gər-kən\ *n* : a small young cucumber used to make pickles; *also* : a small prickly fruit of a vine related to the cucumber used for the same purpose

ghet·to \'get-ō\ *n, pl* **ghettos** *or* **ghettoes** : a quarter of a city in which members of a minority group live because of social, legal, or economic pressure

¹**ghost** \'gōst\ *n* **1** : the seat of life : SOUL **2** : a disembodied soul; *esp* : the soul of a dead person believed to be an inhabitant of the unseen world or to appear in bodily form to living people **3** : SPIRIT, DEMON **4** : a faint trace ⟨a ∼ of a smile⟩ **5** : a false image in a photographic negative or on a television screen — **ghost·ly** *adv*

²**ghost** *vb* : GHOSTWRITE

ghost·write \-ˌrīt\ *vb* **-wrote** \-ˌrōt\; **-writ·ten** \-ˌrit-ᵊn\ : to write for and in the name of another — **ghost·writ·er** *n*

ghoul \'gül\ *n* [Ar *ghūl*] : a legendary evil being that robs graves and feeds on corpses — **ghoul·ish** *adj*

GHQ *abbr* general headquarters

gi *abbr* gill

¹**GI** \(ˈ)jē-'ī\ *adj* [galvanized *iron*; fr. abbr. used in listing such articles as garbage cans, but taken as abbr. for *government issue*] **1** : provided by an official U.S. military supply department ⟨∼ shoes⟩ **2** : of, relating to, or characteristic of U.S. military personnel **3** : conforming to military regulations or customs ⟨a ∼ haircut⟩

²**GI** *n, pl* **GI's** *or* **GIs** \-'īz\ : a member or former member of the U.S. armed forces; *esp* : an enlisted man

³**GI** *abbr* **1** galvanized iron **2** gastrointestinal **3** general issue **4** government issue

gi·ant \'jī-ənt\ *n* **1** : a huge legendary manlike being of great strength **2** : a living being or thing of extraordinary size or powers — **giant** *adj*

gi·ant·ess \-əs\ *n* : a female giant

gib·ber \'jib-ər\ *vb* **gib·bered; gib·ber·ing** \-(ə-)riŋ\ : to speak rapidly, inarticulately, and often foolishly

gib·ber·ish \'jib-(ə-)rish\ *n* : unintelligible or confused speech or language

¹**gib·bet** \'jib-ət\ *n* : GALLOWS

²**gibbet** *vb* **1** : to hang on a gibbet **2** : to expose to public scorn **3** : to execute by hanging

gib·bon \'gib-ən\ *n* : any of several tailless apes of southeastern Asia and the East Indies

gib·bous \'jib-əs, 'gib-\ *adj* **1** : convexly rounded in form : PROTUBERANT **2** : seen with more than half but not all of the apparent disk illuminated ⟨∼ moon⟩ **3** : having a hump : HUMPBACKED

gibe \'jīb\ *vb* **gibed; gib·ing** : to utter taunting words : SNEER — **gibe** *n*

gib·lets \'jib-ləts\ *n pl* : the edible viscera of a fowl

Gib·son \'gib-sən\ *n* : a martini with a small onion

gid·dy \'gid-ē\ *adj* **gid·di·er; -est 1** : DIZZY **2** : causing dizziness **3** : not serious : FRIVOLOUS, SILLY — **gid·di·ness** \'gid-ē-nəs\ *n*

gift \'gift\ *n* **1** : a special ability : TALENT **2** : something given : PRESENT **3** : the act or power of giving

gift·ed \'gif-təd\ *adj* : TALENTED

¹**gig** \'gig\ *n* **1** : a long light ship's boat **2** : a light 2-wheeled one-horse carriage

²**gig** *n* : a pronged spear for catching fish — **gig** *vb*

³**gig** *n* : JOB; *esp* : an entertainer's engagement for a specified time

⁴**gig** *n* : a military demerit — **gig** *vb*

gi·gan·tic \jī-'gant-ik\ *adj* : resembling a giant : IMMENSE, HUGE

gig·gle \'gig-əl\ *vb* **gig·gled; gig·gling** \-(ə-)liŋ\ : to laugh with repeated short catches of the breath — **giggle** *n* — **gig·gly** \-(ə-)lē\ *adj*

GIGO *abbr* garbage in, garbage out

gig·o·lo \'jig-ə-ˌlō\ *n, pl* **-los 1** : a man supported by a woman usu. in return for his attentions **2** : a professional dancing partner or male escort

Gi•la monster \ˌhē-lə-\ *n* : a large orange and black venomous lizard of the southwestern U.S.

¹**gild** \ˈgild\ *vb* **gild•ed** \ˈgil-dəd\ *or* **gilt** \ˈgilt\; **gild•ing** **1** : to overlay with or as if with a thin covering of gold **2** : to give an attractive but often deceptive outward appearance to — **gild•ing** *n*

²**gild** var of GUILD

¹**gill** \ˈjil\ *n* — see WEIGHT table

²**gill** \ˈgil\ *n* : an organ (as of a fish) for obtaining oxygen from water

¹**gilt** \ˈgilt\ *adj* : of the color of gold

²**gilt** *n* : gold or a substance resembling gold laid on the surface of an object

³**gilt** *n* : a young female swine

gim•crack \ˈjim-ˌkrak\ *n* : a showy object of little use or value

gim•let \ˈgim-lət\ *n* : a small tool with screw point and cross handle for boring

gim•mick \ˈgim-ik\ *n* **1** : CONTRIVANCE, GADGET **2** : an important feature that is not immediately apparent : CATCH **3** : a new and ingenious scheme — **gim•micky** \-i-kē\ *adj*

gim•mick•ry \ˈgim-i-krē\ *n, pl* **-ries** : an array of or the use of gimmicks

gimpy \ˈgim-pē\ *adj* : CRIPPLED, LAME

¹**gin** \ˈjin\ *n* [ME *gin,* modif. of OF *engin*] **1** : TRAP, SNARE **2** : a machine to separate seeds from cotton — **gin** *vb*

²**gin** \ˈjin\ *n* [by shortening & alter. fr. *geneva*] : a liquor distilled from a grain mash and flavored with juniper berries

gin•ger \ˈjin-jər\ *n* : the pungent aromatic rootstock of a tropical plant used esp. as a spice and in medicine; *also* : the spice or the plant

ginger ale *n* : a carbonated soft drink flavored with ginger

gin•ger•bread \ˈjin-jər-ˌbred\ *n* **1** : a cake made with molasses and flavored with ginger **2** : tawdry, gaudy, or superfluous ornament

gin•ger•ly \ˈjin-jər-lē\ *adj* : very cautious or careful — **gingerly** *adv*

gin•ger•snap \-ˌsnap\ *n* : a thin brittle molasses cookie flavored with ginger

ging•ham \ˈgiŋ-əm\ *n* : a clothing fabric usu. of yarn-dyed cotton in plain weave

gin•gi•vi•tis \ˌjin-jə-ˈvīt-əs\ *n* : inflammation of the gums

gink•go *also* **ging•ko** \ˈgiŋ-(ˌ)kō\ *n, pl* **ginkgoes** *or* **ginkgos** : a tree of eastern China with fan-shaped leaves often grown as a shade tree

gin•seng \ˈjin-ˌseŋ\ *n* : an aromatic root of a Chinese or No. American herb used esp. in Oriental medicine; *also* : one of these herbs

Gipsy var of GYPSY

gi•raffe \jə-ˈraf\ *n, pl* **giraffes** [It *giraffa,* fr. Ar *zirāfah*] : an African ruminant mammal with an extraordinarily long neck

gird \ˈgərd\ *vb* **gird•ed** \ˈgərd-əd\ *or* **girt** \ˈgərt\; **gird•ing** **1** : to encircle or fasten with or as if with a belt : GIRDLE 〈∼ on a sword〉 **2** : to clothe or invest esp. with power or authority **3** : PREPARE, BRACE

gird•er \ˈgərd-ər\ *n* : a horizontal main supporting beam

gir•dle \ˈgərd-ᵊl\ *n* **1** : something (as a belt or sash) that encircles or confines **2** : a woman's supporting undergarment that extends from the waist to below the hips — **girdle** *vb*

girl \ˈgərl\ *n* **1** : a female child **2** : a typically young woman **3** : a female servant or employee **4** : SWEETHEART — **girl•hood** \-ˌhùd\ *n* — **girl•ish** *adj*

girl Friday *n* : a female assistant (as in an office) entrusted with a wide variety of tasks

girlfriend *n* **1** : a female friend **2** : a frequent or regular female companion of a boy or man

Girl Scout *n* : a member of the Girl Scouts of the United States of America

girth \ˈgərth\ *n* **1** : a band around an animal by which something (as a saddle) may be fastened on its back **2** : a measure around something

gist \ˈjist\ *n* [MF, it lies, fr. *gesir* to lie, fr. L *jacēre*] : the main point of a matter

¹**give** \ˈgiv\ *vb* **gave** \ˈgāv\; **giv•en** \ˈgiv-ən\; **giv•ing** **1** : to make a present of **2** : to bestow by formal action **3** : to accord or yield to another **4** : to put into the possession or keeping of another **5** : PROFFER **6** : DELIVER; *esp* : to deliver in exchange **7** : PAY **8** : to present in public performance or to view **9** : PRO-

VIDE **10** : ATTRIBUTE **11** : to make, form, or yield as a product or result ⟨cows ~ milk⟩ **12** : to deliver by some bodily action ⟨*gave* me a push⟩ **13** : UTTER, PRONOUNCE **14** : DEVOTE **15** : to cause to have or receive **16** : CONTRIBUTE, DONATE **17** : to yield to force, strain, or pressure

²**give** *n* **1** : capacity or tendency to yield to force or strain **2** : the quality or state of being springy

give–and–take \ˌgiv-ən-'tāk\ *n* : an exchange (as of remarks or ideas) esp. on fair or equal terms

give·away \'giv-ə-ˌwā\ *n* **1** : an unintentional revelation or betrayal **2** : something given away free; *esp* : PREMIUM

give in *vb* : SUBMIT, SURRENDER

giv·en \'giv-ən\ *adj* **1** : DISPOSED, INCLINED ⟨~ to swearing⟩ **2** : SPECIFIED, FIXED ⟨at a ~ time⟩ **3** : granted as true : ASSUMED

given name *n* : a name that precedes one's surname

give out *vb* **1** : EMIT **2** : to become exhausted : COLLAPSE **3** : BREAK DOWN

give up *vb* **1** : SURRENDER **2** : to abandon (oneself) to a feeling, influence, or activity **3** : QUIT

giz·mo *or* **gis·mo** \'giz-mō\ *n, pl* **gizmos** *or* **gismos** : GADGET

giz·zard \'giz-ərd\ *n* : a muscular usu. horny-lined enlargement of the alimentary canal of a bird used for churning and grinding up food

gla·brous \'glā-brəs\ *adj* : SMOOTH; *esp* : having a surface without hairs or projections ⟨a ~ leaf⟩

gla·cial \'glā-shəl\ *adj* **1** : extremely cold **2** : of or relating to glaciers **3** : being or relating to a past period of time when a large part of the earth was covered by glaciers **4** *cap* : PLEISTOCENE — **gla·cial·ly** \-ē\ *adv*

gla·ci·ate \'glā-shē-ˌāt\ *vb* **-at·ed; -at·ing** **1** : to subject to glacial action **2** : to produce glacial effects in or on — **gla·ci·a·tion** \ˌglā-s(h)ē-'ā-shən\ *n*

gla·cier \'glā-shər\ *n* : a large body of ice moving slowly down a slope or spreading outward on a land surface

¹**glad** \'glad\ *adj* **glad·der; glad·dest** **1** : experiencing pleasure, joy, or delight **2** : PLEASED **3** : very willing **4** : PLEASANT, JOYFUL **5** : CHEERFUL — **glad·ly** *adv* — **glad·ness** *n*

²**glad** *n* : GLADIOLUS

glad·den \'glad-ᵊn\ *vb* : to make glad

glade \'glād\ *n* : a grassy open space surrounded by woods

glad·i·a·tor \'glad-ē-ˌāt-ər\ *n* **1** : a person engaged in a fight to the death for public entertainment in ancient Rome **2** : a person engaging in a fierce fight or controversy — **glad·i·a·to·ri·al** \ˌglad-ē-ə-'tōr-ē-əl\ *adj*

glad·i·o·lus \ˌglad-ē-'ō-ləs\ *n, pl* **-li** \-(ˌ)lē, -ˌlī\ [L, fr. dim. of *gladius* sword] : any of a genus of chiefly African plants related to the irises and having erect sword-shaped leaves and stalks of brilliantly colored flowers

glad·some \'glad-səm\ *adj* : giving or showing joy : CHEERFUL

glad·stone \'glad-ˌstōn\ *n, often cap* : a traveling bag with flexible sides on a rigid frame that opens flat into two compartments

glam·or·ize *also* **glam·our·ize** \'glam-ə-ˌrīz\ *vb* **-ized; -iz·ing** : to make or look upon as glamorous

glam·our *or* **glam·or** \'glam-ər\ *n* [Sc *glamour*, alter. of E *grammar;* fr. the popular association of erudition with occult practices] : an exciting and often illusory and romantic attractiveness; *esp* : alluring personal attraction — **glam·or·ous** *also* **glam·our·ous** \-(ə-)rəs\ *adj*

¹**glance** \'glans\ *vb* **glanced; glanc·ing** **1** : to strike and fly off to one side **2** : GLEAM **3** : to give a quick look

²**glance** *n* **1** : a quick intermittent flash or gleam **2** : a glancing impact or blow **3** : a quick look

gland \'gland\ *n* : a cell or group of cells that prepares and secretes a substance (as saliva or sweat) for further use in or discharge from the body — **glan·du·lar** \'glan-jə-lər\ *adj*

glans \'glanz\ *n, pl* **glan·des** \'glan-ˌdēz\ [L, lit., acorn] : a conical vascular body forming the extremity of the penis or clitoris

¹**glare** \'glaər\ *vb* **glared; glar·ing** **1** : to shine with a harsh dazzling light **2** : to stare fiercely or angrily — **glar·ing** \'gla(ə)r-iŋ\ *adj* — **glar·ing·ly** *adv*

²**glare** *n* **1** : a harsh dazzling light **2** : an angry or fierce stare

glass \'glas\ *n* **1** : a hard brittle usu. transparent or translucent substance made by melting sand and other materials and cooling to hardness **2** : something made of glass **3** *pl* : a pair of lenses used to correct defects of vision : SPECTACLES **4** : the quantity held by a glass — **glass** *adj* — **glass·ful** \-ˌfül\ *n* — **glass·ware** \-ˌwaər\ *n* — **glassy** *adj*

glass·blow·ing \-ˌblō-iŋ\ *n* : the art of shaping a mass of glass that has been softened by heat by blowing air into it through a tube — **glass·blow·er** \-ˌblō(-ə)r\ *n*

glau·co·ma \glau̇-ˈkō-mə, glȯ-\ *n* : a disease of the eye marked by increased pressure within the eyeball resulting in damage to the retina and gradual loss of vision

¹glaze \ˈglāz\ *vb* **glazed; glaz·ing** **1** : to furnish (as a window frame) with glass **2** : to apply glaze to

²glaze *n* : a glassy coating or surface

gla·zier \ˈglā-zhər\ *n* : a person who sets glass in window frames

¹gleam \ˈglēm\ *n* **1** : a transient subdued or partly obscured light **2** : GLINT **3** : a faint trace ⟨a ~ of hope⟩

²gleam *vb* **1** : to shine with subdued light or moderate brightness **2** : to appear briefly or faintly

glean \ˈglēn\ *vb* **1** : to gather grain left by reapers **2** : to collect little by little or with patient effort — **glean·able** *adj* — **glean·er** *n*

glean·ings \ˈglē-niŋz\ *n pl* : things acquired by gleaning

glee \ˈglē\ *n* [ME, fr. OE *glēo* entertainment, music] **1** : JOY, HILARITY **2** : an unaccompanied song for three or more solo usu. male voices — **glee·ful** *adj*

glee club *n* : a chorus organized for singing usu. short choral pieces

glen \ˈglen\ *n* : a secluded narrow valley

glen·gar·ry \glen-ˈgar-ē\ *n, pl* **-ries** *often cap* : a woolen cap of Scottish origin

glib \ˈglib\ *adj* **glib·ber; glib·best** : speaking or spoken with careless ease — **glib·ly** *adv*

glide \ˈglīd\ *vb* **glid·ed; glid·ing** **1** : to move smoothly and effortlessly **2** : to descend gradually without engine power ⟨~ in an airplane⟩ — **glide** *n*

glid·er \ˈglīd-ər\ *n* **1** : one that glides **2** : an aircraft resembling an airplane but having no engine **3** : a porch seat suspended from an upright framework by short chains or straps

¹glim·mer \ˈglim-ər\ *vb* **glim·mered; glim·mer·ing** \-(ə-)riŋ\ : to shine faintly or unsteadily

²glimmer *n* **1** : a faint unsteady light **2** : INKLING **3** : a small amount : BIT

¹glimpse \ˈglimps\ *vb* **glimpsed; glimps·ing** : to take a brief look : see momentarily or incompletely

²glimpse *n* **1** : a faint idea : GLIMMER **2** : a short hurried look

glint \ˈglint\ *vb* **1** : to shine by reflection : SPARKLE, GLITTER, GLEAM **2** : to appear briefly or faintly — **glint** *n*

glis·san·do \gli-ˈsän-(ˌ)dō\ *n, pl* **-di** \-(ˌ)dē\ *or* **-dos** : a rapid sliding up or down the musical scale

¹glis·ten \ˈglis-ᵊn\ *vb* **glis·tened; glis·ten·ing** \ˈglis-(ᵊ-)niŋ\ : to shine by reflection with a soft luster or sparkle

²glisten *n* : GLITTER, SPARKLE

glis·ter \ˈglis-tər\ *vb* : GLITTER

glitch \ˈglich\ *n* : MALFUNCTION; *also* : SNAG 2

¹glit·ter \ˈglit-ər\ *vb* **1** : to shine with brilliant or metallic luster : SPARKLE **2** : to shine with strong emotion : FLASH ⟨eyes ~*ing* in anger⟩ **3** : to be brilliantly attractive esp. in a superficial way

²glitter *n* **1** : sparkling brilliancy, showiness, or attractiveness **2** : small glittering objects used for ornamentation — **glit·tery** \ˈglit-ə-rē\ *adj*

gloam·ing \ˈglō-miŋ\ *n* : TWILIGHT, DUSK

gloat \ˈglōt\ *vb* : to think about something with great and often malicious delight

glob \ˈgläb\ *n* **1** : a small drop **2** : a large rounded mass

glob·al \ˈglō-bəl\ *adj* **1** : WORLDWIDE **2** : COMPREHENSIVE, GENERAL — **glob·al·ly** \-ē\ *adv*

globe \ˈglōb\ *n* **1** : BALL, SPHERE **2** : EARTH; *also* : a spherical representation of the earth

globe–trot·ter \-ˌträt-ər\ *n* : one that travels widely — **globe–trot·ting** \-ˌträt-iŋ\ *n or adj*

glob·u·lar \ˈgläb-yə-lər\ *adj* : having the shape of a globe or globule

glob·ule \ˈgläb-yül\ *n* : a tiny globe or ball

glob·u·lin \ˈgläb-yə-lən\ *n* : any of a

class of simple proteins insoluble in pure water but soluble in dilute salt solutions that occur widely in plant and animal tissues

glock·en·spiel \'gläk-ən-ˌs(h)pēl\ *n* [G, fr. *glocke* bell + *spiel* play] : a percussion musical instrument consisting of a series of metal bars played with two hammers

gloom \'glüm\ *n* **1** : partial or total darkness **2** : lowness of spirits : DE-JECTION **3** : an atmosphere of despondency — **gloom·i·ly** \'glü-mə-lē\ *adv* — **gloom·i·ness** \-mē-nəs\ *n* — **gloomy** \'glü-mē\ *adj*

glop \'gläp\ *n* : a messy mass or mixture

glo·ri·fy \'glōr-ə-ˌfī\ *vb* **-fied; -fy·ing 1** : to raise to heavenly glory **2** : to light up brilliantly **3** : EXTOL **4** : to give glory to (as in worship) — **glo·ri·fi·ca·tion** \ˌglōr-ə-fə-ˈkā-shən\ *n*

glo·ri·ous \'glōr-ē-əs\ *adj* **1** : possessing or deserving glory : PRAISEWORTHY **2** : conferring glory **3** : RESPLENDENT, MAGNIFICENT **4** : DELIGHTFUL, WONDERFUL — **glo·ri·ous·ly** *adv*

¹glo·ry \'glōr-ē\ *n, pl* **glories 1** : RENOWN **2** : honor and praise rendered in worship **3** : something that secures praise or renown **4** : a distinguishing quality or asset **5** : RESPLENDENCE, MAGNIFICENCE **6** : heavenly bliss **7** : a height of prosperity or achievement

²glory *vb* **glo·ried; glo·ry·ing** : to rejoice proudly : EXULT

¹gloss \'gläs, 'glòs\ *n* **1** : LUSTER, SHEEN, BRIGHTNESS **2** : outward show — **glossy** *adj*

²gloss *vb* **1** : to give a deceptive appearance to **2** : to deal with too lightly or not at all ⟨~ over inadequacies⟩

³gloss *n* [ME *glose*, fr. OF, fr. L *glossa* unusual word requiring explanation, fr. Gk *glōssa, glōtta* tongue, language, unusual word] **1** : an explanatory note (as in the margin of a text) **2** : GLOSSARY **3** : an interlinear translation **4** : a continuous commentary accompanying a text

⁴gloss *vb* : to furnish glosses for

glos·sa·ry \'gläs-(ə-)rē, 'glòs-\ *n, pl* **-ries** : a collection of difficult or specialized terms with their meanings — **glos·sar·i·al** \glä-ˈsar-ē-əl, glò-\ *adj*

glos·so·la·lia \ˌgläs-ə-ˈlā-lē-ə, ˌglòs-\ *n*

[Gk *glōssa* tongue, language + *lalia* chatter, fr. *lalein* to chatter, talk] : TONGUE 6

¹glossy \'gläs-ē, 'glòs-\ *adj* **gloss·i·er; -est** : having a surface luster or brightness — **gloss·i·ly** \-ə-lē\ *adv* — **gloss·i·ness** \-ē-nəs\ *n*

²glossy *n, pl* **gloss·ies** : a photograph printed on smooth shiny paper

glot·tis \'glät-əs\ *n, pl* **glot·tis·es** *or* **glot·ti·des** \-ə-ˌdēz\ : the slitlike opening between the vocal cords in the larynx — **glot·tal** \-ᵊl\ *adj*

glove \'gləv\ *n* **1** : a covering for the hand having separate sections for each finger **2** : a padded leather covering for the hand for use in a sport

¹glow \'glō\ *vb* **1** : to shine with or as if with intense heat **2** : to have a rich warm usu. ruddy color : FLUSH, BLUSH **3** : to feel hot **4** : to show exuberance or elation ⟨~ with pride⟩

²glow *n* **1** : brightness or warmth of color; *esp* : REDNESS **2** : warmth of feeling or emotion **3** : a sensation of warmth **4** : light such as is emitted from a heated substance

glow·er \'glau̇(-ə)r\ *vb* : to stare angrily : SCOWL — **glower** *n*

glow·worm \'glō-ˌwərm\ *n* : any of various insect larvae or adults that give off light

glox·in·ia \gläk-ˈsin-ē-ə\ *n* : any of a genus of Brazilian herbs related to the African violets; *esp* : one with showy bell-shaped or slipper-shaped flowers

gloze \'glōz\ *vb* **glozed; gloz·ing** : to make appear right or acceptable

glu·cose \'glü-ˌkōs\ *n* **1** : a sugar known in three different forms; *esp* : DEXTROSE **2** : a sweet light-colored syrup made from cornstarch

glue \'glü\ *n* : a jellylike protein substance made from animal materials and used for sticking things together; *also* : any of various other strong adhesives — **glue** *vb* — **glu·ey** \'glü-ē\ *adj*

glum \'gləm\ *adj* **glum·mer; glum·mest 1** : MOROSE, SULLEN **2** : DREARY, GLOOMY

¹glut \'glət\ *vb* **glut·ted; glut·ting 1** : to fill esp. with food to satiety : SATIATE **2** : OVERSUPPLY

²glut *n* : an excessive supply

glu·ten \'glüt-ᵊn\ *n* : a gluey protein

substance that causes dough to be sticky

glu·ti·nous \\'glüt-(ə-)nəs\\ *adj* : STICKY

glut·ton \\'glət-ᵊn\\ *n* : one that eats to excess — **glut·ton·ous** \\'glət-(ə-)nəs\\ *adj* — **glut·tony** \\'glət-(ə-)nē\\ *n*

glyc·er·in *or* **glyc·er·ine** \\'glis-(ə-)rən\\ *n* : GLYCEROL

glyc·er·ol \\'glis-ə-ˌrȯl, -ˌrōl\\ *n* : a sweet colorless syrupy liquid obtained from fats or synthesized and used as a solvent, moistener, and lubricant

gly·co·gen \\'glī-kə-jən\\ *n* : a white tasteless substance that is the chief storage carbohydrate of animals

gm *abbr* gram

GM *abbr* 1 general manager 2 guided missile

G–man \\'jē-ˌman\\ *n* : a special agent of the Federal Bureau of Investigation

GMT *abbr* Greenwich mean time

gnarled \\'när-əld\\ *adj* 1 : KNOTTY 2 : GLOOMY, SULLEN

gnash \\'nash\\ *vb* : to grind (as teeth) together

gnat \\'nat\\ *n* : any of various small usu. biting two-winged flies

gnaw \\'nȯ\\ *vb* 1 : to consume, wear away, or make by persistent biting or nibbling 2 : to affect as if by gnawing — **gnaw·er** \\'nȯ(-ə)r\\ *n*

gneiss \\'nīs\\ *n* : a layered granitelike rock

gnome \\'nōm\\ *n* : a dwarf of folklore who lives inside the earth and guards precious ore or treasure — **gnom·ish** \\'nō-mish\\ *adj*

GNP *abbr* gross national product

gnu \\'nü\\ *n, pl* **gnu** *or* **gnus** : any of several large African antelopes with an oxlike head and horns and a horselike mane and tail

¹**go** \\'gō\\ *vb* **went** \\'went\\; **gone** \\'gȯn, 'gän\\; **go·ing** \\'gō-iŋ\\; **goes** \\'gōz\\ 1 : to move on a course : PROCEED ⟨~ slow⟩ 2 : LEAVE, DEPART 3 : to take a certain course or follow a certain procedure 4 : EXTEND, RUN ⟨his land ~es to the river⟩; *also* : LEAD ⟨that door ~es to the cellar⟩ 5 : to be habitually in a certain state ⟨~es armed after dark⟩ 6 : to become lost, consumed, or spent; *also* : DIE 7 : ELAPSE, PASS 8 : to pass by sale ⟨went for a good price⟩ 9 : to become impaired or weakened 10 : to give way under

force or pressure : BREAK 11 : HAPPEN ⟨what's ~ing on⟩ 12 : to be in general or on an average ⟨cheap, as yachts ~⟩ 13 : to become esp. as the result of a contest ⟨the decision *went* against him⟩ 14 : to put or subject oneself ⟨~ to great expense⟩ 15 : RESORT ⟨*went* to court to recover damages⟩ 16 : to begin or maintain an action or motion ⟨here ~es⟩ 17 : to function properly ⟨the clock doesn't ~⟩ 18 : to have currency : CIRCULATE ⟨the report ~es⟩ 19 : to be or act in accordance ⟨a good rule to ~ by⟩ 20 : to come to be applied 21 : to pass by award, assignment, or lot 22 : to contribute to a result ⟨qualities that ~ to make a hero⟩ 23 : to be about, intending, or expecting something ⟨is ~ing to leave town⟩ 24 : to arrive at a certain state or condition ⟨~ to sleep⟩ 25 : to come to be ⟨the tire *went* flat⟩ 26 : to be capable of being sung or played ⟨the tune ~es like this⟩ 27 : to be suitable or becoming : HARMONIZE 28 : to be capable of passing, extending, or being contained or inserted ⟨this coat will ~ in the trunk⟩ 29 : to have a usual or proper place or position : BELONG ⟨these books ~ on the top shelf⟩ 30 : to be capable of being divided ⟨3 ~es into 6 twice⟩ 31 : to have a tendency ⟨that ~es to show that he is honest⟩ 32 : to be acceptable, satisfactory, or adequate 33 : to proceed along or according to : FOLLOW 34 : TRAVERSE 35 : BET, BID ⟨willing to ~ $50⟩ 36 : to assume the function or obligation of ⟨~ bail for a friend⟩ 37 : to participate to the extent of ⟨~ halves⟩ 38 : WEIGH 39 : ENDURE, TOLERATE 40 : AFFORD ⟨can't ~ the price⟩ — **go at** 1 : ATTACK, ATTEMPT 2 : UNDERTAKE — **go back on** 1 : ABANDON 2 : BETRAY 3 : FAIL — **go by the board** : to be discarded — **go down the line** : to give wholehearted support — **go for** 1 : to pass for or serve as 2 : to try to secure 3 : FAVOR — **go one better** : OUTDO, SURPASS — **go over** 1 : EXAMINE 2 : REPEAT 3 : STUDY, REVIEW — **go places** : to be on the way to success — **go to bat for** : DEFEND, CHAMPION — **go to town** 1 : to work or act efficiently 2 : to be very successful

²**go** \\'gō\\ *n, pl* **goes** 1 : the act or manner

of going **2** : the height of fashion ⟨boots are all the ∼⟩ **3** : a turn of affairs : OCCURRENCE **4** : ENERGY, VIGOR **5** : ATTEMPT, TRY **6** : a spell of activity — **no go** : USELESS, HOPELESS — **on the go** : constantly active

³go *adj* : functioning properly

GO *abbr* general order

goad \'gōd\ *n* [ME *gode*, fr. OE *gād* spear, goad] **1** : a pointed rod used to urge on an animal **2** : something that urges : SPUR — **goad** *vb*

go—ahead \'gō-ə-,hed\ *n* : authority to proceed

goal \'gōl\ *n* **1** : the mark set as limit to a race; *also* : an area to be reached safely in children's games **2** : AIM, PURPOSE **3** : an area or object toward which play is directed in order to score; *also* : a successful attempt to score

goal•ie \'gō-lē\ *n* : GOALKEEPER

goal•keep•er \'gōl-,kē-pər\ *n* : a player who defends the goal in various games

goal•post \'gōl-,pōst\ *n* : one of the two vertical posts with a crossbar that constitute the goal (as in soccer)

goat \'gōt\ *n*, *pl* **goats** *or* **goat** : any of various hollow-horned ruminant mammals related to the sheep that have backward-curving horns, a short tail, and usu. straight hair

goa•tee \gō-'tē\ *n* : a small trim pointed or tufted beard on a man's chin

goat•herd \'gōt-,hərd\ *n* : one who tends goats

goat•skin \-,skin\ *n* : the skin of a goat or a leather made from it

¹gob \'gäb\ *n* : LUMP, MASS

²gob *n* : SAILOR

gob•bet \'gäb-ət\ *n* : LUMP, MASS

¹gob•ble \'gäb-əl\ *vb* **gob•bled; gob•bling** \-(ə-)liŋ\ **1** : to swallow or eat greedily **2** : to take eagerly : GRAB

²gobble *vb* **gob•bled; gob•bling** \-(ə-)liŋ\ : to make the natural guttural noise of a male turkey

gob•ble•dy•gook *or* **gob•ble•de•gook** \'gäb-əl-dē-,gůk, -,gük\ *n* : generally unintelligible jargon

gob•bler \'gäb-lər\ *n* : a male turkey

go—be•tween \'gō-bə-,twēn\ *n* : an intermediate agent : BROKER

gob•let \'gäb-lət\ *n* : a drinking glass with a foot and stem

gob•lin \'gäb-lən\ *n* : an ugly or grotesque sprite that is mischievous and sometimes evil and malicious

god \'gäd, 'gȯd\ *n* **1** *cap* : the supreme reality; *esp* : the Being worshiped as the creator and ruler of the universe **2** : a being or object believed to have supernatural attributes and powers and to require worship **3** : a person or thing of supreme value

god•child \-,chīld\ *n* : a person for whom one stands as sponsor at baptism

god•daugh•ter \-,dȯt-ər\ *n* : a female godchild

god•dess \'gäd-əs\ *n* **1** : a female god **2** : a woman whose charm or beauty arouses adoration

god•fa•ther \'gäd-,fäth-ər, 'gȯd-\ *n* : a man who sponsors a person at baptism

god•head \-,hed\ *n* **1** : divine nature or essence **2** *cap* : GOD 1; *also* : the nature of God esp. as existing in three persons

god•hood \-,hůd\ *n* : DIVINITY

god•less \'gäd-ləs, 'gȯd-\ *adj* : not acknowledging a deity or divine law — **god•less•ness** *n*

god•like \-,līk\ *adj* : resembling or having the qualities of God or a god

god•ly \-lē\ *adj* **god•li•er; -est 1** : DIVINE **2** : PIOUS, DEVOUT — **god•li•ness** \-lē-nəs\ *n*

god•moth•er \-,məth-ər\ *n* : a woman who sponsors a person at baptism

god•par•ent \-,par-ənt\ *n* : a sponsor at baptism

god•send \-,send\ *n* : a desirable or needed thing that comes unexpectedly

god•son \-,sən\ *n* : a male godchild

go•fer \'gō-fər\ *n* [alter. of *go for*] : an employee whose duties include running errands

go—get•ter \'gō-'get-ər\ *n* : an aggressively enterprising person — **go—get•ting** \-,get-iŋ\ *adj or n*

gog•gle \'gäg-əl\ *vb* **gog•gled; gog•gling** \-(ə-)liŋ\ : to stare with wide or protuberant eyes

gog•gles \'gäg-əlz\ *n pl* : protective glasses set in a flexible frame that fits snugly against the face

go—go \'gō-,gō\ *adj* [*a-go-go*] **1** : related to, being, or employed to entertain in a discotheque ⟨∼ dancers⟩ **2** : aggressively enterprising and energetic

go·ings–on \ˌgō-iŋz-'ȯn, -'än\ n pl : AC-TIONS, EVENTS

goi·ter \'gȯit-ər\ n : an abnormally enlarged thyroid gland visible as a swelling at the base of the neck — **goi·trous** \-(ə-)rəs\ adj

goi·tre chiefly Brit var of GOITER

gold \'gōld\ n 1 : a malleable yellow metallic chemical element used esp. for coins and jewelry 2 : gold coins; also : MONEY 3 : a yellow color

gold·brick \-ˌbrik\ n : a person (as a soldier) who shirks assigned work — **goldbrick** vb

Gold Coast n : an exclusive residential district

gold digger n : a woman who uses feminine charm to extract money or gifts from men

gold·en \'gōl-dən\ adj 1 : made of or relating to gold 2 : having the color of gold; also : BLOND 3 : SHINING, LUSTROUS 4 : SUPERB 5 : FLOURISHING, PROSPEROUS 6 : radiantly youthful and vigorous 7 : FAVORABLE, ADVANTAGEOUS ⟨a ∼ opportunity⟩ 8 : MELLOW, RESONANT

gold·en–ag·er \'gōl-dən-'ā-jər\ n : an elderly and often retired person usu. engaging in club activities

golden hamster n : a small tawny hamster often kept as a pet

gold·en·rod \'gōl-dən-ˌräd\ n : any of numerous plants related to the daisies but having tall slender stalks with many tiny usu. yellow flower heads

gold·field \'gōld-ˌfēld\ n : a gold-mining district

gold·finch \-ˌfinch\ n 1 : a small largely red, black, and yellow European finch often kept in a cage 2 : any of several small American finches of which the males usu. become bright yellow and black in summer

gold·fish \-ˌfish\ n : a small usu. yellow or golden carp often kept as an aquarium fish

gold·smith \'gōld-ˌsmith\ n : one who makes or deals in articles of gold

golf \'gälf, 'gȯlf\ n : a game played with a small ball and various clubs on a course having 9 or 18 holes — **golf** vb — **golf·er** n

-gon \ˌgän\ n comb form : figure having (so many) angles ⟨hexagon⟩

go·nad \'gō-ˌnad\ n : a sperm- or egg-producing gland : OVARY, TESTIS — **go·nad·al** \gō-'nad-ᵊl\ adj

go·nad·o·trop·ic \gō-ˌnad-ə-'träp-ik\ or **go·nad·o·tro·phic** \-'trō-fik,-'träf-ik\ adj : acting on or stimulating the gonads ⟨∼ hormones⟩

go·nad·o·tro·pin \-'trō-pən\ or **go·nad·o·tro·phin** \-fən\ n : a gonadotropic hormone

gon·do·la \'gän-də-lə (usual for 1), gän-'dō-\ n 1 : a long narrow boat used on the canals of Venice 2 : a railroad car with no top used for hauling loose freight (as coal) 3 : an enclosure attached to the underside of an airship or balloon 4 : an enclosed car suspended from a cable and used esp. for transporting skiers

gon·do·lier \ˌgän-də-'liər\ n : one who propels a gondola

gone \'gȯn\ adj 1 : DEAD 2 : LOST, RUINED 3 : SINKING, WEAK 4 : INVOLVED, ABSORBED 5 : INFATUATED 6 : PREGNANT 7 : PAST

gon·er \'gȯn-ər\ n : one whose case is hopeless

gon·fa·lon \'gän-fə-ˌlän\ n : a flag that hangs from a crosspiece or frame

gong \'gäŋ, 'gȯŋ\ n : a metallic disk that produces a resounding tone when struck

gono·coc·cus \ˌgän-ə-'käk-əs\ n, pl **-coc·ci** \-'käk-ˌ(s)ī, -'käk-(ˌ)(s)ē\ : a pus-producing bacterium that causes gonorrhea — **gono·coc·cal** \-'käk-əl\ or **gono·coc·cic** \-'käk-(s)ik\ adj

gon·or·rhea \ˌgän-ə-'rē-ə\ n : a contagious sexually transmitted inflammation of the genital tract caused by a bacterium — **gon·or·rhe·al** \-'rē-əl\ adj

goo \'gü\ n 1 : a viscid or sticky substance 2 : sentimental tripe — **goo·ey** \-ē\ adj

goo·ber \'gü-bər, 'gub-ər\ n, South & Midland : PEANUT

¹good \'gud\ adj **bet·ter** \'bet-ər\; **best** \'best\ 1 : of a favorable character or tendency 2 : BOUNTIFUL, FERTILE 3 : COMELY, ATTRACTIVE 4 : SUITABLE, FIT 5 : SOUND, WHOLE 6 : AGREEABLE, PLEASANT 7 : SALUTARY, WHOLESOME 8 : CONSIDERABLE, AMPLE 9 : FULL 10 : WELL-FOUNDED 11 : TRUE ⟨holds ∼ for everybody⟩ 12 : recognized or valid esp. in law 13 : ADEQUATE, SATIS-

FACTORY **14** : conforming to a standard **15** : DISCRIMINATING **16** : COMMENDABLE, VIRTUOUS **17** : KIND **18** : UPPER-CLASS **19** : COMPETENT **20** : LOYAL — **good–heart・ed** \-ˈhärt-əd\ *adj* **13** : ADEQUATE, SATISFACTORY — **good・ish** *adj* — **good–look・ing** \ˈgu̇d-ˈlu̇k-iŋ\ *adj* — **good–na・tured** \-ˈnā-chərd\ *adj* — **good–tem・pered** \-ˈtem-pərd\ *adj*

²good *n* **1** : something good **2** : GOODNESS **3** : BENEFIT, WELFARE ⟨for the ~ of mankind⟩ **4** : something that has economic utility **5** *pl* : personal property **6** *pl* : CLOTH **7** *pl* : WARES, COMMODITIES **8** : good persons ⟨the ~ die young⟩ **9** *pl* : proof of wrongdoing — **for good** : FOREVER, PERMANENTLY — **to the good** : in a position of net gain or profit ⟨$10 *to the good*⟩

³good *adv* : WELL

good–bye *or* **good–by** \gu̇d-ˈbī, gə(d)-\ *n* : a concluding remark at parting

good–for–noth・ing \ˈgu̇d-fər-ˌnəth-iŋ\ *n* : an idle worthless person

Good Friday *n* : the Friday before Easter observed as the anniversary of the crucifixion of Christ

good・ly \ˈgu̇d-lē\ *adj* **good・li・er; -est 1** : of pleasing appearance **2** : LARGE, CONSIDERABLE

good・man \ˈgu̇d-mən\ *n, archaic* : MR.

good・ness \ˈgu̇d-nəs\ *n* : EXCELLENCE, VIRTUE

good・wife \ˈgu̇d-ˌwīf\ *n, archaic* : MRS.

good・will \ˈgu̇d-ˈwil\ *n* **1** : BENEVOLENCE **2** : the value of the trade a business has built up over time **3** : cheerful consent **4** : willing effort

goody \ˈgu̇d-ē\ *n, pl* **good・ies** : something that is good esp. to eat

goody–goody \ˌgu̇d-ē-ˈgu̇d-ē\ *adj* : affectedly good — **goody–goody** *n*

goof \ˈgüf\ *vb* **1** : BLUNDER **2** : to spend time idly or foolishly — often used with *off* — **goof** *n*

goof・ball \ˈgüf-ˌbȯl\ *n* **1** *slang* : a barbiturate sleeping pill **2** *slang* : a goofy person

go off *vb* **1** : EXPLODE **2** : to follow a course ⟨the party *went off* well⟩

goof–off \ˈgüf-ˌȯf\ *n* : one who evades work or responsibility

goofy \ˈgü-fē\ *adj* **goof・i・er; -est** : CRAZY, SILLY — **goof・i・ness** \ˈgü-fē-nəs\ *n*

goon \ˈgün\ *n* : a man hired to terrorize or kill opponents

go on *vb* **1** : to continue in a course of action **2** : to take place : HAPPEN

goose \ˈgüs\ *n, pl* **geese** \ˈgēs\ **1** : any of numerous long-necked web-footed birds related to the swans and ducks; *esp* : a female goose as distinguished from a gander **2** : a foolish person **3** *pl* **goos・es** : a tailor's smoothing iron

goose・ber・ry \ˈgüs-ˌber-ē, ˈgüz-, -b(ə-)rē\ *n* : the acid berry of any of several shrubs related to the currant and used esp. in jams and pies

goose・flesh \ˈgüs-ˌflesh\ *n* : a roughening of the skin caused usu. by cold or fear

goose pimples *n pl* : GOOSEFLESH

go out *vb* **1** : to become extinguished **2** : to become a candidate ⟨*went out* for the football team⟩

go over *vb* : SUCCEED

GOP *abbr* Grand Old Party (Republican)

go・pher \ˈgō-fər\ *n* **1** : a burrowing American land tortoise **2** : any of several No. American burrowing rodents with large cheek pouches opening beside the mouth **3** : any of numerous small ground squirrels of the prairie region of No. America

¹gore \ˈgōr\ *n* : BLOOD

²gore *n* : a tapering or triangular piece (as of cloth in a skirt)

³gore *vb* **gored; gor・ing** : to pierce or wound with something pointed

¹gorge \ˈgȯrj\ *n* **1** : THROAT **2** : a narrow ravine **3** : a mass of matter that chokes up a passage

²gorge *vb* **gorged; gorg・ing** : to eat greedily : stuff to capacity : GLUT

gor・geous \ˈgȯr-jəs\ *adj* [ME *gorgayse,* fr. MF *gorgias* elegant] : resplendently beautiful

Gor・gon・zo・la \ˌgȯr-gən-ˈzō-lə\ *n* : a blue cheese of Italian origin

go・ril・la \gə-ˈril-ə\ *n* [fr. Gk *Gorillai,* an African tribe of hairy women] : an African manlike ape related to but much larger than the chimpanzee

gor・man・dize \ˈgȯr-mən-ˌdīz\ *vb* **-dized; -diz・ing** : to eat ravenously — **gor・man・diz・er** *n*

gorp \ˈgȯrp\ *n* : a snack consisting of high-calorie food (as raisins and nuts)

gorse \ˈgȯrs\ *n* : a prickly mostly leafless evergreen Old World shrub of the legume family that bears yellow flowers

gory \\'gōr-ē\ *adj* **gor·i·er; -est 1** : BLOODSTAINED **2** : HORRIBLE, SENSATIONAL

gos·hawk \\'gäs-ˌhȯk\ *n* : any of several long-tailed hawks with short rounded wings

gos·ling \\'gäz-liŋ, 'gȯz-\ *n* : a young goose

¹gos·pel \\'gäs-pəl\ *n* [ME, fr. OE *gōdspel*, fr. *gōd* good + *spell* tale] **1** : the teachings of Christ and the apostles **2** *cap* : any of the first four books of the New Testament **3** : something accepted as infallible truth

²gospel *adj* **1** : of, relating to, or emphasizing the gospel **2** : relating to or being American religious songs associated with evangelism

gos·sa·mer \\'gäs-ə-mər, 'gäz(-ə)-mər\ *n* [ME *gossomer*, fr. *gos* goose + *somer* summer] **1** : a film of cobwebs floating in the air **2** : something light, delicate, or tenuous

¹gos·sip \\'gäs-əp\ *n* **1** : a person who habitually reveals personal or sensational facts **2** : rumor or report of an intimate nature **3** : an informal conversation — **gos·sipy** *adj*

²gossip *vb* : to spread gossip

got past and past part of GET

Goth \\'gäth\ *n* : a member of a Germanic race that early in the Christian era overran the Roman Empire

¹Goth·ic \\'gäth-ik\ *adj* **1** : of or relating to the Goths **2** : of or relating to a style of architecture prevalent in western Europe from the middle 12th to the earth 16th century

²Gothic *n* **1** : the Germanic language of the Goths **2** : the Gothic architectural style or decoration

gotten past part of GET

Gou·da \\'güd-ə\ *n* : a mild Dutch milk cheese shaped in balls

¹gouge \\'gaùj\ *n* **1** : a rounded troughlike chisel **2** : a hole or groove made with or as if with a gouge

²gouge *vb* **gouged; goug·ing 1** : to cut holes or grooves in with or as if with a gouge **2** : DEFRAUD, CHEAT

gou·lash \\'gü-ˌläsh, -ˌlash\ *n* [Hungarian *gulyás*] : a stew made with meat, assorted vegetables, and paprika

go under *vb* : to be overwhelmed, defeated, or destroyed : FAIL

gourd \\'gōrd, 'gùrd\ *n* **1** : any of a family of tendril-bearing vines including the cucumber, squash, and melon **2** : the fruit of a gourd; *esp* : any of various inedible hard-shelled fruits used esp. for ornament or implements

gourde \\'gùrd\ *n* — see MONEY table

gour·mand \\'gùr-ˌmänd\ *n* **1** : one who is excessively fond of eating and drinking **2** : GOURMET

gour·met \\'gùr-ˌmā, gùr-'mā\ *n* [F, fr. MF, fr. *gromet* boy servant, vintner's assistant] : a connoisseur in eating and drinking

gout \\'gaùt\ *n* : a disease marked by painful inflammation and swelling of the joints — **gouty** *adj*

gov *abbr* **1** government **2** governor

gov·ern \\'gəv-ərn\ *vb* **1** : to control and direct the making and administration of policy in : RULE **2** : CONTROL, DIRECT, INFLUENCE **3** : DETERMINE, REGULATE **4** : RESTRAIN — **gov·er·nance** \\'gəv-ər-nəns\ *n*

gov·ern·ess \\'gəv-ər-nəs\ *n* : a woman who teaches and trains a child esp. in a private home

gov·ern·ment \\'gəv-ər(n)-mənt\ *n* **1** : authoritative direction or control : RULE **2** : the making of policy **3** : the organization or agency through which a political unit exercises authority **4** : the complex of institutions, laws, and customs through which a political unit is governed **5** : the governing body — **gov·ern·men·tal** \\ˌgəv-ər(n)-'ment-əl\ *adj*

gov·er·nor \\'gəv(-ə)-nər, 'gəv-ər-nər\ *n* **1** : one that governs; *esp* : a ruler, chief executive, or head of a political unit (as a state) **2** : an attachment to a machine for automatic control of speed — **gov·er·nor·ship** *n*

govt *abbr* government

gown \\'gaùn\ *n* **1** : a loose flowing outer garment **2** : an official robe worn esp. by a judge, clergyman, or teacher **3** : a woman's dress ⟨evening ∼s⟩ **4** : a loose robe — **gown** *vb*

gp *abbr* group

GP *abbr* general practitioner

GPO *abbr* **1** general post office **2** Government Printing Office

GQ *abbr* general quarters

gr *abbr* **1** grade **2** grain **3** gram **4** gravity **5** gross

grab \'grab\ *vb* **grabbed; grab·bing** : to take hastily : SNATCH — **grab** *n*

¹**grace** \'grās\ *n* **1** : help given man by God (as in overcoming temptation) **2** : freedom from sin through divine grace **3** : a virtue coming from God **4** : a short prayer at a meal **5** : a temporary respite (as from the payment of a debt) **6** : APPROVAL, ACCEPTANCE ⟨in his good ∼s⟩ **7** : CHARM **8** : ATTRACTIVENESS, BEAUTY **9** : fitness or proportion of line or expression **10** : ease of movement **11** : a musical trill or ornament **12** — used as a title for a duke, a duchess, or an archbishop — **grace·ful** \-fəl\ *adj* — **grace·ful·ly** \-ē\ *adv* — **grace·ful·ness** *n* — **grace·less** *adj*

²**grace** *vb* **graced; grac·ing** **1** : HONOR **2** : ADORN, EMBELLISH

gra·cious \'grā-shəs\ *adj* **1** : marked by kindness and courtesy **2** : GRACEFUL **3** : characterized by charm and good taste **4** : MERCIFUL — **gra·cious·ly** *adv* — **gra·cious·ness** *n*

grack·le \'grak-əl\ *n* **1** : an Old World starling **2** : an American blackbird with glossy iridescent plumage

grad *abbr* graduate

gra·da·tion \grā-'dā-shən, grə-\ *n* **1** : a series forming successive stages **2** : a step, degree, or stage in a series **3** : an advance by regular degrees **4** : the act or process of grading

¹**grade** \'grād\ *vb* **grad·ed; grad·ing** **1** : to arrange in grades : SORT **2** : to make level or evenly sloping ⟨∼ a highway⟩ **3** : to give a grade to ⟨∼ a pupil in history⟩ **4** : to assign to a grade

²**grade** *n* **1** : a degree or stage in a series, order, or ranking **2** : a position in a scale of rank, quality, or order **3** : a class of persons or things of the same rank or quality **4** : a division of the school course representing one year's work; *also* : the pupils in such a division **5** *pl* : the elementary school system **6** : a mark or rating esp. of accomplishment in school **7** : the degree of slope (as of a road); *also* : SLOPE

grad·er \'grād-ər\ *n* : a machine for leveling earth

grade school *n* : ELEMENTARY SCHOOL

gra·di·ent \'grād-ē-ənt\ *n* : SLOPE, GRADE

grad·u·al \'graj-(ə-w)əl\ *adj* : proceeding or changing by steps or degrees — **grad·u·al·ly** \-ē\ *adv*

grad·u·al·ism \-‚iz-əm\ *n* : the policy of approaching a desired end gradually

¹**grad·u·ate** \'graj-(ə-)wət, -ə-‚wāt\ *n* **1** : a holder of an academic degree or diploma **2** : a graduated container for measuring contents

²**graduate** *adj* **1** : holding an academic degree or diploma **2** : of or relating to studies beyond the first or bachelor's degree ⟨∼ school⟩

³**grad·u·ate** \'graj-ə-‚wāt\ *vb* **-at·ed; -at·ing** **1** : to grant or receive an academic degree or diploma **2** : to admit to a particular standing or grade **3** : to divide into grades, classes, or intervals ⟨*graduated* thermometer⟩

grad·u·a·tion \‚graj-ə-'wā-shən\ *n* **1** : a mark that graduates something **2** : an act or process of graduating **3** : COMMENCEMENT 2

graf·fi·to \gra-'fēt-ō, grə-\ *n, pl* **-ti** \-(‚)ē\ : an inscription or drawing made on a public surface (as a wall)

¹**graft** \'graft\ *n* **1** : a grafted plant; *also* : the point of union in this **2** : material (as skin) used in grafting **3** : the getting of money or advantage dishonestly; *also* : the money or advantage so gained

²**graft** *vb* **1** : to insert a shoot from one plant into another so that they join and grow; *also* : to join one thing to another as in plant grafting ⟨∼ skin over a burn⟩ **2** : to get (as money) dishonestly — **graft·er** *n*

gra·ham cracker \'grā-əm-, 'gram-\ *n* : a slightly sweet cracker made chiefly of whole wheat flour

Grail \'grāl\ *n* : the cup or platter used according to medieval legend by Christ at the Last Supper and thereafter the object of knightly quests

grain \'grān\ *n* **1** : a seed or fruit of a cereal grass **2** : seeds or fruits of various food plants and esp. cereal grasses; *also* : a plant producing grain **3** : a small hard particle **4** : a unit of weight based on the weight of a grain of wheat — see WEIGHT table **5** : TEXTURE; *also* : the arrangement of fibers in wood **6** : natural disposition — **grained** \'grānd\ *adj*

grain alcohol *n* : ALCOHOL 1

grain·field \'grān-ˌfēld\ *n* : a field where grain is grown

grainy \'grā-nē\ *adj* **grain·i·er; -est 1** : resembling or having some characteristic of grain : not smooth or fine **2** *of a photograph* : appearing to be composed of grain-like particles

¹gram \'gram\ *n* [F *gramme,* fr. LL *gramma,* a small weight, fr. Gk *gramma* letter, writing, a small weight, fr. *graphein* to write] : a metric unit of mass and weight equal to ¹/₁₀₀₀ kilogram and nearly equal to one cubic centimeter of water at its maximum density — see METRIC SYSTEM table

²gram *abbr* grammar; grammatical

-gram \ˌgram\ *n comb form* : drawing : writing : record ⟨tele*gram*⟩

gram·mar \'gram-ər\ *n* **1** : the study of the classes of words, their inflections, and their functions and relations in the sentence **2** : a study of what is to be preferred and what avoided in inflection and syntax; *also* : speech or writing evaluated according to its conformity to the principles of grammar — **gram·mar·i·an** \grə-'mer-ē-ən, -'mar-\ *n* — **gram·mat·i·cal** \-'mat-i-kəl\ *adj* — **gram·mat·i·cal·ly** \-k(ə-)lē\ *adv*

grammar school *n* **1** : a secondary school emphasizing Latin and Greek in preparation for college; *also* : a British college preparatory school **2** : a school intermediate between the primary grades and high school **3** : ELEMENTARY SCHOOL

gramme \'gram\ *chiefly Brit* var of GRAM

gram·o·phone \'gram-ə-ˌfōn\ *n* : PHONOGRAPH

gra·na·ry \'grān-(ə-)rē, 'gran-\ *n, pl* **-ries 1** : a storehouse for grain **2** : a region producing grain in abundance

¹grand \'grand\ *adj* **1** : higher in rank or importance : FOREMOST, CHIEF **2** : great in size **3** : INCLUSIVE, COMPLETE ⟨a ∼ total⟩ **4** : MAGNIFICENT, SPLENDID **5** : showing wealth or high social standing **6** : IMPRESSIVE, STATELY **7** : very good : FINE — **grand·ly** \'gran(d)lē\ *adv* — **grand·ness** \'gran(d)-nəs\ *n*

²grand *n, slang* : a thousand dollars

gran·dam \'gran-ˌdam, -dəm\ *or* **gran·dame** \-ˌdām, -dəm\ *n* : an old woman

grand·child \'gran(d)-ˌchīld\ *n* : a child of one's son or daughter

grand·daugh·ter \'gran-ˌdȯt-ər\ *n* : a daughter of one's son or daughter

grande dame \'grän-'däm\ *n, pl* **grandes dames** : a usu. elderly woman of great prestige or ability

gran·dee \gran-'dē\ *n* : a high-ranking Spanish or Portuguese nobleman

gran·deur \'gran-jər\ *n* **1** : the quality or state of being grand : MAGNIFICENCE **2** : something that is grand

grand·fa·ther \'gran(d)-ˌfä<u>th</u>-ər\ *n* : the father of one's father or mother; *also* : ANCESTOR

grandfather clock *n* : a tall clock standing directly on the floor

gran·dil·o·quence \gran-'dil-ə-kwəns\ *n* : pompous eloquence — **gran·dil·o·quent** \-kwənt\ *adj*

gran·di·ose \'gran-dē-ˌōs, ˌgran-dē-'ōs\ *adj* : IMPRESSIVE, IMPOSING; *also* : affectedly splendid — **gran·di·ose·ly** *adv* — **gran·di·os·i·ty** \ˌgran-dē-'äs-ət-ē\ *n*

grand mal \'grän(d)-ˌmäl; 'gran(d)-ˌmal\ *n* [F, lit., great illness] : severe epilepsy

grand·moth·er \'gran(d)-ˌmə<u>th</u>-ər\ *n* : the mother of one's father or mother; *also* : a female ancestor

grand·par·ent \-ˌpar-ənt\ *n* : a parent of one's father or mother

grand piano *n* : a piano with horizontal frame and strings

grand prix \'grän-'prē\ *n, pl* **grand prix** \-'prē(z)\ *often cap G&P* : a long-distance auto race over a road course

grand slam *n* **1** : a total victory or success **2** : a home run hit with three runners on base

grand·son \'gran(d)-ˌsən\ *n* : a son of one's son or daughter

grand·stand \-ˌstand\ *n* : a usu. roofed stand for spectators at a racecourse or stadium

grange \'grānj\ *n* **1** : a farm or farmhouse with its various buildings **2** *cap* : one of the lodges of a national association originally made up of farmers; *also* : the association itself — **grang·er** \'grān-jər\ *n*

gran·ite \'gran-ət\ *n* : a hard igneous rock that takes a polish and is used for building — **gra·nit·ic** \gra-'nit-ik\ *adj*

gran·ite·ware \-ˌwaər\ *n* : enameled ironware

gra·no·la \grə-'nō-lə\ *n* : a mixture of rolled oats and usu. raisins and nuts eaten esp. for breakfast

¹grant \'grant\ *vb* **1** : to consent to : ALLOW, PERMIT **2** : GIVE, BESTOW **3** : to admit as true — **grant·er** \-ər\ *n* — **grant·or** \'grant-ər, -ˌȯr\ *n*

²grant *n* **1** : the act of granting **2** : something granted; *esp* : a gift for a particular purpose ⟨a ∼ for study abroad⟩ **3** : a transfer of property by deed or writing; *also* : the instrument by which such a transfer is made **4** : the property transferred by grant

grant·ee \grant-'ē\ *n* : one to whom a grant is made

grants·man·ship \'grants-mən-ˌship\ *n* : the art of obtaining grants (as for research) — **grants·man** *n*

gran·u·lar \'gran-yə-lər\ *adj* : consisting of or appearing to consist of granules — **gran·u·lar·i·ty** \ˌgran-yə-'lar-ət-ē\ *n*

gran·u·late \'gran-yə-ˌlāt\ *vb* **-lat·ed; -lat·ing** : to form into grains or crystals — **gran·u·la·tion** \ˌgran-yə-'lā-shən\ *n*

gran·ule \'gran-yül\ *n* : a small grain or particle

grape \'grāp\ *n* [ME, fr. OF *crape, grape* hook, grape stalk, bunch of grapes, grape] **1** : a smooth-skinned juicy edible greenish white, deep red, or purple berry that is the chief source of wine **2** : any of numerous woody vines widely grown for their bunches of grapes

grape·fruit \'grāp-ˌfrüt\ *n* : a large edible yellow-skinned citrus fruit; *also* : a tree bearing grapefruit

grape hyacinth *n* : any of several small bulbous spring-flowering herbs with racemes of usu. blue flowers that are related to the lilies

grape·shot \'grāp-ˌshät\ *n* : a cluster of small iron balls formerly fired at people from short range by a cannon

grape·vine \'grāp-ˌvīn\ *n* **1** : GRAPE 2 **2** : RUMOR; *also* : an informal means of circulating information or gossip

graph \'graf\ *n* : a diagram that usu. by means of dots and lines shows relationships between things — **graph** *vb*

-graph \ˌgraf\ *n comb form* **1** : something written ⟨auto*graph*⟩ **2** : instrument for making or transmitting records ⟨seismo*graph*⟩

graph·ic \'graf-ik\ *also* **graph·i·cal** \-i-kəl\ *adj* **1** : being written, drawn, or engraved **2** : vividly described **3** : of or relating to the arts (**graphic arts**) of representation, decoration, and printing on flat surfaces — **graph·i·cal·ly** \-i-k(ə-)lē\ *adv* — **graph·ics** \-iks\ *n*

graphics tablet *n* : a computer input device for entering graphics information by drawing or tracing

graph·ite \'graf-ˌīt\ *n* [G *graphit*, fr. Gk *graphein* to write] : soft carbon used esp. for lead pencils and lubricants

grap·nel \'grap-nᵊl\ *n* : a small anchor with two or more claws used esp. in dragging or grappling operations

¹grap·ple \'grap-əl\ *n* [MF *grappelle*, dim. of *grape* hook] **1** : GRAPNEL **2** : the act of grappling

²grapple *vb* **grap·pled; grap·pling** \'grap-(ə-)liŋ\ **1** : to seize or hold with or as if with a hooked implement **2** : to come to grips with : WRESTLE **3** : COPE ⟨∼ with a problem⟩

¹grasp \'grasp\ *vb* **1** : to make the motion of seizing **2** : to take or seize firmly **3** : to enclose and hold with the fingers or arms **4** : COMPREHEND

²grasp *n* **1** : HANDLE **2** : EMBRACE **3** : HOLD, CONTROL **4** : the reach of the arms **5** : the power of seizing and holding **6** : COMPREHENSION

grasp·ing \-iŋ\ *adj* : GREEDY, AVARICIOUS

grass \'gras\ *n* **1** : herbage for grazing animals **2** : any of a large family of plants (as wheat, bamboo, or sugarcane) with jointed stems and narrow leaves **3** : grass-covered land **4** : MARIJUANA — **grassy** *adj*

grass·hop·per \-ˌhäp-ər\ *n* : any of numerous leaping plant-eating insects

grass·land \-ˌland\ *n* : land covered naturally or under cultivation with grasses and low-growing herbs

grass roots *n pl* : society at the local level as distinguished from the centers of political leadership

¹grate \'grāt\ *vb* **grat·ed; grat·ing** **1** : to pulverize by rubbing against something rough **2** : to grind or rub against with a rasping noise **3** : IRRITATE — **grat·er** *n* — **grat·ing·ly** \'grāt-iŋ-lē\ *adv*

²grate *n* **1** : a framework with bars

across it (as in a window) **2** : a frame of iron bars for holding fuel while it is burning

grate·ful \'grāt-fəl\ *adj* **1** : THANKFUL, APPRECIATIVE; *also* : expressing gratitude **2** : PLEASING — **grate·ful·ly** \-ē\ *adv* — **grate·ful·ness** *n*

grat·i·fy \'grat-ə-ˌfī\ *vb* **-fied; -fy·ing** : to afford pleasure to — **grat·i·fi·ca·tion** \ˌgrat-ə-fə-'kā-shən\ *n*

grat·ing \'grāt-iŋ\ *n* : GRATE

gra·tis \'grat-əs, 'grāt-\ *adv or adj* : without charge or recompense : FREE

grat·i·tude \'grat-ə-ˌt(y)üd\ *n* : THANKFULNESS

gra·tu·itous \grə-'t(y)ü-ət-əs\ *adj* **1** : done or provided without recompense : FREE **2** : UNWARRANTED

gra·tu·ity \-ət-ē\ *n, pl* **-ities** : TIP

gra·va·men \grə-'vā-mən\ *n, pl* **-va·mens** *or* **-vam·i·na** \-'vam-ə-nə\ [LL burden] : the basic or significant part of a grievance or complaint

¹**grave** \'grāv\ *vb* **graved; grav·en** \'grā-vən\ *or* **graved; grav·ing** : SCULPTURE, ENGRAVE

²**grave** *n* : an excavation in the earth as a place of burial; *also* : TOMB

³**grave** \'grāv; 5 *also* 'gräv\ *adj* **1** : IMPORTANT **2** : threatening great harm or danger **3** : DIGNIFIED, SOLEMN **4** : drab in color : SOMBER **5** : of, marked by, or being an accent mark having the form ` — **grave·ly** *adv* — **grave·ness** *n*

grav·el \'grav-əl\ *n* : pebbles and small pieces of rock larger than grains of sand — **grav·el·ly** \-ē\ *adj*

grave·stone \'grāv-ˌstōn\ *n* : a burial monument

grave·yard \-ˌyärd\ *n* : CEMETERY

grav·id \'grav-əd\ *adj* [L *gravidus*, fr. *gravis* heavy] : PREGNANT

gra·vi·me·ter \gra-'vim-ət-ər, 'grav-ə-ˌmēt-\ *n* : a device for measuring variations in a gravitational field

grav·i·tate \'grav-ə-ˌtāt\ *vb* **-tat·ed; -tat·ing** : to move or tend to move toward something

grav·i·ta·tion \ˌgrav-ə-'tā-shən\ *n* **1** : a natural force of attraction that tends to draw bodies together **2** : the action or process of gravitating — **grav·i·ta·tion·al** \-sh(ə-)nəl\ *adj* — **grav·i·ta·tion·al·ly** \-ē\ *adv* — **grav·i·ta·tive** \'grav-ə-ˌtāt-iv\ *adj*

grav·i·ty \'grav-ət-ē\ *n, pl* **-ties** **1** : IMPORTANCE; *esp* : SERIOUSNESS **2** : ²MASS 5 **3** : the gravitational attraction of the mass of a celestial object (as earth) for bodies close to it; *also* : GRAVITATION 1

gra·vure \grə-'vyur\ *n* [F] : PHOTOGRAVURE

gra·vy \'grā-vē\ *n, pl* **gravies** **1** : a sauce made from the thickened and seasoned juices of cooked meat **2** : unearned or illicit gain : GRAFT

¹**gray** \'grā\ *adj* **1** : of the color gray; *also* : dull in color **2** : having gray hair **3** : CHEERLESS, DISMAL **4** : intermediate in position or character — **gray·ish** *adj* — **gray·ness** *n*

²**gray** *n* **1** : something of a gray color **2** : a neutral color ranging between black and white

³**gray** *vb* : to make or become gray

gray·beard \'grā-ˌbiərd\ *n* : an old man

gray birch *n* : a small No. American birch with many lateral branches, grayish white bark, and soft wood

gray·ling \'grā-liŋ\ *n, pl* **grayling** *also* **graylings** : any of several slender freshwater food and sport fishes related to the trouts

gray matter *n* **1** : the grayish part of nervous tissue consisting mostly of nerve cell bodies **2** : INTELLIGENCE

¹**graze** \'grāz\ *vb* **grazed; graz·ing** **1** : to feed on herbage or pasture **2** : to feed (livestock) on grass or pasture — **graz·er** *n*

²**graze** *vb* **grazed; graz·ing** **1** : to touch lightly in passing **2** : SCRATCH, ABRADE

¹**grease** \'grēs\ *n* **1** : rendered animal fat **2** : oily material **3** : a thick lubricant — **greasy** \'grē-sē, -zē\ *adj*

²**grease** \'grēs, 'grēz\ *vb* **greased; greas·ing** : to smear or lubricate with grease

grease·paint \'grēs-ˌpānt\ *n* : theater makeup

great \'grāt\ *adj* **1** : large in size : BIG **2** : ELABORATE, AMPLE **3** : large in number : NUMEROUS **4** : being beyond the average : MIGHTY, INTENSE ⟨a ~ weight⟩ ⟨in ~ pain⟩ **5** : EMINENT, GRAND **6** : long continued ⟨a ~ while⟩ **7** : MAIN, PRINCIPAL **8** : more distant in a family relationship by one generation ⟨a *great*-grandfather⟩ **9** : markedly superior in character, quality, or skill ⟨~ at bridge⟩ **10** : EXCELLENT,

FINE ⟨had a ∼ time⟩ — **great·ly** *adv* — **great·ness** *n*

great circle *n* : a circle on the surface of a sphere that has the same center as the sphere; *esp* : one on the surface of the earth an arc of which is the shortest travel distance between two points

great·coat \'grāt-ˌkōt\ *n* : a heavy overcoat

Great Dane *n* : any of a breed of tall massive powerful smooth-coated dogs

great·heart·ed \'grāt-'härt-əd\ *adj* 1 : COURAGEOUS 2 : MAGNANIMOUS

great power *n, often cap G&P* : one of the nations that figure most decisively in international affairs

great white shark *n* : WHITE SHARK

grebe \'grēb\ *n* : any of a family of lobe-toed diving birds related to the loons

Gre·cian \'grē-shən\ *adj* : GREEK

greed \'grēd\ *n* : acquisitive or selfish desire beyond reason — **greed·i·ly** \'grēd-ᵊl-ē\ *adv* — **greed·i·ness** \-ē-nəs\ *n* — **greedy** \'grēd-ē\ *adj*

¹Greek \'grēk\ *n* 1 : a native or inhabitant of Greece 2 : the ancient or modern language of Greece

²Greek *adj* 1 : of, relating to, or characteristic of Greece, the Greeks, or Greek 2 : ORTHODOX 3

¹green \'grēn\ *adj* 1 : of the color green 2 : covered with verdure; *also* : consisting of green plants or of the leafy parts of plants ⟨a ∼ salad⟩ 3 : UNRIPE; *also* : IMMATURE 4 : having a sickly appearance 5 : not fully processed or treated ⟨∼ liquor⟩ ⟨∼ hides⟩ 6 : INEXPERIENCED; *also* : NAIVE — **green·ish** *adj* — **green·ness** \'grēn-nəs\ *n*

²green *vb* : to make or become green

³green *n* 1 : a color between blue and yellow in the spectrum : the color of growing fresh grass or of the emerald 2 : something of a green color 3 *pl* : leafy parts of plants 4 : a grassy plot; *esp* : a smooth grassy area around the hole into which the ball must be played in golf

green·back \'grēn-ˌbak\ *n* : a U.S. legal-tender note

green bean *n* : a kidney bean that is used as a snap bean when the pods are colored green

green·belt \'grēn-ˌbelt\ *n* : a belt of parkways or farmlands that encircles a community

green·ery \'grēn-(ə-)rē\ *n, pl* **-er·ies** : green foliage or plants

green–eyed \'grēn-'īd\ *adj* : JEALOUS

green·gro·cer \'grēn-ˌgrō-sər\ *n* : a retailer of fresh vegetables and fruit

green·horn \-ˌhȯrn\ *n* : an inexperienced person; *esp* : one easily tricked or cheated

green·house \-ˌhaús\ *n* : a glass structure for the growing of tender plants

green manure *n* : an herbaceous crop (as clover) plowed under when green to enrich the soil

green onion *n* : a young onion pulled before the bulb has enlarged and used esp. in salads

green pepper *n* : SWEET PEPPER

green·room \'grēn-ˌrüm, -ˌrùm\ *n* : a room in a theater or concert hall where actors or musicians relax before, between, or after appearances

green·sward \-ˌswȯrd\ *n* : turf that is green with growing grass

green thumb *n* : an unusual ability to make plants grow

Green·wich mean time \'grin-ij-, 'gren-, -ich-\ *n* [*Greenwich*, England] : GREENWICH TIME

Greenwich time *n* : the time of the meridian of Greenwich used as the basis of worldwide standard time

green·wood \'grēn-ˌwùd\ *n* : a forest green with foliage

greet \'grēt\ *vb* 1 : to address with expressions of kind wishes 2 : to meet or react to in a specified manner 3 : to be perceived by — **greet·er** *n*

greet·ing \-iŋ\ *n* 1 : a salutation on meeting 2 *pl* : best wishes : REGARDS

greeting card *n* : a card that bears a message usu. sent on a special occasion

gre·gar·i·ous \gri-'gar-ē-əs\ *adj* [L *gregarius* of a flock or herd, fr. *greg-, grex* flock, herd] 1 : SOCIAL, COMPANIONABLE 2 : tending to flock together — **gre·gar·i·ous·ly** *adv* — **gre·gar·i·ous·ness** *n*

grem·lin \'grem-lən\ *n* : a small gnome held to be responsible for malfunction of equipment esp. in aircraft

gre·nade \grə-'nād\ *n* [MF, pomegranate, fr. LL *granata*, fr. L *granatus* seedy, fr. *granum* grain] : a small bomb that is thrown by hand or launched (as by a rifle)

gren·a·dier \ˌgren-ə-ˈdiər\ *n* : a member of a European regiment formerly armed with grenades

gren·a·dine \ˌgren-ə-ˈdēn, ˈgren-ə-ˌdēn\ *n* : a syrup flavored with pomegranates and used in mixed drinks

grew past of GROW

grey var of GRAY

grey·hound \ˈgrā-ˌhau̇nd\ *n* : a tall slender dog noted for speed and keen sight

grid \ˈgrid\ *n* **1** : GRATE **2** : a metal plate used as a conductor in a storage battery **3** : an element in an electron tube consisting of a mesh of fine wire **4** : GRIDIRON 2; *also* : FOOTBALL

grid·dle \ˈgrid-ᵊl\ *n* : a flat usu. metal surface for cooking food

griddle cake *n* : PANCAKE

grid·iron \ˈgrid-ˌī(-ə)rn\ *n* **1** : a grate (as of parallel bars) for broiling food **2** : something resembling a gridiron in appearance; *esp* : a football field

grid·lock \ˈgrid-ˌläk\ *n* : a traffic jam in which an intersection is so blocked that no vehicular movement is possible

grief \ˈgrēf\ *n* **1** : emotional suffering caused by or as if by bereavement; *also* : a cause of such suffering **2** : MISHAP **3** : DISASTER

griev·ance \ˈgrē-vəns\ *n* **1** : a cause of distress affording reason for complaint or resistance **2** : COMPLAINT

grieve \ˈgrēv\ *vb* **grieved; griev·ing** [ME *greven*, fr. OF *grever*, fr. L *gravare* to burden, fr. *gravis* heavy, grave] **1** : to cause grief or sorrow to : DISTRESS **2** : to feel grief : SORROW

griev·ous \ˈgrē-vəs\ *adj* **1** : OPPRESSIVE, ONEROUS **2** : causing suffering, grief, or sorrow : SEVERE ⟨a ∼ wound⟩ **3** : SERIOUS, GRAVE — **griev·ous·ly** *adv*

¹grill \ˈgril\ *vb* **1** : to broil on a grill; *also* : to fry or toast on a griddle **2** : to question intensely

²grill *n* **1** : a cooking utensil of parallel bars on which food is grilled **2** : an informal restaurant

grille *or* **grill** \ˈgril\ *n* : a grating that forms a barrier or screen

grill·work \ˈgril-ˌwərk\ *n* : work constituting or resembling a grille

grim \ˈgrim\ *adj* **grim·mer; grim·mest 1** : CRUEL, FIERCE **2** : harsh and forbid-

ding in appearance **3** : RELENTLESS **4** : ghastly or repellent in character — **grim·ly** *adv* — **grim·ness** *n*

gri·mace \ˈgrim-əs, grim-ˈās\ *n* : a facial expression usu. of disgust or disapproval — **grimace** *vb*

grime \ˈgrīm\ *n* : soot, smut, or dirt adhering to or embedded in a surface; *also* : accumulated dirtiness and disorder — **grimy** *adj*

grin \ˈgrin\ *vb* **grinned; grin·ning** : to draw back the lips so as to show the teeth esp. in amusement — **grin** *n*

¹grind \ˈgrīnd\ *vb* **ground** \ˈgrau̇nd\; **grind·ing 1** : to reduce to small particles **2** : to wear down, polish, or sharpen by friction **3** : to press with a grating noise : GRIT ⟨∼ the teeth⟩ **4** : OPPRESS **5** : to operate or produce by turning a crank **6** : DRUDGE; *esp* : to study hard **7** : to move with difficulty or friction ⟨gears ∼ing⟩

²grind *n* **1** : monotonous labor or routine; *esp* : intensive study **2** : one who works or studies excessively

grind·er \ˈgrīn-dər\ *n* **1** : MOLAR **2** *pl* : TEETH **3** : one that grinds **4** : SUBMARINE 2

grind·stone \ˈgrīn-ˌstōn\ *n* : a flat circular stone of natural sandstone that revolves on an axle and is used for grinding, shaping, or smoothing

¹grip \ˈgrip\ *vb* **gripped; grip·ping 1** : to seize or hold firmly **2** : to hold strongly the interest of

²grip *n* **1** : GRASP; *also* : strength in gripping **2** : a firm tenacious hold **3** : UNDERSTANDING **4** : a device for grasping and holding **5** : TRAVELING BAG

gripe \ˈgrīp\ *vb* **griped; grip·ing 1** : SEIZE, GRIP **2** : IRRITATE, VEX **3** : to cause or experience spasmodic pains in the bowels **4** : COMPLAIN — **gripe** *n*

grippe \ˈgrip\ *n* : INFLUENZA

gris–gris \ˈgrē-ˌgrē\ *n, pl* **gris–gris** \-ˌgrēz\ [F] : an amulet or incantation used chiefly by people of African Negro ancestry

gris·ly \ˈgriz-lē\ *adj* **gris·li·er; -est** : HORRIBLE, GRUESOME

grist \ˈgrist\ *n* : grain to be ground or already ground

gris·tle \ˈgris-əl\ *n* : CARTILAGE — **gris·tly** \-(ə-)lē\ *adj*

grist·mill \ˈgrist-ˌmil\ *n* : a mill for grinding grain

¹grit \'grit\ n **1** : a hard sharp granule (as of sand); *also* : material composed of such granules **2** : unyielding courage — **grit·ty** *adj*

²grit *vb* **grit·ted; grit·ting** : GRIND, GRATE

grits \'grits\ *n pl* : coarsely ground hulled grain ⟨hominy ∼⟩

griz·zled \'griz-əld\ *adj* : streaked or mixed with gray

griz·zly \'griz-lē\ *adj* **griz·zli·er; -est** : GRIZZLED

grizzly bear *n* : a large pale-coated bear of western No. America

gro *abbr* gross

groan \'grōn\ *vb* **1** : MOAN **2** : to make a harsh sound under sudden or prolonged strain ⟨the chair ∼ed under his weight⟩ — **groan** *n*

groat \'grōt\ *n* : an old British coin worth four pennies

gro·cer \'grō-sər\ *n* [ME, fr. MF *grossier* wholesaler, fr. *gros* coarse, wholesale, fr. L *grossus* coarse] : a dealer esp. in staple foodstuffs — **gro·cery** \'grōs-(ə-)rē\ *n*

grog \'gräg\ *n* [*Old Grog,* nickname of Edward Vernon †1757 Eng. admiral responsible for diluting the sailors' rum] : alcoholic liquor; *esp* : liquor (as rum) mixed with water

grog·gy \'gräg-ē\ *adj* **grog·gi·er; -est** : weak and unsteady on the feet or in action — **grog·gi·ly** \'gräg-ə-lē\ *adv* — **grog·gi·ness** \-ē-nəs\ *n*

groin \'grȯin\ *n* **1** : the fold marking the juncture of the abdomen and thigh; *also* : the region of this fold **2** : the curved line or rib on a ceiling along which two vaults meet

grom·met \'gräm-ət, 'grəm-\ *n* **1** : a ring of rope **2** : an eyelet of firm material to strengthen or protect an opening

¹groom \'grüm, 'grum\ *n* **1** : a male servant; *esp* : one in charge of horses **2** : BRIDEGROOM

²groom *vb* **1** : to attend to the cleaning of (an animal) **2** : to make neat, attractive, or acceptable : POLISH

grooms·man \'grümz-mən, 'grumz-\ *n* : a male friend who attends a bridegroom at his wedding

groove \'grüv\ *n* **1** : a long narrow channel **2** : a fixed routine — **groove** *vb*

groovy \'grü-vē\ *adj* **groov·i·er; -est** : very good : EXCELLENT

grope \'grōp\ *vb* **groped; grop·ing 1** : to feel about blindly or uncertainly in search ⟨∼ for the right word⟩ **2** : to feel one's way by groping

gros·beak \'grōs-ˌbēk\ *n* : any of several finches of Europe or America with large stout conical bills

gro·schen \'grō-shən\ *n, pl* **groschen** — see *schilling* at MONEY table

gros·grain \'grō-ˌgrān\ *n* [F *gros grain* coarse texture] : a silk or rayon fabric with crosswise cotton ribs

¹gross \'grōs\ *adj* **1** : glaringly noticeable **2** : OUT-AND-OUT, UTTER **3** : BIG, BULKY; *esp* : excessively fat **4** : excessively luxuriant : RANK **5** : GENERAL, BROAD **6** : consisting of an overall total exclusive of deductions ⟨∼ earnings⟩ **7** : EARTHY, CARNAL ⟨∼ pleasures⟩ **8** : lacking knowledge or culture : UNREFINED **9** : OBSCENE — **gross·ly** *adv* — **gross·ness** *n*

²gross *n* : an overall total exclusive of deductions — **gross** *vb*

³gross *n, pl* **gross** : a total of 12 dozen things ⟨a ∼ of pencils⟩

gross national product *n* : the total value of the goods and services produced in a nation during a year

gro·szy \'grȯ-shē\ *n, pl* **groszy** — see *zloty* at MONEY table

grot \'grät\ *n* : GROTTO

gro·tesque \grō-'tesk\ *adj* **1** : FANCIFUL, BIZARRE **2** : absurdly incongruous **3** : ECCENTRIC — **gro·tesque·ly** *adv*

grot·to \'grät-ō\ *n, pl* **grottoes** *also* **grottos 1** : CAVE **2** : an artificial cavelike structure

grouch \'graůch\ *n* **1** : a fit of bad temper **2** : an habitually irritable or complaining person — **grouch** *vb* — **grouchy** *adj*

¹ground \'graůnd\ *n* **1** : the bottom of a body of water **2** *pl* : sediment at the bottom of a liquid : DREGS, LEES **3** : a basis for belief, action, or argument **4** : BACKGROUND **5** : FOUNDATION **6** : the surface of the earth; *also* : SOIL **7** : an area with a particular use ⟨fishing ∼s⟩ **8** *pl* : the area about and belonging to a building **9** : a conductor that makes electrical connection with the earth — **ground·less** \'graůn-(d)ləs\ *adj*

²ground *vb* **1** : to bring to or place on the ground **2** : to provide a reason or justification for **3** : to instruct in fundamental principles **4** : to connect electrically with a ground **5** : to restrict to the ground **6** : to run aground

³**ground** past and past part of GRIND

ground ball *n* : a batted baseball that rolls or bounces along the ground

ground cover *n* : low plants that grow over and cover the soil; *also* : a plant suitable for this use

ground•er \'graún-dər\ *n* : GROUND BALL

ground glass *n* : glass with a light-diffusing surface produced by etching or abrading

ground•hog \'graúnd-ˌhȯg, -ˌhäg\ *n* : WOODCHUCK

ground•ling \'graúnd-liŋ\ *n* **1** : a spectator in the cheaper part of a theater **2** : a person of inferior judgment or taste

ground rule *n* **1** : a sports rule adopted to modify play on a particular field, court, or course **2** : a rule of procedure

ground squirrel *n* : any of various burrowing rodents that are related to the squirrels and live in colonies in open areas

ground swell *n* **1** : a broad deep ocean swell caused by an often distant gale or earthquake **2** : a rapid spontaneous growth (as of political opinion)

ground•wa•ter \'graúnd-ˌwȯt-ər, -ˌwät-\ *n* : water within the earth that supplies wells and springs

ground•work \-ˌwərk\ *n* : FOUNDATION, BASIS

ground zero *n* : the point above, below, or at which a nuclear explosion occurs

¹**group** \'grüp\ *n* **1** : a number of individuals related by a common factor (as physical association, community of interests, or blood) **2** : a combination of atoms commonly found together in a molecule ⟨a methyl ∼⟩

²**group** *vb* : to associate in groups : CLUSTER, AGGREGATE

grou•per \'grü-pər\ *n, pl* **groupers** *also* **grouper** : any of numerous large solitary bottom fishes of warm seas

group•ie \'grü-pē\ *n* : a fan of a rock group who usu. follows the group around on concert tours

group therapy *n* : therapy in the presence of a therapist in which several patients discuss their personal problems

¹**grouse** \'graús\ *n, pl* **grouse** *or* **grouses**
: any of numerous plump-bodied ground-dwelling game birds related to but usu. less brightly colored than the pheasants

²**grouse** *vb* **groused; grous•ing** : COMPLAIN, GRUMBLE

grout \'graút\ *n* : material (as mortar) used for filling spaces — **grout** *vb*

grove \'grōv\ *n* : a small wood usu. without underbrush

grov•el \'gräv-əl, 'grəv-\ *vb* **-eled** *or* **-elled; -el•ing** *or* **-el•ling** \-(ə-)liŋ\ **1** : to creep or lie with the body prostrate in fear or humility **2** : to abase oneself

grow \'grō\ *vb* **grew** \'grü\; **grown** \'grōn\; **grow•ing 1** : to spring up and come to maturity **2** : to be able to grow : THRIVE **3** : to take on some relation through or as if through growth ⟨tree limbs *grown* together⟩ **4** : INCREASE, EXPAND **5** : RESULT, ORIGINATE **6** : to come into existence : ARISE **7** : BECOME **8** : to have an increasing influence **9** : to cause to grow — **grow•er** \'grō(-ə)r\ *n*

growl \'graúl\ *vb* **1** : RUMBLE **2** : to utter a deep throaty threatening sound **3** : GRUMBLE — **growl** *n*

grown–up \'grōn-ˌəp\ *adj* : not childish : ADULT — **grown–up** *n*

growth \'grōth\ *n* **1** : stage or condition attained in growing **2** : a process of growing esp. through progressive development or increase **3** : a result or product of growing ⟨a fine ∼ of hair⟩; *also* : an abnormal mass of tissue (as a tumor)

¹**grub** \'grəb\ *vb* **grubbed; grub•bing 1** : to clear or root out by digging **2** : to dig in the ground usu. for a hidden object **3** : RUMMAGE

²**grub** *n* **1** : a soft thick wormlike larva ⟨beetle ∼s⟩ **2** : DRUDGE; *also* : a slovenly person **3** : FOOD

grub•by \'grəb-ē\ *adj* **grub•bi•er; -est** : DIRTY, SLOVENLY — **grub•bi•ness** \'grəb-ē-nəs\ *n*

grub•stake \'grəb-ˌstāk\ *n* : supplies or funds furnished a mining prospector in return for a share in his finds

¹**grudge** \'grəj\ *vb* **grudged; grudg•ing** : to be reluctant to give : BEGRUDGE

²**grudge** *n* : a feeling of deep-seated resentment or ill will

gru•el \'grü-əl\ *n* : a thin porridge

gru·el·ing *or* **gru·el·ling** \-ə-liŋ\ *adj* : requiring extreme effort : EXHAUSTING

grue·some \'grü-səm\ *adj* [fr. earlier *growsome*, fr. E dial. *grow, grue* to shiver] : inspiring horror or repulsion : GRISLY

gruff \'grəf\ *adj* **1** : rough in speech or manner **2** : being deep and harsh : HOARSE — **gruff·ly** *adv*

grum·ble \'grəm-bəl\ *vb* **grum·bled; grum·bling** \-b(ə-)liŋ\ **1** : to mutter in discontent **2** : GROWL, RUMBLE — **grum·bler** \-b(ə-)lər\ *n*

grumpy \'grəm-pē\ *adj* **grump·i·er; -est** : moodily cross : SURLY — **grump·i·ly** \'grəm-pə-lē\ *adv* — **grump·i·ness** \-pē-nəs\ *n*

grun·gy \'grən-jē\ *adj* **grun·gi·er; -est** : shabby or dirty in character or condition

grun·ion \'grən-yən\ *n* : a fish of the California coast which comes inshore to spawn at nearly full moon

grunt \'grənt\ *n* : a deep throaty sound (as that of a hog) — **grunt** *vb*

GSA *abbr* **1** General Services Administration **2** Girl Scouts of America

G suit *n* [gravity *suit*] : an astronaut's or aviator's suit designed to counteract the physiological effects of acceleration

gt *abbr* great

Gt Brit *abbr* Great Britain

gtd *abbr* guaranteed

GU *abbr* Guam

gua·ca·mo·le \ˌgwäk-ə-'mō-lē\ *n* [AmerSp] : mashed and seasoned avocado

gua·nine \'gwän-ˌēn\ *n* : a purine base that codes genetic information in the molecular chain of DNA or RNA

gua·no \'gwän-ō\ *n* [Sp, fr. Quechua (a South American Indian language) *huanu* dung] : a substance composed chiefly of the excrement of seabirds and used as a fertilizer

gua·ra·ni \ˌgwär-ə-'nē\ *n, pl* **guaranies** *also* **guaranis** — see MONEY table

¹guar·an·tee \ˌgar-ən-'tē\ *n* **1** : GUARANTOR **2** : GUARANTY 1 **3** : an agreement by which one person undertakes to secure another in the possession or enjoyment of something **4** : an assurance of the quality of or of the length of use to be expected from a product offered for sale **5** : GUARANTY 3

²guarantee *vb* **-teed; -tee·ing 1** : to undertake to answer for the debt, failure to perform, or faulty performance of (another) **2** : to undertake an obligation to establish, perform, or continue **3** : to give security to

guar·an·tor \ˌgar-ən-'tȯr\ *n* : one who gives a guarantee

¹guar·an·ty \'gar-ən-tē\ *n, pl* **-ties 1** : an undertaking to answer for another's failure to pay a debt or perform a duty **2** : GUARANTEE 3 **3** : PLEDGE, SECURITY **4** : GUARANTOR

²guaranty *vb* **-tied; -ty·ing** : GUARANTEE

¹guard \'gärd\ *n* **1** : one assigned to protect or oversee another **2** : a man or a body of men on sentinel duty **3** *pl* : troops attached to the person of the sovereign **4** : a defensive position (as in boxing) **5** : the act or duty of protecting or defending **6** : PROTECTION **7** : a football lineman playing between center and tackle; *also* : a basketball player stationed toward the rear **8** : a protective or safety device — **on guard** : WATCHFUL, ALERT

²guard *vb* **1** : PROTECT, DEFEND **2** : to watch over **3** : to be on guard

guard·house \'gärd-ˌhaus\ *n* **1** : a building occupied by a guard or used as a headquarters by soldiers on guard duty **2** : a military jail

guard·ian \'gärd-ē-ən\ *n* **1** : CUSTODIAN **2** : one who has the care of the person or property of another — **guard·ian·ship** *n*

guard·room \'gärd-ˌrüm\ *n* **1** : a room used by a military guard while on duty **2** : a room where military prisoners are confined

guards·man \'gärdz-mən\ *n* : a member of a military body called *guard* or *guards*

gua·va \'gwäv-ə\ *n* : the sweet yellow acid fruit of a shrubby tropical American tree of the myrtle family used esp. for making jam and jelly; *also* : the tree

gu·ber·na·to·ri·al \ˌgüb-ə(r)-nə-'tōr-ē-əl\ *adj* : of or relating to a governor

guer·don \'gərd-ᵊn\ *n* [ME, fr. MF, fr. Old High German *widarlōn*, fr. *widar* back + *lōn* reward] : REWARD, RECOMPENSE

guern·sey \'gərn-zē\ *n, pl* **guernseys** *often cap* : any of a breed of fawn and white dairy cattle that produce rich yellowish milk

guer・ril・la or **gue・ril・la** \gə-'ril-ə\ n [Sp guerrilla, fr. dim. of guerra war, of Gmc origin] : one who engages in irregular warfare esp. as a member of an independent unit

guess \'ges\ vb **1** : to form an opinion from little or no evidence **2** : to conjecture correctly about : DISCOVER **3** : BELIEVE, SUPPOSE — **guess** n

guest \'gest\ n **1** : a person to whom hospitality (as of a house or a club) is extended **2** : a patron of a commercial establishment (as a hotel or restaurant) **3** : a person not a regular member of a cast who appears on a program

guf・faw \gə-'fö\ n : a loud burst of laughter — **guf・faw** \(ˌ)gə-'fö\ vb

guid・ance \'gīd-ᵊns\ n **1** : the act or process of guiding **2** : ADVICE, DIRECTION

¹**guide** \'gīd\ n **1** : one who leads or directs another on a course **2** : one who shows and explains points of interest **3** : something that provides guiding information; also : SIGNPOST **4** : a device to direct the motion of something

²**guide** vb **guid・ed; guid・ing 1** : CONDUCT **2** : MANAGE, DIRECT **3** : to superintend the training of — **guid・able** \'gīd-ə-bəl\ adj

guide・book \'gīd-ˌbuk\ n : a book of information for travelers

guided missile n : a missile whose course may be altered during flight

guide・line \'gīd-ˌlīn\ n : an indication or outline of policy or conduct

guide word n : a term at the head of a page of an alphabetical reference work that indicates the alphabetically first or last word on that page

gui・don \'gīd-ˌän, -ᵊn\ n : a small flag (as of a military unit)

guild \'gild\ n : an association of people with common aims and interests; esp : a medieval association of merchants or craftsmen — **guild・hall** \-ˌhöl\ n

guil・der \'gil-dər\ n : GULDEN

guile \'gīl\ n : deceitful cunning : DUPLICITY — **guile・ful** adj — **guile・less** \'gīl-ləs\ adj — **guile・less・ness** n

guil・lo・tine \'gil-ə-ˌtēn, ˌgē-(y)ə-'tēn\ n : a machine for beheading persons — **guillotine** vb

guilt \'gilt\ n **1** : the fact of having committed an offense esp. against the law **2** : BLAMEWORTHINESS **3** : a feeling of responsibility for wrongdoing — **guilt・less** adj

guilty \'gil-tē\ adj **guilt・i・er; -est 1** : having committed a breach of conduct **2** : suggesting or involving guilt **3** : aware of or suffering from guilt — **guilt・i・ly** \'gil-tə-lē\ adv — **guilt・i・ness** \-tē-nəs\ n

guin・ea \'gin-ē\ n **1** : a British gold coin no longer issued worth 21 shillings **2** : a unit of value equal to 21 shillings

guinea fowl n : a gray and white spotted West African bird related to the pheasants and widely raised for food; also : any of several related birds

guinea hen n : a female guinea fowl; also : GUINEA FOWL

guinea pig n : a small stocky short-eared and nearly tailless So. American rodent

guise \'gīz\ n **1** : a form or style of dress : COSTUME **2** : external appearance : SEMBLANCE

gui・tar \gi-'tär\ n : a musical instrument with usu. six strings plucked with a pick or with the fingers

gulch \'gəlch\ n : RAVINE

gul・den \'gül-dən, 'gùl-\ n, pl **guldens** or **gulden** — see MONEY table

gulf \'gəlf\ n [ME goulf, fr. MF golfe, fr. It golfo, fr. LL colpus, fr. Gk kolpos bosom, gulf] **1** : an extension of an ocean or a sea into the land **2** : ABYSS, CHASM **3** : a wide separation

¹**gull** \'gəl\ n : any of numerous mostly white or gray long-winged web-footed seabirds

²**gull** vb : to make a dupe of : DECEIVE — **gull・ible** adj

³**gull** n : DUPE

gul・let \'gəl-ət\ n : ESOPHAGUS; also : THROAT

gul・ly \'gəl-ē\ n, pl **gullies** : a trench worn in the earth by running water after rains

gulp \'gəlp\ vb **1** : to swallow hurriedly or greedily **2** : SUPPRESS ⟨∼ down a sob⟩ **3** : to catch the breath as if in taking a long drink — **gulp** n

¹**gum** \'gəm\ n : the tissue along the jaws that surrounds the necks of the teeth

²**gum** n **1** : a sticky plant exudate; esp : one that hardens on drying and is soluble in or swells in water and that

includes substances used as emulsifiers, adhesives, and thickeners and in inks **2** : a sticky substance **3** : a preparation usu. of a plant gum sweetened and flavored and used for chewing — **gum·my** *adj*

gum arabic *n* : a water-soluble gum obtained from several acacias and used esp. in adhesives, in confectionery, and in pharmacy

gum·bo \'gəm-bō\ *n* [AmerF *gombo,* of Bantu origin] : a rich thick soup usu. thickened with okra

gum·drop \'gəm-ˌdräp\ *n* : a candy made usu. from corn syrup with gelatin and coated with sugar crystals

gump·tion \'gəmp-shən\ *n* **1** : shrewd common sense **2** : ENTERPRISE, INITIATIVE

gum·shoe \'gəm-ˌshü\ *n* : DETECTIVE — **gumshoe** *vb*

¹gun \'gən\ *n* **1** : CANNON **2** : a portable firearm **3** : a discharge of a gun **4** : something suggesting a gun in shape or function **5** : THROTTLE

²gun *vb* **gunned; gun·ning 1** : to hunt with a gun **2** : SHOOT **3** : to open up the throttle of so as to increase speed

gun·boat \'gən-ˌbōt\ *n* : a small lightly armed ship for use in shallow waters

gun·fight \-ˌfīt\ *n* : a duel with guns — **gun·fight·er** \-ər\ *n*

gun·fire \-ˌfī(ə)r\ *n* : the firing of guns

gung ho \'gəŋ-'hō\ *adj* [*Gung ho!,* motto (interpreted as meaning "work together") of certain U.S. marine raiders in World War II, fr. Chin *kung¹-ho²,* short for *chung¹-kuo² kung¹-yeh⁴ ho²-tso⁴ she⁴* Chinese Industrial Cooperatives Society] : extremely zealous

gun·lock \'gən-ˌläk\ *n* : a device on a firearm by which the charge is ignited

gun·man \-mən\ *n* : a man armed with a gun; *esp* : an armed bandit or gangster

gun·ner \'gən-ər\ *n* **1** : a soldier or airman who operates or aims a gun **2** : one who hunts with a gun

gun·nery \'gən-(ə-)rē\ *n* : the use of guns; *esp* : the science of the flight of projectiles and effective use of guns

gunnery sergeant *n* : a noncommissioned officer in the marine corps ranking next below a first sergeant

gun·ny \'gən-ē\ *n* : coarse jute or hemp material for making sacks

gun·ny·sack \-ˌsak\ *n* : a sack made of gunny

gun·point \-ˌpȯint\ *n* : the muzzle of a gun — **at gunpoint** : under a threat of death by being shot

gun·pow·der \-ˌpaud-ər\ *n* : an explosive powder used in guns and blasting

gun·shot \'gən-ˌshät\ *n* **1** : shot fired from a gun **2** : the range of a gun ⟨within ∼⟩

gun–shy \-ˌshī\ *adj* **1** : afraid of a loud noise **2** : markedly distrustful

gun·sling·er \-ˌsliŋ-ər\ *n* : a gunman esp. in the old West

gun·smith \-ˌsmith\ *n* : one who designs, makes, or repairs firearms

gun·wale *also* **gun·nel** \'gən-ᵊl\ *n* : the upper edge of a ship's or boat's side

gup·py \'gəp-ē\ *n, pl* **guppies** [after R.J.L. *Guppy* †1916 Trinidadian naturalist] : a tiny brightly colored tropical fish

gur·gle \'gər-gəl\ *vb* **gur·gled; gur·gling** \-g(ə-)liŋ\ : to make a sound like that of a flowing and gently splashing liquid — **gurgle** *n*

Gur·kha \'gur-kə, 'gər-\ *n* : a soldier from Nepal in the British or Indian army

gur·ney \'gər-nē\ *n, pl* **gurneys** : a wheeled cot or stretcher

gu·ru \'gur-ü, gə-'rü\ *n, pl* **gurus** [Hindi] **1** : a personal religious and spiritual teacher in Hinduism **2** : a teacher in matters of fundamental concern

gush \'gəsh\ *vb* **1** : to issue or pour forth copiously or violently : SPOUT **2** : to make an effusive display of affection or enthusiasm

gush·er \'gəsh-ər\ *n* : one that gushes; *esp* : an oil well with a large natural flow

gushy \'gəsh-ē\ *adj* **gush·i·er; -est** : marked by effusive sentimentality

gus·set \'gəs-ət\ *n* [ME, piece of armor covering the joints in a suit of armor, fr. MF *gousset*] : a triangular insert (as in a seam of a sleeve) to give width or strength — **gusset** *vb*

gus·sy up \ˌgəs-ē-\ *vb* : to dress up

¹gust \'gəst\ *n* **1** : a sudden brief rush of wind **2** : a sudden outburst : SURGE — **gusty** *adj*

²gust *vb* : to blow in gusts

gus·ta·to·ry \'gəs-tə-ˌtōr-ē\ *adj* : of, relating to, or being the sense or sensation of taste

gus•to \\'gəs-tō\ *n, pl* **gustoes** : RELISH, ZEST

¹gut \\'gət\ *n* **1** *pl* : BOWELS, ENTRAILS **2** : the alimentary canal or a part of it (as the intestine); *also* : BELLY, ABDOMEN **3** *pl* : the inner essential parts **4** *pl* : COURAGE, STAMINA

²gut *vb* **gut•ted; gut•ting 1** : EVISCERATE **2** : to destroy the inside of

gutsy \\'gət-sē\ *adj* **guts•i•er; -est** : aggressively tough : COURAGEOUS

gut•ter \\'gət-ər\ *n* : a channel or low area for carrying off rainwater

gut•ter•snipe \-ˌsnīp\ *n* : a street urchin

gut•tur•al \\'gət-ə-rəl\ *adj* **1** : sounded in the throat **2** : being or marked by an utterance that is strange, unpleasant, or disagreeable — **guttural** *n*

gut•ty \\'gət-ē\ *adj* **gut•ti•er; -est 1** : GUTSY **2** : having a vigorous challenging quality

¹guy \\'gī\ *n* : a rope, chain, or rod attached to something as a brace or guide

²guy *vb* : to steady or reinforce with a guy

³guy *n* : MAN, FELLOW

⁴guy *vb* : to make fun of : RIDICULE

Guy•a•nese \ˌgī-ə-'nēz\ *n, pl* **Guyanese** : a native or inhabitant of Guyana — **Guyanese** *adj*

guz•zle \\'gəz-əl\ *vb* **guz•zled; guz•zling** \-(ə-)liŋ\ : to drink greedily

gym \\'jim\ *n* : GYMNASIUM

gym•kha•na \jim-'kän-ə\ *n* : a meet featuring sports contests; *esp* : a contest of automobile-driving skill

gym•na•si•um *for 1* jim-'nā-zē-əm, -zhəm, *for 2* gim-'nä-zē-əm\ *n, pl* **-na•si•ums** *or* **-na•sia** \-'nā-zē-ə, -'nā-zhə; -'nä-zē-ə\ [L, exercise ground, school, fr. Gk *gymnasion,* fr. *gymnazein* to exercise naked, fr. *gymnos* naked] **1** : a room or building for indoor sports activities **2** : a German secondary school that prepares students for the university

gym•nas•tics \jim-'nas-tiks\ *n* : physical

exercises performed in or adapted to performance in a gymnasium — **gym•nast** \\'jim-ˌnast\ *n* — **gym•nas•tic** *adj*

gym•no•sperm \\'jim-nə-ˌspərm\ *n* : any of a class or subdivision of woody vascular seed plants (as conifers) that produce naked seeds not enclosed in an ovary

gyn *or* **gynecol** *abbr* gynecology

gy•ne•col•o•gy \ˌgīn-ə-'käl-ə-jē, ˌjin-\ *n* : a branch of medicine dealing with the diseases and hygiene of women — **gy•ne•co•log•ic** \ˌgīn-i-kə-'läj-ik, ˌjin-\ *or* **gy•ne•co•log•i•cal** \-i-kəl\ *adj* — **gy•ne•col•o•gist** \ˌgīn-ə-'käl-ə-jəst, ˌjin-\ *n*

gyp \\'jip\ *n* **1** : CHEAT, SWINDLER **2** : FRAUD, SWINDLE — **gyp** *vb*

gyp•sum \\'jip-səm\ *n* : a calcium-containing mineral used in making plaster of paris

Gyp•sy \\'jip-sē\ *n, pl* **Gypsies** [by shortening & altcr. fr. *Egyptian*] : one of a dark Caucasian race coming orig. from India and living chiefly in Europe and the U.S.; *also* : the language of the Gypsies

gypsy moth *n* : an Old World moth that was introduced into the U.S. where its caterpillar is a destructive defoliator of many trees

gy•rate \\'jī-ˌrāt\ *vb* **gy•rat•ed; gy•rat•ing 1** : to revolve around a point or axis **2** : to oscillate with or as if with a circular or spiral motion — **gy•ra•tion** \jī-'rā-shən\ *n*

gyr•fal•con \\'jər-ˌfal-kən, -ˌfȯ(l)-\ *n* : an arctic falcon that is the largest of all falcons and occurs in several forms

gy•ro \\'jī-rō\ *n, pl* **gyros 1** : GYROSCOPE **2** : GYROCOMPASS

gy•ro•com•pass \-ˌkəm-pəs, -ˌkäm-\ *n* : a compass in which the axis of a spinning gyroscope points to the north

gy•ro•scope \-ˌskōp\ *n* : a wheel or disk mounted to spin rapidly about an axis that is free to turn in various directions

Gy Sgt *abbr* gunnery sergeant

gyve \\'jīv, 'gīv\ *n* : FETTER — **gyve** *vb*

H

¹**h** \ˈāch\ *n, pl* **h's** *or* **hs** \ˈā-chəz\ *often cap* : the 8th letter of the English alphabet

²**h** *abbr, often cap* **1** hard; hardness **2** heroin **3** hit **4** husband

H *symbol* hydrogen

ha *abbr* hectare

Hab *abbr* Habacuc; Habakkuk

Ha·ba·cuc \ˈhab-ə-ˌkək, hə-ˈbak-ək\ *n* — see BIBLE table

Ha·bak·kuk \ˈhab-ə-ˌkək, hə-ˈbak-ək\ *n* — see BIBLE table

ha·ba·ne·ra \ˌ(h)äb-ə-ˈner-ə\ *n* [Sp *(danza) habanera*, lit., dance of Havana] : a Cuban dance in slow time; *also* : the music for this dance

ha·be·as cor·pus \ˈhā-bē-əs-ˈkȯr-pəs\ *n* [ME, fr. ML, lit., you should have the body (the opening words of the writ)] : a writ issued to bring a party before a court

hab·er·dash·er \ˈhab-ə(r)-ˌdash-ər\ *n* : a dealer in men's clothing and accessories

hab·er·dash·ery \-ˌdash-(ə-)rē\ *n, pl* **-er·ies 1** : goods sold by a haberdasher **2** : a haberdasher's shop

ha·bil·i·ment \hə-ˈbil-ə-mənt\ *n* **1** *pl* : TRAPPINGS, EQUIPMENT **2** : DRESS; *esp* : the dress characteristic of an occupation or occasion — usu. used in pl.

hab·it \ˈhab-ət\ *n* **1** : DRESS, GARB **2** : BEARING, CONDUCT **3** : PHYSIQUE **4** : mental makeup **5** : a usual manner of behavior : CUSTOM **6** : a behavior pattern acquired by frequent repetition **7** : ADDICTION **8** : mode of growth or occurrence

hab·it·able \ˈhab-ət-ə-bəl\ *adj* : capable of being lived in — **hab·it·abil·i·ty** \ˌhab-ət-ə-ˈbil-ət-ē\ *n*

ha·bi·tant \ˈhab-ət-ənt\ *n* : INHABITANT, RESIDENT

hab·i·tat \ˈhab-ə-ˌtat\ *n* [L, it inhabits] : the place or kind of place where a plant or animal naturally occurs

hab·i·ta·tion \ˌhab-ə-ˈtā-shən\ *n* **1** : OCCUPANCY **2** : a dwelling place : RESIDENCE **3** : SETTLEMENT

hab·it–form·ing \ˈhab-ət-ˌfȯr-miŋ\ *adj* : inducing the formation of an addiction

ha·bit·u·al \hə-ˈbich-(ə-w)əl\ *adj* **1** : CUSTOMARY **2** : doing, practicing, or acting by force of habit **3** : inherent in an individual — **ha·bit·u·al·ly** \-ē\ *adv* — **ha·bit·u·al·ness** *n*

ha·bit·u·ate \hə-ˈbich-ə-ˌwāt\ *vb* **-at·ed; -at·ing 1** : ACCUSTOM **2** : to cause habituation

ha·bit·u·a·tion \hə-ˌbich-ə-ˈwā-shən\ *n* **1** : the process of making habitual **2** : psychological dependence on a drug after a period of use

ha·bi·tué \hə-ˈbich-ə-ˌwā\ *n* [F] : one who frequents a place or class of places

ha·ci·en·da \ˌ(h)äs-ē-ˌen-də\ *n* **1** : a large estate in a Spanish-speaking country **2** : the main building of a farm or ranch

¹**hack** \ˈhak\ *vb* **1** : to cut with repeated irregular blows : CHOP **2** : to cough in a short dry manner **3** : to manage successfully — **hack·er** *n*

²**hack** *n* **1** : an implement for hacking **2** : a short dry cough **3** : a hacking blow

³**hack** *n* **1** : a horse hired or used for varied work **2** : a horse worn out in service **3** : a light easy often 3-gaited saddle horse **4** : HACKNEY 2, TAXICAB **5** : a writer who works mainly for hire **6** : one who serves a cause merely for reward — **hack** *adj*

⁴**hack** *vb* : to operate a taxicab

hack·ie \ˈhak-ē\ *n* : a taxicab driver

hack·le \ˈhak-əl\ *n* **1** : one of the long feathers on the neck or back of a bird **2** *pl* : hairs (as on a dog's neck) that can be erected **3** *pl* : TEMPER, DANDER

hack·man \ˈhak-mən\ *n* : HACKIE

¹**hack·ney** \ˈhak-nē\ *n, pl* **hackneys 1** : a horse for riding or driving **2** : a carriage or automobile kept for hire

²**hackney** *vb* : to make trite

hack·neyed \ˈhak-nēd\ *adj* : lacking in freshness or originality

hack·saw \ˈhak-ˌsȯ\ *n* : a fine-tooth saw in a frame for cutting metal

hack·work \-ˌwərk\ *n* : work done on order usu. according to a formula

had past and past part of HAVE

had·dock \ˈhad-ək\ *n, pl* **haddock** *also*

haddocks : an Atlantic food fish usu. smaller than the related cod

Ha·des \'hād-(ˌ)ēz\ *n* **1** : the abode of the dead in Greek mythology **2** *often not cap* : HELL

haf·ni·um \'haf-nē-əm\ *n* : a gray metallic chemical element

haft \'haft\ *n* : the handle of a weapon or tool

hag \'hag\ *n* **1** : an ugly, slatternly, or evil-looking old woman **2** : WITCH 2

Hag *abbr* Haggai

Hag·gai \'hag-ē-ˌī, 'hag-ˌī\ *n* — see BIBLE table

hag·gard \'hag-ərd\ *adj* : having a worn or emaciated appearance **syn** careworn, wasted, drawn — **hag·gard·ly** *adv*

hag·gis \'hag-əs\ *n* : a traditionally Scottish dish made of the heart, liver, and lungs of a sheep or a calf minced with suet, onions, oatmeal, and seasonings

hag·gle \'hag-əl\ *vb* **hag·gled; hag·gling** \-(ə-)liŋ\ : to argue in bargaining — **hag·gler** \-(ə-)lər\ *n*

ha·gi·og·ra·phy \ˌhag-ē-'äg-rə-fē, ˌhā-jē-\ *n* **1** : biography of saints or venerated persons **2** : idealizing or idolizing biography — **ha·gi·og·ra·pher** \-fər\ *n*

hai·ku \'hī-(ˌ)kü\ *n, pl* **haiku** : an unrhymed Japanese verse form of three lines containing usu. 5, 7, and 5 syllables respectively; *also* : a poem in this form

¹hail \'hāl\ *n* **1** : precipitation in the form of small lumps of ice **2** : something that gives the effect of falling hail

²hail *vb* **1** : to precipitate hail **2** : to hurl forcibly

³hail *interj* [ME, fr. ON *heill*, fr. *heill* healthy] — used to express acclamation

⁴hail *vb* **1** : SALUTE, GREET **2** : SUMMON

⁵hail *n* **1** : an expression of greeting, approval, or praise **2** : hearing distance

Hail Mary *n* : a salutation and prayer to the Virgin Mary

hail·stone \'hāl-ˌstōn\ *n* : a pellet of hail

hail·storm \-ˌstorm\ *n* : a storm accompanied by hail

hair \'haər\ *n* : a threadlike outgrowth esp. of the skin of a mammal; *also* : a covering (as of the head) consisting of

such hairs — **haired** \'haərd\ *adj* — **hair·less** *adj*

hair·breadth \-ˌbredth\ *or* **hairs·breadth** \'haərz-\ *n* : a very small distance or margin

hair·brush \-ˌbrəsh\ *n* : a brush for the hair

hair·cloth \-ˌkloth\ *n* : a stiff wiry fabric used esp. for upholstery

hair·cut \-ˌkət\ *n* : the act, process, or style of cutting and shaping the hair

hair·do \-ˌdü\ *n, pl* **hairdos** : a way of dressing the hair

hair·dress·er \-ˌdres-ər\ *n* : one who dresses or cuts hair — **hair·dress·ing** *n*

hair·line \-'līn\ *n* **1** : a very slender line **2** : the outline of the hair on the head

hair·piece \-ˌpēs\ *n* **1** : TOUPEE **2** : supplementary hair (as a switch) used in some women's hairdos

hair·pin \-ˌpin\ *n* **1** : a U-shaped pin to hold the hair in place **2** : a sharp U-shaped turn in a road — **hairpin** *adj*

hair–rais·ing \'haər-ˌrā-ziŋ\ *adj* : causing terror or astonishment

hair·split·ter \-ˌsplit-ər\ *n* : a person who makes unnecessarily fine distinctions in reasoning or argument — **hair·split·ting** \-ˌsplit-iŋ\ *adj or n*

hair·style \-ˌstīl\ *n* : a way of wearing the hair

hair·styl·ist \-ˌstī-ləst\ *n* : HAIRDRESSER —**hair·styl·ing** \-ˌstī-liŋ\ *n*

hair–trigger *adj* : immediately responsive to the slightest stimulus

hairy \'ha(ə)r-ē\ *adj* **hair·i·er; -est** : covered with or as if with hair — **hair·i·ness** \'har-ē-nəs\ *n*

hairy woodpecker *n* : a common No. American woodpecker with a white back that is larger than the similarly marked downy woodpecker

hajj \'haj\ *n* : the Islamic religious pilgrimage to Mecca

hajji \'haj-ē\ *n* : one who has made a pilgrimage to Mecca — often used as a title

hake \'hāk\ *n* : a marine food fish related to the cod

ha·la·la \hə-'läl-ə\ *n, pl* **halala** *or* **halalas** — see *riyal* at MONEY table

hal·berd \'hal-bərd, 'hol-\ *or* **hal·bert** \-bərt\ *n* : a weapon esp. of the 15th and 16th centuries consisting of a battle-ax and pike on a long handle

hal·cy·on \'hal-sē-ən\ *adj* [Gk *halkyōn*,

a mythical bird believed to nest at sea and to calm the waves] : CALM, PEACEFUL

¹hale \'hāl\ *adj* : free from defect, disease, or infirmity **syn** healthy, sound, robust, well

²hale *vb* **haled; hal·ing 1** : HAUL, PULL **2** : to compel to go ⟨*haled* him into court⟩

ha·ler \'häl-ər\ *n, pl* **ha·le·ru** \'häl-ə-ˌrü\ — see *koruna* at MONEY table

¹half \'haf, 'haf\ *n, pl* **halves** \'havz, 'havz\ **1** : one of two equal parts into which something is divisible **2** : one of a pair

²half *adj* **1** : being one of two equal parts **2** : amounting to nearly half **3** : PARTIAL, IMPERFECT — **half** *adv*

half–and–half \ˌhaf-ən-'haf, ˌhaf-ən-'haf\ *n* : something that is half one thing and half another

half·back \'haf-ˌbak, 'haf-\ *n* **1** : a football back stationed on or near the flank **2** : a player stationed immediately behind the forward line

half–baked \-'bākt\ *adj* **1** : not thoroughly baked **2** : poorly planned; *also* : lacking common sense

half boot *n* : a boot with a top reaching above the ankle

half–breed \'haf-ˌbrēd, 'haf-\ *n* : the offspring of parents of different races — **half–breed** *adj*

half brother *n* : a brother by one parent only

half–caste \'haf-ˌkast, 'haf-\ *n* : one of mixed racial descent — **half–caste** *adj*

half–dol·lar \-'däl-ər\ *n* **1** : a coin representing one half of a dollar **2** : the sum of fifty cents

half·heart·ed \-'härt-əd\ *adj* : lacking spirit or interest — **half·heart·ed·ly** *adv* — **half·heart·ed·ness** *n*

half–life \-ˌlīf\ *n* : the time required for half of something (as atoms or a drug) to undergo a process

half–mast \-'mast\ *n* : a point some distance but not necessarily halfway down below the top of a mast or staff or the peak of a gaff ⟨flags hanging at ∼⟩

half note *n* : a musical note equal in time to ½ of a whole note

half·pen·ny \'hāp-(ə-)nē\ *n, pl* **halfpence** \'hā-pəns\ *or* **halfpennies** : a formerly used British coin representing one half of a penny

half–pint \'haf-ˌpīnt, 'haf-\ *adj* : of less than average size — **half–pint** *n*

half sister *n* : a sister by one parent only

half sole *n* : a shoe sole extending from the shank forward — **half–sole** *vb*

half–staff \'haf-'staf, 'haf-\ *n* : HALF-MAST

half step *n* : the pitch interval between any two adjacent keys on a keyboard instrument

half·time \'haf-ˌtīm, 'haf-\ *n* : an intermission between halves of a game

half–track \-ˌtrak\ *n* **1** : an endless chain-track drive system that propels a vehicle supported in front by a pair of wheels **2** : a motor vehicle propelled by half-tracks; *esp* : such a vehicle lightly armored for military use

half–truth \-ˌtrüth\ *n* : a statement that is only partially true; *esp* : one that deliberately mixes truth and falsehood

half·way \-'wā\ *adj* **1** : midway between two points **2** : PARTIAL — **halfway** *adv*

half–wit \'haf-ˌwit, 'haf-\ *n* : a foolish or imbecilic person — **half–wit·ted** \-'wit-əd\ *adj*

hal·i·but \'hal-ə-bət\ *n, pl* **halibut** *also* **halibuts** [ME *halybutte*, fr. *haly*, *holy* holy + *butte* flatfish, fr. its being eaten on holy days] : a large edible marine flatfish

ha·lite \'hal-ˌīt, 'hā-ˌlīt\ *n* : ROCK SALT

hal·i·to·sis \ˌhal-ə-'tō-səs\ *n* : a condition of having fetid breath

hall \'hol\ *n* **1** : the residence of a medieval king or noble; *also* : the house of a landed proprietor **2** : a large public building **3** : a college or university building **4** : LOBBY; *also* : CORRIDOR **5** : AUDITORIUM

hal·le·lu·jah \ˌhal-ə-'lü-yə\ *interj* [Heb *hallĕlūyāh* praise (ye) the Lord] — used to express praise, joy, or thanks

hall·mark \'hol-ˌmärk\ *n* **1** : a mark put on an article to indicate origin, purity, or genuineness **2** : a distinguishing characteristic

hal·low \'hal-ō\ *vb* **1** : CONSECRATE **2** : REVERE — **hal·lowed** \-ōd, -ə-wəd\ *adj*

Hal·low·een \ˌhal-ə-'wēn, ˌhäl-\ *n* : the evening of October 31 observed esp.

by children in merrymaking and masquerading

hal·lu·ci·nate \hə-ˈlüs-ᵊn-ˌāt\ *vb* **-nat·ed; -nat·ing** : to perceive or experience as an hallucination

hal·lu·ci·na·tion \hə-ˌlüs-ᵊn-ˈā-shən\ *n* : perception of objects or events with no existence in reality due usu. to use of drugs or to disorder of the nervous system; *also* : something so perceived **syn** delusion, illusion, mirage — **hal·lu·ci·na·to·ry** \-ᵊn-ə-ˌtōr-ē\ *adj*

hal·lu·ci·no·gen \hə-ˈlüs-ᵊn-ə-jən\ *n* : a substance that induces hallucinations — **hal·lu·ci·no·gen·ic** \-ˌlüs-ᵊn-ə-ˈjen-ik\ *adj or n*

hall·way \ˈhȯl-ˌwā\ *n* **1** : an entrance hall **2** : CORRIDOR

ha·lo \ˈhā-lo\ *n, pl* **halos** *or* **haloes** [L *halos,* fr. Gk *halōs* threshing floor, disk, halo] **1** : a circle of light appearing to surround a shining body (as the sun) **2** : the aura of glory surrounding an idealized person or thing

¹halt \ˈhȯlt\ *adj* : LAME

²halt *n* : STOP

³halt *vb* **1** : to stop marching or traveling **2** : DISCONTINUE, END

¹hal·ter \ˈhȯl-tər\ *n* **1** : a rope or strap for leading or tying an animal; *also* : HEADSTALL **2** : NOOSE **3** : a brief blouse held in place by straps around the neck and across the back

²halter *vb* **hal·tered; hal·ter·ing** \-t(ə-)riŋ\ **1** : to catch with or as if with a halter; *also* : to put a halter on (as a horse) **2** : IMPEDE, RESTRAIN

halt·ing \ˈhȯl-tiŋ\ *adj* : UNCERTAIN, FALTERING — **halt·ing·ly** *adv*

halve \ˈhav, ˈhȧv\ *vb* **halved; halv·ing** **1** : to divide into two equal parts **2** : to reduce to one half

halv·ers \ˈhav-ərz, ˈhȧv-\ *n pl* : half shares

halves pl of HALF

hal·yard \ˈhal-yərd\ *n* : a rope or tackle for hoisting and lowering something (as sails)

¹ham \ˈham\ *n* **1** : a buttock with its associated thigh **2** : a cut of meat and esp. pork from this region **3** : a showy performer **4** : an operator of an amateur radio station — **ham** *adj*

²ham *vb* **hammed; ham·ming** : to overplay a part : OVERACT

ham·burg·er \ˈham-ˌbər-gər\ *or* **ham-**

burg \-ˌbərg\ *n* [G *Hamburger* of Hamburg, West Germany] **1** : ground beef **2** : a sandwich consisting of a ground-beef patty in a round roll

ham·let \ˈham-lət\ *n* : a small village

¹ham·mer \ˈham-ər\ *n* **1** : a hand tool used for pounding; *also* : something resembling a hammer in form or function **2** : the part of a gun whose striking action causes explosion of the charge **3** : a metal sphere with a flexible wire handle that is hurled for distance in a track-and-field event (**hammer throw**) **4** : ACCELERATOR 2

²hammer *vb* **ham·mered; ham·mer·ing** \ˈham-(ə-)riŋ\ **1** : to beat, drive, or shape with repeated blows of a hammer : POUND **2** : to produce or bring about as if by repeated blows

ham·mer·head \ˈham-ər-ˌhed\ *n* **1** : the striking part of a hammer **2** : any of various medium-sized sharks with eyes at the ends of lateral extensions of the flattened head

ham·mer·lock \-ˌläk\ *n* : a wrestling hold in which an opponent's arm is held bent behind his back

ham·mer·toe \-ˈtō\ *n* : a deformed toe with the 2d and 3d joints permanently flexed

¹ham·mock \ˈham-ək\ *n* [Sp *hamaca,* of AmerInd origin] : a swinging couch hung by cords at each end

²hammock *n* : a fertile elevated area of the southern U.S. and esp. Florida with hardwood vegetation and soil rich in humus

¹ham·per \ˈham-pər\ *vb* **ham·pered; ham·per·ing** \-p(ə-)riŋ\ : IMPEDE **syn** trammel, clog, fetter, shackle

²hamper *n* : a large basket

ham·ster \ˈham-stər\ *n* [G, fr. OHG *hamustro,* of Slavic origin] : a stocky short-tailed Old World rodent with large cheek pouches

¹ham·string \ˈham-ˌstriŋ\ *vb* **-strung** \-ˌstrəŋ\; **-string·ing** \-ˌstriŋ-iŋ\ **1** : to cripple by cutting the leg tendons **2** : to make ineffective or powerless

²hamstring *n* : any of several muscles at the back of the thigh or tendons at the back of the knee

¹hand \ˈhand\ *n* **1** : the end of a front limb when modified (as in humans) for grasping **2** : personal possession — usu. used in pl; *also* : CONTROL **3** : SIDE

5 **4** : a pledge esp. of betrothal **5** : HANDWRITING **6** : SKILL, ABILITY; *also* : a significant part **7** : ASSISTANCE; *also* : PARTICIPATION **8** : an outburst of applause **9** : a single round in a card game; *also* : the cards held by a player after a deal **10** : WORKER, EMPLOYEE; *also* : a member of a ship's crew — **hand·less** \'han-(d)ləs\ *adj* — **at hand** : near in time or place

²**hand** *vb* **1** : to lead, guide, or assist with the hand **2** : to give, pass, or transmit with the hand

hand·bag \'han(d)-ˌbag\ *n* : a bag for carrying small personal articles and money

hand·ball \-ˌbȯl\ *n* : a game played by striking a small rubber ball against a wall with the hand

hand·bar·row \-ˌbar-ō\ *n* : a flat rectangular frame with handles at both ends that is carried by two persons

hand·bill \-ˌbil\ *n* : a small printed sheet for distribution by hand

hand·book \-ˌbu̇k\ *n* : a concise reference book : MANUAL

hand·car \'han(d)-ˌkär\ *n* : a small 4-wheeled railroad car propelled by hand or by a small motor

hand·clasp \-ˌklasp\ *n* : HANDSHAKE

hand·craft \-ˌkraft\ *vb* : to fashion by manual skill

¹**hand·cuff** \-ˌkəf\ *n* : a metal fastening that can be locked around a wrist and is usu. connected with another such fastening

²**handcuff** *vb* : MANACLE

hand·ful \ˌhan(d)-ˌfu̇l\ *n, pl* **hand·fuls** \-ˌfu̇lz\ *also* **hands·ful** \'han(d)z-ˌfu̇l\ **1** : as much or as many as the hand will grasp **2** : a small number ⟨a ∼ of people⟩ **3** : as much as one can manage

hand·gun \-ˌgən\ *n* : a firearm held and fired with one hand

¹**hand·i·cap** \'han-di-ˌkap\ *n* [obs. E *handicap* (a game in which forfeits were held in a cap), fr. *hand in cap*] **1** : a contest in which an artificial advantage is given or disadvantage imposed on a contestant to equalize chances of winning; *also* : the advantage given or disadvantage imposed **2** : a disadvantage that makes achievement difficult

²**handicap** *vb* **-capped; -cap·ping 1** : to give a handicap to **2** : to put at a disadvantage

hand·i·capped *adj* : having a physical or mental disability that limits activity

hand·i·cap·per \-ˌkap-ər\ *n* : one who predicts the winners in a horse race usu. for a publication

hand·i·craft \'han-di-ˌkraft\ *n* **1** : manual skill **2** : an occupation requiring manual skill **3** : the articles fashioned by those engaged in handicraft — **hand·i·craft·er** *n* — **hand·i·crafts·man** \-ˌkrafts-mən\ *n*

hand in glove *or* **hand and glove** *adv* : in an extremely close relationship

hand·i·work \'han-di-ˌwərk\ *n* : work done personally

hand·ker·chief \'haŋ-kər-chəf, -ˌchēf\ *n, pl* **-chiefs** \-chəfs, -ˌchēfs\ *also* **-chieves** \-ˌchēvz\ : a small piece of cloth used for various personal purposes (as the wiping of the face)

¹**han·dle** \'han-dᵊl\ *n* : a part (as of a tool) designed to be grasped by the hand — **han·dled** \-dᵊld\ *adj* — **off the handle** : into a state of sudden and violent anger

²**handle** *vb* **han·dled; han·dling** \'han-dliŋ\ **1** : to touch, hold, or manage with the hands **2** : to have responsibility for **3** : to deal or trade in **4** : to behave in a certain way when managed or directed ⟨a car that ∼s well⟩ — **han·dler** \'han-dlər\ *n*

han·dle·bar \-dᵊl-ˌbär\ *n* : a straight or bent bar with a handle at each end (as for steering a bicycle) — usu. used in pl.

hand·made \'han(d)-'mād\ *adj* : made by hand or a hand process

hand·maid·en \-ˌmād-ᵊn\ *or* **hand·maid** \-ˌmād\ *n* : a female attendant

hand–me–down \-me-ˌdau̇n\ *adj* : used by one person after being used by another ⟨∼ clothes⟩ — **hand–me–down** *n*

hand·out \'hand-ˌau̇t\ *n* **1** : a portion (as of food) given to a beggar **2** : a piece of printed information for free distribution; *also* : a prepared statement released to the press

hand·pick \'han(d)-'pik\ *vb* : to select personally ⟨a ∼ed candidate⟩

hand·rail \'hand-ˌrāl\ *n* : a narrow rail for grasping as a support

hand·saw \'han(d)-ˌsȯ\ *n* : a saw usu. operated with one hand

hands down \'han(d)z-'daun\ *adv* **1** : with little effort **2** : without question

hand·sel \'han-səl\ *n* **1** : a gift made as a token of good luck **2** : a first installment : earnest money

hand·set \'han(d)-ˌset\ *n* : a combined telephone transmitter and receiver mounted on a handle

hand·shake \-ˌshāk\ *n* : a clasping of right hands by two people

hand·some \'han-səm\ *adj* [ME *handsom* easy to manipulate] **1** : SIZABLE, AMPLE **2** : GENEROUS, LIBERAL **3** : pleasing and usu. impressive in appearance **syn** beautiful, lovely, pretty, comely, fair — **hand·some·ly** *adv* — **hand·some·ness** *n*

hands–on \'han(d)-'zȯn, -'zän\ *adj* : being or providing direct practical experience in the operation of something

hand·spring \-ˌspriŋ\ *n* : an acrobatic feat in which the body turns forward or backward in a full circle from a standing position and lands first on the hands and then on the feet

hand·stand \-ˌstand\ *n* : an act of supporting the body on the hands with the trunk and legs balanced in the air

hand–to–hand \ˌhan-tə-ˌhand\ *adj* : being at very close quarters — **hand to hand** *adv*

hand–to–mouth \-ˌmauth\ *adj* : having or providing nothing to spare

hand·wo·ven \'hand-ˌwō-vən\ *adj* : produced on a hand-operated loom

hand·writ·ing \-ˌrīt-iŋ\ *n* : writing done by hand; *also* : the form of writing peculiar to a person — **hand·writ·ten** \-ˌrit-ᵊn\ *adj*

handy \'han-dē\ *adj* **hand·i·er; -est 1** : conveniently near **2** : easily used **3** : DEXTEROUS — **hand·i·ly** \'han-də-lē\ *adv* — **hand·i·ness** \-dē-nəs\ *n*

handy·man \-ˌman\ *n* **1** : one who does odd jobs **2** : one competent in a variety of small skills or repair work

¹**hang** \'haŋ\ *vb* **hung** \'həŋ\ *also* **hanged** \'haŋd\; **hang·ing** \'haŋ-iŋ\ **1** : to fasten or remain fastened to an elevated point without support from below; *also* : to fasten or be fastened so as to allow free motion on the point of suspension ⟨∼ a door⟩ **2** : to put or come to death by suspension (as from a gallows) **3** : DROOP ⟨*hung* his head in shame⟩ **4** : to fasten to a wall ⟨∼ wall-

paper⟩ **5** : to prevent (a jury) from coming to a decision **6** : to display (pictures) in a gallery **7** : to remain stationary in the air **8** : to be imminent **9** : DEPEND **10** : to take hold for support **11** : to be burdensome **12** : to undergo delay **13** : to incline downward; *also* : to fit or fall from the figure in easy lines **14** : to be raptly attentive **15** : LINGER, LOITER — **hang·er** *n*

²**hang** *n* **1** : the manner in which a thing hangs **2** : peculiar and significant meaning **3** : KNACK

han·gar \'haŋ-ər\ *n* [F] : a covered and usu. enclosed area for housing and repairing aircraft

hang·dog \'haŋ-ˌdȯg\ *adj* **1** : ASHAMED, GUILTY **2** : ABJECT, COWED

hang·er–on \'haŋ-ər-'ȯn, -'än\ *n, pl* **hangers–on** : one who hangs around a person or place esp. for personal gain

hang in *vb* : to persist tenaciously

hang·ing \'haŋ-iŋ\ *n* **1** : an execution by strangling or snapping the neck by a suspended noose **2** : something hung — **hanging** *adj*

hang·man \-mən\ *n* : a public executioner

hang·nail \-ˌnāl\ *n* : a bit of skin hanging loose at the side or base of a fingernail

hang on *vb* **1** : HANG IN **2** : to keep a telephone connection open

hang·out \'haŋ-ˌaut\ *n* : a favorite or usual place of resort

hang·over \-ˌō-vər\ *n* **1** : something that remains from what is past **2** : disagreeable physical effects following heavy drinking

hang–up \'haŋ-ˌəp\ *n* : a source of mental or emotional difficulty

hang up \(')haŋ-'əp\ *vb* **1** : to place on a hook or hanger **2** : to end a telephone conversation by replacing the receiver on the cradle **3** : to keep delayed or suspended

hank \'haŋk\ *n* : COIL, LOOP

han·ker \'haŋ-kər\ *vb* **han·kered; han·ker·ing** \-k(ə-)riŋ\ : to desire strongly or persistently : LONG — **han·ker·ing** *n*

han·kie *or* **han·ky** \'haŋ-kē\ *n, pl* **hankies** : HANDKERCHIEF

han·ky–pan·ky \ˌhaŋ-kē-'paŋ-kē\ *n* : questionable or underhanded activity

han·sel var of HANDSEL

han·som \'han-səm\ *n* : a 2-wheeled covered carriage with the driver's seat elevated at the rear

Ha·nuk·kah \'kän-ə-kə, 'hän-\ *n* [Heb *ḥănukkāh* dedication] : an 8-day Jewish holiday commemorating the rededication of the Temple of Jerusalem after its defilement by Antiochus of Syria

hap \'hap\ *n* 1 : HAPPENING 2 : CHANCE, FORTUNE

¹**hap·haz·ard** \hap-'haz-ərd\ *n* : CHANCE

²**haphazard** *adj* : marked by lack of plan or order : AIMLESS — **hap·haz·ard·ly** *adv* — **hap·haz·ard·ness** *n*

hap·less \'hap-ləs\ *adj* : UNFORTUNATE — **hap·less·ly** *adv* — **hap·less·ness** *n*

hap·loid \'hap-ˌlȯid\ *adj* : having the number of chromosomes characteristic of gametic cells — **haploid** *n*

hap·ly \'hap-lē\ *adv* : by chance

hap·pen \'hap-ən\ *vb* **hap·pened; hap·pen·ing** \'hap-(ə-)niŋ\ 1 : to occur by chance 2 : to take place 3 : CHANCE 2

hap·pen·ing \'hap-(ə-)niŋ\ *n* 1 : OCCURRENCE 2 : an event that is especially interesting, entertaining, or important

hap·pi·ly \'hap-ə-lē\ *adv* 1 : LUCKILY 2 : in a happy manner or state ⟨lived ∼ ever after⟩ 3 : APTLY, SUCCESSFULLY

hap·pi·ness \'hap-i-nəs\ *n* 1 : a state of well-being and contentment; *also* : a pleasurable satisfaction 2 : APTNESS

hap·py \'hap-ē\ *adj* **hap·pi·er; -est** 1 : FORTUNATE 2 : APT, FELICITOUS 3 : enjoying well-being and contentment 4 : PLEASANT; *also* : PLEASED, GRATIFIED **syn** glad, cheerful, lighthearted, joyful, joyous

hap·py–go–lucky \ˌhap-ē-gō-'lək-ē\ *adj* : CAREFREE

happy hour *n* : a period of time when the price of drinks at a bar is reduced

hara–kiri \ˌhar-ə-'kir-ē, ˌher-ē-'ker-ē\ *n* [Jp *harakiri*, fr. *hara* belly + *kiri* cutting] : suicide by disembowelment

ha·rangue \hə-'raŋ\ *n* 1 : a bombastic ranting speech 2 : LECTURE — **harangue** *vb* — **ha·rangu·er** \-'raŋ-ər\ *n*

ha·rass \hə-'ras, 'har-əs\ *vb* [F *harasser*, fr. MF, fr. *harer* to set a dog on, fr. OF *hare*, interj. used to incite dogs] 1 : to worry and impede by repeated raids 2 : EXHAUST, FATIGUE 3 : to annoy continually **syn** harry, plague, pester, tease, bedevil — **ha·rass·ment** *n*

har·bin·ger \'här-bən-jər\ *n* : one that announces or foreshadows what is coming : PRECURSOR; *also* : PORTENT

¹**har·bor** \'här-bər\ *n* 1 : a place of security and comfort 2 : a part of a body of water protected and deep enough to furnish anchorage : PORT

²**harbor** *vb* **har·bored; har·bor·ing** \-b(ə-)riŋ\ 1 : to give or take refuge : SHELTER 2 : to be the home or habitat of; *also* : LIVE 3 : to hold a thought or feeling ⟨∼ a grudge⟩

har·bor·age \-bə-rij\ *n* : HARBOR

har·bour *chiefly Brit* var of HARBOR

hard \'härd\ *adj* 1 : not easily penetrated 2 : high in alcoholic content; *also* : containing salts that prevent lathering with soap ⟨∼ water⟩ 3 : stable in value ⟨∼ currency⟩ 4 : physically fit; *also* : free from flaw 5 : FIRM, DEFINITE ⟨∼ agreement⟩; *also* : based on clear fact ⟨∼ evidence⟩ 6 : CLOSE, SEARCHING ⟨∼ look⟩ 7 : REALISTIC ⟨good ∼ sense⟩ 8 : OBDURATE, UNFEELING ⟨∼ heart⟩ 9 : difficult to bear ⟨∼ times⟩; *also* : HARSH, SEVERE 10 : RESENTFUL ⟨∼ feelings⟩ 11 : STRICT, UNRELENTING ⟨∼ bargain⟩ 12 : INCLEMENT ⟨∼ winter⟩ 13 : intense in force or manner ⟨∼ blow⟩ 14 : ARDUOUS, STRENUOUS ⟨∼ work⟩ 15 : sounding as in *arcing* and *geese* respectively — used of *c* and *g* 16 : TROUBLESOME ⟨∼ problem⟩ 17 : having difficulty in doing something ⟨∼ of hearing⟩ 18 : addictive and gravely detrimental to health ⟨∼ drugs⟩ — **hard** *adv* — **hard·ness** *n*

hard–and–fast \ˌhärd-ᵊn-'fast\ *adj* : rigidly binding : STRICT ⟨a ∼ rule⟩

hard·back \'härd-ˌbak\ *n* : a book bound in hard covers

hard·ball \-ˌbȯl\ *n* 1 : BASEBALL 2 : forceful uncompromising methods

hard–bit·ten \-'bit-ᵊn\ *adj* : SEASONED, TOUGH ⟨∼ campaigners⟩

hard·board \-ˌbōrd\ *n* : a very dense fiberboard

hard–boiled \-'bȯild\ *adj* 1 : boiled until both white and yolk have solidified 2 : lacking sentiment : CALLOUS; *also* : HARDHEADED

hard·bound \-ˌbau̇nd\ *adj* : HARDCOVER

hard copy *n* : copy produced on paper in normal-size type

hard–core \'härd-'kōr\ *adj* **1** : extremely resistant to solution or improvement **2** : being the most determined or dedicated members of a specified group **3** : containing explicit depictions of sex acts — **hard core** *n*

hard•cov•er \-'kəv-ər\ *adj* : having rigid boards on the sides covered in cloth or paper ⟨~ books⟩

hard•en \'härd-ᵊn\ *vb* **hard•ened; hard•en•ing** \'härd-(ᵊ-)niŋ\ **1** : to make or become hard or harder **2** : to confirm or become confirmed in disposition or action — **hard•en•er** *n*

hard•hack \'härd-ˌhak\ *n* : an American spirea with rusty hairy leaves and dense clusters of pink or white flowers

hard hat *n* **1** : a protective hat worn esp. by construction workers **2** : a construction worker

hard•head•ed \'härd-'hed-əd\ *adj* **1** : STUBBORN, WILLFUL **2** : SOBER, REALISTIC — **hard•head•ed•ly** *adv* — **hard•head•ed•ness** *n*

hard–heart•ed \-'härt-əd\ *adj* : PITILESS, CRUEL — **hard–heart•ed•ly** *adv* — **hard–heart•ed•ness** *n*

har•di•hood \'härd-ē-ˌhùd\ *n* **1** : resolute courage and fortitude **2** : VIGOR, ROBUSTNESS

hard–line \'härd-'līn\ *adj* : advocating or involving a persistently firm course of action — **hard–lin•er** \-'lī-nər\ *n*

hard•ly \'härd-lē\ *adv* **1** : with force **2** : SEVERELY **3** : with difficulty **4** : only just : BARELY **5** : certainly not

hard palate *n* : the bony anterior part of the palate forming the roof of the mouth

hard•pan \'härd-ˌpan\ *n* : a compact often clayey layer in soil that is impenetrable by roots

hard–pressed \-'prest\ *adj* : HARD PUT; *esp* : being under financial strain

hard put *adj* **1** : barely able **2** : faced with difficulty or perplexity

hard rock *n* : rock music marked by a heavy beat, high amplification, and usu. frenzied performances

hard–shell \'härd-ˌshel\ *adj* : CONFIRMED, UNCOMPROMISING ⟨a ~ conservative⟩

hard•ship \-ˌship\ *n* **1** : SUFFERING, PRI-VATION **2** : something that causes suffering or privation

hard•stand \-ˌstand\ *n* : a hard-surfaced area for parking an airplane

hard–sur•face \-'sər-fəs\ *vb* : to provide (as a road) with a paved surface

hard•tack \-ˌtak\ *n* : a hard biscuit made of flour and water without salt

hard•top \-ˌtäp\ *n* : an automobile resembling a convertible but having a rigid top

hard•ware \-ˌwaər\ *n* **1** : ware (as cutlery or tools) made of metal **2** : the physical components (as electronic devices) of a vehicle (as a spacecraft) or an apparatus (as a computer)

¹hard•wood \'härd-ˌwùd\ *n* : the wood of a broad-leaved usu. deciduous tree as distinguished from that of a conifer; *also* : such a tree

²hardwood *adj* **1** : having or made of hardwood ⟨~ floors⟩ **2** : consisting of mature woody tissue ⟨~ cuttings⟩

hard•work•ing \-'wər-kiŋ\ *adj* : INDUSTRIOUS

har•dy \'härd-ē\ *adj* **har•di•er; -est 1** : BOLD, BRAVE **2** : AUDACIOUS, BRAZEN **3** : ROBUST; *also* : able to withstand adverse conditions (as of weather) ⟨~ shrubs⟩ — **har•di•ly** \'härd-ə-lē\ *adv* — **har•di•ness** \-ē-nəs\ *n*

hare \'haər\ *n, pl* **hare** *or* **hares** : a swift timid long-eared mammal distinguished from the related rabbit by being open-eyed and furry at birth

hare•bell \-ˌbel\ *n* : a slender herb with blue bell-shaped flowers

hare•brained \-'brānd\ *adj* : FLIGHTY, FOOLISH

hare•lip \-'lip\ *n* : a deformity in which the upper lip is vertically split — **harelipped** \-'lipt\ *adj*

ha•rem \'har-əm\ *n* [Ar ḥarīm, lit., something forbidden & ḥaram, lit., sanctuary] **1** : a house or part of a house allotted to women in a Muslim household **2** : the women and servants occupying a harem **3** : a group of females associated with one male

hark \'härk\ *vb* : LISTEN

harken *var of* HEARKEN

har•le•quin \'här-li-k(w)ən\ *n* **1** *cap* : a character (as in comedy) with a shaved head, masked face, variegated tights, and wooden sword **2** : CLOWN 2

har•lot \'här-lət\ *n* : PROSTITUTE

¹**harm** \'härm\ *n* **1** : physical or mental damage : INJURY **2** : MISCHIEF, HURT — **harm・ful** \-fəl\ *adj* — **harm・ful・ly** \-ē\ *adv* — **harm・ful・ness** *n* — **harm・less** *adj* — **harm・less・ly** *adv* — **harm・less・ness** *n*

²**harm** *vb* : to cause harm to : INJURE

¹**har・mon・ic** \här-'män-ik\ *adj* **1** : of or relating to musical harmony or harmonics **2** : pleasing to the ear — **har・mon・i・cal・ly** \-i-k(ə-)lē\ *adv*

²**harmonic** *n* : a musical overtone

har・mon・i・ca \här-'män-i-kə\ *n* : a small wind instrument played by breathing through metallic reeds

har・mo・ni・ous \här-'mō-nē-əs\ *adj* **1** : musically concordant **2** : CONGRUOUS **3** : marked by accord in sentiment or action — **har・mo・ni・ous・ly** *adv* — **har・mo・ni・ous・ness** *n*

har・mo・ni・um \här-'mō-nē-əm\ *n* : a keyboard wind instrument in which the wind acts on a set of metal reeds

har・mo・nize \'här-mə-nīz\ *vb* **-nized; -niz・ing 1** : to play or sing in harmony **2** : to be in harmony **3** : to bring into consonance or accord — **har・mo・ni・za・tion** \här-mə-nə-'zā-shən\ *n*

har・mo・ny \'här-mə-nē\ *n, pl* **-nies 1** : musical agreement of sounds; *esp* : the combination of tones into chords and progressions of chords **2** : a pleasing arrangement of parts; *also* : ACCORD **3** : internal calm

¹**har・ness** \'här-nəs\ *n* **1** : the gear other than a yoke of a draft animal **2** : something that resembles a harness

²**harness** *vb* **1** : to put a harness on; *also* : YOKE **2** : UTILIZE

¹**harp** \'härp\ *n* : a musical instrument consisting of a triangular frame set with strings plucked by the fingers — **harp・ist** *n*

²**harp** *vb* **1** : to play on a harp **2** : to dwell on a subject tiresomely — **harp・er** *n*

har・poon \här-'pün\ *n* : a barbed spear used esp. in hunting large fish or whales — **harpoon** *vb* — **har・poon・er** *n*

harp・si・chord \'härp-si-kȯrd\ *n* : a keyboard instrument producing tones by the plucking of its strings with quills or with leather or plastic points

har・py \'här-pē\ *n, pl* **harpies** [L *Harpyia*, a mythical predatory monster having a woman's head and a vul-

ture's body, fr. Gk] **1** : a predatory person : LEECH **2** : a shrewish woman

har・ri・dan \'har-əd-ᵊn\ *n* : a scolding woman

¹**har・ri・er** \'har-ē-ər\ *n* **1** : a small hound used esp. in hunting rabbits **2** : a runner on a cross-country team

²**harrier** *n* : a slender long-legged hawk

¹**har・row** \'har-ō\ *n* : a cultivating tool that has spikes, spring teeth, or disks and is used esp. to pulverize and smooth the soil

²**harrow** *vb* **1** : to cultivate with a harrow **2** : TORMENT, VEX

har・ry \'har-ē\ *vb* **har・ried; har・ry・ing 1** : RAID, PILLAGE **2** : to torment by or as if by constant attack **syn** worry, annoy, plague, pester

harsh \'härsh\ *adj* **1** : disagreeably rough **2** : causing discomfort or pain **3** : unduly exacting : SEVERE — **harsh・ly** *adv* — **harsh・ness** *n*

hart \'härt\ *n* : STAG

har・um–scar・um \har-əm-'skar-əm\ *adj* : RECKLESS, IRRESPONSIBLE

¹**har・vest** \'här-vəst\ *n* **1** : the season for gathering in crops; *also* : the act of gathering in a crop **2** : a mature crop **3** : the product or reward of exertion

²**harvest** *vb* : to gather in a crop : REAP — **har・vest・er** *n*

has *pres 3d sing of* HAVE

has–been \'haz-bin\ *n* : one that has passed the peak of ability, power, effectiveness, or popularity

¹**hash** \'hash\ *vb* [F *hacher*, fr. OF *hachier*, fr. *hache* battle-ax] **1** : to chop into small pieces **2** : to talk about

²**hash** *n* **1** : chopped meat mixed with potatoes and browned **2** : HODGE-PODGE, JUMBLE

³**hash** *n* : HASHISH

hash browns *n pl* : boiled potatoes that have been diced, mixed with chopped onions and shortening, and fried

hash・ish \'hash-ēsh, ha-'shēsh\ [Ar] *n* : an intoxicating preparation of resin from the hemp plant

hasp \'hasp\ *n* : a fastener (as for a door) consisting of a hinged metal strap that fits over a staple and is secured by a pin or padlock

has・sle \'has-əl\ *n* **1** : WRANGLE; *also* : FIGHT **2** : an annoying or troublesome concern — **hassle** *vb*

has・sock \'has-ək\ *n* [ME, sedge, fr. OE

hassuc] : a cushion that serves as a seat or leg rest; *also* : a cushion to kneel on in prayer

haste \'hāst\ *n* **1** : rapidity of motion or action : SPEED **2** : rash or headlong action **3** : excessive eagerness — **hast·i·ly** \'hā-stə-lē\ *adv* — **hast·i·ness** \-stē-nəs\ *n* — **hasty** \'hā-stē\ *adj*

has·ten \'hās-ᵊn\ *vb* **has·tened; has·ten·ing** \'hās-(ᵊ-)niŋ\ **1** : to urge on **2** : to move or act quickly : HURRY **syn** speed, accelerate, quicken

hat \'hat\ *n* : a covering for the head usu. having a shaped crown and brim

hat·box \'hat-ˌbäks\ *n* : a round piece of luggage esp. for carrying hats

¹hatch \'hach\ *n* **1** : a small door or opening **2** : a door or cover for access down into a compartment of a ship

²hatch *vb* **1** : to produce by incubation; *also* : INCUBATE **2** : to emerge from an egg or pupa; *also* : to give forth young **3** : ORIGINATE — **hatch·ery** \-(ə-)rē\ *n*

hatch·back \'hach-ˌbak\ *n* **1** : a back on an automobile having an upward-opening hatch **2** : an automobile having a hatchback

hatch·et \'hach-ət\ *n* **1** : a short-handled ax with a hammerlike part opposite the blade **2** : TOMAHAWK

hatchet man *n* : a person hired for murder, coercion, or unscrupulous attack

hatch·ing \'hach-iŋ\ *n* : the engraving or drawing of fine lines in close proximity chiefly to give an effect of shading; *also* : the pattern so created

hatch·way \'hach-ˌwā\ *n* : an opening having a hatch

¹hate \'hāt\ *n* **1** : intense hostility and aversion **2** : an object of hatred — **hate·ful** \-fəl\ *adj* — **hate·ful·ly** \-ē\ *adv* — **hate·ful·ness** *n*

²hate *vb* **hat·ed; hat·ing** **1** : to express or feel extreme enmity **2** : to find distasteful **syn** detest, abhor, abominate, loathe — **hat·er** *n*

ha·tred \'hā-trəd\ *n* : HATE; *also* : prejudiced hostility or animosity

hat·ter \'hat-ər\ *n* : one that makes, sells, or cleans and repairs hats

hau·berk \'hȯ-bərk\ *n* : a coat of mail

haugh·ty \'hȯt-ē\ *adj* **haugh·ti·er; -est** [obs. *haught*, fr. ME *haute*, fr. MF *haut*, lit., high, fr. L *altus*] : disdainfully proud **syn** insolent, lordly, overbearing, arrogant — **haugh·ti·ly** \'hȯt-ə-lē\ *adv* — **haugh·ti·ness** \-e-nəs\ *n*

¹haul \'hȯl\ *vb* **1** : to exert traction on : DRAW, PULL **2** : to furnish transportation : CART — **haul·er** *n*

²haul *n* **1** : PULL, TUG **2** : the result of an effort to collect : TAKE **3** : the distance over which a load is transported; *also* : LOAD

haul·age \-ij\ *n* **1** : the act or process of hauling **2** : a charge for hauling

haunch \'hȯnch\ *n* **1** : ¹HIP 1 **2** : HINDQUARTER 2 — usu. used in pl. **3** : HINDQUARTER 1

¹haunt \'hȯnt\ *vb* **1** : to visit often : FREQUENT **2** : to recur constantly and spontaneously to; *also* : to reappear continually in **3** : to visit or inhabit as a ghost — **haunt·er** *n* — **haunt·ing·ly** \-iŋ-lē\ *adv*

²haunt \'hȯnt, *2 is usu* 'hant\ *n* **1** : a place habitually frequented **2** *chiefly dial* : GHOST

haut·bois *or* **haut·boy** \'(h)ō-ˌbȯi\ *n, pl* **hautbois** \-ˌbȯiz\ *or* **hautboys** : OBOE

haute cou·ture \ˌōt-kù-'tü(ə)r\ *n* [F] : the establishments or designers that create fashions for women; *also* : the fashions created

haute cui·sine \-kwi-'zēn\ *n* : artful or elaborate cuisine

hau·teur \hȯ-'tər, (h)ō-\ *n* : HAUGHTINESS

¹have \(')hav, (h)əv, v; *in sense 2 before* "*to*" *usu* 'haf\ *vb* **had** \(')had, (h)əd\; **hav·ing** \'hav-iŋ\; **has** \(')haz, (h)əz, *in sense 2 before* "*to*" *usu* 'has\ **1** : to hold in possession; *also* : to hold in one's use, service, or regard **2** : to be compelled or forced to **3** : to stand in relationship to ⟨*has* many enemies⟩ **4** : OBTAIN; *also* : RECEIVE, ACCEPT **5** : to be marked by **6** : SHOW; *also* : USE, EXERCISE **7** : EXPERIENCE; *also* : TAKE ⟨~ a look⟩ **8** : to entertain in the mind **9** : to cause to **10** : ALLOW **11** : to be competent in **12** : to hold in a disadvantageous position; *also* : TRICK **13** : BEGET **14** : to partake of **15** — used as an auxiliary with the past participle to form the present perfect, past perfect, or future perfect — **have at** : ATTACK — **have coming** : DESERVE — **have done with** : to be finished with — **have had it** : to have endured all one will permit or can stand — **have to do with 1** : to deal with **2** : to have in the way of connection or relation with or effect on

²have \'hav\ *n* : one that has material wealth

ha·ven \'hā-vən\ *n* **1** : HARBOR, PORT **2** : a place of safety **3** : a place offering favorable conditions ⟨a tourist's ∼⟩

have–not \'hav-ˌnät, -'nät\ *n* : one that is poor in material wealth

hav·er·sack \'hav-ər-ˌsak\ *n* [F *havresac,* fr. G *habersack* bag for oats] : a bag similar to a knapsack but worn over one shoulder

hav·oc \'hav-ək\ *n* **1** : wide and general destruction **2** : great confusion and disorder

haw \'hȯ\ *n* : a hawthorn berry; *also* : HAWTHORN

Ha·wai·ian \hə-'wä-yən, -'wī-(y)ən\ *n* : the Polynesian language of Hawaii

¹hawk \'hȯk\ *n* **1** : any of numerous mostly small or medium-sized day‍flying birds of prey (as a falcon or kite) **2** : a supporter of a war or a warlike policy — **hawk·ish** *adj*

²hawk *vb* : to offer goods for sale by calling out in the street — **hawk·er** *n*

hawk·weed \'hȯk-ˌwēd\ *n* : any of several plants related to the daisies usu. having red or orange flower heads

haw·ser \'hȯ-zər\ *n* : a large rope for towing, mooring, or securing a ship

haw·thorn \'hȯ-ˌthȯrn\ *n* : a spiny shrub or tree related to the apple and having white or pink fragrant flowers

¹hay \'hā\ *n* **1** : herbage (as grass) mowed and cured for fodder **2** : REWARD **3** *slang* : BED ⟨hit the ∼⟩ **4** : a small amount of money

²hay *vb* : to cut, cure, and store for hay

hay·cock \'hā-ˌkäk\ *n* : a small conical pile of hay

hay fever *n* : an acute allergic catarrh

hay·fork \'hā-ˌfȯrk\ *n* : a fork for loading or unloading hay

hay·loft \-ˌlȯft\ *n* : a loft for hay

hay·mow \-ˌmau̇\ *n* : a mow of or for hay

hay·rick \-ˌrik\ *n* : a large sometimes thatched outdoor stack of hay

hay·seed \-ˌsēd\ *n, pl* **hayseed** *or* **hayseeds** **1** : clinging bits of straw or chaff from hay **2** : BUMPKIN, YOKEL

hay·stack \-ˌstak\ *n* : a stack of hay

hay·wire \-ˌwī(ə)r\ *adj* : being out of order or control : CRAZY

¹haz·ard \'haz-ərd\ *n* [ME, a dice game, fr. MF *hasard,* fr. Ar *az-zahr* the die] **1** : a source of danger **2** : CHANCE; *also* : ACCIDENT **3** : an obstacle on a golf course — **haz·ard·ous** *adj*

²hazard *vb* : VENTURE, RISK

¹haze \'hāz\ *n* **1** : fine dust, smoke, or light vapor causing lack of transparency in the air **2** : vagueness of mind or perception

²haze *vb* **hazed; haz·ing** : to harass by abusive and humiliating tricks

ha·zel \'hā-zəl\ *n* **1** : any of a genus of shrubs or small trees related to the birches and bearing edible nuts (**ha·zel·nuts** \-ˌnəts\) **2** : a light brown color

hazy \'hā-zē\ *adj* **haz·i·er; -est** **1** : obscured or darkened by haze **2** : VAGUE, INDEFINITE — **haz·i·ly** \'hā-zə-lē\ *adv* — **haz·i·ness** \-zē-nəs\ *n*

Hb *abbr* hemoglobin

HBM *abbr* Her Britannic Majesty; His Britannic Majesty

H–bomb \'āch-ˌbäm\ *n* : HYDROGEN BOMB

HC *abbr* **1** Holy Communion **2** House of Commons

hd *abbr* head

HD *abbr* heavy-duty

hdbk *abbr* handbook

hdkf *abbr* handkerchief

hdwe *abbr* hardware

he \(')hē, ē\ *pron* **1** : that male one **2** : a or the person ⟨∼ who hesitates is lost⟩

He *symbol* helium

HE *abbr* **1** Her Excellency **2** His Eminence **3** His Excellency

¹head \'hed\ *n* **1** : the front or upper part of the body containing the brain, the chief sense organs, and the mouth **2** : MIND; *also* : natural aptitude **3** : POISE **4** : the obverse of a coin **5** : INDIVIDUAL; *also, pl* **head** : one of a number (as of cattle) **6** : the end that is upper or higher or opposite the foot; *also* : either end of something (as a drum) whose two ends need not be distinguished **7** : DIRECTOR, LEADER; *also* : a leading element (as of a procession) **8** : a projecting part; *also* : the striking part of a weapon **9** : the place of leadership or honor **10** : a separate part or topic **11** : the foam on a fermenting or effervescing liquid **12**

: CRISIS — **head·ed** \-əd\ *adj* — **head·less** *adj*

²**head** *adj* : PRINCIPAL, CHIEF

³**head** *vb* **1** : to cut back the upper growth of **2** : to provide with or form a head; *also* : to form the head of **3** : LEAD, CONDUCT **4** : to get in front of esp. so as to stop; *also* : SURPASS **5** : to put or stand at the head **6** : to point or proceed in a certain direction **7** : ORIGINATE

head·ache \-ˌāk\ *n* **1** : pain in the head **2** : a baffling situation or problem

head·band \-ˌband\ *n* : a band worn on or around the head

head·board \-ˌbōrd\ *n* : a board forming the head (as of a bed)

head cold *n* : a common cold centered in the nasal passages and adjacent mucous tissues

head·dress \ˈhed-ˌdres\ *n* : an often elaborate covering for the head

head·first \-ˈfərst\ *adv* : HEADLONG — **headfirst** *adj*

head·gear \-ˌgiər\ *n* : a covering or protective device for the head

head–hunt·ing \-ˌhənt-iŋ\ *n* : the act or custom of seeking out and decapitating enemies and preserving their heads as trophies — **head·hunt·er** \-ər\ *n*

head·ing \ˈhed-iŋ\ *n* **1** : the compass direction in which the longitudinal axis of a ship or airplane points **2** : something that forms or serves as a head

head·land \ˈhed-lənd, -ˌland\ *n* : PROMONTORY

head·light \-ˌlīt\ *n* : a light with a reflector and special lens mounted on the front of a vehicle

head·line \-ˌlīn\ *n* : a head of a newspaper story or article usu. printed in large type

head·lock \-ˌläk\ *n* : a wrestling hold in which one encircles his opponent's head with one arm

¹**head·long** \-ˈlȯŋ\ *adv* **1** : with the head foremost **2** : RECKLESSLY **3** : without delay

²**head·long** \-ˌlȯŋ\ *adj* **1** : PRECIPITATE, RASH **2** : plunging with the head foremost

head·man \ˈhed-ˈman, -ˌman\ *n* : one who is a leader : CHIEF

head·mas·ter \-ˌmas-tər\ *n* : a man heading the staff of a private school

head·mis·tress \-ˌmis-trəs\ *n* : a woman head of a private school

head–on \ˈhed-ˈȯn, -ˈän\ *adj* : having the front facing in the direction of initial contact or line of sight ⟨∼ collision⟩ — **head–on** *adv*

head·phone \-ˌfōn\ *n* : an earphone held on by a band over the head

head·piece \-ˌpēs\ *n* **1** : a covering for the head **2** : an ornament esp. at the beginning of a chapter

head·pin \-ˌpin\ *n* : a bowling pin that stands foremost in the arrangement of pins

head·quar·ters \-ˌkwȯrt-ərz\ *n sing or pl* **1** : a place from which a commander exercises command **2** : the administrative center of an enterprise

head·rest \-ˌrest\ *n* **1** : a support for the head **2** : a pad at the top of the back of an automobile seat

head·room \ˈhed-ˌrüm, -ˌru̇m\ *n* : vertical space in which to stand, sit, or move

head·set \-ˌset\ *n* : a pair of headphones

head·ship \-ˌship\ *n* : the position, office, or dignity of a head

heads·man \ˈhedz-mən\ *n* : EXECUTIONER

head·stall \ˈhed-ˌstȯl\ *n* : an arrangement of straps or rope encircling the head of an animal and forming part of a bridle or halter

head·stone \-ˌstōn\ *n* : a memorial stone at the head of a grave

head·strong \-ˌstrȯŋ\ *adj* **1** : not easily restrained **2** : directed by ungovernable will **syn** unruly, intractable, willful, pertinacious, refractory, stubborn

head·wait·er \-ˈwāt-ər\ *n* : the head of the dining-room staff of a restaurant or hotel

head·wa·ter \-ˌwȯt-ər, -ˌwät-\ *n* : the source of a stream — usu. used in pl.

head·way \-ˌwā\ *n* : forward motion; *also* : PROGRESS

head wind *n* : a wind blowing in a direction opposite to a course esp. of a ship or aircraft

head·word \ˈhed-ˌwərd\ *n* **1** : a word or term placed at the beginning **2** : a word qualified by a modifier

head·work \-ˌwərk\ *n* : mental work or effort : THINKING

heady \ˈhed-ē\ *adj* **head·i·er; -est** **1**

: WILLFUL, RASH; *also* : IMPETUOUS **2** : INTOXICATING **3** : SHREWD

heal \'hēl\ *vb* **1** : to make or become sound or whole; *also* : to restore to health **2** : CURE, REMEDY — **heal·er** *n*

health \'helth\ *n* **1** : sound physical or mental condition; *also* : overall condition of the body ⟨in poor ∼⟩ **2** : WELL-BEING **3** : a toast to someone's health or prosperity

health·ful \'helth-fəl\ *adj* **1** : beneficial to health **2** : HEALTHY — **health·ful·ly** \-ē\ *adv* — **health·ful·ness** *n*

healthy \'hel-thē\ *adj* **health·i·er; -est 1** : enjoying or typical of good health : WELL **2** : evincing or conducive to health **3** : PROSPEROUS; *also* : CONSIDERABLE — **health·i·ly** \'hel-thə-lē\ *adv* — **health·i·ness** \-thē-nəs\ *n*

¹heap \'hēp\ *n* : PILE; *also* : LOT

²heap *vb* **1** : to throw or lay in a heap **2** : to give in large quantities; *also* : to fill more than full

hear \'hiər\ *vb* **heard** \'hərd\; **hear·ing** \'hi(ə)r-iŋ\ **1** : to perceive by the ear **2** : HEED; *also* : ATTEND **3** : to give a legal hearing to or take testimony from **4** : LEARN — **hear·er** \'hir-ər\ *n*

hear·ing *n* **1** : the process, function, or power of perceiving sound; *esp* : the special sense by which noises and tones are received as stimuli **2** : EARSHOT **3** : opportunity to be heard **4** : a listening to arguments (as in a court); *also* : a session in which witnesses are heard (as by a legislative committee)

hear·ken \'här-kən\ *vb* : to give attention : LISTEN **syn** hear, hark, heed

hear·say \'hiər-ˌsā\ *n* : RUMOR

hearse \'hərs\ *n* [ME *herse*, fr. MF *herce* harrow, frame for holding candles] : a vehicle for carrying the dead to the grave

heart \'härt\ *n* **1** : a hollow muscular organ that by rhythmic contraction keeps up the circulation of the blood in the body; *also* : something resembling a heart in shape **2** : any of a suit of playing cards marked with a red figure of a heart; *also, pl* : a card game in which the object is to avoid taking tricks containing hearts **3** : the whole personality; *also* : the emotional or moral as distinguished from the intellectual nature **4** : COURAGE **5** : one's innermost being **6** : CENTER; *also* : the

essential part **7** : the younger central part of a compact leafy cluster (as of lettuce) — **heart·ed** \-əd\ *adj* — **by heart** : by rote or from memory

heart·ache \-ˌāk\ *n* : anguish of mind

heart attack *n* : an acute episode of heart disease due to insufficient blood supply to the heart muscle itself

heart·beat \'härt-ˌbēt\ *n* : one complete pulsation of the heart

heart·break \-ˌbrāk\ *n* : crushing grief

heart·break·ing \-ˌbrā-kiŋ\ *adj* : causing extreme sorrow or distress — **heart·break·er** \-ˌbrā-kər\ *n*

heart·bro·ken \-ˌbrō-kən\ *adj* : overcome by sorrow

heart·burn \-ˌbərn\ *n* : a burning distress behind the lower sternum usu. due to spasm of the esophagus or upper stomach

heart disease *n* : an abnormal organic condition of the heart or of the heart and circulation

heart·en \'härt-ᵊn\ *vb* **heart·ened; heart·en·ing** \'härt-(ᵊ-)niŋ\ : ENCOURAGE

heart·felt \'härt-ˌfelt\ *adj* : deeply felt : SINCERE

hearth \'härth\ *n* **1** : an area (as of brick) in front of a fireplace; *also* : the floor of a fireplace **2** : HOME

hearth·stone \-ˌstōn\ *n* **1** : a stone forming a hearth **2** : HOME

heart·less \'härt-ləs\ *adj* : CRUEL

heart·rend·ing \-ˌren-diŋ\ *adj* : HEARTBREAKING

heart·sick \-ˌsik\ *adj* : very despondent — **heart·sick·ness** *n*

heart·strings \-ˌstriŋz\ *n pl* : the deepest emotions or affections

heart·throb \-ˌthräb\ *n* **1** : the throb of a heart **2** : sentimental emotion **3** : SWEETHEART

heart–to–heart \ˌhärt-tə-ˌhärt\ *adj* : SINCERE, FRANK ⟨a ∼ talk⟩

heart·warm·ing \'härt-ˌwȯr-miŋ\ *adj* : inspiring sympathetic feeling

heart·wood \-ˌwu̇d\ *n* : the older harder nonliving central portion of wood

¹hearty \'härt-ē\ *adj* **heart·i·er; -est 1** : THOROUGHGOING; *also* : JOVIAL **2** : vigorously healthy **3** : ABUNDANT; *also* : NOURISHING **syn** sincere, wholehearted, unfeigned, heartfelt — **heart·i·ly** \'härt-ə-lē\ *adv* — **heart·i·ness** \-ē-nəs\ *n*

²**hearty** *n, pl* **heart•ies** : COMRADE; *also* : SAILOR

¹**heat** \'hēt\ *vb* **1** : to make or become warm or hot **2** : EXCITE — **heat•ed•ly** \-əd-lē\ *adv* — **heat•er** *n*

²**heat** *n* **1** : a condition of being hot : WARMTH **2** : a form of energy that causes a body to rise in temperature, to fuse, to evaporate, or to expand **3** : high temperature **4** : intensity of feeling; *also* : sexual excitement esp. in a female mammal **5** : pungency of flavor **6** : a single continuous effort; *also* : a preliminary race for eliminating less competent contenders **7** : PRESSURE, COERCION; *also* : ABUSE, CRITICISM — **heat•less** *adj*

heat engine *n* : a mechanism for converting heat energy into mechanical energy

heat exchanger *n* : a device (as an automobile radiator) for transferring heat from one fluid to another without allowing them to mix

heat exhaustion *n* : a condition marked by weakness, nausea, dizziness, and profuse sweating that results from physical exertion in a hot environment

heath \'hēth\ *n* **1** : any of a large family of often evergreen shrubby plants (as a blueberry or heather) of wet acid soils **2** : a tract of wasteland — **heathy** *adj*

hea•then \'hē-thən\ *n, pl* **heathens** *or* **heathen 1** : an unconverted member of a people or nation that does not acknowledge the God of the Bible **2** : an uncivilized or irreligious person — **heathen** *adj* — **hea•then•dom** *n* — **hea•then•ish** *adj* — **hea•then•ism** *n*

heath•er \'heth-ər\ *n* : a northern evergreen heath with usu. lavender flowers — **heath•ery** *adj*

heat lightning *n* : flashes of light without thunder ascribed to distant lightning reflected by high clouds

heat•stroke \'hēt-ˌstrōk\ *n* : a disorder marked esp. by high body temperature without sweating and by collapse that follows prolonged exposure to excessive heat

¹**heave** \'hēv\ *vb* **heaved** *or* **hove** \'hōv\; **heav•ing 1** : to rise or lift upward **2** : THROW **3** : to rise and fall rhythmical-ly; *also* : PANT **4** : RETCH **5** : PULL, PUSH — **heav•er** *n*

²**heave** *n* **1** : an effort to lift or raise **2** : THROW, CAST **3** : an upward motion **4** *pl* : a chronic lung disease of horses marked by difficult breathing and persistent cough

heav•en \'hev-ən\ *n* **1** : FIRMAMENT — usu. used in pl. **2** *often cap* : the abode of the Deity and of the blessed dead; *also* : a spiritual state of everlasting communion with God **3** *cap* : GOD 1 **4** : a place of supreme happiness — **heav•en•ly** *adj* — **heav•en•ward** *adv or adj*

¹**heavy** \'hev-ē\ *adj* **heavi•er; -est 1** : having great weight **2** : hard to bear **3** : SERIOUS **4** : DEEP, PROFOUND **5** : burdened with something oppressive; *also* : PREGNANT **6** : SLUGGISH **7** : DRAB; *also* : DOLEFUL **8** : DROWSY **9** : greater than the average of its kind or class **10** : digested with difficulty; *also* : not properly raised or leavened **11** : producing goods (as steel) used in the production of other goods **12** : heavily armed or armored — **heav•i•ly** \'hev-ə-lē\ *adv* — **heavi•ness** \-ē-nəs\ *n*

²**heavy** *n, pl* **heav•ies** : a theatrical role representing a dignified or imposing person; *also* : a villain esp. in a story or a play

heavy–du•ty \ˌhev-ē-'d(y)üt-ē\ *adj* : able to withstand unusual strain

heavy–hand•ed \-'han-dəd\ *adj* **1** : CLUMSY, UNGRACEFUL **2** : OPPRESSIVE, HARSH

heavy•heart•ed \-'härt-əd\ *adj* : SADDENED, DESPONDENT

heavy metal *n* : highly amplified electronic rock with elements of the fantastic

heavy•set \ˌhev-ē-'set\ *adj* : stocky and compact in build

heavy water *n* : water enriched in deuterium

heavy•weight \'hev-ē-ˌwāt\ *n* : one above average in weight; *esp* : a boxer weighing over 175 pounds

Heb *abbr* Hebrews

He•bra•ism \'hē-brā-ˌiz-əm\ *n* : the thought, spirit, or practice characteristic of the Hebrews — **He•bra•ic** \hi-'brā-ik\ *adj*

He·bra·ist \'hē-ˌbrā-əst\ *n* : a specialist in Hebrew and Hebraic studies

He·brew \'hē-brü\ *n* **1** : the language of the Hebrews **2** : a member of or descendant from a group of Semitic peoples; *esp* : ISRAELITE — **Hebrew** *adj*

He·brews \'hē-(ˌ)brüz\ *n* — see BIBLE table

hec·a·tomb \'hek-ə-ˌtōm\ *n* : an ancient Greek and Roman sacrifice of 100 oxen or cattle

heck·le \'hek-əl\ *vb* **heck·led; heck·ling** \-(ə-)liŋ\ : to harass with questions or gibes : BADGER — **heck·ler** \-(ə-)lər\ *n*

hect·are \'hek-ˌtaər\ *n* — see METRIC SYSTEM table

hec·tic \'hek-tik\ *adj* **1** : being hot and flushed **2** : filled with excitement or confusion — **hec·ti·cal·ly** \-ti-k(ə-)lē\ *adv*

hec·to·gram \'hek-tə-ˌgram\ *n* — see METRIC SYSTEM table

hec·to·li·ter \'hek-tə-ˌlēt-ər\ *n* — see METRIC SYSTEM table

hec·to·me·ter \'hek-tə-ˌmēt-ər, hek-ˈtäm-ət-ər\ *n* — see METRIC SYSTEM table

hec·tor \'hek-tər\ *vb* **hec·tored; hec·tor·ing** \-t(ə-)riŋ\ **1** : SWAGGER **2** : to intimidate by bluster or personal pressure

¹hedge \'hej\ *n* **1** : a fence or boundary formed of shrubs or small trees **2** : BARRIER **3** : a means of protection (as against financial loss)

²hedge *vb* **hedged; hedg·ing 1** : ENCIRCLE **2** : HINDER **3** : to protect oneself financially by a counterbalancing transaction **4** : to evade the risk of commitment — **hedg·er** *n*

hedge·hog \-ˌhȯg, -ˌhäg\ *n* : a small Old World insect-eating mammal covered with spines; *also* : PORCUPINE

hedge·hop \-ˌhäp\ *vb* : to fly an airplane very close to the ground

hedge·row \-ˌrō\ *n* : a row of shrubs or trees bounding or separating fields

he·do·nism \'hēd-ᵊn-ˌiz-əm\ *n* [Gk *hēdonē* pleasure] : the doctrine that pleasure is the chief good in life; *also* : a way of life based on this — **he·do·nist** \-ᵊn-əst\ *n* — **he·do·nis·tic** \ˌhēd-ᵊn-ˈis-tik\ *adj*

¹heed \'hēd\ *vb* : to pay attention

²heed *n* : ATTENTION, NOTICE — **heed·ful** \-fəl\ *adj* — **heed·ful·ly** \-ē\ *adv* —

heed·ful·ness *n* — **heed·less** *adj* — **heed·less·ly** *adv* — **heed·less·ness** *n*

¹heel \'hēl\ *n* **1** : the hind part of the foot **2** : one of the crusty ends of a loaf of bread **3** : a solid attachment forming the back of the sole of a shoe **4** : a rear, low, or bottom part **5** : a contemptible person — **heel·less** \'hēl-ləs\ *adj*

²heel *vb* : to tilt to one side : LIST

¹heft \'heft\ *n* : WEIGHT, HEAVINESS

²heft *vb* : to test the weight of by lifting

hefty \'hef-tē\ *adj* **heft·i·er; -est 1** : marked by bigness, bulk, and usu. strength **2** : impressively large

he·ge·mo·ny \hi-ˈjem-ə-nē\ *n* : preponderant influence or authority esp. of one nation over others

he·gi·ra \hi-ˈjī-rə\ *n* [the *Hegira,* flight of Muhammad from Mecca in A.D. 622, fr. ML, fr. Ar *hijrah,* lit., flight] : a journey esp. when undertaken to seek refuge away from a dangerous or undesirable environment

heif·er \'hef-ər\ *n* : a young cow; *esp* : one that has not had a calf

height \'hīt, 'hītth\ *n* **1** : the highest part or point **2** : the distance from the bottom to the top of something standing upright **3** : ALTITUDE

height·en \'hīt-ᵊn\ *vb* **height·ened; height·en·ing** \'hīt-(ᵊ-)niŋ\ **1** : to increase in amount or degree : AUGMENT **2** : to make or become high or higher **syn** enhance, intensify, aggravate, magnify

Heim·lich maneuver \'hīm-lik-\ *n* [Henry J. *Heimlich b*1920 Am. surgeon] : the manual application of sudden upward pressure on the upper abdomen of a choking victim to force a foreign object from the windpipe

hei·nous \'hā-nəs\ *adj* [ME, fr. MF *haineus,* fr. *haine* hate, fr. *hair* to hate] : hatefully or shockingly evil — **hei·nous·ly** *adv* — **hei·nous·ness** *n*

heir \'aər\ *n* : one who inherits or is entitled to inherit property, rank, title, or office — **heir·ship** *n*

heir apparent *n, pl* **heirs apparent** : an heir whose right to succeed (as to a title) cannot be taken away if he or she survives the present holder

heir·ess \'ar-əs\ *n* : a female heir esp. to great wealth

heir·loom \'aər-ˌlüm\ *n* **1** : a piece of

personal property that descends by inheritance **2** : something handed on from one generation to another

heir presumptive *n, pl* **heirs presumptive** : an heir whose present right to inherit could be lost through the birth of a nearer relative

heist \ˈhīst\ *vb, slang* : to commit armed robbery on; *also* : STEAL — **heist** *n, slang*

held past and past part of HOLD

he·li·cal \ˈhel-i-kəl, ˈhē-li-\ *adj* : SPIRAL

he·li·coid \ˈhel-ə-ˌkȯid, ˈhē-lə-\ *or* **he·li·coi·dal** \ˌhel-ə-ˈkȯid-ᵊl, ˌhē-lə-\ *adj* : forming or arranged in a spiral

he·li·cop·ter \ˈhel-ə-ˌkäp-tər, ˈhē-lə-\ *n* [F *hélicoptère*, fr. Gk *helix* spiral + *pteron* wing] : an aircraft that is supported in the air by one or more rotors revolving on substantially vertical axes

he·lio·cen·tric \ˌhē-lē-ō-ˈsen-trik\ *adj* : having or relating to the sun as center

he·lio·trope \ˈhēl-yə-ˌtrōp\ *n* [L *heliotropium*, fr. Gk *hēliotropion*, fr. *hēlio-* sun + *tropos* turn; fr. its flowers' turning toward the sun] : a hairy-leaved garden herb related to the forget-me-not that has clusters of small fragrant white or purple flowers

he·li·port \ˈhel-ə-ˌpȯrt\ *n* : a landing and takeoff place for a helicopter

he·li·um \ˈhē-lē-əm\ *n* [NL, fr. Gk *hēlios* sun; so called from the fact that its existence in the sun's atmosphere was inferred before it was identified on the earth] : a very light nonflammable gaseous chemical element occurring in various natural gases

he·lix \ˈhē-liks\ *n, pl* **he·li·ces** \ˈhel-ə-ˌsēz, ˈhē-lə-\ *also* **he·lix·es** \ˈhē-lik-səz\ : something spiral in form

hell \ˈhel\ *n* **1** : a nether world in which the dead continue to exist **2** : the realm of the devil in which the damned suffer everlasting punishment **3** : a place or state of torment or destruction — **hell·ish** *adj*

hell–bent \-ˌbent\ *adj* : stubbornly determined

hell·cat \-ˌkat\ *n* **1** : WITCH 2 **2** : TORMENTOR; *esp* : SHREW 2

hel·le·bore \ˈhel-ə-ˌbōr\ *n* **1** : a plant related to the buttercup; *also* : its roots used formerly in medicine **2** : a poi-sonous plant related to the lilies; *also* : its dried roots used in medicine and insecticides

Hel·lene \ˈhel-ˌēn\ *n* : GREEK

Hel·le·nism \ˈhel-ə-ˌniz-əm\ *n* : a body of humanistic and classical ideals associated with ancient Greece — **Hel·len·ic** \he-ˈlen-ik\ *adj* — **Hel·le·nist** \ˈhel-ə-nəst\ *n*

Hel·le·nis·tic \ˌhel-ə-ˈnis-tik\ *adj* : of or relating to Greek history, culture, or art after Alexander the Great

hell–for–leather *adv* : at full speed

hell·gram·mite \ˈhel-grə-ˌmīt\ *n* : an aquatic insect larva that is used as bait in fishing

hell·hole \ˈhel-ˌhōl\ *n* : a place of extreme misery or squalor

hel·lion \ˈhel-yən\ *n* : a troublesome or mischievous person

hel·lo \hə-ˈlō, he-\ *n, pl* **hellos** : an expression of greeting — used interjectionally

helm \ˈhelm\ *n* **1** : a lever or wheel for steering a ship **2** : a position of control

hel·met \ˈhel-mət\ *n* : a protective covering for the head

helms·man \ˈhelmz-mən\ *n* : the person at the helm : STEERSMAN

hel·ot \ˈhel-ət\ *n* : SLAVE, SERF

¹help \ˈhelp\ *vb* **1** : AID, ASSIST **2** : REMEDY, RELIEVE **3** : to be of use; *also* : PROMOTE **4** : to change for the better **5** : to refrain from; *also* : PREVENT **6** : to serve with food or drink — **help·er** *n*

²help *n* **1** : AID, ASSISTANCE; *also* : a source of aid **2** : REMEDY, RELIEF **3** : one who assists another **4** : the services of a paid worker — **help·ful** \-fəl\ *adj* — **help·ful·ly** \-ē\ *adv* — **help·ful·ness** *n* — **help·less** *adj* — **help·less·ly** *adv* — **help·less·ness** *n*

help·ing \ˈhel-piŋ\ *n* : a portion of food ⟨asked for a second ∼ of potatoes⟩

help·mate \ˈhelp-ˌmāt\ *n* **1** : HELPER **2** : WIFE

help·meet \-ˌmēt\ *n* : HELPMATE

hel·ter–skel·ter \ˌhel-tər-ˈskel-tər\ *adv* **1** : in headlong disorder **2** : HAPHAZARDLY

helve \ˈhelv\ *n* : a handle of a tool or weapon

Hel·ve·tian \hel-ˈvē-shən\ *adj* : SWISS — **Helvetian** *n*

¹hem \ˈhem\ *n* **1** : a border of an article

(as of cloth) doubled back and stitched down **2** : RIM, MARGIN

²hem *vb* **hemmed; hem·ming 1** : to make a hem in sewing; *also* : BORDER, EDGE **2** : to surround restrictively

he–man \'hē-ˌman\ *n* : a strong virile man

he·ma·tite \'hē-mə-ˌtīt\ *n* : a mineral that consists of an oxide of iron and that constitutes an important iron ore

he·ma·tol·o·gy \ˌhē-mə-'täl-ə-jē\ *n* : a branch of biology that deals with the blood and blood-forming organs — **he·ma·to·log·ic** \-mət-ᵊl-'äj-ik\ *also* **he·ma·to·log·i·cal** \-i-kəl\ *adj* — **he·ma·tol·o·gist** \-'täl-ə-jəst\ *n*

heme \'hēm\ *n* : the deep red iron-containing part of hemoglobin

hemi·sphere \'hem-ə-ˌsfiər\ *n* **1** : one of the halves of the earth as divided by the equator into northern and southern parts (northern hemisphere, southern hemisphere) or by a meridian into two parts so that one half (eastern hemisphere) to the east of the Atlantic ocean includes Europe, Asia, and Africa and the half (western hemisphere) to the west includes No. and So. America and surrounding waters **2** : either of two half spheres formed by a plane through the sphere's center — **hemi·spher·ic** \ˌhem-ə-'sfiər-ik, -'sfer-\ *or* **hemi·spher·i·cal** \-'sfir-i-kəl, -'sfer-\ *adj*

hem·line \'hem-ˌlīn\ *n* : the line formed by the lower edge of a dress, skirt, or coat

hem·lock \'hem-ˌläk\ *n* **1** : any of several poisonous herbs related to the carrot **2** : an evergreen tree related to the pines; *also* : its soft light wood

he·mo·glo·bin \'hē-mə-ˌglō-bən\ *n* : an iron-containing compound found in red blood cells that carries oxygen from the lungs to the body tissues

he·mo·phil·ia \ˌhē-mə-'fil-ē-ə\ *n* : a usu. hereditary tendency to severe prolonged bleeding — **he·mo·phil·i·ac** \-ē-ˌak\ *adj or n* — **he·mo·phil·ic** \-'fil-ik\ *n or adj*

hem·or·rhage \'hem-(ə-)rij\ *n* : a large discharge of blood from the blood vessels — **hemorrhage** *vb* — **hem·or·rhag·ic** \ˌhem-ə-'raj-ik\ *adj*

hem·or·rhoid \'hem-(ə-)ˌröid\ *n* : a swollen mass of dilated veins situated at or just within the anus — usu. used in pl.

hemp \'hemp\ *n* : a tall widely grown Asian herb related to the mulberry that is the source of a tough fiber used in cordage and of marijuana and hashish from its flowers and leaves — **hemp·en** \'hem-pən\ *adj*

hem·stitch \'hem-ˌstich\ *vb* : to embroider (fabric) by drawing out parallel threads and stitching the exposed threads in groups to form designs

hen \'hen\ *n* : a female chicken esp. over a year old; *also* : a female bird

hence \'hens\ *adv* **1** : AWAY **2** : from this time **3** : CONSEQUENTLY **4** : from this source or origin

hence·forth \-ˌfōrth\ *adv* : from this point on

hence·for·ward \hens-'fȯr-wərd\ *adv* : HENCEFORTH

hench·man \'hench-mən\ *n* [ME *hengestman* groom, fr. *hengest* stallion] : a trusted follower or supporter

hen·na \'hen-ə\ *n* **1** : an Old World tropical shrub with fragrant white flowers; *also* : a reddish brown dye obtained from its leaves and used esp. for the hair **2** : the color of henna dye

hen·peck \'hen-ˌpek\ *vb* : to nag and boss one's husband

hep \'hep\ var of HIP

hep·a·rin \'hep-ə-rən\ *n* : a compound found esp. in liver that slows the clotting of blood and is used medically

he·pat·ic \hi-'pat-ik\ *adj* : of, relating to, or associated with the liver

he·pat·i·ca \hi-'pat-i-kə\ *n* : any of a genus of herbs related to the buttercups that have lobed leaves and delicate flowers

hep·a·ti·tis \ˌhep-ə-'tīt-əs\ *n, pl* **-tit·i·des** \-'tit-ə-ˌdēz\ : inflammation of the liver; *also* : an acute virus disease of which this is a feature

hep·tam·e·ter \hep-'tam-ət-ər\ *n* : a line of verse containing seven metrical feet

¹her \(h)ər, ˌhər\ *adj* : of or relating to her or herself

²her \ər, (')hər\ *pron*, objective case of SHE

¹her·ald \'her-əld\ *n* **1** : an official crier or messenger **2** : HARBINGER **3** : ANNOUNCER, SPOKESMAN

²**herald** *vb* **1** : to give notice of **2** : HAIL, GREET; *also* : PUBLICIZE

he·ral·dic \he-'ral-dik, hə-\ *adj* : of or relating to heralds or heraldry

her·ald·ry \'her-əl-drē\ *n, pl* **-ries 1** : the practice of devising and granting armorial insignia and of tracing a person's family to find out its coat of arms **2** : COAT OF ARMS **3** : PAGEANTRY

herb \'(h)ərb\ *n* **1** : a seed plant that lacks woody tissue and dies to the ground at the end of a growing season **2** : a plant or plant part valued for medicinal or savory qualities — **her·ba·ceous** \,(h)ər-'bā-shəs\ *adj*

herb·age \'(h)ər-bij\ *n* : green plants esp. when used or fit for grazing

herb·al·ist \'(h)ər-bə-ləst\ *n* **1** : one that collects, grows, or deals in herbs **2** : one who practices healing by the use of herbs

her·bar·i·um \,(h)ər-'bar-ē-əm\ *n, pl* **-ia** \-ē-ə\ **1** : a collection of dried plant specimens **2** : a place that houses an herbarium

her·bi·cide \'(h)ər-bə-,sīd\ *n* : an agent used to destroy unwanted plants — **her·bi·cid·al** \,(h)ər-bə-'sīd-ᵊl\ *adj*

her·biv·o·rous \,(h)ər-'biv-ə-rəs\ *adj* : feeding on plants — **her·bi·vore** \'(h)ər-bə-,vōr\ *n*

her·cu·le·an \,hər-kyə-'lē-ən, ,hər-'kyü-lē-\ *adj, often cap* : of extraordinary power, size, or difficulty

¹**herd** \'hərd\ *n* **1** : a group of animals of one kind kept or living together **2** : a group of people with a common bond **3** : MOB

²**herd** *vb* : to assemble or move in a herd — **herd·er** *n*

herds·man \'hərdz-mən\ *n* : one who manages, breeds, or tends livestock

¹**here** \'hiər\ *adv* **1** : in or at this place; *also* : NOW **2** : at or in this point, particular, or case **3** : in the present life or state **4** : HITHER

²**here** *n* : this place ⟨get away from ∼⟩

here·abouts \'hir-ə-,bauts\ *or* **here·about** \-,baut\ *adv* : in this vicinity : about or near this place

¹**here·af·ter** \hir-'af-tər\ *adv* **1** : after this in sequence or in time **2** : in some future time or state

²**hereafter** *n, often cap* **1** : FUTURE **2** : an existence beyond earthly life

here·by \hiər-'bī\ *adv* : by means of this

he·red·i·tary \hə-'red-ə-,ter-ē\ *adj* **1** : genetically passed or passable from parent to offspring **2** : passing by inheritance; *also* : having title or possession through inheritance **3** : of a kind established by tradition

he·red·i·ty \-ət-ē\ *n* : the qualities and potentialities genetically derived from one's ancestors; *also* : the passing of these from ancestor to descendant

Her·e·ford \'hər-fərd\ *n* : any of an English breed of hardy red beef cattle with white faces and markings

here·in \hir-'in\ *adv* : in this

here·of \-'əv, -'äv\ *adv* : of this

here·on \-'on, -'än\ *adv* : on this

her·e·sy \'her-ə-sē\ *n, pl* **-sies** [ME *heresie*, fr. OF, fr. LL *haeresis*, fr. LGk *hairesis*, fr. Gk, action of taking, choice, sect, fr. *hairein* to take] **1** : adherence to a religious opinion contrary to church dogma **2** : an opinion or doctrine contrary to church dogma **3** : dissent from a dominant theory, opinion, or practice — **her·e·tic** \-,tik\ *n* — **he·ret·i·cal** \hə-'ret-i-kəl\ *adj*

here·to \hir-'tü\ *adv* : to this document

here·to·fore \'hirt-ə-,fōr\ *adv* : up to this time

here·un·der \hir-'ən-dər\ *adv* : under this or according to this writing

here·un·to \hir-'ən-tü\ *adv* : to this

here·upon \'hir-ə-,pon, -,pän\ *adv* : on this or immediately after this

here·with \'hiər-'with, -'with\ *adv* **1** : with this **2** : HEREBY

her·i·ta·ble \'her-ət-ə-bəl\ *adj* : capable of being inherited

her·i·tage \'her-ət-ij\ *n* **1** : property that descends to an heir **2** : LEGACY **3** : BIRTHRIGHT

her·maph·ro·dite \(,)hər-'maf-rə-,dīt\ *n* : an animal or plant having both male and female reproductive organs — **hermaphrodite** *adj* — **her·maph·ro·dit·ic** \(,)hər-,maf-rə-'dit-ik\ *adj*

her·met·ic \hər-'met-ik\ *also* **her·met·i·cal** \-i-kəl\ *adj* : tightly sealed : AIRTIGHT — **her·met·i·cal·ly** \-i-k(ə-)lē\ *adv*

her·mit \'hər-mət\ *n* [ME *eremite*, fr. OF, fr. LL *eremita*, fr. Gk *erēmitēs*, adj., living in the desert, fr. *erēmia* desert, fr. *erēmos* lonely] : one who lives in solitude esp. for religious reasons

her·mit·age \-ij\ *n* **1** : the dwelling of a hermit **2** : a secluded dwelling

her·nia \'hər-nē-ə\ *n, pl* **-ni·as** *or* **-ni·ae** \-nē-ˌē, -nē-ˌī\ : a protruding of a bodily part (as a loop of intestine) into a pouch of the weakened wall of a cavity in which it is normally enclosed; *also* : the protruded mass — **her·ni·ate** \-nē-ˌāt\ *vb* — **her·ni·a·tion** \ˌhər-nē-'ā-shən\ *n*

he·ro \'hē-rō\ *n, pl* **heroes** **1** : a mythological or legendary figure of great strength or ability **2** : a man admired for his achievements and qualities **3** : the chief male character in a literary or dramatic work **4** *pl usu* **heros** : SUBMARINE 2 — **he·ro·ic** \hi-'rō-ik\ *adj* — **he·ro·i·cal·ly** \-i-k(ə-)lē\ *adv*

heroic couplet *n* : a rhyming couplet in iambic pentameter

he·ro·ics \hi-'rō-iks\ *n pl* : heroic or showy behavior

her·o·in \'her-ə-wən\ *n* : an illicit addictive narcotic drug made from morphine

her·o·ine \'her-ə-wən\ *n* **1** : a woman admired for her achievements and qualities **2** : the chief female character in a literary or dramatic work

her·o·ism \'her-ə-ˌwiz-əm\ *n* **1** : heroic conduct **2** : the qualities of a hero **syn** valor, prowess, gallantry

her·on \'her-ən\ *n, pl* **herons** *also* **heron** : a long-legged long-billed wading bird with soft plumage

her·pes \'hər-pēz\ *n* : any of several virus diseases characterized by the formation of blisters on the skin or mucous membranes

herpes sim·plex \-'sim-ˌpleks\ *n* : either of two forms of herpes marked in one by watery blisters above the waist (as on the mouth and lips) and in the other on the genitalia

herpes zos·ter \-'zäs-tər\ *n* : SHINGLES

her·pe·tol·o·gy \ˌhər-pə-'täl-ə-jē\ *n* : a branch of zoology dealing with reptiles and amphibians — **her·pe·tol·o·gist** \ˌhər-pə-'täl-ə-jəst\ *n*

her·ring \'her-iŋ\ *n, pl* **herring** *or* **herrings** : a soft-finned narrow-bodied food fish of the north Atlantic; *also* : any of various similar or related fishes

her·ring·bone \'her-iŋ-ˌbōn\ *n* : a pattern made up of rows of parallel lines with adjacent rows slanting in reverse directions; *also* : a twilled fabric with this pattern

hers \'hərz\ *pron* : one or the ones belonging to her

her·self \(h)ər-'self\ *pron* : SHE, HER — used reflexively, for emphasis, or in absolute constructions

hertz \'hərts, 'herts\ *n, pl* **hertz** : a unit of frequency equal to one cycle per second

hes·i·tant \'hez-ə-tənt\ *adj* : tending to hesitate — **hes·i·tance** \-tən(t)s\ *n* — **hes·i·tan·cy** \-tən-sē\ *n* — **hes·i·tant·ly** *adv*

hes·i·tate \'hez-ə-ˌtāt\ *vb* **-tat·ed; -tat·ing** **1** : to hold back (as in doubt) **2** : PAUSE **syn** waver, vacillate, falter, shilly-shally — **hes·i·ta·tion** \ˌhez-ə-'tā-shən\ *n*

het·ero·dox \'het-(ə-)rə-ˌdäks\ *adj* **1** : differing from an acknowledged standard **2** : holding unorthodox opinions — **het·er·o·doxy** \-ˌdäk-sē\ *n*

het·er·o·ge·neous \ˌhet-(ə-)rə-'jē-nē-əs, -nyəs\ *adj* : consisting of dissimilar ingredients or constituents : MIXED — **het·er·o·ge·ne·ity** \-jə-'nē-ət-ē\ *n* — **het·er·o·ge·neous·ly** *adv* — **het·er·o·ge·neous·ness** *n*

het·ero·sex·u·al \ˌhet-ə-rō-'sek-sh(ə-w)əl\ *adj* : tending to direct sexual desire toward the opposite sex; *also* : of or relating to different sexes — **heterosexual** *n* — **het·ero·sex·u·al·i·ty** \-ˌsek-shə-'wal-ət-ē\ *n*

hew \'hyü\ *vb* **hewed; hewed** *or* **hewn** \'hyün\; **hew·ing** **1** : to cut or fell with blows (as of an ax) **2** : to give shape to with or as if with an ax **3** : to conform strictly — **hew·er** *n*

HEW *abbr* Department of Health, Education, and Welfare

¹hex \'heks\ *vb* **1** : to practice witchcraft **2** : JINX

²hex *n* : SPELL, JINX

³hex *abbr* hexagon; hexagonal

hexa·gon \'hek-sə-ˌgän\ *n* : a polygon having six angles and six sides — **hex·ag·o·nal** \hek-'sag-ən-ᵊl\ *adj*

hex·am·e·ter \hek-'sam-ət-ər\ *n* : a line of verse containing six metrical feet

hey·day \'hā-ˌdā\ *n* : a period of greatest strength, vigor, or prosperity

hf *abbr* half

Hf *symbol* hafnium

HF *abbr* high frequency

hg *abbr* hectogram

Hg *symbol* [NL *hydrargyrum*, lit., water silver] mercury

hgt *abbr* height

hgwy *abbr* highway

HH *abbr* **1** Her Highness; His Highness **2** His Holiness

HHS *abbr* Department of Health and Human Services

HI *abbr* **1** Hawaii **2** humidity index

hi·a·tus \hī-ˈāt-əs\ *n* [L, fr. *hiatus*, pp. of *hiare* to yawn] **1** : a break in an object : GAP **2** : a lapse in continuity

hi·ba·chi \hi-ˈbäch-ē\ *n* [Jp] : a charcoal brazier

hi·ber·nate \ˈhī-bər-ˌnāt\ *vb* **-nat·ed; -nat·ing** : to pass the winter in a torpid or resting state — **hi·ber·na·tion** \ˌhī-bər-ˈnā-shən\ *n* — **hi·ber·na·tor** \ˈhī-bər-ˌnāt-ər\ *n*

hi·bis·cus \hī-ˈbis-kəs, hə-\ *n* : any of a genus of herbs, shrubs, and trees related to the mallows and noted for large showy flowers

hic·cup *also* **hic·cough** \ˈhik-(ˌ)əp\ *n* : a spasmodic breathing movement checked by sudden closing of the glottis accompanied by a peculiar sound; *also* : this sound — **hiccup** *vb*

hick \ˈhik\ *n* [*Hick*, nickname for *Richard*] : an awkward provincial person — **hick** *adj*

hick·o·ry \ˈhik-(ə-)rē\ *n, pl* **-ries** : any of a genus of No. American hardwood trees related to the walnuts; *also* : the wood of a hickory — **hickory** *adj*

hi·dal·go \hid-ˈal-gō\ *n, pl* **-gos** *often cap* [Sp, fr. earlier *fijo dalgo*, lit., son of something, son of property] : a member of the lower nobility of Spain

hidden tax *n* **1** : a tax ultimately paid by someone other than the person on whom it is formally levied **2** : an economic injustice that reduces one's income or buying power

¹hide \ˈhīd\ *vb* **hid** \ˈhid\; **hid·den** \ˈhid-ᵊn\ *or* **hid; hid·ing** \ˈhīd-iŋ\ **1** : to put or remain out of sight **2** : to conceal for shelter or protection; *also* : to seek protection **3** : to keep secret **4** : to turn away in shame or anger

²hide *n* : the skin of an animal

hide–and–seek \ˌhīd-ᵊn-ˈsēk\ *n* : a children's game in which everyone hides from one player who tries to find them

hide·away \ˈhīd-ə-ˌwā\ *n* : HIDEOUT

hide·bound \-ˌbaund\ *adj* : obstinately conservative

hid·eous \ˈhid-ē-əs\ *adj* [ME *hidous*, fr. OF, fr. *hisde, hide* terror] **1** : offensive to one of the senses : UGLY **2** : morally offensive : SHOCKING — **hid·eous·ly** *adv* — **hid·eous·ness** *n*

hide·out \ˈhīd-ˌaut\ *n* : a place of refuge or concealment

hie \ˈhī\ *vb* **hied; hy·ing** *or* **hie·ing** : HASTEN

hi·er·ar·chy \ˈhī-(ə-)ˌrär-kē\ *n, pl* **-chies** **1** : a ruling body of clergy organized into ranks **2** : persons or things arranged in a graded series — **hi·er·ar·chi·cal** \ˌhī-ə-ˈrär-ki-kəl\ *adj* — **hi·er·ar·chi·cal·ly** \-k(ə-)lē\ *adv*

hi·er·o·glyph·ic \ˌhī-(ə-)rə-ˈglif-ik\ *n* [MF *hieroglyphique*, adj., deriv. of Gk *hieroglyphikos*, fr. *hieros* sacred + *glyphein* to carve] **1** : a character in a system of picture writing (as of the ancient Egyptians) **2** : a symbol or sign difficult to decipher

hi–fi \ˈhī-ˈfī\ *n* **1** : HIGH FIDELITY **2** : equipment for reproduction of sound with high fidelity

hig·gle·dy–pig·gle·dy \ˌhig-əl-dē-ˈpig-əl-dē\ *adv* : in confusion

¹high \ˈhī\ *adj* **1** : ELEVATED; *also* : TALL **2** : advanced toward fullness or culmination; *also* : slightly tainted **3** : long past **4** : SHRILL, SHARP **5** : far from the equator ⟨∼ latitudes⟩ **6** : exalted in character **7** : of greater degree, size, or amount than average **8** : of relatively great importance **9** : FORCIBLE, STRONG ⟨∼ winds⟩ **10** : BOASTFUL, ARROGANT **11** : showing elation or excitement **12** : COSTLY, DEAR **13** : advanced esp. in complexity ⟨∼er mathematics⟩ **14** : INTOXICATED; *also* : excited or stupefied by or as if by a drug (as heroin) — **high·ly** *adv*

²high *adv* **1** : at or to a high place or degree **2** : LUXURIOUSLY ⟨living ∼⟩

³high *n* **1** : an elevated place **2** : a high point or level **3** : the arrangement of gears in an automobile that gives the highest speed **4** : an excited or stupefied state produced by or as if by a drug

high·ball \ˈhī-ˌbȯl\ *n* : a usu. tall drink of liquor mixed with water or a carbonated beverage

high beam *n* : the long-range focus of a vehicle headlight

high·born \'hī-'bȯrn\ *adj* : of noble birth

high·boy \-ˌbȯi\ *n* : a high chest of drawers mounted on a base with legs

high·bred \-'bred\ *adj* : coming from superior stock

high·brow \-ˌbrau̇\ *n* : a person of superior learning or culture — **highbrow** *adj*

high·er–up \ˌhī-ər-'əp\ *n* : a superior officer of official

high·fa·lu·tin \ˌhī-fə-'lüt-ᵊn\ *adj* : PRETENTIOUS, POMPOUS

high fashion *n* **1** : HIGH STYLE **2** : HAUTE COUTURE

high fidelity *n* : the reproduction of sound or image with a high degree of faithfulness to the original

high five *n* : a slapping of upraised right hands by two people (as in celebration) — **high–five** *vb*

high–flown \'hī-'flōn\ *adj* **1** : EXALTED **2** : BOMBASTIC

high frequency *n* : a radio frequency between 3 and 30 megahertz

high gear *n* **1** : HIGH 3 **2** : a state of intense or maximum activity

high–hand·ed \'hī-'han-dəd\ *adj* : OVERBEARING — **high–hand·ed·ly** *adv* — **high–hand·ed·ness** *n*

high–hat \-'hat\ *adj* : SUPERCILIOUS, SNOBBISH — **high–hat** *vb*

high·land \-lənd\ *n* : elevated or mountainous land

high·land·er \-lən-dər\ *n* **1** : an inhabitant of a highland **2** *cap* : an inhabitant of the Scottish Highlands

¹high·light \-ˌlīt\ *n* : an event or detail of major importance

²highlight *vb* **1** : EMPHASIZE **2** : to constitute a highlight of

high–mind·ed \-'mīn-dəd\ *adj* : marked by elevated principles and feelings — **high–mind·ed·ness** *n*

high·ness \'hī-nəs\ *n* **1** : the quality or state of being high **2** — used as a title (as for kings)

high–pres·sure \-'presh-ər\ *adj* : using or involving aggressive and insistent sales techniques

high–rise \-'rīz\ *adj* : having several stories and being equipped with elevators ⟨∼ apartments⟩; *also* : of or relating to high-rise buildings

high·road \-ˌrōd\ *n* : HIGHWAY

high school *n* : a school usu. including grades 9 to 12 or 10 to 12

high sea *n* : the open sea outside territorial waters — usu. used in pl.

high–sound·ing \'hī-'saún-diŋ\ *adj* : POMPOUS, IMPOSING

high–spir·it·ed \-'spir-ət-əd\ *adj* : characterized by a bold or lofty spirit

high–strung \-'strəŋ\ *adj* : having an extremely nervous or sensitive temperament

high style *n* : the newest in fashion or design usu. adopted by a limited number of people

high·tail \'hī-ˌtāl\ *vb* : to retreat at full speed

high tech \-'tek\ *n* : HIGH TECHNOLOGY

high technology *n* : technology involving the use of advanced devices or techniques

high–ten·sion \'hī-'ten-chən\ *adj* : having, using, or relating to high voltage

high–test \-'test\ *adj* : having a high octane number

high–toned \-'tōnd\ *adj* **1** : high in social, moral, or intellectual quality **2** : PRETENTIOUS, POMPOUS

high·way \'hī-ˌwā\ *n* : a main direct road

high·way·man \-mən\ *n* : a person who robs travelers on a road

hi·jack *or* **high–jack** \'hī-ˌjak\ *vb* : to steal esp. by stopping a vehicle on the highway; *also* : to commandeer a flying airplane — **hijack** *n* — **hi·jack·er** *n*

¹hike \'hīk\ *vb* **hiked; hik·ing 1** : to move or raise with a sudden motion **2** : to take a long walk — **hik·er** *n*

²hike *n* **1** : a long walk **2** : RISE, INCREASE

hi·lar·i·ous \hil-'ar-ē-əs, hī-'lar-\ *adj* : marked by or providing boisterous merriment — **hi·lar·i·ous·ly** *adv* — **hi·lar·i·ty** \-ət-ē\ *n*

hill \'hil\ *n* **1** : a usu. rounded elevation of land **2** : a little heap or mound (as of earth) — **hilly** *adj*

hill·bil·ly \'hil-ˌbil-ē\ *n, pl* **-lies** : a person from a backwoods area

hill·ock \'hil-ək\ *n* : a small hill

hill·side \-ˌsīd\ *n* : the part of a hill between the summit and the foot

hill·top \-ˌtäp\ *n* : the top of a hill

hilt \'hilt\ *n* : a handle esp. of a sword or dagger

him \im, (')him\ *pron,* objective case of HE

Hi·ma·la·yan \ˌhim-ə-'lā-ən, him-'äl-yən\ *adj* : of, relating to, or characteristic of the Himalaya mountains or the people living there

him·self \(h)im-'self\ *pron* : HE, HIM — used reflexively, for emphasis, or in absolute constructions

¹hind \'hīnd\ *n, pl* **hinds** *also* **hind** : a female deer : DOE

²hind *adj* : REAR

¹hin·der \'hin-dər\ *vb* **hin·dered; hin·der·ing** \-d(ə-)riŋ\ **1** : to impede the progress of **2** : to hold back **syn** obstruct, block, bar, impede

²hind·er \'hīn-dər\ *adj* : HIND

Hin·di \'hin-dē\ *n* : a literary and official language of northern India

hind·most \'hīn(d)-ˌmōst\ *adj* : farthest to the rear

hind·quar·ter \-ˌkwȯrt-ər\ *n* **1** : one side of the back half of the carcass of a quadruped **2** *pl* : the part of the body of a quadruped behind the junction of hind limbs and trunk

hin·drance \'hin-drəns\ *n* **1** : the state of being hindered; *also* : the action of hindering **2** : IMPEDIMENT

hind·sight \'hīn(d)-ˌsīt\ *n* : understanding of an event after it has happened

Hin·du·ism \'hin-dü-ˌiz-əm\ *n* : a body of religious beliefs and practices native to India — **Hin·du** *n or adj*

hind wing *n* : either of the posterior wings of a 4-winged insect

¹hinge \'hinj\ *n* : a jointed piece on which one piece (as a door, gate, or lid) turns or swings on another

²hinge *vb* **hinged; hing·ing** **1** : to attach by or furnish with hinges **2** : to be contingent on a single consideration

hint \'hint\ *n* **1** : an indirect or summary suggestion **2** : CLUE **3** : a very small amount — **hint** *vb*

hin·ter·land \'hint-ər-ˌland\ *n* **1** : a region behind a coast **2** : a region remote from cities

¹hip \'hip\ *n* : the fruit of a rose

²hip *n* **1** : the part of the body on either side below the waist consisting of the side of the pelvis and the upper thigh **2** : the joint between pelvis and femur

³hip *also* **hep** *adj* **hip·per; hip·pest** : keenly aware of or interested in the newest developments

⁴hip *vb* **hipped; hip·ping** : TELL, INFORM

hip·bone \-'bōn, -ˌbōn\ *n* : the large flaring bone that makes a lateral half of the pelvis in mammals

hip joint *n* : the articulation between the femur and the hipbone

hipped \'hipt\ *adj* : having hips esp. of a specified kind ⟨broad-*hipped*⟩

hip·pie *or* **hip·py** \'hip-ē\ *n, pl* **hippies** : a usu. young person who rejects established mores, advocates nonviolence, and often uses psychedelic drugs or marijuana; *also* : a long-haired unconventionally dressed young person

hip·po·drome \'hip-ə-ˌdrōm\ *n* : an arena for equestrian performances

hip·po·pot·a·mus \ˌhip-ə-'pät-ə-məs\ *n, pl* **-mus·es** *or* **-mi** \-ˌmī\ [L, fr. Gk *hippopotamos,* fr. *hippos* horse + *potamos* river] : a large thick-skinned African river animal related to the swine

¹hire \'hī(ə)r\ *n* **1** : payment for labor or personal services : WAGES **2** : EMPLOYMENT

²hire *vb* **hired; hir·ing** **1** : to employ for pay **2** : to engage the temporary use of for pay

hire·ling \'hī(ə)r-liŋ\ *n* : a hired person; *esp* : one whose motives are mercenary

hir·sute \'hər-ˌsüt, 'hiər-\ *adj* : HAIRY

¹his \(h)iz, ˌhiz\ *adj* : of or relating to him or himself

²his \'hiz\ *pron* : one or the ones belonging to him

His·pan·ic \his-'pan-ik\ *adj* : of or relating to the people, speech, or culture of Spain or Latin America

hiss \'his\ *vb* : to make a sharp sibilant sound; *also* : to express disapproval of by hissing — **hiss** *n*

hist *abbr* historian; historical; history

his·ta·mine \'his-tə-ˌmēn, -mən\ *n* : a chemical compound widespread in animal tissues and playing a major role in allergic reactions

his·to·gram \'his-tə-ˌgram\ *n* : representation of statistical data by means of rectangles whose widths represent class intervals and whose heights represent corresponding frequencies

his·to·ri·an \his-'tōr-ē-ən\ *n* : a student or writer of history

his·to·ric·i·ty \ˌhis-tə-'ris-ət-ē\ *n* : historical actuality

his·to·ri·og·ra·pher \his-ˌtōr-ē-'äg-rə-fər\ *n* : HISTORIAN

his·to·ry \'his-t(ə-)rē\ *n, pl* **-ries** [L *historia*, fr. Gk, inquiry, history, fr. *histōr, istōr* knowing, learned] **1** : a chronological record of significant events often with an explanation of their causes **2** : a branch of knowledge that records and explains past events **3** : events that form the subject matter of history — **his·tor·ic** \his-'tȯr-ik\ *adj* — **his·tor·i·cal** \-i-kəl\ *adj* — **his·tor·i·cal·ly** \-k(ə-)lē\ *adv*

his·tri·on·ic \ˌhis-trē-'än-ik\ *adj* [LL *histrionicus*, fr. L *histrio* actor] **1** : deliberately affected **2** : of or relating to actors or the theater — **his·tri·on·i·cal·ly** \-i-k(ə-)lē\ *adv*

his·tri·on·ics \-iks\ *n pl* **1** : theatrical performances **2** : deliberate display of emotion for effect

¹hit \'hit\ *vb* **hit; hit·ting 1** : to reach with a blow : STRIKE **2** : to make or bring into contact : COLLIDE **3** : to affect detrimentally **4** : to make a request of **5** : to come upon **6** : to accord with : SUIT **7** : REACH, ATTAIN **8** : to indulge in often to excess — **hit·ter** *n*

²hit *n* **1** : BLOW; *also* : COLLISION **2** : something highly successful **3** : a stroke in an athletic contest; *esp* : BASE HIT **4** : a dose of an illegal drug **5** : a murder committed by a gangster

¹hitch \'hich\ *vb* **1** : to move by jerks **2** : to catch or fasten esp. by a hook or knot **3** : HITCHHIKE

²hitch *n* **1** : JERK, PULL **2** : a sudden halt **3** : a connection between something towed and its mover **4** : KNOT

hitch·hike \'hich-ˌhīk\ *vb* : to travel by securing free rides from passing vehicles — **hitch·hik·er** *n*

¹hith·er \'hith-ər\ *adv* : to this place

²hither *adj* : being on the near or adjacent side

hith·er·to \-ˌtü\ *adv* : up to this time

HIV *n* [*human immunodeficiency virus*] : AIDS VIRUS

hive \'hīv\ *n* **1** : a container for housing honeybees **2** : a colony of bees **3** : a place swarming with busy occupants — **hive** *vb*

hives \'hīvz\ *n sing or pl* : an allergic disorder marked by the presence of itching wheals

HJ *abbr* [L *hic jacet*] here lies — used in epitaphs

hl *abbr* hectoliter

HL *abbr* House of Lords

hm *abbr* hectometer

HM *abbr* **1** Her Majesty; Her Majesty's **2** His Majesty; His Majesty's

HMS *abbr* Her Majesty's ship; His Majesty's ship

Ho *symbol* holmium

hoa·gie *also* **hoa·gy** \'hō-gē\ *n, pl* **hoagies** : SUBMARINE 2

hoard \'hōrd\ *n* : a hidden accumulation — **hoard** *vb* — **hoard·er** *n*

hoar·frost \'hōr-ˌfrȯst\ *n* : FROST 2

hoarse \'hōrs\ *adj* **hoars·er; hoars·est 1** : rough and harsh in sound **2** : having a grating voice — **hoarse·ly** *adv* — **hoarse·ness** *n*

hoary \'hōr-ē\ *adj* **hoar·i·er; -est 1** : gray or white with age **2** : ANCIENT — **hoar·i·ness** *n*

hoax \'hōks\ *n* : an act intended to trick or dupe; *also* : something accepted or established by fraud — **hoax** *vb* — **hoax·er** *n*

hob \'häb\ *n* : MISCHIEF, TROUBLE

¹hob·ble \'häb-əl\ *vb* **hob·bled, hob·bling** \-(ə-)liŋ\ **1** : to limp along; *also* : to make lame **2** : FETTER

²hobble *n* **1** : a hobbling movement **2** : something used to hobble an animal

hob·by \'häb-ē\ *n, pl* **hobbies** : a pursuit or interest engaged in for relaxation — **hob·by·ist** \-ē-əst\ *n*

hob·by·horse \'häb-ē-ˌhȯrs\ *n* **1** : a stick with a horse's head on which children pretend to ride **2** : a toy horse mounted on rockers **3** : a favorite topic to which one constantly reverts

hob·gob·lin \'häb-ˌgäb-lən\ *n* **1** : a mischievous goblin **2** : BOGEY 1

hob·nail \-ˌnāl\ *n* : a short large-headed nail for studding shoe soles — **hob·nailed** \-ˌnāld\ *adj*

hob·nob \-ˌnäb\ *vb* **hob·nobbed; hob·nob·bing** : to associate familiarly

ho·bo \'hō-bō\ *n, pl* **hoboes** *also* **hobos** : TRAMP 2

¹hock \'häk\ *n* : a joint or region in the hind limb of a quadruped just above the foot and corresponding to the human ankle

²hock *n* [D *hok* pen, prison] : PAWN; *also* : DEBT **2** — **hock** *vb*

hock·ey \'häk-ē\ *n* **1** : FIELD HOCKEY **2** : ICE HOCKEY

ho·cus–po·cus \,hō-kəs-'pō-kəs\ *n* **1** : SLEIGHT OF HAND **2** : nonsense or sham used to conceal deception

hod \'häd\ *n* **1** : a long-handled tray or trough for carrying a load esp. of mortar or bricks **2** : a coal scuttle

hodge·podge \'häj-,päj\ *n* : a heterogeneous mixture

hoe \'hō\ *n* : a long-handled implement with a thin flat blade used esp. for cultivating, weeding, or loosening the earth around plants — **hoe** *vb*

hoe·cake \'hō-,kāk\ *n* : a small cornmeal cake

hoe·down \-,daůn\ *n* **1** : SQUARE DANCE **2** : a gathering featuring hoedowns

¹hog \'hȯg, 'häg\ *n, pl* **hogs** *also* **hog 1** : a domestic swine esp. when grown **2** : a selfish, gluttonous, or filthy person — **hog·gish** *adj*

²hog *vb* **hogged; hog·ging** : to take or hold selfishly

ho·gan \'hō-,gän\ *n* : an earth-covered dwelling of the Navaho Indians

hog·back \'hȯg-,bak, 'häg-\ *n* : a ridge with a sharp summit and steep sides

hog·nose snake \,hȯg-,nōz-, ,häg-\ *or* **hog·nosed snake** \-,nōz(d)-\ *n* : any of several rather small harmless stout-bodied No. American snakes with an upturned snout that play dead when their threatening display is ineffective

hogs·head \'hȯgz-,hed, 'hägz-\ *n* **1** : a large cask or barrel; *esp* : one holding from 63 to 140 gallons **2** : a liquid measure equal to 63 U.S. gallons

hog–tie \'hȯg-,tī, 'häg-\ *vb* **1** : to tie together the feet of ⟨~ a calf⟩ **2** : to make helpless

hog·wash \-,wȯsh, -,wäsh\ *n* **1** : SWILL 1, SLOP 2 **2** : NONSENSE, BALONEY

hog–wild \-'wīld\ *adj* : lacking in restraint

hoi pol·loi \,hȯi-pə-'lȯi\ *n pl* [Gk, the many] : the general populace

¹hoist \'hȯist\ *vb* : RAISE, LIFT

²hoist *n* **1** : LIFT **2** : an apparatus for hoisting

hoke \'hōk\ *vb* **hoked; hok·ing** : FAKE — usu. used with *up*

ho·kum \'hō-kəm\ *n* : NONSENSE

¹hold \'hōld\ *vb* **held** \'held\; **hold·ing 1**

: POSSESS; *also* : KEEP **2** : RESTRAIN **3** : to have a grasp on **4** : to remain or keep in a particular situation or position **5** : SUSTAIN; *also* : RESERVE **6** : BEAR, COMPORT **7** : to maintain in being or action : PERSIST **8** : CONTAIN, ACCOMMODATE **9** : HARBOR, ENTERTAIN; *also* : CONSIDER, REGARD **10** : to carry on by concerted action; *also* : CONVOKE **11** : to occupy esp. by appointment or election **12** : to be valid **13** : HALT, PAUSE — **hold·er** *n* — **hold forth** : to speak at length — **hold to** : to adhere to : MAINTAIN — **hold with** : to agree with or approve of

²hold *n* **1** : STRONGHOLD **2** : CONFINEMENT; *also* : PRISON **3** : the act or manner of holding : GRIP **4** : a restraining, dominating, or controlling influence **5** : something that may be grasped as a support **6** : an order or indication that something is to be reserved or delayed

³hold *n* **1** : the interior of a ship below decks; *esp* : a ship's cargo deck **2** : an airplane's cargo compartment

hold·ing \'hōl-diŋ\ *n* **1** : land or other property owned **2** : a ruling of a court esp. on an issue of law

holding pattern *n* : a course flown by an aircraft waiting to land

hold out \(')hōl-'daůt\ *vb* **1** : to continue to fight or work **2** : to refuse to come to an agreement — **hold·out** \'hōl-,daůt\ *n*

hold·over \'hōl-,dō-vər\ *n* : a person who continues in office

hold·up \'hōl-,dəp\ *n* **1** : DELAY **2** : robbery at the point of a gun

hole \'hōl\ *n* **1** : an opening into or through something **2** : a hollow place (as a pit or cave) **3** : DEN, BURROW **4** : a unit of play from tee to cup in golf **5** : a wretched or dingy place **6** : an awkward position — **hole** *vb*

hol·i·day \'häl-ə-,dā\ *n* [ME, fr. OE *hāligdæg*, fr. *hālig* holy + *dæg* day] **1** : a day observed in Judaism with commemorative ceremonies **2** : a day of freedom from work; *esp* : one in commemoration of an event **3** : VACATION — **holiday** *vb*

ho·li·ness \'hō-lē-nəs\ *n* **1** : the quality or state of being holy **2** — used as a title for various high religious officials

hol·ler \'häl-ər\ *vb* **hol·lered; hol·ler·ing**

\-(ə-)riŋ\ : to cry out : SHOUT — **holler** *n*

¹**hol·low** \ˈhäl-ō\ *adj* **hol·low·er** \ˈhäl-ə-wər\; **hol·low·est** \-ə-wəst\ **1** : CONCAVE, SUNKEN **2** : having a cavity within **3** : MUFFLED ⟨a ~ sound⟩ **4** : lacking in real value, sincerity, or substance; *also* : FALSE — **hol·low·ness** *n*

²**hollow** *n* **1** : a surface depression **2** : CAVITY, HOLE

³**hollow** *vb* : to make or become hollow

hol·low·ware *or* **hol·lo·ware** \ˈhäl-ə-ˌwaər\ *n* : vessels (as bowls or cups) that have a significant depth and volume

hol·ly \ˈhäl-ē\ *n, pl* **hollies** : a tree or shrub with usu. evergreen glossy spiny-margined leaves and red berries

hol·ly·hock \-ˌhäk, -ˌhȯk\ *n* [ME *holihoc,* fr. *holi* holy + *hoc* mallow] : a tall perennial herb related to the mallows that is widely grown for its showy flowers

hol·mi·um \ˈhōl-mē-əm\ *n* : a metallic chemical element

ho·lo·caust \ˈhäl-ə-ˌkȯst, ˈhō-lə-, ˈhȯ-lə-\ *n* **1** : a thorough destruction esp. by fire **2** *often cap* : the killing of European Jews by the Nazis during World War II

Ho·lo·cene \ˈhō-lə-ˌsēn\ *adj* : RECENT 3 — **Holocene** *n*

ho·lo·gram \ˈhō-lə-ˌgram, ˈhäl-ə-\ *n* : a three-dimensional picture made by reflected laser light on a photographic film without the use of a camera

ho·lo·graph \ˈhō-lə-ˌgraf, ˈhäl-ə-\ *n* : a document wholly in the handwriting of its author

ho·log·ra·phy \hō-ˈläg-rə-fē\ *n* : the process of making or using a hologram — **ho·lo·graph·ic** \ˌhō-lə-ˈgraf-ik, ˌhäl-ə-\ *adj*

hol·stein \ˈhōl-ˌstēn, -ˌstīn\ *n* : any of a breed of large black-and-white dairy cattle that produce large quantities of comparatively low-fat milk

hol·stein–frie·sian \-ˈfrē-zhən\ *n* : HOLSTEIN

hol·ster \ˈhōl-stər\ *n* [Dutch] : a usu. leather case for a firearm

ho·ly \ˈhō-lē\ *adj* **ho·li·er; -est** **1** : worthy of absolute devotion **2** : SACRED **3** : having a divine quality **syn** hallowed, blessed, sacred, sanctified, consecrated

Holy Spirit *n* : the active presence of God in human life constituting the third person of the Trinity

ho·ly·stone \ˈhō-lē-ˌstōn\ *n* : a soft sandstone used to scrub a ship's decks — **holy·stone** *vb*

hom·age \ˈ(h)äm-ij\ *n* [ME, fr. OF *hommage,* fr. *homme* man, vassal, fr. L *homo* man] : reverential regard

hom·bre \ˈäm-brē, ˈəm-, -ˌbrä\ *n* : GUY, FELLOW

hom·burg \ˈhäm-ˌbərg\ *n* [*Homburg,* Germany] : a man's felt hat with a stiff curled brim and a high crown creased lengthwise

¹**home** \ˈhōm\ *n* **1** : one's residence; *also* : HOUSE **2** : the social unit formed by a family living together **3** : a congenial environment; *also* : HABITAT **4** : a place of origin **5** : the objective in various games — **home·less** *adj*

²**home** *vb* **homed; hom·ing** **1** : to go or return home **2** : to proceed to or toward a source of radiated energy used as a guide

home·body \ˈhōm-ˌbäd-ē\ *n* : one whose life centers in the home

home·bred \-ˈbred\ *adj* : produced at home : INDIGENOUS

home·com·ing \-ˌkəm-iŋ\ *n* **1** : a return home **2** : the return of a group of people esp. on a special occasion to a place formerly frequented

home computer *n* : a small inexpensive microcomputer

home economics *n* : the theory and practice of homemaking

home·grown \ˈhōm-ˈgrōn\ *adj* **1** : grown domestically ⟨~ corn⟩ **2** : LOCAL, INDIGENOUS

home·land \-ˌland\ *n* **1** : native land **2** : an area set aside to be a state for a people of a particular national, cultural, or racial origin

home·ly \ˈhōm-lē\ *adj* **home·li·er; -est** **1** : FAMILIAR **2** : unaffectedly natural **3** : lacking beauty or proportion — **home·li·ness** *n*

home·made \ˈhōm-ˌ(m)ād\ *adj* : made in the home, on the premises, or by one's own efforts

home·mak·er \-ˌmā-kər\ *n* : one who manages a household esp. as a wife and mother — **home·mak·ing** \-kiŋ\ *n*

ho•me•op•a•thy \ˌhō-mē-ˈäp-ə-thē\ *n* : a system of medical practice that treats disease esp. with minute doses of a remedy that would in healthy persons produce symptoms of the disease treated — **ho•meo•path** \ˈhō-mē-ə-ˌpath\ *n* — **ho•meo•path•ic** \ˌhō-mē-ə-ˈpath-ik\ *adj*

ho•meo•sta•sis \ˌhō-mē-ō-ˈstā-səs\ *n* : a tendency toward a stable state of equilibrium between interrelated physiological, psychological, or social factors characteristic of an individual or group — **ho•meo•stat•ic** \-ˈstat-ik\ *adj*

home plate *n* : a slab at the apex of a baseball diamond that a base runner must touch in order to score

hom•er \ˈhō-mər\ *n* : HOME RUN — **homer** *vb*

home•room \ˈhōm-ˌrüm, -ˌrùm\ *n* : a classroom where pupils report at the beginning of each school day

home run *n* : a hit in baseball that enables the batter to make a circuit of the bases and score a run

home•sick \ˈhōm-ˌsik\ *adj* : longing for home and family while absent from them — **home•sick•ness** *n*

home•spun \-ˌspən\ *adj* **1** : spun or made at home; *also* : made of a loosely woven usu. woolen or linen fabric **2** : SIMPLE, HOMELY

¹home•stead \ˈhōm-ˌsted\ *n* : the home and land occupied by a family

²homestead *vb* : to acquire or settle on public land — **home•stead•er** \-ˌsted-ər\ *n*

home•stretch \ˈhōm-ˈstrech\ *n* **1** : the part of a racecourse between the last curve and the winning post **2** : a final stage (as of a project)

¹home•ward \ˈhōm-wərd\ *or* **home•wards** \-wərdz\ *adv* : in the direction of home

²homeward *adj* : being or going in the direction of home

home•work \ˈhōm-ˌwərk\ *n* **1** : an assignment given a student to be completed outside the classroom **2** : preparatory reading or research

hom•ey \ˈhō-mē\ *adj* **hom•i•er; -est** : intimate or homelike

ho•mi•cide \ˈhäm-ə-ˌsīd, ˈhō-mə-\ *n* [L *homicida* manslayer & *homicidium* manslaughter; both fr. *homo* man +

caedere to cut, kill] **1** : a person who kills another **2** : a killing of one human being by another — **hom•i•cid•al** \ˌhäm-ə-ˈsīd-ᵊl\ *adj*

hom•i•ly \ˈhäm-ə-lē\ *n, pl* **-lies** : SERMON — **hom•i•let•ic** \ˌhäm-ə-ˈlet-ik\ *adj*

homing pigeon *n* : a racing pigeon trained to return home

hom•i•ny \ˈhäm-ə-nē\ *n* : hulled corn with the germ removed

ho•mo \ˈhō-mō\ *n, pl* **homos** : any of the genus of primate mammals that includes all surviving and various extinct human beings

ho•mo•ge•neous \ˌhō-mə-ˈjē-nē-əs, -nyəs\ *adj* : of the same or a similar kind; *also* : of uniform structure — **ho•mo•ge•ne•i•ty** \-jə-ˈnē-ət-ē\ *n* — **ho•mo•ge•neous•ly** *adv* — **ho•mo•ge•nous•ness** *n*

ho•mog•e•nize \hō-ˈmäj-ə-ˌnīz, hə-\ *vb* **-nized; -niz•ing 1** : to make homogeneous **2** : to reduce the particles in (as milk or paint) to uniform size and distribute them evenly throughout the liquid — **ho•mog•e•ni•za•tion** \-ˌmäj-ə-nə-ˈzā-shən\ *n* — **ho•mog•e•niz•er** *n*

ho•mo•graph \ˈhäm-ə-ˌgraf, ˈhō-mə-\ *n* : one of two or more words spelled alike but different in origin or meaning or pronunciation ⟨the noun *conduct* and the verb *conduct* are ~s⟩

ho•mol•o•gy \hō-ˈmäl-ə-jē, hə-\ *n, pl* **-gies 1** : structural likeness between corresponding parts of different plants or animals due to evolution from a common ancestor **2** : structural likeness between different parts of the same individual — **ho•mol•o•gous** \-ˈmäl-ə-gəs\ *adj*

hom•onym \ˈhäm-ə-ˌnim, ˈhō-mə-\ *n* **1** : HOMOPHONE, HOMOGRAPH **2** : one of two or more words spelled and pronounced alike but different in meaning ⟨*pool* of water and *pool* the game are ~s⟩

ho•mo•phone \ˈhäm-ə-ˌfōn, ˈhō-mə-\ *n* : one of two or more words (as *to, too, two*) pronounced alike but different in meaning or derivation or spelling

Ho•mo sa•pi•ens \ˌhō-mō-ˈsā-pē-ənz, -ˈsap-ē-\ *n* : the totality of human beings : MANKIND 1

ho•mo•sex•u•al \ˌhō-mō-ˈsek-sh(ə-w)əl\ *adj* : of, relating to, or exhibiting sexual desire toward another of the same sex — **homosexual** *n* — **ho·mo·sex·u·al·i·ty** \-ₗsek-shə-'wal-ət-ē\ *n*

hon *abbr* honor; honorable; honorary

hone \'hōn\ *n* : a fine-grit stone for sharpening a cutting implement — **hone** *vb* — **hon·er** *n*

hon·est \'än-əst\ *adj* **1** : free from deception : TRUTHFUL; *also* : GENUINE, REAL **2** : REPUTABLE **3** : CREDITABLE **4** : marked by integrity **5** : FRANK **syn** upright, just, conscientious, honorable — **hon·est·ly** *adv* — **hon·esty** \-ə-stē\ *n*

hon·ey \'hən-ē\ *n, pl* **honeys** : a sweet sticky substance made by bees (**hon·ey·bees** \-ₗbēz\) from the nectar of flowers

¹hon·ey·comb \-ₗkōm\ *n* : a mass of 6-sided wax cells built by honeybees; *also* : something of similar structure or appearance

²honeycomb *vb* : to make or become full of cavities like a honeycomb

hon·ey·dew \-ₗd(y)ü\ *n* : a sweetish deposit secreted on plants by aphids, scale insects, or fungi

honeydew melon *n* : a smooth-skinned muskmelon with sweet green flesh

honey locust *n* : a tall usu. spiny No. American leguminous tree with hard durable wood and long twisted pods

hon·ey·moon \'hən-ē-ₗmün\ *n* **1** : a holiday taken by an newly married couple **2** : a period of harmony esp. just after marriage — **honeymoon** *vb*

hon·ey·suck·le \'hən-ē-ₗsək-əl\ *n* : any of various shrubs, vines, or herbs with tube-shaped flowers rich in nectar

honk \'häŋk, 'hȯŋk\ *n* : the cry of a goose; *also* : a similar sound (as of a horn) — **honk** *vb* — **honk·er** *n*

hon·ky–tonk \'häŋ-kē-ₗtäŋk, 'hȯŋ-kē-ₗtȯŋk\ *n* : a tawdry nightclub or dance hall

¹hon·or \'än-ər\ *n* **1** : good name : REPUTATION; *also* : outward respect **2** : PRIVILEGE **3** : a person of superior standing — used esp. as a title **4** : one who brings respect or fame **5** : an evidence or symbol of distinction **6** : CHASTITY, PURITY **7** : INTEGRITY **syn** homage, reverence, deference, obeisance

²honor *vb* **hon·ored; hon·or·ing** \-(ə-)riŋ\ **1** : to regard or treat with honor **2** : to confer honor on **3** : to fulfill the terms of; *also* : to accept as payment — **hon·or·er** \'än-ər-ər\ *n*

hon·or·able \'än-(ə-)rə-bəl\ *adj* **1** : deserving of honor **2** : accompanied with marks of honor **3** : of great renown **4** : doing credit to the possessor **5** : characterized by integrity — **hon·or·able·ness** *n* — **hon·or·ably** \-blē\ *adv*

hon·o·rar·i·um \ₗän-ə-'rer-ē-əm\ *n, pl* **-ia** \-ē-ə\ *also* **-i·ums** : a reward usu. for services on which custom or propriety forbids a price to be set

hon·or·ary \'än-ə-ₗrer-ē\ *adj* **1** : having or conferring distinction **2** : conferred in recognition of achievement without the usual prerequisites ⟨∼ degree⟩ **3** : UNPAID, VOLUNTARY — **hon·or·ari·ly** \ₗän-ə-'rer-ə-lē\ *adv*

hon·or·if·ic \ₗän-ə-'rif-ik\ *adj* : conferring or conveying honor ⟨∼ titles⟩

hon·our \'än-ər\ *chiefly Brit* var of HONOR

¹hood \'hu̇d\ *n* **1** : a covering for the head and neck and sometimes the face **2** : an ornamental fold (as at the back of an ecclesiastical vestment) **3** : a cover for parts of mechanisms; *esp* : the metal covering over an automobile engine — **hood·ed** \-əd\ *adj*

²hood \'hu̇d, 'hüd\ *n* : HOODLUM

-hood \ₗhu̇d\ *n suffix* **1** : state : condition : quality : character ⟨boy*hood*⟩ ⟨hardi*hood*⟩ **2** : instance of a (specified) state or quality ⟨false*hood*⟩ **3** : individuals sharing a (specified) state or character ⟨brother*hood*⟩

hood·lum \'hüd-ləm, 'hu̇d-\ *n* **1** : THUG **2** : a young ruffian

hoo·doo \'hüd-ü\ *n, pl* **hoodoos** **1** : VOODOO **2** : something that brings bad luck — **hoodoo** *vb*

hood·wink \'hu̇d-ₗwiŋk\ *vb* : to deceive by false appearance

hoo·ey \'hü-ē\ *n* : NONSENSE

hoof \'hu̇f, 'hüf\ *n, pl* **hooves** \'hu̇vz, 'hüvz\ *or* **hoofs** : a horny covering that protects the ends of the toes of ungulate mammals (as horses or cattle); *also* : a hoofed foot — **hoofed** \'hu̇ft, 'hüft\ *adj*

¹hook \'hu̇k\ *n* **1** : a curved or bent device for catching, holding, or pulling **2** : something curved or bent like a hook **3** : a flight of a ball (as in golf) that curves in a direction opposite to the dominant hand of the player propelling it **4** : a short punch delivered with a circular motion and with the elbow bent and rigid

²**hook** *vb* **1** : CURVE, CROOK **2** : to seize or make fast with a hook **3** : STEAL **4** : to work as a prostitute

hoo·kah \'hùk-ə, 'hü-kə\ *n* [Ar *ḥuqqah* bottle of a water pipe] : a pipe for smoking that has a long flexible tube whereby the smoke is cooled by passing through water

hook·er \'hùk-ər\ *n* **1** : one that hooks **2** : PROSTITUTE

hook·up \'hùk-ˌəp\ *n* : an assemblage (as of apparatus or circuits) used for a specific purpose (as in radio)

hook·worm \'hùk-ˌwərm\ *n* : a parasitic intestinal nematode worm having hooks or plates around the mouth

hoo·li·gan \'hü-li-gən\ *n* : RUFFIAN, HOODLUM

hoop \'hùp, 'hüp\ *n* **1** : a circular strip used esp. for holding together the staves of a barrel **2** : a circular figure or object : RING **3** : a circle or flexible material for expanding a woman's skirt

hoop·la \'hüp-ˌlä, 'hùp-ˌlä\ *n* [F *houp-là*, interj.] **1** : TO-DO; *also* : BALLYHOO **2** : bewildering language

hoose·gow \'hüs-ˌgaù\ *n* [Sp *juzgado* panel of judges, courtroom] *slang* : JAIL

hoot \'hüt\ *vb* **1** : to shout or laugh usu. in contempt **2** : to make the natural throat noise of an owl — **hoot** *n* — **hoot·er** *n*

¹**hop** \'häp\ *vb* **hopped; hop·ping 1** : to move by quick springy leaps **2** : to make a quick trip **3** : to ride on esp. surreptitiously and without authorization

²**hop** *n* **1** : a short brisk leap esp. on one leg **2** : DANCE **3** : a short trip by air

³**hop** *n* : a vine related to the mulberry whose ripe dried pistillate catkins are used in medicine and in flavoring malt liquors; *also* : its pistillate catkin

⁴**hop** *vb* **hopped; hop·ping** : to increase the power of ⟨∼ up an engine⟩

¹**hope** \'hōp\ *vb* **hoped; hop·ing** : to desire with expectation of fulfillment

²**hope** *n* **1** : TRUST, RELIANCE **2** : desire accompanied by expectation of fulfillment; *also* : something hoped for **3** : one that gives promise for the future

— **hope·ful** \-fəl\ *adj* — **hope·ful·ly** \-ē\ *adv* — **hope·ful·ness** *n* — **hope·less** *adj* — **hope·less·ly** *adv* — **hope·less·ness** *n*

HOPE *abbr* Health Opportunity for People Everywhere

Ho·pi \'hō-pē\ *n, pl* **Hopi** *also* **Hopis** [Hopi *Hópi*, lit., good, peaceful] : a member of an American Indian people of Arizona; *also* : the language of the Hopi people

hop·per \'häp-ər\ *n* **1** : a usu. immature hopping insect **2** : a usu. funnel-shaped container for delivering material (as grain) **3** : a freight car with hinged doors in a sloping bottom **4** : a box into which a bill to be considered by a legislative body is dropped **5** : a tank holding a liquid and having a device for releasing its contents through a pipe

hop·scotch \'häp-ˌskäch\ *n* : a child's game in which a player tosses an object (as a stone) consecutively into areas of a figure outlined on the ground and hops through the figure and back to regain the object

hor *abbr* horizontal

horde \'hōrd\ *n* : THRONG, SWARM

hore·hound \'hōr-ˌhaùnd\ *n* [ME *horhoune*, fr. OE *hārhūne*, fr. *hār* hoary + *hūne* horehound] : an aromatic bitter mint with downy leaves used esp. in candy or as an extract in cold and cough remedies

ho·ri·zon \hə-'rīz-ᵊn\ *n* [Gk *horizont-, horizōn*, fr. prp. of *horizein* to bound, fr. *horos* limit, boundary] **1** : the line marking the apparent junction of earth and sky **2** : range of outlook or experience

hor·i·zon·tal \ˌhòr-ə-'zänt-ᵊl\ *adj* : parallel to the horizon : LEVEL — **horizontal** *n* — **hor·i·zon·tal·ly** \-ē\ *adv*

hor·mon·al \hòr-'mōn-ᵊl\ *adj* : of, relating to, or resembling a hormone

hor·mone \'hòr-ˌmōn\ *n* [Gk *hormōn*, prp. of *horman* to stir up, fr. *hormē* impulse, assault] : a product of living cells that circulates in body fluids and has a specific effect on some other cells; *esp* : the secretion of an endocrine gland

horn \'hòrn\ *n* **1** : one of the hard projections of bone or keratin on the head of many hoofed animals **2** : something resembling or suggesting a horn **3** : a brass wind instrument **4** : a usu. electrical device that makes a noise ⟨automobile ∼⟩ — **horned** \'hȯrnd\ *adj* — **horn·less** *adj* — **horny** *adj*

horn·book \'hȯrn-ˌbu̇k\ *n* **1** : a child's primer consisting of a sheet of parchment or paper protected by a sheet of transparent horn **2** : a rudimentary treatise

horned toad *n* : any of several small harmless insect-eating lizards with spines on the head resembling horns and spiny scales on the body

hor·net \'hȯr-nət\ *n* : any of the larger social wasps

horn in *vb* : to participate without invitation : INTRUDE

horn·pipe \'hȯrn-ˌpīp\ *n* : a lively folk dance of the British Isles

ho·rol·o·gy \hə-'räl-ə-jē\ *n* : the science of measuring time or constructing time-indicating instruments — **hor·o·log·ic** \ˌhȯr-ə-'läj-ik\ *adj* — **ho·rol·o·gist** \hə-'räl-ə-jəst\ *n*

horo·scope \'hȯr-ə-ˌskōp\ *n* [MF, fr. L *horoscopus*, fr. Gk *hōroskopos*, fr. *hōra* hour + *skopein* to look at] **1** : a diagram of the relative positions of planets and signs of the zodiac at a particular time for use by astrologers to foretell events of a person's life **2** : an astrological forecast

hor·ren·dous \hȯ-'ren-dəs\ *adj* : DREADFUL, HORRIBLE

hor·ri·ble \'hȯr-ə-bəl\ *adj* **1** : marked by or conducive to horror **2** : highly disagreeable — **hor·ri·ble·ness** *n* — **hor·ri·bly** \-blē\ *adv*

hor·rid \'hȯr-əd\ *adj* **1** : HIDEOUS **2** : REPULSIVE — **hor·rid·ly** *adv*

hor·ri·fy \'hȯr-ə-ˌfī\ *vb* **-fied; -fy·ing** : to cause to feel horror **syn** appall, daunt, dismay

hor·ror \'hȯr-ər\ *n* **1** : painful and intense fear, dread, or dismay **2** : intense repugnance **3** : something that horrifies

hors de com·bat \ˌȯrd-ə-kōⁿ-'bä\ *adv or adj* : in a disabled condition

hors d'oeuvre \ȯr-'dərv\ *n, pl* **hors d'oeuvres** *also* **hors d'oeuvre** \-'dərv(z)\ [F *hors-d'oeuvre*, lit., outside of work] : any of various savory foods usu. served as appetizers

horse \'hȯrs\ *n, pl* **hors·es** *also* **horse** **1** : a large solid-hoofed herbivorous

mammal domesticated as a draft and saddle animal **2** : a supporting framework usu. with legs — **horse·less** *adj*

¹horse·back \'hȯrs-ˌbak\ *adv* : on horseback

²horseback *n* : the back of a horse

horse chestnut *n* : a large Asian tree with palmate leaves, erect conical clusters of showy flowers, and large glossy brown seeds enclosed in a prickly bur

horse·flesh \'hȯrs-ˌflesh\ *n* : horses for riding, driving, or racing

horse·fly \-ˌflī\ *n* : any of a group of large two-winged flies with bloodsucking females

horse·hair \-ˌhaȧr\ *n* **1** : the hair of a horse esp. from the mane or tail **2** : cloth made from horsehair

horse·hide \-ˌhīd\ *n* **1** : the dressed or raw hide of a horse **2** : the ball used in baseball

horse latitudes *n pl* : either of two calm regions near 30°N and 30°S latitude

horse·laugh \'hȯrs-ˌlaf, -ˌlȧf\ *n* : a loud boisterous laugh

horse·man \-mən\ *n* **1** : one who rides horseback; *also* : one skilled in managing horses **2** : a breeder or raiser of horses — **horse·man·ship** *n*

horse·play \-ˌplā\ *n* : rough boisterous play

horse·play·er \-ər\ *n* : a bettor on horse races

horse·pow·er \'hȯrs-ˌpau̇(-ə)r\ *n* : a unit of power equal in the U.S. to 746 watts

horse·rad·ish \-ˌrad-ish\ *n* : a tall white-flowered herb related to the mustards whose pungent root is used as a condiment

horse·shoe \'hȯrs(h)-ˌshü\ *n* **1** : a protective metal plate fitted to the rim of a horse's hoof **2** *pl* : a game in which horseshoes are pitched at a fixed object — **horse·sho·er** \-ˌshü-ər\ *n*

horseshoe crab *n* : any of several marine arthropods with a broad crescent-shaped combined head and thorax

horse·tail \'hȯrs-ˌtāl\ *n* : any of a genus of perennial flowerless plants related to the ferns

horse·whip \-ˌhwip\ *vb* : to flog with a whip made to be used on a horse

horse·wom·an \-ˌwu̇m-ən\ *n* : a woman

skilled in riding horseback or in caring for or managing horses; *also* : a woman who breeds or raises horses

hors•ey *or* **horsy** \'hȯr-sē\ *adj* **hors•i•er; -est** **1** : of, relating to, or suggesting a horse **2** : having to do with horses or horse racing

hort *abbr* horticultural; horticulture

hor•ta•tive \'hȯrt-ət-iv\ *adj* : giving exhortation

hor•ta•to•ry \'hȯrt-ə-ˌtōr-ē\ *adj* : HORTATIVE

hor•ti•cul•ture \'hȯrt-ə-ˌkəl-chər\ *n* : the science and art of growing fruits, vegetables, flowers, and ornamental plants — **hor•ti•cul•tur•al** \ˌhȯrt-ə-'kəlch-(-ə)-rəl\ *adj* — **hor•ti•cul•tur•ist** \-rəst\ *n*

Hos *abbr* Hosea

ho•san•na \hō-'zan-ə, -'zän-\ *interj* [Gk *hōsanna,* fr. Heb *hōshī'āh-nnā* pray, save (us)!] — used as a cry of acclamation and adoration

¹hose \'hōz\ *n, pl* **hose** *or* **hos•es 1** *pl* **hose** : STOCKING, SOCK; *also* : a close-fitting garment covering the legs and waist **2** : a flexible tube for conveying fluids (as from a faucet)

²hose *vb* **hosed; hos•ing** : to spray, water, or wash with a hose

Ho•sea \hō-'zā-ə, -'zē-\ *n* — see BIBLE table

ho•siery \'hōzh(-ə)-rē, 'hōz(-ə)-\ *n* : STOCKINGS, SOCKS

hosp *abbr* hospital

hos•pice \'häs-pəs\ *n* **1** : a lodging for travelers or for young persons or the underprivileged **2** : a facility or program supplying a caring environment for those with fatal illnesses

hos•pi•ta•ble \hä-'spit-ə-bəl, 'häs-(ˌ)pit-\ *adj* **1** : given to generous and cordial reception of guests **2** : readily receptive — **hos•pi•ta•bly** \-blē\ *adv*

hos•pi•tal \'häs-ˌpit-ᵊl\ *n* [ME, fr. OF, fr. ML *hospitale,* fr. LL, hospice, fr. L, guest room, fr. *hospit-, hospes* guest, host, fr. *hostis* stranger, enemy] : an institution where the sick or injured receive medical or surgical care

hos•pi•tal•i•ty \ˌhäs-pə-'tal-ət-ē\ *n, pl* **-ties** : hospitable treatment, reception, or disposition

hos•pi•tal•ize \'häs-ˌpit-ᵊl-ˌīz\ *vb* **-ized; -iz•ing** : to place in a hospital for care and treatment — **hos•pi•tal•iza•tion** \ˌhäs-ˌpit-ᵊl-ə-'zā-shən\ *n*

¹host \'hōst\ *n* [ME, fr. OF, fr. LL *hostis,* fr. L, stranger, enemy] **1** : ARMY **2** : MULTITUDE

²host *n* [ME *hoste* host, guest, fr. OF, fr. L *hospit-, hospes*] **1** : one who receives or entertains guests **2** : an animal or plant on or in which a parasite lives — **host** *vb*

³host *n, often cap* [deriv. of L *hostia* sacrifice] : the eucharistic bread

hos•tage \'häs-tij\ *n* : a person kept as a pledge pending the fulfillment of an agreement

hos•tel \'häs-tᵊl\ *n* [ME, fr. OF, fr. LL *hospitale* hospice] **1** : INN **2** : a supervised lodging for youth — **hos•tel•er** *n*

hos•tel•ry \-rē\ *n, pl* **-ries** : INN, HOTEL

host•ess \'hō-stəs\ *n* : a woman who acts as host

hos•tile \'häs-tᵊl, -ˌtīl\ *adj* : marked by usu. overt antagonism : UNFRIENDLY — **hostile** *n* — **hos•tile•ly** \-ē\ *adv*

hos•til•i•ty \hä-'stil-ət-ē\ *n, pl* **-ties 1** : an unfriendly state or action **2** *pl* : overt acts of war

hos•tler \'(h)äs-lər\ *n* : one who takes care of horses or mules

hot \'hät\ *adj* **hot•ter; hot•test 1** : marked by a high temperature or an uncomfortable degree of body heat **2** : giving a sensation of heat or of burning **3** : ARDENT, FIERY **4** : LUSTFUL **5** : EAGER **6** : newly made or received **7** : PUNGENT **8** : unusually lucky or favorable ⟨∼ dice⟩ **9** : recently and illegally obtained ⟨∼ jewels⟩ — **hot** *adv* — **hot•ly** *adv* — **hot•ness** *n*

hot•bed \-ˌbed\ *n* **1** : a glass-covered bed of soil heated (as by fermenting manure) and used esp. for raising seedlings **2** : an environment that favors rapid growth or development

hot–blood•ed \-'bləd-əd\ *adj* : easily roused or excited

hot•box \-ˌbäks\ *n* : a journal bearing (as of a railroad car) overheated by friction

hot•cake \-ˌkāk\ *n* : PANCAKE

hot dog \'hät-ˌdȯg\ *n* : a cooked frankfurter usu. served in a long split roll

ho•tel \hō-'tel\ *n* [F *hôtel,* fr. OF *hostel,* fr. LL *hospitale* hospice] : a building where lodging and usu. meals, entertainment, and various personal services are provided for the public

hot flash *n* : a sudden brief flushing and sensation of heat caused by dilation of skin capillaries usu. associated with menopausal endocrine imbalance

hot·head·ed \'hät-'hed-əd\ *adj* : FIERY, IMPETUOUS — **hot·head** \-ˌhed\ *n* — **hot·head·ed·ly** *adv* — **hot·head·ed·ness** *n*

hot·house \-ˌhaus\ *n* : a heated glass-enclosed house for raising plants

hot line *n* : a telephone line for emergency use (as between governments or to a counseling service)

hot plate *n* : a simple portable appliance for heating or for cooking

hot potato *n* : an embarrassing or controversial issue

hot rod *n* : an automobile modified for high speed and fast acceleration — **hot–rod·der** \'hät-'räd-ər\ *n*

hots \'häts\ *n pl* : strong sexual desire — usu. used with *the*

hot seat *n* : a position of anxiety or embarrassment

hot·shot \'hät-ˌshät\ *n* : a showily skillful person

hot tub *n* : a large wooden tub of hot water for soaking and socializing

hot–wire \'hät-ˌwī(ə)r\ *vb* : to start (an automobile) by short-circuiting the ignition system

¹hound \'haund\ *n* **1** : : a long-eared hunting dog that follows its prey by scent **2** : FAN, ADDICT

²hound *vb* : to pursue relentlessly

hour \'au(ə)r\ *n* **1** : the 24th part of a day **2** : the time of day **3** : a particular or customary time **4** : a class session — **hour·ly** *adv or adj*

hour·glass \'au(ə)r-ˌglas\ *n* : a glass vessel for measuring time in which sand, water, or mercury runs from an upper compartment to a lower compartment in an hour

hou·ri \'hur-ē\ *n* [F, fr. Per *hūri*, fr. Ar *ḥūrīyah*] : one of the beautiful maidens of the Muslim paradise

¹house \'haus\ *n, pl* **hous·es** \'hau-zəz\ **1** : a building for human habitation **2** : a shelter for an animal **3** : a building in which something is stored **4** : HOUSEHOLD; *also* : FAMILY **5** : a residence for a religious community or for students; *also* : those in residence **6** : a legisla-

tive body **7** : a place of business or entertainment **8** : a business organization **9** : the audience in a theater or concert hall — **house·ful** *n*

²house \'hauz\ *vb* **housed; hous·ing 1** : to provide with or take shelter : LODGE **2** : STORE

house·boat \'haus-ˌbōt\ *n* : a roomy pleasure boat fitted for use as a dwelling or for leisurely cruising

house·boy \-ˌboi\ *n* : a boy or man hired to act as a household servant

house·break \-ˌbrāk\ *vb* **-broke; -broken; -break·ing** : to train in excretory habits acceptable in indoor living

house·break·ing \-ˌbrā-kiŋ\ *n* : the act of breaking into a dwelling with the intent of committing a felony

house·clean \-ˌklēn\ *vb* : to clean a house and its furniture — **house·clean·ing** *n*

house·coat \'haus-ˌkōt\ *n* : a woman's often long-skirted informal garment for wear around the house

house·fly \-ˌflī\ *n* : a two-winged fly that is common about human habitations and acts as a vector of diseases (as typhoid fever)

¹house·hold \'haus-ˌhōld\ *n* : those who dwell as a family under the same roof — **house·hold·er** *n*

²household *adj* **1** : DOMESTIC **2** : FAMILIAR, COMMON ⟨a ~ name⟩

house·keep·er \-ˌkē-pər\ *n* : a woman employed to take care of a house — **house·keep·ing** \-piŋ\ *n*

house·lights \-ˌlīts\ *n pl* : the lights that illuminate the parts of a theater occupied by the audience

house·maid \-ˌmād\ *n* : a female servant employed to do housework

house·moth·er \-ˌməth-ər\ *n* : a woman acting as hostess, chaperon, and often housekeeper in a residence for young people

house·plant \'haus-ˌplant\ *n* : a plant grown or kept indoors

house sparrow *n* : a sparrow native to Europe and parts of Asia that has been widely introduced elsewhere

house·top \'haus-ˌtäp\ *n* : ROOF

house·wares \-ˌwaərz\ *n pl* : small articles of household equipment

house·warm·ing \-ˌwor-miŋ\ *n* : a party to celebrate the taking possession of a house or premises

house·wife \'haús-ˌwīf\ *n* : a married woman in charge of a household — **house·wife·ly** \-lē\ *adj* — **house·wif·ery** \-ˌwīf-(ə-)rē\ *n*

house·work \'haús-ˌwərk\ *n* : the work of housekeeping

¹**hous·ing** \'haú-ziŋ\ *n* **1** : SHELTER; *also* : dwellings provided for people **2** : something that covers or protects

²**housing** *n* **1** : CAPARISON 1 **2** *pl* : decorative trappings and harness

hove past and past part of HEAVE

hov·el \'həv-əl, 'häv-\ *n* : a small, wretched, and often dirty house : HUT

hov·er \'həv-ər, 'häv-\ *vb* **hov·ered; hov·er·ing** \-(ə-)riŋ\ **1** : FLUTTER; *also* : to move to and fro **2** : to be in an uncertain state

¹**how** \(ˈ)haú\ *adv* **1** : in what way or manner ⟨~ was it done⟩ **2** : with what meaning ⟨~ do we interpret such behavior⟩ **3** : for what reason ⟨~ could you have done such a thing⟩ **4** : to what extent or degree ⟨~ deep is it⟩ **5** : in what state or condition ⟨~ are you⟩ — **how about** : what do you say to or think of ⟨*how about* coming with me⟩ — **how come** : why is it that

²**how** *conj* **1** : in what manner or condition ⟨remember ~ they fought⟩ **2** : HOWEVER ⟨do it ~ you like⟩

¹**how·be·it** \haú-'bē-ət\ *adv* : NEVERTHELESS

²**howbeit** *conj* : ALTHOUGH

how·dah \'haúd-ə\ *n* [Hindi *hauda*] : a seat or covered pavilion on the back of an elephant or camel

¹**how·ev·er** \haú-'ev-ər\ *conj* : in whatever manner

²**however** *adv* **1** : to whatever degree; *also* : in whatever manner **2** : in spite of that

how·it·zer \'haú-ət-sər\ *n* : a short cannon that shoots shells at a high angle of fire

howl \'haúl\ *vb* **1** : to emit a loud long doleful sound characteristic of dogs **2** : to cry loudly — **howl** *n*

howl·er \'haú-lər\ *n* **1** : one that howls **2** : a humorous and ridiculous blunder

howl·ing \'haú-liŋ\ *adj* **1** : DESOLATE, WILD **2** : very great ⟨a ~ success⟩

how·so·ev·er \ˌhaú-sə-'wev-ər\ *adv* : HOWEVER 1

hoy·den \'hóid-ᵊn\ *n* : a girl or woman of saucy, boisterous, or carefree behavior

HP *abbr* **1** high pressure **2** horsepower

HPF *abbr* highest possible frequency

HQ *abbr* headquarters

hr *abbr* **1** here **2** hour

HR *abbr* House of Representatives

HRH *abbr* Her Royal Highness; His Royal Highness

hrzn *abbr* horizon

HS *abbr* high school

HST *abbr* Hawaiian standard time

ht *abbr* height

HT *abbr* high-tension

hua·ra·che \wə-'räch-ē\ *n* [MexSp] : a sandal with an upper made of interwoven leather thongs

hub \'həb\ *n* **1** : the central part of a wheel, propeller, or fan **2** : a center of activity

hub·bub \'həb-əb\ *n* : UPROAR; *also* : TURMOIL

hub·cap \'həb-ˌkap\ *n* : a removable metal cap over the end of an axle

hu·bris \'hyü-brəs\ *n* : exaggerated pride or self-confidence

huck·le·ber·ry \'hək-əl-ˌber-ē\ *n* **1** : an American shrub related to the blueberry; *also* : its edible dark blue berry **2** : BLUEBERRY

huck·ster \'hək-stər\ *n* : PEDDLER, HAWKER

HUD *abbr* Department of Housing and Urban Development

¹**hud·dle** \'həd-ᵊl\ *vb* **hud·dled; hud·dling** \'həd-(ə-)liŋ\ **1** : to crowd together **2** : CONFER

²**huddle** *n* **1** : a closely packed group **2** : MEETING, CONFERENCE

hue \'hyü\ *n* **1** : a color as distinct from white, gray, and black; *also* : gradation of color **2** : the attribute of colors that permits them to be classed as red, yellow, green, blue, or an intermediate color — **hued** \'hyüd\ *adj*

hue and cry *n* : a clamor of pursuit or protest

huff \'həf\ *n* : a fit of anger or pique — **huffy** *adj*

hug \'həg\ *vb* **hugged; hug·ging** **1** : EMBRACE **2** : to stay close to ⟨the road ~s the river⟩ — **hug** *n*

huge \'hyüj\ *adj* **hug·er; hug·est** : very large or extensive — **huge·ly** *adv* — **huge·ness** *n*

hug·ger–mug·ger \'həg-ər-ˌməg-ər\ *n* **1** : SECRECY **2** : CONFUSION, MUDDLE

Hu·gue·not \'hyü-gə-ˌnät\ *n* : a French Protestant in the 16th and 17th centuries

hu·la \'hü-lə\ *n* : a sinuous Polynesian dance usu. accompanied by chants

hulk \'həlk\ *n* **1** : a heavy clumsy ship **2** : an old ship unfit for service **3** : a bulky or unwieldy person or thing

hulk·ing \'həl-kiŋ\ *adj* : BURLY, MASSIVE

¹**hull** \'həl\ *n* **1** : the outer covering of a fruit or seed **2** : the frame or body esp. of a ship

²**hull** *vb* : to remove the hulls of — **hull·er** *n*

hul·la·ba·loo \'həl-ə-bə-ˌlü\ *n, pl* **-loos** : a confused noise : UPROAR

hum \'həm\ *vb* **hummed; hum·ming 1** : to utter a sound like that of the speech sound \m\ prolonged **2** : DRONE **3** : to be busily active **4** : to sing with closed lips — **hum** *n* — **hum·mer** *n*

hu·man \'(h)yü-mən\ *adj* **1** : of, relating to, being, or characteristic of man **2** : having human form or attributes — **human** *n* — **hu·man·ly** *adv* — **hu·man·ness** \-mən-nəs\ *n*

hu·mane \(h)yü-'mān\ *adj* **1** : marked by compassion, sympathy, or consideration for others **2** : HUMANISTIC — **hu·mane·ly** *adv* — **hu·mane·ness** \-'mān-nəs\ *n*

human immunodeficiency virus *n* : AIDS VIRUS

hu·man·ism \'(h)yü-mə-ˌniz-əm\ *n* **1** : devotion to the humanities; *also* : the revival of classical letters characteristic of the Renaissance **2** : a doctrine or way of life centered on human interests or values — **hu·man·ist** \-nəst\ *n or adj* — **hu·man·is·tic** \ˌ(h)yü-mə-'nis-tik\ *adj*

hu·man·i·tar·i·an \(h)yü-ˌman-ə-'ter-ē-ən\ *n* : one who practices philanthropy — **humanitarian** *adj* — **hu·man·i·tar·i·an·ism** *n*

hu·man·i·ty \(h)yü-'man-ət-ē\ *n, pl* **-ties 1** : the quality or state of being human or humane **2** *pl* : the branches of learning dealing with human concerns (as philosophy) as opposed to natural processes (as physics) **3** : MANKIND 1

hu·man·ize \'(h)yü-mə-ˌnīz\ *vb* **-ized; -iz·ing** : to make human or humane —

hu·man·iza·tion \ˌ(h)yü-mə-nə-'zā-shən\ *n*

hu·man·kind \'(h)yü-mən-ˌkīnd\ *n* : MANKIND 1

hu·man·oid \'(h)yü-mə-ˌnȯid\ *adj* : having human form or characteristics — **humanoid** *n*

¹**hum·ble** \'(h)əm-bəl\ *adj* **hum·bler** \-b(ə-)lər\; **hum·blest** \-b(ə-)ləst\ [ME, fr. OF, fr. L *humilis* low, humble, fr. *humus* earth] **1** : not proud or haughty **2** : not pretentious : UNASSUMING **3** : INSIGNIFICANT **syn** meek, modest, lowly, unassuming — **hum·ble·ness** *n* — **hum·bly** \-blē\ *adv*

²**humble** *vb* **hum·bled; hum·bling** \-b(ə-)liŋ\ **1** : to make humble **2** : to destroy the power or prestige of — **hum·bler** \-b(ə-)lər\ *n*

¹**hum·bug** \'həm-ˌbəg\ *n* **1** : HOAX, FRAUD **2** : NONSENSE

²**humbug** *vb* **hum·bugged; hum·bug·ging** : DECEIVE

hum·ding·er \'həm-'diŋ-ər\ *n* : a person or thing of striking excellence

hum·drum \'həm-ˌdrəm\ *adj* : MONOTONOUS, DULL

hu·mer·us \'hyüm-(ə-)rəs\ *n, pl* **hu·meri** \'hyü-mə-ˌrī, -ˌrē\ : the long bone extending from elbow to shoulder

hu·mid \'(h)yü-məd\ *adj* : containing or characterized by perceptible moisture : DAMP — **hu·mid·ly** *adv*

hu·mid·i·fy \hyü-'mid-ə-ˌfī\ *vb* **-fied; -fy·ing** : to make humid — **hu·mid·i·fi·ca·tion** \-ˌmid-ə-fə-'kā-shən\ *n* — **hu·mid·i·fi·er** \-'mid-ə-ˌfī(-ə)r\ *n*

hu·mid·i·ty \(h)yü-'mid-ət-ē\ *n, pl* **-ties** : the amount of atmospheric moisture

hu·mi·dor \'(h)yü-mə-ˌdȯr\ *n* : a case usu. for storing cigars in which the air is kept properly humidified

hu·mil·i·ate \(h)yü-'mil-ē-ˌāt\ *vb* **-at·ed; -at·ing** : to injure the self-respect of : MORTIFY — **hu·mil·i·at·ing·ly** \-ˌāt-iŋ-lē\ *adv* — **hu·mil·i·a·tion** \-ˌmil-ē-'ā-shən\ *n*

hu·mil·i·ty \(h)yü-'mil-ət-ē\ *n* : the quality or state of being humble

hum·ming·bird \'həm-iŋ-ˌbərd\ *n* : a tiny American bird related to the swifts

hum·mock \'həm-ək\ *n* : a rounded mound : KNOLL

hu·mon·gous \hyü-'məŋ-gəs, -'mäŋ-\

adj [prob. alter. of *huge* + *monstrous*] *slang* : extremely large

¹**hu•mor** \'(h)yü-mər\ *n* **1** : TEMPERAMENT **2** : MOOD **3** : WHIM **4** : a quality that appeals to a sense of the ludicrous or incongruous; *also* : a keen perception of the ludicrous or incongruous **5** : comical or amusing entertainment — **hu•mor•ist** \'(h)yüm-(ə-)rəst\ *n* — **hu•mor•less** \'(h)yü-mər-ləs\ *adj* — **hu•mor•less•ly** *adv* — **hu•mor•less•ness** *n* — **hu•mor•ous** \'(h)yüm-(ə-)rəs\ *adj* — **hu•mor•ous•ly** *adv* — **hu•mor•ous•ness** *n*

²**humor** *vb* **hu•mored**; **hu•mor•ing** \'(h)yüm-(ə-)riŋ\ : to comply with the wishes or mood of

hu•mour *chiefly Brit* var of HUMOR

hump \'həmp\ *n* **1** : a rounded protuberance (as on the back of a camel) **2** : a difficult phase ⟨over the ∼⟩

hump•back \-ˌbak; *1 also* -'bak\ *n* **1** : HUNCHBACK **2** : HUMPBACK WHALE — **hump•backed** *adj*

humpback whale *n* : a large whalebone whale having very long flippers

hu•mus \'(h)yü-məs\ *n* : the dark organic part of soil formed from decaying matter

Hun \'hən\ *n* : a member of an Asian people that invaded Europe in the 5th century A.D.

¹**hunch** \'hənch\ *vb* **1** : to thrust oneself forward **2** : to assume or cause to assume a bent or crooked posture

²**hunch** *n* **1** : PUSH **2** : a strong intuitive feeling as to how something will turn out

hunch•back \'hənch-ˌbak\ *n* : a back with a hump; *also* : a person with a crooked back — **hunch•backed** *adj*

hun•dred \'hən-drəd\ *n, pl* **hundreds** *or* **hundred** : 10 times 10 — **hundred** *adj* — **hun•dredth** \-drədth\ *adj or n*

hun•dred•weight \-ˌwāt\ *n, pl* **hundredweight** *or* **hundredweights** — see WEIGHT table

hung past and past part of HANG

Hung *abbr* Hungarian; Hungary

Hun•gar•i•an \ˌhəŋ-'ger-ē-ən\ *n* **1** : a native or inhabitant of Hungary **2** : the language of Hungary — **Hungarian** *adj*

hun•ger \'həŋ-gər\ *n* **1** : a craving or urgent need for food **2** : a strong desire — **hunger** *vb* — **hun•gri•ly** \-grə-lē\ *adv* — **hun•gry** *adj*

hung over *adj* : having a hangover

hung up *adj* **1** : DELAYED **2** : ENTHUSIASTIC; *also* : PREOCCUPIED

hunk \'həŋk\ *n* **1** : a large piece **2** : an attractive well-built man

hun•ker \'həŋ-kər\ *vb* **hun•kered**; **hun•ker•ing** \-k(ə-)riŋ\ : CROUCH, SQUAT — usu. used with *down*

hun•kers \'həŋ-kərz\ *n pl* : HAUNCHES

hun•ky–do•ry \ˌhəŋ-kē-'dōr-ē\ *adj* : quite satisfactory : FINE

¹**hunt** \'hənt\ *vb* **1** : to pursue for food or in sport; *also* : to take part in a hunt **2** : to try to find : SEEK **3** : to drive or chase esp. by harrying **4** : to traverse in search of prey — **hunt•er** *n*

²**hunt** *n* : an act, practice, or instance of hunting

hunt•ress \'hən-trəs\ *n* : a woman who hunts

hunts•man \'hənts-mən\ *n* **1** : HUNTER **2** : one who manages a hunt and looks after the hounds

hur•dle \'hərd-ᵊl\ *n* **1** : an artificial barrier to leap over in a race **2** : OBSTACLE — **hurdle** *vb* — **hur•dler** \'hərd-(ᵊ-)lər\ *n*

hur•dy–gur•dy \ˌhərd-ē-'gərd-ē, 'hərd-ē-ˌgərd-ē\ *n, pl* **-gur•dies** : a musical instrument in which the sound is produced by turning a crank

hurl \'hərl\ *vb* **1** : to move or cause to move vigorously **2** : to throw down with violence **3** : FLING; *also* : PITCH — **hurl** *n* — **hurl•er** *n*

hur•ly–bur•ly \ˌhər-lē-'bər-lē\ *n* : UPROAR, TUMULT

Hu•ron \'hyùr-ən, 'hyùr-ˌän\ *n, pl* **Hurons** *or* **Huron** : a member of an American Indian people orig. of the St. Lawrence valley

hur•rah \hù-'rȯ, -'rä\ *also* **hur•ray** \hù-'rā\ *interj* — used to express joy, approval, or encouragement

hur•ri•cane \'hər-ə-ˌkān\ *n* [Sp *huracán*, of AmerInd origin] : a tropical cyclone that has winds of 74 miles per hour (117 kilometers per hour) or greater and is usu. accompanied by rain, thunder, and lightning

¹**hur•ry** \'hər-ē\ *vb* **hur•ried**; **hur•ry•ing** **1** : to carry or cause to go with haste **2** : to impel to a greater speed **3** : to

move or act with haste — **hur·ried·ly** *adv* — **hur·ried·ness** *n*

²hurry *n* : extreme haste or eagerness

¹hurt \'hərt\ *vb* **hurt; hurt·ing** **1** : to feel or cause to feel pain **2** : to do harm to : DAMAGE **3** : OFFEND **4** : HAMPER

²hurt *n* **1** : a bodily injury or wound **2** : SUFFERING **3** : HARM, WRONG — **hurt·ful** *adj*

hur·tle \'hərt-ᵊl\ *vb* **hur·tled; hur·tling** \'hərt-(ᵊ-)liŋ\ **1** : to move with a rushing sound **2** : : HURL, FLING

¹hus·band \'həz-bənd\ *n* [ME *husbonde*, fr. OE *hūsbonda* master of a house, fr. ON *hūsbōndi*, fr. *hūs* house + *bōndi* householder] : a married man

²husband *vb* : to manage prudently

hus·band·man \'həz-bən(d)-mən\ *n* : FARMER

hus·band·ry \'həz-bən-drē\ *n* **1** : the control or judicious use of resources **2** : AGRICULTURE

¹hush \'həsh\ *vb* **1** : to make or become quiet or calm **2** : SUPPRESS

²hush *n* : SILENCE, QUIET

hush–hush \'həsh-ˌhəsh\ *adj* : SECRET, CONFIDENTIAL

¹husk \'həsk\ *n* **1** : a usu. thin dry outer covering of a seed or fruit **2** : an outer layer : SHELL

²husk *vb* : to strip the husk from — **husk·er** *n*

¹hus·ky \'həs-kē\ *adj* **hus·ki·er; -est** : HOARSE — **hus·ki·ly** \'həs-kə-lē\ *adv* — **hus·ki·ness** \-kē-nəs\ *n*

²husky *adj* **1** : BURLY, ROBUST **2** : LARGE

³husky *n, pl* **huskies** : a heavy-coated working dog of the New World arctic

hus·sar \(ˌ)hə-'zär\ *n* [Hung *huszár* hussar, (obs.) highway robber, fr. Serb *husar* pirate, fr. ML *cursarius*, fr. *cursus* course] : a member of any of various European cavalry units

hus·sy \'həz-ē, 'həs-\ *n, pl* **hussies** [alter. of *housewife*] **1** : a lewd or brazen woman **2** : a pert or mischievous girl

hus·tings \'həs-tiŋz\ *n pl* : a place where political campaign speeches are made; *also* : the proceedings in an election campaign

hus·tle \'həs-əl\ *vb* **hus·tled; hus·tling** \'həs-(ə-)liŋ\ **1** : JOSTLE, SHOVE **2** : HASTEN, HURRY **3** : to work energetically — **hustle** *n* — **hus·tler** \'həs-lər\ *n*

hut \'hət\ *n* : a small and often temporary dwelling : SHACK

hutch \'həch\ *n* **1** : a chest or compartment for storage **2** : a low cupboard usu. surmounted with open shelves **3** : a pen or coop for an animal **4** : HUT, SHACK

huz·zah *or* **huz·za** \(ˌ)hə-'zä\ *n* : a cheer of acclaim — often used interjectionally to express joy or approbation

HV *abbr* **1** high velocity **2** high voltage

hvy *abbr* heavy

HW *abbr* hot water

hwy *abbr* highway

hy·a·cinth \'hī-ə-(ˌ)sinth\ *n* : a bulbous herb related to the lilies and widely grown for its spikes of fragrant bell≈ shaped flowers

hy·ae·na var of HYENA

hy·brid \'hī-brəd\ *n* **1** : an offspring of genetically differing parents (as members of different breeds or species) **2** : one of mixed origin or composition — **hybrid** *adj* — **hy·brid·iza·tion** \ˌhī-brəd-ə-'zā-shən\ *n* — **hy·brid·ize** \'hī-brəd-ˌīz\ *vb* — **hy·brid·iz·er** \-ˌīz-ər\ *n*

hy·dra \'hī-drə\ *n* : any of numerous small tubular freshwater polyps having at one end a mouth surrounded by tentacles

hy·dran·gea \hī-'drān-jə\ *n* : any of a genus of shrubs related to the currants and grown for their large clusters of white or tinted flowers

hy·drant \'hī-drənt\ *n* : a pipe with a valve and spout at which water may be drawn from a main pipe

hy·drate \'hī-ˌdrāt\ *n* : a compound formed by union of water with some other substance — **hydrate** *vb*

hy·drau·lic \hī-'dro-lik\ *adj* **1** : operated, moved, or effected by means of water **2** : of or relating to hydraulics **3** : operated by the resistance offered or the pressure transmitted when a quantity of liquid is forced through a small orifice or through a tube **4** : hardening or setting under water

hy·drau·lics \hī-'dro-liks\ *n* : a science that deals with practical applications of liquids in motion

hydro \'hī-drō\ *adj* : HYDROELECTRIC

hy·dro·car·bon \ˌhī-drə-'kär-bən\ *n* : an organic compound (as acetylene) containing only carbon and hydrogen

hy·dro·ceph·a·lus \ˌhī-drō-'sef-ə-ləs\ *n* : abnormal increase in the amount of fluid in the cranial cavity accompanied by expansion of the ventricles, enlargement of the skull, and atrophy of the brain

hy·dro·chlo·ric acid \ˌhī-drə-ˌklōr-ik-\ *n* : a sharp-smelling corrosive acid used in the laboratory and in industry and present in dilute form in gastric juice

hy·dro·dy·nam·ics \ˌhī-drō-dī-'nam-iks\ *n* : a science that deals with the motion of fluids and the forces acting on moving bodies immersed in fluids — **hy·dro·dy·nam·ic** *adj*

hy·dro·elec·tric \ˌhī-drō-i-'lek-trik\ *adj* : of, relating to, or used in the production of electricity by waterpower — **hy·dro·elec·tric·i·ty** \-ˌlek-'tris-ət-ē\ *n*

hy·dro·flu·or·ic acid \ˌhī-drō-flu̇-ˌȯr-ik-\ *n* : a weak poisonous acid used esp. in finishing and etching glass

hy·dro·foil \'hī-drə-ˌfȯil\ *n* : a boat that has fins attached to the bottom by struts for lifting the hull clear of the water to allow faster speeds

hy·dro·gen \'hī-drə-jən\ *n* [F *hydro-gène*, fr. Gk *hydōr* water + *-genēs* born, fr. the fact that water is generated by its combustion] : a gaseous colorless odorless highly flammable chemical element that is the lightest of the elements — **hy·drog·e·nous** \hī-'dräj-ə-nəs\ *adj*

hy·dro·ge·nate \hī-'dräj-ə-ˌnāt, hī-drə-jə-\ *vb* **-nat·ed; -nat·ing** : to combine or treat with hydrogen; *esp* : to add hydrogen to the molecule of — **hy·dro·ge·na·tion** \hī-ˌdräj-ə-'nā-shən, ˌhī-drə-jə-\ *n*

hydrogen bomb *n* : a bomb whose violent explosive power is due to the sudden release of atomic energy resulting from the union of light nuclei (as of hydrogen atoms)

hydrogen peroxide *n* : an unstable compound of hydrogen and oxygen used as an oxidizing and bleaching agent, an antiseptic, and a propellant

hy·drog·ra·phy \hī-'dräg-rə-fē\ *n* : the description and study of bodies of water — **hy·drog·ra·pher** \-fər\ *n* — **hy·dro·graph·ic** \ˌhī-drə-'graf-ik\ *adj*

hy·drol·o·gy \hī-'dräl-ə-jē\ *n* : a science dealing with the properties, distribution, and circulation of water — **hy·dro·log·ic** \ˌhī-drə-'läj-ik\ *or* **hy·dro·log·i·cal** \-i-kəl\ *adj* — **hy·drol·o·gist** \hī-'dräl-ə-jəst\ *n*

hy·dro·ly·sis \hī-'dräl-ə-səs\ *n* : a chemical decomposition involving the addition of the elements of water

hy·drom·e·ter \hī-'dräm-ət-ər\ *n* : a floating instrument for determining specific gravities of liquids and hence the strength (as of alcoholic liquors)

hy·dro·pho·bia \ˌhī-drə-'fō-bē-ə\ *n* [LL, fr. Gk, fr. *hydōr* water + *phobos* fear] : RABIES

hy·dro·phone \'hī-drə-ˌfōn\ *n* : an underwater listening device

¹hy·dro·plane \'hī-drə-ˌplān\ *n* **1** : a speedboat usu. with a stepped bottom so that the hull is raised wholly or partly out of the water **2** : SEAPLANE

²hydroplane *vb* : to skid on a wet road due to loss of contact between the tires and road

hy·dro·pon·ics \ˌhī-drə-'pän-iks\ *n* : the growing of plants in nutrient solutions — **hy·dro·pon·ic** *adj*

hy·dro·pow·er \'hī-drə-ˌpau̇(-ə)r\ *n* : hydroelectric power

hy·dro·sphere \'hī-drə-ˌsfiər\ *n* : the water (as vapor or lakes) of the earth

hy·dro·stat·ic \ˌhī-drə-'stat-ik\ *adj* : of or relating to fluids at rest or to the pressures they exert or transmit

hy·dro·ther·a·py \ˌhī-drə-'ther-ə-pē\ *n* : the external application of water in the treatment of disease or disability

hy·dro·ther·mal \ˌhī-drə-'thər-məl\ *adj* : of or relating to hot water

hy·drous \'hī-drəs\ *adj* : containing water

hy·drox·ide \hī-'dräk-ˌsīd\ *n* **1** : a negatively charged ion consisting of one atom of oxygen and one atom of hydrogen **2** : a compound of hydroxide with an element or group

hy·e·na \hī-'ē-nə\ *n* [L *hyaena*, fr. Gk *hyaina*, fr. *hys* hog] : a large nocturnal carnivorous mammal of Asia and Africa

hy·giene \'hī-ˌjēn\ *n* **1** : a science dealing with the establishment and maintenance of health **2** : conditions or practices conducive to health — **hy·gien·ic** \ˌhī-jē-'en-ik, hī-'jen-, hī-'jēn-\ *adj* — **hy·gien·i·cal·ly** \-i-k(ə-)lē\ *adv* — **hy·gien·ist** \hī-'jēn-əst, 'hī-ˌjēn-, hī-'jen-\ *n*

hy·grom·e·ter \hī-'gräm-ət-ər\ *n* : any of several instruments for measuring the humidity of the atmosphere

hy·gro·scop·ic \ˌhī-grə-'skäp-ik\ *adj* : readily taking up and retaining moisture

hying *pres part of* HIE

hy·men \'hī-mən\ *n* : a fold of mucous membrane partly or wholly closing the orifice of the vagina

hy·me·ne·al \ˌhī-mə-'nē-əl\ *adj* : NUPTIAL

hymn \'him\ *n* : a song of praise esp. to God — **hymn** *vb* — **hym·nal** \'him-nəl\ *n*

hyp *abbr* hypothesis; hypothetical

hype \'hīp\ *n* 1 *slang* : HYPODERMIC 2 *slang* : DECEPTION, PUT-ON

hy·per \'hī-pər\ *adj* : EXCITABLE, HIGH-STRUNG

hy·per·acid·i·ty \ˌhī-pə-rə-'sid-ət-ē\ *n* : the condition of containing excessive acid esp. in the stomach — **hy·per·ac·id** \-pə-'ras-əd\ *adj*

hy·per·ac·tive \ˌhī-pə-'rak-tiv\ *adj* : excessively or pathologically active — **hy·per·ac·tiv·i·ty** \-ˌrak-'tiv-ət-ē\ *n*

hy·per·bar·ic \ˌhī-pər-'bar-ik\ *adj* : of, relating to, or utilizing greater than normal pressure esp. of oxygen

hy·per·bo·la \hī-'pər-bə-lə\ *n, pl* **-las** *or* **-lae** \-(ˌ)lē\ : a curve formed by the intersection of a double right circular cone with a plane that cuts both halves of the cone — **hy·per·bol·ic** \ˌhī-pər-'bäl-ik\ *adj*

hy·per·bo·le \hī-'pər-bə-(ˌ)lē\ *n* : extravagant exaggeration used as a figure of speech

hy·per·crit·i·cal \ˌhī-pər-'krit-i-kəl\ *adj* : excessively critical — **hy·per·crit·i·cal·ly** \-k(ə-)lē\ *adv*

hy·per·sen·si·tive \-'sen-sət-iv\ *adj* 1 : excessively or abnormally sensitive 2 : abnormally susceptible physiologically to a specific agent (as a drug or antigen) — **hy·per·sen·si·tive·ness** *n* — **hy·per·sen·si·tiv·i·ty** \-ˌsen-sə-'tiv-ət-ē\ *n*

hy·per·ten·sion \'hī-pər-ˌten-chən\ *n* : high blood pressure — **hy·per·ten·sive** \ˌhī-pər-'ten-siv\ *adj or n*

hy·per·thy·roid·ism \ˌhī-pər-'thī-ˌroid-ˌiz-əm\ *n* : excessive functional activity of the thyroid gland; *also* : the resulting bodily condition — **hy·per·thy·roid** \-'thī-ˌroid\ *adj*

hy·per·tro·phy \hī-'pər-trə-fē\ *n, pl* **-phies** : excessive growth or development of a body part — **hy·per·tro·phic** \ˌhī-pər-'trō-fik\ *adj* — **hypertrophy** *vb*

hy·phen \'hī-fən\ *n* : a punctuation mark - used to divide or to compound words or word elements — **hyphen** *vb*

hy·phen·ate \'hī-fə-ˌnāt\ *vb* **-at·ed; -at·ing** : to connect or divide with a hyphen — **hy·phen·ation** \ˌhī-fə-'nā-shən\ *n*

hyp·no·sis \hip-'nō-səs\ *n, pl* **-no·ses** \-ˌsēz\ : an induced state that resembles sleep and in which the subject is responsive to suggestions of the inducer (hyp·no·tist \'hip-nə-təst\) — **hyp·no·tism** \'hip-nə-ˌtiz-əm\ *n* — **hyp·no·tiz·able** \'hip-nə-ˌtī-zə-bəl\ *adj* — **hyp·no·tize** \-ˌtīz\ *vb*

¹hyp·not·ic \hip-'nät-ik\ *adj* 1 : inducing sleep : SOPORIFIC 2 : of or relating to hypnosis or hypnotism — **hyp·not·i·cal·ly** \-i-k(ə-)lē\ *adv*

²hypnotic *n* : a sleep-inducing drug

¹hy·po \'hī-pō\ *n, pl* **hypos** [short for *hyposulfite*] : SODIUM THIOSULFATE

²hypo *n, pl* **hypos** : HYPODERMIC

hy·po·cen·ter \'hī-pə-ˌsent-ər\ *n* : EPICENTER

hy·po·chon·dria \ˌhī-pə-'kän-drē-ə\ *n* [NL, fr. LL, pl., upper abdomen (formerly regarded as the seat of hypochondria), fr. Gk, lit., the parts under the cartilage (of the breastbone), fr. *hypo*- under + *chondros* cartilage] : depression of mind usu. centered on imaginary physical ailments — **hy·po·chon·dri·ac** \-drē-ˌak\ *adj or n*

hy·poc·ri·sy \hip-'äk-rə-sē\ *n, pl* **-sies** : a feigning to be what one is not or to believe what one does not; *esp* : the false assumption of an appearance of virtue or religion — **hyp·o·crite** \'hip-ə-ˌkrit\ *n* — **hyp·o·crit·i·cal** \ˌhip-ə-'krit-i-kəl\ *adj* — **hyp·o·crit·i·cal·ly** \-k(ə-)lē\ *adv*

¹hy·po·der·mic \ˌhī-pə-'dər-mik\ *adj* : adapted for use in or administered by injection beneath the skin ⟨~ injection⟩ ⟨~ syringe⟩

²hypodermic *n* : a small syringe with a hollow needle for injecting material into or through the skin; *also* : an injection made with this

hypodermic needle *n* 1 : NEEDLE 3 2 : a hypodermic syringe complete with needle

hy•po•gly•ce•mia \ˌhī-pō-glī-'sē-mē-ə\ *n* : abnormal decrease of sugar in the blood — **hy•po•gly•ce•mic** \-mik\ *adj*

hy•pot•e•nuse \hī-'pät-ᵊn-ˌ(y)üs, -ˌ(y)üz\ *n* : the side of a triangle having a right angle that is opposite the right angle

hy•poth•e•sis \hī-'päth-ə-səs\ *n, pl* **-e•ses** \-ˌsēz\ : an assumption made esp. in order to test its logical or empirical consequences — **hy•po•thet•i•cal** \ˌhī-pə-'thet-i-kəl\ *adj* — **hy•po•thet•i•cal•ly** \-k(ə-)lē\ *adv*

hy•poth•e•size \-ˌsīz\ *vb* **-sized; -siz•ing** : to adopt as a hypothesis

hy•po•thy•roid•ism \ˌhī-pō-'thī-ˌroid-ˌiz-əm\ *n* : deficient activity of the thyroid gland; *also* : a resultant lowered metabolic rate and general loss of vigor — **hy•po•thy•roid** *adj*

hys•sop \'his-əp\ *n* : a European mint used in medicine

hys•ter•ec•to•my \ˌhis-tə-'rek-tə-mē\ *n, pl* **-mies** : surgical removal of the uterus

hys•te•ria \his-'ter-ē-ə, -'tir-\ *n* [NL, fr. E *hysteric,* adj., fr. L *hystericus,* fr. Gk *hysterikos,* fr. *hystera* womb; fr. the former notion that hysteric women were suffering from disturbances of the womb] **1** : a nervous disorder marked esp. by defective emotional control **2** : uncontrollable fear or emotion — **hys•ter•i•cal** \-'ter-i-kəl\ *also* **hys•ter•ic** \-ik\ *adj* — **hys•ter•i•cal•ly** \-k(ə-)lē\ *adv*

hys•ter•ics \-'ter-iks\ *n, pl* a fit of uncontrollable laughter or crying

Hz *abbr* hertz

I

¹i \'ī\ *n, pl* **i's** *or* **is** \'īz\ *often cap* : the 9th letter of the English alphabet

²i *abbr, often cap* island; isle

¹I \(')ī, ə\ *pron* : the one speaking or writing

²I *abbr* interstate highway

³I *symbol* iodine

Ia *or* **IA** *abbr* Iowa

iamb \'ī-ˌam\ *or* **iam•bus** \ī-'am-bəs\ *n, pl* **iambs** \'ī-ˌamz\ *or* **iam•bus•es** : a metrical foot of one unaccented syllable followed by one accented syllable — **iam•bic** \ī-'am-bik\ *adj or n*

-ian — see -AN

-i•at•ric \ē-'a-trik\ *also* **-i•at•ri•cal** \-tri-kəl\ *adj comb form* : of or relating to (such) medical treatment or healing

-i•at•rics \ē-'a-triks\ *n pl comb form* : medical treatment

ib *or* **ibid** *abbr* ibidem

ibex \'ī-ˌbeks\ *n, pl* **ibex** *or* **ibex•es** [L] : an Old World wild goat with large curved horns

ibi•dem \'ib-ə-ˌdem, ib-'īd-əm\ *adv* [L] : in the same place

ibis \'ī-bəs\ *n, pl* **ibis** *or* **ibis•es** [L, fr. Gk, fr. Egypt *hyb*] : any of several wading birds related to the herons but having a downwardly curved bill

-ible — see -ABLE

¹-ic \ik\ *adj suffix* **1** : of, relating to, or having the form of : being ⟨panoram*ic*⟩ **2** : related to, derived from, or containing ⟨alcohol*ic*⟩ **3** : in the manner of : like that of : characteristic of **4** : associated or dealing with : utilizing ⟨electron*ic*⟩ **5** : characterized by : exhibiting ⟨nostalg*ic*⟩ : affected with ⟨allerg*ic*⟩ **6** : caused by **7** : tending to produce

²-ic *n suffix* : one having the character or nature of : one belonging to or associated with : one exhibiting or affected by : one that produces

-i•cal \i-kəl\ *adj suffix* : -IC ⟨symmetr*ical*⟩ ⟨geolog*ical*⟩ — **-i•cal•ly** \i-k(ə-)lē\ *adv suffix*

ICBM \ˌī-ˌsē-(ˌ)bē-'em\ *n, pl* **ICBM's** *or* **ICBMs** \-'emz\ : an intercontinental ballistic missile

ICC *abbr* Interstate Commerce Commission

¹ice \'īs\ *n* **1** : frozen water **2** : a state of coldness (as from formality or reserve) **3** : a substance resembling ice **4** : a frozen dessert; *esp* : one containing no milk or cream

²ice *vb* **iced; ic•ing 1** : FREEZE **2** : CHILL **3** : to cover with or as if with icing

ice age *n* : a time of widespread glaciation

ice bag *n* : a waterproof bag to hold ice for local application of cold to the body

ice·berg \\'īs-ˌbərg\\ *n* : a large floating mass of ice broken off from a glacier

iceberg lettuce *n* : any of various crisp light green lettuces that when mature have the leaves arranged in a compact head resembling a cabbage

ice·boat \\'īs-ˌbōt\\ *n* **1** : a boatlike frame on runners propelled on ice usu. by sails **2** : ICEBREAKER 2

ice·bound \\-ˌbaůnd\\ *adj* : surrounded or obstructed by ice

ice·box \\-ˌbäks\\ *n* : REFRIGERATOR

ice·break·er \\-ˌbrā-kər\\ *n* : a ship equipped to make a channel through ice

ice cap *n* : a glacier forming on relatively level land and flowing outward from its center

ice cream *n* : a frozen food containing sweetened or flavored cream or butterfat

ice hockey *n* : a game in which two teams of ice-skating players try to shoot a puck into the opponent's goal

ice·house \\'īs-ˌhaůs\\ *n* : a building in which ice is made or stored

Ice·land·er \\-ˌlan-dər, -lən-\\ *n* : a native or inhabitant of Iceland

¹ice·lan·dic \\īs-'lan-dik\\ *adj* : of, relating to, or characteristic of Iceland, the Icelanders, or their language

²Icelandic *n* : the language of Iceland

ice·man \\'īs-ˌman\\ *n* : one who sells or delivers ice

ice milk *n* : a sweetened frozen food made of skim milk

ice pick *n* : a hand tool ending in a spike for chipping ice

ice–skate \\'īs-ˌskāt\\ *vb* : to skate on ice — **ice skater** *n*

ice storm *n* : a storm in which falling rain freezes on contact

ice water *n* : chilled or iced water esp. for drinking

ich·thy·ol·o·gy \\ˌik-thē-'äl-ə-jē\\ *n* : a branch of zoology dealing with fishes — **ich·thy·ol·o·gist** \\-jəst\\ *n*

ici·cle \\'ī-ˌsik-əl\\ *n* : a hanging mass of ice formed by the freezing of dripping water

ic·ing \\'ī-siŋ\\ *n* : a sweet usu. creamy mixture used to coat baked goods

ICJ *abbr* International Court of Justice

icky \\'ik-ē\\ *adj* **ick·i·er; -est** : OFFENSIVE, DISTASTEFUL

icon \\'ī-ˌkän\\ *n* : IMAGE; *esp* : a religious image painted on a wood panel

icon·o·clasm \\ī-'kän-ə-ˌklaz-əm\\ *n* : the doctrine, practice, or attitude of an iconoclast

icon·o·clast \\-ˌklast\\ *n* [ML *iconoclastes,* fr. MGk *eikonoklastēs,* lit., image destroyer, fr. Gk *eikōn* image + *klan* to break] **1** : one who destroys religious images or opposes their veneration **2** : one who attacks cherished beliefs or institutions

-ics \\iks\\ *n sing or pl suffix* **1** : study : knowledge : skill : practice ⟨linguist*ics*⟩ ⟨electron*ics*⟩ **2** : characteristic actions or activities ⟨acrobat*ics*⟩ **3** : characteristic qualities, operations, or phenomena ⟨mechan*ics*⟩

ic·tus \\'ik-təs\\ *n* : the recurring stress or beat in a rhythmic or metrical series of sounds

ICU *abbr* intensive care unit

icy \\'ī-sē\\ *adj* **ic·i·er; -est** **1** : covered with, abounding in, or consisting of ice **2** : intensely cold **3** : being cold and unfriendly — **ic·i·ly** \\'ī-sə-lē\\ *adv* — **ic·i·ness** \\-sē-nəs\\ *n*

¹id \\'id\\ *n* [L, it] : the part of the psyche in psychoanalytic theory that is completely unconscious and is the source of psychic energy derived from instinctual needs and drives

²id *abbr* idem

ID *abbr* **1** Idaho **2** identification

idea \\ī-'dē-ə\\ *n* **1** : a plan for action : DESIGN, PROJECT **2** : something imagined or pictured in the mind **3** : a central meaning or purpose **syn** concept, conception, notion, impression

¹ide·al \\ī-'dē-(-ə)l\\ *adj* **1** : existing only in the mind : IMAGINARY; *also* : lacking practicality **2** : of or relating to an ideal or to perfection : PERFECT

²ideal *n* **1** : a standard of excellence **2** : one regarded as a model worthy of imitation **3** : GOAL

ide·al·ism \\ī-'dē-(-ə-)ˌliz-əm\\ *n* **1** : the practice of forming or living according to ideals **2** : the tendency to see things as they should be — **ide·al·ist** \\-(-ə-)ləst\\ *n* — **ide·al·is·tic** \\ī-ˌdē-(-ə-)

'lis-tik\ *adj* — **ide·al·is·ti·cal·ly** \-ti-k(ə-)lē\ *adv*

ide·al·ize \ī-'dē-(ə-)ˌlīz\ *vb* **-ized; -iz·ing** : to think of or represent as ideal — **ide·al·iza·tion** \-ˌdē-(ə-)lə-'zā-shən\ *n*

ide·al·ly \ī-'dē-(ə-)lē\ *adv* **1** : in idea or imagination : MENTALLY **2** : in agreement with an ideal : PERFECTLY

ide·ation \ˌīd-ē-'ā-shən\ *n* : the capacity for or process of forming ideas — **ide·ate** \'īd-ē-ˌāt\ *vb* — **ide·ation·al** \ˌīd-ē-'ā-sh(ə-)nəl\ *adj*

idem \'īd-ˌem, 'ēd-, 'id-\ *pron* [L, same] : something previously mentioned

iden·ti·cal \ī-'dent-i-kəl\ *adj* **1** : being the same **2** : exactly or essentially alike **syn** equivalent, equal, tantamount

iden·ti·fi·ca·tion \ī-ˌdent-ə-fə-'kā-shən\ *n* **1** : an act of identifying : the state of being identified **2** : evidence of identity **3** : an unconscious psychological process by which an individual models thoughts, feelings, and actions after another person or an object

iden·ti·fy \ī-'dent-ə-ˌfī\ *vb* **-fied; -fy·ing** **1** : to regard as identical **2** : ASSOCIATE **3** : to establish the identity of **4** : to practice psychological identification — **iden·ti·fi·able** \-ˌfī-ə-bəl\ *adj* — **iden·ti·fi·ably** \-blē\ *adv* — **iden·ti·fi·er** \-ˌfī(-ə)r\ *n*

iden·ti·ty \ī-'dent-ət-ē\ *n, pl* **-ties** **1** : sameness of essential character **2** : INDIVIDUALITY **3** : the fact of being the same person or thing as claimed

identity crisis *n* : psychological conflict esp. in adolescence involving confusion about one's social role and one's personality

ideo·gram \'īd-ē-ə-ˌgram, 'id-\ *n* **1** : a picture or symbol used in a system of writing to represent a thing or an idea **2** : a character or symbol used in a system of writing to represent an entire word

ide·ol·o·gy \ˌīd-ē-'äl-ə-jē, ˌid-\ *also* **ide·al·o·gy** \-'äl-ə-jē, -'al-\ *n, pl* **-gies** **1** : the body of ideas characteristic of a particular individual, group, or culture **2** : the assertions, theories, and aims that constitute a political, social, and economic program — **ide·o·log·i·cal** \ˌīd-ē-ə-'läj-i-kəl, ˌid-\ *adj* — **ide·ol·o·gist** \-ē-'äl-ə-jəst\ *n*

ides \'īdz\ *n sing or pl* : the 15th day of March, May, July, or October or the 13th day of any other month in the ancient Roman calendar

id·i·o·cy \'id-ē-ə-sē\ *n, pl* **-cies** **1** : extreme mental deficiency **2** : something notably stupid or foolish

id·i·om \'id-ē-əm\ *n* **1** : the language peculiar to a person or group **2** : the characteristic form or structure of a language **3** : an expression that cannot be understood from the meanings of its separate words (as *give way*) — **id·i·om·at·ic** \ˌid-ē-ə-'mat-ik\ *adj* — **id·i·om·at·i·cal·ly** \-i-k(ə-)lē\ *adv*

id·io·path·ic \ˌid-ē-ə-'path-ik\ *adj* : arising spontaneously or from an obscure or unknown cause ⟨an ~ disease⟩

id·io·syn·cra·sy \ˌid-ē-ə-'siŋ-krə-sē\ *n, pl* **-sies** : personal peculiarity — **id·io·syn·crat·ic** \ˌid-ē-ō-sin-'krat-ik\ *adj* — **id·io·syn·crat·i·cal·ly** \-'krat-i-k(ə-)lē\ *adv*

id·i·ot \'id-ē-ət\ *n* [ME, fr. L *idiota* ignorant person, fr. Gk *idiōtēs* one in a private station, ignorant person, fr. *idios* one's own, private] **1** : a feebleminded person **2** : a silly or foolish person — **id·i·ot·ic** \ˌid-ē-'ät-ik\ *adj* — **id·i·ot·i·cal·ly** \-i-k(ə-)lē\ *adv*

¹idle \'īd-ᵊl\ *adj* **idler** \'īd-(ə-)lər\; **idlest** \'īd-(ə-)ləst\ **1** : GROUNDLESS, WORTHLESS, USELESS ⟨~ rumor⟩ ⟨~ talk⟩ **2** : not occupied or employed : INACTIVE **3** : LAZY ⟨~ fellows⟩ — **idle·ness** *n* — **idly** \'īd-lē\ *adv*

²idle *vb* **idled; idling** \'īd-(ᵊ-)liŋ\ **1** : to spend time doing nothing **2** : to make idle **3** : to run without being connected so that power is not used for useful work — **idler** \'īd-(ᵊ-)lər\ *n*

idol \'īd-ᵊl\ *n* **1** : an image worshiped as a god **2** : a false god **3** : an object of passionate devotion

idol·a·ter \ī-'däl-ət-ər\ *n* : a worshiper of idols

idol·a·try \-ə-trē\ *n, pl* **-tries** **1** : the worship of a physical object as a god **2** : immoderate devotion — **idol·a·trous** \-trəs\ *adj*

idol·ize \'īd-ᵊl-ˌīz\ *vb* **-ized; -iz·ing** : to make an idol of — **idol·iza·tion** \ˌīd-ᵊl-ə-'zā-shən\ *n*

idyll *or* **idyl** \'īd-ᵊl\ *n* **1** : a simple descriptive or narrative composition; *esp* : a poem about country life **2** : a fit subject for an idyll — **idyl·lic** \ī-'dil-ik\ *adj*

i.e. \<u>th</u>at-'iz, (')ī-'ē\ *abbr* [L *id est* that is]

IE *abbr* **1** Indo-European **2** industrial engineer

-ier — see -ER

if \(ˌ)if, əf\ *conj* **1** : in the event that ⟨∼ he stays, I leave⟩ **2** : WHETHER ⟨ask ∼ he left⟩ **3** — used as a function word to introduce an exclamation expressing a wish ⟨∼ it would only rain⟩ **4** : even though ⟨an interesting ∼ untenable argument⟩

IF *abbr* intermediate freqency

if·fy \'if-ē\ *adj* : full of contingencies or unknown conditions

-i·fy \ə-ˌfī\ *vb suffix* : -FY

IG *abbr* inspector general

ig·loo \'ig-lü\ *n, pl* **igloos** [Eskimo *iglu* house] : an Eskimo house or hut often made of snow blocks and in the shape of a dome

ig·ne·ous \'ig-nē-əs\ *adj* **1** : FIERY **2** : formed by solidification of molten rock

ig·nite \ig-'nīt\ *vb* **ig·nit·ed; ig·nit·ing** : to set afire or catch fire — **ig·nit·able** \-'nīt-ə-bəl\ *n*

ig·ni·tion \ig-'nish-ən\ *n* **1** : a setting on fire **2** : the process or means (as an electric spark) of igniting the fuel mixture in an engine

ig·no·ble \ig-'nō-bəl\ *adj* **1** : of low birth : PLEBEIAN **2** : not honorable : BASE, MEAN — **ig·no·bly** \-blē\ *adv*

ig·no·min·i·ous \ˌig-nə-'min-ē-əs\ *adj* **1** : DISHONORABLE **2** : DESPICABLE **3** : HUMILIATING, DEGRADING — **ig·no·min·i·ous·ly** *adv* — **ig·no·mi·ny** \'ig-nə-ˌmin-ē, ig-'näm-ə-nē\ *n*

ig·no·ra·mus \ˌig-nə-'rā-məs\ *n* [*Ignoramus*, ignorant lawyer in *Ignoramus* (1615), play by George Ruggle] : an utterly ignorant person : DUNCE

ig·no·rance \'ig-nə-rəns\ *n* : the state of being ignorant : lack of knowledge

ig·no·rant \'ig-nə-rənt\ *adj* **1** : lacking knowledge : UNEDUCATED **2** : resulting from or showing lack of knowledge or intelligence **3** : UNAWARE, UNINFORMED — **ig·no·rant·ly** *adv*

ig·nore \ig-'nōr\ *vb* **ig·nored; ig·nor·ing** : to refuse to take notice of **syn** overlook, slight, neglect

igua·na \i-'gwän-ə\ *n* : a large edible tropical American lizard

IGY *abbr* International Geophysical Year

IHP *abbr* indicated horsepower

IHS \ˌī-ˌā-'ches\ [LL, part transliteration of Gk IHΣ, abbreviation for IHΣOYΣ *Iēsous* Jesus] — used as a Christian symbol and monogram for Jesus

ikon var of ICON

IL *abbr* Illinois

il·e·itis \ˌil-ē-'īt-əs\ *n* : inflammation of the ileum

il·e·um \'il-ē-əm\ *n, pl* **il·ea** \-ē-ə\ : the part of the small intestine between the jejunum and the large intestine — **il·e·al** \-ē-əl\ *adj*

il·i·ac \'il-ē-ˌak\ *adj* : of, relating to, or located near the ilium

il·i·um \'il-ē-əm\ *n* : the upper one of the three bones making up either side of the pelvis

ilk \'ilk\ *n* : SORT, FAMILY

¹ill \'il\ *adj* **worse** \'wərs\; **worst** \'wərst\ **1** : not normal or sound ⟨∼ health⟩; *also* : suffering ill health : SICK **2** : BAD, UNLUCKY ⟨∼ omen⟩ **3** : not right or proper ⟨∼ manners⟩ **4** : UNFRIENDLY, HOSTILE ⟨∼ feeling⟩ **5** : HARSH, CRUEL ⟨∼ treatment⟩

²ill *adv* **worse; worst 1** : with displeasure **2** : in a harsh manner **3** : HARDLY, SCARCELY ⟨can ∼ afford it⟩ **4** : BADLY, UNLUCKILY **5** : in a faulty way

³ill *n* **1** : EVIL **2** : MISFORTUNE, DISTRESS **3** : AILMENT, SICKNESS; *also* : TROUBLE

⁴ill *abbr* illustrated; illustration; illustrator

Ill *abbr* Illinois

ill–ad·vised \ˌil-əd-'vīzd\ *adj* : not well counseled ⟨∼ efforts⟩ — **ill–ad·vis·ed·ly** \-'vī-zəd-lē\ *adv*

ill–bred \-'bred\ *adj* : badly brought up : IMPOLITE

il·le·gal \il-'(l)ē-gəl\ *adj* : not lawful; *also* : not sanctioned by official rules — **il·le·gal·i·ty** \ˌil-i-'gal-ət-ē\ *n* — **il·le·gal·ly** \il-'(l)ē-gə-lē\ *adv*

il·leg·i·ble \il-'(l)ej-ə-bəl\ *adj* : not legible — **il·leg·i·bil·i·ty** \il-ˌ(l)ej-ə-'bil-ət-ē\ *n* — **il·leg·i·bly** \il-'(l)ej-ə-blē\ *adv*

il·le·git·i·mate \ˌil-i-'jit-ə-mət\ *adj* **1** : born of unmarried parents **2** : ILLOGICAL **3** : ILLEGAL — **il·le·git·i·ma·cy**

\-'jit-ə-mə-sē\ *n* — **il·le·git·i·mate·ly** \-'jit-ə-mət-lē\ *adv*

ill–fat·ed \'il-'fāt-əd\ *adj* : having or destined to an evil fate : UNFORTUNATE

ill–fa·vored \-'fā-vərd\ *adj* : UGLY, UNATTRACTIVE

ill–got·ten \-'gät-ᵊn\ *adj* : acquired by evil means ⟨∼ gains⟩

ill–hu·mored \-'(h)yü-mərd\ *adj* : SURLY, IRRITABLE

il·lib·er·al \il-'(l)ib-(ə-)rəl\ *adj* : not liberal : NARROW, BIGOTED

il·lic·it \il-'(l)is-ət\ *adj* : not permitted : UNLAWFUL — **il·lic·it·ly** *adv*

il·lim·it·able \il-'(l)im-ət-ə-bəl\ *adj* : BOUNDLESS, MEASURELESS — **il·lim·it·ably** \-blē\ *adv*

Il·li·nois \,il-ə-'nòi *also* -'nòiz\ *n, pl* **Illinois** : a member of an American Indian people of Illinois, Iowa, and Wisconsin

il·lit·er·ate \il-'(l)it-(ə-)rət\ *adj* **1** : having little or no education; *esp* : unable to read or write **2** : showing a lack of familiarity with the fundamentals of a particular field of knowledge — **il·lit·er·a·cy** \-'(l)it-(ə-)rə-sē\ *n* — **illiterate** *n*

ill–man·nered \'il-'man-ərd\ *adj* : marked by bad manners : RUDE

ill–na·tured \-'nā-chərd\ *adj* : CROSS, SURLY — **ill–na·tured·ly** *adv*

ill·ness \'il-nəs\ *n* : SICKNESS

il·log·i·cal \il-'(l)äj-i-kəl\ *adj* : not according to good reasoning; *also* : SENSELESS — **il·log·i·cal·ly** \-i-k(ə-)lē\ *adv*

ill–starred \'il-'stärd\ *adj* : ILL-FATED, UNLUCKY

ill–tem·pered \-'tem-pərd\ *adj* : ILL= NATURED, QUARRELSOME

ill–treat \-'trēt\ *vb* : to treat cruelly or improperly : MALTREAT — **ill–treat·ment** \-mənt\ *n*

il·lume \il-'üm\ *vb* **il·lumed; il·lum·ing** : ILLUMINATE

il·lu·mi·nate \il-'ü-mə-,nāt\ *vb* **-nat·ed; -nat·ing** **1** : to supply or brighten with light : light up **2** : to make clear : ELUCIDATE **3** : to decorate (as a manuscript) with designs or pictures in gold or colors — **il·lu·mi·nat·ing·ly** \-,nāt-iŋ-lē\ *adv* — **il·lu·mi·na·tion** \-,ü-mə-'nā-shən\ *n* — **il·lu·mi·na·tor** \-'ü-mə-,nāt-ər\ *n*

il·lu·mine \il-'ü-mən\ *vb* **-mined; -min·ing** : ILLUMINATE

ill–us·age \'il-'yü-sij, -zij\ *n* : harsh, unkind, or abusive treatment

ill–use \-'yüz\ *vb* : MALTREAT, ABUSE

il·lu·sion \il-'ü-zhən\ *n* [ME, fr. MF, fr. LL *illusio,* fr. L, action of mocking, fr. *illudere* to mock at, fr. *ludere* to play, mock] **1** : a mistaken idea : MISAPPREHENSION, MISCONCEPTION, FANCY **2** : a misleading visual image : HALLUCINATION

il·lu·sion·ist \il-'üzh-(ə-)nəst\ *n* : one that produces illusions; *esp* : a sleight-of-hand performer

il·lu·sive \il-'ü-siv\ *adj* : ILLUSORY

il·lu·so·ry \il-'üs-(ə-)rē, -'üz-\ *adj* : based on or producing illusion

illust *or* **illus** *abbr* illustrated; illustration

il·lus·trate \'il-əs-,trāt\ *vb* **-trat·ed; -trat·ing** [L *illustrare,* fr. *lustrare* to purify, make bright] **1** : to explain by use of examples : CLARIFY; *also* : DEMONSTRATE **2** : to provide with pictures or figures that explain or decorate **3** : to serve to explain or decorate — **il·lus·tra·tor** \'il-əs-,trāt-ər\ *n*

il·lus·tra·tion \,il-əs-'trā-shən\ *n* **1** : the act of illustrating : the condition of being illustrated **2** : an example or instance that helps make something clear **3** : a picture or diagram that explains or decorates

il·lus·tra·tive \il-'əs-trət-iv\ *adj* : serving, tending, or designed to illustrate — **il·lus·tra·tive·ly** *adv*

il·lus·tri·ous \il-'əs trē-əs\ *adj* : notably outstanding because of rank or achievement : EMINENT — **il·lus·tri·ous·ness** *n*

ill will *n* : unfriendly feeling

ILS *abbr* instrument landing system

¹**im·age** \'im-ij\ *n* **1** : a likeness or imitation of a person or thing; *esp* : STATUE **2** : a picture of an object formed by a device (as a mirror or lens) **3** : a person strikingly like another person ⟨he is the ∼ of his father⟩ **4** : a mental picture or conception : IMPRESSION, IDEA, CONCEPT **5** : a vivid representation or description

²**image** *vb* **im·aged; im·ag·ing** **1** : to call up a mental picture of **2** : to describe or portray in words **3** : to create a representation of **4** : REFLECT, MIRROR **5** : to make appear : PROJECT

im·ag·ery \'im-ij-(ə-)rē\ *n* **1** : IMAGES;

also : the art of making images **2** : figurative language **3** : mental images; *esp* : the products of imagination

imag·in·able \im-'aj-(ə-)nə-bəl\ *adj* : capable of being imagined : CONCEIVABLE — **imag·in·ably** \-blē\ *adv*

imag·i·nary \im-'aj-ə-₁ner-ē\ *adj* **1** : existing only in the imagination **2** : containing or relating to the imaginary unit

imaginary number *n* : a complex number (as 2 + 3*i*) whose imaginary part is not zero

imaginary part *n* : the part of a complex number (as 3*i* in 2 + 3*i*) that has the imaginary unit as a factor

imaginary unit *n* : the positive square root of minus 1 : $+\sqrt{-1}$

imag·i·na·tion \im-₁aj-ə-'nā-shən\ *n* **1** : the act or power of forming a mental image of something not present to the senses or not previously known or experienced **2** : creative ability **3** : RESOURCEFULNESS **4** : a mental image : a creation of the mind — **imag·i·na·tive** \im-'aj-(ə-)nət-iv, -ə-₁nāt-iv\ *adj* — **imag·i·na·tive·ly** *adv*

imag·ine \im-'aj-ən\ *vb* **imag·ined; imag·in·ing** \-'aj-(ə-)niŋ\ **1** : to form a mental picture of something not present **2** : THINK, GUESS ⟨I ~ it will rain⟩

im·ag·ism \'im-ij-₁iz-əm\ *n, often cap* : a movement in poetry advocating free verse and the expression of ideas and emotions through clear precise images — **im·ag·ist** \-ij-əst\ *n*

ima·go \im-'ā-gō, -'äg-ō\ *n, pl* **imagoes** *or* **ima·gi·nes** \-'ā-gə-₁nēz, -'äg-ə-\ [L, image] : an insect in its final adult stage — **ima·gi·nal** \im-'ā-gən-ᵊl, -'äg-ən-\ *adj*

im·bal·ance \(')im-'bal-əns\ *n* : lack of balance : the state of being out of equilibrium or out of proportion

im·be·cile \'im-bə-səl, -₁sil\ *n* **1** : a feebleminded person; *esp* : one capable of performing routine personal care under supervision **2** : FOOL, IDIOT — **imbecile** *or* **im·be·cil·ic** \₁im-bə-'sil-ik\ *adj* — **im·be·cil·i·ty** \₁im-bə-'sil-ət-ē\ *n*

imbed *var of* EMBED

im·bibe \im-'bīb\ *vb* **im·bibed; im·bib·ing** **1** : to receive and retain in the mind **2** : DRINK **3** : to drink in : ABSORB — **im·bib·er** *n*

im·bi·bi·tion \₁im-bə-'bish-ən\ *n* : the act or action of imbibing; *esp* : the taking up of fluid by a colloidal system resulting in swelling

im·bri·ca·tion \₁im-brə-'kā-shən\ *n* **1** : an overlapping of edges (as of tiles) **2** : a pattern showing imbrication — **im·bri·cate** \'im-bri-kət\ *adj*

im·bro·glio \im-'brōl-yō\ *n, pl* **-glios** [It, fr. *imbrogliare* to entangle] **1** : a confused mass **2** : a difficult or embarrassing situation; *also* : a serious or embarrassing misunderstanding

im·brue \im-'brü\ *vb* **im·brued; im·bru·ing** : DRENCH, STAIN ⟨a nation *imbrued* with the blood of executed men⟩

im·bue \-'byü\ *vb* **im·bued; im·bu·ing** **1** : to permeate or influence as if by dyeing **2** : to tinge or dye deeply

IMF *abbr* International Monetary Fund

imit *abbr* imitative

im·i·ta·ble \'im-ət-ə-bəl\ *adj* : capable or worthy of being imitated or copied

im·i·tate \'im-ə-₁tāt\ *vb* **-tat·ed; -tat·ing** **1** : to follow as a model : COPY **2** : RESEMBLE **3** : REPRODUCE **4** : MIMIC, COUNTERFEIT — **im·i·ta·tor** \-₁tāt-ər\ *n*

im·i·ta·tion \₁im-ə-'tā-shən\ *n* **1** : an act of imitating **2** : COPY, COUNTERFEIT **3** : a literary work that reproduces the style of another author — **imitation** *adj*

im·i·ta·tive \'im-ə-₁tāt-iv\ *adj* **1** : marked by imitation **2** : exhibiting mimicry **3** : inclined to imitate or copy **4** : COUNTERFEIT

im·mac·u·late \im-'ak-yə-lət\ *adj* **1** : being without stain or blemish : PURE **2** : spotlessly clean ⟨~ linen⟩ — **im·mac·u·late·ly** *adv*

im·ma·nent \'im-ə-nənt\ *adj* : having existence only in the mind — **im·ma·nence** \-nəns\ *n* — **im·ma·nen·cy** \-nən-sē\ *n*

im·ma·te·ri·al \₁im-ə-'tir-ē-əl\ *adj* **1** : not consisting of matter : SPIRITUAL **2** : UNIMPORTANT, TRIFLING — **im·ma·te·ri·al·i·ty** \-₁tir-ē-'al-ət-ē\ *n*

im·ma·ture \₁im-ə-'t(y)ùr\ *adj* : lacking complete development : not yet mature — **im·ma·tu·ri·ty** \-'t(y)ùr-ət-ē\ *n*

im·mea·sur·able \(')im-'ezh-(ə-)rə-bəl\ *adj* : not capable of being measured

: indefinitely extensive : ILLIMITABLE — **im·mea·sur·ably** \-blē\ *adv*

im·me·di·a·cy \im-'ēd-ē-ə-sē\ *n, pl* **-cies** 1 : the quality or state of being immediate 2 : URGENCY 3 : something that is of immediate importance

im·me·di·ate \im-'ēd-ē-ət\ *adj* 1 : acting directly and alone : DIRECT ⟨the ∼ cause of death⟩ 2 : being next in line or relation ⟨members of the ∼ family attended⟩ 3 : not distant : CLOSE 4 : made or done at once ⟨an ∼ response⟩ 5 : near to or related to the present time ⟨the ∼ future⟩ — **im·me·di·ate·ly** *adv*

im·me·mo·ri·al \,im-ə-'mōr-ē-əl\ *adj* : extending beyond the reach of memory, record, or tradition

im·mense \im-'ens\ *adj* [MF, fr. L *immensus* immeasurable, fr. *mensus*, pp. of *metiri* to measure] 1 : very great in size or degree : VAST, HUGE 2 : EXCELLENT — **im·mense·ly** *adv* — **im·men·si·ty** \-'en-sət-ē\ *n*

im·merse \im-'ərs\ *vb* **im·mersed; im·mers·ing** 1 : to plunge or dip esp. into a fluid 2 : ENGROSS, ABSORB 3 : to baptize by immersing — **im·mer·sion** \im-'ər-zhən\ *n*

im·mi·grant \'im-i-grənt\ *n* 1 : a person who immigrates 2 : a plant or animal that becomes established where it did not previously occur

im·mi·grate \'im-ə-,grāt\ *vb* **-grat·ed; -grat·ing** : to come into a foreign country and take up residence — **im·mi·gra·tion** \,im-ə-'grā-shən\ *n*

im·mi·nent \'im-ə-nənt\ *adj* : ready to take place; *esp* : hanging threateningly over one's head — **im·mi·nence** \-nəns\ *n* — **im·mi·nent·ly** *adv*

im·mis·ci·ble \(')im-'is-ə-bəl\ *adj* : incapable of mixing — **im·mis·ci·bil·i·ty** \(,)im-,is-ə-'bil-ət-ē\ *n*

im·mo·bile \(')im-'ō-bəl\ *adj* : incapable of being moved : IMMOVABLE, FIXED — **im·mo·bil·i·ty** \,im-ō-'bil-ət-ē\ *n*

im·mo·bi·lize \im-'ō-bə-,līz\ *vb* : to make immobile — **im·mo·bi·li·za·tion** \im-,ō-bə-lə-'zā-shən\ *n*

im·mod·er·ate \(')im-'äd-(ə-)rət\ *adj* : lacking in moderation : EXCESSIVE — **im·mod·er·a·cy** \-(ə-)rə-sē\ *n* — **im·mod·er·ate·ly** *adv*

im·mod·est \(')im-'äd-əst\ *adj* : not modest : BRAZEN, INDECENT ⟨an ∼ dress⟩ ⟨∼ conduct⟩ — **im·mod·est·ly** *adv* — **im·mod·es·ty** \-ə-stē\ *n*

im·mo·late \'im-ə-,lāt\ *vb* **-lat·ed; -lat·ing** [L *immolare*, fr. *mola* grits; fr. the custom of sprinkling victims with sacrificial meal] : to offer in sacrifice; *esp* : to kill as a sacrificial victim — **im·mo·la·tion** \,im-ə-'lā-shən\ *n*

im·mor·al \(')im-'ȯr-əl\ *adj* : not moral : WICKED — **im·mor·al·ly** \-ē\ *adv*

im·mo·ral·i·ty \,im-ȯ-'ral-ət-ē, ,im-ə-'ral-\ *n* 1 : WICKEDNESS; *esp* : UNCHASTITY 2 : an immoral act or practice

¹**im·mor·tal** \(')im-'ȯrt-ᵊl\ *adj* 1 : not mortal : exempt from death ⟨∼ gods⟩ 2 : exempt from oblivion ⟨those ∼ words⟩ — **im·mor·tal·ly** \-ē\ *adv*

²**immortal** *n* 1 : one exempt from death 2 *pl, often cap* : the gods in Greek and Roman mythology 3 : a person whose fame is lasting ⟨an ∼ of baseball⟩

im·mor·tal·i·ty \,im-,ȯr-'tal-ət-ē\ *n* : the quality or state of being immortal; *esp* : unending existence

im·mor·tal·ize \im-'ȯrt-ᵊl-,īz\ *vb* **-ized; -iz·ing** : to make immortal

im·mov·able \(')im-'ü-və-bəl\ *adj* 1 : firmly fixed, settled, or fastened : FAST, STATIONARY ⟨∼ mountains⟩ 2 : STEADFAST, UNYIELDING 3 : IMPASSIVE — **im·mov·abil·i·ty** \(,)im-,ü-və-'bil-ət-ē\ *n* — **im·mov·ably** \-blē\ *adv*

im·mune \im-'yün\ *adj* 1 : EXEMPT 2 : having a special capacity for resistance (as to a disease) — **im·mu·ni·ty** \im-'yü-nət-ē\ *n*

immune response *n* : a response of the body to an antigen resulting in the formation of antibodies and cells capable of reacting with the antigen and rendering it harmless

im·mu·nize \'im-yə-,nīz\ *vb* **-nized; -niz·ing** : to make immune — **im·mu·ni·za·tion** \,im-yə-nə-'zā-shən\ *n*

im·mu·no·de·fi·cien·cy \,im-yə-nō-di-'fish-ən-sē\ *n* : inability to produce the normal number of antibodies or immunologically sensitized cells esp. in response to specific antigens — **im·mu·no·de·fi·cient** \-ənt\ *adj*

im·mu·no·glob·u·lin \,im-yə-nō-'gläb-yə-lən\ *n* : any of a group of vertebrate serum proteins that include all known antibodies

im·mu·nol·o·gy \,im-yə-'näl-ə-jē\ *n* : a

science that deals with the phenomena and causes of immunity — **im·mu·no·log·ic** \-yən-ᵊl-ˈäj-ik\ *or* **im·mu·no·log·i·cal** \-i-kəl\ *adj* — **im·mu·no·log·i·cal·ly** \-i-k(ə-)lē\ *adv* — **im·mu·nol·o·gist** \ˌim-yə-ˈnäl-ə-jəst\ *n*

im·mu·no·sup·pres·sion \ˌim-yə-nō-sə-ˈpresh-ən\ *n* : suppression (as by drugs) of natural immune responses — **im·mu·no·sup·press** \-sə-ˈpres\ *vb* — **im·mu·no·sup·pres·sant** \-sə-ˈpres-ᵊnt\ *n or adj* — **im·mu·no·sup·pres·sive** \-sə-ˈpres-iv\ *adj*

im·mure \im-ˈyu̇(ə)r\ *vb* **im·mured; im·mur·ing** **1** : to enclose within or as if within walls **2** : to build into a wall; *esp* : to entomb in a wall

im·mu·ta·ble \(ˈ)im-ˈyüt-ə-bəl\ *adj* : UNCHANGEABLE, UNCHANGING — **im·mu·ta·bil·i·ty** \(ˌ)im-ˌyüt-ə-ˈbil-ət-ē\ *n* — **im·mu·ta·bly** \(ˈ)im-ˈyüt-ə-blē\ *adv*

¹imp \ˈimp\ *n* **1** : a small demon : FIEND **2** : a mischievous child

²imp *abbr* **1** imperative **2** imperfect **3** imperial **4** import; imported

¹im·pact \im-ˈpakt\ *vb* **1** : to press together **2** : to have an impact on

²im·pact \ˈim-ˌpakt\ *n* **1** : a forceful contact, collision, or onset; *also* : the impetus communicated in or as if in a collision **2** : EFFECT

im·pact·ed \im-ˈpak-təd\ *adj* : wedged between the jawbone and another tooth

im·pair \im-ˈpa(ə)r\ *vb* : to diminish in quantity, value, excellence, or strength : DAMAGE, LESSEN — **im·pair·ment** *n*

im·pa·la \im-ˈpal-ə\ *n* : a large brownish African antelope that in the male has slender lyre-shaped horns

im·pale \im-ˈpāl\ *vb* **im·paled; im·pal·ing** : to pierce with or as if with something pointed — **im·pale·ment** *n*

im·pal·pa·ble \(ˈ)im-ˈpal-pə-bəl\ *adj* **1** : unable to be felt by touch : INTANGIBLE **2** : not easily seen or understood — **im·pal·pa·bly** \(ˌ)im-ˈpal-pə-blē\ *adv*

im·pan·el \im-ˈpan-ᵊl\ *vb* : to enter in or on a panel : ENROLL ⟨~ a jury⟩

im·part \im-ˈpärt\ *vb* **1** : to give from one's store or abundance ⟨the sun ~s warmth⟩ **2** : to make known

im·par·tial \(ˈ)im-ˈpär-shəl\ *adj* : not partial : UNBIASED, JUST — **im·par·tial·**

i·ty \(ˌ)im-ˌpär-shē-ˈal-ət-ē, -ˌpär-ˈshal-\ *n* — **im·par·tial·ly** \(ˈ)im-ˈpärsh-(ə-)lē\ *adv*

im·pass·able \(ˈ)im-ˈpas-ə-bəl\ *adj* : incapable of being passed, traversed, or circulated ⟨~ roads⟩ — **im·pass·ably** \(ˈ)im-ˈpas-ə-blē\ *adv*

im·passe \ˈim-ˌpas\ *n* **1** : an impassable road or way **2** : a predicament from which there is no obvious escape

im·pas·si·ble \(ˈ)im-ˈpas-ə-bəl\ *adj* : UNFEELING, IMPASSIVE

im·pas·sioned \im-ˈpash-ənd\ *adj* : filled with passion or zeal : showing great warmth or intensity of feeling **syn** passionate, ardent, fervent, fervid

im·pas·sive \(ˈ)im-ˈpas-iv\ *adj* : showing no signs of feeling, emotion, or interest : EXPRESSIONLESS, INDIFFERENT **syn** stoic, phlegmatic, apathetic, stolid — **im·pas·sive·ly** *adv* — **im·pas·siv·i·ty** \ˌim-ˌpas-ˈiv-ət-ē\ *n*

im·pas·to \im-ˈpas-tō, -ˈpäs-\ *n* : the thick application of a pigment to a canvas or panel in painting; *also* : the body of pigment so applied

im·pa·tience \(ˈ)im-ˈpā-shən(t)s\ *n* **1** : restlessness of spirit esp. under irritation, delay, or opposition **2** : restless or eager desire or longing

im·pa·tiens \im-ˈpā-shənz, -shəns\ *n* : any of a genus of watery-juiced annual herbs with spurred flowers and seed capsules that readily split open

im·pa·tient \(ˈ)im-ˈpā-shənt\ *adj* **1** : not patient : restless or short of temper esp. under irritation, delay, or opposition **2** : INTOLERANT ⟨~ of poverty⟩ **3** : prompted or marked by impatience **4** : ANXIOUS — **im·pa·tient·ly** *adv*

im·peach \im-ˈpēch\ *vb* [ME *empechen*, fr. MF *empeechier* to hinder, fr. LL *impedicare* to fetter, fr. L *pedica* fetter, fr. *ped-, pes* foot] **1** : to charge (a public official) before an authorized tribunal with misbehavior in office **2** : to challenge the credibility or validity of — **im·peach·ment** *n*

im·pec·ca·ble \(ˈ)im-ˈpek-ə-bəl\ *adj* **1** : not capable of sinning or wrongdoing **2** : FAULTLESS, FLAWLESS, IRREPROACHABLE ⟨a man of ~ character⟩ — **im·pec·ca·bil·i·ty** \(ˌ)im-ˌpek-ə-ˈbil-ət-ē\ *n* — **im·pec·ca·bly** \(ˈ)im-ˈpek-ə-blē\ *adv*

im·pe·cu·nious \ˌim-pi-ˈkyü-nyəs, -nē-əs\ *adj* : having little or no money — **im·pe·cu·nious·ness** *n*

im·ped·ance \im-ˈpēd-ᵊns\ *n* : the opposition in an electrical circuit to the flow of an alternating current

im·pede \im-ˈpēd\ *vb* **im·ped·ed; im·ped·ing** [L *impedire,* fr. *ped-, pes* foot] : to interfere with the progress of

im·ped·i·ment \im-ˈped-ə-mənt\ *n* : OBSTRUCTION, BLOCK; *esp* : a speech defect

im·ped·i·men·ta \im-ˌped-ə-ˈment-ə\ *n pl* : things that impede

im·pel \im-ˈpel\ *vb* **im·pelled; im·pel·ling** : to urge or drive forward or on : FORCE; *also* : PROPEL

im·pel·ler *also* **im·pel·lor** \im-ˈpel-ər\ *n* : ROTOR

im·pend \im-ˈpend\ *vb* **1** : to hover or hang over threateningly : MENACE **2** : to be about to occur

im·pen·e·tra·ble \(ˈ)im-ˈpen-ə-trə-bəl\ *adj* **1** : incapable of being penetrated or pierced ⟨an ∼ jungle⟩ **2** : incapable of being comprehended : INSCRUTABLE ⟨an ∼ mystery⟩ — **im·pen·e·tra·bil·i·ty** \(ˌ)im-ˌpen-ə-trə-ˈbil-ət-ē\ *n* — **im·pen·e·tra·bly** \(ˈ)im-ˈpen-ə-trə-blē\ *adv*

im·pen·i·tent \(ˈ)im-ˈpen-ə-tənt\ *adj* : not penitent : not repenting of sin — **im·pen·i·tence** \-təns\ *n*

im·per·a·tive \im-ˈper-ət-iv\ *adj* **1** : expressing a command, request, or encouragement ⟨∼ sentence⟩ **2** : having power to restrain, control, or direct **3** : NECESSARY — **imperative** *n* — **im·per·a·tive·ly** *adv*

im·per·cep·ti·ble \ˌim-pər-ˈsep-tə-bəl\ *adj* : not perceptible by the senses or by the mind ⟨∼ changes⟩ — **im·per·cep·ti·bly** \-ˈsep-tə-blē\ *adv*

im·per·cep·tive \ˌim-pər-ˈsep-tiv\ *adj* : not perceptive

imperf *abbr* **1** imperfect **2** imperforate

¹**im·per·fect** \(ˈ)im-ˈpər-fikt\ *adj* **1** : not perfect : DEFECTIVE, INCOMPLETE **2** : of, relating to, or being a verb tense used to designate a continuing state or an incomplete action esp. in the past — **im·per·fect·ly** *adv*

²**imperfect** *n* : the imperfect tense; *also* : a verb form in it

im·per·fec·tion \ˌim-pər-ˈfek-shən\ *n* : the quality or state of being imper-

fect; *also* : DEFICIENCY, FAULT, BLEMISH

im·per·fo·rate \im-ˈpər-fə-rət\ *adj* : lacking perforations or tiny slits ⟨∼ postage stamps⟩

¹**im·pe·ri·al** \im-ˈpir-ē-əl\ *adj* **1** : of, relating to, or befitting an empire or an emperor; *also* : of or relating to the United Kingdom or to the Commonwealth or British Empire **2** : ROYAL, SOVEREIGN; *also* : REGAL, IMPERIOUS **3** : of unusual size or excellence

²**imperial** *n* : a pointed beard growing below the lower lip

im·pe·ri·al·ism \im-ˈpir-ē-ə-ˌliz-əm\ *n* : the policy of seeking to extend the power, dominion, or territories of a nation — **im·pe·ri·al·ist** \-ləst\ *n or adj* — **im·pe·ri·al·is·tic** \-ˌpir-ē-ə-ˈlis-tik\ *adj* — **im·pe·ri·al·is·ti·cal·ly** \-ti-k(ə-)lē\ *adv*

im·per·il \im-ˈper-əl\ *vb* **-iled** *or* **-illed; -il·ing** *or* **-il·ling** : ENDANGER

im·pe·ri·ous \im-ˈpir-ē-əs\ *adj* **1** : COMMANDING, LORDLY **2** : ARROGANT, DOMINEERING **3** : IMPERATIVE, URGENT — **im·pe·ri·ous·ly** *adv*

im·per·ish·able \(ˈ)im-ˈper-ish-ə-bəl\ *adj* : not perishable or subject to decay

im·per·ma·nent \(ˈ)im-ˈpər-mə-nənt\ *adj* : not permanent : TRANSIENT — **im·per·ma·nent·ly** *adv*

im·per·me·able \(ˈ)im-ˈpər-mē-ə-bəl\ *adj* : not permitting passage (as of a fluid) through its substance

im·per·mis·si·ble \ˌim-pər-ˈmis-ə-bəl\ *adj* : not permissible

im·per·son·al \(ˈ)im-ˈpərs-(ᵊ-)nəl\ *adj* **1** : not referring to any particular person or thing **2** : not involving human emotions — **im·per·son·al·i·ty** \(ˌ)im-ˌpərs-ᵊn-ˈal-ət-ē\ *n* — **im·per·son·al·ly** \-ē\ *adv*

im·per·son·ate \im-ˈpərs-ᵊn-ˌāt\ *vb* **-at·ed; -at·ing** : to assume or act the character of — **im·per·son·ation** \-ˌpərs-ᵊn-ˈā-shən\ *n* — **im·per·son·ator** \-ˈpərs-ᵊn-ˌāt-ər\ *n*

im·per·ti·nent \(ˈ)im-ˈpərt-ᵊn-ənt\ *adj* **1** : IRRELEVANT **2** : not restrained within due or proper bounds : RUDE, INSOLENT, SAUCY — **im·per·ti·nence** \-ᵊn-əns\ *n* — **im·per·ti·nent·ly** *adv*

im·per·turb·able \ˌim-pər-ˈtər-bə-bəl\

adj : marked by extreme calm, impassivity, and steadiness : SERENE

im·per·vi·ous \(')im-'pər-vē-əs\ *adj* **1** : incapable of being penetrated (as by moisture) **2** : not capable of being affected or disturbed ⟨∼ to criticism⟩

im·pe·ti·go \,im-pə-'tē-gō, -'tī\ *n* : a contagious skin disease characterized by vesicles, pustules, and yellowish crusts

im·pet·u·ous \im-'pech-(ə-)wəs\ *adj* **1** : marked by impulsive vehemence ⟨∼ temper⟩ **2** : marked by force and violence ⟨with ∼ speed⟩ — **im·pet·u·os·i·ty** \(,)im-,pech-ə-wäs-ət-ē\ *n* — **im·pet·u·ous·ly** *adv*

im·pe·tus \'im-pət-əs\ *n* [L, assault, impetus, fr. *impetere* to attack, fr. *petere* to go to, seek] **1** : a driving force : IMPULSE **2** : INCENTIVE **3** : MOMENTUM

im·pi·ety \(')im-'pī-ət-ē\ *n, pl* **-eties** **1** : the quality or state of being impious **2** : an impious act

im·pinge \im-'pinj\ *vb* **im·pinged; im·ping·ing** **1** : to strike or dash esp. with a sharp collision **2** : ENCROACH, INFRINGE — **im·pinge·ment** \-'pinj-mənt\ *n*

im·pi·ous \'im-pē-əs, (')im-'pī-\ *adj* : not pious : IRREVERENT, PROFANE

imp·ish \'im-pish\ *adj* : of, relating to, or befitting an imp; *esp* : MISCHIEVOUS — **imp·ish·ly** *adv* — **imp·ish·ness** *n*

im·pla·ca·ble \(')im-'plak-ə-bəl, -'plā-kə-\ *adj* : not capable of being appeased, pacified, mitigated, or changed ⟨an ∼ enemy⟩ — **im·pla·ca·bil·i·ty** \(,)im-,plak-ə-'bil-ət-ē, -,plā-kə-\ *n* — **im·pla·ca·bly** \(')im-'plak-ə-blē\ *adv*

im·plant \im-'plant\ *vb* **1** : to set firmly or deeply **2** : to fix in the mind or spirit **3** : to insert in a living site — **im·plant** \'im-,plant\ *n* — **im·plan·ta·tion** \,im-,plan-'tā-shən\ *n*

im·plau·si·ble \(')im-'plȯ-zə-bəl\ *adj* : not plausible — **im·plau·si·bil·i·ty** \(,)im-,plȯ-zə-'bil-ət-ē\ *n* — **im·plau·si·bly** \(')im-'plȯ-zə-blē\ *adv*

¹**im·ple·ment** \'im-plə-mənt\ *n* [ME, fr. LL *implementum* action of filling up, fr. L *implēre* to fill up] : TOOL, UTENSIL, INSTRUMENT

²**im·ple·ment** \-,ment\ *vb* **1** : to carry out; *esp* : to put into practice **2** : to

provide implements for — **im·ple·men·ta·tion** \,im-plə-mən-'tā-shən\ *n*

im·pli·cate \'im-plə-,kāt\ *vb* **-cat·ed; -cat·ing** **1** : IMPLY **2** : INVOLVE — **im·pli·ca·tion** \,im-plə-'kā-shən\ *n*

im·plic·it \im-'plis-ət\ *adj* **1** : understood though not directly stated or expressed : IMPLIED; *also* : POTENTIAL **2** : COMPLETE, UNQUESTIONING, ABSOLUTE ⟨∼ faith⟩ — **im·plic·it·ly** *adv*

im·plode \im-'plōd\ *vb* **im·plod·ed; im·plod·ing** : to burst or collapse inward — **im·plo·sion** \-'plō-zhən\ *n* — **im·plo·sive** \-'plō-siv\ *adj*

im·plore \im-'plōr\ *vb* **im·plored; im·plor·ing** : BESEECH, ENTREAT **syn** supplicate, beg, importune, plead

im·ply \im-'plī\ *vb* **im·plied; im·ply·ing** **1** : to involve or indicate by inference, association, or necessary consequence rather than by direct statement ⟨war *implies* fighting⟩ **2** : to express indirectly : hint at : SUGGEST

im·po·lite \,im-pə-'līt\ *adj* : not polite : RUDE, DISCOURTEOUS

im·pol·i·tic \(')im-'päl-ə-,tik\ *adj* : not politic : RASH

im·pon·der·a·ble \(')im-'pän-d(ə-)rə-bəl\ *adj* : incapable of being weighed or evaluated with exactness — **imponderable** *n*

¹**im·port** \im-'pōrt\ *vb* **1** : MEAN, SIGNIFY **2** : to bring (as merchandise) into a place or country from a foreign or external source — **im·port·er** *n*

²**im·port** \'im-,pōrt\ *n* **1** : IMPORTANCE, SIGNIFICANCE **2** : MEANING, SIGNIFICATION **3** : something (as merchandise) brought in from another country

im·por·tance \im-'pōrt-ᵊns\ *n* : the quality or state of being important : MOMENT, SIGNIFICANCE **syn** consequence, import, weight

im·por·tant \im-'pōrt-ᵊnt\ *adj* **1** : marked by importance : SIGNIFICANT **2** : giving an impression of importance — **im·por·tant·ly** *adv*

im·por·ta·tion \,im-,pōr-'tā-shən, -pər-\ *n* **1** : the act or practice of importing **2** : something imported

im·por·tu·nate \im-'pōrch-(ə-)nət\ *adj* **1** : troublesomely urgent **2** : BURDENSOME, TROUBLESOME

im·por·tune \,im-pər-'t(y)ün, im-'pȯrchən\ *vb* **-tuned; -tun·ing** : to urge or beg with troublesome persistence —

im•por•tu•ni•ty \-ˌim-pər-ˈt(y)ü-nət-ē\ n

im•pose \im-ˈpōz\ vb im•posed; im•pos•ing 1 : to establish or apply by authority ⟨∼ a tax⟩; also : INFLICT ⟨imposed himself as leader⟩ 2 : to make public or offer for sale with intent to deceive ⟨∼ fake antiques on buyers⟩ 3 : OBTRUDE ⟨imposed herself upon others⟩ 4 : to take unwarranted advantage of something ⟨∼ on her good nature⟩ — im•po•si•tion \ˌim-pə-ˈzish-ən\ n

im•pos•ing \im-ˈpō-ziŋ\ adj : impressive because of size, bearing, dignity, or grandeur — im•pos•ing•ly adv

im•pos•si•ble \(ˈ)im-ˈpäs-ə-bəl\ adj 1 : incapable of being or of occurring 2 : felt to be too difficult 3 : extremely undesirable : UNACCEPTABLE — im•pos•si•bil•i•ty \(ˌ)im-ˌpäs-ə-ˈbil-ət-ē\ n — im•pos•si•bly \(ˈ)im-ˈpäs-ə-blē\ adv

¹im•post \ˈim-ˌpōst\ n : TAX, DUTY

²impost n : a block, capital, or molding from which an arch springs

im•pos•tor or im•pos•ter \im-ˈpäs-tər\ n : one that assumes an identity or title not his own in order to deceive

im•pos•ture \im-ˈpäs-chər\ n : DECEPTION; esp : fraudulent impersonation

im•po•tent \ˈim-pət-ənt\ adj 1 : lacking in power or strength : HELPLESS 2 : unable to copulate; also : STERILE — im•po•tence \-pət-əns\ n — im•po•ten•cy \-ən-sē\ n — im•po•tent•ly adv

im•pound \im-ˈpaund\ vb 1 : CONFINE, ENCLOSE ⟨∼ stray dogs⟩ 2 : to seize and hold in legal custody 3 : to collect in a reservoir ⟨∼ water⟩ — im•pound•ment \-ˈpaun(d)-mənt\ n

im•pov•er•ish \im-ˈpäv-(ə-)rish\ vb : to make poor; also : to deprive of strength, richness, or fertility — im•pov•er•ish•ment n

im•prac•ti•ca•ble \(ˈ)im-ˈprak-ti-kə-bəl\ adj : not practicable : incapable of being put into practice or use

im•prac•ti•cal \(ˈ)im-ˈprak-ti-kəl\ adj 1 : not practical 2 : IMPRACTICABLE

im•pre•cate \ˈim-pri-ˌkāt\ vb -cat•ed; -cat•ing : CURSE — im•pre•ca•tion \ˌim-pri-ˈkā-shən\ n

im•pre•cise \ˌim-pri-ˈsīs\ adj : not precise — im•pre•cise•ly adv — im•pre•cise•ness n — im•pre•ci•sion \-ˈsizh-ən\ n

im•preg•na•ble \im-ˈpreg-nə-bəl\ adj : able to resist attack : UNCONQUERABLE, UNASSAILABLE — im•preg•na•bil•i•ty \(ˌ)im-ˌpreg-nə-ˈbil-ət-ē\ n

im•preg•nate \im-ˈpreg-ˌnāt\ vb -nat•ed; -nat•ing 1 : to fertilize or make pregnant 2 : to fill or soak with some other substance — im•preg•na•tion \ˌim-ˌpreg-ˈnā-shən\ n

im•pre•sa•rio \ˌim-prə-ˈsär-ē-ˌō\ n, pl -ri•os [It, fr. impresa undertaking, fr. imprendere to undertake] 1 : the manager or conductor of an opera or concert company 2 : one who puts on an entertainment 3 : MANAGER, PRODUCER

¹im•press \im-ˈpres\ vb 1 : to apply with or produce (as a mark) by pressure : IMPRINT 2 : to press, stamp, or print in or upon 3 : to produce a vivid impression of 4 : to affect esp. forcibly or deeply — im•press•ible adj

²im•press \ˈim-ˌpres\ n 1 : a characteristic or distinctive mark : STAMP 2 : IMPRESSION, EFFECT 3 : a mark made by pressure : IMPRINT 4 : an image of something formed by or as if by pressure; esp : SEAL 5 : a product of pressure or influence

³im•press \im-ˈpres\ vb 1 : to force into naval service 2 : to get the aid or services of by forcible argument or persuasion — im•press•ment n

im•pres•sion \im-ˈpresh-ən\ n 1 : a stamp, form, or figure made by impressing : IMPRINT 2 : an esp. marked influence or effect on feeling, sense, or mind 3 : a characteristic trait or feature resulting from influence : IMPRESS 4 : a single print or copy (as from type or from an engraved plate or book) 5 : all the copies of a publication (as a book) printed for one issue : PRINTING 6 : a usu. vague notion, recollection, belief, or opinion 7 : an imitation in caricature of a noted personality as a form of entertainment

im•pres•sion•able \im-ˈpresh-(ə-)nə-bəl\ adj : capable of being easily impressed : easily molded or influenced

im•pres•sion•ism \im-ˈpresh-ə-ˌniz-əm\ n 1 often cap : a theory or practice in modern art of depicting the natural appearances of objects by dabs or strokes of primary unmixed colors in order to simulate actual reflected light 2 : the depiction of scene, emotion, or character by details intended to achieve a vividness or effectiveness esp. by evoking subjective and sensory impressions — **im·pres·sion·is·tic** \(ˌ)im-ˌpresh-ə-'nis-tik\ *adj*

im·pres·sion·ist \im-'presh-(ə-)nəst\ *n* **1** *often cap* : a painter who practices impressionism **2** : an entertainer who does impressions

im·pres·sive \im-'pres-iv\ *adj* : making or tending to make a marked impression ⟨an ∼ speech⟩ — **im·pres·sive·ly** *adv* — **im·pres·sive·ness** *n*

im·pri·ma·tur \ˌim-prə-'mä-ˌtu̇(ə)r\ *n* [NL, let it be printed] **1** : a license to print or publish; *also* : official approval of a publication by a censor **2** : SANCTION, APPROVAL

¹im·print \im-'print, 'im-ˌprint\ *vb* **1** : to stamp or mark by or as if by pressure : IMPRESS **2** : to fix firmly (as on the memory)

²im·print \'im-ˌprint\ *n* **1** : something imprinted or printed : IMPRESS **2** : a publisher's name printed at the foot of a title page **3** : an indelible distinguishing effect or influence

im·pris·on \im-'priz-ᵊn\ *vb* : to put in or as if in prison : CONFINE — **im·pris·on·ment** \im-'priz-ən-mənt\ *n*

im·prob·a·ble \(')im-'präb-ə-bəl\ *adj* : unlikely to be true or to occur — **im·prob·a·bil·i·ty** \(ˌ)im-ˌpräb-ə-'bil-ət-ē\ *n* — **im·prob·a·bly** \(')im-'präb-ə-blē\ *adv*

im·promp·tu \im-'prämp-t(y)ü\ *adj* [F, fr. *impromptu* extemporaneously, fr. L *in promptu* in readiness] **1** : made or done on or as if on the spur of the moment **2** : EXTEMPORANEOUS, UNREHEARSED — **impromptu** *adv or n*

im·prop·er \(')im-'präp-ər\ *adj* **1** : not proper, fit, or suitable **2** : INCORRECT, INACCURATE **3** : not in accord with propriety, modesty, or good manners — **im·prop·er·ly** *adv*

improper fraction *n* : a fraction whose numerator is equal to or larger than the denominator

im·pro·pri·ety \ˌim-prə-'prī-ət-ē\ *n, pl* **-eties 1** : the quality or state of being improper **2** : an improper act or remark; *esp* : an unacceptable use of a word or of language

im·prove \im-'prüv\ *vb* **im·proved; im·prov·ing 1** : INCREASE, AUGMENT ⟨edu-

cation *improved* his chances⟩ **2** : to enhance or increase in value or quality ⟨∼ farmlands by cultivation⟩ **3** : to grow or become better ⟨∼ in health⟩ **4** : to make good use of ⟨∼ the time by reading⟩ — **im·prov·able** \-'prü-və-bəl\ *adj*

im·prove·ment \im-'prüv-mənt\ *n* **1** : the act or process of improving **2** : increased value or excellence of something **3** : something that adds to the value or appearance of a thing

im·prov·i·dent \(')im-'präv-əd-ənt\ *adj* : not providing for the future — **im·prov·i·dence** \-əns\ *n*

im·pro·vise \'im-prə-ˌvīz\ *vb* **-vised; -vis·ing** [F *improviser,* fr. It *improvvisare,* fr. *improvviso* sudden, fr. L *improvisus,* lit., unforeseen] **1** : to compose, recite, play, or sing on the spur of the moment : EXTEMPORIZE ⟨∼ on the piano⟩ **2** : to make, invent, or arrange offhand ⟨∼ a sail out of shirts⟩ — **im·pro·vi·sa·tion** \im-ˌpräv-ə-'zā-shən, ˌim-prə-və-\ *n* — **im·pro·vis·er** *or* **im·pro·vi·sor** \ˌim-prə-'vī-zər, 'im-prə-ˌvī-\ *n*

im·pru·dent \(')im-'prüd-ᵊnt\ *adj* : not prudent : lacking discretion — **im·pru·dence** \-ᵊns\ *n*

im·pu·dent \'im-pyəd-ənt\ *adj* : marked by contemptuous boldness or disregard of others — **im·pu·dence** \-əns\ *n* — **im·pu·dent·ly** *adv*

im·pugn \im-'pyün\ *vb* [ME, deriv. of L *inpugnare,* deriv. of *pugnare* to fight] : to attack by words or arguments : oppose or attack as false ⟨∼ the motives of an opponent⟩

im·puis·sance \im-'pwis-ᵊns, -'pyü-ə-səns\ *n* [ME, fr. MF] : the quality or state of being powerless : WEAKNESS

im·pulse \'im-ˌpəls\ *n* **1** : a force that starts a body into motion; *also* : the motion produced by such a force **2** : an arousing of the mind and spirit to action; *also* : a wave of nervous excitation **3** : a natural tendency

im·pul·sion \im-'pəl-shən\ *n* **1** : the act of impelling : the state of being impelled **2** : a force that impels **3** : IMPETUS **4** : a sudden inclination

im·pul·sive \im-'pəl-siv\ *adj* **1** : having the power of or actually driving or impelling **2** : acting or prone to act on

impulse ⟨∼ buying⟩ — **im·pul·sive·ly** *adv* — **im·pul·sive·ness** *n*

im·pu·ni·ty \im-'pyü-nət-ē\ *n* [MF or L; MF *impunité,* fr. L *impunitas,* fr. *impune* without punishment, fr. *poena* pain, punishment] : exemption from punishment, harm, or loss

im·pure \(')im-'pyùr\ *adj* 1 : not pure : UNCHASTE, OBSCENE 2 : DIRTY, FOUL 3 : ADULTERATED, MIXED — **im·pu·ri·ty** \-'pyùr-ət-ē\ *n*

im·pute \im-'pyüt\ *vb* **im·put·ed; im·put·ing** 1 : to lay the responsibility or blame for often falsely or unjustly : CHARGE 2 : to credit to a person or a cause : ATTRIBUTE — **im·put·able** \-'pyüt-ə-bəl\ *adj* — **im·pu·ta·tion** \,im-pyə-'tā-shən\ *n*

¹in \(')in, ən, ⁿn\ *prep* 1 — used to indicate physical surroundings ⟨swim ∼ the lake⟩ 2 : INTO 1 ⟨ran ∼ the house⟩ 3 : DURING ⟨∼ the summer⟩ 4 : WITH ⟨written ∼ pencil⟩ 5 — used to indicate one's situation or state of being ⟨∼ luck⟩ ⟨∼ love⟩ 6 — used to indicate manner or purpose ⟨∼ a hurry⟩ ⟨said ∼ reply⟩ 7 : INTO 2 ⟨broke ∼ pieces⟩

²in \'in\ *adv* 1 : to or toward the inside ⟨come ∼⟩ : to or toward some destination or place ⟨flew ∼ from the South⟩ 2 : at close quarters : NEAR ⟨the enemy closed ∼⟩ 3 : into the midst of something ⟨mix ∼ the flour⟩ 4 : to or at its proper place ⟨fit a piece ∼⟩ 5 : WITHIN ⟨locked ∼⟩ 6 : in vogue or season; *also* : at hand 7 : in a completed or terminated state

³in \'in\ *adj* 1 : located inside or within 2 : that is in position, connection, operation, or power ⟨the ∼ party⟩ 3 : directed inward : INCOMING ⟨the ∼ train⟩ 4 : keenly aware of and responsive to what is new and smart ⟨the ∼ crowd⟩; *also* : extremely fashionable ⟨the ∼ thing to do⟩

⁴in \'in\ *n* 1 : one who is in office or power or on the inside 2 : INFLUENCE, PULL ⟨he has an ∼ with the owner⟩

⁵in *abbr* 1 inch 2 inlet

In *symbol* indium

IN *abbr* Indiana

in- \(')in, ,in\ *prefix* 1 : not : NON-, UN- 2 : opposite of : contrary to

inacceptable	inaccuracy
inaccessibility	inaccurate
inaccessible	inaction

inactive	indeterminable
inactivity	indiscernible
inadmissibility	indistinguishable
inadmissible	inedible
inadvisability	ineducable
inadvisable	inefficacious
inapplicable	inefficacy
inapposite	inelastic
inappreciative	inelasticity
inapproachable	inequitable
inappropriate	inequity
inapt	ineradicable
inartistic	inexpedient
inattentive	inexpensive
inaudible	inexpressive
inaudibly	inextinguishable
inauspicious	infeasible
incautious	inharmonious
incomprehension	inhospitable
inconceivable	injudicious
inconclusive	inoffensive
inconsistency	insanitary
inconsistent	insensitive
incoordination	insensitivity
indecipherable	insignificance
indefensible	insignificant
indemonstrable	insuppressible
indestructible	insusceptible

in·abil·i·ty \,in-ə-'bil-ət-ē\ *n* : the quality or state of being unable

in ab·sen·tia \,in-ab-'sen-ch(ē-)ə\ *adv* : in one's absence

in·ac·ti·vate \(')in-'ak-tə-,vāt\ *vb* : to make inactive — **in·ac·ti·va·tion** \(,)in-,ak-tə-'vā-shən\ *n*

in·ad·e·quate \(')in-'ad-i-kwət\ *adj* : not adequate : INSUFFICIENT — **in·ad·e·qua·cy** \-kwə-sē\ *n* — **in·ad·e·quate·ly** *adv* — **in·ad·e·quate·ness** *n*

in·ad·ver·tent \,in-əd-'vərt-ⁿnt\ *adj* 1 : HEEDLESS, INATTENTIVE 2 : UNINTENTIONAL — **in·ad·ver·tence** \-ⁿns\ *n* — **in·ad·ver·ten·cy** \-ⁿn-sē\ *n* — **in·ad·ver·tent·ly** *adv*

in·alien·able \(')in-'āl-yə-nə-bəl, -'ā-lē-ə-nə-\ *adj* : incapable of being alienated, surrendered, or transferred ⟨∼ rights⟩ — **in·alien·abil·i·ty** \(,)in-,āl-yə-nə-'bil-ət-ē, -,ā-lē-ə-nə-\ *n* — **in·alien·ably** \(')in-'āl-yə-nə-blē, -'ā-lē-ə-nə-\ *adv*

in·amo·ra·ta \in-,am-ə-'rät-ə\ *n* : a woman with whom one is in love

inane \in-'ān\ *adj* **inan·er; -est** : EMPTY, INSUBSTANTIAL; *also* : SHALLOW, SILLY — **inan·i·ty** \in-'an-ət-ē\ *n*

in·an·i·mate \(')in-'an-ə-mət\ *adj* : not animate or animated : lacking the qualities of living things — **in·an·i·mate·ly** adv — **in·an·i·mate·ness** n

in·ap·pre·cia·ble \ˌin-ə-'prē-shə-bəl\ adj : too small to be perceived — **in·ap·pre·cia·bly** \-blē\ adv

in·ap·ti·tude \('ˌ)in-'ap-tə-ˌt(y)üd\ n : lack of aptitude

in·ar·tic·u·late \ˌin-är-'tik-yə-lət\ adj 1 : not understandable as spoken words 2 : MUTE 3 : incapable of being expressed by speech; also : UNSPOKEN 4 : not having the power of distinct utterance or effective expression — **in·ar·tic·u·late·ly** adv

in·as·much as \ˌin-əz-ˌməch-əz\ conj : seeing that : SINCE

in·at·ten·tion \ˌin-ə-'ten-chən\ n : failure to pay attention : DISREGARD

¹**in·au·gu·ral** \in-'o-gyə-rəl, -g(ə-)rəl\ adj 1 : of or relating to an inauguration 2 : marking a beginning

²**inaugural** n 1 : an inaugural address 2 : INAUGURATION

in·au·gu·rate \in-'o-g(y)ə-ˌrāt\ vb -rat·ed; -rat·ing 1 : to introduce into an office with suitable ceremonies : INSTALL 2 : to dedicate ceremoniously 3 : BEGIN, INITIATE — **in·au·gu·ra·tion** \-ˌo-g(y)ə-'rā-shən\ n

in·board \'in-ˌbōrd\ adv 1 : inside the hull of a ship 2 : close or closest to the center line of a ship or aircraft — **inboard** adj

in·born \'in-'bȯrn\ adj : present from birth rather than acquired : NATURAL **syn** innate, congenital, native

in·bound \'in-ˌbaund\ adj : inward bound ⟨~ traffic⟩

in·bred \'in-'bred\ adj 1 : INBORN, INNATE 2 : subjected to or produced by inbreeding

in·breed·ing \'in-ˌbrēd-iŋ\ n 1 : the interbreeding of closely related individuals esp. to preserve and fix desirable characters of and to eliminate unfavorable characters from a stock 2 : confinement to a narrow range or a local or limited field of choice — **in·breed** \-'brēd\ vb

inc abbr 1 incomplete 2 incorporated 3 increase

In·ca \'iŋ-kə\ n [Sp, fr. Quechua (a So. American Indian language) inka king, prince] 1 : a noble or a member of the ruling family of an Indian empire of Peru, Bolivia, and Ecuador until the Spanish conquest 2 : a member of any people under Inca influence

in·cal·cu·la·ble \('ˌ)in-'kal-kyə-lə-bəl\ adj : not capable of being calculated; esp : too large or numerous to be calculated — **in·cal·cu·la·bly** \-blē\ adv

in·can·des·cent \ˌin-kən-'des-ᵊnt\ adj 1 : glowing with heat 2 : SHINING, BRILLIANT — **in·can·des·cence** \-ᵊns\ n

incandescent lamp n : a lamp in which an electrically heated filament emits light

in·can·ta·tion \ˌin-ˌkan-'tā-shən\ n : a use of spells or verbal charms spoken or sung as a part of a ritual of magic; also : a formula of words used in or as if in such a ritual

in·ca·pa·ble \('ˌ)in-'kā-pə-bəl\ adj : lacking ability or qualification for a particular purpose; also : UNQUALIFIED — **in·ca·pa·bil·i·ty** \('ˌ)in-ˌkā-pə-'bil-ət-ē\ n

in·ca·pac·i·tate \ˌin-kə-'pas-ə-ˌtāt\ vb -tat·ed; -tat·ing : to make incapable or unfit : DISQUALIFY, DISABLE

in·ca·pac·i·ty \ˌin-kə-'pas-ət-ē\ n, pl -ties : the quality or state of being incapable

in·car·cer·ate \in-'kär-sə-ˌrāt\ vb -at·ed; -at·ing : IMPRISON, CONFINE — **in·car·cer·a·tion** \(ˌ)in-ˌkär-sə-'rā-shən\ n

in·car·na·dine \in-'kär-nə-ˌdīn, -ˌdēn\ vb -dined; -din·ing : REDDEN

in·car·nate \in-'kär-nət, -ˌnāt\ adj 1 : having bodily and esp. human form and substance 2 : PERSONIFIED — **in·car·nate** \-ˌnāt\ vb

in·car·na·tion \ˌin-ˌkär-'nā-shən\ n 1 : the embodiment of a deity or spirit in an earthly form 2 cap : the union of divine and human natures in Jesus Christ 3 : a person showing a trait or typical character to a marked degree 4 : the act of incarnating : the state of being incarnate

incase var of ENCASE

in·cen·di·ary \in-'sen-dē-ˌer-ē\ adj 1 : of or relating to a deliberate burning of property 2 : tending to excite or inflame 3 : designed to kindle fires ⟨an ~ bomb⟩ **incendiary** n

¹**in·cense** \'in-ˌsens\ n 1 : material used to produce a fragrant odor when burned 2 : the perfume or smoke from some spices and gums when burned

²in·cense \in-ˈsens\ *vb* **in·censed; in·cens·ing** : to make extremely angry

in·cen·tive \in-ˈsent-iv\ *n* [ME, fr. LL *incentivum,* fr. *incentivus* stimulating, fr. L, setting the tune, fr. *incinere* to set the tune, fr. *canere* to sing] : something that incites or is likely to incite to determination or action

in·cep·tion \in-ˈsep-shən\ *n* : BEGINNING, COMMENCEMENT

in·cer·ti·tude \(ˈ)in-ˈsərt-ə-ˌt(y)üd\ *n* **1** : UNCERTAINTY, DOUBT, INDECISION **2** : INSECURITY, INSTABILITY

in·ces·sant \(ˈ)in-ˈses-ᵊnt\ *adj* : continuing or flowing without interruption ⟨∼ rains⟩ — **in·ces·sant·ly** *adv*

in·cest \ˈin-ˌsest\ *n* [ME, fr. L *incestum,* fr. *incestus* impure, fr. *castus* pure] : sexual intercourse between persons so closely related that marriage is illegal — **in·ces·tu·ous** \in-ˈses-chə-wəs\ *adj*

¹inch \ˈinch\ *n* [ME, fr. OE *ynce,* fr. L *uncia* twelfth part, inch, ounce] — see WEIGHT table

²inch *vb* : to move by small degrees

in·cho·ate \in-ˈkō-ət, ˈin-kə-ˌwāt\ *adj* [L *inchoatus,* pp. of *inchoare,* lit., to hitch up, fr. *cohum* strap fastening a plow beam to the yoke] : being only partly in existence or operation : INCOMPLETE, INCIPIENT

inch·worm \ˈinch-ˌwərm\ *n* : LOOPER

in·ci·dence \ˈin-səd-əns\ *n* : rate of occurrence or effect

¹in·ci·dent \ˈin-səd-ənt\ *n* **1** : OCCURRENCE, HAPPENING **2** : an action likely to lead to grave consequences esp. in diplomatic matters

²incident *adj* **1** : occurring or likely to occur esp. in connection with some other happening **2** : falling or striking on something ⟨∼ light rays⟩

¹in·ci·den·tal \ˌin-sə-ˈdent-ᵊl\ *adj* **1** : subordinate, nonessential, or attendant in position or significance ⟨∼ expenses⟩ **2** : CASUAL, CHANCE — **in·ci·den·tal·ly** \-ē\ *adv*

²incidental *n* **1** *pl* : minor items (as of expense) that are not individually accounted for **2** : something that is incidental

in·cin·er·ate \in-ˈsin-ə-ˌrāt\ *vb* **-at·ed; -at·ing** : to burn to ashes

in·cin·er·a·tor \in-ˈsin-ə-ˌrāt-ər\ *n* : a furnace for burning waste

in·cip·i·ent \in-ˈsip-ē-ənt\ *adj* : beginning to be or become apparent

in·cise \in-ˈsīz\ *vb* **in·cised; in·cis·ing** : to cut into : CARVE, ENGRAVE

in·ci·sion \in-ˈsizh-ən\ *n* : CUT, GASH; *esp* : a surgical wound

in·ci·sive \in-ˈsī-siv\ *adj* : impressively direct and decisive — **in·ci·sive·ly** *adv*

in·ci·sor \in-ˈsī-zər\ *n* : a tooth for cutting; *esp* : one of the cutting teeth in front of the canines of a mammal

in·cite \in-ˈsīt\ *vb* **in·cit·ed; in·cit·ing** : to arouse to action : stir up — **in·cite·ment** *n*

in·ci·vil·i·ty \ˌin-sə-ˈvil-ət-ē\ *n* **1** : DISCOURTESY, RUDENESS **2** : a rude or discourteous act

incl *abbr* including; inclusive

in·clem·ent \(ˈ)in-ˈklem-ənt\ *adj* : SEVERE, STORMY ⟨∼ weather⟩ — **in·clem·en·cy** \-ən-sē\ *n*

in·cli·na·tion \ˌin-klə-ˈnā-shən\ *n* **1** : PROPENSITY, BENT; *esp* : LIKING **2** : BOW, NOD ⟨an ∼ of the head⟩ **3** : a tilting of something **4** : SLANT, SLOPE

¹in·cline \in-ˈklīn\ *vb* **in·clined; in·clin·ing** **1** : BOW, BEND **2** : to be drawn toward an opinion or course of action **3** : to deviate from the vertical or horizontal : SLOPE **4** : INFLUENCE, PERSUADE

²in·cline \ˈin-ˌklīn\ *n* : SLOPE

inclose, inclosure var of ENCLOSE, ENCLOSURE

in·clude \in-ˈklüd\ *vb* **in·clud·ed; in·clud·ing** : to take in or comprise as a part of a whole ⟨the price ∼s tax⟩ — **in·clu·sion** \in-ˈklü-zhən\ *n* — **in·clu·sive** \-ˈklü-siv\ *adj*

incog *abbr* incognito

¹in·cog·ni·to \ˌin-ˌkäg-ˈnēt-ō, in-ˈkäg-nə-ˌtō\ *adv or adj* [It, fr. L *incognitus* unknown, fr. *cognoscere* to know] : with one's identity concealed

²incognito *n, pl* **-tos** **1** : one appearing or living incognito **2** : the state or disguise of an incognito

in·co·her·ent \ˌin-kō-ˈhir-ənt, -ˈher-\ *adj* **1** : not sticking closely or compactly together : LOOSE **2** : not clearly or logically connected : RAMBLING — **in·co·her·ence** \-əns\ *n* — **in·co·her·ent·ly** *adv*

in·com·bus·ti·ble \ˌin-kəm-ˈbəs-tə-bəl\ *adj* : incapable of being burned — **incombustible** *n*

in·come \ˈin-ˌkəm\ *n* : a gain usu. measured in money that derives from labor, business, or property

income tax \ˌin-(ˌ)kəm-\ *n* : a tax on the net income of an individual or business concern

in·com·ing \ˈin-ˌkəm-iŋ\ *adj* : coming in ⟨the ~ tide⟩ ⟨~ freshmen⟩

in·com·men·su·rate \ˌin-kə-ˈmens-(ə-)rət, -ˈmench-(ə-)rət\ *adj* : not commensurate; *esp* : INADEQUATE

in·com·mode \ˌin-kə-ˈmōd\ *vb* **-mod·ed; -mod·ing** : INCONVENIENCE, DISTURB

in·com·mu·ni·ca·ble \ˌin-kə-ˈmyü-ni-kə-bəl\ *adj* : not communicable : not capable of being communicated or imparted; *also* : UNCOMMUNICATIVE

in·com·mu·ni·ca·do \ˌin-kə-ˌmyü-nə-ˈkäd-ō\ *adv or adj* : without means of communication; *also* : in solitary confinement ⟨a prisoner held ~⟩

in·com·pa·ra·ble \(ˈ)in-ˈkäm-p(ə-)rə-bəl\ *adj* **1** : eminent beyond comparison : MATCHLESS **2** : not suitable for comparison

in·com·pat·i·ble \ˌin-kəm-ˈpat-ə-bəl\ *adj* : incapable of or unsuitable for association or use together ⟨~ colors⟩ ⟨temperamentally ~⟩ — **in·com·pat·i·bil·i·ty** \ˌin-kəm-ˌpat-ə-ˈbil-ət-ē\ *n*

in·com·pe·tent \(ˈ)in-ˈkäm-pət-ənt\ *adj* **1** : not legally qualified **2** : not competent : lacking sufficient knowledge, skill, or ability — **in·com·pe·tence** \-pət-əns\ *n* — **in·com·pe·ten·cy** \-ən-sē\ *n* — **incompetent** *n*

in·com·plete \ˌin-kəm-ˈplēt\ *adj* : lacking a part or parts : UNFINISHED, IMPERFECT — **in·com·plete·ly** *adv* — **in·com·plete·ness** *n*

in·com·pre·hen·si·ble \ˌin-ˌkäm-pē-ˈhen-sə-bəl *adj* : impossible to comprehend : UNINTELLIGIBLE

in·com·press·ible \ˌin-kəm-ˈpres-ə-bəl\ *adj* : not capable of or resistant to compression

in·con·gru·ent \ˌin-kən-ˈgrü-ənt, (ˈ)in-ˈkäŋ-grə-wənt\ *adj* : not congruent

in·con·gru·ous \(ˈ)in-ˈkäŋ-grə-wəs\ *adj* : not consistent with or suitable to the surroundings or associations — **in·con·gru·i·ty** \ˌin-kən-ˈgrü-ət-ē, -ˌkän-\ *n* — **in·con·gru·ous·ly** \(ˈ)in-ˈkäŋ-grə-wəs-lē\ *adv*

in·con·se·quen·tial \ˌin-ˌkän-sə-ˈkwen-chəl\ *adj* **1** : ILLOGICAL; *also* : IRRELE-

VANT **2** : of no significance : UNIMPORTANT — **in·con·se·quence** \(ˈ)in-ˈkän-sə-ˌkwens\ *n* — **in·con·se·quen·tial·ly** \ˌin-ˌkän-sə-ˈkwench-(ə-)lē\ *adv*

in·con·sid·er·able \ˌin-kən-ˈsid-ər-(ə-)bəl, -ˈsid-rə-bəl\ *adj* : SLIGHT, TRIVIAL

in·con·sid·er·ate \ˌin-kən-ˈsid-(ə-)rət\ *adj* : HEEDLESS, THOUGHTLESS; *esp* : not respecting the rights or feelings of others — **in·con·sid·er·ate·ly** *adv* — **in·con·sid·er·ate·ness** *n*

in·con·sol·able \ˌin-kən-ˈsō-lə-bəl\ *adj* : incapable of being consoled — **in·con·sol·ably** \-blē\ *adv*

in·con·spic·u·ous \ˌin-kən-ˈspik-yə-wəs\ *adj* : not readily noticeable — **in·con·spic·u·ous·ly** *adv*

in·con·stant \(ˈ)in-ˈkän-stənt\ *adj* : not constant : CHANGEABLE **syn** fickle, capricious, mercurial, unstable, volatile — **in·con·stan·cy** \-stən-sē\ *n* — **in·con·stant·ly** *adv*

in·con·test·able \ˌin-kən-ˈtes-tə-bəl\ *adj* : not contestable : INDISPUTABLE — **in·con·test·ably** \-ˈtes-tə-blē\ *adv*

in·con·ti·nent \(ˈ)in-ˈkänt-ᵊn-ənt\ *adj* **1** : lacking self-restraint **2** : unable to retain a bodily discharge (as urine) voluntarily — **in·con·ti·nence** \-ᵊn-əns\ *n*

in·con·tro·vert·ible \ˌin-ˌkän-trə-ˈvərt-ə-bəl\ *adj* : not open to question : INDISPUTABLE ⟨~ evidence⟩ — **in·con·tro·vert·ibly** \-blē\ *adv*

¹**in·con·ve·nience** \ˌin-kən-ˈvē-nyəns\ *n* **1** : something that is inconvenient **2** : the quality or state of being inconvenient

²**inconvenience** *vb* : to subject to inconvenience

in·con·ve·nient \ˌin-kən-ˈvē-nyənt\ *adj* : not convenient : causing trouble or annoyance : INOPPORTUNE — **in·con·ve·nient·ly** *adv*

in·cor·po·rate \in-ˈkȯr-pə-ˌrāt\ *vb* **-rat·ed; -rat·ing** **1** : to unite closely or so as to form one body : BLEND **2** : to form, form into, or become a corporation **3** : to give material form to : EMBODY — **in·cor·po·ra·tion** \-ˌkȯr-pə-ˈrā-shən\ *n*

in·cor·po·re·al \ˌin-kȯr-ˈpōr-ē-əl\ *adj* : having no material body or form

in·cor·rect \ˌin-kə-ˈrekt\ *adj* **1** : INACCURATE, FAULTY **2** : not true : WRONG **3** : UNBECOMING, IMPROPER — **in·cor·rect-**

ly \-'rek-(t)lē\ *adv* — **in·cor·rect·ness** \-'rek(t)-nəs\ *n*

in·cor·ri·gi·ble \(')in-'kȯr-ə-jə-bəl\ *adj* : incapable of being corrected, amended, or reformed — **in·cor·ri·gi·bil·i·ty** \(ˌ)in-ˌkȯr-ə-jə-'bil-ət-ē\ *n* — **in·cor·ri·gi·bly** \(')in-'kȯr-ə-jə-blē\ *adv*

in·cor·rupt·ible \ˌin-kə-'rəp-tə-bəl\ *adj* **1** : not subject to decay or dissolution **2** : incapable of being bribed or morally corrupted — **in·cor·rupt·ibil·i·ty** \-ˌrəp-tə-'bil-ət-ē\ *n* —**in·cor·rupt·ibly** \-'rəp-tə-blē\ *adv*

incr *abbr* increase; increased

¹**in·crease** \in-'krēs, 'in-ˌkrēs\ *vb* **in·creased; in·creas·ing 1** : to become greater : GROW **2** : to multiply by the production of young ⟨rabbits ~ rapidly⟩ **3** : to make greater — **in·creas·ing·ly** \-'krē-siŋ-lē\ *adv*

²**in·crease** \'in-ˌkrēs, in-'krēs\ *n* **1** : addition or enlargement in size, extent, or quantity : GROWTH **2** : something (as offspring, produce, or profit) that is added

in·cred·i·ble \(')in-'kred-ə-bəl\ *adj* : too extraordinary and improbable to be believed; *also* : hard to believe — **in·cred·i·bil·i·ty** \(ˌ)in-ˌkred-ə-'bil-ət-ē\ *n* — **in·cred·i·bly** \(')in-'kred-ə-blē\ *adv*

in·cred·u·lous \(')in-'krej-ə-ləs\ *adj* **1** : SKEPTICAL **2** : expressing disbelief — **in·cre·du·li·ty** \ˌin-kri-'d(y)ü-lət-ē\ *n* — **in·cred·u·lous·ly** *adv*

in·cre·ment \'iŋ-krə-mənt, 'in-\ *n* **1** : the action or process of increasing esp. in quantity or value : ENLARGEMENT; *also* : QUANTITY **2** : something gained or added; *esp* : one of a series of regular consecutive additions — **in·cre·men·tal** \ˌiŋ-krə-'ment-ᵊl, ˌin-\ *adj* — **in·cre·men·tal·ly** \-ᵊl-ē\ *adv*

in·crim·i·nate \in-'krim-ə-ˌnāt\ *vb* **-nat·ed; -nat·ing** : to charge with or prove involvement in a crime or fault : AC-CUSE — **in·crim·i·na·tion** \-ˌkrim-ə-'nā-shən\ *n* — **in·crim·i·na·to·ry** \-'krim-(ə-)nə-ˌtōr-ē\ *adj*

incrust *var of* ENCRUST

in·crus·ta·tion \ˌin-ˌkrəs-'tā-shən\ *n* **1** : the act of encrusting : the state of being encrusted **2** : CRUST; *also* : something resembling a crust ⟨~ of habits⟩

in·cu·bate \'iŋ-kyə-ˌbāt, 'in-\ *vb* **-bat·ed; -bat·ing** : to sit on eggs to hatch them;

also : to keep (as eggs) under conditions favorable for development — **in·cu·ba·tion** \ˌiŋ-kyə-'bā-shən, ˌin-\ *n*

in·cu·ba·tor \'iŋ-kyə-ˌbāt-ər, 'in-\ *n* : one that incubates; *esp* : an apparatus providing suitable conditions (as of warmth and moisture) for incubating something

in·cu·bus \'iŋ-kyə-bəs, 'in-\ *n, pl* **-bi** \-ˌbī, -ˌbē\ *also* **-bus·es** [ME, fr. LL, fr. L *incubare* to lie on] **1** : a spirit supposed to work evil on persons in their sleep **2** : NIGHTMARE **3** : one that oppresses like a nightmare

in·cul·cate \in-'kəl-ˌkāt, 'in-(ˌ)kəl-\ *vb* **-cat·ed; -cat·ing** [L *inculcare*, lit., to tread on, fr. *calcare* to trample, fr. *calx* heel] : to teach and impress by frequent repetitions or admonitions — **in·cul·ca·tion** \ˌin-(ˌ)kəl-'kā shən\ *n*

in·cul·pa·ble \(')in-'kəl-pə-bəl\ *adj* : free from guilt : BLAMELESS

in·cul·pate \in-'kəl-ˌpāt, 'in-(ˌ)kəl-\ *vb* **-pat·ed; -pat·ing** : to involve or implicate in guilt : INCRIMINATE

in·cum·ben·cy \in-'kəm-bən-sē\ *n, pl* **-cies 1** : something that is incumbent **2** : the quality of state of being incumbent **3** : the office or period of office of an incumbent

¹**in·cum·bent** \in-'kəm-bənt\ *n* : the holder of an office or position

²**incumbent** *adj* **1** : imposed as a duty **2** : occupying a specified office **3** : lying or resting on something else

incumber *var of* ENCUMBER

in·cu·nab·u·lum \ˌin-kyə-'nab-yə-ləm, iŋ-\ *n, pl* **-la** \-lə\ [NL, fr. L *incunabula*, pl., swaddling clothes, cradle, fr. *cunae* cradle] : a book printed before 1501

in·cur \in-'kər\ *vb* **in·curred; in·cur·ring 1** : to meet with (as an inconvenience) **2** : to become liable or subject to : bring down upon oneself

in·cur·able \(')in-'kyu̇r-ə-bəl\ *adj* : not subject to cure — **in·cur·abil·i·ty** \(ˌ)in-ˌkyu̇r-ə-'bil-ət-ē\ *n* — **incurable** *n* — **in·cur·ably** \(')in-'kyu̇r-ə-blē\ *adv*

in·cu·ri·ous \(')in-'kyu̇r-ē-əs\ *adj* : not curious or inquisitive

in·cur·sion \in-'kər-zhən\ *n* : a sudden usu. temporary invasion : RAID

in·cus \'iŋ-kəs\ *n, pl* **in·cu·des** \iŋ-'kyüd-(ˌ)ēz\ [NL, fr. L, anvil] : the middle of a chain of three small bones in the ear of a mammal

ind *abbr* **1** independent **2** index **3** industrial; industry

Ind *abbr* **1** Indian **2** Indiana

in·debt·ed \in-'det-əd\ *adj* **1** : owing money **2** : owing gratitude or recognition to another — **in·debt·ed·ness** *n*

in·de·cent \(')in-'dēs-ᵊnt\ *adj* : not decent : UNBECOMING, UNSEEMLY; *also* : morally offensive — **in·de·cen·cy** \-ᵊn-sē\ *n* — **in·de·cent·ly** *adv*

in·de·ci·sion \ˌin-di-'sizh-ən\ *n* : a wavering between two or more possible courses of action : IRRESOLUTION

in·de·ci·sive \ˌin-di-'sī-siv\ *adj* **1** : not decisive : INCONCLUSIVE **2** : marked by or prone to indecision **3** : INDEFINITE — **in·de·ci·sive·ly** *adv* — **in·de·ci·sive·ness** *n*

in·de·co·rous \(')in-'dek-(ə-)rəs; ˌin-di-'kōr-əs\ *adj* : not decorous **syn** improper, unseemly, indecent, unbecoming, indelicate — **in·de·co·rous·ly** *adv* — **in·de·co·rous·ness** *n*

in·deed \in-'dēd\ *adv* **1** : without any question : TRULY — often used interjectionally to express irony, disbelief, or surprise **2** : in reality **3** : all things considered

indef *abbr* indefinite

in·de·fat·i·ga·ble \ˌin-di-'fat-i-gə-bəl\ *adj* : UNTIRING — **in·de·fat·i·ga·bly** \-blē\ *adv*

in·de·fea·si·ble \-'fē-zə-bəl\ *adj* : not capable of or not liable to being annulled, made void, or forfeited — **in·de·fea·si·bly** \-'fē-zə-blē\ *adv*

in·de·fin·able \-'fī-nə-bəl\ *adj* : incapable of being precisely described or analyzed

in·def·i·nite \(')in-'def-(ə-)nət\ *adj* **1** : not defining or identifying ⟨*an* is an ∼ article⟩ **2** : not precise : VAGUE **3** : having no fixed limit or amount — **in·def·i·nite·ly** *adv* — **in·def·i·nite·ness** *n*

in·del·i·ble \in-'del-ə-bəl\ *adj* [ML *indelibilis*, fr. L *indelebilis*, fr. *delēre* to delete, destroy] **1** : not capable of being removed or erased ⟨∼ impression⟩ **2** : making marks that cannot easily be removed ⟨an ∼ pencil⟩ — **in·del·i·bly** \in-'del-ə-blē\ *adv*

in·del·i·cate \(')in-'del-i-kət\ *adj* : not delicate; *esp* : IMPROPER, COARSE,

TACTLESS **syn** indecent, unseemly, indecorous, unbecoming — **in·del·i·ca·cy** \in-'del-ə-kə-sē\ *n*

in·dem·ni·fy \in-'dem-nə-ˌfī\ *vb* **-fied; -fy·ing** [L *indemnis* unharmed, fr. *in-* not + *damnum* damage] **1** : to secure against hurt, loss, or damage **2** : to make compensation to for some loss or damage — **in·dem·ni·fi·ca·tion** \-ˌdem-nə-fə-'kā-shən\ *n*

in·dem·ni·ty \in-'dem-nət-ē\ *n, pl* **-ties 1** : security against hurt, loss, or damage; *also* : exemption from incurred penalties or liabilities **2** : something that indemnifies

¹in·dent \in-'dent\ *vb* [ME *indenten*, fr. MF *endenter*, fr. OF, fr. *dent* tooth, fr. L *dent-, dens*] **1** : INDENTURE **2** : to make a toothlike cut on the edge of **3** : to space in (as the first line of a paragraph) from the margin

²indent *vb* **1** : to force inward so as to form a depression : IMPRESS ⟨∼ a pattern in metal⟩ **2** : to form a dent in

in·den·ta·tion \ˌin-ˌden-'tā-shən\ *n* **1** : NOTCH; *also* : a usu. deep recess (as in a coastline) **2** : the action of indenting : the condition of being indented **3** : DENT **4** : INDENTION 2

in·den·tion \in-'den-chən\ *n* **1** : the action of indenting : the condition of being indented **2** : the blank space produced by indenting

¹in·den·ture \in-'den-chər\ *n* **1** : a written certificate or agreement; *esp* : a contract binding one person (as an apprentice) to work for another for a given period of time — usu. used in pl. **2** : INDENTATION 1 **3** : DENT

²indenture *vb* **in·den·tured; in·den·tur·ing** : to bind (as an apprentice) by indentures

in·de·pen·dence \ˌin-də-'pen-dəns\ *n* : the quality or state of being independent : FREEDOM

Independence Day *n* : July 4 observed as a legal holiday in commemoration of the adoption of the Declaration of Independence in 1776

in·de·pen·dent \ˌin-də-'pen-dənt\ *adj* **1** : SELF-GOVERNING; *also* : not affiliated with a larger controlling unit **2** : not requiring or relying on something else or somebody else ⟨an ∼ conclusion⟩ ⟨an ∼ source of income⟩ **3** : not easily influenced : showing self-reliance ⟨an

~ mind⟩ **4** : not committed to a political party ⟨an ~ voter⟩ **5** : refusing or disliking to look to others for help ⟨too ~ to accept charity⟩ **6** : MAIN ⟨an ~ clause⟩ — **independent** *n* — **in·de·pendent·ly** *adv*

in·de·scrib·able \ˌin-di-ˈskrī-bə-bəl\ *adj* **1** : that cannot be described ⟨an ~ sensation⟩ **2** : being too intense or great for description — **in·de·scrib·ably** \-blē\ *adv*

in·de·ter·mi·nate \ˌin-di-ˈtərm-(ə-)nət\ *adj* **1** : VAGUE; *also* : not known in advance **2** : not limited in advance; *also* : not leading to a definite end or result — **in·de·ter·mi·na·cy** \-(ə-)nə-sē\ *n* — **in·de·ter·mi·nate·ly** *adv*

¹**in·dex** \ˈin-ˌdeks\ *n, pl* **in·dex·es** *or* **in·di·ces** \-də-ˌsēz\ **1** : POINTER, INDICATOR **2** : SIGN, TOKEN ⟨an ~ of character⟩ **3** : a guide for facilitating references; *esp* : an alphabetical list of items (as topics or names) treated in a printed work with the page number where each item may be found **4** : a list of restricted or prohibited material ⟨an ~ of forbidden books⟩ **5** *pl usu* **indices** : a number or symbol or expression (as an exponent) associated with another to indicate a mathematical operation or use or position in an arrangement or expansion **6** : a character ☞ used to direct attention (as to a note) **7** : INDEX NUMBER

²**index** *vb* **1** : to provide with or put into an index **2** : to serve as an index of **3** : to regulate by indexation

in·dex·ation \ˌin-ˌdek-ˈsā-shən\ *n* : a system of economic control in which a body of variables (as wages and interest) rise or fall at the same rate as an index of the cost of living

index finger *n* : FOREFINGER

in·dex·ing *n* : INDEXATION

index number *n* : a number used to indicate change in magnitude (as of cost) as compared with the magnitude at some specified time usu. taken as 100

index of refraction : the ratio of the velocity of radiation in the first of two media to its velocity in the second

in·dia ink \ˌin-dē-ə-\ *n, often cap 1st I* **1** : a black solid pigment used in drawing **2** : a fluid made from india ink

In·di·an \ˈin-dē-ən\ *n* **1** : a native or inhabitant of the subcontinent of India **2** : AMERICAN INDIAN — **Indian** *adj*

Indian corn *n* : a tall widely grown American cereal grass bearing seeds on long ears; *also* : its ears or seeds

Indian meal *n* : CORNMEAL

Indian paintbrush *n* : any of a genus of herbaceous plants with brightly colored bracts that are related to the snapdragon

Indian pipe *n* : a waxy white leafless saprophytic herb of Asia and the U.S.

Indian summer *n* : a period of mild weather in late autumn or early winter

In·dia paper \ˌin-dē-ə-\ *n* **1** : a thin absorbent paper used esp. for taking impressions (as of steel engravings) **2** : a thin tough opaque printing paper

indic *abbr* indicative

in·di·cate \ˈin-də-ˌkāt\ *vb* **-cat·ed; -cat·ing** **1** : to point out or to **2** : to state briefly : show indirectly : SUGGEST — **in·di·ca·tion** \ˌin-də-ˈkā-shən\ *n* — **in·di·ca·tor** \ˈin-də-ˌkāt-ər\ *n*

¹**in·dic·a·tive** \in-ˈdik-ət-iv\ *adj* **1** : of, relating to, or being a verb form that represents an act or state as a fact ⟨~ mood⟩ **2** : serving to indicate ⟨actions ~ of fear⟩

²**indicative** *n* **1** : the indicative mood of a language **2** : a form in the indicative mood

in·di·cia \in-ˈdish-(ē-)ə\ *n pl* **1** : distinctive marks **2** : postal markings often imprinted on mail or mailing labels

in·dict \in-ˈdīt\ *vb* **1** : to charge with an offense **2** : to charge with a crime by the finding of a grand jury — **in·dict·able** *adj* — **in·dict·ment** *n*

in·dif·fer·ent \in-ˈdif-ərnt, -ˈdif-(ə-)rənt\ *adj* **1** : UNBIASED, UNPREJUDICED **2** : of no importance one way or the other **3** : marked by no special liking for or dislike of something **4** : being neither excessive nor defective **5** : PASSABLE, MEDIOCRE **6** : being neither right nor wrong — **in·dif·fer·ence** \in-ˈdif-ərns, -ˈdif-(ə-)rəns\ *n* — **in·dif·fer·ent·ly** *adv*

in·dig·e·nous \in-ˈdij-ə-nəs\ *adj* : produced, growing, or living naturally in a particular region

in·di·gent \ˈin-di-jənt\ *adj* : IMPOVERISHED, NEEDY — **in·di·gence** \-jəns\ *n*

in·di·gest·ible \ˌin-dī-ˈjes-tə-bəl, -də-\ *adj* : not readily digested

in·di·ges·tion \-ˈjes-chən\ *n* : inadequate or difficult digestion : DYSPEPSIA

in·dig·nant \in-'dig-nənt\ *adj* : filled with or marked by indignation — **in·dig·nant·ly** *adv*

in·dig·na·tion \,in-dig-'nā-shən\ *n* : anger aroused by something unjust, unworthy, or mean

in·dig·ni·ty \in-'dig-nət-ē\ *n, pl* **-ties** : an offense against personal dignity or self-respect; *also* : humiliating treatment

in·di·go \'in-di-,gō\ *n, pl* **-gos** *or* **-goes** [It dial., fr. L *indicum,* fr. Gk *indikon,* fr. *indikos* Indic, fr. *Indos* India] 1 : a blue dye obtained from plants or synthesized 2 : a color between blue and violet

indigo bunting *n* : a common small finch of the eastern U.S. of which the male is largely indigo-blue

indigo snake *n* : a large harmless blue≠black snake of the southern U.S.

in·di·rect \,in-də-'rekt, -dī-\ *adj* 1 : not straight ⟨an ~ route⟩ 2 : not straightforward and open ⟨~ methods⟩ 3 : not having a plainly seen connection ⟨an ~ cause⟩ 4 : not directly to the point ⟨an ~ answer⟩ — **in·di·rec·tion** \-'rek-shən\ *n* — **in·di·rect·ly** \-'rek-(t)lē\ *adv* — **in·di·rect·ness** \-'rek(t)-nəs\ *n*

in·dis·creet \,in-dis-'krēt\ *adj* : not discreet : IMPRUDENT — **in·dis·cre·tion** \-dis-'kresh-ən\ *n*

in·dis·crim·i·nate \,in-dis-'krim-ə-nət\ *adj* 1 : not marked by discrimination or careful distinction 2 : HAPHAZARD, RANDOM 3 : UNRESTRAINED 4 : JUMBLED, CONFUSED — **in·dis·crim·i·nate·ly** *adv*

in·dis·pens·able \,in-dis-'pen-sə-bəl\ *adj* : absolutely essential : REQUISITE — **in·dis·pens·abil·i·ty** \-,pen-sə-'bil-ət-ē\ *n* — **indispensable** *n* — **in·dis·pens·ably** \-'pen-sə-blē\ *adv*

in·dis·posed \-'pōzd\ *adj* 1 : slightly ill 2 : AVERSE — **in·dis·po·si·tion** \(,)in-,dis-pə-'zish-ən\ *n*

in·dis·put·able \,in-dis-'pyüt-ə-bəl, (')in-,dis-pyət-\ *adj* : not disputable : UNQUESTIONABLE ⟨~ proof⟩ — **in·dis·put·ably** \-blē\ *adv*

in·dis·sol·u·ble \,in-dis-'äl-yə-bəl\ *adj* : not capable of being dissolved, undone, or broken : PERMANENT

in·dis·tinct \,in-dis-'tiŋkt\ *adj* 1 : not sharply outlined or separable : BLURRED, FAINT, DIM 2 : not readily distinguishable : UNCERTAIN — **in·dis·tinct·ly** *adv* — **in·dis·tinct·ness** *n*

in·dite \in-'dīt\ *vb* **in·dit·ed; in·dit·ing** : COMPOSE ⟨~ a poem⟩; *also* : to put in writing ⟨~ a letter⟩

in·di·um \'in-dē-əm\ *n* : a malleable silvery metallic chemical element

indiv *abbr* individual

¹**in·di·vid·u·al** \,in-də-'vij-(ə-w)əl\ *adj* 1 : of, relating to, or used by an individual ⟨~ traits⟩ 2 : being an individual : existing as an indivisible whole 3 : intended for one person ⟨an ~ serving⟩ 4 : SEPARATE ⟨~ copies⟩ 5 : having marked individuality ⟨an ~ style⟩ — **in·di·vid·u·al·ly** \-ē\ *adv*

²**individual** *n* 1 : a single member of a category : a particular person, animal, or thing 2 : PERSON ⟨a disagreeable ~⟩

in·di·vid·u·al·ism \,in-də-'vij-ə(-wə)-,liz-əm\ *n* 1 : EGOISM 2 : a doctrine that the interests of the individual are primary 3 : a doctrine holding that the individual has political or economic rights with which the state must not interfere

in·di·vid·u·al·ist \-ləst\ *n* 1 : one that pursues a markedly independent course in thought or action 2 : one that advocates or practices individualism — **individualist** *or* **in·di·vid·u·al·is·tic** \-,vij-ə(-wə)-'lis-tik\ *adj*

in·di·vid·u·al·i·ty \-,vij-ə-'wal-ət-ē\ *n, pl* **-ties** 1 : the sum of qualities that characterize and distinguish an individual from all others; *also* : PERSONALITY 2 : INDIVIDUAL, PERSON 3 : separate or distinct existence

in·di·vid·u·al·ize \-'vij-ə(-wə)-,līz\ *vb* **-ized; -iz·ing** 1 : to make individual in character 2 : to treat or notice individually : PARTICULARIZE 3 : to adapt to the needs of an individual

in·di·vid·u·ate \,in-də-'vij-ə-,wāt\ *vb* **-at·ed; -at·ing** : to give individuality to : form into an individual — **in·di·vid·u·a·tion** \-,vij-ə-'wā-shən\ *n*

in·di·vis·i·ble \,in-də-'viz-ə-bəl\ *adj* : not divisible — **in·di·vis·i·bil·i·ty** \-,viz-ə-'bil-ət-ē\ *n* — **in·di·vis·i·bly** \-'viz-ə-blē\ *adv*

in·doc·tri·nate \in-'däk-trə-,nāt\ *vb* **-nat·ed; -nat·ing** 1 : to instruct esp. in fundamentals or rudiments : TEACH **2** : to teach the beliefs and doctrines of a particular group — **in•doc•tri•na•tion** \(͵)in-͵däk-trə-'nā-shən\ *n*

In•do—Eu•ro•pe•an \͵in-dō-͵yur-ə-'pē-ən\ *adj* : of, relating to, or constituting a family of languages comprising those spoken in most of Europe and in the parts of the world colonized by Europeans since 1500 and also in Persia, the subcontinent of India, and some other parts of Asia

in•do•lent \'in-də-lənt\ *adj* [LL *indolens* insensitive to pain, fr. L *dolēre* to feel pain] **1** : slow to develop or heal ⟨∼ ulcers⟩ **2** : LAZY — **in•do•lence** \-ləns\ *n*

in•dom•i•ta•ble \in-'däm-ət-ə-bəl\ *adj* : UNCONQUERABLE ⟨∼ courage⟩ — **in•dom•i•ta•bly** \-blē\ *adv*

In•do•ne•sian \͵in-də-'nē-zhən\ *n* : a native or inhabitant of the Republic of Indonesia — **Indonesian** *adj*

in•door \͵in-͵dōr\ *adj* **1** : of or relating to the inside of a building **2** : living, located, or carried on within a building

in•doors \in-'dōrz\ *adv* : in or into a building

indorse var of ENDORSE

in•du•bi•ta•ble \(')in-'d(y)ü-bət-ə-bəl\ *adj* : UNQUESTIONABLE — **in•du•bi•ta•bly** \-blē\ *adv*

in•duce \in-'d(y)üs\ *vb* **in•duced; in•duc•ing 1** : PERSUADE, INFLUENCE **2** : BRING ABOUT ⟨illness *induced* by overwork⟩ **3** : to produce (as an electric current) by induction **4** : to determine by induction; *esp* : to infer from particulars — **in•duc•er** *n*

in•duce•ment \in-'d(y)üs-mənt\ *n* **1** : something that induces : MOTIVE **2** : the act or process of inducing

in•duct \in-'dəkt\ *vb* **1** : to place in office **2** : to admit as a member **3** : to enroll for military training or service

in•duc•tance \in-'dək-təns\ *n* : a property of an electric circuit by which a varying current produces an electromotive force in that circuit or in a nearby circuit

in•duct•ee \(͵)in-͵dək-'tē\ *n* : a person inducted into military service

in•duc•tion \in-'dək-shən\ *n* **1** : INSTALLATION; *also* : INITIATION **2** : the formality by which a civilian is inducted into military service **3** : inference of a generalized conclusion from particular instances; *also* : a conclusion so reached **4** : the act of causing or bringing on or about **5** : the process by which an electric current, an electric charge, or magnetism is produced in a body by the proximity of an electric or magnetic field

in•duc•tive \in-'dək-tiv\ *adj* : of, relating to, or employing induction

indue var of ENDUE

in•dulge \in-'dəlj\ *vb* **in•dulged; in•dulg•ing 1** : to give free rein to : GRATIFY ⟨∼ a taste for exotic dishes⟩ **2** : to yield to the desire of ⟨∼ a sick child⟩ **3** : to gratify one's taste or desire for ⟨∼ in alcohol⟩

in•dul•gence \in-'dəl-jəns\ *n* **1** : remission of temporal punishment due in Roman Catholic doctrine for sins whose eternal punishment has been remitted by reception of the sacrifice of penance **2** : the act of indulging : the state of being indulgent **3** : an indulgent act **4** : the thing indulged in **5** : SELF-INDULGENCE — **in•dul•gent** \-jənt\ *adj* — **in•dul•gent•ly** *adv*

¹in•du•rate \'in-d(y)ə-rət\ *adj* : physically or morally hardened

²in•du•rate \'in-d(y)ə-͵rāt\ *vb* **-rat•ed; -rat•ing 1** : to make unfeeling, stubborn, or obdurate **2** : to make hardy : INURE **3** : to make hard **4** : to grow hard : HARDEN — **in•du•ra•tion** \͵in-d(y)ə-'rā-shən\ *n*

in•dus•tri•al \in-'dəs-trē-əl\ *adj* : of, relating to, or having to do with industry — **in•dus•tri•al•ly** \-ē\ *adv*

in•dus•tri•al•ist \-ə-ləst\ *n* : a person owning or engaged in the management of an industry : MANUFACTURER

in•dus•tri•al•ize \in-'dəs-trē-ə-͵līz\ *vb* **-ized; -iz•ing** : to make or become industrial — **in•dus•tri•al•iza•tion** \-͵dəs-trē-ə-lə-'zā-shən\ *n*

in•dus•tri•ous \in-'dəs-trē-əs\ *adj* : DILIGENT, BUSY — **in•dus•tri•ous•ly** *adv* — **in•dus•tri•ous•ness** *n*

in•dus•try \'in-(͵)dəs-trē\ *n, pl* **-tries 1** : DILIGENCE **2** : a department or branch of a craft, art, business, or manufacture; *esp* : one that employs a large personnel and capital **3** : a distinct group of productive enterprises **4** : manufacturing activity as a whole

in·dwell \(')in-'dwel\ *vb* : to exist within as an activating spirit, force, or principle

¹**ine·bri·ate** \in-'ē-brē-ₐāt\ *vb* -at·ed; -at·ing : to make drunk : INTOXICATE — **ine·bri·a·tion** \-ₐē-brē-'ā-shən\ *n*

²**ine·bri·ate** \-ət\ *n* : one that is drunk; *esp* : an habitual drunkard

in·ef·fa·ble \(')in-'ef-ə-bəl\ *adj* 1 : incapable of being expressed in words : INDESCRIBABLE ⟨∼ joy⟩ 2 : UNSPEAK-ABLE ⟨∼ disgust⟩ 3 : not to be uttered : TABOO ⟨the ∼ name of Jehovah⟩ — **in·ef·fa·bly** \-blē\ *adv*

in·ef·face·able \ₐinə-'fā-sə-bəl\ *adj* : not effaceable : INERADICABLE

in·ef·fec·tive \ₐin-ə-'fek-tiv\ *adj* 1 : not effective : INEFFECTUAL 2 : INCAPABLE — **in·ef·fec·tive·ly** *adv*

in·ef·fec·tu·al \ₐin-ə-'fek-chə-(-wə)l\ *adj* : not producing the proper or usual effect — **in·ef·fec·tu·al·ly** \-ē\ *adv*

in·ef·fi·cient \ₐin-ə-'fish-ənt\ *adj* 1 : not producing the effect intended or desired 2 : INCAPABLE, INCOMPETENT — **in·ef·fi·cien·cy** \-'fish-ən-sē\ *n* — **in·ef·fi·cient·ly** *adv*

in·el·e·gant \(')in-'el-i-gənt\ *adj* : lacking in refinement, grace, or good taste — **in·el·e·gance** \-gəns\ *n*

in·el·i·gi·ble \(')in-'el-ə-jə-bəl\ *adj* : not qualified to be chosen for an office — **in·el·i·gi·bil·i·ty** \(ₐ)in-ₐel-ə-jə-'bil-ət-ē\ *n* — **ineligible** *n*

in·eluc·ta·ble \ₐin-i-'lək-tə-bəl\ *adj* : not to be avoided, changed, or resisted

in·ept \in-'ept\ *adj* 1 : lacking in fitness or aptitude : UNFIT 2 : FOOLISH 3 : being out of place : INAPPROPRIATE 4 : generally incompetent : BUNGLING — **in·ep·ti·tude** \in-'ep-tə-ₐt(y)üd\ *n* — **in·ept·ly** *adv* — **in·ept·ness** *n*

in·equal·i·ty \ₐin-i-'kwäl-ət-ē\ *n* 1 : the quality of being unequal or uneven; *esp* : UNEVENNESS, DISPARITY, CHANGE-ABLENESS 2 : an instance of being unequal

in·er·rant \(')in-'er-ənt\ *adj* : INFALLI-BLE

in·ert \in-'ərt\ *adj* [L *inert-, iners* unskilled, idle, fr. *art-, ars* skill] 1 : powerless to move itself 2 : SLUGGISH 3 : lacking in active properties ⟨chemically ∼⟩ — **in·ert·ly** *adv* — **in·ert·ness** *n*

in·er·tia \in-'ər-sh(ē-)ə\ *n* 1 : a property of matter whereby it remains at rest or continues in uniform motion unless acted upon by some outside force 2 : INERTNESS, SLUGGISHNESS — **in·er·tial** \-shəl\ *adj*

in·es·cap·able \ₐin-ə-'skā-pə-bəl\ *adj* : incapable of being escaped : INEVI-TABLE — **in·es·cap·ably** \-blē\ *adv*

in·es·ti·ma·ble \(')in-'es-tə-mə-bəl\ *adj* 1 : incapable of being estimated or computed ⟨∼ errors⟩ 2 : too valuable or excellent to be fully appreciated — **in·es·ti·ma·bly** \-blē\ *adv*

in·ev·i·ta·ble \in-'ev-ət-ə-bəl\ *adj* : incapable of being avoided or evaded : bound to happen — **in·ev·i·ta·bil·i·ty** \(ₐ)in-ₐev-ət-ə-'bil-ət-ē\ *n* — **in·ev·i·ta·bly** \in-'ev-ət-ə-blē\ *adv*

in·ex·act \ₐin-ig-'zakt\ *adj* 1 : not precisely correct or true : INACCURATE 2 : not rigorous and careful — **in·ex·act·ly** \-'zak-(t)lē\ *adv*

in·ex·cus·able \ₐin-ik-'skyü-zə-bəl\ *adj* : being without excuse or justification — **in·ex·cus·ably** \-blē\ *adv*

in·ex·haust·ible \ₐin-ig-'zö-stə-bəl\ *adj* 1 : incapable of being used up ⟨an ∼ supply⟩ 2 : UNTIRING — **in·ex·haust·ibly** \-blē\ *adv*

in·ex·o·ra·ble \(')in-'eks-(ə-)rə-bəl\ *adj* : not to be moved by entreaty : RE-LENTLESS — **in·ex·o·ra·bly** *adv*

in·ex·pe·ri·ence \ₐin-ik-'spir-ē-əns\ *n* : lack of experience or of knowledge or proficiency gained by experience — **in·ex·pe·ri·enced** \-ənst\ *adj*

in·ex·pert \(')in-'ek-ₐspərt\ *adj* : not expert : UNSKILLED — **in·ex·pert·ly** *adv*

in·ex·pi·a·ble \(')in-'ek-spē-ə-bəl\ *adj* : not capable of being atoned for

in·ex·pli·ca·ble \ₐin-ik-'splik-ə-bəl, (')in-'ek-(ₐ)splik-\ *adj* : incapable of being explained or accounted for — **in·ex·pli·ca·bly** \-blē\ *adv*

in·ex·press·ible \-'spres-ə-bəl\ *adj* : not capable of being expressed — **in·ex·press·ibly** \-blē\ *adv*

in ex·tre·mis \ₐin-ik-'strā-məs, -'strē-\ *adv* : in extreme circumstances; *esp* : at the point of death

in·ex·tri·ca·ble \ₐin-ik-'strik-ə-bəl, (')in-'ek-(ₐ)strik-\ *adj* 1 : forming a maze or tangle from which it is impossible to get free 2 : incapable of being disentangled or untied : UNSOLVABLE — **in·ex·tri·ca·bly** \-blē\ *adv*

inf *abbr* **1** infantry **2** infinitive

in·fal·li·ble \(')in-'fal-ə-bəl\ *adj* **1** : incapable of error : UNERRING **2** : SURE, CERTAIN ⟨an ∼ remedy⟩ — **in·fal·li·bil·i·ty** \(ˌ)in-ˌfal-ə-'bil-ət-ē\ *n* — **in·fal·li·bly** \(')in-'fal-ə-blē\ *adv*

in·fa·mous \'in-fə-məs\ *adj* **1** : having a reputation of the worst kind **2** : DISGRACEFUL — **in·fa·mous·ly** *adv*

in·fa·my \-mē\ *n, pl* **-mies 1** : evil reputation brought about by something grossly criminal, shocking, or brutal **2** : an extreme and publicly known criminal or evil act **3** : the state of being infamous

in·fan·cy \'in-fən-sē\ *n, pl* **-cies 1** : early childhood **2** : a beginning or early period of existence

in·fant \'in-fənt\ *n* [ME *enfaunt,* fr. MF *enfant,* fr. L *infant-, infans,* incapable of speech, young, fr. *fant-, fans,* prp. of *fari* to speak] : BABY; *also* : a person who is a legal minor

in·fan·ti·cide \in-'fant-ə-ˌsīd\ *n* : the killing of an infant; *also* : one who kills an infant

in·fan·tile \'in-fən-ˌtīl, -tᵊl, -ˌtēl\ *adj* : of or relating to infants; *also* : CHILDISH

infantile paralysis *n* : POLIOMYELITIS

in·fan·try \'in-fən-trē\ *n, pl* **-tries** [MF & It; MF *infanterie,* fr. It *infanteria,* fr. *infante* boy, foot soldier] : soldiers trained, armed, and equipped for service on foot — **in·fan·try·man** \-mən\ *n*

in·farct \'in-ˌfärkt\ *n* [L *infarctus,* pp. of *infarcire* to stuff] : an area of dead tissue (as of the heart wall) caused by blocking of local blood circulation — **in·farc·tion** \in-'färk-shən\ *n*

in·fat·u·ate \in-'fach-ə-ˌwāt\ *vb* **-at·ed; -at·ing** : to inspire with a foolish or extravagant love or admiration — **in·fat·u·a·tion** \-ˌfach-ə-'wā-shən\ *n*

in·fect \in-'fekt\ *vb* **1** : to contaminate with disease-producing matter **2** : to communicate a germ or disease to **3** : to cause to share one's feelings

in·fec·tion \in-'fek-shən\ *n* **1** : an act of infecting : the state of being infected **2** : a communicable disease; *also* : an infective agent (as a germ) — **in·fec·tious** \-shəs\ *adj* — **in·fec·tive** \-'fek-tiv\ *adj*

in·fe·lic·i·tous \ˌin-fi-'lis-ət-əs\ *adj* : not apt in application or expression — **in·fe·lic·i·ty** \-ət-ē\ *n*

in·fer \in-'fər\ *vb* **in·ferred; in·fer·ring 1** : to derive as a conclusion from facts or premises **2** : GUESS, SURMISE **3** : to lead to as a conclusion or consequence **4** : HINT, SUGGEST **syn** deduce, conclude, judge, gather — **in·fer·ence** \'in-f(ə-)rəns\ *n* — **in·fer·en·tial** \ˌin-fə-'ren-chəl\ *adj*

in·fe·ri·or \in-'fir-ē-ər\ *adj* **1** : situated lower down **2** : of low or lower degree or rank **3** : of little or less importance, value, or merit — **inferior** *n* — **in·fe·ri·or·i·ty** \(ˌ)in-ˌfir-ē-'or-ət-ē\ *n*

in·fer·nal \in-'fərn-ᵊl\ *adj* **1** : of or relating to hell ⟨∼ fires⟩ **2** : HELLISH, FIENDISH ⟨∼ schemes⟩ **3** : DAMNABLE, DAMNED — **in·fer·nal·ly** \-ē\ *adv*

in·fer·no \in-'fər-nō\ *n, pl* **-nos** [It, hell, fr. LL *infernus* hell, fr. L, lower] : a place or a state that resembles or suggests hell

in·fer·tile \(')in-'fərt-ᵊl\ *adj* : not fertile or productive : BARREN — **in·fer·til·i·ty** \ˌin-fər-'til-ət-ē\ *n*

in·fest \in-'fest\ *vb* : to trouble by spreading or swarming in or over; *also* : to live in or on as a parasite — **in·fes·ta·tion** \ˌin-ˌfes-'tā-shən\ *n*

in·fi·del \'in-fəd-ᵊl, -fə-ˌdel\ *n* **1** : one who is not a Christian or opposes Christianity **2** : an unbeliever esp. with respect to a particular religion

in·fi·del·i·ty \ˌin-fə-'del-ət-ē, -fī-\ *n, pl* **-ties 1** : lack of belief in a religion **2** : UNFAITHFULNESS, DISLOYALTY

in·field \'in-ˌfēld\ *n* : the part of a baseball field inside the baselines — **in·field·er** *n*

in·fight·ing \'in-ˌfīt-iŋ\ *n* **1** : fighting or boxing at close quarters **2** : dissension or rivalry among members of a group

in·fil·trate \in-'fil-ˌtrāt, 'in-(ˌ)fil-\ *vb* **-trat·ed; -trat·ing 1** : to enter or filter into or through something **2** : to pass into or through by or as if by filtering or permeating — **in·fil·tra·tion** \ˌin-(ˌ)fil-'trā-shən\ *n*

in·fi·nite \'in-fə-nət\ *adj* **1** : LIMITLESS, BOUNDLESS, ENDLESS ⟨∼ space⟩ ⟨∼ wisdom⟩ ⟨∼ patience⟩ **2** : VAST, IMMENSE; *also* : INEXHAUSTIBLE ⟨∼ wealth⟩ **3** : greater than any preassigned finite value however large ⟨∼ number of positive integers⟩; *also* : extending to infinity ⟨∼ plane surface⟩ — **infinite** *n* — **in·fi·nite·ly** *adv*

in·fin·i·tes·i·mal \(ˌ)in-ˌfin-ə-ˈtes-ə-məl\ *adj* : immeasurably or incalculably small : very minute — **in·fin·i·tes·i·mal·ly** \-ē\ *adv*

in·fin·i·tive \in-ˈfin-ət-iv\ *n* : a verb form having the characteristics of both verb and noun and in English usu. being used with *to*

in·fin·i·tude \in-ˈfin-ə-ˌt(y)üd\ *n* **1** : the quality or state of being infinite **2** : something that is infinite esp. in extent

in·fin·i·ty \in-ˈfin-ət-ē\ *n, pl* **-ties** **1** : the quality of being infinite **2** : unlimited extent of time, space, or quantity : BOUNDLESSNESS **3** : an indefinitely great number or amount

in·firm \in-ˈfərm\ *adj* **1** : deficient in vitality; *esp* : feeble from age **2** : not solid or stable : INSECURE

in·fir·ma·ry \in-ˈfərm-(ə-)rē\ *n, pl* **-ries** : a place for the care of the infirm or sick

in·fir·mi·ty \in-ˈfər-mət-ē\ *n, pl* **-ties** **1** : FEEBLENESS **2** : DISEASE, AILMENT **3** : a personal failing : FOIBLE

infl *abbr* influenced

in·flame \in-ˈflām\ *vb* **in·flamed; in·flam·ing** **1** : KINDLE **2** : to excite to excessive or uncontrollable action or feeling; *also* : INTENSIFY **3** : to affect or become affected with inflammation

in·flam·ma·ble \in-ˈflam-ə-bəl\ *adj* **1** : FLAMMABLE **2** : easily inflamed, excited, or angered : IRASCIBLE

in·flam·ma·tion \ˌin-flə-ˈmā-shən\ *n* : a bodily response to injury in which an affected area becomes red, hot, and painful and congested with blood

in·flam·ma·to·ry \in-ˈflam-ə-ˌtōr-ē\ *adj* **1** : tending to excite the senses or to arouse anger, disorder, or tumult : SEDITIOUS **2** : causing or accompanied by inflammation ⟨an ∼ disease⟩

in·flate \in-ˈflāt\ *vb* **in·flat·ed; in·flat·ing** **1** : to swell with air or gas ⟨∼ a balloon⟩ **2** : to puff up : ELATE ⟨*inflated* with pride⟩ **3** : to expand or increase abnormally ⟨∼ prices⟩ — **in·flat·able** *adj*

in·fla·tion \in-ˈflā-shən\ *n* **1** : an act of inflating : the state of being inflated **2** : empty pretentiousness : POMPOSITY **3** : an abnormal increase in the volume of money and credit resulting in a sub-

stantial and continuing rise in the general price level

in·fla·tion·ary \-shə-ˌner-ē\ *adj* : of, characterized by, or productive of inflation

in·flect \in-ˈflekt\ *vb* **1** : to turn from a direct line or course : CURVE **2** : to vary a word by inflection **3** : to change or vary the pitch of the voice

in·flec·tion \in-ˈflek-shən\ *n* **1** : the act or result of curving or bending **2** : a change in pitch or loudness of the voice **3** : the change of form that words undergo to mark case, gender, number, tense, person, mood, or voice — **in·flec·tion·al** \-sh(ə-)nəl\ *adj*

in·flex·i·ble \(ˈ)in-ˈflek-sə-bəl\ *adj* **1** : UNYIELDING **2** : RIGID **3** : UNALTERABLE — **in·flex·i·bil·i·ty** \(ˌ)in-ˌflek-sə-ˈbil-ət-ē\ *n* — **in·flex·i·bly** \(ˈ)in-ˈflek-sə-blē\ *adv*

in·flex·ion \in-ˈflek-shən\ *chiefly Brit var of* INFLECTION

in·flict \in-ˈflikt\ *vb* : IMPOSE, AFFLICT; *also* : to give or deliver by or as if by striking — **in·flic·tion** \-ˈflik-shən\ *n*

in·flo·res·cence \ˌin-flə-ˈres-ᵊns\ *n* : the manner of development and arrangement of flowers on a stem; *also* : a flowering stem with its appendages : a flower cluster

in·flow \ˈin-ˌflō\ *n* : a flowing in

¹in·flu·ence \ˈin-ˌflü-əns\ *n* **1** : the act or power of producing an effect without apparent force or direct authority **2** : the power or capacity of causing an effect in indirect or intangible ways ⟨under the ∼ of liquor⟩ **3** : a person or thing that exerts influence — **in·flu·en·tial** \ˌin-flü-ˈen-chəl\ *adj*

²influence *vb* **-enced; -enc·ing** **1** : to affect or alter by influence : SWAY **2** : to have an effect on the condition or development of : MODIFY

in·flu·en·za \ˌin-flü-ˈen-zə\ *n* [It., lit., influence, fr. ML *influentia;* fr. the belief that epidemics were due to the influence of the stars] : an acute and very contagious virus disease marked by fever, prostration, aches and pains, and respiratory inflammation; *also* : any of various feverish usu. virus diseases typically with respiratory symptoms

in·flux \ˈin-ˌfləks\ *n* : a coming in

in·fo \ˈin-(ˌ)fō\ *n* : INFORMATION

in·fold \in-'fōld\ *vb* **1** : ENFOLD **2** : to fold inward or toward one another

in·form \in-'fȯrm\ *vb* **1** : to communicate knowledge to : TELL **2** : to give information or knowledge **3** : to act as an informer **syn** acquaint, apprise, advise, notify

in·for·mal \(')in-'fȯr-məl\ *adj* **1** : conducted or carried out without formality or ceremony ⟨an ~ party⟩ **2** : characteristic of or appropriate to ordinary, casual, or familiar use ⟨~ clothes⟩ — **in·for·mal·i·ty** \,in-fȯr-'mal-ət-ē, -fər-\ *n* — **in·for·mal·ly** \(')in-'fȯr-mə-lē\ *adv*

in·for·mant \in-'fȯr-mənt\ *n* : one who gives information : INFORMER

in·for·ma·tion \,in-fər-'mā-shən\ *n* **1** : the communication or reception of knowledge or intelligence **2** : knowledge obtained from investigation, study, or instruction : FACTS, DATA — **in·for·ma·tion·al** \-sh(ə-)nəl\ *adj*

in·for·ma·tive \in-'fȯr-mət-iv\ *adj* : imparting knowledge : INSTRUCTIVE

in·formed \in-'fȯrmd\ *adj* : EDUCATED, KNOWLEDGEABLE

informed consent *n* : consent to a medical procedure by a subject who understands what is involved

in·form·er \-'fȯr-mər\ *n* : one that informs; *esp* : a person who secretly provides information about the activities of another

in·frac·tion \in-'frak-shən\ *n* [deriv. of L *infractus,* pp. of *infringere* to break off] : the act of infringing : VIOLATION

in·fra dig \,in-frə-'dig\ *adj* [short for L *infra dignitatem*] : being beneath one's dignity

in·fra·red \,in-frə-'red\ *adj* : being, relating to, or using radiation having wavelengths longer than those of red light — **infrared** *n*

in·fra·son·ic \-'sän-ik\ *adj* : having a frequency too low to hear ⟨~ vibration⟩

in·fre·quent \(')in-'frē-kwənt\ *adj* **1** : seldom happening : RARE **2** : placed or occurring at considerable distances or intervals : OCCASIONAL **syn** uncommon, scarce, rare, sporadic — **in·fre·quent·ly** *adv*

in·fringe \in-'frinj\ *vb* **in·fringed; in·fring·ing** [L *infringere*] **1** : VIOLATE, TRANSGRESS ⟨~ a patent⟩ **2** : EN-

CROACH, TRESPASS — **in·fringe·ment** *n*

in·fu·ri·ate \in-'fyur-ē-,āt\ *vb* **-at·ed; -at·ing** : to make furious : ENRAGE — **in·fu·ri·at·ing·ly** \-,āt-iŋ-lē\ *adv*

in·fuse \in-'fyüz\ *vb* **in·fused; in·fus·ing 1** : to instill a principle or quality in : INTRODUCE **2** : INSPIRE, ANIMATE **3** : to steep (as tea) without boiling — **in·fu·sion** \-'fyü-zhən\ *n*

in·fus·ible \(')in-'fyü-zə-bəl\ *adj* : very difficult or impossible to fuse

¹-ing \iŋ\ *vb suffix or adj suffix* — used to form the present participle ⟨sail*ing*⟩ and sometimes to form an adjective resembling a present participle but not derived from a verb ⟨swashbuckl*ing*⟩

²-ing *n suffix* : one of a (specified) kind

³-ing *n suffix* **1** : action or process ⟨sleep*ing*⟩ : instance of an action or process ⟨a meet*ing*⟩ **2** : product or result of an action or process ⟨an engrav*ing*⟩ ⟨earn*ings*⟩ **3** : something used in an action or process ⟨a bed cover*ing*⟩ **4** : something connected with, consisting of, or used in making (a specified thing) ⟨scaffold*ing*⟩ **5** : something related to (a specified concept) ⟨off*ing*⟩

in·gath·er·ing \'in-,gath-(ə-)riŋ\ *n* **1** : COLLECTION, HARVEST **2** : ASSEMBLY

in·ge·nious \in-'jēn-yəs\ *adj* **1** : marked by special aptitude at discovering, inventing, or contriving **2** : marked by originality, resourcefulness, and cleverness in conception or execution — **in·ge·nious·ly** *adv* — **in·ge·nious·ness** *n*

in·ge·nue *or* **in·gé·nue** \'an-jə-,nü, 'än-; 'aⁿ-zhə-\ *n* : a naive girl or young woman; *esp* : an actress representing such a person

in·ge·nu·ity \,in-jə-'n(y)ü-ət-ē\ *n, pl* **-ities** : skill or cleverness in planning or inventing : INVENTIVENESS

in·gen·u·ous \in-'jen-yə-wəs\ *adj* [L *ingenuus* native, freeborn, fr. *gignere* to beget] **1** : STRAIGHTFORWARD, FRANK **2** : NAIVE — **in·gen·u·ous·ly** *adv* — **in·gen·u·ous·ness** *n*

in·gest \in-'jest\ *vb* : to take in for or as if for digestion : ABSORB — **in·ges·tion** \-'jes-chən\ *n*

in·gle·nook \-,nuk\ *n* **1** : a corner by the fire or chimney **2** : a high-backed wooden settee placed close to a fireplace

in·glo·ri·ous \(')in-'glōr-ē-əs\ *adj* **1** : SHAMEFUL **2** : not glorious : lacking fame or honor — **in·glo·ri·ous·ly** *adv*

in·got \'iŋ-gət\ *n* : a mass of metal cast in a form convenient for storage or transportation

¹in·grain \(')in-'grān\ *vb* : to work indelibly into the natural texture or mental or moral constitution : IMBUE — **in·grained** *adj*

²in·grain \ˌin-ˌgrān\ *adj* **1** : made of fiber that is dyed before being spun into yarn **2** : made of yarn that is dyed before being woven or knitted **3** : INNATE — **in·grain** \'in-ˌgrān\ *n*

in·grate \'in-ˌgrāt\ *n* : an ungrateful person

in·gra·ti·ate \in-'grā-shē-ˌāt\ *vb* **-at·ed; -at·ing** : to gain favor by deliberate effort

in·gra·ti·at·ing *adj* **1** : capable of winning favor : PLEASING ⟨an ~ smile⟩ **2** : FLATTERING ⟨an ~ manner⟩

in·grat·i·tude \(')in-'grat-ə-ˌt(y)üd\ *n* : lack of gratitude : UNGRATEFULNESS

in·gre·di·ent \in-'grēd-ē-ənt\ *n* : one of the substances that make up a mixture or compound : CONSTITUENT

in·gress \'in-ˌgres\ *n* : ENTRANCE, ACCESS

in·grow·ing \'in-ˌgrō-iŋ\ *adj* : growing or tending inward

in·grown \-ˌgrōn\ *adj* : grown in; *esp* : having the free tip or edge embedded in the flesh ⟨~ toenail⟩

in·gui·nal \'iŋ-gwən-ᵊl\ *adj* : of, relating to, or situated in the region of the groin

in·hab·it \in-'hab-ət\ *vb* : to live or dwell in — **in·hab·it·able** *adj*

in·hab·it·ant \in-'hab-ət-ənt\ *n* : a permanent resident in a place

in·hal·ant \in-'hā-lənt\ *n* : something (as a medicine) that is inhaled

in·ha·la·tor \'in-(h)ə-ˌlāt-ər\ *n* : a device that provides a mixture of carbon dioxide and oxygen for breathing

in·hale \in-'hāl\ *vb* **in·haled; in·hal·ing** : to draw in by breathing : draw air into the lungs — **in·ha·la·tion** \ˌin-(h)ə-'lā-shən\ *n*

in·hal·er \in-'hā-lər\ *n* : a device by means of which medicinal material is inhaled

in·here \in-'hiər\ *vb* **in·hered; in·her·ing** : to be inherent : BELONG

in·her·ent \in-'hir-ənt, -'her-\ *adj* : established as an essential part of something : INTRINSIC — **in·her·ent·ly** *adv*

in·her·it \in-'her-ət\ *vb* : to receive esp. from one's ancestors — **in·her·it·able** \-ə-bəl\ *adj* — **in·her·i·tance** \-ət-əns\ *n* — **in·her·i·tor** \-ət-ər\ *n*

in·hib·it \in-'hib-ət\ *vb* **1** : PROHIBIT, FORBID **2** : to hold in check : RESTRAIN

in·hi·bi·tion \ˌin-(h)ə-'bish-ən\ *n* **1** : PROHIBITION, RESTRAINT **2** : a usu. inner check on free activity, expression, or functioning

in–house \ˌin-ˌhaús, 'in-ˌhaús\ *adj* : existing, originating, or carried on within a group or organization

in·hu·man \(')in-'(h)yü-mən\ *adj* **1** : lacking pity or kindness : CRUEL, SAVAGE **2** : COLD, IMPERSONAL **3** : not worthy of or conforming to the needs of human beings **4** : of or suggesting a nonhuman class of beings — **in·hu·man·ly** *adv*

in·hu·mane \ˌin-(h)yü-'mān\ *adj* : not humane : INHUMAN 1

in·hu·man·i·ty \-'man-ət-ē\ *n, pl* **-ities** **1** : the quality or state of being cruel or barbarous **2** : a cruel or barbarous act

in·hu·ma·tion \ˌin-hyü-'mā-shən\ *n* : BURIAL

in·im·i·cal \in-'im-i-kəl\ *adj* **1** : being adverse often by reason of hostility **2** : HOSTILE, UNFRIENDLY — **in·im·i·cal·ly** \-ē\ *adv*

in·im·i·ta·ble \(')in-'im-ət-ə-bəl\ *adj* : not capable of being imitated

in·iq·ui·ty \in-'ik-wət-ē\ *n, pl* **-ties** [ME *iniquite,* fr. MF *iniquité,* fr. L *iniquitas,* fr. *iniquus* uneven, fr. *aequus* equal] **1** : WICKEDNESS **2** : a wicked act — **in·iq·ui·tous** \-wət-əs\ *adj*

¹ini·tial \in-'ish-əl\ *adj* **1** : of or relating to the beginning : INCIPIENT **2** : FIRST — **ini·tial·ly** \-ē\ *adv*

²initial *n* : the first letter of a word or name

³initial *vb* **-tialed** *or* **-tialled; -tial·ing** *or* **-tial·ling** \-'ish-(ə-)liŋ\ : to affix an initial to

¹ini·ti·ate \in-'ish-ē-ˌāt\ *vb* **-at·ed; -at·ing** **1** : START, BEGIN **2** : to induct into membership by or as if by special ceremonies **3** : to instruct in the first principles of something — **ini·ti·a·tion** \-ˌish-ē-'ā-shən\ *n*

²ini·tiate \in-'ish-(ē-)ət\ *n* **1** : a person

initiative • inning

who is undergoing or has passed an initation **2** : a person who is instructed or adept in some special field

ini·tia·tive \in-'ish-ət-iv\ *n* **1** : an introductory step **2** : self-reliant enterprise **3** : a process by which laws may be introduced or enacted directly by vote of the people

ini·tia·to·ry \in-'ish-(ē-)ə-ˌtōr-ē\ *adj* **1** : INTRODUCTORY **2** : tending or serving to initiate ⟨∼ rites⟩

in·ject \in-'jekt\ *vb* **1** : to force into something ⟨∼ serum with a needle⟩ **2** : to introduce into some situation or subject ⟨∼ a note of suspicion⟩ — **in·jec·tion** \-'jek-shən\ *n*

in·junc·tion \in-'jəŋk-shən\ *n* **1** : ORDER, ADMONITION **2** : a court writ whereby one is required to do or to refrain from doing a specified act

in·jure \'in-jər\ *vb* **in·jured; in·jur·ing** \'inj-(ə-)riŋ\ : WRONG, DAMAGE, HURT **syn** harm, impair, mar, spoil

in·ju·ry \'inj-(ə-)rē\ *n, pl* **-ries** **1** : an act that damages or hurts : WRONG **2** : hurt, damage, or loss sustained — **in·ju·ri·ous** \in-'jur-ē-əs\ *adj*

in·jus·tice \(')in-'jəs-təs\ *n* **1** : violation of a person's rights : UNFAIRNESS, WRONG **2** : an unjust act or deed

¹ink \'iŋk\ *n* [ME *enke,* fr. OF, fr. LL *encaustum,* fr. L *encaustus* burned in, fr. Gk *enkaustos,* verbal of *enkaiein* to burn in] : a usu. liquid and colored material for writing and printing — **inky** *adj*

²ink *vb* : to put ink on; *esp* : SIGN

ink·blot test \-ˌblät-\ *n* : any of several psychological tests based on the interpretation of irregular figures

ink·horn \'iŋk-ˌhȯrn\ *n* : a small bottle (as of horn) for holding ink

in·kling \'iŋ-kliŋ\ *n* **1** : HINT, INTIMATION **2** : a vague idea

ink·stand \'iŋk-ˌstand\ *n* : INKWELL; *also* : a pen and ink stand

ink·well \-ˌwel\ *n* : a container for ink

in·laid \'in-'lād\ *adj* : decorated with material set into a surface

¹in·land \'in-ˌland, -lənd\ *n* : the interior of a country

²inland *adj* **1** *chiefly Brit* : not foreign : DOMESTIC ⟨∼ revenue⟩ **2** : of or relating to the interior of a country

³inland *adv* : into or toward the interior

in–law \'in-ˌlȯ\ *n* : a relative by marriage

¹in·lay \(')in-'lā, 'in-ˌlā\ *vb* **in·laid** \-'lād\; **in·lay·ing** : to set (one material into another) by way of decoration

²in·lay \'in-ˌlā\ *n* **1** : inlaid work **2** : a shaped filling cemented into a tooth

in·let \'in-ˌlet, -lət\ *n* **1** : a bay in the shore of a sea, lake, or river **2** : a narrow strip of water running into the land

in·mate \'in-ˌmāt\ *n* : a person who lives in the same house or institution with another; *esp* : a person confined to an institution (as a hospital or prison)

in me·di·as res \in-ˌmād-ē-əs-'rās\ *adv* [L, lit., into the midst of things] : in or into the middle of a narrative or plot

in me·mo·ri·am \ˌin-mə-'mōr-ē-əm\ *prep* : in memory of

in·most \'in-ˌmōst\ *adj* : deepest within : INNERMOST

inn \'in\ *n* : HOTEL, TAVERN

in·nards \'in-ərdz\ *n pl* **1** : the internal organs of a man or animal; *esp* : VISCERA **2** : the internal parts of a structure or mechanism

in·nate \in-'āt\ *adj* **1** : existing in, belonging to, or determined by factors present in an individual from birth : NATIVE **2** : belonging to the essential nature of something : INHERENT — **in·nate·ly** *adv*

in·ner \'in-ər\ *adj* **1** : situated farther in ⟨the ∼ bark⟩ **2** : near a center esp. of influence ⟨the ∼ circle⟩ **3** : of or relating to the mind or spirit

in·ner–di·rect·ed \ˌin-ər-də-'rek-təd, -(ˌ)dī-\ *adj* : directed in thought and action by one's own scale of values as opposed to external norms

inner ear *n* : the part of the ear that consists of a complex membranous labyrinth located in a cavity in the temporal bone and contains sense organs of hearing and of awareness of position in space

in·ner·most \'in-ər-ˌmōst\ *adj* : farthest inward : INMOST

in·ner·sole \'in-ər-ˌsōl\ *n* : INSOLE

in·ner·spring \ˌin-ər-ˌspriŋ\ *adj* : having coil springs inside a padded casing

inner tube *n* : TUBE 5

in·ning \'in-iŋ\ *n* : a baseball team's turn at bat; *also* : a division of a baseball game consisting of a turn at bat for each team

in·nings \'in-iŋz\ *n sing or pl* : a division of a cricket match

inn·keep·er \'in-ˌkē-pər\ *n* **1** : the landlord of an inn **2** : a hotel manager

in·no·cence \'in-ə-səns\ *n* **1** : BLAMELESSNESS; *also* : freedom from legal guilt **2** : GUILELESSNESS, SIMPLICITY; *also* : IGNORANCE

in·no·cent \-sənt\ *adj* [ME, fr. MF, fr. L *innocens,* fr. *nocens,* wicked, fr. *nocēre* to harm] **1** : free from guilt or sin : BLAMELESS **2** : harmless in effect or intention; *also* : CANDID **3** : free from legal guilt or fault : LAWFUL **4** : INGENUOUS **5** : DESTITUTE — **innocent** *n* — **in·no·cent·ly** *adv*

in·noc·u·ous \in-'äk-yə-wəs\ *adj* **1** : HARMLESS **2** : INOFFENSIVE, INSIPID

in·nom·i·nate \in-'äm-ə-nət\ *adj* : having no name; *also* : ANONYMOUS

in·no·vate \'in-ə-ˌvāt\ *vb* **-vat·ed; -vat·ing** : to introduce as or as if new : make changes — **in·no·va·tive** \-ˌvāt-iv\ *adj* — **in·no·va·tor** \-ˌvāt-ər\ *n*

in·no·va·tion \ˌin-ə-'vā-shən\ *n* **1** : the introduction of something new **2** : a new idea, method, or device

in·nu·en·do \ˌin-yə-'wen-dō\ *n, pl* **-dos** *or* **-does** [L, by hinting, fr. *innuere* to hint, fr. *nuere* to nod] : HINT, INSINUATION; *esp* : a veiled reflection on character or reputation

in·nu·mer·a·ble \in-'(y)üm(-ə)-rə-bəl\ *adj* : too many to be numbered

in·oc·u·late \in-'äk-yə-ˌlāt\ *vb* **-lat·ed; -lat·ing** [ME *inoculaten* to insert a bud in a plant, fr. L *inoculare,* fr. *oculus* eye, bud] : to introduce something into; *esp* : to treat with a serum or antibody to prevent or cure a disease — **in·oc·u·la·tion** \-ˌäk-yə-'lā-shən\ *n*

in·op·er·a·ble \(')in-'äp-(ə-)rə-bəl\ *adj* **1** : not suitable for surgery **2** : not operable

in·op·er·a·tive \-'äp-(ə-)rət-iv, -'äp-ə-ˌrāt-\ *adj* : not functioning

in·op·por·tune \(ˌ)in-ˌäp-ər-'t(y)ün\ *adj* : happening or coming at the wrong time — **in·op·por·tune·ly** *adv*

in·or·di·nate \in-'ord-(ə-)nət\ *adj* **1** : UNREGULATED, DISORDERLY **2** : EXTRAORDINARY, IMMODERATE ⟨an ∼ curiosity⟩ — **in·or·di·nate·ly** *adv*

in·or·gan·ic \ˌin-ˌor-'gan-ik\ *adj* : being

or composed of matter of other than plant or animal origin : MINERAL

in·pa·tient \'in-ˌpā-shənt\ *n* : a hospital patient who receives lodging and food as well as treatment

in·put \'in-ˌpút\ *n* **1** : something put in **2** : power or energy put into a machine or system **3** : information fed into a data processing system or computer **4** : ADVICE, OPINION — **input** *vb*

in·quest \'in-ˌkwest\ *n* **1** : an official inquiry or examination esp. before a jury **2** : INQUIRY, INVESTIGATION

in·qui·e·tude \(')in-'kwī-ə-ˌt(y)üd\ *n* : UNEASINESS, RESTLESSNESS

in·quire \in-'kwī(ə)r\ *vb* **in·quired; in·quir·ing** **1** : to ask about : ASK **2** : INVESTIGATE, EXAMINE — **in·quir·er** *n* — **in·quir·ing·ly** *adv*

in·qui·ry \'in-ˌkwī(ə)r-ē, in-'kwī(ə)r-ē; 'in-kwə-rē, 'iŋ-\ *n, pl* **-ries** **1** : a request for information; *also* : a search for truth or knowledge **2** : a systematic investigation of a matter of public interest

in·qui·si·tion \ˌin-kwə-'zish-ən, ˌiŋ-\ *n* **1** : a judicial or official inquiry usu. before a jury **2** *cap* : a former Roman Catholic tribunal for the discovery and punishment of heretics **3** : a severe questioning — **in·quis·i·tor** \in-'kwiz-ət-ər\ *n* — **in·quis·i·to·ri·al** \-ˌkwiz-ə-'tōr-ē-əl\ *adj*

in·quis·i·tive \in-'kwiz-ət-iv\ *adj* **1** : given to examination or investigation ⟨an ∼ mind⟩ **2** : unduly curious — **in·quis·i·tive·ly** *adv* — **in·quis·i·tive·ness** *n*

in re \in-'rā, -'rē\ *prep* : in the matter of

INRI *abbr* [L *Iesus Nazarenus Rex Iudaeorum*] Jesus of Nazareth, King of the Jews

in·road \'in-ˌrōd\ *n* **1** : INVASION, RAID **2** : ENCROACHMENT

in·rush \'in-ˌrəsh\ *n* : a crowding or flooding in

ins *abbr* **1** inches **2** insurance

INS *abbr* Immigration and Naturalization Service

in·sa·lu·bri·ous \ˌin-sə-'lü-brē-əs\ *adj* : UNWHOLESOME, NOXIOUS

ins and outs *n pl* : characteristic peculiarities : RAMIFICATIONS

in·sane \(')in-'sān\ *adj* **1** : not mentally sound : MAD; *also* : used by or for the insane **2** : FOOLISH, WILD — **in·sane·ly** *adv* — **in·san·i·ty** \in-'san-ət-ē\ *n*

in·sa·tia·ble \(ˈ)in-ˈsā-shə-bəl\ *adj* : incapable of being satisfied

in·sa·tiate \(ˈ)in-ˈsā-sh(ē-)ət\ *adj* : INSATIABLE

in·scribe \in-ˈskrīb\ *vb* **1** : to write, engrave, or print esp. as a lasting record **2** : ENROLL **3** : to write, engrave, or print characters upon **4** : to dedicate to someone **5** : to stamp deeply or impress esp. on the memory **6** : to draw within a figure so as to touch in as many places as possible — **in·scrip·tion** \-ˈskrip-shən\ *n*

in·scru·ta·ble \in-ˈskrüt-ə-bəl\ *adj* : not readily comprehensible : MYSTERIOUS ⟨an ∼ smile⟩ — **in·scru·ta·bly** \-blē\ *adv*

in·seam \ˈin-ˌsēm\ *n* : the seam on the inside of the leg of a pair of pants; *also* : the length of this seam

in·sect \ˈin-ˌsekt\ *n* [L *insectum*, fr. *insectus*, pp. of *insecare* to cut into, fr. *secare* to cut] : any of a major group of small usu. winged animals (as flies, bees, beetles, and moths) with three pairs of legs

in·sec·ti·cide \in-ˈsek-tə-ˌsīd\ *n* : a preparation for destroying insects — **in·sec·ti·cid·al** \(ˌ)in-ˌsek-tə-ˈsīd-ᵊl\ *adj*

in·sec·tiv·o·rous \ˌin-ˌsek-ˈtiv-(ə-)rəs\ *adj* : depending on insects as food

in·se·cure \ˌin-si-ˈkyùr\ *adj* **1** : UNCERTAIN **2** : UNPROTECTED, UNSAFE **3** : LOOSE, SHAKY **4** : INFIRM **5** : beset by fear or anxiety — **in·se·cure·ly** *adv* — **in·se·cu·ri·ty** \-ˈkyùr-ət-ē\ *n*

in·sem·i·nate \in-ˈsem-ə-ˌnāt\ *vb* **-nat·ed; -nat·ing** : to introduce semen into the genital tract of (a female) — **in·sem·i·na·tion** \-ˌsem-ə-ˈnā-shən\ *n*

in·sen·sate \(ˈ)in-ˈsen-ˌsāt, -sət\ *adj* **1** : INANIMATE **2** : lacking sense or understanding; *also* : FOOLISH **3** : BRUTAL, INHUMAN ⟨∼ rage⟩

in·sen·si·ble \(ˌ)in-ˈsen-sə-bəl\ *adj* **1** : IMPERCEPTIBLE; *also* : SLIGHT, GRADUAL **2** : INANIMATE **3** : UNCONSCIOUS **4** : lacking sensory perception or ability to react ⟨∼ to pain⟩ ⟨∼ from cold⟩ **5** : APATHETIC, INDIFFERENT; *also* : UNAWARE ⟨∼ of their danger⟩ **6** : MEANINGLESS **7** : lacking delicacy or refinement — **in·sen·si·bil·i·ty** \(ˌ)in-ˌsen-sə-ˈbil-ət-ē\ *n* — **in·sen·si·bly** \(ˈ)in-ˈsen-sə-blē\ *adv*

in·sen·tient \(ˈ)in-ˈsen-ch(ē-)ənt\ *adj* : lacking perception, consciousness, or animation — **in·sen·tience** \-ch(ē-)əns\ *n*

in·sep·a·ra·ble \(ˈ)in-ˈsep-(ə-)rə-bəl\ *adj* : incapable of being separated or disjoined — **in·sep·a·ra·bil·i·ty** \(ˌ)in-ˌsep-(ə-)rə-ˈbil-ət-ē\ *n* — **inseparable** *n* — **in·sep·a·ra·bly** \(ˈ)in-ˈsep-(ə-)rə-blē\ *adv*

¹in·sert \in-ˈsərt\ *vb* **1** : to put or thrust in ⟨∼ a key in a lock⟩ ⟨∼ a comma⟩ **2** : INTERPOLATE **3** : to set in (as a piece of fabric) and make fast

²in·sert \ˈin-ˌsərt\ *n* : something that is inserted or is for insertion; *esp* : written or printed material inserted (as between the leaves of a book)

in·ser·tion \in-ˈsər-shən\ *n* **1** : something that is inserted **2** : the act or process of inserting

in·set \ˈin-ˌset\ *vb* **inset** *or* **in·set·ted; in·set·ting** : to set in : INSERT — **inset** *n*

¹in·shore \ˈin-ˈshōr\ *adj* **1** : situated or carried on near shore **2** : moving toward shore

²inshore *adv* : to or toward shore

¹in·side \in-ˈsīd, ˈin-ˌsīd\ *n* **1** : an inner side or surface : INTERIOR **2** : inward nature, thoughts, or feeling **3** *pl* : VISCERA, ENTRAILS **4** : a position of power or confidence — **inside** *adj*

²inside *prep* **1** : in or into the inside of **2** : before the end of ⟨∼ an hour⟩

³inside *adv* **1** : on the inner side **2** : in or into the interior

inside of *prep* : INSIDE

in·sid·er \in-ˈsīd-ər\ *n* : a person who is in a position of power or has access to confidential information

in·sid·i·ous \in-ˈsid-ē-əs\ *adj* [L *insidiosus*, fr. *insidiae* ambush, fr. *insidēre* to sit in, sit on, fr. *sedēre* to sit] **1** : SLY, TREACHEROUS **2** : SEDUCTIVE **3** : having a gradual and cumulative effect : SUBTLE — **in·sid·i·ous·ly** *adv* — **in·sid·i·ous·ness** *n*

in·sight \ˈin-ˌsīt\ *n* : the power or act of seeing into a situation : UNDERSTANDING, PENETRATION; *also* : INTUITION — **in·sight·ful** \ˈin-ˌsīt-fəl, in-ˈsīt-\ *adj*

in·sig·nia \in-ˈsig-nē-ə\ *or* **in·sig·ne** \-(ˌ)nē\ *n, pl* **-nia** *or* **-ni·as** : a distinguishing mark esp. of authority, office, or honor : BADGE, EMBLEM

in·sin·cere \ˌin-sin-ˈsiər\ *adj* : not sin-

cere : HYPOCRITICAL — **in•sin•cere•ly**
adv — **in•sin•cer•i•ty** \-'ser-ət-ē\ *n*

in•sin•u•ate \in-'sin-yə-ˌwāt\ *vb* **-at•ed;
-at•ing** [L *insinuare*, fr. *sinuare* to
bend, curve, fr. *sinus* curve] **1** : to
introduce gradually or in a subtle, indirect, or artful way **2** : to imply in a
subtle or devious way — **in•sin•u•a•
tion** \(ˌ)in-ˌsin-yə-'wā-shən\ *n*

in•sin•u•at•ing *adj* **1** : tending gradually
to cause doubt, distrust, or change of
outlook **2** : winning favor and confidence by imperceptible degrees

in•sip•id \in-'sip-əd\ *adj* **1** : lacking savor **2** : DULL, UNINTERESTING — **in•si•
pid•i•ty** \ˌin-sə-'pid-ət-ē\ *n*

in•sist \in-'sist\ *vb* [MF or L; MF *insis-
ter*, fr. L *insistere* to stand upon, persist, fr. *sistere* to stand] : to take a
resolute stand

in•sis•tence \in-'sis-təns\ *n* : the act of
insisting; *also* : an insistent attitude or
quality : URGENCY

in•sis•tent \in-'sis-tənt\ *adj* : disposed
to insist — **in•sis•tent•ly** *adv*

in si•tu \in-'sī-tü\ *adv or adj* [L, in posi-
tion] : in the natural or original position

in•so•far as \ˌin-sə-ˌfär-əz\ *conj* : to the
extent or degree that

insol *abbr* insoluble

in•so•la•tion \ˌin-(ˌ)sō-'lā-shən\ *n* : solar radiation that has been received

in•sole \'in-ˌsōl\ *n* **1** : an inside sole of a
shoe **2** : a loose thin strip placed inside a shoe for warmth or comfort

in•so•lent \'in-sə-lənt\ *adj* : contemptuous, rude, disrespectful, or brutal in
behavior or language : OVERBEARING,
BOLD — **in•so•lence** \-ləns\ *n*

in•sol•u•ble \(')in-'säl-yə-bəl\ *adj* **1**
: having or admitting of no solution or
explanation **2** : difficult or impossible
to dissolve — **in•sol•u•bil•i•ty** \(ˌ)in-
ˌsäl-yə-'bil-ət-ē\ *n*

in•solv•able \(')in-'säl-və-bəl\ *adj* : not
capable of being solved

in•sol•vent \(')in-'säl-vənt\ *adj* **1** : un-
able to pay one's debts **2** : insufficient
to pay all debts charged against it ⟨an
∼ estate⟩ **3** : IMPOVERISHED, DEFICIENT
— **in•sol•ven•cy** \-vən-sē\ *n*

in•som•nia \in-'säm-nē-ə\ *n* : prolonged
and usu. abnormal sleeplessness

in•so•much as \ˌin-sə-ˌməch-əz\ *conj*
: INASMUCH AS

insomuch that *conj* : to such a degree
that : SO

in•sou•ci•ance \in-'sü-sē-əns, aⁿ-süs-
yäⁿs\ *n* [F] : lighthearted unconcern
— **in•sou•ci•ant** \in-'sü-sē-ənt, aⁿ-süs-
yäⁿ\ *adj*

insp *abbr* inspector

in•spect \in-'spekt\ *vb* : to view closely
and critically : EXAMINE — **in•spec•tion**
\-'spek-shən\ *n* — **in•spec•tor** \-tər\ *n*

in•spi•ra•tion \ˌin-spə-'rā-shən\ *n* **1** : IN-
HALATION **2** : the act or power of moving the intellect or emotions **3** : the
quality or state of being inspired; *also*
: something that is inspired **4** : an inspiring agent or influence — **in•spi•ra•
tion•al** \-sh(ə-)nəl\ *adj*

in•spire \in-'spī(ə)r\ *vb* **in•spired; in•
spir•ing 1** : INHALE **2** : to influence,
move, or guide by divine or supernatural inspiration **3** : exert an animating, enlivening, or exalting influence upon **4** : AFFECT **5** : to
communicate to an agent supernatu-
rally; *also* : CREATE **6** : to bring about;
also : INCITE **7** : to spread by indirect
means — **in•spir•er** *n*

in•spir•it \in-'spir-ət\ *vb* : ANIMATE,
HEARTEN

inst *abbr* **1** instant **2** institute; institution; institutional

in•sta•bil•i•ty \ˌin-stə-'bil-ət-ē\ *n* : lack
of firmness or steadiness

in•stall *or* **in•stal** \in-'stól\ *vb* **in•stalled;
in•stall•ing 1** : to place formally in of-
fice : induct into an office, rank, or
order **2** : to establish in an indicated
place, condition, or status **3** : to set
up for use or service — **in•stal•la•tion**
\ˌin-stə-'lā-shən\ *n*

¹**in•stall•ment** *or* **in•stal•ment** \in-'stól-
mənt\ *n* : INSTALLATION

²**installment** *also* **instalment** *n* **1** : one of
the parts into which a debt or sum is
divided for payment **2** : one of several
parts presented at intervals

¹**in•stance** \'in-stəns\ *n* **1** : INSTIGATION,
REQUEST ⟨entered the contest at the ∼
of friends⟩ **2** : EXAMPLE ⟨an ∼ of her-
oism⟩ ⟨for ∼⟩ **3** : an event or step that
is part of a process or series **syn** case,
illustration, sample, specimen

²**instance** *vb* **in•stanced; in•stanc•ing** : to
mention as a case or example

¹**in•stant** \'in-stənt\ *n* **1** : MOMENT ⟨the ∼

we met⟩ **2** : the present or current month ⟨your letter of the 10th ∼⟩

²instant *adj* **1** : URGENT **2** : PRESENT, CURRENT **3** : IMMEDIATE ⟨∼ relief⟩ **4** : partially prepared by the manufacturer to make final preparation easy ⟨∼ cake mix⟩; *also* : immediately soluble in water ⟨∼ coffee⟩

in•stan•ta•neous \‚in-stən-'tā-nē-əs\ *adj* : done or occurring in an instant or without delay — **in•stan•ta•neous•ly** *adv*

in•stan•ter \in-'stant-ər\ *adv* : at once

in•stan•ti•ate \in-'stan-chē-‚āt\ *vb* **-at•ed; -at•ing** : to represent by a concrete example — **in•stan•ti•a•tion** \-‚stan-chē-'ā-shən\ *n*

in•stant•ly \'in-stənt-lē\ *adv* : at once : IMMEDIATELY

in•state \in-'stāt\ *vb* : to establish in a rank or office : INSTALL

in•stead \in-'sted\ *adv* **1** : as a substitute or equivalent **2** : as an alternative : RATHER

instead of \in-‚sted-ə(v), -‚stid-\ *prep* : as a substitute for or alternative to

in•step \'in-‚step\ *n* : the arched part of the human foot in front of the ankle joint

in•sti•gate \'in-stə-‚gāt\ *vb* **-gat•ed; -gat•ing** : to goad or urge forward : PROVOKE, INCITE ⟨∼ a revolt⟩ — **in•sti•ga•tion** \‚in-stə-'gā-shən\ *n* — **in•sti•ga•tor** \'in-stə-‚gāt-ər\ *n*

in•still *also* **in•stil** \in-'stil\ *vb* **in•stilled; in•still•ing 1** : to cause to enter drop by drop **2** : to impart gradually

¹in•stinct \'in-‚stiŋkt\ *n* **1** : a natural aptitude **2** : a largely inheritable and unalterable tendency of an organism to make a complex and specific response to environmental stimuli without involving reason; *also* : behavior originating below the conscious level — **in•stinc•tive** \in-'stiŋk-tiv\ *adj* — **in•stinc•tive•ly** *adv*

²in•stinct \in-'stiŋkt, 'in-‚stiŋkt\ *adj* : IMBUED, INFUSED

in•stinc•tu•al \in-'stiŋ(k)-chə(-wə)l\ *adj* : of, relating to, or based on instinct

¹in•sti•tute \'in-stə-‚t(y)üt\ *vb* **-tut•ed; -tut•ing 1** : to establish in a position or office **2** : to originate and get established : ORGANIZE **3** : INAUGURATE, INITIATE

²institute *n* **1** : an elementary principle

recognized as authoritative; *also, pl* : a collection of such principles and precepts **2** : an organization for the promotion of a cause : ASSOCIATION **3** : an educational institution **4** : a meeting for instruction or a brief course of such meetings

in•sti•tu•tion \‚in-stə-'t(y)ü-shən\ *n* **1** : an act of originating, setting up, or founding **2** : an established practice, law, or custom **3** : a society or corporation esp. of a public character ⟨a charitable ∼⟩; *also* : the building which houses it — **in•sti•tu•tion•al** \-'t(y)ü-sh(ə-)nəl\ *adj* — **in•sti•tu•tion•al•ize** \-‚īz\ *vb* — **in•sti•tu•tion•al•ly** \-ē\ *adv*

instr *abbr* **1** instructor **2** instrument; instrumental

in•struct \in-'strəkt\ *vb* [ME *instructen,* fr. L *instructus,* pp. of *instruere,* fr. *struere* to build] **1** : TEACH **2** : INFORM **3** : to give directions or commands to

in•struc•tion \in-'strək-shən\ *n* **1** : LESSON, PRECEPT **2** : COMMAND, ORDER **3** *pl* : DIRECTIONS **4** : the action, practice, or profession of a teacher — **in•struc•tion•al** \-sh(ə-)nəl\ *adj*

in•struc•tive \in-'strək-tiv\ *adj* : carrying a lesson : ENLIGHTENING

in•struc•tor \in-'strək-tər\ *n* : one that instructs; *esp* : a college teacher below professorial rank — **in•struc•tor•ship** *n*

¹in•stru•ment \'in-strə-mənt\ *n* **1** : a device used to produce music **2** : a means by which something is done **3** : TOOL, UTENSIL **4** : a legal document (as a deed) **5** : a device used in navigating an airplane

²in•stru•ment \-‚ment\ *vb* : to equip with instruments

in•stru•men•tal \‚in-strə-'ment-ᵊl\ *adj* **1** : acting as an agent or means **2** : of, relating to, or done with an instrument **3** : relating to, composed for, or performed on a musical instrument

in•stru•men•tal•ist \-əst\ *n* : a player on a musical instrument

in•stru•men•tal•i•ty \‚in-strə-mən-'tal-ət-ē, -‚men-\ *n, pl* **-ties 1** : the quality or state of being instrumental **2** : MEANS, AGENCY

in•stru•men•ta•tion \‚in-strə-mən-'tā-shən, -‚men-\ *n* **1** : the arrangement or composition of music for instruments (as for an orchestra) **2** : the use or application of instruments

instrument flying *n* : airplane navigation by instruments only

instrument panel *n* : DASHBOARD

in·sub·or·di·nate \ˌin-sə-ˈbȯrd-(ə-)nət\ *adj* : disobedient to authority — **in·sub·or·di·na·tion** \-ˌbȯrd-ᵊn-ˈā-shən\ *n*

in·sub·stan·tial \ˌin-səb-ˈstan-chəl\ *adj* **1** : lacking substance or reality **2** : lacking firmness or solidity

in·suf·fer·able \(ˈ)in-ˈsəf-(ə-)rə-bəl\ *adj* : not to be endured : INTOLERABLE ⟨an ~ bore⟩ — **in·suf·fer·ably** \-blē\ *adv*

in·suf·fi·cient \ˌin-sə-ˈfish-ənt\ *adj* : not sufficient; *also* : INCOMPETENT — **in·suf·fi·cien·cy** \-ˈfish-ən-sē\ *n* — **in·suf·fi·cient·ly** *adv*

in·su·lar \ˈins-(y)ə-lər, ˈin-shə-lər\ *adj* **1** : of, relating to, or forming an island **2** : ISOLATED, DETACHED **3** : of or relating to island people **4** : NARROW, PREJUDICED — **in·su·lar·i·ty** \ˌins-(y)ə-ˈlar-ət-ē, ˌin-shə-ˈlar-\ *n*

in·su·late \ˈin-sə-ˌlāt\ *vb* **-lat·ed; -lat·ing** [L *insula* island] : ISOLATE; *esp* : to separate a conductor of electricity, heat, or sound from other conducting bodies by means of a nonconductor — **in·su·la·tion** \ˌin-sə-ˈlā-shən\ *n* — **in·su·la·tor** \ˈin-sə-ˌlāt-ər\ *n*

in·su·lin \ˈin-s(ə-)lən\ *n* : a pancreatic hormone essential for bodily use of sugars and used in the control of diabetes mellitus

insulin shock *n* : hypoglycemia associated with the presence of excessive insulin in the system

¹**in·sult** \in-ˈsəlt\ *vb* [MF or L; MF *insulter,* fr. L *insultare,* lit., to spring upon, fr. *saltare* to leap] : to treat with insolence or contempt : AFFRONT — **in·sult·ing·ly** \-iŋ-lē\ *adv*

²**in·sult** \ˈin-ˌsəlt\ *n* : a gross indignity

in·su·per·a·ble \(ˈ)in-ˈsü-p(ə-)rə-bəl\ *adj* : incapable of being surmounted, overcome, or passed over — **in·su·per·a·bly** \-blē\ *adv*

in·sup·port·able \ˌin-sə-ˈpōrt-ə-bəl\ *adj* **1** : UNENDURABLE **2** : UNJUSTIFIABLE

in·sur·able \in-ˈshùr-ə-bəl\ *adj* : capable of being or proper to be insured

in·sur·ance \in-ˈshùr-əns\ *n* **1** : the business of insuring persons or property **2** : coverage by contract whereby one

party agrees to indemnify or guarantee another against loss by a specified contingent event or peril **3** : the state of being insured; *also* : means of insuring **4** : the sum for which something is insured

in·sure \in-ˈshùr\ *vb* **in·sured; in·sur·ing** **1** : to provide or obtain insurance on or for : UNDERWRITE **2** : to make certain : ENSURE

in·sured \in-ˈshùrd\ *n* : a person whose life or property is insured

in·sur·er \in-ˈshùr-ər\ *n* : one that insures; *esp* : a company issuing insurance

in·sur·gent \in-ˈsər-jənt\ *n* **1** : a person who revolts against civil authority or an established government : REBEL **2** : one who acts contrary to the policies and decisions of his political party — **in·sur·gence** \-jəns\ *n* — **in·sur·gen·cy** \-jən-sē\ *n* — **in·sur·gent** *adj*

in·sur·mount·able \ˌin-sər-ˈmaùnt-ə-bəl\ *adj* : INSUPERABLE — **in·sur·mount·ably** \-blē\ *adv*

in·sur·rec·tion \ˌin-sə-ˈrek-shən\ *n* : an act or instance of revolting against civil authority or an established government — **in·sur·rec·tion·ist** *n*

int *abbr* **1** interest **2** interior **3** intermediate **4** internal **5** international **6** intransitive

in·tact \in-ˈtakt\ *adj* : untouched esp. by anything that harms or diminishes

in·ta·glio \in-ˈtal-yō\ *n, pl* **-glios** [It] : an engraving cut deeply into the surface of a hard material

in·take \ˈin-ˌtāk\ *n* **1** : an opening through which fluid enters **2** : the act of taking in **3** : the amount taken in

in·tan·gi·ble \(ˈ)in-ˈtan-jə-bəl\ *adj* **1** : incapable of being touched : not tangible : IMPALPABLE **2** : impossible to define or determine with certainty or precision : VAGUE — **intangible** *n* — **in·tan·gi·bly** \-blē\ *adv*

in·te·ger \ˈint-i-jər\ *n* [L, adj., whole, entire] : a number (as 1, 2, 3, 12, 432) that is not a fraction and does not include a fraction, is the negative of such a number, or is 0

in·te·gral \ˈint-i-grəl\ *adj* **1** : essential to completeness : CONSTITUENT **2** : formed as a unit with another part **3** : composed of parts that make up a whole **4** : ENTIRE

in•te•grate \'int-ə-ˌgrāt\ *vb* **-grat•ed; -grat•ing 1** : to form, coordinate, or blend into a functioning or unified whole : UNITE **2** : to incorporate into a larger unit **3** : to end the segregation of and bring into common and equal membership in society or an organization; *also* : DESEGREGATE — **in•te•gra•tion** \ˌint-ə-'grā-shən\ *n*

integrated circuit *n* : a group of tiny electronic components and their connections in or on a small slice of material (as silicon)

in•teg•ri•ty \in-'teg-rət-ē\ *n* **1** : SOUND-NESS **2** : adherence to a code of values : utter sincerity, honesty, and candor **3** : COMPLETENESS

in•teg•u•ment \in-'teg-yə-mənt\ *n* : a covering layer (as a skin or cuticle) of an organism

in•tel•lect \'int-ᵊl-ˌekt\ *n* **1** : the power of knowing : the capacity for knowledge **2** : the capacity for rational or intelligent thought esp. when highly developed **3** : a person with great intellectual powers

in•tel•lec•tu•al \ˌint-ᵊl-'ek-ch(ə-w)əl\ *adj* **1** : of, relating to, or performed by the intellect : RATIONAL **2** : given to study, reflection, and speculation **3** : engaged in activity requiring the creative use of the intellect — **intellectual** *n* — **in•tel•lec•tu•al•ly** \-ē\ *adv*

in•tel•lec•tu•al•ism \-chə-(wə)-ˌliz-əm\ *n* : devotion to the exercise of intellect or to intellectual pursuits

in•tel•li•gence \in-'tel-ə-jəns\ *n* **1** : ability to learn and understand or to deal with new or trying situations **2** : relative intellectual capacity **3** : INFORMATION, NEWS **4** : an agency engaged in obtaining information esp. concerning an enemy or possible enemy; *also* : the information so gained

intelligence quotient *n* : a number expressing the intelligence of a person determined by dividing the person's mental age by his or her chronological age and multiplying by 100

in•tel•li•gent \in-'tel-ə-jənt\ *adj* : having or showing intelligence or intellect — **in•tel•li•gent•ly** *adv*

in•tel•li•gen•tsia \in-ˌtel-ə-'jent-sē-ə, -'gent-\ *n* [Russ *intelligentsiya*, fr. L *intelligentia* intelligence] : intellec-

tual people as a group : the educated class

in•tel•li•gi•ble \in-'tel-ə-jə-bəl\ *adj* : capable of being understood or comprehended — **in•tel•li•gi•bil•i•ty** \-ˌtel-ə-jə-'bil-ət-ē\ *n* — **in•tel•li•gi•bly** \-'tel-ə-jə-blē\ *adv*

in•tem•per•ance \(')in-'tem-p(ə-)rəns\ *n* : lack of moderation; *esp* : habitual or excessive drinking of intoxicants — **in•tem•per•ate** \-p(ə-)rət\ *adj* — **in•tem•per•ate•ness** *n*

in•tend \in-'tend\ *vb* [ME *entenden, intenden*, fr. MF *entendre* to purpose, fr. L *indendere* to stretch out, to purpose, fr. *tendere* to stretch] **1** : to have in mind as a purpose or aim **2** : to design for a specified use or future

in•ten•dant \in-'ten-dənt\ *n* : a governor or similar administrative official esp. under the French, Spanish, or Portuguese monarchies

¹**in•tend•ed** \-'ten-dəd\ *adj* **1** : expected to be such in the future; *esp* : BE-TROTHED **2** : INTENTIONAL

²**intended** *n* : an affianced person

in•tense \in-'tens\ *adj* **1** : existing in an extreme degree **2** : very large : CON-SIDERABLE **3** : strained or straining to the utmost **4** : feeling deeply; *also* : deeply felt — **in•tense•ly** *adv*

in•ten•si•fy \in-'ten-sə-ˌfī\ *vb* **-fied; -fy-ing 1** : to make or become intense or more intensive **2** : to make more acute : SHARPEN **syn** aggravate, heighten, enhance, magnify — **in•ten•si•fi•ca•tion** \-ˌten-sə-fə-'kā-shən\ *n*

in•ten•si•ty \in-'ten-sət-ē\ *n, pl* **-ties 1** : the quality or state of being intense **2** : degree of strength, energy, or force

¹**in•ten•sive** \in-'ten-siv\ *adj* **1** : involving or marked by special effort **2** : serving to give emphasis — **in•ten•sive•ly** *adv*

²**intensive** *n* : an intensive word, particle, or prefix

intensive care *adj* : having special medical facilities, services, and equipment to meet the needs of gravely ill patients — **intensive care** *n*

¹**in•tent** \in-'tent\ *n* **1** : PURPOSE, AIM **2** : the state of mind with which an act is done : VOLITION **3** : MEANING, SIGNIFI-CANCE

²**intent** *adj* **1** : directed with keen or eager attention ⟨an ∼ gaze⟩ **2** : EN-

GROSSED; *also* : DETERMINED — **in·tent·ly** *adv* — **in·tent·ness** *n*

in·ten·tion \in-'ten-chən\ *n* **1** : a determination to act in a certain way **2** : PURPOSE, AIM, END **syn** intent, design, object, objective, goal

in·ten·tion·al \in-'tench-(ə-)nəl\ *adj* : done by intention or design : INTENDED — **in·ten·tion·al·ly** *adv*

in·ter \in-'tər\ *vb* **in·terred; in·ter·ring** [ME *enteren,* fr. OF *enterrer,* fr. L *in* in + *terra* earth] : BURY

in·ter·ac·tion \,int-ər-'ak-shən\ *n* : mutual or reciprocal action or influence — **in·ter·act** \-'akt\ *vb*

in·ter·ac·tive \-'ak-tiv\ *adj* **1** : mutually or reciprocally active **2** : allowing two-way electronic communications (as between a person and a computer) — **in·ter·ac·tive·ly** *adv*

in·ter alia \,int-ər-'ā-lē-ə, -'äl-ē-\ *adv* : among other things

in·ter·atom·ic \,int-ər-ə-'täm-ik\ *adj* : existing or acting between atoms

in·ter·breed \-'brēd\ *vb* **-bred** \-'bred\; **-breed·ing** : to breed together

in·ter·ca·la·ry \in-'tər-kə-,ler-ē\ *adj* **1** : INTERCALATED ⟨February 29 is an ∼ day⟩ **2** : INTERPOLATED

in·ter·ca·late \-,lāt\ *vb* **-lat·ed; -lat·ing** **1** : to insert (as a day) in a calendar **2** : to insert between or among existing elements or layers — **in·ter·ca·la·tion** \-,tər-kə-'lā-shən\ *n*

in·ter·cede \,int-ər-'sēd\ *vb* **-ced·ed; -ced·ing** : to act between parties with a view to reconciling differences

¹**in·ter·cept** \,int-ər-'sept\ *vb* **1** : to stop or interrupt the progress or course of **2** : to include (as part of a curve or solid) between two points, curves, or surfaces **3** : to gain possession of (an opponent's pass in football) — **in·ter·cep·tion** \-'sep-shən\ *n*

²**in·ter·cept** \'int-ər-,sept\ *n* : INTERCEPTION; *esp* : the interception of a target by an interceptor or missile

in·ter·cep·tor \,int-ər-'sep-tər\ *n* : a fighter plane or missile designed for defense against attacking bombers or missiles

in·ter·ces·sion \,int-ər-'sesh-ən\ *n* **1** : MEDIATION **2** : prayer or petition in favor of another — **in·ter·ces·sor** \-'ses-ər\ *n* — **in·ter·ces·so·ry** \-'ses-(ə-)rē\ *adj*

¹**in·ter·change** \,int-ər-'chānj\ *vb* **1** : to put each in the place of the other **2** : EXCHANGE **3** : to change places mutually — **in·ter·change·able** \-'chān-jə-bəl\ *adj* — **in·ter·change·ably** \-blē\ *adv*

²**in·ter·change** \'int-ər-,chānj\ *n* **1** : EXCHANGE **2** : a highway junction that by separated levels permits passage between highways without crossing traffic streams

in·ter·col·le·giate \,int-ər-kə-'lē-j(ē-)ət\ *adj* : existing or carried on between colleges

in·ter·com \'int-ər-,käm\ *n* : INTERCOMMUNICATION SYSTEM

in·ter·com·mun·i·ca·tion system \,int-ər-kə-,myü-nə-'kā-shən-\ *n* : a two-way communication system with microphone and loudspeaker at each station for localized use

in·ter·con·ti·nen·tal \-,känt-ᵊn-'ent-ᵊl\ *adj* **1** : extending among or carried on between continents ⟨∼ trade⟩ **2** : capable of traveling between continents ⟨∼ ballistic missiles⟩

in·ter·course \'int-ər-,kōrs\ *n* **1** : connection or dealings between persons or nations **2** : physical sexual contact between individuals that involves the genitalia of at least one person ⟨oral ∼⟩ ⟨heterosexual ∼⟩; *esp* : SEXUAL INTERCOURSE

in·ter·de·nom·i·na·tion·al \,int-ər-di-,näm-ə-'nā-sh(ə-)nəl\ *adj* : involving different denominations

in·ter·de·part·men·tal \,int-ər-di-,pärt-'ment-ᵊl, -,dē-\ *adj* : carried on between or involving different departments (as of a college)

in·ter·de·pen·dent \,int-ər-di-'pen-dənt\ *adj* : dependent upon one another — **in·ter·de·pen·dence** \-dəns\ *n*

in·ter·dict \,int-ər-'dikt\ *vb* **1** : to prohibit by decree **2** : to destroy, cut, or damage (as an enemy line of supply) — **in·ter·dic·tion** \-'dik-shən\ *n*

in·ter·dis·ci·plin·ary \-'dis-ə-plə-,ner-ē\ *adj* : involving two or more academic, scientific, or artistic disciplines

¹**in·ter·est** \'in-t(ə-)rəst, -tə-,rest\ *n* **1** : right, title, or legal share in something **2** : a charge for borrowed money that is generally a percentage of the amount borrowed : the return received by capital on its investment **3**

: WELFARE, BENEFIT; *also* : SELF-INTEREST **4** *pl* : a group financially interested in an industry or enterprise **5** : CURIOSITY, CONCERN **6** : readiness to be concerned with or moved by an object or class of objects **7** : a quality in a thing that arouses interest

²**interest** *vb* **1** : to persuade to participate or engage **2** : to engage the attention of

in·ter·est·ing *adj* : holding the attention — **in·ter·est·ing·ly** *adv*

in·ter·face \'int-ər-ˌfās\ *n* **1** : a surface forming a common boundary of two bodies, spaces, or phases ⟨an oil-water ∼⟩ **2** : the place at which two independent systems meet and act on or communicate with each other ⟨the man-machine ∼⟩ **3** : the means by which interaction or communication is effected at an interface — **in·ter·fa·cial** \ˌint-ər-'fā-shəl\ *adj*

in·ter·faith \ˌint-ər-'fāth\ *adj* : involving persons of different religious faiths

in·ter·fere \ˌint-ə(r)-fiər\ *vb* -**fered**; -**fering** [MF *(s')entreferir* to strike one another, fr. OF, fr. *entre* between, among + *ferir* to strike, fr. L *ferire*] **1** : to come in collision or be in opposition : CLASH **2** : to enter into the affairs of others **3** : to affect one another

in·ter·fer·ence \-'fir-əns\ *n* **1** : the act or process of interfering **2** : something that interferes : OBSTRUCTION **3** : the mutual effect on meeting of two waves resulting in areas of increased and decreased amplitude **4** : the blocking of an opponent in football to make way for the ballcarrier **5** : the illegal hindering of an opponent in sports

in·ter·fer·om·e·ter \ˌint-ə(r)-fə-'räm-ət-ər\ *n* : a device that uses the interference of waves for making precise measurements — **in·ter·fer·om·e·try** \-fə-'räm-ə-trē\ *n*

in·ter·fer·on \ˌint-ər-'fiər-ˌän\ *n* : an antiviral protein of low molecular weight produced usu. by animal cells in response to a virus, a parasite in the cell, or a chemical

in·ter·fuse \ˌint-ər-'fyüz\ *vb* **1** : to combine by fusing : BLEND **2** : INFUSE

in·ter·ga·lac·tic \ˌint-ər-gə-'lak-tik\ *adj* : relating to or situated in the spaces between galaxies

in·ter·gla·cial \-'glā-shəl\ *adj* : occurring between successive glaciations

in·ter·gov·ern·men·tal \-ˌgəv-ər(n)-'ment-ᵊl\ *adj* : existing or occurring between two governments or levels of government

in·ter·im \'in-tə-rəm\ *n* [L, adv., meanwhile, fr. *inter* between] : a time intervening : INTERVAL — **interim** *adj*

¹**in·te·ri·or** \in-'tir-ē-ər\ *adj* **1** : lying, occurring, or functioning within the limiting boundaries : INSIDE, INNER **2** : remote from the surface, border, or shore : INLAND

²**interior** *n* **1** : INSIDE **2** : the inland part (as of a country) **3** : the internal affairs of a state or nation **4** : a scene or view of the interior of a building

interior decoration *n* : INTERIOR DESIGN — **interior decorator** *n*

interior design *n* : the art or practice of planning and supervising the design and execution of architectural interiors and their furnishings — **interior designer** *n*

interj *abbr* interjection

in·ter·ject \ˌint-ər-'jekt\ *vb* : to throw in between or among other things

in·ter·jec·tion \ˌint-ər-'jek-shən\ *n* : an exclamatory word (as *ouch*) — **in·ter·jec·tion·al·ly** \-sh(ə-)nəl-ē\ *adv*

in·ter·lace \ˌint-ər-'lās\ *vb* **1** : to unite by or as if by lacing together : INTERWEAVE **2** : INTERSPERSE

in·ter·lard \ˌint-ər-'lärd\ *vb* : to insert or introduce at intervals : INTERSPERSE

in·ter·leave \ˌint-ər-'lēv\ *vb* -**leaved**; -**leav·ing** : to arrange in alternate layers

¹**in·ter·line** \ˌint-ər-'līn\ *vb* : to insert between lines already written or printed

²**interline** *vb* : to provide (as a coat) with an interlining

in·ter·lin·ear \ˌint-ər-'lin-ē-ər\ *adj* : inserted between lines already written or printed ⟨an ∼ translation of a text⟩

in·ter·lin·ing \'int-ər-ˌlī-niŋ\ *n* : a lining (as of a coat) between the ordinary lining and the outside fabric

in·ter·link \ˌint-ər-'liŋk\ *vb* : to link together

in·ter·lock \ˌint-ər-'läk\ *vb* **1** : to engage or interlace together : lock together : UNITE **2** : to connect in such a way that action of one part affects action of another part — **in·ter·lock** \ˈint-ər-ˌläk\ n

in·ter·loc·u·tor \ˌint-ər-ˈläk-yət-ər\ n : one who takes part in dialogue or conversation

in·ter·loc·u·to·ry \-yə-ˌtōr-ē\ adj : pronounced during the progress of a legal action and having only provisional force ⟨an ∼ decree⟩

in·ter·lope \ˌint-ər-ˈlōp\ vb **-loped; -loping** 1 : to encroach on the rights (as in trade) of others 2 : INTRUDE, INTERFERE — **in·ter·lop·er** n

in·ter·lude \ˈint-ər-ˌlüd\ n 1 : a usu. short simple play or dramatic entertainment 2 : an intervening period, space, or event 3 : a short piece of music inserted between the parts of a longer composition or a religious service

in·ter·mar·riage \ˌint-ər-ˈmar-ij\ n : marriage between members of different groups; *also* : marriage within one's own group

in·ter·mar·ry \-ˈmar-ē\ vb 1 : to marry each other 2 : to marry within a group 3 : to become connected by intermarriage

in·ter·med·dle \ˌint-ər-ˈmed-ᵊl\ vb : MEDDLE, INTERFERE

¹**in·ter·me·di·ary** \ˌint-ər-ˈmēd-ē-ˌer-ē\ adj 1 : INTERMEDIATE 2 : acting as a mediator

²**intermediary** n, pl **-ar·ies** : MEDIATOR, GO-BETWEEN

¹**in·ter·me·di·ate** \ˌint-ər-ˈmēd-ē-ət\ adj : being or occurring at the middle place or degree or between extremes

²**intermediate** n 1 : an intermediate term, object, or class 2 : INTERMEDIARY

intermediate school n 1 : JUNIOR HIGH SCHOOL 2 : a school usu. comprising grades 4–6

in·ter·ment \in-ˈtər-mənt\ n : BURIAL

in·ter·mez·zo \ˌint-ər-ˈmet-sō, -ˈmed-zō\ n, pl **-zi** \-sē, -zē\ or **-zos** [It, deriv. of L *intermedius* intermediate] : a short movement connecting major sections of an extended musical work (as a symphony); *also* : a short independent instrumental composition

in·ter·mi·na·ble \(ˈ)in-ˈtərm-(ə-)nə-bəl\ adj : ENDLESS; *esp* : wearisomely protracted — **in·ter·mi·na·bly** \-blē\ adv

in·ter·min·gle \ˌint-ər-ˈmiŋ-gəl\ vb : to mingle or mix together

in·ter·mis·sion \ˌint-ər-ˈmish-ən\ n 1 : INTERRUPTION, BREAK 2 : a temporary halt esp. in a public performance

in·ter·mit \-ˈmit\ vb **-mit·ted; -mit·ting** : DISCONTINUE; *also* : to be intermittent

in·ter·mit·tent \-ˈmit-ᵊnt\ adj : coming and going at intervals **syn** recurrent, periodic, alternate — **in·ter·mit·tent·ly** adv

in·ter·mix \ˌint-ər-ˈmiks\ vb : to mix together : INTERMINGLE — **in·ter·mix·ture** \-ˈmiks-chər\ n

in·ter·mo·lec·u·lar \-mə-ˈlek-yə-lər\ adj : existing or acting between molecules

in·ter·mon·tane \ˌint-ər-ˈmän-ˌtān\ or **in·ter·mont** \ˈint-ər-ˌmänt\ adj : situated between mountains

¹**in·tern** \ˈin-ˌtərn, in-ˈtərn\ vb : to confine or impound esp. during a war — **in·tern·ee** \(ˌ)in-ˌtər-ˈnē\ n — **in·tern·ment** \in-ˈtərn-mənt\ n

²**in·tern** or **in·terne** \ˈin-ˌtərn\ n : an advanced student or recent graduate (as in medicine) gaining supervised practical experience — **in·tern·ship** n

³**in·tern** \ˈin-ˌtərn\ vb : to act as an intern

in·ter·nal \in-ˈtərn-ᵊl\ adj 1 : INWARD, INTERIOR 2 : having to do with or situated in the inside of the body ⟨∼ pain⟩ 3 : of or relating to the domestic affairs of a country or state ⟨∼ revenue⟩ 4 : of, relating to, or existing within the mind 5 : INTRINSIC, INHERENT — **in·ter·nal·ly** \-ē\ adv

internal–combustion engine n : a heat engine in which the combustion that generates the heat takes place inside the engine proper

internal medicine n : a branch of medicine that deals with the diagnosis and treatment of nonsurgical diseases

¹**in·ter·na·tion·al** \ˌint-ər-ˈnash-(ə-)nəl\ adj 1 : common to or affecting two or more nations ⟨∼ trade⟩ 2 : of, relating to, or constituting a group having members in two or more nations — **in·ter·na·tion·al·ly** \-ē\ adv

²**international** n : one that is internation-

al; *esp* : an organization of international scope

in·ter·na·tion·al·ism \-'nash-(ə-)nəl-,iz-əm\ *n* : a policy of political and economic cooperation among nations; *also* : an attitude favoring such a policy

in·ter·na·tion·al·ize \,int-ər-'nash-(ə-)nəl-,īz\ *vb* : to make international; *esp* : to place under international control

in·ter·ne·cine \,int-ər-'nes-,ēn, -'nē-,sīn\ *adj* [L *internecinus*, fr. *internecare* to destroy, kill, fr. *necare* to kill, fr. *nec-, nex* violent death] **1** : DEADLY; *esp* : mutually destructive **2** : of, relating to, or involving conflict within a group ⟨∼ feuds⟩

in·ter·nist \'in-,tər-nəst\ *n* : a specialist in internal medicine esp. as distinguished from a surgeon

in·ter·node \'int-ər-,nōd\ *n* : an interval or part between two nodes (as of a stem)

in·ter·nun·cio \,int-ər-'nən-sē-,ō, -'nùn-\ *n* [It *internunzio*] : a papal legate of lower rank than a nuncio

in·ter·of·fice \-'òf-əs\ *adj* : functioning or communicating between the offices of an organization

in·ter·per·son·al \-'pərs-(ə-)nəl\ *adj* : being, relating to, or involving relations between persons — **in·ter·per·son·al·ly** \-ē\ *adv*

in·ter·plan·e·tary \,int-ər-'plan-ə-,ter-ē\ *adj* : existing, carried on, or operating between planets ⟨∼ space⟩

in·ter·play \'int-ər-,plā\ *n* : INTERACTION

in·ter·po·late \in-'tər-pə-,lāt\ *vb* **-lat·ed; -lat·ing 1** : to change (as a text) by inserting new or foreign matter **2** : to insert (as words) into a text or into a conversation **3** : to estimate values of (a function) between two known values — **in·ter·po·la·tion** \-,tər-pə-'lā-shən\ *n*

in·ter·pose \,int-ər-'pōz\ *vb* **-posed; -pos·ing 1** : to place between **2** : to thrust in : INTRUDE, INTERRUPT **3** : to inject between parts of a conversation or argument **4** : to be or come between **syn** interfere, intercede, intermediate, intervene — **in·ter·po·si·tion** \-pə-'zish-ən\ *n*

in·ter·pret \in-'tər-prət\ *vb* **1** : to explain the meaning of; *also* : to act as an interpreter : TRANSLATE **2** : to understand according to individual belief, judgment, or interest **3** : to represent artistically — **in·ter·pret·er** *n* — **in·ter·pre·tive** \-'tər-prət-iv\ *adj*

in·ter·pre·ta·tion \in-,tər-prə-'tā-shən\ *n* **1** : EXPLANATION **2** : an instance of artistic interpretation in performance or adaptation — **in·ter·pre·ta·tive** \-'tər-prə-,tāt-iv\ *adj*

in·ter·ra·cial \-'rā-shəl\ *adj* : of, involving, or designed for members of different races

in·ter·reg·num \,int-ə-'reg-nəm\ *n, pl* **-nums** *or* **-na** \-nə\ **1** : the time during which a throne is vacant between two successive reigns or regimes **2** : a pause in a continuous series

in·ter·re·late \,int-ə(r)-ri-'lāt\ *vb* : to bring into or have a mutual relationship — **in·ter·re·lat·ed·ness** \-lāt-əd-nəs\ *n* — **in·ter·re·la·tion** \-'lā-shən\ *n* — **in·ter·re·la·tion·ship** *n*

interrog *abbr* interrogative

in·ter·ro·gate \in-'ter-ə-,gāt\ *vb* **-gat·ed; -gat·ing** : to question esp. formally and systematically : ASK — **in·ter·ro·ga·tion** \-,ter-ə-'gā-shən\ *n* — **in·ter·ro·ga·tor** \-'ter-ə-,gāt-ər\ *n*

in·ter·rog·a·tive \,int-ə-'räg-ət-iv\ *adj* : asking a question ⟨∼ sentence⟩ — **interrogative** *n*

in·ter·rog·a·to·ry \,int-ə-'räg-ə-,tōr-ē\ *adj* : INTERROGATIVE

in·ter·rupt \,int-ə-'rəpt\ *vb* **1** : to stop or hinder by breaking in **2** : to break the uniformity or continuity of **3** : to break in with questions or remarks while another is speaking — **in·ter·rupt·er** *n* — **in·ter·rup·tion** \-'rəp-shən\ *n* — **in·ter·rup·tive** \-'rəp-tiv\ *adv*

in·ter·scho·las·tic \,int-ər-skə-'las-tik\ *adj* : existing or carried on between schools

in·ter·sect \,int-ər-'sekt\ *vb* : to cut or divide by passing through : cut across : meet and cross : OVERLAP — **in·ter·sec·tion** \-'sek-shən\ *n*

in·ter·sperse \,int-ər-'spərs\ *vb* **-spersed; -spers·ing 1** : to place something at intervals in or among **2** : to insert at intervals among other things — **in·ter·sper·sion** \-'spər-zhən\ *n*

¹in·ter·state \,int-ər-'stāt\ *adj* : relating

to, including, or connecting two or more states esp. of the U.S.

²in·ter·state \ˈint-ər-ˌstāt\ *n* : an interstate highway

in·ter·stel·lar \ˌint-ər-ˈstel-ər\ *adj* : located or taking place among the stars

in·ter·stice \in-ˈtər-stəs\ *n, pl* **-stic·es** \-stə-ˌsēz, -stə-səz\ : a space that intervenes between things : CHINK — **in·ter·sti·tial** \ˌint-ər-ˈstish-əl\ *adj*

in·ter·tid·al \ˌint-ər-ˈtīd-ᵊl\ *adj* : of, relating to, or being the area that is above low-tide mark but exposed to tidal flooding

in·ter·twine \-ˈtwīn\ *vb* : to twine or cause to twine about one another : INTERLACE

in·ter·twist \-ˈtwist\ *vb* : INTERTWINE

in·ter·ur·ban \-ˈər-bən\ *adj* : going between cities or towns

in·ter·val \ˈint-ər-vəl\ *n* [ME *intervalle*, fr. MF, fr. L *intervallum* space between ramparts, interval, fr. *inter-* between + *vallum* rampart] 1 : a space of time between events or states : PAUSE 2 : a space between objects, units, or states 3 : the difference in pitch between two tones

in·ter·vene \ˌint-ər-ˈvēn\ *vb* **-vened; -ven·ing** 1 : to occur, fall, or come between points of time or between events 2 : to enter or appear as an unrelated feature or circumstance ⟨rain *intervened* and we postponed the trip⟩ 3 : to come in or between in order to stop, settle, or modify ⟨~ in a quarrel⟩ 4 : to occur or lie between two things — **in·ter·ven·tion** \-ˈven-chən\ *n*

in·ter·ven·tion·ism \-ˈven-chə-ˌniz-əm\ *n* : interference by one country in the political affairs of another — **in·ter·ven·tion·ist** \-ˈvench-(ə-)nəst\ *n or adj*

in·ter·view \ˈint-ər-ˌvyü\ *n* 1 : a formal consultation 2 : a meeting at which a writer or reporter obtains information from a person; *also* : the recorded or written account of such a meeting — **interview** *vb* — **in·ter·view·er** *n*

in·ter·vo·cal·ic \ˌint-ər-vō-ˈkal-ik\ *adj* : immediately preceded and immediately followed by a vowel

in·ter·weave \ˌint-ər-ˈwēv\ *vb* **-wove** \-ˈwōv\ *also* **-weaved; -wo·ven** \-ˈwō-vən\ *also* **-weaved; -weav·ing** : to weave or blend together : INTER-

TWINE, INTERMINGLE — **in·ter·wo·ven** \-ˈwō-vən\ *adj*

in·tes·tate \in-ˈtes-ˌtāt, -tət\ *adj* 1 : having made no valid will ⟨died ~⟩ 2 : not disposed of by will ⟨~ estate⟩

in·tes·tine \in-ˈtes-tən\ *n* : the. tubular part of the alimentary canal that extends from stomach to anus and consists of a long narrow upper part (**small intestine**) followed by a broader shorter lower part (**large intestine**) — — **in·tes·ti·nal** \-tən-ᵊl\ *adj*

in·ti \ˈint-ē\ *n* — see MONEY table

¹in·ti·mate \ˈint-ə-ˌmāt\ *vb* **-mat·ed; -mat·ing** 1 : ANNOUNCE, NOTIFY 2 : to communicate indirectly : HINT — **in·ti·ma·tion** \ˌint-ə-mā-shən\ *n*

²in·ti·mate \ˈint-ə-mət\ *adj* 1 : INTRINSIC; *also* : INNERMOST 2 : marked by very close association, contact, or familiarity 3 : marked by a warm friendship 4 : suggesting informal warmth or privacy 5 : of a very personal or private nature — **in·ti·ma·cy** \ˈint-ə-mə-sē\ *n* — **in·ti·mate·ly** *adv*

³in·ti·mate \ˈint-ə-mət\ *n* : an intimate friend, associate, or confidant

in·tim·i·date \in-ˈtim-ə-ˌdāt\ *vb* **-dat·ed; -dat·ing** : to make timid or fearful : FRIGHTEN; *esp* : to compel or deter by or as if by threats **syn** cow, bulldoze, bully, browbeat — **in·tim·i·da·tion** \-ˌtim-ə-ˈdā-shən\ *n*

intl *or* **intnl** *abbr* international

in·to \ˌin-tə, ˈin-tü\ *prep* 1 : to the inside of ⟨ran ~ the house⟩ 2 : to the state, condition, or form of ⟨got ~ trouble⟩ 3 : AGAINST ⟨ran ~ a wall⟩

in·tol·er·a·ble \(ˈ)in-ˈtäl-(ə-)rə-bəl\ *adj* 1 : UNBEARABLE 2 : EXCESSIVE — **in·tol·er·a·bly** \-blē\ *adv*

in·tol·er·ant \(ˈ)in-ˈtäl-ə-rənt\ *adj* 1 : unable to endure 2 : unwilling to endure 3 : unwilling to grant equality, freedom, or other social rights : BIGOTED — **in·tol·er·ance** \-rəns\ *n*

in·to·na·tion \ˌin-tə-ˈnā-shən\ *n* 1 : the act of intoning and esp. of chanting 2 : something that is intoned 3 : the manner of singing, playing, or uttering tones 4 : the rise and fall in pitch of the voice in speech

in·tone \in-ˈtōn\ *vb* **in·toned; in·ton·ing** : to utter in musical or prolonged tones : CHANT

in to·to \in-ˈtōt-ō\ *adv* [L, on the whole] : TOTALLY, ENTIRELY

in·tox·i·cant \in-ˈtäk-si-kənt\ *n* : something that intoxicates; *esp* : an alcoholic drink — **intoxicant** *adj*

in·tox·i·cate \-sə-ˌkāt\ *vb* -**cat·ed; -cat·ing** [ML *intoxicare*, fr. L *toxicum* poison] **1** : to make drunk **2** : to excite or elate greatly — **in·tox·i·ca·tion** \-ˌtäk-sə-ˈkā-shən\ *n*

in·trac·ta·ble \(ˈ)in-ˈtrak-tə-bəl\ *adj* : not easily controlled : OBSTINATE

in·tra·mo·lec·u·lar \ˌin-trə-mə-ˈlek-yə-lər\ *adj* : exciting or acting within a molecule

in·tra·mu·ral \-ˈmyùr-əl\ *adj* : being or occurring within the walls or limits (as of a city or college) ⟨∼ sports⟩

in·tra·mus·cu·lar \-ˈməs-kyə-lər\ *adj* : situated within or administered by entering a muscle — **in·tra·mus·cu·lar·ly** *adv*

intrans *abbr* intransitive

in·tran·si·geance \in-ˈtrans-ə-jəns, -ˈtranz-\ *n* : INTRANSIGENCE

in·tran·si·gence \-jəns\ *n* : the quality or state of being intransigent

in·tran·si·gent \-jənt\ *adj* : UNCOMPROMISING; *also* : IRRECONCILABLE — **intransigent** *n*

in·tran·si·tive \(ˈ)in-ˈtrans-ət-iv, -ˈtranz-\ *adj* : not transitive; *esp* : not having or containing an object ⟨an ∼ verb⟩ — **in·tran·si·tive·ly** *adv* — **in·tran·si·tive·ness** *n*

in·tra·state \ˌin-trə-ˈstāt\ *adj* : existing or occurring within a state

in·tra·uter·ine device \-ˈyüt-ə-rən-, -ˌrīn\ *n* : a device (as a spiral of plastic or a ring of stainless steel) inserted and left in the uterus to prevent pregnancy

in·tra·ve·nous \ˌin-trə-ˈvē-nəs\ *adj* : being within or entering by way of the veins — **in·tra·ve·nous·ly** *adv*

intrench *var of* ENTRENCH

in·trep·id \in-ˈtrep-əd\ *adj* : characterized by resolute fearlessness, fortitude, and endurance — **in·tre·pid·i·ty** \ˌin-trə-ˈpid-ət-ē\ *n*

in·tri·cate \ˈin-tri-kət\ *adj* [ME, fr. L *intricatus,* pp. of *intricare* to entangle, fr. *tricae* trifles, impediments] **1** : having many complexly interrelated parts : COMPLICATED **2** : difficult to fol-

low, understand, or solve — **in·tri·ca·cy** \-tri-kə-sē\ *n* — **in·tri·cate·ly** *adv*

¹in·trigue \in-ˈtrēg\ *vb* **in·trigued; in·trigu·ing 1** : to accomplish by intrigue **2** : to carry on an intrigue; *esp* : PLOT, SCHEME **3** : to arouse the interest, desire, or curiosity of — **in·trigu·ing·ly** \-iŋ-lē\ *adv*

²in·trigue \ˈin-ˌtrēg, in-ˈtrēg\ *n* **1** : a secret scheme : MACHINATION **2** : a clandestine love affair

in·trin·sic \in-ˈtrin-zik, -sik\ *adj* : belonging to the essential nature or constitution of a thing — **in·trin·si·cal·ly** \-zi-k(ə-)lē, -si-\ *adv*

introd *abbr* introduction

in·tro·duce \ˌin-trə-ˈd(y)üs\ *vb* -**duced; -duc·ing 1** : to lead or bring in esp. for the first time **2** : to bring into practice or use **3** : to cause to be acquainted **4** : to present for discussion **5** : to put in **syn** insinuate, interpolate, interpose, interject — **in·tro·duc·tion** \-ˈdək-shən\ *n* — **in·tro·duc·to·ry** \-ˈdək-t(ə-)rē\ *adj*

in·troit \ˈin-ˌtrō-ət, -ˌtroit\ *n* **1** *often cap* : the first part of the traditional proper of the Mass **2** : a piece of music sung or played at the beginning of a worship service

in·tro·mit \ˌin-trə-ˈmit\ *vb* -**mit·ted; -mit·ting** : to send or put in : INSERT — **in·tro·mis·sion** \-ˈmish-ən\ *n*

in·tro·spec·tion \-ˈspek-shən\ *n* : a reflective looking inward : an examination of one's own thoughts or feelings — **in·tro·spect** \ˌin-trə-ˈspekt\ *vb* — **in·tro·spec·tive** \-ˈspek-tiv\ *adj* — **in·tro·spec·tive·ly** *adv*

in·tro·vert \ˈin-trə-ˌvərt\ *n* : a person more interested in his own mental life than in the world about him — **in·tro·ver·sion** \ˌin-trə-ˈvər-zhən\ *n* — **introvert** *adj* — **in·tro·vert·ed** \ˈin-trə-ˌvərt-əd\ *adj*

in·trude \in-ˈtrüd\ *vb* **in·trud·ed; in·trud·ing 1** : to thrust, enter, or force in or upon **2** : ENCROACH, TRESPASS — **in·trud·er** *n* — **in·tru·sion** \-ˈtrü-zhən\ *n* — **in·tru·sive** \-ˈtrü-siv\ *adj* — **in·tru·sive·ness** *n*

intrust *var of* ENTRUST

in·tu·it \in-ˈt(y)ü-ət\ *vb* : to apprehend by intuition

in·tu·ition \ˌin-t(y)ù-ˈish-ən\ *n* **1** : the power or faculty of knowing things without conscious reasoning **2** : quick and ready insight — **in·tu·i·tive** \in-ˈt(y)ü-ət-iv\ adj — **in·tu·i·tive·ly** adv

in·tu·mes·cence \ˌin-t(y)u̇-ˈmes-ᵊns\ n **1** : the state of being or the action of becoming swollen **2** : something swollen or enlarged — **in·tu·mesce** \-ˈmes\ vb — **in·tu·mes·cent** \-ᵊnt\ adj

In·u·it \ˈin-(y)ə-wət\ n [Aleut inuit, pl. of inuk person] **1** : a member of the Eskimo people of America **2** : the language of the Inuit people

in·un·date \ˈin-ən-ˌdāt\ vb **-dat·ed; -dat·ing** : to cover with or as if with a flood : OVERFLOW — **in·un·da·tion** \ˌin-ən-ˈdā-shən\ n

in·ure \in-ˈ(y)u̇r\ vb **in·ured; in·ur·ing** [ME enuren, fr. en- in + ure, n., use, custom, fr. MF uevre work, practice, fr. L opera work] **1** : to accustom to accept something undesirable **2** : to become of advantage : ACCRUE

inv abbr **1** inventor **2** invoice

in vac·uo \in-ˈvak-yə-ˌwō\ adv [L] : in a vacuum

in·vade \in-ˈvād\ vb **in·vad·ed; in·vad·ing** **1** : to enter for conquest or plunder **2** : to encroach upon **3** : to spread through and usu. harm ⟨germs ∼ the tissues⟩ — **in·vad·er** n

¹in·val·id \(ˈ)in-ˈval-əd\ adj : being without foundation or force in fact, reason, or law — **in·va·lid·i·ty** \ˌin-və-ˈlid-ət-ē\ n — **in·val·id·ly** adv

²in·va·lid \ˈin-və-ləd\ adj : defective in health : SICKLY

³invalid \ˈin-və-ləd\ n : a person in usu. chronic ill health — **in·va·lid·ism** \-ˌiz-əm\ n

⁴in·va·lid \ˈin-və-ləd, -ˌlid\ vb **1** : to remove from active duty by reason of sickness or disability **2** : to make sickly or disabled

in·val·i·date \(ˈ)in-ˈval-ə-ˌdāt\ vb : to make invalid; esp : to weaken or make valueless

in·valu·able \(ˈ)in-ˈval-yə(-wə)-bəl\ adj : valuable beyond estimation

in·vari·able \(ˈ)in-ˈver-ē-ə-bəl\ adj : not changing or capable of change : CONSTANT — **in·vari·ably** \-blē\ adv

in·va·sion \in-ˈvā-zhən\ n : an act or instance of invading; esp : entry of an army into a country for conquest

in·vec·tive \in-ˈvek-tiv\ n **1** : an abusive expression or speech **2** : abusive language — **invective** adj

in·veigh \in-ˈvā\ : to protest or complain bitterly or vehemently : RAIL

in·vei·gle \in-ˈvā-gəl, -ˈvē-\ vb **in·vei·gled; in·vei·gling** \-g(ə-)liŋ\ [modif. of MF aveugler to blind, hoodwink] **1** : to win over by flattery : ENTICE **2** : to acquire by ingenuity or flattery

in·vent \in-ˈvent\ vb **1** : to think up **2** : to create or produce for the first time — **in·ven·tor** \-ˈvent-ər\ n

in·ven·tion \in-ˈven-chən\ n **1** : INVENTIVENESS **2** : a creation of the imagination; esp : a false conception **3** : a device, contrivance, or process originated after study and experiment **4** : the act or process of inventing

in·ven·tive \in-ˈvent-iv\ adj **1** : CREATIVE, INGENIOUS ⟨an ∼ composer⟩ **2** : characterized by invention ⟨an ∼ turn of mind⟩ — **in·ven·tive·ness** n

in·ven·to·ry \ˈin-vən-ˌtōr-ē\ n, pl **-ries** **1** : an itemized list of current goods or assets **2** : SURVEY, SUMMARY **3** : STOCK, SUPPLY **4** : the act or process of taking an inventory — **inventory** vb

in·verse \(ˈ)in-ˈvərs, ˈin-ˌvərs\ adj : opposite in order, nature, or effect : REVERSED — **in·verse·ly** adv

in·ver·sion \in-ˈvər-zhən\ n **1** : a reversal of position, order, or relationship; esp : an increase of temperature with altitude through a layer of air **2** : the act or process of inverting

in·vert \in-ˈvərt\ vb **1** : to reverse in position, order, or relationship **2** : to turn upside down or inside out **3** : to turn inward

¹in·ver·te·brate \(ˈ)in-ˈvərt-ə-brət, -ˌbrāt\ adj : lacking a backbone; also : of or relating to invertebrates

²invertebrate n : an invertebrate animal

¹in·vest \in-ˈvest\ vb **1** : to install formally in an office or honor **2** : to furnish with power or authority : VEST **3** : to cover completely : ENVELOP **4** : CLOTHE, ADORN **5** : BESIEGE **6** : to endow with a quality or characteristic

²invest vb **1** : to commit money in order to earn a financial return **2** : to expend for future benefits or advantages **3** : to make an investment — **in·ves·tor** \-ˈves-tər\ n

in·ves·ti·gate \in-ˈves-tə-ˌgāt\ vb **-gat·ed; -gat·ing** [L investigare to track, investigate, fr. vestigium footprint, track] : to study by close examination and systematic inquiry — **in·ves·ti·ga·tion** \-ˌves-tə-ˈgā-shən\ *n* — **in·ves·ti·ga·tor** \-ˈves-tə-ˌgāt-ər\ *n*

in·ves·ti·ture \in-ˈves-tə-ˌchŭr, -chər\ *n* **1** : the act of ratifying or establishing in office : CONFIRMATION **2** : something that covers or adorns

¹**in·vest·ment** \in-ˈves(t)-mənt\ *n* **1** : an outer layer : ENVELOPE **2** : INVESTITURE 1 **3** : BLOCKADE, SIEGE

²**investment** *n* : the outlay of money for income or profit; *also* : the sum invested or the property purchased

in·vet·er·ate \in-ˈvet-(ə-)rət\ *adj* **1** : firmly established by age or long persistence **2** : confirmed in a habit — **in·vet·er·a·cy** \-(ə-)rə-sē\ *n*

in·vi·a·ble \(ˈ)in-ˈvī-ə-bəl\ *adj* : incapable of surviving

in·vid·i·ous \in-ˈvid-ē-əs\ *adj* **1** : tending to cause discontent, animosity, or envy **2** : ENVIOUS **3** : INJURIOUS — **in·vid·i·ous·ly** *adv*

in·vig·o·rate \in-ˈvig-ə-ˌrāt\ *vb* **-rat·ed**; **-rat·ing** : to give life and energy to : ANIMATE — **in·vig·o·ra·tion** \-ˌvig-ə-ˈrā-shən\ *n*

in·vin·ci·ble \(ˈ)in-ˈvin-sə-bəl\ *adj* : incapable of being conquered, overcome, or subdued — **in·vin·ci·bil·i·ty** \(ˌ)in-ˌvin-sə-ˈbil-ət-ē\ *n* — **in·vin·ci·bly** \(ˈ)in-ˈvin-sə-blē\ *adv*

in·vi·o·la·ble \(ˈ)in-ˈvī-ə-lə-bəl\ *adj* **1** : safe from violation or profanation **2** : UNASSAILABLE — **in·vi·o·la·bil·i·ty** \(ˌ)in-ˌvī-ə-lə-ˈbil-ət-ē\ *n*

in·vi·o·late \(ˈ)in-ˈvī-ə-lət\ *adj* : not violated or profaned : PURE

in·vis·i·ble \(ˈ)in-ˈviz-ə-bəl\ *adj* **1** : incapable of being seen ⟨∼ to the naked eye⟩ **2** : HIDDEN **3** : IMPERCEPTIBLE, INCONSPICUOUS — **in·vis·i·bil·i·ty** \(ˌ)in-ˌviz-ə-ˈbil-ət-ē\ *n* — **in·vis·i·bly** \(ˈ)in-ˈviz-ə-blē\ *adv*

in·vi·ta·tion·al \ˌin-və-ˈtā-sh(ə-)nəl\ *adj* : limited to invited participants

in·vite \in-ˈvīt\ *vb* **in·vit·ed**; **in·vit·ing** **1** : ENTICE, TEMPT **2** : to increase the likelihood of **3** : to request the presence or participation of : ASK **4** : to request formally **5** : ENCOURAGE — **in·vi·ta·tion** \ˌin-və-ˈtā-shən\ *n*

in·vit·ing \in-ˈvīt-iŋ\ *adj* : ATTRACTIVE, TEMPTING

in·vo·ca·tion \ˌin-və-ˈkā-shən\ *n* **1** : SUPPLICATION; *esp* : a prayer at the beginning of a service **2** : a formula for conjuring : INCANTATION

¹**in·voice** \ˈin-ˌvȯis\ *n* [modif. of MF *envois*, pl. of *envoi* message] **1** : an itemized list of goods shipped usu. specifying the price and the terms of sale : BILL **2** : a consignment of merchandise

²**invoice** *vb* **in·voiced**; **in·voic·ing** : to make an invoice for : BILL

in·voke \in-ˈvōk\ *vb* **in·voked**; **in·vok·ing** **1** : to petition for help or support **2** : to appeal to or cite as authority ⟨∼ a law⟩ **3** : to call forth by incantation : CONJURE ⟨∼ spirits⟩ **4** : to make an earnest request for : SOLICIT **5** : to put into effect or operation **6** : to bring about : CAUSE

in·vo·lu·cre \ˈin-və-ˌlü-kər\ *n* : one or more whorls of bracts below and close to a flower or fruit

in·vol·un·tary \(ˈ)in-ˈväl-ən-ˌter-ē\ *adj* **1** : done contrary to or without choice **2** : COMPULSORY **3** : not subject to control by the will ⟨∼ muscles⟩ — **in·vol·un·tari·ly** \(ˌ)in-ˌväl-ən-ˈter-ə-lē\ *adv*

in·vo·lute \ˈin-və-ˌlüt\ *adj* **1** : curled spirally and usu. closely ⟨∼ shell⟩ **2** : INVOLVED, INTRICATE

in·vo·lu·tion \ˌin-və-ˈlü-shən\ *n* **1** : the act or an instance of enfolding or entangling **2** : COMPLEXITY, INTRICACY

in·volve \in-ˈvälv\ *vb* **in·volved**; **in·volv·ing** **1** : to draw in as a participant **2** : ENVELOP **3** : to relate closely : CONNECT **4** : to have as part of itself : INCLUDE **5** : ENTAIL, IMPLY **6** : to have an effect on — **in·volve·ment** *n*

in·volved \-ˈvälvd\ *adj* : INTRICATE, COMPLEX ⟨an ∼ assassination plot⟩

in·vul·ner·a·ble \(ˈ)in-ˈvəl-nə-rə-bəl\ *adj* **1** : incapable of being wounded, injured, or damaged **2** : immune to or proof against attack — **in·vul·ner·a·bil·i·ty** \(ˌ)in-ˌvəl-nə-rə-ˈbil-ət-ē\ *n* — **in·vul·ner·a·bly** \(ˈ)in-ˈvəl-nə-rə-blē\ *adv*

¹**in·ward** \ˈin-wərd\ *adj* **1** : situated on the inside **2** : MENTAL; *also* : SPIRITUAL **3** : directed toward the interior

²**inward** *or* **in·wards** \-wərdz\ *adv* **1** : toward the inside, center, or interior **2** : toward the inner being

in·ward·ly \ˈin-wərd-lē\ *adv* **1** : MENTALLY, SPIRITUALLY **2** : INTERNALLY ⟨bled ∼⟩ **3** : to oneself ⟨cursed ∼⟩ **4** : toward the center or interior

IOC *abbr* International Olympic Committee

io•dide \'ī-ə-ˌdīd\ *n* : a compound of iodine with another element or group

io•dine \'ī-ə-ˌdīn, -əd-ᵊn\ *n* : a nonmetallic chemical element used in medicine and photography

io•dize \'ī-ə-ˌdīz\ *vb* **io•dized; io•diz•ing** : to treat with iodine or an iodide

ion \'ī-ən, 'ī-ˌän\ *n* [Gk, neut. of *iōn*, prp. of *ienai* to go; so called because in electrolysis it goes to one of the two poles] : an electrically charged particle or group of atoms — **ion•ic** \ī-'än-ik\ *adj*

ion•ize \'ī-ə-ˌnīz\ *vb* **ion•ized; ion•iz•ing 1** : to convert wholly or partly into ions **2** : to become ionized — **ion•iz•able** \-ˌnī-zə-bəl\ *adj* — **ion•iza•tion** \ˌī-ə-nə-'zā-shən\ *n* — **ion•iz•er** \'ī-ə-ˌnī-zər\ *n*

ion•o•sphere \ī-'än-ə-ˌsfiər\ *n* : the part of the earth's atmosphere beginning at an altitude of about 30 miles and extending outward 300 miles or more that contains free electrically charged particles — **ion•o•spher•ic** \ī-ˌän-ə-'sfi(ə)r-ik, -'sfer-\ *adj*

IOOF *abbr* Independent Order of Odd Fellows

io•ta \ī-'ōt-ə\ *n* [L, fr. Gk *iōta*, the 9th letter of the Greek alphabet] : a very small quantity : JOT

IOU \ˌī-(ˌ)ō-'yü\ *n* : an acknowledgement of a debt

IP *abbr* innings pitched

ip•e•cac \'ip-i-ˌkak\ *n* [Pg *ipecacuanha*] **1** : the dried rhizome and roots of ipecac used esp. as the source of an emetic **2** : a tropical So. American creeping plant related to the madder

ip•so fac•to \ˌip-sō-'fak-tō\ *adv* [NL, lit., by the fact itself] : by the very nature of the case

iq *abbr* [L *idem quod*] the same as

IQ \'ī-'kyü\ *n* : INTELLIGENCE QUOTIENT

¹Ir *abbr* Irish

²Ir *symbol* iridium

IR *abbr* **1** information retrieval **2** internal revenue

IRA *abbr* **1** individual retirement account **2** Irish Republican Army

Ira•ni•an \ir-'ā-nē-ən *also* -'ä-\ *n* : a native or inhabitant of Iran — **Iranian** *adj*

Iraqi \i-'räk-ē, -'rak-\ *n* : a native or inhabitant of Iraq — **Iraqi** *adj*

iras•ci•ble \ir-'as-ə-bəl, ī-'ras-\ *adj* : marked by hot temper and easily provoked anger **syn** choleric, testy, touchy, cranky, cross — **iras•ci•bil•i•ty** \-ˌas-ə-'bil-ət-ē, -ˌras-\ *n*

irate \ī-'rāt\ *adj* **1** : roused to ire **2** : arising from anger ⟨∼ words⟩ — **irate•ly** *adv*

IRBM *abbr* intermediate range ballistic missile

ire \'ī(ə)r\ *n* : ANGER, WRATH — **ire•ful** *adj*

Ire *abbr* Ireland

ire•nic \ī-'ren-ik\ *adj* : conducive to or operating toward peace or conciliation

ir•i•des•cence \ˌir-ə-'des-ᵊns\ *n* : a rainbowlike play of colors — **ir•i•des•cent** \-ᵊnt\ *adj*

irid•i•um \ir-'id-ē-əm\ *n* : a hard brittle very heavy metallic chemical element used in alloys

iris \'ī-rəs\ *n, pl* **iris•es** *or* **iri•des** \'ī-rə-ˌdēz, 'ir-ə-\ [ME, fr. L *iris* rainbow, iris plant, fr. Gk, rainbow, iris plant, iris of the eye] **1** : the colored part around the pupil of the eye **2** : any of a large genus of plants with linear basal leaves and large showy flowers

Irish \'īr-ish\ *n* **1 Irish** *pl* : the people of Ireland **2** : the Celtic language of Ireland — **Irish** *adj* — **Irish•man** \-mən\ *n* — **Irish•wom•an** \-ˌwùm-ən\ *n*

Irish bull *n* : an incongruous statement (as ''it was hereditary in his family to have no children'')

Irish coffee *n* : hot sugared coffee with Irish whiskey and whipped cream

Irish moss *n* : the dried and bleached plants of two red algae; *also* : either of these two red algae

Irish setter *n* : any of a breed of bird dogs with a mahogany-red coat

irk \'ərk\ *vb* : to make weary, irritated, or bored : ANNOY

irk•some \'ərk-səm\ *adj* : tending to irk : ANNOYING — **irk•some•ly** *adv*

¹iron \'ī(-ə)rn\ *n* **1** : a heavy magnetic metallic chemical element that rusts easily, can be readily shaped, and is vital to biological processes **2** : something made of metal and esp. iron; *also* : something (as handcuffs) used to bind or restrain ⟨put them in ∼s⟩ **3**

: a household device with a flat base that is heated and used for pressing cloth **4** : STRENGTH, HARDNESS

²**iron** *vb* **1** : to press or smooth with or as if with a heated flatiron **2** : to remove (as wrinkles) by ironing — **iron·er** *n*

iron·bound \'ī(-ə)rn-'baùnd\ *adj* **1** : HARSH, RUGGED ⟨∼ coast⟩ **2** : STERN, RIGOROUS ⟨∼ traditions⟩

¹**iron·clad** \-'klad\ *adj* **1** : sheathed in iron armor **2** : so firm or secure as to be unbreakable

²**iron·clad** \-ˌklad\ *n* : an armored naval vessel

iron curtain *n* : a political, military, and ideological barrier that cuts off and isolates an area; *esp* : one between an area under Soviet control and other areas

iron·ic \ī-'rän-ik\ *or* **iron·i·cal** \-i-kəl\ *adj* **1** : of, relating to, or marked by irony **2** : given to irony — **iron·i·cal·ly** \-i-k(ə-)lē\ *adv*

iron·ing \'ī(-ə)r-niŋ\ *n* : clothes ironed or to be ironed

iron lung *n* : a device for artificial respiration (as in polio) that encloses the chest or body in a chamber in which changes of pressure force air into and out of the lungs

iron out *vb* : to remove or lessen difficulties in or extremes of

iron oxide *n* : FERRIC OXIDE

iron·stone \'ī(-ə)rn-ˌstōn\ *n* **1** : a hard iron-rich sedimentary rock **2** : a hard heavy durable pottery developed in England in the 19th century

iron·ware \-ˌwaər\ *n* : articles made of iron

iron·weed \-ˌwēd\ *n* : any of several weedy American plants related to the daisy that have terminal heads of red or purple tubular flowers

iron·wood \-ˌwùd\ *n* : a tree or shrub with exceptionally hard wood; *also* : its wood

iron·work \-ˌwərk\ *n* **1** : work in iron **2** *pl* : a mill or building where iron or steel is smelted or heavy iron or steel products are made — **iron·work·er** *n*

iro·ny \'ī-rə-nē\ *n, pl* **-nies** [L *ironia*, fr. Gk *eirōnia*, fr. *eirōn* dissembler] **1** : the use of words to express the opposite of what one really means **2** : incongruity between the actual result of a sequence of events and the expected result

Ir·o·quois \'ir-ə-ˌkwòi\ *n, pl* **Iroquois** \-ˌkwòi(z)\ [F, fr. Algonquin (a No. American Indian dialect) *Irinakhoiw*, lit., real adders] **1** *pl* : an American Indian confederacy of New York that consisted of the Cayuga, Mohawk, Oneida, Onondaga, and Seneca and later included the Tuscarora **2** : a member of any of the Iroquois peoples

ir·ra·di·ate \ir-'ād-ē-ˌāt\ *vb* **-at·ed; -at·ing** **1** : ILLUMINATE **2** : ENLIGHTEN **3** : to treat by exposure to radiation **4** : RADIATE — **ir·ra·di·a·tion** \-ˌād-ē-'ā-shən\ *n*

¹**ir·ra·tio·nal** \(')ir-'ash-(ə-)nəl\ *adj* **1** : incapable of reasoning ⟨∼ beasts⟩; *also* : defective in mental power ⟨∼ with fever⟩ **2** : not based on reason ⟨∼ fears⟩ **3** : relating to, consisting of, or being one or more irrational numbers — **ir·ra·tio·nal·i·ty** \(ˌ)ir-ˌash-ə-'nal-ət-ē\ *n* — **ir·ra·tio·nal·ly** \(')ir-'ash-(ə-)nə-lē\ *adv*

²**irrational** *n* : IRRATIONAL NUMBER

irrational number *n* : a real number that cannot be expressed as the quotient of two integers

ir·rec·on·cil·able \(ˌ)ir-ˌek-ən-'sī-lə-bəl, (')ir-'ek-ən-ˌsī-\ *adj* : impossible to reconcile, adjust, or harmonize — **ir·rec·on·cil·abil·i·ty** \(ˌ)ir-ˌek-ən-ˌsī-lə-'bil-ət-ē\ *n*

ir·re·cov·er·able \ˌir-i-'kəv-(ə-)rə-bəl\ *adj* : not capable of being recovered or rectified : IRREPARABLE — **ir·re·cov·er·ably** \-blē\ *adv*

ir·re·deem·able \ˌir-i-'dē-mə-bəl\ *adj* **1** : not redeemable; *esp* : not terminable by payment of the principal ⟨an ∼ bond⟩ **2** : not convertible into gold or silver at the will of the holder **3** : being beyond remedy : HOPELESS

ir·re·den·tism \-'den-ˌtiz-əm\ *n* : a principle or policy directed toward the incorporation of a territory historically or ethnically part of another into that other — **ir·re·den·tist** \-'dent-əst\ *n or adj*

ir·re·duc·ible \ˌir-i-'d(y)ü-sə-bəl\ *adj* : not reducible — **ir·re·duc·ibly** \-'d(y)ü-sə-blē\ *adv*

ir·re·fra·ga·ble \(')ir-'(r)ef-rə-gə-bəl\ *adj* : IRREFUTABLE

ir·re·fut·able \ˌir-i-ˈfyüt-ə-bəl, (ˈ)ir-ˈ(r)ef-yət-\ *adj* : impossible to refute

irreg *abbr* irregular

ir·reg·u·lar \(ˈ)ir-ˈeg-yə-lər\ *adj* **1** : not regular : not natural or uniform **2** : not conforming to the normal or usual manner of inflection ⟨∼ verbs⟩ **3** : not belonging to a regular or organized army organization ⟨∼ troops⟩ — **irregular** *n* — **ir·reg·u·lar·i·ty** \(ˌ)ir-ˌeg-yə-ˈlar-ət-ē\ *n* — **ir·reg·u·lar·ly** \(ˈ)ir-ˈeg-yə-lər-lē\ *adv*

ir·rel·e·vant \(ˈ)ir-ˈel-ə-vənt\ *adj* : not relevant — **ir·rel·e·vance** \-vəns\ *n*

ir·re·li·gious \ˌir-i-ˈlij-əs\ *adj* : lacking religious emotions, doctrines, or practices

ir·re·me·di·a·ble \ˌir-i-ˈmēd-ē-ə-bəl\ *adj* : impossible to remedy or correct : INCURABLE

ir·re·mov·able \-ˈmü-və-bəl\ *adj* : not removable

ir·rep·a·ra·ble \(ˈ)ir-ˈep-(ə-)rə-bəl\ *adj* : impossible to make good, undo, repair, or remedy ⟨∼ damage⟩

ir·re·place·able \ˌir-i-ˈplā-sə-bəl\ *adj* : not replaceable

ir·re·press·ible \-ˈpres-ə-bəl\ *adj* : impossible to repress or control

ir·re·proach·able \-ˈprō-chə-bəl\ *adj* : not reproachable : BLAMELESS

ir·re·sist·ible \ˌir-i-ˈzis-tə-bəl\ *adj* : impossible to successfully resist — **ir·re·sist·ibly** \-blē\ *adv*

ir·res·o·lute \(ˈ)ir-ˈez-ə-ˌlüt\ *adj* : uncertain how to act or proceed : VACILLATING — **ir·res·o·lute·ly** \-ˌlüt-lē; (ˌ)ir-ˌez-ə-ˈlüt\ *adv* — **ir·res·o·lu·tion** \(ˌ)ir-ˌez-ə-ˈlü-shən\ *n*

ir·re·spec·tive of \ˌir-i-ˈspek-tiv-\ *prep* : without regard to

ir·re·spon·si·ble \-ˈspän-sə-bəl\ *adj* : not responsible — **ir·re·spon·si·bil·i·ty** \-ˌspän-sə-ˈbil-ət-ē\ *n* — **ir·re·spon·si·bly** \-ˈspän-sə-blē\ *adv*

ir·re·triev·able \ˌir-i-ˈtrē-və-bəl\ *adj* : not retrievable : IRRECOVERABLE

ir·rev·er·ence \(ˈ)ir-ˈev-(ə-)rəns\ *n* **1** : lack of reverence **2** : an irreverent act or utterance — **ir·rev·er·ent** \-(ə-)rənt\ *adj*

ir·re·vers·ible \ˌir-i-ˈvər-sə-bəl\ *adj* : incapable of being reversed

ir·rev·o·ca·ble \(ˈ)ir-ˈev-ə-kə-bəl\ *adj* : incapable of being revoked or recalled — **ir·rev·o·ca·bly** \-blē\ *adv*

ir·ri·gate \ˈir-ə-ˌgāt\ *vb* **-gat·ed; -gat·ing** : to supply (as land) with water by artificial means; *also* : to flush with liquid — **ir·ri·ga·tion** \ˌir-ə-ˈgā-shən\ *n*

ir·ri·ta·ble \ˈir-ət-ə-bəl\ *adj* : capable of being irritated; *esp* : readily or easily irritated — **ir·ri·ta·bil·i·ty** \ˌir-ət-ə-ˈbil-ət-ē\ *n* — **ir·ri·ta·bly** \ˈir-ət-ə-blē\ *adv*

ir·ri·tate \ˈir-ə-ˌtāt\ *vb* **-tat·ed; -tat·ing 1** : to excite to anger : EXASPERATE **2** : to act as a stimulus toward : STIMULATE; *also* : to make sore or inflamed — **ir·ri·tant** \ˈir-ə-tənt\ *adj or n* — **ir·ri·tat·ing·ly** \-ˌtāt-iŋ-lē\ *adv* — **ir·ri·ta·tion** \ˌir-ə-ˈtā-shən\ *n*

ir·rupt \(ˈ)ir-ˈəpt\ *vb* **1** : to rush in forcibly or violently **2** : to increase suddenly in numbers ⟨rabbits ∼ in cycles⟩ — **ir·rup·tion** \-ˈəp-shən\ *n*

IRS *abbr* Internal Revenue Service

is pres 3d sing of BE

Isa *or* **Is** *abbr* Isaiah

Isa·iah \ī-ˈzā-ə\ *n* — see BIBLE table

Isa·ias \ī-ˈzā-əs\ *n* — see BIBLE table

ISBN *abbr* International Standard Book Number

-ish \ish\ *adj suffix* **1** : of, relating to, or being ⟨Finn*ish*⟩ **2** : characteristic of ⟨boy*ish*⟩ ⟨mul*ish*⟩ **3** : having a touch or trace of : somewhat ⟨purpl*ish*⟩ **4** : having the approximate age of ⟨forty*ish*⟩ **5** : being or occurring at the approximate time of ⟨eight*ish*⟩

isin·glass \ˈīz-ᵊn-ˌglas, ˈī-ziŋ-\ *n* **1** : a gelatin obtained from various fish **2** : MICA

isl *abbr* island

Is·lam \is-ˈläm, iz-, -ˈlam, ˈis-ˌ, ˈiz-ˌ\ *n* [Ar *islām* submission (to the will of God)] : the religious faith of Muslims; *also* : the civilization built on this faith — **Is·lam·ic** \is-ˈläm-ik, iz-, -ˈlam-\ *adj*

is·land \ˈī-lənd\ *n* **1** : a body of land surrounded by water and smaller than a continent **2** : something resembling an island in its isolation

is·land·er \ˈī-lən-dər\ *n* : a native or inhabitant of an island

isle \ˈīl\ *n* : ISLAND; *esp* : a small island

is·let \ˈī-lət\ *n* : a small island

ism \ˈiz-əm\ *n* : a distinctive doctrine, cause, or theory

-ism \ˌiz-əm\ *n suffix* **1** : act : practice : process ⟨critic*ism*⟩ **2** : manner of action or behavior characteristic of a (specified) person or thing **3** : state : condition : property ⟨barbarian*ism*⟩ **4** : abnormal state or condition resulting from excess of a (specified) thing or marked by resemblance to (such) a person or thing ⟨alcohol*ism*⟩ ⟨mongol*ism*⟩ **5** : doctrine : theory : cult ⟨Buddh*ism*⟩ **6** : adherence to a set of principles ⟨stoic*ism*⟩ **7** : characteristic or peculiar feature or trait ⟨colloquial*ism*⟩

iso·bar \ˈī-sə-ˌbär\ *n* : a line on a map connecting places of equal barometric pressure — **iso·bar·ic** \ˌī-sə-ˈbär-ik, -ˈbar-\ *adj*

iso·late \ˈī-sə-ˌlāt, ˈis-ə-\ *vb* **-lat·ed; -lat·ing** [fr. *isolated* set apart, fr. F *isolé*, fr. It *isolato*, fr. *isola* island, fr. L *insula*] : to place or keep by itself : separate from others — **iso·la·tion** \ˌī-sə-ˈlā-shən, ˌis-ə-\ *n*

iso·lat·ed *adj* **1** : occurring alone or once : UNIQUE **2** : SPORADIC

iso·la·tion·ism \ˌī-sə-ˈlā-shə-ˌniz-əm, ˌis-ə-\ *n* : a policy of national isolation by abstention from international political and economic relations — **iso·la·tion·ist** \-sh(ə-)nəst\ *n or adj*

iso·mer \ˈī-sə-mər\ *n* : any of two or more chemical compounds that contain the same numbers of atoms of the same elements but differ in structural arrangement and properties — **iso·mer·ic** \ˌī-sə-ˈmer-ik\ *adj* — **isom·er·ism** \ī-ˈsäm-ə-ˌriz-əm\ *n*

iso·met·rics \ˌī-sə-ˈme-triks\ *n sing or pl* : exercise involving contraction of muscles taking place against resistance but without significant shortening of muscle fibers — **isometric** *adj*

iso·prene \ˈī-sə-ˌprēn\ *n* : a hydrocarbon used esp. in making synthetic rubber

isos·ce·les \ī-ˈsäs-ə-ˌlēz\ *adj* : having two equal sides ⟨an ∼ triangle⟩

isos·ta·sy \ī-ˈsäs-tə-sē\ *n* : general equilibrium in the earth's crust maintained by the gravity-induced flow of deep rock material — **iso·stat·ic** \ˌī-sə-ˈstat-ik\ *adj* — **iso·stat·i·cal·ly** \-i-k(ə-)lē\ *adv*

iso·therm \ˈī-sə-ˌthərm\ *n* : a line on a map connecting points having the same temperature

iso·ther·mal \ˌī-sə-ˈthər-məl\ *adj* : of, relating to, or marked by equality of temperature

iso·ton·ic \ˌī-sə-ˈtän-ik\ *adj* : having the same or equal osmotic pressure ⟨a salt solution ∼ with red blood cells⟩

iso·tope \ˈī-sə-ˌtōp\ *n* [Gk *isos* equal + *topos* place] : any of the forms of a chemical element that differ chiefly in the number of neutrons in an atom — **iso·to·pic** \ˌī-sə-ˈtäp-ik, -ˈtō-pik\ *adj* — **iso·to·pi·cal·ly** \-ˈtäp-i-k(ə-)lē, -ˈtō-pi-\ *adv*

Isr *abbr*\ Israel; Israeli

Is·rae·li \iz-ˈrā-lē\ *n, pl* **Israelis** *also* **Israeli** : a native or inhabitant of Israel — **Israeli** *adj*

Is·ra·el·ite \ˈiz-rē-ə-ˌlīt\ *n* : a member of the Hebrew people descended from Jacob

is·su·ance \ˈish-ə-wəns\ *n* : the act of issuing or giving out esp. officially

¹is·sue \ˈish-ü\ *n* **1** *pl* : proceeds from a source of revenue (as an estate) **2** : the action of going, coming, or flowing out : EGRESS, EMERGENCE **3** : EXIT, OUTLET, VENT **4** : OFFSPRING, PROGENY **5** : OUTCOME, RESULT **6** : a point of debate or controversy; *also* : the point at which an unsettled matter is ready for a decision **7** : a discharge (as of blood) from the body **8** : something coming forth from a specified source **9** : the act of officially giving out or printing : PUBLICATION; *also* : the quantity of things given out at one time

²issue *vb* **is·sued; is·su·ing** **1** : to go, come, or flow out **2** : to come forth or cause to come forth : EMERGE, DISCHARGE, EMIT **3** : ACCRUE **4** : to descend from a specified parent or ancestor **5** : to result in **6** : to put forth or distribute officially **7** : PUBLISH **8** : EMANATE, RESULT — **is·su·er** *n*

¹-ist \əst\ *n suffix* **1** : one that performs a (specified) action ⟨cycl*ist*⟩ : one that makes or produces ⟨novel*ist*⟩ **2** : one that plays a (specified) musical instrument ⟨harp*ist*⟩ **3** : one that operates a (specified) mechanical instrument or contrivance ⟨automobil*ist*⟩ **4** : one that specializes in a (specified) art or science or skill ⟨geolog*ist*⟩ **5** : one that adheres to or advocates a (specified) doctrine or system or code of behavior ⟨social*ist*⟩ or that of a (specified) individual ⟨Darwin*ist*⟩

²**-ist** *adj suffix* : -ISTIC

isth•mi•an \'is-mē-ən\ *adj* : of, relating to, or situated in or near an isthmus

isth•mus \'is-məs\ *n* : a narrow strip of land connecting two larger portions of land

-is•tic \'is-tik\ *or* **-is•ti•cal** \'is-ti-kəl\ *adj suffix* : of, relating to, or characteristic of ⟨altru*istic*⟩

ISV *abbr* International Scientific Vocabulary

¹**it** \('')it, ət\ *pron* **1** : that one — used of a lifeless thing, a plant, a person or animal, or an abstract entity ⟨~'s a big building⟩ ⟨~'s a shade tree⟩ ⟨who is ~⟩ ⟨beauty is everywhere and ~ is a source of joy⟩ **2** — used as an anticipatory subject or object ⟨~'s good to see you⟩

²**it** \'it\ *n* : the player in a game who performs a function (as trying to catch others in a game of tag) essential to the nature of the game

It *abbr* Italian; Italy

ital *abbr* italic; italicized

Ital *abbr* Italian

Ital•ian \ə-'tal-yən, i-\ *n* **1** : a native or inhabitant of Italy **2** : the language of Italy — **Italian** *adj*

Italian sandwich *n* : SUBMARINE 2

ital•ic \i-'tal-ik, ī-\ *adj* : relating to type in which the letters slope up toward the right (as in ''*italic*'') — **italic** *n*

ital•i•cize \i-'tal-ə-ˌsīz, ī-\ *vb* **-cized; -ciz•ing** : to print in italics

itch \'ich\ *n* **1** : an uneasy irritating skin sensation related to pain **2** : a skin disorder accompanied by an itch **3** : a persistent desire — **itch** *vb* — **itchy** *adj*

-ite \ˌīt\ *n suffix* **1** : native : resident ⟨Brooklyn*ite*⟩ **2** : descendant ⟨Ishmael*ite*⟩ **3** : adherent : follower ⟨Lenin*ite*⟩ **4** : product ⟨metabol*ite*⟩ **5** : mineral : rock ⟨quartz*ite*⟩

item \'īt-əm\ *n* [L, likewise, also] **1** : a separate particular in a list, account, or series : ARTICLE **2** : a separate piece of news (as in a newspaper)

item•ize \'īt-ə-ˌmīz\ *vb* **-ized; -iz•ing** : to set down in detail : LIST — **item•iza•tion** \ˌīt-ə-mə-'zā-shən\ *n*

it•er•ate \'it-ə-ˌrāt\ *vb* **-at•ed; -at•ing** : REITERATE, REPEAT

it•er•a•tion \ˌit-ə-'rā-shən\ *n* : REPETITION; *esp* : a computational process in which a series of operations is repeated a number of times

itin•er•ant \ī-'tin-ə-rənt, ə-\ *adj* : traveling from place to place; *esp* : covering a circuit ⟨an ~ preacher⟩

itin•er•ary \ī-'tin-ə-ˌrer-ē, ə-\ *n, pl* **-aries 1** : the route of a journey or the proposed outline of one **2** : a travel diary **3** : GUIDEBOOK

its \('')its, əts\ *adj* : of or relating to it or itself

it•self \it-'self, ət-\ *pron* : that identical one — used reflexively, for emphasis, or in absolute constructions

-ity \ət-ē\ *n suffix* : quality : state : degree ⟨alkalin*ity*⟩

IUD \ˌī-ˌyü-'dē\ *n* : INTRAUTERINE DEVICE

IV *abbr* intravenous; intravenously

-ive \iv\ *adj suffix* : that performs or tends toward an (indicated) action ⟨correct*ive*⟩

ivo•ry \'īv-(ə-)rē\ *n, pl* **-ries** [ME *ivorie*, fr. OF *ivoire*, fr. L *eboreus* of ivory, fr. *ebur* ivory] **1** : the hard creamy=white material composing elephants' tusks **2** : a variable door averaging a pale yellow **3** : something made of ivory or of a similar substance

ivory tower *n* **1** : an impractical lack of concern with urgent problems **2** : a place of learning

ivy \'ī-vē\ *n, pl* **ivies** : a trailing woody vine with evergreen leaves and small black berries

IWW *abbr* Industrial Workers of the World

-ize \ˌīz\ *vb suffix* **1** : cause to be or conform to or resemble ⟨American*ize*⟩ : cause to be formed into ⟨union*ize*⟩ **2** : subject to a (specified) action ⟨satir*ize*⟩ **3** : saturate, treat, or combine with ⟨macadam*ize*⟩ **4** : treat like ⟨idol*ize*⟩ **5** : become : become like ⟨crystall*ize*⟩ **6** : be productive in or of : engage in a (specified) activity ⟨philosoph*ize*⟩ **7** : adopt or spread the manner of activity or the teaching of ⟨Christian*ize*⟩

J

¹j \ˈjā\ *n, pl* **j's** *or* **js** \ˈjāz\ *often cap* : the 10th letter of the English alphabet

²j *abbr, often cap* **1** jack **2** journal **3** judge **4** justice

¹jab \ˈjab\ *vb* **jabbed; jab·bing** : to thrust quickly or abruptly : POKE

²jab *n* : a usu. short straight punch

jab·ber \ˈjab-ər\ *vb* **jab·bered; jab·ber·ing** \ˈjab-(ə-)riŋ\ : to talk rapidly, indistinctly, or unintelligibly : CHATTER — **jabber** *n*

jab·ber·wocky \ˈjab-ər-ˌwäk-ē\ *n* : meaningless speech or writing

ja·bot \zha-ˈbō, ˈjab-ˌō\ *n* : a ruffle worn down the front of a dress or shirt

jac·a·ran·da \ˌjak-ə-ˈran-də\ *n* : any of a genus of pinnate-leaved tropical American trees with clusters of showy blue flowers

ja·cinth \ˈjās-ᵊnth\ *n* : HYACINTH

¹jack \ˈjak\ *n* **1** : a mechanical device; *esp* : one used to raise a heavy body a short distance **2** : a male donkey **3** : a small target ball in lawn bowling **4** : a small national flag flown by a ship **5** : a small 6-pointed metal object used in a game (**jacks**) **6** : a playing card bearing the figure of a soldier or servant **7** : a socket into which a plug is inserted for connecting electric circuits

²jack *vb* **1** : to raise by means of a jack **2** : INCREASE ⟨∼ up prices⟩

jack·al \ˈjak-əl, -ˌȯl\ *n* [Turk *çakal,* fr. Per *shagāl,* fr. Skt *sṛgāla*] : an Old World wild dog smaller than the related wolves

jack·a·napes \ˈjak-ə-ˌnāps\ *n* **1** : MONKEY, APE **2** : an impudent or conceited person

jack·ass \-ˌas\ *n* **1** : a male ass; *also* : DONKEY **2** : a stupid person : FOOL

jack·boot \-ˌbüt\ *n* **1** : a heavy military boot of glossy black leather extending above the knee **2** : a military boot reaching to the calf and having no laces

jack·daw \ˈjak-ˌdȯ\ *n* : a black and gray Eurasian crowlike bird

jack·et \ˈjak-ət\ *n* [ME *jaket,* fr. MF *jaquet,* dim. of *jaque* short jacket, fr. *jacque* peasant, fr. the name *Jacques* James] **1** : a garment for the upper body usu. having a front opening, collar, and sleeves **2** : an outer covering or casing ⟨a book ∼⟩

Jack Frost *n* : frost or frosty weather personified

jack·ham·mer \ˈjak-ˌham-ər\ *n* : a pneumatic percussion tool for drilling rock or breaking pavement

jack–in–the–box \ˈjak-ən-thə-ˌbäks\ *n, pl* **jack–in–the–box·es** *or* **jacks–in–the–box** : a toy consisting of a small box out of which a figure springs when the lid is raised

jack–in–the–pul·pit \ˌjak-ən-thə-ˈpùl-ˌpit, -ˌpət, -ˈpəl-\ *n, pl* **jack–in–the–pulpits** *or* **jacks–in–the–pulpit** : an American spring-flowering woodland herb having an upright club-shaped spadix arched over by a green and purple spathe

¹jack·knife \ˈjak-ˌnīf\ *n* **1** : a large pocketknife **2** : a dive in which the diver bends from the waist and touches his ankles before straightening out

²jackknife *vb* : to fold like a jackknife ⟨the trailer truck *jackknifed*⟩

jack·leg \ˈjak-ˌleg\ *adj* **1** : lacking skill or training **2** : MAKESHIFT

jack–of–all–trades \ˌjak-əv-ˌȯl-ˈtrādz\ *n, pl* **jacks–of–all–trades** : one who is able to do passable work at various tasks

jack–o'–lan·tern \ˈjak-ə-ˌlant-ərn\ *n* : a lantern made of a pumpkin cut to look like a human face

jack·pot \ˈjak-ˌpät\ *n* **1** : a large sum of money formed by the accumulation of stakes from previous play (as in poker) **2** : an impressive and often unexpected success or reward

jack·rab·bit \-ˌrab-ət\ *n* : a large hare of western No. America with very long hind legs

jack·screw \-ˌskrü\ *n* : a screw-operated jack

jack·straw \-ˌstrȯ\ *n* **1** : a straw or a thin strip used in the game of jackstraws **2** *pl* : a game in which jackstraws are let fall in a heap and each player in turn tries to remove them one at a time without disturbing the rest

jack–tar \-ˈtär\ *n, often cap* : SAILOR

Ja·cob's ladder \ˌjā-kəbz-\ *n* : any of several perennial herbs related to phlox that have pinnate leaves and bright blue or white bell-shaped flowers

jac·quard \ˈjak-ˌärd\ *n, often cap* : a fabric of intricate variegated weave or pattern

¹jade \ˈjād\ *n* **1** : a broken-down, vicious, or worthless horse **2** : a disreputable woman

²jade *vb* **jad·ed; jad·ing 1** : to wear out by overwork or abuse **2** : to become weary **syn** exhaust, fatigue, tire

³jade *n* [F, fr. obs. Sp (*piedra de la*) *ijada*, lit., loin stone; fr. the belief that jade cures renal colic] : a usu. green gemstone that takes a high polish

jad·ed \ˈjād-əd\ *adj* : dulled by a surfeit or excess

¹jag \ˈjag\ *n* : a sharp projecting part

²jag *n* : SPREE

jag·ged \ˈjag-əd\ *adj* : sharply notched

jag·uar \ˈjag(-yə)-ˌwär\ *n* : a black=spotted tropical American cat that is larger and stockier than the Old World leopard

jai alai \ˈhī-ˌlī\ *n* [Sp, fr. Basque, fr. *jai* festival + *alai* merry] : a court game played by usu. two or four players with a ball and a curved wicker basket strapped to the right wrist

¹jail \ˈjāl\ *n* [ME *jaiole*, fr. OF, fr. LL *caveola*, dim. of L *cavea* cage] : PRISON; *esp* : one for persons held in lawful custody

²jail *vb* : to confine in a jail

jail·bird \-ˌbərd\ *n* : an habitual criminal

jail·break \-ˌbrāk\ *n* : a forcible escape from jail

jail·er *or* **jail·or** \ˈjā-lər\ *n* : a keeper of a jail

jal·ap \ˈjal-əp, ˈjäl-\ *n* : a purgative drug from the root of a Mexican plant related to the morning glory; *also* : this root or plant

ja·la·pe·ño \ˌhäl-ə-ˈpān-(ˌ)yō\ *n* : a Mexican hot pepper

ja·lopy \jə-ˈläp-ē\ *n, pl* **ja·lop·ies** : a dilapidated automobile

jal·ou·sie \ˈjal-ə-sē\ *n* [F, lit., jealousy] : a blind, window, or door with adjustable horizontal slats or louvers

¹jam \ˈjam\ *vb* **jammed; jam·ming 1** : to press into a close or tight position **2** : to cause to become wedged so as to be unworkable; *also* : to make or become unworkable through the jamming of a movable part **3** : to push forcibly ⟨~ on the brakes⟩ **4** : CRUSH, BRUISE **5** : to make unintelligible by sending out interfering signals or messages **6** : to take part in a jam session

²jam *n* **1** : a crowded mass that impedes or blocks ⟨traffic ~⟩ **2** : a difficult state of affairs

³jam *n* : a food made by boiling fruit and sugar to a thick consistency

Jam *abbr* Jamaica

jamb \ˈjam\ *n* [ME *jambe*, fr. MF, lit., leg] : an upright piece forming the side of an opening (as of a door)

jam·ba·laya \ˌjəm-bə-ˈlī-ə\ *n* [LaF] : rice cooked with ham, sausage, chicken, shrimp, or oysters and seasoned with herbs

jam·bo·ree \ˌjam-bə-ˈrē\ *n* : a large festive gathering

James \ˈjāmz\ *n* — see BIBLE table

jam–pack \ˈjam-ˈpak\ *vb* : to pack tightly or to excess

jam session *n* : an impromptu performance by jazz musicians

Jan *abbr* January

jan·gle \ˈjaŋ-gəl\ *vb* **jan·gled; jan·gling** \-g(ə-)liŋ\ : to make a harsh or discordant sound — **jangle** *n*

jan·i·tor \ˈjan-ət-ər\ *n* [L, fr. *janua* door] : a person who has the care of a building — **jan·i·to·ri·al** \ˌjan-ə-ˈtōr-ē-əl\ *adj*

Jan·u·ary \ˈjan-yə-ˌwer-ē\ *n* [ME *Januarie*, fr. L *Januarius*, first month of the ancient Roman year, fr. *Janus*, two-faced god of gates and beginnings] : the 1st month of the year having 31 days

¹ja·pan \jə-ˈpan\ *n* : a varnish giving a hard brilliant finish

²japan *vb* **ja·panned; ja·pan·ning** : to cover with a coat of japan

Jap·a·nese \ˌjap-ə-ˈnēz, -ˈnēs\ *n, pl* **Japanese 1** : a native or inhabitant of Japan **2** : the language of Japan — **Japanese** *adj*

Japanese beetle *n* : a small metallic green and brown beetle introduced from Japan that is a pest on the roots of grasses as a grub and on foliage and fruits as an adult

¹jape \'jāp\ *vb* **japed; jap·ing 1** : JOKE **2** : MOCK

²jape *n* : JEST, GIBE

¹jar \'jär\ *vb* **jarred; jar·ring 1** : to make a harsh or discordant sound **2** : to have a harsh or disagreeable effect **3** : VIBRATE, SHAKE

²jar *n* **1** : a harsh discordant sound **2** : QUARREL, DISPUTE **3** : JOLT **4** : a painful effect : SHOCK

³jar *n* : a broad-mouthed container usu. of glass or earthenware

jar·di·niere \ˌjärd-³n-'iər\ *n* : an ornamental stand or pot for plants or flowers

jar·gon \'jär-gən, -ˌgän\ *n* **1** : confused unintelligible language **2** : the special vocabulary of a particular group or activity **3** : obscure and often pretentious language

Jas *abbr* James

jas·mine \'jaz-mən\ *n* [F *jasmin,* fr. Ar *yāsumīn*] : any of various climbing shrubs with fragrant flowers

jas·per \'jas-pər\ *n* : a red, yellow, or brown opaque quartz

jaun·dice \'jȯn-dəs\ *n* : yellowish discoloration of skin, tissues, and body fluids by bile pigments; *also* : a disorder marked by jaundice

jaun·diced \-dəst\ *adj* **1** : affected with or as if with jaundice **2** : exhibiting envy, distaste, or hostility

jaunt \'jȯnt\ *n* : a short trip usu. for pleasure

jaun·ty \'jȯnt-ē\ *adj* **jaun·ti·er; -est** : sprightly in manner or appearance : LIVELY — **jaun·ti·ly** \'jȯnt-³l-ē\ *adv* — **jaun·ti·ness** \-ē-nəs\ *n*

Ja·va·nese \ˌjav-ə-'nēz, ˌjäv-, -'nēs\ *n* : a native or inhabitant of the Indonesian island of Java

jav·e·lin \'jav-(ə-)lən\ *n* **1** : a light spear **2** : a slender shaft thrown for distance in a track-and-field contest

¹jaw \'jȯ\ *n* **1** : either of the bony or cartilaginous structures that support the soft tissues enclosing the mouth and that usu. bear teeth **2** : the parts forming the walls of the mouth and serving to open and close it — usu. used in pl. **3** : one of a pair of movable parts for holding or crushing something — **jaw·bone** \-'bōn, -ˌbōn\ *n* — **jawed** \'jȯd\ *adj*

²jaw *vb* : to talk abusively, indignantly, or at length

jaw·break·er \-ˌbrā-kər\ *n* **1** : a word difficult to pronounce **2** : a round hard candy

jay \'jā\ *n* : any of various noisy brightly colored birds smaller than the related crows

jay·bird \'jā-ˌbərd\ *n* : JAY

jay·gee \'jā-'jē\ *n* : LIEUTENANT JUNIOR GRADE

jay·vee \'jā-'vē\ *n* **1** : JUNIOR VARSITY **2** : a member of a junior varsity team

jay·walk \'jā-ˌwȯk\ *vb* : to cross a street carelessly without regard for traffic regulations — **jay·walk·er** *n*

¹jazz \'jaz\ *n* **1** : American music characterized by improvisation, syncopated rhythms, and contrapuntal ensemble playing **2** : empty talk **3** : similar but unspecified things : STUFF

²jazz *vb* : ENLIVEN ⟨∼ things up⟩

jazzy \'jaz-ē\ *adj* **jazz·i·er; -est 1** : having the characteristics of jazz **2** : marked by unrestraint, animation, or flashiness

JCS *abbr* joint chiefs of staff

jct *abbr* junction

JD *abbr* **1** [L *juris doctor*] doctor of jurisprudence; doctor of law **2** [L *jurum doctor*] doctor of laws **3** justice department **4** juvenile delinquent

jeal·ous \'jel-əs\ *adj* **1** : demanding complete devotion **2** : suspicious of a rival or of one believed to enjoy an advantage **3** : VIGILANT — **jeal·ous·ly** *adv* — **jeal·ou·sy** \-ə-sē\ *n*

jeans \'jēnz\ *n pl* [short for *jean fustian,* fr. ME *Gene* Genoa] : pants made of durable twilled cotton cloth

jeep \'jēp\ *n* [alter. of *gee pee,* fr. *general-purpose*] : a small four-wheel drive general-purpose motor vehicle used by the U.S. army in World War II

¹jeer \'jiər\ *vb* : to speak or cry out in derision : MOCK

²jeer *n* : TAUNT

Je·ho·vah \ji-'hō-və\ *n* : GOD 1

je·hu \'jē-h(y)ü\ *n* : a driver of a coach or cab

je·june \ji-'jün\ *adj* : lacking interest or significance : DULL

je·ju·num \ji-'jü-nəm\ *n* [L] : the section of the small intestine between the duodenum and the ileum — **je·ju·nal** \-ˈjün-ᵊl\ *adj*

jell \ˈjel\ *vb* **1** : to come to the consistency of jelly **2** : to take shape

jel·ly \ˈjel-ē\ *n, pl* **jellies** **1** : a food with a soft elastic consistency due usu. to the presence of gelatin or pectin; *esp* : a fruit product made by boiling sugar and the juice of a fruit **2** : a substance resembling jelly — **jelly** *vb*

jelly bean *n* : a bean-shaped candy

jel·ly·fish \ˈjel-ē-ˌfish\ *n* : an invertebrate sea animal with a saucer-shaped jellylike body

jen·net \ˈjen-ət\ *n* **1** : a small Spanish horse **2** : a female donkey

jen·ny \ˈjen-ē\ *n, pl* **jennies** : a female bird or donkey

je·on \jā-ˈòn\ *n, pl* **jeon** — see *won* at MONEY table

jeop·ar·dy \ˈjep-ərd-ē\ *n* [ME *jeopardie,* fr. OF *jeu parti* alternative, lit., divided game] : exposure to death, loss, or injury **syn** peril, hazard, risk, danger — **jeop·ar·dize** \-ər-ˌdīz\ *vb*

Jer *abbr* Jeremiah; Jeremias

jer·e·mi·ad \ˌjer-ə-ˈmī-əd, -ˌad\ *n* : a prolonged lamentation or complaint

Jer·e·mi·ah \ˌjer-ə-ˈmī-ə\ *n* — see BIBLE table

Jer·e·mi·as \ˌjer-ə-ˈmī-əs\ *n* — see BIBLE table

¹**jerk** \ˈjərk\ *n* **1** : a short quick pull or twist : TWITCH **2** : a stupid, foolish, or eccentric person — **jerk·i·ly** \ˈjər-kə-lē\ *adv* — **jerky** \ˈjər-kē\ *adj*

²**jerk** *vb* **1** : to give a sharp quick push, pull, or twist **2** : to move in short abrupt motions

jer·kin \ˈjər-kən\ *n* : a close-fitting usu. sleeveless jacket

jerk·wa·ter \ˈjərk-ˌwȯt-ər, -ˌwät-\ *adj* [fr. *jerkwater* (rural train); fr. the fact that it took on water carried in buckets from the source of supply] : of minor importance : INSIGNIFICANT ⟨∼ towns⟩

jer·ry–built \ˈjer-ē-ˌbilt\ *adj* : built cheaply and flimsily

jer·sey \ˈjər-zē\ *n, pl* **jerseys** [*Jersey,* one of the Channel islands] **1** : a plain weft-knitted fabric **2** : a close fitting knitted shirt **3** : any of a breed of small usu. fawn-colored dairy cattle

jess \ˈjes\ *n* : a leg strap by which a captive bird of prey may be controlled

jes·sa·mine \ˈjes-ə-mən\ var of JASMINE

jest \ˈjest\ *n* **1** : an act intended to provoke laughter **2** : a witty remark **3** : a frivolous mood ⟨spoken in ∼⟩ — **jest** *vb*

jest·er \ˈjes-tər\ *n* : a retainer formerly kept to provide casual entertainment

¹**jet** \ˈjet\ *n* : a velvet-black coal that takes a good polish and is used for jewelry

²**jet** *vb* **jet·ted; jet·ting** : to spout or emit in a stream

³**jet** *n* **1** : a forceful rush (as of liquid or gas) through a narrow opening; *also* : a nozzle for a jet of fluid **2** : a jet-propelled airplane

⁴**jet** *vb* **jet·ted; jet·ting** : to travel by jet

jet lag *n* : a condition that is marked esp. by fatigue and irritability and occurs following a long flight through several time zones

jet·lin·er \ˈjet-ˌlī-nər\ *n* : a jet-propelled airliner

jet·port \ˈjet-ˌpōrt\ *n* : an airport designed to handle jets

jet–propelled \ˌjet-prə-ˈpeld\ *adj* : driven by an engine (**jet engine**) that produces propulsion (**jet propulsion**) by the rearward discharge of a jet of fluid (as heated air and exhaust gases)

jet·sam \ˈjet-səm\ *n* : jettisoned goods; *esp* : such goods washed ashore

jet set *n* : an international group of wealthy people who frequent fashionable resorts

jet stream *n* : a long narrow high-altitude current of high-speed winds blowing generally from the west

jet·ti·son \ˈjet-ə-sən\ *vb* **1** : to throw (goods) overboard to lighten a ship or aircraft in distress **2** : DISCARD — **jettison** *n*

jet·ty \ˈjet-ē\ *n, pl* **jetties** **1** : a pier built to influence the current or to protect a harbor **2** : a landing wharf

jeu d'es·prit \zhœ-des-prē\ *n, pl* **jeux d'esprit** *same*\ [F, lit., play of the mind] : a witty comment or composition

Jew \ˈjü\ *n* **1** : ISRAELITE **2** : one whose religion is Judaism — **Jew·ish** *adj*

¹**jew·el** \ˈjü-əl\ *n* [ME *juel,* fr. OF, dim. of *jeu* game, play, fr. L *jocus* game, joke] **1** : an ornament of precious metal **2** : GEMSTONE, GEM

²jewel *vb* **-eled** *or* **-elled; -el•ing** *or* **-el•ling** : to adorn or equip with jewels

jew•el•er *or* **jew•el•ler** \'jü-ə-lər\ *n* : a person who makes or deals in jewelry and related articles

jew•el•ry \'jü-əl-rē\ *n* : JEWELS; *esp* : objects of precious metal set with gems and worn for personal adornment

jew•el•weed \-ˌwēd\ *n* : IMPATIENS

Jew•ry \'ju̇(ə)r-ē, 'jü-rē\ *n* : the Jewish people

jg *abbr* junior grade

¹jib \'jib\ *n* : a triangular sail set on a line running from the bow to the mast

²jib *vb* **jibbed; jib•bing** : to refuse to proceed further

jibe \'jīb\ *vb* **jibed; jib•ing** : to be in accord : AGREE

jif•fy \'jif-ē\ *n, pl* **jiffies** : MOMENT, INSTANT ⟨I'll be ready in a ∼⟩

¹jig \'jig\ *n* **1** : a lively dance in triple rhythm **2** : TRICK, GAME ⟨the ∼ is up⟩ **3** : a device used to hold work during manufacture or assembly

²jig *vb* **jigged; jig•ging** : to dance a jig

jig•ger \'jig-ər\ *n* : a measure usu. holding 1½ ounces used in mixing drinks

jig•gle \'jig-əl\ *vb* **jig•gled; jig•gling** \-(ə-)liŋ\ : to move with quick little jerks — **jiggle** *n*

jig•saw \'jig-ˌsȯ\ *n* : a machine saw with a narrow vertically reciprocating blade for cutting curved lines

jigsaw puzzle *n* : a puzzle consisting of small irregularly cut pieces to be fitted together to form a picture

ji•had \ji-'häd, -'had\ *n* **1** : a Muslim holy war **2** : CRUSADE 2

¹jilt \'jilt\ *vb* : to drop (one's lover) unfeelingly

²jilt *n* : one who jilts a lover

jim crow \'jim-'krō\ *n, often cap J&C* : discrimination against blacks esp. by legal enforcement or traditional sanctions — **jim crow** *adj, often cap J&C* — **jim crow•ism** *n, often cap J&C*

jim–dan•dy \'jim-'dan-dē\ *n* : something excellent of its kind

jim•mies \'jim-ēz\ *n pl* : tiny rod-shaped bits of usu. chocolate-flavored candy often sprinkled on ice cream

¹jim•my \'jim-ē\ *n, pl* **jimmies** : a small crowbar

²jimmy *vb* **jim•mied; jim•my•ing** : to force open with a jimmy

jim•son•weed \'jim-sən-ˌwēd\ *n, often cap* : a coarse poisonous weed that is related to the potato and tomato and has large trumpet-shaped white or violet flowers

¹jin•gle \'jiŋ-gəl\ *vb* **jin•gled; jin•gling** \-g(ə-)liŋ\ : to make a light clinking or tinkling sound

²jingle *n* **1** : a light clinking or tinkling sound **2** : a short verse or song with catchy repetition

jin•go•ism \'jiŋ-gō-ˌiz-əm\ *n* : extreme chauvinism or nationalism marked esp. by a belligerent foreign policy — **jin•go•ist** \-əst\ *n* — **jin•go•is•tic** \ˌjiŋ-gō-'is-tik\ *adj*

jin•rik•i•sha \jin-'rik-ˌshȯ\ *n* : RICKSHA

¹jinx \'jiŋks\ *n* : one that brings bad luck

²jinx *vb* : to foredoom to failure or misfortune

jit•ney \'jit-nē\ *n, pl* **jitneys** : a small bus that serves a regular route according to a flexible schedule

jit•ter•bug \'jit-ər-ˌbəg\ *n* : a dance in which couples two-step, balance, and twirl vigorously in standardized patterns — **jitterbug** *vb*

jit•ters \'jit-ərz\ *n pl* : extreme nervousness — **jit•tery** \-ə-rē\ *adj*

¹jive \'jīv\ *n* **1** : swing music or dancing performed to it **2** : glib, deceptive, or foolish talk **3** : the jargon of jazz enthusiasts

²jive *vb* **jived; jiv•ing** **1** : KID, TEASE; *also* : DECEIVE, SWINDLE **2** : to dance to or play jive

Jn *or* **Jno** *abbr* John

Jo *abbr* Joel

¹job \'jäb\ *n* **1** : a piece of work **2** : something that has to be done : DUTY **3** : a regular remunerative position — **job•less** *adj*

²job *vb* **jobbed; job•bing** **1** : to do occasional pieces of work for hire **2** : to hire or let by the job

Job \'jōb\ *n* — see BIBLE table

job action *n* : a protest action by workers to force compliance with demands

job•ber \'jäb-ər\ *n* **1** : a person who buys goods and then sells them to other dealers : MIDDLEMAN **2** : a person who does work by the job

job•hold•er \'jäb-ˌhōl-dər\ *n* : one having a regular job

jock \'jäk\ *n* [*jockstrap*] : ATHLETE; *esp* : a college athlete

¹jock•ey \'jäk-ē\ *n, pl* **jockeys** : one who

rides a horse esp. as a professional in a race

²jockey *vb* **jock·eyed; jock·ey·ing** : to maneuver or manipulate by adroit or devious means

jock·strap \'jäk-ˌstrap\ *n* [E slang *jock* (penis)] : ATHLETIC SUPPORTER

jo·cose \jō-'kōs\ *adj* : MERRY, HUMOROUS **syn** jocular, facetious, witty

joc·u·lar \'jäk-yə-lər\ *adj* : marked by jesting : PLAYFUL — **joc·u·lar·i·ty** \ˌjäk-yə-'lar-ət-ē\ *n*

jo·cund \'jäk-ənd\ *adj* : marked by mirth or cheerfulness

jodh·pur \'jäd-pər\ *n* **1** *pl* : riding breeches loose above the knee and tight-fitting below **2** : an ankle-high boot fastened with a strap

Jo·el \'jō-əl\ *n* — see BIBLE table

¹jog \'jäg\ *vb* **jogged; jog·ging 1** : to give a slight shake or push to **2** : to go at a slow monotonous pace **3** : to run or ride at a slow trot — **jog·ger** *n*

²jog *n* **1** : a slight shake **2** : a jogging movement or pace

³jog *n* **1** : a projecting or retreating part of a line or surface **2** : a brief abrupt change in direction

jog·gle \'jäg-əl\ *vb* **jog·gled; jog·gling** \-(ə-)liŋ\ : to shake slightly — **joggle** *n*

john \'jän\ *n* **1** : TOILET **2** : a prostitute's client

John \'jän\ *n* — see BIBLE table

john·ny \'jän-ē\ *n, pl* **johnnies** : a short gown opening in the back that is worn by hospital patients

John·ny–jump–up \ˌjän-ē-'jəm-ˌpəp\ *n* : any of various small-flowered culti- vated pansies

joie de vi·vre \ˌzhwäd-ə-'vēvrᵊ\ *n* [F] : keen enjoyment of life

join \'jȯin\ *vb* **1** : to come or bring to- gether so as to form a unit **2** : to come or bring into close association **3** : to become a member of ⟨∼ a church⟩ **4** : ADJOIN **5** : to take part in a collective activity

join·er \'jȯi-nər\ *n* **1** : a worker who constructs articles by joining pieces of wood **2** : a gregarious person who joins many organizations

¹joint \'jȯint\ *n* **1** : the point of contact between bones of an animal skeleton with the parts that surround and sup- port it **2** : a cut of meat suitable for roasting **3** : a place where two things

or parts are connected **4** : ESTABLISH- MENT; *esp* : a shabby or disreputable establishment **5** : a marijuana ciga- rette

²joint *adj* **1** : UNITED **2** : common to two or more — **joint·ly** *adv*

³joint *vb* **1** : to unite by or provide with a joint **2** : to separate the joints of

joist \'jȯist\ *n* : any of the small beams ranged parallel from wall to wall in a building to support the floor or ceiling

¹joke \'jōk\ *n* : something said or done to provoke laughter; *esp* : a brief nar- rative with a humorous climax

²joke *vb* **joked; jok·ing** : to make jokes — **jok·ing·ly** \'jō-kiŋ-lē\ *adv*

jok·er \'jō-kər\ *n* **1** : a person who jokes **2** : an extra card used in some card games **3** : a misleading part of an agreement that works to one party's disadvantage

jol·li·fi·ca·tion \ˌjäl-i-fə-'kā-shən\ *n* : a festive celebration

jol·li·ty \'jäl-ət-ē\ *n, pl* **-ties** : GAIETY, MERRIMENT

jol·ly \'jäl-ē\ *adj* **jol·li·er; -est** : full of high spirits : MERRY

¹jolt \'jōlt\ *vb* **1** : to give a quick hard knock or blow to **2** : to move with a sudden jerky motion — **jolt·er** *n*

²jolt *n* **1** : an abrupt jerky blow or move- ment **2** : a sudden shock

Jo·nah \'jō-nə\ *n* — see BIBLE table

Jo·nas \'jō-nəs\ *n* — see BIBLE table

jon·gleur \zhōⁿ-'glər\ *n* : an itinerant medieval minstrel

jon·quil \'jän-kwəl\ *n* [F *jonquille*, fr. Sp *junquillo*, dim. of *junco* reed, fr. L *juncus*] : a narcissus with fragrant clustered white or yellow flowers

josh \'jäsh\ *vb* : TEASE, JOKE

Josh *abbr* Joshua

Josh·ua \'jäsh-(ə-)wə\ *n* — see BIBLE ta- ble

Joshua tree *n* : a tall branched yucca of the southwestern U.S.

jos·tle \'jäs-əl\ *vb* **jos·tled; jos·tling** \-(ə-)liŋ\ **1** : to come in contact or into collision **2** : to make one's way by pushing and shoving

Jos·ue \'jäsh-ə-ˌwē\ *n* — see BIBLE table

¹jot \'jät\ *n* : the least bit : IOTA

²jot *vb* **jot·ted; jot·ting** : to write briefly and hurriedly

jot·ting \'jät-iŋ\ *n* : a brief note

joule \'jül\ *n* : a unit of work or energy

equal to the work done by a force of one newton acting through a distance of one meter

jounce \\'jaúns\ *vb* **jounced; jounc·ing** : JOLT — **jounce** *n*

jour *abbr* 1 journal 2 journeyman

jour·nal \\'jərn-ᵊl\ *n* [ME, service book containing the day hours, fr. MF, fr. *journal* daily, fr. L *diurnalis*, fr. *dies* day] 1 : a brief account of daily events 2 : a record of proceedings (as of a legislative body) 3 : a periodical (as a newspaper) dealing esp. with current events 4 : the part of a rotating axle or spindle that turns in a bearing

jour·nal·ese \ˌjərn-ᵊl-'ēz, -'ēs\ *n* : a style of writing held to be characteristic of newspapers

jour·nal·ism \\'jərn-ᵊl-ˌiz-əm\ *n* 1 : the business of writing for, editing, or publishing periodicals (as newspapers) 2 : writing designed for or characteristic of newspapers — **jour·nal·ist** \-əst\ *n* — **jour·nal·is·tic** \ˌjərn-ᵊl-'is-tik\ *adj*

¹**jour·ney** \\'jər-nē\ *n, pl* **journeys** [ME, fr. OF *journee* day's journey, fr. *jour* day] : travel from one place to another

²**journey** *vb* **jour·neyed; jour·ney·ing** : to go on a journey : TRAVEL

jour·ney·man \-mən\ *n* 1 : a worker who has learned a trade and works for another person 2 : an experienced reliable worker

¹**joust** \\'jaúst\ *n* : a combat on horseback between two knights with lances esp. as part of a tournament

²**joust** *vb* : to engage in a joust

jo·vial \\'jō-vē-əl\ *adj* : marked by good humor — **jo·vi·al·i·ty** \ˌjō-vē-'al-ət-ē\ *n* — **jo·vi·al·ly** \\'jō-vē-ə-lē\ *adv*

¹**jowl** \\'jaúl\ *n* 1 : the lower jaw 2 : CHEEK

²**jowl** *n* : loose flesh about the lower jaw or throat

¹**joy** \\'jói\ *n* [ME, fr. OF *joie*, fr. L *gaudia*] 1 : a feeling of happiness that comes from success, good fortune, or a sense of well-being 2 : a source of happiness **syn** bliss, delight, enjoyment, pleasure — **joy·less** *adj*

²**joy** *vb* : REJOICE

joy·ful \-fəl\ *adj* : experiencing, causing, or showing joy — **joy·ful·ly** \-ē\ *adv*

joy·ous \\'jói-əs\ *adj* : JOYFUL — **joy·ous·ly** *adv* — **joy·ous·ness** *n*

joy·ride \-ˌrīd\ *n* : a ride for pleasure often marked by reckless driving — **joy·rid·er** *n* — **joy·rid·ing** *n*

JP *abbr* 1 jet propulsion 2 justice of the peace

Jr *abbr* junior

JRC *abbr* Junior Red Cross

jt *or* **jnt** *abbr* joint

ju·bi·lant \\'jü-bə-lənt\ *adj* [L *jubilans*, prp. of *jubilare* to rejoice] : EXULTANT — **ju·bi·lant·ly** *adv*

ju·bi·la·tion \ˌjü-bə-'lā-shən\ *n* : EXULTATION

ju·bi·lee \\'jü-bə-ˌlē\ *n* [ME, fr. MF & LL; MF *jubilé*, fr. LL *jubilaeus*, fr. LGk *iōbēlaios*, fr. Heb *yōbhēl* ram's horn, trumpet, jubilee] 1 : a 50th anniversary 2 : a season or occasion of celebration

Jud *abbr* Judith

Ju·da·ic \jü-'dā-ik\ *also* **Ju·da·ical** \-'dā-ə-kəl\ *adj* : of, relating to, or characteristic of Jews or Judaism

Ju·da·ism \\'jüd-ə-ˌiz-əm\ *n* : a religion developed among the ancient Hebrews and marked by belief in one God and by the moral and ceremonial laws of the Old Testament and the rabinic tradition

Ju·das tree \\'jüd-əs-\ *n* : a Eurasian leguminous tree with purplish rosy flowers

Jude \\'jüd\ *n* — see BIBLE table

Judg *abbr* Judges

¹**judge** \\'jəj\ *vb* **judged; judg·ing** 1 : to form an authoritative opinion 2 : to decide as a judge : TRY 3 : to form an estimate or evaluation about something : THINK **syn** conclude, deduce, gather, infer

²**judge** *n* 1 : a public official authorized to decide questions brought before a court 2 : UMPIRE 3 : one who gives an authoritative opinion : CRITIC — **judge·ship** *n*

Judges *n* — see BIBLE table

judg·ment *or* **judge·ment** \\'jəj-mənt\ *n* 1 : a decision or opinion given after judging; *esp* : a formal decision given by a court 2 *cap* : the final judging of mankind by God 3 : the process of forming an opinion by discerning and comparing 4 : the capacity for judging : DISCERNMENT

Judgment Day *n* : the day of the final judging of all human beings by God

ju·di·ca·ture \\'jüd-i-kə-ˌchůr\ *n* **1** : the administration of justice **2** : JUDICIARY 1

ju·di·cial \jů-'dish-əl\ *adj* **1** : of or relating to the administration of justice or the judiciary **2** : ordered or enforced by a court **3** : CRITICAL — **ju·di·cial·ly** \-ē\ *adv*

ju·di·cia·ry \jů-'dish-ē-ˌer-ē, -'dish-ə-rē\ *n* **1** : a system of courts of law; *also* : the judges of these courts **2** : a branch of government in which judicial power is vested — **judiciary** *adj*

ju·di·cious \jů-'dish-əs\ *adj* : having, exercising, or characterized by sound judgment **syn** prudent, sage, sane, sensible, wise — **ju·di·cious·ly** *adv*

Ju·dith \'jüd-əth\ *n* — see BIBLE table

ju·do \'jüd-ō\ *n* [Jp, lit., gentleness art] : a sport derived from jujitsu that emphasizes the use of quick movement and leverage to throw an opponent — **ju·do·ist** *n*

¹jug \'jəg\ *n* **1** : a large deep container with a narrow mouth and a handle **2** : JAIL, PRISON

²jug *vb* **jugged; jug·ging** : JAIL, IMPRISON

jug·ger·naut \'jəg-ər-ˌnòt\ *n* [Hindi *Jagannāth,* title of Vishnu (a Hindu god), lit., lord of the world] : a massive inexorable force or object that crushes everything in its path

jug·gle \'jəg-əl\ *vb* **jug·gled; jug·gling** \-(ə-)liŋ\ **1** : to keep several objects in motion in the air at the same time **2** : to manipulate esp. in order to achieve a desired and often fraudulent end — **jug·gler** \'jəg-lər\ *n*

jug·u·lar \'jəg-yə-lər\ *adj* : of, relating to, or situated in or on the throat or neck ⟨the ∼ veins⟩

juice \'jüs\ *n* **1** : the extractable fluid contents of cells or tissues **2** *pl* : the natural fluids of an animal body **3** : a medium (as electricity) that supplies power

juic·er \'jü-sər\ *n* : an appliance for extracting juice (as from fruit)

juice up *vb* : to give life, energy, or spirit to

juicy \'jü-sē\ *adj* **juic·i·er; -est 1** : SUCCULENT **2** : rich in interest; *also* : RACY — **juic·i·ly** \'jü-sə-lē\ *adv* — **juic·i·ness** \-sē-nəs\ *n*

ju·jit·su *or* **ju·jut·su** \jü-'jit-sü\ *n* [Jp *jūjutsu,* fr. *jū* weakness, gentleness + *jutsu* art, skill] : an art of fighting employing holds, throws, and paralyzing blows

ju·jube \'jü-ˌjüb, 'jü-jů-ˌbē\ *n* : a fruit= flavored gumdrop or lozenge

juke·box \'jük-ˌbäks\ *n* : a coin-operated automatic record player

Jul *abbr* July

ju·lep \'jü-ləp\ *n* [ME sweetened water, fr. MF, fr. Ar *julāb,* fr. Per *gulāb,* fr. *gul* rose + *āb* water] : a drink made of bourbon, sugar, and mint served over crushed ice in a tall glass

Ju·ly \jů-'lī\ *n* [ME *Julie,* fr. OE *Julius,* fr. L, fr. Gaius *Julius* Caesar] : the 7th month of the year having 31 days

¹jum·ble \'jəm-bəl\ *vb* **jum·bled; jum·bling** \-b(ə-)liŋ\ : to mix in a confused mass

²jumble *n* : a disorderly mass or pile

jum·bo \'jəm-bō\ *n, pl* **jumbos** [*Jumbo,* a huge elephant exhibited by P.T. Barnum] : a very large specimen of its kind — **jumbo** *adj*

¹jump \'jəmp\ *vb* **1** : to spring into the air : leap over **2** : to give a start **3** : to rise or increase suddenly or sharply **4** : to make a sudden attack **5** : ANTICIPATE ⟨∼ the gun⟩ **6** : to leave hurriedly and often furtively ⟨∼ town⟩ **7** : to act or move before (as a signal)

²jump *n* **1** : a spring into the air; *esp* : one made for height or distance in a track meet **2** : a sharp sudden increase **3** : an initial advantage

¹jump·er \'jəm-pər\ *n* : one that jumps

²jumper *n* **1** : a loose blouse **2** : a sleeveless one-piece dress worn usu. with a blouse **3** *pl* : a child's sleeveless coverall

jumping bean *n* : a seed of any of several Mexican shrubs that tumbles about because of the movements of the larva of a small moth inside it

jumping–off place \ˌjəm-piŋ-'òf-\ *n* **1** : a remote or isolated place **2** : a place from which an enterprise is launched

jump·suit \'jəmp-ˌsüt\ *n* **1** : a uniform worn by parachutists in jumping **2** : a one-piece garment consisting of a blouse or shirt with attached trousers or shorts

jumpy \'jəm-pē\ *adj* **jump·i·er; -est** : NERVOUS, JITTERY

¹**jun** \'jən\ *n, pl* **jun** — see *won* at MONEY table

²**jun** *abbr* junior

Jun *abbr* June

junc *abbr* junction

jun•co \'jəŋ-kō\ *n, pl* **juncos** *or* **juncoes** : any of several small common pink‑ billed American finches that are largely gray with conspicuous white feathers in the tail

junc•tion \'jəŋk-shən\ *n* **1** : an act of joining **2** : a place or point of meeting ⟨a railroad ∼⟩

junc•ture \'jeŋk-chər\ *n* **1** : JOINT, CONNECTION **2** : UNION **3** : a critical time or state of affairs

June \'jün\ *n* [ME, fr. L *Junius*] : the 6th month of the year having 30 days

jun•gle \'jəŋ-gəl\ *n* **1** : a thick tangled mass of tropical vegetation; *also* : a tract overgrown with vegetation **2** : a place of ruthless struggle for survival

¹**ju•nior** \'jü-nyər\ *adj* **1** : YOUNGER **2** : lower in rank **3** : of or relating to juniors

²**junior** *n* **1** : a person who is younger or of lower rank than another **2** : a student in his next-to-last year (as at a college)

junior college *n* : a school that offers studies corresponding to those of the 1st two years of college

junior high school *n* : a school usu. including grades 7-9

junior varsity *n* : a team whose members lack the experience or qualifications required for the varsity

ju•ni•per \'jü-nə-pər\ *n* : any of various evergreen shrubs or trees related to the pines

¹**junk** \'jəŋk\ *n* **1** : old iron, glass, paper, or waste; *also* : discarded articles **2** : a shoddy product **3** *slang* : NARCOTICS; *esp* : HEROIN — **junky** *adj*

²**junk** *vb* : DISCARD, SCRAP

³**junk** *n* : a ship of Chinese waters with a high poop and overhanging stem

junk•er \'jəŋ-kər\ *n* : something (as an old automobile) ready for scrapping

Jun•ker \'yüŋ-kər\ *n* [G] : a member of the Prussian landed aristocracy

jun•ket \'jəŋ-kət\ *n* **1** : a dessert of sweetened flavored milk set by rennet as a pudding **2** : a trip made by an official at public expense

junk food *n* : food that is high in calories but low in nutritional content

junk•ie *or* **junky** \'jəŋ-kē\ *n, pl* **junkies 1** *slang* : a narcotics peddler or addict **2** : one that derives inordinate pleasure from or is dependent on something ⟨sugar ∼⟩

jun•ta \'hün-tə, 'jənt-ə, 'hən-tə\ *n* [Sp, fr. *junto* joined, fr. L *jungere* to join] : a group of persons controlling a government esp. after a revolutionary seizure of power

Ju•pi•ter \'jü-pət-ər\ *n* : the largest of the planets and the one 5th in order of distance from the sun

Ju•ras•sic \jù-'ras-ik\ *adj* : of, relating to, or being the period of the Mesozoic era between the Triassic and the Cretaceous — **Jurassic** *n*

ju•rid•i•cal \jù-'rid-i-kəl\ *or* **ju•rid•ic** \-ik\ *adj* **1** : of or relating to the administration of justice **2** : LEGAL — **ju•rid•i•cal•ly** \-i-k(ə-)lē\ *adv*

ju•ris•dic•tion \ˌjür-əs-'dik-shən\ *n* **1** : the power, right, or authority to interpret and apply the law **2** : the authority of a sovereign power **3** : the limits or territory within which authority may be exercised — **ju•ris•dic•tion•al** \-sh(ə-)nəl\ *adj*

ju•ris•pru•dence \-'prüd-³ns\ *n* **1** : a system of laws **2** : the science or philosophy of law

ju•rist \'jür-əst\ *n* : one having a thorough knowledge of law

ju•ris•tic \jù-'ris-tik\ *adj* **1** : of or relating to a jurist or jurisprudence **2** : of, relating to, or recognized in law

ju•ror \'jür-ər\ *n* : a member of a jury

¹**ju•ry** \'jür-ē\ *n, pl* **juries 1** : a body of persons sworn to inquire into a matter submitted to them and to give their verdict **2** : a committee for judging and awarding prizes (as at a contest)

²**jury** *adj* : improvised for temporary use esp. in an emergency ⟨a ∼ mast⟩

jury–rig \'jür-ē-ˌrig\ *vb* : to erect, construct, or arrange in a makeshift fashion

¹**just** \'jəst\ *adj* **1** : having a basis in or conforming to fact or reason : REASONABLE ⟨∼ comment⟩ **2** : CORRECT, PROPER ⟨∼ proportions⟩ **3** : morally or legally right ⟨a ∼ title⟩ **4** : DESERVED, MERITED ⟨∼ punishment⟩ **syn** upright,

honorable, conscientious, honest — **just·ly** adv — **just·ness** n

²**just** \(ˌ)jəst, (ˌ)jist\ adv **1** : EXACTLY ⟨~ right⟩ **2** : very recently ⟨has ~ left⟩ **3** : BARELY ⟨lives ~ outside the city⟩ **4** : DIRECTLY ⟨~ across the street⟩ **5** : ONLY ⟨~ a note⟩ **6** : VERY

jus·tice \'jəs-təs\ n **1** : the administration of what is just (as by assigning merited rewards or punishments) **2** : JUDGE **3** : the administration of law **4** : FAIRNESS; also : RIGHTEOUSNESS

justice of the peace : a local magistrate empowered chiefly to try minor cases, to administer oaths, and to perform marriages

jus·ti·fy \'jəs-tə-ˌfī\ vb **-fied; -fy·ing 1** : to prove to be just, right, or reasonable **2** : to pronounce free from guilt or blame **3** : to adjust or arrange spaces in a line of printed text so the

margins are even — **jus·ti·fi·able** adj — **jus·ti·fi·ca·tion** \ˌjəs-tə-fə-'kā-shən\ n

jut \'jət\ vb **jut·ted; jut·ting** : PROJECT, PROTRUDE

jute \'jüt\ n : a strong glossy fiber from a tropical herb used esp. for making sacks and twine

juv abbr juvenile

¹**ju·ve·nile** \'jü-və-ˌnīl, -vən-ᵊl\ adj **1** : showing incomplete development **2** : of, relating to, or characteristic of children or young people

²**juvenile** n **1** : a young person **2** : a young lower animal (as a fish or a bird) **3** : an actor or actress who plays youthful parts

jux·ta·pose \'jək-stə-ˌpōz\ vb **-posed; -pos·ing** : to place side by side — **jux·ta·po·si·tion** \ˌjək-stə-pə-'zish-ən\ n

JV abbr junior varsity

K

¹**k** \'kā\ n, pl **k's** or **ks** \'kāz\ often cap : the 11th letter of the English alphabet

²**k** abbr **1** karat **2** kilogram **3** kitchen **4** knit **5** kosher

¹**K** abbr Kelvin

²**K** symbol **1** [NL kalium] potassium **2** strikeout

ka·bob \'kā-ˌbäb, kə-'bäb\ n : cubes of meat cooked with vegetables usu. on a skewer

Ka·bu·ki \kə-'bü-kē\ n : traditional Japanese popular drama with highly stylized singing and dancing

kad·dish \'käd-ish\ n, often cap : a Jewish prayer recited in the daily synagogue ritual and by mourners at public services after the death of a close relative

kaf·fee·klatsch \'kȯf-ē-ˌklach, 'käf-\ n, often cap [G] : an informal social gathering for coffee and talk

kai·ser \'kī-zər\ n : EMPEROR; esp : the ruler of Germany from 1871 to 1918

kale \'kāl\ n : a hardy cabbage with curled leaves that do not form a head

ka·lei·do·scope \kə-'līd-ə-ˌskōp\ n : an instrument containing loose bits of colored glass between two flat plates and two plane mirrors so placed that

changes of position of the bits of glass are reflected in an endless variety of patterns — **ka·lei·do·scop·ic** \-ˌlīd-ə-'skäp-ik\ adj — **ka·lei·do·scop·i·cal·ly** \-i-k(ə-)lē\ adv

ka·ma·ai·na \ˌkäm-ə-'ī-nə\ n [Hawaiian kama'āina, fr. kama child + 'āina land] : one who has lived in Hawaii for a long time

kame \'kām\ n [Sc, lit., comb] : a short ridge or mound of material deposited by glacial meltwater

ka·mi·ka·ze \ˌkäm-i-'käz-ē\ n [Jp, lit., divine wind] : a member of a corps of Japanese pilots assigned to make a suicidal crash on a target; also : an airplane flown in such an attack

Kan or **Kans** abbr Kansas

kan·ga·roo \ˌkaŋ-gə-'rü\ n, pl **-roos** : any of several large leaping marsupial mammals of Australia with powerful hind legs and a long thick tail

kangaroo court n : a court or an illegal self-appointed tribunal characterized by irresponsible, perverted, or irregular procedures

ka·olin \'kā-ə-lən\ n : a fine usu. white clay used in ceramics and refractories and in medicine in the treatment of diarrhea

ka·pok \ˈkā-ˌpäk\ *n* : silky fiber from the seeds of a tropical tree used esp. as a filling (as for life preservers)

Kap·o·si's sar·co·ma \ˈkap-ə-sēz-sär-ˈkō-mə\ *n* : a serious disease now usu. associated with AIDS that affects esp. the skin and mucous membranes and is characterized usu. by the formation of pink to reddish brown or bluish plaques

ka·put *also* **ka·putt** \kä-ˈpùt, kə-, -ˈpüt\ *adj* [G, fr. F *capot* not having made a trick at piquet] **1** : utterly defeated or destroyed **2** : made useless or unable to function

kar·a·kul \ˈkar-ə-kəl\ *n* : the dark tightly curled pelt of the newborn lamb of an Asian sheep

kar·at \ˈkar-ət\ *n* : a unit for expressing proportion of gold in an alloy equal to 1/24 part of pure gold

ka·ra·te \kə-ˈrät-ē\ *n* [Jp, lit., empty hand] : an art of self-defense in which an attacker is disabled by crippling kicks and punches

kar·ma \ˈkär-mə\ *n, often cap* [Skt] : the force generated by a person's actions held in Hinduism and Buddhism to perpetuate transmigration and to determine his destiny in his next existence — **kar·mic** \-mik\ *adj, often cap*

karst \ˈkärst\ *n* [G] : an irregular limestone region with sinks, underground streams, and caverns

ka·ty·did \ˈkāt-ē-ˌdid\ *n* : any of several large green tree-dwelling American grasshoppers

kay·ak \ˈkī-ˌak\ *n* : an Eskimo canoe made of a skin-covered frame with a small opening and propelled by a double-bladed paddle; *also* : a similar portable boat

kayo \(ˈ)kā-ˈō, ˈkā-ō\ *n* : KNOCKOUT — **kayo** *vb*

ka·zoo \kə-ˈzü\ *n, pl* **kazoos** : a toy musical instrument consisting of a tube with a membrane sealing one end and a side hole to sing or hum into

KB *abbr* kilobyte

kc *abbr* kilocycle

KC *abbr* **1** Kansas City **2** King's Counsel **3** Knights of Columbus

kc/s *abbr* kilocycles per second

KD *abbr* knocked down

ke·bab *or* **ke·bob** \kə-ˈbäb\ *var of* KABOB

¹kedge \ˈkej\ *vb* **kedged; kedg·ing** : to move a ship by hauling on a line attached to a small anchor dropped at the distance and in the direction desired

²kedge *n* : a small anchor

keel \ˈkēl\ *n* **1** : a timber or plate running lengthwise along the center of the bottom of a ship **2** : something (as a bird's breastbone) like a ship's keel in form or use — **keeled** \ˈkēld\ *adj*

keel·boat \ˈkēl-ˌbōt\ *n* : a shallow covered keeled riverboat for freight that is usu. rowed, poled, or towed

keel·haul \-ˌhȯl\ *vb* : to haul under the keel of a ship as punishment

keel over *vb* **1** : OVERTURN, CAPSIZE **2** : FAINT, SWOON

keel·son \ˈkel-sən, ˈkēl-\ *n* : a reinforcing structure above and fastened to a ship's keel

¹keen \ˈkēn\ *adj* **1** : SHARP ⟨a ∼ knife⟩ **2** : SEVERE ⟨a ∼ wind⟩ **3** : ENTHUSIASTIC ⟨∼ about swimming⟩ **4** : mentally alert ⟨a ∼ mind⟩ **5** : STRONG, ACUTE ⟨∼ eyesight⟩ **6** : WONDERFUL, EXCELLENT — **keen·ly** *adv* — **keen·ness** \ˈkēn-nəs\ *n*

²keen *n* : a lamentation for the dead uttered in a loud wailing voice or in a wordless cry — **keen** *vb*

¹keep \ˈkēp\ *vb* **kept** \ˈkept\; **keep·ing** **1** : FULFILL, OBSERVE ⟨∼ a promise⟩ ⟨∼ a holiday⟩ **2** : GUARD ⟨∼ us from harm⟩; *also* : to take care of ⟨∼ a neighbor's children⟩ **3** : MAINTAIN ⟨∼ silence⟩ **4** : to have in one's service or at one's disposal ⟨∼ a horse⟩ **5** : to preserve a record in ⟨∼ a diary⟩ **6** : to have in stock for sale **7** : to retain in one's possession ⟨∼ what you find⟩ **8** : to carry on (as a business) : CONDUCT **9** : HOLD, DETAIN ⟨∼ him in jail⟩ **10** : to refrain from revealing ⟨∼ a secret⟩ **11** : to continue in good condition ⟨meat will ∼ in a freezer⟩ **12** : ABSTAIN, REFRAIN — **keep·er** *n*

²keep *n* **1** : FORTRESS **2** : the means or provisions by which one is kept — **for keeps** **1** : with the provision that one keeps what he wins ⟨play marbles *for keeps*⟩ **2** : PERMANENTLY

keep·ing \ˈkē-piŋ\ *n* : CONFORMITY ⟨in ∼ with good taste⟩

keep·sake \ˈkēp-ˌsāk\ *n* : MEMENTO

keep up *vb* **1** : to persevere in **2** : MAIN-

TAIN, SUSTAIN **3** : to keep informed **4** : to continue without interruption

keg \\'keg\ *n* : a small cask or barrel

keg·ler \\'keg-lər\ *n* : [1]BOWLER

kelp \\'kelp\ *n* : any of various coarse brown seaweeds; *also* : a mass of these or their ashes often used as fertilizer

Kelt \\'kelt\ var of CELT

kel·vin \\'kel-vən\ *n* : a unit of temperature equal to 1/273.16 of the Kelvin scale temperature of the triple point of water and equal to the Celsius degree in size

Kelvin *adj* : relating to, conforming to, or being a temperature scale according to which absolute zero is 0 K, the equivalent of —273.15°C

ken \\'ken\ *n* **1** : range of vision : SIGHT **2** : range of understanding

ken·nel \\'ken-ºl\ *n* : a shelter for a dog or cat; *also* : an establishment for the breeding or boarding of dogs or cats — **kennel** *vb*

ke·no \\'kē-nō\ *n* : a game resembling bingo

Ken·tucky bluegrass \kən-₁tək-ē-\ *n* : a valuable pasture and meadow grass of both Europe and America

Ke·ogh plan \\'kē-(₁)ō-\ *n* [Eugene James *Keogh b*1907 Am. politician] : an individual retirement account for the self-employed

ke·pi \\'kā-pē, 'kep-ē\ *n* [F] : a military cap with a round flat top sloping toward the front and a visor

ker·a·tin \\'ker-ət-ºn\ *n* : any of various sulfur-containing fibrous proteins that form the chemical basis of hair and horny tissues — **ke·ra·ti·nous** \kə-'rat-ºn-əs, ₁ker-ə-'tī-nəs\ *adj*

kerb \\'kərb\ *n, Brit* : CURB

ker·chief \\'kər-chəf, -₁chéf\ *n, pl* **ker·chiefs** \-chəfs, -₁chéfs\ *also* **kerchieves** \-₁chēvz\ [ME *courchef,* fr. OF *cuevrechief,* fr. *covrir* to cover + *chief* head] **1** : a square of cloth worn by women esp. as a head covering **2** : HANDKERCHIEF

kerf \\'kərf\ *n* : a slit or notch made by a saw or cutting torch

ker·nel \\'kərn-ºl\ *n* **1** : the inner softer part of a seed, fruit stone, or nut **2** : a whole seed of a cereal **3** : a central or essential part : CORE

ker·o·sene *or* **ker·o·sine** \\'ker-ə-₁sēn, ₁ker-ə-'sēn, 'kar-, ₁kar-\ *n* : a thin oil produced from petroleum and used for a fuel and as a solvent

ketch \\'kech\ *n* : a large fore-and-aft rigged boat with two masts

ketch·up var of CATSUP

ket·tle \\'ket-ºl\ *n* : a metallic vessel for boiling liquids

ket·tle·drum \-₁drəm\ *n* : a brass or copper drum with parchment stretched across the top

[1]**key** \\'kē\ *n* **1** : a usu. metal instrument by which the bolt of a lock is turned; *also* : a device having the form or function of a key **2** : a means of gaining or preventing entrance, possession, or control **3** : EXPLANATION, SOLUTION **4** : one of the levers pressed by a finger in operating or playing an instrument **5** : a leading individual or principle **6** : a system of seven tones based on their relationship to a tonic; *also* : the tone or pitch of a voice **7** : a small switch for opening or closing an electric circuit

[2]**key** *vb* **1** : SECURE, FASTEN **2** : to regulate the musical pitch of **3** : to bring into harmony or conformity **4** : to make nervous — usu. used with *up*

[3]**key** *adj* : BASIC, CENTRAL ⟨∼ issues⟩

[4]**key** *n* : a low island or reef (as off the southern coast of Florida)

[5]**key** *n, slang* : a kilogram esp. of marijuana or heroin

key·board \-₁bōrd\ *n* **1** : a row of keys (as on a piano) **2** : an assemblage of keys for operating a machine

key club *n* : a private club serving liquor and providing entertainment

key·hole \\'kē-₁hōl\ *n* : a hole for receiving a key

[1]**key·note** \-₁nōt\ *n* **1** : the first and harmonically fundamental tone of a scale **2** : the central fact, idea, or mood

[2]**keynote** *vb* **1** : to set the keynote of **2** : to deliver the major address (as at a convention) — **key·not·er** *n*

key·punch \\'kē-₁pənch\ *n* : a machine with a keyboard used to cut holes or notches in punch cards — **keypunch** *vb* — **key·punch·er** *n*

key·stone \\'kē-₁stōn\ *n* : the wedge-shaped piece at the crown of an arch that locks the other pieces in place

key word *n* : a word that is a key; *esp*

: a word exemplifying the meaning or value of a letter or symbol

kg *abbr* kilogram

KGB *abbr* [Russ *Komitet Gosudarstvennoi Bezopasnosti*] (Soviet) State Security Committee

kha·ki \'kak-ē, 'käk-\ *n* [Hindi *khaki* dust-colored, fr. *khāk* dust, fr. Per] **1** : a light yellowish brown **2** : a khaki‑colored cloth; *also* : a military uniform of this cloth

khan \'kän, 'kan\ *n* : a Mongol leader; *esp* : a successor of Genghis Khan

khe·dive \kə-'dēv\ *n* : a ruler of Egypt from 1867 to 1914 governing as a viceroy of the sultan of Turkey

khoum \'küm\ *n* — see *ouguiya* at MONEY table

kHz *abbr* kilohertz

KIA *abbr* killed in action

kib·ble \'kib-əl\ *vb* **kib·bled; kib·bling** : to grind coarsely — **kibble** *n*

kib·butz \kib-'üts, -'üts\ *n, pl* **kib·but·zim** \-ˌüt-'sēm, -ˌüt-\ [NHeb *qibbūṣ*] : a collective farm or settlement in Israel

ki·bitz·er \'kib-ət-sər, kə-'bit-\ *n* [Yiddish] : one who looks on and usu. offers unwanted advice esp. at a card game — **kib·itz** \'kib-əts\ *vb*

ki·bosh \'kī-ˌbäsh\ *n* : something that serves as a check or stop ⟨put the ~ on his plan⟩

¹kick \'kik\ *vb* **1** : to strike out or hit with the foot; *also* : to score by kicking a ball **2** : to object strongly **3** : to recoil when fired — **kick·er** *n*

²kick *n* **1** : a blow or thrust with the foot; *esp* : a propelling of a ball with the foot **2** : the recoil of a gun **3** : a feeling or expression of objection **4** : stimulating effect esp. of pleasure

kick·back \'kik-ˌbak\ *n* **1** : a sharp violent reaction **2** : a secret return of a part of a sum received

kick in *vb* **1** : CONTRIBUTE **2** *slang* : DIE

kick·off \'kik-ˌöf\ *n* **1** : a kick that puts the ball in play (as in football) **2** : COMMENCEMENT

kick off *vb* **1** : to start or resume play with a placekick **2** : to begin proceedings **3** *slang* : DIE

kick over *vb* : to begin or cause to begin to fire — used of an internal-combustion engine

kick·shaw \'kik-ˌshö\ *n* [fr. F *quelque chose* something] **1** : DELICACY **2** : BAUBLE

kick·stand \'kik-ˌstand\ *n* : a swiveling metal bar attached to a 2-wheeled vehicle for holding it up when not in use

kicky \'kik-ē\ *adj* : providing a kick or thrill : EXCITING

¹kid \'kid\ *n* **1** : a young goat **2** : the flesh, fur, or skin of a young goat; *also* : something (as leather) made of kid **3** : CHILD, YOUNGSTER — **kid·dish** \'kid-ish\ *adj*

²kid *vb* **kid·ded; kid·ding 1** : FOOL **2** : TEASE — **kid·der** *n* — **kid·ding·ly** \'kid-iŋ-lē\ *adv*

kid·nap \'kid-ˌnap\ *vb* **-napped** *or* **-naped** \-ˌnapt\; **-nap·ping** *or* **-nap·ing** : to hold or carry a person away by unlawful force or by fraud and against his will — **kid·nap·per** *or* **kid·nap·er** *n*

kid·ney \'kid-nē\ *n, pl* **kidneys 1** : either of a pair of organs lying near the backbone that excrete waste products of the body in the form of urine **2** : TEMPERAMENT; *also* : SORT

kidney bean *n* **1** : an edible seed of the common cultivated bean; *esp* : one that is large and dark red **2** : a plant bearing kidney beans

kid·skin \'kid-ˌskin\ *n* : the skin of a young goat used for leather

kiel·ba·sa \k(y)el-'bäs-ə, kil-\ *n, pl* **-basas** *also* **-ba·sy** \-'bäs-ē\ : a smoked sausage of Polish origin

kie·sel·guhr *or* **kie·sel·gur** \'kē-zəl-ˌgùr\ *n* : loose or porous diatomite

¹kill \'kil\ *vb* **1** : to deprive of life **2** : to put an end to ⟨~ competition⟩; *also* : DEFEAT ⟨~ a proposed amendment⟩ **3** : USE UP ⟨~ time⟩ **4** : to mark for omission **syn** slay, murder, assassinate, execute — **kill·er** *n*

²kill *n* **1** : an act of killing **2** : an animal or animals killed (as in a hunt); *also* : an aircraft, ship, or vehicle destroyed by military action

kill·deer \'kil-ˌdiər\ *n, pl* **killdeers** *or* **killdeer** [imit.] : a plover of temperate No. America with a plaintive penetrating cry

kill·ing \'kil-iŋ\ *n* : a sudden notable gain or profit

kill·joy \'kil-ˌjöi\ *n* : one who spoils the pleasures of others

kiln \'kil(n)\ *n* : a heated enclosure (as an oven) for processing a substance by burning, firing, or drying — **kiln** *vb*

ki·lo \'kē-lō\ *n, pl* **kilos** : KILOGRAM

ki·lo·byte \'kil-ə-ˌbīt, 'kē-lə-\ *n* : 1024 bytes

kilo·cy·cle \'kil-ə-ˌsī-kəl\ *n* : KILOHERTZ

ki·lo·gram \'kē-lə-ˌgram, 'kil-ə-\ *n* : the basic metric unit of mass and weight — see METRIC SYSTEM table

ki·lo·hertz \'kil-ə-ˌhərts, 'kē-lə-, -ˌherts\ *n* : 1000 hertz

kilo·li·ter \'kil-ə-ˌlēt-ər\ *n* — see METRIC SYSTEM table

ki·lo·me·ter \kil-'äm-ət-ər, 'kil-ə-ˌmēt-\ *n* — see METRIC SYSTEM table

ki·lo·ton \'kil-ə-ˌtən, 'kē-lō-\ *n* **1** : 1000 tons **2** : an explosive force equivalent to that of 1000 tons of TNT

ki·lo·volt \-ˌvōlt\ *n* : 1000 volts

kilo·watt \'kil-ə-ˌwät\ *n* : 1000 watts

kilowatt–hour *n* : a unit of energy equal to that expended by one kilowatt in one hour

kilt \'kilt\ *n* : a knee-length pleated skirt usu. of tartan worn by men in Scotland

kil·ter \'kil-tər\ *n* : proper condition ⟨out of ∼⟩

ki·mo·no \kə-'mō-nə\ *n, pl* **-nos 1** : a loose robe with wide sleeves traditionally worn with a wide sash as an outer garment by the Japanese **2** : a loose dressing gown or jacket

kin \'kin\ *n* **1** : an individual's relatives **2** : KINSMAN

ki·na \'kē-nə\ *n* — see MONEY table

¹**kind** \'kīnd\ *n* **1** : essential quality or character **2** : a group united by common traits or interests : CATEGORY; *also* : VARIETY **3** : goods or commodities as distinguished from money

²**kind** *adj* **1** : of a sympathetic, forbearing, or pleasant nature ⟨∼ friends⟩ **2** : arising from sympathy or forbearance ⟨∼ deeds⟩ **syn** benevolent, benign, benignant, kindly — **kind·ness** \'kīn(d)-nəs\ *n*

kin·der·gar·ten \'kin-dər-ˌgärt-ᵊn\ *n* [Ger, lit., children's garden] : a school or class for children usu. from four to six years old

kin·der·gart·ner \-ˌgärt-nər\ *n* **1** : a kindergarten pupil **2** : a kindergarten teacher

kind·heart·ed \'kīnd-'härt-əd\ *adj* : marked by a sympathetic nature

kin·dle \'kin-dᵊl\ *vb* **kin·dled; kin·dling**

\-(d)liŋ, -dᵊl-iŋ\ **1** : to set on fire : start burning **2** : to stir up : AROUSE **3** : ILLUMINATE, GLOW

kin·dling \'kin-(d)liŋ, 'kin-lən\ *n* : easily combustible material for starting a fire

¹**kind·ly** \'kīn-dlē\ *adj* **kind·li·er; -est 1** : of an agreeable or beneficial nature **2** : of a sympathetic or generous nature ⟨∼ men⟩ — **kind·li·ness** *n*

²**kindly** *adv* **1** : READILY ⟨does not take ∼ to criticism⟩ **2** : SYMPATHETICALLY **3** : COURTEOUSLY, OBLIGINGLY

kind of \ˌkīn-də(v)\ *adv* : to a moderate degree ⟨it's *kind of* late to begin⟩

¹**kin·dred** \'kin-drəd\ *n* **1** : a group of related individuals **2** : one's relatives

²**kindred** *adj* : of a like nature or character

kine \'kīn\ *archaic* pl of COW

ki·ne·mat·ics \ˌkin-ə-'mat-iks\ *n* : a science that deals with motion apart from considerations of mass and force — **ki·ne·mat·ic** \-ik\ *or* **ki·ne·mat·i·cal** \-i-kəl\ *adj*

kin·e·scope \'kin-ə-ˌskōp\ *n* **1** : PICTURE TUBE **2** : a moving picture made from the image on a picture tube

kin·es·the·sia \ˌkin-əs-'thē-zh(ē-)ə\ *or* **kin·es·the·sis** \-'thē-səs\ *n, pl* **-the·sias** *or* **-the·ses** \-ˌsēz\ : a sense mediated by nervous elements in muscles, tendons, and joints and stimulated by bodily movements and tensions; *also* : sensory experience derived from this source — **kin·es·thet·ic** \-'thet-ik\ *adj*

ki·net·ic \kə-'net-ik\ *adj* : of or relating to the motion of material bodies and the forces and energy (**kinetic energy**) associated with them

ki·net·ics \kə-'net-iks\ *n sing or pl* : a science that deals with the effects of forces upon the motions of material bodies or with changes in a physical or chemical system

kin·folk \'kin-ˌfōk\ *or* **kinfolks** *n pl* : RELATIVES

king \'kiŋ\ *n* **1** : a male sovereign **2** : a chief among competitors ⟨home-run ∼⟩ **3** : the principal piece in the game of chess **4** : a playing card bearing the figure of a king **5** : a checker that has been crowned — **king·less** *adj* — **king·ly** *adj* — **king·ship** *n*

king·bolt \-ˌbōlt\ *n* : a vertical bolt by

which the forward axle and wheels of a vehicle are connected to the other parts

king crab *n* **1** : HORSESHOE CRAB **2** : any of several very large crabs

king·dom \'kiŋ-dəm\ *n* **1** : a country whose head is a king or queen **2** : a realm or region in which something or someone is dominant ⟨a cattle ∼⟩ **3** : one of the three primary divisions of lifeless material, plants, and animals into which natural objects are grouped

king·fish·er \-ˌfish-ər\ *n* : a bright-colored crested bird that feeds chiefly on fish

king·pin \'kiŋ-ˌpin\ *n* **1** : any of several bowling pins **2** : the leader in a group or undertaking **3** : KINGBOLT

Kings *n* — see BIBLE table

king–size \'kiŋ-ˌsīz\ *or* **king–sized** \-ˌsīzd\ *adj* **1** : longer than the regular or standard size **2** : unusually large **3** : having dimensions of about 76 by 80 inches ⟨a ∼ bed⟩; *also* : of a size that fits a king-size bed

kink \'kiŋk\ *n* **1** : a short tight twist or curl **2** : a mental peculiarity : QUIRK **3** : CRAMP ⟨a ∼ in the back⟩ **4** : an imperfection likely to cause difficulties in operation — **kinky** *adj*

kin·ship \'kin-ˌship\ *n* : RELATIONSHIP

kins·man \'kinz-mən\ *n* : RELATIVE; *esp* : a male relative

kins·wom·an \-ˌwum-ən\ *n* : a female relative

ki·osk \'kē-ˌäsk\ *n* : a small structure with one or more open sides

Ki·o·wa \'kī-ə-ˌwȯ, -ˌwä, -ˌwā\ *n, pl* **Kiowa** *or* **Kiowas** : a member of an American Indian people of Colorado, Kansas, New Mexico, Oklahoma, and Texas

¹kip \'kip\ *n* : the undressed hide of a young or small animal

²kip \'kip, 'gip\ *n, pl* **kip** *or* **kips** — see MONEY table

kip·per \'kip-ər\ *n* : a fish (as a herring) preserved by salting and drying or smoking — **kipper** *vb*

kirk \'kərk, 'kirk\ *n, chiefly Scot* : CHURCH

kir·tle \'kərt-ᵊl\ *n* : a long gown or dress worn by women

kis·met \'kiz-ˌmet, -mət\ *n, often cap*

[Turk, fr. Ar *qismah* portion, lot] : FATE

¹kiss \'kis\ *vb* **1** : to touch or caress with the lips as a mark of affection or greeting **2** : to touch gently or lightly

²kiss *n* **1** : a caress with the lips **2** : a gentle touch or contact **3** : a bite-size candy

kiss·er \'kis-ər\ *n* **1** : one that kisses **2** *slang* : MOUTH **3** *slang* : FACE

kit \'kit\ *n* **1** : a set of articles for personal use; *also* : a set of tools or implements or of parts to be assembled **2** : a container (as a case) for a kit

kitch·en \'kich-ən\ *n* **1** : a room with cooking facilities **2** : the personnel that prepares, cooks, and serves food

kitch·en·ette \ˌkich-ə-'net\ *n* : a small kitchen or an alcove containing cooking facilities

kitchen police *n* **1** : KP **2** : the work of KPs

kitch·en·ware \'kich-ən-ˌwaər\ *n* : utensils and appliances for use in a kitchen

kite \'kīt\ *n* **1** : any of various hawks with deeply forked tails **2** : a light frame covered with paper or cloth and designed to be flown in the air at the end of a long string

kith \'kith\ *n* [ME, fr. OE *cȳthth*, fr. *cūth* known] : familiar friends, neighbors, or relatives ⟨∼ and kin⟩

kitsch \'kich\ *n* [G] : shoddy or cheap artistic or literary material

kit·ten \'kit-ᵊn\ *n* : a young cat — **kitten·ish** *adj*

¹kit·ty \'kit-ē\ *n, pl* **kitties** : CAT; *esp* : KITTEN

²kitty *n, pl* **kitties** : a fund in a poker game made up of contributions from each pot; *also* : POOL

kit·ty–cor·ner *or* **kit·ty–cor·nered** *var of* CATERCORNER

ki·wi \'kē-(ˌ)wē\ *n* : a flightless New Zealand bird

ki·wi·fruit \-ˌfrüt\ *n* : a brownish hairy egg-shaped fruit with sweet bright green flesh and small edible black seeds

KJV *abbr* King James Version

KKK *abbr* Ku Klux Klan

kl *abbr* kiloliter

klatch *or* **klatsch** \'klach\ *n* [G *klatsch* gossip] : a gathering marked by informal conversation

klep·to·ma·nia \ˌklep-tə-'mā-nē-ə\ *n* : a persistent neurotic impulse to steal esp. without economic motive — **klep·to·ma·ni·ac** \-nē-ˌak\ *n*

klieg light *or* **kleig light** \'klēg-\ *n* : a very bright lamp used in making motion pictures

km *abbr* kilometer

kn *abbr* knot

knack \'nak\ *n* **1** : a clever way of doing something **2** : natural aptitude

knap·sack \'nap-ˌsak\ *n* : a usu. canvas or leather bag or case strapped on the back and used esp. for carrying supplies (as on a hike)

knave \'nāv\ *n* **1** : ROGUE **2** : JACK 6 — **knav·ery** \'nāv-(ə-)rē\ *n* — **knav·ish** \'nā-vish\ *adj*

knead \'nēd\ *vb* : to work and press into a mass with the hands; *also* : MASSAGE — **knead·er** *n*

knee \'nē\ *n* : the joint in the middle part of the leg — **kneed** \'nēd\ *adj*

knee·cap \'nē-ˌkap\ *n* : a thick flat movable bone forming the front of the knee

knee·hole \-ˌhōl\ *n* : a space (as under a desk) for the knees

kneel \'nēl\ *vb* **knelt** \'nelt\ *or* **kneeled; kneel·ing** : to bend the knee : fall or rest on the knees

¹knell \'nel\ *vb* **1** : to ring esp. for a death or disaster **2** : to summon, announce, or proclaim by a knell

²knell *n* **1** : a stroke of a bell esp. when tolled (as for a funeral) **2** : an indication of the end or failure of something

knew past of KNOW

knick·ers \'nik-ərz\ *n pl* : loose-fitting short pants gathered at the knee

knick·knack \'nik-ˌnak\ *n* : a small trivial article intended for ornament

¹knife \'nīf\ *n, pl* **knives** \'nīvz\ **1** : a cutting instrument consisting of a sharp blade fastened to a handle **2** : a sharp cutting tool in a machine

²knife *vb* **knifed; knif·ing** : to stab, slash, or wound with a knife

¹knight \'nīt\ *n* **1** : a mounted warrior of feudal times serving a king **2** : a man honored by a sovereign for merit and in Great Britain ranking below a baronet **3** : a man devoted to the service of a lady **4** : a member of an order or society **5** : a chess piece having a move of two squares to a square of the opposite color — **knight·ly** *adj*

²knight *vb* : to make a knight of

knight·hood \'nīt-ˌhud\ *n* **1** : the rank, dignity, or profession of a knight **2** : CHIVALRY **3** : knights as a class or body

knish \kə-'nish\ *n* [Yiddish] : a small round or square of dough stuffed with a filling (as of meat or fruit) and baked or fried

¹knit \'nit\ *vb* **knit** *or* **knit·ted; knit·ting 1** : to link firmly or closely **2** : WRINKLE ⟨∼ her brows⟩ **3** : to form a fabric by interlacing yarn or thread in connected loops with needles **4** : to grow together — **knit·ter** *n*

²knit *n* **1** : a basic knitting stitch **2** : a knitted garment or fabric

knit·wear \-ˌwaər\ *n* : knitted clothing

knob \'näb\ *n* **1** : a rounded protuberance; *also* : a small rounded ornament or handle **2** : a rounded usu. isolated hill — **knobbed** \'näbd\ *adj* — **knob·by** \'näb-ē\ *adj*

¹knock \'näk\ *vb* **1** : to strike with a sharp blow **2** : BUMP, COLLIDE **3** : to make a pounding noise; *esp* : to have engine knock **4** : to find fault with

²knock *n* **1** : a sharp blow **2** : a pounding noise; *esp* : one caused by abnormal ignition in an engine

knock·down \'näk-ˌdaun\ *n* **1** : the action of knocking down **2** : something (as a blow) that knocks down **3** : something that can be easily assembled or disassembled

knock down \-'daun\ *vb* **1** : to strike to the ground with or as if with as sharp blow **2** : to take apart : DISASSEMBLE **3** : to receive an income or salary : EARN **4** : to make a reduction in

knock·er \'näk-ər\ *n* : one that knocks; *esp* : a device hinged to a door for use in knocking

knock–knee \'näk-'nē, -ˌnē\ *n* : a condition in which the legs curve inward at the knees — **knock–kneed** \-'nēd\ *adj*

knock off *vb* **1** : to stop doing something **2** : to do quickly, carelessly, or routinely **3** : to deduct from a price **4** : KILL **5** : ROB

knock·out \'näk-ˌaut\ *n* **1** : a blow that fells and immobilizes an opponent (as in boxing) **2** : something sensationally striking or attractive

knock out \-'aút\ *vb* **1** : to defeat by a knockout **2** : to make unconscious or inoperative **3** : to tire out : EXHAUST

knock•wurst *or* **knack•wurst** \'näk-ˌwərst, -ˌvú(r)st\ *n* : a short thick heavily seasoned sausage

knoll \'nōl\ *n* : a small round hill

¹**knot** \'nät\ *n* **1** : an interlacing (as of string or ribbon) that forms a lump or knob **2** : PROBLEM **3** : a bond of union; *esp* : the marriage bond **4** : a protuberant lump or swelling in tissue; *also* : the base of a woody branch enclosed in the stem from which it arises **5** : GROUP, CLUSTER **6** : an ornamental bow of ribbon **7** : one nautical mile per hour; *also* : one nautical mile — **knot•ty** *adj*

²**knot** *vb* **knot•ted; knot•ting 1** : to tie in or with a knot **2** : ENTANGLE

knot•hole \-ˌhōl\ *n* : a hole in a board or tree trunk where a knot has come out

knout \'naút, 'nüt\ *n* : a whip used for flogging

know \'nō\ *vb* **knew** \'n(y)ü\; **known** \'nōn\; **know•ing 1** : to perceive directly : have understanding or direct cognition of; *also* : to recognize the nature of **2** : to be acquainted or familiar with **3** : to be aware of the truth of **4** : to have a practical understanding of — **know•able** *adj* — **know•er** *n* — **in the know** : possessing confidential information

know–how \'nō-ˌhaú\ *n* : knowledge of how to do something smoothly and efficiently

know•ing \'nō-iŋ\ *adj* **1** : having or reflecting knowledge, intelligence, or information **2** : shrewdly and keenly alert **3** : DELIBERATE, INTENTIONAL **syn** intelligent, clever, bright, smart — **know•ing•ly** *adv*

knowl•edge \'näl-ij\ *n* **1** : understanding gained by actual experience ⟨a ∼ of carpentry⟩ **2** : range of information ⟨within my ∼⟩ **3** : clear perception of truth **4** : something learned and kept in the mind

knowl•edge•able \-ə-bəl\ *adj* : having or showing knowledge or intelligence

knuck•le \'nək-əl\ *n* : the rounded knob at a joint and esp. at a finger joint

knuck•le•bone \'nək-əl-ˌbōn\ *n* : one of the bones forming a knuckle

knuckle down *vb* : to apply oneself earnestly

knuckle under *vb* : SUBMIT, SURRENDER

knurl \'nərl\ *n* **1** : KNOB **2** : one of a series of small ridges on a metal surface to aid in gripping — **knurled** \'nərld\ *adj*

¹**KO** \(')kā-'ō, 'kā-ō\ *n* : KNOCKOUT

²**KO** *vb* **KO'd** \kā-'ōd, 'kā-ōd\; **KO'•ing** \-'ō-iŋ, -ō-\ : to knock out in boxing

ko•ala \kō-'äl-ə\ *n* : a gray furry Australian marsupial with large hairy ears that feeds on eucalyptus leaves

ko•bo \'kō-(ˌ)bō\ *n, pl* **kobo** — see *naira* at MONEY table

K of C *abbr* Knights of Columbus

kohl•ra•bi \kōl-'räb-ē\ *n, pl* **-bies** [G, fr. It *cavolo rapa*, lit., cabbage turnip] : a cabbage that forms no head but has a swollen fleshy edible stem

ko•lin•sky \kə-'lin-skē\ *n, pl* **-skies** : the fur of various Asian minks

kook \'kük\ *n* : SCREWBALL 2

kooky *also* **kook•ie** \'kü-kē\ *adj* **kook•i•er; -est** : having the characteristics of a kook — **kook•i•ness** *n*

ko•peck *or* **ko•pek** \'kō-ˌpek\ *n* — see *ruble* at MONEY table

Ko•ran \kə-'ran, -'rän\ *n* [Ar *qur'ān*] : a book of sacred writings accepted by Muslims as revelations made to Muhammad by Allah

Ko•re•an \kə-'rē-ən\ *n* : a native or inhabitant of Korea — **Korean** *adj*

ko•ru•na \'kòr-ə-ˌnä\ *n, pl* **ko•ru•ny** \-ə-nē\ *or* **korunas** *or* **ko•rum** \'kòr-əm\ — see MONEY table

ko•sher \'kō-shər\ *adj* [Yiddish, fr. Heb *kāshēr* fit, proper] : ritually fit for use according to Jewish law; *also* : selling or serving such food

kow•tow \kaú-'taú, 'kaú-ˌtaú\ *vb* [Chin *k'o¹ t'ou²*, fr. *k'o¹* to bump + *t'ou²* head] **1** : to show obsequious deference **2** : to kneel and touch the forehead to the ground as a sign of homage or deep respect

KP \(')kā-'pē\ *n* **1** : enlisted persons detailed to help the cooks in a military mess **2** : the work of KPs

kph *abbr* kilometers per hour

Kr *symbol* krypton

kraal \'kräl, 'kròl\ *n* **1** : a village of southern African natives **2** : an enclosure for domestic animals in southern Africa

kraut \'kraut\ *n* : SAUERKRAUT

Krem·lin \'krem-lən\ *n* : the Russian government

Krem·lin·ol·o·gist \ˌkrem-lə-'näl-ə-jəst\ *n* : a specialist in the policies and practices of the Soviet government

¹**kro·na** \'krō-nə\ *n, pl* **kro·nor** \-ˌnȯr\ [Sw] — see MONEY table

²**kro·na** \'krō-nə\ *n, pl* **kro·nur** \-nər\ [Icel] — see MONEY table

kro·ne \'krō-nə\ *n, pl* **kro·ner** \-nər\ — see MONEY table

Kru·ger·rand \'krü-gə(r)-ˌrand, -ˌränd\ *n* : a 1-ounce gold coin of the Republic of South Africa equal in bullion value to 25 rand and having an official price of 31 rand

kryp·ton \'krip-ˌtän\ *n* : a gaseous chemical element that occurs in small quantities in air and is used in electric lamps

KS *abbr* Kansas

kt *abbr* 1 karat 2 knight

ku·do \'k(y)üd-ō\ *n, pl* **kudos** [fr. *kudos* (taken as pl.)] 1 : AWARD, HONOR 2 : COMPLIMENT, PRAISE

ku·dos \'k(y)ü-ˌdäs\ *n* : fame and renown resulting from achievement

kud·zu \'kùd-zü\ *n* [Jp *kuzu*] : a creeping vine widely grown for hay and forage and for erosion control

ku·lak \k(y)ü-'lak\ *n* [Russ., lit., fist] 1 : a wealthy peasant farmer in 19th century Russia 2 : a farmer characterized by Communists as too wealthy

kum·quat \'kəm-ˌkwät\ *n* [Chin *kam kwat*, fr. *kam* gold + *kwat* orange] : a small citrus fruit with sweet spongy rind and acid pulp

kung fu \ˌkəŋ-'fü, ˌkuŋ-\ *n* : a Chinese art of self-defense resembling karate

ku·rus \kə-'rüsh\ *n, pl* **kurus** — see *lira* at MONEY table

kv *abbr* kilovolt

kw *abbr* kilowatt

kwa·cha \'kwäch-ə\ *n, pl* **kwacha** — see MONEY table

kwan·za \'kwän-zə\ *n, pl* **kwanzas** *or* **kwanza** — see MONEY table

kwash·i·or·kor \ˌkwäsh-ē-'ȯr-kȯr, -ȯr-'kȯr\ *n* : a disease of young children resulting from deficient intake of protein

kwhr *or* **kwh** *abbr* kilowatt-hour

Ky *or* **KY** *abbr* Kentucky

kyat \'chät\ *n* — see MONEY table

L

¹**l** \'el\ *n, pl* **l's** *or* **ls** \'elz\ *often cap* : the 12th letter of the English alphabet

²**l** *abbr, often cap* 1 lake 2 large 3 left 4 [L *libra*] pound 5 line 6 liter

¹**La** *abbr* Louisiana

²**La** *symbol* lanthanum

LA *abbr* 1 law agent 2 Los Angeles 3 Louisiana

lab \'lab\ *n* : LABORATORY

Lab *abbr* Labrador

¹**la·bel** \'lā-bəl\ *n* 1 : a slip attached to something for identification or description 2 : a descriptive or identifying word or phrase 3 : BRAND 3

²**label** *vb* **-beled** *or* **-belled; -bel·ing** *or* **-bel·ling** \-b(ə-)liŋ\ 1 : to affix a label to 2 : to describe or name with a label

la·bi·al \'lā-bē-əl\ *adj* : of or relating to the lips or labia

la·bia ma·jo·ra \ˌlā-bē-ə-mə-'jȯr-ə\ *n pl* : the outer fatty folds of the vulva

labia mi·no·ra \-mə-'nōr-ə\ *n pl* : the inner highly vascular folds of the vulva

la·bile \'lā-ˌbīl, -bəl\ *adj* 1 : UNSTABLE 2 : ADAPTABLE

la·bi·um \'lā-bē-əm\ *n, pl* **la·bia** \-ə\ [NL, fr. L, lip] : any of the folds at the margin of the vulva

¹**la·bor** \'lā-bər\ *n* 1 : physical or mental effort; *also* : human activity that provides the goods or services in an economy 2 : the physical activities involved in parturition 3 : TASK 4 : those who do manual labor or work for wages; *also* : labor unions or their officials

²**labor** *vb* **la·bored; la·bor·ing** \-b(ə-)riŋ\ 1 : WORK 2 : to move with great effort 3 : to be in the labor of giving birth 4 : to suffer from some disadvantage or distress ⟨∼ under a delusion⟩ 5 : to treat or work out laboriously — **la·bor·er** *n*

lab·o·ra·to·ry \'lab-(ə-)rə-ˌtōr-ē\ *n, pl*

-ries : a place equipped for making scientific experiments or tests

Labor Day *n* : the 1st Monday in September observed as a legal holiday in recognition of the working people

la·bored \'lā-bərd\ *adj* : not freely or easily done ⟨∼ breathing⟩

la·bo·ri·ous \lə-'bōr-ē-əs\ *adj* **1** : INDUSTRIOUS **2** : requiring great effort — **la·bo·ri·ous·ly** *adv*

la·bor·sav·ing \'lā-bər-ˌsā-viŋ\ *adj* : designed to replace or decrease labor

la·bour *chiefly Brit var of* LABOR

lab·ra·dor·ite \'lab-rə-ˌdȯr-ˌīt\ *n* : a feldspar showing a play of several colors

Lab·ra·dor retriever \'lab-rə-ˌdȯr-\ *n* : a strongly built retriever having a short dense black, yellow, or chocolate coat

la·bur·num \lə-'bər-nəm\ *n* : a leguminous shrub or tree with hanging clusters of yellow flowers

lab·y·rinth \'lab-ə-ˌrinth\ *n* : a place constructed of or filled with confusing intricate passageways : MAZE — **lab·y·rin·thine** \ˌlab-ə-'rin-thən\ *adj*

lac \'lak\ *n* : a resinous substance secreted by a scale insect and used in the manufacture of shellac and lacquers

¹lace \'lās\ *vb* **laced; lac·ing 1** : TIE **2** : to adorn with lace **3** : INTERTWINE **4** : BEAT, LASH **5** : to give zest or savor to

²lace *n* [ME, fr. OF *laz,* fr. L *laqueus* snare, noose] **1** : a cord or string used for drawing together two edges **2** : an ornamental braid **3** : a fine openwork usu. figured fabric made of thread — **lacy** \'lā-sē\ *adj*

lac·er·ate \'las-ə-ˌrāt\ *vb* **-at·ed; -at·ing** : to tear roughly — **lac·er·a·tion** \ˌlas-ə-'rā-shən\ *n*

lace·wing \'lās-ˌwiŋ\ *n* : any of various insects with delicate wing veins, long antennae, and brilliant eyes

lach·ry·mose \'lak-rə-ˌmōs\ *adj* **1** : TEARFUL **2** : MOURNFUL

¹lack \'lak\ *vb* **1** : to be wanting or missing **2** : to be deficient in

²lack *n* : the fact or state of being wanting or deficient : NEED

lack·a·dai·si·cal \ˌlak-ə-'dā-zi-kəl\ *adj* : lacking life, spirit, or zest — **lack·a·dai·si·cal·ly** \-k(ə-)lē\ *adv*

lack·ey \'lak-ē\ *n, pl* **lackeys 1** : a liveried retainer **2** : TOADY

lack·lus·ter \'lak-ˌləs-tər\ *adj* : DULL

la·con·ic \lə-'kän-ik\ *adj* [L *laconicus* Spartan, fr. Gk *lakōnikos;* fr. the Spartan reputation for terseness of speech] : sparing of words : TERSE — **la·con·i·cal·ly** \-i-k(ə-)lē\ *adv*

lac·quer \'lak-ər\ *n* : a clear or colored usu. glossy and quick-drying surface coating that contains natural or synthetic substances — **lacquer** *vb*

lac·ri·mal *also* **lach·ry·mal** \'lak-rə-məl\ *adj* : of, relating to, or being the glands that produce tears

lac·ri·ma·tion \ˌlak-rə-'mā-shən\ *n* : secretion of tears

la·crosse \lə-'krȯs\ *n* [CanF *la crosse,* lit., the crosier] : a game played on a field by two teams with a hard ball and long-handled rackets

lac·tate \'lak-ˌtāt\ *vb* **lac·tat·ed; lac·tat·ing** : to secrete milk — **lac·ta·tion** \lak-'tā-shən\ *n*

lac·tic \'lak-tik\ *adj* **1** : of or relating to milk **2** : formed in the souring of milk

lactic acid *n* : a syrupy acid present in blood and muscle tissue, produced by bacterial fermentation of carbohydrates, and used in food and medicine

lac·tose \'lak-ˌtōs\ *n* : a sugar present in milk

la·cu·na \lə-'k(y)ü-nə\ *n, pl* **la·cu·nae** \-nē\ *or* **la·cu·nas** [L, pool, pit, gap, fr. *lacus* lake] : a blank space or missing part : GAP

lad \'lad\ *n* : YOUTH; *also* : FELLOW

lad·der \'lad-ər\ *n* : a device for climbing that consists of two parallel sidepieces joined at intervals by crosspieces

lad·die \'lad-ē\ *n* : a young lad

lad·en \'lād-ᵊn\ *adj* : LOADED, BURDENED

lad·ing \'lād-iŋ\ *n* : CARGO, FREIGHT

la·dle \'lād-ᵊl\ *n* : a deep-bowled long-handled spoon used in taking up and conveying liquids — **ladle** *vb*

la·dy \'lād-ē\ *n, pl* **ladies** [ME, fr. OE *hlǣfdīge,* fr. *hlāf* bread + *-dīge* (akin to *dǣge* kneader of bread)] **1** : a woman of property, rank, or authority; *also* : a woman of superior social position or of refinement **2** : WOMAN **3** : WIFE

lady beetle *n* : LADYBUG

la·dy·bird \'lād-ē-ˌbərd\ *n* : LADYBUG

la•dy•bug \-ˌbəg\ *n* : any of various small nearly hemispherical and usu. brightly colored beetles that feed mostly on other insects

la•dy•fin•ger \ˈlād-ē-ˌfiŋ-gər\ *n* : a small finger-shaped sponge cake

la•dy–in–wait•ing \ˌlād-ē-in-ˈwāt-iŋ\ *n*, *pl* **ladies–in–waiting** : a lady appointed to attend or wait on a queen or princess

la•dy•like \ˈlād-ē-ˌlīk\ *adj* : WELL-BRED

la•dy•love \-ˌləv\ *n* : SWEETHEART

la•dy•ship \ˈlād-ē-ˌship\ *n* : the condition of being a lady : rank of lady

lady's slipper \ˈlād-ē(z)-ˌslip-ər\ *n* : any of several No. American orchids with slipper-shaped flowers

¹lag \ˈlag\ *n* **1** : a slowing up or falling behind; *also* : the amount by which one lags **2** : INTERVAL

²lag *vb* **lagged; lag•ging 1** : to fail to keep up : stay behind **2** : to slacken gradually **syn** dawdle, dally, tarry, loiter

la•ger \ˈläg-ər\ *n* : a light-colored usu. dry beer

¹lag•gard \ˈlag-ərd\ *adj* : DILATORY, SLOW — **lag•gard•ly** *adv or adj* — **lag•gard•ness** *n*

²laggard *n* : one that lags or lingers

la•gniappe \ˈlan-ˌyap\ *n* : something given free esp. with a purchase

la•goon \lə-ˈgün\ *n* : a shallow sound, channel, or pond near or communicating with a larger body of water

laid past and past part of LAY

laid–back \ˈlād-ˈbak\ *adj* : having a relaxed style or character ⟨∼ music⟩

lain past part of ¹LIE

lair \ˈlaər\ *n* : the resting or living place of a wild animal : DEN

laird \ˈlaərd\ *n*, *Scot* : a landed proprietor

lais•sez–faire \ˌles-ˌā-ˈfar\ *n* [F *laissez faire* let do] : a doctrine opposing governmental interference in economic affairs beyond that necessary to maintain peace and property rights

la•ity \ˈlā-ət-ē\ *n* **1** : the people of a religious faith who are not members of its clergy **2** : the mass of people who are of a particular field

lake \ˈlāk\ *n* : an inland body of standing water of considerable size; *also* : a pool of liquid (as lava or pitch)

¹lam \ˈlam\ *vb* **lammed; lam•ming** : to flee hastily — **lam** *n*

²lam *abbr* laminated

Lam *abbr* Lamentations

la•ma \ˈläm-ə\ *n* : a Buddhist monk of Tibet or Mongolia

la•ma•sery \ˈläm-ə-ˌser-ē\ *n*, *pl* **-ser•ies** : a monastery for lamas

¹lamb \ˈlam\ *n* **1** : a young sheep; *also* : its flesh used as food **2** : an innocent or gentle person

²lamb *vb* : to bring forth a lamb

lam•baste *or* **lam•bast** \lam-ˈbāst, -ˈbast\ *vb* **1** : BEAT **2** : EXCORIATE

lam•bent \ˈlam-bənt\ *adj* [L *lambens*, prp. of *lambere* to lick] **1** : FLICKERING **2** : softly radiant ⟨∼ eyes⟩ **3** : marked by lightness or brilliance ⟨∼ humor⟩ — **lam•ben•cy** \-bən-sē\ *n* — **lam•bent•ly** *adv*

lamb•skin \ˈlam-ˌskin\ *n* : a lamb's skin or a small fine-grade sheepskin or the leather made from either

¹lame \ˈlām\ *adj* **lam•er; lam•est 1** : having a body part and usu. a limb so disabled as to impair freedom of movement; *also* : marked by stiffness and soreness **2** : lacking substance : WEAK — **lame•ly** *adv* — **lame•ness** *n*

²lame *vb* **lamed; lam•ing** : to make lame : CRIPPLE

la•mé \lä-ˈmā, la-\ *n* [F] : a brocaded clothing fabric with tinsel filling threads (as of gold or silver)

lame•brain \ˈlām-ˌbrān\ *n* : a stupid person

lame duck *n* : an elected official continuing to hold office between an election and the inauguration of a successor

¹la•ment \lə-ˈment\ *vb* **1** : to mourn aloud : WAIL **2** : to express sorrow for : BEWAIL — **lam•en•ta•ble** \ˈlam-ən-tə-bəl, lə-ˈment-ə-\ *adj* — **lam•en•ta•bly** \-blē\ *adv* — **lam•en•ta•tion** \ˌlam-ən-ˈtā-shən\ *n*

²lament *n* **1** : a crying out in grief : WAIL **2** : DIRGE, ELEGY

Lamentations *n* — see BIBLE table

la•mia \ˈlā-mē-ə\ *n* : a female demon

lam•i•na \ˈlam-ə-nə\ *n*, *pl* **-nae** \-ˌnē\ *or* **-nas** : a thin plate or scale

lam•i•nar \ˈlam-ə-nər\ *adj* : arranged in or consisting of laminae

lam•i•nat•ed \-ˌnāt-əd\ *adj* : consisting of laminae; *esp* : composed of layers of firmly united material — **lam•i•nate**

\-ˌnāt\ *vb* — **lam•i•nate** \-nət\ *n or adj* — **lam•i•na•tion** \ˈlam-ə-ˈnā-shən\ *n*

lamp \ˈlamp\ *n* **1** : a vessel with a wick for burning a flammable liquid (as oil) to produce light **2** : a device for producing light or heat

lamp•black \-ˌblak\ *n* : black soot made by incomplete burning of carbonaceous matter and used esp. as a pigment

lamp•light•er \-ˌlīt-ər\ *n* : a person employed to light gas streetlights

lam•poon \lam-ˈpün\ *n* : SATIRE; *esp* : one that is harsh and usu. directed against an individual — **lampoon** *vb*

lam•prey \ˈlam-prē\ *n, pl* **lampreys** : an eellike aquatic vertebrate animal with sucking mouth and no jaws

la•nai \lə-ˈnī\ *n* [Hawaiian] : a porch furnished for use as a living room

¹lance \ˈlans\ *n* **1** : a spear carried by mounted soldiers **2** : any of various sharp-pointed implements; *esp* : LANCET

²lance *vb* **lanced; lanc•ing** : to pierce or open with a lance ⟨~ a boil⟩

lance corporal *n* : an enlisted man in the marine corps ranking above a private first class and below a corporal

lanc•er \ˈlan-sər\ *n* : a cavalryman of a unit formerly armed with lances

lan•cet \ˈlan-sət\ *n* : a sharp-pointed and usu. 2-edged surgical instrument

¹land \ˈland\ *n* **1** : the solid part of the surface of the earth; *also* : a part of the earth's surface ⟨fenced ~⟩ ⟨marshy ~⟩ **2** : NATION **3** : REALM, DOMAIN — **land•less** *adj*

²land *vb* **1** : DISEMBARK; *also* : to touch at a place on shore **2** : to alight or cause to alight on a surface **3** : to bring to or arrive at a destination **4** : to catch with a hook and bring in ⟨~ a fish⟩; *also* : GAIN, SECURE ⟨~ a job⟩

lan•dau \ˈlan-ˌdaů\ *n* **1** : a 4-wheeled carriage with a top divided into two sections that can be lowered, thrown back, or removed **2** : an automobile with a folding top over the rear passenger compartment

land•ed \ˈlan-dəd\ *adj* : having an estate in land ⟨~ gentry⟩

land•er \ˈlan-dər\ *n* : a space vehicle designed to land on a celestial body

land•fall \ˈlan(d)-ˌfȯl\ *n* : a sighting or making of land (as after a voyage); *also* : the land first sighted

land•fill \-ˌfil\ *n* : a low-lying area on which trash and garbage is buried between layers of earth

land•form \-ˌfȯrm\ *n* : a natural feature of a land surface

land•hold•er \ˈland-ˌhōl-dər\ *n* : a holder or owner of land — **land•hold•ing** \-diŋ\ *adj or n*

land•ing \ˈlan-diŋ\ *n* **1** : the action of one that lands **2** : a place for discharging or taking on passengers and cargo **3** : a level part of a staircase

landing gear *n* : the part that supports the weight of an airplane or spacecraft

land•la•dy \ˈland-ˌlād-ē\ *n* : a woman who is a landlord

land•locked \-ˌläkt\ *adj* **1** : enclosed or nearly enclosed by land ⟨a ~ country⟩ **2** : confined to fresh water by some barrier ⟨~ salmon⟩

land•lord \-ˌlȯrd\ *n* **1** : the owner of property leased or rented to another **2** : a person who rents lodgings : INNKEEPER

land•lub•ber \-ˌləb-ər\ *n* : one who knows little of the sea or seamanship

land•mark \ˈlan(d)-ˌmärk\ *n* **1** : an object that marks a course or boundary or serves as a guide **2** : an event that marks a turning point **3** : a structure of unusual historical and usu. aesthetic interest

land•mass \-ˌmas\ *n* : a large area of land

land•own•er \ˈland-ˌō-nər\ *n* : an owner of land

¹land•scape \ˈlan(d)-ˌskāp\ *n* **1** : a picture of natural inland scenery **2** : a portion of land that can be seen in one glance

²landscape *vb* **land•scaped; land•scap•ing** : to improve the natural beauties of a tract of land by grading, clearing, or decorative planting

land•slide \ˈlan(d)-ˌslīd\ *n* **1** : the slipping down of a mass of rocks or earth on a steep slope; *also* : the mass of material that slides **2** : an overwhelming victory esp. in a political contest

lands•man \ˈlan(d)z-mən\ *n* : a person who lives or works on land

land•ward \ˈland-wərd\ *adv or adj* : to or toward the land

lane \ˈlān\ *n* **1** : a narrow passageway

(as between fences) **2** : a relatively narrow way or track ⟨traffic ∼⟩

lang *abbr* language

lan·guage \'laŋ-gwij\ *n* [ME, fr. OF, fr. *langue* tongue, language, fr. L *lingua*] **1** : the words, their pronunciation, and the methods of combining them used and understood by a considerable community **2** : form or style of verbal expression **3** : a system of signs and symbols and rules for using them that is used to carry information

lan·guid \'laŋ-gwəd\ *adj* **1** : WEAK **2** : sluggish in character or disposition : LISTLESS **3** : SLOW — **lan·guid·ly** *adv* — **lan·guid·ness** *n*

lan·guish \'laŋ-gwish\ *vb* **1** : to become languid **2** : to become dispirited : PINE **3** : to appeal for sympathy by assuming an expression of grief

lan·guor \'laŋ-(g)ər\ *n* **1** : a languid feeling **2** : SLUGGISHNESS **syn** lethargy, lassitude, torpidity, torpor — **lan·guor·ous** *adj* — **lan·guor·ous·ly** *adv*

lank \'laŋk\ *adj* **1** : not well filled out **2** : hanging straight and limp

lanky \'laŋ-kē\ *adj* **lank·i·er; -est** : ungracefully tall and thin

lan·o·lin \'lan-əl-ən\ *n* : the fatty coating of sheep's wool esp. when refined for use in ointments and cosmetics

lan·ta·na \lan-'tän-ə\ *n* : any of a genus of tropical shrubs related to the vervains with heads of small bright flowers

lan·tern \'lant-ərn\ *n* **1** : a usu. portable light with a protective covering **2** : the chamber in a lighthouse containing the light **3** : a projector for slides

lan·tha·num \'lan-thə-nəm\ *n* : a soft malleable metallic chemical element

lan·yard \'lan-yərd\ *n* : a piece of rope for fastening something in ships; *also* : any of various cords

¹lap \'lap\ *n* **1** : a loose panel of a garment **2** : the clothing that lies on the knees, thighs, and lower part of the trunk when one sits; *also* : the front part of the lower trunk and thighs of a seated person **3** : an environment of nurture ⟨the ∼ of luxury⟩ **4** : CHARGE, CONTROL ⟨in the ∼ of the gods⟩

²lap *vb* **lapped; lap·ping 1** : FOLD **2** : WRAP **3** : to lay over or near so as to partly cover

³lap *n* **1** : the amount by which an object overlaps another; *also* : the part of an object that overlaps another **2** : a smoothing and polishing tool **3** : one circuit around a racecourse **4** : one complete turn (as of a rope around a drum)

⁴lap *vb* **lapped; lap·ping 1** : to scoop up food or drink with the tip of the tongue; *also* : DEVOUR — usu. used with *up* **2** : to splash gently ⟨*lapping* waves⟩

⁵lap *n* **1** : an act or instance of lapping **2** : a gentle splashing sound

lap·board \'lap-ˌbōrd\ *n* : a board used on the lap as a table or desk

lap·dog \-ˌdȯg\ *n* : a small dog that may be held in the lap

la·pel \lə-'pel\ *n* : the fold of the front of a coat that is usu. a continuation of the collar

¹lap·i·dary \'lap-ə-ˌder-ē\ *n, pl* **-dar·ies** : one who cuts, polishes, and engraves precious stones

²lapidary *adj* **1** : of, relating to, or suitable for engraved inscriptions **2** : of or relating to precious stones or the art of cutting them

lap·in \'lap-ən\ *n* : rabbit fur usu. sheared and dyed

la·pis la·zu·li \ˌlap-əs-'laz(h)-ə-lē\ *n* : a usu. blue semiprecious stone often having sparkling bits of pyrite

Lapp \'lap\ *n* : a member of a people of northern Scandinavia, Finland, and the Kola peninsula of Russia

lap·pet \'lap-ət\ *n* : a fold or flap on a garment

¹lapse \'laps\ *n* [L *lapsus*, fr. *labi* to slip] **1** : a slight error **2** : a fall from a higher to a lower state **3** : the termination of a right or privilege through failure to meet requirements **4** : a passage of time; *also* : INTERVAL

²lapse *vb* **lapsed; laps·ing 1** : to commit apostasy **2** : to sink or slip gradually : SUBSIDE **3** : CEASE

lap·wing \'lap-ˌwiŋ\ *n* : an Old World crested plover

lar·board \'lär-bərd\ *n* : ⁵PORT

lar·ce·ny \'lärs(-ə)-nē\ *n, pl* **-nies** [ME, fr. MF *larcin* theft, fr. L *latrocinium* robbery, fr. *latro* mercenary soldier] : THEFT — **lar·ce·nous** \-nəs\ *adj*

larch \'lärch\ *n* : a conical tree related to the pines that sheds its needles in the fall

¹lard \\'lärd\ *vb* **1** : to insert strips of usu. pork fat into (meat) before cooking; *also* : GREASE **2** *obs* : ENRICH

²lard *n* : a soft white fat obtained by rendering fatty tissue of the hog

lar·der \\'lärd-ər\ *n* : a place where foods (as meat) are kept

lar·es and pe·na·tes \\,lar-ēz-ən-pə-'nāt-ēz\ *n pl* **1** : household gods **2** : personal or household effects

large \\'lärj\ *adj* **larg·er; larg·est** **1** : having more than usual power, capacity, or scope **2** : exceeding most other things of like kind in quantity or size **syn** big, great, oversize — **large·ness** *n* — **at large** **1** : UNCONFINED **2** : as a whole

large·ly \\'lärj-lē\ *adv* : to a large extent

lar·gess *or* **lar·gesse** \\lär-'zhes, -'jes\ *n* **1** : liberal giving **2** : a generous gift

¹lar·go \\'lär-gō\ *adv or adj* [It, slow, broad, fr. L *largus* abundant] : in a very slow and stately manner — used as a direction in music

²largo *n, pl* **largos** : a largo movement

lar·i·at \\'lar-ē-ət\ *n* [AmerSp *la reata* the lasso, fr. Sp *la* the + AmerSp *reata* lasso, fr. Sp *reatar* to tie again] : a long rope used to catch or tether livestock

¹lark \\'lärk\ *n* : any of various small songbirds; *esp* : SKYLARK

²lark *n* : something done solely for fun or adventure : ESCAPADE

³lark *vb* : to engage in harmless fun or mischief — usu. used with *about*

lark·spur \\'lärk-,spər\ *n* : any of various mostly annual delphiniums

lar·va \\'lär-və\ *n, pl* **lar·vae** \\-(,)vē\ *also* **larvas** [L, specter, mask] : the wingless often wormlike form in which insects hatch from the egg; *also* : any young animal (as a tadpole) that is fundamentally unlike its parent — **lar·val** \\-vəl\ *adj*

lar·yn·gi·tis \\,lar-ən-'jīt-əs\ *n* : inflammation of the larynx

lar·ynx \\'lar-iŋks\ *n, pl* **la·ryn·ges** \\lə-'rin-,jēz\ *or* **lar·ynx·es** : the upper part of the trachea containing the vocal cords — **la·ryn·ge·al** \\,lar-ən-'jē-əl, lə-'rin-jē-əl\ *adj*

la·sa·gna \\lə-'zän-yə\ *n* [It] : boiled broad flat noodles baked with a sauce usu. of tomatoes, cheese, and meat

las·car \\'las-kər\ *n* : an Indian sailor

las·civ·i·ous \\lə-'siv-ē-əs\ *adj* : LEWD, LUSTFUL — **las·civ·i·ous·ness** *n*

la·ser \\'lā-zər\ *n* [*l*ight *a*mplification by *s*timulated *e*mission of *r*adiation] : a device that produces an intense monochromatic beam of light

¹lash \\'lash\ *vb* **1** : to move vigorously **2** : WHIP **3** : to attack verbally

²lash *n* **1** : a stroke esp. with a whip **2** : a stinging rebuke **3** : EYELASH

³lash *vb* : to bind with a rope, cord, or chain

lass \\'las\ *n* : GIRL

lass·ie \\'las-ē\ *n* : LASS

las·si·tude \\'las-ə-,t(y)üd\ *n* **1** : WEARINESS, FATIGUE **2** : LANGUOR

las·so \\'las-ō, la-'sü\ *n, pl* **lassos** *or* **lassoes** [Sp *lazo*] : a rope or long leather thong with a noose used for catching livestock — **lasso** *vb*

¹last \\'last\ *vb* **1** : to continue in existence or operation **2** : to remain valid, valuable, or important : ENDURE **3** : to be enough for the needs of

²last *n* : a foot-shaped form on which a shoe is shaped or repaired

³last *vb* : to shape with a last

⁴last *adj* **1** : following all the rest : FINAL **2** : next before the present **3** : least likely ⟨the ∼ thing he wants⟩ **4** : CONCLUSIVE; *also* : SUPREME — **last·ly** *adv*

⁵last *adv* **1** : at the end **2** : most recently **3** : in conclusion

⁶last *n* : something that is last — **at last** : FINALLY

Last Supper *n* : the supper eaten by Jesus and his disciples on the night of his betrayal

lat *abbr* latitude

Lat *abbr* Latin

lat·a·kia \\,lat-ə-'kē-ə\ *n* : an aromatic Turkish smoking tobacco

¹latch \\'lach\ *vb* : to catch or get hold

²latch *n* : a catch that holds a door or gate closed

³latch *vb* : CATCH, FASTEN

latch·et \\'lach-ət\ *n* : a strap, thong, or lace for fastening a shoe or sandal

latch·key \\'lach-,kē\ *n* : a key for opening a door latch esp. from the outside

latch·string \\-,striŋ\ *n* : a string on a latch that may be left hanging outside the door for raising the latch

¹late \\'lāt\ *adj* **lat·er; lat·est** **1** : coming or remaining after the due, usual, or proper time : TARDY **2** : far advanced toward the close or end **3** : recently deceased ⟨her ∼ husband⟩ **4** : made, appearing, or happening just previous to the present : RECENT — **late·ly** adv — **late·ness** n

²**late** adv **lat·er; lat·est 1** : after the usual or proper time; also : at or to an advanced point in time **2** : RECENTLY

late·com·er \\'lāt-ˌkəm-ər\ n : one who arrives late

la·teen \lə-'tēn\ adj : relating to or being a triangular sail extended by a long spar slung to a low mast

la·tent \\'lāt-ᵊnt\ adj : present but not visible or active **syn** dormant, quiescent, potential — **la·ten·cy** \-ᵊn-sē\ n

¹**lat·er·al** \\'lat-(ə-)rəl\ adj : situated on, directed toward, or coming from the side — **lat·er·al·ly** \-ē\ adv

²**lateral** n **1** : a lateral passage (as a drainage ditch) **2** : a football pass thrown parallel to the line of scrimmage or away from the opponent's goal

la·tex \\'lā-ˌteks\ n, pl **la·ti·ces** \\'lāt-ə-ˌsēz, 'lat-\ or **la·tex·es 1** : a milky plant juice esp. of members of the milkweed group ⟨rubber is made from a ∼⟩ **2** : a water emulsion of a synthetic rubber or plastic used esp. as a paint

lath \\'lath, 'lath\ n, pl **laths** or **lath** : a thin narrow strip of wood used esp. as a base for plaster; also : a building material in sheets used for the same purpose — **lath·ing** \-iŋ\ n

lathe \\'lāth\ n : a machine in which a piece of material is held and turned while being shaped by a tool

¹**lath·er** \\'lath-ər\ n **1** : a foam or froth formed when a detergent is agitated in water; also : foam from profuse sweating (as by a horse) **2** : DITHER

²**lather** vb **lath·ered; lath·er·ing** \-(ə-)riŋ\ : to spread lather over; also : to form a lather

Lat·in \\'lat-ᵊn\ n **1** : the language of ancient Rome **2** : a member of any of the peoples whose languages derive from Latin — **Latin** adj

Latin American n : a native or inhabitant of any of the countries of No., Central, or So. America whose official language is Spanish or Portuguese — **Latin–American** adj

La·ti·no \lə-'tē-nō\ n, pl **-nos** : a native or inhabitant of Latin America; also

: a person of Latin-American origin living in the U.S.

lat·i·tude \\'lat-ə-ˌt(y)üd\ n **1** : angular distance north or south from the earth's equator measured in degrees **2** : a region marked by its latitude **3** : freedom of action or choice

lat·i·tu·di·nar·i·an \ˌlat-ə-ˌt(y)üd-ᵊn-'er-ē-ən\ n : a person who is broad and liberal in religious belief and conduct

la·trine \lə-'trēn\ n : TOILET

lat·ter \\'lat-ər\ adj **1** : more recent; also : FINAL **2** : of, relating to, or being the second of two things referred to — **lat·ter·ly** adv

lat·ter–day adj **1** : of present or recent times **2** : of a later or subsequent time

Latter–day Saint n : a member of a religious body founded by Joseph Smith in 1830 and accepting the Book of Mormon as divine revelation : MORMON

lat·tice \\'lat-əs\ n **1** : a framework of crossed wood or metal strips; also : a window, door, or gate having a lattice **2** : a regular geometrical arrangement

lat·tice·work \-ˌwərk\ n : LATTICE; also : work made of lattices

¹**laud** \\'lȯd\ n : PRAISE, ACCLAIM

²**laud** vb : PRAISE, EXTOL — **laud·able** adj — **laud·ably** adv

lau·da·num \\'lȯd-(ᵊ-)nəm\ n : OPIATE; esp : a tincture of opium

lau·da·to·ry \\'lȯd-ə-ˌtōr-ē\ adj : of, relating to, or expressive of praise

¹**laugh** \\'laf, 'låf\ vb : to show mirth, joy, or scorn with a smile and chuckle or explosive sound; also : to become amused or derisive — **laugh·able** adj — **laugh·ing·ly** \-iŋ-lē\ adv

²**laugh** n **1** : the act of laughing **2** : JOKE; also : JEER

laugh·ing·stock \\'laf-iŋ-ˌstäk, 'låf-\ n : an object of ridicule

laugh·ter \\'laf-tər, 'låf-\ n : the action or sound of laughing

¹**launch** \\'lȯnch\ vb [ME launchen, fr. OF lancher, fr. LL lanceare to wield a lance] **1** : THROW, HURL; also : to send off ⟨∼ a rocket⟩ **2** : to set afloat **3** : to set in operation : START

²**launch** n : an act or instance of launching

³**launch** n : a small open or half-decked motorboat

launch·er \\'lȯn-chər\ n **1** : one that

launches **2** : a device for firing a grenade from a rifle **3** : a device for launching a rocket or rocket shell

launch•pad \\'lȯnch-ˌpad\ *n* : a platform from which a rocket is launched

laun•der \\'lȯn-dər\ *vb* **laun•dered; laun•der•ing** \-d(ə-)riŋ\ : to wash or wash and iron clothing and household linens — **laun•der•er** *n* — **laun•dress** \-drəs\ *n*

laun•dry \\'lȯn-drē\ *n, pl* **laundries** [fr. obs. *launder* launderer, fr. MF *lavandier*, fr. ML *lavandarius*, fr. L *lavandus* needing to be washed, fr. *lavare* to wash] **1** : a place where laundering is done **2** : clothes or linens that have been or are to be laundered — **laun•dry•man** \-mən\ *n* — **laun•dry•wom•an** \-ˌwùm-ən\ *n*

lau•re•ate \\'lȯr-ē-ət\ *n* : the recipient of honor for achievement in an art or science — **lau•re•ate•ship** *n*

lau•rel \\'lȯ-rəl\ *n* **1** : any of several trees or shrubs related to the sassafras and cinnamon; *esp* : a small evergreen tree of southern Europe **2** : MOUNTAIN LAUREL **3** : a crown of laurel : HONOR, DISTINCTION — usu. used in pl.

lav *abbr* lavatory

la•va \\'läv-ə, 'lav-\ *n* [It] : melted rock coming from a volcano; *also* : such rock solidified

la•vage \lə-'väzh\ *n* [F] : WASHING; *esp* : the washing out (as of an organ) for medicinal reasons

la•va•liere *or* **la•val•liere** \ˌläv-ə-'liər\ *n* [F *lavallière* necktie with a large bow] : a pendant on a fine chain that is worn as a necklace

lav•a•to•ry \\'lav-ə-ˌtōr-ē\ *n, pl* **-ries** **1** : a fixed washbowl with running water and drainpipe **2** : BATHROOM

lave \\'lāv\ *vb* **laved; lav•ing** : WASH

lav•en•der \\'lav-ən-dər\ *n* **1** : a European mint or its dried leaves and flowers used to perfume clothing and bed linen **2** : a pale purple

¹lav•ish \\'lav-ish\ *adj* [ME *lavas* abundance, fr. MF *lavasse* downpour, fr. *laver* to wash] **1** : expending or bestowing profusely **2** : expended or produced in abundance — **lav•ish•ly** *adv*

²lavish *vb* : to expend or give freely

law \\'lȯ\ *n* **1** : a rule of conduct or action established by custom or laid down and enforced by a governing authority; *also* : the whole body of such rules **2** : the control brought about by enforcing rules **3** *cap* : the revelation of the divine will set forth in the Old Testament; *also* : the first part of the Jewish scriptures **4** : a rule or principle of construction or procedure **5** : the science that deals with laws and their interpretation and application **6** : the profession of a lawyer **7** : a rule or principle stating something that always works in the same way under the same conditions

law•break•er \\'lȯ-ˌbrā-kər\ *n* : one who violates the law

law•ful \\'lȯ-fəl\ *adj* **1** : permitted by law **2** : RIGHTFUL — **law•ful•ly** \-ē\ *adv*

law•giv•er \-ˌgiv-ər\ *n* : LEGISLATOR

law•less \\'lȯ-ləs\ *adj* **1** : having no laws **2** : UNRULY, DISORDERLY ⟨a ~ mob⟩ — **law•less•ness** *n*

law•mak•er \-ˌmā-kər\ *n* : LEGISLATOR

law•man \\'lȯ-mən\ *n* : a law enforcement official (as a sheriff or marshal)

¹lawn \\'lȯn\ *n* : ground (as around a house) covered with closely mowed grass

²lawn *n* : a fine sheer linen or cotton fabric

law•ren•ci•um \lȯ-'ren-sē-əm\ *n* : a short-lived radioactive element

law•suit \\'lȯ-ˌsüt\ *n* : a suit in law

law•yer \\'lȯ-yər\ *n* : one who conducts lawsuits for clients or advises as to legal rights and obligations in other matters

lax \\'laks\ *adj* **1** : not strict ⟨~ discipline⟩ **2** : not tense or rigid **syn** remiss, negligent, neglectful, delinquent, derelict — **lax•i•ty** \\'lak-sət-ē\ *n* — **lax•ly** *adv*

¹lax•a•tive \\'lak-sət-iv\ *adj* : relieving constipation

²laxative *n* : a usu. mild laxative drug

¹lay \\'lā\ *vb* **laid** \\'lād\; **lay•ing** **1** : to beat or strike down **2** : to put on or against a surface : PLACE **3** : to produce and deposit eggs **4** : SETTLE; *also* : ALLAY **5** : SPREAD **6** : PREPARE, CONTRIVE **7** : WAGER **8** : to impose esp. as a duty or burden **9** : to set in order or position **10** : to bring to a specified condition **11** : to put forward : SUBMIT

²lay *n* : the way in which something lies or is laid in relation to something else

³**lay** past of ¹LIE

⁴**lay** *n* **1** : a simple narrative poem **2** : SONG

⁵**lay** *adj* : of or relating to the laity

lay·away \ˈlā-ə-ˌwā\ *n* : a purchasing agreement by which a retailer agrees to hold merchandise secured by a deposit until the price is paid in full by the customer

lay·er \ˈlā-ər\ *n* **1** : one that lays **2** : one thickness, course, or fold laid or lying over or under another

lay·ette \lā-ˈet\ *n* [F, fr. MF, dim. of *laye* box] : an outfit of clothing and equipment for a newborn infant

lay·man \ˈlā-mən\ *n* : a member of the laity

lay·off \ˈlā-ˌȯf\ *n* **1** : the act of dismissing an employee temporarily **2** : a period of inactivity

lay·out \ˈlā-ˌaut\ *n* **1** : ARRANGEMENT **2** : SET, OUTFIT

lay·wom·an \ˈlā-ˌwum-ən\ *n* : a woman who is a member of the laity

la·zar \ˈlaz-ər, ˈlā-zər\ *n* : LEPER

laze \ˈlāz\ *vb* **lazed; laz·ing** : to pass time in idleness or relaxation

la·zy \ˈlā-zē\ *adj* **la·zi·er; -est 1** : disliking activity or exertion **2** : SLUGGISH — **la·zi·ly** \ˈlā-zə-lē\ *adv* — **la·zi·ness** \-zē-nəs\ *n*

la·zy·bones \ˈlā-zē-ˌbōnz\ *n* : a lazy person

lazy Su·san \ˌlā-zē-ˈsüz-ᵊn\ *n* : a revolving tray placed on a dining table

lb *abbr* [L *libra*] pound

lc *abbr* lowercase

LC *abbr* Library of Congress

¹**LCD** \ˈel-ˈsē-ˈdē\ *n* [*liquid crystal display*] : a display (as of the time in a watch) that consists of segments of a liquid crystal whose reflectivity varies with the voltage applied to them

²**LCD** *abbr* least common denominator; lowest common denominator

LCDR *abbr* lieutenant commander

LCM *abbr* least common multiple; lowest common multiple

LCpl *abbr* lance corporal

ld *abbr* **1** load **2** lord

LD *abbr* lethal dose

LDC *abbr* less developed country

ldg *abbr* **1** landing **2** loading

LDS *abbr* Latter-day Saints

lea \ˈlē, ˈlā\ *n* : PASTURE, MEADOW

leach \ˈlēch\ *vb* : to pass a liquid (as water) through to carry off the soluble components; *also* : to dissolve out by such means ⟨∼ alkali from ashes⟩

¹**lead** \ˈlēd\ *vb* **led** \ˈled\; **lead·ing 1** : to guide on a way; *also* : to run in a specified direction **2** : LIVE ⟨∼ a quiet life⟩ **3** : to direct the operations, activity, or performance of ⟨∼ an orchestra⟩ **4** : to go at the head of : be first ⟨∼ a parade⟩ **5** : to begin play with; *also* : BEGIN, OPEN **6** : to tend toward a definite result ⟨study ∼*ing* to a degree⟩ — **lead·er** *n* — **lead·er·less** *adj* — **lead·er·ship** *n*

²**lead** \ˈlēd\ *n* **1** : a position at the front; *also* : a margin by which one leads **2** : the privilege of leading in cards; *also* : the card or suit led **3** : EXAMPLE **4** : one that leads **5** : a principal role (as in a play); *also* : one who plays such a role **6** : INDICATION, CLUE **7** : an insulated electrical conductor

³**lead** \ˈled\ *n* **1** : a heavy bluish white chemical element that is easily bent and shaped **2** : an article made of lead; *esp* : a weight for sounding at sea **3** : a thin strip of metal used to separate lines of type in printing **4** : a thin stick of marking substance in or for a pencil

⁴**lead** \ˈled\ *vb* **1** : to cover, line, or weight with lead **2** : to fix (glass) in position with lead **3** : to treat or mix with lead or a lead compound

lead·en \ˈled-ᵊn\ *adj* **1** : made of lead; *also* : of the color of lead **2** : SLUGGISH, DULL

lead off \(ˈ)lēd-ˈȯf\ *vb* : OPEN, BEGIN; *esp* : to bat first in an inning — **lead·off** \ˈlēd-ˌȯf\ *adj*

lead poisoning *n* : chronic intoxication produced by the absorption of lead into the system

¹**leaf** \ˈlēf\ *n, pl* **leaves** \ˈlēvz\ **1** : a usu. flat and green outgrowth of a plant stem that is a unit of foliage and functions esp. in photosynthesis; *also* : FOLIAGE **2** : something that is suggestive of a leaf — **leaf·less** *adj* — **leafy** *adj*

²**leaf** *vb* **1** : to produce leaves **2** : to turn the pages of a book

leaf·age \ˈlē-fij\ *n* : FOLIAGE

leafed \ˈlēft\ *adj* : LEAVED

leaf·hop·per \ˈlēf-ˌhäp-ər\ *n* : any of numerous small leaping insects related to the cicadas that suck the juices of plants

leaf·let \'lēf-lət\ *n* **1** : a division of a compound leaf **2** : PAMPHLET, FOLDER

leaf mold *n* : a compost or layer composed chiefly of decayed vegetable matter

leaf·stalk \'lēf-ˌstȯk\ *n* : PETIOLE

¹league \'lēg\ *n* : a measure of distance equal to about three miles

²league *n* **1** : an association or alliance for a common purpose **2** : CLASS, CATEGORY — **league** *vb*

leagu·er \'lē-gər\ *n* : a member of a league

¹leak \'lēk\ *vb* **1** : to enter or escape through a leak **2** : to let a substance in or out through an opening **3** : to become or make known

²leak *n* **1** : a crack or hole that accidentally admits a fluid or light or lets it escape; *also* : something that secretly or accidentally permits the admission or escape of something else **2** : LEAKAGE — **leaky** *adj*

leak·age \'lē-kij\ *n* **1** : the act of leaking **2** : the thing or amount that leaks

leal \'lēl\ *adj, chiefly Scot* : LOYAL

¹lean \'lēn\ *vb* **1** : to bend from a vertical position : INCLINE **2** : to cast one's weight to one side for support **3** : to rely on for support **4** : to incline in opinion, taste, or desire — **lean** *n*

²lean *adj* **1** : lacking or deficient in flesh and esp. in fat **2** : lacking richness or productiveness **3** : low in fuel content — **lean·ness** \'lēn-nəs\ *n*

lean–to \'lēn-ˌtü\ *n, pl* **lean–tos** \-ˌtüz\ : a wing or extension of a building having a roof of only one slope; *also* : a rough shed or shelter with a similar roof

¹leap \'lēp\ *vb* **leapt** \'lēpt, 'lept\ *or* **leaped; leap·ing** : to spring free from a surface or over an obstacle : JUMP

²leap *n* : JUMP

leap·frog \'lēp-ˌfrȯg, -ˌfräg\ *n* : a game in which one player bends down and another vaults over him — **leapfrog** *vb*

leap year *n* : a year containing 366 days with February 29 as the extra day

learn \'lərn\ *vb* **learned** \'lərnd, 'lərnt\; **learn·ing** **1** : to gain knowledge, understanding, or skill by study or experience; *also* : MEMORIZE **2** : to find out : ASCERTAIN — **learn·er** *n*

learn·ed \'lər-nəd\ *adj* : SCHOLARLY, ERUDITE

learn·ing \'lər-niŋ\ *n* : KNOWLEDGE, ERUDITION

learnt \'lərnt\ *chiefly Brit* past & past part of LEARN

¹lease \'lēs\ *n* : a contract transferring real estate for a term of years or at will usu. for a specified rent

²lease *vb* **leased; leas·ing** **1** : to grant by lease **2** : to hold under a lease **syn** let, charter, hire, rent

lease·hold \'lēs-ˌhōld\ *n* **1** : a tenure by lease **2** : land held by lease — **lease·hold·er** *n*

leash \'lēsh\ *n* [ME *lees, leshe,* fr. OF *laisse,* fr. *laissier* to let go, fr. L *laxare* to loosen, fr. *laxus* slack] : a line for leading or restraining an animal — **leash** *vb*

¹least \'lēst\ *adj* **1** : lowest in importance or position **2** : smallest in size or degree **3** : SLIGHTEST

²least *n* : one that is least

³least *adv* : in the smallest or lowest degree

least common denominator *n* : the least common multiple of two or more denominators

least common multiple *n* : the smallest common multiple of two or more numbers

least·wise \'lēst-ˌwīz\ *adv* : at least

leath·er \'leth-ər\ *n* : animal skin dressed for use — **leath·ern** \-ərn\ *adj* — **leath·ery** *adj*

leath·er·neck \-ˌnek\ *n* : MARINE

¹leave \'lēv\ *vb* **left** \'left\; **leav·ing** **1** : to allow or cause to remain behind; *also* : DELIVER **2** : to have as a remainder **3** : BEQUEATH **4** : to let stay without interference **5** : to go away : depart from **6** : to give up : ABANDON

²leave *n* **1** : PERMISSION; *also* : authorized absence from duty **2** : DEPARTURE

³leave *vb* **leaved; leav·ing** : LEAF

leaved \'lēvd\ *adj* : having leaves

¹leav·en \'lev-ən\ *n* **1** : a substance (as yeast) used to produce fermentation (as in dough) **2** : something that modifies or lightens a mass or aggregate

²leaven *vb* **leav·ened; leav·en·ing** \'lev-(ə-)niŋ\ : to raise (dough) with a leaven; *also* : to permeate with a modifying or vivifying element

leav·en·ing \ˈlev-(ə-)niŋ\ *n* : LEAVEN

leaves pl of LEAF

leave–tak·ing \ˈlēv-ˌtā-kiŋ\ *n* : DEPARTURE, FAREWELL

leav·ings \ˈlē-viŋz\ *n pl* : REMNANT, RESIDUE

lech·ery \ˈlech-ə-rē\ *n* : inordinate indulgence in sexual activity — **lech·er** \ˈlech-ər\ *n* — **lech·er·ous** *adj* — **lech·er·ous·ness** *n*

lec·i·thin \ˈles-ə-thən\ *n* : any of several waxy phosphorus-containing substances that are common in animals and plants, form colloidal solutions in water, and have emulsifying and wetting properties

lect *abbr* lecture; lecturer

lec·tern \ˈlek-tərn\ *n* : a desk to support a book in a convenient position for a standing reader

lec·tor \-tər\ *n* : one whose chief duty is to read the lessons in a church service

lec·ture \ˈlek-chər\ *n* 1 : a discourse given before an audience or a class esp. for instruction 2 : REPRIMAND — **lec·ture** *vb* — **lec·tur·er** *n* — **lec·ture·ship** *n*

led past and past part of LEAD

LED \ˈel-ˈē-ˈdē\ *n* [*light-emitting diode*] : a semiconductor diode that emits light when a voltage is applied to it and is used esp. for electronic displays

le·der·ho·sen \ˈlād-ər-ˌhōz-ᵊn\ *n pl* : leather shorts often with suspenders worn esp. in Bavaria

ledge \ˈlej\ *n* [ME *legge* bar of a gate] 1 : a shelflike projection from a top or an edge 2 : REEF

led·ger \ˈlej-ər\ *n* : a book containing accounts to which debits and credits are transferred in final form

lee \ˈlē\ *n* 1 : a protecting shelter 2 : the side (as of a ship) that is sheltered from the wind — **lee** *adj*

leech \ˈlēch\ *n* [ME *leche* physician, fr. OE *læce*] 1 : any of various segmented usu. freshwater worms related to the earthworms; *esp* : one formerly used by physicians to draw blood 2 : a hanger-on who seeks gain

leek \ˈlēk\ *n* : an onionlike herb grown for its mildly pungent leaves and stalk

leer \ˈliər\ *n* : a suggestive, knowing, or malicious look — **leer** *vb*

leery \ˈli(ə)r-ē\ *adj* : SUSPICIOUS, WARY

lees \ˈlēz\ *n pl* : DREGS

¹lee·ward \ˈlē-wərd, ˈlü-ərd\ *n* : the lee side

²leeward *adj* : situated away from the wind

lee·way \ˈlē-ˌwā\ *n* 1 : lateral movement of a ship when under way 2 : an allowable margin of freedom or variation

¹left \ˈleft\ *adj* [ME, fr. OE, weak; fr. the left hand's being the weaker in most individuals] 1 : of, relating to, or being the side of the body in which the heart is mostly located; *also* : located nearer to this side than to the right 2 *often cap* : of, adhering to, or constituted by the political Left — **left** *adv*

²left *n* 1 : the left hand; *also* : the side or part that is on or toward the left side 2 *cap* : those professing political views marked by desire to reform the established order and usu. to give greater freedom to the common man

³left past and past part of LEAVE

left–hand *adj* 1 : LEFT-HANDED 2 : situated on the left

left–hand·ed \ˈleft-ˈhan-dəd\ *adj* 1 : using the left hand habitually or better than the right 2 : designed for or done with the left hand 3 : INSINCERE, BACKHANDED 4 : COUNTERCLOCKWISE — **left–handed** *adv*

left·ism \ˈlef-ˌtiz-əm\ *n* 1 : the principles and views of the Left; *also* : the movement embodying these principles 2 : advocacy of or adherence to the doctrines of the Left — **left·ist** \-təst\ *n or adj*

left·over \ˈleft-ˌō-vər\ *n* : an unused or unconsumed residue

¹leg \ˈleg\ *n* 1 : a limb of an animal used esp. for supporting the body and in walking; *esp* : the part of the vertebrate leg between knee and foot 2 : something resembling or analogous to an animal leg ⟨table ∼⟩ 3 : the part of an article of clothing that covers the leg 4 : a portion of a trip — **legged** \ˈleg-əd\ *adj* — **leg·less** *adj*

²leg *vb* **legged; leg·ging** : to use the legs in walking or esp. in running

³leg *abbr* 1 legal 2 legislative; legislature

leg·a·cy \ˈleg-ə-sē\ *n, pl* **-cies** : INHERITANCE, BEQUEST; *also* : something that has come from an ancestor or predecessor or the past

le•gal \'lē-gəl\ *adj* **1** : of or relating to law or lawyers **2** : LAWFUL; *also* : STATUTORY **3** : enforced in courts of law — **le•gal•i•ty** \li-'gal-ət-ē\ *n* — **le•gal•ize** \'lē-gə-ˌlīz\ *vb* — **le•gal•ly** \-gə-lē\ *adv*

le•gal•ism \'lē-gə-ˌliz-əm\ *n* : strict, literal, or excessive conformity to the law or to a religious or moral code — **le•gal•is•tic** \ˌlē-gə-'lis-tik\ *adj*

leg•ate \'leg-ət\ *n* : an official representative; *esp* : AMBASSADOR

leg•a•tee \ˌleg-ə-'tē\ *n* : a person to whom a legacy is bequeathed

le•ga•tion \li-'gā-shən\ *n* **1** : a diplomatic mission headed by a minister **2** : the official residence and office of a minister to a foreign government

le•ga•to \li-'gät-ō\ *adv or adj* [It, lit., tied] : in a smooth and connected manner — used as a direction in music

leg•end \'lej-ənd\ *n* [ME *legende*, fr. MF & ML; MF *legende*, fr. ML *legenda*, fr. L *legere* to gather, select, read] **1** : a story coming down from the past; *esp* : one popularly accepted as historical though not verifiable **2** : an inscription on an object; *also* : CAPTION **3** : an explanatory list of the symbols on a map or chart

leg•end•ary \'lej-ən-ˌder-ē\ *adj* : of, relating to, or characteristic of a legend

leg•er•de•main \ˌlej-ərd-ə-'mān\ *n* [ME, fr. MF *leger de main* light of hand] : SLEIGHT OF HAND

leg•ging *or* **leg•gin** \'leg-ən, -iŋ\ *n* : a covering for the leg

leg•gy \'leg-ē\ *adj* **leg•gi•er; -est 1** : having unusually long legs **2** : having attractive legs **3** : SPINDLY — used of a plant

leg•horn \'leg-ˌ(h)ȯrn, 'leg-ərn\ *n* **1** : a fine plaited straw; *also* : a hat made of this straw **2** : any of a Mediterranean breed of small hardy fowls

leg•i•ble \'lej-ə-bəl\ *adj* : capable of being read : CLEAR — **leg•i•bil•i•ty** \ˌlej-ə-'bil-ət-ē\ *n* — **leg•i•bly** \'lej-ə-blē\ *adv*

¹le•gion \'lē-jən\ *n* **1** : a unit of the Roman army comprising 3000 to 6000 soldiers **2** : MULTITUDE **3** : an association of ex-servicemen — **le•gion•ary** \-ˌer-ē\ *n* — **le•gion•naire** \ˌlē-jən-'aər\ *n*

²legion *adj* : MANY, NUMEROUS

Le•gion•naires' disease *also* **Le•gion-**naire's **disease** \ˌlē-jə-'nerz-\ *n* [so called fr. its first recognized occurrence during the 1976 American Legion convention] : a pneumonia that is caused by a bacterium and affects one or more lobes of the lung

legis *abbr* legislation; legislative; legislature

leg•is•late \'lej-ə-ˌslāt\ *vb* **-lat•ed; -lat•ing** : to make or enact laws; *also* : to bring about by legislation — **leg•is•la•tor** \-ˌslāt-ər\ *n*

leg•is•la•tion \ˌlej-ə-'slā-shən\ *n* **1** : the action of legislating **2** : laws made by a legislative body

leg•is•la•tive \'lej-ə-ˌslāt-iv\ *adj* **1** : having the power of legislating **2** : of or relating to a legislature

leg•is•la•ture \'lej-ə-ˌslā-chər\ *n* : an organized body of persons having the authority to make laws

le•git \li-'jit\ *adj, slang* : LEGITIMATE

le•git•i•mate \li-'jit-ə-mət\ *adj* **1** : lawfully begotten **2** : GENUINE **3** : LAWFUL **4** : conforming to recognized principles or accepted rules or standards — **le•git•i•ma•cy** \-mə-sē\ *n* — **le•git•i•mate•ly** *adv*

le•git•i•mize \li-'jit-ə-ˌmīz\ *vb* **-mized; -miz•ing** : LEGITIMATE

leg•man \'leg-ˌman\ *n* **1** : a reporter assigned usu. to gather information **2** : an assistant who gathers information and runs errands

le•gume \'leg-ˌyüm, li-'gyüm\ *n* [F] **1** : any of a large group of plants having fruits that are dry pods and split when ripe and including important food and forage plants (as beans and clover) **2** : the part of a legume used as food; *also* : VEGETABLE **2** — **le•gu•mi•nous** \li-'gyü-mə-nəs\ *adj*

¹lei \'lā(-ˌē)\ *n* : a wreath or necklace usu. of flowers

²lei \'lā\ *pl of* LEU

lei•sure \'lēzh-ər, 'lezh-, 'lāzh-\ *n* **1** : time free from work or duties **2** : EASE; *also* : CONVENIENCE **syn** relaxation, rest, repose — **lei•sure•ly** *adj*

leit•mo•tiv *or* **leit•mo•tif** \'līt-mō-ˌtēf\ *n* [G *leitmotiv*, fr. *leiten* to lead + *motiv* motive] : a dominant recurring theme

lek \'lek\ *n, pl* **leks** *or* **le•ke** *also* **lek** *or* **le•ku** — see MONEY table

lem•ming \'lem-iŋ\ *n* [Norw] : any of several short-tailed northern rodents

lem·on \\'lem-ən\\ *n* **1** : an acid yellow usu. nearly oblong citrus fruit; *also* : a citrus tree that bears lemons **2** : something unsatisfactory or defective (as an automobile) : DUD — **lem·ony** *adj*

lem·on·ade \\,lem-ə-'nād\\ *n* : a beverage of lemon juice, sugar, and water

lem·pi·ra \\lem-'pir-ə\\ *n* — see MONEY table

le·mur \\'lē-mər\\ *n* : any of numerous arboreal mammals largely of Madagascar usu. with a muzzle like a fox, large eyes, very soft woolly fur, and a long furry tail

lend \\'lend\\ *vb* **lent** \\'lent\\; **lend·ing 1** : to give for temporary use on condition that the same or its equivalent be returned **2** : AFFORD, FURNISH **3** : ACCOMMODATE — **lend·er** *n*

lend–lease \\-'lēs\\ *n* : the transfer of goods and services to an ally to aid in a common cause with payment being made by a return of the items or their use in the common cause or by a similar transfer of other goods and services

length \\'leŋth\\ *n* **1** : the longer or longest dimension of an object; *also* : a measured distance **2** : duration or extent in time or space **3** : the length of something taken as a unit of measure ⟨the horse won by a ~⟩ **4** : PIECE; *esp* : one in a series of pieces designed to be joined

length·en \\'leŋ-thən\\ *vb* **length·ened; length·en·ing** \\'leŋth-(ə-)niŋ\\ : to make or become longer **syn** extend, elongate, prolong, protract

length·wise \\-,wīz\\ *adv* : in the direction of the length — **lengthwise** *adj*

lengthy \\'leŋ-thē\\ *adj* **length·i·er; -est 1** : protracted excessively **2** : EXTENDED, LONG

le·nient \\'lē-nē-ənt, -nyənt\\ *adj* : of mild and tolerant disposition or effect **syn** indulgent, forbearing, merciful, tolerant — **le·ni·en·cy** \\'lē-nē-ən-sē, -nyən-sē\\ *n* — **le·ni·ent·ly** *adv*

len·i·tive \\'len-ət-iv\\ *adj* : alleviating pain or acrimony

len·i·ty \\'len-ət-ē\\ *n* : LENIENCY, MILDNESS

lens \\'lenz\\ *n* [L *lent-, lens* lentil; so called fr. the shape of a convex lens] **1** : a curved piece of glass or plastic used singly or combined in an optical instrument for forming an image; *also* : a device for focusing radiation other than light **2** : a transparent body in the eye that focuses light rays on receptors at the back of the eye

Lent \\'lent\\ *n* : a 40-day period of penitence and fasting observed from Ash Wednesday to Easter by many churches — **Lent·en** \\-ᵊn\\ *adj*

len·til \\'lent-ᵊl\\ *n* : an Old World legume grown for its flat edible seeds and for fodder; *also* : its seed

Leo \\'lē-ō\\ *n* [L, lit., lion] : the 5th sign of the zodiac in astrology

le·one \\lē-'ōn\\ *n, pl* **leones** *or* **leone** — see MONEY table

le·o·nine \\'lē-ə-,nīn\\ *adj* : of, relating to, or resembling a lion

leop·ard \\'lep-ərd\\ *n* : a large strong usu. tawny and black-spotted cat of southern Asia and Africa

le·o·tard \\'lē-ə-,tärd\\ *n* : a close-fitting garment worn esp. by dancers and people doing exercises

lep·er \\'lep-ər\\ *n* **1** : a person affected with leprosy **2** : OUTCAST

lep·re·chaun \\'lep-rə-,kän\\ *n* : a mischievous elf of Irish folklore

lep·ro·sy \\'lep-rə-sē\\ *n* : a chronic bacterial disease marked esp. by slow-growing swellings with deformity and loss of sensation of affected parts — **lep·rous** \\-rəs\\ *adj*

lep·ton \\lep-'tän\\ *n, pl* **lep·ta** \\-'tä\\ — see *drachma* at MONEY table

les·bi·an \\'lez-bē-ən\\ *n, often cap* [fr. the reputed homosexual group associated with the poet Sappho of Lesbos] : a female homosexual — **lesbian** *adj* — **les·bi·an·ism** \\-,iz-əm\\ *n*

lèse ma·jes·té *or* **lese maj·es·ty** \\'lēz-'maj-ə-stē\\ *n* [MF *lese majesté,* fr. L *laesa majestas,* lit., injured majesty] : an offense violating the dignity of a sovereign

le·sion \\'lē-zhən\\ *n* : an abnormal structural change in the body due to injury or disease

¹less \\'les\\ *adj* **1** : FEWER ⟨~ than six⟩ **2** : of lower rank, degree, or importance **3** : SMALLER; *also* : more limited in quantity

²less *adv* : to a lesser extent or degree

³less *prep* : diminished by : MINUS

⁴**less** *n, pl* **less 1** : a smaller portion **2** : something of less importance

-less \ləs\ *adj suffix* **1** : destitute of : not having ⟨child*less*⟩ **2** : unable to be acted on or to act (in a specified way) ⟨daunt*less*⟩

les•see \le-'sē\ *n* : a tenant under a lease

less•en \'les-ᵊn\ *vb* **less•ened; less•en•ing** \'les-(ᵊ-)niŋ\ : to make or become less **syn** decrease, diminish, dwindle, abate

less•er \'les-ər\ *adj* : of less size, quality, or significance

les•son \'les-ᵊn\ *n* **1** : a passage from sacred writings read in a service of worship **2** : a reading or exercise to be studied by a pupil; *also* : something learned **3** : a period of instruction **4** : an instructive example

les•sor \'les-ˌor, le-'sor\ *n* : one who conveys property by a lease

lest \ˌlest\ *conj* : for fear that

¹**let** \'let\ *n* [ME *lette*, fr. *letten* to delay, hinder, fr. OE *lettan*] **1** : HINDRANCE, OBSTACLE **2** : a shot or point in racket games that does not count

²**let** *vb* **let; let•ting** [ME *leten*, fr. OE *lǣtan*] **1** : to cause to : MAKE ⟨∼ it be known⟩ **2** : RENT, LEASE; *also* : to assign esp. after bids **3** : ALLOW, PERMIT ⟨∼ me go⟩

-let \lət\ *n suffix* **1** : small one ⟨book*let*⟩ **2** : article worn on ⟨wrist*let*⟩

let•down \'let-ˌdau̇n\ *n* **1** : DISAPPOINTMENT **2** : a slackening of effort **3** : the descent of an aircraft to the beginning of a landing approach

le•thal \'lē-thəl\ *adj* : DEADLY, FATAL — **le•thal•ly** \-ē\ *adv*

leth•ar•gy \'leth-ər-jē\ *n* **1** : abnormal drowsiness **2** : the quality or state of being lazy or indifferent **syn** languor, lassitude, torpidity, torpidness — **le•thar•gic** \li-'thär-jik\ *adj*

let on *vb* **1** : REVEAL, ADMIT **2** : PRETEND

¹**let•ter** \'let-ər\ *n* **1** : a symbol that stands for a speech sound and constitutes a unit of an alphabet **2** : a written or printed communication **3** *pl* : LITERATURE; *also* : LEARNING **4** : the literal meaning ⟨the ∼ of the law⟩ **5** : a single piece of type

²**letter** *vb* : to mark with letters : INSCRIBE — **let•ter•er** *n*

let•ter•head \'let-ər-ˌhed\ *n* : stationery with a printed or engraved heading; *also* : the heading itself

let•ter–per•fect \ˌlet-ər-'pər-fikt\ *adj* : correct to the smallest detail

let•ter•press \'let-ər-ˌpres\ *n* **1** : printing done directly by impressing the paper on an inked raised surface **2** *chiefly Brit* : TEXT

letters patent *n pl* : a written grant from a government to a person in a form readily open for inspection by all

let•tuce \'let-əs\ *n* [ME *letuse*, fr. OF *laitues*, pl. of *laitue*, fr. L *lactuca*, fr. *lac* milk; fr. its milky juice] : a garden plant with crisp leaves used esp. in salads

let•up \'let-ˌəp\ *n* : a lessening of effort

leu \'leu̇\ *n, pl* **lei** \'lā\ — see MONEY table

leu•ke•mia \lü-'kē-mē-ə\ *n* : a cancerous disease in which white blood cells increase greatly — **leu•ke•mic** \-mik\ *adj or n*

leu•ko•cyte *also* **leu•co•cyte** \'lü-kə-ˌsīt\ *n* : WHITE BLOOD CELL

lev \'lef\ *n, pl* **le•va** \'lev-ə\ — see MONEY table

Lev *or* **Levit** *abbr* Leviticus

¹**le•vee** \'lev-ē; lə-'vē, -'vā\ *n* [F *lever* act of arising] : a reception held by a person of distinction

²**lev•ee** \'lev-ē\ *n* : an embankment to prevent or confine flooding (as by a river); *also* : a river landing place

¹**lev•el** \'lev-əl\ *n* **1** : a device for establishing a horizontal line or plane **2** : horizontal condition **3** : a horizontal position, line, or surface often taken as an index of altitude; *also* : a flat area of ground **4** : height, position, rank, or size in a scale

²**level** *vb* **-eled** *or* **-elled; -el•ling** *or* **-el•ing** \-(ə-)liŋ\ **1** : to make flat or level; *also* : to come to a level **2** : AIM, DIRECT **3** : EQUALIZE **4** : RAZE — **lev•el•er** *n*

³**level** *adj* **1** : having a flat even surface **2** : HORIZONTAL **3** : of the same height or rank; *also* : UNIFORM **4** : steady and cool in judgment — **lev•el•ly** \'lev-əl-(l)ē\ *adv* — **lev•el•ness** *n*

lev•el•head•ed \ˌlev-əl-'hed-əd\ *adj* : having sound judgment : SENSIBLE

le•ver \'lev-ər, 'lē-vər\ *n* **1** : a bar used for prying or dislodging something; *also* : a means for achieving one's purpose **2** : a rigid piece turning about an axis and used for transmitting and changing force and motion

le·ver·age \'lev-(ə-)rij, 'lēv-\ *n* : the action or mechanical effect of a lever

le·vi·a·than \li-'vī-ə-thən\ *n* **1** : a large sea animal **2** : something very large or formidable of its kind

lev·i·tate \'lev-ə-ˌtāt\ *vb* **-tat·ed; -tat·ing** : to rise or cause to rise in the air in seeming defiance of gravitation — **lev·i·ta·tion** \ˌlev-ə-'tā-shən\ *n*

Le·vit·i·cus \li-'vit-ə-kəs\ *n* — see BIBLE table

lev·i·ty \'lev-ət-ē\ *n* : lack of earnestness **syn** lightness, flippancy, frivolity

¹levy \'lev-ē\ *n, pl* **lev·ies 1** : the imposition or collection of an assessment; *also* : an amount levied **2** : the enlistment of men for military service; *also* : troops raised by levy

²levy *vb* **lev·ied; levy·ing 1** : to impose or collect by legal authority **2** : to enlist for military service **3** : WAGE ⟨~ war⟩ **4** : to seize property in satisfaction of a legal claim

lewd \'lüd\ *adj* [ME *lewed* vulgar, fr. OE *lǣwede* lay, ignorant] **1** : sexually unchaste **2** : OBSCENE, SALACIOUS — **lewd·ly** *adv* — **lewd·ness** *n*

lex·i·cog·ra·phy \ˌlek-sə-'käg-rə-fē\ *n* **1** : the editing or making of a dictionary **2** : the principles and practices of dictionary making — **lex·i·cog·ra·pher** \-fər\ *n* — **lex·i·co·graph·i·cal** \-kō-'graf-i-kəl\ *or* **lex·i·co·graph·ic** \-ik\ *adj*

lex·i·con \'lek-sə-ˌkän\ *n, pl* **lex·i·ca** \-si-kə\ *or* **lexicons** : DICTIONARY

LF *abbr* low frequency

lg *abbr* **1** large **2** long

LH *abbr* **1** left hand **2** lower half

li *abbr* link

Li *symbol* lithium

LI *abbr* Long Island

li·a·bil·i·ty \ˌlī-ə-'bil-ət-ē\ *n, pl* **-ties 1** : the quality or state of being liable **2** *pl* : DEBTS **3** : DISADVANTAGE

li·a·ble \'lī-ə-bəl\ *adj* **1** : legally obligated : RESPONSIBLE **2** : LIKELY, APT ⟨~ to fall⟩ **3** : SUSCEPTIBLE

li·ai·son \'lē-ə-ˌzän, lē-'ā-\ *n* [F] **1** : a close bond : INTERRELATIONSHIP **2** : an illicit sexual relationship **3** : communication for mutual understanding (as between parts of an armed force)

li·ar \'lī-ər\ *n* : a person who lies

¹lib \'lib\ *n* : LIBERATION

²lib *abbr* **1** liberal **2** librarian; library

li·ba·tion \lī-'bā-shən\ *n* **1** : an act of pouring a liquid as a sacrifice (as to a god); *also* : the liquid poured **2** : DRINK — **li·ba·tion·ary** *adj*

¹li·bel \'lī-bəl\ *n* [ME, written declaration, fr. MF, fr. L *libellus,* dim. of *liber* book] **1** : a spoken or written statement or a representation that gives an unjustly unfavorable impression of a person or thing **2** : the action or crime of publishing a libel — **li·bel·ous** *or* **li·bel·lous** \-bə-ləs\ *adj*

²libel *vb* **-beled** *or* **-belled; -bel·ing** *or* **-bel·ling** : to make or publish a libel — **li·bel·er** *n* — **li·bel·ist** *n*

¹lib·er·al \'lib(-ə)-rəl\ *adj* [ME, fr. MF, fr. L *liberalis* suitable for a freeman, generous, fr. *liber* free] **1** : of, relating to, or based on the liberal arts **2** : GENEROUS, BOUNTIFUL **3** : not literal **4** : not narrow in opinion or judgment : TOLERANT; *also* : not orthodox **5** : not conservative — **lib·er·al·i·ty** \ˌlib-ə-'ral-ət-ē\ *n* — **lib·er·al·ize** \'lib-(ə-)rə-ˌlīz\ *vb* — **lib·er·al·ly** \-rə-lē\ *adv*

²liberal *n* : a person who holds liberal views

liberal arts *n pl* : the studies (as language, philosophy, history, literature, or abstract science) in a college or university intended to provide chiefly general knowledge and to develop the general intellectual capacities

lib·er·al·ism \'lib(-ə)-rə-ˌliz-əm\ *n* : liberal principles and theories

lib·er·ate \'lib-ə-ˌrāt\ *vb* **-at·ed; -at·ing 1** : to free from bondage or restraint; *also* : to raise to equal rights and status **2** : to free (as a gas) from combination — **lib·er·a·tion** \ˌlib-ə-'rā-shən\ *n* — **lib·er·a·tor** \'lib-ə-ˌrāt-ər\ *n*

lib·er·at·ed *adj* : freed from or opposed to traditional social and sexual attitudes or roles ⟨a ~ woman⟩

lib·er·tar·i·an \ˌlib-ər-'ter-ē-ən\ *n* **1** : an advocate of the doctrine of free will **2** : one who upholds the principles of liberty

lib·er·tine \'lib-ər-ˌtēn\ *n* : one who leads a dissolute life

lib·er·ty \'lib-ərt-ē\ *n, pl* **-ties 1** : FREEDOM **2** : an action going beyond normal limits; *esp* : FAMILIARITY **3** : a short leave from naval duty

li·bid·i·nous \lə-'bid-ᵊn-əs\ *adj* **1** : LASCIVIOUS **2** : LIBIDINAL

li·bi·do \lə-'bēd-ō, -'bīd-\ *n, pl* **-dos** [NL, fr. L, desire, lust] : psychic energy derived from basic biological urges; *also* : sexual drive — **li·bid·i·nal** \lə-'bid-ᵊn-əl\ *adj*

Li·bra \'lē-brə\ *n* [L, lit., scales] : the 7th sign of the zodiac in astrology

li·brar·i·an \lī-'brer-ē-ən\ *n* : a specialist in the management of a library

li·brary \'lī-ˌbrer-ē\ *n, pl* **-brar·ies 1** : a place in which books and related materials are kept for use but not for sale **2** : a collection of books

li·bret·to \lə-'bret-ō\ *n, pl* **-tos** *or* **-ti** \-ē\ [It, dim. of *libro* book, fr. L *liber*] : the text of a work (as an opera) for the musical theater — **li·bret·tist** \-əst\ *n*

Lib·y·an \'lib-ē-ən\ *n* : a native or inhabitant of Libya — **Libyan** *adj*

lice pl of LOUSE

li·cense *or* **li·cence** \'līs-ᵊns\ *n* **1** : permission to act; *esp* : legal permission to engage in an activity **2** : a document, plate, or tag evidencing a license granted **3** : freedom used irresponsibly — **license** *vb*

licensed practical nurse *n* : a specially trained person who is licensed (as by a state) to provide routine care for the sick

li·cens·ee \ˌlīs-ᵊn-'sē\ *n* : a licensed person

li·cen·te \lə-'sent-ē\ *n, pl* **licente** *or* **li·cen·ti** \-ē\ — see *loti* at MONEY table

li·cen·ti·ate \lī-'sen-chē-ət\ *n* : one licensed to practice a profession

li·cen·tious \lī-'sen-chəs\ *adj* : LEWD, LASCIVIOUS — **li·cen·tious·ly** *adv* — **li·cen·tious·ness** *n*

li·chee var of LITCHI

li·chen \'lī-kən\ *n* : any of various complex lower plants made up of an alga and a fungus growing as a unit on a solid surface — **li·chen·ous** *adj*

lic·it \'lis-ət\ *adj* : LAWFUL

¹lick \'lik\ *vb* **1** : to draw the tongue over; *also* : to flicker over like a tongue **2** : THRASH; *also* : DEFEAT

²lick *n* **1** : a stroke of the tongue **2** : a small amount **3** : a hasty careless effort **4** : BLOW **5** : a natural deposit of salt that animals lick

lick·e·ty–split \ˌlik-ət-ē-'split\ *adv* : at great speed

lick·spit·tle \'lik-ˌspit-ᵊl\ *n* : a fawning subordinate : TOADY

lic·o·rice \'lik(-ə)-rish, -rəs\ *n* [ME *licorice*, fr. OF, fr. LL *liquiritia*, alter. of L *glycyrrhiza*, fr. Gk *glykyrrhiza*, fr. *glykys* sweet + *rhiza* root] **1** : the dried root of a European leguminous plant; *also* : an extract from it used esp. as a flavoring and in medicine **2** : a confection flavored with licorice **3** : a plant yielding licorice

lid \'lid\ *n* **1** : a movable cover **2** : EYELID **3** : a force that represses — **lid·ded** \'lid-əd\ *adj*

li·do \'lēd-ō\ *n, pl* **lidos** : a fashionable beach resort

¹lie \'lī\ *vb* **lay** \'lā\; **lain** \'lān\; **ly·ing** \'lī-iŋ\ **1** : to be in, stay at rest in, or assume a horizontal position; *also* : to be in a helpless or defenseless state **2** : EXTEND **3** : to occupy a certain relative position **4** : to have an effect esp. through mere presence

²lie *n* : the position in which something lies

³lie *vb* **lied; ly·ing** \'lī-iŋ\ : to tell a lie

⁴lie *n* : an untrue statement made with intent to deceive

lied \'lēt\ *n, pl* **lie·der** \'lēd-ər\ [G] : a German song esp. of the 19th century

lief \'lēv, 'lēf\ *adv* : GLADLY, WILLINGLY

¹liege \'lēj\ *adj* [ME, fr. OF, fr. LL *laeticus*, fr. *laetus* serf] : LOYAL, FAITHFUL

²liege *n* **1** : VASSAL **2** : a feudal superior

lien \'lēn, 'lē-ən\ *n* : a legal claim on the property of another for the satisfaction of a debt or the fulfillment of a duty

lieu \'lü\ *n, archaic* : PLACE, STEAD — **in lieu of** : in the place of

lieut *abbr* lieutenant

lieu·ten·ant \lü-'ten-ənt\ *n* [ME, fr. MF, fr. *lieu* place + *tenant* holding, fr. *tenir* to hold, fr. L *tenēre*] **1** : a representative of another in the performance of duty **2** : FIRST LIEUTENANT; *also* : SECOND LIEUTENANT **3** : a commissioned officer in the navy ranking next below a lieutenant commander — **lieu·ten·an·cy** \-ən-sē\ *n*

lieutenant colonel *n* : a commissioned officer (as in the army) ranking next below a colonel

lieutenant commander *n* : a commissioned officer in the navy ranking next below a commander

lieutenant general *n* : a commissioned officer (as in the army) ranking next below a general

lieutenant governor *n* : a deputy or subordinate governor

lieutenant junior grade *n, pl* **lieutenants junior grade** : a commissioned officer in the navy ranking next below a lieutenant

life \'līf\ *n, pl* **lives** \'līvz\ **1** : the quality that distinguishes a vital and functional being from a dead body or inanimate matter; *also* : a state of an organism characterized esp. by capacity for metabolism, growth, reaction to stimuli, and reproduction **2** : the physical and mental experiences of an individual **3** : BIOGRAPHY **4** : the period of existence **5** : manner of living **6** : PERSON **7** : ANIMATION, SPIRIT; *also* : LIVELINESS **8** : animate activity ⟨signs of ∼⟩ **9** : one providing interest and vigor — **life•less** *adj* — **life•like** *adj*

life•blood \'līf-'bləd, -ˌbləd\ *n* : a basic source of strength and vitality

life•boat \-ˌbōt\ *n* : a sturdy boat designed for use in saving lives at sea

life•guard \-ˌgärd\ *n* : a usu. expert swimmer employed to safeguard bathers

life•line \-ˌlīn\ *n* **1** : a line to which persons may cling for safety **2** : a trade route or means of communication considered indispensable

life•long \-ˌlȯŋ\ *adj* : continuing through life

life preserver *n* : a device designed to save a person from drowning by providing buoyancy in water

lif•er \'lī-fər\ *n* **1** : a person sentenced to life imprisonment **2** : a person who makes a career in the armed forces

life raft *n* : a raft for use by people forced into the water

life•sav•ing \'līf-ˌsā-viŋ\ *n* : the skill or practice of saving or protecting lives esp. of drowning persons — **life•sav•er** \-ˌsā-vər\ *n*

life science *n* : a branch of science (as biology, medicine, anthropology, or sociology) that deals with living organisms and life processes — usu. used in pl

life•time \-ˌtīm\ *n* : the duration of an individual's existence

life•work \-'wərk\ *n* : the entire or principal work of one's lifetime; *also* : a work extending over a lifetime

LIFO *abbr* last in, first out

¹lift \'lift\ *vb* **1** : RAISE, ELEVATE; *also* : RISE, ASCEND **2** : to put an end to : STOP **3** : to pay off ⟨∼ a mortgage⟩

²lift *n* **1** : LOAD **2** : the action or an instance of lifting **3** : HELP; *also* : a ride along one's way **4** : RISE, ADVANCE **5** *chiefly Brit* : ELEVATOR **6** : an elevation of the spirits **7** : the upward force that is developed by a moving airfoil and that opposes the pull of gravity

lift–off \'lif-ˌtȯf\ *n* : a vertical takeoff (as by a rocket)

lift truck *n* : a small truck for lifting and transporting loads

lig•a•ment \'lig-ə-mənt\ *n* : a band of tough tissue that holds bones together

li•gate \'lī-ˌgāt\ *vb* **li•gat•ed; li•gat•ing** : to tie with a ligature — **li•ga•tion** \lī-'gā-shən\ *n*

lig•a•ture \'lig-ə-ˌchůr, -chər\ *n* **1** : something that binds or ties; *also* : a thread used in surgery esp. for tying blood vessels **2** : a printed or written character consisting of two or more letters or characters (as *æ*) united

¹light \'līt\ *n* **1** : something that makes vision possible : electromagnetic radiation visible to the human eye; *also* : BRIGHTNESS **2** : DAYLIGHT **3** : a source of light (as a candle) **4** : ENLIGHTENMENT; *also* : TRUTH **5** : public knowledge **6** : a particular aspect or appearance presented to view ⟨now saw the matter in a different ∼⟩ **7** : WINDOW **8** *pl* : STANDARDS ⟨according to his ∼s⟩ **9** : CELEBRITY **10** : LIGHTHOUSE, BEACON; *also* : a traffic signal **11** : a flame for lighting something

²light *adj* **1** : BRIGHT **2** : PALE ⟨∼ blue⟩ — **light•ness** *n*

³light *vb* **light•ed** *or* **lit** \'lit\; **light•ing 1** : to make or become light **2** : to cause to burn : BURN **3** : to conduct with a light **4** : ILLUMINATE

⁴light *adj* **1** : not heavy **2** : not serious ⟨∼ reading⟩ **3** : SCANTY ⟨∼ rain⟩ **4** : GENTLE ⟨a ∼ blow⟩ **5** : easily endurable ⟨∼ cold⟩ ; *also* : requiring little effort ⟨∼ exercise⟩ **6** : SWIFT, NIMBLE **7** : FRIVOLOUS **8** : DIZZY **9** : producing goods for direct consumption by the consumer ⟨∼ industry⟩ — **light•ly** *adv* — **light•ness** *n*

⁵light *adv* **1** : LIGHTLY **2** : with little baggage ⟨travel ∼⟩

⁶light *vb* **light•ed** *or* **lit** \'lit\; **light•ing 1** : SETTLE, ALIGHT **2** : to fall unexpectedly **3** : HAPPEN

light adaptation *n* : the whole process by which the eye adapts to seeing in strong light — **light–adapt•ed** \'līt-ə-ˌdap-təd\ *adj*

light–emitting diode *n* : LED

¹light•en \'līt-ᵊn\ *vb* **light•ened; light•en•ing** \'līt-(ə-)niŋ\ **1** : ILLUMINATE, BRIGHTEN **2** : to give out flashes of lightning

²lighten *vb* **light•ened; light•en•ing** \'līt-(ə-)niŋ\ **1** : to relieve of a burden **2** : GLADDEN **3** : to become lighter

¹ligh•ter \'līt-ər\ *n* : a barge used esp. in loading or unloading ships

²light•er \'līt-ər\ *n* : a device for lighting ⟨a cigarette ∼⟩

light•face \'līt-ˌfās\ *n* : a type having light thin lines — **light•faced** \-ˈfāst\ *adj*

light–head•ed \'līt-ˈhed-əd\ *adj* **1** : feeling confused or dizzy **2** : lacking maturity or seriousness

light•heart•ed \-ˈhärt-əd\ *adj* : free from worry — **light•heart•ed•ly** *adv* — **light•heart•ed•ness** *n*

light•house \-ˌhaús\ *n* : a structure with a powerful light for guiding mariners

light meter *n* : a small portable device for measuring illumination; *esp* : a device for indicating correct photographic exposure

¹light•ning \'līt-niŋ\ *n* : the flashing of light produced by a discharge of atmospheric electricity from one cloud to another or between a cloud and the earth; *also* : the discharge itself

²lightning *adj* : extremely fast

lightning bug *n* : FIREFLY

lightning rod *n* : a grounded metallic rod set up on a structure to protect it from lightning

light out *vb* : to leave in a hurry

light•proof \'līt-ˈprüf\ *adj* : impenetrable by light

lights \'līts\ *n pl* : the lungs esp. of a slaughtered animal

light•ship \'līt-ˌship\ *n* : a ship with a powerful light moored at a place dangerous to navigation

light show *n* : a kaleidoscopic display (as of colored lights) imitating the effects of psychedelic drugs

light•some \'līt-səm\ *adj* **1** : free from care **2** : NIMBLE

¹light•weight \'līt-ˌwāt\ *n* : one of less than average weight; *esp* : a boxer weighing more than 126 but not over 135 pounds

²lightweight *adj* **1** : INCONSEQUENTIAL **2** : of less than average weight

light–year \'līt-ˌyiər\ *n* **1** : an astronomical unit of distance equal to the distance that light travels in one year or about 5,878,000,000,000 miles **2** : an extremely long distance esp. as a measure of progress

lig•ne•ous \'lig-nē-əs\ *adj* : WOODY

lig•ni•fy \'lig-nə-ˌfī\ *vb* **-fied; -fy•ing** : to convert into or become wood or woody tissue — **lig•ni•fi•ca•tion** \ˌlig-nə-fə-ˈkā-shən\ *n*

lig•nite \'lig-ˌnīt\ *n* : brownish black soft coal esp. of a slightly woody texture

¹like \'līk\ *vb* **liked; lik•ing 1** : ENJOY ⟨∼s baseball⟩ **2** : WANT **3** : CHOOSE ⟨does as she ∼s⟩ — **lik•able** *or* **like•able** \'lī-kə-bəl\ *adj*

²like *n* : PREFERENCE

³like *adj* : SIMILAR **syn** alike, analogous, comparable, parallel, uniform

⁴like *prep* **1** : similar or similarly to **2** : typical of **3** : inclined to ⟨looks ∼ rain⟩ **4** : such as ⟨a subject ∼ physics⟩

⁵like *n* : COUNTERPART

⁶like *conj* : in the same way that

-like \ˌlīk\ *adj comb form* : resembling or characteristic of ⟨lady*like* behavior⟩ ⟨a life*like* statue⟩

like•li•hood \'lī-klē-ˌhúd\ *n* : PROBABILITY

¹like•ly \'lī-klē\ *adj* **like•li•er; -est 1** : PROBABLE **2** : BELIEVABLE **3** : PROMISING ⟨a ∼ place to fish⟩

²likely *adv* : in all probability

lik•en \'lī-kən\ *vb* **lik•ened; lik•en•ing** \'līk-(ə-)niŋ\ : COMPARE

like•ness \'līk-nəs\ *n* **1** : COPY, PORTRAIT **2** : APPEARANCE, GUISE **3** : RESEMBLANCE

like•wise \-ˌwīz\ *adv* **1** : in like manner **2** : in addition : ALSO

lik•ing \\'lī-kiŋ\ *n* : favorable regard; *also* : TASTE

li•ku•ta \li-'küt-ə\ *n, pl* **ma•ku•ta** \mä-\ — see MONEY table

li•lac \\'lī-lək, -ˌlak, -ˌläk\ *n* [obs. F (now *lilas*), fr. Ar *līlak*, fr. Per *nīlak* bluish, fr. *nīl* blue, fr. Skt *nīla* dark blue] **1** : a shrub with large clusters of fragrant grayish pink, purple, or white flowers **2** : a moderate purple

lil•an•ge•ni \ˌlil-ən-'gen-ē\ *n, pl* **em•a•lan•ge•ni** \ˌem-ə-lən-'gen-ē\ — see MONEY table

lil•li•pu•tian \ˌlil-ə-'pyü-shən\ *adj, often cap* **1** : SMALL, MINIATURE **2** : PETTY

lilt \\'lilt\ *n* **1** : a cheerful lively song or tune **2** : a rhythmical swing, flow, or cadence

lily \\'lil-ē\ *n, pl* **lil•ies** : any of numerous tall bulbous herbs with leafy stems and usu. funnel-shaped flowers; *also* : any of various related plants (as the onion, amaryllis, or iris)

lily of the valley : a low perennial herb of the lily family that produces a raceme of fragrant nodding bell≠ shaped white flowers

li•ma bean \ˌlī-mə-\ *n* : any of various bushy or tall-growing beans that have flat edible usu. pale green or whitish seeds; *also* : the seed of a lima bean

limb \\'lim\ *n* **1** : one of the projecting paired appendages (as legs, arms, or wings) that an animal uses esp. in moving or grasping **2** : a large branch of a tree : BOUGH — **limb•less** *adj*

¹lim•ber \\'lim-bər\ *adj* **1** : FLEXIBLE, SUPPLE **2** : LITHE, NIMBLE

²limber *vb* **lim•bered; lim•ber•ing** \-b(ə-)riŋ\ : to make or become limber

¹lim•bo \\'lim-bō\ *n, pl* **limbos** [ME, fr. ML, abl. of *limbus* limbo, fr. L, border] **1** *often cap* : an abode of souls barred from heaven through no fault of their own **2** : a place or state of confinement or oblivion

²limbo *n, pl* **limbos** [native name in West Indies] : a West Indian acrobatic dance orig. for men

Lim•burg•er \\'lim-ˌbər-gər\ *n* : a creamy semisoft surface-ripened cheese with a pungent odor and strong flavor

¹lime \\'līm\ *n* : a caustic infusible white substance that consists of calcium and oxygen, is obtained by heating lime- stone or shells until they crumble to powder, and is used in making cement and in fertilizer — **limy** \\'lī-mē\ *adj*

²lime *n* : a small lemonlike greenish yellow citrus fruit with juicy acid pulp

lime•ade \ˌlīm-'ād\ *n* : a beverage of lime juice, sugar, and water

lime•light \\'līm-ˌlīt\ *n* **1** : a device in which flame is directed against a cylinder of lime formerly used in the theater to cast a strong white light on the stage **2** : the center of public attention

lim•er•ick \\'lim-(ə-)rik\ *n* : a light or humorous poem of 5 lines

lime•stone \\'līm-ˌstōn\ *n* : a rock that is formed by accumulation of organic remains (as shells), is used in building, and yields lime when burned

¹lim•it \\'lim-ət\ *vb* **1** : to set limits to **2** : to reduce in quantity or extent — **lim•i•ta•tion** \ˌlim-ə-'tā-shən\ *n*

²limit *n* **1** : BOUNDARY; *also, pl* : BOUNDS **2** : something that restrains or confines; *also* : the utmost extent **3** : a prescribed maximum or minimum — **lim•it•less** *adj*

lim•it•ed \\'lim-ət-əd\ *adj* **1** : confined within limits **2** : offering superior and faster service and transportation

limn \\'lim\ *vb* **limned; limn•ing** \lim-(n)iŋ\ **1** : DRAW; *also* : PAINT **2** : DELINEATE **3** : DESCRIBE

li•mo•nite \\'lī-mə-ˌnīt\ *n* : a ferric oxide that is a major ore of iron — **li•mo•nit•ic** \ˌlī-mə-'nit-ik\ *adj*

lim•ou•sine \\'lim-ə-ˌzēn, ˌlim-ə-'zēn\ *n* [F] **1** : a large luxurious often chauffeur-driven sedan **2** : a large vehicle for transporting passengers to and from an airport

¹limp \\'limp\ *vb* : to walk lamely; *also* : to proceed with difficulty

²limp *n* : a limping movement or gait

³limp *adj* **1** : having no defined shape; *also* : not stiff or rigid **2** : lacking in strength or firmness — **limp•ly** *adv* — **limp•ness** *n*

lim•pet \\'lim-pət\ *n* : a sea mollusk with a conical shell that clings to rocks or timbers

lim•pid \\'lim-pəd\ *adj* [F or L; F *limpide*, fr. L *limpidus*, fr. *lympha, limpa* water] : CLEAR, TRANSPARENT

lin *abbr* **1** lineal **2** linear

lin•age \\'lī-nij\ *n* : the number of lines of written or printed matter

linch·pin \\'linch-ˌpin\ *n* : a locking pin inserted crosswise (as through the end of an axle)

lin·den \\'lin-dən\ *n* : any of a genus of trees with large heart-shaped leaves and clustered yellowish flowers rich in nectar

¹line \\'līn\ *vb* **lined; lin·ing** : to cover the inner surface of

²line *n* **1** : CORD, ROPE, WIRE; *also* : a length of material used in measuring and leveling **2** : pipes for conveying a fluid ⟨a gas ∼⟩ **3** : a horizontal row of written or printed characters; *also* : VERSE **4** : NOTE **5** : the words making up a part in a drama — usu. used in pl. **6** : something distinct, long, and narrow; *also* : ROUTE **7** : a state of agreement **8** : a course of conduct, action, or thought; *also* : OCCUPATION **9** : LIMIT **10** : an arrangement of persons or objects of one kind in an orderly series ⟨a ∼ of trees⟩ ⟨waiting in ∼⟩ **11** : a transportation system **12** : the football players who are stationed on the line of scrimmage **13** : a long narrow mark; *also* : EQUATOR **14** : a geometric element that is the path of a moving point **15** : CONTOUR **16** : a general plan **17** : an indication based on insight or investigation

³line *vb* **lined; lin·ing** **1** : to mark with a line **2** : to place or form a line along **3** : ALIGN

lin·eage \\'lin-ē-ij\ *n* : lineal descent from a common progenitor; *also* : FAMILY

lin·eal \\'lin-ē-əl\ *adj* **1** : LINEAR **2** : consisting of or being in a direct line of ancestry; *also* : HEREDITARY

lin·ea·ment \\'lin-ē-ə-mənt\ *n* : an outline, feature, or contour of a body and esp. of a face — usu. used in pl.

lin·ear \\'lin-ē-ər\ *adj* **1** : of, relating to, or consisting of a line : STRAIGHT **2** : composed of simply drawn lines with little attempt at pictorial representation ⟨∼ script⟩ **3** : being long and uniformly narrow

line·back·er \\'līn-ˌbak-ər\ *n* : a defensive football player who lines up immediately behind the line of scrimmage

line drive *n* : a baseball hit in a nearly straight line not far above the ground

line·man \\'līn-mən\ *n* **1** : one who sets up or repairs communication or power lines **2** : a player in the line in football

lin·en \\'lin-ən\ *n* **1** : cloth made of flax; *also* : thread or yarn spun from flax **2** : clothing or household articles made of linen cloth or similar fabric

line of scrimmage : an imaginary line in football parallel to the goal lines and tangent to the nose of the ball laid on the ground before a scrimmage

¹lin·er \\'lī-nər\ *n* : a ship or airplane of a regular transportation line

²liner *n* : one that lines or is used as a lining

line score *n* : a score of a baseball game giving the runs, hits, and errors made by each team

lines·man \\'līnz-mən\ *n* **1** : LINEMAN **2** : an official who assists a referee

line·up \\'līn-ˌəp\ *n* **1** : a list of players taking part in a game (as of baseball) **2** : a line of persons arranged esp. for identification by police

ling \\'liŋ\ *n* : any of several fishes related to the cod

lin·ger \\'liŋ-gər\ *vb* **lin·gered; lin·ger·ing** \-g(ə-)riŋ\ : TARRY; *also* : PROCRASTINATE

lin·ge·rie \ˌlän-jə-'rā, ˌlaⁿ-zhə-, -'rē\ *n* [F, fr. MF, fr. *linge* linen, fr. L *lineus* made of linen, fr. *linum* flax, linen] : women's intimate apparel

lin·go \\'liŋ-gō\ *n, pl* **lingoes** : usu. strange or incomprehensible language

lin·gua fran·ca \ˌliŋ-gwə-'fraŋ-kə\ *n, pl* **lingua francas** *or* **lin·guae fran·cae** \-gwē-'fraŋ-ˌkē\ [It] **1** : a common language that consists of Italian mixed with French, Spanish, Greek, and Arabic and is spoken in Mediterranean ports **2** : any of various languages used as common or commercial tongues among speakers of different languages

lin·gual \\'liŋ-gwəl\ *adj* : of, relating to, or produced by the tongue

lin·guist \\'liŋ-gwəst\ *n* **1** : a person skilled in languages **2** : one who specializes in linguistics

lin·guis·tics \liŋ-'gwis-tiks\ *n* : the study of human speech including the units, nature, structure, and development of language or a language — **lin·guis·tic** *adj*

lin·i·ment \\'lin-ə-mənt\ *n* : a liquid

preparation rubbed on the skin esp. to relieve pain

lin·ing \'lī-niŋ\ n : material used to line esp. an inner surface

link \'liŋk\ n **1** : a connecting structure; *esp* : a single ring of a chain **2** : BOND, TIE — **link** vb

link·age \'liŋ-kij\ n **1** : the manner or style of being united **2** : the quality or state of being linked **3** : a system of links

linking verb n : a word or expression (as a form of *be, become, feel,* or *seem*) that links a subject with its predicate

links \'liŋks\ n pl : a golf course

link·up \'liŋk-,əp\ n **1** : MEETING **2** : something that serves as a linking device or factor

lin·net \'lin-ət\ n : an Old World finch

li·no·leum \lə-'nō-lē-əm\ n [L *lin*um flax + *oleum* oil] : a floor covering with a canvas back and a surface of hardened linseed oil and a filler (as cork dust)

lin·seed \'lin-,sēd\ n : the seeds of flax yielding a yellowish oil (**linseed oil**) used esp. in paints and linoleum

lin·sey–wool·sey \,lin-zē-'wùl-zē\ n : a coarse sturdy fabric of wool and linen or cotton

lint \'lint\ n **1** : linen made into a soft fleecy substance for use in surgical dressings **2** : fine ravels, fluff, or loose short fibers from yarn or fabrics **3** : the fibers that surround cotton seeds and form the cotton staple

lin·tel \'lint-ᵊl\ n : a horizontal piece across the top of an opening (as of a door) that carries the weight of the structure above it

li·on \'lī-ən\ n, pl **lions** : a large flesh–eating cat of Africa and southern Asia with a shaggy mane in the male

li·on·ess \'lī-ə-nəs\ n : a female lion

li·on·heart·ed \,lī-ən-'härt-əd\ adj : COURAGEOUS, BRAVE

li·on·ize \'lī-ə-,nīz\ vb -ized; iz·ing : to treat as an object of great interest or importance — **li·on·iza·tion** \lī-ə-nə-'zā-shən\ n

lip \'lip\ n **1** : either of the two fleshy folds that surround the mouth; *also* : a part or projection suggesting such a lip **2** : the edge of a hollow vessel or cavity — **lipped** \'lipt\ adj

lip·read·ing \'lip-,rēd-iŋ\ n : the interpreting of a speaker's words without hearing the voice by watching lip and facial movements

lip service n : avowal of allegiance that goes no further than verbal expression

lip·stick \'lip-,stik\ n : a waxy solid colored cosmetic in stick form for the lips

liq abbr **1** liquid **2** liquor

liq·ue·fy also **liq·ui·fy** \'lik-wə-,fī\ vb -fied; -fy·ing : to make or become liquid — **liq·ue·fac·tion** \,lik-wə-'fak-shən\ n — **liq·ue·fi·able** \-,fī-ə-bəl\ adj — **liq·ue·fi·er** \-,fī(-ə)r\ n

li·queur \li-'kər\ n [F] : a distilled alcoholic liquor flavored with aromatic susbtances and usu. sweetened

¹liq·uid \'lik-wəd\ adj **1** : flowing freely like water **2** : neither solid nor gaseous **3** : shining and clear ⟨large ~ eyes⟩ **4** : smooth and musical in tone; *also* : smooth and unconstrained in movement **5** : consisting of or capable of ready conversion into cash ⟨~ assets⟩ — **li·quid·i·ty** \lik-'wid-ət-ē\ n

²liquid n : a liquid substance

liq·ui·date \'lik-wə-,dāt\ vb -dat·ed; -dat·ing **1** : to pay off ⟨~ a debt⟩ **2** : to settle the accounts and distribute the assets of (as a business) **3** : to get rid of; *esp* : KILL — **liq·ui·da·tion** \,lik-wə-'dā-shən\ n

liquid crystal n : an organic liquid that resembles a crystal in having ordered molecular arrays

liquid crystal display n : LCD

liquid measure n : a unit or series of units for measuring liquid capacity — see METRIC SYSTEM table, WEIGHT table

li·quor \'lik-ər\ n : a liquid substance; *esp* : a distilled alcoholic beverage

li·ra \'lir-ə, 'lē-rə\ n — see MONEY table

lisle \'līl\ n : a smooth tightly twisted thread usu. made of long-staple cotton

lisp \'lisp\ vb : to pronounce \s\ and \z\ imperfectly esp. by giving them the sounds of \th\ and \t͟h\; *also* : to speak childishly — **lisp** n

lis·some also **lis·som** \'lis-əm\ adj : LITHE; *also* : NIMBLE

¹list \'list\ vb, archaic : PLEASE; *also* : WISH

²list vb, archaic : LISTEN

³list n **1** : a simple series of words or

numerals; *also* : an official roster **2** : CATALOG, CHECKLIST

⁴list *vb* : to make a list of; *also* : to include on a list

⁵list *vb* : TILT

⁶list *n* : a leaning to one side : TILT

lis·ten \'lis-ᵊn\ *vb* **lis·tened; lis·ten·ing** \'lis-(ᵊ-)niŋ\ **1** : to pay attention in order to hear **2** : HEED — **lis·ten·er** \'lis-(ᵊ-)nər\ *n*

lis·ten·er·ship \'lis-(ᵊ-)nər-ˌship\ *n* : the audience for a radio program or record album

list·ing \'lis-tiŋ\ *n* **1** : an act or instance of making or including in a list **2** : something that is listed

list·less \'list-ləs\ *adj* : LANGUID, SPIRITLESS — **list·less·ly** *adv* — **list·less·ness** *n*

list price *n* : the price of an item as published in a catalog, price list, or advertisement but subject to discounts

lists \'lists\ *n pl* : an arena for combat (as jousting)

¹lit \'lit\ past and past part of LIGHT

²lit *abbr* **1** liter **2** literal; literally **3** literary **4** literature

lit·a·ny \'lit-ᵊn-ē\ *n, pl* **-nies** [ME *letanie*, fr. OF, fr. LL *litania*, fr. LGk *litaneia*, fr. Gk, entreaty, fr. *litanos* entreating] : a prayer consisting of a series of supplications and responses said alternately by a leader and a group

li·tchi \'lī-chē, 'lē-\ *n* [Chin (Peking dialect) *li⁴ chih¹*] **1** : an oval fruit with a hard scaly outer covering, a small hard seed, and edible flesh **2** : a tree bearing litchis

li·ter \'lēt-ər\ *n* — see METRIC SYSTEM table

lit·er·al \'lit-(ə-)rəl\ *adj* **1** : adhering to fact or to the ordinary or usual meaning (as of a word) **2** : UNADORNED; *also* : PROSAIC **3** : VERBATIM

lit·er·al·ism \'lit-(ə-)rə-ˌliz-əm\ *n* **1** : adherence to the explicit substance (as of an idea) **2** : fidelity to observable fact — **lit·er·al·is·tic** \ˌlit-(ə-)rə-'lis-tik\ *adj*

lit·er·al·ly \'lit-ər-(ə-)lē, 'li-trə-lē\ *adv* **1** : ACTUALLY ⟨was ∼ insane⟩ **2** : VIRTUALLY ⟨∼ poured out new ideas⟩

lit·er·ary \'lit-ə-ˌrer-ē\ *adj* **1** : of or relating to literature **2** : versed in literature : WELL-READ

lit·er·ate \'lit-(ə-)rət\ *adj* **1** : EDUCATED; *also* : able to read and write **2** : LITERARY; *also* : POLISHED, LUCID — **lit·er·a·cy** \'lit-(ə-)rə-sē\ *n*

li·te·ra·ti \ˌlit-ə-'rät-ē\ *n pl* **1** : the educated class **2** : persons interested in literature or the arts

lit·er·a·tim \ˌlit-ə-'rāt-əm, -'rät-\ *adv or adj* : letter for letter

lit·er·a·ture \'lit-(ə-)rə-ˌchùr, -chər\ *n* **1** : the production of written works having excellence of form or expression and dealing with ideas of permanent interest **2** : the written works produced in a particular language, country, or age

lithe \'līth̄, 'līth\ *adj* **1** : SUPPLE, RESILIENT **2** : characterized by effortless grace

lithe·some \'līth̄-səm, 'līth-\ *adj* : LISSOME

lith·i·um \'lith-ē-əm\ *n* : a light silver-white chemical element

li·thog·ra·phy \lith-'äg-rə-fē\ *n* : the process of printing from a plane surface (as a smooth stone or metal plate) on which the image to be printed is ink-receptive and the blank area ink-repellent — **lith·o·graph** \'lith-ə-ˌgraf\ *vb* — **lithograph** *n* — **li·thog·ra·pher** \lith-'äg-rə-fər, 'lith-ə-ˌgraf-ər\ *n* — **lith·o·graph·ic** \ˌlith-ə-'graf-ik\ *adj* — **lith·o·graph·i·cal·ly** \-i-k(ə-)lē\ *adv*

li·thol·o·gy \lith-'äl-ə-jē\ *n, pl* **-gies** : the study of rocks — **lith·o·log·ic** \ˌlith-ə-'läj-ik\ *adj*

lith·o·sphere \'lith-ə-ˌsfiər\ *n* : the outer part of the solid earth

Lith·u·a·nian \ˌlith-(y)ə-'wā-nē-ən\ *n* **1** : a native or inhabitant of Lithuania **2** : the language of the Lithuanians — **Lithuanian** *adj*

lit·i·gant \'lit-i-gənt\ *n* : a party to a lawsuit

lit·i·gate \'lit-ə-ˌgāt\ *vb* **-gat·ed; -gat·ing** : to carry on a legal contest by judicial process; *also* : to contest at law — **lit·i·ga·tion** \ˌlit-ə-'gā-shən\ *n*

li·ti·gious \lə-'tij-əs\ *adj* **1** : CONTENTIOUS **2** : prone to engage in lawsuits **3** : of or relating to litigation — **li·ti·gious·ness** *n*

lit·mus \'lit-məs\ *n* : a coloring matter from lichens that turns red in acid solutions and blue in alkaline

litmus test *n* : a test in which a single factor (as an attitude) is decisive

Litt D *or* **Lit D** *abbr* [ML *litterarum doctor*] : doctor of letters; doctor of literature

¹**lit·ter** \ˈlit-ər\ *n* [ME, fr. OF *litiere*, fr. *lit* bed, fr. L *lectus*] **1** : a covered and curtained couch with shafts used to carry a single passenger; *also* : a device (as a stretcher) for carrying a sick or injured person **2** : material used as bedding for animals; *also* : the uppermost layer of organic debris on the forest floor **3** : the offspring of an animal at one birth **4** : RUBBISH

²**litter** *vb* **1** : to give birth to young **2** : to strew with litter

lit·ter·a·teur \ˌlit-ə-rə-ˈtər\ *n* [F] : a literary person; *esp* : a professional writer

lit·ter·bug \ˈlit-ər-ˌbəg\ *n* : one who litters a public area

¹**lit·tle** \ˈlit-ᵊl\ *adj* **lit·tler** \ˈlit-(ᵊ-)lər\ *or* **less** \ˈles\ *or* **less·er** \ˈles-ər\; **lit·tlest** \ˈlit-(ᵊ-)ləst\ *or* **least** \ˈlēst\ **1** : not big **2** : not important **3** : not much **4** : NARROW, MEAN — **lit·tle·ness** *n*

²**little** *adv* **less** \ˈles\; **least** \ˈlēst\ **1** : SLIGHTLY; *also* : not at all **2** : INFREQUENTLY

³**little** *n* **1** : a small amount or quantity **2** : a short time or distance

Little Dipper *n* : DIPPER 4

little theater *n* : a small theater for low-cost usu. experimental drama designed for a limited audience

lit·to·ral \ˈlit-ə-rəl; ˌlit-ə-ˈral\ *adj* : of, relating to, or growing on or near a shore esp. of the sea — **littoral** *n*

lit·ur·gy \ˈlit-ər-jē\ *n, pl* **-gies** : a rite or body of rites prescribed for public worship — **li·tur·gi·cal** \lə-ˈtər-ji-kəl\ *adj* — **li·tur·gi·cal·ly** \-k(ə-)lē\ *adv* — **lit·ur·gist** \ˈlit-ər-jəst\ *n*

liv·able *also* **live·able** \ˈliv-ə-bəl\ *adj* **1** : suitable for living in or with **2** : ENDURABLE — **liv·a·bil·i·ty** \ˌliv-ə-ˈbil-ət-ē\ *n*

¹**live** \ˈliv\ *vb* **lived**; **liv·ing** **1** : to be or continue alive **2** : SUBSIST **3** : RESIDE **4** : to conduct one's life **5** : to remain in human memory or record

²**live** \ˈlīv\ *adj* **1** : having life **2** : BURNING, GLOWING ⟨a ∼ cigar⟩ **3** : connected to electric power ⟨a ∼ wire⟩ **4** : UNEXPLODED ⟨a ∼ bomb⟩ **5** : of continuing interest ⟨a ∼ issue⟩ **6** : of or involving the actual presence of real people ⟨∼ audience⟩; *also* : broadcast directly at the time of production ⟨a ∼ radio program⟩ **7** : being in play ⟨a ∼ ball⟩

lived–in \ˈlivd-ˌin\ *adj* : of or suggesting long-term human habitation or use

live down *vb* : to live so as to wipe out the memory or effects of

live in \(ˈ)liv-ˈin\ *vb* : to live in one's place of employment — used of a servant — **live–in** \ˌliv-ˌin\ *adj*

live·li·hood \ˈlīv-lē-ˌhu̇d\ *n* : means of support or subsistence

live·long \ˌliv-ˌlȯŋ\ *adj* [ME *lef long*, fr. *lef* dear + *long* long] : WHOLE, ENTIRE ⟨the ∼ day⟩

live·ly \ˈlīv-lē\ *adj* **live·li·er; -est** **1** : full of life **2** : KEEN, VIVID ⟨∼ interest⟩ **3** : ANIMATED ⟨∼ debate⟩ **4** : showing activity or vigor ⟨a ∼ manner⟩ **5** : quick to rebound ⟨a ∼ ball⟩ **syn** vivacious, sprightly, gay, animated, spirited — **live·li·ness** *n*

liv·en \ˈlī-vən\ *vb* **liv·ened; liv·en·ing** \ˈlīv-(ə-)niŋ\ : ENLIVEN

¹**liv·er** \ˈliv-ər\ *n* : a large glandular organ of vertebrates that secretes bile and is a center of metabolic activity — **liv·ered** \ˈliv-ərd\ *adj*

²**liver** *n* : one that lives esp. in a specified way ⟨a fast ∼⟩

liv·er·ish \ˈliv-(ə-)rish\ *adj* **1** : resembling liver esp. in color **2** : BILIOUS **3** : MELANCHOLY

liv·er·wort \ˈliv-ər-ˌwərt\ *n* : any of various plants resembling the related mosses

liv·er·wurst \-ˌwərst, -ˌwu̇(r)st\ *n* [part trans. of G *leberwurst*, fr. *leber* liver + *wurst* sausage] : a sausage consisting chiefly of liver

liv·ery \ˈliv-(ə-)rē\ *n, pl* **-er·ies** **1** : a special uniform worn by the servants of a wealthy household; *also* : distinctive dress **2** : the feeding, care, and stabling of horses for pay; *also* : the keeping of horses and vehicles for hire — **liv·er·ied** \-rēd\ *adj*

liv·ery·man \-mən\ *n* : the keeper of a livery stable

lives *pl of* LIFE

live·stock \ˈlīv-ˌstäk\ *n* : farm animals kept for use and profit

live wire *n* : an alert active aggressive person

liv·id \'liv-əd\ *adj* [F *livide*, fr. L *lividus*, fr. *livēre* to be blue] **1** : discolored by bruising **2** : ASHEN, PALLID **3** : REDDISH **4** : ENRAGED

¹**liv·ing** \'liv-iŋ\ *adj* **1** : having life **2** : NATURAL **3** : full of life and vigor; *also* : VIVID

²**living** *n* **1** : the condition of being alive; *also* : manner of life **2** : LIVELIHOOD

living room *n* : a room in a residence used for the common social activities of the occupants

living wage *n* : a wage sufficient to provide the necessities and comforts held to comprise an acceptable standard of living

liz·ard \'liz-ərd\ *n* : a 4-legged scaly reptile with a long tapering tail

Lk *abbr* Luke

ll *abbr* lines

lla·ma \'läm-ə\ *n* [Sp] : any of several wild or domesticated So. American mammals related to the camel but smaller and without a hump

lla·no \'län-ō\ *n, pl* **llanos** : an open grassy plain esp. of Latin America

LLD *abbr* [NL *legum doctor*] doctor of laws

LNG *abbr* liquefied natural gas

¹**load** \'lōd\ *n* **1** : PACK; *also* : CARGO **2** : a mass of weight supported by something **3** : something that burdens the mind or spirits **4** : a large quantity — usu. used in pl. **5** : a standard, expected, or authorized burden

²**load** *vb* **1** : to put a load in or on; *also* : to receive a load **2** : BURDEN **3** : to increase the weight of by adding something **4** : to supply abundantly **5** : to put a charge in (as a firearm)

load·ed \'lōd-əd\ *adj* **1** *slang* : DRUNK **2** : having a large amount of money

load·stone var of LODESTONE

¹**loaf** \'lōf\ *n, pl* **loaves** \'lōvz\ : a shaped or molded mass esp. of bread

²**loaf** *vb* : to spend time in idleness : LOUNGE — **loaf·er** *n*

loam \'lōm, 'lüm\ *n* : SOIL; *esp* : a loose soil of mixed clay, sand, and silt — **loamy** *adj*

¹**loan** \'lōn\ *n* **1** : money lent at interest; *also* : something lent for the borrower's temporary use **2** : the grant of temporary use

²**loan** *vb* : LEND

loan shark *n* : a person who lends money at excessive rates of interest — **loan·shark·ing** \'lōn-ˌshär-kiŋ\ *n*

loan·word \'lōn-ˌwərd\ *n* : a word taken from another language and at least partly naturalized

loath \'lōth, 'lōth\ *also* **loathe** \lōth, lōth\ *adj* : RELUCTANT

loathe \'lōth\ *vb* **loathed; loath·ing** : to dislike greatly **syn** abominate, abhor, detest, hate

loath·ing \'lō-thiŋ\ *n* : extreme disgust

loath·some \'lōth-səm, 'lōth-\ *adj* : exciting loathing : REPULSIVE

lob \'läb\ *vb* **lobbed; lob·bing** : to throw, hit, or propel something in a high arc — **lob** *n*

¹**lob·by** \'läb-ē\ *n, pl* **lobbies 1** : a corridor or hall used esp. as a passageway or waiting room **2** : a group of persons engaged in lobbying

²**lobby** *vb* **lob·bied; lob·by·ing** : to try to influence public officials and esp. legislators — **lob·by·ist** *n*

lobe \'lōb\ *n* : a curved or rounded projection or division — **lo·bar** \'lō-bər\ *adj* — **lobed** \'lōbd\ *adj*

lo·bot·o·my \lō-'bät-ə-mē\ *n, pl* **-mies** : severance of nerve fibers by incision into the brain for the relief of some mental disorders

lob·ster \'läb-stər\ *n* [ME, fr. OE *loppestre*, fr. *loppe* spider] : an edible marine crustacean with two large pincerlike claws and four other pairs of legs; *also* : SPINY LOBSTER

lob·ule \'läb-yül\ *n* : a small lobe; *also* : a subdivision of a lobe — **lob·u·lar** \'läb-yə-lər\ *adj*

¹**lo·cal** \'lō-kəl\ *adj* **1** : of, relating to, or occupying a particular place **2** : serving a particular limited district; *also* : making all stops ⟨a ~ train⟩ **3** : affecting a small part of the body ⟨~ infection⟩ — **lo·cal·ly** \-ē\ *adv*

²**local** *n* : one that is local

lo·cale \lō-'kal\ *n* : a place that is the setting for a particular event

lo·cal·i·ty \lō-'kal-ət-ē\ *n, pl* **-ties** : a particular spot, situation, or location

lo·cal·ize \'lō-kə-ˌlīz\ *vb* **-ized; -iz·ing** : to fix in or confine to a definite place or locality — **lo·cal·iza·tion** \ˌlō-kə-lə-'zā-shən\ *n*

lo·cate \'lō-ˌkāt, lō-'kāt\ *vb* **lo·cat·ed; lo-**

cat·ing 1 : STATION, SETTLE **2** : to determine the site of **3** : to find or fix the place of in a sequence

lo·ca·tion \lō-'kā-shən\ *n* **1** : SITUATION, PLACE **2** : the process of locating **3** : a place outside a studio where a motion picture is filmed

loc cit *abbr* [L *loco citato*] in the place cited

loch \'läk, 'läk\ *n, Scot* : LAKE; *also* : a bay or arm of the sea esp. when nearly landlocked

¹lock \'läk\ *n* : a tuft, strand, or ringlet of hair; *also* : a cohering bunch (as of wool or flax)

²lock *n* **1** : a fastening in which a bolt is operated **2** : the mechanism of a firearm by which the charge is exploded **3** : an enclosure (as in a canal) used in raising or lowering boats from level to level **4** : a wrestling hold

³lock *vb* **1** : to fasten the lock of; *also* : to make fast with a lock **2** : to confine or exclude by means of a lock **3** : INTERLOCK

lock·er \'läk-ər\ *n* **1** : a drawer, cupboard, or compartment for individual storage use **2** : an insulated compartment for storing frozen food

lock·et \'läk-ət\ *n* : a small usu. metal case for a memento worn suspended from a chain or necklace

lock·jaw \'läk-ˌjȯ\ *n* : TETANUS

lock·nut \-ˌnət\ *n* **1** : a nut screwed tight on another to prevent it from slacking back **2** : a nut designed to lock itself when screwed tight

lock·out \'läk-ˌau̇t\ *n* : the suspension of work by an employer during a labor dispute in order to make employees accept the terms being offered

lock·smith \'läk-ˌsmith\ *n* : one who makes or repairs locks

lock·step \'läk-ˌstep\ *n* : a mode of marching in step by a body of men moving in a very close single file

lock·up \'läk-ˌəp\ *n* : JAIL

lo·co \'lō-kō\ *adj, slang* [Sp] : CRAZY, FRENZIED

lo·co·mo·tion \ˌlō-kə-'mō-shən\ *n* **1** : the act or power of moving from place to place **2** : TRAVEL

¹lo·co·mo·tive \ˌlō-kə-'mōt-iv\ *adj* : of or relating to locomotion or a locomotive

²locomotive *n* : a self-propelled vehicle used to move railroad cars

lo·co·mo·tor \ˌlō-kə-'mōt-ər\ *adj* : of or relating to locomotion or organs used in locomotion

lo·co·weed \'lō-kō-ˌwēd\ *n* : any of several leguminous plants of western No. America that are poisonous to livestock

lo·cus \'lō-kəs\ *n, pl* **lo·ci** \'lō-ˌsī\ [L] **1** : PLACE, LOCALITY **2** : the set of all points whose location is determined by stated conditions

lo·cust \'lō-kəst\ *n* **1** : a usu. destructive migratory grasshopper **2** : CICADA **3** : any of various leguminous trees with hard wood

lo·cu·tion \lō-'kyü-shən\ *n* : a particular form of expression; *also* : PHRASEOLOGY

lode \'lōd\ *n* : an ore deposit

lode·star \'lōd-ˌstär\ *n* [ME *lode sterre*, fr. *lode* course, fr. OE *lād*] : a guiding star; *esp* : NORTH STAR

lode·stone \-ˌstōn\ *n* : an iron-containing rock with magnetic properties

¹lodge \'läj\ *vb* **lodged**; **lodg·ing 1** : to provide quarters for; *also* : to settle in a place **2** : CONTAIN **3** : to come to a rest and remain **4** : to deposit for safekeeping **5** : to vest (as authority) in an agent **6** : FILE ⟨∼ a complaint⟩

²lodge *n* **1** : a house set apart for residence in a special season or by an employee on an estate; *also* : INN **2** : the meeting place of a branch of a fraternal organization; *also* : the members of such a branch **3** : a den or lair esp. of gregarious animals

lodg·er \'läj-ər\ *n* : a person who occupies a rented room in another's house

lodg·ing \'läj-iŋ\ *n* **1** : DWELLING **2** : a room or suite of rooms in another's house rented as a dwelling place — usu. used in pl.

lodg·ment *or* **lodge·ment** \'läj-mənt\ *n* **1** : a lodging place **2** : the act or manner of lodging **3** : DEPOSIT

loess \'les, 'lə(r)s, 'lō-əs\ *n* : a usu. yellowish brown loamy deposit believed to be chiefly deposited by the wind

¹loft \'lȯft\ *n* [ME, fr. OE, fr. ON *lopt* air] **1** : ATTIC **2** : GALLERY ⟨organ ∼⟩ **3** : an upper floor (as in a warehouse or barn) esp. when not partitioned **4** : the thickness of a fabric or insulated material (as of a sleeping bag)

²**loft** *vb* : to strike or throw a ball so that it rises high in the air

lofty \\'lȯf-tē\ *adj* **loft·i·er; -est 1** : NOBLE; *also* : SUPERIOR **2** : extremely proud **3** : HIGH, TALL — **loft·i·ly** \\'lȯf-tə-lē\ *adv* — **loft·i·ness** \-tē-nəs\ *n*

¹**log** \\'lȯg, 'läg\ *n* **1** : a bulky piece of unshaped timber **2** : an apparatus for measuring a ship's speed **3** : the daily record of a ship's progress; *also* : a regularly kept record of performance (as of an airplane)

²**log** *vb* **logged; log·ging 1** : to cut trees for lumber **2** : to enter in a log **3** : to sail a ship or fly an airplane for (an indicated distance or period of time) **4** : to have (an indicated record) to one's credit : ACHIEVE — **log·ger** \\'lȯg-ər, 'läg-\ *n*

³**log** *n* : LOGARITHM

lo·gan·ber·ry \\'lō-gən-ˌber-ē\ *n* : a red= fruited upright-growing dewberry; *also* : its fruit

log·a·rithm \\'lȯg-ə-ˌri<u>th</u>-əm, 'läg-\ *n* : the exponent that indicates the power to which a base number is raised to produce a given number ⟨the ∼ of 100 to the base number of 10 is 2⟩ — **log·a·rith·mic** \ˌlȯg-ə-'ri<u>th</u>-mik, ˌläg-\ *adj*

loge \\'lōzh\ *n* **1** : a small compartment; *also* : a box in a theater **2** : a small partitioned area; *also* : the forward section of a theater mezzanine

log·ger·head \\'lȯg-ər-ˌhed, 'läg-\ *n* : a large sea turtle of the warmer parts of the Atlantic — **at loggerheads** : in a state of quarrelsome disagreement

log·gia \\'lō-jē-ə, 'lȯ-jä\ *n, pl* **loggias** \\'lō-jē-əz, 'lȯ-jäz\ : a roofed open gallery

log·ic \\'läj-ik\ *n* **1** : a science that deals with the rules and tests of sound thinking and proof by reasoning **2** : sound reasoning **3** : the fundamental principles and the connection of circuit elements for arithmetical computation in a computer — **log·i·cal** \-i-kəl\ *adj* — **log·i·cal·ly** \-i-k(ə-)lē\ *adv* — **lo·gi·cian** \lō-'jish-ən\ *n*

lo·gis·tics \lō-'jis-tiks\ *n sing or pl* : the procurement, maintenance, and transportation of matériel, facilities, and personnel — **lo·gis·tic** *adj*

log·jam \\'lȯg-ˌjam, 'läg-\ *n* **1** : a deadlocked jumble of logs in a watercourse **2** : DEADLOCK

logo \\'lȯg-ō, 'läg-\ *n, pl* **log·os** \-ōz\ : LOGOTYPE

logo·type \\'lȯg-ə-ˌtīp, 'läg-\ *n* : an identifying symbol (as for advertising)

log·roll·ing \-ˌrō-liŋ\ *n* : the trading of votes by legislators to secure favorable action on projects of individual interest

lo·gy \\'lō-gē\ *also* **log·gy** \\'lȯg-ē, 'läg-\ *adj* **lo·gi·er; -est** : deficient in vitality : SLUGGISH

loin \\'lȯin\ *n* **1** : the part of the body on each side of the spinal column and between the hip and the lower ribs; *also* : a cut of meat from this part of an animal **2** *pl* : the upper and lower abdominal regions and the region about the hips

loin·cloth \-ˌklȯth\ *n* : a cloth worn about the loins often as the sole article of clothing in warm climates

loi·ter \\'lȯit-ər\ *vb* **1** : LINGER **2** : to hang around idly **syn** dawdle, dally, procrastinate, lag, tarry — **loi·ter·er** *n*

loll \\'läl\ *vb* **1** : DROOP, DANGLE **2** : LOUNGE

lol·li·pop *or* **lol·ly·pop** \\'läl-i-ˌpäp\ *n* : a lump of hard candy on a stick

lol·ly·gag \\'läl-ē-ˌgag\ *vb* **-gagged; -gagging** : DAWDLE

Lond *abbr* London

lone \\'lōn\ *adj* **1** : SOLITARY ⟨a ∼ sentinel⟩ **2** : SOLE, ONLY ⟨the ∼ theater in town⟩ **3** : ISOLATED ⟨a ∼ tree⟩

lone·ly \\'lōn-lē\ *adj* **lone·li·er; -est 1** : being without company **2** : UNFREQUENTED ⟨a ∼ spot⟩ **3** : LONESOME — **lone·li·ness** *n*

lon·er \\'lō-nər\ *n* : one that avoids others

lone·some \\'lōn-səm\ *adj* **1** : sad from lack of companionship **2** : REMOTE; *also* : SOLITARY — **lone·some·ly** *adv* — **lone·some·ness** *n*

¹**long** \\'lȯŋ\ *adj* **lon·ger** \\'lȯŋ-gər\; **lon·gest** \\'lȯŋ-gəst\ **1** : extending for a considerable distance; *also* : TALL, ELONGATED **2** : having a specified length **3** : extending over a considerable time; *also* : TEDIOUS **4** : containing many items in a series **5** : being a syllable or speech sound of relatively great duration **6** : extending far into the future **7** : well furnished with something — used with *on*

²**long** *adv* : for or during a long time

³**long** *n* : a long period of time

⁴**long** *vb* **longed; long·ing** \ˈlȯŋ-iŋ\ : to feel a strong desire or wish **syn** yearn, hanker, pine, hunger, thirst

⁵**long** *abbr* longitude

long·boat \ˈlȯŋ-ˌbōt\ *n* : the largest boat carried by a merchant sailing ship

long·bow \-ˌbō\ *n* : a wooden bow drawn by hand and usu. 5 to 6 feet long

lon·gev·i·ty \län-ˈjev-ət-ē\ *n* [LL *longaevitas,* fr. L *longaevus* long-lived, fr. *longus* long + *aevum* age] : a long duration of individual life; *also* : length of life

long·hair \ˈlȯŋ-ˌhaər\ *n* **1** : a lover of classical music **2** : HIPPIE **3** : a domestic cat having long outer fur

long·hand \-ˌhand\ *n* : HANDWRITING

long·horn \-ˌhȯrn\ *n* : any of the cattle with long horns formerly common in the southwestern U.S.

long hundredweight *n* — see WEIGHT table

long·ing \ˈlȯŋ-iŋ\ *n* : an eager desire esp. for something unattainable — **long·ing·ly** *adv*

lon·gi·tude \ˈlän-jə-ˌt(y)üd\ *n* : angular distance expressed usu. in degrees east or west from the meridian that runs between the north and south poles and passes through Greenwich, England

lon·gi·tu·di·nal \ˌlän-jə-ˈt(y)üd-(ə-)nəl\ *adj* **1** : extending lengthwise **2** : of or relating to length — **lon·gi·tu·di·nal·ly** \-ē\ *adv*

long·shore·man \ˈlȯŋ-ˈshōr-mən\ *n* : a laborer at a wharf who loads and unloads cargo

long–suf·fer·ing \-ˈsəf(-ə)-riŋ\ *n* : long and patient endurance of offense

long–term \ˈlȯŋ-ˈtərm\ *adj* **1** : extending over or involving a long period of time **2** : constituting a financial obligation based on a term usu. of more than 10 years ⟨a ∼ mortgage⟩

long·time \ˌlȯŋ-ˌtīm\ *adj* : of long duration ⟨∼ friends⟩

long ton *n* — see WEIGHT table

lon·gueur \lōⁿ-gœr\ *n, pl* **longueurs** \-gœr(z)\ [F, lit., length] : a dull tedious passage or section

long–wind·ed \ˈlȯŋ-ˈwin-dəd\ *adj* : tediously long in speaking or writing

loo·fah \ˈlü-fə\ *n* : a sponge consisting of the fibrous skeleton of a gourd

¹**look** \ˈluk\ *vb* **1** : to exercise the power of vision : SEE **2** : EXPECT **3** : to have an appearance that befits ⟨∼s the part⟩ **4** : SEEM ⟨∼s thin⟩ **5** : to direct one's attention : HEED **6** : POINT, FACE **7** : to show a tendency — **look after** : to take care of — **look for** : EXPECT

²**look** *n* **1** : the action of looking : GLANCE **2** : EXPRESSION; *also* : physical appearance **3** : ASPECT

look down \(ˈ)luk-ˈdaun\ *vb* : DESPISE — used with *on* or *upon*

looking glass *n* : MIRROR

look·out \ˈluk-ˌaut\ *n* **1** : a person assigned to watch (as on a ship) **2** : a careful watch **3** : VIEW **4** : a matter of concern

look up \(ˈ)luk-ˈəp\ *vb* **1** : IMPROVE ⟨business is *looking up*⟩ **2** : to search for in or as if in a reference work **3** : to seek out esp. for a brief visit

¹**loom** \ˈlüm\ *n* : a frame or machine for weaving together threads or yarns into cloth

²**loom** *vb* **1** : to come into sight in an unnaturally large, indistinct, or distorted form **2** : to appear in an impressively exaggerated form

loon \ˈlün\ *n* : a web-footed black-and-white fish-eating diving bird

loo·ny *or* **loo·ney** \ˈlü-nē\ *adj* **loo·ni·er; -est** : CRAZY, FOOLISH

loony bin *n* : an insane asylum

loop \ˈlüp\ *n* **1** : a fold or doubling of a line through which another line or hook can be passed; *also* : a loop-shaped figure or course ⟨a ∼ in a river⟩ **2** : a circular airplane maneuver involving flying upside down **3** : a ring-shaped intrauterine device **4** : a piece of film whose ends are spliced together to project continuously — **loop** *vb*

loop·er \ˈlü-pər\ *n* : any of numerous rather small hairless moth caterpillars that move with a looping movement

loop·hole \ˈlüp-ˌhōl\ *n* **1** : a small opening in a wall through which firearms may be discharged **2** : a means of escape; *esp* : an ambiguity or omission that allows one to evade the intent of a law or contract

¹**loose** \ˈlüs\ *adj* **loos·er; loos·est 1** : not rigidly fastened **2** : free from restraint

or obligation **3** : not dense or compact in structure **4** : not chaste : LEWD **5** : SLACK **6** : not precise or exact — **loose•ly** *adv* — **loose•ness** *n*

²**loose** *vb* **loosed; loos•ing 1** : RELEASE **2** : UNTIE **3** : DETACH **4** : DISCHARGE **5** : RELAX, SLACKEN

³**loose** *adv* : LOOSELY

loos•en \'lüs-ᵊn\ *vb* **loos•ened; loos•en•ing** \'lüs-(ᵊ-)niŋ\ **1** : FREE **2** : to make or become loose **3** : to relax the severity of

loot \'lüt\ *n* [Hindi *lūṭ*, fr. Skt *luṇṭati* he robs] : goods taken in war or by robbery : PLUNDER — **loot** *vb* — **loot•er** *n*

¹**lop** \'läp\ *vb* **lopped; lop•ping** : to cut branches or twigs from : TRIM; *also* : to cut off

²**lop** *vb* **lopped; lop•ping** : to hang downward; *also* : to flop or sway loosely

lope \'lōp\ *n* : an easy bounding gait — **lope** *vb*

lop•sid•ed \'läp-'sīd-əd\ *adj* **1** : leaning to one side **2** : UNSYMMETRICAL — **lop•sid•ed•ly** *adv* — **lop•sid•ed•ness** *n*

lo•qua•cious \lō-'kwā-shəs\ *adj* : excessively talkative — **lo•quac•i•ty** \-'kwas-ət-ē\ *n*

¹**lord** \'lȯrd\ *n* [ME *loverd, lord,* fr. OE *hlāford,* fr. *hlāf* loaf + *weard* keeper] **1** : one having power and authority over others; *esp* : a person from whom a feudal fee or estate is held **2** : a man of rank or high position; *esp* : a British nobleman **3** *pl, cap* : the upper house of the British parliament **4** : a person of great power in some field

²**lord** *vb* : to act like a lord; *esp* : to put on airs — usu. used with *it*

lord chancellor *n, pl* **lords chancellor** : a British officer of state who presides over the House of Lords, serves as head of the British judiciary, and is usu. a leading member of the cabinet

lord•ly \-lē\ *adj* **lord•li•er; -est 1** : DIGNIFIED; *also* : NOBLE **2** : HAUGHTY

lord•ship \-ˌship\ *n* **1** : the rank or dignity of a lord — used as a title **2** : the authority or territory of a lord

Lord's Supper *n* : COMMUNION

lore \'lōr\ *n* : KNOWLEDGE; *esp* : traditional knowledge or belief

lor•gnette \lȯrn-'yet\ *n* [F, fr. *lorgner* to take a sidelong look at, fr. MF, fr. *lorgne* cross-eyed] : a pair of eye-

glasses or opera glasses with a handle

lorn \'lȯrn\ *adj* : FORSAKEN, DESOLATE

lor•ry \'lȯr-ē\ *n, pl* **lorries 1** : a large low horse-drawn wagon without sides **2** *Brit* : MOTORTRUCK

lose \'lüz\ *vb* **lost** \'lȯst\; **los•ing** \'lü-ziŋ\ **1** : DESTROY **2** : to miss from a customary place : MISLAY **3** : to suffer deprivation of **4** : to fail to use : WASTE **5** : to fail to win or obtain ⟨~ the game⟩ **6** : to fail to keep or maintain ⟨~ his balance⟩ **7** : to wander from ⟨~ his way⟩ **8** : to get rid of ⟨~ weight⟩ — **los•er** *n*

loss \'lȯs\ *n* **1** : the harm resulting from losing **2** : something that is lost **3** *pl* : killed, wounded, or captured soldiers **4** : failure to win **5** : an amount by which the cost exceeds the selling price **6** : decrease in amount or degree **7** : RUIN

loss leader *n* : an article sold at a loss in order to draw customers

lost \'lȯst\ *adj* **1** : not used, won, or claimed **2** : no longer possessed or known **3** : ruined or destroyed physically or morally **4** : DENIED; *also* : HARDENED **5** : unable to find the way; *also* : HELPLESS **6** : ABSORBED, RAPT

lot \'lät\ *n* **1** : an object used in deciding something by chance; *also* : the use of lots to decide something **2** : SHARE, PORTION; *also* : FORTUNE, FATE **3** : a plot of land **4** : a group of individuals : SET **5** : a considerable quantity

loth \'lōth, 'lō<u>th</u>\ *var of* LOATH

lo•ti \'lōt-ē\ *n, pl* **ma•lo•ti** \mə-'lōt-ē\ — see MONEY table

lo•tion \'lō-shən\ *n* : a liquid preparation for cosmetic and external medicinal use

lot•tery \'lät-ə-rē\ *n, pl* **-ter•ies 1** : a drawing of lots in which prizes are given to the winning names or numbers **2** : a matter determined by chance

lo•tus \'lōt-əs\ *n* **1** : a fruit held in Greek legend to cause dreamy content and forgetfulness **2** : a water lily used in ancient Egyptian and Hindu art and religious symbolism **3** : any of several forage plants related to the clovers

loud \'laȯd\ *adj* **1** : marked by intensity or volume of sound **2** : CLAMOROUS, NOISY **3** : obtrusive or offensive in color or pattern ⟨a ~ suit⟩ — **loud** *adv* — **loud·ly** *adv* — **loud·ness** *n*

loud·mouthed \-'maůth̲d, -'maůtht\ *adj* : given to loud offensive talk

loud·speak·er \'laůd-'spē-kər\ *n* : a device that changes electrical signals into sound

¹**lounge** \'laůnj\ *vb* **lounged; loung·ing** : to act or move lazily or listlessly

²**lounge** *n* **1** : a room with comfortable furniture; *also* : a room (as in a theater) with lounging, smoking, and toilet facilities **2** : a long couch

lour \'laů(-ə)r\ , **loury** \'laů(ə)r-ē\ var of LOWER, LOWERY

louse \'laůs\ *n, pl* **lice** \'līs\ **1** : a small wingless insect parasitic on warm≈blooded animals **2** : a plant pest (as an aphid) **3** : a contemptible person

lousy \'laů-zē\ *adj* **lous·i·er; -est 1** : infested with lice **2** : POOR, INFERIOR **3** : amply supplied ⟨~ with money⟩ — **lous·i·ly** \'laů-zə-lē\ *adv* — **lous·i·ness** \-zē-nəs\ *n*

lout \'laůt\ *n* : a stupid awkward fellow — **lout·ish** *adj* — **lout·ish·ly** *adv*

lou·ver *or* **lou·vre** \'lü-vər\ *n* **1** : an opening having parallel slanted slats to allow flow of air but to exclude rain or sun or to provide privacy; *also* : a slat in such an opening **2** : a device with movable slats for controlling the flow of air or light

¹**love** \'ləv\ *n* **1** : strong affection **2** : warm attachment ⟨~ of the sea⟩ **3** : attraction based on sexual desire **4** : a beloved person **5** : a score of zero in tennis — **love·less** *adj*

²**love** *vb* **loved; lov·ing 1** : CHERISH **2** : to feel a passion, devotion, or tenderness for **3** : CARESS **4** : to take pleasure in ⟨~s to play bridge⟩ — **lov·able** \'ləv-ə-bəl\ *adj* — **lov·er** *n*

love·bird \'ləv-ˌbərd\ *n* : any of various small usu. gray or green parrots that seemingly show great affection for their mates

love·lorn \-ˌlȯrn\ *adj* : deprived of love or of a lover

love·ly \'ləv-lē\ *adj* **love·li·er; -est** : BEAUTIFUL — **love·li·ness** *n*

love·mak·ing \-ˌmā-kiŋ\ *n* **1** : COURTSHIP **2** : sexual activity; *esp* : COPULATION

love·sick \-ˌsik\ *adj* **1** : YEARNING **2** : expressing a lover's longing — **love·sick·ness** *n*

lov·ing \'ləv-iŋ\ *adj* : AFFECTIONATE — **lov·ing·ly** *adv*

¹**low** \'lō\ *vb* : MOO

²**low** *n* : MOO

³**low** *adj* **low·er** \'lō(-ə)r\; **low·est** \'lō-əst\ **1** : not high or tall ⟨~ wall⟩; *also* : DÉCOLLETÉ **2** : situated or passing below the normal level or surface ⟨~ ground⟩ ; *also* : marking a nadir **3** : STRICKEN, PROSTRATE **4** : not loud ⟨~ voice⟩ **5** : being near the equator **6** : humble in status **7** : WEAK; *also* : DEPRESSED **8** : less than usual **9** : falling short of a standard **10** : UNFAVORABLE — **low** *adv* — **low·ness** *n*

⁴**low** *n* **1** : something that is low **2** : a region of low barometric pressure **3** : the arrangement of gears in an automobile transmission that gives the slowest speed and greatest power

low beam *n* : the short-range focus of a vehicle headlight

low blow *n* : an unprincipled attack

low·brow \'lō-ˌbraů\ *n* : a person without intellectual interests or culture

low·down \'lō-ˌdaůn\ *n* : pertinent and esp. guarded information

low–down \'lō-daůn\ *adj* **1** : MEAN, CONTEMPTIBLE **2** : deeply emotional

low–end \-ˌənd\ *adj* : of, relating to, or being the lowest-priced merchandise in a manufacturer's line

¹**low·er** \'laů(-ə)r\ *vb* **1** : FROWN **2** : to become dark, gloomy, and threatening

²**low·er** \'lō(-ə)r\ *adj* **1** : relatively low (as in rank) **2** : constituting the popular and more representative branch of a bicameral legislative body **3** : situated beneath the earth's surface

³**low·er** \'lō(-ə)r\ *vb* **1** : DROP; *also* : DIMINISH **2** : to let descend by its own weight; *also* : to reduce the height of **3** : to reduce in value, number, or amount **4** : DEGRADE; *also* : HUMBLE

low·er·case \ˌlō(-ə)r-'kās\ *adj* : being a letter that belongs to or conforms to the series a, b, c, etc., rather than A, B, C, etc. — **lowercase** *n*

lower class *n* : a social class occupying a position below the middle class and having the lowest status in a society — **lower–class** \-'klas\ *adj*

low·er·most \'lō(-ə)r-ˌmōst\ *adj* : LOWEST

low•ery \\'laŭ-(ə-)rē\ *adj* : GLOOMY, LOW-ERING

lowest common denominator *n* **1** : LEAST COMMON DENOMINATOR **2** : something acceptable to the greatest number of people

lowest common multiple *n* : LEAST COMMON MULTIPLE

low frequency *n* : a frequency of a radio wave in the range between 30 and 300 kilohertz

low–key \\'lō-'kē\ *also* **low–keyed** \-'kēd\ *adj* : of low intensity : restrained

low•land \\'lō-lənd, -ˌland\ *n* : low and usu. level country

low•life \\'lō-ˌlīf\ *n, pl* **low•lifes** \-ˌlīfs\ *also* **low•lives** \-ˌlīvz\ : a person of low social status or moral character

low•ly \\'lō-lē\ *adj* **low•li•er; -est 1** : HUMBLE, MEEK **2** : ranking low in some hierarchy — **low•li•ness** *n*

low–rise \\'lō-'rīz\ *adj* : being one or two stories and not equipped with elevators ⟨a ∼ building⟩

¹lox \\'läks\ *n* : liquid oxygen

²lox *n, pl* **lox** *or* **lox•es** : smoked salmon

loy•al \\'lȯi(-ə)l\ *adj* [MF, fr. OF *leial, leel,* fr. L *legalis* legal] **1** : faithful in allegiance to one's government **2** : faithful esp. to a cause or ideal : CONSTANT — **loy•al•ly** \\'lȯi-ə-lē\ *adv* — **loy•al•ty** \\'lȯi(-ə)l-tē\ *n*

loy•al•ist \\'lȯi-ə-ləst\ *n* : one who is or remains loyal to a political party, government, or sovereign

loz•enge \\'läz-ᵊnj\ *n* **1** : a diamond-shaped figure **2** : a small flat often medicated candy

LP *abbr* low pressure

LPG *abbr* liquefied petroleum gas

LPN \\'el-'pē-'en\ *n* : LICENSED PRACTICAL NURSE

LSD \ˌel-ˌes-'dē\ *n* [*l*ysergic acid *d*iethylamide] : a crystalline compound that causes psychotic symptoms similar to those of schizophrenia

lt *abbr* light

Lt *abbr* lieutenant

LT *abbr* long ton

LTC *or* **Lt Col** *abbr* lieutenant colonel

Lt Comdr *abbr* lieutenant commander

ltd *abbr* limited

LTG *or* **Lt Gen** *abbr* lieutenant general

LTJG *abbr* lieutenant, junior grade

ltr *abbr* letter

Lu *symbol* lutetium

lu•au \\'lü-ˌaŭ\ *n* : a Hawaiian feast

lub *abbr* lubricant; lubricating

lub•ber \\'ləb-ər\ *n* **1** : LOUT **2** : an unskilled seaman — **lub•ber•ly** *adj*

lube \\'lüb\ *n* : lubricant; *also* : an application of a lubricant

lu•bri•cant \\'lü-bri-kənt\ *n* : a material (as grease) capable of reducing friction when applied between moving parts

lu•bri•cate \\'lü-brə-ˌkāt\ *vb* **-cat•ed; -cat•ing** : to apply a lubricant to — **lu•bri•ca•tion** \ˌlü-brə-'kā-shən\ *n* — **lu•bri•ca•tor** \\'lü-brə-ˌkāt-ər\ *n*

lu•bri•cious \lü-'brish-əs\ *or* **lu•bri•cous** \\'lü-bri-kəs\ *adj* **1** : SMOOTH, SLIPPERY **2** : LECHEROUS; *also* : SALACIOUS — **lu•bric•i•ty** \lü-'bris-ət-ē\ *n*

lu•cent \\'lüs-ᵊnt\ *adj* **1** : LUMINOUS **2** : CLEAR, LUCID

lu•cerne \lü-'sərn\ *n, chiefly Brit* : ALFALFA

lu•cid \\'lü-səd\ *adj* **1** : SHINING **2** : clear-minded **3** : easily understood — **lu•cid•i•ty** \lü-'sid-ət-ē\ *n* — **lu•cid•ly** *adv* — **lu•cid•ness** *n*

Lu•ci•fer \\'lü-sə-fər\ *n* [ME, the morning star, a fallen rebel archangel, the Devil, fr. OE, fr. L, the morning star, fr. *lucifer* light-bearing] : DEVIL, SATAN

¹luck \\'lək\ *n* **1** : CHANCE, FORTUNE **2** : good fortune — **luck•less** *adj*

²luck *vb* **1** : to prosper or succeed esp. through chance or good fortune **2** : to come upon something desirable by chance — usu. used with *out, on, onto,* or *into*

lucky \\'lək-ē\ *adj* **luck•i•er; -est 1** : favored by luck : FORTUNATE **2** : FORTUITOUS **3** : seeming to bring good luck — **luck•i•ly** \\'lək-ə-lē\ *adv* — **luck•i•ness** \-ē-nəs\ *n*

lu•cra•tive \\'lü-krət-iv\ *adj* : PROFITABLE — **lu•cra•tive•ly** *adv* — **lu•cra•tive•ness** *n*

lu•cre \\'lü-kər\ *n* [ME, fr. L *lucrum*] : PROFIT; *also* : MONEY

lu•cu•bra•tion \ˌlü-k(y)ə-'brā-shən\ *n* : laborious study : MEDITATION

lu•di•crous \\'lüd-ə-krəs\ *adj* : LAUGHABLE, RIDICULOUS — **lu•di•crous•ly** *adv* — **lu•di•crous•ness** *n*

luff \\'ləf\ *vb* : to sail a ship closer to the wind — **luff** *n*

¹**lug** \\'ləg\ *vb* **lugged; lug•ging 1** : DRAG, PULL **2** : to carry laboriously

²**lug** *n* **1** : a projecting piece (as for fastening, support, or traction) **2** : a heavy nut used with a bolt

lug•gage \\'ləg-ij\ *n* **1** : BAGGAGE **2** : containers (as suitcases) for carrying personal belongings

lu•gu•bri•ous \lü-'gü-brē-əs\ *adj* : mournful often to an exaggerated degree — **lu•gu•bri•ous•ly** *adv* — **lu•gu•bri•ous•ness** *n*

Luke \\'lük\ *n* — see BIBLE table

luke•warm \\'lük-'wȯrm\ *adj* **1** : moderately warm : TEPID **2** : not enthusiastic — **luke•warm•ly** *adv*

¹**lull** \\'ləl\ *vb* **1** : SOOTHE, CALM **2** : to cause to relax vigilance

²**lull** *n* **1** : a temporary calm (as during a storm) **2** : a temporary drop in activity

lul•la•by \\'ləl-ə-ˌbī\ *n, pl* **-bies** : a song to lull children to sleep

lum•ba•go \ˌləm-'bā-gō\ *n* : rheumatic pain in the lower back and loins

lum•bar \\'ləm-bər, -ˌbär\ *adj* : of, relating to, or constituting the loins or the vertebrae between the thoracic vertebrae and sacrum ⟨∼ region⟩

¹**lum•ber** \\'ləm-bər\ *vb* **lum•bered; lum•ber•ing** \-b(ə-)riŋ\ : to move heavily or clumsily

²**lumber** *n* **1** : surplus or disused articles that arc stored away **2** : timber esp. when dressed for use

³**lumber** *vb* **lum•bered; lum•ber•ing** \-b(ə-)riŋ\ : to cut logs; *also* : to saw logs into lumber — **lum•ber•man** \-mən\ *n*

lum•ber•jack \-ˌjak\ *n* : LOGGER

lum•ber•yard \-ˌyärd\ *n* : a place where lumber is kept for sale

lu•mi•nary \\'lü-mə-ˌner-ē\ *n, pl* **-nar•ies 1** : a very famous person **2** : a source of light; *esp* : a celestial body

lu•mi•nes•cence \-'nes-ᵊns\ *n* : the low-temperature emission of light (as by a chemical or physiological process) — **lu•mi•nes•cent** \-ᵊnt\ *adj*

lu•mi•nous \\'lü-mə-nəs\ *adj* **1** : emitting light; *also* : LIGHTED **2** : CLEAR, INTELLIGIBLE — **lu•mi•nance** \-nəns\ *n* — **lu•mi•nos•i•ty** \ˌlü-mə-'näs-ət-ē\ *n* — **lu•mi•nous•ly** *adv*

lum•mox \\'ləm-əks\ *n* : a clumsy person

¹**lump** \\'ləmp\ *n* **1** : a piece or mass of irregular shape **2** : AGGREGATE, TOTALITY **3** : a usu. abnormal swelling — **lump•ish** *adj* — **lumpy** *adj*

²**lump** *vb* **1** : to leap together in a.lump **2** : to form into lumps

³**lump** *adj* : not divided into parts ⟨a ∼ sum⟩

lu•na•cy \\'lü-nə-sē\ *n, pl* **-cies 1** : INSANITY **2** : extreme folly

lu•nar \\'lü-nər\ *adj* : of or relating to the moon

lu•na•tic \\'lü-nə-ˌtik\ *adj* [ME *lunatik*, fr. LL *lunaticus*, fr. L *luna*; fr. the belief that lunacy fluctuated with the phases of the moon] **1** : INSANE; *also* : used for insane persons **2** : extremely foolish — **lunatic** *n*

¹**lunch** \\'lənch\ *n* **1** : a light meal usu. eaten in the middle of the day **2** : the food prepared for a lunch

²**lunch** *vb* : to eat lunch

lun•cheon \\'lən-chən\ *n* : a usu. formal lunch

lun•cheon•ette \ˌlən-chə-'net\ *n* : a small restaurant serving light lunches

lunch•room \\'lənch-ˌrüm, -ˌrům\ *n* **1** : LUNCHEONETTE **2** : a room (as in a school) where lunches are sold and eaten or lunches brought from home may be eaten

lu•nette \lü-'net\ *n* : something shaped like a crescent

lung \\'ləŋ\ *n* **1** : one of the usu. paired baglike breathing organs in the chest of an air-breathing vertebrate **2** : a mechanical device for introducing fresh air into and removing stale air from the lungs — **lunged** \\'ləŋd\ *adj*

lunge \\'lənj\ *n* **1** : a sudden thrust or pass (as with a sword) **2** : a sudden forward stride or leap — **lunge** *vb*

lu•pine \\'lü-pən\ *n* : any of a genus of leguminous plants with long upright clusters of pealike flowers

lu•pus \\'lü-pəs\ *n* [ML, fr. L *wolf*] : any of several diseases (as systemic lupus erythematosus) characterized by skin lesions

lupus er•y•the•ma•to•sus \-ˌer-ə-ˌthē-mə-'tō-səs\ *n* : a disorder characterized by skin inflammation; *esp* : SYSTEMIC LUPUS ERYTHEMATOSUS

lurch \\'lərch\ *n* : a sudden swaying or tipping movement — **lurch** *vb*

¹**lure** \\'lůr\ *n* **1** : ENTICEMENT; *also* : AP-

PEAL **2** : an artificial bait for catching fish

²lure *vb* **lured; lur·ing** : to draw on with a promise of pleasure or gain

lu·rid \ˈlu̇r-əd\ *adj* **1** : LIVID **2** : shining with the red glow of fire seen through smoke or cloud **3** : GRUESOME; *also* : SENSATIONAL **syn** ghastly, grisly, grim, horrible, macabre — **lu·rid·ly** *adv*

lurk \ˈlərk\ *vb* **1** : to move furtively : SNEAK **2** : to lie concealed

lus·cious \ˈləsh-əs\ *adj* **1** : having a pleasingly sweet taste or smell **2** : sensually appealing — **lus·cious·ly** *adv* — **lus·cious·ness** *n*

¹lush \ˈləsh\ *adj* : having or covered with abundant growth ⟨∼ pastures⟩

²lush *n* : an habitual heavy drinker

lust \ˈləst\ *n* **1** : sexual desire often to an intense or unrestrained degree **2** : an intense longing — **lust** *vb* — **lust·ful** *adj*

lus·ter *or* **lus·tre** \ˈləs-tər\ *n* **1** : a shine or sheen esp. from reflected light **2** : BRIGHTNESS, GLITTER **3** : GLORY, SPLENDOR — **lus·ter·less** *adj* — **lus·trous** \-trəs\ *adj*

lus·tral \ˈləs-trəl\ *adj* : PURIFICATORY

lusty \ˈləs-tē\ *adj* **lust·i·er; -est** : full of vitality : ROBUST — **lust·i·ly** \ˈləs-tə-lē\ *adv* — **lust·i·ness** \-tē-nəs\ *n*

lute \ˈlüt\ *n* : a stringed musical instrument with a large pear-shaped body and a fretted fingerboard — **lu·te·nist** *or* **lu·ta·nist** \ˈlüt-ᵊn-əst\ *n*

lu·te·tium *also* **lu·te·cium** \lü-ˈtē-sh(ē-)əm\ *n* : a rare metallic chemical element

Lu·ther·an \ˈlü-th(ə-)rən\ *n* : a member of a Protestant denomination adhering to the doctrines of Martin Luther — **Lu·ther·an·ism** \-ˌiz-əm\ *n*

lux·u·ri·ant \ˌləg-ˈzhu̇r-ē-ənt, ˌlək-ˈshu̇r-\ *adj* **1** : yielding or growing abundantly : LUSH, PRODUCTIVE **2** : abundantly rich and varied; *also* : FLORID — **lux·u·ri·ance** \-ē-əns\ *n* — **lux·u·ri·ant·ly** *adv*

lux·u·ri·ate \-ē-ˌāt\ *vb* **-at·ed; -at·ing 1** : to grow profusely **2** : REVEL

lux·u·ry \ˈləksh-(ə-)rē, ˈləgzh-\ *n, pl* **-ries 1** : great ease and comfort **2** : something desirable but costly or hard to get **3** : something adding to pleasure or comfort but not absolutely

necessary — **lux·u·ri·ous** \ˌləg-ˈzhu̇r-ē-əs, ˌlək-ˈshu̇r-\ *adj* — **lux·u·ri·ous·ly** *adv*

lv *abbr* leave

lwei \lə-ˈwā\ *n, pl* **lwei** — see *kwanza* at MONEY table

LWV *abbr* League of Women Voters

¹-ly \lē\ *adj suffix* **1** : like in appearance, manner, or nature ⟨queen*ly*⟩ **2** : characterized by regular recurrence in (specified) units of time : every ⟨hour*ly*⟩

²-ly \lē (*corresponding adjectives may end in* əl, *as* "double"); *-ically is* i-k(ə-)lē\ *adv suffix* **1** : in a (specified) manner ⟨slow*ly*⟩ **2** : from a (specified) point of view ⟨grammatical*ly*⟩

ly·ce·um \lī-ˈsē-əm, ˈlī-sē-\ *n* **1** : a hall for public lectures **2** : an association providing public lectures, concerts, and entertainments

lye \ˈlī\ *n* : a white crystalline corrosive alkaline substance used in making rayon and soap

ly·ing \ˈlī-iŋ\ *adj* : UNTRUTHFUL, FALSE

ly·ing-in \ˌlī-iŋ-ˈin\ *n, pl* **lyings-in** *or* **lying-ins** : the state during and consequent to childbirth : CONFINEMENT

lymph \ˈlimf\ *n* [L *lympha*, water goddess, water, fr. Gk *nymphē* nymph] : a pale liquid consisting chiefly of blood plasma and white blood cells, circulating in thin-walled tubes (**lymphatic vessels**), and bathing the body tissues — **lym·phat·ic** \lim-ˈfat-ik\ *adj*

lymph·ade·nop·a·thy \ˌlim-ˌfad-ᵊn-ˈäp-ə-thē\ *n, pl* **-thies** : abnormal enlargement of the lymph nodes

lymph node *n* : one of the rounded masses of lymphoid tissue surrounded by a capsule

lym·pho·cyte \ˈlim-fə-ˌsīt\ *n* : any of the weakly motile leukocytes produced in lymphoid tissue that are the typical cells in lymph and include the cellular mediators (as a B cell or a T cell) of immunity

lym·phoid \ˈlim-ˌfȯid\ *adj* **1** : of, relating to, or constituting the tissue characteristic of the lymph nodes **2** : of, relating to, or resembling lymph

lynch \ˈlinch\ *vb* : to put to death by mob action without legal sanction or due process of law — **lynch·er** *n*

lynx \ˈliŋks\ *n, pl* **lynx** *or* **lynx·es** : a

wildcat with a short tail, long legs, and usu. tufted ears

lyre \ˈlī(ə)r\ *n* : a stringed musical instrument of the harp class used by the ancient Greeks

¹**lyr·ic** \ˈlir-ik\ *n* **1** : a lyric poem **2** *pl* : the words of a popular song — **lyr·i·cal** \-i-kəl\ *adj*

²**lyric** *adj* **1** : suitable for singing : MELODIC **2** : expressing direct and usu. intense personal emotion

ly·ser·gic acid di·eth·yl·am·ide \lə-ˌsər-jik . . . ˌdī-ˌeth-ə-ˈlam-ˌīd, lī-, -ˈlam-əd\ *n* : LSD

LZ *abbr* landing zone

M

¹**m** \ˈem\ *n, pl* **m's** *or* **ms** \ˈemz\ *often cap* : the 13th letter of the English alphabet

²**m** *abbr, often cap* **1** Mach **2** male **3** married **4** masculine **5** medium **6** [L *meridies*] noon **7** meter **8** mile **9** [L *mille*] thousand **10** minute **11** month **12** moon

ma \ˈmä, ˈmȯ\ *n* : MOTHER

MA *abbr* **1** [ML *magister artium*] master of arts **2** Massachusetts **3** mental age

ma'am \ˈmam, *after* "yes" *often* əm\ *n* : MADAM

Mac *or* **Macc** *abbr* Maccabees

ma·ca·bre \mə-ˈkäb(-rə), -ˈkäb-ər\ *adj* [F] **1** : having death as a subject **2** : GRUESOME **3** : HORRIBLE

mac·ad·am \mə-ˈkad-əm\ *n* **1** : a roadway or pavement of small closely packed broken stone **2** : the broken stone used in macadamizing — **mac·ad·am·ize** \-ˌīz\ *vb*

ma·caque \mə-ˈkak, -ˈkäk\ *n* : any of several short-tailed Asian and East Indian monkeys

mac·a·ro·ni \ˌmak-ə-ˈrō-nē\ *n* **1** : a food made chiefly of wheat flour dried in the form of usu. slender tubes **2** *pl* **-nis** *or* **-nies** : FOP, DANDY

mac·a·roon \ˌmak-ə-ˈrün\ *n* : a small cookie made chiefly of egg whites, sugar, and ground almonds or coconut

ma·caw \mə-ˈkȯ\ *n* : a large long-tailed parrot of Central and So. America

Mac·ca·bees \ˈmak-ə-ˌbēz\ *n* — see BIBLE table

Mc·Coy \mə-ˈkȯi\ *n* [alter. of *Mackay* (in the phrase *the real Mackay* the true chief of the Mackay clan, a position often disputed)] : something that is neither imitation nor substitute ⟨the real ∼⟩

¹**mace** \ˈmās\ *n* **1** : a heavy often spiked club used as a weapon esp. in the Middle Ages **2** : an ornamental staff carried as a symbol of authority

²**mace** *n* : a spice from the fibrous coating of the nutmeg

mac·er·ate \ˈmas-ə-ˌrāt\ *vb* **-at·ed; -at·ing 1** : to cause to waste away **2** : to soften by steeping or soaking so as to separate the parts — **mac·er·a·tion** \ˌmas-ə-ˈrā-shən\ *n*

mach *abbr* machine; machinery; machinist

Mach \ˈmäk\ *n* : MACH NUMBER

Mach·a·bees \ˈmak-ə-ˌbēz\ *n* — see BIBLE table

ma·chete \mə-ˈshet-ē\ *n* : a large heavy knife used for cutting sugarcane and underbrush and as a weapon

Ma·chi·a·vel·lian \ˌmak-ē-ə-ˈvel-ē-ən\ *adj* [Niccolo *Machiavelli*, †1527 Ital. political philosopher] : characterized by cunning, duplicity, and bad faith — **Ma·chi·a·vel·lian·ism** *n*

mach·i·na·tion \ˌmak-ə-ˈnā-shən, ˌmash-ə-\ *n* : an act of planning esp. to do harm; *esp* : PLOT — **mach·i·nate** \ˈmak-ə-ˌnāt, ˈmash-\ *vb*

¹**ma·chine** \mə-ˈshēn\ *n* **1** : CONVEYANCE, VEHICLE; *esp* : AUTOMOBILE **2** : a combination of mechanical parts that transmit forces, motion, and energy to do some desired work ⟨a sewing ∼⟩ **3** : an instrument (as a pulley or lever) for transmitting or modifying force or motion **4** : an electrical, electronic, or mechanical device for performing a task ⟨a calculating ∼⟩ **5** : a highly organized political group under the leadership of a boss or small clique

²**machine** *vb* **ma•chined; ma•chin•ing** : to shape or finish by machine-operated tools — **ma•chin•able** \-ˈshē-nə-bəl\ *adj*

machine gun *n* : an automatic gun capable of rapid continuous firing — **machine–gun** *vb* — **machine gunner** *n*

machine language *n* : the set of symbolic instruction codes usu. in binary form that is used to represent operations and data in a machine (as a computer)

machine–readable *adj* : directly usable by a computer

ma•chin•ery \mə-ˈshēn-(ə-)rē\ *n, pl* **-er•ies** 1 : MACHINES; *also* : the working parts of a machine 2 : the means by which something is done

ma•chin•ist \mə-ˈshē-nəst\ *n* : a person who makes or works on machines

ma•chis•mo \mä-ˈchēz-(ˌ)mō, -ˈchiz-\ *n* : a strong or exaggerated pride in one's masculinity

Mach number \ˈmäk-\ *n* : a number representing the ratio of the speed of a body to the speed of sound in the surrounding atmosphere ⟨a *Mach number* of 2 indicates a speed that is twice the speed of sound⟩

ma•cho \ˈmä-chō\ *adj* [Sp, male, fr. L *masculus*] : characterized by machismo

mack•er•el \ˈmak-(ə-)rəl\ *n, pl* **mackerel** *or* **mackerels** : a No. Atlantic food fish greenish above and silvery below

mack•i•naw \ˈmak-ə-ˌnȯ\ *n* : a short heavy plaid coat

mack•in•tosh *also* **mac•in•tosh** \ˈmak-ən-ˌtäsh\ *n* 1 *chiefly Brit* : RAINCOAT 2 : a lightweight waterproof fabric

mac•ra•mé *also* **mac•ra•me** \ˈmak-rə-ˌmā\ *n* [deriv. of Ar *miqramah* embroidered veil] : a coarse lace or fringe made by knotting threads or cords in a geometrical pattern

mac•ro \ˈmak-(ˌ)rō\ *adj* : very large; *also* : involving large quantities or being on a large scale

mac•ro•bi•ot•ic \ˌmak-rō-bī-ˈät-ik, -bē-\ *adj* : relating to or being a very restricted diet (as one containing chiefly whole grains)

mac•ro•cosm \ˈmak-rə-ˌkäz-əm\ *n* : the great world : UNIVERSE

ma•cron \ˈmāk-ˌrän, ˈmak-\ *n* : a mark ¯ placed over a vowel (as in \māk\) to show that the vowel is long

mac•ro•scop•ic \ˌmak-rə-ˈskäp-ik\ *adj* : visible to the naked eye — **mac•ro•scop•i•cal•ly** \-i-k(ə-)lē\ *adv*

mad \ˈmad\ *adj* **mad•der; mad•dest** 1 : disordered in mind : INSANE 2 : being rash and foolish 3 : FURIOUS, ENRAGED 4 : carried away by enthusiasm 5 : RABID 6 : marked by wild gaiety and merriment 7 : FRANTIC — **mad•ly** *adv* — **mad•ness** *n*

Mad•a•gas•can \ˌmad-ə-ˈgas-kən\ *n* : a native or inhabitant of Madagascar

mad•am \ˈmad-əm\ *n* 1 *pl* **mes•dames** \mā-ˈdäm\ — used as a form of polite address to a woman 2 *pl* **madams** : the female head of a house of prostitution

ma•dame \mə-ˈdam, *before a surname also* ˌmad-əm\ *n, pl* **mes•dames** \mā-ˈdäm\ : MISTRESS — used as a title for a woman not of English-speaking nationality

mad•cap \ˈmad-ˌkap\ *adj* : WILD, RECKLESS — **madcap** *n*

mad•den \ˈmad-ᵊn\ *vb* **mad•dened; mad•den•ing** \ˈmad-(ᵊ-)niŋ\ : to make mad — **mad•den•ing•ly** *adv*

mad•der \ˈmad-ər\ *n* : a Eurasian plant with yellow flowers and fleshy red roots; *also* : its root or a dye prepared from it

made past and past part of MAKE

Ma•dei•ra \mə-ˈdir-ə\ *n* : an amber-colored dessert wine

ma•de•moi•selle \ˌmad-(ə-)m(w)ə-ˈzel, mam-ˈzel\ *n, pl* **ma•de•moi•selles** \-ˈzelz\ *or* **mes•de•moi•selles** \ˌmād-(ə-)m(w)e-ˈzel\ : an unmarried girl or woman — used as a title for an unmarried woman not of English-speaking and esp. of French nationality

made–up \ˈmād-ˈəp\ *adj* 1 : marked by the use of makeup 2 : fancifully conceived or falsely devised

mad•house \ˈmad-ˌhaùs\ *n* 1 : a place for the detention and care of the insane 2 : a place of great uproar

mad•man \ˈmad-ˌman, -mən\ *n* : LUNATIC

ma•don•na \mə-ˈdän-ə\ *n* : a representation (as a picture or statue) of the Virgin Mary

ma•dras \ˈmad-rəs; mə-ˈdras, -ˈdräs\ *n* [*Madras,* India] : a fine usu. cotton fabric with various designs (as plaid)

mad·ri·gal \\'mad-ri-gəl\ *n* [It *madrigale*] : a somewhat elaborate part-song esp. of the 16th century; *also* : a love poem suitable for a musical setting

mad·wom·an \\'mad-ˌwùm-ən\ *n* : a woman who is insane

mael·strom \\'māl-strəm\ *n* : a violent whirlpool

mae·stro \\'mī-strō\ *n, pl* **maestros** *or* **mae·stri** \-ˌstrē\ [It] : a master in an art; *esp* : an eminent composer, conductor, or teacher of music

Ma·fia \\'mäf-ē-ə\ *n* [It] **1** : a secret society of political terrorists **2** : a secret criminal organization

ma·fi·o·so \ˌmäf-ē-'ō-(ˌ)sō\ *n, pl* **-si** \-(ˌ)sē,\ : a member of the Mafia

¹mag *abbr* **1** magnetism **2** magneto **3** magnitude

²mag \\'mag\ *n* : MAGAZINE

mag·a·zine \\'mag-ə-ˌzēn\ *n* **1** : a storehouse esp. for military supplies **2** : a place for keeping gunpowder in a fort or ship **3** : a publication usu. containing stories, articles, or poems and issued periodically **4** : a container in a gun for holding cartridges; *also* : a chamber (as on a camera) for film

ma·gen·ta \mə-'jent-ə\ *n* : a deep purplish red

mag·got \\'mag-ət\ *n* : the legless wormlike larva of a two-winged fly — **mag·goty** *adj*

ma·gi \\'mā-jī\ *n pl, often cap* : the three wise men from the East who paid homage to the infant Jesus

mag·ic \\'maj-ik\ *n* **1** : the art of persons who claim to be able to do things by the help of supernatural powers or by their own knowledge of nature's secrets **2** : an extraordinary power or influence seemingly from a supernatural force **3** : SLEIGHT OF HAND — **magic** *adj* — **mag·i·cal** \-i-kəl\ *adj* — **mag·i·cal·ly** \-i-k(ə-)lē\ *adv*

ma·gi·cian \mə-'jish-ən\ *n* : one skilled in magic

mag·is·te·ri·al \ˌmaj-ə-'stir-ē-əl\ *adj* **1** : AUTHORITATIVE **2** : of or relating to a magistrate or his office or duties

ma·gis·tral \\'maj-ə-strəl\ *adj* : AUTHORITATIVE

mag·is·trate \\'maj-ə-ˌstrāt\ *n* : an official entrusted with administration of the laws — **mag·is·tra·cy** \-strə-sē\ *n*

mag·ma \\'mag-mə\ *n* : molten rock material within the earth — **mag·mat·ic** \mag-'mat-ik\ *adj*

mag·nan·i·mous \mag-'nan-ə-məs\ *adj* **1** : showing or suggesting a lofty and courageous spirit **2** : NOBLE, GENEROUS — **mag·na·nim·i·ty** \ˌmag-nə-'nim-ət-ē\ *n* — **mag·nan·i·mous·ly** *adv* — **mag·nan·i·mous·ness** *n*

mag·nate \\'mag-ˌnāt\ *n* : a person of rank, influence, or distinction

mag·ne·sia \mag-'nē-shə, -zhə\ *n* [NL, fr. *magnes carneus,* a white earth, lit., flesh magnet] : a light white substance that is an oxide of magnesium and is used as a laxative

mag·ne·sium \mag-'nē-zē-əm, -zhəm\ *n* : a silver-white light and easily worked metallic chemical element

mag·net \\'mag-nət\ *n* **1** : LODESTONE **2** : a body that is able to attract iron **3** : something that attracts

mag·net·ic \mag-'net-ik\ *adj* **1** : of or relating to a magnet or magnetism **2** : magnetized or capable of being magnetized **3** : having an unusual ability to attract ⟨a ∼ leader⟩ — **mag·net·i·cal·ly** \-i-k(ə-)lē\ *adv*

magnetic disk *n* : DISK 3

magnetic north *n* : the northerly direction in the earth's magnetic field indicated by the north-seeking pole of a horizontal magnetic needle

magnetic tape *n* : a ribbon coated with a magnetic material on which information (as sound) may be stored

mag·ne·tism \\'mag-nə-ˌtiz-əm\ *n* **1** : the power to attract as possessed by a magnet **2** : the science that deals with magnetic phenomena **3** : an ability to attract

mag·ne·tite \\'mag-nə-ˌtīt\ *n* : a black mineral that is an important iron ore

mag·ne·tize \\'mag-nə-ˌtīz\ *vb* **-tized; -tiz·ing** **1** : to induce magnetic properties in **2** : to attract like a magnet : CHARM — **mag·ne·tiz·able** *adj* — **mag·ne·ti·za·tion** \ˌmag-nət-ə-'zā-shən\ *n* — **mag·ne·tiz·er** *n*

mag·ne·to \mag-'nēt-ō\ *n, pl* **-tos** : a generator used to produce sparks in an internal-combustion engine

mag·ne·tom·e·ter \ˌmag-nə-'täm-ət-ər\ *n* : an instrument for measuring the strength of a magnetic field

mag·ne·to·sphere \mag-'nēt-ə-ˌsfiər,

-ˈnet-\ *n* : a region of the upper atmosphere that extends out for thousands of miles and in which charged particles are trapped by the earth's magnetic field — **mag·ne·to·spher·ic** \-ˌnēt-ə-ˈsfiər-ik, -ˈsfer-\ *adj*

mag·nif·i·cent \mag-ˈnif-ə-sənt\ *adj* **1** : characterized by grandeur or beauty : SPLENDID **2** : EXALTED, NOBLE **syn** imposing, stately, noble, grand, majestic — **mag·nif·i·cence** \-səns\ *n* — **mag·nif·i·cent·ly** *adv*

mag·nif·i·co \mag-ˈnif-i-ˌkō\ *n, pl* **-coes** *or* **-cos 1** : a nobleman of Venice **2** : a person of high position

mag·ni·fy \ˈmag-nə-ˌfī\ *vb* **-fied; -fy·ing 1** : EXTOL, LAUD; *also* : to cause to be held in greater esteem **2** : INTENSIFY; *also* : EXAGGERATE **3** : to enlarge in fact or in appearance ⟨a microscope *magnifies* an object⟩ — **mag·ni·fi·ca·tion** \ˌmag-nə-fə-ˈkā-shən\ *n* — **mag·ni·fi·er** \ˈmag-nə-ˌfī(-ə)r\ *n*

mag·nil·o·quent \mag-ˈnil-ə-kwənt\ *adj* : characterized by an exalted and often bombastic style or manner — **mag·nil·o·quence** \-kwəns\ *n*

mag·ni·tude \ˈmag-nə-ˌt(y)üd\ *n* **1** : greatness of size or extent **2** : SIZE **3** : QUANTITY **4** : a number representing the brightness of a celestial body

mag·no·lia \mag-ˈnōl-yə\ *n* : any of several spring-flowering shrubs and trees with large often fragrant flowers

mag·num opus \ˌmag-nəm-ˈō-pəs\ *n* [L] : the greatest achievement of an artist or writer

mag·pie \ˈmag-ˌpī\ *n* : a long-tailed black-and-white bird related to the jays

Mag·yar \ˈmag-ˌyär, ˈmäg-; ˈmäj-ˌär\ *n* : a member of the dominant people of Hungary — **Magyar** *adj*

ma·ha·ra·ja *or* **ma·ha·ra·jah** \ˌmä-hə-ˈräj-ə\ *n* : a Hindu prince ranking above a raja

ma·ha·ra·ni *or* **ma·ha·ra·nee** \-ˈrän-ē\ *n* : the wife of a maharaja; *also* : a Hindu princess ranking above a rani

ma·ha·ri·shi \ˌmä-hə-ˈrē-shē\ *n* : a Hindu teacher of mystical knowledge

ma·hat·ma \mə-ˈhät-mə, -ˈhat-\ *n* [Skt *mahātman*, fr. *mahātman* great=souled, fr. *mahat* great + *ātman* soul] : a person revered for high-mindedness, wisdom, and selflessness

Ma·hi·can \mə-ˈhē-kən\ *n, pl* **Mahican** *or* **Mahicans** : a member of an American Indian people of the upper Hudson river valley

ma·hog·a·ny \mə-ˈhäg-ə-nē\ *n, pl* **-nies** : any of various tropical trees with reddish wood used in furniture; *esp* : an American evergreen tree or its durable lustrous reddish brown wood

ma·hout \mə-ˈhaut\ *n* [Hindi *mahāut*] : a keeper and driver of an elephant

maid \ˈmād\ *n* **1** : an unmarried girl or young woman **2** : a female servant

¹**maid·en** \ˈmād-ᵊn\ *n* : MAID 1 — **maid·en·ly** *adj*

²**maiden** *adj* **1** : UNMARRIED; *also* : VIRGIN **2** : of, relating to, or befitting a maiden **3** : FIRST ⟨∼ voyage⟩

maid·en·hair \-ˌhaər\ *n* : a fern with delicate feathery fronds

maid·en·head \ˈmād-ᵊn-ˌhed\ *n* **1** : VIRGINITY **2** : HYMEN

maid·en·hood \-ˌhud\ *n* : the condition or time of being a maiden

maid–in–wait·ing \ˌmād-ᵊn-ˈwāt-iŋ\ *n, pl* **maids–in–wait·ing** \ˌmād-zən-\ : a young woman appointed to attend a queen or princess

maid of honor : a bride's principal unmarried wedding attendant

maid·ser·vant \ˈmād-ˌsər-vənt\ *n* : a female servant

¹**mail** \ˈmāl\ *n* [ME *male*, fr. OF] **1** : something sent or carried in the postal system **2** : a nation's postal system — often used in pl.

²**mail** *vb* : to send by mail

³**mail** *n* [ME *maille*, fr. MF, fr. L *macula* spot, mesh] : armor made of metal links or plates

mail·box \-ˌbäks\ *n* **1** : a public box for the collection of mail **2** : a private box for the delivery of mail

mail·man \-ˌman\ *n* : a man who delivers mail

maim \ˈmām\ *vb* : to mutilate, disfigure, or wound seriously : CRIPPLE

¹**main** \ˈmān\ *n* **1** : FORCE ⟨with might and ∼⟩ **2** : MAINLAND; *also* : HIGH SEA **3** : the chief part **4** : a principal pipe, duct, or circuit of a utility system

²**main** *adj* **1** : CHIEF, PRINCIPAL **2** : fully exerted ⟨∼ force⟩ **3** : expressing the chief predication in a complex sentence ⟨the ∼ clause⟩ — **main·ly** *adv*

main·frame \'mān-ˌfrām\ *n* : a large fast computer

main·land \'mān-ˌland, -lənd\ *n* : a continuous body of land constituting the chief part of a country or continent

main·line \'mān-'līn\ *vb, slang* : to inject a narcotic drug into a vein

main line *n* : a principal highway or railroad line

main·mast \'mān-ˌmast, -məst\ *n* : the principal mast on a sailing ship

main·sail \'mān-ˌsāl, -səl\ *n* : the largest sail on the mainmast

main·spring \-ˌspriŋ\ *n* **1** : the chief spring in a mechanism (as of a watch) **2** : the chief motive, agent, or cause

main·stay \-ˌstā\ *n* **1** : a stay running from the head of the mainmast to the foot of the foremast **2** : a chief support

main·stream \-ˌstrēm\ *n* : a prevailing current or direction of activity or influence — **mainstream** *adj*

main·tain \mān-'tān\ *vb* [ME *mainteinen*, fr. OF *maintenir*, fr. ML *manutenēre*, fr. L *manu tenēre* to hold in the hand] **1** : to keep in an existing state (as of repair) **2** : to sustain against opposition or danger **3** : to continue in : CARRY ON **4** : to provide for : SUPPORT **5** : ASSERT — **main·tain·abil·i·ty** \-ˌtā-nə-'bil-ət-ē\ *n* — **main·tain·able** \-'tā-nə-bəl\ *adj* — **main·te·nance** \'mānt-(ə-)nəns\ *n*

main·top \'mān-ˌtäp\ *n* : a platform at the head of the mainmast of a square-rigged ship

mai·son·ette \ˌmāz-ᵊn-'et\ *n* **1** : a small house **2** : an apartment often on two floors

maî·tre d' *or* **mai·tre d'** \ˌmā-trə-'dē, ˌme-\ *n, pl* **maître d's** *or* **maitre d's** \-'dēz\ : MAÎTRE D'HÔTEL

maî·tre d'hô·tel \ˌmā-trə-dō-'tel, ˌme-\ *n, pl* **maîtres d'hôtel** *same*\ [F, lit., master of house] **1** : MAJORDOMO **2** : the head of a dining-room staff (as of a hotel)

maize \'māz\ *n* : INDIAN CORN

Maj *abbr* major

maj·es·ty \'maj-ə-stē\ *n, pl* **-ties** **1** : sovereign power, authority, or dignity; *also* : the person of a sovereign — used as a title **2** : GRANDEUR, SPLENDOR — **ma·jes·tic** \mə-'jes-tik\ *adj* — **ma·jes·ti·cal·ly** \-ti-k(ə-)lē\ *adv*

Maj Gen *abbr* Major General

ma·jol·i·ca \mə-'jäl-i-kə\ *also* **ma·iol·i·ca** \-'yäl-\ *n* : any of several faiences; *esp* : an Italian tin-glazed pottery

¹ma·jor \'mā-jər\ *adj* **1** : greater in number, extent, or importance ⟨a ~ poet⟩ **2** : notable or conspicuous in effect or scope ⟨a ~ improvement⟩ **3** : SERIOUS ⟨a ~ illness⟩ **4** : having half steps between the 3d and 4th and the 7th and 8th degrees ⟨~ scale⟩; *also* : based on a major scale ⟨~ key⟩ ⟨~ chord⟩

²major *n* **1** : a commissioned officer (as in the army) ranking next below a lieutenant colonel **2** : a subject of academic study chosen as a field of specialization; *also* : a student specializing in such a field

³major *vb* **ma·jored; ma·jor·ing** \'māj-(ə-)riŋ\ : to pursue an academic major

ma·jor·do·mo \ˌmā-jər-'dō-mō\ *n, pl* **-mos** [Sp *mayordomo* or obs. It *maiordomo*, fr. ML *major domus*, lit., chief of the house] **1** : a head steward **2** : BUTLER

majorette *n* : DRUM MAJORETTE

major general *n* : a commissioned officer (as in the army) ranking next below a lieutenant general

ma·jor·i·ty \mə-'jòr-ət-ē\ *n, pl* **-ties** **1** : the age at which full civil rights are accorded; *also* : the status of one who has attained this age **2** : a number greater than half of a total; *also* : the excess of this greater number over the remainder **3** : the military rank of a major

major–medical *adj* : of, relating to, or being a form of insurance designed to pay all or part of the medical bills of major illnesses usu. after deduction of a fixed initial sum

ma·jus·cule \'maj-əs-ˌkyül, mə-'jəs-\ *n* : a large letter (as a capital)

¹make \'māk\ *vb* **made** \'mād\; **mak·ing** **1** : to cause to exist, occur, or appear; *also* : DESTINE ⟨was *made* to be an actor⟩ **2** : FASHION ⟨~ a dress⟩; *also* : COMPOSE **3** : to formulate in the mind ⟨~ plans⟩ **4** : CONSTITUTE ⟨house *made* of stone⟩ **5** : to compute to be **6** : to set in order : PREPARE ⟨~ a bed⟩ **7** : to cause to be or become; *also* : APPOINT **8** : ENACT; *also* : EXECUTE ⟨~ a will⟩ **9** : CONCLUDE ⟨didn't know what to ~ of it⟩ **10** : to carry out : PERFORM ⟨~ a speech⟩ **11** : COMPEL **12** : to assure the success of ⟨anyone he likes is *made*⟩ **13** : to amount to in significance ⟨∼*s* no difference⟩ **14** : to be capable of developing or being fashioned into **15** : REACH, ATTAIN; *also* : GAIN **16** : to start out : GO **17** : to have weight or effect ⟨courtesy ∼*s* for safer driving⟩ **syn** form, shape, fabricate, manufacture — **mak·er** *n* — **make believe** : PRETEND — **make do** : to manage with the means at hand — **make fun of** : RIDICULE, MOCK — **make good 1** : INDEMNIFY ⟨*make good* the loss⟩; *also* : to carry out successfully ⟨*make good* his promise⟩ **2** : SUCCEED — **make way 1** : to give room for passing, entering, or occupying **2** : to make progress

²make *n* **1** : the manner or style of construction; *also* : BRAND 3 **2** : MAKEUP **3** : the action of manufacturing — **on the make** : in search of wealth, social status, or sexual adventure

¹make–be·lieve \'māk-bə-ˌlēv\ *n* : a pretending to believe : PRETENSE

²make–believe *adj* : IMAGINED, PRETENDED

make–do \-ˌdü\ *adj* : MAKESHIFT

make out *vb* **1** : to draw up in writing ⟨*make out* a shopping list⟩ **2** : to find or grasp the meaning of ⟨how do you *make* that *out*⟩ **3** : to pretend to be true **4** : DISCERN ⟨*make out* a form in the fog⟩ **5** : GET ALONG, FARE ⟨*make out* well in business⟩ **6** : to engage in amorous kissing and caressing

make over *vb* : REMAKE, REMODEL

make·shift \'māk-ˌshift\ *n* : a temporary expedient — **makeshift** *adj*

make·up \-ˌəp\ *n* **1** : the way in which something is put together; *also* : physical, mental, and moral constitution **2** : cosmetics esp. for the face; *also* : materials (as wigs and cosmetics) used in costuming (as for a play)

make up \(ˈ)māk-ˈəp\ *vb* **1** : FORM, COMPOSE **2** : to compensate for a deficiency **3** : SETTLE ⟨*made up* my mind⟩ **4** : INVENT, IMPROVISE **5** : to become reconciled **6** : to put on makeup

make–work \'māk-ˌwərk\ *n* : assigned busywork

mak·ings \'mā-kiŋz\ *n pl* : the material from which something is made

makuta pl of LIKUTA

Mal *abbr* Malachi

Mal·a·chi \'mal-ə-ˌkī\ *n* — see BIBLE table

Mal·a·chi·as \ˌmal-ə-ˈkī-əs\ *n* — see BIBLE table

mal·a·chite \'mal-ə-ˌkīt\ *n* : a mineral that is a green carbonate of copper used for making ornamental objects

mal·adapt·ed \ˌmal-ə-ˈdap-təd\ *adj* : poorly suited to a particular use, purpose, or situation

mal·ad·just·ed \ˌmal-ə-ˈjəs-təd\ *adj* : poorly or inadequately adjusted (as to one's environment) — **mal·ad·just·ment** \-ˈjəs(t)-mənt\ *n*

mal·adroit \ˌmal-ə-ˈdroit\ *adj* : not adroit : INEPT

mal·a·dy \'mal-əd-ē\ *n, pl* **-dies** : a disease or disorder of body or mind

mal·aise \mə-ˈlāz, ma-\ *n* [F] : a vague feeling of bodily or mental disorder

mal·a·mute \'mal-ə-ˌmyüt\ *n* : a dog often used to draw sleds esp. in northern No. America

mal·a·prop·ism \'mal-ə-ˌpräp-ˌiz-əm\ *n* : a usu. humorous misuse of a word

mal·ap·ro·pos \ˌmal-ˌap-rə-ˈpō, mal-ˈap-rə-ˌpō\ *adv* : in an inappropriate or inopportune way — **malapropos** *adj*

ma·lar·ia \mə-ˈler-ē-ə\ *n* [It, fr. *mala aria* bad air] : a disease marked by recurring chills and fever and caused by a parasite carried by a mosquito — **ma·lar·i·al** \-əl\ *adj*

ma·lar·key \mə-ˈlär-kē\ *n* : insincere or foolish talk

mal·a·thi·on \ˌmal-ə-ˈthī-ən, -ˌän\ *n* : an insecticide with a relatively low toxicity for mammals

Ma·la·wi·an \mə-ˈlä-wē-ən\ *n* : a native or inhabitant of Malawi — **Malawian** *adj*

Ma·lay \mə-ˈlā, ˈmā-ˌlā\ *n* **1** : a member of a people of the Malay peninsula and archipelago **2** : the language of the Malays — **Malay** *adj* — **Ma·lay·an** \mə-ˈlā-ən, ˈmā-ˌlā-\ *n or adj*

Ma·lay·sian \mə-ˈlā-zhən, -shən\ *n* : a native or inhabitant of Malaysia — **Malaysian** *adj*

mal·con·tent \ˌmal-kən-ˈtent\ *adj* : marked by a dissatisfaction with the existing state of affairs : DISCONTENTED — **malcontent** *n*

mal de mer \ˌmal-də-ˈmeər\ *n* : SEASICKNESS

¹male \'māl\ *adj* **1** : of, relating to, or

being the sex that begets young; *also* : STAMINATE **2** : MASCULINE — **male-ness** *n*

²**male** *n* : a male individual

male·dic·tion \ˌmal-ə-ˈdik-shən\ *n* : CURSE, EXECRATION

male·fac·tor \ˈmal-ə-ˌfak-tər\ *n* : EVIL-DOER; *esp* : one who commits an offense against the law — **mal·e·fac·tion** \ˌmal-ə-ˈfak-shən\ *n*

ma·lef·ic \mə-ˈlef-ik\ *adj* **1** : BALEFUL **2** : MALICIOUS

ma·lef·i·cent \-ə-sənt\ *adj* : working or productive of harm or evil

ma·lev·o·lent \mə-ˈlev-ə-lənt\ *adj* : having, showing, or arising from ill will, spite, or hatred **syn** malignant, malign, malicious, spiteful — **ma·lev·o·lence** \-ləns\ *n*

mal·fea·sance \mal-ˈfēz-ᵊns\ *n* : wrongful conduct esp. by a public official

mal·for·ma·tion \ˌmal-fȯr-ˈmā-shən\ *n* : an irregular or faulty formation or structure — **mal·formed** \mal-ˈfȯrmd\ *adj*

mal·func·tion \mal-ˈfəŋk-shən\ *vb* : to fail to operate in the normal or usual manner — **malfunction** *n*

Ma·li·an \ˈmäl-ē-ən\ *n* : a native or inhabitant of Mali — **Malian** *adj*

mal·ice \ˈmal-əs\ *n* : ILL WILL — **ma·li·cious** \mə-ˈlish-əs\ *adj* — **ma·li·cious·ly** *adv*

¹**ma·lign** \mə-ˈlīn\ *adj* **1** : evil in nature, influence, or effect ⟨hindered by ∼ influences⟩; *also* : MALIGNANT **2** **2** : moved by ill will toward others

²**malign** *vb* : to speak evil of : DEFAME

ma·lig·nant \mə-ˈlig-nənt\ *adj* **1** : INJURIOUS, MALIGN **2** : tending or likely to cause death : VIRULENT — **ma·lig·nan·cy** \-nən-sē\ *n* — **ma·lig·nant·ly** *adv* — **ma·lig·ni·ty** \-nət-ē\ *n*

ma·lin·ger \mə-ˈliŋ-gər\ *vb* **-gered; -ger·ing** \-g(ə-)riŋ\ [F *malingre* sickly] : to pretend illness so as to avoid duty — **ma·lin·ger·er** *n*

mal·i·son \ˈmal-ə-sən, -zən\ *n* : CURSE

mall \ˈmȯl, ˈmal\ *n* **1** : a shaded walk : PROMENADE **2** : an urban shopping area featuring a variety of shops surrounding a concourse **3** : a usu. large enclosed suburban shopping area containing various shops

mal·lard \ˈmal-ərd\ *n, pl* **mallard** *or*

mallards : a common wild duck that is the ancestor of domestic ducks

mal·lea·ble \ˈmal-ē-ə-bəl\ *adj* **1** : capable of being extended or shaped by beating with a hammer or by the pressure of rollers **2** : ADAPTABLE, PLIABLE **syn** plastic, pliant, ductile, supple — **mal·le·a·bil·i·ty** \ˌmal-ē-ə-ˈbil-ət-ē\ *n*

mal·let \ˈmal-ət\ *n* **1** : a tool with a large head for driving another tool or for striking a surface without marring it **2** : a hammerlike implement for striking a ball (as in polo or croquet)

mal·le·us \ˈmal-ē-əs\ *n, pl* **mal·lei** \-ē-ˌī -ē-ˌē\ [NL, fr. L, hammer] : the outermost of the three small bones of the mammalian ear

mal·low \ˈmal-ō\ *n* : any of several tall herbs with lobed leaves and 5-petaled white, yellow, rose, or purplish flowers

malm·sey \ˈmä(l)m-zē\ *n, often cap* : the sweetest variety of Madeira wine

mal·nour·ished \mal-ˈnər-isht\ *adj* : poorly nourished

mal·nu·tri·tion \ˌmal-n(y)ü-ˈtrish-ən\ *n* : faulty and esp. inadequate nutrition

mal·oc·clu·sion \ˌmal-ə-ˈklü-zhən\ *n* : faulty coming together of teeth in biting

mal·odor·ous \mal-ˈōd-ə-rəs\ *adj* : ill-smelling — **mal·odor·ous·ly** *adv* — **mal·odor·ous·ness** *n*

ma·lo·ti \mə-ˈlōt-ē\ *pl of* LOTI

mal·prac·tice \mal-ˈprak-təs\ *n* : a dereliction of professional duty or a failure of professional skill that results in injury, loss, or damage

malt \ˈmȯlt\ *n* **1** : grain and esp. barley steeped in water until it has sprouted and used in brewing and distilling **2** : liquor made with malt — **malty** *adj*

malted milk \ˌmȯl-təd-\ *n* : a powder prepared from dried milk and an extract from malt; *also* : a beverage of this powder in milk or other liquid

Mal·thu·sian \mal-ˈth(y)ü-zhən\ *adj* : of or relating to Malthus or his theory that population unless checked (as by war) tends to increase faster than its means of subsistence — **Malthusian** *n* — **Mal·thu·sian·ism** \-zhə-ˌniz-əm\ *n*

malt·ose \ˈmȯl-ˌtōs\ *n* : a sugar formed esp. from starch by the action of enzymes and used in brewing and distilling

mal·treat \mal-'trēt\ *vb* : to treat cruelly or roughly : ABUSE — **mal·treatment** *n*

ma·ma *or* **mam·ma** \'mäm-ə\ *n* : MOTHER

mam·bo \'mäm-bō\ *n, pl* **mambos** : a dance of Cuban origin related to the rumba — **mambo** *vb*

mam·mal \'mam-əl\ *n* : any of the group of vertebrate animals that includes man and all others which nourish their young with milk — **mam·ma·li·an** \mə-'mā-lē-ən, ma-\ *adj or n*

mam·ma·ry \'mam-ə-rē\ *adj* : of, relating to, or being the glands (**mammary glands**) that in female mammals secrete milk

mam·mo·gram \'mam-ə-ˌgram\ *n* : a photograph of the breasts made by X rays

mam·mog·ra·phy \ma-'mäg-rə-fē\ *n, pl* **-phies** : X-ray examination of the breasts (as for early detection of cancer)

mam·mon \'mam-ən\ *n, often cap* : material wealth having a debasing influence

¹mam·moth \'mam-əth\ *n* : any of various large hairy extinct elephants

²mammoth *adj* : of very great size : GIGANTIC **syn** colossal, enormous, immense, vast, elephantine

¹man \'man\ *n, pl* **men** \'men\ **1** : a human being; *esp* : an adult male **2** : MANKIND **3** : one possessing in high degree the qualities considered distinctive of manhood; *also* : HUSBAND **4** : an adult male servant or employee **5** : one of the pieces with which various games (as chess) are played **6** *often cap* : white society or people

²man *vb* **manned; man·ning 1** : to supply with men ⟨~ a fleet⟩ **2** : FORTIFY, BRACE

³man *abbr* manual

Man *abbr* Manitoba

man–about–town \ˌman-ə-ˌbaut-'taun\ *n, pl* **men–about–town** \ˌmen-\ : a worldly and socially active man

man·a·cle \'man-i-kəl\ *n* **1** : a shackle for the hand or wrist **2** : something used as a restraint

man·age \'man-ij\ *vb* **man·aged; man·ag·ing 1** : HANDLE, CONTROL; *also* : to direct or carry on business or affairs **2** : to make and keep submissive **3** : to

treat with care : HUSBAND **4** : to achieve one's purpose : CONTRIVE — **man·age·abil·i·ty** \ˌman-ij-ə-'bil-ət-ē\ *n* — **man·age·able** \'man-ij-ə-bəl\ *adj* — **man·age·able·ness** *n* — **man·age·ably** \-blē\ *adv*

man·age·ment \'man-ij-mənt\ *n* **1** : the act or art of managing : CONTROL **2** : judicious use of means to accomplish an end **3** : executive ability **4** : the group of those who manage or direct an enterprise

man·ag·er \'man-ij-ər\ *n* : one that manages — **man·a·ge·ri·al** \ˌman-ə-'jir-ē-əl\ *adj*

ma·ña·na \mən-'yän-ə\ [Sp., lit., tomorrow] *n* : an indefinite time in the future

man–at–arms \ˌman-ət-'ärmz\ *n, pl* **men–at–arms** \ˌmen-\ : SOLDIER; *esp* : one who is heavily armed and mounted

Man·chu·ri·an \man-'chur-ē-ən\ *n* : a native or inhabitant of Manchuria, China — **Manchurian** *adj*

man·ci·ple \'man-sə-pəl\ *n* : a steward or purveyor esp. for a college or monastery

man·da·mus \man-'dā-məs\ *n* [L, we enjoin, fr. *mandare*] : a writ issued by a superior court commanding that an official act or duty be performed

man·da·rin \'man-də-rən\ *n* **1** : a public official of high rank under the Chinese Empire **2** *cap* : the chief dialect of China **3** : a reddish orange to yellow loose-skinned citrus fruit; *also* : a tree that bears mandarins

man·date \'man-ˌdāt\ *n* **1** : an authoritative command **2** : an authorization to act given to a representative **3** : a commission granted by the League of Nations to a member nation for governing conquered territory; *also* : a territory so governed

man·da·to·ry \'man-də-ˌtōr-ē\ *adj* **1** : containing or constituting a command : OBLIGATORY **2** : of or relating to a League of Nations mandate

man·di·ble \'man-də-bəl\ *n* **1** : JAW; *esp* : a lower jaw **2** : either segment of a bird's bill — **man·dib·u·lar** \man-'dib-yə-lər\ *adj*

man·do·lin \'man-də-'lin, 'man-dᵊl-ən\ *n* : a stringed musical instrument with a pear-shaped body and a fretted neck

man·drag·o·ra \man-'drag-ə-rə\ *n* : MANDRAKE 1

man·drake \'man-ˌdrāk\ *n* **1** : an Old World herb of the nightshade family or its large forked root superstitiously credited with human and medicinal attributes **2** : MAYAPPLE

man·drel *also* **man·dril** \'man-drəl\ *n* **1** : an axle or spindle inserted into a hole in a piece of work to support it during machining **2** : a metal bar used as a core around which material may be cast, shaped, or molded

man·drill \'man-drəl\ *n* : a large fierce gregarious baboon of western Africa

mane \'mān\ *n* : long heavy hair growing about the neck of some mammals (as a horse) — **maned** \'mānd\ *adj*

man–eat·er \'man-ˌēt-ər\ *n* : one (as a shark or cannibal) that has or is thought to have an appetite for human flesh — **man–eat·ing** \-ˌēt-iŋ\ *adj*

ma·nège \ma-'nezh, mə-\ *n* : the art of horsemanship or of training horses

ma·nes \'män-ˌās, 'mā-ˌnēz\ *n pl, often cap* : the spirits of the dead and gods of the lower world in ancient Roman belief

ma·neu·ver \mə-'n(y)ü-vər\ *n* [F *manœuvre,* fr. OF *maneuvre* work done by hand, fr. ML *manuopera,* fr. L *manu operare* to work by hand] **1** : a military or naval movement; *also* : an armed forces training exercise — often used in pl. **2** : a procedure involving expert physical movement **3** : an evasive movement or shift of tactics; *also* : an action taken to gain a tactical end — **maneuver** *vb* — **ma·neu·ver·abil·i·ty** \-ˌn(y)üv-(ə-)rə-'bil-ət-ē\ *n*

man Fri·day \'man-'frīd-ē\ *n* : an efficient and devoted aide or employee

man·ful \'man-fəl\ *adj* : having or showing courage and resolution — **man·ful·ly** \-ē\ *adv*

man·ga·nese \'maŋ-gə-ˌnēz, -ˌnēs\ *n* : a grayish white metallic chemical element resembling iron but not magnetic

mange \'mānj\ *n* : a contagious itchy skin disease esp. of domestic animals — **mangy** \'mān-jē\ *adj*

man·ger \'mān-jər\ *n* : a trough or open box for livestock feed or fodder

¹man·gle \'maŋ-gəl\ *vb* **man·gled; man·gling** \-g(ə-)liŋ\ **1** : to cut, bruise, or hack with repeated blows **2** : to spoil or injure in making or performing — **man·gler** \-g(ə-)lər\ *n*

²mangle *n* : a machine for ironing laundry by passing it between heated rollers

man·go \'maŋ-gō\ *n, pl* **mangoes** *also* **mangos** [Pg *manga*] : a yellowish red tropical fruit with juicy slightly acid pulp; *also* : an evergreen tree related to the sumacs that bears this fruit

man·grove \'man-ˌgrōv\ *n* : a tropical maritime tree that sends out many prop roots and forms dense thickets important in coastal land building

man·han·dle \'man-ˌhan-d³l\ *vb* : to handle roughly

man·hat·tan \man-'hat-³n\ *n, often cap* : a cocktail made of whiskey and vermouth

man·hole \'man-ˌhōl\ *n* : a hole through which a person may go esp. to gain access to an underground or enclosed structure

man·hood \-ˌhud\ *n* **1** : the condition of being an adult male **2** : manly qualities : COURAGE **3** : MEN ⟨the nation's ∼⟩

man–hour \-'au̇(-ə)r\ *n* : a unit of one hour's work by one person

man·hunt \-ˌhənt\ *n* : an organized hunt for a person and esp. for one charged with a crime

ma·nia \'mā-nē-ə, -nyə\ *n* **1** : insanity esp. when marked by extreme excitement **2** : excessive enthusiasm

ma·ni·ac \'mā-nē-ˌak\ *n* : LUNATIC, MADMAN

ma·ni·a·cal \mə-'nī-ə-kəl\ *also* **ma·ni·ac** \'mā-nē-ak\ *adj* **1** : affected with or suggestive of madness **2** : FRANTIC

man·ic \'man-ik\ *adj* : affected with, relating to, or resembling mania — **manic** *n*

man·ic–de·pres·sive \ˌman-ik-di-'pres-iv\ *adj* : characterized by mania, by psychotic depression, or by alternating mania and depression — **manic–depressive** *n*

¹man·i·cure \'man-ə-ˌkyu̇ər\ *n* **1** : MANICURIST **2** : a treatment for the care of the hands and nails

²manicure *vb* **-cured; -cur·ing** **1** : to do manicure work on **2** : to trim closely and evenly

man•i•cur•ist \-ˌkyu̇r-əst\ *n* : a person who gives manicure treatments

¹man•i•fest \ˈman-ə-ˌfest\ *adj* [ME, fr. MF or L; MF *manifeste,* fr. L *manifestus,* lit., hit by the hand, fr. *manus* hand + *-festus* (akin to L in*festus* hostile)] **1** : readily perceived by the senses and esp. by the sight **2** : easily understood : OBVIOUS — **man•i•fest•ly** *adv*

²manifest *vb* : to make evident or certain by showing or displaying **syn** evidence, evince, demonstrate, exhibit

³manifest *n* : a list of passengers or an invoice of cargo for a ship or plane

man•i•fes•ta•tion \ˌman-ə-fə-ˈstā-shən\ *n* : DISPLAY, DEMONSTRATION

man•i•fes•to \ˌman-ə-ˈfes-tō\ *n, pl* **-tos** *or* **-toes** : a public declaration of intentions, motives, or views

¹man•i•fold \ˈman-ə-ˌfōld\ *adj* **1** : marked by diversity or variety **2** : consisting of or operating many of one kind combined

²manifold *n* : a pipe fitting with several lateral outlets for connecting it with other pipes

³manifold *vb* **1** : to make a number of copies of (as a letter) **2** : MULTIPLY

man•i•kin *or* **man•ni•kin** \ˈman-i-kən\ *n* **1** : MANNEQUIN **2** : a little man : DWARF, PYGMY

Ma•nila hemp \mə-ˌnil-ə-\ *n* : a tough fiber from a Philippine banana plant used esp. for cordage

manila paper \mə-ˌnil-ə-\ *n, often cap* **M** : a tough brownish paper made orig. from Manila hemp

man•i•oc \ˈman-ē-ˌäk\ *n* : CASSAVA

ma•nip•u•late \mə-ˈnip-yə-ˌlāt\ *vb* **-lat•ed; -lat•ing** [fr. *manipulation,* fr. F, fr. *manipule* handful, fr. L *manipulus*] **1** : to treat or operate manually or mechanically esp. with skill **2** : to manage or use skillfully **3** : to influence esp. with intent to deceive — **ma•nip•u•la•tion** \mə-nip-yə-ˈlā-shən\ *n* — **ma•nip•u•la•tive** \-ˈnip-yə-ˌlāt-iv\ *adj* — **ma•nip•u•la•tor** \-ˌlāt-ər\ *n*

man•kind *n* **1** \ˈman-ˈkīnd\ : the human race **2** \-ˌkīnd\ : men as distinguished from women

¹man•ly \ˈman-lē\ *adj* **man•li•er; -est** : having qualities appropriate to or generally associated with a man : BOLD, RESOLUTE — **man•li•ness** *n*

²manly *adv* : in a manly manner

man–made \ˈman-ˈmād\ *adj* : made by man rather than nature ⟨∼ systems⟩; *esp* : SYNTHETIC ⟨∼ fibers⟩

man•na \ˈman-ə\ *n* **1** : food miraculously supplied to the Israelites in the wilderness **2** : something of value that comes unexpectedly : WINDFALL

manned \ˈmand\ *adj* : carrying or performed by a person ⟨∼ spaceflight⟩

man•ne•quin \ˈman-i-kən\ *n* **1** : a form representing the human figure used esp. for displaying clothes **2** : a person employed to model clothing

man•ner \ˈman-ər\ *n* **1** : KIND, SORT **2** : a way of acting or proceeding ⟨worked in a brisk ∼⟩; *also* : normal behavior ⟨spoke bluntly as was his ∼⟩ **3** : a method of artistic execution **4** *pl* : social conduct; *also* : BEARING **5** *pl* : BEHAVIOR ⟨taught the child good ∼s⟩

man•nered \ˈman-ərd\ *adj* **1** : having manners of a specified kind ⟨well= *mannered*⟩ **2** : having an artificial character ⟨a highly ∼ style⟩

man•ner•ism \ˈman-ə-ˌriz-əm\ *n* **1** : ARTIFICIALITY, PRECIOSITY **2** : a peculiarity of action, bearing, or treatment **syn** pose, air, affectation

man•ner•ly \ˈman-ər-lē\ *adj* : showing good manners : POLITE — **man•ner•li•ness** *n*

man•nish \ˈman-ish\ *adj* **1** : resembling or suggesting a man rather than a woman **2** : generally associated with or characteristic of a man — **man•nish•ly** *adv* — **man•nish•ness** *n*

ma•noeu•vre \mə-ˈn(y)ü-vər\ *chiefly Brit* var of MANEUVER

man–of–war \ˌman-ə(v)-ˈwȯr\ *n, pl* **men–of–war** \ˌmen-\ : WARSHIP

ma•nom•e•ter \mə-ˈnäm-ət-ər\ *n* : an instrument for measuring the pressure of gases — **mano•met•ric** \ˌman-ə-ˈme-trik\ *adj*

man•or \ˈman-ər\ *n* **1** : the house or hall of an estate; *also* : a landed estate **2** : an English estate of a feudal lord — **ma•no•ri•al** \mə-ˈnȯr-ē-əl\ *adj* — **ma•no•ri•al•ism** \-ə-ˌliz-əm\ *n*

man power *n* **1** : power available from or supplied by the physical effort of human beings **2** *usu* **man•pow•er** : the total supply of persons available and fitted for service

man•qué \mänⁿ-ˈkā\ *adj* [F, fr. pp. of

manquer to lack, fail] : short of or frustrated in the fulfillment of one's aspirations or talents ⟨a poet ∼⟩

man·sard \\'man-ˌsärd, -sərd\ *n* : a roof having two slopes on all sides with the lower slope steeper than the upper one

manse \\'mans\ *n* : the residence esp. of a Presbyterian clergyman

man·ser·vant \\'man-ˌsər-vənt\ *n, pl* **men·ser·vants** \\'men-ˌsər-vənts\ : a male servant

man·sion \\'man-chən\ *n* : a large imposing residence; *also* : a separate apartment in a large structure

man–size \\'man-ˌsīz\ *or* **man–sized** \-ˌsīzd\ *adj* : suitable for or requiring a man

man·slaugh·ter \-ˌslȯt-ər\ *n* : the unlawful killing of a human being without express or implied malice

man·slay·er \-ˌslā-ər\ *n* : one who slays a man

man·ta \\'mant-ə\ *n* : a square piece of cloth or blanket used in southwestern U.S. and Latin America as a cloak or shawl

man·teau \man-ˈtō\ *n* : a loose cloak, coat, or robe

man·tel \\'mant-ᵊl\ *n* : a beam, stone, or arch serving as a lintel to support the masonry above a fireplace; *also* : a shelf above a fireplace

man·tel·piece \\'mant-ᵊl-ˌpēs\ *n* : the shelf of a mantel

man·til·la \man-ˈtē-(y)ə, -ˈtil-ə\ *n* : a light scarf worn over the head and shoulders esp. by Spanish and Latin-American women

man·tis \\'mant-əs\ *n, pl* **man·tis·es** *or* **man·tes** \\'man-ˌtēz\ [NL, fr. Gk, lit., divener, prophet] : a large insect related to the grasshoppers that feeds on other insects which it holds in forelimbs folded as if in prayer

man·tis·sa \man-ˈtis-ə\ *n* : the decimal part of a logarithm

¹man·tle \\'mant-ᵊl\ *n* **1** : a loose sleeveless garment worn over other clothes **2** : something that covers, enfolds, or envelopes **3** : a lacy sheath that gives light by incandescence when placed over a flame **4** : the portion of the earth lying between the crust and the core **5** : MANTEL

²mantle *vb* **man·tled; man·tling** \\'mant-

(ᵊ-)liŋ\ **1** : to cover with a mantle **2** : BLUSH

man·tra \\'man-trə\ *n* : a Hindu or Buddhist mystical formula of incantation

¹man·u·al \\'man-yə(-wə)l\ *adj* **1** : of, relating to, or involving the hands; *also* : worked by hand ⟨a ∼ choke⟩ **2** : requiring or using physical skill and energy — **man·u·al·ly** \-ē\ *adv*

²manual *n* **1** : a small book; *esp* : HANDBOOK **2** : the prescribed movements in the handling of a military item and esp. a weapon during a drill or ceremony ⟨the ∼ of arms⟩ **3** : a keyboard esp. of an organ

man·u·fac·to·ry \ˌman-(y)ə-ˈfak-t(ə-)rē\ *n* : FACTORY

¹man·u·fac·ture \ˌman-(y)ə-ˈfak-chər\ *n* [MF, fr. L *manu factus* made by hand] **1** : something made from raw materials **2** : the process of making wares by hand or by machinery; *also* : a productive industry using mechanical power and machinery

²manufacture *vb* **-tured; -tur·ing 1** : to make from raw materials by hand or by machinery; *also* : to engage in manufacture **2** : INVENT, FABRICATE; *also* : CREATE — **man·u·fac·tur·er** *n*

man·u·mit \ˌman-yə-ˈmit\ *vb* **-mit·ted; -mit·ting** : to free from slavery — **man·u·mis·sion** \-ˈmish-ən\ *n*

¹ma·nure \mə-ˈn(y)u̇r\ *vb* **ma·nured; ma·nur·ing** : to fertilize land with manure

²manure *n* : FERTILIZER; *esp* : refuse from stables and barnyards — **ma·nu·ri·al** \-ˈn(y)u̇r-ē-əl\ *adj*

man·u·script \\'man-yə-ˌskript\ *n* [L *manu scriptus* written by hand] **1** : a written or typewritten composition or document **2** : writing as opposed to print

Manx \\'maŋks\ *n pl* : the people of the Isle of Man — **Manx** *adj*

¹many \\'men-ē\ *adj* **more** \\'mōr\; **most** \\'mōst\ : consisting of or amounting to a large but indefinite number

²many *pron* : a large number

³many *n* : a large but indefinite number

many·fold \ˌmen-ē-ˈfōld\ *adv* : by many times

many–sid·ed \-ˈsīd-əd\ *adj* **1** : having many sides or aspects **2** : VERSATILE

Mao·ism \\'mau̇-ˌiz-əm\ *n* : the theory and practice of Communism developed in China chiefly by Mao Tse≠

tung — **Mao•ist** \'mau̇-əst\ *n or adj*
Mao•ri \'mau̇(ə)r-ē\ *n, pl* **Maori** *or*
Maoris : a member of a Polynesian
people native to New Zealand
¹**map** \'map\ *n* [ML *mappa,* fr. L, napkin, towel] **1** : a representation usu.
on a flat surface of the whole or part of
an area **2** : a representation of the celestial sphere or part of it
²**map** *vb* **mapped; map•ping 1** : to make
a map of **2** : to plan in detail ⟨∼ out a
program⟩ — **map•pa•ble** \'map-ə-bəl\
adj — **map•per** *n*
ma•ple \'mā-pəl\ *n* : any of various
trees or shrubs with 2-winged dry fruit
and opposite leaves; *also* : the hard
light-colored wood of a maple used
esp. for floors and furniture
maple sugar *n* : sugar made by boiling
maple syrup
maple syrup *n* : syrup made by concentrating the sap of maple trees and esp.
the sugar maple
mar \'mär\ *vb* **marred; mar•ring** : to detract from the wholeness or perfection
of : SPOIL **syn** injure, hurt, harm, damage, impair, blemish
Mar *abbr* March
ma•ra•ca \mə-'räk-ə, -'rak-\ *n* [Pg
maracá] : a dried gourd or a rattle like
a gourd that contains dried seeds or
pebbles and is used as a percussion
instrument
mar•a•schi•no \ˌmar-ə-'skē-nō, -'shē-\
n, pl **-nos** *often cap* [It] : a cherry preserved in a true or imitation sweet
cherry liqueur
mar•a•thon \'mar-ə-ˌthän\ *n* [*Marathon,* Greece, site of a victory of
Greeks over Persians in 490 B.C. the
news of which was carried to Athens
by a long-distance runner] **1** : a
long-distance race esp. on foot **2** : an
endurance contest
mar•a•thon•er \'mar-ə-ˌthän-ər\ *n* : one
who takes part in a marathon — **mar-
a•thon•ing** *n*
ma•raud \mə-'rȯd\ *vb* : to roam about
and raid in search of plunder : PILLAGE
— **ma•raud•er** *n*
mar•ble \'mär-bəl\ *n* **1** : a limestone
that can be polished and used in fine
building work **2** : something resembling marble (as in coldness) **3** : a
small ball (as of glass) used in various
games; *also, pl* : a children's game

played with these small balls —
marble *adj*
mar•bling \-b(ə-)liŋ\ *n* : an intermixture
of fat through the lean of a cut of meat
mar•cel \mär-'sel\ *n* : a deep soft wave
made in the hair by the use of a heated
curling iron — **marcel** *vb*
¹**march** \'märch\ *n* : a border region
: FRONTIER
²**march** *vb* **1** : to move along in or as if in
military formation **2** : to walk in a direct purposeful manner; *also* : PROG-
RESS, ADVANCE **3** : TRAVERSE — **march-
er** *n*
³**march** *n* **1** : the action of marching;
also : the distance covered (as by a
military unit) in a march **2** : a regular
measured stride or rhythmic step used
in marching **3** : forward movement **4**
: a piece of music with marked rhythm
suitable for marching to
March *n* [ME, fr. OF, fr. L *martius,* fr.
Mart-, Mars, Roman god of war] : the
third month of the year having 31 days
mar•chio•ness \'mär-shə-nəs\ *n* **1** : the
wife or widow of a marquess **2** : a
woman holding the rank of a marquess in her own right
march–past \'märch-ˌpast\ *n* : a marching by esp. of troops in review
Mar•di Gras \'märd-ē-ˌgrä\ *n* [F, lit.,
fat Tuesday] : the Tuesday before
Ash Wednesday often observed with
parades and merrymaking
¹**mare** \'maər\ *n* : a female of an animal
of the horse group
²**ma•re** \'mär-(ˌ)ā\ *n, pl* **ma•ria** \'mär-ē-
ə\ : any of several large dark areas on
the surface of the moon or Mars
mar•ga•rine \'märj-(ə-)rən, -ə-ˌrēn\ *n*
: a food product made usu. from vegetable oils churned with skimmed milk
and used as a substitute for butter
mar•gin \'mär-jən\ *n* **1** : the part of a
page outside the main body of printed
or written matter **2** : EDGE **3** : a spare
amount, measure, or degree allowed
for use if needed **4** : measure or degree of difference ⟨passed the bill by a
∼ of one vote⟩ — **mar•gin•al** \-ᵊl\ *adj*
— **mar•gin•al•ly** \-ē\ *adv*
mar•gi•na•lia \ˌmär-jə-'nā-lē-ə\ *n pl*
: marginal notes
mar•grave \'mär-ˌgrāv\ *n* : the military
governor esp. of a medieval German
border province

mar·gue·rite \ˌmär-g(y)ə-'rēt\ *n* [F] : any of several daisies or chrysanthemums

ma·ri·a·chi \ˌmär-ē-'äch-ē\ *n* : a Mexican street band; *also* : a member of or the music of such a band

mari·gold \'mar-ə-ˌgōld, 'mer-\ *n* : a garden plant related to the daisies with double yellow, orange, or reddish flower heads

mar·i·jua·na *also* **mar·i·hua·na** \ˌmar-ə-'(h)wän-ə\ *n* [MexSp *marihuana*] : the dried leaves and flowering tops of the female hemp plant that are sometimes smoked for their intoxicating effect; *also* : HEMP

ma·rim·ba \mə-'rim-bə\ *n* : a xylophone of southern Africa and Central America; *also* : a modern version of it

ma·ri·na \mə-'rē-nə\ *n* : a dock or basin providing secure moorings for motorboats and yachts

mar·i·na·ra \ˌmar-ə-'nar-ə\ *adj* [It (*alla*) *marinara*, lit., in sailor style] : made with tomatoes, onions, garlic, and spices; *also* : served with marinara sauce

mar·i·nate \'mar-ə-ˌnāt\ *vb* **-nat·ed; -nat·ing** : to steep (as meat or fish) in a brine or pickle

¹ma·rine \mə-'rēn\ *adj* **1** : of or relating to the sea or its navigation or commerce **2** : of or relating to marines

²marine 1 : the mercantile and naval shipping of a country **2** : any of a class of soldiers serving on shipboard or with a naval force

mar·i·ner \'mar-ə-nər\ *n* : SAILOR

mar·i·o·nette \ˌmar-ē-ə-'net, ˌmer-\ *n* : a puppet moved by strings or by hand

mar·i·tal \'mar-ət-ᵊl\ *adj* : of or relating to marriage : CONJUGAL **syn** matrimonial, connubial, nuptial

mar·i·time \'mar-ə-ˌtīm\ *adj* **1** : of, relating to, or bordering on the sea **2** : of or relating to navigation or commerce of the sea

mar·jo·ram \'märj-(ə-)rəm\ *n* : a fragrant aromatic mint used esp. as a seasoning

¹mark \'märk\ *n* **1** : TARGET; *also* : GOAL, OBJECT **2** : something (as a line or fixed object) designed to record position; *also* : the starting line or position in a track event **3** : an object of abuse or ridicule **4** : the question under discussion **5** : NORM ⟨not up to the ∼⟩ **6** : a visible sign : INDICATION; *also* : CHARACTERISTIC **7** : a written or printed symbol **8** : GRADE ⟨a ∼ of B +⟩ **9** : IMPORTANCE, DISTINCTION **10** : a lasting impression ⟨made his ∼ in the world⟩; *also* : a damaging impression left on a surface

²mark *vb* **1** : to set apart by a line or boundary **2** : to designate by a mark or make a mark on **3** : CHARACTERIZE ⟨the vehemence that ∼s his speeches⟩; *also* : SIGNALIZE ⟨this year ∼s the 50th anniversary⟩ **4** : to take notice of : OBSERVE — **mark·er** *n*

³mark *n* — see MONEY table

Mark \'märk\ *n* — see BIBLE table

mark·down \'märk-ˌdaủn\ *n* **1** : a lowering of price **2** : the amount by which an original price is reduced

mark down \(')märk-'daủn\ *vb* : to put a lower price on

marked \'märkt\ *adj* : NOTICEABLE — **mark·ed·ly** \'mär-kəd-lē\ *adv*

¹mar·ket \'mär-kət\ *n* **1** : a meeting together of people for trade by purchase and sale; *also* : a public place where such a meeting is held **2** : the rate or price offered for a commodity or security **3** : a geographical area of demand for commodities; *also* : extent of demand **4** : a retail establishment usu. of a specific kind ⟨a meat ∼⟩

²market *vb* : to go to a market to buy or sell; *also* : SELL — **mar·ket·able** *adj*

mar·ket·place \'mär-kət-ˌplās\ *n* **1** : an open square in a town where markets are held **2** : the world of trade or economic activity

mark·ka \'mär-ˌkä\ *n, pl* **mark·kaa** \'mär-ˌkä\ *or* **markkas** \-ˌkäz\ — see MONEY table

marks·man \'märks-mən\ *n* : a person skillful at hitting a target — **marks·man·ship** *n*

mark·up \'märk-ˌəp\ *n* **1** : a raising of price **2** : an amount added to the cost price of an article to determine the selling price

mark up \(')märk-'əp\ *vb* : to put a higher price on

marl \'märl\ *n* : an earthy deposit rich in lime used as fertilizer — **marly** \'mär-lē\ *adj*

mar·lin \\'mär-lən\ *n* : a large oceanic sport fish

mar·line·spike *also* **mar·lin·spike** \\'mär-lən-ˌspīk\ *n* : a pointed iron tool used to separate strands of rope or wire (as in splicing)

mar·ma·lade \\'mär-mə-ˌlād\ *n* : a clear jelly holding in suspension pieces of fruit and fruit rind

mar·mo·re·al \mär-'mōr-ē-əl\ *adj* : of, relating to, or resembling marble

mar·mo·set \\'mär-mə-ˌset\ *n* : any of various small bushy-tailed tropical American monkeys

mar·mot \\'mär-mət\ *n* : a stout short-legged burrowing No. American rodent

¹**ma·roon** \mə-'rün\ *vb* **1** : to put ashore (as on a desolate island) and leave to one's fate **2** : to leave in isolation and without hope of escape

²**maroon** *n* : a dark red

mar·plot \\'mär-ˌplät\ *n* : one who endangers the success of an enterprise by his meddling

mar·quee \mär-'kē\ *n* [modif. of F *marquise*, lit., marchioness] **1** : a large tent set up (as for an outdoor party) **2** : a usu. metal and glass canopy over an entrance (as of a theater)

mar·quess \\'mär-kwəs\ *n* **1** : a nobleman of hereditary rank in Europe and Japan **2** : a member of the British peerage ranking below a duke and above an earl

mar·que·try \\'mär-kə-trē\ *n* : inlaid work of wood, shell, or ivory (as on a table or cabinet)

mar·quis \\'mär-kwəs, mär-'kē\ *n* : MARQUESS

mar·quise \mär-'kēz\ *n, pl* **mar·quises** \-'kēz(-əz)\ : MARCHIONESS

mar·qui·sette \ˌmär-k(w)ə-'zet\ *n* : a sheer meshed fabric

mar·riage \\'mar-ij\ *n* **1** : the state of being married **2** : a wedding ceremony and attendant festivities **3** : a close union — **mar·riage·able** *adj*

mar·row \\'mar-ō\ *n* : a soft vascular tissue that fills the cavities of most bones

mar·row·bone \\'mar-ə-ˌbōn, -ō-ˌbōn\ *n* : a bone (as a shinbone) rich in marrow

mar·ry \\'mar-ē\ *vb* **mar·ried; mar·ry·ing 1** : to join as husband and wife according to law or custom **2** : to take as husband or wife : WED **3** : to enter into a close union — **mar·ried** *adj or n*

Mars \\'märz\ *n* : the planet fourth from the sun conspicuous for its red appearance

marsh \\'märsh\ *n* : a tract of soft wet land — **marshy** *adj*

¹**mar·shal** \\'mär-shəl\ *n* **1** : a high official in a medieval household; *also* : a person in charge of the ceremonial aspects of a gathering **2** : a general officer of the highest military rank **3** : an administrative officer (as of a U.S. judicial district) having duties similar to a sheriff's **4** : the administrative head of a city police or fire department

²**marshal** *vb* **-shaled** *or* **-shalled; -shal·ing** *or* **-shal·ling** \\'märsh-(ə-)liŋ\ **1** : to arrange in order, rank, or position **2** : to lead with ceremony : USHER

marsh gas *n* : METHANE

marsh·mal·low \\'märsh-ˌmel-ō, -ˌmal-\ *n* : a light creamy confection made from corn syrup, sugar, albumen, and gelatin

marsh marigold *n* : a swamp herb related to the buttercups that has bright yellow flowers

mar·su·pi·al \mär-'sü-pē-əl\ *n* : any of a large group of mostly Australian primitive mammals that bear very immature young which are nourished in a pouch on the abdomen of the female — **marsupial** *adj*

mart \\'märt\ *n* : MARKET

mar·ten \\'märt-ᵊn\ *n, pl* **marten** *or* **martens** : a slender weasel-like mammal with fine gray or brown fur; *also* : this fur

mar·tial \\'mär-shəl\ *adj* [L *martialis* of Mars, fr. *Mart-, Mars* Mars, Roman god of war] **1** : of, relating to, or suited for war or a warrior ⟨∼ music⟩ **2** : of or relating to an army or military life **3** : WARLIKE

martial law *n* **1** : the law applied in occupied territory by the occupying military forces **2** : the established law of a country administered by military forces in an emergency when civilian law enforcement agencies are unable to maintain public order and safety

mar·tian \\'mär-shən\ *adj, often cap* : of or relating to the planet Mars or its hypothetical inhabitants — **martian** *n, often cap*

mar·tin \\'märt-ᵊn\\ *n* : any of several small swallows and flycatchers

mar·ti·net \\,märt-ᵊn-'et\\ *n* : a strict disciplinarian

mar·tin·gale \\'märt-ᵊn-,gāl\\ *n* : a strap connecting a horse's girth to the bit or reins so as to hold down its head

mar·ti·ni \\mär-'tē-nē\\ *n* : a cocktail made of gin or vodka and dry vermouth

¹mar·tyr \\'märt-ər\\ *n* [ME, fr. OE, fr. LL, fr. Gk *martyr-, martys,* lit., witness] **1** : a person who dies rather than renounce his religion; *also* : one who makes a great sacrifice for the sake of principle **2** : a great or constant sufferer

²martyr *vb* **1** : to put to death for adhering to a belief **2** : TORTURE

mar·tyr·dom \\'märt-ər-dəm\\ *n* **1** : the suffering and death of a martyr **2** : TORTURE

¹mar·vel \\'mär-vəl\\ *n* **1** : something that causes wonder or astonishment **2** : intense surprise or interest

²marvel *vb* **-veled** *or* **-velled; -vel·ing** *or* **-vel·ling** \\'märv-(ə-)liŋ\\ : to feel surprise, wonder, or amazed curiosity

mar·vel·ous *or* **mar·vel·lous** \\'märv-(ə-)ləs\\ *adj* **1** : causing wonder **2** : of the highest kind or quality : SPLENDID — **mar·vel·ous·ly** *adv* — **mar·vel·ous·ness** *n*

Marx·ism \\'märk-,siz-əm\\ *n* : the political, economic, and social principles and policies advocated by Karl Marx — **Marx·ist** \\-səst\\ *n or adj*

mar·zi·pan \\'märt-sə-,pän, -,pan; 'mär-zə-,pan\\ *n* [G] : a confection of almond paste, sugar, and egg whites

masc *abbr* masculine

mas·cara \\mas-'kar-ə\\ *n* : a cosmetic for coloring the eyelashes and eyebrows

mas·cot \\'mas-,kät, -kət\\ *n* [F *mascotte,* fr. Provençal *mascoto,* fr. *masco* witch, fr. ML *masca*] : a person, animal, or object believed to bring good luck

¹mas·cu·line \\'mas-kyə-lən\\ *adj* **1** : MALE; *also* : MANLY **2** : of, relating to, or constituting the gender that includes most words or grammatical

forms referring to males — **mas·cu·lin·i·ty** \\,mas-kyə-'lin-ət-ē\\ *n*

²masculine *n* **1** : a male person **2** : a noun, pronoun, adjective, or inflectional form or class of the masculine gender; *also* : the masculine gender

ma·ser \\'mā-zər\\ *n* [*m*icrowave *a*mplification by *s*timulated *e*mission of *r*adiation] : a device that utilizes the natural oscillation of atoms or molecules between energy levels for generating microwaves

¹mash \\'mash\\ *n* **1** : crushed malt or grain steeped in hot water to make wort **2** : a mixture of ground feeds for livestock **3** : a soft pulpy mass

²mash *vb* **1** : to reduce to a soft pulpy state **2** : CRUSH, SMASH ⟨∼ a finger⟩ — **mash·er** *n*

MASH *abbr* mobile army surgical hospital

¹mask \\'mask\\ *n* **1** : a cover for the face usu. for disguise or protection **2** : MASQUE **3** : a figure of a head worn on the stage in antiquity **4** : a copy of a face made by means of a mold ⟨death ∼⟩ **5** : something that conceals or disguises **6** : the face of an animal (as a fox)

²mask *vb* **1** : to conceal from view : DISGUISE **2** : to cover for protection

mask·er \\'mas-kər\\ *n* : a participant in a masquerade

mas·och·ism \\'mas-ə-,kiz-əm, 'maz-\\ *n* **1** : a sexual perversion characterized by pleasure in being subjected to pain and humiliation **2** : pleasure in being abused or dominated — **mas·och·ist** \\-kəst\\ *n* — **mas·och·is·tic** \\,mas-ə-'kis-tik, ,maz-\\ *adj*

ma·son \\'mās-ᵊn\\ *n* **1** : a skilled worker who builds with stone, brick, or concrete **2** *cap* : FREEMASON

Ma·son·ic \\mə-'sän-ik\\ *adj* : of or relating to Freemasons or Freemasonry

ma·son·ry \\'mās-ᵊn-rē\\ *n, pl* **-ries 1** : something constructed of materials used by masons **2** : the art, trade, or work of a mason **3** *cap* : FREEMASONRY

masque \\'mask\\ *n* **1** : MASQUERADE **2** : a short allegorical dramatic performance (as of the 17th century)

¹mas·quer·ade \\,mas-kə-'rād\\ *n* **1** : a social gathering of persons wearing masks; *also* : a costume for wear at such a gathering **2** : DISGUISE

²**masquerade** *vb* **-ad•ed; -ad•ing 1** : to disguise oneself : POSE **2** : to take part in a masquerade — **mas•quer•ad•er** *n*

¹**mass** \'mas\ *n* **1** *cap* : a sequence of prayers and ceremonies forming the eucharistic service of the Roman Catholic Church **2** *often cap* : a celebration of the Eucharist **3** : a musical setting for parts of the Mass

²**mass** *n* **1** : a quantity or aggregate of matter usu. of considerable size **2** : EXPANSE, BULK; *also* : MASSIVENESS **3** : the principal part **4** : AGGREGATE, WHOLE ⟨people in the ∼⟩ **5** : the quantity of matter that a body possesses as evidenced by inertia **6** : a large quantity, amount, or number **7** : the great body of people — usu. used in pl. — **massy** *adj*

³**mass** *vb* : to form or collect into a mass

Mass *abbr* Massachusetts

mas•sa•cre \'mas-i-kər\ *n* **1** : the killing of many persons under cruel or atrocious circumstances **2** : a wholesale slaughter — **massacre** *vb*

¹**mas•sage** \mə-'säzh, -'säj\ *n* : remedial or hygienic treatment of the body by manipulation (as rubbing and kneading)

²**massage** *vb* **mas•saged; mas•sag•ing 1** : to subject to massage **2** : to treat flatteringly; *also* : MANIPULATE ⟨∼ data⟩

mas•seur \ma-'sər\ *n* : a man who practices massage

mas•seuse \-'sə(r)z, -'süz\ *n* : a woman who practices massage

mas•sif \ma-'sēf\ *n* : a principal mountain mass

mas•sive \'mas-iv\ *adj* **1** : forming or consisting of a large mass **2** : large in structure, scope, or degree — **mas•sive•ly** *adv* — **mas•sive•ness** *n*

mass•less \'mas-ləs\ *adj* : having no mass ⟨∼ particles⟩

mass medium *n, pl* **mass media** : a medium of communication (as the newspapers or television) that is designed to reach the mass of the people

mass–pro•duce \ˌmas-prə-'d(y)üs\ *vb* : to produce in quantity usu. by machinery — **mass production** *n*

¹**mast** \'mast\ *n* **1** : a long pole or spar rising from the keel or deck of a ship and supporting the yards, booms, and

rigging **2** : a vertical pole — **mast•ed** \'mas-təd\ *adj*

²**mast** *n* : nuts (as acorns) accumulated on the forest floor and often serving as food for hogs

¹**mas•ter** \'mas-tər\ *n* **1** : a male teacher; *also* : a person holding an academic degree higher than a bachelor's but lower than a doctor's **2** : one highly skilled (as in an art or profession) **3** : one having authority or control **4** : VICTOR, SUPERIOR **5** : the commander of a merchant ship **6** : a youth or boy too young to be called *mister* — used as a title **7** : an original (as of a phonograph record) from which copies are made

²**master** *vb* **mas•tered; mas•ter•ing** \-t(ə-)riŋ\ **1** : OVERCOME, SUBDUE **2** : to become skilled or proficient in **3** : to produce a master record or tape of (as a musical performance)

master chief petty officer *n* : a petty officer of the highest rank in the navy

mas•ter•ful \'mas-tər-fəl\ *adj* **1** : inclined and usu. competent to act as a master **2** : having or reflecting the skill of a master ⟨did a ∼ job of reporting⟩ — **mas•ter•ful•ly** \-ē\ *adv*

master gunnery sergeant *n* : a noncommissioned officer in the marine corps ranking above a master sergeant

master key *n* : a key designed to open several different locks

mas•ter•ly \'mas-tər-lē\ *adj* : indicating thorough knowledge or superior skill ⟨∼ performance⟩

mas•ter•mind \-ˌmīnd\ *n* : a person who provides the directing or creative intelligence for a project — **mastermind** *vb*

master of ceremonies : a person who acts as host at a formal event or a program of entertainment

mas•ter•piece \'mas-tər-ˌpēs\ *n* : a work done with extraordinary skill

master plan *n* : an overall plan

master sergeant *n* **1** : a noncommissioned officer in the army ranking next below a sergeant major **2** : a noncommissioned officer in the air force ranking next below a senior master sergeant **3** : a noncommissioned officer in the marine corps ranking next below a master gunnery sergeant

mas·ter·stroke \\'mas-tər-ˌstrōk\ *n* : a masterly performance or move

mas·ter·work \-ˌwərk\ *n* : MASTERPIECE

mas·tery \\'mas-t(ə-)rē\ *n* 1 : DOMINION; *also* : SUPERIORITY 2 : possession or display of great skill or knowledge

mast·head \\'mast-ˌhed\ *n* 1 : the top of a mast 2 : the printed matter in a newspaper giving the title and details of ownership and rates

mas·tic \\'mas-tik\ *n* : a pasty material used as a protective coating or cement

mas·ti·cate \\'mas-tə-ˌkāt\ *vb* -cat·ed; -cat·ing : CHEW — **mas·ti·ca·tion** \ˌmas-tə-'kā-shən\ *n*

mas·tiff \\'mas-təf\ *n* : a large smooth-coated dog used esp. as a guard dog

mast·odon \\'mas-tə-ˌdän\ *n* [NL, fr. Gk *mastos* breast + *odōn, odous* tooth] : a huge elephantlike extinct animal

mas·toid \\'mas-ˌtȯid\ *n* : a bony prominence behind the ear — **mastoid** *adj*

mas·tur·ba·tion \ˌmas-tər-'bā-shən\ *n* : stimulation of the genital organs to a climax of excitement by contact (as manual) exclusive of sexual intercourse — **mas·tur·bate** \\'mas-tər-ˌbāt\ *vb*

¹mat \\'mat\ *n* 1 : a piece of coarse woven or plaited fabric 2 : something made up of many intertwined strands 3 : a large thick pad used as a surface for wrestling and gymnastics

²mat *vb* **mat·ted; mat·ting** : to form into a tangled mass

³mat *or* **matt** *or* **matte** *adj* [F, fr. OF, defeated, fr. L *mattus* drunk] : not shiny : DULL

⁴mat *or* **matt** *or* **matte** *n* 1 : a border going around a picture between picture and frame or serving as the frame 2 : a dull finish

mat·a·dor \\'mat-ə-ˌdȯr\ *n* [Sp, fr. *matar* to kill] : a bullfighter whose role is to kill the bull in a bullfight

¹match \\'mach\ *n* 1 : a person or thing equal or similar to another : COUNTERPART 2 : a pair of persons or objects that harmonize 3 : a contest or game between two or more individuals 4 : a marriage union; *also* : a prospective marriage partner — **match·less** *adj*

²match *vb* 1 : to meet as an antagonist; *also* : PIT ⟨*~ing* his strength against his enemy's⟩ 2 : to provide with a worthy competitor; *also* : to set in comparison with 3 : MARRY 4 : to combine suitably or congenially; *also* : ADAPT, SUIT 5 : to provide with a counterpart

³match *n* : a short slender piece of flammable material (as wood) tipped with a combustible mixture that ignites through friction

match·book \-ˌbu̇k\ *n* : a small folder containing rows of paper matches

match·lock \-ˌläk\ *n* : a musket with a slow-burning cord lowered over a hole in the breech to ignite the charge

match·mak·er \-ˌmā-kər\ *n* : one who arranges a match and esp. a marriage

match·wood \-ˌwu̇d\ *n* : small pieces of wood

¹mate \\'māt\ *vb* **mat·ed; mat·ing** : CHECKMATE — **mate** *n*

²mate *n* 1 : ASSOCIATE, COMPANION; *also* : HELPER 2 : a deck officer on a merchant ship ranking below the captain 3 : one of a pair; *esp* : either member of a married couple or a breeding pair of animals

³mate *vb* **mat·ed; mat·ing** 1 : to join or fit together : COUPLE 2 : to come or bring together as mates

ma·té *or* **ma·te** \\'mä-ˌtā\ *n* : a tealike beverage used esp. in So. America

¹ma·te·ri·al \mə-'tir-ē-əl\ *adj* 1 : PHYSICAL ⟨*~* world⟩; *also* : BODILY ⟨*~* needs⟩ 2 : of or relating to matter rather than form ⟨*~* cause⟩; *also* : EMPIRICAL ⟨*~* knowledge⟩ 3 : highly important : SIGNIFICANT 4 : of a physical or worldly nature ⟨*~* progress⟩ — **ma·te·ri·al·ly** \-ē\ *adv*

²material *n* 1 : the elements or substance of which something is composed or made 2 : apparatus necessary for doing or making something

ma·te·ri·al·ism \mə-'tir-ē-ə-ˌliz-əm\ *n* 1 : a theory that everything can be explained as being or coming from matter 2 : a preoccupation with material rather than intellectual or spiritual things — **ma·te·ri·al·ist** \-ləst\ *n or adj* — **ma·te·ri·al·is·tic** \-ˌtir-ē-ə-'lis-tik\ *adj* — **ma·te·ri·al·is·ti·cal·ly** \-ti-k(ə-)lē\ *adv*

ma·te·ri·al·ize \mə-'tir-ē-ə-ˌlīz\ *vb* -ized; -iz·ing 1 : to give material form to; *also* : to assume bodily form 2 : to make an often unexpected appearance — **ma·te·ri·al·iza·tion** \mə-ˌtir-ē-ə-lə-ˈzā-shən\ *n*

ma·té·ri·el *or* **ma·te·ri·el** \mə-ˌtir-ē-ˈel\ *n* [F *matériel*] : equipment, apparatus, and supplies used by an organization

ma·ter·nal \mə-ˈtərn-ᵊl\ *adj* **1** : MOTHERLY **2** : related through or inherited or derived from a mother — **ma·ter·nal·ly** \-ē\ *adv*

ma·ter·ni·ty \mə-ˈtər-nət-ē\ *n, pl* **-ties 1** : the quality or state of being a mother; *also* : MOTHERLINESS **2** : a hospital facility for the care of women before and during childbirth and for newborn babies — **maternity** *adj*

¹**math** \ˈmath\ *n* : MATHEMATICS

²**math** *abbr* mathematical; mathematician

math·e·mat·ics \ˌmath-ə-ˈmat-iks\ *n pl* : the science of numbers and their operations and the relations between them and of space configurations and their structure and measurement — **math·e·mat·i·cal** \-ˈmat-i-kəl\ *adj* — **math·e·mat·i·cal·ly** \-i-k(ə-)lē\ *adv* — **math·e·ma·ti·cian** \ˌmath-ə-mə-ˈtish-ən\ *n*

mat·i·nee *or* **mat·i·née** \ˌmat-ᵊn-ˈā\ *n* [F *matinée*, lit., morning, fr. OF, fr. *matin* morning, fr. L *matutinum*, fr. neut. of *matutinus* of the morning, fr. *Matuta*, goddess of morning] : a musical or dramatic performance usu. in the afternoon

mat·ins \ˈmat-ᵊnz\ *n pl, often cap* **1** : special prayers said between midnight and 4 a.m. **2** : a morning service of liturgical prayer in Anglican churches

ma·tri·arch \ˈmā-trē-ˌärk\ *n* : a female who rules or dominates a family, group, or state — **ma·tri·ar·chal** \ˌmā-trē-ˈär-kəl\ *adj* — **ma·tri·ar·chy** \ˈmā-trē-ˌär-kē\ *n*

ma·tri·cide \ˈma-trə-ˌsīd, ˈmā-\ *n* **1** : the murder of a mother by her child **2** : one who kills his mother — **ma·tri·cid·al** \ˌma-trə-ˈsīd-ᵊl, ˌmā-\ *adj*

ma·tric·u·late \mə-ˈtrik-yə-ˌlāt\ *vb* **-lat·ed; -lat·ing** : to enroll as a member of a body and esp. of a college or university — **ma·tric·u·la·tion** \-ˌtrik-yə-ˈlā-shən\ *n*

mat·ri·mo·ny \ˈmat-rə-ˌmō-nē\ *n* [ME, fr. MF *matremoine*, fr. L *matrimonium*, fr. *mater* mother, matron] : MAR-RIAGE — **mat·ri·mo·nial** \ˌmat-rə-ˈmō-nē-əl\ *adj* —**mat·ri·mo·nial·ly** *adv*

ma·trix \ˈmā-triks\ *n, pl* **ma·tri·ces** \ˈmā-trə-ˌsēz, ˈma-\ *or* **ma·trix·es** \ˈmā-trik-səz\ **1** : something within which something else originates or develops **2** : a mold from which a relief surface (as a piece of type) is made

ma·tron \ˈmā-trən\ *n* **1** : a married woman usu. of dignified maturity or social distinction **2** : a woman supervisor (as in a school or police station) — **ma·tron·ly** *adj*

Matt *abbr* Matthew

¹**mat·ter** \ˈmat-ər\ *n* **1** : a subject of interest or concern **2** *pl* : events or circumstances of a particular situation; *also* : elements that constitute material for treatment (as in writing) **3** : TROUBLE, DIFFICULTY ⟨what's the ~⟩ **4** : the substance of which a physical object is composed **5** : PUS **6** : an indefinite amount or quantity ⟨a ~ of a few days⟩ **7** : something written or printed **8** : MAIL

²**matter** *vb* : to be of importance : SIGNIFY

mat·ter–of–fact \ˌmat-ə-rə(v)-ˈfakt\ *adj* : adhering to or concerned with fact — **mat·ter–of–fact·ly** *adv* — **mat·ter–of–fact·ness** *n*

Mat·thew \ˈmath-yü\ *n* — see BIBLE table

mat·tins *often cap, chiefly Brit* var of MATINS

mat·tock \ˈmat-ək\ *n* : a digging and grubbing tool with features of an adz and an ax or pick

mat·tress \ˈma-trəs\ *n* **1** : a fabric case filled with resilient material used either alone as a bed or on a bedstead **2** : an inflatable airtight sack for use as a mattress

mat·u·rate \ˈmach-ə-ˌrāt\ *vb* **-rat·ed; -rat·ing** : MATURE

mat·u·ra·tion \ˌmach-ə-ˈrā-shən\ *n* **1** : the process of becoming mature **2** : the emergence of personal and behavioral characteristics through growth processes — **mat·u·ra·tion·al** \-sh(ə-)nəl\ *adj*

¹**ma·ture** \mə-ˈt(y)ùr\ *adj* **ma·tur·er; -est 1** : based on slow careful consideration **2** : having attained a final or desired state ⟨~ wine⟩ **3** : of or relating

to a condition of full development **4** : due for payment ⟨a ∼ loan⟩

²**mature** *vb* **ma·tured; ma·tur·ing** : to bring to maturity or completion

ma·tu·ri·ty \mə-ˈt(y)ùr-ət-ē\ *n* : the quality or state of being mature; *esp* : full development

ma·tu·ti·nal \ˌmach-ù-ˈtīn-ᵊl; mə-ˈt(y)üt-(ᵊ-)nəl\ *adj* : of, relating to, or occurring in the morning : EARLY

mat·zo \ˈmät-sə\ *n, pl* **mat·zoth** \-ˌsōt(h), -sōs\ *or* **mat·zos** [Yiddish *matse*] : unleavened bread eaten esp. at the Passover

maud·lin \ˈmȯd-lən\ *adj* [alter. of Mary *Magdalene;* fr. the practice of depicting her as a weeping, penitent sinner] **1** : weakly and effusively sentimental **2** : drunk enough to be emotionally silly : FUDDLED

¹**maul** \ˈmȯl\ *n* : a heavy hammer often with a wooden head used esp. for driving wedges or piles

²**maul** *vb* **1** : BEAT, BRUISE; *also* : MANGLE **2** : to handle roughly

maun·der \ˈmȯn-dər\ *vb* **maun·dered; maun·der·ing** \-d(ə-)riŋ\ **1** : to wander slowly and idly **2** : to speak indistinctly or disconnectedly

mau·so·le·um \ˌmȯ-sə-ˈlē-əm, ˌmȯ-zə-\ *n, pl* **-leums** *or* **-lea** \-ˈlē-ə\ [L, fr. Gk *mausōleion,* fr. *Mausōlos* Mausolus † *ab* 353 B.C. ruler of Caria whose tomb was one of the seven wonders of the ancient world] : a large tomb; *esp* : a usu. stone building for entombment of the dead above ground

mauve \ˈmōv, ˈmȯv\ *n* : a moderate purple, violet, or lilac color

ma·ven *or* **ma·vin** \ˈmā-vən\ *n* [Yiddish *meyvn,* fr. LHeb *mēbhīn,* fr. Heb *l'havin* to understand] : EXPERT

mav·er·ick \ˈmav-(ə-)rik\ *n* [Samuel A. *Maverick* † 1870 Am. pioneer who did not brand his calves] **1** : an unbranded range animal **2** : NONCONFORMIST

ma·vis \ˈmā-vəs\ *n* : an Old World thrush

maw \ˈmȯ\ *n* **1** : STOMACH; *also* : the crop of a bird **2** : the throat, gullet, or jaws usu. of a carnivore

mawk·ish \ˈmȯ-kish\ *adj* [ME *mawke* maggot, fr. ON *mathkr*] : sickly sentimental — **mawk·ish·ly** *adv* — **mawk·ish·ness** *n*

max *abbr* maximum

maxi \ˈmak-sē\ *n, pl* **max·is** : a long skirt, dress, or coat that usu. extends to the ankle

maxi- *comb form* **1** : extra long ⟨*maxi*-kilt⟩ **2** : extra large ⟨*maxi*-problems⟩

max·il·la \mak-ˈsil-ə\ *n, pl* **max·il·lae** \-ˈsil-(ˌ)ē\ *or* **maxillas** : JAW 1; *esp* : an upper jaw — **max·il·lary** \ˈmak-sə-ˌler-ē\ *adj*

max·im \ˈmak-səm\ *n* : a proverbial saying

max·i·mal \ˈmak-s(ə-)məl\ *adj* : MAXIMUM — **max·i·mal·ly** \-ē\ *adv*

max·i·mize \ˈmak-sə-ˌmīz\ *vb* **-mized; -miz·ing** **1** : to increase to a maximum **2** : to make the most of

max·i·mum \ˈmak-s(ə-)məm\ *n, pl* **max·i·ma** \-sə-mə\ *or* **maximums** \-s(ə-)məmz\ **1** : the greatest quantity, value, or degree **2** : an upper limit allowed by authority **3** : the largest of a set of numbers — **maximum** *adj*

may \(ˈ)mā\ *verbal auxiliary, past* **might** \(ˈ)mīt\; *pres sing & pl* **may** **1** : have permission or liberty to ⟨you ∼ go now⟩ **2** : be in some degree likely to ⟨you ∼ be right⟩ **3** — used as an auxiliary to express a wish, purpose, contingency, or concession

May \ˈmā\ *n* [ME, fr. OF *mai,* fr. L *Maius,* fr. *Maia,* Roman goddess] : the fifth month of the year having 31 days

Ma·ya \ˈmī-ə\ *n, pl* **Maya** *or* **Mayas** : a member of a group of peoples of the Yucatan peninsula and adjacent areas — **Ma·yan** \ˈmī-ən\ *adj*

may·ap·ple \ˈmā-ˌap-əl\ *n* : a No. American woodland herb related to the barberry that has a poisonous root, large leaf, and edible but insipid yellow fruit

may·be \ˈmā-bē, ˈmeb-ē\ *adv* : PERHAPS

May Day \ˈmā-ˌdā\ *n* : May 1 celebrated as a springtime festival and in some countries as Labor Day

may·flow·er \ˈmā-ˌflaù(-ə)r\ *n* : any of several spring blooming herbs (as the trailing arbutus or anemone)

may·fly \ˈmā-flī\ *n* : any of an order of insects with an aquatic nymph and a short-lived fragile adult having membranous wings

may·hem \ˈmā-ˌhem, ˈmā-əm\ *n* **1** : willful and permanent crippling, mutilation, or disfigurement of a person **2** : needless or willful damage

may·on·naise \\'mā-ə-ˌnāz\ *n* [F] : a dressing made of raw eggs or egg yolks, vegetable oil, and vinegar or lemon juice

may·or \\'mā-ər\ *n* : an official elected to act as chief executive or nominal head of a city or borough — **may·or·al** \-əl\ *adj* — **may·or·al·ty** \-əl-tē\ *n*

may·pole \\'mā-ˌpōl\ *n, often cap* : a tall flower-wreathed pole forming a center for May Day sports and dances

maze \\'māz\ *n* : a confusing intricate network of passages — **mazy** *adj*

ma·zur·ka \mə-'zər-kə\ *n* : a Polish dance in moderate triple measure

MB *abbr* Manitoba

MBA *abbr* master of business administration

mc *abbr* megacycle

¹MC *n* : MASTER OF CEREMONIES

²MC *abbr* member of Congress

MCPO *abbr* master chief petty officer

¹Md *abbr* Maryland

²Md *symbol* mendelevium

MD *abbr* **1** [NL *medicinae doctor*] doctor of medicine **2** Maryland **3** muscular dystrophy

mdnt *abbr* midnight

mdse *abbr* merchandise

MDT *abbr* mountain daylight (saving) time

me \(')mē\ *pron, objective case of* 1

Me *abbr* Maine

ME *abbr* **1** Maine **2** mechanical engineer **3** medical examiner **4** Middle English

¹mead \\'mēd\ *n* : an alcoholic beverage brewed from water and honey, malt, and yeast

²mead *n, archaic* : MEADOW

mead·ow \\'med-ō\ *n* : land in or mainly in grass; *esp* : a tract of moist low-lying usu. level grassland — **mead·ow·land** \-ˌland\ *n* — **mead·owy** \\'med-ə-wē\ *adj*

mead·ow·lark \\'med-ō-ˌlärk\ *n* : any of several No. American songbirds that are largely brown and buff above and have a yellow breast marked with a black crescent

mead·ow·sweet \-ˌswēt\ *n* : a No. American native or naturalized spirea

mea·ger *or* **mea·gre** \\'mē-gər\ *adj* **1** : THIN **2** : lacking richness, fertility, or

strength : POOR **syn** scanty, scant, spare, sparse — **mea·ger·ly** *adv* — **mea·ger·ness** *n*

¹meal \\'mēl\ *n* **1** : the portion of food taken at one time : REPAST **2** : an act or the time of eating a meal

²meal *n* **1** : usu. coarsely ground seeds of a cereal (as Indian corn) **2** : a product resembling seed meal — **mealy** *adj*

meal·time \\'mēl-ˌtīm\ *n* : the usual time at which a meal is served

mealy·bug \\'mē-lē-ˌbəg\ *n* : any of numerous scale insects with a white powdery covering that are destructive pests esp. of fruit trees

mealy·mouthed \ˌmē-lē-'mauᵗh̲d, -'mauᵗht\ *adj* : not plain and straightforward : DEVIOUS

¹mean \\'mēn\ *adj* **1** : HUMBLE **2** : lacking power or acumen : ORDINARY **3** : SHABBY, CONTEMPTIBLE **4** : IGNOBLE, BASE **5** : STINGY **6** : pettily selfish or malicious — **mean·ly** *adv* — **mean·ness** \\'mēn-nəs\ *n*

²mean \\'mēn\ *vb* **meant** \\'ment\; **mean·ing** \\'mē-niŋ\ **1** : to have in the mind as a purpose **2** : to serve to convey, show, or indicate : SIGNIFY **3** : to have importance to the degree of ⟨health ~s everything⟩ **4** : to direct to a particular individual

³mean *adj* **1** : occupying a middle position (as in space, order, or time) **2** : being a mean ⟨a ~ value⟩

⁴mean *n* **1** : a middle point between extremes **2** *pl* : something helpful in achieving a desired end **3** *pl* : material resources affording a secure life **4** : ARITHMETIC MEAN

¹me·an·der \mē-'an-dər\ *n* [L *maeander*, fr. Gk *maiandros*, fr. *Maiandros* (now *Menderes*), river in Asia Minor] **1** : a turn or winding of a stream **2** : a winding course

²meander *vb* **-dered; -der·ing** \-d(ə-)riŋ\ **1** : to follow a winding course **2** : to wander aimlessly or casually

mean·ing \\'mē-niŋ\ *n* **1** : the thing one intends to convey esp. by language; *also* : the thing that is thus conveyed **2** : PURPOSE **3** : SIGNIFICANCE **4** : CONNOTATION; *also* : DENOTATION — **mean·ing·ful** \-fəl\ *adj* — **mean·ing·ful·ly** \-ē\ *adv* — **mean·ing·less** *adj*

¹mean·time \\'mēn-ˌtīm\ *n* : the intervening time

²meantime *adv* : MEANWHILE

¹mean•while \-ˌhwīl\ *n* : MEANTIME

²meanwhile *adv* : during the intervening time

meas *abbr* measure

mea•sles \ˈmē-zəlz\ *n pl* : an acute virus disease marked by fever and an eruption of distinct circular red spots

mea•sly \ˈmēz-(ə-)lē\ *adj* **mea•sli•er; -est** : contemptibly small or insignificant

¹mea•sure \ˈmezh-ər, ˈmāzh-\ *n* **1** : an adequate or moderate portion; *also* : a suitable limit **2** : the dimensions, capacity, or amount of something ascertained by measuring; *also* : an instrument for measuring **3** : a unit of measurement; *also* : a system of such units ⟨metric ∼⟩ **4** : the act or process of measuring **5** : rhythmic structure or movement **6** : the part of a musical staff between two adjacent bars **7** : CRITERION **8** : a means to an end **9** : a legislative bill — **mea•sure•less** *adj*

²measure *vb* **mea•sured; mea•sur•ing** \ˈmezh-(ə-)riŋ, ˈmāzh-\ **1** : to regulate esp. by a standard **2** : to apportion by measure **3** : to mark off by making measurements **4** : to ascertain the measurements of **5** : to bring into comparison or competition **6** : to serve as a means of measuring **7** : to have a specified measurement — **mea•sur•able** \ˈmezh-(ə-)rə-bəl, ˈmāzh-\ *adj* — **mea•sur•ably** \-blē\ *adv* — **mea•sur•er** *n*

mea•sure•ment \ˈmezh-ər-mənt, ˈmāzh-\ *n* **1** : the act or process of measuring **2** : a figure, extent, or amount obtained by measuring

measure up *vb* **1** : to have necessary qualifications **2** : to equal esp. in ability

meat \ˈmēt\ *n* **1** : FOOD; *esp* : solid food as distinguished from drink **2** : animal and esp. mammal flesh considered as food **3** : the edible part inside a covering (as a shell or rind) — **meaty** *adj*

meat•ball \-ˌbȯl\ *n* : a small ball of chopped or ground meat

mec•ca \ˈmek-ə\ *n, often cap* [*Mecca*, Saudi Arabia, birthplace of Muhammad and holy city of Islam] : a center of activity sought as a goal by people sharing a common interest

mech *abbr* mechanical; mechanics

¹me•chan•ic \mi-ˈkan-ik\ *adj* : of or relating to manual work or skill

²mechanic *n* **1** : a manual worker **2** : MACHINIST; *esp* : one who repairs machines

me•chan•i•cal \mi-ˈkan-i-kəl\ *adj* **1** : of or relating to machinery, to manual operations, or to mechanics **2** : done as if by a machine : AUTOMATIC **syn** instinctive, impulsive, spontaneous — **me•chan•i•cal•ly** \-k(ə-)lē\ *adv*

mechanical drawing *n* : drawing done with the aid of instruments

me•chan•ics \mi-ˈkan-iks\ *n sing or pl* **1** : a branch of physics that deals with energy and forces and their effect on bodies **2** : the practical application of mechanics (as to the operation of machines) **3** : mechanical or functional details

mech•a•nism \ˈmek-ə-ˌniz-əm\ *n* **1** : a piece of machinery; *also* : a process or technique for achieving a result **2** : mechanical operation or action **3** : the fundamental processes involved in or responsible for a natural phenomenon ⟨the visual ∼⟩

mech•a•nis•tic \ˌmek-ə-ˈnis-tik\ *adj* : mechanically determined ⟨∼ universe⟩ — **mech•a•nis•ti•cal•ly** \-ti-k(ə-)lē\ *adv*

mech•a•nize \ˈmek-ə-ˌnīz\ *vb* **-nized; -niz•ing** **1** : to make mechanical **2** : to equip with machinery esp. in order to replace human or animal labor **3** : to equip with armed and armored motor vehicles — **mech•a•ni•za•tion** \ˌmek-ə-nə-ˈzā-shən\ *n* — **mech•a•niz•er** \ˈmek-ə-ˌnī-zər\ *n*

med *abbr* **1** medical; medicine **2** medieval **3** medium

MEd *abbr* master of education

med•al \ˈmed-ᵊl\ *n* [MF *medaille,* fr. OIt *medaglia* coin worth half a denarius, medal, fr. (assumed) VL *medalis* half, fr. LL *medialis* middle, fr. L *medius*] **1** : a small usu. metal object bearing a religious emblem or picture **2** : a piece of metal issued to commemorate a person or event or awarded for excellence or achievement

med•al•ist *or* **med•al•list** \ˈmed-ᵊl-əst\ *n* **1** : a designer or maker of medals **2** : a recipient of a medal

me•dal•lion \mə-ˈdal-yən\ *n* **1** : a large

medal 2 : a tablet or panel bearing a portrait or an ornament

med•dle \'med-əl\ *vb* **med•dled; med•dling** \'med-(ə-)liŋ\ : to interfere without right or propriety — **med•dler** \'med-(ə-)lər\ *n*

med•dle•some \'med-əl-səm\ *adj* : inclined to meddle in the affairs of others

me•dia \'mēd-ē-ə\ *n, pl* **me•di•as** : MEDIUM 4

me•di•al \'mēd-ē-əl\ *adj* **1** : occurring in or extending toward the middle : MEDIAN **2** : MEAN, AVERAGE

¹**me•di•an** \'mēd-ē-ən\ *n* **1** : a medial part **2** : a value in an ordered set of values below and above which there are an equal number of values

²**median** *adj* **1** : MEDIAL 1 **2** : relating to or constituting a statistical median

median strip *n* : a strip dividing a highway into lanes according to the direction of travel

¹**me•di•ate** \'mēd-ē-ət\ *adj* **1** : occupying a middle or mediating position **2** : acting through a mediate agency — **me•di•ate•ly** *adv*

²**me•di•ate** \'mēd-ē-ˌāt\ *vb* **-at•ed; -at•ing** : to act as an intermediary (as in settling a dispute or promoting a chemical or physiological result or activity) **syn** intercede, intervene, interpose, interfere — **me•di•a•tion** \ˌmēd-ē-'ā-shən\ *n* — **me•di•a•tor** \'mēd-ē-ˌāt-ər\ *n*

med•ic \'med-ik\ *n* : one engaged in medical work; *esp* : CORPSMAN

med•i•ca•ble \'med-i-kə-bəl\ *adj* : CURABLE, REMEDIABLE — **med•i•ca•bly** \-blē\ *adv*

med•ic•aid \'med-i-ˌkād\ *n, often cap* : a program of financial assistance for medical care designed for those unable to afford regular medical service and financed jointly by the state and federal governments

med•i•cal \'med-i-kəl\ *adj* : of or relating to the science or practice of medicine or the treatment of disease — **med•i•cal•ly** \-k(ə-)lē\ *adv*

medical examiner *n* : a public officer who makes postmortem examinations of bodies to find the cause of death

me•di•ca•ment \mi-'dik-ə-mənt, 'med-i-kə-\ *n* : a medicine or healing application

medi•care \'med-i-ˌkeər\ *n, often cap* : a government program of financial assistance for medical care esp. for the aged

med•i•cate \'med-ə-ˌkāt\ *vb* **-cat•ed; -cat•ing** : to treat with medicine — **med•i•ca•tion** \ˌmed-ə-'kā-shən\ *n*

me•dic•i•nal \mə-'dis-(ə-)nəl\ *adj* : tending or used to cure disease or relieve pain — **me•dic•i•nal•ly** \-ē\ *adv*

med•i•cine \'med-ə-sən\ *n* **1** : a substance or preparation used in treating disease **2** : a science or art dealing with the prevention or cure of disease

medicine ball *n* : a heavy stuffed leather ball used for conditioning exercises

medicine man *n* : a priestly healer or sorcerer esp. among the American Indians

med•i•co \'med-i-ˌkō\ *n, pl* **-cos** : a medical practitioner or student

me•di•eval *or* **me•di•ae•val** \ˌmēd-ē-'ē-vəl, ˌmed-, mē-'dē-vəl\ *adj* : of, relating to, or characteristic of the Middle Ages — **me•di•e•val•ism** \-ˌiz-əm\ *n* — **me•di•e•val•ist** \-əst\ *n*

me•di•o•cre \ˌmēd-ē-'ō-kər\ *adj* [MF, fr. L *mediocris,* lit., halfway up a mountain, fr. *medius* middle + *ocris* stony mountain] : of moderate or low quality : ORDINARY — **me•di•oc•ri•ty** \-'äk-rət-ē\ *n*

med•i•tate \'med-ə-ˌtāt\ *vb* **-tat•ed; -tat•ing** **1** : to muse over : CONTEMPLATE, PONDER **2** : INTEND, PURPOSE — **med•i•ta•tion** \ˌmed-ə-'tā-shən\ *n* — **med•i•ta•tive** \'med-ə-ˌtāt-iv\ *adj* — **med•i•ta•tive•ly** *adv*

Med•i•ter•ra•nean \ˌmed-ə-tə-'rā-nē-ən, -'rā-nyən\ *adj* : of or relating to the Mediterranean sea or to the lands or people around it

¹**me•di•um** \'mēd-ē-əm\ *n, pl* **mediums** *or* **me•dia** \-ē-ə\ [L] **1** : something in a middle position; *also* : a middle position or degree **2** : a means of effecting or conveying something **3** : a surrounding or enveloping substance **4** : a channel or system of communication, information, or entertainment **5** : a mode of artistic expression **6** : an individual held to be a channel of communication between the earthly world and a world of spirits **7** : a condition in which something may function or flourish

²medium *adj* : intermediate in amount, quality, position, or degree

me·di·um·is·tic \ˌmēd-ē-ə-ˈmis-tik\ *adj* : of, relating to, or being a spiritualistic medium

med·ley \ˈmed-lē\ *n, pl* **medleys 1** : HODGEPODGE **2** : a musical composition made up esp. of a series of songs

me·dul·la \mə-ˈdəl-ə\ *n, pl* **-las** *or* **-lae** \-(ˌ)ē, -ˌī\ [L] : an inner or deep anatomical part; *also* : the posterior part (**medulla ob·lon·ga·ta** \-ˌäb-ˌlȯŋ-ˈgät-ə\) of the brain

meed \ˈmēd\ *n* **1** *archaic* : REWARD **2** : a fitting return

meek \ˈmēk\ *adj* **1** : characterized by patience and long-suffering **2** : deficient in spirit and courage **3** : MODERATE — **meek·ly** *adv* — **meek·ness** *n*

meer·schaum \ˈmiər-shəm, -ˌshȯm\ *n* [G, fr. *meer* sea + *schaum* foam] : a tobacco pipe made of a light white clayey mineral

¹meet \ˈmēt\ *vb* **met** \ˈmet\; **meet·ing 1** : to come upon : FIND **2** : JOIN, INTERSECT **3** : to appear to the perception of **4** : OPPOSE, FIGHT **5** : to join in conversation or discussion; *also* : ASSEMBLE **6** : to conform to **7** : to pay fully **8** : to cope with **9** : to provide for **10** : to be introduced to

²meet *n* : an assembling esp. for a hunt or for competitive sports

³meet *adj* : SUITABLE, PROPER

meet·ing \ˈmēt-iŋ\ *n* **1** : an act of coming together : ASSEMBLY **2** : JUNCTION, INTERSECTION

meet·ing·house \-ˌhaůs\ *n* : a building for public assembly and esp. for Protestant worship

mega·byte \ˈmeg-ə-ˌbīt\ *n* : a unit of computer storage capacity approximately equal to one million bytes

mega·cy·cle \-ˌsī-kəl\ *n* : MEGAHERTZ

mega·death \-ˌdeth\ *n* : one million deaths — used as a unit in reference to atomic warfare

mega·hertz \ˈmeg-ə-ˌhərts, -ˌheərts\ *n* : a unit of frequency equal to one million hertz

mega·lith \ˈmeg-ə-ˌlith\ *n* : one of the huge stones used in various prehistoric monuments — **mega·lith·ic** \ˌmeg-ə-ˈlith-ik\ *adj*

meg·a·lo·ma·nia \ˌmeg-ə-lō-ˈmā-nē-ə, -nyə\ *n* : a disorder of mind marked by feelings of personal omnipotence and grandeur — **meg·a·lo·ma·ni·ac** \-ˈmā-nē-ˌak\ *adj or n*

meg·a·lop·o·lis \ˌmeg-ə-ˈläp-ə-ləs\ *n* : a very large urban unit

mega·phone \ˈmeg-ə-ˌfōn\ *n* : a cone-shaped device used to intensify or direct the voice — **megaphone** *vb*

mega·ton \-ˌtən\ *n* : an explosive force equivalent to that of one million tons of TNT

mega·vi·ta·min \-ˌvīt-ə-mən\ *adj* : relating to or consisting of very large doses of vitamins — **mega·vi·ta·mins** *n pl*

mei·o·sis \mī-ˈō-səs\ *n* : the cellular process that results in the number of chromosomes in gamete-producing cells being reduced to one half — **mei·ot·ic** \mī-ˈät-ik\ *adj*

mel·an·cho·lia \ˌmel-ən-ˈkō-lē-ə\ *n* : a mental condition marked by extreme depression often with delusions

mel·an·chol·ic \ˌmel-ən-ˈkäl-ik\ *adj* **1** : DEPRESSED **2** : of or relating to melancholia

mel·an·choly \ˈmel-ən-ˌkäl-ē\ *n, pl* **-chol·ies** [ME *malencolie*, fr. MF *melancolie*, fr. LL *melancholia*, fr. Gk, fr. *melan-, melas* black + *cholē* bile; so called fr. the former belief that it was caused by an excess in the system of black bile, a substance supposedly secreted by the kidneys or spleen] : depression of spirits : DEJECTION, GLOOM — **melancholy** *adj*

Mel·a·ne·sian \ˌmel-ə-ˈnē-zhən\ *n* : a member of the dominant native group of the Pacific island grouping of Melanesia — **Melanesian** *adj*

mé·lange \mā-ˈläⁿzh, -ˈlänj\ *n* : a mixture esp. of incongruous elements

me·lan·ic \mə-ˈlan-ik\ *adj* **1** : having black pigment **2** : affected with or characterized by melanism — **melanic** *n*

mel·a·nin \ˈmel-ə-nən\ *n* : a dark brown or black animal or plant pigment

mel·a·nism \ˈmel-ə-ˌniz-əm\ *n* : an increased amount of black or nearly black pigmentation

mel·a·no·ma \ˌmel-ə-ˈnō-mə\ *n, pl* **-mas** *also* **-ma·ta** \-mət-ə\ : a usu. malignant tumor containing black pigment

¹meld \ˈmeld\ *vb* : to show or announce for a score in a card game

²**meld** *n* : a card or combination of cards that is or can be melded

me·lee \'mā-ˌlā, mā-'lā\ *n* [F *mêlée*] : a confused struggle **syn** fracas, row, brawl, donnybrook

me·lio·rate \'mēl-yə-ˌrāt, 'mē-lē-ə-\ *vb* **-rat·ed; -rat·ing** : to make or become better — **me·lio·ra·tion** \ˌmēl-yə-'rā-shən, ˌmē-lē-ə-\ *n* — **me·lio·ra·tive** \'mēl-yə-ˌrāt-iv, 'mē-lē-ə-\ *adj*

mel·lif·lu·ous \me-'lif-lə-wəs, mə-\ *adj* [LL *mellifluus*, fr. L *mel* honey + *fluere* to flow] : sweetly flowing — **mel·lif·lu·ous·ly** *adv* — **mel·lif·lu·ous·ness** *n*

¹**mel·low** \'mel-ō\ *adj* **1** : soft and sweet because of ripeness ⟨~ apple⟩; *also* : well aged and pleasingly mild ⟨~ wine⟩ **2** : made gentle by age or experience **3** : being rich and full but not garish or strident ⟨~ colors⟩ **4** : of soft loamy consistency ⟨~ soil⟩ — **mel·low·ness** *n*

²**mellow** *vb* : to make or become mellow

me·lo·de·on \mə-'lōd-ē-ən\ *n* : a small reed organ in which a suction bellows draws air inward through the reeds

me·lo·di·ous \mə-'lōd-ē-əs\ *adj* : pleasing to the ear — **me·lo·di·ous·ly** *adv* — **me·lo·di·ous·ness** *n*

melo·dra·ma \'mel-ə-ˌdräm-ə, -ˌdram-\ *n* : an extravagantly theatrical play in which action and plot predominate over characterization — **melo·dra·mat·ic** \ˌmel-ə-drə-'mat-ik\ *adj* — **melo·dra·ma·tist** \ˌmel-ə-'dram-ət-əst, -'dräm-\ *n*

mel·o·dy \'mel-əd-ē\ *n, pl* **-dies 1** : sweet or agreeable sound ⟨birds making ~⟩ **2** : a particular succession of notes : TUNE, AIR — **me·lod·ic** \mə-'läd-ik\ *adj* — **me·lod·i·cal·ly** \-i-k(ə-)lē\ *adv*

mel·on \'mel-ən\ *n* : any of certain fruits (as a muskmelon or watermelon) of the gourd family usu. eaten raw

¹**melt** \'melt\ *vb* **1** : to change from a solid to a liquid state usu. by heat **2** : DISSOLVE, DISINTEGRATE; *also* : to cause to disperse or disappear **3** : to make or become tender or gentle

²**melt** *n* : a melted substance

melt·down \'melt-ˌdaùn\ *n* : the melting of the core of a nuclear reactor

melt·wa·ter \'melt-ˌwȯt-ər, -ˌwät-\ *n* : water derived from the melting of ice and snow

mem *abbr* **1** member **2** memoir **3** memorial

mem·ber \'mem-bər\ *n* **1** : a part (as an arm, leg, or branch) of a person, lower animal, or plant **2** : one of the individuals composing a group **3** : a constituent part of a whole

mem·ber·ship \-ˌship\ *n* **1** : the state or status of being a member **2** : the body of members

mem·brane \'mem-ˌbrān\ *n* : a thin pliable layer esp. of animal or plant tissue — **mem·bra·nous** \-brə-nəs\ *adj*

me·men·to \mə-'ment-ō\ *n, pl* **-tos** or **-toes** [ME, fr. L remember] : something that serves to warn or remind : SOUVENIR

memo \'mem-ō\ *n, pl* **mem·os** : MEMORANDUM

mem·oir \'mem-ˌwär\ *n* **1** : MEMORANDUM **2** : AUTOBIOGRAPHY — usu. used in pl. **3** : an account of something noteworthy; *also, pl* : the record of the proceedings of a learned society

mem·o·ra·bil·ia \ˌmem-ə-rə-'bil-ē-ə, -'bil-yə\ *n pl* [L] : things worthy of remembrance; *also* : a record of such things

mem·o·ra·ble \'mem-(ə-)rə-bəl\ *adj* : worth remembering : NOTABLE — **mem·o·ra·bil·i·ty** \ˌmem-ə-rə-'bil-ət-ē\ *n* — **mem·o·ra·ble·ness** *n* — **mem·o·ra·bly** \-blē\ *adv*

mem·o·ran·dum \ˌmem-ə-'ran-dəm\ *n, pl* **-dums** or **-da** \-də\ **1** : an informal record; *also* : a written reminder **2** : an informal written note

¹**me·mo·ri·al** \mə-'mōr-ē-əl\ *adj* : serving to preserve remembrance

²**memorial** *n* **1** : something designed to keep remembrance alive; *esp* : MONUMENT **2** : a statement of facts often accompanied with a petition — **me·mo·ri·al·ize** *vb*

Memorial Day *n* : the last Monday in May or formerly May 30 observed as a legal holiday in honor of those who died in war

mem·o·rize \'mem-ə-ˌrīz\ *vb* **-rized; -riz·ing** : to learn by heart — **mem·o·ri·za·tion** \ˌmem-(ə-)rə-'zā-shən\ *n* — **mem·o·riz·er** \'mem-ə-ˌrīz-ər\ *n*

mem·o·ry \'mem-(ə-)rē\ *n, pl* **-ries 1** : the power or process of remembering **2** : the store of things remembered **3** : COMMEMORATION **4** : something remembered **5** : the time within which past events are remembered **6** : a device (as in a computer) in which information can be stored **syn** remembrance, recollection, reminiscence

men pl of MAN

¹men•ace \ˈmen-əs\ n **1** : THREAT **2** : DANGER; also : NUISANCE

²menace vb **men•aced; men•ac•ing 1** : THREATEN **2** : ENDANGER — **men•ac•ing•ly** adv

mé•nage \mā-ˈnäzh\ n [F] : HOUSEHOLD

me•nag•er•ie \mə-ˈnaj-(ə-)rē\ n : a collection of wild animals esp. for exhibition

¹mend \ˈmend\ vb **1** : to improve in manners or morals **2** : to put into good shape : REPAIR **3** : to restore to health : HEAL — **mend•er** n

²mend n **1** : an act of mending **2** : a mended place

men•da•cious \men-ˈdā-shəs\ adj : given to deception or falsehood : UNTRUTHFUL **syn** dishonest, deceitful — **men•da•cious•ly** adv — **men•dac•i•ty** \-ˈdas-ət-ē\ n

men•de•le•vi•um \ˌmen-də-ˈlē-vē-əm, -ˈlā-\ n : a radioactive chemical element artificially produced

men•di•cant \ˈmen-di-kənt\ n **1** : BEGGAR **2** often cap : FRIAR — **men•di•can•cy** \-kən-sē\ n — **mendicant** adj

men•folk \ˈmen-ˌfōk\ or **men•folks** \-ˌfōks\ n pl **1** : men in general **2** : the men of a family or community

men•ha•den \men-ˈhād-ᵊn, mən-\ n, pl **-den** also **-dens** : a marine fish related to the herring that is abundant along the Atlantic coast of the U.S.

¹me•nial \ˈmē-nē-əl, -nyəl\ adj **1** : of or relating to servants **2** : HUMBLE; also : SERVILE — **me•ni•al•ly** \-ē\ adv

²menial n : a domestic servant

men•in•gi•tis \ˌmen-ən-ˈjīt-əs\ n, pl **-git•i•des** \-ˈjit-ə-ˌdēz\ : inflammation of the membranes enclosing the brain and spinal cord; also : a usu. bacterial disease marked by this

me•ninx \ˈmē-niŋks, ˈmen-iŋks\ n, pl **me•nin•ges** \mə-ˈnin-(ˌ)jēz\ : any of the three membranes that envelop the brain and spinal cord — **men•in•ge•al** \ˌmen-ən-ˈjē-əl\ adj

me•nis•cus \mə-ˈnis-kəs\ n, pl **me•nis•ci** \-ˈnis-ˌ(k)ī, -ˌkē\ also **me•nis•cus•es 1** : CRESCENT **2** : the curved upper surface of a column of liquid

meno•pause \ˈmen-ə-ˌpoz\ n : the period of natural cessation of menstruation — **meno•paus•al** \ˌmen-ə-ˈpo-zəl\ adj

men•ses \ˈmen-ˌsēz\ n pl : the menstrual flow

men•stru•a•tion \ˌmen-strə-ˈwā-shən, men-ˈstrā-\ n : a discharging of bloody matter at approximately monthly intervals from the uterus of breeding-age nonpregnant primate females — **men•stru•al** \ˈmen-strə(-wə)l\ adj — **men•stru•ate** \ˈmen-strə-ˌwāt, -ˌstrāt\ vb

men•su•ra•ble \ˈmens-(ə-)rə-bəl, ˈmench-(ə-)rə-\ adj : MEASURABLE

men•su•ra•tion \ˌmen-sə-ˈrā-shən, ˌmen-chə-\ n : MEASUREMENT

-ment \mənt\ n suffix **1** : concrete result, object, or agent of a (specified) action ⟨embank*ment*⟩ ⟨entangle*ment*⟩ **2** : concrete means or instrument of a (specified) action ⟨entertain*ment*⟩ **3** : action : process ⟨encircle*ment*⟩ ⟨develop*ment*⟩ **4** : place of a (specified) action ⟨encamp*ment*⟩ **5** : state : condition ⟨amaze*ment*⟩

men•tal \ˈment-ᵊl\ adj **1** : of or relating to the mind **2** : of, relating to, or affected with a disorder of the mind — **men•tal•ly** \-ē\ adv

mental age n : a measure used in psychological testing that expresses a person's mental attainment in terms of the number of years it takes the average child to reach the same level

mental deficiency n : failure in intellectual development that results in social incompetence and is considered to be the result of a defective central nervous system

men•tal•i•ty \men-ˈtal-ət-ē\ n, pl **-ties 1** : mental power or capacity **2** : mode or way of thought

men•thol \ˈmen-ˌthol, -ˌthōl\ n : a white soothing substance from oil of peppermint — **men•tho•lat•ed** \-thə-ˌlāt-əd\ adj

¹men•tion \ˈmen-chən\ n **1** : a brief or casual reference **2** : a formal citation for outstanding achievement

²mention vb **men•tioned; men•tion•ing** \ˈmench-(ə-)niŋ\ **1** : to refer to : CITE

2 : to cite for outstanding achievement — **not to mention** : AS WELL AS

men·tor \'men-ˌtȯr, 'ment-ər\ *n* : a trusted counselor or guide; *also* : TUTOR, COACH

menu \'men-yü, 'mān-\ *n, pl* **menus** [F, fr. *menu* small, detailed, fr. L *minutus* minute (adj.)] : a list of the dishes available (as in a restaurant) for a meal; *also* : the dishes served

me·ow \mē-'aü\ *vb* : to make the characteristic cry of a cat — **meow** *n*

me·phit·ic \mə-'fit-ik\ *adj* : foul-smelling

mer *abbr* meridian

mer·can·tile \'mər-kən-ˌtēl, -ˌtīl\ *adj* : of or relating to merchants or trading

¹mer·ce·nary \'mərs-ᵊn-ˌer-ē\ *n, pl* **-nar·ies** : one who serves merely for wages; *esp* : a soldier serving in a foreign army

²mercenary *adj* **1** : serving merely for pay or gain **2** : hired for service in a foreign army — **mer·ce·nari·ly** \ˌmərs-ᵊn-'er-ə-lē\ *adv* — **mer·ce·nari·ness** \'mərs-ᵊn-ˌer-ē-nəs\ *n*

mer·cer \'mər-sər\ *n* : a dealer in usu. expensive fabrics

mer·cer·ize \'mər-sə-ˌrīz\ *vb* **-ized; -iz·ing** : to treat cotton yarn or cloth with alkali so that it looks silky or takes a better dye

¹mer·chan·dise \'mər-chən-ˌdīz, -ˌdīs\ *n* : the commodities or goods that are bought and sold in business

²mer·chan·dise \-ˌdīz\ *vb* **-dised; -dis·ing** : to buy and sell in business : TRADE — **mer·chan·dis·er** *n*

mer·chant \'mər-chənt\ *n* **1** : a buyer and seller of commodities for profit **2** : STOREKEEPER

mer·chant·able \'mər-chənt-ə-bəl\ *adj* : acceptable to buyers : MARKETABLE

mer·chant·man \'mər-chənt-mən\ *n* : a ship used in commerce

merchant marine *n* : the commercial ships of a nation

merchant ship *n* : MERCHANTMAN

mer·cu·ri·al \ˌmər-'kyùr-ē-əl\ *adj* **1** : unpredictably changeable **2** : MERCURIC — **mer·cu·ri·al·ly** \-ē\ *adv* — **mer·cu·ri·al·ness** *n*

mer·cu·ric \ˌmər-'kyùr-ik\ *adj* : of, relating to, or containing mercury

mercuric chloride *n* : a poisonous compound of mercury and chlorine used as an antiseptic and fungicide

mer·cu·ry \'mər-kyə-rē\ *n, pl* **-ries 1** : a heavy silver-white liquid metallic chemical element used esp. in scientific instruments **2** *cap* : the planet nearest the sun

mer·cy \'mər-sē\ *n, pl* **mercies** [ME, fr. OF *merci*, fr. ML *merces*, fr. L, price paid, wages, fr. *merc-, merx* merchandise] **1** : compassion shown to an offender; *also* : imprisonment rather than death for first-degree murder **2** : a blessing resulting from divine favor or compassion; *also* : a fortunate circumstance **3** : compassion shown to victims of misfortune — **mer·ci·ful** \-si-fəl\ *adj* — **mer·ci·ful·ly** \-ē\ *adv* — **mer·ci·less** \-si-ləs\ *adj* — **mer·ci·less·ly** *adv* — **mercy** *adj*

mercy killing *n* : the act or practice of killing or permitting the death of hopelessly sick or injured persons or animals with as little pain as possible for reasons of mercy

¹mere \'miər\ *n* : LAKE, POOL

²mere *adj* **mer·est 1** : being nothing more than : BARE **2** : not diluted : PURE — **mere·ly** *adv*

mer·e·tri·cious \ˌmer-ə-'trish-əs\ *adj* [L *meretricius*, fr. *meretrix* prostitute, fr. *merēre* to earn] : tawdrily attractive; *also* : SPECIOUS — **mer·e·tri·cious·ly** *adv* — **mer·e·tri·cious·ness** *n*

mer·gan·ser \(ˌ)mər-'gan-sər\ *n* : any of various fish-eating ducks with a crested head and a slender bill hooked at the end and serrated along the margins

merge \'mərj\ *vb* **merged; merg·ing 1** : to blend gradually **2** : to combine, unite, or coalesce into one **syn** mingle, amalgamate, fuse, interfuse, intermingle

merg·er \'mər-jər\ *n* **1** : the act or process of merging **2** : absorption by a corporation of one or more others

me·rid·i·an \mə-'rid-ē-ən\ *n* [ME, fr. MF *meridien*, fr. *meridien* of noon, fr. L *meridianus*, fr. *meridies* noon, south, irreg. fr. *medius* mid + *dies* day] **1** : the highest point : CULMINATION **2** : one of the imaginary circles on the earth's surface passing through the north and south poles — **meridian** *adj*

me·ringue \mə-'raŋ\ *n* [F] : a dessert topping of baked beaten egg whites and powdered sugar

me·ri·no \mə-'rē-nō\ *n, pl* **-nos** [Sp] **1** : any of a breed of sheep noted for fine soft wool; *also* : its wool or fleece **2** : a fine soft fabric or yarn of wool or wool and cotton

¹mer·it \'mer-ət\ *n* **1** : laudable or blameworthy traits or actions **2** : a praiseworthy quality; *also* : character or conduct deserving reward or honor **3** *pl* : the intrinsic nature of a legal case; *also* : legal significance

²merit *vb* : EARN, DESERVE

mer·i·toc·ra·cy \ˌmer-ə-'täk-rə-sē\ *n, pl* **-cies** : an educational system whereby the talented are chosen and moved ahead on the basis of their achievement; *also* : leadership by the talented

mer·i·to·ri·ous \ˌmer-ə-'tōr-ē-əs\ *adj* : deserving honor or esteem — **mer·i·to·ri·ous·ly** *adv* — **mer·i·to·ri·ous·ness** *n*

mer·maid \'mər-ˌmād\ *n* : a legendary sea creature with a woman's upper body and a fish's tail

mer·man \-ˌman, -mən\ *n* : a legendary sea creature with a man's upper body and a fish's tail

mer·ri·ment \'mer-i-mənt\ *n* **1** : HILARITY **2** : FESTIVITY

mer·ry \'mer-ē\ *adj* **mer·ri·er; -est** **1** : full of gaiety or high spirits **2** : marked by festivity **3** : BRISK ⟨a ∼ pace⟩ **syn** blithe, jocund, jovial, jolly, mirthful — **mer·ri·ly** \'mer-ə-lē\ *adv*

merry–go–round \'mer-ē-gō-ˌraủnd\ *n* **1** : a circular revolving platform with benches and figures of animals on which people sit for a ride **2** : a busy round of activities

mer·ry·mak·ing \'mer-ē-ˌmā-kiŋ\ *n* **1** : CONVIVIALITY **2** : a festive occasion — **mer·ry·mak·er** \-ˌmā-kər\ *n*

me·sa \'mā-sə\ *n* [Sp, lit., table, fr. L *mensa*] : a flat-topped hill with steep sides

més·al·liance \ˌmā-ˌzal-'yäⁿs, ˌmā-zə-'lī- əns\ *n, pl* **més·al·liances** \-'yäⁿs (-əz), -ˌlī-ən-səz\ [F] : a marriage with a person of inferior social position

mes·cal \me-'skal, mə-\ *n* **1** : a small cactus that is the source of a stimulant used esp. by Mexican Indians **2** : a

usu. colorless liquor distilled from the leaves of an agave; *also* : AGAVE

mes·ca·line \'mes-kə-lən, -ˌlēn\ *n* : a hallucinatory alkaloid from the mescal cactus

mesdames *pl of* MADAM *or of* MADAME *or of* MRS.

mesdemoiselles *pl of* MADEMOISELLE

¹mesh \'mesh\ *n* **1** : one of the openings between the threads or cords of a net; *also* : one of the similar spaces in a network **2** : the fabric of a net **3** : NETWORK **4** : working contact (as of the teeth of gears) ⟨in ∼⟩ — **meshed** \'mesht\ *adj*

²mesh *vb* **1** : to catch in or as if in a mesh **2** : to be in or come into mesh : ENGAGE **3** : to fit together properly

mesh·work \'mesh-ˌwərk\ *n* : NETWORK

me·si·al \'mē-zē-əl, -sē-\ *adj* : of, relating to, or being the surface of a tooth that is closest to the middle of the front of the jaw

mes·mer·ize \'mez-mə-ˌrīz\ *vb* **-ized; -iz·ing** : HYPNOTIZE — **mes·mer·ic** \mez-'mer-ik\ *adj* — **mes·mer·ism** \'mez-mə-ˌriz-əm\ *n*

Me·so·lith·ic \ˌmez-ə-'lith-ik\ *adj* : of, relating to, or being a transitional period of the Stone Age between the Paleolithic and the Neolithic periods

me·so·sphere \'mez-ə-ˌsfiər\ *n* : a layer of the atmosphere above the stratosphere

Me·so·zo·ic \ˌmez-ə-'zō-ik, ˌmēz-\ *adj* : of, relating to, or being the era of geologic history between the Paleozoic and the Cenozoic and extending from about 230 million years ago to about 70 million years ago — **Mesozoic** *n*

mes·quite \mə-'skēt, me-\ *n* : a thorny leguminous shrub of Mexico and the southwestern U.S. with sugar-rich pods important as fodder

¹mess \'mes\ *n* **1** : a quantity of food; *also* : enough food of a specified kind for a dish or meal ⟨a ∼ of beans⟩ **2** : a group of persons who regularly eat together; *also* : a meal eaten by such a group **3** : a confused, dirty, or offensive state — **messy** *adj*

²mess *vb* **1** : to supply with meals; *also* : to take meals with a mess **2** : to make dirty or untidy; *also* : BUNGLE **3**

: INTERFERE, MEDDLE 4 : PUTTER, TRIFLE

mes·sage \'mes-ij\ *n* : a communication sent by one person to another

messeigneurs *pl of* MONSEIGNEUR

mes·sen·ger \'mes-ᵊn-jər\ *n* : one who carries a message or does an errand

messenger RNA *n* : an RNA that carries the code for a particular protein from the nuclear DNA to a ribosome in the cytoplasm and acts as a template for the formation of that protein

Mes·si·ah \mə-'sī-ə\ *n* 1 : the expected king and deliverer of the Jews 2 : Jesus 3 *not cap* : a professed or accepted leader of a cause — **mes·si·an·ic** \ˌmes-ē-'an-ik\ *adj*

messieurs *pl of* MONSIEUR

mess·mate \'mes-ˌmāt\ *n* : a member of a group who eat regularly together

Messrs. \ˌmes-ərz\ *pl of* MR.

mes·ti·zo \me-'stē-zō\ *n, pl* **-zos** [Sp, fr. *mestizo* mixed, fr. LL *mixticius*, fr. L *mixtus*, pp. of *miscēre* to mix] : a person of mixed blood

¹met past and past part of MEET

²met *abbr* metropolitan

me·tab·o·lism \mə-'tab-ə-ˌliz-əm\ *n* : the sum of the processes in the building up and breaking down of the substance of plants and animals incidental to life; *also* : the processes by which a substance is handled in the body ⟨∼ of sugar⟩ — **met·a·bol·ic** \ˌmet-ə-'bäl-ik\ *adj* — **me·tab·o·lize** \mə-'tab-ə-ˌlīz\ *vb*

me·tab·o·lite \-ˌlīt\ *n* 1 : a product of metabolism 2 : a substance essential to the metabolism of a particular organism

meta·car·pal \ˌmet-ə-'kär-pəl\ *n* : any of usu. five more or less elongated bones of the part of the hand or forefoot between the carpus and the bones of the digits — **metacarpal** *adj*

meta·car·pus \-'kär-pəs\ *n* : the part of the hand or forefoot that contains the metacarpals

met·al \'met-ᵊl\ *n* 1 : any of various opaque, fusible, ductile, and typically lustrous substances; *esp* : one that is a chemical element 2 : METTLE; *also* : the material out of which a person or thing is made — **me·tal·lic** \mə-'tal-ik\ *adj* — **met·al·loid** \'met-ᵊl-ˌóid\ *n or adj*

met·al·lur·gy \'met-ᵊl-ˌər-jē\ *n* : the science and technology of metals — **met·al·lur·gi·cal** \ˌmet-ᵊl-'ər-ji-kəl\ *adj* — **met·al·lur·gist** \'met-ᵊl-ˌər-jəst\ *n*

met·al·ware \'met-ᵊl-ˌwaər\ *n* : metal utensils for household use

met·al·work \-ˌwərk\ *n* : work and esp. artistic work made of metal — **met·al·work·er** \-ˌwər-kər\ *n* — **met·al·work·ing** \-ˌwər-kiŋ\ *n*

meta·mor·phism \ˌmet-ə-'mór-ˌfiz-əm\ *n* : a change in the structure of rock; *esp* : a change to a more compact highly crystalline condition produced by pressure, heat, and water — **met·a·mor·phic** \-'mór-fik\ *adj*

meta·mor·pho·sis \ˌmet-ə-'mór-fə-səs\ *n, pl* **-pho·ses** \-ˌsēz\ 1 : a change of physical form, structure, or substance esp. by supernatural means; *also* : a striking alteration (as in appearance or character) 2 : a fundamental change in form and often habits of an animal accompanying the transformation of a larva into an adult — **met·a·mor·phose** \-ˌfōz, -ˌfōs\ *vb*

met·a·phor \'met-ə-ˌfór\ *n* : a figure of speech in which a word denoting one subject or idea is used in place of another to suggest a likeness between them (as in ''the ship plows the sea'') — **met·a·phor·i·cal** \ˌmet-ə-'fór-i-kəl\ *adj*

meta·phys·ics \ˌmet-ə-'fiz-iks\ *n* [ML *Metaphysica*, title of Aristotle's treatise on the subject, fr. Gk (*ta*) *meta* (*ta*) *physika*, lit., the (works) after the physical (works); fr. its position in his collected works] : the part of philosophy concerned with the study of the ultimate causes and underlying nature of things — **meta·phys·i·cal** \-'fiz-i-kəl\ *adj* — **meta·phy·si·cian** \-fə-'zish-ən\ *n*

me·tas·ta·sis \mə-'tas-tə-səs\ *n, pl* **-ta·ses** \-ˌsēz\ : transfer of a health-impairing agency (as tumor cells) to a new site in the body; *also* : a secondary growth of a malignant tumor — **met·a·stat·ic** \ˌmet-ə-'stat-ik\ *adj*

meta·tar·sal \ˌmet-ə-'tär-səl\ *n* : any of the bones of the foot between the tarsus and the bones of the digits that in human beings include five more or less elongated bones — **metatarsal** *adj*

meta·tar·sus \-'tär-səs\ *n* : the part of the foot in man or of the hind foot in quadrupeds that contains the metatarsals

¹**mete** \'mēt\ *vb* **met•ed; met•ing 1** *archaic* : MEASURE **2** : ALLOT

²**mete** *n* : BOUNDARY ⟨∼s and bounds⟩

me•tem•psy•cho•sis \mə-,tem(p)-si-'kō-səs, ,met-əm-,sī-\ *n* : the passing of the soul at death into another body either human or animal

me•te•or \'mēt-ē-ər, -ē-,ȯr\ *n* **1** : a usu. small particle of matter in the solar system observable only when it falls into the earth's atmosphere where friction causes it to glow **2** : the streak of light produced by passage of a meteor

me•te•or•ic \,mēt-ē-'ȯr-ik\ *adj* **1** : of, relating to, or resembling a meteor **2** : transiently brilliant ⟨a ∼ career⟩ — **me•te•or•i•cal•ly** \-i-k(ə-)lē\ *adv*

me•te•or•ite \'mēt-ē-ə-,rīt\ *n* : a meteor that reaches the surface of the earth

me•te•or•oid \'mēt-ē-ə-,rȯid\ *n* : a meteor in orbit around the sun

me•te•o•rol•o•gy \,mēt-ē-ə-'räl-ə-jē\ *n* : a science that deals with the atmosphere and its phenomena and esp. with weather and weather forecasting — **me•te•o•ro•log•ic** \,mēt-ē-,ȯr-ə-'läj-ik\ *or* **me•te•o•ro•log•i•cal** \-'läj-i-kəl\ *adj* — **me•te•o•rol•o•gist** \,mēt-ē-ə-'räl-ə-jəst\ *n*

¹**me•ter** \'mēt-ər\ *n* : rhythm in verse or music

²**met•er** \'mēt-ər\ *n* : the basic metric unit of length — see METRIC SYSTEM table

³**me•ter** \'mēt-ər\ *n* : a measuring and sometimes recording instrument

⁴**me•ter** *vb* **1** : to measure by means of a meter **2** : to print postal indicia on by means of a postage meter ⟨∼ed mail⟩

meter–kilogram–second *adj* : MKS

meter maid *n* : a female member of a police department who is assigned to write tickets for parking violations

meth•a•done \'meth-ə-,dōn\ *also* **meth•a•don** \-,dän\ *n* : a synthetic addictive narcotic drug used esp. as a substitute narcotic in the treatment of heroin addiction

meth•am•phet•amine \,meth-am-'fet-ə-,mēn, ,meth-əm-, -mən\ *n* : a drug used in the form of its hydrochloride as a stimulant for the central nervous system and in the treatment of obesity

meth•ane \'meth-,ān\ *n* : a colorless odorless flammable gas produced by decomposition of organic matter (as in marshes) or from coal and used as a fuel

meth•a•nol \'meth-ə-,nȯl, -,nōl\ *n* : a volatile flammable poisonous liquid alcohol that consists of carbon, hydrogen, and oxygen and that is used esp. as a solvent and as an antifreeze

meth•aqua•lone \me-'thak-wə-,lōn\ *n* : a sedative and hypnotic habit-forming drug that is not a barbiturate

meth•od \'meth-əd\ *n* [MF *methode*, fr. L *methodus*, fr. Gk *methodos*, fr. *meta* with + *hodos* way] **1** : a procedure or process for achieving an end **2** : orderly arrangement : PLAN **syn** mode, manner, way, fashion, system — **me•thod•i•cal** \mə-'thäd-i-kəl\ *adj* — **me•thod•i•cal•ly** \-k(ə-)lē\ *adv* — **me•thod•i•cal•ness** *n*

Meth•od•ist \'meth-əd-əst\ *n* : a member of a Protestant denomination adhering to the doctrines of John Wesley — **Meth•od•ism** \-ə-,diz-əm\ *n*

meth•od•ize \'meth-ə-,dīz\ *vb* **-ized; -iz•ing** : SYSTEMATIZE

meth•od•ol•o•gy \,meth-ə-'däl-ə-jē\ *n, pl* **-gies 1** : a body of methods and rules followed in a science or discipline **2** : the study of the principles or procedures of inquiry in a particular field

meth•yl \'meth-əl\ *n* : a chemical group consisting of carbon and hydrogen

methyl alcohol *n* : METHANOL

meth•yl•mer•cury \,meth-əl-'mər-kyə-rē\ *n* : any of various toxic compounds of mercury that tend to accumulate in animals esp. at the top of a food chain

met•i•cal \'met-i-kəl\ *n* — see MONEY table

me•tic•u•lous \mə-'tik-yə-ləs\ *adj* [L *meticulosus* timid, fr. *metus* fear] : extremely careful in attending to details — **me•tic•u•lous•ly** *adv* — **me•tic•u•lous•ness** *n*

mé•tier \'me-,tyā, me-'tyā\ *n* : an area of activity in which one is expert or successful

me•tre \'mēt-ər\ *chiefly Brit var of* METER

met•ric \'me-trik\ *adj* **1** : of or relating to measurement; *esp* : of or relating to the metric system **2** : METRICAL 1

met·ri·cal \'me-tri-kəl\ adj 1 : of, relating to, or composed in meter 2 : METRIC 1 — **met·ri·cal·ly** \-tri-k(ə-)lē\ adv

met·ri·ca·tion \ˌme-tri-'kā-shən\ n : the act or process of converting into or expressing in the metric system

met·ri·cize \'me-trə-ˌsīz\ vb **-cized; -cizing** : to change into or express in the metric system

metric system n : a decimal system of weights and measures based on the meter and on the kilogram

metric ton n — see METRIC SYSTEM table

¹**met·ro** \'me-trō\ n, pl **metros** : SUBWAY

²**metro** adj : of, relating to, or characteristic of a metropolis and sometimes including its suburbs

me·trol·o·gy \me-'träl-ə-jē\ n : the science of weights and measures or of measurement

met·ro·nome \'me-trə-ˌnōm\ n : an instrument for marking exact time by a regularly repeated tick

me·trop·o·lis \mə-'träp-(ə-)ləs\ n [LL, fr. Gk *mētropolis*, fr. *mētēr* mother + *polis* city] : the chief or capital city of a country, state, or region — **met·ro·pol·i·tan** \ˌme-trə-'päl-ət-ᵊn\ adj

met·tle \'met-ᵊl\ n 1 : quality of temperament 2 : SPIRIT, COURAGE

met·tle·some \'met-ᵊl-səm\ adj : full of mettle

MeV abbr million electron volts

mew \'myü\ vb : CONFINE

mews \'myüz\ n pl, chiefly Brit : stables usu. with living quarters built around a court; also : a narrow street with dwellings converted from stables

Mex abbr Mexican; Mexico

Mex·i·can \'mek-si-kən\ n : a native or inhabitant of Mexico — **Mexican** adj

mez·za·nine \'mez-ᵊn-ˌēn, ˌmez-ᵊn-'ēn\ n 1 : a low-ceilinged story between two main stories of a building 2 : the lowest balcony in a theater; also : the first few rows of such a balcony

mez·zo–so·pra·no \ˌmet-sō-sə-'pran-ō, ˌme(d)z-\ n : a woman's voice having a range between that of the soprano and contralto; also : a singer having such a voice

MF abbr medium frequency

MFA abbr master of fine arts

mg abbr milligram

Mg symbol magnesium

MG abbr 1 machine gun 2 major general 3 military government

mgr abbr 1 manager 2 monseigneur 3 monsignor

mgt or **mgmt** abbr management

MGy Sgt abbr master gunnery sergeant

MHz abbr megahertz

mi abbr 1 mile; mileage 2 mill

MI abbr 1 Michigan 2 military intelligence

MIA \ˌem-ˌī-'ā\ n [missing in action] : a member of the armed forces whose whereabouts following a combat mission are unknown

Mi·ami \mī-'am-ē, -'am-ə\ n, pl **Mi·ami** or **Mi·am·is** : a member of an American Indian people orig. of Wisconsin and Indiana

mi·as·ma \mī-'az-mə, mē-\ n, pl **-mas** also **-ma·ta** \-mət-ə\ : an exhalation formerly held to cause disease : a noxious vapor — **mi·as·mic** \-mik\ adj

Mic abbr Micah

mi·ca \'mī-kə\ n [NL, fr. L, grain, crumb] : any of various minerals readily separable into thin transparent sheets

Mi·cah \'mī-kə\ n — see BIBLE table

mice pl of MOUSE

Mich abbr Michigan

Mi·che·as \'mī-kē-əs, mī-'kē-əs\ n — see BIBLE table

Mic·mac \'mik-ˌmak\ n, pl **Micmac** or **Micmacs** : a member of an American Indian people of eastern Canada

micr- or **micro-** comb form 1 : small : minute 2 : one millionth part of a specified unit ⟨*micro*second⟩

¹**mi·cro** \'mī-krō\ adj 1 : very small; esp : MICROSCOPIC 2 : involving minute quantities or variations

²**micro** n : MICROCOMPUTER

mi·crobe \'mī-ˌkrōb\ n : MICROORGANISM; esp : one causing disease — **mi·cro·bi·al** \mī-'krō-bē-əl\ adj

mi·cro·bi·ol·o·gy \ˌmī-krō-bī-'äl-ə-jē\ n : a branch of biology dealing esp. with microscopic forms of life — **mi·cro·bi·o·log·i·cal** \ˌmī-krō-ˌbī-ə-'läj-i-kəl\ adj — **mi·cro·bi·ol·o·gist** \ˌmī-krō-bī-'äl-ə-jəst\ n

mi·cro·bus \'mī-krō-ˌbəs\ n : a station wagon shaped like a bus

mi·cro·cap·sule \-ˌkap-səl, -ˌsül\ n : a tiny capsule containing material (as a medicine) that is released when the capsule is broken, melted, or dissolved

mi·cro·chip \-ˌchip\ *n* : INTEGRATED CIRCUIT

mi·cro·cir·cuit \-ˌsər-kət\ *n* : a compact electronic circuit

mi·cro·com·put·er \-kəm-ˌpyüt-ər\ *n* : a very small computer

mi·cro·copy \-ˌkäp-ē\ *n* : a photographic copy (as of print) on a reduced scale — **microcopy** *vb*

mi·cro·cosm \ˈmī-krə-ˌkäz-əm\ *n* : an individual or community thought of as a miniature world or universe

mi·cro·elec·tron·ics \ˈmī-krō-i-ˌlek-ˈträn-iks\ *n* : a branch of electronics that deals with the miniaturization of electronic circuits and components — **mi·cro·elec·tron·ic** \-ik\ *adj*

mi·cro·en·cap·su·late \ˌmī-krō-in-ˈkap-sə-ˌlāt\ *vb* : to enclose in a microcapsule ⟨*microencapsulated* aspirin⟩ — **mi·cro·en·cap·su·la·tion** \-in-ˌkap-sə-ˈlā-shən\ *n*

mi·cro·fiche \ˈmī-krō-ˌfēsh, -ˌfish\ *n, pl* **-fiche** *or* **-fiches** \-ˌfēsh(-əz), -ˌfish(-əz)\ : a sheet of microfilm containing rows of images of pages of printed matter

mi·cro·film \-ˌfilm\ *n* : a film bearing a photographic record (as of print) on a reduced scale — **microfilm** *vb*

mi·cro·graph \ˈmī-krə-ˌgraf\ *n* : a graphic reproduction of the image of an object formed by a microscope — **micrograph** *vb*

mi·cro·me·te·or·ite \ˌmī-krō-ˈmēt-ē-ə-ˌrīt\ *n* **1** : a meteorite particle of very small size **2** : a very small particle in interplanetary space

mi·crom·e·ter \mī-ˈkräm-ət-ər\ *n* : an instrument used with a telescope or microscope for measuring minute distances

mi·cro·min·ia·ture \ˌmī-krō-ˈmin-ē-ə-ˌchùr, -ˈmin-i-ˌchùr, -chər\ *adj* : MICROMINIATURIZED

mi·cro·min·ia·tur·iza·tion \-ˌmin-ē-ə-ˌchùr-ə-ˈzā-shən, -ˌmin-i-ˌchùr-, -chər-\ *n* : the process of producing microminiaturized things

mi·cro·min·ia·tur·ized \-ˈmin-ē-ə-chə-ˌrīzd, -ˈmin-i-chə-\ *adj* : reduced to or produced in a very small size and esp. in a size smaller than one considered miniature

mi·cron \ˈmī-ˌkrän\ *n, pl* **microns** *also* **mi·cra** \-krə\ : one millionth of a meter

mi·cro·or·gan·ism \ˌmī-krō-ˈòr-gə-ˌniz-əm\ *n* : a living being (as a bacterium) too tiny to be seen by the unaided eye

mi·cro·phone \ˈmī-krə-ˌfōn\ *n* : an instrument for converting sound waves into variations of an electric current for transmitting or recording sound

mi·cro·pho·to·graph \ˌmī-krə-ˈfōt-ə-ˌgraf\ *n* : PHOTOMICROGRAPH

mi·cro·pro·ces·sor \ˌmī-krō-ˈpräs-ˌes-ər\ *n* : a computer processor contained on a microchip

mi·cro·scope \ˈmī-krə-ˌskōp\ *n* : an instrument for making magnified images of minute objects usu. using light — **mi·cros·co·py** \mī-ˈkräs-kə-pē\ *n*

mi·cro·scop·ic \ˌmī-krə-ˈskäp-ik\ *or* **mi·cro·scop·i·cal** \-i-kəl\ *adj* **1** : of, relating to, or involving the use of the microscope **2** : too tiny to be seen without the use of a microscope : very small — **mi·cro·scop·i·cal·ly** \-i-k(ə-)lē\ *adv*

mi·cro·sec·ond \ˌmī-krō-ˈsek-ənd\ *n* : one millionth of a second

mi·cro·state \ˈmī-krō-ˌstāt\ *n* : a nation that is extremely small in area and population

mi·cro·sur·gery \ˌmī-krō-ˈsərj-(ə-)rē\ *n* : minute dissection or manipulation (as by a laser beam) of living structures (as cells) for surgical or experimental purposes — **mi·cro·sur·gi·cal** \-ˈsər-ji-kəl\ *adj*

mi·cro·wave \ˈmī-krə-ˌwāv\ *n* : a radio wave between one millimeter and one meter in wavelength

microwave oven *n* : an oven in which food is cooked by the heat produced from microwave penetration of the food

¹mid \ˈmid\ *adj* : MIDDLE

²mid *abbr* middle

mid·air \ˈmid-ˈaər\ *n* : a point or region in the air well above the ground

mid·day \ˈmid-ˌdā, -ˈdā\ *n* : NOON

mid·den \ˈmid-ᵊn\ *n* : a refuse heap

¹mid·dle \ˈmid-ᵊl\ *adj* **1** : equally distant from the extremes : MEDIAL, CENTRAL **2** : being at neither extreme : INTERMEDIATE **3** *cap* : constituting an intermediate period

²**middle** *n* **1** : a middle part, point, or position **2** : WAIST

middle age *n* : the period of life from about 40 to about 60 — **mid·dle–aged** \ˌmid-ᵊl-ˈājd\ *adj*

Middle Ages *n pl* : the period of European history from about A.D. 500 to about 1500

mid·dle·brow \ˈmid-ᵊl-ˌbrau̇\ *n* : a person who is moderately but not highly cultivated

middle class *n* : a social class holding a position between the upper class and the lower class — **middle-class** *adj*

middle ear *n* : a small membrane-lined cavity of the ear through which sound waves are transmitted by a chain of tiny bones

middle finger *n* : the midmost of the five digits of the hand

mid·dle·man \ˈmid-ᵊl-ˌman\ *n* : INTERMEDIARY; *esp* : one intermediate between the producer of goods and the retailer or consumer

middle–of–the–road *adj* : standing for or following a course of action midway between extremes; *esp* : being neither liberal nor conservative in politics — **mid·dle–of–the–road·er** \-ˈrōd-ər\ *n* — **midd·dle–of–the–road·ism** \-ˈrod-ˌiz-əm\ *n*

middle school *n* : a school usu. including grades 5 to 8 or 6 to 8

mid·dle·weight \ˈmid-ᵊl-ˌwāt\ *n* : one of average weight; *esp* : a boxer weighing more than 147 but not over 160 pounds

mid·dling \ˈmid-liŋ, -lən\ *adj* **1** : of middle, medium, or moderate size, degree, or quality **2** : MEDIOCRE

mid·dy \ˈmid-ē\ *n, pl* **middies** : MIDSHIPMAN

midge \ˈmij\ *n* : a very small fly : GNAT

midg·et \ˈmij-ət\ *n* **1** : a very small person : DWARF **2** : something (as an animal) very small of its kind

midi \ˈmid-ē\ *n* : a calf-length dress, coat, or skirt

mid·land \ˈmid-lənd, -ˌland\ *n* : the interior or central region of a country

mid–life \ˈmid-ˈlīf\ *n* : MIDDLE AGE

mid·most \-ˌmōst\ *adj* : being in or near the exact middle — **midmost** *adv*

mid·night \-ˌnīt\ *n* : 12 o'clock at night

midnight sun *n* : the sun above the horizon at midnight in the arctic or antarctic summer

mid·point \ˈmid-ˌpȯint, -ˈpȯint\ *n* : a point at or near the center or middle

mid·riff \ˈmid-ˌrif\ *n* [ME *midrif*, fr. OE *midhrif*, fr. *midde* mid + *hrif* belly] **1** : DIAPHRAGM 1 **2** : the mid-region of the human torso

mid·ship·man \ˈmid-ˌship-mən, (ˈ)mid-ˈship-mən\ *n* : a student in a naval academy

mid·ships \-ˌships\ *adv* : AMIDSHIPS

midst \ˈmidst\ *n* **1** : the interior or central part or point **2** : a position of proximity to the members of a group ⟨in our ∼⟩ **3** : the condition of being surrounded or beset — **midst** *prep*

mid·stream \ˈmid-ˈstrēm, -ˌstrēm\ *n* : the middle of a stream

mid·sum·mer \-ˈsəm-ər, -ˌsəm-\ *n* **1** : the middle of summer **2** : the summer solstice

mid·town \ˈmid-ˌtau̇n, -ˈtau̇n\ *n* : a central section of a city; *esp* : one situated between sections called *downtown* and *uptown* — **midtown** *adj*

¹**mid·way** \ˈmid-ˌwā, -ˈwā\ *adv* : in the middle of the way or distance

²**mid·way** \-ˌwā\ *n* : an avenue (as at a carnival) for concessions and light amusements

mid·week \-ˌwēk\ *n* : the middle of the week — **mid·week·ly** \-ˌwē-klē, -ˈwē-\ *adj or adv*

mid·wife \ˈmid-ˌwīf\ *n* : a woman who helps other women in childbirth — **mid·wife·ry** \-ˌwī-f(ə-)rē\ *n*

mid·win·ter \ˈmid-ˈwint-ər, -ˌwint-\ *n* **1** : the middle of winter **2** : the winter solstice

mid·year \-ˌyiər\ *n* **1** : the middle of a year **2** : a midyear examination — **midyear** *adj*

mien \ˈmēn\ *n* **1** : air or bearing esp. as expressive of mood or personality : DEMEANOR **2** : APPEARANCE, ASPECT

miff \ˈmif\ *vb* : to put into an ill humor

¹**might** \(ˈ)mīt\ past of MAY — used as an auxiliary to express permission or possibility in the past, a present condition contrary to fact, less probability or possibility than *may,* or as a polite alternative to *may, ought,* or *should*

²**might** \ˈmīt\ *n* : the power, authority,

or resources of an individual or a group

mighty \ˈmīt-ē\ *adj* **might·i·er; -est** **1** : very strong : POWERFUL **2** : GREAT, NOTABLE — **might·i·ly** \ˈmīt-ə-lē\ *adv* — **might·i·ness** \-ē-nəs\ *n* — **mighty** *adv*

mi·gnon·ette \ˌmin-yə-ˈnet\ *n* : a garden plant with spikes of tiny fragrant flowers

mi·graine \ˈmī-ˌgrān\ *n* [F, fr. LL *hemicrania* pain in one side of the head, fr. Gk *hēmikrania*, fr. *hēmi-* half + *kranion* cranium] : a condition marked by recurrent severe headache and often nausea

mi·grant \ˈmī-grənt\ *n* : one that migrates; *esp* : a person who moves in order to find work (as picking crops)

mi·grate \ˈmī-ˌgrāt\ *vb* **mi·grat·ed; mi·grat·ing** **1** : to move from one country or place to another **2** : to pass usu. periodically from one region or climate to another for feeding or breeding — **mi·gra·tion** \mī-ˈgrā-shən\ *n* — **mi·gra·tion·al** \-sh(ə-)nəl\ *adj* — **mi·gra·to·ry** \ˈmī-grə-ˌtōr-ē\ *adj*

mi·ka·do \mə-ˈkäd-ō\ *n, pl* **-dos** : an emperor of Japan

mike \ˈmīk\ *n* : MICROPHONE

¹mil \ˈmil\ *n* **1** : a unit of length equal to ¹⁄₁₀₀₀ inch **2** — see *pound* at MONEY table

²mil *abbr* military

milch \ˈmilk, ˈmilch\ *adj* : giving milk ⟨∼ cow⟩

mild \ˈmīld\ *adj* **1** : gentle in nature or behavior **2** : moderate in action or effect **3** : TEMPERATE **syn** easy, complaisant, amiable, lenient — **mild·ly** *adv* — **mild·ness** *n*

mil·dew \ˈmil-ˌd(y)ü\ *n* : a superficial usu. whitish growth produced on organic matter and on plants by a fungus; *also* : a fungus producing this growth — **mildew** *vb*

mile \ˈmīl\ *n* [ME, fr. OE *mīl*, fr. L *milia* miles, fr. *milia passuum*, lit., thousands of paces] **1** — see WEIGHT table **2** : NAUTICAL MILE

mile·age \ˈmī-lij\ *n* **1** : an allowance for traveling expenses at a certain rate per mile **2** : distance in miles traveled (as in a day) **3** : the amount of service yielded (as by a tire) expressed in terms of miles of travel **4** : the average number of miles a car will travel on a gallon of gasoline

mile·post \ˈmīl-ˌpōst\ *n* : a post indicating the distance in miles from a given point

mile·stone \ˈmīl-ˌstōn\ *n* **1** : a stone serving as a milepost **2** : a significant point in development

mi·lieu \mēl-ˈyə(r), -ˈyü\ *n, pl* **mi·lieus** *or* **mi·lieux** \-ˈyə(r)(z), -ˈyüz\ [F] : ENVIRONMENT, SETTING

mil·i·tant \ˈmil-ə-tənt\ *adj* **1** : engaged in warfare **2** : aggressively active esp. in a cause — **mil·i·tance** \-təns\ *n* — **mil·i·tan·cy** \-tən-sē\ *n* — **militant** *n* — **mil·i·tant·ly** *adv*

mil·i·ta·rism \ˈmil-ə-tə-ˌriz-əm\ *n* **1** : predominance of the military class or its ideals **2** : a policy of aggressive military preparedness — **mil·i·ta·rist** \-rəst\ *n* — **mil·i·ta·ris·tic** \ˌmil-ə-tə-ˈris-tik\ *adj*

mil·i·ta·rize \ˈmil-ə-tə-ˌrīz\ *vb* **-rized; -riz·ing** **1** : to equip with military forces and defenses **2** : to give a military character to

¹mil·i·tary \ˈmil-ə-ˌter-ē\ *adj* **1** : of or relating to soldiers, arms, war, or the army **2** : performed by armed forces; *also* : supported by armed force **syn** martial, warlike — **mil·i·tar·i·ly** \ˌmil-ə-ˈter-ə-lē\ *adv*

²military *n, pl* **military** *also* **mil·i·tar·ies** **1** : the military, naval, and air forces of a nation **2** : military persons

mil·i·tate \ˈmil-ə-ˌtāt\ *vb* **-tat·ed; -tat·ing** : to have weight or effect

mi·li·tia \mə-ˈlish-ə\ *n* : a part of the organized armed forces of a country liable to call only in emergency — **mi·li·tia·man** \-mən\ *n*

¹milk \ˈmilk\ *n* **1** : a nutritive usu. whitish fluid secreted by female mammals for feeding their young **2** : a milklike liquid (as a plant juice) — **milk·i·ness** \-ē-nəs\ *n* — **milky** *adj*

²milk *vb* **1** : to draw off the milk of ⟨∼ a cow⟩ **2** : to draw something from as if by milking — **milk·er** *n*

milk·maid \ˈmilk-ˌmād\ *n* : DAIRYMAID

milk·man \-ˌman, -mən\ *n* : a person who sells or delivers milk

milk of magnesia : a milk-white mixture of hydroxide of magnesium and water used as an antacid and laxative

milk shake *n* : a thoroughly blended

drink made of milk, a flavoring syrup, and often ice cream

milk·sop \'milk-ˌsäp\ *n* : an unmanly man

milk·weed \-ˌwēd\ *n* : any of a genus of coarse herbs with milky juice and clustered flowers

Milky Way *n* **1** : a broad irregular band of light that stretches across the sky and is caused by the light of a very great number of faint stars **2** : MILKY WAY GALAXY

Milky Way galaxy *n* : the galaxy of which the sun is a member and which includes the stars that comprise the Milky Way

¹**mill** \'mil\ *n* **1** : a building with machinery for grinding grain into flour **2** : a machine used in processing (as by grinding, stamping, cutting, or finishing) raw material **3** : FACTORY

²**mill** *vb* **1** : to process in a mill **2** : to move in a circle or in an eddying mass

³**mill** *n* : one tenth of a cent

mill·age \'mil-ij\ *n* : a rate (as of taxation) expressed in mills

mill·dam \'mil-ˌdam\ *n* : a dam to make a millpond; *also* : MILLPOND

mil·len·ni·um \mə-'len-ē-əm\ *n, pl* **-nia** \-ē-ə\ *or* **-niums 1** : a period of 1000 years; *also* : a 1000th anniversary or its celebration **2** : the 1000 years mentioned in Revelation 20 when holiness is to prevail and Christ is to reign on earth **3** : a period of great happiness or perfect government

mill·er \'mil-ər\ *n* **1** : one that operates a mill and esp. a flour mill **2** : any of various moths having powdery wings

mil·let \'mil-ət\ *n* : any of several small-seeded cereal and forage grasses cultivated for grain or hay; *also* : the grain of a millet

mil·li·am·pere \ˌmil-ē-'am-ˌpiər\ *n* : one thousandth of an ampere

mil·liard \'mil-ˌyärd, 'mil-ē-ˌärd\ *n, Brit* : a thousand millions

mil·li·bar \'mil-ə-ˌbär\ *n* : a unit of atmospheric pressure

mil·li·gram \'mil-ə-ˌgram\ *n* — see METRIC SYSTEM table

mil·li·li·ter \-ˌlēt-ər\ *n* — see METRIC SYSTEM table

mil·lime \mə-'lēm\ *n* — see *dinar* at MONEY table

mil·li·me·ter \'mil-ə-ˌmēt-ər\ *n* — see METRIC SYSTEM table

mil·li·ner \'mil-ə-nər\ *n* [fr. *Milan*, Italy; fr. the importation of women's finery from Italy in the 16th century] : one who designs, makes, trims, or sells women's hats

mil·li·nery \'mil-ə-ˌner-ē\ *n* **1** : women's apparel for the head **2** : the business or work of a milliner

mill·ing \'mil-iŋ\ *n* : a corrugated edge on a coin

mil·lion \'mil-yən\ *n, pl* **millions** *or* **million** : a thousand thousands — **million** *adj* — **mil·lionth** \-yənth\ *adj or n*

mil·lion·aire \ˌmil-yə-'ner, 'mil-yə-ˌner\ *n* : one whose wealth is estimated at a million or more (as of dollars or pounds)

mil·li·pede \'mil-ə-ˌpēd\ *n* : any of a class of arthropods related to the centipedes and having a long segmented body with a hard covering, two pairs of legs on most segments, and no poison fangs

mil·li·sec·ond \'mil-ə-ˌsek-ənd\ *n* : one thousandth of a second

mil·li·volt \-ˌvōlt\ *n* : one thousandth of a volt

mill·pond \'mil-ˌpänd\ *n* : a pond made by damming a stream to produce a fall of water for operating a mill

mill·race \-ˌrās\ *n* : a canal in which water flows to and from a mill wheel

mill·stone \-ˌstōn\ *n* : either of two round flat stones used for grinding grain

mill·stream \-ˌstrēm\ *n* : a stream whose flow is used to run a mill; *also* : the stream in a millrace

mill wheel *n* : a waterwheel that drives a mill

mill·wright \'mil-ˌrīt\ *n* : one whose occupation is planning and building mills or setting up their machinery

milt \'milt\ *n* : the male reproductive glands of fishes when filled with secretion; *also* : the secretion itself

mime \'mīm, 'mēm\ *n* **1** : MIMIC **2** : the art of characterization or of narration by body movement; *also* : a performance of mime — **mime** *vb*

mim·eo·graph \'mim-ē-ə-ˌgraf\ *n* : a machine for making many copies by means of a stencil through which ink is pressed — **mimeograph** *vb*

mi·me·sis \mə-'mē-səs, mī-\ *n* : IMITATION, MIMICRY

mi·met·ic \-'met-ik\ *adj* **1** : IMITATIVE **2** : relating to, characterized by, or exhibiting mimicry

¹**mim·ic** \'mim-ik\ *n* : one that mimics

²**mimic** *vb* **mim·icked** \-ikt\; **mim·ick·ing** **1** : to imitate closely **2** : to ridicule by imitation **3** : to resemble by biological mimicry

mim·ic·ry \'mim-i-krē\ *n, pl* **-ries 1** : an instance of mimicking **2** : a superficial resemblance of one organism to another or to natural objects among which it lives that gives it an advantage (as protection from predation)

mi·mo·sa \mə-'mō-sə, mī-, -zə\ *n* : any of various leguminous trees, shrubs, and herbs of warm regions with globular heads of small white or pink flowers

min *abbr* **1** minim **2** minimum **3** mining **4** minister **5** minor **6** minute

min·a·ret \ˌmin-ə-'ret\ *n* [F, fr. Turk *minare*, fr. Ar *manārah* lighthouse] : a slender lofty tower attached to a mosque

mi·na·to·ry \'min-ə-ˌtōr-ē, 'mī-nə-\ *adj* : THREATENING, MENACING

mince \'mins\ *vb* **minced; minc·ing 1** : to cut into small pieces **2** : to restrain (words) within the bounds of decorum **3** : to walk in a prim affected manner — **minc·ing** *adj*

mince·meat \'mins-ˌmēt\ *n* : a finely chopped mixture esp. of raisins, apples, spices, and often meat used as a filling for a pie

mince pie *n* : a pie filled with mincemeat

¹**mind** \'mīnd\ *n* **1** : MEMORY **2** : the part of an individual that feels, perceives, thinks, wills, and esp. reasons **3** : INTENTION, DESIRE **4** : normal mental condition **5** : OPINION, VIEW **6** : mental qualities of a person or group **7** : intellectual ability

²**mind** *vb* **1** *chiefly dial* : REMEMBER **2** : to attend to ⟨~ your own business⟩ **3** : HEED, OBEY **4** : to be concerned about : WORRY; *also* : DISLIKE **5** : to be careful or cautious **6** : to take charge of **7** : to regard with attention

mind–bend·ing \'mīn(d)-ˌben-diŋ\ *adj* : MIND-BLOWING

mind–blow·ing \-ˌblō-iŋ\ *adj* : PSYCHEDELIC; *also* : MIND-BOGGLING

mind–bog·gling \-ˌbäg-(ə-)liŋ\ *adj* : mentally or emotionally exciting

mind·ed \'mīn-dəd\ *adj* **1** : having a mind of a specified kind — usu. used in combination ⟨narrow-*minded*⟩ **2** : INCLINED, DISPOSED

mind·ful \'mīnd-fəl\ *adj* : bearing in mind : AWARE — **mind·ful·ly** \-ē\ *adv* — **mind·ful·ness** *n*

mind·less \'mīn-dləs\ *adj* **1** : destitute of mind or consciousness; *esp* : UNINTELLIGENT **2** : UNTHINKING, HEEDLESS — **mind·less·ly** *adv* — **mind·less·ness** *n*

¹**mine** \'mīn\ *pron* : one or the ones belonging to me

²**mine** \'mīn\ *n* **1** : an excavation in the earth from which mineral substances are taken; *also* : an ore deposit **2** : a subterranean passage under an enemy position; *also* : an encased explosive for destroying enemy personnel, vehicles, or ships **3** : a rich source of supply

³**mine** \'mīn\ *vb* **mined; min·ing 1** : to dig a mine **2** : UNDERMINE **3** : to get ore from the earth **4** : to place military mines in — **min·er** *n*

mine·lay·er \'mīn-ˌlā-ər\ *n* : a naval vessel for laying underwater mines

min·er·al \'min(-ə)-rəl\ *n* **1** : a solid homogeneous crystalline substance (as diamond, gold, or quartz) not of animal or vegetable origin **2** : any of various naturally occurring homogeneous substances (as coal, salt, water, or gas) obtained usu. from the ground **3** *pl, Brit* : MINERAL WATER — **mineral** *adj*

min·er·al·ize \'min-(ə-)rə-ˌlīz\ *vb* **-ized; -iz·ing 1** : to transform (a metal) into an ore **2** : to impregnate or supply with minerals

min·er·al·o·gy \ˌmin-ə-'räl-ə-jē, -'ral-\ *n* : a science dealing with minerals — **min·er·al·og·i·cal** \ˌmin(-ə)-rə-'läj-i-kəl\ *adj* — **min·er·al·o·gist** \ˌmin-ə-'räl-ə-jəst, -'ral-\ *n*

mineral oil *n* : an oil of mineral origin; *esp* : a refined petroleum oil used as a laxative

mineral water *n* : water infused with mineral salts or gases

min•e•stro•ne \ˌmin-ə-ˈstrō-nē, -ˈstrōn\ *n* [It, fr. *minestra,* fr. *minestrare* to serve, dish up, fr. L *ministrare,* fr. *minister* servant] : a rich thick vegetable soup

mine•sweep•er \ˈmīn-ˌswē-pər\ *n* : a warship designed for removing or neutralizing underwater mines

min•gle \ˈmiŋ-gəl\ *vb* **min•gled; min•gling** \-g(ə-)liŋ\ **1** : to bring or combine together : MIX **2** : CONCOCT

ming tree \ˈmiŋ-\ *n* : a dwarfed usu. evergreen tree grown in a pot; *also* : an artificial imitation of this made from plant materials

mini \ˈmin-ē\ *n, pl* **min•is** : something small of its kind — **mini** *adj*

mini- *comb form* : miniature : of small dimensions

min•ia•ture \ˈmin-ē-ə-ˌchùr, ˈmin-i-ˌchùr, -chər\ *n* [It *miniatura* art of illuminating a manuscript, fr. ML, fr. L *miniare* to color with red lead, fr. *minium* red lead] **1** : a copy on a much reduced scale; *also* : something small of its kind **2** : a small painting (as on ivory or metal) — **miniature** *adj* — **min•ia•tur•ist** \-ˌchùr-əst, -chər-\ *n*

min•ia•tur•ize \ˈmin-ē-ə-ˌchə-ˌrīz, ˈmin-i-\ *vb* **-ized; iz•ing** : to design or construct in small size — **min•ia•tur•iza•tion** \ˌmin-ē-ə-ˌchùr-ə-ˈzā-shən, ˌmin-i-, -chər-\ *n*

mini•bike \ˈmin-ē-ˌbīk\ *n* : a small one-passenger motorcycle

mini•bus \-ˌbəs\ *n* : a small bus

mini•com•put•er \-kəm-ˌpyüt-ər\ *n* : a computer intermediate between a mainframe and a microcomputer in size and speed

min•im \ˈmin-əm\ *n* — see WEIGHT table

min•i•mal \ˈmin-ə-məl\ *adj* **1** : relating to or being a minimum : LEAST **2** : of or relating to minimal art — **min•i•mal•ly** \-ē\ *adv*

minimal art *n* : an impersonal style of abstract art and esp. sculpture consisting primarily of simple geometric forms — **minimal artist** *n*

min•i•mal•ist \ˈmin-ə-mə-ləst\ *n* : MINIMAL ARTIST

min•i•mize \ˈmin-ə-ˌmīz\ *vb* **-mized; -miz•ing** **1** : to reduce to a minimum **2** : to estimate at a minimum; *also* : BELITTLE **syn** depreciate, decry, disparage

min•i•mum \ˈmin-ə-məm\ *n, pl* **-ma** \-mə\ *or* **-mums** **1** : the least quantity assignable, admissible, or possible **2** : the least of a set of numbers **3** : the lowest degree or amount of variation (as of temperature) reached or recorded — **minimum** *adj*

min•ion \ˈmin-yən\ *n* [MF *mignon* darling] **1** : a servile dependent **2** : one highly favored **3** : a subordinate official

min•is•cule \ˈmin-əs-ˌkyül\ var of MINUSCULE

mini•se•ries \ˈmin-ē-ˌsir-ēz\ *n* : a motion picture made for television and presented in several parts

mini•skirt \-ˌskərt\ *n* : a skirt with the hemline several inches above the knee

mini•state \-ˌstāt\ *n* : MICROSTATE

¹min•is•ter \ˈmin-ə-stər\ *n* **1** : AGENT **2** : CLERGYMAN; *esp* : a Protestant clergyman **3** : a high officer of state who heads a division of governmental activities **4** : a diplomatic representative to a foreign state — **min•is•te•ri•al** \ˌmin-ə-ˈstir-ē-əl\ *adj*

²minister *vb* **min•is•tered; min•is•ter•ing** \-st(ə-)riŋ\ **1** : to perform the functions of a minister of religion **2** : to give aid — **min•is•tra•tion** \ˌmin-ə-ˈstrā-shən\ *n*

min•is•trant \ˈmin-ə-strənt\ *adj, archaic* : performing service as a minister — **ministrant** *n*

min•is•try \ˈmin-ə-strē\ *n, pl* **-tries** **1** : MINISTRATION **2** : the office, duties, or functions of a minister; *also* : his period of service or office **3** : CLERGY **4** : AGENCY **5** *often cap* : the body of ministers governing a nation or state; *also* : a government department headed by a minister

mink \ˈmiŋk\ *n, pl* **mink** *or* **minks** : a slender mammal resembling the related weasels; *also* : its soft lustrous typically dark brown fur

Minn *abbr* Minnesota

min•ne•sing•er \ˈmin-i-ˌsiŋ-ər, ˈmin-ə-ˌziŋ-\ *n* [G, fr. Middle High German, fr. *minne* love + *singer*] : one of a class of German lyric poets and musicians of the 12th to the 14th centuries

min•now \ˈmin-ō\ *n, pl* **minnows** *also* **minnow** : any of numerous small freshwater fishes

¹**mi·nor** \'mī-nər\ *adj* **1** : inferior in importance, size, or degree **2** : not having reached majority **3** : having the third, sixth, and sometimes the seventh degrees lowered by a half step ⟨∼ scale⟩; *also* : based on a minor scale ⟨∼ key⟩

²**minor** *n* **1** : a person who has not attained majority **2** : a subject of academic study chosen as a secondary field of specialization

³**minor** *vb* : to pursue an academic minor

mi·nor·i·ty \mə-'nȯr-ət-ē, mī-\ *n, pl* **-ties 1** : the period or state of being a minor **2** : the smaller in number of two groups; *esp* : a group having less than the number of votes necessary for control **3** : a part of a population differing from others (as in race or religion); *also* : a member of a minority

min·ster \'min-stər\ *n* **1** : a church attached to a monastery **2** : a large or important church

min·strel \'min-strəl\ *n* **1** : a medieval singer of verses; *also* : MUSICIAN, POET **2** : one of a group of performers in a program usu. of black American songs, jokes, and impersonations — **min·strel·sy** \-sē\ *n*

¹**mint** \'mint\ *n* **1** : a place where coins are made **2** : a vast sum — **mint** *vb* — **mint·age** \-ij\ *n* — **mint·er** *n*

²**mint** *adj* : unmarred as if fresh from a mint ⟨∼ coins⟩

³**mint** *n* : any of a large family of square-stemmed herbs and shrubs; *esp* : one (as spearmint) with fragrant aromatic foliage used in flavoring — **minty** *adj*

min·u·end \'min-yə-ˌwend\ *n* : a number from which another is to be subtracted

min·u·et \ˌmin-yə-'wet\ *n* : a slow graceful dance

¹**mi·nus** \'mī-nəs\ *prep* **1** : diminished by : LESS ⟨7 ∼ 3 equals 4⟩ **2** : LACKING, WITHOUT ⟨∼ his hat⟩

²**minus** *n* : a negative quantity or quality

³**minus** *adj* **1** : requiring subtraction **2** : algebraically negative ⟨∼ quantity⟩ **3** : having negative qualities

¹**mi·nus·cule** \'min-əs-ˌkyül\ *n* : a lower-case letter

²**minuscule** *adj* : very small

minus sign *n* : a sign — used in math-ematics to indicate subtraction or a negative quantity

¹**min·ute** \'min-ət\ *n* **1** : the 60th part of an hour or of a degree **2** : a short space of time **3** *pl* : the official record of the proceedings of a meeting

²**mi·nute** \mī-'n(y)üt, mə-\ *adj* **mi·nut·er; -est 1** : very small **2** : of little importance : TRIFLING **3** : marked by close attention to details **syn** diminutive, tiny, miniature, wee — **mi·nute·ly** *adv* — **mi·nute·ness** *n*

min·ute·man \'min-ət-ˌman\ *n* : a member of a group of armed men pledged to take the field at a minute's notice during and immediately before the American Revolution

mi·nu·tia \mə-'n(y)ü-sh(ē-)ə, mī-\ *n, pl* **-ti·ae** \-shē-ˌē\ [L] : a minute or minor detail — usu. used in pl.

minx \'miŋks\ *n* : a pert girl

Mio·cene \'mī-ə-ˌsēn\ *adj* : of, relating to, or being the epoch of the Tertiary between the Oligocene and the Pliocene — **Miocene** *n*

mir·a·cle \'mir-i-kəl\ *n* **1** : an extraordinary event manifesting a supernatural work of God **2** : an unusual event, thing, or accomplishment : WONDER, MARVEL — **mi·rac·u·lous** \mə-'rak-yə-ləs\ *adj* — **mi·rac·u·lous·ly** *adv*

miracle drug *n* : a usu. newly discovered drug capable of producing a marked and favorable change in a patient's condition

mi·rage \mə-'räzh\ *n* **1** : an illusion visible at sea, in deserts, or above a hot pavement of some distant object often in distorted form as a result of atmospheric conditions **2** : something illusory and unattainable

¹**mire** \'mī(ə)r\ *n* : heavy and often deep mud or slush — **miry** *adj*

²**mire** *vb* **mired; mir·ing** : to stick or sink in or as if in mire

¹**mir·ror** \'mir-ər\ *n* **1** : a polished or smooth substance (as of glass) that forms images by reflection **2** : a true representation; *also* : MODEL

²**mirror** *vb* : to reflect in or as if in a mirror

mirth \'mərth\ *n* : gladness or gaiety accompanied with laughter **syn** glee, jollity, hilarity, merriment — **mirth·ful** \-fəl\ *adj* — **mirth·ful·ly** \-ē\ *adv* — **mirth·ful·ness** *n* — **mirth·less** *adj*

MIRV \\'mərv\ *n* [*m*ultiple *i*ndependently targeted *r*eentry *v*ehicle] : an ICBM with multiple warheads that have different targets — **MIRV** *vb*

mis·ad·ven·ture \\,mis-əd-'ven-chər\ *n* : MISFORTUNE, MISHAP

mis·aligned \\,mis-ə-'līnd\ *adj* : not properly aligned — **mis·align·ment** \\-'līn-mənt\ *n*

mis·al·li·ance \\,mis-ə-'lī-əns\ *n* : MÉSALLIANCE; *also* : a marriage between persons unsuited to each other

mis·al·lo·ca·tion \\,mis-,al-ə-'kā-shən\ *n* : faulty or improper allocation

mis·an·thrope \\'mis-ᵊn-,thrōp\ *n* : one who hates mankind — **mis·an·throp·ic** \\,mis-ᵊn-'thräp-ik\ *adj* — **mis·an·throp·i·cal·ly** \\-i-k(ə-)lē\ *adv* — **mis·an·thro·py** \\mis-'an-thrə-pē\ *n*

mis·ap·ply \\,mis-ə-'plī\ *vb* : to apply wrongly — **mis·ap·pli·ca·tion** \\,mis-,ap-lə-'kā-shən\ *n*

mis·ap·pre·hend \\,mis-,ap-ri-'hend\ *vb* : MISUNDERSTAND — **mis·ap·pre·hen·sion** \\-'hen-chən\ *n*

mis·ap·pro·pri·ate \\,mis-ə-'prō-prē-,āt\ *vb* : to appropriate wrongly; *esp* : to take dishonestly for one's own use — **mis·ap·pro·pri·a·tion** \\-,prō-prē-'ā-shən\ *n*

mis·be·got·ten \\-bi-'gät-ᵊn\ *adj* : ILLEGITIMATE

mis·be·have \\,mis-bi-'hāv\ *vb* : to behave improperly — **mis·be·hav·er** *n* — **mis·be·hav·ior** \\-'hā-vyər\ *n*

mis·be·liev·er \\-bə-'lē-vər\ *n* : one who holds a false or unorthodox belief

mis·brand \\mis-'brand\ *vb* : to brand falsely or in a misleading manner

misc *abbr* miscellaneous

mis·cal·cu·late \\mis-'kal-kyə-,lāt\ *vb* : to calculate wrongly — **mis·cal·cu·la·tion** \\,mis-,kal-kyə-'lā-shən\ *n*

mis·call \\mis-'kȯl\ *vb* : MISNAME

mis·car·riage \\-'kar-ij\ *n* 1 : a corrupt or incompetent administration ⟨∼ of justice⟩ 2 : expulsion of a fetus before it is capable of independent life

mis·car·ry \\-'kar-ē\ *vb* 1 : to give birth prematurely and esp. before the fetus is capable of living independently 2 : to go wrong; *also* : to be unsuccessful

mis·ce·ge·na·tion \\mis-,ej-ə-'nā-shən, ,mis-i-jə-'nā-\ *n* [L *miscēre* to mix + *genus* race] : a mixture of races; *esp* : marriage or cohabitation between a white person and a member of another race

mis·cel·la·neous \\,mis-ə-'lā-nē-əs\ *adj* 1 : consisting of diverse things or members; *also* : having various traits 2 : dealing with or interested in diverse subjects — **mis·cel·la·neous·ly** *adv* — **mis·cel·la·neous·ness** *n*

mis·cel·la·ny \\'mis-ə-,lā-nē\ *n, pl* **-nies** 1 : a collection of writings on various subjects 2 : HODGEPODGE

mis·chance \\mis'chans\ *n* : bad luck; *also* : MISHAP

mis·chief \\'mis-chəf\ *n* 1 : injury caused by a human agency 2 : a source of harm or irritation 3 : action that annoys; *also* : MISCHIEVOUSNESS

mis·chie·vous \\'mis-chə-vəs\ *adj* 1 : HARMFUL, INJURIOUS 2 : causing annoyance or minor injury 3 : irresponsibly playful — **mis·chie·vous·ly** *adv* — **mis·chie·vous·ness** *n*

mis·ci·ble \\'mis-ə-bəl\ *adj* : capable of being mixed or dissolved

mis·com·mu·ni·ca·tion \\,mis-kə-,myü-nə-'kā-shən\ *n* : failure to communicate clearly

mis·con·ceive \\,mis-kən-'sēv\ *vb* : to interpret incorrectly — **mis·con·cep·tion** \\-'sep-shən\ *n*

mis·con·duct \\mis-'kän-(,)dəkt\ *n* 1 : MISMANAGEMENT 2 : intentional wrongdoing 3 : improper behavior

mis·con·strue \\,mis-kən-'strü\ *vb* : MISINTERPRET — **mis·con·struc·tion** \\-'strək-shən\ *n*

mis·count \\mis-'kaunt\ *vb* : to count incorrectly : MISCALCULATE

mis·cre·ant \\'mis-krē-ənt\ *n* : one who behaves criminally or viciously — **miscreant** *adj*

mis·cue \\mis-'kyü\ *n* : MISTAKE, ERROR — **miscue** *vb*

mis·deed \\mis-'dēd\ *n* : a wrong deed

mis·de·mean·or \\,mis-di-'mē-nər\ *n* 1 : a crime less serious than a felony 2 : MISDEED

mis·di·rect \\,mis-də-'rekt, -dī-\ *vb* : to give a wrong direction to — **mis·di·rec·tion** \\-'rek-shən\ *n*

mis·do·ing \\mis-'dü-iŋ\ *n* : WRONGDOING — **mis·do·er** \\-'dü-ər\ *n*

mise–en–scène \\,mē-,zän-'sen, -'sän\ *n, pl* **mise–en–scènes** \\-'sen(z), -'sän(z)\ [F] 1 : the arrangement of the scenery, property, and actors on a stage **2** : SETTING; *also* : ENVIRONMENT

mi·ser \'mī-zər\ *n* [L *miser* miserable] : a person who hoards his money — **mi·ser·li·ness** \-lē-nəs\ *n* — **mi·ser·ly** *adj*

mis·er·a·ble \'miz-(ə-)rə-bəl, 'miz-ər-bəl\ *adj* **1** : wretchedly deficient; *also* : causing extreme discomfort **2** : extremely poor **3** : SHAMEFUL — **mis·er·a·ble·ness** *n* — **mis·er·a·bly** \-blē\ *adv*

mis·ery \'miz-(ə-)rē\ *n, pl* **-er·ies 1** : suffering and want caused by poverty or affliction **2** : a cause of suffering or discomfort **3** : emotional distress

mis·fea·sance \mis-'fēz-³ns\ *n* : the performance of a lawful action in an illegal or improper manner

mis·file \-'fīl\ *vb* : to file in an inappropriate place

mis·fire \-'fī(ə)r\ *vb* **1** : to fail to fire **2** : to miss an intended effect — **misfire** *n*

mis·fit \'mis-ˌfit, mis-'fit\ *n* **1** : an imperfect fit **2** : a person poorly adjusted to his environment

mis·for·tune \mis-'fȯr-chən\ *n* **1** : bad fortune : ill luck **2** : an unfortunate condition or event

mis·giv·ing \-'giv-iŋ\ *n* : a feeling of doubt or suspicion esp. concerning a future event

mis·gov·ern \-'gəv-ərn\ *vb* : to govern badly — **mis·gov·ern·ment** \-'gəv-ər(n)-mənt\ *n*

mis·guid·ance \mis-'gīd-³ns\ *n* : faulty guidance — **mis·guide** \-'gīd\ *vb* — **mis·guid·ed·ly** \-'gīd-əd-lē\ *adv*

mis·han·dle \-'han-d³l\ *vb* **1** : MALTREAT **2** : to manage wrongly

mis·hap \'mis-ˌhap\ *n* : an unfortunate accident

mish·mash \'mish-ˌmash, -ˌmäsh\ *n* : HODGEPODGE, JUMBLE

mis·in·form \ˌmis-³n-'fȯrm\ *vb* : to give false or misleading information to — **mis·in·for·ma·tion** \ˌmis-ˌin-fər-'mā-shən\ *n*

mis·in·ter·pret \ˌmis-³n-'tər-prət\ *vb* : to understand or explain wrongly — **mis·in·ter·pre·ta·tion** \-ˌtər-prə-'tā-shən\ *n*

mis·judge \mis-'jəj\ *vb* **1** : to estimate wrongly **2** : to have an unjust opinion of — **mis·judg·ment** \mis-'jəj-mənt\ *n*

mis·la·bel \-'lā-bəl\ *vb* : to label incorrectly or falsely

mis·lay \mis-'lā\ *vb* **-laid** \-'lād\; **-lay·ing** : MISPLACE, LOSE

mis·lead \mis-'lēd\ *vb* **-led** \-'led\; **-lead·ing** : to lead in a wrong direction or into a mistaken action or belief — **mis·lead·ing·ly** *adv*

mis·like \-'līk\ *vb* : DISLIKE — **mis·like** *n*

mis·man·age \-'man-ij\ *vb* : to manage badly — **mis·man·age·ment** *n*

mis·match \-'mach\ *vb* : to match unsuitably or badly — **mis·match** \mis-'mach, 'mis-ˌmach\ *n*

mis·name \-'nām\ *vb* : to name incorrectly : MISCALL

mis·no·mer \mis-'nō-mər\ *n* : a wrong name or designation

mi·sog·y·nist \mə-'säj-ə-nəst\ *n* : one who hates women — **mi·sog·y·nis·tic** \mə-ˌsäj-ə-'nis-tik\ *adj* — **mi·sog·y·ny** \mə-'säj-ə-nē\ *n*

mis·ori·ent \mis-'ōr-ē-ˌent\ *vb* : to orient improperly or incorrectly — **mis·ori·en·ta·tion** \mis-ˌōr-ē-ən-'tā-shən\ *n*

mis·place \-'plās\ *vb* **1** : to put in a wrong place; *also* : MISLAY **2** : to set on a wrong object ⟨~ trust⟩

mis·play \-'plā\ *n* : a wrong or unskillful play — **mis·play** \mis-'plā, 'mis-ˌplā\ *vb*

mis·print \mis-'print\ *vb* : to print incorrectly — **mis·print** \'mis-ˌprint, mis-'print\ *n*

mis·pro·nounce \ˌmis-prə-'naůns\ *vb* : to pronounce incorrectly — **mis·pro·nun·ci·a·tion** \-prə-ˌnən-sē-'ā-shən\ *n*

mis·quote \mis-'kwōt\ *vb* : to quote incorrectly — **mis·quo·ta·tion** \ˌmis-kwō-'tā-shən\ *n*

mis·read \-'rēd\ *vb* **-read** \-'red\; **-read·ing** \-'rēd-iŋ\ : to read or interpret incorrectly

mis·rep·re·sent \ˌmis-ˌrep-ri-'zent\ *vb* : to represent falsely or unfairly — **mis·rep·re·sen·ta·tion** \-ˌzen-'tā-shən\ *n*

¹mis·rule \mis-'rül\ *vb* : MISGOVERN

²mis·rule *n* **1** : MISGOVERNMENT **2** : DISORDER

¹miss \'mis\ *vb* **1** : to fail to hit, reach, or contact **2** : to feel the absence of **3** : to fail to obtain **4** : AVOID ⟨just ~ed hitting the other car⟩ **5** : OMIT **6** : to fail to understand **7** : to fail to perform or attend; *also* : MISFIRE

²**miss** *n* **1** : a failure to hit or to attain a result **2** : MISFIRE

³**miss** *n* **1** *cap* — used as a title prefixed to the name of an unmarried woman or girl **2** : a young unmarried woman or girl

Miss *abbr* Mississippi

mis·sal \'mis-əl\ *n* : a book containing all that is said or sung at mass during the entire year

mis·send \mis-'send\ *vb* : to send incorrectly ⟨*missent* mail⟩

mis·shap·en \-'shā-pən\ *adj* : badly shaped : having an ugly shape

mis·sile \'mis-əl\ *n* [L, fr. neut. of *missilis* capable of being thrown, fr. *mittere* to let go, send] : an object (as a stone, bullet, or rocket) thrown or projected usu. so as to strike a target

mis·sile·ry *also* **mis·sil·ry** \'mis-əl-rē\ *n* **1** : MISSILES **2** : the science of the making and use of guided missiles

miss·ing \'mis-iŋ\ *adj* : ABSENT; *also* : LOST

mis·sion \'mish-ən\ *n* **1** : a group of missionaries; *also* : a place where missionaries work **2** : a group of envoys to a foreign country; *also* : a team of specialists or cultural leaders sent to a foreign country **3** : TASK

¹**mis·sion·ary** \'mish-ə-ˌner-ē\ *adj* : of, relating to, or engaged in church missions

²**missionary** *n, pl* **-ar·ies** : a person commissioned by a church to propagate its faith or carry on humanitarian work

mis·sion·er \'mish-(ə-)nər\ *n* : MISSIONARY

Mis·sis·sip·pi·an \ˌmis-ə-'sip-ē-ən\ *adj* : of, relating to, or being the period of the Paleozoic era between the Devonian and the Pennsylvanian — **Mississippian** *n*

mis·sive \'mis-iv\ *n* : LETTER

mis·spell \mis-'spel\ *vb* : to spell incorrectly — **mis·spell·ing** *n*

mis·spend \mis-'spend\ *vb* **-spent** \-'spent\; **-spend·ing** : WASTE, SQUANDER ⟨a *misspent* youth⟩

mis·state \-'stāt\ *vb* : to state incorrectly — **mis·state·ment** *n*

mis·step \-'step\ *n* **1** : a wrong step **2** : MISTAKE, BLUNDER

mist \'mist\ *n* **1** : water in the form of particles suspended or falling in the air **2** : something that dims or obscures

mis·tak·able \mə-'stā-kə-bəl\ *adj* : capable of being misunderstood or mistaken

mis·take \mə-'stāk\ *n* **1** : a misunderstanding of the meaning or implication of something **2** : a wrong action or statement : ERROR — **mistake** *vb*

mis·tak·en \-'stā-kən\ *adj* **1** : MISUNDERSTOOD **2** : having a wrong opinion or incorrect information **3** : ERRONEOUS — **mis·tak·en·ly** *adv*

mis·ter \'mis-tər\ *n* **1** *cap* — used sometimes instead of *Mr.* **2** : SIR — used without a name in addressing a man

mis·tle·toe \'mis-əl-ˌtō\ *n* : a parasitic green plant with yellowish flowers and waxy white berries that grows on trees

mis·tral \'mis-trəl, mi-'sträl\ *n* [F, fr. Provençal, fr. *mistral* masterful, fr. L *magistralis,* fr. *magister* master] : a strong cold dry northerly wind of southern Europe

mis·treat \mis-'trēt\ *vb* : to treat badly : ABUSE — **mis·treat·ment** *n*

mis·tress \'mis-trəs\ *n* **1** : a woman who has power, authority, or ownership ⟨~ of the house⟩ **2** : a country or state having supremacy ⟨~ of the seas⟩ **3** : a woman with whom a man has sexual relations outside of marriage; *also, archaic* : SWEETHEART **4** — used archaically as a title prefixed to the name of a married or unmarried woman

mis·tri·al \'mis-ˌtrīl\ *n* : a trial that has no legal effect (as by reason of an error)

¹**mis·trust** \mis-'trəst\ *n* : a lack of confidence : DISTRUST — **mis·trust·ful** \-fəl\ *adj* — **mis·trust·ful·ly** \-ē\ *adv* — **mis·trust·ful·ness** *n*

²**mistrust** *vb* : to have no trust or confidence in : SUSPECT

misty \'mis-tē\ *adj* **mist·i·er; -est** : obscured by or as if by mist : INDISTINCT — **mist·i·ly** \'mis-tə-lē\ *adv* — **mist·i·ness** \-tē-nəs\ *n*

mis·un·der·stand \ˌmis-ˌən-dər-'stand\ *vb* **-stood** \-'stůd\; **-stand·ing** **1** : to fail to understand **2** : to interpret incorrectly

mis·un·der·stand·ing \-'stan-diŋ\ *n* **1**

: MISINTERPRETATION **2** : DISAGREE-
MENT, QUARREL

mis·us·age \mish-ˈü-sij, mis(h)-ˈyü-, -zij\ *n* **1** : bad treatment : ABUSE **2** : wrong or improper use

mis·use \mish-ˈüz, mis(h)-ˈyüz\ *vb* **1** : to use incorrectly **2** : ABUSE, MIS-TREAT — **mis·use** \-ˈyüs\ *n*

mite \ˈmīt\ *n* **1** : any of various tiny animals related to the spiders that often live and feed on animals or plants **2** : a small coin or sum of money **3** : a small amount : BIT

¹**mi·ter** *or* **mi·tre** \ˈmīt-ər\ *n* [ME *mitre,* fr. MF, fr. L *mitra* headband, turban, fr. Gk] **1** : a headdress worn by bishops and abbots **2** : a joint or corner made by cutting two pieces of wood at an angle and fitting the cut edges together

²**miter** *or* **mitre** *vb* **mi·tered** *or* **mi·tred; mi·ter·ing** *or* **mi·tring** \ˈmīt-ə-riŋ\ **1** : to match or fit together in a miter joint **2** : to bevel the ends of for making a miter joint

mit·i·gate \ˈmit-ə-ˌgāt\ *vb* **-gat·ed; -gat·ing** **1** : to make less harsh or hostile **2** : to make less severe or painful — **mit·i·ga·tion** \ˌmit-ə-ˈgā-shən\ *n* — **mit·i·ga·tive** \ˈmit-ə-ˌgāt-iv\ *adj*

mi·to·sis \mī-ˈtō-səs\ *n, pl* **-to·ses** \-ˌsēz\ : a process that takes place in the nucleus of a dividing cell and results in the formation of two new nuclei each having the same number of chromosomes as the parent nucleus; *also* : cell division in which mitosis occurs — **mi·tot·ic** \-ˈtät-ik\ *adj*

mitt \ˈmit\ *n* : a baseball glove (as for a catcher)

mit·ten \ˈmit-ᵊn\ *n* : a covering for the hand having a separate section for the thumb only

¹**mix** \ˈmiks\ *vb* **1** : to combine into one mass **2** : ASSOCIATE **3** : to form by mingling components **4** : to produce (a recording) by electronically combining sounds from different sources **5** : CROSSBREED **6** : CONFUSE ⟨∼es up the facts⟩ **7** : to become involved **syn** blend, merge, coalesce, amalgamate, fuse — **mix·able** *adj* — **mix·er** *n*

²**mix** *n* : a product of mixing; *esp* : a commercially prepared mixture of food ingredients

mixed number *n* : a number (as 5⅔)

composed of an integer and a fraction

mixed–up \ˈmikst-ˈəp\ *adj* : marked by bewilderment, perplexity, or disorder : CONFUSED

mixt *abbr* mixture

mix·ture \ˈmiks-chər\ *n* **1** : the act or process of mixing; *also* : the state of being mixed **2** : a product of mixing

mix–up \ˈmiks-ˌəp\ *n* : an instance of confusion ⟨a ∼ about the train⟩

miz·zen *or* **miz·en** \ˈmiz-ᵊn\ *n* **1** : a fore-and-aft sail set on the mizzen-mast **2** : MIZZENMAST — **mizzen** *or* **mizen** *adj*

miz·zen·mast \-ˌmast, -məst\ *n* : the mast aft or next aft of the mainmast

mk *abbr* **1** mark **2** markka

Mk *abbr* Mark

mks \ˈem-ˈkā-ˈes\ *adj, often cap M&K&S* : of, relating to, or being a system of units based on the meter, the kilogram, and the second

mktg *abbr* marketing

ml *abbr* milliliter

MLD *abbr* **1** median lethal dose **2** minimum lethal dose

Mlle *abbr* [F] mademoiselle

Mlles *abbr* [F] mesdemoiselles

mm *abbr* millimeter

MM *abbr* [F] messieurs

Mme *abbr* [F] madame

Mn *symbol* manganese

MN *abbr* Minnesota

mne·mon·ic \nə-ˈmän-ik\ *adj* : assisting or designed to assist memory

mo *abbr* month

¹**Mo** *abbr* Missouri

²**Mo** *symbol* molybdenum

MO *abbr* **1** mail order **2** medical officer **3** Missouri **4** modus operandi **5** money order

moan \ˈmōn\ *n* : a low prolonged sound indicative of pain or grief — **moan** *vb*

moat \ˈmōt\ *n* : a deep wide usu. water-filled trench around a castle

¹**mob** \ˈmäb\ *n* [L *mobile vulgus* vacillating crowd] **1** : MASSES, RABBLE **2** : a large disorderly crowd **3** : a criminal gang

²**mob** *vb* **mobbed; mob·bing** **1** : to crowd around and attack or annoy **2** : to crowd into or around ⟨shoppers *mobbed* the stores⟩

¹**mo·bile** \ˈmō-bəl, -ˌbīl, -ˌbēl\ *adj* **1** : capable of moving or being moved **2** : changeable in appearance, mood, or

purpose; *also* : ADAPTABLE **3** : having the opportunity for or undergoing a shift in social status **4** : using vehicles for transportation ⟨~ warfare⟩ — **mo·bil·i·ty** \mō-ˈbil-ət-ē\ *n*

²**mo·bile** \ˈmō-ˌbēl\ *n* : a construction (as of wire and sheet metal) with parts that can be set in motion by air currents; *also* : a similar structure suspended so that it is moved by a current of air

mobile home *n* : a trailer used as a permanent dwelling

mo·bi·lize \ˈmō-bə-ˌlīz\ *vb* **-lized; -lizing 1** : to put into movement or circulation **2** : to assemble and make ready for action ⟨~ army reserves⟩ — **mo·bi·li·za·tion** \ˌmō-bə-lə-ˈzā-shən\ *n* — **mo·bi·liz·er** \ˈmō-bə-ˌlī-zər\ *n*

mob·ster \ˈmäb-stər\ *n* : a member of a criminal gang

moc·ca·sin \ˈmäk-ə-sən\ *n* **1** : a soft leather heelless shoe **2** : WATER MOCCASIN

¹**mock** \ˈmäk, ˈmȯk\ *vb* **1** : to treat with contempt or ridicule **2** : DELUDE **3** : DEFY **4** : to mimic in sport or derision — **mock·er** *n* — **mock·ery** \-(ə-)rē\ *n* — **mock·ing·ly** *adv*

²**mock** *adj* : SHAM, PSEUDO

mock–he·ro·ic \ˌmäk-hi-ˈrō-ik, ˌmȯk-\ *adj* : ridiculing or burlesquing the heroic style, character, or action ⟨a ~ poem⟩

mock·ing·bird \ˈmäk-iŋ-ˌbərd, ˈmȯk-\ *n* : a songbird of the southern U.S. that mimics the calls of other birds

mock–up \ˈmäk-ˌəp, ˈmȯk-\ *n* : a full-sized structural model built for study, testing, or display ⟨a ~ of an airplane⟩

¹**mod** \ˈmäd\ *adj* : MODERN; *esp* : bold, free, and unconventional in style, behavior, or dress

²**mod** *abbr* **1** moderate **2** modern

mode \ˈmōd\ *n* **1** : a particular form or variety of something; *also* : STYLE **2** : a manner of doing something **3** : the most frequent value of a set of data — **mod·al** \ˈmōd-ᵊl\ *adj*

¹**mod·el** \ˈmäd-ᵊl\ *n* **1** : structural design **2** : a miniature representation; *also* : a pattern of something to be made **3** : an example for imitation or emulation **4** : one who poses for an artist; *also* : MANNEQUIN **5** : TYPE, DESIGN — **model** *adj*

²**model** *vb* **-eled** *or* **-elled; -el·ing** *or* **-el·ling** \-(ə-)liŋ\ **1** : SHAPE, FASHION, CONSTRUCT **2** : to work as a fashion model

³**model** *adj* **1** : serving as or worthy of being a pattern ⟨a ~ student⟩ **2** : being a miniature representation of something ⟨a ~ airplane⟩

¹**mod·er·ate** \ˈmäd-(ə-)rət\ *adj* **1** : avoiding extremes; *also* : TEMPERATE **2** : AVERAGE; *also* : MEDIOCRE **3** : limited in scope or effect **4** : not expensive — **moderate** *n* — **mod·er·ate·ly** *adv* — **mod·er·ate·ness** *n*

²**mod·er·ate** \ˈmäd-ə-ˌrāt\ *vb* **-at·ed; -at·ing 1** : to lessen the intensity of : TEMPER **2** : to act as a moderator — **mod·er·a·tion** \ˌmäd-ə-ˈrā-shən\ *n*

mod·er·a·tor \ˈmäd-ə-ˌrāt-ər\ *n* **1** : MEDIATOR **2** : one who presides over an assembly, meeting, or discussion

mod·ern \ˈmäd-ərn\ *adj* [LL *modernus,* fr. L *modo* just now, fr. *modus* measure] : of, relating to, or characteristic of the present or the immediate past : CONTEMPORARY — **modern** *n* — **mo·der·ni·ty** \mə-ˈdər-nət-ē\ *n* — **mod·ern·ly** \ˈmäd-ərn-lē\ *adv* — **mod·ern·ness** \-ərn-nəs\ *n*

mod·ern·ism \ˈmäd-ər-ˌniz-əm\ *n* : a practice, movement, or belief peculiar to modern times

mod·ern·ize \ˈmäd-ər-ˌnīz\ *vb* **-ized; -iz·ing** : to make or become modern — **mod·ern·iza·tion** \ˌmäd-ər-nə-ˈzā-shən\ *n* — **mod·ern·iz·er** \ˈmäd-ər-ˌnī-zər\ *n*

mod·est \ˈmäd-əst\ *adj* **1** : having a moderate estimate of oneself; *also* : DIFFIDENT **2** : observing the proprieties of dress and behavior **3** : limited in size, amount, or scope — **mod·est·ly** *adv* — **mod·es·ty** \-ə-stē\ *n*

mod·i·cum \ˈmäd-i-kəm\ *n* : a small amount

modif *abbr* modification

mod·i·fy \ˈmäd-ə-ˌfī\ *vb* **-fied; -fy·ing 1** : MODERATE **2** : to limit the meaning of esp. in a grammatical construction **3** : CHANGE, ALTER — **mod·i·fi·ca·tion** \ˌmäd-ə-fə-ˈkā-shən\ *n* — **mod·i·fi·er** \ˈmäd-ə-ˌfī(-ə)r\ *n*

mod·ish \ˈmōd-ish\ *adj* : FASHIONABLE, STYLISH — **mod·ish·ly** *adv* — **mod·ish·ness** *n*

mo·diste \mō-ˈdēst\ *n* : a maker of fashionable dresses

mod·u·lar \'mäj-ə-lər\ *adj* : constructed with standardized units

mod·u·lar·ized \'mäj-ə-lə-ˌrīzd\ *adj* : containing or consisting of modules

mod·u·late \'mäj-ə-ˌlāt\ *vb* **-lat·ed; -lat·ing 1** : to tune to a key or pitch **2** : to keep in proper measure or proportion : TEMPER **3** : to vary the amplitude or frequency of a carrier wave for the transmission of intelligence (as in radio or television) — **mod·u·la·tion** \ˌmäj-ə-'lā-shən\ *n* — **mod·u·la·tor** \'mäj-ə-ˌlāt-ər\ *n* — **mod·u·la·to·ry** \-lə-ˌtōr-ē\ *adj*

mod·ule \'mäj-ül\ *n* **1** : any in a series of standardized units for use together **2** : an assembly of wired electronic parts for use with other such assemblies **3** : an independent unit that constitutes a part of the total structure of a space vehicle ⟨a propulsion ∼⟩

mo·dus ope·ran·di \ˌmōd-əs-ˌäp-ə-'ran-dē, -ˌdī\ *n, pl* **mo·di operandi** \'mō-ˌdē-ˌäp-, 'mō-ˌdī-\ [NL] : a method of procedure

¹mo·gul \'mō-gəl, mō-'gəl\ *n* [fr. *Mogul,* one of the Mongol conquerors of India or their descendants, fr. Per *Mughul* Mongol, fr. Mongolian *Mongol*] : an important person : magnate

²mogul \'mō-gəl\ *n* : a bump in a ski run

mo·hair \'mō-ˌhaər\ *n* [modif. of obs. It *mocaiarro,* fr. Ar *mukhayyar,* lit., choice] : a fabric or yarn made wholly or in part from the long silky hair of the Angora goat

Mo·ham·med·an var of MUHAMMADAN

Mo·hawk \'mō-ˌhök\ *n, pl* **Mohawk** or **Mohawks** : a member of an American Indian people of the Mohawk river valley, New York; *also* : the language of the Mohawk people

Mo·he·gan \mō-'hē-gən, mə-\ or **Mo·hi·can** \-'hē-kən\ *n, pl* **Mohegan** or **Mohegans** or **Mohican** or **Mohicans** : a member of an American Indian people of southeastern Connecticut

Mo·hi·can \mō-'hē-kən, mə-\ var of MAHICAN

moi·ety \'mòi-ət-ē\ *n, pl* **-eties** : one of two equal or approximately equal parts

moil \'mòil\ *vb* : to work hard : DRUDGE — **moil** *n* — **moil·er** *n*

moi·ré \mò-'rā, mwä-\ or **moire** \same, or 'mòi(-ə)r, 'mwär\ *n* : a fabric (as silk) having a watered appearance

moist \'mòist\ *adj* : slightly or moderately wet — **moist·ly** *adv* — **moist·ness** *n*

moist·en \'mòis-ᵊn\ *vb* **moist·ened; moist·en·ing** \'mòis-(ᵊ-)niŋ\ : to make or become moist — **moist·en·er** \'mòis-(ᵊ-)nər\ *n*

mois·ture \'mòis-chər\ *n* : the small amount of liquid that causes dampness

mol *abbr* molecular; molecule

mo·lar \'mō-lər\ *n* [L *molaris,* fr. *molaris* of a mill, fr. *mola* millstone] : one of the broad teeth adapted to grinding food and located in the back of the jaw — **molar** *adj*

mo·las·ses \mə-'las-əz\ *n* : the thick brown syrup that is separated from raw sugar in sugar manufacture

¹mold \'mōld\ *n* : crumbly soil rich in organic matter

²mold *n* **1** : distinctive nature or character **2** : the frame on or around which something is constructed **3** : a cavity in which something is shaped; *also* : an object so shaped **4** : MOLDING

³mold *vb* **1** : to shape in or as if in a mold **2** : to ornament with molding — **mold·er** *n*

⁴mold *n* : a surface growth of fungus on damp or decaying matter; *also* : a fungus that forms molds — **mold·i·ness** \'mōl-dē-nəs\ *n* — **moldy** *adj*

⁵mold *vb* : to become moldy

mold·board \'mōl(d)-ˌbōrd\ *n* : a curved iron plate attached above the plowshare to lift and turn the soil

mold·er \'mōl-dər\ *vb* **mold·ered; mold·er·ing** \-d(ə-)riŋ\ : to crumble into small pieces

mold·ing \'mōl-diŋ\ *n* **1** : an act or process of shaping in a mold; *also* : an object so shaped **2** : a decorative surface, plane, or curved strip

¹mole \'mōl\ *n* : a small often pigmented spot or protuberance on the skin

²mole *n* : a small burrowing mammal with tiny eyes, hidden ears, and soft fur

³mole *n* : a massive breakwater or jetty

mo·lec·u·lar biology \mə-'lek-yə-lər-\ *n* : a branch of biology dealing with the ultimate physical and chemical organization of living matter and esp. with the molecular basis of inheritance and protein synthesis — **molecular biologist** *n*

mol·e·cule \\'mäl-i-ˌkyül\\ *n* : the smallest particle of matter that is the same chemically as the whole mass — **mo·lec·u·lar** \\mə-'lek-yə-lər\\ *adj*

mole·hill \\'mōl-ˌhil\\ *n* : a little ridge of earth thrown up by a mole

mole·skin \\-ˌskin\\ *n* 1 : the skin of the mole used as fur 2 : a heavy durable cotton fabric for industrial, medical, or clothing use

mo·lest \\mə-'lest\\ *vb* 1 : ANNOY, DISTURB 2 : to make annoying sexual advances to — **mo·les·ta·tion** \\ˌmōl-ˌes-'tā-shən\\ *n* — **mo·lest·er** \\mə-'les-tər\\ *n*

moll \\'mäl\\ *n* : a gangster's girlfriend

mol·li·fy \\'mäl-ə-ˌfī\\ *vb* **-fied; -fy·ing** 1 : to soothe in temper : APPEASE 2 : SOFTEN 3 : to reduce in intensity : ASSUAGE — **mol·li·fi·ca·tion** \\ˌmäl-ə-fə-'kā-shən\\ *n*

mol·lusk *or* **mol·lusc** \\'mäl-əsk\\ *n* : any of a large group of mostly shelled and aquatic invertebrate animals including snails, clams, and squids — **mol·lus·can** *also* **mol·lus·kan** \\mə-'ləs-kən\\ *adj*

¹**mol·ly·cod·dle** \\'mäl-ē-ˌkäd-ᵊl\\ *n* : a pampered man or boy

²**mollycoddle** *vb* **mol·ly·cod·dled; mol·ly·cod·dling** \\-ˌkäd-(ə-)liŋ\\ : PAMPER

Mo·lo·tov cocktail \\ˌmäl-ə-ˌtóf-, ˌmól-\\ *n* : a crude bomb made of a bottle filled usu. with gasoline and fitted with a wick or saturated rag and ignited usu. just prior to hurling

¹**molt** \\'mōlt\\ *vb* : to shed hair, feathers, outer skin, or horns periodically with the parts being replaced by new growth — **molt·er** *n*

²**molt** *n* : the act or process of molting

mol·ten \\'mōlt-ᵊn\\ *adj* 1 : fused or liquefied by heat 2 : GLOWING

mo·ly \\'mō-lē\\ *n* : a mythical herb with black root, white flowers, and magic powers

mo·lyb·de·num \\mə-'lib-də-nəm\\ *n* : a metallic chemical element used in strengthening and hardening steel

mom \\'mäm, 'məm\\ *n* : MOTHER

mom–and–pop *adj* : being a small owner-operated business

mo·ment \\'mō-mənt\\ *n* 1 : a minute portion of time : INSTANT 2 : a time of excellence ⟨he has his ∼*s*⟩ 3 : IMPORTANCE **syn** consequence, significance, weight, import

mo·men·tari·ly \\ˌmō-mən-'ter-ə-lē\\ *adv* 1 : for a moment 2 : INSTANTLY 3 : at any moment : SOON

mo·men·tary \\'mō-mən-ˌter-ē\\ *adj* 1 : continuing only a moment; *also* : EPHEMERAL 2 : recurring at every moment — **mo·men·tar·i·ness** \\'mō-mən-ˌter-ē-nəs\\ *n*

mo·men·tous \\mō-'ment-əs\\ *adj* : very important — **mo·men·tous·ly** *adv* — **mo·men·tous·ness** *n*

mo·men·tum \\mō-'ment-əm\\ *n, pl* **mo·men·ta** \\-'ment-ə\\ *or* **momentums** : a property that a moving body has due to its mass and motion; *also* : IMPETUS

mom·my \\'mäm-ē, 'məm-\\ *n, pl* **mommies** : MOTHER

Mon *abbr* Monday

mon·arch \\'män-ərk, -ˌärk\\ *n* 1 : a person who reigns over a kingdom or an empire 2 : one holding preeminent position or power — **mo·nar·chi·cal** \\mə-'när-ki-kəl\\ *also* **mo·nar·chic** \\-'när-kik\\ *adj*

monarch butterfly *n* : a large orange and black migratory American butterfly whose larva feeds on milkweed

mon·ar·chist \\'män-ər-kəst\\ *n* : a believer in monarchical government — **mon·ar·chism** \\-ˌkiz-əm\\ *n*

mon·ar·chy \\'män-ər-kē\\ *n, pl* **-chies** : a nation or state governed by a monarch

mon·as·tery \\'män-ə-ˌster-ē\\ *n, pl* **-ter·ies** : a house for persons under religious vows (as monks)

mo·nas·tic \\mə-'nas-tik\\ *adj* : of or relating to monasteries or to monks or nuns — **monastic** *n* — **mo·nas·ti·cal·ly** \\-ti-k(ə-)lē\\ *adv*

mo·nas·ti·cism \\mə-'nas-tə-ˌsiz-əm\\ *n* : the monastic life, system, or condition

mon·au·ral \\mä-'nór-əl\\ *adj* : MONOPHONIC — **mon·au·ral·ly** \\-ē\\ *adv*

Mon·day \\'mən-dē, -ˌdā\\ *n* : the second day of the week

mon·e·tary \\'män-ə-ˌter-ē, 'mən-\\ *adj* : of or relating to money or to the mechanisms by which it is supplied and circulated in the economy

mon·ey \\'mən-ē\\ *n, pl* **moneys** *or* **monies** \\'mən-ēz\\ 1 : something (as metal currency) accepted as a medium of exchange **2** : wealth reckoned in monetary terms **3** : the 1st, 2d, and 3d places in a horse or dog race

mon·eyed \'mən-ēd\ *adj* **1** : having money : WEALTHY **2** : consisting in or derived from money

mon·ey·lend·er \'mən-ē-ˌlen-dər\ *n* : one whose business is lending money; *specif* : PAWNBROKER

money market *n* : the trade in short-term negotiable financial instruments

money of account : a denominator of value or basis of exchange used in keeping accounts

money order *n* : an order purchased at a post office, bank, or telegraph office directing another office to pay a sum of money to a party named on it

mon·ger \'məŋ-gər, 'mäŋ-\ *n* **1** : DEALER **2** : one who tries to stir up or spread something

mon·go \'mäŋ-(ˌ)gō\ *n, pl* **mongo** — see *tugrik* at MONEY table

Mon·gol \'mäŋ-gəl, 'män-ˌgōl\ *n* : a person of Mongoloid racial stock and esp. of the chiefly pastoral Mongoloid peoples of Mongolia — **Mongol** *adj*

Mon·go·lian \män-'gōl-yən, mäŋ-, -'gō-lē-ən\ *n* **1** : a native or inhabitant of Mongolia **2** : a member of the Mongoloid racial stock — **Mongolian** *adj*

mon·gol·ism \'mäŋ-gə-ˌliz-əm\ *n* : DOWN'S SYNDROME

Mon·gol·oid \'mäŋ-gə-ˌlȯid\ *adj* **1** : of or relating to a major racial stock native to Asia that includes peoples of northern and eastern Asia, Malaysians, Eskimos, and often American Indians **2** *often not cap* : of, relating to, or affected with Down's syndrome — **Mongoloid** *n*

mon·goose \'mäŋ-ˌgüs, 'mäŋ-\ *n, pl* **mon·goos·es** *also* **mon·geese** \-ˌgēs\ : a small agile mammal of India that is related to the civet cats and feeds on snakes and rodents

mon·grel \'mäŋ-grəl, 'məŋ-\ *n* : an offspring of parents of different breeds or uncertain ancestry

mo·nism \'mō-ˌniz-əm, 'män-iz-\ *n* : a view that reality is basically one — **mo·nist** \'mō-nəst, 'män-əst\ *n*

mo·ni·tion \mō-'nish-ən, mə-\ *n* : WARNING, CAUTION

mon·i·tor \'män-ət-ər\ *n* **1** : a student appointed to assist a teacher **2** : one that monitors; *esp* : a video display screen (as for a computer)

monitor *vb* **mon·i·tored; mon·i·tor·ing** \'män-ət-ə-riŋ, 'män-ə-triŋ\ : to watch, check, or observe for a special purpose

mon·i·to·ry \'män-ə-ˌtōr-ē\ *adj* : giving admonition : WARNING

monk \'məŋk\ *n* [ME, fr. OE *munuc*, fr. LL *monachus*, fr. LGk *monachos*, fr. Gk, adj., single, fr. *monos* single, alone] : a man belonging to a religious order and living in a monastery — **monk·ish** *adj*

monk *n* : MONKEY

mon·key \'məŋ-kē\ *n, pl* **monkeys** : a primate mammal other than man; *esp* : one of the smaller, longer-tailed, and usu. more arboreal primates as contrasted with the apes

monkey *vb* **mon·keyed; mon·key·ing 1** : FOOL, TRIFLE **2** : TAMPER

monkey bars *n pl* : a framework of bars on which children can play

mon·key·shine \'mən-kē-ˌshīn\ *n* : PRANK — usu. used in pl.

monkey wrench *n* : a wrench with one fixed and one adjustable jaw at right angles to a handle

monks·hood \'məŋks-ˌhu̇d\ *n* : any of a genus of poisonous plants related to the buttercups; *esp* : a tall Old World plant grown for its white or purplish flowers or as a source of drugs (as aconite)

mono \'män-ō\ *adj* : MONOPHONIC

mono *n* : MONONUCLEOSIS

mono·chro·mat·ic \ˌmän-ə-krō-'mat-ik\ *adj* **1** : having or consisting of one color **2** : consisting of radiation (as light) of a single wavelength

mono·chrome \'män-ə-ˌkrōm\ *adj* : characterized by the reproduction or transmission of visual images in tones of gray ⟨~ television⟩

mon·o·cle \'män-i-kəl\ *n* : an eyeglass for one eye

mono·clo·nal \ˌmän-ə-'klō-nəl\ *adj* : produced by, being, or composed of cells derived from a single cell ⟨~ antibodies⟩

mono·cot·y·le·don \ˌmän-ə-ˌkät-ᵊl-'ēd-ᵊn\ *n* : any of a subclass of seed plants having an embryo with a single cotyle-

don and usu. parallel-veined leaves —
mono·cot·y·le·don·ous *adj*

mon·o·dy \\'män-əd-ē\ *n, pl* **-dies** : ELE-GY, DIRGE — **mo·nod·ic** \mə-'näd-ik\ *or* **mo·nod·i·cal** \-i-kəl\ *adj* — **mon·o·dist** \\'män-əd-əst\ *n*

mo·nog·a·my \mə-'näg-ə-mē\ *n* : marriage with but one person at a time — **mo·nog·a·mist** \mə-'näg-ə-məst\ *n* — **mo·nog·a·mous** \mə-'näg-ə-məs\ *adj*

mono·gram \\'män-ə-ˌgram\ *n* : a sign of identity composed of the combined initials of a name — **monogram** *vb*

mono·graph \\'män-ə-ˌgraf\ *n* : a learned treatise on a small area of learning

mono·lin·gual \ˌmän-ə-'liŋ-gwəl\ *adj* : expressed in or knowing or using only one language

mono·lith \\'män-ᵊl-ˌith\ *n* **1** : a single great stone often in the form of a monument or column **2** : something large and powerful that acts as a single unified force — **mono·lith·ic** \ˌmän-ᵊl-'ith-ik\ *adj*

mono·logue *also* **mono·log** \\'män-ᵊl-ˌȯg\ *n* : a dramatic soliloquy; *also* : a long speech monopolizing conversation — **mono·logu·ist** \-ˌȯg-əst\ *or* **mo·no·lo·gist** \mə-'näl-ə-jəst; 'män-ᵊl-ˌȯg-əst\ *n*

mono·ma·nia \ˌmän-ə-'mā-nē-ə, -nyə\ *n* **1** : mental derangement involving a single idea or area of thought **2** : excessive concentration on a single object or idea — **mono·ma·ni·ac** \-nē-ˌak\ *n or adj*

mono·mer \\'män-ə-mər\ *n* : a simple chemical compound that can be polymerized

mono·nu·cle·o·sis \ˌmän-ō-ˌn(y)ü-klē-'ō-səs\ *n* : an acute infectious disease characterized by fever, swelling of lymph glands, and increased numbers of lymph cells in the blood

mono·phon·ic \ˌmän-ə-'fän-ik\ *adj* : of or relating to sound transmission, recording, or reproduction by techniques that provide a single transmission path

mono·plane \\'män-ə-ˌplān\ *n* : an airplane with only one set of wings

mo·nop·o·ly \mə-'näp-(ə-)lē\ *n, pl* **-lies** [L *monopolium*, fr. Gk *monopōlion*, fr. *monos* alone, single + *pōlein* to sell] **1** : exclusive ownership (as through command of supply) **2** : a commodity controlled by one party **3** : one that has a monopoly — **mo·nop·o·list** \-ləst\ *n* — **mo·nop·o·lis·tic** \mə-ˌnäp-ə-'lis-tik\ *adj* — **mo·nop·o·li·za·tion** \-lə-'zā-shən\ *n* — **mo·nop·o·lize** \mə-'näp-ə-ˌlīz\ *vb*

mono·rail \\'män-ə-ˌrāl\ *n* : a single rail serving as a track for a wheeled vehicle; *also* : a vehicle traveling on such a track

mono·so·di·um glu·ta·mate \ˌmän-ə-ˌsōd-ē-əm-'glüt-ə-ˌmāt\ *n* : a crystalline salt used for seasoning foods

mono·syl·la·ble \\'män-ə-'sil-ə-bəl\ *n* : a word of one syllable — **mono·syl·lab·ic** \ˌmän-ə-sə-'lab-ik\ *adj* — **mono·syl·lab·i·cal·ly** \-i-k(ə-)lē\ *adv*

mono·the·ism \\'män-ə-(ˌ)thē-ˌiz-əm\ *n* : a doctrine or belief that there is only one deity — **mono·the·ist** \-ˌthē-əst\ *n*

mono·tone \\'män-ə-ˌtōn\ *n* : a succession of syllables, words, or sentences in one unvaried key or pitch

mo·not·o·nous \mə-'nät-ᵊn-əs\ *adj* **1** : uttered or sounded in one unvarying tone **2** : tediously uniform — **mo·not·o·nous·ly** *adv* — **mo·not·o·nous·ness** *n* — **mo·not·o·ny** \-ᵊn-ē\ *n*

mon·ox·ide \mə-'näk-ˌsīd\ *n* : an oxide containing one atom of oxygen in the molecule

mon·sei·gneur \ˌmōⁿ-ˌsān-'yər\ *n, pl* **mes·sei·gneurs** \ˌmā-ˌsān-'yər(z)\ : a French dignitary — used as a title

mon·sieur \məs-'yə(r), *Fr* mə-'syœ\ *n, pl* **mes·sieurs** \məs(h)-(ˌ)yə(r)(z), mäs-; mə-'si(ə)r(z)\ : a Frenchman of high rank or station — used as a title equivalent to *Mister*

mon·si·gnor \män-'sē-nyər\ *n, pl* **monsignors** *or* **mon·si·gno·ri** \ˌmän-ˌsēn-'yōr-ē\ [It *monsignore*] : a Roman Catholic prelate — used as a title

mon·soon \män-'sün\ *n* [obs. Dutch *monssoen*, fr. Pg *monção*, fr. Ar *mawsim* time, season] **1** : a periodic wind esp. in the Indian ocean and southern Asia **2** : the season of the southwest monsoon esp. in India **3** : rainfall associated with the monsoon

¹**mon·ster** \\'män-stər\ *n* **1** : an abnormally developed plant or animal **2** : an animal of strange or terrifying shape; *also* : one unusually large of its kind **3** : an extremely ugly, wicked, or cruel person — **mon·stros·i·ty** \män-'sträs-

ət-ē\ *n* — **mon·strous** \'män-strəs\ *adj* — **mon·strous·ly** *adv*

²**monster** *adj* : very large : ENORMOUS

mon·strance \'män-strəns\ *n* : a vessel in which the consecrated Host is exposed for the adoration of the faithful

Mont *abbr* Montana

mon·tage \män-'täzh\ *n* [F] **1** : a composite photograph made by combining several separate pictures **2** : an artistic composition made up of several different kinds of items (as strips of newspaper, pictures, bits of wood) arranged together

month \'mənth\ *n, pl* **months** \'məns, 'mənths\ [OE *mōnath*, fr. *mōna* moon] : one of the 12 parts into which the year is divided — **month·ly** *adv or adj or n*

month·long \'mənth-'loṅ\ *adj* : lasting a month

mon·u·ment \'män-yə-mənt\ *n* **1** : a lasting reminder; *esp* : a structure erected in remembrance of a person or event **2** : a natural feature or area of special interest set aside by the government as public property

mon·u·men·tal \,män-yə-'ment-ᵊl\ *adj* **1** : of or relating to a monument **2** : MASSIVE; *also* : OUTSTANDING **3** : very great — **mon·u·men·tal·ly** \-ē\ *adv*

moo \'mü\ *vb* : to make the natural throat noise of a cow — **moo** *n*

¹**mood** \'müd\ *n* **1** : a conscious state of mind or predominant emotion : FEELING **2** : a prevailing attitude : DISPOSITION

²**mood** *n* : distinction of form of a verb to express whether its action or state is conceived as fact or in some other manner (as wish)

moody \'müd-ē\ *adj* **mood·i·er; -est 1** : GLOOMY **2** : subject to moods : TEMPERAMENTAL — **mood·i·ly** \'müd-ᵊl-ē\ *adv* — **mood·i·ness** \-ē-nəs\ *n*

¹**moon** \'mün\ *n* **1** : the earth's natural satellite **2** : SATELLITE 2

²**moon** *vb* : to engage in idle reverie

moon·beam \'mün-,bēm\ *n* : a ray of light from the moon

¹**moon·light** \-,līt\ *n* : the light of the moon — **moon·lit** \-,lit\ *adj*

²**moonlight** *vb* **moon·light·ed; moon·light·ing** : to hold a second job in addition to a regular one — **moon·light·er** *n*

moon·scape \-,skāp\ *n* : the surface of the moon as seen or as pictured

moon·shine \-,shīn\ *n* **1** : MOONLIGHT **2** : empty talk **3** : intoxicating liquor usu. illegally distilled

moon·stone \-,stōn\ *n* : a transparent or translucent feldspar of pearly luster used as a gem

moon·struck \-,strək\ *adj* **1** : mentally unbalanced **2** : romantically sentimental

¹**moor** \'mùr\ *n* : an area of open and usu. infertile and wet or peaty wasteland

²**moor** *vb* : to make fast with or as if with cables, lines, or anchors

Moor \'mùr\ *n* : one of a North African people of Arab and Berber ancestry that conquered Spain in the 8th century — **Moor·ish** *adj*

moor·ing \'mùr-iṅ\ *n* **1** : a place where or an object to which a craft can be made fast **2** : an established practice or stabilizing influence — usu. used in pl.

moor·land \-lənd, -,land\ *n* : land consisting of moors

moose \'müs\ *n, pl* **moose** : a large heavy-antlered American deer; *also* : the European elk

¹**moot** \'müt\ *vb* : to bring up for debate or discussion; *also* : DEBATE

²**moot** *adj* **1** : open to question; *also* : DISPUTED **2** : having no practical significance

¹**mop** \'mäp\ *n* : an implement made of absorbent material fastened to a handle and used esp. for cleaning floors

²**mop** *vb* **mopped; mop·ping** : to use a mop on : clean with a mop

mope \'mōp\ *vb* **moped; mop·ing 1** : to become dull, dejected, or listless **2** : DAWDLE

mop·pet \'mäp-ət\ *n* [obs. E *mop* fool, child] : CHILD

mop–up \'mäp-,əp\ *n* : a final clearance or disposal

mo·raine \mə-'rān\ *n* : an accumulation of earth and stones left by a glacier

¹**mor·al** \'mȯr-əl\ *adj* **1** : of or relating to principles of right and wrong **2** : conforming to a standard of right behavior; *also* : capable of right and wrong action **3** : probable but not proved ⟨a ~ certainty⟩ **4** : having the effects of such on the mind, confidence, or will

⟨a ∼ victory⟩ **syn** virtuous, righteous, noble, ethical, principled — **mor•al•ly** \-ē\ *adv*

²**moral** *n* **1** : the practical meaning (as of a story) **2** *pl* : moral practices or teachings

mo•rale \mə-'ral\ *n* **1** : MORALITY **2** : the mental and emotional attitudes of an individual to the tasks at hand; *also* : ESPRIT DE CORPS

mor•al•ist \'mȯr-ə-ləst\ *n* **1** : a teacher or student of morals **2** : one concerned with regulating the morals of others — **mor•al•is•tic** \ˌmȯr-ə-'lis-tik\ *adj* — **mor•al•is•ti•cal•ly** \-ti-k(ə-)lē\ *adv*

mo•ral•i•ty \mə-'ral-ət-ē\ *n, pl* **-ties** : moral conduct : VIRTUE

mor•al•ize \'mȯr-ə-ˌlīz\ *vb* **-ized; -iz•ing** : to make moral reflections — **mor•al•iza•tion** \ˌmȯr-ə-lə-'zā-shən\ *n* — **mor•al•iz•er** \'mȯr-ə-ˌlī-zər\ *n*

mo•rass \mə-'ras\ *n* : SWAMP

mor•a•to•ri•um \ˌmȯr-ə-'tōr-ē-əm\ *n, pl* **-ri•ums** *or* **-ria** \-ē-ə\ [deriv. of L *mora* delay] : a suspension of activity

mo•ray \mə-'rā, 'mȯr-ˌā\ *n* : any of numerous often brightly colored savage eels occurring in warm seas

mor•bid \'mȯr-bəd\ *adj* **1** : of, relating to, or typical of disease; *also* : DISEASED, SICKLY **2** : characterized by gloomy or unwholesome ideas or feelings **3** : GRISLY, GRUESOME ⟨∼ details⟩ — **mor•bid•i•ty** \mȯr-'bid-ət-ē\ *n* — **mor•bid•ly** \'mȯr-bəd-lē\ *adv* — **mor•bid•ness** *n*

mor•dant \'mȯrd-ᵊnt\ *adj* **1** : INCISIVE **2** : BURNING, PUNGENT — **mor•dant•ly** *adv*

¹**more** \'mōr\ *adj* **1** : GREATER **2** : ADDITIONAL

²**more** *adv* **1** : in addition ⟨a couple of times ∼⟩ **2** : to a greater or higher degree

³**more** *n* **1** : a greater quantity, number, or amount ⟨the ∼ the merrier⟩ **2** : an additional amount ⟨too full to eat ∼⟩

⁴**more** *pron* : additional persons or things ⟨∼ were found in the road⟩

mo•rel \mə-'rel\ *n* : any of several pitted edible fungi

more•over \mōr-'ō-vər\ *adv* : in addition : FURTHER

mo•res \'mȯr-ˌāz\ *n pl* **1** : the fixed mor-

ally binding customs of a group **2** : HABITS, MANNERS

Mor•gan \'mȯr-gən\ *n* : any of an American breed of lightly built horses

morgue \'mȯrg\ *n* : a place where the bodies of dead persons are kept until released for burial

mor•i•bund \'mȯr-ə-(ˌ)bənd\ *adj* : being in a dying condition — **mor•i•bun•di•ty** \ˌmȯr-ə-'bən-dət-ē\ *n*

Mor•mon \'mȯr-mən\ *n* : a member of the Church of Jesus Christ of Latter-day Saints — **Mor•mon•ism** \-mə-ˌniz-əm\ *n*

morn \'mȯrn\ *n* : MORNING

morn•ing \'mȯr-niŋ\ *n* **1** : the early part of the day; *esp* : the time from the sunrise to noon **2** : BEGINNING

morning glory *n* : any of various twining plants related to the sweet potato that have often showy bell-shaped or funnel-shaped flowers

morning sickness *n* : nausea and vomiting that occur in the morning esp. during early pregnancy

morning star *n* : a bright planet (as Venus) seen in the eastern sky before or at sunrise

Mo•roc•can \mə-'räk-ən\ *n* : a native or inhabitant of Morocco

mo•roc•co \mə-'räk-ō\ *n* : a fine leather made of goatskins tanned with sumac

mo•ron \'mōr-ˌän\ *n* : a defective person having a potential mental age of between 8 and 12 years and capable of doing routine work under supervision; *also* : a stupid person — **mo•ron•ic** \mə-'rän-ik\ *adj* — **mo•ron•i•cal•ly** \-i-k(ə-)lē\ *adv*

mo•rose \mə-'rōs\ *adj* [L *morosus*, lit., capricious, fr. *mor-, mos* will] : having a sullen disposition; *also* : GLOOMY — **mo•rose•ly** *adv* — **mo•rose•ness** *n*

mor•pheme \'mȯr-ˌfēm\ *n* : a meaningful linguistic unit that contains no smaller meaningful parts — **mor•phe•mic** \mȯr-'fē-mik\ *adj*

mor•phia \'mȯr-fē-ə\ *n* : MORPHINE

mor•phine \'mȯr-ˌfēn\ *n* [F, fr. Gk *Morpheus* Greek god of dreams] : an addictive drug obtained from opium and used to ease pain or induce sleep

mor•phol•o•gy \mȯr-'fäl-ə-jē\ *n* **1** : a branch of biology dealing with the form and structure of organisms **2** : a study and description of word formation in a language — **mor·pho·log·i·cal** \ˌmȯr-fə-'läj-i-kəl\ *adj* — **mor·phol·o·gist** \mȯr-'fäl-ə-jəst\ *n*

mor·ris \'mȯr-əs\ *n* : a vigorous English dance performed traditionally by men wearing costumes and bells

mor·row \'mär-ō\ *n* : the next day

Morse code \'mȯrs-\ *n* : either of two codes consisting of dots and dashes or long and short sounds used for transmitting messages

mor·sel \'mȯr-səl\ *n* [ME, fr. OF, dim. of *mors* bite, fr. L *morsus*, fr. *mordēre* to bite] **1** : a small piece or quantity **2** : a tasty dish

mor·tal \'mȯrt-ᵊl\ *adj* **1** : causing death : FATAL; *also* : leading to eternal punishment ⟨~ sin⟩ **2** : subject to death ⟨~ man⟩ **3** : implacably hostile ⟨~ foe⟩ **4** : very great : EXTREME ⟨~ fear⟩ **5** : HUMAN ⟨~ limitations⟩ — **mortal** *n* — **mor·tal·i·ty** \mȯr-'tal-ət-ē\ *n* — **mor·tal·ly** \'mȯrt-ᵊl-ē\ *adv*

¹mor·tar \'mȯrt-ər\ *n* **1** : a strong bowl in which substances are pounded or crushed with a pestle **2** : a short-barreled cannon used to fire shells at high angles

²mortar *n* : a plastic building material (as a mixture of cement, lime, or gypsum plaster with sand and water) that is spread between bricks or stones to bind them together as it hardens — **mortar** *vb*

mor·tar·board \'mȯrt-ər-ˌbōrd\ *n* **1** : a board or platform about three feet square for holding mortar **2** : an academic cap with a broad square top

mort·gage \'mȯr-gij\ *n* [ME *morgage*, fr. MF, fr. OF, fr. *mort* dead + *gage* gage] : a transfer of rights to a piece of property usu. as security for the payment of a loan or debt that becomes void when the debt is paid — **mortgage** *vb* — **mort·gag·ee** \ˌmȯr-gi-'jē\ *n* — **mort·ga·gor** \ˌmȯr-gi-'jȯr\ *n*

mor·ti·cian \mȯr-'tish-ən\ *n* [L *mort-, mors* death + E *-ician* (as in *physician*)] : UNDERTAKER

mor·ti·fy \'mȯrt-ə-ˌfī\ *vb* **-fied; -fy·ing 1** : to subdue (as the body) esp. by abstinence or self-inflicted pain **2** : HUMILIATE **3** : to become necrotic or gangrenous — **mor·ti·fi·ca·tion** \ˌmȯrt-ə-fə-'kā-shən\ *n*

mor·tise *also* **mor·tice** \'mȯrt-əs\ *n* : a

hole cut in a piece of wood into which another piece fits to form a joint

mor·tu·ary \'mȯr-chə-ˌwer-ē\ *n, pl* **-aries** : a place in which dead bodies are kept until burial

mos *abbr* months

mo·sa·ic \mō-'zā-ik\ *n* : a surface decoration made by inlaying small pieces (as of colored glass or stone) to form figures or patterns; *also* : a design made in mosaic

mo·sey \'mō-zē\ *vb* **mo·seyed; mo·sey·ing** : SAUNTER

Mos·lem \'mäz-ləm\ var of MUSLIM

mosque \'mäsk\ *n* : a building used for public worship by Muslims

mos·qui·to \mə-'skēt-ō\ *n, pl* **-toes** *also* **-tos** : a two-winged fly the female of which sucks the blood of man and lower animals

mosquito net *n* : a net or screen for keeping out mosquitoes

moss \'mȯs\ *n* : any of a large group of green plants without flowers but with small leafy stems growing in clumps — **mossy** *adj*

moss·back \'mȯs-ˌbak\ *n* : an extremely conservative person : FOGY

¹most \'mōst\ *adj* **1** : the majority of ⟨~ people⟩ **2** : GREATEST ⟨the ~ ability⟩

²most *adv* **1** : to the greatest or highest degree ⟨~ beautiful⟩ **2** : to a very great degree ⟨a ~ careful driver⟩

³most *n* : the greatest amount ⟨the ~ he can do⟩

⁴most *pron* : the greatest number or part ⟨~ became discouraged⟩

-most \ˌmōst\ *adj suffix* : most ⟨inner*most*⟩

most·ly \'mōst-lē\ *adv* : MAINLY

mot \'mō\ *n, pl* **mots** \'mō(z)\ [F, word, saying, fr. L *muttum* grunt] : a witty saying

mote \'mōt\ *n* : a small particle

mo·tel \mō-'tel\ *n* [blend of *motor* and *hotel*] : a hotel in which the rooms are accessible from an outdoor parking area

mo·tet \mō-'tet\ *n* : a choral work on a sacred text for several voices usu. without instrumental accompaniment

moth \'mȯth\ *n, pl* **moths** \'mȯthz, 'mȯths\ : any of various insects belonging to the same order as the butterflies but usu. night-flying and with a stouter body and smaller wings; *esp* : CLOTHES MOTH

moth·ball \\'moth-ˌból\ *n* **1** : a ball (as of naphthalene) used to keep moths out of clothing **2** *pl* : protective storage ⟨ships put in ∼s after the war⟩

¹moth·er \\'məth-ər\ *n* **1** : a female parent **2** : the superior of a religious community of women **3** : SOURCE, ORIGIN — **moth·er·hood** \-ˌhüd\ *n* — **moth·er·less** *adj* — **moth·er·li·ness** \-lē-nəs\ *n* — **moth·er·ly** *adj*

²mother *vb* **moth·ered;** **moth·er·ing** \\'məth-(ə-)riŋ\ **1** : to give birth to; *also* : PRODUCE **2** : to protect like a mother

moth·er–in–law \\'məth-ə-rən-ˌló, 'məth-ərn-ˌló\ *n, pl* **mothers–in–law** \\'məth-ər-zən-\ : the mother of one's spouse

moth·er–land \\'məth-ər-ˌland\ *n* **1** : the land of origin of something **2** : the native land of one's ancestors

moth·er–of–pearl \ˌməth-ə-rə(v)-'pərl\ *n* : the hard pearly matter forming the inner layer of a mollusk shell

mo·tif \mō-'tēf\ *n* [F, motive, motif] : a dominant idea or central theme (as in a work of art)

mo·tile \\'mōt-ᵊl, 'mō-ˌtīl\ *adj* : capable of spontaneous movement — **mo·til·i·ty** \mō-'til-ət-ē\ *n*

¹mo·tion \\'mō-shən\ *n* **1** : a proposal for action (as by a deliberative body) **2** : an act, process, or instance of moving **3** *pl* : ACTIVITIES, MOVEMENTS — **mo·tion·less** *adj* — **mo·tion·less·ly** *adv* — **mo·tion·less·ness** *n*

²motion *vb* **mo·tioned;** **mo·tion·ing** \\'mō-sh(ə-)niŋ\ : to direct or signal by a motion

motion picture *n* : a series of pictures thrown on a screen so rapidly that they produce a continuous picture in which persons and objects seem to move

motion sickness *n* : sickness induced by motion and characterized by nausea

mo·ti·vate \\'mōt-ə-ˌvāt\ *vb* **-vat·ed; -vat·ing** : to provide with a motive : IMPEL — **mo·ti·va·tion** \ˌmōt-ə-'vā-shən\ *n*

¹mo·tive \\'mōt-iv, 2 *also* mō-'tēv\ *n* **1** : something (as a need or desire) that causes a person to act **2** : a recurrent theme in a musical composition — **mo·tive·less** *adj*

²mo·tive \\'mōt-iv\ *adj* **1** : moving to action **2** : of or relating to motion

mot·ley \\'mät-lē\ *adj* **1** : variegated in color **2** : made up of diverse often incongruous elements **syn** heterogeneous, miscellaneous, assorted, mixed, varied

¹mo·tor \\'mōt-ər\ *n* **1** : one that imparts motion **2** : a machine that produces motion or power for doing work **3** : AUTOMOBILE

²motor *vb* : to travel or transport by automobile : DRIVE — **mo·tor·ist** *n*

mo·tor·bike \\'mōt-ər-ˌbīk\ *n* : a small lightweight motorcycle

mo·tor·boat \-ˌbōt\ *n* : a boat propelled by a motor

mo·tor·cade \-ˌkād\ *n* : a procession of motor vehicles

mo·tor·car \-ˌkär\ *n* : AUTOMOBILE

motor court *n* : MOTEL

mo·tor·cy·cle \\'mōt-ər-ˌsī-kəl\ *n* : a 2-wheeled automotive vehicle — **mo·tor·cy·clist** \-k(ə-)ləst\ *n*

motor home *n* : a motor vehicle built on a truck or bus chassis and equipped as a self-contained traveling home

mo·tor·ize \\'mōt-ə-ˌrīz\ *vb* **-ized; -iz·ing** **1** : to equip with a motor **2** : to equip with motor-driven vehicles

mo·tor·man \\'mōt-ər-mən\ *n* : an operator of a motor-driven vehicle (as a streetcar or subway train)

motor scooter *n* : a low 2- or 3-wheeled automotive vehicle resembling a child's scooter but having a seat

mo·tor·truck \\'mōt-ər-ˌtrək\ *n* : an automotive truck

motor vehicle *n* : an automotive vehicle (as an automobile) not operated on rails

mot·tle \\'mät-ᵊl\ *vb* **mot·tled;** **mot·tling** \\'mät-(ᵊ-)liŋ\ : to mark with spots of different color : BLOTCH

mot·to \\'mät-ō\ *n, pl* **mottoes** *also* **mottos** [It, fr. L *muttum* grunt, fr. *muttire* to mutter] **1** : a sentence, phrase, or word inscribed on something to indicate its character or use **2** : a short expression of a guiding rule of conduct

moue \\'mü\ *n* : a little grimace

mould \\'mōld\ var of MOLD

moult \\'mōlt\ var of MOLT

mound \\'maund\ *n* **1** : an artificial bank or hill of earth or stones **2** : KNOLL

¹**mount** \'maůnt\ *n* : a high hill

²**mount** *vb* **1** : to increase in amount or extent; *also* : RISE, ASCEND **2** : to get up on something; *esp* : to seat oneself on (as a horse) for riding **3** : to put in position ⟨~ artillery⟩ **4** : to set on something that elevates **5** : to attach to a support **6** : to prepare esp. for examination or display : ARRANGE — **mount•able** *adj* — **mount•er** *n*

³**mount** *n* **1** : FRAME, SUPPORT **2** : a means of conveyance; *esp* : SADDLE HORSE

moun•tain \'maůnt-ᵊn\ *n* : a landmass higher than a hill — **moun•tain•ous** \-(ᵊ-)nəs\ *adj*

mountain ash *n* : any of various trees related to the roses that have pinnate leaves and red or orange-red fruits

moun•tain•eer \ₗmaůnt-ᵊn-'iər\ *n* **1** : a native or inhabitant of a mountainous region **2** : one who climbs mountains for sport

mountain goat *n* : an antelope of mountainous northwestern No. America that resembles a goat

mountain laurel *n* : a No. American evergreen shrub of the heath family that has glossy leaves and clusters of rose-colored or white flowers

mountain lion *n* : COUGAR

moun•tain•side \'maůnt-ᵊn-ₗsīd\ *n* : the side of a mountain

moun•tain•top \-ₗtäp\ *n* : the summit of a mountain

moun•te•bank \'maůnt-i-ₗbaŋk\ *n* [It *montimbanco*, fr. *montare* to mount + *in* in, on + *banco, banca* bench] : QUACK, CHARLATAN

Mount•ie \'maůnt-ē\ *n* : a member of the Royal Canadian Mounted Police

mount•ing \'maůnt-iŋ\ *n* : something that serves as a frame or support

mourn \'mōrn\ *vb* : to feel or express grief or sorrow — **mourn•er** *n*

mourn•ful \-fəl\ *adj* : expressing, feeling, or causing sorrow — **mourn•ful•ly** \-ē\ *adv* — **mourn•ful•ness** *n*

mourn•ing \'mōr-niŋ\ *n* **1** : an outward sign (as black clothes) of grief for a person's death **2** : a period of time during which signs of grief are shown

mouse \'maůs\ *n, pl* **mice** \'mīs\ : any of various small rodents with pointed snout, long body, and slender tail

mous•er \'maů-zər\ *n* : a cat proficient at catching mice

mouse•trap \'maůs-ₗtrap\ *n* **1** : a trap for catching mice **2** : a stratagem that lures one to defeat or destruction — **mousetrap** *vb*

mousse \'müs\ *n* [F, lit., froth] : a molded chilled dessert made with sweetened and flavored whipped cream or egg whites and gelatin

mous•tache \'məs-ₗtash, (ₗ)məs-'tash\ var of MUSTACHE

mousy *or* **mous•ey** \'maů-sē, -zē\ *adj* **mous•i•er; -est 1** : QUIET, STEALTHY **2** : TIMID — **mous•i•ness** \'maů-sē-nəs, -zē-\ *n*

¹**mouth** \'maůth\ *n, pl* **mouths** \'maůthz, 'maůths\ **1** : the opening through which an animal takes in food; *also* : the space between the mouth and the pharynx **2** : something resembling a mouth (as in affording entrance) — **mouthed** \'maůthd, 'maůtht\ *adj* — **mouth•ful** *n*

²**mouth** \'maůth\ *vb* : SPEAK; *also* : DECLAIM

mouth•part \'maůth-ₗpärt\ *n* : a structure or appendage near the mouth (as of an insect) esp. when adapted for eating

mouth•piece \-ₗpēs\ *n* **1** : a part (as of a musical instrument) that goes in the mouth or to which the mouth is applied **2** : SPOKESMAN

mouth•wash \-ₗwȯsh, -ₗwäsh\ *n* : a usu. antiseptic liquid preparation for cleaning the mouth and teeth

mou•ton \'mü-ₗtän\ *n* : processed sheepskin that has been sheared or dyed to resemble beaver or seal

¹**move** \'müv\ *vb* **moved; mov•ing 1** : to change or cause to change position or posture : SHIFT **2** : to go or cause to go from one point to another : ADVANCE; *also* : DEPART **3** : to take or cause to take action : PROMPT **4** : to show marked activity **5** : to stir the emotions **6** : to make a formal request, application, or appeal **7** : to change one's residence **8** : EVACUATE **2** — **mov•able** *or* **move•able** \-ə-bəl\ *adj*

²**move** *n* **1** : an act of moving **2** : a calculated procedure : MANEUVER

move•ment \'müv-mənt\ *n* **1** : the act or process of moving : MOVE **2** : TENDENCY, TREND; *also* : a series of organized activities working toward an objective **3** : the moving parts of a mechanism (as of a watch) **4** : RHYTHM **5** : a unit or division of an extended musical composition **6** : CADENCE **7** : an act of voiding the bowels; *also* : STOOL **4**

mov•er \'mü-vər\ *n* : one that moves; *esp* : a person or company that moves the belongings of others from one home or place of business to another

mov•ie \'mü-vē\ *n* **1** : MOTION PICTURE **2** *pl* : a showing of a motion picture **3** *pl* : the motion-picture industry

¹mow \'maù\ *n* : the part of a barn where hay or straw is stored

²mow \'mō\ *vb* **mowed; mowed** *or* **mown** \'mōn\; **mow•ing** **1** : to cut (as grass) with a scythe or machine **2** : to cut the standing herbage of ⟨~ the lawn⟩ — **mow•er** *n*

Mo•zam•bi•can \ˌmō-zəm-'bē-kən\ *n* : a native or inhabitant of Mozambique

moz•za•rel•la \ˌmät-sə-'rel-ə\ *n* [It] : a moist white unsalted unripened mild cheese of a smooth rubbery texture

MP *abbr* **1** melting point **2** member of parliament **3** metropolitan police **4** military police; military policeman

mpg *abbr* miles per gallon

mph *abbr* miles per hour

Mr. \ˌmis-tər\ *n, pl* **Messrs.** \ˌmes-ərz\ — used as a conventional title of courtesy before a man's surname or his title of office

Mrs. \ˌmis-əz, -əs, *esp Southern* ˌmiz-əz, -əs, *or* (ˌ)miz, *or before given names* (ˌ)mis\ *n, pl* **Mes•dames** \mā-'däm, -'dam\ — used as a conventional title of courtesy before a married woman's surname

Ms. \(')miz\ *n* — used instead of *Miss* or *Mrs.*

MS *abbr* **1** manuscript **2** master of science **3** military science **4** Mississippi **5** motor ship **6** multiple sclerosis

msec *abbr* millisecond

msg *abbr* message

MSG *abbr* **1** master sergeant **2** monosodium glutamate

msgr *abbr* **1** monseigneur **2** monsignor

MSgt *abbr* master sergeant

MSS *abbr* manuscripts

MST *abbr* mountain standard time

mt *abbr* mount; mountain

Mt *abbr* Matthew

MT *abbr* **1** metric ton **2** Montana **3** mountain time

mtg *abbr* **1** meeting **2** mortgage

mtge *abbr* mortgage

¹much \'məch\ *adj* **more** \'mōr\; **most** \'mōst\ : great in quantity, amount, extent, or degree ⟨~ money⟩

²much *adv* **more; most** **1** : to a great degree or extent ⟨~ happier⟩ **2** : APPROXIMATELY, NEARLY ⟨looks ~ as he did years ago⟩

³much *n* **1** : a great quantity, amount, extent, or degree **2** : something considerable or impressive

mu•ci•lage \'myü-s(ə-)lij\ *n* : a watery sticky solution (as of a gum) used esp. as an adhesive — **mu•ci•lag•i•nous** \ˌmyü-sə-'laj-ə-nəs\ *adj*

muck \'mək\ *n* **1** : soft moist barnyard manure **2** : FILTH, DIRT **3** : a dark richly organic soil; *also* : MUD, MIRE — **mucky** *adj*

muck•rak•er \-ˌrā-kər\ *n* : one who exposes publicly real or apparent misconduct of prominent individuals — **muck•rak•ing** \-ˌrā-kiŋ\ *n*

mu•cus \'myü-kəs\ *n* : a slimy slippery protective secretion of membranes (**mucous membranes**) lining some body cavities — **mu•cous** \-kəs\ *adj*

mud \'məd\ *n* : soft wet earth : MIRE — **mud•di•ly** \'məd-ᵊl-ē\ *adv* — **mud•di•ness** \-ē-nəs\ *n* — **mud•dy** *adj or vb*

mud•dle \'məd-ᵊl\ *vb* **mud•dled; mud•dling** \'məd-(ə-)liŋ\ **1** : to make muddy **2** : to confuse esp. with liquor **3** : to mix up or make a mess of **4** : to think or act in a confused way

mud•dle•head•ed \ˌməd-ᵊl-'hed-əd\ *adj* **1** : mentally confused **2** : INEPT

mud•guard \'məd-ˌgärd\ *n* : a guard over or a flap behind a wheel of a vehicle to catch or deflect mud

mud•room \'məd-ˌrüm, -ˌrùm\ *n* : a room in a house for removing dirty or wet footwear and clothing

mud•sling•er \-ˌsliŋ-ər\ *n* : one who uses invective esp. against a political opponent — **mud•sling•ing** \-ˌsliŋ-iŋ\ *n*

Muen•ster \'mən-stər, 'm(y)ün-, 'mùn-\ *n* : a semisoft bland or sharp cheese

mu•ez•zin \m(y)ü-'ez-ᵊn\ *n* : a Muslim crier who calls the hour of daily prayer

¹muff \'məf\ *n* : a warm tubular covering for the hands

²muff *n* : a bungling performance; *esp*

: a failure to hold a ball in attempting a catch — **muff** *vb*

muf•fin \\'məf-ən\ *n* : a small soft biscuit baked in a small cup-shaped container

muf•fle \\'məf-əl\ *vb* **muf•fled; muf•fling** \\'məf-(ə-)liŋ\ **1** : to wrap up so as to conceal or protect **2** : to wrap or pad with something to dull the sound of **3** : to keep down : SUPPRESS

muf•fler \\'məf-lər\ *n* **1** : a scarf worn around the neck **2** : a device to deaden noise

muf•ti \\'məf-tē\ *n* : civilian clothes

¹mug \\'məg\ *n* : a usu. metal or earthenware cylindrical drinking cup

²mug *vb* **mugged; mug•ging 1** : to make faces esp. in order to attract the attention of an audience **2** : PHOTOGRAPH

³mug *vb* **mugged; mug•ging** : to assault usu. with intent to rob — **mug•ger** *n*

mug•gy \\'məg-ē\ *adj* **mug•gi•er; -est** : being warm and humid — **mug•gi•ness** \\'məg-ē-nəs\ *n*

mug•wump \\'məg-,wəmp\ *n* [obs. slang *mugwump* (kingpin), fr. Natick (a No. American Indian dialect) *mugwomp* captain] : an independent in politics

Mu•ham•mad•an \mō-'ham-əd-ən, -'häm-; mü-\ *n* : MUSLIM — **Mu•ham•mad•an•ism** \-,iz-əm\ *n*

muk•luk \\'mək-,lək\ *n* [Esk *muklok* large seal] **1** : an Eskimo boot of sealskin or reindeer skin **2** : a boot with a soft leather sole worn over several pairs of socks

mu•lat•to \m(y)ù-'lat-ō, -'lät-\ *n, pl* **-toes** *or* **-tos** [Sp *mulato,* fr. *mulo* mule, fr. L *mulus;* so called because the mule is the offspring of parents of different species] : a first-generation offspring of a Negro and a white; *also* : a person of mixed Caucasian and Negro ancestry

mul•ber•ry \\'məl-,ber-ē\ *n* : a tree grown for its leaves that are used as food for silkworms or for its edible berrylike fruit; *also* : this fruit

mulch \\'məlch\ *n* : a protective covering (as of straw or leaves) spread on the ground esp. to reduce evaporation or control weeds — **mulch** *vb*

¹mulct \\'məlkt\ *vb* **1** : FINE **2** : DEFRAUD

²mulct *n* : FINE, PENALTY

¹mule \\'myül\ *n* **1** : a hybrid offspring of a male donkey and a female horse **2**

: a very stubborn person — **mul•ish** \\'myü-lish\ *adj* — **mul•ish•ly** *adv* — **mu•lish•ness** *n*

²mule *n* : a slipper whose upper does not extend around the heel of the foot

mule deer *n* : a long-eared deer of western No. America

mu•le•teer \,myü-lə-'tiər\ *n* : one who drives mules

¹mull \\'məl\ *vb* : PONDER, MEDITATE

²mull *vb* : to heat, sweeten, and flavor (as wine) with spices

mul•lein \\'məl-ən\ *n* : a tall herb with coarse woolly leaves and flowers in spikes

mul•let \\'məl-ət\ *n, pl* **mullet** *or* **mullets 1** : any of various largely gray marine food fishes **2** : any of various red or golden mostly tropical marine food fishes

mul•li•gan stew \,məl-i-gən-\ *n* : a stew made from whatever ingredients are available

mul•li•ga•taw•ny \,məl-i-gə-'tô-nē\ *n* : a soup usu. of chicken stock seasoned with curry

mul•lion \\'məl-yən\ *n* : a vertical strip separating windowpanes

multi- *comb form* **1** : many : multiple ⟨*multi*unit⟩ **2** : many times over ⟨*mul-ti*millionaire⟩

mul•ti•col•ored \,məl-ti-'kəl-ərd\ *adj* : having many colors

mul•ti•di•men•sion•al \-ti-də-'mench-nəl, -dī-; -,tī-də-\ *adj* : of, relating to, or having many dimensions ⟨a ∼ problem⟩

mul•ti•fac•et•ed \-'fas-ət-əd\ *adj* : having several distinct facets

mul•ti•fam•i•ly \-'fam-(ə-)lē\ *adj* : designed for use by several families

mul•ti•far•i•ous \,məl-tə-'far-ē-əs\ *adj* : having great variety : DIVERSE — **mul•ti•far•i•ous•ly** *adv*

mul•ti•flo•ra rose \,məl-tə-'flōr-ə-\ *n* : a vigorous thorny rose with clusters of small flowers

mul•ti•form \\'məl-ti-,fôrm\ *adj* : having many forms or appearances — **mul•ti•for•mi•ty** \,məl-ti-'fôr-mət-ē\ *n*

mul•ti•lat•er•al \,məl-ti-'lat-ə-rəl, -,tī-, -'la-trəl\ *adj* : having many sides or participants ⟨∼ treaty⟩

mul•ti•lev•el \-'lev-əl\ *adj* : having several levels

mul•ti•lin•gual \-'liŋ-gwəl\ *adj* : containing, expressed in, or able to use several languages — **mul·ti·lin·gual·ism** \-gwə-ˌliz-əm\ *n*

mul·ti·me·dia \-ˈmēd-ē-ə\ *adj* : using, involving, or encompassing several media ⟨a ∼ advertising campaign⟩

mul·ti·mil·lion·aire \ˌməl-ti-ˌmil-yə-ˈnaər, -ˌtī-, -ˈmil-yə-ˌnaər\ *n* : a person worth several million dollars

mul·ti·na·tion·al \-ˈnash-(ə-)nəl\ *adj* **1** : of or relating to several nationalities ⟨a ∼ society⟩ **2** : relating to or involving several nations **3** : having divisions in several countries

¹**mul·ti·ple** \ˈməl-tə-pəl\ *adj* **1** : more than one; *also* : MANY **2** : VARIOUS, COMPLEX

²**multiple** *n* : the product of a quantity by an integer ⟨35 is a ∼ of 7⟩

multiple–choice *adj* : having several answers given from which the correct one is to be chosen ⟨a ∼ question⟩

multiple sclerosis *n* : a disease marked by patches of hardened tissue in the brain or spinal cord resulting in partial or complete paralysis and muscular twitching

mul·ti·pli·cand \ˌməl-tə-pli-ˈkand\ *n* : a number that is to be multiplied by another

mul·ti·pli·ca·tion \ˌməl-tə-plə-ˈkā-shən\ *n* **1** : INCREASE **2** : a short method of finding out what would be the result of adding a figure the number of times indicated by another figure

multiplication sign *n* **1** : TIMES SIGN **2** : a centered dot used to indicate multiplication

mul·ti·plic·i·ty \ˌməl-tə-ˈplis-ət-ē\ *n, pl* **-ties** : a great number or variety

mul·ti·pli·er \ˈməl-tə-ˌplī(-ə)r\ *n* : one that multiplies; *esp* : a number by which another number is multiplied

mul·ti·ply \ˈməl-tə-ˌplī\ *vb* **-plied; -ply·ing 1** : to increase in number (as by breeding) **2** : to find the product of by multiplication

mul·ti·pur·pose \ˌməl-ti-ˈpər-pəs, -ˌtī-\ *adj* : having or serving several purposes

mul·ti·ra·cial \-ˈrā-shəl\ *adj* : composed of, involving, or representing several races

mul·ti·sense \-ˌsen(t)s\ *adj* : having several meanings ⟨∼ words⟩

mul·ti·stage \-ˌstāj\ *adj* : having successive operating stages ⟨∼ rockets⟩

mul·ti·story \-ˌstōr-ē\ *adj* : having several stories ⟨∼ buildings⟩

mul·ti·tude \ˈməl-tə-ˌt(y)üd\ *n* : a great number — **mul·ti·tu·di·nous** \ˌməl-tə-ˈt(y)üd-(ə-)nəs\ *adj*

mul·ti·unit \ˌməl-ti-ˈyü-nət, -ˌtī-\ *adj* : having several units

mul·ti·ver·si·ty \ˌməl-ti-ˈvər-s(ə-)tē\ *n, pl* **-ties** : a very large university with many divisions and diverse functions

mul·ti·vi·ta·min \-ˈvīt-ə-mən\ *adj* : containing several vitamins and esp. all known to be essential to health

¹**mum** \ˈməm\ *adj* : SILENT

²**mum** *n* : CHRYSANTHEMUM

mum·ble \ˈməm-bəl\ *vb* **mum·bled; mum·bling** \-b(ə-)liŋ\ : to speak in a low indistinct manner — **mumble** *n* — **mum·bler** \-b(ə-)lər\ *n* — **mum·bly** \-b(ə-)lē\ *adj*

mum·ble·ty·peg *or* **mum·ble-the-peg** \ˈməm-bəl-(tē-)ˌpeg\ *n* : a game in which the players try to flip a knife from various positions so that the blade will stick into the ground

mum·bo jum·bo \ˌməm-bō-ˈjəm-bō\ *n* **1** : a complicated ritual with elaborate trappings **2** : confusing or meaningless talk : NONSENSE

mum·mer \ˈməm-ər\ *n* **1** : an actor esp. in a pantomime **2** : one who goes merrymaking in disguise during festivals — **mum·mery** *n*

mum·my \ˈməm-ē\ *n, pl* **mummies** [ME *mummie* powdered parts of a mummified body used as a drug, fr. MF *momie*, fr. ML *mumia* mummy, powdered mummy, fr. Ar *mūmiyah* bitumen, mummy, fr. Per *mūm* wax] : a body embalmed for burial in the manner of the ancient Egyptians — **mum·mi·fi·ca·tion** \ˌməm-i-fə-ˈkā-shən\ *n* — **mum·mi·fy** \ˈməm-i-ˌfī\ *vb*

mumps \ˈməmps\ *n sing or pl* [fr. pl. of obs. *mump* (grimace)] : a virus disease marked by fever and swelling esp. of the salivary glands

mun *or* **munic** *abbr* municipal

munch \ˈmənch\ *vb* : to chew with a crunching sound

munch·ies \ˈmən-chēz\ *n pl* **1** : hunger pangs **2** : light snack foods

mun·dane \ˌmən-ˈdān, ˈmən-ˌdān\ *adj*

1 : of or relating to the world **2** : concerned with the practical details of everyday life — **mun·dane·ly** adv

mu·nic·i·pal \myu̇-'nis-ə-pəl\ adj **1** : of, relating to, or characteristic of a municipality **2** : restricted to one locality — **mu·nic·i·pal·ly** \-ē\ adv

mu·nic·i·pal·i·ty \myu̇-ˌnis-ə-'pal-ət-ē\ n, pl **-ties** : an urban political unit with corporate status and usu. powers of self-government

mu·nif·i·cent \myu̇-'nif-ə-sənt\ adj : liberal in giving : GENEROUS — **mu·nif·i·cence** \-səns\ n

mu·ni·tions \myu̇-'nish-ənz\ n pl : military materiel; esp : AMMUNITION

¹mu·ral \'myu̇r-əl\ adj **1** : of or relating to a wall **2** : applied to and made part of a wall surface

²mural n : a mural painting — **mu·ral·ist** n

¹mur·der \'mərd-ər\ n **1** : the crime of unlawfully killing a person esp. with malice aforethought **2** : something unusually difficult or dangerous

²murder vb **1** : to commit a murder; also : to kill brutally **2** : to put an end to **3** : to spoil by performing poorly ⟨∼ a song⟩ — **mur·der·er** n

mur·der·ess \'mərd-ə-rəs\ n : a woman who murders

mur·der·ous \'mərd-ər-əs\ adj **1** : marked by or causing murder or bloodshed ⟨∼ gunfire⟩ **2** : having or appearing to have the purpose of murder — **mur·der·ous·ly** adv

murk \'mərk\ n : DARKNESS, GLOOM — **murk·i·ly** \'mər-kə-lē\ adv — **murk·i·ness** \-kē-nəs\ n — **murky** adj

mur·mur \'mər-mər\ n **1** : a muttered complaint **2** : a low indistinct often continuous sound — **murmur** vb — **mur·mur·er** n — **mur·mur·ous** adj

mur·rain \'mər-ən\ n : PLAGUE

mus abbr **1** museum **2** music

mus·ca·tel \ˌməs-kə-'tel\ n : a sweet dessert wine

¹mus·cle \'məs-əl\ n [MF, fr. L musculus, fr. dim. of mus mouse] **1** : body tissue consisting of long cells that contract when stimulated; also : an organ consisting of this tissue and functioning in moving a body part **2** : STRENGTH, BRAWN — **mus·cled** \'məs-əld\ adj — **mus·cu·lar** \'məs-kyə-lər\ adj — **mus·cu·lar·i·ty** \ˌməs-kyə-'lar-ət-ē\ n

²muscle vb **mus·cled; mus·cling** \'məs-(ə-)liŋ\ : to force one's way ⟨∼ in on another racketeer⟩

mus·cle–bound \'məs-əl-ˌbau̇nd\ adj : having some of the muscles abnormally enlarged and lacking in elasticity (as from excessive athletic exercise)

muscular dystrophy n : a disease characterized by progressive wasting of muscles

mus·cu·la·ture \'məs-kyə-lə-ˌchu̇r\ n : the muscles of the body or its parts

¹muse \'myüz\ vb **mused; mus·ing** [ME musen, fr. MF muser to gape, idle, muse, fr. muse mouth of an animal, fr. ML musus] : to become absorbed in thought — **mus·ing·ly** adv

²muse n [fr. Muse any of the nine sister goddesses of learning and the arts in Greek mythology, fr. ME, fr. MF, fr. L Musa, fr. Gk Mousa] : a source of inspiration

mu·sette \myu̇-'zet\ n [F] : a small knapsack with a shoulder strap used esp. by soldiers for carrying provisions and personal belongings

musette bag n : MUSETTE

mu·se·um \myu̇-'zē-əm\ n : an institution devoted to the procurement, care, and display of objects of lasting interest or value

¹mush \'məsh\ n **1** : cornmeal boiled in water **2** : sentimental drivel

²mush vb : to travel esp. over snow with a sled drawn by dogs

¹mush·room \'məsh-ˌrüm, -ˌru̇m\ n : the fleshy usu. caplike spore-bearing organ of various fungi esp. when edible

²mushroom vb **1** : to grow rapidly **2** : to spread out : EXPAND

mushy \'məsh-ē\ adj **mush·i·er; -est 1** : soft like mush **2** : weakly sentimental

mu·sic \'myü-zik\ n **1** : the science or art of combining tones into a composition having structure and continuity; also : vocal or instrumental sounds having rhythm, melody, or harmony **2** : an agreeable sound **3** : the unpleasant consequences of one's actions ⟨face the ∼⟩

¹mu·si·cal \'myü-zi-kəl\ adj **1** : of or relating to music or musicians **2** : hav-

ing the pleasing tonal qualities of music **3** : having an interest in or a talent for music — **mu·si·cal·ly** \-k(ə-)lē\ *adv*
²**musical** *n* : a film or theatrical production consisting of musical numbers and dialogue based on a unifying plot
mu·si·cale \ˌmyü-zi-ˈkal\ *n* : a usu. private social gathering featuring music
mu·si·cian \myü-ˈzish-ən\ *n* : a composer, conductor, or performer of music — **mu·si·cian·ly** *adj* — **mu·si·cian·ship** *n*
mu·si·col·o·gy \ˌmyü-zi-ˈkäl-ə-jē\ *n* : a study of music as a field of knowledge or research — **mu·si·co·log·i·cal** \-kə-ˈläj-i-kəl\ *adj* — **mu·si·col·o·gist** \-ˈkäl-ə-jəst\ *n*
musk \ˈməsk\ *n* : a substance obtained esp. from a small Asian deer (**musk deer**) and used as a perfume fixative — **musk·i·ness** \ˈməs-kē-nəs\ *n* — **musky** *adj*
mus·keg \ˈməs-ˌkeg\ *n* : BOG; *esp* : a mossy bog in northern No. America
mus·kel·lunge \ˈməs-kə-ˌlənj\ *n, pl* **muskellunge** : a large No. American pike prized as a sport fish
mus·ket \ˈməs-kət\ *n* [MF *mousquet*, fr. It *moschetto* arrow for a crossbow, musket, fr. dim. of *mosca* fly, fr. L *musca*] : a heavy large-caliber usu. muzzle-loading shoulder firearm — **mus·ke·teer** \ˌməs-kə-ˈtiər\ *n*
mus·ket·ry \ˈməs-kə-trē\ *n* **1** : MUSKETS **2** : MUSKETEERS **3** : musket fire
musk·mel·on \ˈməsk-ˌmel-ən\ *n* : a small round to oval melon that has usu. a sweet edible green or orange flesh
musk–ox \ˈməsk-ˌäks\ *n* : a heavyset shaggy-coated wild ox of Greenland and the arctic tundra of northern No. America
musk·rat \ˈməs-ˌkrat\ *n, pl* **muskrat** or **muskrats** : a large No. American water rodent with webbed feet and dark brown fur; *also* : its fur
Mus·lim \ˈməz-ləm\ *n* : an adherent of the religion founded by the Arab prophet Muhammad
mus·lin \ˈməz-lən\ *n* : a plain-woven sheer to coarse cotton fabric
¹**muss** \ˈməs\ *n* : a state of disorder — **muss·i·ly** \ˈməs-ə-lē\ *adv* — **muss·i·ness** \-ē-nəs\ *n* — **mussy** *adj*
²**muss** *vb* : to make untidy : DISARRANGE

mus·sel \ˈməs-əl\ *n* **1** : a dark edible saltwater bivalve mollusk **2** : any of various freshwater bivalve mollusks of the central U.S. having shells with a pearly lining
¹**must** \(ˈ)məst\ *vb* — used as an auxiliary esp. to express a command, requirement, obligation, or necessity
²**must** \ˈməst\ *n* **1** : an imperative duty **2** : an indispensable item
mus·tache \ˈməs-ˌtash, (ˌ)məs-ˈtash\ *n* : the hair growing on the human upper lip
mus·tang \ˈməs-ˌtaŋ\ *n* [MexSp *mestengo*, fr. Sp, stray, fr. *mesteño* strayed, fr. *mesta* annual roundup of cattle that disposed of strays, fr. ML (*animalia*) *mixta* mixed animals] : a small hardy naturalized horse of the western plains of America
mus·tard \ˈməs-tərd\ *n* **1** : a pungent yellow powder obtained from the seeds of an herb related to the turnips and used as a condiment or in medicine **2** : the mustard plant; *also* : a closely related plant
mustard gas *n* : an irritant vesicant poisonous gas used in warfare
¹**mus·ter** \ˈməs-tər\ *vb* **mus·tered; mus·ter·ing** \-t(ə-)riŋ\ [ME *mustren* to show, muster, fr. OF *monstrer*, fr. L *monstrare* to show, fr. *monstrum* evil omen, monster] **1** : CONVENE, ASSEMBLE; *also* : to call the roll of **2** : ACCUMULATE **3** : to call forth : ROUSE **4** : to amount to : COMPRISE
²**muster** *n* **1** : an act of assembling (as for military inspection); *also* : critical examination **2** : an assembled group
muster out *vb* : to discharge from military service
musty \ˈməs-tē\ *adj* **mus·ti·er; -est** : MOLDY, STALE; *also* : tasting or smelling of damp or decay — **must·i·ly** \ˈməs-tə-lē\ *adv* — **must·i·ness** \-tē-nəs\ *n*
mu·ta·ble \ˈmyüt-ə-bəl\ *adj* **1** : prone to change : FICKLE **2** : liable to mutation : VARIABLE — **mu·ta·bil·i·ty** \ˌmyüt-ə-ˈbil-ət-ē\ *n*
mu·tant \ˈmyüt-ᵊnt\ *adj* : of, relating to, or produced by mutation — **mutant** *n*
mu·tate \ˈmyü-ˌtāt\ *vb* **mu·tat·ed; mu·tat·ing** : to undergo or cause to undergo mutation — **mu·ta·tive** \ˈmyü-ˌtāt-iv, ˈmyüt-ət-\ *adj*

mu·ta·tion \myü-'tā-shən\ *n* **1** : CHANGE **2** : a sudden and relatively permanent change in a hereditary character; *also* : the process of producing a mutation **3** : an individual or strain resulting from mutation — **mu·ta·tion·al** *adj*

¹mute \'myüt\ *adj* **mut·er; mut·est 1** : unable to speak : DUMB **2** : SILENT — **mute·ly** *adv* — **mute·ness** *n*

²mute *n* **1** : a person who cannot or does not speak **2** : a device on a musical instrument that reduces, softens, or muffles the tone

³mute *vb* **mut·ed; mut·ing** : to muffle or reduce the sound of

mu·ti·late \'myüt-ᵊl-ˌāt\ *vb* **-lat·ed; -lat·ing 1** : MAIM, CRIPPLE **2** : to cut up or alter radically so as to make imperfect — **mu·ti·la·tion** \ˌmyüt-ᵊl-'ā-shən\ *n* — **mu·ti·la·tor** \'myüt-ᵊl-ˌāt-ər\ *n*

mu·ti·ny \'myüt-(ə-)nē\ *n, pl* **-nies** : willful refusal to obey constituted authority; *esp* : revolt against a superior officer — **mu·ti·neer** \ˌmyüt-ᵊn-'iər\ *n* — **mu·ti·nous** \'myüt-ᵊn-əs\ *adj* — **mu·ti·nous·ly** *adv*

mutt \'mət\ *n* : MONGREL, CUR

mut·ter \'mət-ər\ *vb* **1** : to speak indistinctly or with a low voice and lips partly closed **2** : GRUMBLE — **mutter** *n*

mut·ton \'mət-ᵊn\ *n* [ME *motoun*, fr. OF *moton* ram] : the flesh of a mature sheep used for food — **mut·tony** *adj*

mut·ton·chops \'mət-ᵊn-ˌchäps\ *n pl* : whiskers on the side of the face that are narrow at the temple and broad and round by the lower jaws

mu·tu·al \'myü-chə(-wə)l\ *adj* **1** : given and received in equal amount ⟨∼ trust⟩ **2** : having the same feelings one for the other ⟨∼ enemies⟩ **3** : COMMON, JOINT ⟨a ∼ friend⟩ — **mu·tu·al·ly** \-ē\ *adv*

mutual fund *n* : an investment company that invests money of its shareholders in a usu. diversified group of securities of other corporations

muu·muu \'mü-ˌmü\ *n* : a loose dress of Hawaiian origin for informal wear

¹muz·zle \'məz-əl\ *n* **1** : the nose and jaws of an animal; *also* : a covering for the muzzle to prevent the animal from biting or eating **2** : the mouth of a gun

²muzzle *vb* **muz·zled; muz·zling** \-(ə-)liŋ\ **1** : to put a muzzle on **2** : to restrain from expression : GAG

mv *or* **mV** *abbr* millivolt

MV *abbr* motor vessel

MVP *abbr* most valuable player

MW *abbr* megawatt

my \(')mī, mə\ *adj* **1** : of or relating to me or myself **2** — used interjectionally esp. to express surprise

my·col·o·gy \mī-'käl-ə-jē\ *n* : the study of fungi — **my·co·log·i·cal** \ˌmī-kə-'läj-i-kəl\ *adj* — **my·col·o·gist** \mī-'käl-ə-jəst\ *n*

my·elo·ma \ˌmī-ə-'lō-mə\ *n, pl* **-mas** *or* **-ma·ta** \-mət-ə\ : a primary tumor of the bone marrow

my·nah *or* **my·na** \'mī-nə\ *n* : any of several Asian starlings; *esp* : a dark brown slightly crested bird sometimes taught to mimic speech

my·o·pia \mī-'ō-pē-ə\ *n* : SHORTSIGHTEDNESS — **my·o·pic** \-'ō-pik, -'äp-ik\ *adj* — **my·o·pi·cal·ly** \-(ə-)lē\ *adv*

¹myr·i·ad \'mir-ē-əd\ *n* [Gk *myriad-, myrias,* fr. *myrioi* countless, ten thousand] : an indefinitely large number

²myriad *adj* : consisting of a very great but indefinite number

myr·mi·don \'mər-mə-ˌdän\ *n* : a loyal follower; *esp* : one who executes orders without protest or pity

myrrh \'mər\ *n* : a fragrant aromatic plant gum used in perfumes and formerly for incense

myr·tle \'mərt-ᵊl\ *n* : an evergreen shrub of southern Europe with shiny leaves, fragrant flowers, and black berries; *also* : PERIWINKLE

my·self \mī-'self, mə-\ *pron* : I, ME — used reflexively, for emphasis, or in absolute constructions ⟨I hurt ∼⟩ ⟨I ∼ did it⟩ ⟨∼ busy, I sent him instead⟩

mys·tery \'mis-t(ə-)rē\ *n, pl* **-ter·ies 1** : a religious truth known by revelation alone **2** : something not understood or beyond understanding **3** : enigmatic quality or character **4** : a work of fiction dealing with the solution of a mysterious crime — **mys·te·ri·ous** \mis-'tir-ē-əs\ *adj* — **mys·te·ri·ous·ly** *adv* — **mys·te·ri·ous·ness** *n*

¹mys·tic \'mis-tik\ *adj* **1** : of or relating to mystics or mysticism **2** : MYSTERIOUS; *also* : MYSTIFYING

²mystic *n* : a person who experiences

mystical union or direct communion with God or ultimate reality

mys·ti·cal \'mis-ti-kəl\ *adj* **1** : SPIRITUAL, SYMBOLIC **2** : of or relating to an intimate knowledge of or direct communion with God (as through contemplation or visions)

mys·ti·cism \'mis-tə-ˌsiz-əm\ *n* : the belief that direct knowledge of God or ultimate reality is attainable through immediate intuition or insight

mys·ti·fy \'mis-tə-ˌfī\ *vb* **-fied; -fy·ing** **1** : to perplex the mind of **2** : to make mysterious — **mys·ti·fi·ca·tion** \ˌmis-tə-fə-'kā-shən\ *n*

mys·tique \mis-'tēk\ *n* [F] **1** : an air or attitude of mystery and reverence developing around something **2** : the special esoteric skill essential in a calling or activity

myth \'mith\ *n* **1** : a usu. legendary narrative that presents part of the beliefs of a people or explains a practice or natural phenomenon **2** : an imaginary or unverifiable person or thing — **myth·i·cal** \-i-kəl\ *adj*

my·thol·o·gy \mith-'äl-ə-jē\ *n, pl* **-gies** : a body of myths and esp. of those dealing with the gods and heroes of a people — **myth·o·log·i·cal** \ˌmith-ə-'läj-i-kəl\ *adj* — **my·thol·o·gist** \mith-'äl-ə-jəst\ *n*

N

¹n \'en\ *n, pl* **n's** *or* **ns** \'enz\ *often cap* **1** : the 14th letter of the English alphabet **2** : an unspecified quantity

²n *abbr, often cap* **1** net **2** neuter **3** noon **4** normal **5** north; northern **6** note **7** noun **8** number

N *symbol* nitrogen

-n — see -EN

Na *symbol* [NL *natrium*] sodium

NA *abbr* **1** no account **2** North America **3** not applicable **4** not available

NAACP \ˌen-ˌdəb-əl-ˌā-ˌsē-'pē, ˌen-ˌā-ˌā-ˌsē-\ *abbr* National Association for the Advancement of Colored People

nab \'nab\ *vb* **nabbed; nab·bing** : SEIZE; *esp* : ARREST

na·bob \'nā-ˌbäb\ *n* [Hindi & Urdu *nawwāb*, fr. Ar *nuwwāb*, pl. of *nā'ib* governor] : a man of great wealth or prominence

na·celle \nə-'sel\ *n* : an enclosed shelter on an aircraft (as for an engine)

na·cre \'nā-kər\ *n* : MOTHER-OF-PEARL

na·dir \'nā-ˌdir, 'nād-ər\ *n* [ME, fr. MF, fr. Ar *naẓīr* opposite] **1** : the point of the celestial sphere that is directly opposite the zenith and directly beneath the observer **2** : the lowest point

¹nag \'nag\ *n* : HORSE; *esp* : an old or decrepit horse

²nag *vb* **nagged; nag·ging** **1** : to find fault incessantly : COMPLAIN **2** : to irritate by constant scolding or urging **3** : to be a continuing source of annoyance ⟨a *nagging* toothache⟩

³nag *n* : one who nags habitually

Nah *abbr* Nahum

Na·huatl \'nä-ˌwät-ᵊl\ *n* : an American Indian language of southern Mexico

Na·hum \'nā-(h)əm\ *n* — see BIBLE table

na·iad \'nā-əd, 'nī-, -ˌad\ *n, pl* **naiads** *or* **na·ia·des** \-ə-ˌdēz\ **1** : one of the nymphs in ancient mythology living in lakes, rivers, springs, and fountains **2** : an aquatic young of some insects (as a dragonfly)

na·if *or* **na·if** \nä-'ēf\ *adj* : NAIVE

¹nail \'nāl\ *n* **1** : a horny sheath protecting the end of each finger and toe in man and related primates **2** : a slender pointed fastener with a head designed to be pounded in

²nail *vb* : to fasten with or as if with a nail — **nail·er** *n*

nail down *vb* : to settle or establish clearly and unmistakably

nain·sook \'nān-ˌsůk\ *n* [Hindi *nainsukh*, fr. *nain* eye + *sukh* delight] : a soft lightweight muslin

nai·ra \'nī-rə\ *n* — see MONEY table

na·ive *or* **na·ïve** \nä-'ēv\ *adj* **na·iv·er; -est** [F *naïve*, fem. of *naïf*, fr. OF, inborn, natural, fr. L *nativus* native] **1** : marked by unaffected simplicity : ARTLESS, INGENUOUS **2** : CREDULOUS — **na·ive·ly** *adv* — **na·ive·ness** *n*

na·ive·té *also* **na·ive·té** *or* **na·ive·te** \ˌnä-ˌēv(-ə)-'tä, nä-'ē-və-ˌtä\ *n* **1** : a naive remark or action **2** : the quality or state of being naive

na·ive·ty also **na·ïve·ty** \nä-ˈēv-(ə-)tē\ n, pl **-ties** : NAÏVETÉ

na·ked \ˈnā-kəd\ adj **1** : having no clothes on : NUDE **2** : UNSHEATHED ⟨a ∼ sword⟩ **3** : lacking a usual or natural covering (as of foliage or feathers) **4** : PLAIN, UNADORNED ⟨the ∼ truth⟩ **5** : not aided by artificial means ⟨seen by the ∼ eye⟩ — **na·ked·ly** adv — **na·ked·ness** n

nam·by–pam·by \ˌnam-bē-ˈpam-bē\ adj **1** : INSIPID **2** : WEAK, INDECISIVE

¹**name** \ˈnām\ n **1** : a word or words by which a person or thing is known **2** : a disparaging epithet ⟨call someone ∼s⟩ **3** : REPUTATION; esp : distinguished reputation ⟨made a ∼ for himself⟩ **4** : FAMILY, CLAN ⟨was a disgrace to his ∼⟩ **5** : appearance as opposed to reality ⟨a friend in ∼ only⟩

²**name** vb **named; nam·ing 1** : to give a name to : CALL **2** : to mention or identify by name **3** : NOMINATE, APPOINT **4** : to decide on : CHOOSE **5** : to speak about : MENTION ⟨∼ a price⟩ — **name·able** adj

³**name** adj **1** : of, relating to, or bearing a name ⟨∼ tag⟩ **2** : having an established reputation ⟨∼ brands⟩

name day n : the church feast day of the saint after whom one is named

name·less \ˈnām-ləs\ adj **1** : having no name **2** : not marked with a name ⟨a ∼ grave⟩ **3** : not known by name ⟨a ∼ hero⟩ **4** : too distressing to be described ⟨∼ fears⟩ — **name·less·ly** adv

name·ly \ˈnām-lē\ adv : that is to say : AS ⟨the cat family, ∼, lions, tigers, and similar animals⟩

name·plate \-ˌplāt\ n : a plate or plaque bearing a name (as of a resident)

name·sake \-ˌsāk\ n : one that has the same name as another; esp : one named after another

nan·keen \nan-ˈkēn\ n : a durable brownish yellow cotton fabric orig. woven by hand in China

nan·ny goat \ˈnan-ē-\ n : a female domestic goat

nano·me·ter \ˈnan-ə-ˌmēt-ər\ n : one billionth of a meter

nano·sec·ond \-ˌsek-ənd\ n : one billionth of a second

¹**nap** \ˈnap\ vb **napped; nap·ping 1** : to

sleep briefly esp. during the day : DOZE **2** : to be off guard ⟨was caught napping⟩

²**nap** n : a short sleep esp. during the day

³**nap** n : a soft downy fibrous surface (as on yarn and cloth) — **nap·less** adj

na·palm \ˈnā-ˌpä(l)m\ n [naphthalene + palmitate salt of a fatty acid] **1** : a thickener used in jelling gasoline (as for incendiary bombs) **2** : fuel jelled with napalm

nape \ˈnāp, ˈnap\ n : the back of the neck

na·pery \ˈnā-p(ə-)rē\ n : household linen esp. for the table

naph·tha \ˈnaf-thə, ˈnap-\ n : any of various liquid hydrocarbon mixtures used chiefly as solvents

naph·tha·lene \-ˌlēn\ n : a crystalline substance obtained from coal tar used in organic synthesis and as a moth repellent

nap·kin \ˈnap-kən\ n **1** : a piece of material (as cloth) used at table to wipe the lips or fingers and protect the clothes **2** : a small cloth or towel

na·po·leon \nə-ˈpōl-yən, -ˈpō-lē-ən\ n : an oblong pastry with a filling of cream, custard, or jelly between layers of puff paste

Na·po·le·on·ic \nə-ˌpō-lē-ˈän-ik\ adj : of, relating to, or characteristic of Napoleon I or his family

narc \ˈnärk\ n, slang : one (as a government agent) who investigates narcotics violations

nar·cis·sism \ˈnär-sə-ˌsiz-əm\ n [G narzissismus, fr. Narziss Narcissus, fr. L Narcissus, fr. Gk Narkissos, beautiful youth of Greek mythology who fell in love with his own image] **1** : undue dwelling on one's own self or attainments **2** : love of or sexual desire for one's own body — **nar·cis·sist** \-səst\ n or adj — **nar·cis·sis·tic** \ˌnär-sə-ˈsis-tik\ adj

nar·cis·sus \när-ˈsis-əs\ n, pl **-cis·sus** or **-cis·sus·es** or **-cis·si** \-ˈsis-ˌī, -ē\ : DAFFODIL; esp : one with short-tubed flowers usu. borne separately

nar·co·sis \när-ˈkō-səs\ n, pl **-co·ses** \-ˌsēz\ : a state of stupor, unconsciousness, or arrested activity produced by the influence of chemicals (as narcotics)

nar·cot·ic \när-ˈkät-ik\ n [ME narkotik,

fr. MF *narcotique,* fr. *narcotique,* adj., fr. ML *narcoticus,* fr. Gk *narkōtikos,* fr. *narkoun* to benumb, fr. *narkē* numbness] : a drug (as opium) that dulls the senses and induces sleep — **narcotic** *adj*

nar·co·tize \'när-kə-ˌtīz\ *vb* **-tized; -tiz·ing 1** : to treat with or subject to a narcotic; *also* : to put into a state of narcosis **2** : to soothe to unconsciousness or unawareness

nard \'närd\ *n* : a fragment ointment of the ancients

na·ris \'nar-əs\ *n, pl* **na·res** \'nar-(ˌ)ēz\ [L] : an opening of the nose : NOSTRIL

nark var of NARC

Nar·ra·gan·set \ˌnar-ə-'gan-sət\ *n, pl* **Narraganset** *or* **Narragansets** : a member of an American Indian people of Rhode Island

nar·rate \'nar-ˌāt\ *vb* **nar·rat·ed; nar·rat·ing** : to recite the details of (as a story) : RELATE, TELL — **nar·ra·tion** \na-'rā-shən\ *n* — **nar·ra·tor** \'nar-ˌāt-ər\ *n*

nar·ra·tive \'nar-ət-iv\ *n* **1** : something that is narrated : STORY **2** : the art or practice of narrating

¹**nar·row** \'nar-ō\ *adj* **1** : of slender or less than standard width **2** : limited in size or scope : RESTRICTED **3** : not liberal in views : PREJUDICED **4** : interpreted or interpreting strictly **5** : CLOSE ⟨a ~ escape⟩ ; *also* : barely successful ⟨won by a ~ margin⟩ — **nar·row·ly** *adv* — **nar·row·ness** *n*

²**narrow** *n* : a narrow passage : STRAIT — usu. used in pl.

³**narrow** *vb* : to lessen in width or extent

nar·row–mind·ed \ˌnar-ō-'mīn-dəd\ *adj* : not liberal or broad-minded

nar·whal \'när-ˌhwäl, 'när-wəl\ *n* : an arctic sea animal about 20 feet (6 meters) long that is related to the dolphin and in the male has a long twisted ivory tusk

NAS *abbr* naval air station

NASA \'nas-ə\ *abbr* National Aeronautics and Space Administration

¹**na·sal** \'nā-zəl\ *n* **1** : a nasal part **2** : a nasal consonant or vowel

²**nasal** *adj* **1** : of or relating to the nose **2** : uttered through the nose — **na·sal·ly** \-ē\ *adv*

na·sal·ize \'nā-zə-ˌlīz\ *vb* **-ized; -iz·ing 1** : to make nasal **2** : to speak in a nasal manner — **na·sal·iza·tion** \ˌnā-zə-lə-'zā-shən\ *n*

na·scent \'nas-ᵊnt, 'nās\ *adj* : coming into existence : beginning to grow or develop — **na·scence** \-ᵊns\ *n*

nas·tur·tium \nə-'stər-shəm, na-\ *n* : a watery-stemmed herb with showy spurred flowers and pungent seeds

nas·ty \'nas-tē\ *adj* **nas·ti·er; -est 1** : FILTHY **2** : INDECENT, OBSCENE **3** : DISHONORABLE ⟨a ~ trick⟩ **4** : HARMFUL, DANGEROUS ⟨took a ~ fall⟩ **5** : DISAGREEABLE ⟨~ weather⟩ **6** : MEAN, ILL-NATURED ⟨a ~ temper⟩ — **nas·ti·ly** \'nas-tə-le\ *adv* — **nas·ti·ness** \-tē-nəs\ *n*

nat *abbr* **1** national **2** native **3** natural

na·tal \'nāt-ᵊl\ *adj* **1** : NATIVE **2** : of, relating to, or present at birth

na·tal·i·ty \nā-'tal-ət-ē, nə-\ *n, pl* **-ties** : BIRTHRATE

na·ta·to·ri·um \ˌnāt-ə-'tōr-ē-əm, ˌnat-\ *n* : a swimming pool esp. indoors

na·tion \'nā-shən\ *n* [ME *nacioun,* fr. MF *nation,* fr. L *nation-, natio* birth, race, nation, fr. *natus,* pp. of *nasci* to be born] **1** : NATIONALITY 5; *also* : a politically organized nationality **2** : a community of people composed of one or more nationalities with its own territory and government **3** : the territory of a nation **4** : a federation of tribes (as of American Indians) — **na·tion·hood** *n*

¹**na·tion·al** \'nash-(ə-)nəl\ *adj* **1** : of or relating to a nation **2** : comprising or characteristic of a nationality **3** : FEDERAL **3** — **na·tion·al·ly** \-ē\ *adv*

²**national** *n* **1** : one who is under the protection of a nation without regard to the more formal status of citizen or subject **2** : an organization (as a labor union) having local units throughout a nation **3** : a competition that is national in scope — usu. used in pl.

National Guard *n* **1** : a militia force recruited by each state, equipped by the federal government, and jointly maintained subject to the call of either **2** : a military force serving as a national constabulary and defense force

na·tion·al·ism \'nash-(ə-)nəl-ˌiz-əm\ *n* : devotion to national interests, unity, and independence

na·tion·al·ist \-əst\ *n* **1** : an advocate of or believer in nationalism **2** *cap* : a member of a political party or group advocating national independence or strong national government — **nationalist** *adj, often cap* — **na·tion·al·is·tic** \ˌnash-(ə-)nəl-'is-tik\ *adj*

na·tion·al·i·ty \ˌnash-(ə-)'nal-ət-ē\ *n, pl* **-ties 1** : national character **2** : a legal relationship involving allegiance of an individual and his protection by the state **3** : membership in a particular nation **4** : political independence or existence as a separate nation **5** : a people having a common origin, tradition, and language and capable of forming a state **6** : an ethnic group within a larger unit (as a nation)

na·tion·al·ize \'nash-(ə-)nəl-ˌīz\ *vb* **-ized; -iz·ing 1** : to make national : make a nation of **2** : to remove from private ownership and place under government control — **na·tion·al·iza·tion** \ˌnash-(ə-)nəl-ə-'zā-shən\ *n*

national park *n* : an area of special scenic, historical, or scientific importance set aside and maintained by a national government esp. for recreation or study

national seashore *n* : a recreational area adjacent to a seacoast and maintained by the federal government

na·tion·wide \ˌnā-shən-'wīd\ *adj* : extending throughout a nation

¹**na·tive** \'nāt-iv\ *adj* **1** : INBORN, NATURAL **2** : born in a particular place or country **3** : belonging to a person because of the place or circumstances of his birth ⟨his ∼ language⟩ **4** : grown, produced, or originating in a particular place : INDIGENOUS

²**native** *n* : one that is native; *esp* : a person who belongs to a particular country by birth

Native American *n* : AMERICAN INDIAN

na·tiv·ism \'nāt-iv-ˌiz-əm\ *n* **1** : a policy of favoring native inhabitants over immigrants **2** : the revival or perpetuation of a native culture esp. in opposition to acculturation

Na·tiv·i·ty \nə-'tiv-ət-ē, nā-\ *n, pl* **-ties 1** : the birth of Christ **2** *not cap* : the process or circumstances of being born : BIRTH

natl *abbr* national

NATO \'nāt-(ˌ)ō\ *abbr* North Atlantic Treaty Organization

nat·ty \'nat-ē\ *adj* **nat·ti·er; -est** : trimly neat and tidy : SMART — **nat·ti·ly** \'nat-ᵊl-ē\ *adv* — **nat·ti·ness** \-ē-nəs\ *n*

¹**nat·u·ral** \'nach-(ə-)rəl\ *adj* **1** : determined by nature : INBORN, INNATE ⟨∼ ability⟩ **2** : BORN ⟨a ∼ fool⟩ **3** : ILLEGITIMATE **4** : HUMAN **5** : of or relating to nature **6** : not artificial **7** : being simple and sincere : not affected **8** : LIFELIKE **9** : having neither sharps nor flats in the key signature **syn** ingenuous, naive, unsophisticated, artless, guileless — **nat·u·ral·ness** *n*

²**natural** *n* **1** : IDIOT **2** : a character placed on a line or space of the musical staff to nullify the effect of a preceding sharp or flat **3** : one obviously suitable for a specific purpose **4** : AFRO

natural childbirth *n* : a system of managing childbirth in which the mother prepares to remain conscious and assist in delivery with little or no use of drugs

natural gas *n* : gas coming from the earth's crust through natural openings or bored wells; *esp* : a combustible mixture of hydrocarbons and esp. methane used chiefly as a fuel and raw material

natural history *n* **1** : a treatise on some aspect of nature **2** : the study of natural objects esp. from an amateur or popular point of view

nat·u·ral·ism \'nach-(ə-)rə-ˌliz-əm\ *n* **1** : action or thought based only on natural desires and instincts **2** : a doctrine that denies a supernatural explanation of the origin or development of the universe and holds that scientific laws account for all of nature **3** : realism in art and literature — **nat·u·ral·is·tic** \ˌnach-(ə-)rə-'lis-tik\ *adj*

nat·u·ral·ist \-ləst\ *n* **1** : one that advocates or practices naturalism **2** : a student of animals or plants esp. in the field

nat·u·ral·ize \-ˌlīz\ *vb* **-ized; -iz·ing 1** : to become or cause to become established as if native ⟨∼ new forage crops⟩ **2** : to confer the rights of a citizen on — **nat·u·ral·iza·tion** \ˌnach-(ə-)rə-lə-'zā-shən\ *n*

nat·u·ral·ly \'nach-(ə-)rə-lē, 'nach-ər-lē\ *adv* **1** : by nature : by natural character or ability **2** : as might be expected **3** : without artificial aid; *also*

: without affectation **4** : REALIS-
TICALLY

natural science *n* : a science (as physics, chemistry, or biology) that deals
with matter, energy, and their interre-
lations and transformations or with
objectively measurable phenomena
— **natural scientist** *n*

natural selection *n* : the natural process
that results in the survival of individuals or groups best adjusted to the
conditions under which they live

na•ture \'nā-chər\ *n* [ME, fr. MF, fr. L
natura, fr. *natus*, pp. of *nasci* to be
born] **1** : the inherent quality or basic
constitution of a person or thing **2**
: KIND, SORT **3** : DISPOSITION, TEMPERA-
MENT **4** : the physical universe **5**
: one's natural instincts or way of life
⟨quirks of human ∼⟩; *also* : primitive
state ⟨a return to ∼⟩ **6** : natural scenery or environment ⟨beauties of ∼⟩

naught \'not, 'nät\ *n* **1** : NOTHING **2** : the
arithmetical symbol 0 : ZERO

naugh•ty \'not-ē, 'nät-\ *adj* **naugh•ti•er**;
-est 1 : guilty of disobedience or misbehavior **2** : lacking in taste or propriety — **naugh•ti•ly** \'not-ᵊl-ē, 'nät-\ *adv*
— **naugh•ti•ness** \-ē-nəs\ *n*

nau•sea \'no-zē-ə, 'no-shə\ *n* [L, seasickness, nausea, fr. Gk *nautia*,
nausia, fr. *nautēs* sailor] **1** : sickness
of the stomach with a desire to vomit
2 : extreme disgust

nau•se•ate \'no-z(h)ē-,āt, -s(h)ē-\ *vb* **-at-
ed**; **-at•ing** : to affect or become affected with nausea — **nau•se•at•ing•ly**
\-,āt-iŋ-lē\ *adv*

nau•seous \'no-shəs, -zē-əs\ *adj* **1**
: causing nausea or disgust **2** : affected with nausea or disgust

naut *abbr* nautical

nau•ti•cal \'not-i-kəl\ *adj* : of or relating
to seamen, navigation, or ships —
nau•ti•cal•ly \-k(ə-)lē\ *adv*

nautical mile *n* : a unit of distance equal
to about 6076.115 feet

nau•ti•lus \'not-ᵊl-əs\ *n, pl* **-lus•es** *or* **-li**
\-ᵊl-,ī, -,ē\ : a sea mollusk related to
the octopuses but having a spiral shell
divided into chambers

nav *abbr* **1** naval **2** navigable; navigation

Na•va•ho *or* **Na•va•jo** \'nav-ə-,hō, 'näv-\
n, pl **Navaho** *or* **Navahos** *or* **Navajo** *or*
Navajos : a member of an American

Indian people of northern New Mexico and Arizona; *also* : their language

na•val \'nā-vəl\ *adj* : of, relating to, or
possessing a navy

naval stores *n pl* : products (as pitch,
turpentine, or rosin) obtained from
resinous conifers (as pines)

nave \'nāv\ *n* [ML *navis*, fr. L, ship]
: the central part of a church running
lengthwise

na•vel \'nā-vəl\ *n* : a depression in the
middle of the abdomen that marks the
point of attachment of fetus and mother

navel orange *n* : a seedless orange having a pit at the blossom end where the
fruit encloses a small secondary fruit

nav•i•ga•ble \'nav-i-gə-bəl\ *adj* **1** : capable of being navigated ⟨a ∼ river⟩ **2**
: capable of being steered ⟨a ∼ bal-
loon⟩ — **nav•i•ga•bil•i•ty** \,nav-i-gə-
'bil-ət-ē\ *n*

nav•i•gate \'nav-ə-,gāt\ *vb* **-gat•ed; -gat-
ing 1** : to sail on or through ⟨∼ the
Atlantic ocean⟩ **2** : to steer or direct
the course of a ship or aircraft **3**
: MOVE; *esp* : WALK ⟨could hardly ∼⟩
— **nav•i•ga•tion** \,nav-ə-'gā-shən\ *n* —
nav•i•ga•tor \'nav-ə-,gāt-ər\ *n*

na•vy \'nā-vē\ *n, pl* **navies 1** : FLEET;
also : the warships belonging to a nation **2** *often cap* : a nation's organization for naval warfare

navy exchange *n* : a post exchange at a
navy installation

navy yard *n* : a yard where naval vessels are built or repaired

¹nay \'nā\ *adv* **1** : NO **2** : not merely this
but also : not only so but ⟨the letter
made him happy, ∼, ecstatic⟩

²nay *n* : a negative vote; *also* : a person
casting such a vote

nay•say•er \'nā-,sā-ər\ *n* : one who denies, refuses, or opposes something

Na•zi \'nät-sē, 'nat-\ *n* [G, fr. *national-
sozialist*, lit., national socialist] : a
member of a German fascist party
controlling Germany from 1933 to
1945 under Adolf Hitler — **Nazi** *adj* —
Na•zism \'nät-,siz-əm, 'nat-\ *or* **Na•zi-
ism** \-sē-,iz-əm\ *n*

Nb *symbol* niobium

NB *abbr* **1** New Brunswick **2** nota bene

NBA *abbr* **1** National Basketball Association **2** National Boxing Association

NBC *abbr* National Broadcasting Company

NBS *abbr* National Bureau of Standards

NC *abbr* **1** no charge **2** North Carolina

NCAA *abbr* National Collegiate Athletic Association

NCE *abbr* New Catholic Edition

NCO \ˌen-ˌsē-ˈō\ *n* : NONCOMMISSIONED OFFICER

Nd *symbol* neodymium

ND *abbr* **1** no date **2** North Dakota

N Dak *abbr* North Dakota

Ne *symbol* neon

NE *abbr* **1** Nebraska **2** New England **3** northeast

Ne·an·der·thal \nē-ˈan-dər-ˌt(h)ȯl, nā-ˈän-dər-ˌtäl\ *adj* : of, relating to, or being an extinct primitive Old World man; *also* : crudely primitive (as in manner or conduct) — **Neanderthal** *n*

neap tide \ˈnēp-\ *n* : a tide of minimum range occurring at the first and third quarters of the moon

¹**near** \ˈniər\ *adv* **1** : at, within, or to a short distance or time **2** : ALMOST

²**near** *prep* : close to

³**near** *adj* **1** : closely related or associated; *also* : INTIMATE **2** : not far away; *also* : being the closer or left-hand member of a pair **3** : barely avoided ⟨a ~ accident⟩ **4** : DIRECT, SHORT ⟨by the ~*est* route⟩ **5** : STINGY **6** : not real but very like ⟨~ silk⟩ — **near·ly** *adv* — **near·ness** *n*

⁴**near** *vb* : APPROACH

near beer *n* : any of various malt liquors low in alcohol

near·by \niər-ˈbī, ˈniər-ˌbī\ *adv or adj* : close at hand

near·sight·ed \ˈniər-ˈsīt-əd\ *adj* : seeing distinctly at short distances only : SHORTSIGHTED — **near·sight·ed·ly** *adv* — **near·sight·ed·ness** *n*

neat \ˈnēt\ *adj* [MF *net*, fr. L *nitidus* bright, neat, fr. *nitēre* to shine] **1** : being orderly and clean **2** : not mixed or diluted ⟨~ brandy⟩ **3** : marked by tasteful simplicity **4** : PRECISE, SYSTEMATIC **5** : SKILLFUL, ADROIT **6** : FINE, ADMIRABLE — **neat** *adv* — **neat·ly** *adv* — **neat·ness** *n*

neath \ˈnēth\ *prep, dial* : BENEATH

neat's–foot oil \ˈnēts-ˌfut-\ *n* [*neat* (bovine)] : a pale yellow fatty oil made

esp. from the bones of cattle and used chiefly as a leather dressing

neb \ˈneb\ *n* **1** : the beak of a bird or tortoise; *also* : NOSE, SNOUT **2** : NIB

Neb *or* **Nebr** *abbr* Nebraska

NEB *abbr* New English Bible

neb·u·la \ˈneb-yə-lə\ *n, pl* **-las** *or* **-lae** \-ˌlē, -ˌlī\ [NL, fr. L, mist, cloud] **1** : any of many vast cloudlike masses of gas or dust among the stars **2** : GALAXY — **neb·u·lar** \-lər\ *adj*

neb·u·lize \ˈneb-yə-ˌlīz\ *vb* **-lized; -lizing** : to reduce to a fine spray — **neb·u·liz·er** \-ˌlī-zər\ *n*

neb·u·los·i·ty \ˌneb-yə-ˈläs-ət-ē\ *n, pl* **-ties** **1** : the quality or state of being nebulous **2** : nebulous matter

neb·u·lous \ˈneb-yə-ləs\ *adj* **1** : of or relating to a nebula **2** : HAZY, INDISTINCT ⟨a ~ memory⟩

¹**nec·es·sary** \ˈnes-ə-ˌser-ē\ *n, pl* **-saries** : an indispensable item

²**necessary** *adj* [ME *necessarie*, fr. L *necessarius*, fr. *necesse* necessary, fr. *ne-* not + *cedere* to withdraw] **1** : INEVITABLE, INESCAPABLE; *also* : CERTAIN **2** : PREDETERMINED **3** : COMPULSORY **4** : positively needed : INDISPENSABLE *syn* imperative, necessitous, essential — **nec·es·sar·i·ly** \ˌnes-ə-ˈser-ə-lē\ *adv*

ne·ces·si·tate \ni-ˈses-ə-ˌtāt\ *vb* **-tat·ed; -tat·ing** : to make necessary

ne·ces·si·tous \ni-ˈses-ət-əs\ *adj* **1** : NEEDY, IMPOVERISHED **2** : URGENT **3** : NECESSARY

ne·ces·si·ty \ni-ˈses-ət-ē\ *n, pl* **-ties** **1** : conditions that cannot be changed **2** : WANT, POVERTY **3** : something that is necessary **4** : very great need

¹**neck** \ˈnek\ *n* **1** : the part of the body connecting the head and the trunk **2** : the part of a garment covering or near to the neck **3** : a relatively narrow part suggestive of a neck ⟨~ of a bottle⟩ ⟨~ of land⟩ **4** : a narrow margin esp. of victory ⟨won by a ~⟩ — **necked** \ˈnekt\ *adj*

²**neck** *vb* : to kiss and caress amorously

neck and neck *adv or adj* : very close (as in a race)

neck·er·chief \ˈnek-ər-chəf, -ˌchēf\ *n, pl* **-chiefs** \-chəfs, -ˌchēfs\ *also* **-chieves** \-ˌchēvz\ : a square of cloth worn folded about the neck like a scarf

neck·lace \ˈnek-ləs\ *n* : an ornamental

chain or a string (as of jewels or beads) worn around the neck

neck·line \-ˌlīn\ *n* : the outline of the neck opening of a garment

neck·tie \-ˌtī\ *n* : a strip of cloth worn around the neck and tied in front

ne·crol·o·gy \nə-ˈkräl-ə-jē\ *n, pl* **-gies 1** : a list of the recently dead **2** : OBITUARY

nec·ro·man·cy \ˈnek-rə-ˌman-sē\ *n* **1** : the art or practice of conjuring up the spirits of the dead for purposes of magically revealing the future **2** : MAGIC, SORCERY — **nec·ro·man·cer** \-sər\ *n*

ne·crop·o·lis \nə-ˈkräp-ə-ləs, ne-\ *n, pl* **-lis·es** *or* **-les** \-ˌlēz\ *or* **-leis** \-ˌlās\ *or* **-li** \-ˌlī, -ˌlē\ : CEMETERY; *esp* : a large elaborate cemetery of an ancient city

ne·cro·sis \nə-ˈkrō-səs, ne-\ *n, pl* **ne·cro·ses** \-ˌsēz\ : usu. local death of body tissue — **ne·crot·ic** \-ˈkrät-ik\ *adj*

nec·tar \ˈnek-tər\ *n* **1** : the drink of the Greek and Roman gods; *also* : any delicious drink **2** : a sweet plant secretion that is the raw material of honey

nec·tar·ine \ˌnek-tə-ˈrēn\ *n* : a smooth-skinned peach

née *or* **nee** \ˈnā\ *adj* [F, lit., born] — used to identify a woman by her maiden family name

¹need \ˈnēd\ *n* **1** : OBLIGATION ⟨no ~ to hurry⟩ **2** : a lack of something requisite, desirable, or useful **3** : a condition requiring supply or relief ⟨when the ~ arises⟩ **4** : POVERTY **syn** necessity, exigency

²need *vb* **1** : to be in want **2** : to have cause or occasion for : REQUIRE ⟨he ~s advice⟩ **3** : to be under obligation or necessity ⟨we ~ to know the truth⟩

need·ful \ˈnēd-fəl\ *adj* : NECESSARY, REQUISITE

¹nee·dle \ˈnēd-ᵊl\ *n* **1** : a slender pointed usu. steel implement used in sewing **2** : a slender rod (as for knitting, controlling a small opening, or transmitting vibrations to or from a recording) ⟨a phonograph ~⟩ **3** : a slender hollow instrument by which material is introduced into or withdrawn from the body **4** : a slender indicator on a dial **5** : a needle-shaped leaf (as of a pine)

²needle *vb* **nee·dled; nee·dling** \ˈnēd-(ᵊ-)liŋ\ : PROD, GOAD; *esp* : to incite to action by repeated gibes

nee·dle·point \ˈnēd-ᵊl-ˌpȯint\ *n* **1** : lace worked with a needle over a paper pattern **2** : embroidery done on canvas across counted threads — **needlepoint** *adj*

need·less \ˈnēd-ləs\ *adj* : UNNECESSARY — **need·less·ly** *adv* — **need·less·ness** *n*

nee·dle·wom·an \ˈnēd-ᵊl-ˌwüm-ən\ *n* : a woman who does needlework; *esp* : SEAMSTRESS

nee·dle·work \-ˌwərk\ *n* : work done with a needle; *esp* : work (as embroidery) other than plain sewing

needs \ˈnēdz\ *adv* : of necessity : NECESSARILY ⟨must ~ be recognized⟩

needy \ˈnēd-ē\ *adj* **need·i·er; -est** : being in want : POVERTY-STRICKEN

ne'er \ˈneər\ *adv* : NEVER

ne'er–do–well \ˈneər-dü-ˌwel\ *n* : an idle worthless person — **ne'er–do–well** *adj*

ne·far·i·ous \ni-ˈfar-ē-əs\ *adj* [L *nefarius,* fr. *nefas* crime, fr. *ne-* not + *fas* right, divine law] : very wicked : EVIL — **ne·far·i·ous·ly** *adv*

neg *abbr* negative

ne·gate \ni-ˈgāt\ *vb* **ne·gat·ed; ne·gat·ing 1** : to deny the existence or truth of **2** : to cause to be ineffective or invalid : NULLIFY

ne·ga·tion \ni-ˈgā-shən\ *n* **1** : the action or operation of negating or making negative **2** : a negative doctrine or statement

¹neg·a·tive \ˈneg-ət-iv\ *adj* **1** : marked by denial, prohibition, or refusal ⟨a ~ reply⟩ **2** : not positive or constructive; *esp* : not affirming the presence of what is sought or suspected to be present ⟨a ~ test⟩ **3** : less than zero ⟨a ~ number⟩ **4** : being, relating to, or charged with electricity of which the electron is the elementary unit ⟨a ~ particle⟩ **5** : having the light and dark parts opposite to what they were in the original photographic subject — **neg·a·tive·ly** *adv*

²negative *n* **1** : a negative word or statement **2** : a negative vote or reply; *also* : REFUSAL **3** : something that is the opposite or negation of something else **4** : the side that votes or argues for the opposition (as in a debate) **5** : a negative photographic image on transparent material

³**negative** *vb* **-tived; -tiv·ing 1** : to refuse to accept or approve **2** : to vote against **3** : DISPROVE

negative income tax *n* : a system of federal subsidy payments to families with incomes below a stipulated level

neg·a·tiv·ism \'neg-ət-iv-ˌiz-əm\ *n* : an attitude of skepticism and denial of nearly everything affirmed or suggested by others

¹**ne·glect** \ni-'glekt\ *vb* [L *neglegere, neclegere,* fr. *nec*- not + *legere* to gather] **1** : DISREGARD **2** : to leave undone or unattended to esp. through carelessness **syn** omit, ignore, overlook, slight, forget, miss

²**neglect** *n* **1** : an act or instance of neglecting something **2** : the condition of being neglected — **ne·glect·ful** *adj*

neg·li·gee *also* **neg·li·gé** \ˌneg-lə-'zhā\ *n* : a woman's long flowing dressing gown

neg·li·gent \'neg-li-jənt\ *adj* : marked by neglect **syn** neglectful, remiss, delinquent, derelict — **neg·li·gence** \-jəns\ *n* — **neg·li·gent·ly** *adv*

neg·li·gi·ble \'neg-li-jə-bəl\ *adj* : so small as to be neglected or disregarded

ne·go·tiant \ni-'gō-sh(ē-)ənt\ *n* : NEGOTIATOR

ne·go·ti·ate \ni-'gō-shē-ˌāt\ *vb* **-at·ed; -at·ing** [L *negotiari* to carry on business, fr. *negotium* business, fr. *neg*- not + *otium* leisure] **1** : to confer with another so as to arrive at the settlement of some matter; *also* : to arrange for or bring about by such conferences ⟨~ a treaty⟩ **2** : to transfer to another by delivery or endorsement in return for equivalent value ⟨~ a check⟩ **3** : to get through, around, or over successfully ⟨~ a turn⟩ — **ne·go·tia·ble** \-sh(ē-)ə-bəl\ *adj* — **ne·go·ti·a·tion** \ni-ˌgō-s(h)ē-'ā-shən\ *n* — **ne·go·ti·a·tor** \-'gō-shē-ˌāt-ər\ *n*

ne·gri·tude \'neg-rə-ˌt(y)üd, 'nē-grə-\ *n* : a consciousness of and pride in one's African heritage

Ne·gro \'nē-grō\ *n, pl* **Negroes** [Sp or Pg, fr. *negro* black] : a member of the black race — **Negro** *adj* — **Ne·groid** \'nē-ˌgroid\ *n or adj, often not cap*

Neh *abbr* Nehemiah

Ne·he·mi·ah \ˌnē-(h)ə-'mī-ə\ *n* — see BIBLE table

NEI *abbr* not elsewhere included

neigh \'nā\ *n* : a loud prolonged cry of a horse — **neigh** *vb*

¹**neigh·bor** \'nā-bər\ *n* **1** : one living or located near another **2** : FELLOWMAN

²**neighbor** *vb* **neigh·bored; neigh·bor·ing** \-b(ə-)riŋ\ : to be next to or near to : border on

neigh·bor·hood \'nā-bər-ˌhùd\ *n* **1** : NEARNESS **2** : a place or region near : VICINITY; *also* : a number or amount near ⟨costs in the ~ of $10⟩ **3** : the people living near one another **4** : a section lived in by neighbors and usu. having distinguishing characteristics

neigh·bor·ly \-lē\ *adj* : befitting congenial neighbors; *esp* : FRIENDLY — **neigh·bor·li·ness** *n*

¹**nei·ther** \'nē-thər, 'nī-\ *pron* : neither one : not the one and not the other ⟨~ of the two⟩

²**neither** *conj* **1** : not either ⟨~ good nor bad⟩ **2** : NOR ⟨~ did I⟩

³**neither** *adj* : not either ⟨~ hand⟩

nel·son \'nel-sən\ *n* : a wrestling hold in which one applies leverage against an opponent's arm, neck, and head

nem·a·tode \'nem-ə-ˌtōd\ *n* : any of a group of elongated cylindrical worms parasitic in animals or plants or free-living in soil or water

nem·e·sis \'nem-ə-səs\ *n, pl* **-e·ses** \-ə-ˌsēz\ [L *Nemesis,* goddess of divine retribution, fr. Gk] **1** : one that inflicts retribution or vengeance **2** : a formidable and usu. victorious rival **3** : an act or effect of retribution; *also* : CURSE

neo·clas·sic \ˌnē-ō-'klas-ik\ *or* **neo·clas·si·cal** \-i-kəl\ *adj* : of or relating to a revival or adaptation of the classical style esp. in literature, art, or music

neo·co·lo·nial·ism \ˌnē-ō-kə-'lō-nyəl-ˌiz-əm, -'lō-nē-ə-ˌliz-əm\ *n* : the economic and political policies by which a nation indirectly maintains or extends its influence over other areas or peoples — **neo·co·lo·nial** *adj* — **neo·co·lo·nial·ist** \-əst\ *n or adj*

neo·con·ser·va·tive \-kən-'sər-vət-iv\ *n* : a former liberal espousing political conservatism — **neo·con·ser·va·tism** \-və-ˌtiz-əm\ *n* — **neoconservative** *adj*

neo•dym•i•um \ˌnē-ō-'dim-ē-əm\ *n* : a yellow metallic chemical element

neo—im•pres•sion•ism \ˌnē-ō-im-'presh-ə-ˌniz-əm\ *n, often cap N&I* : a late 19th century French art movement that attempted to make impressionism more precise and to use a pointillist painting technique

Neo•lith•ic \ˌnē-ə-'lith-ik\ *adj* : of or relating to the latest period of the Stone Age characterized by polished stone implements

ne•ol•o•gism \nē-'äl-ə-ˌjiz-əm\ *n* : a new word or expression

ne•on \'nē-ˌän\ *n* [Gk, neut. of *neos* new] 1 : a gaseous colorless chemical element used in electric lamps 2 : a lamp in which a discharge through neon gives a reddish glow — **neon** *adj*

neo•na•tal \ˌnē-ō-'nāt-ᵊl\ *adj* : of, relating to, or affecting the newborn — **neo•na•tal•ly** \-ē\ *adv* — **ne•o•nate** \'nē-ō-ˌnāt\ *n*

neo•phyte \'nē-ə-ˌfīt\ *n* 1 : a new convert : PROSELYTE 2 : NOVICE 3 : BEGINNER

neo•plasm \'nē-ə-ˌplaz-əm\ *n* : TUMOR — **neo•plas•tic** \ˌnē-ə-'plas-tik\ *adj*

Ne•pali \nə-'pȯl-ē, -'päl-\ *n, pl* **Nepali** : a native or inhabitant of Nepal

ne•pen•the \nə-'pen-thē\ *n* 1 : a potion used by the ancients to dull pain and sorrow 2 : something capable of making one forget grief or suffering

neph•ew \'nef-yü, *chiefly Brit* 'nev-\ *n* : a son of one's brother, sister, brother-in-law, or sister-in-law

ne•phrit•ic \ni-'frit-ik\ *adj* 1 : RENAL 2 : of, relating to, or affected with nephritis

ne•phri•tis \ni-'frīt-əs\ *n, pl* **ne•phrit•i•des** \-'frit-ə-ˌdēz\ : kidney inflammation

ne plus ul•tra \ˌnē-ˌpləs-'əl-trə\ *n* [NL, (go) no more beyond] : the highest point capable of being attained

nep•o•tism \'nep-ə-ˌtiz-əm\ *n* [F *népotisme,* fr. It *nepotismo,* fr. *nepote* nephew, fr. L *nepot-, nepos* grandson, nephew] : favoritism shown to a relative (as in the granting of jobs)

Nep•tune \'nep-ˌt(y)ün\ *n* : the 8th planet in order of distance from the sun — **Nep•tu•ni•an** \nep-'t(y)ü-nē-ən\ *adj*

nep•tu•ni•um \nep-'t(y)ü-nē-əm\ *n* : a short-lived radioactive chemical element artificially produced as a by≠product in the production of plutonium

Ne•re•id \'nir-ē-əd\ *n* : a sea nymph in Greek mythology

¹**nerve** \'nərv\ *n* 1 : one of the strands of nervous tissue that carry nervous impulses between the brain and spinal cord and every part of the body 2 : power of endurance or control : FORTITUDE; *also* : BOLDNESS, DARING 3 *pl* : NERVOUSNESS 4 : a vein of a leaf or insect wing — **nerved** \'nərvd\ *adj* — **nerve•less** *adj*

²**nerve** *vb* **nerved; nerv•ing** : to give strength or courage to

nerve cell *n* : NEURON; *also* : the nucleus-containing central part of a neuron exclusive of its processes

nerve gas *n* : a war gas damaging esp. to the nervous and respiratory systems

nerve—rack•ing *or* **nerve—wrack•ing** \'nərv-ˌrak-iŋ\ *adj* : extremely trying on the nerves

ner•vous \'nər-vəs\ *adj* 1 : FORCIBLE, SPIRITED 2 : of, relating to, or made up of nerve cells or nerves 3 : easily excited or annoyed : JUMPY 4 : TIMID, APPREHENSIVE ⟨a ∼ smile⟩ 5 : UNEASY, UNSTEADY — **ner•vous•ly** *adv* — **ner•vous•ness** *n*

nervous breakdown *n* : an attack of mental or emotional disorder of sufficient severity to be incapacitating esp. when requiring hospitalization

nervous system *n* : a bodily system that in vertebrates is made up of the brain and spinal cord, nerves, ganglia, and parts of the sense organs and that receives and interprets stimuli and transmits impulses

nervy \'nər-vē\ *adj* **nerv•i•er; -est** 1 : showing calm courage 2 : marked by impudence or presumption ⟨a ∼ salesman⟩ 3 : EXCITABLE, NERVOUS

-ness \nəs\ *n suffix* : state : condition : quality : degree ⟨good*ness*⟩

¹**nest** \'nest\ *n* 1 : the shelter prepared by a bird for its eggs and young 2 : a place where eggs (as of insects or fish) are laid and hatched 3 : a place of rest, retreat, or lodging 4 : DEN, HANGOUT ⟨a ∼ of theives⟩ 5 : the occupants of a nest 6 : a series of objects (as

bowls or tables) fitting inside or under one another

²**nest** *vb* **1** : to build or occupy a nest **2** : to fit compactly together or within one another

nest egg *n* : a fund of money accumulated as a reserve

nes·tle \'nes-əl\ *vb* **nes·tled; nes·tling** \-(ə-)liŋ\ **1** : to settle snugly or comfortably **2** : to press closely and affectionately : CUDDLE **3** : to settle, shelter, or house as if in a nest

nest·ling \'nest-liŋ\ *n* : a bird too young to leave its nest

¹**net** \'net\ *n* **1** : a meshed fabric twisted, knotted, or woven together at regular intervals; *esp* : a device of net used esp. to catch birds, fish, or insects **2** : something made of net used esp. for protecting, confining, carrying, or dividing ⟨a tennis ∼⟩ **3** : SNARE, TRAP

²**net** *vb* **net·ted; net·ting 1** : to cover or enclose with or as if with a net **2** : to catch in or as if in a net

³**net** *adj* : free from all charges or deductions ⟨∼ profit⟩ ⟨∼ weight⟩

⁴**net** *vb* **net·ted; net·ting** to gain or produce as profit : CLEAR, YIELD ⟨his business *netted* $50,000 a year⟩

⁵**net** *n* : a net amount, profit, weight, or price

NET *abbr* National Educational Television

Neth *abbr* Netherlands

neth·er \'neth-ər\ *adj* : situated down or below ⟨the ∼ regions of the earth⟩

Neth·er·land·er \'neth-ər-ₘland-ər\ *n* : a native or inhabitant of the Netherlands

neth·er·most \-ₘmōst\ *adj* : LOWEST

neth·er·world \-ₘwərld\ *n* **1** : the world of the dead **2** : UNDERWORLD

net·ting \'net-iŋ\ *n* **1** : NETWORK **2** : the act or process of making a net or network **3** : the act, process, or right of fishing with a net

¹**net·tle** \'net-³l\ *n* : any of various coarse herbs with stinging hairs

²**nettle** *vb* **net·tled; net·tling** : PROVOKE, VEX, IRRITATE

net·tle·some \'net-³l-səm\ *adj* : causing vexation : IRRITATING

net·work \'net-ₘwərk\ *n* **1** : NET **2** : a system of elements (as lines or channels) that cross in the manner of the threads in a net **3** : a group or system of related or connected parts; *esp* : a chain of radio or television stations

net·work·ing \'net-ₘwərk-iŋ\ *n* : the exchange of information or services among individuals, groups, or institutions

neu·ral \'n(y)ùr-əl\ *adj* : of, relating to, or involving a nerve or the nervous system

neu·ral·gia \n(y)ù-'ral-jə\ *n* : acute pain that follows the course of a nerve — **neu·ral·gic** \-jik\ *adj*

neur·as·the·nia \ₘn(y)ùr-əs-'thē-nē-ə\ *n* : an emotional and psychic disorder characterized esp. by easy susceptibility to fatigue and often by lack of motivation, feelings of inadequacy, and psychosomatic symptoms — **neur·as·then·ic** \-'then-ik\ *adj or n*

neu·ri·tis \n(y)ù-'rīt-əs\ *n, pl* **-rit·i·des** \-'rit-ə-ₘdēz\ *or* **-ri·tis·es** : inflammation of a nerve — **neu·rit·ic** \-'rit-ik\ *adj or n*

neu·rol·o·gy \n(y)ù-'räl-ə-jē\ *n* : the scientific study of the nervous system — **neu·ro·log·i·cal** \ₘn(y)ùr-ə-'läj-i-kəl\ *or* **neu·ro·log·ic** \-ik\ *adj* — **neu·ro·log·i·cal·ly** \-i-k(ə-)lē\ *adv* — **neu·rol·o·gist** \n(y)ù-'räl-ə-jəst\ *n*

neu·ron \'n(y)ü-ₘrän\ *also* **neu·rone** \-ₘrōn\ *n* : a cell with specialized processes that is the fundamental functional unit of nervous tissue

neu·ro·sci·ence \ₘn(y)ùr-ō-'sī-ən(t)s\ *n* : a branch of the life sciences that deals with the anatomy, physiology, biochemistry, or molecular biology of nerves and nervous tissue and esp. with their relation to behavior and learning — **neu·ro·sci·en·tist** \-ənt-əst\ *n*

neu·ro·sis \n(y)ù-'rō-səs\ *n, pl* **-ro·ses** \-ₘsēz\ : a mental and emotional disorder that is less serious than a psychosis, is not characterized by disturbance of the use of language, and is accompanied by various bodily and mental disturbances (as visceral symptoms, anxieties, or phobias)

¹**neu·rot·ic** \n(y)ù-'rät-ik\ *adj* : of, relating to, being, or affected with a neurosis; *also* : NERVOUS — **neu·rot·i·cal·ly** \-i-k(ə-)lē\ *adv*

²**neurotic** *n* : an emotionally unstable or neurotic person

neut *abbr* neuter

¹neu·ter \'n(y)üt-ər\ *adj* [ME *neutre*, fr. MF & L; MF *neutre*, fr. L *neuter*, lit., neither, fr. *ne-* not + *uter* which of two] **1** : of, relating to, or constituting the gender that includes most words or grammatical forms referring to things classed as neither masculine nor feminine **2** : having imperfectly developed or no sex organs

²neuter *n* **1** : a noun, pronoun, adjective, or inflectional form or class of the neuter gender; *also* : the neuter gender **2** : WORKER 2; *also* : a spayed or castrated animal

¹neu·tral \'n(y)ü-trəl\ *n* **1** : one that is neutral **2** : a neutral color **3** : the position of machine gears in which power is not transmitted

²neutral *adj* **1** : not favoring either side in a quarrel, contest, or war **2** : of or relating to a neutral state or power **3** : MIDDLING, INDIFFERENT **4** : having no hue : GRAY; *also* : not decided in color **5** : neither acid nor basic ⟨a ∼ solution⟩ **6** : not electrically charged

neu·tral·ism \'n(y)ü-trə-ˌliz-əm\ *n* : a policy or the advocacy of neutrality esp. in international affairs

neu·tral·i·ty \n(y)ü-ˈtral-ət-ē\ *n* : the quality or state of being neutral; *esp* : immunity from invasion or from use by belligerents

neu·tral·ize \'n(y)ü-trə-ˌlīz\ *vb* **-ized; -iz·ing** : to make neutral; *esp* : COUNTERACT — **neu·tral·iza·tion** \ˌn(y)ü-trə-lə-ˈzā-shən\ *n*

neu·tri·no \n(y)ü-ˈtrē-nō\ *n, pl* **-nos** : an uncharged elementary particle held to be massless

neu·tron \'n(y)ü-ˌträn\ *n* : an uncharged atomic particle that is nearly equal in mass to the proton and is present in all atomic nuclei except hydrogen

neutron bomb *n* : a nuclear bomb designed to produce lethal neutrons but less blast and fire damage than other nuclear bombs

Nev *abbr* Nevada

nev·er \'nev-ər\ *adv* **1** : not ever **2** : not in any degree, way, or condition

nev·er·more \ˌnev-ər-ˈmōr\ *adv* : never again

nev·er–nev·er land \ˌnev-ər-ˈnev-ər-\ *n* : an ideal or imaginary place

nev·er·the·less \ˌnev-ər-thə-ˈles\ *adv* : in spite of that : HOWEVER

ne·vus \'nē-vəs\ *n, pl* **ne·vi** \-ˌvī\ : a usu. pigmented birthmark

¹new \'n(y)ü\ *adj* **1** : not old : RECENT, MODERN **2** : recently discovered, recognized, or learned about ⟨∼ drugs⟩ **3** : not formerly known or experienced : UNFAMILIAR **4** : different from the former **5** : not accustomed ⟨∼ to the work⟩ **6** : beginning as a repetition of a previous act or thing ⟨a ∼ year⟩ **7** : REFRESHED, REGENERATED ⟨rest made a ∼ man of him⟩ **8** : being in a position or place for the first time ⟨a ∼ member⟩ **9** *cap* : having been in use after medieval times : MODERN ⟨*New* Latin⟩ **syn** novel, modern, newfangled, fresh — **new·ish** *adj* — **new·ness** *n*

²new *adv* : NEWLY ⟨*new*-mown hay⟩

¹new·born \-ˈbȯrn\ *adj* **1** : recently born **2** : born anew ⟨∼ hope⟩

²newborn *n, pl* **newborn** *or* **newborns** : a newborn individual

new·com·er \'n(y)ü-ˌkəm-ər\ *n* **1** : one recently arrived **2** : BEGINNER

New Deal *n* : the legislative and administrative program of President F. D. Roosevelt to promote economic recovery and social reform during the 1930s — **New Deal·er** \-ˈdē-lər\ *n*

new·el \'n(y)ü-əl\ *n* [ME *nowell*, fr. MF *nouel* stone of a fruit, fr. LL *nucalis* like a nut, fr. L *nuc-, nux* nut] : a post about which the steps of a circular staircase wind; *also* : a post at the foot of a stairway or one at a landing

new·fan·gled \'n(y)ü-ˈfaŋ-gəld\ *adj* [ME, fr. *newefangel,* fr. *new* + OE *fangen,* pp. of *fōn* to take, seize] **1** : attracted to novelty **2** : of the newest style : NOVEL

new–fash·ioned \-ˈfash-ənd\ *adj* **1** : made in a new fashion or form **2** : UP-TO-DATE

new·found \-ˈfau̇nd\ *adj* : newly found

New Left *n* : a political movement originating in the 1960s that advocates radical change in prevailing political, social, and educational practices

new·ly \'n(y)ü-lē\ *adv* **1** : LATELY, RECENTLY **2** : ANEW, AFRESH

new·ly·wed \-ˌwed\ *n* : one recently married

new math *n* : mathematics based on the theory of sets

new mathematics *n* : NEW MATH

new moon *n* : the phase of the moon with its dark side toward the earth; *also* : the thin crescent moon seen for a few days after the new moon phase

news \\'n(y)üz\\ *n* **1** : a report of recent events : TIDINGS **2** : material reported in a newspaper or news periodical or on a newscast

news・boy \\'n(y)üz-ˌbȯi\\ *n* : one who delivers or sells newspapers

news・cast \\-ˌkast\\ *n* : a radio or television broadcast of news — **news・cast・er** \\-ˌkas-tər\\ *n*

news・let・ter \\-ˌlet-ər\\ *n* : a small newspaper containing news or information of interest chiefly to a special group

news・mag・a・zine \\'n(y)üz-ˌmag-ə-ˌzēn\\ *n* : a usu. weekly magazine devoted chiefly to summarizing and analyzing the news

news・man \\-mən, -ˌman\\ *n* : one who gathers, reports, or comments on the news

news・pa・per \\-ˌpā-pər\\ *n* : a paper that is published at regular intervals and contains news, articles of opinion, features, and advertising

news・pa・per・man \\'n(y)üz-ˌpā-pər-ˌman\\ *n* : one who owns or is employed by a newspaper

news・print \\'n(y)üz-ˌprint\\ *n* : cheap paper made chiefly from wood pulp and used mostly for newspapers

news・reel \\-ˌrēl\\ *n* : a short motion picture portraying current events

news・stand \\-ˌstand\\ *n* : a place where newspapers and periodicals are sold

news・week・ly \\-ˌwēk-lē\\ *n* : a weekly newspaper or newsmagazine

news・wor・thy \\-ˌwər-ˌt͟hē\\ *adj* : sufficiently interesting to the general public to warrant reporting (as in a newspaper)

newsy \\'n(y)ü-zē\\ *adj* **news・i・er; -est** : filled with news; *esp* : CHATTY

newt \\'n(y)üt\\ *n* : any of various small salamanders living chiefly in the water

New Testament *n* : the second of the two chief divisions of the Bible — see BIBLE table

new・ton \\'n(y)üt-ᵊn\\ *n* : the unit of force in the metric system equal to the force required to impart an acceleration of one meter per second per second to a mass of one kilogram

new wave *n, often cap N&W* : a cinematic movement characterized by improvisation, abstraction, subjective symbolism, and often experimental photographic techniques

New World *n* : the western hemisphere; *esp* : the continental landmass of No. and So. America

New Year *n* : NEW YEAR'S DAY; *also* : the first days of the year

New Year's Day *n* : January 1 observed as a legal holiday

New Zea・land・er \\n(y)ü-'zē-lən-dər\\ *n* : a native or inhabitant of New Zealand

¹**next** \\'nekst\\ *adj* : immediately preceding or following : NEAREST

²**next** *prep* : nearest or adjacent to

³**next** *adv* **1** : in the time, place, or order nearest or immediately succeeding **2** : on the first occasion to come

nex・us \\'nek-səs\\ *n, pl* **nex・us・es** \\-sə-səz\\ *or* **nex・us** \\-səs, -ˌsüs\\ : CONNECTION, LINK

Nez Percé \\'nez-'pərs, F nā-per-sā\\ *n* : a member of an American Indian people of Idaho, Washington, and Oregon

NF *abbr* Newfoundland

NFC *abbr* National Football Conference

NFL *abbr* National Football League

Nfld *abbr* Newfoundland

NG *abbr* **1** National Guard **2** no good

ngul・trum \\eŋ-'gùl-trəm\\ *n* — see MONEY table

ngwee \\eŋ-'gwē\\ *n, pl* **ngwee** — see *kwacha* at MONEY table

NH *abbr* New Hampshire

NHL *abbr* National Hockey League

Ni *symbol* nickel

ni・a・cin \\'nī-ə-sən\\ *n* : NICOTINIC ACID

nib \\'nib\\ *n* : POINT; *esp* : a pen point

¹**nib・ble** \\'nib-əl\\ *vb* **nib・bled; nib・bling** \\-(ə-)liŋ\\ : to bite gently or bit by bit

²**nibble** *n* : a small or cautious bite

nice \\'nīs\\ *adj* **nic・er; nic・est** [ME, foolish, wanton, fr. OF, fr. L *nescius* ignorant, fr. *nescire* not to know] **1** : FASTIDIOUS, DISCRIMINATING **2** : marked by delicate discrimination or treatment **3** : PLEASING, AGREEABLE; *also* : well-executed **4** : WELL-BRED

⟨~ people⟩ **5** : VIRTUOUS, RESPECTABLE — **nice·ly** adv — **nice·ness** n

nice–nel·ly \'nīs-'nel-ē\ adj, often cap 2d N **1** : PRUDISH **2** : having the nature of or containing a euphemism — **nice nelly** n, often cap 2d N — **nice–nel·ly·ism** \-ˌiz-əm\ n, often cap 2d N

nice·ty \'nī-sət-ē\ n, pl **-ties 1** : a dainty, delicate, or elegant thing ⟨enjoy the *niceties* of life⟩ **2** : a fine detail ⟨*niceties* of workmanship⟩ **3** : EXACTNESS, PRECISION, ACCURACY

niche \'nich\ n [F] **1** : a recess (as for a statue) in a wall **2** : a place, work, or use for which a person or thing is best fitted

¹nick \'nik\ n **1** : a small notch or groove **2** : the final critical moment ⟨in the ~ of time⟩

²nick vb : NOTCH, CHIP

¹nick·el \'nik-əl\ n **1** : a hard silver-white metallic chemical element capable of a high polish and used in alloys **2** also **nick·le** : the U.S. 5-cent piece made of copper and nickel; also : the Canadian 5-cent piece

²nick·el vb **-eled** or **-elled; -el·ing** or **-el·ling** : to plate with nickel

nick·el·ode·on \ˌnik-ə-'lōd-ē-ən\ n **1** : an early movie theater charging an admission price of five cents **2** : a coin-operated musical device

nickel silver n : a silver-white alloy of copper, zinc, and nickel

nick·er \'nik-ər\ vb **nick·ered; nick·er·ing** : NEIGH, WHINNY

nick·name \'nik-ˌnām\ n [ME *nekename* additional name, alter. (resulting from incorrect division of *an ekename*) of *ekename*, fr. *eke* addition + *name*] **1** : a usu. descriptive name given instead of or in addition to the one belonging to a person, place, or thing **2** : a familiar form of a proper name — **nickname** vb

nic·o·tine \'nik-ə-ˌtēn\ n : a poisonous substance found in tobacco and used as an insecticide

nicotinic acid n : an organic acid of the vitamin B complex found in plants and animals and used against pellagra

niece \'nēs\ n : a daughter of one's brother, sister, brother-in-law, or sister-in-law

nif·ty \'nif-tē\ adj **nif·ti·er; -est** : very good : very attractive

Ni·ge·ri·an \nī-'jir-ē-ən\ n : a native or inhabitant of Nigeria — **Nigerian** adj

Ni·ge·rois \ˌnē-zhər-'wä\ n, pl **Nigerois** : a native or inhabitant of Niger

nig·gard \'nig-ərd\ n : a stingy person : MISER — **nig·gard·li·ness** \-lē-nəs\ n — **nig·gard·ly** adj or adv

nig·gling \'nig-(ə-)liŋ\ adj **1** : PETTY **2** : bothersome in a petty way

¹nigh \'nī\ adv **1** : near in place, time, or relationship **2** : NEARLY, ALMOST

²nigh adj : CLOSE, NEAR

³nigh prep : NEAR

night \'nīt\ n **1** : the period between dusk and dawn **2** : the darkness of night **3** : a period of misery or unhappiness **4** : NIGHTFALL — **night** adj

night blindness n : reduced visual capacity in faint light (as at night)

night·cap \'nīt-ˌkap\ n **1** : a cloth cap worn with nightclothes **2** : a usu. alcoholic drink taken at bedtime

night·clothes \-ˌklō(th)z\ n pl : garments worn in bed

night·club \-ˌkləb\ n : a place of entertainment open at night usu. serving food and liquor and providing music for dancing

night crawler n : EARTHWORM; esp : a large earthworm found on the soil surface at night

night·dress \'nīt-ˌdres\ n : NIGHTGOWN

night·fall \-ˌfȯl\ n : the coming of night

night·gown \-ˌgaủn\ n : a loose garment designed for wear in bed

night·hawk \-ˌhȯk\ n : any of several birds related to and resembling the whippoorwill

night·in·gale \'nīt-ᵊn-ˌgāl, -iŋ-\ n [ME, fr. OE *nihtegale*, fr. *niht* night + *galan* to sing] : any of several Old World thrushes noted for the sweet nocturnal song of the male

night·life \'nīt-ˌlīf\ n : the activity of pleasure-seekers at night

night·ly \'nīt-lē\ adj **1** : happening, done, or produced by night or every night **2** : of or relating to the night or every night — **nightly** adv

night·mare \'nīt-ˌmar\ n : a frightening oppressive dream or state occurring during sleep — **nightmare** adj — **night·mar·ish** \-ˌmar-ish\ adj

night rider n : a member of a secret band who ride masked at night doing violence to punish or terrorize

night·shade \'nīt-ˌshād\ *n* : any of a large genus of woody or herbaceous plants having alternate leaves, flowers in clusters, and fruits that are berries and including poisonous forms (as belladonna) and important food plants (as potato, tomato, or eggplant)

night·shirt \-ˌshərt\ *n* : a nightgown esp. for a man or a boy

night soil *n* : human excrement collected for fertilizing the soil

night·stick \'nīt-ˌstik\ *n* : a policeman's club

night·time \-ˌtīm\ *n* : the time from dusk to dawn

night·walk·er \-ˌwȯ-kər\ *n* : a person who roves about at night esp. with criminal or immoral intent

ni·hil·ism \'nī-(h)ə-ˌliz-əm, 'nē-\ *n* 1 : an attitude or doctrine that traditional values and beliefs are unfounded and that existence is senseless and useless 2 : ANARCHISM 3 : TERRORISM — **ni·hil·ist** \-ləst\ *n or adj* — **ni·hil·is·tic** \ˌnī-(h)ə-'lis-tik, ˌnē-\ *adj*

nil \'nil\ *n* : NOTHING, ZERO

nim·ble \'nim-bəl\ *adj* **nim·bler** \-b(ə-)lər\; **nim·blest** \-b(ə-)ləst\ [ME *nimel*, fr. OE *numol* holding much, fr. *niman* to take] 1 : quick and light in motion : AGILE ⟨a ∼ dancer⟩ 2 : quick in understanding and learning : CLEVER ⟨a ∼ mind⟩ — **nim·ble·ness** *n* — **nim·bly** \-blē\ *adv*

nim·bus \'nim-bəs\ *n, pl* **nim·bi** \-ˌbī, -bē\ *or* **nim·bus·es** 1 : a figure (as a disk) suggesting radiant light about the head of a drawn or sculptured divinity, saint, or sovereign 2 : a rain cloud that is of uniform grayness and extends over the entire sky

nim·rod \'nim-ˌräd\ *n* : HUNTER

nin·com·poop \'nin-kəm-ˌpüp\ *n* : FOOL, SIMPLETON

nine \'nīn\ *n* 1 : one more than eight 2 : the 9th in a set or series 3 : something having nine units; *esp* : a baseball team — **nine** *adj or pron* — **ninth** \'nīnth\ *adj or adv or n*

nine days' wonder *n* : something that creates a short-lived sensation

nine·pins \'nīn-ˌpinz\ *n* : tenpins played without the headpin

nine·teen \'nīn-'tēn\ *n* : one more than 18 — **nineteen** *adj or pron* — **nine·teenth** \-'tēnth\ *adj or n*

nine·ty \'nīnt-ē\ *n, pl* **nineties** : nine times 10 — **nine·ti·eth** \-ē-əth\ *adj or n* — **ninety** *adj or pron*

nin·ny \'nin-ē\ *n, pl* **ninnies** : FOOL

ni·o·bi·um \nī-'ō-bē-əm\ *n* : a gray metallic chemical element used in alloys

¹**nip** \'nip\ *vb* **nipped; nip·ping** 1 : to catch hold of and squeeze tightly between two surfaces, edges, or points 2 : CLIP 3 : to destroy the growth, progress, or fulfillment of ⟨*nipped* in the bud⟩ 4 : to injure or make numb with cold : CHILL 5 : SNATCH, STEAL

²**nip** *n* 1 : a sharp stinging cold 2 : a biting or pungent flavor 3 : PINCH, BITE 4 : a small portion : BIT

³**nip** *n* : a small quantity of liquor : SIP

⁴**nip** *vb* **nipped; nip·ping** : to take liquor in nips : TIPPLE

nip and tuck \ˌnip-ən-'tək\ *adj or adv* : so close that the lead shifts rapidly from one contestant to another

nip·per \'nip-ər\ *n* 1 : one that nips 2 *pl* : PINCERS 3 : a small boy

nip·ple \'nip-əl\ *n* : the protuberance of a mammary gland through which milk is drawn off : TEAT; *also* : something resembling a nipple

nip·py \'nip-ē\ *adj* **nip·pi·er; -est** 1 : PUNGENT, SHARP 2 : CHILLY

nir·va·na \nir-'vän-ə\ *n, often cap* [Skt *nirvāṇa*, lit., act of extinguishing, fr. *nis-* out + *vāti* it blows] 1 : the final freeing of a soul from all that enslaves it; *esp* : the supreme happiness that according to Buddhism comes when all passion, hatred, and delusion die out and the soul is released from the necessity of further purification 2 : OBLIVION; *also* : PARADISE

ni·sei \'nē-'sā\ *n, pl* **nisei** *also* **niseis** : a son or daughter of immigrant Japanese parents who is born and educated in America

ni·si \'nī-ˌsī\ *adj* [L, unless, fr. *ne-* not + *si* if] : taking effect at a specified time unless previously modified or voided ⟨a divorce decree ∼⟩

nit \'nit\ *n* : the egg of a parasitic insect (as a louse); *also* : the young insect

ni·ter \'nīt-ər\ *n* 1 : POTASSIUM NITRATE 2 : SODIUM NITRATE

nit–pick·ing \'nit-ˌpik-iŋ\ *n* : minute and usu. unjustified criticism — **nit·pick·er** \-ər\ *n*

¹**ni·trate** \'nī-ˌtrāt, -trət\ *n* 1 : a salt or

ester of nitric acid **2** : sodium nitrate or potassium nitrate used as a fertilizer

²ni•trate \-ˌtrāt\ *vb* **ni•trat•ed; ni•trat•ing** : to treat or combine with nitric acid or a nitrate — **ni•tra•tion** \nī-ˈtrā-shən\ *n*

ni•tric acid \ˌnī-trik-\ *n* : a corrosive liquid acid used in making dyes, explosives, and fertilizers

ni•tri•fi•ca•tion \ˌnī-trə-fə-ˈkā-shən\ *n* : the process of nitrifying; *esp* : the oxidation (as by bacteria) of ammonium salts to nitrites and then to nitrates

ni•tri•fy \ˈnī-trə-ˌfī\ *vb* **-fied; -fy•ing 1** : to combine with nitrogen or a nitrogen compound **2** : to subject to or produce by nitrification

ni•trite \ˈnī-ˌtrīt\ *n* : a salt of nitrous acid

ni•tro \ˈnī-trō\ *n, pl* **nitros** : any of various nitrated products; *esp* : NITROGLYCERIN

ni•tro•gen \ˈnī-trə-jən\ *n* : a tasteless odorless gaseous chemical element constituting 78 percent of the atmosphere by volume — **ni•trog•e•nous** \nī-ˈträj-ə-nəs\ *adj*

ni•tro•glyc•er•in *or* **ni•tro•glyc•er•ine** \ˌnī-trə-ˈglis-(ə-)rən\ *n* : a heavy oily explosive liquid used in making dynamite and in medicine

ni•trous acid \ˌnī-trəs-\ *n* : an unstable nitrogen-containing acid known only in solution or in the form of its salts

nitrous oxide *n* : a colorless gas used esp. as an anesthetic in dentistry

nit•ty–grit•ty \ˈnit-ē-ˌgrit-ē, ˌnit-ē-ˈgrit-ē\ *n* : the actual state of things : what is ultimately essential and true

nit•wit \ˈnit-ˌwit\ *n* : a flighty stupid person

¹nix \ˈniks\ *n* : NOTHING

²nix *vb* : VETO, REJECT

³nix *adv* : NO

NJ *abbr* New Jersey

NL *abbr* National League

NLRB *abbr* National Labor Relations Board

NM *abbr* **1** nautical mile **2** New Mexico

N Mex *abbr* New Mexico

NNE *abbr* north-northeast

NNW *abbr* north-northwest

¹no \(ˈ)nō\ *adv* **1** — used to express the negative of an alternative ⟨shall we continue or ∼⟩ **2** : in no respect or degree ⟨he is ∼ better than the others⟩ **3** : not so ⟨∼, I'm not ready⟩ **4** — used with adjective to imply a meaning opposite to the positive statement ⟨in ∼ uncertain terms⟩ **5** — used to introduce a more emphatic or explicit statement ⟨has the right, ∼, the duty to continue⟩ **6** — used as an interjection to express surprise or doubt ⟨∼ —you don't say⟩ **7** — used in combination with a verb to form a compound adjective ⟨*no*-bake pie⟩

²no *adj* **1** : not any; *also* : hardly any **2** : not a ⟨she's ∼ expert⟩

³no \ˈnō\ *n, pl* **noes** *or* **nos** \ˈnōz\ **1** : REFUSAL, DENIAL **2** : a negative vote or decision; *also, pl* : persons voting in the negative

⁴no *abbr* **1** north; northern **2** [L *numero,* abl. of *numerus*] number

¹No *or* **Noh** \ˈnō\ *n, pl* **No** *or* **Noh** : classic Japanese dance-drama having a heroic theme, a chorus, and highly stylized action, costuming, and scenery

²No *symbol* nobelium

No•bel•ist \nō-ˈbel-əst\ *n* : a winner of a Nobel prize

no•bel•i•um \nō-ˈbel-ē-əm\ *n* : a radioactive chemical element produced artificially

No•bel prize \(ˌ)nō-ˌbel-\ *n* : any of various annual prizes (as in peace, literature, or medicine) established by the will of Alfred Nobel for the encouragement of persons who work for the interests of humanity

no•bil•i•ty \nō-ˈbil-ət-ē\ *n* **1** : the quality or state of being noble ⟨∼ of character⟩ **2** : nobles considered as forming a class

¹no•ble \ˈnō-bəl\ *adj* **no•bler** \-b(ə-)lər\; **no•blest** \-b(ə-)ləst\ [ME, fr. OF, fr. L *nobilis* knowable, well known, noble, fr. *noscere* to come to know] **1** : ILLUSTRIOUS; *also* : FAMOUS, NOTABLE **2** : of high birth, rank, or station : ARISTOCRATIC **3** : EXCELLENT **4** : STATELY, IMPOSING ⟨a ∼ edifice⟩ **5** : of a magnanimous nature — **no•ble•ness** *n* — **no•bly** \-blē\ *adv*

²noble *n* : a person of noble rank or birth

no•ble•man \ˈnō-bəl-mən\ *n* : a member of the nobility : PEER

no•blesse oblige \nō-ˌbles-ə-ˈblēzh\ *n* : the obligation of honorable, generous, and responsible behavior associated with high rank or birth

¹no·body \'nō-ˌbäd-ē, -bəd-ē\ *pron* : no person

²nobody *n, pl* **no·bod·ies** : a person of no influence, importance, or worth

noc·tur·nal \näk-'tərn-ᵊl\ *adj* **1** : of, relating to, or occurring in the night **2** : active at night ⟨a ~ bird⟩

noc·turne \'näk-ˌtərn\ *n* **1** : a dreamy pensive composition for the piano **2** : a work of art dealing with night

noc·u·ous \'näk-yə-wəs\ *adj* : likely to cause injury : HARMFUL

nod \'näd\ *vb* **nod·ded; nod·ding 1** : to bend the head downward or forward (as in bowing, going to sleep, or giving assent) **2** : to move up and down ⟨tulips *nodding* in the breeze⟩ **3** : to show by a nod of the head ⟨~ agreement⟩ **4** : to make a slip or error in a moment of abstraction — **nod** *n*

nod·dle \'näd-ᵊl\ *n* : HEAD

nod·dy \'näd-ē\ *n, pl* **noddies 1** : SIMPLETON **2** : a stout-bodied tropical tern

node \'nōd\ *n* : a thickened, swollen, or differentiated area (as of tissue); *esp* : the part of a stem from which a leaf arises — **nod·al** \-ᵊl\ *adj*

nod·ule \'näj-ül\ *n* : a small lump or swelling — **nod·u·lar** \'näj-ə-lər\ *adj*

no·el \nō-'el\ *n* [F *noël* Christmas, carol, fr. L *natalis* birthday] **1** : a Christmas carol **2** *cap* : the Christmas season

noes *pl of* NO

no–fault \'nō-ˌfȯlt\ *adj* **1** : of, relating to, or being a motor vehicle insurance plan under which an accident victim is compensated usu. up to a stipulated limit for actual losses by his own insurance company regardless of who is responsible **2** : of, relating to, or being a divorce law according to which neither party is held responsible for the breakup of the marriage

nog·gin \'näg-ən\ *n* **1** : a small mug or cup; *also* : a small quantity of drink **2** : a person's head

no–good \ˌnō-ˌgud\ *adj* : having no worth, use, or chance of success — **no–good** \'nō-ˌgud\ *n*

Noh *var of* NO

no–hit·ter \(ˈ)nō-'hit-ər\ *n* : a baseball game or part of a game in which a pitcher allows the opposition no base hits

no·how \'nō-ˌhau\ *adv* : in no manner

¹noise \'nȯiz\ *n* [ME, fr. OF, strife, quarrel, noise, fr. L *nausea* nausea] **1** : loud, confused, or senseless shouting or outcry **2** : SOUND; *esp* : one that lacks agreeable musical quality or is noticeably unpleasant **3** : unwanted electronic signal or disturbance — **noise·less** *adj* — **noise·less·ly** *adv*

²noise *vb* **noised; nois·ing** : to spread by rumor or report ⟨the story was *noised* abroad⟩

noise·mak·er \'nȯiz-ˌmā-kər\ *n* : one that makes noise; *esp* : a device used to make noise at parties

noise pollution *n* : environmental pollution consisting of annoying or harmful noise

noi·some \'nȯi-səm\ *adj* **1** : HARMFUL, UNWHOLESOME **2** : offensive to the senses (as smell) : DISGUSTING

noisy \'nȯi-zē\ *adj* **nois·i·er; -est 1** : making loud noises **2** : full of noises : LOUD — **nois·i·ly** \'nȯi-zə-lē\ *adv* — **nois·i·ness** \-zē-nəs\ *n*

nol·le pro·se·qui \ˌnäl-ē-'präs-ə-ˌkwī\ *n* [L, to be unwilling to pursue] : an entry on the record of a legal action that the prosecutor or plaintiff will proceed no further in an action or suit or in some aspect of it

no·lo con·ten·de·re \ˌnō-lō-kən-'ten-də-rē\ *n* [L, I do not wish to contend] : a plea in a criminal prosecution that subjects the defendant to conviction but does not admit guilt or preclude denying the charges in another proceeding

nol–pros \'näl-'präs\ *vb* **nol–prossed; nol–pros·ing** : to discontinue by entering a nolle prosequi

nom *abbr* nominative

no·mad \'nō-ˌmad\ *n* **1** : a member of a people with no fixed residence but wandering from place to place **2** : an individual who roams about aimlessly — **nomad** *adj* — **no·mad·ic** \nō-'mad-ik\ *adj*

no–man's–land \'nō-ˌmanz-ˌland\ *n* **1** : an area of unowned, unclaimed, or uninhabited land **2** : an unoccupied area between opposing troops

nom de guerre \ˌnäm-di-'geər\ *n, pl*

noms de guerre \ˌnäm(z)-di-\ [F, lit., war name] : PSEUDONYM

nom de plume \-ˈplüm\ *n, pl* **noms de plume** \ˌnäm(z)-di-\ [F *nom* name + *de* of + *plume* pen] : PSEUDONYM

no·men·cla·ture \ˈnō-mən-ˌklā-chər\ *n* **1** : NAME, DESIGNATION **2** : a system of names used in a science or art

nom·i·nal \ˈnäm-ən-ᵊl\ *adj* **1** : being something in name or form only ⟨∼ head of a party⟩ **2** : TRIFLING ⟨a ∼ price⟩ — **nom·i·nal·ly** \-ē\ *adv*

nom·i·nate \ˈnäm-ə-ˌnāt\ *vb* **-nat·ed; -nat·ing** : to choose as a candidate for election, appointment, or honor — **nom·i·na·tion** \ˌnäm-ə-ˈnā-shən\ *n*

nom·i·na·tive \ˈnäm-(ə-)nət-iv\ *adj* : of, relating to, or constituting a grammatical case marking typically the subject of a verb — **nominative** *n*

nom·i·nee \ˌnäm-ə-ˈnē\ *n* : a person nominated for an office, duty, or position

non- \(ˈ)nän, ˌnän\ *prefix* : not : reverse of : absence of

nonabrasive	noncompetitive
nonabsorbent	noncompliance
nonacademic	noncomplying
nonacceptance	nonconcurrence
nonacid	nonconcurrent
nonactivated	nonconducting
nonadaptive	nonconflicting
nonaddicting	nonconformance
nonadhesive	nonconforming
nonadjacent	nonconstructive
nonadjustable	noncontagious
nonaggression	noncontinuous
nonalcoholic	noncontributing
nonappearance	noncorroding
nonaromatic	noncorrosive
nonathletic	noncrystalline
nonattendance	nondeductible
nonbeliever	nondelivery
nonbelligerent	nondemocratic
nonbreakable	nondenominational
nonburnable	nondepartmental
noncancerous	nondestructive
noncandidate	nondevelopment
noncellular	nondiscrimination
nonchargeable	nondiscriminitory
nonclerical	nondistinctive
noncoital	nondistribution
noncombat	nondivided
noncombustible	nondurable
noncommercial	noneconomic
noncommunicable	noneducational
non-Communist	nonelastic
noncompeting	nonelection
nonelective	nonnegotiable
nonelectric	nonobservance
nonelectrical	nonoccurrence
nonemotional	nonofficial
nonenforceable	nonoily
nonenforcement	nonorthodox
nonessential	nonparallel
nonethical	nonparasitic
nonexchangeable	nonparticipant
nonexempt	nonparticipating
nonexistence	nonpathogenic
nonexistent	nonpaying
nonexplosive	nonpayment
nonfarm	nonperformance
nonfatal	nonperishable
nonfattening	nonphysical
nonfederated	nonpoisonous
nonferrous	nonpolar
nonfiction	nonpolitical
nonfictional	nonporous
nonfilamentous	nonpregnant
nonfilterable	nonproductive
nonflammable	nonprofessional
nonflowering	nonprotein
nonfood	nonradioactive
nonfreezing	nonrandom
nonfulfillment	nonreactive
nonfunctional	nonreciprocal
nongraded	nonrecognition
nonhereditary	nonrecoverable
nonhomogeneous	nonrecurrent
nonhomologous	nonrecurring
nonhuman	nonrefillable
nonidentical	nonreligious
nonimportation	nonrenewable
nonindustrial	nonresidential
noninfectious	nonrestricted
noninflammable	nonreturnable
nonintellectual	nonreversible
nonintercourse	nonruminant
noninterference	nonsalable
nonintoxicant	nonscientific
nonintoxicating	nonscientist
nonionizing	nonseasonal
nonirritating	nonsectarian
nonlegal	nonsegregated
nonlife	nonselective
nonlinear	non-self-governing
nonliterary	nonsexist
nonliving	nonsexual
nonlogical	nonshrinkable
nonmagnetic	nonsinkable
nonmalignant	nonskid
nonmaterial	nonslip
nonmember	nonsmoker
nonmembership	nonsmoking
nonmigratory	nonsocial
nonmilitary	nonspeaking
nonmoral	nonspecialist
nonmotile	nonspecialized
nonmoving	nonstaining

nonstriated
nonstriker
nonsubscriber
nonsuccess
nonsurgical
nontaxable
nonteaching
nontechnical
nontemporal
nontenured
nontheistic
nonthreatening
nontoxic
nontraditional
nontransferable
nontransparent

nontypical
nonuniform
nonuser
nonvascular
nonvenomous
nonviable
nonviolation
nonvisual
nonvocal
nonvolatile
nonvoter
nonvoting
nonworker
nonworking
nonzero

non·age \'nän-ij, 'nō-nij\ *n* **1** : legal minority **2** : a period of youth **3** : IMMATURITY

no·na·ge·nar·i·an \,nō-nə-jə-'ner-ē-ən, ,nän-ə-\ *n* : a person who is in his nineties

non·aligned \,nän-ᵊl-'īnd\ *adj* : not allied with other nations

non·book \'nän-,bùk\ *n* : a book of little literary merit which is often a compilation (as of press clippings)

¹nonce \'näns\ *n* : the one, particular, or present occasion or purpose ⟨for the ∼⟩

²nonce *adj* : occurring, used, or made only once or for a special occasion ⟨a ∼ word⟩

non·cha·lant \,nän-shə-'länt\ *adj* [F, fr. OF, fr. prp. of *nonchaloir* to disregard, fr. *non-* not + *chaloir* to concern, fr. L *calēre* to be warm] : giving an effect of unconcern or indifference — **non·cha·lance** \-'läns\ *n* — **non·cha·lant·ly** *adv*

non·com \'nän-,käm\ *n* : NONCOMMISSIONED OFFICER

non·com·ba·tant \,nän-kəm-'bat-ᵊnt, nän-'käm-bət-ənt\ *n* : a member (as a chaplain) of the armed forces whose duties do not include fighting; *also* : CIVILIAN — **noncombatant** *adj*

non·com·mis·sioned officer \,nän-kə-,mish-ənd-\ *n* : a subordinate officer in the armed forces appointed from enlisted personnel

non·com·mit·tal \,nän-kə-'mit-ᵊl\ *adj* : indicating neither consent nor dissent

non com·pos men·tis \,nän-,käm-pəs-'ment-əs\ *adj* : not of sound mind

non·con·duc·tor \,nän-kən-'dək-tər\ *n* : a substance that is a very poor conductor of heat, electricity, or sound

non·con·form·ist \-kən-'fòr-məst\ *n* **1** *often cap* : a person who does not conform to an established church and esp. the Church of England **2** : a person who does not conform to a generally accepted pattern of thought or action — **non·con·for·mi·ty** \-'fòr-mət-ē\ *n*

non·co·op·er·a·tion \,nän-kō-,äp-ə-'rā-shən\ *n* : failure or refusal to cooperate; *esp* : refusal through civil disobedience of a people to cooperate with the government of a country

non·cred·it \(')nän-'kred-ət\ *adj* : not offering credit toward a degree

non·dairy \'nän-'de(ə)r-ē\ *adj* : containing no milk or milk products

non·de·script \,nän-di-'skript\ *adj* : not belonging to any particular class or kind : not easily described

non·drink·er \-'driŋ-kər\ *n* : one who abstains from alcoholic beverages

¹none \'nən\ *pron* **1** : not any ⟨∼ of them went⟩ **2** : not one ⟨∼ of the family⟩ **3** : not any such thing or person ⟨half a loaf is better than ∼⟩

²none *adj, archaic* : not any : NO

³none *adv* : by no means : not at all ⟨he got there ∼ too soon⟩

non·en·ti·ty \,nän-'ent-ət-ē\ *n* **1** : something that does not exist or exists only in the imagination **2** : one of no consequence or significance

nones \'nōnz\ *n sing or pl* : the 7th day of March, May, July, or October or the 5th day of any other month in the ancient Roman calendar

none·such \'nən-,səch\ *n* : one without an equal — **nonesuch** *adj*

none·the·less \,nən-thə-'les\ *adv* : NEVERTHELESS

non–eu·clid·e·an \,nän-yü-'klid-ē-ən\ *adj, often cap E* : not assuming or in accordance with all the postulates of Euclid's *Elements* ⟨∼ geometry⟩

non·event \'nän-i-,vent\ *n* **1** : an event that fails to take place or to satisfy expectations **2** : a highly promoted event of little or no consequence

non·fat \-'fat\ *adj* : lacking fat solids : having fat solids removed ⟨∼ milk⟩

non·gono·coc·cal \'nän-,gän-ə-'käk-əl\ *adj* : not caused by the gonococcus

non·he·ro \-'hē-rō\ *n* : ANTIHERO

non·in·ter·ven·tion \,nän-,int-ər-'ven-chən\ *n* : refusal or failure to intervene (as in the affairs of another state)

non•met•al \'nän-'met-ᵊl\ *n* : a chemical element (as carbon, phosphorus, or oxygen) that lacks metallic properties — **non•me•tal•lic** \ˌnän-mə-'tal-ik\ *adj*

non•neg•a•tive \-'neg-ət-iv\ *adj* : not negative : being either positive or zero

non•ob•jec•tive \ˌnän-əb-'jek-tiv\ *adj* **1** : not objective **2** : representing no natural or actual object, figure, or scene ⟨∼ art⟩

¹**non•pa•reil** \ˌnän-pə-'rel\ *adj* : having no equal : PEERLESS

²**nonpareil** *n* **1** : an individual of unequaled excellence : PARAGON **2** : a small flat disk of chocolate covered with white sugar pellets

non•par•ti•san \'nän-'pärt-ə-zən\ *adj* : not partisan; *esp* : not influenced by political party spirit or interests

non•per•son \-'pərs-ᵊn\ *n* **1** : UNPERSON **2** : a person having no social or legal status

non•plus \'nän-'pləs\ *vb* **-plussed** *also* **-plused** \-'pləst\; **-plus•sing** *also* **-plus•ing** : PUZZLE, PERPLEX

non•pre•scrip•tion \ˌnän-pri-'skrip-shən\ *adj* : available for sale legally without a doctor's prescription

non•prof•it \'nän-'präf-ət\ *adj* : not conducted or maintained for the purpose of making a profit

non•pro•lif•er•a•tion \ˌnän-prə-ˌlif-ə-'rā-shən\ *adj* : providing for the stoppage of proliferation (as of nuclear arms) ⟨a ∼ treaty⟩

non•read•er \'nän-'rēd-ər\ *n* : one who does not read

non•rep•re•sen•ta•tion•al \ˌnän-ˌrep-ri-ˌzen-'tā-sh(ə-)nəl\ *adj* : NONOBJECTIVE 2

non•res•i•dent \'nän-'rez-əd-ənt\ *adj* : not living in a particular place — **non•res•i•dence** \-əd-əns\ *n* — **nonresident** *n*

non•re•sis•tance \ˌnän-ri-'zis-təns\ *n* : the principles or practice of passive submission to authority even when unjust or oppressive

non•re•stric•tive \-ri-'strik-tiv\ *adj* **1** : not serving or tending to restrict **2** : not limiting the reference of the word or phrase modified ⟨a ∼ clause⟩

non•rig•id \nän-'rij-əd\ *adj* : maintain-

ing form by pressure of contained gas ⟨a ∼ airship⟩

non•sched•uled \'nän-'skej-üld\ *adj* : licensed to carry passengers or freight by air without a regular schedule

non•sense \'nän-ˌsens, -səns\ *n* **1** : foolish or meaningless words or actions **2** : things of no importance or value : TRIFLES — **non•sen•si•cal** \nän-'sen-si-kəl\ *adj* — **non•sen•si•cal•ly** \-k(ə-)lē\ *adv*

non seq *abbr* non sequitur

non se•qui•tur \nän-'sek-wət-ər\ *n* [L, it does not follow] : an inference that does not follow from the premises

non•sked \'nän-'sked\ *n* : a nonscheduled airline or transport plane

non•stan•dard \ˌnän-'stan-dərd\ *adj* **1** : not standard **2** : not conforming to the usage characteristic of educated native speakers of a language

non•start•er \'nän-'stärt-ər\ *n* : one that does not start or gets off to a poor start

non•stick \-'stik\ *adj* : allowing easy removal of cooked food particles

non•stop \-'stäp\ *adj* : done or made without a stop — **nonstop** *adv*

non•sup•port \ˌnän-sə-'pōrt\ *n* : failure to support; *esp* : failure on the part of one under obligation to provide maintenance

non trop•po \'nän-'trȯ-pō\ *adv or adj* [It] : not too much so : moderately so — used as a direction in music

non–U \'nän-'yü\ *adj* : not characteristic of the upper classes

non•union \-'yü-nyən\ *adj* **1** : not belonging to a trade union ⟨∼ carpenters⟩ **2** : not recognizing or favoring trade unions or their members ⟨∼ employers⟩

non•us•er \-'yü-zər\ *n* : one who does not make use of something (as drugs)

non•vi•o•lence \-'nän-'vī-ə-ləns\ *n* **1** : abstention from violence as a matter of principle **2** : avoidance of violence **3** : nonviolent political demonstrations — **non•vi•o•lent** \-lənt\ *adj*

non•white \ˌnän-'hwīt, -'wīt\ *adj* : a person whose features and esp. skin color are different from those of Caucasians of northwestern Europe — **nonwhite** *adj*

non•wo•ven \'nän-'wō-vən\ *adj* : made of fibers held together by interlocking or bonding (as by chemical or thermal means) — **nonwoven** *n*

noo•dle \ˈnüd-ᵊl\ *n* : a food paste made with egg and shaped typically in ribbon form

nook \ˈnu̇k\ *n* **1** : an interior angle or corner formed usu. by two walls ⟨a chimney ~⟩ **2** : a sheltered or hidden place ⟨a shady ~⟩

noon \ˈnün\ *n* : the middle of the day : 12 o'clock in the daytime — **noon** *adj*

noon•day \-ˌdā\ *n* : NOON, MIDDAY

no one *pron* : NOBODY

noon•tide \ˈnün-ˌtīd\ *n* : NOON

noon•time \-ˌtīm\ *n* : NOON

noose \ˈnüs\ *n* : a loop with a running knot (as in a lasso) that binds closer the more it is drawn

no–par \ˈno-ˈpär\ *or* **no–par–val•ue** *adj* : having no nominal value ⟨~ stock⟩

nope \ˈnōp\ *adv* : NO

nor \nər, (ˈ)nȯr\ *conj* : and not ⟨not for you ~ for me⟩ — used esp. to introduce and negate the second member and each later member of a series of items preceded by *neither* ⟨neither here ~ there⟩

Nor *abbr* Norway; Norwegian

Nor•dic \ˈnȯrd-ik\ *adj* **1** : of or relating to the Germanic peoples of northern Europe and esp. of Scandinavia **2** : of or relating to a physical type characterized by tall stature, long head, light skin and hair, and blue eyes — **Nordic** *n*

nor•epi•neph•rine \ˈnȯr-ˌep-ə-ˈnef-rən\ *n* [*nor*mal + *epinephrine*] : a nitrogen-containing compound that is the chemical means of transmission across synapses in parts of the sympathetic and central nervous systems

norm \ˈnȯrm\ *n* [L *norma*, lit., carpenter's square] : AVERAGE; *esp* : a set standard of development or achievement usu. derived from the average or median achievement of a large group

¹**nor•mal** \ˈnȯr-məl\ *adj* **1** : REGULAR, STANDARD, NATURAL **2** : of average intelligence; *also* : sound in mind and body — **nor•mal•cy** \-sē\ *n* — **nor•mal•i•ty** \nȯr-ˈmal-ət-ē\ *n* — **nor•mal•ly** \ˈnȯr-mə-lē\ *adv*

²**normal** *n* **1** : one that is normal **2** : the usual condition, level, or quantity

nor•mal•ize \ˈnȯr-mə-ˌlīz\ *vb* **-ized; -izing** : to make normal or average —

nor•mal•iza•tion \ˌnȯr-mə-lə-ˈzā-shən\ *n*

normal school *n* : a usu. 2-year school for training chiefly elementary teachers

Nor•man \ˈnȯr-mən\ *n* **1** : a native or inhabitant of Normandy **2** : one of the 10th century Scandinavian conquerors of Normandy **3** : one of the Norman-French conquerors of England in 1066 — **Norman** *adj*

nor•ma•tive \ˈnȯr-mət-iv\ *adj* : of, relating to, or prescribing norms — **nor•ma•tive•ly** *adv* — **nor•ma•tive•ness** *n*

Norse \ˈnȯrs\ *n, pl* **Norse 1** *pl* : SCANDINAVIANS; *also* : NORWEGIANS **2** : NORWEGIAN; *also* : any of the western Scandinavian dialects or languages

Norse•man \-mən\ *n* : one of the ancient Scandinavians

¹**north** \ˈnȯrth\ *adv* : to or toward the north

²**north** *adj* **1** : situated toward or at the north **2** : coming from the north

³**north** *n* **1** : the direction to the left of one facing east **2** : the compass point directly opposite to south **3** *cap* : regions or countries north of a specified or implied point — **north•er•ly** \ˈnȯrth-ər-lē\ *adv or adj* — **north•ern** \-ərn\ *adj* — **North•ern•er** \-ə(r)n-ər\ *n* — **north•ern•most** \-ərn-ˌmōst\ *adj* — **north•ward** \ˈnȯrth-wərd\ *adv or adj* — **north•wards** \-wərdz\ *adv*

north•east \nȯrth-ˈēst\ *n* **1** : the general direction between north and east **2** : the compass point midway between north and east **3** *cap* : regions or countries northeast of a specified or implied point — **northeast** *adj or adv* — **north•east•er•ly** \-ər-lē\ *adv or adj* — **north•east•ern** \-ərn\ *adj*

north•east•er \-ər\ *n* **1** : a strong northeast wind **2** : a storm with northeast winds

north•er \ˈnȯr-thər\ *n* **1** : a strong north wind **2** : a storm with north winds

northern lights *n pl* : AURORA BOREALIS

north pole *n, often cap N&P* : the northernmost point of the earth

North Star *n* : the star toward which the northern end of the earth's axis points

north•west \nȯrth-ˈwest\ *n* **1** : the general direction between north and west

2 : the compass point midway between north and west **3** *cap* : regions or countries northwest of a specified or implied point — **northwest** *adj or adv* — **north·west·er·ly** \-ər-lē\ *adv or adj* — **north·west·ern** \-ərn\ *adj*

Norw *abbr* Norway; Norwegian

Nor·we·gian \nȯr-ˈwē-jən\ *n* **1** : a native or inhabitant of Norway **2** : the language of Norway — **Norwegian** *adj*

nos *abbr* numbers

¹**nose** \ˈnōz\ *n* **1** : the part of the face containing the nostrils and covering the front of the nasal cavity **2** : the organ or sense of smell **3** : something (as a point, edge, or projecting front part) that resembles a nose ⟨the ～ of a plane⟩ — **nosed** \ˈnōzd\ *adj*

²**nose** *vb* **nosed; nos·ing** **1** : to detect by or as if by smell : SCENT **2** : to push or move with the nose **3** : to touch or rub with the nose : NUZZLE **4** : PRY **5** : to move ahead slowly ⟨the ship *nosed* into her berth⟩

nose·bleed \-ˌblēd\ *n* : a bleeding from the nose

nose cone *n* : a protective cone constituting the forward end of a rocket or missile

nose dive *n* **1** : a downward nose-first plunge (as of an airplane) **2** : a sudden extreme drop (as in prices)

nose·gay \ˈnōz-ˌgā\ *n* : a small bunch of flowers : POSY

nose out *vb* : to defeat by a narrow margin

nose·piece \-ˌpēs\ *n* **1** : a fitting at the lower end of a microscope tube to which the objectives are attached **2** : the bridge of a pair of eyeglasses

no–show \ˈnō-ˈshō\ *n* : a person who reserves space (as on an airplane or at a concert) but neither uses nor cancels the reservation

nos·tal·gia \nä-ˈstal-jə\ *n* [NL, fr. Gk *nostos* return home + *algos* pain, grief] **1** : HOMESICKNESS **2** : a wistful yearning for something past or irrecoverable — **nos·tal·gic** \-jik\ *adj*

nos·tril \ˈnäs-trəl\ *n* [ME *nosethirl,* fr. OE *nosthyrl,* fr. *nosu* nose + *thyrel* hole] : an external naris usu. with the adjoining nasal wall and passage

nos·trum \ˈnäs-trəm\ *n* [L, neut. of *noster* our, ours, fr. *nos* we] : a questionable medicine or remedy

nosy *or* **nos·ey** \ˈnō-zē\ *adj* **nos·i·er; -est** : INQUISITIVE, PRYING

not \(ˈ)nät\ *adv* **1** — used to make negative a group of words or a word ⟨the boys are ～ here⟩ **2** — used to stand for the negative of a preceding group of words ⟨sometimes hard to see and sometimes ～⟩

no·ta be·ne \ˌnōt-ə-ˈbē-nē, -ˈben-ē\ [L, mark well] — used to call attention to something important

no·ta·bil·i·ty \ˌnōt-ə-ˈbil-ət-ē\ *n, pl* **-ties** **1** : the quality or state of being notable **2** : NOTABLE

¹**no·ta·ble** \ˈnōt-ə-bəl\ *adj* **1** : NOTEWORTHY, REMARKABLE ⟨a ～ achievement⟩ **2** : DISTINGUISHED, PROMINENT ⟨two ～ politicians made speeches⟩

²**no·ta·ble** *n* : a person of note

no·ta·bly \ˈnōt-ə-blē\ *adv* **1** : in a notable manner **2** : ESPECIALLY, PARTICULARLY

no·tar·i·al \nō-ˈter-ē-əl\ *adj* : of, relating to, or done by a notary public

no·ta·rize \ˈnōt-ə-ˌrīz\ *vb* **-rized; -riz·ing** : to acknowledge or make legally authentic as a notary public

no·ta·ry public \ˌnōt-ə-rē-\ *n, pl* **notaries public** *or* **notary publics** : a public official who attests or certifies writings (as deeds) to make them legally authentic

no·ta·tion \nō-ˈtā-shən\ *n* **1** : ANNOTATION, NOTE **2** : the act, process, or method of representing data by marks, signs, figures, or characters; *also* : a system of symbols (as letters, numerals, or musical notes) used in such notation

¹**notch** \ˈnäch\ *n* **1** : a V-shaped hollow in an edge or surface **2** : a narrow pass between two mountains

²**notch** *vb* **1** : to cut or make notches in **2** : to score or record by or as if by cutting a series of notches ⟨～ed 20 points for the team⟩

notch·back \ˈnäch-ˌbak\ *n* : an automobile with a trunk whose lid forms a distinct deck

¹**note** \ˈnōt\ *vb* **not·ed; not·ing** **1** : to notice or observe with care; *also* : to record or preserve in writing **2** : to make special mention of : REMARK

²**note** *n* **1** : a musical sound **2** : a cry, call, or sound esp. of a bird **3** : a special tone in a person's words or voice

⟨a ∼ of fear⟩ **4** : a character in music used to indicate duration of a tone by its shape and pitch by its position on the staff **5** : a characteristic feature : MOOD, QUALITY ⟨a ∼ of optimism⟩ **6** : MEMORANDUM **7** : a brief and informal record; *also* : a written or printed comment or explanation **8** : a written promise to pay a debt **9** : a piece of paper money **10** : a short informal letter **11** : a formal diplomatic or official communication **12** : DISTINCTION, REPUTATION ⟨an artist of ∼⟩ **13** : OBSERVATION, NOTICE, HEED ⟨take ∼ of the time⟩

note·book \'nōt-₁bùk\ *n* : a book for notes or memoranda

not·ed \'nōt-əd\ *adj* : well known by reputation : EMINENT, CELEBRATED

note·wor·thy \-₁wər-thē\ *adj* : worthy of note : REMARKABLE

¹**noth·ing** \'nəth-iŋ\ *pron* **1** : no thing ⟨leaves ∼ to the imagination⟩ **2** : no part **3** : one of no interest, value, or importance ⟨she's ∼ to me⟩

²**nothing** *adv* : not at all : in no degree

³**nothing** *n* **1** : something that does not exist **2** : ZERO **3** : a person or thing of little or no value or importance

⁴**nothing** *adj* : of no account : worthless

noth·ing·ness \-nəs\ *n* **1** : the quality or state of being nothing **2** : NONEXISTENCE; *also* : utter insignificance **3** : something insignificant or valueless

¹**no·tice** \'nōt-əs\ *n* **1** : WARNING, ANNOUNCEMENT **2** : notification of the termination of an agreement or contract at a specified time **3** : ATTENTION, HEED ⟨bring the matter to my ∼⟩ **4** : a written or printed announcement **5** : a short critical account or examination (as of a play) : REVIEW

²**notice** *vb* **no·ticed; no·tic·ing 1** : to make mention of : remark on : NOTE **2** : to take notice of : OBSERVE, MARK

no·tice·able \'nōt-ə-sə-bəl\ *adj* **1** : worthy of notice **2** : capable of being or likely to be noticed — **not·tice·ably** \-blē\ *adv*

no·ti·fy \'nōt-ə-₁fī\ *vb* **-fied; -fy·ing 1** : to give notice of : report the occurrence of **2** : to give notice to — **no·ti·fi·ca·tion** \₁nōt-ə-fə-'kā-shən\ *n*

no·tion \'nō-shən\ *n* **1** : IDEA, CONCEPTION ⟨have a ∼ of what he means⟩ **2** : a belief held : OPINION, VIEW **3**

: WHIM, FANCY ⟨a sudden ∼ to go⟩ **4** *pl* : small useful articles (as pins, needles, or thread)

no·tion·al \'nō-sh(ə-)nəl\ *adj* **1** : existing in the mind only : IMAGINARY, UNREAL **2** : given to foolish or fanciful moods or ideas : WHIMSICAL

no·to·ri·ous \nō-'tōr-ē-əs\ *adj* : generally known and talked of; *esp* : widely and unfavorably known — **no·to·ri·ety** \₁nōt-ə-'rī-ət-ē\ *n* — **no·to·ri·ous·ly** \nō-'tōr-ē-əs-lē\ *adv*

¹**not·with·stand·ing** \₁nät-with-'stan-diŋ, -with-\ *prep* : in spite of

²**notwithstanding** *adv* : NEVERTHELESS

³**notwithstanding** *conj* : ALTHOUGH

nou·gat \'nü-gət\ *n* [F, fr. Provençal, fr. Old Provençal *nogat*, fr. *noga* nut, fr. L *nuc-, nux*] : a confection of nuts or fruit pieces in a sugar paste

nought \'nòt, 'nät\ *var of* NAUGHT

noun \'naùn\ *n* : a word that is the name of a subject of discourse (as a person or place)

nour·ish \'nər-ish\ *vb* : to cause to grow and develop (as by care and feeding)

nour·ish·ing *adj* : giving nourishment

nour·ish·ment \'nər-ish-mənt\ *n* **1** : FOOD, NUTRIMENT **2** : the action or process of nourishing

nou·veau riche \₁nü-₁vō-'rēsh\ *n, pl* **nou·veaux riches** *same*\ [F] : a person newly rich : PARVENU

Nov *abbr* November

no·va \'nō-və\ *n, pl* **novas** *or* **no·vae** \-(₁)vē, -₁vī\ [NL, fem. of L *novus* new] : a star that suddenly increases greatly in brightness and then within a few months or years grows dim again

¹**nov·el** \'näv-əl\ *adj* **1** : having no precedent : NEW **2** : STRANGE, UNUSUAL

²**novel** *n* : a long invented prose narrative dealing with human experience through a connected sequence of events — **nov·el·ist** \-(ə-)ləst\ *n*

nov·el·ette \₁näv-ə-'let\ *n* : a brief novel or long short story

nov·el·ize \'näv-ə-₁līz\ *vb* **-ized; -iz·ing** : to convert into the form of a novel — **nov·el·iza·tion** \₁näv-ə-lə-'zā-shən\ *n*

no·vel·la \nō-'vel-ə\ *n, pl* **novellas** *or* **no·vel·le** \-'vel-ē\ : NOVELETTE

nov·el·ty \'näv-əl-tē\ *n, pl* **-ties 1** : something new or unusual **2** : NEWNESS **3** : a small manufactured article intended mainly for personal or household adornment — usu. used in pl.

No•vem•ber \nō-'vem-bər\ *n* [ME *Novembre,* fr. OF, fr. L *November* (ninth month), fr. *novem* nine] : the 11th month of the year having 30 days

no•ve•na \nō-'vē-nə\ *n* : a Roman Catholic nine days' devotion

nov•ice \'näv-əs\ *n* **1** : a new member of a religious order who is preparing to take the vows of religion **2** : one who is inexperienced or untrained

no•vi•tiate \nō-'vish-ət\ *n* **1** : the period or state of being a novice **2** : NOVICE **3** : a house where novices are trained

¹now \(')naù\ *adv* **1** : at the present time or moment **2** : in the time immediately before the present **3** : FORTHWITH **4** — used with the sense of present time weakened or lost (as to express command, introduce an important point, or indicate a transition) ⟨∼ hear this⟩ **5** : SOMETIMES ⟨∼ one and ∼ another⟩ **6** : under the present circumstances **7** : at the time referred to

²now *conj* : in view of the fact ⟨∼ that you're here, we'll start⟩

³now \'naù\ *n* : the present time or moment : PRESENT

⁴now \'naù\ *adj* **1** : of or relating to the present time ⟨the ∼ president⟩ **2** : excitingly new ⟨∼ clothes⟩; *also* : constantly aware of what is new ⟨∼ people⟩

NOW *abbr* **1** National Organization for Women **2** negotiable order of withdrawal

now•a•days \'naù-(ə-)ˌdāz\ *adv* : at the present time

no•way \'nō-ˌwā\ *or* **no•ways** \-ˌwāz\ *adv* : NOWISE

no•where \-ˌhweər\ *adv* : not anywhere — **no•where** *n*

nowhere near *adv* : not nearly

no•wise \'nō-ˌwīz\ *adv* : in no way

nox•ious \'näk-shəs\ *adj* : harmful esp. to health or morals

noz•zle \'näz-əl\ *n* : a short tube constricted in the middle or at one end and used (as on a hose) to speed up or direct a flow of fluid

np *abbr* **1** no pagination **2** no place (of publication)

Np *symbol* neptunium

NP *abbr* **1** notary public **2** noun phrase

NS *abbr* **1** not specified **2** Nova Scotia **3** nuclear ship

NSA *abbr* National Security Agency

NSC *abbr* National Security Council

NSF *abbr* **1** National Science Foundation **2** not sufficient funds

NSW *abbr* New South Wales

NT *abbr* **1** New Testament **2** Northern Territory **3** Northwest Territories

nth \'enth\ *adj* **1** : numbered with an unspecified or indefinitely large ordinal number **2** : EXTREME, UTMOST ⟨to the ∼ degree⟩

NTP *abbr* normal temperature and pressure

nt wt *or* **n wt** *abbr* net weight

NU *abbr* name unknown

nu•ance \'n(y)ü-ˌäns, n(y)ü-'äns\ *n* [F] : a shade of difference : a delicate variation (as in tone or meaning)

nub \'nəb\ *n* **1** : KNOB, LUMP **2** : GIST, POINT ⟨the ∼ of the story⟩

nub•bin \'nəb-ən\ *n* **1** : something (as an ear of Indian corn) that is small for its kind, stunted, undeveloped, or imperfect **2** : a small projecting bit

nub•ble \'nəb-əl\ *n* : a small knob or lump — **nub•bly** \-(ə-)lē\ *adj*

nu•bile \'n(y)ü-bəl, -ˌbīl\ *adj* : of marriageable condition or age ⟨∼ girls⟩

nu•cle•ar \'n(y)ü-klē-ər\ *adj* **1** : of, relating to, or constituting a nucleus **2** : of, relating to, or using the atomic nucleus or energy derived from it

nu•cle•ate \'n(y)ü-klē-ˌāt\ *vb* **-at•ed; -at•ing** : to form, act as, or have a nucleus — **nu•cle•ation** \ˌn(y)ü-klē-'ā-shən\ *n*

nu•cle•ic acid \n(y)ü-ˌklē-ik, -ˌklā-\ *n* : any of various complex organic acids (as DNA) found esp. in cell nuclei

nu•cle•on \'n(y)ü-klē-ˌän\ *n* : a proton or a neutron esp. in the atomic nucleus — **nu•cle•on•ic** \ˌn(y)ü-klē-'än-ik\ *adj*

nu•cle•us \'n(y)ü-klē-əs\ *n, pl* **nu•clei** \-klē-ˌī\ *also* **nu•cle•us•es** [NL, fr. L, kernel, dim. of *nuc-, nux* nut] **1** : a central mass or part about which matter gathers or is collected : CORE **2** : a cell part that is characteristic of all living things except viruses, bacteria, and certain algae, that is necessary for heredity and for making proteins, that contains the chromosomes with their genes, and that is enclosed in a membrane **3** : a mass of gray matter or group of nerve cells in the central nervous system **4** : the central part of an atom that comprises nearly all of the atomic mass

nu·clide \'n(y)ü-ˌklīd\ *n* : a species of atom characterized by the constitution of its nucleus

¹nude \'n(y)üd\ *adj* **nud·er; nud·est** : BARE, NAKED, UNCLOTHED — **nu·di·ty** \'n(y)üd-ət-ē\ *n*

²nude *n* **1** : a nude human figure esp. as depicted in art **2** : the condition of being nude ⟨in the ∼⟩

nudge \'nəj\ *vb* **nudged; nudg·ing** : to touch or push gently (as with the elbow) usu. in order to seek attention — **nudge** *n*

nud·ism \'n(y)üd-ˌiz-əm\ *n* : the practice of going nude esp. in mixed groups at specially secluded places — **nud·ist** \'n(y)üd-əst\ *n*

nu·ga·to·ry \'n(y)ü-gə-ˌtōr-ē\ *adj* **1** : INCONSEQUENTIAL, WORTHLESS **2** : having no force : INOPERATIVE

nug·get \'nəg-ət\ *n* : a lump of precious metal (as gold)

nui·sance \'n(y)üs-ᵊns\ *n* : an annoying or troublesome person or thing

nuisance tax *n* : an excise tax collected in small amounts directly from the consumer

null \'nəl\ *adj* **1** : having no legal or blinding force : INVALID, VOID **2** : amounting to nothing **2** : INSIGNIFICANT — **nul·li·ty** \'nəl-ət-ē\ *n*

null and void *adj* : having no force, binding power, or validity

nul·li·fy \'nəl-ə-ˌfī\ *vb* **-fied; -fy·ing** : to make null or valueless; *also* : ANNUL — **nul·li·fi·ca·tion** \ˌnəl-ə-fə-ˈkā-shən\ *n*

num *abbr* numeral

Num *or* **Numb** *abbr* Numbers

numb \'nəm\ *adj* : lacking sensation or emotion : BENUMBED — **numb** *vb* — **numb·ly** *adv* — **numb·ness** *n*

¹num·ber \'nəm-bər\ *n* **1** : the total of individuals or units taken together **2** : a group or aggregate not specif. enumerated ⟨a small ∼ of tickets remain unsold⟩ **3** : the possibility of being counted ⟨the sands of the desert are without ∼⟩ **4** : a distinction of word form to denote reference to one or more than one **5** : a unit belonging to

a mathematical system and subject to its laws; *also, pl* : ARITHMETIC **6** : a symbol used to represent a mathematical number; *also* : such a number used to identify or designate ⟨a phone ∼⟩ **7** : one in a series ⟨the best ∼ on the program⟩

²number *vb* **num·bered; num·ber·ing** \-b(ə-)riŋ\ **1** : COUNT, ENUMERATE **2** : to include with or be one of a group **3** : to restrict to a small or definite number **4** : to assign a number to **5** : to comprise in number : TOTAL

num·ber·less \-ləs\ *adj* : INNUMERABLE, COUNTLESS

Numbers *n* — see BIBLE table

nu·mer·al \'n(y)üm-(ə-)rəl\ *n* : a word or symbol representing a number — **numeral** *adj*

nu·mer·ate \'n(y)ü-mə-ˌrāt\ *vb* **-at·ed; -at·ing** : ENUMERATE

nu·mer·a·tor \'n(y)ü-mə-ˌrāt-ər\ *n* : the part of a fraction above the line

nu·mer·ic \n(y)ü-ˈmer-ik\ *adj* : NUMERICAL; *esp* : denoting a number or a system of numbers

nu·mer·i·cal \n(y)ü-ˈmer-i-kəl\ *adj* **1** : of or relating to numbers **2** : denoting a number or expressed in numbers — **nu·mer·i·cal·ly** \-k(ə-)lē\ *adv*

nu·mer·ol·o·gy \ˌn(y)ü-mə-ˈräl-ə-jē\ *n* : the study of the occult significance of numbers — **nu·mer·ol·o·gist** \-jəst\ *n*

nu·mer·ous \'n(y)üm-(ə-)rəs\ *adj* : consisting of, including, or relating to a great number : MANY

nu·mis·mat·ics \ˌn(y)ü-məz-ˈmat-iks\ *n* : the study or collection of monetary objects — **nu·mis·mat·ic** \-ik\ *adj* — **nu·mis·ma·tist** \n(y)ü-ˈmiz-mət-əst\ *n*

num·skull \'nəm-ˌskəl\ *n* : a stupid person : DUNCE

nun \'nən\ *n* : a woman belonging to a religious order; *esp* : one under solemn vows of poverty, chastity, and obedience

nun·cio \'nən-sē-ˌō, 'nùn-\ *n, pl* **-ci·os** [It, fr. L *nuntius* messenger] : a permanent high-ranking papal representative to a civil government

nun·nery \'nən-ə-rē\ *n, pl* **-ner·ies** : a convent of nuns

¹nup·tial \'nəp-shəl\ *adj* : of or relating to marriage or a wedding

²nuptial *n* : MARRIAGE, WEDDING — usu. used in pl.

¹nurse \'nərs\ *n* [ME, fr. OF *nurice*, fr. LL *nutricia*, fr. L, fem. of *nutricius* nourishing] **1** : a girl or woman employed to take care of children **2** : a person trained to care for sick people

²nurse *vb* **nursed; nurs·ing 1** : SUCKLE **2** : to take charge of and watch over **3** : TEND ⟨∼ an invalid⟩ **4** : to treat with special care ⟨∼ a headache⟩ **5** : to hold in one's mind or consideration ⟨∼ a grudge⟩ **6** : to act or serve as a nurse

nurse·maid \-₁mād\ *n* : a girl or woman employed to look after children

nurs·ery \'nərs-(ə-)rē\ *n, pl* **-er·ies 1** : a room for children **2** : a place where children are temporarily cared for in their parents' absence **3** : a place where young plants are grown usu. for transplanting

nurs·ery·man \-mən\ *n* : a man who keeps or works in a plant nursery

nursery school *n* : a school for children under kindergarten age

nursing home *n* : a private establishment where care is provided for persons (as the chronically ill) who are unable to care for themselves

nurs·ling \'nərs-liŋ\ *n* **1** : one that is solicitously cared for **2** : a nursing child

¹nur·ture \'nər-chər\ *n* **1** : TRAINING, UP-BRINGING; *also* : the influences that modify the expression of an individual's heredity **2** : FOOD, NOURISHMENT

²nurture *vb* **nur·tured; nur·tur·ing 1** : to care for : FEED, NOURISH **2** : EDUCATE, TRAIN **3** : FOSTER

nut \'nət\ *n* **1** : a dry fruit or seed with a hard shell and a firm inner kernel; *also* : its kernel **2** : a metal block with a hole through it that is fastened to a bolt or screw by means of a screw thread within the hole **3** : the ridge on the upper end of the fingerboard in a stringed musical instrument over which the strings pass **4** : a foolish, eccentric, or crazy person **5** : ENTHUSIAST

nut·crack·er \-₁krak-ər\ *n* : an instrument for cracking nuts

nut·hatch \'nət-₁hach\ *n* [ME *note-hache*, fr. *note* nut + *hache* ax, fr. OF, battle-ax] : any of various small birds that creep on tree trunks in search of food and resemble titmice

nut·meg \'nət-₁meg, -₁māg\ *n* [ME *notemuge*, deriv. of Old Provençal *noz muscada*, fr. *noz* nut (fr. L *nuc-, nux*) + *muscada*, fem. of *muscat* musky] : the nutlike aromatic seed of a tropical tree that is ground for use as a spice; *also* : this spice

nut·pick \'nət-₁pik\ *n* : a small sharp-pointed table implement for extracting the kernels from nuts

nu·tria \'n(y)ü-trē-ə\ *n* [Sp] **1** : the durable usu. light brown fur of a nutria **2** : a So. American aquatic rodent with webbed feet and dorsal mammary glands

¹nu·tri·ent \'n(y)ü-trē-ənt\ *adj* : NOUR-ISHING

²nutrient *n* : a nutritive substance or ingredient

nu·tri·ment \-trə-mənt\ *n* : NUTRIENT

nu·tri·tion \n(y)ü-'trish-ən\ *n* : the act or process of nourishing; *esp* : the processes by which an individual takes in and utilizes food material — **nu·tri·tion·al** \-'trish-(ə-)nəl\ *adj* — **nu·tri·tious** \-'trish-əs\ *adj* — **nu·tri·tive** \'n(y)ü-trət-iv\ *adj*

nuts \'nəts\ *adj* **1** : ENTHUSIASTIC, KEEN **2** : CRAZY, DEMENTED

nut·shell \'nət-₁shel\ *n* : the shell of a nut — **in a nutshell** : in a few words ⟨that's the story *in a nutshell*⟩

nut·ty \'nət-ē\ *adj* **nut·ti·er; -est 1** : containing or suggesting nuts ⟨a ∼ flavor⟩ **2** : mentally unbalanced

nuz·zle \'nəz-əl\ *vb* **nuz·zled; nuz·zling** \-(ə-)liŋ\ **1** : to root around, push, or touch with or as if with the nose **2** : NESTLE, SNUGGLE

NV *abbr* Nevada

NW *abbr* northwest

NWT *abbr* Northwest Territories

NY *abbr* New York

NYC *abbr* New York City

ny·lon \'nī-₁län\ *n* **1** : any of numberous strong tough elastic synthetic materials used esp. in textiles and plastics **2** *pl* : stockings made of nylon

nymph \'nimf\ *n* **1** : any of the lesser goddesses in ancient mythology represented as maidens living in the mountains, forests, meadows, and waters **2** : an immature insect; *esp* : one that resembles the adult but is smaller and less differentiated and usu. lacks wings

nym·pho·ma·nia \₁nim-fə-'mā-nē-ə, -nyə\ *n* : excessive sexual desire by a

O

¹**o** \'ō\ *n, pl* **o's** *or* **os** \'ōz\ *often cap* : the 15th letter of the English alphabet
²**o** *abbr, often cap* **1** ocean **2** Ohio **3** ohm
¹**O** \'ō\ *var of* OH
²**O** *symbol* oxygen
o/a *abbr* on or about
oaf \'ōf\ *n* : a stupid or awkward person — **oaf·ish** \'ō-fish\ *adj*
oak \'ōk\ *n, pl* **oaks** *or* **oak** : any of various trees or shrubs related to the beech and chestnut and having a rounded thin-shelled nut surrounded at the base by a hardened cup; *also* : the usu. tough hard durable wood of an oak — **oak·en** \'ō-kən\ *adj*
oa·kum \'ō-kəm\ *n* : loosely twisted hemp or jute fiber impregnated with tar and used esp. in caulking ships
oar \'ōr\ *n* : a long pole with a broad blade at one end used for propelling or steering a boat
oar·lock \-₁läk\ *n* : a U-shaped device for holding an oar in place
oars·man \'ōrz-mən\ *n* : one who rows esp. in a racing crew
OAS *abbr* Organization of American States
oa·sis \ō-'ā-səs\ *n, pl* **oa·ses** \-₁sēz\ : a fertile or green area in an arid region
oat \'ōt\ *n* : a cereal grass widely grown for its edible seed; *also* : this seed — **oat·en** \-ᵊn\ *adj*
oat·cake \'ōt-₁kāk\ *n* : a thin flat oatmeal cake
oath \'ōth\ *n, pl* **oaths** \'ōthz, 'ōths\ **1** : a solemn appeal to God to witness to the truth of a statement or the sacredness of a promise **2** : an irreverent or careless use of a sacred name
oat·meal \'ōt-₁mēl\ *n* **1** : meal made from oats **2** : porridge made from ground or rolled oats
Ob *or* **Obad** *abbr* Obadiah
Oba·di·ah \₁ō-bə-'dī-əh\ *n* — see BIBLE table
ob·bli·ga·to \₁äb-lə-'gät-ō\ *n, pl* **-tos** *also* **-ti** \-'gät-ē\ [It] : an accompanying

part usu. played by a solo instrument
ob·du·rate \'äb-d(y)ə-rət\ *adj* : stubbornly resistant : UNYIELDING **syn** inflexible, adamant, rigid, uncompromising — **ob·du·ra·cy** \-rə-sē\ *n*
obe·di·ent \ō-'bēd-ē-ənt\ *adj* : submissive to the restraint or command of authority **syn** docile, tractable, amenable, biddable — **obe·di·ence** \-əns\ *n* — **obe·di·ent·ly** *adv*
obei·sance \ō-'bās-əns, -'bēs-\ *n* : a bow made to show respect or submission; *also* : DEFERENCE, HOMAGE
obe·lisk \'äb-ə-₁lisk\ *n* [MF *obelisque*, fr. L *obeliscus*, fr. Gk *obeliskos*, fr. dim. of *obelos* spit, pointed pillar] : a 4-sided pillar that tapers toward the top and ends in a pyramid
obese \ō-'bēs\ *adj* [L *obesus*, fr. pp. of *obedere* to eat up, fr. *ob-* against + *edere* to eat] : excessively fat — **obe·si·ty** \-'bē-sət-ē\ *n*
obey \ō-'bā\ *vb* **obeyed; obey·ing 1** : to follow the commands or guidance of : behave obediently **2** : to comply with ⟨∼ orders⟩
ob·fus·cate \'äb-fə-₁skāt\ *vb* **-cat·ed; -cat·ing 1** : to make dark or obscure **2** : CONFUSE — **ob·fus·ca·tion** \₁äb-fəs-'kā-shən\ *n*
obi \'ō-bē\ *n* : a broad sash worn with a Japanese kimono
obit \ō-'bit, 'ō-bət\ *n* : OBITUARY
obi·ter dic·tum \₁ō-bət-ər-'dik-təm\ *n, pl* **obiter dic·ta** \-tə\ [LL, lit., something said in passing] : an incidental remark or observation
obit·u·ary \ə-'bich-ə-₁wer-ē\ *n, pl* **-ar·ies** : a notice of a person's death usu. with a short biographical account
obj *abbr* object; objective
¹**ob·ject** \'äb-jikt\ *n* **1** : something that may be seen or felt; *also* : something that may be perceived or examined mentally **2** : something that arouses an emotional response (as of affection or pity) **3** : AIM, PURPOSE **4** : a word or

female — **nym·pho·ma·ni·ac** \-nē-₁ak\ *n or adj*
NZ *abbr* New Zealand

word group denoting that on or toward which the action of a verb is directed; *also* : a noun or noun equivalent in a prepositional phrase

²**ob•ject** \əb-'jekt\ *vb* 1 : to offer in opposition 2 : to oppose something; *also* : DISAPPROVE **syn** protest, remonstrate, expostulate — **ob•jec•tor** \-'jek-tər\ *n*

ob•jec•ti•fy \əb-'jek-tə-ˌfī\ *vb* **-fied; -fy•ing** : to make objective

ob•jec•tion \əb-'jek-shən\ *n* 1 : the act of objecting 2 : a reason for or a feeling of disapproval

ob•jec•tion•able \əb-'jek-sh(ə-)nə-bəl\ *adj* : UNDESIRABLE, OFFENSIVE — **ob•jec•tion•ably** \-blē\ *adv*

¹**ob•jec•tive** \əb-'jek-tiv\ *adj* 1 : of or relating to an object or end 2 : existing outside and independent of the mind 3 : of, relating to, or constituting a grammatical case marking typically the object of a verb or preposition 4 : treating or dealing with facts without distortion by personal feelings or prejudices — **ob•jec•tive•ly** *adv* — **ob•jec•tive•ness** *n* — **ob•jec•tiv•i•ty** \ˌäb-ˌjek-'tiv-ət-ē\ *n*

²**objective** *n* 1 : the lens (as in a microscope) nearest the object and forming an image of it 2 : an aim, goal, or end of action

ob•jet d'art \ˌȯb-ˌzhā-'där\ *n, pl* **ob•jets d'art** *same*\ [F] : an article of artistic worth; *also* : CURIO

ob•jet trou•vé \'ȯb-ˌzhā-trü-'vā\ *n, pl* **objets trouvés** *same*\ [F, lit., found object] : a found natural object (as a piece of driftwood) held to have aesthetic value; *also* : an artifact not orig. intended as art but displayed as a work of art

ob•jur•gate \'äb-jər-ˌgāt\ *vb* **-gat•ed; -gat•ing** : to denounce harshly — **ob•jur•ga•tion** \ˌäb-jər-'gā-shən\ *n*

obl *abbr* 1 oblique 2 oblong

ob•late \äb-'lāt\ *adj* : flattened or depressed at the poles ⟨an ~ spheroid⟩

ob•la•tion \ə-'blā-shən\ *n* : a religious offering

ob•li•gate \'äb-lə-ˌgāt\ *vb* **-gat•ed; -gat•ing** : to bind legally or morally; *also* : to bind by a favor

ob•li•ga•tion \ˌäb-lə-'gā-shən\ *n* 1 : an act of obligating oneself to a course of action 2 : something (as a promise or a contract) that binds one to a course

of action 3 : INDEBTEDNESS; *also* : LIABILITY 4 : DUTY — **oblig•a•to•ry** \ə-'blig-ə-ˌtōr-ē, 'äb-li-gə-\ *adj*

oblige \ə-'blīj\ *vb* **obliged; oblig•ing** 1 : FORCE, COMPEL 2 : to bind by a favor; *also* : to do a favor for or do something as a favor

oblig•ing \ə-'blī-jiŋ\ *adj* : willing to do favors — **oblig•ing•ly** *adv*

oblique \ō-'blēk *also* ō-'blīk\ *adj* 1 : neither perpendicular nor parallel : SLANTING 2 : not straightforward : INDIRECT — **oblique•ly** *adv* — **oblique•ness** *n* — **obliq•ui•ty** \-'blik-wət-ē\ *n*

oblit•er•ate \ə-'blit-ə-ˌrāt\ *vb* **-at•ed; -at•ing** [L *oblitterare*, fr. *ob* in the way of + *littera* letter] 1 : to make undecipherable by wiping out or covering over 2 : to remove from recognition or memory 3 : CANCEL — **oblit•er•a•tion** \-ˌblit-ə-'rā-shən\ *n*

obliv•i•on \ə-'bliv-ē-ən\ *n* 1 : the condition of being oblivious 2 : the condition or state of being forgotten

obliv•i•ous \-ē-əs\ *adj* 1 : lacking memory or mindful attention 2 : UNAWARE — **obliv•i•ous•ly** *adv* — **obliv•i•ous•ness** *n*

ob•long \'äb-ˌlȯŋ\ *adj* : deviating from a square, circular, or spherical form by elongation in one dimension ⟨the ~ fruit of a lemon tree⟩ — **oblong** *n*

ob•lo•quy \'äb-lə-kwē\ *n, pl* **-quies** 1 : strongly condemnatory utterance or language 2 : bad repute : DISGRACE **syn** dishonor, shame, infamy, disrepute, ignominy

ob•nox•ious \äb-'näk-shəs, əb-\ *adj* : REPUGNANT, OFFENSIVE — **ob•nox•ious•ly** *adv* — **ob•nox•ious•ness** *n*

oboe \'ō-bō\ *n* [It, fr. F *hautbois*, fr. *haut* high + *bois* wood] : a woodwind instrument shaped like a slender conical tube with holes and keys and a reed mouthpiece — **obo•ist** \'ō-bō-əst\ *n*

ob•scene \äb-'sēn, əb-\ *adj* 1 : REPULSIVE 2 : deeply offensive to morality or decency; *esp* : designed to incite to lust or depravity **syn** gross, vulgar, coarse, crude, indecent — **ob•scene•ly** *adv* — **ob•scen•i•ty** \-'sen-ət-ē\ *n*

ob•scu•ran•tism \äb-'skyu̇r-ən-ˌtiz-əm, ˌäb-skyu̇-'ran-\ *n* 1 : opposition to the spread of knowledge 2 : deliberate vagueness or abstruseness — **ob•scu-**

ran·tist \-ən-təst, -'rant-əst\ *n or adj*

¹**ob·scure** \äb-'skyür, əb-\ *adj* **1** : DIM, GLOOMY **2** : not readily understood : VAGUE **3** : REMOTE; *also* : HUMBLE — **ob·scure·ly** *adv* — **ob·scu·ri·ty** \-'skyür-ət-ē\ *n*

²**obscure** *vb* **ob·scured; ob·scur·ing 1** : to make dark, dim, or indistinct **2** : to conceal or hide by or as if by covering

ob·se·qui·ous \əb-'sē-kwē-əs\ *adj* : humbly or excessively attentive (as to a person in authority) : FAWNING, SYCOPHANTIC — **ob·se·qui·ous·ly** *adv* — **ob·se·qui·ous·ness** *n*

ob·se·quy \'äb-sə-kwē\ *n, pl* **-quies** : a funeral or burial rite — usu. used in pl.

ob·serv·able \əb-'zər-və-bəl\ *adj* **1** : necessarily or customarily observed **2** : NOTICEABLE

ob·ser·vance \əb-'zər-vəns\ *n* **1** : a customary practice or ceremony **2** : an act or instance of following a custom, rule, or law **3** : OBSERVATION

ob·ser·vant \-vənt\ *adj* **1** : WATCHFUL ⟨~ spectators⟩ **2** : KEEN, PERCEPTIVE **3** : MINDFUL ⟨~ of the amenities⟩

ob·ser·va·tion \,äb-sər-'vā-shən, -zər-\ *n* **1** : an act or the power of observing **2** : the gathering of information (as for scientific studies) by noting facts or occurrences **3** : a conclusion drawn from observing; *also* : REMARK, STATEMENT **4** : the fact of being observed

ob·ser·va·to·ry \əb-'zər-və-,tōr-ē\ *n, pl* **-ries** : a place or institution equipped for observation of natural phenomena (as in astronomy)

ob·serve \əb-'zərv\ *vb* **ob·served; ob·serv·ing 1** : to conform one's action or practice to **2** : CELEBRATE **3** : to make a scientific observation of **4** : to see or sense esp. through careful attention **5** : to come to realize esp. through consideration of noted facts **6** : REMARK — **ob·serv·er** *n*

ob·sess \əb-'ses\ *vb* : to preoccupy intensely or abnormally

ob·ses·sion \äb-'sesh-ən, əb-\ *n* : a persistent disturbing preoccupation with an idea or feeling; *also* : an emotion or idea causing such a preoccupation — **ob·ses·sive** \-'ses-iv\ *adj or n* — **ob·ses·sive·ly** *adv*

ob·sid·i·an \əb-'sid-ē-ən\ *n* : a dark natural glass formed by the cooling of molten lava

ob·so·les·cent \,äb-sə-'les-ᵊnt\ *adj* : going out of use : becoming obsolete — **ob·so·les·cence** \-ᵊns\ *n*

ob·so·lete \,äb-sə-'lēt, 'äb-sə-,lēt\ *adj* : no longer in use; *also* : OLD-FASHIONED **syn** extinct, outworn, passé, superseded

ob·sta·cle \'äb-sti-kəl\ *n* : something that stands in the way or opposes

ob·stet·rics \əb-'stet-riks\ *n sing or pl* : a branch of medicine that deals with childbirth — **ob·stet·ric** \-rik\ *or* **ob·stet·ri·cal** \-ri-kəl\ *adj* — **ob·ste·tri·cian** \,äb-stə-'trish-ən\ *n*

ob·sti·nate \'äb-stə-nət\ *adj* : fixed and unyielding (as in an opinion or course) despite reason or persuasion : STUBBORN — **ob·sti·na·cy** \-nə-sē\ *n* — **ob·sti·nate·ly** *adv*

ob·strep·er·ous \əb-'strep-(ə-)rəs\ *adj* **1** : uncontrollably noisy **2** : stubbornly resistant to control : UNRULY — **ob·strep·er·ous·ness** *n*

ob·struct \əb-'strəkt\ *vb* **1** : to block by an obstacle **2** : to impede the passage, action, or operation of **3** : to shut off from sight — **ob·struc·tive** \-'strək-tiv\ *adj* — **ob·struc·tor** \-tər\ *n*

ob·struc·tion \əb-'strək-shən\ *n* **1** : an act of obstructing : the state of being obstructed **2** : something that obstructs : HINDRANCE

ob·struc·tion·ist \-sh(ə-)nəst\ *n* : a person who hinders progress or business esp. in a legislative body — **ob·struc·tion·ism** \-shə-,niz-əm\ *n*

ob·tain \əb-'tān\ *vb* **1** : to gain or attain usu. by planning or effort **2** : to be generally recognized or established **syn** procure, secure, win, earn, acquire — **ob·tain·able** *adj*

ob·trude \əb-'trüd\ *vb* **ob·trud·ed; ob·trud·ing 1** : to thrust out **2** : to thrust forward without warrant or request **3** : INTRUDE — **ob·tru·sion** \-'trü-zhən\ *n* — **ob·tru·sive** \-'trü-siv\ *adj* — **ob·tru·sive·ly** *adv* — **ob·tru·sive·ness** *n*

ob·tuse \äb-'t(y)üs, əb-\ *adj* **ob·tus·er; -est 1** : not sharp or quick of wit **2** : exceeding 90 degrees but less than 180 degrees ⟨~ angle⟩ **3** : not pointed or acute : BLUNT — **ob·tuse·ly** *adv* — **ob·tuse·ness** *n*

obv *abbr* obverse

¹**ob·verse** \äb-'vərs, 'äb-,vərs\ *adj* **1** : facing the observer or opponent **2**

: having the base narrower than the top **3** : being a counterpart or complement — **ob·verse·ly** *adv*

²ob·verse \'äb-ˌvərs, äb-'vərs\ *n* **1** : the side (as of a coin) bearing the principal design and lettering **2** : a front or principal surface **3** : a similar but contrasting element or condition

ob·vi·ate \'äb-vē-ˌāt\ *vb* **-at·ed; -at·ing** : to anticipate and prevent (as a situation) or make unnecessary (as an action) **syn** prevent, avert, forestall, forfend, preclude — **ob·vi·a·tion** \ˌäb-vē-'ā-shən\ *n*

ob·vi·ous \'äb-vē-əs\ *adj* [L *obvius,* fr. *obviam* in the way, fr. *ob* in the way of + *viam,* acc. of *via* way] : easily found, seen, or understood : PLAIN **syn** evident, manifest, patent, clear — **ob·vi·ous·ly** *adv* — **ob·vi·ous·ness** *n*

OC *abbr* officer candidate

oc·a·ri·na \ˌäk-ə-'rē-nə\ *n* [It, fr. *oca* goose, fr. LL *auca,* deriv. of L *avis* bird] : a simple wind instrument with holes that may be opened or closed by the finger to vary the pitch

occas *abbr* occasionally

¹oc·ca·sion \ə-'kā-zhən\ *n* **1** : a favorable opportunity **2** : a direct or indirect cause **3** : the time of an event **4** : EXIGENCY **5** *pl* : AFFAIRS, BUSINESS **6** : a special event : CELEBRATION

²occasion *vb* **-sioned; -sion·ing** \-'kāzh-(ə-)niŋ\ : CAUSE

oc·ca·sion·al \ə-'kāzh-(ə-)nəl\ *adj* **1** : happening or met with now and then ⟨∼ references to the war⟩ **2** : used or designed for a special occasion ⟨∼ verse⟩ **syn** infrequent, rare, sporadic — **oc·ca·sion·al·ly** \-ē\ *adv*

oc·ci·den·tal \ˌäk-sə-'dent-ᵊl\ *adj, often cap* [fr. *Occident* West, fr. ME, fr. L *occident-, occidens,* fr. prp. of *occidere* to fall, set (of the sun)] : WESTERN — **Occidental** *n*

oc·clude \ə-'klüd\ *vb* **oc·clud·ed; oc·clud·ing** **1** : OBSTRUCT **2** : to shut in or out **3** : to come together with opposing surfaces in contact — **oc·clu·sion** \-'klü-zhən\ *n* — **oc·clu·sive** \-'klü-siv\ *adj*

¹oc·cult \ə-'kəlt\ *adj* **1** : not revealed : SECRET **2** : ABSTRUSE, MYSTERIOUS **3** : of or relating to supernatural agencies, their effects, or knowledge of them

²occult *n* : occult matters — used with *the*

oc·cult·ism \ə-'kəl-ˌtiz-əm\ *n* : occult theory or practice — **oc·cult·ist** \-təst\ *n*

oc·cu·pan·cy \'äk-yə-pən-sē\ *n, pl* **-cies** **1** : the act of occupying : the state of being occupied **2** : an occupied building or part of a building

oc·cu·pant \-pənt\ *n* : one who occupies something; *esp* : RESIDENT

oc·cu·pa·tion \ˌäk-yə-'pā-shən\ *n* **1** : an activity in which one engages; *esp* : VOCATION **2** : the taking possession of property; *also* : the taking possession of an area by a foreign military force — **oc·cu·pa·tion·al** \-sh(ə-)nəl\ *adj* — **oc·cu·pa·tion·al·ly** \-ē\ *adv*

occupational therapy *n* : therapy by means of activity; *esp* : creative activity prescribed for its effect in promoting recovery or rehabilitation — **occupational therapist** *n*

oc·cu·py \'äk-yə-ˌpī\ *vb* **-pied; -py·ing** **1** : to engage the attention or energies of **2** : to fill up (an extent in space or time) **3** : to take or hold possession of **4** : to reside in as owner or tenant — **oc·cu·pi·er** \-ˌpī(-ə)r\ *n*

oc·cur \ə-'kər\ *vb* **oc·curred; oc·cur·ring** \-'kər-iŋ\ **1** : to be found or met with : APPEAR **2** : HAPPEN **3** : to come to mind

oc·cur·rence \ə-'kər-əns\ *n* **1** : something that takes place **2** : the action or process of occurring

ocean \'ō-shən\ *n* **1** : the whole body of salt water that covers nearly three fourths of the surface of the earth **2** : one of the large bodies of water into which the great ocean is divided — **oce·an·ic** \ˌō-shē-'an-ik\ *adj*

ocean·ar·i·um \ˌō-shə-'nar-ē-əm\ *n, pl* **-iums** *or* **-ia** \-ē-ə\ : a large marine aquarium

ocean·front \'ō-shən-ˌfrənt\ *n* : a shore area on the ocean

ocean·go·ing \-ˌgō-iŋ\ *adj* : of, relating to, or suitable for travel on the ocean

ocean·og·ra·phy \ˌō-shə-'näg-rə-fē\ *n* : a science dealing with the ocean and its phenomena — **ocean·og·ra·pher** \-fər\ *n* — **ocean·o·graph·ic** \-nə-'graf-ik\ *adj*

ocean·ol·o·gy \ˌō-shə-'näl-ə-jē\ *n*

: OCEANOGRAPHY — **ocean·ol·o·gist** \-jəst\ *n*

oce·lot \ˈäs-ə-ˌlät, ˈō-sə-\ *n* : a medium-sized American wildcat ranging southward from Texas and having a tawny yellow or gray coat with black markings

ocher *or* **ochre** \ˈō-kər\ *n* : an earthy usu. red or yellow iron ore used as a pigment; *also* : the color esp. of yellow ocher

o'·clock \ə-ˈkläk\ *adv* : according to the clock

OCS *abbr* officer candidate school

oct *abbr* octavo

Oct *abbr* October

oc·ta·gon \ˈäk-tə-ˌgän\ *n* : a polygon of eight angles and eight sides — **oc·tag·o·nal** \äk-ˈtag-ən-ᵊl\ *adj*

oc·tane \ˈäk-ˌtān\ *n* **1** : any of several isomeric liquid hydrocarbons containing 8 carbon atoms per molecule **2** : OCTANE NUMBER

octane number *n* : a number that is used to measure the antiknock properties of gasoline and that increases as the likelihood of knocking decreases

oc·tave \ˈäk-tiv\ *n* **1** : a musical interval embracing eight degrees; *also* : a tone or note at this interval or the whole series of notes, tones, or keys within this interval **2** : a group of eight

oc·ta·vo \äk-ˈtā-vō, -ˈtäv-ō\ *n, pl* **-vos 1** : the size of a piece of paper cut eight from a sheet **2** : a book printed on octavo pages

oc·tet \äk-ˈtet\ *n* **1** : a musical composition for eight voices or eight instruments; *also* : the performers of such a composition **2** : a group or set of eight

Oc·to·ber \äk-ˈtō-bər\ *n* [ME *Octobre*, fr. OF, fr. L *October* (eighth month), fr. *octo* eight] : the 10th month of the year having 31 days

oc·to·ge·nar·i·an \ˌäk-tə-jə-ˈner-ē-ən\ *n* : a person who is in his eighties

oc·to·pus \ˈäk-tə-pəs\ *n, pl* **-pus·es** *or* **-pi** \-ˌpī\ : any of various sea mollusks with eight long arms furnished with two rows of suckers

oc·to·syl·lab·ic \ˌäk-tə-sə-ˈlab-ik\ *adj* : having or composed of verses having eight syllables — **octosyllabic** *n*

¹**oc·u·lar** \ˈäk-yə-lər\ *adj* **1** : VISUAL **2** : of or relating to the eye or the eyesight

²**ocular** *n* : EYEPIECE

oc·u·list \ˈäk-yə-ləst\ *n* **1** : OPHTHALMOLOGIST **2** : OPTOMETRIST

¹**OD** \(ˈ)ō-ˈdē\ *n* : an overdose of a narcotic

²**OD** *abbr* **1** doctor of optometry **2** [L *oculus dexter*] right eye **3** officer of the day **4** olive drab **5** overdraft **6** overdrawn

odd \ˈäd\ *adj* [ME *odde*, fr. ON *oddi* point of land, triangle, odd number] **1** : being only one of a pair or set ⟨an ∼ shoe⟩ **2** : somewhat more than the number mentioned ⟨forty ∼ years ago⟩ **3** : not divisible by two without leaving a remainder ⟨∼ numbers⟩ **4** : additional to what is usual ⟨∼ jobs⟩ **5** : STRANGE ⟨an ∼ way of behaving⟩ — **odd·ly** *adv* — **odd·ness** *n*

odd·ball \ˈäd-ˌbȯl\ *n* : one that is eccentric

odd·i·ty \ˈäd-ət-ē\ *n, pl* **-ties 1** : one that is odd **2** : the quality or state of being odd

odd·ment \ˈäd-mənt\ *n* : something left over : REMNANT

odds \ˈädz\ *n pl* **1** : a difference by which one thing is favored over another **2** : DISAGREEMENT — usu. used with *at* **3** : an equalizing allowance made to one believed to have a smaller chance of winning

odds and ends *n pl* : miscellaneous things or matters

odds–on \ˈädz-ˈȯn, -ˈän\ *adj* : having a better than even chance to win

ode \ˈōd\ *n* : a lyric poem that expresses a noble feeling with dignity

odi·ous \ˈōd-ē-əs\ *adj* : causing or deserving hatred or repugnance — **odi·ous·ly** *adv* — **odi·ous·ness** *n*

odi·um \ˈōd-ē-əm\ *n* **1** : merited loathing : HATRED **2** : DISGRACE

odom·e·ter \ō-ˈdäm-ət-ər\ *n* [F *odomètre*, fr. Gk *hodometron*, fr. *hodos* way, road + *metron* measure] : an instrument for measuring distance traveled (as by a vehicle)

odor \ˈōd-ər\ *n* **1** : the quality of something that stimulates the sense of smell; *also* : a sensation resulting from such stimulation **2** : REPUTE, ESTIMATION — **odor·less** *adj* — **odor·ous** *adj*

od·ys·sey \ˈäd-ə-sē\ *n, pl* **-seys** [the *Odyssey*, epic poem attributed to Homer recounting the long wanderings of Odysseus] : a long wandering marked usu. by many changes of fortune

OED *abbr* Oxford English Dictionary

oe·di·pal \\'ed-ə-pəl, 'ēd-\\ *adj, often cap* : of or relating to the Oedipus complex

Oe·di·pus complex \\-pəs-\\ *n* : the positive sexual feelings of a child toward the parent of the opposite sex that may be a source of adult personality disorder when unresolved

OEO *abbr* Office of Economic Opportunity

o'er \\'ō(ə)r\\ *adv or prep* : OVER

OES *abbr* Order of the Eastern Star

oe·soph·a·gus *chiefly Brit* var of ESOPHAGUS

oeu·vre \\œvr³\\ *n, pl* **oeuvres** *same*\\ : a substantial body of work constituting the lifework of a writer, an artist, or a composer

of \\(')əv, 'äv\\ *prep* **1** : FROM ⟨a man ∼ the West⟩ **2** : having as a significant background or character element ⟨a man ∼ noble birth⟩ ⟨a woman ∼ ability⟩ **3** : owing to ⟨died ∼ flu⟩ **4** : BY ⟨the plays ∼ Shakespeare⟩ **5** : having as component parts or material, contents, or members ⟨a house ∼ brick⟩ ⟨a glass ∼ water⟩ ⟨a pack ∼ fools⟩ **6** : belonging to or included by ⟨the front ∼ the house⟩ ⟨a time ∼ life⟩ ⟨one ∼ you⟩ ⟨the best ∼ his kind⟩ ⟨the son ∼ a doctor⟩ **7** : ABOUT ⟨tales ∼ the West⟩ **8** : connected with : OVER ⟨the king ∼ England⟩ **9** : that is : signified as ⟨the city ∼ Rome⟩ **10** — used to indicate apposition of the words it joins ⟨that fool ∼ a husband⟩ **11** : as concerns : FOR ⟨love ∼ country⟩ **12** — used to indicate the application of an adjective ⟨fond ∼ candy⟩ **13** : BEFORE ⟨five minutes ∼ ten⟩

OF *abbr* outfield

¹off \\'òf\\ *adv* **1** : from a place or position ⟨drove ∼ in a new car⟩; *also* : ASIDE ⟨turned ∼ into a side road⟩ **2** : at a distance in time or space ⟨stood ∼ a few yards⟩ ⟨several years ∼⟩ **3** : so as to be unattached or removed ⟨the lid blew ∼⟩ **4** : to a state of discontinuance, exhaustion, or completion ⟨shut the radio ∼⟩ **5** : away from regular work ⟨took time ∼ for lunch⟩

²off \\(')òf\\ *prep* **1** : away from ⟨just ∼ the highway⟩ ⟨take it ∼ the table⟩ **2** : to seaward of ⟨sail ∼ the Maine coast⟩ **3** : FROM ⟨borrowed a dollar ∼ me⟩ **4** : at the expense of ⟨lives ∼ his sister⟩ **5** : not now engaged in ⟨∼ duty⟩ **6** : abstaining from ⟨∼ liquor⟩ **7** : below the usual level of ⟨∼ his game⟩

³off \\(')òf\\ *adj* **1** : more removed or distant **2** : started on the way **3** : not operating **4** : not correct **5** : REMOTE, SLIGHT **6** : INFERIOR **7** : provided for ⟨well ∼⟩

⁴off *abbr* office; officer; official

of·fal \\'ò-fəl\\ *n* : the waste or by-product of a process; *esp* : the viscera and trimmings of a butchered animal removed in dressing

off and on *adv* : with periodic cessation

¹off·beat \\'òf-ˌbēt\\ *n* : the unaccented part of a musical measure

²offbeat *adj* : ECCENTRIC, UNCONVENTIONAL

off–col·or \\'òf-'kəl-ər\\ *or* **off–col·ored** \\-ərd\\ *adj* **1** : not having the right or standard color **2** : of doubtful propriety : RISQUÉ

of·fend \\ə-'fend\\ *vb* **1** : SIN, TRANSGRESS **2** : to cause discomfort or pain : HURT **3** : to cause dislike or vexation : ANNOY **syn** affront, insult, outrage — **of·fend·er** *n*

of·fense *or* **of·fence** \\ə-'fens, *esp for 2 &* 3 'äf-ˌens\\ *n* **1** : something that outrages the senses **2** : ATTACK, ASSAULT **3** : the offensive team or members of a team playing offensive positions **4** : DISPLEASURE **5** : SIN, MISDEED **6** : an infraction of law : CRIME

¹of·fen·sive \\ə-'fen-siv *esp for 1 & 2* 'äf-ˌen-\\ *adj* **1** : AGGRESSIVE **2** : of or relating to an attempt to score in a game; *also* : of or relating to a team in possession of the ball or puck **3** : OBNOXIOUS **4** : INSULTING — **of·fen·sive·ly** *adv* — **of·fen·sive·ness** *n*

²offensive *n* : ATTACK

¹of·fer \\'òf-ər\\ *vb* **of·fered**; **of·fer·ing** \\-(ə-)riŋ\\ **1** : SACRIFICE **2** : to present for acceptance : TENDER; *also* : to propose as payment **3** : PROPOSE, SUGGEST; *also* : to declare one's readiness **4** : to try or begin to exert ⟨∼ resistance⟩ **5** : to place on sale — **of·fer·ing** *n*

²offer *n* **1** : PROPOSAL **2** : BID **3** : TRY

of・fer・to・ry \\'óf-ə(r)-ˌtōr-ē\ *n, pl* **-ries** : the presentation of offerings at a church service; *also* : the musical accompaniment during it

off・hand \\'óf-'hand\ *adv or adj* : without previous thought or preparation

off・hour \-ˌaú(-ə)r\ *n* : a period of time other than a rush hour; *also* : a period of time other than business hours

of・fice \\'óf-əs\ *n* **1** : a special duty or position; *esp* : a position of authority in government ⟨run for ∼⟩ **2** : a prescribed form or service of worship; *also* : RITE **3** : an assigned or assumed duty or role **4** : a place where a business is transacted or a service is supplied

of・fice・hold・er \-ˌhōl-dər\ *n* : one holding a public office

of・fi・cer \\'óf-ə-sər\ *n* **1** : one charged with the enforcement of law **2** : one who holds an office of trust or authority **3** : one who holds a commission in the armed forces

¹of・fi・cial \ə-'fish-əl\ *n* : OFFICER

²official *adj* **1** : of or relating to an office or to officers **2** : AUTHORIZED, AUTHORITATIVE **3** : befitting or characteristic of a person in office — **of・fi・cial・ly** \-ē\ *adv*

of・fi・cial・dom \ə-'fish-əl-dəm\ *n* : officials as a class

of・fi・cial・ism \ə-'fish-ə-ˌliz-əm\ *n* : lack of flexibility and initiative combined with excessive adherence to regulations

of・fi・ci・ant \ə-'fish-ē-ənt\ *n* : an officiating clergyman

of・fi・ci・ate \ə-'fish-ē-ˌāt\ *vb* **-at・ed; -at・ing** **1** : to perform a ceremony, function, or duty **2** : to act in an official capacity

of・fi・cious \ə-'fish-əs\ *adj* : volunteering one's services where they are neither asked for nor needed — **of・fi・cious・ly** *adv* — **of・fi・cious・ness** *n*

off・ing \\'óf-iŋ\ *n* : the near or foreseeable future

off・ish \\'óf-ish\ *adj* : inclined to stand aloof

off–line \\'óf-'līn\ *adj or adv* : not controlled directly by a computer

off of *prep* : OFF

off・print \\'óf-ˌprint\ *n* : a separately printed excerpt (as from a magazine)

off–sea・son \-ˌsēz-ᵊn\ *n* : a time of suspended or reduced activity

¹off・set \-ˌset\ *n* **1** : a sharp bend (as in a pipe) by which one part is turned aside out of line **2** : a printing process in which an inked impression is first made on a rubber-blanketed cylinder and then transferred to the paper

²off・set *vb* **-set; -set・ting** **1** : to place over against : BALANCE **2** : to compensate for **3** : to form an offset in (as a wall)

off・shoot \\'óf-ˌshüt\ *n* **1** : a collateral or derived branch, descendant, or member **2** : a branch of a main stem (as of a plant)

¹off・shore \\'óf-'shōr\ *adv* : at a distance from the shore

²off・shore \\'óf-ˌshōr\ *adj* **1** : moving away from the shore **2** : situated off the shore but within waters under a country's control

off・side \-'sīd\ *adv or adj* : illegally in advance of the ball or puck

off・spring \-ˌspriŋ\ *n, pl* **offspring** *also* **offsprings** : PROGENY, YOUNG

off・stage \\'óf-'stāj, -ˌstāj\ *adv or adj* : off or away from the stage

off–the–record *adj* : given or made in confidence and not for publication

off–the–shelf *adj* : available as a stock item : not specially designed or made

off–white \\'óf-'hwīt\ *n* : a yellowish or grayish white

off year *n* **1** : a year in which no major election is held **2** : a year of diminished activity or production

oft \\'óft\ *adv* : OFTEN

of・ten \\'óf-(t)ən\ *adv* : many times : FREQUENTLY

of・ten・times \-ˌtīmz\ *or* **oft・times** \\'óf(t)-ˌtīmz\ *adv* : OFTEN

ogle \\'ōg-əl\ *vb* **ogled; ogling** \-(ə-)liŋ\ : to look at in a flirtatious way — **ogle** *n* — **ogler** \-(ə-)lər\ *n*

ogre \\'ō-gər\ *n* **1** : a monster of fairy tales and folklore that feeds on human beings **2** : a dreaded person or object

ogress \\'ō-g(ə-)rəs\ *n* : a female ogre

oh \(')ō\ *interj* **1** — used to express an emotion or in response to physical stimuli **2** — used in direct address

OH *abbr* Ohio

ohm \\'ōm\ *n* : a unit of electrical resistance equal to the resistance of a circuit in which a potential difference of one volt produces a current of one ampere — **ohm·ic** \\'ō-mik\ *adj*

ohm·me·ter \\'ō(m)-₁mēt-ər\ *n* : an instrument for indicating resistance in ohms directly

¹**oil** \\'oil\ *n* [ME *oile,* fr. OF, fr. L *oleum* olive oil, fr. Gk *elaion,* fr. *elaia* olive] **1** : a fatty or greasy liquid substance obtained from plants, animals, or minerals and used for fuel, food, medicines, and manufacturing **2** : PE-TROLEUM **3** : artists' colors made with oil; *also* : a painting in such colors — **oil·i·ness** \\'oi-lē-nəs\ *n* — **oily** \\'oi-lē\ *adj*

²**oil** *vb* : to put oil in or on — **oil·er** *n*

oil·cloth \-₁klòth\ *n* : cloth treated with oil or paint and used for table and shelf coverings

oil shale *n* : a rock (as shale) from which oil can be recovered by distillation

oil·skin \\'oil-₁skin\ *n* **1** : an oiled waterproof cloth **2** : an oilskin raincoat **3** *pl* : an oilskin coat and trousers

oink \\'oiŋk\ *n* : the natural noise of a hog — **oink** *vb*

oint·ment \\'oint-mənt\ *n* : a medicinal or cosmetic preparation usu. with a fatty or greasy base for use on the skin

OJ *abbr* orange juice

Ojib·wa *or* **Ojib·way** \ō-'jib-₁wā\ *n, pl* **Ojibwa** *or* **Ojibwas** *or* **Ojibway** *or* **Ojibways** : a member of an American Indian people orig. of Michigan

OJT *abbr* on-the-job training

¹**OK** *or* **okay** \ō-'kā\ *adv or adj* : all right

²**OK** *or* **okay** *vb* **OK'd** *or* **okayed; OK'-ing** *or* **okay·ing** : APPROVE, AUTHORIZE — **OK** *or* **okay** *n*

³**OK** *abbr* Oklahoma

Okla *abbr* Oklahoma

okra \\'ō-krə, *Southern also* -krē\ *n* : a tall annual plant related to the hollyhocks that has edible green pods; *also* : these pods

¹**old** \\'ōld\ *adj* **1** : ANCIENT; *also* : of long standing **2** *cap* : belonging to an early period ⟨*Old* Irish⟩ **3** : having existed for a specified period of time **4** : of or relating to a past era **5** : advanced in years **6** : showing the effects of age or use **7** : no longer in use — **old·ish** \\'ōl-dish\ *adj*

²**old** *n* : old or earlier time ⟨days of ∼⟩

old·en \\'ōl-dən\ *adj* : of or relating to a bygone era

¹**old–fash·ioned** \\'ōl(d)-'fash-ənd\ *adj* **1** : OUT-OF-DATE, ANTIQUATED **2** : CONSERVATIVE

²**old–fashioned** *n* : a cocktail usu. made with whiskey, bitters, sugar, a twist of lemon peel, and water or soda water

old guard *n, often cap O&G* : the conservative members of an organization

old hat *adj* **1** : OLD-FASHIONED **2** : STALE, TRITE

old·ie \\'ōl-dē\ *n* : something old; *esp* : a popular song from the past

old–line \\'ōl(d)-'līn\ *adj* **1** : ORIGINAL, ESTABLISHED ⟨an ∼ business⟩ **2** : adhering to old policies or practices

old maid *n* **1** : SPINSTER **2** : a prim fussy person — **old–maid·ish** \\'ōl(d)-'mād-ish\ *adj*

old man *n* **1** : HUSBAND **2** : FATHER

old·ster \\'ōl(d)-stər\ *n* : an old or elderly person

Old Testament *n* : the first of the two chief divisions of the Bible — see BIBLE table

old–time \\'ōl(d)-₁tīm\ *adj* **1** : of, relating to, or characteristic of an earlier period **2** : of long standing

old–tim·er \ōl(d)-'tī-mər\ *n* VETERAN; *also* : OLDSTER

old–world \\'ōl(d)-'wərld\ *adj* : having old fashioned charm

Old World *n* : the eastern hemisphere; *esp* : continental Europe

ole·ag·i·nous \₁ō-lē-'aj-ə-nəs\ *adj* : OILY

ole·an·der \\'ō-lē-₁an-dər\ *n* : a poisonous evergreen shrub often grown for its fragrant red or white flowers

oleo \\'ō-lē-₁ō\ *n, pl* **oleos** : MARGARINE

oleo·mar·ga·rine \₁ō-lē-ō-'märj-(ə-)rən, -'märj-ə-₁rēn\ *n* : MARGARINE

ol·fac·to·ry \äl-'fak-t(ə-)rē, ōl-\ *adj* : of or relating to the sense of smell

oli·gar·chy \\'äl-ə-₁gär-kē, 'ō-lə-\ *n, pl* **-chies 1** : a government in which power is in the hands of a few **2** : a state having an oligarchy; *also* : the group holding power in such a state — **oli·garch** \-₁gärk\ *n* — **oli·gar·chic** \₁äl-ə-'gär-kik, ₁ō-lə-\ *or* **oli·gar·chi·cal** \-ki-kəl\ *adj*

Oli·go·cene \\'äl-i-gō-₁sēn, ə-'lig-ə-₁sēn\ *adj* : of, relating to, or being the epoch of the Tertiary between the Eocene and the Miocene — **Oligocene** *n*

olio \\'ō-lē-₁ō\ *n, pl* **oli·os** : HODGEPODGE, MEDLEY

ol·ive \'äl-iv, -əv\ *n* **1** : an Old World evergreen tree grown in warm regions for its fruit that is important as food and for its edible oil (**olive oil**) **2** : a dull yellow to yellowish green color

olive drab *n* **1** : a variable color averaging a grayish olive **2** : a wool or cotton fabric of an olive drab color; *also* : a uniform of this fabric

ol·iv·ine \'äl-ə-ˌvēn\ *n* : a usu. greenish mineral that is a complex silicate of magnesium and iron

Olym·pic Games \ə-'lim-pik-, ō-\ *n pl* : a modified revival of an ancient Greek festival held every four years and consisting of international athletic contests

om \'ōm\ *n* : a mantra consisting of the sound "om" used in contemplating ultimate reality

Oma·ha \'ō-mə-ˌhä, -ˌho\ *n, pl* **Omaha** *or* **Omahas** : a member of an American Indian people of northeastern Nebraska

om·buds·man \'äm-ˌbudz-mən, äm-'budz-\ *n, pl* **-men** \-mən\ **1** : a government official appointed to investigate complaints made by individuals against abuses or capricious acts of public officials **2** : one that investigates reported complaints (as from students or consumers)

om·elet *or* **om·elette** \'äm-(ə-)lət\ *n* [F *omelette,* alter. of MF *alumelle,* lit., knife blade, modif. of L *lamella,* dim. of *lamina* thin plate] : eggs beaten with milk or water, cooked without stirring until set, and folded over

omen \'ō-mən\ *n* : an event or phenomenon believed to be a sign or warning of a future occurrence

om·i·nous \'äm-ə-nəs\ *adj* : foretelling evil : THREATENING — **om·i·nous·ly** *adv* — **om·i·nous·ness** *n*

omis·sion \ō-'mish-ən\ *n* **1** : something neglected or left undone **2** : the act of omitting : the state of being omitted

omit \ō-'mit\ *vb* **omit·ted; omit·ting 1** : to leave out or leave unmentioned **2** : to fail to perform : NEGLECT

¹om·ni·bus \'äm-ni-(ˌ)bəs\ *n* : BUS

²omnibus *adj* : of, relating to, or providing for many things at once (an ~ bill)

om·nip·o·tent \äm-'nip-ət-ənt\ *adj* : having unlimited authority or influence : ALMIGHTY — **om·nip·o·tence** \-əns\ *n* — **om·nip·o·tent·ly** *adv*

om·ni·pres·ent \ˌäm-ni-'prez-ᵊnt\ *adj* : present in all places at all times — **om·ni·pres·ence** \-ᵊns\ *n*

om·ni·scient \äm-'nish-ənt\ *adj* : having infinite awareness, understanding, and insight — **om·ni·science** \-əns\ *n* — **om·ni·scient·ly** *adv*

om·ni·um–gath·er·um \ˌäm-nē-əm-'gath-ə-rəm\ *n, pl* **omnium–gatherums** : a miscellaneous collection

om·niv·o·rous \äm-'niv-(ə-)rəs\ *adj* : feeding on both animal and vegetable substances; *also* : AVID (an ~ reader) — **om·niv·o·rous·ly** *adv*

¹on \(')on, (')än\ *prep* **1** : in or to a position over and in contact with (a book ~ the table) (jumped ~ his horse) **2** : touching the surface of (shadows ~ the wall) **3** : AT, TO (~ the right were the mountains) **4** : IN, ABOARD (went ~ the train) **5** : during or at the time of (came ~ Monday) (every hour ~ the hour) **6** : through the agency of (was cut ~ a tin can) **7** : in a state or process of (~ fire) (~ the wane) **8** : connected with as a member or participant (~ a committee) (~ tour) **9** — used to indicate a basis, source, or standard of computation (has it ~ good authority) (10 cents ~ the dollar) **10** : with regard to (a monopoly ~ wheat) **11** : at or toward as an object (crept up ~ her) (smiled ~ him) **12** : ABOUT, CONCERNING (a book ~ minerals)

²on \'on, 'än\ *adv* **1** : in or into a position of contact with or attachment to a surface **2** : FORWARD **3** : into operation

³on \'on, 'än\ *adj* : being in operation or in progress

ON *abbr* Ontario

¹once \'wəns\ *adv* **1** : one time only **2** : at any one time **3** : FORMERLY **4** : by one degree of relationship

²once *n* : one single time — **at once 1** : at the same time **2** : IMMEDIATELY

³once *adj* : FORMER

⁴once *conj* : AS SOON AS

once–over \-ˌō-vər\ *n* : a swift examination or survey

on·com·ing \'on-ˌkəm-iŋ, 'än-\ *adj* : APPROACHING (~ traffic)

¹one \'wən\ *adj* **1** : being a single unit or

thing ⟨∼ person went⟩ **2** : being one in particular ⟨early ∼ morning⟩ **3** : being the same in kind or quality ⟨members of ∼ race⟩; *also* : UNITED **4** : being not specified or fixed ⟨at ∼ time or another⟩

²one *n* **1** : the number denoting unity **2** : the 1st in a set or series **3** : a single person or thing — **one·ness** \ˈwən-nəs\ *n*

³one *pron* **1** : a single member or specimen ⟨saw ∼ of his friends⟩ **2** : a person in general ⟨∼ never knows⟩ **3** — used in place of a first-person pronoun

Onei·da \ō-ˈnīd-ə\ *n, pl* **Oneida** *or* **Oneidas** : a member of an American Indian people orig. of New York

oner·ous \ˈän-ə-rəs, ˈō-nə-\ *adj* : imposing or constituting a burden : TROUBLESOME **syn** oppressive, exacting, burdensome, weighty

one·self \(ˌ)wən-ˈself\ *also* **one's self** \(ˌ)wən-, ˌwənz-\ *pron* : one's own self — usu. used reflexively or for emphasis

one–sid·ed \ˈwən-ˈsīd-əd\ *adj* **1** : having or occurring on one side only; *also* : having one side prominent or more developed **2** : UNEQUAL ⟨a ∼ game⟩ **3** : PARTIAL ⟨a ∼ attitude⟩

one·time \ˈwən-ˌtīm\ *adj* : FORMER

one–to–one \ˌwən-tə-ˈwən\ *adj* : pairing each element of a class uniquely with an element of another class

one up *adj* : being in a position of advantage ⟨was *one up* on the others⟩

one–way *adj* : moving, allowing movement, or functioning in only one direction ⟨∼ streets⟩

on·go·ing \ˈȯn-ˌgō-iŋ, ˈän-\ *adj* : continuously moving forward

on·ion \ˈən-yən\ *n* : a plant related to the lilies and grown for its pungent edible bulb; *also* : this bulb

on·ion·skin \-ˌskin\ *n* : a thin strong translucent paper of very light weight

on–line *adj or adv* : controlled directly by a computer ⟨∼ equipment⟩

on·look·er \ˈȯn-ˌlu̇k-ər, ˈän-\ *n* : SPECTATOR

¹on·ly \ˈōn-lē\ *adj* **1** : unquestionably the best **2** : SOLE

²only *adv* **1** : MERELY, JUST ⟨∼ $2⟩ **2** : SOLELY ⟨known ∼ to me⟩ **3** : at the very least ⟨was ∼ too true⟩ **4** : as a final result ⟨will ∼ make you sick⟩

³only *conj* : except that

on·o·mato·poe·ia \ˌän-ə-ˌmat-ə-ˈpē-(y)ə\ *n* **1** : formation of words in imitation of natural sounds (as *buzz* or *hiss*) **2** : the use of words whose sound suggests the sense — **on·o·mato·poe·ic** \-ˈpē-ik\ *or* **on·o·mato·po·et·ic** \-pō-ˈet-ik\ *adj* — **on·o·mato·poe·i·cal·ly** \-ˈpē-ə-k(ə-)lē\ *or* **on·o·mato·po·et·i·cal·ly** \-pō-ˈet-i-k(ə-)lē\ *adv*

On·on·da·ga \ˌän-ə(n)-ˈdȯ-gə\ *n, pl* **-ga** *or* **-gas** : a member of an American Indian people of New York and Canada

on·rush \ˈȯn-ˌrəsh, ˈän-\ *n* : a rushing onward — **on·rush·ing** \-iŋ\ *adj*

on·set \-ˌset\ *n* **1** : ATTACK **2** : BEGINNING

on·shore \-ˌshȯr\ *adj* **1** : moving toward the shore **2** : situated on or near the shore — **on·shore** \-ˈshȯr\ *adv*

on·slaught \ˈȯn-ˌslȯt, ˈän-\ *n* : a fierce attack

Ont *abbr* Ontario

on·to \ˈȯn-tə, ˈän-; ˈȯn-ˌtü, ˈän-\ *prep* : to a position or point on

onus \ˈō-nəs\ *n* **1** : BURDEN **2** : OBLIGATION **3** : BLAME

¹on·ward \ˈȯn-wərd, ˈän-\ *also* **on·wards** \-wərdz\ *adv* : FORWARD

²onward *adj* : directed or moving onward : FORWARD

on·yx \ˈän-iks\ *n* [ME *onix,* fr. OF & L; OF, fr. L *onyx,* fr. Gk, lit., claw, nail] : a translucent chalcedony in parallel layers of different colors

oo·dles \ˈüd-ᵊlz\ *n pl* : a great quantity

oo·lite \ˈō-ə-ˌlīt\ *n* : a rock consisting of small round grains cemented together — **oo·lit·ic** \ˌō-ə-ˈlit-ik\ *adj*

¹ooze \ˈüz\ *n* **1** : a soft deposit (as of mud) on the bottom of a body of water **2** : soft wet ground : MUD — **oozy** \ˈü-zē\ *adj*

²ooze *n* : something that oozes

³ooze *vb* **oozed; ooz·ing** **1** : to flow or leak out slowly or imperceptibly **2** : EXUDE

op *abbr* opus

OP *abbr* **1** observation post **2** out of print

opac·i·ty \ō-ˈpas-ət-ē\ *n, pl* **-ties** **1** : the quality or state of being opaque **2** : obscurity of meaning **3** : mental dullness **4** : an opaque spot in a normally transparent structure

opal \\'ō-pəl\ *n* : a mineral with soft changeable colors that is used as a gem

opal·es·cent \,ō-pə-'les-³nt\ *adj* : IRIDESCENT — **opal·es·cence** \-³ns\ *n*

opaque \ō-'pāk\ *adj* **1** : not allowing radiant energy and esp. light to pass through **2** : not easily understood **3** : OBTUSE — **opaque·ly** *adv* — **opaqueness** *n*

op art \'äp-\ *n* : OPTICAL ART — **op artist** *n*

op cit *abbr* [L *opere citato*] in the work cited

ope \'ōp\ *vb* **oped; op·ing** *archaic* : OPEN

OPEC *abbr* Organization of Petroleum Exporting Countries

¹open \'ō-pən\ *adj* **open·er** \'ōp-(ə-)nər\; **open·est** \'ōp-(ə-)nəst\ **1** : not shut or shut up ⟨an ∼ door⟩ **2** : not secret or hidden; *also* : FRANK **3** : not enclosed or covered ⟨an ∼ fire⟩; *also* : not protected **4** : free to be entered or used ⟨an ∼ tournament⟩ **5** : easy to get through or see ⟨∼ country⟩ **6** : spread out : EXTENDED **7** : not decided ⟨an ∼ question⟩ **8** : readily accessible and cooperative; *also* : GENEROUS **9** : having components separated by a space in writing and printing ⟨the name *Spanish moss* is an ∼ compound⟩ **10** : ready to operate ⟨stores are ∼⟩ **11** : free from restraints or controls ⟨∼ season⟩ — **open·ly** *adv* — **open·ness** \-pən-nəs\ *n*

²open \'ō-pən\ *vb* **opened** \'ō-pənd\; **open·ing** \'ōp-(ə-)niŋ\ **1** : to change or move from a shut position; *also* : to make open by clearing away obstacles **2** : to make accessible **3** : to make openings in **4** : to make or become functional ⟨∼ a store⟩ **5** : REVEAL; *also* : ENLIGHTEN **6** : BEGIN — **open·er** \'ōp-(ə-)nər\ *n*

³open *n* **1** : OUTDOORS **2** : a contest or tournament open to all

open–air *adj* : OUTDOOR ⟨∼ theaters⟩

open·hand·ed \,ō-pən-'han-dəd\ *adj* : GENEROUS

open–heart *adj* : of, relating to, or performed on a heart temporarily relieved of circulatory function and laid open for inspection and treatment

open–hearth *adj* : of, relating to, or being a process of making steel in a furnace that reflects the heat from the roof onto the material

open·ing \'ōp-(ə-)niŋ\ *n* **1** : an act or instance of making or becoming open **2** : BEGINNING **3** : something that is open **4** : OCCASION; *also* : an opportunity for employment

open–mind·ed \,ō-pən-'mīn-dəd\ *adj* : free from rigidly fixed preconceptions

open sentence *n* : a statement (as in mathematics) containing at least one blank or unknown so that when the blank is filled or a quantity substituted for the unknown the statement becomes a complete statement that is either true or false

open shop *n* : an establishment having members and nonmembers of a labor union on the payroll

open·work \'ō-pən-,wərk\ *n* : work so made as to show openings through its substance ⟨a railing of wrought-iron ∼⟩ — **open–worked** \-,wərkt\ *adj*

¹opera *pl of* OPUS

²op·era \'äp-(ə-)rə\ *n* : a drama set to music — **op·er·at·ic** \,äp-ə-'rat-ik\ *adj*

op·er·a·ble \'äp-(ə-)rə-bəl\ *adj* **1** : fit, possible, or desirable to use **2** : likely to result in a favorable outcome upon surgical treatment

opera glasses *n pl* : small binoculars for use in a theater

op·er·ate \'äp-ə-,rāt\ *vb* **-at·ed; -at·ing** **1** : to perform work : FUNCTION **2** : to produce an effect **3** : to put or keep in operation **4** : to perform an operation — **op·er·a·tor** \-,rāt-ər\ *n*

op·er·a·tion \,äp-ə-'rā-shən\ *n* **1** : a doing or performing of a practical work **2** : an exertion of power or influence; *also* : method or manner of functioning **3** : a surgical procedure **4** : a process of deriving one mathematical expression from others according to a rule **5** : a military action or mission — **op·er·a·tion·al** \-sh(ə-)nəl\ *adj*

¹op·er·a·tive \'äp-(ə-)rət-iv, 'äp-ə-,rāt-\ *adj* **1** : producing an appropriate effect **2** : OPERATING ⟨an ∼ force⟩ **3** : having to do with physical operations; *also* : WORKING ⟨an ∼ craftsman⟩ **4** : based on or consisting of an operation

²**operative** *n* : OPERATOR; *esp* : a secret agent

op·er·et·ta \ˌäp-ə-'ret-ə\ *n* [It, dim. of *opera*] : a light musical-dramatic work with a romantic plot, spoken dialogue, and dancing scenes

oph·thal·mic \äf-'thal-mik, äp-\ *adj* : of, relating to, or located near the eye

oph·thal·mol·o·gy \ˌäf-ˌthal-'mäl-ə-jē, ˌäp-\ *n* : a branch of medicine dealing with the structure, functions, and diseases of the eye — **oph·thal·mol·o·gist** \-jəst\ *n*

oph·thal·mo·scope \äf-'thal-mə-ˌskōp, äp-\ *n* : an instrument with a mirror centrally perforated for use in viewing the interior of the eye

opi·ate \'ō-pē-ət, -pē-ˌāt\ *n* : a preparation or derivative of opium; *also* : NARCOTIC — **opiate** *adj*

opine \ō-'pīn\ *vb* **opined; opin·ing** : to express an opinion : STATE

opin·ion \ə-'pin-yən\ *n* **1** : a belief stronger than impression and less strong than positive knowledge **2** : JUDGMENT **3** : a formal statement by an expert after careful study

opin·ion·at·ed \ə-'pin-yə-ˌnāt-əd\ *adj* : obstinately adhering to personal opinions

opi·um \'ō-pē-əm\ *n* [ME, fr. L, fr. Gk *opion*, fr. dim. of *opos* sap] : an addictive narcotic drug that is the dried juice of a poppy

opos·sum \ə-'päs-əm\ *n, pl* **opossums** *also* **opossum** [fr. *âpäsûm*, lit., white animal (in some American Indian language of Virginia)] : any of various American marsupial mammals; *esp* : a common omnivorous tree-dwelling animal of the eastern U.S.

opp *abbr* opposite

op·po·nent \ə-'pō-nənt\ *n* : one that opposes : ADVERSARY

op·por·tune \ˌäp-ər-'t(y)ün\ *adj* [ME, fr. MF *opportun*, fr. L *opportunus*, fr. *ob-* toward + *portus* port, harbor] : SUITABLE — **op·por·tune·ly** *adv*

op·por·tun·ism \ˌäp-ər-'t(y)ü-ˌniz-əm\ *n* : a taking advantage of opportunities or circumstances esp. with little regard for principles or ultimate consequences — **op·por·tun·ist** \-nəst\ *n* — **op·por·tu·nis·tic** \-t(y)ü-'nis-tik\ *adj*

op·por·tu·ni·ty \ˌäp-ər-'t(y)ü-nət-ē\ *n, pl* **-ties 1** : a favorable combination of circumstances, time, and place **2** : a chance for advancement or progress

op·pose \ə-'pōz\ *vb* **op·posed; op·pos·ing 1** : to place opposite or against something (as to provide resistance or contrast) **2** : to strive against : RESIST — **op·po·si·tion** \ˌäp-ə-'zish-ən\ *n*

¹**op·po·site** \'äp-ə-zət\ *n* : one that is opposed or contrary

²**opposite** *adj* **1** : set over against something that is at the other end or side **2** : OPPOSED, HOSTILE; *also* : CONTRARY **3** : contrarily turned or moving — **op·po·site·ly** *adv* — **op·po·site·ness** *n*

³**opposite** *adv* : on opposite sides

⁴**opposite** *prep* : across from and usu. facing ⟨the house ∼ ours⟩

op·press \ə-'pres\ *vb* **1** : to crush by abuse of power or authority **2** : to weigh down : BURDEN **syn** aggrieve, wrong, persecute — **op·pres·sive** \-'pres-iv\ *adj* — **op·pres·sive·ly** *adv* — **op·pres·sor** \-'pres-ər\ *n*

op·pres·sion \ə-'presh-ən\ *n* **1** : unjust or cruel exercise of power or authority **2** : DEPRESSION

op·pro·bri·ous \ə-'prō-brē-əs\ *adj* : expressing or deserving opprobrium — **op·pro·bri·ous·ly** *adv*

op·pro·bri·um \-brē-əm\ *n* **1** : something that brings disgrace **2** : INFAMY

¹**opt** \'äpt\ *vb* : to make a choice

²**opt** *abbr* **1** optical; optician; optics **2** optional

op·tic \'äp-tik\ *adj* : of or relating to vision or the eye

op·ti·cal \'äp-ti-kəl\ *adj* **1** : relating to optics **2** : OPTIC **3** : of, relating to, or using light **4** : of or relating to optical art

optical art *n* : nonobjective art characterized by the use of geometric patterns often for an illusory effect

optical disc *n* : a disc on which information has been recorded digitally and which is read using a laser

optical fiber *n* : a single fiber-optic strand

op·ti·cian \äp-'tish-ən\ *n* **1** : a maker of or dealer in optical items and instruments **2** : one that grinds lenses to prescription and dispenses spectacles

op·tics \'äp-tiks\ *n pl* : a science that deals with the nature and properties of light and the effects that it undergoes and produces

op·ti·mal \\'äp-tə-məl\\ *adj* : most desirable or satisfactory — **op·ti·mal·ly** \\-ē\\ *adv*

op·ti·mism \\'äp-tə-ˌmiz-əm\\ *n* [F *optimisme,* fr. L *optimum,* n., best, fr. neut. of *optimus* best] **1** : a doctrine that this world is the best possible world **2** : an inclination to anticipate the best possible outcome of actions or events — **op·ti·mist** \\-məst\\ *n* — **op·ti·mis·tic** \\ˌäp-tə-'mis-tik\\ *adj* — **op·ti·mis·ti·cal·ly** \\-ti-k(ə-)lē\\ *adv*

op·ti·mum \\'äp-tə-məm\\ *n, pl* **-ma** \\-mə\\ *also* **-mums** [L] : the amount or degree of something most favorable to an end; *also* : greatest degree attained under implied or specified conditions

op·tion \\'äp-shən\\ *n* **1** : the power or right to choose **2** : a right to buy or sell something at a specified price during a specified period **3** : something offered for choice — **op·tion·al** \\-sh(ə-)nəl\\ *adj*

op·tom·e·try \\äp-'täm-ə-trē\\ *n* : the art or profession of examining the eyes for defects of refraction and of prescribing lenses to correct these — **op·tom·e·trist** \\-trəst\\ *n*

opt out *vb* : to choose not to participate

op·u·lence \\'äp-yə-ləns\\ *n* **1** : WEALTH **2** : ABUNDANCE

op·u·lent \\'äp-yə-lənt\\ *adj* **1** : WEALTHY **2** : richly abundant

opus \\'ō-pəs\\ *n, pl* **opera** \\'ō-pə-rə, 'äp-ə-\\ *also* **opus·es** \\'ō-pə-səz\\ : WORK; *esp* : a musical composition

or \\ər, (ˌ)ȯr\\ *conj* — used as a function word to indicate an alternative ⟨sink ∼ swim⟩

OR *abbr* **1** operating room **2** Oregon

-or \\ər\\ *n suffix* : one that does a (specified) thing ⟨calculat*or*⟩ ⟨elevat*or*⟩

or·a·cle \\'ȯr-ə-kəl\\ *n* **1** : one held to give divinely inspired answers or revelations **2** : an authoritative or wise utterance; *also* : a person of great authority or wisdom — **orac·u·lar** \\ȯ-'rak-yə-lər\\ *adj*

¹oral \\'ȯr-əl, 'ȯr-\\ *adj* **1** : SPOKEN **2** : of or relating to the mouth **3** : of, relating to, or characterized by the first stage of psychosexual development in which libidinal gratification is derived from intake (as of food), by sucking, and later by biting **4** : relating to or characterized by personality traits of passive dependency and aggressiveness — **oral·ly** \\'ȯr-ə-lē, 'ȯr-\\ *adv*

²oral *n* : an oral examination — usu. used in pl.

orang \\ə-'raŋ\\ *n* : ORANGUTAN

or·ange \\'ȯr-inj\\ *n* **1** : a juicy citrus fruit with reddish yellow rind; *also* : the evergreen tree with fragrant white flowers that bears this fruit **2** : a color between red and yellow

or·ange·ade \\ˌȯr-inj-'ād\\ *n* : a beverage of orange juice, sugar, and water

orange hawkweed *n* : a weedy herb related to the daisies with bright orange-red flower heads

or·ange·ry \\'ȯr-inj-(ə-)rē\\ *n, pl* **-ries** : a protected place (as a greenhouse) for raising oranges in cool climates

orang·utan \\ə-'raŋ-ə-ˌtaŋ, -ˌtan\\ *n* [Malay *orang hutan,* fr. *orang* man + *hutan* forest] : a reddish brown manlike tree-living ape of Borneo and Sumatra

orate \\ȯ-'rāt\\ *vb* **orat·ed; orat·ing** : to speak in a declamatory manner

ora·tion \\ə-'rā-shən\\ *n* : an elaborate discourse delivered in a formal dignified manner

or·a·tor \\'ȯr-ət-ər\\ *n* : one noted for skill and power as a public speaker

or·a·tor·i·cal \\ˌȯr-ə-'tȯr-i-kəl\\ *adj* : of, relating to, or characteristic of an orator or oratory

or·a·to·rio \\ˌȯr-ə-'tȯr-ē-ˌō\\ *n, pl* **-rios** : a lengthy choral work usu. on a scriptural subject

¹or·a·to·ry \\'ȯr-ə-ˌtȯr-ē\\ *n, pl* **-ries** : a private or institutional chapel

²oratory *n* : the art of speaking eloquently and effectively in public **syn** rhetoric, elocution

orb \\'ȯrb\\ *n* : a spherical body; *esp* : a celestial body (as a planet)

or·bic·u·lar \\ȯr-'bik-yə-lər\\ *adj* : SPHERICAL

¹or·bit \\'ȯr-bət\\ *n* [L *orbita,* lit., track, rut] **1** : a path described by one body or object in its revolution about another **2** : range or sphere of activity — **or·bit·al** \\-ᵊl\\ *adj*

²orbit *vb* **1** : CIRCLE **2** : to send up and make revolve in an orbit ⟨∼ a satellite⟩ — **or·bit·er** \\-bət-ər\\ *n*

orch *abbr* orchestra

or·chard \\'ȯr-chərd\\ *n* : a place where fruit trees or nut trees are grown; *also*

: the trees of such a place — **or·chard·ist** \-əst\ *n*

or·ches·tra \ˈȯr-kə-strə\ *n* [L, fr. Gk *orchēstra,* fr. *orcheisthai* to dance] **1** : a group of instrumentalists organized to perform ensemble music **2** : the front section of seats on the main floor of a theater — **or·ches·tral** \ȯr-ˈkes-trəl\ *adj*

or·ches·trate \ˈȯr-kə-ˌstrāt\ *vb* **-trat·ed; -trat·ing** : to compose or arrange for an orchestra — **or·ches·tra·tion** \ˌȯr-kə-ˈstrā-shən\ *n*

or·chid \ˈȯr-kəd\ *n* [irreg. from L *orchis,* fr. Gk, testicle] : any of numerous related plants having often showy flowers with three petals of which the middle one is enlarged into a lip; *also* : a flower of an orchid

ord *abbr* **1** order **2** ordnance

or·dain \ȯr-ˈdān\ *vb* **1** : to admit to the ministry or priesthood by the ritual of a church **2** : DECREE, ENACT; *also* : DESTINE

or·deal \ȯr-ˈdē(-ə)l, ˈȯr-ˌdē(-ə)l\ *n* : a severe trial or experience

¹**or·der** \ˈȯrd-ər\ *vb* **or·dered; or·der·ing** \ˈȯrd-(ə-)riŋ\ **1** : ARRANGE, REGULATE **2** : COMMAND **3** : to place an order

²**order** *n* **1** : a group of people formally united; *also* : a badge or medal of such a group **2** : any of the several grades of the Christian ministry; *also, pl* : ORDINATION **3** : a rank, class, or special group of persons or things **4** : a category of biological classification ranking above the family and below the class **5** : ARRANGEMENT, SEQUENCE; *also* : the prevailing mode of things **6** : a customary mode of procedure; *also* : the rule of law or proper authority **7** : a specific rule, regulation, or authoritative direction **8** : a style of building; *also* : an architectural column forming the unit of a style **9** : condition esp. with regard to repair **10** : a written direction to pay money or to buy or sell goods; *also* : goods bought or sold

¹**or·der·ly** \ˈȯrd-ər-lē\ *adj* **1** : arranged according to some order; *also* : NEAT, TIDY **2** : well behaved ⟨an ~ crowd⟩ **syn** methodical, systematic, regular — **or·der·li·ness** *n*

²**orderly** *n, pl* **-lies 1** : a soldier who attends a superior officer **2** : a hospital attendant who does general work

¹**or·di·nal** \ˈȯrd-(ə-)nəl\ *n* : an ordinal number

²**ordinal** *adj* : indicating order or rank (as sixth) in a series

or·di·nance \ˈȯrd-(ə-)nəns\ *n* : an authoritative decree or law; *esp* : a municipal regulation

or·di·nary \ˈȯrd-ᵊn-ˌer-ē\ *adj* **1** : to be expected : USUAL **2** : of common quality, rank, or ability; *also* : POOR, INFERIOR **syn** customary, routine, normal, everyday — **or·di·nar·i·ly** \ˌȯrd-ᵊn-ˈer-ə-lē\ *adv*

or·di·nate \ˈȯrd-(ə-)nət, ˈȯrd-ᵊn-ˌāt\ *n* : the coordinate of a point in a plane coordinate system that is the distance of the point from the horizontal axis found by measuring along a line parallel to the vertical axis

or·di·na·tion \ˌȯrd-ᵊn-ˈā-shən\ *n* : the act or ceremony by which a person is ordained

ord·nance \ˈȯrd-nəns\ *n* **1** : military supplies (as weapons, ammunition, or vehicles) **2** : CANNON, ARTILLERY

Or·do·vi·cian \ˌȯrd-ə-ˈvish-ən\ *adj* : of, relating to, or being the period of the Paleozoic era between the Cambrian and the Silurian — **Ordovician** *n*

or·dure \ˈȯr-jər\ *n* : EXCREMENT

¹**ore** \ˈōr\ *n* : a mineral mined to obtain a substance that it contains

²**ore** \ˈər-ə\ *n, pl* **ore** — see *krona, krone* at MONEY table

Oreg *or* **Ore** *abbr* Oregon

oreg·a·no \ə-ˈreg-ə-ˌnō\ *n* [AmerSp] : a bushy perennial mint used as a seasoning and a source of oil

org *abbr* organization; organized

or·gan \ˈȯr-gən\ *n* **1** : a musical instrument having sets of pipes sounded by compressed air and controlled by keyboards; *also* : an instrument in which the sounds of the pipe organ are approximated by electronic devices **2** : a differentiated animal or plant structure made up of cells and tissues and performing some bodily function **3** : a means of performing a function or accomplishing an end **4** : PERIODICAL

or·gan·dy *also* **or·gan·die** \ˈȯr-gən-dē\ *n, pl* **-dies** [F *organdi*] : a fine transparent muslin with a stiff finish

or·gan·ic \ȯr-'gan-ik\ *adj* **1** : of, relating to, or arising in a bodily organ **2** : ORGANIZED ⟨an ∼ whole⟩ **3** : of, relating to, or derived from living things **4** : of, relating to, or containing carbon compounds **5** : of or relating to a branch of chemistry dealing with carbon compounds **6** : involving, producing, or dealing in foods produced without the use of laboratory-made fertilizers, growth substances, antibiotics, or pesticides ⟨∼ gardeners⟩ — **or·gan·i·cal·ly** \-i-k(ə-)lē\ *adv*

or·gan·ism \'ȯr-gə-,niz-əm\ *n* : a living person, animal, or plant — **or·gan·is·mic** \,ȯr-gə-'niz-mik\ *adj*

or·gan·ist \'ȯr-gə-nəst\ *n* : one who plays an organ

or·ga·ni·za·tion \,ȯrg-(ə-)nə-'zā-shən\ *n* **1** : the act or process of organizing or of being organized; *also* : the condition or manner of being organized **2** : ASSOCIATION, SOCIETY **3** : MANAGEMENT — **or·ga·ni·za·tion·al** *adj*

or·ga·nize \'ȯr-gə-,nīz\ *vb* **-nized; -niz·ing** **1** : to develop an organic structure **2** : to arrange or form into a complete and functioning whole **3** : to set up an administrative structure for **4** : to arrange by systematic planning and united effort **5** : to join in a union; *also* : UNIONIZE **syn** institute, found, establish, constitute — **or·ga·niz·er** *n*

or·gano·chlo·rine \ȯr-,gan-ə-'klȯr-,ēn\ *adj* : of or relating to the chlorinated hydrocarbon pesticides (as DDT) — **organochlorine** *n*

or·gano·phos·phate \-'fäs-,fāt\ *n* : an organophosphorus pesticide — **organophosphate** *adj*

or·gano·phos·pho·rus \-'fäs-f(ə-)rəs\ *also* **or·gano·phos·pho·rous** \-fäs-'fōr-əs\ *adj* : of, relating to, or being a phosphorus-containing organic pesticide (as malathion)

or·gan·za \ȯr-'gan-zə\ *n* : a sheer dress fabric resembling organdy and usu. made of silk, rayon, or nylon

or·gasm \'ȯr-,gaz-əm\ *n* : a climax of sexual excitement

or·gi·as·tic \,ȯr-jē-'as-tik\ *adj* : of, relating to, or marked by orgies

or·gu·lous \'ȯr-g(y)ə-ləs\ *adj* : PROUD

or·gy \'ȯr-jē\ *n, pl* **orgies** : a gathering marked by unrestrained indulgence (as in alcohol, drugs, or sexual practices)

ori·el \'ōr-ē-əl\ *n* : a window built out from a wall and usu. supported by a bracket

ori·ent \'ōr-ē-,ent\ *vb* **1** : to set in a definite position esp. in relation to the points of the compass **2** : to acquaint with an existing situation or environment — **ori·en·ta·tion** \,ōr-ē-ən-'tā-shən\ *n*

Orient *n* : EAST 3; *esp* : the countries of eastern Asia

ori·en·tal \,ōr-ē-'ent-ᵊl\ *adj* [fr. *Orient* East, fr. ME, fr. MF, fr. L *orient-, oriens*, fr. prp. of *oriri* to rise] *often cap* : of or situated in the Orient — **Oriental** *n*

ori·en·tate \'ōr-ē-ən-,tāt\ *vb* **-tat·ed; -tat·ing** **1** : ORIENT **2** : to face east

or·i·fice \'ȯr-ə-fəs\ *n* : OPENING, MOUTH

ori·flamme \'ȯr-ə-,flam\ *n* : a brightly colored banner used as a standard or ensign in battle

orig *abbr* original; originally

ori·ga·mi \,ȯr-ə-'gäm-ē\ *n* : the art or process of Japanese paper folding

or·i·gin \'ȯr-ə-jən\ *n* **1** : ANCESTRY **2** : rise, beginning, or derivation from a source; *also* : CAUSE **3** : the intersection of coordinate axes

¹orig·i·nal \ə-'rij-(ə-)nəl\ *n* : something from which a copy, reproduction, or translation is made : PROTOTYPE

²original *adj* **1** : FIRST, INITIAL **2** : not copied from something else : FRESH **3** : INVENTIVE — **orig·i·nal·i·ty** \-,rij-ə-'nal-ət-ē\ *n* — **orig·i·nal·ly** \-'rij-ən-ᵊl-ē\ *adv*

orig·i·nate \ə-'rij-ə-,nāt\ *vb* **-nat·ed; -nat·ing** **1** : to give rise to : INITIATE **2** : to come into existence : BEGIN — **orig·i·na·tor** \-,nāt-ər\ *n*

ori·ole \'ōr-ē-,ōl\ *n* [F *oriol*, fr. L *aureolus*, dim. of *aureus* golden, fr. *aurum* gold] : any of a family of New World birds of which the males are usually black and yellow or orange and the females chiefly greenish or yellowish

or·i·son \'ȯr-ə-sən\ *n* : PRAYER

or·mo·lu \'ȯr-mə-,lü\ *n* : a brass made to imitate gold and used for decorative purposes

¹or·na·ment \'ȯr-nə-mənt\ *n* : something that lends grace or beauty — **or·na·men·tal** \,ȯr-nə-'ment-ᵊl\ *adj*

²**or·na·ment** \-ˌment\ *vb* : to provide with ornament : ADORN — **or·na·men·ta·tion** \ˌȯr-nə-mən-ˈtā-shən\ *n*

or·nate \ȯr-ˈnāt\ *adj* : elaborately decorated — **or·nate·ly** *adv* — **or·nate·ness** *n*

or·nery \ˈȯrn-(ə-)rē, ˈän-\ *adj* : having an irritable disposition

ornith *abbr* ornithology

or·ni·thol·o·gy \ˌȯr-nə-ˈthäl-ə-jē\ *n, pl* **-gies** : a branch of zoology dealing with birds — **or·ni·tho·log·i·cal** \-thə-ˈläj-i-kəl\ *adj* — **or·ni·thol·o·gist** \-ˈthäl-ə-jəst\ *n*

oro·tund \ˈȯr-ə-ˌtənd\ *adj* **1** : SONOROUS **2** : POMPOUS

or·phan \ˈȯr-fən\ *n* : a child deprived by death of one or usu. both parents — **orphan** *vb*

or·phan·age \ˈȯrf-(ə-)nij\ *n* : an institution for the care of orphans

or·ris \ˈȯr-əs\ *n* : a European iris with a fragrant rootstock (**orrisroot**) used in perfume and sachets

orth·odon·tia \ˌȯr-thə-ˈdän-ch(ē-)ə\ *n* : ORTHODONTICS

or·tho·don·tics \ˌȯr-thə-ˈdänt-iks\ *n* : a branch of dentistry dealing with faulty tooth occlusion and its correction — **or·tho·don·tist** \-ˈdänt-əst\ *n*

or·tho·dox \ˈȯr-thə-ˌdäks\ *adj* [MF or LL; MF *orthodoxe,* fr. LL *orthodoxus,* fr. LGk *orthodoxos,* fr. Gk *orthos* right + *doxa* opinion] **1** : conforming to established doctrine esp. in religion **2** : CONVENTIONAL **3** *cap* : of or relating to a Christian church originating in the church of the Eastern Roman Empire — **or·tho·doxy** \-ˌdäk-sē\ *n*

or·thog·ra·phy \ȯr-ˈthäg-rə-fē\ *n* : SPELLING — **or·tho·graph·ic** \ˌȯr-thə-ˈgraf-ik\ *adj*

or·tho·pe·dics \ˌȯr-thə-ˈpēd-iks\ *n sing or pl* : the correction or prevention of skeletal deformities — **or·tho·pe·dic** \-ik\ *adj* — **or·tho·pe·dist** \-ˈpēd-əst\ *n*

or·to·lan \ˈȯrt-ᵊl-ən\ *n* : a European bunting valued as a table delicacy

-ory \ˌōr-ē, (ə-)rē\ *adj suffix* **1** : of, relating to, or characterized by **2** : serving for, producing, or maintaining

Os *symbol* osmium

OS *abbr* **1** [L *oculus sinister*] left eye **2** out of stock

Osage \ō-ˈsāj\ *n, pl* **Osag·es** *or* **Osage** : a member of an American Indian people orig. of Missouri

os·cil·late \ˈäs-ə-ˌlāt\ *vb* **-lat·ed; -lat·ing** **1** : to swing backward and forward like a pendulum **2** : to move or travel back and forth between two points **3** : VARY, FLUCTUATE — **os·cil·la·tion** \ˌäs-ə-ˈlā-shən\ *n* — **os·cil·la·tor** \ˈäs-ə-ˌlāt-ər\ *n* — **os·cil·la·to·ry** \ä-ˈsil-ə-ˌtōr-ē\ *adj*

os·cil·lo·scope \ä-ˈsil-ə-ˌskōp\ *n* : an instrument in which variations in current or voltage appear as a visible wave form on a fluorescent screen

os·cu·late \ˈäs-kyə-ˌlāt\ *vb* **-lat·ed; -lat·ing** : KISS — **os·cu·la·tion** \ˌäs-kyə-ˈlā-shən\ *n*

Osee \ˈō-ˌzē, ō-ˈzā-ə\ *n* — see BIBLE table

OSHA *abbr* Occupational Safety and Health Administration

osier \ˈō-zhər\ *n* : a willow tree with pliable twigs used esp. in making baskets and furniture; *also* : a twig from an osier

os·mi·um \ˈäz-mē-əm\ *n* : a heavy hard brittle metallic chemical element used in alloys

os·mo·sis \äz-ˈmō-səs, äs-\ *n* : diffusion of a solvent through a partially permeable membrane into a solution of higher concentration that tends to equalize the concentrations of the solutions on either side of the membrane — **os·mot·ic** \-ˈmät-ik\ *adj*

os·prey \ˈäs-prē, -ˌprā\ *n, pl* **ospreys** : a large brown and white fish-eating hawk

os·si·fy \ˈäs-ə-ˌfī\ *vb* **-fied; -fy·ing** : to change into bone — **os·si·fi·ca·tion** \ˌäs-ə-fə-ˈkā-shən\ *n*

os·su·ary \ˈäsh-ə-ˌwer-ē, ˈäs-(y)ə-\ *n, pl* **-ar·ies** : a depository for the bones of the dead

os·ten·si·ble \ä-ˈsten-sə-bəl\ *adj* : shown outwardly : PROFESSED, APPARENT — **os·ten·si·bly** \-blē\ *adv*

os·ten·ta·tion \ˌäs-tən-ˈtā-shən\ *n* : pretentious or excessive display — **os·ten·ta·tious** \-shəs\ *adj* — **os·ten·ta·tious·ly** *adv*

os·teo·path \ˈäs-tē-ə-ˌpath\ *n* : a practitioner of osteopathy

os·te·op·a·thy \ˌäs-tē-ˈäp-ə-thē\ *n* : a system of healing that emphasizes manipulation (as of joints) but does not exclude other agencies (as the use of medicine and surgery) — **os·teo·path·ic** \ˌäs-tē-ə-ˈpath-ik\ adj

os·teo·po·ro·sis \ˌäs-tē-ō-pə-ˈrō-səs\ n, pl **-ro·ses** \-ˌsēz\ : a bodily disorder occurring esp. after age 45, characterized by fragile and porous bones, and caused by faulty nutrition and mineral metabolism

ostler var of HOSTLER

ost·mark \ˈōst-ˌmärk, ˈost-\ n — see MONEY table

os·tra·cize \ˈäs-trə-ˌsīz\ vb **-cized; -ciz·ing** [Gk ostrakizein to banish by voting with potsherds, fr. ostrakon shell, potsherd] : to exclude from a group by common consent — **os·tra·cism** \-ˌsiz-əm\ n

os·trich \ˈäs-trich, ˈós-\ n : a very large swift-footed flightless bird of Africa and Arabia

Os·we·go tea \ä-ˌswē-gō-\ n : a No. American mint with showy scarlet flowers

OT abbr 1 Old Testament 2 overtime

¹**oth·er** \ˈəth-ər\ adj 1 : being the one left; also : being the ones distinct from those first mentioned 2 : ALTERNATE ⟨every ~ day⟩ 3 : DIFFERENT 4 : ADDITIONAL 5 : recently past ⟨the ~ night⟩

²**other** pron 1 : remaining one or ones ⟨one foot and then the ~⟩ 2 : a different or additional one ⟨something or ~⟩

oth·er·wise \-ˌwīz\ adv 1 : in a different way 2 : in different circumstances 3 : in other respects — **otherwise** adj

oth·er·world \-ˌwərld\ n : a world beyond death or beyond present reality

oth·er·world·ly \-ˌwərl-(d)lē\ adj : not worldly : concerned with spiritual, intellectual, or imaginative matters

oti·ose \ˈō-shē-ˌōs, ˈōt-ē-\ adj 1 : IDLE 2 : STERILE 3 : USELESS

oto·lar·yn·gol·o·gist \ˈōt-ō-ˌlar-ən-ˈgäl-ə-jəst\ n : a specialist in otorhinolaryngology — **oto·lar·yn·gol·o·gy** \-ə-jē\ n

oto·rhi·no·lar·yn·gol·o·gy \ˌōt-ō-ˌrī-nō-ˌlar-ən-ˈgäl-ə-jē\ n : a medical specialty concerned esp. with the ear, nose, and throat — **oto·rhi·no·lar·yn·gol·o·gist** \-jəst\ n

OTS abbr officers' training school

Ot·ta·wa \ˈät-ə-wə, -ˌwä, -ˌwó\ n, pl **Ottawas** or **Ottawa** : a member of an American Indian people of Michigan and southern Ontario

ot·ter \ˈät-ər\ n, pl **otters** also **otter** : a web-footed fish-eating mammal that is related to the weasels and has dark brown fur; also : its fur

ot·to·man \ˈät-ə-mən\ n : an upholstered seat or couch; also : an overstuffed footstool

ou·bli·ette \ˌü-blē-ˈet\ n [F, fr. MF, fr. oublier to forget, fr. L oblivisci] : a dungeon with an opening at the top

ought \ˈót\ verbal auxiliary — used to express moral obligation, advisability, natural expectation, or logical consequence

ou·gui·ya \ü-ˈg(w)ē-(y)ə\ n, pl **ouguiya** — see MONEY table

ounce \ˈauns\ n [ME, fr. MF unce, fr. L uncia twelfth part, ounce, fr. unus one] : a unit of avoirdupois, troy, and apothecaries' weight — see WEIGHT table

our \är, (ˈ)au(ə)r\ adj : of or relating to us or ourselves

ours \(ˈ)au(ə)rz, ärz\ pron : one or the ones belonging to us

our·selves \är-ˈselvz, au(ə)r-\ pron : our own selves — used reflexively, for emphasis, or in absolute constructions ⟨we pleased ~⟩ ⟨we'll do it ~⟩ ⟨~ tourists, we avoided other tourists⟩

-ous \əs\ adj suffix : full of : abounding in : having : possessing the qualities of ⟨clamorous⟩ ⟨poisonous⟩

oust \ˈaust\ vb : to eject from or deprive of property or position : EXPEL syn evict, dismiss, banish, deport

oust·er \ˈaus-tər\ n : EXPULSION

¹**out** \ˈaut\ adv 1 : in a direction away from the inside or center 2 : beyond control 3 : to extinction, exhaustion, or completion 4 : in or into the open 5 : so as to retire a batter or base runner; also : so as to be retired

²**out** vb : to become known ⟨the truth will ~⟩

³**out** prep 1 : out through ⟨looked ~ the window⟩ 2 : outward on or along ⟨drive ~ the river road⟩

⁴**out** adj 1 : situated outside or at a distance 2 : not in : ABSENT; also : not being in power 3 : not successful in

reaching base **4** : not being in vogue or fashion : not up-to-date

⁵**out** *n* **1** : one who is out of office **2** : the retiring of a batter or base runner

out–and–out \ˌaůt-³n(d)-'aůt\ *adj* : COMPLETE, THOROUGHGOING ⟨an ∼ fraud⟩

out·bid \'aůt-'bid\ *vb* : to make a higher bid than

¹**out·board** \'aůt-ˌbōrd\ *adj* **1** : situated outboard **2** : having or using an outboard motor

²**outboard** *adv* **1** : outside a ship's hull : away from the long axis of a ship **2** : in a position closer to the wing tip of an airplane

outboard motor *n* : a small internal-combustion engine with propeller attached for mounting at the stern of a small boat

out·bound \'aůt-ˌbaůnd\ *adj* : outward bound ⟨∼ traffic⟩

out·break \-ˌbrāk\ *n* **1** : a sudden or violent breaking out **2** : something (as an epidemic) that breaks out

out·build·ing \-ˌbil-diŋ\ *n* : a building separate from but accessory to a main house

out·burst \-ˌbərst\ *n* : ERUPTION; *esp* : a violent expression of feeling

out·cast \-ˌkast\ *n* : one who is cast out by society : PARIAH

out·class \aůt-'klas\ *vb* : SURPASS

out·come \'aůt-ˌkəm\ *n* : a final consequence : RESULT

out·crop \-ˌkräp\ *n* : a coming out of bedrock to the surface of the ground; *also* : the part of a rock formation that thus appears — **outcrop** *vb*

out·cry \-ˌkrī\ *n* : a loud cry : CLAMOR

out·dat·ed \aůt-'dāt-əd\ *adj* : OUTMODED

out·dis·tance \-'dis-təns\ *vb* : to go far ahead of (as in a race) : OUTSTRIP

out·do \-'dü\ *vb* **-did** \-'did\; **-done** \-'dən\; **-do·ing** \-'dü-iŋ\; **-does** \-'dəz\ : to go beyond in action or performance : EXCEL

out·door \ˌaůt-'dōr\ *also* **out·doors** \-ˌdōrz\ *adj* **1** : of or relating to the outdoors **2** : performed outdoors **3** : not enclosed (as by a roof)

¹**out·doors** \aůt-'dōrz\ *adv* : in or into the open air

²**outdoors** *n* **1** : the open air **2** : the world away from human habitation

out·draw \aůt-'drȯ\ *vb* **-drew** \-'drü\;

-drawn \-'drȯn\; **-draw·ing** **1** : to attract a larger audience than **2** : to draw a handgun more quickly than

out·er \'aůt-ər\ *adj* **1** : EXTERNAL **2** : situated farther out; *also* : being away from a center

out·er·most \-ˌmōst\ *adj* : farthest out

outer space *n* : SPACE 5; *esp* : the region beyond the solar system

out·face \aůt-'fās\ *vb* **1** : to cause to waver or submit **2** : DEFY

out·field \'aůt-ˌfēld\ *n* : the part of a baseball field beyond the infield and within the foul lines; *also* : players in the outfield — **out·field·er** \-ˌfēl-dər\ *n*

out·fight \aůt-'fīt\ *vb* : to surpass in fighting : DEFEAT

¹**out·fit** \'aůt-ˌfit\ *n* **1** : the equipment or apparel for a special purpose or occasion **2** : GROUP

²**outfit** *vb* **out·fit·ted; out·fit·ting** : EQUIP — **out·fit·ter** *n*

out·flank \aůt-'flaŋk\ *vb* : to get around the flank of (an opposing force)

out·flow \'aůt-ˌflō\ *n* **1** : a flowing out **2** : something that flows out

out·fox \aůt-'fäks\ *vb* : OUTWIT

out·gen·er·al \-'jen-(ə-)rəl\ *vb* : to surpass in generalship

out·go \'aůt-ˌgō\ *n, pl* **outgoes** : EXPENDITURES, OUTLAY

out·go·ing \-ˌgō-iŋ\ *adj* **1** : going out ⟨∼ tide⟩ **2** : retiring from a place or position **3** : FRIENDLY

out·grow \aůt-'grō\ *vb* **-grew** \-'grü\; **-grown** \-'grōn\; **-grow·ing** **1** : to grow faster than **2** : to grow too large for

out·growth \'aůt-ˌgrōth\ *n* : a product of growing out : OFFSHOOT; *also* : CONSEQUENCE

out·guess \aůt-'ges\ *vb* : OUTWIT

out·gun \-'gən\ *vb* : to surpass in firepower

out·house \'aůt-ˌhaůs\ *n* : OUTBUILDING; *esp* : an outdoor toilet

out·ing \'aůt-iŋ\ *n* : a brief stay or trip in the open

out·land·ish \aůt-'lan-dish\ *adj* **1** : of foreign appearance or manner; *also* : BIZARRE **2** : remote from civilization — **out·land·ish·ly** *adv*

out·last \-'last\ *vb* : to last longer than

¹**out·law** \'aůt-ˌlȯ\ *n* **1** : a person excluded from the protection of the law **2** : a lawless person

²**outlaw** *vb* **1** : to deprive of the protec-

tion of the law **2** : to make illegal —
out·law·ry \'aut-ˌlȯ(ə)r-ē\ n
out·lay \'aut-ˌlā\ n **1** : the act of spending **2** : EXPENDITURE
out·let \'aut-ˌlet, -lət\ n **1** : EXIT, VENT **2** : a means of release (as for an emotion) **3** : a market for a commodity **4** : a receptacle for the plug of an electrical device
¹out·line \'aut-ˌlīn\ n **1** : a line marking the outer limits of an object or figure **2** : a drawing in which only contours are marked **3** : SUMMARY, SYNOPSIS **4** : PLAN
²outline vb **1** : to draw the outline of **2** : to indicate the chief features or parts of
out·live \aut-'liv\ vb : to live longer than **syn** outlast, survive
out·look \'aut-ˌluk\ n **1** : a place offering a view; also : VIEW **2** : STANDPOINT **3** : the prospect for the future
out·ly·ing \-ˌlī-iŋ\ adj : distant from a center or main body
out·ma·neu·ver \ˌaut-mə-'n(y)ü-vər\ vb **1** : to defeat by more skillful maneuvering **2** : to surpass in maneuverability
out·mod·ed \aut-'mōd-əd\ adj **1** : being out of style **2** : no longer acceptable or approved
out·num·ber \-'nəm-bər\ vb : to exceed in number
out of prep **1** : out from within or behind ⟨walk out of the room⟩ ⟨look out of the window⟩ **2** : from a state of ⟨wake up out of a deep sleep⟩ **3** : beyond the limits of ⟨out of sight⟩ **4** : BECAUSE OF ⟨came out of curiosity⟩ **5** : FROM, WITH ⟨built it out of scrap⟩ **6** : in or into a state of loss or not having ⟨cheated him out of $5000⟩ ⟨we're out of matches⟩ **7** : from among ⟨one out of four⟩ — **out of it** : SQUARE, OLD=
FASHIONED
out–of–bounds \ˌaut-ə(v)-'baun(d)z\ adv or adj : outside the prescribed boundaries or limits
out–of–date \-'dāt\ adj : no longer in fashion or in use : OUTMODED
out–of–door \-'dōr\ or **out–of–doors** \-'dōrz\ adj : OUTDOOR
out–of–the–way \-thə-'wā\ adj **1** : being off the beaten track **2** : UNUSUAL
out·pa·tient \'aut-ˌpā-shənt\ n : a per-

son not an inmate of a hospital who visits it for diagnosis or treatment
out·per·form \ˌaut-pər-'förm\ vb : to perform better than
out·play \aut-'plā\ vb : to play more skillfully than
out·point \-'point\ vb : to win more points than
out·post \'aut-ˌpōst\ n **1** : a military detachment stationed at some distance from a main force to protect it from surprise attack; also : a military base established (as by treaty) in a foreign country **2** : an outlying or frontier settlement
out·pour·ing \-ˌpōr-iŋ\ n : something that pours out or is poured out
out·pull \aut-'pul\ vb : OUTDRAW 1
¹out·put \'aut-ˌput\ n **1** : the amount produced (as by a machine or factory) : PRODUCTION **2** : the information fed out by a computer
²output vb **out·put·ted** or **output**; **out·put·ting** : to produce as output
¹out·rage \'aut-ˌrāj\ n [ME, fr. OF, excess, outrage, fr. outre beyond, in excess, fr. L ultra] **1** : a violent or shameful act **2** : INJURY, INSULT **3** : the anger or resentment aroused by an outrage
²outrage vb **out·raged**; **out·rag·ing** **1** : RAPE **2** : to subject to violent injury or gross insult **3** : to arouse to extreme resentment
out·ra·geous \aut-'rā-jəs\ adj : extremely offensive, insulting, or shameful : SHOCKING — **out·ra·geous·ly** adv
out·rank \-'raŋk\ vb : to rank higher than
ou·tré \ü-'trā\ adj [F] : violating convention or propriety : BIZARRE
¹out·reach \aut-'rēch\ vb **1** : to surpass in reach **2** : to get the better of by trickery
²out·reach \'aut-ˌrēch\ n **1** : the act of reaching out **2** : the extent of reach **3** : the extending of services beyond usual limits
out·rid·er \-ˌrīd-ər\ n : a mounted attendant
out·rig·ger \-ˌrig-ər\ n **1** : a frame that extends from the side of a canoe or boat to prevent upsetting **2** : a craft equipped with an outrigger
¹out·right \(')aut-'rīt\ adv **1** : COMPLETELY **2** : INSTANTANEOUSLY

²**outright** *adj* **1** : being exactly what is stated ⟨~ lie⟩ **2** : given or made without reservation or encumbrance ⟨~ sale⟩

out•run \aut-'rən\ *vb* **-ran** \-'ran\; **-run; -run•ning** : to run faster than; *also* : EXCEED

out•sell \-'sel\ *vb* **-sold** \-'sōld\; **-sell•ing** : to exceed in sales

out•set \'aut-₁set\ *n* : BEGINNING, START

out•shine \aut-'shīn\ *vb* **-shone** \-'shōn\ *or* **-shined; -shin•ing** **1** : to shine brighter than **2** : SURPASS

¹**out•side** \aut-'sīd, 'aut-₁sīd\ *n* **1** : a place or region beyond an enclosure or boundary **2** : EXTERIOR **3** : the utmost limit or extent

²**outside** *adj* **1** : OUTER **2** : coming from without ⟨~ influences⟩ **3** : being apart from one's regular duties ⟨~ activities⟩ **4** : REMOTE ⟨an ~ chance⟩

³**outside** *adv* : on or to the outside

⁴**outside** *prep* **1** : on or to the outside of **2** : beyond the limits of **3** : EXCEPT

outside of *prep* **1** : OUTSIDE **2** : BESIDES

out•sid•er \aut-'sīd-ər\ *n* : one who does not belong to a group

out•size \'aut-₁sīz\ *n* : an unusual size; *esp* : a size larger than the standard

out•skirts \-₁skərts\ *n pl* : the outlying parts (as of a city) : BORDERS

out•smart \aut-'smärt\ *vb* : OUTWIT

out•spend \-'spend\ *vb* **1** : to exceed the limits of in spending ⟨~s his income⟩ **2** : to surpass in spending

out•spo•ken \aut-'spō-kən\ *adj* : direct and open in speech or expression — **out•spo•ken•ness** \-kən-nəs\ *n*

out•spread \-'spred\ *vb* **-spread; -spread•ing** : to spread out : EXTEND

out•stand•ing \-'stan-diŋ\ *adj* **1** : PROJECTING **2** : UNPAID; *also* : UNRESOLVED **3** : publicly issued and sold **4** : CONSPICUOUS; *also* : DISTINGUISHED — **out•stand•ing•ly** *adv*

out•stay \-'stā\ *vb* **1** : OVERSTAY **2** : to surpass in endurance

out•stretched \-'strecht\ *adj* : stretched out : EXTENDED

out•strip \-'strip\ *vb* **1** : to go faster than **2** : EXCEL, SURPASS

out•vote \-'vōt\ *vb* : to defeat by a majority of votes

¹**out•ward** \'aut-wərd\ *adj* **1** : moving or directed toward the outside **2** : showing outwardly

²**outward** *or* **out•wards** \-wərdz\ *adv* : toward the outside

out•ward•ly \-wərd-lē\ *adv* : on the outside : EXTERNALLY

out•wear \aut-'waər\ *vb* **-wore** \-'wōr\; **-worn** \-'wōrn\; **-wear•ing** : to wear longer than : OUTLAST

out•weigh \-'wā\ *vb* : to exceed in weight, value, or importance

out•wit \-'wit\ *vb* : to get the better of by superior cleverness

¹**out•work** \-'wərk\ *vb* : to outdo in working

²**out•work** \'aut-₁wərk\ *n* : a minor defensive position outside a fortified area

out•worn \aut-'wōrn\ *adj* : OUTMODED

ou•zo \'ü-(₁)zō, -(₁)zȯ\ *n* : a colorless anise-flavored unsweetened Greek liqueur

ova *pl of* OVUM

oval \'ō-vəl\ *adj* [ML *ovalis,* fr. LL, of an egg, fr. L *ovum*] : egg-shaped; *also* : broadly elliptical — **oval** *n*

ova•ry \'ōv-(ə-)rē\ *n, pl* **-ries** **1** : a usu. paired organ of a female animal in which eggs and often sex hormones are produced **2** : the part of a flower in which seeds are produced — **ovar•i•an** \ō-'var-ē-ən, -'ver-\ *adj*

ovate \'ō-₁vāt\ *adj* : egg-shaped

ova•tion \ō-'vā-shən\ *n* [L *ovation-, ovatio,* fr. *ovatus,* pp. of *ovare* to exult] : an enthusiastic popular tribute

ov•en \'əv-ən\ *n* : a chamber (as in a stove) for baking, heating, or drying

oven•bird \-₁bərd\ *n* : a large American warbler that builds its dome-shaped nest on the ground

¹**over** \'ō-vər\ *adv* **1** : across a barrier or intervening space **2** : across the brim ⟨boil ~⟩ **3** : so as to bring the underside up **4** : out of a vertical position **5** : beyond some quantity, limit, or norm **6** : ABOVE **7** : at an end **8** : THROUGH; *also* : THOROUGHLY **9** : AGAIN

²**over** \₁ō-vər, 'ō-\ *prep* **1** : above in position, authority, or scope ⟨towered ~ her⟩ ⟨obeyed those ~ him⟩ ⟨the talk was ~ their heads⟩ **2** : more than ⟨paid ~ $100 for it⟩ **3** : ON, UPON ⟨a cape ~ his shoulders⟩ **4** : along the length of ⟨~ the road⟩ **5** : through the medium of : ON ⟨spoke ~ TV⟩ **6** : all through ⟨showed me ~ the house⟩ **7**

: on or above so as to cross ⟨walk ∼ the bridge⟩ ⟨jump ∼ a ditch⟩ **8** : DURING ⟨∼ the past 25 years⟩ **9** : on account of ⟨fought ∼ a woman⟩

³**over** \'ō-vər, ˌō-\ *adj* **1** : UPPER, HIGHER **2** : REMAINING **3** : ENDED

over- *prefix* **1** : so as to exceed or surpass **2** : excessive; excessively

overabundance	overindulgence
overabundant	overindulgent
overactive	overlarge
overaggressive	overlearn
overambitious	overliberal
overanxious	overload
overbid	overlong
overbold	overmodest
overbuild	overnice
overburden	overoptimism
overbuy	overoptimistic
overcapacity	overpay
overcapitalize	overpopulated
overcareful	overpopulation
overcautious	overpraise
overcompensation	overprice
overconfidence	overproduce
overconfident	overproduction
overconscientious	overprotect
overcook	overproud
overcritical	overrate
overcrowd	overreact
overdecorated	overrefinement
overdetermined	overrepresented
overdevelop	overripe
overdose	oversell
overdress	oversensitive
overeager	oversensitiveness
overeat	oversimple
overemphasis	oversimplification
overemphasize	oversimplify
overenthusiastic	overspecialization
overestimate	overspecialize
overexcite	overspend
overexert	overstock
overexertion	overstrict
overextend	oversubtle
overfatigued	oversupply
overfeed	overtax
overfill	overtired
overgenerous	overtrain
overgraze	overuse
overhasty	overvalue
overheat	overzealous
overindulge	

over·act \ˌō-vər-'akt\ *vb* : to exaggerate in acting

¹**over·age** \-'āj\ *adj* **1** : too old to be useful **2** : older than is normal for one's position, function, or grade

²**over·age** \'ōv-(ə-)rij\ *n* : SURPLUS

over·all \ˌō-vər-'ȯl\ *adj* : including everything ⟨∼ expenses⟩

over·alls \'ō-vər-ˌȯlz\ *n pl* : trousers of strong material usu. with a piece extending up to cover the chest

over·arm \-ˌärm\ *adj* : done with the arm raised above the shoulder

over·awe \ˌō-vər-'ȯ\ *vb* : to restrain or subdue by awe

over·bal·ance \-'bal-əns\ *vb* **1** : OUTWEIGH **2** : to cause to lose balance

over·bear·ing \-'ba(ə)r-iŋ\ *adj* : ARROGANT, DOMINEERING

over·blown \-'blōn\ *adj* **1** : PORTLY **2** : INFLATED, PRETENTIOUS

over·board \'ō-vər-ˌbōrd\ *adv* **1** : over the side of a ship into the water **2** : to extremes of enthusiasm

¹**over·cast** \'ō-vər-ˌkast\ *adj* : clouded over : GLOOMY

²**over·cast** *n* : COVERING; *esp* : a covering of clouds

over·charge \ˌō-vər-'chärj\ *vb* **1** : to charge too much **2** : to fill or load too full — **over·charge** \'ō-vər-ˌchärj\ *n*

over·coat \'ō-vər-ˌkōt\ *n* : a warm coat worn over indoor clothing

over·come \ˌō-vər-'kəm\ *vb* **-came** \-'kām\; **-come; -com·ing** **1** : CONQUER **2** : to make helpless or exhausted

over·do \ˌō-vər-'dü\ *vb* **-did** \-'did\; **-done** \-'dən\; **-do·ing** \-'dü-iŋ\; **-does** \-'dəz\ **1** : to do too much; *also* : to tire oneself **2** : EXAGGERATE **3** : to cook too long

over·draft \'ō-vər-ˌdraft, -ˌdraft\ *n* : an overdrawing of a bank account; *also* : the sum overdrawn

over·draw \ˌō-vər-'drȯ\ *vb* **-drew** \-'drü\; **-drawn** \-'drȯn\; **-draw·ing** **1** : to draw checks on a bank account for more than the balance **2** : EXAGGERATE

over·drive \'ō-vər-ˌdrīv\ *n* : an automotive transmission gear that transmits to the drive shaft a speed greater than the engine speed

over·dub \ˌō-vər-'dəb\ *vb* : to transfer (recorded sound) onto an earlier recording for a combined effect — **over·dub** \'ō-vər-ˌdəb\ *n*

over·due \-'d(y)ü\ *adj* **1** : unpaid when due; *also* : not appearing or presented on time **2** : more than ready

over·ex·pose \ˌō-vər-ik-'spōz\ *vb* : to expose (a photographic plate or film) for more time than is needed — **over·ex·po·sure** \-'spō-zhər\ n

¹over·flow \-'flō\ vb **1** : INUNDATE; *also* : to pour forth in a flood **2** : to flow over the brim or top of

²over·flow \'ō-vər-ˌflō\ n **1** : FLOOD; *also* : SURPLUS **2** : an outlet for surplus liquid

over·fly \ˌō-vər-'flī\ vb **-flew** \-'flü\; **-flown** \-'flōn\; **-fly·ing** : to fly over in an airplane or spacecraft — **over·flight** \'ō-vər-ˌflīt\ n

over·grow \ˌō-vər-'grō\ vb **-grew** \-'grü\; **-grown** \-'grōn\; **-grow·ing** **1** : to grow over so as to cover **2** : OUTGROW **3** : to grow excessively

over·hand \'ō-vər-ˌhand\ adj : made with the hand brought down from above — **overhand** adv

¹over·hang \'ō-vər-ˌhaŋ, ˌō-vər-'haŋ\ vb **-hung** \-ˌhəŋ, -'həŋ\; **-hang·ing** **1** : to project over : jut out **2** : to hang over threateningly

²over·hang \'ō-vər-ˌhaŋ\ n : a part (as of a roof) that overhangs

over·haul \ˌō-vər-'hȯl\ vb **1** : to examine thoroughly and make necessary repairs and adjustments **2** : OVERTAKE

¹over·head \ˌō-vər-'hed\ adv : ALOFT

²over·head \'ō-vər-ˌhed\ adj : operating or lying above ⟨~ door⟩

³over·head \'ō-vər-ˌhed\ n : business expenses not chargeable to a particular part of the work

over·hear \ˌō-vər-'hiər\ vb **-heard** \-'hərd\; **-hear·ing** \-'hi(ə)r-iŋ\ : to hear without the speaker's knowledge or intention

over·joyed \ˌō-vər-'jȯid\ adj : filled with great joy

over·kill \'ō-vər-ˌkil\ n **1** : a capacity for destruction of a target greatly exceeding that required **2** : a large excess

over·land \'ō-vər-ˌland, -lənd\ adv or adj : by, on, or across land

over·lap \ˌō-vər-'lap\ vb **1** : to lap over **2** : to have something in common

over·lay \ˌō-vər-'lā\ vb **-laid** \-'lād\; **-lay·ing** : to lay or spread over or across — **over·lay** \'ō-vər-ˌlā\ n

over·leap \ˌō-vər-'lēp\ vb **-leaped** or **-leapt** \-'lēpt, -'lept\; **-leap·ing** \-'lē-piŋ\ **1** : to leap over or across **2** : to defeat (oneself) by going too far

over·lie \ˌō-vər-'lī\ vb **-lay** \-'lā\; **-lain** \-'lān\; **-ly·ing** \-'lī-iŋ\ : to lie over or upon

¹over·look \ˌō-vər-'lük\ vb **1** : INSPECT **2** : to look down on from above **3** : to fail to see **4** : IGNORE; *also* : EXCUSE **5** : SUPERVISE

²over·look \'ō-vər-ˌlük\ n : a place from which to look down upon a scene below

over·lord \-ˌlȯrd\ n : a lord who has supremacy over other lords

over·ly \'ō-vər-lē\ adv : EXCESSIVELY

over·mas·ter \ˌō-vər-'mas-tər\ vb : OVERPOWER, SUBDUE

over·match \-'mach\ vb : to be more than a match for : DEFEAT

over·much \-'məch\ adj or adv : too much

¹over·night \-'nīt\ adv **1** : on or during the night **2** : SUDDENLY ⟨became famous ~⟩

²overnight adj : of, lasting, or staying the night ⟨~ guests⟩

over·pass \'ō-vər-ˌpas\ n **1** : a crossing (as of two highways) at different levels by means of a bridge **2** : the upper level of an overpass

over·play \ˌō-vər-'plā\ vb **1** : EXAGGERATE; *also* : OVEREMPHASIZE **2** : to rely too much on the strength of

over·pow·er \-'paů(-ə)r\ vb **1** : to overcome by superior force **2** : OVERWHELM ⟨~ed by hunger⟩

over·print \-'print\ vb : to print over with something additional — **over·print** \'ō-vər-ˌprint\ n

over·qual·i·fied \-'kwäl-ə-ˌfīd\ adj : having more education, training, or experience than a job calls for

over·reach \ˌō-və(r)-'rēch\ vb **1** : to reach above or beyond **2** : to defeat (oneself) by too great an effort

over·ride \-'rīd\ vb **-rode** \-'rōd\; **-rid·den** \-'rid-ᵊn\; **-rid·ing** \-'rīd-iŋ\ **1** : to ride over or across **2** : to prevail over; *also* : to set aside

over·rule \-'rül\ vb **1** : to prevail over **2** : to rule against **3** : to set aside

¹over·run \-'rən\ vb **-ran** \-'ran\; **-run·ning** **1** : to defeat and occupy the positions of **2** : OVERSPREAD; *also* : INFEST **3** : to go beyond **4** : to flow over

²over·run \'ō-və(r)-ˌrən\ n **1** : an act or instance of overrunning; *esp* : an exceeding of estimated costs **2** : the amount by which something overruns

over•sea \ˌō-vər-ˈsē, ˈō-vər-ˌsē\ *adj or adv* : OVERSEAS

over•seas \ˌō-vər-ˈsēz, -ˌsēz\ *adv or adj* : beyond or across the sea : ABROAD

over•see \ˌō-vər-ˈsē\ *vb* **-saw** \-ˈsȯ\; **-seen** \-ˈsēn\; **-see•ing 1** : OVERLOOK **2** : INSPECT; *also* : SUPERVISE — **over•seer** \ˈō-vər-ˌsiər\ *n*

over•sexed \ˌō-vər-ˈsekst\ *adj* : exhibiting excessive sexual drive or interest

over•shad•ow \-ˈshad-ō\ *vb* **1** : DARKEN **2** : to exceed in importance

over•shoe \ˈō-vər-ˌshü\ *n* : a protective outer shoe; *esp* : GALOSH

over•shoot \ˌō-vər-ˈshüt\ *vb* **-shot** \-ˈshät\; **-shoot•ing 1** : to pass swiftly beyond **2** : to shoot over or beyond (as a target)

over•sight \ˈō-vər-ˌsīt\ *n* **1** : SUPERVISION **2** : an inadvertent omission or error

over•size \ˌō-vər-ˈsīz\ *or* **over•sized** \-ˈsīzd\ *adj* : of more than ordinary size

over•sleep \ˌō-vər-ˈslēp\ *vb* **-slept** \-ˈslept\; **-sleep•ing** : to sleep beyond the time for waking

over•spread \-ˈspred\ *vb* **-spread**; **-spread•ing** : to spread over or above

over•state \-ˈstāt\ *vb* : EXAGGERATE — **over•state•ment** *n*

over•stay \-ˈstā\ *vb* : to stay beyond the time or limits of

over•step \-ˈstep\ *vb* : EXCEED

over•sub•scribe \-səb-ˈskrīb\ *vb* : to subscribe for more of than is available, asked for, or offered for sale

overt \ō-ˈvərt, ˈō-ˌvərt\ *adj* [ME, fr. MF *ouvert, overt,* fr. pp. of *ouvrir* to open] : not secret

over•take \ˌō-vər-ˈtāk\ *vb* **-took** \-ˈtu̇k\; **-tak•en** \-ˈtā-kən\; **-tak•ing** : to catch up with; *also* : to catch up with and pass by

over•throw \ˌō-vər-ˈthrō\ *vb* **-threw** \-ˈthrü\; **-thrown** \-ˈthrōn\; **-throw•ing 1** : UPSET **2** : to bring down : DEFEAT ⟨∼ a government⟩ **3** : to throw over or past — **over•throw** \ˈō-vər-ˌthrō\ *n*

over•time \ˈō-vər-ˌtīm\ *n* : time beyond a set limit; *esp* : working time in excess of a standard day or week — **overtime** *adv*

over•tone \-ˌtōn\ *n* **1** : one of the higher tones in a complex musical tone **2** : IMPLICATION, SUGGESTION

over•top \ˌō-vər-ˈtäp\ *vb* **1** : to tower above **2** : SURPASS

over•trick \ˈō-vər-ˌtrik\ *n* : a card trick won in excess of the number bid

over•ture \ˈō-vər-ˌchu̇r, -chər\ *n* [ME, lit., opening, fr. MF, fr. (assumed) VL *opertura,* alter. of L *apertura*] **1** : an opening offer **2** : an orchestral introduction to a musical dramatic work

over•turn \ˌō-vər-ˈtərn\ *vb* **1** : to turn over : UPSET **2** : OVERTHROW

over•view \ˈō-vər-ˌvyü\ *n* : a general survey : SUMMARY

over•ween•ing \ˌō-vər-ˈwē-niŋ\ *adj* **1** : ARROGANT **2** : IMMODERATE

over•weigh \-ˈwā\ *vb* **1** : to exceed in weight **2** : OPPRESS

over•weight \ˈō-vər-ˌwāt\ *n* **1** : weight above what is required or allowed **2** : bodily weight greater than normal for one's age, height, and build — **overweight** *adj*

over•whelm \ˌō-vər-ˈhwelm\ *vb* **1** : OVERTHROW **2** : SUBMERGE **3** : to overcome completely

over•whelm•ing *adj* : EXTREME, GREAT ⟨∼ indifference⟩ — **over•whelm•ing•ly** *adv*

over•win•ter \-ˈwint-ər\ *vb* : to survive the winter

over•work \-ˈwərk\ *vb* **1** : to work or cause to work too hard or long **2** : to use too much — **overwork** *n*

over•wrought \ˌō-və(r)-ˈrȯt\ *adj* **1** : extremely excited **2** : elaborated to excess

ovi•duct \ˈō-və-ˌdəkt\ *n* : a tube that serves for the passage of eggs from an ovary

ovip•a•rous \ō-ˈvip-ə-rəs\ *adj* : reproducing by eggs that hatch outside the parent's body

ovoid \ˈō-ˌvȯid\ *or* **ovoi•dal** \ō-ˈvȯid-əl\ *adj* : egg-shaped : OVAL

ovu•late \ˈäv-yə-ˌlāt, ˈōv-\ *vb* **-lat•ed**; **-lat•ing** : to produce eggs or discharge them from an ovary — **ovu•la•tion** \ˌäv-yə-ˈlā-shən, ˌōv-\ *n*

ovule \ˈäv-yül, ˈōv-\ *n* : any of the bodies in a plant ovary that after fertilization become seeds

ovum \ˈō-vəm\ *n, pl* **ova** \-və\ : EGG 2

ow \ˈau̇\ *interj* — used esp. to express sudden pain

owe \ˈō\ *vb* **owed**; **ow•ing 1** : to be under obligation to pay or render **2** : to be indebted to or for; *also* : to be in debt

owing to *prep* : BECAUSE OF

owl \'aul\ *n* : a nocturnal bird of prey with large head and eyes and strong talons — **owl•ish** *adj* — **owl•ish•ly** *adv*

owl•et \'au-lət\ *n* : a young or small owl

¹own \'ōn\ *adj* : belonging to oneself — used as an intensive after a possessive adjective ⟨his ~ car⟩

²own *vb* **1** : to have or hold as property **2** : ACKNOWLEDGE; *also* : CONFESS — **own•er** *n* — **own•er•ship** *n*

³own *pron* : one or ones belonging to oneself

ox \'äks\ *n, pl* **ox•en** \'äk-sən\ *also* **ox** : one of the common large domestic cattle kept for milk, draft, and meat; *esp* : an adult castrated male

ox•blood \'äks-ˌbləd\ *n* : a moderate reddish brown

ox•bow \'äks-ˌbō\ *n* **1** : a U-shaped collar worn by a draft ox **2** : a U-shaped bend in a river — **oxbow** *adj*

ox•ford \'äks-fərd\ *n* : a low shoe laced or tied over the instep

ox•i•dant \'äk-səd-ənt\ *n* : OXIDIZING AGENT — **oxidant** *adj*

ox•i•da•tion \ˌäk-sə-'dā-shən\ *n* : the act or process of oxidizing; *also* : the condition of being oxidized — **ox•i•da•tive** \'äk-sə-ˌdāt-iv\ *adj*

ox•ide \'äk-ˌsīd\ *n* : a compound of oxygen with another element or group

ox•i•dize \'äk-sə-ˌdīz\ *vb* **-dized; -diz•ing** : to combine with oxygen ⟨iron rusts because it is *oxidized* by exposure to the air⟩ — **ox•i•diz•er** *n*

oxidizing agent *n* : a substance (as oxygen or nitric acid) that oxidizes by taking up electrons

oxy•acet•y•lene \ˌäk-sē-ə-'set-ᵊl-ən, -ᵊl-ˌēn\ *adj* : of, relating to, or utilizing a mixture of oxygen and acetylene

ox•y•gen \'äk-si-jən\ *n* [F *oxygène,* fr. Gk *oxys,* adj., acid, lit., sharp + *-genēs* born; so called because it was once thought to be an essential element of all acids] : a colorless odorless gaseous chemical element that is found in the air, is essential to life, and is involved in combustion

ox•y•gen•ate \'äk-si-jə-ˌnāt\ *vb* **-at•ed; -at•ing** : to impregnate, combine, or supply with oxygen — **ox•y•gen•ation** \ˌäk-si-jə-'nā-shən\ *n*

oxygen tent *n* : a canopy which can be placed over a bedridden person and within which a flow of oxygen can be maintained

oys•ter \'ȯi-stər\ *n* : any of various mollusks with an irregular 2-valved shell that live on stony bottoms in shallow seas and include edible shellfish and pearl producers — **oys•ter•ing** \'ȯi-st(ə-)riŋ\ *n* — **oys•ter•man** \'ȯi-stər-mən\ *n*

oz *abbr* [obs. It *onza* (now *oncia*)] ounce; ounces

ozone \'ō-ˌzōn\ *n* **1** : a faintly blue form of oxygen that is produced by the silent discharge of electricity in air or oxygen and is used for disinfecting, deodorizing, and bleaching **2** : pure and refreshing air

P

¹p \'pē\ *n, pl* **p's** *or* **ps** \'pēz\ *often cap* : the 16th letter of the English alphabet

²p *abbr, often cap* **1** page **2** participle **3** past **4** pawn **5** pence; penny **6** per **7** petite **8** pint **9** pressure **10** purl

P *symbol* phosphorus

pa \'pä, 'pȯ\ *n* : FATHER

¹Pa *abbr* Pennsylvania

²Pa *symbol* protactinium

PA *abbr* **1** Pennsylvania **2** per annum **3** physician's assistant **4** power of attorney **5** press agent **6** private account **7** professional association **8** public address **9** purchasing agent

pa•'an•ga \pä-'äŋ-(g)ə\ *n* — see MONEY table

pab•u•lum \'pab-yə-ləm\ *n* [L, food, fodder] : usu. soft digestible food

Pac *abbr* Pacific

PAC *abbr* political action committee

¹pace \'pās\ *n* **1** : rate of movement or progress (as in walking or working) **2** : a step in walking; *also* : the length of such a step **3** : GAIT; *esp* : a horse's gait in which the legs on the same side move together

²**pace** *vb* **paced; pac•ing 1** : to go or cover at a pace or with slow steps **2** : to measure off by paces **3** : to set or regulate the pace of

³**pace** \ˈpā-sē\ *prep* : with due respect to

pace•mak•er \ˈpās-ˌmā-kər\ *n* **1** : one that sets the pace for another **2** : a body part (as of the heart) that serves to establish and maintain a rhythmic activity **3** : an electrical device for stimulating or steadying the heartbeat

pac•er \ˈpā-sər\ *n* **1** : a horse that paces **2** : PACEMAKER

pachy•derm \ˈpak-i-ˌdərm\ *n* [F *pachyderme,* fr. Gk *pachydermos* thick-skinned, fr. *pachys* thick + *derma* skin] : any of various thick≠skinned hoofed mammals (as an elephant)

pach•ys•an•dra \ˌpak-i-ˈsan-drə\ *n* : any of a genus of low evergreen plants used as a ground cover

pa•cif•ic \pə-ˈsif-ik\ *adj* **1** : tending to lessen conflict **2** : CALM, PEACEFUL **3** *cap* : of or relating to the Pacific Ocean

pac•i•fi•er \ˈpas-ə-ˌfī(-ə)r\ *n* : one that pacifies; *esp* : a device for a baby to chew or suck on

pac•i•fism \ˈpas-ə-ˌfiz-əm\ *n* : opposition to war or violence as a means of settling disputes — **pac•i•fist** \-fəst\ *n or adj* — **pac•i•fis•tic** \ˌpas-ə-ˈfis-tik\ *adj*

pac•i•fy \ˈpas-ə-ˌfī\ *vb* **-fied; -fy•ing 1** : to allay anger or agitation in **2** : SETTLE; *also* : SUBDUE — **pac•i•fi•ca•tion** \ˌpas-ə-fə-ˈkā-shən\ *n*

¹**pack** \ˈpak\ *n* **1** : a compact bundle; *also* : a flexible container for carrying a bundle esp. on the back **2** : a large amount : HEAP **3** : a set of playing cards **4** : a group or band of people or animals **5** : wet absorbent material for application to the body

²**pack** *vb* **1** : to stow goods in for transportation **2** : to fill in or surround so as to prevent passage of air, steam, or water **3** : to put into a protective container **4** : to load with a pack ⟨~ a mule⟩ **5** : to crowd in **6** : to make into a pack **7** : to cause to go without ceremony ⟨~ them off to school⟩ **8** : WEAR, CARRY ⟨~ a gun⟩

³**pack** *vb* : to make up fraudulently so as to secure a desired result ⟨~ a jury⟩

¹**pack•age** \ˈpak-ij\ *n* **1** : BUNDLE, PARCEL **2** : a group of related things offered as a whole

²**package** *vb* **pack•aged; pack•ag•ing** : to make into or enclose in a package

package deal *n* : an offer containing several items all or none of which must be accepted

package store *n* : a store that sells alcoholic beverages in sealed containers for consumption off the premises

pack•er \ˈpak-ər\ *n* : one that packs; *esp* : a wholesale food dealer

pack•et \ˈpak-ət\ *n* **1** : a passenger boat carrying mail and cargo on a regular schedule **2** : a small bundle or package

pack•horse \ˈpak-ˌhȯrs\ *n* : a horse used to carry goods or supplies

pack•ing \ˈpak-iŋ\ *n* : material used to pack something

pack•ing•house \-ˌhaús\ *n* : an establishment for processing and packing food and esp. meat and its by-products

pack rat *n* : a bushy-tailed rodent of the Rocky Mountain area that hoards food and miscellaneous objects

pack•sad•dle \ˈpak-ˌsad-ᵊl\ *n* : a saddle for supporting packs on the back of an animal

pack•thread \-ˌthred\ *n* : strong thread for tying

pact \ˈpakt\ *n* : AGREEMENT, TREATY

¹**pad** \ˈpad\ *n* **1** : a cushioning part or thing : CUSHION **2** : the cushioned part of the foot of some mammals **3** : the floating leaf of a water plant **4** : a writing tablet **5** : LAUNCHPAD **6** : living quarters; *also* : BED

²**pad** *vb* **pad•ded; pad•ding 1** : to furnish with a pad or padding **2** : to expand with needless or fraudulent matter

pad•ding \ˈpad-iŋ\ *n* : the material with which something is padded

¹**pad•dle** \ˈpad-ᵊl\ *vb* **pad•dled; pad•dling** : to move the hands and feet about in shallow water

²**paddle** *n* **1** : an implement with a flat blade used in propelling and steering a small craft (as a canoe) **2** : an implement used for stirring, mixing, or beating **3** : a broad board on the outer rim of a waterwheel or a paddle wheel

³**paddle** *vb* **pad•dled; pad•dling** \ˈpad-(ᵊ-)liŋ\ **1** : to move on or through wa-

ter by or as if by using a paddle **2** : to beat or stir with a paddle

paddle wheel *n* : a wheel with boards around its outer edge used to move a water craft

paddle wheeler *n* : a steam-driven vessel propelled by a paddle wheel

pad·dock \\'pad-ək\\ *n* : a usu. enclosed area for pasturing or exercising animals; *esp* : one where racehorses are saddled and paraded before a race

pad·dy \\'pad-ē\\ *n, pl* **paddies** : wet land where rice is grown

pad·dy wagon \\'pad-ē-\\ *n* : PATROL WAGON

pad·lock \\'pad-,läk\\ *n* : a removable lock with a curved piece that snaps into a catch — **padlock** *vb*

pa·dre \\'päd-rā\\ *n* [Sp or It or Pg, lit., father, fr. L *pater*] **1** : PRIEST, CLERGYMAN **2** : a military chaplain

pae·an \\'pē-ən\\ *n* : an exultant song of praise or thanksgiving

pa·gan \\'pā-gən\\ *n* [ME, fr. LL *paganus*, fr. L, country dweller, fr. *pagus* country district] : HEATHEN — **pagan** *adj* — **pa·gan·ism** \\-,iz-əm\\ *n*

¹page \\'pāj\\ *n* : ATTENDANT; *esp* : one employed to deliver messages

²page *vb* **paged; pag·ing** : to summon by repeatedly calling out the name of

³page *n* : a single leaf (as of a book); *also* : a single side of such a leaf

⁴page *vb* **paged; pag·ing** : to mark or number the pages of

pag·eant \\'paj-ənt\\ *n* [ME *pagyn, padgeant*, lit., scene of a play, fr. ML *pagina*, fr. L, page] : an elaborate spectacle, show, or procession esp. with tableaux or floats — **pag·eant·ry** \\-ən-trē\\ *n*

page·boy \\'pāj-,bȯi\\ *n* [¹*page*] : an often shoulder-length hairdo with the ends of the hair turned under in a smooth roll

pag·er \\'pā-jər\\ *n* : one that pages; *esp* : BEEPER

pag·i·nate \\'paj-ə-,nāt\\ *vb* **-nat·ed; -nat·ing** : ⁴PAGE

pag·i·na·tion \\,paj-ə-'nā-shən\\ *n* **1** : the paging of written or printed matter **2** : the number and arrangement of pages (as of a book)

pa·go·da \\pə-'gōd-ə\\ *n* : a tower with roofs curving upward at the division of each of several stories ⟨Chinese ~⟩

paid past and past part of PAY

pail \\'pāl\\ *n* : a usu. cylindrical vessel with a handle — **pail·ful** \\-,ful\\ *n*

¹pain \\'pān\\ *n* **1** : PUNISHMENT, PENALTY **2** : suffering or distress of body or mind; *also* : a sensation marked by discomfort (as throbbing or aching) **3** *pl* : great care — **pain·ful** \\-fəl\\ *adj* — **pain·ful·ly** \\-ē\\ *adv* — **pain·less** *adj* — **pain·less·ly** *adv*

²pain *vb* : to cause or experience pain

pain·kill·er \\'pān-,kil-ər\\ *n* : something (as a drug) that relieves pain — **pain·kill·ing** \\-iŋ\\ *adj*

pains·tak·ing \\'pān-,stā-kiŋ\\ *adj* : taking pains : showing care — **pains·taking** *n* — **pains·tak·ing·ly** *adv*

¹paint \\'pānt\\ *vb* **1** : to apply color, pigment, or paint to **2** : to produce or portray in lines or colors on a surface; *also* : to practice the art of painting **3** : to decorate with colors **4** : to use cosmetics **5** : to describe vividly **6** : SWAB — **paint·er** *n*

²paint *n* **1** : something produced by painting **2** : MAKEUP **3** : a mixture of a pigment and a liquid that forms a thin adherent coating when spread on a surface; *also* : the dry pigment used in making this mixture **4** : an applied coating of paint

paint·brush \\'pānt-,brəsh\\ *n* : a brush for applying paint

paint·ing \\'pānt-iŋ\\ *n* **1** : a work (as a picture) produced by painting **2** : the art or occupation of painting

¹pair \\'paər\\ *n, pl* **pairs** *also* **pair** [ME *paire*, fr. OF, fr. L *paria* equal things, fr. neut. pl. of *par* equal] **1** : two things of a kind designed for use together **2** : something made up of two corresponding pieces ⟨a ~ of trousers⟩ **3** : a set of two people or animals ⟨a carriage and ~⟩ ⟨a married ~⟩

²pair *vb* **1** : to arrange in pairs **2** : to form a pair : MATCH **3** : to become associated with another

pai·sa \\pī-'sä\\ *n, pl* **paisa** *or* **pai·se** \\-'sä\\ — see *rupee, taka* at MONEY table

pais·ley \\'pāz-lē\\ *adj, often cap* : decorated with colorful curved abstract figures ⟨a ~ shawl⟩

Pai·ute \\'pī-,(y)üt\\ *n* : a member of an American Indian people orig. of Utah, Arizona, Nevada, and California

pa·ja·mas \pə-'jäm-əz, -'jam-\ *n pl* : a loose suit for sleeping or lounging

Pak·i·stani \ˌpak-i-'stan-ē, ˌpäk-i-'stän-ē\ *n* : a native or inhabitant of Pakistan — **Pakistani** *adj*

pal \'pal\ *n* : a close friend

pal·ace \'pal-əs\ *n* [ME *palais*, fr. OF, fr. L *palatium*, fr. *Palatium*, the Palatine Hill in Rome where the emperors' residences were built] **1** : the official residence of a sovereign **2** : MANSION

pal·a·din \'pal-əd-ən\ *n* : a knightly supporter of a medieval prince

pa·laes·tra \pə-'les-trə\ *n, pl* **-trae** \-(ˌ)trē\ : a school in ancient Greece or Rome for sports (as wrestling)

pa·lan·quin \ˌpal-ən-'kēn\ *n* : an enclosed couch for one person borne on the shoulders of men by means of poles

pal·at·able \'pal-ət-ə-bəl\ *adj* : agreeable to the taste **syn** appetizing, savory, tasty, toothsome

pal·a·tal \'pal-ət-ᵊl\ *adj* **1** : of or relating to the palate **2** : pronounced with the front of the tongue near or touching the hard palate ⟨the \y\ in *yeast* and the \sh\ in *she* are ~ sounds⟩

pal·a·tal·ize \'pal-ət-ᵊl-ˌīz\ *vb* **-ized; -iz·ing** : to pronounce as or change into a palatal sound — **pal·a·tal·iza·tion** \ˌpal-ət-ᵊl-ə-'zā-shən\ *n*

pal·ate \'pal-ət\ *n* **1** : the roof of the mouth consisting of an anterior bony part and a posterior membranous fold **2** : TASTE

pa·la·tial \pə-'lā-shəl\ *adj* **1** : of, relating to, or being a palace **2** : MAGNIFICENT

pa·lat·i·nate \pə-'lat-ᵊn-ət\ *n* : the territory of a palatine

¹pal·a·tine \'pal-ə-ˌtīn\ *adj* **1** : of or relating to a palace : PALATIAL **2** : possessing royal privileges; *also* : of or relating to a palatine or a palatinate

²palatine *n* **1** : a high officer of an imperial palace **2** : a feudal lord having sovereign power within his domains

pa·la·ver \pə-'lav-ər, -'läv-\ *n* [Pg *palavra* word, speech, fr. LL *parabola* parable, speech] : a long parley : TALK — **palaver** *vb*

¹pale \'pāl\ *adj* **pal·er; pal·est 1** : deficient in color : WAN ⟨~ face⟩ **2** : lacking in brightness : DIM ⟨~ star⟩ **3** : light in color or shade ⟨~ blue⟩ — **pale·ness** *n*

²pale *vb* **paled; pal·ing** : to make or become pale

³pale *vb* **paled; pal·ing** : to enclose with or as if with pales : FENCE

⁴pale *n* **1** : a stake or picket of a fence **2** : an enclosed place; *also* : a district or territory within certain bounds or under a particular jurisdiction **3** : LIMITS, BOUNDS ⟨conduct beyond the ~⟩

pale·face \'pāl-ˌfās\ *n* : a white person

Pa·leo·cene \'pā-lē-ə-ˌsēn\ *adj* : of, relating to, or being the earliest epoch of the Tertiary — **Paleocene** *n*

pa·le·og·ra·phy \ˌpā-lē-'äg-rə-fē\ *n* : the study of ancient writings and inscriptions — **pa·le·og·ra·pher** \-fər\ *n*

Pa·leo·lith·ic \ˌpā-lē-ə-'lith-ik\ *adj* : of or relating to an early period of the Stone Age characterized by rough or chipped stone implements

pa·le·on·tol·o·gy \ˌpā-lē-ˌän-'täl-ə-jē\ *n* : a science dealing with the life of past geologic periods esp. as known from fossil remains — **pa·le·on·tol·o·gist** \-ˌän-'täl-ə-jəst, -ən-\ *n*

Pa·leo·zo·ic \ˌpā-lē-ə-'zō-ik\ *adj* : of, relating to, or being the era of geologic history between the Proterozoic and Mesozoic and extending from about 620 million years ago to about 230 million years ago — **Paleozoic** *n*

pal·ette \'pal-ət\ *n* : a thin often oval board on which a painter lays and mixes colors; *also* : the colors on a palette

pal·frey \'pȯl-frē\ *n, pl* **palfreys** *archaic* : a saddle horse; *esp* : one suitable for a woman

pa·limp·sest \'pal-əmp-ˌsest\ *n* [L *palimpsestus*, fr. Gk *palimpsēstos* scraped again] : writing material (as a parchment) used after the erasure of earlier writing

pal·in·drome \'pal-ən-ˌdrōm\ *n* : a word, verse, or sentence (as 'Able was I ere I saw Elba') that reads the same backward or forward

pal·ing \'pā-liŋ\ *n* **1** : a fence of pales **2** : material for pales **3** : PALE, PICKET

pal·in·ode \'pal-ə-ˌnōd\ *n* : an ode or song of recantation or retraction

pal·i·sade \ˌpal-ə-'sād\ *n* **1** : a high fence of stakes esp. for defense **2** : a line of steep cliffs

¹pall \'pȯl\ *vb* **1** : to lose in interest or attraction **2** : SATIATE, CLOY

²pall *n* **1** : a heavy cloth draped over a coffin **2** : something that produces a gloomy atmosphere

pal·la·di·um \pə-'lād-ē-əm\ *n* : a silver-white metallic chemical element used esp. as a catalyst and in alloys

pall·bear·er \'pȯl-ˌbar-ər\ *n* : a person who attends the coffin at a funeral

¹pal·let \'pal-ət\ *n* : a small, hard, or makeshift bed

²pallet *n* : a portable platform for transporting and storing materials

pal·li·ate \'pal-ē-ˌāt\ *vb* **-at·ed; -at·ing 1** : to ease without curing **2** : to cover by excuses and apologies — **pal·li·a·tion** \ˌpal-ē-'ā-shən\ *n* — **pal·li·a·tive** \'pal-ē-ˌāt-iv\ *adj or n*

pal·lid \'pal-əd\ *adj* : PALE, WAN

pal·lor \'pal-ər\ *n* : PALENESS

¹palm \'päm, 'pälm\ *n* [ME, fr. OE, fr. L *palma* palm of the hand, palm tree; fr. the resemblance of the tree's leaves to the outstretched hand] **1** : any of a family of mostly tropical trees, shrubs, or vines usu. with a tall unbranched stem topped by a crown of large leaves **2** : a symbol of victory; *also* : VICTORY

²palm *n* : the underpart of the hand between the fingers and the wrist

³palm *vb* **1** : to conceal in or with the hand ⟨~ a card⟩ **2** : to impose by fraud

pal·mate \'pal-ˌmāt, 'pä(l)m-ˌāt\ *also* **pal·mat·ed** \-ˌmāt-əd, -ˌāt-\ *adj* : resembling a hand with the fingers spread

palm·er \'päm-ər, 'päl-mər\ *n* : a person wearing two crossed palm leaves as a sign of having gone on a pilgrimage to the Holy Land

pal·met·to \pal-'met-ō\ *n, pl* **-tos** *or* **-toes** : any of several usu. small palms with fan-shaped leaves

palm·ist·ry \'päm-ə-strē, 'päl-mə-\ *n* : the practice of reading a person's character or future from the markings on the palms — **palm·ist** \'päm-əst, 'päl-məst\ *n*

Palm Sunday *n* : the Sunday preceding Easter and commemorating Christ's triumphal entry into Jerusalem

palmy \'päm-ē, 'päl-mē\ *adj* **palm·i·er; -est 1** : abounding in or bearing palms **2** : FLOURISHING, PROSPEROUS

pal·o·mi·no \ˌpal-ə-'mē-nō\ *n, pl* **-nos** [AmerSp, fr. Sp, like a dove, fr. L *palumbinus,* fr. *palumbes* wood pigeon] : a horse with a pale cream to golden coat and cream or white mane and tail

pal·pa·ble \'pal-pə-bəl\ *adj* **1** : capable of being touched or felt : TANGIBLE **2** : OBVIOUS, PLAIN **syn** perceptible, sensible, appreciable, tangible, detectable — **pal·pa·bly** \-blē\ *adv*

pal·pate \'pal-ˌpāt\ *vb* **pal·pat·ed; pal·pat·ing** : to examine by touch esp. medically — **pal·pa·tion** \pal-'pā-shən\ *n*

pal·pi·tate \'pal-pə-ˌtāt\ *vb* **-tat·ed; -tat·ing** : to beat strongly and irregularly : THROB, QUIVER — **pal·pi·ta·tion** \ˌpal-pə-'tā-shən\ *n*

pal·sy \'pȯl-zē\ *n, pl* **palsies 1** : PARALYSIS **2** : a condition marked by tremor — **pal·sied** \-zēd\ *adj*

pal·ter \'pȯl-tər\ *vb* **pal·tered; pal·ter·ing** \-t(ə-)riŋ\ **1** : to act insincerely : EQUIVOCATE **2** : HAGGLE

pal·try \'pȯl-trē\ *adj* **pal·tri·er; -est 1** : TRASHY ⟨a ~ pamphlet⟩ **2** : MEAN ⟨a ~ trick⟩ **3** : TRIVIAL ⟨~ excuses⟩ **4** : MEAGER, MEASLY ⟨a ~ sum⟩

pam *abbr* pamphlet

pam·pa \'pam-pə, 'päm-\ *n, pl* **pam·pas** \-pəz, -pəs\ : a grassy So. American plain

pam·per \'pam-pər\ *vb* **pam·pered; pam·per·ing** \-p(ə-)riŋ\ : to treat with excessive attention : INDULGE **syn** coddle, humor, baby, spoil

pam·phlet \'pam-flət\ *n* [ME *pamflet* unbound booklet, fr. *Pamphilus seu De Amore* Pamphilus or On Love, popular Latin love poem of the 12th cent.] : an unbound printed publication

pam·phle·teer \ˌpam-flə-'tir\ *n* : a writer of pamphlets attacking something or urging a cause

¹pan \'pan\ *n* **1** : a usu. broad, shallow, and open container for domestic use; *also* : something resembling such a container **2** : a basin or depression in land **3** : HARDPAN

²pan *vb* **panned; pan·ning 1** : to wash earth or gravel in a pan in searching for gold **2** : to criticize severely ⟨a new play *panned* by the critics⟩

Pan *abbr* Panama

pan·a·cea \ˌpan-ə-'sē-ə\ *n* : a remedy for all ills or difficulties

pa·nache \pə-'nash, -'näsh\ *n* [MF *pennache,* deriv. of LL *pinnaculum* small wing] **1** : an ornamental tuft (as of feathers) esp. on a helmet **2** : dash or flamboyance in style and action

pan·a·ma \'pan-ə-ˌmä, -ˌmȯ\ *n, often cap* : a handmade hat braided from strips of the leaves from a tropical American tree

pan·a·tela \ˌpan-ə-'tel-ə\ *n* [Sp, fr. AmerSp, a long thin biscuit, deriv. of L *panis* bread] : a long slender cigar with straight sides rounded off at the sealed end

pan·cake \'pan-ˌkāk\ *n* : a flat cake made of thin batter and fried on both sides

pan·chro·mat·ic \ˌpan-krō-'mat-ik\ *adj* : sensitive to light of all colors ⟨∼ film⟩

pan·cre·as \'paŋ-krē-əs, 'pan-\ *n* : a large gland that produces insulin and discharges enzymes into the intestine — **pan·cre·at·ic** \ˌpaŋ-krē-'at-ik, ˌpan-\ *adj*

pan·da \'pan-də\ *n* **1** : a long-tailed Himalayan mammal related to and resembling the racoon **2** : a large black-and-white mammal of western China usu. classified with the bears

pan·dem·ic \pan-'dem-ik\ *n* : a widespread outbreak of disease — **pandemic** *adj*

pan·de·mo·ni·um \ˌpan-də-'mō-nē-əm\ *n* : a wild uproar : TUMULT

¹pan·der \'pan-dər\ *n* **1** : a go-between in love intrigues **2** : PIMP **3** : someone who caters to or exploits others' desires or weaknesses

²pander *vb* **pan·dered; pan·der·ing** \-d(ə-)riŋ\ : to act as a pander

P and L *abbr* profit and loss

pan·dow·dy \pan-'daȯd-ē\ *n, pl* **-dies** : a deep-dish apple dessert spiced, sweetened, and covered with a crust

pane \'pān\ *n* : a sheet of glass (as in a door or window)

pan·e·gyr·ic \ˌpan-ə-'jir-ik\ *n* : a eulogistic oration or writing — **pan·e·gyr·ist** \-'jir-əst\ *n*

¹pan·el \'pan-ᵊl\ *n* **1** : a list of persons appointed for special duty ⟨a jury ∼⟩; *also* : a group of people taking part in a discussion or quiz program **2** : a sec-

tion of something (as a wall or door) often sunk below the level of the frame; *also* : a flat piece of construction material **3** : a flat piece of wood on which a picture is painted **4** : a board mounting instruments or controls

²panel *vb* **-eled** *or* **-elled; -el·ing** *or* **-el·ling** : to decorate with panels

pan·el·ing \'pan-ᵊl-iŋ\ *n* : decorative panels

pan·el·ist \'pan-ᵊl-əst\ *n* : a member of a discussion or quiz panel

panel truck *n* : a small motortruck with a fully enclosed body

pang \'paŋ\ *n* : a sudden sharp attack (as of pain)

¹pan·han·dle \'pan-ˌhan-dᵊl\ *n* : a narrow projection of a larger territory (as a state)

²panhandle *vb* **-dled; -dling** \-ˌhan-d(ə-)liŋ\ : to ask for money on the street — **pan·han·dler** \-d(ə-)lər\ *n*

¹pan·ic \'pan-ik\ *n* : a sudden overpowering fright **syn** terror, consternation, dismay, alarm, dread, fear — **pan·icky** \-i-kē\ *adj*

²panic *vb* **pan·icked** \-ikt\; **pan·ick·ing** : to affect or be affected with panic

pan·i·cle \'pan-i-kəl\ *n* : a compound loosely branched racemose flower cluster

pan·jan·drum \pan-'jan-drəm\ *n, pl* **-drums** *also* **-dra** \-drə\ : a powerful personage or pretentious official

pan·nier *also* **pan·ier** \'pan-yər\ *n* : a large basket esp. for bearing on the back

pan·o·ply \'pan-ə-plē\ *n, pl* **-plies 1** : a full suit of armor **2** : a protective covering **3** : an impressive array

pan·ora·ma \ˌpan-ə-'ram-ə, -'räm-\ *n* **1** : a picture unrolled before one's eyes **2** : a complete view in every direction — **pan·oram·ic** \-'ram-ik\ *adj*

pan out *vb* : TURN OUT; *esp* : SUCCEED

pan·sy \'pan-zē\ *n, pl* **pansies** [MF *pensée,* fr. *pensée* thought, fr. *penser* to think, fr. L *pensare* to ponder] : a low-growing garden herb related to the violet; *also* : its showy flower

¹pant \'pant\ *vb* [ME *panten,* fr. MF *pantaisier,* fr. (assumed) VL *phantasiare* to have hallucinations, fr. Gk *phantasioun,* fr. *phantasia* appearance, imagination] **1** : to breathe in a labored manner 2 : YEARN 3 : THROB

²pant *n* : a panting breath or sound

³pant *n* **1** : an outer garment covering each leg separately and usu. extending from the waist to the ankle — usu. used in pl. **2** *pl* : PANTIE

pan·ta·loons \ˌpant-ᵊl-'ünz\ *n pl* **1** : close-fitting trousers of the 19th century usu. having straps passing under the instep **2** : loose-fitting usu. shorter than ankle-length trousers

pan·the·ism \'pan-thē-ˌiz-əm\ *n* : a doctrine that equates God with the forces and laws of the universe — **pan·the·ist** \-əst\ *n* — **pan·the·is·tic** \ˌpan-thē-'is-tik\ *adj*

pan·the·on \'pan-thē-ˌän, -ən\ *n* **1** : a temple dedicated to all the gods **2** : a building serving as the burial place of or containing memorials to famous dead **3** : the gods of a people

pan·ther \'pan-thər\ *n, pl* **panthers** *also* **panther 1** : LEOPARD; *esp* : one of a black form **2** : COUGAR **3** : JAGUAR

pant·ie *or* **panty** \'pant-ē\ *n, pl* **pant·ies** : a woman's or child's undergarment covering the lower trunk and made with closed crotch — usu. used in pl.

pan·to·mime \'pant-ə-ˌmīm\ *n* **1** : a play in which the actors use no words **2** : expression of something by bodily or facial movements only — **pantomime** *vb* — **pan·to·mim·ic** \ˌpant-ə-'mim-ik\ *adj*

pan·try \'pan-trē\ *n, pl* **pantries** : a storage room for food or dishes

pant·suit \'pant-ˌsüt\ *n* : a woman's outfit consisting usu. of a long jacket and pants of the same material

panty hose *n pl* : a one-piece undergarment for women consisting of hosiery combined with a panty

panty·waist \'pant-ē-ˌwāst\ *n* : SISSY

pap \'pap\ *n* : soft food for infants or invalids

pa·pa \'päp-ə\ *n* : FATHER

pa·pa·cy \'pā-pə-sē\ *n, pl* **-cies 1** : the office of pope **2** : a succession of popes **3** : the term of a pope's reign **4** *cap* : the system of government of the Roman Catholic Church

pa·pa·in \pə-'pā-ən, -'pī-ən\ *n* : an enzyme in the juice of unripe papayas that is used esp. as a meat tenderizer and in medicine

pa·pal \'pā-pəl\ *adj* : of or relating to the pope or to the Roman Catholic Church

pa·paw *n* **1** \pə-'pȯ\ : PAPAYA **2** \'päp-ˌȯ\ : a No. American tree with yellow edible fruit; *also* : its fruit

pa·pa·ya \pə-'pī-ə\ *n* : a tropical American tree with large yellow black-seeded edible fruit; *also* : its fruit

pa·per \'pā-pər\ *n* [ME *papir*, fr. MF *papier*, fr. L *papyrus* papyrus, paper, fr. Gk *papyros* papyrus] **1** : a pliable substance made usu. of vegetable matter and used to write or print on, to wrap things in, or to cover walls; *also* : a single sheet of this substance **2** : a printed or written document **3** : NEWSPAPER **4** : WALLPAPER — **paper** *adj or vb* — **pa·pery** \'pā-p(ə-)rē\ *adj*

pa·per·back \-ˌbak\ *n* : a paper-covered book

pa·per·board \-ˌbōrd\ *n* : a material made from cellulose fiber (as wood pulp) like paper but usu. thicker

pa·per·hang·er \'pā-pər-ˌhaŋ-ər\ *n* : one that applies wallpaper — **pa·per·hang·ing** \-iŋ\ *n*

pa·per·weight \-ˌwāt\ *n* : an object used to hold down loose papers by its weight

pa·pier–mâ·ché \ˌpā-pər-mə-'shā, ˌpap-ˌyā-mə-, -ma-\ *n* [F, lit., chewed paper] : a molding material of waste paper and additives (as glue) — **papier–mâché** *adj*

pa·pil·la \pə-'pil-ə\ *n, pl* **pa·pil·lae** \-'pil-(ˌ)ē, -ˌī\ [L, nipple] : a small projecting bodily part — **pap·il·lary** \'pap-ə-ˌler-ē, pə-'pil-ə-rē\ *adj*

pa·pil·lote \ˌpäp-ē-'(y)ōt\ *n* [F] : a greased paper wrapper in which food is cooked

pa·poose \pa-'püs, pə-\ *n* : a young child of No. American Indian parents

pa·pri·ka \pə-'prē-kə, pa-\ *n* [Hung] : a mild red spice made from the fruit of some sweet peppers

Pap smear \'pap-\ *n* : a method for the early detection of cancer

Pap test \'pap-\ *n* : PAP SMEAR

pap·ule \'pap-yül\ *n* : a small solid usu. conical lesion of the skin — **pap·u·lar** \-yə-lər\ *adj*

pa·py·rus \pə-'pī-rəs\ *n, pl* **pa·py·rus·es** *or* **pa·py·ri** \-(ˌ)rē, -ˌrī\ **1** : a tall grassy Egyptian sedge **2** : paper made from papyrus pith

¹par \'pär\ *n* **1** : a stated value (as of a security) **2** : a common level : EQUALITY **3** : an accepted standard or normal condition **4** : the score standard set for each hole of a golf course — **par** *adj*

²par *abbr* **1** paragraph **2** parallel **3** parish

pa•ra \'pär-ə\ *n, pl* **paras** *or* **para** — see *dinar* at MONEY table

par•a•ble \'par-ə-bəl\ *n* : a simple story told to illustrate a moral truth

pa•rab•o•la \pə-'rab-ə-lə\ *n* : a plane curve generated by a point moving so that its distance from a fixed point is equal to its distance from a fixed line : a curve formed by the intersection of a cone with a plane parallel to its side — **par•a•bol•ic** \,par-ə-'bäl-ik\ *adj*

para•chute \'par-ə-,shüt\ *n* : a device for slowing the descent of a person or object through the air that consists of a usu. hemispherical canopy beneath which the person or object is suspended — **parachute** *vb* — **par•a•chut•ist** \-,shüt-əst\ *n*

¹pa•rade \pə-'rād\ *n* **1** : a pompous display : EXHIBITION ⟨a ~ of wealth⟩ **2** : MARCH, PROCESSION; *esp* : a ceremonial formation and march (as of troops) **3** : a place for strolling

²parade *vb* **pa•rad•ed; pa•rad•ing 1** : to march in a parade **2** : PROMENADE **3** : SHOW OFF **4** : MASQUERADE

par•a•digm \'par-ə-,dīm, -,dim\ *n* **1** : MODEL, PATTERN **2** : a systematic inflection of a verb or noun showing a complete conjugation or declension

par•a•dise \'par-ə-,dīs, -,dīz\ *n* [ME *paradis*, fr. OF, fr. LL *paradisus*, fr. Gk *paradeisos*, lit., enclosed park, of Iranian origin] **1** : HEAVEN **2** : a place or state of bliss

par•a•di•si•a•cal \,par-ə-də-'sī-ə-kəl\ *or* **par•a•dis•i•ac** \-'diz-ē-,ak, -'dis-\ *adj* : of, relating to, or resembling paradise

par•a•dox \'par-ə-,däks\ *n* : a statement that seems contrary to common sense and yet is perhaps true — **par•a•dox•i•cal** \,par-ə-'däk-si-kəl\ *adj* — **par•a•dox•i•cal•ly** \-k(ə-)lē\ *adv*

par•af•fin \'par-ə-fən\ *n* : a waxy substance used esp. for making candles and sealing foods

par•a•gon \'par-ə-,gän, -gən\ *n* : a model of perfection : PATTERN

¹para•graph \'par-ə-,graf\ *n* : a subdivision of a written composition that deals with one point or gives the words of one speaker; *also* : a character (as ¶) marking the beginning of a paragraph

²paragraph *vb* : to divide into paragraphs

par•a•keet \'par-ə-,kēt\ *n* : any of numerous usu. small slender parrots with a long graduated tail

para•le•gal \,par-ə-'lē-gəl\ *adj* : of, relating to, or being a paraprofessional who assists a lawyer — **paralegal** *n*

Par•a•li•pom•e•non \,par-ə-lə-'päm-ə-,nän\ *n* — see BIBLE table

par•al•lax \'par-ə-,laks\ *n* : the difference in apparent direction of an object as seen from two different points

¹par•al•lel \'par-ə-,lel\ *adj* [L *parallelus*, fr. Gk *parallēlos*, fr. *para* beside + *allēlōn* of one another, fr. *allos* . . . *allos* one . . . another, fr. *allos* other] **1** : lying or moving in the same direction but always the same distance apart **2** : similar in essential parts : LIKE — **par•al•lel•ism** \-,iz-əm\ *n*

²parallel *n* **1** : a parallel line, curve, or surface **2** : one of the imaginary circles on the earth's surface that parallel the equator and mark the latitude **3** : something essentially similar to another **4** : LIKENESS, SIMILARITY

³parallel *vb* **1** : COMPARE **2** : to correspond to **3** : to extend in a parallel direction with

par•al•lel•o•gram \,par-ə-'lel-ə-,gram\ *n* : a 4-sided geometrical figure with opposite sides equal and parallel

pa•ral•y•sis \pə-'ral-ə-səs\ *n, pl* **-y•ses** \-,sēz\ : loss of function and esp. of feeling or the power of voluntary motion — **par•a•lyt•ic** \,par-ə-'lit-ik\ *adj or n*

par•a•lyze \'par-ə-,līz\ *vb* **-lyzed; -lyz•ing 1** : to affect with paralysis **2** : to make powerless or inactive — **par•a•lyz•ing•ly** \-,lī-ziŋ-lē\ *adv*

par•a•me•cium \,par-ə-'mē-sh(ē-)əm, -sē-əm\ *n, pl* **-cia** \-sh(ē-)ə, -sē-ə\ *also* **-ci•ums** : any of a genus of slipper-shaped protozoans that move by cilia

para•med•i•cal \,par-ə-'med-i-kəl\ *adj* : concerned with supplementing the work of trained medical professionals — **para•med•ic** \,par-ə-'med-ik\ *n*

pa·ram·e·ter \pə-'ram-ət-ər\ *n* **1** : an arbitrary constant whose value characterizes a member of a system (as a family of curves) **2** : a physical property whose value determines the characteristics or behavior of a system **3** : a characteristic element : FACTOR — **para·met·ric** \ˌpar-ə-'me-trik\ *adj*

para·mil·i·tary \ˌpar-ə-'mil-ə-ˌter-ē\ *adj* : formed on a military pattern esp. as an auxiliary military force

par·a·mount \'par-ə-ˌmaunt\ *adj* : superior to all others : SUPREME **syn** preponderant, predominant, dominant, chief, sovereign

par·amour \'par-ə-ˌmur\ *n* : an illicit lover

para·noia \ˌpar-ə-'noi-ə\ *n* : a psychosis marked by delusions and irrational suspicion usu. without hallucinations — **par·a·noid** \'par-ə-ˌnoid\ *adj or n*

par·a·pet \'par-ə-pət, -ˌpet\ *n* **1** : a protecting rampart **2** : a low wall or railing (as at the edge of a bridge)

par·a·pher·na·lia \ˌpar-ə-fə(r)-'nāl-yə\ *n sing or pl* **1** : personal belongings **2** : EQUIPMENT, APPARATUS

para·phrase \'par-ə-ˌfrāz\ *n* : a restatement of a text giving the meaning in different words — **paraphrase** *vb*

para·ple·gia \ˌpar-ə-'plē-j(ē-)ə\ *n* : paralysis of the lower trunk and legs — **para·ple·gic** \-jik\ *adj or n*

para·pro·fes·sion·al \-prə-'fesh-(ə-)nəl\ *n* : a trained aide who assists a professional

para·psy·chol·o·gy \ˌpar-ə-sī-'käl-ə-jē\ *n* : a branch of study involving the investigation of telepathy and related subjects — **para·psy·chol·o·gist** \-jəst\ *n*

par·a·site \'par-ə-ˌsīt\ *n* [MF, fr. L *parasitus,* fr. Gk *parasitos,* fr. *para-* beside + *sitos* grain, food] **1** : a plant or animal living in or on another organism usu. to its harm **2** : one depending on another and not making adequate return — **par·a·sit·ic** \ˌpar-ə-'sit-ik\ *adj* — **par·a·sit·ism** \'par-ə-sə-ˌtiz-əm, -ˌsīt-ˌiz-\ *n* — **par·a·sit·ize** \-sə-ˌtīz\ *vb*

par·a·si·tol·o·gy \ˌpar-ə-sə-'täl-ə-jē\ *n* : a branch of biology dealing with parasites and parasitism esp. among animals — **par·a·si·tol·o·gist** \-jəst\ *n*

para·sol \'par-ə-ˌsol\ *n* [F, fr. It *para-* sole, fr. *parare* to shield + *sole* sun, fr. L *sol*] : a lightweight umbrella used as a shield against the sun

para·sym·pa·thet·ic nervous system \ˌpar-ə-ˌsim-pə-'thet-ik-\ *n* : the part of the autonomic nervous system that tends to induce secretion, to increase the tone and contractility of smooth muscle, and to cause the dilatation of blood vessels

para·thi·on \ˌpar-ə-'thī-ən, -ˌän\ *n* : an extremely toxic insecticide

para·thy·roid \-'thī-ˌroid\ *n* : PARATHYROID GLAND — **parathyroid** *adj*

parathyroid gland *n* : any of usu. four small endocrine glands that are adjacent to or embedded in the thyroid gland and produce a hormone concerned with calcium metabolism

para·troop·er \'par-ə-ˌtrü-pər\ *n* : a member of the paratroops

para·troops \-ˌtrüps\ *n pl* : troops trained to parachute from an airplane

para·ty·phoid \ˌpar-ə-'tī-ˌfoid, -tī-'foid\ *n* : a food poisoning resembling typhoid fever

par·boil \'pär-ˌboil\ *vb* : to boil briefly

¹**par·cel** \'pär-səl\ *n* **1** : a tract or plot of land **2** : COLLECTION, LOT **3** : a wrapped bundle : PACKAGE

²**parcel** *vb* **-celed** *or* **-celled; -cel·ing** *or* **-cel·ling** \'pär-s(ə-)liŋ\ : to divide into portions

parcel post *n* **1** : a mail service handling parcels **2** : packages handled by parcel post

parch \'pärch\ *vb* **1** : to toast under dry heat **2** : to shrivel with heat

parch·ment \'pärch-mənt\ *n* : the skin of an animal prepared for writing on; *also* : a writing on such material

pard \'pärd\ *n* : LEOPARD

¹**par·don** \'pärd-ᵊn\ *n* : excuse of an offense without penalty; *esp* : an official release from legal punishment

²**pardon** *vb* **par·doned; par·don·ing** \'pärd-(ᵊ-)niŋ\ : to free from penalty : EXCUSE, FORGIVE — **par·don·able** \'pärd-(ᵊ-)nə-bəl\ *adj*

par·don·er \'pärd-(ᵊ-)nər\ *n* **1** : a medieval preacher delegated to raise money for religious works by soliciting offerings and granting indulgences **2** : one that pardons

pare \'paər\ *vb* **pared; par·ing** **1** : to trim or shave off an outside part (as the skin or rind) of ⟨∼ an apple⟩ **2** : to reduce as if by paring ⟨∼ expenses⟩ — **par·er** *n*

par·e·go·ric \ˌpar-ə-ˈgȯr-ik\ *n* : an alcoholic preparation of opium and camphor

par·ent \ˈpar-ənt\ *n* **1** : one that begets or brings forth offspring : FATHER, MOTHER **2** : SOURCE, ORIGIN — **par·ent·age** \-ij\ *n* — **pa·ren·tal** \pə-ˈrent-ᵊl\ *adj* — **par·ent·hood** *n*

pa·ren·the·sis \pə-ˈren-thə-səs\ *n, pl* **-the·ses** \-ˌsēz\ **1** : a word, phrase, or sentence inserted in a passage to explain or modify the thought **2** : one of a pair of punctuation marks () used esp. to enclose parenthetic matter — **par·en·thet·ic** \ˌpar-ən-ˈthet-ik\ *or* **par·en·thet·i·cal** \-i-kəl\ *adj* — **par·en·thet·i·cal·ly** \-k(ə-)lē\ *adv*

pa·ren·the·size \pə-ˈren-thə-ˌsīz\ *vb* **-sized; -siz·ing** : to make a parenthesis of

par·ent·ing \ˈpar-ənt-iŋ, ˈper-\ *n* : the raising of a child by its parents

pa·re·sis \pə-ˈrē-səs, ˈpar-ə-\ *n, pl* **pa·re·ses** \-ˌsēz\ : a usu. incomplete paralysis; *also* : insanity caused by syphilitic alteration of the brain that leads to dementia and paralysis

par ex·cel·lence \ˌpär-ˌek-sə-ˈläⁿs\ *adj* [F, lit., by excellence] : being the best of a kind : PREEMINENT

par·fait \pär-ˈfā\ *n* [F, lit., something perfect, fr. *parfait* perfect, fr. L *perfectus*] **1** : a flavored custard containing whipped cream and a syrup frozen without stirring **2** : a cold dessert made of layers of fruit, syrup, ice cream, and whipped cream

pa·ri·ah \pə-ˈrī-ə\ *n* : OUTCAST

pa·ri·etal \pə-ˈrī-ət-ᵊl\ *adj* **1** : of, relating to, or forming the walls of an anatomical structure **2** : of or relating to college living or its regulation

pari–mu·tu·el \ˌpar-i-ˈmyü-chə(-wə)l\ *n* : a betting system in which winners share the total stakes minus a percentage for the management

par·ing \ˈpar-iŋ\ *n* : something pared off ⟨potato ∼s⟩

pa·ri pas·su \ˌpar-i-ˈpas-ü\ *adv or adj* [L, with equal step] : at an equal rate or pace

Par·is green \ˌpar-əs-\ *n* : a poisonous bright green powder used as a pigment and as an insecticide

par·ish \ˈpar-ish\ *n* **1** : a church district in the care of one pastor; *also* : the residents of such an area **2** : a local church community **3** : a civil division of the state of Louisiana : COUNTY

pa·rish·io·ner \pə-ˈrish-(ə-)nər\ *n* : a member or resident of a parish

par·i·ty \ˈpar-ət-ē\ *n, pl* **-ties** : EQUALITY, EQUIVALENCE

¹park \ˈpärk\ *n* **1** : a tract of ground kept as a game preserve or recreation area **2** : a level valley between mountain ranges **3** : a place where vehicles (as automobiles) are parked **4** : an enclosed stadium used esp. for ball games

²park *vb* **1** : to leave a vehicle temporarily (as in a parking lot or garage) **2** : to set and leave temporarily

par·ka \ˈpär-kə\ *n* : a very warm jacket with a hood

Par·kin·son's disease \ˈpär-kən-sənz-\ *n* : a chronic progressive nervous disease of later life that is marked by tremor and weakness of resting muscles and by a peculiar gait

Par·kin·son's Law *n* **1** : an observation in office organization: the number of subordinates increases at a fixed rate regardless of the amount of work produced **2** : an observation in office organization: work expands so as to fill the time available for its completion

park·way \ˈpärk-ˌwā\ *n* : a broad landscaped thoroughfare

par·lance \ˈpär-ləns\ *n* **1** : SPEECH **2** : manner of speaking ⟨military ∼⟩

¹par·lay \ˈpär-ˌlā, -lē\ *vb* : to increase or change into something of much greater value

²parlay *n* : a series of bets in which the original stake plus its winnings are risked on successive wagers

par·ley \ˈpär-lē\ *n, pl* **parleys** : a conference usu. over matters in dispute : DISCUSSION — **parley** *vb*

par·lia·ment \ˈpär-lə-mənt\ *n* **1** : a formal governmental conference **2** *cap* : an assembly that constitutes the supreme legislative body of a country (as the United Kingdom) — **par·lia·men·ta·ry** \ˌpär-lə-ˈmen-t(ə-)rē\ *adj*

par·lia·men·tar·i·an \ˌpär-lə-ˌmen-ˈter-ē-ən\ *n* **1** *often cap* : an adherent of the parliament in opposition to the king during the English Civil War **2** : an expert in parliamentary procedure

par·lor \'pär-lər\ *n* **1** : a room for conversation or the reception of guests **2** : a place of business ⟨beauty ∼⟩

par·lour \'pär-lər\ *chiefly Brit* var of PARLOR

par·lous \'pär-ləs\ *adj* : full of danger or risk : PRECARIOUS ⟨∼ state of a country's finances⟩ — **par·lous·ly** *adv*

Par·me·san \'pär-mə-ˌzän, -ˌzan\ *n* : a hard dry cheese with a sharp flavor

par·mi·gia·na \ˌpär-mi-'jän-ə, ˌpär-mi-'zhän\ *or* **par·mi·gia·no** \-'jän-(ˌ)ō\ *adj* : made or covered with Parmesan cheese ⟨veal ∼⟩

pa·ro·chi·al \pə-'rō-kē-əl\ *adj* **1** : of or relating to a church parish **2** : limited in scope : NARROW, PROVINCIAL — **pa·ro·chi·al·ism** \-ə-ˌliz-əm\ *n*

parochial school *n* : a school maintained by a religious body

par·o·dy \'par-əd-ē\ *n, pl* **-dies** [L *parodia*, fr. Gk *parōidia*, fr. *para-* beside + *aidein* to sing] : a humorous or satirical imitation — **parody** *vb*

pa·role \pə-'rōl\ *n* : a conditional release of a prisoner before his sentence expires — **parole** *vb* — **pa·rol·ee** \-ˌrō-'lē, -'rō-ˌlē\ *n*

par·ox·ysm \'par-ək-ˌsiz-əm, pə-'räk-\ *n* : a sudden sharp attack (as of pain or coughing) : SPASM **syn** convulsion, fit — **par·ox·ys·mal** \ˌpar-ək-'siz-məl, pə-ˌräk-\ *adj*

par·quet \'pär-ˌkā, pär-'kā\ *n* [F] **1** : a flooring of parquetry **2** : the lower floor of a theater; *esp* : the forward part of the orchestra

par·que·try \'pär-kə-trē\ *n, pl* **-tries** : fine woodwork inlaid in patterns

par·ra·keet var of PARAKEET

par·ri·cide \'par-ə-ˌsīd\ *n* **1** : one that murders his or her father, mother, or a close relative **2** : the act of a parricide

par·rot \'par-ət\ *n* : any of numerous bright-colored tropical birds that have a stout hooked bill

parrot fever *n* : an infectious disease of birds that is marked by diarrhea and wasting and is transmissible to man

par·ry \'par-ē\ *vb* **par·ried; par·ry·ing 1** : to ward off a weapon or blow **2** : to evade esp. by an adroit answer — **parry** *n*

parse \'pärs *also* 'pärz\ *vb* **parsed; pars·ing** : to give a grammatical description of a word or a group of words

par·sec \'pär-ˌsek\ *n* : a unit of measure for interstellar space equal to 3.26 light-years or 19.2 trillion miles

par·si·mo·ny \'pär-sə-ˌmō-nē\ *n* : extreme or excessive frugality — **par·si·mo·ni·ous** \ˌpär-sə-'mō-nē-əs\ *adj* — **par·si·mo·ni·ous·ly** *adv*

pars·ley \'pär-slē\ *n* : a garden plant with finely divided leaves used as a seasoning or garnish

pars·nip \'pär-snəp\ *n* : a garden plant with a long edible root; *also* : this root

par·son \'pärs-ᵊn\ *n* [ME *persone*, fr. OF, fr. ML *persona*, lit., person, fr. L] : a usu. Protestant clergyman

par·son·age \'pärs-(ᵊ-)nij\ *n* : a house provided by a church for its pastor

¹part \'pärt\ *n* **1** : a division or portion of a whole **2** : the melody or score for a particular voice or instrument ⟨the alto ∼⟩ **3** : a spare piece for a machine **4** : DUTY, FUNCTION **5** : one of the sides in a dispute ⟨took his friend's ∼⟩ **6** : ROLE; *also* : an actor's lines in a play **7** *pl* : TALENTS, ABILITY **8** : the line where one's hair divides (as in combing)

²part *vb* **1** : to take leave of someone **2** : to divide or break into parts : SEPARATE **3** : to go away : DEPART; *also* : DIE **4** : to give up possession ⟨∼ed with her jewels⟩ **5** : APPORTION, SHARE

³part *abbr* **1** participial; participle **2** particular

par·take \pär-'tāk, pər-\ *vb* **-took** \-'tůk\; **-tak·en** \-'tā-kən\; **-tak·ing 1** : to have a share or part **2** : to take a portion (as of food) — **par·tak·er** *n*

par·terre \pär-'tear\ *n* [F, fr. MF, fr. *par terre* on the ground] **1** : an ornamental arrangement of flower beds **2** : the part of a theater floor behind the orchestra

par·the·no·gen·e·sis \ˌpär-thə-nō-'jen-ə-səs\ *n* [NL, fr. Gk *parthenos* virgin + L *genesis* genesis] : development of a new individual from an unfertilized egg — **par·the·no·ge·net·ic** \-jə-'net-ik\ *adj*

par·tial \'pär-shəl\ *adj* **1** : favoring one party over the other : BIASED **2**

: markedly or foolishly fond — used with *to* **3** : not total or general : affecting a part only — **par·tial·i·ty** \ˌpärsh-(ē-)ˈal-ət-ē\ *n* — **par·tial·ly** \ˈpärsh-(ə-)lē\ *adv*

par·tic·i·pate \pər-ˈtis-ə-ˌpāt, pär-\ *vb* **-pat·ed; -pat·ing 1** : to take part in something ⟨∼ in a game⟩ **2** : SHARE — **par·tic·i·pant** \-pənt\ *adj or n* — **par·tic·i·pa·tion** \-ˌtis-ə-ˈpā-shən\ *n* — **par·tic·i·pa·tor** \-ˈtis-ə-ˌpāt-ər\ *n* — **par·tic·i·pa·to·ry** \-ˈtis-ə-pə-ˌtōr-ē\ *adj*

par·ti·ci·ple \ˈpärt-ə-ˌsip-əl\ *n* : a word having the characteristics of both verb and adjective — **par·ti·cip·i·al** \ˌpärt-ə-ˈsip-ē-əl\ *adj*

par·ti·cle \ˈpärt-i-kəl\ *n* **1** : a very small bit of matter **2** : ELEMENTARY PARTICLE **3** : a unit of speech (as an article, preposition, or conjunction) expressing some general aspect of meaning or some connective or limiting relation

par·ti·cle·board \-ˌbōrd\ *n* : a board made of very small pieces of wood bonded together

par·ti–col·or \ˌpärt-ē-ˈkəl-ər\ *or* **par·ti–col·ored** \-ərd\ *adj* : showing different colors or tints; *esp* : having patches of two or more colors

¹**par·tic·u·lar** \pə(r)-ˈtik-yə-lər\ *adj* **1** : of or relating to a specific person or thing ⟨the laws of a ∼ state⟩ **2** : DISTINCTIVE, SPECIAL ⟨the ∼ point of his talk⟩ **3** : SEPARATE, INDIVIDUAL ⟨each ∼ hair⟩ **4** : attentive to details : PRECISE **5** : hard to please : EXACTING **syn** single, sole, unique, lone, solitary — **par·tic·u·lar·i·ty** \-ˌtik-yə-ˈlar-ət-ē\ *n* — **par·tic·u·lar·ly** \-ˈtik-yə-lər-lē\ *adv*

²**particular** *n* : an individual fact or detail

par·tic·u·lar·ize \pə(r)-ˈtik-yə-lə-ˌrīz\ *vb* **-ized; -iz·ing 1** : to state in detail : SPECIFY **2** : to go into details

par·tic·u·late \pər-ˈtik-yə-lət, pär-, -ˌlāt\ *adj* : relating to or existing as minute separate particles

¹**part·ing** \ˈpärt-iŋ\ *n* **1** : SEPARATION, DIVISION **2** : the action of leaving one another ⟨lovers' ∼⟩ **3** : a place of separation or divergence

²**parting** *adj* : given, taken, or performed at parting ⟨a ∼ kiss⟩

par·ti·san *or* **par·ti·zan** \ˈpärt-ə-zən, -sən\ *n* **1** : one that takes the part of

another : ADHERENT **2** : GUERRILLA — **partisan** *adj* — **par·ti·san·ship** *n*

par·tite \ˈpär-ˌtīt\ *adj* : divided into a usu. specified number of parts

par·ti·tion \pər-ˈtish-ən, pär-\ *n* **1** : DIVISION **2** : something that divides or separates; *esp* : an interior wall dividing one part of a house from another — **partition** *vb*

par·ti·tive \ˈpärt-ət-iv\ *adj* : of, relating to, or denoting a part ⟨a ∼ construction⟩

part·ly \ˈpärt-lē\ *adv* : in part : in some measure or degree

part·ner \ˈpärt-nər\ *n* **1** : ASSOCIATE, COLLEAGUE **2** : either of two persons who dance together **3** : one who plays on the same team with another **4** : HUSBAND, WIFE **5** : one of two or more persons contractually associated as joint principals in a business — **part·ner·ship** *n*

part of speech : a traditional class of words distinguished according to the kind of idea denoted and the function performed in a sentence

par·tridge \ˈpär-trij\ *n, pl* **partridge** *or* **par·tridg·es** : any of various stout≠bodied game birds

part–song \ˈpärt-ˌsȯŋ\ *n* : a song with two or more voice parts

part–time \-ˈtīm\ *adj or adv* : involving or working less than a full or regular schedule

par·tu·ri·tion \ˌpärt-ə-ˈrish-ən, ˌpär-chə-, ˌpär-tyu̇-\ *n* : CHILDBIRTH

part·way \ˈpärt-ˈwā\ *adv* : to some extent : PARTLY

par·ty \ˈpärt-ē\ *n, pl* **parties 1** : a person or group taking one side of a question; *esp* : a group of persons organized for the purpose of directing the policies of a government **2** : a person or group concerned in an action or affair : PARTICIPANT **3** : a group of persons detailed for a common task **4** : a social gathering

par·ve·nu \ˈpär-və-ˌn(y)ü\ *n* [F, fr. pp. of *parvenir* to arrive, fr. L *pervenire*, fr. *per* through + *venire* to come] : one who has recently or suddenly risen to wealth or power and has not yet secured the social position associated with it

pas \ˈpä\ *n, pl* **pas** \ˈpä(z)\ *n* : a dance step or combination of steps

pas•cal \pas-'kal\ *n* : a unit of pressure in the metric system equal to one newton per square meter

pas•chal \'pas-kəl\ *adj* [deriv. of Heb *pesaḥ* Passover] : of, relating to, appropriate for, or used during Passover or Easter ceremonies

pa•sha \'päsh-ə, 'pash-; pə-'shä\ *n* : a man (as formerly a governor in Turkey) of high rank

¹**pass** \'pas\ *vb* **1** : MOVE, PROCEED **2** : to go away; *also* : DIE **3** : to move past, beyond, or over **4** : to allow to elapse : SPEND **5** : to go or make way through **6** : to go or allow to go unchallenged **7** : to undergo transfer **8** : to render a legal judgment **9** : OCCUR **10** : to secure the approval of (as a legislature) **11** : to go or cause to go through an inspection, test, or course of study successfully **12** : to be regarded **13** : CIRCULATE **14** : VOID **15** : to transfer the ball or puck to another player **16** : to decline to bid or bet on one's hand in a card game **17** : to permit to reach first base by a base on balls — **pass•er** *n*

²**pass** *n* : a gap in a mountain range

³**pass** *n* **1** : the act or an instance of passing **2** : REALIZATION, ACCOMPLISHMENT **3** : a state of affairs **4** : a written authorization to leave, enter, or move about freely **5** : a transfer of a ball or puck from one player to another **6** : BASE ON BALLS **7** : EFFORT, TRY **8** : a sexually inviting gesture or approach

⁴**pass** *abbr* **1** passenger **2** passive

pass•able \'pas-ə-bəl\ *adj* **1** : capable of being passed or traveled on **2** : just good enough : TOLERABLE — **pass•ably** \-blē\ *adv*

pas•sage \'pas-ij\ *n* **1** : the action or process of passing **2** : a means (as a road or corridor) of passing **3** : a voyage esp. by sea or air **4** : a right or permission to pass **5** : ENACTMENT **6** : a mutual act (as an exchange of blows) **7** : a usu. brief portion or section (as of a book)

pas•sage•way \-ˌwā\ *n* : a way that allows passage

pass•book \'pas-ˌbu̇k\ *n* : BANKBOOK

pas•sé \pa-'sā\ *adj* **1** : past one's prime **2** : not up-to-date : OUTMODED

pas•sel \'pas-əl\ *n* : a large number

pas•sen•ger \'pas-ᵊn-jər\ *n* : a traveler in a public or private conveyance

passe–par•tout \ˌpas-pər-'tü\ *n* [F] : something that passes or enables one to pass everywhere

pass•er•by \'pas-ər-ˌbī\ *n, pl* **pass•ers•by** \-ərz-\ : one who passes by

pas•ser•ine \'pas-ə-ˌrīn\ *adj* : of or relating to the large order of birds comprising singing birds that perch

pas•sim \'pas-əm\ *adv* [L, fr. *passus* scattered, fr. pp. of *pandere* to spread] : here and there : THROUGHOUT

pass•ing \'pas-iŋ\ *n* : the act of one that passes or causes to pass; *esp* : DEATH

pas•sion \'pash-ən\ *n* **1** *often cap* : the sufferings of Christ between the night of the Last Supper and his death **2** : strong feeling; *also pl* : the emotions as distinguished from reason **3** : RAGE, ANGER **4** : LOVE; *also* : an object of affection or enthusiasm **5** : sexual desire — **pas•sion•ate** \'pash-(ə-)nət\ *adj* — **pas•sion•ate•ly** *adv* — **pas•sion•less** *adj*

pas•sion•flow•er \'pash-ən-ˌflau̇(-ə)r\ *n* [trans. of L *flos passionis;* fr. the fancied resemblance of parts of the flower to the instruments of Christ's crucifixion] : any of a genus of chiefly tropical woody climbing vines or erect herbs with showy flowers and pulpy often edible berries

passion fruit *n* : the edible fruit of a passionflower

pas•sive \'pas-iv\ *adj* **1** : not active : acted upon **2** : asserting that the grammatical subject is subjected to or affected by the action represented by the verb ⟨∼ voice⟩ **3** : making use of the sun's heat usu. without the aid of mechanical devices **4** : SUBMISSIVE, PATIENT — **passive** *n* — **pas•sive•ly** *adv* — **pas•siv•i•ty** \pa-'siv-ət-ē\ *n*

pass•key \'pas-ˌkē\ *n* : a key for opening two or more locks

pass out *vb* : to lose consciousness

Pass•over \'pas-ˌō-vər\ *n* [fr. the exemption of the Israelites from the slaughter of the firstborn in Egypt (Exod 12:23–27)] : a Jewish holiday celebrated in March or April in commemoration of the Hebrews' liberation from slavery in Egypt

pass•port \'pas-ˌpōrt\ *n* : an official

document issued by a country upon request to a citizen requesting protection during travel abroad

pass up *vb* : DECLINE, REJECT

pass·word \'pas-₁wərd\ *n* **1** : a word or phrase that must be spoken by a person before he is allowed to pass a guard **2** : a sequence of characters required for access to a computer system

¹past \'past\ *adj* **1** : AGO ⟨10 years ∼⟩ **2** : just gone or elapsed ⟨the ∼ month⟩ **3** : having existed or taken place in a period before the present : BYGONE **4** : of, relating to, or constituting a verb tense that expresses time gone by

²past *prep or adv* : BEYOND

³past *n* **1** : time gone by **2** : something that happened or was done in a former time **3** : the past tense; *also* : a verb form in it **4** : a secret past life

pas·ta \'päs-tə\ *n* [It] **1** : a paste in processed form (as spaghetti) or in the form of fresh dough (as ravioli) **2** : a dish of cooked pasta

¹paste \'pāst\ *n* **1** : DOUGH **2** : a smooth food product made by evaporation or grinding ⟨almond ∼⟩ **3** : a shaped dough (as spaghetti or ravioli) **4** : a preparation (as of flour and water) for sticking things together **5** : a brilliant glass of high lead content used in imitation gems

²paste *vb* **past·ed; past·ing** : to cause to adhere by paste : STICK

paste·board \'pās(t)-₁bōrd\ *n* : a stiff material made of sheets of paper pasted together; *also* : PAPERBOARD

¹pas·tel \pas-'tel\ *n* **1** : a paste made of powdered pigment; *also* : a crayon of such paste **2** : a drawing in pastel **3** : a pale or light color

²pastel *adj* **1** : of or relating to a pastel **2** : pale and light in color

pas·tern \'pas-tərn\ *n* : the part of a horse's foot extending from the fetlock to the top of the hoof

pas·teur·i·za·tion \₁pas-chə-rə-'zā-shən, ₁pas-tə-\ *n* : partial sterilization of a substance (as milk) by heat or radiation — **pas·teur·ize** \'pas-chə-₁rīz, 'pas-tə-\ *vb* — **pas·teur·iz·er** *n*

pas·tiche \pas-'tēsh\ *n* : a composition (as in literature or music) made up of selections from different works

pas·tille \pas-'tēl\ *n* **1** : a small mass of

aromatic paste for fumigating or scenting the air of a room **2** : an aromatic or medicated lozenge

pas·time \'pas-₁tīm\ *n* : DIVERSION

pas·tor \'pas-tər\ *n* [ME *pastour*, fr. OF, fr. L *pastor*, herdsman, fr. *pastus*, pp. of *pascere* to feed] : a clergyman serving a local church or parish — **pas·tor·ate** \-t(ə-)rət\ *n*

¹pas·to·ral \'pas-t(ə-)rəl\ *adj* **1** : of or relating to shepherds or to rural life **2** : of or relating to spiritual guidance esp. of a congregation **3** : of or relating to the pastor of a church

²pastoral \'pas-t(ə-)rəl\ *n* : a literary work dealing with shepherds or rural life

pas·to·rale \₁pas-tə-'räl, -'ral\ *n* [It] : a musical composition having a pastoral theme

past participle *n* : a participle that typically expresses completed action, that is one of the principal parts of the verb, and that is used in the formation of perfect tenses in the active voice and of all tenses in the passive voice

pas·tra·mi *also* **pas·tro·mi** \pə-'sträm-ē\ *n* [Yiddish] : a highly seasoned smoked beef prepared esp. from shoulder cuts

pas·try \'pā-strē\ *n, pl* **pastries** : sweet baked goods made of dough or with a crust made of enriched dough

pas·tur·age \'pas-chə-rij\ *n* : PASTURE

¹pas·ture \'pas-chər\ *n* **1** : plants (as grass) for the feeding of grazing livestock **2** : land or a plot of land used for grazing

²pasture *vb* **pas·tured; pas·tur·ing 1** : GRAZE **2** : to use as pasture

pasty \'pā-stē\ *adj* **past·i·er; -est** : resembling paste; *esp* : pallid and unhealthy in appearance

¹pat \'pat\ *n* **1** : a light tap esp. with the hand or a flat instrument; *also* : the sound made by it **2** : something (as butter) shaped into a small flat usu. square individual portion

²pat *adv* : in a pat manner : APTLY, PERFECTLY

³pat *vb* **pat·ted; pat·ting 1** : to strike lightly with a flat instrument **2** : to flatten, smooth, or put into place or shape with a pat **3** : to tap gently or lovingly with the hand

⁴pat *adj* **1** : exactly suited to the occa-

sion **2** : memorized exactly **3** : UN-
YIELDING
⁵**pat** *abbr* patent
pa•ta•ca \pə-'täk-ə\ *n* — see MONEY table
¹**patch** \'pach\ *n* **1** : a piece used to cover a torn or worn place; *also* : one
worn on a garment as an ornament or
insignia **2** : a small area distinct from
that about it **3** : a shield worn over the
socket of an injured or missing eye
²**patch** *vb* **1** : to mend or cover with a
patch **2** : to make of fragments **3** : to
repair usu. in hasty fashion
patch test *n* : a test for allergic sensitivity made by applying to the unbroken
skin small pads soaked with the aller-
gen to be tested
patch•work \'pach-ˌwərk\ *n* : something made of pieces of different materials, shapes, or colors
pate \'pāt\ *n* : HEAD; *esp* : the crown of
the head
pâ•té \pä-'tā\ *n* [F] **1** : a meat or fish pie
or patty **2** : a spread of finely mashed
seasoned and spiced meat
pa•tel•la \pə-'tel-ə\ *n, pl* **-lae** \-'tel-(ˌ)ē,
-ˌī\ *or* **-las** [L] : KNEECAP
pat•en \'pat-ᵊn\ *n* **1** : PLATE; *esp* : one of
precious metal for the eucharistic
bread **2** : a thin disk
¹**pa•tent** *1 & 4 are* 'pat-ᵊnt, *Brit also*
'pāt-, *2 & 3 are* 'pat-ᵊnt, 'pāt-\ *adj* **1**
: open to public inspection — used
chiefly in the phrase *letters patent* **2**
: free from obstruction **3** : EVIDENT,
OBVIOUS **4** : protected by a patent **syn**
manifest, distinct, apparent, palpable,
plain, clear — **pat•ent•ly** *adv*
²**pat•ent** \'pat-ᵊnt, *Brit also* 'pāt-\ *n* **1** : an
official document conferring a right or
privilege **2** : a document securing to
an inventor for a term of years exclusive right to his invention **3** : something patented — **pat•en•tee** \ˌpat-
ᵊn-'tē, *Brit also* ˌpāt-\ *n*
³**pat•ent** *vb* : to secure by patent
pa•ter•fa•mil•i•as \ˌpāt-ər-fə-'mil-ē-əs\
n, pl **pa•tres•fa•mil•i•as** \ˌpā-ˌtrēz-\ [L]
: the father of a family : the male head
of a household
pa•ter•nal \pə-'tərn-ᵊl\ *adj* **1** : FATHERLY
2 : related through or inherited or
derived from a father — **pa•ter•nal•ly**
\-ē\ *adv*
pa•ter•nal•ism \-ˌiz-əm\ *n* : a system un-

der which an authority treats those
under its control paternally (as by
regulating their conduct and supplying their needs)
pa•ter•ni•ty \pə-'tər-nət-ē\ *n* **1** : FATHER-
HOOD **2** : descent from a father
¹**path** \'path, 'pȧth\ *n, pl* **paths** \'pathz,
'paths, 'pȧthz, 'pȧths\ **1** : a trodden
way **2** : ROUTE, COURSE — **path•less** *adj*
²**path** *or* **pathol** *abbr* pathology
pa•thet•ic \pə-'thet-ik\ *adj* : evoking
tenderness, pity, or sorrow **syn** pitiful,
piteous, pitiable, poor — **pa•thet•i•cal-**
ly \-i-k(ə-)lē\ *adv*
path•find•er \'path-ˌfīn-dər, 'pȧth-\ *n*
: one that discovers a way; *esp* : one
that explores untraveled regions to
mark out a new route
patho•gen \'path-ə-jən\ *n* : a specific
cause (as a bacterium or virus) of disease — **patho•gen•ic** \ˌpath-ə-'jen-ik\
adj — **patho•ge•nic•i•ty** \-jə-'nis-ət-ē\ *n*
pa•thol•o•gy \pə-'thäl-ə-jē\ *n, pl* **-gies 1**
: the study of the essential nature of
disease **2** : the abnormality of structure and function characteristic of a
disease — **path•o•log•i•cal** \ˌpath-ə-
'läj-i-kəl\ *adj* — **pa•thol•o•gist**
\pə-'thäl-ə-jəst\ *n*
pa•thos \'pā-ˌthäs\ *n* : an element in experience or artistic representation
evoking pity or compassion
path•way \'path-ˌwā, 'pȧth-\ *n* : PATH
pa•tience \'pā-shəns\ *n* **1** : the capacity,
habit, or fact of being patient **2** *chiefly*
Brit : SOLITAIRE 2
¹**pa•tient** \'pā-shənt\ *adj* **1** : bearing pain
or trials without complaint **2** : showing self-control : CALM **3** : STEADFAST,
PERSEVERING — **pa•tient•ly** *adv*
²**patient** *n* : a person under medical care
pa•ti•na \'pat-ə-nə, pə-'tē-nə\ *n, pl* **pa-**
ti•nas \-nəz\ *or* **pa•ti•nae** \'pat-ə-ˌnē,
-ˌnī\ : a green film formed on copper
and bronze by exposure to moist air
pa•tio \'pat-ē-ˌō, 'pät-\ *n, pl* **pa•ti•os 1**
: COURTYARD **2** : a paved recreation
area near a house
pa•tois \'pa-ˌtwä\ *n, pl* **pa•tois** \-ˌtwäz\
[F] **1** : a dialect other than the standard dialect; *esp* : illiterate or provincial speech **2** : JARGON 2
pa•tri•arch \'pā-trē-ˌärk\ *n* **1** : a man
revered as father or founder (as of a
tribe) **2** : a venerable old man **3** : an
ecclesiastical dignitary (as the bishop

of an Eastern Orthodox see) — **pa·tri·ar·chal** \ˌpā-trē-'är-kəl\ *adj* — **pa·tri·arch·ate** \'pā-trē-ˌär-kət, -ˌkāt\ *n* — **pa·tri·ar·chy** \-ˌär-kē\ *n*

pa·tri·cian \pə-'trish-ən\ *n* : a person of high birth : ARISTOCRAT — **patrician** *adj*

pat·ri·cide \'pa-trə-ˌsīd\ *n* **1** : one who murders his own father **2** : the murder of one's own father

pat·ri·mo·ny \'pa-trə-ˌmō-nē\ *n* : something (as an estate) inherited or derived esp. from one's father : HERITAGE — **pat·ri·mo·ni·al** \ˌpat-rə-'mō-nē-əl\ *adj*

pa·tri·ot \'pā-trē-ət, -ˌät\ *n* [MF *patriote*, fr. LL *patriota*, fr. Gk *patriōtēs*, fr. *patrios* of one's father, fr. *patr-, patēr* father] : one who loves his country — **pa·tri·ot·ic** \ˌpā-trē-'ät-ik\ *adj* — **pa·tri·ot·i·cal·ly** \-i-k(ə-)lē\ *adv* — **pa·tri·o·tism** \'pā-trē-ə-ˌtiz-əm\ *n*

pa·tris·tic \pə-'tris-tik\ *adj* : of or relating to the church fathers or their writings

¹pa·trol \pə-'trōl\ *n* : the action of going the rounds (as of an area) for observation or the maintenance of security; *also* : a person or group performing such an action

²patrol *vb* **pa·trolled; pa·trol·ling** [F *patrouiller*, fr. MF, to tramp around in the mud, fr. *patte* paw] : to carry out a patrol

pa·trol·man \pə-'trōl-mən\ *n* : a policeman assigned to a beat

patrol wagon *n* : an enclosed motortruck for carrying prisoners

pa·tron \'pā-trən\ *n* [ME, fr. MF, fr. ML & L; ML *patronus* patron saint, patron of a benefice, pattern, fr. L, defender, fr. *patr-, pater* father] **1** : a person chosen or named as special protector **2** : a wealthy or influential supporter ⟨∼ of poets⟩; *also* : BENEFACTOR **3** : a regular client or customer **syn** sponsor, guarantor, angel, backer

pa·tron·ess \'pā-trə-nəs\ *n* : a woman who is a patron

pa·tron·age \'pa-trə-nij, 'pā-\ *n* **1** : the support or influence of a patron **2** : the trade of customers **3** : control of appointment to government jobs

pa·tron·ize \'pā-trə-ˌnīz, 'pa-\ *vb* **-ized;**

-iz·ing 1 : to be a customer of **2** : to treat condescendingly

pat·ro·nym·ic \ˌpa-trə-'nim-ik\ *n* : a name derived from the name of one's father or paternal ancestor usu. by the addition of a prefix or suffix

pa·troon \pə-'trün\ *n* : the proprietor of a manorial estate esp. in New York under Dutch rule

pat·sy \'pat-sē\ *n, pl* **pat·sies** : one who is duped or victimized

¹pat·ter \'pat-ər\ *vb* : to talk glibly or mechanically **syn** chatter, prate, chat, prattle, babble

²patter *n* **1** : a specialized lingo **2** : extremely rapid talk ⟨a comedian's ∼⟩

³patter *vb* : to strike, pat, or tap rapidly

⁴patter *n* : a quick succession of taps or pats ⟨the ∼ of rain⟩

¹pat·tern \'pat-ərn\ *n* [ME *patron*, fr. MF, fr. ML *patronus*, fr. L, defender, fr. *patr-, pater* father] **1** : an ideal model **2** : something used as a model for making things ⟨a dressmaker's ∼⟩ **3** : SAMPLE **4** : an artistic design **5** : CONFIGURATION

²pattern *vb* : to form according to a pattern

pat·ty *also* **pat·tie** \'pat-ē\ *n, pl* **patties 1** : a little pie **2** : a small flat cake esp. of chopped food

pau·ci·ty \'pȯ-sət-ē\ *n* : smallness of number or quantity

paunch \'pȯnch\ *n* : a usu. large belly : POTBELLY — **paunchy** *adj*

pau·per \'pȯ-pər\ *n* : a person without means of support except from charity — **pau·per·ism** \-pə-ˌriz-əm\ *n* — **pau·per·ize** \-pə-ˌrīz\ *vb*

¹pause \'pȯz\ *n* **1** : a temporary stop; *also* : a period of inaction **2** : a brief suspension of the voice **3** : a sign ⌢ or ⌣ above or below a musical note or rest to show it is to be prolonged **4** : a reason for pausing

²pause *vb* **paused; paus·ing** : to stop, rest, or linger for a time

pave \'pāv\ *vb* **paved; pav·ing** : to cover (as a road) with hard material in order to smooth or firm the surface

pave·ment \'pāv-mənt\ *n* **1** : a paved surface **2** : the material with which something is paved

pa·vil·ion \pə-'vil-yən\ *n* [ME *pavilon*, fr. OF *paveillon*, fr. L *papilion-, papilio* butterfly] **1** : a large tent **2** : a light structure (as in a park) used for entertainment or shelter

pav·ing \'pā-viŋ\ *n* : PAVEMENT

¹**paw** \'pȯ\ *n* : the foot of a quadruped (as a dog or lion) having claws

²**paw** *vb* **1** : to feel or handle clumsily or rudely **2** : to touch or strike with a paw; *also* : to scrape with a hoof **3** : to flail about or grab for with the hands

pawl \'pȯl\ *n* : a pivoted tongue or sliding bolt designed to fall into notches on another machine part to permit motion in one direction only

¹**pawn** \'pȯn\ *n* **1** : goods deposited as security for a loan; *also* : HOSTAGE **2** : the state of being pledged

²**pawn** *vb* : to deposit as a pledge

³**pawn** *n* [ME *pown*, fr. MF *poon*, fr. ML *pedon-*, *pedo* foot soldier, fr. LL, one with broad feet, fr. L *ped-*, *pes* foot] : a chessman of the least value

pawn·bro·ker \'pȯn-ˌbrō-kər\ *n* : one who loans money on goods pledged

Paw·nee \pȯ-'nē\ *n*, *pl* **Pawnee** *or* **Pawnees** : a member of an American Indian people orig. of Kansas and Nebraska

pawn·shop \'pȯn-ˌshäp\ *n* : a pawnbroker's place of business

paw·paw var of PAPAW

¹**pay** \'pā\ *vb* **paid** \'pād\ *also in sense 7* **payed; pay·ing** [ME *payen*, fr. OF *paier*, fr. L *pacare* to pacify, fr. *pac-*, *pax* peace] **1** : to make due return to for goods or services **2** : to discharge indebtedness for : SETTLE ⟨~ a bill⟩ **3** : to give in forfeit ⟨~ the penalty⟩ **4** : REQUITE **5** : to give, offer, or make freely or as fitting ⟨~ attention⟩ **6** : to be profitable to : RETURN **7** : to make slack and allow to run out ⟨~ out a rope⟩ — **pay·able** *adj* — **pay·ee** \pā-'ē\ *n* — **pay·er** *n*

²**pay** *n* **1** : the status of being paid by an employer : EMPLOY **2** : something paid; *esp* : WAGES

³**pay** *adj* **1** : containing something valuable (as gold) ⟨~ dirt⟩ **2** : equipped to receive a fee for use ⟨~ telephone⟩

pay·check \'pā-ˌchek\ *n* **1** : a check in payment of wages or salary **2** : WAGES, SALARY

pay·load \'pā-ˌlōd\ *n* : the load carried by a vehicle in addition to what is necessary for its operation

pay·mas·ter \-ˌmas-tər\ *n* : one who distributes the payroll

pay·ment \'pā-mənt\ *n* **1** : the act of paying **2** : something paid

pay·off \-ˌȯf\ *n* **1** : payment at the outcome of an enterprise ⟨a big ~ from an investment⟩ **2** : the climax of an incident or enterprise ⟨the ~ of a story⟩

pay·roll \'pā-ˌrōl\ *n* : a list of persons entitled to receive pay; *also* : the money to pay those on such a list

payt *abbr* payment

pay up *vb* : to pay what is due; *also* : to pay in full

Pb *symbol* [L *plumbum*] lead

PBX *abbr* private branch exchange

PC *abbr* **1** Peace Corps **2** percent; percentage **3** personal computer **4** postcard **5** [L *post cibum*] after meals **6** professional corporation

PCB \ˌpē-ˌsē-'bē\ *n* : POLYCHLORINATED BIPHENYL

PCP \ˌpē-ˌsē-'pē\ *n* : PHENCYCLIDINE

pct *abbr* percent; percentage

pd *abbr* paid

Pd *symbol* palladium

PD *abbr* **1** per diem **2** police department **3** potential difference

PDQ \ˌpē-ˌdē-'kyü\ *adv*, *often not cap* [abbr. of *pretty damned quick*] : IMMEDIATELY

PDT *abbr* Pacific daylight time

PE *abbr* **1** physical education **2** printer's error **3** professional engineer

pea \'pē\ *n*, *pl* **peas** *also* **pease** \'pēz\ **1** : the round edible protein-rich seed borne in the pod of a widely grown leguminous vine; *also* : this vine **2** : any of various plants resembling or related to the pea

peace \'pēs\ *n* **1** : a state of calm and quiet; *esp* : public security under law **2** : freedom from disturbing thoughts or emotions **3** : a state of concord (as between persons or governments); *also* : an agreement to end hostilities — **peace·able** \-ə-bəl\ *adj* — **peace·ably** \-blē\ *adv* — **peace·ful** \-fəl\ *adj* — **peace·ful·ly** \-ē\ *adv*

peace·keep·ing \'pēs-ˌkē-piŋ\ *n* : the preserving of peace; *esp* : international enforcement and supervision of a truce — **peace·keep·er** \-pər\ *n*

peace·mak·er \-ˌmā-kər\ *n* : one who settles an argument or stops a fight

peace·time \-ˌtīm\ *n* : a time when a nation is not at war

peach \ˈpēch\ *n* [ME *peche,* fr. MF (the fruit), fr. LL *persica,* fr. L *persicum,* fr. neut. of *persicus* Persian, fr. *Persia*] : a sweet juicy fruit of a low tree with pink blossoms; *also* : this tree

pea·cock \ˈpē-ˌkäk\ *n* : the male peafowl having long tail coverts which can be spread at will displaying brilliant colors

pea·fowl \-ˌfaul\ *n* : a very large domesticated Asian pheasant

pea·hen \-ˌhen\ *n* : the female peafowl

¹**peak** \ˈpēk\ *n* **1** : a pointed or projecting part **2** : the top of a hill or mountain; *also* : MOUNTAIN **3** : the front projecting part of a cap **4** : the narrow part of a ship's bow or stern **5** : the highest level or greatest degree — **peak** *adj*

²**peak** *vb* : to bring to or reach a maximum

peak·ed \ˈpē-kəd\ *adj* : THIN, SICKLY

¹**peal** \ˈpēl\ *n* **1** : the loud ringing of bells **2** : a set of tuned bells **3** : a loud sound or succession of sounds

²**peal** *vb* : to give out peals : RESOUND

pea·nut \ˈpē-(ˌ)nət\ *n* : an annual herb related to the pea but having pods that ripen underground; *also* : this pod or one of the edible seeds it bears

pear \ˈpaər\ *n* : the fleshy fruit of a tree related to the apple; *also* : this tree

pearl \ˈpərl\ *n* **1** : a small hard often lustrous body formed within the shell of some mollusks and used as a gem **2** : one that is choice or precious ⟨~s of wisdom⟩ **3** : a slightly bluish medium gray — **pearly** \ˈpər-lē\ *adj*

peas·ant \ˈpez-ᵊnt\ *n* **1** : any of a class of small landowners or laborers tilling the soil **2** : a person of low social or cultural status — **peas·ant·ry** \-ᵊn-trē\ *n*

pea·shoot·er \ˈpē-ˌshüt-ər\ *n* : a toy blowgun for shooting peas

peat \ˈpēt\ *n* : a dark substance formed by partial decay of plants (as mosses) in water — **peaty** *adj*

peat moss *n* : SPHAGNUM

¹**peb·ble** \ˈpeb-əl\ *n* : a small usu. round stone — **peb·bly** \-(ə-)lē\ *adj*

²**pebble** *vb* **peb·bled; peb·bling** \-(ə-)liŋ\ : to produce a rough surface texture in ⟨~ leather⟩

pe·can \pi-ˈkän, -ˈkan\ *n* : a large American hickory tree bearing a smooth-shelled edible nut; *also* : this nut

pec·ca·dil·lo \ˌpek-ə-ˈdil-ō\ *n, pl* **-loes** *or* **-los** : a slight offense

pec·ca·ry \ˈpek-ə-rē\ *n, pl* **-ries** : an American chiefly tropical mammal resembling but smaller than the related pigs

pec·ca·vi \pe-ˈkä-ˌvē\ *n* [L, I have sinned, fr. *peccare* to sin] : an acknowledgment of sin

¹**peck** \ˈpek\ *n* — see WEIGHT table

²**peck** *vb* **1** : to strike or pierce with or as if with the bill **2** : to make (as a hole) by pecking **3** : to pick up with or as if with the bill

³**peck** *n* **1** : an impression made by pecking **2** : a quick sharp stroke; *also* : KISS

pecking order *also* **peck order** *n* : a basic pattern of social organization within a flock of poultry in which each bird pecks another lower in the scale without fear of retaliation and submits to pecking by one of higher rank; *also* : a social hierarchy

pec·tin \ˈpek-tən\ *n* : any of various water-soluble plant substances that cause fruit jellies to set — **pec·tic** \-tik\ *adj*

pec·to·ral \ˈpek-t(ə-)rəl\ *adj* : of or relating to the breast or chest

pec·u·late \ˈpek-yə-ˌlāt\ *vb* **-lat·ed; -lat·ing** : EMBEZZLE — **pec·u·la·tion** \ˌpek-yə-ˈlā-shən\ *n*

pe·cu·liar \pi-ˈkyül-yər\ *adj* [ME *peculier,* fr. L *peculiaris* of private property, special, fr. *peculium* private property, fr. *pecus* cattle] **1** : belonging exclusively to one person or group **2** : CHARACTERISTIC, DISTINCTIVE **3** : QUEER, ODD **syn** idiosyncratic, eccentric, singular, strange, weird — **pe·cu·liar·i·ty** \-ˌkyül-ˈyar-ət-ē, -ē-ˈar-\ *n* — **pe·cu·liar·ly** \-ˈkyül-yər-lē\ *adv*

pe·cu·ni·ary \pi-ˈkyü-nē-ˌer-ē\ *adj* : of or relating to money : MONETARY

ped·a·gogue *also* **ped·a·gog** \ˈped-ə-ˌgäg\ *n* : TEACHER, SCHOOLMASTER

ped·a·go·gy \ˈped-ə-ˌgōj-ē, -ˌgäj-\ *n* : the art or profession of teaching; *esp* : EDUCATION **2** — **ped·a·gog·ic** \ˌped-ə-ˈgäj-ik, -ˈgōj-\ *or* **ped·a·gog·i·cal** \-i-kəl\ *adj*

¹**pedal**\'ped-ᵊl\ *n* : a lever worked by the foot

²**ped·al** *adj* : of or relating to the foot

³**ped·al** \'ped-ᵊl\ *vb* **-aled** *also* **-alled; -al·ing** *also* **-al·ling** \-(ᵊ-)liŋ\ **1** : to use or work a pedal (as of a piano or bicycle) **2** : to ride a bicycle

ped·ant \'ped-ᵊnt\ *n* **1** : a person who makes a display of his learning **2** : a formal uninspired teacher — **pe·dan·tic** \pi-'dant-ik\ *adj* — **ped·ant·ry** \'ped-ᵊn-trē\ *n*

ped·dle \'ped-ᵊl\ *vb* **ped·dled; ped·dling** \'ped-(ᵊ-)liŋ\ : to sell or offer for sale from place to place — **ped·dler** *also* **ped·lar** \'ped-lər\ *n*

ped·er·ast \'ped-ə-ˌrast\ *n* [Gk *paiderastēs*, lit., lover of boys] : one that practices anal intercourse esp. with a boy — **ped·er·as·ty** \'ped-ə-ˌras-tē\ *n*

ped·es·tal \'ped-əs-tᵊl\ *n* : the support or foot of something (as a column, statue, or vase) that is upright

¹**pe·des·tri·an** \pə-'des-trē-ən\ *adj* **1** : COMMONPLACE **2** : going on foot

²**pedestrian** *n* : WALKER

pe·di·at·rics \ˌpēd-ē-'a-triks\ *n* : a branch of medicine dealing with the care and diseases of children — **pe·di·at·ric** \-trik\ *adj* — **pe·di·a·tri·cian** \ˌpēd-ē-ə-'trish-ən\ *n*

pedi·cab \'ped-i-ˌkab\ *n* : a pedal-driven tricycle with seats for a driver and two passengers

ped·i·cure \'ped-i-ˌkyur\ *n* : care of the feet, toes, and nails; *also* : a single treatment of these parts — **ped·i·cur·ist** \-ˌkyur-əst\ *n*

ped·i·gree \'ped-ə-ˌgrē\ *n* [ME *pedegru*, fr. MF *pie de grue* crane's foot; fr. the shape made by the lines of genealogical chart] **1** : a record of a line of ancestors **2** : an ancestral line — **ped·i·greed** \-grēd\ *adj*

ped·i·ment \'ped-ə-mənt\ *n* : a low triangular gablelike decoration (as over a door or window) on a building

pe·dom·e·ter \pi-'däm-ət-ər\ *n* : an instrument that measures the distance one walks

pe·dun·cle \'pē-ˌdəŋ-kəl\ *n* : a narrow supporting stalk

peek \'pēk\ *vb* **1** : to look furtively **2** : to peer from a place of concealment **3** : GLANCE — **peek** *n*

¹**peel** \'pēl\ *n* : a skin or rind esp. of a fruit

²**peel** *vb* [ME *pelen*, fr. MF *peler*, fr. L *pilare* to remove the hair from, fr. *pilus* hair] **1** : to strip the skin, bark, or rind from **2** : to strip off (as a coat); *also* : to come off **3** : to lose the skin, bark, or rind

peel·ing \'pē-liŋ\ *n* : a peeled-off piece or strip (as of skin or rind)

peen \'pēn\ *n* : the usu. hemispherical or wedge-shaped end of the head of a hammer opposite the face

¹**peep** \'pēp\ *vb* : to utter a feeble shrill sound

²**peep** *n* : a feeble shrill sound

³**peep** *vb* **1** : to look slyly esp. through an aperture : PEEK **2** : to begin to emerge — **peep·er** *n*

⁴**peep** *n* **1** : a first faint appearance **2** : a brief or furtive look

peep·hole \'pēp-ˌhōl\ *n* : a hole to peep through

¹**peer** \'piər\ *n* **1** : one of equal standing with another : EQUAL **2** : NOBLE — **peer·age** \-ij\ *n*

²**peer** *vb* **1** : to look intently or curiously **2** : to come slightly into view

peer·ess \'pir-əs\ *n* : a woman who is a peer

peer·less \'piər-ləs\ *adj* : having no equal : MATCHLESS **syn** supreme, unequalled, unparalleled, incomparable

¹**peeve** \'pēv\ *vb* **peeved; peev·ing** : to make resentful : ANNOY

²**peeve** *n* **1** : a feeling or mood of resentment **2** : a particular grievance

pee·vish \'pē-vish\ *adj* : querulous in temperament : FRETFUL **syn** irritable, petulant, huffy — **pee·vish·ly** *adv* — **pee·vish·ness** *n*

pee·wee \'pē-(ˌ)wē\ *n* : one that is diminutive or tiny

¹**peg** \'peg\ *n* **1** : a small pointed piece (as of wood) used to pin down or fasten things or to fit into holes **2** : a projecting piece used as a support or boundary marker **3** : SUPPORT, PRETEXT **4** : STEP, DEGREE **5** : THROW

²**peg** *vb* **pegged; peg·ging** **1** : to put a peg into : fasten, pin down, or attach with or as if with pegs **2** : to work hard and steadily : PLUG **3** : HUSTLE **4** : to mark by pegs **5** : to hold (as prices) at a set level or rate **6** : THROW

peg·ma·tite \'peg-mə-ˌtīt\ *n* : a coarse

variety of granite occurring in veins

PEI *abbr* Prince Edward Island

pei·gnoir \pān-ˈwär, pen-\ *n* [F, lit., garment worn while combing the hair, fr. MF, fr. *peigner* to comb the hair, fr. L *pectinare,* fr. *pectin-, pecten* comb] : NEGLIGEE

pe·jo·ra·tive \pi-ˈjȯr-ət-iv, ˈpej-(ə-)rət-\ *adj* : having a tendency to make or become worse : DISPARAGING

peke \ˈpēk\ *n, often cap* : PEKINGESE

Pe·king·ese *or* **Pe·kin·ese** \ˌpē-kən-ˈēz, -kiŋ-, -ˈēs\ *n, pl* **Pekingese** *or* **Pekinese** : a small short-legged long-haired Chinese dog

pe·koe \ˈpē-(ˌ)kō\ *n* : a black tea made from small-sized tea leaves esp. in India and Ceylon

pel·age \ˈpel-ij\ *n* : the hairy covering of a mammal

pe·lag·ic \pə-ˈlaj-ik\ *adj* : OCEANIC

pelf \ˈpelf\ *n* : MONEY, RICHES

pel·i·can \ˈpel-i-kən\ *n* : a large web‑footed bird having a pouched lower bill used to scoop in fish

pel·la·gra \pə-ˈlag-rə, -ˈlāg-\ *n* : a chronic disease marked by skin and digestive disorders and nervous symptoms and caused by a faulty diet

pel·let \ˈpel-ət\ *n* **1** : a little ball (as of medicine) **2** : BULLET — **pel·let·al** \-ᵊl\ *adj* — **pel·let·ize** \-ˌīz\ *vb*

pell–mell \ˈpel-ˈmel\ *adv* **1** : in mingled confusion **2** : HEADLONG

pel·lu·cid \pə-ˈlü-səd\ *adj* : extremely clear : LIMPID, TRANSPARENT **syn** translucent, lucid, lucent

¹pelt \ˈpelt\ *n* : a skin esp. of a fur-bearing animal

²pelt *vb* : to strike with a succession of blows or missiles

pel·vis \ˈpel-vəs\ *n, pl* **pel·vis·es** \-və-səz\ *or* **pel·ves** \-ˌvēz\ : a basin‑shaped part of the vertebrate skeleton consisting chiefly of the two large bones of the hip — **pel·vic** \-vik\ *adj*

pem·mi·can *also* **pem·i·can** \ˈpem-i-kən\ *n* : dried meat pounded fine and mixed with melted fat

¹pen \ˈpen\ *n* **1** : a small enclosure for animals **2** : a small place of confinement or storage

²pen *vb* **penned; pen·ning** : to shut in a pen : ENCLOSE

³pen *n* : an instrument with a split point

to hold ink used for writing; *also* : a fluid-using writing instrument

⁴pen *vb* **penned; pen·ning** : WRITE

⁵pen *n* : PENITENTIARY

⁶pen *abbr* peninsula

PEN *abbr* International Association of Poets, Playwrights, Editors, Essayists and Novelists

pe·nal \ˈpēn-ᵊl\ *adj* : of or relating to punishment

pe·nal·ize \ˈpēn-ᵊl-ˌīz, ˈpen-\ *vb* **-ized; -iz·ing** : to put a penalty on

pen·al·ty \ˈpen-ᵊl-tē\ *n, pl* **-ties 1** : punishment for crime or offense **2** : something forfeited when a person fails to do something agreed to **3** : disadvantage, loss, or hardship due to some action

pen·ance \ˈpen-əns\ *n* **1** : an act performed to show sorrow or repentance for sin **2** : a sacrament (as in the Roman Catholic Church) consisting of repentance, confession, a penance, and absolution

Pe·na·tes \pə-ˈnāt-ēz\ *n pl* : the Roman gods of the household

pence \ˈpens\ *pl of* PENNY

pen·chant \ˈpen-chənt\ *n* [F, fr. prp. of *pencher* to incline, fr. (assumed) VL *pendicare,* fr. L *pendere* to weigh] : a strong inclination : LIKING **syn** leaning, propensity, predilection, predisposition

¹pen·cil \ˈpen-səl\ *n* : a writing or drawing tool consisting of or having a slender cylinder of a solid marking substance

²pencil *vb* **-ciled** *or* **-cilled; -cil·ing** *or* **-cil·ling** \-s(ə-)liŋ\ : to paint, draw, or write with a pencil

pen·dant *also* **pen·dent** \ˈpen-dənt\ *n* : a hanging ornament (as an earring)

pen·dent *or* **pen·dant** \ˈpen-dənt\ *adj* : SUSPENDED, OVERHANGING

¹pend·ing \ˈpen-diŋ\ *prep* **1** : DURING **2** : while awaiting

²pending *adj* **1** : not yet decided **2** : IMMINENT

pen·du·lous \ˈpen-jə-ləs, -də-\ *adj* : hanging loosely : DROOPING

pen·du·lum \-ləm\ *n* : a body that swings freely from a fixed point

pe·ne·plain *also* **pe·ne·plane** \ˈpēn-i-ˌplān\ *n* : a large almost flat land surface shaped by erosion

pen·e·trate \ˈpen-ə-ˌtrāt\ *vb* **-trat·ed;**

-trat·ing 1 : to enter into : PIERCE 2 : PERMEATE 3 : to see into : UNDERSTAND 4 : to affect deeply — **pen·e·tra·ble** \-trə-bəl\ *adj* — **pen·e·tra·tion** \ˌpen-ə-ˈtrā-shən\ *n* — **pen·e·tra·tive** \ˈpen-ə-ˌtrāt-iv\ *adj*

pen·e·trat·ing \-ˌtrāt-iŋ\ *adj* 1 : having the power of entering, piercing, or pervading ⟨a ∼ shriek⟩ ⟨a ∼ odor⟩ 2 : ACUTE, DISCERNING ⟨a ∼ look⟩

pen·guin \ˈpen-gwən, ˈpeŋ-\ *n* : any of several erect short-legged flightless seabirds of the southern hemisphere

pen·hold·er \ˈpen-ˌhōl-dər\ *n* : a holder or handle for a pen

pen·i·cil·lin \ˌpen-ə-ˈsil-ən\ *n* : any of several antibiotics produced by a green mold and used against various bacteria

pen·in·su·la \pə-ˈnin-sə-lə\ *n* [L *paeninsula*, fr. *paene* almost + *insula* island] : a long narrow portion of land extending out into the water — **pen·in·su·lar** \-lər\ *adj*

pe·nis \ˈpē-nəs\ *n, pl* **pe·nes** \-ˌnēz\ *or* **pe·nis·es** [L, penis, tail] : a male organ of copulation that in the human male also functions as the channel by which urine leaves the body

¹**pen·i·tent** \ˈpen-ə-tənt\ *adj* : feeling sorrow for sins or offenses : REPENTANT — **pen·i·tence** \-təns\ *n* — **pen·i·ten·tial** \ˌpen-ə-ˈten-chəl\ *adj*

²**penitent** *n* : a penitent person

¹**pen·i·ten·tia·ry** \ˌpen-ə-ˈtench-(ə-)rē\ *n, pl* **-ries** : a state or federal prison

²**pen·i·ten·tia·ry** *adj* : of, relating to, or incurring confinement in a penitentiary

pen·knife \ˈpen-ˌnīf\ *n* : a small pocketknife

pen·light *or* **pen·lite** \ˈpen-ˌlīt\ *n* : a small flashlight resembling a fountain pen in size or shape

pen·man \ˈpen-mən\ *n* 1 : COPYIST 2 : one skilled in penmanship 3 : AUTHOR

pen·man·ship \-ˌship\ *n* : the art or practice of writing with the pen

Penn *or* **Penna** *abbr* Pennsylvania

pen name *n* : an author's pseudonym

pen·nant \ˈpen-ənt\ *n* 1 : a tapering flag used esp. for signaling 2 : a flag symbolic of championship

pen·ni \ˈpen-ē\ *n, pl* **pen·nia** \-ē-ə\ *or*

pen·nis \-ēz\ — see *markka* at MONEY table

pen·non \ˈpen-ən\ *n* 1 : a long narrow ribbonlike flag borne on a lance 2 : WING

Penn·syl·va·nian \ˌpen-səl-ˈvā-nyən\ *adj* : of, relating to, or being the period of the Paleozoic era between the Mississippian and the Permian — **Pennsylvanian** *n*

pen·ny \ˈpen-ē\ *n, pl* **pennies** \-ēz\ *or* **pence** \ˈpens\ 1 : a British monetary unit formerly equal to ¹/₁₂ shilling but now equal to ¹/₁₀₀ pound; *also* : a coin of this value — see *pound* at MONEY table 2 *pl* **pennies** : a cent of the U.S. or Canada — **pen·ni·less** \ˈpen-i-ləs\ *adj*

pen·ny–pinch·ing \ˈpen-ē-ˌpin-chiŋ\ *n* : FRUGALITY, PARSIMONY — **pen·ny–pinch·er** \-chər\ *n* — **penny–pinching** *adj*

pen·ny·roy·al \ˌpen-ē-ˈrȯi-əl, ˈpen-i-ˌrīl\ *n* : a hairy perennial mint with small pungently aromatic leaves

pen·ny·weight \ˈpen-ē-ˌwāt\ *n* — see WEIGHT table

pen·ny–wise \ˈpen-ē-ˌwīz\ *adj* : wise or prudent only in small matters

pe·nol·o·gy \pi-ˈnäl-ə-jē\ *n* : a branch of criminology dealing with prisons and the treatment of offenders

¹**pen·sion** \ˈpen-chən\ *n* : a fixed sum paid regularly esp. to a person retired from service

²**pen·sion** \ˈpen-chən\ *vb* **pen·sioned; pen·sion·ing** \ˈpench-(ə-)niŋ\ : to pay a pension to — **pen·sion·er** *n*

pen·sive \ˈpen-siv\ *adj* : musingly, dreamily, or sadly thoughtful **syn** reflective, speculative, contemplative, meditative — **pen·sive·ly** *adv*

pen·stock \ˈpen-ˌstäk\ *n* 1 : a sluice or gate for regulating a flow 2 : a conduit for conducting water

pent \ˈpent\ *adj* : shut up : CONFINED

pen·ta·gon \ˈpent-ə-ˌgän\ *n* : a polygon of five angles and five sides — **pen·tag·o·nal** \pen-ˈtag-ən-ᵊl\ *adj*

pen·tam·e·ter \pen-ˈtam-ət-ər\ *n* : a line consisting of five metrical feet

Pen·te·cost \ˈpent-i-ˌkȯst\ *n* : the 7th Sunday after Easter observed as a church festival commemorating the descent of the Holy Spirit on the apostles — **Pen·te·cos·tal** \ˌpent-i-ˈkäst-ᵊl\ adj

Pentecostal n : a member of a fundamentalist Christian religious body that stresses religious revivals — **Pen·te·cos·tal·ism** \ˌpent-i-ˈkäst-ᵊl-ˌiz-əm\ n

pent·house \ˈpent-ˌhaùs\ n [ME pentis, fr. MF appentis, prob. fr. ML appenticium appendage, fr. L appendic-, appendix] 1 : a shed or sloping roof attached to a wall or building 2 : an apartment built on the roof of a building

pen·ul·ti·mate \pi-ˈnəl-tə-mət\ adj : next to the last ⟨~ syllable⟩

pen·um·bra \pə-ˈnəm-brə\ n, pl **-brae** \-(ˌ)brē\ or **-bras** : the partial shadow surrounding a complete shadow (as in an eclipse)

pe·nu·ri·ous \pə-ˈn(y)ùr-ē-əs\ adj 1 : marked by penury 2 : MISERLY syn stingy, close, tightfisted, parsimonious

pen·u·ry \ˈpen-yə-rē\ n : extreme poverty

pe·on \ˈpē-ˌän, -ən\ n, pl **peons** or **pe·o·nes** \pā-ˈō-nēz\ 1 : a member of the landless laboring class in Spanish America 2 : one bound to service for payment of a debt — **pe·on·age** \-ə-nij\ n

pe·o·ny \ˈpē-ə-nē\ n, pl **-nies** : a garden plant with large usu. double red, pink, or white flowers; also : its flower

¹**peo·ple** \ˈpē-pəl\ n, pl **people** [ME peple, fr. OF peuple, fr. L populus] 1 pl : human beings making up a group or linked by a common characteristic or interest 2 pl : human beings — often used in compounds instead of persons ⟨salespeople⟩ 3 pl : the mass of persons in a community : POPULACE; also : ELECTORATE ⟨the ~'s choice⟩ 4 pl **peoples** : a body of persons (as a tribe, nation, or race) united by a common culture, sense of kinship, or political organization

²**people** vb **peo·pled; peo·pling** \-p(ə-)liŋ\ : to supply or fill with or as if with people

¹**pep** \ˈpep\ n : brisk energy or initiative — **pep·py** adj

²**pep** vb **pepped; pep·ping** : to put pep into : STIMULATE

¹**pep·per** \ˈpep-ər\ n 1 : a pungent condiment from the berry (**pep·per·corn** \-ˌkórn\) of an East Indian climbing plant; also : this plant 2 : a plant related to the tomato and widely grown for its hot or mild sweet fruit; also : this fruit

²**pepper** vb **pep·pered; pep·per·ing** \ˈpep-(ə-)riŋ\ 1 : to sprinkle or season with or as if with pepper 2 : to shower with missiles or rapid blows

pep·per·mint \-ˌmint, -mənt\ n : a pungent aromatic mint; also : candy flavored with its oil

pep·per·o·ni \ˌpep-ə-ˈrō-nē\ n : a highly seasoned beef and pork sausage

pep·pery \ˈpep-(ə-)rē\ adj 1 : having the qualities of pepper : PUNGENT, HOT 2 : having a hot temper 3 : FIERY

pep·sin \ˈpep-sən\ n : an enzyme of the stomach that begins the digestion of proteins; also : a preparation of this used medicinally

pep·tic \ˈpep-tik\ adj 1 : relating to or promoting digestion 2 : resulting from the action of digestive juices ⟨a ~ ulcer⟩

Pe·quot \ˈpē-ˌkwät\ n : a member of an American Indian people of eastern Connecticut

¹**per** \(ˈ)pər\ prep 1 : by means of 2 : to or for each 3 : ACCORDING TO

²**per** adv : for each : APIECE

³**per** abbr 1 period 2 person

¹**per·ad·ven·ture** \ˈpər-əd-ˌven-chər\ adv, archaic : PERHAPS

²**peradventure** n : DOUBT, CHANCE

per·am·bu·late \pə-ˈram-byə-ˌlāt\ vb **-lat·ed; -lat·ing** : to travel over esp. on foot — **per·am·bu·la·tion** \-ˌram-byə-ˈlā-shən\ n

per·am·bu·la·tor \pə-ˈram-byə-ˌlāt-ər\ n, chiefly Brit : a baby carriage

per an·num \(ˌ)pər-ˈan-əm\ adv [ML] : in or for each year : ANNUALLY

per·cale \(ˌ)pər-ˈkāl, ˈpər-ˌ; (ˌ)pər-ˈkal\ n : a fine woven cotton cloth

per cap·i·ta \(ˌ)pər-ˈkap-ət-ə\ adv or adj [ML, by heads] : by or for each person

per·ceive \pər-ˈsēv\ vb **per·ceived; per·ceiv·ing** 1 : to attain awareness : REALIZE 2 : to become aware of through the senses — **per·ceiv·able** adj

¹**per·cent** \pər-ˈsent\ adv [fr. per + L centum hundred] : in each hundred

²**percent** n, pl **percent** or **percents** 1 : one

part in a hundred : HUNDREDTH **2** : PERCENTAGE

per·cent·age \pər-'sent-ij\ *n* **1** : a part of a whole expressed in hundredths **2** : the result obtained by multiplying a number by a percent **3** : ADVANTAGE, PROFIT **4** : PROBABILITY; *also* : favorable odds

per·cen·tile \pər-'sen-ˌtīl\ *n* : a statistical measure expressing the standing of a score or grade in terms of the percentage of scores or grades falling with or below it

per·cept \'pər-ˌsept\ *n* : a sense impression of an object accompanied by an understanding of what it is

per·cep·ti·ble \pər-'sep-tə-bəl\ *adj* : capable of being perceived — **per·cep·ti·bly** \-blē\ *adv*

per·cep·tion \pər-'sep-shən\ *n* **1** : an act or result of perceiving **2** : awareness of environment through physical sensation **3** : ability to perceive : INSIGHT, COMPREHENSION **syn** penetration, discernment, discrimination

per·cep·tive \pər-'sep-tiv\ *adj* : of or relating to perception : having perception; *also* : DISCERNING — **per·cep·tive·ly** *adv*

per·cep·tu·al \-chə(-wə)l\ *adj* : of, relating to, or involving sensory stimulus as opposed to abstract concept — **per·cep·tu·al·ly** \-ē\ *adv*

¹perch \'pərch\ *n* **1** : a roost for birds **2** : a high station or vantage point

²perch *vb* : ROOST

³perch *n, pl* **perch** *or* **perch·es** : either of two small freshwater spiny-finned food fishes; *also* : any of various fishes resembling or related to these

per·chance \pər-'chans\ *adv* : PERHAPS

per·cip·i·ent \pər-'sip-ē-ənt\ *adj* : capable of or characterized by perception — **per·cip·i·ence** \-əns\ *n*

per·co·late \'pər-kə-ˌlāt\ *vb* **-lat·ed; -lat·ing 1** : to trickle or filter through a permeable substance **2** : to filter hot water through to extract the essence ⟨~ coffee⟩ — **per·co·la·tor** \-ˌlāt-ər\ *n*

per con·tra \(ˌ)pər-'kän-trə\ *adv* [It, by the opposite side (of the ledger)] **1** : on the contrary **2** : by way of contrast

per·cus·sion \pər-'kəsh-ən\ *n* **1** : a sharp blow : IMPACT; *esp* : a blow upon a cap (**percussion cap**) filled with pow-

der and designed to explode the charge in a firearm **2** : the beating or striking of a musical instrument; *also* : instruments sounded by striking, shaking, or scraping

per di·em \-'dē-əm, -'dī-\ *adv* [ML] : by the day — **per diem** *adj or n*

per·di·tion \pər-'dish-ən\ *n* [ME *perdicion*, fr. LL *perdition-, perditio*, fr. L *perdere* to destroy, fr. *per-* to destruction + *dare* to give] **1** : eternal damnation **2** : HELL

per·du·ra·ble \(ˌ)pər-'d(y)ùr-ə-bəl\ *adj* : very durable — **per·du·ra·bil·i·ty** \-ˌd(y)ùr-ə-'bil-ət-ē\ *n*

per·e·gri·na·tion \ˌper-ə-grə-'nā-shən\ *n* : a journeying about from place to place

pe·remp·to·ry \pə-'remp-t(ə-)rē\ *adj* **1** : barring a right of action or delay : FINAL **2** : expressive of urgency or command : IMPERATIVE **3** : marked by self-assurance : DECISIVE **syn** imperious, masterful, domineering, magisterial — **pe·remp·to·ri·ly** \-t(ə-)rə-lē\ *adv*

¹pe·ren·ni·al \pə-'ren-ē-əl\ *adj* **1** : present at all seasons of the year ⟨~ streams⟩ **2** : continuing to live from year to year ⟨~ plants⟩ **3** : recurring regularly : PERMANENT ⟨~ problems⟩ **syn** lasting, perpetual, enduring, everlasting — **pe·ren·ni·al·ly** \-ē\ *adv*

²perennial *n* : a plant that lives for an indefinite number of years

perf *abbr* **1** perfect **2** perforated

¹per·fect \'pər-fikt\ *adj* **1** : being without fault or defect **2** : EXACT, PRECISE **3** : COMPLETE **4** : relating to or being a verb tense that expresses an action or state completed at the time of speaking or at a time spoken of **syn** whole, entire, intact — **per·fect·ly** \-fik-(t)lē\ *adv* — **per·fect·ness** \-fik(t)-nəs\ *n*

²per·fect \pər-'fekt\ *vb* : to make perfect

³per·fect \'pər-fikt\ *n* : the perfect tense; *also* : a verb form in it

per·fect·ible \pər-'fek-tə-bəl, 'pər-fik-\ *adj* : capable of improvement or perfection — **per·fect·ibil·i·ty** \pər-ˌfek-tə-'bil-ət-ē, ˌpər-fik-\ *n*

per·fec·tion \pər-'fek-shən\ *n* **1** : the quality or state of being perfect **2** : the highest degree of excellence **3** : the act or process of perfecting **syn** virtue, merit, excellence

per·fec·tion·ist \-sh(ə-)nəst\ *n* : a person who will not accept or be content with anything less than perfection

per·fec·to \pər-'fek-tō\ *n, pl* **-tos** : a cigar that is thick in the middle and tapers almost to a point at each end

per·fi·dy \'pər-fəd-ē\ *n, pl* **-dies** [L *perfidia,* fr. *perfidus* faithless, fr. *per fidem decipere* to betray, lit., to deceive by trust] : violation of faith or loyalty : TREACHERY — **per·fid·i·ous** \pər-'fid-ē-əs\ *adj* — **per·fid·i·ous·ly** *adv*

per·fo·rate \'pər-fə-ˌrāt\ *vb* **-rat·ed; -rat·ing** : to bore through : PIERCE; *esp* : to make a line of holes in to facilitate separation **syn** puncture, punch, prick — **per·fo·ra·tion** \ˌpər-fə-'rā-shən\ *n*

per·force \pər-'fōrs\ *adv* : of necessity

per·form \pə(r)-'fȯrm\ *vb* **1** : FULFILL **2** : to carry out : ACCOMPLISH **3** : FUNCTION **4** : to do in a set manner **5** : to give a performance : PLAY **syn** execute, discharge, achieve — **per·form·er** *n*

per·for·mance \pər-'fȯr-ˌməns\ *n* **1** : the act or process of performing **2** : DEED, FEAT **3** : a public presentation

¹**per·fume** \pər-'fyüm, 'pər-ˌfyüm\ *n* **1** : a usu. pleasant odor : FRAGRANCE **2** : a preparation used for scenting

²**per·fume** \pər-'fyüm, 'pər-ˌfyüm\ *vb* **per·fumed; per·fum·ing** : to treat with a perfume; *also* : SCENT

per·fum·ery \ˌpər-'fyüm-(ə-)rē\ *n, pl* **-er·ies** : PERFUMES

per·func·to·ry \pər-'fəŋk-t(ə-)rē\ *adj* : done merely as a duty — **per·func·to·ri·ly** \-t(ə-)rə-lē\ *adv*

per·go·la \'pər-gə-lə\ *n* [It] : a structure consisting of posts supporting an open roof in the form of a trellis

perh *abbr* perhaps

per·haps \pər-'(h)aps, 'praps\ *adv* : possibly but not certainly

per·i·gee \'per-ə-ˌjē\ *n* [fr. *perigee* point in the orbit of a satellite of the earth when it is nearest the earth, fr. NL *perigeum,* fr. Gk *perigeion,* fr. *peri* around, near + *gē* earth] : the point at which an orbiting object is nearest the body (as the earth) being orbited

peri·he·lion \ˌper-ə-'hēl-yən\ *n, pl* **-he·lia** \-'hēl-yə\ : the point in the path of a celestial body (as a planet) that is nearest to the sun

per·il \'per-əl\ *n* : DANGER; *also* : a source of danger : RISK **syn** jeopardy, hazard — **per·il·ous** *adj* — **per·il·ous·ly** *adv*

peri·lune \'per-ə-ˌlün\ *n* : the point in a lunar orbit closest to the moon's surface

pe·rim·e·ter \pə-'rim-ət-ər\ *n* : the outer boundary of a body or figure; *also* : the length of a perimeter

¹**pe·ri·od** \'pir-ē-əd\ *n* **1** : SENTENCE; *also* : the full pause closing the utterance of a sentence **2** : END, STOP **3** : a punctuation mark . used esp. to mark the end of a declarative sentence or an abbreviation **4** : an extent of time; *esp* : one regarded as a stage or division in a process or development **5** : a portion or division of time in which something comes to an end and is ready to begin again **6** : a single cyclic occurrence of menstruation **syn** epoch, era, age

²**period** *adj* : of or relating to a particular historical period ⟨∼ furniture⟩

pe·ri·od·ic \ˌpir-ē-'äd-ik\ *adj* **1** : occurring at regular intervals of time **2** : happening repeatedly **3** : of or relating to a sentence that has no trailing elements following full grammatical statement of the essential idea

¹**pe·ri·od·i·cal** \ˌpir-ē-'äd-i-kəl\ *adj* **1** : PERIODIC **2** : published at regular intervals **3** : of or relating to a periodical — **pe·ri·od·i·cal·ly** \-k(ə-)lē\ *adv*

²**periodical** *n* : a periodical publication

peri·odon·tal \ˌper-ē-ō-'dänt-ᵊl\ *adj* : surrounding or occurring about the teeth

per·i·pa·tet·ic \ˌper-ə-pə-'tet-ik\ *adj* : performed or performing while moving about : ITINERANT

pe·riph·er·al \pə-'rif-(ə-)rəl\ *n* : a device connected to a computer to provide communication or auxiliary functions

peripheral nervous system *n* : the part of the nervous system that is outside the central nervous system and comprises the spinal nerves, the cranial nerves except the one supplying the retina, and the autonomic nervous system

pe·riph·ery \pə-'rif-(ə-)rē\ *n, pl* **-er·ies** **1** : the boundary of a rounded fgure **2**

: outward bounds : border area — **pe-riph-er-al** \-(ə-)rəl\ *adj*

pe-riph-ra-sis \pə-'rif-rə-səs\ *n, pl* **-ra-ses** \-ˌsēz\ : CIRCUMLOCUTION

pe-rique \pə-'rēk\ *n* [LaF] : a strong-flavored Louisiana tobacco used in smoking mixtures

peri-scope \'per-ə-ˌskōp\ *n* : a tubular optical instrument enabling an observer to get an otherwise blocked field of view

per-ish \'per-ish\ *vb* : to become destroyed or ruined : DIE

per-ish-able \'per-ish-ə-bəl\ *adj* : easily spoiled ⟨∼ foods⟩ — **perishable** *n*

peri-stal-sis \ˌper-ə-'stól-səs, -'stal-\ *n, pl* **-stal-ses** : waves of contraction passing along the intestine and forcing its contents onward — **per-i-stal-tic** \-'stól-tik, -'stal-\ *adj*

peri-style \'per-ə-ˌstīl\ *n* : a row of columns surrounding a building or court

peri-to-ne-um \ˌper-ət-ᵊn-'ē-əm\ *n, pl* **-ne-ums** *or* **-nea** : the smooth transparent serous membrane that lines the cavity of the abdomen — **peri-to-ne-al** \-'ē-əl\ *adj*

peri-to-ni-tis \ˌper-ət-ᵊn-'īt-əs\ *n* : inflammation of the membrane lining the cavity of the abdomen

peri-wig \'per-i-ˌwig\ *n* : WIG

¹**per-i-win-kle** \'per-i-ˌwiŋ-kəl\ *n* : a usu. blue-flowered creeping plant cultivated as a ground cover

²**periwinkle** *n* : any of various small edible seashore snails

per-ju-ry \'pərj-(ə-)rē\ *n* : the voluntary violation of an oath to tell the truth : false swearing — **per-jure** \'pər-jər\ *vb* — **per-jur-er** *n*

¹**perk** \'pərk\ *vb* **1** : to thrust (as the head) up impudently or jauntily **2** : to make trim or brisk : FRESHEN **3** : to regain vigor or spirit — **perky** *adj*

²**perk** *vb* : PERCOLATE

per-lite \'pər-ˌlīt\ *n* : volcanic glass that when expanded by heat forms a lightweight material used esp. in concrete and plaster and for potting plants

¹**perm** \'pərm\ *n* : PERMANENT

²**perm** *vb* : to give (hair) a permanent

³**perm** *abbr* permanent

per-ma-frost \'pər-mə-ˌfróst\ *n* : a permanently frozen layer below the surface in frigid regions of a planet (as earth)

¹**per-ma-nent** \'pər-mə-nənt\ *adj* : LASTING, STABLE — **per-ma-nence** \-nəns\ *n* — **per-ma-nen-cy** \-nən-sē\ *n* — **per-ma-nent-ly** *adv*

²**permanent** *n* : a long-lasting hair wave or straightening

permanent press *n* : the process of treating fabrics with chemicals (as resin) and heat for setting the shape and for aiding wrinkle resistance

per-me-able \'pər-mē-ə-bəl\ *adj* : having small openings that permit liquids or gases to seep through — **per-me-a-bil-i-ty** \ˌpər-mē-ə-'bil-ət-ē\ *n*

per-me-ate \'pər-mē-ˌāt\ *vb* **-at-ed; -at-ing 1** : PERVADE **2** : to seep through the pores of : PENETRATE — **per-me-ation** \ˌpər-mē-'ā-shən\ *n*

Perm-ian \'pər-mē-ən\ *adj* : of, relating to, or being the latest period of the Paleozoic era — **Permian** *n*

per-mis-si-ble \pər-'mis-ə-bəl\ *adj* : that may be permitted : ALLOWABLE

per-mis-sion \pər-'mish-ən\ *n* : formal consent : AUTHORIZATION

per-mis-sive \pər-'mis-iv\ *adj* : granting permission; *esp* : INDULGENT — **per-mis-sive-ness** *n*

¹**per-mit** \pər-'mit\ *vb* **per-mit-ted; per-mit-ting 1** : to consent to : ALLOW **2** : to make possible

²**per-mit** \'pər-ˌmit, pər-'mit\ *n* : a written permission : LICENSE

per-mu-ta-tion \ˌpər-myù-'tā-shən\ *n* **1** : TRANSFORMATION **2** : any one of the total number of changes in position or order possible among the units or members of a group ⟨∼s of the alphabet⟩ **syn** innovation, mutation, vicissitude

per-ni-cious \pər-'nish-əs\ *adj* [MF *pernicieus,* fr. L *perniciosus,* fr. *pernicies* destruction, fr. *per-* through + *nec-, nex* violent death] : very destructive or injurious — **per-ni-cious-ly** *adv*

per-ora-tion \'per-ər-ˌā-shən, 'pər-\ *n* : the concluding part of a speech

¹**per-ox-ide** \pə-'räk-ˌsīd\ *n* : an oxide containing a large proportion of oxygen; *esp* : HYDROGEN PEROXIDE

²**peroxide** *vb* **-id-ed; -id-ing** : to bleach with hydrogen peroxide

perp *abbr* perpendicular

per-pen-dic-u-lar \ˌpər-pən-'dik-yə-lər\ *adj* **1** : standing at right angles to the plane of the horizon **2** : meeting another line at a right angle — **pependicular** *n* — **per·pen·dic·u·lar·i·ty** \-ˌdik-yə-ˈlar-ət-ē\ *n* — **per·pen·dic·u·lar·ly** *adv*

per·pe·trate \ˈpər-pə-ˌtrāt\ *vb* **-trat·ed; -trat·ing** : to be guilty of : COMMIT — **per·pe·tra·tion** \ˌpər-pə-ˈtrā-shən\ *n* — **per·pe·tra·tor** \ˈpər-pə-ˌtrāt-ər\ *n*

per·pet·u·al \pər-ˈpech-(ə-w)əl\ *adj* **1** : continuing forever : EVERLASTING **2** : occurring continually : CONSTANT ⟨∼ annoyance⟩ **syn** ceaseless, unceasing, continual, continuous, incessant, unremitting — **per·pet·u·al·ly** \-ē\ *adv*

per·pet·u·ate \pər-ˈpech-ə-ˌwāt\ *vb* **-at·ed; -at·ing** : to make perpetual : cause to last indefinitely — **per·pet·u·a·tion** \-ˌpech-ə-ˈwā-shən\ *n*

per·pe·tu·ity \ˌpər-pə-ˈt(y)ü-ət-ē\ *n, pl* **-it·ies 1** : endless time : ETERNITY **2** : the quality or state of being perpetual

per·plex \pər-ˈpleks\ *vb* : to disturb mentally; *esp* : CONFUSE — **per·plex·i·ty** \-ət-ē\ *n*

per·plexed \-ˈplekst\ *adj* **1** : filled with uncertainty : PUZZLED **2** : full of difficulty : COMPLICATED — **per·plexed·ly** \-ˈplek-səd-lē\ *adv*

per·qui·site \ˈpər-kwə-zət\ *n* : a privilege or profit beyond regular pay

pers *abbr* person; personal

per se \(ˌ)pər-ˈsā\ *adv* [L] : by, of, or in itself : as such

per·se·cute \ˈpər-si-ˌkyüt\ *vb* **-cut·ed; -cut·ing** : to pursue in such a way as to injure or afflict : HARASS; *esp* : to cause to suffer because of belief **syn** oppress, wrong, aggrieve — **per·se·cu·tion** \ˌpər-si-ˈkyü-shən\ *n* — **per·se·cu·tor** \ˈpər-si-ˌkyüt-ər\ *n*

per·se·vere \ˌpər-sə-ˈviər\ *vb* **-vered; -ver·ing** : to persist (as in an undertaking) in spite of difficulties — **per·se·ver·ance** \-ˈvir-əns\ *n*

Per·sian \ˈpər-zhən\ *n* **1** : a native or inhabitant of ancient Persia **2** : a member of one of the peoples of modern Iran **3** : the language of the Persians

Persian cat *n* : a stocky round-headed domestic cat that has long and silky fur

Persian lamb *n* : a pelt that is obtained from lambs that are older than those

yielding broadtail and that has very silky tightly curled fur

per·si·flage \ˈpər-si-ˌfläzh, ˈper-\ *n* [F, fr. *persifler* to banter, fr. *per-* thoroughly + *siffler* to whistle, hiss, boo, fr. L *sibilare*] : lightly jesting or mocking talk

per·sim·mon \pər-ˈsim-ən\ *n* : a tree related to the ebony; *also* : its edible orange-red plumlike fruit

per·sist \pər-ˈsist, -ˈzist\ *vb* **1** : to go on resolutely or stubbornly in spite of difficulties : PERSEVERE **2** : to continue to exist — **per·sis·tence** \-ˈsis-təns, -ˈzis-\ *n* — **per·sis·ten·cy** \-tən-sē\ *n* — **per·sis·tent** \-tənt\ *adj* — **per·sis·tent·ly** *adv*

per·snick·e·ty \pər-ˈsnik-ət-ē\ *adj* : fussy about small details

per·son \ˈpərs-ᵊn\ *n* [ME, fr. OF *persone*, fr. L *persona* actor's mask, character in a play, person, prob. fr. Etruscan *phersu* mask] **1** : a human being : INDIVIDUAL — used in combination esp. by those who prefer to avoid *man* in compounds applicable to both sexes ⟨chair*person*⟩ **2** : one of the three modes of being in the Godhead as understood by Trinitarians **3** : the body of a human being **4** : the individual personality of a human being : SELF **5** : reference of a segment of discourse to the speaker, to one spoken to, or to one spoken of esp. as indicated by certain pronouns

per·son·able \ˈpərs-(ᵊ-)nə-bəl\ *adj* : pleasing in person : ATTRACTIVE

per·son·age \ˈpərs-(ᵊ-)nij\ *n* : a person of rank, note, or distinction

¹per·son·al \ˈpərs-(ᵊ-)nəl\ *adj* **1** : of, relating to, or affecting a person : PRIVATE ⟨∼ correspondence⟩ **2** : done in person ⟨a ∼ inquiry⟩ **3** : relating to the person or body ⟨∼ injuries⟩ **4** : relating to an individual esp. in an offensive way ⟨resented such ∼ remarks⟩ **5** : of or relating to temporary or movable property as distinguished from real estate **6** : denoting grammatical person — **per·son·al·ly** \-ē\ *adv*

²personal *n* **1** : a short newspaper paragraph relating to a person or group or to personal matters **2** : a short personal or private communication in the classified ads section of a newspaper

personal computer *n* : MICROCOMPUTER

per·son·al·i·ty \ˌpərs-ᵊn-ˈal-ət-ē\ *n, pl*

-ties 1 : an offensively personal remark ⟨indulges in *personalities*⟩ **2** : distinctive personal character **3** : distinction of personal and social traits; *also* : a person having such quality **syn** individuality, temperament, disposition, makeup

per·son·al·ize \'pǝrs-(ǝ-)nǝ-ˌlīz\ *vb* **-ized; -iz·ing** : to make personal or individual; *esp* : to mark as belonging to a particular person

per·son·al·ty \'pǝrs-(ǝ-)nǝl-tē\ *n, pl* **-ties** : personal property

per·so·na non gra·ta \pǝr-ˌsō-nǝ-ˌnän-'grat-ǝ, -'grät-\ *adj* [L] : being personally unacceptable or unwelcome

per·son·ate \'pǝrs-ǝn-ˌāt\ *vb* **-at·ed; -at·ing** : IMPERSONATE, REPRESENT

per·son·i·fy \pǝr-'sän-ǝ-ˌfī\ *vb* **-fied; -fy·ing 1** : to think of or represent as a person **2** : to be the embodiment of : INCARNATE ⟨∼ the law⟩ — **per·son·i·fi·ca·tion** \-ˌsän-ǝ-fǝ-'kā-shǝn\ *n*

per·son·nel \ˌpǝrs-ǝn-'el\ *n* : a body of persons employed in a service or an organization

per·spec·tive \pǝr-'spek-tiv\ *n* **1** : the science of painting and drawing so that objects represented have apparent depth and distance **2** : the aspect in which a subject or its parts are mentally viewed; *esp* : a view of things (as objects or events) in their true relationship or relative importance

per·spi·cac·i·ty \ˌpǝr-spǝ-'kas-ǝt-ē\ *n* : acuteness of understanding or judgment — **per·spi·ca·cious** \-'kā-shǝs\ *adj*

per·spic·u·ous \pǝr-'spik-yǝ-wǝs\ *adj* : plain to the understanding — **per·spi·cu·i·ty** \ˌpǝr-spǝ-'kyü-ǝt-ē\ *n*

per·spire \pǝr-'spīr\ *vb* **per·spired; per·spir·ing** : SWEAT — **per·spi·ra·tion** \ˌpǝr-spǝ-'rā-shǝn\ *n*

per·suade \pǝr-'swād\ *vb* **per·suad·ed; per·suad·ing** : to move by argument or entreaty to a belief or course of action — **per·sua·sive** \-'swā-siv, -ziv\ *adj* — **per·sua·sive·ly** *adv* — **per·sua·sive·ness** *n*

per·sua·sion \pǝr-'swā-zhǝn\ *n* **1** : the act or process of persuading **2** : OPINION, BELIEF

¹pert \'pǝrt\ *adj* [ME, open, bold, pert, modif. of OF *apert,* fr. L *apertus* open, fr. pp. of *aperire* to open] **1**

: saucily free and forward : IMPUDENT **2** : stylishly trim : JAUNTY **3** : LIVELY

²pert *abbr* pertaining

per·tain \pǝr-'tān\ *vb* **1** : to belong to as a part, quality, or function ⟨duties ∼ing to the office⟩ **2** : to have reference : RELATE ⟨facts that ∼ to the case⟩ **syn** bear, appertain, apply

per·ti·na·cious \ˌpǝrt-ǝn-'ā-shǝs\ *adj* **1** : holding resolutely to an opinion or purpose **2** : obstinately persistent : TENACIOUS ⟨a ∼ bill collector⟩ **syn** obstinate, dogged, mulish, headstrong, perverse — **per·ti·nac·i·ty** \-'as-ǝt-ē\ *n*

per·ti·nent \'pǝrt-ǝn-ǝnt\ *adj* : relating to the matter under consideration **syn** relevant, germane, applicable, apropos — **per·ti·nence** \-ǝns\ *n*

per·turb \pǝr-'tǝrb\ *vb* : to disturb greatly esp. in mind : UPSET — **per·tur·ba·tion** \ˌpǝrt-ǝr-'bā-shǝn\ *n*

per·tus·sis *n* : WHOOPING COUGH

pe·ruke \pǝ-'rük\ *n* : WIG

pe·ruse \pǝ-'rüz\ *vb* **pe·rused; pe·rus·ing** : READ; *esp* : to read attentively — **pe·rus·al** \-'rü-zǝl\ *n*

Pe·ru·vi·an \pǝ-'rü-vē-ǝn\ *n* : a native or inhabitant of Peru

per·vade \pǝr-'vād\ *vb* **per·vad·ed; per·vad·ing** : to spread through every part of : PERMEATE, PENETRATE — **per·va·sive** \-ˌvā-siv, -ziv\ *adj*

per·verse \pǝr-'vǝrs\ *adj* **1** : turned away from what is right or good : CORRUPT **2** : obstinate in opposing what is reasonable or accepted — **per·verse·ly** *adv* — **per·verse·ness** *n* — **per·ver·si·ty** \-'vǝr-sǝt-ē\ *n*

per·ver·sion \pǝr-'vǝr-zhǝn\ *n* **1** : the action of perverting : the condition of being perverted **2** : a perverted form of something; *esp* : aberrant sexual behavior

¹per·vert \pǝr-'vǝrt\ *vb* **1** : to lead astray : CORRUPT ⟨∼ the young⟩ **2** : to divert to a wrong purpose : MISAPPLY ⟨∼ evidence⟩ **syn** deprave, debase, debauch, demoralize

²per·vert \'pǝr-ˌvǝrt\ *n* : one that is perverted; *esp* : a person given to sexual perversion

pe·se·ta \pǝ-'sāt-ǝ\ *n* — see MONEY table

pe·se·wa \pǝ-'sā-wǝ\ *n* — see *cedi* at MONEY table

pes·ky \'pes-kē\ *adj* **pes·ki·er; -est** : causing annoyance : TROUBLESOME

pe·so \'pā-sō\ *n, pl* **pesos** — see MONEY table

pes·si·mism \'pes-ə-ˌmiz-əm\ *n* [F *pessimisme,* fr. L *pessimus* worst] : an inclination to take the least favorable view (as of events) or to expect the worst possible outcome — **pes·si·mist** \-məst\ *n* — **pes·si·mis·tic** \ˌpes-ə-'mis-tik\ *adj*

pest \'pest\ *n* **1** : a destructive epidemic disease : PLAGUE **2** : a plant or animal detrimental to man **3** : one that pesters : NUISANCE

pes·ter \'pes-tər\ *vb* **pes·tered; pes·ter·ing** \-t(ə-)riŋ\ : to harass with petty irritations : ANNOY

pes·ti·cide \'pes-tə-ˌsīd\ *n* : an agent used to kill pests

pes·tif·er·ous \pes-'tif-(ə-)rəs\ *adj* **1** : PESTILENT **2** : ANNOYING

pes·ti·lence \'pes-tə-ləns\ *n* : a destructive infectious swiftly spreading disease; *esp* : PLAGUE

pes·ti·lent \-lənt\ *adj* **1** : dangerous to life : DEADLY; *also* : spreading or causing pestilence **2** : PERNICIOUS, HARMFUL **3** : TROUBLESOME

pes·ti·len·tial \ˌpes-tə-'len-chəl\ *adj* **1** : causing or tending to cause pestilence : DEADLY **2** : morally harmful — **pes·ti·len·tial·ly** \-ē\ *adv*

pes·tle \'pes-əl, 'pes-t³l\ *n* : an implement for grinding substances in a mortar

¹pet \'pet\ *n* **1** : FAVORITE, DARLING **2** : a domesticated animal kept for pleasure rather than utility

²pet *adj* **1** : kept or treated as a pet ⟨∼ dog⟩ **2** : expressing fondness ⟨∼ name⟩ **3** : particularly liked or favored

³pet *vb* **pet·ted; pet·ting** **1** : to stroke gently or lovingly **2** : to make a pet of : PAMPER **3** : to engage in amorous kissing and caressing

⁴pet *n* : a fit of peevishness, sulkiness, or anger

Pet *abbr* Peter

pet·al \'pet-³l\ *n* : one of the modified leaves of a flower's corolla

pe·tard \pə-'tär(d)\ *n* : a case containing an explosive to break down a door or gate or breach a wall

pe·ter \'pēt-ər\ *vb* : to diminish gradually and come to an end ⟨his energy ∼ed out⟩

Pe·ter \'pēt-ər\ *n* — see BIBLE table

pet·i·ole \'pet-ē-ˌōl\ *n* : a stalk that supports a leaf

pe·tite \pə-'tēt\ *adj* [F] : small and trim of figure ⟨a ∼ woman⟩

pe·tit four \ˌpet-ē-'fōr\ *n, pl* **petits fours** *or* **petit fours** \-'fōrz\ [F, lit., small oven] : a small cake cut from pound or sponge cake and frosted

¹pe·ti·tion \pə-'tish-ən\ *n* : an earnest request : ENTREATY; *esp* : a formal written request made to a superior

²petition *vb* **-tioned; -tion·ing** \-'tish-(ə-)niŋ\ : to make a petition — **pe·ti·tion·er** \-(ə-)nər\ *n*

pet·nap·ping \'pet-ˌnap-iŋ\ *n* : the act of stealing a pet

pe·trel \'pe-trəl\ *n* : any of various small seabirds that fly far from land

pet·ri·fy \'pe-trə-ˌfī\ *vb* **-fied; -fy·ing** **1** : to change into stony material **2** : to make rigid or inactive (as from fear or awe) — **pet·ri·fac·tion** \ˌpe-trə-'fak-shən\ *n*

pet·ro·chem·i·cal \ˌpe-trō-'kem-i-kəl\ *n* : a chemical isolated or derived from petroleum or natural gas — **pet·ro·chem·is·try** \-'kem-ə-strē\ *n*

pet·rol \'pe-trəl\ *n, Brit* : GASOLINE

pet·ro·la·tum \ˌpe-trə-'lāt-əm\ *n* : a tasteless, odorless, and oily or greasy substance from petroleum that is used esp. in ointments and dressings

pe·tro·leum \pə-'trō-lē-əm\ *n* [ML, fr. L *petr-* stone, rock (fr. Gk, fr. *petros* stone & *petra* rock) + *oleum* oil] : an oily flammable liquid obtained from wells drilled in the ground and refined into gasoline, fuel oils, and other products

petroleum jelly *n* : PETROLATUM

¹pet·ti·coat \'pet-ē-ˌkōt\ *n* **1** : a skirt worn under a dress **2** : an outer skirt

²petticoat *adj* : FEMALE ⟨∼ government⟩

pet·ti·fog \'pet-ē-ˌfòg, -ˌfäg\ *vb* **-fogged; -fog·ging** **1** : to engage in legal trickery **2** : to quibble over insignificant details — **pet·ti·fog·ger** *n*

pet·tish \'pet-ish\ *adj* : PEEVISH **syn** irritable, petulant, fretful, huffy, querulous

pet·ty \'pet-ē\ *adj* **pet·ti·er; -est** [ME *pety* small, minor, alter. of *petit,* fr. MF, small] **1** : having secondary rank : MINOR ⟨∼ prince⟩ **2** : of little importance : TRIFLING ⟨∼ faults⟩ **3** : marked by narrowness or meanness — **pet·ti-**

ly \\'pet-ᵊl-ē\\ *adv* — **pet·ti·ness** \\-ē-nəs\\ *n*

petty officer *n* : a subordinate officer in the navy or coast guard appointed from among the enlisted men

petty officer first class *n* : a petty officer ranking below a chief petty officer

petty officer second class *n* : a petty officer ranking below a petty officer first class

petty officer third class *n* : a petty officer ranking below a petty officer second class

pet·u·lant \\'pech-ə-lənt\\ *adj* : marked by capricious ill humor **syn** irritable, peevish, fretful, fractious, querulous — **pet·u·lance** \\-ləns\\ *n* — **pet·u·lant·ly** *adv*

pe·tu·nia \\pi-'t(y)ün-yə\\ *n* : a garden plant with bright funnel-shaped flowers

pew \\'pyü\\ *n* [ME *pewe*, fr. MF *puie* balustrade, fr. L *podia*, pl. of *podium* parapet, podium, fr. Gk *podion* base, dim. of *pod-*, *pous* foot] : one of the benches with backs fixed in rows in a church

pe·wee \\'pē-(ˌ)wē\\ *n* : any of various small flycatchers

pew·ter \\'pyüt-ər\\ *n* : an alloy of tin usu. with lead used esp. for kitchen or table utensils

pey·o·te \\pā-'ōt-ē\\ *also* **pey·otl** \\-'ōt-ᵊl\\ *n* : a stimulant drug derived from an American cactus; *also* : this cactus

pf *abbr* **1** pfennig **2** preferred

PFC *abbr* private first class

pfd *abbr* preferred

pfen·nig \\'fen-ig\\ *n, pl* **pfennig** *also* **pfennigs** *or* **pfen·ni·ge** \\'fen-i-gə\\ — see *deutsche mark, mark* at MONEY table

pg *abbr* page

PG *abbr* postgraduate

PGA *abbr* Professional Golfers' Association

pH \\(ˌ)pē-'āch\\ *n* : a value used to express acidity and alkalinity; *also* : the condition represented by such a value

PH *abbr* **1** pinch hit **2** public health

pha·eton \\'fā-ət-ᵊn\\ *n* [F *phaéton*, fr. Gk Phaethōn, son of the sun god who persuaded his father to let him drive the chariot of the sun but who lost control of the horses with disastrous consequences] **1** : a light 4-wheeled horse‑

drawn vehicle **2** : an open automobile with two cross seats

phage \\'fāj\\ *n* : BACTERIOPHAGE

pha·lanx \\'fā-ˌlaŋks\\ *n, pl* **pha·lanx·es** *or* **pha·lan·ges** \\fə-'lan-ˌjēz\\ **1** : a group or body (as of troops) in compact formation **2** *pl phalanges* : one of the digital bones of the hand or foot of a vertebrate

phal·a·rope \\'fal-ə-ˌrōp\\ *n, pl* **-ropes** *also* **-rope** : any of several small shorebirds

phal·lic \\'fal-ik\\ *adj* **1** : of, relating to, or resembling a phallus **2** : relating to or being the stage of psychosexual development in psychoanalytic theory during which children become interested in their own sexual organs

phal·lus \\'fal-əs\\ *n, pl* **phal·li** \\'fal-ˌī\\ *or* **phal·lus·es** : PENIS; *also* : a symbolic representation of the penis

phan·tasm \\'fan-ˌtaz-əm\\ *n* : a product of the imagination : ILLUSION

phan·tas·ma·go·ria \\fan-ˌtaz-mə-'gōr-ē-ə\\ *n* : a constantly shifting complex succession of things seen or imagined; *also* : a scene that constantly changes or fluctuates

phantasy *var of* FANTASY

phan·tom \\'fant-əm\\ *n* [deriv. of L *phantasma*] **1** : something (as a specter) that is apparent to sense but has no substantial existence **2** : a mere show : SHADOW **3** : a representation of something abstract, ideal, or incorporeal — **phantom** *adj* — **phan·tom·like** *adv or adj*

pha·raoh \\'fe(ə)r-ō, 'fā-rō\\ *n, often cap* : a ruler of ancient Egypt

phar·i·sa·ical \\ˌfar-ə-'sā-ə-kəl\\ *adj* : hypocritically self-righteous — **phar·i·sa·ical·ly** \\-k(ə-)lē\\ *adv*

phar·i·see \\'far-ə-ˌsē\\ *n* **1** *cap* : a member of an ancient Jewish sect noted for strict observance of rites and ceremonies of the traditional law **2** : a self‑righteous or hypocritical person — **phar·i·sa·ic** \\ˌfar-ə-'sā-ik\\ *adj*

pharm *abbr* pharmaceutical; pharmacist; pharmacy

phar·ma·ceu·ti·cal \\ˌfär-mə-'süt-i-kəl\\ *adj* **1** : of or relating to pharmacy or pharmacists **2** : MEDICINAL — **pharmaceutical** *n*

phar·ma·col·o·gy \\ˌfär-mə-'käl-ə-jē\\ *n* **1** : the science of drugs esp. as related to medicinal uses **2** : the reactions and properties of a drug — **phar·ma·co·log·i·cal** \-i-kəl\ *also* **phar·ma·co·log·ic** \-kə-'läj-ik\ *adj* — **phar·ma·col·o·gist** \-'käl-ə-jəst\ *n*

phar·ma·co·poe·ia *also* **phar·ma·co·pe·ia** \-kə-'pē-(y)ə\ *n* **1** : a book describing drugs and medicinal preparations **2** : a stock of drugs

phar·ma·cy \'fär-mə-sē\ *n, pl* **-cies** **1** : the art or practice of preparing and dispensing drugs **2** : DRUGSTORE — **phar·ma·cist** \-səst\ *n*

phar·os \'faər-ˌäs\ *n* : LIGHTHOUSE

phar·ynx \'far-iŋks\ *n, pl* **pha·ryn·ges** \fə-'rin-ˌjēz\ *also* **phar·ynx·es** : the space just back of the mouth into which the nostrils, esophagus, and trachea open — **pha·ryn·ge·al** \fə-'rin-j(ē-)əl, ˌfar-ən-'jē-əl\ *adj*

phase \'fāz\ *n* **1** : a particular appearance in a recurring series of changes ⟨~s of the moon⟩ **2** : a stage or interval in a process or cycle ⟨first ~ of an experiment⟩ **3** : an aspect or part under consideration

phase in *vb* : to introduce in stages

phase·out \'fāz-ˌaut\ *n* : a gradual stopping of operations or production

phase out \'fāz-'aut\ *vb* : to stop production or use of in stages

PhD *abbr* [L *philosophiae doctor*] doctor of philosophy

pheas·ant \'fez-ᵊnt\ *n, pl* **pheasant** *or* **pheasants** : any of various long-tailed brilliantly colored game birds related to the domestic fowl

phen·cy·cli·dine \ˌfen-'sī-klə-ˌdēn\ *n* : a drug used medicinally as an anesthetic and sometimes illicitly to induce vivid mental imagery

phe·no·bar·bi·tal \ˌfē-nō-'bär-bə-ˌtol\ *n* : a crystalline drug used as a hypnotic and sedative

phe·nol \'fē-ˌnōl, -ˌnol, fi-'nōl, -'nol\ *n* : a caustic poisonous acidic compound in tar used as a disinfectant

phe·nom·e·non \fi-'näm-ə-ˌnän, -nən\ *n, pl* **-na** \-nə\ *or* **-nons** [LL *phaenomenon*, fr. Gk *phainomenon*, fr. neut. of *phainomenos*, prp. of *phainesthai* to appear] **1** *pl* **-na** : an observable fact or event **2** : an outward sign of the working of a law of nature **3** *pl* **-nons** : an extraordinary person or thing : PRODIGY — **phe·nom·e·nal** \-'näm-ən-ᵊl\ *adj*

pher·o·mone \'fer-ə-ˌmōn\ *n* : a chemical substance that is produced by an animal and serves to stimulate a behavioral response in other individuals of the same species — **pher·o·mon·al** \ˌfer-ə-'mōn-ᵊl\ *adj*

phi·al \'fī-(-ə)l\ *n* : VIAL

Phil *abbr* Philippians

phi·lan·der \fə-'lan-dər\ *vb* **-dered; -der·ing** \-d(ə-)riŋ\ : to make love without serious intent : FLIRT — **phi·lan·der·er** *n*

phi·lan·thro·py \fə-'lan-thrə-pē\ *n, pl* **-pies** **1** : goodwill to fellowmen; *esp* : effort to promote human welfare **2** : a charitable act or gift; *also* : an organization that distributes or is supported by donated funds — **phil·an·throp·ic** \ˌfil-ən-'thräp-ik\ *adj* — **phi·lan·thro·pist** \fə-'lan-thrə-pəst\ *n*

phi·lat·e·ly \fə-'lat-ᵊl-ē\ *n* : the collection and study of postage and imprinted stamps — **phi·lat·e·list** \-ᵊl-əst\ *n*

Phi·le·mon \fə-'lē-mən, fī-\ *n* — see BIBLE table

Phi·lip·pi·ans \fə-'lip-ē-ənz\ *n* — see BIBLE table

phi·lip·pic \fə-'lip-ik\ *n* : TIRADE

phi·lis·tine \'fil-ə-ˌstēn; fə-'lis-tən\ *n, often cap* [*Philistine*, inhabitant of ancient Philistia (Palestine)] : a materialistic person; *esp* : one who is smugly insensitive or indifferent to intellectual or artistic values — **philistine** *adj, often cap*

philo·den·dron \ˌfil-ə-'den-drən\ *n, pl* **-drons** *or* **-dra** \-drə\ [NL, fr. Gk, neut. of *philodendros* loving trees, fr. *philos* dear, friendly + *dendron* tree] : any of various arums grown for their showy foliage

phi·lol·o·gy \fə-'läl-ə-jē\ *n* **1** : the study of literature and relevant fields **2** : LINGUISTICS; *esp* : historical and comparative linguistics — **phil·o·log·i·cal** \ˌfil-ə-'läj-i-kəl\ *adj* — **phi·lol·o·gist** \fə-'läl-ə-jəst\ *n*

philos *abbr* philosopher; philosophy

phi·los·o·pher \fə-'läs-ə-fər\ *n* **1** : a reflective thinker : SCHOLAR **2** : a student of or specialist in philosophy **3** : one whose philosophical perspective enables him to meet trouble calmly

phi·los·o·phize \fə-'läs-ə-ˌfīz\ *vb* **-phized; -phiz·ing** **1** : to reason like a philosopher : THEORIZE **2** : to expound a philosophy esp. superficially

phi·los·o·phy \fə-'läs-ə-fē\ *n, pl* **-phies** **1** : a critical study of fundamental beliefs and the grounds for them **2** : sciences and liberal arts exclusive of medicine, law, and theology ⟨doctor of ∼⟩ **3** : a system of philosophical concepts ⟨Aristotelian ∼⟩ **4** : a basic theory concerning a particular subject or sphere of activity **5** : the sum of the ideas and convictions of an individual or group ⟨his ∼ of life⟩ **6** : calmness of temper and judgment — **phil·o·soph·ic** \ˌfil-ə-'säf-ik\ *or* **phil·o·soph·i·cal** \-i-kəl\ *adj* — **phil·o·soph·i·cal·ly** \-k(ə-)lē\ *adv*

phil·ter *or* **phil·tre** \'fil-tər\ *n* **1** : a potion, drug, or charm held to arouse sexual passion **2** : a magic potion

phle·bi·tis \fli-'bīt-əs\ *n* : inflammation of a vein

phle·bot·o·my \fli-'bät-ə-mē\ *n, pl* **-mies** : the opening of a vein for removing or releasing blood

phlegm \'flem\ *n* : thick mucus secreted in abnormal quantity esp. in the nose and throat

phleg·mat·ic \fleg-'mat-ik\ *adj* : having or showing a slow and stolid temperament **syn** impassive, apathetic, stoic, stolid

phlo·em \'flō-ˌem\ *n* : a vascular plant tissue external to the xylem that carries dissolved food material downward

phlox \'fläks\ *n, pl* **phlox** *or* **phlox·es** : any of several American herbs; *esp* : one that has tall stalks with showy spreading terminal clusters of flowers

pho·bia \'fō-bē-ə\ *n* : an irrational persistent fear or dread

phoe·be \'fē-(ˌ)bē\ *n* : a flycatcher of the eastern U.S. that has a slight crest and is grayish brown above and yellowish white below

phoe·nix \'fē-niks\ *n* : a legendary bird held to live for centuries and then to burn itself to death and rise fresh and young from its ashes

phon *abbr* phonetics

¹phone \'fōn\ *n* **1** : EARPHONE **2** : TELEPHONE

²phone *vb* **phoned; phon·ing** : TELEPHONE

pho·neme \'fō-ˌnēm\ *n* : one of the smallest units of speech that distinguish one utterance from another — **pho·ne·mic** \fō-'nē-mik\ *adj*

pho·net·ics \fə-'net-iks\ *n* : the study and systematic classification of the sounds made in spoken utterance — **pho·net·ic** \-ik\ *adj* — **pho·ne·ti·cian** \ˌfō-nə-'tish-ən\ *n*

pho·nic \'fän-ik\ *adj* **1** : of, relating to, or producing sound **2** : of or relating to the sounds of speech or to phonics — **pho·ni·cal·ly** \-i-k(ə-)lē\ *adv*

pho·nics \'fän-iks\ *n* : a method of teaching people to read and pronounce words by learning the phonetic value of letters, letter groups, and esp. syllables

pho·no·graph \'fō-nə-ˌgraf\ *n* : an instrument for reproducing sounds by means of the vibration of a needle following a spiral groove on a revolving disc — **pho·no·graph·ic** \ˌfō-nə-'graf-ik\ *adj* — **pho·no·graph·i·cal·ly** \-i-k(ə-)lē\ *adv*

pho·nol·o·gy \fə-'näl-ə-jē\ *n* : a study and description of the sound changes in a language — **pho·no·log·i·cal** \ˌfōn-ᵊl-'äj-i-kəl\ *adj* — **pho·nol·o·gist** \fə-'näl-ə-jəst\ *n*

pho·ny *or* **pho·ney** \'fō-nē\ *adj* **pho·ni·er; -est** : marked by empty pretension : FAKE — **phony** *n*

phosph- *or* **phospho-** *comb form* **1** : phosphorus **2** : phosphate

phos·phate \'fäs-ˌfāt\ *n* : a salt of a phosphoric acid — **phos·phat·ic** \fäs-'fat-ik\ *adj*

phos·phor \'fäs-fər\ *also* **phos·phore** \-ˌfōr, -fər\ *n* : a phosphorescent substance

phos·pho·res·cence \ˌfäs-fə-'res-ᵊns\ *n* **1** : luminescence caused by radiation absorption that continues after the radiation has stopped **2** : an enduring luminescence without sensible heat — **phos·pho·res·cent** \-ᵊnt\ *adj* — **phos·pho·res·cent·ly** *adv*

phosphoric acid \ˌfäs-ˌfòr-ik-, -ˌfär-\ *n* : any of several oxygen-containing acids of phosphorus

phos·pho·rus \'fäs-f(ə-)rəs\ *n* [NL, fr. Gk *phōsphoros* light-bearing, fr. *phōs* light + *pherein* to carry, bring] : a nonmetallic chemical element that has characteristics similar to nitrogen and occurs widely esp. as phosphates — **phos•phor•ic** \fäs-ˈfȯr-ik, -ˈfär-\ *adj* — **phos•pho•rous** \ˈfäs-f(ə-)rəs; fäs-ˈfȯr-əs, -ˈfȯr-\ *adj*

phot- *or* **photo-** *comb form* **1** : light **2** : photograph : photographic **3** : photoelectric

pho•to \ˈfōt-ō\ *n, pl* **photos** : PHOTOGRAPH — **photo** *vb or adj*

pho•to•cell \ˈfōt-ə-ˌsel\ *n* : PHOTOELECTRIC CELL

pho•to•chem•i•cal \ˌfōt-ō-ˈkem-i-kəl\ *adj* : of, relating to, or resulting from the chemical action of radiant energy

pho•to•com•pose \-kəm-ˈpōz\ *vb* : to compose reading matter for reproduction by means of characters photographed on film — **pho•to•com•po•si•tion** \-ˌkäm-pə-ˈzish-ən\ *n*

pho•to•copy \ˈfōt-ə-ˌkäp-ē\ *n* : a photographic reproduction of graphic matter — **photocopy** *vb*

pho•to•elec•tric \ˌfōt-ō-i-ˈlek-trik\ *adj* : relating to an electrical effect due to the interaction of light with matter — **pho•to•elec•tri•cal•ly** \-tri-k(ə-)lē\ *adv*

photoelectric cell *n* : a device in which variations in light are converted into variations in an electric current

pho•to•en•grave \ˌfōt-ō-in-ˈgrāv\ *vb* : to make a photoengraving of

pho•to•en•grav•ing \-ˈgrā-viŋ\ *n* : a process by which an etched printing plate is made from a photograph or drawing; *also* : a print made from such a plate

photo finish *n* : a race finish so close that a photograph of the finish is used to determine the winner

¹pho•tog \fə-ˈtäg\ *n* : PHOTOGRAPHER

²photog *abbr* photographic; photography

pho•to•ge•nic \ˌfōt-ə-ˈjen-ik\ *adj* : eminently suitable esp. aesthetically for being photographed

pho•to•graph \ˈfōt-ə-ˌgraf\ *n* : a picture taken by photography — **pho•to•graph** *vb* — **pho•tog•ra•pher** \fə-ˈtäg-rə-fər\ *n*

pho•tog•ra•phy \fə-ˈtäg-rə-fē\ *n* : the art or process of producing images on a sensitized surface (as film in a camera) by the action of light — **pho•to•graph•ic** \ˌfōt-ə-ˈgraf-ik\ *adj* — **pho•to•graph•i•cal•ly** \-i-k(ə-)lē\ *adv*

pho•to•gra•vure \ˌfōt-ə-grə-ˈvyu̇r\ *n* : a process for making prints from an in-

taglio plate prepared by photographic methods

pho•to•li•thog•ra•phy \ˌfōt-ō-lith-ˈäg-rə-fē\ *n* : the process of photographically transferring a pattern to a surface for etching (as in making an integrated circuit)

pho•tom•e•ter \fō-ˈtäm-ət-ər\ *n* : an instrument for measuring luminous intensity — **pho•to•met•ric** \ˌfōt-ə-ˈme-trik\ *adj* — **pho•tom•e•try** \fō-ˈtäm-ə-trē\ *n*

pho•to•mi•cro•graph \ˌfōt-ə-ˈmī-krə-ˌgraf\ *n* : a photograph of a magnified image of a small object — **pho•to•mi•crog•ra•phy** \-mī-ˈkräg-rə-fē\ *n*

pho•ton \ˈfō-ˌtän\ *n* : a quantum of radiant energy

pho•to•play \ˈfōt-ō-ˌplā\ *n* : MOTION PICTURE

pho•to•sen•si•tive \ˌfōt-ə-ˈsen-sət-iv\ *adj* : sensitive or sensitized to the action of radiant energy

pho•to•sphere \ˈfōt-ə-ˌsfiər\ *n* **1** : a sphere of light **2** : the luminous surface of a star — **pho•to•spher•ic** \ˌfōt-ə-ˈsfi(ə)r-ik, -ˈsfer-\ *adj*

pho•to•syn•the•sis \ˌfōt-ō-ˈsin-thə-səs\ *n* : formation of carbohydrates by chlorophyll-containing plants exposed to sunlight — **pho•to•syn•the•size** \-ˌsīz\ *vb* — **pho•to•syn•thet•ic** \-sin-ˈthet-ik\ *adj*

phr *abbr* phrase

¹phrase \ˈfrāz\ *n* **1** : a brief expression **2** : a group of two or more grammatically related words that form a sense unit expressing a thought

²phrase *vb* **phrased; phras•ing** : to express in words

phrase•ol•o•gy \ˌfrā-zē-ˈäl-ə-jē\ *n, pl* **-gies** : a manner of phrasing : STYLE

phras•ing \ˈfrā-ziŋ\ *n* : style of expression

phre•net•ic \fri-ˈnet-ik\ *adj* : FRENETIC

phren•ic \ˈfren-ik\ *adj* : of or relating to the diaphragm ⟨∼ nerves⟩

phre•nol•o•gy \fri-ˈnäl-ə-jē\ *n* : the study of the conformation of the skull as indicative of mental faculties and character traits

phy•lac•tery \fə-ˈlak-t(ə-)rē\ *n, pl* **-ter•ies** **1** : one of two small square leather boxes containing slips inscribed with scripture passages and traditionally worn on the left arm and forehead by

Jewish men during morning weekday prayers **2** : AMULET

phy·lum \ˈfī-ləm\ *n, pl* **phy·la** \-lə\ : a major division of the animal and in some classifications the plant kingdom; *also* : a group (as of people) apparently of common origin

phys *abbr* **1** physical **2** physics

¹phys·ic \ˈfiz-ik\ *n* **1** : the profession of medicine **2** : MEDICINE; *esp* : CATHARTIC

²physic *vb* **phys·icked; phys·ick·ing** : PURGE

¹phys·i·cal \ˈfiz-i-kəl\ *adj* **1** : of or relating to nature or the laws of nature **2** : material as opposed to mental or spiritual **3** : of, relating to, or produced by the forces and operations of physics **4** : of or relating to the body — **phys·i·cal·ly** \-k(ə-)lē\ *adv*

²physical *n* : an examination of the bodily functions and condition of an individual

physical education *n* : instruction in the development and care of the body ranging from simple calisthenics to training in hygiene, gymnastics, and the performance and management of athletic games

physical examination *n* : PHYSICAL

physical science *n* : any of the sciences (as physics and astronomy) that deal primarily with nonliving materials — **physical scientist** *n*

physical therapy *n* : the treatment of disease by physical and mechanical means (as massage, exercise, water, or heat) — **physical therapist** *n*

phy·si·cian \fə-ˈzish-ən\ *n* : a doctor of medicine

phys·i·cist \ˈfiz-ə-səst\ *n* : a specialist in physics

phys·ics \ˈfiz-iks\ *n* **1** : the science of matter and energy and their interactions **2** : physical properties and composition

phys·i·og·no·my \ˌfiz-ē-ˈä(g)-nə-mē\ *n, pl* **-mies** : facial appearance esp. as a reflection of inner character

phys·i·og·ra·phy \ˌfiz-ē-ˈäg-rə-fē\ *n* : geography dealing with physical features of the earth — **phys·io·graph·ic** \ˌfiz-ē-ō-ˈgraf-ik\ *adj*

phys·i·ol·o·gy \ˌfiz-ē-ˈäl-ə-jē\ *n* **1** : a science dealing with the functions and functioning of living matter and be-

ings **2** : functional processes in an organism or any of its parts — **phys·i·o·log·i·cal** \-ē-ə-ˈläj-i-kəl\ *or* **phys·i·o·log·ic** \-ik\ *adj* — **phys·i·o·log·i·cal·ly** \-i-k(ə-)lē\ *adv* — **phys·i·ol·o·gist** \-ē-ˈäl-ə-jəst\ *n*

phys·io·ther·a·py \ˌfiz-ē-ō-ˈther-ə-pē\ *n* : treatment of disease by physical means (as massage or exercise) — **phys·io·ther·a·pist** \-pəst\ *n*

phy·sique \fə-ˈzēk\ *n* : the build of a person's body : bodily constitution

phy·to·plank·ton \ˈfīt-ō-ˌplaŋk-tən\ *n* : plant life of the plankton

¹pi *also* **pie** \ˈpī\ *n, pl* **pies** : jumbled type

²pi *n, pl* **pis** \ˈpīz\ : the symbol π denoting the ratio of the circumference of a circle to its diameter; *also* : the ratio itself

pi·a·nis·si·mo \ˌpē-ə-ˈnis-ə-ˌmō\ *adv or adj* : very softly — used as a direction in music

pi·a·nist \pē-ˈan-əst, ˈpē-ə-nəst\ *n* : one who plays the piano

¹pi·a·no \pē-ˈän-ō\ *adv or adj* : SOFTLY — used as a direction in music

²piano \pē-ˈan-ō\ *n, pl* **pianos** [It, short for *pianoforte,* fr. *piano e forte* soft and loud, fr. *piano* soft (fr. L *planus* level, flat) + *forte* loud, fr. L *fortis* strong; fr. the fact that its tones could be varied in loudness] : a musical instrument having steel strings sounded by felt covered hammers operated from a keyboard

pi·ano·forte \pē-ˌan-ō-ˈfȯr-ˌtā, -tē; pē-ˈan-ə-ˌfȯrt\ *n* : PIANO

pi·as·ter *or* **pi·as·tre** \pē-ˈas-tər\ *n* — see *lira, pound* at MONEY table

pi·az·za \pē-ˈaz-ə, *esp for 1* -ˈat-sə\ *n, pl* **piazzas** *or* **pi·az·ze** \-ˈat-(ˌ)sā, -ˈät-\ [It, fr. L *platea* broad street] **1** : an open square esp. in an Italian town **2** : a long hall with an arched roof; *also, dial* : VERANDA

pi·broch \ˈpē-ˌbräk\ *n* : a set of variations for the bagpipe

pic \ˈpik\ *n, pl* **pics** *or* **pix** \ˈpiks\ **1** : PHOTOGRAPH **2** : MOTION PICTURE

pi·ca \ˈpī-kə\ *n* : a typewriter type providing 10 characters to the inch

pic·a·resque \ˌpik-ə-ˈresk, ˌpē-kə-\ *adj* : of or relating to rogues ⟨∼ fiction⟩

pic·a·yune \ˌpik-ē-ˈ(y)ün\ *adj* [F *picaillon* halfpenny] : of little value : TRIVIAL; *also* : PETTY

pic·ca·lil·li \ˌpik-ə-'lil-ē\ *n* : a pungent relish of chopped vegetables and spices

pic·co·lo \'pik-ə-ˌlō\ *n, pl* **-los** [It, short for *piccolo flauto* small flute] : a small shrill flute pitched an octave higher than the ordinary flute

pice \'pīs\ *n, pl* **pice** : PAISA

¹**pick** \'pik\ *vb* **1** : to pierce or break up with a pointed instrument **2** : to remove bit by bit ⟨∼ meat from bones⟩; *also* : to remove covering matter from **3** : to gather by plucking ⟨∼ apples⟩ **4** : CULL, SELECT **5** : ROB ⟨∼ a pocket⟩ **6** : PROVOKE ⟨∼ a quarrel⟩ **7** : to dig into or pull lightly at **8** : to pluck with fingers or a plectrum **9** : to loosen or pull apart with a sharp point ⟨∼ wool⟩ **10** : to unlock with a wire **11** : to eat sparingly — **pick·er** *n*

²**pick** *n* **1** : the act or privilege of choosing **2** : the best or choicest one **3** : the part of a crop gathered at one time

³**pick** *n* **1** : PICKAX **2** : a pointed implement used for picking **3** : a small thin piece (as of metal) used to pluck the strings of a stringed instrument

pick·a·back \'pig-ē-ˌbak, 'pik-ə-\ var of PIGGYBACK

pick·ax \'pik-ˌaks\ *n* : a tool with a wooden handle and a blade pointed at one end or at both ends that is used by diggers and miners

pick·er·el \'pik(-ə)-rəl\ *n, pl* **pickerel** *or* **pickerels** : any of various small pikes; *also* : WALLEYE 2

pick·er·el·weed \-rəl-ˌwēd\ *n* : a blue-flowered American shallow-water herb

¹**pick·et** \'pik-ət\ *n* **1** : a pointed stake (as for a fence) **2** : a detached body of soldiers on outpost duty; *also* : SENTINEL **3** : a person posted by a labor union where workers are on strike; *also* : a person posted for a demonstration

²**picket** *vb* **1** : to guard with pickets **2** : TETHER **3** : to post pickets at ⟨∼ a factory⟩ **4** : to serve as a picket

pick·ings \'pik-iŋz, -ənz\ *n pl* **1** : gleanable or eatable fragments : SCRAPS **2** : yield for effort expended : RETURN; *also* : share of spoils

pick·le \'pik-əl\ *n* **1** : a brine or vinegar solution for preserving foods; *also* : a

food preserved in a pickle **2** : a difficult situation : PLIGHT — **pickle** *vb*

pick·lock \'pik-ˌläk\ *n* **1** : a tool for picking locks **2** : BURGLAR, THIEF

pick·pock·et \'pik-ˌpäk-ət\ *n* : one who steals from pockets

pick·up \'pik-ˌəp\ *n* **1** : a picking up **2** : revival of activity : IMPROVEMENT **3** : ACCELERATION **4** : a temporary chance acquaintance **5** : the conversion of mechanical movements into electrical impulses in the reproduction of sound; *also* : a device for making such conversion **6** : a light truck having an enclosed cab and an open body with low sides and a tailgate

pick up \(')pik-'əp\ *vb* **1** : to take hold of and lift **2** : IMPROVE **3** : to put in order

picky \'pik-ē\ *adj* **pick·i·er; -est** : FUSSY, FINICKY

¹**pic·nic** \'pik-ˌnik\ *n* : an outing with food usu. provided by members of the group and eaten in the open

²**picnic** *vb* **pic·nicked; pic·nick·ing** : to go on a picnic : eat in picnic fashion

pi·co·sec·ond \'pē-kō-ˌsek-ənd\ *n* : one trillionth of a second

pi·cot \'pē-ˌkō\ *n* : one of a series of small loops forming an edging on ribbon or lace

pic·to·ri·al \pik-'tōr-ē-əl\ *adj* : of, relating to, or consisting of pictures

¹**pic·ture** \'pik-chər\ *n* **1** : a representation made by painting, drawing, or photography **2** : a vivid description in words **3** : IMAGE, COPY **4** : a transitory visual image or reproduction **5** : MOTION PICTURE **6** : SITUATION

²**picture** *vb* **pic·tured; pic·tur·ing** **1** : to paint or draw a picture of **2** : to describe vividly in words **3** : to form a mental image of

pic·tur·esque \ˌpik-chə-'resk\ *adj* **1** : resembling a picture ⟨a ∼ landscape⟩ **2** : CHARMING, QUAINT ⟨a ∼ character⟩ **3** : GRAPHIC, VIVID ⟨a ∼ account⟩ — **pic·tur·esque·ness** *n*

picture tube *n* : a cathode-ray tube on which the picture in a television set appears

pid·dle \'pid-ᵊl\ *vb* **pid·dled; pid·dling** \'pid-(ᵊ-)liŋ\ : to act or work idly : DAWDLE

pid·dling \-(ᵊ-)lən, -(ᵊ-)liŋ\ *adj* : TRIVIAL, PALTRY

pid·gin \'pij-ən\ *n* [fr. *Pidgin English*, Pidgin E, modif. of E *business English*] : a simplified speech used for communication between people with different languages; *esp* : an English-based pidgin used in the Orient

¹**pie** \'pī\ *n* : a dish consisting of a pastry crust and a filling (as of fruit or meat)

²**pie** var of PI

¹**pie·bald** \'pī-₁bȯld\ *adj* : of different colors; *esp* : blotched with white and black

²**piebald** *n* : a piebald animal (as a horse)

¹**piece** \'pēs\ *n* **1** : a part of a whole : FRAGMENT **2** : one of a group, set, or mass ⟨chess ∼⟩; *also* : a single item ⟨a ∼ of news⟩ **3** : a length, weight, or size in which something is made or sold **4** : a product (as an essay) of creative work **5** : FIREARM **6** : COIN

²**piece** *vb* **pieced; piec·ing 1** : to repair or complete by adding pieces : PATCH **2** : to join into a whole

pièce de ré·sis·tance \pē-₁es-də-rä-₁zē-'stäns\ *n, pl* **pièces de ré·sis·tance** *same*\ **1** : the chief dish of a meal **2** : an outstanding item

piece·meal \'pēs-₁mēl\ *adv or adj* : one piece at a time : GRADUALLY

piece·work \-₁wərk\ *n* : work done and paid for by the piece — **piece·work·er** *n*

pied \'pīd\ *adj* : of two or more colors in blotches : VARIEGATED

pied–à–terre \pē-₁ȧd-ə-'ter\ *n, pl* **pieds–à–terre** *same*\ [F, lit., foot to the ground] : a temporary or second lodging

pier \'piər\ *n* **1** : a support for a bridge span **2** : a structure built out into the water for use as a landing place or a promenade or to protect or form a harbor **3** : an upright supporting part (as a pillar) of a building or structure

pierce \'piərs\ *vb* **pierced; pierc·ing 1** : to enter or thrust into sharply or painfully : STAB **2** : to make a hole in or through : PERFORATE **3** : to force or make a way into or through : PENETRATE **4** : to see through : DISCERN

pies *pl of* PI *or of* PIE

pi·ety \'pī-ət-ē\ *n, pl* **pi·et·ies 1** : fidelity to natural obligations (as to parents) **2** : dutifulness in religion : DEVOUTNESS **3** : a pious act **syn** allegiance, devotion, loyalty

pif·fle \'pif-əl\ *n* : trifling talk or action

pig \'pig\ *n* **1** : SWINE; *esp* : a young swine **2** : PORK **3** : one thought to resemble a pig (as in dirtiness or greed) **4** : a casting of metal (as iron or lead) run directly from a smelting furnace into a mold

pi·geon \'pij-ən\ *n* : any of numerous stout-bodied short-legged birds with smooth thick plumage

¹**pi·geon·hole** \'pij-ən-₁hōl\ *n* : a small open compartment (as in a desk) for keeping letters or documents

²**pigeonhole** *vb* **1** : to place in or as if in a pigeonhole : FILE **2** : to lay aside **3** : CLASSIFY

pi·geon–toed \'pij-ən-₁tōd\ *adj* : having the toes turned in

pig·gish \'pig-ish\ *adj* **1** : GREEDY **2** : STUBBORN

pig·gy·back \'pig-ē-₁bak\ *adv or adj* **1** : up on the back and shoulders **2** : on a railroad flatcar

pig·head·ed \'pig-'hed-əd\ *adj* : OBSTINATE, STUBBORN

pig latin *n, often cap L* : a jargon that is made by systematic alteration of English

pig·let \'pig-lət\ *n* : a small usu. young hog

pig·ment \'pig-mənt\ *n* **1** : coloring matter **2** : a powder mixed with a suitable liquid to give color (as in paints and enamels)

pig·men·ta·tion \₁pig-mən-'tā-shən\ *n* : coloration with or deposition of pigment; *esp* : an excessive deposition of bodily pigment

pigmy var of PYGMY

pig·nut \'pig-₁nət\ *n* : any of several bitter hickory nuts; *also* : a tree bearing these

pig·pen \-₁pen\ *n* **1** : a pen for pigs **2** : a dirty place

pig·skin \-₁skin\ *n* **1** : the skin of a pig; *also* : leather made from it **2** : FOOTBALL 2

pig·sty \-₁stī\ *n* : PIGPEN

pig·tail \-₁tāl\ *n* : a tight braid of hair

pi·ka \'pī-kə\ *n* : any of various small short-eared mammals of the rocky uplands of Asia and western No. America that are related to the rabbits

¹**pike** \'pīk\ *n* : a sharp point or spike

²**pike** *n, pl* **pike** *or* **pikes** : a large slender

long-snouted freshwater food fish; *also* : a related fish

³pike *n* : a long wooden shaft with a pointed steel head formerly used as a foot soldier's weapon

⁴pike *n* : TURNPIKE

pik·er \'pī-kər\ *n* 1 : one who does things in a small way or on a small scale 2 : TIGHTWAD, CHEAPSKATE

pike·staff \'pīk-ˌstaf\ *n* : the staff of a foot soldier's pike

pi·laf *or* **pi·laff** \pi-'läf, 'pē-ˌläf\ *or* **pi·lau** \pi-'lō, -'lò, 'pē-lō, -lò\ *n* : a dish made of seasoned rice often with meat

pi·las·ter \pi-'las-tər, 'pī-ˌlas-tər\ *n* : a slightly projecting upright column that ornaments or helps to support a wall

pil·chard \'pil-chərd\ *n* : any of several fishes related to the herrings and often packed as sardines

¹pile \'pīl\ *n* : a long slender column (as of wood or steel) driven into the ground to support a vertical load

²pile *n* 1 : a quantity of things heaped together 2 : PYRE 3 : a great number or quantity : LOT

³pile *vb* **piled; pil·ing** 1 : to lay in a pile : STACK 2 : to heap up : ACCUMULATE 3 : to press forward in a mass : CROWD

⁴pile *n* : a velvety surface of fine short hairs or threads (as on cloth) — **piled** \'pīld\ *adj* — **pile·less** *adj*

piles \'pīlz\ *n pl* : HEMORRHOIDS

pil·fer \'pil-fər\ *vb* **pil·fered; pil·fer·ing** \-f(ə-)riŋ\ : to steal in small quantities

pil·grim \'pil-grəm\ *n* [ME, fr. OF *peligrin*, fr. LL *pelegrinus*, alter. of L *peregrinus* foreigner, fr. *peregrinus* foreign, fr. *pereger* being abroad, fr. *per* through + *ager* land] 1 : one who journeys in foreign lands : WAYFARER 2 : one who travels to a shrine or holy place as an act of devotion 3 *cap* : one of the English settlers founding Plymouth colony in 1620

pil·grim·age \-grə-mij\ *n* : a journey of a pilgrim esp. to a shrine or holy place

pil·ing \'pī-liŋ\ *n* : a structure of piles

pill \'pil\ *n* 1 : a medicine prepared in a little ball to be taken whole 2 : a disagreeable or tiresome person 3 : an oral contraceptive — usu. used with *the*

pil·lage \'pil-ij\ *vb* **pil·laged; pil·lag·ing** : to take booty : LOOT, PLUNDER — **pillage** *n*

pil·lar \'pil-ər\ *n* 1 : a strong upright support (as for a roof) 2 : a column or shaft standing alone esp. as a monument — **pil·lared** \-ərd\ *adj*

pill·box \'pil-ˌbäks\ *n* 1 : a low usu. round box to hold pills 2 : something (as a low concrete emplacement for machine guns) shaped like a pillbox

pil·lion \'pil-yən\ *n* 1 : a pad or cushion placed behind a saddle for an extra rider 2 : a motorcycle or bicycle saddle for a passenger

¹pil·lo·ry \'pil-(ə-)rē\ *n, pl* **-ries** : a wooden frame for public punishment having holes in which the head and hands can be locked

²pillory *vb* **-ried; -ry·ing** 1 : to set in a pillory 2 : to expose to public scorn

¹pil·low \'pil-ō\ *n* : a case filled with springy material (as feathers) and used to support the head of a resting person

²pillow *vb* : to rest or place on or as if on a pillow; *also* : to serve as a pillow for

pil·low·case \'pil-ə-ˌkās, -ō-\ *n* : a removable covering for a pillow

¹pi·lot \'pī-lət\ *n* 1 : HELMSMAN, STEERSMAN 2 : a person qualified and licensed to take ships into and out of a port 3 : GUIDE, LEADER 4 : one that flies an aircraft or spacecraft 5 : a television show filmed or taped as a sample of a proposed series — **pi·lot·less** *adj*

²pilot *vb* : CONDUCT, GUIDE; *esp* : to act as pilot of

³pilot *adj* : serving as a guiding or activating device or as a testing or trial unit ⟨a ~ light⟩ ⟨a ~ factory⟩

pi·lot·house \'pī-lət-ˌhaùs\ *n* : an enclosed place forward on the upper deck of a ship that shelters the steering gear and the helmsman

pil·sner *also* **pil·sen·er** \'pilz-(ə-)nər\ *n* [G, lit., of Pilsen, city in Czechoslovakia (now Plzeň)] 1 : a light beer with a strong flavor of hops 2 : a tall slender footed glass for beer

pi·men·to \pə-'ment-ō\ *n, pl* **pimentos** *or* **pimento** [Sp *pimienta* allspice, pepper, fr. LL *pigmenta*, pl. of *pigmentum* plant juice, fr. L, pigment] 1 : PIMIENTO 2 : ALLSPICE

pi·mien·to \pə-'m(y)ent-ō\ *n, pl* **-tos** : a

mild red sweet pepper fruit that yields paprika

pimp \'pimp\ *n* : a man who solicits clients for a prostitute — **pimp** *vb*

pim·per·nel \'pim-pər-ˌnel, -pər-nəl\ *n* : any of a genus of herbs related to the primroses and having flowers that close in rainy or cloudy weather

pim·ple \'pim-pəl\ *n* : a small inflamed swelling on the skin often containing pus — **pim·ply** \-p(ə-)lē\ *adj*

¹**pin** \'pin\ *n* **1** : a piece of wood or metal used esp. for fastening articles together or as a support by which one article may be suspended from another; *esp* : a small pointed piece of wire with a head used for fastening clothes or attaching papers **2** : an ornament or emblem fastened to clothing with a pin **3** : one of the wooden pieces constituting the target (as in bowling); *also* : the staff of the flag marking a hole on a golf course **4** : LEG

²**pin** *vb* **pinned; pin·ning 1** : to fasten with a pin **2** : to press together and hold fast **3** : to make dependent ⟨*pinned* their hopes on one man⟩ **4** : to assign the blame for ⟨∼ a crime on someone⟩ **5** : to define clearly : ESTABLISH ⟨∼ down an idea⟩ **6** : to hold fast or immobile in a spot or position

pi·ña co·la·da \ˌpēn-yə-kō-'läd-ə\ *n* [Sp, lit., strained pineapple] : a tall drink made of rum, cream of coconut, and pineapple juice mixed with ice

pin·afore \'pin-ə-ˌfōr\ *n* : a sleeveless dress or apron fastened at the back

pince–nez \paⁿs-'nā\ *n, pl* **pince–nez** \-'nā(z)\ [F, lit., pinch-nose] : eyeglasses clipped to the nose by a spring

pin·cer \'pin-sər\ *n* **1** *pl* : a gripping instrument with two handles and two grasping jaws **2** : a claw (as of a lobster) resembling pincers

¹**pinch** \'pinch\ *vb* **1** : to squeeze between the finger and thumb or between the jaws of an instrument **2** : to compress painfully : CRAMP **3** : CONTRACT, SHRIVEL **4** : to be miserly; *also* : to subject to strict economy **5** : STEAL **6** : ARREST

²**pinch** *n* **1** : a critical point **2** : painful effect **3** : an act of pinching **4** : a very small quantity **5** : ARREST

³**pinch** *adj* : SUBSTITUTE ⟨a ∼ runner⟩

pinch–hit \(ˈ)pinch-'hit\ *vb* **1** : to bat in the place of another player esp. when a hit is particularly needed **2** : to act or serve in place of another — **pinch hit** *n* — **pinch hitter** *n*

pin curl *n* : a curl made usu. by dampening a strand of hair, coiling it, and securing it by a hairpin or clip

pin·cush·ion \'pin-ˌkush-ən\ *n* : a cushion for pins not in use

¹**pine** \'pīn\ *n* : any of a genus of evergreen cone-bearing trees; *also* : the light durable resinous wood of a pine

²**pine** *vb* **pined; pin·ing 1** : to lose vigor or health through distress **2** : to long for something intensely

pi·ne·al \'pī-nē-əl, pī-'nē-əl\ *n* : PINEAL GLAND — **pineal** *adj*

pineal gland *n* : a small usu. conical appendage of the brain of all vertebrates with a cranium that is variously postulated to be a vestigial third eye, an endocrine organ, or the seat of the soul

pine·ap·ple \'pīn-ˌap-əl\ *n* : a tropical plant bearing an edible juicy fruit; *also* : its fruit

pin·feath·er \'pin-ˌfeth-ər\ *n* : a new feather just coming through the skin

ping \'piŋ\ *n* **1** : a sharp sound like that of a bullet striking **2** : engine knock

pin·hole \'pin-ˌhōl\ *n* : a small hole made by, for, or as if by a pin

¹**pin·ion** \'pin-yən\ *n* : the end section of a bird's wing; *also* : WING

²**pinion** *vb* : to restrain by binding the arms; *also* : SHACKLE

³**pinion** *n* : a gear with a small number of teeth designed to mesh with a larger wheel or rack

¹**pink** \'piŋk\ *n* **1** : any of a genus of plants with narrow leaves often grown for their showy flowers **2** : the highest degree : HEIGHT ⟨the ∼ of condition⟩

²**pink** *n* : a light tint of red

³**pink** *adj* **1** : of the color pink **2** : holding socialistic views — **pink·ish** *adj*

⁴**pink** *vb* **1** : PIERCE, STAB **2** : to perforate in an ornamental pattern **3** : to cut a saw-toothed edge on

pink elephants *n pl* : any of various hallucinations arising esp. from heavy drinking or use of narcotics

pink·eye \'piŋk-ˌī\ *n* : an acute contagious eye inflammation

pin·kie *or* **pin·ky** \'piŋ-kē\ *n, pl* **pinkies** : the smallest finger of the hand

pin·nace \'pin-əs\ *n* **1** : a light sailing ship **2** : a ship's boat

pin·na·cle \'pin-i-kəl\ *n* [ME *pinacle*, fr. MF, fr. LL *pinnaculum* gable, fr. dim. of L *pinna* wing, battlement] **1** : a turret ending in a small spire **2** : a lofty peak **3** : the highest point : ACME

pin·nate \'pin-ˌāt\ *adj* : having similar parts arranged on each side of an axis — **pin·nate·ly** *adv*

pi·noch·le \'pē-ˌnək-əl\ *n* : a card game played with a 48-card deck

pi·ñon *or* **pin·yon** \'pin-ˌyōn, -ˌyän\ *n, pl* **pi·ñons** *or* **pin·yons** *or* **pi·ño·nes** \pin-'yō-nēz\ [AmerSp *piñón*] : any of various low-growing pines of western No. America with edible seeds; *also* : the edible seed of a piñon

pin·point \'pin-ˌpȯint\ *vb* : to locate, hit, or aim with great precision

pin·prick \-ˌprik\ *n* **1** : a small puncture made by or as if by a pin **2** : a petty irritation or annoyance

pins and needles *n pl* : a pricking tingling sensation in a limb growing numb or recovering from numbness — **on pins and needles** : in a nervous or jumpy state of anticipation

pin·stripe \'pin-ˌstrīp\ *n* : a narrow stripe on a fabric; *also* : a suit with such stripes — **pin–striped** \-ˌstrīpt\ *adj*

pint \'pīnt\ *n* — see WEIGHT table

pin·to \'pin-ˌtō\ *n, pl* **pintos** *also* **pintoes** : a spotted horse

pinto bean *n* : a mottled kidney bean that is grown in the southwestern U.S. for food and for stock feed

pin·up \'pin-ˌəp\ *adj* : suitable for pinning up on an admirer's wall ⟨∼ photo⟩; *also* : suited (as by beauty) to be the subject of a pinup photograph

pin·wheel \-ˌhwēl\ *n* **1** : a toy consisting of lightweight vanes that revolve at the end of a stick **2** : a fireworks device in the form of a revolving wheel of colored fire

pin·worm \-ˌwərm\ *n* : a small worm parasitic in the intestines of man

pin·yin \'pin-'yin\ *n, often cap* : a system for writing Chinese ideograms by using Roman letters to represent the sounds

¹pi·o·neer \ˌpī-ə-'niər\ *n* [MF *pionier*, fr. OF *peonier* foot soldier, fr. *peon* foot soldier, fr. ML *pedon-*, *pedo*, fr. LL one with broad feet, fr. L *ped-*, *pes* foot] **1** : one that originates or helps open up a new line of thought or activity **2** : an early settler in a territory

²pioneer *vb* **1** : to act as a pioneer **2** : to open or prepare for others to follow; *esp* : SETTLE

pi·ous \'pī-əs\ *adj* **1** : marked by reverence for deity : DEVOUT **2** : excessively or affectedly religious **3** : SACRED, DEVOTIONAL **4** : marked by sham or hypocrisy **5** : showing loyal reverence for a person or thing : DUTIFUL — **pi·ous·ly** *adv*

¹pip \'pip\ *n* **1** : a disease of birds **2** : a usu. minor human ailment

²pip *n* : one of the dots or figures used chiefly to indicate numerical value (as of a playing card)

³pip *n* : a small fruit seed (as of an apple)

¹pipe \'pīp\ *n* **1** : a musical instrument having a tube played by forcing air through it **2** : BAGPIPE **3** : a tube designed to conduct something (as water, steam, or oil) **4** : a device for smoking having a tube with a bowl at one end and a mouthpiece at the other

²pipe *vb* **piped**; **pip·ing** **1** : to play on a pipe **2** : to speak in a high or shrill voice **3** : to convey by or as if by pipes — **pip·er** *n*

pipe down *vb* : to stop talking or making noise

pipe dream *n* : an illusory or fantastic hope

pipe·line \'pīp-ˌlīn\ *n* **1** : a line of pipe with pumps, valves, and control devices for conveying liquids, gases, or fine solids **2** : a channel for information

pi·pette *or* **pi·pet** \pī-'pet\ *n* : a device for measuring and transferring small volumes of liquid

pipe up *vb* : to begin to play, sing, or speak

pip·ing \'pī-piŋ\ *n* **1** : the music of pipes **2** : a narrow fold of material used to decorate edges or seams

piping hot *adj* : so hot as to sizzle or hiss : very hot

pip·pin \'pip-ən\ *n* : any of several yellowish apples

pip–squeak \'pip-ˌskwēk\ *n* : one that is small or insignificant

pi·quant \'pē-kənt\ *adj* **1** : pleasantly savory : PUNGENT **2** : engagingly provocative; *also* : having a lively charm — **pi·quan·cy** \-kən-sē\ *n*

¹**pique** \'pēk\ *n* [F] : offense taken by one slighted; *also* : a fit of resentment

²**pique** *vb* **piqued; piqu·ing 1** : to offend esp. by slighting **2** : to arouse by a provocation or challenge : GOAD

pi·qué *or* **pi·que** \pi-'kā\ *n* : a durable ribbed clothing fabric

pi·quet \pi-'kā\ *n* : a 2-handed card game played with 32 cards

pi·ra·cy \'pī-rə-sē\ *n, pl* **-cies 1** : robbery on the high seas or in the air **2** : the unauthorized use of another's production or invention

pi·ra·nha \pə-'ran-yə, -'rän-(y)ə\ *n* [Pg] : a small So. American fish that often attacks human beings and large animals

pi·rate \'pī-rət\ *n* [ME, fr. MF or L; MF, fr. L *pirata,* fr. Gk *peiratēs,* fr. *peiran* to attempt, attack] : one who commits piracy — **pirate** *vb* — **pi·rat·i·cal** \pə-'rat-i-kəl, pī-\ *adj*

pir·ou·ette \ˌpir-ə-'wet\ *n* [F] : a full turn on the toe or ball of one foot in ballet; *also* : a rapid whirling about of the body — **pirouette** *vb*

pis *pl of* PI

pis·ca·to·ri·al \ˌpis-kə-'tōr-ē-əl\ *adj* : of or relating to fishing

Pi·sces \'pī-sēz\ *n* [ME, fr. L, lit., fishes] **1** : a zodiacal constellation between Aquarius and Aries usu. pictured as a fish **2** : the 12th sign of the zodiac in astrology; *also* : one born under this sign

pis·mire \'pis-ˌmī(ə)r\ *n* : ANT

pis·ta·chio \pə-'stash-(ē-ˌ)ō, -'stäsh-\ *n, pl* **-chios** : the greenish edible seed of a small tree related to the sumacs; *also* : the tree

pis·til \'pis-t°l\ *n* : the female reproductive organ in a flower — **pis·til·late** \'pis-tə-ˌlāt\ *adj*

pis·tol \'pis-t°l\ *n* : a handgun whose chamber is integral with the barrel

pistol–whip \-ˌhwip\ *vb* : to beat with a pistol

pis·ton \'pis-tən\ *n* : a sliding piece that receives and transmits motion and that usu. consists of a short cylinder inside a large cylinder

¹**pit** \'pit\ *n* **1** : a hole, shaft, or cavity in the ground **2** : an often sunken area designed for a particular use; *also* : an enclosed place (as for cockfights) **3** : HELL; *also, pl* : WORST ⟨it's the ∼s⟩ **4** : a hollow or indentation esp. in the surface of the body **5** : a small indented scar (as from smallpox)

²**pit** *vb* **pit·ted; pit·ting 1** : to form pits in or become marred with pits **2** : to match for fighting

³**pit** *n* : the stony seed of some fruits (as the cherry, peach, and date)

⁴**pit** *vb* **pit·ted; pit·ting** : to remove the pit from

pi·ta \'pēt-ə\ *n* [NGk] : a thin flat bread

pit–a–pat \ˌpit-i-'pat\ *n* : PITTER-PATTER — **pit–a–pat** *adv or adj*

pit bull *n* : a powerful compact short-haired dog developed for fighting

¹**pitch** \'pich\ *n* **1** : a dark sticky substance left over esp. from distilling tar or petroleum **2** : resin from various conifers — **pitchy** *adj*

²**pitch** *vb* **1** : to erect and fix firmly in place ⟨∼ a tent⟩ **2** : THROW, FLING **3** : to deliver a baseball to a batter **4** : to toss (as coins) toward a mark **5** : to set at a particular level ⟨∼ the voice low⟩ **6** : to fall headlong **7** : to have the front end (as of a ship) alternately plunge and rise **8** : to incline downward : SLOPE

³**pitch** *n* **1** : the action or a manner of pitching **2** : degree of slope ⟨∼ of a roof⟩ **3** : the relative level of some quality or state ⟨a high ∼ of excitement⟩ **4** : highness or lowness of sound **5** : an often high-pressure sales talk **6** : the delivery of a baseball to a batter; *also* : the baseball delivered

pitch·blende \'pich-ˌblend\ *n* : a dark mineral that is the chief source of uranium

¹**pitch·er** \'pich-ər\ *n* : a container for liquids that usu. has a lip and a handle

²**pitcher** *n* : one that pitches esp. in a baseball game

pitcher plant *n* : a plant with leaves modified to resemble pitchers in which insects are trapped and digested

pitch·fork \'pich-ˌfork\ *n* : a long-handled fork used esp. in pitching hay

pitch in *vb* **1** : to begin to work **2** : to contribute to a common effort

pitch·man \'pich-mən\ *n* : SALESMAN; *esp* : one who vends novelties on the streets or from a concession

pit·e·ous \'pit-ē-əs\ *adj* : arousing pity : PITIFUL — **pit·e·ous·ly** *adv*

pit·fall \'pit-,fȯl\ *n* **1** : TRAP, SNARE; *esp* : a covered pit used for capturing animals **2** : a hidden danger or difficulty

pith \'pith\ *n* **1** : loose spongy tissue esp. in the center of the stem of vascular plants **2** : the essential part : CORE

pithy \'pith-ē\ *adj* **pith·i·er; -est 1** : consisting of or filled with pith **2** : being brief and to the point

piti·able \'pit-ē-ə-bəl\ *adj* : PITIFUL

piti·ful \'pit-i-fəl\ *adj* **1** : arousing or deserving pity ⟨a ∼ sight⟩ **2** : MEAN, MEAGER — **piti·ful·ly** \-f(ə-)lē\ *adv*

piti·less \'pit-i-ləs\ *adj* : devoid of pity : MERCILESS — **pit·i·less·ly** *adv*

pi·ton \'pē-,tän\ *n* [F] : a spike, wedge, or peg that can be driven into a rock or ice surface as a support

pit·tance \'pit-ᵊns\ *n* : a small portion, amount, or allowance

pit·ter–pat·ter \'pit-ər-,pat-ər, 'pit-ē-\ *n* : a rapid succession of light taps or sounds — **pitter–patter** \,pit-ər-'pat-ər, ,pit-ē-\ *adv or adj* — **pitter–patter** \like *adv*\ *vb*

pi·tu·itary \pə-'t(y)ü-ə-,ter-ē\ *n, pl* **-itar·ies** : PITUITARY GLAND — **pituitary** *adj*

pituitary gland *n* : a small oval endocrine gland attached to the brain which produces various hormones that affect most basic bodily functions

pit viper *n* : any of various mostly New World specialized venomous snakes with a sensory pit on each side of the head and hollow perforated fangs

¹pity \'pit-ē\ *n, pl* **pit·ies** [ME *pite*, fr. OF *pité*, fr. L *pietas* piety, pity, fr. *pius* pious] **1** : sympathetic sorrow : COMPASSION **2** : something to be regretted

²pity *vb* **pit·ied; pity·ing** : to feel pity for

¹piv·ot \'piv-ət\ *n* : a fixed pin on which something turns — **pivot** *adj* — **piv·ot·al** \'piv-ət-ᵊl\ *adj*

²pivot *vb* : to turn on or as if on a pivot

pix *pl of* PIC

pix·el \'pik-səl, -,sel\ *n* : any of the small elements that together make up an image (as on a television screen)

pix·ie *or* **pixy** \'pik-sē\ *n, pl* **pix·ies** : FAIRY; *esp* : a mischievous sprite

piz·za \'pēt-sə\ *n* [It] : an open pie made of rolled bread dough spread with a spiced mixture (as of tomatoes, cheese, and ground meat) and baked

piz·zazz *or* **pi·zazz** \pə-'zaz\ *n* **1** : GLAMOUR **2** : VITALITY

piz·ze·ria \,pēt-sə-'rē-ə\ *n* : an establishment where pizzas are made and sold

piz·zi·ca·to \,pit-si-'kät-ō\ *adv or adj* [It] : by means of plucking instead of bowing — used as a direction in music

pj's \(')pē-'jāz\ *n pl* : PAJAMAS

pk *abbr* **1** park **2** peak **3** peck **4** pike

pkg *abbr* package

pkt *abbr* **1** packet **2** pocket

pkwy *abbr* parkway

pl *abbr* **1** place **2** plate **3** plural

¹plac·ard \'plak-ərd, -,ärd\ *n* : a notice posted in a public place : POSTER

²plac·ard \-,ärd, -ərd\ *vb* **1** : to cover with or as if with placards **2** : to announce by posting

pla·cate \'plā-,kāt, 'plak-,āt\ *vb* **pla·cat·ed; pla·cat·ing** : to soothe esp. by concessions : APPEASE — **pla·ca·ble** \'plak-ə-bəl, 'plā-kə-\ *adj*

¹place \'plās\ *n* [ME, fr. MF, open space, fr. L *platea* broad street, fr. Gk *plateia* (*hodos*), fr. fem. of *platys* broad, flat] **1** : SPACE, ROOM **2** : an indefinite region : AREA **3** : a building or locality used for a speical purpose **4** : a center of population **5** : a particular part of a surface : SPOT **6** : relative position in a scale or sequence; *also* : high and esp. 2d position at the end of a competition **7** : ACCOMMODATION; *esp* : SEAT **8** : the position of a figure in a numeral ⟨12 is a two ∼ number⟩ **9** : JOB; *esp* : public office **10** : a public square

²place *vb* **placed; plac·ing 1** : to distribute in an orderly manner : ARRANGE **2** : to put in a particular place : SET **3** : IDENTIFY **4** : to give an order for ⟨∼ a bet⟩ **5** : to rank high and esp. 2d at the end of a competition

pla·ce·bo \plə-'sē-bō\ *n, pl* **-bos** [L, I shall please] : an inert medication used for its psychological effect or for purposes of comparison in an experiment

place·hold·er \'plās-,hōl-dər\ *n* : a symbol in a mathematical or logical expression that may be replaced by the name of any element of a set

place·kick \-,kik\ *n* : the kicking of a

ball placed or held on the ground — **placekick** *vb* — **place·kick·er** *n*

place·ment \'plās-mənt\ *n* : an act or instance of placing

pla·cen·ta \plə-'sent-ə\ *n, pl* **-centas** *or* **-cen·tae** \-'sent-(ˌ)ē\ [NL, fr. L, flat cake] : the organ in most mammals by which the fetus is joined to the uterus of the mother and is nourished — **pla·cen·tal** \-'sent-ᵊl\ *adj*

plac·er \'plas-ər\ *n* : an alluvial or glacial deposit containing particles of valuable mineral

plac·id \'plas-əd\ *adj* : UNDISTURBED, PEACEFUL **syn** tranquil, serene, calm — **pla·cid·i·ty** \pla-'sid-ət-ē\ *n* — **plac·id·ly** \'plas-əd-lē\ *adv*

plack·et \'plak-ət\ *n* : a slit in a garment

pla·gia·rize \'plā-jə-ˌrīz\ *vb* **-rized; -riz·ing** : to present the ideas or words of another as one's own — **pla·gia·rism** \-ˌriz-əm\ *n* — **pla·gia·rist** \-rəst\ *n*

¹plague \'plāg\ *n* **1** : a disastrous evil or influx; *also* : NUISANCE **2** : PESTILENCE; *esp* : a destructive contagious bacterial disease (as bubonic plague)

²plague *vb* **plagued; plagu·ing 1** : to afflict with or as if with disease or disaster **2** : TEASE, TORMENT, HARASS

plaid \'plad\ *n* **1** : a rectangular length of tartan worn esp. over the left shoulder as part of the Scottish national costume **2** : a twilled woolen fabric with a tartan pattern **3** : a pattern of unevenly spaced repeated stripes crossing at right angles — **plaid** *adj*

¹plain \'plān\ *n* : an extensive area of level or rolling treeless country

²plain *adj* **1** : lacking ornament ⟨a ~ dress⟩ **2** : free of extraneous matter **3** : OPEN, UNOBSTRUCTED ⟨~ view⟩ **4** : EVIDENT, OBVIOUS **5** : easily understood : CLEAR **6** : CANDID, BLUNT **7** : SIMPLE, UNCOMPLICATED ⟨~ cooking⟩ **8** : lacking beauty — **plain·ly** *adv* — **plain·ness** \'plān-nəs\ *n*

plain·clothes·man \'plān-'klō(th)z-mən, -ˌman\ *n* : a police officer who does not wear a uniform while on duty : DETECTIVE

plain·spo·ken \-'spō-kən\ *adj* : speaking or spoken plainly and esp. bluntly

plaint \'plānt\ *n* **1** : LAMENTATION, WAIL **2** : PROTEST, COMPLAINT

plain·tiff \'plānt-əf\ *n* : the complaining party in a lawsuit

plain·tive \'plānt-iv\ *adj* : expressive of suffering or woe : MELANCHOLY — **plain·tive·ly** *adv*

plait \'plāt, 'plat\ *n* **1** : PLEAT **2** : a braid esp. of hair or straw — **plait** *vb*

¹plan \'plan\ *n* **1** : a drawing or diagram showing the parts or outline of something **2** : a method for accomplishing something **3** : GOAL, AIM — **plan·less** *adj*

²plan *vb* **planned; plan·ning 1** : to form a plan of ⟨~ a new city⟩ **2** : INTEND ⟨*planned* to go⟩ — **plan·ner** *n*

¹plane \'plān\ *vb* **planed; plan·ing** : to smooth or level off with or as if with a plane — **plan·er** *n*

²plane *n* : PLANE TREE

³plane *n* : a tool for smoothing or shaping a wood surface

⁴plane *n* **1** : a level or flat surface **2** : a level of existence, consciousness, or development **3** : one of the main supporting surfaces of an airplane; *also* : AIRPLANE

⁵plane *adj* **1** : FLAT, LEVEL **2** : dealing with flat surfaces or figures ⟨~ geometry⟩

plane·load \'plān-ˌlōd\ *n* : a load that fills an airplane

plan·et \'plan-ət\ *n* [ME *planete*, fr. OF, fr. LL *planeta*, modif. of Gk *planēt-, planēs*, lit., wanderer, fr. *planasthai* to wander] : a celestial body other than a comet, asteroid, or satellite that revolves around the sun — **plan·e·tary** \-ə-ˌter-ē\ *adj*

plan·e·tar·i·um \ˌplan-ə-'ter-ē-əm\ *n, pl* **-iums** *or* **-ia** \-ē-ə\ : a building or room housing a device to project images of celestial bodies

plan·e·tes·i·mal \ˌplan-ə-'tes-ə-məl\ *n* : any of numerous small solid celestial bodies which may have existed during the formation of the solar system

plan·e·toid \'plan-ə-ˌtȯid\ *n* : a body resembling a planet; *esp* : ASTEROID

plane tree *n* : SYCAMORE 2; *esp* : one of or introduced from the Old World

plan·gent \'plan-jənt\ *adj* **1** : having a loud reverberating sound **2** : having an expressive esp. plaintive quality — **plan·gen·cy** \-jən-sē\ *n*

¹plank \'plaŋk\ *n* **1** : a heavy thick board **2** : an article in the platform of a political party

²plank *vb* **1** : to cover with planks **2** : to

set or lay down forcibly **3** : to cook and serve on a board

plank·ing \\'plaŋ-kiŋ\ *n* : a quantity or covering of planks

plank·ton \\'plaŋk-tən\ *n* : the passively floating or weakly swimming animal and plant life of a body of water — **plank·ton·ic** \plaŋk-'tän-ik\ *adj*

¹**plant** \\'plant\ *vb* **1** : to set in the ground to grow **2** : ESTABLISH, SETTLE **3** : to stock or provide with something **4** : to place firmly or forcibly **5** : to hide or arrange with intent to deceive

²**plant** *n* **1** : any of a kingdom of living things that usu. have no locomotor ability or obvious sense organs and have cellulose cell walls and usu. capacity for indefinite growth **2** : the land, buildings, and machinery used in carrying on a trade or business

¹**plan·tain** \\'plant-ən\ *n* [ME, fr. OF, fr. L *plantagin-, plantago,* fr. *planta* sole of the foot; fr. its broad leaves] : any of a genus of short-stemmed weedy herbs with spikes of tiny greenish flowers

²**plantain** *n* [Sp *plántano* plane tree, banana tree, fr. ML *plantanus* plane tree, alter. of L *platanus*] : a banana plant with starchy greenish fruit; *also* : its fruit

plan·tar \\'plant-ər, 'plan-ˌtär\ *adj* : of or relating to the sole of the foot

plan·ta·tion \plan-'tā-shən\ *n* **1** : a large group of trees under cultivation **2** : an agricultural estate worked by resident laborers

plant·er \\'plant-ər\ *n* **1** : one that plants or sows; *esp* : an owner or operator of a plantation **2** : a container for a plant

plant louse *n* : APHID

plaque \\'plak\ *n* [F] **1** : an ornamental brooch **2** : a flat thin piece (as of metal) used for decoration; *also* : a commemorative tablet **3** : a bacteria-containing film on a tooth

plash \\'plash\ *n* : SPLASH — **plash** *vb*

plas·ma \\'plaz-mə\ *n* **1** : the watery part of blood, lymph, or milk **2** : a gas composed of ionized particles — **plas·mat·ic** \plaz-'mat-ik\ *adj*

¹**plas·ter** \\'plas-tər\ *n* **1** : a dressing consisting of a backing spread with an often medicated substance that clings to the skin ⟨adhesive ∼⟩ **2** : a paste that hardens as it dries and is used for coating walls and ceilings

²**plaster** *vb* **plas·tered; plas·ter·ing** \-t(ə-)riŋ\ : to cover with or as if with plaster — **plas·ter·er** *n*

plas·ter·board \\'plas-tər-ˌbōrd\ *n* : a wallboard consisting of fiberboard, paper, or felt over a plaster core

plaster of par·is \-'par-əs\ *often cap 2d P* : a white powder made from gypsum and used as a quick-setting paste with water for casts and molds

¹**plas·tic** \\'plas-tik\ *adj* [L *plasticus* of molding, fr. Gk *plastikos,* fr. *plassein* to mold, form] **1** : capable of being molded ⟨∼ clay⟩ **2** : characterized by or using modeling ⟨∼ arts⟩ **3** : made or consisting of a plastic **syn** pliable, pliant, ductile, malleable, adaptable — **plas·tic·i·ty** \plas-'tis-ət-ē\ *n*

²**plastic** *n* : a plastic substance; *esp* : a synthetic or processed material that can be formed into rigid objects or into films or filaments

plastic surgery *n* : a branch of surgery concerned with the repair, restoration, or improvement of lost, injured, defective, or misshapen body parts — **plastic surgeon** *n*

¹**plat** \\'plat\ *n* **1** : a small plot of ground **2** : a plan of a piece of land with actual or proposed features (as lots)

²**plat** *vb* **plat·ted; plat·ting** : to make a plat of

¹**plate** \\'plāt\ *n* **1** : a flat thin piece of material **2** : domestic hollowware made of or plated with gold, silver, or base metals **3** : DISH **4** : HOME PLATE **5** : the molded metal or plastic cast of a page of type to be printed from **6** : a thin sheet of material (as glass) that is coated with a chemical sensitive to light and is used in photography **7** : the part of a denture that fits to the mouth and holds the teeth **8** : something printed from an engraving **9** : a huge mobile segment of the earth's crust

²**plate** *vb* **plat·ed; plat·ing** **1** : to arm with armor plate **2** : to overlay with metal (as gold or silver) **3** : to make a printing plate of

pla·teau \pla-'tō\ *n, pl* **plateaus** *or* **plateaux** \-'tōz\ [F] : a large level area raised above adjacent land on at least one side : TABLELAND

plate glass *n* : rolled, ground, and polished sheet glass

plat·en \'plat-ən\ *n* **1** : a flat plate of metal; *esp* : one (as the part of a printing press which presses the paper against the type) that exerts or receives pressure **2** : the roller of a typewriter

plat·form \'plat-ˌfȯrm\ *n* **1** : a raised flooring or stage for speakers, performers, or workers **2** : a declaration of the principles on which a group of persons (as a political party) stands

plat·ing \'plāt-iŋ\ *n* : a coating of metal plates or plate ⟨the ∼ of a ship⟩

plat·i·num \'plat-(ə-)nəm\ *n* : a heavy silver-white metallic chemical element

plat·i·tude \'plat-ə-ˌt(y)üd\ *n* : a flat or trite remark — **plat·i·tu·di·nous** \-'t(y)üd-(ə-)nəs\ *adj*

pla·ton·ic love \plə-ˌtän-ik-, plā-\ *n, often cap P* : a close relationship between two persons in which sexual desire has been suppressed or sublimated

pla·toon \plə-'tün\ *n* [F *peloton* small detachment, lit., ball, fr. *pelote* little ball] **1** : a subdivision of a company-size military unit usu. consisting of two or more squads or sections **2** : a group of football players trained either for offense or for defense and sent into the game as a body

platoon sergeant *n* : a noncommissioned officer in the army ranking below a first sergeant

plat·ter \'plat-ər\ *n* **1** : a large serving plate **2** : a phonograph record

platy \'plat-ē\ *n, pl* **platy** *or* **plat·ys** *or* **plat·ies** : any of various small stocky often brilliantly colored fish that are popular for tropical aquariums

platy·pus \'plat-i-pəs\ *n, pl* **platy·pus·es** *also* **platy·pi** \-ˌpī\ [NL, fr. Gk *platypous* flat-footed, fr. *platys* broad, flat + *pous* foot] : a small aquatic egg-laying marsupial mammal of Australia with webbed feet and a fleshy bill like a duck's

plau·dit \'plȯd-ət\ *n* : an act of applause

plau·si·ble \'plȯ-zə-bəl\ *adj* [L *plausibilis* worthy of applause, fr. *plausus*, pp. of *plaudere*] : seemingly worthy of belief : PERSUASIVE — **plau·si·bil·i·ty** \ˌplȯ-zə-'bil-ət-ē\ *n* — **plau·si·bly** \'plȯ-zə-blē\ *adv*

¹play \'plā\ *n* **1** : brisk handling of something (as a weapon) **2** : the course of a game; *also* : a particular act or maneuver in a game **3** : recreational activity; *esp* : the spontaneous activity of children **4** : JEST ⟨said in ∼⟩ **5** : the act or an instance of punning **6** : GAMBLING **7** : OPERATION ⟨bring extra force into ∼⟩ **8** : a brisk or light movement **9** : free motion (as of part of a machine) **10** : scope for action **11** : PUBLICITY **12** : an effort to arouse liking ⟨made a ∼ for her⟩ **13** : a stage representation of a drama; *also* : a dramatic composition — **play·ful** \-fəl\ *adj* — **play·ful·ly** \-ē\ *adv* — **play·ful·ness** *n* — **in play** : in condition or position to be played

²play *vb* **1** : to engage in recreation : FROLIC **2** : to handle or behave lightly or absentmindedly **3** : to make a pun ⟨∼ on words⟩ **4** : to take advantage ⟨∼ on fears⟩ **5** : to move or operate in a brisk or irregular manner ⟨a flashlight ∼ed over the wall⟩ **6** : to perform music ⟨∼ on a violin⟩; *also* : to perform (music) on an instrument ⟨∼ a waltz⟩ **7** : to perform music upon ⟨∼ the piano⟩; *also* : to sound in performance ⟨the organ is ∼ing⟩ **8** : to cause to emit sounds ⟨∼ a radio⟩ **9** : to act in a dramatic medium; *also* : to act in the character of ⟨∼ the hero⟩ **10** : GAMBLE **11** : to behave in a specified way ⟨∼ safe⟩; *also* : COOPERATE ⟨∼ along with him⟩ **12** : to deal with; *also* : EMPHASIZE ⟨∼ up her good qualities⟩ **13** : to perform for amusement ⟨∼ a trick⟩ **14** : WREAK **15** : to contend with in a game; *also* : to fill (a certain position) on a team **16** : to make wagers on ⟨∼ the races⟩ **17** : WIELD, PLY **18** : to keep in action — **play·er** *n*

play·act·ing \'plā-ˌak-tiŋ\ *n* **1** : performance in theatrical productions **2** : insincere or artificial behavior

play·back \'plā-ˌbak\ *n* : an act of reproducing a sound recording often immediately after recording — **play back** \(ˈ)plā-'bak\ *vb*

play·bill \-ˌbil\ *n* : a poster advertising the performance of a play

play·book \-ˌbu̇k\ *n* : a notebook containing diagramed football plays

play·boy \-ˌbȯi\ *n* : a man whose chief interest is the pursuit of pleasure

play·go·er \-ˌgō(-ə)r\ *n* : a person who frequently attends plays

play·ground \-ˌgraund\ *n* : an area used for games and recreation esp. by children

play·house \-ˌhaus\ *n* **1** : THEATER **2** : a small house for children to play in

playing card *n* : one of a set of 24 to 78 cards marked to show its rank and suit and used to play a game of cards

play·let \ˈplā-lət\ *n* : a short play

play·mate \-ˌmāt\ *n* : a companion in play

play–off \-ˌȯf\ *n* : a contest or series of contests to break a tie or determine a championship

play·pen \-ˌpen\ *n* : a portable enclosure in which a young child may play

play·suit \-ˌsüt\ *n* : a sports and play outfit for women and children

play·thing \-ˌthiŋ\ *n* : TOY

play·wright \-ˌrīt\ *n* : a writer of plays

pla·za \ˈplaz-ə, ˈpläz-\ *n* [Sp, fr. L *platea* broad street] **1** : a public square in a city or town **2** : a shopping center

plea \ˈplē\ *n* **1** : a defendant's answer in law to charges made against him **2** : something alleged as an excuse : PRETEXT **3** : ENTREATY, APPEAL

plead \ˈplēd\ *vb* **plead·ed** \ˈplēd-əd\ *or* **pled** \ˈpled\; **plead·ing** **1** : to argue before a court or authority ⟨∼ a case⟩ **2** : to answer to a charge or indictment ⟨∼ guilty⟩ **3** : to argue for or against something ⟨∼ for acquittal⟩ **4** : to appeal earnestly ⟨∼s for help⟩ **5** : to offer as a plea (as in defense) ⟨∼ed illness⟩ — **plead·er** *n*

pleas·ant \ˈplez-ᵊnt\ *adj* **1** : giving pleasure : AGREEABLE ⟨a ∼ experience⟩ **2** : marked by pleasing behavior or appearance ⟨a ∼ person⟩ — **pleas·ant·ly** *adv* — **pleas·ant·ness** *n*

pleas·ant·ry \-ᵊn-trē\ *n, pl* **-ries** : a pleasant and casual act or speech

¹please \ˈplēz\ *vb* **pleased; pleas·ing** **1** : to give pleasure or satisfaction to **2** : LIKE ⟨do as you ∼⟩ **3** : to be the will or pleasure of ⟨may it ∼ his Majesty⟩

²please *adv* — used as a function word to express politeness or emphasis in a request ⟨∼ come in⟩

pleas·ing \ˈplē-ziŋ\ *adj* : giving pleasure — **pleas·ing·ly** *adv*

plea·sur·able \ˈplezh-(ə-)rə-bəl\ *adj* : PLEASANT, GRATIFYING — **plea·sur·ably** \-blē\ *adv*

plea·sure \ˈplezh-ər\ *n* **1** : DESIRE, INCLINATION ⟨await your ∼⟩ **2** : a state of gratification : ENJOYMENT **3** : a source of delight or joy

¹pleat \ˈplēt\ *vb* **1** : FOLD; *esp* : to arrange in pleats **2** : BRAID

²pleat *n* : a fold (as in cloth) made by doubling material over on itself : PLAIT

plebe \ˈplēb\ *n* : a freshman at a military or naval academy

¹ple·be·ian \pli-ˈbē-ən\ *n* **1** : a member of the Roman plebs **2** : one of the common people

²plebeian *adj* **1** : of or relating to plebeians **2** : COMMON, VULGAR

pleb·i·scite \ˈpleb-ə-ˌsīt, -sət\ *n* : a vote of the people (as of a country) on a proposal submitted to them

plebs \ˈplebz\ *n, pl* **ple·bes** \ˈplē-bēz\ **1** : the common people of ancient Rome **2** : the general populace

plec·trum \ˈplek-trəm\ *n, pl* **plec·tra** \-trə\ *or* **plec·trums** [L] : ³PICK 3

¹pledge \ˈplej\ *n* **1** : something given as security for the performance of an act **2** : the state of being held as a security or guaranty **3** : TOAST 3 **4** : PROMISE, VOW

²pledge *vb* **pledged; pledg·ing** **1** : to deposit as a pledge **2** : TOAST 3 **3** : to bind by a pledge : PLIGHT **4** : PROMISE

Pleis·to·cene \ˈplī-stə-ˌsēn\ *adj* : of, relating to, or being the earlier epoch of the Quaternary — **Pleistocene** *n*

ple·na·ry \ˈplē-nə-rē, ˈplen-ə-\ *adj* **1** : FULL ⟨∼ power⟩ **2** : including all entitled to attend ⟨∼ session⟩

pleni·po·ten·tia·ry \ˌplen-ə-pə-ˈtench-(ə-)rē, -ˈten-chē-ˌer-ē\ *n, pl* **-ries** : a diplomatic agent having full authority — **plenipotentiary** *adj*

plen·i·tude \ˈplen-ə-ˌt(y)üd\ *n* **1** : COMPLETENESS **2** : ABUNDANCE

plen·te·ous \ˈplent-ē-əs\ *adj* **1** : FRUITFUL **2** : existing in plenty

plen·ti·ful \ˈplent-i-fəl\ *adj* **1** : containing or yielding plenty **2** : ABUNDANT — **plen·ti·ful·ly** \-ē\ *adv*

plen·ty \ˈplent-ē\ *n* : a more than adequate number or amount

ple·num \ˈplen-əm, ˈplēn-əm\ *n, pl* **-nums** *or* **-na** \-ə\ : a general assembly of all members esp. of a legislative body

pleth·o·ra \'pleth-ə-rə\ *n* : an excessive quantity or fullness; *also* : PROFUSION

pleu·ri·sy \'plùr-ə-sē\ *n* : inflammation of the membrane that lines the chest and covers the lungs

plex·us \'plek-səs\ *n* : an interlacing network esp. of blood vessels or nerves

pli·able \'plī-ə-bəl\ *adj* 1 : FLEXIBLE 2 : yielding easily to others **syn** plastic, pliant, ductile, malleable, adaptable — **pli·abil·i·ty** \ˌplī-ə-'bil-ət-ē\ *n*

pli·ant \'plī-ənt\ *adj* 1 : FLEXIBLE 2 : easily influenced : PLIABLE — **pli·an·cy** \-ən-sē\ *n*

pli·ers \'plī-(-ə)rz\ *n pl* : small pincers for bending wire or handling small objects

¹plight \'plīt\ *vb* : to put or give in pledge : ENGAGE

²plight *n* : CONDITION, STATE; *esp* : a bad state

plinth \'plinth\ *n* : the lowest part of the base of an architectural column

Plio·cene \'plī-ə-ˌsēn\ *adj* : of, relating to, or being the latest epoch of the Tertiary — **Pliocene** *n*

plod \'pläd\ *vb* **plod·ded; plod·ding** 1 : to walk heavily or slowly : TRUDGE 2 : to work laboriously and monotonously : DRUDGE — **plod·der** *n* — **plod·ding·ly** \-iŋ-lē\ *adv*

plop \'pläp\ *vb* **plopped; plop·ping** 1 : to make or move with a sound like that of something dropping into water 2 : to set, drop, or throw heavily — **plop** *n*

¹plot \'plät\ *n* 1 : a small area of ground 2 : a ground plan (as of an area) 3 : the main story (as of a book or movie) 4 : a secret scheme : INTRIGUE

²plot *vb* **plot·ted; plot·ting** 1 : to make a plot or plan of 2 : to mark on or as if on a chart 3 : to plan or contrive esp. secretly — **plot·ter** *n*

plo·ver \'pləv-ər, 'plō-vər\ *n, pl* **plover** *or* **plovers** : any of various shorebirds related to the sandpipers but with shorter stouter bills

¹plow *or* **plough** \'plaù\ *n* 1 : an implement used to cut, turn over, and partly break up soil 2 : a device operating like a plow; *esp* : SNOWPLOW

²plow *or* **plough** *vb* 1 : to open, break up,

or work with a plow 2 : to cleave or move through like a plow ⟨a ship ~*ing* the waves⟩ 3 : to proceed laboriously — **plow·able** *adj* — **plow·er** *n*

plow·boy \'plaù-ˌbòi\ *n* : a boy who guides a plow or leads the horse drawing it

plow·man \-mən, -ˌman\ *n* 1 : a man who guides a plow 2 : a farm laborer

plow·share \-ˌshear\ *n* : the part of a plow that cuts the earth

ploy \'plòi\ *n* : a tactic intended to embarrass or frustrate an opponent

¹pluck \'plək\ *vb* 1 : to pull off or out : PICK; *also* : to pull something from 2 : to play (an instrument) by pulling the strings 3 : TUG, TWITCH

²pluck *n* 1 : an act or instance of plucking 2 : SPIRIT, COURAGE

plucky \'plək-ē\ *adj* **pluck·i·er; -est** : COURAGEOUS, SPIRITED

¹plug \'pləg\ *n* 1 : STOPPER; *also* : an obstructing mass 2 : a cake of tobacco 3 : a poor or worn-out horse 4 : a device on the end of a cord for making an electrical connection 5 : a piece of favorable publicity

²plug *vb* **plugged; plug·ging** 1 : to stop, make tight, or secure by inserting a plug 2 : HIT, SHOOT 3 : to publicize insistently 4 : PLOD, DRUDGE

plum \'pləm\ *n* [ME, fr. OE *plūme*, fr. L *prunum* plum] 1 : a smooth-skinned juicy fruit borne by trees related to the peach and cherry; *also* : a tree bearing plums 2 : a raisin when used in desserts (as puddings) 3 : something excellent; *esp* : something desirable given in return esp. for a political favor

plum·age \'plü-mij\ *n* : the feathers of a bird

¹plumb \'pləm\ *n* : a weight on the end of a line (**plumb line**) used esp. by builders to show vertical direction

²plumb *adv* 1 : VERTICALLY 2 : EXACTLY; *also* : IMMEDIATELY 3 : COMPLETELY

³plumb *vb* : to sound, adjust, or test with a plumb ⟨~ the depth of a well⟩

⁴plumb *adj* 1 : VERTICAL 2 : THOROUGH, COMPLETE

plumb·er \'pləm-ər\ *n* [ME, fr. MF *plombier*, fr. L *plumbarius*, deriv. of *plumbum* lead] : a worker who fits or repairs water and gas pipes and fixtures

plumb·ing \'pləm-iŋ\ *n* : a system of pipes in a building for supplying and carrying off water

¹**plume** \'plüm\ *n* : FEATHER; *esp* : a large, conspicuous, or showy feather — **plumed** \'plümd\ *adj* — **plumy** \'plü-mē\ *adj*

²**plume** *vb* **plumed; plum·ing** 1 : to provide or deck with feathers 2 : to indulge (oneself) in pride

¹**plum·met** \'pləm-ət\ *n* : PLUMB; *also* : PLUMB LINE

²**plummet** *vb* : to drop or plunge straight down

¹**plump** \'pləmp\ *vb* 1 : to drop or fall suddenly or heavily 2 : to favor something strongly ⟨~s for the new method⟩

²**plump** *n* : a sudden heavy fall or blow; *also* : the sound made by it

³**plump** *adv* 1 : straight down; *also* : straight ahead 2 : UNQUALIFIEDLY

⁴**plump** *adj* : having a full rounded usu. pleasing form : CHUBBY **syn** fleshy, stout, roly-poly, rotund — **plump·ness** *n*

¹**plun·der** \'plən-dər\ *vb* **plun·dered; plun·der·ing** \-d(ə-)riŋ\ : to take the goods of by force or wrongfully : PILLAGE — **plun·der·er** *n*

²**plunder** *n* : something taken by force or theft : LOOT

¹**plunge** \'plənj\ *vb* **plunged; plung·ing** 1 : IMMERSE, SUBMERGE 2 : to enter or cause to enter a state or course of action suddenly or violently ⟨~ into war⟩ 3 : to cast oneself into or as if into water 4 : to gamble heavily and recklessly 5 : to descend suddenly

²**plunge** *n* : a sudden dive, leap, or rush

plung·er \'plən-jər\ *n* 1 : one that plunges 2 : a sliding piece driven by or against fluid pressure : PISTON 3 : a rubber cup on a handle pushed against an opening to free a waste outlet of an obstruction

plunk \'pləŋk\ *vb* 1 : to make or cause to make a hollow metallic sound 2 : to drop heavily or suddenly — **plunk** *n*

plu·per·fect \(')plü-'pər-fikt\ *adj* [modif. of LL *plusquamperfectus*, lit., more than perfect] : of, relating to, or constituting a verb tense that denotes an action or state as completed at or before a past time spoken of — **pluperfect** *n*

plu·ral \'plúr-əl\ *adj* [ME, fr. MF & L; MF *plurel*, fr. L *pluralis*, fr. *plur-*, *plus* more] : of, relating to, or constituting a word form used to denote more than one — **plural** *n*

plu·ral·i·ty \plù-'ral-ət-ē\ *n, pl* **-ties** 1 : the state of being plural 2 : an excess of votes over those cast for an opposing candidate 3 : the greatest number of votes cast when not a majority

plu·ral·ize \'plúr-ə-,līz\ *vb* **-ized; -iz·ing** : to make plural or express in the plural form — **plu·ral·iza·tion** \,plúr-ə-lə-'zā-shən\ *n*

¹**plus** \'pləs\ *adj* [L, more] 1 : requiring addition 2 : having or being in addition to what is anticipated or specified ⟨~ values⟩

²**plus** *n, pl* **plus·es** \'pləs-əz\ *also* **plus·ses** 1 : a sign + (**plus sign**) used in mathematics to require addition or designate a positive quantity 2 : an added quantity; *also* : a positive quantity 3 : ADVANTAGE

³**plus** *prep* : increased by : with the addition of ⟨3 ~ 4 equals 7⟩

¹**plush** \'pləsh\ *n* : a fabric with a pile longer and less dense than velvet pile — **plushy** *adj*

²**plush** *adj* : notably luxurious — **plush·ly** *adv*

Plu·to \'plüt-ō\ *n* : the planet farthest from the sun

plu·toc·ra·cy \plü-'täk-rə-sē\ *n, pl* **-cies** 1 : government by the wealthy 2 : a controlling class of the wealthy — **plu·to·crat** \'plüt-ə-,krat\ *n* — **plu·to·crat·ic** \,plüt-ə-'krat-ik\ *adj*

plu·to·ni·um \plü-'tō-nē-əm\ *n* : a radioactive chemical element formed by the decay of neptunium

plu·vi·al \'plü-vē-əl\ *adj* 1 : of or relating to rain 2 : characterized by abundant rain

¹**ply** \'plī\ *vb* **plied; ply·ing** : to twist together ⟨~ yarns⟩

²**ply** *n, pl* **plies** : one of the folds, thicknesses, or strands of which something (as plywood or yarn) is made

³**ply** *vb* **plied; ply·ing** 1 : to use, practice, or work diligently ⟨*plies* her needle⟩ ⟨~ a trade⟩ 2 : to keep supplying something to ⟨*plied* them with liquor⟩ 3 : to go or travel regularly esp. by sea

Plym·outh Rock \,plim-əth-\ *n* : any of

an American breed of medium-sized single-combed domestic fowls

ply·wood \'plī-ˌwu̇d\ *n* : material made of thin sheets of wood glued and pressed together

pm *abbr* premium

Pm *symbol* promethium

PM *abbr* **1** paymaster **2** police magistrate **3** postmaster **4** *often not cap* post meridiem **5** postmortem **6** prime minister **7** provost marshal

pmk *abbr* postmark

pmt *abbr* payment

PN *abbr* promissory note

pneu·mat·ic \n(y)u̇-'mat-ik\ *adj* **1** : of, relating to, or using air or wind **2** : moved by air pressure **3** : filled with compressed air — **pneu·mat·i·cal·ly** \-i-k(ə-)lē\ *adv*

pneu·mo·co·ni·o·sis \'n(y)ü-mō-ˌkō-nē-'ō-səs\ *n* : a disease of the lungs caused by habitual inhalation of irritant mineral or metallic particles

pneu·mo·nia \n(y)u̇-'mō-nyə\ *n* : an inflammatory disease of the lungs

Po *symbol* polonium

PO *abbr* **1** petty officer **2** post office

¹poach \'pōch\ *vb* [ME *pochen,* fr. MF *pocher,* fr. OF *pochier,* lit., to put into a bag, fr. *poche* bag, pocket, of Gmc origin] : to cook (as an egg or fish) in simmering liquid

²poach *vb* : to hunt or fish unlawfully — **poach·er** *n*

POC *abbr* port of call

pock \'päk\ *n* : a small swelling on the skin (as in smallpox); *also* : its scar

¹pock·et \'päk-ət\ *n* **1** : a small bag open at the top or side inserted in a garment **2** : supply of money : MEANS **3** : RECEPTACLE, CONTAINER **4** : a small isolated area or group **5** : a small body of ore — **pock·et·ful** *n*

²pocket *vb* **1** : to put in or as if in a pocket **2** : STEAL

³pocket *adj* **1** : small enough to fit in a pocket; *also* : SMALL, MINIATURE **2** : carried in or paid from one's own pocket

¹pock·et·book \-ˌbu̇k\ *n* **1** : PURSE; *also* : HANDBAG **2** : financial resources

²pocketbook *adj* : relating to money

pocket gopher *n* : GOPHER 2

pock·et·knife \'päk-ət-ˌnīf\ *n* : a knife with a folding blade to be carried in the pocket

pocket veto *n* : an indirect veto of a legislative bill by an executive through retention of the bill unsigned until after adjournment of the legislature

pock·mark \'päk-ˌmärk\ *n* : a pit or scar caused by smallpox or acne — **pock·marked** \-ˌmärkt\ *adj*

po·co \ˌpō-kō, ˌpȯ-\ *adv* [It, little, fr. L *paucus*] : SOMEWHAT — used to qualify a direction in music ⟨∼ allegro⟩

po·co a po·co \ˌpō-kō-ä-'pō-kō, ˌpȯ-kō-ä-'pȯ-\ *adv* : little by little : by small degrees : GRADUALLY

pod \'päd\ *n* **1** : a dry fruit (as of a pea) that splits open when ripe **2** : an external streamlined compartment (as for a jet engine) on an airplane **3** : a detachable compartment (as for personnel, a power unit, or an instrument) on a spacecraft

POD *abbr* pay on delivery

po·di·a·try \pə-'dī-ə-trē, pō-\ *n* : the care and treatment of the human foot in health and disease — **po·di·a·trist** \pə-'dī-ə-trəst, pō-\ *n*

po·di·um \'pōd-ē-əm\ *n, pl* **podiums** *or* **po·dia** \-ē-ə\ **1** : a dais esp. for an orchestral conductor **2** : LECTERN

POE *abbr* **1** port of embarkation **2** port of entry

po·em \'pō-əm\ *n* : a composition in verse

po·esy \'pō-ə-zē\ *n* : POETRY

po·et \'pō-ət\ *n* [ME, fr. OF *poete,* fr. L *poeta,* fr. Gk *poiētēs* maker, poet, fr. *poiein* to make, create] : a writer of poetry; *also* : a creative artist of great sensitivity

po·et·as·ter \'pō-ət-ˌas-tər\ *n* : an inferior poet

po·et·ess \'pō-ət-əs\ *n* : a girl or woman who writes poetry

poetic justice *n* : an outcome in which vice is punished and virtue rewarded usu. in a manner peculiarly or ironically appropriate

po·et·ry \'pō-ə-trē\ *n* **1** : metrical writing **2** : POEMS — **po·et·ic** \pō-'et-ik\ *or* **po·et·i·cal** \-i-kəl\ *adj*

po·grom \'pō-grəm, pō-'gräm\ *n* [Yiddish, fr. Russ, lit., devastation] : an organized massacre of helpless people and esp. of Jews

poi \'pȯi\ *n, pl* **poi** *or* **pois** : a Hawaiian

food of taro root cooked, pounded, and kneaded to a paste and often allowed to ferment

poi·gnant \\'pȯi-nyənt\ *adj* **1** : painfully affecting the feelings ⟨∼ grief⟩ **2** : deeply moving ⟨∼ scene⟩ — **poi·gnan·cy** \\-nyən-sē\ *n*

poi·lu \pwäl-'(y)ü\ *n* : a French soldier

poin·ci·ana \ˌpȯin-sē-'an-ə\ *n* : any of a genus of ornamental tropical leguminous trees or shrubs with bright orange or red flowers

poin·set·tia \pȯin-'set-ē-ə, -'set-ə\ *n* : a showy tropical American spurge that has scarlet bracts around its small greenish flowers

¹point \\'pȯint\ *n* **1** : an individual detail; *also* : the most important essential **2** : PURPOSE **3** : a geometric element that has position but no size **4** : a particular place : LOCALITY **5** : a particular stage or degree **6** : a sharp end : TIP **7** : a projecting piece of land **8** : a punctuation mark; *esp* : PERIOD **9** : DECIMAL POINT **10** : one of the divisions of the compass **11** : a unit of counting (as in a game score) — **point·less** *adj* — **beside the point** : IRRELEVANT — **in point** : to the point — **to the point** : RELEVANT, PERTINENT

²point *vb* **1** : to furnish with a point : SHARPEN **2** : PUNCTUATE **3** : to separate (a decimal fraction) from an integer by a decimal point **4** : to indicate the position of esp. by extending a finger **5** : to direct attention to ⟨∼ out an error⟩ **6** : AIM, DIRECT **7** : to lie extended, aimed, or turned in a particular direction : FACE, LOOK

point–blank \\'pȯint-'blaŋk\ *adj* **1** : so close to the target that a missile fired will travel in a straight line to the mark **2** : DIRECT, BLUNT — **point–blank** *adv*

point·ed \\'pȯint-əd\ *adj* **1** : having a point **2** : being to the point : DIRECT **3** : aimed at a particular person or group; *also* : CONSPICUOUS, MARKED — **point·ed·ly** *adv*

point·er \\'pȯint-ər\ *n* **1** : one that points out : INDICATOR **2** : a large short-haired hunting dog **3** : HINT, TIP

poin·til·lism \\'pwaⁿ(n)-tē-ˌ(y)iz-əm, 'pȯint-ᵊl-ˌiz-əm\ *n* [F *pointillisme*, fr. *pointiller* to stipple] : the theory or practice in painting of applying small strokes or dots of color to a surface so

that from a distance they blend together — **poin·til·list** *also* **poin·til·liste** \ˌpwaⁿ(n)-tē-'(y)ēst, 'pȯint-ᵊl-əst\ *n or adj*

point of no return : a critical point (as in a course of action) at which turning back or reversal is not possible

point of view : a position from which something is considered or evaluated

¹poise \\'pȯiz\ *vb* **poised; pois·ing** : BALANCE

²poise *n* **1** : BALANCE **2** : self-possessed calmness; *also* : a particular way of carrying oneself

¹poi·son \\'pȯiz-ᵊn\ *n* [ME, fr. OF, drink, poisonous drink, poison, fr. L *potion-, potio* drink] : a substance that through its chemical action can injure or kill — **poi·son·ous** \\-(ə-)nəs\ *adj*

²poison *vb* **poi·soned; poi·son·ing** \\'pȯiz-(ə-)niŋ\ **1** : to injure or kill with poison **2** : to treat or taint with poison **3** : to affect destructively : CORRUPT ⟨∼ed her mind⟩ — **poi·son·er** \\'pȯiz-(ə-)nər\ *n*

poison hemlock *n* : a large branching poisonous herb with finely divided leaves and white flowers that is related to the carrot

poison ivy *n* : a usu. climbing plant related to sumac that has leaves composed of three shiny leaflets and produces an irritating oil causing a usu. intensely itching skin rash; *also* : any of several related plants

poison oak *n* : any of several plants closely related to poison ivy and with similar properties

poison sumac *n* : a smooth shrubby American swamp plant with pinnate leaves, greenish flowers, greenish white berries, and irritating properties similar to the related poison ivy

¹poke \\'pōk\ *n* : BAG, SACK

²poke *vb* **poked; pok·ing** **1** : PROD; *also* : to stir up by prodding **2** : to make a prodding or jabbing movement esp. repeatedly **3** : HIT, PUNCH **4** : to thrust forward obtrusively **5** : RUMMAGE **6** : MEDDLE, PRY **7** : DAWDLE — **poke fun at** : RIDICULE, MOCK

³poke *n* : a quick thrust; *also* : PUNCH

¹pok·er \\'pō-kər\ *n* : a metal rod for stirring a fire

²po·ker \\'pō-kər\ *n* : any of several card games played with a deck of 52 cards in which each player bets on the superiority of his hand

poke·weed \\'pōk-ˌwēd\ *n* : a coarse American perennial herb with clusters of white flowers and dark purple juicy berries

poky *or* **pok·ey** \\'pō-kē\ *adj* **pok·i·er; -est 1** : small and cramped **2** : SHABBY, DULL **3** : annoyingly slow

pol \\'päl\ *n* : POLITICIAN

po·lar \\'pō-lər\ *adj* **1** : of or relating to a geographical pole **2** : of or relating to a pole (as of a magnet)

polar bear *n* : a large creamy-white bear that inhabits arctic regions

Po·lar·is \pə-'lar-əs\ *n* : NORTH STAR

po·lar·i·ty \pō-'lar-ət-ē, pə-\ *n, pl* **-ties** : the condition of having poles and esp. magnetic or electrical poles

po·lar·iza·tion \ˌpō-lə-rə-'zā-shən\ *n* **1** : the action of polarizing : the state of being polarized **2** : concentration about opposing extremes

po·lar·ize \\'pō-lə-ˌrīz\ *vb* **-ized; -iz·ing 1** : to cause (light waves) to vibrate in a definite way **2** : to give physical polarity to **3** : to break up into opposing groups

pol·der \\'pōl-dər, 'päl-\ *n* [D] : a tract of low land reclaimed from the sea

¹**pole** \\'pōl\ *n* : a long slender piece of wood or metal ⟨telephone ∼⟩

²**pole** *vb* **poled; pol·ing** : to impel or push with a pole

³**pole** *n* **1** : either end of an axis esp. of the earth **2** : either of the terminals of an electric battery **3** : one of two or more regions in a magnetized body at which the magnetism is concentrated

Pole \\'pōl\ *n* : a native or inhabitant of Poland

pole·ax \\'pōl-ˌaks\ *n* : a battle-ax with a short handle and a hook or point opposite the blade

pole·cat \\'pōl-ˌkat\ *n, pl* **polecats** *or* **polecat 1** : a European carnivorous mammal of which the ferret is considered a domesticated variety **2** : SKUNK

po·lem·ic \pə-'lem-ik\ *n* : the art or practice of disputation — usu. used in pl. — **po·lem·i·cal** \-i-kəl\ *also* **po·lem·ic** \-ik\ *adj* — **po·lem·i·cist** \-səst\ *n*

pole·star \\'pōl-ˌstär\ *n* **1** : NORTH STAR **2** : a directing principle : GUIDE

pole vault *n* : a field contest in which each contestant uses a pole to vault for height over a crossbar — **pole–vault** *vb* — **pole–vault·er** *n*

¹**po·lice** \pə-'lēs\ *vb* **po·liced; po·lic·ing 1** : to control, regulate, or keep in order esp. by use of police ⟨∼ a highway⟩ **2** : to make clean and put in order ⟨∼ a camp⟩

²**police** *n, pl* **police** [MF, government, fr. LL *politia*, fr. Gk *politeia*, fr. *politeuein* to be a citizen, engage in political activity, fr. *politēs* citizen, fr. *polis* city, state] **1** : the department of government that keeps public order and safety and enforces the laws; *also* : the members of this department **2** : a private organization resembling a police force; *also* : its members **3** : military personnel detailed to clean and put in order

po·lice·man \-mən\ *n* : a member of a police force

police state *n* : a state characterized by repressive, arbitrary, totalitarian rule by means of secret police

po·lice·wom·an \pə-'lēs-ˌwu̇-mən\ *n* : a woman who is a member of a police force

¹**pol·i·cy** \\'päl-ə-sē\ *n, pl* **-cies** : a definite course or method of action selected to guide and determine present and future decisions

²**policy** *n, pl* **-cies** : a writing whereby a contract of insurance is made

pol·i·cy·hold·er \\'päl-ə-sē-ˌhōl-dər\ *n* : one granted an insurance policy

po·lio \\'pō-lē-ˌō\ *n* : POLIOMYELITIS — **polio** *adj*

po·lio·my·eli·tis \-ˌmī-ə-'līt-əs\ *n* : an acute virus disease marked by inflammation of the nerve cells of the spinal cord

¹**pol·ish** \\'päl-ish\ *vb* **1** : to make smooth and glossy usu. by rubbing **2** : to refine or improve in manners, condition, or style

²**polish** *n* **1** : a smooth glossy surface : LUSTER **2** : REFINEMENT, CULTURE **3** : the action or process of polishing

Pol·ish \\'pō-lish\ *n* : the Slavic language of the Poles — **Polish** *adj*

polit *abbr* political; politician

po·lit·bu·ro \\'päl-ət-ˌbyu̇r-ō, 'pō-lət-, pə-'lit-\ *n* [Russ *politbyuro*] : the principal policy-making committee of a Communist party

po·lite \pə-'līt\ *adj* **po·lit·er; -est 1** : RE-

FINED, CULTIVATED ⟨∼ society⟩ **2** : marked by correct social conduct : COURTEOUS; *also* : CONSIDERATE, TACTFUL — **po·lite·ly** *adv* — **po·lite·ness** *n*

po·li·tesse \ˌpäl-i-ˈtes\ *n* [F] : formal politeness

pol·i·tic \ˈpäl-ə-ˌtik\ *adj* **1** : wise in promoting a policy ⟨a ∼ statesman⟩ **2** : shrewdly tactful ⟨a ∼ move⟩

po·lit·i·cal \pə-ˈlit-i-kəl\ *adj* **1** : of or relating to government or politics **2** : involving or charged or concerned with acts against a government or a political system ⟨∼ criminals⟩ — **po·lit·i·cal·ly** \-k(ə-)lē\ *adv*

pol·i·ti·cian \ˌpäl-ə-ˈtish-ən\ *n* : a person actively engaged in government or politics

pol·i·tick \ˈpäl-ə-ˌtik\ *vb* : to engage in political discussion or activity

po·lit·i·co \pə-ˈlit-i-ˌkō\ *n, pl* **-cos** *also* **-coes** : POLITICIAN

pol·i·tics \ˈpäl-ə-ˌtiks\ *n sing or pl* **1** : the art or science of government, of guiding or influencing governmental policy, or of winning and holding control over a government **2** : political affairs or business; *esp* : competition between groups or individuals for power and leadership **3** : political opinions

pol·i·ty \ˈpäl-ət-ē\ *n, pl* **-ties** : a politically organized unit; *also* : the form or constitution of such a unit

pol·ka \ˈpōl-kə, ˈpō-kə\ *n* [Czech, fr. Pol *Polka* Polish woman, fem. of *Polak* Pole] : a lively couple dance of Bohemian origin; *also* : music for this dance — **polka** *vb*

pol·ka dot \ˈpō-kə-ˌdät\ *n* : a dot in a pattern of regularly distributed dots — **polka–dot** *or* **polka–dot·ted** \-ˌdät-əd\ *adj*

¹**poll** \ˈpōl\ *n* **1** : HEAD **2** : the casting and recording of votes; *also* : the total vote cast **3** : the place where votes are cast — usu. used in pl. **4** : a questioning of persons to obtain information or opinions to be analyzed

²**poll** *vb* **1** : to cut off or shorten a growth or part of : CLIP, SHEAR **2** : to receive and record the votes of **3** : to receive (as votes) in an election **4** : to question in a poll

pol·lack *or* **pol·lock** \ˈpäl-ək\ *n, pl*

pollack *or* **pollock** : an important Atlantic food fish that is related to the cods

pol·len \ˈpäl-ən\ *n* [NL fr. L, fine flour] : a mass of male spores of a seed plant usu. appearing as a yellow dust

pol·li·na·tion \ˌpäl-ə-ˈnā-shən\ *n* : the carrying of pollen to the female part of a plant to fertilize the seed — **pol·li·nate** \ˈpäl-ə-ˌnāt\ *vb* — **pol·li·na·tor** \-ər\ *n*

poll·ster \ˈpōl-stər\ *n* : one that conducts a poll or compiles data obtained by a poll

poll tax *n* : a tax of a fixed amount per person levied on adults

pol·lute \pə-ˈlüt\ *vb* **pol·lut·ed; pol·lut·ing** : to make impure; *esp* : to contaminate with man-made waste — **pol·lut·ant** \-ˈlüt-ᵊnt\ *n* — **pol·lut·er** *n* — **pol·lu·tion** \-ˈlü-shən\ *n*

pol·ly·wog *or* **pol·li·wog** \ˈpäl-ē-ˌwäg\ *n* : TADPOLE

po·lo \ˈpō-lō\ *n* : a game played by two teams on horseback using long-handled mallets to drive a wooden ball

po·lo·ni·um \pə-ˈlō-nē-əm\ *n* [NL, fr. ML *Polonia* Poland, birthplace of its discoverer, Mme. Curie] : a radioactive metallic chemical element

pol·ter·geist \ˈpōl-tər-ˌgīst\ *n* [G, fr. *poltern* to knock + *geist* spirit] : a noisy usu. mischievous ghost held to be responsible for unexplained noises

pol·troon \päl-ˈtrün\ *n* : COWARD

poly·chlo·ri·nat·ed bi·phe·nyl \ˌpäl-i-ˈklōr-ə-ˌnāt-əd-ˌbī-ˈfen-ᵊl, -ˈfēn-\ *n* : any of several industrial compounds that are poisonous environmental pollutants

poly·clin·ic \ˌpäl-i-ˈklin-ik\ *n* : a clinic or hospital treating diseases of many sorts

poly·es·ter \ˈpäl-ē-ˌes-tər\ *n* : a polymer composed of ester groups used esp. in making fibers or plastics

poly·eth·yl·ene \ˌpäl-ē-ˈeth-ə-ˌlēn\ *n* : a lightweight plastic resistant to chemicals and moisture and used chiefly in packaging

po·lyg·a·my \pə-ˈlig-ə-mē\ *n* : the practice of having more than one wife or husband at one time — **po·lyg·a·mist** \-məst\ *n* — **po·lyg·a·mous** \-məs\ *adj*

poly·glot \ˈpäl-i-ˌglät\ *adj* **1** : speaking or writing several languages **2** : containing or made up of several languages — **polyglot** *n*

poly·gon \'päl-i-ˌgän\ *n* : a closed plane figure bounded by straight lines — **po·lyg·o·nal** \pə-'lig-ən-ᵊl\ *adj*

poly·graph \'päl-i-ˌgraf\ *n* : an instrument for recording variations of several bodily functions (as blood pressure) simultaneously — **po·lyg·ra·pher** \pə-'lig-rə-fər, 'päl-i-ˌgraf-ər\ *n*

poly·he·dron \ˌpäl-i-'hē-drən\ *n* : a solid formed by plane faces — **poly·he·dral** \-drəl\ *adj*

poly·math \'päl-i-ˌmath\ *n* : a person of encyclopedic learning

poly·mer \'päl-ə-mər\ *n* : a chemical compound formed by union of small molecules of the same kind — **poly·mer·ic** \ˌpäl-ə-'mer-ik\ *adj*

po·lym·er·iza·tion \pə-ˌlim-ə-rə-'zā-shən\ *n* : a chemical reaction in which two or more small molecules combine to form larger molecules with repeating structural units — **po·lym·er·ize** \pə-'lim-ə-ˌrīz\ *vb*

Poly·ne·sian \ˌpäl-ə-'nē-zhən\ *n* **1** : a member of any of the native peoples of Polynesia **2** : a group of Austronesian languages spoken in Polynesia — **Polynesian** *adj*

poly·no·mi·al \ˌpäl-ə-'nō-mē-əl\ *n* : an algebraic expression having two or more terms each of which consists of a constant multiplied by one or more variables raised to a nonnegative integral power — **polynomial** *adj*

pol·yp \'päl-əp\ *n* **1** : an invertebrate animal (as a coral) that is a coelenterate having a hollow cylindrical body closed at one end **2** : a projecting mass of swollen and hypertrophied or tumorous membrane ⟨a rectal ∼⟩

po·lyph·o·ny \pə-'lif-ə-nē\ *n* : music consisting of two or more melodically independent but harmonizing voice parts — **poly·phon·ic** \ˌpäl-i-'fän-ik\ *adj*

poly·sty·rene \ˌpäl-i-'stīr-ˌēn\ *n* : a rigid transparent nonconducting thermoplastic used esp. in molded products and foams

poly·syl·lab·ic \ˌpäl-i-sə-'lab-ik\ *adj* **1** : having more than three syllables **2** : characterized by polysyllabic words

poly·syl·la·ble \'päl-i-ˌsil-ə-bəl\ *n* : a polysyllabic word

poly·tech·nic \ˌpäl-i-'tek-nik\ *adj* : of, relating to, or instructing in many technical arts or applied sciences

poly·the·ism \'päl-i-thē-ˌiz-əm\ *n* : belief in or worship of many gods — **poly·the·ist** \-ˌthē-əst\ *adj or n* — **poly·the·is·tic** \ˌpäl-i-thē-'is-tik\ *adj*

poly·un·sat·u·rat·ed \'päl-ē-ˌən-'sach-ə-ˌrāt-əd\ *adj, of an oil or fatty acid* : having many unsaturated chemical bonds between carbon atoms

poly·vi·nyl \ˌpäl-i-'vīn-ᵊl\ *adj* : of, relating to, or being a polymerized vinyl compound, resin, or plastic — often used in combination

po·made \pō-'mäd, -'mād\ *n* : a perfumed ointment esp. for the hair or scalp

pome·gran·ate \'päm-(ə-)ˌgran-ət\ *n* [ME *poumgarnet*, fr. MF *pomme grenate*, lit., seedy apple, fr. *pomme* apple (fr. LL *pomum*, fr. L, fruit) + *grenate* seedy, fr. L *granatus*, fr. *granum* grain] : a tropical reddish fruit with many seeds and an edible crimson pulp; *also* : the tree that bears it

¹**pom·mel** \'pəm-əl, 'päm-\ *n* **1** : the knob on the hilt of a sword **2** : the knoblike bulge at the front and top of a saddlebow

²**pom·mel** \'pəm-əl\ *vb* **-meled** *or* **-melled**; **-mel·ing** *or* **-mel·ling** \-(ə-)liŋ\ : PUMMEL

pomp \'pämp\ *n* **1** : brilliant display : SPLENDOR **2** : OSTENTATION

pom·pa·dour \'päm-pə-ˌdōr\ *n* : a style of dressing the hair high over the forehead

pom·pa·no \'päm-pə-ˌnō, 'pəm-\ *n, pl* **-no** *or* **-nos** : a food fish of the southern Atlantic coast

pom–pom \'päm-ˌpäm\ *n* : an ornamental ball or tuft used on a cap or costume

pom·pon \'päm-ˌpän\ *n* **1** : POM-POM **2** : a chrysanthemum or dahlia with small rounded flower heads

pomp·ous \'päm-pəs\ *adj* **1** : suggestive of pomp; *esp* : OSTENTATIOUS **2** : pretentiously dignified **3** : excessively elevated or ornate **syn** arrogant, magisterial, self-important — **pom·pos·i·ty** \päm-'päs-ət-ē\ *n* — **pomp·ous·ly** *adv*

pon·cho \'pän-chō\ *n, pl* **ponchos** [AmerSp] **1** : a cloak like a blanket with a slit in the middle for the head **2**

: a waterproof garment resembling a poncho

pond \'pänd\ *n* : a small body of water

pon·der \'pän-dər\ *vb* **pon·dered; pon·der·ing** \-d(ə-)riŋ\ **1** : to weigh in the mind **2** : to consider carefully

pon·der·o·sa pine \ˌpän-də-ˌrō-sə-, -zə-\ *n* : a tall timber tree of western No. America with long needles; *also* : its wood

pon·der·ous \'pän-d(ə-)rəs\ *adj* **1** : of very great weight ⟨a ∼ stone⟩ **2** : UNWIELDY, CLUMSY ⟨a ∼ weapon⟩ **3** : oppressively dull ⟨a ∼ speech⟩ **syn** cumbrous, cumbersome, weighty

pone \'pōn\ *n, Southern & Midland* : an oval-shaped cornmeal cake; *also* : corn bread in the form of pones

pon·gee \pän-'jē\ *n* : a thin soft silk, cotton, or rayon fabric

pon·iard \'pän-yərd\ *n* : DAGGER

pon·tiff \'pänt-əf\ *n* : BISHOP; *esp* : POPE — **pon·tif·i·cal** \pän-'tif-i-kəl\ *adj*

pon·tif·i·cals \pän-'tif-i-kəlz\ *n pl* : the insignia worn by a bishop when celebrating a pontifical mass

¹pon·tif·i·cate \pän-'tif-i-kət, -ə-ˌkāt\ *n* : the state, office, or term of office of a pontiff

²pon·tif·i·cate \pän-'tif-ə-ˌkāt\ *vb* **-cat·ed; -cat·ing** : to deliver dogmatic opinions

pon·toon \pän-'tün\ *n* **1** : a flat-bottomed boat **2** : a boat or float used in building a floating temporary bridge **3** : a float of an airplane

po·ny \'pō-nē\ *n, pl* **ponies** : a small horse

po·ny·tail \-ˌtāl\ *n* : a style of arranging hair to resemble the tail of a pony

pooch \'püch\ *n* : DOG

poo·dle \'püd-ᵊl\ *n* [G *pudel*, short for *pudelhund*, fr. *pudeln* to splash (fr. *pudel* puddle) + *hund* dog] : an active dog with a heavy curly coat

pooh–pooh \'pü-'pü\ *also* **pooh** \'pü\ *vb* **1** : to express contempt or impatience **2** : DERIDE, SCORN

¹pool \'pül\ *n* **1** : a small deep body of usu. fresh water **2** : a small body of standing liquid **3** : SWIMMING POOL

²pool *n* **1** : all the money bet on the result of a particular event **2** : any of several games of billiards played on a table having six pockets **3** : the amount contributed by the participants in a joint venture **4** : a combination between competing firms for mutual profit **5** : a readily available supply

³pool *vb* : to contribute to a common fund or effort

¹poop \'püp\ *n* : an enclosed superstructure at the stern of a ship

²poop *n, slang* : INFORMATION

poop deck *n* : a partial deck above a ship's main afterdeck

poor \'pùr\ *adj* **1** : lacking material possessions ⟨∼ people⟩ **2** : less than adequate : MEAGER ⟨∼ crop⟩ **3** : arousing pity ⟨∼ fellows⟩ **4** : inferior in quality or value ⟨∼ sportsmanship⟩ **5** : UNPRODUCTIVE, BARREN ⟨∼ soil⟩ **6** : fairly unsatisfactory ⟨∼ prospects⟩; *also* : UNFAVORABLE ⟨∼ opinion⟩ **syn** bad, wrong, unsatisfactory, rotten — **poorly** *adv*

poor boy \'pō(r)-ˌbói\ *n* : SUBMARINE 2

poor·house \'pùr-ˌhaùs\ *n* : a publicly supported home for needy or dependent persons

poor–mouth \-ˌmaùth, -ˌmaùth\ *vb* : to plead poverty as a defense or excuse

¹pop \'päp\ *vb* **popped; pop·ping** **1** : to go, come, enter, or issue forth suddenly or quickly ⟨∼ into bed⟩ **2** : to put or thrust suddenly ⟨∼ questions⟩ **3** : to burst or cause to burst with or make a sharp sound **4** : to protrude from the sockets **5** : SHOOT **6** : to hit a pop-up

²pop *n* **1** : a sharp explosive sound **2** : SHOT **3** : a flavored soft drink

³pop *n* : FATHER

⁴pop *adj* **1** : POPULAR ⟨∼ music⟩ **2** : of or relating to pop music ⟨∼ singer⟩ **3** : of or relating to the popular culture disseminated through the mass media ⟨∼ psychology⟩ **4** : of, relating to, or imitating pop art ⟨∼ painter⟩

⁵pop *n* : pop music, art, or culture

⁶pop *abbr* population

pop art *n* : art in which commonplace objects (as comic strips or soup cans) are used as subject matter — **pop artist** *n*

pop·corn \'päp-ˌkòrn\ *n* : an Indian corn whose kernels burst open into a white starchy mass when heated; *also* : the burst kernels

pope \'pōp\ *n, often cap* : the head of the Roman Catholic Church

pop–eyed \'päp-,īd\ *adj* : having eyes that bulge (as from disease)

pop fly *n* : a short high fly in baseball

pop·gun \'päp-,gən\ *n* : a toy gun for shooting pellets with compressed air

pop·in·jay \'päp-ən-,jā\ *n* [ME *papejay* parrot, fr. MF *papegai, papejai*, fr. Ar *babghā'*] : a strutting supercilious person

pop·lar \'päp-lər\ *n* : any of various slender quick-growing trees related to the willows

pop·lin \'päp-lən\ *n* : a strong plain-woven fabric with crosswise ribs

pop·over \'päp-,ō-vər\ *n* : a biscuit made from a thin batter rich in egg and expanded by baking into a hollow shell

pop·per \'päp-ər\ *n* : a utensil for popping corn

pop·py \'päp-ē\ *n, pl* **poppies** : any of several herbs that have showy flowers including one that yields opium

pop·py·cock \'päp-ē-,käk\ *n* : empty talk : NONSENSE

pop·u·lace \'päp-yə-ləs\ *n* **1** : the common people **2** : POPULATION

pop·u·lar \'päp-yə-lər\ *adj* **1** : of or relating to the general public ⟨∼ government⟩ **2** : easy to understand : PLAIN ⟨∼ style⟩ **3** : INEXPENSIVE ⟨∼ rates⟩ **4** : frequently encountered or widely accepted ⟨∼ notion⟩ **5** : commonly liked or approved ⟨∼ teacher⟩ — **pop·u·lar·i·ty** \,päp-yə-'lar-ət-ē\ *n* — **pop·u·lar·ize** \'päp-yə-lə-,rīz\ *vb* — **pop·u·lar·ly** \-lər-lē\ *adv*

pop·u·late \'päp-yə-,lāt\ *vb* **-lat·ed; -lat·ing** **1** : to have a place in : INHABIT **2** : PEOPLE

pop·u·la·tion \,päp-yə-'lā-shən\ *n* **1** : the people or number of people in an area **2** : the individuals under consideration (as in statistical sampling)

population explosion *n* : a pyramiding of numbers of a biological population; *esp* : the recent great increase in human numbers resulting from both increased survival and exponential population growth

pop·u·list \'päp-yə-ləst\ *n* : a believer in or advocate of the rights, wisdom, or virtues of the common people — **pop·u·lism** \-,liz-əm\ *n*

pop·u·lous \'päp-yə-ləs\ *adj* **1** : densely populated; *also* : having a large popu-

lation **2** : CROWDED — **pop·u·lous·ness** *n*

pop–up \'päp-,əp\ *n* : a short high fly in baseball

POR *abbr* pay on return

por·ce·lain \'pōr-s(ə-)lən\ *n* : a fine-grained translucent ceramic ware

porch \'pōrch\ *n* : a covered entrance usu. with a separate roof : VERANDA

por·cine \'pȯr-,sīn\ *adj* : of, relating to, or suggesting swine

por·cu·pine \'pȯr-kyə-,pīn\ *n* [ME *porkepin*, fr. MF *porc espin*, fr. It *porcospino*, fr. L *porcus* pig + *spina* spine, prickle] : a mammal having stiff sharp easily detachable spines mingled with its hair

¹pore \'pōr\ *vb* **pored; por·ing** **1** : to read studiously or attentively ⟨∼ over a book⟩ **2** : PONDER, REFLECT

²pore *n* : a tiny hole or space (as in the skin or soil) — **pored** \'pōrd\ *adj*

pork \'pōrk\ *n* : the flesh of swine dressed for use as food

pork barrel *n* : a government project or appropriation yielding rich patronage benefits

pork·er \'pōr-kər\ *n* : HOG; *esp* : a young pig suitable for use as fresh pork

por·nog·ra·phy \pȯr-'näg-rə-fē\ *n* [Gk *pornographos* writing of harlots] : the depiction of erotic behavior designed primarily to cause sexual excitement — **por·no·graph·ic** \,pȯr-nə-'graf-ik\ *adj*

po·rous \'pōr-əs\ *adj* **1** : full of pores **2** : permeable to fluids : ABSORPTIVE — **po·ros·i·ty** \pə-'räs-ət-ē\ *n*

por·phy·ry \'pȯr-f(ə-)rē\ *n, pl* **-ries** : a rock consisting of feldspar crystals embedded in a compact fine-grained base material — **por·phy·rit·ic** \,pȯr-fə-'rit-ik\ *adj*

por·poise \'pȯr-pəs\ *n* [ME *porpoys*, fr. MF *porpois*, fr. ML *porcopiscis*, fr. L *porcus* pig + *piscis* fish] **1** : any of several small blunt-snouted whales **2** : any of several dolphins

por·ridge \'pȯr-ij\ *n* : a soft food made by boiling meal of grains or legumes in milk or water

por·rin·ger \-ən-jər\ *n* : a low one-handled metal bowl or cup

¹port \'pōrt\ *n* **1** : HARBOR **2** : a city with a harbor **3** : AIRPORT

²**port** *n* **1** : an inlet or outlet (as in an engine) for a fluid **2** : PORTHOLE

³**port** *n* : BEARING, CARRIAGE

⁴**port** *vb* : to turn or put a helm to the left

⁵**port** *n* : the left side of a ship or airplane looking forward — **port** *adj*

⁶**port** *n* : a sweet fortified wine

por·ta·ble \'pōrt-ə-bəl\ *adj* : capable of being carried — **portable** *n*

¹**por·tage** \'pōrt-ij, pȯr-'täzh\ *n* [ME, fr. MF] : the carrying of boats and goods overland between navigable bodies of water; *also* : a route for such carrying

²**por·tage** \'pōrt-ij, pȯr-'täzh\ *vb* **por·taged; por·tag·ing** : to carry gear over a portage

por·tal \'pōrt-ᵊl\ *n* : DOOR, ENTRANCE; *esp* : a grand or imposing one

portal–to–portal *adj* : of or relating to the time spent by a worker in traveling from the entrance to his employer's property to his actual working place (as in a mine) and in returning after the work shift

port·cul·lis \pōrt-'kəl-əs\ *n* : a grating at the gateway of a castle or fortress that can be let down to stop entrance

porte co·chere \ˌpōrt-kō-'sher\ *n* [F *porte cochère,* lit., coach door] : a roofed structure extending from the entrance of a building over an adjacent driveway and sheltering those getting in or out of vehicles

por·tend \pȯr-'tend\ *vb* **1** : to give a sign or warning of beforehand **2** : INDICATE, SIGNIFY **syn** augur, prognosticate, foretell, predict, forecast, prophesy

por·tent \'pȯr-ˌtent\ *n* **1** : something that foreshadows a coming event : OMEN **2** : MARVEL, PRODIGY

por·ten·tous \pȯr-'tent-əs\ *adj* **1** : of, relating to, or constituting a portent **2** : PRODIGIOUS **3** : self-consciously weighty : POMPOUS

¹**por·ter** \'pōrt-ər\ *n, chiefly Brit* : DOORKEEPER

²**porter** *n* **1** : one that carries burdens; *esp* : one employed (as at a terminal) to carry baggage **2** : an attendant in a railroad car **3** : a dark heavy ale

por·ter·house \'pōrt-ər-ˌhaus\ *n* : a choice beefsteak with a large tenderloin

port·fo·lio \pōrt-'fō-lē-ˌō\ *n, pl* **-li·os 1** : a portable case for papers or drawings **2** : the office and functions of a minister of state **3** : the securities held by an investor

port·hole \'pōrt-ˌhōl\ *n* : an opening in the side of a ship or aircraft

por·ti·co \'pōrt-i-ˌkō\ *n, pl* **-coes** *or* **-cos** [It] : a row of columns supporting a roof around or at the entrance of a building

por·tiere \pōr-'tye(ə)r, -'ti(ə)r; 'pōrt-ē-ər\ *n* : a curtain hanging across a doorway

¹**por·tion** \'pōr-shən\ *n* **1** : one's part or share ⟨a ∼ of food⟩ **2** : DOWRY **3** : an individual's lot **4** : a part of a whole ⟨a ∼ of the sky⟩

²**portion** *vb* **por·tioned; por·tion·ing** \-sh(ə-)niŋ\ **1** : to divide into portions **2** : to allot to as a portion

port·land cement \ˌpōrt-lən(d)-\ *n* : a cement made by calcining and grinding a mixture of clay and limestone

port·ly \'pōrt-lē\ *adj* **port·li·er; -est** : somewhat stout

port·man·teau \pōrt-'man-ˌtō\ *n, pl* **-teaus** *or* **-teaux** \-ˌtōz\ [MF *portemanteau,* fr. *porter* to carry + *manteau* mantle, fr. L *mantellum*] : a large traveling bag

port of call : an intermediate port where ships customarily stop for supplies, repairs, or transshipment of cargo

port of entry 1 : a place where foreign goods may be cleared through a customhouse **2** : a place where an alien may enter a country

por·trait \'pōr-trət, -ˌtrāt\ *n* : a picture (as a painting or photograph) of a person usu. showing the face

por·trait·ist \-əst\ *n* : a maker of portraits

por·trai·ture \'pōr-trə-ˌchur\ *n* : the practice or art of making portraits

por·tray \pōr-'trā\ *vb* **1** : to make a picture of : DEPICT **2** : to describe in words **3** : to play the role of — **por·tray·al** *n*

Por·tu·guese \'pōr-chə-ˌgēz, -ˌgēs; ˌpōr-chə-'gēz, -'gēs\ *n, pl* **Portuguese 1** : a native or inhabitant of Portugal **2** : the language of Portugal and Brazil — **Portuguese** *adj*

Portuguese man–of–war *n* : any of several large colonial invertebrate animals that are related to the jellyfishes and have a large sac resembling a bladder by means of which the colony floats at the surface of the sea

por·tu·laca \\ˌpōr-chə-'lak-ə\ *n* : a tropical succulent herb cultivated for its showy flowers

pos *abbr* 1 position 2 positive

¹pose \\'pōz\ *vb* **posed; pos·ing** 1 : to assume or cause to assume a posture usu. for artistic purposes 2 : to set forth : PROPOSE ⟨∼ a question⟩ 3 : to affect an attitude or character

²pose *n* 1 : a sustained posture; *esp* : one assumed by a model 2 : an attitude assumed for effect : PRETENSE

¹pos·er \\'pō-zər\ *n* : a puzzling question

²poser *n* : a person who poses

po·seur \\pō-'zər\ *n* [F, lit., poser] : an affected or insincere person

posh \\'päsh\ *adj* : FASHIONABLE

pos·it \\'päs-ət\ *vb* : to assume the existence of : POSTULATE

po·si·tion \\pə-'zish-ən\ *n* 1 : an arranging in order 2 : the stand taken on a question 3 : the point or area occupied by something : SITUATION 4 : the arrangement of parts (as of the body) in relation to one another : POSTURE 5 : RANK, STATUS 6 : EMPLOYMENT, JOB — **position** *vb*

¹pos·i·tive \\'päz-ət-iv\ *adj* 1 : expressed definitely ⟨∼ views⟩ 2 : CONFIDENT, CERTAIN 3 : of, relating to, or constituting the degree of grammatical comparison that denotes no increase in quality, quantity, or relation 4 : not fictitious : REAL 5 : active and effective in function ⟨∼ leadership⟩ 6 : having the light and shade as existing in the original subject ⟨a ∼ photograph⟩ 7 : numerically greater than zero ⟨a ∼ number⟩ 8 : being, relating to, or charged with electricity of which the proton is the elementary unit 9 : AFFIRMATIVE ⟨a ∼ response⟩ — **pos·i·tive·ly** *adv* — **pos·i·tive·ness** *n*

²positive *n* 1 : the positive degree or a positive form in a language 2 : a positive photograph

pos·i·tron \\'päz-ə-ˌträn\ *n* : a positively charged particle having the same mass and magnitude of charge as the electron

poss *abbr* possessive

pos·se \\'päs-ē\ *n* [ML *posse comitatus*, lit., power or authority of the country]

: a body of persons organized to assist a sheriff in an emergency

pos·sess \\pə-'zes\ *vb* 1 : to have as property : OWN 2 : to have as an attribute, knowledge, or skill 3 : to enter into and control firmly ⟨∼ed by a devil⟩ — **pos·ses·sor** \\-'zes-ər\ *n*

pos·ses·sion \\-'zesh-ən\ *n* 1 : control or occupancy of property 2 : OWNERSHIP 3 : something owned : PROPERTY 4 : domination by something 5 : SELF≠ CONTROL

pos·ses·sive \\pə-'zes-iv\ *adj* 1 : of, relating to, or constituting a grammatical case denoting ownership 2 : showing the desire to possess ⟨a ∼ nature⟩ — **possessive** *n* — **pos·ses·sive·ness** *n*

pos·si·ble \\'päs-ə-bəl\ *adj* 1 : being within the limits of ability, capacity, or realization ⟨a ∼ task⟩ 2 : being something that may or may not occur ⟨∼ dangers⟩ 3 : able or fitted to become ⟨a ∼ site for a bridge⟩ — **pos·si·bil·i·ty** \\ˌpäs-ə-'bil-ət-ē\ *n* — **pos·si·bly** \\'päs-ə-blē\ *adv*

pos·sum \\'päs-əm\ *n* : OPOSSUM

¹post \\'pōst\ *n* 1 : an upright piece of timber or metal serving esp. as a support : PILLAR 2 : a pole or stake set up as a mark or indicator

²post *vb* 1 : to affix to a usual place (as a wall) for public notices ⟨∼ no bills⟩ 2 : to publish or announce by or as if by a public notice ⟨∼ grades⟩ 3 : to forbid (property) to trespassers by putting up a notice 4 : SCORE 4

³post *n* 1 *obs* : COURIER 2 *chiefly Brit* : MAIL; *also* : POST OFFICE

⁴post *vb* 1 : to ride or travel with haste : HURRY 2 : MAIL ⟨∼ a letter⟩ 3 : to enter in a ledger 4 : INFORM ⟨kept him ∼ed on new developments⟩

⁵post *n* 1 : the place at which a soldier is stationed; *esp* : a sentry's beat or station 2 : a station or task to which a person is assigned 3 : the place at which a body of troops is stationed : CAMP 4 : OFFICE, POSITION 5 : a trading settlement or station

⁶post *vb* 1 : to station in a given place 2 : to put up (as bond)

post·age \\'pōs-tij\ *n* : the fee for postal service; *also* : stamps representing this fee

post·al \\'pōs-tᵊl\ *adj* : of or relating to the mails or the post office

postal card *n* : POSTCARD

postal service *n* : a government agency or department handling the transmission of mail

post·boy \'pōst-ˌbȯi\ *n* : POSTILION

post·card \-ˌkärd\ *n* : a card on which a message may be written for mailing without an envelope

post chaise *n* : a 4-wheeled closed carriage for two to four persons

post·con·so·nan·tal \ˌpōst-ˌkän-sə-'nant-ᵊl\ *adj* : immediately following a consonant

post·date \(')pōs(t)-'dāt\ *vb* : to date with a date later than that of execution

post·doc·tor·al \(')pōs(t)-'däk-t(ə-)rəl\ *also* **post·doc·tor·ate** \-t(ə-)rət\ *adj* : of, relating to, or engaged in advanced academic or professional work beyond a doctor's degree

post·er \'pō-stər\ *n* : a bill or placard for posting in a public place

¹**pos·te·ri·or** \pō-'stir-ē-ər, pä-\ *adj* **1** : later in time **2** : situated behind

²**pos·te·ri·or** \pä-'stir-ē-ər, pō-\ *n* : the hinder parts of the body : BUTTOCKS

pos·ter·i·ty \pä-'ster-ət-ē\ *n* **1** : the descendants from one ancestor **2** : succeeding generations; *also* : future time

pos·tern \'pōs-tərn, 'päs-\ *n* **1** : a back door or gate **2** : a private or side entrance

post exchange *n* : a store at a military post that sells to military personnel and authorized civilians

post·grad·u·ate \(')pōst-'graj-ə-wət\ *adj* : of or relating to studies beyond the bachelor's degree — **postgraduate** *n*

post·haste \'pōst-'hāst\ *adv* : with all possible speed

post·hole \'pōst-ˌhōl\ *n* : a hole for a post and esp. a fence post

post·hu·mous \'päs-chə-məs\ *adj* **1** : born after the death of the father **2** : published after the death of the author

post·hyp·not·ic \ˌpōst-hip-'nät-ik\ *adj* : of, relating to, or characteristic of the period following a hypnotic trance

pos·til·ion *or* **pos·til·lion** \pō-'stil-yən, pə-\ *n* : a rider on the left-hand horse of a pair drawing a coach

Post·im·pres·sion·ism \ˌpōst-im-'presh-ə-ˌniz-əm\ *n* : a late 19th century French theory or practice of art that stresses variously volume, picture structure, or expressionism

post·lude \'pōst-ˌlüd\ *n* : an organ solo played at the end of a church service

post·man \'pōst-mən, -ˌman\ *n* : MAILMAN

post·mark \-ˌmärk\ *n* : an official postal marking on a piece of mail; *esp* : the mark canceling the postage stamp — **postmark** *vb*

post·mas·ter \-ˌmas-tər\ *n* : one who has charge of a post office

postmaster general *n, pl* **postmasters general** : an official in charge of a national postal service

post me·ri·di·em \'pōst-mə-'rid-ē-əm\ *adj* [L] : being after noon

post·mis·tress \-ˌmis-trəs\ *n* : a woman in charge of a post office

¹**post·mor·tem** \(')pōst-'mȯrt-əm\ *adj* [L *post mortem* after death] **1** : done, occurring, or collected after death **2** : relating to a postmortem examination

²**postmortem** *n* : AUTOPSY

post·na·sal drip \'pōst-'nā-zəl-\ *n* : flow of mucous secretion from the posterior part of the nasal cavity onto the wall of the pharynx

post·na·tal \(')pōst-'nāt-ᵊl\ *adj* : subsequent to birth; *also* : of or relating to a newborn child

post office *n* **1** : POSTAL SERVICE **2** : a local branch of a post office department

post·op·er·a·tive \(')pōst-'äp-(ə-)rət-iv, -'äp-ə-ˌrāt-\ *adj* : following a surgical operation ⟨~ care⟩

post·paid \'pōst-'pād\ *adv* : with the postage paid by the sender and not chargeable to the receiver

post·par·tum \(')pōst-'pärt-əm\ *adj* [NL *post partum* after birth] : following parturition — **postpartum** *adv*

post·pone \pōs(t)-'pōn\ *vb* **post·poned**; **post·pon·ing** : to hold back to a later time — **post·pone·ment** *n*

post road *n* : a road over which mail is carried

post·script \'pōs(t)-ˌskript\ *n* : a note added esp. to a completed letter

post time *n* : the designated time for the start of a horse race

pos·tu·lant \'päs-chə-lənt\ *n* : a probationary candidate for membership in a religious house

¹pos·tu·late \\'päs-chə-ˌlāt\ *vb* **-lat·ed; -lat·ing** : to assume as true

²pos·tu·late \\'päs-chə-lət, -ˌlāt\ *n* : a proposition taken for granted as true and made the starting point in a chain of reasoning

¹pos·ture \\'päs-chər\ *n* **1** : the position or bearing of the body or one of its parts **2** : STATE, CONDITION **3** : ATTITUDE

²posture *vb* **pos·tured; pos·tur·ing** : to strike a pose esp. for effect

post·war \\'pōst-'wȯr\ *adj* : of or relating to the period after a war

po·sy \\'pō-zē\ *n, pl* **posies 1** : a brief sentiment : MOTTO **2** : a bunch of flowers; *also* : FLOWER

¹pot \\'pät\ *n* **1** : a rounded container used chiefly for domestic purposes **2** : the total of the bets at stake at one time **3** : RUIN ⟨go to ∼⟩ **4** : MARIJUANA — **pot·ful** *n*

²pot *vb* **pot·ted; pot·ting 1** : to preserve in a pot **2** : SHOOT

po·ta·ble \\'pōt-ə-bəl\ *adj* : suitable for drinking — **po·ta·bil·i·ty** \ˌpōt-ə-'bil-ət-ē\ *n*

po·tage \pȯ-'täzh\ *n* : a thick soup

pot·ash \\'pät-ˌash\ *n* [sing. of *pot ashes*] : potassium or any of its various compounds

po·tas·si·um \pə-'tas-ē-əm\ *n* : a silver-white metallic chemical element that occurs abundantly in nature esp. combined in minerals

potassium bromide *n* : a crystalline salt used as a sedative and in photography

potassium carbonate *n* : a white salt used in making glass and soap

potassium nitrate *n* : a soluble salt used in making gunpowder, in preserving meat, and in medicine

po·ta·tion \pō-'tā-shən\ *n* : a usu. alcoholic drink; *also* : the act of drinking

po·ta·to \pə-'tāt-ō\ *n, pl* **-toes** : the edible starchy tuber of a plant related to the tomato; *also* : this plant

potato beetle *n* : COLORADO POTATO BEETLE

potato bug *n* : COLORADO POTATO BEETLE

pot·bel·ly \\'pät-ˌbel-ē\ *n* : a protruding abdomen — **pot·bel·lied** \-ēd\ *adj*

pot·boil·er \-ˌbȯi-lər\ *n* : a usu. inferior work of art or literature produced only to earn money

po·tent \\'pōt-ᵊnt\ *adj* **1** : having authority or influence : POWERFUL **2** : chemically or medicinally effective **3** : able to copulate **syn** forceful, forcible, mighty, puissant — **po·ten·cy** \-ᵊn-sē\ *n*

po·ten·tate \\'pōt-ᵊn-ˌtāt\ *n* : one who wields controlling power : RULER

¹po·ten·tial \pə-'ten-chəl\ *adj* : existing in possibility : capable of becoming actual ⟨a ∼ champion⟩ **syn** dormant, latent, quiescent — **po·ten·ti·al·i·ty** \pə-ˌten-chē-'al-ət-ē\ *n* — **po·ten·tial·ly** \-'tench-(ə-)lē\ *adv*

²potential *n* **1** : something that can develop or become actual **2** : the work required to move a unit positive charge from infinity to a point in question; *also* : POTENTIAL DIFFERENCE

potential difference *n* : the difference in potential between two points that represents the work involved in the transfer of a unit quantity of electricity from one point to the other

po·ten·ti·ate \pə-'ten-chē-ˌāt\ *vb* **-at·ed; -at·ing** : to make potent; *esp* : to augment the activity of (as a drug) synergistically — **po·ten·ti·a·tion** \-ˌten-chē-'ā-shən\ *n*

pot·head \\'pät-ˌhed\ *n* : an individual who smokes marijuana

poth·er \\'päth-ər\ *n* : a noisy disturbance; *also* : FUSS

pot·herb \\'pät-ˌ(h)ərb\ *n* : an herb whose leaves or stems are boiled for greens or used to season food

pot·hole \\'pät-ˌhōl\ *n* : a large pit or hole (as in a road surface)

pot·hook \-ˌhu̇k\ *n* : an S-shaped hook for hanging pots and kettles over an open fire

po·tion \\'pō-shən\ *n* : a mixture of liquids (as liquor or medicine)

pot·luck \\'pät-'lək\ *n* : the regular meal available to a guest for whom no special preparations have been made

pot·pie \-'pī\ *n* : pastry-covered meat and vegetables cooked in a deep dish

pot·pour·ri \ˌpō-pu̇-'rē\ *n* [F *pot pourri*, lit., rotten pot] : a miscellaneous collection : MEDLEY

pot·sherd \\'pät-ˌshərd\ *n* : a pottery fragment

pot·shot \-ˌshät\ *n* **1** : a shot taken from ambush or at a random or easy target

2 : a critical remark made in a random or sporadic manner

pot·tage \'pät-ij\ *n* : a thick soup of vegetables or vegetables and meat

¹pot·ter \'pät-ər\ *n* : one that makes pottery

²potter *vb* : PUTTER

pot·tery \'pät-ə-rē\ *n, pl* **-ter·ies 1** : a place where earthen pots and dishes are made **2** : the art of the potter **3** : dishes, pots, and vases made from clay

¹pouch \'paùch\ *n* **1** : a small bag (as for tobacco) carried on the person **2** : a bag for storing or transporting goods ⟨mail ∼⟩ ⟨diplomatic ∼⟩ **3** : an anatomical sac; *esp* : one for carrying the young on the abdomen of a female marsupial (as a kangaroo)

²pouch *vb* : to make puffy or protuberant

poult \'pōlt\ *n* : a young fowl; *esp* : a young turkey

poul·ter·er \'pōl-tər-ər\ *n* : one that deals in poultry

poul·tice \'pōl-təs\ *n* : a soft usu. heated and medicated mass spread on cloth and applied to a sore or injury — **poultice** *vb*

poul·try \'pōl-trē\ *n* : domesticated birds kept for eggs or meat — **poul·try·man** \-mən\ *n*

pounce \'paùns\ *vb* **pounced; pounc·ing** : to spring or swoop upon and seize something

¹pound \'paùnd\ *n, pl* **pounds** *also* **pound 1** : a unit of avoirdupois, troy, and apothecaries' weight — see WEIGHT table **2** — see MONEY table

²pound *vb* **1** : to crush to a powder or pulp by beating **2** : to strike or beat heavily or repeatedly **3** : DRILL **4** : to move or move along heavily

³pound *n* : a public enclosure where stray animals are kept

pound·age \'paùn-dij\ *n* : POUNDS; *also* : weight in pounds

pound cake *n* : a rich cake made with a large amount of eggs and shortening in proportion to the flour used

pound–fool·ish \'paùnd-'fü-lish\ *adj* : imprudent in dealing with large sums or large matters

pour \'pōr\ *vb* **1** : to flow or cause to flow in a stream or flood **2** : to rain hard **3** : to supply freely and copiously

pour·boire \pùr-'bwär\ *n* [F, fr. *pour boire* for drinking] : TIP, GRATUITY

pout \'paùt\ *vb* : to show displeasure by thrusting out the lips; *also* : to look sullen — **pout** *n*

pov·er·ty \'päv-ərt-ē\ *n* [ME *poverte*, fr. OF *poverté*, fr. L *paupertat-, paupertas*, fr. *pauper* poor] **1** : lack of money or material possessions : WANT **2** : poor quality (as of soil)

poverty line *n* : a level of personal or family income below which one is classified as poor according to government standards

pov·er·ty–strick·en \'päv-ərt-ē-,strik-ən\ *adj* : very poor : DESTITUTE

POW \,pē-(,)ō-'dəb-əl-(,)yü\ *abbr* prisoner of war

¹pow·der \'paùd-ər\ *n* [ME *poudre*, fr. OF, fr. L *pulver-, pulvis* dust] **1** : dry material made up of fine particles; *also* : a usu. medicinal or cosmetic preparation in this form **2** : a solid explosive (as gunpowder) — **pow·dery** *adj*

²powder *vb* **pow·dered; pow·der·ing** \'paùd-(ə-)riŋ\ **1** : to sprinkle or cover with or as if with powder **2** : to reduce to powder

powder room *n* : a rest room for women

¹pow·er \'paù(-ə)r\ *n* **1** : a position of ascendancy over others : AUTHORITY **2** : the ability to act or produce an effect **3** : one that has control or authority; *esp* : a sovereign state **4** : physical might; *also* : mental or moral vigor **5** : the number of times as indicated by an exponent a number is to be multiplied by itself **6** : force or energy used to do work; *also* : the time rate at which work is done or energy transferred **7** : the amount by which an optical lens magnifies — **pow·er·ful** \-fəl\ *adj* — **pow·er·ful·ly** \-ē\ *adv* — **pow·er·less** *adj*

²power *vb* : to supply with power and esp. motive power

pow·er·boat \-'bōt\ *n* : MOTORBOAT

pow·er·house \'paù(-ə)r-,haùs\ *n* **1** : POWER PLANT 1 **2** : one having great drive, energy, or ability

power plant *n* **1** : a building in which electric power is generated **2** : an engine and related parts supplying the motive power of a self-propelled vehicle

pow·wow \'pau̇-ˌwau̇\ *n* **1** : a No. American Indian ceremony (as for victory in war) **2** : a meeting for discussion : CONFERENCE

pox \'päks\ *n, pl* **pox** *or* **pox·es** : any of various diseases (as smallpox or syphilis) marked by a rash on the skin

pp *abbr* **1** pages **2** pianissimo

PP *abbr* **1** parcel post **2** past participle **3** postpaid **4** prepaid

ppd *abbr* **1** postpaid **2** prepaid

PPS *abbr* [L *post postscriptum*] an additional postscript

ppt *abbr* precipitate

PQ *abbr* Province of Quebec

pr *abbr* **1** pair **2** price

Pr *symbol* praseodymium

PR *abbr* **1** payroll **2** public relations **3** Puerto Rico

prac·ti·ca·ble \'prak-ti-kə-bəl\ *adj* : capable of being put into practice, done, or accomplished — **prac·ti·ca·bil·i·ty** \ˌprak-ti-kə-'bil-ət-ē\ *n*

prac·ti·cal \'prak-ti-kəl\ *adj* **1** : of, relating to, or shown in practice ⟨∼ questions⟩ **2** : VIRTUAL ⟨∼ control⟩ **3** : capable of being put to use ⟨a ∼ knowledge of French⟩ **4** : inclined to action as opposed to speculation ⟨a ∼ person⟩ **5** : qualified by practice ⟨a good ∼ mechanic⟩ — **prac·ti·cal·i·ty** \ˌprak-ti-'kal-ət-ē\ *n* — **prac·ti·cal·ly** \'prak-ti-k(ə-)lē\ *adv*

practical joke *n* : a prank intended to trick or embarrass someone or cause him physical discomfort

practical nurse *n* : a nurse who cares for the sick professionally without having the training or experience required of a registered nurse

¹prac·tice *or* **prac·tise** \'prak-təs\ *vb* **prac·ticed** *or* **prac·tised; prac·tic·ing** *or* **prac·tis·ing** **1** : to perform or work at repeatedly so as to become proficient ⟨∼ tennis strokes⟩ **2** : CARRY OUT, APPLY ⟨∼s what he preaches⟩ **3** : to do or perform customarily ⟨∼ politeness⟩ **4** : to be professionally engaged in ⟨∼ law⟩

²practice *also* **practise** *n* **1** : actual performance or application **2** : customary action : HABIT **3** : systematic exercise for proficiency **4** : the exercise of

a profession; *also* : a professional business

prac·ti·tio·ner \prak-'tish-(ə-)nər\ *n* : one that practices a profession

prae·tor \'prēt-ər\ *n* : an ancient Roman magistrate ranking below a consul — **prae·to·ri·an** \prē-'tōr-ē-ən, -'tȯr-\ *adj*

prag·mat·ic \prag-'mat-ik\ *also* **prag·mat·i·cal** \-i-kəl\ *adj* **1** : of or relating to practical affairs **2** : concerned with the practical consequences of actions or beliefs

prag·ma·tism \'prag-mə-ˌtiz-əm\ *n* : a practical approach to problems and affairs

prai·rie \'prer-ē\ *n* : a broad tract of level or rolling grassland

prairie dog *n* : an American burrowing rodent related to the marmots and living in colonies

prairie schooner *n* : a covered wagon used by pioneers in cross-country travel

praise \'prāz\ *vb* **praised; prais·ing** **1** : to express approval of : COMMEND **2** : to glorify (a divinity or a saint) esp. in song — **praise** *n* — **praise·wor·thy** \-ˌwər-thē\ *adj*

pra·line \'prä-ˌlēn, 'prā-\ *n* [F] : a candy of nut kernels embedded in boiled brown sugar or maple sugar

pram \'pram\ *n, chiefly Brit* : PERAMBULATOR

prance \'prans\ *vb* **pranced; pranc·ing** **1** : to spring from the hind legs ⟨a *prancing* horse⟩ **2** : SWAGGER; *also* : CAPER — **prance** *n* — **pranc·er** *n*

prank \'praŋk\ *n* : a playful or mildly mischievous act : TRICK — **prank·ster** \-stər\ *n*

pra·seo·dym·i·um \ˌprā-zē-ō-'dim-ē-əm\ *n* : a white metallic chemical element

prate \'prāt\ *vb* **prat·ed; prat·ing** : to talk long and idly : chatter foolishly

prat·fall \'prat-ˌfȯl\ *n* **1** : a fall on the buttocks **2** : a humiliating blunder

¹prat·tle \'prat-ᵊl\ *vb* **prat·tled; prat·tling** \'prat-(ᵊ-)liŋ\ : PRATE, BABBLE

²prattle *n* : trifling or childish talk

prawn \'prȯn\ *n* : any of numerous edible shrimplike crustaceans; *also* : SHRIMP 1

pray \'prā\ *vb* **1** : ENTREAT, IMPLORE **2** : to ask earnestly for something **3** : to address a divinity esp. with supplication

prayer \\'praər\\ *n* **1** : a supplication or expression addressed to God; *also* : a set order of words used in praying **2** : an earnest request or wish **3** : the act or practice of praying to God **4** : a religious service consisting chiefly of prayers — often used in pl. **5** : something prayed for **6** : a slight chance

prayer book *n* : a book containing prayers and often directions for worship

prayer·ful \\'praər-fəl\\ *adj* **1** : DEVOUT **2** : EARNEST — **prayer·ful·ly** \\-ē\\ *adv*

praying mantis *n* : MANTIS

preach \\'prēch\\ *vb* **1** : to deliver a sermon **2** : to set forth in a sermon **3** : to advocate earnestly — **preach·er** *n* — **preach·ment** *n*

pre·ad·o·les·cence \\'prē-ˌad-ᵊl-'es-ᵊns\\ *n* : the period of human development just preceding adolescence — **pre·ad·o·les·cent** \\-ᵊnt\\ *adj or n*

pre·am·ble \\'prē-ˌam-bəl\\ *n* [ME, fr. MF *preambule*, fr. ML *preambulum*, fr. LL, neut. of *praeambulus* walking in front of, fr. L *prae* in front of + *ambulare* to walk] : an introductory part ⟨the ∼ to a constitution⟩

pre·am·pli·fi·er \\(')prē-'am-plə-ˌfī(-ə)r\\ *n* : an amplifier that increases extremely weak signals before they are fed to additional amplifier circuits

pre·ar·range \\ˌprē-ə-'rānj\\ *vb* : to arrange beforehand — **pre·ar·range·ment** *n*

pre·as·signed \\ˌprē-ə-'sīnd\\ *adj* : assigned beforehand

prec *abbr* preceding

Pre·cam·bri·an \\'prē-'kam-brē-ən, -'kām-\\ *adj* : of, relating to, or being the period of geologic history preceding the Paleozoic era — **Precambrian** *n*

¹pre·can·cel \\(')prē-'kan-səl\\ *vb* : to cancel (a postage stamp) in advance of use — **pre·can·cel·la·tion** \\ˌprē-ˌkan-sə-'lā-shən\\ *n*

²precancel *n* : a precanceled postage stamp

pre·can·cer·ous \\(')prē-'kans-(ə-)rəs\\ *adj* : likely to become cancerous

pre·car·i·ous \\pri-'kar-ē-əs\\ *adj* : dependent on uncertain conditions : dangerously insecure : UNSTABLE ⟨a

∼ foothold⟩ ⟨∼ prosperity⟩ **syn** delicate, sensitive, ticklish, touchy, tricky — **pre·car·i·ous·ly** *adv* — **pre·car·i·ous·ness** *n*

pre·cau·tion \\pri-'ko-shən\\ *n* : a measure taken beforehand to prevent harm or secure good — **pre·cau·tion·ary** \\-shə-ˌner-ē\\ *adj*

pre·cede \\pri-'sēd\\ *vb* **pre·ced·ed; pre·ced·ing** : to be, go, or come ahead or in front of (as in rank, sequence, or time)

pre·ce·dence \\'pres-əd-əns, pri-'sēd-ᵊns\\ *n* **1** : the act or fact of preceding **2** : consideration based on order of importance : PRIORITY

¹pre·ce·dent \\pri-'sēd-ᵊnt, 'pres-əd-ənt\\ *adj* : prior in time, order, or significance

²prec·e·dent \\'pres-əd-ənt\\ *n* : something said or done that may serve to authorize or justify further words or acts of the same or a similar kind

pre·ced·ing \\pri-'sēd-iŋ\\ *adj* : that precedes **syn** antecedent, foregoing, prior, former, anterior

pre·cen·tor \\pri-'sent-ər\\ *n* : a leader of the singing of a choir or congregation

pre·cept \\'prē-ˌsept\\ *n* : a command or principle intended as a general rule of action or conduct

pre·cep·tor \\pri-'sep-tər, 'prē-ˌsep-\\ *n* : TUTOR

pre·ces·sion \\prē-'sesh-ən\\ *n* : a slow gyration of the rotation axis of a spinning body (as the earth) — **pre·cess** \\prē-'ses\\ *vb*

pre·cinct \\'prē-ˌsiŋkt\\ *n* **1** : an administrative subdivision (as of a city) : DISTRICT ⟨police ∼⟩ ⟨electoral ∼⟩ **2** : an enclosure bounded by the limits of a building or place — often used in pl. **3** *pl* : ENVIRONS

pre·ci·os·i·ty \\ˌpres(h)-ē-'äs-ət-ē\\ *n, pl* **-ties** : fastidious refinement

pre·cious \\'presh-əs\\ *adj* **1** : of great value ⟨∼ jewels⟩ **2** : greatly cherished : DEAR ⟨∼ memories⟩ **3** : AFFECTED ⟨∼ language⟩

prec·i·pice \\'pres-ə-pəs\\ *n* : a steep cliff

pre·cip·i·tan·cy \\pri-'sip-ət-ən-sē\\ *n* : undue hastiness or suddenness

¹pre·cip·i·tate \\pri-'sip-ə-ˌtāt\\ *vb* **-tat·ed; -tat·ing** **1** : to throw violently **2** : to throw down **3** : to cause to happen quickly or abruptly ⟨∼ a quarrel⟩ **4**

: to cause to separate from solution or suspension **5** : to fall as rain, snow, or hail **syn** speed, accelerate, quicken, hasten, hurry

²**pre·cip·i·tate** \pri-'sip-ət-ət, -ə-ˌtāt\ *n* : the solid matter that separates from a solution or suspension

³**pre·cip·i·tate** \pri-'sip-ət-ət\ *adj* **1** : showing extreme or unwise haste : RASH **2** : falling with steep descent; *also* : PRECIPITOUS — **pre·cip·i·tate·ly** *adv* — **pre·cip·i·tate·ness** *n*

pre·cip·i·ta·tion \pri-ˌsip-ə-'tā-shən\ *n* **1** : rash haste **2** : the process of precipitating or forming a precipitate **3** : water that falls to earth esp. as rain or snow; *also* : the quantity of this water

pre·cip·i·tous \pri-'sip-ət-əs\ *adj* **1** : PRECIPITATE **2** : having the character of a precipice : very steep ⟨a ∼ slope⟩; *also* : containing precipices ⟨∼ trails⟩ — **pre·cip·i·tous·ly** *adv*

pré·cis \prā-'sē\ *n, pl* **pré·cis** \-'sēz\ [F] : a concise summary of essential points

pre·cise \pri-'sīs\ *adj* **1** : exactly defined or stated : DEFINITE **2** : highly accurate : EXACT **3** : conforming strictly to a standard : SCRUPULOUS — **pre·cise·ly** *adv* — **pre·cise·ness** *n*

pre·ci·sion \pri-'sizh-ən\ *n* : the quality or state of being precise

pre·clude \pri-'klüd\ *vb* **pre·clud·ed; pre·clud·ing** : to make impossible : BAR, PREVENT

pre·co·cious \pri-'kō-shəs\ *adj* [L *praecoc-, praecox* early ripening, precocious, fr. *prae-* ahead + *coquere* to cook] : early in development and esp. in mental development — **pre·co·cious·ly** *adv* — **pre·coc·i·ty** \pri-'käs-ət-ē\ *n*

pre·con·ceive \ˌprē-kən-'sēv\ *vb* : to form an opinion of beforehand — **pre·con·cep·tion** \-'sep-shən\ *n*

pre·con·cert·ed \-'sərt-əd\ *adj* : arranged or agreed on in advance

pre·con·di·tion \-'dish-ən\ *vb* : to put in proper or desired condition or frame of mind in advance

pre·cook \'prē-'kůk\ *vb* : to cook partially or entirely before final cooking or reheating

pre·cur·sor \pri-'kər-sər\ *n* : one that precedes and indicates the approach of another : FORERUNNER

pred *abbr* predicate

pre·da·ceous *or* **pre·da·cious** \pri-'dā-shəs\ *adj* : living by preying on others : PREDATORY

pre·date \'prē-'dāt\ *vb* : ANTEDATE

pre·da·tion \pri-'dā-shən\ *n* **1** : the act of preying or plundering **2** : a mode of life in which food is primarily obtained by killing and consuming animals

pred·a·tor \'pred-ət-ər\ *n* : an animal that lives by killing and consuming other animals

pred·a·to·ry \'pred-ə-ˌtōr-ē\ *adj* **1** : of or relating to plunder ⟨∼ warfare⟩ **2** : disposed to exploit others **3** : preying upon other animals

pre·de·cease \ˌprē-di-'sēs\ *vb* **-ceased; -ceas·ing** : to die before another person

pre·de·ces·sor \'pred-ə-ˌses-ər, 'prēd-\ *n* : one that has previously held a position to which another has succeeded

pre·des·ig·nate \(')prē-'dez-ig-ˌnāt\ *vb* : to designate beforehand

pre·des·ti·na·tion \ˌprē-ˌdes-tə-'nā-shən\ *n* : the act of foreordaining to an earthly lot or eternal destiny by divine decree; *also* : the state of being so foreordained — **pre·des·ti·nate** \prē-'des-tə-ˌnāt\ *vb*

pre·des·tine \prē-'des-tən\ *vb* : to settle beforehand : FOREORDAIN

pre·de·ter·mine \ˌprē-di-'tər-mən\ *vb* : to determine beforehand

pred·i·ca·ble \'pred-i-kə-bəl\ *adj* : capable of being predicated or affirmed

pre·dic·a·ment \pri-'dik-ə-mənt\ *n* : a difficult or trying situation **syn** dilemma, pickle, quagmire, jam

¹**pred·i·cate** \'pred-i-kət\ *n* : the part of a sentence or clause that expresses what is said of the subject

²**pred·i·cate** \'pred-ə-ˌkāt\ *vb* **-cat·ed; -cat·ing** **1** : AFFIRM **2** : to assert to be a quality or attribute ⟨∼ intelligence of man⟩ **3** : FOUND, BASE — **pred·i·ca·tion** \ˌpred-ə-'kā-shən\ *n*

pre·dict \pri-'dikt\ *vb* : to declare in advance — **pre·dict·able** \-'dik-tə-bəl\ *adj* — **pre·dict·ably** \-blē\ *adv* — **pre·dic·tion** \-'dik-shən\ *n*

pre·di·ges·tion \ˌprē-dī-'jes-chən, -də-\ *n* : artificial partial digestion of food esp. for use in cases of illness or impaired digestion — **pre·di·gest** \-'jest\ vb

pre·di·lec·tion \ˌpred-ᵊl-'ek-shən, ˌprēd-\ n : a favorable inclination

pre·dis·pose \ˌprē-dis-'pōz\ vb : to incline in advance : make susceptible — **pre·dis·po·si·tion** \ˌprē-ˌdis-pə-'zish-ən\ n

pre·dom·i·nant \pri-'däm-ə-nənt\ adj : greater in importance, strength, influence, or authority — **pre·dom·i·nance** \-nəns\ n

pre·dom·i·nant·ly \-nənt-lē\ adv : for the most part : MAINLY

pre·dom·i·nate \pri-'däm-ə-ˌnāt\ vb : to be superior esp. in power or numbers : PREVAIL

pree·mie \'prē-mē\ n : a baby born prematurely

pre·em·i·nent \prē-'em-ə-nənt\ adj : having highest rank : OUTSTANDING — **pre·em·i·nence** \-nəns\ n — **pre·em·i·nent·ly** adv

pre·empt \prē-'empt\ vb 1 : to settle upon (public land) with the right to purchase before others; also : to take by such right 2 : to seize upon before someone else can 3 : to take the place of syn usurp, confiscate, appropriate, expropriate — **pre·emp·tion** \-'emp-shən\ n

pre·emp·tive \prē-'emp-tiv\ adj : marked by the seizing of the initiative : initiated by oneself ⟨~ attack⟩

preen \'prēn\ vb 1 : to dress or smooth up : PRIMP 2 : to trim or dress with the beak 3 : to pride (oneself) for achievement

pre·ex·ist \ˌprē-ig-'zist\ vb : to exist before — **pre·ex·is·tence** \-'zis-təns\ n — **pre·ex·is·tent** \-tənt\ adj

pref abbr 1 preface 2 preference 3 preferred 4 prefix

pre·fab \'prē-'fab, 'prē-ˌfab\ n : a prefabricated structure

pre·fab·ri·cate \'prē-'fab-rə-ˌkāt\ vb : to manufacture the parts of (a structure) beforehand for later assembly — **pre·fab·ri·ca·tion** \ˌprē-ˌfab-ri-'kā-shən\ n

¹pref·ace \'pref-əs\ n : introductory comments : FOREWORD — **pref·a·to·ry** \'pref-ə-ˌtōr-ē\ adj

²preface vb **pref·aced**; **pref·ac·ing** : to introduce with a preface

pre·fect \'prē-ˌfekt\ n 1 : a high official; esp : a chief officer or magistrate 2 : a student monitor — **pre·fec·ture** \-ˌfek-chər\ n

pre·fer \pri-'fər\ vb **pre·ferred**; **pre·fer·ring** 1 archaic : PROMOTE 2 : to like better : choose above another 3 : to bring (as a charge) against a person — **pref·er·a·ble** \'pref-(ə-)rə-bəl\ adj — **pref·er·a·bly** \-blē\ adv

pref·er·ence \'pref-(ə-)rəns\ n 1 : a special liking for one thing over another 2 : CHOICE, SELECTION — **pref·er·en·tial** \ˌpref-ə-'ren-chəl\ adj

pre·fer·ment \pri-'fər-mənt\ n : PROMOTION, ADVANCEMENT

pre·fig·ure \prē-'fig-yər\ vb 1 : FORESHADOW 2 : to imagine beforehand

¹pre·fix \'prē-ˌfiks, prē-'fiks\ vb : to place before ⟨~ a title to a name⟩

²pre·fix \'prē-ˌfiks\ n : an affix occurring at the beginning of a word

pre·flight \'prē-'flīt\ adj : preparing for or preliminary to flight

pre·form \'prē-'fòrm\ vb : to form or shape beforehand

preg·na·ble \'preg-nə-bəl\ adj : vulnerable to capture ⟨a ~ fort⟩

preg·nant \'preg-nənt\ adj 1 : containing unborn young within the body 2 : rich in significance : MEANINGFUL — **preg·nan·cy** \-nən-sē\ n

pre·heat \'prē-'hēt\ vb : to heat beforehand; esp : to heat (an oven) to a designated temperature before using

pre·hen·sile \prē-'hen-səl, -ˌsīl\ adj : adapted for grasping esp. by wrapping around ⟨a monkey with a ~ tail⟩

pre·his·tor·ic \ˌprē-(h)is-'tòr-ik\ or **pre·his·tor·i·cal** \-i-kəl\ adj : of, relating to, or existing in the period before written history began

pre·ig·ni·tion \ˌprē-ig-'nish-ən\ n : ignition in an internal-combustion engine before the proper time

pre·in·duc·tion \ˌprē-in-'dək-shən\ adj : occurring prior to induction into military service

pre·judge \'prē-'jəj\ vb : to judge before full hearing or examination

¹prej·u·dice \'prej-əd-əs\ n 1 : DAMAGE; esp : detriment to one's rights or claims 2 : an opinion for or against something without adequate basis — **prej·u·di·cial** \ˌprej-ə-'dish-əl\ adj

²prejudice vb **-diced**; **-dic·ing** 1 : to damage by a judgment or action esp. at law **2** : to cause to have prejudice

prel·ate \'prel-ət\ *n* : an ecclesiastic (as a bishop) of high rank — **prel·a·cy** \-ə-sē\ *n*

pre·launch \'prē-'lonch\ *adj* : preparing for or preliminary to launch

pre·lim \'prē-₁lim, pri-'lim\ *n or adj* : PRELIMINARY

¹pre·lim·i·nary \pri-'lim-ə-₁ner-ē\ *n, pl* **-nar·ies** : something that precedes or introduces the main business or event

²preliminary *adj* : preceding the main discourse or business

pre·lude \'prel-₁(y)üd, 'prā-₁lüd\ *n* **1** : an introductory performance or event **2** : a musical section or movement introducing the main theme; *also* : an organ solo played at the beginning of a church service

prem *abbr* premium

pre·mar·i·tal \(')prē-'mar-ət-ᵊl\ *adj* : existing or occurring before marriage

pre·ma·ture \₁prē-mə-'t(y)ùər, -'chù(ə)r\ *adj* : happening, coming, born, or done before the usual or proper time **syn** untimely, early — **pre·ma·ture·ly** *adv*

pre·med \'prē-'med\ *adj* : PREMEDICAL — **premed** *n*

pre·med·i·cal \(')prē-'med-i-kəl\ *adj* : preceding and preparing for the professional study of medicine

pre·med·i·tate \pri-'med-ə-₁tāt\ *vb* : to consider and plan beforehand — **pre·med·i·ta·tion** \-₁med-ə-'tā-shən\ *n*

pre·men·stru·al \(')prē-'men-strə(-wə)l\ *adj* : of, relating to, or occurring in the period just preceding menstruation

¹pre·mier \pri-'m(y)iər, 'prē-mē-ər\ *adj* [ME *primier*, fr. MF *premier* first, chief, fr. L *primarius* of the first rank] : first in rank or importance : CHIEF; *also* : first in time : EARLIEST

²premier *n* : PRIME MINISTER — **pre·mier·ship** *n*

¹pre·miere \pri-'myer, -'miər\ *n* : a first performance

²premiere *or* **pre·mier** *like* ¹PREMIERE\ *vb* **pre·miered; pre·mier·ing** : to give or receive a first public performance

prem·ise \'prem-əs\ *n* **1** : a statement of fact or a supposition made or implied as a basis of argument **2** *pl* : a piece of land with the structures on it; *also* : the place of business of an enterprise

pre·mi·um \'prē-mē-əm\ *n* **1** : REWARD, PRIZE **2** : a sum over and above the stated value **3** : something paid over and above a fixed wage or price **4** : something given with a purchase **5** : the sum paid for a contract of insurance **6** : an unusually high value

pre·mix \'prē-'miks\ *vb* : to mix before use

¹pre·mo·lar \(')prē-'mō-lər\ *adj* : situated in front of or preceding the molar teeth

²premolar *n* : either of two double-pointed premolar teeth behind the canine on each side of each jaw in man

pre·mo·ni·tion \₁prē-mə-'nish-ən, ₁prem-ə-\ *n* : previous notice : FOREWARNING; *also* : PRESENTIMENT — **pre·mon·i·to·ry** \pri-'män-ə-₁tōr-ē\ *adj*

pre·na·tal \'prē-'nāt-ᵊl\ *adj* : occurring, existing, or taking place before birth

pre·oc·cu·pa·tion \prē-₁äk-yə-'pā-shən\ *n* : complete absorption of the mind or interests; *also* : something that causes such absorption

pre·oc·cu·pied \prē-'äk-yə-₁pīd\ *adj* **1** : last in thought; *also* : absorbed in some preoccupation **2** : already occupied **syn** abstracted, absent, absent-minded

pre·oc·cu·py \-₁pī\ *vb* **1** : to occupy the attention of beforehand **2** : to take possession of before another

pre·op·er·a·tive \(')prē-'äp-(ə-)rət-iv, -'äp-ə-₁rāt-\ *adj* : occurring before and usu. soon before a surgical operation

pre·or·dain \₁prē-ór-'dān\ *vb* : FOREORDAIN

pre–owned \'prē-'ōnd\ *adj* : SECONDHAND

prep *abbr* **1** preparatory **2** preposition

pre·pack·age \(')prē-'pak-ij\ *vb* : to package (as food) before offering for sale to the customer

preparatory school *n* **1** : a usu. private school preparing students primarily for college **2** *Brit* : a private elementary school preparing students primarily for public schools

pre·pare \pri-'paər\ *vb* **pre·pared; pre·par·ing** **1** : to make or get ready ⟨∼ dinner⟩ ⟨∼ a boy for college⟩ **2** : to get ready beforehand : PROVIDE **3** : to put together : COMPOUND ⟨∼ a vaccine⟩ —

prep·a·ra·tion \,prep-ə-'rā-shən\ *n* — **pre·par·a·to·ry** \pri-'par-ə-,tōr-ē\ *adj*

pre·pared·ness \pri-'par-əd-nəs\ *n* : a state of adequate preparation

pre·pay \'prē-'pā\ *vb* **-paid** \-'pād\; **-pay·ing** : to pay or pay the charge on in advance

pre·pon·der·ant \pri-'pän-d(ə-)rənt\ *adj* : having greater weight, force, influence, or frequency — **pre·pon·der·ance** \-d(ə-)rəns\ *n* — **pre·pon·der·ant·ly** *adv*

pre·pon·der·ate \pri-'pän-də-,rāt\ *vb* **-at·ed; -at·ing** [L *praeponderare,* fr. *prae-* ahead + *ponder-, pondus* weight] : to exceed in weight, force, influence, or frequency : PREDOMINATE

prep·o·si·tion \,prep-ə-'zish-ən\ *n* : a word that combines with a noun or pronoun to form a phrase — **prep·o·si·tion·al** \-'zish-(ə-)nəl\ *adj*

pre·pos·sess \,prē-pə-'zes\ *vb* **1** : to influence beforehand for or against someone or something **2** : to induce to a favorable opinion beforehand

pre·pos·sess·ing *adj* : tending to create a favorable impression : ATTRACTIVE ⟨a ~ manner⟩

pre·pos·ses·sion \-'zesh-ən\ *n* **1** : PREJUDICE **2** : an exclusive concern with one idea or object

pre·pos·ter·ous \pri-'päs-t(ə-)rəs\ *adj* : contrary to nature or reason : ABSURD

prep·py *or* **prep·pie** \'prep-ē\ *n, pl* **preppies 1** : a student at or a graduate of a preparatory school **2** : a person deemed to dress or behave like a preppy

pre·puce \'prē-,pyüs\ *n* : FORESKIN

pre·re·cord \,prē-ri-'kȯrd\ *vb* : to record for later broadcast

pre·req·ui·site \prē-'rek-wə-zət\ *n* : something required beforehand or for the end in view — **prerequisite** *adj*

pre·rog·a·tive \pri-'räg-ət-iv\ *n* : an exclusive or special right, power, or privilege

pres *abbr* **1** present **2** president

¹pres·age \'pres-ij\ *n* **1** : something that foreshadows a future event : OMEN **2** : FOREBODING

²pre·sage \'pres-ij, pri-'sāj\ *vb* **pre·saged; pre·sag·ing 1** : to give an omen or warning of : FORESHADOW **2** : FORETELL, PREDICT

pres·by·opia \,prez-bē-'ō-pē-ə\ *n* : a visual condition in which loss of elasticity of the lens of the eye causes defective accommodation and inability to focus sharply for near vision — **pres·by·opic** \-'ō-pik, -'äp-ik\ *adj or n*

pres·by·ter \'prez-bət-ər\ *n* **1** : PRIEST, MINISTER **2** : an elder in a Presbyterian church

¹Pres·by·te·ri·an \,prez-bə-'tir-ē-ən\ *adj* **1** *often not cap* : characterized by a graded system of representative ecclesiastical bodies (as presbyteries) exercising legislative and judicial powers **2** : of or relating to a group of Protestant Christian bodies that are presbyterian in government

²Presbyterian *n* : a member of a Presbyterian church — **Pres·by·te·ri·an·ism** \-,iz-əm\ *n*

pres·by·tery \'prez-bə-,ter-ē\ *n, pl* **-ter·ies 1** : the part of a church reserved for the officiating clergy **2** : a ruling body in Presbyterian churches consisting of the ministers and representative elders of a district

pre·school \'prē-'skül\ *adj* : of, relating to, or constituting the period in a child's life from infancy to the age of five or six — **pre·school·er** \-'skü-lər\ *n*

pre·science \'presh-əns, 'prēsh-\ *n* : foreknowledge of events; *also* : FORESIGHT — **pre·scient** \-(ē-)ənt\ *adj*

pre·scribe \pri-'skrīb\ *vb* **pre·scribed; pre·scrib·ing 1** : to lay down as a guide or rule of action **2** : to direct the use of something as a remedy

pre·scrip·tion \pri-'skrip-shən\ *n* **1** : the action of prescribing rules or directions **2** : a written direction for the preparation and use of a medicine; *also* : a medicine prescribed

pres·ence \'prez-ᵊns\ *n* **1** : the fact or condition of being present **2** : the space immediately around a person **3** : one that is present **4** : the bearing of a person; *esp* : stately bearing

¹pres·ent \'prez-ᵊnt\ *n* : something presented : GIFT

²pre·sent \pri-'zent\ *vb* **1** : to bring into the presence or acquaintance of : INTRODUCE **2** : to bring before the public ⟨~ a play⟩ **3** : to make a gift to **4** : to give formally **5** : to lay (as a charge) before a court for inquiry **6** : to aim or direct (as a weapon) so as to face in a particular direction — **pre·sent·able** *adj* — **pre·sen·ta·tion** \ˌprē-ˌzen-'tā-shən, ˌprez-ᵊn-\ *n* — **pre·sent·ment** \pri-'zent-mənt\ *n*

³**pres·ent** \'prez-ᵊnt\ *adj* **1** : now existing or in progress ⟨∼ conditions⟩ **2** : being in view or at hand ⟨∼ at the meeting⟩ **3** : under consideration ⟨the ∼ problem⟩ **4** : of, relating to, or constituting a verb tense that expresses present time or the time of speaking

⁴**pres·ent** \'prez-ᵊnt\ *n* **1** *pl* : the present legal document **2** : the present tense; *also* : a verb form in it **3** : the present time

pres·ent–day \'prez-ᵊnt-'dā\ *adj* : now existing or occurring : CURRENT

pre·sen·ti·ment \pri-'zent-ə-mənt\ *n* : a feeling that something is about to happen : PREMONITION

pres·ent·ly \'prez-ᵊnt-lē\ *adv* **1** : SOON **2** : NOW

present participle *n* : a participle that typically expresses present action and that in English is formed with the suffix *-ing* and is used in the formation of the progressive tenses

¹**pre·serve** \pri-'zərv\ *vb* **pre·served; pre·serv·ing** **1** : to keep safe : GUARD, PROTECT **2** : to keep from decaying; *esp* : to process food (as by canning or pickling) to prevent spoilage **3** : MAINTAIN ⟨∼ silence⟩ — **pres·er·va·tion** \ˌprez-ər-'vā-shən\ *n* — **pre·ser·va·tive** \pri-'zər-vət-iv\ *adj or n* — **pre·serv·er** \-'zər-vər\ *n*

²**preserve** *n* **1** : preserved fruit — often used in pl. **2** : an area for the protection of natural resources (as animals)

pre·set \'prē-'set\ *vb* **-set; -set·ting** : to set beforehand

pre·shrunk \'prē-'shrəŋk\ *adj* : of, relating to, or being a fabric subjected to a shrinking process during manufacture usu. to reduce later shrinking

pre·side \pri-'zīd\ *vb* **pre·sid·ed; pre·sid·ing** [L *praesidēre* to guard, preside over, lit., to sit in front of, sit at the head of, fr. *prae* in front of + *sedēre* to sit] **1** : to occupy the place of authority; *esp* : to act as chairman **2** : to exercise guidance or control

pres·i·dent \'prez-əd-ənt\ *n* **1** : one cho-

sen to preside ⟨∼ of the assembly⟩ **2** : the chief officer of an organization (as a corporation or society) **3** : an elected official serving as both chief of state and chief political executive; *also* : a chief of state often with only minimal political powers — **pres·i·den·cy** \-ən-sē\ *n* — **pres·i·den·tial** \ˌprez-ə-'den-chəl\ *adj*

pre·si·dio \pri-'sēd-ē-ˌō, -'sid-\ *n, pl* **-di·os** [Sp] : a garrisoned place; *esp* : a military post or fortified settlement in areas currently or orig. under Spanish control

pre·sid·i·um \pri-'sid-ē-əm\ *n, pl* **-ia** \-ē-ə\ *or* **-iums** [Russ *prezidium*, fr. L *praesidium* garrison] : a permanent executive committee selected in Communist countries to act for a larger body

¹**pre·soak** \(')prē-'sōk\ *vb* : to soak beforehand

²**pre·soak** \'prē-'sōk\ *n* **1** : an instance of presoaking **2** : a preparation used in presoaking clothes

¹**press** \'pres\ *n* **1** : a crowded condition : THRONG **2** : a machine for exerting pressure; *esp* : PRINTING PRESS **3** : CLOSET, CUPBOARD **4** : PRESSURE **5** : the properly creased condition of a freshly pressed garment **6** : the act or the process of printing **7** : a printing or publishing establishment **8** : the media (as newspapers and magazines) of public news and comment; *also* : persons (as reporters) employed in these media **9** : comment in newspapers and periodicals **10** : a pressure device (as for keeping a tennis racket from warping)

²**press** *vb* **1** : to bear down upon : push steadily against **2** : ASSAIL, COMPEL **3** : to squeeze out the juice or contents of ⟨∼ grapes⟩ **4** : to squeeze to a desired density, shape, or smoothness; *esp* : IRON **5** : to try hard to persuade : URGE **6** : to follow through : PROSECUTE **7** : CROWD **8** : to force one's way **9** : to require haste or speed in action **10** : to make (a phonograph record) from a matrix — **press·er** *n*

press agent *n* : an agent employed to maintain good public relations through publicity

press·ing \'pres-iŋ\ *adj* : URGENT

press·man \'pres-mən, -ˌman\ *n* : the

operator of a press and esp. a printing press

press·room \\'pres-₁rüm, -₁rüm\\ *n* : a room in a printing plant containing the printing presses; *also* : a room for the use of reporters

¹**pres·sure** \\'presh-ər\\ *n* **1** : the burden of physical or mental distress : OPPRESSION **2** : the action of pressing; *esp* : the application of force to something by something else in direct contact with it **3** : the condition of being pressed or of exerting force over a surface **4** : the stress or urgency of matters demanding attention **syn** stress, strain, tension

²**pressure** *vb* **pres·sured; pres·sur·ing** \\-(ə-)riŋ\\ : to apply pressure to

pressure group *n* : a group that seeks to influence governmental policy but not to elect candidates to office

pressure suit *n* : an inflatable suit for high-altitude or space flight to protect the body from low pressure

pres·sur·ize \\'presh-ə-₁rīz\\ *vb* **-ized; -izing 1** : to maintain normal atmospheric pressure within (an airplane cabin) during high-altitude flight **2** : to apply pressure to **3** : to design to withstand pressure — **pres·sur·iza·tion** \\₁presh-(ə-)rə-'zā-shən\\ *n*

pres·ti·dig·i·ta·tion \\₁pres-tə-₁dij-ə-'tā-shən\\ *n* : SLEIGHT OF HAND

pres·tige \\pres-'tēzh, -'tēj\\ *n* [F, fr. MF, conjuror's trick, illusion, fr. LL *praestigium*, fr. L *praestigiae*, pl., conjuror's tricks, irreg. fr. *praestringere* to tie up, blindfold, fr. *prae-* in front of + *stringere* to bind tight] : standing or estimation in the eyes of people : REPUTATION **syn** influence, authority, weight — **pres·ti·gious** \\-'tij-əs, -'tēj-\\ *adj*

pres·to \\'pres-tō\\ *adv or adj* [It] : suddenly as if by magic : IMMEDIATELY

pre·stress \\(')prē-'stres\\ *vb* : to introduce internal stresses into (as a structural beam) to counteract later load stresses

pre·sume \\pri-'züm\\ *vb* **pre·sumed; pre·sum·ing 1** : to take upon oneself without leave or warrant : DARE **2** : to take for granted : ASSUME **3** : to act or behave with undue boldness — **pre·sum·able** \\-'zü-mə-bəl\\ *adj* — **pre·sum·ably** \\-blē\\ *adv*

pre·sump·tion \\pri-'zəmp-shən\\ *n* **1** : presumptuous attitude or conduct : AUDACITY **2** : an attitude or belief dictated by probability; *also* : the grounds lending probability to a belief — **pre·sump·tive** \\-tiv\\ *adj*

pre·sump·tu·ous \\pri-'zəmp-chə-(wə)s\\ *adj* : overstepping due bounds : taking liberties : OVERBOLD

pre·sup·pose \\₁prē-sə-'pōz\\ *vb* **1** : to suppose beforehand **2** : to require beforehand as a necessary condition **syn** presume, assume — **pre·sup·po·si·tion** \\(₁)prē-₁səp-ə-'zish-ən\\ *n*

pre·teen \\'prē-'tēn\\ *n* : a boy or girl not yet 13 years old — **preteen** *adj*

pre·tend \\pri-'tend\\ *vb* **1** : PROFESS ⟨doesn't ∼ to be scientific⟩ **2** : FEIGN ⟨∼ to be angry⟩ **3** : to lay claim ⟨∼ to a throne⟩ — **pre·tend·er** *n*

pre·tense *or* **pre·tence** \\'prē-₁tens, pri-'tens\\ *n* **1** : CLAIM; *esp* : one not supported by fact **2** : mere display : SHOW **3** : an attempt to attain a certain condition ⟨made a ∼ at discipline⟩ **4** : false show : PRETEXT — **pre·ten·sion** \\pri-'ten-chən\\ *n*

pre·ten·tious \\pri-'ten-chəs\\ *adj* **1** : making or possessing claims (as to excellence) : OSTENTATIOUS ⟨a ∼ literary style⟩ **2** : making demands on one's ability or means : AMBITIOUS ⟨too ∼ an undertaking⟩ — **pre·ten·tious·ly** *adv* — **pre·ten·tious·ness** *n*

pret·er·it *or* **pret·er·ite** \\'pret-ə-rət\\ *adj* : PAST **3** — **preterit** *n*

pre·ter·nat·u·ral \\₁prēt-ər-'nach(-ə)-rəl\\ *adj* **1** : exceeding what is natural **2** : inexplicable by ordinary means — **pre·ter·nat·u·ral·ly** \\-ē\\ *adv*

pre·text \\'prē-₁tekst\\ *n* : a purpose stated or assumed to cloak the real intention or state of affairs

pret·ti·fy \\'prit-i-₁fī, 'pùrt-\\ *vb* **-fied; -fying** : to make pretty — **pret·ti·fi·ca·tion** \\₁prit-i-fə-'kā-shən, ₁pùrt-\\ *n*

¹**pret·ty** \\'prit-ē, 'pùrt\\ *adj* **pret·ti·er; -est** [ME *praty, prety*, fr. OE *prættig* tricky, fr. *prætt* trick] **1** : pleasing by delicacy or grace : superficially appealing rather than strikingly beautiful ⟨∼ flowers⟩ **2** : FINE, GOOD ⟨a ∼ profit⟩ — often used ironically ⟨a ∼ state of affairs⟩ **syn** comely, fair, beautiful, attractive, lovely — **pret·ti·ly**

\'prit-ᵊl-ē\ *adv* — **pret·ti·ness** \-ē-nəs\ *n*

²**pret·ty** \ˌpùrt-ē, pərt-, ˌprit-\ *adv* : in some degree : MODERATELY

³**pret·ty** \'prit-ē, 'pùrt-ē\ *vb* **pret·tied; pret·ty·ing** : to make pretty

pret·zel \'pret-səl\ *n* [G *brezel*, deriv. of L *brachiatus* having branches like arms, fr. *brachium* arm] : a usu. brittle, glazed, salted, and usu. twisted cracker

prev *abbr* previous; previously

pre·vail \pri-'vāl\ *vb* **1** : to win mastery : TRIUMPH **2** : to be or become effective : SUCCEED **3** : to urge successfully ⟨~ed upon her to sing⟩ **4** : to be frequent : PREDOMINATE — **pre·vail·ing·ly** \-iŋ-lē\ *adv*

prev·a·lent \'prev-ə-lənt\ *adj* : generally or widely existent : WIDESPREAD — **prev·a·lence** \-ləns\ *n*

pre·var·i·cate \pri-'var-ə-ˌkāt\ *vb* **-cat·ed; -cat·ing** : to deviate from the truth : EQUIVOCATE — **pre·var·i·ca·tion** \-ˌvar-ə-'kā-shən\ *n* — **pre·var·i·ca·tor** \-'var-ə-ˌkāt-ər\ *n*

pre·vent \pri-'vent\ *vb* **1** : to keep from happening or existing ⟨steps to ~ war⟩ **2** : to hold back : HINDER, STOP ⟨~ us from going⟩ — **pre·vent·able** *also* **pre·vent·ible** \-ə-bəl\ *adj* — **pre·ven·tion** \-'ven-chən\ *n* — **pre·ven·tive** \-'vent-iv\ *or* **pre·ven·ta·tive** \-'vent-ət-iv\ *adj or n*

pre·ver·bal \(')prē-'vər-bəl\ *adj* : having not yet acquired the faculty of speech

¹**pre·view** \'prē-ˌvyü\ *vb* : to see or discuss beforehand; *esp* : to view or show in advance of public presentation

²**preview** *n* **1** : an advance showing or viewing **2** *also* **pre·vue** \-ˌvyü\ : a showing of snatches from a motion picture advertised for future appearance **3** : FORETASTE

pre·vi·ous \'prē-vē-əs\ *adj* : going before : EARLIER, FORMER **syn** foregoing, prior, preceding, former, antecedent — **pre·vi·ous·ly** *adv*

pre·vi·sion \prē-'vizh-ən\ *n* **1** : FORESIGHT, PRESCIENCE **2** : FORECAST, PREDICTION

pre·war \'prē-'wȯr\ *adj* : occurring or existing before a war

¹**prey** \'prā\ *n, pl* **preys 1** : an animal taken for food by another; *also* : VICTIM **2** : the act or habit of preying

²**prey** *vb* **1** : to raid for booty **2** : to seize and devour something as prey **3** : to have a harmful or wearing effect

prf *abbr* proof

¹**price** \'prīs\ *n* **1** *archaic* : VALUE **2** : the amount of money paid or asked for the sale of a specified thing; *also* : the cost at which something is obtained

²**price** *vb* **priced; pric·ing 1** : to set a price on **2** : to ask the price of **3** : to drive by raising prices ⟨*priced* themselves out of the market⟩

price–fix·ing \'prīs-ˌfik-siŋ\ *n* : the setting of prices artificially (as by producers or government)

price·less \'prīs-ləs\ *adj* : having a value beyond any price : INVALUABLE **syn** precious, costly, expensive

price support *n* : artificial maintenance of prices of a commodity at a level usu. fixed through government action

price war *n* : a period of commercial competition in which prices are repeatedly cut by the competitors

pric·ey *also* **pricy** \'prī-sē\ *adj* **pric·i·er; -est** : EXPENSIVE

¹**prick** \'prik\ *n* **1** : a mark or small wound made by a pointed instrument **2** : something sharp or pointed **3** : an instance of pricking; *also* : a sensation of being pricked

²**prick** *vb* **1** : to pierce slightly with a sharp point; *also* : to have or cause a pricking sensation **2** : to affect with anguish or remorse ⟨~s his conscience⟩ **3** : to outline with punctures ⟨~ out a pattern⟩ **4** : to cause to stand erect ⟨the dog ~ed up his ears⟩ **syn** punch, puncture, perforate, bore, drill

prick·er \'prik-ər\ *n* : BRIAR, THORN

¹**prick·le** \'prik-əl\ *n* **1** : a small sharp point (as on a plant) **2** : a slight stinging pain — **prick·ly** \'prik-lē\ *adj*

²**prickle** *vb* **prick·led; prick·ling** \-(ə-)liŋ\ **1** : to prick lightly **2** : TINGLE

prickly heat *n* : a red cutaneous eruption with intense itching and tingling caused by inflammation around the ducts of the sweat glands

prickly pear *n* : any of a genus of cacti with usu. yellow flowers and prickly flat or rounded joints; *also* : the pulpy pear-shaped edible fruit of a prickly pear

¹pride \'prīd\ *n* **1** : CONCEIT **2** : justifiable self-respect **3** : elation over an act or possession **4** : haughty behavior : DISDAIN **5** : ostentatious display — **pride·ful** *adj*

²pride *vb* **prid·ed; prid·ing** : to indulge in pride

priest \'prēst\ *n* [ME *preist,* fr. OE *prēost,* fr. LL *presbyter,* fr. Gk *presbyteros* elder, priest, fr. compar. of *presbys* old] : a person having authority to perform the sacred rites of a religion; *esp* : an Anglican, Eastern, or Roman Catholic clergyman ranking below a bishop and above a deacon — **priest·hood** *n* — **priest·li·ness** \-lē-nəs\ *n* — **priest·ly** *adj*

priest·ess \'prē-stəs\ *n* : a woman authorized to perform the sacred rites of a religion

prig \'prig\ *n* : one who irritates by rigid or pointed observance of proprieties — **prig·gish** \'prig-ish\ *adj* — **prig·gish·ly** *adv*

¹prim \'prim\ *adj* **prim·mer; prim·mest** : stiffly formal and precise — **prim·ly** *adv* — **prim·ness** *n*

²prim *abbr* **1** primary **2** primitive

pri·ma·cy \'prī-mə-sē\ *n* **1** : the state of being first (as in rank) **2** : the office, rank, or character of an ecclesiastical primate

pri·ma don·na \ˌprim-ə-'dän-ə\ *n, pl* **prima donnas** [It, lit., first lady] **1** : a principal female singer (as in an opera company) **2** : an extremely sensitive, vain, or undisciplined person

pri·ma fa·cie \ˌprī-mə-'fā-shə, -s(h)ē\ *adj or adv* [L, at first view] **1** : based on immediate impression : APPARENT **2** : SELF-EVIDENT

pri·mal \'prī-məl\ *adj* **1** : ORIGINAL, PRIMITIVE **2** : first in importance

pri·mar·i·ly \prī-'mer-ə-lē\ *adv* **1** : FUNDAMENTALLY **2** : ORIGINALLY

¹pri·ma·ry \'prī-ˌmer-ē, 'prīm-(ə-)rē\ *adj* **1** : first in order of time or development; *also* : PREPARATORY **2** : of first rank or importance; *also* : FUNDAMENTAL **3** : not derived from or dependent on something else ⟨~ sources⟩

²primary *n, pl* **-ries** : a preliminary election in which voters nominate or express a preference among candidates usu. of their own party

primary school *n* **1** : a school usu. including grades 1-3 and sometimes kindergarten **2** : ELEMENTARY SCHOOL

pri·mate \'prī-ˌmāt *or esp for 1* -mət\ *n* **1** *often cap* : the highest-ranking bishop of a province or nation **2** : any of an order of mammals that includes man, the apes, and monkeys

¹prime \'prīm\ *n* **1** : the earliest stage of something; *esp* : SPRINGTIME **2** : the most active, thriving, or successful stage or period (as of one's life) **3** : the best individual; *also* : the best part of something **4** : any integer that is not 0, +1, or −1 and is divisible by no integer except +1, −1, and plus or minus itself; *esp* : any such integer that is positive

²prime *adj* **1** : standing first (as in time, rank, significance, or quality) ⟨~ requisite⟩ **2** : not capable of being divided without a remainder by any number except itself or 1 ⟨a ~ number⟩

²prime *vb* **primed; prim·ing** **1** : FILL, LOAD **2** : to lay a preparatory coating upon (as in painting) **3** : to put in working condition **4** : to instruct beforehand : COACH

prime meridian *n* : the meridian of 0° longitude from which other longitudes are reckoned east and west

prime minister *n* **1** : the chief minister of a ruler or state **2** : the chief executive of a parliamentary government

¹prim·er \'prim-ər\ *n* **1** : a small book for teaching children to read **2** : a small introductory book on a subject

²prim·er \'prī-mər\ *n* **1** : one that primes **2** : a device for igniting an explosive **3** : material for priming a surface

prime rate *n* : an interest rate announced by a bank to be the lowest available to its most credit-worthy customers

prime time *n* : the evening period generally from 7 to 11 p.m. during which television has its largest number of viewers

pri·me·val \prī-'mē-vəl\ *adj* : of or relating to the earliest ages : PRIMITIVE

¹prim·i·tive \'prim-ət-iv\ *adj* **1** : ORIGINAL, PRIMEVAL **2** : of, relating to, or characteristic of an early stage of development or a relatively simple people or culture **3** : ELEMENTAL, NATURAL **4** : SELF-TAUGHT; *also* : produced by a self-taught artist — **prim·i·tive·ly** *adv* — **prim·i·tive·ness** *n* — **prim·i·tiv·i·ty** \ˌprim-ə-'tiv-ət-ē\ *n*

²**primitive** *n* **1** : a primitive artist **2** : a member of a primitive people

prim·i·tiv·ism \'prim-ət-iv-ˌiz-əm\ *n* : the style of art of primitive peoples or primitive artists

pri·mo·gen·i·tor \ˌprī-mō-'jen-ət-ər\ *n* : ANCESTOR, FOREFATHER

pri·mo·gen·i·ture \-'jen-ə-ˌchu̇r\ *n* **1** : the state of being the firstborn of a family **2** : an exclusive right of inheritance belonging to the eldest son

pri·mor·di·al \prī-'mȯrd-ē-əl\ *adj* : first created or developed : existing in its original state : PRIMEVAL

primp \'primp\ *vb* : to dress in a careful or finicky manner

prim·rose \'prim-ˌrōz\ *n* : any of a genus of herbs with large leaves arranged at the base of the stem and clusters of showy flowers on leafless stalks

prin *abbr* **1** principal **2** principle

prince \'prins\ *n* [ME, fr. OF, fr. L *princeps*, lit., one who takes the first part, fr. *primus* first + *capere* to take] **1** : MONARCH, KING **2** : a male member of a royal family; *esp* : a son of the monarch **3** : a person of high standing (as in a class) ⟨a ∼ of poets⟩ — **prince·dom** \-dəm\ *n* — **prince·ly** *adj*

prince·ling \-liŋ\ *n* : a petty prince

prin·cess \'prin-səs, -ˌses\ *n* **1** : a female member of a royal family **2** : the consort of a prince

¹**prin·ci·pal** \'prin-sə-pəl\ *adj* : most important — **prin·ci·pal·ly** \-ē\ *adv*

²**principal** *n* **1** : a leading person (as in a play) **2** : the chief officer of an educational institution **3** : the person from whom an agent's authority derives **4** : a capital sum placed at interest or used as a fund

prin·ci·pal·i·ty \ˌprin-sə-'pal-ət-ē\ *n, pl* **-ties** : the position, territory, or jurisdiction of a prince

principal parts *n pl* : the inflected forms of a verb

prin·ci·ple \'prin-sə-pəl\ *n* **1** : a general or fundamental law, doctrine, or assumption **2** : a rule or code of con-

duct; *also* : devotion to such a code **3** : the laws or facts of nature underlying the working of an artificial device **4** : a primary source : ORIGIN; *also* : an underlying faculty or endowment **5** : the active part (as of a drug)

prin·ci·pled \-sə-pəld\ *adj* : exhibiting, based on, or characterized by principle ⟨high-*principled*⟩

prink \'priŋk\ *vb* : PRIMP

¹**print** \'print\ *n* **1** : a mark made by pressure **2** : something stamped with an impression **3** : printed state or form **4** : printed matter **5** : a copy made by printing **6** : cloth with a pattern applied by printing

²**print** *vb* **1** : to stamp (as a mark) in or on something **2** : to produce impressions of (as from type) **3** : to write in letters like those of printer's type **4** : to make (a positive picture) from a photographic negative — **print·er** *n*

print·able \'print-ə-bəl\ *adj* **1** : capable of being printed or of being printed from **2** : worthy or fit to be published

print·ing \'print-iŋ\ *n* **1** : reproduction in printed form **2** : the art, practice, or business of a printer **3** : IMPRESSION 5

printing press *n* : a machine that produces printed copies

print·out \'print-ˌau̇t\ *n* : a printed record produced by a computer — **print out** \(')print-'au̇t\ *vb*

¹**pri·or** \'prī(-ə)r\ *n* : the superior of a religious house

²**pri·or** *adj* **1** : earlier in time or order **2** : taking precedence logically or in importance — **pri·or·i·ty** \prī-'ȯr-ət-ē\ *n*

pri·or·ess \'prī-ə-rəs\ *n* : a nun corresponding in rank to a prior

pri·or·i·tize \prī-'ȯr-ə-ˌtīz, 'prī-ə-rə-ˌtīz\ *vb* **-tized; -tiz·ing** : to list or rate in order of priority

prior to *prep* : in advance of : BEFORE

pri·o·ry \'prī-(ə-)rē\ *n, pl* **-ries** : a religious house under a prior or prioress

prism \'priz-əm\ *n* [LL *prisma*, fr. Gk, lit., anything sawed, fr. *priein* to saw] **1** : a solid whose sides are parallelograms and whose ends are parallel and alike in shape and size **2** : a usu. 3-sided transparent object that breaks up light into rainbow colors — **pris·mat·ic** \priz-'mat-ik\ *adj*

pris·on \'priz-ᵊn\ *n* : a place or state of confinement esp. for criminals

pris·on·er \'priz-(ə-)nər\ *n* : a person deprived of his liberty; *esp* : one on trial or in prison

pris·sy \'pris-ē\ *adj* **pris·si·er; -est** : being overly prim and precise : PRIGGISH — **pris·si·ness** \'pris-ē-nəs\ *n*

pris·tine \'pris-,tēn\ *adj* **1** : PRIMITIVE **2** : having the purity of its original state : UNSPOILED

prith·ee \'prith-ē\ *interj, archaic* — used to express a wish or request

pri·va·cy \'prī-və-sē\ *n, pl* **-cies 1** : the quality or state of being apart from others **2** : SECRECY

¹pri·vate \'prī-vət\ *adj* **1** : belonging to or intended for a particular individual or group ⟨~ property⟩ **2** : restricted to the individual : PERSONAL ⟨~ opinion⟩ **3** : carried on by the individual independently ⟨~ study⟩ **4** : not holding public office ⟨a ~ citizen⟩ **5** : withdrawn from company or observation ⟨a ~ place⟩ **6** : not known publicly ⟨~ dealings⟩ — **pri·vate·ly** *adv*

²private *n* : an enlisted man of the lowest rank in the marine corps or of one of the two lowest ranks in the army — **in private** : not openly or in public

pri·va·teer \,prī-və-'tiər\ *n* : an armed private ship licensed to attack enemy shipping; *also* : a sailor on such a ship

private first class *n* : an enlisted man ranking next below a corporal in the army and next below a lance corporal in the marine corps

pri·va·tion \prī-'vā-shən\ *n* **1** : DEPRIVATION **2** : the state of being deprived; *esp* : lack of what is needed for existence

priv·et \'priv-ət\ *n* : a nearly evergreen shrub related to the olive and widely used for hedges

¹priv·i·lege \'priv(-ə)-lij\ *n* [ME, fr. OF, fr. L *privilegium* law for or against a private person, fr. *privus* private + *leg-, lex* law] : a right or immunity granted as an advantage or favor esp. to some and not others

²privilege *vb* **-leged; -leg·ing** : to grant a privilege to

priv·i·leged \-lijd\ *adj* **1** : having or enjoying one or more privileges ⟨~ classes⟩ **2** : not subject to disclosure in a court of law ⟨a ~ communication⟩

¹privy \'priv-ē\ *adj* **1** : PERSONAL, PRIVATE **2** : SECRET **3** : admitted as one

sharing in a secret ⟨~ to the conspiracy⟩ — **priv·i·ly** \'priv-ə-lē\ *adv*

²privy *n, pl* **priv·ies** : TOILET; *esp* : OUTHOUSE

¹prize \'prīz\ *n* **1** : something offered or striven for in competition or in contests of chance **2** : something exceptionally desirable

²prize *adj* **1** : awarded or worthy of a prize ⟨a ~ essay⟩; *also* : awarded as a prize ⟨a ~ medal⟩ **2** : OUTSTANDING

³prize *vb* **prized; priz·ing** : to value highly : ESTEEM **syn** treasure, cherish, appreciate

⁴prize *n* : property (as a ship) lawfully captured in time of war

⁵prize \'prīz\ *vb* **prized; priz·ing** : PRY

prize·fight \'prīz-,fīt\ *n* : a professional boxing match — **prize·fight·er** *n* — **prize·fight·ing** \-iŋ\ *n*

prize·win·ner \'prīz-,win-ər\ *n* : a winner of a prize — **prize·win·ning** \-,win-iŋ\ *adj*

¹pro \'prō\ *n, pl* **pros** : a favorable argument, person, or position

²pro *adv* : in favor : FOR

³pro *n or adj* : PROFESSIONAL

PRO *abbr* public relations officer

prob *abbr* **1** probable; probably **2** problem

prob·a·ble \'präb-ə-bəl\ *adj* **1** : apparently or presumably true ⟨a ~ hypothesis⟩ **2** : likely to be or become true or real ⟨a ~ result⟩ — **prob·a·bil·i·ty** \,präb-ə-'bil-ət-ē\ *n* — **prob·a·bly** \'präb-ə-blē, 'präb-lē\ *adv*

¹pro·bate \'prō-,bāt\ *n* : the judicial determination of the validity of a will

²pro·bate *vb* **pro·bat·ed; pro·bat·ing** : to establish (a will) by probate as genuine and valid

pro·ba·tion \prō-'bā-shən\ *n* **1** : subjection of an individual to a period of testing and trial to ascertain fitness (as for a job) **2** : the action of giving a convicted offender freedom during good behavior under the supervision of a probation officer — **pro·ba·tion·ary** \-shə-,ner-ē\ *adj*

pro·ba·tion·er \-sh(ə-)nər\ *n* **1** : one (as a newly admitted student nurse) whose fitness is being tested during a trial period **2** : a convicted offender on probation

pro·ba·tive \'prō-bət-iv\ *adj* **1** : serving to test or try **2** : serving to prove

¹probe \ˈprōb\ *n* **1** : a slender instrument for examining a cavity (as a wound) **2** : an information-gathering device sent into outer space **3** : a penetrating investigation **syn** inquiry, inquest, research, inquisition

²probe *vb* **probed; prob•ing 1** : to examine with a probe **2** : to investigate thoroughly

pro•bi•ty \ˈprō-bət-ē\ *n* : UPRIGHTNESS, HONESTY

prob•lem \ˈpräb-ləm\ *n* **1** : a question raised for consideration or solution **2** : an intricate unsettled question **3** : a source of perplexity or vexation — **problem** *adj*

prob•lem•at•ic \ˌpräb-lə-ˈmat-ik\ *or* **prob•lem•at•i•cal** \-i-kəl\ *adj* **1** : difficult to solve or decide : PUZZLING **2** : DUBIOUS, QUESTIONABLE

pro•bos•cis \prə-ˈbäs-əs, -kəs\ *n, pl* **-bos•cis•es** *also* **-bos•ci•des** \-ˈbäs-ə-ˌdēz\ [L, fr. Gk *proboskis,* fr. *pro-* before + *boskein* to feed] : a long flexible snout (as the trunk of an elephant)

proc *abbr* proceedings

pro•caine \ˈprō-ˌkān\ *n* : a compound used esp. as a local anesthetic

pro•ca•the•dral \ˌprō-kə-ˈthē-drəl\ *n* : a parish church used as a cathedral

pro•ce•dure \prə-ˈsē-jər\ *n* **1** : a particular way of doing something ⟨democratic ~⟩ **2** : a series of steps followed in a regular order ⟨surgical ~⟩ — **pro•ce•dur•al** \-ˈsēj-(ə-)rəl\ *adj*

pro•ceed \prō-ˈsēd\ *vb* **1** : to come forth : ISSUE **2** : to go on in an orderly way; *also* : CONTINUE **3** : to begin and carry on an action **4** : to take legal action **5** : to go forward : ADVANCE

pro•ceed•ing \-iŋ\ *n* **1** : PROCEDURE **2** *pl* : DOINGS **3** *pl* : legal action **4** : TRANSACTION **5** *pl* : an official record of things said or done

pro•ceeds \ˈprō-ˌsēdz\ *n pl* : the total amount or the profit arising from a business deal : RETURN

¹pro•cess \ˈpräs-ˌes, ˈprōs-\ *n, pl* **pro•cess•es** \-ˌes-əz, -ə-səz, -ə-ˌsēz\ **1** : PROGRESS, ADVANCE **2** : something going on : PROCEEDING **3** : a natural phenomenon marked by gradual changes that lead toward a particular result ⟨the ~ of growth⟩ **4** : a series of actions or operations directed toward a particular result ⟨a manufacturing ~⟩ **5** : legal action **6** : a mandate issued by a court; *esp* : SUMMONS **7** : a projecting part of an organism or organic structure

²process *vb* : to subject to a special process

pro•ces•sion \prə-ˈsesh-ən\ *n* : a group of individuals moving along in an orderly often ceremonial way : PARADE

pro•ces•sion•al \-ˈsesh-(ə-)nəl\ *n* **1** : music for a procession **2** : a ceremonial procession

pro•ces•sor \ˈpräs-ˌes-ər, ˈprōs-\ *n* **1** : one that processes **2** : the part of a computer that operates on data

pro•claim \prō-ˈklām\ *vb* : to make known publicly : DECLARE — **proc•la•ma•tion** \ˌpräk-lə-ˈmā-shən\ *n*

pro•cliv•i•ty \prō-ˈkliv-ət-ē\ *n, pl* **-ties** : an inherent inclination esp. toward something objectionable

pro•con•sul \prō-ˈkän-səl\ *n* **1** : a governor or military commander of an ancient Roman province **2** : an administrator in a modern colony, dependency, or occupied area usu. with wide powers — **pro•con•su•lar** \-sə-lər\ *adj* — **pro•con•su•late** \-sə-lət\ *n* — **pro•con•sul•ship** *n*

pro•cras•ti•nate \prə-ˈkras-tə-ˌnāt\ *vb* **-nat•ed; -nat•ing** [L *procrastinare,* fr. *pro-* forward + *crastinus* of tomorrow, fr. *cras* tomorrow] : to put off usu. habitually the doing of something that should be done **syn** dawdle, delay, loiter, linger — **pro•cras•ti•na•tion** \-ˌkras-tə-ˈnā-shən\ *n* — **pro•cras•ti•na•tor** \-ˈkras-tə-ˌnāt-ər\ *n*

pro•cre•ate \ˈprō-krē-ˌāt\ *vb* **-at•ed; -at•ing** : to beget or bring forth offspring **syn** reproduce, breed, generate, propagate — **pro•cre•ation** \ˌprō-krē-ˈā-shən\ *n* — **pro•cre•ative** \ˈprō-krē-ˌāt-iv\ *adj* — **pro•cre•ator** \-ˌāt-ər\ *n*

pro•crus•te•an \prə-ˈkrəs-tē-ən\ *adj, often cap* [deriv. of *Procrustes,* villain of Greek mythology who made victims fit his bed by stretching them or cutting off their legs] : marked by arbitrary often ruthless disregard of individual differences or special circumstances

proc•tor \ˈpräk-tər\ *n* : one appointed to supervise students (as at an examination) — **proctor** *vb* — **proc·to·ri·al** \präk-'tōr-ē-əl\ *adj*

proc·u·ra·tor \'präk-yə-ˌrāt-ər\ *n* : ADMINISTRATOR; *esp* : an official of ancient Rome administering a province

pro·cure \prə-'kyu̇(ə)r\ *vb* **pro·cured; pro·cur·ing** 1 : to get possession of : OBTAIN 2 : to make women available for promiscuous sexual intercourse 3 : to cause to happen or be done : ACHIEVE **syn** secure, acquire, gain, win, earn — **pro·cur·able** \-'kyu̇r-ə-bəl\ *adj* — **pro·cure·ment** \-'kyu̇(ə)r-mənt\ *n* — **pro·cur·er** *n*

¹**prod** \'präd\ *vb* **prod·ded; prod·ding** 1 : to thrust a pointed instrument into : GOAD 2 : INCITE, STIR — **prod** *n*

²**prod** *abbr* product; production

prod·i·gal \'präd-i-gəl\ *adj* 1 : recklessly extravagant; *also* : LUXURIANT 2 : WASTEFUL, LAVISH **syn** profuse, lavish, lush, opulent — **prodigal** *n* — **prod·i·gal·i·ty** \ˌpräd-ə-'gal-ət-ē\ *n*

pro·di·gious \prə-'dij-əs\ *adj* 1 : exciting wonder 2 : extraordinary in size or degree : ENORMOUS **syn** monstrous, tremendous, stupendous, monumental — **pro·di·gious·ly** *adv*

prod·i·gy \'präd-ə-jē\ *n, pl* **-gies** 1 : something extraordinary : WONDER 2 : a highly talented child

¹**pro·duce** \prə-'d(y)üs\ *vb* **pro·duced; pro·duc·ing** 1 : to present to view : EXHIBIT 2 : to give birth or rise to : YIELD 3 : EXTEND, PROLONG 4 : to give being or form to : BRING ABOUT, MAKE; *esp* : MANUFACTURE 5 : to cause to accrue ⟨∼ a profit⟩ — **pro·duc·er** *n*

²**pro·duce** \'präd-(ˌ)üs, 'prōd- *also* -(ˌ)yüs\ *n* : PRODUCT 2; *also* : agricultural products and esp. fresh fruits and vegetables

prod·uct \'präd-(ˌ)əkt\ *n* 1 : the number resulting from multiplication 2 : something produced (as by labor, thought, or growth)

pro·duc·tion \prə-'dək-shən\ *n* 1 : something produced : PRODUCT 2 : the act or process of producing — **pro·duc·tive** \-'dək-tiv\ *adj* — **pro·duc·tive·ness** *n* — **pro·duc·tiv·i·ty** \(ˌ)prō-ˌdək-'tiv-ət-ē, ˌpräd-(ˌ)ək-\ *n*

pro·em \'prō-ˌem\ *n* 1 : preliminary comment : PREFACE 2 : PRELUDE

prof *abbr* 1 professional 2 professor

¹**pro·fane** \prō-'fān\ *vb* **pro·faned; pro-**

fan·ing 1 : to treat (something sacred) with irreverence or contempt : DESECRATE 2 : to debase by an unworthy use — **prof·a·na·tion** \ˌpräf-ə-'nā-shən\ *n*

²**profane** *adj* [ME *prophane,* fr. MF, fr. L *profanus,* fr. *pro-* before + *fanum* temple] 1 : not concerned with religion : SECULAR 2 : not holy because unconsecrated, impure, or defiled 3 : serving to debase what is holy : IRREVERENT ⟨∼ language⟩ — **pro·fane·ly** *adv* — **pro·fane·ness** \-'fān-nəs\ *n*

pro·fan·i·ty \prō-'fan-ət-ē\ *n, pl* **-ties** 1 : the quality or state of being profane 2 : the use of profane language 3 : profane language

pro·fess \prə-'fes\ *vb* 1 : to declare or admit openly : AFFIRM 2 : to declare in words only : PRETEND 3 : to confess one's faith in 4 : to practice or claim to be versed in (a calling or occupation) — **pro·fess·ed·ly** \-əd-lē\ *adv*

pro·fes·sion \prə-'fesh-ən\ *n* 1 : an open declaration or avowal of a belief or opinion 2 : a calling requiring specialized knowledge and often long academic preparation 3 : the whole body of persons engaged in a calling

¹**pro·fes·sion·al** \prə-'fesh-(ə-)nəl\ *adj* 1 : of, relating to, or characteristic of a profession 2 : engaged in one of the learned professions 3 : participating for gain in an activity often engaged in by amateurs — **pro·fes·sion·al·ly** \-ē\ *adv*

²**professional** *n* : one that engages in an activity professionally

pro·fes·sion·al·ism \-ˌiz-əm\ *n* 1 : the conduct, aims, or qualities that characterize or mark a profession or a professional person 2 : the following of a profession (as athletics) for gain or livelihood

pro·fes·sion·al·ize \-ˌīz\ *vb* **-ized; -iz·ing** : to give a professional nature to

pro·fes·sor \prə-'fes-ər\ *n* : a teacher at a university or college; *esp* : a faculty member of the highest academic rank — **pro·fes·so·ri·al** \ˌprō-fə-'sōr-ē-əl, ˌpräf-ə-\ *adj* — **pro·fes·sor·ship** *n*

prof·fer \'präf-ər\ *vb* **prof·fered; prof·fer·ing** \-(ə-)riŋ\ : to present for acceptance : OFFER — **proffer** *n*

pro·fi·cient \prə-'fish-ənt\ *adj* : well advanced in an art, occupation, or branch of knowledge **syn** adept, skillful, expert, masterful, masterly — **pro·fi·cien·cy** \-ən-sē\ n — **proficient** n — **pro·fi·cient·ly** adv

¹**pro·file** \'prō-ˌfīl\ n [It profilo, fr. profilare to draw in outline, fr. pro- forward (fr. L) + filare to spin, fr. LL, fr. L filum thread] **1** : a representation of something in outline; esp : a human head seen in side view **2** : a concise biographical sketch **3** : degree or level of public exposure ⟨keep a low ∼⟩ **syn** contour, silhouette, outline

²**profile** vb **pro·filed; pro·fil·ing** : to write or draw a profile of

¹**prof·it** \'präf-ət\ n **1** : a valuable return : GAIN **2** : the excess of the selling price of goods over their cost — **prof·it·less** adj

²**profit** vb **1** : to be of use : BENEFIT **2** : to derive benefit : GAIN — **prof·it·able** \'präf-ət-ə-bəl, 'präf-tə-bəl\ adj — **prof·it·ably** \-blē\ adv

prof·i·teer \ˌpräf-ə-'tiər\ n : one who makes what is considered an unreasonable profit — **profiteer** vb

prof·li·gate \'präf-li-gət, -lə-ˌgāt\ adj **1** : completely given up to dissipation and licentiousness **2** : wildly extravagant — **prof·li·ga·cy** \-gə-sē\ n — **profligate** n — **prof·li·gate·ly** adv

pro for·ma \prō-'för-mə\ adj : done or existing as a matter of form

pro·found \prə-'faund\ adj **1** : marked by intellectual depth or insight ⟨a ∼ thought⟩ **2** : coming from or reaching to a depth ⟨a ∼ sigh⟩ **3** : deeply felt : INTENSE ⟨∼ sympathy⟩ — **pro·found·ly** adv — **pro·fun·di·ty** \-'fən-dət-ē\ n

pro·fuse \prə-'fyüs\ adj : pouring forth liberally : ABUNDANT **syn** lavish, prodigal, luxuriant, exuberant — **pro·fuse·ly** adv — **pro·fu·sion** \-'fyü-zhən\ n

pro·gen·i·tor \prō-'jen-ət-ər\ n **1** : a direct ancestor : FOREFATHER **2** : ORIGINATOR, PRECURSOR

prog·e·ny \'präj-ə-nē\ n, pl **-nies** : OFFSPRING, CHILDREN, DESCENDANTS

prog·na·thous \'präg-nə-thəs\ adj : having the jaws projecting beyond the upper part of the face

prog·no·sis \präg-'nō-səs\ n, pl **-no·ses** \-ˌsēz\ : a forecast esp. of the course of a disease

prog·nos·tic \präg-'näs-tik\ n **1** : POR-

TENT **2** : PROPHECY — **prognostic** adj

prog·nos·ti·cate \präg-'näs-tə-ˌkāt\ vb **-cat·ed; -cat·ing** : to foretell from signs or symptoms — **prog·nos·ti·ca·tion** \-ˌnäs-tə-'kā-shən\ n — **prog·nos·ti·ca·tor** \-'näs-tə-ˌkāt-ər\ n

¹**pro·gram** \'prō-ˌgram, -grəm\ n **1** : a brief outline of the order to be pursued or the subjects included (as in a public entertainment); also : PERFORMANCE **2** : a plan of procedure **3** : coded instructions for a computer — **pro·gram·mat·ic** \ˌprō-grə-'mat-ik\ adj

²**program** also **programme** vb **-grammed** or **-gramed; -gram·ming** or **-gram·ing** **1** : to enter in a program **2** : to provide (as a computer) with a program — **pro·gram·ma·bil·i·ty** \(ˌ)prō-ˌgram-ə-'bil-ət-ē\ n — **pro·gram·ma·ble** \'prō-ˌgram-ə-bəl\ adj — **pro·gram·mer** or **pro·gram·er** \'prō-ˌgram-ər, -grə-mər\ n

programmed instruction n : instruction through information given in small steps with each requiring a correct response by the learner before going on to the next step

pro·gram·ming or **pro·gram·ing** \-ˌgram-iŋ, -grə-miŋ\ n **1** : the process of instructing or learning by means of an instruction program **2** : the process of preparing an instruction program

¹**prog·ress** \'präg-rəs, -ˌres\ n **1** : a forward movement : ADVANCE **2** : a gradual betterment

²**pro·gress** \prə-'gres\ vb **1** : to move forward : PROCEED **2** : to develop to a more advanced stage : IMPROVE

pro·gres·sion \prə-'gresh-ən\ n **1** : an act of progressing : ADVANCE **2** : a continuous and connected series

¹**pro·gres·sive** \prə-'gres-iv\ adj **1** : of, relating to, or characterized by progress ⟨a ∼ city⟩ **2** : advancing by stages ⟨a ∼ disease⟩ **3** often cap : of or relating to political Progressives **4** : of, relating to, or constituting a verb form that expresses action in progress at the time of speaking or a time spoken of — **pro·gres·sive·ly** adv

²**progressive** n **1** : one that is progressive **2** : a person believing in moderate political change and social improvement by government action; esp, cap : a member of a Progressive Party (as in

the presidential campaigns of 1912, 1924, and 1948) in the U.S.

pro·hib·it \prō-'hib-ət\ vb **1** : to forbid by authority **2** : to prevent from doing something

pro·hi·bi·tion \ˌprō-ə-'bish-ən\ n **1** : the act of prohibiting **2** : the forbidding by law of the sale or manufacture of alcoholic beverages — **pro·hi·bi·tion·ist** \-'bish-(ə-)nəst\ n — **pro·hib·i·tive** \prō-'hib-ət-iv\ adj — **pro·hib·i·tive·ly** adv — **pro·hib·i·to·ry** \-'hib-ə-ˌtōr-ē\ adj

¹proj·ect \'präj-ˌekt, -ikt\ n **1** : a specific plan or design : SCHEME **2** : a planned undertaking ⟨a research ~⟩

²pro·ject \prə-'jekt\ vb **1** : to devise in the mind : DESIGN **2** : to throw forward **3** : PROTRUDE **4** : to cause (light or shadow) to fall into space or (an image) to fall on a surface ⟨~ a beam of light⟩ **5** : to attribute (a thought, feeling, or personal characteristic) to a person, group, or object — **pro·jec·tion** \-'jek-shən\ n

pro·jec·tile \prə-'jek-t²l\ n **1** : a body hurled or projected by external force; esp : a missile for a firearm **2** : a self-propelling weapon

pro·jec·tion·ist \prə-'jek-sh(ə-)nəst\ n : one that operates a motion-picture projector or television equipment

pro·jec·tor \-'jek-tər\ n : one that projects; esp : a device for projecting pictures on a screen

pro·le·gom·e·non \ˌprō-li-'gäm-ə-ˌnän, -nən\ n, pl **-e·na** \-nə\ : prefatory remarks

pro·le·tar·i·an \ˌprō-lə-'ter-ē-ən\ n : a member of the proletariat — **proletarian** adj

pro·le·tar·i·at \-ē-ət\ n : the laboring class; esp : industrial workers who sell their labor to live

pro·lif·er·ate \prə-'lif-ə-ˌrāt\ vb **-at·ed**; **-at·ing** : to grow or increase by rapid production of new units (as cells or offspring) — **pro·lif·er·a·tion** \-ˌlif-ə-'rā-shən\ n

pro·lif·ic \prə-'lif-ik\ adj **1** : producing young or fruit abundantly **2** : marked by abundant inventiveness or productivity ⟨a ~ writer⟩ — **pro·lif·i·cal·ly** \-i-k(ə-)lē\ adv

pro·lix \prō-'liks, 'prō-ˌliks\ adj : VER-

BOSE **syn** wordy, diffuse, redundant — **pro·lix·i·ty** \prō-'lik-sət-ē\ n

pro·logue also **pro·log** \'prō-ˌlòg, -ˌläg\ n : PREFACE ⟨~ of a play⟩

pro·long \prə-'lòŋ\ vb **1** : to lengthen in time : CONTINUE ⟨~ a meeting⟩ **2** : to lengthen in extent or range **syn** protract, extend, elongate, stretch — **pro·lon·ga·tion** \ˌprō-ˌlòŋ-'gā-shən\ n

prom \'präm\ n : a formal dance given by a high school or college class

¹prom·e·nade \ˌpräm-ə-'nād, -'näd\ n [F, fr. promener to take for a walk, fr. L prominare to drive forward] **1** : a leisurely walk for pleasure or display **2** : a place for strolling **3** : an opening grand march at a formal ball

²promenade vb **-nad·ed**; **-nad·ing** **1** : to take a promenade **2** : to walk about in or on

pro·me·thi·um \prə-'mē-thē-əm\ n : a metallic chemical element obtained from uranium or neodymium

prom·i·nence \'präm(-ə)-nəns\ n **1** : something prominent **2** : the quality, state, or fact of being prominent or conspicuous **3** : a mass of cloudlike gas that arises from the sun's chromosphere

prom·i·nent \-nənt\ adj **1** : jutting out : PROJECTING **2** : readily noticeable : CONSPICUOUS **3** : DISTINGUISHED, EMINENT **syn** remarkable, outstanding, striking, salient — **prom·i·nent·ly** adv

pro·mis·cu·ous \prə-'mis-kyə-wəs\ adj **1** : consisting of various sorts and kinds : MIXED **2** : not restricted to one class or person; esp : not restricted to one sexual partner **syn** miscellaneous, assorted, heterogeneous, motley, varied — **prom·is·cu·i·ty** \ˌpräm-is-'kyü-ət-ē, ˌprō-ˌmis-\ n — **pro·mis·cu·ous·ly** adv — **pro·mis·cu·ous·ness** n

¹prom·ise \'präm-əs\ n **1** : a pledge to do or not to do something specified **2** : ground for expectation of success or improvement **3** : something promised

²promise vb **prom·ised**; **prom·is·ing** **1** : to engage to do, bring about, or provide ⟨~ help⟩ **2** : to suggest beforehand ⟨dark clouds ~ rain⟩ **3** : to give ground for expectation ⟨the book ~s to be good⟩

prom·is·ing \'präm-ə-siŋ\ adj : likely to succeed or yield good results — **prom·is·ing·ly** adv

prom·is·so·ry \'präm-ə-ˌsōr-ē\ *adj* : containing a promise

prom·on·to·ry \'präm-ən-ˌtōr-ē\ *n, pl* **-ries** : a point of land jutting into the sea : HEADLAND

pro·mote \prə-'mōt\ *vb* **pro·mot·ed; pro·mot·ing 1** : to advance in station, rank, or honor **2** : to contribute to the growth or prosperity of : FURTHER **3** : LAUNCH — **pro·mo·tion** \-'mō-shən\ *n* — **pro·mo·tion·al** \-'mōsh-(ə-)nəl\ *adj*

pro·mot·er \-'mōt-ər\ *n* : one that promotes; *esp* : one that assumes the financial responsibilities of a sports event

¹**prompt** \'prämpt\ *vb* **1** : INCITE **2** : to assist (one acting or reciting) by suggesting the next words **3** : INSPIRE, URGE — **prompt·er** *n*

²**prompt** *adj* **1** : being ready and quick to act; *also* : PUNCTUAL **2** : performed readily or immediately ⟨∼ service⟩ — **prompt·ly** *adv* — **prompt·ness** *n*

prompt·book \-ˌbu̇k\ *n* : a copy of a play with directions for performance used by a theater prompter

promp·ti·tude \'prämp-tə-ˌt(y)üd\ *n* : the quality or habit of being prompt : PROMPTNESS

pro·mul·gate \'präm-əl-ˌgāt; prō-'məl-\ *vb* **-gat·ed; -gat·ing** : to make known or put into force by open declaration — **prom·ul·ga·tion** \ˌpräm-əl-'gā-shən, ˌprō-(ˌ)məl-\ *n*

pron *abbr* **1** pronoun **2** pronounced **3** pronunciation

prone \'prōn\ *adj* **1** : having a tendency or inclination : DISPOSED **2** : lying face downward; *also* : lying flat or prostrate **syn** subject, exposed, open, liable, susceptible — **prone·ness** \'prōn-nəs\ *n*

prong \'prȯŋ\ *n* : one of the sharp points of a fork : TINE; *also* : a slender projecting part (as of an antler)

prong·horn \'prȯŋ-ˌhȯrn\ *n, pl* **pronghorn** *also* **pronghorns** : a ruminant mammal of treeless parts of western No. America that resembles an antelope

pro·noun \'prō-ˌnau̇n\ *n* : a word used as a substitute for a noun

pro·nounce \prə-'nau̇ns\ *vb* **pro·nounced; pro·nounc·ing 1** : to utter officially or as an opinion ⟨∼ sentence⟩ **2** : to employ the organs of speech in order to produce ⟨∼ a word⟩; *esp* : to say or speak correctly ⟨she can't ∼ his name⟩ — **pro·nounce·able** *adj* — **pro·nun·ci·a·tion** \-ˌnən-sē-'ā-shən\ *n*

pro·nounced \-'nau̇nst\ *adj* : strongly marked : DECIDED

pro·nounce·ment \prə-'nau̇ns-mənt\ *n* : a formal declaration of opinion; *also* : ANNOUNCEMENT

pron·to \'prän-ˌtō\ *adv* [Sp, fr. L *promptus* prompt] : QUICKLY

pro·nu·clear \'prō-'n(y)ü-klē-ər\ *adj* : supporting the use of nuclear-powered electric generating stations

pro·nun·ci·a·men·to \prō-ˌnən-sē-ə-'ment-ō\ *n, pl* **-tos** *or* **-toes** : PROCLAMATION, MANIFESTO

¹**proof** \'prüf\ *n* **1** : the evidence that compels acceptance by the mind of a truth or fact **2** : a process or operation that establishes validity or truth : TEST **3** : a trial impression (as from type) **4** : a trial print from a photographic negative **5** : alcoholic content (as of a beverage) indicated by a number that is twice the percent by volume of alcohol present ⟨whiskey of 90 ∼ is 45% alcohol⟩

²**proof** *adj* **1** : successful in resisting or repelling ⟨∼ against tampering⟩ **2** : of standard strength or quality or alcoholic content

proof·read \-ˌrēd\ *vb* : to read and mark corrections in (as a printer's proof) — **proof·read·er** *n*

¹**prop** \'präp\ *n* : something that props

²**prop** *vb* **propped; prop·ping 1** : to support by placing something under or against ⟨∼ up a wall⟩ **2** : SUSTAIN, STRENGTHEN

³**prop** *n* : PROPERTY 4

⁴**prop** *n* : PROPELLER

⁵**prop** *abbr* **1** property **2** proposition **3** proprietor

pro·pa·gan·da \ˌpräp-ə-'gan-də, ˌprō-pə-\ *n* [NL, fr. *Congregatio de propaganda fide* Congregation for propagating the faith, organization established by Pope Gregory XV] : the spreading of ideas or information to further or damage a cause; *also* : ideas or allegations spread for such a purpose — **pro·pa·gan·dist** \-dəst\ *n*

pro·pa·gan·dize \-ˌdīz\ *vb* **-dized; -diz·ing** : to subject to or carry on propaganda

prop·a·gate \\'präp-ə-ˌgāt\ *vb* **-gat·ed; -gat·ing 1** : to reproduce or cause to reproduce biologically : MULTIPLY **2** : to cause to spread — **prop·a·ga·tion** \ˌpräp-ə-'gā-shən\ *n*

pro·pane \\'prō-ˌpān\ *n* : a heavy flammable gas found in petroleum and natural gas and used as a fuel

pro·pel \prə-'pel\ *vb* **pro·pelled; pro·pel·ling 1** : to drive forward or onward **2** : to urge on : MOTIVATE **syn** push, shove, thrust, drive

pro·pel·lant *also* **pro·pel·lent** \-'pel-ənt\ *n* : something (as an explosive or fuel) that propels — **propellant** *or* **propellent** *adj*

pro·pel·ler \prə-'pel-ər\ *n* : a device consisting of a hub fitted with blades that is used to propel a vehicle (as a motorboat or an airplane)

pro·pen·si·ty \prə-'pen-sət-ē\ *n, pl* **-ties** : an often intense natural inclination or preference

¹**prop·er** \\'präp-ər\ *adj* **1** : referring to one individual only ⟨∼ noun⟩ **2** : belonging characteristically to a species or individual : PECULIAR **3** : very satisfactory : EXCELLENT **4** : strictly limited to a specified thing ⟨the city ∼⟩ **5** : CORRECT ⟨the ∼ way to proceed⟩ **6** : strictly decorous : GENTEEL **7** : marked by suitability or rightness ⟨∼ punishment⟩ **syn** meet, appropriate, fitting, seemly — **prop·er·ly** *adv*

²**proper** *n* : the parts of the Mass that vary according to the liturgical calendar

prop·er·tied \\'präp-ərt-ēd\ *adj* : owning property and esp. much property

prop·er·ty \\'präp-ərt-ē\ *n, pl* **-ties 1** : a quality peculiar to an individual or thing **2** : something owned; *esp* : a piece of real estate **3** : OWNERSHIP **4** : an article or object used in a play other than painted scenery and actor's costumes

proph·e·cy *also* **proph·e·sy** \\'präf-ə-sē\ *n, pl* **-cies** *also* **-sies 1** : an inspired utterance of a prophet **2** : PREDICTION

proph·e·sy \-ˌsī\ *vb* **-sied; -sy·ing 1** : to speak or utter by divine inspiration **2** : PREDICT — **proph·e·si·er** \-ˌsī(-ə)r\ *n*

proph·et \\'präf-ət\ *n* [ME *prophete*, fr. OF, fr. L *propheta*, fr. Gk *prophētēs*, fr. *pro* for + *phanai* to speak] **1** : one who utters divinely inspired revela-

tions **2** : one who foretells future events

proph·et·ess \\'präf-ət-əs\ *n* : a woman who is a prophet

pro·phet·ic \prə-'fet-ik\ *or* **pro·phet·i·cal** \-i-kəl\ *adj* : of, relating to, or characteristic of a prophet or prophecy — **pro·phet·i·cal·ly** \-i-k(ə-)lē\ *adv*

¹**pro·phy·lac·tic** \ˌprō-fə-'lak-tik, ˌpräf-ə-\ *adj* **1** : preventing or guarding from disease **2** : PREVENTIVE

²**prophylactic** *n* : something (as a drug or device) that protects from disease

pro·phy·lax·is \-'lak-səs\ *n, pl* **-lax·es** \-'lak-ˌsēz\ : measures designed to preserve health and prevent the spread of disease

pro·pin·qui·ty \prə-'piŋ-kwət-ē\ *n* **1** : KINSHIP **2** : nearness in place or time : PROXIMITY

pro·pi·ti·ate \prō-'pish-ē-ˌāt\ *vb* **-at·ed; -at·ing** : to gain or regain the favor of : APPEASE — **pro·pi·ti·a·tion** \-ˌpis(h)-ē-'ā-shən\ *n* — **pro·pi·tia·to·ry** \-'pish-(ē-)ə-ˌtōr-ē\ *adj*

pro·pi·tious \prə-'pish-əs\ *adj* **1** : favorably disposed ⟨∼ deities⟩ **2** : being of good omen ⟨∼ circumstances⟩

prop·man \\'präp-ˌman\ *n* : one who is in charge of theater or motion-picture stage properties

pro·po·nent \prə-'pō-nənt\ *n* : one who argues in favor of something

¹**pro·por·tion** \prə-'pōr-shən\ *n* **1** : the relation of one part to another or to the whole with respect to magnitude, quantity, or degree : RATIO **2** : BALANCE, SYMMETRY **3** : SHARE, QUOTA **4** : SIZE, DEGREE — **in proportion** : PROPORTIONAL

²**proportion** *vb* **-tioned; -tion·ing** \-sh(ə-)niŋ\ **1** : to adjust (a part or thing) in size relative to other parts or things **2** : to make the parts of harmonious

pro·por·tion·al \prə-'pȯr-sh(ə-)nəl\ *adj* : corresponding in size, degree, or intensity; *also* : having the same or a constant ratio — **pro·por·tion·al·ly** \-ē\ *adv*

pro·por·tion·ate \prə-'pȯr-sh(ə-)nət\ *adj* : PROPORTIONAL — **pro·por·tion·ate·ly** *adv*

pro·pose \prə-'pōz\ *vb* **pro·posed; pro·pos·ing 1** : PLAN, INTEND ⟨∼s to buy a house⟩ **2** : to make an offer of marriage **3** : to offer for consideration : SUGGEST ⟨∼ a policy⟩ — **pro·pos·al** \-ᵖō-zəl\ *n* — **pro·pos·er** *n*

¹**prop·o·si·tion** \ˌpräp-ə-ᵖzish-ən\ *n* **1** : something proposed for consideration : PROPOSAL; *esp* : a request for sexual intercourse **2** : a statement of something to be discussed, proved, or explained **3** : SITUATION, AFFAIR ⟨a tough ∼⟩ — **prop·o·si·tion·al** \-ᵖzish-(ə-)nəl\ *adj*

²**proposition** *vb* **-tioned; -tion·ing** \-ᵖzish-(ə-)niŋ\ : to make a proposal to; *esp* : to suggest sexual intercourse to

pro·pound \prə-ᵖpaùnd\ *vb* : to set forth for consideration ⟨∼ a doctrine⟩

pro·pri·e·tary \prə-ᵖprī-ə-ˌter-ē\ *adj* **1** : of, relating to, or characteristic of a proprietor ⟨∼ control⟩ **2** : made and sold by one with the sole right to do so ⟨∼ medicines⟩

pro·pri·etor \prə-ᵖprī-ət-ər\ *n* : OWNER — **pro·pri·etor·ship** *n*

pro·pri·etress \-ᵖprī-ə-trəs\ *n* : a woman who is a proprietor

pro·pri·ety \prə-ᵖprī-ət-ē\ *n, pl* **-eties 1** : the standard of what is socially acceptable in conduct or speech **2** *pl* : the customs of polite society

pro·pul·sion \prə-ᵖpəl-shən\ *n* **1** : the action or process of propelling **2** : something that propels — **pro·pul·sive** \-siv\ *adj*

pro ra·ta \prō-ᵖrāt-ə, -ᵖrät-\ *adv* : in proportion to the share of each : PROPORTIONATELY

pro·rate \ᵖprō-ᵖrāt\ *vb* **pro·rat·ed; pro·rat·ing** : to divide, distribute, or assess proportionately

pro·rogue \prə-ᵖrōg\ *vb* **pro·rogued; pro·rogu·ing** : to suspend or end a session of (a legislative body) **syn** adjourn, dissolve, recess — **pro·ro·ga·tion** \ˌprōr-ō-ᵖgā-shən\ *n*

pros *pl of* PRO

pro·sa·ic \prō-ᵖzā-ik\ *adj* : lacking imagination or excitement : DULL

pro·sce·ni·um \prō-ᵖsē-nē-əm\ *n* **1** : the part of a stage in front of the curtain **2** : the wall containing the arch that frames the stage

pro·scribe \prō-ᵖskrīb\ *vb* **pro·scribed; pro·scrib·ing 1** : OUTLAW **2** : to condemn or forbid as harmful — **pro·scrip·tion** \-ᵖskrip-shən\ *n*

prose \ᵖprōz\ *n* [ME, fr. MF, fr. L

prosa, fr. fem. of *prorsus, prosus*, straightforward, being in prose, fr. *proversus*, pp. of *provertere* to turn forward] : the ordinary language people use in speaking or writing

pros·e·cute \ᵖpräs-i-ˌkyüt\ *vb* **-cut·ed; -cut·ing 1** : to follow to the end ⟨∼ an investigation⟩ **2** : to seek legal punishment of ⟨∼ a forger⟩ — **pros·e·cu·tion** \ˌpräs-i-ᵖkyü-shən\ *n* — **pros·e·cu·tor** \ᵖpräs-i-ˌkyüt-ər\ *n*

¹**pros·e·lyte** \ᵖpräs-ə-ˌlīt\ *n* : a new convert to a religion, belief, or party — **pros·e·lyt·ism** \-ˌlīt-ˌiz-əm\ *n*

²**proselyte** *vb* **-lyt·ed; -lyt·ing** : PROSELYTIZE

pros·e·ly·tize \ᵖpräs-(ə-)lə-ˌtīz\ *vb* **-tized; -tiz·ing 1** : to induce someone to convert to one's faith **2** : to recruit someone to join one's party, institution, or cause

pros·o·dy \ᵖpräs-əd-ē\ *n, pl* **-dies** : the study of versification and esp. of metrical structure

¹**pros·pect** \ᵖpräs-ˌpekt\ *n* **1** : an extensive view; *also* : OUTLOOK **2** : the act of looking forward **3** : a mental vision of something to come **4** : something that is awaited or expected : POSSIBILITY **5** : a potential buyer or customer; *also* : a likely candidate — **pro·spec·tive** \prə-ᵖspek-tiv, ᵖpräs-ˌpek-\ *adj* — **pro·spec·tive·ly** *adv*

²**pros·pect** \ᵖpräs-ˌpekt\ *vb* : to explore esp. for mineral deposits — **pros·pec·tor** \-ˌpek-tər, -ᵖpek-\ *n*

pro·spec·tus \prə-ᵖspek-təs\ *n* : a preliminary statement that describes an enterprise and is distributed to prospective buyers or participants

pros·per \ᵖpräs-pər\ *vb* **pros·pered; pros·per·ing** \-p(ə-)riŋ\ : SUCCEED; *esp* : to achieve economic success

pros·per·i·ty \präs-ᵖper-ət-ē\ *n* : thriving condition : SUCCESS; *esp* : economic well-being

pros·per·ous \ᵖpräs-p(ə-)rəs\ *adj* **1** : FAVORABLE ⟨∼ winds⟩ **2** : marked by success or economic well-being ⟨a ∼ business⟩

pros·tate \ᵖpräs-ˌtāt\ *also* **pros·tat·ic** \prä-ᵖstat-ik\ *adj* : of, relating to, or being the prostate gland — **prostate** *n*

prostate gland *n* : a glandular body about the base of the male urethra that produces a secretion which is a major part of the fluid ejaculated during an orgasm

pros·ta·ti·tis \ˌpräs-tə-ˈtīt-əs\ *n* : inflammation of the prostate gland

pros·the·sis \präs-ˈthē-səs, ˈpräs-thə-\ *n, pl* **-the·ses** \-ˌsēz\ : an artificial replacement for a missing body part — **pros·thet·ic** \präs-ˈthet-ik\ *adj*

pros·thet·ics \-ˈthet-iks\ *n pl* : the surgical and dental specialties concerned with the artificial replacement of missing parts

¹**pros·ti·tute** \ˈpräs-tə-ˌt(y)üt\ *vb* **-tut·ed; -tut·ing** **1** : to offer indiscriminately for sexual intercourse esp. for money **2** : to devote to corrupt or unworthy purposes — **pros·ti·tu·tion** \ˌpräs-tə-ˈt(y)ü-shən\ *n*

²**prostitute** *n* : one who engages in promiscuous sexual intercourse for pay

¹**pros·trate** \ˈpräs-ˌtrāt\ *adj* **1** : stretched out with face on the ground in adoration or submission **2** : lying flat **3** : completely overcome ⟨∼ with a cold⟩

²**pros·trate** \ˈpräs-ˌtrāt\ *vb* **pros·trat·ed; pros·trat·ing** **1** : to throw or put into a prostrate position **2** : to reduce to a weak or powerless condition — **pros·tra·tion** \präs-ˈtrā-shən\ *n*

prosy \ˈprō-zē\ *adj* **pros·i·er; -est** **1** : PROSAIC **2** : TEDIOUS

Prot *abbr* Protestant

prot·ac·tin·i·um \ˌprōt-ˌak-ˈtin-ē-əm\ *n* : a metallic radioactive element of relatively short life

pro·tag·o·nist \prō-ˈtag-ə-nəst\ *n* **1** : the principal character in a drama or story **2** : a spokesman for a cause : CHAMPION

pro·te·an \ˈprōt-ē-ən\ *adj* : able to assume different shapes or roles

pro·tect \prə-ˈtekt\ *vb* : to shield from injury : GUARD

pro·tec·tion \prə-ˈtek-shən\ *n* **1** : the act of protecting : the state of being protected **2** : one that protects ⟨wear a helmet as a ∼⟩ **3** : the supervision or support of one that is smaller and weaker **4** : the freeing of producers from foreign competition in their home market by high duties on foreign competitive goods — **pro·tec·tive** \-ˈtek-tiv\ *adj*

pro·tec·tion·ist \-sh(ə-)nəst\ *n* : an advocate of government economic protection for domestic producers through restrictions on foreign competitors — **pro·tec·tion·ism** \-shə-ˌniz-əm\ *n*

pro·tec·tor \prə-ˈtek-tər\ *n* **1** : one that protects : GUARDIAN **2** : a device used to prevent injury : GUARD **3** : REGENT 1

pro·tec·tor·ate \-t(ə-)rət\ *n* **1** : government by a protector **2** : the relationship of superior authority assumed by one state over a dependent one; *also* : the dependent political unit in such a relationship

pro·té·gé \ˈprōt-ə-ˌzhā\ *n* [F] : one who is protected, trained, or guided by an influential person

pro·tein \ˈprō-ˌtēn, ˈprōt-ē-ən\ *n* [F *protéine*, fr. LGk *prōteios* primary, fr. Gk *prōtos* first] : any of numerous complex nitrogen-containing substances that consist of chains of amino acids, are present in all living matter, and are an essential part of the human diet

pro tem \prō-ˈtem\ *adv* : PRO TEMPORE

pro tem·po·re \prō-ˈtem-pə-rē\ *adv* [L] : for the time being

Pro·tero·zo·ic \ˌprät-ə-rə-ˈzō-ik, ˌprōt-\ *adj* : of, relating to, or being the era of geologic history between the Archeozoic and the Paleozoic and extending from about 1.4 billion years ago to about 620 million years ago — **Proterozoic** *n*

¹**pro·test** \ˈprō-ˌtest\ *n* **1** : the act of protesting; *esp* : an organized public demonstration of disapproval **2** : a complaint or objection against an idea, an act, or a course of action

²**pro·test** \prə-ˈtest\ *vb* **1** : to assert positively : make solemn declaration of ⟨∼s his innocence⟩ **2** : to object strongly : make a protest against ⟨∼ a ruling⟩ — **prot·es·ta·tion** \ˌprät-əs-ˈtā-shən\ *n* — **pro·test·er** *or* **pro·tes·tor** \-ər\ *n*

Prot·es·tant \ˈprät-əs-tənt, *3 also* prə-ˈtes-\ *n* **1** : a member or adherent of one of the Christian churches deriving from the Reformation **2** : a Christian not of a Catholic or Orthodox church **3** *not cap* : one who makes a protest — **Prot·es·tant·ism** \ˈprät-əs-tənt-ˌiz-əm\ *n*

pro·tha·la·mi·on \ˌprō-thə-ˈlā-mē-ən\ *or* **pro·tha·la·mi·um** \-mē-əm\ *n, pl* **-mia**

\-mē-ə\ : a song in celebration of a marriage

pro•to•col \\'prōt-ə-ˌkȯl\ *n* [MF *pro-thocole*, fr. ML *protocollum*, fr. LGk *prōtokollon* first sheet of a papyrus roll bearing data of manufacture, fr. Gk *prōtos* first + *kollan* to glue together, fr. *kolla* glue] 1 : an original draft or record 2 : a preliminary memorandum of diplomatic negotiation 3 : a code of diplomatic or military etiquette

pro•ton \\'prō-ˌtän\ *n* [Gk *prōton*, neut. of *prōtos* first] : a positively charged atomic particle present in all atomic nuclei

pro•to•plasm \\'prōt-ə-ˌplaz-əm\ *n* : the complex colloidal largely protein substance of living plant and animal cells that is regarded as the only form of matter in which the vital phenomena are manifested — **pro•to•plas•mic** \ˌprōt-ə-ˈplaz-mik\ *adj*

pro•to•type \\'prōt-ə-ˌtīp\ *n* : an original model : ARCHETYPE

pro•to•zo•an \ˌprōt-ə-ˈzō-ən\ *n* : any of a phylum or subkingdom of lower invertebrate animals that are not divided into cells or are considered as made up of a single cell

pro•tract \prō-ˈtrakt\ *vb* : to prolong in time or space **syn** extend, lengthen, elongate, stretch

pro•trac•tor \-ˈtrak-tər\ *n* : an instrument for drawing and measuring angles

pro•trude \prō-ˈtrüd\ *vb* **pro•trud•ed; pro•trud•ing** : to stick out or cause to stick out : jut out — **pro•tru•sion** \-ˈtrü-zhən\ *n*

pro•tu•ber•ance \prō-ˈt(y)ü-b(ə-)rəns\ *n* : something that protrudes

pro•tu•ber•ant \-b(ə-)rənt\ *adj* : extending beyond the surrounding surface in a bulge

proud \\'praud\ *adj* 1 : having or showing excessive self-esteem : HAUGHTY 2 : highly pleased : EXULTANT 3 : having proper self-respect ⟨too ∼ to beg⟩ 4 : GLORIOUS ⟨a ∼ occasion⟩ 5 : SPIRITED ⟨a ∼ steed⟩ **syn** arrogant, insolent, overbearing, disdainful — **proud•ly** *adv*

prov *abbr* 1 province; provincial 2 provisional

Prov *abbr* Proverbs

prove \\'prüv\ *vb* **proved; proved** *or* **prov•en** \\'prü-vən\; **prov•ing** \\'prü-viŋ\ 1 : to test by experiment or by a standard 2 : to establish the truth of by argument or evidence 3 : to show to be correct, valid, or genuine 4 : to turn out esp. after trial or test ⟨the car *proved* to be a good choice⟩ — **prov•able** \\'prü-və-bəl\ *adj*

prov•e•nance \\'präv-ə-nəns\ *n* : ORIGIN, SOURCE

Pro•ven•çal \ˌprō-ˌvän-ˈsäl, ˌpräv-ən-\ *n* 1 : a native or inhabitant of Provence 2 : a Romance language spoken in southeastern France — **Provençal** *adj*

prov•en•der \\'präv-ən-dər\ *n* 1 : dry food for domestic animals : FEED 2 : FOOD, VICTUALS

pro•ve•nience \prə-ˈvē-nyəns\ *n* : ORIGIN, SOURCE

prov•erb \\'präv-ˌərb\ *n* : a pithy popular saying : ADAGE

pro•ver•bi•al \prə-ˈvər-bē-əl\ *adj* 1 : of, relating to, or resembling a proverb 2 : commonly spoken of

Proverbs *n* — see BIBLE table

pro•vide \prə-ˈvīd\ *vb* **pro•vid•ed; pro•vid•ing** [ME *providen*, fr. L *providēre*, lit., to see ahead, fr. *pro-* forward + *vidēre* to see] 1 : to take measures beforehand ⟨∼ against inflation⟩ 2 : to make a proviso or stipulation 3 : to supply what is needed ⟨∼ for a family⟩ 4 : EQUIP 5 : to supply for use : YIELD — **pro•vid•er** *n*

pro•vid•ed \prə-ˈvīd-əd\ *conj* : on condition that : IF

prov•i•dence \\'präv-əd-əns\ *n* 1 *often cap* : divine guidance or care 2 *cap* : GOD 1 3 : the quality or state of being provident

prov•i•dent \-əd-ənt\ *adj* 1 : making provision for the future : PRUDENT 2 : FRUGAL — **prov•i•dent•ly** *adv*

prov•i•den•tial \ˌpräv-ə-ˈden-chəl\ *adj* 1 : of, relating to, or determined by Providence 2 : OPPORTUNE, LUCKY

prov•ince \\'präv-əns\ *n* 1 : an administrative district or division of a country 2 *pl* : all of a country except the metropolis 3 : proper business or scope : SPHERE

pro•vin•cial \prə-ˈvin-chəl\ *adj* 1 : of or relating to a province 2 : confined to a region : NARROW ⟨~ ideas⟩ — **pro·vin·cial·ism** \-ˌiz-əm\ *n*

proving ground *n* : a place for scientific experimentation or testing

¹pro·vi·sion \prə-ˈvizh-ən\ *n* **1** : the act or process of providing; *also* : a measure taken beforehand **2** : a stock of needed supplies; *esp* : a stock of food — usu. used in pl. **3** : PROVISO

²provision *vb* **-sioned; -sion·ing** \-ˈvizh-(ə-)niŋ\ : to supply with provisions

pro·vi·sion·al \-ˈvizh-(ə-)nəl\ *adj* : provided for a temporary need : CONDITIONAL

pro·vi·so \prə-ˈvī-zō\ *n, pl* **-sos** *or* **-soes** [ME, fr. ML *proviso quod* provided that] : an article or clause that introduces a condition : STIPULATION

prov·o·ca·tion \ˌpräv-ə-ˈkā-shən\ *n* **1** : the act of provoking **2** : something that provokes

pro·voke \prə-ˈvōk\ *vb* **pro·voked; pro·vok·ing** **1** : to incite to anger : INCENSE **2** : to call forth : EVOKE ⟨a sally that *provoked* laughter⟩ **3** : to stir up on purpose ⟨~ an argument⟩ **syn** irritate, exasperate, aggravate, inflame, rile, pique — **pro·voc·a·tive** \prə-ˈväk-ət-iv\ *adj*

pro·vo·lo·ne \ˌprō-və-ˈlō-nē\ *n* : a hard smooth often smoked Italian cheese that is made from heated and kneaded curd

pro·vost \ˈprō-ˌvōst, ˈpräv-əst\ *n* : a high official : DIGNITARY; *esp* : a high-ranking university administrative officer

provost marshal \ˌprō-ˌvō-ˈmär-shəl\ *n* : an officer who supervises the military police of a command

prow \ˈprau̇\ *n* : the bow of a ship

prow·ess \ˈprau̇-əs\ *n* **1** : military valor and skill **2** : extraordinary ability

prowl \ˈprau̇l\ *vb* : to roam about stealthily — **prowl** *n* — **prowl·er** *n*

prowl car *n* : SQUAD CAR

prox·i·mal \ˈpräk-sə-məl\ *adj* **1** : next to or nearest the point of attachment or origin; *esp* : located toward the center of the body **2** : of, relating to, or being the mesial and distal surfaces of a tooth

prox·i·mate \ˈpräk-sə-mət\ *adj* **1** : very near **2** : DIRECT ⟨the ~ cause⟩

prox·im·i·ty \präk-ˈsim-ət-ē\ *n* : NEARNESS

prox·i·mo \ˈpräk-sə-ˌmō\ *adj* [L *proximo mense* in the next month] : of or occurring in the next month after the present

proxy \ˈpräk-sē\ *n, pl* **prox·ies** : the authority or power to act for another; *also* : a document giving such authorization — **proxy** *adj*

prude \ˈprüd\ *n* : one who shows or affects extreme modesty — **prud·ery** \ˈprüd-ə-rē\ *n* — **prud·ish** \ˈprüd-ish\ *adj*

pru·dent \ˈprüd-ᵊnt\ *adj* **1** : shrewd in the management of practical affairs **2** : CAUTIOUS, DISCREET **3** : PROVIDENT, FRUGAL **syn** judicious, foresighted, sensible, sane — **pru·dence** \-ᵊns\ *n* — **pru·den·tial** \prü-ˈden-chəl\ *adj* — **pru·dent·ly** \ˈprüd-ᵊnt-lē\ *adv*

¹prune \ˈprün\ *n* : a dried plum

²prune *vb* **pruned; prun·ing** : to cut off unwanted parts (as of a tree)

pru·ri·ent \ˈprur-ē-ənt\ *adj* : LASCIVIOUS; *also* : exciting to lasciviousness — **pru·ri·ence** \-ē-əns\ *n*

¹pry \ˈprī\ *vb* **pried; pry·ing** : to look closely or inquisitively; *esp* : SNOOP

²pry *vb* **pried; pry·ing** **1** : to raise, move, or pull apart with a pry or lever **2** : to detach or open with difficulty

³pry *n* : a tool for prying

Ps *or* **Psa** *abbr* Psalms

PS *abbr* **1** [L *postscriptum*] postscript **2** public school

psalm \ˈsäm, ˈsälm\ *n, often cap* [ME, fr. OE *psealm*, fr. LL *psalmus*, fr. Gk *psalmos*, lit., twanging of a harp, fr. *psallein* to pluck, play a stringed instrument] : a sacred song or poem; *esp* : one of the hymns collected in the Book of Psalms — **psalm·ist** *n*

psalm·o·dy \ˈsäm-əd-ē, ˈsäl-məd-\ *n* **1** : the singing of psalms in worship **2** : a collection of psalms

Psalms *n* — see BIBLE table

Psal·ter \ˈsȯl-tər\ *n* : the Book of Psalms; *also* : a collection of the Psalms arranged for devotional use

pseud *abbr* pseudonym; pseudonymous

pseu·do \ˈsüd-ō\ *adj* : SPURIOUS, SHAM

pseud·onym \ˈsüd-ᵊn-ˌim\ *n* : a fictitious name — **pseud·on·y·mous** \sü-ˈdän-ə-məs\ *adj*

PSG *abbr* platoon sergeant

psi *abbr* pounds per square inch

psi particle \\'sī-, 'psī-\\ *n* [*psi* (Greek letter)] : J PARTICLE

pso·ri·a·sis \\sə-'rī-ə-səs\\ *n* : a chronic skin disease characterized by red patches covered with white scales

PST *abbr* Pacific standard time

¹psych *also* **psyche** \\'sīk\\ *vb* **psyched; psych·ing 1** : OUTGUESS; *also* : to analyze beforehand **2** : INTIMIDATE; *also* : to prepare oneself psychologically ⟨get *psyched* up for the game⟩

²psych *abbr* psychology

psy·che \\'sī-kē\\ *n* : SOUL, SELF; *also* : MIND

psy·che·del·ic \\ˌsī-kə-'del-ik\\ *adj* **1** : of, relating to, or causing abnormal psychic effects ⟨∼ drugs⟩ **2** : relating to the taking of psychedelic drugs ⟨∼ experience⟩ **3** : imitating, suggestive of, or reproducing the effects of psychedelic drugs ⟨∼ art⟩ ⟨∼ colors⟩ — **psychedelic** *n* — **psy·che·del·i·cal·ly** \\-i-k(ə-)lē\\ *adv*

psy·chi·a·try \\sə-'kī-ə-trē, sī-\\ *n* : a branch of medicine dealing with mental disorders — **psy·chi·at·ric** \\ˌsī-kē-'a-trik\\ *adj* — **psy·chi·a·trist** \\sə-'kī-ə-trəst, sī-\\ *n*

¹psy·chic \\'sī-kik\\ *also* **psy·chi·cal** \\-ki-kəl\\ *adj* **1** : of or relating to the psyche **2** : lying outside the sphere of physical science **3** : sensitive to nonphysical or supernatural forces — **psy·chi·cal·ly** \\-k(ə-)lē\\ *adv*

²psychic *n* : a person apparently sensitive to nonphysical forces; *also* : MEDIUM 6

psychic energizer *n* : ANTIDEPRESSANT

psy·cho \\'sī-kō\\ *n, pl* **psychos** : a mentally disturbed person — **psycho** *adj*

psy·cho·ac·tive \\ˌsī-kō-'ak-tiv\\ *adj* : affecting the mind or behavior

psy·cho·anal·y·sis \\ˌsī-kō-ə-'nal-ə-səs\\ *n* : a method of dealing with psychic disorders by having the patient talk freely about himself and esp. about dreams, problems, and early childhood memories and experiences — **psy·cho·an·a·lyst** \\-'an-ᵊl-əst\\ *n* — **psy·cho·an·a·lyt·ic** \\-ˌan-ᵊl-'it-ik\\ *adj* — **psy·cho·an·a·lyze** \\-'an-ᵊl-ˌīz\\ *vb*

psy·cho·dra·ma \\ˌsī-kə-'dräm-ə, -'dram-\\ *n* : an extemporized dramatization designed esp. to afford catharsis for one or more of the participants from whose life history the plot is abstracted

psy·cho·gen·ic \\-'jen-ik\\ *adj* : originating in the mind or in mental or emotional conflict

psychol *abbr* psychologist; psychology

psy·chol·o·gy \\sī-'käl-ə-jē\\ *n, pl* **-gies 1** : the science of mind and behavior **2** : the mental and behavioral characteristics of an individual or group — **psy·cho·log·i·cal** \\ˌsī-kə-'läj-i-kəl\\ *adj* — **psy·cho·log·i·cal·ly** \\-i-k(ə-)lē\\ *adv* — **psy·chol·o·gist** \\sī-'käl-ə-jəst\\ *n*

psy·cho·path \\'sī-kə-ˌpath\\ *n* : a mentally ill or unstable person; *esp* : one who has a poorly balanced personality and does not feel guilty about not living up to normal moral and social responsibilities — **psy·cho·path·ic** \\ˌsī-kə-'path-ik\\ *adj*

psy·cho·sex·u·al \\ˌsī-kō-'sek-sh(ə-w)əl\\ *adj* **1** : of or relating to the mental, emotional, and behavioral aspects of sexual development **2** : of or relating to the physiological psychology of sex

psy·cho·sis \\sī-'kō-səs\\ *n, pl* **-cho·ses** \\-ˌsēz\\ : a serious mental illness (as schizophrenia) characterized by defective or lost contact with reality — **psy·chot·ic** \\-'kät-ik\\ *adj or n*

psy·cho·so·mat·ic \\ˌsī-kə-sə-'mat-ik\\ *adj* : of, relating to, or caused by the interaction of mental and bodily phenomena ⟨∼ ulcers⟩

psy·cho·ther·a·py \\ˌsī-kō-'ther-ə-pē\\ *n* : treatment of mental or emotional disorder or of related bodily ills by psychological means — **psy·cho·ther·a·pist** \\-pəst\\ *n*

psy·cho·tro·pic \\ˌsī-kə-'trō-pik\\ *adj* : acting on the mind ⟨∼ drugs⟩

pt *abbr* **1** part **2** payment **3** pint **4** point **5** port

Pt *symbol* platinum

PT *abbr* **1** Pacific time **2** physical therapy **3** physical training

PTA *abbr* Parent-Teacher Association

ptar·mi·gan \\'tär-mi-gən\\ *n, pl* **-gan** *or* **-gans** : any of various grouses of northern regions with completely feathered feet

PT boat \\(')pē-'tē-\\ *n* [*patrol torpedo*] : a fast motorboat usu. armed with torpedos, machine guns, and depth charges

pte *abbr, Brit* private

ptg *abbr* printing

PTO *abbr* **1** Parent-Teacher Organization **2** please turn over

pto・maine \'tō-ˌmān\ *n* : any of various chemical substances formed by bacteria in decaying matter (as meat)

ptomaine poisoning *n* : food poisoning caused usu. by bacteria or their products

PTV *abbr* public television

Pu *symbol* plutonium

¹pub \'pəb\ *n, chiefly Brit* : PUBLIC HOUSE, TAVERN

²pub *abbr* **1** public **2** publication **3** published; publisher; publishing

pu・ber・ty \'pyü-bərt-ē\ *n* : the condition of being or period of becoming first capable of reproducing sexually — **pu・ber・tal** \-bərt-ᵊl\ *adj*

pu・bes \'pyü-bēz\ *n, pl* **pubes 1** : the hair that appears upon the lower middle region of the abdomen at puberty **2** : the pubic region

pu・bes・cence \pyü-'bes-ᵊns\ *n* **1** : the quality or state of being pubescent **2** : a pubescent covering or surface

pu・bes・cent \-ᵊnt\ *adj* **1** : arriving at or having reached puberty **2** : covered with fine soft short hairs

pu・bic \'pyü-bik\ *adj* : of, relating to, or situated near the pubes or the pubis

pu・bis \'pyü-bəs\ *n, pl* **pu・bes** \-bēz\ : the ventral and anterior of the three principal bones composing either half of the pelvis

publ *abbr* **1** publication **2** published; publisher

¹pub・lic \'pəb-lik\ *adj* **1** : of, relating to, or affecting the people as a whole 〈~ opinion〉 **2** : CIVIC, GOVERNMENTAL 〈~ expenditures〉 **3** : of, relating to, or serving the community 〈~ officials〉 **4** : not private : SOCIAL 〈~ morality〉 **5** : open to all 〈~ library〉 **6** : exposed to general view 〈the story became ~〉 **7** : well known : PROMINENT 〈~ figures〉 — **pub・lic・ly** *adv*

²public *n* **1** : the people as a whole : POPULACE **2** : a group of people having common interests 〈wrote for his ~〉

pub・li・can \'pəb-li-kən\ *n* **1** : a Jewish tax collector for the ancient Romans **2** *chiefly Brit* : the licensee of a public house

pub・li・ca・tion \ˌpəb-lə-'kā-shən\ *n* **1**

: the act or process of publishing **2** : a published work

public house *n* **1** : INN **2** *chiefly Brit* : a licensed saloon or bar

pub・li・cist \'pəb-lə-səst\ *n* : one that publicizes; *esp* : PRESS AGENT

pub・lic・i・ty \(ˌ)pə-'blis-ət-ē\ *n* **1** : information with news value issued to gain public attention or support **2** : public attention or acclaim

pub・li・cize \'pəb-lə-ˌsīz\ *vb* **-cized; -cizing** : to give publicity to

public relations *n sing or pl* : the business of fostering public goodwill toward a person, firm, or institution; *also* : the degree of goodwill and understanding achieved

public school *n* **1** : an endowed secondary boarding school in Great Britain offering a classical curriculum and preparation for the universities or public service **2** : a free tax-supported school controlled by a local governmental authority

pub・lic–spir・it・ed \ˌpəb-lik-'spir-ət-əd\ *adj* : motivated by devotion to the general or national welfare

public television *n* : television that provides cultural, informational, and instructive programs without commercials

pub・lish \'pəb-lish\ *vb* **1** : to make generally known : announce publicly **2** : to produce or release literature, information, musical scores or sometimes recordings, or art for sale to the public — **pub・lish・er** *n*

¹puck \'pək\ *n* : a mischievous sprite — **puck・ish** *adj*

²puck *n* : a disk used in ice hockey

¹puck・er \'pək-ər\ *vb* **puck・ered; puck・er・ing** \-(ə-)riŋ\ : to contract into folds or wrinkles

²pucker *n* : FOLD, WRINKLE

pud・ding \'pùd-iŋ\ *n* : a soft, spongy, or thick creamy dessert

pud・dle \'pəd-ᵊl\ *n* : a very small pool of usu. dirty or muddy water

pu・den・dum \pyü-'den-dəm\ *n, pl* **-da** \-də\ [NL, deriv. of L *pudēre* to be ashamed] : the human external genital organs esp. of a woman

pudgy \'pəj-ē\ *adj* **pudg・i・er; -est** : being short and plump : CHUBBY

pueb・lo \pü-'eb-lō, 'pweb-\ *n, pl* **-los** [Sp, village, lit., people, fr. L *popu-*

lus] **1** : an American Indian village of Arizona or New Mexico consisting of flat-roofed stone or adobe houses **2** *cap* : a member of an American Indian people of the southwestern U.S.

pu·er·ile \'pyü-ə-rəl\ *adj* : CHILDISH, SILLY — **pu·er·il·i·ty** \ˌpyü-ə-'ril-ət-ē\ *n*

pu·er·per·al \pyü-'ər-p(ə-)rəl\ *adj* : of, relating to, or occurring during childbirth or the period immediately following ⟨~ infection⟩

puerperal fever *n* : an abnormal condition that results from infection of the placental site following childbirth or abortion

Puer·to Ri·can \ˌpōrt-ə-'rē-kən, ˌpwert-\ *n* : a native or inhabitant of Puerto Rico — **Puerto Rican** *adj*

¹puff \'pəf\ *vb* **1** : to blow in short gusts **2** : PANT **3** : to emit small whiffs or clouds **4** : BLUSTER, BRAG **5** : INFLATE, SWELL **6** : to make proud or conceited **7** : to praise extravagantly

²puff *n* **1** : a short discharge (as of air or smoke); *also* : a slight explosive sound accompanying it **2** : a light fluffy pastry **3** : a slight swelling **4** : a fluffy mass; *esp* : a small pad for applying cosmetic powder **5** : a laudatory notice or review — **puffy** *adj*

puff·ball \'pəf-ˌbȯl\ *n* : any of various globe-shaped and often edible fungi

puf·fin \'pəf-ən\ *n* : any of several seabirds having a short neck and a red-tipped triangular bill

¹pug \'pəg\ *n* **1** : any of a breed of small stocky short-haired dogs **2** : a close coil of hair

²pug *n* : ¹BOXER

pu·gi·lism \'pyü-jə-ˌliz-əm\ *n* : BOXING — **pu·gi·list** \-ləst\ *n* — **pu·gi·lis·tic** \ˌpyü-jə-'lis-tik\ *adj*

pug·na·cious \ˌpəg-'nā-shəs\ *adj* : fond of fighting : COMBATIVE **syn** belligerent, quarrelsome, bellicose, contentious, truculent — **pug·nac·i·ty** \-'nas-ət-ē\ *n*

puis·sance \'pwis-ᵊns, 'pyü-ə-səns\ *n* : POWER, STRENGTH — **puis·sant** \-ᵊnt, -sənt\ *adj*

puke \'pyük\ *vb* **puked; puk·ing** : VOMIT — **puke** *n*

puk·ka \'pək-ə\ *adj* [Hindi *pakkā* cooked, ripe, solid, fr. Skt *pakva*] : GENUINE, AUTHENTIC; *also* : FIRST-CLASS, COMPLETE

pul \'pül\ *n, pl* **puls** \'pülz\ *or* **pul** — see *afghani* at MONEY table

pu·la \'p(y)ü-lə\ *n, pl* **pula** — see MONEY table

pul·chri·tude \'pəl-krə-ˌt(y)üd\ *n* : BEAUTY — **pul·chri·tu·di·nous** \ˌpəl-krə-'t(y)üd-(ᵊ-)nəs\ *adj*

pule \'pyül\ *vb* **puled; pul·ing** : WHINE, WHIMPER

¹pull \'pül\ *vb* **1** : PLUCK; *also* : EXTRACT ⟨~ a tooth⟩ **2** : to exert force so as to draw (something) toward the force; *also* : MOVE ⟨~ out of a driveway⟩ **3** : STRETCH, STRAIN ⟨~ a tendon⟩ **4** : to draw apart : TEAR **5** : to make (as a proof) by printing **6** : REMOVE **7** : DRAW ⟨~ a gun⟩ **8** : to carry out esp. with daring ⟨~ a robbery⟩ **9** : to be guilty of : PERPETRATE **10** : ATTRACT **11** : to express strong sympathy — **pull·er** *n*

²pull *n* **1** : the act or an instance of pulling **2** : the effort expended in moving **3** : ADVANTAGE; *esp* : special influence **4** : a device for pulling something or for operating by pulling **5** : a force that attracts or compels

pull·back \'pül-ˌbak\ *n* : an orderly withdrawal of troops

pul·let \'pül-ət\ *n* : a young hen esp. of the domestic chicken when less than a year old

pul·ley \'pül-ē\ *n, pl* **pulleys** **1** : a wheel with a grooved rim that forms part of a tackle for hoisting or for changing the direction of a force **2** : a wheel used to transmit power by means of a band, belt, rope, or chain

Pull·man \'pül-mən\ *n* : a railroad passenger car with comfortable furnishings esp. for night travel

pull off *vb* : to accomplish successfully

pull·out \'pül-ˌaut\ *n* : PULLBACK

pull·over \'pül-ˌō-vər\ *adj* : put on by being pulled over the head ⟨~ sweater⟩ — **pull·over** \'pül-ˌō-vər\ *n*

pull–up \'pül-ˌəp\ *n* : CHIN-UP

pull up \pül-'əp\ *vb* : to bring or come to a halt : STOP

pul·mo·nary \'pül-mə-ˌner-ē, 'pəl-\ *adj* : of, relating to, or carried on by the lungs ⟨the ~ circulation⟩

pul·mo·tor \-ˌmōt-ər\ *n* : an apparatus for pumping oxygen or air into and out of the lungs

pulp \'pəlp\ *n* **1** : the soft juicy or fleshy

part of a fruit or vegetable **2** : a soft moist mass **3** : the soft sensitive tissue that fills the central cavity of a tooth **4** : a material (as from wood or rags) used in making paper **5** : a magazine using rough-surfaced paper and often dealing with sensational material — **pulpy** *adj*

pul·pit \'pul-ˌpit\ *n* : a raised platform or high reading desk used in preaching or conducting a worship service

pulp·wood \'pəlp-ˌwud\ *n* : wood (as of aspen or pine) used in making pulp for paper

pul·sar \'pəl-ˌsär\ *n* : a celestial source of pulsating electromagnetic radiation (as radio waves)

pul·sate \'pəl-ˌsāt\ *vb* **pul·sat·ed; pul·sat·ing** : to expand and contract rhythmically : BEAT — **pul·sa·tion** \ˌpəl-'sā-shən\ *n*

pulse \'pəls\ *n* **1** : the regular throbbing in the arteries caused by the contractions of the heart **2** : a brief change in electrical current or voltage — **pulse** *vb*

pul·ver·ize \'pəl-və-ˌrīz\ *vb* **-ized; -iz·ing** **1** : to reduce (as by crushing or grinding) or be reduced to very small particles **2** : DEMOLISH

pu·ma \'p(y)ü-mə\ *n, pl* **pumas** *also* **puma** : COUGAR

pum·ice \'pəm-əs\ *n* : a light porous volcanic glass used esp. for smoothing and polishing

pum·mel \'pəm-əl\ *vb* **-meled** *also* **-melled; -mel·ing** *also* **-mel·ling** \-(ə-)liŋ\ : POUND, BEAT

¹pump \'pəmp\ *n* : a device for raising, transferring, or compressing fluids esp. by suction or pressure

²pump *vb* **1** : to raise (as water) with a pump **2** : to draw water or air from by means of a pump; *also* : to fill by means of a pump ⟨∼ up a tire⟩ **3** : to force or propel in the manner of a pump — **pump·er** *n*

³pump *n* : a low shoe that grips the foot chiefly at the toe and heel

pum·per·nick·el \'pəm-pər-ˌnik-əl\ *n* : a dark coarse somewhat sour rye bread

pump·kin \'pəm(p)-kən, 'pəŋ-kən\ *n* : the large usu. orange fruit of a vine of the gourd family that is widely used as food; *also* : this vine

pun \'pən\ *n* : the humorous use of a word in a way that suggests two interpretations — **pun** *vb*

¹punch \'pənch\ *vb* **1** : PROD, POKE; *also* : DRIVE, HERD ⟨∼ing cattle⟩ **2** : to strike with the fist **3** : to emboss, perforate, or make with a punch — **punch·er** *n*

²punch *n* **1** : a quick blow with or as if with the fist **2** : effective energy or forcefulness

³punch *n* : a tool for piercing, stamping, cutting, or forming

⁴punch *n* [perh. fr. Hindi *pãc* five, fr. Skt *pañca:* fr. the number of ingredients] : a drink usu. composed of wine or alcoholic liquor and nonalcoholic beverages; *also* : a drink composed of nonalcoholic beverages (as fruit juices)

punch card *n* : a card with holes punched in particular positions to represent data

pun·cheon \'pən-chən\ *n* : a large cask

punch line *n* : the sentence or phrase in a joke that makes the point

punc·til·io \ˌpəŋk-'til-ē-ˌō\ *n, pl* **-i·os** **1** : a nice detail of conduct in a ceremony or in observance of a code **2** : careful observance of forms (as in social conduct)

punc·til·i·ous \ˌpəŋk-'til-ē-əs\ *adj* : marked by precise accordance with codes or conventions **syn** meticulous, scrupulous, careful, punctual

punc·tu·al \'pəŋk-chə(-wə)l\ *adj* : acting or habitually acting at an appointed time : PROMPT — **punc·tu·al·i·ty** \ˌpəŋk-chə-'wal-ət-ē\ *n* — **punc·tu·al·ly** \'pəŋk-chə(-wə)-lē\ *adv*

punc·tu·ate \'pəŋk-chə-ˌwāt\ *vb* **-at·ed; -at·ing** **1** : to mark or divide (written matter) with punctuation marks **2** : to break into at intervals **3** : EMPHASIZE

punc·tu·a·tion \ˌpəŋk-chə-'wā-shən\ *n* : the act, practice, or system of inserting standardized marks in written matter to clarify the meaning and separate structural units

¹punc·ture \'pəŋk-chər\ *n* **1** : an act of puncturing **2** : a small hole made by puncturing

²puncture *vb* **punc·tured; punc·tur·ing** **1** : to make a hole in : PIERCE **2** : to make useless as if by a puncture

pun·dit \'pən-dət\ *n* **1** : a learned person : TEACHER **2** : AUTHORITY

pun·gent \\'pən-jənt\\ *adj* **1** : having a sharp incisive quality : CAUSTIC ⟨a ~ editorial⟩ **2** : causing a sharp or irritating sensation; *esp* : ACRID ⟨~ smell of burning leaves⟩ — **pun·gen·cy** \\-jən-sē\\ *n* — **pun·gent·ly** *adv*

pun·ish \\'pən-ish\\ *vb* **1** : to impose a penalty on for a fault or crime ⟨~ an offender⟩ **2** : to inflict a penalty for ⟨~ treason with death⟩ **3** : to inflict injury on : HURT **syn** chastise, castigate, chasten, discipline, correct — **pun·ish·able** *adj*

pun·ish·ment \\-mənt\\ *n* **1** : retributive suffering, pain, or loss : PENALTY **2** : rough treatment

pu·ni·tive \\'pyü-nət-iv\\ *adj* : inflicting, involving, or aiming at punishment

¹punk \\'pəŋk\\ *n* **1** : a young inexperienced person **2** : a petty hoodlum

²punk *adj* : very poor : INFERIOR

³punk *n* : dry crumbly wood useful for tinder; *also* : a substance made from fungi for use as tinder

pun·kin \\'pəŋ-kən\\ *var of* PUMPKIN

pun·ster \\'pən-stər\\ *n* : one who is given to punning

¹punt \\'pənt\\ *n* : a long narrow flat-bottomed boat with square ends

²punt *vb* : to propel (as a punt) with a pole

³punt *vb* : to kick a football or soccer ball dropped from the hands before it touches the ground

⁴punt *n* : the act or an instance of punting a ball

pu·ny \\'pyü-nē\\ *adj* **pu·ni·er; -est** [MF *puisné* younger, lit., born afterward, fr. *puis* afterward (fr. L *post*) + *né* born, fr. L *natus*] : slight in power, size, or importance : WEAK

pup \\'pəp\\ *n* : a young dog; *also* : one of the young of some other animals

pu·pa \\'pyü-pə\\ *n, pl* **pu·pae** \\-(ˌ)pē\\ *or* **pupas** [NL, fr. L *pupa* girl, doll] : a form of some insects (as a bee, moth, or beetle) that occurs between the larva and the adult and is usu. enclosed in a cocoon or case — **pu·pal** \\-pəl\\ *adj*

¹pu·pil \\'pyü-pəl\\ *n* **1** : a child or young person in school or in the charge of a tutor **2** : DISCIPLE

²pupil *n* : the dark central opening of the iris of the eye

pup·pet \\'pəp-ət\\ *n* [ME *popet*, fr. MF, deriv. of L *pupa*] **1** : a small figure of a person or animal moved by hand or by strings or wires **2** : DOLL **3** : one whose acts are controlled by an outside force

pup·pe·teer \\ˌpəp-ə-'tiər\\ *n* : one who manipulates puppets

pup·py \\'pəp-ē\\ *n, pl* **puppies** : a young dog

pur·blind \\'pər-ˌblīnd\\ *adj* **1** : partly blind **2** : lacking in insight : OBTUSE

¹pur·chase \\'pər-chəs\\ *vb* **pur·chased; pur·chas·ing** : to obtain by paying money or its equivalent : BUY — **pur·chas·er** *n*

²purchase *n* **1** : an act or instance of purchasing **2** : something purchased **3** : a secure hold or grasp; *also* : advantageous leverage

pur·dah \\'pərd-ə\\ *n* : seclusion of women from public observation among Muslims and some Hindus esp. in India

pure \\'pyu̇r\\ *adj* **pur·er; pur·est 1** : unmixed with any other matter: : free from taint ⟨~ gold⟩ ⟨~ water⟩ **2** : SHEER, ABSOLUTE ⟨~ nonsense⟩ **3** : ABSTRACT, THEORETICAL ⟨~ mathematics⟩ **4** : free from what vitiates, weakens, or pollutes ⟨speaks a ~ French⟩ **5** : free from moral fault : INNOCENT **6** : CHASTE, CONTINENT — **pure·ly** *adv*

pure–blood·ed \\-'bləd-əd\\ *or* **pure–blood** *adj* : of unmixed ancestry : PUREBRED — **pure·blood** *n*

pure·bred \\-'bred\\ *adj* : bred from members of a recognized breed, strain, or kind without crossbreeding over many generations — **pure·bred** \\-ˌbred\\ *n*

¹pu·ree \\pyu̇-'rā, -'rē\\ *n* [F, fr. MF, fr. fem. of *puré*, pp of *purer* to purify, strain, fr. L *purare* to purify] : a paste or thick liquid suspension usu. produced by rubbing cooked food through a sieve; *also* : a thick soup having vegetables so prepared as a base

²puree *vb* **pu·reed; pu·ree·ing** : to make a puree of

pur·ga·tion \\ˌpər-'gā-shən\\ *n* : the act or result of purging

¹pur·ga·tive \\'pər-gət-iv\\ *adj* : purging or tending to purge; *also* : being a purgative

²purgative *n* : a strong laxative : CA-
THARTIC

pur·ga·to·ry \\'pər-gə-ˌtōr-ē\ *n, pl* **-ries 1**
: an intermediate state after death for
expiatory purification **2** : a place or
state of temporary punishment —
pur·ga·tor·i·al \ˌpər-gə-'tōr-ē-əl\ *adj*

¹purge \\'pərj\ *vb* **purged; purg·ing 1** : to
cleanse or purify esp. from sin **2** : to
have or cause strong and usu. repeated emptying of the bowels **3** : to rid
(as a political party) by a purge

²purge *n* **1** : something that purges; *esp*
: PURGATIVE **2** : an act or result of
purging; *esp* : a ridding of persons regarded as treacherous or disloyal

pu·ri·fy \\'pyur-ə-ˌfī\ *vb* **-fied; -fy·ing** : to
make or become pure — **pu·ri·fi·ca-
tion** \ˌpyur-ə-fə-'kā-shən\ *n* — **pu·rif-
i·ca·to·ry** \pyu̇-'rif-i-kə-ˌtōr-ē\ *adj* —
pu·ri·fi·er \-ˌfī(-ə)r\ *n*

Pu·rim \\'pu̇r-(ˌ)im\ *n* : a Jewish holiday
celebrated in February or March in
commemoration of the deliverance of
the Jews from the massacre plotted by
Haman

pu·rine \\'pyu̇r-ˌēn\ *n* **1** : a base that is
the parent of compounds of the uric
acid group **2** : a derivative of purine;
esp : a base (as adenine or guanine)
that is a constituent of DNA or RNA

pur·ism \\'pyu̇r-ˌiz-əm\ *n* : rigid adherence to or insistence on purity or nicety esp. in use of words — **pur·ist** \-əst\
n

pu·ri·tan \\'pyu̇r-ət-ᵊn\ *n* **1** *cap* : a member of a 16th and 17th century Protes-
tant group in England and New England opposing the ceremonies and
government of the Church of England
2 : one who practices or preaches a
stricter or professedly purer moral
code than that which prevails — **pu·ri-
tan·i·cal** \ˌpyu̇r-ə-'tan-i-kəl\ *adj*

pu·ri·ty \\'pyu̇r-ət-ē\ *n* : the quality or
state of being pure

¹purl \\'pərl\ *vb* : to knit in purl stitch

²purl *n* : a stitch in knitting

³purl *n* : a gentle murmur or movement
(as of purling water)

⁴purl *vb* **1** : EDDY, SWIRL **2** : to make a
soft murmuring sound

pur·lieu \\'pərl-(y)ü\ *n* **1** : an outlying
district : SUBURB **2** *pl* : ENVIRONS

pur·loin \(ˌ)pər-'lȯin, 'pər-ˌlȯin\ *vb* : to
appropriate wrongfully : FILCH

¹pur·ple \\'pər-pəl\ *adj* **pur·pler**
\-p(ə-)lər\; **pur·plest** \-p(ə-)ləst\ **1** : of
the color purple **2** : highly rhetorical
⟨a ∼ passage⟩ **3** : PROFANE ⟨∼ lan-
guage⟩ — **pur·plish** \\'pər-p(ə-)lish\ *adj*

²purple *n* **1** : a bluish red color **2** : a
purple robe emblematic esp. of regal
rank or authority

¹pur·port \\'pər-ˌpōrt\ *n* : meaning conveyed or implied; *also* : GIST

²pur·port \(ˌ)pər-'pōrt\ *vb* : to convey
or profess outwardly as the meaning
or intention : CLAIM — **pur·port·ed·ly**
\-əd-lē\ *adv*

¹pur·pose \\'pər-pəs\ *n* **1** : an object or
result aimed at : INTENTION **2** : RESO-
LUTION, DETERMINATION — **pur·pose-
ful** \-fəl\ *adj* — **pur·pose·ful·ly** \-ē\ *adv*
— **pur·pose·less** *adj* — **pur·pose·ly** *adv*

²purpose *vb* **pur·posed; pur·pos·ing** : to
propose as an aim to oneself

purr \\'pər\ *n* : a low murmur typical of
a contented cat — **purr** *vb*

¹purse \\'pərs\ *n* **1** : a receptacle (as a
pouch) to carry money and often oth-
er small objects in **2** : RESOURCES **3** : a
sum of money offered as a prize or
present

²purse *vb* **pursed; purs·ing** : PUCKER

purs·er \\'pər-sər\ *n* : an official on a
ship who keeps accounts and attends
to the comfort of passengers

purs·lane \\'pər-slən, -ˌslān\ *n* : a
fleshy-leaved weedy trailing plant
with tiny yellow flowers that is sometimes used in salads

pur·su·ance \pər-'sü-əns\ *n* : the act of
carrying into effect

pur·su·ant to \-'sü-ənt-\ *prep* : in carrying out : ACCORDING TO ⟨*pursuant to*
your instructions⟩

pur·sue \pər-'sü\ *vb* **pur·sued; pur·su-
ing 1** : to follow in order to overtake
or overcome : CHASE **2** : to seek to
accomplish ⟨∼s his aims⟩ **3** : to proceed along ⟨∼ a course⟩ **4** : to engage
in ⟨∼ a vocation⟩ — **pur·su·er** *n*

pur·suit \pər-'süt\ *n* **1** : the act of pursuing **2** : OCCUPATION, BUSINESS

pu·ru·lent \\'pyu̇r-(y)ə-lənt\ *adj* : containing or accompanied by pus — **pu-
ru·lence** \-ləns\ *n*

pur·vey \(ˌ)pər-'vā\ *vb* **pur·veyed; pur-
vey·ing** : to supply (as provisions)
usu. as a business — **pur·vey·ance**
\-əns\ *n* — **pur·vey·or** \-ər\ *n*

pur·view \\'pər-ˌvyü\ *n* **1** : the range or limit esp. of authority, responsibility, or intention **2** : range of vision, understanding, or cognizance

pus \\'pəs\ *n* : thick yellowish white fluid matter (as in a boil) formed at a place of inflammation and infection (as an abscess) and containing germs, blood cells, and tissue debris

¹push \\'pùsh\ *vb* [ME *pusshen*, fr. OF *poulser* to beat, push, fr. L *pulsare*, fr. *pulsus*, pp. of *pellere* to drive, strike] **1** : to press against with force in order to drive or impel **2** : to thrust forward, downward, or outward **3** : to urge on : press forward **4** : to urge or press the advancement, adoption, or practice of; *esp* : to make aggressive efforts to sell **5** : to engage in the illicit sale of narcotics

²push *n* **1** : a vigorous effort : DRIVE **2** : an act of pushing : SHOVE **3** : vigorous enterprise : ENERGY

push–button *adj* : using or dependent on complex and more or less automatic mechanisms ⟨∼ warfare⟩

push button *n* : a small button or knob that when pushed operates something esp. by closing an electric circuit

push·cart \\'pùsh-ˌkärt\ *n* : a cart or barrow pushed by hand

push·er \-ər\ *n* : one that pushes; *esp* : one that pushes illegal drugs

push·over \-ˌō-vər\ *n* **1** : an opponent easy to defeat **2** : SUCKER **3** : something easily accomplished

push–up \-ˌəp\ *n* : a conditioning exercise performed in a prone position by raising and lowering the body with the straightening and bending of the arms while keeping the back straight and supporting the body on the hands and toes

pushy \\'pùsh-ē\ *adj* **push·i·er; -est** : aggressive often to an objectionable degree

pu·sil·lan·i·mous \ˌpyü-sə-'lan-ə-məs\ *adj* [LL *pusillanimis*, fr. L *pusillus* very small (dim. of *pusus* small child) + *animus* spirit] : contemptibly timid : COWARDLY — **pu·sil·la·nim·i·ty** \ˌpyü-sə-lə-'nim-ət-ē\ *n*

¹puss \\'pùs\ *n* : CAT

²puss *n* : FACE

¹pussy \\'pùs-ē\ *n, pl* **puss·ies** : CAT

²pus·sy \\'pəs-ē\ *adj* **pus·si·er; -est** : full of or resembling pus

pussy·cat \\'pùs-ē-ˌkat\ *n* : CAT

pussy·foot \\'pùs-ē-ˌfùt\ *vb* **1** : to tread or move warily or stealthily **2** : to refrain from committing oneself

pussy willow \ˌpùs-ē-\ *n* : a willow having large silky catkins

pus·tule \\'pəs-chül\ *n* : a pus-filled pimple

put \\'pùt\ *vb* **put; put·ting** **1** : to bring into a specified position : PLACE ⟨∼ the book on the table⟩ **2** : SEND, THRUST **3** : to throw with an upward pushing motion ⟨∼ the shot⟩ **4** : to bring into a specified state ⟨∼ the plan into effect⟩ **5** : SUBJECT ⟨∼ traitors to death⟩ **6** : IMPOSE **7** : to set before one for decision ⟨∼ the question⟩ **8** : EXPRESS, STATE **9** : TRANSLATE, ADAPT **10** : APPLY, ASSIGN ⟨∼ them to work⟩ **11** : to give as an estimate ⟨∼ the number at 20⟩ **12** : ATTACH, ATTRIBUTE ⟨∼ a high value on it⟩ **13** : to take a specified course ⟨the ship ∼ out to sea⟩

pu·ta·tive \\'pyüt-ət-iv\ *adj* **1** : commonly accepted **2** : INFERRED

put–down \\'pùt-ˌdaùn\ *n* : a humiliating remark : SQUELCH

put in *vb* **1** : to come in with : INTERPOSE ⟨*put in* a good word for me⟩ **2** : to spend time at some occupation or job ⟨*put in* eight hours at the office⟩

put off *vb* : POSTPONE, DELAY

¹put–on \ˌpùt-ˌón, -ˌän\ *adj* : PRETENDED, ASSUMED

²put–on \\'pùt-ˌón, -ˌän\ *n* : a deliberate act of misleading someone; *also* : PARODY, SPOOF

put·out \\'pùt-ˌaùt\ *n* : the retiring of a base runner or batter in baseball

put out \ˌpùt-'aùt\ *vb* **1** : EXTINGUISH **2** : ANNOY; *also* : INCONVENIENCE **3** : to cause to be out (as in baseball)

pu·tre·fy \\'pyü-trə-ˌfī\ *vb* **-fied; -fy·ing** : to make or become putrid : ROT — **pu·tre·fac·tion** \ˌpyü-trə-'fak-shən\ *n* — **pu·tre·fac·tive** \-tiv\ *adj*

pu·tres·cent \pyü-'tres-ᵊnt\ *adj* : becoming putrid : ROTTING — **pu·tres·cence** \-ᵊns\ *n*

pu·trid \\'pyü-trəd\ *adj* **1** : ROTTEN, DECAYED **2** : VILE, CORRUPT — **pu·trid·i·ty** \pyü-'trid-ət-ē\ *n*

putsch \\'pùch\ *n* [G] : a secretly plotted

and suddenly executed attempt to overthrow a government

putt \'pət\ *n* : a golf stroke made on the green to cause the ball to roll into the hole — **putt** *vb*

put·tee \ˌpə-'tē, 'pət-ē\ *n* [Hindi *paṭṭī* strip of cloth] **1** : a cloth strip wrapped around the lower leg **2** : a leather legging

¹put·ter \'pùt-ər\ *n* : one that puts

²putt·er \'pət-ər\ *n* **1** : a golf club used in putting **2** : one that putts

³put·ter \'pət-ər\ *vb* **1** : to move or act aimlessly or idly **2** : TINKER

put·ty \'pət-ē\ *n, pl* **putties** [F *potée*, lit., potful, fr. OF, fr. *pot*, of Gmc origin] : a doughlike cement usu. of whiting and linseed oil used esp. to fasten glass in sashes — **putty** *vb*

¹puz·zle \'pəz-əl\ *vb* **puz·zled; puz·zling** \-(ə-)liŋ\ **1** : to bewilder mentally : CONFUSE, PERPLEX **2** : to solve with difficulty or ingenuity ⟨∼ out a mystery⟩ **3** : to be in a quandary ⟨∼ over what to do⟩ **4** : to attempt a solution of a puzzle ⟨∼ over a person's words⟩ **syn** mystify, bewilder, nonplus, confound — **puz·zle·ment** *n* — **puz·zler** \-(ə-)ler\ *n*

²puzzle *n* **1** : something that puzzles **2** : a question, problem, or contrivance designed for testing ingenuity

PVC *abbr* polyvinyl chloride

pvt *abbr* private

PW *abbr* prisoner of war

PX *abbr* post exchange

pya \pē-'ä\ *n* — see *kyat* at MONEY table

pyg·my \'pig-mē\ *n, pl* **pygmies** [ME *pigmei*, fr. L *pygmaeus* of a pygmy, dwarfish, fr. Gk *pygmaios*, fr. *pygmē* fist, measure of length] **1** *cap* : any of a small people of equatorial Africa **2** : DWARF — **pygmy** *adj*

py·ja·mas \pə-'jä-məz\ *chiefly Brit var* of PAJAMAS

py·lon \'pī-ˌlän, -lən\ *n* **1** : a usu. massive gateway; *esp* : an Egyptian one flanked by flat-topped pyramids **2** : a tower that supports a long span of wire **3** : a post or tower marking a prescribed course of flight for an airplane

py·or·rhea \ˌpī-ə-'rē-ə\ *n* : an inflammation with pus of the sockets of the teeth

¹pyr·a·mid \'pir-ə-ˌmid\ *n* **1** : a massive structure with a square base and four triangular faces meeting at a point **2** : a geometrical solid having a polygon for its base and three or more triangles for its sides that meet at a point to form the top — **py·ra·mi·dal** \pə-'ram-əd-ᵊl, ˌpir-ə-'mid-\ *adj*

²pyramid *vb* **1** : to build up in the form of a pyramid : heap up **2** : to increase rapidly on a broadening base

pyre \'pī(ə)r\ *n* : a combustible heap for burning a dead body as a funeral rite

py·re·thrum \pī-'rē-thrəm\ *n* : an insecticide consisting of the dried heads of any of several Old World chrysanthemums

py·rim·i·dine \pī-'rim-ə-ˌdēn\ *n* : any of a group of bases including several (as cytosine, thymine, or uracil) that are constituents of DNA or RNA

py·rite \'pī-ˌrīt\ *n* : a mineral containing sulfur and iron that is brass-yellow in color

py·rol·y·sis \pī-'räl-ə-səs\ *n* : chemical change brought about by the action of heat

py·ro·ma·nia \ˌpī-rō-'mā-nē-ə\ *n* : an irresistible impulse to start fires — **py·ro·ma·ni·ac** \-nē-ˌak\ *n*

py·ro·tech·nics \ˌpī-rə-'tek-niks\ *n pl* **1** : a display of fireworks **2** : a spectacular display (as of oratory) — **py·ro·tech·nic** \-nik\ *also* **py·ro·tech·ni·cal** \-ni-kəl\ *adj*

py·rox·ene \pī-'räk-ˌsēn\ *n* : any of various minerals that are silicates and usu. contain aluminum, calcium, sodium, magnesium, or iron

Pyr·rhic victory \ˌpir-ik-\ *n* [*Pyrrhus*, king of Epirus who sustained heavy losses in defeating the Romans] : a victory won at excessive cost

py·thon \'pī-ˌthän, -thən\ *n* [L, monstrous serpent killed by the god Apollo, fr. Gk *Pythōn*] : a large snake (as a boa) that squeezes and suffocates its prey; *esp* : any of an Old World genus including the largest snakes living at the present time

pyx \'piks\ *n* : a small case used to carry the Eucharist to the sick

Q

¹**q** \\'kyü\ *n, pl* **q's** *or* **qs** \\'kyüz\ *often cap*
: the 17th letter of the English alphabet

²**q** *abbr, often cap* **1** quart **2** quarto **3** queen **4** query **5** question

QC *abbr* Queen's Counsel

QED *abbr* [L *quod erat demonstrandum*] which was to be demonstrated

QEF *abbr* [L *quod erat faciendum*] which was to be done

QEI *abbr* [L *quod erat inveniendum*] which was to be found out

qin·tar \kin-'tär\ *n, pl* **qin·dar·ka** \kin-'där kə\ *or* **qintar** — see *lek* at MONEY table

qi·vi·ut \\'kē-vē-ˌüt\ *n* [Esk] : the wool of the undercoat of the musk-ox

Qld *or* **Q'land** *abbr* Queensland

QM *abbr* quartermaster

QMC *abbr* quartermaster corps

QMG *abbr* quartermaster general

qq v *abbr* [L *quae vide*] which (*pl*) see

qr *abbr* quarter

¹**qt** \\'kyü-'tē\ *n, often cap Q&T* : QUIET — usu. used in the phrase *on the qt*

²**qt** *abbr* **1** quantity **2** quart

qto *abbr* quarto

qty *abbr* quantity

qu *or* **ques** *abbr* question

¹**quack** \\'kwak\ *vb* : to make the characteristic cry of a duck

²**quack** *n* : the cry of a duck

³**quack** *n* **1** : CHARLATAN **2** : a pretender to medical skill **syn** faker, impostor, mountebank — **quack** *adj* — **quack·ery** \-ə-rē\ *n* — **quack·ish** *adj*

¹**quad** \\'kwäd\ *n* : QUADRANGLE

²**quad** *n* : QUADRUPLET

³**quad** *abbr* quadrant

quad·ran·gle \\'kwäd-ˌraŋ-gəl\ *n* **1** : a flat geometrical figure having four angles and four sides **2** : a 4-sided courtyard or enclosure — **quad·ran·gu·lar** \kwä-'draŋ-gyə-lər\ *adj*

quad·rant \\'kwäd-rənt\ *n* **1** : an instrument for measuring angular elevation used esp. in astronomy and surveying **2** : one quarter of a circle : an arc of 90° **3** : any of the four quarters into which something is divided by two lines intersecting each other at right angles

quad·ra·phon·ic \ˌkwäd-rə-'fän-ik\ *adj* : of or relating to the transmission, recording, or reproduction of sound using four transmission channels

qua·drat·ic \kwä-'drat-ik\ *adj* : having or being a term in which the variable (as *x*) is squared but containing no term in which the variable is raised to a higher power than a square ⟨a ~ equation⟩ — **quadratic** *n*

qua·dren·ni·al \kwä-'dren-ē-əl\ *adj* **1** : consisting of or lasting for four years **2** : occurring every four years

qua·dren·ni·um \-ē-əm\ *n, pl* **-ni·ums** *or* **-nia** \-ē-ə\ : a period of four years

¹**quad·ri·lat·er·al** \ˌkwäd-rə-'lat-(ə-)rəl\ *n* : a polygon of four sides

²**quadrilateral** *adj* : having four sides

qua·drille \kwä-'dril, k(w)ə-\ *n* : a square dance made up of five or six figures in various rhythms

quad·ri·par·tite \ˌkwäd-rə-'pär-ˌtīt\ *adj* **1** : consisting of four parts **2** : shared by four parties or persons

quad·ri·phon·ics \-'fän-iks\ *n* : QUADRIPHONY

quad·ri·phony \\'kwäd-rə-ˌfän-ē\ *n* : quadraphonic transmission, recording, or reproduction of sound

qua·driv·i·um \kwä-'driv-ē-əm\ *n* : the four liberal arts of arithmetic, music, geometry, and astronomy in a medieval university

quad·ru·ped \\'kwäd-rə-ˌped\ *n* : an animal having four feet — **qua·dru·pe·dal** \kwä-'drü-pəd-ᵊl, ˌkwäd-rə-'ped-\ *adj*

¹**qua·dru·ple** \kwä-'drüp-əl, -'drəp-; 'kwäd-rəp-\ *vb* **qua·dru·pled; qua·dru·pling** \-(ə-)liŋ\ : to make or become four times as great or as many

²**quadruple** *adj* : FOURFOLD

qua·dru·plet \kwä-'drəp-lət, -'drüp-; 'kwäd-rəp-\ *n* **1** : one of four offspring born at one birth **2** : a group of four of a kind

¹**qua·dru·pli·cate** \kwä-'drü-pli-kət\ *adj* **1** : repeated four times **2** : FOURTH

²**qua·dru·pli·cate** \-plə-ˌkāt\ *vb* **-cat·ed; -cat·ing** **1** : QUADRUPLE **2** : to provide in quadruplicate — **qua·dru·pli·ca·tion** \-ˌdrü-plə-'kā-shən\ *n*

³**qua·dru·pli·cate** \-'drü-pli-kət\ *n* **1**

: four copies all alike ⟨typed in ∼⟩ **2** : one of four like things

quaff \'kwäf, 'kwaf\ *vb* : to drink deeply or repeatedly — **quaff** *n*

quag·mire \'kwag-ˌmī(ə)r, 'kwäg-\ *n* **1** : soft miry land that yields under the foot **2** : a difficult situation from which it is hard to escape

qua·hog \'kō-ˌhȯg, 'kwȯ-, 'kwō-, -ˌhäg\ *n* : a round thick-shelled American clam

quai \'kā\ *n* : QUAY

¹quail \'kwāl\ *n, pl* **quail** *or* **quails** [ME *quaille*, fr. MF, fr. ML *quaccula*, of imit. origin] : any of various short‑winged stout-bodied game birds (as a bobwhite) related to the domestic chicken

²quail *vb* [ME *quailen* to curdle, fr. MF *quailler*, fr. L *coagulare*, fr. *coagulum* curdling agent, fr. *cogere* to drive together] : to lose heart : COWER **syn** recoil, shrink, flinch, wince, blanch

quaint \'kwānt\ *adj* : unusual or different in character or appearance; *esp* : pleasingly old-fashioned or unfamiliar **syn** odd, queer, curious, strange — **quaint·ly** *adv* — **quaint·ness** *n*

¹quake \'kwāk\ *vb* **quaked; quak·ing 1** : to shake usu. from shock or instability **2** : to tremble usu. from cold or fear

²quake *n* : a shaking or trembling; *esp* : EARTHQUAKE

Quak·er \'kwā-kər\ *n* : FRIEND 5

quaking aspen *n* : an aspen of the U.S. and Canada that has small nearly circular leaves with flattened petioles and finely serrate margins

qual *abbr* quality

qual·i·fi·ca·tion \ˌkwäl-ə-fə-'kā-shən\ *n* **1** : LIMITATION, MODIFICATION **2** : a special skill that fits a person for some work or position

qual·i·fied \'kwäl-ə-ˌfīd\ *adj* **1** : fitted for a given purpose **2** : limited in some way

qual·i·fi·er \'kwäl-ə-ˌfī-ər\ *n* **1** : one that satisfies requirements **2** : a word or word group that limits the meaning of another word or word group

qual·i·fy \'kwäl-ə-ˌfī\ *vb* **-fied; -fy·ing 1** : to reduce from a general to a particular form : MODIFY **2** : to make less harsh **3** : to limit the meaning of (as a noun) **4** : to fit by skill or training for some purpose **5** : to give or have a

legal right to do something **6** : to demonstrate the necessary ability (as in a preliminary race) **syn** moderate, temper

qual·i·ta·tive \'kwäl-ə-ˌtāt-iv\ *adj* : of, relating to, or involving quality — **qual·i·ta·tive·ly** *adv*

¹qual·i·ty \'kwäl-ət-ē\ *n, pl* **-ties 1** : peculiar and essential character : NATURE **2** : degree of excellence **3** : high social status **4** : a distinguishing attribute

²quality *adj* : being of high quality

qualm \'kwäm\ *n* **1** : a sudden attack (as of nausea) **2** : a sudden misgiving **3** : SCRUPLE

qualm·ish \-ish\ *adj* **1** : feeling qualms : NAUSEATED **2** : overly scrupulous : SQUEAMISH **3** : of, relating to, or producing qualms

quan·da·ry \'kwän-d(ə-)rē\ *n, pl* **-ries** : a state of perplexity or doubt

quan·ti·ta·tive \'kwän-tə-ˌtāt-iv\ *adj* : of, relating to, or involving quantity — **quan·ti·ta·tive·ly** *adv*

quan·ti·ty \'kwän-tət-ē\ *n, pl* **-ties 1** : AMOUNT, NUMBER **2** : a considerable amount

quan·tize \'kwän-ˌtīz\ *vb* **quan·tized; quan·tiz·ing** : to subdivide (as energy) into small units

quan·tum \'kwänt-əm\ *n, pl* **quan·ta** \-ə\ [L, neut. of *quantus* how much] **1** : QUANTITY, AMOUNT **2** : an elemental unit of energy

quantum mechanics *n sing or pl* : a general mathematical theory dealing with the interactions of matter and radiation in terms of observable quantities only — **quantum mechanical** *adj* — **quantum mechanically** *adv*

quar·an·tine \'kwȯr-ən-ˌtēn\ *n* [It *quarantina*, lit., period of forty days, fr. MF *quarantaine*, fr. OF, fr. *quarante* forty, fr. L *quadraginta*] **1** : a period during which a ship suspected of carrying contagious disease is forbidden contact with the shore **2** : a restraint on the movements of persons or goods to prevent the spread of pests or disease **3** : a place or period of quarantine — **quarantine** *vb*

quark \'kwȯrk, 'kwärk\ *n* : a hypothetical particle that carries a fractional charge and is held to be a constituent of heavier particles (as protons and neutrons)

¹quar·rel \'kwȯr(-ə)l\ *n* **1** : a ground of dispute **2** : a verbal clash : CONFLICT — **quar·rel·some** \-səm\ *adj*

²quarrel *vb* **-reled** *or* **-relled; -rel·ing** *or* **-rel·ling** **1** : to find fault **2** : to dispute angrily : WRANGLE

¹quar·ry \'kwȯr-ē\ *n, pl* **quarries** [ME *querre* entrails of game given to the hounds, fr. MF *cuiree*] **1** : game hunted with hawks **2** : PREY

²quarry *n, pl* **quarries** [ME *quarey*, alter. of *quarrere*, fr. MF *quarriere*, fr. (assumed) OF *quarre* squared stone, fr. L *quadrum* square] : an open excavation usu. for obtaining building stone, slate, or limestone — **quarry** *vb*

¹quart \'kwȯrt\ *n* — see WEIGHT table

²quart *abbr* quarterly

¹quar·ter \'kwȯrt-ər\ *n* **1** : one of four equal parts **2** : a fourth of a dollar; *also* : a coin of this value **3** : a district of a city **4** *pl* : LODGINGS ⟨moved into new ~s⟩ **5** : MERCY, CLEMENCY ⟨gave no ~⟩ **6** : a fourth part of the moon's period

²quarter *vb* **1** : to divide into four equal parts **2** : to provide with shelter

¹quar·ter·back \-ˌbak\ *n* : a football player who calls the signals for his team

²quarterback *vb* **1** : to direct the offensive play of a football team **2** : LEAD, BOSS

quar·ter·deck \-ˌdek\ *n* : the stern area of a ship's upper deck

quarter horse *n* : a compact muscular saddle horse characterized by great endurance and by high speed for short distances

¹quar·ter·ly \'kwȯrt-ər-lē\ *adv* : at 3-month intervals

²quarterly *adj* : occurring, issued, or payable at 3-month intervals

³quarterly *n, pl* **-lies** : a periodical published four times a year

quar·ter·mas·ter \-ˌmas-tər\ *n* **1** : a petty officer who attends to a ship's helm, binnacle, and signals **2** : an army officer who provides clothing and subsistence for troops

quar·ter·staff \-ˌstaf\ *n, pl* **-staves** \-ˌstavz, -ˌstāvz\ : a long stout staff formerly used as a weapon

quar·tet *also* **quar·tette** \kwȯr-'tet\ *n* **1** : a musical composition for four instruments or voices **2** : a group of four and esp. of four musicians

quar·to \'kwȯrt-ō\ *n, pl* **quartos** **1** : the size of a piece of paper cut four from a sheet **2** : a book printed on quarto pages

quartz \'kwȯrts\ *n* : a common often transparent crystalline mineral that is a form of silica

quartz heater *n* : a portable electric heater whose heating elements are sealed in quartz-glass tubes

quartz·ite \'kwȯrt-ˌsīt\ *n* : a compact granular rock composed of quartz and derived from sandstone

qua·sar \'kwā-ˌzär, -ˌsär\ *n* : any of various distant starlike celestial objects that are powerful emitters of electromagnetic radiation (as blue light and radio waves)

quash \'kwäsh, 'kwȯsh\ *vb* **1** : to set aside by judicial action : VOID **2** : to suppress or extinguish summarily and completely : QUELL

qua·si \'kwā-ˌzī, -ˌsī; 'kwäz-ē, 'kwäs-\ *adj* : being in some sense or degree ⟨a ~ corporation⟩

quasi- *comb form* [L, as if, as it were, approximately, fr. *quam* as + *si* if] : in some sense or degree ⟨*quasi*-historical⟩

Qua·ter·na·ry \'kwät-ər-ˌner-ē, kwə-'tər-nə-rē\ *adj* : of, relating to, or being the geologic period from the end of the Tertiary to the present — **Quaternary** *n*

qua·train \'kwä-ˌtrān\ *n* : a unit of four lines of verse

qua·tre·foil \'kat-ər-ˌfȯil, 'kat-rə-\ *n* : a conventionalized representation of a flower with four petals or of a leaf with four leaflets

qua·ver \'kwā-vər\ *vb* **qua·vered; qua·ver·ing** \'kwāv-(ə-)riŋ\ **1** : TREMBLE, SHAKE **2** : TRILL **3** : to speak in tremulous tones **syn** shudder, quake, twitter, quiver, shiver — **quaver** *n*

quay \'kē, 'k(w)ā\ *n* : WHARF

Que *abbr* Quebec

quean \'kwēn\ *n* : PROSTITUTE

quea·sy \'kwē-zē\ *adj* **quea·si·er; -est** : NAUSEATED — **quea·si·ly** \-zə-lē\ *adv* — **quea·si·ness** \-zē-nəs\ *n*

queen \'kwēn\ *n* **1** : the wife or widow of a king **2** : a female monarch **3** : a woman notable for rank, power, or attractiveness **4** : the most privileged piece in the game of chess **5** : a playing card bearing the figure of a queen **6** : a fertile female of a social insect (as a bee or termite) — **queen•ly** *adj*

Queen Anne's lace \-ˈanz-\ *n* : WILD CARROT

queen consort *n, pl* **queens consort** : the wife of a reigning king

queen mother *n* : a dowager queen who is mother of the reigning sovereign

queen–size *adj* : having dimensions of approximately 60 inches by 80 inches ⟨∼ bed⟩; *also* : of a size that fits a queen-size bed

¹queer \ˈkwiər\ *adj* **1** : differing from the usual or normal : PECULIAR, STRANGE **2** : COUNTERFEIT **syn** weird, bizarre, eccentric, curious — **queer** *n* — **queer•ly** *adv* — **queer•ness** *n*

²queer *vb* : to spoil the effect of : DISRUPT ⟨∼ed our plans⟩

quell \ˈkwel\ *vb* : to put an end to by force : CRUSH ⟨∼ a riot⟩

quench \ˈkwench\ *vb* **1** : PUT OUT, EXTINGUISH **2** : SUBDUE **3** : SLAKE, SATISFY ⟨∼ed his thirst⟩ **4** : to cool (as heated steel) suddenly by immersion esp. in water or oil — **quench•able** *adj* — **quench•less** *adj*

quer•u•lous \ˈkwer-(y)ə-ləs\ *adj* **1** : constantly complaining **2** : FRETFUL, WHINING **syn** petulant, pettish, irritable, peevish, huffy — **quer•u•lous•ly** *adv* — **quer•u•lous•ness** *n*

que•ry \ˈkwi(ə)r-ē, ˈkwe(ə)r-\ *n, pl* **queries** : QUESTION — **query** *vb*

quest \ˈkwest\ *n* : SEARCH — **quest** *vb*

¹ques•tion \ˈkwes-chən\ *n* **1** : an interrogative expression : QUERY **2** : a subject for discussion or debate; *also* : a proposition to be voted on in a meeting **3** : INQUIRY **4** : DISPUTE

²question *vb* **1** : to ask questions **2** : DOUBT, DISPUTE **3** : to subject to analysis : EXAMINE **syn** ask, interrogate, quiz, query — **ques•tion•er** *n*

ques•tion•able \ˈkwes-chə-nə-bəl\ *adj* **1** : not certain or exact : DOUBTFUL **2** : not believed to be true, sound, or moral **syn** dubious, problematical, moot, debatable

question mark *n* : a punctuation mark ? used esp. at the end of a sentence to indicate a direct question

ques•tion•naire \ˌkwes-chə-ˈna(ə)r\ *n*

: a set of questions for obtaining information

quet•zal \ket-ˈsäl, -ˈsal\ *n, pl* **quetzals** *or* **quet•za•les** \-ˈsäl-ās, -ˈsal-\ **1** : a Central American bird with brilliant plumage **2** *pl* **quetzales** — see MONEY table

¹queue \ˈkyü\ *n* [F, lit., tail, fr. L *cauda, coda*] **1** : a braid of hair usu. worn hanging at the back of the head **2** : a line esp. of persons or vehicles

²queue *vb* **queued; queu•ing** *or* **queue•ing** : to line up in a queue

quib•ble \ˈkwib-əl\ *n* **1** : an evasion of or shifting from the point at issue **2** : a minor objection — **quibble** *vb*

¹quick \ˈkwik\ *adj* **1** *archaic* : LIVING **2** : RAPID, SPEEDY ⟨∼ steps⟩ **3** : prompt to understand, think, or perceive : ALERT **4** : easily aroused ⟨a ∼ temper⟩ **5** : turning or bending sharply ⟨a ∼ turn in the road⟩ **syn** fleet, fast, hasty, expeditious — **quick** *adv* — **quick•ly** *adv* — **quick•ness** *n*

²quick *n* **1** : sensitive living flesh **2** : a vital part : HEART

quick bread *n* : a bread made with a leavening agent that permits immediate baking of the dough or batter mixture

quick•en \ˈkwik-ən\ *vb* **quick•ened; quick•en•ing** \-(ə-)niŋ\ **1** : to come to life : REVIVE **2** : AROUSE, STIMULATE **3** : to increase in speed : HASTEN **4** : to show vitality (as by growing or moving) **syn** animate, enliven, liven, vivify

quick–freeze \ˈkwik-ˈfrēz\ *vb* **-froze** \-ˈfrōz\; **-fro•zen** \-ˈfrōz-ᵊn\; **-freez•ing** : to freeze (food) for preservation so rapidly that ice crystals formed are too small to rupture the cells

quick•ie \ˈkwik-ē\ *n* : something hurriedly done or made

quick•lime \ˈkwik-ˌlīm\ *n* : the first solid product obtained by calcining limestone

quick•sand \-ˌsand\ *n* : a deep mass of loose sand mixed with water

quick•sil•ver \-ˌsil-vər\ *n* : MERCURY

quick•step \-ˌstep\ *n* : a spirited march tune esp. accompanying a march in quick time

quick time *n* : a rate of marching in which 120 steps each 30 inches in length are taken in one minute

quick–wit•ted \ˈkwik-ˈwit-əd\ *adj*

: mentally alert **syn** clever, bright, smart, intelligent

quid \'kwid\ *n* : a cut or wad of something chewable ⟨a ∼ of tobacco⟩

quid pro quo \,kwid-,prō-'kwō\ *n* [NL, something for something] : something given or received for something else

qui·es·cent \kwī-'es-ᵊnt\ *adj* : being at rest : QUIET **syn** latent, dormant, potential — **qui·es·cence** \-ᵊns\ *n*

¹qui·et \'kwī-ət\ *n* : REPOSE

²quiet *adj* **1** : marked by little motion or activity : CALM **2** : GENTLE, MILD ⟨a man of ∼ disposition⟩ **3** : enjoyed in peace and relaxation ⟨a ∼ cup of tea⟩ **4** : free from noise or uproar **5** : not showy : MODEST ⟨∼ clothes⟩ **6** : SECLUDED ⟨a ∼ nook⟩ — **quiet** *adv* — **qui·et·ly** *adv* — **qui·et·ness** *n*

³quiet *vb* **1** : CALM, PACIFY **2** : to become quiet ⟨∼ down⟩

qui·etude \'kwī-ə-,t(y)üd\ *n* : QUIETNESS, REPOSE

qui·etus \kwī-'ēt-əs\ *n* [ME *quietus est*, fr. ML, he is quit, formula of discharge from obligation] **1** : final settlement (as of a debt) **2** : DEATH

quill \'kwil\ *n* **1** : a large stiff feather; *also* : the hollow tubular part of a feather **2** : one of the hollow sharp spines of a hedgehog or porcupine **3** : a pen made from a feather

¹quilt \'kwilt\ *n* : a padded bed coverlet

²quilt *vb* **1** : to fill, pad, or line like a quilt **2** : to stitch or sew in layers with padding in between **3** : to make quilts

quince \'kwins\ *n* : a hard yellow apple-like fruit; *also* : a tree related to the roses that bears this fruit

qui·nine \'kwī-,nīn\ *n* : a bitter white drug obtained from cinchona bark and used esp. in treating malaria

quin·sy \'kwin-zē\ *n* : a severe inflammation of the throat or adjacent parts with swelling and fever

quint \'kwint\ *n* : QUINTUPLET

quin·tal \'kwint-ᵊl, 'kant-\ *n* : HUNDREDWEIGHT

quin·tes·sence \kwin-'tes-ᵊns\ *n* **1** : the purest essence of something **2** : the most typical example — **quint·es·sen·tial** \,kwint-ə-'sen-chəl\ *adj*

quin·tet *also* **quin·tette** \kwin-'tet\ *n* **1** : a musical composition for five instruments or voices **2** : a group of five

and esp. of five musicians; *also* : a basketball team

¹quin·tu·ple \kwin-'t(y)üp-əl, -'təp-; 'kwint-əp-\ *adj* **1** : having five units or members **2** : being five times as great or as many — **quintuple** *n*

²quintuple *vb* **quin·tu·pled; quin·tu·pling** : to make or become five times as great or as many

quin·tu·plet \kwin-'təp-lət, -'t(y)üp-; 'kwint-əp-\ *n* **1** : a group of five of a kind **2** : one of five offspring born at one birth

¹quin·tu·pli·cate \kwin-'t(y)ü-pli-kət\ *adj* **1** : repeated five times **2** : FIFTH

²quintuplicate *n* **1** : one of five like things **2** : five copies all alike ⟨typed in ∼⟩

³quin·tu·pli·cate \-plə-,kāt\ *vb* **-cat·ed; -cat·ing 1** : QUINTUPLE **2** : to provide in quintuplicate

¹quip \'kwip\ *n* : a clever remark : GIBE

²quip *vb* **quipped; quip·ping 1** : to make quips : GIBE **2** : to jest or gibe at

quire \'kwī(ə)r\ *n* : a set of 24 or sometimes 25 sheets of paper of the same size and quality

quirk \'kwərk\ *n* : a peculiarity of action or behavior — **quirky** *adj*

quirt \'kwərt\ *n* : a riding whip with a short handle and a rawhide lash

quis·ling \'kwiz-liŋ\ *n* [Vidkun *Quisling* †1945 Norw. politician who collaborated with the Nazis] : a traitor who collaborates with the invaders of his country

quit \'kwit\ *vb* **quit** *also* **quit·ted; quit·ting 1** : CONDUCT, BEHAVE ⟨∼ themselves well⟩ **2** : to depart from : LEAVE, ABANDON **syn** acquit, comport, deport, demean — **quit·ter** *n*

quite \'kwīt\ *adv* **1** : COMPLETELY, WHOLLY **2** : to an extreme : POSITIVELY **3** : to a considerable extent : RATHER

quits \'kwits\ *adj* : even or equal with another ⟨call it ∼⟩

quit·tance \'kwit-ᵊns\ *n* : REQUITAL

¹quiv·er \'kwiv-ər\ *n* : a case for carrying arrows

²quiver *vb* **quiv·ered; quiv·er·ing** \-(ə-)riŋ\ : to shake with a slight trembling motion **syn** shiver, shudder, quaver, quake, tremble

³quiver *n* : the act or action of quivering : TREMOR

qui vive \kē-'vēv\ *n* [F *qui-vive*, fr. *qui*

vive? long live who?, challenge of a French sentry] : ALERT ⟨on the *qui vive* for prowlers⟩

quix•ot•ic \kwik-**'**sät-ik\ *adj* [fr. Don *Quixote,* hero of the novel *Don Quixote de la Mancha* by Cervantes] : foolishly impractical esp. in the pursuit of ideals

¹quiz **'**kwiz\ *n, pl* **quiz•zes 1** : an eccentric person **2** : PRACTICAL JOKE **3** : a short oral or written test

²quiz *vb* **quizzed; quiz•zing 1** : MOCK **2** : to look at inquisitively **3** : to question closely : EXAMINE **syn** ask, interrogate, query

quiz•zi•cal **'**kwiz-i-kəl\ *adj* **1** : slightly eccentric **2** : marked by bantering or teasing **3** : INQUISITIVE, QUESTIONING

quoit **'**kwāt, **'**k(w)ȯit\ *n* **1** : a flattened ring of iron or circle of rope used in a throwing game **2** *pl* : a game in which quoits are thrown at an upright pin in an attempt to ring the pin

quon•dam **'**kwän-dəm, -ˌdam\ *adj* [L, at one time, formerly, fr. *quom, cum* when] : FORMER

quo•rum **'**kwȯr-əm\ *n* : the number of members required to be present for business to be legally transacted

quot *abbr* quotation

quo•ta **'**kwōt-ə\ *n* : a proportional part esp. when assigned : SHARE

quot•able **'**kwōt-ə-bəl\ *adj* : fit for or worth quoting

quo•ta•tion \kwō-**'**tā-shən\ *n* **1** : the act or process of quoting **2** : the price currently bid or offered for something **3** : something that is quoted

quotation mark *n* : one of a pair of punctuation marks " " or ' ' used esp. to indicate the beginning and end of a quotation in which exact phraseology is directly cited

quote **'**kwōt\ *vb* **quot•ed; quot•ing** [ML *quotare* to mark the number of, number references, fr. L *quotus* of what number or quantity, fr. *quot* how many, (as) many as] **1** : to speak or write a passage from another usu. with acknowledgment; *also* : to repeat a passage in substantiation or illustration **2** : to state the market price of a commodity, stock, or bond **3** : to inform a hearer or reader that matter following is quoted — **quote** *n*

quoth \(**'**)kwōth\ *vb past* [ME, past of *quethen* to say, fr. OE *cwethan*] *archaic* : SAID — usu. used in the 1st and 3d persons with the subject following

quo•tid•i•an \kwō-**'**tid-ē-ən\ *adj* **1** : DAILY **2** : COMMONPLACE, ORDINARY

quo•tient **'**kwō-shənt\ *n* : the number obtained by the division of one number by another

qursh *n, pl* **qursh** **'**kȯrsh\ — see *riyal* at MONEY table

qv *abbr* [L *quod vide*] which see

qy *abbr* query

R

¹r **'**är\ *n, pl* **r's** *or* **rs** **'**ärz\ *often cap* : the 18th letter of the English alphabet

²r *abbr, often cap* **1** rabbi **2** radius **3** rare **4** Republican **5** rerun **6** resistance **7** right **8** river **9** roentgen **10** rook **11** run

Ra *symbol* radium

RA *abbr* **1** regular army **2** Royal Academy

¹rab•bet **'**rab-ət\ *n* : a groove in the edge or face of a board esp. to receive another piece

²rabbet *vb* : to cut a rabbet in; *also* : to join by means of a rabbet

rab•bi **'**rab-ˌī\ *n* [LL, fr. Gk *rhabbi,* fr. Heb *rabbī* my master, fr. *rabh* master + -*ī* my] **1** : MASTER, TEACHER — used

by Jews as a term of address **2** : a Jew trained and ordained for professional religious leadership — **rab•bin•ic** \rə-**'**bin-ik\ *or* **rab•bin•i•cal** \-i-kəl\ *adj*

rab•bin•ate **'**rab-ə-nət, -ˌnāt\ *n* **1** : the office of a rabbi **2** : the whole body of rabbis

rab•bit **'**rab-ət\ *n, pl* **rabbit** *or* **rabbits** : a long-eared burrowing mammal related to the hare; *also* : its pelt

rabble **'**rab-əl\ *n* **1** : MOB 2 **2** : the lowest class of people

rab•ble–rous•er **'**rab-əl-ˌraȯ-zər\ *n* : one that stirs up (as to hatred or violence) the masses of the people

ra•bid **'**rab-əd\ *adj* **1** : VIOLENT, FURIOUS **2** : being fanatical or extreme **3**

: affected with rabies — **ra·bid·ly** *adv*

ra·bies \'rā-bēz\ *n, pl* **rabies** [NL, fr. L, madness] : an acute deadly virus disease of the nervous system transmitted by the bite of an affected animal

rac·coon \ra-'kün\ *n, pl* **raccoon** *or* **raccoons** : a gray No. American chiefly tree-dwelling mammal with a bushy ringed tail and nocturnal habits; *also* : its fur

¹race \'rās\ *n* **1** : a strong current of running water; *also* : its channel **2** : an onward course (as of time or life) **3** : a contest in speed **4** : a contest for a desired end (as election to office)

²race *vb* **raced; rac·ing** **1** : to run in a race **2** : to run swiftly : RUSH **3** : to engage in a race with **4** : to drive at high speed — **rac·er** *n*

³race *n* **1** : a family, tribe, people, or nation of the same stock; *also* : MANKIND **2** : a group of individuals within a biological species able to breed together — **ra·cial** \'rā-shəl\ *adj* — **ra·cial·ly** \-ē\ *adv*

race·course \'rās-ˌkōrs\ *n* : a course for racing

race·horse \-ˌhȯrs\ *n* : a horse bred or kept for racing

ra·ceme \rā-'sēm\ *n* [L *racemus* bunch of grapes] : a flower cluster with flowers borne along a stem and blooming from the base toward the tip — **rac·e·mose** \'ras-ə-ˌmōs\ *adj*

race·track \'rās-ˌtrak\ *n* : a usu. oval course on which races are run

race·way \-ˌwā\ *n* **1** : a channel for a current of water **2** : RACECOURSE

ra·cial·ism \'rā-shə-ˌliz-əm\ *n* : RACISM — **ra·cial·ist** \-ləst\ *n* — **ra·cial·is·tic** \ˌrā-shə-'lis-tik\ *adj*

racing form *n* : an information sheet giving data about racehorses for use by bettors

rac·ism \'rās-ˌiz-əm\ *n* : a belief that some races are by nature superior to others; *also* : discrimination based on such belief — **rac·ist** \-əst\ *n*

¹rack \'rak\ *n* **1** : an instrument of torture on which a body is stretched **2** : a framework on or in which something may be placed (as for display or storage) **3** : a bar with teeth on one side to mesh with a pinion or worm gear

²rack *vb* **1** : to torture with or as if with a rack **2** : to stretch or strain by force

3 : TORMENT **4** : to place on or in a rack

¹rack·et *also* **rac·quet** \'rak-ət\ *n* [MF *raquette*, fr. Ar *rāḥah* palm of the hand] : a light bat made of netting stretched across an oval open frame and used for striking a ball

²racket *n* **1** : confused noise : DIN **2** : a fraudulent or dishonest scheme or activity

³racket *vb* : to make a racket

rack·e·teer \ˌrak-ə-'tiər\ *n* : a person who obtains money by an illegal enterprise usu. involving intimidation — **rack·e·teer·ing** *n*

rack up *vb* : SCORE

ra·con·teur \ˌrak-ˌän-'tər\ *n* : one good at telling anecdotes

racy \'rā-sē\ *adj* **rac·i·er; -est** **1** : having the quality of something in its original or most characteristic form **2** : full of zest **3** : PUNGENT, SPICY **4** : RISQUÉ, SUGGESTIVE — **rac·i·ly** \'rā-sə-lē\ *adv* — **rac·i·ness** \-sē-nəs\ *n*

rad *abbr* **1** radical **2** radio **3** radius

ra·dar \'rā-ˌdär\ *n* [*radio detecting and ranging*] : a device that emits radio waves for detecting and locating an object by the reflection of the radio waves and that may use this reflection to determine the object's direction and speed

ra·dar·scope \'rā-ˌdär-ˌskōp\ *n* : a visual display for a radar receiver

¹ra·di·al \'rād-ē-əl\ *adj* : arranged or having parts arranged like rays coming from a common center ⟨the ∼ form of a starfish⟩ — **ra·di·al·ly** \-ē\ *adv*

²radial *n* : a pneumatic tire with cords laid perpendicular to the center line

radial engine *n* : an internal-combustion engine with cylinders arranged radially like the spokes of a wheel

ra·di·ant \'rād-ē-ənt\ *adj* **1** : SHINING, GLOWING **2** : beaming with happiness **3** : transmitted by radiation **syn** brilliant, bright, luminous, lustrous — **ra·di·ance** \-əns\ *n* — **ra·di·ant·ly** *adv*

radiant energy *n* : energy transmitted as electromagnetic waves

ra·di·ate \'rād-ē-ˌāt\ *vb* **-at·ed; -at·ing** **1** : to send out rays : SHINE, GLOW **2** : to issue in rays ⟨light ∼s⟩ ⟨heat ∼s⟩ **3** : to spread around as from a center — **ra·di·a·tion** \ˌrād-ē-'ā-shən\ *n*

radiation sickness *n* : sickness that results from exposure to radiation and is commonly marked by fatigue, nausea, vomiting, loss of teeth and hair, and in more severe cases by damage to blood-forming tissue

ra·di·a·tor \'rād-ē-ˌāt-ər\ *n* : any of various devices (as a set of pipes or tubes) for transferring heat from a fluid within to an area or object outside

¹rad·i·cal \'rad-i-kəl\ *adj* [ME, fr. LL *radicalis*, fr. L *radic-, radix* root] **1** : FUNDAMENTAL, EXTREME, THOROUGHGOING **2** : of or relating to radicals in politics — **rad·i·cal·ism** \-ˌiz-əm\ *n* — **rad·i·cal·ly** \-ē\ *adv*

²radical *n* **1** : a person who favors rapid and sweeping changes in laws and methods of government **2** : a group of atoms that is replaceable by a single atom or remains unchanged during reactions **3** : a mathematical expression indicating a root by means of a radical sign; *also* : RADICAL SIGN

rad·i·cal·ize \-kə-ˌlīz\ *vb* **-ized; -iz·ing** : to make radical esp. in politics — **rad·i·cal·iza·tion** \ˌrad-i-kə-lə-'zā-shən\ *n*

radical sign *n* : the sign √‾ placed over a mathematical expression to indicate that its root is to be taken

radii pl of RADIUS

¹ra·dio \'rād-ē-ˌō\ *n, pl* **ra·di·os 1** : transmission or reception of signals using electromagnetic waves without a connecting wire **2** : a radio receiving set **3** : the radio broadcasting industry — **radio** *adj*

²radio *vb* : to communicate or send a message to by radio

ra·dio·ac·tiv·i·ty \ˌrād-ē-ō-ˌak-'tiv-ət-ē\ *n* : the property that some elements have of spontaneously emitting energetic particles by the disintegration of atomic nuclei — **ra·dio·ac·tive** \-'ak-tiv\ *adj*

radio astronomy *n* : astronomy dealing with radio waves received from outside the earth's atmosphere

ra·dio·car·bon \ˌrād-ē-ō-'kär-bən\ *n* : CARBON 14

radio frequency *n* : an electromagnetic wave frequency intermediate between audio frequency and infrared frequency used esp. in radio and television transmission

ra·dio·gen·ic \ˌrād-ē-ō-'jen-ik\ *adj* : produced by radioactivity

ra·dio·gram \'rād-ē-ō-ˌgram\ *n* **1** : RADIOGRAPH **2** : a message transmitted by radiotelegraphy

ra·dio·graph \-ˌgraf\ *n* : a photograph made by some form of radiation other than light; *esp* : an X-ray photograph — **radiograph** *vb* — **ra·dio·graph·ic** \ˌrād-ē-ō-'graf-ik\ *adj* — **ra·dio·graph·i·cal·ly** \-i-k(ə-)lē\ *adv* — **ra·di·og·ra·phy** \ˌrād-ē-'äg-rə-fē\ *n*

ra·dio·iso·tope \ˌrād-ē-ō-'ī-sə-ˌtōp\ *n* : a radioactive isotope

ra·di·ol·o·gy \ˌrād-ē-'äl-ə-jē\ *n* : the use of radiant energy (as X rays and radium radiations) in medicine — **ra·di·ol·o·gist** \-jəst\ *n*

ra·dio·man \'rād-ē-ō-ˌman\ *n* : a radio operator or technician

ra·di·om·e·ter \ˌrād-ē-'äm-ət-ər\ *n* : an instrument for measuring the intensity of radiant energy — **ra·di·om·e·try** \-ə-trē\ *n* — **ra·dio·met·ric** \ˌrād-ē-ō-'me-trik\ *adj*

ra·dio·phone \'rād-ē-ə-ˌfōn\ *n* : RADIOTELEPHONE

ra·dio·sonde \'rād-ē-ō-ˌsänd\ *n* : a small radio transmitter carried aloft (as by balloon) and used to transmit meteorological data

ra·dio·tele·graph \ˌrād-ē-ō-'tel-ə-ˌgraf\ *n* : wireless telegraphy — **ra·dio·tele·graph·ic** \-ˌtel-ə-'graf-ik\ *adj* — **ra·dio·te·leg·ra·phy** \-tə-'leg-rə-fē\ *n*

ra·dio·tele·phone \-'tel-ə-ˌfōn\ *n* : a telephone that uses radio waves wholly or partly instead of connecting wires — **ra·dio·te·le·pho·ny** \-tə-'lef-ə-nē, -'tel-ə-ˌfō-nē\ *n*

radio telescope *n* : a radio receiver-antenna combination used for observation in radio astronomy

ra·dio·ther·a·py \ˌrād-ē-ō-'ther-ə-pē\ *n* : the treatment of disease by means of X rays or radioactive substances — **ra·dio·ther·a·pist** \-pəst\ *n*

rad·ish \'rad-ish\ *n* [ME, alter. of OE *rædic*, fr. L *radic-, radix* root, radish] : a pungent fleshy root usu. eaten raw; *also* : a plant related to the mustards that produces this root

ra·di·um \'rād-ē-əm\ *n* : a strongly radioactive metallic chemical element that is used in the treatment of cancer

ra·di·us \'rād-ē-əs\ *n, pl* **ra·dii** \-ē-ˌī\

also **ra·di·us·es 1** : the one of the two bones of the human forearm that is on the thumb side; **2** : a straight line extending from the center of a circle or a sphere to the circumference or surface **3** : a circular area defined by the length of its radius **syn** range, reach, scope, compass

RADM *abbr* rear admiral

ra·don \ˈrā-ˌdän\ *n* : a heavy radioactive gaseous chemical element

RAF *abbr* Royal Air Force

raf·fia \ˈraf-ē-ə\ *n* : fiber used esp. for making baskets and hats and obtained from the stalks of the leaves of a Madagascar palm (raffia palm)

raff·ish \ˈraf-ish\ *adj* : jaunty or sporty esp. in a flashy or vulgar manner — **raff·ish·ly** *adv* — **raff·ish·ness** *n*

¹raf·fle \ˈraf-əl\ *n* : a lottery in which the prize is won by one of a number of persons buying chances

²raffle *vb* **raf·fled; raf·fling** \ˈraf-(ə-)liŋ\ : to dispose of by a raffle

¹raft \ˈraft\ *n* **1** : a number of logs or timbers fastened together to form a float **2** : a flat structure for support or transportation on water

²raft *vb* **1** : to travel or transport by raft **2** : to make into a raft

³raft *n* : a large amount or number

raf·ter \ˈraf-tər\ *n* : a usu. sloping timber of a roof

¹rag \ˈrag\ *n* : a waste piece of cloth

²rag *n* : a composition in ragtime

ra·ga \ˈräg-ə\ *n* **1** : an ancient traditional melodic pattern or mode in Indian music **2** : an improvisation based on a raga

rag·a·muf·fin \ˈrag-ə-ˌməf-ən\ *n* [*Ragamoffyn,* a demon in *Piers Plowman* (1393), attributed to William Langland] : a ragged dirty person

¹rage \ˈrāj\ *n* **1** : violent and uncontrolled anger **2** : VOGUE, FASHION

²rage *vb* **raged; rag·ing 1** : to be furiously angry : RAVE **2** : to be in violent tumult ⟨the storm *raged*⟩ **3** : to continue out of control

rag·ged \ˈrag-əd\ *adj* **1** : TORN, TATTERED; *also* : wearing tattered clothes **2** : done in an uneven way ⟨a ∼ performance⟩ — **rag·ged·ly** *adv* — **rag·ged·ness** *n*

rag·lan \ˈrag-lən\ *n* : an overcoat with sleeves (raglan sleeves) sewn in with seams slanting from neck to underarm

ra·gout \ra-ˈgü\ *n* [F *ragoût,* fr. *ragoûter* to revive the taste, fr. *re-* + *a-* to (fr. L *ad-*) + *goût* taste, fr. L *gustus*] : a highly seasoned meat stew with vegetables

rag·pick·er \ˈrag-ˌpik-ər\ *n* : one who collects rags and refuse for a livelihood

rag·time \ˈrag-ˌtīm\ *n* : rhythm in which there is more or less continuous syncopation in the melody

rag·weed \-ˌwēd\ *n* : any of several coarse weedy herbs with allergenic pollen

¹raid \ˈrād\ *n* : a sudden usu. surprise attack or invasion : FORAY

²raid *vb* : to make a raid on — **raid·er** *n*

¹rail \ˈrāl\ *n* [ME *raile,* fr. MF *reille* ruler, bar, fr. L *regula* ruler, fr. *regere* to keep straight, direct, rule] **1** : a bar extending from one support to another as a guard or barrier **2** : a bar forming a track for wheeled vehicles **3** : RAILROAD

²rail *vb* : to provide with a railing : FENCE

³rail *n, pl* **rail** *or* **rails** : any of a family of small wading birds related to the cranes and often hunted as game birds

⁴rail *vb* [ME *railen,* fr. MF *railler* to mock, fr. Old Provençal *ralhar* to babble, joke] : to complain angrily : SCOLD, REVILE — **rail·er** *n*

rail·ing \ˈrā-liŋ\ *n* : a barrier of rails

rail·lery \ˈrā-lə-rē\ *n, pl* **-ler·ies** : good-natured ridicule : BANTER

¹rail·road \ˈrāl-ˌrōd\ *n* : a permanent road with rails fixed to ties providing a track for cars; *also* : such a road and its assets constituting a property

²railroad *vb* **1** : to send by rail **2** : to work on a railroad **3** : to put through (as a law) too hastily **4** : to convict hastily or with insufficient or improper evidence — **rail·road·er** *n* — **rail·road·ing** *n*

rail·way \-ˌwā\ *n* **1** : a line of track providing a runway for wheels **2** : RAILROAD

rai·ment \ˈrā-mənt\ *n* : CLOTHING

¹rain \ˈrān\ *n* **1** : water falling in drops from the clouds **2** : a shower of objects ⟨a ∼ of bullets⟩ — **rainy** *adj*

²rain *vb* **1** : to fall as or like rain **2** : to send down rain **3** : to pour down

rain·bow \-ˌbō\ *n* : an arc or circle of colors formed by the refraction and reflection of the sun's rays in rain, spray, or mist

rainbow trout *n* : a large stout-bodied trout of western No. America that usu. has red or pink stripes with black dots along its sides

rain check *n* **1** : a ticket stub good for a later performance when the scheduled one is rained out **2** : an assurance of a deferred extension of an offer

rain·coat \ˈrān-ˌkōt\ *n* : a waterproof or water-repellent coat

rain·drop \-ˌdräp\ *n* : a drop of rain

rain·fall \-ˌfȯl\ *n* **1** : a fall of rain **2** : amount of precipitation ⟨an annual ∼ of 50 centimeters⟩

rain forest *n* : a tropical woodland that has an annual rainfall of at least 100 inches and that is marked by lofty broad-leaved evergreen trees forming a continuous canopy

rain·mak·ing \ˈrān-ˌmā-kiŋ\ *n* : the action or process of producing or attempting to produce rain by artificial means — **rain·mak·er** \-kər\ *n*

rain out *vb* : to interrupt or prevent by rain

rain·storm \ˈrān-ˌstȯrm\ *n* : a storm of or with rain

rain·wa·ter \-ˌwȯt-ər, -ˌwät-\ *n* : water fallen as rain

¹raise \ˈrāz\ *vb* **raised; rais·ing 1** : to cause or help to rise : LIFT ⟨∼ a window⟩ **2** : AWAKEN, AROUSE ⟨enough to ∼ the dead⟩ **3** : BUILD, ERECT ⟨∼ a monument⟩ **4** : PROMOTE ⟨was *raised* to captain⟩ **5** : COLLECT ⟨∼ money⟩ **6** : BREED, GROW ⟨∼ cattle⟩ ⟨∼ corn⟩; *also* : BRING UP ⟨∼ a family⟩ **7** : PROVOKE ⟨∼ a laugh⟩ **8** : to bring to notice ⟨∼ an objection⟩ **9** : INCREASE ⟨∼ prices⟩; *also* : to bet more than **10** : to make light and spongy ⟨∼ dough⟩ **11** : END ⟨∼ a siege⟩ **12** : to cause to form ⟨∼ a blister⟩ **syn** lift, hoist, boost, elevate — **rais·er** *n*

²raise *n* : an increase in amount (as of a bid or bet); *also* : an increase in pay

rai·sin \ˈrāz-ᵊn\ *n* [ME, fr. MF, grape, fr. L *racemus* cluster of grapes or berries] : a grape dried for food

rai·son d'être \ˌrā-ˌzōⁿ-ˈdetrᵊ\ *n* : reason or justification for existence

ra·ja *or* **ra·jah** \ˈräj-ə\ *n* [Hindi *rājā*, fr. Skt *rājan* king] : an Indian prince

¹rake \ˈrāk\ *n* : a long-handled garden tool having a crossbar with prongs

²rake *vb* **raked; rak·ing 1** : to gather, loosen, or smooth with or as if with a rake **2** : to sweep the length of (as a trench or ship) with gunfire

³rake *n* : inclination from either perpendicular or horizontal : SLANT, SLOPE

⁴rake *n* : a dissolute man : LIBERTINE

rake–off \ˈrāk-ˌȯf\ *n* : a percentage or cut taken

¹rak·ish \ˈrā-kish\ *adj* : DISSOLUTE — **rak·ish·ly** *adv* — **rak·ish·ness** *n*

²rakish *adj* **1** : having a smart appearance indicative of speed ⟨a ∼ sloop⟩ ⟨∼ masts⟩ **2** : JAUNTY, SPORTY — **rak·ish·ly** *adv* — **rak·ish·ness** *n*

¹ral·ly \ˈral-ē\ *vb* **ral·lied; ral·ly·ing 1** : to bring together for a common purpose; *also* : to bring back to order ⟨a leader ∼*ing* his forces⟩ **2** : to arouse to activity or from depression or weakness : REVIVE, RECOVER **3** : to come together again to renew an effort **syn** stir, rouse, awaken, waken, kindle

²rally *n, pl* **rallies 1** : an act of rallying **2** : a mass meeting to arouse enthusiasm **3** : a competitive automobile event run over public roads

³rally *vb* **ral·lied; ral·ly·ing** : BANTER

¹ram \ˈram\ *n* **1** : a male sheep **2** : BATTERING RAM

²ram *vb* **rammed; ram·ming 1** : to force or drive in or through **2** : CRAM, CROWD **3** : to strike against violently

¹ram·ble \ˈram-bəl\ *vb* **ram·bled; ram·bling** \-b(ə-)liŋ\ : to go about aimlessly : ROAM, WANDER

²ramble *n* : a leisurely excursion; *esp* : an aimless walk

ram·bler \ˈram-blər\ *n* **1** : a person who rambles **2** : a hardy climbing rose with large clusters of small flowers

ram·bunc·tious \ram-ˈbəŋk-shəs\ *adj* : UNRULY

ra·mie \ˈrā-mē, ˈram-ē\ *n* : a strong lustrous bast fiber from an Asian nettle

ram·i·fy \ˈram-ə-ˌfī\ *vb* **-fied; -fy·ing** : to branch out — **ram·i·fi·ca·tion** \ˌram-ə-fə-ˈkā-shən\ *n*

ramp \ˈramp\ *n* : a sloping passage or roadway connecting different levels

¹ram·page \ˈram-ˌpāj, (ˈ)ram-ˈpāj\ *vb*

ram·paged; ram·pag·ing : to rush about wildly

²**ram·page** \'ram-ˌpāj\ *n* : a course of violent or riotous action or behavior — **ram·pa·geous** \ram-'pā-jəs\ *adj*

ram·pan·cy \'ram-pən-sē\ *n* : the quality or state of being rampant

ram·pant \'ram-pənt\ *adj* : unchecked in growth or spread : RIFE ⟨fear was ∼ in the town⟩ — **ram·pant·ly** *adv*

ram·part \'ram-ˌpärt\ *n* **1** : a broad embankment raised as a fortification **2** : a protective barrier **3** : a wall-like ridge

¹**ram·rod** \'ram-ˌräd\ *n* **1** : a rod used to ram a charge into a muzzle-loading gun **2** : a cleaning rod for small arms **3** : BOSS, OVERSEER

²**ramrod** *vb* : to direct, supervise, and control

ram·shack·le \'ram-ˌshak-əl\ *adj* : RICKETY, TUMBLEDOWN

ran past of RUN

¹**ranch** \'ranch\ *n* [MexSp *rancho* small ranch, fr. Sp, camp, hut & Sp dial., small farm, fr. Old Spanish *ranchear* (*se*) to take up quarters, fr. MF (*se*) *ranger* to take up a position, fr. *ranger* to set in a row] **1** : an establishment for the raising and grazing of livestock (as cattle, sheep, or horses) **2** : a large farm devoted to a specialty

²**ranch** *vb* : to live or work on a ranch — **ranch·er** *n*

ranch house *n* : a one-story house typically with a low-pitched roof

ran·cho \'ran-chō, 'rän-\ *n, pl* **ranchos** : RANCH

ran·cid \'ran-səd\ *adj* **1** : having a rank smell or taste **2** : ROTTEN, SPOILED — **ran·cid·i·ty** \ran-'sid-ət-ē\ *n*

ran·cor \'raŋ-kər\ *n* : deep hatred : intense ill will **syn** antagonism, animosity, antipathy, enmity, hostility — **ran·cor·ous** *adj*

rand \'rand, 'ränd, 'ränt\ *n, pl* **rand** — see MONEY table

R & B *abbr* rhythm and blues

R & D *abbr* research and development

ran·dom \'ran-dəm\ *adj* : CHANCE, HAPHAZARD — **ran·dom·ly** *adv* — **ran·dom·ness** *n*

random–access *adj* : allowing access to stored data in any order the user desires

random–access memory \ˌran-dəm-'ak-ˌses-\ *n* : a computer memory that provides the main internal storage available to the user for programs and data

ran·dom·ize \'ran-də-ˌmīz\ *vb* **-ized; -iz-ing** : to distribute, treat, or perform in a random way — **ran·dom·iza·tion** \ˌran-də-mə-'zā-shən\ *n*

R and R *abbr* rest and recreation; rest and recuperation

rang past of RING

¹**range** \'rānj\ *n* **1** : a series of things in a row **2** : the act of ranging or roaming **3** : open land where animals (as livestock) may roam and graze **4** : a cooking stove **5** : a variation within limits **6** : the distance a weapon will shoot or is to be shot **7** : a place where shooting is practiced; *also* : a course over which missiles are tested **8** : the space or extent included, covered, or used : SCOPE **syn** reach, compass, radius, circle

²**range** *vb* **ranged; rang·ing** **1** : to set in a row or in proper order **2** : to set in place among others of the same kind **3** : to roam over or through : EXPLORE **4** : to roam at large or freely **5** : to correspond in direction or line **6** : to vary within limits **7** : to find the range of an object by instrument (as radar)

rang·er \'rān-jər\ *n* **1** : a warden who patrols forest lands **2** : a member of a body of troops who range over a region **3** : an expert in close-range fighting and raiding tactics

rangy \'rān-jē\ *adj* **rang·i·er; -est** : being long-limbed and slender — **rang·i·ness** \'rān-jē-nəs\ *n*

ra·ni *or* **ra·nee** \rä-'nē, 'rän-ˌē\ *n* : a raja's wife

¹**rank** \'raŋk\ *adj* **1** : strong and vigorous and usu. coarse in growth ⟨∼ weeds⟩ **2** : unpleasantly strong-smelling — **rank·ly** *adv* — **rank·ness** *n*

²**rank** *n* **1** : ROW **2** : a line of soldiers ranged side by side **3** *pl* : the body of enlisted men ⟨rose from the ∼s⟩ **4** : an orderly arrangement **5** : CLASS, DIVISION **6** : a grade of official standing (as in an army) **7** : position in a group **8** : superior position

³**rank** *vb* **1** : to arrange in lines or in regular formation **2** : to arrange according to classes **3** : to take or have

a relative position **4** : to rate above (as in official standing)

rank and file *n* **1** : the enlisted men of an armed force **2** : the general membership of a body as contrasted with its leaders

rank·ing \'raŋ-kiŋ\ *adj* **1** : having a high position : FOREMOST **2** : being next to the chairman in seniority

ran·kle \'raŋ-kəl\ *vb* **ran·kled; ran·kling** \-k(ə-)liŋ\ [ME *ranclen* to fester, fr. MF *rancler*, fr. OF *draoncler, raoncler*, fr. *draoncle, raoncle* festering sore, fr. (assumed) VL *dracunculus*, fr. L, dim. of *draco* serpent] : to cause anger, irritation, or bitterness

ran·sack \'ran-ˌsak\ *vb* : to search thoroughly; *esp* : to search through and rob

¹ran·som \'ran-səm\ *n* [ME *ransoun*, fr. OF *rançon*, fr. L *redemption-, redemptio* act of buying back, fr. *redimere* to buy back, redeem] **1** : something paid or demanded for the freedom of a captive **2** : the act of ransoming

²ransom *vb* : to free from captivity or punishment by paying a price — **ran·som·er** *n*

rant \'rant\ *vb* **1** : to talk loudly and wildly **2** : to scold violently — **rant·er** *n* — **rant·ing·ly** \-iŋ-lē\ *adv*

¹rap \'rap\ *n* **1** : a sharp blow **2** : a sharp rebuke **3** *slang* : responsibility for or consequences of an action

²rap *vb* **rapped; rap·ping 1** : to strike sharply : KNOCK **2** : to utter sharply **3** : to criticize sharply

³rap *vb* **rapped; rap·ping** : to talk freely and frankly — **rap** *n*

ra·pa·cious \rə-'pā-shəs\ *adj* **1** : excessively greedy or covetous **2** : living on prey **3** : RAVENOUS — **ra·pa·cious·ly** *adv* — **ra·pa·cious·ness** *n* — **ra·pac·i·ty** \-'pas-ət-ē\ *n*

¹rape \'rāp\ *n* : a European herb related to the mustards that is grown as a forage crop and for its seeds (**rapeseed** \-ˌsēd\)

²rape *vb* **raped; rap·ing** : to commit rape on : RAVISH — **rap·er** *n* — **rap·ist** \'rā-pəst\ *n*

³rape *n* **1** : a carrying away by force **2** : sexual intercourse by a man with a woman without her consent and chiefly by force or deception; *also* : unlaw-

ful sexual intercourse of any kind by force or threat

¹rap·id \'rap-əd\ *adj* [L *rapidus* seizing, sweeping, rapid, fr. *rapere* to seize, sweep away] : very fast : SWIFT **syn** fleet, quick, speedy — **ra·pid·i·ty** \rə-'pid-ət-ē\ *n* — **rap·id·ly** \'rap-əd-lē\ *adv*

²rapid *n* : a place in a stream where the current flows very fast usu. over obstructions — usu. used in pl.

rapid eye movement *n* : rapid conjugate movement of the eyes associated with REM sleep

rapid transit *n* : fast passenger transportation (as by subway) in urban areas

ra·pi·er \'rā-pē-ər\ *n* : a straight 2-edged sword with a narrow pointed blade

rap·ine \'rap-ən, -ˌīn\ *n* : PILLAGE, PLUNDER

rap·pen \'räp-ən\ *n, pl* **rappen** : the centime of Switzerland

rap·port \ra-'pōr\ *n* : RELATION; *esp* : relation characterized by harmony

rap·proche·ment \ˌrap-ˌrōsh-'mäⁿ, ra-'prōsh-ˌmäⁿ\ *n* : the establishment of or a state of having cordial relations

rap·scal·lion \rap-'skal-yən\ *n* : RASCAL, SCAMP

rapt \'rapt\ *adj* **1** : carried away with emotion **2** : ABSORBED, ENGROSSED — **rapt·ly** \'rap-(t)lē\ *adv* — **rapt·ness** \'rap(t)-nəs\ *n*

rap·ture \'rap-chər\ *n* : spiritual or emotional ecstasy — **rap·tur·ous** \-chə-rəs\ *adj*

rapture of the deep : a confused mental state caused by nitrogen forced into a diver's bloodstream from atmospheric air under pressure

ra·ra avis \ˌrar-ə-'ā-vəs\ *n* [L, rare bird] : a rare person or thing : RARITY

¹rare \'ra(ə)r\ *adj* **rar·er; rar·est 1** : not thick or dense : THIN ⟨~ air⟩ **2** : unusually fine : EXCELLENT, SPLENDID **3** : seldom met with — **rare·ly** *adv* — **rare·ness** *n* — **rar·i·ty** \'rar-ət-ē\ *n*

²rare *adj* **rar·er; rar·est** : cooked so that the inside is still red ⟨~ beef⟩

rare·bit \'ra(ə)r-bət\ *n* : WELSH RABBIT

rar·efac·tion \ˌrar-ə-'fak-shən\ *n* **1** : the action or process of rarefying **2** : the state of being rarefied **3** : a state or region of minimum pressure in a substance (as air) being traveled through by a wave formed by compression (as sound)

rar•efy *also* **rar•i•fy** \\'rar-ə-ˌfī\ *vb* **-efied; -efy•ing** : to make or become rare, thin, or less dense

rar•ing \\'rar-ən, -iŋ\ *adj* : full of enthusiasm or eagerness

ras•cal \\'ras-kəl\ *n* **1** : a mean or dishonest person **2** : a mischievous person — **ras•cal•i•ty** \ras-'kal-ət-ē\ *n* — **ras•cal•ly** \\'ras-kə-lē\ *adj*

¹**rash** \\'rash\ *adj* : having or showing little regard for consequences : too hasty in decision, action, or speech : RECKLESS **syn** daring, foolhardy, adventurous, venturesome — **rash•ly** *adv* — **rash•ness** *n*

²**rash** *n* : an eruption on the body

rash•er \\'rash-ər\ *n* : a thin slice of bacon or ham broiled or fried; *also* : a portion consisting of several such slices

¹**rasp** \\'rasp\ *vb* **1** : to rub with or as if with a rough file **2** : to grate harshly on (as one's nerves) **3** : to speak in a grating tone

²**rasp** *n* : a coarse file with cutting points instead of ridges

rasp•ber•ry \\'raz-ˌber-ē, -b(ə-)rē\ *n* **1** : an edible red or black berry produced by some brambles; *also* : such a bramble **2** : a sound of contempt made by protruding the tongue through the lips and expelling air forcibly

¹**rat** \\'rat\ *n* **1** : any of numerous scaly-tailed rodents larger than the related mice **2** : a contemptible person; *esp* : one that betrays his associates

²**rat** *vb* **rat•ted; rat•ting** **1** : to betray one's associates **2** : to hunt or catch rats

rat cheese *n* : CHEDDAR

ratch•et \\'rach-ət\ *n* : a device that consists of a bar or wheel having slanted teeth into which a pawl drops so as to allow motion in only one direction

ratchet wheel *n* : a toothed wheel held in position or turned by a pawl

¹**rate** \\'rāt\ *vb* **rat•ed; rat•ing** : to scold violently

²**rate** *n* **1** : quantity, amount, or degree measured by some standard **2** : an amount (as of payment) measured by its relation to some other amount (as

of time) **3** : a charge, payment, or price fixed according to a ratio, scale, or standard ⟨tax ~⟩ **4** : RANK, CLASS

³**rate** *vb* **rat•ed; rat•ing** **1** : CONSIDER, REGARD **2** : ESTIMATE **3** : to settle the relative rank or class of **4** : to be classed : RANK **5** : to be of consequence **6** : to have a right to : DESERVE — **rat•er** *n*

rath•er \\'rath-ər, 'räth-, 'rəth-\ *adv* [ME, fr. OE *hrathor*, compar. of *hrathe* quickly] **1** : more properly **2** : PREFERABLY **3** : more correctly speaking **4** : to the contrary : INSTEAD **5** : SOMEWHAT

raths•kel•ler \\'rät-ˌskel-ər, 'rat(h)-\ *n* [obs. G (now *ratskeller*), city-hall basement restaurant, fr. *rat* council + *keller* cellar] : a usu. basement tavern or restaurant

rat•i•fy \\'rat-ə-ˌfī\ *vb* **-fied; -fy•ing** : to approve and accept formally — **rat•i•fi•ca•tion** \ˌrat-ə-fə-'kā-shən\ *n*

rat•ing \\'rāt-iŋ\ *n* **1** : a classification according to grade : RANK **2** *Brit* : a naval enlisted man **3** : an estimate of the credit standing and business responsibility of a person or firm

ra•tio \\'rā-sh(ē-)ō\ *n, pl* **ra•tios** **1** : the quotient of two numbers or mathematical expressions **2** : the relation in number, quantity, or degree between things

ra•ti•o•ci•na•tion \ˌrat-ē-ˌōs-ᵊn-'ā-shən, ˌrash-, -ˌäs-\ *n* : exact thinking : REASONING — **ra•ti•o•ci•nate** \-'ōs-ᵊn-ˌāt, -'äs-\ *vb* — **ra•ti•o•ci•na•tive** \-'ōs-ᵊn-ˌāt-iv, -'äs-\ *adj* — **ra•ti•o•ci•na•tor** \-'ōs-ᵊn-ˌāt-ər, -'äs-\ *n*

¹**ra•tion** \\'rash-ən, 'rā-shən\ *n* **1** : a food allowance for one day **2** : FOOD, PROVISIONS, DIET — usu. used in pl. **3** : SHARE, ALLOTMENT

²**ration** *vb* **ra•tioned; ra•tion•ing** \\'rash-(ə-)niŋ, 'rāsh-\ **1** : to supply with or allot as rations **2** : to use or allot sparingly **syn** apportion, portion, prorate, parcel

¹**ra•tio•nal** \\'rash-(ə-)nəl\ *adj* **1** : having reason or understanding; *also* : SANE **2** : of or relating to reason **3** : relating to, consisting of, or being one or more rational numbers — **ra•tio•nal•ly** \-ē\ *adv*

²**rational** *n* : RATIONAL NUMBER

ra•tio•nale \ˌrash-ə-'nal\ *n* **1** : an explanation of principles controlling belief or practice **2** : an underlying reason

ra·tio·nal·ism \'rash-(ə-)nə-ˌliz-əm\ *n* : the practice of guiding one's actions and opinions solely by what seems reasonable — **ra·tio·nal·ist** \-ləst\ *n* — **rationalist** *or* **ra·tio·nal·is·tic** \ˌrash-(ə-)nə-'lis-tik\ *adj*

ra·tio·nal·i·ty \ˌrash-ə-'nal-ət-ē\ *n, pl* **-ties** : the quality or state of being rational

ra·tio·nal·ize \'rash-(ə-)nə-ˌlīz\ *vb* **-ized; -iz·ing 1** : to make (something irrational) appear rational or reasonable **2** : to provide a natural explanation of (as a myth) **3** : to justify (as one's behavior or weaknesses) esp. to oneself **4** : to find plausible but untrue reasons for conduct — **ra·tio·nal·iza·tion** \ˌrash-(ə-)nə-lə-'zā-shən\ *n*

rational number *n* : an integer or the quotient of two integers

rat·line \'rat-lən\ *n* : one of the small transverse ropes fastened to the shrouds of a ship and forming the steps of a rope ladder

rat race *n* : strenuous, tiresome, and usu. competitive activity or rush

rat·tan \ra-'tan, rə-\ *n* : an Asian climbing palm with long stems

rat·ter \'rat-ər\ *n* : a rat-catching dog or cat

¹rat·tle \'rat-ᵊl\ *vb* **rat·tled; rat·tling** \'rat-(ᵊ-)liŋ\ **1** : to make or cause to make a series of clattering sounds **2** : to move with a clattering sound **3** : to say or do in a brisk lively fashion ⟨∼ off the answers⟩ **4** : CONFUSE, UPSET ⟨∼ a witness⟩

²rattle *n* **1** : a series of clattering and knocking sounds **2** : a toy that produces a rattle when shaken **3** : a rattling organ at the end of a rattlesnake's tail made up of horny joints

rat·tler \'rat-lər\ *n* : RATTLESNAKE

rat·tle·snake \'rat-ᵊl-ˌsnāk\ *n* : any of various American venomous snakes with a rattle at the end of the tail

rat·tle·trap \'rat-ᵊl-ˌtrap\ *n* : something rickety and full of rattles; *esp* : an old car

rat·tling \'rat-liŋ\ *adj* **1** : LIVELY, BRISK **2** : FIRST-RATE, SPLENDID

rat·trap \'rat-ˌtrap\ *n* **1** : a trap for rats **2** : a dilapidated building

rat·ty \'rat-ē\ *adj* **rat·ti·er; -est 1** : in-

fested with rats **2** : of, relating to, or suggestive of rats **3** : SHABBY

rau·cous \'ro-kəs\ *adj* **1** : HARSH, HOARSE, STRIDENT **2** : boisterously disorderly — **rau·cous·ly** *adv* — **rau·cous·ness** *n*

raun·chy \'ron-chē, 'rän-\ *adj* **raun·chi·er; -est 1** : SLOVENLY, DIRTY **2** : OBSCENE, SMUTTY — **raun·chi·ness** \-chē-nəs\ *n*

rau·wol·fia \raù-'wùl-fē-ə, rò-\ *n* : a medicinal extract from the root of an Indian tree; *also* : this tree

¹rav·age \'rav-ij\ *n* [F] : an act or result of ravaging : DEVASTATION

²ravage *vb* **rav·aged; rav·ag·ing** : to lay waste : DEVASTATE — **rav·ag·er** *n*

¹rave \'rāv\ *vb* **raved; rav·ing** [ME *raven*] **1** : to talk wildly in or as if in delirium : STORM, RAGE **2** : to talk with extreme enthusiasm

²rave *n* **1** : an act or instance of raving **2** : an extravagantly favorable criticism

¹rav·el \'rav-əl\ *vb* **-eled** *or* **-elled; -el·ing** *or* **-el·ling** \-(ə-)liŋ\ **1** : UNRAVEL, UNTWIST **2** : TANGLE, CONFUSE

²ravel *n* **1** : something tangled **2** : something raveled out; *esp* : a loose thread

¹ra·ven \'rā-vən\ *n* : a large black bird related to the crow

²raven *adj* : black and glossy like a raven's feathers

rav·en·ing \'rav-(ə-)niŋ\ *adj* : GREEDY

rav·en·ous \'rav-(ə-)nəs\ *adj* **1** : RAPACIOUS, VORACIOUS **2** : eager for food : very hungry — **rav·en·ous·ly** *adv* — **rav·en·ous·ness** *n*

ra·vine \rə-'vēn\ *n* : a small narrow steep-sided valley larger than a gully and smaller than a canyon

rav·i·o·li \ˌrav-ē-'ō-lē\ *n* [It, fr. It dial., pl. of *raviolo,* lit., little turnip, dim. of *rava* turnip, fr. L *rapa*] : small cases of dough with a savory filling (as of meat or cheese)

rav·ish \'rav-ish\ *vb* **1** : to seize and take away by violence **2** : to overcome with emotion and esp. with joy or delight **3** : RAPE — **rav·ish·er** *n* — **rav·ish·ment** *n*

¹raw \'ro\ *adj* **raw·er** \'ro(-ə)r\; **raw·est** \'ro-əst\ **1** : not cooked **2** : changed little from the original form : not processed ⟨∼ materials⟩ **3** : having the skin abraded or irritated ⟨a ∼ sore⟩ **4** : not trained or experienced ⟨∼ recruits⟩ **5** : VULGAR, COARSE **6** : disagreeably cold and damp ⟨a ∼ day⟩ **7** : UNFAIR ⟨∼ deal⟩ — **raw·ness** n

²raw n : a raw place or state; *esp* : NUDITY

raw·boned \'rȯ-'bōnd\ *adj* **1** : LEAN, GAUNT **2** : having a heavy frame that seems to have little flesh

raw·hide \'rȯ-ˌhīd\ n : the untanned skin of cattle; *also* : a whip made of this

¹ray \'rā\ n : any of numerous large flat fishes that are related to the sharks and have the eyes on the upper surface and the hind end of the body slender and taillike

²ray n [ME, fr. MF *rai*, fr. L *radius* rod, ray] **1** : one of the lines of light that appear to radiate from a bright object **2** : a thin beam of radiant energy (as light) **3** : light from a beam **4** : a thin line like a beam of light **5** : an animal or plant structure resembling a ray **6** : a tiny bit : PARTICLE ⟨a ∼ of hope⟩

ray·on \'rā-ˌän\ n : a yarn, thread, or fabric made from fibers produced chemically from cellulose

raze \'rāz\ *vb* **razed; raz·ing** **1** : to destroy to the ground : DEMOLISH **2** : to scrape, cut, or shave off

ra·zor \'rā-zər\ n : a sharp cutting instrument used to shave off hair

ra·zor–backed \ˌrā-zər-'bakt\ *or* **ra·zor·back** \'rā-zər-ˌbak\ *adj* : having a sharp narrow back ⟨∼ horse⟩

razor clam n : any of numerous marine bivalve mollusks having a long narrow curved thin shell

¹razz \'raz\ n : RASPBERRY 2

²razz *vb* : RIDICULE, TEASE

Rb *symbol* rubidium

RBC *abbr* red blood cells; red blood count

RBI \ˌär-(ˌ)bē-'ī, 'rib-ē\ n, pl **RBIs** or **RBI** [*r*un *b*atted *i*n] : a run in baseball that is driven in by a batter

RC *abbr* **1** Red Cross **2** Roman Catholic

RCAF *abbr* Royal Canadian Air Force

RCMP *abbr* Royal Canadian Mounted Police

rct *abbr* recruit

rd *abbr* **1** road **2** rod **3** round

RD *abbr* rural delivery

RDA *abbr* recommended daily allowance; recommended dietary allowance

re \(')rā, (')rē\ *prep* : with regard to

Re *symbol* rhenium

re- \rē, ˌrē, 'rē\ *prefix* **1** : again : anew **2** : back : backward

reabsorb	reattain
reaccommodate	reattempt
reacquire	reauthorization
reactivate	reauthorize
reactivation	reawake
readapt	reawaken
readdress	rebaptism
readjust	rebaptize
readjustment	rebid
readmission	rebind
readmit	reboil
readmittance	rebroadcast
readopt	reburial
reaffirm	rebury
reaffirmation	recalculate
realign	recalculation
realignment	rechannel
reallocate	recharge
reallocation	recharter
reanalysis	recheck
reanalyze	rechristen
reanimate	reclean
reanimation	recoin
reannex	recolonization
reannexation	recolonize
reappear	recolor
reappearance	recomb
reapplication	recombine
reapply	recommence
reappoint	recommission
reappointment	recommit
reapportion	recompile
reapportionment	recompose
reappraisal	recompress
reappraise	recompression
rearm	recomputation
rearmament	recompute
rearouse	reconceive
rearrange	reconcentrate
rearrangement	reconception
rearrest	recondensation
reascend	recondense
reassail	recondition
reassemble	reconfirm
reassembly	reconfirmation
reassert	reconnect
reassess	reconquer
reassessment	reconquest
reassign	reconsecrate
reassignment	reconsecration
reassume	reconsult
reattach	reconsultation
reattachment	recontact
reattack	recontaminate

recontamination
recontract
reconvene
reconvert
recook
recopy
recouple
recross
recrystallize
recut
redecorate
redecoration
rededicate
rededication
redefine
redefinition
redeposit
redesign
redetermination
redetermine
redevelop
redevelopment
redigest
redip
redirect
rediscount
rediscover
rediscovery
redissolve
redistill
redistillation
redistribute
redistribution
redouble
redraft
redraw
reecho
reedit
reelect
reelection
reembodiment
reembody
reemerge
reemergence
reemphasis
reemphasize
reemploy
reemployment
reenact
reenactment
reenergize
reenlist
reenlistment
reenter
reequip
reestablish
reestablishment
reevaluate
reevaluation
reexamination
reexamine

reexchange
reexport
refashion
refasten
refight
refigure
refilm
refilter
refinance
refinish
refit
refix
refloat
refly
refold
reforge
reformulate
reformulation
refortify
refound
refreeze
refuel
refurnish
regather
regild
regive
reglue
regrade
regrind
regrowth
rehandle
rehear
reheat
rehouse
reimpose
reimposition
reincorporate
reinsert
reinsertion
reintegrate
reinterpret
reinterpretation
reintroduce
reintroduction
reinvent
reinvention
reinvest
reinvestment
reinvigorate
reinvigoration
reissue
rejudge
rekindle
reknit
relaunch
relearn
reletter
relight
reline
reload
remanufacture

remap
remarriage
remarry
remelt
remigration
remix
remold
rename
renegotiate
renegotiation
renominate
renomination
renumber
reoccupy
reopen
reorder
reorganization
reorganize
reorient
reorientation
repack
repaint
repass
repeople
rephotograph
rephrase
replant
repopulate
reprice
reprocess
republication
republish
repurchase
reradiate
reread
rerecord
resay
rescore
rescreen
reseal
reseed
resell
reset
resettle
resettlement
resew
reshipment
reshow
resow
respell

restaff
restate
restatement
restock
restraighten
restrengthen
restrike
restring
restructure
restudy
restuff
restyle
resubmit
resummon
resupply
resurface
resurvey
resynthesis
resynthesize
retaste
retell
retest
rethink
retool
retrain
retransmission
retransmit
retrial
reunification
reunify
reunite
reusable
reuse
revaluate
revaluation
revalue
reverify
revictual
revisit
rewarm
rewash
reweave
rewed
reweigh
reweld
rewind
rewire
rewrite
rezone

¹**reach** \'rēch\ *vb* **1** : to stretch out **2** : to touch or attempt to touch or seize **3** : to extend to **4** : to arrive at **5** : to communicate with **syn** gain, realize, achieve, attain — **reach•able** *adj* — **reach•er** *n*

²**reach** *n* **1** : an unbroken stretch or expanse; *esp* : a straight part of a river **2** : the act of reaching **3** : the distance

or extent of reaching or of ability to reach **4** : power to comprehend

re·act \rē-'akt\ *vb* **1** : to exert a return or counteracting influence **2** : to respond to a stimulus **3** : to act in opposition to a force or influence **4** : to turn back or revert to a former condition **5** : to undergo chemical reaction

re·ac·tant \-tənt\ *n* : a chemically reacting substance

re·ac·tion \rē-'ak-shən\ *n* **1** : a return or reciprocal action **2** : a counter tendency; *esp* : a tendency toward a former esp. outmoded political or social order or policy **3** : bodily, mental, or emotional response to a stimulus **4** : chemical change **5** : a process involving change in atomic nuclei

¹re·ac·tion·ary \rē-'ak-shə-ˌner-ē\ *adj* : relating to, marked by, or favoring esp. political reaction

²reactionary *n, pl* **-ar·ies** : a reactionary person

re·ac·tive \rē-'ak-tiv\ *adj* : reacting or tending to react

re·ac·tor \rē-'ak-tər\ *n* **1** : one that reacts **2** : a vessel for a chemical reaction **3** : a device for the controlled release of nuclear energy

¹read \'rēd\ *vb* **read** \'red\; **read·ing** \'rēd-iŋ\ **1** : to understand language by interpreting written symbols for speech sounds **2** : to utter aloud written or printed words **3** : to learn by observing ⟨~ nature's signs⟩ **4** : to discover the meaning of ⟨~ the clues⟩ **5** : to attribute (a meaning) to something ⟨~ guilt in his manner⟩ **6** : INDICATE ⟨thermometer ~s 10°⟩ **7** : to study by a course of reading ⟨~s law⟩ **8** : to consist in phrasing or meaning ⟨the two versions ~ differently⟩ — **read·abil·i·ty** \ˌrēd-ə-'bil-ət-ē\ *n* — **read·able** \'rēd-ə-bəl\ *adj* — **read·ably** \-blē\ *adv* — **read·er** *n*

²read \'red\ *adj* : informed by reading ⟨a widely ~ man⟩

read·er·ship \'rēd-ər-ˌship\ *n* : the mass or a particular group of readers

read·ing \'rēd-iŋ\ *n* **1** : something read or for reading **2** : a particular version **3** : a particular interpretation (as of a law) **4** : a particular performance (as of a musical work) **5** : an indication of a certain state of affairs; *also* : an indi-

cation of data made by an instrument ⟨thermometer ~⟩

read–only memory \ˌrēd-'ōn-lē-\ *n* : a usu. small computer memory that contains special-purpose information (as a program) which cannot be altered

read·out \'rēd-ˌaut\ *n* : the process of removing information from an automatic device (as a computer) and displaying it in an understandable form; *also* : the information removed from such a device

read out \(')rēd-'aut\ *vb* : to expel from an organization

¹ready \'red-ē\ *adj* **readi·er; -est** **1** : prepared for use or action **2** : likely to do something indicated; *also* : willingly disposed : INCLINED **3** : spontaneously prompt **4** : notably dexterous, adroit, or skilled **5** : immediately available : HANDY — **read·i·ly** \'red-ə-lē\ *adv* — **read·i·ness** \-ē-nəs\ *n*

²ready *vb* **read·ied; ready·ing** : to make ready : PREPARE

³ready *n* : the state of being ready

ready–made \ˌred-ē-'mād\ *adj* : already made up for general sale : not specially made — **ready–made** *n*

ready room *n* : a room in which pilots are briefed and await orders

re·agent \rē-'ā-jənt\ *n* : a substance that takes part in or brings about a particular chemical reaction

¹re·al \'rē(-ə)l\ *adj* [ME, real, relating to things (in law), fr. MF, fr. ML & LL; ML *realis* relating to things (in law), fr. LL, real, fr. L *res* thing, fact] **1** : actually being or existent **2** : not artificial : GENUINE — **re·al·ness** *n* — **for real 1** : in earnest **2** : GENUINE

²real *adv* : VERY

real estate *n* : property in buildings and land

real image *n* : an image formed by rays of light coming to a focus

re·al·ism \'rē-ə-ˌliz-əm\ *n* **1** : the disposition to face facts and to deal with them practically **2** : true and faithful portrayal of nature and of people in art or literature — **re·al·ist** \-ləst\ *adj or n* — **re·al·is·tic** \ˌrē-ə-'lis-tik\ *adj* — **re·al·is·ti·cal·ly** \-ti-k(ə-)lē\ *adv*

re·al·i·ty \rē-'al-ət-ē\ *n, pl* **-ties 1** : the quality or state of being real **2** : something real **3** : the totality of real things and events

re·al·ize \'rē-ə-ˌlīz\ vb **-ized; -iz·ing 1** : to make actual : ACCOMPLISH **2** : OBTAIN, GAIN ⟨~ a profit⟩ **3** : to convert into money ⟨~ assets⟩ **4** : to be aware of : UNDERSTAND — **re·al·iz·able** adj — **re·al·iza·tion** \ˌrē-ə-lə-'zā-shən\ n

re·al·ly \'rē-(ə-)lē, 'ril-ē\ adv : in truth : in fact : ACTUALLY

realm \'relm\ n **1** : KINGDOM **2** : SPHERE, DOMAIN

real number n : any of the numbers (as $-2, 3, 7/8, .25, \pi$) that are rational or irrational

re·al·po·li·tik \rā-'äl-ˌpō-li-ˌtēk\ n [G] : politics based on practical and material factors rather than on theoretical or ethical objectives

real time n : the actual time during which something takes place — **real-time** adj

re·al·ty \'rē-(ə)l-tē\ n : REAL ESTATE

¹ream \'rēm\ n [ME reme, fr. MF raime, fr. Ar rizmah, lit., bundle] : a quantity of paper that is variously 480, 500, or 516 sheets

²ream vb **1** : to enlarge or shape with a reamer **2** : to clean or clear with a reamer

ream·er \'rē-mər\ n : a tool with cutting edges that is used to enlarge or shape a hole

reap \'rēp\ vb **1** : to cut or clear with a scythe, sickle, or machine **2** : to gather by or as if by cutting : HARVEST ⟨~ a reward⟩ — **reap·er** n

¹rear \'riər\ vb **1** : to erect by building **2** : to set or raise upright **3** : to breed and raise for use or market ⟨~ livestock⟩ **4** : BRING UP, FOSTER **5** : to lift or rise up; esp : to rise on the hind legs

²rear n **1** : the unit (as of an army) or area farthest from the enemy **2** : BACK; also : the position at the back of something

³rear adj : being at the back

rear admiral n : a commissioned officer in the navy or coast guard ranking next below a vice admiral

¹rear·ward \'riər-wərd\ adj **1** : being at or toward the rear **2** : directed toward the rear

²rear·ward also **rear·wards** \-wərdz\ adv : at or toward the rear

¹rea·son \'rēz-ᵊn\ n [ME resoun, fr. OF raison, fr. L ration-, ratio reason, computation] **1** : a statement offered in explanation or justification **2** : GROUND, CAUSE **3** : the power to think : INTELLECT **4** : a sane or sound mind **5** : due exercise of the faculty of logical thought

²reason vb **rea·soned; rea·son·ing** \'rēz-(ᵊ-)niŋ\ **1** : to talk with another to cause a change of mind **2** : to use the faculty of reason : THINK **3** : to discover or formulate by the use of reason — **rea·son·er** n — **rea·son·ing** n

rea·son·able \'rēz-(ᵊ-)nə-bəl\ adj **1** : being within the bounds of reason : not extreme : MODERATE, FAIR **2** : INEXPENSIVE **3** : able to reason : RATIONAL — **rea·son·able·ness** n — **rea·son·ably** \-blē\ adv

re·as·sure \ˌrē-ə-'shùr\ vb **1** : to assure again **2** : to restore confidence to : free from fear — **re·as·sur·ance** \-'shùr-əns\ n — **re·as·sur·ing·ly** \-'shùr-iŋ-lē\ adv

¹re·bate \'rē-ˌbāt\ vb **re·bat·ed; re·bat·ing** : to make or give a rebate

²re·bate n : a return of part of a payment **syn** deduction, abatement, discount

¹reb·el \'reb-əl\ adj [ME, fr. OF rebelle, fr. L rebellis, fr. re- + bellum war, fr. OL duellum] : of or relating to rebels

²rebel n : one that rebels against authority

³re·bel \ri-'bel\ vb **re·belled; re·bel·ling 1** : to resist the authority of one's government **2** : to act in or show disobedience **3** : to feel or exhibit anger or revulsion

re·bel·lion \ri-'bel-yən\ n : resistance to authority; esp : defiance against a government through uprising or revolt

re·bel·lious \-yəs\ adj **1** : given to or engaged in rebellion **2** : inclined to resist authority — **re·bel·lious·ly** adv — **re·bel·lious·ness** n

re·birth \'rē-'bərth\ n **1** : a new or 2d birth **2** : RENAISSANCE, REVIVAL

re·born \-'bȯrn\ adj : born again : REGENERATED, REVIVED

¹re·bound \'rē-'baùnd, ri-\ vb **1** : to spring back on or as if on striking another body **2** : to recover from a setback or frustration

²re·bound \'rē-ˌbaùnd\ n **1** : the action of rebounding **2** : a rebounding ball **3**

: immediate spontaneous reaction to setback or frustration

re·buff \ri-'bəf\ *vb* : to reject or criticize sharply : SNUB — **rebuff** *n*

re·build \(')rē-'bild\ *vb* -**built** \-'bilt\; -**build·ing** **1** : REPAIR, RECONSTRUCT; *also* : REMODEL **2** : to build again

¹**re·buke** \ri-'byük\ *vb* **re·buked; re·buk·ing** : to reprimand sharply : REPROVE

²**rebuke** *n* : a sharp reprimand

re·bus \'rē-bəs\ *n* [L, by things, abl. pl. of *res* thing] : a representation of syllables or words by means of pictures; *also* : a riddle composed of such pictures

re·but \ri-'bət\ *vb* **re·but·ted; re·but·ting** : to refute esp. formally (as in debate) by evidence and arguments **syn** disprove, controvert, confute — **re·but·ter** *n*

re·but·tal \ri-'bət-ᵊl\ *n* : the act of rebutting

rec *abbr* **1** receipt **2** record; recording **3** recreation

re·cal·ci·trant \ri-'kal-sə-trənt\ *adj* [LL *recalcitrant-, recalcitrans,* prp. of *recalcitrare* to be stubbornly disobedient, fr. L, to kick back, fr. *re-* back, again + *calcitrare* to kick, fr. *calc-, calx* heel] **1** : stubbornly resisting authority **2** : resistant to handling or treatment **syn** refractory, headstrong, willful, unruly, ungovernable — **re·cal·ci·trance** \-trəns\ *n*

¹**re·call** \ri-'kȯl\ *vb* **1** : to call back **2** : REMEMBER, RECOLLECT **3** : REVOKE, ANNUL

²**re·call** \ri-'kȯl, 'rē-ˌkȯl\ *n* **1** : a summons to return **2** : the procedure of removing an official by popular vote **3** : remembrance of things learned or experienced **4** : the act of revoking

re·cant \ri-'kant\ *vb* : to take back (something one has said) publicly : make an open confession of error — **re·can·ta·tion** \ˌrē-ˌkan-'tā-shən\ *n*

¹**re·cap** \'rē-ˌkap, ri-'kap\ *vb* **re·capped; re·cap·ping** : RECAPITULATE — **re·cap** \'rē-ˌkap\ *n*

²**re·cap** \'rē-ˌkap\ *vb* **re·capped; re·cap·ping** : RETREAD — **re·cap** \'rē-ˌkap\ *n*

re·ca·pit·u·late \ˌrē-kə-'pich-ə-ˌlāt\ *vb* -**lat·ed; -lat·ing** : to restate briefly : SUMMARIZE — **re·ca·pit·u·la·tion** \-ˌpich-ə-'lā-shən\ *n*

re·cap·ture \(')rē-'kap-chər\ *vb* **1** : to

capture again **2** : to experience again ⟨~ happy times⟩

re·cast \(')rē-'kast\ *vb* **1** : to cast again **2** : REVISE, REMODEL ⟨~ a sentence⟩

recd *abbr* received

re·cede \ri-'sēd\ *vb* **re·ced·ed; re·ced·ing** **1** : to move back or away : WITHDRAW **2** : to slant backward **3** : DIMINISH, CONTRACT

¹**re·ceipt** \ri-'sēt\ *n* **1** : RECIPE **2** : the act of receiving **3** : something received — usu. used in pl. **4** : a written acknowledgment of something received

²**receipt** *vb* **1** : to give a receipt for **2** : to mark as paid

re·ceiv·able \ri-'sē-və-bəl\ *adj* **1** : capable of being received; *esp* : acceptable as legal ⟨~ certificates⟩ **2** : subject to call for payment ⟨notes ~⟩

re·ceive \ri-'sēv\ *vb* **re·ceived; re·ceiv·ing** **1** : to take in or accept (as something sent or paid) : come into possession of : GET **2** : CONTAIN, HOLD **3** : to permit to enter : GREET, WELCOME **4** : to be at home to visitors **5** : to accept as true or authoritative **6** : to be the subject of : UNDERGO, EXPERIENCE ⟨~ a shock⟩ **7** : to change incoming radio waves into sounds or pictures

re·ceiv·er \ri-'sē-vər\ *n* **1** : one that receives **2** : a person legally appointed to receive and have charge of property or money involved in a lawsuit **3** : a device for converting electromagnetic waves or signals into audio or visual form ⟨telephone ~⟩

re·ceiv·er·ship \-ˌship\ *n* **1** : the office or function of a receiver **2** : the condition of being in the hands of a receiver

re·cen·cy \'rēs-ᵊn-sē\ *n* : RECENTNESS

re·cent \'rēs-ᵊnt\ *adj* **1** : of the present time or time just past ⟨~ history⟩ **2** : lately made or used : NEW, FRESH **3** *cap* : of, relating to, or being the present geologic epoch — **re·cent·ly** *adv* — **re·cent·ness** *n*

re·cep·ta·cle \ri-'sep-ti-kəl\ *n* **1** : something used to receive and hold something else : CONTAINER **2** : the enlarged end of a flower stalk upon which the parts of the flower grow **3** : an electrical fitting containing the live parts of a circuit

re·cep·tion \ri-'sep-shən\ *n* **1** : the act of receiving **2** : a social gathering at which guests are formally welcomed

re·cep·tion·ist \-sh(ə-)nəst\ *n* : one employed to greet callers

re·cep·tive \ri-'sep-tiv\ *adj* : able or inclined to receive; *esp* : open and responsive to ideas, impressions, or suggestions — **re·cep·tive·ly** *adv* — **re·cep·tive·ness** *n* — **re·cep·tiv·i·ty** \ˌrē-ˌsep-'tiv-ət-ē\ *n*

re·cep·tor \ri-'sep-tər\ *n* **1** : one that receives; *esp* : SENSE ORGAN **2** : a molecule in the outer cell membrane or in the cell interior that has an affinity for a specific chemical group, molecule, or virus

¹re·cess \'rē-ˌses, ri-'ses\ *n* **1** : a secret or secluded place **2** : an indentation in a line or surface (as an alcove in a room) **3** : a suspension of business or procedure for rest or relaxation

²recess *vb* **1** : to put into a recess **2** : to make a recess in **3** : to interrupt for a recess **4** : to take a recess

re·ces·sion \ri-'sesh-ən\ *n* **1** : the act of receding : WITHDRAWAL **2** : a departing procession (as at the end of a church service) **3** : a period of reduced economic activity

re·ces·sion·al \-(ə-)nəl\ *n* **1** : a hymn or musical piece at the conclusion of a service or program **2** : RECESSION 2

¹re·ces·sive \ri-'ses-iv\ *adj* **1** : tending to go back : RECEDING **2** : producing or being a bodily characteristic that is masked or not expressed when a contrasting dominant gene or trait is present ⟨∼ genes⟩

²recessive *n* **1** : a recessive characteristic or gene **2** : an individual that has one or more recessive characteristics

re·cher·ché \rə-ˌsher-'shā, -'she(ə)r-ˌshā\ *adj* [F] **1** : CHOICE, RARE **2** : excessively refined

re·cid·i·vism \ri-'sid-ə-ˌviz-əm\ *n* : a tendency to relapse into a previous condition; *esp* : relapse into criminal behavior — **re·cid·i·vist** \-vəst\ *n*

recip *abbr* reciprocal; reciprocity

rec·i·pe \'res-ə-(ˌ)pē\ *n* [L, take, imperative of *recipere* to receive, fr. *re-* back + *capere* to take] **1** : a set of instructions for making something (as a food dish) from various ingredients **2** : a method of procedure : FORMULA

re·cip·i·ent \ri-'sip-ē-ənt\ *n* : one that receives

¹re·cip·ro·cal \ri-'sip-rə-kəl\ *adj* **1** : inversely related **2** : MUTUAL, JOINT, SHARED **3** : so related to each other that one completes the other or is equivalent to the other **syn** correspondent, complementary — **re·cip·ro·cal·ly** \-k(ə-)lē\ *adv*

²reciprocal *n* **1** : something in a reciprocal relationship to another **2** : one of a pair of numbers (as ²⁄₃, ³⁄₂) whose product is one

re·cip·ro·cate \-ˌkāt\ *vb* **-cat·ed; -cat·ing 1** : to move backward and forward alternately ⟨a *reciprocating* piston⟩ **2** : to give and take mutually **3** : to make a return for something done or given — **re·cip·ro·ca·tion** \-ˌsip-rə-'kā-shən\ *n*

rec·i·proc·i·ty \ˌres-ə-'präs-ət-ē\ *n, pl* **-ties 1** : the quality or state of being reciprocal **2** : mutual exchange of privileges (as trade advantages between countries)

re·cit·al \ri-'sīt-ᵊl\ *n* **1** : an act or instance of reciting : ACCOUNT **2** : a public reading or recitation ⟨a poetry ∼⟩ **3** : a concert given by a musician, dancer, or dance troupe **4** : a public exhibition of skill given by music or dance pupils — **re·cit·al·ist** \-ᵊl-əst\ *n*

rec·i·ta·tion \ˌres-ə-'tā-shən\ *n* **1** : RECITING, RECITAL **2** : delivery before an audience of something memorized **3** : a classroom exercise in which pupils answer questions on a lesson they have studied

re·cite \ri-'sīt\ *vb* **re·cit·ed; re·cit·ing 1** : to repeat verbatim (as something memorized) **2** : to recount in some detail : RELATE **3** : to reply to a teacher's questions on a lesson — **re·cit·er** *n*

reck·less \'rek-ləs\ *adj* : lacking caution : RASH **syn** hasty, brash, hotheaded, thoughtless — **reck·less·ly** *adv* — **reck·less·ness** *n*

reck·on \'rek-ən\ *vb* **reck·oned; reck·on·ing** \-(ə-)niŋ\ **1** : COUNT, CALCULATE, COMPUTE **2** : CONSIDER, REGARD **3** *chiefly dial* : THINK, SUPPOSE, GUESS

reck·on·ing \-iŋ\ *n* **1** : an act or instance of reckoning **2** : a settling of accounts ⟨day of ∼⟩

re·claim \ri-'klām\ *vb* **1** : to recall from wrong conduct : REFORM **2** : to put into a desired condition (as by labor or discipline) ⟨∼ marshy land⟩ **3** : to obtain from a waste product or by-product **4** : to demand or obtain the return of **syn** save, redeem, rescue — **re·claim·able** *adj* — **rec·la·ma·tion** \ˌrek-lə-ˈmā-shən\ *n*

re·cline \ri-ˈklīn\ *vb* **re·clined; re·clin·ing 1** : to lean or incline backward **2** : to lie down : REST

re·clin·er \ri-ˈklī-nər\ *n* : a chair with an adjustable back and footrest

rec·luse \ˈrek-ˌlüs, ri-ˈklüs\ *n* : a person who lives in seclusion or leads a solitary life : HERMIT

rec·og·ni·tion \ˌrek-əg-ˈnish-ən\ *n* **1** : the act of recognizing : the state of being recognized : ACKNOWLEDGMENT **2** : special notice or attention

re·cog·ni·zance \ri-ˈkä(g)-nə-zəns\ *n* : a promise recorded before a court or magistrate to do something (as to appear in court or to keep the peace) usu. under penalty of a money forfeiture

rec·og·nize \ˈrek-əg-ˌnīz\ *vb* **-nized; -niz·ing 1** : to acknowledge (as a speaker in a meeting) as one entitled to be heard at the time **2** : to acknowledge the existence or the independence of (a country or government) **3** : to take notice of **4** : to acknowledge with appreciation **5** : to acknowledge acquaintance with **6** : to identify as previously known **7** : to perceive clearly : REALIZE — **rec·og·niz·able** \ˈrek-əg-ˌnī-zə-bəl\ *adj* — **rec·og·niz·ably** \-blē\ *adv*

¹**re·coil** \ri-ˈkȯil\ *vb* **1** : to draw back : RETREAT **2** : to spring back to or as if to a starting point **syn** shrink, flinch, wince, quail, blanch

²**re·coil** \ˈrē-ˌkȯil, ri-ˈkȯil\ *n* : the action of recoiling (as by a gun or spring)

re·coil·less \-ˌkȯil-ləs, -ˈkȯil-\ *adj* : venting expanding propellant gas before recoil is produced ⟨~ gun⟩

rec·ol·lect \ˌrek-ə-ˈlekt\ *vb* : to recall to mind : REMEMBER **syn** recall, remind, reminisce, bethink

rec·ol·lec·tion \ˌrek-ə-ˈlek-shən\ *n* **1** : the act or power of recollecting **2** : something recollected

re·com·bi·nant DNA \(ˈ)rē-ˈkäm-bə-nənt-\ *n* : DNA prepared in the laboratory by breaking up and splicing together DNA from several different species of organisms

rec·om·mend \ˌrek-ə-ˈmend\ *vb* **1** : to

present as deserving of acceptance or trial **2** : to give in charge : COMMIT **3** : to cause to receive favorable attention **4** : ADVISE, COUNSEL — **rec·om·mend·able** \-ˈmen-də-bəl\ *adj*

rec·om·men·da·tion \ˌrek-ə-mən-ˈdā-shən\ *n* **1** : the act of recommending **2** : a thing or a course of action recommended **3** : something that recommends

¹**rec·om·pense** \ˈrek-əm-ˌpens\ *vb* **-pensed; -pens·ing 1** : to give compensation to : pay for **2** : to return in kind : REQUITE **syn** reimburse, indemnify, repay, compensate

²**recompense** *n* : COMPENSATION

rec·on·cile \ˈrek-ən-ˌsīl\ *vb* **-ciled; -cil·ing 1** : to cause to be friendly or harmonious again **2** : ADJUST, SETTLE ⟨~ differences⟩ **3** : to bring to submission or acceptance **syn** conform, accommodate, harmonize, coordinate — **rec·on·cil·able** *adj* — **rec·on·cile·ment** *n* — **rec·on·cil·er** *n* — **rec·on·cil·i·a·tion** \ˌrek-ən-ˌsil-ē-ˈā-shən\ *n*

re·con·dite \ˈrek-ən-ˌdīt\ *adj* **1** : hard to understand : PROFOUND, ABSTRUSE **2** : little known : OBSCURE

re·con·nais·sance \ri-ˈkän-ə-zəns, -səns\ *n* [F, lit., recognition] : a preliminary survey of an area; *esp* : an exploratory military survey of enemy territory

re·con·noi·ter *or* **re·con·noi·tre** \ˌrē-kə-ˈnȯit-ər, ˌrek-ə-\ *vb* **-noi·tered** *or* **-noi·tred; -noi·ter·ing** *or* **-noi·tring** : to make a reconnaissance of : engage in reconnaissance

re·con·sid·er \ˌrē-kən-ˈsid-ər\ *vb* : to consider again with a view to changing or reversing; *esp* : to take up again in a meeting — **re·con·sid·er·a·tion** \-ˌsid-ə-ˈrā-shən\ *n*

re·con·sti·tute \ˈrē-ˈkän-stə-ˌt(y)üt\ *vb* : to restore to a former condition by adding water ⟨~ powdered milk⟩

re·con·struct \ˌrē-kən-ˈstrəkt\ *vb* : to construct again : REBUILD

re·con·struc·tion \ˌrē-kən-ˈstrək-shən\ *n* **1** : the action of reconstructing : the state of being reconstructed **2** *often cap* : the reorganization and reestablishment of the seceded states in the Union after the American Civil War **3** : something reconstructed

¹**re·cord** \ri-ˈkȯrd\ *vb* **1** : to set down (as proceedings in a meeting) in writing **2**

: to register permanently **3** : INDICATE, READ **4** : to give evidence of **5** : to cause (as sound or visual images) to be registered (as on magnetic tape) in a form that permits reproduction

²rec·ord \'rek-ərd\ *n* **1** : the act of recording **2** : a written account of proceedings **3** : known facts about a person **4** : an attested top performance **5** : something on which sound or visual images have been recorded

re·cord·er \ri-'kord-ər\ *n* **1** : a judge in some city courts **2** : one who records transactions officially **3** : a recording device **4** : a wind instrument with a whistle mouthpiece and eight finger-holes

re·cord·ing \ri-'kord-iŋ\ *n* : RECORD 5

re·cord·ist \ri-'kord-əst\ *n* : one who records sound esp. on film

¹re·count \ri-'kaunt\ *vb* : to relate in detail : TELL **syn** recite, rehearse, narrate, describe, state, report

²re·count \'rē-'kaunt\ *vb* : to count again

³re·count \'rē-,kaunt, (')rē-'kaunt\ *n* : a second or fresh count

re·coup \ri-'küp\ *vb* : to get an equivalent or compensation for : make up for something lost **syn** retrieve, regain, recover

re·course \'rē-,kōrs, ri-'kōrs\ *n* **1** : a turning to someone or something for assistance or protection **2** : a source of aid : RESORT

re·cov·er \ri-'kəv-ər\ *vb* **-ered; -er·ing** \-(ə-)riŋ\ **1** : to get back again : REGAIN, RETRIEVE **2** : to regain normal health, poise, or status **3** : to make up for : RECOUP ⟨∼ed all his losses⟩ **4** : RECLAIM ⟨∼ land from the sea⟩ **5** : to obtain a legal judgment in one's favor — **re·cov·er·able** *adj* — **re·cov·ery** \-'kəv-(ə-)rē\ *n*

re·cov·er \'rē-'kəv-ər\ *vb* : to cover again

¹rec·re·ant \'rek-rē-ənt\ *adj* [ME, fr. MF, fr. prp. of *recroire* to renounce one's cause in a trial by battle, fr. *re-* back + *croire* to believe, fr. L *credere*] **1** : COWARDLY **2** : UNFAITHFUL

²recreant *n* **1** : COWARD **2** : DESERTER

rec·re·ate \'rek-rē-,āt\ *vb* **-at·ed; -at·ing** **1** : to give new life or freshness to **2** : to take recreation — **rec·re·ative** \-,āt-iv\ *adj*

re·cre·ate \,rē-krē-'āt\ *vb* : to create

again — **re·cre·ation** \-'ā-shən\ *n* — **re·cre·ative** \-'āt-iv\ *adj*

rec·re·ation \,rek-rē-'ā-shən\ *n* : a refreshing of strength or spirits after work; *also* : a means of refreshment **syn** diversion, entertainment, amusement — **rec·re·ation·al** \-sh(ə-)nəl\ *adj*

recreational vehicle *n* : a vehicle designed for recreational use (as camping)

re·crim·i·nate \ri-'krim-ə-,nāt\ *vb* **-nat·ed; -nat·ing** : to make an accusation against an accuser — **re·crim·i·na·tion** \-,krim-ə-'nā-shən\ *n* — **re·crim·i·na·to·ry** \-'krim-(ə-)nə-,tōr-ē\ *adj*

re·cru·des·cence \,rē-krü-'des-°ns\ *n* : a new outbreak esp. of something unhealthful or dangerous after a period of abatement or inactivity — **re·cru·desce** \,rē-krü-'des\ *vb*

¹re·cruit \ri-'krüt\ *vb* **1** : to form or strengthen with new members ⟨∼ an army⟩ **2** : to secure the services of ⟨∼ engineers⟩ **3** : to restore or increase in health or vigor ⟨resting to ∼ his strength⟩ — **re·cruit·er** *n* — **re·cruit·ment** *n*

²recruit *n* [F *recrute, recrue* fresh growth, new levy of soldiers, fr. MF, fr. *recroistre* to grow up again, fr. L *recrescere*] : a newcomer to an activity or field; *esp* : a newly enlisted member of the armed forces

rec sec *abbr* recording secretary

rect *abbr* **1** receipt **2** rectangle; rectangular **3** rectified

rec·tal \'rek-t°l\ *adj* : of or relating to the rectum — **rec·tal·ly** \-ē\ *adv*

rect·an·gle \'rek-,taŋ-gəl\ *n* : a 4-sided figure with four right angles; *esp* : one with adjacent sides of unequal length — **rect·an·gu·lar** \rek-'taŋ-gyə-lər\ *adj*

rec·ti·fi·er \'rek-tə-,fī(-ə)r\ *n* : one that rectifies; *esp* : a device for converting alternating current into direct current

rec·ti·fy \'rek-tə-,fī\ *vb* **-fied; -fy·ing** **1** : to make or set right : CORRECT **2** : to convert alternating current into direct current **syn** emend, amend, mend, right — **rec·ti·fi·ca·tion** \,rek-tə-fə-'kā-shən\ *n*

rec·ti·lin·ear \,rek-tə-'lin-ē-ər\ *adj* **1** : moving in a straight line ⟨∼ motion⟩ **2** : characterized by straight lines

rec·ti·tude \'rek-tə-,t(y)üd\ *n* **1** : moral integrity **2** : correctness of procedure

syn virtue, goodness, morality, probity

rec·to \\'rek-tō\\ *n, pl* **rectos** : a right-hand page

rec·tor \\'rek-tər\\ *n* **1** : a clergyman in charge of a parish **2** : the head of a university or school — **rec·to·ri·al** \\rek-'tōr-ē-əl\\ *adj*

rec·to·ry \\'rek-t(ə-)rē\\ *n, pl* **-ries** : the residence of a rector or a parish priest

rec·tum \\'rek-təm\\ *n, pl* **rectums** *or* **rec·ta** \\-tə\\ [NL, fr. *rectum intestinum,* lit., straight intestine] : the last part of the intestine joining colon and anus

re·cum·bent \\ri-'kəm-bənt\\ *adj* : lying down : RECLINING

re·cu·per·ate \\ri-'k(y)ü-pə-,rāt\\ *vb* **-at·ed; -at·ing** : to get back (as health, strength, or losses) : RECOVER — **re·cu·per·a·tion** \\-,k(y)ü-pə-'rā-shən\\ *n* — **re·cu·per·a·tive** \\-'k(y)ü-pə-,rāt-iv\\ *adj*

re·cur \\ri-'kər\\ *vb* **re·curred; re·cur·ring** **1** : to go or come back in thought or discussion **2** : to occur or appear again esp. after an interval — **re·cur·rence** \\-'kər-əns\\ *n* — **re·cur·rent** \\-ənt\\ *adj*

re·cy·cle \\rē-'sī-kəl\\ *vb* **1** : to pass again through a cycle of changes or treatment **2** : to process (as liquid body waste, glass, or cans) in order to regain materials for human use — **recycle** *n*

¹red \\'red\\ *adj* **red·der; red·dest** **1** : of the color red **2** : endorsing radical social or political change esp. by force **3** *often cap* : of or relating to the U.S.S.R. or its allies — **red·ly** *adv* — **red·ness** *n*

²red *n* **1** : the color of blood or of the ruby **2** : a revolutionary in politics **3** *cap* : COMMUNIST **4** : the condition of showing a loss ⟨in the ~⟩

re·dact \\ri-'dakt\\ *vb* **1** : to put in writing : FRAME **2** : EDIT — **re·dac·tor** \\-'dak-tər\\ *n*

re·dac·tion \\-'dak-shən\\ *n* **1** : an act or instance of redacting **2** : EDITION

red alga *n* : any of several reddish usu. marine algae

red blood cell *n* : one of the hemoglobin-containing cells that carry oxygen from the lungs to the tissues and are responsible for the red color of vertebrate blood

red·breast \\'red-,brest\\ *n* : ROBIN

red·cap \\'red-,kap\\ *n* : a baggage porter (as at a railroad station)

red–carpet *adj* : marked by ceremonial courtesy

red cedar *n* : an American juniper with fragrant close-grained red wood; *also* : its wood

red clover *n* : a Eurasian clover with globe-shaped heads of reddish flowers widely cultivated for hay and forage

red·coat \\'red-,kōt\\ *n* : a British soldier esp. during the Revolutionary War

red·den \\'red-ᵊn\\ *vb* : to make or become red or reddish : FLUSH, BLUSH

red·dish \\'red-ish\\ *adj* : tinged with red — **red·dish·ness** *n*

re·deem \\ri-'dēm\\ *vb* [ME *redemen,* modif. of MF *redimer,* fr. L *redimere,* fr. *re-, red-* re- + *emere* to take, buy] **1** : to recover (property) by discharging an obligation **2** : to ransom, free, or rescue by paying a price **3** : to free from the consequences of sin **4** : to remove the obligation of by payment ⟨the government ~s savings bonds⟩; *also* : to convert into something of value **5** : to make good (a promise) by performing : FULFILL **6** : to atone for — **re·deem·able** *adj* — **re·deem·er** *n*

re·demp·tion \\ri-'demp-shən\\ *n* : the act of redeeming : the state of being redeemed — **re·demp·tive** \\-tiv\\ *adj* — **re·demp·to·ry** \\-t(ə-)rē\\ *adj*

re·de·ploy \\,rēd-i-'plȯi\\ *vb* **1** : to transfer from one area or activity to another **2** : to relocate men or equipment — **re·de·ploy·ment** \\-mənt\\ *n*

red fox *n* : a fox with orange-red to reddish brown fur

red–hand·ed \\'red-'han-dəd\\ *adv or adj* : in the act of committing a misdeed

red·head \\-,hed\\ *n* : a person having red hair — **red·head·ed** \\-'hed-əd\\ *adj*

red herring *n* : a diversion intended to distract attention from the real issue

red–hot \\'red-'hät\\ *adj* **1** : glowing red with heat ⟨~ iron⟩ **2** : EXCITED, FURIOUS **3** : very new ⟨~ news⟩

re·dis·trict \\'rē-'dis-(,)trikt\\ *vb* : to organize into new territorial and esp. political divisions

red–let·ter \\,red-,let-ər\\ *adj* : of special significance : MEMORABLE

red–light district *n* : a district with many houses of prostitution

re·do \(')rē-'dü\ *vb* : to do over or again; *esp* : REDECORATE

red oak *n* : any of various American oaks with leaves usu. having spiny= tipped lobes and acorns that take two years to mature; *also* : the wood of a red oak

red·o·lent \'red-ᵊl-ənt\ *adj* **1** : FRAGRANT, AROMATIC **2** : having a specified fragrance **3** : REMINISCENT, SUGGESTIVE — **red·o·lence** \-əns\ *n* — **red·o·lent·ly** *adv*

re·doubt \ri-'daut\ *n* [F *redoute*, fr. It *ridotto*, fr. ML *reductus* secret place, fr. L, withdrawn, fr. *reducere* to lead back, fr. *re-* back + *ducere* to lead] : a small usu. temporary fortification

re·doubt·able \ri-'daut-ə-bəl\ *adj* [ME *redoutable*, fr. MF, fr. *redouter* to dread, fr. *re-* re- + *douter* to doubt] : arousing dread or fear : FORMIDABLE

re·dound \ri-'daund\ *vb* **1** : to have an effect **2** : to become added or transferred : ACCRUE

red pepper *n* : CAYENNE PEPPER

¹re·dress \ri-'dres\ *vb* **1** : to set right : REMEDY **2** : COMPENSATE **3** : to remove the cause of (a grievance) **4** : AVENGE

²re·dress *n* **1** : relief from distress **2** : a means or possibility of seeking a remedy **3** : compensation for loss or injury **4** : an act or instance of redressing

red snapper *n* : any of various fishes including several food fishes

red spider *n* : any of several small web-spinning mites that attack forage and crop plants

red squirrel *n* : a common American squirrel with the upper parts chiefly red

red–tailed hawk \ˌred-ˌtāld-\ *n* : a common hawk of eastern No. America with a rather short typically reddish tail

red tape *n* [fr. the red tape formerly used to bind legal documents in England] : official routine or procedure marked by excessive complexity which results in delay or inaction

red tide *n* : seawater discolored by the presence of large numbers of dinoflagellates which produce a toxin poisonous to many forms of marine life

and to human beings who consume infected shellfish

re·duce \ri-'d(y)üs\ *vb* **re·duced; re·duc·ing** **1** : LESSEN **2** : to bring to a specified state or condition ⟨∼ chaos to order⟩ **3** : to put in a lower rank or grade **4** : CONQUER ⟨∼ a fort⟩ **5** : to bring into a certain order or classification **6** : to correct (as a fracture) by restoration of displaced parts **7** : to lessen one's weight **syn** decrease, diminish, abate, dwindle, lessen, recede — **re·duc·er** *n* — **re·duc·ible** \-'d(y)üs-ə-bəl\ *adj*

re·duc·tion \ri-'dək-shən\ *n* **1** : the act of reducing : the state of being reduced **2** : something made by reducing **3** : the amount taken off in reducing something

re·dun·dan·cy \ri-'dən-dən-sē\ *n, pl* **-cies 1** : the quality or state of being redundant : SUPERFLUITY **2** : something redundant or in excess **3** : the use of surplus words

re·dun·dant \-dənt\ *adj* : exceeding what is needed or normal : SUPERFLUOUS; *esp* : using more words than necessary — **re·dun·dant·ly** *adv*

red–winged blackbird \'red-ˌwiŋd-\ *n* : a No. American blackbird of which the adult male is black with a patch of bright scarlet on the wings

red·wood \'red-ˌwud\ *n* : a tall coniferous timber tree of California or its durable wood

reed \'rēd\ *n* **1** : any of various tall slender grasses of wet areas; *also* : a stem or growth of reed **2** : a musical instrument made from the hollow stem of a reed **3** : an elastic tongue of cane, wood, or metal by which tones are produced in organ pipes and certain other wind instruments — **reedy** *adj*

re·ed·u·cate \(')rē-'ej-ə-ˌkāt\ *vb* : to train again; *esp* : to rehabilitate through education — **re·ed·u·ca·tion** *n*

¹reef \'rēf\ *n* **1** : a part of a sail taken in or let out in regulating the sail's size **2** : the reduction in sail area made by reefing

²reef *vb* : to reduce the area of a sail by rolling or folding part of it

³reef *n* : a ridge of rocks or sand at or near the surface of the water

¹reef·er \'rē-fər\ *n* **1** : one that reefs **2** : a close-fitting thick jacket

²reefer *n* : a marijuana cigarette

¹reek \'rēk\ *n* : a strong or disagreeable fume or odor

²reek *vb* **1** : to give off or become permeated with a strong or offensive odor **2** : to give a strong impression of some constituent quality — **reek·er** *n* — **reeky** \'rē-kē\ *adj*

¹reel \'rēl\ *n* : a revolvable device on which something flexible (as film, tape, cord, or wire) may be wound; *also* : a quantity of something wound on such a device

²reel *vb* **1** : to wind on or as if on a reel **2** : to pull or draw (as a fish) by reeling a line — **reel·able** *adj* — **reel·er** *n*

³reel *vb* **1** : WHIRL; *also* : to be giddy **2** : to waver or fall back from a blow : RECOIL **3** : to walk or move unsteadily

⁴reel *n* : a reeling motion

⁵reel *n* : a lively Scottish dance or its music

re·en·force \ˌrē-ən-'fōrs\ var of REIN-FORCE

re·en·try \rē-'en-trē\ *n* **1** : a second or new entry **2** : the action of reentering the earth's atmosphere from space

reeve \'rēv\ *vb* **rove** \'rōv\ *or* **reeved; reev·ing** : to pass (as a rope) through a hole in a block or cleat

¹ref \'ref\ *n* : REFEREE 2

²ref *abbr* **1** reference **2** referred **3** reformed **4** refunding

re·fec·tion \ri-'fek-shən\ *n* **1** : refreshment esp. after hunger or fatigue **2** : food and drink together : REPAST

re·fec·to·ry \ri-'fek-t(ə-)rē\ *n, pl* **-ries** : a dining hall (as in a monastery or college)

re·fer \ri-'fər\ *vb* **re·ferred; re·fer·ring 1** : to assign to a certain source, cause, or relationship **2** : to direct or send to some person or place (as for information or help) **3** : to submit to someone else for consideration or action **4** : to have recourse (as for information or aid) **5** : to have connection : RELATE **6** : to direct attention : speak of : MENTION, ALLUDE **syn** recur, repair, resort, apply, go, turn — **re·fer·able** \'ref-(ə-)rə-bəl, ri-'fər-ə-\ *adj*

¹ref·er·ee \ˌref-ə-'rē\ *n* **1** : a person to whom an issue esp. in law is referred for investigation or settlement **2** : an umpire in certain games

²referee *vb* **-eed; -ee·ing** : to act as referee

ref·er·ence \'ref-ərns, 'ref-(ə-)rəns\ *n* **1** : the act of referring **2** : RELATION, RESPECT **3** : ALLUSION, MENTION **4** : a direction of the attention to another passage or book **5** : consultation esp. for obtaining information ⟨books for ∼⟩ **6** : a person of whom inquiries as to character or ability can be made **7** : a written recommendation of a person for employment

ref·er·en·dum \ˌref-ə-'ren-dəm\ *n, pl* **-da** \-də\ *or* **-dums** [NL, fr. L] : the referring of legislative measures to the voters for approval or rejection; *also* : a vote on a measure so submitted

ref·er·ent \'ref-(ə-)rənt\ *n* [L *referent-, referens,* prp. of *referre*] : one that refers or is referred to; *esp* : the thing a word stands for — **referent** *adj*

re·fer·ral \ri-'fər-əl\ *n* **1** : the act or an instance of referring **2** : one that is referred

¹re·fill \'rē-'fil\ *vb* : to fill again : REPLENISH — **re·fill·able** *adj*

²re·fill \'rē-ˌfil\ *n* : a new or fresh supply of something

re·fine \ri-'fīn\ *vb* **re·fined; re·fin·ing 1** : to free from impurities or waste matter **2** : IMPROVE, PERFECT **3** : to free or become free of what is coarse or uncouth **4** : to make improvements by introducing subtle changes — **re·fin·er** *n*

re·fined \ri-'fīnd\ *adj* **1** : freed from impurities **2** : CULTURED, CULTIVATED **3** : SUBTLE

re·fine·ment \ri-'fīn-mənt\ *n* **1** : the action of refining **2** : the quality or state of being refined **3** : a refined feature or method; *also* : something intended to improve or perfect

re·fin·ery \ri-'fīn-(ə-)rē\ *n, pl* **-er·ies** : a building and equipment for refining metals, oil, or sugar

refl *abbr* reflex; reflexive

re·flect \ri-'flekt\ *vb* [ME *reflecten,* fr. L *reflectere* to bend back, fr. *re-* back + *flectere* to bend] **1** : to bend or cast back (as light, heat, or sound) **2** : to give back a likeness or image of as a mirror does **3** : to bring as a result ⟨∼ed credit on him⟩ **4** : to cast reproach or blame ⟨their bad conduct ∼ed on their training⟩ **5** : PONDER,

MEDITATE — **re·flec·tion** \-'flek-shən\ *n* — **re·flec·tive** \-tiv\ *adj* — **re·flec·tiv·ity** \(ˌ)rē-ˌflek-'tiv-ət-ē\ *n*

re·flec·tor \ri-'flek-tər\ *n* : one that reflects; *esp* : a polished surface for reflecting radiation (as light)

¹**re·flex** \'rē-ˌfleks\ *n* **1** : an automatic and usu. inborn response to a stimulus not involving higher mental centers **2** *pl* : the power of acting or responding with enough speed ⟨an athlete with great ~es⟩

²**reflex** *adj* **1** : bent or directed back **2** : of or relating to a reflex — **re·flex·ly** *adv*

¹**re·flex·ive** \ri-'flek-siv\ *adj* : of or relating to an action directed back upon the doer or the grammatical subject ⟨a ~ verb⟩ ⟨the ~ pronoun *himself*⟩ — **re·flex·ive·ly** *adv* — **re·flex·ive·ness** *n*

²**reflexive** *n* : a reflexive verb or pronoun

re·fo·cus \(')rē-'fō-kəs\ *vb* **1** : to focus again **2** : to change the emphasis or direction of ⟨~ed her life⟩

re·for·es·ta·tion \ˌrē-ˌfȯr-ə-'stā-shən\ *n* : the action of renewing a forest by planting seeds or young trees — **re·for·est** \rē-'fȯr-əst\ *vb*

¹**re·form** \ri-'fȯrm\ *vb* **1** : to make better or improve by removal of faults **2** : to correct or improve one's own character or habits **syn** correct, rectify, emend, remedy, redress, revise — **re·form·able** *adj* — **re·for·ma·tive** \-'fȯr-mət-iv\ *adj*

²**reform** *n* : improvement or correction of what is corrupt or defective

re–form \'rē-'fȯrm\ *vb* : to form again

ref·or·ma·tion \ˌref-ər-'mā-shən\ *n* **1** : the act of reforming : the state of being reformed **2** *cap* : a 16th century religious movement marked by the establishment of the Protestant churches

¹**re·for·ma·to·ry** \ri-'fȯr-mə-ˌtōr-ē\ *adj* : aiming at or tending toward reformation : REFORMATIVE

²**reformatory** *n, pl* **-ries** : a penal institution for reforming young or first offenders or women

re·form·er \ri-'fȯr-mər\ *n* **1** : one that works for or urges reform **2** *cap* : a leader of the Protestant Reformation

refr *abbr* refraction

re·fract \ri-'frakt\ *vb* [L *refractus,* pp. of *refringere* to break open, break up, refract, fr. *re-* back + *frangere* to break] : to subject to refraction

re·frac·tion \ri-'frak-shən\ *n* : the bending of a ray (as of light) when it passes obliquely from one medium into another in which its speed is different — **re·frac·tive** \-tiv\ *adj*

re·frac·to·ry \ri-'frak-t(ə-)rē\ *adj* **1** : OBSTINATE, STUBBORN, UNMANAGEABLE **2** : difficult to melt, corrode, or draw out; *esp* : capable of enduring high temperature ⟨~ bricks⟩ **syn** recalcitrant, intractable, ungovernable, unruly, headstrong, willful — **re·frac·to·ri·ness** \ri-'frak-t(ə-)rē-nəs\ *n* — **refractory** *n*

¹**re·frain** \ri-'frān\ *vb* : to hold oneself back : FORBEAR — **re·frain·ment** *n*

²**refrain** *n* : a phrase or verse recurring regularly in a poem or song

re·fresh \ri-'fresh\ *vb* **1** : to make or become fresh or fresher **2** : to revive by or as if by renewal of supplies ⟨~ one's memory⟩ **3** : to freshen up **4** : to supply or take refreshment **syn** restore, rejuvenate, renovate, refurbish — **re·fresh·er** *n* — **re·fresh·ing·ly** *adv*

re·fresh·ment \-mənt\ *n* **1** : the act of refreshing : the state of being refreshed **2** : something that refreshes **3** *pl* : a light meal

re·fried beans \(ˌ)rē-ˌfrīd-\ *n pl* : beans cooked with seasonings, fried, then mashed and fried again

refrig *abbr* refrigerating; refrigeration

re·frig·er·ate \ri-'frij-ə-ˌrāt\ *vb* **-at·ed; -at·ing** : to make cool; *esp* : to chill or freeze (food) for preservation — **re·frig·er·ant** \-(ə-)rənt\ *adj or n* — **re·frig·er·a·tion** \-ˌfrij-ə-'rā-shən\ *n* — **re·frig·er·a·tor** \-'frij-ə-ˌrāt-ər\ *n*

ref·uge \'ref-ˌyüj\ *n* **1** : shelter or protection from danger or distress **2** : a place that provides protection

ref·u·gee \ˌref-yü-'jē\ *n* : one who flees for safety esp. to a foreign country

re·ful·gence \ri-'fùl-jəns, -'fəl-\ *n* : radiant or shining quality or state — **re·ful·gent** \-jənt\ *adj*

¹**re·fund** \ri-'fənd, 'rē-ˌfənd\ *vb* : to give or put back (money) : REPAY — **re·fund·able** *adj*

²**re·fund** \'rē-ˌfənd\ *n* **1** : the act of refunding **2** : a sum refunded

re·fur·bish \ri-'fər-bish\ *vb* : to brighten or freshen up : RENOVATE

¹re·fuse \ri-'fyüz\ *vb* **re·fused; re·fus·ing**
1 : to decline to accept : REJECT **2** : to decline to do, give, or grant : DENY — **re·fus·al** \-'fyü-zəl\ *n*

²ref·use \'ref-ˌyüs, -ˌyüz\ *n* : rejected or worthless matter : RUBBISH, TRASH

re·fuse·nik *or* **re·fus·nik** \ri-'fyüz-nik\ *n* : a Soviet citizen who is refused permission to emigrate

re·fute \ri-'fyüt\ *vb* **re·fut·ed; re·fut·ing** [L *refutare,* fr. *re-* back + *-futare* to beat] : to prove to be false by argument or evidence — **ref·u·ta·tion** \ˌref-yù-'tā-shən\ *n* — **re·fut·er** \ri-'fyüt-ər\ *n*

¹reg \'reg\ *n* : REGULATION

²reg *abbr* **1** region **2** register; registered; registration **3** regular

re·gain \ri-'gān\ *vb* **1** : to gain or get again : get back ⟨∼ed his health⟩ **2** : to get back to : reach again ⟨∼ the shore⟩ **syn** recover, retrieve, recoup, repossess

re·gal \'rē-gəl\ *adj* **1** : of, relating to, or befitting a king : ROYAL **2** : STATELY, SPLENDID — **re·gal·ly** \-ē\ *adv*

re·gale \ri-'gāl\ *vb* **re·galed; re·gal·ing** **1** : to entertain richly or agreeably **2** : to give pleasure or amusement to **syn** gratify, delight, please, rejoice, gladden

re·ga·lia \ri-'gāl-yə\ *n pl* **1** : the emblems, symbols, or paraphernalia of royalty (as the crown and scepter) **2** : the insignia of an office or order **3** : special costume : FINERY

¹re·gard \ri-'gärd\ *n* **1** : CONSIDERATION, HEED; *also* : CARE, CONCERN **2** : GAZE, GLANCE, LOOK **3** : RESPECT, ESTEEM **4** *pl* : friendly greetings implying respect and esteem **5** : an aspect to be considered : PARTICULAR — **re·gard·ful** *adj* — **re·gard·less** *adj*

²regard *vb* **1** : to pay attention to **2** : to show respect for : HEED **3** : to hold in high esteem : care for **4** : to look at : gaze upon **5** *archaic* : to relate to **6** : to think of : CONSIDER

re·gard·ing \-iŋ\ *prep* : CONCERNING

regardless of \ri-'gärd-ləs-\ *prep* : in spite of

re·gat·ta \ri-'gät-ə, -'gat-\ *n* : a boat race or a series of boat races

regd *abbr* registered

re·gen·cy \'rē-jən-sē\ *n, pl* **-cies** **1** : the office or government of a regent or body of regents **2** : a body of regents **3** : the period during which a regent governs

re·gen·er·a·cy \ri-'jen-(ə-)rə-sē\ *n* : the state of being regenerated

¹re·gen·er·ate \ri-'jen-(ə-)rət\ *adj* **1** : formed or created again **2** : spiritually reborn or converted

²re·gen·er·ate \ri-'jen-ə-ˌrāt\ *vb* **1** : to cause to experience spiritual renewal **2** : to reform completely **3** : to give or gain new life; *also* : to renew by a new growth of tissue — **re·gen·er·a·tion** \-ˌjen-ə-'rā-shən\ *n* — **re·gen·er·a·tive** \-'jen-ə-ˌrāt-iv\ *adj* — **re·gen·er·a·tor** \-ˌrāt-ər\ *n*

re·gent \'rē-jənt\ *n* **1** : a person who rules during the childhood, absence, or incapacity of the sovereign **2** : a member of a governing board (as of a state university)

reg·gae \'reg-ˌā\ *n* : popular music that originated in Jamaica and combines indigenous styles with elements of rock and roll and soul music

reg·i·cide \'rej-ə-ˌsīd\ *n* **1** : one who murders a king **2** : murder of a king

re·gime *also* **ré·gime** \rā-'zhēm, ri-\ *n* **1** : REGIMEN **2** : a form or system of government **3** : a government in power; *also* : a period of rule

reg·i·men \'rej-ə-mən\ *n* **1** : a systematic course of treatment or behavior ⟨a strict dietary ∼⟩ **2** : GOVERNMENT

¹reg·i·ment \'rej-ə-mənt\ *n* : a military unit consisting usu. of a number of battalions — **reg·i·men·tal** \ˌrej-ə-'ment-ᵊl\ *adj*

²reg·i·ment \'rej-ə-ˌment\ *vb* : to organize rigidly esp. for regulation or central control — **reg·i·men·ta·tion** \ˌrej-ə-mən-'tā-shən\ *n*

reg·i·men·tals \ˌrej-ə-'ment-ᵊlz\ *n pl* **1** : a regimental uniform **2** : military dress

re·gion \'rē-jən\ *n* [ME, fr. MF, fr. L *region-, regio,* fr. *regere* to rule] : an often indefinitely defined part or area

re·gion·al \'rēj-(ə-)nəl\ *adj* **1** : of or relating to a geographical region **2** : of or relating to a bodily region : LOCALIZED — **re·gion·al·ly** \-ē\ *adv*

¹reg·is·ter \'rej-ə-stər\ *n* **1** : a record of items or details; *also* : a book or system for keeping such a record **2** : the range of a voice or instrument **3** : a device to regulate ventilation or heating **4** : an automatic device recording a number or quantity

²**register** *vb* **-tered; -ter·ing** \-st(ə-)riŋ\ **1** : to enter in a register (as in a list of guests) **2** : to record automatically **3** : to secure special care for (mail matter) by paying additional postage **4** : to show (emotions) by facial expression or gestures **5** : to correspond or adjust so as to correspond exactly

registered nurse *n* : a graduate trained nurse who has been licensed to practice by a state authority after passing qualifying examinations

reg·is·trant \ˈrej-ə-strənt\ *n* : one that registers or is registered

reg·is·trar \-ˌsträr\ *n* : an official recorder or keeper of records (as at an educational institution)

reg·is·tra·tion \ˌrej-ə-ˈstrā-shən\ *n* **1** : the act of registering **2** : an entry in a register **3** : the number of persons registered : ENROLLMENT **4** : a document certifying an act of registering

reg·is·try \ˈrej-ə-strē\ *n, pl* **-tries 1** : ENROLLMENT, REGISTRATION **2** : the state or fact of being entered in a register **3** : a place of registration **4** : an official record book or an entry in one

reg·nant \ˈreg-nənt\ *adj* **1** : REIGNING **2** : DOMINANT **3** : of common or widespread occurrence : PREVALENT

rego·lith \ˈreg-ə-ˌlith\ *n* : unconsolidated residual or transported material that overlies the solid rock on the earth, moon, or a planet

¹**re·gress** \ˈrē-ˌgres\ *n* **1** : WITHDRAWAL **2** : RETROGRESSION

²**re·gress** \ri-ˈgres\ *vb* : to go or cause to go back or to a lower level — **re·gres·sive** *adj* — **re·gres·sor** \-ˈgres-ər\ *n*

re·gres·sion \ri-ˈgresh-ən\ *n* : the act or an instance of regressing; *esp* : reversion to an earlier mental or behavioral level

¹**re·gret** \ri-ˈgret\ *vb* **re·gret·ted; re·gret·ting 1** : to mourn the loss or death of **2** : to be keenly sorry for **3** : to experience regret — **re·gret·ta·ble** \-ə-bəl\ *adj* — **re·gret·ta·bly** \-blē\ *adv* — **re·gret·ter** *n*

²**regret** *n* **1** : mental distress caused by something beyond one's power to remedy **2** : an expression of sorrow **3** *pl* : a note or oral message politely

declining an invitation — **re·gret·ful** \-fəl\ *adj* — **re·gret·ful·ly** \-ē\ *adv*

re·group \(ˈ)rē-ˈgrüp\ *vb* : to form into a new grouping

regt *abbr* regiment

¹**reg·u·lar** \ˈreg-yə-lər\ *adj* [ME *reguler*, fr. MF, fr. LL *regularis* regular, fr L, of a bar, fr. *regula* rule, straightedge, fr. *regere* to guide straight, rule] **1** : belonging to a religious order **2** : made, built, or arranged according to a rule, standard, or type; *also* : even or symmetrical in form or structure **3** : ORDERLY, METHODICAL ⟨∼ habits⟩; *also* : not varying : STEADY ⟨a ∼ pace⟩ **4** : made, selected, or conducted according to rule or custom **5** : properly qualified ⟨not a ∼ lawyer⟩ **6** : conforming to the normal or usual manner or inflection **7** : belonging to a permanent standing army and esp. to one maintained by a national government **syn** systematic, orderly, methodical — **reg·u·lar·i·ty** \ˌreg-yə-ˈlar-ət-ē\ *n* — **reg·u·lar·ize** \ˈreg-yə-lə-ˌrīz\ *vb* — **reg·u·lar·ly** *adv*

²**regular** *n* **1** : one that is regular (as in attendance) **2** : a member of the regular clergy **3** : a soldier in a regular army **4** : a player on an athletic team who is usu. in the starting lineup

reg·u·late \ˈreg-yə-ˌlāt\ *vb* **-lat·ed; -lat·ing 1** : to govern or direct according to rule : CONTROL **2** : to bring under the control of law or authority **3** : to put in good order **4** : to fix or adjust the time, amount, degree, or rate of — **reg·u·la·tive** \-ˌlāt-iv\ *adj* — **reg·u·la·tor** \-ˌlāt-ər\ *n* — **reg·u·la·to·ry** \-lə-ˌtōr-ē\ *adj*

reg·u·la·tion \ˌreg-yə-ˈlā-shən\ *n* **1** : the act of regulating : the state of being regulated **2** : a rule dealing with details of procedure **3** : an order issued by an executive authority of a government and having the force of law

re·gur·gi·tate \rē-ˈgər-jə-ˌtāt\ *vb* **-tat·ed; -tat·ing** [ML *regurgitare*, fr. L *re-* re- + LL *gurgitare* to engulf, fr. L *gurgit-, gurges* whirlpool] : to throw or be thrown back or out; *esp* : VOMIT — **re·gur·gi·ta·tion** \-ˌgər-jə-ˈtā-shən\ *n*

re·hab \ˈrē-ˌhab\ *n* **1** : REHABILITATION **2** : a rehabilitated building — **rehab** *vb*

re·ha·bil·i·tate \ˌrē-(h)ə-ˈbil-ə-ˌtāt\ *vb* **-tat·ed; -tat·ing 1** : to restore to a former capacity, rank, or right : REIN-STATE **2** : to put into good condition again — **re·ha·bil·i·ta·tion** \-ˌbil-ə-ˈtā-shən\ *n* — **re·ha·bil·i·ta·tive** \-ˌtāt-iv\ *adj*

re·hash \ˈrē-ˈhash\ *vb* : to present again in another form without real change or improvement — **rehash** *n*

re·hear·ing \ˈrē-ˈhi(ə)r-iŋ\ *n* : a second or new hearing by the same tribunal

re·hears·al \ri-ˈhər-səl\ *n* **1** : something told again : RECITAL **2** : a private performance or practice session preparatory to a public appearance

re·hearse \ri-ˈhərs\ *vb* **re·hearsed; re·hears·ing 1** : to say again : REPEAT **2** : to recount in order : ENUMERATE **3** : to give a rehearsal of ⟨∼ a play⟩ **4** : to train by rehearsal ⟨∼ an actor⟩ **5** : to engage in a rehearsal — **re·hears·er** *n*

¹**reign** \ˈrān\ *n* **1** : the authority or rule of a sovereign **2** : the time during which a sovereign rules

²**reign** *vb* **1** : to rule as a sovereign **2** : to be predominant or prevalent

re·im·burse \ˌrē-əm-ˈbərs\ *vb* **-bursed; -burs·ing** [*re-* re- + obs. E *imburse* (to put in the pocket, pay), fr. ML *imbursare* to put into a purse, fr. L *in-* in + ML *bursa* purse, fr. LL, hide of an ox, fr. Gk *byrsa*] : to pay back : make restitution : REPAY **syn** indemnify, recompense, requite, compensate — **re·im·burs·able** *adj* — **re·im·burse·ment** *n*

¹**rein** \ˈrān\ *n* **1** : a line of a bridle by which a rider or driver directs an animal **2** : a restraining influence : CHECK **3** : position of control or command **4** : complete freedom — usu. used in the phrase *give rein to*

²**rein** *vb* : to check or direct by reins

re·in·car·na·tion \ˌrē-ˌin-ˌkär-ˈnā-shən\ *n* : rebirth of the soul in a new body — **re·in·car·nate** \ˌrē-in-ˈkär-ˌnāt\ *vb*

rein·deer \ˈrān-ˌdiər\ *n* [ME *reindere,* fr. ON *hreinn* reindeer + ME *deer*] : any of several large deer of northern regions that are used for draft and meat, have antlers in both sexes, and are grouped with the caribou in a single species

reindeer moss *n* : a gray, erect, tufted, and much-branched lichen of northern regions that is consumed by reindeer and sometimes by man

re·in·fec·tion \ˌrē-ən-ˈfek-shən\ *n* : infection following another infection of the same type

re·in·force \ˌrē-ən-ˈfōrs\ *vb* **1** : to strengthen with additional forces (as troops or ships) **2** : to strengthen with new force, aid, material, or support — **re·in·force·ment** *n* — **re·in·forc·er** *n*

re·in·state \ˌrē-ən-ˈstāt\ *vb* **-stat·ed; -stat·ing** : to restore to a former position, condition, or capacity — **re·in·state·ment** *n*

re·it·er·ate \rē-ˈit-ə-ˌrāt\ *vb* **-at·ed; -at·ing** : to state or do over again or repeatedly **syn** repeat, iterate, reprise — **re·it·er·a·tion** \-ˌit-ə-ˈrā-shən\ *n*

¹**re·ject** \ri-ˈjekt\ *vb* **1** : to refuse to acknowledge or submit to **2** : to refuse to take or accept **3** : to refuse to grant, consider, or accede to **4** : to throw out esp. as useless or unsatisfactory — **re·jec·tion** \-ˈjek-shən\ *n*

²**re·ject** \ˈrē-ˌjekt\ *n* : a rejected person or thing

re·joice \ri-ˈjȯis\ *vb* **re·joiced; re·joic·ing 1** : to give joy to : GLADDEN **2** : to feel joy or great delight — **re·joic·er** *n*

re·join \ˈrē-ˈjȯin *for 1,* ri- *for 2*\ *vb* **1** : to join again : come together again : REUNITE **2** : to say in answer (as to a plaintiff's plea in court) : REPLY

re·join·der \ri-ˈjȯin-dər\ *n* : REPLY; *esp* : an answer to a reply

re·ju·ve·nate \ri-ˈjü-və-ˌnāt\ *vb* **-nat·ed; -nat·ing** : to make young or youthful again : give new vigor to **syn** renew, refresh, renovate, restore — **re·ju·ve·na·tion** \-ˌjü-və-ˈnā-shən\ *n*

rel *abbr* relating; relative

¹**re·lapse** \ri-ˈlaps, ˈrē-ˌlaps\ *n* : the action or process of relapsing; *esp* : a recurrence of illness after a period of improvement

²**re·lapse** \ri-ˈlaps\ *vb* **re·lapsed; re·laps·ing** : to slip back into a former condition (as of illness) after a change for the better

re·late \ri-ˈlāt\ *vb* **re·lat·ed; re·lat·ing 1** : to give an account of : TELL, NARRATE **2** : to show or establish logical or causal connection between **3** : to be connected : have reference **4** : to have meaningful social relationships **5** : to respond favorably — **re·lat·able** *adj* — **re·lat·er** *or* **re·la·tor** *n*

re·lat·ed \-əd\ *adj* **1** : connected by

some understood relationship **2** : connected through membership in the same family — **re·lat·ed·ness** *n*

re·la·tion \ri-'lā-shən\ *n* **1** : NARRATION, ACCOUNT **2** : CONNECTION, RELATIONSHIP **3** : connection by blood or marriage : KINSHIP; *also* : RELATIVE **4** : REFERENCE, RESPECT ⟨in ~ to this matter⟩ **5** : the state of being mutually interested or involved (as in social or commercial matters) **6** *pl* : DEALINGS, AFFAIRS **7** *pl* : SEXUAL INTERCOURSE — **re·la·tion·al** \-sh(ə-)nəl\ *adj*

re·la·tion·ship \-ˌship\ *n* : the state of being related or interrelated

¹**rel·a·tive** \'rel-ət-iv\ *n* **1** : a word referring grammatically to an antecedent **2** : a thing having a relation to or a dependence upon another thing **3** : a person connected with another by blood or marriage; *also* : an animal or plant related to another by common descent

²**relative** *adj* **1** : introducing a subordinate clause qualifying an expressed or implied antecedent ⟨~ pronoun⟩; *also* : introduced by such a connective ⟨~ clause⟩ **2** : PERTINENT, RELEVANT **3** : not absolute or independent : COMPARATIVE **4** : expressed as the ratio of the specified quantity to the total magnitude or to the mean of all quantities involved **syn** dependent, contingent, conditional — **rel·a·tive·ly** *adv* — **rel·a·tive·ness** *n*

relative humidity *n* : the ratio of the amount of water vapor actually present in the air to the greatest amount possible at the same temperature

rel·a·tiv·is·tic \ˌrel-ət-iv-'is-tik\ *adj* **1** : of, relating to, or characterized by relativity **2** : moving at a velocity that is a significant fraction of the speed of light so that effects predicted by the theory of relativity become evident ⟨a ~ electron⟩ — **rel·a·tiv·is·ti·cal·ly** \-ti-k(ə-)lē\ *adv*

rel·a·tiv·i·ty \ˌrel-ə-'tiv-ət-ē\ *n, pl* **-ties 1** : the quality or state of being relative **2** : a theory in physics that considers mass and energy to be equivalent and that states that a moving object will experience changes in size and time which are related to its speed but are only noticeable at speeds approaching that of light

re·lax \ri-'laks\ *vb* **1** : to make or become less firm, tense, or rigid **2** : to make less severe or strict **3** : to seek rest or recreation — **re·lax·er** *n*

¹**re·lax·ant** \ri-'lak-sənt\ *adj* : producing relaxation

²**relaxant** *n* : a relaxing agent; *esp* : a drug that induces muscular relaxation

re·lax·ation \ˌrē-ˌlak-'sā-shən\ *n* **1** : the act of relaxing or state of being relaxed : a lessening of tension **2** : DIVERSION, RECREATION **syn** rest, repose, leisure, ease

¹**re·lay** \'rē-ˌlā\ *n* **1** : a fresh supply (as of horses or men) arranged beforehand to relieve or replace others at various stages **2** : a race between teams in which each team member covers a specified part of a course **3** : an electromagnetic device in which the opening or closing of one circuit activates another device (as a switch in another circuit) **4** : the act of passing along by stages

²**re·lay** \'rē-ˌlā, ri-'lā\ *vb* **re·layed; re·lay·ing 1** : to place in or provide with relays **2** : to pass along by relays **3** : to control or operate by a relay

³**re·lay** \'rē-'lā\ *vb* **-laid** \-'lād\; **-lay·ing** : to lay again

¹**re·lease** \ri-'lēs\ *vb* **re·leased; re·leas·ing 1** : to set free from confinement or restraint **2** : to relieve from something (as pain, trouble, or penalty) that oppresses or burdens **3** : RELINQUISH ⟨~ a claim⟩ **4** : to permit publication or performance (as of a news story or a motion picture) on but not before a specified date **syn** emancipate, discharge, free, liberate

²**release** *n* **1** : relief or deliverance from sorrow, suffering, or trouble **2** : discharge from an obligation or responsibility **3** : an act of setting free : the state of being freed **4** : a document effecting a legal release **5** : a device for holding or releasing a mechanism as required **6** : a releasing for performance or publication; *also* : the matter released (as to the press)

rel·e·gate \'rel-ə-ˌgāt\ *vb* **-gat·ed; -gat·ing 1** : to send into exile : BANISH **2** : to remove or dismiss to some less prominent position **3** : to assign to a particular class or sphere **4** : to submit or refer for judgment, decision, or execution : DELEGATE **syn** commit, entrust, consign, commend — **rel·e·ga·tion** \ˌrel-ə-ˈgā-shən\ n

re·lent \ri-ˈlent\ vb **1** : to become less stern, severe, or harsh **2** : SLACKEN

re·lent·less \-ləs\ adj : mercilessly hard or harsh : immovably stern or persistent — **re·lent·less·ly** adv — **re·lent·less·ness** n

rel·e·vance \ˈrel-ə-vəns\ n : relation to the matter at hand : practical and esp. social applicability

rel·e·van·cy \-vən-sē\ n : RELEVANCE

rel·e·vant \ˈrel-ə-vənt\ adj : bearing on the matter at hand : PERTINENT **syn** germane, material, applicable, apropos — **rel·e·vant·ly** adv

re·li·able \ri-ˈlī-ə-bəl\ adj : fit to be trusted or relied on : DEPENDABLE, TRUSTWORTHY — **re·li·a·bil·i·ty** \-ˌlī-ə-ˈbil-ət-ē\ n — **re·li·able·ness** n — **re·li·ably** \-ˈlī-ə-blē\ adv

re·li·ance \ri-ˈlī-əns\ n **1** : the act of relying **2** : the state of being reliant **3** : one relied on — **re·li·ant** \-ənt\ adj

rel·ic \ˈrel-ik\ n **1** : an object venerated because of its association with a saint or martyr **2** : SOUVENIR, MEMENTO **3** pl : REMAINS, RUINS **4** : a remaining trace : VESTIGE

rel·ict \ˈrel-ikt\ n : WIDOW

re·lief \ri-ˈlēf\ n **1** : removal or lightening of something oppressive, painful, or distressing **2** : aid in the form of money or necessities (as for the aged or handicapped) **3** : military assistance in or rescue from a position of difficulty **4** : release from a post or from performance of a duty; also : one that relieves another by taking his place **5** : legal remedy or redress **6** : projection of figures or ornaments from the background (as in sculpture) **7** : the elevations of a land surface

relief pitcher n : a baseball pitcher who takes over for another during a game

re·lieve \ri-ˈlēv\ vb **re·lieved; re·liev·ing** **1** : to free partly or wholly from a burden or from distress **2** : to bring about the removal or alleviation of : MITIGATE **3** : to release from a post or duty; also : to take the place of **4** : to break the monotony of (as by contrast in color) **5** : to raise in relief **syn** alleviate, lighten, assuage, allay — **re·liev·er** n

relig abbr religion

re·li·gion \ri-ˈlij-ən\ n **1** : the service and worship of God or the supernatural **2** : devotion to a religious faith **3** : an organized system of faith and worship; also : a personal set of religious beliefs and practices **4** : a cause, principle, or belief held to with faith and ardor — **re·li·gion·ist** n

¹**re·li·gious** \ri-ˈlij-əs\ adj **1** : relating or devoted to the divine or that which is held to be of ultimate importance **2** : of or relating to religious beliefs or observances **3** : scrupulously and conscientiously faithful **4** : FERVENT, ZEALOUS — **re·li·gious·ly** adv

²**religious** n, pl **religious** : one (as a monk) bound by vows and devoted to a life of piety

re·lin·quish \ri-ˈliŋ-kwish, -ˈlin-\ vb **1** : to withdraw or retreat from : ABANDON, QUIT **2** : GIVE UP ⟨~ a title⟩ **3** : to let go of : RELEASE **syn** yield, leave, resign, surrender, cede, waive — **re·lin·quish·ment** n

rel·i·quary \ˈrel-ə-ˌkwer-ē\ n, pl **-quar·ies** : a container for religious relics

¹**rel·ish** \ˈrel-ish\ n [ME reles aftertaste, fr. OF, release, something left over, fr. relessier to relax, release, fr. L relaxare] **1** : a characteristic flavor (as of food) : SAVOR **2** : keen enjoyment or delight in something : GUSTO **3** : APPETITE, INCLINATION **4** : a highly seasoned sauce (as of pickles) eaten with other food to add flavor

²**relish** vb **1** : to add relish to **2** : to take pleasure in : ENJOY **3** : to eat with pleasure — **rel·ish·able** adj

re·live \(ˈ)rē-ˈliv\ vb : to live again or over again; esp : to experience again in the imagination

re·lo·cate \(ˈ)rē-ˈlō-ˌkāt, ˌrē-lō-ˈkāt\ vb **1** : to locate again **2** : to move to a new location — **re·lo·ca·tion** \ˌrē-lō-ˈkā-shən\ n

re·luc·tant \ri-ˈlək-tənt\ adj : holding back (as from acting) : UNWILLING; also : showing unwillingness ⟨~ obedience⟩ **syn** disinclined, indisposed, hesitant, loath, averse — **re·luc·tance** \-təns\ — **re·luc·tant·ly** adv

re·ly \ri-ˈlī\ vb **re·lied; re·ly·ing** [ME relien to rally, fr. MF relier to connect, rally, fr. L *religare* to tie back, fr. *re-* back + *ligare* to tie] : to place faith or confidence : DEPEND **syn** trust, count

REM \'rem\ *n* : RAPID EYE MOVEMENT

re·main \ri-'mān\ *vb* **1** : to be left after others have been removed, subtracted, or destroyed **2** : to be something yet to be shown, done, or treated ⟨it ~s to be seen⟩ **3** : to stay after others have gone **4** : to continue unchanged

re·main·der \ri-'mān-dər\ *n* **1** : that which is left over : a remaining group, part, or trace **2** : the number left after a subtraction **3** : the number that is left over from the dividend after division and that is less than the divisor **4** : a book sold at a reduced price by the publisher after sales have slowed **syn** leavings, rest, balance, remnant, residue

re·mains \-'mānz\ *n pl* **1** : a remaining part or trace ⟨the ~ of a meal⟩ **2** : writings left unpublished at an author's death **3** : a dead body

¹**re·make** \(')rē-'māk\ *vb* **-made** \-'mād\; **-mak·ing** : to make anew or in a different form

²**re·make** \(')rē-,māk\ *n* : one that is remade; *esp* : a new version of a motion picture

re·mand \ri-'mand\ *vb* : to order back; *esp* : to return to custody pending trial or for further detention

¹**re·mark** \ri-'märk\ *vb* **1** : to take notice of : OBSERVE **2** : to express as an observation or comment : SAY

²**remark** *n* **1** : the act of remarking : OBSERVATION, NOTICE **2** : a passing observation or comment

re·mark·able \ri-'mär-kə-bəl\ *adj* : worthy of being or likely to be noticed : UNUSUAL, EXTRAORDINARY, NOTEWORTHY — **re·mark·able·ness** *n* — **re·mark·ably** \-blē\ *adv*

re·me·di·a·ble \ri-'mēd-ē-ə-bəl\ *adj* : capable of being remedied ⟨~ speech defects⟩

re·me·di·al \ri-'mēd-ē-əl\ *adj* : intended to remedy or improve

¹**rem·e·dy** \'rem-əd-ē\ *n, pl* **-dies 1** : a medicine or treatment that cures or relieves **2** : something that corrects or counteracts an evil or compensates for a loss

²**remedy** *vb* **-died; -dy·ing** : to provide or serve as a remedy for

re·mem·ber \ri-'mem-bər\ *vb* **-bered; -ber·ing** \-b(ə-)riŋ\ **1** : to have come into the mind again : think of again : RECOLLECT **2** : to keep from forgetting : keep in mind **3** : to convey greetings from **4** : COMMEMORATE

re·mem·brance \-brəns\ *n* **1** : an act of remembering : RECOLLECTION **2** : the ability to remember : MEMORY **3** : the power of remembering; *also* : the period over which one's memory extends **4** : a memory of a person, thing, or event **5** : something that serves to bring to mind : REMINDER, MEMENTO **6** : a greeting or gift recalling or expressing friendship or affection

re·mind \ri-'mīnd\ *vb* : to put in mind of someone or something : cause to remember — **re·mind·er** *n*

rem·i·nisce \,rem-ə-'nis\ *vb* **-nisced; -nisc·ing** : to indulge in reminiscence

rem·i·nis·cence \-'nis-ᵊns\ *n* **1** : a recalling or telling of a past experience **2** : an account of a memorable experience

rem·i·nis·cent \-ᵊnt\ *adj* **1** : of or relating to reminiscence **2** : marked by or given to reminiscence **3** : serving to remind : SUGGESTIVE — **rem·i·nis·cent·ly** *adv*

re·miss \ri-'mis\ *adj* **1** : negligent or careless in the performance of work or duty **2** : showing neglect or inattention **syn** lax, neglectful, delinquent, derelict — **re·miss·ly** *adv* — **re·miss·ness** *n*

re·mis·sion \ri-'mish-ən\ *n* **1** : the act or process of remitting **2** : a state or period during which something is remitted

re·mit \ri-'mit\ *vb* **re·mit·ted; re·mit·ting 1** : FORGIVE, PARDON **2** : to give or gain relief from (as pain) **3** : to refer for consideration, report, or decision **4** : to refrain from exacting or enforcing (as a penalty) **5** : to send (money) in payment of a bill **syn** excuse, condone

re·mit·tal \ri-'mit-ᵊl\ *n* : REMISSION

re·mit·tance \ri-'mit-ᵊns\ *n* **1** : a sum of money remitted **2** : transmittal of money (as to a distant place)

rem·nant \'rem-nənt\ *n* **1** : a usu. small part or trace remaining **2** : an unsold or unused end of fabrics that are sold by the yard **syn** remainder, residue, rest

re·mod·el \'rē-'mäd-ᵊl\ *vb* : to alter the structure of : MAKE OVER

re·mon·strance \ri-'män-strəns\ *n* : an act or instance of remonstrating

re·mon·strant \-strənt\ *adj* : vigorously objecting or opposing — **remonstrant** *n* — **re·mon·strant·ly** *adv*

re·mon·strate \ri-'män-ˌstrāt\ *vb* -**strat·ed; -strat·ing** : to plead in opposition to something : speak in protest or reproof **syn** expostulate, object, protest — **re·mon·stra·tion** \ri-ˌmän-'strā-shən, ˌrem-ən-\ *n* — **re·mon·stra·tive** \ri-'män-strət-iv\ *adj* — **re·mon·stra·tor** \ri-'män-ˌstrāt-ər\ *n*

rem·o·ra \'rem-ə-rə\ *n* : any of several fishes with sucking organs on the head by means of which they cling to other fishes and ships

re·morse \ri-'mȯrs\ *n* [ME, fr. MF *remors,* fr. ML *remorsus,* fr. LL, act of biting again, fr. L *remorsus,* pp. of *remordēre* to bite again, fr. *re-* again + *mordēre* to bite] : regret for one's sins or for acts that wrong others : distress arising from a sense of guilt **syn** penitence, repentance, contrition — **re·morse·ful** *adj*

re·morse·less \-ləs\ *adj* **1** : MERCILESS **2** : PERSISTENT, RELENTLESS

re·mote \ri-'mōt\ *adj* **re·mot·er; -est 1** : far off in place or time : not near **2** : not closely related : DISTANT **3** : located out of the way : SECLUDED **4** : small in degree : SLIGHT ⟨a ∼ chance⟩ **5** : distant in manner — **re·mote·ly** *adv* — **re·mote·ness** *n*

¹**re·mount** \'rē-'maunt\ *vb* **1** : to mount again **2** : to furnish remounts to

²**re·mount** \'rē-ˌmaunt\ *n* : a fresh horse to replace one disabled or exhausted

¹**re·move** \ri-'müv\ *vb* **re·moved; re·mov·ing 1** : to move from one place to another : TRANSFER **2** : to move by lifting or taking off or away **3** : DISMISS, DISCHARGE **4** : to get rid of : ELIMINATE ⟨∼ a fire hazard⟩ **5** : to change one's residence or location **6** : to go away : DEPART **7** : to be capable of being removed — **re·mov·able** *adj* — **re·mov·al** \-vəl\ *n* — **re·mov·er** *n*

²**remove** *n* **1** : a transfer from one location to another : MOVE **2** : a degree or stage of separation

REM sleep *n* : a state of sleep associated with rapid eye movements and oc-

curring approximately at 90-minute intervals that is characterized by changes in the electrical activity of the brain, changes in heart rhythm, relaxed muscles, vascular congestion of the sex organs, and dreaming

re·mu·ner·ate \ri-'myü-nə-ˌrāt\ *vb* -**at·ed; -at·ing** : to pay an equivalent for or to : RECOMPENSE — **re·mu·ner·a·tor** \-ˌrāt-ər\ *n*

re·mu·ner·a·tion \ri-ˌmyü-nə-'rā-shən\ *n* : COMPENSATION, PAYMENT

re·mu·ner·a·tive \ri-'myü-nə-rət-iv, -ˌrāt-\ *adj* : serving to remunerate : GAINFUL

re·nais·sance \ˌren-ə-'säns, -'zäns\ *n* **1** *cap* : the revival of classical influences in art and literature and the beginnings of modern science in Europe in the 14th-17th centuries; *also* : the period of the Renaissance **2** *often cap* : a movement or period of vigorous artistic and intellectual activity **3** : REBIRTH, REVIVAL

re·nal \'rēn-ᵊl\ *adj* : of, relating to, or located in or near the kidneys

re·na·scence \ri-'nas-ᵊns, -'nās-\ *n, often cap* : RENAISSANCE

rend \'rend\ *vb* **rent** \'rent\; **rend·ing 1** : to remove by violence : WREST **2** : to tear forcibly apart : SPLIT

ren·der \'ren-dər\ *vb* **ren·dered; ren·der·ing** \-d(ə-)riŋ\ **1** : to extract (as lard) by heating **2** : to give to another; *also* : YIELD **3** : to give in return **4** : to do (a service) for another ⟨∼ aid⟩ **5** : to cause to be or become : MAKE **6** : to reproduce or represent by artistic or verbal means **7** : TRANSLATE ⟨∼ into English⟩

¹**ren·dez·vous** \'rän-di-ˌvü, -dā-\ *n, pl* **ren·dez·vous** \-ˌvüz\ [MF, fr. *rendez vous* present yourselves] **1** : a place appointed for a meeting; *also* : a meeting at an appointed place **2** : a place of popular resort **3** : the process of bringing two spacecraft together **syn** tryst, engagement, appointment

²**rendezvous** *vb* -**voused** \-ˌvüd\; **-vous·ing** \-ˌvü-iŋ\; **-vouses** \-ˌvüz\ : to come or bring together at a rendezvous

ren·di·tion \ren-'dish-ən\ *n* : an act or a result of rendering ⟨first ∼ of the work into English⟩

ren·e·gade \'ren-i-ˌgād\ *n* [Sp *renega-*

do, fr. ML *renegatus,* fr. pp. of *renegare* to deny, fr. L *re-* re- + *negare* to deny] : one who deserts a faith, cause, principle, or party for another

re•nege \ri-'nig, -'neg, -'nēg, -'nāg\ *vb* **re•neged; re•neg•ing 1** : to fail to follow suit when able in a card game in violation of the rules **2** : to go back on a promise or commitment — **re•neg•er** *n*

re•new \ri-'n(y)ü\ *vb* **1** : to make or become new, fresh, or strong again **2** : to restore to existence : RECREATE, REVIVE **3** : to make or do again : REPEAT ⟨∼ a complaint⟩ **4** : to begin again : RESUME ⟨∼ed his efforts⟩ **5** : REPLACE ⟨∼ the lining of a coat⟩ **6** : to grant or obtain an extension of or on ⟨∼ a lease⟩ ⟨∼ a subscription⟩ — **re•new•er** *n*

re•new•able \ri-'n(y)ü-ə-bəl\ *adj* **1** : capable of being renewed **2** : capable of being replaced by natural ecological cycles or sound management procedures ⟨water, wildlife, and forests are ∼ resources⟩

re•new•al \ri-'n(y)ü-əl\ *n* **1** : the act of renewing : the state of being renewed **2** : something renewed

ren•net \'ren-ət\ *n* **1** : the contents of the stomach of an unweaned animal (as a calf) or the lining membrane of the stomach used for curdling milk **2** : rennin or a substitute used to curdle milk

ren•nin \'ren-ən\ *n* : a stomach enzyme that coagulates casein and is used commercially to curdle milk in the making of cheese

re•nounce \ri-'nau̇ns\ *vb* **re•nounced; re•nounc•ing 1** : to give up, refuse, or resign usu. by formal declaration **2** : to refuse further to follow, obey, or recognize : REPUDIATE **syn** abdicate, resign — **re•nounce•ment** *n*

ren•o•vate \'ren-ə-,vāt\ *vb* **-vat•ed; -vat•ing 1** : to make like new again : put in good condition : REPAIR **2** : to restore to vigor or activity — **ren•o•va•tion** \-,ren-ə-'vā-shən\ *n* — **ren•o•va•tor** \'ren-ə-,vāt-ər\ *n*

re•nown \ri-'nau̇n\ *n* : a state of being widely acclaimed and honored : FAME, CELEBRITY **syn** honor, glory, reputation, repute — **re•nowned** \-'nau̇nd\ *adj*

¹rent \'rent\ *n* **1** : money or the amount of money paid or due (as monthly) for the use of another's property **2** : property rented or for rent

²rent *vb* **1** : to take and hold under an agreement to pay rent **2** : to give possession and use of in return for rent **3** : to be for rent ⟨∼s for $100 a month⟩ — **rent•er** *n*

³rent *n* **1** : a tear in cloth **2** : a split in a party or organized group : SCHISM

¹rent•al \'rent-ᵊl\ *n* **1** : an amount paid or collected as rent **2** : a property rented **3** : an act of renting

²rental *adj* : of or relating to rent

re•nun•ci•a•tion \ri-,nən-sē-'ā-shən\ *n* : the act of renouncing : REPUDIATION

rep *abbr* **1** repair **2** report; reporter **3** representative **4** republic

Rep *abbr* Republican

re•pack•age \(')rē-'pak-ij\ *vb* : to package again or anew; *esp* : to put into a more attractive form

¹re•pair \ri-'paər\ *vb* [ME *repairen,* fr. MF *repairier* to go back to one's country, fr. LL *repatriare,* fr. L *re-* re- + *patria* native country] : to make one's way : GO ⟨∼ed to his den⟩

²repair *vb* [ME *repairen,* fr. MF *reparer,* fr. L *reparare,* fr. *re-* re- + *parare* to prepare] **1** : to restore to good condition **2** : to restore to a healthy state **3** : REMEDY ⟨∼ a wrong⟩ — **re•pair•er** *n* — **re•pair•man** \-,man\ *n*

³repair *n* **1** : an act of repairing **2** : a result of repairing **3** : condition with respect to need of repairing ⟨in bad ∼⟩

rep•a•ra•tion \,rep-ə-'rā-shən\ *n* **1** : the act of making amends for a wrong **2** : amends made for a wrong; *esp* : money paid by a defeated nation in compensation for damages caused during hostilities — usu. used in pl. **syn** redress, restitution, indemnity

re•par•a•tive \ri-'par-ət-iv\ *adj* **1** : of, relating to, or effecting repairs **2** : serving to make amends

rep•ar•tee \,rep-ər-'tē\ *n* **1** : a witty reply **2** : a succession of clever replies; *also* : skill in making such replies

re•past \ri-'past, 'rē-,past\ *n* : a supply of food and drink served as a meal

re•pa•tri•ate \rē-'pā-trē-,āt\ *vb* **-at•ed; -at•ing** : to send or bring back to the country of origin or citizenship ⟨∼ profits⟩ ⟨∼ prisoners of war⟩ — **re•pa-**

759

tri·ate \-trē-ət, -trē-ˌāt\ *n* — **re·pa·tri·a·tion** \-ˌpā-trē-'ā-shən\ *n*

re·pay \rē-'pā\ *vb* **-paid** \-'pād\; **-pay·ing** **1** : to pay back : REFUND **2** : to give or do in return or requital **3** : to make a return payment to : RECOMPENSE, REQUITE **syn** remunerate, compensate, reimburse, indemnify — **re·pay·able** *adj* — **re·pay·ment** *n*

re·peal \ri-'pēl\ *vb* : to annul by authoritative and esp. legislative action — **repeal** *n* — **re·peal·er** *n*

¹re·peat \ri-'pēt\ *vb* **1** : to say again **2** : to do again **3** : to say over from memory **syn** iterate, reiterate, reprise — **re·peat·able** *adj* — **re·peat·er** *n*

²re·peat \ri-'pēt, 'rē-ˌpēt\ *n* **1** : the act of repeating **2** : something repeated or to be repeated (as a radio or television program)

re·peat·ed \ri-'pēt-əd\ *adj* : done or recurring again and again : FREQUENT — **re·peat·ed·ly** *adv*

repeating decimal *n* : a decimal in which a particular digit or sequence of digits repeats itself indefinitely

re·pel \ri-'pel\ *vb* **re·pelled**; **re·pel·ling** **1** : to drive away : REPULSE **2** : to fight against : RESIST **3** : to turn away : REJECT **4** : to cause aversion in : DISGUST

¹re·pel·lent *also* **re·pel·lant** \ri-'pel-ənt\ *adj* **1** : tending to drive away ⟨a mosquito-*repellent* spray⟩ **2** : causing disgust

²repellent *also* **repellant** *n* : something that repels; *esp* : a substance used to prevent insect attacks

re·pent \ri-'pent\ *vb* **1** : to turn from sin and resolve to reform one's life **2** : to feel sorry for (something done) : REGRET — **re·pen·tance** \ri-'pent-ᵊns\ *n* — **re·pen·tant** \-ᵊnt\ *adj*

re·per·cus·sion \ˌrē-pər-'kəsh-ən, ˌrep-ər-\ *n* **1** : REVERBERATION **2** : a reciprocal action or effect **3** : a widespread, indirect, or unforeseen effect of something done or said

rep·er·toire \'rep-ə(r)-ˌtwär\ *n* [F] **1** : a list of plays, operas, pieces, or parts which a company or performer is prepared to present **2** : a list of the skills or devices possessed by a person or needed in his occupation

rep·er·to·ry \'rep-ə(r)-ˌtōr-ē\ *n, pl* **-ries** **1** : REPOSITORY **2** : REPERTOIRE **3** : a company that presents its repertoire

in the course of one season at one theater

rep·e·ti·tion \ˌrep-ə-'tish-ən\ *n* **1** : the act or an instance of repeating **2** : the fact of being repeated

rep·e·ti·tious \-'tish-əs\ *adj* : marked by repetition; *esp* : tediously repeating — **rep·e·ti·tious·ly** *adv* — **rep·e·ti·tious·ness** *n*

re·pet·i·tive \ri-'pet-ət-iv\ *adj* : REPETITIOUS — **re·pet·i·tive·ly** *adv* — **re·pet·i·tive·ness** *n*

re·pine \ri-'pīn\ *vb* **re·pined**; **re·pin·ing** **1** : to feel or express discontent or dejection **2** : to long for something

repl *abbr* replace; replacement

re·place \ri-'plās\ *vb* **1** : to restore to a former place or position **2** : to take the place of : SUPPLANT **3** : to put something new in the place of — **re·place·able** *adj* — **re·plac·er** *n*

re·place·ment \ri-'plās-mənt\ *n* **1** : the act of replacing : the state of being replaced : SUBSTITUTION **2** : one that replaces; *esp* : one assigned to a military unit to replace a loss or fill a quota

¹re·play \'rē-'plā\ *vb* : to play again or over

²re·play \'rē-ˌplā\ *n* **1** : an act or instance of replaying **2** : the playing of a tape (as a videotape)

re·plen·ish \ri-'plen-ish\ *vb* : to fill or build up again : stock or supply anew — **re·plen·ish·ment** *n*

re·plete \ri-'plēt\ *adj* **1** : fully provided **2** : FULL; *esp* : full of food — **re·plete·ness** *n*

re·ple·tion \ri-'plē-shən\ *n* : the state of being replete

rep·li·ca \'rep-li-kə\ *n* [It, repetition, fr. *replicare* to repeat, fr. LL, fr. L, to fold back, fr. *re-* back + *plicare* to fold] **1** : a close reproduction or facsimile (as of a painting or statue) esp. by the maker of the original **2** : COPY, DUPLICATE

¹rep·li·cate \'rep-lə-ˌkāt\ *vb* **-cat·ed**; **-cat·ing** : DUPLICATE, REPEAT

²rep·li·cate \-li-kət\ *n* : one of several identical experiments or procedures

rep·li·ca·tion \ˌrep-lə-'kā-shən\ *n* **1** : ANSWER, REPLY **2** : precise copying or reproduction; *also* : an act or process of this

¹**re•ply** \ri-ˈplī\ *vb* **re•plied; re•ply•ing** : to say or do in answer : RESPOND

²**reply** *n, pl* **replies** : ANSWER, RESPONSE

¹**re•port** \ri-ˈpōrt\ *n* [ME, fr. MF, fr. OF, fr. *reporter* to report, fr. L *reportare*, fr. *re-* back + *portare* to carry] **1** : common talk : RUMOR **2** : FAME, REPUTATION **3** : a usu. detailed account or statement **4** : an explosive noise

²**report** *vb* **1** : to give an account of : RELATE, TELL **2** : to serve as carrier of (a message) **3** : to prepare or present (as an account of an event) for a newspaper or a broadcast **4** : to make a charge of misconduct against **5** : to present oneself (as for work) **6** : to make known to the authorities ⟨∼ a fire⟩ **7** : to return or present (as a matter referred to a committee) with conclusions and recommendations — **re•port•able** *adj*

re•port•age \ri-ˈpōrt-ij, *esp for 2* ˌrep-ər-ˈtäzh, ˌrep-ˌȯr-ˈ\ *n* [F] **1** : the act or process of reporting news **2** : writing intended to give an account of observed or documented events

report card *n* : a periodic report on a student's grades

re•port•ed•ly \ri-ˈpōrt-əd-lē\ *adv* : according to report

re•port•er \ri-ˈpōrt-ər\ *n* : one that reports; *esp* : a person who gathers and reports news for a news medium — **re•por•to•ri•al** \ˌrep-ə(r)-ˈtōr-ē-əl\ *adj*

¹**re•pose** \ri-ˈpōz\ *vb* **re•posed; re•pos•ing** **1** : to lay at rest **2** : to lie at rest **3** : to lie dead **4** : to take a rest **5** : to rest for support : LIE

²**repose** *n* **1** : a state of resting (as after exertion); *esp* : SLEEP **2** : CALM, PEACE **3** : cessation or absence of activity, movement, or animation **4** : composure of manner : POISE — **re•pose•ful** *adj*

³**repose** *vb* **re•posed; re•pos•ing** **1** : to place (as trust) in someone or something **2** : to place for control, management, or use

re•pos•i•to•ry \ri-ˈpäz-ə-ˌtōr-ē\ *n, pl* **-ries** **1** : a place where something is deposited or stored **2** : a person to whom something is entrusted

re•pos•sess \ˌrē-pə-ˈzes\ *vb* **1** : to regain possession of **2** : to resume possession of in default of the payment of installments due — **re•pos•ses•sion** \-ˈzesh-ən\ *n*

rep•re•hend \ˌrep-ri-ˈhend\ *vb* : to express disapproval of : CENSURE **syn** criticize, condemn, denounce, blame, pan — **rep•re•hen•sion** \-ˈhen-chən\ *n*

rep•re•hen•si•ble \-ˈhen-sə-bəl\ *adj* : deserving blame or censure : CULPABLE — **rep•re•hen•si•bly** \-blē\ *adv*

rep•re•sent \ˌrep-ri-ˈzent\ *vb* **1** : to present a picture or a likeness of : PORTRAY, DEPICT **2** : to serve as a sign or symbol of **3** : to act the role of **4** : to stand in the place of : act or speak for **5** : to be a member or example of : TYPIFY **6** : to serve as an elected representative of **7** : to describe as having a specified quality or character **8** : to state with the purpose of affecting judgment or action

rep•re•sen•ta•tion \ˌrep-ri-ˌzen-ˈtā-shən\ *n* **1** : the act of representing **2** : one (as a picture or image) that represents something else **3** : the state of being represented in a legislative body; *also* : the body of persons representing a constituency **4** : a usu. formal statement made to effect a change

¹**rep•re•sen•ta•tive** \ˌrep-ri-ˈzent-ət-iv\ *adj* **1** : serving to represent **2** : standing or acting for another **3** : founded on the principle of representation : carried on by elected representatives ⟨∼ government⟩ — **rep•re•sen•ta•tive•ly** *adv* — **rep•re•sen•ta•tive•ness** *n*

²**representative** *n* **1** : a typical example of a group, class, or quality **2** : one that represents another; *esp* : one representing a district in a legislative body usu. as a member of a lower house

re•press \ri-ˈpres\ *vb* **1** : CURB, SUBDUE **2** : RESTRAIN, SUPPRESS; *esp* : to exclude from consciousness — **re•pres•sion** \-ˈpresh-ən\ *n* — **re•pres•sive** \-ˈpres-iv\ *adj*

¹**re•prieve** \ri-ˈprēv\ *vb* **re•prieved; re•priev•ing** **1** : to delay the punishment or execution of **2** : to give temporary relief to

²**reprieve** *n* **1** : the act of reprieving : the state of being reprieved **2** : a formal temporary suspension of a sentence esp. of death **3** : a temporary respite

¹**rep•ri•mand** \'rep-rə-ˌmand\ *n* : a severe or formal reproof

²**reprimand** *vb* : to reprove severely or formally

¹**re•print** \'rē-'print\ *vb* : to print again

²**re•print** \'rē-ˌprint\ *n* : a reproduction of printed matter

re•pri•sal \ri-'prī-zəl\ *n* : an act in retaliation for something done by another

re•prise \ri-'prēz\ *n* : a recurrence, renewal, or resumption of an action; *also* : a musical repetition

¹**re•proach** \ri-'prōch\ *n* **1** : a cause or occasion of blame or disgrace **2** : DIS-GRACE, DISCREDIT **3** : the act of reproaching : REBUKE — **re•proach•ful** \-fəl\ *adj* — **re•proach•ful•ly** \-ē\ *adv* — **re•proach•ful•ness** *n*

²**reproach** *vb* **1** : CENSURE, REBUKE **2** : to cast discredit on **syn** chide, admonish, reprove, reprimand — **re•proach•able** *adj*

rep•ro•bate \'rep-rə-ˌbāt\ *n* **1** : a person foreordained to damnation **2** : a thoroughly bad person : SCOUNDREL — **reprobate** *adj*

rep•ro•ba•tion \ˌrep-rə-'bā-shən\ *n* : strong disapproval : CONDEMNATION

re•pro•duce \ˌrē-prə-'d(y)üs\ *vb* **1** : to produce again or anew **2** : to bear offspring — **re•pro•duc•ible** \-'d(y)ü-sə-bəl\ *adj* — **re•pro•duc•tion** \-'dək-shən\ *n* — **re•pro•duc•tive** \-'dək-tiv\ *adj*

re•proof \ri-'prüf\ *n* : blame or censure for a fault

re•prove \ri-'prüv\ *vb* **re•proved; re•prov•ing 1** : to administer a rebuke to **2** : to express disapproval of **syn** reprimand, admonish, reproach, chide — **re•prov•er** *n*

rept *abbr* report

rep•tile \'rep-t³l, -ˌtīl\ *n* [ME *reptil,* fr. MF or LL; MF *reptile,* fr. LL *reptile,* fr. L *repere* to creep] : any of a large class of air-breathing scaly vertebrates including snakes, lizards, alligators, and turtles — **rep•til•i•an** \rep-'til-ē-ən\ *adj or n*

re•pub•lic \ri-'pəb-lik\ *n* [F *république,* fr. MF *republique,* fr. L *respublica,* fr. *res* thing, wealth + *publica,* fem. of *publicus* public] **1** : a government having a chief of state who is not a monarch and is usu. a president; *also*

: a nation or other political unit having such a government **2** : a government in which supreme power is held by the citizens entitled to vote and is exercised by elected officers and representatives governing according to law; *also* : a nation or other political unit having such a form of government

¹**re•pub•li•can** \-li-kən\ *adj* **1** : of, relating to, or resembling a republic **2** : favoring or supporting a republic **3** *cap* : of, relating to, or constituting one of the two major political parties in the U.S. evolving in the mid-19th century — **re•pub•li•can•ism** *n, often cap*

²**republican** *n* **1** : one that favors or supports a republican form of government **2** *cap* : a member of a republican party and esp. of the Republican party of the U.S.

re•pu•di•ate \ri-'pyüd-ē-ˌāt\ *vb* **-at•ed; -at•ing** [L *repudiare* to cast off, divorce, fr. *repudium* divorce] **1** : to cast off : DISOWN **2** : to refuse to have anything to do with : refuse to acknowledge, accept, or pay ⟨∼ a charge⟩ ⟨∼ a debt⟩ **syn** spurn, reject, decline — **re•pu•di•a•tion** \-ˌpyüd-ē-'ā-shən\ *n* — **re•pu•di•a•tor** \-'pyüd-ē-ˌāt-ər\ *n*

re•pug•nance \ri-'pəg-nəns\ *n* **1** : the quality or fact of being contradictory or inconsistent **2** : strong dislike, distaste, or antagonism

re•pug•nant \-nənt\ *adj* **1** : marked by repugnance **2** : contrary to a person's tastes or principles : exciting distaste or aversion **syn** repellent, abhorrent, distasteful, obnoxious, revolting, loathsome — **re•pug•nant•ly** *adv*

¹**re•pulse** \ri-'pəls\ *vb* **re•pulsed; re•puls•ing 1** : to drive or beat back : REPEL **2** : to repel by discourtesy or denial : REBUFF **3** : to cause a feeling of repulsion in : DISGUST

²**repulse** *n* **1** : REBUFF, REJECTION **2** : a repelling or being repelled in hostile encounter

re•pul•sion \ri-'pəl-shən\ *n* **1** : the action of repulsing : the state of being repulsed **2** : the force with which bodies, particles, or like forces repel one another **3** : a feeling of aversion

re•pul•sive \-siv\ *adj* **1** : serving or tending to repel or reject **2** : arousing aversion or disgust **syn** repugnant, revolting, loathsome, noisome — **re·pul·sive·ly** adv — **re·pul·sive·ness** n

rep·u·ta·ble \'rep-yət-ə-bəl\ adj : having a good reputation : ESTIMABLE — **rep·u·ta·bly** \-blē\ adv

rep·u·ta·tion \ˌrep-yə-'tā-shən\ n **1** : overall quality or character as seen or judged by people in general **2** : place in public esteem or regard

¹re·pute \ri-'pyüt\ vb **re·put·ed; re·put·ing** : CONSIDER, ACCOUNT

²repute n **1** : REPUTATION **2** : the state of being favorably known or spoken of

re·put·ed \ri-'pyüt-əd\ adj **1** : REPUTABLE **2** : according to reputation : SUPPOSED — **re·put·ed·ly** adv

req abbr **1** request **2** require; required **3** requisition

¹re·quest \ri-'kwest\ n **1** : an act or instance of asking for something **2** : a thing asked for **3** : the fact or condition of being asked for ⟨available on ∼⟩

²request vb **1** : to make a request to or of **2** : to ask for — **re·quest·er** n

re·qui·em \'rek-wē-əm, 'rāk-\ n [ME, fr. L (first word of the requiem mass), acc. of requies rest, fr. quies quiet, rest] **1** : a mass for a dead person; also : a musical setting for this **2** : a musical service or hymn in honor of the dead

re·quire \ri-'kwī(ə)r\ vb **re·quired; re·quir·ing 1** : to demand as necessary or essential **2** : COMMAND, ORDER

re·quire·ment \-mənt\ n **1** : something (as a condition or quality) required ⟨entrance ∼⟩ **2** : NECESSITY

req·ui·site \'rek-wə-zət\ adj : REQUIRED, NECESSARY — **requisite** n

req·ui·si·tion \ˌrek-wə-'zish-ən\ n **1** : formal application or demand (as for supplies) **2** : the state of being in demand or use — **requisition** vb

re·quite \ri-'kwīt\ vb **re·quit·ed; re·quit·ing 1** : to make return for : REPAY **2** : to make retaliation for : AVENGE **3** : to make return to for a benefit or service or for an injury — **re·quit·al** \-'kwīt-ᵊl\ n

rere·dos \'rer-ə-ˌdäs\ n : a usu. ornamental wood or stone screen or partition wall behind an altar

re·run \'rē-ˌrən, 'rē-'rən\ n : the act or an instance of running again or anew;

esp : a showing of a motion picture or television program after its first run — **re·run** \'rē-'rən\ vb

res abbr **1** research **2** reservation; reserve **3** residence **4** resolution

re·sale \'rē-ˌsāl, -'sāl\ n : the act of selling again usu. to a new party — **re·sal·able** \'rē-'sā-lə-bəl\ adj

re·scind \ri-'sind\ vb : REPEAL, CANCEL, ANNUL — **re·scind·er** n — **re·scis·sion** \-'sizh-ən\ n

re·script \'rē-ˌskript\ n : an official or authoritative order or decree

res·cue \'res-kyü\ vb **res·cued; res·cu·ing** [ME rescuen, fr. MF rescourre, fr. OF, fr. re- re- + escourre to shake out, fr. L excutere] : to free from danger, harm, or confinement **syn** deliver, save — **rescue** n — **res·cu·er** n

re·search \ri-'sərch, 'rē-ˌsərch\ n **1** : careful or diligent search **2** : studious and critical inquiry and examination aimed at the discovery and interpretation of new knowledge **3** : the collecting of information about a particular subject — **research** vb — **re·search·er** n

re·sec·tion \ri-'sek-shən\ n : the surgical removal of part of an organ or structure

re·sem·blance \ri-'zem-bləns\ n : the quality or state of resembling

re·sem·ble \ri-'zem-bəl\ vb **-bled; -bling** \-b(ə-)liŋ\ : to be like or similar to

re·sent \ri-'zent\ vb : to feel or exhibit annoyance or indignation at — **re·sent·ful** \-fəl\ adj — **re·sent·ful·ly** \-ē\ adv — **re·sent·ment** n

re·ser·pine \ri-'sər-ˌpēn, -pən\ n : a drug obtained from rauwolfia and used in treating high blood pressure and nervous tension

res·er·va·tion \ˌrez-ər-'vā-shən\ n **1** : an act of reserving **2** : something (as a room in a hotel) arranged for in advance **3** : something reserved; esp : a tract of public land set aside for a special use **4** : a limiting condition

¹re·serve \ri-'zərv\ vb **re·served; re·serv·ing 1** : to store for future or special use **2** : to hold back for oneself **3** : to set aside or arrange to have set aside or held for special use

²reserve n **1** : something reserved : STOCK, STORE **2** : a military force withheld from action for later use —

usu. used in pl. **3** : the military forces of a country not part of the regular services; *also* : RESERVIST **4** : a tract set apart : RESERVATION **5** : an act of reserving **6** : restraint or caution in one's words or bearing **7** : money or its equivalent kept in hand or set apart to meet liabilities

re·served \ri-'zərvd\ *adj* **1** : restrained in words and actions **2** : set aside for future or special use — **re·serv·ed·ly** \-'zər-vəd-lē\ *adv* — **re·serv·ed·ness** \-vəd-nəs\ *n*

re·serv·ist \ri-'zər-vəst\ *n* : a member of a military reserve

res·er·voir \'rez-ə(r)v-ˌwär, -ə(r)v-ˌ(w)ȯr\ *n* [F] : a place where something is kept in store; *esp* : an artificial lake where water is collected as a water supply

re·shuf·fle \rē-'shəf-əl\ *vb* **1** : to shuffle again **2** : to reorganize usu. by redistribution of existing elements — **reshuffle** *n*

re·side \ri-'zīd\ *vb* **re·sid·ed; re·sid·ing** **1** : to make one's home : DWELL **2** : to be present as a quality or vested as a right

res·i·dence \'rez-əd-əns\ *n* **1** : the act or fact of residing in a place as a dweller or in discharge of a duty or an obligation **2** : the place where one actually lives **3** : a building used as a home : DWELLING **4** : the period of living in a place

res·i·den·cy \'rez-əd-ən-sē\ *n, pl* **-cies** **1** : the residence of or the territory under a diplomatic resident **2** : a period of advanced training in a medical specialty

¹res·i·dent \-ənt\ *adj* **1** : RESIDING **2** : being in residence **3** : not migratory

²resident *n* **1** : one who resides in a place **2** : a diplomatic representative with governing powers (as in a protectorate) **3** : a physician serving a residency

res·i·den·tial \ˌrez-ə-'den-chəl\ *adj* **1** : used as a residence or by residents **2** : occupied by or restricted to residences — **res·i·den·tial·ly** \-ē\ *adv*

¹re·sid·u·al \ri-'zij-(ə-w)əl\ *adj* : being a residue or remainder

²residual *n* **1** : a residual product or substance **2** : a payment (as to an actor or

writer) for each rerun after an initial showing (as of a taped TV show)

re·sid·u·ary \ri-'zij-ə-ˌwer-ē\ *adj* : of, relating to, or constituting a residue esp. of an estate

res·i·due \'rez-ə-ˌd(y)ü\ *n* : a part remaining after another part has been taken away : REMAINDER

re·sid·u·um \ri-'zij-ə-wəm\ *n, pl* **re·sid·ua** \-ə-wə\ [L] **1** : something remaining or residual after certain deductions are made **2** : a residual product **syn** remainder, rest, balance, remnant

re·sign \ri-'zīn\ *vb* [ME *resignen*, fr. MF *resigner*, fr. L *resignare*, lit., to unseal, cancel, fr. *signare* to sign, seal] **1** : to give up deliberately (as one's position) esp. by a formal act **2** : to give (oneself) over (as to grief or despair) without resistance — **re·sign·ed·ly** \-'zī-nəd-lē\ *adv*

re–sign \'rē-'sīn\ *vb* : to sign again

res·ig·na·tion \ˌrez-ig-'nā-shən\ *n* **1** : an act or instance of resigning; *also* : a formal notification of such an act **2** : the quality or state of being resigned

re·sil·ience \ri-'zil-yəns\ *n* **1** : the ability of a body to regain its original size and shape after being compressed, bent, or stretched **2** : an ability to recover from or adjust easily to change or misfortune

re·sil·ien·cy \-yən-sē\ *n* : RESILIENCE

re·sil·ient \-yənt\ *adj* : marked by resilience **syn** flexible, supple

res·in \'rez-ᵊn\ *n* : a substance obtained from the gum or sap of some trees and used esp. in varnishes, plastics, and medicine; *also* : a comparable synthetic product — **res·in·ous** *adj*

¹re·sist \ri-'zist\ *vb* **1** : to fight against : OPPOSE ⟨∼ aggression⟩ **2** : to withstand the force or effect of ⟨∼ disease⟩ **syn** combat, withstand, repel — **re·sist·ible** \-'zis-tə-bəl\ *adj* — **re·sist·less** *adj*

²resist *n* : something (as a coating) that resists or prevents a particular action

re·sis·tance \ri-'zis-təns\ *n* **1** : the act or an instance of resisting : OPPOSITION **2** : the opposition offered by a body to the passage through it of a steady electric current

re·sis·tant \-tənt\ *adj* : giving or capable of resistance

re·sis·tiv·i·ty \ri-ˌzis-'tiv-ət-ē, ˌrē-\ *n, pl* **-ties** : capacity for resisting

re·sis·tor \ri-'zis-tər\ *n* : a device used to provide resistance to the flow of an electric current

res·o·lute \'rez-ə-ˌlüt\ *adj* : firmly determined in purpose : RESOLVED **syn** steadfast, staunch, faithful, true, loyal — **res·o·lute·ly** *adv* — **res·o·lute·ness** *n*

res·o·lu·tion \ˌrez-ə-'lü-shən\ *n* **1** : the act or process of resolving **2** : the action of solving; *also* : SOLUTION **3** : the quality of being resolute : FIRMNESS, DETERMINATION **4** : a formal statement expressing the opinion, will, or intent of a body of persons

¹re·solve \ri-'zälv\ *vb* **re·solved; re·solving 1** : to break up into constituent parts : ANALYZE **2** : to find an answer to : SOLVE **3** : DETERMINE, DECIDE **4** : to make or pass a formal resolution — **re·solv·able** *adj*

²resolve *n* **1** : something resolved **2** : fixity of purpose

res·o·nance \'rez-ᵊn-əns\ *n* **1** : the quality or state of being resonant **2** : a reinforcement of sound in a vibrating body caused by waves from another body vibrating at nearly the same rate

res·o·nant \'rez-ᵊn-ənt\ *adj* **1** : continuing to sound : RESOUNDING **2** : relating to or exhibiting resonance **3** : intensified and enriched by or as if by resonance — **res·o·nant·ly** *adv*

res·o·nate \'rez-ᵊn-ˌāt\ *vb* **-nat·ed; -nating 1** : to produce or exhibit resonance **2** : REVERBERATE, RESOUND

res·o·na·tor \-ᵊn-ˌāt-ər\ *n* : something that resounds or exhibits resonance

re·sorp·tion \rē-'sȯrp-shən, -'zȯrp-\ *n* : the action or process of breaking down and assimilating something (as a tooth or an embryo)

¹re·sort \ri-'zȯrt\ *n* [ME, fr. MF, resource, recourse, fr. *resortir* to rebound, resort, fr. OF, fr. *sortir* to escape, sally] **1** : one looked to for help : REFUGE **2** : RECOURSE **3** : frequent or general visiting ⟨place of ~⟩ **4** : a frequently visited place : HAUNT **5** : a place providing recreation esp. to vacationers

²resort *vb* **1** : to go often or habitually **2** : to have recourse (as for aid)

re·sound \ri-'zau̇nd\ *vb* **1** : to become filled with sound : REVERBERATE, RING **2** : to sound loudly

re·sound·ing \-iŋ\ *adj* **1** : RESONATING, RESONANT **2** : impressively sonorous ⟨~ name⟩ **3** : EMPHATIC, UNEQUIVOCAL ⟨a ~ success⟩ — **re·sound·ing·ly** *adv*

re·source \'rē-ˌsȯrs, ri-'sȯrs\ *n* [F *ressource*, fr. OF *ressourse* relief, resource, fr. *resourdre* to relieve, lit., to rise again, fr. L *resurgere*, fr. *re-* again + *surgere* to rise] **1** : a source of supply or support — usu. used in pl. **2** *pl* : available funds **3** : a possibility of relief or recovery **4** : a means of spending leisure time **5** : ability to meet and handle situations — **resource·ful** \ri-'sȯrs-fəl\ *adj* — **resource·ful·ness** *n*

resp *abbr* respective; respectively

¹re·spect \ri-'spekt\ *n* **1** : relation to something usu. specified : REFERENCE, REGARD **2** : high or special regard : ESTEEM **3** *pl* : an expression of respect or deference **4** : DETAIL, PARTICULAR — **re·spect·ful** \-fəl\ *adj* — **re·spect·ful·ly** \-ē\ *adv* — **re·spect·ful·ness** *n*

²respect *vb* **1** : to consider deserving of high regard : ESTEEM **2** : to refrain from interfering with ⟨~ another's privacy⟩ **3** : to have reference to : CONCERN — **re·spect·er** *n*

re·spect·able \ri-'spek-tə-bəl\ *adj* **1** : worthy of respect : ESTIMABLE **2** : decent or correct in conduct : PROPER **3** : fair in size, quantity, or quality : MODERATE, TOLERABLE **4** : fit to be seen : PRESENTABLE — **re·spect·a·bil·i·ty** \-ˌspek-tə-'bil-ət-ē\ *n* — **re·spect·ably** \-'spek-tə-blē\ *adv*

re·spect·ing \-tiŋ\ *prep* : with regard to

re·spec·tive \-tiv\ *adj* : PARTICULAR, SEPARATE ⟨returned to their ~ homes⟩

re·spec·tive·ly \-lē\ *adv* **1** : as relating to each **2** : each in the order given

res·pi·ra·tion \ˌres-pə-'rā-shən\ *n* **1** : an act or the process of breathing **2** : the physical and chemical processes (as breathing and oxidation) by which a living thing obtains the oxygen and eliminates waste gases (as carbon dioxide) — **res·pi·ra·to·ry** \'res-p(ə-)rə-ˌtōr-ē, ri-'spī-rə-\ *adj* — **re·spire** \ri-'spī(ə)r\ *vb*

res·pi·ra·tor \'res-pə-ˌrāt-ər\ *n* **1** : a device covering the mouth or nose esp.

to prevent inhaling harmful vapors **2** : a device for artificial respiration

re·spite \'res-pət\ *n* **1** : a temporary delay **2** : an interval of rest or relief

re·splen·dent \ri-'splen-dənt\ *adj* : shining brilliantly : gloriously bright : SPLENDID — **re·splen·dence** \-dəns\ *n* — **re·splen·dent·ly** *adv*

re·spond \ri-'spänd\ *vb* **1** : ANSWER, REPLY **2** : REACT ⟨~ to a stimulus⟩ **3** : to show favorable reaction ⟨~ to medication⟩ — **re·spond·er** *n*

re·spon·dent \ri-'spän-dənt\ *n* : one who responds; *esp* : one who answers in various legal proceedings — **respondent** *adj*

re·sponse \ri-'späns\ *n* **1** : an act of responding **2** : something constituting a reply or a reaction

re·spon·si·bil·i·ty \ri-ˌspän-sə-'bil-ət-ē\ *n, pl* **-ties 1** : the quality or state of being responsible **2** : something for which one is responsible

re·spon·si·ble \ri-'spän-sə-bəl\ *adj* **1** : liable to be called upon to answer for one's acts or decisions : ANSWERABLE **2** : able to fulfull one's obligations : RELIABLE, TRUSTWORTHY **3** : able to choose for oneself between right and wrong **4** : involving accountability or important duties ⟨~ position⟩ — **re·spon·si·ble·ness** *n* — **re·spon·si·bly** \-blē\ *adv*

re·spon·sive \-siv\ *adj* **1** : RESPONDING **2** : quick to respond : SENSITIVE **3** : using responses ⟨~ readings⟩ — **re·spon·sive·ly** *adv* — **re·spon·sive·ness** *n*

¹rest \'rest\ *n* **1** : REPOSE, SLEEP **2** : freedom from work or activity **3** : a state of motionlessness or inactivity **4** : a place of shelter or lodging **5** : a silence in music equivalent in duration to a note of the same value; *also* : a character indicating this **6** : something used as a support — **rest·ful** \-fəl\ *adj* — **rest·ful·ly** \-ē\ *adv*

²rest *vb* **1** : to get rest by lying down; *esp* : SLEEP **2** : to cease from action or motion **3** : to give rest to : set at rest **4** : to sit or lie fixed or supported **5** : to place on or against a support **6** : to remain based or founded **7** : to cause to be firmly fixed : GROUND **8** : to remain for action : DEPEND

³rest *n* : something that remains over

res·tau·rant \'res-t(ə-)rənt, -tə-ˌränt\ *n* [F, fr. prp. of *restaurer* to restore, fr. L *restaurare*] : a public eating place

res·tau·ra·teur \ˌres-tə-rə-'tər\ *also* **res·tau·ran·teur** \-ˌrän-\ *n* : the operator or proprietor of a restaurant

rest home *n* : an establishment that gives care for the aged or convalescent

res·ti·tu·tion \ˌres-tə-'t(y)ü-shən\ *n* : the act of restoring : the state of being restored; *esp* : restoration of something to its rightful owner **syn** amends, redress, reparation, indemnity, compensation

res·tive \'res-tiv\ *adj* [ME, fr. MF *restif*, fr. *rester* to stop behind, remain, fr. L *restare,* fr. *re-* back + *stare* to stand] **1** : BALKY **2** : UNEASY, FIDGETY **syn** restless, impatient, nervous — **res·tive·ly** *adv* — **res·tive·ness** *n*

rest·less \'rest-ləs\ *adj* **1** : lacking or denying rest **2** : never resting or ceasing : UNQUIET ⟨the ~ sea⟩ **3** : marked by or showing unrest esp. of mind : DISCONTENTED **syn** restive, impatient, nervous, fidgety — **rest·less·ly** *adv* — **rest·less·ness** *n*

re·stor·able \ri-'stōr-ə-bəl\ *adj* : fit for restoring or reclaiming

res·to·ra·tion \ˌres-tə-'rā-shən\ *n* **1** : an act of restoring : the state of being restored **2** : something that is restored; *esp* : a reconstruction or representation of an original form (as of a building)

re·stor·ative \ri-'stōr-ət-iv\ *n* : something that restores esp. to consciousness or health — **restorative** *adj*

re·store \ri-'stōr\ *vb* **re·stored; re·stor·ing 1** : to give back : RETURN **2** : to put back into use or service **3** : to put or bring back into a former or original state : REPAIR, RENEW **4** : to put again in possession of something — **re·stor·er** *n*

re·strain \ri-'strān\ *vb* **1** : to prevent from doing something **2** : to limit, restrict, or keep under control : CURB **3** : to place under restraint or arrest — **re·strain·able** *adj* — **re·strain·er** *n*

re·strained \ri-'strānd\ *adj* : marked by restraint : DISCIPLINED — **re·strain·ed·ly** \-'strā-nəd-lē\ *adv*

re·straint \ri-'strānt\ *n* **1** : an act of restraining : the state of being restrained **2** : a restraining force, agency, or device **3** : deprivation or limitation of liberty : CONFINEMENT **4** : control over one's feelings : RESERVE

re·strict \ri-'strikt\ vb **1** : to confine within bounds : LIMIT **2** : to place under restriction as to use — **re·stric·tive** adj — **re·stric·tive·ly** adv

re·stric·tion \ri-'strik-shən\ n **1** : something (as a law or rule) that restricts **2** : an act of restricting : the state of being restricted

rest room n : a room or suite of rooms providing personal facilities (as toilets)

¹re·sult \ri-'zəlt\ vb [ME resulten, fr. ML resultare, fr. L, to rebound, fr. re- + saltare to leap] : to proceed or come about as an effect or consequence — **re·sul·tant** \-'zəlt-ᵊnt\ adj or n

²result n **1** : something that results : EFFECT, CONSEQUENCE **2** : beneficial or discernible effect **3** : something obtained by calculation or investigation

re·sume \ri-'züm\ vb **re·sumed; re·sum·ing** **1** : to take or assume again **2** : to return to or begin again after interruption **3** : to take back to oneself — **re·sump·tion** \-'zəmp-shən\ n

ré·su·mé or **re·su·me** or **re·su·mé** \'rez-ə-ˌmā, ˌrez-ə-'mā\ n [F résumé] : SUMMARY; esp : a short account of one's career and qualifications usu. prepared by a job applicant

re·sur·gence \ri-'sər-jəns\ n : a rising again into life, activity, or prominence — **re·sur·gent** \-jənt\ adj

res·ur·rect \ˌrez-ə-'rekt\ vb **1** : to raise from the dead **2** : to bring to attention or use again

res·ur·rec·tion \ˌrez-ə-'rek-shən\ n **1** cap : the rising of Christ from the dead **2** often cap : the rising to life of all human dead before the final judgment **3** : REVIVAL

re·sus·ci·tate \ri-'səs-ə-ˌtāt\ vb **-tat·ed; -tat·ing** : to revive from a condition resembling death — **re·sus·ci·ta·tion** \ri-ˌsəs-ə-'tā-shən, ˌrē-\ n — **re·sus·ci·ta·tor** \-ˌtāt-ər\ n

ret abbr **1** retain **2** retired **3** return

¹re·tail \'rē-ˌtāl, esp for 2 also ri-'tāl\ vb **1** : to sell in small quantities directly to the ultimate consumer **2** : to tell in detail or to one person after another — **re·tail·er** n

²re·tail \'rē-ˌtāl\ n : the sale of goods in small amounts to ultimate consumers — **retail** adj or adv

re·tain \ri-'tān\ vb **1** : to hold in possession or use **2** : to engage (as a lawyer) by paying a fee in advance **3** : to keep in a fixed place or position **syn** detain, withhold, reserve

¹re·tain·er \-ər\ n **1** : one that retains **2** : a servant in a wealthy household; also : EMPLOYEE

²retainer n : a fee paid to secure services (as of a lawyer)

¹re·take \'rē-'tāk\ vb **-took** \-'tûk\; **-tak·en** \-'tā-kən\; **-tak·ing** **1** : to take or seize again **2** : to photograph again

²re·take \'rē-ˌtāk\ n : a second photographing of a motion-picture scene

re·tal·i·ate \ri-'tal-ē-ˌāt\ vb **-at·ed; -at·ing** : to return like for like; esp : to get revenge — **re·tal·i·a·tion** \-ˌtal-ē-'ā-shən\ n — **re·tal·ia·to·ry** \-'tal-yə-ˌtōr-ē\ adj

re·tard \ri-'tärd\ vb : to hold back : delay the progress of **syn** slow, slacken, detain — **re·tar·da·tion** \ˌrē-ˌtär-'dā-shən, ri-\ n — **re·tard·er** n

re·tar·date \-'tärd-ˌāt, -ət\ n : a mentally retarded person

re·tard·ed \ri-'tärd-əd\ adj : slow or limited in intellectual, emotional, or academic development ⟨a ∼ child⟩

retch \'rech, 'rēch\ vb : to try to vomit

re·ten·tion \ri-'ten-chən\ n **1** : the act of retaining : the state of being retained **2** : the power of retaining esp. in the mind : RETENTIVENESS

re·ten·tive \-'tent-iv\ adj : having the power of retaining; esp : retaining knowledge easily — **re·ten·tive·ness** n

ret·i·cent \'ret-ə-sənt\ adj : inclined to be silent or secretive : UNCOMMUNICATIVE **syn** reserved, taciturn, close-mouthed — **ret·i·cence** \-səns\ n — **ret·i·cent·ly** adv

ret·i·na \'ret-ᵊn-ə\ n, pl **retinas** or **ret·i·nae** \-ᵊn-ˌē\ : the sensory membrane lining the eye and receiving the image formed by the lens — **ret·i·nal** \'ret-ᵊn-əl\ adj

ret·i·nue \'ret-ᵊn-ˌ(y)ü\ n : the body of attendants or followers of a distinguished person

re·tire \ri-'tī(ə)r\ vb **retired; re·tir·ing** **1** : RETREAT **2** : to withdraw esp. for privacy **3** : to withdraw from one's occupation or position **4** : to go to bed **5** : to withdraw from circulation or from the market or from usual use or service **6** : to cause to be out in baseball — **re•tire•ment** *n*

re•tired \ri-ˈtī(ə)rd\ *adj* **1** : SECLUDED, QUIET **2** : withdrawn from active duty or from one's occupation **3** : received by or due to one who has retired

re•tir•ee \ri-ˌtī-ˈrē\ *n* : a person who has retired from an occupation

re•tir•ing \ri-ˈtīr-iŋ\ *adj* : SHY, RESERVED

¹**re•tort** \ri-ˈtȯrt\ *vb* [L *retortus,* pp. of *retorquēre,* lit., to twist back, hurl back, fr. *re-* back + *torquēre* to twist] **1** : to say in reply : answer back usu. sharply **2** : to answer (an argument) by a counter argument **3** : RETALIATE

²**retort** *n* : a quick, witty, or cutting reply

³**re•tort** \ri-ˈtȯrt, ˈrē-ˌtȯrt\ *n* [MF *retorte,* fr. ML *retorta,* fr. L, fem. of *retortus,* pp. of *retorquēre* to twist back; fr. its shape] : a vessel in which substances are distilled or broken up by heat

re•touch \ˈrē-ˈtəch\ *vb* : TOUCH UP; *esp* : to change (as a photographic negative) in order to produce a more desirable appearance

re•trace \(ˈ)rē-ˈtrās\ *vb* : to trace again or in a reverse direction ⟨*retraced* his steps⟩

re•tract \ri-ˈtrakt\ *vb* **1** : to draw back or in **2** : to withdraw (as a charge or promise) : DISAVOW — **re•tract•able** *adj* — **re•trac•tion** \-ˈtrak-shən\ *n*

re•trac•tile \ri-ˈtrak-tᵊl, -ˌtīl\ *adj* : capable of being drawn back or in ⟨∼ claws⟩

¹**re•tread** \ˈrē-ˈtred\ *vb* **re•tread•ed; re•tread•ing** : to put a new tread on (a worn tire)

²**re•tread** \ˈrē-ˌtred\ *n* **1** : a new tread on a tire **2** : a retreaded tire **3** : one pressed into service again; *also* : REMAKE

¹**re•treat** \ri-ˈtrēt\ *n* **1** : an act of withdrawing esp. from something dangerous, difficult, or disagreeable **2** : a military signal for withdrawal; *also* : a military flag-lowering ceremony **3** : a place of privacy or safety : REFUGE **4** : a period of group withdrawal for prayer, meditation, and study

²**retreat** *vb* **1** : to make a retreat : WITHDRAW **2** : to slope backward

re•trench \ri-ˈtrench\ *vb* [obs. F *retrencher* (now *retrancher*), fr. MF *retrenchier,* fr. *re-* + *trenchier* to cut] **1** : to cut down or pare away : REDUCE, CURTAIL **2** : to cut down expenses : ECONOMIZE — **re•trench•ment** *n*

ret•ri•bu•tion \ˌre-trə-ˈbyü-shən\ *n* : something administered or exacted in recompense; *esp* : PUNISHMENT **syn** reprisal, vengeance, revenge, retaliation — **re•trib•u•tive** \ri-ˈtrib-yət-iv\ *adj* — **re•trib•u•to•ry** \-yə-ˌtȯr-ē\ *adj*

re•trieve \ri-ˈtrēv\ *vb* **re•trieved; re•triev•ing** **1** : to search about for and bring in (killed or wounded game) **2** : RECOVER, RESTORE — **re•triev•able** *adj* — **re•triev•al** \-ˈtrē-vəl\ *n*

re•triev•er \ri-ˈtrē-vər\ *n* : one that retrieves; *esp* : a dog of any of several breeds used esp. for retrieving game

ret•ro•ac•tive \ˌre-trō-ˈak-tiv\ *adj* : made effective as of a date prior to enactment ⟨a ∼ pay raise⟩ — **ret•ro•ac•tive•ly** *adv*

ret•ro•fire \ˈre-trō-ˌfī(ə)r\ *vb* : to ignite a retro-rocket — **retrofire** *n*

ret•ro•fit \ˌre-trō-ˈfit\ *vb* : to furnish (as an aircraft) with newly available equipment

¹**ret•ro•grade** \ˈre-trə-ˌgrād\ *adj* **1** : moving or tending backward **2** : tending toward or resulting in a worse condition

²**retrograde** *vb* **1** : RETREAT **2** : DETERIORATE, DEGENERATE

ret•ro•gres•sion \ˌre-trə-ˈgresh-ən\ *n* : return to a former and less complex level of development or organization — **ret•ro•gress** \ˌre-trə-ˈgres\ *vb* — **ret•ro•gres•sive** \ˌre-trə-ˈgres-iv\ *adj*

ret•ro–rock•et \ˈre-trō-ˌräk-ət\ *n* : an auxiliary rocket (as on a spacecraft) used to slow forward motion

ret•ro•spect \ˈre-trə-ˌspekt\ *n* : a review of past events — **ret•ro•spec•tion** \ˌre-trə-ˈspek-shən\ *n* — **ret•ro•spec•tive** \-ˈspek-tiv\ *adj* — **ret•ro•spec•tive•ly** *adv*

ret•ro•vi•rus \ˈre-trō-ˌvī-rəs\ *n* : any of a group of RNA-containing viruses (as the AIDS virus) that make DNA using RNA instead of the reverse and include numerous viruses causing tumors in animals including man

¹re•turn \ri-ˈtərn\ *vb* **1** : to go or come back **2** : to pass, give, or send back to an earlier possessor **3** : to put back to or in a former place or state **4** : REPLY, ANSWER **5** : to report esp. officially **6** : to elect to office **7** : to bring in (as profit) : YIELD **8** : to give or perform in return — **re•turn•er** *n*

²return *n* **1** : an act of coming or going back to or from a former place or state **2** : RECURRENCE **3** : a report of the results of balloting **4** : a formal statement of taxable income **5** : the profit from labor, investment, or business : YIELD **6** : the act of returning something **7** : something that returns or is returned; *also* : a means (as a pipe) of returning **8** : something given in repayment or reciprocation; *also* : ANSWER, RETORT **9** : an answering play — **return** *adj*

¹re•turn•able \ri-ˈtərn-ə-bəl\ *adj* : capable of being returned (as for reuse or recycling); *also* : permitted to be returned

²returnable *n* : a returnable beverage container

re•turn•ee \ri-ˌtər-ˈnē\ *n* : one who returns

re•union \rē-ˈyü-nyən\ *n* **1** : an act of reuniting : the state of being reunited **2** : a meeting again of persons who have been separated

¹rev \ˈrev\ *n* : a revolution of a motor

²rev *vb* **revved; rev•ving** : to increase the revolutions per minute of (a motor)

³rev *abbr* **1** revenue **2** reverse **3** review; reviewed **4** revised; revision **5** revolution

Rev *abbr* **1** Revelation **2** Reverend

re•vamp \(ˈ)rē-ˈvamp\ *vb* : RECONSTRUCT, REVISE; *esp* : to give a new form to old materials

re•vanche \rə-ˈvänsh\ *n* [F] : REVENGE; *esp* : a usu. political policy designed to recover lost territory or status

re•veal \ri-ˈvēl\ *vb* **1** : to make known **2** : to show plainly : open up to view

rev•eil•le \ˈrev-ə-lē\ *n* [modif. of F *réveillez*, imper. pl. of *réveiller* to awaken, fr. *eveiller* to awaken, fr. (assumed) VL *exvigilare*, fr. L *vigilare* to keep watch, stay awake] : a military signal sounded at about sunrise

¹rev•el \ˈrev-əl\ *vb* **-eled** *or* **-elled; -el•ing** *or* **-el•ling** \-(ə-)liŋ\ **1** : to take part in a revel **2** : to take great delight — **rev•el•er** *or* **rev•el•ler** \-ər\ *n* — **rev•el•ry** \-əl-rē\ *n*

²revel *n* : a usu. wild party or celebration

rev•e•la•tion \ˌrev-ə-ˈlā-shən\ *n* **1** : an act of revealing **2** : something revealed; *esp* : an enlightening or astonishing disclosure

Rev•e•la•tion \ˌrev-ə-ˈlā-shən\ *n* — see BIBLE table

¹re•venge \ri-ˈvenj\ *vb* **re•venged; re•veng•ing** : to inflict harm or injury in return for (a wrong) : AVENGE — **re•veng•er** *n*

²revenge *n* **1** : the act of revenging **2** : a desire to return evil for evil **3** : an opportunity for getting satisfaction **syn** vengeance, retaliation, retribution, reprisal — **re•venge•ful** *adj*

rev•e•nue \ˈrev-ə-ˌn(y)ü\ *n* [ME, fr. MF, fr. *revenir* to return, fr. L *revenire*, fr. *re-* back + *venire* to come] **1** : investment income **2** : money collected by a government (as through taxes)

rev•e•nu•er \ˈrev-ə-ˌn(y)ü-ər\ *n* : a revenue officer or boat

re•verb \ri-ˈvərb, ˈrē-ˌvərb\ *n* : an electronically produced echo effect in recorded music; *also* : a device for producing reverb

re•ver•ber•ate \ri-ˈvər-bə-ˌrāt\ *vb* **-at•ed; -at•ing 1** : REFLECT ⟨∼ light or heat⟩ **2** : to resound in or as if in a series of echoes — **re•ver•ber•a•tion** \-ˌvər-bə-ˈrā-shən\ *n*

¹re•vere \ri-ˈviər\ *vb* **re•vered; re•ver•ing** : to show honor and devotion to : VENERATE **syn** reverence, worship, adore

²revere *n* : REVERS

¹rev•er•ence \ˈrev-(ə-)rəns\ *n* **1** : honor and respect mixed with love and awe **2** : a sign (as a bow or curtsy) of respect

²reverence *vb* **-enced; -enc•ing** : to regard or treat with reverence

¹rev•er•end \-rənd\ *adj* **1** : worthy of reverence : REVERED **2** : being a member of the clergy — used as a title

²reverend *n* : a member of the clergy

rev•er•ent \-rənt\ *adj* : expressing reverence — **rev•er•ent•ly** *adv*

rev•er•en•tial \ˌrev-ə-ˈren-chəl\ *adj* : REVERENT

rev•er•ie *also* **rev•ery** \\'rev-(ə-)rē\ *n, pl* **-er•ies** **1** : DAYDREAM **2** : the state of being lost in thought

re•vers \ri-'viər, -'veər\ *n, pl* **re•vers** \-'viərz, -'veərz\ [F] : a lapel esp. on a woman's garment

re•ver•sal \ri-'vər-səl\ *n* : an act or process of reversing

¹re•verse \ri-'vərs\ *adj* **1** : opposite to a previous or normal condition **2** : acting or operating in a manner opposite or contrary **3** : effecting reverse movement — **re•verse•ly** *adv*

²reverse *vb* **re•versed; re•vers•ing** **1** : to turn upside down or completely about in position or direction **2** : to set aside or change (as a legal decision) **3** : to change to the contrary ⟨∼ a policy⟩ **4** : to go or cause to go in the opposite direction **5** : to put (as a car) in reverse — **re•vers•ible** \-'vər-sə-bəl\ *adj*

³reverse *n* **1** : something contrary to something else : OPPOSITE **2** : an act or instance of reversing; *esp* : a change for the worse **3** : the back of something **4** : a gear that reverses something

re•ver•sion \ri-'vər-zhən\ *n* **1** : the right of succession or future possession (as to a title or property) **2** : return toward some former or ancestral condition; *also* : a product of this — **re•ver•sion•ary** \-zhə-,ner-ē\ *adj*

re•vert \ri-'vərt\ *vb* **1** : to come or go back ⟨∼ed to savagery⟩ **2** : to return to a proprietor or his or her heirs **3** : to return to an ancestral type

¹re•view \ri-'vyü\ *n* **1** : an act of revising **2** : a formal military inspection **3** : a general survey **4** : INSPECTION, EXAMINATION; *esp* : REEXAMINATION **5** : a critical evaluation (as of a book) **6** : a magazine devoted to reviews and essays **7** : a renewed study of previously studied material **8** : REVUE

²re•view \ri-'vyü, *1 also* 'rē-\ *vb* **1** : to examine or study again; *esp* : to reexamine judicially **2** : to hold a review of ⟨∼ troops⟩ **3** : to write a critical examination of ⟨∼ a novel⟩ **4** : to view retrospectively : look back over ⟨∼ed his life⟩ **5** : to study material again

re•view•er \ri-'vyü-ər\ *n* : one that reviews; *esp* : a writer of critical reviews

re•vile \ri-'vīl\ *vb* **re•viled; re•vil•ing** : to abuse verbally : rail at **syn** vituperate, berate, rate, upbraid, scold — **re•vile•ment** *n* — **re•vil•er** *n*

re•vise \ri-'vīz\ *vb* **re•vised; re•vis•ing** **1** : to look over something written in order to correct or improve **2** : to make a new version of — **re•vis•able** *adj* — **re•vise** *n* — **re•vis•er** *or* **re•vi•sor** \-'vī-zər\ *n* — **re•vi•sion** \-'vizh-ən\ *n*

re•vi•tal•ize \'rē-'vīt-ᵊl-,īz\ *vb* **-ized; -iz•ing** : to give new life or vigor to — **re•vi•tal•iza•tion** \,rē-,vīt-ᵊl-ə-'zā-shən\ *n*

re•viv•al \ri-'vī-vəl\ *n* **1** : an act of reviving : the state of being revived **2** : a new publication or presentation (as of a book or play) **3** : an evangelistic meeting or series of meetings

re•vive \ri-'vīv\ *vb* **re•vived; re•viv•ing** **1** : to return or restore to consciousness or life : become or make active or flourishing again **2** : to bring back into use **3** : to renew mentally — **re•viv•er** *n*

re•viv•i•fy \rē-'viv-ə-,fī\ *vb* : REVIVE — **re•viv•i•fi•ca•tion** \-,viv-ə-fə-'kā-shən\ *n*

re•vo•ca•ble \'rev-ə-kə-bəl *also* ri-'vō-kə-bəl\ *adj* : capable of being revoked

re•vo•ca•tion \,rev-ə-'kā-shən\ *n* : an act or instance of revoking

re•voke \ri-'vōk\ *vb* **re•voked; re•vok•ing** **1** : to annul by recalling or taking back : REPEAL, RESCIND **2** : RENEGE 1 — **re•vok•er** *n*

¹re•volt \ri-'vōlt\ *vb* **1** : to throw off allegiance to a ruler or government : REBEL **2** : to experience disgust or shock **3** : to turn or cause to turn away with disgust or abhorrence — **re•volt•er** *n*

²revolt *n* : REBELLION, INSURRECTION

re•volt•ing \-iŋ\ *adj* : extremely offensive — **re•volt•ing•ly** *adv*

rev•o•lu•tion \,rev-ə-'lü-shən\ *n* **1** : the action by a heavenly body of going round in an orbit **2** : ROTATION **3** : a sudden, radical, or complete change; *esp* : the overthrow or renunciation of one ruler or government and substitution of another by the governed

¹rev•o•lu•tion•ary \-shə-,ner-ē\ *adj* **1** : of or relating to revolution **2** : tending to or promoting revolution **3** : constituting or bringing about a major change

²revolutionary *n, pl* **-ar•ies** : one who

takes part in a revolution or who advocates revolutionary doctrines

rev・o・lu・tion・ist \ˌrev-ə-ˈlü-sh(ə-)nəst\ n : REVOLUTIONARY — **revolutionist** adj

rev・o・lu・tion・ize \-shə-ˌnīz\ vb **-ized; -iz-ing** : to change fundamentally or completely : make revolutionary — **rev・o・lu・tion・iz・er** n

re・volve \ri-ˈvälv\ vb **re・volved; re・volv-ing 1** : to turn over in the mind : reflect upon : PONDER **2** : to move in an orbit; also : ROTATE — **re・volv・able** adj

re・volv・er \ri-ˈväl-vər\ n : a pistol with a revolving cylinder of several chambers

re・vue \ri-ˈvyü\ n : a theatrical production consisting typically of brief often satirical sketches and songs

re・vul・sion \ri-ˈvəl-shən\ n **1** : a strong sudden reaction or change of feeling **2** : a feeling of complete distaste or repugnance

revved past and past part of REV

revving pres part of REV

¹re・ward \ri-ˈwȯrd\ vb **1** : to give a reward to or for **2** : RECOMPENSE

²reward n **1** : something given in return for good or evil done or received; esp : something given or offered for some service or attainment **2** : a stimulus that is administered to an organism after a response and that increases the probability of occurrence of the response **syn** premium, prize, award

re・work \(ˈ)rē-ˈwərk\ vb **1** : REVISE **2** : to reprocess for further use

RF abbr radio frequency

RFD abbr rural free delivery

Rh symbol rhodium

RH abbr right hand

rhap・so・dy \ˈrap-səd-ē\ n, pl **-dies** [L rhapsodia portion of an epic poem adapted for recitation, fr. Gk rhapsōidia recitation of selections from epic poetry, rhapsody, fr. rhaptein to sew, stitch together + aidein to sing] **1** : an expression of extravagant praise or ecstasy **2** : an instrumental composition of irregular form — **rhap・sod・ic** \rap-ˈsäd-ik\ adj — **rhap・sod・i・cal・ly** \-i-k(ə-)lē\ adv — **rhap・so・dize** \ˈrap-sə-ˌdīz\ vb

rhea \ˈrē-ə\ n : any of several large flightless 3-toed So. American birds that resemble but are smaller than the African ostrich

rhe・ni・um \ˈrē-nē-əm\ n : a rare heavy hard metallic chemical element

rheo・stat \ˈrē-ə-ˌstat\ n : a resistor for regulating an electric current by means of variable resistances — **rheo・stat・ic** \ˌrē-ə-ˈstat-ik\ adj

rhe・sus monkey \ˌrē-səs-\ n : a pale brown Indian monkey often used in medical research

rhet・o・ric \ˈret-ə-rik\ n [ME rethorik, fr. MF rethorique, fr. L rhetorica, fr. Gk rhētorikē, lit., art of oratory] : the art of speaking or writing effectively — **rhe・tor・i・cal** \ri-ˈtȯr-i-kəl\ adj — **rhet・o・ri・cian** \ˌret-ə-ˈrish-ən\ n

rheum \ˈrüm\ n : a watery discharge from the mucous membranes esp. of the eyes or nose — **rheumy** adj

rheu・mat・ic fever \rù-ˌmat-ik-\ n : an acute disease chiefly of children and young adults that is characterized by fever, by inflammation and pain in and around the joints, and by inflammation of the membranes surrounding the heart and the heart valves

rheu・ma・tism \ˈrü-mə-ˌtiz-əm, ˈrùm-ə-\ n : any of various conditions marked by stiffness, pain, or swelling in muscles or joints — **rheu・mat・ic** \rù-ˈmat-ik\ adj

rheu・ma・toid arthritis \-ˌtȯid-\ n : a progressive constitutional disease characterized by inflammation and swelling of joint structures

Rh factor \ˈär-ˈāch-\ n [rhesus monkey (in which it was first detected)] : any of one or more inherited substances in red blood cells that may cause dangerous reactions in some infants or in transfusions

rhine・stone \ˈrīn-ˌstōn\ n : a colorless imitation stone of high luster made of glass, paste, or gem quartz

rhi・no \ˈrī-nō\ n, pl **rhino** or **rhinos** : RHINOCEROS

rhi・noc・er・os \rī-ˈnäs-(ə-)rəs\ n, pl **-noc・er・os・es** or **-noc・er・os** or **-noc・eri** \-ˈnäs-ə-ˌrī\ [ME rinoceros, fr. L rhinoceros, fr. Gk rhinokerōs, fr. rhin-, rhis nose + keras horn] : a large thick-skinned mammal of Africa and Asia with one or two upright horns of keratin on the snout and three toes on each foot

rhi・zome \ˈrī-ˌzōm\ n : a specialized rootlike plant stem that forms shoots above and roots below — **rhi·zom·a·tous** \rī-'zäm-ət-əs\ adj

Rh–neg·a·tive \ˌär-ˌāch-'neg-ət-iv\ adj : lacking Rh factors in the red blood cells

rho·di·um \'rōd-ē-əm\ n : a hard ductile metallic chemical element

rho·do·den·dron \ˌrōd-ə-'den-drən\ n : any of various shrubs or trees of the heath family grown for their clusters of large bright flowers

rhom·boid \'räm-ˌbȯid\ n : a parallelogram with unequal adjacent sides and angles that are not right angles

rhom·bus \'räm-bəs\ n, pl **rhom·bus·es** or **rhom·bi** \-ˌbī\ : a parallelogram having all four sides equal

Rh–pos·i·tive \ˌär-ˌāch-'päz-ət-iv\ adj : containing Rh factors in the red blood cells

rhu·barb \'rü-ˌbärb\ n [ME rubarbe, fr. MF reubarbe, fr. ML reubarbarum, alter. of rha barbarum, lit., barbarian rhubarb] : a garden plant related to the buckwheat and having thick juicy edible pink and red stems on the leaves

¹rhyme \'rīm\ n 1 : a composition in verse that rhymes; also : POETRY 2 : correspondence in terminal sounds (as of two lines of verse)

²rhyme vb **rhymed; rhym·ing** 1 : to make rhymes; also : to write poetry 2 : to have rhymes : be in rhyme

rhy·o·lite \'rī-ə-ˌlīt\ n : a very acid volcanic rock

rhythm \'rith-əm\ n 1 : regular rise and fall in the flow of sound in speech 2 : a movement or activity in which some action or element recurs regularly — **rhyth·mic** \'rith-mik\ or **rhyth·mi·cal** \-mi-kəl\ adj — **rhyth·mi·cal·ly** \-k(ə-)lē\ adv

rhythm and blues n : popular music based on blues and Negro folk music

rhythm method n : a method of birth control in which a couple does not have sexual intercourse during the time when ovulation is most likely to occur

RI abbr Rhode Island

ri·al \rē-'ȯl, -'äl\ n — see MONEY table

¹rib \'rib\ n 1 : any of the series of curved bones of the chest of most vertebrates that are joined to the backbone in pairs and help to support

the body wall and protect the organs inside 2 : something resembling a rib in shape or function 3 : an elongated ridge

²rib vb **ribbed; rib·bing** 1 : to furnish or strengthen with ribs 2 : to mark with ridges in knitting

³rib vb **ribbed; rib·bing** : to poke fun at : TEASE — **rib·ber** n

rib·ald \'rib-əld\ adj : coarse or indecent esp. in language ⟨~ jokes⟩ — **rib·ald·ry** \-əl-drē\ n

rib·and \'rib-ənd\ n : RIBBON

rib·bon \'rib-ən\ n 1 : a narrow fabric typically of silk or velvet used for trimming and for badges 2 : a strip of inked cloth (as in a typewriter) 3 : TATTER ⟨torn to ~s⟩

ri·bo·fla·vin \ˌrī-bə-'flā-vən, 'rī-bə-ˌflā-vən\ n : a growth-promoting vitamin of the vitamin B complex occurring in milk and liver

ri·bo·nu·cle·ic acid \ˌrī-bō-n(y)ù-ˌklē-ik-, -ˌklä-\ n : RNA

ri·bose \'rī-ˌbōs\ n : a sugar with five carbon atoms and five oxygen atoms in each molecule that is part of RNA

ri·bo·some \'rī-bə-ˌsōm\ n : any of the RNA-rich cytoplasmic granules in a cell that are sites of protein synthesis — **ri·bo·som·al** \ˌrī-bə-'sō-məl\ adj

rice \'rīs\ n : an annual grass grown in warm wet areas for its edible seed; also : this seed

rich \'rich\ adj 1 : possessing or controlling great wealth : WEALTHY 2 : COSTLY, VALUABLE 3 : deep and pleasing in color or tone 4 : ABUNDANT 5 : containing much sugar, fat, or seasoning; also : high in combustible content 6 : FRUITFUL, FERTILE — **rich·ly** adv — **rich·ness** n

rich·es \'rich-əz\ n pl [ME, sing. or pl., fr. richesse, lit., richness, fr. OF, fr. riche rich] : things that make one rich : WEALTH

Rich·ter scale \'rik-tər-\ n : a scale for expressing the magnitude of a seismic disturbance (as an earthquake) in terms of the energy dissipated in it

rick \'rik\ n : a large stack (as of hay) in the open air

rick·ets \'rik-əts\ n : a deficiency disease of children marked esp. by soft deformed bones and caused by inadequate sunlight or inadequate vitamin D

rick·ett·sia \ri-'ket-sē-ə\ *n, pl* **-si·as** *or* **-si·ae** \-sē-ˌē\ : any of a family of rod-shaped microorganisms that cause various diseases (as typhus)

rick·ety \'rik-ət-ē\ *adj* **1** : affected with rickets **2** : FEEBLE **3** : SHAKY

rick·sha *or* **rick·shaw** \'rik-ˌshȯ\ *n* : a small covered 2-wheeled vehicle pulled by one person and used orig. in Japan

¹ric·o·chet \'rik-ə-ˌshā, *Brit also* -ˌshet\ *n* : a glancing rebound or skipping (as of a bullet off a wall)

²ricochet *vb* **-cheted** \-ˌshād\ *or* **-chet·ted** \-ˌshet-əd\; **-chet·ing** \-ˌshā-iŋ\ *or* **-chet·ting** \-ˌshet-iŋ\ : to skip with or as if with glancing rebounds

rid \'rid\ *vb* **rid** *also* **rid·ded**; **rid·ding** : to make free : CLEAR, RELIEVE — **rid·dance** \'rid-ᵊns\ *n*

rid·den \'rid-ᵊn\ *adj* **1** : being harassed, oppressed, or obsessed by ⟨debt-*ridden*⟩ ⟨conscience-*ridden*⟩ **2** : excessively full of or supplied with ⟨slum=*ridden*⟩

¹rid·dle \'rid-ᵊl\ *n* : a puzzling question to be solved or answered by guessing

²riddle *vb* **rid·dled**; **rid·dling** \'rid-(ᵊ-)liŋ\ **1** : EXPLAIN, SOLVE **2** : to speak in riddles

³riddle *n* : a coarse sieve

⁴riddle *vb* **rid·dled**; **rid·dling** \'rid-(ᵊ-)liŋ\ **1** : to sift with a riddle **2** : to fill as full of holes as a sieve **3** : PERMEATE

¹ride \'rīd\ *vb* **rode** \'rōd\; **rid·den** \'rid-ᵊn\; **rid·ing** \'rīd-iŋ\ **1** : to go on an animal's back or in a conveyance (as a boat, car, or airplane); *also* : to sit on and control so as to be carried along ⟨∼ a bicycle⟩ **2** : to float or move on water ⟨∼ at anchor⟩; *also* : to move like a floating object **3** : to bear along : CARRY ⟨*rode* her on their shoulders⟩ **4** : to travel over a surface ⟨car ∼s well⟩ **5** : to proceed over on horseback **6** : to torment by nagging or teasing

²ride *n* **1** : an act of riding; *esp* : a trip on horseback or by vehicle **2** : a way (as a lane) suitable for riding **3** : a mechanical device (as a merry-go-round) for riding on **4** : a means of transportation

rid·er \'rīd-ər\ *n* **1** : one that rides **2** : an addition to a document often attached on a separate piece of paper **3** : a clause dealing with an unrelated matter attached to a legislative bill during passage — **rid·er·less** *adj*

¹ridge \'rij\ *n* **1** : a range of hills **2** : a raised line or strip **3** : the line made where two sloping surfaces meet — **ridgy** *adj*

²ridge *vb* **ridged**; **ridg·ing** **1** : to form into a ridge **2** : to extend in ridges

ridge·pole \'rij-ˌpōl\ *n* : the highest horizontal timber in a sloping roof to which the upper ends of the rafters are fastened

¹rid·i·cule \'rid-ə-ˌkyül\ *n* : the act of exposing to laughter : DERISION

²ridicule *vb* **-culed**; **-cul·ing** : to laugh at or make fun of mockingly or contemptuously **syn** deride, taunt, twit, mock

ri·dic·u·lous \rə-'dik-yə-ləs\ *adj* : arousing or deserving ridicule : ABSURD, PREPOSTEROUS **syn** laughable, ludicrous, farcical, risible — **ri·dic·u·lous·ly** *adv* — **ri·dic·u·lous·ness** *n*

ri·el \rē-'el\ *n* — see MONEY table

rife \'rīf\ *adj* : WIDESPREAD, PREVALENT, ABOUNDING — **rife** *adv*

riff \'rif\ *n* : a repeated phrase in jazz typically supporting a solo improvisation; *also* : a piece based on such a phrase — **riff** *vb*

riff·raff \'rif-ˌraf\ *n* [ME *riffe raffe*, fr. *rif and raf* every single one, fr. MF *rif et raf* completely] **1** : RABBLE **2** : REFUSE, RUBBISH

¹ri·fle \'rī-fəl\ *vb* **ri·fled**; **ri·fling** \-f(ə-)liŋ\ : to ransack esp. in order to steal — **ri·fler** \-f(ə-)lər\ *n*

²rifle *vb* **ri·fled**; **ri·fling** \-f(ə-)liŋ\ : to cut spiral grooves into the bore of ⟨*rifled* arms⟩ — **rifling** *n*

³rifle *n* **1** : a shoulder weapon with a rifled bore **2** *pl* : a body of soldiers armed with rifles — **ri·fle·man** \-fəl-mən\ *n*

rift \'rift\ *n* **1** : CLEFT, FISSURE **2** : ESTRANGEMENT, SEPARATION — **rift** *vb*

¹rig \'rig\ *vb* **rigged**; **rig·ging** **1** : to fit out (as a ship) with rigging **2** : CLOTHE, DRESS **3** : EQUIP **4** : to set up esp. as a makeshift ⟨∼ up a shelter⟩

²rig *n* **1** : the distinctive shape, number, and arrangement of sails and masts of a ship **2** : a carriage with its horse or horses **3** : CLOTHING, DRESS **4** : EQUIPMENT

³**rig** *vb* **rigged; rig•ging 1** : to manipulate or control esp. by deceptive or dishonest means **2** : to fix in advance for a desired result — **rig•ger** \\'rig-ər\\ *n*

rig•ging \\'rig-iŋ, -ən\\ *n* **1** : the ropes and chains that hold and move masts, sails, and spars of a ship **2** : a network (as in theater scenery) used for support and manipulation

¹**right** \\'rīt\\ *adj* **1** : RIGHTEOUS, UPRIGHT **2** : JUST, PROPER **3** : conforming to truth or fact : CORRECT **4** : APPROPRIATE, SUITABLE **5** : STRAIGHT ⟨a ∼ line⟩ **6** : GENUINE, REAL **7** : of, relating to, or being the stronger hand in most persons **8** : located nearer to the right hand; *esp* : being on the right when facing in the same direction as the observer **9** : made to be placed or worn outward ⟨∼ side of a rug⟩ **10** : NORMAL, SOUND ⟨not in her ∼ mind⟩ **syn** correct, accurate, exact, precise, nice — **right•ness** *n*

²**right** *n* **1** : qualities that constitute what is correct, just, proper, or honorable **2** : something (as a power or privilege) to which one has a just or lawful claim **3** : just action or decision : the cause of justice **4** : the side or part that is on or toward the right side **5** *cap* : political conservatives **6** *often cap* : a conservative position — **right•ward** \\-wərd\\ *adj*

³**right** *adv* **1** : according to what is right ⟨live ∼⟩ **2** : EXACTLY, PRECISELY ⟨∼ here and now⟩ **3** : DIRECTLY ⟨went ∼ home⟩ **4** : according to fact or truth ⟨guess ∼⟩ **5** : all the way : COMPLETELY ⟨∼ to the end⟩ **6** : IMMEDIATELY ⟨∼ after lunch⟩ **7** : QUITE, VERY ⟨∼ nice weather⟩ **8** : on or to the right ⟨looked ∼ and left⟩

⁴**right** *vb* **1** : to relieve from wrong **2** : to adjust or restore to a proper state or position **3** : to bring or restore to an upright position **4** : to become upright — **right•er** *n*

right angle *n* : an angle whose measure is 90° : an angle whose sides are perpendicular to each other — **right–angled** \\'rīt-'aŋ-gəld\\ *or* **right–an•gle** \\-gəl\\ *adj*

right circular cone *n* : CONE 2

righ•teous \\'rī-chəs\\ *adj* : acting or being in accordance with what is just, honorable, and free from guilt or wrong : UPRIGHT **syn** virtuous, noble, moral, ethical — **righ•teous•ly** *adv* — **righ•teous•ness** *n*

right•ful \\'rīt-fəl\\ *adj* **1** : JUST; *also* : FITTING **2** : having or held by a legally just claim — **right•ful•ly** \\-ē\\ *adv* — **right•ful•ness** *n*

right–hand \\'rīt-,hand\\ *adj* **1** : situated on the right **2** : RIGHT-HANDED **3** : chiefly relied on ⟨his ∼ man⟩

right–hand•ed \\-'han-dəd\\ *adj* **1** : using the right hand habitually or better than the left **2** : designed for or done with the right hand **3** : CLOCKWISE ⟨a ∼ twist⟩ — **right–handed** *adv* — **right–hand•ed•ly** *adv* — **right–hand•ed•ness** *n*

right•ly \\'rīt-lē\\ *adv* **1** : FAIRLY, JUSTLY **2** : PROPERLY **3** : CORRECTLY, EXACTLY

right–of–way \\,rīt-ə(v)-'wā\\ *n, pl* **rights–of–way 1** : a legal right of passage over another person's ground **2** : the area over which a right-of-way exists **3** : the land on which a public road is built **4** : the land occupied by a railroad **5** : the land used by a public utility **6** : the right of traffic to take precedence over other traffic

right on *interj* — used to express agreement or give encouragement

right–to–life *adj* : opposed to abortion — **right–to–lif•er** \\'rīt-tə-'lī-fər\\ *n*

right triangle *n* : a triangle having one right angle

rig•id \\'rij-əd\\ *adj* **1** : lacking flexibility : STIFF **2** : strictly observed **syn** severe, stern, rigorous, stringent — **ri•gid•i•ty** \\rə-'jid-ət-ē\\ *n* — **rig•id•ly** *adv*

rig•ma•role \\'rig-(ə-)mə-,rōl\\ *n* [alter. of obs. *ragman roll* (long list, catalog)] **1** : confused or senseless talk **2** : a complex largely meaningless procedure

rig•or \\'rig-ər\\ *n* **1** : the quality of being inflexible or unyielding : STRICTNESS **2** : HARSHNESS, SEVERITY **3** : a tremor caused by a chill **4** : strict precision : EXACTNESS **syn** difficulty, hardship, vicissitude — **rig•or•ous** *adj* — **rig•or•ous•ly** *adv*

rig•or mor•tis \\,rig-ər-'mȯrt-əs\\ *n* [NL, stiffness of death] : temporary rigidity of muscles occurring after death

rile \\'rīl\\ *vb* **riled; ril•ing 1** : to make angry **2** : ROIL 1

¹**rill** \\'ril\\ *n* : a very small brook

²**rill** \\'ril\\ *or* **rille** \\'ril, 'ril-ə\\ *n* : a long narrow valley on the moon

¹rim \\'rim\\ *n* **1** : the outer part of a wheel **2** : an outer edge esp. of something curved : BORDER, MARGIN

²rim *vb* **rimmed; rim•ming 1** : to furnish with a rim **2** : to run around the rim of

¹rime \\'rīm\\ *n* **1** : FROST 2 **2** : frostlike ice tufts formed from fog or cloud on the windward side of exposed objects — **rimy** \\'rī-mē\\ *adj*

²rime *var of* RHYME

rind \\'rīnd\\ *n* : a usu. hard or tough outer layer ⟨lemon ∼⟩

¹ring \\'riŋ\\ *n* **1** : a circular band worn as an ornament or token or used for holding or fastening ⟨wedding ∼⟩ ⟨key ∼⟩ **2** : something circular in shape ⟨smoke ∼⟩ **3** : a place for contest or display ⟨boxing ∼⟩; *also* : PRIZEFIGHTING **4** : a group of people who work together for selfish or dishonest purposes — **ring•like** \\'riŋ-ˌlīk\\ *adj*

²ring *vb* **ringed; ring•ing** \\'riŋ-iŋ\\ **1** : ENCIRCLE **2** : to move in a ring or spirally **3** : to throw a ring over (a mark) in a game (as quoits)

³ring *vb* **rang** \\'raŋ\\; **rung** \\'rəŋ\\; **ring•ing** \\'riŋ-iŋ\\ **1** : to sound resonantly when struck; *also* : to feel as if filled with such sound **2** : to cause to make a clear metallic sound by striking **3** : to announce or call by or as if by striking a bell ⟨∼ an alarm⟩ **4** : to repeat loudly and persistently **5** : to sound a bell ⟨∼ for the butler⟩

⁴ring *n* **1** : a set of bells **2** : the clear resonant sound of vibrating metal **3** : resonant tone : SONORITY **4** : a sound or character expressive of a particular quality **5** : an act or instance of ringing; *esp* : a telephone call

¹ring•er \\'riŋ-ər\\ *n* **1** : one that sounds by ringing **2** : one that enters a competition under false representations **3** : one that closely resembles another

²ringer *n* : one that encircles or puts a ring around

ring•git \\'riŋ-git\\ *n* — see MONEY table

ring•lead•er \\'riŋ-ˌlēd-ər\\ *n* : a leader esp. of a group of troublemakers

ring•let \\'riŋ-lət\\ *n* : a long curl

ring•mas•ter \\'riŋ-ˌmas-tər\\ *n* : one in charge of performances in a circus ring

ring up *vb* **1** : to total and record esp. by means of a cash register **2** : ACHIEVE ⟨*rang up* many triumphs⟩

ring•worm \\'riŋ-ˌwərm\\ *n* : a contagious skin disease caused by fungi and marked by ring-shaped discolored patches

rink \\'riŋk\\ *n* : a level extent of ice marked off for skating or various games; *also* : a similar surface (as of wood) marked off or enclosed for a sport or game ⟨roller-skating ∼⟩

¹rinse \\'rins\\ *vb* **rinsed; rins•ing** [ME *rincen,* fr. MF *rincer,* fr. (assumed) VL *recentiare,* fr. L *recent-, recens* fresh, recent] **1** : to wash lightly or in water only **2** : to cleanse (as of soap) with clear water **3** : to treat (hair) with a rinse — **rins•er** *n*

²rinse *n* **1** : an act of rinsing **2** : a liquid used for rinsing **3** : a solution that temporarily tints hair

ri•ot \\'rī-ət\\ *n* **1** *archaic* : disorderly behavior **2** : disturbance of the public peace; *esp* : a violent public disorder **3** : random or disorderly profusion ⟨a ∼ of color⟩ — **riot** *vb* — **ri•ot•er** *n* — **ri•ot•ous** *adj*

¹rip \\'rip\\ *vb* **ripped; rip•ping 1** : to cut or tear open **2** : to saw or split (wood) with the grain — **rip•per** *n*

²rip *n* : a rent made by ripping

RIP *abbr* [L *requiescat in pace*] may he rest in peace, may she rest in peace; [L *requiescant in pace*] may they rest in peace

ri•par•i•an \\rə-'per-ē-ən\\ *adj* : of or relating to the bank of a stream, river, or lake

rip cord *n* : a cord that is pulled to release the pilot parachute which lifts a main parachute out of its container

ripe \\'rīp\\ *adj* **rip•er; rip•est 1** : fully grown and developed : MATURE ⟨∼ fruit⟩ **2** : fully prepared for some use or object : READY — **ripe•ly** *adv* — **ripe•ness** *n*

rip•en \\'rī-pən\\ *vb* **rip•ened; rip•en•ing** \\'rīp-(ə-)niŋ\\ **1** : to grow or make ripe **2** : to bring to completeness or perfection; *also* : to age or cure (cheese) to develop characteristic flavor, odor, body, texture, and color

rip—off \\'rip-ˌȯf\\ *n* **1** : an act of stealing : THEFT **2** : a cheap imitation — **rip off** \\(')rip-'ȯf\\ *vb*

ri•poste \\ri-'pōst\\ *n* [F, modif. of It *risposta,* lit., answer] **1** : a fencer's return thrust after a parry **2** : a retaliatory maneuver or response; *esp* : a quick retort — **riposte** *vb*

rip·ple \'rip-əl\ *vb* **rip·pled; rip·pling** \-(ə-)liŋ\ **1** : to become lightly ruffled on the surface **2** : to make a sound like that of rippling water — **ripple** *n*

rip·saw \'rip-ˌso\ *n* : a coarse-toothed saw used to cut wood in the direction of the grain

rip·stop \'rip-ˌstäp\ *adj* : being a fabric woven in such a way that small tears do not spread ⟨∼ nylon⟩

¹**rise** \'rīz\ *vb* **rose** \'rōz\; **ris·en** \'riz-ᵊn\; **ris·ing** \'rī-ziŋ\ **1** : to get up from sitting, kneeling, or lying **2** : to get up from sleep or from one's bed **3** : to return from death **4** : to take up arms : go to war; *also* : REBEL **5** : to end a session : ADJOURN **6** : to appear above the horizon **7** : to move upward : ASCEND **8** : to extend above other objects **9** : to attain a higher level or rank **10** : to increase in quantity or in intensity **11** : to come into being : HAPPEN, BEGIN, ORIGINATE

²**rise** *n* **1** : an act of rising : a state of being risen **2** : BEGINNING, ORIGIN **3** : the elevation of one point above another **4** : an increase in amount, number, or volume **5** : an upward slope **6** : a spot higher than surrounding ground **7** : an angry reaction

ris·er \'rī-zər\ *n* **1** : one that rises **2** : the upright part between stair treads

ris·i·bil·i·ty \ˌriz-ə-'bil-ət-ē\ *n, pl* **-ties** : the ability or inclination to laugh — often used in pl.

ris·i·ble \'riz-ə-bəl\ *adj* **1** : able or inclined to laugh **2** : arousing laughter : FUNNY **3** : of or relating to laughter ⟨∼ muscles⟩

¹**risk** \'risk\ *n* : exposure to possible loss or injury : DANGER, PERIL — **risk·i·ness** \'ris-kē-nəs\ *n* — **risky** *adj*

²**risk** *vb* **1** : to expose to danger ⟨∼ed his life⟩ **2** : to incur the danger of

ris·qué \ris-'kā\ *adj* [F] : verging on impropriety or indecency

rite \'rīt\ *n* **1** : a set form of conducting a ceremony **2** : the liturgy of a church **3** : a ceremonial act or action

rit·u·al \'rich-(ə-w)əl\ *n* **1** : the established form esp. for a religious ceremony **2** : a system of rites **3** : a ceremonial act or action **4** : a customarily repeated act or series of acts — **ritual** *adj* — **rit·u·al·ism** \-ˌiz-əm\ *n* — **rit·u·al·is·tic** \ˌrich-(ə-w)əl-'is-tik\ *adj* — **rit·u·al·is·ti·cal·ly** \-ti-k(ə-)lē\ *adv* — **rit·u·al·ly** \'rich-(ə-w)ə-lē\ *adv*

riv *abbr* river

¹**ri·val** \'rī-vəl\ *n* [MF or L; MF, fr. L *rivalis* one using the same stream as another, rival in love, fr. *rivalis* of a stream, fr. *rivus* stream] **1** : one of two or more trying to get what only one can have **2** : one striving for competitive advantage **3** : one that equals another esp. in desired qualities : MATCH, PEER

²**rival** *adj* : COMPETING

³**rival** *vb* **-valed** *or* **-valled; -val·ing** *or* **-val·ling** \'rīv-(ə-)liŋ\ **1** : to be in competition with **2** : to try to equal or excel **3** : to have qualities that equal another's : MATCH

ri·val·ry \'rī-vəl-rē\ *n, pl* **-ries** : COMPETITION

rive \'rīv\ *vb* **rived** \'rīvd\; **riv·en** \'riv-ən\ *also* **rived; riv·ing** \'rī-viŋ\ **1** : SPLIT, REND **2** : SHATTER

riv·er \'riv-ər\ *n* : a natural stream larger than a brook

riv·er·bank \-ˌbaŋk\ *n* : the bank of a river

riv·er·bed \-ˌbed\ *n* : the channel occupied by a river

riv·er·boat \-ˌbōt\ *n* : a boat for use on a river

riv·er·front \-ˌfrənt\ *n* : the land or area along a river

riv·er·side \'riv-ər-ˌsīd\ *n* : the side or bank of a river

¹**riv·et** \'riv-ət\ *n* : a metal bolt with a head at one end used to fasten things together by being put through holes in them and then being flattened on the plain end to make another head

²**rivet** *vb* : to fasten with or as if with a rivet — **riv·et·er** *n*

riv·u·let \'riv-(y)ə-lət\ *n* : a small stream

ri·yal \rē-'(y)äl, -'(y)al\ *n* — see MONEY table

rm *abbr* **1** ream **2** room

Rn *symbol* radon

RN *abbr* **1** registered nurse **2** Royal Navy

RNA \ˌär-ˌen-'ā\ *n* : any of various nucleic acids (as messenger RNA) that are found esp. in the cytoplasm of cells, have ribose as the 5-carbon sugar, and are associated with protein synthesis

rnd *abbr* round

¹**roach** \'rōch\ *n, pl* **roach** *also* **roach·es** : any of various fishes related to the carp; *also* : any of several sunfishes

²**roach** *n* **1** : COCKROACH **2** : the butt of a marijuana cigarette

road \'rōd\ *n* **1** : ROADSTEAD — often used in pl. **2** : an open way for vehicles, persons, and animals : HIGHWAY **3** : ROUTE, PATH **4** : a series of scheduled visits (as games or performances) in several locations or the travel necessary to make these visits ⟨the team is on the ∼⟩

road·abil·i·ty \ˌrōd-ə-'bil-ət-ē\ *n* : the qualities (as steadiness and balance) desirable in an automobile on the road

road·bed \'rōd-ˌbed\ *n* **1** : the foundation of a road or railroad **2** : the part of the surface of a road on which vehicles travel

road·block \-ˌbläk\ *n* **1** : a barricade on the road ⟨a police ∼⟩ **2** : an obstruction to progress

road·run·ner \-ˌrən-ər\ *n* : a largely terrestrial bird of the southwestern U.S. and Mexico that is a speedy runner

road·side \'rōd-ˌsīd\ *n* : the strip of land along a road — **roadside** *adj*

road·stead \-ˌsted\ *n* : an anchorage for ships usu. less sheltered than a harbor

road·ster \'rōd-stər\ *n* **1** : a driving horse **2** : an open automobile with one cross seat

road·way \'rōd-ˌwā\ *n* : ROAD; *esp* : ROADBED

road·work \-ˌwərk\ *n* : conditioning for an athletic contest (as a boxing match) consisting mainly of long runs

roam \'rōm\ *vb* **1** : WANDER, ROVE **2** : to range or wander over or about

¹**roan** \'rōn\ *adj* : of dark color (as black, red, or brown) sprinkled with white ⟨a ∼ horse⟩

²**roan** *n* : an animal (as a horse) with a roan coat; *also* : its color

¹**roar** \'rōr\ *vb* **1** : to utter a full loud prolonged sound **2** : to make a loud confused sound (as of wind or waves) — **roar·er** *n*

²**roar** *n* : a sound of roaring

¹**roast** \'rōst\ *vb* **1** : to cook by dry heat (as before a fire or in an oven) **2** : to criticize severely or kiddingly

²**roast** *n* **1** : a piece of meat suitable for roasting **2** : an outing at which food is roasted ⟨corn ∼⟩ **3** : severe criticism or kidding

³**roast** *adj* : ROASTED

roast·er \'rō-stər\ *n* **1** : one that roasts **2** : a device for roasting **3** : something adapted to roasting

rob \'räb\ *vb* **robbed; rob·bing** **1** : to steal from **2** : to commit robbery **3** : to deprive of something due or expected — **rob·ber** *n*

robber fly *n* : any of numerous predaceous flies

rob·bery \'räb-(ə-)rē\ *n, pl* **-ber·ies** : the act or practice of robbing; *esp* : theft of something from a person by use of violence or threat

¹**robe** \'rōb\ *n* **1** : a long flowing outer garment; *esp* : one used for ceremonial occasions **2** : a wrap or covering for the lower body (as for sitting outdoors)

²**robe** *vb* **robed; rob·ing** **1** : to clothe with or as with a robe **2** : DRESS

rob·in \'räb-ən\ *n* **1** : a small European thrush with a yellowish red throat and breast **2** : a large No. American thrush with a grayish back, a streaked throat, and a chiefly dull reddish breast

ro·bot \'rō-ˌbät, -bət\ *n* [Czech, fr. *robota* work] **1** : a machine that looks and acts like a human being **2** : an efficient but insensitive person **3** : an automatic apparatus **4** : something guided by automatic controls

ro·bust \rō-'bəst, 'rō-(ˌ)bəst\ *adj* [L *robustus* oaken, strong, fr. *robur* oak, strength] : strong and vigorously healthy — **ro·bust·ly** *adv* — **ro·bust·ness** *n*

¹**rock** \'räk\ *vb* **1** : to move back and forth in or as if in a cradle **2** : to sway or cause to sway back and forth

²**rock** *n* **1** : a rocking movement **2** : popular music usu. played on electric instruments and characterized by a strong beat and much repetition

³**rock** *n* **1** : a mass of stony material; *also* : broken pieces of stone **2** : solid mineral deposits **3** : something like a rock in firmness — **rock** *adj* — **rock·like** *adj* — **rocky** *adj*

rock and roll *n* : ²ROCK 2

rock•bound \\'räk-ˌbaủnd\ *adj* : fringed or covered with rocks

rock•er \\'räk-ər\ *n* **1** : one of the curved pieces on which something (as a chair or cradle) rocks **2** : a chair that rocks on rockers **3** : a device that works with a rocking motion **4** : a rock performer, song, or enthusiast

¹rock•et \\'räk-ət\ *n* [It *rocchetta*, lit., small distaff] **1** : a firework that is propelled through the air by the gases produced by a burning substance **2** : a jet engine that operates on the same principle as a firework rocket but carries the oxygen needed for burning its fuel **3** : a rocket-propelled bomb or missile

²rocket *vb* **1** : to convey by means of a rocket **2** : to rise abruptly and rapidly

rock•et•ry \\'räk-ə-trē\ *n* : the study or use of rockets

rocket ship *n* : a rocket-propelled spacecraft

rock•fall \\'räk-ˌfȯl\ *n* : a mass of falling or fallen rocks

rock•fish \\'räk-ˌfish\ *n* : any of various important market fishes that live among rocks or on rocky bottoms

rock 'n' roll \ˌräk-ən-'rōl\ *n* : ²ROCK 2

rock salt *n* : common salt in rocklike masses or large crystals

rock wool *n* : woollike insulation made from molten rock or slag

Rocky Mountain sheep *n* : BIGHORN

ro•co•co \rə-'kō-kō\ *adj* [F, irreg. fr. *rocaille* rock work] : of or relating to an artistic style esp. of the 18th century marked by fanciful curved forms and elaborate ornamentation — **rococo** *n*

rod \\'räd\ *n* **1** : a straight slender stick **2** : a stick or bundle of twigs used in punishing a person; *also* : PUNISHMENT **3** : a staff borne to show rank **4** — see WEIGHT table **5** *slang* : PISTOL

rode past of RIDE

ro•dent \\'rōd-ᵊnt\ *n* [fr. L *rodent-, rodens,* prp. of *rodere* to gnaw] : any of a large order of relatively small mammals (as mice, squirrels, and beavers) with sharp front teeth used for gnawing

ro•deo \\'rōd-ē-ˌō, rə-'dā-ō\ *n, pl* **ro•deos** [Sp, fr. *rodear* to surround, fr. *rueda* wheel, fr. L *rota*] **1** : ROUNDUP 1 **2** : a public performance featuring cowboy skills (as riding and roping)

¹roe \\'rō\ *n, pl* **roe** *or* **roes** : DOE

²roe *n* : the eggs of a fish esp. while bound together in a mass

roe•buck \\'rō-ˌbək\ *n, pl* **roebuck** *or* **roebucks** : a male roe deer

roe deer *n* : a small nimble European and Asian deer that is reddish brown in summer and grayish in the winter

roent•gen ray \ˌrent-gən-\ *n, often cap 1st R* : X RAY

rog•er \\'räj-ər\ *interj* — used esp. in radio and signaling to indicate that a message has been received and understood

rogue \\'rōg\ *n* **1** : a dishonest person : SCOUNDREL **2** : a mischievous person : SCAMP — **rogu•ery** \\'rō-gə-rē\ *n* — **rogu•ish** \\'rō-gish\ *adj* — **rogu•ish•ly** *adv* — **rogu•ish•ness** *n*

roil \\'rȯil, *for 2 also* 'rīl\ *vb* **1** : to make cloudy or muddy by stirring up **2** : RILE 1

rois•ter \\'rȯi-stər\ *vb* **rois•tered; rois•ter•ing** \-st(ə-)riŋ\ : to engage in noisy revelry : CAROUSE — **rois•ter•er** \-stər-ər\ *n*

role *also* **rôle** \\'rōl\ *n* **1** : an assigned or assumed character; *also* : a part played (as by an actor) **2** : FUNCTION

role model *n* : a person whose behavior in a particular role is imitated by others

¹roll \\'rōl\ *n* **1** : a document containing an official record **2** : an official list of names **3** : something (as a bun) that is rolled up or rounded as if rolled **4** : something that rolls : ROLLER

²roll *vb* **1** : to move by turning over and over **2** : to press with a roller **3** : to move on wheels **4** : to sound with a full reverberating tone **5** : to make a continuous beating sound (as on a drum) **6** : to move onward as if by completing a revolution ⟨years ~ed by⟩ **7** : to flow or seem to flow in a continuous stream or with a rising and falling motion ⟨the river ~ed on⟩ **8** : to swing or sway from side to side **9** : to shape or become shaped in rounded form **10** : to utter with a trill

³roll *n* **1** : a sound produced by rapid strokes on a drum **2** : a heavy reverberating sound **3** : a rolling movement or action **4** : a swaying movement (as of a ship) **5** : SOMERSAULT

roll·back \'rōl-ˌbak\ *n* : the act or an instance of rolling back

roll back \'rōl-'bak\ *vb* 1 : to reduce (as a commodity price) on a national scale 2 : to cause to withdraw : push back

roll bar *n* : an overhead metal bar in an automobile designed to protect riders in case the automobile overturns

roll call *n* : the act or an instance of calling off a list of names (as of soldiers); *also* : a time for a roll call

roll·er \'rō-lər\ *n* 1 : a revolving cylinder used for moving, pressing, shaping, applying, or smoothing something 2 : a rod on which something is rolled up 3 : a long heavy wave on a coast

roll·er coast·er \'rō-lər-ˌkō-stər\ *n* : an elevated railway (as in an amusement park) constructed with sharp curves and steep slopes

roller skate *n* : a skate with wheels instead of a runner — **roller–skate** *vb* — **roller skater** *n*

rol·lick \'räl-ik\ *vb* : ROMP, FROLIC

rol·lick·ing \-iŋ\ *adj* : full of fun and good spirits

roly–poly \ˌrō-lē-'pō-lē\ *adj* : ROTUND

Rom *abbr* 1 Roman 2 Romance 3 Romania; Romanian 4 Romans

ROM *abbr* read-only memory

ro·maine \rō-'mān\ *n* [F, lit., Roman] : a lettuce with a tall loose head of long crisp leaves

¹Ro·man \'rō-mən\ *n* 1 : a native or resident of Rome 2 : a citizen of the Roman Empire

²Roman *adj* 1 : of or relating to Rome or the Romans 2 *not cap* : relating to type in which the letters are upright (as in this definition) 3 : of or relating to the Roman Catholic Church

Roman candle *n* : a cylindrical firework that discharges balls of fire

Roman Catholic *adj* : of or relating to the body of Christians in communion with the pope and having a liturgy centered in the Mass — **Roman Catholicism** *n*

¹ro·mance \rō-'mans, 'rō-ˌmans\ *n* [ME *romauns*, fr. OF *romans* French, something written in French, fr. L *romanice* in the Roman manner, fr. *romanicus* Roman, fr. *Romanus*] 1 : a medieval tale of knightly adventure 2 : a prose narrative dealing with heroic or mysterious events set in a remote time or place 3 : a love story 4 : a romantic attachment or episode between lovers — **ro·manc·er** *n*

²romance *vb* **ro·manced; ro·manc·ing** 1 : to exaggerate or invent detail or incident 2 : to have romantic fancies 3 : to carry on a romantic episode with

Ro·mance \rō-'mans, 'rō-ˌmans\ *adj* : of or relating to any of several languages developed from Latin

Ro·ma·nian \rù-'mā-nē-ən, rō-, -nyən\ *n* 1 : a native or inhabitant of Romania 2 : RUMANIAN 2

Roman numeral *n* : a numeral in a system of notation that is based on the ancient Roman system

Ro·ma·no \rə-'män-ō, rō-\ *n* : a hard Italian cheese that is sharper than Parmesan

¹ro·man·tic \rō-'mant-ik\ *n* : a romantic person; *esp* : a romantic writer, composer, or artist

²romantic *adj* 1 : IMAGINARY 2 : VISIONARY 3 : having an imaginative or emotional appeal 4 : of, relating to, or having the characteristics of romanticism — **ro·man·ti·cal·ly** \-i-k(ə-)lē\ *adv*

ro·man·ti·cism \rō-'mant-ə-ˌsiz-əm\ *n, often cap* : a literary movement (as in early 19th century England) marked esp. by emphasis on the imagination and the emotions and by the use of autobiographical material — **ro·man·ti·cist** \-səst\ *n, often cap*

romp \'rämp\ *vb* 1 : to play actively and noisily 2 : to win a contest easily — **romp** *n*

romp·er \'räm-pər\ *n* 1 : one that romps 2 : a child's one-piece garment with the lower part shaped like bloomers — usu. used in pl.

rood \'rüd\ *n* : CROSS, CRUCIFIX

¹roof \'rüf, 'rùf\ *n, pl* **roofs** \'rüfs, 'rùfs; 'rüvz, 'rùvz\ 1 : the upper covering part of a building 2 : something suggesting a roof of a building — **roofed** \'rüft, 'rùft\ *adj* — **roof·ing** *n* — **roof·less** *adj*

²roof *vb* : to cover with a roof

roof·top \-ˌtäp\ *n* : a roof esp. of a house

roof·tree \-ˌtrē\ *n* : RIDGEPOLE

¹rook \'rùk\ *n* : a common Old World bird resembling the related crow

²rook *vb* : CHEAT, SWINDLE

³**rook** *n* : a chess piece that can move parallel to the sides of the board across any number of unoccupied squares

rook•ery \ˈrùk-ə-rē\ *n, pl* **-er•ies** : a breeding ground or haunt of gregarious birds or mammals; *also* : a colony of such birds or mammals

rook•ie \ˈrùk-ē\ *n* : BEGINNER, RECRUIT; *esp* : a first-year player in a professional sport

¹**room** \ˈrüm, ˈrùm\ *n* **1** : an extent of space occupied by or sufficient or available for something **2** : a partitioned part of a building : CHAMBER; *also* : the people in a room **3** : OPPORTUNITY, CHANCE ⟨∼ to develop his talents⟩ — **room•ful** *n* — **roomy** *adj*

²**room** *vb* : to occupy lodgings : LODGE — **room•er** *n*

room•ette \rü-ˈmet, rùm-ˈet\ *n* : a small private room on a railroad sleeping car

room•mate \ˈrüm-ˌmāt, ˈrùm-\ *n* : one of two or more persons sharing the same room or dwelling

¹**roost** \ˈrüst\ *n* : a support on which or a place where birds perch

²**roost** *vb* : to settle on or as if on a roost

roost•er \ˈrüs-tər, ˈrùs-\ *n* : an adult male domestic fowl : COCK

¹**root** \ˈrüt, ˈrùt\ *n* **1** : the leafless usu. underground part of a seed plant that functions in absorption, aeration, and storage or as a means of anchorage; *also* : an underground plant part esp. when fleshy and edible **2** : something (as the basal part of a tooth or hair) resembling a root **3** : SOURCE, ORIGIN **4** : the essential core : HEART ⟨get to the ∼ of the matter⟩ **5** : a number that when taken as a factor an indicated number of times gives a specified number **6** : the lower part — **root•less** *adj* — **root•like** *adj*

²**root** *vb* **1** : to form roots **2** : to fix or become fixed by or as if by roots : ESTABLISH **3** : UPROOT

³**root** *vb* **1** : to turn up or dig with the snout ⟨pigs ∼ing⟩ **2** : to poke or dig around (as in search of something)

⁴**root** \ˈrüt\ *vb* **1** : to applaud or encourage noisily : CHEER **2** : to wish success or lend support to — **root•er** *n*

root beer *n* : a sweetened effervescent beverage flavored with extracts of roots and herbs

root•let \ˈrüt-lət, ˈrùt-\ *n* : a small root

root•stock \-ˌstäk\ *n* : an underground part of a plant that resembles a rhizome

¹**rope** \ˈrōp\ *n* **1** : a large strong cord made of strands of fiber **2** : a hangman's noose **3** : a thick string (as of pearls) made by twisting or braiding

²**rope** *vb* **roped; rop•ing** **1** : to bind, tie, or fasten together with a rope **2** : to separate or divide off by means of a rope **3** : LASSO

Ror•schach test \ˈrȯr-ˌshäk-\ *n* : a personality and intelligence test in which a subject interprets ink-blot designs in terms that reveal intellectual and emotional factors

ro•sa•ry \ˈrō-zə-rē\ *n, pl* **-ries** **1** *often cap* : a Roman Catholic devotion consisting of meditation on sacred mysteries during recitation of Hail Marys **2** : a string of beads used in praying

¹**rose** past of RISE

²**rose** \ˈrōz\ *n* **1** : any of a genus of usu. prickly often climbing shrubs with divided leaves and bright often fragrant flowers; *also* : one of these flowers **2** : something resembling a rose in form **3** : a moderate purplish red color — **rose** *adj*

ro•sé \rō-ˈzā\ *n* [F] : a light pink wine

ro•se•ate \ˈrō-zē-ət, -zē-ˌāt\ *adj* **1** : resembling a rose esp. in color **2** : OPTIMISTIC ⟨a ∼ view of the future⟩

rose•bud \ˈrōz-ˌbəd\ *n* : the flower of a rose when it is at most partly open

rose•bush \-ˌbùsh\ *n* : a shrubby rose

rose•mary \ˈrōz-ˌmer-ē\ *n, pl* **-mar•ies** [ME *rosmarine*, fr. L *rosmarinus*, fr. *ros* dew + *marinus* of the sea, fr. *mare* sea] : a fragrant shrubby mint with evergreen leaves used in perfumery and cooking

ro•sette \rō-ˈzet\ *n* [F] **1** : a usu. small badge or ornament of ribbon gathered in the shape of a rose **2** : a circular ornament filled with representations of leaves

rose•wa•ter \ˈrōz-ˌwȯt-ər, -ˌwät-\ *adj* : a watery solution of the fragrant constituents of the rose used as a perfume

rose•wood \-ˌwùd\ *n* : any of various tropical trees with dark red wood streaked with black; *also* : this wood

Rosh Ha·sha·nah \ˌrōsh-(h)ə-ˈshō-nə\ *n* [Heb *rōsh hashshānāh*, lit., beginning of the year] : the Jewish New Year observed as a religious holiday in September or October

ros·in \ˈräz-ᵊn\ *n* : a hard brittle resin obtained esp. from pine trees and used in varnishes and on violin bows

ros·ter \ˈräs-tər\ *n* **1** : a list of personnel; *also* : the persons listed on a roster **2** : an itemized list

ros·trum \ˈräs-trəm\ *n, pl* **rostrums** *or* **ros·tra** \-trə\ [L *Rostra*, pl., a platform for speakers in the Roman Forum decorated with the beaks of captured ships, fr. pl. of *rostrum* beak, ship's beak, fr. *rodere* to gnaw] : a stage or platform for public speaking

rosy \ˈrō-zē\ *adj* **ros·i·er; -est 1** : of the color rose **2** : HOPEFUL, PROMISING — **ros·i·ly** \ˈrō-zə-lē\ *adv* — **ros·i·ness** \-zē-nəs\ *n*

¹rot \ˈrät\ *vb* **rot·ted; rot·ting** : to undergo decomposition : DECAY

²rot *n* **1** : DECAY **2** : a disease of plants or animals in which tissue breaks down **3** : NONSENSE

¹ro·ta·ry \ˈrōt-ə-rē\ *adj* **1** : turning on an axis like a wheel **2** : having a rotating part

²rotary *n, pl* **-ries 1** : a rotary machine **2** : a circular road junction

ro·tate \ˈrō-ˌtāt\ *vb* **ro·tat·ed; ro·tat·ing 1** : to turn or cause to turn about an axis or a center : REVOLVE **2** : to alternate in a series **syn** turn, circle, spin, whirl, twirl — **ro·ta·tion** \rō-ˈtā-shən\ *n* — **ro·ta·tor** \ˈrō-ˌtāt-ər\ *n* — **ro·ta·to·ry** \ˈrōt-ə-ˌtōr-ē\ *adj*

ROTC *abbr* Reserve Officers' Training Corps

rote \ˈrōt\ *n* **1** : repetition from memory often without attention to meaning **2** : fixed routine or repetition — **rote** *adj*

ro·tis·ser·ie \rō-ˈtis-(ə-)rē\ *n* [F] **1** : a restaurant specializing in broiled and barbecued meats **2** : an appliance fitted with a spit on which food is rotated before or over a source of heat

ro·to·gra·vure \ˌrōt-ə-grə-ˈvyùr\ *n* : PHOTOGRAVURE

ro·tor \ˈrōt-ər\ *n* **1** : a part that rotates **2** : a system of rotating horizontal blades for supporting a helicopter

rot·ten \ˈrät-ᵊn\ *adj* **1** : having rotted **2** : CORRUPT **3** : extremely unpleasant or inferior — **rot·ten·ness** \-ᵊn-(n)əs\ *n*

rot·ten·stone \ˈrät-ᵊn-ˌstōn\ *n* : a decomposed siliceous limestone used for polishing

ro·tund \rō-ˈtənd\ *adj* : rounded out **syn** plump, chubby, portly, stout — **ro·tun·di·ty** \-ˈtən-dət-ē\ *n*

ro·tun·da \rō-ˈtən-də\ *n* **1** : a round building; *esp* : one covered by a dome **2** : a large round room

rou·ble \ˈrü-bəl\ var of RUBLE

roué \rü-ˈā\ *n* [F, lit., broken on the wheel, fr. pp. of *rouer* to break on the wheel, fr. ML *rotare*, fr. L, to rotate; fr. the feeling that such a person deserves this punishment] : a man devoted to a life of sensual pleasure : RAKE

rouge \ˈrüzh, ˈrüj\ *n* [F, lit., red] **1** : a cosmetic used to give a red color to cheeks and lips **2** : a red powder used in polishing glass, gems, and metal — **rouge** *vb*

¹rough \ˈrəf\ *adj* **rough·er; rough·est 1** : uneven in surface : not smooth **2** : SHAGGY **3** : not calm : TURBULENT, TEMPESTUOUS **4** : marked by harshness or violence **5** : DIFFICULT, TRYING **6** : coarse or rugged in character or appearance **7** : marked by lack of refinement **8** : CRUDE, UNFINISHED **9** : done or made hastily or tentatively — **rough·ly** *adv* — **rough·ness** *n*

²rough *n* **1** : uneven ground covered with high grass esp. along a golf fairway **2** : a crude, unfinished, or preliminary state; *also* : something in such a state **3** : ROWDY, TOUGH

³rough *vb* **1** : ROUGHEN **2** : MANHANDLE **3** : to make or shape roughly esp. in a preliminary way — **rough·er** *n*

rough·age \ˈrəf-ij\ *n* : coarse bulky food (as bran) whose bulk stimulates the intestine to move its contents along

rough–and–ready \ˌrəf-ən-ˈred-ē\ *adj* : rude or unpolished in nature, method, or manner but effective in action or use

rough–and–tum·ble \-ˈtəm-bəl\ *n* : rough unrestrained fighting or struggling — **rough–and–tumble** *adj*

rough·en \ˈrəf-ən\ *vb* **rough·ened; rough·en·ing** \-(ə-)niŋ\ : to make or become rough

rough–hewn \ˈrəf-ˈhyün\ *adj* **1** : being

rough and unfinished ⟨∼ beams⟩ **2** : lacking smooth manners or social grace

rough·house \'rəf-ˌhau̇s\ *vb* **rough·housed; rough·hous·ing** : to participate in rough noisy behavior — **roughhouse** *n*

rough·neck \'rəf-ˌnek\ *n* **1** : ROWDY, TOUGH **2** : a worker on a crew drilling oil wells

rough·shod \'rəf-ˌshäd\ *adv* : with no consideration for the wishes or feelings of others ⟨rode ∼ over the opposition⟩

rou·lette \rü-'let\ *n* [F, lit., small wheel] **1** : a gambling game in which a whirling wheel is used **2** : a wheel or disk with teeth around the outside

¹round \'rau̇nd\ *adj* **1** : having every part of the surface or circumference the same distance from the center **2** : CYLINDRICAL **3** : COMPLETE, FULL **4** : approximately correct; *esp* : exact only to a specific decimal or place ⟨use the ∼ number 1400 for the exact figure 1411⟩ **5** : liberal or ample in size or amount **6** : BLUNT, OUTSPOKEN **7** : moving in or forming a circle **8** : of or relating to handwriting that is predominantly curved rather than angular — **round·ish** *adj* — **round·ly** \'rau̇n-(d)lē\ *adv* — **round·ness** \'rau̇n(d)-nəs\ *n*

²round *prep or adv* : AROUND

³round *n* **1** : something round (as a circle, globe, or ring) **2** : a curved or rounded part (as a rung of a ladder) **3** : a circuitous path or course; *also* : an habitually covered route (as of a watchman) **4** : a series or cycle of recurring actions or events **5** : one shot fired by a soldier or a gun; *also* : ammunition for one shot **6** : a period of time or a unit of play in a game or contest **7** : a cut of beef esp. between the rump and the lower leg — **in the round 1** : FREESTANDING **2** : with a center stage surrounded by an audience on all sides ⟨theater *in the round*⟩

⁴round *vb* **1** : to make or become round **2** : to go or pass around or part way around **3** : COMPLETE, FINISH **4** : to become plump or shapely **5** : to express as a round number **6** : to follow a winding course : BEND

¹round·about \'rau̇n-də-ˌbau̇t\ *n, Brit* : MERRY-GO-ROUND

²roundabout *adj* : INDIRECT, CIRCUITOUS

roun·de·lay \'rau̇n-də-ˌlā\ *n* **1** : a simple song with refrain **2** : a poem with a refrain recurring frequently or at fixed intervals

round·house \'rau̇nd-ˌhau̇s\ *n* : a circular building for housing and repairing locomotives

round–shoul·dered \'rau̇n(d)-'shōl-dərd\ *adj* : having the shoulders stooping or rounded

round–trip *n* : a trip to a place and back

round·up \'rau̇nd-ˌəp\ *n* **1** : the gathering together of cattle on the range by riding around them and driving them in; *also* : the men and horses engaged in a roundup **2** : a gathering in of scattered persons or things **3** : SUMMARY ⟨news ∼⟩ — **round up** \'rau̇nd-'əp\ *vb*

round·worm \-ˌwərm\ *n* : NEMATODE

rouse \'rau̇z\ *vb* **roused; rous·ing 1** : to wake from sleep **2** : to excite to activity : stir up

roust·about \'rau̇s-tə-ˌbau̇t\ *n* : one who does heavy unskilled labor (as on a dock or in an oil field)

¹rout \'rau̇t\ *n* **1** : MOB 1, 2 **2** : DISTURBANCE **3** : a fashionable gathering

²rout *vb* **1** : RUMMAGE **2** : to gouge out **3** : to expel by force

³rout *n* **1** : a state of wild confusion or disorderly retreat **2** : a disastrous defeat

⁴rout *vb* **1** : to put to flight **2** : to defeat decisively

¹route \'rüt, 'rau̇t\ *n* **1** : a traveled way **2** : CHANNEL **3** : a line of travel

²route *vb* **rout·ed; rout·ing 1** : to send by a selected route **2** : to arrange and direct the order of

route·man \-mən, -ˌman\ *n* : one who sells and makes deliveries on an assigned route

rou·tine \rü-'tēn\ *n* [F, fr. MF, fr. *route* traveled way] **1** : a round (as of work or play) regularly followed **2** : any regular course of action — **routine** *adj* — **rou·tine·ly** *adv* — **rou·tin·ize** \-'tēn-ˌīz\ *vb*

¹rove \'rōv\ *vb* **roved; rov·ing** : to wander over or through : RAMBLE, ROAM — **rov·er** *n*

²rove past and past part of REEVE

¹row \'rō\ *vb* **1** : to propel a boat with

oars **2** : to travel or convey in a row-boat **3** : to match rowing skill against — **row·er** \ˈrō-(-ə)r\ *n*

²**row** *n* : an act or instance of rowing

³**row** *n* **1** : a number of objects in an orderly sequence **2** : WAY, STREET

⁴**row** \ˈraů\ *n* : a noisy quarrel

⁵**row** \ˈraů\ *vb* : to engage in a row

row·boat \ˈrō-ˌbōt\ *n* : a small boat designed to be rowed

row·dy \ˈraůd-ē\ *adj* **row·di·er; -est** : coarse or boisterous in behavior : ROUGH — **row·di·ness** \ˈraůd-ē-nəs\ *n* — **rowdy** *n* — **row·dy·ish** *adj* — **row·dy·ism** *n*

row·el \ˈraů(-ə)l\ *n* : a small pointed wheel on a spur used to urge on a horse — **rowel** *vb*

roy·al \ˈrȯi-əl\ *adj* **1** : of or relating to a king or sovereign **2** : resembling or befitting a king — **roy·al·ly** \-ē\ *adv*

roy·al·ist \-ə-ləst\ *n* : an adherent of a king or of monarchical government

roy·al·ty \ˈrȯi-əl-tē\ *n, pl* **-ties** **1** : the state of being royal **2** : a royal person : royal persons **3** : a share of a product or profit (as of a mine or oil well) claimed by the owner for allowing another person to use the property **4** : a payment made to an author or composer for each copy of a work sold or to an inventor for each article sold under a patent

RP *abbr* relief pitcher

RPM *abbr* revolutions per minute

RPS *abbr* revolutions per second

rpt *abbr* **1** repeat **2** report

RR *abbr* **1** railroad **2** rural route

RS *abbr* **1** recording secretary **2** revised statutes **3** right side **4** Royal Society

RSV *abbr* Revised Standard Version

RSVP *abbr* [F *répondez s'il vous plaît*] please reply

RSWC *abbr* right side up with care

rt *abbr* right

RT *abbr* radiotelephone

rte *abbr* route

Ru *symbol* ruthenium

¹**rub** \ˈrəb\ *vb* **rubbed; rub·bing** **1** : to use pressure and friction on a body or object **2** : to fret or chafe with friction **3** : to scour, polish, erase, or smear by pressure and friction

²**rub** *n* **1** : DIFFICULTY, OBSTRUCTION **2** : something grating to the feelings

¹**rub·ber** \ˈrəb-ər\ *n* **1** : one that rubs **2** : ERASER **3** : a flexible waterproof elastic substance made from the juice of various tropical plants or synthetically; *also* : something made of this material — **rubber** *adj* — **rub·ber·ize** \-ˌīz\ *vb* — **rub·bery** *adj*

²**rubber** *n* **1** : a contest that consists of an odd number of games and is won by the side that takes a majority **2** : an extra game played to decide a tie

rub·ber·neck \-ˌnek\ *vb* : to look about, stare, or listen with excessive curiosity

rub·ber·neck·er \-ər\ *also* **rubberneck** *n* **1** : an idly or overly inquisitive person **2** : a person on a guided tour

rub·bish \ˈrəb-ish\ *n* **1** : useless waste or rejected matter : TRASH **2** : something worthless or nonsensical

rub·ble \ˈrəb-əl\ *n* : broken stones or bricks used in masonry; *also* : a mass of such material

ru·bel·la \rü-ˈbel-ə\ *n* : GERMAN MEASLES

ru·bi·cund \ˈrü-bi-(ˌ)kənd\ *adj* : RED, RUDDY

ru·bid·i·um \rü-ˈbid-ē-əm\ *n* : a soft silvery metallic chemical element

ru·ble \ˈrü-bəl\ *n* — see MONEY table

ru·bric \ˈrü-brik\ *n* [ME *rubrike* red ocher, heading in red letters of part of a book, fr. MF *rubrique*, fr. L *rubrica*, fr. *ruber* red] **1** : HEADING, TITLE; *also* : CLASS, CATEGORY **2** : a rule esp. for the conduct of a religious service

ru·by \ˈrü-bē\ *n, pl* **rubies** : a precious stone of a clear red color

ru·by–throat·ed hummingbird \ˌrü-bē-ˌthrōt-əd-\ *n* : a bright green and whitish hummingbird of eastern No. America with a red throat in the male

ruck·us \ˈrək-əs\ *n* : ROW, DISTURBANCE

rud·der \ˈrəd-ər\ *n* : a movable flat piece attached vertically at the rear of a boat or aircraft for steering

rud·dy \ˈrəd-ē\ *adj* **rud·di·er; -est** : REDDISH; *esp* : of a healthy reddish complexion — **rud·di·ness** \ˈrəd-ē-nəs\ *n*

rude \ˈrüd\ *adj* **rud·er; rud·est** **1** : roughly made : CRUDE **2** : UNDEVELOPED, PRIMITIVE **3** : IMPOLITE, DISCOURTEOUS **4** : UNSKILLED — **rude·ly** *adv* — **rude·ness** *n*

ru·di·ment \ˈrüd-ə-mənt\ *n* **1** : an elementary principle or basic skill — usu. used in pl. **2** : something not fully developed — usu. used in pl. — **ru·di·men·ta·ry** \ˌrüd-ə-ˈmen-t(ə-)rē\ *adj*

¹rue \ˈrü\ *vb* **rued; ru·ing** : to feel regret, remorse, or penitence for

²rue *n* : REGRET, SORROW — **rue·ful** \-fəl\ *adj* — **rue·ful·ly** \-ē\ *adv* — **rue·ful·ness** *n*

³rue *n* : a European strong-scented woody herb with bitter-tasting leaves

rue anemone *n* : a delicate herb of the buttercup family with white flowers

ruff \ˈrəf\ *n* **1** : a wheel-shaped frilled collar worn about 1600 **2** : a fringe of hair or feathers around the neck of an animal — **ruffed** \ˈrəft\ *adj*

ruf·fi·an \ˈrəf-ē-ən\ *n* [MF *rufian*] : a brutal person — **ruf·fi·an·ly** *adj*

¹ruf·fle \ˈrəf-əl\ *vb* **ruf·fled; ruf·fling** \-(ə-)liŋ\ **1** : to roughen the surface of **2** : IRRITATE, VEX **3** : to erect (as hair or feathers) in or like a ruff **4** : to draw into or provide with plaits or folds **5** : to flip through (as pages)

²ruffle *n* **1** : RIPPLE **2** : a strip of fabric gathered or pleated on one edge **3** : RUFF 2

rug \ˈrəg\ *n* **1** : a piece of heavy fabric usu. with a nap or pile used as a floor covering **2** : a covering for the legs, lap, and feet

rug·by \ˈrəg-bē\ *n, often cap* [*Rugby* School, Rugby, England, where it was first played] : a football game in which play is continuous and interference and forward passing are not permitted

rug·ged \ˈrəg-əd\ *adj* **1** : having a rough uneven surface **2** : TURBULENT, STORMY **3** : HARSH, STERN **4** : ROBUST, STURDY — **rug·ged·ly** *adv* — **rug·ged·ness** *n*

¹ru·in \ˈrü-ən\ *n* **1** : complete collapse or destruction **2** : the remains of something destroyed — usu. used in pl. **3** : a cause of destruction **4** : the action of destroying

²ruin *vb* **1** : DESTROY **2** : to damage beyond repair **3** : BANKRUPT

ru·in·ation \ˌrü-ə-ˈnā-shən\ *n* : RUIN, DESTRUCTION

ru·in·ous \ˈrü-ə-nəs\ *adj* **1** : RUINED, DILAPIDATED **2** : causing ruin — **ru·in·ous·ly** *adv*

¹rule \ˈrül\ *n* **1** : a guide or principle for governing action : REGULATION **2** : the usual way of doing something **3** : the exercise of authority or control : GOVERNMENT **4** : RULER 2

²rule *vb* **ruled; rul·ing 1** : CONTROL, GOVERN **2** : to be preeminent in : DOMINATE, PREVAIL **3** : to give or state as a considered decision **4** : to mark on paper with or as if with a ruler

rul·er \ˈrü-lər\ *n* **1** : SOVEREIGN **2** : a straight strip of material (as wood or metal) marked off in units and used for measuring or as a straightedge

rum \ˈrəm\ *n* **1** : a liquor distilled from a fermented cane product (as molasses) **2** : alcoholic liquor

Rum *abbr* Rumania; Rumanian

Ru·ma·nian \rü-ˈmā-nē-ən, -nyən\ *n* **1** : ROMANIAN 1 **2** : the language of the Romanians — **Rumanian** *adj*

rum·ba \ˈrəm-bə, ˈrùm-\ *n* : a dance of Cuban origin marked by strong rhythmic movements

¹rum·ble \ˈrəm-bəl\ *vb* **rum·bled; rum·bling** \-b(ə-)liŋ\ : to make a low heavy rolling sound; *also* : to travel or move along with such a sound — **rum·bler** \-b(ə-)lər\ *n*

²rumble *n* **1** : a low heavy rolling sound **2** : a street fight esp. among gangs

rumble seat *n* : a folding seat in the back of an automobile that is not covered by the top

rum·bling \ˈrəm-bliŋ\ *n* **1** : RUMBLE **2** : widespread talk or complaints — usu. used in pl.

¹ru·mi·nant \ˈrü-mə-nənt\ *n* : a ruminant mammal

²ruminant *adj* **1** : chewing the cud; *also* : of or relating to a group of hoofed mammals (as cattle, deer, and camels) that chew the cud and have a complex 3- or 4-chambered stomach **2** : given to or engaged in contemplation : MEDITATIVE

ru·mi·nate \ˈrü-mə-ˌnāt\ *vb* **-nat·ed; -nat·ing** [L *ruminari* to chew the cud, muse upon, fr. *rumin-, rumen* gullet] **1** : MEDITATE, MUSE **2** : to chew the cud — **ru·mi·na·tion** \ˌrü-mə-ˈnā-shən\ *n*

¹rum·mage \ˈrəm-ij\ *vb* **rum·maged; rum·mag·ing** : to poke around in all corners looking for something — **rum·mag·er** *n*

²rummage *n* **1** : a miscellaneous collection **2** : an act of rummaging

rum·my \ˈrəm-ē\ *n* : any of several card games for two or more players

ru·mor \'rü-mər\ *n* **1** : common talk **2** : a statement or report current but not authenticated — **rumor** *vb*

rump \'rəmp\ *n* **1** : the rear part of an animal; *also* : a cut of beef behind the upper sirloin **2** : a small remaining fragment : REMNANT

rum·ple \'rəm-pəl\ *vb* **rum·pled; rum·pling** \-p(ə-)liŋ\ : TOUSLE, MUSS, WRINKLE — **rumple** *n* — **rum·ply** \'rəm-p(ə-)lē\ *adj*

rum·pus \'rəm-pəs\ *n* : DISTURBANCE, FRACAS

rumpus room *n* : a room usu. in the basement of a home that is used for games, parties, and recreation

¹**run** \'rən\ *vb* **ran** \'ran\; **run; run·ning 1** : to go at a pace faster than a walk **2** : to take to flight : FLEE **3** : to go without restraint ⟨lets his children ∼⟩ **4** : to go rapidly or hurriedly : HASTEN, RUSH **5** : to perform or bring about by running **6** : to make a quick or casual trip or visit **7** : to contend in a race; *esp* : to enter an election **8** : to put forward as a candidate for office **9** : to move on or as if on wheels : pass or slide freely **10** : to go back and forth : PLY **11** : to move in schools esp. to a spawning ground ⟨shad are *running*⟩ **12** : FUNCTION, OPERATE ⟨left his car *running*⟩ **13** : to continue in force ⟨two years to ∼⟩ **14** : to flow rapidly or under pressure : MELT, FUSE, DISSOLVE; *also* : DISCHARGE **15** : to tend to produce or to recur ⟨family ∼s to blonds⟩ **16** : to take a certain direction **17** : to be current ⟨rumors *running* wild⟩ **18** : to be worded or written **19** : to cause to run **20** : TRACE ⟨∼ down a rumor⟩ **21** : to cause to pass ⟨∼ a wire from the antenna⟩ **22** : to cause to collide **23** : SMUGGLE **24** : MANAGE, CONDUCT, OPERATE ⟨∼ a business⟩ **25** : INCUR ⟨∼ a risk⟩ **26** : to permit to accumulate before settling ⟨∼ a charge account⟩

²**run** *n* **1** : an act or the action of running **2** : a school of migrating fish **3** : a score in baseball **4** : BROOK, CREEK **5** : a continuous series esp. of similar things **6** : persistent heavy demands from depositors, creditors, or customers **7** : the quantity of work turned out in a continuous operation; *also* : a period of operation (as of a machine or plant) **8** : the usual or normal kind ⟨the ordinary ∼ of students⟩ **9** : the distance covered in continuous travel or sailing **10** : a regular course or route; *also* : TRIP, JOURNEY **11** : freedom of movement in a place or area ⟨has the ∼ of the house⟩ **12** : an enclosure for animals **13** : an inclined course (as for skiing) **14** : a lengthwise ravel (as in a stocking) — **run·less** *adj*

run·about \'rən-ə-ˌbaùt\ *n* : a light wagon, automobile, or motorboat

run·a·gate \'rən-ə-ˌgāt\ *n* **1** : VAGABOND **2** : FUGITIVE

run·around \'rən-ə-ˌraùnd\ *n* : evasive or delaying action esp. in reply to a request

¹**run·away** \'rən-ə-ˌwā\ *n* **1** : one that runs away : FUGITIVE **2** : the act of running away or out of control; *also* : something (as a horse) that is running out of control

²**runaway** *adj* **1** : FUGITIVE **2** : accomplished by elopement ⟨∼ marriage⟩ **3** : won by a long lead **4** : subject to uncontrolled changes ⟨∼ inflation⟩ **5** : operating out of control ⟨a ∼ locomotive⟩

run·down \'rən-ˌdaùn\ *n* : an item-by=item report : SUMMARY

run–down \'rən-'daùn\ *adj* **1** : EXHAUSTED **2** : completely unwound **3** : being in poor repair : DILAPIDATED

run down \'rən-'daùn\ *vb* **1** : to collide with and knock down **2** : to chase until exhausted or captured **3** : to find by search **4** : DISPARAGE **5** : to cease to operate for lack of motive power **6** : to decline in physical condition

rune \'rün\ *n* **1** : any of the characters of any of several alphabets formerly used by the Germanic peoples **2** : MYSTERY, MAGIC **3** : a poem esp. in Finnish or Old Norse — **ru·nic** \'rü-nik\ *adj*

¹**rung** past part of RING

²**rung** \'rəŋ\ *n* **1** : a rounded crosspiece between the legs of a chair **2** : one of the crosspieces of a ladder **3** : a spoke of a wheel

run–in \'rən-ˌin\ *n* **1** : something run in **2** : ALTERCATION, QUARREL

run in \'rən-'in\ *vb* **1** : to insert as additional matter **2** : to arrest esp. for a minor offense **3** : to pay a casual visit

run·nel \'rən-ᵊl\ *n* : BROOK, STREAMLET

run·ner \'rən-ər\ *n* **1** : one that runs **2** : a baseball player on base or attempting to reach base **3** : BALLCARRIER **4** : a thin piece or part on which something (as a sled or an ice skate) slides **5** : the support of a drawer or a sliding door **6** : a horizontal branch from the base of a plant that produces new plants **7** : a plant producing runners **8** : a long narrow carpet **9** : a narrow decorative cloth cover for a table or dresser top

run·ner–up \'rən-ər-ˌəp\ *n, pl* **runners–up** *also* **runner–ups** : the competitor in a contest who finishes next to the winner

¹run·ning \'rən-iŋ\ *adj* **1** : FLOWING **2** : FLUID, RUNNY **3** : CONTINUOUS, INCESSANT **4** : measured in a straight line ⟨cost per ∼ foot⟩ **5** : of or relating to an act of running **6** : fitted or trained for running ⟨∼ horse⟩

²running *adv* : in succession

running light *n* : one of the lights carried by a vehicle (as a ship) at night

run·ny \'rən-ē\ *adj* : having a tendency to run ⟨a ∼ nose⟩

run·off \'rən-ˌȯf\ *n* : a final contest (as an election) to a previous indecisive contest

run–of–the–mill \ˌrən-ə(v)-thə-'mil\ *adj* : not outstanding : AVERAGE

run on \'rən-'ȯn, -'än\ *vb* **1** : to continue (matter in type) without a break or a new paragraph **2** : to place or add (as an entry in a dictionary) at the end of a paragraphed item — **run–on** \-ˌȯn, -ˌän\ *n*

runt \'rənt\ *n* : an unusually small person or animal : DWARF — **runty** *adj*

run·way \'rən-ˌwā\ *n* **1** : a beaten path made by animals; *also* : a passage for animals **2** : a paved strip of ground for the landing and takeoff of aircraft **3** : a narrow platform from a stage into an auditorium **4** : a support on which something runs

ru·pee \rü-'pē, 'rü-ˌpē\ *n* — see MONEY table

ru·pi·ah \rü-'pē-ə\ *n, pl* **rupiah** *or* **rupiahs** — see MONEY table

¹rup·ture \'rəp-chər\ *n* : a breaking or tearing apart; *also* : HERNIA

²rupture *vb* **rup·tured; rup·tur·ing** : to cause or undergo rupture

ru·ral \'rür-əl\ *adj* : of or relating to the country, country people, or agriculture

ruse \'rüs, 'rüz\ *n* : a wily subterfuge : TRICK, ARTIFICE

¹rush \'rəsh\ *n* : a hollow-stemmed grasslike marsh plant — **rushy** *adj*

²rush *vb* [ME *russhen*, fr. MF *ruser* to put to flight, deceive] **1** : to move forward or act with too great haste or eagerness or without preparation **2** : to perform in a short time or at high speed **3** : ATTACK, CHARGE — **rush·er** *n*

³rush *n* **1** : a violent forward motion **2** : unusual demand or activity **3** : a crowding of people to one place **4** : a running play in football

⁴rush *adj* : requiring or marked by special speed or urgency ⟨∼ orders⟩

rush hour *n* : a time when the amount of traffic or business is at a peak

rusk \'rəsk\ *n* : a sweet or plain bread baked, sliced, and baked again until dry and crisp

Russ *abbr* Russia; Russian

rus·set \'rəs-ət\ *n* **1** : a coarse reddish brown cloth **2** : a variable reddish brown or yellowish brown color **3** : any of various winter apples with rough russet skins — **russet** *adj*

Rus·sian \'rəsh-ən\ *n* **1** : a native or inhabitant of Russia or the U.S.S.R. **2** : the chief language of the U.S.S.R. — **Russian** *adj*

rust \'rəst\ *n* **1** : a reddish coating formed on iron when it is exposed to esp. moist air **2** : any of various diseases causing reddish spots on plants **3** : a reddish orange color — **rust** *vb* — **rusty** *adj*

¹rus·tic \'rəs-tik\ *adj* **1** : RURAL **2** : made of the rough limbs of trees ⟨∼ furniture⟩ **3** : AWKWARD, BOORISH **4** : PLAIN, SIMPLE — **rus·ti·cal·ly** \'rəs-ti-k(ə-)lē\ *adv* — **rus·tic·i·ty** \ˌrəs-'tis-ət-ē\ *n*

²rustic *n* : a rustic person

rus·ti·cate \'rəs-ti-ˌkāt\ *vb* **-cat·ed; -cat·ing** : to go into or reside in the country — **rus·ti·ca·tion** \ˌrəs-ti-'kā-shən\ *n*

¹rus·tle \'rəs-əl\ *vb* **rus·tled; rus·tling** \'rəs-(ə-)liŋ\ **1** : to make or cause a rustle **2** : to cause to rustle ⟨∼ a newspaper⟩ **3** : to act or move with energy or speed; *also* : to procure in this way **4** : to forage food **5** : to steal cattle from the range — **rus·tler** \-(ə-)lər\ *n*

²**rustle** *n* : a quick succession or confusion of small sounds ⟨∼ of leaves⟩

¹**rut** \'rət\ *n* : state or period of sexual excitement esp. in male deer — **rut** *vb*

²**rut** *n* **1** : a track worn by wheels or by habitual passage of something **2** : a usual or fixed routine

ru•ta•ba•ga \ˌrüt-ə-'bā-gə, ˌrùt-\ *n* : a turnip with a large yellowish root

Ruth \'rüth\ *n* — see BIBLE table

ru•the•ni•um \rü-'thē-nē-əm\ *n* : a hard brittle metallic chemical element

ruth•less \'rüth-ləs\ *adj* [fr. *ruth* compassion, pity, fr. ME *ruthe,* fr. *ruen* to rue, fr. OE *hrēowan*] : having no pity

: MERCILESS, CRUEL — **ruth•less•ly** *adv* — **ruth•less•ness** *n*

RV *abbr* recreational vehicle

R–value \'är-ˌval-yü\ *n* : a measure of the resistance of a substance (as insulation) to heat flow

RW *abbr* **1** right worshipful **2** right worthy

rwy *or* **ry** *abbr* railway

-ry \rē\ *n suffix* : -ERY ⟨bigot*ry*⟩

rye \'rī\ *n* **1** : a hardy cereal grass grown for grain or as a cover crop; *also* : its seed **2** : a whiskey distilled from a rye mash

S

¹**s** \'es\ *n, pl* **s's** *or* **ss** \'es-əz\ *often cap* : the 19th letter of the English alphabet

²**s** *abbr, often cap* **1** saint **2** second **3** senate **4** series **5** shilling **6** singular **7** small **8** son **9** south; southern

¹**-s** \s *after sounds* f, k, k̲, p, t, th; əz *after sounds* ch, j, s, sh, z, zh; z *after other sounds*\ *n pl suffix* — used to form the plural of most nouns that do not end in *s, z, sh, ch,* or postconsonantal *y* ⟨head*s*⟩ ⟨book*s*⟩ ⟨boy*s*⟩ ⟨belief*s*⟩ , to form the plural of proper nouns that end in postconsonantal *y* ⟨Mary*s*⟩ , and with or without a preceding apostrophe to form the plural of abbreviations, numbers, letters, and symbols used as nouns ⟨MC*s*⟩ ⟨4*s*⟩ ⟨#*s*⟩ ⟨B'*s*⟩

²**-s** *adv suffix* — used to form adverbs denoting usual or repeated action or state ⟨works night*s*⟩

³**-s** *vb suffix* — used to form the third person singular present of most verbs that do not end in *s, z, sh, ch,* or postconsonantal *y* ⟨fall*s*⟩ ⟨take*s*⟩ ⟨play*s*⟩

S *symbol* sulfur

SA *abbr* **1** Salvation Army **2** seaman apprentice **3** sex appeal **4** [L *sine anno* without year] without date **5** South Africa **6** South America **7** subject to approval

Sab•bath \'sab-əth\ *n* [ME *sabat,* fr. OF & OE, fr. L *sabbatum,* fr. Gk *sabbaton,* fr. Heb *shabbāth,* lit., rest] **1**

: the 7th day of the week observed as a day of worship by Jews and some Christians **2** : Sunday observed among Christians as a day of worship

sab•bat•i•cal \sə-'bat-i-kəl\ *n* : a leave often with pay granted (as to a college professor) usu. every 7th year for rest, travel, or research

sa•ber *or* **sa•bre** \'sā-bər\ *n* [F *sabre*] : a cavalry sword with a curved blade and thick back

saber saw *n* : a light portable electric saw with a pointed reciprocating blade

sa•ble \'sā-bəl\ *n, pl* **sables 1** : the color black **2** *pl* : mourning garments **3** : a dark brown mammal of northern Europe and Asia related to the martens and valued for its fur; *also* : this fur

¹**sab•o•tage** \'sab-ə-ˌtäzh\ *n* [F] **1** : deliberate destruction of an employer's property or hindering of production by workers **2** : destructive or hampering action by enemy agents or sympathizers in time of war

²**sabotage** *vb* **-taged; -tag•ing** : to practice sabotage on : WRECK

sab•o•teur \ˌsab-ə-'tər\ *n* : a person who commits sabotage

sac \'sak\ *n* : a baglike part of an animal or plant

SAC \'sak\ *abbr* Strategic Air Command

sac•cha•rin \'sak-(ə-)rən\ *n* : a white

crystalline compound used as an artificial sweetener

sac·cha·rine \'sak-(ə-)rən\ *adj* : nauseatingly sweet ⟨~ poetry⟩

sac·er·do·tal \,sas-ər-'dōt-ᵊl, ,sak-\ *adj* : PRIESTLY — **sac·er·do·tal·ism** *n*

sa·chem \'sā-chəm\ *n* : a No. American Indian chief

sa·chet \sa-'shā\ *n* [F, fr. OF, dim. of *sac* bag] : a small bag filled with perfumed powder for scenting clothes

¹**sack** \'sak\ *n* **1** : a large coarse bag; *also* : a small container esp. of paper **2** : a loose jacket or short coat

²**sack** *vb* : DISMISS, FIRE

³**sack** *n* [modif. of MF *sec* dry, fr. L *siccus*] : a white wine popular in England in the 16th and 17th centuries

⁴**sack** *vb* : to plunder a captured town

sack·cloth \-,klȯth\ *n* : a rough garment worn as a sign of penitence

sac·ra·ment \'sak-rə-mənt\ *n* **1** : a formal religious act or rite; *esp* : one (as baptism or the Eucharist) held to have been instituted by Christ **2** : the elements of the Eucharist — **sac·ra·men·tal** \,sak-rə-'ment-ᵊl\ *adj*

sa·cred \'sā-krəd\ *adj* **1** : set apart for the service or worship of deity **2** : devoted exclusively to one service or use **3** : worthy of veneration or reverence **4** : of or relating to religion : RELIGIOUS **syn** blessed, divine, hallowed, holy, sanctified — **sa·cred·ly** *adv* — **sa·cred·ness** *n*

sacred cow *n* : one that is often unreasonably immune from criticism

¹**sac·ri·fice** \'sak-rə-,fīs\ *n* **1** : the offering of something precious to deity **2** : something offered in sacrifice **3** : LOSS, DEPRIVATION **4** : a bunt allowing a base runner to advance while the batter is put out; *also* : a fly ball allowing a runner to score after the catch — **sac·ri·fi·cial** \,sak-rə-'fish-əl\ *adj* — **sac·ri·fi·cial·ly** \-ē\ *adv*

²**sac·ri·fice** *vb* **-ficed; -fic·ing 1** : to offer up or kill as a sacrifice **2** : to accept the loss or destruction of for an end, cause, or ideal **3** : to make a sacrifice in baseball

sac·ri·lege \'sak-rə-lij\ *n* [ME, fr. OF, fr. L *sacrilegium*, fr. *sacrilegus* one who steals sacred things, fr. *sacr-, sacer* sacred + *legere* to gather, steal] **1** : violation of something consecrated

to God **2** : gross irreverence toward a hallowed person, place, or thing — **sac·ri·le·gious** \,sak-rə-'lij-əs, -'lē-jəs\ *adj* — **sac·ri·le·gious·ly** *adv*

sac·ris·tan \'sak-rə-stən\ *n* **1** : a church officer in charge of the sacristy **2** : SEXTON

sac·ris·ty \'sak-rə-stē\ *n, pl* **-ties** : VESTRY

sac·ro·il·i·ac \,sak-rō-'il-ē-,ak\ *n* : the joint between the upper part of the hipbone and the sacrum

sac·ro·sanct \'sak-rō-,saŋkt\ *adj* : SACRED, INVIOLABLE

sa·crum \'sak-rəm, 'sā-krəm\ *n, pl* **sa·cra** \'sak-rə, 'sā-krə\ : the part of the vertebral column that is directly connected with or forms a part of the pelvis and in man consists of five fused vertebrae

sad \'sad\ *adj* **sad·der; sad·dest 1** : GRIEVING, MOURNFUL, DOWNCAST **2** : causing sorrow **3** : DULL, SOMBER — **sad·ly** *adv* — **sad·ness** *n*

sad·den \'sad-ᵊn\ *vb* **sad·dened; sad·den·ing** \'sad-(ᵊ-)niŋ\ : to make sad

¹**sad·dle** \'sad-ᵊl\ *n* **1** : a usu. padded leather-covered seat (as for a rider on horseback) **2** : the upper back portion of a carcass (as of mutton)

²**saddle** *vb* **sad·dled; sad·dling** \'sad-(ᵊ-)liŋ\ **1** : to put a saddle on **2** : BURDEN

sad·dle·bow \'sad-ᵊl-,bō\ *n* : the arch in the front of a saddle

saddle horse *n* : a horse suited for or trained for riding

Sad·du·cee \'saj-ə-,sē, 'sad-yə-\ *n* : a member of an ancient Jewish sect opposed to the Pharisees — **Sad·du·ce·an** \,saj-ə-'sē-ən, ,sad-yə-\ *adj*

sad·iron \'sad-,ī(-ə)rn\ *n* : a flatiron with a removable handle

sa·dism \'sā-,diz-əm, 'sad-,iz-\ *n* : a sexual perversion in which gratification is associated with inflicting physical or mental pain on others — **sa·dist** \'sād-əst, 'sad-\ *n* — **sa·dis·tic** \sə-'dis-tik\ *adj* — **sa·dis·ti·cal·ly** \-ti-k(ə-)lē\ *adv*

SAE *abbr* **1** self-addressed envelope **2** stamped addressed envelope

sa·fa·ri \sə-'fär-ē, -'far-\ *n* [Ar *safarīy* of a trip] **1** : a hunting expedition esp. in eastern Africa **2** : JOURNEY, TRIP

¹**safe** \'sāf\ *adj* **saf·er; saf·est 1** : freed

from injury or risk **2** : affording safety; *also* : secure from danger or loss **3** : RELIABLE, TRUSTWORTHY — **safe•ly** *adv*

²**safe** *n* : a container for keeping articles (as valuables) safe

safe–con•duct \-'kän-(ˌ)dəkt\ *n* : a pass permitting a person to go through enemy lines

¹**safe•guard** \-ˌgärd\ *n* : a measure or device for preventing accident or injury

²**safeguard** *vb* : to provide a safeguard for : PROTECT

safe•keep•ing \'sāf-'kē-piŋ\ *n* : a keeping or being kept in safety

safe•ty \'sāf-tē\ *n, pl* **safeties** **1** : freedom from danger : SECURITY **2** : a protective device **3** : a football play in which the ball is downed by the offensive team behind its own goal line **4** : a defensive football back in the deepest position — **safety** *adj*

safety glass *n* : shatter-resistant material formed of two sheets of glass with a sheet of clear plastic between them

safety match *n* : a match that ignites only when struck on a special surface

saf•flow•er \'saf-ˌlau̇(-ə)r\ *n* : a widely grown Old World herb related to the daisies that has large orange or red flower heads yielding a dyestuff and seeds rich in edible oil

saf•fron \'saf-rən\ *n* : an aromatic deep orange powder from the flower of a crocus used to color and flavor foods

sag \'sag\ *vb* **sagged; sag•ging** **1** : to bend down at the middle **2** : to become flabby : DROOP — **sag** *n*

sa•ga \'säg-ə\ *n* [ON] : a narrative of heroic deeds; *esp* : one recorded in Iceland in the 12th and 13th centuries

sa•ga•cious \sə-'gā-shəs\ *adj* : of keen mind : SHREWD — **sa•gac•i•ty** \-'gas-ət-ē\ *n*

sag•a•more \'sag-ə-ˌmōr\ *n* : a subordinate No. American Indian chief

¹**sage** \'sāj\ *adj* [ME, fr. OF, fr. (assumed) VL *sapius*, fr. L *sapere* to taste, have good taste, be wise] : WISE, PRUDENT — **sage•ly** *adv*

²**sage** *n* : a wise man : PHILOSOPHER

³**sage** *n* [ME, fr. MF *sauge*, fr. L *salvia*, fr. *salvus* healthy; fr. its use as a medicinal herb] **1** : a shrublike mint with leaves used in flavoring **2** : SAGE-BRUSH

sage•brush \'sāj-ˌbrəsh\ *n* : any of several low shrubby No. American plants related to the daisies; *esp* : one of the western U.S. with a sagelike odor

Sag•it•tar•i•us \ˌsaj-ə-'ter-ē-əs\ *n* [L, lit., archer] **1** : a zodiacal constellation between Scorpio and Capricorn usu. pictured as a centaur archer **2** : the 9th sign of the zodiac in astrology; *also* : one born under this sign

sa•go \'sā-gō\ *n, pl* **sagos** : a dry granulated starch esp. from the pith of an East Indian palm (**sago palm**)

sa•gua•ro \sə-'wär-ə\ *n, pl* **-ros** [MexSp] : a desert cactus of the southwestern U.S. and Mexico with a tall columnar simple or sparsely branched trunk of up to 60 feet (20 meters)

said past and past part of SAY

¹**sail** \'sāl\ *n* **1** : a piece of fabric by means of which the wind is used to propel a ship **2** : a sailing ship **3** : something resembling a sail **4** : a trip on a sailboat

²**sail** *vb* **1** : to travel on a sailing ship **2** : to pass over in a ship **3** : to manage or direct the course of a ship **4** : to glide through the air

sail•boat \-ˌbōt\ *n* : a boat usu. propelled by sail

sail•cloth \-ˌklȯth\ *n* : a heavy canvas used for sails, tents, or upholstery

sail•fish \-ˌfish\ *n* : any of a genus of large sea fishes with a very large dorsal fin that are related to the swordfish

sail•ing \'sā-liŋ\ *n* : the action, fact, or pastime of cruising or racing in a sailboat

sail•or \'sā-lər\ *n* : one that sails; *esp* : a member of a ship's crew

sail•plane \'sāl-ˌplān\ *n* : a glider designed to rise in an upward air current

saint \'sānt, *before a name* (ˌ)sānt *or* sənt\ *n* **1** : one officially recognized as preeminent for holiness **2** : one of the spirits of the departed in heaven **3** : a holy or godly person — **saint•ed** \-əd\ *adj* — **saint•hood** \-ˌhu̇d\ *n*

Saint Ber•nard \-bər-'närd\ *n* : any of a Swiss alpine breed of tall powerful working dogs used esp. formerly in aiding lost travelers

saint•ly \'sānt-lē\ *adj* : relating to, resembling, or befitting a saint — **saint•li•ness** *n*

Saint Val•en•tine's Day \-'val-ən-ˌtīnz\

n : February 14 observed in honor of St. Valentine and as a time for exchanging valentines

¹sake \\'sāk\ *n* **1** : MOTIVE, PURPOSE **2** : personal or social welfare, safety, or well-being

²sa·ke *or* **sa·ki** \\'säk-ē\ *n* : a Japanese alcoholic beverage of fermented rice

sa·laam \sə-'läm\ *n* [Ar *salām,* lit., peace] **1** : a salutation or ceremonial greeting in the East **2** : an obeisance performed by bowing very low and placing the right palm on the forehead — **salaam** *vb*

sa·la·cious \sə-'lā-shəs\ *adj* **1** : arousing sexual desire or imagination **2** : LUSTFUL — **sa·la·cious·ly** *adv* — **sa·la·cious·ness** *n*

sal·ad \\'sal-əd\ *n* : a cold dish (as of lettuce, vegetables, fish, eggs, or fruit) served with dressing

sal·a·man·der \\'sal-ə-,man-dər\ *n* : any of an order of amphibians that look like lizards but have scaleless usu. smooth moist skin

sa·la·mi \sə-'läm-ē\ *n* [It] : a highly seasoned sausage of pork and beef

sal·a·ry \\'sal(-ə)-rē\ *n, pl* **-ries** [ME *salarie,* fr. L *salarium* salt money, pension, salary, fr. neut. of *salarius* of salt, fr. *sal* salt] : payment made at regular intervals for services

sale \\'sāl\ *n* **1** : transfer of ownership of property from one person to another in return for money **2** : ready market : DEMAND **3** : AUCTION **4** : a selling of goods at bargain prices — **sal·able** *or* **sale·able** \\'sā-lə-bəl\ *adj*

sales·girl \\'sālz-,gərl\ *n* : SALESWOMAN

sales·man \-mən\ *n* : a person who sells in a store or to outside customers — **sales·man·ship** *n*

sales·per·son \-,pər-sən\ *n* : a salesman or saleswoman

sales·wom·an \-,wùm-ən\ *n* : a woman who sells merchandise

sal·i·cyl·ic acid \,sal-ə-,sil-ik-\ *n* : a crystalline organic acid used in the form of its salts to relieve pain and fever

¹sa·lient \\'sāl-yənt\ *adj* : jutting forward beyond a line; *also* : PROMINENT **syn** conspicuous, striking, noticeable

²salient *n* : a projecting part in a line of defense

¹sa·line \\'sā-,lēn, -,līn\ *adj* : consisting

of or containing salt : SALTY — **sa·lin·i·ty** \sā-'lin-ət-ē, sə-\ *n*

²saline *n* **1** : a metallic salt esp. with a purgative action **2** : a saline solution

sa·li·va \sə-'lī-və\ *n* : a liquid secreted into the mouth that helps digestion — **sal·i·vary** \\'sal-ə-,ver-ē\ *adj*

sal·i·vate \\'sal-ə-,vāt\ *vb* **-vat·ed; -vat·ing** : to produce saliva esp. in excess — **sal·i·va·tion** \,sal-ə-'vā-shən\ *n*

Salk vaccine \\'sò(l)k-\ *n* [after Jonas *Salk* b1914 American physician] : a polio vaccine that contains inactivated virus and is given by injection

sal·low \\'sal-ō\ *adj* : of a yellowish sickly color ⟨a ∼ liverish skin⟩

sal·ly \\'sal-ē\ *n, pl* **sallies 1** : a rushing attack on besiegers by troops of a besieged place **2** : a witty remark or retort **3** : a brief excursion — **sally** *vb*

salm·on \\'sam-ən\ *n, pl* **salmon** *also* **salmons 1** : any of several food fishes with pinkish flesh related to the trouts **2** : a strong yellowish pink

sa·lon \sə-'län, 'sal-,än, sa-'lōⁿ\ *n* [F] : an elegant drawing room; *also* : a fashionable shop ⟨beauty ∼⟩

sa·loon \sə-'lün\ *n* **1** : a large drawing room or ballroom esp. on a passenger ship **2** : a place where liquors are sold and drunk : BARROOM **3** *Brit* : SEDAN 2

sal soda \\'sal-'sōd-ə\ *n* : SODIUM CARBONATE

¹salt \\'sòlt\ *n* **1** : a white crystalline substance that consists of sodium and chlorine and is used in seasoning foods **2** : a saltlike cathartic substance (as Epsom salts) **3** : a compound formed usu. by action of an acid on metal **4** : SAILOR — **salt·i·ness** \\'sòl-tē-nəs\ *n* — **salty** \\'sòl-tē\ *adj*

²salt *vb* : to preserve, season, or feed with salt

³salt *adj* : preserved or treated with salt; *also* : SALTY

SALT *abbr* Strategic Arms Limitation Talks

salt away *vb* : to lay away safely : SAVE

salt·box \\'sòlt-,bäks\ *n* : a frame dwelling with two stories in front and one behind and a long sloping roof

salt·cel·lar \\'sòlt-,sel-ər\ *n* : a small vessel for holding salt at the table

sal·tine \sòl-'tēn\ *n* : a thin crisp cracker sprinkled with salt

salt lick *n* : LICK 5

salt·pe·ter \'sȯlt-ˈpēt-ər\ *n* [fr. earlier *saltpeter,* fr. ME, fr. MF *saltpetre,* fr. ML *sal petrae,* lit., salt of the rock] **1** : POTASSIUM NITRATE **2** : SODIUM NITRATE

salt·wa·ter \ˌsȯlt-ˌwȯt-ər, -ˌwät-\ *adj* : of, relating to, or living in salt water

sa·lu·bri·ous \sə-ˈlü-brē-əs\ *adj* : favorable to health

sal·u·tary \'sal-yə-ˌter-ē\ *adj* : health= giving; *also* : BENEFICIAL

sal·u·ta·tion \ˌsal-yə-ˈtā-shən\ *n* : an expression of greeting, goodwill, or courtesy usu. by word or gesture

sa·lu·ta·to·ri·an \sə-ˌlüt-ə-ˈtōr-ē-ən\ *n* : the student having the 2nd highest rank in a graduating class who delivers the salutatory address

sa·lu·ta·to·ry \sə-ˈlüt-ə-ˌtōr-ē\ *adj* : relating to or being the welcoming oration delivered at an academic commencement

¹sa·lute \sə-ˈlüt\ *vb* **sa·lut·ed; sa·lut·ing 1** : GREET **2** : to honor by special ceremonies **3** : to show respect to (a superior officer) by a formal position of hand, rifle, or sword

²salute *n* **1** : GREETING **2** : the formal position assumed in saluting a superior

¹sal·vage \'sal-vij\ *n* **1** : money paid for saving a ship, its cargo, or passengers when the ship is wrecked or in danger **2** : the saving of a ship **3** : the saving of possessions in danger of being lost **4** : things saved from loss or destruction (as by a wreck or fire)

²salvage *vb* **sal·vaged; sal·vag·ing** : to rescue from destruction

sal·va·tion \sal-ˈvā-shən\ *n* **1** : the saving of a person from sin or its consequences esp. in the life after death **2** : the saving from danger, difficulty, or evil **3** : something that saves

¹salve \'sav, 'såv\ *n* : a medicinal ointment

²salve *vb* **salved; salv·ing** : EASE, SOOTHE

sal·ver \'sal-vər\ *n* [F *salve,* fr. Sp *salva* sampling of food to detect poison, tray, fr. *salvar* to save, sample food to detect poison, fr. LL *salvare* to save, fr. L *salvus* safe] : a small serving tray

sal·vo \'sal-vō\ *n, pl* **salvos** *or* **salvoes** : a simultaneous discharge of guns

Sam *or* **Saml** *abbr* Samuel

SAM \'sam, ˌes-ˌā-ˈem\ *n* [surface-to-

air missile] : a guided missile for use against aircraft by ground units

sa·mar·i·um \sə-ˈmer-ē-əm\ *n* : a pale gray lustrous metallic chemical element

¹same \'sām\ *adj* **1** : being the one referred to : not different **2** : SIMILAR **syn** identical, equivalent, equal, tantamount — **same·ness** *n*

²same *pron* : the same one or ones

³same *adv* : in the same manner

sam·o·var \'sam-ə-ˌvär\ *n* [Russ, fr. *samo*- self + *varit'* to boil] : an urn with a spigot at the base used esp. in Russia to boil water for tea

sam·pan \'sam-ˌpan\ *n* : a flat-bottomed skiff of the Far East usu. propelled by two short oars

¹sam·ple \'sam-pəl\ *n* : a piece or item that shows the quality of the whole from which it was taken : EXAMPLE, SPECIMEN

²sample *vb* **sam·pled; sam·pling** \-p(ə-)liŋ\ : to judge the quality of by a sample

sam·pler \'sam-plər\ *n* : a piece of needlework; *esp* : one testing skill in embroidering

Sam·u·el \'sam-yə(-wə)l\ *n* — see BIBLE table

sam·u·rai \'sam-(y)ə-ˌrī\ *n, pl* **samurai** : a member of a Japanese feudal warrior class practicing a chivalric code

san·a·to·ri·um \ˌsan-ə-ˈtōr-ē-əm\ *n, pl* **-riums** *or* **-ria** \-ē-ə\ **1** : a health resort **2** : an establishment for the care esp. of convalescents or the chronically ill

sanc·ti·fy \'saŋk-tə-ˌfī\ *vb* **-fied; -fy·ing 1** : to make holy : CONSECRATE **2** : to free from sin — **sanc·ti·fi·ca·tion** \ˌsaŋk-tə-fə-ˈkā-shən\ *n*

sanc·ti·mo·nious \ˌsaŋk-tə-ˈmō-nē-əs\ *adj* : hypocritically pious — **sanc·ti·mo·nious·ly** *adv*

¹sanc·tion \'saŋk-shən\ *n* **1** : authoritative approval **2** : a measure (as a threat or fine) designed to enforce a law or standard ⟨economic ∼s⟩

²sanction *vb* **sanc·tioned; sanc·tion·ing** \-sh(ə-)niŋ\ : to give approval to : RATIFY **syn** endorse, accredit, certify, approve

sanc·ti·ty \'saŋk-tət-ē\ *n, pl* **-ties 1** : GODLINESS **2** : SACREDNESS

sanc·tu·ary \'saŋk-chə-ˌwer-ē\ *n, pl* **-aries 1** : a consecrated place (as the part of a church in which the altar is placed) **2** : a place of refuge ⟨bird ∼⟩

sanc•tum \'saŋk-təm\ *n, pl* **sanctums** *also* **sanc•ta** \-tə\ : a private office or study : DEN ⟨an editor's ∼⟩

¹**sand** \'sand\ *n* : loose particles of hard broken rock — **sandy** *adj*

²**sand** *vb* **1** : to cover or fill with sand **2** : to scour, smooth, or polish with an abrasive (as sandpaper) — **sand•er** *n*

san•dal \'san-dᵊl\ *n* : a shoe consisting of a sole strapped to the foot; *also* : a low or open slipper or rubber overshoe

san•dal•wood \-ˌwu̇d\ *n* : the fragrant yellowish heartwood of a parasitic tree of southeastern Asia that is much used in ornamental carving and cabinetwork; *also* : the tree

sand•bag \'san(d)-ˌbag\ *n* : a bag filled with sand and used in fortifications, as ballast, or as a weapon

sand•bank \-ˌbaŋk\ *n* : a deposit of sand (as in a bar or shoal)

sand•bar \-ˌbär\ *n* : a ridge of sand formed in water by tides or currents

sand•blast \-ˌblast\ *n* : sand blown (as for cleaning stone) by air or steam — **sandblast** *vb* — **sand•blast•er** *n*

sand•hog \'sand-ˌhȯg, -ˌhäg\ *n* : a laborer who builds underwater tunnels

sand•lot \'san(d)-ˌlät\ *n* : a vacant lot esp. when used for the unorganized sports of children — **sand•lot** *adj* — **sand•lot•ter** *n*

sand•man \-ˌman\ *n* : the genie of folklore who makes children sleepy

sand•pa•per \-ˌpā-pər\ *n* : paper with abrasive (as sand) glued on one side used in smoothing and polishing surfaces — **sandpaper** *vb*

sand•pip•er \-ˌpī-pər\ *n* : any of numerous shorebirds with a soft-tipped bill longer than that of the related plovers

sand•stone \-ˌstōn\ *n* : rock made of sand held together by a natural cement

sand•storm \-ˌstȯrm\ *n* : a windstorm that drives clouds of sand

sand trap *n* : a hazard on a golf course consisting of a hollow containing sand

¹**sand•wich** \'sand-(ˌ)wich\ *n* [after John Montagu, 4th Earl of *Sandwich* †1792 Eng. diplomat] **1** : two or more slices of bread with a layer (as of meat or cheese) spread between them **2** : something resembling a sandwich

²**sandwich** *vb* : to squeeze or crowd in

sane \'sān\ *adj* **san•er; san•est** : mentally sound and healthy; *also* : SENSIBLE, RATIONAL — **sane•ly** *adv*

sang *past of* SING

sang•froid \'sän-'frwä\ *n* [F *sang-froid*, lit., cold blood] : self-possession or an imperturbable state esp. under strain

san•gui•nary \'saŋ-gwə-ˌner-ē\ *adj* : BLOODY ⟨∼ battle⟩

san•guine \'saŋ-gwən\ *adj* **1** : RUDDY **2** : CHEERFUL, HOPEFUL

sanit *abbr* sanitary; sanitation

san•i•tar•i•an \ˌsan-ə-'ter-ē-ən\ *n* : a specialist in sanitation and public health

san•i•tar•i•um \ˌsan-ə-'ter-ē-əm\ *n, pl* **-i•ums** *or* **-ia** \-ē-ə\ : SANATORIUM

san•i•tary \'san-ə-ˌter-ē\ *adj* **1** : of or relating to health : HYGIENIC **2** : free from filth or infective matter

sanitary napkin *n* : a disposable absorbent pad used to absorb uterine flow (as during menstruation)

san•i•ta•tion \ˌsan-ə-'tā-shən\ *n* : a making sanitary; *also* : protection of health by maintenance of sanitary conditions

san•i•tize \'san-ə-ˌtīz\ *vb* **-tized; -tiz•ing** **1** : to make sanitary **2** : to make more acceptable by removing unpleasant features

san•i•ty \'san-ət-ē\ *n* : soundness of mind

sank *past of* SINK

sans \(ˌ)sanz\ *prep* : WITHOUT

San•skrit \'san-ˌskrit\ *n* : an ancient language that is the classical language of India and of Hinduism — **Sanskrit** *adj*

San•ta Ana \ˌsant-ə-'an-ə\ *n* [*Santa Ana* mountains in southern Calif.] : a hot dry wind from the north, northeast, or east in southern California

¹**sap** \'sap\ *n* : a vital fluid; *esp* : a watery fluid that circulates through a vascular plant — **sap•less** *adj*

²**sap** *vb* **sapped; sap•ping** **1** : UNDERMINE **2** : to weaken gradually

sa•pi•ent \'sā-pē-ənt, 'sap-ē-\ *adj* : WISE, DISCERNING — **sa•pi•ence** \-əns\ *n*

sap•ling \'sap-liŋ\ *n* : a young tree

sap·phire \\'saf-ˌī(ə)r\ *n* [ME *safir*, fr. OF, fr. L *sapphirus*, fr. Gk *sappheiros*, fr. Heb *sappīr*, fr. Skt *śanipriya*, lit., dear to the planet Saturn, fr. *Śani* Saturn + *priya* dear] : a hard transparent bright blue precious stone

sap·py \\'sap-ē\ *adj* **sap·pi·er; -est 1** : full of sap **2** : SILLY, FOOLISH

sap·ro·phyte \\'sap-rə-ˌfīt\ *n* : a living thing and esp. a plant living on dead or decaying organic matter — **sap·ro·phyt·ic** \ˌsap-rə-'fit-ik\ *adj*

sap·suck·er \\'sap-ˌsek-ər\ *n* : any of several small American woodpeckers

sap·wood \-ˌwud\ *n* : the younger active and usu. lighter and softer outer layer of wood (as of a tree trunk)

sar·casm \\'sär-ˌkaz-əm\ *n* **1** : a cutting or contemptuous remark **2** : ironic criticism or reproach — **sar·cas·tic** \sär-'kas-tik\ *adj* — **sar·cas·ti·cal·ly** \-ti-k(ə)lē\ *adv*

sar·coph·a·gus \sär-'käf-ə-gəs\ *n, pl* **-gi** \-ˌgī, -ˌjī\ *also* **-gus·es** [L *sarcophagus* (*lapis*) limestone used for coffins, fr. Gk (*lithos*) *sarkophagos*, lit., flesh≠eating stone, fr. *sark-*, *sarx* flesh + *phagein* to eat] : a large stone coffin

sar·dine \sär-'dēn\ *n, pl* **sardines** *also* **sardine** : a young or small fish preserved esp. in oil for use as food

sar·don·ic \sär-'dän-ik\ *adj* : expressing scorn or mockery : bitterly disdainful **syn** ironic, satiric, sarcastic — **sar·don·i·cal·ly** \-i-k(ə)lē\ *adv*

sa·ri *also* **sa·ree** \\'sär-ē\ *n* [Hindi *sāṛī*] : a garment of southern Asian women that consists of a long cloth draped around the body and head or shoulder

sa·rong \sə-'róŋ, -'räŋ\ *n* : a loose skirt wrapped around the body and worn by men and women of the Malay archipelago and the Pacific islands

sar·sa·pa·ril·la \ˌsas-(ə-)pe-'ril-ə, ˌsärs-\ *n* **1** : the root of a tropical American smilax used esp. for flavoring; *also* : the plant **2** : a sweetened carbonated beverage flavored with sassafras and an oil from a birch

sar·to·ri·al \sär-'tōr-ē-əl\ *adj* : of or relating to a tailor or tailored clothes — **sar·to·ri·al·ly** \-ē\ *adv*

SASE *abbr* self-addressed stamped envelope

¹sash \\'sash\ *n* : a broad band worn around the waist or over the shoulder

²sash *n, pl* **sash** *also* **sash·es** : a frame for a pane of glass in a door or window; *also* : the movable part of a window

sa·shay \sa-'shā\ *vb* **1** : WALK, GLIDE, GO **2** : to strut or move about in an ostentatious manner **3** : to proceed in a diagonal or sideways manner

Sask *abbr* Saskatchewan

Sas·quatch \\'sas-ˌkwach, -ˌkwäch\ *n* [from Salish (an American Indian language) *se'sxac* wild men] : a hairy manlike creature reported to exist in the northwestern U.S. and western Canada and said to be a very tall primate

sas·sa·fras \\'sas-ə-ˌfras\ *n* [Sp *sasafrás*] : a No. American tree related to the laurel; *also* : its dried bark now known to have carcinogenic properties

sassy \\'sas-ē\ *adj* **sass·i·er; -est** : SAUCY

¹sat past and past part of SIT

²sat *abbr* saturate; saturated; saturation

Sat *abbr* Saturday

Sa·tan \\'sāt-ᵊn\ *n* : DEVIL

sa·tang \sə-'täŋ\ *n, pl* **satang** *or* **satangs** — see *baht* at MONEY table

sa·tan·ic \sə-'tan-ik, sā-\ *adj* **1** : of or resembling Satan **2** : extremely malicious or wicked — **sa·tan·i·cal·ly** \-i-k(ə-)lē\ *adv*

satch·el \\'sach-əl\ *n* : TRAVELING BAG

sate \\'sāt\ *vb* **sat·ed; sat·ing** : to satisfy to the full; *also* : SURFEIT, GLUT

sa·teen \sa-'tēn, sə-\ *n* : a cotton cloth finished to resemble satin

sat·el·lite \\'sat-ᵊl-ˌīt\ *n* **1** : an obsequious follower of a prince or distinguished person : TOADY **2** : a celestial body that orbits a larger body **3** : a man-made object that orbits a celestial body

sa·ti·ate \\'sā-shē-ˌāt\ *vb* **-at·ed; -at·ing** : to satisfy fully or to excess

sa·ti·ety \sə-'tī-ət-ē\ *n* : fullness to the point of excess

sat·in \\'sat-ᵊn\ *n* : a fabric (as of silk) with a glossy surface — **sat·iny** *adj*

sat·in·wood \\'sat-ᵊn-ˌwud\ *n* : a hard yellowish brown wood of satiny luster; *also* : a tree yielding this wood

sat·ire \\'sa-ˌtī(ə)r\ *n* : biting wit, irony, or sarcasm used to expose vice or folly; *also* : a literary work having these qualities — **sa·tir·ic** \sə-'tir-ik\ *or* **sa·tir·i·cal** \-i-kəl\ *adj* — **sa·tir·i·cal·ly** \-ē\ *adv* — **sat·i·rist** \'sat-ə-rəst\ *n* — **sat·i·rize** \-ə-ˌrīz\ *vb*

sat·is·fac·tion \ˌsat-əs-'fak-shən\ *n* **1** : payment through penance of punishment incurred by sin **2** : CONTENTMENT, GRATIFICATION **3** : reparation for an insult **4** : settlement of a claim

sat·is·fac·to·ry \-'fak-t(ə-)rē\ *adj* : giving satisfaction : ADEQUATE — **sat·is·fac·to·ri·ly** \-'fak-t(ə-)rə-lē\ *adv*

sat·is·fy \'sat-əs-ˌfī\ *vb* **-fied; -fy·ing 1** : to make happy : GRATIFY **2** : to pay what is due to **3** : to answer or discharge (a claim) in full **4** : CONVINCE **5** : to meet the requirements of — **sat·is·fy·ing·ly** *adv*

sa·trap \'sā-ˌtrap, 'sa-\ *n* [ME, fr. L *satrapes*, fr. Gk *satrapēs*, fr. OPer *xshathrapāvan*, lit., protector of the dominion] : a petty prince : subordinate ruler

sat·u·rate \'sach-ə-ˌrāt\ *vb* **-rat·ed; -rat·ing 1** : to soak thoroughly **2** : to treat or charge with something to the point where no more can be absorbed, dissolved, or retained ⟨water *saturated* with salt⟩ — **sat·u·ra·ble** \'sach-(ə-)rə-bəl\ *adj* — **sat·u·ra·tion** \ˌsach-ə-'rā-shən\ *n*

Sat·ur·day \'sat-ər-dē, -ˌdā\ *n* : the 7th day of the week

Saturday night special *n* : a cheap easily concealed handgun

Sat·urn \'sat-ərn\ *n* : the planet 6th in order from the sun

sat·ur·nine \'sat-ər-ˌnīn\ *adj* : SULLEN, SARDONIC

sa·tyr \'sāt-ər\ *n* **1** *often cap* : a woodland deity in Greek mythology having certain characteristics of a horse or goat **2** : a lecherous man

¹sauce \'sȯs, *3 usu* 'sas\ *n* **1** : a dressing for salads, meats, or puddings **2** : stewed fruit **3** : IMPUDENCE

²sauce \'sȯs, *2 usu* 'sas\ *vb* **sauced; sauc·ing 1** : to add zest to **2** : to be impudent to

sauce·pan \'sȯs-ˌpan\ *n* : a cooking pan with a long handle

sau·cer \'sȯ-sər\ *n* : a rounded shallow dish for use under a cup

saucy \'sas-ē, 'sȯs-ē\ *adj* **sauc·i·er; -est** : IMPUDENT, PERT — **sauc·i·ly** \-ə-lē\ *adv* — **sauc·i·ness** \-ē-nəs\ *n*

sau·er·kraut \'saů(-ə)r-ˌkraůt\ *n* [G, fr. *sauer* sour + *kraut* cabbage] : finely cut cabbage fermented in brine

sau·na \'saů-nə\ *n* **1** : a Finnish steam bath in which the steam is provided by water thrown on hot stones **2** : a dry heat bath; *also* : a room or cabinet used for such a bath

saun·ter \'sȯnt-ər, 'sänt-\ *vb* : STROLL

sau·sage \'sȯ-sij\ *n* [deriv. of LL *salsicia*, fr. L *salsus* salted] : minced and highly seasoned meat (as pork) usu. enclosed in a tubular casing

S Aust *abbr* South Australia

sau·té \sȯ-'tā, sō-\ *vb* **sau·téed** *or* **sau·téd; sau·té·ing** [F] : to fry lightly in a little fat — **sauté** *n*

sau·terne \sō-'tərn, sȯ-\ *n, often cap* [F *sauternes*] : a usu. semisweet white wine

¹sav·age \'sav-ij\ *adj* [ME *sauvage*, fr. MF, fr. ML *salvaticus*, fr. L *silvaticus* of the woods, wild, fr. *silva* wood, forest] **1** : WILD, UNTAMED **2** : UNCIVILIZED, BARBAROUS **3** : CRUEL, FIERCE — **sav·age·ly** *adv* — **sav·age·ness** *n* — **sav·age·ry** \-(ə-)rē\ *n*

²savage *n* **1** : a member of a primitive human society **2** : a rude, unmannerly, or brutal person

sa·van·na *or* **sa·van·nah** \sə-'van-ə\ *n* [Sp *zavana*] : grassland containing scattered trees

sa·vant \sa-'vänt, sə-, 'sav-ənt\ *n* : a learned man : SCHOLAR

¹save \'sāv\ *vb* **saved; sav·ing 1** : to redeem from sin **2** : to rescue from danger **3** : to preserve or guard from destruction or loss **4** : to put aside as a store or reserve — **sav·er** *n*

²save *n* : a play that prevents an opponent from scoring or winning

³save \(ˌ)sāv\ *prep* : EXCEPT

⁴save \(ˌ)sāv\ *conj* : BUT

savings and loan association *n* : a cooperative association that holds savings of members in the form of dividend-bearing shares and that invests chiefly in mortgage loans

savings bank *n* : a bank that holds funds of individual depositors in interest-bearing accounts and makes long-term investments (as in mortgage loans)

savings bond *n* : a registered U.S. bond

issued in denominations of $50 to $10,000

sav·ior *or* **sav·iour** \'sāv-yər\ *n* **1** : one who saves **2** *cap* : Jesus Christ

sa·voir faire \ˌsav-ˌwär-'far\ *n* [F *savoir-faire,* lit., knowing how to do] : readiness in knowing how to act : TACT

¹sa·vor *also* **sa·vour** \'sā-vər\ *n* **1** : the taste and odor of something **2** : a special flavor or quality — **sa·vory** *adj*

²savor *also* **savour** *vb* **sa·vored; sa·vor·ing** \'sāv-(ə-)riŋ\ **1** : to have a specified taste, smell, or quality **2** : to taste with pleasure

sa·vo·ry \'sāv-(ə-)rē\ *n, pl* **-ries** : any of several aromatic mints used in cooking

¹sav·vy \'sav-ē\ *vb* **sav·vied; sav·vy·ing** [modif. of Sp *sabe* he knows] : COMPREHEND, UNDERSTAND

²savvy *n* : practical know-how ⟨political ∼⟩

¹saw past of SEE

²saw \'sȯ\ *n* : a cutting tool with a blade having a line of teeth along its edge

³saw *vb* **sawed** \'sȯd\; **sawed** *or* **sawn** \'sȯn\; **saw·ing** \'sȯ(-)iŋ\ : to cut or divide with or as if with a saw — **saw·yer** \-yər\ *n*

⁴saw *n* : a common saying : MAXIM

saw·dust \'sȯ-(ˌ)dəst\ *n* : fine particles made by a saw in cutting

saw·fly \'sȯ-ˌflī\ *n* : any of numerous insects belonging to the same order as bees and wasps and including many whose larvae are plant-feeding pests

saw·horse \'sȯ-ˌhȯrs\ *n* : a rack on which wood is rested while being sawed by hand

saw·mill \-ˌmil\ *n* : a mill for sawing logs

saw palmetto *n* : any of several shrubby palms with spiny-toothed petioles

sax·i·frage \'sak-sə-frij, -ˌfrāj\ *n* [deriv. of LL *saxifraga,* fr. L, lit., breaking rocks] : any of a genus of plants with showy 5-parted flowers and usu. with leaves growing in tufts close to the ground

sax·o·phone \'sak-sə-ˌfōn\ *n* : a musical instrument consisting of a conical metal tube with a reed mouthpiece and finger keys — **sax·o·phon·ist** \-əst\ *n*

¹say \'sā\ *vb* **said** \'sed\; **say·ing** \'sā-iŋ\;

says \'sez\ **1** : to express in words ⟨∼ what you mean⟩ **2** : to state as opinion or belief **3** : PRONOUNCE; *also* : RECITE, REPEAT ⟨∼ your prayers⟩ **4** : INDICATE ⟨the clock ∼s noon⟩

²say *n, pl* **says** \'sāz\ **1** : an expression of opinion **2** : power of decision

say·ing \'sā-iŋ\ *n* : a commonly repeated statement

say–so \'sā-(ˌ)sō\ *n* : an esp. authoritative assertion or decision; *also* : the right to decide

sb *abbr* substantive

Sb *symbol* [L *stibium*] antimony

SB *abbr* [NL *scientiae baccalaureus*] bachelor of science

SBA *abbr* Small Business Administration

sc *abbr* **1** scale **2** scene **3** science

Sc *symbol* scandium

SC *abbr* **1** South Carolina **2** Supreme Court

¹scab \'skab\ *n* **1** : scabies of domestic animals **2** : a protective crust over a sore or wound **3** : a worker who replaces a striker or works under conditions not authorized by a union **4** : a plant disease in which crusted spots form on stems or leaves — **scab·by** *adj*

²scab *vb* **scabbed; scab·bing** **1** : to become covered with a scab **2** : to work as a scab

scab·bard \'skab-ərd\ *n* : a sheath for the blade of a weapon (as a sword)

sca·bies \'skā-bēz\ *n* [L] : contagious itch or mange caused by mites living as parasites under the skin

sca·brous \'skab-rəs, 'skāb-\ *adj* **1** : DIFFICULT, KNOTTY **2** : rough to the touch : SCALY, SCURFY ⟨a ∼ leaf⟩ **3** : dealing with suggestive, indecent, or scandalous themes; *also* : SQUALID

scad \'skad\ *n* **1** : a large number or quantity **2** *pl* : a great abundance

scaf·fold \'skaf-əld, -ˌōld\ *n* **1** : a raised platform for workers to sit or stand on **2** : a platform on which a criminal is executed (as by hanging)

scaf·fold·ing \-iŋ\ *n* : a system of scaffolds; *also* : materials for scaffolds

scal·a·wag \'skal-i-ˌwag\ *n* : RASCAL

¹scald \'skȯld\ *vb* **1** : to burn with or as if with hot liquid or steam **2** : to heat to just below the boiling point

²scald *n* : a burn caused by scalding

¹scale \'skāl\ *n* **1** : either pan of a balance **2** : BALANCE — usu. used in pl. **3** : a weighing instrument

²**scale** *vb* **scaled; scal·ing** : WEIGH

³**scale** *n* **1** : one of the small thin plates that cover the body esp. of a fish or reptile **2** : a thin plate **3** : a thin coating, layer, or incrustation **4** : SCALE INSECT — **scaled** \'skāld\ *adj* — **scaleless** \'skāl-ləs\ *adj* — **scaly** *adj*

⁴**scale** *vb* **scaled; scal·ing** : to strip of scales

⁵**scale** *n* [ME, fr. LL *scala* ladder, staircase, fr. L *scalae*, pl., stairs, rungs, ladder] **1** : something divided into regular spaces as a help in drawing or measuring **2** : a graduated series **3** : the size of a sample (as a model) in proportion to the size of the actual thing **4** : a standard of estimation or judgment **5** : a series of musical tones going up or down in pitch according to a specified scheme

⁶**scale** *vb* **scaled; scal·ing 1** : to go up by or as if by a ladder **2** : to arrange in a graded series

scale insect *n* : any of numerous small insects that live and are often pests on plants and have wingless scale-covered females

scale·pan \'skāl-₁pan\ *n* : ¹SCALE 1

scal·lion \'skal-yən\ *n* [deriv. of L *ascalonia* (*caepa*) onion of Ascalon (seaport in Palestine)] : an onion without an enlarged bulb

¹**scal·lop** \'skäl-əp, 'skal-\ *n* **1** : any of a family of marine mollusks with radially ridged shell valves; *also* : a large edible muscle of this mollusk **2** : one of a continuous series of rounded projections forming an edge (as in lace)

²**scallop** *vb* **1** : to edge (as lace) with scallops **2** : to bake in a casserole

¹**scalp** \'skalp\ *n* : the part of the skin and flesh of the head usu. covered with hair

²**scalp** *vb* **1** : to remove the scalp from **2** : to obtain for the sake of reselling at greatly increased prices — **scalp·er** *n*

scal·pel \'skal-pəl\ *n* : a small straight knife with a thin blade used esp. in surgery

scam \'skam\ *n* : a fraudulent or deceptive act or operation

scamp \'skamp\ *n* : RASCAL

scam·per \'skam-pər\ *vb* **scam·pered;**

scam·per·ing \-p(ə-)riŋ\ : to run nimbly and playfully — **scamper** *n*

scam·pi \'skam-pē\ *n, pl* **scampi** [It] : SHRIMP; *esp* : large shrimp prepared with a garlic-flavored sauce

¹**scan** \'skan\ *vb* **scanned; scan·ning 1** : to read (verses) so as to show metrical structure **2** : to examine closely **3** : to move an electromagnetic beam across esp. in a regular pattern **4** : to make a scan of (as the human body) **syn** scrutinize, inspect, examine — **scan·ner** \'skan-ər\ *n*

²**scan** *n* **1** : the act or process of scanning **2** : a picture of the distribution of radioactive material in something; *also* : a picture of part of the body made by combining separate pictures taken from different angles or of different sections

Scand *abbr* Scandinavia; Scandinavian

scan·dal \'skan-dᵊl\ *n* [LL *scandalum* stumbling block, offense, fr. Gk *skandalon*] **1** : DISGRACE, DISHONOR **2** : malicious gossip : SLANDER — **scan·dal·ize** *vb* — **scan·dal·ous** *adj* — **scan·dal·ous·ly** *adv*

scan·dal·mon·ger \-₁məŋ-gər, -₁mäŋ-\ *n* : a person who circulates scandal

Scan·di·na·vian \₁skan-də-'nā-vē-ən\ *n* : a native or inhabitant of Scandinavia — **Scandinavian** *adj*

scan·di·um \'skan-dē-əm\ *n* : a white metallic chemical element

¹**scant** \'skant\ *adj* **1** : barely sufficient **2** : having scarcely enough **syn** scanty, skimpy, meager, sparse, exiguous

²**scant** *vb* **1** : SKIMP **2** : STINT

scant·ling \'skant-liŋ\ *n* : a piece of lumber; *esp* : one used for an upright in building

scanty \'skant-ē\ *adj* **scant·i·er; -est** : barely sufficient : SCANT — **scant·i·ly** \'skant-ə-lē\ *adv* — **scant·i·ness** \-ē-nəs\ *n*

scape·goat \'skāp-₁gōt\ *n* : one that bears the blame for others

scape·grace \-₁grās\ *n* [*scape* (escape)] : an incorrigible rascal

scap·u·la \'skap-yə-lə\ *n, pl* **-lae** \-₁lē\ *or* **-las** [L] : SHOULDER BLADE

scap·u·lar \-lər\ *adj* : of or relating to the shoulder or shoulder blade

scar \'skär\ *n* : a mark left after injured tissue has healed — **scar** *vb*

scar·ab \'skar-əb\ *n* [MF *scarabee*, fr.

L *scarabaeus*] : any of a family of large stout beetles; *also* : an ornament (as a gem) representing such a beetle

scarce \'skeərs\ *adj* **scarc·er; scarc·est 1** : not plentiful **2** : RARE — **scar·ci·ty** \'sker-sət-ē\ *n*

scarce·ly \'skeərs-lē\ *adv* **1** : BARELY **2** : almost not **3** : very probably not

¹**scare** \'skeər\ *vb* **scared; scar·ing** : FRIGHTEN, STARTLE

²**scare** *n* : FRIGHT — **scary** *adj*

scare·crow \'skeər-ˌkrō\ *n* : a crude figure set up to scare birds away from crops

¹**scarf** \'skärf\ *n, pl* **scarves** \'skärvz\ *or* **scarfs 1** : a broad band (as of cloth) worn about the shoulders, around the neck, over the head, or about the waist **2** : a long narrow cloth cover for a table or dresser top

²**scarf** *vb* [alter. of earlier *scoff* eat greedily] : to eat greedily

scar·i·fy \'skar-ə-ˌfī\ *vb* **-fied; -fy·ing 1** : to make scratches or small cuts in : wound superficially ⟨∼ skin for vaccination⟩ ⟨∼ seeds to help them germinate⟩ **2** : to lacerate the feelings of : FLAY — **scar·i·fi·ca·tion** \ˌskar-ə-fə-'kā-shən\ *n*

scar·la·ti·na \ˌskär-lə-'tē-nə\ *n* : SCARLET FEVER

scar·let \'skär-lət\ *n* : a bright red — **scarlet** *adj*

scarlet fever *n* : an acute contagious disease marked by fever, sore throat, and red rash and caused by certain streptococci

scarp \'skärp\ *n* : a line of cliffs produced by faulting or erosion

scath·ing \'skā-thiŋ\ *adj* : bitterly severe

scat·o·log·i·cal \ˌskat-ᵊl-'äj-i-kəl\ *adj* : concerned with obscene matters

scat·ter \'skat-ər\ *vb* **1** : to distribute or strew about irregularly **2** : DISPERSE

scav·enge \'skav-ənj\ *vb* **scav·enged; scav·eng·ing** : to work or function as a scavenger

scav·en·ger \'skav-ən-jər\ *n* [alter. of earlier *scavager*, fr. ME *skawager* collector of a toll on goods sold by nonresident merchants, fr. *skawage* toll on goods sold by nonresident merchants, fr. OF *escauwage* inspection] : a person or animal that collects or disposes of refuse or waste

sce·nar·io \sə-'nar-ē-ˌō\ *n, pl* **-i·os** : the plot or outline of a dramatic work; *also* : an account of a projected action

scene \'sēn\ *n* [MF, stage, fr. L *scena, scaena* stage, scene, fr. Gk *skēnē* temporary shelter, tent, building forming the background for a dramatic performance, stage] **1** : a division of one act of a play **2** : a single situation or sequence in a play or motion picture **3** : a stage setting **4** : VIEW, PROSPECT **5** : the place of an occurrence or action **6** : a display of strong feeling and esp. anger **7** : a sphere of activity ⟨the fashion ∼⟩ — **sce·nic** \'sēn-ik\ *adj*

scen·ery \'sēn-(ə-)rē\ *n, pl* **-er·ies 1** : the painted scenes or hangings of a stage and the fittings that go with them **2** : a picturesque view or landscape

¹**scent** \'sent\ *n* **1** : ODOR, SMELL **2** : sense of smell **3** : course of pursuit : TRACK **4** : PERFUME **2** — **scent·less** *adj*

²**scent** *vb* **1** : SMELL **2** : to imbue or fill with odor

scep·ter \'sep-tər\ *n* : a staff borne by a sovereign as an emblem of authority

scep·tic \'skep-tik\ *var of* SKEPTIC

sch *abbr* school

¹**sched·ule** \'skej-ül, *esp Brit* 'shed-yül\ *n* **1** : a list of items or details **2** : TIMETABLE

²**schedule** *vb* **sched·uled; sched·ul·ing** : to make a schedule of; *also* : to enter on a schedule

sche·mat·ic \ski-'mat-ik\ *adj* : of or relating to a scheme or diagram : DIAGRAMMATIC — **schematic** *n* — **sche·mat·i·cal·ly** \-i-k(ə-)lē\ *adv*

¹**scheme** \'skēm\ *n* **1** : a plan for doing something; *esp* : a crafty plot **2** : a systematic design

²**scheme** *vb* **schemed; schem·ing** : to form a plot : INTRIGUE — **schem·er** *n* — **schem·ing** *adj*

Schick test \'shik-\ *n* : a serological test for susceptibility to diphtheria

schil·ling \'shil-iŋ\ *n* — see MONEY table

schism \'siz-əm, 'skiz-\ *n* **1** : DIVISION, SPLIT; *also* : DISCORD, DISSENSION **2** : a formal division in or separation from a religious body **3** : the offense of promoting schism

schis·mat·ic \siz-'mat-ik, skiz-\ *n* : one who creates or takes part in schism — **schismatic** *adj*

schist \'shist\ *n* : a metamorphic crystalline rock

schizo·phre·nia \,skit-sə-'frē-nē-ə\ *n* [NL, fr. Gk *schizein* to split + *phrēn* diaphragm, mind] : a psychotic disorder that is characterized by a twisted view of the real world, by a greatly reduced ability to carry out one's daily tasks, and by abnormal ways of thinking, feeling, and behaving — **schiz·oid** \'skit-,sȯid\ *adj or n* — **schizo·phren·ic** \,skit-sə-'fren-ik\ *adj or n*

schle·miel \shlə-'mēl\ *n* : an unlucky bungler : CHUMP

schmaltz *also* **schmalz** \'shmȯlts, 'shmälts\ *n* [Yiddish *shmalts,* lit., rendered fat] : sentimental or florid music or art — **schmaltzy** *adj*

schnau·zer \'shnaut-sər, 's(h)naú-zər\ *n* [G, fr. *schnauze* snout] : a dog of any of three breeds that are characterized by a long head, small ears, heavy eyebrows, mustache and beard, and a wiry coat

schol·ar \'skäl-ər\ *n* **1** : STUDENT, PUPIL **2** : a learned man : SAVANT — **schol·ar·ly** *adj*

schol·ar·ship \-,ship\ *n* **1** : the qualities or learning of a scholar **2** : money awarded to a student to help pay for further education

scho·las·tic \skə-'las-tik\ *adj* : of or relating to schools, scholars, or scholarship

¹school \'skül\ *n* **1** : an institution for teaching and learning; *also* : the pupils in attendance **2** : a body of persons of like opinions or beliefs ⟨the radical ∼⟩

²school *vb* : TEACH, TRAIN, DRILL

³school *n* : a large number of one kind of water animal swimming and feeding together

school·boy \-,bȯi\ *n* : a boy attending school

school·fel·low \-,fel-ō\ *n* : SCHOOLMATE

school·girl \-,gərl\ *n* : a girl attending school

school·house \-,haús\ *n* : a building used as a school

school·marm \-,mä(r)m\ *or* **school-ma'am** \-,mäm, -,mam\ *n* **1** : a woman schoolteacher **2** : a person who exhibits characteristics popularly attributed to schoolteachers

school·mas·ter \-,mas-tər\ *n* : a male schoolteacher

school·mate \-,māt\ *n* : a school companion

school·mis·tress \-,mis-trəs\ *n* : a woman schoolteacher

school·room \-,rüm, -,rúm\ *n* : CLASSROOM

school·teach·er \-,tē-chər\ *n* : one who teaches in a school

schoo·ner \'skü-nər\ *n* : a fore-and-aft rigged sailing ship

schuss \'shús, 'shüs\ *vb* [G] : to ski down a slope at high speed — **schuss** *n*

sci *abbr* science; scientific

sci·at·i·ca \sī-'at-i-kə\ *n* : pain in the region of the hips or along the course of the nerve at the back of the thigh

sci·ence \'sī-əns\ *n* [ME, fr. MF, fr. L *scientia,* fr. *scient-, sciens* having knowledge, fr. prp. of *scire* to know] **1** : an area of knowledge that is an object of study; *esp* : NATURAL SCIENCE **2** : knowledge covering general truths or the operation of general laws especially as obtained and tested through the scientific method — **sci·en·tif·ic** \,sī-ən-'tif-ik\ *adj* — **sci·en·tif·i·cal·ly** \-i-k(ə-)lē\ *adv* — **sci·en·tist** \'sī-ənt-əst\ *n*

science fiction *n* : fiction dealing principally with the impact of actual or imagined science on society or individuals

scientific method *n* : the rules and methods for the pursuit of knowledge involving the finding and stating of a problem, the collection of facts through observation and experiment, and the making and testing of ideas that need to be proven right or wrong

scim·i·tar \'sim-ət-ər\ *n* : a curved sword used chiefly by Arabs and Turks

scin·til·la \sin-'til-ə\ *n* : SPARK, TRACE

scin·til·late \'sint-ᵊl-,āt\ *vb* **-lat·ed; -lat·ing** : SPARKLE, GLEAM — **scin·til·la·tion** \,sint-ᵊl-'ā-shən\ *n*

sci·on \'sī-ən\ *n* **1** : a shoot of a plant joined to a stock in grafting **2** : DESCENDANT

scis·sors \'siz-ərz\ *n pl* : a cutting instrument like shears but usu. smaller

scissors kick *n* : a swimming kick in which the legs move like scissors

scle·ro·sis \sklə-'rō-səs\ *n* : a usu. abnormal hardening of tissue (as of an artery) — **scle·rot·ic** \-'rät-ik\ *adj*

scoff \'skäf\ *vb* : MOCK, JEER — **scoff·er** *n*

scoff·law \-,lȯ\ *n* : a contemptuous law violator

¹**scold** \'skōld\ *n* : a person who scolds

²**scold** *vb* : to censure severely or angrily

sconce \'skäns\ *n* : a candlestick or an electric light fixture bracketed to a wall

scone \'skōn, 'skän\ *n* : a biscuit (as of oatmeal) baked on a griddle

¹**scoop** \'sküp\ *n* 1 : a large shovel; *also* : a shovellike utensil ⟨a sugar ∼⟩ 2 : an act of scooping 3 : information of immediate interest

²**scoop** *vb* 1 : to take out or up or empty with or as if with a scoop 2 : to make hollow 3 : to report a news item in advance of

scoot \'sküt\ *vb* : to go suddenly and swiftly

scoot·er \'sküt-ər\ *n* 1 : a child's vehicle consisting of a narrow board mounted between two wheels tandem with an upright steering handle attached to the front wheel 2 : MOTOR SCOOTER

¹**scope** \'skōp\ *n* [It *scopo* purpose, goal, fr. Gk *skopos*, fr. *skeptesthai* to watch, look at] 1 : space or opportunity for action or thought 2 : extent covered : RANGE

²**scope** *n* : an instrument (as a microscope or radarscope) for viewing

scorch \'skȯrch\ *vb* : to burn the surface of; *also* : to dry or shrivel with heat ⟨∼ed lawns⟩

¹**score** \'skōr\ *n, pl* **scores** 1 *or pl* **score** : TWENTY 2 : CUT, SCRATCH, SLASH 3 : a record of points made (as in a game) 4 : DEBT 5 : REASON, GROUND 6 : the music of a composition or arrangement with different parts indicated 7 : success in obtaining something (as drugs) esp. illegally

²**score** *vb* **scored; scor·ing** 1 : RECORD 2 : to keep score in a game 3 : to mark with lines, grooves, scratches, or notches 4 : to gain or tally in or as if in a game ⟨*scored* a point⟩ 5 : to assign a grade or score to ⟨∼ the tests⟩ 6 : to compose a score for 7 : SUCCEED — **score·less** *adj* — **scor·er** *n*

sco·ria \'skōr-ē-ə\ *n, pl* **-ri·ae** \-ē-,ē\ [L] : a rough cindery lava

¹**scorn** \'skȯrn\ *n* : an emotion involving both anger and disgust : CONTEMPT — **scorn·ful** \-fəl\ *adj* — **scorn·ful·ly** \-ē\ *adv*

²**scorn** *vb* : to hold in contempt : DISDAIN — **scorn·er** *n*

Scor·pio \'skȯr-pē-,ō\ *n* [L, lit., scorpion] 1 : a zodiacal constellation between Libra and Sagittarius usu. pictured as a scorpion 2 : the 8th sign of the zodiac in astrology; *also* : one born under this sign

scor·pi·on \'skȯr-pē-ən\ *n* : any of an order of arthropods related to the spiders and having a poisonous sting at the tip of a long jointed tail

¹**Scot** \'skät\ *n* : a native or inhabitant of Scotland

²**Scot** *abbr* Scotland; Scottish

Scotch \'skäch\ *n* 1 : SCOTS 2 **Scotch** *pl* : the people of Scotland 3 : a whiskey distilled in Scotland esp. from malted barley — **Scotch** *adj* — **Scotch·man** \-mən\ *n* — **Scotch·wom·an** \-,wu̇m-ən\ *n*

Scotch pine *n* : a pine that is naturalized in the U.S. from northern Europe and Asia and is a valuable timber tree

scot–free \'skät-'frē\ *adj* : free from obligation, harm, or penalty

Scots \'skäts\ *n* : the English language of Scotland

Scots·man \'skäts-mən\ *n* : SCOTCHMAN

Scots·wom·an \-,wu̇-mən\ *n* : SCOTCHWOMAN

Scot·tish \'skät-ish\ *adj* : SCOTCH

scoun·drel \'skau̇n-drəl\ *n* : a mean or wicked person : VILLAIN

¹**scour** \'skau̇(ə)r\ *vb* 1 : to move rapidly through : RUSH 2 : to examine thoroughly

²**scour** *vb* 1 : to rub (as with a gritty substance) in order to clean 2 : to cleanse by or as if by rubbing

¹**scourge** \'skərj\ *n* 1 : LASH, WHIP 2 : PUNISHMENT; *also* : a cause of affliction (as a plague)

²**scourge** *vb* **scourged; scourg·ing** 1 : LASH, FLOG 2 : to punish severely

¹**scout** \'skau̇t\ *vb* [ME *scouten*, fr. MF *escouter* to listen, fr. L *auscultare*] 1 : to look around : RECONNOITER 2 : to inspect or observe to get information

²**scout** *n* 1 : a person sent out to get information; *also* : a soldier, airplane, or ship sent out to reconnoiter 2 : a

member of either of two youth organizations (**Boy Scouts, Girl Scouts**) — **scout·mas·ter** \-ˌmas-tər\ *n*

³**scout** *vb* : SCORN, SCOFF

scow \ˈskaů\ *n* : a large flat-bottomed boat with square ends

scowl \ˈskaůl\ *vb* : to draw down the forehead and make a face in expression of displeasure — **scowl** *n*

SCPO *abbr* senior chief petty officer

scrab·ble \ˈskrab-əl\ *vb* **scrab·bled; scrab·bling** \-(ə-)liŋ\ **1** : SCRAPE, SCRATCH **2** : CLAMBER, SCRAMBLE **3** : to work hard and long **4** : SCRIBBLE — **scrabble** *n* — **scrab·bler** \(ə-)lər\ *n*

scrag·gly \ˈskrag-lē\ *adj* : IRREGULAR; *also* : RAGGED, UNKEMPT

scram \ˈskram\ *vb* **scrammed; scramming** : to go away at once

scram·ble \ˈskram-bəl\ *vb* **scram·bled; scram·bling** \-b(ə-)liŋ\ **1** : to clamber clumsily around **2** : to struggle for or as if for possession of something **3** : to spread irregularly **4** : to mix together **5** : to prepare (eggs) by stirring during frying — **scramble** *n*

¹**scrap** \ˈskrap\ *n* **1** : FRAGMENT, PIECE **2** : discarded material : REFUSE

²**scrap** *vb* **scrapped; scrap·ping 1** : to make into scrap ⟨∼ a battleship⟩ **2** : to get rid of as useless

³**scrap** *n* : FIGHT

⁴**scrap** *vb* **scrapped; scrap·ping** : FIGHT, QUARREL — **scrap·per** *n*

scrap·book \ˈskrap-ˌbůk\ *n* : a blank book in which mementos are kept

¹**scrape** \ˈskrāp\ *vb* **scraped; scrap·ing 1** : to remove by drawing a knife over; *also* : to clean or smooth by rubbing off the covering **2** : GRATE; *also* : to damage or injure the surface of by contact with something rough **3** : to scrape something with a grating sound **4** : to get together (money) by strict economy **5** : to get along with difficulty — **scrap·er** *n*

²**scrape** *n* **1** : the act or the effect of scraping **2** : a bow accompanied by a drawing back of the foot **3** : an unpleasant predicament

¹**scrap·py** \ˈskrap-ē\ *adj* **scrap·pi·er; -est** : DISCONNECTED, FRAGMENTARY

²**scrappy** *adj* **scrap·pi·er; -est 1** : QUARRELSOME **2** : having an aggressive and determined spirit

¹**scratch** \ˈskrach\ *vb* **1** : to scrape, dig, or rub with or as if with claws or nails ⟨a dog ∼*ing* at the door⟩ ⟨∼*ed* his arm on thorns⟩ **2** : to cause to move or strike roughly and gratingly ⟨∼*ed* his nails across the blackboard⟩ **3** : to scrape (as money) together **4** : to cancel or erase by or as if by drawing a line through — **scratchy** *adj*

²**scratch** *n* **1** : a mark made by or as if by scratching; *also* : a sound so made **2** : the starting line in a race **3** : a point at the beginning of a project at which nothing has been done ahead of time ⟨built from ∼⟩

³**scratch** *adj* **1** : made as or used for a trial attempt ⟨∼ paper⟩ **2** : made or done by chance ⟨a ∼ hit⟩

scrawl \ˈskrȯl\ *vb* : to write hastily and carelessly — **scrawl** *n*

scraw·ny \ˈskrȯ-nē\ *adj* **scraw·ni·er; -est** : very thin : SKINNY

¹**scream** \ˈskrēm\ *vb* : to cry out loudly and shrilly

²**scream** *n* : a loud shrill cry

scream·ing \ˈskrēm-iŋ\ *adj* : so striking as to attract notice as if by screaming ⟨∼ headlines⟩

screech \ˈskrēch\ *vb* : SHRIEK — **screech** *n* — **screechy** \ˈskrē-chē\ *adj*

¹**screen** \ˈskrēn\ *n* **1** : a device or partition used to hide, restrain, protect, or decorate ⟨a wire-mesh window ∼⟩; *also* : something that shelters, protects, or conceals **2** : a sieve or perforated material for separating finer from coarser parts (as of sand) **3** : a surface on which an image is made to appear (as in television) **4** : the motion-picture industry

²**screen** *vb* **1** : to shield with or as if with a screen **2** : to separate with or as if with a screen **3** : to present (as a motion picture) on the screen **syn** hide, conceal, secrete, cover

screen·ing \-iŋ\ *n* : metal or plastic mesh (as for window screens)

¹**screw** \ˈskrü\ *n* [ME, fr. MF *escroe* nut, fr. ML *scrofa*, fr. L, sow] **1** : a simple machine consisting of a solid cylinder with a spiral groove around it and a corresponding hollow cylinder into which it fits **2** : a naillike metal piece with a spiral groove and a head with a slot used to fasten pieces of solid material together **3** : PROPELLER

²**screw** *vb* **1** : to fasten or close by means

of a screw **2** : to operate or adjust by means of a screw **3** : to move or cause to move spirally; *also* : to close or set in position by such an action

screw•ball \'skrü-ˌbȯl\ *n* **1** : a baseball pitch breaking in a direction opposite to a curve **2** : a whimsical, eccentric, or crazy person

screw•driv•er \'skrü-ˌdrī-vər\ *n* **1** : a tool for turning screws **2** : a drink made of vodka and orange juice

screwy \'skrü-ē\ *adj* **screw•i•er; -est 1** : crazily absurd, eccentric, or unusual **2** : : CRAZY, INSANE

scrib•ble \'skrib-əl\ *vb* **scrib•bled; scrib•bling** \-(ə-)liŋ\ : to write hastily or carelessly — **scribble** *n* — **scrib•bler** \-(ə-)lər\ *n*

scribe \'skrīb\ *n* **1** : one of a learned class in ancient Palestine serving as copyists, teachers, and jurists **2** : a person whose business is the copying of writing **3** : AUTHOR; *esp* : JOURNALIST

scrim \'skrim\ *n* : a light loosely woven cotton or linen cloth

scrim•mage \'skrim-ij\ *n* : the play between two football teams beginning with the snap of the ball; *also* : practice play between a team's squads — **scrimmage** *vb*

scrimp \'skrimp\ *vb* : to be niggardly : economize greatly ⟨∼ and save⟩

scrim•shaw \'skrim-ˌshȯ\ *n* : carved or engraved articles made esp. by American whalers usu. from whalebone or whale ivory — **scrimshaw** *vb*

scrip \'skrip\ *n* **1** : a certificate showing its holder is entitled to something (as stock or land) **2** : paper money issued for temporary use in an emergency

¹**script** \'skript\ *n* **1** : written matter (as lines for a play or broadcast) **2** : HANDWRITING

²**script** *abbr* scripture

scrip•ture \'skrip-chər\ *n* **1** *cap* : the books of the Bible — often used in pl. **2** : the sacred writings of a religion — **scrip•tur•al** \'skrip-chə-rəl\ *adj* — **scrip•tur•al•ly** \-ē\ *adv*

scriv•en•er \'skriv-(ə-)nər\ *n* : SCRIBE, WRITER, AUTHOR

scrod \'skräd\ *n* : a young fish (as a cod or haddock); *esp* : one split and boned for cooking

scrof•u•la \'skrȯf-yə-lə\ *n* : tuberculosis of lymph nodes esp. in the neck

scroll \'skrōl\ *n* : a roll of paper or parchment for writing a document; *also* : a spiral or coiled ornamental form suggesting a loosely or partly rolled scroll

scroll saw *n* : JIGSAW

scro•tum \'skrōt-əm\ *n, pl* **scro•ta** \-ə\ *or* **scrotums** [L] : a pouch that in most mammals contains the testes

scrounge \'skraünj\ *vb* **scrounged; scroung•ing** : to collect by or as if by foraging

¹**scrub** \'skrəb\ *n* **1** : a thick growth of stunted trees or shrubs; *also* : an area of land covered with scrub **2** : an inferior domestic animal **3** : a person of insignificant size or standing; *esp* : a player not on the first team — **scrub** *adj* — **scrub•by** *adj*

²**scrub** *vb* **scrubbed; scrub•bing 1** : to rub in washing ⟨∼ clothes⟩ **2** : to wash by rubbing ⟨∼ out a spot⟩ **3** : CANCEL

³**scrub** *n* : an act or instance of scrubbing ⟨gave the clothes a good ∼⟩

scruff \'skrəf\ *n* : the loose skin of the back of the neck : NAPE

scruffy \'skrəf-ē\ *adj* **scruff•i•er; -est** : UNKEMPT, SLOVENLY

scrump•tious \'skrəm(p)-shəs\ *adj* : DELIGHTFUL, EXCELLENT — **scrump•tious•ly** *adv*

¹**scru•ple** \'skrü-pəl\ *n* [MF *scrupule*, fr. L *scrupulus* small sharp stone, cause of mental discomfort, scruple, dim. of *scrupus* sharp stone] **1** : a point of conscience or honor **2** : hesitation due to ethical considerations

²**scruple** *vb* **scru•pled; scru•pling** \-p(ə-)liŋ\ : to be reluctant on grounds of conscience : HESITATE

scru•pu•lous \'skrü-pyə-ləs\ *adj* **1** : having moral integrity **2** : PAINSTAKING — **scru•pu•lous•ly** *adv* — **scru•pu•lous•ness** *n*

scru•ti•nize \'skrüt-ən-ˌīz\ *vb* **-nized; -niz•ing** : to examine closely

scru•ti•ny \'skrüt-ᵊn-ē\ *n, pl* **-nies** [L *scrutinium,* fr. *scrutari* to search, examine, fr. *scruta* trash] : a careful looking over **syn** inspection, examination, analysis

scu•ba \'sk(y)ü-bə\ *n* [*s*elf-*c*ontained *u*nderwater *b*reathing *a*pparatus] : an apparatus for breathing while swimming under water

scuba diver *n* : one who swims under water with the aid of scuba gear

¹**scud** \'skəd\ *vb* **scud·ded; scud·ding** : to move speedily

²**scud** *n* : light clouds driven by the wind

¹**scuff** \'skəf\ *vb* **1** : to scrape the feet while walking : SHUFFLE **2** : to scratch or become scratched or worn away

²**scuff** *n* **1** : a mark or injury caused by scuffing **2** : a flat-soled slipper without quarter or heel strap

scuf·fle \'skəf-əl\ *vb* **scuf·fled; scuf·fling** \-(ə-)liŋ\ **1** : to struggle confusedly at close quarters **2** : to shuffle one's feet — **scuffle** *n*

¹**scull** \'skəl\ *n* **1** : an oar for use in sculling; *also* : one of a pair of short oars for a single oarsman **2** : a racing shell propelled by one or two persons using sculls

²**scull** *vb* : to propel (a boat) by an oar over the stern

scul·lery \'skəl-(ə-)rē\ *n, pl* **-ler·ies** [ME, department of household in charge of dishes, fr. MF *escuelerie,* fr. *escuelle* bowl, fr. L *scutella* drinking bowl] : a small room near the kitchen used for cleaning dishes, culinary utensils, and vegetables

scul·lion \'skəl-yən\ *n* [ME *sculion,* fr. MF *escouillon* dishcloth, alter. of *escouvillon,* fr. *escouve* broom, fr. L *scopa,* lit., twig] : a kitchen helper

sculpt \'skəlpt\ *vb* : CARVE, SCULPTURE

sculp·tor \'skəlp-tər\ *n* : one who produces works of sculpture

¹**sculp·ture** \'skəlp-chər\ *n* : the act, process, or art of carving or molding material (as stone, wood, or plastic); *also* : work produced this way — **sculp·tur·al** \'skəlp-chə-rəl\ *adj*

²**sculpture** *vb* **sculp·tured; sculp·tur·ing** : to form or alter as or as if a work of sculpture

scum \'skəm\ *n* **1** : a foul filmy covering on the surface of a liquid **2** : waste matter **3** : RABBLE

scup·per \'skəp-ər\ *n* : an opening in the side of a ship through which water on deck is drained overboard

scurf \'skərf\ *n* : thin dry scales of skin (as dandruff); *also* : a scaly deposit or covering — **scurfy** \'skər-fē\ *adj*

scur·ri·lous \'skər-ə-ləs\ *adj* : coarsely jesting : OBSCENE, VULGAR

scur·ry \'skər-ē\ *vb* **scur·ried; scur·ry·ing** : SCAMPER

¹**scur·vy** \'skər-vē\ *n* : a disease marked by spongy gums, loosened teeth, and bleeding into the tissues and caused by lack of vitamin C

²**scurvy** *adj* : MEAN, CONTEMPTIBLE — **scur·vi·ly** \'skər-və-lē\ *adv*

scutch·eon \'skəch-ən\ *n* : ESCUTCHEON

¹**scut·tle** \'skət-ᵊl\ *n* : a pail for carrying coal

²**scuttle** *n* : a small opening with a lid esp. in the deck, side, or bottom of a ship

³**scuttle** *vb* **scut·tled; scut·tling** \'skət-(ᵊ-)liŋ\ : to cut a hole in the deck, side, or bottom of (a ship) in order to sink

⁴**scuttle** *vb* **scut·tled; scut·tling** \'skət-(ᵊ-)liŋ\ : SCURRY, SCAMPER

scut·tle·butt \'skət-ᵊl-ˌbət\ *n* : GOSSIP

scythe \'sīth\ *n* : an implement for mowing (as grass or grain) by hand — **scythe** *vb*

SD *abbr* **1** South Dakota **2** special delivery

S Dak *abbr* South Dakota

Se *symbol* selenium

SE *abbr* southeast

sea \'sē\ *n* **1** : a large body of salt water **2** : OCEAN **3** : rough water; *also* : a heavy wave **4** : something likened to the sea esp. in vastness — **sea** *adj* — **at sea** : LOST, BEWILDERED

sea anemone *n* : any of numerous coelenterate polyps whose form, bright and varied colors, and cluster of tentacles superficially resemble a flower

sea·bird \'sē-ˌbərd\ *n* : a bird (as a gull) frequenting the open ocean

sea·board \-ˌbōrd\ *n* : SEACOST; *also* : the land bordering a coast

sea·coast \-ˌkōst\ *n* : the shore of the sea

sea·far·er \-ˌfar-ər\ *n* : SEAMAN

sea·far·ing \-ˌfar-iŋ\ *n* : a mariner's calling — **seafaring** *adj*

sea·food \-ˌfüd\ *n* : edible marine fish and shellfish

sea·go·ing \-ˌgō-iŋ\ *adj* : OCEANGOING

sea horse *n* : any of numerous small sea fishes with the head and forepart of the body sharply flexed like the head and neck of a horse

¹**seal** \'sēl\ *n, pl* **seals** *also* **seal 1** : any of

various large sea mammals occurring chiefly in cold regions and having limbs adapted for swimming **2** : the pelt of a seal

²**seal** *vb* : to hunt seals

³**seal** *n* **1** : something that fastens or secures; *also* : GUARANTEE, PLEDGE **2** : a device having a raised design that can be stamped on clay or wax; *also* : the impression made by stamping with such a device **3** : a mark acceptable as having the legal effect of an official seal

⁴**seal** *vb* **1** : to affix a seal to; *also* : AUTHENTICATE **2** : to fasten with a seal; *esp* : to enclose securely **3** : to determine irrevocably

sea–lane \'sē-ˌlān\ *n* : an established sea route

seal·ant \'sē-lənt\ *n* : a sealing agent

seal·er \'sē-lər\ *n* : a coat applied to prevent subsequent coats of paint or varnish from sinking in

sea level *n* : the level of the surface of the sea esp. at its mean position midway between mean high and low water

sea lion *n* : any of several large Pacific seals with external ears

seal·skin \'sēl-ˌskin\ *n* **1** : ¹SEAL 2 **2** : a garment of sealskin

¹**seam** \'sēm\ *n* **1** : the line of junction of two edges and esp. of edges of fabric sewn together **2** : layer of mineral matter ⟨coal ∼s⟩ **3** : WRINKLE — **seamless** *adj*

²**seam** *vb* **1** : to join by or as if by sewing **2** : WRINKLE, FURROW

sea·man \'sē-mən\ *n* **1** : one who assists in the handling of ships : MARINER **2** : an enlisted man in the navy ranking next below a petty officer third class

seaman apprentice *n* : an enlisted man in the navy ranking next below a seaman

seaman recruit *n* : an enlisted man of the lowest rank in the navy

sea·man·ship \'sē-mən-ˌship\ *n* : the art or skill of handling a ship

sea·mount \'sē-ˌmaůnt\ *n* : an underwater mountain

seam·stress \'sēm-strəs\ *n* : a woman who does sewing

seamy \'sē-mē\ *adj* **seam·i·er; -est 1** : UNPLEASANT **2** : DEGRADED, SORDID

sé·ance \'sā-ˌäns\ *n* [F] : a spiritualist meeting to receive communications from spirits

sea·plane \'sē-ˌplān\ *n* : an airplane that can take off from and land on water

sea·port \-ˌpōrt\ *n* : a port for oceangoing ships

sear \'siər\ *vb* **1** : WITHER **2** : to burn or scorch esp. on the surface; *also* : BRAND

¹**search** \'sərch\ *vb* [ME *cerchen*, fr. MF *cerchier* to go about, survey, search, fr. LL *circare* to go about, fr. L *circum* round about] **1** : to look through in trying to find something **2** : SEEK **3** : PROBE — **search·er** *n*

²**search** *n* : the act of searching

search·light \-ˌlīt\ *n* : an apparatus for projecting a beam of light; *also* : the light projected

sea·scape \'sē-ˌskāp\ *n* **1** : a view of the sea **2** : a picture representing a scene at sea

sea·shore \-ˌshōr\ *n* : the shore of a sea : SEACOAST

sea·sick \-ˌsik\ *adj* : nauseated by or as if by the motion of a ship — **sea·sick·ness** *n*

sea·side \'sē-ˌsīd\ *n* : SEASHORE

¹**sea·son** \'sēz-ⁿn\ *n* [ME, fr. OF *saison*, fr. L *sation-, satio* action of sowing, fr. *satus*, pp. of *serere* to sow] **1** : one of the divisions of the year (as spring or summer) **2** : a special period ⟨the Easter ∼⟩ — **sea·son·al** \'sēz-(ə-)nəl\ *adj* — **sea·son·al·ly** \-ē\ *adv*

²**season** *vb* **sea·soned; sea·son·ing** \'sēz-(ə-)niŋ\ **1** : to make pleasant to the taste by use of salt, pepper, or spices **2** : to make (as by aging or drying) suitable for use **3** : to accustom or habituate to something (as hardship) **syn** harden, inure, acclimatize, toughen — **sea·son·er** \'sēz-(ə-)nər\ *n*

sea·son·able \'sēz-(ə-)nə-bəl\ *adj* : occurring at a fit time **syn** timely, propitious, opportune — **sea·son·ably** \-blē\ *adv*

sea·son·ing \'sēz-(ə-)niŋ\ *n* : something that seasons : CONDIMENT

¹**seat** \'sēt\ *n* **1** : a chair, bench, or stool for sitting on **2** : a place which serves as a capital or center

²**seat** *vb* **1** : to place in or on a seat **2** : to provide seats for

seat belt *n* : straps designed to hold a person steady in a seat

SEATO \'sē-ˌtō\ *abbr* Southeast Asia Treaty Organization

seat–of–the–pants *adj* : employing or based on personal experience, judgment, and effort rather than technological aids ⟨~ navigation⟩

sea urchin *n* : any of a class of oblate spiny marine echinoderms having thin brittle shells

sea·wall \'sē-ˌwȯl\ *n* : an embankment to protect the shore from erosion

¹**sea·ward** \'sē-wərd\ *n* : the direction or side away from land and toward the open sea

²**seaward** *adj* **1** : directed or situated toward the sea **2** : coming from the sea

³**seaward** *also* **sea·wards** \-wərdz\ *adv* : toward the sea

sea·wa·ter \'sē-ˌwȯt-ər, -ˌwät-\ *n* : water in or from the sea

sea·way \-ˌwā\ *n* : an inland waterway that admits ocean shipping

sea·weed \-ˌwēd\ *n* : a marine alga (as a kelp); *also* : a mass of marine algae

sea·wor·thy \'sē-ˌwər-ᵵẖē\ *adj* : fit for a sea voyage

se·ba·ceous \si-'bā-shəs\ *adj* : of, relating to, or secreting fatty material

sec *abbr* **1** second; secondary **2** secretary **3** section **4** [L *secundum*] according to

SEC *abbr* Securities and Exchange Commission

se·cede \si-'sēd\ *vb* **se·ced·ed; se·ced·ing** : to withdraw from an organized body and esp. from a political body

se·ces·sion \si-'sesh-ən\ *n* : the act of seceding — **se·ces·sion·ist** *n*

se·clude \si-'klüd\ *vb* **se·clud·ed; se·clud·ing** : to keep or shut away from others

se·clu·sion \si-'klü-zhən\ *n* : the act of secluding : the state of being secluded — **se·clu·sive** \-siv\ *adj*

¹**sec·ond** \'sek-ənd\ *adj* [ME, fr. OF, fr. L *secundus* second, following, favorable, fr. *sequi* to follow] **1** : being number two in a countable series **2** : next after the first **3** : ALTERNATE ⟨every ~ year⟩ — **second** *or* **sec·ond·ly** *adv*

²**second** *n* [ME *secunde*, fr. ML *secunda*, fr. L, fem. of *secundus* second; fr. its being the second division of a unit into 60 parts, as a minute is the first] **1** : the 60th part of a minute of time or angular measure **2** : an instant of time

³**second** *n* **1** : one that is second **2** : one who assists another (as in a duel) **3** : an inferior or flawed article (as of merchandise) **4** : the second forward gear in a motor vehicle

⁴**second** *vb* **1** : to encourage or give support to **2** : to act as a second to **3** : to support (a motion) by adding one's voice to that of a proposer

sec·ond·ary \'sek-ən-ˌder-ē\ *adj* **1** : second in rank, value, or occurrence : INFERIOR, LESSER **2** : belonging to a second or later stage of development **3** : coming after the primary or elementary ⟨~ schools⟩ **syn** subordinate, collateral, dependent

secondary sex characteristic *n* : a physical characteristic (as the breasts of a female mammal or the showy feathers of a male bird) that appears in members of one sex at puberty or in seasonal breeders at breeding season and is not directly concerned with reproduction

second fiddle *n* : one that plays a supporting or subserviant role

sec·ond–guess \ˌsek-ᵊŋ-'ges, -ən-\ *vb* : to think out other strategies or explanations for after the event

sec·ond·hand \ˌsek-ən-'hand\ *adj* **1** : not original **2** : not new : USED ⟨~ clothes⟩ **3** : dealing in used goods

second lieutenant *n* : a commissioned officer (as in the army) ranking next below a first lieutenant

sec·ond–rate \ˌsek-ən(d)-'rāt\ *adj* : INFERIOR

second–story man *n* : a burglar who enters by an upstairs window

sec·ond–string \ˌsek-ən-ˌstriŋ, ˌsek-ᵊŋ-\ *adj* : being a substitute (as on a ball team)

se·cre·cy \'sē-krə-sē\ *n, pl* **-cies** **1** : the habit or practice of being secretive **2** : the quality or state of being secret

¹**se·cret** \'sē-krət\ *adj* **1** : HIDDEN, CONCEALED ⟨a ~ panel⟩ **2** : COVERT, STEALTHY; *also* : engaged in detecting or spying ⟨a ~ agent⟩ **3** : kept from general knowledge — **se·cret·ly** *adv*

²**secret** *n* **1** : MYSTERY **2** : something kept from the knowledge of others

sec·re·tar·i·at \ˌsek-rə-'ter-ē-ət\ *n* **1** : the office of a secretary **2** : the body of secretaries in an office **3** : the administrative department of a governmental organization ⟨the UN ∼⟩

sec·re·tary \'sek-rə-ˌter-ē\ *n, pl* **-tar·ies** **1** : a person employed to handle records, correspondence, and routine work for another person **2** : an officer of a corporation or business who is in charge of correspondence and records **3** : an official at the head of a department of government **4** : a writing desk — **sec·re·tari·al** \ˌsek-rə-'ter-ē-əl\ *adj* — **sec·re·tary·ship** \'sek-rə-ˌter-ē-ˌship\ *n*

¹se·crete \si-'krēt\ *vb* **se·cret·ed; se·cret·ing** : to produce and emit as a secretion

²se·crete \si-'krēt, 'sē-krət\ *vb* **se·cret·ed; se·cret·ing** : HIDE, CONCEAL

se·cre·tion \si-'krē-shən\ *n* **1** : an act or process of secreting **2** : a product of glandular activity; *esp* : one (as a hormone) useful in the organism — **se·cre·to·ry** \-'krēt-ə-rē\ *adj*

se·cre·tive \'sē-krət-iv, si-'krēt-\ *adj* : tending to keep secrets or to act secretly — **se·cre·tive·ly** *adv* — **se·cre·tive·ness** *n*

¹sect \'sekt\ *n* **1** : a dissenting religious body **2** : a religious denomination **3** : a group adhering to a distinctive doctrine or to a leader

²sect *abbr* section

¹sec·tar·i·an \sek-'ter-ē-ən\ *adj* **1** : of or relating to a sect or sectarian **2** : limited in character or scope — **sec·tar·i·an·ism** *n*

²sectarian *n* **1** : an adherent of a sect **2** : a narrow or bigoted person

sec·ta·ry \'sek-tə-rē\ *n, pl* **-ries** : a member of a sect

¹sec·tion \'sek-shən\ *n* **1** : a part cut off or separated **2** : a distinct part **3** : the appearance that a thing has or would have if cut straight through

²section *vb* **1** : to separate or become separated into sections **2** : to represent in sections

sec·tion·al \'sek-sh(ə-)nəl\ *adj* **1** : of, relating to, or characteristic of a section **2** : local or regional rather than general in character **3** : divided into sections — **sec·tion·al·ism** *n*

sec·tor \'sek-tər\ *n* **1** : a part of a circle between two radii **2** : an area assigned to a military leader to defend

sec·u·lar \'sek-yə-lər\ *adj* **1** : not sacred or ecclesiastical **2** : not bound by monastic vows ⟨∼ priest⟩

sec·u·lar·ism \'sek-yə-lə-ˌriz-əm\ *n* : indifference to or exclusion of religion — **sec·u·lar·ist** \-rəst\ *n* — **secularist** *or* **sec·u·lar·is·tic** \ˌsek-yə-lə-'ris-tik\ *adj*

sec·u·lar·ize \'sek-yə-lə-ˌrīz\ *vb* **-ized; -iz·ing** **1** : to make secular **2** : to transfer from ecclesiastical to civil or lay use, possession, or control — **sec·u·lar·iza·tion** \ˌsek-yə-lə-rə-'zā-shən\ *n* — **sec·u·lar·iz·er** \'sek-yə-lə-ˌrī-zər\ *n*

¹se·cure \si-'kyúr\ *adj* **se·cur·er; -est** [L *securus* safe, secure, fr. *se* without + *cura* care] **1** : easy in mind : free from fear **2** : free from danger or risk of loss : SAFE **3** : CERTAIN, SURE — **se·cure·ly** *adv*

²secure *vb* **se·cured; se·cur·ing** **1** : to make safe : GUARD **2** : to assure payment of by giving a pledge or collateral **3** : to fasten safely ⟨∼ a door⟩ **4** : GET, ACQUIRE

se·cu·ri·ty \si-'kyúr-ət-ē\ *n, pl* **-ties** **1** : SAFETY **2** : freedom from worry **3** : something (as collateral) given as pledge of payment **4** *pl* : bond or stock certificates **5** : PROTECTION

secy *abbr* secretary

se·dan \si-'dan\ *n* **1** : a covered chair borne on poles by two men **2** : an enclosed automobile usu. with front and back seats and a permanent top

se·date \si-'dāt\ *adj* : quiet and dignified in behavior **syn** staid, sober, serious, solemn — **se·date·ly** *adv*

¹sed·a·tive \'sed-ət-iv\ *adj* : serving or tending to relieve tension — **se·da·tion** \si-'dā-shən\ *n*

²sedative *n* : a sedative drug

sed·en·tary \'sed-ᵊn-ˌter-ē\ *adj* : characterized by or requiring much sitting

sedge \'sej\ *n* : any of a family of plants that are related to the grasses, grow in marshes, and often have three-sided stems — **sedgy** \'sej-ē\ *adj*

sed·i·ment \'sed-ə-mənt\ *n* **1** : the material that settles to the bottom of a liquid : LEES, DREGS **2** : material (as stones and sand) deposited by water, wind, or a glacier — **sed·i·men·ta·ry** \ˌsed-ə-'men-t(ə-)rē\ *adj* — **sed·i·men·ta·tion** \-ˌmən-'tā-shən, -ˌmen-\ *n*

se·di·tion \si-'dish-ən\ *n* : the causing of discontent, insurrection, or resistance against a government — **se·di·tious** \-əs\ *adj*

se·duce \si-'d(y)üs\ *vb* **se·duced; se·duc·ing 1** : to persuade to disobedience or disloyalty **2** : to lead astray **3** : to entice to unlawful sexual intercourse without the use of force **syn** tempt, entice, inveigle, lure — **se·duc·er** *n* — **se·duc·tion** \-'dək-shən\ *n* — **se·duc·tive** \-tiv\ *adj*

sed·u·lous \'sej-ə-ləs\ *adj* [L *sedulus,* fr. *sedulo* sincerely, diligently, fr. *se* without + *dolus* guile] : DILIGENT, PAINSTAKING

¹**see** \'sē\ *vb* **saw** \'sȯ\; **seen** \'sēn\; **see·ing** \'sē-iŋ\ **1** : to perceive by the eye : have the power of sight **2** : EXPERIENCE **3** : UNDERSTAND **4** : to make sure ⟨∼ that order is kept⟩ **5** : to meet with **6** : to keep company with esp. in dating **7** : ACCOMPANY, ESCORT **syn** behold, descry, espy, view, observe, note, discern

²**see** *n* : the authority or jurisdiction of a bishop

¹**seed** \'sēd\ *n, pl* **seed** *or* **seeds 1** : the grains of plants used for sowing **2** : a ripened ovule of a plant that may develop into a new plant; *also* : a plant structure (as a spore or small dry fruit) capable of producing a new plant **3** : DESCENDANTS **4** : SOURCE, ORIGIN — **seed·bed** \-ˌbed\ *n* — **seed·less** *adj* — **go to seed** *or* **run to seed 1** : to develop seed **2** : DECAY

²**seed** *vb* **1** : SOW, PLANT ⟨∼ land to grass⟩ **2** : to bear or shed seeds **3** : to remove seeds from — **seed·er** *n*

seed·ling \'sēd-liŋ\ *n* **1** : a plant grown from seed **2** : a young plant; *esp* : a tree smaller than a sapling

seed·time \'sēd-ˌtīm\ *n* : the season for sowing

seedy \'sēd-ē\ *adj* **seed·i·er; -est 1** : containing or full of seeds **2** : inferior in condition or quality : SHABBY

seek \'sēk\ *vb* **sought** \'sȯt\; **seek·ing 1** : to search for **2** : to try to reach or obtain ⟨∼ fame⟩ **3** : ATTEMPT — **seek·er** *n*

seem \'sēm\ *vb* **1** : to give the impression of being : APPEAR **2** : to appear to the observation or understanding

seem·ing \-iŋ\ *adj* : outwardly apparent — **seem·ing·ly** *adv*

seem·ly \'sēm-lē\ *adj* **seem·li·er; -est** : PROPER, DECENT

seep \'sēp\ *vb* : to leak through fine pores or cracks : percolate slowly — **seep·age** \'sē-pij\ *n*

seer \'siər\ *n* : a person who foresees or predicts events : PROPHET

seer·suck·er \'siər-ˌsək-ər\ *n* [Hindi *śīrśaker,* fr. Per *shīr-o-shakar,* lit., milk and sugar] : a light fabric of linen, cotton, or rayon usu. striped and slightly puckered

see·saw \'sē-ˌsȯ\ *n* **1** : a contest in which now one side now the other has the lead **2** : a children's sport of riding up and down on the ends of a plank supported in the middle; *also* : the plank so used — **seesaw** *vb*

seethe \'sēth\ *vb* **seethed; seeth·ing** [archaic *seethe* boil] : to become violently agitated

seg·ment \'seg-mənt\ *n* **1** : a division of a thing : SECTION ⟨∼ of an orange⟩ **2** : a part cut off from a geometrical figure (as a circle) by a line — **seg·ment·ed** \-ˌment-əd\ *adj*

seg·re·gate \'seg-ri-ˌgāt\ *vb* **-gat·ed; -gat·ing** [L *segregare,* fr. *se-* apart + *greg-, grex* herd, flock] : to cut off from others : ISOLATE — **seg·re·ga·tion** \ˌseg-ri-'gā-shən\ *n*

seg·re·ga·tion·ist \ˌseg-ri-'gā-sh(ə-)nəst\ *n* : one who believes in or practices the segregation of races

sei·gneur \sān-'yər\ *n, often cap* [MF, fr. ML *senior,* fr. L, adj., elder] : a feudal lord

¹**seine** \'sān\ *n* : a large weighted fishing net

²**seine** *vb* **seined; sein·ing** : to fish or catch with a seine

seis·mic \'sīz-mik, 'sīs-\ *adj* : of, relating to, resembling, or caused by an earthquake — **seis·mic·i·ty** \sīz-'mis-ət-ē, sīs-\ *n*

seis·mo·gram \'sīz-mə-ˌgram, 'sīs-\ *n* : the record of an earth tremor made by a seismograph

seis·mo·graph \-ˌgraf\ *n* : an apparatus for recording earthquake data — **seis·mo·graph·ic** \ˌsīz-mə-'graf-ik, ˌsīs-\ *adj* — **seis·mog·ra·phy** \sīz-'mäg-rə-fē, sīs-\ *n*

seis·mol·o·gy \sīz-'mäl-ə-jē, sīs-\ *n* : a science that deals with earthquakes — **seis·mo·log·i·cal** \ˌsīz-mə-'läj-i-kəl,

ˌsīs-\ *adj* — **seis·mol·o·gist** \sīz-ˈmäl-ə-jəst, sīs-\ *n*

seis·mom·e·ter \sīz-ˈmäm-ət-ər, sīs-\ *n* : a seismograph measuring the actual movement of the ground

seize \ˈsēz\ *vb* **seized; seiz·ing 1** : to lay hold of or take possession of by force **2** : ARREST **3** : UNDERSTAND **4** : to attack or overwhelm physically : AFFLICT **syn** take, grasp, clutch, snatch, grab

sei·zure \ˈsē-zhər\ *n* **1** : the act of seizing : the state of being seized **2** : a sudden attack (as of disease)

sel *abbr* select; selected; selection

sel·dom \ˈsel-dəm\ *adv* : not often : RARELY

¹**se·lect** \sə-ˈlekt\ *adj* **1** : CHOSEN, PICKED; *also* : CHOICE **2** : judicious or restrictive in choice : DISCRIMINATING

²**select** *vb* : to take by preference from a number or group : pick out : CHOOSE

se·lec·tion \sə-ˈlek-shən\ *n* **1** : the act of selecting **2** : something selected : CHOICE **3** : a natural or artificial process that increases the chance of propagation of some organisms and decreases that of others

se·lec·tive \sə-ˈlek-tiv\ *adj* : of or relating to selection : selecting or tending to select ⟨∼ shoppers⟩

selective service *n* : a system for calling men up for military service

se·lect·man \si-ˈlek(t)-ˌman, -mən\ *n* : one of a board of officials elected in towns of most New England states to administer town affairs

sel·e·nite \ˈsel-ə-ˌnīt\ *n* [L *selenites,* fr. Gk *selēnitēs (lithos),* lit., stone of the moon, fr. *selēnē* moon; fr. the belief that it waxed and waned with the moon] : a variety of transparent crystalline gypsum

se·le·ni·um \sə-ˈlē-nē-əm\ *n* : a nonmetallic chemical element that varies in electrical conductivity with the intensity of its illumination

self \ˈself\ *n, pl* **selves** \ˈselvz\ **1** : the essential person distinct from all other persons in identity **2** : a particular side of a person's character **3** : personal interest : SELFISHNESS

self- *comb form* **1** : oneself : itself **2** : of oneself or itself **3** : by oneself; *also* : automatic **4** : to, for, or toward oneself

self-abasement
self-accusation
self-acting
self-addressed
self-adjusting
self-administer
self-advancement
self-aggrandize-
  ment
self-aggrandizing
self-analysis
self-appointed
self-asserting
self-assertion
self-assertive
self-assurance
self-assured
self-awareness
self-betrayal
self-closing
self-command
self-complacent
self-conceit
self-concern
self-condemned
self-confessed
self-confidence
self-confident
self-congratulation
self-congratulatory
self-constituted
self-contradiction
self-contradictory
self-control
self-correcting
self-created
self-criticism
self-cultivation
self-deceit
self-deceiving
self-deception
self-defeating
self-defense
self-delusion
self-denial
self-denying
self-depreciation
self-despair
self-destruction
self-destructive
self-determination
self-discipline
self-distrust
self-doubt
self-educated
self-employed
self-employment
self-esteem
self-evident
self-examination
self-explaining

self-explanatory
self-expression
self-forgetful
self-fulfilling
self-giving
self-governing
self-government
self-help
self-hypnosis
self-identity
self-image
self-importance
self-important
self-imposed
self-improvement
self-incrimination
self-induced
self-indulgence
self-inflicted
self-interest
self-limiting
self-love
self-lubricating
self-luminous
self-mastery
self-operating
self-perception
self-perpetuating
self-pity
self-portrait
self-possessed
self-possession
self-preservation
self-proclaimed
self-propelled
self-propelling
self-protection
self-realization
self-regard
self-registering
self-reliance
self-reliant
self-reproach
self-respect
self-respecting
self-restraint
self-rule
self-sacrifice
self-satisfaction
self-satisfied
self-seeking
self-service
self-serving
self-starting
self-styled
self-sufficiency
self-sufficient
self-supporting
self-sustaining
self-taught
self-torment

self-winding   self-worth

self–cen·tered \'self-'sent-ərd\ *adj* : concerned only with one's own self — **self–cen·tered·ness** *n*

self–com·posed \ˌself-kəm-'pōzd\ *adj* : having control over one's emotions

self–con·scious \'self-'kän-chəs\ *adj* **1** : aware of oneself as an individual **2** : uncomfortably conscious of oneself as an object of observation by others — **self–con·scious·ly** *adv* — **self–con·scious·ness** *n*

self–con·tained \ˌself-kən-'tānd\ *adj* **1** : complete in itself **2** : showing self≈ command; *also* : reserved in manner

self–de·struct \-di-'strəkt\ *vb* : to destroy itself

self–ef·fac·ing \-ə-'fā-siŋ\ *adj* : RETIRING, SHY

self–fer·til·iza·tion \ˌself-ˌfərt-ᵊl-ə-'zā-shən\ *n* : fertilization of a plant or animal by its own pollen or sperm

self·ish \'sel-fish\ *adj* : taking care of one's own comfort, pleasure, or interest excessively or without regard for others — **self·ish·ly** *adv* — **self·ish·ness** *n*

self·less \'self-ləs\ *adj* : UNSELFISH — **self·less·ness** *n*

self–made \'self-'mād\ *adj* : rising from poverty or obscurity by one's own efforts ⟨~ man⟩

self–pol·li·na·tion \ˌself-ˌpäl-ə-'nā-shən\ *n* : pollination of a flower by its own pollen or sometimes by pollen from another flower on the same plant

self–reg·u·lat·ing \'self-'reg-yə-ˌlāt-iŋ\ *adj* : AUTOMATIC

self–righ·teous \-'rī-chəs\ *adj* : strongly convinced of one's own righteousness — **self–righ·teous·ly** *adv*

self·same \'self-ˌsām\ *adj* : precisely the same : IDENTICAL

self–seal·ing \'self-'sē-liŋ\ *adj* : capable of sealing itself (as after puncture)

self–start·er \-'stärt-ər\ *n* : a person who has initiative

self–will \'self-'wil\ *n* : OBSTINACY

sell \'sel\ *vb* **sold** \'sōld\; **sell·ing** **1** : to transfer (property) in return for money or something else of value **2** : to deal in as a business **3** : to be sold ⟨cars are ~ing well⟩ — **sell·er** *n*

selling climax *n* : a sharp decline in stock prices for a short time on very heavy trading volume followed by a rally

sell out \(')sel-'aüt\ *vb* **1** : to dispose of entirely by sale; *esp* : to sell one's business **2** : BETRAY — **sell·out** \'sel-ˌaüt\ *n*

selt·zer \'selt-sər\ *n* [modif. of G *Selterser (wasser)* water of Selters, fr. Nieder *Selters,* Germany] : an artificially prepared water charged with carbon dioxide

sel·vage *or* **sel·vedge** \'sel-vij\ *n* : the edge of a woven fabric so formed as to prevent raveling

selves *pl of* SELF

sem *abbr* **1** semicolon **2** seminar **3** seminary

se·man·tic \si-'mant-ik\ *also* **se·man·ti·cal** \-i-kəl\ *adj* : of or relating to meaning

se·man·tics \si-'mant-iks\ *n sing or pl* **1** : the study of meanings in language **2** : connotative meaning

sema·phore \'sem-ə-ˌfōr\ *n* **1** : a visual signaling apparatus with movable arms **2** : signaling by hand-held flags

sem·blance \'sem-bləns\ *n* **1** : outward appearance **2** : IMAGE, LIKENESS

se·men \'sē-mən\ *n* [NL, fr. L, seed] : a sticky whitish fluid of the male reproductive tract that contains the sperm

se·mes·ter \sə-'mes-tər\ *n* [G, fr. L *semestris* half-yearly, fr. *sex* six + *mensis* month] : half a year; *esp* : one of the two terms into which many colleges divide the school year

semi- \ˌsem-i, 'sem-, -ˌī\ *prefix* **1** : precisely half of **2** : half in quantity or value; *also* : half of or occurring halfway through a specified period **3** : partly : incompletely **4** : partial : incomplete **5** : having some of the characteristics of

semiannual	semiliterate
semiarid	semimonthly
semicentennial	semiofficial
semicircle	semipermanent
semicircular	semipolitical
semicivilized	semiprecious
semiclassical	semiprivate
semiconscious	semiprofessional
semidarkness	semireligious
semidivine	semiretired
semiformal	semiskilled
semigloss	semisweet
semi–independent	semitransparent
semiliquid	semiweekly

semiyearly

semi·au·to·mat·ic \ˌsem-ē-ˌȯt-ə-ˈmat-ik\ *adj, of a firearm* : employing recoil or gas pressure to eject an empty cartridge case and to load before firing again

semi·co·lon \ˈsem-i-ˌkō-lən\ *n* : a punctuation mark ; used esp. to separate major sentence elements

semi·con·duc·tor \ˌsem-i-kən-ˈdək-tər\ *n* : a substance whose electrical conductivity is between that of a conductor and an insulator — **semi·con·duct·ing** \-ˈdək-tiŋ\ *adj*

semi·dry·ing \ˌsem-i-ˈdrī-iŋ\ *adj* : that dries imperfectly or slowly ⟨a ~ oil⟩

¹semi·fi·nal \ˌsem-i-ˈfīn-ᵊl\ *adj* : being next to the last in an elimination tournament

²semi·fi·nal \ˈsem-i-ˌfīn-ᵊl\ *n* : a semifinal round or match

semi·flu·id \ˌsem-i-ˈflü-əd, -ˌī-\ *adj* : SEMISOLID

semi·lu·nar \-ˈlü-nər\ *adj* : crescent-shaped

sem·i·nal \ˈsem-ən-ᵊl\ *adj* **1** : of, relating to, or consisting of seed or semen **2** : containing or contributing the seeds of later development : CREATIVE, ORIGINAL — **sem·i·nal·ly** \-ē\ *adv*

sem·i·nar \ˈsem-ə-ˌnär\ *n* **1** : a course of study pursued by a group of advanced students doing original research under a professor **2** : CONFERENCE

sem·i·nary \ˈsem-ə-ˌner-ē\ *n, pl* **-nar·ies** [ME, seedbed, nursery, fr. L *seminarium*, fr. *semen* seed] : an educational institution; *esp* : one that gives theological training — **sem·i·nar·i·an** \ˌsem-ə-ˈner-ē-ən\ *n*

Sem·i·nole \ˈsem-ə-ˌnōl\ *n, pl* **Seminoles** *or* **Seminole** : a member of an American Indian people of Florida

semi·per·me·able \ˌsem-i-ˈpər-mē-ə-bəl\ *adj* : partially but not freely or wholly permeable; *esp* : permeable to some usu. small molecules but not to other usu. larger particles ⟨a ~ membrane⟩ — **semi·per·me·abil·i·ty** \-ˌpər-mē-ə-ˈbil-ət-ē\ *n*

semi·soft \-ˈsȯft\ *adj* : moderately soft; *esp* : firm but easily cut ⟨~ cheese⟩

semi·sol·id \-ˈsäl-əd\ *adj* : having the qualities of both a solid and a liquid

Sem·ite \ˈsem-ˌīt\ *n* : a member of any of a group of peoples (as the Jews or Arabs) of southwestern Asia — **Se·mit·ic** \sə-ˈmit-ik\ *adj*

semi·trail·er \ˈsem-i-ˌtrā-lər, ˈsem-ˌī-\ *n* : a freight trailer that when attached is supported at its forward end by the truck tractor; *also* : a semitrailer with attached tractor

semi·works \ˈsem-i-ˌwərks, ˈsem-ˌī-\ *n pl* : a manufacturing plant operating on a limited commercial scale to provide final tests of a new product or process

semp·stress \ˈsemp-strəs\ *var of* SEAMSTRESS

¹sen \ˈsen\ *n, pl* **sen** — see *yen* at MONEY table

²sen *n, pl* **sen** — see *rupiah* at MONEY table

³sen *n, pl* **sen** — see *dollar, riel* at MONEY table

⁴sen *n, pl* **sen** — see *ringgit* at MONEY table

⁵sen *abbr* **1** senate; senator **2** senior

sen·ate \ˈsen-ət\ *n* [ME *senat,* fr. OF, fr. L *senatus*, lit., council of elders, fr. *senex* old, old man] : the upper branch of a legislature

sen·a·tor \ˈsen-ət-ər\ *n* : a member of a senate — **sen·a·to·ri·al** \ˌsen-ə-ˈtōr-ē-əl\ *adj*

send \ˈsend\ *vb* **sent** \ˈsent\; **send·ing 1** : to cause to go **2** : EMIT **3** : to propel or drive esp. with force **4** : to put or bring into a certain condition — **send·er** *n*

send–off \ˈsend-ˌȯf\ *n* : a demonstration of goodwill and enthusiasm for the beginning of a new venture (as a trip)

se·ne \ˈsā-(ˌ)nā\ *n, pl* **sene** — see *tala* at MONEY table

Sen·e·ca \ˈsen-i-kə\ *n, pl* **Seneca** *or* **Senecas** : a member of an American Indian people of western New York

Sen·e·ga·lese \ˌsen-i-gə-ˈlēz, -ˈlēs\ *n, pl* **Senegalese** : a native or inhabitant of Senegal — **Senegalese** *adj*

se·nes·cence \si-ˈnes-ᵊns\ *n* : the state of being old; *also* : the process of becoming old — **se·nes·cent** \-ᵊnt\ *adj*

sen·gi \ˈseŋ-gē\ *n, pl* **sengi** — see *zaire* at MONEY table

se·nile \ˈsēn-ˌīl, ˈsen-\ *adj* : OLD, AGED; *esp* : exhibiting loss of mental ability usu. associated with old age — **se•nil•i•ty** \si-'nil-ət-ē\ n

¹se•nior \'sē-nyər\ n **1** : a person older or of higher rank than another **2** : a member of the graduating class of a high school or college

²senior adj [ME, fr. L, older, elder, compar. of senex old] **1** : ELDER **2** : more advanced in dignity or rank **3** : belonging to the final year of a school or college course

senior chief petty officer n : a petty officer in the navy ranking next below a master chief petty officer

senior citizen n : an elderly person; esp : one who has retired

senior high school n : a school usu. including grades 10 to 12

se•nior•i•ty \sēn-'yȯr-ət-ē\ n **1** : the quality or state of being senior **2** : a privileged status owing to length of continuous service

senior master sergeant n : a noncommissioned officer in the air force ranking next below a chief master sergeant

sen•i•ti \'sen-ə-tē\ n, pl **seniti** — see pa'anga at MONEY table

sen•na \'sen-ə\ n **1** : any of various cassias **2** : the dried leaflets or pods of a cassia used as a purgative

sen•sa•tion \sen-'sā-shən\ n **1** : awareness (as of noise or heat) or a mental process (as seeing or hearing) due to stimulation of a sense organ; also : an indefinite bodily feeling **2** : a condition of excitement; also : the thing that causes this condition

sen•sa•tion•al \-sh(ə-)nəl\ adj **1** : of or relating to sensation or the senses **2** : arousing an intense and usu. superficial interest or emotional reaction — **sen•sa•tion•al•ly** \-ē\ adv

sen•sa•tion•al•ism \-ˌiz-əm\ n : the use or effect of sensational subject matter or treatment

sen•sa•tion•al•ize \-ˌīz\ vb **-ized; -iz•ing** : to present in a sensational manner

¹sense \'sens\ n **1** : semantic content : MEANING **2** : the faculty of perceiving by means of sense organs; also : a bodily function or mechanism based on this ⟨the pain ∼⟩ **3** : SENSATION, AWARENESS **4** : INTELLIGENCE, JUDGMENT **5** : OPINION ⟨the ∼ of the meeting⟩ — **sense•less** adj — **sense•less•ly** adv

²sense vb **sensed; sens•ing 1** : to be or become aware of : perceive by the senses **2** : to detect (as radiation) automatically

sense organ n : a bodily structure (as an eye or ear) that responds to a stimulus (as heat or light) and sends impulses to the brain where they are interpreted as sensations

sen•si•bil•i•ty \ˌsen-sə-'bil-ət-ē\ n, pl **-ties** : delicacy of feeling : SENSITIVITY

sen•si•ble \'sen-sə-bəl\ adj **1** : capable of being perceived by the senses or by reason; also : capable of receiving sense impressions **2** : AWARE, CONSCIOUS **3** : REASONABLE, INTELLIGENT — **sen•si•bly** \-blē\ adv

sen•si•tive \'sen-sət-iv\ adj **1** : subject to excitation by or responsive to stimuli **2** : having power of feeling **3** : of such a nature as to be easily affected — **sen•si•tive•ness** n — **sen•si•tiv•i•ty** \ˌsen-sə-'tiv-ət-ē\ n

sensitive plant n : any of several mimosas with leaves that fold or droop when touched

sen•si•tize \'sen-sə-ˌtīz\ vb **-tized; -tiz•ing** : to make or become sensitive or hypersensitive — **sen•si•ti•za•tion** \ˌsen-sət-ə-'zā-shən\ n

sen•si•tom•e•ter \ˌsen-sə-'täm-ət-ər\ n : an instrument for measuring sensitivity of photographic material — **sen•si•to•met•ric** \-sət-ə-'me-trik\ adj — **sen•si•tom•e•try** \-sə-'täm-ə-trē\ n

sen•sor \'sen-ˌsȯr, -sər\ n : a device that responds to a physical stimulus

sen•so•ry \'sens-(ə-)rē\ adj : of or relating to sensation or the senses

sen•su•al \'sench-(ə-)wəl\ adj **1** : relating to the pleasing of the senses **2** : devoted to the pleasures of the senses — **sen•su•al•ist** n — **sen•su•al•i•ty** \ˌsen-chə-'wal-ət-ē\ n — **sen•su•al•ly** \'sench-(ə-)wə-lē, 'sen-shə-lē\ adv

sen•su•ous \'sench-(ə-)wəs\ adj **1** : relating to the senses or to things that can be perceived by the senses **2** : VOLUPTUOUS — **sen•su•ous•ly** adv — **sen•su•ous•ness** n

sent past and past part of SEND

¹sen•tence \'sent-ᵊns, -ᵊnz\ n [ME, fr. OF, fr. L sententia, lit., feeling, opinion, fr. sentire to feel] **1** : the punishment set by a court **2** : a grammatically self-contained speech unit that expresses an assertion, a question, a command, a wish, or an exclamation

²**sentence** *vb* **sen·tenced; sen·tenc·ing** : to impose a sentence on **syn** condemn, damn, doom

sen·ten·tious \sen-'ten-chəs\ *adj* : using wise sayings or proverbs; *also* : using pompous language

sen·ti \'sent-ē\ *n, pl* **senti** — see *shilling* at MONEY table

sen·tient \'sen-ch(ē-)ənt\ *adj* : capable of feeling : having perception

sen·ti·ment \'sent-ə-mənt\ *n* **1** : FEEL-ING; *also* : thought and judgment influenced by feeling : emotional attitude **2** : OPINION, NOTION

sen·ti·men·tal \sent-ə-'ment-ᵊl\ *adj* **1** : influenced by tender feelings **2** : affecting the emotions **syn** bathetic, maudlin, mawkish, mushy — **sen·ti·men·tal·ism** *n* — **sen·ti·men·tal·ist** *n* — **sen·ti·men·tal·i·ty** \-ˌmen-'tal-ət-ē, -mən-\ *n* — **sen·ti·men·tal·ly** \-'ment-ᵊl-ē\ *adv*

sen·ti·men·tal·ize \-'ment-ᵊl-ˌīz\ *vb* **-ized; -iz·ing** **1** : to indulge in sentiment **2** : to look upon or imbue with sentiment — **sen·ti·men·tal·iza·tion** \-ˌment-ᵊl-ə-'zā-shən\ *n*

sen·ti·mo \sen-'tē-(ˌ)mō\ *n, pl* **-mos** — see *peso* at MONEY table

sen·ti·nel \'sent-(ᵊ-)nəl\ *n* [MF *sentinelle*, fr. It *sentinella*, fr. *sentina* vigilance, fr. *sentire* to perceive, fr. L] : one that watches or guards

sen·try \'sen-trē\ *n, pl* **sentries** : SENTI-NEL, GUARD

sep *abbr* separate, separated

Sep *abbr* September

se·pal \'sēp-əl, 'sep-\ *n* : one of the modified leaves comprising a flower calyx

sep·a·ra·ble \'sep-(ə-)rə-bəl\ *adj* : capable of being separated

¹**sep·a·rate** \'sep-ə-ˌrāt\ *vb* **-rat·ed; -rat·ing** **1** : to set or keep apart : DISUNITE, DISCONNECT, SEVER **2** : to keep apart by something intervening **3** : to cease to be together : PART

²**sep·a·rate** \'sep-(ə-)rət\ *adj* **1** : not connected **2** : divided from each other **3** : SINGLE, PARTICULAR ⟨the ~ pieces of the puzzle⟩ — **sep·a·rate·ly** *adv*

³**sep·a·rate** *n* : an article of dress designed to be worn interchangeably

with others to form various combinations

sep·a·ra·tion \ˌsep-ə-'rā-shən\ *n* **1** : the act or process of separating : the state of being separated **2** : a point, line, means, or area of division

sep·a·rat·ist \'sep-(ə-)rət-əst, 'sep-ə-ˌrāt-\ *n* : an advocate of separation (as from a political body) — **sep·a·rat·ism** \-rə-ˌtiz-əm\ *n*

sep·a·ra·tive \'sep-ə-ˌrāt-iv, 'sep-(ə-)rət-\ *adj* : tending toward, causing or expressing separation

sep·a·ra·tor \'sep-(ə-)ˌrāt-ər\ *n* : one that separates; *esp* : a device for separating cream from milk

se·pia \'sē-pē-ə\ *n* : a brownish gray to dark brown

sep·sis \'sep-səs\ *n, pl* **sep·ses** \'sep-ˌsēz\ : a poisoned condition due to spread of bacteria or their products in the body

Sept *abbr* September

Sep·tem·ber \sep-'tem-bər\ *n* : the 9th month of the year having 30 days

sep·tic \'sep-tik\ *adj* **1** : PUTREFACTIVE **2** : relating to or characteristic of sepsis

sep·ti·ce·mia \ˌsep-tə-'sē-mē-ə\ *n* : BLOOD POISONING

septic tank *n* : a tank in which sewage is disintegrated by bacteria

sep·tu·a·ge·nar·i·an \sep-ˌt(y)ü-ə-jə-'ner-ē-ən\ *n* : a person who is 70 or more but less than 80 years old — **septuagenarian** *adj*

Sep·tu·a·gint \sep-'t(y)ü-ə-jənt, 'sep-tə-wə-ˌjint\ *n* : a Greek version of the Old Testament used by Greek-speaking Christians

¹**sep·ul·cher** *or* **sep·ul·chre** \'sep-əl-kər\ *n* : burial vault : TOMB

²**sepulcher** *or* **sepulchre** *vb* **-chered** *or* **-chred; -cher·ing** *or* **-chring** \-k(ə-)riŋ\ : BURY, ENTOMB

se·pul·chral \sə-'pəl-krəl\ *adj* **1** : relating to burial or the grave **2** : GLOOMY

sep·ul·ture \'sep-əl-ˌchùr\ *n* **1** : BURIAL, INTERMENT **2** : SEPULCHER

seq *abbr* [L *sequens, sequentes, sequentia*] the following

seqq *abbr* [L *sequentia*] the following ones

se·quel \'sē-kwəl\ *n* **1** : logical consequence **2** : a literary or cinematic work continuing a story begun in a preceding one

se•quence \'sē-kwəns\ *n* **1** : SERIES **2** : chronological order of events **3** : RESULT, SEQUEL **syn** succession, chain, progression, series, train — **se•quen•tial** \si-'kwen-chəl\ *adj*

se•quent \'sē-kwənt\ *adj* **1** : SUCCEEDING, CONSECUTIVE **2** : RESULTANT

se•ques•ter \si-'kwes-tər\ *vb* : to set apart : SEGREGATE

se•ques•trate \'sēk-wəs-ˌtrāt, si-'kwes-\ *vb* **-trat•ed; -trat•ing** : SEQUESTER — **se•ques•tra•tion** \ˌsēk-wəs-'trā-shən, ˌsek-\ *n*

se•quin \'sē-kwən\ *n* **1** : an old gold coin of Turkey and Italy **2** : a small metal or plastic plate used for ornamentation esp. on clothing

se•quoia \si-'kwȯi-ə\ *n* : either of two huge California coniferous trees

ser *abbr* **1** serial **2** series

sera pl of SERUM

se•ra•glio \sə-'ral-yō\ *n, pl* **-glios** [It *serraglio*] : HAREM

se•ra•pe \sə-'räp-ē\ *n* : a colorful woolen shawl worn over the shoulders esp. by Mexican men

ser•a•phim \'ser-ə-ˌfim\ *n, pl* **seraphim** : an angel of a high order of celestial beings — **se•raph•ic** \sə-'raf-ik\ *adj*

Serb \'sərb\ *n* **1** : a native or inhabitant of Serbia, republic, Yugoslavia **2** : a Slavic language of Serbia

sere \'siər\ *adj* : DRY, WITHERED

¹ser•e•nade \ˌser-ə-'nād\ *n* [F, fr. It *serenata*, fr. *sereno* clear] : music sung or played as a compliment esp. outdoors at night for a lady

²serenade *vb* **-nad•ed; -nad•ing** : to entertain with or perform a serenade

ser•en•dip•i•ty \ˌser-ən-'dip-ət-ē\ *n* [fr. its possession by the heroes of the Persian fairy tale *The Three Princes of Serendip*] : the gift of finding valuable or agreeable things not sought for — **ser•en•dip•i•tous** \-əs\ *adj*

se•rene \sə-'rēn\ *adj* **1** : QUIET, CALM **2** : CLEAR ⟨~ skies⟩ **syn** tranquil, peaceful, placid — **se•rene•ly** *adv* — **se•ren•i•ty** \sə-'ren-ət-ē\ *n*

serf \'sərf\ *n* : a peasant bound to the land and subject in some degree to the owner — **serf•dom** \-dəm\ *n*

serg *or* **sergt** *abbr* sergeant

serge \'sərj\ *n* : a twilled woolen cloth

ser•geant \'sär-jənt\ *n* [ME, servant, attendant, officer who keeps order, fr.

OF *sergent, serjant,* fr. L *servient-, serviens,* prp. of *servire* to serve] **1** : a noncommissioned officer (as in the army) ranking next below a staff sergeant **2** : an officer in a police force

sergeant first class *n* : a noncommissioned officer in the army ranking next below a master sergeant

sergeant major *n, pl* **sergeants major** *or* **sergeant majors 1** : a noncommissioned officer in the army, air force, or marine corps serving as chief administrative assistant in a headquarters **2** : a noncommissioned officer in the marine corps ranking above a first sergeant

¹se•ri•al \'sir-ē-əl\ *adj* : appearing in parts that follow regularly ⟨a ~ story⟩ — **se•ri•al•ly** *adv*

²serial *n* : a serial story or other writing — **se•ri•al•ist** \-ə-ləst\ *n*

se•ries \'si(ə)r-ēz\ *n, pl* **series** : a number of things or events arranged in order and connected by being alike in some way **syn** succession, progression, sequence, chain, train, string

seri•graph \'ser-ə-ˌgraf\ *n* : an original silk-screen print — **se•rig•ra•pher** \sə-'rig-rə-fər\ *n* — **se•rig•ra•phy** \-fē\ *n*

se•ri•ous \'sir-ē-əs\ *adj* **1** : thoughtful or subdued in appearance or manner : SOBER **2** : requiring much thought or work **3** : EARNEST, DEVOTED **4** : DANGEROUS, HARMFUL **syn** grave, sedate, sober, staid — **se•ri•ous•ly** *adv* — **se•ri•ous•ness** *n*

ser•mon \'sər-mən\ *n* [ME, fr. OF, fr. ML *sermon, sermo,* fr. L, speech, conversation, fr. *serere* to link together] **1** : a religious discourse esp. as part of a worship service **2** : a lecture on conduct or duty

se•rol•o•gy \sə-'räl-ə-jē\ *n* : a science dealing with serums and esp. their reactions and properties — **se•ro•log•i•cal** \ˌsir-ə-'läj-i-kəl\ *or* **se•ro•log•ic** \-ik\ *adj*

se•rous \'sir-əs\ *adj* : of, relating to, resembling, or producing serum; *esp* : thin and watery

ser•pent \'sər-pənt\ *n* : SNAKE

¹ser•pen•tine \'sər-pən-ˌtēn, -ˌtīn\ *adj* **1** : SLY, CRAFTY **2** : WINDING, TURNING

²ser•pen•tine \-ˌtēn\ *n* : a dull-green mineral having a mottled appearance

ser·rate \\'ser-ˌāt\ *adj* : having a saw‑toothed edge ⟨a ∼ leaf⟩

ser·ried \\'ser-ēd\ *adj* : DENSE

se·rum \\'sir-əm\ *n, pl* **serums** *or* **se·ra** \-ə\ [L, whey, serum] : the liquid anti‑body-containing part that can be sepa‑rated from blood when it clots; *also* : a preparation of animal serum con‑taining specific antibodies and used to prevent or cure disease

serv *abbr* service

ser·vant \\'sər-vənt\ *n* : a person em‑ployed esp. for domestic work

¹serve \\'sərv\ *vb* **served; serv·ing 1** : to work as a servant **2** : to render obedi‑ence and worship to (God) **3** : to com‑ply with the commands or demands of **4** : to work through or perform a term of service (as in the army) **5** : PUT IN ⟨*served* five years in jail⟩ **6** : to be of use : ANSWER ⟨pine boughs *served* for a bed⟩ **7** : BENEFIT **8** : to prove ade‑quate or satisfactory for ⟨a pie that ∼*s* eight people⟩ **9** : to make ready and pass out ⟨∼ drinks⟩ **10** : to furnish or supply with something ⟨one power company *serving* the whole state⟩ **11** : to wait on ⟨∼ a customer⟩ **12** : to treat or act toward in a specified way **13** : to put the ball in play (as in tennis) — **serv·er** *n*

²serve *n* : the act of serving a ball (as in tennis)

¹ser·vice \\'sər-vəs\ *n* **1** : the occupation of a servant **2** : HELP, BENEFIT **3** : a meeting for worship; *also* : a form fol‑lowed in worship or in a ceremony ⟨burial ∼⟩ **4** : the act, fact, or means of serving **5** : performance of official or professional duties **6** : a serving of the ball (as in tennis) **7** : a set of dishes or silverware **8** : a branch of public employment; *also* : the persons in it ⟨civil ∼⟩ **9** : military or naval duty **syn** use, advantage, account, avail

²service *vb* **ser·viced; ser·vic·ing** : to do maintenance or repair work on or for

ser·vice·able \\'sər-və-sə-bəl\ *adj* : pre‑pared for service : USEFUL, USABLE

ser·vice·man \\'sər-vəs-ˌman, -mən\ *n* **1** : a male member of the armed forces **2** : a man employed to repair or main‑tain equipment

service station *n* : a retail station for servicing motor vehicles

ser·vice·wom·an \\'sər-vəs-ˌwum-ən\ *n* : a female member of the armed forces

ser·vile \\'sər-vəl, -ˌvīl\ *adj* **1** : befitting a slave or servant **2** : behaving like a slave : SUBMISSIVE — **ser·vil·i·ty** \ˌsər-'vil-ət-ē\ *n*

serv·ing \\'sər-viŋ\ *n* : HELPING

ser·vi·tor \\'sər-vət-ər\ *n* : a male ser‑vant

ser·vi·tude \\'sər-və-ˌt(y)üd\ *n* : SLAV‑ERY, BONDAGE

ser·vo \\'sər-vō\ *n, pl* **servos 1** : SER‑VOMOTOR **2** : SERVOMECHANISM

ser·vo·mech·a·nism \\'sər-vō-ˌmek-ə-ˌniz-əm\ *n* : a device for auto‑matically correcting the performance of a mechanism

ser·vo·mo·tor \\'sər-vō-ˌmōt-ər\ *n* : a motor in a servomechanism that sup‑plements a primary control by cor‑recting position or motion

ses·a·me \\'ses-ə-mē\ *n* : an East Indian annual herb; *also* : its seeds that yield an edible oil (**sesame oil**) and are used in flavoring

ses·qui·cen·ten·ni·al \ˌses-kwi-sen-'ten-ē-əl\ *n* [L *sesqui*- one and a half, half again] : a 150th anniversary or its cel‑ebration — **sesquicentennial** *adj*

ses·qui·pe·da·lian \ˌses-kwə-pə-'dāl-yən\ *adj* **1** : having many syl‑lables : LONG **2** : using long words

ses·sile \\'ses-īl, -əl\ *adj* : attached by the base ⟨a ∼ leaf⟩

ses·sion \\'sesh-ən\ *n* **1** : a meeting or series of meetings of a body (as a court or legislature) for the transac‑tion of business **2** : a meeting or peri‑od devoted to a particular activity

¹set \\'set\ *vb* **set; set·ting 1** : to cause to sit **2** : PLACE **3** : ARRANGE, ADJUST **4** : to cause to be or do **5** : SETTLE, DE‑CREE **6** : to fix in a frame **7** : ESTIMATE **8** : WAGER, STAKE **9** : to make fast or rigid **10** : to adapt (as words) to some‑thing (as music) **11** : to become fixed or firm or solid **12** : to be suitable : FIT **13** : BROOD **14** : to have a certain di‑rection **15** : to pass below the horizon **16** : to defeat in bridge — **set about** : to begin to do — **set forth** : to begin a trip — **set off 1** : to start out on a course or a trip **2** : to cause to explode — **set out** : to begin a trip or undertak‑ing — **set sail** : to begin a voyage

²set *n* **1** : a setting or a being set **2** : DI‑

RECTION, COURSE; *also* : TENDENCY **3** : FORM, BUILD **4** : the fit of something (as a coat) **5** : an artificial setting for the scene of a play or motion picture **6** : a group of tennis games in which one side wins at least six to an opponent's four or less **7** : a group of persons or things of the same kind or having a common characteristic usu. classed together **8** : a collection of things and esp. of mathematical elements (as numbers or points) **9** : an electronic apparatus ⟨a television ∼⟩

³set *adj* **1** : fixed by authority or custom **2** : DELIBERATE **3** : RIGID **4** : PERSISTENT

set•back \'set-ˌbak\ *n* : a temporary defeat : REVERSE

set back \'set-'bak\ *vb* : HINDER, DELAY; *also* : REVERSE

set•screw \'set-ˌskrü\ *n* : a screw screwed through one part tightly upon or into another part to prevent relative movement

set•tee \se-'tē\ *n* : a bench or sofa with a back and arms

set•ter \'set-ər\ *n* : a large long-coated hunting dog

set•ting \'set-iŋ\ *n* **1** : the frame in which a gem is set **2** : BACKGROUND, ENVIRONMENT; *also* : SCENERY **3** : music written for a text (as of a poem) **4** : the eggs that a fowl sits on for hatching at one time

set•tle \'set-ᵊl\ *vb* **set•tled; set•tling** \'set-(ᵊ-)liŋ\ [ME *settlen* to seat, bring to rest, come to rest, fr. OE *setlan*, fr. *setl* seat] **1** : to put in place **2** : to locate permanently **3** : to make compact **4** : QUIET, CALM **5** : to establish in life, business, or a home **6** : to direct one's efforts **7** : to fix by agreement **8** : to give legally **9** : ADJUST, ARRANGE **10** : DECIDE, DETERMINE **11** : to make a final disposition of ⟨∼ an account⟩ **12** : to come to rest **13** : to reach an agreement on **14** : to sink gradually to a lower level **15** : to become clear by depositing sediment **syn** set, fix, establish, place — **set•tler** \-(ᵊ-)lər\ *n*

set•tle•ment \'set-ᵊl-mənt\ *n* **1** : the act or process of settling **2** : BESTOWAL ⟨a marriage ∼⟩ **3** : payment of an account **4** : COLONY **5** : a small village **6** : an institution in a poor district of a city to give aid to the community **7** : adjustment of doubts and differences

set–to \'set-ˌtü\ *n, pl* **set–tos** : FIGHT

set•up \'set-ˌəp\ *n* **1** : the manner or act of arranging **2** : glass, ice, and nonalcoholic beverage for mixing served to patrons who supply their own liquor

set up \'set-'əp\ *vb* **1** : to place in position; *also* : ASSEMBLE **2** : CAUSE **3** : FOUND, ESTABLISH

sev•en \'sev-ən\ *n* **1** : one more than six **2** : the 7th in a set or series **3** : something having seven units — **seven** *adj or pron* — **sev•enth** \-ənth\ *adj or adv or n*

sev•en•teen \ˌsev-ən-'tēn\ *n* : one more than 16 — **seventeen** *adj or pron* — **sev•en•teenth** \-'tēnth\ *adj or n*

seventeen–year locust *n* : a cicada of the U.S. that has in the North a life of 17 years and in the South of 13 years of which most is spent underground as a nymph and only a few weeks as a winged adult

sev•en•ty \'sev-ən-tē\ *n, pl* **-ties** : seven times 10 — **sev•en•ti•eth** \-tē-əth\ *adj or n* — **seventy** *adj or pron*

sev•en•ty–eight \ˌsev-ən-tē-'āt\ *n* : a phonograph record designed to be played at 78 revolutions per minute

sev•er \'sev-ər\ *vb* **sev•ered; sev•er•ing** \-(ə-)riŋ\ : DIVIDE; *esp* : to separate by force (as by cutting or tearing) — **sev•er•ance** \-(ə-)rəns\ *n*

sev•er•al \'sev-(ə-)rəl\ *adj* [ME, fr. ML *separalis*, fr. L *separ* separate, fr. *separare* to separate] **1** : INDIVIDUAL, DISTINCT ⟨federal union of the ∼ states⟩ **2** : consisting of an indefinite number but yet not very many — **sev•er•al•ly** \-ē\ *adv*

severance pay *n* : extra pay given an employee upon leaving a job permanently

se•vere \sə-'viər\ *adj* **se•ver•er; -est** **1** : marked by strictness or sternness : AUSTERE **2** : strict in discipline **3** : causing distress and esp. physical discomfort or pain ⟨∼ weather⟩ ⟨a ∼ wound⟩ **4** : hard to endure ⟨∼ trials⟩ **syn** stern, ascetic, astringent, austere — **se•vere•ly** *adv* — **se•ver•i•ty** \-'ver-ət-ē\ *n*

sew \'sō\ *vb* **sewed; sewn** \'sōn\ *or* **sewed; sew•ing** **1** : to fasten by stitches made with thread and needle **2** : to engage in sewing

sew·age \ˈsü-ij\ *n* : waste materials carried off by sewers

¹**sew·er** \ˈsō(-ə)r\ *n* : one that sews

²**sew·er** \ˈsü-ər\ *n* : an artificial pipe or channel to carry off waste matter

sew·er·age \ˈsü-ə-rij\ *n* **1** : SEWAGE **2** : a system of sewers

sew·ing \ˈsō-iŋ\ *n* **1** : the activity of one who sews **2** : material that has been or is to be sewed

sex \ˈseks\ *n* **1** : either of two groups into which many living things are divided according to their roles in reproduction and which are distinguished as male and female; *also* : the qualities by which these sexes are differentiated and which directly or indirectly function in reproduction involving two parents **2** : sexual activity or intercourse — **sexed** \ˈsekst\ *adj* — **sex·less** *adj*

sex·a·ge·nar·i·an \ˌsek-sə-jə-ˈner-ē-ən\ *n* : a person who is 60 or more but less than 70 years old — **sexagenarian** *adj*

sex cell *n* : an egg cell or sperm cell

sex chromosome *n* : one of usu. a pair of chromosomes that are usu. similar in one sex but different in the other sex and are concerned with the inheritance of sex

sex hormone *n* : a hormone (as from the gonads or adrenal cortex) that affects the growth or function of the reproductive organs or the development of secondary sex characteristics

sex·ism \ˈsek-ˌsiz-əm\ *n* : prejudice or discrimination based on sex; *esp* : discrimination against women — **sex·ist** \ˈsek-səst\ *adj or n*

sex·pot \ˈseks-ˌpät\ *n* : a sexually stimulating woman

sex symbol *n* : a usu. renowned person (as an entertainer) noted and admired for conspicuous attractiveness

sex·tant \ˈsek-stənt\ *n* [NL *sextant-, sextans* sixth part of a circle, fr. L, sixth part, fr. *sextus* sixth] : a navigational instrument for measuring the angle between the horizon and the sun or a star in order to determine latitude

sex·tet \sek-ˈstet\ *n* **1** : a musical composition for six voices or six instruments; *also* : the six performers of such a composition **2** : a group or set of six

sex·ton \ˈsek-stən\ *n* : one who takes care of church property

sex·u·al \ˈsek-sh(ə-w)əl\ *adj* : of, relating to, or involving sex or the sexes ⟨a ∼ spore⟩ ⟨∼ relations⟩ — **sex·u·al·i·ty** \ˌsek-shə-ˈwal-ət-ē\ *n* — **sex·u·al·ly** \ˈsek-shə-(wə-)lē\ *adv*

sexual intercourse *n* **1** : intercourse between a male and a female in which the penis is inserted into the vagina **2** : intercourse between individuals which involves genital contact but in which the penis is not inserted into the vagina

sexually transmitted disease *n* : a disease (as syphilis, gonorrhea, or the genital form of herpes simplex) usu. or often transmitted by direct sexual contact

sexy \ˈsek-sē\ *adj* **sex·i·er; -est** : sexually suggestive or stimulating : EROTIC

SF *abbr* **1** sacrifice fly **2** science fiction

SFC *abbr* sergeant first class

SG *abbr* **1** senior grade **2** sergeant **3** solicitor general **4** surgeon general

sgd *abbr* signed

Sgt *abbr* sergeant

Sgt Maj *abbr* sergeant major

sh *abbr* share

shab·by \ˈshab-ē\ *adj* **shab·bi·er; -est 1** : dressed in worn clothes **2** : threadbare and faded from wear **3** : MEAN ⟨∼ treatment⟩ — **shab·bi·ly** \ˈshab-ə-lē\ *adv* — **shab·bi·ness** \-ē-nəs\ *n*

shack \ˈshak\ *n* : HUT, SHANTY

¹**shack·le** \ˈshak-əl\ *n* **1** : something (as a manacle or fetter) that confines the legs or arms **2** : a check on free action made as if by fetters **3** : a device for making something fast or secure

²**shackle** *vb* **shack·led; shack·ling** \-(ə-)liŋ\ : to fasten with shackles

shad \ˈshad\ *n, pl* **shad** : any of several sea fishes related to the herrings that swim up rivers to spawn and are important food fish

¹**shade** \ˈshād\ *n* **1** : partial obscurity **2** : space sheltered from the light esp. of the sun **3** : PHANTOM **4** : something that shelters from or intercepts light or heat; *also, pl* : SUNGLASSES **5** : a dark color or a variety of a color **6** : a small difference — **shady** *adj*

²**shade** *vb* **shad·ed; shad·ing 1** : to shelter

from light and heat **2** : DARKEN, OB-
SCURE **3** : to mark with degrees of light
or color **4** : to show slight differences
esp. in color or meaning
shad·ing \'shād-iŋ\ *n* : the color and
lines representing darkness or shadow in a drawing or painting
¹shad·ow \'shad-ō\ *n* **1** : partial darkness
in a space from which light rays are
cut off **2** : SHELTER **3** : shade cast
upon a surface by something intercepting rays from a light ⟨the ~ of a
tree⟩ **4** : PHANTOM **5** : a shaded portion
of a picture **6** : a small portion or degree : TRACE ⟨a ~ of doubt⟩ **7** : a
source of gloom or unhappiness —
shad·owy *adj*
²shadow *vb* **1** : to cast a shadow on **2** : to
represent faintly or vaguely **3** : to follow and watch closely : TRAIL
shad·ow·box \'shad-ō-ˌbäks\ *vb* : to
box with an imaginary opponent esp.
for training
¹shaft \'shaft\ *n, pl* **shafts** **1** : the long
handle of a spear or lance **2** : SPEAR,
LANCE **3** *or pl* **shaves** \'shavz\ : POLE;
esp : one of two poles between which
a horse is hitched to pull a vehicle **4**
: something (as a column) long and
slender **5** : a bar to support a rotating
piece or to transmit power by rotation
6 : an inclined opening in the ground
(as for finding or mining ore) **7** : a
vertical opening (as for an elevator)
through the floors of a building
²shaft *vb* : to fit with a shaft
shag \'shag\ *n* **1** : a shaggy tangled mat
(as of wool) **2** : tobacco cut into fine
shreds
shag·gy \'shag-ē\ *adj* **shag·gi·er; -est** **1**
: rough with or as if with long hair or
wool **2** : tangled or rough in surface
shah \'shä, 'shȯ\ *n, often cap* : a sovereign of Iran
Shak *abbr* Shakespeare
¹shake \'shāk\ *vb* **shook** \'shu̇k\; **shak·en**
\'shā-kən\; **shak·ing** **1** : to move or
cause to move jerkily or irregularly **2**
: BRANDISH, WAVE ⟨*shaking* his fist⟩ **3**
: to disturb emotionally ⟨*shaken* by
her death⟩ **4** : WEAKEN ⟨*shook* his
faith⟩ **5** : to bring or come into a certain position, condition, or arrangement by or as if by moving jerkily **6**
: to clasp (hands) in greeting or as a
sign of goodwill or agreement **syn**

tremble, quake, quaver, shiver, quiver — **shak·able** \'shā-kə-bəl\ *adj*
²shake *n* **1** : the act or a result of shaking
2 : DEAL, TREATMENT ⟨a fair ~⟩
shake·down \'shāk-ˌdau̇n\ *n* **1** : an improvised bed **2** : EXTORTION **3** : a process or period of adjustment **4** : a test
(as of a new ship or airplane) under
operating conditions
shake down \(ˈ)shāk-ˈdau̇n\ *vb* **1** : to
take up temporary quarters **2** : to occupy a makeshift bed **3** : to become
accustomed esp. to new surroundings
or duties **4** : to settle down **5** : to give
a shakedown test to **6** : to obtain money from in a dishonest or illegal manner **7** : to bring about a reduction of
shak·er \'shā-kər\ *n* **1** : one that shakes
⟨pepper ~⟩ **2** *cap* : a member of a
religious sect founded in England in
1747
shake–up \'shāk-ˌəp\ *n* : an extensive
often drastic reorganization
shaky \'shā-kē\ *adj* **shak·i·er; -est** : UN-
SOUND, WEAK — **shak·i·ly** \'shā-kə-lē\
adv — **shak·i·ness** \-kē-nəs\ *n*
shale \'shāl\ *n* : a rock made up of fine
layers and formed from clay, mud, or
silt
shall \shəl, (ˈ)shal\ *vb, past* **should**
\shəd, (ˈ)shu̇d\; *pres sing & pl* **shall** —
used as an auxiliary to express a command, what seems inevitable or likely
in the future, simple futurity, or determination
shal·lop \'shal-əp\ *n* : a light open boat
shal·lot \shə-ˈlät\ *n* [modif. of F
échalote] **1** : the bulb of a perennial
herb that is produced in clusters,
resembles an onion, and is used in
seasoning; *also* : this herb **2** : GREEN
ONION
¹shal·low \'shal-ō\ *adj* **1** : not deep **2**
: not intellectually profound **syn**
superficial, sketchy
²shallow *n* : a shallow place in a body of
water — usu. used in pl.
¹sham \'sham\ *n* **1** : something resembling an article of household linen and
used in its place as a decoration ⟨a
pillow ~⟩ **2** : COUNTERFEIT, IMITATION
²sham *vb* **shammed; sham·ming** : FEIGN,
PRETEND — **sham·mer** *n*
³sham *adj* : FALSE ⟨~ pearls⟩
sha·man \'shäm-ən, 'shā-mən\ *n* [Russ,
fr. Tungusic (a language of Siberia)]

: a priest who uses magic to cure the sick, to divine the hidden, and to control events

sham·ble \\'sham-bəl\\ *vb* **sham·bled; sham·bling** \\-b(ə-)liŋ\\ : to shuffle along — **sham·ble** *n*

sham·bles \\'sham-bəlz\\ *n* [*shamble* (meat market) & obs. E *shamble* (table for exhibition of meat for sale)] **1** : a scene of great slaughter **2** : a scene or state of great destruction or disorder

¹shame \\'shām\\ *n* **1** : a painful sense of having done something wrong, improper, or immodest **2** : DISGRACE, DISHONOR **3** : a cause of feeling shame — **shame·ful** \\-fəl\\ *adj* — **shame·ful·ly** \\-ē\\ *adv* — **shame·less** *adj* — **shame·less·ly** *adv*

²shame *vb* **shamed; sham·ing** **1** : DISGRACE **2** : to make ashamed

shame·faced \\'shām-'fāst\\ *adj* : ASHAMED, ABASHED — **shame·faced·ly** \\-'fā-səd-lē, -'fāst-lē\\ *adv*

¹sham·poo \\sham-'pü\\ *vb* [Hindi *cąpo*, imper. of *cąpnā* to press, shampoo] : to wash (as the hair) with soap and water or with a special preparation; *also* : to clean (as a rug) similarly

²shampoo *n, pl* **shampoos** **1** : the act or process of shampooing **2** : a preparation for use in shampooing

sham·rock \\'sham-ˌräk\\ *n* [IrGael *seamrōg*, dim. of *seamar* clover, honeysuckle] : a plant with three leaflets used as an Irish floral emblem

shang·hai \\shaŋ-'hī\\ *vb* **shang·haied; shang·hai·ing** [*Shanghai*, China] : to force aboard a ship for service as a sailor; *also* : to trick or force into something

Shan·gri–la \\ˌshaŋ-gri-'lä\\ *n* [*Shangri=La*, imaginary land depicted in the novel *Lost Horizon* (1933) by James Hilton] : a remote idyllic hideaway

shank \\'shaŋk\\ *n* **1** : the part of the leg between the knee and ankle in man or a corresponding part of a quadruped **2** : a cut of meat from the leg **3** : the narrow part of the sole of a shoe beneath the instep **4** : the part of a tool or instrument (as a key or anchor) connecting the functioning part with a part by which it is held or moved

shan·tung \\'shan-'təŋ\\ *n* : a fabric in plain weave having a slightly irregular surface

shan·ty \\'shant-ē\\ *n, pl* **shanties** : a small roughly built shelter or dwelling

¹shape \\'shāp\\ *vb* **shaped; shap·ing** **1** : to form esp. in a particular shape **2** : DESIGN **3** : ADAPT, ADJUST **4** : REGULATE **syn** make, fashion, fabricate, manufacture, frame, mold

²shape *n* **1** : APPEARANCE **2** : surface configuration : FORM **3** : bodily contour apart from the head and face : FIGURE **4** : PHANTOM **5** : CONDITION

shape·less \\'shāp-ləs\\ *adj* **1** : having no definite shape **2** : not shapely — **shape·less·ly** *adv* — **shape·less·ness** *n*

shape·ly \\'shāp-lē\\ *adj* **shape·li·er; -est** : having a pleasing shape — **shape·li·ness** *n*

shard \\'shärd\\ *also* **sherd** \\'shərd\\ *n* : a broken piece : FRAGMENT

¹share \\'sheər\\ *n* **1** : a portion belonging to one person or group **2** : any of the equal interests into which the capital stock of a corporation is divided

²share *vb* **shared; shar·ing** **1** : APPORTION **2** : to use or enjoy with others **3** : PARTICIPATE — **shar·er** *n*

³share *n* : PLOWSHARE

share·crop·per \\-ˌkräp-ər\\ *n* : a farmer who works another's land in return for a share of the crop — **share·crop** *vb*

share·hold·er \\-ˌhōl-dər\\ *n* : STOCKHOLDER

¹shark \\'shärk\\ *n* : any of various active, predaceous, and mostly large marine fishes with skeletons of cartilage

²shark *n* : a greedy crafty person

shark·skin \\-ˌskin\\ *n* **1** : the hide of a shark or leather made from it **2** : a fabric (as of cotton or rayon) woven from strands of many fine threads and having a sleek appearance and silky feel

¹sharp \\'shärp\\ *adj* **1** : having a thin cutting edge or fine point : not dull or blunt **2** : COLD, NIPPING ⟨a ∼ wind⟩ **3** : keen in intellect, perception, or attention **4** : BRISK, ENERGETIC **5** : IRRITABLE ⟨a ∼ temper⟩ **6** : causing intense distress ⟨a ∼ pain⟩ **7** : HARSH, CUTTING ⟨∼ words⟩ **8** : affecting the senses as if cutting or piercing ⟨a ∼ sound⟩ ⟨a ∼ smell⟩ **9** : not smooth or rounded ⟨∼ features⟩ **10** : involving an abrupt or extreme change ⟨a ∼

turn⟩ **11** : CLEAR, DISTINCT ⟨mountains in ~ relief⟩; *also* : easy to perceive ⟨a ~ contrast⟩ **12** : higher than the true pitch; *also* : raised by a half step **13** : STYLISH ⟨a ~ dresser⟩ **syn** keen, acute, quick-witted, penetrative — **sharp·ly** *adv* — **sharp·ness** *n*

²sharp *adv* **1** : in a sharp manner **2** : EXACTLY, PRECISELY ⟨left at 8 ~⟩

³sharp *n* **1** : a sharp edge or point **2** : a character ♯ indicating a note a half step higher than the note named **3** : SHARPER

⁴sharp *vb* : to raise in pitch by a half step

sharp·en \'shär-pən\ *vb* **sharp·ened; sharp·en·ing** \'shärp-(ə-)niŋ\ : to make or become sharp — **sharp·en·er** \'shärp-(ə-)nər\ *n*

sharp·er \'shär-pər\ *n* : SWINDLER; *esp* : a cheating gambler

sharp·ie *or* **sharpy** \'shär-pē\ *n, pl* **sharp·ies 1** : SHARPER **2** : a person who is exceptionally keen or alert

sharp·shoot·er \'shärp-,shüt-ər\ *n* : a good marksman — **sharp·shoot·ing** \-iŋ\ *n*

shat·ter \'shat-ər\ *vb* : to dash or burst into fragments — **shat·ter·proof** \,shat-ər-'prüf\ *adj*

¹shave \'shāv\ *vb* **shaved; shaved** *or* **shav·en** \'shā-vən\; **shav·ing 1** : to slice in thin pieces **2** : to make bare or smooth by cutting the hair from **3** : to cut or pare off by the sliding movement of a razor **4** : to skim along or near the surface of

²shave *n* **1** : any of various tools for cutting thin slices **2** : an act or process of shaving

shav·er \'shā-vər\ *n* : an electric-powered razor

shaves pl of SHAFT

shav·ing \'shā-viŋ\ *n* **1** : the act of one that shaves **2** : something shaved off

shawl \'shȯl\ *n* : a square or oblong piece of fabric used esp. by women as a loose covering for the head or shoulders

Shaw·nee \shȯ-'nē, shä-\ *n, pl* **Shawnee** *or* **Shawnees** : a member of an American Indian people orig. of the central Ohio valley; *also* : their language

she \(')shē\ *pron* : that female one ⟨who is ~⟩; *also* : that one regarded as feminine ⟨~'s a fine ship⟩

sheaf \'shēf\ *n, pl* **sheaves** \'shēvz\ **1** : a bundle of stalks and ears of grain **2** : a group of things bound together

¹shear \'shiər\ *vb* **sheared; sheared** *or* **shorn** \'shȯrn\; **shear·ing 1** : to cut the hair or wool from : CLIP, TRIM **2** : to deprive by or as if by cutting **3** : to cut or break sharply

²shear *n* **1** : any of various cutting tools that consist of two blades fastened together so that the edges slide one by the other — usu. used in pl. **2** *chiefly Brit* : the act, an instance, or the result of shearing **3** : an action or stress caused by applied forces that causes two parts of a body to slide on each other

sheath \'shēth\ *n, pl* **sheaths** \'shēthz, 'shēths\ **1** : a case for a blade (as of a knife); *also* : an anatomical covering suggesting such a case **2** : a close-fitting dress usu. worn without a belt

sheathe \'shēth\ *also* **sheath** \'shēth\ *vb* **sheathed; sheath·ing 1** : to put into a sheath **2** : to cover with something that guards or protects

sheath·ing \'shē-thiŋ, -thiŋ\ *n* : material used to sheathe something; *esp* : the first covering of boards or of waterproof material on the outside wall of a frame house or on a timber roof

sheave \'shiv, 'shēv\ *n* : a grooved wheel or pulley (as on a pulley block)

she·bang \shi-'baŋ\ *n* : CONTRIVANCE, AFFAIR, CONCERN ⟨blew up the whole ~⟩

¹shed \'shed\ *vb* **shed; shed·ding 1** : to cause to flow from a cut or wound ⟨~ blood⟩ **2** : to pour down in drops ⟨~ tears⟩ **3** : to give out (as light) : DIFFUSE **4** : to throw off (as a natural covering) : DISCARD

²shed *n* : a slight structure built for shelter or storage

sheen \'shēn\ *n* : a subdued luster

sheep \'shēp\ *n, pl* **sheep 1** : any of a genus of cud-chewing mammals that are stockier than the related goats and lack a beard in the male; *esp* : one raised for meat or for its wool or skin **2** : a timid or defenseless person **3** : SHEEPSKIN

sheep dog *n* : a dog used to tend, drive, or guard sheep

sheep·fold \'shēp-,fōld\ *n* : a pen or shelter for sheep

sheep·herd·er \'shēp-,hərd-ər\ *n* : a

worker in charge of sheep esp. on open range — **sheep·herd·ing** \-iŋ\ *n*

sheep·ish \'shē-pish\ *adj* : BASHFUL, TIMID; *esp* : embarrassed by consciousness of a fault — **sheep·ish·ly** *adv*

sheep·skin \'shēp-ˌskin\ *n* **1** : the hide of a sheep or leather prepared from it; *also* : PARCHMENT **2** : DIPLOMA

¹sheer \'shiər\ *adj* **1** : very thin or transparent **2** : UNQUALIFIED ⟨∼ folly⟩ **3** : very steep **syn** pure, simple, absolute, unadulterated, unmitigated — **sheer** *adv*

²sheer *vb* : to turn from a course

¹sheet \'shēt\ *n* **1** : a broad piece of plain cloth (as for a bed) **2** : a single piece of paper **3** : a broad flat surface ⟨a ∼ of water⟩ **4** : something broad and long and relatively thin

²sheet *n* **1** : a rope that regulates the angle at which a sail is set to catch the wind **2** *pl* : spaces at either end of an open boat

sheet·ing \'shēt-iŋ\ *n* : material in the form of sheets or suitable for forming into sheets

sheikh *or* **sheik** \'shēk, 'shāk\ *n* : an Arab chief — **sheikh·dom** *or* **sheik·dom** \-dəm\ *n*

shek·el \'shek-əl\ *n* — see MONEY table

shelf \'shelf\ *n, pl* **shelves** \'shelvz\ **1** : a thin flat usu. long and narrow structure fastened horizontally (as on a wall) above the floor to hold things **2** : something (as a sandbar) that suggests a shelf

shelf life *n* : the period of storage time during which a material will remain useful

¹shell \'shel\ *n* **1** : a hard or tough outer covering of an animal (as a beetle, turtle, or mollusk) or of an egg or a seed or fruit (as a nut); *also* : something that resembles a shell ⟨a pastry ∼⟩ **2** : a light narrow racing boat propelled by oarsmen **3** : a case holding an explosive and designed to be fired from a cannon; *also* : a case holding the charge of powder and shot or bullet for small arms **4** : a plain usu. sleeveless blouse or sweater — **shelled** \'sheld\ *adj* — **shelly** \'shel-ē\ *adj*

²shell *vb* **1** : to remove from a shell or husk **2** : BOMBARD — **shell·er** *n*

¹shel·lac \shə-'lak\ *n* **1** : a purified lac

used esp. in varnishes **2** : lac dissolved in alcohol and used as a varnish

²shellac *vb* **shel·lacked; shel·lack·ing 1** : to coat or treat with shellac **2** : to defeat decisively

shel·lack·ing \shə-'lak-iŋ\ *n* : a sound drubbing

shell bean *n* : a bean grown esp. for its edible seeds; *also* : its edible seed

shell·fish \-ˌfish\ *n* : a water animal (as an oyster or lobster) with a shell

shell out *vb* : PAY

shell shock *n* : any of various nervous disorders appearing in soldiers exposed to modern warfare

¹shel·ter \'shel-tər\ *n* : something that gives protection : REFUGE

²shelter *vb* **shel·tered; shel·ter·ing** \-t(ə-)riŋ\ : to give protection or refuge to **syn** harbor, lodge, house

shelve \'shelv\ *vb* **shelved; shelv·ing 1** : to slope gradually **2** : to store on shelves **3** : to dismiss from service or use **4** : to put aside : DEFER ⟨∼ a proposal⟩

shelv·ing \'shel-viŋ\ *n* : material for shelves

she·nan·i·gan \shə-'nan-i-gən\ *n* **1** : an underhand trick **2** : questionable conduct — usu. used in pl. **3** : high-spirited or michievous activity — usu. used in pl.

¹shep·herd \'shep-ərd\ *n* : one who tends sheep

²shepherd *vb* : to tend as or in the manner of a shepherd

shep·herd·ess \'shep-ərd-əs\ *n* : a woman who tends sheep

sher·bet \'shər-bət\ *n* [Turk *serbet,* fr. Per *sharbat,* fr. Ar *sharbah* drink] **1** : a drink of sweetened diluted fruit juice **2** *or* **sher·bert** \-bərt\ : a frozen dessert of fruit juices, sugar, milk or water, and egg whites or gelatin

sherd var of SHARD

sher·iff \'sher-əf\ *n* [ME *shirreve,* fr. OE *scīrgerēfa,* lit., shire reeve (local official)] : a county officer charged with the execution of the law and the preservation of order

sher·ry \'sher-ē\ *n, pl* **sherries** [alter. of earlier *sherris* (taken as pl.), fr. *Xeres* (now *Jerez*), Spain] : a fortified wine with a nutty flavor

Shet·land pony \ˌshet-lən(d)-\ *n* : any of

a breed of small stocky shaggy hardy ponies

shew \\'shō\ *Brit* var of SHOW

shi·at·su *also* **shi·at·zu** \shē-'ät-sü\ *n* [short for Jp *Shiatsuryōhō*] : a finger massage of those bodily areas used in acupuncture

shib·bo·leth \\'shib-ə-ləth\ *n* [Heb *shibbōleth* stream; fr. the use of this word as a test to distinguish the men of Gilead from members of the tribe of Ephraim, who pronounced it *sibbōleth* (Judges 12:5, 6)] **1** : a pet phrase **2** : language that is a criterion for distinguishing members of a group

shied past and past part of SHY

¹shield \\'shēld\ *n* **1** : a broad piece of defensive armor carried on the arm **2** : something that protects or hides

²shield *vb* : to protect or hide with a shield **syn** protect, guard, safeguard

shier comparative of SHY

shiest superlative of SHY

¹shift \\'shift\ *vb* **1** : EXCHANGE, REPLACE **2** : to change place, position, or direction : MOVE; *also* : to change the arrangement of gears transmitting power in an automobile **3** : GET BY, MANAGE **syn** remove, ship, transfer

²shift *n* **1** : SCHEME, TRICK **2** : a woman's slip or loose-fitting dress **3** : a group working together alternating with other groups **4** : TRANSFER **5** : GEARSHIFT

shift·less \\'shif(t)-ləs\ *adj* : LAZY, INEFFICIENT — **shift·less·ness** *n*

shifty \\'shif-tē\ *adj* **shift·i·er; -est 1** : TRICKY; *also* : ELUSIVE **2** : indicative of a tricky nature ⟨∼ eyes⟩

Shih Tzu \\'shēd-'zü\ *n* : a small short-legged dog of an ancient Chinese breed that has a short muzzle and a long dense coat

shi·lingi \shil-'iŋ-ē\ *n, pl* **shi·lingi** : the shilling of Tanzania

shill \\'shil\ *n* : one who acts as a decoy (as for a cheater) — **shill** *vb*

shil·le·lagh *also* **shil·la·lah** \shə-'lā-lē\ *n* [*Shillelagh*, town in Ireland famed for its oaks] : CUDGEL, CLUB

shil·ling \\'shil-iŋ\ *n* — see MONEY TABLE

shilly–shally \\'shil-ē-ˌshal-ē\ *vb* **shilly–shall·ied; shilly–shally·ing 1** : to show hesitation or lack of decisiveness **2** : to waste time

shim \\'shim\ *n* : a thin often tapered piece of wood, metal, or stone used (as in leveling something) to fill in

shim·mer \\'shim-ər\ *vb* **shim·mered; shim·mer·ing** \-(ə-)riŋ\ : to shine waveringly or tremulously : GLIMMER **syn** flash, gleam, glint, sparkle, glitter — **shimmer** *n* — **shim·mery** *adj*

shim·my \\'shim-ē\ *n, pl* **shimmies** : an abnormal vibration esp. in the front wheels of a motor vehicle — **shimmy** *vb*

¹shin \\'shin\ *n* : the front part of the leg below the knee

²shin *vb* **shinned; shin·ning** : to climb (as a pole) by gripping alternately with arms or hands and legs

shin·bone \\'shin-'bōn, -ˌbōn\ *n* : TIBIA

¹shine \\'shīn\ *vb* **shone** \\'shōn\ *or* **shined; shin·ing 1** : to give light **2** : GLEAM, GLITTER **3** : to be eminent **4** : to cause to shed light **5** : POLISH

²shine *n* **1** : BRIGHTNESS, RADIANCE **2** : LUSTER, BRILLIANCE **3** : SUNSHINE

shin·er \\'shī-nər\ *n* **1** : a small silvery fish; *esp* : any of numerous small freshwater American fishes related to the carp **2** : a bruised eye

¹shin·gle \\'shiŋ-gəl\ *n* **1** : a small thin piece of building material (as wood or an asbestos composition) used in overlapping rows for covering a roof or outside wall **2** : a small sign

²shingle *vb* **shin·gled; shin·gling** \-g(ə-)liŋ\ : to cover with shingles

³shingle *n* : a beach strewn with gravel; *also* : coarse gravel (as on a beach)

shin·gles \\'shiŋ-gəlz\ *n pl* : acute inflammation of the spinal and cranial nerves caused by the chicken pox virus and associated with eruptions and pain along the course of the affected nerves

shin·ny \\'shin-ē\ *vb* **shin·nied; shin·ny·ing** : SHIN

Shin·to \\'shin-ˌtō\ *n* : the indigenous religion of Japan consisting esp. in reverence of the spirits of natural forces and imperial ancestors — **Shin·to·ism** *n* — **Shin·to·ist** *n or adj*

shiny \\'shī-nē\ *adj* **shin·i·er; -est** : BRIGHT, RADIANT; *also* : POLISHED

¹ship \\'ship\ *n* **1** : a large oceangoing boat **2** : a ship's officers and crew **3** : AIRSHIP, AIRCRAFT, SPACECRAFT

²ship *vb* **shipped; ship·ping 1** : to put or receive on board a ship for transportation **2** : to have transported by a carrier **3** : to take or draw into a boat ⟨~ oars⟩ ⟨~ water⟩ **4** : to engage to serve on a ship — **ship・per** *n*

-ship \ˌship\ *n suffix* **1** : state : condition : quality ⟨friend*ship*⟩ **2** : office : dignity : profession ⟨lord*ship*⟩ ⟨clerk*ship*⟩ **3** : art : skill ⟨horseman*ship*⟩ **4** : something showing, exhibiting, or embodying a quality or state ⟨town*ship*⟩ **5** : one entitled to a (specified) rank, title, or appellation ⟨his Lord*ship*⟩ **6** : the body of persons engaged in a specified activity ⟨reader*ship*⟩

ship・board \ˈship-ˌbōrd\ *n* : SHIP

ship・build・er \ˈship-ˌbil-dər\ *n* : one who designs or builds ships

ship・fit・ter \ˈship-ˌfit-ər\ *n* **1** : one who constructs ships **2** : a naval enlisted man who works as a plumber

ship・mate \-ˌmāt\ *n* : a fellow sailor

ship・ment \-mənt\ *n* : the process of shipping; *also* : the goods shipped

ship・ping \ˈship-iŋ\ *n* **1** : SHIPS; *esp* : ships in one port or belonging to one country **2** : transportation of goods

ship・shape \ˈship-ˈshāp\ *adj* : TRIM, TIDY

ship・worm \-ˌwərm\ *n* : any of various wormlike marine clams that burrow in wood and damage wooden ships and wharves

¹ship・wreck \-ˌrek\ *n* **1** : a wrecked ship **2** : destruction or loss of a ship **3** : total loss or failure : RUIN

²shipwreck *vb* : to cause or meet disaster at sea through destruction or foundering

ship・wright \ˈship-ˌrīt\ *n* : a carpenter skilled in ship construction and repair

ship・yard \-ˌyärd\ *n* : a place where ships are built or repaired

shire \ˈshī(ə)r, *in place-name compounds* ˌshiər, shər\ *n* : a county in Great Britain

shirk \ˈshərk\ *vb* : to avoid performing (duty or work) — **shirk・er** *n*

shirr \ˈshər\ *vb* **1** : to make shirring in **2** : to bake (eggs removed from the shell) until set

shirr・ing \ˈshər-iŋ\ *n* : a decorative gathering in cloth made by drawing up parallel lines of stitches

shirt \ˈshərt\ *n* **1** : a loose cloth garment usu. having a collar, sleeves, a front opening, and a tail long enough

to be tucked inside trousers or a skirt **2** : UNDERSHIRT — **shirt・less** *adj*

shirt・ing \-iŋ\ *n* : cloth suitable for making shirts

shish ke・bab \ˈshish-kə-ˌbäb\ *n* : kabob cooked on skewers

shiv \ˈshiv\ *n, slang* : KNIFE

¹shiv・er \ˈshiv-ər\ *vb* **shiv・ered; shiv・er・ing** \-(ə-)riŋ\ : TREMBLE, QUIVER **syn** shudder, quaver, shake, quake

²shiver *n* : an instance of shivering — **shiv・ery** *adj*

¹shoal \ˈshōl\ *n* **1** : a shallow place in a sea, lake, or river **2** : a sandbank or bar creating a shallow

²shoal *n* : a large group (as of fish)

shoat \ˈshōt\ *n* : a weaned young pig

¹shock \ˈshäk\ *n* : a pile of sheaves of grain set up in the field

²shock *n* [MF *choc*, fr. *choquer* to strike against] **1** : a sharp impact or violent shake or jar **2** : a sudden violent mental or emotional disturbance **3** : the effect of a charge of electricity passing through the body **4** : a state of bodily collapse caused esp. by crushing wounds, blood loss, or burns **5** : an attack of apoplexy or heart disease **6** : SHOCK ABSORBER — **shock・proof** \-ˈprüf\ *adj*

³shock *vb* **1** : to strike with surprise, horror, or disgust **2** : to subject to the action of an electrical discharge

⁴shock *n* : a thick bushy mass (as of hair)

shock absorber *n* : any of several devices for absorbing the energy of sudden shocks in machinery

shock・er \ˈshäk-ər\ *n* : one that shocks; *esp* : a sensational work of fiction or drama

shock・ing \-iŋ\ *adj* : extremely startling and offensive — **shock・ing・ly** *adv*

shock therapy *n* : the treatment of mental disorder by induction of coma or convulsion through the use of drugs or electricity

¹shod・dy \ˈshäd-ē\ *n* **1** : wool reclaimed from old rags; *also* : a fabric made from it **2** : inferior or imitation material **3** : pretentious vulgarity

²shoddy *adj* **shod・di・er; -est 1** : made of shoddy **2** : cheaply imitative : INFERIOR, SHAM — **shod・di・ly** \ˈshäd-ᵊl-ē\ *adv* — **shod・di・ness** \-ē-nəs\ *n*

¹shoe \ˈshü\ *n* **1** : a covering for the human foot **2** : HORSESHOE **3** : the part of a brake that presses on the wheel **4** : the casing of an automobile tire

²shoe *vb* **shod** \'shäd\ *also* **shoed** \'shüd\; **shoe·ing** \'shü-iŋ\ : to put a shoe or shoes on

shoe·lace \-ˌlās\ *n* : a lace or string for fastening a shoe

shoe·mak·er \-ˌmā-kər\ *n* : one who makes or repairs shoes

shoe·string \'shü-ˌstriŋ\ *n* **1** : SHOELACE **2** : a small sum of money

shone past and past part of SHINE

shook past of SHAKE

shook–up \(ˈ)shůk-ˈəp\ *adj* : nervously upset : AGITATED

¹shoot \'shüt\ *vb* **shot** \'shät\; **shoot·ing 1** : to drive (as an arrow or bullet) forward quickly or forcibly **2** : to hit, kill, or wound with a missile **3** : to cause a missile to be driven forth or forth from ⟨~ a gun⟩ ⟨~ an arrow⟩ **4** : to send forth (as a ray of light) **5** : to thrust forward or out **6** : to pass rapidly along ⟨~ the rapids⟩ **7** : PHOTOGRAPH, FILM **8** : to drive or rush swiftly : DART **9** : to grow by or as if by sending out shoots; *also* : MATURE, DEVELOP — **shoot·er** *n*

²shoot *n* **1** : the aerial part of a plant; *also* : a plant part (as a branch) developed from one bud **2** : an act of shooting (as with a bow or a firearm) **3** : a shooting match

shooting iron *n* : FIREARM

shooting star *n* : METEOR 2

shoot up *vb* : to inject a narcotic into a vein

¹shop \'shäp\ *n* [ME *shoppe*, fr. OE *sceoppa* booth] **1** : a place where things are made or worked on : FACTORY, MILL **2** : a retail store ⟨dress ~⟩

²shop *vb* **shopped; shop·ping** : to visit stores for purchasing or examining goods — **shop·per** *n*

shop·keep·er \'shäp-ˌkē-pər\ *n* : a retail merchant

shop·lift \-ˌlift\ *vb* : to steal goods on display from a store — **shop·lift·er** \-ˌlif-tər\ *n*

shop·worn \-ˌwōrn\ *adj* : soiled or frayed from much handling in a store

¹shore \'shōr\ *n* : land along the edge of a body of water — **shore·less** *adj*

²shore *vb* **shored; shor·ing** : to give support to : BRACE, PROP

³shore *n* : ¹PROP

shore·bird \-ˌbərd\ *n* : any of a large group of birds (as the plovers and sandpipers) mostly found along the seashore

shore patrol *n* : a branch of a navy that exercises guard and police functions

shor·ing \'shōr-iŋ\ *n* : the act of supporting with or as if with a prop

shorn past part of SHEAR

¹short \'shȯrt\ *adj* **1** : not long or tall **2** : not great in distance **3** : brief in time **4** : not coming up to standard or to an expected amount **5** : CURT, ABRUPT **6** : insufficiently supplied **7** : made with shortening : FLAKY **8** : consisting of or relating to a sale of securities or commodities that the seller does not possess or has not contracted for at the time of the sale ⟨~ sale⟩ — **short·ness** *n*

²short *adv* **1** : ABRUPTLY, CURTLY **2** : at some point before a goal aimed at

³short *n* **1** : something shorter than normal or standard **2** *pl* : drawers or trousers of less than knee length **3** : SHORT CIRCUIT

⁴short *vb* : SHORT-CIRCUIT

short·age \'shȯrt-ij\ *n* : LACK, DEFICIT

short·cake \'shȯrt-ˌkāk\ *n* : a dessert consisting of short biscuit spread with sweetened fruit

short·change \-ˈchānj\ *vb* : to cheat esp. by giving less than the correct amount of change

short circuit *n* : a connection made between points in an electric circuit between which current does not normally flow — **short–circuit** *vb*

short·com·ing \'shȯrt-ˌkəm-iŋ\ *n* : FAILING, DEFECT

short·cut \-ˌkət\ *n* **1** : a route more direct than that usu. taken **2** : a quicker way of doing something

short·en \'shȯrt-ᵊn\ *vb* **short·ened, short·en·ing** \'shȯrt-(ə-)niŋ\ : to make or become short **syn** curtail, abbreviate, abridge, retrench

short·en·ing \'shȯrt-(ə-)niŋ\ *n* : a substance (as lard or butter) that makes pastry tender and flaky

short·hand \'shȯrt-ˌhand\ *n* : a method of writing rapidly by using symbols and abbreviations for letters, words, or phrases : STENOGRAPHY

short·hand·ed \-ˈhan-dəd\ *adj* : short of the needed number of people

short·horn \-ˌhȯrn\ *n, often cap* : any of a breed of mostly red cattle of English origin

short hundredweight *n* — see WEIGHT table

short–lived \ˈshȯrt-ˈlīvd, -ˌlivd\ *adj* : of short life or duration

short·ly \ˈshȯrt-lē\ *adv* **1** : in a few words **2** : in a short time : SOON

short order *n* : an order for food that can be quickly cooked

short shrift *n* **1** : a brief respite from death **2** : little consideration

short·sight·ed \ˈshȯrt-ˈsīt-əd\ *adj* **1** : NEARSIGHTED **2** : lacking foresight — **short·sight·ed·ness** *n*

short·stop \-ˌstäp\ *n* : a baseball player defending the area between second and third base

short story *n* : a short invented prose narrative usu. dealing with a few characters and aiming at unity of effect

short–tem·pered \ˈshȯrt-ˈtem-pərd\ *adj* : having a quick temper

short–term \-ˈtərm\ *adj* **1** : occurring over or involving a relatively short period of time **2** : of or relating to a financial transaction based on a term usu. of less than a year

short ton *n* — see WEIGHT table

short·wave \ˈshȯrt-ˈwāv\ *n* : a radio wave with a wavelength between 10 and 100 meters

Sho·sho·ne *or* **Sho·sho·ni** \shə-ˈshō-nē\ *n, pl* **Shoshones** *or* **Shoshoni** : a member of an American Indian people orig. ranging through California, Colorado, Idaho, Nevada, Utah, and Wyoming

¹shot \ˈshät\ *n* **1** : an act of shooting **2** : a stroke or throw in some games **3** : something that is shot : MISSILE, PROJECTILE; *esp* : small pellets forming a charge for a shotgun **4** : a metal sphere that is thrown for distance in the shot put **5** : RANGE, REACH **6** : MARKSMAN **7** : a single photographic exposure **8** : a single sequence of a motion picture or a television program made by one camera **9** : an injection (as of medicine) into the body **10** : a portion (as of liquor or medicine) taken at one time

²shot past and past part of SHOOT

shot·gun \ˈshät-ˈgən\ *n* : a gun with a smooth bore used to fire small shot at short range

shot put *n* : a field event consisting in putting the shot for distance

should \shəd, (ˈ)shu̇d\ *past of* SHALL — used as an auxiliary to express condition, obligation or propriety, probability, or futurity from a point of view in the past

¹shoul·der \ˈshōl-dər\ *n* **1** : the part of the body of a person or animal where the arm or foreleg joins the body **2** : a projecting part resembling a human shoulder

²shoulder *vb* **shoul·dered; shoul·der·ing** \-d(ə-)riŋ\ **1** : to push or thrust with the shoulder **2** : to take upon the shoulder **3** : to take the responsibility of

shoulder belt *n* : an automobile safety belt worn across the torso and over the shoulder

shoulder blade *n* : the flat triangular bone at the back of the shoulder

shout \ˈshau̇t\ *vb* : to utter a sudden loud cry — **shout** *n*

shove \ˈshəv\ *vb* **shoved; shov·ing** : to push along, aside, or away — **shove** *n*

¹shov·el \ˈshəv-əl\ *n* **1** : a broad long-handled scoop used to lift and throw loose material **2** : the amount of something held by a shovel

²shovel *vb* **-eled** *or* **-elled; -el·ing** *or* **-el·ling** \-(ə-)liŋ\ **1** : to take up and throw with a shovel **2** : to dig or clean out with a shovel

¹show \ˈshō\ *vb* **showed** \ˈshōd\; **shown** \ˈshōn\ *or* **showed; show·ing** [ME *shewen, showen,* fr. OE *scēawian* to look, look at, see] **1** : to cause or permit to be seen : EXHIBIT ⟨∼ anger⟩ **2** : CONFER, BESTOW ⟨∼ mercy⟩ **3** : REVEAL, DISCLOSE ⟨∼ed courage in battle⟩ **4** : INSTRUCT ⟨∼ed me how to do it⟩ **5** : PROVE ⟨∼s he was guilty⟩ **6** : APPEAR **7** : to be noticeable **8** : to be third in a horse race

²show *n* **1** : a demonstrative display **2** : outward appearance ⟨a ∼ of resistance⟩ **3** : SPECTACLE **4** : a theatrical presentation **5** : a radio or television program **6** : third place in a horse race

¹show·case \ˈshō-ˌkās\ *n* : a cabinet for displaying items (as in a store)

²showcase *vb* **show·cased; show·cas·ing** : EXHIBIT

show·down \'shō-ˌdau̇n\ *n* : the final settlement of a contested issue; *also* : the test of strength by which a contested issue is resolved

¹show·er \'shau̇(-ə)r\ *n* **1** : a brief fall of rain **2** : a bath in which water is showered on the person **3** : a party given by friends who bring gifts — **show·ery** *adj*

²shower *vb* **1** : to fall in a shower **2** : to bathe in a shower

show·man \'shō-mən\ *n* : one having a gift for dramatization and visual effectiveness — **show·man·ship** *n*

show-off \'shō-ˌȯf\ *n* : one that seeks to attract attention by conspicuous behavior

show off \(ˈ)shō-ˈȯf\ *vb* **1** : to display proudly **2** : to act as a show-off

show·piece \'shō-ˌpēs\ *n* : an outstanding example used for exhibition

show·place \-ˌplās\ *n* : an estate or building that is a showpiece

show up *vb* : ARRIVE

showy \'shō-ē\ *adj* **show·i·er; -est** : superficially impressive or striking — **show·i·ly** \'shō-ə-lē\ *adv* — **show·i·ness** \-ē-nəs\ *n*

shpt *abbr* shipment

shrap·nel \'shrap-n°l\ *n, pl* **shrapnel** [Henry *Shrapnel* †1842 E artillery officer] **1** : a case filled with shot and having a bursting charge which explodes it in flight **2** : bomb, mine, or shell fragments

¹shred \'shred\ *n* : a narrow strip cut or torn off : a small fragment

²shred *vb* **shred·ded; shred·ding** : to cut or tear into shreds

shrew \'shrü\ *n* **1** : any of numerous very small mammals with velvety fur that are related to the moles **2** : a scolding woman

shrewd \'shrüd\ *adj* : KEEN, ASTUTE — **shrewd·ly** *adv* — **shrewd·ness** *n*

shrew·ish \'shrü-ish\ *adj* : having an irritable disposition : ILL-TEMPERED

shriek \'shrēk\ *n* : a shrill cry : SCREAM, YELL — **shriek** *vb*

shrift \'shrift\ *n, archaic* : the act of shriving

shrike \'shrīk\ *n* : a grayish or brownish bird that often impales its usu. insect prey upon thorns before devouring it

¹shrill \'shril\ *vb* : to make a high-pitched piercing sound

²shrill *adj* : high-pitched : PIERCING ⟨∼ whistle⟩ — **shril·ly** \'shril-lē\ *adv*

shrimp \'shrimp\ *n, pl* **shrimps** *or* **shrimp 1** : any of various small marine crustaceans related to the lobsters **2** : a small or puny person

shrine \'shrīn\ *n* [ME, receptacle for the relics of a saint, fr. OE *scrīn*, fr. L *scrinium* case, chest] **1** : the tomb of a saint; *also* : a place where devotion is paid to a saint or deity **2** : a place or object hallowed by its associations

¹shrink \'shriŋk\ *vb* **shrank** \'shraŋk\ *also* **shrunk** \'shrəŋk\; **shrunk** *or* **shrunk·en** \'shrəŋ-kən\ **1** : to draw back or away **2** : to become smaller or more compact **3** : to lessen in value **syn** contract, constrict, compress, condense — **shrink·able** *adj*

²shrink *n* : PSYCHIATRIST

shrink·age \'shriŋ-kij\ *n* **1** : the act of shrinking **2** : a decrease in value **3** : the amount by which something contracts or lessens in extent

shrive \'shrīv\ *vb* **shrived** *or* **shrove** \'shrōv\; **shriv·en** \'shriv-ən\ *or* **shrived** : to minister the sacrament of penance to

shriv·el \'shriv-əl\ *vb* **-eled** *or* **-elled; -el·ing** *or* **-el·ling** \-(ə-)liŋ\ : to shrink and draw together into wrinkles : wither up

¹shroud \'shrau̇d\ *n* **1** : something that covers or screens **2** : a cloth placed over a dead body **3** : one of the ropes leading usu. in pairs from the masthead of a ship to the side to support the mast

²shroud *vb* : to veil or screen from view

shrub \'shrəb\ *n* : a low usu. several-stemmed woody plant — **shrub·by** *adj*

shrub·bery \'shrəb-(ə-)rē\ *n, pl* **-ber·ies** : a planting or growth of shrubs

shrug \'shrəg\ *vb* **shrugged; shrug·ging** : to hunch (the shoulders) up to express doubt, indifference, or dislike — **shrug** *n*

shrug off *vb* **1** : to brush aside : MINIMIZE **2** : to shake off **3** : to remove (a garment) by wriggling out

sht *abbr* sheet

shtg *abbr* shortage

¹shuck \'shək\ *n* : SHELL, HUSK

²shuck *vb* : to strip of shucks

shud·der \'shəd-ər\ *vb* **shud·dered;**

shud·der·ing \-(ə-)riŋ\ : TREMBLE, QUAKE — **shudder** n

shuf·fle \'shəf-əl\ vb **shuf·fled; shuf·fling** \-(ə-)liŋ\ 1 : to mix in a disorderly mass 2 : to rearrange the order of (cards in a pack) by mixing two parts of the pack together 3 : to move with a sliding or dragging gait 4 : to shift from place to place 5 : to dance in a slow lagging manner — **shuffle** n

shuf·fle·board \'shəf-əl-ˌbōrd\ n : a game in which players use long-handled cues to shove wooden disks into scoring areas marked on a smooth surface

shun \'shən\ vb **shunned; shun·ning** : to avoid deliberately or habitually **syn** evade, elude, escape, duck

¹**shunt** \'shənt\ vb [ME *shunten* to flinch] : to turn off to one side; *esp* : to switch (a train) from one track to another

²**shunt** n 1 : a method or device for turning or thrusting aside 2 : a conductor joining two points in an electrical circuit forming a parallel path through which a portion of the current may pass

shut \'shət\ vb **shut; shut·ting** 1 : CLOSE 2 : to forbid entrance into 3 : to lock up 4 : to fold together ⟨∼ a penknife⟩ 5 : to cease or suspend activity ⟨∼ down an assembly line⟩

shut·down \-ˌdaùn\ n : a temporary cessation of activity (as in a factory)

shut–in \'shət-ˌin\ n : an invalid confined to his home, room, or bed

shut·out \'shət-ˌaùt\ n : a game or contest in which one side fails to score

shut out \ˌshət-'aùt\ vb 1 : EXCLUDE 2 : to prevent (an opponent) from scoring in a game or contest

shut·ter \'shət-ər\ n 1 : a movable cover for a door or window for privacy or to keep out light or air : BLIND 2 : the part of a camera that opens and closes to expose the film

shut·ter·bug \'shət-ər-ˌbəg\ n : a photography enthusiast

¹**shut·tle** \'shət-ᵊl\ n 1 : an instrument used in weaving for passing the horizontal threads between the vertical threads 2 : a vehicle traveling back and forth over a short route ⟨a ∼ bus⟩ 3 : SPACE SHUTTLE

²**shuttle** vb **shut·tled; shut·tling** \'shət-(ᵊ-)liŋ\ : to move back and forth rapidly or frequently

shut·tle·cock \'shət-ᵊl-ˌkäk\ n : a light feathered object (as of cork or plastic) used in badminton

shut up vb : to cease or cause to cease talking

¹**shy** \'shī\ adj **shi·er** or **shy·er** \'shī(-ə)r\; **shi·est** or **shy·est** \'shī-əst\ 1 : easily frightened : TIMID 2 : WARY 3 : BASHFUL 4 : DEFICIENT, LACKING — **shy·ly** adv — **shy·ness** n

²**shy** vb **shied; shy·ing** 1 : to shrink back : RECOIL 2 : to start suddenly aside through fright ⟨the horse *shied*⟩

shy·ster \'shī-stər\ n : an unscrupulous lawyer or politician

Si symbol silicon

Si·a·mese \ˌsī-ə-'mēz, -'mēs\ n, pl **Siamese** : THAI — **Siamese** adj

Siamese twin n [fr. Chang †1874 and Eng †1874 twins born in Siam with bodies united] : one of a pair of twins with bodies joined together at birth

¹**sib·i·lant** \'sib-ə-lənt\ adj : having, containing, or producing the sound of or a sound resembling that of the *s* or the *sh* in *sash*

²**sibilant** n : a sibilant speech sound (as English \s\, \z\, \sh\, \zh\, \ch (= tsh)\, or \j (= dzh)\)

sib·ling \'sib-liŋ\ n : one of two or more offspring of the same parents

sib·yl \'sib-əl\ n, often cap : PROPHETESS — **sib·yl·line** \-ə-ˌlīn, -ˌlēn\ adj

sic \'sik, 'sēk\ adv : intentionally so written — used after a printed word or passage to indicate that it exactly reproduces an original ⟨said he seed [*sic*] it all⟩

sick \'sik\ adj 1 : not in good health : ILL; *also* : of, relating to, or intended for the sick ⟨∼ pay⟩ 2 : NAUSEATED 3 : LANGUISHING, PINING 4 : DISGUSTED 5 : MACABRE, SADISTIC ⟨∼ jokes⟩ — **sick·ly** adj

sick·bed \'sik-ˌbed\ n : a bed on which one lies sick

sick·en \'sik-ən\ vb **sick·ened; sick·en·ing** \-(ə-)niŋ\ : to make or become sick — **sick·en·ing·ly** adv

sick·le \'sik-əl\ n : a cutting tool consisting of a curved metal blade with a short handle

sickle–cell anemia n : an inherited anemia in which red blood cells tend to become crescent-shaped and cannot carry oxygen properly and which occurs esp. in blacks

sick·ness \\'sik-nəs\\ *n* **1** : ill health; *also* : a specific disease **2** : NAUSEA

side \\'sīd\\ *n* **1** : a border of an object; *esp* : one of the longer borders as contrasted with an end **2** : an outer surface of an object **3** : the right or left part of the trunk of a body **4** : a place away from a central point or line **5** : a position regarded as opposite to another **6** : a body of contestants — **side** *adj*

side·arm \\-,ärm\\ *adj* : made with a sideways sweep of the arm — **sidearm** *adv*

side arm *n* : a weapon worn at the side or in the belt

side·bar \\'sīd-,bär\\ *n* : a short news story accompanying a major story and presenting related topics or additional details

side·board \\-,bōrd\\ *n* : a piece of dining-room furniture for holding articles of table service

side·burns \\-,bərnz\\ *n pl* : whiskers on the side of the face in front of the ears

side·car \\-,kär\\ *n* : a one-wheeled passenger car attached to the side of a motorcycle

side effect *n* : a secondary and usu. adverse effect (as of a drug)

side·kick \\'sīd-,kik\\ *n* : PAL, PARTNER

¹side·long \\'sīd-,lȯŋ\\ *adv* : in the direction of or along the side : OBLIQUELY

²side·long \\,sīd-,lȯŋ\\ *adj* : directed to one side : SLANTING ⟨∼ look⟩

side·man \\'sīd-,man\\ *n* : a member of a jazz or swing orchestra

side·piece \\-,pēs\\ *n* : a piece forming or contained in the side of something

si·de·re·al \\sī-'dir-ē-əl, sə-\\ *adj* **1** : of or relating to the stars **2** : measured by the apparent motion of the stars

sid·er·ite \\'sid-ə-,rīt\\ *n* : a native carbonate of iron that is a valuable iron ore

side·show \\'sīd-,shō\\ *n* **1** : a minor show offered in addition to a main exhibition (as of a circus) **2** : an incidental diversion

side·step \\-,step\\ *vb* **1** : to step aside **2** : AVOID, EVADE

side·stroke \\-,strōk\\ *n* : a swimming stroke which is executed on the side and in which the arms are swept backward and downward and the legs do a scissors kick

side·swipe \\-,swīp\\ *vb* : to strike with a glancing blow along the side — **sideswipe** *n*

¹side·track \\-,trak\\ *n* : SIDING 1

²sidetrack *vb* **1** : to switch from a main railroad line to a siding **2** : to turn aside from a purpose

side·walk \\'sīd-,wȯk\\ *n* : a paved walk at the side of a road or street

side·wall \\-,wȯl\\ *n* **1** : a wall forming the side of something **2** : the side of an automobile tire

side·ways \\-,wāz\\ *adv or adj* **1** : from the side **2** : with one side to the front **3** : to, toward, or at one side

side·wind·er \\-,wīn-dər\\ *n* : a small pale-colored desert rattlesnake of the southwestern U.S.

sid·ing \\'sīd-iŋ\\ *n* **1** : a short railroad track connected with the main track **2** : material (as boards) covering the outside of frame buildings

si·dle \\'sīd-ᵊl\\ *vb* **si·dled; si·dling** \\'sīd-(ᵊ-)liŋ\\ : to move sideways or side foremost

SIDS *abbr* sudden infant death syndrome

siege \\'sēj\\ *n* [ME *sege,* fr. OF, seat, blockade] **1** : the placing of an army around or before a fortified place to force its surrender **2** : a persistent attack (as of illness)

sie·mens \\'sē-mənz, 'zē-\\ *n* : a unit of conductance equivalent to one ampere per volt

si·er·ra \\sē-'er-ə\\ *n* [Sp, lit., saw, fr. L *serra*] : a range of mountains esp. with jagged peaks

si·es·ta \\sē-'es-tə\\ *n* [Sp, fr. L *sexta (hora)* noon, lit., sixth hour] : a midday rest or nap

sieve \\'siv\\ *n* : a utensil with meshes or holes to separate finer particles from coarser or solids from liquids

sift \\'sift\\ *vb* **1** : to pass through a sieve **2** : to separate with or as if with a sieve **3** : to examine carefully **4** : to scatter by or as if by passing through a sieve — **sift·er** *n*

sig *abbr* **1** signal **2** signature

sigh \\'sī\\ *vb* **1** : to let out a deep audible breath (as in weariness or sorrow) **2** : GRIEVE, YEARN — **sigh** *n*

¹sight \\'sīt\\ *n* **1** : something seen or

worth seeing **2** : the process or power of seeing; *esp* : the sense of which the eye is the receptor and by which qualities of appearance (as position, shape, and color) are perceived **3** : INSPECTION **4** : a device (as a small bead on a gun barrel) that aids the eye in aiming **5** : VIEW, GLIMPSE **6** : the range of vision — **sight·less** *adj*

²**sight** *vb* **1** : to get sight of **2** : to aim by means of a sight

sight·ed \'sīt-əd\ *adj* : having sight

sight·ly \-lē\ *adj* : pleasing to the sight

sight–see·ing \'sīt-,sē-iŋ\ *adj* : engaged in or used for seeing sights of interest — **sight·seer** \-,sē-ər\ *n*

¹**sign** \'sīn\ *n* **1** : SYMBOL **2** : a gesture expressing a command, wish, or thought **3** : a notice publicly displayed for advertising purposes or for giving direction or warning **4** : OMEN, PORTENT **5** : TRACE, VESTIGE

²**sign** *vb* **1** : to mark with a sign **2** : to represent by a sign **3** : to make a sign or signal **4** : to write one's name on in token of assent or obligation **5** : to assign legally **6** : to use sign language — **sign·er** *n*

¹**sig·nal** \'sig-nᵊl\ *n* **1** : a sign agreed on as the start of some joint action **2** : a sign giving warning or notice of something **3** : the message, sound, or image transmitted in electronic communication (as radio)

²**signal** *vb* **-naled** *or* **-nalled; -nal·ing** *or* **-nal·ling** \-nə-liŋ\ **1** : to communicate by signals **2** : to notify by a signal

³**signal** *adj* **1** : DISTINGUISHED, OUTSTANDING ⟨a ∼ honor⟩ **2** : used in signaling — **sig·nal·ly** \-ē\ *adv*

sig·nal·ize \'sig-nə-,līz\ *vb* **-ized; -iz·ing** : to point out or make conspicuous — **sig·nal·iza·tion** \,sig-nə-lə-'zā-shən\ *n*

sig·nal·man \'sig-nᵊl-mən, -,man\ *n* : one who signals or works with signals

sig·na·to·ry \'sig-nə-,tōr-ē\ *n, pl* **-ries** : a person or government that signs jointly with others — **signatory** *adj*

sig·na·ture \'sig-nə-,chur\ *n* **1** : the name of a person written by himself **2** : the sign placed after the clef to indicate the key or the meter of a piece of music

sign·board \'sīn-,bōrd\ *n* : a board bearing a sign or notice

sig·net \'sig-nət\ *n* : a small intaglio seal (as in a ring)

sig·nif·i·cance \sig-'nif-i-kəns\ *n* **1** : something signified : MEANING **2** : SUGGESTIVENESS **3** : CONSEQUENCE, IMPORTANCE

sig·nif·i·cant \-kənt\ *adj* **1** : having meaning; *esp* : having a hidden or special meaning **2** : having or likely to have considerable influence or effect : IMPORTANT — **sig·nif·i·cant·ly** *adv*

sig·ni·fy \'sig-nə-,fī\ *vb* **-fied; -fy·ing 1** : to show by a sign **2** : MEAN, IMPORT **3** : to have significance — **sig·ni·fi·ca·tion** \,sig-nə-fə-'kā-shən\ *n*

sign in *vb* : to make a record of arrival (as by signing a register)

sign language *n* : a formal system of hand gestures used by the deaf to communicate

sign off *vb* : to announce the end (as of a program or broadcast)

sign of the cross : a gesture of the hand forming a cross (as to invoke divine blessing)

sign on *vb* **1** : ENLIST **2** : to announce the start of broadcasting for the day

sign out *vb* : to indicate departure by signing a register or punching a clock

sign·post \'sīn-,pōst\ *n* : a post bearing a sign

Sikh \'sēk\ *n* : an adherent of a religion of India marked by rejection of caste — **Sikh·ism** *n*

si·lage \'sī-lij\ *n* : chopped fodder stored in a silo to ferment for use as a rich moist animal feed

¹**si·lence** \'sī-ləns\ *n* **1** : the state of being silent **2** : STILLNESS **3** : SECRECY

²**silence** *vb* **si·lenced; si·lenc·ing 1** : to reduce to silence : STILL **2** : to cause to cease hostile firing or criticism

si·lenc·er \'sī-lən-sər\ *n* : a device for muffling the noise of a gunshot

si·lent \'sī-lənt\ *adj* **1** : not speaking : MUTE; *also* : TACITURN **2** : STILL, QUIET **3** : performed or borne without utterance **syn** reticent, reserved, close-mouthed, close — **si·lent·ly** *adv*

¹**sil·hou·ette** \,sil-ə-'wet\ *n* [F] **1** : a representation of the outlines of an object filled in with black or some other uniform color **2** : OUTLINE ⟨∼ of a ship⟩

²**silhouette** *vb* **-ett·ed; -ett·ing** : to represent by a silhouette; *also* : to show against a light background

sil·i·ca \'sil-i-kə\ *n* : a mineral that consists of silicon and oxygen

sil·i·cate \'sil-ə-ˌkāt, 'sil-i-kət\ *n* : a chemical salt that consists of a metal combined with silicon and oxygen

si·li·ceous *or* **si·li·cious** \sə-'lish-əs\ *adj* : of, relating to, or containing silica or a silicate

sil·i·con \'sil-i-kən, 'sil-ə-ˌkän\ *n* : a nonmetallic chemical element that occurs in combination as the most abundant element next to oxygen in the earth's crust and is used esp. in electronics

sil·i·cone \'sil-ə-ˌkōn\ *n* : an organic silicon compound used esp. for lubricants and varnishes

sil·i·co·sis \ˌsil-ə-'kō-səs\ *n* : a lung disease caused by prolonged inhaling of silica dusts

silk \'silk\ *n* **1** : a fine strong lustrous protein fiber produced by insect larvae for their cocoons; *esp* : one from moth larvae (**silk·worms** \-ˌwərmz\) used for cloth **2** : thread or cloth made from silk — **silk·en** \'sil-kən\ *adj* — **silky** *adj*

silk screen *n* : a stencil process in which coloring matter is forced through the meshes of a prepared silk or organdy screen; *also* : a print made by this process — **silk–screen** *vb*

sill \'sil\ *n* **1** : a heavy crosspiece (as of wood or stone) that forms the bottom member of a window frame or a doorway; *also* : a horizontal supporting piece at the base of a structure **2** : a flat mass of igneous rock injected while molten between other rocks

sil·ly \'sil-ē\ *adj* **sil·li·er; -est** [ME *sely, silly* happy, innocent, pitiable, feeble, fr. OE *sælig*] FOOLISH, ABSURD, STUPID — **sil·li·ness** *n*

si·lo \'sī-lō\ *n, pl* **silos** [Sp] : a trench, pit, or tall cylinder in which silage is stored

¹silt \'silt\ *n* **1** : fine earth; *esp* : particles of such soil floating in rivers, ponds, or lakes **2** : a deposit (as by a river) of silt — **silty** *adj*

²silt *vb* : to obstruct or cover with silt — **silt·ation** \sil-'tā-shən\ *n*

Si·lu·ri·an \sī-'lùr-ē-ən\ *adj* : of, relating to, or being the period of the Paleozoic era between the Ordovician and the Devonian — **Silurian** *n*

¹sil·ver \'sil-vər\ *n* **1** : a white ductile metallic chemical element that takes a high polish and is a better conductor of heat and electricity than any other substance **2** : coin made of silver **3** : FLATWARE **4** : a grayish white color — **sil·very** *adj*

²silver *adj* **1** : relating to, made of, or coated with silver **2** : SILVERY

³silver *vb* **sil·vered; sil·ver·ing** \'silv-(ə-)riŋ\ : to coat with or as if with silver — **sil·ver·er** *n*

silver bromide *n* : a light-sensitive compound used esp. in photography

silver chloride *n* : a light-sensitive compound used esp. in photography

sil·ver·fish \'sil-vər-ˌfish\ *n* : a small wingless insect found in houses and sometimes injurious to sized paper and starched clothes

silver iodide *n* : a light-sensitive compound used in photography, rainmaking, and medicine

silver maple *n* : a No. American maple with deeply cut leaves that are green above and silvery white below

silver nitrate *n* : a soluble compound used in photography and as an antiseptic

sil·ver·ware \'sil-vər-ˌwaər\ *n* : FLATWARE

sim·i·an \'sim-ē-ən\ *n* : MONKEY, APE — **simian** *adj*

sim·i·lar \'sim-ə-lər\ *adj* : marked by correspondence or resemblance **syn** alike, akin, comparable, parallel — **sim·i·lar·i·ty** \ˌsim-ə-'lar-ət-ē\ *n* — **sim·i·lar·ly** \'sim-ə-lər-lē\ *adv*

sim·i·le \'sim-ə-(ˌ)lē\ *n* [L, likeness, comparison, fr. neut. of *similis* like, similar] : a figure of speech in which two dissimilar things are compared by the use of *like* or *as* (as in "cheeks like roses")

si·mil·i·tude \sə-'mil-ə-ˌt(y)üd\ *n* : LIKENESS, RESEMBLANCE **syn** similarity, semblance

sim·mer \'sim-ər\ *vb* **sim·mered; sim·mer·ing** \-(ə-)riŋ\ **1** : to stew at or just below the boiling point **2** : to be on the point of bursting out with violence or emotional disturbance — **simmer** *n*

si·mo·nize \'sī-mə-ˌnīz\ *vb* **-nized; -niz·ing** : to polish with or as if with wax

si·mo·ny \'sī-mə-nē, 'sim-ə-\ *n* [LL *simonia*, fr. *Simon* Magus 1st cent. A.D.

sorcerer of Samaria (Acts 8:9–24)] : the buying or selling of a church office

sim·pa·ti·co \sim-'pät-i-ˌkō, -'pat-\ *adj* : CONGENIAL, LIKABLE

sim·per \'sim-pər\ *vb* **sim·pered; sim·per·ing** \-p(ə-)riŋ\ : to smile in a silly manner — **simper** *n*

sim·ple \'sim-pəl\ *adj* **sim·pler** \-p(ə-)lər\; **sim·plest** \-p(ə-)ləst\ [ME, fr. OF, plain, uncomplicated, artless, fr. L *simplus, simplex*, lit., single; L *simplus* fr. *sim-* one + *-plus* multiplied by; L *simplex* fr. *sim-* + *-plex* -fold] **1** : not combined with anything else **2** : not other than : MERE **3** : not complex : PLAIN **4** : ABSOLUTE ⟨land held in fee ∼⟩ **5** : STRAIGHTFORWARD; *also* : ARTLESS **6** : UNADORNED **7** : lacking education, experience, or intelligence **8** : developing from a single ovary ⟨a ∼ fruit⟩ **syn** easy, facile, light, effortless — **sim·ple·ness** *n* — **sim·ply** \-plē\ *adv*

sim·ple·ton \'sim-pəl-tən\ *n* : FOOL

sim·plic·i·ty \sim-'plis-ət-ē\ *n* **1** : lack of complication : CLEARNESS **2** : CANDOR, ARTLESSNESS **3** : plainness in manners or way of life **4** : IGNORANCE, FOOLISHNESS

sim·pli·fy \'sim-plə-ˌfī\ *vb* **-fied; -fy·ing** : to make simple : make less complex : CLARIFY — **sim·pli·fi·ca·tion** \ˌsim-plə-fə-'kā-shən\ *n*

sim·plis·tic \sim-'plis-tik\ *adj* : excessively simple : tending to overlook complexities ⟨a ∼ solution⟩

sim·u·late \'sim-yə-ˌlāt\ *vb* **-lat·ed; -lat·ing** : to create the effect or appearance of : FEIGN — **sim·u·la·tion** \ˌsim-yə-'lā-shən\ *n* — **sim·u·la·tor** \'sim-yə-ˌlāt-ər\ *n*

si·mul·ta·ne·ous \ˌsī-məl-'tā-nē-əs, ˌsim-əl-\ *adj* : occurring or operating at the same time — **si·mul·ta·ne·ous·ly** *adv* — **si·mul·ta·ne·ous·ness** *n*

¹sin \'sin\ *n* **1** : an offense esp. against God **2** : FAULT **3** : a weakened state of human nature in which the self is estranged from God — **sin·less** *adj*

²sin *vb* **sinned; sin·ning** : to commit a sin — **sin·ner** *n*

¹since \(')sins\ *adv* **1** : from a past time until now **2** : backward in time : AGO

²since *prep* **1** : in the period after ⟨changes made ∼ the war⟩ **2** : contin-

uously from ⟨has been here ∼ 1980⟩

³since *conj* **1** : from the time when **2** : seeing that : BECAUSE

sin·cere \sin-'siər\ *adj* **sin·cer·er; sin·cer·est 1** : free from hypocrisy : HONEST **2** : GENUINE, REAL — **sin·cere·ly** *adv* — **sin·cer·i·ty** \-'ser-ət-ē\ *n*

si·ne·cure \'sī-ni-ˌkyùr, 'sin-i-\ *n* : a well-paid job that requires little work

si·ne die \ˌsī-ni-'dī-ˌē, ˌsin-ā-'dē-ˌā\ *adv* [L, without day] : INDEFINITELY

si·ne qua non \ˌsin-i-ˌkwä-'nän, -'nōn\ *n* [LL, without which not] : an indispensable or essential thing

sin·ew \'sin-yü\ *n* **1** : TENDON **2** : physical strength — **sin·ewy** *adj*

sin·ful \'sin-fəl\ *adj* : marked by or full of sin : WICKED — **sin·ful·ly** \-ē\ *adv* — **sin·ful·ness** *n*

¹sing \'siŋ\ *vb* **sang** \'saŋ\ *or* **sung** \'səŋ\; **sung; sing·ing** \'siŋ-iŋ\ **1** : to produce musical tones with the voice; *also* : to utter with musical tones **2** : to produce harmonious sustained sounds ⟨birds ∼*ing*⟩ **3** : CHANT, INTONE **4** : to make a prolonged shrill sound ⟨locusts ∼*ing*⟩ **5** : to write poetry; *also* : to celebrate in song or verse **6** : to give information or evidence — **sing·er** *n*

²sing *abbr* singular

singe \'sinj\ *vb* **singed; singe·ing** \'sin-jiŋ\ : to scorch lightly the outside of; *esp* : to remove the hair or down from (a plucked fowl) with flame

¹sin·gle \'siŋ-gəl\ *adj* **1** : UNMARRIED **2** : being alone : being the only one **3** : having only one feature or part **4** : made for one person or family **syn** sole, unique, lone, solitary, separate, particular — **sin·gle·ness** *n* — **sin·gly** \-glē\ *adv*

²single *vb* **sin·gled; sin·gling** \-g(ə-)liŋ\ **1** : to select (one) from a group **2** : to hit a single

³single *n* **1** : a separate person or thing **2** : a hit in baseball that enables the batter to reach first base **3** *pl* : a tennis match with one player on each side

single bond *n* : a chemical bond in which one pair of electrons is shared by two atoms in a molecule

single–lens reflex *n* : a camera having a single lens that forms an image which is either reflected to the viewfinder or recorded on film

sin·gle·ton \'siŋ-gəl-tən\ *n* : a card that is the only one of its suit orig. held in a hand

sin·gle·tree \-₁trē\ *n* : WHIFFLETREE

sin·gu·lar \'siŋ-gyə-lər\ *adj* **1** : of, relating to, or constituting a word form denoting one person, thing, or instance **2** : of unusual quality **3** : OUTSTANDING, EXCEPTIONAL **4** : ODD, STRANGE — **singular** *n* — **sin·gu·lar·i·ty** \₁siŋ-gyə-'lar-ət-ē\ *n* — **sin·gu·lar·ly** \'siŋ-gyə-lər-lē\ *adv*

sin·is·ter \'sin-əs-tər\ *adj* [ME, fr. L on the left side, inauspicious] **1** : threatening or foreboding evil or disaster **2** : indicative of lurking evil **syn** baleful, malign, malefic, maleficent

¹sink \'siŋk\ *vb* **sank** \'saŋk\ *or* **sunk** \'səŋk\; **sunk; sink·ing 1** : SUBMERGE **2** : to descend lower and lower **3** : to grow less in volume or height **4** : to slope downward **5** : to penetrate downward **6** : to fail in health or strength **7** : LAPSE, DEGENERATE **8** : to cause (a ship) to descend to the bottom **9** : to make (a hole or shaft) by digging, boring, or cutting **10** : INVEST — **sink·able** *adj*

²sink *n* **1** : DRAIN, SEWER **2** : a basin connected with a drain **3** : an extensive depression in the land surface

sink·er \'siŋ-kər\ *n* : a weight for sinking a fishing line or net

sink·hole \'siŋk-₁hōl\ *n* : a hollow place in which drainage collects

sin·u·ous \'sin-yə-wəs\ *adj* : bending in and out : WINDING — **sin·u·os·i·ty** \₁sin-yə-'wäs-ət-ē\ *n*

si·nus \'sī-nəs\ *n* [NL, fr. L curve, hollow] **1** : any of several cavities of the skull mostly connecting with the nostrils **2** : a space forming a channel (as for the passage of blood)

si·nus·itis \₁sī-nə-'sīt-əs\ *n* : inflammation of a sinus esp. of the skull

Sioux \'sü\ *n, pl* **Sioux** \'sü(z)\ [F] : DAKOTA

sip \'sip\ *vb* **sipped; sip·ping** : to drink in small quantities — **sip** *n*

¹si·phon \'sī-fən\ *n* [F] **1** : a bent tube through which a liquid can be transferred by means of air pressure up and over the edge of one container and into another container placed at a lower level **2** *usu* **sy·phon** : a bottle that ejects soda water through a tube when a valve is opened

²siphon *vb* **si·phoned; si·phon·ing** \'sīf-(ə-)niŋ\ : to draw off by means of a siphon

sir \(')sər\ *n* [ME *sire* sire, fr. OF, fr. L *senior*, compar. of *senex* old, old man] **1** : a man of rank or position — used as a title before the given name of a knight or baronet **2** — used in addressing a man without using his name

¹sire \'sī(ə)r\ *n* **1** : FATHER; *also, archaic* : FOREFATHER **2** *archaic* : LORD — used as a title of respect esp. in addressing a sovereign **3** : the male parent of an animal (as a horse or dog)

²sire *vb* **sired; sir·ing** : BEGET, PROCREATE

si·ren \'sī-rən\ *n* **1** : a seductive or alluring woman **2** : an electrically operated device for producing a loud shrill warning signal — **siren** *adj*

sir·loin \'sər-₁lȯin\ *n* [alter. of earlier *surloin*, modif. of MF *surlonge*, fr. *sur* over (fr. L *super*) + *longe* loin] : a cut of beef taken from the part in front of the round

sirup var of SYRUP

si·sal \'sī-səl, -zəl\ *n* : a strong cordage fiber from an agave; *also* : this agave

sis·sy \'sis-ē\ *n, pl* **sissies** : an effeminate boy or man; *also* : a timid or cowardly person

sis·ter \'sis-tər\ *n* **1** : a female having one or both parents in common with another individual **2** : a member of a religious order of women : NUN **3** *chiefly Brit* : NURSE — **sis·ter·ly** *adj*

sis·ter·hood \-₁hu̇d\ *n* **1** : the state of being sisters or a sister **2** : a community or society of sisters

sis·ter–in–law \'sis-t(ə-)rən-₁lȯ\ *n, pl* **sisters–in–law** \-tər-zən-\ : the sister of one's husband or wife; *also* : the wife of one's brother

sit \'sit\ *vb* **sat** \'sat\; **sit·ting 1** : to rest upon the buttocks or haunches **2** : ROOST, PERCH **3** : to occupy a seat **4** : to hold a session **5** : to cover eggs for hatching : BROOD **6** : to pose for a portrait **7** : to remain quiet or inactive **8** : FIT **9** : to cause (oneself) to be seated **10** : to place in position **11** : to keep one's seat on ⟨∼ a horse⟩ **12** : BABY= SIT — **sit·ter** *n*

si·tar \si-'tär\ *n* [Hindi] : an Indian lute

with a long neck and a varying number of strings

site \\'sīt\ *n* : LOCATION

sit–in \\'sit-ˌin\ *n* : an act of sitting in the seats or on the floor of an establishment as a means of organized protest

sit·u·at·ed \\'sich-ə-ˌwāt-əd\ *adj* : LOCATED, PLACED

sit·u·a·tion \ˌsich-ə-'wā-shən\ *n* 1 : LOCATION, SITE 2 : JOB 3 : CONDITION, CIRCUMSTANCES

sit–up \\'sit-ˌəp\ *n* : an exercise performed from a supine position by raising the trunk to a sitting position usu. while keeping the legs straight and returning to the original position

six \\'siks\ *n* 1 : one more than five 2 : the 6th in a set or series 3 : something having six units; *esp* : a 6-cylinder engine or automobile — **six** *adj or pron* — **sixth** \\'siksth\ *adj or adv or n*

six–gun \\'siks-ˌgən\ *n* : a 6-chambered revolver

six–pack \\'siks-ˌpak\ *n* : six bottles or cans (as of beer) packaged and purchased together; *also* : the contents of a six-pack

six·pence \-pəns, *US also* -ˌpens\ *n* : the sum of six pence; *also* : an English silver coin of this value — **six·pen·ny** \-pən-ē, *US also* -ˌpen-ē\ *adj*

six–shoot·er \\'sik(s)-'shüt-ər\ *n* : SIX= GUN

six·teen \\'siks-'tēn\ *n* : one more than 15 — **sixteen** *adj or pron* — **six·teenth** \-'tēnth\ *adj or n*

six·ty \\'siks-tē\ *n, pl* **sixties** : six times 10 — **six·ti·eth** \\'siks-tē-əth\ *adj or n* — **sixty** *adj or pron*

siz·able *or* **size·able** \\'sī-zə-bəl\ *adj* : quite large — **siz·ably** \-blē\ *adv*

¹**size** \\'sīz\ *n* : physical extent or bulk : DIMENSIONS; *also* : MAGNITUDE

²**size** *vb* **sized; siz·ing** : to grade or classify according to size

³**size** *n* : a gluey material used for filling the pores in paper, plaster, or textiles — **siz·ing** \\'sī-ziŋ\ *n*

⁴**size** *vb* **sized; siz·ing** : to cover, stiffen, or glaze with size

siz·zle \\'siz-əl\ *vb* **siz·zled; siz·zling** \-(ə-)liŋ\ : to fry or shrivel up with a hissing sound — **sizzle** *n*

SJ *abbr* Society of Jesus

SK *abbr* Saskatchewan

¹**skate** \\'skāt\ *n, pl* **skates** *also* **skate**

: any of numerous rays with thick broad fins

²**skate** *n* 1 : a metal runner with a frame fitting on a shoe used for gliding over ice 2 : ROLLER SKATE — **skate** *vb* — **skat·er** *n*

skate·board \\'skāt-ˌbōrd\ *n* : a short board mounted on roller-skate wheels — **skate·board·er** \-ər\ *n* — **skate·board·ing** \-iŋ\ *n*

skeet \\'skēt\ *n* : trapshooting in which clay targets are thrown in such a way that their angle of flight simulates that of a flushed game bird

skein \\'skān\ *n* : a loosely twisted quantity (as of yarn) as it is taken from the reel

skel·e·ton \\'skel-ət-ᵊn\ *n* 1 : the usu. bony supporting framework of an animal body 2 : a bare minimum 3 : FRAMEWORK — **skel·e·tal** \-ət-ᵊl\ *adj*

skep·tic \\'skep-tik\ *n* 1 : one who believes in skepticism 2 : one having a critical or doubting attitude 3 : one who doubts or disbelieves in religious tenets — **skep·ti·cal** \-ti-kəl\ *adj*

skep·ti·cism \\'skep-tə-ˌsiz-əm\ *n* 1 : a doubting state of mind 2 : a doctrine that certainty of knowledge cannot be attained 3 : unbelief in religion

sketch \\'skech\ *n* 1 : a rough drawing or outline 2 : a short or slight literary composition (as a story or essay); *also* : a vaudeville act — **sketch** *vb* — **sketchy** *adj*

¹**skew** \\'skyü\ *vb* : TWIST, SWERVE

²**skew** *n* : SLANT

skew·er \\'skyü-ər\ *n* : a pin for holding meat in form while roasting — **skewer** *vb*

¹**ski** \\'skē\ *n, pl* **skis** [Norw, fr. ON *skīth* stick of wood, ski] : one of a pair of long strips (as of wood) bound one on each foot for gliding over snow

²**ski** *vb* **skied** \\'skēd\; **ski·ing** : to glide on skis — **ski·er** *n*

¹**skid** \\'skid\ *n* 1 : a plank for supporting something above the ground 2 : a device placed under a wheel to prevent turning 3 : a timber or rail over or on which something is slid or rolled 4 : the action of skidding 5 : a runner on the landing gear of an aircraft 6 : ²PALLET

²**skid** *vb* **skid·ded; skid·ding** 1 : to slide without rotating ⟨a *skidding* wheel⟩ 2

: to slide sideways on the road ⟨the car *skidded* on ice⟩

skid row *n* : a district of cheap saloons frequented by vagrants and alcoholics

skiff \'skif\ *n* : a small open boat

ski lift *n* : CHAIR LIFT

skill \'skil\ *n* **1** : ability to use one's knowledge effectively in doing something **2** : developed or acquired ability **syn** art, craft, cunning, dexterity, expertise, know-how — **skilled** \'skild\ *adj*

skil·let \'skil-ət\ *n* : a frying pan

skill·ful *or* **skil·ful** \'skil-fəl\ *adj* **1** : having or displaying skill : EXPERT **2** : accomplished with skill — **skill·ful·ly** \-ē\ *adv* — **skill·ful·ness** *n*

¹skim \'skim\ *vb* **skimmed; skim·ming 1** : to take off from the top of a liquid; *also* : to remove (scum or cream) from ⟨~ milk⟩ **2** : to read rapidly and superficially **3** : to pass swiftly over — **skim·mer** *n*

²skim *adj* **1** : having the cream removed **2** : made of skim milk

skim·ming \'skim-iŋ\ *n* : the practice of concealing gambling profits so as to avoid tax payments

ski·mo·bile \'skē-mō-₁bēl\ *n* : SNOWMOBILE

skimp \'skimp\ *vb* : to give insufficient attention, effort, or funds; *also* : to save by skimping

skimpy \'skim-pē\ *adj* **skimp·i·er; -est** : deficient in supply or execution

¹skin \'skin\ *n* **1** : the outer limiting layer of an animal body; *also* : the usu. thin tough tissue of which this is made **2** : an outer or surface layer (as a rind or peel) — **skin·less** *adj* — **skinned** *adj*

²skin *vb* **skinned; skin·ning** : to free from skin : remove the skin of

³skin *adj* : devoted to showing nudes ⟨~ magazines⟩

skin–dive \'skin-₁dīv\ *vb* : to swim below the surface of water with a face mask and portable breathing device — **skin diver** *n* — **skin diving** *n*

skin·flint \'skin-₁flint\ *n* : a very stingy person

skin graft *n* : skin that is taken from one area to replace skin in another area — **skin grafting** *n*

skin·ny \'skin-ē\ *adj* **skin·ni·er; -est 1** : resembling skin **2** : very thin

skin·ny–dip·ping \-₁dip-iŋ\ *n* : swimming in the nude

skin·tight \'skin-'tīt\ *adj* : closely fitted to the figure

¹skip \'skip\ *vb* **skipped; skip·ping 1** : to move with leaps and bounds **2** : to leap lightly over **3** : to pass from point to point (as in reading) disregarding what is in between **4** : to pass over without notice or mention

²skip *n* : a light bouncing step; *also* : a gait of alternate hops and steps

skip·jack \'skip-₁jak\ *n* : a small sailboat with bottom similar to a flat V and sides vertical

skip·per \'skip-ər\ *n* [ME, fr. Middle Dutch *schipper*, fr. *schip* ship] : the master of a ship — **skipper** *vb*

skir·mish \'skər-mish\ *n* : a minor engagement in war; *also* : a minor dispute or contest — **skirmish** *vb*

¹skirt \'skərt\ *n* : a free-hanging part of a garment extending from the waist down

²skirt *vb* **1** : to pass around the outer edge of **2** : BORDER

skit \'skit\ *n* : a brief dramatic sketch

ski tow *n* : SKI LIFT

skit·ter \'skit-ər\ *vb* : to glide or skip lightly or quickly : skim along a surface

skit·tish \'skit-ish\ *adj* **1** : CAPRICIOUS, IRRESPONSIBLE **2** : easily frightened ⟨a ~ horse⟩

skiv·vy \'skiv-ē\ *n, pl* **skivvies** : men's underwear; *esp* : a T-shirt and briefs or shorts — usu. used in pl.

ski·wear \'skē-₁waər\ *n* : clothing suitable for wear while skiing

skulk \'skəlk\ *vb* : to move furtively : SNEAK, LURK — **skulk·er** *n*

skull \'skəl\ *n* : the bony or cartilaginous case that protects the brain and supports the jaws

skull·cap \'skəl-₁kap\ *n* : a close-fitting brimless cap

¹skunk \'skəŋk\ *n, pl* **skunks** *also* **skunk 1** : any of various No. American mammals related to the weasels that can forcibly eject an ill-smelling fluid when startled **2** : a contemptible person

²skunk *vb* : to defeat decisively; *esp* : to shut out in a game

skunk cabbage *n* : a perennial herb of eastern No. America with an unpleasant-smelling early spring flower; *also* : a related herb of the Pacific coast region

sky \\'skī\\ *n, pl* **skies 1** : the upper air **2** : HEAVEN — **sky·ey** \\'skī-ē\\ *adj*

sky·cap \\-ˌkap\\ *n* : a person employed to carry luggage at an airport

sky·div·ing \\-ˌdī-viŋ\\ *n* : the sport of jumping from an airplane and executing various body maneuvers before opening a parachute — **sky diver** *n*

sky·jack \\-ˌjak\\ *vb* : to take control of an airplane in flight by threat of violence — **sky·jack·er** *n* — **sky·jack·ing** *n*

¹**sky·lark** \\-ˌlärk\\ *n* : a European lark noted for its song and its steep upward flight

²**skylark** *vb* : to frolic boisterously or recklessly

sky·light \\'skī-ˌlīt\\ *n* : a window in a roof or ceiling — **sky·light·ed** \\-ˌlīt-əd\\ *adj*

sky·line \\-ˌlīn\\ *n* **1** : HORIZON **2** : an outline against the sky

¹**sky·rock·et** \\-ˌräk-ət\\ *n* : ¹ROCKET 1

²**skyrocket** *vb* : ²ROCKET 2

sky·scrap·er \\-ˌskrā-pər\\ *n* : a very tall building

sky·walk \\-ˌwȯk\\ *n* : a usu. enclosed aerial walkway connecting two buildings

sky·ward \\-wərd\\ *adv* : toward the sky

sky·writ·ing \\-ˌrīt-iŋ\\ *n* : writing in the sky formed by smoke emitted from an airplane — **sky·writ·er** \\-ər\\ *n*

slab \\'slab\\ *n* : a thick flat piece or slice

¹**slack** \\'slak\\ *adj* **1** : CARELESS, NEGLIGENT **2** : SLUGGISH, LISTLESS **3** : not taut : LOOSE **4** : not busy or active **syn** lax, remiss, neglectful, delinquent, derelict — **slack·ly** *adv* — **slack·ness** *n*

²**slack** *vb* **1** : to make or become slack : LOOSEN, RELAX **2** : SLAKE 2

³**slack** *n* **1** : cessation of movement or flow : LETUP **2** : a part that hangs loose without strain ⟨~ of a rope⟩ **3** : trousers for casual wear — usu. used in pl.

slack·en \\'slak-ən\\ *vb* **slack·ened; slack·en·ing** \\-(ə-)niŋ\\ : to make or become slack

slack·er \\'slak-ər\\ *n* : one that shirks work or evades military duty

slag \\'slag\\ *n* : the waste left after the melting of ores and the separation of metal from them

slain past part of SLAY

slake \\'slāk, *for 2 also* 'slak\\ *vb* **slaked; slak·ing 1** : to cause to subside with or as if with refreshing drink ⟨~ thirst⟩ **2** : to cause (lime) to crumble by mixture with water

sla·lom \\'släl-əm\\ *n* [Norw., lit., sloping track] : skiing in a zigzag course between obstacles

¹**slam** \\'slam\\ *n* : the winning of every trick or of all tricks but one in bridge

²**slam** *n* : a heavy jarring impact : BANG

³**slam** *vb* **slammed; slam·ming 1** : to shut violently and noisily **2** : to throw or strike with a loud impact

¹**slan·der** \\'slan-dər\\ *n* [ME *sclaundre, slaundre,* fr. OF *esclandre,* fr. LL *scandalum* stumbling block, offense] : a false report maliciously uttered and tending to injure the reputation of a person — **slan·der·ous** *adj*

²**slander** *vb* **slan·dered; slan·der·ing** \\-d(ə-)riŋ\\ : to utter slander against : DEFAME — **slan·der·er** *n*

slang \\'slaŋ\\ *n* : an informal nonstandard vocabulary composed typically of invented words, arbitrarily changed words, and extravagant figures of speech — **slangy** *adj*

¹**slant** \\'slant\\ *n* **1** : a sloping direction, line, or plane **2** : a particular or personal viewpoint — **slant** *adj* — **slant·wise** \\-ˌwīz\\ *adv or adj*

²**slant** *vb* **1** : SLOPE **2** : to interpret or present in accordance with a special viewpoint **syn** incline, lean, list, tilt, heel — **slant·ing·ly** *adv*

slap \\'slap\\ *vb* **slapped; slap·ping 1** : to strike sharply with the open hand **2** : REBUFF, INSULT — **slap** *n*

¹**slash** \\'slash\\ *vb* **1** : to cut with sweeping strokes **2** : to cut slits in (a garment) **3** : to reduce sharply

²**slash** *n* **1** : GASH **2** : an ornamental slit in a garment **3** : a clearing in a forest littered with debris; *also* : the debris present

slat \\'slat\\ *n* : a thin narrow flat strip

¹**slate** \\'slāt\\ *n* **1** : a dense fine-grained rock that splits into thin layers **2** : a roofing tile or a writing tablet made from this rock **3** : a list of candidates for election

²**slate** *vb* **slat·ed; slat·ing 1** : to cover with slate **2** : to designate for action or appointment

slath•er \'slat͟h-ər\ *vb* **slath•ered; slath-er•ing** \-(ə-)riŋ\ : to spread with or on thickly or lavishly

slat•tern \'slat-ərn\ *n* : a slovenly woman — **slat•tern•ly** *adj*

¹slaugh•ter \'slȯt-ər\ *n* **1** : the butchering of livestock for market **2** : great destruction of lives esp. in battle

²slaughter *vb* **1** : to kill (animals) for food : BUTCHER **2** : to kill in large numbers or in a bloody way : MASSACRE

slaugh•ter•house \-ˌhaùs\ *n* : an establishment where animals are butchered

Slav \'släv, 'slav\ *n* : a person speaking a Slavic language

¹slave \'slāv\ *n* [ME *sclave*, fr. OF or ML; OF *esclave*, fr. ML *sclavus*, fr. *Sclavus* Slav; fr. the reduction to slavery of many Slavic peoples of central Europe] **1** : a person held in servitude as property **2** : a device (as the typewriter unit of a computer) that is directly responsive to another — **slave** *adj*

²slave *vb* **slaved; slav•ing** : to work like a slave : DRUDGE

¹sla•ver \'slav-ər, 'slāv-\ *n* : SLOBBER — **slaver** *vb*

²slav•er \'slā-vər\ *n* : a ship or a person engaged in transporting slaves

slav•ery \'slāv-(ə-)rē\ *n* **1** : wearisome drudgery **2** : the condition of being a slave **3** : the practice of owning slaves **syn** servitude, bondage, enslavement

¹Slav•ic \'slav-lik, 'släv-\ *adj* : of or relating to the Slavs or their languages

²Slavic *n* : a branch of the Indo-European language family including various languages (as Russian or Polish) of eastern Europe

slav•ish \'slā-vish\ *adj* **1** : SERVILE **2** : obeying or imitating with no freedom of judgment or choice — **slav•ish•ly** *adv*

slaw \'slȯ\ *n* : COLESLAW

slay \'slā\ *vb* **slew** \'slü\; **slain** \'slān\; **slay•ing** : KILL — **slay•er** *n*

sleaze \'slēz\ *n* : a sleazy quality or appearance

slea•zy \'slē-zē, 'slā-\ *adj* **slea•zi•er; -est 1** : FLIMSY, SHODDY **2** : marked by cheapness of character or quality

¹sled \'sled\ *n* : a vehicle on runners adapted esp. for sliding on snow

²sled *vb* **sled•ded, sled•ding** : to ride or carry on a sled

¹sledge \'slej\ *n* : SLEDGEHAMMER

²sledge *n* : a strong heavy sled

sledge•ham•mer \'slej-ˌham-ər\ *n* : a large heavy hammer usu. wielded with both hands — **sledgehammer** *adj or vb*

¹sleek \'slēk\ *vb* **1** : to make smooth or glossy **2** : to gloss over

²sleek *adj* : having a smooth well≈ groomed look

¹sleep \'slēp\ *n* **1** : a natural periodic suspension of consciousness **2** : a state (as death or coma) suggesting sleep — **sleep•less** *adj* — **sleep•less•ness** *n*

²sleep *vb* **slept** \'slept\; **sleep•ing 1** : to rest or be in a state of sleep; *also* : to spend in sleep **2** : to have sexual intercourse **3** : to provide sleeping space for

sleep•er \'slē-pər\ *n* **1** : one that sleeps **2** : a horizontal beam to support something on or near ground level **3** : SLEEPING CAR **4** : someone or something unpromising or unnoticed that suddenly attains prominence or value

sleeping bag *n* : a warmly lined bag for sleeping esp. outdoors

sleeping car *n* : a railroad car with berths for sleeping

sleeping pill *n* : a drug in tablet or capsule form taken to induce sleep

sleeping sickness *n* : a serious disease that is prevalent in tropical Africa, is marked by fever, lethargy, tremors, and loss of weight, and is caused by protozoans transmitted by the tsetse fly

sleep•walk•er \'slēp-ˌwȯ-kər\ *n* : one who walks in his sleep

sleepy \'slē-pē\ *adj* **sleep•i•er; -est 1** : ready for sleep **2** : quietly inactive — **sleep•i•ly** \'slē-pə-lē\ *adv* — **sleep•i•ness** \-pē-nəs\ *n*

sleet \'slēt\ *n* : frozen or partly frozen rain — **sleet** *vb* — **sleety** *adj*

sleeve \'slēv\ *n* **1** : a part of a garment covering an arm **2** : a tubular part designed to fit over another part — **sleeve•less** *adj*

¹sleigh \'slā\ *n* : an open usu. horse≈ drawn vehicle on runners for use on snow or ice

²sleigh *vb* : to drive or travel in a sleigh

sleight \\'slīt\ *n* **1** : TRICK **2** : DEXTERITY

sleight of hand : a trick requiring skillful manual manipulation

slen·der \\'slen-dər\ *adj* **1** : SLIM, THIN **2** : WEAK, SLIGHT **3** : MEAGER, INADEQUATE

slen·der·ize \-də-ˌrīz\ *vb* **-ized; -iz·ing** : to make slender

sleuth \\'slüth\ *n* [short for *sleuthhound* bloodhound, fr. ME, fr. *sleuth* track of an animal or person, fr. ON *slōth*] : DETECTIVE

¹slew \\'slü\ past of SLAY

²slew *vb* : TURN, VEER, SKID

¹slice \\'slīs\ *n* **1** : a thin flat piece cut from something **2** : a wedge-shaped blade (as for serving fish) **3** : a flight of a ball (as in golf) that curves in the direction of the dominant hand of the player propelling it

²slice *vb* **sliced; slic·ing** **1** : to cut a slice from; *also* : to cut into slices **2** : to hit (a ball) so that a slice results

¹slick \\'slik\ *vb* : to make smooth or sleek

²slick *adj* **1** : very smooth : SLIPPERY **2** : CLEVER, SMART

³slick *n* **1** : a smooth patch of water covered with a film of oil **2** : a popular magazine printed on coated paper

slick·er \\'slik-ər\ *n* **1** : a long loose raincoat **2** : a sly tricky person **3** : a city dweller esp. of natty appearance or sophisticated mannerisms

¹slide \\'slīd\ *vb* **slid** \\'slid\; **slid·ing** \\'slīd-iŋ\ **1** : to move smoothly along a surface **2** : to fall by a loss of support **3** : to slip along quietly

²slide *n* **1** : an act or instance of sliding **2** : something (as a cover or fastener) that operates by sliding **3** : a fall of a mass of earth or snow down a hillside **4** : a surface on which something slides **5** : a glass plate on which a specimen is mounted for examination under a microscope **6** : a small transparent image that can be projected on a screen

slid·er \\'slīd-ər\ *n* **1** : one that slides **2** : a baseball pitch that looks like a fastball but curves slightly

slide rule *n* : an instrument for calculation consisting of a ruler and a medial slide graduated with logarithmic scales

slier comparative of SLY

sliest superlative of SLY

¹slight \\'slīt\ *adj* **1** : SLENDER; *also* : FRAIL **2** : UNIMPORTANT **3** : SCANTY, MEAGER — **slight·ly** *adv*

²slight *vb* **1** : to treat as unimportant **2** : to ignore discourteously **3** : to perform or attend to carelessly **syn** neglect, overlook, disregard

³slight *n* : a humiliating discourtesy

¹slim \\'slim\ *adj* **slim·mer; slim·mest** [Dutch, bad, inferior, fr. Middle Dutch *slimp* crooked, bad] **1** : SLENDER, SLIGHT, THIN **2** : SCANTY, MEAGER

²slim *vb* **slimmed; slim·ming** : to make or become slender

slime \\'slīm\ *n* **1** : sticky mud **2** : a slippery substance (as on the skin of a slug or catfish) — **slimy** *adj*

slim–jim \\'slim-'jim, -ˌjim\ *adj* : notably slender

¹sling \\'sliŋ\ *vb* **slung** \\'sləŋ\; **sling·ing** \\'sliŋ-iŋ\ **1** : to throw forcibly : FLING **2** : to hurl with a sling

²sling *n* **1** : a short strap with strings attached for hurling stones or shot **2** : a strap, rope, or chain for holding securely something being lifted, lowered, or carried

sling·shot \\'sliŋ-ˌshät\ *n* : a forked stick with elastic bands for shooting small stones or shot

slink \\'sliŋk\ *vb* **slunk** \\'sləŋk\ *also* **slinked** \\'sliŋkt\; **slink·ing** **1** : to move stealthily or furtively **2** : to move sinuously — **slinky** *adj*

¹slip \\'slip\ *vb* **slipped; slip·ping** **1** : to escape quietly or secretly **2** : to slide along or cause to slide along smoothly **3** : to make a mistake **4** : to pass unnoticed or undone **5** : to fall off from a standard or level

²slip *n* **1** : a ramp for repairing ships **2** : a ship's berth between two piers **3** : secret or hurried departure, escape, or evasion **4** : BLUNDER **5** : a sudden mishap **6** : a woman's one-piece garment worn under a dress **7** : PILLOWCASE

³slip *n* **1** : a shoot or twig from a plant for planting or grafting **2** : a long narrow strip; *esp* : one of paper used for a record ⟨deposit ∼⟩

⁴slip *vb* **slipped; slip·ping** : to take slips from (a plant)

slip·knot \\'slip-ˌnät\ *n* : a knot that slips along the rope around which it is made

slipped disk *n* : a protrusion of one of the disks of cartilage between vertebrae with pressure on spinal nerves resulting esp. in low back pain

slip·per \'slip-ər\ *n* : a light low shoe that may be easily slipped on and off

slip·pery \'slip-(ə-)rē\ *adj* **slip·peri·er; -est** **1** : icy, wet, smooth, or greasy enough to cause one to fall or lose one's hold **2** : TRICKY, UNRELIABLE — **slip·peri·ness** *n*

slip·shod \'slip-'shäd\ *adj* : SLOVENLY, CARELESS ⟨~ work⟩

slip·stream \'slip-ˌstrēm\ *n* : the stream of air driven aft by the propeller of an aircraft

slip·up \'slip-ˌəp\ *n* **1** : MISTAKE **2** : ACCIDENT

¹**slit** \'slit\ *vb* **slit; slit·ting** **1** : SLASH **2** : to cut off or away

²**slit** *n* : a long narrow cut or opening

slith·er \'slith-ər\ *vb* : to slip or glide along like a snake — **slith·ery** *adj*

sliv·er \'sliv-ər\ *n* : SPLINTER

slob \'släb\ *n* : a slovenly or boorish person

slob·ber \'släb-ər\ *vb* **slob·bered; slob·ber·ing** \-(ə-)riŋ\ : to dribble saliva — **slobber** *n*

sloe \'slō\ *n* : the fruit of the blackthorn

slog *vb* **slogged; slog·ging** **1** : to hit hard : BEAT **2** : to work hard and steadily

slo·gan \'slō-gən\ *n* [alter. of earlier *slogorn*, fr. ScGael *sluagh-ghairm* army cry] : a word or phrase expressing the spirit or aim of a party, group, or cause

sloop \'slüp\ *n* : a single-masted sailboat with a jib and a fore-and-aft mainsail

¹**slop** \'släp\ *n* **1** : thin tasteless drink or liquid food — usu. used in pl. **2** : food waste or gruel for animal feed **3** : body and toilet waste — usu. used in pl.

²**slop** *vb* **slopped; slop·ping** **1** : SPILL **2** : to feed with slop ⟨~ hogs⟩

¹**slope** \'slōp\ *vb* **sloped; slop·ing** : SLANT, INCLINE

²**slope** *n* **1** : upward or downward slant or degree of slant **2** : ground that forms an incline **3** : the part of a landmass draining into a particular ocean

slop·py \'släp-ē\ *adj* **slop·pi·er; -est** **1** : MUDDY, SLUSHY **2** : SLOVENLY, MESSY

slosh \'släsh\ *vb* **1** : to flounder through or splash about in or with water, mud, or slush **2** : to move with a splashing motion

slot \'slät\ *n* **1** : a long narrow opening or groove **2** : a position in a sequence

slot car *n* : an electric toy racing car that runs on a grooved track

sloth \'slöth, 'slōth\ *n, pl* **sloths** *with* ths *or* thz\ **1** : LAZINESS, INDOLENCE **2** : a slow-moving So. and Central American mammal related to the armadillos — **sloth·ful** *adj*

slot machine *n* **1** : a machine whose operation is begun by dropping a coin into a slot **2** : a coin-operated gambling machine that pays off according to the matching of symbols on wheels spun by a handle

¹**slouch** \'slau̇ch\ *n* **1** : a lazy or incompetent person **2** : a loose or drooping gait or posture

²**slouch** *vb* : to walk, stand, or sit with a slouch : SLUMP

¹**slough** \'slü, *2 usu* 'slau̇\ *n* **1** : a wet and marshy or muddy place (as a swamp) **2** : a discouraged state of mind

²**slough** \'sləf\ *or* **sluff** *n* : something (as a snake's skin) that may be shed

³**slough** \'sləf\ *or* **sluff** *vb* : to cast off

slov·en \'sləv-ən\ *n* [ME *sloveyn* rascal, perh. fr. Flem *sloovin* woman of low character] : an untidy person

slov·en·ly \'sləv-ən-lē\ *adj* **1** : untidy in dress or person **2** : lazily or carelessly done : SLIPSHOD

¹**slow** \'slō\ *adj* **1** : SLUGGISH; *also* : dull in mind : STUPID **2** : moving, flowing, or proceeding at less than the usual speed **3** : taking more than the usual time **4** : registering behind the correct time **5** : not lively : BORING **syn** dilatory, laggard, deliberate, leisurely — **slow** *adv* — **slow·ly** *adv* — **slow·ness** *n*

²**slow** *vb* **1** : to make slow : hold back **2** : to go slower

slow motion *n* : motion-picture action photographed so as to appear much slower than normal — **slow–motion** *adj*

SLR *abbr* single-lens reflex

sludge \'sləj\ *n* : a slushy mass : OOZE; *esp* : solid matter produced by sewage treatment processes

slue *var of* ²SLEW

¹**slug** \'sləg\ *n* **1** : a small mass of metal; *esp* : BULLET **2** : a metal disk for use

(as in a slot machine) in place of a coin **3** : any of numerous slimy wormlike mollusks related to the snails **4** : a quantity of liquor drunk

²**slug** *vb* **slugged; slug•ging** : to strike forcibly and heavily — **slug•ger** *n*

slug•gard \'sləg-ərd\ *n* : a lazy person

slug•gish \'sləg-ish\ *adj* **1** : SLOTHFUL, LAZY **2** : slow in movement or flow **3** : STAGNANT, DULL — **slug•gish•ly** *adv* — **slug•gish•ness** *n*

¹**sluice** \'slüs\ *n* **1** : an artificial passage for water with a gate for controlling the flow; *also* : the gate so used **2** : a channel that carries off surplus water **3** : an inclined trough or flume for washing ore or floating logs

²**sluice** *vb* **sluiced; sluic•ing** **1** : to draw off through a sluice **2** : to wash with running water : FLUSH

sluice•way \'slüs-ˌwā\ *n* : an artificial channel into which water is let by a sluice

¹**slum** \'sləm\ *n* : a thickly populated area marked by poverty and dirty or deteriorated houses

²**slum** *vb* **slummed; slum•ming** : to visit slums esp. out of curiosity; *also* : to go somewhere or do something that might be considered beneath one's station

¹**slum•ber** \'sləm-bər\ *vb* **slum•bered; slum•ber•ing** \-b(ə-)riŋ\ **1** : DOZE; *also* : SLEEP **2** : to be in a sluggish or torpid state

²**slumber** *n* : SLEEP

slum•ber•ous *or* **slum•brous** \'sləmb(ə-)rəs\ *adj* **1** : SLUMBERING, SLEEPY **2** : PEACEFUL, INACTIVE

slum•lord \'sləm-ˌlȯrd\ *n* : a landlord who receives unusually large profits from substandard properties

slump \'sləmp\ *vb* **1** : to sink down suddenly : COLLAPSE **2** : SLOUCH **3** : to decline sharply — **slump** *n*

slung past and past part of SLING

slunk past and past part of SLINK

¹**slur** \'slər\ *vb* **slurred; slur•ring** **1** : to slide or slip over without due mention or emphasis **2** : to perform two or more successive notes of different pitch in a smooth or connected way

²**slur** *n* : a curved line ⌣ or ⌢ connecting notes to be slurred; *also* : a group of slurred notes

³**slur** *n* : a slighting remark : ASPERSION

slurp \'slərp\ *vb* : to eat or drink noisily — **slurp** *n*

slur•ry \'slər-ē\ *n*, *pl* **slur•ries** : a watery mixture of insoluble matter

slush \'sləsh\ *n* **1** : partly melted or watery snow **2** : soft mud — **slushy** *adj*

slut \'slət\ *n* **1** : a slovenly woman **2** : PROSTITUTE — **slut•tish** \'slət-ish\ *adj*

sly \'slī\ *adj* **sli•er** *also* **sly•er** \'slī(-ə)r\; **sli•est** *also* **sly•est** \'slī-əst\ **1** : CRAFTY, CUNNING **2** : SECRETIVE, FURTIVE **3** : ROGUISH **syn** tricky, wily, artful, foxy, guileful — **sly•ly** *adv* — **sly•ness** *n*

sm *abbr* small

Sm *symbol* samarium

SM *abbr* **1** [NL *scientiae magister*] master of science **2** sergeant major

SMA *abbr* sergeant major of the army

¹**smack** \'smak\ *n* : characteristic flavor; *also* : a slight trace

²**smack** *vb* **1** : to have a taste **2** : to have a trace or suggestion

³**smack** *vb* **1** : to move (the lips) so as to make a sharp noise **2** : to kiss or slap with a loud noise

⁴**smack** *n* **1** : a sharp noise made by the lips **2** : a noisy slap

⁵**smack** *adv* : squarely and sharply

⁶**smack** *n* : a sailing ship used in fishing

⁷**smack** *n, slang* : HEROIN

SMaj *abbr* sergeant major

¹**small** \'smȯl\ *adj* **1** : little in size or amount **2** : operating on a limited scale **3** : few in number **4** : made up of little things **5** : TRIFLING, UNIMPORTANT **6** : MEAN, PETTY **syn** diminutive, petite, wee, tiny, minute — **small•ish** *adj* — **small•ness** *n*

²**small** *n* : a small part or product ⟨the ~ of the back⟩

small•pox \'smȯl-ˌpäks\ *n* : a contagious virus disease marked by fever and a skin eruption

small–time \'smȯl-'tīm\ *adj* : insignificant in performance and standing : MINOR — **small–tim•er** \-'tī-mər\ *n*

¹**smart** \'smärt\ *vb* **1** : to cause or feel a stinging pain **2** : to feel or endure distress — **smart** *n*

²**smart** *adj* **1** : making one smart ⟨a ~ blow⟩ **2** : mentally quick : BRIGHT **3** : WITTY, CLEVER **4** : STYLISH **5** : being a guided missile **6** : containing a microprocessor for limited computing capability ⟨~ terminal⟩ **syn** knowing, quick-witted, intelligent, brainy,

sharp — **smart·ly** *adv* — **smart·ness** *n*

smart al·eck \'smärt-ˌal-ik\ *n* : a person given to obnoxious cleverness

¹**smash** \'smash\ *n* **1** : a smashing blow; *esp* : a hard overhand stroke in tennis **2** : the act or sound of smashing **3** : collision of vehicles : CRASH **4** : COLLAPSE, RUIN; *esp* : BANKRUPTCY **5** : a striking success : HIT — **smash** *adj*

²**smash** *vb* **1** : to break or be broken into pieces **2** : to move forward with force and shattering effect **3** : to destroy utterly : WRECK

smat·ter·ing \'smat-ə-riŋ\ *n* **1** : superficial knowledge **2** : a small scattered number or amount

¹**smear** \'smiər\ *n* : a spot left by an oily or sticky substance

²**smear** *vb* **1** : to overspread with something oily or sticky **2** : SMUDGE, SOIL **3** : to injure by slander or insults

¹**smell** \'smel\ *vb* **smelled** \'smeld\ *or* **smelt** \'smelt\; **smell·ing** **1** : to perceive the odor of by sense organs of the nose; *also* : to detect or seek with or as if with these organs **2** : to have or give off an odor

²**smell** *n* **1** : the process or power of perceiving odor; *also* : the special sense by which one perceives odor **2** : ODOR, SCENT **3** : an act of smelling — **smelly** *adj*

smelling salts *n pl* : an aromatic preparation used as a stimulant and restorative (as to relieve faintness)

¹**smelt** \'smelt\ *n, pl* **smelts** *or* **smelt** : any of several small food fishes of coastal or fresh waters that are related to the trouts

²**smelt** *vb* : to melt or fuse (ore) in order to separate the metal; *also* : REFINE

smelt·er \'smel-tər\ *n* **1** : one that smelts **2** : an establishment for smelting

smid·gen *also* **smid·geon** *or* **smid·gin** \'smij-ən\ *n* : a small amount : BIT

smi·lax \'smī-ˌlaks\ *n* **1** : any of various mostly climbing and prickly plants related to the lilies **2** : an ornamental plant related to the asparagus

¹**smile** \'smīl\ *vb* **smiled**; **smil·ing** **1** : to look with a smile **2** : to be favorable **3** : to express by a smile

²**smile** *n* : a change of facial expression to express amusement, pleasure, or affection

smirch \'smərch\ *vb* **1** : to make dirty or stained **2** : to bring disgrace on — **smirch** *n*

smirk \'smərk\ *vb* : to wear a self-conscious or conceited smile : SIMPER — **smirk** *n*

smite \'smīt\ *vb* **smote** \'smōt\; **smit·ten** \'smit-ᵊn\ *or* **smote**; **smit·ing** \'smīt-iŋ\ **1** : to strike heavily; *also* : to kill by striking **2** : to affect as if by a heavy blow

smith \'smith\ *n* : a worker in metals; *esp* : BLACKSMITH

smith·er·eens \ˌsmith-ə-'rēnz\ *n pl* [Ir-Gael *smidirín*] : FRAGMENTS, BITS

smithy \'smith-ē\ *n, pl* **smith·ies** : a smith's workshop

¹**smock** \'smäk\ *n* : a loose garment worn over other clothes as a protection

²**smock** *vb* : to gather (cloth) in regularly spaced tucks — **smock·ing** *n*

smog \'smäg, 'smȯg\ *n* [blend of *smoke* and *fog*] : a thick haze caused by the action of sunlight on air polluted by smoke and automobile exhaust fumes — **smog·gy** *adj*

¹**smoke** \'smōk\ *n* **1** : the gas from burning material (as coal, wood, or tobacco) in which are suspended particles of soot **2** : a mass or column of smoke **3** : something (as a cigarette) to smoke; *also* : the act of smoking — **smoke·less** *adj* — **smoky** *adj*

²**smoke** *vb* **smoked**; **smok·ing** **1** : to emit smoke **2** : to inhale and exhale the fumes of burning tobacco; *also* : to use in smoking ⟨~ a pipe⟩ **3** : to stupefy or drive away by smoke **4** : to discolor with smoke **5** : to cure (as meat) with smoke — **smok·er** *n*

smoke detector *n* : an alarm that sounds automatically when it detects smoke

smoke jumper *n* : a forest-fire fighter who parachutes to locations otherwise difficult to reach

smoke·stack \'smōk-ˌstak\ *n* : a pipe or funnel through which smoke and gases are discharged

smol·der *or* **smoul·der** \'smōl-dər\ *vb* **smol·dered** *or* **smoul·dered**; **smol·der·ing** *or* **smoul·der·ing** \-d(ə-)riŋ\ **1** : to burn and smoke without flame **2** : to burn inwardly — **smolder** *n*

smooch \'smüch\ *vb* : KISS, PET — **smooch** *n*

¹smooth \'smüth\ *adj* **1** : not rough or uneven **2** : not jarring or jolting **3** : BLAND, MILD **4** : fluent in speech and agreeable in manner **syn** even, flat, level, plane — **smooth·ly** *adv* — **smooth·ness** *n*

²smooth *vb* **1** : to make smooth **2** : to free from trouble or difficulty

smooth muscle *n* : muscle with no cross striations that is typical of visceral organs (as the stomach and bladder) and is not under voluntary control

smor·gas·bord \'smor-gəs-ˌbord\ *n* [Sw *smörgasbord*, fr. *smörgas* open sandwich + *bord* table] : a luncheon or supper buffet consisting of many foods

smote past and past part of SMITE

¹smoth·er \'sməth-ər\ *n* **1** : thick stifling smoke **2** : dense fog, spray, foam, or dust **3** : a confused multitude of things : WELTER

²smother *vb* **smoth·ered; smoth·er·ing** \-(ə-)riŋ\ **1** : to kill by depriving of air **2** : SUPPRESS **3** : to cover thickly

SMSgt *abbr* senior master sergeant

¹smudge \'sməj\ *vb* **smudged; smudg·ing** : to soil or blur by rubbing or smearing

²smudge *n* : a dirty or blurred spot — **smudgy** *adj*

smug \'sməg\ *adj* **smug·ger; smug·gest** : conscious of one's virtue and importance : SELF-SATISFIED — **smug·ly** *adv* — **smug·ness** *n*

smug·gle \'sməg-əl\ *vb* **smug·gled; smug·gling** \-(ə-)liŋ\ **1** : to import or export secretly, illegally, or without paying the duties required by law **2** : to convey secretly — **smug·gler** \'sməg-lər\ *n*

smut \'smət\ *n* **1** : something (as soot) that smudges; *also* : SMUDGE, SPOT **2** : any of various destructive fungous diseases of plants; *also* : a fungus causing smut **3** : indecent language or matter — **smut·ty** *adj*

smutch \'sməch\ *n* : SMUDGE

Sn *symbol* [LL *stannum*] tin

snack \'snak\ *n* : a light meal : BITE

snaf·fle \'snaf-əl\ *n* : a simple jointed bit for a horse's bridle

¹snag \'snag\ *n* **1** : a stump or piece of a tree esp. when under water **2** : an unexpected difficulty **syn** obstacle, obstruction, impediment, bar

²snag *vb* **snagged; snag·ging 1** : to become caught on or as if on a snag **2** : to seize quickly : SNATCH

snail \'snāl\ *n* : a small mollusk with a spiral shell into which it can withdraw

snake \'snāk\ *n* **1** : any of numerous long-bodied limbless crawling reptiles : SERPENT **2** : a treacherous person **3** : something that resembles a snake — **snaky** *adj*

snake·bird \'snāk-ˌbərd\ *n* : any of several fish-eating birds related to the cormorants but having a long slender neck and sharp-pointed bill

snake·bite \-ˌbīt\ *n* : the bite of a snake and esp. a venomous snake

¹snap \'snap\ *vb* **snapped; snapping 1** : to grasp or slash at something with the teeth **2** : to get or buy quickly **3** : to utter sharp or angry words **4** : to break suddenly with a sharp sound **5** : to give a sharp cracking noise **6** : to throw with a quick motion **7** : FLASH ⟨her eyes *snapped*⟩ **8** : to put a football into play — **snap·per** *n* — **snap·pish** *adj* — **snap·py** *adj*

²snap *n* **1** : the act or sound of snapping **2** : something very easy to do : CINCH **3** : a short period of cold weather **4** : a catch or fastening that closes with a click **5** : a thin brittle cookie **6** : ENERGY, VIM; *also* : smartness of movement **7** : the putting of the ball into play in football

snap bean *n* : a bean grown primarily for its young tender pods that are usu. broken in pieces and cooked as a vegetable

snap·drag·on \'snap-ˌdrag-ən\ *n* : any of several garden plants with long spikes of showy 2-lipped flowers

snapping turtle *n* : either of two large edible American turtles with powerful jaws and a strong musky odor

snap·shot \'snap-ˌshät\ *n* : a photograph taken usu. with an inexpensive hand-held camera

snare \'snaər\ *n* : a trap often consisting of a noose for catching birds or mammals — **snare** *vb*

¹snarl \'snärl\ *n* : TANGLE

²snarl *vb* : to cause to become knotted and intertwined

³snarl *vb* : to growl angrily or threateningly

⁴snarl *n* : an angry ill-tempered growl

¹snatch \'snach\ *vb* **1** : to try to grasp

something suddenly **2** : to seize or take away suddenly **syn** clutch, seize, grab, nab

²snatch *n* **1** : a short period **2** : an act of snatching **3** : something brief or fragmentary 〈~*es* of song〉

¹sneak \\'snēk\\ *vb* **sneaked** \\'snēkt\\ *or* **snuck** \\'snək\\; **sneak·ing** : to move, act, or take in a furtive manner — **sneak·ing·ly** *adv*

²sneak *n* **1** : one who acts in a furtive or shifty manner **2** : a stealthy or furtive move or escape — **sneaky** *adj*

sneak·er \\'snē-kər\\ *n* : a usu. canvas sports shoe with a pliable rubber sole

sneer \\'sniər\\ *vb* : to show scorn or contempt by curling the lip or by a jeering tone — **sneer** *n*

sneeze \\'snēz\\ *vb* **sneezed; sneez·ing** : to force the breath out suddenly and violently as a reflex act — **sneeze** *n*

snick·er \\'snik-ər\\ *n* : a partly suppressed laugh — **snicker** *vb*

snide \\'snīd\\ *adj* **1** : MEAN, LOW 〈a ~ trick〉 **2** : slyly disparaging 〈a ~ remark〉

sniff \\'snif\\ *vb* **1** : to draw air audibly up the nose **2** : to show disdain or scorn **3** : to detect by or as if by smelling — **sniff** *n*

snif·fle \\'snif-əl\\ *n* **1** *pl* : a head cold marked by nasal discharge **2** : SNUFFLE — **sniffle** *vb*

¹snip \\'snip\\ *n* **1** : a fragment snipped off **2** : a simple stroke of the scissors or shears

²snip *vb* **snipped; snip·ping** : to cut off by bits : CLIP; *also* : to remove by cutting off

¹snipe \\'snīp\\ *n, pl* **snipes** *or* **snipe** : any of several long-billed game birds that occur esp. in marshy areas and resemble the related woodcocks

²snipe *vb* **sniped; snip·ing** : to shoot at an exposed enemy from a concealed position usu. at long range — **snip·er** *n*

snip·py \\'snip-ē\\ *adj* **snip·pi·er; -est** : CURT, SNAPPISH

snips \\'snips\\ *n pl* : hand shears used esp. for cutting sheet metal 〈tin ~〉

snitch \\'snich\\ *vb* **1** : INFORM, TATTLE **2** : PILFER, SNATCH

sniv·el \\'sniv-əl\\ *vb* **-eled** *or* **-elled; -el·ing** *or* **-el·ling** \\-(ə-)liŋ\\ **1** : to have a running nose; *also* : SNUFFLE **2** : to whine in a snuffling manner — **snivel** *n*

snob \\'snäb\\ *n* [obs. *snob* member of the lower classes, fr. E dial., shoemaker] : one who seeks association with persons of higher social position and looks down on those he considers inferior — **snob·bish** *adj* — **snob·bish·ly** *adv* — **snob·bish·ness** *n*

snob·bery \\'snäb-(ə-)rē\\ *n, pl* **-ber·ies** : snobbish conduct

¹snoop \\'snüp\\ *vb* [D *snoepen* to buy or eat on the sly] : to pry in a furtive or meddlesome way

²snoop *n* : a prying meddlesome person

snooty \\'snüt-ē\\ *adj* **snoot·i·er; -est** : DISDAINFUL, SNOBBISH

snooze \\'snüz\\ *vb* **snoozed; snooz·ing** : to take a nap : DOZE — **snooze** *n*

snore \\'snōr\\ *vb* **snored; snor·ing** : to breathe with a rough hoarse noise while sleeping — **snore** *n*

snor·kel \\'snȯr-kəl\\ *n* [G *schnorchel*] : a tube projecting above the water used by swimmers for breathing with the face under water — **snorkel** *vb*

snort \\'snȯrt\\ *vb* : to force air violently and noisily through the nose 〈his horse ~*ed*〉 — **snort** *n*

snout \\'snaut\\ *n* **1** : a long projecting muzzle (as of a pig) **2** : a usu. large or grotesque nose

¹snow \\'snō\\ *n* **1** : crystals of ice formed from the vapor of water in the air **2** : a descent or shower of snow crystals — **snowy** *adj*

²snow *vb* **1** : to fall or cause to fall in or as snow **2** : to cover or shut in with or as if with snow

snow·ball \\'snō-ˌbȯl\\ *vb* : to increase or expand at a rapidly accelerating rate

snow·bank \\-ˌbaŋk\\ *n* : a mound or slope of snow

snow·belt \\-ˌbelt\\ *n, often cap* : a region that receives an appreciable amount of annual snowfall

snow·blow·er \\-ˌblō-ər\\ *n* : a machine in which a rotating spiral blade picks up and propels snow aside

snow·drift \\-ˌdrift\\ *n* : a bank of drifted snow

snow·drop \\-ˌdräp\\ *n* : a plant with narrow leaves and a nodding white flower that blooms early in the spring

snow·fall \\-ˌfȯl\\ *n* : a fall of snow

snow fence *n* : a fence across the path of prevailing winds to protect something (as a road) from drifting snow

snow·field \'snō-ˌfēld\ *n* : a mass of perennial snow at the head of a glacier

snow·mo·bile \'snō-mō-ˌbēl\ *n* : any of various automotive vehicles for travel on snow — **snow·mo·bil·er** \-ˌbē-lər\ *n* — **snow·mo·bil·ing** \-liŋ\ *n*

snow pea *n* : any of a variety of the cultivated pea with edible pods

snow·plow \'snō-ˌplaù\ *n* : a device for clearing away snow

¹**snow·shoe** \-ˌshü\ *n* : a light frame of wood strung with thongs that is attached to a shoe or boot to prevent sinking down into soft snow

²**snowshoe** *vb* **snow·shoed; snow·shoe·ing** : to travel on snowshoes

snow·storm \-ˌstórm\ *n* : a storm of falling snow

snow thrower *n* : SNOWBLOWER

snowy \'snō-ē\ *adj* **snow·i·er; -est 1** : marked by snow **2** : white as snow

snub \'snəb\ *vb* **snubbed; snub·bing** : to treat with disdain : SLIGHT — **snub** *n*

snub–nosed \'snəb-'nōzd\ *adj* : having a nose slightly turned up at the end

snuck past and past part of SNEAK

¹**snuff** \'snəf\ *vb* **1** : to pinch off the charred end of (a candle) **2** : to put out (a candle) — **snuff·er** *n*

²**snuff** *vb* **1** : to draw forcibly into or through the nose **2** : SMELL

³**snuff** *n* : SNIFF

⁴**snuff** *n* : pulverized tobacco

snuf·fle \'snəf-əl\ *vb* **snuf·fled; snuf·fling** \-(ə-)liŋ\ **1** : to snuff or sniff audibly and repeatedly **2** : to breathe with a sniffing sound — **snuf·fle** *n*

snug \'snəg\ *adj* **snug·ger; snug·gest 1** : fitting closely and comfortably **2** : CONCEALED — **snug·ly** *adv* — **snug·ness** *n*

snug·gle \'snəg-əl\ *vb* **snug·gled; snug·gling** \-(ə-)liŋ\ : to curl up or draw close comfortably : NESTLE

¹**so** \(')sō\ *adv* **1** : in the manner indicated **2** : in the same way **3** : THUS **4** : FINALLY **5** : to the extent indicated **6** : THEREFORE

²**so** *conj* : for that reason ⟨he wanted it, ∼ he took it⟩

³**so** \ˌsō, 'sō\ *pron* **1** : the same ⟨became chairman and remained ∼⟩ **2** : approximately that ⟨I'd like a dozen or ∼⟩

⁴**so** *abbr* south; southern

SO *abbr* strikeout

¹**soak** \'sōk\ *vb* **1** : to remain in a liquid **2** : WET, SATURATE **3** : to draw in by or as if by absorption **syn** drench, steep, impregnate, saturate

²**soak** *n* **1** : the act of soaking **2** : the liquid in which something is soaked **3** : DRUNKARD

soap \'sōp\ *n* : a cleansing substance made usu. by action of alkali on fat — **soap** *vb* — **soapy** *adj*

soap opera *n* [fr. its frequently being sponsored by soap manufacturers] : a radio or television daytime serial drama

soap·stone \'sōp-ˌstōn\ *n* : a soft stone having a soapy feel and containing talc

soar \'sōr\ *vb* : to fly upward or at a height on as if on wings

sob \'säb\ *vb* **sobbed; sob·bing** : to weep with convulsive heavings of the chest or contractions of the throat — **sob** *n*

so·ber \'sō-bər\ *adj* **so·ber·er** \-bər-ər\; **so·ber·est** \-b(ə-)rəst\ **1** : temperate in the use of liquor **2** : not drunk **3** : serious or grave in mood or disposition **4** : not affected by passion or prejudice **syn** solemn, earnest, staid, sedate — **so·ber·ly** *adv* — **so·ber·ness** *n*

so·bri·ety \sə-'brī-ət-ē, sō-\ *n* : the quality or state of being sober

so·bri·quet \'sō-bri-ˌkā, -ˌket\ *n* [F] : NICKNAME

soc *abbr* social; society

so–called \'sō-'kóld\ *adj* : commonly or popularly but often inaccurately so termed

soc·cer \'säk-ər\ *n* [by shortening & alter. fr. *association football*] : a football game played on a field by two teams with a round inflated ball

¹**so·cia·ble** \'sō-shə-bəl\ *adj* **1** : liking companionship : FRIENDLY **2** : characterized by pleasant social relations **syn** gracious, cordial, affable, genial — **so·cia·bil·i·ty** \ˌsō-shə-'bil-ət-ē\ *n* — **so·cia·bly** \'sō-shə-blē\ *adv*

²**sociable** *n* : an informal social gathering

¹**so·cial** \'sō-shəl\ *adj* **1** : marked by pleasant companionship with one's friends **2** : naturally living or growing in groups or communities ⟨∼ insects⟩ **3** : of or relating to human society, the interaction of the group and its members, and the welfare of these members ⟨∼ behavior⟩ **4** : of, relating to,

or based on rank in a particular society ⟨∼ circles⟩; *also* : of or relating to fashionable society — **so•cial•ly** \-ē\ *adv*

²social *n* : a social gathering

social disease *n* : VENEREAL DISEASE

so•cial•ism \'sō-shə-,liz-əm\ *n* : a theory of social organization based on government ownership, management, and control of the means of production and the distribution and exchange of goods — **so•cial•ist** \'sōsh-(ə-)ləst\ *n or adj* — **so•cial•is•tic** \,sō-shə-'lis-tik\ *adj*

so•cial•ite \'sō-shə-,līt\ *n* : a person prominent in fashionable society

so•cial•ize \'sō-shə-,līz\ *vb* **-ized; -iz•ing** 1 : to regulate according to the theory and practice of socialism 2 : to adapt to social needs or uses 3 : to participate actively in a social gathering — **so•cial•iza•tion** \,sōsh-(ə-)lə-'zā-shən\ *n*

socialized medicine *n* : medical and hospital services administered by an organized group (as a state agency) and paid for by funds obtained usu. by assessments, taxation, or philanthropy

social science *n* : a science that deals with human society or its elements (as family, state, or race), institutions, and relationships or with a particular aspect of human society — **social scientist** *n*

social work *n* : services, activities, or methods concerned with aiding the economically underprivileged and socially maladjusted — **social worker** *n*

so•ci•ety \sə-'sī-ət-ē\ *n, pl* **-et•ies** [MF *societé* fr. L *societat-, societas,* fr. *socius* companion] 1 : COMPANIONSHIP 2 : a voluntary association of persons for common ends 3 : a part of a community bound together by common interests and standards; *esp* : a leisure class indulging in social affairs

sociol *abbr* sociologist; sociology

so•ci•ol•o•gy \,sō-s(h)ē-'äl-ə-jē\ *n* : the study of the development and structure of society and social relationships — **so•ci•o•log•i•cal** \-ə-'läj-i-kəl\ *adj* — **so•ci•ol•o•gist** \-'äl-ə-jəst\ *n*

so•cio•re•li•gious \,sō-s(h)ē-ō-ri-'lij-əs\ *adj* : of, relating to, or involving both social and religious factors

¹sock \'säk\ *n, pl* **socks** *or* **sox** \'säks\ : a stocking with a short leg

²sock *vb* : to hit, strike, or apply forcefully

³sock *n* : a vigorous blow : PUNCH

sock•et \'säk-ət\ *n* : an opening or hollow that receives and holds something

socket wrench *n* : a wrench usu. in the form of a bar and removable socket made to fit a bolt or nut

sock in *vb* : to close to takeoffs or landings by aircraft

¹sod \'säd\ *n* : the surface layer of the soil filled with roots (as of grass)

²sod *vb* **sod•ded; sod•ding** : to cover with sod or turfs

so•da \'sōd-ə\ *n* 1 : SODIUM CARBONATE 2 : SODIUM BICARBONATE 3 : SODIUM 4 : SODA WATER 5 : SODA POP 6 : a sweet drink of soda water, flavoring, and often ice cream

soda pop *n* : a carbonated, sweetened, and flavored soft drink

soda water *n* : a beverage of water charged with carbon dioxide

sod•den \'säd-ᵊn\ *adj* 1 : lacking spirit : DULLED 2 : SOAKED, DRENCHED 3 : heavy or doughy from being improperly cooked ⟨∼ biscuits⟩

so•di•um \'sōd-ē-əm\ *n* : a soft waxy silver white metallic chemical element occurring in nature in combined form (as in salt)

sodium bicarbonate *n* : a white crystalline salt used in cooking and in medicine

sodium carbonate *n* : a carbonate of sodium used esp. in washing and bleaching textiles

sodium chloride *n* : SALT 1

sodium hydroxide *n* : a white brittle caustic substance used in making soap and rayon and in bleaching

sodium nitrate *n* : a crystalline salt used as a fertilizer and in curing meat

sodium thiosulfate *n* : a hygroscopic crystalline salt used as a photographic fixing agent

sod•omy \'säd-ə-mē\ *n* [ME, fr. OF *sodomie,* fr. LL *Sodoma* Sodom; fr. the homosexual proclivities of the men of the city (Gen 19:1–11)] 1 : copulation with a member of the same sex or with an animal 2 : non-coital and esp. anal or oral copulation

with a member of the opposite sex —
sod·om·ize \'säd-ə-ˌmīz\ vb
so·ev·er \sō-'ev-ər\ adv **1** : in any degree or manner ⟨how bad ∼⟩ **2** : at all
: of any kind ⟨any help ∼⟩
so·fa \'sō-fə\ n [Ar ṣuffah long bench]
: a couch usu. with upholstered back
and arms
soft \'sȯft\ adj **1** : not hard or rough
: NONVIOLENT **2** : RESTFUL, GENTLE,
SOOTHING **3** : emotionally susceptible
4 : not prepared to endure hardship **5**
: not containing certain salts that prevent lathering ⟨∼ water⟩ **6** : occurring
at such a speed as to avoid destructive
impact ⟨∼ landing of a spacecraft on
the moon⟩ **7** : BIODEGRADABLE ⟨a ∼ de-
tergent⟩ **8** : not alcoholic; also : less
detrimental than a hard narcotic **syn**
bland, mild, gentle, balmy — **soft·ly**
\'sȯft-lē\ adv — **soft·ness** \'sȯf(t)-nəs\
n
soft·ball \'sȯf(t)-ˌbȯl\ n : a game similar
to baseball played with a ball larger
and softer than a baseball; also : the
ball used in this game
soft·bound \-ˌbau̇nd\ adj : not bound in
hard covers ⟨∼ books⟩
soft coal n : bituminous coal
soft·en \'sȯ-fən\ vb **soft·ened; soft·en·ing**
\'sȯf-(ə-)niŋ\ : to make or become soft
— **soft·en·er** \-(ə-)nər\ n
soft palate n : the fold at the back of the
hard palate that partially separates the
mouth and the pharynx
soft·ware \'sȯft-ˌwaər\ n : the entire set
of programs, procedures, and related
documentation associated with a system; esp : computer programs
soft·wood \-ˌwu̇d\ n **1** : the wood of a
coniferous tree (as a pine or fir) as
compared to that of a tree producing
enclosed seeds **2** : a tree that yields
softwood — **softwood** adj
sog·gy \'säg-ē\ adj **sog·gi·er; -est** : heavy
with moisture : SOAKED, SODDEN —
sog·gi·ly \'säg-ə-lē\ adv — **sog·gi·ness**
\-ē-nəs\ n
soi·gné or **soi·gnée** \swän-'yā\ adj : elegantly maintained; esp : WELL≈
GROOMED
¹soil \'sȯil\ vb **1** : CORRUPT, POLLUTE **2**
: to make or become dirty **3** : STAIN,
DISGRACE
²soil n **1** : STAIN, DEFILEMENT **2** : EXCRE-
MENT, WASTE

³soil n **1** : firm land : EARTH **2** : the loose
surface material of the earth in which
plants grow **3** : COUNTRY, REGION
soi·ree or **soi·rée** \swä-'rā\ n [F soirée
evening period, evening party, fr.
MF, fr. soir evening, fr. L sero at a
late hour] : an evening party
so·journ \'sō-ˌjərn, sō-'jərn\ vb : to
dwell in a place temporarily — **sojourn** n — **so·journ·er** n
¹sol \'säl, 'sȯl\ n : a fluid colloidal system
²sol abbr **1** solicitor **2** soluble **3** solution
Sol \'säl\ n : SUN
¹sol·ace \'säl-əs\ n : COMFORT
²solace vb **so·laced; so·lac·ing** : to give
solace to : CONSOLE
so·lar \'sō-lər\ adj **1** : of, derived from,
or relating to the sun **2** : measured by
the earth's course in relation to the
sun ⟨the ∼ year⟩ **3** : operated by or
utilizing the sun's heat ⟨∼ house⟩
solar cell n : a photoelectric cell that
converts sunlight into electrical energy and is used as a power source
solar collector n : any of various devices for the absorption of solar radiation for the heating of water or buildings or the production of electricity
solar flare n : a sudden temporary outburst of energy from a small area of
the sun's surface
so·lar·i·um \sō-'lar-ē-əm, sə-\ n, pl **-ia**
\-ē-ə\ also **-ums** : a room exposed to
the sun; esp : a room (as in a hospital)
for exposure of the body to sunshine
solar plexus \'sō-lər-'plek-səs\ n **1** : a
network of nerves situated behind the
stomach **2** : the general area of the
stomach below the sternum
solar system n : the sun with the group
of celestial bodies that revolve about
it
solar wind n : the continuous radiation
of charged particles from the sun's
surface
sold past and past part of SELL
¹sol·der \'säd-ər, 'sȯd-\ n : a metallic alloy used when melted to mend or join
metallic surfaces
²solder vb **sol·dered; sol·der·ing** \-(ə-)riŋ\
1 : to unite or repair with solder **2** : to
join securely : CEMENT
soldering iron n : a metal device for applying heat in soldering
¹sol·dier \'sōl-jər\ n [ME soudier, fr.

OF, fr. *soulde* pay, fr. LL *solidus* a Roman coin, fr. L, solid] : a person in military service; *esp* : an enlisted man — **sol·dier·ly** *adj or adv*

²**soldier** *vb* **sol·diered; sol·dier·ing** \ˌsōlj-(ə-)riŋ\ **1** : to serve as a soldier **2** : to pretend to work while actually doing nothing

soldier of fortune : ADVENTURER

sol·diery \ˈsōlj-(ə-)rē\ *n* **1** : a body of soldiers **2** : the profession of soldiering

¹**sole** \ˈsōl\ *n* **1** : the undersurface of the foot **2** : the bottom of a shoe

²**sole** *vb* **soled; sol·ing** : to furnish (a shoe) with a sole

³**sole** *n* : any of various mostly small= mouthed flatfishes valued as food

⁴**sole** *adj* : ONLY, SINGLE — **sole·ly** \ˈsō(l)-lē\ *adv*

so·le·cism \ˈsäl-ə-ˌsiz-əm, ˈsō-lə-\ *n* **1** : a mistake in grammar **2** : a breach of etiquette

sol·emn \ˈsäl-əm\ *adj* **1** : marked by or observed with full religious ceremony **2** : FORMAL, CEREMONIOUS **3** : highly serious : GRAVE **4** : SOMBER, GLOOMY **syn** ceremonial, conventional, stately — **so·lem·ni·ty** \sə-ˈlem-nət-ē\ *n* — **sol·emn·ly** \ˈsäl-əm-lē\ *adv* — **sol·emn·ness** *n*

sol·em·nize \ˈsäl-əm-ˌnīz\ *vb* **-nized; -niz·ing** **1** : to observe or honor with solemnity **2** : to celebrate (a marriage) with religious rites — **sol·em·ni·az·tion** \ˈsäl-əm-nə-ˈzā-shən\ *n*

so·le·noid \ˈsō-lə-ˌnȯid, ˈsäl-\ *n* : a coil of wire usu. in cylindrical form that when carrying a current acts like a magnet

so·lic·it \sə-ˈlis-ət\ *vb* **1** : ENTREAT, BEG **2** : to approach with a request or plea **3** : TEMPT, LURE **syn** ask, request, desire — **so·lic·i·ta·tion** \-ˌlis-ə-ˈtā-shən\ *n*

so·lic·i·tor \sə-ˈlis-ət-ər\ *n* **1** : one that solicits **2** : LAWYER; *esp* : a legal official of a city or state

so·lic·i·tous \sə-ˈlis-ət-əs\ *adj* **1** : WORRIED, CONCERNED **2** : EAGER, WILLING **syn** avid, impatient, keen, anxious — **so·lic·i·tous·ly** *adv*

so·lic·i·tude \sə-ˈlis-ə-ˌt(y)üd\ *n* : CONCERN, ANXIETY

¹**sol·id** \ˈsäl-əd\ *adj* **1** : not hollow; *also* : written as one word without a hy-

phen ⟨a ∼ compound⟩ **2** : having, involving, or dealing with three dimensions or with solids **3** : not loose or spongy : COMPACT ⟨a ∼ mass of rock⟩; *also* : neither gaseous nor liquid : HARD, RIGID ⟨∼ ice⟩ **4** : of good substantial quality or kind ⟨∼ comfort⟩ **5** : thoroughly dependable : RELIABLE ⟨a ∼ citizen⟩; *also* : serious in purpose or character ⟨∼ reading⟩ **6** : UNANIMOUS, UNITED ⟨∼ for pay increases⟩ **7** : of one substance or character — **solid** *adv* — **so·lid·i·ty** \sə-ˈlid-ət-ē\ *n* — **sol·id·ly** \ˈsäl-əd-lē\ *adv* — **sol·id·ness** *n*

²**solid** *n* **1** : a geometrical figure (as a cube or sphere) having three dimensions **2** : a solid substance

sol·i·dar·i·ty \ˌsäl-ə-ˈdar-ət-ē\ *n* : unity based on shared interests, objectives, or standards

solid geometry *n* : a branch of geometry that deals with figures of three-dimensional space

so·lid·i·fy \sə-ˈlid-ə-ˌfī\ *vb* **-fied; -fy·ing** : to make or become solid — **so·lid·i·fi·ca·tion** \-ˌlid-ə-fə-ˈkā-shən\ *n*

solid–state *adj* **1** : relating to the structure and properties of solid material **2** : not using vacuum tubes

so·lil·o·quize \sə-ˈlil-ə-ˌkwīz\ *vb* **-quized; -quiz·ing** : to talk to oneself : utter a soliloquy

so·lil·o·quy \sə-ˈlil-ə-kwē\ *n, pl* **-quies** [LL *soliloquium,* fr. L *solus* alone + *loqui* to speak] **1** : the act of talking to oneself **2** : a dramatic monologue that gives the illusion of being a series of unspoken reflections

sol·i·taire \ˈsäl-ə-ˌtaər\ *n* **1** : a single gem (as a diamond) set alone **2** : a card game played by one person alone

sol·i·tary \ˈsäl-ə-ˌter-ē\ *adj* **1** : being or living apart from others **2** : LONELY, SECLUDED **3** : SOLE, ONLY

sol·i·tude \ˈsäl-ə-ˌt(y)üd\ *n* **1** : the state of being alone : SECLUSION **2** : a lonely place **syn** isolation

soln *abbr* solution

¹**so·lo** \ˈsō-lō\ *n, pl* **solos** [It, fr. *solo* alone, fr. L *solus*] **1** : a piece of music for a single voice or instrument with or without accompaniment **2** : an action in which there is only one performer — **solo** *adj or vb* — **so·lo·ist** *n*

²**solo** *adv* : without a companion : ALONE

so·lon \\'sō-lən\ *n* **1** : a wise and skillful lawgiver **2** : a member of a legislative body

sol·stice \\'säl-stəs\ *n* [ME, fr. OF, fr. L *solstitium*, fr. *sol* sun + *status*, pp. of *sistere* to come to a stop, cause to stand] : the time of the year when the sun is farthest north of the equator (**summer solstice**) about June 22 or farthest south (**winter solstice**) about Dec. 22 — **sol·sti·tial** \säl-'stish-əl\ *adj*

sol·u·ble \\'säl-yə-bəl\ *adj* **1** : capable of being dissolved in or as if in a fluid **2** : capable of being solved or explained — **sol·u·bil·i·ty** \,säl-yə-'bil-ət-ē\ *n*

sol·ute \\'säl-,yüt\ *n* : a dissolved substance

so·lu·tion \sə-'lü-shən\ *n* **1** : an action or process of solving a problem; *also* : an answer to a problem **2** : an act or the process by which one substance is homogenously mixed with another usu. liquid substance; *also* : a mixture thus formed

solve \\'sälv\ *vb* **solved; solv·ing** : to find the answer to or a solution for — **solv·able** *adj*

sol·ven·cy \\'säl-vən-sē\ *n* : the condition of being solvent

¹sol·vent \-vənt\ *adj* **1** : able or sufficient to pay all legal debts **2** : dissolving or able to dissolve

²solvent *n* : a usu. liquid substance capable of dissolving or dispersing one or more other substances

som·ber *or* **som·bre** \\'säm-bər\ *adj* **1** : DARK, GLOOMY **2** : GRAVE, MELANCHOLY — **som·ber·ly** *adv*

som·bre·ro \səm-'brer-ō\ *n, pl* **-ros** [Sp, fr. *sombra* shade] : a broad-brimmed felt hat worn esp. in the Southwest and in Mexico

¹some \(')səm\ *adj* **1** : one unspecified ⟨~ man called⟩ **2** : an unspecified or indefinite number of ⟨~ berries are ripe⟩ **3** : at least a few or a little ⟨~ years ago⟩

²some \\'səm\ *pron* : a certain number or amount ⟨~ of them are here⟩ ⟨~ of it is missing⟩

¹-some \səm\ *adj suffix* : characterized by a (specified) thing, quality, state, or action ⟨awe*some*⟩ ⟨burden*some*⟩

²-some *n suffix* : a group of (so many) members and esp. persons ⟨four*some*⟩

¹some·body \\'səm-,bäd-ē, -bəd-\ *pron* : some person

²somebody *n* : a person of importance

some·day \\'səm-,dā\ *adv* : at some future time

some·how \-,haů\ *adv* : by some means

some·one \-(,)wən\ *pron* : some person

som·er·sault \\'səm-ər-,sȯlt\ *n* [MF *sombresaut* leap, deriv. of L *super* over + *saltus* leap, fr. *salire* to jump] : a leap or roll in which a person turns the heels over the head — **somersault** *vb*

som·er·set \-,set\ *n or vb* : SOMERSAULT

some·thing \\'səm-thiŋ\ *pron* : some undetermined or unspecified thing

some·time \\'səm-,tīm\ *adv* **1** : at a future time **2** : at an unknown or unnamed time

some·times \\'səm-,tīmz\ *adv* : OCCASIONALLY

¹some·what \-,hwät, -,hwət\ *pron* : SOMETHING

²somewhat *adv* : in some degree

some·where \-,hweər\ *adv* : in, at, or to an unknown or unnamed place

som·nam·bu·lism \säm-'nam-byə-,liz-əm\ *n* : activity (as walking about) during sleep — **som·nam·bu·list** \-ləst\ *n*

som·no·lent \\'säm-nə-lənt\ *adj* : SLEEPY, DROWSY — **som·no·lence** \-ləns\ *n*

son \\'sən\ *n* **1** : a male offspring or descendant **2** *cap* : Jesus Christ **3** : a person deriving from a particular source (as a country, race, or school)

so·nar \\'sō-,när\ *n* [*sound na*vigation *r*anging] : an apparatus that detects the presence and location of submerged objects (as submarines) by sound waves

so·na·ta \sə-'nät-ə\ *n* [It] : an instrumental composition with three or four movements differing in rhythm and mood but related in key

son·a·ti·na \,sän-ə-'tē-nə\ *n* [It, dim. of *sonata*] : a short usu. simplified sonata

song \\'sȯŋ\ *n* **1** : vocal music; *also* : a short composition of words and music **2** : poetic composition **3** : a distinctive or characteristic sound (as of a bird) **4** : a small amount ⟨sold for a ~⟩

song·bird \\'sȯŋ-,bərd\ *n* : a bird that utters a series of musical tones

Song of Sol·o·mon \-'säl-ə-mən\ *n* — see BIBLE table

Song of Songs *n* — see BIBLE table

song•ster \-stər\ *n* : one that sings

song•stress \-strəs\ *n* : a female singer

son•ic \'sän-ik\ *adj* : of or relating to sound waves or the speed of sound

sonic boom *n* : an explosive sound produced by an aircraft traveling at supersonic speed

son–in–law \'sȯn-ən-ˌlȯ\ *n, pl* **sons–in–law** : the husband of one's daughter

son•net \'sän-ət\ *n* : a poem of 14 lines usu. in iambic pentameter with a definite rhyme scheme

so•no•rous \sə-'nōr-əs, 'sän-ə-rəs\ *adj* **1** : giving out sound when struck **2** : loud, deep, or rich in sound : RESONANT **3** : high-sounding : IMPRESSIVE — **so•nor•i•ty** \sə-'nȯr-ət-ē\ *n*

soon \'sün\ *adv* **1** : before long **2** : PROMPTLY, QUICKLY **3** *archaic* : EARLY **4** : WILLINGLY, READILY

soot \'sut, 'sət, 'süt\ *n* : a fine black powder consisting chiefly of carbon that is formed when something burns and that colors smoke — **sooty** *adj*

sooth \'süth\ *n, archaic* : TRUTH

soothe \'süth\ *vb* **soothed; sooth•ing 1** : to please by flattery or attention **2** : to calm down : COMFORT — **sooth•er** *n* — **sooth•ing•ly** *adv*

sooth•say•er \'süth-ˌsā-ər\ *n* : one that foretells events — **sooth•say•ing** \-iŋ\ *n*

¹**sop** \'säp\ *n* : a conciliatory bribe, gift, or concession

²**sop** *vb* **sopped; sop•ping 1** : to steep or dip in or as if in a liquid **2** : to wet thoroughly : SOAK; *also* : to mop up (a liquid)

SOP *abbr* standard operating procedure; standing operating procedure

soph *abbr* sophomore

soph•ism \'säf-ˌiz-əm\ *n* **1** : an argument correct in form but embodying a subtle fallacy **2** : SOPHISTRY

soph•ist \'säf-əst\ *n* : PHILOSOPHER; *esp* : a captious or fallacious reasoner

so•phis•tic \sä-'fis-tik, sə-\ *or* **so•phis•ti•cal** \-ti-kəl\ *adj* : of or characteristic of sophists or sophistry **syn** fallacious, illogical, unreasonable, unreasoned

so•phis•ti•cat•ed \-tə-ˌkāt-əd\ *adj* **1** : COMPLEX ⟨∼ instruments⟩ **2** : made wise or worldly-wise by experience or disillusionment **3** : intellectually appealing ⟨∼ novel⟩ — **so•phis•ti•ca•tion** \-ˌfis-tə-'kā-shən\ *n*

soph•ist•ry \'säf-ə-strē\ *n* : subtly deceptive reasoning or argument

soph•o•more \'säf-(ə-)ˌmȯr\ *n* : a student in his or her second year of college or secondary school

soph•o•mor•ic \ˌsäf-ə-'mȯr-ik\ *adj* **1** : being overconfident of knowledge but poorly informed and immature **2** : of, relating to, or characteristic of a sophomore

So•pho•ni•as \ˌsäf-ə-'nī-əs, ˌsō-fə-\ *n* — see BIBLE table

sop•o•rif•ic \ˌsäp-ə-'rif-ik\ *adj* **1** : causing sleep or drowsiness **2** : LETHARGIC

so•pra•no \sə-'pran-ō\ *n, pl* **-nos** [It, fr. *sopra* above, fr. L *supra*] **1** : the highest singing voice; *also* : a part for this voice **2** : a singer with a soprano voice — **soprano** *adj*

sorb \'sȯrb\ *vb* : to take up and hold by adsorption or absorption

sor•bet \'sȯr-bət\ *n* : ice having a fruit flavor and typically served between courses as a palate refresher

sor•cery \'sȯrs-(ə-)rē\ *n* [ME *sorcerie,* fr. OF, fr. *sorcier* sorcerer, fr. (assumed) VL *sortiarius,* fr. L *sort-, sors* chance, lot] : the use of magic : WITCHCRAFT — **sor•cer•er** \-rər\ *n* — **sor•cer•ess** \-rəs\ *n*

sor•did \'sȯrd-əd\ *adj* **1** : FILTHY, DIRTY **2** : marked by baseness or grossness : VILE — **sor•did•ly** *adv* — **sor•did•ness** *n*

¹**sore** \'sōr\ *adj* **sor•er; sor•est 1** : causing pain or distress ⟨a ∼ bruise⟩ **2** : painfully sensitive ⟨∼ eyes⟩ **3** : SEVERE, INTENSE **4** : IRRITATED, ANGRY — **sore•ly** *adv* — **sore•ness** *n*

²**sore** *n* **1** : a sore spot on the body; *esp* : one (as an ulcer) with the tissues broken and usu. infected **2** : a source of pain or vexation

sore•head \'sō(ə)r-ˌhed, 'sȯ(ə)r-\ *n* : a person easily angered or discontented

sore throat *n* : painful throat due to inflammation

sor•ghum \'sȯr-gəm\ *n* : a tall variable Old World tropical grass grown widely for its edible seed, for forage, or for its sweet juice which yields a syrup

so•ror•i•ty \sə-'rȯr-ət-ē\ *n, pl* **-ties** [ML *sororitas* sisterhood, fr. L *soror* sister] : a club of girls or women esp. at a college

sorp·tion \'sȯrp-shən\ *n* : the process of sorbing : the state of being sorbed

sor·rel \'sȯr-əl\ *n* : any of several sour-juiced herbs

sor·row \'sär-ō\ *n* **1** : deep distress and regret **2** : a cause of grief or sadness **3** : a display of grief or sadness — **sor·row** *vb* — **sor·row·ful** \-fəl\ *adj* — **sor·row·ful·ly** \-f(ə-)lē\ *adv*

sor·ry \'sär-ē\ *adj* **sor·ri·er; -est 1** : feeling sorrow, regret, or penitence **2** : MOURNFUL, SAD **3** : causing sorrow, pity, or scorn : WRETCHED

¹sort \'sȯrt\ *n* **1** : a group of persons or things that have similar characteristics : CLASS **2** : WAY, MANNER **3** : QUALITY, NATURE — **out of sorts 1** : somewhat ill **2** : GROUCHY, IRRITABLE

²sort *vb* **1** : to put in a certain place according to kind, class, or nature **2** : to be in accord : AGREE

sor·tie \'sȯrt-ē, sȯr-'tē\ *n* **1** : a sudden issuing of troops from a defensive position against the enemy **2** : one mission or attack by one airplane

SOS \,es-(,)ō-'es\ *n* : a call or request for help or rescue

so—so \'sō-'sō\ *adv or adj* : PASSABLY

sot \'sät\ *n* : a habitual drunkard — **sot·tish** *adj*

sou·brette \sü-'bret\ *n* [F] : a coquettish maidservant or a frivolous young woman in a comedy

souf·flé \sü-'flā\ *n* [F, fr. *soufflé*, pp. of *souffler* to blow, puff up, fr. L *sufflare*, fr. *sub-* up + *flare* to blow] : a spongy dish made light in baking by stiffly beaten egg whites

sough \'saù, 'səf\ *vb* : to make a moaning or sighing sound — **sough** *n*

sought past and past part of SEEK

¹soul \'sōl\ *n* **1** : the immaterial essence of an individual life **2** : the spiritual principle embodied in human beings or the universe **3** : an active or essential part **4** : man's moral and emotional nature **5** : spiritual or moral force **6** : PERSON ⟨a kindly ∼⟩ **7** : a strong, positive feeling (as of intense sensitivity and emotional fervor) conveyed esp. by black American performers; *also* : NEGRITUDE — **souled** \'sōld\ *adj* — **soul·less** \'sōl-ləs\ *adj*

²soul *adj* **1** : of, relating to, or characteristic of black Americans or their culture ⟨∼ food⟩ ⟨∼ music⟩ **2** : designed for or controlled by blacks ⟨∼ radio stations⟩

soul brother *n* : a black male

soul·ful \'sōl-fəl\ *adj* : full of or expressing deep feeling — **soul·ful·ly** \-ē\ *adv*

¹sound \'saùnd\ *adj* **1** : not diseased or sickly **2** : free from flaw or defect **3** : FIRM, STRONG **4** : free from error : RIGHT **5** : LEGAL, VALID **6** : THOROUGH **7** : UNDISTURBED ⟨∼ sleep⟩ **8** : showing good judgment — **sound·ly** *adv* — **sound·ness** *n*

²sound *n* **1** : the sensation of hearing; *also* : mechanical energy transmitted by longitudinal pressure waves (as in air) that is the stimulus to hearing **2** : something heard : NOISE, TONE; *also* : hearing distance : EARSHOT **3** : a musical style — **sound·less** *adj* — **sound·proof** \-,prüf\ *adj or vb*

³sound *vb* **1** : to make or cause to make a noise **2** : to order or proclaim by a sound ⟨∼ the alarm⟩ **3** : to convey a certain impression : SEEM **4** : to examine the condition of by causing to give out sounds

⁴sound *n* : a long passage of water wider than a strait often connecting two larger bodies of water ⟨Long Island ∼⟩

⁵sound *vb* **1** : to measure the depth of (water) esp. by a weighted line dropped from the surface : FATHOM **2** : PROBE **3** : to dive down suddenly ⟨the hooked fish ∼ed⟩ — **sound·ing** *n*

sound·er \'saùn-dər\ *n* : one that sounds; *esp* : a device for making soundings

sound·stage \'saùn(d)-,stāj\ *n* : the part of a motion-picture studio in which a production is filmed

soup \'süp\ *n* **1** : a liquid food with stock as its base and often containing pieces of solid food **2** : something having the consistency of soup **3** : an unfortunate predicament ⟨in the ∼⟩

soup up *vb* : to increase the power of

soup·çon \süp-'sōⁿ\ *n* [F] : a little bit : TRACE

soupy \'sü-pē\ *adj* **soup·i·er; -est 1** : having the consistency of soup **2** : densely foggy or cloudy

¹sour \'saù(ə)r\ *adj* **1** : having an acid or tart taste ⟨∼ as vinegar⟩ **2** : SPOILED, PUTRID ⟨a ∼ odor⟩ **3** : UNPLEASANT,

DISAGREEABLE ⟨∼ disposition⟩ — **sour-ish** *adj* — **sour•ly** *adv* — **sour•ness** *n*

²sour *vb* : to become or make sour

source \'sōrs\ *n* **1** : ORIGIN, BEGINNING **2** : the beginning of a stream of water **3** : a supplier of information

¹souse \'saùs\ *vb* **soused; sous•ing 1** : PICKLE **2** : to plunge into a liquid **3** : DRENCH **4** : to make drunk

²souse *n* **1** : something (as pigs' feet) steeped in pickle **2** : a soaking in liquid **3** : DRUNKARD

¹south \'saùth\ *adv* : to or toward the south

²south *adj* **1** : situated toward or at the south **2** : coming from the south

³south *n* **1** : the direction to the right of one facing east **2** : the compass point directly opposite to north **3** *cap* : regions or countries south of a specified or implied point; *esp* : the southeastern part of the U.S. — **south•er•ly** \'sə<u>th</u>-ər-lē\ *adj or adv* — **south•ern** \'sə<u>th</u>-ərn\ *adj* — **South•ern•er** *n* — **south•ern•most** \-ˌmōst\ *adj* — **south-ward** \'saùth-wərd\ *adv or adj* — **south•wards** \-wərdz\ *adv*

South African *n* : a native or inhabitant of the Republic of South Africa — **South African** *adj*

south•east \saùth-'ēst, *naut* saù-'ēst\ *n* **1** : the general direction between south and east **2** : the compass point midway between south and east **3** *cap* : regions or countries southeast of a specified or implied point — **southeast** *adj or adv* — **south•east•er•ly** *adv or adj* — **south•east•ern** \-ərn\ *adj*

south•paw \'saùth-ˌpò\ *n* : a left-handed baseball pitcher — **southpaw** *adj*

south pole *n, often cap S&P* : the southernmost point of the earth

south•west \saùth-'west, *naut* saù-'west\ *n* **1** : the general direction between south and west **2** : the compass point midway between south and west **3** *cap* : regions or countries southwest of a specified or implied point — **southwest** *adj or adv* — **south•west•er•ly** *adv or adj* — **south•west•ern** \-ərn\ *adj*

sou•ve•nir \ˌsü-və-'nir\ *n* [F] : something serving as a reminder

sou'•west•er \saù-'wes-tər\ *n* : a waterproof hat worn at sea in stormy weather; *also* : a long waterproof coat

¹sov•er•eign \'säv-(ə-)rən\ *n* **1** : one possessing the supreme power and authority in a state **2** : a gold coin of the United Kingdom

²sovereign *adj* **1** : EXCELLENT, FINE **2** : supreme in power or authority **3** : CHIEF, HIGHEST **4** : having independent authority **syn** dominant, predominant, paramount, preponderant

sov•er•eign•ty \-tē\ *n, pl* **-ties 1** : supremacy in rule or power **2** : power to govern without external control **3** : the supreme political power in a state

so•vi•et \'sōv-ē-ˌet, 'säv-, -ē-ət\ *n* **1** : an elected governmental council in a Communist country **2** *pl, cap* : the people and esp. the leaders of the U.S.S.R. — **so•vi•et•ism** *n, often cap* — **so•vi•et•ize** *vb, often cap*

¹sow \'saù\ *n* : an adult female swine

²sow \'sō\ *vb* **sowed; sown** \'sōn\ *or* **sowed; sow•ing 1** : to plant seed for growing esp. by scattering **2** : to strew with or as if with seed **3** : to scatter abroad — **sow•er** \'sō(-ə)r\ *n*

sow bug \'saù-\ *n* : WOOD LOUSE

sox pl of SOCK

soy \'sòi\ *n* : a sauce made from soybeans fermented in brine

soy•bean \'sòi-ˌbēn\ *n* : an Asian legume widely grown for forage and for its edible seeds that yield a valuable oil (**soybean oil**); *also* : its seed

sp *abbr* **1** special **2** species **3** specimen **4** spelling **5** spirit

Sp *abbr* Spain

SP *abbr* **1** shore patrol; shore patrolman **2** shore police **3** specialist

spa \'spä\ *n* [*Spa*, watering place in Belgium] **1** : a mineral spring; *also* : a resort with mineral springs **2** : a commercial establishment with facilities for healthful exercise

¹space \'spās\ *n* **1** : a period of time **2** : some small measurable part of space **3** : the limitless area in which all things exist and move **4** : an empty place **5** : the region beyond the earth's atmosphere **6** : a definite place (as a seat or stateroom on a train or ship)

²space *vb* **spaced; spac•ing** : to place at intervals

space–age \'spās-ˌāj\ *adj* : of, relating

to, or befitting the age of space exploration ⟨∼ technology⟩

space·craft \-ˌkraft\ *n* : a vehicle for travel beyond the earth's atmosphere

space·flight \-ˌflīt\ *n* : flight beyond the earth's atmosphere

space heater *n* : a device for heating an enclosed space

space·man \'spās-ˌman, -mən\ *n* : one who travels outside the earth's atmosphere

space·ship \'spās(h)-ˌship\ *n* : a spacecraft designed to carry one or more passengers

space shuttle *n* : a reusable spacecraft designed to transport people and cargo between earth and space

space station *n* : a manned artificial satellite in a fixed orbit serving as a base (as for scientific observation)

space suit *n* : a suit equipped to make life in space possible for its wearer

space walk *n* : a period of movement in space outside a spacecraft by an astronaut — **space walk** *vb* — **space·walk·er** \'spās-ˌwȯ-kər\ *n* — **space·walk·ing** \-kiŋ\ *n*

spa·cious \'spā-shəs\ *adj* : very large in extent : ROOMY **syn** commodious, capacious, ample — **spa·cious·ly** *adv* — **spa·cious·ness** *n*

¹spade \'spād\ *n* : a shovel with a flat blade — **spade·ful** *n*

²spade *vb* **spad·ed; spad·ing** : to dig with a spade

³spade *n* : any of a suit of playing cards marked with a black figure resembling an inverted heart with a short stem at the bottom

spa·dix \'spād-iks\ *n, pl* **spa·di·ces** \'spād-ə-ˌsēz\ : a floral spike with a fleshy or succulent axis usu. enclosed in a spathe

spa·ghet·ti \spə-'get-ē\ *n* [It, fr. pl. of *spaghetto,* dim. of *spago* cord, string] : a dough made chiefly from wheat flour and formed in thin solid strings

¹span \'span\ *n* **1** : an English unit of length equal to nine inches (about 23 centimeters) **2** : a limited portion of time **3** : the spread (as of an arch) from one support to another

²span *vb* **spanned; span·ning 1** : MEASURE **2** : to extend across

³span *n* : a pair of animals (as mules) driven together

Span *abbr* Spanish

span·dex \'span-ˌdeks\ *n* : an elastic synthetic textile fiber

span·gle \'spaŋ-gəl\ *n* : a small disk of shining metal used esp. on a dress for ornament — **spangle** *vb*

Span·iard \'span-yərd\ *n* : a native or inhabitant of Spain

span·iel \'span-yəl\ *n* [ME *spaniell,* fr. MF *espaignol,* lit., Spaniard, fr. L *Hispania* Spain] : any of numerous mostly small and short-legged dogs usu. with long wavy hair and large drooping ears

Span·ish \'span-ish\ *n* **1** : the chief language of Spain and of many countries colonized by the Spanish **2 Spanish** *pl* : the people of Spain — **Spanish** *adj*

Spanish American *n* : a native or inhabitant of one of the countries of America in which Spanish is the national language; *also* : a resident of the U.S. whose native language is Spanish — **Spanish–American** *adj*

Spanish fly *n* : a dried preparation of green European beetles with diuretic and aphrodisiac effects produced by irritating the urinary tract; *also* : this beetle

Spanish moss *n* : a plant related to the pineapple that grows in pendent tufts of grayish green filaments on trees in the southern U.S. and the West Indies

spank \'spaŋk\ *vb* : to strike the buttocks of with the open hand — **spank** *n*

spank·ing \'spaŋ-kiŋ\ *adj* : BRISK, LIVELY ⟨∼ breeze⟩

¹spar \'spär\ *n* : a rounded wood or metal piece (as a mast, yard, boom, or gaff) for supporting sail rigging

²spar *vb* **sparred; spar·ring** : to box for practice without serious hitting; *also* : SKIRMISH, WRANGLE

SPAR \'spär\ *n* : a member of the women's reserve of the U.S. Coast Guard

¹spare \'spaər\ *vb* **spared; spar·ing 1** : to refrain from punishing or injuring : show mercy to **2** : to exempt from something **3** : to get along without **4** : to use frugally or rarely

²spare *adj* **spar·er; spar·est 1** : held in reserve **2** : SUPERFLUOUS **3** : not liberal or profuse **4** : LEAN, THIN **5** : SCANTY **syn** meager, sparse, skimpy, exiguous, scant

³**spare** *n* **1** : a duplicate kept in reserve; *esp* : a spare tire **2** : the knocking down of all the bowling pins with the first two balls

spar·ing \'spar-iŋ\ *adj* : SAVING, FRUGAL **syn** thrifty, economical, provident — **spar·ing·ly** *adv*

¹**spark** \'spärk\ *n* **1** : a small particle of a burning substance or a hot glowing particle struck from a mass (as by steel on flint) **2** : a short bright flash of electricity between two points **3** : SPARKLE **4** : a particle capable of being kindled or developed : GERM

²**spark** *vb* **1** : to emit or produce sparks **2** : to stir to activity : INCITE

³**spark** *vb* : WOO, COURT

¹**spar·kle** \'spär-kəl\ *vb* **spar·kled; spar·kling** \-k(ə-)liŋ\ **1** : FLASH, GLEAM **2** : to perform brilliantly **3** : EFFERVESCE — **spar·kler** \-k(ə-)lər\ *n*

²**sparkle** *n* **1** : GLEAM **2** : ANIMATION

spark plug *n* : a device that produces a spark to ignite the fuel mixture in an engine cylinder

spar·row \'spar-ō\ *n* : any of several small dull singing birds

sparrow hawk *n* : any of various small hawks or falcons

sparse \'spärs\ *adj* **spars·er; spars·est** : thinly scattered : SCANTY **syn** meager, spare, skimpy, exiguous, scant — **sparse·ly** *adv*

spasm \'spaz-əm\ *n* **1** : an involuntary and abnormal muscular contraction **2** : a sudden, violent, and temporary effort or feeling — **spas·mod·ic** \spaz-'mäd-ik\ *adj* — **spas·mod·i·cal·ly** \-i-k(ə-)lē\ *adv*

spas·tic \'spas-tik\ *adj* : of, relating to, or marked by muscular spasm ⟨∼ paralysis⟩ — **spastic** *n*

¹**spat** \'spat\ past and past part of SPIT

²**spat** *n, pl* **spat** *or* **spats** : a young bivalve mollusk (as an oyster)

³**spat** *n* : a gaiter covering instep and ankle

⁴**spat** *n* : a brief petty quarrel : DISPUTE

⁵**spat** *vb* **spat·ted; spat·ting** : to quarrel briefly

spate \'spāt\ *n* : a sudden outburst

spathe \'spāth\ *n* : a sheathing bract or pair of bracts enclosing an inflorescence (as of the calla lily) and esp. a spadix on the same axis

spa·tial \'spā-shəl\ *adj* : of or relating to space — **spa·tial·ly** \-ē\ *adv*

spat·ter \'spat-ər\ *vb* **1** : to splash with drops of liquid **2** : to sprinkle around — **spatter** *n*

spat·u·la \'spach-ə-lə\ *n* : a flexible knifelike implement for scooping, spreading, or mixing soft substances

spav·in \'spav-ən\ *n* : a bony enlargement of the hock of a horse — **spav·ined** \-ənd\ *adj*

¹**spawn** \'spȯn\ *vb* [ME *spawnen,* fr. OF *espandre* to spread out, expand; fr. L *expandere,* fr. *ex-* out + *pandere* to spread] **1** : to produce eggs or offspring esp. in large numbers **2** : GENERATE

²**spawn** *n* **1** : the eggs of water animals (as fishes or oysters) that lay many small eggs **2** : offspring esp. when produced in great quantities

spay \'spā\ *vb* **spayed; spay·ing** : to remove the ovaries from (a female animal)

SPCA *abbr* Society for the Prevention of Cruelty to Animals

SPCC *abbr* Society for the Prevention of Cruelty to Children

speak \'spēk\ *vb* **spoke** \'spōk\; **spo·ken** \'spō-kən\; **speak·ing** **1** : to utter words **2** : to express orally **3** : to mention in speech or writing **4** : to address an audience **5** : to use or be able to use (a language) in speech

speak·easy \'spē-ˌkē-zē\ *n, pl* **-eas·ies** : an illicit drinking place

speak·er \'spē-kər\ *n* **1** : one that speaks **2** : the presiding officer of a deliberative assembly **3** : LOUDSPEAKER

¹**spear** \'spiər\ *n* **1** : a long-shafted weapon with a sharp point for thrusting or throwing **2** : a sharp-pointed instrument with barbs (as for spearing fish) — **spear·man** \-mən\ *n*

²**spear** *vb* : to strike or pierce with or as if with a spear

³**spear** *n* : a young shoot (as of asparagus)

spear·head \-ˌhed\ *n* : a leading force, element, or influence — **spearhead** *vb*

spear·mint \-ˌmint\ *n* : a common highly aromatic garden mint

spec *abbr* **1** special **2** specifically

spe·cial \'spesh-əl\ *adj* **1** : UNCOMMON, NOTEWORTHY **2** : particularly favored

3 : INDIVIDUAL, UNIQUE **4** : EXTRA, ADDITIONAL **5** : confined to or designed for a definite field of action, purpose, or occasion — **special** *n* — **spe·cial·ly** \-ē\ *adv*

special delivery *n* : delivery of mail by messenger for an extra fee

Special Forces *n pl* : a branch of the army composed of men specially trained in guerrilla warfare

spe·cial·ist \'spesh-(ə-)ləst\ *n* **1** : one who devotes himself to some special branch of learning or activity **2** : any of four enlisted ranks in the army corresponding to the grades of corporal through sergeant first class

spe·cial·ize \'spesh-ə-ˌlīz\ *vb* **-ized; -iz·ing** : to concentrate one's efforts in a special activity or field; *also* : to change in an adaptive manner — **spe·cial·iza·tion** \ˌspesh-ə-lə-'zā-shən\ *n*

spe·cial·ty \'spesh-əl-tē\ *n, pl* **-ties** **1** : a particular quality or detail **2** : a product of a special kind or of special excellence **3** : a branch of knowledge, business, or professional work in which one specializes

spe·cie \'spē-shē, -sē\ *n* : money in coin

spe·cies \'spē-shēz, -sēz\ *n, pl* **spe·cies** [L, appearance, kind, species, fr. *specere* to look] **1** : SORT, KIND **2** : a category of biological classification ranking just below the genus or subgenus and comprising closely related organisms potentially able to breed with one another

specif *abbr* specific; specifically

¹spe·cif·ic \spi-'sif-ik\ *adj* **1** : DEFINITE, EXACT **2** : having a unique relation to something ⟨∼ antibodies⟩; *esp* : exerting a distinctive and usu. curative or causative influence **3** : of, relating to, or constituting a species — **spe·cif·i·cal·ly** \-i-k(ə-)lē\ *adv*

²specific *n* : a specific remedy

spec·i·fi·ca·tion \ˌspes-ə-fə-'kā-shən\ *n* **1** : the act or process of specifying **2** : a description of work to be done and materials to be used (as in building) — usu. used in pl.

specific gravity *n* : the ratio of the density of a substance to the density of some substance (as water) taken as a standard when both densities are obtained by weighing in air

spec·i·fy \'spes-ə-ˌfī\ *vb* **-fied; -fy·ing** : to mention or name explicitly

spec·i·men \'spes-ə-mən\ *n* : an item or part typical of a group or whole

spe·cious \'spē-shəs\ *adj* : seeming to be genuine, correct, or beautiful but not really so ⟨∼ reasoning⟩

speck \'spek\ *n* **1** : a small spot or blemish **2** : a small particle : BIT — **speck** *vb*

speck·le \'spek-əl\ *n* : a little speck — **speck·le** *vb*

spec·ta·cle \'spek-ti-kəl\ *n* **1** : something exhibited to view; *esp* : an impressive public display **2** *pl* : GLASSES — **spec·ta·cled** \-kəld\ *adj*

¹spec·tac·u·lar \spek-'tak-yə-lər\ *adj* : SENSATIONAL, STRIKING, SHOWY

²spectacular *n* : an elaborate spectacle

spec·ta·tor \'spek-ˌtāt-ər\ *n* : one who looks on (as at a sports event) **syn** observer, witness, bystander, onlooker, eyewitness

spec·ter *or* **spec·tre** \'spek-tər\ *n* : a visible disembodied spirit : GHOST

spec·tral \'spek-trəl\ *adj* **1** : of, relating to, or resembling a specter **2** : of, relating to, or made by a spectrum

spec·tro·gram \'spek-trə-ˌgram\ *n* : a photograph or diagram of a spectrum

spec·tro·graph \-ˌgraf\ *n* : an instrument for dispersing radiation into a spectrum and photographing or mapping the spectrum — **spec·tro·graph·ic** \ˌspek-trə-'graf-ik\ *adj* — **spec·tro·graph·i·cal·ly** \-i-k(ə-)lē\ *adv*

spec·trom·e·ter \spek-'träm-ət-ər\ *n* : a spectroscope fitted for measuring spectra — **spec·tro·met·ric** \ˌspek-trə-'me-trik\ *adj*

spec·tro·scope \'spek-trə-ˌskōp\ *n* : an optical instrument that produces spectra from or by the use of electromagnetic radiation — **spec·tro·scop·ic** \ˌspek-trə-'skäp-ik\ *adj* — **spec·tro·scop·i·cal·ly** \-i-k(ə-)lē\ *adv* — **spec·tros·co·pist** \spek-'träs-kə-pəst\ *n* — **spec·tros·co·py** \-pē\ *n*

spec·trum \'spek-trəm\ *n, pl* **spec·tra** \-trə\ *or* **spectrums** [NL, fr. L, appearance, specter, fr. *specere* to look] **1** : a series of colors formed when a beam of white light is dispersed (as by a prism) so that its parts are arranged in the order of their wavelengths **2** : a series of radiations arranged in regular order **3** : a continuous sequence or range ⟨a wide ∼ of political opinions⟩

spec•u•late \'spek-yə-ˌlāt\ *vb* **-lat•ed; -lat•ing** [L *speculari* to spy out, examine, fr. *specula* watchtower, fr. *specere* to look, look at] **1** : REFLECT, MEDITATE **2** : to engage in a business deal where a good profit may be made at considerable risk **syn** reason, think, deliberate, cogitate — **spec•u•la•tion** \ˌspek-yə-'lā-shən\ *n* — **spec•u•la•tive** \'spek-yə-ˌlāt-iv\ *adj* — **spec•u•la•tive•ly** *adv* — **spec•u•la•tor** \-ˌlāt-ər\ *n*

speech \'spēch\ *n* **1** : the act of speaking **2** : TALK, CONVERSATION **3** : a public discourse **4** : LANGUAGE, DIALECT **5** : an individual manner of speaking **6** : the power of speaking — **speech•less** *adj*

¹speed \'spēd\ *n* **1** *archaic* : SUCCESS **2** : SWIFTNESS, RAPIDITY **3** : rate of motion or performance **4** : a transmission gear in an automotive vehicle or bicycle **5** : METHAMPHETAMINE; *also* : a related drug **syn** haste, hurry, dispatch, celerity — **speed•i•ly** \'spēd-ᵊl-ē\ *adv* — **speedy** *adj*

²speed *vb* **sped** \'sped\ *or* **speed•ed; speed•ing 1** *archaic* : PROSPER; *also* : GET ALONG, FARE **2** : to go fast; *esp* : to go at an excessive or illegal speed **3** : to cause to go faster — **speed•er** *n*

speed•boat \-ˌbōt\ *n* : a fast motorboat

speed•om•e•ter \spi-'däm-ət-ər\ *n* : an instrument for indicating speed or speed and distance traveled

speed•up \'spēd-ˌəp\ *n* **1** : ACCELERATION **2** : an employer's demand for accelerated output without increased pay

speed•way \'spēd-ˌwā\ *n* : a racecourse for motor vehicles

speed•well \'spēd-ˌwel\ *n* : a low creeping plant that bears spikes of small usu. bluish flowers and is related to the snapdragon

¹spell \'spel\ *n* [ME, talk, tale, fr. OE] **1** : a magic formula : INCANTATION **2** : a controlling influence

²spell *vb* **spelled** \'speld\; **spell•ing** : to take the place of for a time in work or duty : RELIEVE

³spell *vb* **spelled** \'speld, 'spelt\; **spell•ing 1** : to name, write, or print in order the letters of a word **2** : MEAN

⁴spell *n* **1** *archaic* : the relief of one person by another in any work or duty **2** : one's turn at work or duty **3** : a stretch of a specified kind of weather **4** : a period of bodily or mental distress or disorder : ATTACK

spell•bind•er \-ˌbīn-dər\ *n* : a speaker of compelling eloquence

spell•bound \-ˌbaund\ *adj* : held by or as if by a spell : FASCINATED

spell•er \'spel-ər\ *n* **1** : one who spells words **2** : a book with exercises for teaching spelling

spe•lunk•er \spi-'ləŋ-kər, 'spē-ˌləŋ-kər\ *n* : one who makes a hobby of exploring caves — **spe•lunk•ing** \-kiŋ\ *n*

spend \'spend\ *vb* **spent** \'spent\; **spend•ing 1** : to pay out : USE UP **2** : WEAR OUT, EXHAUST; *also* : to consume wastefully **3** : to cause or permit to elapse : PASS **4** : to make use of — **spend•er** *n*

spend•thrift \'spen(d)-ˌthrift\ *n* : one who spends wastefully or recklessly

spent \'spent\ *adj* : drained of energy

sperm \'spərm\ *n, pl* **sperm** *or* **sperms 1** : SEMEN **2** : a male gamete

sper•ma•to•zo•on \(ˌ)spər-ˌmat-ə-'zō-ˌän, -'zō-ən\ *n, pl* **-zoa** \-'zō-ə\ : a motile male gamete of an animal usu. with a rounded or elongated head and a long posterior flagellum

sperm cell *n* : SPERM 2

sperm whale \'spərm-\ *n* : a whale with conical teeth, no whalebone, and a large fluid-containing cavity in the head

spew \'spyü\ *vb* : VOMIT

sp gr *abbr* specific gravity

sphag•num \'sfag-nəm\ *n* : any of a genus of atypical mosses that grow in wet acid areas where their remains become compacted with other plant debris to form peat; *also* : a mass of these mosses

sphere \'sfiər\ *n* [ME *spere* globe, celestial sphere, fr. MF *espere*, fr. L *sphaera*, fr. Gk *sphaira*, lit., ball] **1** : a globular body **2** : a celestial body **3** : a solid figure so shaped that every point on its surface is an equal distance from the center **4** : range of action or influence : FIELD — **spher•i•cal** \'sfir-i-kəl, 'sfer-\ *adj* — **spher•i•cal•ly** \-i-k(ə-)lē\ *adv*

spher•oid \'sfi(ə)r-ˌoid, 'sfe(ə)r-\ *n* : a figure similar to a sphere but not perfectly round — **sphe·roi·dal** \sfir-'ȯid-ᵊl\ *adj*

sphinc·ter \'sfiŋk-tər\ *n* : a muscular ring that closes a bodily opening

sphinx \'sfiŋks\ *n, pl* **sphinx·es** *or* **sphin·ges** \'sfin-ˌjēz\ 1 : a winged monster in Greek mythology having a woman's head and a lion's body and noted for killing anyone unable to answer its riddle 2 : an enigmatic or mysterious person 3 : an ancient Egyptian image having the body of a lion and the head of man, ram, or hawk

spice \'spīs\ *n* 1 : any of various aromatic plant products (as pepper or nutmeg) used to season or flavor foods 2 : something that adds interest and relish — **spice** *vb* — **spicy** *adj*

spice·bush \'spīs-ˌbu̇sh\ *n* : an aromatic shrub related to the laurels that bears dense clusters of small yellow flowers followed by scarlet or yellow berries

spick–and–span *or* **spic–and–span** \ˌspik-ən-'span\ *adj* : quite new; *also* : spotlessly clean

spic·ule \'spik-yül\ *n* : a slender pointed body esp. of calcium or silica ⟨sponge ∼s⟩

spi·der \'spīd-ər\ *n* 1 : any of numerous arachnids that have a 2-part body, eight legs, and two or more pairs of abdominal organs for spinning threads of silk used esp. in making webs for catching prey 2 : a cast-iron frying pan — **spi·dery** *adj*

spider plant *n* : a houseplant of the lily family having long green leaves usu. striped with white and producing tufts of small plants on long hanging stems

spiderweb *n* : the web spun by a spider

spiel \'spēl\ *vb* : to talk volubly or extravagantly — **spiel** *n*

spig·ot \'spig-ət, 'spik-ət\ *n* : FAUCET

¹**spike** \'spīk\ *n* 1 : a very large nail 2 : any of various pointed projections (as on the sole of a shoe to prevent slipping) — **spiky** *adj*

²**spike** *vb* **spiked; spik·ing** 1 : to fasten with spikes 2 : to put an end to : QUASH ⟨∼ a rumor⟩ 3 : to pierce with or impale on a spike 4 : to add alcoholic liquor to (a drink)

³**spike** *n* 1 : an ear of grain 2 : a long cluster of usu. stemless flowers

¹**spill** \'spil\ *vb* **spilled** \'spild, 'spilt\ *also* **spilt** \'spilt\; **spill·ing** 1 : to cause or allow esp. unintentionally to fall, flow, or run out 2 : to lose or allow to be scattered 3 : to cause (blood) to flow 4 : to run out or over with resulting loss or waste — **spill·able** *adj*

²**spill** *n* 1 : an act of spilling; *also* : a fall from a horse or vehicle or in running 2 : something spilled 3 : SPILLWAY

spill·way \-ˌwā\ *n* : a passage for surplus water to run over or around an obstruction (as a dam)

¹**spin** \'spin\ *vb* **spun** \'spən\; **spin·ning** 1 : to draw out (fiber) and twist into thread; *also* : to form (thread) by such means 2 : to form thread by extruding a sticky quickly hardening fluid; *also* : to construct from such thread ⟨spiders ∼ their webs⟩ 3 : to produce slowly and by degrees ⟨∼ a story⟩ 4 : TWIRL 5 : WHIRL, REEL ⟨my head is *spinning*⟩ 6 : to move rapidly along — **spin·ner** *n*

²**spin** *n* 1 : a rapid rotating motion 2 : an excursion in a wheeled vehicle

spin·ach \'spin-ich\ *n* : a dark green herb grown for its edible leaves

spi·nal \'spīn-ᵊl\ *adj* : of or relating to the backbone or spinal cord — **spi·nal·ly** \-ē\ *adv*

spinal column *n* : BACKBONE

spinal cord *n* : the thick cord of nervous tissue that extends from the brain along the back in the cavity of the backbone and carries nerve impulses to and from the brain

spinal nerve *n* : any of the paired nerves which arise from the spinal cord and pass to various parts of the body and of which there are normally 31 pairs in human beings

spin·dle \'spin-dᵊl\ *n* 1 : a round tapering stick or rod by which fibers are twisted in spinning 2 : a turned part of a piece of furniture ⟨the ∼s of a chair⟩ 3 : a slender pin or rod which turns or on which something else turns

spin·dling \'spin-(d)liŋ\ *adj* : SPINDLY

spin·dly \'spin-(d)lē\ *adj* : being long or tall and thin and usu. weak

spin·drift \'spin-ˌdrift\ *n* : spray blown from waves

spine \'spīn\ *n* 1 : BACKBONE 2 : a stiff sharp process esp. on a plant or animal — **spine·less** *adj* — **spiny** *adj*

spi·nel \spə-'nel\ *n* : a hard crystalline

mineral of variable color used as a gem

spin·et \'spin-ət\ *n* **1** : an early harpsichord having a single keyboard and only one string for each note **2** : a small upright piano

spin·na·ker \'spin-i-kər\ *n* : a large triangular sail set on a long light pole

spinning jen·ny \-ˌjen-ē\ *n* : an early multiple-spindle machine for spinning wool or cotton

spinning wheel *n* : a small machine for spinning thread or yarn in which a large wheel drives a single spindle

spin–off \'spin-ˌȯf\ *n* **1** : the distribution by a business to its stockholders of particular assets and esp. of stock of another company **2** : a usu. useful by-product ⟨~s from missile research⟩ — **spin off** *vb*

spin·ster \'spin-stər\ *n* : an unmarried woman past the common age for marrying — **spin·ster·hood** \-ˌhu̇d\ *n*

spiny lobster *n* : an edible crustacean differing from the related lobster in lacking the large front claws and in having a very spiny carapace

¹spi·ral \'spī-rəl\ *adj* **1** : circling around a center like the thread of a screw **2** : winding or coiling around a center or pole in gradually enlarging circles — **spi·ral·ly** \-ē\ *adv*

²spiral *n* **1** : something that has a spiral form; *also* : a single turn in a spiral object **2** : a continuously spreading and accelerating increase or decrease

³spiral *vb* **-raled** *or* **-ralled; -ral·ing** *or* **-ral·ling** **1** : to move in a spiral course **2** : to form into a spiral

spi·rant \'spī-rənt\ *n* : a consonant (as \f\, \s\, \sh\) uttered with decided friction of the breath against some part of the oral passage — **spirant** *adj*

spire \'spī(ə)r\ *n* **1** : a slender tapering stalk (as of grass) **2** : a pointed tip (as of a tree or antler) **3** : STEEPLE — **spiry** *adj*

spi·rea *or* **spi·raea** \spī-'rē-ə\ *n* : any of a genus of shrubs related to the roses with dense clusters of small white or pink flowers

¹spir·it \'spir-ət\ *n* [ME, fr. OF or L; OF, fr. L *spiritus,* lit., breath] **1** : a life≠giving force; *also* : the animating principle : SOUL **2** *cap* : HOLY SPIRIT **3** : SPECTER, GHOST **4** : PERSON **5** : DISPO-

SITION, MOOD **6** : VIVACITY, ARDOR **7** : essential or real meaning : INTENT **8** : distilled alcoholic liquor **9** : LOYALTY ⟨school ~⟩ — **spir·it·less** *adj*

²spirit *vb* : to carry off secretly or mysteriously

spir·it·ed \'spir-ət-əd\ *adj* **1** : ANIMATED, LIVELY **2** : COURAGEOUS

¹spir·i·tu·al \'spir-ich-(ə-w)əl\ *adj* **1** : of, relating to, consisting of, or affecting the spirit : INCORPOREAL **2** : of or relating to sacred matters **3** : ecclesiastical rather than lay or temporal — **spir·i·tu·al·i·ty** \ˌspir-i-chə-'wal-ət-ē\ *n* — **spir·i·tu·al·ize** \'spir-ich-(ə-w)ə-ˌlīz\ *vb* — **spir·i·tu·al·ly** \-lē\ *adv*

²spiritual *n* : a religious song originating among blacks of the southern U.S.

spir·i·tu·al·ism \'spir-ich-(ə-w)ə-ˌliz-əm\ *n* : a belief that spirits of the dead communicate with the living usu. through a medium — **spir·i·tu·al·ist** \-ləst\ *n, often cap* — **spir·i·tu·al·is·tic** \ˌspir-ich-(ə-w)ə-'lis-tik\ *adj*

spir·i·tu·ous \'spir-ich-(ə-w)əs, 'spir-ət-əs\ *adj* : containing alcohol ⟨~ liquors⟩

spi·ro·chete *also* **spi·ro·chaete** \'spī-rə-ˌkēt\ *n* : any of an order of spiral bacteria including one that causes syphilis

spirt var of SPURT

¹spit \'spit\ *n* **1** : a thin pointed rod for holding meat over a fire **2** : a point of land that runs out into the water

²spit *vb* **spit·ted; spit·ting** : to pierce with or as if with a spit

³spit *vb* **spit** *or* **spat** \'spat\; **spit·ting** **1** : to eject (saliva) from the mouth **2** : to send forth forcefully, defiantly, or disgustedly **3** : to rain or snow lightly

⁴spit *n* **1** : SALIVA **2** : perfect likeness ⟨~ and image of his father⟩ **3** : a sprinkle of rain or flurry of snow

spit·ball \'spit-ˌbȯl\ *n* **1** : paper chewed and rolled into a ball to be thrown as a missile **2** : a baseball pitch delivered after the ball has been moistened with saliva or sweat

¹spite \'spīt\ *n* : ill will with a wish to annoy, anger, or defeat : petty malice **syn** malignity, spleen, grudge, malevolence — **spite·ful** \-fəl\ *adj* — **spite·ful·ly** \-ē\ *adv* — **spite·ful·ness** *n* — **in spite of** : in defiance or contempt of : NOTWITHSTANDING

²**spite** *vb* **spit·ed; spit·ing** : to treat maliciously (as by insulting or thwarting)

spit·tle \ˈspit-ᵊl\ *n* : SALIVA

spit·tle·bug \-ˌbəg\ *n* : any of numerous leaping insects with froth-secreting larvae that are related to the aphids

spit·toon \spi-ˈtün\ *n* : a receptacle for spit

splash \ˈsplash\ *vb* **1** : to dash a liquid about **2** : to scatter a liquid on : SPATTER **3** : to fall or strike with a splashing noise **syn** sprinkle, bespatter, douse, splatter — **splash** *n*

splash·down \ˈsplash-ˌdaùn\ *n* : the landing of a manned spacecraft in the ocean — **splash down** \(ˈ)splash-ˈdaùn\ *vb*

splat·ter \ˈsplat-ər\ *vb* : SPATTER — **splatter** *n*

¹**splay** \ˈsplā\ *vb* **1** : to spread out **2** : to slope or slant outward ⟨∼ed doorway⟩ — **splay** *n*

²**splay** *adj* **1** : spread out : turned outward **2** : AWKWARD, CLUMSY

spleen \ˈsplēn\ *n* **1** : a vascular organ located near the stomach in most vertebrates that is concerned esp. with the storage, formation, and destruction of blood cells **2** : SPITE, MALICE **syn** malignity, grudge, malevolence, ill will, spitefulness

splen·did \ˈsplen-dəd\ *adj* [L *splendidus,* fr. *splendēre* to shine] **1** : SHINING, BRILLIANT **2** : SHOWY, GORGEOUS **3** : ILLUSTRIOUS **4** : EXCELLENT **syn** resplendent, glorious, sublime, superb — **splen·did·ly** *adv*

splen·dor \ˈsplen-dər\ *n* **1** : BRILLIANCE **2** : POMP, MAGNIFICENCE

sple·net·ic \spli-ˈnet-ik\ *adj* : marked by bad temper or spite

splen·ic \ˈsplen-ik\ *adj* : of, relating to, or located in the spleen

splice \ˈsplīs\ *vb* **spliced; splic·ing** **1** : to unite (as two ropes) by weaving the strands together **2** : to unite (as two timbers or pieces of film) by connecting the ends together — **splice** *n*

splint \ˈsplint\ *n* **1** : a thin strip of wood interwoven with others to make something (as a basket) **2** : material or a device used to protect and keep in place an injured body part (as a broken arm)

¹**splin·ter** \ˈsplint-ər\ *n* : a thin piece of something split off lengthwise : SLIVER

²**splinter** *vb* : to split into splinters

split \ˈsplit\ *vb* **split; split·ting** **1** : to divide lengthwise or along a grain or seam **2** : to burst or break in pieces **3** : to divide into parts or sections **4** : LEAVE **syn** rend, cleave, rip, tear — **split** *n*

split–lev·el \ˈsplit-ˈlev-əl\ *n* : a house divided so that the floor in one part is about halfway between two floors in the other

split personality *n* : SCHIZOPHRENIA; *also* : a mental and emotional disorder which is a neurosis and in which the personality becomes separated into two or more parts each of which controls behavior part of the time

split·ting \ˈsplit-iŋ\ *adj* : causing a piercing sensation ⟨∼ headache⟩

splotch \ˈspläch\ *n* : BLOTCH

splurge \ˈsplərj\ *n* : a showy display or expense — **splurge** *vb*

splut·ter \ˈsplət-ər\ *n* : SPUTTER — **splutter** *vb*

¹**spoil** \ˈspóil\ *n* : PLUNDER, BOOTY

²**spoil** *vb* **spoiled** \ˈspóild, ˈspóilt\ *or* **spoilt** \ˈspóilt\; **spoil·ing** **1** : ROB, PILLAGE **2** : to damage seriously : RUIN **3** : to impair the quality or effect of **4** : to damage the disposition of by pampering; *also* : INDULGE, CODDLE **5** : DECAY, ROT **6** : to have an eager desire ⟨∼ing for a fight⟩ **syn** injure, harm, hurt, mar — **spoil·age** \ˈspói-lij\ *n*

spoil·er \ˈspói-lər\ *n* **1** : one that spoils **2** : a device (as on an airplane or automobile) used to disrupt airflow and decrease lift

spoil·sport \ˈspóil-ˌspōrt\ *n* : one who spoils the sport or pleasure of others

¹**spoke** \ˈspōk\ past & archaic past part of SPEAK

²**spoke** *n* **1** : any of the rods extending from the hub of a wheel to the rim **2** : a rung of a ladder

spo·ken \ˈspō-kən\ past part of SPEAK

spokes·man \ˈspōks-mən\ *n* : one who speaks as the representative of another or others

spokes·per·son \-ˌpər-sən\ *n* : SPOKESMAN

spokes·wom·an \-ˌwùm-ən\ *n* : a woman who speaks as the representative of another or others

spo·li·a·tion \ˌspō-lē-ˈā-shən\ *n* : the act

of plundering : the state of being plundered

¹**sponge** \'spənj\ *n* **1** : the elastic porous mass of fibers that forms the skeleton of any of a phylum of primitive sea animals; *also* : one of the animals **2** : the act of washing or wiping with a sponge **3** : a spongelike or porous mass or material (as used for sponging) — **spongy** \'spən-jē\ *adj*

²**sponge** *vb* **sponged; spong·ing 1** : to gather sponges **2** : to bathe or wipe with a sponge **3** : to live at another's expense — **spong·er** *n*

sponge cake *n* : a cake made without shortening

sponge rubber *n* : a cellular rubber resembling natural sponge

spon·sor \'spän-sər\ *n* [LL, fr. L, guarantor, surety, fr. *sponsus*, pp. of *spondēre* to promise] **1** : one who takes the responsibility for some other person or thing : SURETY **2** : GODPARENT **3** : a business firm that pays the cost of a radio or television program usu. in return for advertising time during its course **syn** patron, guarantor, backer — **sponsor** *vb* — **spon·sor·ship** *n*

spon·ta·ne·ous \spän-'tā-nē-əs\ *adj* [LL *spontaneus*, fr. L *sponte* of one's free will, voluntarily] **1** : done or produced freely or naturally **2** : acting or taking place without external force or cause **syn** impulsive, instinctive, automatic, unpremeditated — **spon·ta·ne·ity** \ˌspänt-ən-'ē-ət-ē\ *n* — **spon·ta·ne·ous·ly** \spän-'tā-nē-əs-lē\ *adv*

spontaneous combustion *n* : a bursting into flame of material through heat produced within itself by chemical action (as oxidation)

spoof \'spüf\ *vb* **1** : DECEIVE, HOAX **2** : to make good-natured fun of — **spoof** *n*

¹**spook** \'spük\ *n* : GHOST, APPARITION — **spooky** *adj*

²**spook** *vb* : FRIGHTEN

spool \'spül\ *n* : a cylinder on which flexible material (as thread) is wound

spoon \'spün\ *n* [ME, fr. OE *spōn* splinter, chip] **1** : an eating or cooking implement consisting of a shallow bowl with a handle **2** : a metal piece used on a fishing line as a lure — **spoon** *vb* — **spoon·ful** *n*

spoon·bill \'spün-ˌbil\ *n* : any of several wading birds related to the ibises that have a bill with a broad flat tip

spoon–feed \'spün-ˌfēd\ *vb* **-fed** \-ˌfed\; **-feed·ing 1** : to feed by means of a spoon **2** : to present (information) so completely as to preclude independent thought

spoor \'spu̇r, 'spōr\ *n* : a track, a trail, a scent, or droppings esp. of a wild animal

spo·rad·ic \spə-'rad-ik\ *adj* : occurring in scattered single instances **syn** occasional, rare, scarce, infrequent, uncommon — **spo·rad·i·cal·ly** \-i-k(ə-)lē\ *adv*

spore \'spōr\ *n* : a primitive usu. one-celled reproductive body produced by plants and some lower animals

¹**sport** \'spōrt\ *vb* [ME *sporten* to divert, disport, short for *disporten*, fr. MF *desporter*, fr. *des*- (fr. L *dis*- apart) + *porter* to carry, fr. L *portare*] **1** : to amuse oneself : FROLIC **2** : to wear or display ostentatiously — **sport·ive** *adj*

²**sport** *n* **1** : a source of diversion : PASTIME **2** : physical activity engaged in for pleasure **3** : JEST **4** : MOCKERY ⟨make ∼ of his efforts⟩ **5** : BUTT, LAUGHINGSTOCK **6** : one who accepts results cheerfully whether favoring his interests or not **7** : an individual distinguished by a mutation **syn** play, frolic, fun, recreation — **sporty** *adj*

³**sport** *or* **sports** *adj* : of, relating to, or suitable for sport or casual wear ⟨∼ coats⟩

sport fish *n* : a fish important for the sport it affords anglers

sports·cast \'spōrts-ˌkast\ *n* : a broadcast dealing with sports events — **sports·cast·er** \-ˌkas-tər\ *n*

sports·man \'spōrts-mən\ *n* **1** : a person who engages in sports and esp. in hunting and fishing **2** : one who plays fairly and wins or loses gracefully — **sports·man·ship** *n*

sports·wom·an \-ˌwu̇m-ən\ *n* : a woman who engages in sports

sports·writ·er \-ˌrīt-ər\ *n* : one who writes about sports esp. for a newspaper — **sports·writ·ing** \-iŋ\ *n*

¹**spot** \'spät\ *n* **1** : STAIN, BLEMISH **2** : a small part different (as in color) from the main part **3** : LOCATION, SITE — **spot·less** *adj* — **spot·less·ly** *adv* — **on the spot** : in difficulty or danger

²**spot** *vb* **spot·ted; spot·ting 1** : to mark or disfigure with spots **2** : to pick out : RECOGNIZE, IDENTIFY

³**spot** *adj* **1** : being, done, or originating on the spot ⟨a ∼ broadcast⟩ **2** : paid upon delivery **3** : made at random or at a few key points ⟨a ∼ check⟩

spot–check \'spät-ˌchek\ *vb* : to make a spot check of

spot·light \-ˌlīt\ *n* **1** : a circle of brilliant light projected upon a particular area, person, or object (as on a stage); *also* : the device that produces this light **2** : public notice — **spotlight** *vb*

spot·ter \'spät-ər\ *n* **1** : one that keeps watch : OBSERVER **2** : one that removes spots

spot·ty \'spät-ē\ *adj* **spot·ti·er; -est** : uneven in quality; *also* : sparsely distributed ⟨∼ attendance⟩

spou·sal \'spau̇-zəl, -səl\ *n* : NUPTIALS — usu. used in pl.

spouse \'spau̇s\ *n* : one's husband or wife

¹**spout** \'spau̇t\ *vb* **1** : to eject or issue forth forcibly and freely ⟨wells ∼ing oil⟩ **2** : to speak pompously

²**spout** *n* **1** : a pipe or hole through which liquid spouts **2** : a jet of liquid; *esp* : WATERSPOUT 2

spp *abbr, pl* species

¹**sprain** \'sprān\ *n* : a sudden or severe twisting of a joint with stretching or tearing of ligaments; *also* : a sprained condition

²**sprain** *vb* : to subject to sprain

sprat \'sprat\ *n* : a small European herring; *also* : a young herring

sprawl \'sprȯl\ *vb* **1** : to lie or sit with limbs spread out awkwardly **2** : to spread out irregularly — **sprawl** *n*

¹**spray** \'sprā\ *n* : a usu. flowering branch or a decorative arrangement of flowers and foliage

²**spray** *n* **1** : liquid flying in small drops like water blown from a wave **2** : a jet of fine vapor (as from an atomizer) **3** : an instrument (as an atomizer) for scattering fine liquid

³**spray** *vb* **1** : to scatter or let fall in a spray **2** : to discharge spray on or into — **spray·er** *n*

spray can *n* : a pressurized container from which aerosols are sprayed

spray gun *n* : a device for spraying liquids (as paint or insecticide)

¹**spread** \'spred\ *vb* **spread; spread·ing 1** : to scatter over a surface **2** : to flatten out : open out **3** : to stretch, force, or push apart **4** : to distribute over a period of time or among many persons **5** : to pass on from person to person **6** : to cover with something ⟨∼ a floor with rugs⟩ **7** : to prepare for a meal ⟨∼ a table⟩ — **spread·er** *n*

²**spread** *n* **1** : the act or process of spreading **2** : EXPANSE, EXTENT **3** : a prominent display in a magazine or newspaper **4** : a food to be spread on bread or crackers **5** : a cloth cover for a bed **6** : distance between two points : GAP

spree \'sprē\ *n* : an unrestrained outburst ⟨buying ∼⟩; *esp* : a drinking bout

sprig \'sprig\ *n* : a small shoot or twig

spright·ly \'sprīt-lē\ *adj* **spright·li·er; -est** : LIVELY, SPIRITED **syn** animated, vivacious, gay — **spright·li·ness** *n*

¹**spring** \'spriŋ\ *vb* **sprang** \'spraŋ\ *or* **sprung** \'sprəŋ\; **sprung; spring·ing** \'spriŋ-iŋ\ **1** : to move suddenly upward or forward **2** : to shoot up ⟨weeds ∼ up overnight⟩ **3** : to move quickly by elastic force **4** : to make lame : STRAIN **5** : WARP **6** : to develop (a leak) through the seams **7** : to make known suddenly ⟨∼ a surprise⟩ **8** : to cause to close suddenly ⟨∼ a trap⟩

²**spring** *n* **1** : a source of supply; *esp* : an issuing of water from the ground **2** : SOURCE, ORIGIN; *also* : MOTIVE **3** : the season between winter and summer **4** : an elastic body or device that recovers its original shape when it is released after being distorted **5** : the act or an instance of leaping up or forward **6** : RESILIENCE — **springy** *adj*

spring·board \'spriŋ-ˌbōrd\ *n* : a springy board used in jumping or vaulting or for diving

spring fever *n* : a lazy or restless feeling often associated with the onset of spring

spring tide *n* : a tide of greater-than-average range that occurs at each new moon and full moon

spring·time \'spriŋ-ˌtīm\ *n* : the season of spring

¹**sprin·kle** \'spriŋ-kəl\ *vb* **sprin·kled; sprin·kling** \-k(ə-)liŋ\ : to scatter in

small drops or particles — **sprin·kler** \-k(ə-)lər\ *n*

²**sprinkle** *n* : a light rainfall

sprin·kling \'spriŋ-kliŋ\ *n* : SMATTERING

¹**sprint** \'sprint\ *vb* : to run at top speed esp. for a short distance — **sprint·er** *n*

²**sprint** *n* 1 : a short run at top speed 2 : a short distance race

sprite \'sprīt\ *n* 1 : GHOST, SPIRIT 2 : ELF, FAIRY

spritz *vb* : SPRAY

sprock·et \'spräk-ət\ *n* : a tooth on a wheel (**sprocket wheel**) shaped so as to interlock with a chain

¹**sprout** \'spraut\ *vb* : to send out new growth esp. rapidly ⟨~*ing* seeds⟩

²**sprout** *n* : a usu. young and growing plant shoot

¹**spruce** \'sprüs\ *vb* **spruced; spruc·ing** : to make or become spruce

²**spruce** *adj* **spruc·er; spruc·est** : neat and smart in appearance **syn** stylish, fashionable, modish, dapper, natty

³**spruce** *n* : any of a genus of evergreen pyramid-shaped trees related to the pines and having soft light wood; *also* : the wood of a spruce

sprung past and past part of SPRING

spry \'sprī\ *adj* **spri·er** *or* **spry·er** \'sprī(-ə)r\; **spri·est** *or* **spry·est** \'sprī-əst\ : NIMBLE, ACTIVE **syn** agile, brisk, lively, sprightly

spud \'spəd\ *n* 1 : a sharp narrow spade 2 : POTATO

spume \'spyüm\ *n* : frothy matter on liquids : FOAM

spu·mo·ni *or* **spu·mo·ne** \spu̇-'mō-nē\ *n* [It *spumone*, deriv. of *spuma* foam] : ice cream in layers of different colors, flavors, and textures often with candied fruits and nuts

spun past and past part of SPIN

spun glass *n* : FIBERGLASS

spunk \'spəŋk\ *n* [fr. *spunk* tinder, fr. ScGael *spong* sponge, tinder, fr. L *spongia* sponge] : PLUCK, COURAGE — **spunky** *adj*

¹**spur** \'spər\ *n* 1 : a pointed device fastened to a rider's boot and used to urge on a horse 2 : something that urges to action 3 : a stiffly projecting part or process (as on the leg of a cock or on some flowers) 4 : a ridge extending sideways from a mountain 5 : a branch of railroad track extending from the main line **syn** goad, motive,

impulse, incentive, inducement — **spurred** \'spərd\ *adj* — **on the spur of the moment** : on hasty impulse

²**spur** *vb* **spurred; spur·ring** 1 : to urge a horse on with spurs 2 : INCITE

spurge \'spərj\ *n* : any of various herbs and woody plants with bitter milky juice

spu·ri·ous \'spyu̇r-ē-əs\ *adj* [LL *spurius* false, fr. L, of illegitimate birth, fr. *spurius*, n., bastard] : not genuine : FALSE

spurn \'spərn\ *vb* 1 : to kick away or trample on 2 : to reject with disdain **syn** repudiate, refuse, decline

¹**spurt** \'spərt\ *vb* : to gush out : spout forth

²**spurt** *n* : a sudden gushing or spouting

³**spurt** *n* 1 : a sudden brief burst of effort or speed 2 : a sharp increase of activity ⟨~ in sales⟩

⁴**spurt** *vb* : to make a spurt

sput·ter \'spət-ər\ *vb* 1 : to spit small scattered particles : SPLUTTER 2 : to utter words hastily or explosively in excitement or confusion 3 : to make small popping sounds — **sputter** *n*

spu·tum \'spyüt-əm\ *n, pl* **spu·ta** \-ə\ [L] : material that is spit or coughed up and consists of saliva and mucus

¹**spy** \'spī\ *vb* **spied; spy·ing** 1 : to watch or search for information secretly : act as a spy 2 : to get a momentary or quick glimpse of : SEE

²**spy** *n, pl* **spies** 1 : one who secretly watches others 2 : one who secretly tries to obtain information for his own country in the territory of an enemy

spy·glass \'spī-ˌglas\ *n* : a small telescope

sq *abbr* 1 squadron 2 square

squab \'skwäb\ *n, pl* **squabs** *or* **squab** : a young pigeon

squab·ble \'skwäb-əl\ *n* : a noisy altercation : WRANGLE **syn** quarrel, spat, row, tiff — **squabble** *vb*

squad \'skwäd\ *n* 1 : a small organized group of military personnel 2 : a small group engaged in a common effort

squad car *n* : a police car connected by two-way radio with headquarters

squad·ron \'skwäd-rən\ *n* 1 : a body of men in regular formation 2 : any of several units of military organization

squal·id \'skwäl-əd\ *adj* 1 : filthy or degraded through neglect or poverty 2

: SORDID, DEBASED **syn** nasty, foul, dirty, grubby

squall \\'skwȯl\ *n* : a sudden violent gust of wind often with rain or snow — **squally** *adj*

squa·lor \\'skwäl-ər\ *n* : the quality or state of being squalid

squan·der \\'skwän-dər\ *vb* **squan·dered; squan·der·ing** \-d(ə-)riŋ\ : to spend wastefully or foolishly

¹square \\'skwaər\ *n* **1** : an instrument used to lay out or test right angles **2** : a rectangle with all four sides equal **3** : something square **4** : the product of a number multiplied by itself **5** : an area bounded by four streets **6** : an open area in a city where streets meet **7** : a highly conventional person

²square *adj* **squar·er; squar·est 1** : having four equal sides and four right angles **2** : forming a right angle ⟨cut a ∼ corner⟩ **3** : multiplied by itself : SQUARED ⟨X² is the symbol for X ∼⟩ **4** : being a unit of square measure equal to a square each side of which measures one unit ⟨a ∼ foot⟩ **5** : being of a specified length in each of two dimensions ⟨an area 10 feet ∼⟩ **6** : exactly adjusted **7** : JUST, FAIR ⟨a ∼ deal⟩ **8** : leaving no balance ⟨make accounts ∼⟩ **9** : SUBSTANTIAL ⟨a ∼ meal⟩ **10** : highly conservative or conventional — **square·ly** *adv*

³square *vb* **squared; squar·ing 1** : to form with four equal sides and right angles or with flat surfaces ⟨∼ a timber⟩ **2** : to multiply a number by itself **3** : CONFORM, AGREE **4** : BALANCE, SETTLE ⟨∼ an account⟩

square dance *n* : a dance for four couples arranged to form a square

square measure *n* : a unit or system of units for measuring area — see METRIC SYSTEM table, WEIGHT table

square–rigged \\'skwaər-'rigd\ *adj* : having the chief sails extended on yards that are fastened to the masts horizontally and at their center

square–rig·ger \-'rig-ər\ *n* : a square-rigged craft

square root *n* : either of the two numbers whose squares are equal to a given number ⟨either +3 or −3 is the *square root* of 9⟩

¹squash \\'skwäsh, 'skwȯsh\ *vb* **1** : to beat or press into a pulp or flat mass **2** : QUASH, SUPPRESS

²squash *n* **1** : the impact of something soft and heavy; *also* : the sound of such impact **2** : a crushed mass **3** : SQUASH RACQUETS

³squash *n, pl* **squash·es** *or* **squash** : a fruit of any of various plants related to the gourds that is used esp. as a vegetable; *also* : a plant bearing squashes

squash racquets *n* : a game played on a 4-wall court with a racket and rubber ball

¹squat \\'skwät\ *vb* **squat·ted; squat·ting 1** : to sit down upon the hams or heels **2** : to settle on land without right or title; *also* : to settle on public land with a view to acquiring title — **squatter** *n*

²squat *n* : the act or posture of squatting

³squat *adj* **squat·ter; squat·test** : low to the ground; *also* : short and thick in stature **syn** thickset, stocky, heavyset, stubby

squaw \\'skwȯ\ *n* : an American Indian woman

squawk \\'skwȯk\ *n* : a harsh loud cry; *also* : a noisy protest — **squawk** *vb*

squeak \\'skwēk\ *vb* **1** : to utter or speak in a weak shrill tone **2** : to make a thin high-pitched sound — **squeak** *n* — **squeaky** *adj*

¹squeal \\'skwēl\ *vb* **1** : to make a shrill sound or cry **2** : COMPLAIN, PROTEST **3** : to betray a secret or turn informer

²squeal *n* : a shrill sharp somewhat prolonged cry

squea·mish \\'skwē-mish\ *adj* **1** : easily nauseated; *also* : NAUSEATED **2** : easily disgusted **syn** fussy, nice, dainty, fastidious, persnickety — **squea·mish·ness** *n*

squee·gee \\'skwē-ˌjē\ *n* : a blade set crosswise on a handle and used for spreading or wiping liquid on, across, or off a surface — **squeegee** *vb*

¹squeeze \\'skwēz\ *vb* **squeezed; squeez·ing 1** : to exert pressure on the opposite sides or parts of **2** : to obtain by pressure ⟨∼ juice from a lemon⟩ **3** : to force, thrust, or cause to pass by pressure — **squeez·er** *n*

²squeeze *n* **1** : an act of squeezing **2** : a quantity squeezed out

squeeze bottle *n* : a flexible plastic bottle that dispenses its contents by being pressed

squelch \'skwelch\ *vb* **1** : to suppress completely : CRUSH **2** : to move in soft mud — **squelch** *n*

squib \'skwib\ *n* **1** : a small firecracker; *esp* : one that fizzes instead of exploding **2** : a brief witty writing or speech

squid \'skwid\ *n, pl* **squid** *or* **squids** : any of numerous 10-armed long-bodied sea mollusks usu. having a slender internal shell

squint \'skwint\ *vb* **1** : to look or aim obliquely **2** : to close the eyes partly ⟨the glare made him ∼⟩ **3** : to be cross-eyed — **squint** *n or adj*

¹squire \'skwī(ə)r\ *n* [ME *squier*, fr. OF *esquier*, fr. LL *scutarius*, fr. L *scutum* shield] **1** : an armor-bearer of a knight **2** : a man gallantly devoted to a lady **3** : a member of the British gentry ranking below a knight and above a gentleman; *also* : a prominent landowner **4** : a local magistrate

²squire *vb* **squired; squir·ing** : to attend as a squire or escort

squirm \'skwərm\ *vb* : to twist about like a worm : WRIGGLE

squir·rel \'skwər(-ə)l\ *n, pl* **squirrels** *also* **squirrel** [ME *squirel*, fr. MF *esquireul*, fr. VL *scurius*, alter. of L *sciurus*, fr. Gk *skiouros*, fr. *skia* shadow + *oura* tail] : any of various rodents usu. with a long bushy tail and strong hind legs; *also* : the fur of a squirrel

¹squirt \'skwərt\ *vb* : to eject liquid in a thin spurt

²squirt *n* **1** : an instrument (as a syringe) for squirting **2** : a small forcible jet of liquid

¹Sr *abbr* **1** senior **2** sister

²Sr *symbol* strontium

SR *abbr* seaman recruit

SRO *abbr* **1** single-room occupancy **2** standing room only

SS *abbr* **1** saints **2** Social Security **3** steamship **4** sworn statement

SSA *abbr* Social Security Administration

SSE *abbr* south-southeast

SSG *or* **SSgt** *abbr* staff sergeant

ssp *abbr* subspecies

SSR *abbr* Soviet Socialist Republic

SSS *abbr* Selective Service System

SST \'es-'es-'tē\ *n* [*supersonic transport*] : a supersonic passenger airplane

SSW *abbr* south-southwest

st *abbr* **1** stanza **2** state **3** stitch **4** stone **5** street

St *abbr* saint

ST *abbr* **1** short ton **2** standard time

-st — see -EST

sta *abbr* station; stationary

¹stab \'stab\ *n* **1** : a wound given by a pointed weapon **2** : a quick thrust; *also* : a brief attempt

²stab *vb* **stabbed; stab·bing** : to pierce or wound with or as if with a pointed weapon; *also* : THRUST, DRIVE

sta·bile \'stā-ˌbēl\ *n* : a stable abstract sculpture or construction typically made of sheet metal, wire, and wood

sta·bi·lize \'stā-bə-ˌlīz\ *vb* **-lized; -liz·ing** **1** : to make stable **2** : to hold steady ⟨∼ prices⟩ **syn** steady — **sta·bi·li·za·tion** \ˌstā-bə-lə-'zā-shən\ *n* — **sta·bi·liz·er** \'stā-bə-ˌlī-zər\ *n*

¹sta·ble \'stā-bəl\ *n* : a building in which livestock is sheltered and fed — **sta·ble·man** \-mən, -ˌman\ *n*

²stable *vb* **sta·bled; sta·bling** \-b(ə-)liŋ\ : to put or keep in a stable

³stable *adj* **sta·bler** \-b(ə-)lər\; **sta·blest** \-b(ə-)ləst\ **1** : firmly established; *also* : mentally healthy and well-balanced **2** : steady in purpose : CONSTANT **3** : DURABLE, ENDURING **4** : resistant to chemical or physical change **syn** lasting, permanent, perpetual, perdurable — **sta·bil·i·ty** \stə-'bil-ət-ē\ *n*

stac·ca·to \stə-'kät-ō\ *adj* [It] : cut short so as not to sound connected ⟨∼ notes⟩

¹stack \'stak\ *n* **1** : a large pile (as of hay) **2** : a large quantity **3** : a vertical pipe : SMOKESTACK **4** : an orderly pile (as of poker chips) **5** : a rack with shelves for storing books

²stack *vb* **1** : to pile up **2** : to arrange (cards) secretly for cheating

stack up *vb* : MEASURE UP

sta·di·um \'stād-ē-əm\ *n, pl* **-dia** \-ē-ə\ *or* **-di·ums** : a structure with tiers of seats for spectators built around a field for sports events

¹staff \'staf\ *n, pl* **staffs** \'stafs, 'stavz\ *or* **staves** \'stavz, 'stāvz\ **1** : a pole, stick, rod, or bar used for supporting, for measuring, or as a symbol of authority; *also* : CLUB, CUDGEL **2** : something that sustains ⟨bread is the ∼ of life⟩ **3** : the five horizontal lines on which music is written **4** : a body of assistants to an executive **5** : a group of officers holding no command but having duties concerned with planning and managing

²**staff** *vb* : to supply with a staff or with workers

staff•er \'staf-ər\ *n* : a member of a staff (as of a newspaper)

staff sergeant *n* : a noncommissioned officer ranking in the army next below a sergeant first class, in the air force next below a technical sergeant, and in the marine corps next below a gunnery sergeant

¹**stag** \'stag\ *n, pl* **stags** *or* **stag** : an adult male of various large deer

²**stag** *adj* : restricted to or intended for men ⟨a ∼ party⟩ ⟨∼ movies⟩

³**stag** *adv* : unaccompanied by a date

¹**stage** \'stāj\ *n* **1** : a raised platform on which an orator may speak or a play may be presented **2** : the acting profession : THEATER **3** : the scene of a notable action or event **4** : a station or resting place on a traveled road **5** : STAGECOACH **6** : a degree of advance in an undertaking, process, or development **7** : a propulsion unit in a rocket — **stagy** \'stā-jē\ *adj*

²**stage** *vb* **staged; stag•ing** : to produce or perform on or as if on a stage — **stage•able** *adj*

stage•coach \'stāj-,kōch\ *n* : a horse⹀drawn coach that runs regularly between stations

stag•fla•tion \,stag-'flā-shən\ *n* : inflation with stagnant economic activity and high unemployment

¹**stag•ger** \'stag-ər\ *vb* **stag•gered; stag•ger•ing** \-(ə-)riŋ\ **1** : to reel from side to side : TOTTER **2** : to begin to doubt : WAVER **3** : to cause to reel or waver **4** : to arrange in overlapping or alternating positions or times ⟨∼ working hours⟩ **5** : ASTONISH — **stag•ger•ing•ly** *adv*

²**stagger** *n* **1** *pl* : an abnormal condition of domestic mammals and birds associated with damage to the central nervous system and marked by lack of coordination and a reeling unsteady gait **2** : a reeling or unsteady gait or stance

stag•ing \'stā-jiŋ\ *n* **1** : SCAFFOLDING **2** : the assembling of troops and matériel in transit in a particular place

stag•nant \'stag-nənt\ *adj* **1** : not flowing : MOTIONLESS ⟨∼ water in a pond⟩ **2** : DULL, INACTIVE ⟨∼ business⟩

stag•nate \'stag-,nāt\ *vb* **stag•nat•ed; stag•nat•ing** : to be or become stagnant — **stag•na•tion** \stag-'nā-shən\ *n*

staid \'stād\ *adj* : SOBER, SEDATE **syn** grave, serious, earnest

¹**stain** \'stān\ *vb* **1** : DISCOLOR, SOIL **2** : to color (as wood, paper, or cloth) by processes affecting the material itself **3** : TAINT, CORRUPT **4** : DISGRACE

²**stain** *n* **1** : SPOT, DISCOLORATION **2** : a taint of guilt : STIGMA **3** : a preparation (as a dye or pigment) used in staining — **stain•less** *adj*

stainless steel *n* : steel alloyed with chromium that is highly resistant to stain, rust, and corrosion

stair \'staər\ *n* **1** : a series of steps or flights of steps for passing from one level to another — often used in pl. **2** : one step of a stairway

stair•case \-,kās\ *n* : a flight of steps with their supporting framework, casing, and balusters

stair•way \-,wā\ *n* : one or more flights of stairs with connecting landings

stair•well \-,wel\ *n* : a vertical shaft in which stairs are located

¹**stake** \'stāk\ *n* **1** : a pointed piece of material (as of wood) driven into the ground as a marker or a support **2** : a post to which a person is bound for death by burning; *also* : such a death **3** : something that is staked for gain or loss **4** : the prize in a contest

²**stake** *vb* **staked; stak•ing** **1** : to mark the limits of with stakes **2** : to tether to a stake **3** : to support or secure with stakes **4** : to place as a bet

stake•out \'stāk-,aut\ *n* : a surveillance by police (as of an area)

sta•lac•tite \stə-'lak-,tīt\ *n* [NL *stalactites,* fr. Gk *stalaktos* dripping] : an icicle-shaped deposit hanging from the roof or sides of a cavern

sta•lag•mite \stə-'lag-,mīt\ *n* [NL *stalagmites,* fr. Gk *stalagma* drop or *stalagmos* dripping] : a deposit resembling an inverted stalactite rising from the floor of a cavern

stale \'stāl\ *adj* **stal•er; stal•est** **1** : flat

and tasteless from age ⟨∼ beer⟩ **2** : not freshly made ⟨∼ bread⟩ **3** : COMMONPLACE, TRITE — **stale** *vb*

stale·mate \'stāl-ˌmāt\ *n* : a drawn contest : DEADLOCK — **stalemate** *vb*

¹**stalk** \'stȯk\ *vb* **1** : to approach (game) stealthily **2** : to walk stiffly or haughtily

²**stalk** *n* : a plant stem; *also* : any slender usu. upright supporting or connecting part — **stalked** \'stȯkt\ *adj*

¹**stall** \'stȯl\ *n* **1** : a compartment in a stable or barn for one animal **2** : a booth or counter where articles may be displayed for sale **3** : a seat in a church choir; *also* : a church pew **4** *Brit* : a front orchestra seat in a theater

²**stall** *vb* : to bring or come to a standstill unintentionally ⟨∼ an engine⟩

³**stall** *n* : the condition of an airfoil or aircraft in which lift is lost and the airfoil or aircraft tends to drop

stal·lion \'stal-yən\ *n* : a male horse

stal·wart \'stȯl-wərt\ *adj* : STOUT, STRONG; *also* : BRAVE, VALIANT

sta·men \'stā-mən\ *n* : an organ of a flower that produces pollen

stam·i·na \'stam-ə-nə\ *n* [L, pl. of *stamen* warp, thread of life spun by the Fates] : VIGOR, ENDURANCE

sta·mi·nate \'stā-mə-nət, 'stam-ə-, -ˌnāt\ *adj* **1** : having or producing stamens **2** : having stamens but no pistils

stam·mer \'stam-ər\ *vb* **stam·mered; stam·mer·ing** \-(ə-)riŋ\ : to hesitate or stumble in speaking — **stammer** *n* — **stam·mer·er** *n*

¹**stamp** \'stamp; *for 2 also* 'stämp *or* 'stȯmp\ *vb* **1** : to pound or crush with a heavy instrument **2** : to strike or beat with the bottom of the foot **3** : to impress or imprint with a mark **4** : to cut out or indent with a stamp or die **5** : to attach a postage stamp to

²**stamp** *n* **1** : a device or instrument for stamping **2** : the mark made by stamping; *also* : a distinctive mark or quality **3** : the act of stamping **4** : a paper or a mark put on a thing to show that a required charge has been paid

¹**stam·pede** \stam-'pēd\ *n* : a wild headlong rush or flight esp. of frightened animals

²**stampede** *vb* **stam·ped·ed; stam·ped·ing 1** : to flee or cause to flee in panic **2**

: to act or cause to act together suddenly and heedlessly

stance \'stans\ *n* : a way of standing

¹**stanch** \'stȯnch, 'stänch\ *vb* : to check the flowing of (as blood); *also* : to cease flowing or bleeding

²**stanch** *var of* ²STAUNCH

stan·chion \'stan-chən\ *n* : an upright bar, post, or support

¹**stand** \'stand\ *vb* **stood** \'stu̇d\; **standing 1** : to take or be at rest in an upright or firm position **2** : to assume a specified position **3** : to remain stationary or unchanged **4** : to be steadfast **5** : to act in resistance ⟨∼ against a foe⟩ **6** : to maintain a relative position or rank **7** : to gather slowly and remain briefly ⟨tears *stood* in her eyes⟩ **8** : to set upright **9** : ENDURE, TOLERATE ⟨I won't ∼ for that⟩ **10** : to submit to ⟨∼ trial⟩ — **stand pat** : to oppose or resist change

²**stand** *n* **1** : an act of standing, staying, or resisting **2** : a stop made to give a performance **3** : POSITION, VIEWPOINT **4** : a place taken by a witness to testify in court **5** *pl* : tiered seats for spectators **6** : a raised platform (as for speakers) **7** : a structure for a small retail business **8** : a structure for supporting or holding something upright ⟨music ∼⟩ **9** : a group of plants growing in a continuous area

stand–alone \'stand-ə-ˌlōn\ *adj* : SELF-CONTAINED; *esp* : capable of operation independent of a computer

stan·dard \'stan-dərd\ *n* **1** : a figure adopted as an emblem by a people **2** : the personal flag of a ruler; *also* : FLAG **3** : something set up as a rule for measuring or as a model to be followed **4** : an upright support ⟨lamp ∼⟩ — **standard** *adj*

stan·dard–bear·er \-ˌbar-ər\ *n* : the leader of a cause

stan·dard·ize \'stan-dərd-ˌīz\ *vb* **-ized; -iz·ing** : to make standard or uniform — **stan·dard·iza·tion** \ˌstan-dərd-ə-'zā-shən\ *n*

standard of living : the necessities, comforts, and luxuries that a person or group is accustomed to

standard time *n* : the time established by law or by general usage over a region or country

stand·by \'stan(d)-ˌbī\ *n, pl* **stand·bys**

\-‚bīz\ **1** : one that can be relied on **2** : a substitute in reserve — **on standby** : ready or available for immediate action or use

stand–in \ˈstan-‚din\ n **1** : someone employed to occupy an actor's place while lights and camera are readied **2** : SUBSTITUTE

¹**stand•ing** \ˈstan-diŋ\ adj **1** : ERECT **2** : not flowing : STAGNANT **3** : remaining at the same level or amount for an indefinite period ⟨∼ offer⟩ **4** : PERMANENT **5** : done from a standing position ⟨a ∼ jump⟩

²**standing** n **1** : length of service; also : relative position in society or in a profession : RANK **2** : DURATION

stand•off \ˈstand-‚ȯf\ n : TIE, DRAW

stand•out \ˈstand-‚au̇t\ n : something conspicuously excellent

stand•pipe \ˈstan(d)-‚pīp\ n : a high vertical pipe or reservoir for water used to produce a uniform pressure

stand•point \-‚pȯint\ n : a position from which objects or principles are judged

stand•still \-‚stil\ n : a state of rest

stank \ˈstaŋk\ past of STINK

stan•za \ˈstan-zə\ n [It] : a group of lines forming a division of a poem

sta•pes \ˈstā-‚pēz\ n, pl **stapes** or **sta•pe•des** \ˈstā-pə-‚dēz\ : the small innermost bone of the ear of mammals

staph•y•lo•coc•cus \‚staf-ə-lō-ˈkäk-əs\ n, pl **-coc•ci** \-ˈkäk-‚(s)ī\ : any of various spherical bacteria including some that cause purulent infections — **staph•y•lo•coc•cal** \-ˈkäk-əl\ adj

¹**sta•ple** \ˈstā-pəl\ n : a U-shaped piece of metal or wire with sharp points to be driven into or through objects and sometimes bent at the ends to hold or fasten one object to another — **staple** vb — **sta•pler** \-p(ə-)lər\ n

²**staple** n **1** : a chief commodity or product **2** : the main part of a thing : chief item **3** : unmanufactured or raw material **4** : a textile fiber suitable for spinning into yarn

³**staple** adj **1** : regularly produced in large quantities **2** : PRINCIPAL, MAIN

¹**star** \ˈstär\ n **1** : a celestial body that appears as a fixed point of light; esp : such a body that is gaseous, self≈luminous, and of great mass **2** : a planet or configuration of planets that is held in astrology to influence one's fortune — usu. used in pl. **3** obs : DESTINY, FORTUNE **4** : a conventional figure representing a star; esp : ASTERISK **5** : an actor or actress playing the leading role **6** : a brilliant performer — **star•dom** \ˈstärd-əm\ n — **star•less** adj — **star•like** adj — **star•ry** adj

²**star** vb **starred; star•ring** **1** : to adorn with stars **2** : to mark with an asterisk **3** : to play the leading role

star•board \ˈstär-bərd\ n [ME sterbord, fr. OE stēorbord, fr. stēor- steering oar + bord ship's side] : the right side of a ship or airplane looking forward — **starboard** adj

¹**starch** \ˈstärch\ vb : to stiffen with starch

²**starch** n : a complex carbohydrate that is stored in plants, is an important foodstuff, and is used in adhesives and sizes, in laundering, and in pharmacy — **starchy** adj

stare \ˈstaər\ vb **stared; star•ing** : to look fixedly with wide-open eyes — **stare** n — **star•er** n

star•fish \ˈstär-‚fish\ n : any of a class of echinoderms usu. having five arms arranged around a central disk and feeding largely on mollusks

stark \ˈstärk\ adj **1** archaic : STRONG, ROBUST **2** : rigid as if in death; also : STRICT **3** : SHEER, UTTER **4** : BARREN, DESOLATE ⟨∼ landscape⟩; also : UNADORNED ⟨∼ realism⟩ **5** : sharply delineated — **stark** adv — **stark•ly** adv

star•light \ˈstär-‚līt\ n : the light given by the stars

star•ling \ˈstär-liŋ\ n : a dark brown or in summer glossy greenish black European bird related to the crows that is naturalized and often a pest in No. America

¹**start** \ˈstärt\ vb **1** : to give an involuntary twitch or jerk (as from surprise) **2** : BEGIN, COMMENCE **3** : to set going **4** : to enter (as a horse) in a contest **5** : TAP ⟨∼ a cask⟩ — **start•er** n

²**start** n **1** : a sudden involuntary motion : LEAP **2** : a spasmodic and brief effort or action **3** : BEGINNING; also : the place of beginning

star•tle \ˈstärt-ᵊl\ vb **star•tled; star•tling** \ˈstärt-(ᵊ-)liŋ\ : to frighten or surprise suddenly : cause to start

star•tling adj : causing sudden fear, surprise, or anxiety

starve \\'stärv\ *vb* **starved; starv•ing**
[ME *sterven* to die, fr. OE *steorfan*] **1**
: to perish from hunger **2** : to suffer
extreme hunger **3** : to kill with hunger; *also* : to distress or subdue by
famine — **star•va•tion** \stär-'vā-shən\
n

starve•ling \\'stärv-liŋ\ *n* : one that is
thin from lack of nourishment

stash \\'stash\ *vb* : to store in a secret
place — **stash** *n*

stat *abbr* **1** [L *statim*] immediately **2**
statute

¹state \\'stāt\ *n* [ME *stat*, fr. OF & L; OF
estat, fr. L *status*, fr. *stare* to stand] **1**
: mode or condition of being ⟨gaseous
∼ of water⟩ **2** : condition of mind **3**
: social position **4** : a body of people
occupying a definite territory and organized under one government; *also*
: the government of such a body of
people **5** : one of the constituent units
of a nation having a federal government — **state•hood** \-ₓhùd\ *n*

²state *vb* **stat•ed; stat•ing 1** : FIX ⟨*stated*
intervals⟩ **2** : to express in words

state•craft \\'stāt-ₓkraft\ *n* : state management : STATESMANSHIP

state•house \-ₓhaús\ *n* : the building in
which a state legislature meets

state•ly \\'stāt-lē\ *adj* **state•li•er; -est 1**
: having lofty dignity : HAUGHTY **2**
: IMPRESSIVE, MAJESTIC **syn** magnificent, imposing, august — **state•li•ness**
n

state•ment \\'stāt-mənt\ *n* **1** : the act or
result of presenting in words **2** : a
summary of a financial account

state•room \\'stāt-ₓrüm, -ₓrùm\ *n* : a private room on a ship or railroad car

state•side \\'stāt-ₓsīd\ *adj* : of or relating
to the U.S. as regarded from outside
its continental limits ⟨∼ mail⟩ —
stateside *adv*

states•man \\'stāts-mən\ *n* : one skilled
in government and wise in handling
public affairs; *also* : one influential in
shaping public policy — **states•man•-
like** *adj* — **states•man•ship** *n*

¹stat•ic \\'stat-ik\ *adj* **1** : acting by mere
weight without motion ⟨∼ pressure⟩ **2**
: relating to bodies or forces at rest or
in equilibrium **3** : not moving : not active **4** : of or relating to stationary
charges of electricity **5** : of, relating
to, or caused by radio static

²static *n* : noise produced in a radio or
television receiver by atmospheric or
other electrical disturbances

¹sta•tion \\'stā-shən\ *n* **1** : the place
where a person or thing stands or is
appointed to remain **2** : a regular
stopping place on a transportation
route ⟨a railroad ∼⟩ ⟨a bus ∼⟩; *also*
: DEPOT **3** : a place where a fleet is
assigned for duty **4** : a stock farm or
ranch in Australia or New Zealand **5**
: social standing **6** : a complete assemblage of radio or television equipment for sending or receiving

²station *vb* **sta•tioned; sta•tion•ing** \\'stā-
sh(ə-)niŋ\ : to assign to a station

sta•tion•ary \\'stā-shə-ₓner-ē\ *adj* **1**
: fixed in a certain place or position **2**
: not changing condition : neither improving nor getting worse

station break *n* : a pause in a radio or
television broadcast for announcement of the identity of the network or
station

sta•tio•ner \\'stā-sh(ə-)nər\ *n* : one that
sells stationery

sta•tio•nery \\'stā-shə-ₓner-ē\ *n* : materials (as paper, pens, or ink) for writing;
esp : letter paper with envelopes

station wagon *n* : an automobile having
an interior longer than a sedan's, one
or more folding or removable seats to
make carrying light cargo easier, and
no trunk

sta•tis•tic \stə-'tis-tik\ *n* **1** : a single
term or datum in a collection of statistics **2** : a quantity (as the mean) that is
computed from a sample

sta•tis•tics \stə-'tis-tiks\ *n pl* [G *statistik*
study of political facts and figures, fr.
NL *statisticus* of politics, fr. L *status*
state] **1** : a branch of mathematics
dealing with the analysis and interpretation of masses of numerical data **2**
: facts collected and arranged in an
orderly way for study — **sta•tis•ti•cal**
\-ti-kəl\ *adj* — **sta•tis•ti•cal•ly** \-ti-
k(ə-)lē\ *adv* — **stat•is•ti•cian** \ₓstat-ə-
'stish-ən\ *n*

stat•u•ary \\'stach-ə-ₓwer-ē\ *n, pl* **-ar•ies**
1 : the art of making statues **2** : STAT-
UES

stat•ue \\'stach-ü\ *n* : a likeness of a living being sculptured in a solid substance

stat•u•esque \ₓstach-ə-'wesk\ *adj* : resembling a statue esp. in well-proportioned or massive dignity

stat·u·ette \ˌstach-ə-ˈwet\ *n* : a small statue

stat·ure \ˈstach-ər\ *n* **1** : natural height (as of a person) **2** : quality or status gained (as by achievement)

sta·tus \ˈstāt-əs, ˈstat-\ *n* **1** : the state or condition of a person in the eyes of others **2** : condition of affairs

sta·tus quo \-ˈkwō\ *n* [L, state in which] : the existing state of affairs

stat·ute \ˈstach-üt\ *n* : a law enacted by a legislative body

stat·u·to·ry \ˈstach-ə-ˌtōr-ē\ *adj* : imposed by statute : LAWFUL

¹**staunch** \ˈstȯnch\ var of ¹STANCH

²**staunch** *adj* **1** : WATERTIGHT ⟨a ∼ ship⟩ **2** : FIRM, STRONG; *also* : STEADFAST, LOYAL **syn** resolute, constant, true, faithful — **staunch·ly** *adv*

¹**stave** \ˈstāv\ *n* **1** : CUDGEL, STAFF **2** : any of several narrow strips of wood placed edge to edge to make something (as a barrel or bucket) **3** : STANZA

²**stave** *vb* **staved** *or* **stove** \ˈstōv\; **stav·ing** **1** : to break in the staves of; *also* : to break a hole in **2** : to drive or thrust away ⟨∼ off trouble⟩

staves pl of STAFF

¹**stay** \ˈstā\ *n* : a strong rope or wire used to support or steady something (as a ship's mast)

²**stay** *vb* **stayed** \ˈstād\ *also* **staid** \ˈstād\; **stay·ing** **1** : PAUSE, WAIT **2** : to stand firm **3** : LIVE, DWELL **4** : DELAY, POSTPONE **5** : to last out (as a race) **6** : STOP, CHECK **7** : to satisfy (as hunger) for a time **syn** remain, abide, linger, tarry

³**stay** *n* **1** : STOP, HALT **2** : a residence or sojourn in a place

⁴**stay** *n* **1** : PROP, SUPPORT **2** : CORSET — usu. used in pl.

⁵**stay** *vb* : to hold up : PROP

staying power *n* : STAMINA

stbd *abbr* starboard

std *abbr* standard

STD \ˈes-ˈtē-ˈdē\ *n* : SEXUALLY TRANSMITTED DISEASE

Ste *abbr* [F *sainte*] saint (female)

stead \ˈsted\ *n* **1** : ADVANTAGE, AVAIL ⟨stood him in good ∼⟩ **2** : the place or function ordinarily occupied or carried out by another ⟨her brother served in her ∼⟩

stead·fast \ˈsted-ˌfast\ *adj* **1** : firmly fixed in place **2** : not subject to change **3** : firm in belief, determination, or adherence : LOYAL **syn** resolute, true, faithful, staunch — **stead·fast·ly** *adv* — **stead·fast·ness** *n*

¹**steady** \ˈsted-ē\ *adj* **steadi·er; -est** **1** : FIRM, FIXED **2** : not faltering or swerving; *also* : CALM **3** : STABLE **4** : CONSTANT, RESOLUTE **5** : REGULAR **6** : RELIABLE, SOBER **syn** uniform, even, stable, constant — **steadi·ly** \ˈsted-ᵊl-ē\ *adv* — **steadi·ness** \-ē-nəs\ *n* — **steady** *adv*

²**steady** *vb* **stead·ied; steady·ing** : to make or become steady

steak \ˈstāk\ *n* : a slice of meat cut from a fleshy part esp. of a beef carcass

¹**steal** \ˈstēl\ *vb* **stole** \ˈstōl\; **sto·len** \ˈstō-lən\; **steal·ing** **1** : to come or go secretly or gradually **2** : to take and carry away without right or permission **3** : to get for oneself slyly or secretly **4** : to gain a base in baseball by running without the aid of a hit or an error **syn** pilfer, filch, purloin, swipe

²**steal** *n* **1** : an act of stealing **2** : BARGAIN

stealth \ˈstelth\ *n* : secret or underhanded procedure : FURTIVENESS

stealthy \ˈstel-thē\ *adj* **stealth·i·er; -est** : done by stealth : FURTIVE, SLY **syn** secret, covert, clandestine, surreptitious, underhanded — **stealth·i·ly** \ˈstel-thə-lē\ *adv*

¹**steam** \ˈstēm\ *n* **1** : the vapor into which water is changed when heated to the boiling point **2** : water vapor when compressed so that it supplies heat and power **3** : POWER, FORCE, ENERGY — **steamy** *adj*

²**steam** *vb* **1** : to pass off as vapor **2** : to emit vapor **3** : to move by or as if by the agency of steam — **steam·er** *n*

steam·boat \ˈstēm-ˌbōt\ *n* : a boat driven by steam power

steam engine *n* : a reciprocating engine having a piston driven in a closed cylinder by steam

steam·fit·ter \ˈstēm-ˌfit-ər\ *n* : a workman who puts in or repairs equipment (as steam pipes) for heating, ventilating, or refrigerating systems — **steam fitting** *n*

steam·roll·er \-ˈrō-lər\ *n* : a machine for compacting roads or pavements — **steam·roll·er** *also* **steam·roll** \-ˌrōl\ *vb*

steam•ship \-ˌship\ *n* : a ship driven by steam

steed \'stēd\ *n* : HORSE

¹**steel** \'stēl\ *n* **1** : iron treated with intense heat and mixed with carbon to make it hard and tough **2** : an article made of steel **3** : a quality (as hardness of mind) that suggests steel — **steel** *adj* — **steely** *adj*

²**steel** *vb* **1** : to sheathe, point, or edge with steel **2** : to make able to resist

steel wool *n* : long fine steel shavings used esp. for scouring and smoothing

steel•yard \'stēl-ˌyärd\ *n* : a balance in which the object to be weighed is hung from the shorter arm of a lever and is balanced by a weight that slides along the longer arm

¹**steep** \'stēp\ *adj* **1** : having a very sharp slope : PRECIPITOUS **2** : too great or too high ⟨∼ prices⟩ — **steep•ly** *adv* — **steep•ness** *n*

²**steep** *n* : a steep slope

³**steep** *vb* **1** : to soak in a liquid; *esp* : to extract the essence of by soaking ⟨∼ tea⟩ **2** : SATURATE ⟨∼ed in learning⟩

stee•ple \'stē-pəl\ *n* : a tall tapering structure built on top of a church tower; *also* : a church tower

stee•ple•chase \-ˌchās\ *n* [fr. the use of church steeples as landmarks to guide the riders] : a race across country by horsemen; *also* : a race over a course obstructed by hurdles

¹**steer** \'stiər\ *n* : a male bovine animal castrated before sexual maturity and usu. raised for beef

²**steer** *vb* **1** : to direct the course of (as by a rudder or wheel) **2** : GUIDE, CONTROL **3** : to pursue a course of action **4** : to be subject to guidance or direction — **steers•man** \'stiərz-mən\ *n*

steer•age \'sti(ə)r-ij\ *n* **1** : DIRECTION, GUIDANCE **2** : a section in a passenger ship for passengers paying the lowest fares

stein \'stīn\ *n* : an earthenware mug

stel•lar \'stel-ər\ *adj* : of or relating to stars : resembling a star

¹**stem** \'stem\ *n* **1** : the main stalk of a plant; *also* : a plant part that supports another part (as a leaf or fruit) **2** : the bow of a ship **3** : a line of ancestry : STOCK **4** : that part of an inflected word which remains unchanged throughout a given inflection **5**

: something resembling the stem of a plant — **stem•less** *adj*

²**stem** *vb* **stemmed; stem•ming** : to have a specified source : DERIVE

³**stem** *vb* **stemmed; stem•ming** : to make headway against ⟨∼ the tide⟩

⁴**stem** *vb* **stemmed; stem•ming** : to stop or check by or as if by damming

stemmed \'stemd\ *adj* : having a stem

stench \'stench\ *n* : STINK

sten•cil \'sten-səl\ *n* [ME *stanselen* to ornament with sparkling colors, fr. MF *estanceler*, fr. *estancele* spark, fr. (assumed) VL *stincilla*, fr. L *scintilla*] : a piece of thin impervious material (as metal or paper) that is perforated with lettering or a design through which a substance (as ink or paint) is applied to a surface to be printed — **stencil** *vb*

ste•nog•ra•phy \stə-'näg-rə-fē\ *n* : the art or process of writing in shorthand — **ste•nog•ra•pher** \-fər\ *n* — **steno•graph•ic** \ˌsten-ə-'graf-ik\ *adj*

sten•to•ri•an \sten-'tōr-ē-ən\ *adj* : extremely loud

¹**step** \'step\ *n* **1** : a rest for the foot in ascending or descending : STAIR **2** : an advance made by raising one foot and putting it down in a different spot **3** : manner of walking **4** : a small space or distance **5** : a degree, rank, or plane in a series **6** : a sequential measure leading to a result

²**step** *vb* **stepped; step•ping** **1** : to advance or recede by steps **2** : to go on foot : WALK **3** : to move along briskly **4** : to press down with the foot **5** : to measure by steps **6** : to construct or arrange in or as if in steps

step•broth•er \'step-ˌbrəth-ər\ *n* : the son of one's stepparent by a former marriage

step•child \-ˌchīld\ *n* : a child of one's husband or wife by a former marriage

step•daugh•ter \-ˌdȯt-ər\ *n* : a daughter of one's wife or husband by a former marriage

step down *vb* **1** : to lower the voltage of (a current) by means of a transformer **2** : RETIRE, RESIGN

step•fa•ther \-ˌfäth-ər\ *n* : the husband of one's mother by a subsequent marriage

step•lad•der \'step-ˌlad-ər\ *n* : a light portable set of steps in a hinged frame

step·moth·er \-ˌməth̲-ər\ *n* : the wife of one's father by a subsequent marriage

step·par·ent \-ˌpar-ənt\ *n* : the husband or wife of one's mother or father by a subsequent marriage

steppe \'step\ *n* [Russ *step'*] : dry level grass-covered land in regions of wide temperature range esp. in southeastern Europe and Asia

step·sis·ter \'step-ˌsis-tər\ *n* : the daughter of one's stepparent by a former marriage

step·son \-ˌsən\ *n* : a son of one's wife or husband by a former marriage

step up \(ˈ)step-'əp\ *vb* 1 : to increase the voltage of (a current) by means of a transformer 2 : INCREASE, ACCELERATE — **step–up** \'step-ˌəp\ *n*

ster *abbr* sterling

ste·reo \'ster-ē-ˌō, 'stir-\ *n, pl* **ste·re·os** 1 : stereophonic reproduction 2 : a stereophonic sound system — **stereo** *adj*

ste·reo·phon·ic \ˌster-ē-ə-'fän-ik, ˌstir-\ *adj* : of or relating to sound reproduction designed to create the effect of listening to the original — **ste·reo·phon·i·cal·ly** \-i-k(ə-)lē\ *adv*

ster·e·o·scope \'ster-ē-ə-ˌskōp, 'stir-\ *n* [Gk *stereos* solid + *skopein* to look at] : an optical instrument that blends two slightly different pictures of the same subject to give the effect of depth

ste·reo·scop·ic \ˌster-ē-ə-'skäp-ik, ˌstir-\ *adj* 1 : of or relating to the stereoscope 2 : characterized by stereoscopy ⟨~ vision⟩ — **ste·reo·scop·i·cal·ly** \-i-k(ə-)lē\ *adv*

ste·re·os·co·py \ˌster-ē-'äs-kə-pē, ˌstir-\ *n* : the seeing of objects in three dimensions

ste·reo·type \'ster-ē-ə-ˌtīp, 'stir-\ *n* 1 : a metal printing plate cast from a mold made from set type 2 : something agreeing with a pattern; *esp* : an idea that many people have about a thing or a group and that may often be untrue or only partly true

ste·reo·typed \-ˌtīpt\ *adj* : repeated without variation : lacking originality or individuality **syn** trite, clichéd, commonplace, hackneyed, stale, threadbare

ster·ile \'ster-əl\ *adj* 1 : unable to bear fruit, crops, or offspring 2 : free from living things and esp. germs — **ste·ril·i·ty** \stə-'ril-ət-ē\ *n*

ster·il·ize \'ster-ə-ˌlīz\ *vb* **-ized; -iz·ing** : to make sterile; *esp* : to free from germs — **ster·il·iza·tion** \ˌster-ə-lə-'zā-shən\ *n* — **ster·il·iz·er** \'ster-ə-ˌlī-zər\ *n*

¹ster·ling \'stər-liŋ\ *n* 1 : British money 2 : sterling silver

²sterling *adj* 1 : of, relating to, or calculated in terms of British sterling 2 : having a fixed standard of purity represented by an alloy of 925 parts of silver with 75 parts of copper 3 : made of sterling silver 4 : EXCELLENT

¹stern \'stərn\ *adj* 1 : SEVERE, AUSTERE 2 : STOUT, STURDY ⟨~ resolve⟩ — **stern·ly** *adv* — **stern·ness** *n*

²stern *n* : the rear end of a boat

ster·num \'stər-nəm\ *n, pl* **sternums** *or* **ster·na** \-nə\ : a long flat bone or cartilage at the center front of the chest connecting the ribs of the two sides

ste·roid \'stir-ˌȯid\ *n* : any of numerous compounds containing a 17-carbon 4-ring system and including various hormones and sugar derivatives — **steroid** *or* **ste·roi·dal** \stə-'rȯid-ᵊl\ *adj*

stetho·scope \'steth-ə-ˌskōp\ *n* : an instrument for listening to sounds produced in the body and esp. in the chest

ste·ve·dore \'stē-və-ˌdōr\ *n* [Sp *estibador*, fr. *estibar* to pack, fr. L *stipare* to press together] : one who works at loading and unloading ships

¹stew \'st(y)ü\ *n* 1 : a dish of stewed meat and vegetables served in gravy 2 : a state of excitement, worry, or confusion

²stew *vb* 1 : to boil slowly : SIMMER 2 : to become excited or worried

stew·ard \'st(y)ü-ərd\ *n* [ME, fr. OE *stīweard*, fr. *stī* hall, sty + *weard* ward] 1 : one employed on a large estate to manage domestic concerns (as keeping accounts and directing servants) 2 : one actively concerned with the direction of the affairs of an organization 3 : one who supervises the provision and distribution of food (as on a ship); *also* : an employee on a ship or airplane who serves passengers — **stew·ard·ship** *n*

stew·ard·ess \-əs\ *n* : a woman who is a steward

stg *abbr* sterling

¹**stick** \'stik\ *n* **1** : a cut or broken branch or twig; *also* : a long slender piece of wood **2** : ROD, STAFF **3** : something resembling a stick **4** : a dull uninteresting person

²**stick** *vb* **stuck** \'stək\; **stick·ing 1** : STAB, PRICK **2** : IMPALE **3** : ATTACH, FASTEN **4** : to thrust or project in some direction or manner **5** : to be unable to proceed or move freely **6** : to hold fast by or as if by gluing : ADHERE **7** : to hold to something firmly or closely : CLING **8** : to become jammed or blocked

stick·er \'stik-ər\ *n* : one that sticks (as a bur) or causes sticking (as glue); *esp* : a gummed label

stick insect *n* : any of various usu. wingless insects (as a walkingstick) with a long round body resembling a stick

stick·ler \'stik-(ə-)lər\ *n* : one who insists on exactness or completeness

stick shift *n* : a manually operated gearshift mounted on the steering-wheel column or floor of an automobile

stick–to–it·ive·ness \stik-'tü-ət-iv-nəs\ *n* : dogged perseverance : TENACITY

stick up \(')stik-'əp\ *vb* : to rob at gunpoint — **stick·up** \'stik-,əp\ *n*

sticky \'stik-ē\ *adj* **stick·i·er; -est 1** : ADHESIVE **2** : VISCOUS, GLUEY **3** : tending to stick ⟨~ valve⟩

¹**stiff** \'stif\ *adj* **1** : not pliant : RIGID **2** : not limber ⟨~ joints⟩; *also* : TENSE, TAUT **3** : not flowing or working easily ⟨~ paste⟩ **4** : not natural and easy : FORMAL **5** : STRONG, FORCEFUL ⟨~ breeze⟩ **6** : HARSH, SEVERE **syn** inflexible, rigid, inelastic — **stiff·ly** *adv* — **stiff·ness** *n*

²**stiff** *vb* : to refrain from tipping ⟨~ a waiter⟩

stiff·en \'stif-ən\ *vb* **stiff·ened; stiff·en·ing** \-(ə-)niŋ\ : to make or become stiff — **stiff·en·er** \-(ə-)nər\ *n*

stiff–necked \-'nekt\ *adj* : STUBBORN, HAUGHTY

sti·fle \'stī-fəl\ *vb* **sti·fled; sti·fling** \-f(ə-)liŋ\ **1** : SUFFOCATE **2** : QUENCH, SUPPRESS **3** : SMOTHER, MUFFLE **4** : to die because of obstruction of the breath

stig·ma \'stig-mə\ *n, pl* **stig·ma·ta** \stig-'mät-ə, 'stig-mət-ə\ *or* **stigmas** [L] **1** : a mark of disgrace or discredit **2** *pl* : bodily marks resembling the wounds

of the crucified Christ **3** : the upper part of the pistil of a flower that receives the pollen in fertilization — **stig·mat·ic** \stig-'mat-ik\ *adj*

stig·ma·tize \'stig-mə-,tīz\ *vb* **-tized; -tiz·ing 1** : to mark with a stigma **2** : to set a mark of disgrace upon

stile \'stīl\ *n* : steps used for crossing a fence or wall

sti·let·to \stə-'let-ō\ *n, pl* **-tos** *or* **-toes** [It, dim. of *stilo* stylus, dagger] : a slender dagger

¹**still** \'stil\ *adj* **1** : MOTIONLESS **2** : making no sound : QUIET, SILENT — **still·ness** *n*

²**still** *vb* : to make or become still : QUIET

³**still** *adv* **1** : without motion ⟨sit ~⟩ **2** : up to and during this or that time **3** : in spite of that : NEVERTHELESS **4** : EVEN ⟨ran ~ faster⟩ **5** : BESIDES, YET

⁴**still** *n* **1** : STILLNESS, SILENCE **2** : a static photograph esp. of an instant in a motion picture

⁵**still** *n* **1** : DISTILLERY **2** : apparatus used in distillation

still·birth \'stil-,bərth\ *n* : the birth of a dead fetus

still·born \-'bȯrn\ *adj* : born dead

still life *n, pl* **still lifes** : a picture of inanimate objects

stilt \'stilt\ *n* : one of a pair of poles for walking with each having a step or loop for the foot; *also* : a polelike support of a structure above ground or water level

stilt·ed \'stil-təd\ *adj* : FORMAL, POMPOUS ⟨~ writing⟩

Stil·ton \'stilt-ᵊn\ *n* : a blue-veined cheese with wrinkled rind

stim·u·lant \'stim-yə-lənt\ *n* **1** : an agent (as a drug) that temporarily increases the activity of an organism or any of its parts **2** : STIMULUS **3** : an alcoholic beverage — **stimulant** *adj*

stim·u·late \-,lāt\ *vb* **-lat·ed; -lat·ing** : to make active or more active : ANIMATE, AROUSE **syn** excite, provoke, motivate, quicken — **stim·u·la·tion** \,stim-yə-'lā-shən\ *n* — **stim·u·la·tive** \'stim-yə-,lāt-iv\ *adj*

stim·u·lus \'stim-yə-ləs\ *n, pl* **-li** \-,lī\ [L] : something that stimulates : SPUR

¹**sting** \'stiŋ\ *vb* **stung** \'stəŋ\; **sting·ing** \'stiŋ-iŋ\ **1** : to prick painfully esp. with a sharp or poisonous process **2**

: to cause to suffer acutely — **sting·er** n

²sting n **1** : an act of stinging; *also* : a resultant sore, pain, or mark **2** : a pointed often venom-bearing organ (as of a bee)

stin·gy \'stin-jē\ *adj* **stin·gi·er; -est** : not generous : SPARING, NIGGARDLY — **stin·gi·ness** n

stink \'stiŋk\ *vb* **stank** \'staŋk\ *or* **stunk** \'stəŋk\; **stunk; stink·ing** : to give forth a strong and offensive smell; *also* : to be extremely bad in quality or repute — **stink** n — **stink·er** n

stink·bug \'stiŋk-ˌbəg\ n : any of various true bugs that emit a disagreeable odor

¹stint \'stint\ *vb* **1** : to be sparing or frugal **2** : to restrict to a scant allowance : cut short in amount

²stint n **1** : RESTRAINT, LIMITATION **2** : an assigned amount of work **3** : a period of time spent at a particular activity

sti·pend \'stī-ˌpend, -pənd\ n [alter. of ME *stipendy*, fr. L *stipendium*, fr. *stips* gift + *pendere* to weigh, pay] : a fixed sum of money paid periodically for services or to defray expenses

stip·ple \'stip-əl\ *vb* **stip·pled; stip·pling** \-(ə-)liŋ\ **1** : to engrave by means of dots and light strokes instead of by lines **2** : to apply (as paint or ink) with small short touches that together produce an even and softly graded shadow — **stipple** n

stip·u·late \'stip-yə-ˌlāt\ *vb* **-lat·ed; -lat·ing** : to make an agreement; *esp* : to make a special demand for something as a condition in an agreement — **stip·u·la·tion** \ˌstip-yə-'lāsh-ən\ n

¹stir \'stər\ *vb* **stirred; stir·ring** **1** : to move slightly **2** : AROUSE, EXCITE **3** : to mix, dissolve, or make by continued circular movement ⟨~ eggs into cake batter⟩ **4** : to move to activity (as by pushing, beating, or prodding)

²stir n **1** : a state of agitation or activity **2** : an act of stirring

³stir n, slang : PRISON

stir–fry \'stər-ˌfrī\ *vb* : to fry quickly over high heat while stirring continuously

stir·ring \'stər-iŋ\ *adj* **1** : ACTIVE, BUSTLING **2** : ROUSING, INSPIRING

stir·rup \'stər-əp\ n [OE *stigrāp*, lit., mounting rope] **1** : a light frame hung from a saddle to support the foot of a horseback rider **2** : STAPES

¹stitch \'stich\ n **1** : a sudden sharp pain esp. in the side **2** : one of the series of loops formed by or over a needle in sewing **syn** twinge, pang, throe

²stitch *vb* **1** : to fasten or join with stitches **2** : to decorate with stitches **3** : SEW

stk *abbr* stock

stoat \'stōt\ n, pl **stoats** also **stoat** : the European ermine esp. in its brown summer coat

¹stock \'stäk\ n **1** *archaic* : a block of wood **2** : a stupid person **3** : a wooden part of a thing serving as its support, frame, or handle **4** pl : a device for publicly punishing offenders consisting of a wooden frame with holes in which the feet and hands can be locked **5** : the original from which others derive; *also* : a group having a common origin : FAMILY **6** : farm animals **7** : the supply of goods kept by a merchant **8** : the proprietorship element in a corporation divided to give the owners an interest and usu. voting power **9** : a company of actors playing at a particular theater and presenting a series of plays **10** : liquid in which meat, fish, or vegetables have been simmered that is used as a basis for soup, gravy, or sauce **11** : raw material

²stock *vb* : to provide with stock

³stock *adj* : kept regularly for sale or use; *also* : used regularly : STANDARD

stock·ade \stä-'kād\ n [Sp *estacada*, fr. *estaca* stake, pale] : an enclosure of posts and stakes for defense or confinement

stock·bro·ker \-ˌbrō-kər\ n : one who executes orders to buy and sell securities

stock car n : a racing car having the basic chassis of a commercially produced regular model

stock exchange n **1** : a place where trading in securities is accomplished under an organized system **2** : an association of stockbrokers

stock·hold·er \'stäk-ˌhōl-dər\ n : one who owns corporate stock

stock·i·nette *or* **stock·i·net** \ˌstäk-ə-'net\ n : an elastic knitted textile fabric used esp. for infants' wear and bandages

stock•ing \'stäk-iŋ\ *n* : a close-fitting knitted covering for the foot and leg

stock market *n* 1 : STOCK EXCHANGE 1 2 : a market for stocks

stock•pile \'stäk-ˌpīl\ *n* : a reserve supply esp. of something essential — **stockpile** *vb*

stocky \'stäk-ē\ *adj* **stock•i•er; -est** : being short and relatively thick : STURDY **syn** thickset, squat, heavyset, stubby

stock•yard \'stäk-ˌyärd\ *n* : a yard for stock; *esp* : one for livestock about to be slaughtered or shipped

stodgy \'stäj-ē\ *adj* **stodg•i•er; -est** : HEAVY, DULL, UNINSPIRED

¹**sto•ic** \'stō-ik\ *n* [ME, fr. L *stoicus*, fr. Gk *stōikos*, lit., of the portico, fr. *Stoa* (*Poikilē*) the Painted Portico, portico at Athens where Zeno taught] : one who suffers without complaining

²**stoic** *or* **sto•i•cal** \-i-kəl\ *adj* : not affected by passion or feeling; *esp* : showing indifference to pain **syn** impassive, phlegmatic, apathetic, stolid — **sto•ical•ly** \-i-k(ə-)lē\ *adv* — **sto•icism** \'stō-ə-ˌsiz-əm\ *n*

stoke \'stōk\ *vb* **stoked; stok•ing** 1 : to stir up a fire 2 : to tend and supply fuel to a furnace — **stok•er** *n*

STOL *abbr* short takeoff and landing

¹**stole** \'stōl\ past of STEAL

²**stole** *n* 1 : a long narrow band worn round the neck by some clergymen 2 : a long wide scarf or similar covering worn by women

stolen past part of STEAL

stol•id \'stäl-əd\ *adj* : not easily aroused or excited : showing little or no emotion **syn** phlegmatic, apathetic, impassive, stoic — **sto•lid•i•ty** \stä-ˈlid-ət-ē\ *n* — **stol•id•ly** \'stäl-əd-lē\ *adv*

sto•lon \'stō-lən, -ˌlän\ *n* : RUNNER 6

¹**stom•ach** \'stəm-ək\ *n* 1 : a saclike digestive organ of a vertebrate into which food goes from the mouth by way of the throat and which opens below into the intestine 2 : a cavity in an invertebrate animal that is analogous to a stomach 3 : ABDOMEN 4 : desire for food caused by hunger : APPETITE 5 : INCLINATION, DESIRE

²**stomach** *vb* : to bear without overt resentment : BROOK

stom•ach•ache \-ˌāk\ *n* : pain in or in the region of the stomach

stom•ach•er \'stəm-i-kər, -i-chər\ *n* : the front of a bodice often appearing between the laces of an outer garment (as in 16th century costume)

¹**stomp** \'stämp, 'stȯmp\ *vb* : STAMP

²**stomp** *n* 1 : STAMP 3 2 : a jazz dance marked by heavy stamping

¹**stone** \'stōn\ *n* 1 : hardened earth or mineral matter : ROCK 2 : a small piece of rock 3 : a precious stone : GEM 4 : a hard abnormal mass in a bodily cavity or duct 5 : a hard stony seed or one (as of a plum) with a stony covering 6 *pl usu* **stone** : a British unit of weight equal to 14 pounds — **stony** *also* **ston•ey** \'stō-nē\ *adj*

²**stone** *vb* **stoned; ston•ing** 1 : to pelt or kill with stones 2 : to remove the stones of (a fruit)

Stone Age *n* : the first known period of prehistoric human culture characterized by the use of stone tools

stoned \'stōnd\ *adj* 1 : DRUNK 2 : being under the influence of a drug

stood past and past part of STAND

stooge \'stüj\ *n* 1 : a person who plays a subordinate or compliant role to a principal 2 : STRAIGHT MAN

stool \'stül\ *n* 1 : a seat usu. without back or arms 2 : FOOTSTOOL 3 : a seat used while urinating or defecating 4 : a discharge of fecal matter

stool pigeon *n* : DECOY, INFORMER

¹**stoop** \'stüp\ *vb* 1 : to bend over 2 : CONDESCEND 3 : to humiliate or lower oneself socially or morally

²**stoop** *n* 1 : an act of bending over 2 : a bent position of head and shoulders

³**stoop** *n* : a porch or platform at a house door

¹**stop** \'stäp\ *vb* **stopped; stop•ping** 1 : to close (an opening or hole) by filling or covering closely 2 : BLOCK, HALT 3 : to cease to go on 4 : to cease activity or operation 5 : STAY, TARRY **syn** quit, discontinue, desist, halt, cease

²**stop** *n* 1 : END, CESSATION 2 : a set of organ pipes of one tone quality; *also* : a control knob for such a set 3 : OBSTRUCTION 4 : PLUG, STOPPER 5 : an act of stopping : CHECK 6 : a delay in a journey : STAY 7 : a place for stopping 8 *chiefly Brit* : any of several punctuation marks

stop·gap \\'stäp-ˌgap\ *n* : something that serves as a temporary expedient

stop·light \-ˌlīt\ *n* : TRAFFIC LIGHT

stop·page \\'stäp-ij\ *n* : the act of stopping : the state of being stopped

stop·per \\'stäp-ər\ *n* : something (as a cork or plug) for sealing an opening

stop·watch \\'stäp-ˌwäch\ *n* : a watch having a component (as a hand) that can be started or stopped at will for exact timing

stor·age \\'stōr-ij\ *n* **1** : space for storing; *also* : cost of storing **2** : the act of storing; *esp* : the safekeeping of goods (as in a warehouse)

storage battery *n* : a group of connected cells that converts chemical energy into electrical energy by reversible chemical reactions and that may be recharged by electrical means

¹store \\'stōr\ *vb* **stored; stor·ing 1** : to provide esp. for a future need **2** : to place or leave in a safe location for preservation or future use

²store *n* **1** : something accumulated and kept for future use **2** : a large or ample quantity **3** : STOREHOUSE **4** : a retail business establishment

store·house \-ˌhaús\ *n* : a building for storing goods or supplies; *also* : an abundant source or supply

store·keep·er \-ˌkē-pər\ *n* : one who operates a retail store

store·room \-ˌrüm, -ˌrúm\ *n* : a room for storing goods or supplies

sto·ried \\'stōr-ēd\ *adj* : celebrated in story or history

stork \\'stórk\ *n* : any of various large stout-billed Old World wading birds related to the herons and ibises

¹storm \\'stórm\ *n* **1** : a heavy fall of rain, snow, or hail with high wind **2** : a violent outbreak or disturbance **3** : a mass attack on a defended position — **storm·i·ly** \\'stór-mə-lē\ *adv* — **storm·i·ness** \-mē-nəs\ *n* — **stormy** *adj*

²storm *vb* **1** : to blow with violence; *also* : to rain, snow, or hail heavily **2** : to make a mass attack against **3** : to be violently angry : RAGE **4** : to rush along furiously

¹sto·ry \\'stōr-ē\ *n, pl* **stories 1** : NARRATIVE, ACCOUNT **2** : REPORT, STATEMENT **3** : ANECDOTE **4** : LIE, FALSEHOOD **syn** lie, falsehood, untruth, tale, canard

²story *also* **sto·rey** \\'stōr-ē\ *n, pl* **stories** *also* **storeys** : a floor of a building or the space between two adjacent floor levels

sto·ry·tell·er \-ˌtel-ər\ *n* : a teller of stories

sto·tin·ka \stō-'tiŋ-kə, stə-\ *n, pl* **-tin·ki** \-kē\ — see *lev* at MONEY table

¹stout \\'staút\ *adj* **1** : BRAVE **2** : FIRM **3** : STURDY **4** : STAUNCH, ENDURING **5** : SOLID **6** : FORCEFUL **7** : BULKY, THICKSET **syn** fleshy, fat, portly, corpulent, obese, plump — **stout·ly** *adv* — **stout·ness** *n*

²stout *n* : a dark heavy alcoholic beverage brewed from roasted malt and hops

¹stove \\'stōv\ *n* : an apparatus that burns fuel or uses electricity to provide heat (as for cooking or room heating)

²stove past and past part of STAVE

stow \\'stō\ *vb* **1** : HIDE, STORE **2** : to pack in a compact mass

stow·away \\'stō-ə-ˌwā\ *n* : one who hides on a vehicle to ride free

¹STP \ˌes-ˌtē-'pē\ *n* : a psychotropic drug chemically related to amphetamine

²STP *abbr* standard temperature and pressure

strad·dle \\'strad-ᵊl\ *vb* **strad·dled; strad·dling** \\'strad-(ᵊ-)liŋ\ **1** : to stand, sit, or walk with legs spread apart **2** : to favor or seem to favor two apparently opposite sides — **straddle** *n*

strafe \\'strāf\ *vb* **strafed; straf·ing** : to fire upon with machine guns from a low-flying airplane

strag·gle \\'strag-əl\ *vb* **strag·gled; straggling** \-(ə-)liŋ\ **1** : to wander from the direct course : ROVE, STRAY **2** : to become separated from others of the same kind — **strag·gler** \-(ə-)lər\ *n* — **strag·gly** \-(ə-)lē\ *adj*

¹straight \\'strāt\ *adj* **1** : free from curves, bends, angles, or irregularities : DIRECT **2** : not wandering from the main point or proper course ⟨~ thinking⟩ **3** : HONEST, UPRIGHT **4** : not marked by confusion : correctly arranged or ordered **5** : UNMIXED, UNDILUTED ⟨~ whiskey⟩ **6** : CONVENTIONAL, SQUARE; *also* : HETEROSEXUAL

²straight *adv* : in a straight manner

³straight *n* **1** : a straight line, course, or arrangement **2** : the part of a racetrack between the last turn and the finish **3** : a sequence of five cards in a poker hand

straight–arm \'strāt-ˌärm\ *vb* : to ward off an opponent with the arm held straight — **straight–arm** *n*

straight·away \'strāt-ə-ˌwā\ *n* : a straight stretch (as at a racetrack)

straight·edge \'strāt-ˌej\ *n* : a piece of material with a straight edge for testing straight lines and surfaces or drawing straight lines

straight·en \'strāt-ᵊn\ *vb* **straight·ened; straight·en·ing** \'strāt-(ᵊ-)niŋ\ : to make or become straight

straight·for·ward \strāt-'fȯr-wərd\ *adj* **1** : CANDID, HONEST **2** : proceeding in a straight course or manner

straight man *n* : an entertainer who feeds lines to a comedian

straight·way \'strāt-'wā, -ˌwā\ *adv* : IMMEDIATELY

¹strain \'strān\ *n* [ME *streen* progeny, lineage, fr. OE *strēon* gain, acquisition] **1** : LINEAGE, ANCESTRY **2** : a group (as of people or plants) of presumed common ancestry **3** : an inherited or inherent character or quality ⟨a ~ of madness in the family⟩ **4** : STREAK, TRACE **5** : MELODY **6** : the general style or tone

²strain *vb* [ME *strainen*, fr. MF *estraindre*, fr. L *stringere* to bind or draw tight, press together] **1** : to draw taut **2** : to exert to the utmost **3** : to strive violently **4** : to injure by improper or excessive use **5** : to filter or remove by filtering **6** : to stretch beyond a proper limit — **strain·er** *n*

³strain *n* **1** : excessive tension or exertion (as of body or mind) **2** : bodily injury from excessive tension, effort, or use; *esp* : one in which muscles or ligaments are unduly stretched usu. from a wrench or twist **3** : deformation of a material body under the action of applied forces

¹strait \'strāt\ *adj* [ME, fr. OF *estreit*, fr. L *strictus* strait, strict] **1** *archaic* : NARROW **2** *archaic* : CONSTRICTED **3** *archaic* : STRICT **4** : DIFFICULT, STRAITENED

²strait *n* **1** : a narrow channel connecting two bodies of water **2** *pl* : DISTRESS

strait·en \'strāt-ᵊn\ *vb* **strait·ened; strait·en·ing** \'strāt-(ᵊ-)niŋ\ **1** : to hem in

: CONFINE **2** : to make distressing or difficult

strait·jack·et *or* **straight·jack·et** \'strāt-ˌjak-ət\ *n* : a cover or garment of strong material (as canvas) used to bind the body and esp. the arms closely in restraining a violent prisoner or patient — **straitjacket** *or* **straightjacket** *vb*

strait·laced *or* **straight·laced** \-'lāst\ *adj* : strict in observing moral or religious laws

¹strand \'strand\ *n* : SHORE; *esp* : a shore of a sea or ocean

²strand *vb* **1** : to run, drift, or drive upon the shore ⟨a ~ed ship⟩ **2** : to place or leave in a helpless position

³strand *n* **1** : one of the fibers twisted or plaited together into a cord, rope, or cable; *also* : a cord, rope, or cable made up of such fibers **2** : a twisted or plaited ropelike mass ⟨a ~ of pearls⟩ — **strand·ed** \'stran-dəd\ *adj*

strange \'strānj\ *adj* **strang·er; strang·est** [ME, fr. OF *estrange*, fr. L *extraneus*, lit., external, fr. *extra* outside] **1** : of external origin, kind, or character **2** : NEW, UNFAMILIAR **3** : SHY **4** : UNACCUSTOMED, INEXPERIENCED **syn** singular, peculiar, eccentric, erratic, odd, queer, quaint, curious — **strange·ly** *adv* — **strange·ness** *n*

strang·er \'strān-jər\ *n* **1** : FOREIGNER **2** : INTRUDER **3** : a person with whom one is unacquainted

stran·gle \'straŋ-gəl\ *vb* **stran·gled; stran·gling** \-g(ə-)liŋ\ **1** : to choke to death : THROTTLE **2** : STIFLE, SUFFOCATE — **stran·gler** \-g(ə-)lər\ *n*

stran·gu·late \'straŋ-gyə-ˌlāt\ *vb* **-lat·ed; -lat·ing 1** : STRANGLE, CONSTRICT **2** : to become so constricted as to stop circulation

stran·gu·la·tion \ˌstraŋ-gyə-'lā-shən\ *n* : the act or process of strangling or strangulating : the state of being strangled or strangulated

¹strap \'strap\ *n* : a narrow strip of flexible material used esp. for fastening, holding together, or wrapping

²strap *vb* **strapped; strap·ping 1** : to secure with a strap **2** : BIND, CONSTRICT **3** : to flog with a strap **4** : STROP

strap·less \-ləs\ *adj* : having no straps; *esp* : having no shoulder straps

¹**strap·ping** \'strap-iŋ\ *adj* : LARGE, STRONG, HUSKY

²**strap·ping** *n* : material for a strap

strat·a·gem \'strat-ə-jəm, -ˌjem\ *n* **1** : a trick in war to deceive or outwit the enemy; *also* : a deceptive scheme **2** : skill in deception

strat·e·gy \'strat-ə-jē\ *n, pl* **-gies** [Gk *stratēgia* generalship, fr. *stratēgos* general, fr. *stratos* army + *agein* to lead] **1** : the science and art of military command aimed at meeting the enemy under conditions advantageous to one's own force **2** : a careful plan or method esp. for achieving an end — **stra·te·gic** \strə-'tē-jik\ *adj* — **strat·e·gist** \'strat-ə-jəst\ *n*

strat·i·fy \'strat-ə-ˌfī\ *vb* **-fied; -fy·ing** : to form or arrange in layers — **strat·i·fi·ca·tion** \ˌstrat-ə-fə-'kā-shən\ *n*

stra·tig·ra·phy \strə-'tig-rə-fē\ *n* : geology that deals with rock strata — **strati·graph·ic** \ˌstrat-ə-'graf-ik\ *adj*

strato·sphere \'strat-ə-ˌsfiər\ *n* : the portion of the earth's atmosphere higher than 7 miles (11 kilometers) above the earth — **strato·spher·ic** \ˌstrat-ə-'sfi(ə)r-ik, -'sfer-\ *adj*

stra·tum \'strāt-əm, 'strat-\ *n, pl* **stra·ta** \'strāt-ə, 'strat-\ [NL, fr. L, spread, bed, fr. neut. of *stratus,* pp. of *sternere* to spread out] **1** : a bed, layer, or sheetlike mass (as of one kind of rock lying between layers of other kinds of rock) **2** : a level of culture; *also* : a group of people representing one stage in cultural development

¹**straw** \'strȯ\ *n* **1** : stalks of grain after threshing; *also* : a single coarse dry stem (as of a grass) **2** : a thing of small worth : TRIFLE **3** : a prepared tube for sucking up a beverage

²**straw** *adj* **1** : made of straw **2** : having no real force or validity ⟨a ∼ vote⟩

straw·ber·ry \'strȯ-ˌber-ē, -b(ə-)rē\ *n* : an edible juicy usu. red pulpy fruit borne by a low herb with white flowers and long slender runners; *also* : this plant

straw boss *n* : a foreman of a small gang of workers

straw·flow·er \'strȯ-ˌflau̇(-ə)r\ *n* : any of several plants whose flowers can be dried with little loss of form or color

¹**stray** \'strā\ *n* **1** : a domestic animal wandering at large or lost **2** : WAIF

²**stray** *vb* **1** : ROVE, ROAM **2** : to wander from a course : DEVIATE

³**stray** *adj* **1** : having strayed : separated from the group or the main body **2** : occurring at random ⟨∼ remarks⟩

¹**streak** \'strēk\ *n* **1** : a line or mark of a different color or texture from its background **2** : a narrow band of light; *also* : a lightning bolt **3** : a slight admixture : TRACE **4** : a brief run (as of luck); *also* : an unbroken series

²**streak** *vb* **1** : to form streaks in or on **2** : to move very swiftly

¹**stream** \'strēm\ *n* **1** : a body of water (as a river) flowing on the earth; *also* : any body of flowing fluid (as water or gas) **2** : a continuous procession ⟨the ∼ of history⟩

²**stream** *vb* **1** : to flow in or as if in a stream **2** : to pour out streams of liquid **3** : to trail out in length **4** : to move forward in a steady stream

stream·bed \'strēm-ˌbed\ *n* : the channel occupied or formerly occupied by a stream

stream·er \'strē-mər\ *n* **1** : a long narrow ribbonlike flag **2** : a long ribbon on a dress or hat **3** : a newspaper headline that runs across the entire sheet **4** *pl* : AURORA

stream·let \'strēm-lət\ *n* : a small stream

stream·lined \-ˌlīnd\ *adj* **1** : made with contours to reduce resistance to motion through water or air **2** : SIMPLIFIED **3** : MODERNIZED — **streamline** *vb*

street \'strēt\ *n* [ME *strete,* fr. OE *strǣt,* fr. LL *strata* paved road, fr. L, fem. of *stratus,* pp. of *sternere* to spread out] **1** : a thoroughfare esp. in a city, town, or village **2** : the occupants of the houses on a street

street·car \-ˌkär\ *n* : a passenger vehicle running on rails on city streets

street railway *n* : a company operating streetcars or buses

street·walk·er \'strēt-ˌwȯ-kər\ *n* : PROSTITUTE

strength \'streŋth\ *n* **1** : the quality of being strong : ability to do or endure : POWER **2** : TOUGHNESS, SOLIDITY **3** : power to resist attack **4** : INTENSITY **5** : force as measured in numbers ⟨the ∼ of an army⟩

strength•en \'streŋ-thən\ vb **strength-ened; strength•en•ing** \'streŋth-(ə-)niŋ\ : to make, grow, or become stronger — **strength•en•er** \'streŋth-(ə-)nər\ n

stren•u•ous \'stren-yə-wəs\ adj 1 : VIGOROUS, ENERGETIC 2 : requiring energetic effort or stamina — **stren•u•ous•ly** adv

strep throat \'strep-\ n : an inflammatory sore throat cause by streptococci and marked by fever, prostration, and toxemia

strep•to•coc•cus \,strep-tə-'käk-əs\ n, pl **-coc•ci** \-'käk-,(s)ī, -'käk-(,)(s)ē\ : any of various spherical bacteria that usu. grow in chains and include some causing serious diseases — **strep•to•coc•cal** \-əl\ adj

strep•to•my•cin \-'mīs-ᵊn\ n : an antibiotic produced by soil bacteria and used esp. in treating tuberculosis

¹**stress** \'stres\ n 1 : PRESSURE, STRAIN; esp : a force that tends to distort a body 2 : a factor that induces bodily or mental tension; also : a state induced by such a stress 3 : URGENCY, EMPHASIS 4 : relative prominence of sound 5 : ACCENT; also : any syllable carrying the accent

²**stress** vb 1 : to put pressure or strain on 2 : to put emphasis on : ACCENT

¹**stretch** \'strech\ vb 1 : to spread or reach out : EXTEND 2 : to draw out in length or breadth : EXPAND 3 : to make tense : STRAIN 4 : EXAGGERATE 5 : to become extended without breaking ⟨rubber ∼es easily⟩

²**stretch** n 1 : an act of extending or drawing out beyond ordinary or normal limits 2 : a continuous extent in length, area, or time 3 : the extent to which something may be stretched 4 : either of the straight sides of a racecourse

³**stretch** adj : easily stretched ⟨∼ pants⟩

stretch•er \'strech-ər\ n 1 : one that stretches 2 : a litter (as of canvas) esp. for carrying a disabled person

stretch•er–bear•er \-,bar-ər\ n : one who carries one end of a stretcher

strew \'strü\ vb **strewed; strewed** or **strewn** \'strün\; **strew•ing** 1 : to spread by scattering 2 : to cover by or as if by scattering something over or on 3 : DISSEMINATE

stria \'strī-ə\ n, pl **stri•ae** \'strī-,ē\ 1

: STRIATION 3 2 : a stripe or line (as in the skin)

stri•at•ed muscle \'strī-,āt-əd-\ n : muscle tissue made up of long thin cells with many nuclei and alternate light and dark stripes that usually connects to and moves the vertebrate skeleton and is mostly under voluntary control

stri•a•tion \strī-'ā-shən\ n 1 : the state of being marked with stripes or lines 2 : arrangement of striations or striae 3 : a minute groove, scratch, or channel esp. when one of a parallel series

strick•en \'strik-ən\ adj 1 : WOUNDED 2 : afflicted with disease, misfortune, or sorrow

strict \'strikt\ adj 1 : allowing no evasion or escape : RIGOROUS ⟨∼ discipline⟩ 2 : ACCURATE, PRECISE **syn** stringent, rigid, rigorous — **strict•ly** \'strik-(t)lē\ adv — **strict•ness** \'strik(t)-nəs\ n

stric•ture \'strik-chər\ n 1 : an abnormal narrowing of a bodily passage; also : the narrowed part 2 : hostile criticism : a critical remark

¹**stride** \'strīd\ vb **strode** \'strōd\; **stridden** \'strid-ᵊn\; **strid•ing** \'strīd-iŋ\ : to walk or run with long regular steps — **strid•er** n

²**stride** n 1 : a long step; also : the distance covered by such a step 2 : manner of striding : GAIT

stri•dent \'strīd-ᵊnt\ adj : harsh sounding : GRATING, SHRILL

strife \'strīf\ n : CONFLICT, FIGHT, STRUGGLE **syn** discord, contention, dissension

¹**strike** \'strīk\ vb **struck** \'strək\; **struck** also **strick•en** \'strik-ən\; **strik•ing** \'strī-kiŋ\ 1 : to take a course : GO ⟨∼ out for home⟩ 2 : to touch or hit sharply; also : to deliver a blow 3 : to produce by or as if by a blow ⟨struck terror in the foe⟩ 4 : to lower (as a flag or sail) 5 : to collide with; also : to injure or destroy by collision 6 : DELETE, CANCEL 7 : to produce by impressing ⟨struck a medal⟩; also : COIN ⟨∼ a new cent⟩ 8 : to cause to sound ⟨∼ a bell⟩ 9 : to afflict suddenly : lay low ⟨stricken with a high fever⟩ 10 : to appear to; also : to appear to as remarkable : IMPRESS 11 : to reach by reckoning ⟨∼ an average⟩ 12 : to stop work in order to obtain a change in conditions of em-

ployment **13** : to cause (a match) to ignite by rubbing **14** : to come upon ⟨~ a detour from the main road⟩ **15** : TAKE ON, ASSUME ⟨~ a pose⟩ — **strik·er** *n*

²**strike** *n* **1** : an act or instance of striking **2** : a sudden discovery of rich ore or oil deposits **3** : a pitched baseball recorded against a batter **4** : the knocking down of all the bowling pins with the 1st ball **5** : a military attack

strike·break·er \-ˌbrā-kər\ *n* : one hired to replace a striking worker

strike·out \-ˌau̇t\ *n* : an out in baseball as a result of a batter's being charged with three strikes

strike out \(ˈ)strīk-ˈau̇t\ *vb* **1** : to enter upon a course of action **2** : to start out vigorously **3** : to make an out in baseball by a strikeout

strike up *vb* **1** : to begin or cause to begin to sing or play **2** : BEGIN

strike zone *n* : the area over home plate through which a pitched baseball must pass to be called a strike

strik·ing \ˈstrī-kiŋ\ *adj* : attracting attention : very noticeable **syn** arresting, salient, conspicuous, outstanding, remarkable, prominent — **strik·ing·ly** *adv*

¹**string** \ˈstriŋ\ *n* **1** : a line usu. composed of twisted threads **2** : a series of things arranged as if strung on a cord **3** : a plant fiber (as a leaf vein) **4** *pl* : the stringed instruments of an orchestra **syn** succession, progression, sequence, chain, train

²**string** *vb* **strung** \ˈstrəŋ\; **string·ing** \ˈstriŋ-iŋ\ **1** : to provide with strings ⟨~ a racket⟩ **2** : to thread on or as if on a string ⟨~ pearls⟩ **3** : to take the strings out of ⟨~ beans⟩ **4** : to hang, tie, or fasten by a string **5** : to make taut **6** : to extend like a string

string bean *n* : a bean of one of the older varieties of kidney bean that have stringy fibers on the lines of separation of the pods; *also* : SNAP BEAN

stringed instrument *n* : a musical instrument (as a violin, guitar, or piano) sounded by plucking or striking or by drawing a bow across tense strings

strin·gen·cy \ˈstrin-jən-sē\ *n* **1** : STRICTNESS, SEVERITY **2** : SCARCITY ⟨~ of money⟩ — **strin·gent** \-jənt\ *adj*

string·er \ˈstriŋ-ər\ *n* **1** : a long horizon-

tal member in a framed structure or a bridge **2** : a news correspondent paid by the amount of copy

stringy \ˈstriŋ-ē\ *adj* **string·i·er; -est 1** : resembling string esp. in tough, fibrous, or disordered quality ⟨~ meat⟩ ⟨~ hair⟩ **2** : lean and sinewy in build

¹**strip** \ˈstrip\ *vb* **stripped** \ˈstript\ *also* **stript; strip·ping 1** : to take the covering or clothing from **2** : to take off one's clothes **3** : to pull or tear off **4** : to make bare or clear (as by cutting or grazing) **5** : PLUNDER, PILLAGE **syn** divest, denude, deprive, dismantle — **strip·per** *n*

²**strip** *n* **1** : a long narrow flat piece **2** : AIRSTRIP

¹**stripe** \ˈstrīp\ *vb* **striped** \ˈstrīpt\; **strip·ing** : to make stripes on

²**stripe** *n* **1** : a line or long narrow division having a different color from the background **2** : a strip of braid (as on a sleeve) indicating military rank or length of service **3** : TYPE, CHARACTER **syn** description, nature, kind, sort

striped bass \ˈstrīpt-, ˈstrī-pəd-\ *n* : a large marine food and sport fish of the Atlantic and Pacific coasts of the U.S.

strip·ling \ˈstrip-liŋ\ *n* : YOUTH, LAD

strip mine *n* : a mine that is worked from the earth's surface by the stripping of the topsoil — **strip–mine** *vb*

strip·tease \ˈstrip-ˌtēz\ *n* : a burlesque act in which a performer removes his or her clothing piece by piece — **strip·teas·er** *n*

strive \ˈstrīv\ *vb* **strove** \ˈstrōv\ *also* **strived** \ˈstrīvd\; **striv·en** \ˈstriv-ən\ *or* **strived; striv·ing** \ˈstrī-viŋ\ **1** : to struggle in opposition : CONTEND **2** : to make effort : labor hard **syn** endeavor, attempt, try, assay

strobe \ˈstrōb\ *n* **1** : STROBOSCOPE **2** : a device for high-speed intermittent illumination

stro·bo·scope \ˈstrō-bə-ˌskōp\ *n* : an instrument for studying rapid motion by means of a rapidly flashing light

strode past of STRIDE

¹**stroke** \ˈstrōk\ *vb* **stroked; strok·ing 1** : to rub gently **2** : to flatter in a manner designed to persuade

²**stroke** *n* **1** : the act of striking : BLOW, KNOCK **2** : a sudden action or process producing an impact ⟨~ of lightning⟩ **3** : sudden weakening or loss of con-

sciousness or the power to feel caused by rupture or obstruction of an artery of the brain **4** : a vigorous effort **5** : the sound of striking (as of a clock) **6** : one of a series of movements against air or water to get through or over it ⟨the ∼ of a bird's wing⟩ **7** : a single movement with or as if with a tool or implement (as a pen) **8** : a rower who sets the pace for a crew

stroll \\'strōl\ *vb* : to walk in a leisurely or idle manner **syn** saunter, amble, mosey — **stroll** *n* — **stroll•er** *n*

strong \\'stroŋ\ *adj* **stron•ger** \\'stroŋ-gər\\; **stron•gest** \\'stroŋ-gəst\ **1** : POWERFUL, VIGOROUS **2** : HEALTHY, ROBUST **3** : of a specified number ⟨an army 10 thousand ∼⟩ **4** : not mild or weak **5** : VIOLENT ⟨∼ wind⟩ **6** : ZEALOUS **7** : not easily broken **8** : FIRM, SOLID **syn** stout, sturdy, stalwart, tough — **strong•ly** *adv*

strong–arm \\'stroŋ-'ärm\ *adj* : having or using undue force ⟨∼ methods⟩

strong•hold \\'stroŋ-ˌhōld\ *n* : a fortified place : FORTRESS

strong•man \\'stroŋ-ˌman\ *n* : one who leads or controls by force of will and character or by military strength

stron•tium \\'strän-ch(ē-)əm, 'stränt-ē-əm\ *n* : a soft malleable metallic chemical element

¹**strop** \\'sträp\ *n* : STRAP; *esp* : one for sharpening a razor

²**strop** *vb* **stropped; strop•ping** : to sharpen a razor on a strop

stro•phe \\'strō-fē\ *n* [Gk *strophē,* lit., act of turning] : a division of a poem — **stroph•ic** \\'sträf-ik\ *adj*

strove past of STRIVE

struck past and past part of STRIKE

¹**struc•ture** \\'strək-chər\ *n* [ME, fr. L *structura,* fr. *structus,* pp. of *struere* to heap up, build] **1** : the manner of building : CONSTRUCTION **2** : something built (as a house or a dam); *also* : something made up of interdependent parts in a definite pattern of organization **3** : arrangement or relationship of elements in a substance, body, or system — **struc•tur•al** *adj*

²**structure** *vb* **struc•tured; struc•tur•ing** : to make into a structure

stru•del \\'s(h)trüd-ᵊl\ *n* [G] : a pastry made of a thin sheet of dough rolled up with filling and baked ⟨apple ∼⟩

¹**strug•gle** \\'strəg-əl\ *vb* **strug•gled; strug•gling** \-(ə-)liŋ\ **1** : to make strenuous efforts against opposition : STRIVE **2** : to proceed with difficulty or with great effort **syn** endeavor, attempt, try, assay

²**struggle** *n* **1** : CONTEST, STRIFE **2** : a violent effort or exertion

strum \\'strəm\ *vb* **strummed; strum•ming** : to play on a stringed instrument by brushing the strings with the fingers ⟨∼ a guitar⟩

strum•pet \\'strəm-pət\ *n* : PROSTITUTE

strung \\'strəŋ\ past and past part of STRING

¹**strut** \\'strət\ *vb* **strut•ted; strut•ting** : to walk with an affectedly proud gait **syn** swagger

²**strut** *n* **1** : a haughty or pompous gait **2** : a bar or rod for resisting lengthwise pressure

strych•nine \\'strik-ˌnīn, -nən, -ˌnēn\ *n* : a bitter poisonous alkaloid from some plants used as a poison (as for rats) and medicinally as a stimulant to the central nervous system

¹**stub** \\'stəb\ *n* **1** : STUMP 2 **2** : a short blunt end **3** : a small part of each leaf (as of a checkbook) kept as a memorandum of the items on the detached part

²**stub** *vb* **stubbed; stub•bing** : to strike (as one's toe) against something

stub•ble \\'stəb-əl\ *n* **1** : the cut stem ends of herbs and esp. grasses left in the soil after harvest **2** : a rough surface or growth resembling stubble — **stub•bly** \-(ə-)lē\ *adj*

stub•born \\'stəb-ərn\ *adj* **1** : FIRM, DETERMINED **2** : done or continued in a willful, unreasonable, or persistent manner **3** : not easily controlled or remedied ⟨a ∼ fever⟩ — **stub•born•ly** *adv* — **stub•born•ness** *n*

stub•by \\'stəb-ē\ *adj* : short, blunt, and thick like a stub

¹**stuc•co** \\'stək-ō\ *n, pl* **stuccos** *or* **stuccoes** [It] : plaster for coating exterior walls

²**stucco** *vb* : to coat with stucco

stuck past and past part of STICK

stuck–up \\'stək-'əp\ *adj* : CONCEITED

¹**stud** \\'stəd\ *n* : a male animal and esp. a horse (**stud•horse** \-ˌhȯrs\\) kept for breeding

²**stud** *n* **1** : one of the smaller uprights in a building to which the wall materials

are fastened **2** : a removable device like a button used as a fastener or ornament ⟨shirt ∼s⟩ **3** : a projecting nail, pin, or rod

³**stud** *vb* **stud·ded; stud·ding 1** : to supply with or adorn with studs **2** : DOT

⁴**stud** *abbr* student

stud·book \'stəd-ˌbůk\ *n* : an official record of the pedigree of purebred animals

stud·ding \'stəd-iŋ\ *n* **1** : the studs in a building or wall **2** : material for studs

stu·dent \'st(y)üd-ᵊnt\ *n* : SCHOLAR, PUPIL; *esp* : one who attends a school

stud·ied \'stəd-ēd\ *adj* : INTENTIONAL ⟨a ∼ insult⟩ **syn** deliberate, considered, premeditated, designed

stu·dio \'st(y)üd-ē-ˌō\ *n, pl* **-dios 1** : a place where an artist works; *also* : a place for the study of an art **2** : a place where motion pictures are made **3** : a place equipped for the transmission of radio or television programs

stu·di·ous \'st(y)üd-ē-əs\ *adj* : devoted to study — **stu·di·ous·ly** *adv*

¹**study** \'stəd-ē\ *n, pl* **stud·ies 1** : the use of the mind to gain knowledge **2** : the act or process of learning about something **3** : careful examination **4** : INTENT, PURPOSE **5** : a branch of learning **6** : a room esp. for reading and writing

²**study** *vb* **stud·ied; study·ing 1** : to engage in study or the study of **2** : to consider attentively or in detail **syn** consider, contemplate, weigh

¹**stuff** \'stəf\ *n* **1** : personal property **2** : raw material **3** : a finished textile fabric; *esp* : a worsted fabric **4** : writing, talk, or ideas of little or transitory worth **5** : an aggregate of matter; *also* : matter of a particular often unspecified kind **6** : fundamental material **7** : special knowledge or capability

²**stuff** *vb* **1** : to fill by packing something into : CRAM **2** : to eat greedily : GORGE **3** : to prepare (as meat) by filling with seasoned bread crumbs and spices **4** : to stop up : PLUG

stuffed shirt \'stəft-\ *n* : a smug, conceited, and usu. pompous and inflexibly conservative person

stuff·ing \'stəf-iŋ\ *n* : material used to fill tightly; *esp* : a mixture of bread crumbs and spices used to stuff meat and poultry

stuffy \'stəf-ē\ *adj* **stuff·i·er; -est 1** : lacking fresh air : CLOSE; *also* : blocked up ⟨a ∼ nose⟩ **2** : STODGY

stul·ti·fy \'stəl-tə-ˌfī\ *vb* **-fied; -fy·ing 1** : to cause to appear foolish or stupid **2** : to make untrustworthy; *also* : to make ineffective **3** : to have a dulling effect on — **stul·ti·fi·ca·tion** \ˌstəl-tə-fə-ˈkā-shən\ *n*

stum·ble \'stəm-bəl\ *vb* **stum·bled; stum·bling** \-b(ə-)liŋ\ **1** : to trip in walking or running **2** : to walk unsteadily; *also* : to speak or act in a blundering or clumsy manner **3** : to blunder morally; *also* : to come or happen by chance — **stumble** *n*

stumbling block *n* : an obstacle to belief, understanding, or progress

¹**stump** \'stəmp\ *n* **1** : the base of a bodily part (as a leg or tooth) left after the rest is removed **2** : the part of a plant and esp. a tree remaining with the root after the top is cut off **3** : a place or occasion for political public speaking — **stumpy** *adj*

²**stump** *vb* **1** : to clear (land) of stumps **2** : to tour (a region) making political speeches **3** : BAFFLE, PERPLEX **4** : to walk clumsily and heavily

stun \'stən\ *vb* **stunned; stun·ning 1** : to make senseless or dizzy by or as if by a blow **2** : BEWILDER, STUPEFY

stung past and past part of STING

stunk past and past part of STINK

stun·ning \'stən-iŋ\ *adj* : strikingly beautiful — **stun·ning·ly** *adv*

¹**stunt** \'stənt\ *vb* : to hinder the normal growth of : DWARF

²**stunt** *n* : an unusual or spectacular feat

stu·pe·fy \'st(y)ü-pə-ˌfī\ *vb* **-fied; -fy·ing 1** : ASTONISH **2** : to make stupid, groggy, or insensible — **stu·pe·fac·tion** \ˌst(y)ü-pə-ˈfak-shən\ *n*

stu·pen·dous \st(y)ü-ˈpen-dəs\ *adj* : causing astonishment esp. because of great size or height **syn** tremendous, prodigious, monumental, monstrous — **stu·pen·dous·ly** *adv*

stu·pid \'st(y)ü-pəd\ *adj* [MF *stupide,* fr. L *stupidus,* fr. *stupēre* to be benumbed, be astonished] **1** : very dull in mind **2** : showing or resulting from dullness of mind — **stu·pid·i·ty** \st(y)ü-ˈpid-ət-ē\ *n* — **stu·pid·ly** \'st(y)ü-pəd-lē\ *adv*

stu·por \'st(y)ü-pər\ *n* **1** : a condition of greatly dulled or completely suspended sense or feeling **2** : a torpid state often following stress or shock — **stu·por·ous** *adj*

stur·dy **'**stərd-ē\\ *adj* **stur·di·er; -est** [ME, reckless, brave, fr. OF *estourdi* stunned, fr. pp. of *estourdir* to stun] **1** : RESOLUTE, UNYIELDING **2** : STRONG, ROBUST **syn** stout, stalwart, tough, tenacious — **stur·di·ly** **'**stərd-ᵊl-ē\\ *adv* — **stur·di·ness** \\-ē-nəs\\ *n*

stur·geon **'**stər-jən\\ *n* : any of various large food fishes whose roe is made into caviar

stut·ter **'**stət-ər\\ *vb* : to speak with involuntary disruption or blocking of sounds — **stutter** *n*

STV *abbr* subscription television

¹sty **'**stī\\ *n, pl* **sties** : a pen or housing for swine

²sty *or* **stye** **'**stī\\ *n, pl* **sties** *or* **styes** : an inflamed swelling of a skin gland on the edge of an eyelid

¹style **'**stīl\\ *n* **1** : a slender pointed instrument or process; *esp* : STYLUS **2** : a way of speaking or writing; *esp* : one characteristic of an individual, period, school, or nation ⟨ornate ∼⟩ **3** : the custom followed in spelling, capitalization, punctuation, and typography **4** : mode of address : TITLE **5** : manner or method of acting, making, or performing; *also* : a distinctive or characteristic manner **6** : a fashionable manner or mode **7** : overall excellence, skill, or grace in performance, manner, or appearance — **sty·lis·tic** \\stī-**'**lis-tik\\ *adj*

²style *vb* **styled; styl·ing 1** : NAME, DESIGNATE **2** : to make or design in accord with a prevailing mode

styl·ing **'**stī-liŋ\\ *n* : the way in which something is styled

styl·ish **'**stī-lish\\ *adj* : conforming to an accepted standard of style : FASHIONABLE **syn** modish, smart, chic — **styl·ish·ly** *adv* — **styl·ish·ness** *n*

styl·ist **'**stī-ləst\\ *n* **1** : a master of style esp. in writing **2** : a developer or designer of styles

styl·ize **'**stīl-ˌīz\\ *vb* **styl·ized; styl·iz·ing** : to conform to a style; *esp* : to represent or design according to a pattern or style rather than according to nature

sty·lus **'**stī-ləs\\ *n, pl* **sty·li** **'**stī(ə)l-ˌī\\ *also* **sty·lus·es** **'**stī-lə-səz\\ [modif. of L

stilus stake, stylus] **1** : a pointed implement used by the ancients for writing on wax **2** : a phonograph needle

sty·mie **'**stī-mē\\ *vb* **sty·mied; sty·mie·ing** : BLOCK, FRUSTRATE

styp·tic **'**stip-tik\\ *adj* : tending to check bleeding — **styptic** *n*

suave **'**swäv\\ *adj* [MF, pleasant, sweet, fr. L *suavis*] : persuasively pleasing : smoothly agreeable **syn** urbane, smooth, bland — **suave·ly** *adv* — **sua·vi·ty** **'**swäv-ət-ē\\ *n*

¹sub **'**səb\\ *n* : SUBSTITUTE — **sub** *vb*

²sub *n* : SUBMARINE

³sub *abbr* **1** subtract **2** suburb

sub- \\ˌsəb, **'**səb\\ *prefix* **1** : under : beneath **2** : subordinate : secondary **3** : subordinate portion of : subdivision of **4** : with repetition of a process described in a simple verb so as to form, stress, or deal with subordinate parts or relations **5** : somewhat **6** : falling nearly in the category of : bordering on

subacute	subminimal
subagency	subminimum
subagent	suboptimal
subaqueous	suborder
subarctic	subparagraph
subarea	subparallel
subatmospheric	subphylum
subaverage	subplot
subbasement	subpolar
subcategory	subprincipal
subclass	subproblem
subclassify	subprofessional
subclinical	subprogram
subcontract	subregion
subcontractor	subroutine
subculture	subsaturated
subdeacon	subsection
subdean	subsense
subdiscipline	subspecies
subentry	substage
subfamily	subsystem
subfreezing	subteen
subgenus	subtemperate
subgroup	subthreshold
subhead	subtopic
subheading	subtotal
subhuman	subtreasury
subindex	subtype
subinterval	subunit
subkingdom	subvariety
sublease	subvisible
sublethal	subvocal
subliterate	subzero

sub·al·pine \\ˌsəb-**'**al-ˌpīn, **'**səb-\\ *adj* **1**

: of or relating to the region about the foot and lower slopes of the Alps **2** *cap* : of, relating to, or growing on high upland slopes

sub·al·tern \sə-'bȯl-tərn\ *n* : SUBORDINATE; *also* : a commissioned officer in the British army below the rank of captain

sub·as·sem·bly \ˌsəb-ə-'sem-blē\ *n* : an assembled unit to be incorporated with other units in a finished product

sub·atom·ic \ˌsəb-ə-'täm-ik\ *adj* : of or relating to the inside of the atom or to particles smaller than atoms

sub·com·mit·tee \'səb-kə-ˌmit-ē, ˌsəb-kə-'mit-ē\ *n* : a subordinate division of a committee

sub·com·pact \'səb-'käm-ˌpakt\ *n* : an automobile smaller than a compact

¹sub·con·scious \ˌsəb-'kän-chəs, 'səb-\ *adj* : existing in the mind and affecting thought and behavior without entering conscious awareness — **sub·con·scious·ly** *adv* — **sub·con·scious·ness** *n*

²subconscious *n* : mental activities just below the threshold of consciousness

sub·con·ti·nent \'səb-'känt-(ə-)nənt\ *n* : a vast subdivision of a continent — **sub·con·ti·nen·tal** \ˌsəb-ˌkänt-ᵊn-'ent-ᵊl\ *adj*

sub·cu·ta·ne·ous \ˌsəb-kyu̇-'tā-nē-əs\ *adj* : located, made, or used under the skin ⟨~ fat⟩ ⟨~ needle⟩

sub·di·vide \ˌsəb-də-'vīd, 'səb-də-ˌvīd\ *vb* : to divide into several parts; *esp* : to divide (a tract of land) into building lots — **sub·di·vi·sion** \-'vizh-ən, -ˌvizh-\ *n*

sub·duc·tion \səb-'dək-shən\ *n* : the descent of the edge of one crustal plate beneath the edge of an adjacent plate

sub·due \səb-'d(y)ü\ *vb* **sub·dued; sub·du·ing 1** : to bring into subjection : VANQUISH **2** : to bring under control : CURB **3** : to reduce the intensity of

subj *abbr* **1** subject **2** subjunctive

¹sub·ject \'səb-jikt\ *n* [ME, fr. MF, fr. L *subjectus* one under authority & *subjectum* subject of a proposition, fr. *subicere* to subject, lit., to throw under, fr. *sub-* under + *jacere* to throw] **1** : a person under the authority of another **2** : a person subject to a sovereign **3** : an individual subjected to an operation or process **4** : the person or thing discussed or treated : TOPIC,

THEME **5** : a word or word group denoting that of which something is predicated

²subject *adj* **1** : being under the power or rule of another **2** : LIABLE, EXPOSED ⟨~ to floods⟩ **3** : dependent on some act or condition ⟨appointment ~ to senate approval⟩ **syn** subordinate, secondary, tributary, collateral, dependent

³sub·ject \səb-'jekt\ *vb* **1** : to bring under control : CONQUER **2** : to make liable **3** : to cause to undergo or submit to — **sub·jec·tion** \-'jek-shən\ *n*

sub·jec·tive \(ˌ)səb-'jek-tiv\ *adj* **1** : of, relating to, or constituting a subject **2** : of, relating to, or arising within one's self or mind in contrast to what is outside : PERSONAL — **sub·jec·tive·ly** *adv* — **sub·jec·tiv·i·ty** \-ˌjek-'tiv-ət-ē\ *n*

subject matter *n* : matter presented for consideration, discussion, or study

sub·join \(ˌ)səb-'jȯin\ *vb* : APPEND

sub ju·di·ce \(')su̇b-'yüd-i-ˌkā, 'səb-'jüd-ə-(ˌ)sē\ *adv* [L] : before a judge or court : not yet legally decided

sub·ju·gate \'səb-ji-ˌgāt\ *vb* **-gat·ed; -gat·ing** : CONQUER, SUBDUE; *also* : ENSLAVE **syn** reduce, overcome, overthrow, vanquish, defeat, beat — **sub·ju·ga·tion** \ˌsəb-ji-'gā-shən\ *n*

sub·junc·tive \səb-'jəŋk-tiv\ *adj* : of, relating to, or constituting a verb form that represents an act or state as contingent or possible or viewed emotionally (as with desire) ⟨~ mood⟩ — **subjunctive** *n*

sub·let \'səb-'let\ *vb* **-let; -let·ting** : to let all or a part of (a leased property) to another; *also* : to rent (a property) from a lessee

sub·li·mate \'səb-lə-ˌmāt\ *vb* **-mat·ed; -mat·ing 1** : SUBLIME **2** : to direct the expression of (as an instinctual desire or impulse) from a primitive to a more socially and culturally acceptable form — **sub·li·ma·tion** \ˌsəb-lə-'mā-shən\ *n*

¹sub·lime \sə-'blīm\ *vb* **sub·limed; sub·lim·ing** : to pass or cause to pass directly from the solid to the vapor state

²sublime *adj* **1** : EXALTED, NOBLE **2** : having awe-inspiring beauty or grandeur **syn** glorious, splendid, superb, resplendent, gorgeous — **sub·lim·i·ty** \-'blim-ət-ē\ *n*

sub·lim·i·nal \(ˌ)səb-ˈlim-ən-ᵊl, ˈsəb-\ *adj* **1** : inadequate to produce a sensation or a perception ⟨∼ stimuli⟩ **2** : existing or functioning below the threshold of conscious awareness ⟨the ∼ mind⟩ ⟨∼ techniques in advertising⟩

sub·ma·chine gun \ˌsəb-mə-ˈshēn-ˌgən\ *n* : an automatic firearm fired from the shoulder or hip

¹sub·ma·rine \ˈsəb-mə-ˌrēn, ˌsəb-mə-ˈrēn\ *adj* : UNDERWATER; *esp* : UNDERSEA

²submarine *n* **1** : a naval vessel designed to operate underwater **2** : a large sandwich made from a long split roll with any of a variety of fillings

sub·merge \səb-ˈmərj\ *vb* **sub·merged; sub·merg·ing 1** : to put or plunge under the surface of water **2** : INUNDATE **syn** immerse, duck, dip, dunk — **sub·mer·gence** \-ˈmər-jəns\ *n*

sub·merse \səb-ˈmərs\ *vb* **sub·mersed; sub·mers·ing** : SUBMERGE — **sub·mer·sion** \-ˈmər-zhən\ *n*

¹sub·mers·ible \səb-ˈmər-sə-bəl\ *adj* : capable of being submerged

²submersible *n* : something that is submersible; *esp* : SUBMARINE 1

sub·mi·cro·scop·ic \ˌsəb-ˌmī-krə-ˈskäp-ik\ *adj* : too small to be seen in an ordinary microscope

sub·min·ia·ture \ˌsəb-ˈmin-ē-ə-ˌchùr, ˈsəb-, -ˈmin-i-ˌchùr, -chər\ *adj* : very small

sub·mit \səb-ˈmit\ *vb* **sub·mit·ted; sub·mit·ting 1** : to commit to the discretion or decision of another or of others **2** : YIELD, SURRENDER **3** : to put forward as an opinion — **sub·mis·sion** \-ˈmish-ən\ *n* — **sub·mis·sive** \-ˈmis-iv\ *adj*

sub·nor·mal \ˌsəb-ˈnòr-məl\ *adj* : falling below what is normal — **sub·nor·mal·i·ty** \ˌsəb-nòr-ˈmal-ət-ē\ *n*

sub·or·bit·al \ˌsəb-ˈòr-bət-ᵊl, ˈsəb-\ *adj* : being or involving less than one orbit

¹sub·or·di·nate \sə-ˈbòrd-(ᵊ-)nət\ *adj* **1** : of lower class or rank **2** : INFERIOR **3** : submissive to authority **4** : subordinated to other elements in a sentence : DEPENDENT ⟨∼ clause⟩ **syn** secondary, subject, tributary, collateral

²subordinate *n* : one that is subordinate

³sub·or·di·nate \sə-ˈbòrd-ᵊn-ˌāt\ *vb* **-nat·ed; -nat·ing 1** : to place in a lower rank

or class **2** : SUBDUE — **sub·or·di·na·tion** \-ˌbòrd-ᵊn-ˈā-shən\ *n*

sub·orn \sə-ˈbòrn\ *vb* **1** : to induce secretly to do an unlawful thing **2** : to induce to commit perjury — **sub·or·na·tion** \ˌsəb-ˌòr-ˈnā-shən\ *n*

¹sub·poe·na \sə-ˈpē-nə\ *n* [ME *suppena,* fr. L *sub poena* under penalty] : a writ commanding the person named in it to attend court under penalty for failure to do so

²subpoena *vb* **-naed; -na·ing** : to summon with a subpoena

sub·scribe \səb-ˈskrīb\ *vb* **sub·scribed; sub·scrib·ing 1** : to sign one's name to a document **2** : to give consent by or as if by signing one's name **3** : to promise to contribute by signing one's name with the amount promised **4** : to place an order by signing **5** : FAVOR, APPROVE **syn** agree, acquiesce, assent, accede — **sub·scrib·er** *n*

sub·script \ˈsəb-ˌskript\ *n* : a symbol (as a letter or number) immediately below or below and to the right or left of another written character — **subscript** *adj*

sub·scrip·tion \səb-ˈskrip-shən\ *n* **1** : the act of subscribing : SIGNATURE **2** : a purchase by signed order

sub·se·quent \ˈsəb-si-kwənt, -sə-ˌkwent\ *adj* : following after : SUCCEEDING — **sub·se·quent·ly** \-ˌkwent-lē, -kwənt-\ *adv*

sub·ser·vi·ence \səb-ˈsər-vē-əns\ *n* **1** : a subordinate place or condition; *also* : willingness to serve in a subordinate capacity **2** : SERVILITY — **sub·ser·vi·en·cy** \-ən-sē\ *n* — **sub·er·vi·ent** \-ənt\ *adj*

sub·set \ˈsəb-ˌset\ *n* : a set each of whose elements is an element of an inclusive set

sub·side \səb-ˈsīd\ *vb* **sub·sid·ed; sub·sid·ing** [L *subsidere,* fr. *sub-* under + *sidere* to sit down, sink] **1** : to settle to the bottom of a liquid **2** : to tend downward : DESCEND **3** : SINK, SUBMERGE **4** : to become quiet and tranquil **syn** abate, wane, moderate, slacken — **sub·sid·ence** \səb-ˈsīd-ᵊns, ˈsəb-səd-əns\ *n*

¹sub·sid·iary \səb-ˈsid-ē-ˌer-ē\ *adj* **1** : furnishing aid or support; *also* : owned or controlled by some main company **2** : of or relating to a subsidy **syn** auxiliary, contributory, subservient, accessory

²subsidiary *n, pl* **-iar·ies** : one that is subsidiary; *esp* : a company controlled by another

sub·si·dize \'səb-sə-ˌdīz\ *vb* **-dized; -dizing** : to aid or furnish with a subsidy

sub·si·dy \'səb-səd-ē\ *n, pl* **-dies** [ME, fr. L *subsidium* reserve troops, support, assistance, fr. *sub-* near + *sedēre* to sit] : a gift of public money to a private person or company or to another government **syn** grant, appropriation, subvention

sub·sist \səb-'sist\ *vb* **1** : EXIST, PERSIST **2** : to receive the means (as food and clothing) of maintaining life

sub·sis·tence \səb-'sis-təns\ *n* **1** : EXISTENCE **2** : means of subsisting : the minimum (as of food and clothing) necessary to support life

sub·soil \'səb-ˌsȯil\ *n* : a layer of weathered material just under the surface soil

sub·son·ic \ˌsəb-'sän-ik, 'səb-\ *adj* **1** : being or relating to a speed less than that of sound; *also* : moving at such a speed **2** : INFRASONIC

sub·stance \'səb-stəns\ *n* **1** : essential nature : ESSENCE ⟨divine ∼⟩; *also* : the fundamental or essential part or quality ⟨the ∼ of his speech⟩ **2** : physical material from which something is made or which has discrete existence; *also* : matter of particular or definite chemical constitution **3** : material possessions : PROPERTY, WEALTH

sub·stan·dard \ˌsəb-'stan-dərd, 'səb-\ *adj* : falling short of a standard or norm

sub·stan·tial \səb-'stan-chəl\ *adj* **1** : existing as or in substance : MATERIAL; *also* : not illusory : REAL **2** : IMPORTANT, ESSENTIAL **3** : NOURISHING, SATISFYING ⟨∼ meal⟩ **4** : having means : WELL-TO-DO **5** : CONSIDERABLE ⟨∼ profit⟩ **6** : STRONG, FIRM — **sub·stan·tial·ly** \-ē\ *adv*

sub·stan·ti·ate \səb-'stan-chē-ˌāt\ *vb* **-at·ed; -at·ing** **1** : to give substance or body to **2** : VERIFY, PROVE — **sub·stan·ti·a·tion** \-ˌstan-chē-'ā-shən\ *n*

sub·stan·tive \'səb-stən-tiv\ *n* : NOUN; *also* : a word or phrase used as a noun

sub·sta·tion \'səb-ˌstā-shən\ *n* : a station (as a post-office branch) subordinate to another station

¹sub·sti·tute \'səb-stə-ˌt(y)üt\ *n* : a person or thing replacing another — **substitute** *adj*

²substitute *vb* **-tut·ed; -tut·ing** **1** : to put or use in the place of another **2** : to serve as a substitute — **sub·sti·tu·tion** \ˌsəb-stə-'t(y)ü-shən\ *n*

sub·stra·tum \'səb-ˌstrāt-əm, -ˌstrat-\ *n, pl* **-stra·ta** \-ə\ : the layer or structure lying underneath

sub·struc·ture \'səb-ˌstrək-chər\ *n* : FOUNDATION, GROUNDWORK

sub·sur·face \'səb-ˌsər-fəs\ *n* : earth material near the surface of the ground — **subsurface** *adj*

sub·ter·fuge \'səb-tər-ˌfyüj\ *n* : a trick or device used in order to conceal, escape, or evade **syn** fraud, deception, trickery

sub·ter·ra·nean \ˌsəb-tə-'rā-nē-ən\ *adj* **1** : lying or being underground **2** : SECRET, HIDDEN

sub·tile \'sət-ᵊl\ *adj* **sub·til·er** \'sət-lər, -ᵊl-ər\; **sub·til·est** \'sət-ləst, -ᵊl-əst\ : SUBTLE

sub·ti·tle \'səb-ˌtīt-ᵊl\ *n* **1** : a secondary or explanatory title (as of a book) **2** : printed matter projected on a motion-picture screen during or between the scenes

sub·tle \'sət-ᵊl\ *adj* **sub·tler** \'sət-(ᵊ-)lər\; **sub·tlest** \'sət-(ᵊ-)ləst\ **1** : hardly noticeable : DELICATE, REFINED **2** : SHREWD, KEEN **3** : CLEVER, SLY — **sub·tle·ty** \-tē\ *n* — **sub·tly** \'sət-(ᵊ-)lē\ *adv*

sub·tract \səb-'trakt\ *vb* : to take away (as one number from another); *also* : to perform the operation of deducting one number from another — **sub·trac·tion** \-'trak-shən\ *n*

sub·tra·hend \'səb-trə-ˌhend\ *n* : a number that is to be subtracted from another

sub·trop·i·cal \ˌsəb-'träp-i-kəl, 'səb-\ *also* **sub·trop·ic** \-ik\ *adj* : of, relating to, or being regions bordering on the tropical zone

sub·urb \'səb-ˌərb\ *n* **1** : an outlying part of a city; *also* : a small community adjacent to a city **2** *pl* : a residential area adjacent to a city — **sub·ur·ban** \sə-'bər-bən\ *adj or n*

sub·ur·ban·ite \sə-'bər-bə-ˌnīt\ *n* : one living in a suburb

sub·ur·bia \sə-'bər-bē-ə\ *n* **1** : SUBURBS **2** : suburban people or customs

sub·ven·tion \səb-'ven-chən\ *n* : SUBSIDY, ENDOWMENT

sub·vert \səb-'vərt\ *vb* **1** : OVERTHROW, RUIN **2** : CORRUPT **syn** sabotage, undermine — **sub·ver·sion** \-'vər-zhən\ *n* — **sub·ver·sive** \-'vər-siv\ *adj*

sub·way \'səb-ˌwā\ *n* : an underground way; *esp* : an underground electric railway

suc·ceed \sək-'sēd\ *vb* **1** : to follow next in order or next after another; *esp* : to inherit sovereignty, rank, title, or property **2** : to attain a desired object or end : be successful

suc·cess \sək-'ses\ *n* **1** : satisfactory completion of something **2** : the gaining of wealth and fame **3** : one that succeeds — **suc·cess·ful** \-fəl\ *adj* — **suc·cess·ful·ly** \-ē\ *adv*

suc·ces·sion \sək-'sesh-ən\ *n* **1** : the order, act, or right of succeeding to a property, title, or throne **2** : the act or process of following in order **3** : a series of persons or things that follow one after another **syn** progression, sequence, chain, train, string

suc·ces·sive \sək-'ses-iv\ *adj* : following in order : CONSECUTIVE — **suc·ces·sive·ly** *adv*

suc·ces·sor \sək-'ses-ər\ *n* : one that succeeds (as to a throne, title, estate, or office)

suc·cinct \(ˌ)sək-'siŋkt, sə-'siŋkt\ *adj* : BRIEF, CONCISE **syn** terse, laconic, summary, curt, short — **suc·cinct·ly** *adv* — **suc·cinct·ness** *n*

suc·cor \'sək-ər\ *n* [ME *succur*, fr. earlier *sucurs*, taken as pl., fr. OF *sucors*, fr. ML *succursus*, fr. L *succursus*, pp. of *succurrere* to run up, run to help] : AID, HELP, RELIEF — **succor** *vb*

suc·co·tash \'sək-ə-ˌtash\ *n* [from an American Indian language] : beans and kernels of sweet corn cooked together

¹suc·cu·lent \'sək-yə-lənt\ *adj* : full of juice : JUICY; *also* : having fleshy tissues that conserve moisture — **suc·cu·lence** \-ləns\ *n*

²succulent *n* : a succulent plant (as a cactus)

suc·cumb \sə-'kəm\ *vb* **1** : to give up **2** : DIE **syn** submit, capitulate, relent, defer

¹such \(ˈ)səch, (ˌ)sich\ *adj* **1** : of this or that kind **2** : having a quality just specified or to be specified

²such *pron* **1** : such a one or ones ⟨he's the boss, and had the right to act as ~⟩ **2** : that or those similar or related thereto ⟨boards and nails and ~⟩

³such *adv* : to that degree : so

such·like \'səch-ˌlīk\ *adj* : SIMILAR

¹suck \'sək\ *vb* **1** : to draw in liquid and esp. mother's milk with the mouth **2** : to draw liquid from by action of the mouth ⟨~ an orange⟩ **3** : to take in or up or remove by or as if by suction

²suck *n* : the act of sucking : SUCTION

suck·er \'sək-ər\ *n* **1** : one that sucks **2** : a part of an animal's body used for sucking or for clinging **3** : a fish with thick soft lips for sucking in food **4** : a shoot from the roots or lower part of a plant **5** : a person easily deceived

suck·le \'sək-əl\ *vb* **suck·led**; **suck·ling** \-(ə-)liŋ\ : to give or draw milk from the breast or udder; *also* : NURTURE, REAR

suck·ling \'sək-liŋ\ *n* : a young unweaned mammal

su·cre \'sü-(ˌ)krā\ *n* — see MONEY table

su·crose \'sü-ˌkrōs, -ˌkrōz\ *n* : a sweet sugar obtained esp. from sugarcane or sugar beets

suc·tion \'sək-shən\ *n* **1** : the act of sucking **2** : the act or process of drawing something (as liquid or dust) into a space (as in a vacuum cleaner or a pump) by partially exhausting the air in the space — **suc·tion·al** \-sh(ə-)nəl\ *adj*

sud·den \'səd-ən\ *adj* [ME *sodain*, fr. MF, fr. L *subitaneus*, fr. *subitus* sudden, fr. pp. of *subire* to come up] **1** : happening or coming quickly or unexpectedly ⟨~ shower⟩; *also* : changing angle or character all at once ⟨~ turn in the road⟩ ⟨~ descent to the sea⟩ **2** : HASTY, RASH ⟨~ decision⟩ **3** : made or brought about in a short time : PROMPT ⟨~ cure⟩ **syn** precipitate, headlong, impetuous, hasty — **sud·den·ly** *adv* — **sud·den·ness** *n*

sudden infant death syndrome *n* : death due to unknown causes of an infant in apparently good health that occurs usu. before one year of age

suds \'sədz\ *n pl* : soapy water esp. when frothy — **sudsy** \'səd-zē\ *adj*

sue \'sü\ *vb* **sued; su·ing 1** : PETITION, SOLICIT **2** : to seek justice or right by bringing legal action **syn** appeal

suede *or* **suède** \'swād\ *n* [F *gants de Suède* Swedish gloves] **1** : leather with a napped surface **2** : a fabric with a suedelike nap

su·et \'sü-ət\ *n* : the hard fat from beef and mutton that yields tallow

suff *abbr* **1** sufficient **2** suffix

suf·fer \'səf-ər\ *vb* **suf·fered; suf·fer·ing** \-(ə-)riŋ\ **1** : to feel or endure pain **2** : EXPERIENCE, UNDERGO **3** : to bear loss, damage, or injury **4** : ALLOW, PERMIT **syn** endure, abide, tolerate, stand, brook, stomach — **suf·fer·er** *n*

suf·fer·ance \'səf-(ə-)rəns\ *n* **1** : consent or approval implied by lack of interference or resistance **2** : ENDURANCE, PATIENCE

suf·fer·ing \-(ə-)riŋ\ *n* : PAIN, MISERY, HARDSHIP

suf·fice \sə-'fīs\ *vb* **suf·ficed; suf·fic·ing 1** : to satisfy a need : be sufficient **2** : to be capable or competent

suf·fi·cien·cy \sə-'fish-ən-sē\ *n* **1** : a sufficient quantity to meet one's needs **2** : ADEQUACY

suf·fi·cient \sə-'fish-ənt\ *adj* : adequate to accomplish a purpose or meet a need — **suf·fi·cient·ly** *adv*

¹**suf·fix** \'səf-ˌiks\ *n* : an affix occurring at the end of a word

²**suf·fix** \'səf-iks, (ˌ)sə-'fiks\ *vb* : to attach as a suffix — **suf·fix·ation** \ˌsəf-ˌik-'sā-shən\ *n*

suf·fo·cate \'səf-ə-ˌkāt\ *vb* **-cat·ed; -cat·ing** : STIFLE, SMOTHER, CHOKE — **suf·fo·cat·ing·ly** *adv* — **suf·fo·ca·tion** \ˌsəf-ə-'kā-shən\ *n*

suf·fra·gan \'səf-ri-gən\ *n* : an assistant bishop; *esp* : one not having the right of succession — **suffragan** *adj*

suf·frage \'səf-rij\ *n* [L *suffragium*] **1** : VOTE **2** : the right to vote : FRANCHISE

suf·frag·ette \ˌsəf-ri-'jet\ *n* : a woman who advocates suffrage for her sex

suf·frag·ist \'səf-ri-jəst\ *n* : one who advocates extension of the suffrage esp. to women

suf·fuse \sə-'fyüz\ *vb* **suf·fused; suf·fus·ing** : to spread over or through in the manner of a fluid or light **syn** infuse, imbue, ingrain, steep — **suf·fu·sion** \-'fyü-zhən\ *n*

¹**sug·ar** \'shug-ər\ *n* **1** : a sweet substance that is colorless or white when pure and is chiefly derived from sugarcane or sugar beets **2** : a water-soluble compound (as glucose) similar to sucrose — **sug·ary** *adj*

²**sugar** *vb* **sug·ared; sug·ar·ing** \'shug-(ə-)riŋ\ **1** : to mix, cover, or sprinkle with sugar **2** : SWEETEN ⟨~ advice with flattery⟩ **3** : to form sugar ⟨a syrup that ~s⟩ **4** : GRANULATE

sugar beet *n* : a large beet with a white root from which sugar is made

sug·ar·cane \'shug-ər-ˌkān\ *n* : a tall grass widely grown in warm regions for the sugar in its stalks

sugar daddy *n* **1** : a well-to-do usu. older man who supports or spends lavishly on a mistress or girlfriend **2** : a generous benefactor of a cause

sugar maple *n* : a maple with a sweet sap; *esp* : one of eastern No. America with sap that is the chief source of maple syrup and maple sugar

sugar pea *n* : SNOW PEA

sug·ar·plum \'shug-ər-ˌpləm\ *n* : a small ball of candy

sug·gest \sə(g)-'jest\ *vb* **1** : to put (as a thought, plan, or desire) into a person's mind **2** : to remind or evoke by association of ideas **syn** imply, hint, intimate, insinuate, connote

sug·gest·ible \sə(g)-'jes-tə-bəl\ *adj* : easily influenced by suggestion

sug·ges·tion \-'jes-chən\ *n* **1** : an act or instance of suggesting; *also* : something suggested **2** : a slight indication

sug·ges·tive \-'jes-tiv\ *adj* : tending to suggest something; *esp* : suggesting something improper or indecent — **sug·ges·tive·ly** *adv* — **sug·ges·tive·ness** *n*

sui·cide \'sü-ə-ˌsīd\ *n* **1** : the act of killing oneself purposely **2** : one that commits or attempts suicide — **sui·cid·al** \ˌsü-ə-'sīd-ᵊl\ *adj*

sui ge·ner·is \ˌsü-ˌī-'jen-ə-rəs; ˌsü-ē-'jen-\ *adj* [L, of its own kind] : being in a class by itself : UNIQUE

¹**suit** \'süt\ *n* **1** : an action in court to recover a right or claim **2** : an act of suing or entreating; *esp* : COURTSHIP **3** : a number of things used together ⟨~ of clothes⟩ **4** : one of the four sets of playing cards in a pack **syn** prayer, plea, petition, appeal

²**suit** *vb* **1** : to be appropriate or fitting **2**

: to be becoming to **3** : to meet the needs or desires of : PLEASE

suit•able \'süt-ə-bəl\ *adj* : FITTING, PROPER, APPROPRIATE **syn** fit, meet, apt, happy — **suit•abil•i•ty** \ˌsüt-ə-'bil-ət-ē\ *n* — **suit•able•ness** \'süt-ə-bəl-nəs\ *n* — **suit•ably** \-ə-blē\ *adv*

suit•case \'süt-ˌkās\ *n* : a flat rectangular traveling bag

suite \'swēt, *for 4 also* 'süt\ *n* **1** : a personal staff attending a dignitary or ruler : RETINUE **2** : a group of rooms occupied as a unit : APARTMENT **3** : a modern instrumental composition free in its character and number of movements; *also* : a long orchestral concert arrangement in suite form of material drawn from a longer work **4** : a set of matched furniture for a room

suit•ing \'süt-iŋ\ *n* : fabric for suits of clothes

suit•or \'süt-ər\ *n* **1** : one who sues or petitions **2** : one who seeks to marry a woman

su•ki•ya•ki \skē-'(y)äk-ē; ˌsük-ē-'(y)äk-ē, ˌsük-\ *n* : thin slices of meat, bean curd, and vegetables cooked in soy sauce, sake, and sugar

sul•fa \'səl-fə\ *adj* **1** : related chemically to sulfanilamide **2** : of, relating to, or using sulfa drugs ⟨∼ therapy⟩

sulfa drug *n* : any of various synthetic organic bacteria-inhibiting drugs that are closely related chemically to sulfanilamide

sul•fa•nil•amide \ˌsəl-fə-'nil-ə-ˌmīd\ *n* : a sulfur-containing organic compound that is the parent compound of most sulfa drugs

sul•fate \'səl-ˌfāt\ *n* : a salt or ester of sulfuric acid

sul•fide \'səl-'fīd\ *n* : a compound of sulfur

sul•fur *or* **sul•phur** \'səl-fər\ *n* : a nonmetallic element that occurs in nature combined or free in vulcanizing rubber and in medicine

sulfur dioxide *n* : a heavy pungent toxic gas that is used esp. in bleaching, as a preservative, and as a refrigerant, and is a major air pollutant

sul•fu•ric \ˌsəl-'fyùr-ik\ *adj* : of, relating to, or containing sulfur

sulfuric acid *n* : a heavy corrosive oily strong acid

sul•fu•rous \'səl-f(y)ə-rəs, *also esp for 1* ˌsəl-'fyùr-əs\ *adj* **1** : of, relating to, or containing sulfur **2** *or* **sul•phu•rous** : of or relating to brimstone or the fire of hell : INFERNAL **3** *or* **sulphurous** : FIERY, INFLAMED ⟨∼ sermons⟩

¹sulk \'səlk\ *vb* : to be or become moodily silent

²sulk *n* : a sulky mood or spell

¹sulky \'səl-kē\ *adj* : inclined to sulk : MOROSE, MOODY **syn** surly, glum, sullen, gloomy — **sulk•i•ly** \'səl-kə-lē\ *adv* — **sulk•i•ness** \-kē-nəs\ *n*

²sulky *n, pl* **sulkies** : a light 2-wheeled vehicle with a seat for the driver and usu. no body

sul•len \'səl-ən\ *adj* **1** : gloomily silent : MOROSE **2** : DISMAL, GLOOMY ⟨a ∼ sky⟩ **syn** glum, surly, dour, saturnine — **sul•len•ly** *adv* — **sul•len•ness** \'səl-ən-(n)əs\ *n*

sul•ly \'səl-ē\ *vb* **sul•lied; sul•ly•ing** : SOIL, SMIRCH, DEFILE

sul•tan \'səlt-ᵊn\ *n* : a sovereign esp. of a Muslim state — **sul•tan•ate** \-ˌāt\ *n*

sul•ta•na \ˌsəl-'tan-ə\ *n* **1** : a female member of a sultan's family **2** : a pale seedless grape; *also* : a raisin of this grape

sul•try \'səl-trē\ *adj* **sul•tri•er; -est** [obs. E *sulter* to swelter, alter. of E *swelter*] : very hot and moist : SWELTERING; *also* : burning hot : TORRID

¹sum \'səm\ *n* [ME *summe*, fr. OF, fr. L *summa*, fr. fem. of *summus* highest] **1** : a quantity of money **2** : the whole amount **3** : GIST **4** : the result obtained by adding numbers **5** : a problem in arithmetic **syn** aggregate, total, whole

²sum *vb* **summed; sum•ming** : to find the sum of by adding or counting

su•mac *also* **su•mach** \'s(h)ü-ˌmak\ *n* : any of a genus of trees, shrubs, and woody vines with pinnate compound leaves and spikes of red or whitish berries

sum•ma•rize \'səm-ə-ˌrīz\ *vb* **-rized; -riz•ing** : to tell in a summary

¹sum•ma•ry \'səm-ə-rē\ *adj* **1** : covering the main points briefly : CONCISE **2** : done without delay or formality ⟨∼ punishment⟩ **syn** terse, succinct, laconic — **sum•mar•i•ly** \(ˌ)sə-'mer-ə-lē, 'səm-ə-rə-lē\ *adv*

²sum•ma•ry *n, pl* **-ries** : a concise statement of the main points

sum•ma•tion \(ˌ)sə-'mā-shən\ *n* : a summing up; *esp* : a speech in court summing up the arguments in a case

sum·mer \\'səm-ər\\ *n* : the season of the year in a region in which the sun shines most directly : the warmest period of the year — **sum·mery** *adj*

sum·mer·house \\'səm-ər-ˌhaus\\ *n* : a covered structure in a garden or park to provide a shady retreat

summer squash *n* : any of various garden squashes (as zucchini) used as a vegetable while immature

sum·mit \\'səm-ət\\ *n* : the highest point

sum·mon \\'səm-ən\\ *vb* **sum·moned; sum·mon·ing** \\-(ə-)niŋ\\ [ME *somonen,* fr. OF *somondre,* fr. (assumed) VL *summonere,* alter. of L *summonēre* to remind secretly] **1** : to call to a meeting : CONVOKE **2** : to send for; *also* : to order to appear in court **3** : to evoke esp. by an act of the will ⟨~ up courage⟩ — **sum·mon·er** *n*

sum·mons \\'səm-ənz\\ *n, pl* **sum·mons·es** **1** : an authoritative call to appear at a designated place or to attend to a duty **2** : a warning or citation to appear in court at a specified time to answer charges

sump·tu·ous \\'səmp-chə-(-wə)s\\ *adj* : LAVISH, LUXURIOUS

sum up *vb* : SUMMARIZE

¹sun \\'sən\\ *n* **1** : the shining celestial body around which the earth and other planets revolve and from which they receive light and heat **2** : a celestial body like the sun **3** : SUNSHINE — **sun·less** *adj* — **sun·ny** *adj*

²sun *vb* **sunned; sun·ning 1** : to expose to or as if to the rays of the sun **2** : to sun oneself

Sun *abbr* Sunday

sun·bath \\'sən-ˌbath, -ˌbath\\ *n* : an exposure to sunlight or a sunlamp — **sun·bathe** \\-ˌbāth\\ *vb*

sun·beam \\-ˌbēm\\ *n* : a ray of sunlight

sun·bon·net \\-ˌbän-ət\\ *n* : a bonnet with a wide brim to shield the face and neck from the sun

¹sun·burn \\-ˌbərn\\ *vb* **-burned** \\-ˌbərnd\\ *or* **-burnt** \\-ˌbərnt\\; **-burn·ing** : to burn or discolor by the sun

²sunburn *n* : a skin inflammation caused by overexposure to sunlight

sun·dae \\'sən-dē\\ *n* : ice cream served with topping

Sun·day \\'sən-dē, -ˌdā\\ *n* : the 1st day of the week : the Christian Sabbath

sun·der \\'sən-dər\\ *vb* **sun·dered; sun·der·ing** \\-d(ə-)riŋ\\ : to force apart **syn** sever, part, disjoin, disunite

sun·di·al \\-ˌdī(-ə)l\\ *n* : a device for showing the time of day from the shadow cast on a plate by an object with a straight edge

sun·down \\-ˌdaun\\ *n* : SUNSET 2

sun·dries \\'sən-drēz\\ *n pl* : various small articles or items

sun·dry \\'sən-drē\\ *adj* : SEVERAL, DIVERS, VARIOUS **syn** many, numerous

sun·fish \\'sən-ˌfish\\ *n* **1** : a huge sea fish with a deep flattened body **2** : any of a family of American freshwater fishes that are related to the perches, are often brightly colored, and usu. have the body flattened from side to side

sun·flow·er \\-ˌflau(-ə)r\\ *n* : any of a genus of tall plants related to the daisies and often grown for the oil-rich seeds of their yellow-petaled dark-centered flower heads

sung past and past part of SING

sun·glasses \\'sən-ˌglas-əz\\ *n pl* : glasses to protect the eyes from the sun

sunk past and past part of SINK

sunk·en \\'səŋ-kən\\ *adj* **1** : SUBMERGED **2** : fallen in : HOLLOW ⟨~ cheeks⟩ **3** : lying in a depression ⟨~ garden⟩; *also* : constructed below the general floor level ⟨~ living room⟩

sun·lamp \\'sən-ˌlamp\\ *n* : an electric lamp designed to emit radiation of wavelengths from ultraviolet to infrared

sun·light \\-ˌlīt\\ *n* : SUNSHINE

sun·lit \\-ˌlit\\ *adj* : lighted by or as if by the sun

sun·rise \\-ˌrīz\\ *n* **1** : the apparent rising of the sun above the horizon **2** : the time at which the sun rises

sun·roof \\-ˌrüf, -ˌruf\\ *n* : an automobile roof having a panel that can be opened

sun·screen \\-ˌskrēn\\ *n* : a substance used in suntan preparations to protect the skin

sun·set \\-ˌset\\ *n* **1** : the apparent descent of the sun below the horizon **2** : the time at which the sun sets

sun·shade \\'sən-ˌshād\\ *n* : something (as a parasol or awning) used as a protection from the sun's rays

sun·shine \-ˌshīn\ *n* : the direct light of the sun — **sun·shiny** *adj*

sun·spot \-ˌspät\ *n* : one of the dark spots that appear from time to time on the sun's surface

sun·stroke \-ˌstrōk\ *n* : a bodily condition often marked by a high fever and collapse and caused by staying in the sun for too long

sun·tan \-ˌtan\ *n* : a browning of the skin from exposure to the sun's rays

sun·up \-ˌəp\ *n* : SUNRISE 2

¹**sup** \ˈsəp\ *vb* **supped; sup·ping** : to take or drink in swallows or gulps

²**sup** *n* : a mouthful esp. of liquor or broth; *also* : a small quantity of liquid

³**sup** *vb* **supped; sup·ping 1** : to eat the evening meal **2** : to make one's supper ⟨*supped* on roast beef⟩

⁴**sup** *abbr* **1** superior **2** supplement; supplementary **3** supply **4** supra

¹**su·per** \ˈsü-pər\ *n* : SUPERINTENDENT

²**super** *adj* **1** : very fine : EXCELLENT **2** : EXTREME, EXCESSIVE

super- \ˌsü-pər, ˈsü-\ *prefix* **1** : over and above : higher in quantity, quality, or degree than : more than **2** : in addition : extra **3** : exceeding a norm **4** : in excessive degree or intensity **5** : surpassing all or most others of its kind **6** : situated above, on, or at the top of **7** : next above or higher **8** : more inclusive than **9** : superior in status or position

superachiever	superpower
superagency	superrich
superblock	supersalesman
superbomb	supersecret
supercity	supersize
supereminent	supersized
superfine	supersophisticated
supergalaxy	superspectacle
supergovernment	superspy
superheat	superstar
superhuman	superstate
superhumanly	superstratum
superindividual	superstrength
superliner	superstrong
superman	supersubtle
supermom	supersubtlety
supernormal	supersystem
superpatriot	supertanker
superpatriotic	supertax
superpatriotism	superwoman
superphysical	

su·per·abun·dant \ˌsü-pər-ə-ˈbən-dənt\ *adj* : more than ample — **su·per·abun·dance** \-dəns\ *n*

su·per·an·nu·ate \ˌsü-pər-ˈan-yə-ˌwāt\ *vb* **-at·ed; -at·ing** : to retire and pension because of age or infirmity — **su·per·an·nu·at·ed** *adj*

su·perb \su̇-ˈpərb\ *adj* [L *superbus* excellent, proud, fr. *super* above] : marked to the highest degree by grandeur, excellence, brilliance, or competence **syn** resplendent, glorious, gorgeous, sublime — **su·perb·ly** *adv*

su·per·car·go \ˌsü-pər-ˈkär-gō, ˈsü-pər-ˌkär-gō\ *n* : an officer on a merchant ship who manages the business part of the voyage

su·per·charg·er \ˈsü-pər-ˌchär-jər\ *n* : a device for increasing the amount of air supplied to an internal-combustion engine

su·per·cil·ious \ˌsü-pər-ˈsil-ē-əs\ *adj* [L *superciliosus*, fr. *supercilium* eyebrow, haughtiness] : haughtily contemptuous **syn** disdainful, overbearing, arrogant, lordly, superior

su·per·con·duc·tiv·i·ty \ˈsü-pər-ˌkän-ˌdək-ˈtiv-ət-ē\ *n* : a complete disappearance of electrical resistance in a substance at temperatures near absolute zero — **su·per·con·duc·tive** \ˌsü-pər-kən-ˈdək-tiv\ *adj* — **su·per·con·duc·tor** \-ˈdək-tər\ *n*

su·per·con·ti·nent \ˈsü-pər-ˌkänt-ᵊn-ənt\ *n* : a hypothetical former large continent from which other continents broke off and drifted away

su·per–du·per \ˈsü-pər-ˈdü-pər\ *adj* : of the greatest excellence, size, effectiveness, or impressiveness

su·per·ego \ˌsü-pər-ˈē-gō\ *n* : the one of the three divisions of the psyche in psychoanalytic theory that functions to reward and punish through a system of moral attitudes, conscience, and a sense of guilt

su·per·fi·cial \ˌsü-pər-ˈfish-əl\ *adj* **1** : of or relating to the surface or appearance only **2** : not thorough : SHALLOW **syn** cursory, sketchy — **su·per·fi·ci·al·i·ty** \-ˌfish-ē-ˈal-ət-ē\ *n* — **su·per·fi·cial·ly** \-ˈfish-(ə-)lē\ *adv*

su·per·flu·ous \su̇-ˈpər-flə-wəs\ *adj* : exceeding what is sufficient or necessary : SURPLUS **syn** extra, spare, supernumerary — **su·per·flu·i·ty** \ˌsü-pər-ˈflü-ət-ē\ n

su·per·high·way \ˌsü-pər-ˈhī-ˌwā\ n : a broad highway designed for high-speed traffic

su·per·im·pose \-im-ˈpōz\ vb : to lay (one thing) over and above something else

su·per·in·tend \ˌsü-p(ə-)rin-ˈtend\ vb : to have or exercise the charge and oversight of : DIRECT — **su·per·in·ten·dence** \-ˈten-dəns\ n — **su·per·in·ten·den·cy** \-dən-sē\ n — **su·per·in·ten·dent** \-dənt\ n

¹**su·pe·ri·or** \su̇-ˈpir-ē-ər\ adj 1 : situated higher up; also : higher in rank or numbers 2 : of greater value or importance 3 : courageously indifferent (as to pain or misfortune) 4 : better than most others of its kind 5 : ARROGANT, HAUGHTY — **su·pe·ri·or·i·ty** \-ˌpir-ē-ˈȯr-ət-ē\ n

²**superior** n 1 : one who is above another in rank, office, or station; esp : the head of a religious house or order 2 : one higher in quality or merit

¹**su·per·la·tive** \su̇-ˈpər-lət-iv\ adj 1 : of, relating to, or constituting the degree of grammatical comparison that denotes an extreme or unsurpassed level or extent 2 : surpassing others : SUPREME syn peerless, incomparable, superb — **su·per·la·tive·ly** adv

²**superlative** n 1 : the superlative degree or a superlative form in a language 2 : the utmost degree : ACME

su·per·mar·ket \ˈsü-pər-ˌmär-kət\ n : a self-service retail market selling foods and household merchandise

su·per·nal \su̇-ˈpərn-əl\ adj 1 : of or from on high : TOWERING 2 : of heavenly or spiritual character : ETHEREAL

su·per·nat·u·ral \ˌsü-pər-ˈnach-(ə-)rəl\ adj : of or relating to phenomena beyond or outside of nature; esp : relating to or attributed to a divinity, ghost, or infernal spirit — **su·per·nat·u·ral·ly** \-ē\ adv

su·per·no·va \ˌsü-pər-ˈnō-və\ n : the explosion of a very large star

¹**su·per·nu·mer·ary** \-ˈn(y)ü-mə-ˌrer-ē\ adj : exceeding the usual or required number : EXTRA syn surplus, superfluous, spare

²**supernumerary** n, pl **-ar·ies** : an extra person or thing; esp : an actor hired for a nonspeaking part

su·per·pose \ˌsü-pər-ˈpōz\ vb **-posed; -pos·ing** : SUPERIMPOSE — **su·per·po·si·tion** \-pə-ˈzish-ən\ n

su·per·sat·u·rat·ed \ˌsü-pər-ˈsach-ə-ˌrāt-əd\ adj : containing an amount of a substance greater than that required for saturation

su·per·scribe \ˈsü-pər-ˌskrīb, ˌsü-pər-ˈskrīb\ vb **-scribed; -scrib·ing** : to write on the top or outside : ADDRESS — **su·per·scrip·tion** \ˌsü-pər-ˈskrip-shən\ n

su·per·script \ˈsü-pər-ˌskript\ n : a symbol (as a numeral or letter) written immediately above or above and to one side of another character

su·per·sede \ˌsü-pər-ˈsēd\ vb **-sed·ed; -sed·ing** [MF superseder to refrain from, fr. L supersedēre to be superior to, refrain from, fr. super- above + sedēre to sit] : to take the place of : REPLACE syn displace, supplant

su·per·son·ic \-ˈsän-ik\ adj 1 : ULTRASONIC 2 : being or relating to speeds from one to five times the speed of sound; also : capable of moving at such a speed ⟨a ～ airplane⟩

su·per·son·ics \-ˈsän-iks\ n : the science of supersonic phenomena

su·per·sti·tion \ˌsü-pər-ˈstish-ən\ n 1 : beliefs or practices resulting from ignorance, fear of the unknown, or trust in magic or chance 2 : an irrationally abject attitude of mind toward nature, the unknown, or God resulting from superstition — **su·per·sti·tious** \-əs\ adj

su·per·struc·ture \ˈsü-pər-ˌstrək-chər\ n : something built on a base or as a vertical extension

su·per·vene \ˌsü-pər-ˈvēn\ vb **-vened; -ven·ing** : to occur as something additional or unexpected syn follow, succeed, ensue

su·per·vise \ˈsü-pər-ˌvīz\ vb **-vised; -vis·ing** : OVERSEE, SUPERINTEND — **su·per·vi·sion** \ˌsü-pər-ˈvizh-ən\ n — **su·per·vi·sor** \ˈsü-pər-ˌvī-zər\ n — **su·per·vi·so·ry** \ˌsü-pər-ˈvīz-(ə-)rē\ adj

su·pine \su̇-ˈpīn\ adj 1 : lying on the back with face upward 2 : LETHARGIC, SLUGGISH; also : ABJECT syn inactive, inert, passive, idle

supp or **suppl** abbr supplement; supplementary

sup·per \'səp-ər\ n : the evening meal esp. when dinner is taken at midday — **sup·per·time** \-ˌtīm\ n

sup·plant \sə-'plant\ vb 1 : to take the place of (another) esp. by force or trickery 2 : REPLACE syn displace, supersede

sup·ple \'səp-əl\ adj **sup·pler** \-(ə-)lər\; **sup·plest** \-(ə-)ləst\ 1 : COMPLIANT, ADAPTABLE 2 : capable of bending without breaking or creasing : LIMBER syn resilient, elastic, flexible

¹**sup·ple·ment** \'səp-lə-mənt\ n 1 : something that supplies a want or makes an addition 2 : a continuation (as of a book) containing corrections or additional material — **sup·ple·men·tal** \ˌsəp-lə-'ment-ᵊl\ adj — **sup·ple·men·ta·ry** \-'men-t(ə-)rē\ adj

²**sup·ple·ment** \'səp-lə-ˌment\ vb : to fill up the deficiencies of : add to

sup·pli·ant \'səp-lē-ənt\ n : one who supplicates : PETITIONER, PLEADER

sup·pli·cant \'səp-li-kənt\ n : SUPPLIANT

sup·pli·cate \'səp-lə-ˌkāt\ vb **-cat·ed; -cat·ing** 1 : to make a humble entreaty; esp : to pray to God 2 : to ask earnestly and humbly : BESEECH syn implore, beg, entreat, plead — **sup·pli·ca·tion** \ˌsəp-lə-'kā-shən\ n

¹**sup·ply** \sə-'plī\ vb **sup·plied; sup·ply·ing** [ME supplien, fr. MF soupleier, fr. L supplēre to fill up, supplement, supply, fr. sub- up + plēre to fill] 1 : to add as a supplement 2 : to satisfy the needs of 3 : FURNISH, PROVIDE — **sup·pli·er** \-'plī(-ə)r\ n

²**supply** n, pl **supplies** 1 : the quantity or amount (as of a commodity) needed or available; also : PROVISIONS, STORES — usu. used in pl. 2 : the act or process of filling a want or need : PROVISION 3 : the quantities of goods or services offered for sale at a particular time or at one price

sup·ply–side \sə-'plī-ˌsīd\ adj : of, relating to, or being an economic theory that recommends the reduction of tax rates to expand economic activity

¹**sup·port** \sə-'pōrt\ vb 1 : BEAR, TOLERATE 2 : to take sides with : BACK, ASSIST 3 : to provide with food, clothing, and shelter 4 : to hold up or serve as a foundation for syn uphold, advocate, champion — **sup·port·able** adj — **sup·port·er** n

²**support** n 1 : the act of supporting : the state of being supported 2 : one that supports : PROP, BASE

sup·pose \sə-'pōz\ vb **sup·posed; sup·pos·ing** 1 : to assume to be true (as for the sake of argument) 2 : EXPECT ⟨I am supposed to go⟩ 3 : to think probable — **sup·pos·al** n

sup·posed \sə-'pōz(-ə)d\ adj : BELIEVED; also : mistakenly believed — **sup·pos·ed·ly** \-'pō-zəd-lē, -'pōz-dlē\ adv

sup·pos·ing \sə-'pō-ziŋ\ conj : if by way of hypothesis : on the assumption that

sup·po·si·tion \ˌsəp-ə-'zish-ən\ n 1 : something that is supposed : HYPOTHESIS 2 : the act of supposing

sup·pos·i·to·ry \sə-'päz-ə-ˌtōr-ē\ n, pl **-ries** [ML suppositorium, lit., placed beneath] : a small easily melted mass of usu. medicated material for insertion (as into the rectum)

sup·press \sə-'pres\ vb 1 : to put down by authority or force : SUBDUE ⟨∼ a revolt⟩ 2 : to keep from being known; also : to stop the publication or circulation of 3 : to exclude from consciousness : REPRESS — **sup·press·ible** \-'pres-ə-bəl\ adj — **sup·pres·sion** \-'presh-ən\ n

sup·pres·sant \sə-'pres-ᵊnt\ n : an agent (as a drug) that tends to suppress rather than eliminate something (as appetite)

sup·pu·rate \'səp-yə-ˌrāt\ vb **-rat·ed; -rat·ing** : to form or give off pus — **sup·pu·ra·tion** \ˌsəp-yə-'rā-shən\ n

su·pra \'sü-prə, -ˌprä\ adv : earlier in this writing : ABOVE

su·pra·na·tion·al \ˌsü-prə-'nash-(ə-)nəl, -ˌprä-\ adj : transcending national boundaries, authority, or interests ⟨∼ organizations⟩

su·prem·a·cist \su̇-'prem-ə-səst\ n : an advocate of group supremacy

su·prem·a·cy \su̇-'prem-ə-sē\ n, pl **-cies** : supreme rank, power, or authority

su·preme \su̇-'prēm\ adj [L supremus, superl. of superus upper, fr. super over, above] 1 : highest in rank or authority 2 : highest in degree or quality ⟨he is ∼ among poets⟩ 3 : ULTIMATE ⟨the ∼ sacrifice⟩ syn superlative, surpassing, peerless, incomparable — **su·preme·ly** *adv* — **su·preme·ness** *n*

Supreme Being *n* : GOD 1

supt *abbr* superintendent

supvr *abbr* supervisor

sur·cease \'sər-ˌsēs\ *n* : CESSATION, RESPITE

¹**sur·charge** \'sər-ˌchärj\ *vb* 1 : to fill to excess : OVERLOAD 2 : to print or write a surcharge on (postage stamps)

²**surcharge** *n* 1 : an extra fee or cost 2 : an excessive load or burden 3 : something officially printed on a postage stamp to give it a new value or use

sur·cin·gle \'sər-ˌsiŋ-gəl\ *n* : a band passing around a horse's body to make something (as a saddle or pack) fast

¹**sure** \'shur\ *adj* **sur·er; sur·est** [ME, fr. MF *sur*, fr. L *securus* secure] 1 : firmly established 2 : TRUSTWORTHY, RELIABLE 3 : CONFIDENT 4 : not to be disputed : UNDOUBTED 5 : bound to happen 6 : careful to remember or attend to something ⟨be ∼ to lock the door⟩ **syn** certain, cocksure, positive — **sure·ly** *adv* — **sure·ness** *n*

²**sure** *adv* : SURELY

sure·fire \ˌshur-ˌfī(ə)r\ *adj* : certain to get results : DEPENDABLE

sure·ty \'shur-ət-ē\ *n, pl* **-ties** 1 : SURENESS, CERTAINTY 2 : something that makes sure : GUARANTEE 3 : one who becomes a guarantor for another person **syn** security, bond, bail

¹**surf** \'sərf\ *n* : waves that break upon the shore; *also* : the sound or foam of breaking waves

²**surf** *vb* : to ride the surf (as on a surfboard) — **surf·er** *n* — **surf·ing** *n*

¹**sur·face** \'sər-fəs\ *n* 1 : the outside of an object or body 2 : outward aspect or appearance

²**surface** *vb* **sur·faced; sur·fac·ing** 1 : to give a surface to : make smooth 2 : to rise to the surface

surf·board \'sərf-ˌbōrd\ *n* : a buoyant board used in riding the crests of waves

¹**sur·feit** \'sər-fət\ *n* 1 : EXCESS, SUPERABUNDANCE 2 : excessive indulgence (as in food or drink) 3 : disgust caused by excess (as in eating and drinking)

²**surfeit** *vb* : to feed, supply, or indulge to the point of surfeit : CLOY

surg *abbr* surgeon; surgery; surgical

¹**surge** \'sərj\ *vb* **surged; surg·ing** 1 : to rise and fall actively : TOSS 2 : to move in waves 3 : to rise suddenly to a high value

²**surge** *n* 1 : a sweeping onward like a wave of the sea ⟨a ∼ of emotion⟩ 2 : a large billow 3 : a transient sudden increase of current in an electrical circuit

sur·geon \'sər-jən\ *n* : a physician who specializes in surgery

sur·gery \'sərj-(ə-)rē\ *n, pl* **-ger·ies** [ME *surgerie*, fr. OF *cirurgie, surgerie*, fr. L *chirurgia*, fr. Gk *cheirourgia*, fr. *cheirourgos* surgeon, fr. *cheirourgos* working with the hand, fr. *cheir* hand + *ergon* work] 1 : a branch of medicine concerned with the correction of physical defects, the repair of injuries, and the treatment of disease esp. by operations 2 : a surgeon's operating room or laboratory 3 : work done by a surgeon

sur·gi·cal \'sər-ji-kəl\ *adj* : of, relating to, or associated with surgeons or surgery — **sur·gi·cal·ly** \-k(ə-)lē\ *adv*

sur·ly \'sər-lē\ *adj* **sur·li·er; -est** [alter. of ME *sirly* lordly, imperious, fr. *sir*] : ILL-NATURED, CRABBED **syn** morose, glum, sullen, sulky, gloomy — **sur·li·ness** *n*

sur·mise \sər-'mīz\ *vb* **sur·mised; sur·mis·ing** : GUESS **syn** conjecture, presume, suppose — **surmise** *n*

sur·mount \sər-'maunt\ *vb* 1 : to rise superior to : OVERCOME 2 : to get to or lie at the top of **syn** conquer, lick, master

sur·name \'sər-ˌnām\ *n* 1 : NICKNAME 2 : the name borne in common by members of a family

sur·pass \sər-'pas\ *vb* 1 : to be superior to in quality, degree, or performance : EXCEL 2 : to be beyond the reach or powers of **syn** transcend, outdo, outstrip, exceed — **sur·pass·ing·ly** *adv*

sur·plice \'sər-pləs\ *n* : a loose white outer ecclesiastical vestment usu. of knee length with large open sleeves

sur·plus \'sər-(ˌ)pləs\ *n* 1 : quantity left over : EXCESS 2 : the excess of assets over liabilities **syn** superfluity, overabundance, surfeit

¹**sur·prise** \sə(r)-'prīz\ *n* 1 : an attack made without warning 2 : a taking un-

awares **3** : something that surprises **4** : AMAZEMENT, ASTONISHMENT

²surprise *also* **sur·prize** *vb* **sur·prised; sur·pris·ing 1** : to come upon and attack unexpectedly **2** : to take unawares **3** : AMAZE **4** : to effect or accomplish by means of a surprise **syn** astonish, astound, amaze, dumbfound — **sur·pris·ing** *adj* — **sur·pris·ing·ly** *adv*

sur·re·al·ism \sə-'rē-ə-ˌliz-əm\ *n* : art, literature, or theater characterized by fantastic or incongruous imagery or effects produced by unnatural juxtapositions and combinations — **sur·re·al·ist** \-ləst\ *n or adj* — **sur·re·al·is·tic** \sə-ˌrē-ə-'lis-tik\ *adj* — **sur·re·al·is·ti·cal·ly** \-ti-k(ə-)lē\ *adv*

¹sur·ren·der \sə-'ren-dər\ *vb* **-dered; -der·ing** \-d(ə-)riŋ\ **1** : to yield to the power of another : give up under compulsion **2** : RELINQUISH

²surrender *n* : the act of giving up or yielding oneself or the possession of something to another **syn** submission, capitulation

sur·rep·ti·tious \ˌsər-əp-'tish-əs\ *adj* : done, made, or acquired by stealth : CLANDESTINE **syn** underhand, covert, furtive — **sur·rep·ti·tious·ly** *adv*

sur·rey \'sər-ē\ *n, pl* **surreys** : a 4-wheeled 2-seated horse-drawn carriage

sur·ro·gate \'sər-ə-ˌgāt, -gət\ *n* **1** : DEPUTY, SUBSTITUTE **2** : a law officer in some states with authority in the probate of wills, the settlement of estates, and the appointment of guardians

sur·round \sə-'raùnd\ *vb* **1** : to enclose on all sides : ENCIRCLE **2** : to enclose so as to cut off retreat or escape

sur·round·ings \sə-'raùn-diŋz\ *n pl* : conditions by which one is surrounded

sur·tax \'sər-ˌtaks\ *n* : an additional tax over and above a normal tax

sur·tout \(ˌ)sər-'tü\ *n* [F, fr. *sur* over (fr. L *super*) + *tout* all, fr. L *totus* whole] : a man's long close-fitting overcoat

surv *abbr* survey; surveying; surveyor

sur·veil·lance \sər-'vā-ləns, -'vāl-yəns, -'vā-əns\ *n* [F] : close watch; *also* : SUPERVISION

¹sur·vey \sər-'vā\ *vb* **sur·veyed; sur·vey·ing 1** : to look over and examine closely **2** : to find and represent the

contours, measurements, and position of a part of the earth's surface (as a tract of land) **3** : to view or study something as a whole **syn** scrutinize, examine, inspect, study — **sur·vey·or** \-ər\ *n*

²sur·vey \'sər-ˌvā\ *n, pl* **surveys** : the act or an instance of surveying; *also* : something that is surveyed

sur·vey·ing \sər-'vā-iŋ\ *n* : the branch of mathematics that teaches the art of making surveys

sur·vive \sər-'vīv\ *vb* **sur·vived; sur·viv·ing 1** : to remain alive or existent **2** : OUTLIVE, OUTLAST — **sur·viv·al** *n* — **sur·vi·vor** \-'vī-vər\ *n*

sus·cep·ti·ble \sə-'sep-tə-bəl\ *adj* **1** : of such a nature as to permit ⟨words ~ of being misunderstood⟩ **2** : having little resistance to a stimulus or agency ⟨~ to colds⟩ **3** : easily affected or emotionally moved : RESPONSIVE **syn** sensitive, subject, exposed, prone, liable, open — **sus·cep·ti·bil·i·ty** \-ˌsep-tə-'bil-ət-ē\ *n*

su·shi \'sü-shē\ *n* [Jp] : cold rice shaped into small cakes and topped or wrapped with garnishes (as of raw fish)

¹sus·pect \'səs-ˌpekt, sə-'spekt\ *adj* : regarded with suspicion

²sus·pect \'səs-ˌpekt\ *n* : one who is suspected (as of a crime)

³sus·pect \sə-'spekt\ *vb* **1** : to have doubts of : MISTRUST **2** : to imagine to be guilty without proof **3** : SURMISE

sus·pend \sə-'spend\ *vb* **1** : to bar temporarily from a privilege, office, or function **2** : to stop temporarily : make inactive for a time **3** : to withhold (judgment) for a time **4** : HANG; *esp* : to hang so as to be free except at one point; *also* : to keep from falling or sinking by some invisible support **syn** stay, postpone, defer

sus·pend·er \sə-'spen-dər\ *n* **1** : one of two supporting straps which pass over the shoulders and to which the trousers are fastened **2** *Brit* : a fastener attached to a garment or garter to hold up a stocking or sock

sus·pense \sə-'spens\ *n* **1** : SUSPENSION **2** : mental uncertainty : ANXIETY **3** : excitement as to an outcome — **sus·pense·ful** *adj*

sus·pen·sion \sə-'spen-chən\ *n* **1** : the

act of suspending : the state or period of being suspended **2** : the state of a substance when its particles are mixed with but undissolved in a fluid or solid; *also* : a substance in this state **3** : something suspended **4** : a device by which something is suspended

sus·pen·so·ry \sə-'spens-(ə-)rē\ *adj* **1** : SUSPENDED; *also* : fitted or serving to suspend something **2** : temporarily leaving undetermined

sus·pi·cion \sə-'spish-ən\ *n* **1** : the act or an instance of suspecting something wrong without proof **2** : a slight trace **syn** mistrust, uncertainty, doubt, skepticism

sus·pi·cious \sə-'spish-əs\ *adj* **1** : open to or arousing suspicion **2** : inclined to suspect **3** : showing suspicion — **sus·pi·cious·ly** *adv*

sus·tain \sə-'stān\ *vb* **1** : to provide with nourishment **2** : to keep going : PROLONG ⟨~ed effort⟩ **3** : to hold up : PROP **4** : to hold up under : ENDURE **5** : SUFFER ⟨~ a broken arm⟩ **6** : to support as true, legal, or valid **7** : PROVE, CORROBORATE

sus·te·nance \'səs-tə-nəns\ *n* **1** : FOOD, NOURISHMENT **2** : a supplying with the necessities of life **3** : something that sustains or supports

su·ture \'sü-chər\ *n* **1** : material or a stitch for sewing a wound together **2** : a seam or line along which two things or parts are joined by or as if by sewing ⟨the ~s of the skull⟩

su·zer·ain \'süz-(ə-)rən, -ə-,rān\ *n* [F] **1** : a feudal lord **2** : a nation that has political control over another nation — **su·zer·ain·ty** \-tē\ *n*

svc *or* **svce** *abbr* service

svelte \'sfelt\ *adj* [F, fr. It *svelto,* fr. *svellere* to pluck out, modif. of L *evellere,* fr. *e-* out + *vellere* to pluck] : SLENDER, LITHE

svgs *abbr* savings

SW *abbr* **1** shortwave **2** southwest

¹swab \'swäb\ *n* **1** : MOP **2** : a wad of absorbent material esp. for applying medicine or for cleaning; *also* : a sample taken with a swab **3** : SAILOR

²swab *vb* **swabbed; swab·bing** : to use a swab on : MOP

swad·dle \'swäd-ᵊl\ *vb* **swad·dled; swad·dling** \'swäd-(ᵊ-)liŋ\ **1** : to bind (an in-

fant) in bands of cloth **2** : to wrap up : SWATHE

swaddling clothes *n pl* : bands of cloth wrapped around an infant

swag \'swag\ *n* : stolen goods : LOOT

swage \'swāj, 'swej\ *n* : a tool used by metal workers for shaping their work — **swage** *vb*

swag·ger \'swag-ər\ *vb* **swag·gered; swag·ger·ing** \-(ə-)riŋ\ **1** : to walk with a conceited swing or strut **2** : BOAST, BRAG — **swagger** *n*

Swa·hi·li \swä-'hē-lē\ *n, pl* **Swahili** *or* **Swahilis** : a language that is a trade and governmental language over much of East Africa and the Congo region

swain \'swān\ *n* [ME *swein* boy, servant, fr. ON *sveinn*] **1** : RUSTIC; *esp* : SHEPHERD **2** : ADMIRER, SUITOR

¹swal·low \'swäl-ō\ *n* : any of various small long-winged migratory birds that often have a deeply forked tail

²swallow *vb* **1** : to take into the stomach through the throat **2** : to envelop or take in as if by swallowing **3** : to accept or believe without question, protest, or anger

³swallow *n* **1** : an act of swallowing **2** : as much as can be swallowed at one time

swal·low·tail \'swäl-ō-,tāl\ *n* **1** : a deeply forked and tapering tail like that of a swallow **2** : TAILCOAT **3** : any of various large butterflies with the border of the hind wing drawn out into a process resembling a tail — **swal·low·tailed** \,swäl-ō-'tāld\ *adj*

swam *past of* SWIM

swa·mi \'swäm-ē\ *n* [Hindi *svāmī,* fr. Skt *svāmin* owner, lord] : a Hindu ascetic or religious teacher

¹swamp \'swämp\ *n* : wet spongy land — **swamp** *adj* — **swampy** *adj*

²swamp *vb* **1** : to fill or become filled with or as if with water **2** : OVERWHELM **3**

swamp·land \-,land\ *n* : SWAMP

swan \'swän\ *n, pl* **swans** *also* **swan** : any of several heavy-bodied long-necked mostly pure white swimming birds related to the geese

¹swank \'swaŋk\ *or* **swanky** \'swaŋ-kē\ *adj* **swank·er** *or* **swank·i·er; -est** : showily smart and dashing; *also* : fashionably elegant

²**swank** *n* **1** : PRETENTIOUSNESS **2** : ELE-
GANCE
swans·down \'swänz-ˌdau̇n\ *n* **1** : the
very soft down of a swan used esp. for
trimming or powder puffs **2** : a soft
thick cotton flannel
swan song *n* : a farewell appearance,
act, or pronouncement
swap \'swäp\ *vb* **swapped; swap·ping**
: TRADE, EXCHANGE — **swap** *n*
sward \'swȯrd\ *n* : the grassy surface of
land
¹**swarm** \'swȯrm\ *n* **1** : a great number of
honeybees leaving together from a
hive with a queen to start a new colony; *also* : a hive of bees **2** : a large
crowd
²**swarm** *vb* **1** : to form in a swarm and
depart from a hive **2** : to throng together : gather in great numbers
swart \'swȯrt\ *adj* : SWARTHY
swar·thy \'swȯr-ᵺē, -ᵺē\ *adj* **swar·thi·
er; -est** : dark in color or complexion
: dark-skinned
swash \'swäsh\ *vb* : to move about with
a splashing sound — **swash** *n*
swash·buck·ler \-ˌbək-lər\ *n* : a boasting blustering soldier or daredevil —
swash·buck·ling \-ˌbək-(ə-)liŋ\ *adj*
swas·ti·ka \'swäs-ti-kə, swä-'stē-\ *n*
[Skt *svastika,* fr. *svasti* welfare, fr. *su*-
well + *asti* he is] : a symbol or ornament in the form of a cross with the
ends of the arms bent at right angles
swat \'swät\ *vb* **swat·ted; swat·ting** : to
hit sharply ⟨~ a fly⟩ ⟨~ a ball⟩ — **swat**
n — **swat·ter** *n*
SWAT *abbr* Special Weapons and Tactics
swatch \'swäch\ *n* : a sample piece (as
of fabric) or a collection of samples
swath \'swäth, 'swȯth\ *or* **swathe**
\'swäᵺ, 'swȯᵺ, 'swäᵺ\ *n* [ME, fr.
OE *swæth* footstep, trace] **1** : a row of
cut grass or grain **2** : the sweep of a
scythe or mowing machine or the path
cut in mowing
swathe \'swäᵺ, 'swȯᵺ, 'swäᵺ\ *vb*
swathed; swath·ing : to bind or wrap
with or as if with a bandage
¹**sway** \'swā\ *n* **1** : a gentle swinging
from side to side **2** : a controlling influence **3** : sovereign power : DOMIN-
ION
²**sway** *vb* **1** : to swing gently from side to
side **2** : RULE, GOVERN **3** : to cause to

swing from side to side **4** : BEND,
SWERVE; *also* : INFLUENCE **syn** oscillate, fluctuate, vibrate, waver
sway·back \'swā-'bak, -ˌbak\ *n* : a sagging of the back found esp. in horses
— **sway·backed** \-'bakt\ *adj*
swear \'swaər\ *vb* **swore** \'swōr\; **sworn**
\'swōrn\; **swear·ing** **1** : to make a solemn statement or promise under oath
: VOW **2** : to assert emphatically as
true with an appeal to God or one's
honor **3** : to administer an oath to **4**
: to charge or confirm under oath;
also : to bind by or as if by an oath **5**
: to use profane or obscene language
— **swear·er** *n*
swear in *vb* : to induct into office by
administration of an oath
¹**sweat** \'swet\ *vb* **sweat** *or* **sweat·ed;
sweat·ing** **1** : to excrete salty moisture
from glands of the skin : PERSPIRE **2**
: to form drops of moisture on the surface **3** : to work so that one sweats
: TOIL **4** : to cause to sweat **5** : to draw
out or get rid of by perspiring **6** : to
make a person overwork
²**sweat** *n* **1** : perceptible liquid exuded
through pores from glands (**sweat
glands**) of the skin : PERSPIRATION **2**
: moisture issuing from or gathering
on the surface in drops — **sweaty** *adj*
sweat·er \'swet-ər\ *n* **1** : one that
sweats **2** : a knitted or crocheted jacket or pullover
sweat·shop \'swet-ˌshäp\ *n* : a shop or
factory in which workers are employed for long hours at low wages
and under unhealthy conditions
Swed *abbr* Sweden; Swedish
swede \'swēd\ *n* **1** *cap* : a native or inhabitant of Sweden **2** : RUTABAGA
Swed·ish \'swēd-ish\ *n* **1** : the language
of Sweden **2 Swedish** *pl* : the people of
Sweden — **Swedish** *adj*
¹**sweep** \'swēp\ *vb* **swept** \'swept\;
sweep·ing **1** : to remove or clean by
brushing **2** : to remove or destroy by
vigorous continuous action **3** : to strip
or clear by gusts of wind or rain **4** : to
move over with speed and force ⟨the
tide *swept* over the shore⟩ **5** : to gather in with a single swift movement **6**
: to move or extend in a wide curve —
sweep·er *n* — **sweep·ing** *adj*
²**sweep** *n* **1** : something (as a long oar)
that operates with a sweeping motion

2 : a clearing off or away **3** : a winning of all the contests or prizes in a competition **4** : a sweeping movement ⟨∼ of a scythe⟩ **5** : CURVE, BEND **6** : RANGE, SCOPE

sweep·ing *n* **1** : the act or action of one that sweeps **2** *pl* : things collected by sweeping : REFUSE

sweep–sec·ond \'swēp-ˌsek-ənd\ *n* : a hand marking seconds on a timepiece

sweep·stakes \'swēp-ˌstāks\ *also* **sweep·stake** \-ˌstāk\ *n, pl* **sweepstakes** **1** : a race or contest in which the entire prize may go to the winner; *esp* : a horse race in which the stakes are contributed at least in part by the owners of the horses **2** : any of various lotteries

¹**sweet** \'swēt\ *adj* **1** : being or causing the one of the four basic taste sensations that is caused esp. by table sugar and is identified esp. by the taste buds at the front of the tongue; *also* : pleasing to the taste **2** : KINDLY, MILD **3** : pleasing to a sense other than taste ⟨a ∼ smell⟩ ⟨∼ music⟩ **4** : not stale or spoiled : WHOLESOME ⟨∼ milk⟩ **5** : not salted ⟨∼ butter⟩ — **sweet·ish** *adj* — **sweet·ly** *adv* — **sweet·ness** *n*

²**sweet** *n* **1** : something sweet : CANDY **2** : DARLING

sweet·bread \'swēt-ˌbred\ *n* : the pancreas or thymus of an animal (as a calf or lamb) used for food

sweet·bri·er *also* **sweet·bri·ar** \-ˌbrī(-ə)r\ *n* : a thorny European rose with fragrant white to deep pink flowers

sweet clover *n* : any of a genus of erect legumes widely grown for soil improvement or hay

sweet corn *n* : an Indian corn with kernels rich in sugar and cooked as a vegetable while immature

sweet·en \'swēt-ᵊn\ *vb* **sweet·ened; sweet·en·ing** \'swēt-(ᵊ-)niŋ\ : to make sweet — **sweet·en·er** \'swēt-(ᵊ-)nər\ *n* — **sweet·en·ing** *n*

sweet fern *n* : a small No. American shrub with sweet-scented or aromatic leaves

sweet·heart \'swēt-ˌhärt\ *n* : one who is loved

sweet·meat \'swēt-ˌmēt\ *n* : CANDY

sweet pea *n* : a garden plant of the legume family with climbing stems

and fragrant flowers of many colors; *also* : its flower

sweet pepper *n* : a large mild thick=walled fruit of a pepper; *also* : a plant related to the potato that bears sweet peppers

sweet potato *n* : a tropical vine related to the morning glory; *also* : its sweet yellow edible root

sweet–talk \'swēt-ˌtȯk\ *vb* : FLATTER, COAX — **sweet talk** *n*

sweet tooth *n* : a craving or fondness for sweet food

sweet wil·liam \swēt-'wil-yəm\ *n, often cap W* : a widely cultivated Eurasian pink with small white to deep red or purple flowers often showily spotted, banded, or mottled

¹**swell** \'swel\ *vb* **swelled; swelled** *or* **swol·len** \'swō-lən\; **swell·ing** **1** : to grow big or make bigger **2** : to expand or distend abnormally or excessively ⟨a *swollen* joint⟩; *also* : BULGE **3** : to fill or be filled with emotion (as pride) **syn** expand, amplify, distend, inflate, dilate — **swell·ing** *n*

²**swell** *n* **1** : a long crestless wave or series of waves in the open sea **2** : sudden or gradual increase in size or value **3** : a person dressed in the height of fashion; *also* : a person of high social position or outstanding competence

³**swell** *adj* **1** : FASHIONABLE, STYLISH; *also* : socially prominent **2** : EXCELLENT, FIRST-RATE

swelled head *n* : an exaggerated opinion of oneself : SELF-CONCEIT

swell·head \'swel-ˌhed\ *n* : one who has a swelled head — **swell·head·ed** \-'hed-əd\ *adj*

swel·ter \'swel-tər\ *vb* **swel·tered; swel·ter·ing** \-t(ə-)riŋ\ [ME *sweltren,* fr. *swelten* to die, be overcome by heat, fr. OE *sweltan* to die] : to be faint or oppressed with the heat

swept past and past part of SWEEP

swerve \'swərv\ *vb* **swerved; swerv·ing** : to move abruptly aside from a straight line or course **syn** digress, deviate, diverge — **swerve** *n*

¹**swift** \'swift\ *adj* **1** : moving or capable of moving with great speed **2** : occurring suddenly **3** : READY, ALERT — **swift·ly** *adv* — **swift·ness** \'swif(t)-nəs\ *n*

²**swift** *n* : any of numerous small in-

sect-eating birds with long narrow wings

swig \'swig\ *vb* **swigged; swig·ging** : to drink in long drafts — **swig** *n*

¹**swill** \'swil\ *vb* **1** : to swallow greedily : GUZZLE **2** : to feed (as hogs) on swill

²**swill** *n* **1** : food for animals composed of edible refuse mixed with liquid **2** : GARBAGE

¹**swim** \'swim\ *vb* **swam** \'swam\; **swum** \'swəm\; **swim·ming 1** : to propel one-self along in water by natural means (as by hands and legs, by tail, or by fins) **2** : to glide smoothly along **3** : FLOAT **4** : to be covered with or as if with a liquid **5** : to be dizzy ⟨his head *swam*⟩ **6** : to cross or go over by swimming — **swim·mer** *n*

²**swim** *n* **1** : an act of swimming **2** : the main current of activity or fashion ⟨in the social ∼⟩

swim·ming \'swim-iŋ\ *n* : the action, art, or sport of swimming and diving

swimming pool *n* : a tank of concrete or plastic designed for swimming

swim·suit \'swim-,süt\ *n* : a suit for swimming or bathing

swin·dle \'swin-dᵊl\ *vb* **swin·dled; swin·dling** \-(d)liŋ, -dᵊl-iŋ\ [fr. *swindler*, fr. G *schwindler* giddy person, fr. *schwindeln* to be dizzy] : CHEAT, DE-FRAUD — **swindle** *n* — **swin·dler** \-d(ᵊ-)lər\ *n*

swine \'swīn\ *n, pl* **swine 1** : any of a family of stout short-legged hoofed mammals with bristly skin and a long flexible snout; *esp* : one widely raised as a meat animal **2** : a contemptible person — **swin·ish** \'swī-nish\ *adj*

¹**swing** \'swiŋ\ *vb* **swung** \'swəŋ\; **swing·ing** \'swiŋ-iŋ\ **1** : to move rapidly in an arc **2** : to sway or cause to sway back and forth **3** : to hang so as to move freely back and forth or in a curve **4** : to be executed by hanging **5** : to move or turn on a hinge or pivot **6** : to manage or handle successfully **7** : to march or walk with free swaying movements **8** : to have a steady pulsing rhythm **9** : to be lively and up≠to-date; *also* : to engage freely in sex **syn** wield, manipulate, ply, maneuver — **swing·er** *n* — **swing·ing** *adj*

²**swing** *n* **1** : the act of swinging **2** : a swinging blow, movement, or rhythm **3** : the distance through which some-thing swings : FLUCTUATION **4** : a seat suspended by a rope or chain for swinging back and forth for pleasure **5** : jazz music played esp. by a large band and marked by a steady lively rhythm, simple harmony, and a basic melody often submerged in improvi-sation — **swing** *adj*

swing–by \'swiŋ-,bī\ *n, pl* **swing–bys** : an interplanetary mission in which a spacecraft uses the gravitational field of a planet near which it passes for changing course

¹**swipe** \'swīp\ *vb* **swiped; swip·ing 1** : to strike or wipe with a sweeping motion **2** : PILFER, SNATCH

²**swipe** *n* : a strong sweeping blow

swirl \'swərl\ *vb* : EDDY — **swirl** *n*

swish \'swish\ *n* **1** : a prolonged hissing sound **2** : a light sweeping or brushing sound — **swish** *vb*

Swiss \'swis\ *n* **1** *pl* **Swiss** : a native or inhabitant of Switzerland **2** : a hard cheese with large holes

Swiss chard *n* : CHARD

¹**switch** \'swich\ *n* **1** : a slender flexible whip, rod, or twig **2** : a blow with a switch **3** : a shift from one thing to another **4** : a device for adjusting the rails of a track so that a locomotive or train may be turned from one track to another; *also* : a railroad siding **5** : a device for making, breaking, or changing the connections in an elec-trical circuit **6** : a heavy strand of hair often used in addition to a person's own hair for some coiffures

²**switch** *vb* **1** : to punish or urge on with a switch **2** : WHISK ⟨a cow ∼*ing* her tail⟩ **3** : to shift or turn by operating a switch **4** : CHANGE, EXCHANGE

switch·back \'swich-,bak\ *n* : a zig-zag road or arrangement of railroad tracks for climbing a steep grade

switch·blade \-,blād\ *n* : a pocket-knife with a spring-operated blade

switch·board \-,bōrd\ *n* : a panel on which is mounted a group of electric switches so arranged that a number of circuits may be connected, combined, and controlled

switch–hit·ter \-'hit-ər\ *n* : a baseball player who bats either right-handed or left-handed — **switch–hit** \-'hit\ *vb*

switch·man \'swich-mən\ *n* : one who attends a railroad switch

Switz *abbr* Switzerland

¹**swiv·el** \'swiv-əl\ *n* : a device joining two parts so that one or both can turn freely

²**swivel** *vb* **-eled** *or* **-elled**; **-el·ing** *or* **-el·ling** \-(ə-)liŋ\ : to swing or turn on or as if on a swivel

swiz·zle stick \'swiz-əl-\ *n* : a stick used to stir mixed drinks

swollen past part of SWELL

swoon \'swün\ *vb* : FAINT — **swoon** *n*

swoop \'swüp\ *vb* : to descend or pounce swiftly like a hawk on its prey — **swoop** *n*

sword \'sȯrd\ *n* **1** : a weapon with a long pointed blade and sharp cutting edges **2** : the use of force

sword·fish \-ˌfish\ *n* : a very large ocean food fish with the bones of the upper jaw prolonged in a long sword-like beak

sword·play \-ˌplā\ *n* : the art or skill of wielding a sword

swords·man \'sȯrdz-mən\ *n* : one skilled in wielding a sword; *esp* : FENCER

sword·tail \'sȯrd-ˌtāl\ *n* : a small brightly marked Central American fish

swore past of SWEAR

sworn past part of SWEAR

swum past part of SWIM

swung past and past part of SWING

syb·a·rite \'sib-ə-ˌrīt\ *n* : a lover of luxury : VOLUPTUARY

syc·a·more \'sik-ə-ˌmōr\ *n* **1** : a Eurasian maple with yellowish green flowers widely planted as a shade tree **2** : a large spreading tree of eastern and central No. America that has light brown flaky bark and small round fruits hanging on long stalks

sy·co·phant \'sik-ə-fənt\ *n* : a servile flatterer — **syc·o·phan·tic** \ˌsik-ə-'fant-ik\ *adj*

syl *or* **syll** *abbr* syllable

sy·li \'sē-lē\ *n, pl* **sylis** — see MONEY table

syl·lab·i·ca·tion \sə-ˌlab-ə-'kā-shən\ *n* : the dividing of words into syllables

syl·lab·i·fy \sə-'lab-ə-ˌfī\ *vb* **-fied**; **-fy·ing** : to form or divide into syllables — **syl·lab·i·fi·ca·tion** \-ˌlab-ə-fə-'kā-shən\ *n*

syl·la·ble \'sil-ə-bəl\ *n* [ME, fr. MF *sillabe*, fr. L *syllaba*, fr. Gk *syllabē*, fr. *syllambanein* to gather together, fr. *syn* with + *lambanein* to take] : a unit of spoken language consisting of an uninterrupted utterance and forming either a whole word (as *cat*) or a commonly recognized division of a word (as *syl* in *syl·la·ble*); *also* : one or more letters representing such a unit — **syl·lab·ic** \sə-'lab-ik\ *adj*

syl·la·bus \'sil-ə-bəs\ *n, pl* **-bi** \-ˌbī\ *or* **-bus·es** : a summary containing the heads or main topics of a speech, book, or course of study

syl·lo·gism \'sil-ə-ˌjiz-əm\ *n* : a logical scheme of a formal argument consisting of a major and a minor premise and a conclusion which must logically be true if the premises are true — **syl·lo·gis·tic** \ˌsil-ə-'jis-tik\ *adj*

sylph \'silf\ *n* **1** : an imaginary being inhabiting the air **2** : a slender graceful woman

syl·van \'sil-vən\ *adj* **1** : living or located in a wooded area; *also* : of, relating to, or characteristic of forest **2** : abounding in woods or trees : WOODED

sym *abbr* **1** symbol **2** symmetrical

sym·bi·o·sis \ˌsim-ˌbī-'ō-səs, -bē-\ *n, pl* **-o·ses** \-ˌsēz\ : the living together in close association of two dissimilar organisms esp. when mutually beneficial — **sym·bi·ot·ic** \-'ät-ik\ *adj*

sym·bol \'sim-bəl\ *n* **1** : something that stands for something else; *esp* : something concrete that represents or suggests another thing that cannot in itself be pictured ⟨the lion is a ∼ of bravery⟩ **2** : a letter, character, or sign used in writing or printing relating to a particular field (as mathematics or music) to represent operations, quantities, elements, sounds, or other ideas — **sym·bol·ic** \sim-'bäl-ik\ *also* **sym·bol·i·cal** \-i-kəl\ *adj* — **sym·bol·i·cal·ly** \-k(ə-)lē\ *adv*

sym·bol·ism \'sim-bə-ˌliz-əm\ *n* : representation of abstract or intangible things by means of symbols or emblems

sym·bol·ize \'sim-bə-ˌlīz\ *vb* **-ized**; **-iz·ing** **1** : to serve as a symbol of **2** : to represent by symbols — **sym·bol·iza·tion** \ˌsim-bə-lə-'zā-shən\ *n*

sym·me·try \'sim-ə-trē\ *n, pl* **-tries 1** : an arrangement marked by regularity and balanced proportions **2** : correspondence in size, shape, and position of parts that are on opposite sides of a dividing line or center **syn** proportion, balance, harmony — **sym·met·ri·cal** \sə-'me-tri-kəl\ *or* **sym·met·ric** \sə-'me-trik\ *adj* — **sym·met·ri·cal·ly** \-k(ə-)lē\ *adv*

sympathetic nervous system *n* : the part of the autonomic nervous system that is concerned esp. with preparing the body to react to situations of stress or emergency and that tends to depress secretion, decrease the tone and contractility of muscle not under direct voluntary control, and cause the contraction of blood vessels

sym·pa·thize \'sim-pə-ˌthīz\ *vb* **-thized; -thiz·ing** : to feel or show sympathy — **sym·pa·thiz·er** *n*

sym·pa·thy \'sim-pə-thē\ *n, pl* **-thies 1** : a relationship between persons or things wherein whatever affects one similarly affects the others **2** : harmony of interests and aims **3** : FAVOR, SUPPORT **4** : the capacity for entering into and sharing the feelings or interests of another; *also* : COMPASSION, PITY **5** : an expression of sorrow for another's loss, grief, or misfortune — **sym·pa·thet·ic** \ˌsim-pə-'thet-ik\ *adj* — **sym·pa·thet·i·cal·ly** \-i-k(ə-)lē\ *adv*

sym·pho·ny \'sim-fə-nē\ *n, pl* **-nies 1** : harmony of sounds **2** : a large and complex composition for a full orchestra **3** : a large orchestra of a kind that plays symphonies — **sym·phon·ic** \sim-'fän-ik\ *adj*

sym·po·sium \sim-'pō-zē-əm\ *n, pl* **-sia** \-zē-ə\ *or* **-siums** [L, fr. Gk *symposion,* fr. *sympinein* to drink together, fr. *syn-* together + *pinein* to drink] : a conference at which a particular topic is discussed by various speakers; *also* : a collection of opinions about a subject

symp·tom \'simp-təm\ *n* **1** : a change in an organism indicative of disease or abnormality; *esp* : one (as a headache) that can be sensed only by the individual affected **2** : SIGN, INDICATION — **symp·tom·at·ic** \ˌsimp-tə-'mat-ik\ *adj*

syn *abbr* synonym; synonymous; synonymy

syn·a·gogue *or* **syn·a·gog** \'sin-ə-ˌgäg\ *n* [ME *synagoge,* fr. OF, fr. LL *synago-*

ga, fr. Gk *synagōgē* assembly, synagogue, fr. *synagein* to bring together] **1** : a Jewish congregation **2** : the house of worship of a Jewish congregation

syn·apse \'sin-ˌaps, sə-'naps\ *n* : the point at which a nervous impulse passes from one neuron to another

¹**sync** *also* **synch** \'siŋk\ *vb* **synced** *also* **synched** \'siŋkt\; **sync·ing** *also* **synch·ing** \'siŋ-kiŋ\ : SYNCHRONIZE

²**sync** *also* **synch** *n* : SYNCHRONIZATION, SYNCHRONISM — **sync** *adj*

syn·chro·mesh \'siŋ-krō-ˌmesh, 'sin-\ *adj* : designed for effecting synchronized shifting of gears — **synchromesh** *n*

syn·chro·nize \'siŋ-krə-ˌnīz, 'sin-\ *vb* **-nized; -niz·ing 1** : to occur or cause to occur at the same instant **2** : to represent, arrange, or tabulate according to dates or time **3** : to cause to agree in time **4** : to make synchronous in operation — **syn·chro·nism** \-ˌniz-əm\ *n* — **syn·chro·ni·za·tion** \ˌsiŋ-krə-nə-'zā-shən, ˌsin-\ *n* — **syn·chro·niz·er** \'siŋ-krə-ˌnī-zər, 'sin-\ *n*

syn·chro·nous \'siŋ-krə-nəs, 'sin-\ *adj* **1** : happening at the same time : CONCURRENT **2** : working, moving, or occurring together at the same rate and at the proper time

syn·co·pa·tion \ˌsiŋ-kə-'pā-shən, ˌsin-\ *n* : a shifting of the regular musical accent : occurrence of accented notes on the weak beat — **syn·co·pate** \'siŋ-kə-ˌpāt, 'sin-\ *vb*

syn·co·pe \'siŋ-kə-(ˌ)pē, 'sin-\ *n* : the loss of one or more sounds or letters in the interior of a word (as in *fo'c'sle* from *forecastle*)

¹**syn·di·cate** \'sin-di-kət\ *n* **1** : a group of persons who combine to carry out a financial or industrial undertaking **2** : a business concern that sells materials for publication in many newspapers and periodicals at the same time

²**syn·di·cate** \-də-ˌkāt\ *vb* **-cat·ed; -cat·ing 1** : to combine into or manage as a syndicate **2** : to publish through a syndicate — **syn·di·ca·tion** \ˌsin-də-'kā-shən\ *n*

syn·drome \'sin-ˌdrōm\ *n* : a group of signs and symptoms that occur together and characterize a particular abnormality

syn·er·gism \'sin-ər-ˌjiz-əm\ n : interaction of discrete agencies (as industrial firms) or agents (as drugs) such that the total effect is greater than the sum of the individual effects — **syn·er·gist** \-jəst\ n — **syn·er·gis·tic** \-'jis-tik\ adj — **syn·er·gis·ti·cal·ly** \-ti-k(ə-)lē\ adv

syn·fuel \'sin-ˌfyül\ n [synthetic] : a fuel derived from a fossil fuel or from fermentation (as of grain)

syn·od \'sin-əd\ n : COUNCIL, ASSEMBLY; esp : a religious governing body — **syn·od·al** \-əd-ᵊl, -ˌäd-ᵊl\ adj **syn·od·ic** \-ik\ or **syn·od·i·cal** \sə-'näd-i-kəl\ adj

syn·onym \'sin-ə-ˌnim\ n : one of two or more words in the same language which have the same or very nearly the same meaning — **syn·on·y·mous** \sə-'nän-ə-məs\ adj — **syn·on·y·my** \-mē\ n

syn·op·sis \sə-'näp-səs\ n, pl **-op·ses** \-ˌsēz\ : a condensed statement or outline (as of a treatise) : ABSTRACT

syn·op·tic \sə-'näp-tik\ also **syn·op·ti·cal** \-ti-kəl\ adj : characterized by or affording a comprehensive view

syn·tax \'sin-ˌtaks\ n : the way in which words are put together to form phrases, clauses, or sentences — **syn·tac·tic** \sin-'tak-tik\ or **syn·tac·ti·cal** \-ti-kəl\ adj

syn·the·sis \'sin-thə-səs\ n, pl **-the·ses** \-ˌsēz\ : the combination of parts or elements into a whole; esp : the production of a substance by union of chemically simpler substances — **syn·the·size** \-ˌsīz\ vb — **syn·the·siz·er** n

syn·thet·ic \sin-'thet-ik\ adj : produced artificially esp. by chemical means; also : not genuine — **synthetic** n — **syn·thet·i·cal·ly** \-i-k(ə-)lē\ adv

syph·i·lis \'sif-(ə-)ləs\ n [NL, fr. poem *Syphilis sive Morbus Gallicus (Syphilis or the French disease)* (1530) by Girolamo Fracastoro †1553 Ital. physician] : a destructive contagious usu. venereal disease caused by a spirochete — **syph·i·lit·ic** \ˌsif-ə-'lit-ik\ adj or n

sy·phon var of SIPHON

¹sy·ringe \sə-'rinj, 'sir-inj\ n : a device used esp. for injecting liquids into or withdrawing them from the body

²syringe vb **sy·ringed; sy·ring·ing** : to inject or cleanse with or as if with a syringe

syr·up \'sər-əp, 'sir-əp\ n **1** : a thick sticky solution of sugar and water often flavored or medicated **2** : the concentrated juice of a fruit or plant — **syr·upy** adj

syst abbr system

sys·tem \'sis-təm\ n **1** : a group of units so combined as to form a whole and to operate in unison **2** : the body as a functioning whole; also : a group of bodily organs (as the nervous system) that together carry on some vital function **3** : a definite scheme or method of procedure or classification **4** : regular method or order — **sys·tem·at·ic** \ˌsis-tə-'mat-ik\ also **sys·tem·at·i·cal** \-i-kəl\ adj — **sys·tem·at·i·cal·ly** \-k(ə-)lē\ adv

sys·tem·atize \'sis-tə-mə-ˌtīz\ vb **-atized; -atiz·ing** : to make into a system : arrange methodically

¹sys·tem·ic \sis-'tem-ik\ adj **1** : of, relating to, or affecting the whole body ⟨∼ disease⟩ **2** : acting through the bodily systems after absorption or ingestion by making the organism toxic to a pest (as a mite or insect)

²systemic n : a systemic pesticide

systemic lupus erythematosus n : a disease characterized by fever, skin rash, and arthritis, often by anemia, by small hemorrhages of the skin and mucous membranes, and in serious cases by involvement of various internal organs

sys·tem·ize \'sis-tə-ˌmīz\ vb **-ized; -iz·ing** : SYSTEMATIZE

systems analyst n : a person who studies a procedure or business to determine its goals or purposes and to discover the best ways to accomplish them — **systems analysis** n

sys·to·le \'sis-tə-(ˌ)lē\ n : a rhythmically recurrent contraction esp. of the heart — **sys·tol·ic** \sis-'täl-ik\ adj

Szech·uan or **Szech·wan** \'sech-ˌwän\ adj : of, relating to, or being a style of Chinese cooking that is spicy, oily, and esp. peppery

T

¹t \'tē\ *n, pl* t's *or* ts \'tēz\ *often cap* : the 20th letter of the English alphabet

²t *abbr, often cap* 1 tablespoon 2 teaspoon 3 temperature 4 ton 5 transitive 6 troy 7 true

Ta *symbol* tantalum

TA *abbr* teaching assistant

¹tab \'tab\ *n* 1 : a short projecting flap, loop, or tag; *also* : a small insert or addition 2 : close surveillance : WATCH ⟨keep ∼s on him⟩ 3 : BILL, CHECK

²tab *vb* tabbed; tab•bing : DESIGNATE

tab•bou•leh \tə-'bü-lə\ *n* [Ar] : a salad consisting chiefly of wheat, tomatoes, parsley, mint, onions, lemon juice, and olive oil

tab•by \'tab-ē\ *n, pl* tabbies : a usu. striped or mottled domestic cat; *also* : a female domestic cat

tab•er•na•cle \'tab-ər-ˌnak-əl\ *n* [deriv. of L *taberna* hut] 1 *often cap* : a tent sanctuary used by the Israelites during the Exodus 2 : a receptacle for the consecrated elements of the Eucharist 3 : a house of worship

¹ta•ble \'tā-bəl\ *n* 1 : a flat slab or plaque : TABLET 2 : a piece of furniture consisting of a smooth flat slab fixed on legs 3 : a supply of food : BOARD, FARE 4 : a group of people assembled at or as if at a table 5 : a systematic arrangement of data for ready reference 6 : a condensed enumeration — ta•ble•top \-ˌtäp\ *n*

²table *vb* ta•bled; ta•bling \-b(ə-)liŋ\ 1 *Brit* : to place on the agenda 2 : to remove (a parliamentary motion) from consideration indefinitely

tab•leau \'tab-ˌlō\ *n, pl* tab•leaux \-ˌlōz\ *also* tableaus [F] 1 : a graphic description : PICTURE 2 : a striking or artistic grouping 3 : a static depiction of a scene usu. presented on a stage by costumed participants

ta•ble•cloth \'tā-bəl-ˌklȯth\ *n* : a covering spread over a dining table before the table is set

ta•ble d'hôte \ˌtäb-əl-'dōt\ *n* [F, lit., host's table] : a complete meal of several courses offered at a fixed price

ta•ble•land \'tā-bəl-ˌ(l)and\ *n* : PLATEAU

ta•ble•spoon \-ˌspün\ *n* 1 : a large spoon used esp. for serving 2 : TABLESPOON-FUL

ta•ble•spoon•ful \'tā-bəl-ˌspün-ˌful\ *n, pl* -spoonfuls \-ˌfulz\ *also* -spoons•ful \-ˌspünz-ˌful\ : a unit of measure equal to one half fluidounce

tab•let \'tab-lət\ *n* 1 : a flat slab suited for or bearing an inscription 2 : a collection of sheets of paper glued together at one edge 3 : a compressed or molded block of material; *esp* : a usu. disk-shaped medicated mass

table tennis *n* : a game resembling tennis played on a tabletop with wooden paddles and a small hollow plastic ball

ta•ble•ware \'tā-bəl-ˌwaər\ *n* : utensils (as of china or silver) for table use

¹tab•loid \'tab-ˌlȯid\ *adj* : condensed into small scope

²tabloid *n* : a newspaper marked by small pages, condensation of the news, and usu. many photographs; *esp* : one characterized by sensationalism

¹ta•boo *also* ta•bu \tə-'bü, ta-\ *adj* [fr. Tongan, a Polynesian language] 1 : set apart as charged with a dangerous supernatural power : INVIOLABLE 2 : banned esp. as immoral or dangerous

²taboo *also* tabu *n, pl* taboos *also* tabus 1 : a prohibition against touching, saying, or doing something for fear of immediate harm from a mysterious superhuman force 2 : a prohibition imposed by social usage or as a protection

ta•bor *also* ta•bour \'tā-bər\ *n* : a small drum used to accompany a pipe or fife played by the same person

tab•u•lar \'tab-yə-lər\ *adj* 1 : having a flat surface 2 : arranged in a table; *esp* : set up in rows and columns 3 : computed by means of a table

tab•u•late \-ˌlāt\ *vb* -lat•ed; -lat•ing : to put into tabular form — tab•u•la•tion \ˌtab-yə-'lā-shən\ *n* — tab•u•la•tor \'tab-yə-ˌlāt-ər\ *n*

TAC \'tak\ *abbr* Tactical Air Command

tach \'tak\ *n* : TACHOMETER

ta·chom·e·ter \ta-'käm-ət-ər, tə-\ *n* [deriv. of Gk *tachys* rapid] : a device to indicate speed of rotation

tachy·car·dia \ˌtak-i-'kärd-ē-ə\ *n* : rapid heart action

tachy·on \'tak-ē-ˌän\ *n* : a hypothetical particle held to travel faster than light

tac·it \'tas-ət\ *adj* [F or L; F *tacite*, fr. L *tacitus* silent, fr. *tacēre* to be silent] **1** : expressed without words or speech **2** : implied or indicated but not actually expressed ⟨∼ consent⟩ — **tac·it·ly** *adv* — **tac·it·ness** *n*

tac·i·turn \'tas-ə-ˌtərn\ *adj* : disinclined to talk : habitually silent **syn** uncommunicative, reserved, reticent, closemouthed — **tac·i·tur·ni·ty** \ˌtas-ə-'tər-nət-ē\ *n*

¹tack \'tak\ *vb* **1** : to fasten with tacks; *also* : to add on **2** : to change the direction of (a sailing ship) from one tack to another **3** : to follow a zigzag course

²tack *n* **1** : a small sharp nail with a broad flat head **2** : the direction a ship is sailing as shown by the way the sails are trimmed; *also* : the run of a ship on one tack **3** : a change of course from one tack to another **4** : a zigzag course **5** : a course of action

³tack *n* : gear for harnessing a horse

¹tack·le \'tak-əl, *naut often* 'tāk-\ *n* **1** : GEAR, APPARATUS, EQUIPMENT **2** : the rigging of a ship **3** : an arrangement of ropes and pulleys for hoisting or pulling heavy objects **4** : the act or an instance of tackling; *also* : a football lineman playing between guard and end

²tackle *vb* **tack·led; tack·ling** \-(ə-)liŋ\ **1** : to attach and secure with or as if with tackle **2** : to seize, grapple with, or throw down with the intention of subduing or stopping **3** : to set about dealing with ⟨∼ a problem⟩

¹tacky \'tak-ē\ *adj* **tack·i·er; -est** : sticky to the touch

²tacky *adj* **tack·i·er; -est** **1** : SHABBY, SEEDY **2** : marked by lack of style or good taste; *also* : cheaply showy : GAUDY

ta·co \'täk-ō\ *n, pl* **tacos** \-ōz, -ōs\ [MexSp] : a tortilla rolled up with or folded over a filling

tact \'takt\ *n* [F, sense of touch, fr. L *tactus*, fr. *tactus*, pp. of *tangere* to touch] : a keen sense of what to do or say to keep good relations with others — **tact·ful** \-fəl\ *adj* — **tact·ful·ly** \-ē\ *adv* — **tact·less** *adj* — **tact·less·ly** *adv*

tac·tic \'tak-tik\ *n* : a planned action for accomplishing an end

tac·tics \'tak-tiks\ *n sing or pl* **1** : the science of maneuvering forces in combat **2** : the skill of using available means to reach an end — **tac·ti·cal** \-ti-kəl\ *adj* — **tac·ti·cian** \tak-'tish-ən\ *n*

tac·tile \'tak-t⁹l, -ˌtīl\ *adj* : of, relating to, or perceptible through the sense of touch

tad·pole \'tad-ˌpōl\ *n* [ME *taddepol*, fr. *tode* toad + *polle* head] : an aquatic larva of a frog or toad that has a tail and gills

tae kwon do \'tī-'kwän-'dō\ *n* : a Korean martial art resembling karate

taf·fe·ta \'taf-ət-ə\ *n* : a crisp lustrous fabric (as of silk or rayon)

taff·rail \'taf-ˌrāl, -rəl\ *n* : the rail around a ship's stern

taf·fy \'taf-ē\ *n, pl* **taffies** : a candy usu. of molasses or brown sugar stretched until porous and light-colored

¹tag \'tag\ *n* **1** : a metal or plastic binding on an end of a shoelace **2** : a piece of hanging or attached material **3** : a hackneyed quotation or saying **4** : a descriptive or identifying epithet

²tag *vb* **tagged; tag·ging** **1** : to provide or mark with or as if with a tag; *esp* : IDENTIFY **2** : to attach as an addition **3** : to follow closely and persistently ⟨∼s along everywhere we go⟩ **4** : to hold responsible for something

³tag *n* : a game in which one player chases others and tries to touch one of them

⁴tag *vb* **tagged; tag·ging** **1** : to touch in or as if in a game of tag **2** : SELECT

TAG *abbr* the adjutant general

tag sale *n* : GARAGE SALE

Ta·hi·tian \tə-'hē-shən\ *n* **1** : a native or inhabitant of Tahiti **2** : the Polynesian language of the Tahitians — **Tahitian** *adj*

tai·ga \'tī-gä\ *n* [Russ] : swampy coniferous northern forest (as of parts of Canada) beginning where the tundra ends

¹tail \'tāl\ *n* **1** : the rear end or a process extending from the rear end of an animal **2** : something resembling an animal's tail **3** *pl* : full evening dress for men **4** : the back, last, lower, or inferior part of something; *esp* : the reverse of a coin **5** : one who follows or keeps watch on someone — **tailed** \'tāld\ *adj* — **tail·less** \'tāl-ləs\ *adj*

²**tail** *vb* : FOLLOW; *esp* : to follow for the purpose of surveillance **syn** dog, shadow, trail, tag

tail·coat \-'kōt\ *n* : a coat with tails; *esp* : a man's full-dress coat with two long tapering skirts at the back

¹**tail·gate** \-,gāt\ *n* : a board or gate at the back end of a vehicle that can be let down (as for loading)

²**tailgate** *adj* : relating to or being a picnic set up on the tailgate esp. of a station wagon

³**tailgate** *vb* **tail·gat·ed; tail·gat·ing** : to drive dangerously close behind another vehicle

tail·light \-,līt\ *n* : a usu. red warning light mounted at the rear of a vehicle

¹**tai·lor** \'tā-lər\ *n* [ME *taillour*, fr. OF *tailleur*, fr. *taillier* to cut, fr. LL *taliare*, fr. L *talea* twig, cutting] : one whose occupation is making or altering garments

²**tailor** *vb* **1** : to make or fashion as the work of a tailor **2** : to make or adapt to suit a special purpose

tail pipe *n* : an outlet by which the exhaust gases are removed from an engine

tail·spin \'tāl-,spin\ *n* : a rapid descent or downward spiral

tail wind *n* : a wind blowing in the same general direction as the course of a moving airplane or ship

¹**taint** \'tānt\ *vb* **1** : to affect or become affected with something bad and esp. putrefaction **2** : CORRUPT, CONTAMINATE **syn** pollute, defile, soil

²**taint** *n* : a contaminating mark or influence

ta·ka \'täk-ə\ *n* — see MONEY table

¹**take** \'tāk\ *vb* **took** \'tuk\; **tak·en** \'tā-kən\; **tak·ing 1** : to get into one's hands or possession : GRASP, SEIZE **2** : CAPTURE; *also* : DEFEAT **3** : to obtain or secure for use **4** : to catch or attack through the effect of a sudden force or influence ⟨*taken* ill⟩ **5** : CAPTIVATE, DELIGHT **6** : to bring into a relation ⟨~ a wife⟩ **7** : REMOVE, SUBTRACT **8** : to pick out : CHOOSE **9** : ASSUME, UNDERTAKE

10 : RECEIVE, ACCEPT **11** : to use for transportation ⟨~ a bus⟩ **12** : to become impregnated with : ABSORB ⟨~s a dye⟩ **13** : to receive into one's body (as by eating) ⟨~ a pill⟩ **14** : ENDURE, UNDERGO **15** : to lead, carry, or cause to go along to another place **16** : NEED, REQUIRE **17** : to obtain as the result of a special procedure ⟨~ a snapshot⟩ **18** : to undertake and do, make, or perform ⟨~ a walk⟩ **19** : to take effect : ACT, OPERATE **syn** grab, clutch, snatch, seize, nab, grapple — **tak·er** *n* — **take advantage of 1** : to profit by **2** : EXPLOIT — **take after** : RESEMBLE — **take care** : to be careful — **take care of** : to care for : attend to — **take effect** : to become operative — **take exception** : OBJECT — **take for** : to suppose to be; *esp* : to mistake for — **take place** : HAPPEN — **take to 1** : to go to **2** : to apply or devote oneself to **3** : to conceive a liking for

²**take** *n* **1** : the number or quantity taken; *also* : PROCEEDS, RECEIPTS **2** : an act or the action of taking **3** : a television or movie scene filmed or taped at one time; *also* : a sound recording made at one time **4** : mental response

take·off \-,óf\ *n* **1** : IMITATION; *esp* : PARODY **2** : an act or instance of taking off

take off \'tāk-'óf\ *vb* **1** : REMOVE **2** : DEDUCT **3** : to set out : go away **4** : to leave the surface; *esp* : to begin flight

take on *vb* **1** : to begin to perform or deal with; *also* : to contend with as an opponent **2** : ENGAGE, HIRE **3** : to assume or acquire as or as if one's own **4** : to make an unusual show of one's feelings esp. of grief or anger

take over \'tāk-'ō-vər\ *vb* : to assume control or possession of or responsibility for — **take·over** \-,ō-vər\ *n*

take up *vb* **1** : PICK UP **2** : to begin to occupy **3** : to absorb or incorporate into itself ⟨plants *taking up* nutrients⟩ **4** : to begin to engage in ⟨*took up* jogging⟩ **5** : to make tighter or shorter ⟨*take up* the slack⟩

tak·ings \'tā-kiŋz\ *n pl* : receipts esp. of money

ta·la \'täl-ə\ *n, pl* **tala** — see MONEY table

talc \'talk\ *n* : a soft mineral with a soapy feel used esp. in making toilet powder (**tal·cum powder** \'tal-kəm-\)

tale \'tāl\ *n* **1** : a relation of a series of events **2** : a report of a confidential matter **3** : idle talk; *esp* : harmful gossip **4** : a usu. imaginative narrative **5** : FALSEHOOD **6** : COUNT, TALLY

tal·ent \'tal-ənt\ *n* **1** : an ancient unit of weight and value **2** : the natural endowments of a person **3** : a special often creative or artistic aptitude **4** : mental power : ABILITY **5** : a person of talent **syn** genius, gift, faculty, aptitude, knack — **tal·ent·ed** \-əd\ *adj*

ta·ler \'täl-ər\ *n* : any of numerous silver coins issued by German states from the 15th to the 19th centuries

tales·man \'tālz-mən\ *n* [ME *tales* talesmen, fr. ML *tales de circumstantibus* such (persons) of the bystanders; fr. the wording of the writ summoning them] : a person summoned for jury duty

tal·is·man \'tal-əs-mən, -əz-\ *n, pl* -**mans** [F *talisman* or Sp *talismán* or It *talismano*, fr. Ar *ṭilsam*, fr. MGk *telesma*, fr. Gk, consecration, fr. *telein* to initiate into the mysteries, complete, fr. *telos* end] : an object thought to act as a charm

¹talk \'tȯk\ *vb* **1** : to express in speech : utter words : SPEAK **2** : DISCUSS ⟨~ business⟩ **3** : to influence or cause by talking ⟨~ed him into agreeing⟩ **4** : to use (a language) for communicating **5** : CONVERSE **6** : to reveal confidential information; *also* : GOSSIP **7** : to give a talk : LECTURE — **talk·er** *n* — **talk back** : to answer impertinently

²talk *n* **1** : the act of talking **2** : a way of speaking **3** : a formal discussion **4** : REPORT, RUMOR **5** : the topic of comment or gossip ⟨the ~ of the town⟩ **6** : an informal address or lecture

talk·ative \'tȯ-kət-iv\ *adj* : given to talking **syn** loquacious, chatty, gabby, garrulous — **talk·ative·ly** *adv* — **talk·ative·ness** *n*

talk·ing–to \'tȯ-kiŋ-ˌtü\ *n* : REPRIMAND, REPROOF

tall \'tȯl\ *adj* **1** : high in stature; *also* : of a specified height ⟨six feet ~⟩ **2** : LARGE, FORMIDABLE ⟨a ~ order⟩ **3** : UNBELIEVABLE, IMPROBABLE ⟨a ~ story⟩ **syn** lofty, high — **tall·ness** *n*

tal·low \'tal-ō\ *n* : a hard white fat rendered usu. from cattle or sheep tissues and used esp. in soap and lubricants

¹tal·ly \'tal-ē\ *n, pl* **tallies** [ME *talye*, fr. ML *talea*, fr. L, twig, cutting] **1** : a device for visibly recording or accounting esp. business transactions **2** : a recorded account **3** : a corresponding part; *also* : CORRESPONDENCE

²tally *vb* **tal·lied; tal·ly·ing 1** : to mark on or as if on a tally **2** : to make a count of : RECKON; *also* : SCORE **3** : CORRESPOND, MATCH **syn** square, accord, harmonize, conform, jibe

tal·ly·ho \ˌtal-ē-'hō\ *n, pl* -**hos 1** : a call of a huntsman at sight of the fox **2** : a four-in-hand coach

Tal·mud \'täl-ˌmu̇d, 'tal-məd\ *n* [Heb *talmūdh*, lit., instruction] : the authoritative body of Jewish tradition — **Tal·mu·dic** \tal-'m(y)üd-ik, -'məd-; täl-'mu̇d-\ *adj* — **Tal·mud·ist** \'täl-ˌmu̇d-əst, 'tal-məd-\ *n*

tal·on \'tal-ən\ *n* : the claw of an animal and esp. of a bird of prey

ta·lus \'tā-ləs, 'tal-əs\ *n* : rock debris at the base of a cliff

tam \'tam\ *n* : TAM-O'-SHANTER

ta·ma·le \tə-'mäl-ē\ *n* [MexSp *tamales*, pl. of *tamal* tamale] : ground meat seasoned with chili, rolled in cornmeal dough, wrapped in corn husks, and steamed

tam·a·rack \'tam-ə-ˌrak\ *n* : a larch of the northern U.S. and Canada; *also* : its hard resinous wood

tam·a·rind \'tam-ə-rənd, -ˌrind\ *n* [Sp & Pg *tamarindo*, fr. Ar *tamr hindī*, lit., Indian date] : a tropical tree of the legume family with hard yellowish wood and feathery leaves; *also* : its acid brown fruit

tam·ba·la \täm-'bäl-ə\ *n, pl* -**la** *or* -**las** — see *kwacha* at MONEY table

tam·bou·rine \ˌtam-bə-'rēn\ *n* : a small shallow drum with loose disks at the sides played by shaking or striking with the hand

¹tame \'tām\ *adj* **tam·er; tam·est 1** : reduced from a state of native wildness esp. so as to be useful to man : DOMESTICATED **2** : made docile : SUBDUED **3** : lacking spirit or interest : INSIPID **syn** submissive, domestic, domesticated — **tame·ly** *adv* — **tame·ness** *n*

²tame *vb* **tamed; tam·ing 1** : to make or become tame; *also* : to subject (land) to cultivation **2** : HUMBLE, SUBDUE —

tam·able *or* **tame·able** \'tā-mə-bəl\ *adj* — **tame·less** *adj* — **tam·er** *n*

tam–o’–shan·ter \'tam-ə-ˌshant-ər\ *n* [fr. poem *Tam o’ Shanter* (1790) by Robert Burns †1796 Scot. poet] : a Scottish woolen cap with a wide flat circular crown and usu. a pompon in the center

tamp \'tamp\ *vb* : to drive down or in by a series of light blows

tam·per \'tam-pər\ *vb* **tam·pered; tam·per·ing** \-p(ə-)riŋ\ **1** : to carry on underhand negotiations (as by bribery) ⟨~ with a witness⟩ **2** : to interfere so as to weaken or change for the worse ⟨~ with a document⟩ **3** : to try foolish or dangerous experiments

tam·pon \'tam-ˌpän\ *n* : a plug (as of cotton) introduced into a cavity usu. to check bleeding or absorb secretions

¹tan \'tan\ *vb* **tanned; tan·ning 1** : to change (hide) into leather esp. by soaking in a liquid containing tannin **2** : to make or become brown (as by exposure to the sun) **3** : WHIP, THRASH

²tan *n* **1** : TANBARK; *also* : a tanning material **2** : a brown skin color induced by sun or weather **3** : a light yellowish brown color

³tan *abbr* tangent

tan·a·ger \'tan-i-jər\ *n* : any of numerous American passerine birds with brightly colored males

tan·bark \'tan-ˌbärk\ *n* : bark (as of oak or sumac) that is rich in tannin and used in tanning

¹tan·dem \'tan-dəm\ *n* [L, at last, at length (taken to mean “lengthwise”), fr. *tam* so] **1** : a 2-seated carriage with horses hitched tandem; *also* : its team **2** : a bicycle for two persons sitting one behind the other — **in tandem** : in a tandem arrangement

²tandem *adv* : one behind another

³tandem *adj* **1** : consisting of things arranged one behind the other **2** : working in conjunction with each other

tang \'taŋ\ *n* **1** : a part in a tool that connects the blade with the handle **2** : a sharp distinctive flavor; *also* : a pungent odor — **tangy** *adj*

¹tan·gent \'tan-jənt\ *adj* [L *tangent-, tangens*, prp. of *tangere* to touch] : TOUCHING; *esp* : meeting a curve or surface and not cutting it if extended

²tangent *n* **1** : a tangent line, curve, or surface **2** : an abrupt change of course — **tan·gen·tial** \tan-'jen-chəl\ *adj*

tan·ger·ine \'tan-jə-ˌrēn, ˌtan-jə-'rēn\ *n* : a deep orange loose-skinned citrus fruit; *also* : a tree that bears tangerines

¹tan·gi·ble \'tan-jə-bəl\ *adj* **1** : perceptible esp. by the sense of touch : PALPABLE **2** : substantially real : MATERIAL ⟨~ rewards⟩ **3** : capable of being appraised **syn** appreciable, perceptible, sensible, discernible — **tan·gi·bil·i·ty** \ˌtan-jə-'bil-ət-ē\ *n*

²tangible *n* : something tangible; *esp* : a tangible asset

¹tan·gle \'taŋ-gəl\ *vb* **tan·gled; tan·gling** \-g(ə-)liŋ\ **1** : to involve so as to hamper or embarrass; *also* : ENTRAP **2** : to unite or knit together in intricate confusion : ENTANGLE

²tangle *n* **1** : a tangled twisted mass (as of vines) **2** : a confusedly complicated state : MUDDLE

tan·go \'taŋ-gō\ *n, pl* **tangos** : a dance of Spanish-American origin — **tango** *vb*

tank \'taŋk\ *n* **1** : a large artificial receptacle for liquids **2** : a heavily armed and armored combat vehicle that moves on beltlike tracks — **tank·ful** *n*

tan·kard \'taŋ-kərd\ *n* : a tall one-handled drinking vessel

tank·er \'taŋ-kər\ *n* : a vehicle equipped for transporting a liquid

tank top *n* : a sleeveless collarless pullover shirt with shoulder straps

tank town *n* **1** : a town at which trains stop for water **2** : a small town

tan·ner \'tan-ər\ *n* : one that tans hides

tan·nery \'tan-(ə-)rē\ *n, pl* **-ner·ies** : a place where tanning is carried on

tan·nic acid \ˌtan-ik-\ *n* : TANNIN

tan·nin \'tan-ən\ *n* : any of various substances of plant origin used in tanning and dyeing, in inks, and as astringents

tan·sy \'tan-zē\ *n, pl* **tansies** [ME *tanesey*, fr. OF *tanesie*, fr. ML *athanasia*, fr. Gk, immortality, fr. *athanatos* immortal, fr. *a-* not + *thanatos* death] : a common weedy herb related to the daisies with an aromatic odor and very bitter taste

tan·ta·lize \'tant-ᵊl-ˌīz\ *vb* **-lized; -liz·ing** [fr. *Tantalus*, mythical Greek king punished in Hades by having to stand up to his chin in water that receded as he bent to drink] : to tease or torment by presenting something desirable but keeping it out of reach — **tan·ta·liz·er** *n* — **tan·ta·liz·ing·ly** *adv*

tan·ta·lum \\'tant-ᵊl-əm\\ *n* : a hard ductile acid-resisting chemical element

tan·ta·mount \\'tant-ə-ˌmaůnt\\ *adj* : equivalent in value or meaning **syn** same, equal, identical

tan·trum \\'tan-trəm\\ *n* : a fit of bad temper

Tan·za·ni·an \\ˌtan-zə-'nē-ən\\ *n* : a native or inhabitant of Tanzania — **Tanzanian** *adj*

Tao·ism \\'taů-ˌiz-əm, 'daů-\\ *n* : a religion developed from a Chinese mystic philosophy and Buddhist religion — **Tao·ist** \\-əst\\ *adj or n*

¹**tap** \\'tap\\ *n* **1** : FAUCET, COCK **2** : liquor drawn through a tap **3** : the removing of fluid from a container or cavity by tapping **4** : a tool for forming an internal screw thread **5** : a point in an electric circuit where a connection may be made

²**tap** *vb* **tapped; tap·ping 1** : to release or cause to flow by piercing or by drawing a plug from a container or cavity **2** : to pierce so as to let out or draw off a fluid **3** : to draw from ⟨∼ resources⟩ **4** : to cut in on (a telephone wire) to get information; *also* : to cut in (an electrical circuit) on another circuit **5** : to form an internal screw thread in by means of a tap **6** : to connect (as a gas or water main) with a local supply — **tap·per** *n*

³**tap** *vb* **tapped; tap·ping 1** : to rap lightly **2** : to make (as a hole) by repeated light blows **3** : to repair by putting a half sole on **4** : SELECT; *esp* : to elect to membership

⁴**tap** *n* **1** : a light blow or stroke; *also* : its sound **2** : a small metal plate for the sole or heel of a shoe

¹**tape** \\'tāp\\ *n* **1** : a narrow band of woven fabric **2** : a narrow flexible strip; *esp* : MAGNETIC TAPE

²**tape** *vb* **taped; tap·ing 1** : to fasten or support with tape **2** : to measure with a tape measure **3** : to record on magnetic tape

tape deck *n* : a device used to play back and often to record on magnetic tapes

that usu. has to be connected to a separate audio system

tape measure *n* : a tape marked off in units (as inches) for measuring

tape player *n* : a self-contained device for the playback of recorded magnetic tapes

¹**ta·per** \\'tā-pər\\ *n* **1** : a slender wax candle; *also* : a long waxed wick **2** : a gradual lessening of thickness or width in a long object ⟨the ∼ of a steeple⟩

²**taper** *vb* **ta·pered; ta·per·ing** \\'tā-p(ə-)riŋ\\ **1** : to make or become gradually smaller toward one end **2** : to diminish gradually

tape–re·cord \\ˌtāp-ri-'kȯrd\\ *vb* : to make a recording of on magnetic tape — **tape recorder** *n* — **tape recording** *n*

tap·es·try \\'tap-ə-strē\\ *n, pl* **-tries** : a heavy reversible textile that has designs or pictures woven into it and is used esp. as a wall hanging

tape·worm \\'tāp-ˌwərm\\ *n* : a long flat segmented worm that lives as a parasite in the intestines

tap·i·o·ca \\ˌtap-ē-'ō-kə\\ *n* : a usu. granular preparation of cassava starch used esp. in puddings; *also* : a dish (as pudding) that contains tapioca

ta·pir \\'tā-pər\\ *n, pl* **tapir** *or* **tapirs** : any of several large harmless hoofed mammals of tropical America and southeast Asia related to the horses

tap·pet \\'tap-ət\\ *n* : a lever or projection moved by some other piece (as a cam) or intended to tap or touch something else to cause a particular motion

tap·room \\'tap-ˌrüm, -ˌrům\\ *n* : BARROOM

tap·root \\-ˌrüt, -ˌrůt\\ *n* : a large main root growing vertically downward and giving off small lateral roots

taps \\'taps\\ *n sing or pl* : the last bugle call at night blown as a signal that lights are to be put out; *also* : a similar call blown at military funerals and memorial services

tap·ster \\'tap-stər\\ *n* : BARTENDER

¹**tar** \\'tär\\ *n* **1** : a thick dark sticky liquid distilled from organic material (as wood or coal) **2** : SAILOR, SEAMAN

²**tar** *vb* **tarred; tar·ring** : to smear with or as if with tar

tar·an·tel·la \ˌtar-ən-ˈtel-ə\ *n* : a lively folk dance of southern Italy in 6/8 time

ta·ran·tu·la \tə-ˈranch-(ə-)lə, -ˈrant-ᵊl-ə\ *n, pl* **tarantulas** *also* **ta·ran·tu·lae** \-ˈran-chə-ˌlē, -ˈrant-ᵊl-ˌē\ **1** : a large European spider once thought very dangerous **2** : any of a family of large hairy American spiders with a sharp bite that is not very poisonous to human beings

tar·dy \ˈtärd-ē\ *adj* **tar·di·er; -est 1** : moving slowly : SLUGGISH **2** : LATE; *also* : DILATORY **syn** behindhand, overdue, belated — **tar·di·ness** \-ē-nəs\ *n*

¹tare \ˈtaər\ *n* : a weed of fields where grain is grown

²tare *n* : a deduction from the gross weight of a substance and its container made in allowance for the weight of the container — **tare** *vb*

¹tar·get \ˈtär-gət\ *n* [ME, fr. MF *targette,* dim. of *targe* light shield, of Gmc origin] **1** : a mark to shoot at **2** : an object of ridicule or criticism **3** : a goal to be achieved

²target *vb* : to make a target of

tar·iff \ˈtar-əf\ *n* [It *tariffa,* fr. Ar *taʿrīf* notification] **1** : a schedule of duties imposed by a government esp. on imported goods; *also* : a duty or rate of duty imposed in such a schedule **2** : a schedule of rates or charges **syn** duty, toll, tax, levy, assessment

tar·mac \ˈtär-ˌmak\ *n* : a surface paved with crushed stone covered with tar

tarn \ˈtärn\ *n* : a small mountain lake

tar·nish \ˈtär-nish\ *vb* : to make or become dull or discolored — **tarnish** *n*

ta·ro \ˈtär-ō, ˈtar-\ *n, pl* **taros** : a tropical plant grown for its edible starchy fleshy root; *also* : this root

tar·ot \ˈtar-ō\ *n* : one of a set of 22 pictorial playing cards used esp. for fortune-telling

tar·pau·lin \tär-ˈpȯ-lən, ˈtär-pə-\ *n* : a piece of material (as waterproof canvas) used for protecting exposed objects

tar·pon \ˈtär-pən\ *n, pl* **tarpon** *or* **tarpons** : a large silvery sport fish common in warm coastal waters of the Atlantic esp. off Florida

tar·ra·gon \ˈtar-ə-gən\ *n* : a small European perennial wormwood with pungent aromatic foliage used as a flavoring

¹tar·ry \ˈtar-ē\ *vb* **tar·ried; tar·ry·ing 1** : to be tardy : DELAY; *esp* : to be slow in leaving **2** : to stay in or at a place : SOJOURN **syn** remain, wait, linger, abide

²tar·ry \ˈtär-ē\ *adj* : of, resembling, or smeared with tar

tar sand *n* : sand or sandstone that is naturally soaked with the heavy sticky portions of petroleum

tar·sus \ˈtär-səs\ *n, pl* **tar·si** \-ˌsī\ [NL] : the part of the foot of a vertebrate between the metatarsus and the leg; *also* : the small bones that support this part of the limb — **tar·sal** \-səl\ *adj or n*

¹tart \ˈtärt\ *adj* **1** : agreeably sharp to the taste : PUNGENT **2** : BITING, CAUSTIC **syn** sour, acid, acerb — **tart·ly** *adv* — **tart·ness** *n*

²tart *n* **1** : a small pie or pastry shell containing jelly, custard, or fruit **2** : PROSTITUTE

tar·tan \ˈtärt-ᵊn\ *n* : a twilled woolen fabric with a plaid design of Scottish origin consisting of stripes of varying width and color against a solid background

tar·tar \ˈtärt-ər\ *n* **1** : a substance in the juice of grapes deposited (as in wine casks) as a reddish crust or sediment **2** : a hard crust of saliva, debris, and calcium salts on the teeth

tar·tar sauce *or* **tar·tare sauce** \ˌtärt-ər-\ *n* : mayonnaise with chopped pickles, olives, or capers

¹task \ˈtask\ *n* [ME *taske,* fr. OF *tasque,* fr. ML *tasca* tax or service imposed by a feudal superior, fr. *taxare* to tax] : a piece of assigned work **syn** job, duty, chore, stint, assignment

²task *vb* : to oppress with great labor

task force *n* : a temporary grouping to accomplish a particular objective

task·mas·ter \ˈtask-ˌmas-tər\ *n* : one that imposes a task or burdens another with labor

¹tas·sel \ˈtas-əl, ˈtäs-\ *n* **1** : a hanging ornament made of a bunch of cords of even length fastened at one end **2** : something suggesting a tassel; *esp* : a male flower cluster of Indian corn

²tassel *vb* **-seled** *or* **-selled; -sel·ing** *or* **-sel·ling** \-(ə-)liŋ\ : to adorn with or put forth tassels

¹taste \ˈtāst\ *vb* **tast·ed; tast·ing 1** : EXPE-

RIENCE, UNDERGO **2** : to try or determine the flavor of by taking a bit into the mouth **3** : to eat or drink esp. in small quantities : SAMPLE **4** : to have a specific flavor

²taste *n* **1** : a small amount tasted **2** : BIT; *esp* : a sample of experience **3** : the special sense that identifies sweet, sour, bitter, or salty qualities and is mediated by receptors in the tongue **4** : a quality perceptible to the sense of taste; *also* : a complex sensation involving true taste, smell, and touch **5** : individual preference **6** : critical judgment, discernment, or appreciation; *also* : aesthetic quality **syn** tang, relish, flavor, savor — **taste·ful** \-fəl\ *adj* — **taste·ful·ly** \-ē\ *adv* — **taste·less** *adj* — **taste·less·ly** *adv* — **tast·er** *n*

taste bud *n* : a sense organ mediating the sensation of taste

tasty \'tā-stē\ *adj* **tast·i·er; -est** : pleasing to the taste : SAVORY **syn** palatable, appetizing, toothsome, flavorsome — **tast·i·ness** \'tā-stē-nəs\ *n*

tat \'tat\ *vb* **tat·ted; tat·ting** : to work at or make by tatting

¹tat·ter \'tat-ər\ *vb* : to make or become ragged

²tatter *n* **1** : a part torn and left hanging **2** *pl* : tattered clothing

tat·ter·de·ma·lion \ˌtat-ərd-i-'māl-yən\ *n* : one that is ragged or disreputable

tat·ter·sall \'tat-ər-ˌsȯl, -səl\ *n* : a pattern of colored lines forming squares on solid background; *also* : a fabric in a tattersall pattern

tat·ting \'tat-iŋ\ *n* : a delicate handmade lace formed usu. by looping and knotting with a single thread and a small shuttle; *also* : the act or process of making such lace

tat·tle \'tat-ᵊl\ *vb* **tat·tled; tat·tling** \'tat-(ᵊ-)liŋ\ **1** : CHATTER, PRATE **2** : to tell secrets; *also* : to inform against another — **tat·tler** \'tat-(ᵊ-)lər\ *n*

tat·tle·tale \'tat-ᵊl-ˌtāl\ *n* : one that tattles : INFORMER

¹tat·too \ta-'tü\ *n, pl* **tattoos** [alter. of earlier *taptoo*, fr. D *taptoe*, fr. the phrase *tap toe!* taps shut!] **1** : a call sounded before taps as notice to go to quarters **2** : a rapid rhythmic rapping

²tattoo *vb* : to mark (the skin) with tattoos

³tattoo *n, pl* **tattoos** [Tahitian *tatau*] : an indelible figure fixed upon the body esp. by insertion of pigment under the skin

taught past and past part of TEACH

¹taunt \'tȯnt\ *n* : a sarcastic challenge or insult

²taunt *vb* : to reproach or challenge in a mocking manner : jeer at **syn** mock, deride, ridicule, twit — **taunt·er** *n*

taupe \'tōp\ *n* : a brownish gray

Tau·rus \'tȯr-əs\ *n* [L, lit., bull] **1** : a zodiacal constellation between Aries and Gemini usu. pictured as a bull **2** : the 2d sign of the zodiac in astrology; *also* : one born under this sign

taut \'tȯt\ *adj* **1** : tightly drawn : not slack **2** : extremely nervous : TENSE **3** : TRIM, TIDY ⟨a ~ ship⟩ — **taut·ly** *adv* — **taut·ness** *n*

tau·tol·o·gy \tȯ-'täl-ə-jē\ *n, pl* **-gies** : needless repetition of an idea, statement, or word; *also* : an instance of such repetition — **tau·to·log·i·cal** \ˌtȯt-ᵊl-'äj-i-kəl\ *adj* — **tau·to·log·i·cal·ly** \-i-k(ə-)lē\ *adv* — **tau·tol·o·gous** \tȯ-'täl-ə-gəs\ *adj* — **tau·tol·o·gous·ly** *adv*

tav·ern \'tav-ərn\ *n* [ME *taverne*, fr. OF, fr. L *taberna*, lit., hut, shop] **1** : an establishment where alcoholic liquors are sold to be drunk on the premises **2** : INN

taw \'tȯ\ *n* **1** : a marble used as a shooter **2** : the line from which players shoot at marbles

taw·dry \'tȯ-drē\ *adj* **taw·dri·er; -est** [fr. *tawdry lace* (a tie of lace for the neck), fr. *St. Audrey* (St. Etheldreda) †679 queen of Northumbria] : cheap and gaudy in appearance and quality **syn** garish, flashy, chintzy, meretricious — **taw·dri·ly** *adv*

taw·ny \'tȯ-nē\ *adj* **taw·ni·er; -est** : of a brownish orange color

¹tax \'taks\ *vb* **1** : to levy a tax on **2** : CHARGE, ACCUSE **3** : to put under pressure — **tax·able** \'tak-sə-bəl\ *adj* — **tax·a·tion** \tak-'sā-shən\ *n*

²tax *n* **1** : a charge usu. of money imposed by authority on persons or property for public purposes **2** : a heavy charge : STRAIN **syn** assessment, levy, duty, tariff

¹taxi \'tak-sē\ *n, pl* **tax·is** \-sēz\ *also* **tax·ies** : TAXICAB; *also* : a similarly operated boat or airplane

²taxi *vb* **tax·ied; taxi·ing** *or* **taxy·ing; tax·is**

or **tax•ies 1** : to move along the ground or on the water under an airplane's own power when starting or after a landing **2** : to go by taxicab

taxi•cab \'tak-sē-ˌkab\ *n* : an automobile that carries passengers for a fare usu. based on the distance traveled

taxi•der•my \'tak-sə-ˌdər-mē\ *n* : the art of preparing, stuffing, and mounting skins of animals — **taxi•der•mist** \-məst\ *n*

tax•on•o•my \tak-'sän-ə-mē\ *n* : classification esp. of animals or plants according to natural relationships — **tax•o•nom•ic** \ˌtak-sə-'näm-ik\ *adj* — **tax•on•o•mist** \tak-'sän-ə-məst\ *n*

tax•pay•er \'taks-ˌpā-ər\ *n* : one who pays or is liable for a tax — **tax•pay•ing** \-iŋ\ *adj*

Tay–Sachs disease \'tā-'saks-\ *n* : a fatal hereditary disease caused by the absence of an enzyme needed to break down fatty material and characterized by a buildup of lipids in the nervous tissue

tb *abbr* tablespoon; tablespoonful

Tb *symbol* terbium

TB \(')tē-'bē\ *n* : TUBERCULOSIS

TBA *abbr, often not cap* to be announced

T–bar lift \ˌtē-ˌbär-\ *n* : a chair lift with a series of T-shaped bars

tbs *or* **tbsp** *abbr* tablespoon; tablespoonful

Tc *symbol* technetium

TC *abbr* teachers college

T cell *n* : a lymphocyte specialized esp. for promoting immunity (as against viruses and in the rejection of foreign tissues) or for helping make antibodies

TD *abbr* **1** touchdown **2** Treasury Department

TDY *abbr* temporary duty

Te *symbol* tellurium

tea \'tē\ *n* **1** : the cured leaves and leaf buds of a shrub grown chiefly in China, Japan, India, and Sri Lanka; *also* : this shrub **2** : a drink made by steeping tea in boiling water **3** : refreshments usu. including tea served in late afternoon; *also* : a reception at which tea is served

teach \'tēch\ *vb* **taught** \'tȯt\; **teach•ing** **1** : to cause to know a subject : act as a teacher **2** : to show how 〈~ a child to swim〉 **3** : to make to know the disagreeable consequences of an action **4** : to guide the studies of **5** : to impart the knowledge of 〈~ algebra〉 — **teach•able** *adj* — **teach•er** *n*

teach•ing \-iŋ\ *n* **1** : the act, practice, or profession of a teacher **2** : something taught; *esp* : DOCTRINE

tea•cup \'tē-ˌkəp\ *n* : a small cup used with a saucer for hot beverages

teak \'tēk\ *n* : a tall East Indian timber tree; *also* : its hard durable yellowish brown wood

tea•ket•tle \'tē-ˌket-ᵊl\ *n* : a covered kettle with a handle and spout for boiling water

teal \'tēl\ *n, pl* **teal** *or* **teals** : any of several small short-necked wild ducks

¹team \'tēm\ *n* [ME *teme*, fr. OE *tēam* offspring, lineage, group of draft animals] **1** : two or more draft animals harnessed to the same vehicle or implement **2** : a number of persons associated in work or activity; *esp* : a group on one side in a match — **team•mate** \'tēm-ˌmāt\ *n*

²team *vb* **1** : to haul with or drive a team **2** : to form a team : join forces

³team *adj* : of or performed by a team

team•ster \'tēm-stər\ *n* : one that drives a team or truck

team•work \-ˌwərk\ *n* : the work or activity of a number of persons acting in close association as members of a unit

tea•pot \'tē-ˌpät\ *n* : a vessel with a spout for brewing and serving tea

¹tear \'tiər\ *n* : a drop of the salty liquid that moistens the eye and inner side of the eyelids — **tear•ful** \-fəl\ *adj* — **tear•ful•ly** \-ē\ *adv*

²tear \'taər\ *vb* **tore** \'tȯr\; **torn** \'tȯrn\; **tear•ing** **1** : to separate parts of or pull apart by force : REND **2** : LACERATE **3** : to disrupt by the pull of contrary forces **4** : to remove by force : WRENCH **5** : to move or act with violence, haste, or force **syn** rip, split, cleave, rend

³tear \'taər\ *n* **1** : the act of tearing **2** : a hole or flaw made by tearing : RENT

tear gas \'tiər-\ *n* : a substance that on dispersion in the atmosphere blinds the eyes with tears — **tear gas** *vb*

tear•jerk•er \'tiər-ˌjər-kər\ *n* : an extravagantly pathetic story, song, play, movie, or broadcast

¹tease \'tēz\ *vb* **teased; teas·ing 1 :** to disentangle and lay parallel by combing or carding ⟨~ wool⟩ **2 :** to scratch the surface of (cloth) so as to raise a nap **3 :** to annoy persistently esp. in fun by goading, coaxing, or tantalizing **4 :** to comb (hair) by taking a strand and pushing the short hairs toward the scalp with the comb **syn** harass, worry, pester, annoy

²tease *n* **1 :** the act of teasing or state of being teased **2 :** one that teases

tea·sel *also* **tea·zel** *or* **tea·zle** \'tē-zəl\ *n* **:** a prickly herb or its flower head covered with stiff bracts and used to raise the nap on cloth; *also* **:** an artificial device used for this purpose

tea·spoon \'tē-ˌspün\ *n* **1 :** a small spoon suitable for stirring beverages **2 :** TEASPOONFUL

tea·spoon·ful \-ˌfùl\ *n, pl* **-spoonfuls** *also* **-spoons·ful** \-ˌspünz-ˌfùl\ **:** a unit of measure equal to one-sixth fluidounce (about 5 milliliters) or one third of a tablespoonful

teat \'tit, 'tēt\ *n* **:** the protuberance through which milk is drawn from an udder or breast

tech *abbr* **1** technical; technically; technician **2** technological; technology

tech·ne·tium \tek-'nē-sh(ē-)əm\ *n* **:** a metallic chemical element produced in certain nuclear reactions

tech·nic \'tek-nik, tek-'nēk\ *n* **:** TECHNIQUE 1

tech·ni·cal \'tek-ni-kəl\ *adj* [Gk *technikos* of art, skillful, fr. *technē* art, craft, skill] **1 :** having special knowledge esp. of a mechanical or scientific subject ⟨~ experts⟩ **2 :** of or relating to a particular and esp. a practical or scientific subject ⟨~ training⟩ **3 :** according to a strict interpretation of the rules **4 :** of or relating to technique — **tech·ni·cal·ly** \-k(ə-)lē\ *adv*

tech·ni·cal·i·ty \ˌtek-nə-'kal-ət-ē\ *n, pl* **-ties 1 :** a detail meaningful only to a specialist **2 :** the quality or state of being technical

technical sergeant *n* **:** a noncommissioned officer in the air force ranking next below a master sergeant

tech·ni·cian \tek-'nish-ən\ *n* **:** a person who has acquired the technique of a specialized skill or subject

tech·nique \tek-'nēk\ *n* [F] **1 :** the manner in which technical details are treated or basic physical movements are used **2 :** technical methods

tech·noc·ra·cy \tek-'näk-rə-sē\ *n* **:** management of society by technical experts — **tech·no·crat** \'tek-nə-ˌkrat\ *n* — **tech·no·crat·ic** \ˌtek-nə-'krat-ik\ *adj*

tech·nol·o·gy \tek-'näl-ə-jē\ *n, pl* **-gies :** applied science; *also* **:** a technical method of achieving a practical purpose — **tech·no·log·i·cal** \ˌtek-nə-'läj-i-kəl\ *adj*

tec·ton·ics \tek-'tän-iks\ *n sing or pl* **1 :** geological structural features **2 :** geology dealing with faulting and folding **3 :** DIASTROPHISM — **tec·ton·ic** \-ik\ *adj*

ted·dy bear \'ted-ē-ˌbaər\ *n* [*Teddy* Roosevelt, fr. a cartoon depicting the president sparing the life of a bear cub while hunting] **:** a stuffed toy bear

te·dious \'tēd-ē-əs, 'tē-jəs\ *adj* **:** tiresome because of length or dullness **syn** boring, tiring, irksome — **te·dious·ly** *adv* — **te·dious·ness** *n*

te·di·um \'tēd-ē-əm\ *n* **:** TEDIOUSNESS; *also* **:** BOREDOM

¹tee \'tē\ *n* **:** a small mound or peg on which a golf ball is placed to be hit at the beginning of play on a hole; *also* **:** the area from which the ball is hit to begin play

²tee *vb* **teed; tee·ing :** to place (a ball) on a tee

teem \'tēm\ *vb* **:** to become filled to overflowing **:** ABOUND **syn** swarm, crawl, flow

teen *adj* **:** TEENAGE

teen·age \'tēn-ˌāj\ *or* **teen·aged** \-ˌājd\ *adj* **:** of, being, or relating to people in their teens — **teen·ag·er** \-ˌā-jər\ *n*

teens \'tēnz\ *n pl* **:** the numbers 13 to 19 inclusive; *esp* **:** the years 13 to 19 in a person's life

tee·ny \'tē-nē\ *adj* **tee·ni·er; -est :** TINY

tee·pee *var of* TEPEE

tee shirt *var of* T-SHIRT

tee·ter \'tēt-ər\ *vb* **1 :** to move unsteadily **2 :** SEESAW — **teeter** *n*

teeth *pl of* TOOTH

teethe \'tēth\ *vb* **teethed; teeth·ing :** to grow teeth **:** cut one's teeth

teeth·ing \'tē-thiŋ\ *n* **:** the process of growth of the first set of teeth through the gums with its accompanying phenomena

tee•to•tal \'tē-'tōt-ᵊl, -₁tōt-\ *adj* : of or relating to the practice of complete abstinence from alcoholic drinks — **tee•to•tal•er** *or* **tee•to•tal•ler** \-'tōt-ᵊl-ər\ *n* — **tee•to•tal•ism** \-ᵊl-₁iz-əm\ *n*

TEFL *abbr* teaching English as a foreign language

tek•tite \'tek-₁tīt\ *n* : a glassy body of probably meteoric origin

tel *abbr* **1** telegram **2** telegraph **3** telephone

tele•cast \'tel-i-₁kast\ *vb* **-cast** *also* **-casted; -cast•ing** : to broadcast by television — **telecast** *n* — **tele•cast•er** *n*

tele•com•mu•ni•ca•tion \₁tel-i-kə-₁myü-nə-'kā-shən\ *n* : communication at a distance (as by telephone or radio)

tele•con•fer•ence \'tel-i-₁kän-f(ə-)rəns\ *n* : a conference among people remote from one another held using telecommunications — **tele•con•fer•enc•ing** *n*

teleg *abbr* telegraphy

tele•gen•ic \₁tel-ə-'jen-ik, -'jēn-\ *adj* : markedly attractive to television viewers

tele•gram \'tel-ə-₁gram\ *n* : a message sent by telegraph

¹**tele•graph** \-₁graf\ *n* : an electric apparatus or system for sending messages by a code over wires — **tele•graph•ic** \₁tel-ə-'graf-ik\ *adj*

²**telegraph** *vb* : to send or communicate by or as if by telegraph — **te•leg•ra•pher** \tə-'leg-rə-fər\ *n*

te•leg•ra•phy \tə-'leg-rə-fē\ *n* : the use or operation of a telegraph apparatus or system

te•lem•e•try \tə-'lem-ə-trē\ *n* : the transmission esp. by radio of measurements made by automatic instruments to a distant station — **tele•me•ter** \'tel-ə-₁mēt-ər\ *n*

te•lep•a•thy \tə-'lep-ə-thē\ *n* : apparent communication from one mind to another by extrasensory means — **tele•path•ic** \₁tel-ə-'path-ik\ *adj* — **tele•path•i•cal•ly** \-i-k(ə-)lē\ *adv*

¹**tele•phone** \'tel-ə-₁fōn\ *n* : an instrument for transmitting and receiving sounds over long distances by electricity

²**telephone** *vb* **-phoned; -phon•ing 1** : to send or communicate by telephone **2**

: to speak to (a person) by telephone — **tele•phon•er** *n*

te•le•pho•ny \tə-'lef-ə-nē, 'tel-ə-₁fō-\ *n* : use or operation of apparatus for transmission of sounds between distant points — **tel•e•phon•ic** \₁tel-ə-'fän-ik\ *adj*

tele•pho•to \₁tel-ə-'fōt-ō\ *adj* : being a camera lens giving a large image of a distant object — **tele•pho•to•graph•ic** \-₁fōt-ə-'graf-ik\ *adj* — **tele•pho•tog•ra•phy** \-fə-'täg-rə-fē\ *n*

tele•play \'tel-i-₁plā\ *n* : a play written for television

tele•print•er \'tel-ə-₁print-ər\ *n* : TELETYPEWRITER

¹**tele•scope** \'tel-ə-₁skōp\ *n* : a cylindrical instrument equipped with lenses or mirrors for viewing distant objects

²**telescope** *vb* **-scoped; -scop•ing 1** : to slide or pass or cause to slide or pass one within another like the sections of a hand telescope **2** : COMPRESS, CONDENSE

tele•scop•ic \₁tel-ə-'skäp-ik\ *adj* **1** : of or relating to a telescope **2** : seen only by a telescope **3** : able to discern objects at a distance **4** : having parts that telescope — **tele•scop•i•cal•ly** \-i-k(ə-)lē\ *adv*

tele•text \'tel-ə-₁tekst\ *n* : an electronic system in which printed matter is broadcast by a television station and displayed on a subscriber's television set having a decoder

tele•thon \'tel-ə-₁thän\ *n* : a long television program usu. to solicit funds for a charity

tele•type•writ•er \₁tel-ə-'tīp-₁rīt-ər\ *n* : a printing device resembling a typewriter used to send and receive signals over telephone lines

tele•vise \'tel-ə-₁vīz\ *vb* **-vised; -vis•ing** : to pick up and usu. broadcast by television

tele•vi•sion \'tel-ə-₁vizh-ən\ *n* [F *télévision*, fr. Gk *tēle* far, at a distance + F *vision* vision] : transmission and reproduction of images by a device that converts light waves into radio waves and then converts these back into visible light rays

tell \'tel\ *vb* **told** \'tōld\; **tell•ing 1** : COUNT, ENUMERATE **2** : to relate in detail : NARRATE **3** : SAY, UTTER **4** : to make known : REVEAL **5** : to report to

: INFORM **6** : ORDER, DIRECT **7** : to ascertain by observing **8** : to have a marked effect **9** : to serve as evidence **syn** reveal, disclose, discover, betray

tell·er \\'tel-ər\\ *n* **1** : one that relates : NARRATOR **2** : one that counts **3** : a bank employee handling money received or paid out

tell·ing \\'tel-iŋ\\ *adj* : producing a marked effect : EFFECTIVE **syn** cogent, convincing, sound

tell off *vb* : REPRIMAND, SCOLD

tell·tale \\'tel-ˌtāl\\ *n* **1** : INFORMER, TATTLETALE **2** : something that serves to disclose : INDICATION — **telltale** *adj*

tel·lu·ri·um \\tə-'lùr-ē-əm\\ *n* : a chemical element that resembles sulfur in properties

te·mer·i·ty \\tə-'mer-ət-ē\\ *n, pl* **-ties** : rash or presumptuous daring : BOLDNESS **syn** audacity, effrontery, gall, nerve, cheek

temp *abbr* **1** temperature **2** temporary

¹tem·per \\'tem-pər\\ *vb* **tem·pered; tem·per·ing** \\-p(ə-)riŋ\\ **1** : to dilute or soften by the addition of something else ⟨~ justice with mercy⟩ **2** : to bring (as steel) to a desired hardness by reheating and cooling **3** : to toughen (glass) by gradual heating and cooling **4** : TOUGHEN **5** : TUNE

²temper *n* **1** : characteristic tone : TENDENCY **2** : the hardness or toughness of a substance ⟨~ of a knife blade⟩ **3** : a characteristic frame of mind : DISPOSITION **4** : calmness of mind : COMPOSURE **5** : state of feeling or frame of mind at a particular time **6** : heat of mind or emotion **syn** temperament, character, personality, makeup

tem·pera \\'tem-pə-rə\\ *n* [It] : a painting process using an albuminous or colloidal medium as a vehicle; *also* : a painting done in tempera

tem·per·a·ment \\'tem-p(ə-)rə-mənt\\ *n* **1** : characteristic or habitual inclination or mode of emotional response : DISPOSITION ⟨nervous ~⟩ **2** : excessive sensitiveness or irritability **syn** character, personality, nature, makeup — **tem·per·a·men·tal** \\ˌtem-p(ə-)rə-'ment-ᵊl\\ *adj*

tem·per·ance \\'tem-p(ə-)rəns\\ *n* : habitual moderation in the indulgence of the appetites or passions; *esp*

: moderation in or abstinence from the use of intoxicating drink

tem·per·ate \\'tem-p(ə-)rət\\ *adj* **1** : not extreme or excessive : MILD **2** : moderate in indulgence of appetite or desire **3** : moderate in the use of intoxicating liquors **4** : having a moderate climate **syn** sober, continent, abstemious

temperate zone *n, often cap T&Z* : the region between the tropic of Cancer and the arctic circle or between the tropic of Capricorn and the antarctic circle

tem·per·a·ture \\'tem-pər-ˌchùr, -p(ə-)rə-ˌchùr, -chər\\ *n* **1** : degree of hotness or coldness of something (as air, water, or the body) as shown by a thermometer **2** : FEVER

tem·pest \\'tem-pəst\\ *n* [ME, fr. OF *tempeste*, fr. L *tempestas* season, weather, storm, fr. *tempus* time] : a violent wind esp. with rain, hail, or snow

tem·pes·tu·ous \\tem-'pes-chə-wəs\\ *adj* : of, involving, or resembling a tempest : STORMY — **tem·pes·tu·ous·ly** *adv* — **tem·pes·tu·ous·ness** *n*

tem·plate *also* **tem·plet** \\'tem-plət\\ *n* : a gauge, mold, or pattern used as a guide to the form of a piece being made

¹tem·ple \\'tem-pəl\\ *n* **1** : an edifice for the worship of a deity **2** : a place devoted to a special or exalted purpose

²temple *n* : the flattened space on each side of the forehead esp. of man

tem·po \\'tem-pō\\ *n, pl* **tem·pi** \\-(ˌ)pē\\ *or* **tempos** [It, lit., time] **1** : the rate of speed of a musical piece or passage **2** : rate of motion or activity : PACE

¹tem·po·ral \\'tem-p(ə-)rəl\\ *adj* **1** : of, relating to, or limited by time ⟨~ and spatial bounds⟩ **2** : of or relating to earthly life or secular concerns ⟨~ power⟩ **syn** profane, secular, lay

²temporal *adj* : of or relating to the temples or the sides of the skull

¹tem·po·rary \\'tem-pə-ˌrer-ē\\ *adj* : lasting for a time only : TRANSITORY **syn** transient, ephemeral, momentary, impermanent — **tem·po·rar·i·ly** \\ˌtem-pə-'rer-ə-lē\\ *adv*

²temporary *n, pl* **-rar·ies** : one serving for a limited time

tem·po·rize \\'tem-pə-ˌrīz\\ *vb* **-rized; -riz·ing** **1** : to adapt one's actions to the time or the dominant opinion : COMPROMISE **2** : to draw out matters so as to gain time — **tem·po·riz·er** *n*

tempt \'tempt\ *vb* **1** : to entice to do wrong by promise of pleasure or gain **2** : PROVOKE **3** : to risk the dangers of **4** : to induce to do something : INCITE **syn** inveigle, decoy, seduce, lure — **tempt·er** *n* — **tempt·ing·ly** *adv*

temp·ta·tion \temp-'tā-shən\ *n* **1** : the act of tempting : the state of being tempted **2** : something that tempts

tempt·ress \'temp-trəs\ *n* : a woman who tempts

ten \'ten\ *n* **1** : one more than nine **2** : the 10th in a set or series **3** : something having 10 units — **ten** *adj or pron* — **tenth** \'tenth\ *adj or adv or n*

ten·a·ble \'ten-ə-bəl\ *adj* : capable of being held, maintained, or defended — **ten·a·bil·i·ty** \,ten-ə-'bil-ət-ē\ *n*

te·na·cious \tə-'nā-shəs\ *adj* **1** : not easily pulled apart : COHESIVE, TOUGH ⟨steel is a ∼ metal⟩ **2** : holding fast ⟨∼ of his rights⟩ **3** : RETENTIVE ⟨∼ memory⟩ — **te·na·cious·ly** *adv* — **te·nac·i·ty** \tə-'nas-ət-ē\ *n*

ten·an·cy \'ten-ən-sē\ *n, pl* **-cies** : the temporary possession or occupancy of something (as a house) that belongs to another; *also* : the period of a tenant's occupancy

ten·ant \'ten-ənt\ *n* **1** : one who rents or leases (as a house) from a landlord **2** : DWELLER, OCCUPANT — **tenant** *vb* — **ten·ant·less** *adj*

tenant farmer *n* : a farmer who works land owned by another and pays rent either in cash or in shares of produce

ten·ant·ry \'ten-ən-trē\ *n, pl* **-ries** : the body of tenants esp. on a great estate

Ten Commandments *n pl* : the commandments of God given to Moses on Mount Sinai

¹tend \'tend\ *vb* **1** : to apply oneself ⟨∼ to your affairs⟩ **2** : to take care of ⟨∼ a plant⟩ **3** : to manage the operations of ⟨∼ a machine⟩ **syn** mind, watch, attend

²tend *vb* **1** : to move or develop one's course in a particular direction **2** : to show an inclination or tendency

ten·den·cy \'ten-dən-sē\ *n, pl* **-cies** **1** : DRIFT, TREND **2** : a proneness to or readiness for a particular kind of thought or action : PROPENSITY **syn**

bent, leaning, disposition, inclination

ten·den·tious \ten-'den-chəs\ *adj* : marked by a tendency in favor of a particular point of view : BIASED — **ten·den·tious·ly** *adv* — **ten·den·tious·ness** *n*

¹ten·der \'ten-dər\ *adj* **1** : having a soft texture : easily broken, chewed, or cut **2** : physically weak : DELICATE; *also* : IMMATURE **3** : expressing or responsive to love or sympathy : LOVING, COMPASSIONATE **4** : SENSITIVE, TOUCHY **syn** sympathetic, warm, warmhearted — **ten·der·ly** *adv* — **ten·der·ness** *n*

²tender *n* **1** : an offer or proposal made for acceptance; *esp* : an offer of a bid for a contract **2** : something (as money) that may be offered in payment

³tender *vb* : to present for acceptance

⁴tend·er \'ten-dər\ *n* **1** : one that tends or takes care **2** : a boat carrying passengers and freight to a larger ship **3** : a car attached to a steam locomotive for carrying fuel and water

ten·der·foot \'ten-dər-,fut\ *n, pl* **-feet** \-,fēt\ *also* **-foots** \-,futs\ **1** : one not hardened to frontier or rough outdoor life **2** : an inexperienced beginner : NEOPHYTE

ten·der·heart·ed \,ten-dər-'härt-əd\ *adj* : easily moved to love, pity, or sorrow : COMPASSIONATE

ten·der·ize \'ten-də-,rīz\ *vb* **-ized; -iz·ing** : to make (meat) tender — **ten·der·iz·er** \'ten-də-,rī-zər\ *n*

ten·der·loin \'ten-dər-,loin\ *n* **1** : a tender strip of beef or pork from near the backbone **2** : a district of a city largely devoted to vice

ten·di·ni·tis *or* **ten·don·itis** \,ten-də-'nīt-əs\ *n* : inflammation of a tendon

ten·don \'ten-dən\ *n* : a tough cord of dense tissue uniting a muscle with another part (as a bone) — **ten·di·nous** \-də-nəs\ *adj*

ten·dril \'ten-drəl\ *n* : a slender coiling organ by which some climbing plants attach themselves to a support

ten·e·brous \'ten-ə-brəs\ *adj* : shut off from the light : GLOOMY, OBSCURE

ten·e·ment \'ten-ə-mənt\ *n* **1** : a house used as a dwelling **2** : a building divided into apartments for rent to families; *esp* : one meeting only minimum stan-

dards of safety and comfort **3** : APART-
MENT, FLAT

te·net \'ten-ət\ *n* [L, he holds, fr. *tenēre*
to hold] : one of the principles or doctrines held in common by members of
an organized group (as a church or
profession) **syn** doctrine, dogma, belief

ten·fold \'ten-,fōld, -'fōld\ *adj* : being
10 times as great or as many — **ten-
fold** \-'fōld\ *adv*

ten–gallon hat *n* : a wide-brimmed hat
with a large soft crown

Tenn *abbr* Tennessee

ten·nis \'ten-əs\ *n* : a game played with
a ball and racket on a court divided by
a net

ten·on \'ten-ən\ *n* : a projecting part in
a piece of material (as wood) for insertion into a mortise to make a joint

ten·or \'ten-ər\ *n* **1** : the general drift of
something spoken or written : PUR-
PORT **2** : the highest natural adult male
voice **3** : TREND, TENDENCY

ten·pen·ny \,ten-,pen-ē\ *adj* : amounting to, worth, or costing 10 pennies

tenpenny nail *n* : a nail three inches
(about 7.6 centimeters) long

ten·pin \'ten-,pin\ *n* : a bottle-shaped
bowling pin set in groups of 10 and
bowled at in a game **(tenpins)**

¹tense \'tens\ *n* [ME *tens* time, tense, fr.
MF, fr. L *tempus*] : distinction of
form of a verb to indicate the time of
the action or state

²tense *adj* **tens·er; tens·est** [L *tensus,* fr.
pp. of *tendere* to stretch] **1** : stretched
tight : TAUT **2** : feeling or marked by
nervous tension **syn** stiff, rigid, inflexible — **tense·ly** *adv* — **tense·ness** *n* —
ten·si·ty \'ten-sət-ē\ *n*

³tense *vb* **tensed; tens·ing** : to make or
become tense

ten·sile \'ten-səl, -,sīl\ *adj* : of or relating to tension ⟨~ strength⟩

ten·sion \'ten-chən\ *n* **1** : the act of
straining or stretching; *also* : the condition of being strained or stretched **2**
: a state of mental unrest often with
signs of bodily stress **3** : a state of
latent hostility or opposition **4** : VOLT-
AGE

ten–speed \'ten-,spēd\ *n* : a bicycle
with 10 possible combinations of
gears

¹tent \'tent\ *n* **1** : a collapsible shelter of

material stretched and supported by
poles **2** : a canopy placed over the
head and shoulders to retain vapors or
oxygen being medically administered

²tent *vb* **1** : to lodge in tents **2** : to cover
with or as if with a tent

ten·ta·cle \'tent-i-kəl\ *n* : any of the long
flexible projections about the head or
mouth (as of an insect, mollusk, or
fish) — **ten·ta·cled** \-kəld\ *adj* — **ten-
tac·u·lar** \ten-'tak-yə-lər\ *adj*

ten·ta·tive \'tent-ət-iv\ *adj* **1** : not fully
worked out or developed ⟨~ plans⟩ **2**
: HESITANT, UNCERTAIN ⟨a ~ smile⟩ —
ten·ta·tive·ly *adv*

ten·u·ous \'ten-yə-wəs\ *adj* **1** : not
dense : RARE ⟨a ~ fluid⟩ **2** : not thick
: SLENDER ⟨a ~ rope⟩ **3** : having little
substance : FLIMSY, WEAK ⟨~ influ-
ences⟩ **syn** thin, slim, slight — **te·nu·i-
ty** \te-'n(y)ü-ət-ē, tə-\ *n* — **ten·u·ous·ly**
\'ten-yə-wəs-lē\ *adv* — **ten·u·ous·ness**
n

ten·ure \'ten-yər\ *n* : the act, right,
manner, or period of holding something (as a landed property or a position)

ten·ured \'ten-yərd\ *adj* : having tenure
⟨~ faculty members⟩

te·o·sin·te \,tā-ō-'sint-ē\ *n* : a large annual grass of Mexico and Central
America closely related to maize

te·pee \'tē-(,)pē\ *n* [Dakota *tipi,* fr. *ti* to
dwell + *pi* to use for] : an American
Indian conical tent usu. of skins

tep·id \'tep-əd\ *adj* **1** : moderately
warm : LUKEWARM **2** : HALFHEARTED

te·qui·la \tə-'kē-lə, tā-\ *n* : a Mexican
liquor made from mescal

ter *abbr* **1** terrace **2** territory

ter·bi·um \'tər-bē-əm\ *n* : a metallic
chemical element

ter·cen·te·na·ry \,tər-,sen-'ten-ə-rē, tər-
'sent-ⁿn-,er-ē\ *n, pl* **-ries** : a 300th anniversary; *also* : its celebration —
tercentenary *adj*

ter·cen·ten·ni·al \,tər-,sen-'ten-ē-əl\ *adj
or n* : TERCENTENARY

te·re·do \tə-'rēd-ō, -'rad-\ *n, pl* **teredos**
or **te·red·i·nes** \-'red-ⁿn-,ēz\ [L] : SHIP-
WORM

¹term \'tərm\ *n* **1** : END, TERMINATION **2**
: DURATION; *esp* : a period of time
fixed esp. by law or custom **3** : a
mathematical expression connected
with another by a plus or minus sign;

also : any of the members of a ratio or of a series **4** : a word or expression that has a precise meaning in some uses or is limited to a particular subject or field **5** *pl* : PROVISIONS, CONDITIONS ⟨~s of a contract⟩ **6** *pl* : mutual relationship ⟨on good ~s⟩ **7** : AGREEMENT, CONCORD

²term *vb* : to apply a term to : CALL

ter•ma•gant \'tər-mə-gənt\ *n* : an overbearing or nagging woman : SHREW **syn** virago, vixen, scold

¹ter•mi•nal \'tər-mən-ᵊl\ *adj* : of, relating to, or forming an end, limit, or terminus **syn** final, concluding, last, latest

²terminal *n* **1** : EXTREMITY, END **2** : a device at the end of a wire or on electrical equipment for making a connection **3** : either end of a transportation line (as a railroad) with its offices and freight and passenger stations; *also* : a freight or passenger station **4** : a device connected to a communication network used to enter, receive, and display data

ter•mi•nate \'tər-mə-ˌnāt\ *vb* **-nat•ed; -nat•ing** : to bring or come to an end **syn** conclude, finish, complete — **ter•mi•na•ble** \-nə-bəl\ *adj* — **ter•mi•na•tion** \ˌtər-mə-'nā-shən\ *n* — **ter•mi•na•tor** \'tər-mə-ˌnāt-ər\ *n*

ter•mi•nol•o•gy \ˌtər-mə-'näl-ə-jē\ *n, pl* **-gies** : the technical or special terms used in a business, art, science, or special subject

ter•mi•nus \'tər-mə-nəs\ *n, pl* **-ni** \-ˌnī\ *or* **-nus•es** [L] **1** : final goal : END **2** : either end of a transportation line, travel route, pipeline, or canal; *also* : the station or city at such a place

ter•mite \'tər-ˌmīt\ *n* : any of a large group of pale soft-bodied social insects that feed on wood

tern \'tərn\ *n* : any of numerous small seabirds with narrow wings and often a black cap

ter•na•ry \'tər-nə-rē\ *adj* **1** : of, relating to, or proceeding by threes **2** : having or consisting of three elements or parts **3** : having a mathematical base of three ⟨a ~ logarithm⟩

terr *abbr* territory

¹ter•race \'ter-əs\ *n* **1** : a flat roof or open platform **2** : a level area next to a building **3** : an embankment with level top **4** : a bank or ridge on a slope to conserve moisture and soil **5** : a row of houses on raised land; *also* : a street with such a row of houses **6** : a strip of park in the middle of a street

²terrace *vb* **ter•raced; ter•rac•ing** : to form into a terrace or supply with terraces

ter•ra–cot•ta \ˌter-ə-'kät-ə\ *n* [It *terra cotta,* lit., baked earth] : a reddish brown earthenware used for vases and small statues

terra fir•ma \-'fər-mə\ *n* [NL] : solid ground

ter•rain \tə-'rān\ *n* : the surface features of an area of land ⟨a rough ~⟩

ter•ra in•cog•ni•ta \'ter-ə-ˌin-ˌkäg-'nēt-ə\ *n, pl* **ter•rae in•cog•ni•tae** \'ter-ˌī-ˌin-ˌkäg-'nē-tī\ [L] : an unexplored area or field of knowledge

ter•ra•pin \'ter-ə-pən\ *n* : any of various No. American edible turtles of fresh or brackish water

ter•rar•i•um \tə-'rar-ē-əm\ *n, pl* **-ia** \-ē-ə\ *or* **-i•ums** : a vivarium without standing water

ter•res•tri•al \tə-'res-t(r)ē-əl\ *adj* **1** : of or relating to the earth or its inhabitants **2** : living or growing on land ⟨~ plants⟩ **syn** mundane, earthly, worldly

ter•ri•ble \'ter-ə-bəl\ *adj* **1** : exciting terror : FEARFUL, DREADFUL ⟨~ weapons⟩ **2** : hard to bear : DISTRESSING ⟨a ~ situation⟩ **3** : extreme in degree : INTENSE ⟨~ heat⟩ **4** : of very poor quality : AWFUL ⟨a ~ play⟩ **syn** frightful, horrible, shocking, appalling — **ter•ri•bly** \-blē\ *adv*

ter•ri•er \'ter-ē-ər\ *n* [F (*chien*) *terrier,* lit., earth dog, fr. *terrier* of earth, fr. ML *terrarius,* fr. L *terra* earth] : any of various usu. small dogs orig. used by hunters to drive small game from holes

ter•rif•ic \tə-'rif-ik\ *adj* **1** : exciting terror **2** : EXTRAORDINARY, ASTOUNDING ⟨~ speed⟩ **3** : unusually good ⟨makes ~ chili⟩ **syn** terrible, frightful, dreadful, fearful, horrible, awful

ter•ri•fy \'ter-ə-ˌfī\ *vb* **-fied; -fy•ing** : to fill with terror : FRIGHTEN **syn** scare, terrorize, startle, alarm — **ter•ri•fy•ing•ly** *adv*

ter•ri•to•ri•al \ˌter-ə-'tōr-ē-əl\ *adj* **1** : of or relating to a territory ⟨~ government⟩ **2** : of or relating to an assigned area ⟨∼ commanders⟩

ter·ri·to·ry \'ter-ə-ˌtōr-ē\ *n, pl* **-ries 1** : a geographical area belonging to or under the jurisdiction of a governmental authority **2** : a part of the U.S. not included within any state but organized with a separate legislature **3** : REGION, DISTRICT; *also* : a region in which one feels at home **4** : a field of knowledge or interest **5** : an assigned area

ter·ror \'ter-ər\ *n* **1** : a state of intense fear : FRIGHT **2** : one that inspires fear **syn** panic, consternation, dread, alarm, dismay, horror, trepidation

ter·ror·ism \'ter-ər-ˌiz-əm\ *n* : the systematic use of terror esp. as a means of coercion — **ter·ror·ist** \-əst\ *adj or n*

ter·ror·ize \'ter-ər-ˌīz\ *vb* **-ized; -iz·ing 1** : to fill with terror : SCARE **2** : to coerce by threat or violence **syn** terrify, frighten, alarm, startle

ter·ry \'ter-ē\ *n, pl* **terries** : an absorbent fabric with a loose pile of uncut loops

terse \'tərs\ *adj* **ters·er; ters·est** [L *tersus* clean, neat, fr. pp. of *tergēre* to wipe off] : effectively brief : CONCISE — **terse·ly** *adv* — **terse·ness** *n*

ter·tia·ry \'tər-shē-ˌer-ē\ *adj* **1** : of third rank, importance, or value **2** *cap* : of, relating to, or being the earlier period of the Cenozoic era **3** : occurring in or being the third stage

Tertiary *n* : the Tertiary period

TESL *abbr* teaching English as a second language

tes·sel·late \'tes-ə-ˌlāt\ *vb* **-lat·ed; -lat·ing** : to form into or adorn with mosaic

¹test \'test\ *n* [ME, vessel in which metals were assayed, fr. MF, fr. L *testum* earthen vessel] **1** : a critical examination or evaluation : TRIAL **2** : a means or result of testing

²test *vb* **1** : to put to test : TRY, EXAMINE **2** : to undergo or score on tests ⟨an ore that ∼s high in gold⟩

tes·ta·ment \'tes-tə-mənt\ *n* **1** *cap* : either of two main divisions of the Bible **2** : EVIDENCE, WITNESS **3** : CREDO **4** : an act to determine the disposition of one's property after death : WILL — **tes·ta·men·ta·ry** \ˌtes-tə-'ment-(ə-)rē\ *adj*

tes·tate \'tes-ˌtāt, -tət\ *adj* : having left a valid will

tes·ta·tor \'tes-ˌtāt-ər, tes-'tāt-\ *n* : a person who dies leaving a valid will

tes·ta·trix \tes-'tā-triks\ *n* : a female testator

¹tes·ter \'tēs-tər, 'tes-\ *n* : a canopy over a bed, pulpit, or altar

²test·er \'tes-tər\ *n* : one that tests

tes·ti·cle \'tes-ti-kəl\ *n* : TESTIS

tes·ti·fy \'tes-tə-ˌfī\ *vb* **-fied; -fy·ing 1** : to make a statement based on personal knowledge or belief : bear witness **2** : to serve as evidence or proof **syn** attest, affirm

tes·ti·mo·ni·al \ˌtes-tə-'mō-nē-əl\ *n* **1** : a statement testifying to a person's good character or to the worth of something **2** : an expression of appreciation : TRIBUTE — **testimonial** *adj*

tes·ti·mo·ny \'tes-tə-ˌmō-nē\ *n, pl* **-nies 1** : a solemn declaration made by a witness under oath esp. in a court **2** : evidence based on observation or knowledge **3** : an outward sign : SYMBOL **syn** evidence, confirmation, proof, testament

tes·tis \'tes-təs\ *n, pl* **tes·tes** \'tes-ˌtēz\ [L, witness, testis] : an oval-shaped male reproductive organ which is usu. located in the scrotum, which produces and secretes various male hormones and esp. testosterone, and in which sperm are produced

tes·tos·ter·one \te-'stäs-tə-ˌrōn\ *n* : a male sex hormone that causes development of the male reproductive system and secondary sex character

test tube *n* : a glass tube closed at one end and used esp. in chemistry and biology

tes·ty \'tes-tē\ *adj* **tes·ti·er; -est** [ME *testif*, fr. Anglo-French (the French of medieval England), headstrong, fr. OF *teste* head, fr. LL *testa* skull, fr. L, shell] : marked by ill humor : easily annoyed

tet·a·nus \'tet-ᵊn-əs\ *n* : a disease caused by bacterial poisons and marked by stiffness and spasms of the muscles with locking of the jaws — **tet·a·nal** \-əl\ *adj*

tetchy \'tech-ē\ *adj* **tetchi·er; -est** : irritably or peevishly sensitive

¹tête–à–tête \'tāt-ə-ˌtāt\ *n* [F, lit., head

to head] : a private conversation between two persons

²tête–à–tête \ˌtāt-ə-ˈtāt\ *adv* : PRIVATELY, FAMILIARLY

³tête–à–tête \ˌtāt-ə-ˌtāt\ *adj* : being face-to-face : PRIVATE

¹teth·er \ˈteth-ər\ *n* 1 : a line by which something (as an animal or balloon) is fastened 2 : the limit of one's strength or resources

²tether *vb* : to fasten or restrain by or as if by a tether

tet·ra·eth·yl lead \ˌte-trə-ˌeth-əl-\ *n* : a heavy oily poisonous liquid used as an antiknock agent in gasoline

tet·ra·he·dron \-ˈhē-drən\ *n, pl* **-drons** *or* **-dra** \-drə\ : a polyhedron that has four faces — **tet·ra·he·dral** \-drəl\ *adj*

tet·ra·hy·dro·can·nab·i·nol \-ˌhī-drə-kə-ˈnab-ə-ˌnȯl, -ˌnōl\ *n* : THC

te·tram·e·ter \te-ˈtram-ət-ər\ *n* : a line consisting of four metrical feet

Teu·ton·ic \t(y)ü-ˈtän-ik\ *adj* : GERMANIC

Tex *abbr* Texas

text \ˈtekst\ *n* 1 : the actual words of an author's work 2 : the main body of printed or written matter on a page 3 : a scriptural passage chosen as the subject esp. of a sermon 4 : THEME, TOPIC 5 : TEXTBOOK — **tex·tu·al** \ˈteks-chə(-wə)l\ *adj*

text·book \ˈteks(t)-ˌbu̇k\ *n* : a book used in the study of a subject

tex·tile \ˈtek-ˌstīl, ˈteks-t⁹l\ *n* : CLOTH; *esp* : a woven or knit cloth

tex·ture \ˈteks-chər\ *n* 1 : the visual or tactile surface characteristics and appearance of something ⟨a coarse ∼⟩ 2 : essential part 3 : basic scheme or structure : FABRIC 4 : overall structure

TGIF *abbr* thank God it's Friday

¹Th *abbr* Thursday

²Th *symbol* thorium

¹-th — see ¹-ETH

²-th *or* **-eth** *adj suffix* — used in forming ordinal numbers ⟨hundred*th*⟩

³-th *n suffix* 1 : act or process 2 : state or condition ⟨dear*th*⟩

Thai \ˈtī\ *n, pl* **Thai** *or* **Thais** : a native or inhabitant of Thailand — **Thai** *adj*

thal·a·mus \ˈthal-ə-məs\ *n, pl* **-mi** \-ˌmī\ [NL] : a subdivision of the brain that receives nerve impulses and sends them to appropriate parts of the brain cortex

thal·li·um \ˈthal-ē-əm\ *n* : a poisonous metallic chemical element

¹than \thən, (ˈ)than\ *conj* 1 — used after a comparative adjective or adverb to introduce the second part of a comparison expressing inequality ⟨older ∼ I am⟩ 2 — used after *other* or a word of similar meaning to express a difference of kind, manner, or identity ⟨adults other ∼ parents⟩

²than *prep* : in comparison with ⟨older ∼ me⟩

thane \thān\ *n* 1 : a free retainer of an Anglo-Saxon lord 2 : a Scottish feudal lord

thank \ˈthaŋk\ *vb* : to express gratitude to ⟨∼*ed* him for the present⟩

thank·ful \ˈthaŋk-fəl\ *adj* 1 : conscious of benefit received 2 : expressive of thanks 3 : GLAD — **thank·ful·ly** \-ē\ *adv* — **thank·ful·ness** *n*

thank·less \ˈthaŋ-kləs\ *adj* 1 : UNGRATEFUL 2 : UNAPPRECIATED

thanks \ˈthaŋks\ *n pl* : an expression of gratitude

thanks·giv·ing \thaŋks-ˈgiv-iŋ\ *n* 1 : the act of giving thanks 2 : prayer expressing gratitude 3 *cap* : the 4th Thursday in November observed as a legal holiday for giving thanks for divine goodness

¹that \(ˈ)that\ *pron, pl* **those** \(ˈ)thōz\ 1 : the one indicated, mentioned, or understood ⟨∼'s my wife⟩ 2 : the one farther away or first mentioned ⟨this is an elm, ∼'s a maple⟩ 3 : what has been indicated or mentioned ⟨after ∼, we left⟩ 4 : the one or ones : IT, THEY ⟨*those* who wish to leave may do so⟩

²that *adj, pl* **those** 1 : being the one mentioned, indicated, or understood ⟨∼ boy⟩ ⟨*those* people⟩ 2 : being the one farther away or first mentioned ⟨this chair or ∼ one⟩

³that \thət, (ˌ)that\ *conj* 1 : the following, namely ⟨he said ∼ he would⟩; *also* : which is, namely ⟨there's a chance ∼ it may fail⟩ 2 : to this end or purpose ⟨shouted ∼ all might hear⟩ 3 : as to result in the following, namely ⟨so heavy ∼ it can't be moved⟩ 4 : for this reason, namely : BECAUSE ⟨we're glad ∼ you came⟩ 5 : I wish this, or I am surprised or indignant at this, namely ⟨~ it should come to this⟩

⁴that \thət, (ˌ)that\ *pron* **1** : WHO, WHOM, WHICH ⟨the man ~ saw you⟩ ⟨the man ~ you saw⟩ ⟨the money ~ was spent⟩ **2** : in, on, or at which ⟨the way ~ he drives⟩ ⟨the day ~ it rained⟩

⁵that \ˈthat\ *adv* : to such an extent or degree ⟨I like it, but not ~ much⟩

¹thatch \ˈthach\ *vb* : to cover with or as if with thatch

²thatch *n* **1** : plant material (as straw) for use as roofing **2** : a mat of grass clippings accumulated next to the soil on a lawn **3** : a covering of or as if of thatch ⟨a ~ of white hair⟩

thaw \ˈthȯ\ *vb* **1** : to melt or cause to melt **2** : to become so warm as to melt ice or snow **3** : to abandon aloofness or hostility **syn** liquefy — **thaw** *n*

THC \ˌtē-ˌach-ˈsē\ *n* [*tetra*hydro*cannabinol*] : a physiologically active chemical from hemp plant resin that is the chief intoxicant in marijuana

¹the \thə, *before vowel sounds usu* thē\ *definite article* **1** : that in particular **2** — used before adjectives functioning as nouns ⟨a word to ~ wise⟩

²the *adv* **1** : to what extent ⟨~ sooner, the better⟩ **2** : to that extent ⟨the sooner, ~ better⟩

theat *abbr* theater; theatrical

the·ater *or* **the·atre** \ˈthē-ət-ər\ *n* **1** : a building for dramatic performances; *also* : a building or area for showing motion pictures **2** : a place of enactment of significant events ⟨~ of war⟩ **3** : a place (as a lecture room) resembling a theater **4** : dramatic literature or performance

theater–in–the–round *n* : a theater with the stage in the center of the auditorium

the·at·ri·cal \thē-ˈa-tri-kəl\ *also* **the·atric** \-trik\ *adj* **1** : of or relating to the theater **2** : marked by artificiality of emotion : HISTRIONIC **3** : marked by extravagant display : SHOWY **syn** dramatic, melodramatic

the·at·ri·cals \-kəlz\ *n pl* : the performance of plays

the·at·rics \thē-ˈa-triks\ *n pl* **1** : THEATRICALS **2** : staged or contrived effects

the·be \ˈthä-bā\ *n, pl* **thebe** — see *pula* at MONEY table

thee \(ˈ)thē\ *pron, objective case of* THOU

theft \ˈtheft\ *n* : the act of stealing

thegn \ˈthān\ *n* : THANE 1

their \thər, (ˌ)theər\ *adj* : of or relating to them or themselves

theirs \ˈtheərz\ *pron* : their one : their ones

the·ism \ˈthē-ˌiz-əm\ *n* : belief in the existence of a god or gods — **the·ist** \-əst\ *n or adj* — **the·is·tic** \thē-ˈis-tik\ *adj*

them \(th)əm, (ˈ)them\ *pron, objective case of* THEY

theme \ˈthēm\ *n* **1** : a subject or topic of discourse or of artistic representation **2** : a written exercise : COMPOSITION **3** : a melodic subject of a musical composition or movement — **the·mat·ic** \thi-ˈmat-ik\ *adj*

them·selves \thəm-ˈselvz, them-\ *pron pl* : THEY, THEM — used reflexively, for emphasis, or in absolute constructions ⟨they govern ~⟩ ⟨they ~ couldn't come⟩ ⟨~ busy, they sent me⟩

¹then \(ˈ)then\ *adv* **1** : at that time **2** : soon after that : NEXT **3** : in addition : BESIDES **4** : in that case **5** : CONSEQUENTLY

²then \ˈthen\ *n* : that time ⟨since ~⟩

³then \ˈthen\ *adj* : existing or acting at that time ⟨the ~ king⟩

thence \ˈthens, thens\ *adv* **1** : from that place **2** *archaic* : THENCEFORTH **3** : from that fact : THEREFROM

thence·forth \-ˌfōrth\ *adv* : from that time forward : THEREAFTER

thence·for·ward \thens-ˈfȯr-wərd, thens-\ *also* **thence·for·wards** \-wərdz\ *adv* : onward from that place or time : THENCEFORTH

the·oc·ra·cy \thē-ˈäk-rə-sē\ *n, pl* **-cies** **1** : government by officials regarded as divinely inspired **2** : a state governed by a theocracy — **the·o·crat·ic** \ˌthē-ə-ˈkrat-ik\ *adj*

theol *abbr* theological; theology

the·ol·o·gy \thē-ˈäl-ə-jē\ *n, pl* **-gies** **1** : the study of religion and of religious ideas and beliefs; *esp* : a branch of theology treating of God and his relation to the world **2** : a theory or system of theology — **the·o·lo·gian** \ˌthē-ə-ˈlō-jən\ *n* — **the·o·log·i·cal** \-ˈläj-i-kəl\ *adj*

the·o·rem \\'thē-ə-rəm, 'thir-əm\\ *n* **1** : a statement in mathematics that has been or is to be proved **2** : an idea accepted or proposed as a demonstrable truth : PROPOSITION

the·o·ret·i·cal \\ˌthē-ə-'ret-i-kəl\\ *also* **the·o·ret·ic** \\-ik\\ *adj* **1** : relating to or having the character of theory **2** : existing only in theory — **the·o·ret·i·cal·ly** \\-i-k(ə-)lē\\ *adv*

the·o·rize \\'thē-ə-ˌrīz\\ *vb* **-rized; -riz·ing** : to form a theory : SPECULATE — **the·o·rist** \\-rəst\\ *n*

the·o·ry \\'thē-ə-rē, 'thir-ē\\ *n, pl* **-ries 1** : abstract thought **2** : the general principles of a subject **3** : a plausible or scientifically acceptable general principle offered to explain observed facts **4** : HYPOTHESIS, GUESS

theory of games : GAME THEORY

the·os·o·phy \\thē-'äs-ə-fē\\ *n* : belief about God and the world held to be based on mystical insight — **theo·soph·i·cal** \\ˌthē-ə-'säf-i-kəl\\ *adj* — **the·os·o·phist** \\thē-'äs-ə-fəst\\ *n*

ther·a·peu·tic \\ˌther-ə-'pyüt-ik\\ *adj* [Gk *therapeutikos,* fr. *therapeuein* to attend, treat, fr. *theraps* attendant] : of, relating to, or dealing with healing and esp. with remedies for diseases — **ther·a·peu·ti·cal·ly** \\-i-k(ə-)lē\\ *adv*

ther·a·peu·tics \\ˌther-ə-'pyüt-iks\\ *n* : a branch of medical science dealing with the use of remedies

ther·a·py \\'ther-ə-pē\\ *n, pl* **-pies** : treatment of bodily or mental disorders or maladjustment — **ther·a·pist** \\-pəst\\ *n*

¹**there** \\'tha͟ər, 'theər\\ *adv* **1** : in or at that place — often used interjectionally **2** : to or into that place : THITHER **3** : in that matter or respect

²**there** \\(ˌ)thar, (ˌ)ther, thər\\ *pron* — used as a function word to introduce a sentence or clause ⟨∼'s a man here⟩

³**there** \\'tha͟ər, 'theər\\ *n* **1** : that place ⟨get away from ∼⟩ **2** : that point ⟨you take it from ∼⟩

there·abouts *or* **there·about** \\ˌthar-ə-'bau̇t(s), 'thar-ə-ˌbau̇t(s), ˌther-ə-'bau̇t(s), 'ther-ə-ˌ\\ *adv* **1** : near that place or time **2** : near that number, degree, or quantity

there·af·ter \\thar-'af-tər, ther-\\ *adv* : after that : AFTERWARD

there·at \\-'at\\ *adv* **1** : at that place **2** : at that occurrence : on that account

there·by \\thar-'bī, ther-, 'tha(ə)r-ˌbī, 'the(ə)r-ˌbī\\ *adv* **1** : by that : by that means **2** : connected with or with reference to that

there·for \\thar-'fȯr, ther-\\ *adv* : for or in return for that

there·fore \\'tha(ə)r-ˌfȯr, 'the(ə)r-\\ *adv* : for that reason : CONSEQUENTLY

there·from \\thar-'frəm, ther-\\ *adv* : from that or it

there·in \\thar-'in, ther-\\ *adv* **1** : in or into that place, time, or thing **2** : in that respect

there·of \\-'əv, -'äv\\ *adv* **1** : of that or it **2** : from that : THEREFROM

there·on \\-'ȯn, -'än\\ *adv* **1** : on that **2** *archaic* : THEREUPON **3**

there·to \\thar-'tü, ther-\\ *adv* : to that

there·un·to \\thar-'ən-(ˌ)tü; ˌthar-ən-'tü, ˌther-\\ *adv, archaic* : THERETO

there·upon \\'thar-ə-ˌpȯn, 'ther-, -ˌpän; ˌthar-ə-'pȯn, -'pän, ˌther-\\ *adv* **1** : on that matter : THEREON **2** : THEREFORE **3** : immediately after that : at once

there·with \\thar-'with, ther-, -with\\ *adv* **1** : with that **2** *archaic* : THEREUPON, FORTHWITH

there·with·al \\'tha(ə)r-with-ˌȯl, 'the(ə)r-, -with-\\ *adv* **1** *archaic* : BESIDES **2** : THEREWITH

therm *abbr* thermometer

ther·mal \\'thər-məl\\ *adj* **1** : of, relating to, or caused by heat **2** : designed to prevent the loss of body heat ⟨∼ underwear⟩ — **ther·mal·ly** \\-ē\\ *adv*

thermal pollution *n* : the discharge of liquid (as waste water from a factory) into a natural body of water at a temperature harmful to the environment

therm·is·tor \\'thər-ˌmis-tər\\ *n* : an electrical resistor whose resistance varies sharply with temperature

ther·mo·cline \\'thər-mə-ˌklīn\\ *n* : a transition layer in a thermally stratified body of water that separates zones of widely different temperature

ther·mo·dy·nam·ics \\ˌthər-mə-dī-'nam-iks\\ *n* : physics that deals with the mechanical action or relations of heat — **ther·mo·dy·nam·ic** \\-ik\\ *adj* — **ther·mo·dy·nam·i·cal·ly** \\-i-k(ə-)lē\\ *adv*

ther·mom·e·ter \\thə(r)-'mäm-ət-ər\\ *n* [F *thermomètre,* fr. Gk *thermē* heat +

metron measure] : an instrument for measuring temperature commonly by means of the expansion or contraction of mercury or alcohol as indicated by its rise or fall in a thin glass tube — **ther·mo·met·ric** \ˌthər-mə-'me-trik\ *adj* — **ther·mo·met·ri·cal·ly** \-tri-k(ə-)lē\ *adv*

ther·mo·nu·cle·ar \ˌthər-mō-'n(y)ü-klē-ər\ *adj* **1** : of or relating to changes in the nucleus of atoms of low atomic weight (as hydrogen) that require a very high temperature (as in the hydrogen bomb) **2** : utilizing or relating to a thermonuclear bomb ⟨∼ war⟩

ther·mo·plas·tic \ˌthər-mə-'plas-tik\ *adj* : capable of softening when heated and of hardening again when cooled ⟨∼ resins⟩ — **thermoplastic** *n*

ther·mo·reg·u·la·tor \ˌthər-mō-'reg-yə-ˌlāt-ər\ *n* : a device for the regulation of temperature

ther·mos \'thər-məs\ *n* : VACUUM BOTTLE

ther·mo·sphere \'thər-mə-ˌsfiər\ *n* : the part of the earth's atmosphere that begins at about 50 miles (about 80 kilometers) above the earth's surface, extends to outer space, and is characterized by steadily increasing temperature with height

ther·mo·stat \'thər-mə-ˌstat\ *n* : a device that automatically controls temperature — **ther·mo·stat·ic** \ˌthər-mə-'stat-ik\ *adj* — **ther·mo·stat·i·cal·ly** \-i-k(ə-)lē\ *adv*

the·sau·rus \thi-'sȯr-əs\ *n, pl* **-sau·ri** \-'sȯr-ˌī\ *or* **-sau·rus·es** \-'sȯr-ə-səz\ [NL, fr. L, treasure, collection, fr. Gk *thēsauros*] : a book of words and their synonyms — **the·sau·ral** \-'sȯr-əl\ *adj*

these pl of THIS

the·sis \'thē-səs\ *n, pl* **the·ses** \'thē-ˌsēz\ **1** : a proposition that a person advances and offers to maintain by argument **2** : an essay embodying results of original research; *esp* : one written for an academic degree

¹**thes·pi·an** \'thes-pē-ən\ *adj, often cap* [fr. *Thespis*, 6th cent. B.C. Greek poet and reputed originator of tragedy] : relating to the drama : DRAMATIC

²**thespian** *n* : ACTOR

Thess *abbr* Thessalonians

Thes·sa·lo·nians \ˌthes-ə-'lō-nyənz, -nē-ənz\ *n* — see BIBLE table

thew \'th(y)ü\ *n* : MUSCLE, SINEW — usu. used in pl.

they \(')thā\ *pron* **1** : those individuals under discussion : the ones previously mentioned or referred to **2** : unspecified persons : PEOPLE

thi·a·mine \'thī-ə-mən, -ˌmēn\ *also* **thi·a·min** \-mən\ *n* : a vitamin of the vitamin B complex that is essential to normal metabolism and nerve function

¹**thick** \'thik\ *adj* **1** : having relatively great depth or extent from one surface to its opposite ⟨a ∼ plank⟩; *also* : heavily built : THICKSET **2** : densely massed : CROWDED; *also* : FREQUENT, NUMEROUS **3** : dense or viscous in consistency ⟨∼ syrup⟩ **4** : marked by haze, fog, or mist ⟨∼ weather⟩ **5** : measuring in thickness ⟨one meter ∼⟩ **6** : imperfectly articulated : INDISTINCT ⟨∼ speech⟩ **7** : STUPID, OBTUSE **8** : associated on close terms : INTIMATE **9** : EXCESSIVE **syn** compact, close, dense, crowded, tight — **thick·ly** *adv*

²**thick** *n* **1** : the most crowded or active part **2** : the part of greatest thickness

thick·en \'thik-ən\ *vb* **thick·ened; thick·en·ing** \-(ə-)niŋ\ : to make or become thick — **thick·en·er** \-(ə-)nər\ *n*

thick·et \'thik-ət\ *n* : a dense growth of bushes or small trees

thick·ness \-nəs\ *n* **1** : the quality or state of being thick **2** : the smallest of three dimensions ⟨length, width, and ∼⟩ **3** : LAYER, SHEET ⟨a single ∼ of canvas⟩

thick·set \'thik-'set\ *adj* **1** : closely placed or planted **2** : having a thick body : BURLY

thick–skinned \-'skind\ *adj* **1** : having a thick skin **2** : not easily bothered by criticism or insult

thief \'thēf\ *n, pl* **thieves** \'thēvz\ : one that steals esp. secretly

thieve \'thēv\ *vb* **thieved; thiev·ing** : STEAL, ROB **syn** filch, pilfer, purloin, swipe

thiev·ery \'thēv-(ə-)rē\ *n, pl* **-er·ies** : the act of stealing : THEFT

thigh \'thī\ *n* : the part of the vertebrate hind limb between the knee and the hip

thigh·bone \'thī-ˌbōn\ *n* : FEMUR

thim·ble \'thim-bəl\ *n* : a cap or guard used in sewing to protect the finger when pushing the needle — **thim·ble·ful** *n*

¹thin \'thin\ *adj* **thin·ner; thin·nest 1** : having little extent from one surface through to its opposite : not thick : SLENDER **2** : not closely set or placed : SPARSE ⟨∼ hair⟩ **3** : not dense or not dense enough : more fluid or rarefied than normal ⟨∼ air⟩ ⟨∼ syrup⟩ **4** : lacking substance, fullness, or strength ⟨∼ broth⟩ **5** : FLIMSY **syn** slim, slight, tenuous — **thin·ly** *adv* — **thin·ness** \'thin-nəs\ *n*

²thin *vb* **thinned; thin·ning** : to make or become thin

thine \'thīn\ *pron, archaic* : one or the ones belonging to thee

thing \'thiŋ\ *n* **1** : a matter of concern : AFFAIR ⟨∼s to do⟩ **2** *pl* : state of affairs ⟨∼s are improving⟩ **3** : EVENT, CIRCUMSTANCE ⟨the crime was a terrible ∼⟩ **4** : DEED, ACT ⟨expected great ∼s of him⟩ **5** : a distinct entity : OBJECT **6** : an inanimate object distinguished from a living being **7** *pl* : POSSESSIONS, EFFECTS ⟨packed his ∼s⟩ **8** : an article of clothing **9** : DETAIL, POINT **10** : IDEA, NOTION **11** : something one likes to do : SPECIALTY ⟨doing his ∼⟩

think \'thiŋk\ *vb* **thought** \'thȯt\; **think·ing 1** : to form or have in the mind **2** : to have as an opinion : BELIEVE **3** : to reflect on : PONDER **4** : to call to mind : REMEMBER **5** : REASON **6** : to form a mental picture of : IMAGINE **7** : to devise by thinking ⟨*thought* up a plan to escape⟩ **syn** conceive, fancy, realize, envisage — **think·er** *n*

think tank *n* : an institute, corporation, or group organized for interdisciplinary research (as in technological or social problems)

thin·ner \'thin-ər\ *n* : a volatile liquid (as turpentine) used to thin paint

thin–skinned \'thin-'skind\ *adj* **1** : having a thin skin **2** : extremely sensitive to criticism or insult

¹third \'thərd\ *adj* : next after the second — **third** *or* **third·ly** *adv*

²third *n* **1** : one of three equal parts of something **2** : one that is third **3** : the 3d forward gear in an automotive vehicle

third degree *n* : the subjection of a pris-

oner to mental or physical torture to force a confession

third dimension *n* **1** : thickness, depth, or apparent thickness or depth that confers solidity on an object **2** : a quality that confers reality — **third–dimensional** *adj*

third world *n, often cap T&W* **1** : a group of nations esp. in Africa and Asia that are not aligned with either the Communist or the non-Communist blocs **2** : an aggregate of minority groups within a larger predominant culture **3** : the aggregate of the underdeveloped nations of the world

¹thirst \'thərst\ *n* **1** : a feeling of dryness in the mouth and throat associated with a wish to drink; *also* : a bodily condition producing this **2** : an ardent desire : CRAVING ⟨a ∼ for knowledge⟩ — **thirsty** *adj*

²thirst *vb* **1** : to need drink : suffer thirst **2** : to have a strong desire : CRAVE

thir·teen \ˌthər-'tēn, 'thər-\ *n* : one more than 12 — **thirteen** *adj or pron* — **thir·teenth** \-'tēnth\ *adj or n*

thir·ty \'thərt-ē\ *n, pl* **thirties** : three times 10 — **thir·ti·eth** \-ē-əth\ *adj or n* — **thirty** *adj or pron*

¹this \(')this\ *pron, pl* **these** \(')thēz\ **1** : the one close or closest in time or space ⟨∼ is your book⟩ **2** : what is in the present or under immediate observation or discussion ⟨∼ is a mess⟩; *also* : what is happening or being done now ⟨after ∼ we'll leave⟩

²this *adj, pl* **these 1** : being the one near, present, just mentioned, or more immediately under observation ⟨∼ book⟩ **2** : constituting the immediate past or future ⟨friends all *these* years⟩

³this \'this\ *adv* : to such an extent or degree ⟨we need a book about ∼ big⟩

this·tle \'this-əl\ *n* : any of several tall prickly herbs

this·tle·down \-ˌdau̇n\ *n* : the down from the ripe flower head of a thistle

¹thith·er \'thith-ər\ *adv* : to that place

²thither *adj* : being on the farther side

thith·er·ward \-wərd\ *adv* : toward that place : THITHER

thole \'thōl\ *n* : a pin set in the gunwale of a boat against which an oar pivots in rowing

thong \'thȯŋ\ *n* **1** : a strip esp. of leather

or hide **2** : a sandal held on the foot by a thong between the toes

tho·rax \'thōr-ˌaks\ *n, pl* **tho·rax·es** *or* **tho·ra·ces** \'thōr-ə-ˌsēz\ **1** : the part of the body of a mammal between the neck and the abdomen; *also* : its cavity **2** : the middle of the three main divisions of the body of an insect — **tho·rac·ic** \thə-'ras-ik\ *adj*

tho·ri·um \'thōr-ē-əm\ *n* : a radioactive metallic chemical element

thorn \'thȯrn\ *n* **1** : a woody plant bearing sharp processes **2** : a sharp rigid plant process that is usu. a modified leafless branch **3** : something that causes distress — **thorny** *adj*

thor·ough \'thər-ō\ *adj* **1** : COMPLETE, EXHAUSTIVE 〈a ～ search〉 **2** : very careful : PAINSTAKING 〈a ～ scholar〉 **3** : having full mastery — **thor·ough·ly** *adv* — **thor·ough·ness** *n*

¹thor·ough·bred \'thər-ə-ˌbred\ *adj* **1** : bred from the best blood through a long line **2** *cap* : of or relating to the Thoroughbred breed of horses **3** : marked by high-spirited grace

²thoroughbred *n* **1** *cap* : any of an English breed of light speedy horses kept chiefly for racing **2** : one (as a pedigreed animal) of excellent quality

thor·ough·fare \-ˌfaər\ *n* : a public road or street

thor·ough·go·ing \ˌthər-ə-'gō-iŋ\ *adj* : marked by thoroughness or zeal

thorp \'thȯrp\ *n, archaic* : village

those pl of THAT

¹thou \(')thaú\ *pron, archaic* : the person addressed

²thou \'thaú\ *n, pl* **thou** : a thousand of something (as dollars)

¹though \'thō\ *adv* : HOWEVER, NEVERTHELESS 〈not for long, ～〉

²though \(ˌ)thō\ *conj* **1** : despite the fact that 〈～ the odds are hopeless, they fight on〉 **2** : granting that 〈～ it may look bad, still, all is not lost〉

¹thought \'thȯt\ past and past part of THINK

²thought *n* **1** : the process of thinking **2** : serious consideration : REGARD **3** : reasoning power **4** : the power to imagine : CONCEPTION **5** : IDEA, NOTION **6** : OPINION, BELIEF

thought·ful \'thȯt-fəl\ *adj* **1** : absorbed in thought **2** : marked by careful thinking 〈a ～ essay〉 **3** : considerate

of others 〈a ～ host〉 — **thought·ful·ly** \-ē\ *adv* — **thought·ful·ness** *n*

thought·less \-ləs\ *adj* **1** : insufficiently alert : CARELESS 〈a ～ worker〉 **2** : RECKLESS 〈a ～ act〉 **3** : lacking concern for others : INCONSIDERATE 〈～ remarks〉 — **thought·less·ly** *adv* — **thought·less·ness** *n*

thou·sand \'thaúz-ənd\ *n, pl* **thousands** *or* **thousand** : 10 times 100 — **thousand** *adj* — **thou·sandth** \-ᵊnth\ *adj or n*

thousands digit *n* : the numeral (as 1 in 1456) occupying the thousands place in a number

thousands place *n* : the place four to the left of the decimal point in an Arabic number

thrall \'thrȯl\ *n* **1** : SLAVE, BONDMAN **2** : THRALLDOM

thrall·dom *or* **thral·dom** \'thrȯl-dəm\ *n* : the condition of a thrall

thrash \'thrash\ *vb* **1** : THRESH 1 **2** : BEAT, WHIP; *also* : DEFEAT **3** : to move about violently **4** : to go over again and again 〈～ over the matter〉; *also* : to hammer out 〈～ out a plan〉

¹thrash·er \'thrash-ər\ *n* : one that thrashes or threshes

²thrasher *n* : a long-tailed bird resembling a thrush

¹thread \'thred\ *n* **1** : a thin continuous strand of spun and twisted textile fibers **2** : something resembling a textile thread **3** : the ridge or groove that winds around a screw **4** : a train of thought **5** : a continuing element

²thread *vb* **1** : to pass a thread through the eye of (a needle) **2** : to pass (as film) through something **3** : to make one's way through or between **4** : to put together on a thread 〈～ beads〉 **5** : to form a screw thread on or in

thread·bare \-ˌbaər\ *adj* **1** : worn so that the thread shows : SHABBY **2** : TRITE

thready \-ē\ *adj* **1** : consisting of or bearing fibers of filaments 〈a ～ bark〉 **2** : lacking in fullness, body, or vigor

threat \'thret\ *n* **1** : an expression of intent to do harm **2** : one that threatens

threat·en \'thret-ᵊn\ *vb* **threat·ened**; **threat·en·ing** \'thret-(ᵊ-)niŋ\ **1** : to utter threats against **2** : to give signs or warning of : PORTEND **3** : to hang over as a threat : MENACE — **threat·en·ing·ly** *adv*

three \\'thrē\ *n* **1** : one more than two **2** : the 3d in a set or series **3** : something having three units — **three** *adj or pron*

3–D \\'thrē-'dē\ *n* : three-dimensional form

three–dimensional *adj* **1** : relating to or having three dimensions **2** : giving the illusion of varying distances ⟨a ∼ picture⟩

three·fold \\'thrē-,fōld, -'fold\ *adj* **1** : having three parts : TRIPLE **2** : being three times as great or as many — **three·fold** \-'fōld\ *adv*

three·pence \\'threp-əns,'thrip-, 'thrəp-, *US also* 'thrē-pens\ *n* **1** *pl* **threepence** *or* **three·penc·es** : a coin worth three pennies **2** : the sum of three British pennies

three·score \\'thrē-'skōr\ *adj* : being three times twenty : SIXTY

three·some \\'thrē-səm\ *n* : a group of three persons or things

thren·o·dy \\'thren-əd-ē\ *n, pl* **-dies** : a song of lamentation : ELEGY

thresh \\'thrash, 'thresh\ *vb* **1** : to separate (as grain from straw) by beating **2** : THRASH — **thresh·er** *n*

thresh·old \\'thresh-,ōld\ *n* **1** : the sill of a door **2** : a point or place of beginning or entering : OUTSET **3** : a point at which a physiological or psychological effect begins to be produced

threw past of THROW

thrice \\'thrīs\ *adv* **1** : three times **2** : in a threefold manner or degree

thrift \\'thrift\ *n* [ME fr. ON, prosperity, fr. *thrīfask* to thrive] : careful management esp. of money : FRUGALITY — **thrift·i·ly** \\'thrif-tə-lē\ *adv* — **thrift·less** *adj* — **thrifty** *adj*

thrill \\'thril\ *vb* [ME *thirlen, thrillen* to pierce, fr. OE *thyrlian,* fr. *thyrel* hole, fr. *thurh* through] **1** : to have or cause to have sudden sharp feeling of excitement; *also* : TINGLE, SHIVER **2** : TREMBLE, VIBRATE — **thrill** *n* — **thrill·er** *n* — **thrill·ing·ly** \-iŋ-lē\ *adv*

thrive \\'thrīv\ *vb* **throve** \\'thrōv\ *or* **thrived; thriv·en** \\'thriv-ən\ *also* **thrived; thriv·ing** \\'thrī-viŋ\ **1** : to grow luxuriantly : FLOURISH **2** : to gain in wealth or possessions : PROSPER

throat \\'thrōt\ *n* : the part of the neck in front of the spinal column; *also* : the passage through it to the stomach and lungs — **throat·ed** \-əd\ *adj*

throaty \\'thrōt-ē\ *adj* **throat·i·er; -est** **1** : uttered or produced from low in the throat ⟨a ∼ voice⟩ **2** : heavy, thick, or deep as if from the throat ⟨∼ notes of a horn⟩ — **throat·i·ly** \\'thrōt-ᵊl-ē\ *adv* — **throat·i·ness** \-ē-nəs\ *n*

¹throb \\'thräb\ *vb* **throbbed; throb·bing** : to pulsate or pound esp. with abnormal force or rapidity : BEAT, VIBRATE

²throb *n* : BEAT, PULSE

throe \\'thrō\ *n* **1** : PANG, SPASM **2** *pl* : a hard or painful struggle

throm·bo·sis \thräm-'bō-səs\ *n, pl* **-bo·ses** \-,sēz\ : the formation or presence of a clot in a blood vessel during life — **throm·bot·ic** \-'bät-ik\ *adj*

throm·bus \\'thräm-bəs\ *n, pl* **throm·bi** \-,bī\ : a clot of blood formed within a blood vessel and remaining attached to its place of origin

throne \\'thrōn\ *n* **1** : the chair of state esp. of a king or bishop **2** : royal power : SOVEREIGNTY

¹throng \\'throŋ\ *n* **1** : MULTITUDE **2** : a crowding together of many persons

²throng *vb* **thronged; throng·ing** \\'throŋ-iŋ\ : CROWD

¹throt·tle \\'thrät-ᵊl\ *vb* **throt·tled; throt·tling** \\'thrät-(ᵊ-)liŋ\ [ME *throtlen,* fr. *throte* throat] **1** : CHOKE, STRANGLE **2** : SUPPRESS **3** : to reduce the speed of (an engine) by closing the throttle — **throt·tler** \-(ᵊ-)lər\ *n*

²throttle *n* : a valve regulating the flow of steam or fuel to an engine; *also* : the lever controlling this valve

¹through \('\)thrü\ *prep* **1** : into at one side and out at the other side of ⟨go ∼ the door⟩ **2** : by way of ⟨entered ∼ a skylight⟩ **3** : AMONG ⟨a path ∼ the trees⟩ **4** : by means of ⟨succeeded ∼ hard work⟩ **5** : over the whole of ⟨rumors swept ∼ the office⟩ **6** : during the whole of ⟨∼ the night⟩ **7** : to and including ⟨Monday ∼ Friday⟩

²through \\'thrü\ *adv* **1** : from one end or side to the other **2** : from beginning to end : to completion ⟨see it ∼⟩ **3** : to the core : THOROUGHLY ⟨he was wet ∼⟩ **4** : into the open : OUT ⟨break ∼⟩

³through \\'thrü\ *adj* **1** : permitting free passage ⟨a ∼ street⟩ **2** : going from point of origin to destination without change or transfer ⟨∼ train⟩ **3** : coming from or going to points outside a local area ⟨∼ traffic⟩ **4** : FINISHED ⟨∼ with the job⟩

¹through·out \thrü-'aut\ *adv* **1** : EVERYWHERE **2** : from beginning to end

²throughout *prep* **1** : in or to every part of **2** : during the whole period of

through·put \'thrü-ˌput\ *n* : OUTPUT, PRODUCTION ⟨the ∼ of a computer⟩

through·way var of THRUWAY

throve past of THRIVE

¹throw \'thrō\ *vb* **threw** \'thrü\; **thrown** \'thrōn\; **throw·ing** **1** : to propel through the air esp. with a forward motion of the hand and arm ⟨∼ a ball⟩ **2** : to cause to fall or fall off **3** : to put suddenly in a certain position or condition ⟨∼ into panic⟩ **4** : to put on or take off hastily ⟨∼ on a coat⟩ **5** : to move (a lever) so as to connect or disconnect parts of something (as a clutch) **6** : to lose intentionally ⟨∼ a game⟩ **7** : to act as host for ⟨∼ a party⟩ **syn** toss, fling, pitch, sling — **throw·er** \'thrō(-ə)r\ *n*

²throw *n* **1** : an act of throwing, hurling, or flinging; *also* : CAST **2** : the distance a missile may be thrown **3** : a light coverlet **4** : a woman's scarf or light wrap

throw·away \'thrō-ə-ˌwā\ *n* : something that is or is designed to be thrown away esp. after one use

throw·back \'thrō-ˌbak\ *n* : reversion to an earlier type or phase; *also* : an instance or product of this

throw up *vb* **1** : to build hurriedly **2** : VOMIT

thrum \'thrəm\ *vb* **thrummed; thrumming** : to play or pluck a stringed instrument idly : STRUM

thrush \'thrəsh\ *n* : any of a large family of small or medium-sized songbirds that are mostly of a plain color often with spotted underparts

¹thrust \'thrəst\ *vb* **thrust; thrust·ing** **1** : to push or drive with force : SHOVE **2** : STAB, PIERCE **3** : INTERJECT **4** : to press the acceptance of upon someone

²thrust *n* **1** : a lunge with a pointed weapon **2** : ATTACK **3** : the pressure of one part of a construction against another (as of an arch against an abut-

ment) **4** : the force produced by a propeller or jet or rocket engine that drives a vehicle (as an aircraft) forward **5** : a violent push : SHOVE

thrust·er *also* **thrust·or** \'thrəs-tər\ *n* : one that thrusts; *esp* : a rocket engine

thru·way \'thrü-ˌwā\ *n* : EXPRESSWAY

¹thud \'thəd\ *vb* **thud·ded; thud·ding** : to move or strike so as to make a thud

²thud *n* **1** : BLOW **2** : a dull sound

thug \'thəg\ *n* [Hindi *thag*, lit., thief, fr. Skt *sthaga* rogue] : a brutal ruffian or assassin

thu·li·um \'th(y)ü-lē-əm\ *n* : a rare metallic chemical element

¹thumb \'thəm\ *n* **1** : the short thick first digit of the human hand or a corresponding digit of a lower animal **2** : the part of a glove or mitten that covers the thumb

²thumb *vb* **1** : to leaf through (pages) with the thumb **2** : to wear or soil with the thumb by frequent handling **3** : to request or obtain (a ride) in a passing automobile by signaling with the thumb

thumb index *n* : a series of notches cut in the fore edge of a book to facilitate reference

¹thumb·nail \'thəm-ˌnāl\ *n* : the nail of the thumb

²thumb·nail \ˌthəm-ˌnāl\ *adj* : BRIEF, CONCISE ⟨a ∼ description⟩

thumb·print \'thəm-ˌprint\ *n* : an impression made by the thumb

thumb·screw \'thəm-ˌskrü\ *n* **1** : a screw with a head that may be turned by the thumb and forefinger **2** : a device of torture for squeezing the thumb

thumb·tack \-ˌtak\ *n* : a tack with a broad flat head for pressing with one's thumb into a board or wall

¹thump \'thəmp\ *vb* **1** : to strike with or as if with something thick or heavy so as to cause a dull heavy sound **2** : POUND

²thump *n* : a blow with or as if with something blunt or heavy; *also* : the sound made by such a blow

¹thun·der \'thən-dər\ *n* **1** : the sound following a flash of lightning; *also* : a noise like such a sound **2** : a loud utterance or threat

²thunder *vb* **thun·dered; thun·der·ing**

\-d(ə-)riŋ\ **1** : to produce thunder **2** : ROAR, SHOUT

thun•der•bolt \-ˌbōlt\ *n* : a flash of lightning with its accompanying thunder

thun•der•clap \-ˌklap\ *n* : a crash of thunder

thun•der•cloud \-ˌklaud\ *n* : a dark storm cloud producing lightning and thunder

thun•der•head \-ˌhed\ *n* : a large cumulus cloud often appearing before a thunderstorm

thun•der•ous \'thən-d(ə-)rəs\ *adj* : producing thunder; *also* : making a noise like thunder — **thun•der•ous•ly** *adv*

thun•der•show•er \'thən-dər-ˌshau(-ə)r\ *n* : a shower accompanied by thunder and lightning

thun•der•storm \-ˌstorm\ *n* : a storm accompanied by thunder and lightning

thun•der•struck \-ˌstrək\ *adj* : stunned as if struck by a thunderbolt

Thurs *or* **Thu** *abbr* Thursday

Thurs•day \'thərz-dē, -ˌdā\ *n* [deriv. of ON *thōrsdagr*, lit., day of Thor (Norse god)] : the fifth day of the week

thus \'thəs\ *adv* **1** : in this or that manner **2** : to this degree or extent : SO **3** : because of this or that : HENCE

¹thwack \'thwak\ *vb* : to strike with something flat or heavy

²thwack *n* : a heavy blow : WHACK

¹thwart \'thwort\ *vb* **1** : BAFFLE **2** : BLOCK, DEFEAT **syn** balk, foil, outwit, frustrate

²thwart \'thwort, *naut often* 'thort\ *adv* : ATHWART

³thwart *adj* : situated or placed across something else

⁴thwart \'th(w)ort\ *n* : a rower's seat extending across a boat

thy \(ˌ)thī\ *adj, archaic* : of, relating to, or done by or to thee or thyself

thyme \'tīm, 'thīm\ *n* [ME, fr. MF *thym*, fr. L *thymum*, fr. Gk *thymon*, fr. *thyein* to make a burnt offering, sacrifice] : any of several mints with aromatic leaves used esp. in seasoning

thy•mine \'thī-ˌmēn\ *n* : a pyrimidine base that is one of the four bases coding genetic information in the molecular chain of DNA

thy•mus \'thī-məs\ *n* : a glandular organ of the neck that is composed largely of lymphoid tissue, functions esp. in the development of the body's immune system, and tends to disappear or become rudimentary in the adult

thy•ris•tor \thī-'ris-tər\ *n* : a semiconductor device that acts as a switch, rectifier, or voltage regulator

thy•roid \'thī-ˌroid\ *also* **thy•roi•dal** \thī-'roid-ᵊl\ *adj* [NL *thyroides*, fr. Gk *thyreoeidēs* shield-shaped, thyroid, fr. *thyreos* shield shaped like a door, fr. *thyra* door] : of, relating to, or being a large endocrine gland that lies at the base of the neck and produces several iodine-containing hormones that affect growth, development, and metabolism — **thyroid** *n*

thy•rox•ine *or* **thy•rox•in** \thī-'räk-ˌsēn, -sən\ *n* : an iodine-containing amino acid that is the active principle of the thyroid gland and is used to treat thyroid disorders

thy•self \thī-'self\ *pron, archaic* : YOURSELF

Ti *symbol* titanium

ti•ara \tē-'ar-ə, -'er-, -'är-\ *n* **1** : the pope's triple crown **2** : a decorative headband or semicircle for formal wear by women

Ti•bet•an \tə-'bet-ᵊn\ *n* : a native or inhabitant of Tibet — **Tibetan** *adj*

tib•ia \'tib-ē-ə\ *n, pl* **-i•ae** \-ē-ˌē\ *also* **-i•as** [L] : the inner of the two bones of the vertebrate hind limb between the knee and the ankle

tic \'tik\ *n* : a local and habitual twitching of muscles esp. of the face

ti•cal \ti-'käl, 'tik-əl\ *n, pl* **ticals** *or* **tical** : BAHT

¹tick \'tik\ *n* : any of numerous small 8-legged blood-sucking arachnid arthropods

²tick *n* : the fabric case of a mattress or pillow; *also* : a mattress consisting of a tick and its filling

³tick *n* **1** : a light rhythmic audible tap or beat **2** : a small mark used to draw attention to or check something

⁴tick *vb* **1** : to make the sound of a tick or series of ticks **2** : to mark, count, or announce by or as if by ticking beats **3** : to function as an operating mechanism : RUN **4** : to mark or check with a tick

⁵tick *n* : CREDIT; *also* : a credit account

tick•er \'tik-ər\ *n* **1** : something (as a

watch) that ticks **2** : a telegraph instrument that prints information (as stock prices) on paper tape **3** *slang* : HEART

ticker tape *n* : the paper ribbon on which a telegraphic ticker prints

¹**tick·et** \'tik-ət\ *n* **1** : CERTIFICATE, LICENSE, PERMIT; *esp* : a certificate or token showing that a fare or admission fee has been paid **2** : TAG, LABEL **3** : SLATE 3 **4** : a summons issued to a traffic offender

²**ticket** *vb* **1** : to attach a ticket to **2** : to furnish or serve with a ticket

tick·ing \'tik-iŋ\ *n* : a strong fabric used in upholstering and as a mattress covering

tick·le \'tik-əl\ *vb* **tick·led; tick·ling** \-(ə-)liŋ\ **1** : to have a tingling sensation **2** : to excite or stir up agreeably : PLEASE, AMUSE **3** : to touch (as a body part) lightly so as to cause uneasiness, laughter, or spasmodic movements — **tickle** *n*

tick·lish \'tik-(ə-)lish\ *adj* **1** : OVERSENSITIVE, TOUCHY **2** : UNSTABLE ⟨a ∼ foothold⟩ **3** : requiring delicate handling ⟨∼ subject⟩ **4** : sensitive to tickling — **tick·lish·ly** *adv* — **tick·lish·ness** *n*

tid·al wave \'tīd-ᵊl-\ *n* **1** : an unusually high sea wave that sometimes follows an earthquake **2** : an unusual rise of water alongshore due to strong winds

tid·bit \'tid-ˌbit\ *n* : a choice morsel

¹**tide** \'tīd\ *n* [ME, time, fr. OE *tīd*] **1** : the alternate rising and falling of the surface of the ocean **2** : something that fluctuates like the tides of the sea — **tid·al** \'tīd-ᵊl\ *adj*

²**tide** *vb* **tid·ed; tid·ing** : to carry through or help along as if by the tide ⟨a loan to ∼ him over⟩

tide·land \'tīd-ˌland, -lənd\ *n* **1** : land overflowed during flood tide **2** : land under the ocean within a nation's territorial waters — often used in pl.

tide·wa·ter \-ˌwȯt-ər, -ˌwät-\ *n* **1** : water overflowing land at flood tide **2** : low-lying coastal land

tid·ings \'tīd-iŋz\ *n pl* : NEWS, MESSAGE

¹**ti·dy** \'tīd-ē\ *adj* **ti·di·er; -est 1** : well ordered and cared for : NEAT **2** : LARGE, SUBSTANTIAL ⟨a ∼ sum⟩ — **ti·di·ness** \'tīd-ē-nəs\ *n*

²**tidy** *vb* **ti·died; ti·dy·ing 1** : to put in order **2** : to make things tidy

³**tidy** *n, pl* **tidies** : a piece of decorated cloth or needlework used to protect the back or arms of a chair from wear or soil

¹**tie** \'tī\ *n* **1** : a line, ribbon, or cord used for fastening, uniting, or closing **2** : a structural element (as a beam or rod) holding two pieces together **3** : one of the cross supports to which railroad rails are fastened **4** : a connecting link : BOND ⟨family ∼s⟩ **5** : an equality in number (as of votes or scores); *also* : an undecided or deadlocked contest **6** : NECKTIE

²**tie** *vb* **tied; ty·ing** \'tī-iŋ\ *or* **tie·ing 1** : to fasten, attach, or close by means of a tie **2** : to bring together firmly : UNITE **3** : to form a knot or bow in ⟨∼ a scarf⟩ **4** : to restrain from freedom of action : CONSTRAIN **5** : to make or have an equal score with

tie·back \'tī-ˌbak\ *n* : a decorative strip for draping a curtain to the side of a window

tie–dye·ing \'tī-ˌdī-iŋ\ *n* : a method of producing patterns in textiles by tying parts of the fabric so that they will not absorb the dye — **tie–dyed** \-ˌdīd\ *adj*

tie–in \'tī-ˌin\ *n* : CONNECTION

tier \'tiər\ *n* : ROW, LAYER; *esp* : one of two or more rows arranged one above another

tie–rod \'tī-ˌräd\ *n* : a rod used as a connecting member or brace

tie–up \'tī-ˌəp\ *n* **1** : a slowing or stopping of traffic or business **2** : CONNECTION

tiff \'tif\ *n* : a petty quarrel — **tiff** *vb*

tif·fin \'tif-ən\ *n, chiefly Brit* : LUNCHEON

ti·ger \'tī-gər\ *n* : a large tawny black-striped Asian flesh-eating mammal related to the cat — **ti·ger·ish** \-g(ə-)rish\ *adj*

¹**tight** \'tīt\ *adj* **1** : so close in structure as not to permit passage of a liquid or gas **2** : fixed or held very firmly in place **3** : TAUT **4** : fitting usu. too closely ⟨∼ shoes⟩ **5** : set close together : COMPACT ⟨a ∼ formation⟩ **6** : DIFFICULT, TRYING ⟨get in a ∼ spot⟩ **7** : STINGY, MISERLY **8** : evenly contested : CLOSE **9** : INTOXICATED **10** : low in supply : hard to get ⟨money is ∼⟩ — **tight·ly** *adv* — **tight·ness** *n*

²tight *adv* **1** : TIGHTLY, FIRMLY **2** : SOUNDLY 〈sleep ∼〉

tight・en \'tīt-ᵊn\ *vb* **tight・ened; tight・en・ing** \'tīt-(ᵊ-)niŋ\ : to make or become tight

tight・fist・ed \'tīt-'fis-təd\ *adj* : STINGY

tight・rope \'tīt-ˌrōp\ *n* : a taut rope or wire for acrobats to perform on

tights \'tīts\ *n pl* : skintight garments covering the body esp. below the waist

tight・wad \'tīt-ˌwäd\ *n* : a stingy person

ti・gress \'tī-grəs\ *n* : a female tiger

til・de \'til-də\ *n* [Sp, fr. ML *titulus* tittle] : a mark ˜ placed esp. over the letter *n* (as in Spanish *señor* sir) to denote the sound \nʸ\ or over vowels (as in Portuguese *irmã* sister) to indicate nasal quality

¹tile \'tīl\ *n* **1** : a thin piece of fired clay, stone, or concrete used for roofs, floors, or walls; *also* : a hollow or concave earthenware or concrete piece used for a drain **2** : a thin piece (as of a rubber composition) used for covering walls or floors — **til・ing** \-iŋ\ *n*

²tile *vb* **tiled; til・ing 1** : to cover with tiles **2** : to install drainage tile in — **til・er** *n*

¹till \(ˌ)til\ *prep or conj* : UNTIL

²till \'til\ *vb* : to work by plowing, sowing, and raising crops : CULTIVATE — **till・able** *adj* — **till・er** *n*

³till \'til\ *n* : DRAWER; *esp* : a money drawer in a store or bank

till・age \'til-ij\ *n* **1** : the work of tilling land **2** : cultivated land

¹til・ler \'til-ər\ *n* [OE *telgor, telgra* twig, shoot] : a sprout or stalk esp. from the base or lower part of a plant

²til・ler \'til-ər\ *n* [ME *tiler* stock of a crossbow, fr. MF *telier*, lit., beam of a loom, fr. ML *telarium*, fr. L *tela* web] : a lever used for turning a boat's rudder from side to side

¹tilt \'tilt\ *n* **1** : a military exercise in which two combatants charging usu. with lances try to unhorse each other : JOUST; *also* : a tournament of tilts **2** : a verbal contest **3** : SLANT, TIP

²tilt *vb* **1** : to move or shift so as to incline : TIP **2** : to engage in or as if in combat with lances : JOUST

tilth \'tilth\ *n* **1** : TILLAGE 2 **2** : the state of aggregation of the soil esp. in relation to its suitability for crop growth

Tim *abbr* Timothy

¹tim・ber \'tim-bər\ *n* [ME, fr. OE, building, wood] **1** : wooded land or growing trees from which timber may be obtained **2** : wood for use in making something **3** : a usu. large squared or dressed piece of wood — **tim・ber・land** \-bər-ˌland\ *n*

²timber *vb* **tim・bered; tim・ber・ing** \-b(ə-)riŋ\ : to cover, frame, or support with timbers

tim・bered \'tim-bərd\ *adj* **1** : having walls framed by exposed timbers **2** : covered with growing timber

tim・ber・ing \'tim-b(ə-)riŋ\ *n* : a set or arrangement of timbers

tim・ber・line \'tim-bər-ˌlīn\ *n* : the upper limit of tree growth on mountains or in high latitudes

timber rattlesnake *n* : a moderate-sized rattlesnake widely distributed through the eastern half of the U.S.

timber wolf *n* : a large usu. gray No. American wolf

tim・bre *also* **tim・ber** \'tam-bər, 'tim-\ *n* [F, fr. MF, bell struck by a hammer, fr. OF, drum, fr. MGk *tymbanon* kettledrum, fr. Gk *tympanon*] : the distinctive quality given to a sound by its overtones

tim・brel \'tim-brəl\ *n* : a small hand drum or tambourine

¹time \'tīm\ *n* **1** : a period during which an action, process, or condition exists or continues 〈gone a long ∼〉 **2** : LEISURE 〈found ∼ to read〉 **3** : a point or period when something occurs : OCCASION 〈the last ∼ we met〉 **4** : a set or customary moment or hour for something to occur 〈arrived on ∼〉 **5** : AGE, ERA **6** : state of affairs : CONDITIONS 〈hard ∼s〉 **7** : a rate of speed : TEMPO **8** : a moment, hour, day, or year as indicated by a clock or calendar 〈what ∼ is it〉 **9** : a system of reckoning time 〈solar ∼〉 **10** : one of a series of recurring instances; *also, pl* : added or accumulated quantities or examples 〈five ∼s greater〉 **11** : a person's experience during a particular period 〈had a good ∼ at the beach〉

²time *vb* **timed; tim・ing 1** : to arrange or set the time of : SCHEDULE 〈∼s his calls conveniently〉 **2** : to set the tempo or duration of 〈∼ a performance〉 **3** : to cause to keep time with 〈∼s her steps to the music⟩ **4** : to determine or record the time, duration, or rate of ⟨∼ a sprinter⟩ — **tim·er** *n*

time bomb *n* **1** : a bomb so made as to explode at a predetermined time **2** : something having the potential of a dangerous delayed reaction

time clock *n* : a clock that records the times of arrival and departure of workers

time frame *n* : a period of time esp. with respect to some action or project

time–hon·ored \'tīm-ˌän-ərd\ *adj* : honored because of age or long usage

time·keep·er \'tīm-ˌkē-pər\ *n* **1** : a clerk who keeps records of the time worked by employees **2** : one appointed to mark and announce the time in an athletic game or contest

time·less \'tīm-ləs\ *adj* **1** : UNENDING **2** : not limited or affected by time ⟨∼ works of art⟩ — **time·less·ly** *adv* — **time·less·ness** *n*

time·ly \'tīm-lē\ *adj* **time·li·er; -est 1** : coming early or at the right time : OPPORTUNE ⟨a ∼ arrival⟩ **2** : appropriate to the time ⟨a ∼ book⟩ — **time·li·ness** *n*

time–out \'tīm-ˈaut\ *n* : a brief suspension of activity esp. in an athletic game

time·piece \'tīm-ˌpēs\ *n* : a device (as a clock) to show the passage of time

times \ˌtīmz\ *prep* : multiplied by ⟨2 ∼ 2 is 4⟩

time–shar·ing \'tīm-ˌsheər-iŋ\ *n* : simultaneous access to a computer by many users

times sign *n* : the symbol × used to indicate multiplication

time·ta·ble \'tīm-ˌtā-bəl\ *n* **1** : a table of the departure and arrival times (as of trains) **2** : a schedule showing a planned order or sequence

time warp *n* : an anomaly, discontinuity, or suspension held to occur in the progress of time

time·worn \-ˌwōrn\ *adj* **1** : worn by time **2** : HACKNEYED, STALE

tim·id \'tim-əd\ *adj* : lacking in courage or self-confidence : FEARFUL — **ti·mid·i·ty** \tə-ˈmid-ət-ē\ *n* — **tim·id·ly** \'tim-əd-lē\ *adv*

tim·o·rous \'tim-(ə-)rəs\ *adj* : of a timid disposition : AFRAID — **tim·o·rous·ly** *adv* — **tim·o·rous·ness** *n*

tim·o·thy \'tim-ə-thē\ *n* : a grass with long cylindrical spikes widely grown for hay

Tim·o·thy \'tim-ə-thē\ *n* — see BIBLE table

tim·pa·ni \'tim-pə-nē\ *n pl* [It] : a set of kettledrums played by one performer in an orchestra — **tim·pa·nist** \-nəst\ *n*

¹tin \'tin\ *n* **1** : a soft white crystalline metallic element malleable at ordinary temperatures but brittle when heated that is used in solders and alloys **2** : a container (as a can) made of tinplate

²tin *vb* **tinned; tin·ning 1** : to cover or plate with tin **2** *chiefly Brit* : to pack in tins : CAN

tinct \'tiŋkt\ *n* : TINCTURE, TINGE

¹tinc·ture \'tiŋk-chər\ *n* **1** : a substance that colors or dyes **2** : a slight admixture : TRACE **3** : an alcoholic solution of a medicinal substance **syn** touch, suggestion, suspicion, soupçon

²tincture *vb* **tinc·tured; tinc·tur·ing** : COLOR, TINGE

tin·der \'tin-dər\ *n* : something that catches fire easily; *esp* : a substance used to kindle a fire from a slight spark

tin·der·box \'tin-dər-ˌbäks\ *n* **1** : a metal box for holding tinder and usu. flint and steel for striking a spark **2** : a highly flammable object or place

tine \'tīn\ *n* : a slender pointed part (as of a fork or an antler) : PRONG

tin·foil \'tin-ˌfȯil\ *n* : a thin metal sheeting usu. of aluminum or tin-lead alloy

¹tinge \'tinj\ *vb* **tinged; tinge·ing** *or* **ting·ing** \'tin-jiŋ\ **1** : to color slightly : TINT **2** : to affect or modify esp. with a slight odor or taste

²tinge *n* : a slight coloring, flavor, or quality : TRACE **syn** touch, suggestion, suspicion, tincture

tin·gle \'tin-gəl\ *vb* **tin·gled; tin·gling** \-g(ə-)liŋ\ **1** : to feel a prickling or thrilling sensation **2** : TINKLE — **tingle** *n*

¹tin·ker \'tiŋ-kər\ *n* **1** : a usu. itinerant mender of household utensils **2** : an unskillful mender : BUNGLER

²tinker *vb* **tin·kered; tin·ker·ing** \-k(ə-)riŋ\ : to repair or adjust something in an unskillful or experimental manner — **tin·ker·er** *n*

¹tin·kle \'tiŋ-kəl\ *vb* **tin·kled; tin·kling**

\-k(ə-)liŋ\ : to make or cause to make a tinkle

²tinkle *n* : a series of short high ringing or clinking sounds

tin·ny \'tin-ē\ *adj* **tin·ni·er; -est 1** : abounding in or yielding tin **2** : resembling tin; *also* : LIGHT, CHEAP **3** : thin in tone ⟨a ∼ voice⟩ — **tin·ni·ly** \'tin-ᵊl-ē\ *adv* — **tin·ni·ness** \-ē-nəs\ *n*

tin·plate \'tin-'plāt\ *n* : thin sheet iron or steel coated with tin — **tin–plate** *vb*

tin·sel \'tin-səl\ *n* [MF *etincelle* spark, glitter] **1** : a thread, strip, or sheet of metal, paper, or plastic used to produce a glittering appearance (as in fabrics) **2** : something superficially attractive but of little worth

tin·smith \'tin-ˌsmith\ *n* : one that works with sheet metal (as tinplate)

¹tint \'tint\ *n* **1** : a slight or pale coloration : HUE **2** : any of various shades of a color

²tint *vb* : to impart a tint to : COLOR

tin·tin·nab·u·la·tion \ˌtin-tə-ˌnab-yə-'lā-shən\ *n* **1** : the ringing of bells **2** : a tingling sound as if of bells

tin·ware \'tin-ˌwaər\ *n* : articles made of tinplate

ti·ny \'tī-nē\ *adj* **ti·ni·er; -est** : very small : MINUTE **syn** miniature, diminutive, wee, lilliputian

¹tip \'tip\ *vb* **tipped; tip·ping 1** : OVERTURN, UPSET **2** : LEAN, SLANT; *also* : TILT

²tip *n* : the act or an instance of tipping

³tip *n* **1** : the usu. pointed end of something **2** : a small piece or part serving as an end, cap, or point

⁴tip *vb* **tipped, tip·ping 1** : to furnish with a tip **2** : to cover or adorn the tip of

⁵tip *n* : a light touch or blow

⁶tip *vb* **tipped; tip·ping** : to strike lightly : TAP

⁷tip *n* : a piece of expert of confidential information : HINT

⁸tip *vb* **tipped; tip·ping** : to impart a piece of information about or to

⁹tip *vb* **tipped; tip·ping** : to give a gratuity to

¹⁰tip *n* : a gift or small sum given for a service performed or anticipated

tip–off \'tip-ˌòf\ *n* : WARNING, TIP

tip·pet \'tip-ət\ *n* : a long scarf or shoulder cape

tip·ple \'tip-əl\ *vb* **tip·pled; tip·pling** \-(ə-)liŋ\ : to drink intoxicating liquor esp. habitually or excessively — **tip·pler** \-(ə-)lər\ *n*

tip·ster \'tip-stər\ *n* : one who gives or sells tips esp. for gambling

tip·sy \'tip-sē\ *adj* **tip·si·er; -est** : unsteady or foolish from the effects of alcohol

¹tip·toe \'tip-ˌtō\ *n* : the tip of a toe; *also* : the ends of the toes

²tiptoe *adv or adj* : on or as if on tiptoe

³tiptoe *vb* **tip·toed; tip·toe·ing** : to walk or proceed on or as if on tiptoe

¹tip–top \'tip-'täp\ *n* : the highest point

²tip–top *adj* : EXCELLENT, FIRST-RATE

ti·rade \tī-'rād, 'tī-ˌrād\ *n* [F, shot, tirade, fr. MF, fr. It *tirata*, fr. *tirare* to draw, shoot] : a prolonged speech of abuse or condemnation

¹tire \'tī(ə)r\ *vb* **tired; tir·ing 1** : to make or become weary : FATIGUE **2** : to wear out the patience of : BORE

²tire *n* **1** : a wheel band that forms the tread of a wheel **2** : a rubber cushion usu. containing compressed air that encircles a wheel (as of an automobile)

tired \'tī(ə)rd\ *adj* **1** : WEARY, FATIGUED **2** : HACKNEYED

tire·less \'tī(ə)r-ləs\ *adj* : not tiring : UNTIRING, INDEFATIGABLE —**tire·less·ly** *adv* — **tire·less·ness** *n*

tire·some \'tī(ə)r-səm\ *adj* : tending to bore : WEARISOME, TEDIOUS — **tire·some·ly** *adv* — **tire·some·ness** *n*

tis·sue \'tish-ü\ *n* [ME *tissu*, a rich fabric, fr. OF, fr. *tistre* to weave, fr. L *texere*] **1** : a fine lightweight often sheer fabric **2** : NETWORK, WEB **3** : a soft absorbent paper **4** : a mass or layer of cells forming a basic structural element of an animal or plant body

¹tit \'tit\ *n* : TEAT

²tit *n* : TITMOUSE

Tit *abbr* Titus

ti·tan \'tīt-ᵊn\ *n* **1** *cap* : one of a family of giants overthrown by the gods of ancient Greece **2** : one gigantic in size or power

ti·tan·ic \tī-'tan-ik, tə-\ *adj* : enormous in size, force, or power **syn** immense, huge, gigantic, giant, colossal, mammoth

ti·ta·ni·um \tī-'tān-ē-əm, tə-\ *n* : a gray light strong metallic chemical element used in alloys

tit·bit \'tit-ˌbit\ *var of* TIDBIT

tithe \\'tīth\ *n* : a 10th part paid or given esp. for the support of a church — **tithe** *vb* — **tith·er** *n*

tit·il·late \\'tit-ᵊl-ˌāt\ *vb* -**lat·ed; -lat·ing** 1 : TICKLE 2 : to excite pleasurably — **tit·il·la·tion** \ˌtit-ᵊl-'ā-shən\ *n*

tit·i·vate *or* **tit·ti·vate** \\'tit-ə-ˌvāt\ *vb* -**vat·ed; -vat·ing** : to dress up : spruce up

ti·tle \\'tīt-ᵊl\ *n* 1 : CLAIM, RIGHT; *esp* : a legal right to the ownership of property 2 : the distinguishing name esp. of an artistic production (as a book) 3 : an appellation of honor, rank, or office 4 : CHAMPIONSHIP **syn** designation, denomination, appellation

ti·tled \\'tīt-ᵊld\ *adj* : having a title esp. of nobility

title page *n* : a page of a book bearing the title and usu. the names of the author and publisher

tit·mouse \\'tit-ˌmaůs\ *n, pl* **tit·mice** \-ˌmīs\ : any of numerous small long-tailed insect-eating birds

tit·ter \\'tit-ər\ *vb* : to laugh in an affected or in a nervous or half-suppressed manner — **titter** *n*

tit·tle \\'tit-ᵊl\ *n* : a tiny piece : JOT

tit·tle–tat·tle \\'tit-ᵊl-ˌtat-ᵊl\ *n* : idle talk : GOSSIP

tit·u·lar \\'tich-(ə-)lər\ *adj* 1 : existing in title only : NOMINAL ⟨~ ruler⟩ 2 : of, relating to, or bearing a title ⟨~ role⟩

Ti·tus \\'tīt-əs\ *n* — see BIBLE table

tiz·zy \\'tiz-ē\ *n, pl* **tizzies** : a highly excited and distracted state of mind

tk *abbr* 1 tank 2 truck

TKO \\'tē-kā-'ō\ *n* [*technical knockout*] : the termination of a boxing match when a boxer is declared unable to continue the fight

tkt *abbr* ticket

Tl *symbol* thallium

TLC *abbr* tender loving care

T lymphocyte *n* : T CELL

Tm *symbol* thulium

TM *abbr* trademark

T-man \\'tē-ˌman\ *n* : a special agent of the U.S. Treasury Department

tn *abbr* 1 ton 2 town

TN *abbr* Tennessee

tng *abbr* training

tnpk *abbr* turnpike

TNT \ˌtē-ˌen-'tē\ *n* : a flammable toxic compound used as a high explosive

¹to \tə, (')tü\ *prep* 1 : in the direction of and reaching ⟨drove ~ town⟩ 2 : in the direction of : TOWARD ⟨walking ~ school⟩ 3 : ON, AGAINST ⟨apply salve ~ a burn⟩ 4 : as far as ⟨can pay up ~ a dollar⟩ 5 : so as to become or bring about ⟨beaten ~ death⟩ ⟨broken ~ pieces⟩ 6 : BEFORE ⟨it's five minutes ~ six⟩ 7 : UNTIL ⟨from May ~ December⟩ 8 : fitting or being a part of : FOR ⟨key ~ the lock⟩ 9 : with the accompaniment of ⟨sing ~ the music⟩ 10 : in relation or comparison with ⟨similar ~ that one⟩ ⟨won 10 ~ 6⟩ 11 : in accordance with ⟨add salt ~ taste⟩ 12 : within the range of ⟨~ my knowledge⟩ 13 : contained, occurring, or included in ⟨two pints ~ a quart⟩ 14 : as regards ⟨agreeable ~ everyone⟩ 15 : affecting as the receiver or beneficiary ⟨whispered ~ her⟩ ⟨gave it ~ me⟩ 16 : for no one except ⟨a room ~ myself⟩ 17 : into the action of ⟨we got ~ talking⟩ 18 — used for marking the following verb as an infinitive ⟨wants ~ go⟩ ⟨easy ~ like⟩ ⟨the man ~ beat⟩ and often used by itself at the end of a clause in place of an infinitive suggested by the preceding context ⟨goes to town whenever he wants ~⟩ ⟨can leave if you'd like ~⟩

²to \\'tü\ *adv* 1 : in a direction toward ⟨run ~ and fro⟩ ⟨wrong side ~⟩ 2 : into contact esp. with the frame of a door ⟨the door slammed ~⟩ 3 : to the matter in hand ⟨fell ~ and ate heartily⟩ 4 : to a state of consciousness or awareness ⟨came ~ hours after the accident⟩

TO *abbr* turn over

toad \\'tōd\ *n* : a leaping amphibian differing typically from the related frogs in shorter stockier build, rough dry warty skin, and less aquatic habits

toad·stool \-ˌstül\ *n* : MUSHROOM; *esp* : one that is poisonous or inedible

toady \\'tōd-ē\ *n, pl* **toad·ies** : one who flatters in the hope of gaining favors : SYCOPHANT — **toady** *vb*

to–and–fro \ˌtü-ən-'frō\ *adj* : forward and backward

¹toast \\'tōst\ *vb* 1 : to warm thoroughly 2 : to make (as bread) crisp, hot, and brown by heat

²toast *n* 1 : sliced toasted bread 2 : someone or something in whose honor persons drink **3** : an act of drinking in honor of a toast

³**toast** *vb* : to propose or drink to as a toast

toast·er \'tō-stər\ *n* : one that toasts; *esp* : an electrical appliance for toasting

toaster oven *n* : a small electrical appliance that bakes, toasts, and usu. broils

toast·mas·ter \'tōst-₁mas-tər\ *n* : one that presides at a banquet and introduces the after-dinner speakers — **toast·mis·tress** \-₁mis-trəs\ *n*

to·bac·co \tə-'bak-ō\ *n, pl* **-cos** [Sp *tabaco*] **1** : a tall broad-leaved herb related to the potato; *also* : its leaves prepared for smoking or chewing or as snuff **2** : manufactured tobacco products

to·bac·co·nist \tə-'bak-ə-nəst\ *n* : a dealer in tobacco

To·bi·as \tə-'bī-əs\ *n* — see BIBLE table

To·bit \'tō-bət\ *n* — see BIBLE table

¹**to·bog·gan** \tə-'bäg-ən\ *n* [CanF *tobogan*] : a long flat-bottomed light sled made of thin boards curved up at one end

²**toboggan** *vb* **1** : to coast on a toboggan **2** : to decline suddenly (as in value)

toc·sin \'täk-sən\ *n* **1** : an alarm bell **2** : a warning signal

¹**to·day** \tə-'dā\ *adv* **1** : on or for this day **2** : at the present time

²**today** *n* : the present day, time, or age

tod·dle \'täd-ᵊl\ *vb* **tod·dled; tod·dling** \'täd-(ᵊ-)liŋ\ : to walk with short tottering steps in the manner of a young child — **toddle** *n* — **tod·dler** \-(ᵊ-)lər\ *n*

tod·dy \'täd-ē\ *n, pl* **toddies** [Hindi *tārī* juice of a palm, fr. *tār* a palm, fr. Skt *tāla*] : a drink made of liquor, sugar, spices, and hot water

to—do \tə-'dü\ *n, pl* **to—dos** \-'düz\ : BUSTLE, STIR

¹**toe** \'tō\ *n* **1** : one of the jointed parts of the front end of a foot **2** : the front part of a foot or hoof

²**toe** *vb* **toed; toe·ing** : to touch, reach, or drive with the toes

toea \'toi-ə\ *n* — see *kina* at MONEY table

toe·hold \'tō-₁hōld\ *n* **1** : a place of support for the toes **2** : a slight footing

toe·nail \'tō-₁nāl\ *n* : a nail of a toe

tof·fee *or* **tof·fy** \'tȯ-fē, 'täf-ē\ *n, pl*

toffees *or* **toffies** : candy of brittle but tender texture made by boiling sugar and butter together

tog \'täg, 'tȯg\ *vb* **togged; tog·ging** : to put togs on : DRESS

to·ga \'tō-gə\ *n* : the loose outer garment worn in public by citizens of ancient Rome — **to·gaed** \-gəd\ *adj*

¹**to·geth·er** \tə-'ge<u>th</u>-ər\ *adv* **1** : in or into one place or group **2** : in or into contact or association ⟨mix ∼⟩ **3** : at one time : SIMULTANEOUSLY ⟨talk and work ∼⟩ **4** : in succession ⟨for days ∼⟩ **5** : in or into harmony or coherence ⟨get ∼ on a plan⟩ **6** : as a group : JOINTLY — **to·geth·er·ness** *n*

²**together** *adj* : composed in mind or manner

tog·gery \'täg-(ə-)rē, 'tȯg-\ *n* : CLOTHING

tog·gle switch \'täg-əl-\ *n* : an electric switch operated by pushing a projecting lever through a small arc

togs \'tägz, 'tȯgz\ *n pl* : CLOTHING; *esp* : clothes for a specified use ⟨riding ∼⟩

¹**toil** \'tȯil\ *n* **1** : laborious effort **2** : long fatiguing labor : DRUDGERY — **toil·some** *adj*

²**toil** *vb* [ME *toilen* to argue, struggle, fr. OF *toeillier* to stir, disturb, dispute, fr. L *tudiculare* to crush, grind, fr. *tudicula* machine for crushing olives, dim. of *tudes* hammer] **1** : to work hard and long **2** : to proceed with laborious effort : PLOD — **toil·er** *n*

³**toil** *n* [ME *toile* cloth, net, fr. L *tela* web, fr. *texere* to weave, construct] : NET, TRAP — usu. used in pl.

toi·let \'tȯi-lət\ *n* **1** : the act or process of dressing and grooming oneself **2** : BATHROOM **3** : a fixture for use in urinating and defacating; *esp* : one consisting essentially of a water-flushed bowl and seat

toi·let·ry \'tȯi-lə-trē\ *n, pl* **-ries** : an article or preparation used in making one's toilet — usu. used in pl.

toi·lette \twä-'let\ *n* **1** : TOILET 1 **2** : formal attire; *also* : a particular costume

toilet training *n* : the process of training a child to control bladder and bowel movements and to use the toilet — **toilet train** *vb*

toil·worn \'tȯil-₁wōrn\ *adj* : showing the effects of toil

To·kay \tō-'kā\ *n* : naturally sweet wine from Hungary

toke \\'tōk\ *n, slang* : a puff on a marijuana cigarette

¹to•ken \\'tō-kən\ *n* **1** : an outward sign **2** : SYMBOL, EMBLEM **3** : SOUVENIR, KEEPSAKE **4** : a small part representing the whole **5** : a piece resembling a coin issued as money or for use by a particular group on specified terms

²token *adj* **1** : done or given as a token esp. in partial fulfillment of an obligation **2** : MINIMAL, PERFUNCTORY

to•ken•ism \\'tō-kə-ˌniz-əm\ *n* : the policy or practice of making only a token effort (as to desegregate)

told past and past part of TELL

tole \\'tōl\ *n* : sheet metal and esp. tinplate for use in domestic and ornamental wares

tol•er•a•ble \\'täl-(ə-)rə-bəl\ *adj* **1** : capable of being borne or endured **2** : moderately good : PASSABLE — **tol•er•a•bly** \-blē\ *adv*

tol•er•ance \\'täl(-ə)-rəns\ *n* **1** : the act or practice of tolerating; *esp* : sympathy or indulgence for beliefs or practices differing from one's own **2** : the allowable deviation from a standard (as of size) **3** : capacity for enduring or adapting (as to a poor environment) **syn** forbearance, leniency, clemency — **tol•er•ant** *adj* — **tol•er•ant•ly** *adv*

tol•er•ate \\'täl-ə-ˌrāt\ *vb* **-at•ed; -at•ing** **1** : to allow to be or to be done without hindrance **2** : to endure or resist the action of (as a drug) **syn** abide, bear, suffer, stand, brook — **tol•er•a•tion** \ˌtäl-ə-'rā-shən\ *n*

¹toll \\'tōl\ *n* **1** : a tax paid for a privilege (as for passing over a bridge) **2** : a charge for a service (as for a long-distance telephone call) **3** : the cost in loss or suffering at which something is achieved **syn** levy, assessment, duty, tariff

²toll *vb* **1** : to give signal of : SOUND **2** : to cause the slow regular sounding of (a bell) esp. by pulling a rope **3** : to sound with slow measured strokes **4** : to announce by tolling

³toll *n* : the sound of a tolling bell

toll•booth \\'tōl-ˌbüth\ *n* : a booth where tolls are paid

toll•gate \\'tōl-ˌgāt\ *n* : a point where vehicles stop to pay a toll

toll•house \-ˌhaus\ *n* : a house or booth where tolls are paid

tol•u•ene \\'täl-yə-ˌwēn\ *n* : a liquid hydrocarbon used as a solvent and as an antiknock agent

tom \\'täm\ *n* : the male of various animals; *esp* : TOMCAT

¹tom•a•hawk \\'täm-ə-ˌhok\ *n* : a light ax used as a missile and as a hand weapon by No. American Indians

²tomahawk *vb* : to strike or kill with a tomahawk

to•ma•to \tə-'māt-ō, -'mät-\ *n, pl* **-toes** : a usu. large, rounded, and red or yellow pulpy edible berry of a widely grown tropical herb related to the potato; *also* : this herb

tomb \\'tüm\ *n* **1** : a place of burial : GRAVE **2** : a house, chamber, or vault for the dead

tom•boy \\'täm-ˌboi\ *n* : a girl of boyish behavior

tomb•stone \\'tüm-ˌstōn\ *n* : a stone marking a grave

tom•cat \\'täm-ˌkat\ *n* : a male cat

Tom Col•lins \\'täm-'käl-ənz\ *n* : a tall iced drink with a base of gin

tome \\'tōm\ *n* : BOOK; *esp* : a large or weighty one

tom•fool•ery \täm-'fül-(ə-)rē\ *n* : foolish trifling : NONSENSE

tom•my gun \\'täm-ē-ˌgən\ *n* : SUBMACHINE GUN

to•mog•ra•phy \tō-'mäg-rə-fē\ *n* : a diagnostic technique using X-ray photographs in which the shadows of structures before and behind the section under study do not show — **to•mo•graph•ic** \ˌtō-mə-'graf-ik\ *adj*

to•mor•row \tə-'mär-ō\ *adv* : on or for the day after today — **tomorrow** *n*

tom•tit \\'täm-ˌtit, täm-'tit\ *n* : any of several small active birds

tom–tom \\'täm-ˌtäm\ *n* : a small-headed drum beaten with the hands

ton \\'tən\ *n, pl* **tons** *also* **ton** **1** — see WEIGHT table **2** : a unit equal to the volume of a long-ton weight of seawater or 35 cubic feet used in reckoning the displacement of ships

to•nal•i•ty \tō-'nal-ət-ē\ *n, pl* **-ties** : tonal quality

¹tone \\'tōn\ *n* [ME, fr. L *tonus* tension, tone, fr. Gk *tonos*, lit., act of stretching; fr. the dependence of the pitch of a musical string on its tension] **1** : vocal or musical sound; *esp* : sound quality **2** : a sound of definite pitch **3**

: WHOLE STEP **4** : accent or inflection expressive of an emotion **5** : the pitch of a word often used to express differences of meaning **6** : style or manner of expression **7** : color quality; *also* : SHADE, TINT **8** : the effect in painting of light and shade together with color **9** : the healthy and vigorous condition of a living body or bodily part **10** : general character, quality, or trend **syn** atmosphere, feeling, mood, vein — **ton·al** \'tōn-ᵊl\ *adj*

²**tone** *vb* **toned; ton·ing 1** : to give a particular intonation or inflection to **2** : to impart tone to **3** : SOFTEN, MELLOW **4** : to harmonize in color : BLEND

tone·arm *n* : the movable part of a record player that carries the pickup and the needle

tong \'täŋ, 'tȯŋ\ *n* : a Chinese secret society in the U.S.

tongs \'täŋz, 'tȯŋz\ *n pl* : a grasping device consisting of two pieces joined at one end by a pivot or hinged like scissors

¹**tongue** \'təŋ\ *n* **1** : a fleshy movable process of the floor of the mouth used in tasting and in taking and swallowing food and in man as a speech organ **2** : the flesh of a tongue (as of the ox) used as food **3** : the power of communication **4** : LANGUAGE 1 **5** : manner or quality of utterance; *also* : intended meaning **6** : ecstatic usu. unintelligible utterance accompanying religious excitation — usu. used in pl. **7** : something resembling an animal's tongue in being elongated and fastened at one end only — **tongued** \'təŋd\ *adj* — **tongue·less** *adj*

²**tongue** *vb* **tongued; tongu·ing** \'təŋ-iŋ\ **1** : to touch or lick with the tongue **2** : to articulate notes on a wind instrument

tongue–in–cheek *adj* : with insincerity, irony, or whimsical exaggeration — **tongue in cheek** *adv*

tongue–lash \'təŋ-ˌlash\ *vb* : CHIDE, REPROVE — **tongue–lash·ing** \-iŋ\ *n*

tongue–tied \'təŋ-ˌtīd\ *adj* : unable to speak clearly or freely usu. from shortness of the membrane under the tongue or from shyness

tongue twister *n* : an utterance that is difficult to articulate because of a succession of similar consonants

¹**ton·ic** \'tän-ik\ *adj* **1** : of, relating to, or producing a healthy physical or mental condition : INVIGORATING **2** : relating to or based on the 1st tone of a scale

²**tonic** *n* **1** : something (as a drug) that invigorates, restores, or refreshes **2** : the 1st degree of a musical scale

¹**to·night** \tə-'nīt\ *adv* : on this present night or the night following this present day

²**tonight** *n* : the present or the coming night

ton·nage \'tən-ij\ *n* **1** : a duty on ships based on tons carried **2** : ships in terms of the number of tons registered or carried **3** : total weight in tons shipped, carried, or mined

ton·sil \'tän-səl\ *n* : either of a pair of oval masses of spongy tissue that lie one on each side of the throat at the back of the mouth

ton·sil·lec·to·my \ˌtän-sə-'lek-tə-mē\ *n, pl* **-mies** : the surgical removal of the tonsils

ton·sil·li·tis \-'līt-əs\ *n* : inflammation of the tonsils

ton·so·ri·al \tän-'sōr-ē-əl\ *adj* : of or relating to a barber or his work

ton·sure \'tän-chər\ *n* [ME, fr. ML *tonsura*, fr. L, act of shearing, fr. *tonsus*, pp. of *tondēre* to shear] **1** : the rite of admission to the clerical state by the clipping or shaving of the head **2** : the shaven crown or patch worn by clerics (as monks)

too \(')tü\ *adv* **1** : in addition : ALSO **2** : EXCESSIVELY **3** : to such a degree as to be regrettable **4** : VERY

took past of TAKE

¹**tool** \'tül\ *n* **1** : a hand instrument used to aid in mechanical operations **2** : the cutting or shaping part in a machine; *also* : a machine for shaping metal in any way **3** : something used in doing a job ⟨a scholar's books are his ~s⟩; *also* : a means to an end **4** : a person used by another : DUPE

²**tool** *vb* **1** : to shape, form, or finish with a tool; *esp* : to letter or decorate (as a book cover) by means of hand tools **2** : to equip a plant or industry with machines and tools for production **3** : DRIVE, RIDE ⟨~ing along at 60⟩

¹**toot** \'tüt\ *vb* **1** : to sound or cause to sound esp. in short blasts **2** : to blow a wind instrument (as a horn)

²toot *n* : a short blast (as on a horn)

tooth \'tüth\ *n, pl* **teeth** \'tēth\ **1** : one of the hard bony structures borne esp. on the jaws of vertebrates and used for seizing and chewing food and as weapons; *also* : a hard sharp structure esp. around the mouth of an invertebrate **2** : something resembling an animal's tooth **3** : one of the projections on the edge of a wheel that fits into corresponding projections on another wheel — **toothed** \'tütht\ *adj* — **tooth·less** *adj*

tooth·ache \'tüth-ˌāk\ *n* : pain in or about a tooth

tooth·brush \-ˌbrəsh\ *n* : a brush for cleaning the teeth

tooth·paste \-ˌpāst\ *n* : a paste for cleaning the teeth

tooth·pick \-ˌpik\ *n* : a pointed instrument for removing substances caught between the teeth

tooth powder *n* : a powder for cleaning the teeth

tooth·some \'tüth-səm\ *adj* **1** : ATTRACTIVE ⟨a ∼ blond⟩ **2** : pleasing to the taste : DELICIOUS **syn** palatable, appetizing, savory, tasty

toothy \'tü-thē\ *adj* **tooth·i·er; -est** : having or showing prominent teeth

¹top \'täp\ *n* **1** : the highest part, point, or level of something **2** : the stalks and leaves of a plant with edible roots ⟨beet ∼s⟩ **3** : the upper end, edge, or surface ⟨the ∼ of a page⟩ **4** : an upper piece, lid, or covering **5** : a platform around the head of the lower mast **6** : the highest degree, pitch, or rank

²top *vb* **topped; top·ping 1** : to remove or trim the top of : PRUNE ⟨∼ a tree⟩ **2** : to cover with a top or on the top : CROWN, CAP **3** : to be superior to : EXCEL, SURPASS **4** : to go over the top of **5** : to strike (a golf ball) above the center **6** : to make an end or conclusion ⟨∼ off a meal with coffee⟩

³top *adj* : of, relating to, or being at the top : HIGHEST

⁴top *n* : a child's toy that has a tapering point on which it is made to spin

to·paz \'tō-ˌpaz\ *n* : a hard silicate mineral that when occurring as perfect yellow crystals is valued as a gem

top·coat \'täp-ˌkōt\ *n* : a lightweight overcoat

top–dress \'täp-ˌdres\ *vb* : to apply material to (as land) without working it in; *esp* : to scatter fertilizer over

top·dress·ing \-iŋ\ *n* : a material used to top-dress soil

tope \'tōp\ *vb* **toped; top·ing** : to drink intoxicating liquor to excess

top·er \'tō-pər\ *n* : one that topes; *esp* : DRUNKARD

top flight *n* : the highest level of excellence or rank — **top·flight** *adj*

top hat *n* : a man's tall-crowned hat usu. of beaver or silk

top–heavy \'täp-ˌhev-ē\ *adj* : having the top part too heavy for the lower part

top·ic \'täp-ik\ *n* **1** : a heading in an outlined argument **2** : the subject of a discourse or a section of it : THEME

top·i·cal \-i-kəl\ *adj* **1** : of, relating to, or arranged by topics ⟨a ∼ outline⟩ **2** : relating to current or local events — **top·i·cal·ly** \-k(ə-)lē\ *adv*

top·knot \'täp-ˌnät\ *n* **1** : an ornament (as a knot of ribbons) forming a headdress **2** : a crest of feathers or hair on the top of the head

top·less \-ləs\ *adj* **1** : wearing no clothing on the upper body **2** : featuring topless waitresses or entertainers

top·mast \'täp-ˌmast, -məst\ *n* : the 2d mast above a ship's deck

top·most \'täp-ˌmōst\ *adj* : highest of all : UPPERMOST

top–notch \-'näch\ *adj* : of the highest quality : FIRST-RATE

topog *abbr* topography

to·pog·ra·phy \tə-'päg-rə-fē\ *n* **1** : the art of showing in detail on a map or chart the physical features of a place or region **2** : the outline of the form of a place showing its relief and the position of features (as rivers, roads, or cities) — **to·pog·ra·pher** \-fər\ *n* — **top·o·graph·ic** \ˌtäp-ə-'graf-ik\ *or* **top·o·graph·i·cal** \-i-kəl\ *adj*

top·ping \'täp-iŋ\ *n* : something (as a garnish or sauce) that forms a top

top·ple \'täp-əl\ *vb* **top·pled; top·pling** \-(ə-)liŋ\ **1** : to fall from or as if from being top-heavy **2** : to push over : OVERTURN; *also* : OVERTHROW

tops \'täps\ *adj* : topmost in quality or eminence ⟨is considered ∼ in his field⟩

top·sail \'täp-ˌsāl, -səl\ *also* **top·s'l** \-səl\ *n* : the sail next above the lowest sail on a mast in a square-rigged ship

top secret *adj* : demanding inviolate secrecy among those concerned

top•side \'täp-'sīd\ *adv or adj* **1** : to or on the top or surface **2** : on deck

top•sides \-'sīdz\ *n pl* : the top portion of the outer surface of a ship on each side above the waterline

top•soil \'täp-ˌsȯil\ *n* : surface soil usu. including the organic layer in which plants have most of their roots

top•sy–tur•vy \ˌtäp-sē-'tər-vē\ *adv* **1** : in utter confusion **2** : UPSIDE DOWN — **topsy–turvy** *adj*

toque \'tōk\ *n* : a woman's small hat without a brim

tor \'tȯr\ *n* : a high craggy hill

To•rah \'tōr-ə\ *n* **1** : a scroll of the first five books of the Old Testament used in a synagogue; *also* : these five books **2** : the body of divine knowledge and law found in the Jewish scriptures and tradition

torch \'tȯrch\ *n* **1** : a flaming light made of something that burns brightly and usu. carried in the hand **2** : something that resembles a torch in giving light, heat, or guidance **3** *chiefly Brit* : FLASHLIGHT — **torch•bear•er** \-ˌbar-ər\ *n* — **torch•light** \-ˌlīt\ *n*

torch song *n* : a popular sentimental song of unrequited love

tore past of TEAR

to•re•ador \'tȯr-ē-ə-ˌdȯr\ *n* : BULLFIGHTER

to•re•ro \tə-'rer-ō\ *n, pl* **-ros** [Sp] : BULLFIGHTER

¹**tor•ment** \'tȯr-ˌment\ *n* **1** : extreme pain or anguish of body or mind **2** : a source of vexation or pain

²**tor•ment** \tȯr-'ment\ *vb* **1** : to cause severe suffering of body or mind to **2** : VEX, HARASS **syn** rack, afflict, try, torture — **tor•men•tor** \-ər\ *n*

torn past part of TEAR

tor•na•do \tȯr-'nād-ō\ *n, pl* **-does** *or* **-dos** [modif of Sp *tronada* thunderstorm, fr. *tronar* to thunder, fr. L *tonare*] : a violent destructive whirling wind accompanied by a funnel-shaped cloud that moves over a narrow path

¹**tor•pe•do** \tȯr-'pēd-ō\ *n, pl* **-does** : a thin cylindrical self-propelled submarine weapon

²**torpedo** *vb* **tor•pe•doed; tor•pe•do•ing** \-'pēd-ə-wiŋ\ : to hit or destroy with or as if with a torpedo

torpedo boat *n* : a small very fast boat for firing torpedoes

tor•pid \'tȯr-pəd\ *adj* **1** : having lost motion or the power of exertion **2** : SLUGGISH **3** : lacking vigor : DULL — **tor•pid•i•ty** \tȯr-'pid-ət-ē\ *n*

tor•por \'tȯr-pər\ *n* **1** : DULLNESS, APATHY **2** : extreme sluggishness : STAGNATION **syn** stupor, lethargy, languor, lassitude

¹**torque** \'tȯrk\ *n* : a force that produces or tends to produce rotation or torsion

²**torque** *vb* **torqued; torqu•ing** : to impart torque to : cause to twist (as about an axis)

tor•rent \'tȯr-ənt\ *n* [F, fr. L *torrent-, torrens*, fr. *torrent-, torrens* burning, seething, rushing, fr. prp. of *torrēre* to parch, burn] **1** : a rushing stream (as of water) **2** : a tumultuous outburst

tor•ren•tial \tȯ-'ren-chəl, tə-\ *adj* : relating to or resembling a torrent ⟨∼ rains⟩

tor•rid \'tȯr-əd\ *adj* **1** : parched with heat esp. of the sun : HOT **2** : ARDENT

torrid zone *n* : the region of the earth between the tropic of Cancer and the tropic of Capricorn

tor•sion \'tȯr-shən\ *n* **1** : a twisting of a bodily organ on its own axis **2** : a wrenching by which one part of a body is under pressure to turn about a longitudinal axis while the other part is held fast or is under pressure to turn in the opposite direction — **tor•sion•al** \'tȯr-sh(ə-)nəl\ *adj* — **tor•sion•al•ly** \-ē\ *adv*

tor•so \'tȯr-sō\ *n, pl* **torsos** *or* **tor•si** \'tȯr-ˌsē\ [It, lit., stalk] : the trunk of the human body

tort \'tȯrt\ *n* : a wrongful act which does not involve a breach of contract and for which the injured party can recover damages in a civil action

tor•ti•lla \tȯr-'tē-(y)ə\ *n* : a round thin cake of unleavened cornmeal bread usu. eaten hot with a topping of ground meat or cheese

tor•toise \'tȯrt-əs\ *n* : TURTLE; *esp* : a land turtle

¹**tor•toise•shell** \'tȯrt-ə-ˌshel, -əs(h)-ˌshel\ *n* **1** : the mottled horny substance of the shell of some turtles used in inlaying and in making various

ornamental articles **2** : any of several showy butterflies

²tortoiseshell *adj* : made of or resembling tortoiseshell esp. in spotted brown and yellow coloring

tor·to·ni \tȯr-ˈtō-nē\ *n* : ice cream made of heavy cream often with minced almonds and chopped cherries and flavored with rum

tor·tu·ous \ˈtȯrch-(ə-)wəs\ *adj* **1** : marked by twists or turns : WINDING **2** : DEVIOUS, TRICKY

¹tor·ture \ˈtȯr-chər\ *n* **1** : anguish of body or mind : AGONY **2** : the infliction of severe pain esp. to punish or coerce

²torture *vb* **tor·tured; tor·tur·ing** \ˈtȯrch-(ə-)riŋ\ **1** : to cause intense suffering to : TORMENT **2** : to punish or coerce by inflicting severe pain **3** : TWIST, DISTORT **syn** rack, harrow, afflict, try — **tor·tur·er** *n*

To·ry \ˈtōr-ē\ *n, pl* **Tories** [IrGael *tōraidhe* pursued man, robber] **1** : a member of a chiefly 18th century British party upholding the established church and the traditional political structure **2** : an American supporter of the British during the American Revolution **3** *often not cap* : an extreme conservative — **Tory** *adj*

¹toss \ˈtȯs, ˈtäs\ *vb* **1** : to fling to and fro or up and down **2** : to throw with a quick light motion; *also* : BANDY **3** : to fling or lift with a sudden motion ⟨~ed her head angrily⟩ **4** : to move restlessly or turbulently ⟨~es on the waves⟩ **5** : to twist and turn repeatedly **6** : FLOUNCE **7** : to accomplish readily ⟨~ off an article⟩ **8** : to decide an issue by flipping a coin

²toss *n* : an act or instance of tossing; *esp* : TOSS-UP 1

toss–up \-ˌəp\ *n* **1** : a deciding by flipping a coin **2** : an even chance **3** : something that offers no clear basis for choice

¹tot \ˈtät\ *n* **1** : a small child **2** : a small drink of alcoholic liquor : SHOT

²tot *vb* **tot·ted; tot·ting** : to add up

³tot *abbr* total

¹to·tal \ˈtōt-ᵊl\ *adj* **1** : making up a whole : ENTIRE ⟨~ amount⟩ **2** : COMPLETE, UTTER ⟨a ~ failure⟩ **3** : involving a complete and unified effort esp. to

achieve a desired effect — **to·tal·ly** \-ē\ *adv*

²total *n* **1** : SUM 4 **2** : the entire amount **syn** aggregate, whole, gross, totality

³total *vb* **to·taled** *or* **to·talled; to·tal·ing** *or* **to·tal·ling** **1** : to add up : COMPUTE **2** : to amount to : NUMBER **3** : to make a total wreck of (a car)

to·tal·i·tar·i·an \tō-ˌtal-ə-ˈter-ē-ən\ *adj* : of or relating to a political regime based on subordination of the individual to the state and strict control of all aspects of life esp. by coercive measures; *also* : advocating, constituting, or characteristic of such a regime — **totalitarian** *n* — **to·tal·i·tar·i·an·ism** \-ē-ə-ˌniz-əm\ *n*

to·tal·i·ty \tō-ˈtal-ət-ē\ *n, pl* **-ties** **1** : an aggregate amount : SUM, WHOLE **2** : ENTIRETY, WHOLENESS

to·tal·iza·tor *or* **to·tal·isa·tor** \ˈtōt-ᵊl-ə-ˌzāt-ər\ *n* : a machine for registering and indicating the number of bets and the odds on a horse or dog race

¹tote \ˈtōt\ *vb* **tot·ed; tot·ing** : CARRY

²tote *vb* **tot·ed; tot·ing** : ADD, TOTAL — usu. used with *up*

to·tem \ˈtōt-əm\ *n* : an object (as an animal or plant) serving as the emblem of a family or clan and often as a reminder of its ancestry; *also* : something usu. carved or painted to represent such an object

totem pole *n* : a pole that is carved with a series of totems and is erected before the houses of some northwest American Indians

tot·ter \ˈtät-ər\ *vb* **1** : to tremble or rock as if about to fall : SWAY **2** : to move unsteadily : STAGGER

tou·can \ˈtü-ˌkan\ *n* : any of a family of fruit-eating birds of tropical America with brilliant coloring and a very large beak

¹touch \ˈtəch\ *vb* **1** : to bring a bodily part (as the hand) into contact with so as to feel **2** : to be or cause to be in contact **3** : to strike or push lightly esp. with the hand or foot **4** : DISTURB, HARM **5** : to make use of ⟨never ~es alcohol⟩ **6** : to induce to give or lend **7** : to get to : REACH **8** : to refer to in passing : MENTION **9** : to affect the interest of : CONCERN **10** : to leave a mark on; *also* : BLEMISH **11** : to move to sympathetic feeling **12** : to come close : VERGE **13** : to have a bearing : RELATE **14** : to make a usu. brief or incidental stop in port **syn** affect, influence, impress, strike, sway

²**touch** *n* **1** : a light stroke or tap **2** : the act or fact of touching or being touched **3** : the sense by which pressure or traction on the skin or mucous membrane is perceived; *also* : a particular sensation conveyed by this sense **4** : mental or moral sensitiveness : TACT **5** : a small quantity : HINT **6** : a manner of striking or touching esp. the keys of a keyboard instrument **7** : an improving detail ⟨add a few ∼es to the painting⟩ **8** : distinctive manner or skill ⟨∼ of a master⟩ **9** : the state of being in contact ⟨keep in ∼⟩ **syn** suggestion, suspicion, tincture, tinge

touch•down \'təch-ˌdaún\ *n* : the act of scoring six points in American football by being lawfully in possession of the ball on, above, or behind an opponent's goal line

tou•ché \tü-'shā\ *interj* [F] — used to acknowledge a hit in fencing or the success of an argument, an accusation, or a witty point

touch football *n* : football played informally and chiefly characterized by the substitution of touching for tackling

touch•ing \'təch-iŋ\ *adj* : capable of stirring emotions **syn** moving, impressive, poignant, affecting

touch off *vb* **1** : to describe with precision **2** : to cause to explode **3** : to release or initiate with sudden intensity

touch•stone \'təch-ˌstōn\ *n* : a test or criterion of genuineness or quality **syn** standard, gauge, benchmark, yardstick

touch up \(')təch-'əp\ *vb* : to improve or perfect by small additional strokes or alterations

touchy \'təch-ē\ *adj* **touch•i•er; -est 1** : easily offended : PEEVISH **2** : calling for tact in treatment ⟨a ∼ subject⟩ **syn** irascible, cranky, cross, tetchy, testy

¹**tough** \'təf\ *adj* **1** : strong or firm in texture but flexible and not brittle **2** : not easily chewed **3** : characterized by severity and determination ⟨a ∼ policy⟩ **4** : capable of enduring strain or hardship : ROBUST **5** : hard to influ-

ence : STUBBORN **6** : difficult to accomplish, resolve, or cope with ⟨a ∼ problem⟩ **7** : ROWDYISH **syn** tenacious, stout, sturdy, stalwart — **tough•ly** *adv* — **tough•ness** *n*

²**tough** *n* : a tough person : ROWDY

tough•en \'təf-ən\ *vb* **tough•ened; tough•en•ing** \-(ə-)niŋ\ : to make or become tough

tou•pee \tü-'pā\ *n* [F *toupet* forelock] : a small wig for a bald spot

¹**tour** \'túr, *1 is also* 'taú(ə)r\ *n* **1** : one's turn : SHIFT **2** : a journey in which one returns to the starting point

²**tour** *vb* : to travel over as a tourist

tour de force \ˌtúrd-ə-'fōrs\ *n, pl* **tours de force** *same*\ [F] : a feat of strength, skill, or ingenuity

tour•ist \'túr-əst\ *n* : one that makes a tour for pleasure or culture

tourist class *n* : economy accommodation on a ship, airplane, or train

tour•ma•line \'túr-mə-lən, -ˌlēn\ *n* : a mineral that when transparent is valued as a gem

tour•na•ment \'túr-nə-mənt, 'tər-\ *n* **1** : a medieval sport in which mounted armored knights contended with blunted lances or swords; *also* : the whole series of knightly sports, jousts, and tilts occurring at one time and place **2** : a championship series of games or athletic contests

tour•ney \-nē\ *n, pl* **tourneys** : TOURNAMENT

tour•ni•quet \'túr-ni-kət, 'tər-\ *n* : a device (as a bandage twisted tight with a stick) for stopping bleeding or blood flow

tou•sle \'taú-zəl\ *vb* **tou•sled; tou•sling** \'taúz-(ə-)liŋ\ : to disorder by rough handling : DISHEVEL, MUSS

¹**tout** \'taút\ *vb* : to give a tip or solicit bets on a racehorse — **tout** *n*

²**tout** \'taút, 'tüt\ *vb* : to praise or publicize loudly

¹**tow** \'tō\ *vb* : to draw or pull along behind **syn** tug, haul, drag, lug

²**tow** *n* **1** : an act of towing or condition of being towed **2** : something (as a barge) that is towed

³**tow** *n* : short or broken fiber (as of flax or hemp) used esp. for yarn, twine, or stuffing

to•ward *or* **to•wards** \(')tō(-ə)rd(z), tə-'wórd(z)\ *prep* **1** : in the direction of ⟨heading ∼ the river⟩ **2** : along a course leading to ⟨efforts ∼ reconciliation⟩ **3** : in regard to ⟨tolerance ∼ minorities⟩ **4** : FACING ⟨the gun's muzzle was ∼ him⟩ **5** : close upon ⟨it was getting along ∼ sundown⟩ **6** : for part payment of ⟨paid $100 ∼ his tuition⟩

tow·boat \'tō-ˌbōt\ *n* : TUGBOAT

tow·el \'taủ(-ə)l\ *n* : an absorbent cloth or paper for wiping or drying

tow·el·ing *or* **tow·el·ling** \'taủ-(ə-)liŋ\ *n* : a cotton or linen fabric often used for making towels

¹**tow·er** \'taủ(-ə)r\ *n* **1** : a tall structure either isolated or built upon a larger structure ⟨an observation ∼⟩ ⟨a bell ∼ of a church⟩ **2** : a towering citadel — **tow·ered** \'taủ(-ə)rd\ *adj*

²**tower** *vb* : to reach or rise to a great height **syn** overlook, dominate

tow·er·ing \-iŋ\ *adj* **1** : LOFTY ⟨∼ pines⟩ **2** : reaching high intensity ⟨a ∼ rage⟩ **3** : EXCESSIVE ⟨∼ ambition⟩

tow·head \'tō-ˌhed\ *n* : a person having flaxen hair — **tow·head·ed** \-ˌhed-əd\ *adj*

to·whee \'tō-ˌhē, 'tō-(ˌ)ē, tō-'hē\ *n* : a common finch of eastern No. America having the male black, white, and reddish; *also* : any of several related finches

to wit \tə-'wit\ *adv* : NAMELY

town \'taủn\ *n* **1** : a compactly settled area usu. larger than a village but smaller than a city **2** : CITY **3** : the inhabitants of a town **4** : a New England territorial and political unit usu. containing both rural and urban areas; *also* : a New England community in which matters of local government are decided by a general assembly **(town meeting)** of qualified voters

town house *n* **1** : the city residence of a person having a country home **2** : a single-family house of two or sometimes three stories connected to another house by a common wall

town·ie *or* **towny** \'taủ-nē\ *n, pl* **townies** : a permanent resident of a town as distinguished from a member of another group

towns·folk \'taủnz-ˌfōk\ *n pl* : TOWNS-PEOPLE

town·ship \'taủn-ˌship\ *n* **1** : TOWN 4 **2** : a unit of local government in some states **3** : an unorganized subdivision

of a county; *also* : an administrative division **4** : a division of territory in surveys of U.S. public land containing 36 square miles

towns·man \'taủnz-mən\ *n* **1** : a native or resident of a town or city **2** : a fellow citizen of a town

towns·peo·ple \-ˌpē-pəl\ *n pl* **1** : the inhabitants of a town or city **2** : town≠ bred persons

tow·path \'tō-ˌpath, -ˌpȧth\ *n* : a path (as along a canal) traveled by men or animals towing boats

tow truck *n* : WRECKER 2

tox·emia \täk-'sē-mē-ə\ *n* : a bodily disorder associated with the presence of toxic matter in the blood

tox·ic \'täk-sik\ *adj* [LL *toxicus,* fr. L *toxicum* poison, fr. Gk *toxikon* arrow poison, fr. neut. of *toxikos* of a bow, fr. *toxon* bow, arrow] : of, relating to, or caused by poison or a toxin : POISONOUS — **tox·ic·i·ty** \täk-'sis-ət-ē\ *n*

tox·i·col·o·gy \ˌtäk-sə-'käl-ə-jē\ *n* : a science that deals with poisons and esp. with problems of their use and control — **tox·i·co·log·i·cal** \-'läj-i-kəl\ *or* **tox·i·co·log·ic** \ˌtäk-si-kə-'läj-ik\ *adj* — **tox·i·col·o·gist** \-'käl-ə-jəst\ *n*

toxic shock syndrome *n* : an acute disease probably of bacterial origin that is characterized by fever, sore throat, and diffuse erythema and occurs esp. in menstruating females using tampons

tox·in \'täk-sən\ *n* : a substance produced by a living organism that is very poisonous when introduced into the tissues but is usu. destroyed by digestive processes when taken by mouth

¹**toy** \'tȯi\ *n* **1** : something trifling **2** : a small ornament : BAUBLE **3** : something for a child to play with

²**toy** *vb* **1** : FLIRT **2** : to deal with something lightly : TRIFLE **3** : to amuse oneself as if with a plaything

³**toy** *adj* **1** : DIMINUTIVE **2** : designed for use as a toy

tp *abbr* **1** title page **2** township

tpk *or* **tpke** *abbr* turnpike

tr *abbr* **1** translated; translation; translator **2** transpose **3** troop

¹**trace** \'trās\ *n* **1** : a mark (as a footprint or track) left by something that has passed : VESTIGE **2** : a minute or barely detectable amount

²trace *vb* **traced; trac·ing 1** : to mark out : SKETCH **2** : to form (as letters) carefully **3** : to copy (a drawing) by marking lines on transparent paper laid over the drawing to be copied **4** : to follow the trail of : track down **5** : to study out and follow the development of — **trace·able** *adj* — **trac·er** *n*

³trace *n* : either of two lines of a harness for fastening a draft animal to a vehicle

trac·ery \ˈtrās(-ə)-rē\ *n, pl* **-er·ies** : ornamental work having a design with branching or interlacing lines

tra·chea \ˈtrā-kē-ə\ *n, pl* **-che·ae** \-kē-ˌē\ *also* **-che·as** : the main tube by which air enters the lungs : WINDPIPE — **tra·che·al** \-kē-əl\ *adj*

trac·ing \ˈtrā-siŋ\ *n* **1** : the act of one that traces **2** : something that is traced **3** : a graphic record made by an instrument for measuring vibrations or pulsations

¹track \ˈtrak\ *n* **1** : a mark left in passing **2** : PATH, ROUTE, TRAIL **3** : a course laid out for racing; *also* : track-and-field sports **4** : one of a series of paths along which material (as music) is recorded (as on magnetic tape) **5** : the course along which something moves; *esp* : a way made by two parallel lines of metal rails **6** : awareness of a fact or progression ⟨lost ∼ of his movements⟩ **7** : either of two endless metal belts on which a vehicle (as a tractor) travels

²track *vb* **1** : to follow the tracks or traces of : TRAIL **2** : to make tracks on **3** : to carry on the feet and deposit ⟨∼ed mud on the floor⟩ — **track·er** *n*

track·age \ˈtrak-ij\ *n* : lines of railway track

track–and–field \ˌtrak-ən-ˈfēld\ *adj* : of or relating to athletic contests held on a running track or on the adjacent field

¹tract \ˈtrakt\ *n* **1** : a stretch of land without precise boundaries ⟨broad ∼s of prairie⟩ **2** : a defined area of land ⟨a garden ∼⟩ **3** : a system of body parts or organs together serving some special purpose ⟨the digestive ∼⟩

²tract *n* : a pamphlet of political or religious propaganda

trac·ta·ble \ˈtrak-tə-bəl\ *adj* **1** : easily controlled : DOCILE **2** : easily wrought : MALLEABLE **syn** amenable, obedient, biddable

trac·tate \ˈtrak-ˌtāt\ *n* : TREATISE

tract house *n* : any of many similarly designed houses built on a tract of land

trac·tion \ˈtrak-shən\ *n* **1** : the act of drawing : the state of being drawn **2** : the drawing of a vehicle by motive power; *also* : the particular form of motive power used **3** : the adhesive friction of a body on a surface on which it moves **4** : a pulling force applied to a skeletal structure (as a broken bone) by using a special device; *also* : a state of tension created by such a pulling force ⟨a leg in ∼⟩ — **trac·tion·al** \-sh(ə-)nəl\ *adj* — **trac·tive** \ˈtrak-tiv\ *adj*

trac·tor \ˈtrak-tər\ *n* **1** : an automotive vehicle that is borne on four wheels or beltlike metal tracks and is used esp. for drawing farm equipment **2** : a motortruck with short chassis for hauling a trailer

¹trade \ˈtrād\ *n* **1** : one's regular business or work : OCCUPATION **2** : an occupation requiring manual or mechanical skill **3** : the persons engaged in a business or industry **4** : the business of buying and selling or bartering commodities **5** : an act of trading : TRANSACTION **syn** craft, profession, calling, vocation

²trade *vb* **trad·ed; trad·ing 1** : to give in exchange for another commodity : BARTER **2** : to engage in the exchange, purchase, or sale of goods **3** : to deal regularly as a customer — **trade on** : EXPLOIT ⟨*trades on* his family name⟩

trade–in \ˈtrād-ˌin\ *n* : an item of merchandise taken as part payment of a purchase

trade in \(ˈ)trād-ˈin\ *vb* : to turn in as part payment for a purchase

¹trade·mark \ˈtrād-ˌmärk\ *n* : a device (as a word or mark) that points distinctly to the origin or ownership of merchandise to which it is applied and that is legally reserved for the exclusive use of the owner

²trademark *vb* : to secure the trademark rights for

trade name *n* : a name that is given by a manufacturer or merchant to a product to distinguish it as made or sold by him and that may be used and protected as a trademark

trad·er \'trād-ər\ *n* **1** : a person whose business is buying or selling **2** : a ship engaged in trade

trades·man \'trādz-mən\ *n* **1** : one who runs a retail store : SHOPKEEPER **2** : CRAFTSMAN

trades·peo·ple \-ˌpē-pəl\ *n pl* : people engaged in trade

trade wind *n* : a wind blowing almost constantly in one direction

trading stamp *n* : a printed stamp of value given as a premium to a retail customer and when accumulated in numbers redeemed in merchandise

tra·di·tion \trə-'dish-ən\ *n* **1** : an inherited, established, or customary pattern of thought or action **2** : the handing down of beliefs and customs by word of mouth or by example without written instruction; *also* : a belief or custom thus handed down — **tra·di·tion·al** \-ˌdish(ə-)nəl\ *adj* — **tra·di·tion·al·ly** \-ē\ *adv*

tra·duce \trə-'d(y)üs\ *vb* **tra·duced; tra·duc·ing** : to lower the reputation of : DEFAME, SLANDER **syn** malign, libel, calumniate — **tra·duc·er** *n*

¹traf·fic \'traf-ik\ *n* **1** : the business of bartering or buying and selling **2** : communication or dealings between individuals or groups **3** : the movement (as of vehicles) along a route **4** : the passengers or cargo carried by a transportation system

²traffic *vb* **traf·ficked; traf·fick·ing** : to carry on traffic — **traf·fick·er** *n*

traffic circle *n* : ROTARY 2

traffic light *n* : an electrically operated visual signal for controlling traffic

tra·ge·di·an \trə-'jēd-ē-ən\ *n* **1** : a writer of tragedies **2** : an actor who plays tragic roles

tra·ge·di·enne \trə-ˌjēd-ē-'en\ *n* [F] : an actress who plays tragic roles

trag·e·dy \'traj-əd-ē\ *n, pl* **-dies** [ME *tragedie*, fr. MF, fr. L *tragoedia*, fr. Gk *tragōidia*, fr. *tragos* goat + *aeidein* to sing] **1** : a serious drama describing a conflict between the protagonist and a superior force (as destiny) and having a sad end that excites pity or terror **2** : a disastrous

event : CALAMITY; *also* : MISFORTUNE **3** : tragic quality or element

trag·ic \'traj-ik\ *also* **trag·i·cal** \-i-kəl\ *adj* **1** : of, relating to, or expressive of tragedy **2** : appropriate to tragedy **3** : LAMENTABLE, UNFORTUNATE — **trag·i·cal·ly** \-i-k(ə-)lē\ *adv*

¹trail \'trāl\ *vb* **1** : to hang down so as to drag along or sweep the ground **2** : to draw or drag along behind **3** : to extend over a surface in a straggling manner **4** : to follow slowly : lag behind **5** : to follow upon the track of : PURSUE **6** : DWINDLE ⟨her voice ~ed off⟩ **syn** tag, tail, dog, shadow

²trail *n* **1** : something that trails or is trailed ⟨a ~ of smoke⟩ **2** : a trace or mark left by something that has passed or been drawn along : TRACK ⟨a ~ of blood⟩ **3** : a beaten path; *also* : a marked path through woods **4** : SCENT

trail bike *n* : a small motorcycle for use other than on highways

trail·blaz·er \-ˌblā-zər\ *n* : PATHFINDER, PIONEER — **trail·blaz·ing** \-ziŋ\ *adj or n*

trail·er \'trā-lər\ *n* **1** : one that trails; *esp* : a creeping plant (as an ivy) **2** : a vehicle that is hauled by another (as a tractor) **3** : a vehicle equipped to serve wherever parked as a dwelling or as a place of business

trailing arbutus *n* : a trailing spring-flowering plant of the heath family with fragrant pink or white flowers; *also* : its flower

¹train \'trān\ *n* **1** : a part of a gown that trails behind the wearer **2** : RETINUE **3** : a moving file of persons, vehicles, or animals **4** : a connected series ⟨a ~ of thought⟩ **5** : AFTERMATH **6** : a connected line of railroad cars usu. hauled by a locomotive **syn** succession, sequence, procession, chain

²train *vb* **1** : to cause to grow as desired ⟨~ a vine on a trellis⟩ **2** : to form by instruction, discipline, or drill **3** : to make or become prepared (as by exercise) for a test of skill **4** : to aim or point at an object ⟨~ guns on a fort⟩ **syn** discipline, school, educate, instruct — **train·er** *n*

train·ee \trā-'nē\ *n* : one who is being trained for a job

train·ing \'trā-niŋ\ *n* **1** : the act, process, or method of one who trains **2**

: the knowledge or experience gained by one who trains

train·load \'trān-ˌlōd\ *n* : the full freight or passenger capacity of a railroad train

train·man \-mən\ *n* : a member of a train crew

traipse \'trāps\ *vb* **traipsed; traips·ing** : TRAMP, WALK

trait \'trāt\ *n* : a distinguishing quality (as of personality) : CHARACTERISTIC

trai·tor \'trāt-ər\ *n* [ME *traitre,* fr. OF, fr. L *traditor,* fr. *traditus,* pp. of *tradere* to hand over, deliver, betray, fr. *trans-* across + *dare* to give] 1 : one who betrays another's trust or is false to an obligation 2 : one who commits treason — **trai·tor·ous** *adj*

tra·jec·to·ry \trə-'jek-t(ə-)rē\ *n, pl* **-ries** : the curve that a body (as a planet in its orbit) describes in space

tram \'tram\ *n* 1 *chiefly Brit* : STREETCAR 2 : a boxlike car running on a railway (**tram·way** \-ˌwā\) in a mine or a logging camp

¹tram·mel \'tram-əl\ *n* [ME *tramayle,* a kind of net, fr. MF *tremail,* fr. LL *tremaculum,* fr. L *tres* three + *macula* mesh, spot] : something impeding activity, progress, or freedom

²trammel *vb* **-meled** *or* **-melled; -mel·ing** *or* **-mel·ling** \-(ə-)liŋ\ 1 : to catch and hold in or as if in a net 2 : HAMPER **syn** clog, fetter, shackle, hobble

¹tramp \'tramp, *1 & 3 are also* 'trämp, 'tromp\ *vb* 1 : to walk, tread, or step heavily 2 : to walk about or through; *also* : HIKE 3 : to tread on forcibly and repeatedly

²tramp \'tramp, *5 is also* 'trämp, 'tromp\ *n* 1 : a foot traveler 2 : a begging or thieving vagrant 3 : an immoral woman; *esp* : PROSTITUTE 4 : a walking trip : HIKE 5 : the succession of sounds made by the beating of feet on a road 6 : a ship that does not follow a regular course but takes cargo to any port

tram·ple \'tram-pəl\ *vb* **tram·pled; tram·pling** \-p(ə-)liŋ\ 1 : to tread heavily so as to bruise, crush, or injure 2 : to inflict injury or destruction 3 : to press down or crush by or as if by treading : STAMP — **trample** *n* — **tram·pler** \-p(ə-)lər\ *n*

tram·po·line \ˌtram-pə-'lēn, 'tram-pə-ˌlēn\ *n* [Sp *trampolín*] : a resilient can-

vas sheet or web supported by springs in a metal frame used as a springboard in tumbling — **tram·po·lin·ist** \-nəst\ *n*

trance \'trans\ *n* [ME, fr. MF *transe,* fr. *transir* to pass away, swoon, fr. L *transire* to pass, pass away, fr. *trans-* across + *ire* go] 1 : DAZE, STUPOR 2 : a prolonged and profound sleeplike condition (as of deep hypnosis) 3 : a state of mystical absorption

tran·quil \'traŋ-kwəl, 'tran-\ *adj* : free from agitation or disturbance : QUIET **syn** serene, placid, peaceful — **tran·quil·li·ty** *or* **tran·quil·i·ty** \tran-'kwil-ət-ē, traŋ-\ *n* — **tran·quil·ly** \'traŋ-kwə-lē, 'tran-\ *adv*

tran·quil·ize *also* **tran·quil·lize** \'traŋ-kwə-ˌlīz, 'tran-\ *vb* **-ized** *also* **-lized; -iz·ing** *also* **-liz·ing** : to make or become tranquil; *esp* : to relieve of mental tension and anxiety

tran·quil·iz·er *also* **tran·quil·liz·er** \-ˌlī-zər\ *n* : a drug used to relieve tension and anxiety

trans *abbr* 1 transaction 2 transitive 3 translated; translation; translator 4 transportation 5 transverse

trans·act \trans-'akt, tranz-\ *vb* : CARRY OUT, PERFORM; *also* : CONDUCT

trans·ac·tion \-'ak-shən\ *n* 1 : something transacted; *esp* : a business deal 2 : an act or process of transacting 3 *pl* : the records of the proceedings of a society or organization

trans·at·lan·tic \ˌtrans-ət-'lant-ik, ˌtranz-\ *adj* : crossing or extending across or situated beyond the Atlantic ocean

trans·ceiv·er \trans-'ē-vər, tranz-\ *n* : a radio transmitter-receiver that uses many of the same components for transmission and reception

tran·scend \trans-'end\ *vb* 1 : to rise above the limits of 2 : SURPASS **syn** exceed, outdo, outshine, outstrip

tran·scen·dent \-'en-dənt\ *adj* 1 : exceeding usual limits : SURPASSING 2 : transcending material existence **syn** superlative, supreme, peerless, incomparable

tran·scen·den·tal \ˌtrans-ˌen-'dent-ᵊl, -ən-\ *adj* 1 : TRANSCENDENT 2 : of, relating to, or characteristic of transcendentalism; *also* : ABSTRUSE

tran·scen·den·tal·ism \-ᵊl-ˌiz-əm\ *n* : a philosophy holding that ultimate reality is unknowable or asserting the primacy of the spiritual over the material and empirical — **tran·scen·den·tal·ist** \-ᵊl-əst\ *adj or n*

trans·con·ti·nen·tal \ˌtrans-ˌkänt-ᵊn-ᶦent-ᵊl\ *adj* : extending or going across a continent

tran·scribe \trans-ᶦkrīb\ *vb* **tran·scribed; tran·scrib·ing 1** : to write a copy of **2** : to make a copy of (dictated or recorded matter) in longhand or on a typewriter **3** : to represent (speech sounds) by means of phonetic symbols; *also* : to make a musical transcription of

tran·script \ᶦtrans-ˌkript\ *n* **1** : a written, printed, or typed copy **2** : an official copy esp. of a student's educational record

tran·scrip·tion \trans-ᶦkrip-shən\ *n* **1** : an act or process of transcribing **2** : COPY, TRANSCRIPT **3** : an arrangement of a musical composition for some instrument or voice other than the original

trans·duc·er \-ᶦd(y)ü-sər\ *n* : a device that is actuated by power from one system and supplies power usu. in another form to a second system

tran·sept \ᶦtrans-ˌept\ *n* : the part of a cruciform church that crosses at right angles to the greatest length; *also* : either of the projecting ends

¹**trans·fer** \trans-ᶦfər, ᶦtrans-ˌfər\ *vb* **trans·ferred; trans·fer·ring 1** : to pass or cause to pass from one person, place, or situation to another : TRANSPORT, TRANSMIT **2** : to make over the possession of : CONVEY **3** : to print or copy from one surface to another by contact **4** : to change from one vehicle or transportation line to another — **trans·fer·able** \trans-ᶦfər-ə-bəl\ *adj* — **trans·fer·al** \-əl\ *n*

²**trans·fer** \ᶦtrans-ˌfər\ *n* **1** : conveyance of right, title, or interest in property from one person to another **2** : an act or process of transferring **3** : one that transfers or is transferred **4** : a ticket entitling a passenger to continue a journey on another route

trans·fer·ence \trans-ᶦfər-əns\ *n* : an act, process, or instance of transferring

trans·fig·ure \trans-ᶦfig-yər\ *vb* **-ured; -ur·ing 1** : to change the form or ap-

pearance of **2** : EXALT, GLORIFY — **trans·fig·u·ra·tion** \ˌtrans-ˌfig-(y)ə-ᶦrā-shən\ *n*

trans·fix \trans-ᶦfiks\ *vb* **1** : to pierce through with or as if with a pointed weapon **2** : to hold motionless by or as if by piercing

trans·form \trans-ᶦförm\ *vb* **1** : to change in structure, appearance, or character **2** : to change (an electric current) in potential or type **syn** transmute, transfigure, transmogrify — **trans·for·ma·tion** \ˌtrans-fər-ᶦmā-shən\ *n* — **trans·form·er** \trans-ᶦför-mər\ *n*

trans·fuse \trans-ᶦfyüz\ *vb* **trans·fused; trans·fus·ing 1** : to cause to pass from one to another **2** : to diffuse into or through **3** : to transfer (as blood) into a vein of a person or animal — **trans·fu·sion** \-ᶦfyü-zhən\ *n*

trans·gress \trans-ᶦgres, tranz-\ *vb* [F *transgresser,* fr. L *transgressus,* pp. of *transgredi* to step beyond or across, fr. *trans-* across + *gradi* to step] **1** : to go beyond the limits set by ⟨∼ the divine law⟩ **2** : to go beyond : EXCEED **3** : SIN — **trans·gres·sion** \-ᶦgresh-ən\ *n* — **trans·gres·sor** \-ᶦgres-ər\ *n*

¹**tran·sient** \ᶦtranch-ənt\ *adj* **1** : not lasting long : SHORT-LIVED **2** : passing through a place with only a brief stay **syn** transitory, passing, momentary, fleeting — **tran·sient·ly** *adv*

²**transient** *n* : one that is transient; *esp* : a transient guest

tran·sis·tor \tranz-ᶦis-tər, trans-\ *n* [*trans*fer + re*sistor:* fr. its transferring an electrical signal across a resistor] **1** : a small electronic semiconductor device similar in use to a vacuum tube **2** : a radio having transistors

tran·sis·tor·ize \-tə-ˌrīz\ *vb* **-ized; -iz·ing** : to equip (a device) with transistors

tran·sit \ᶦtrans-ət, ᶦtranz-\ *n* **1** : a passing through, across, or over : PASSAGE **2** : conveyance of persons or things from one place to another **3** : usu. local transportation esp. of people by public conveyance **4** : a surveyor's instrument for measuring angles

tran·si·tion \trans-ᶦish-ən, tranz-\ *n* : passage from one state, place, stage,

or subject to another : CHANGE —
tran·si·tion·al \-'ish-(ə-)nəl\ *adj*

tran·si·tive \'trans-ət-iv, 'tranz-\ *adj* **1** : having or containing an object required to complete the meaning **2** : TRANSITIONAL — **tran·si·tive·ly** *adv* — **tran·si·tive·ness** *n* — **tran·si·tiv·i·ty** \ˌtrans-ə-'tiv-ət-ē, ˌtranz-\ *n*

tran·si·to·ry \'trans-ə-ˌtōr-ē, 'tranz-\ *adj* : of brief duration : SHORT-LIVED, TEMPORARY **syn** transient, passing, momentary, fleeting

transl *abbr* translated; translation

trans·late \trans-'lāt, tranz-\ *vb* **trans·lat·ed; trans·lat·ing 1** : to bear or change from one place, state, or form to another **2** : to convey to heaven without death **3** : to transfer (a bishop) from one see to another **4** : to turn into one's own or another language — **trans·lat·able** *adj* — **trans·la·tion** \-'lā-shən\ *n* — **trans·la·tor** \-'lāt-ər\ *n*

trans·lit·er·ate \trans-'lit-ə-ˌrāt, tranz-\ *vb* **-at·ed; -at·ing** : to represent or spell in the characters of another alphabet — **trans·lit·er·a·tion** \ˌtrans-ˌlit-ə-'rā-shən, ˌtranz-\ *n*

trans·lu·cent \trans-'lüs-ᵊnt, tranz-\ *adj* : admitting and diffusing light so that objects beyond cannot be clearly distinguished : partly transparent — **trans·lu·cence** \-ᵊns\ *n* — **trans·lu·cen·cy** \-ᵊn-sē\ *n* — **trans·lu·cent·ly** *adv*

trans·mi·grate \-'mī-ˌgrāt\ *vb* : to pass at death from one body or being to another — **trans·mi·gra·tion** \ˌtrans-mī-'grā-shən, ˌtranz-\ *n* — **trans·mi·gra·to·ry** \trans-'mī-grə-ˌtōr-ē\ *adj*

trans·mis·sion \-'mish-ən\ *n* **1** : an act or process of transmitting **2** : the passage of radio waves between transmitting stations and receiving stations **3** : the gears by which power is transmitted from the engine of an automobile to the axle that propels the vehicle **4** : something transmitted

trans·mit \-'mit\ *vb* **trans·mit·ted; trans·mit·ting 1** : to transfer from one person or place to another : FORWARD **2** : to pass on by or as if by inheritance **3** : to cause or allow to spread abroad or to another ⟨∼ a disease⟩ **4** : to cause (as light, electricity, or force) to pass through space or a medium **5** : to send out (radio or television signals) **syn** convey, communicate, impart —

trans·mis·si·ble \-'mis-ə-bəl\ *adj* —
trans·mit·ta·ble \-'mit-ə-bəl\ *adj* —
trans·mit·tal \-'mit-ᵊl\ *n*

trans·mit·ter \-'mit-ər\ *n* **1** : one that transmits **2** : the part of a telephone into which one speaks **3** : an apparatus for transmitting telegraph, radio, or television signals

trans·mog·ri·fy \trans-'mäg-rə-ˌfī, tranz-\ *vb* **-fied; -fy·ing** : to change or alter often with grotesque or humorous effect — **trans·mog·ri·fi·ca·tion** \-ˌmäg-rə-fə-'kā-shən\ *n*

trans·mute \-'myüt\ *vb* **trans·muted; trans·mut·ing** : to change or alter in form, appearance, or nature **syn** transform, convert, transfigure, metamorphose — **trans·mu·ta·tion** \ˌtrans-myü-'tā-shən, ˌtranz-\ *n*

trans·na·tion·al \-'nash-(ə-)nəl\ *adj* : extending beyond national boundaries

trans·oce·an·ic \ˌtrans-ˌō-shē-'an-ik, ˌtranz-\ *adj* **1** : lying or dwelling beyond the ocean **2** : crossing or extending across the ocean

tran·som \'tran-səm\ *n* **1** : a piece (as a crossbar in the frame of a window or door) that lies crosswise in a structure **2** : a window above an opening (as a door) built on and often hinged to a horizontal crossbar

tran·son·ic *also* **trans–son·ic** \tran(s)-'sän-ik\ *adj* : being, relating to, or moving at a speed that is about that of sound in air or about 741 miles (1185 kilometers) per hour

transp *abbr* transportation

trans·pa·cif·ic \ˌtrans-pə-'sif-ik\ *adj* : crossing, extending across, or situated beyond the Pacific ocean

trans·par·ent \trans-'par-ənt\ *adj* **1** : transmitting light : clear enough to be seen through **2** : SHEER, DIAPHANOUS ⟨a ∼ fabric⟩ **3** : readily understood : CLEAR; *also* : easily detected ⟨a ∼ lie⟩ **syn** lucid, translucent, lucent — **trans·par·en·cy** \-ən-sē\ *n* — **trans·par·ent·ly** *adv*

tran·spire \trans-'pī(ə)r\ *vb* **trans·pired; trans·pir·ing** [MF *transpirer,* fr. L *trans-* across + *spirare* to breathe] **1** : to pass off (as watery vapor) through pores or a membrane **2** : to become known : come to light **3** : to take place : OCCUR — **tran·spi·ra·tion** \ˌtrans-pə-'rā-shən\ *n*

¹**trans·plant** \trans-'plant\ *vb* **1** : to take up and set again in another soil or location **2** : to remove from one place and settle or introduce elsewhere : TRANSPORT **3** : to transfer (an organ or tissue) from one part or individual to another **4** : to tolerate or adapt to being transplanted — **trans·plan·ta·tion** \ˌtrans-ˌplan-'tā-shən\ *n*

²**trans·plant** \'trans-ˌplant\ *n* **1** : something transplanted **2** : the act or process of transplanting

trans·po·lar \trans-'pō-lər\ *adj* : going or extending across either of the polar regions

¹**trans·port** \trans-'pōrt\ *vb* **1** : to convey from one place to another : CARRY **2** : to carry away by strong emotion : ENRAPTURE **3** : to send to a penal colony overseas **syn** bear, carry, convey, ferry — **trans·por·ta·tion** \ˌtrans-pər-'tā-shən\ *n* — **trans·port·er** \trans-'pōrt-ər\ *n*

²**trans·port** \'trans-ˌpōrt\ *n* **1** : an act of transporting : TRANSPORTATION **2** : strong or intensely pleasurable emotion : RAPTURE **3** : a ship used in transporting troops or supplies; *also* : a vehicle (as a truck or plane) used to transport persons or goods

trans·pose \trans-'pōz\ *vb* **trans·posed**; **trans·pos·ing** **1** : to change the position or sequence of ⟨∼ the letters in a word⟩ **2** : to write or perform (a musical composition) in a diffcrent key **syn** reverse, invert — **trans·po·si·tion** \ˌtrans-pə-'zish-ən\ *n*

trans·ship \tran(ch)-'ship, trans-\ *vb* : to transfer for further transportation from one ship or conveyance to another — **trans·ship·ment** *n*

tran·sub·stan·ti·a·tion \ˌtrans-əb-ˌstan-chē-'ā-shən\ *n* : the change in the eucharistic elements from the substance of bread and wine to the substance of the body of Christ with only the appearances of bread and wine remaining

trans·verse \trans-'vərs, tranz-\ *adj* : lying across : set crosswise — **transverse** \'trans-ˌvərs, 'tranz-\ *n* — **trans·verse·ly** *adv*

trans·ves·tite \trans-'ves-ˌtīt, tranz-\ *n* : a person and esp. a male who adopts the dress and often the behavior of the opposite sex — **transvestite** *adj* — **trans·ves·tism** \-ˌtiz-əm\ *n*

¹**trap** \'trap\ *n* **1** : a device for catching animals **2** : something by which one is caught unawares **3** : a machine for throwing objects into the air to be targets for shooters; *also* : a hazard on a golf course consisting of a depression containing sand **4** : a light one-horse carriage on springs **5** : a device to allow some one thing to pass through while keeping other things out ⟨a ∼ in a drainpipe⟩ **6** *pl* : a group of percussion instruments used in a jazz or dance orchestra

²**trap** *vb* **trapped**; **trap·ping** **1** : to catch in or as if in a trap; *also* : CONFINE **2** : to provide or set (a place) with traps **3** : to set traps for animals esp. as a business **syn** snare, entrap, ensnare, bag, lure, decoy — **trap·per** *n*

³**trap** *n* : any of various dark fine‑grained igneous rocks used esp. in making roads

trap·door \'trap-ˌdōr\ *n* : a lifting or sliding door covering an opening in a floor or roof

tra·peze \tra-'pēz\ *n* : a gymnastic apparatus consisting of a horizontal bar suspended by two parallel ropes

trap·e·zoid \'trap-ə-ˌzōid\ *n* [NL *trapezoïdes,* fr. Gk *trapezoeidēs* trapezoid-shaped, fr. *trapeza* table, fr. *tra-* four + *peza* foot] : a plane 4-sided figure with two and only two sides parallel — **trap·e·zoi·dal** \ˌtrap-ə-'zōid-ᵊl\ *adj*

trap·pings \'trap-iŋz\ *n pl* **1** : an ornamental covering esp. for a horse **2** : outward decoration or dress

trap·rock \'trap-ˌräk\ *n* : ³TRAP

traps \'traps\ *n pl* : personal belongings : LUGGAGE

trap·shoot·ing \'trap-ˌshüt-iŋ\ *n* : shooting at clay pigeons sprung from a trap into the air away from the shooter

trash \'trash\ *n* **1** : something of little worth : RUBBISH **2** : a worthless person; *also* : such persons as a group : RIFFRAFF — **trashy** *adj*

trau·ma \'traù-mə, 'trò-\ *n, pl* **trau·ma·ta** \-mət-ə\ *or* **traumas** [Gk] : a bodily or mental injury usu. caused by an external agent; *also* : a cause of trau-ma — **trau·mat·ic** \trə-'mat-ik, trȯ-, traủ-\ *adj*

¹tra·vail \trə-'vāl, 'trav-ˌāl\ *n* **1** : painful work or exertion : TOIL **2** : AGONY, TORMENT **3** : CHILDBIRTH, LABOR **syn** work, drudgery, grind

²travail *vb* : to labor hard : TOIL

¹trav·el \'trav-əl\ *vb* **-eled** *or* **-elled; -el·ing** *or* **-el·ling** \-(ə-)liŋ\ **1** : to go on or as if on a trip or tour : JOURNEY **2** : to move as if by traveling : PASS ⟨news ∼s fast⟩ **3** : ASSOCIATE **4** : to go from place to place as a salesman **5** : to move from point to point ⟨light waves ∼ very fast⟩ **6** : to journey over or through ⟨∼*ing* the highways⟩ — **trav·el·er** *or* **trav·el·ler** *n*

²travel *n* **1** : the act of traveling : PASSAGE **2** : JOURNEY, TRIP — often used in pl. **3** : the number traveling : TRAFFIC **4** : the motion of a piece of machinery and esp. when to and fro; *also* : length of motion (as of a piston)

traveling bag *n* : a bag carried by hand and designed to hold a traveler's clothing and personal articles

trav·el·ogue *or* **trav·el·og** \'trav-ə-ˌlȯg, -ˌläg\ *n* : a usu. illustrated lecture on travel

¹tra·verse \'trav-ərs\ *n* : something (as a crosswise beam) that crosses or lies across

²tra·verse \trə-'vərs, tra-'vərs *or* 'trav-ərs\ *vb* **tra·versed; tra·vers·ing** **1** : to pass through : PENETRATE **2** : to go or travel across or over **3** : to extend over **4** : SWIVEL

³tra·verse \'tra-ˌvərs\ *adj* : TRANSVERSE

trav·er·tine \'trav-ər-ˌtēn, -tən\ *n* : a crystalline mineral formed by deposition from spring waters

¹trav·es·ty \'trav-ə-stē\ *vb* **-tied; -ty·ing** : to make a travesty of

²travesty *n, pl* **-ties** [obs. E *travesty*, disguised, parodied, fr. F *travesti*, pp. of *travestir* to disguise, fr. It *travestire*, fr. *tra-* across (fr. L *trans-*) + *vestire* to dress] : a burlesque and usu. grotesque translation or imitation

¹trawl \'trȯl\ *vb* : to fish or catch with a trawl — **trawl·er** *n*

²trawl *n* **1** : a large conical net dragged along the sea bottom in fishing **2** : a long fishing line anchored at both ends and equipped with many hooks

tray \'trā\ *n* : an open receptacle with flat bottom and low rim for holding, carrying, or exhibiting articles

treach·er·ous \'trech-(ə-)rəs\ *adj* **1** : characterized by treachery **2** : UNTRUSTWORTHY, UNRELIABLE **3** : providing insecure footing or support **syn** traitorous, faithless, false, disloyal — **treach·er·ous·ly** *adv*

treach·ery \'trech-(ə-)rē\ *n, pl* **-er·ies** : violation of allegiance or trust

trea·cle \'trē-kəl\ *n* [ME *triacle* a medicinal compound, fr. MF, fr. L *theriaca*, fr. Gk *thēriakē* antidote against a poisonous bite, fr. *thērion* wild animal] **1** *chiefly Brit* : MOLASSES **2** : something heavily sweet and cloying

¹tread \'tred\ *vb* **trod** \'träd\; **trod·den** \'träd-ᵊn\ *or* **trod; tread·ing** **1** : to step or walk on or over **2** : to move on foot : WALK; *also* : DANCE **3** : to beat or press with the feet

²tread *n* **1** : a mark made by or as if by treading **2** : the manner or sound of stepping **3** : the part of a wheel that makes contact with a road **4** : the horizontal part of a step

trea·dle \'tred-ᵊl\ *n* : a lever device pressed by the foot to drive a machine

tread·mill \'tred-ˌmil\ *n* **1** : a mill worked by persons who tread on steps around the edge of a wheel or by animals that walk on an endless belt **2** : a wearisome routine

treas *abbr* treasurer; treasury

trea·son \'trēz-ᵊn\ *n* : the offense of attempting to overthrow the government of one's country or of assisting its enemies in war — **trea·son·able** \-(ᵊ-)nə-bəl\ *adj* — **trea·son·ous** \-(ᵊ-)nəs\ *adj*

¹trea·sure \'trezh-ər, 'trāzh-\ *n* **1** : wealth stored up or held in reserve **2** : something of great value

²treasure *vb* **trea·sured; trea·sur·ing** \-(ə-)riŋ\ **1** : HOARD **2** : to keep as precious : CHERISH **syn** prize, value, appreciate, esteem

trea·sur·er \'trezh-rər, 'trezh-ər-ər, 'trāzh-\ *n* : an officer entrusted with the receipt, care, and disbursement of funds

treasure trove \-ˌtrōv\ *n* **1** : treasure (as money in gold) which is found hidden and whose ownership is unknown **2** : a valuable discovery

trea·sury \\'trezh-(ə-)rē, 'trāzh-\ *n, pl* **-sur·ies** **1** : a place in which stores of wealth are kept **2** : the place of deposit and disbursement of collected funds; *esp* : one where public revenues are deposited, kept, and disbursed **3** *cap* : a governmental department in charge of finances

¹treat \\'trēt\ *vb* **1** : NEGOTIATE **2** : to deal with esp. in writing; *also* : HANDLE **3** : to pay for the food or entertainment of **4** : to behave or act toward ⟨∼ them well⟩ **5** : to regard in a specified manner ⟨∼ as inferiors⟩ **6** : to care for medically or surgically **7** : to subject to some action (as of a chemical) ⟨∼ soil with lime⟩

²treat *n* **1** : food or entertainment paid for by another **2** : a source of joy or amusement

trea·tise \\'trēt-əs\ *n* : a systematic written exposition or argument

treat·ment \\'trēt-mənt\ *n* : the act or manner or an instance of treating someone or something; *also* : a substance or method used in treating

trea·ty \\'trēt-ē\ *n, pl* **treaties** : an agreement made by negotiation or diplomacy esp. between two or more states or governments **syn** contract, bargain, pact, convention

¹tre·ble \\'treb-əl\ *n* **1** : the highest of the four voice parts in vocal music : SOPRANO **2** : a high-pitched or shrill voice or sound **3** : the upper half of the musical pitch range

²treble *adj* **1** : triple in number or amount **2** : relating to or having the range of a musical treble **3** : high=pitched : SHRILL — **tre·bly** \\'treb-(ə-)lē\ *adv*

³treble *vb* **tre·bled; tre·bling** \\'treb-(ə-)liŋ\ : to make or become three times the size, amount, or number

¹tree \\'trē\ *n* **1** : a woody perennial plant usu. with a single main stem and a head of branches and leaves at the top **2** : a piece of wood adapted to a particular use ⟨a shoe ∼⟩ **3** : something resembling a tree ⟨a genealogical ∼⟩ — **tree·less** *adj*

²tree *vb* **treed; tree·ing** : to drive to or up a tree ⟨∼ a raccoon⟩

tree farm *n* : an area of forest land managed to ensure continuous commercial production

tree line *n* : TIMBERLINE

tree of heaven : an Asian ailanthus that is widely grown as a shade and ornamental tree

tree surgery *n* : operative treatment of diseased trees esp. for control of decay — **tree surgeon** *n*

tre·foil \\'trē-ˌfȯil, 'tref-ˌȯil\ *n* **1** : a clover or related herb with leaves with three leaflets **2** : a decorative design with three leaflike parts

¹trek \\'trek\ *vb* **trekked; trek·king** **1** : to travel or migrate by ox wagon **2** : to make one's way arduously

²trek *n* **1** : a migration esp. of settlers by ox wagon **2** : TRIP; *esp* : one involving difficulties or complex organization

¹trel·lis \\'trel-əs\ *n* [ME *trelis,* fr. MF *treliz* fabric of coarse weave, trellis, fr. (assumed) VL *trilicius* woven with triple thread, fr. L *tres* three + *liceum* thread] : a structure of latticework

²trellis *vb* : to train (as a vine) on a trellis

trem·a·tode \\'trem-ə-ˌtōd\ *n* : any of a class of parasitic worms

¹trem·ble \\'trem-bəl\ *vb* **trem·bled; trem·bling** \-b(ə-)liŋ\ **1** : to shake involuntarily (as with fear or cold) : SHIVER **2** : to move, sound, pass, or come to pass as if shaken or tremulous **3** : to be affected with fear or doubt

²tremble *n* : a spell of shaking or quivering : TREMOR

tre·men·dous \tri-'men-dəs\ *adj* **1** : such as may excite trembling : TERRIFYING **2** : astonishingly large, powerful, great, or excellent **syn** stupendous, monumental, monstrous — **tre·men·dous·ly** *adv*

trem·o·lo \\'trem-ə-ˌlō\ *n, pl* **-los** [It] : a rapid fluttering of a tone or alternating tones to produce a tremulous effect

trem·or \\'trem-ər\ *n* **1** : a trembling or shaking esp. from weakness or disease **2** : a quivering motion of the earth (as during an earthquake)

trem·u·lous \\'trem-yə-ləs\ *adj* **1** : marked by trembling or tremors : QUIVERING **2** : TIMOROUS, TIMID — **trem·u·lous·ly** *adv*

¹trench \\'trench\ *n* [ME *trenche* track cut through a wood, fr. MF, act of cutting, fr. *trenchier* to cut] **1** : a long narrow cut in the ground : DITCH; *esp* : a ditch protected by banks of earth and used to shelter soldiers **2** : a long narrow steep-sided depression in the ocean floor

²trench *vb* **1** : to cut or dig trenches in; *also* : to drain by trenches **2** : to protect (troops) with trenches **3** : to come close : VERGE

tren·chant \'tren-chənt\ *adj* **1** : vigorously effective; *also* : CAUSTIC **2** : sharply perceptive : KEEN **3** : CLEAR-CUT, DISTINCT **syn** incisive, biting, crisp

tren·cher \'tren-chər\ *n* : a wooden platter for serving food

tren·cher·man \'tren-chər-mən\ *n* : a hearty eater

trench foot *n* : a painful foot disorder resembling frostbite and resulting from exposure to cold and wet

trench mouth *n* : a contagious infection of the mouth and adjacent parts that is marked by ulceration and caused by bacteria

¹trend \'trend\ *vb* **1** : to have or take a general direction : TEND **2** : to show a tendency : INCLINE

²trend *n* **1** : a general direction taken (as by a stream or mountain range) **2** : a prevailing tendency : DRIFT **3** : a current style or preference : VOGUE

tre·pan \tri-'pan\ *vb* **tre·panned; tre·pan·ning** : to remove surgically a disk of bone from (the skull) — **trep·a·na·tion** \ˌtrep-ə-'nā-shən\ *n*

tre·phine \'trē-ˌfīn\ *n* : a surgical instrument for cutting out circular sections (as of bone or corneal tissue) — **trephine** *vb*

trep·i·da·tion \ˌtrep-ə-'dā-shən\ *n* : nervous agitation : APPREHENSION **syn** horror, terror, panic, consternation, dread, fright, dismay

¹tres·pass \'tres-pəs, -ˌpas\ *n* **1** : SIN, OFFENSE **2** : wrongful entry on real property **syn** transgression, violation, infraction, infringement

²trespass *vb* **1** : to commit an offense : ERR, SIN **2** : INTRUDE, ENCROACH; *esp* : to enter unlawfully upon the land of another — **tres·pass·er** *n*

tress \'tres\ *n* : a long lock of hair — usu. used in pl.

tres·tle *also* **tres·sel** \'tres-əl\ *n* **1** : a supporting framework consisting usu. of a horizontal piece with spreading legs at each end **2** : a braced framework of timbers, piles, or steel for carrying a road or railroad over a depression

trey \'trā\ *n, pl* **treys** : a card or the side of a die with three spots

tri·ad \'trī-ˌad, -əd\ *n* : a union or group of three usu. closely related persons or things

tri·age \trē-'äzh, 'trē-ˌäzh\ *n* [F, sifting] : the sorting of and allocation of treatment to patients and esp. battle and disaster victims according to a system of priorities designed to maximize the number of survivors

¹tri·al \'trī(-ə)l\ *n* **1** : the action or process of trying or putting to the proof : TEST **2** : the hearing and judgment of a matter in issue before a competent tribunal **3** : a source of vexation or annoyance **4** : a temporary use or experiment to test quality or usefulness **5** : EFFORT, ATTEMPT **syn** cross, ordeal, tribulation, affliction

²trial *adj* **1** : of, relating to, or used in a trial **2** : made or done as a test

tri·an·gle \'trī-ˌaŋ-gəl\ *n* **1** : a figure that has three sides and three angles : a polygon having three sides **2** : something shaped like a triangle — **tri·an·gu·lar** \trī-'aŋ-gyə-lər\ *adj* — **tri·an·gu·lar·ly** *adv*

tri·an·gu·la·tion \(ˌ)trī-ˌaŋ-gyə-'lā-shən\ *n* : a trigonometric operation for finding a position using bearings from two fixed points a known distance apart — **tri·an·gu·late** \trī-'aŋ-gyə-ˌlāt\ *vb*

Tri·as·sic \trī-'as-ik\ *adj* : of, relating to, or being the earliest period of the Mesozoic era — **Triassic** *n*

trib *abbr* tributary

tribe \'trīb\ *n* **1** : a social group comprising numerous families, clans, or generations **2** : a group of persons having a common character, occupation, or interest **3** : a group of related plants or animals ⟨the cat ∼⟩ — **trib·al** \'trī-bəl\ *adj*

tribes·man \'trībz-mən\ *n* : a member of a tribe

trib·u·la·tion \ˌtrib-yə-'lā-shən\ *n* [ME *tribulacion,* fr. OF, fr. L *tribulatio,* fr. *tribulare* to press, oppress, fr. *tribulum* drag used in threshing] : distress or suffering resulting from oppression or persecution; *also* : a trying experience **syn** trial, affliction, cross, ordeal

tri·bu·nal \trī-'byün-ᵊl, trib-'yün-\ *n* **1** : the seat of a judge **2** : a court of justice **3** : something that decides or determines ⟨the ∼ of public opinion⟩

tri·bune \'trib-,yün, trib-'yün\ *n* **1** : an official in ancient Rome with the function of protecting the interests of plebeian citizens from the patricians **2** : a defender of the people

¹trib·u·tary \'trib-yə-,ter-ē\ *adj* **1** : paying tribute : SUBJECT **2** : flowing into a larger stream or a lake **syn** subordinate, secondary, dependent

²tributary *n, pl* **-tar·ies** **1** : a ruler or state that pays tribute **2** : a tributary stream

trib·ute \'trib-(,)yüt, -yət\ *n* **1** : a payment by one ruler or nation to another as an act of submission or price of protection **2** : a usu. excessive tax, rental, or levy exacted by a sovereign or superior **3** : a gift or service showing respect, gratitude, or affection; *also* : PRAISE **syn** eulogy, citation, encomium, panegyric

trice \'trīs\ *n* : INSTANT, MOMENT

tri·ceps \'trī-,seps\ *n, pl* **tri·ceps·es** *also* **triceps** : a large muscle along the back of the upper arm that is attached at its upper end by three main parts and acts to extend the arm at the elbow joint

tri·chi·na \trik-'ī-nə\ *n, pl* **-nae** \-(,)nē\ *also* **-nas** : a small slender nematode worm that in the larval state is parasitic in the voluntary muscles of flesh≠eating mammals (as the hog and human beings)

trich·i·no·sis \,trik-ə-'nō-səs\ *n* : a disease caused by infestation of muscle tissue by trichinae and marked by pain, fever, and swelling

¹trick \'trik\ *n* **1** : a crafty procedure meant to deceive **2** : a mischievous action : PRANK **3** : a childish action **4** : a deceptive or ingenious feat designed to puzzle or amuse **5** : PECULIARITY, MANNERISM **6** : a quick or artful way of getting a result : KNACK **7** : the cards played in one round of a card game **8** : a tour of duty : SHIFT **syn** ruse, maneuver, artifice, wile, feint

²trick *vb* **1** : to deceive by cunning or artifice : CHEAT **2** : to dress ornately

trick·ery \'trik-(ə-)rē\ *n* : deception by tricks and stratagems

trick·le \'trik-əl\ *vb* **trick·led; trick·ling** \-(ə-)liŋ\ **1** : to run or fall in drops **2** : to flow in a thin gentle stream — **trickle** *n*

trick·ster \'trik-stər\ *n* : one who tricks or cheats

tricky \'trik-ē\ *adj* **trick·i·er; -est** **1** : inclined to trickery ⟨a ∼ person⟩ **2** : requiring skill or caution ⟨a ∼ situation to handle⟩ **3** : UNRELIABLE

tri·col·or \'trī-,kəl-ər\ *n* : a flag of three colors ⟨the French ∼⟩

tri·cy·cle \'trī-(,)sik-əl\ *n* : a 3-wheeled vehicle usu. propelled by pedals

tri·dent \'trīd-ᵊnt\ *n* [L *trident-, tridens,* fr. *tres* three + *dent-, dens* tooth] : a 3-pronged spear

tried \'trīd\ *adj* **1** : found trustworthy through testing **2** : subjected to trials **syn** reliable, dependable, trusty

tri·en·ni·al \'trī-'en-ē-əl\ *adj* **1** : lasting for three years **2** : occurring or being done every three years — **tri·ennial** *n*

¹tri·fle \'trī-fəl\ *n* : something of little value or importance; *esp* : an insignificant amount (as of money)

²trifle *vb* **tri·fled; tri·fling** \-f(ə-)liŋ\ **1** : to talk in a jesting or mocking manner **2** : to act frivolously or playfully **3** : DALLY, FLIRT **4** : to handle idly : TOY — **tri·fler** \-f(ə-)lər\ *n*

tri·fling \'trī-fliŋ\ *adj* **1** : FRIVOLOUS **2** : TRIVIAL, INSIGNIFICANT **syn** petty, paltry, measly, inconsequential

tri·fo·cals \trī-'fō-kəlz\ *n pl* : eyeglasses with lenses having one part for close focus, one for intermediate focus, and one for distant focus

tri·fo·li·ate \trī-'fō-lē-ət\ *adj* : having three leaves or leaflets

¹trig \'trig\ *adj* : stylishly trim : SMART **syn** tidy, spruce, shipshape

²trig *n* : TRIGONOMETRY

¹trig·ger \'trig-ər\ *n* [alter. of earlier *tricker,* fr. Dutch *trekker,* fr. Middle Dutch *trecker* one that pulls, fr. *trecken* to pull] : a movable lever that activates a device when it is squeezed; *esp* : the part of a firearm lock moved by the finger to release the hammer in firing — **trigger** *adj* — **trig·gered** \-ərd\ *adj*

²trigger *vb* **1** : to fire by pulling a trigger **2** : to initiate, actuate, or set off as if by a trigger

trig·o·nom·e·try \,trig-ə-'näm-ə-trē\ *n*

: the branch of mathematics dealing with the relations of the sides and angles of triangles and of methods of deducing from given parts other required parts — **trig·o·no·met·ric** \-nə-'me-trik\ *also* **trig·o·no·met·ri·cal** \-trik-əl\ *adj*

¹**trill** \'tril\ *n* **1** : the alternation of two musical tones a scale degree apart **2** : WARBLE **3** : the rapid vibration of one speech organ against another (as of the tip of the tongue against the teeth)

²**trill** *vb* : to utter as or with a trill

tril·lion \'tril-yən\ *n* **1** : a thousand billions **2** *Brit* : a million billions — **trillion** *adj* — **tril·lionth** \-yənth\ *adj or n*

tril·li·um \'tril-ē-əm\ *n* : any of a genus of herbs of the lily family with an erect stem bearing a whorl of three leaves and a large solitary flower with three petals

tril·o·gy \'tril-ə-jē\ *n, pl* **-gies** : a series of three dramas or literary or musical compositions that are closely related and develop one theme

¹**trim** \'trim\ *vb* **trimmed; trim·ming** [OE *trymian, trymman* to strengthen, arrange, fr. *trum* strong, firm] **1** : to put ornaments on : ADORN **2** : to defeat esp. resoundingly **3** : to make trim, neat, regular, or less bulky by or as if by cutting ⟨∼ a beard⟩ ⟨∼ a budget⟩ **4** : to cause (a boat) to assume a desired position in the water by arrangement of ballast, cargo, or passengers; *also* : to adjust (as a submarine or airplane) esp. for horizontal motion **5** : to adjust (a sail) to a desired position **6** : to change one's views for safety or expediency — **trim·ly** *adv* — **trim·mer** *n* — **trim·ness** *n*

²**trim** *adj* **trim·mer; trim·mest** : showing neatness, good order, or compactness ⟨∼ figure⟩ **syn** tidy, trig, smart, spruce, shipshape

³**trim** *n* **1** : good condition : FITNESS **2** : material used for ornament or trimming; *esp* : the woodwork in the finish of a house esp. around doors and windows **3** : the position of a ship or boat esp. with reference to the horizontal; *also* : the relation between the plane of a sail and the direction of a ship **4** : the position of an airplane at which it will continue in level flight

with no adjustments to the controls **5** : something that is trimmed off

tri·ma·ran \'trī-mə-ˌran, ˌtrī-mə-'ran\ *n* : a fast pleasure sailboat with three hulls side by side

tri·mes·ter \trī-'mes-tər, 'trī-ˌmes-tər\ *n* **1** : a period of three or about three months **2** : one of three terms into which an academic year is sometimes divided

trim·e·ter \'trim-ət-ər\ *n* : a line consisting of three metrical feet

trim·ming \'trim-iŋ\ *n* **1** : DEFEAT **2** : the action of one that trims **3** : something that trims, ornaments, or completes

tri·month·ly \trī-'mənth-lē\ *adj* : occurring every three months

trine \'trīn\ *adj* : THREEFOLD, TRIPLE

Trin·i·da·di·an \ˌtrin-ə-'dād-ē-ən, -'dad-\ *n* : a native or inhabitant of the island of Trinidad — **Trinidadian** *adj*

Trin·i·tar·i·an \ˌtrin-ə-'ter-ē-ən\ *n* : a believer in the doctrine of the Trinity — **Trin·i·tar·i·an·ism** \-ē-ə-ˌniz-əm\ *n*

Trin·i·ty \'trin-ət-ē\ *n* **1** : the unity of Father, Son, and Holy Spirit as three persons in one Godhead **2** *not cap* : TRIAD

trin·ket \'triŋ-kət\ *n* **1** : a small ornament (as a jewel or ring) **2** : TRIFLE

trio \'trē-ō\ *n, pl* **tri·os** **1** : a musical composition for three voices or three instruments **2** : the performers of a musical or dance trio **3** : a group or set of three

tri·ode \'trī-ˌōd\ *n* : a vacuum tube with three electrodes

¹**trip** \'trip\ *vb* **tripped; trip·ping** **1** : to move with light quick steps **2** : to catch the foot against something so as to stumble or cause to stumble **3** : to make a mistake : SLIP; *also* : to detect in a misstep : EXPOSE **4** : to release (as a spring or switch) by moving a catch; *also* : ACTIVATE **5** : to get high on a psychedelic drug

²**trip** *n* **1** : JOURNEY, VOYAGE **2** : a quick light step **3** : a false step : STUMBLE; *also* : ERROR **4** : the action of tripping mechanically; *also* : a device for tripping **5** : an intense drug-induced hallucinatory experience **6** : pursuit of an obsessive interest ⟨an ego ∼⟩

tri·par·tite \trī-'pär-ˌtīt\ *adj* **1** : divided into three parts **2** : having three corresponding parts or copies **3** : made between three parties ⟨a ~ treaty⟩

tripe \ˈtrīp\ *n* **1** : stomach tissue of a ruminant and esp. an ox used as food **2** : something poor, worthless, or offensive : TRASH

¹tri·ple \ˈtrip-əl\ *vb* **tri·pled; tri·pling** \-(ə-)liŋ\ **1** : to make or become three times as great or as many **2** : to hit a triple

²triple *n* **1** : a triple quantity **2** : a group of three **3** : a hit in baseball that lets the batter reach third base

³triple *adj* **1** : being three times as great or as many **2** : having three units or members **3** : repeated three times

triple bond *n* : a chemical bond in which three pairs of electrons are shared by two atoms in a molecule

triple point *n* : the condition of temperature and pressure under which the gaseous, liquid, and solid forms of a substance can exist in equilibrium

trip·let \ˈtrip-lət\ *n* **1** : a unit of three lines of verse **2** : a group of three of a kind **3** : one of three offspring born at one birth

tri·plex \ˈtrip-ˌleks, ˈtrī-ˌpleks\ *adj* : THREEFOLD, TRIPLE

¹trip·li·cate \ˈtrip-li-kət\ *adj* : made in three identical copies

²trip·li·cate \-lə-ˌkāt\ *vb* **-cat·ed; -cat·ing** **1** : TRIPLE **2** : to provide three copies of ⟨~ a document⟩

³trip·li·cate \-li-kət\ *n* : three copies all alike — used with *in* ⟨typed in ~⟩

tri·ply \ˈtrip-(ə-)lē\ *adv* : in a triple degree, amount, or manner

tri·pod \ˈtrī-ˌpäd\ *n* : something (as a caldron, stool, or camera stand) that rests on three legs — **tripod** *or* **tri·po·dal** \ˈtrip-əd-ᵊl, ˈtrī-ˌpäd-\ *adj*

trip·tych \ˈtrip-tik\ *n* : a picture or carving (as an altarpiece) in three panels side by side

tri·reme \ˈtrī-ˌrēm\ *n* : an ancient galley having three banks of oars

tri·sect \ˈtrī-ˌsekt, trī-ˈsekt\ *vb* : to divide into three usu. equal parts — **tri·sec·tion** \ˈtrī-ˌsek-shən\ *n*

trite \ˈtrīt\ *adj* **trit·er; trit·est** [L *tritus,* fr. pp. of *terere* to rub, wear away] : used so commonly that the novelty is worn off : STALE **syn** hackneyed, stereotyped, commonplace, clichéd

tri·ti·um \ˈtrit-ē-əm, ˈtrish-ē-\ *n* : a ra-

dioactive form of hydrogen with atoms of three times the mass of ordinary hydrogen atoms

tri·ton \ˈtrīt-ᵊn\ *n* : any of various large marine mollusks with a heavy elongated conical shell; *also* : the shell of a triton

trit·u·rate \ˈtrich-ə-ˌrāt\ *vb* **-rat·ed; -rat·ing** : to rub or grind to a fine powder

¹tri·umph \ˈtrī-əmf\ *n, pl* **tri·umphs** \-əmfs, -əm(p)s\ **1** : the joy or exultation of victory or success **2** : VICTORY, CONQUEST — **tri·um·phal** \trī-ˈəm-fəl\ *adj*

²triumph *vb* **1** : to celebrate victory or success exultantly **2** : to obtain victory : PREVAIL — **tri·um·phant** \trī-ˈəm-fənt\ *adj* — **tri·um·phant·ly** *adv*

tri·um·vir \trī-ˈəm-vər\ *n, pl* **-virs** *also* **-vi·ri** \-və-ˌrī\ : a member of a triumvirate

tri·um·vi·rate \-və-rət\ *n* : a ruling body of three persons

tri·une \ˈtrī-ˌ(y)ün\ *adj, often cap* : being three in one ⟨the ~ God⟩

triv·et \ˈtriv-ət\ *n* **1** : a 3-legged stand : TRIPOD **2** : a metal stand with short feet for use under a hot dish

triv·ia \ˈtriv-ē-ə\ *n sing or pl* : unimportant matters : TRIFLES

triv·i·al \ˈtriv-ē-əl\ *adj* [L *trivialis* found everywhere, commonplace, trivial, fr. *trivium* crossroads, fr. *tres* three + *via* way] : of little importance — **triv·i·al·i·ty** \ˌtriv-ē-ˈal-ət-ē\ *n*

triv·i·um \ˈtriv-ē-əm\ *n, pl* **triv·ia** \-ē-ə\ : the three liberal arts of grammar, rhetoric, and logic in a medieval university

tri·week·ly \trī-ˈwē-klē\ *adj* **1** : occurring or appearing three times a week **2** : occurring or appearing every three weeks — **triweekly** *adv*

tro·che \ˈtrō-kē\ *n* : a medicinal lozenge

tro·chee \ˈtrō-(ˌ)kē\ *n* : a metrical foot of one accented syllable followed by one unaccented syllable — **tro·cha·ic** \trō-ˈkā-ik\ *adj*

trod past and past part of TREAD

trodden past part of TREAD

troi·ka \ˈtroi-kə\ *n* [Russ *troĭka* a vehicle drawn by three horses, fr. *troe* three] : a group of three; *esp* : an administrative or ruling body of three

¹troll \ˈtrōl\ *vb* **1** : to sing the parts of (a song) in succession **2** : to angle for with a hook and line drawn through the water **3** : to sing or play jovially

²troll *n* : a lure used in trolling; *also* : the line with its lure

³troll *n* : a dwarf or giant in Teutonic folklore inhabiting caves or hills

trol·ley *or* **trol·ly** \'träl-ē\ *n, pl* **trolleys** *or* **trollies 1** : a device (as a grooved wheel on the end of a pole) to carry current from a wire to an electrically driven vehicle **2** : TROLLEY CAR **3** : a wheeled carriage running on an overhead rail or track

trol·ley·bus \'träl-ē-ˌbəs\ *n* : a bus powered electrically from two overhead wires

trolley car *n* : a streetcar powered electrically through a trolley

trol·lop \'träl-əp\ *n* **1** : a slovenly woman **2** : a loose woman : WANTON

trom·bone \träm-'bōn, 'träm-ˌbōn\ *n* [It, lit., big trumpet, fr. *tromba* trumpet] : a brass wind instrument that consists of a long metal tube with two turns and a flaring end and that has a movable slide to vary the pitch — **trom·bon·ist** \-'bō-nəst, -ˌbō-\ *n*

tromp \'trämp, 'trȯmp\ *vb* **1** : TRAMP, MARCH **2** : to stamp with the foot **3** : DEFEAT

¹troop \'trüp\ *n* **1** : a cavalry unit corresponding to an infantry company **2** *pl* : armed forces : SOLDIERS **3** : a collection of people or things **4** : a unit of Girl Scouts or Boy Scouts under an adult leader **syn** band, troupe, party, corps

²troop *vb* : to move or gather in crowds

troop·er \'trü-pər\ *n* **1** : an enlisted cavalryman; *also* : a cavalry horse **2** : a mounted or state policeman

troop·ship \'trüp-ˌship\ *n* : a ship for carrying troops

trope \'trōp\ *n* : the use of a word or expression in a figurative sense

tro·phy \'trō-fē\ *n, pl* **trophies** : something gained or given in conquest or victory esp. when preserved or mounted as a memorial

trop·ic \'träp-ik\ *n* [ME *tropik*, fr. L *tropicus* of the solstice, fr. Gk *tropikos*, fr. *tropē* turn] **1** : either of the two parallels of latitude one approximately 23½ degrees north of the equator (**tropic of Cancer** \-'kan-ser\) and one approximately 23½ degrees south

of the equator (**tropic of Capricorn** \-'kap-rə-ˌkȯrn\) where the sun is directly overhead when apparently at its greatest distance north or south of the equator **2** *pl, often cap* : the region lying between the tropics of Cancer and Capricorn — **trop·i·cal** \-i-kəl\ *or* **tropic** *adj*

tro·pism \'trō-ˌpiz-əm\ *n* : involuntary orientation of an organism in response to a source of stimulation; *also* : a reflex reaction involving this

tro·po·sphere \'trōp-ə-ˌsfiər, 'träp-\ *n* : the portion of the atmosphere which extends outward about 10 miles (16 kilometers) from the earth's surface and in which most weather occurs — **tro·po·spher·ic** \ˌtrōp-ə-'sfi(ə)r-ik, ˌträp-, -'sfer-\ *adj*

¹trot \'trät\ *n* **1** : a moderately fast gait of a 4-footed animal (as a horse) in which the legs move in diagonal pairs **2** : a jogging gait of a man between a walk and a run

²trot *vb* **trot·ted; trot·ting 1** : to ride, drive, or go at a trot **2** : to proceed briskly : HURRY — **trot·ter** *n*

troth \'träth, 'trȯth, 'trōth\ *n* **1** : pledged faithfulness : FIDELITY **2** : one's pledged word; *also* : BETROTHAL

trou·ba·dour \'trü-bə-ˌdȯr\ *n* [F, fr. Old Provençal *trobador*] : one of a class of poet musicians flourishing esp. in southern France and northern Italy during the 11th, 12th, and 13th centuries

¹trou·ble \'trəb-əl\ *vb* **trou·bled; trou·bling** \'trəb-(ə-)liŋ\ **1** : to agitate mentally or spiritually : DISTURB, WORRY **2** : to produce physical disorder in : AFFLICT **3** : to put to inconvenience **4** : RUFFLE ⟨~ the waters⟩ **5** : to make an effort **syn** distress, ail, upset, worry — **trou·ble·some** *adj* — **trou·ble·some·ly** *adv* — **trou·blous** \-(ə-)ləs\ *adj*

²trouble *n* **1** : the quality or state of being troubled esp. mentally **2** : an instance of distress or annoyance **3** : DISEASE, AILMENT ⟨heart ~⟩ **4** : EXERTION, PAINS ⟨took the ~ to phone⟩ **5** : a cause of disturbance or distress

trou·ble·mak·er \-ˌmā-kər\ *n* : a person who causes trouble

trou·ble·shoot·er \-ˌshüt-ər\ *n* **1** : a worker employed to locate trouble and make repairs in equipment **2** : an expert in resolving disputes or problems — **trou·ble·shoot** vb

trough \'tròf, 'tròth, *by bakers often* 'trò\ *n, pl* **troughs** \'tròfs, 'tròvz; 'tròths, 'trò(th)z; 'tròz\ **1** : a long shallow open boxlike container esp. for water or feed for livestock **2** : a gutter along the eaves of a house **3** : a long channel or depression (as between waves or hills)

trounce \'traùns\ vb **trounced; trounc·ing 1** : to thrash or punish severely **2** : to defeat decisively

troupe \'trüp\ *n* : COMPANY; *esp* : a group of performers on the stage — **troup·er** *n*

trou·sers \'traù-zərz\ *n pl* [alter. of earlier *trouse,* fr. ScGael *triubhas*] : an outer garment extending from the waist to the ankle or sometimes only to the knee, covering each leg separately, and worn esp. by males — **trouser** *adj*

trous·seau \'trü-sō, trü-'sō\ *n, pl* **trousseaux** \-sōz, -'sōz\ *or* **trous·seaus** [F] : the personal outfit of a bride

trout \'traùt\ *n, pl* **trout** *also* **trouts** [ME, fr. OE *trūht,* fr. LL *tructa,* a fish with sharp teeth, fr. Gk *trōktēs,* lit., gnawer] : any of various mostly freshwater food and game fishes usu. smaller than the related salmons

trout lily *n* : DOGTOOTH VIOLET

trow \'trō\ vb, *archaic* : THINK, SUPPOSE

trow·el \'traù(-ə)l\ *n* **1** : any of various hand implements used for spreading, shaping, or smoothing loose or plastic material (as mortar or plaster) **2** : a small flat or scooplike implement used in gardening — **trowel** vb

troy \'tròi\ *adj* : expressed in troy weight ⟨~ ounce⟩

troy weight *n* : a system of weights based on a pound of 12 ounces and an ounce of 480 grains and used in the U.S. esp. for precious metals and gems — see WEIGHT table

tru·ant \'trü-ənt\ *n* [ME, vagabond, idler, fr. OF, vagrant] : one who shirks duty; *esp* : one who stays out of school without permission — **tru·an·cy** \-ən-sē\ *n* — **truant** *adj*

truce \'trüs\ *n* **1** : ARMISTICE **2** : a respite esp. from a disagreeable state or action

¹**truck** \'trək\ vb **1** : EXCHANGE, BARTER **2** : to have dealings : TRAFFIC

²**truck** *n* **1** : BARTER **2** : small goods or merchandise; *esp* : vegetables grown for market **3** : DEALINGS

³**truck** *n* **1** : a vehicle (as a strong heavy automobile) designed for carrying heavy articles or hauling a trailer **2** : a swiveling frame with springs and one or more pairs of wheels used to carry and guide one end of a locomotive or of a railroad or electric car — **truck·load** \-,lōd\ *n*

⁴**truck** vb **1** : to transport on a truck **2** : to be employed in driving a truck — **truck·er** *n*

truck·age \'trək-ij\ *n* : transportation by truck; *also* : the cost of such transportation

truck farm *n* : a farm growing vegetables for market — **truck farmer** *n*

truck garden *n* : a garden where vegetables are raised for market

truck·le \'trək-əl\ vb **truck·led; truck·ling** \-(ə-)liŋ\ : to yield slavishly to the will of another : SUBMIT **syn** fawn, toady, cringe, cower

truc·u·lent \'trək-yə-lənt\ *adj* **1** : feeling or showing ferocity : SAVAGE **2** : aggressively self-assertive : PUGNACIOUS — **truc·u·lence** \-ləns\ *n* — **truc·u·len·cy** \-lən-sē\ *n* — **truc·u·lent·ly** *adv*

trudge \'trəj\ vb **trudged; trudg·ing** : to walk or march steadily and usu. laboriously

¹**true** \'trü\ *adj* **tru·er; tru·est 1** : STEADFAST, LOYAL **2** : conformable to fact or reality ⟨a ~ description⟩ **3** : CONSISTENT ⟨~ to expectations⟩ **4** : properly so called ⟨the ~ stomach⟩ **5** : RIGHTFUL ⟨~ and lawful king⟩ **6** : conformable to a standard or pattern; *also* : placed or formed accurately **syn** constant, staunch, resolute, steadfast

²**true** *adv* **1** : TRUTHFULLY **2** : ACCURATELY ⟨the bullet flew straight and ~⟩; *also* : without variation from type ⟨breed ~⟩

³**true** *n* **1** : TRUTH, REALITY — usu. used with *the* **2** : the state of being accurate (as in alignment) ⟨out of ~⟩

⁴**true** vb **trued; true·ing** *also* **tru·ing** : to make level, square, balanced, or concentric

true–blue *adj* : marked by unswerving loyalty

true bug *n* : BUG 2

true·heart·ed \\'trü-'härt-əd\\ *adj* : FAITHFUL, LOYAL

truf·fle \\'trəf-əl, 'trüf-\\ *n* **1** : a European underground fungus; *also* : its dark wrinkled edible fruit **2** : a candy made of chocolate, butter, and sugar shaped into balls and coated with cocoa

tru·ism \\'trü-ˌiz-əm\\ *n* : an undoubted or self-evident truth **syn** commonplace, platitude, bromide, cliché

tru·ly \\'trü-lē\\ *adv* **1** : in all sincerity **2** : in agreement with fact **3** : ACCURATELY **4** : in a proper or suitable manner

¹trump \\'trəmp\\ *n* : TRUMPET

²trump *n* : a card of a designated suit any of whose cards will win over a card that is not of this suit; *also* : the suit itself — often used in pl.

³trump *vb* : to take with a trump

trumped–up \\'trəm(p)t-'əp\\ *adj* : fraudulently concocted : SPURIOUS

trum·pery \\'trəm-p(ə-)rē\\ *n* **1** : NONSENSE **2** : trivial articles : JUNK

¹trum·pet \\'trəm-pət\\ *n* **1** : a wind instrument consisting of a long curved metal tube flaring at one end and with a cup-shaped mouthpiece at the other **2** : something that resembles a trumpet or its tonal quality **3** : a funnel-shaped instrument for collecting, directing, or intensifying sound

²trumpet *vb* **1** : to blow a trumpet **2** : to proclaim on or as if on a trumpet — **trum·pet·er** *n*

¹trun·cate \\'trəŋ-ˌkāt, 'trən-\\ *adj* : having the end square or blunt

²truncate *vb* **trun·cat·ed; trun·cat·ing** : to shorten by or as if by cutting : LOP — **trun·ca·tion** \\ˌtrəŋ-'kā-shən\\ *n*

trun·cheon \\'trən-chən\\ *n* : a policeman's club

trun·dle \\'trən-dᵊl\\ *vb* **trun·dled; trun·dling** : to roll along : WHEEL

trundle bed *n* : a low bed that can be slid under a higher bed when not in use

trunk \\'trəŋk\\ *n* **1** : the main stem of a tree **2** : the body of a person or animal apart from the head and limbs **3** : the main or basal part of something **4** : a box or chest used to hold usu. clothes or personal effects (as of a traveler); *also* : the enclosed luggage space in the rear of an automobile **5** : the long

muscular nose of an elephant **6** *pl* : men's shorts worn chiefly for sports **7** : a usu. major channel or passage **8** : a circuit between telephone exchanges

trunk line *n* : a system handling long-distance through traffic

¹truss \\'trəs\\ *vb* **1** : to secure tightly : BIND **2** : to arrange for cooking by binding close the wings or legs of (a fowl) **3** : to support, strengthen, or stiffen by a truss

²truss *n* **1** : a collection of structural parts (as beams) forming a rigid framework (as in bridge or building construction) **2** : a device worn to reduce a hernia by pressure

¹trust \\'trəst\\ *n* **1** : assured reliance on the character, strength, or truth of someone or something **2** : a basis of reliance, faith, or hope **3** : confident hope **4** : financial credit **5** : a property interest held by one person for the benefit of another **6** : a combination of firms formed by a legal agreement; *esp* : one that reduces competition **7** : something entrusted to one to be cared for in the interest of another **8** : CARE, CUSTODY **syn** confidence, dependence, faith, reliance

²trust *vb* **1** : to place confidence : DEPEND **2** : to be confident : HOPE **3** : ENTRUST **4** : to permit to stay or go or to do something without fear or misgiving **5** : to rely on or on the truth of : BELIEVE **6** : to extend credit to

trust·ee \\ˌtrəs-'tē\\ *n* **1** : a person to whom property is legally committed in trust **2** : a country charged with the supervision of a trust territory

trust·ee·ship \\ˌtrəs-'tē-ˌship\\ *n* **1** : the office or function of a trustee **2** : supervisory control by one or more nations over a trust territory

trust·ful \\'trəst-fəl\\ *adj* : full of trust : CONFIDING — **trust·ful·ly** \\-ē\\ *adv* — **trust·ful·ness** *n*

trust territory *n* : a non-self-governing territory placed under a supervisory authority by the Trusteeship Council of the United Nations

trust·wor·thy \\-ˌwər-thē\\ *adj* : worthy of confidence : DEPENDABLE **syn** trusty, tried, reliable — **trust·wor·thi·ness** *n*

¹trusty \'trəs-tē\ *adj* **trust·i·er; -est**
: TRUSTWORTHY, DEPENDABLE
²trusty \'trəs-tē, ˌtrəs-'tē\ *n, pl* **trust·ies**
: a trusted person; *esp* : a convict considered trustworthy and allowed special privileges
truth \'trüth\ *n, pl* **truths** \'trüthz, 'trüths\ **1** : TRUTHFULNESS, HONESTY **2** : the real state of things : FACT **3** : the body of real events or facts : ACTUALITY **4** : a true or accepted statement or proposition ⟨the ∼s of science⟩ **5** : agreement with fact or reality : CORRECTNESS **syn** veracity, verity, truthfulness
truth·ful \'trüth-fəl\ *adj* : telling or disposed to tell the truth — **truth·ful·ly** \-ē\ *adv* — **truth·ful·ness** *n*
truth serum *n* : a drug held to induce a subject under questioning to talk freely
¹try \'trī\ *vb* **tried; try·ing 1** : to examine or investigate judicially **2** : to conduct the trial of **3** : to put to test or trial **4** : to subject to strain, affliction, or annoyance **5** : to extract or clarify (as lard) by melting **6** : to make an effort to do something : ATTEMPT, ENDEAVOR **syn** essay, assay, strive, struggle
²try *n, pl* **tries** : an experimental trial
try·ing \'trī-iŋ\ *adj* : severely straining the powers of endurance
try on *vb* : to put on (a garment) to test the fit and looks
try out \(')trī-'aut\ *vb* : to participate in competition esp. for a position on an athletic team or a part in a play — **try·out** \'trī-ˌaut\ *n*
tryst \'trist, 'trīst\ *n* : an agreement (as between lovers) to meet; *also* : an appointed place of meeting **syn** rendezvous, engagement, assignation
tsar \'zär, '(t)sär\ var of CZAR
tset·se fly \'t(s)et-sē-, 't(s)ēt-sē-\ *n* : any of several flies that occur in Africa south of the Sahara desert and include the vector of sleeping sickness
TSgt *abbr* technical sergeant
T–shirt \'tē-ˌshərt\ *n* : a collarless short-sleeved or sleeveless cotton undershirt for men; *also* : an outer shirt of similar design
tsp *abbr* teaspoon; teaspoonful
T square *n* : a ruler with a crosspiece at one end for making parallel lines
tsu·na·mi \(t)su̇-'näm-ē\ *n* [Jp] : a tidal

wave caused by an earthquake or volcanic eruption
TT *abbr* Trust Territories
Tu *abbr* Tuesday
tub \'təb\ *n* **1** : a wide low bucketlike vessel **2** : BATHTUB; *also* : BATH **3** : the amount that a tub will hold
tu·ba \'t(y)ü-bə\ *n* : a large low-pitched brass wind instrument
tube \'t(y)üb\ *n* **1** : a hollow cylinder to convey fluids : CHANNEL, DUCT **2** : any of various usu. cylindrical structures or devices **3** : a round metal container from which a paste is squeezed **4** : a tunnel for vehicular or rail travel **5** : an airtight tube of rubber inside a tire to hold air under pressure **6** : ELECTRON TUBE **7** : TELEVISION — **tubed** \'t(y)übd\ *adj* — **tube·less** *adj*
tu·ber \'t(y)ü-bər\ *n* : a short fleshy usu. underground stem (as of a potato plant) bearing minute scalelike leaves each with a bud at its base
tu·ber·cle \'t(y)ü-bər-kəl\ *n* **1** : a small knobby prominence or outgrowth esp. on an animal or plant **2** : a small abnormal lump in an organ or on the skin; *esp* : one caused by tuberculosis
tubercle bacillus *n* : a bacterium that is the cause of tuberculosis
tu·ber·cu·lar \t(y)u̇-'bər-kyə-lər\ *adj* **1** : of, resembling, or being a tubercle : TUBERCULATED **2** : TUBERCULOUS
tu·ber·cu·lat·ed \t(y)u̇-'bər-kyə-ˌlāt-əd\ *also* **tu·ber·cu·late** \-lət\ *adj* : having or covered with tubercles
tu·ber·cu·lin \t(y)u̇-'bər-kyə-lən\ *n* : a sterile liquid extracted from the tubercle bacillus and used in the diagnosis of tuberculosis esp. in children and cattle
tu·ber·cu·lo·sis \t(y)u̇-ˌbər-kyə-'lō-səs\ *n, pl* **-lo·ses** \-ˌsēz\ : a communicable bacterial disease typically marked by wasting, fever, and formation of cheesy tubercles often in the lungs — **tu·ber·cu·lous** \-'bər-kyə-ləs\ *adj*
tube·rose \'t(y)üb-ˌrōz\ *n* : a bulbous herb related to the amaryllis and often grown for its spike of fragrant waxy white flowers
tu·ber·ous \'t(y)ü-b(ə-)rəs\ *adj* : of, resembling, or being a plant tuber
tub·ing \'t(y)ü-biŋ\ *n* **1** : material in the form of a tube; *also* : a length of tube **2** : a series of tubes

tu·bu·lar \\'t(y)ü-byə-lər\ *adj* : having the form of or consisting of a tube; *also* : made with tubes

tu·bule \\'t(y)ü-byül\ *n* : a small tube

¹tuck \\'tək\ *n* : a fold stitched into cloth to shorten, decorate, or control fullness

²tuck *vb* **1** : to pull up into a fold ⟨~ed up her skirt⟩ **2** : to make tucks in **3** : to put into a snug often concealing place ⟨~ a book under the arm⟩ **4** : to secure in place by pushing the edges under ⟨~ in a blanket⟩ **5** : to cover by tucking in bedclothes

tuck·er \\'tək-ər\ *vb* **tuck·ered; tuck·er·ing** \\'tək-(ə-)riŋ\ : EXHAUST, FATIGUE

Tues *or* **Tue** *abbr* Tuesday

Tues·day \\'t(y)üz-dē\ *n* : the 3d day of the week

tu·fa \\'t(y)ü-fə\ *n* : a porous rock formed as a deposit from springs or streams

tuff \\'təf\ *n* : a rock composed of volcanic detritus

¹tuft \\'təft\ *n* **1** : a small cluster of long flexible outgrowths (as hairs); *also* : a bunch of soft fluffy threads cut off short and used as ornament **2** : CLUMP, CLUSTER — **tuft·ed** \\'təf-təd\ *adj*

²tuft *vb* **1** : to provide or adorn with a tuft **2** : to make (as a mattress) firm by stitching at intervals and sewing on tufts

¹tug \\'təg\ *vb* **tugged; tug·ging** **1** : to pull hard **2** : to struggle in opposition : CONTEND **3** : to move by pulling hard : HAUL **4** : to tow with a tugboat

²tug *n* **1** : a harness trace **2** : an act of tugging : PULL **3** : a straining effort **4** : a struggle between opposing people or forces **5** : TUGBOAT

tug·boat \-ˌbōt\ *n* : a strongly built boat used for towing or pushing

tug–of–war \ˌtəg-ə(v)-'wȯr\ *n, pl* **tugs–of–war** **1** : a struggle for supremacy **2** : an athletic contest in which two teams pull against each other at opposite ends of a rope

tu·grik *or* **tu·ghrik** \\'tü-grik\ *n* — see MONEY table

tu·ition \t(y)ü-'ish-ən\ *n* **1** : INSTRUCTION **2** : the price of or payment for instruction

tu·la·re·mia \ˌt(y)ü-lə-'rē-mē-ə\ *n* : an infectious bacterial disease esp. of wild rabbits, rodents, humans, and some domestic animals that in humans is marked by symptoms (as fever) of toxemia

tu·lip \\'t(y)ü-ləp\ *n* [NL *tulipa,* fr. Turk *tülbend* turban] : any of a genus of Eurasian bulbous herbs related to the lilies and grown for their large showy erect cup-shaped flowers; *also* : a flower or bulb of a tulip

tulip tree *n* : a tall American timber tree with greenish tulip-shaped flowers and soft white wood

tulle \\'tül\ *n* : a sheer silk, rayon, or nylon net ⟨a bridal veil of ~⟩

¹tum·ble \\'təm-bəl\ *vb* **tum·bled; tum·bling** \-b(ə-)liŋ\ [ME *tumblen,* fr. *tumben* to dance, fr. OE *tumbian*] **1** : to perform gymnastic feats of rolling and turning **2** : to fall or cause to fall suddenly and helplessly **3** : to fall into ruin **4** : to roll over and over : TOSS **5** : to issue forth hurriedly and confusedly **6** : to come to understand **7** : to throw together in a confused mass

²tumble *n* **1** : a disorderly state **2** : an act or instance of tumbling

tum·ble·down \ˌtəm-bəl-ˌdaůn\ *adj* : DILAPIDATED, RAMSHACKLE

tum·bler \\'təm-blər\ *n* **1** : one that tumbles; *esp* : ACROBAT **2** : a drinking glass without foot or stem **3** : a movable obstruction in a lock that must be adjusted to a particular position (as by a key) before the bolt can be thrown

tum·ble·weed \\'təm-bəl-ˌwēd\ *n* : a plant that breaks away from its roots in autumn and is driven about by the wind

tum·bril *also* **tum·brel** \\'təm-brəl\ *n* **1** : CART **2** : a vehicle carrying condemned persons (as political prisoners during the French Revolution) to a place of execution

tu·mid \\'t(y)ü-məd\ *adj* **1** : SWOLLEN, DISTENDED **2** : BOMBASTIC, TURGID

tum·my \\'təm-ē\ *n, pl* **tummies** : BELLY, ABDOMEN, STOMACH

tu·mor \\'t(y)ü-mər\ *n* : an abnormal and functionless mass of tissue that is not inflammatory and arises from pre-existent tissue — **tu·mor·ous** *adj*

tu·mult \\'t(y)ü-ˌməlt\ *n* **1** : disorderly agitation of a crowd usu. with uproar and confusion of voices **2** : DISTURBANCE, RIOT **3** : a confusion of loud noise and usu. turbulent movement **4** : violent agitation of mind or feelings

tu•mul•tu•ous \t(y)ů-'məlch-(ə-)wəs, -'məl-chəs\ *adj* **1** : marked by tumult **2** : tending to incite a tumult **3** : marked by violent upheaval

tun \'tən\ *n* : a large cask

tu•na \'t(y)ü-nə\ *n, pl* **tuna** *or* **tunas** [Sp] : any of several mostly large sea fishes related to the mackerels and important for food and sport

tun•able \'t(y)ü-nə-bəl\ *adj* : capable of being tuned — **tun•abil•i•ty** \,t(y)ü-nə-'bil-ət-ē\ *n*

tun•dra \'tən-drə\ *n* : a treeless plain of arctic and subarctic regions

¹tune \'t(y)ün\ *n* **1** : an easily remembered melody **2** : correct musical pitch **3** : harmonious relationship : AGREEMENT ⟨in ~ with the times⟩ **4** : general attitude ⟨changed his ~⟩ **5** : AMOUNT, EXTENT ⟨in debt to the ~ of millions⟩

²tune *vb* **tuned; tun•ing** **1** : to adjust in musical pitch **2** : to bring or come into harmony : ATTUNE **3** : to adjust a radio or television receiver so as to receive a broadcast **4** : to put in good working order **5** : to adjust the frequency of the output of (a device) to a chosen frequency — **tun•er** *n*

tune•ful \-fəl\ *adj* : MELODIOUS, MUSICAL — **tune•ful•ly** \-ē\ *adv* — **tune•ful•ness** *n*

tune•less \-ləs\ *adj* **1** : UNMELODIOUS **2** : not producing music — **tune•less•ly** *adv*

tune–up \'t(y)ün-,əp\ *n* : an adjustment to ensure efficient functioning ⟨an engine ~⟩

tung•sten \'təŋ-stən\ *n* [Sw, fr. *tung* heavy + *sten* stone] : a white hard heavy ductile metallic element used for electrical purposes and in hardening alloys (as steel)

tu•nic \'t(y)ü-nik\ *n* **1** : a usu. knee= length belted under or outer garment worn by ancient Greeks and Romans **2** : a hip-length or longer blouse or jacket

tuning fork *n* : a 2-pronged metal implement that gives a fixed tone when struck and is useful for tuning musical instruments

Tu•ni•sian \t(y)ü-'nēzh-ən, -'nizh-\ *n* : a native or inhabitant of Tunisia — **Tunisian** *adj*

¹tun•nel \'tən-³l\ *n* : an enclosed passage (as a tube or conduit); *esp* : one underground (as in a mine)

²tunnel *vb* **-neled** *or* **-nelled; -nel•ing** *or* **-nel•ling** \'tən-(³-)liŋ\ : to make a tunnel through or under

tun•ny \'tən-ē\ *n, pl* **tunnies** *also* **tunny** : TUNA

-tu•ple \,təp-əl, ,tüp-\ *n comb form* : set of (so many) elements

tuque \'t(y)ük\ *n* [CanF] : a warm knitted cone-shaped cap with a tassel or pom-pom worn esp. for winter sports or play

tur•ban \'tər-bən\ *n* **1** : a headdress worn esp. by Muslims and made of a cap around which is wound a long cloth **2** : a headdress resembling a Muslim turban; *esp* : a woman's close-fitting hat without a brim

tur•bid \'tər-bəd\ *adj* [L *turbidus* confused, turbid, fr. *turba* confusion, crowd] **1** : thick with roiled sediment ⟨a ~ stream⟩ **2** : heavy with smoke or mist : DENSE **3** : CONFUSED, MUDDLED — **tur•bid•i•ty** \,tər-'bid-ət-ē\ *n*

tur•bine \'tər-bən, -,bīn\ *n* [F, fr. L *turbin-, turbo* top, whirlwind, whirl] : an engine whose central drive shaft is fitted with curved vanes whirled by the pressure of water, steam, or gas

tur•bo•elec•tric \'tər-bō-i-'lek-trik\ *adj* : involving or depending as a power source on electricity produced by turbine generators

tur•bo•fan \-,fan\ *n* **1** : a fan that is directly connected to and driven by a turbine and is used to supply air for cooling, ventilation, or combustion **2** : a jet engine having a turbofan

tur•bo•jet \-,jet\ *n* : an airplane powered by a jet engine (**turbojet engine**) having a turbine-driven air compressor supplying compressed air to the combustion chamber

tur•bo•prop \-,präp\ *n* : an airplane powered by a jet engine (**turbo–propeller engine**) having a turbine-driven propeller but usu. obtaining additional thrust from the discharge of a jet of hot gases

tur•bot \'tər-bət\ *n, pl* **turbot** *also* **turbots** : a European flatfish that is a popular food fish; *also* : any of several similar flatfishes

tur·bu·lence \\'tər-byə-ləns\ *n* : the quality or state of being turbulent

tur·bu·lent \-lənt\ *adj* **1** : causing violence or disturbance **2** : marked by agitation or tumult : TEMPESTUOUS — **tur·bu·lent·ly** *adv*

tu·reen \tə-'rēn, tyū-\ *n* [F *terrine*, fr. MF, fr. fem. of *terrin* of earth, fr. L *terra* earth] : a deep bowl from which foods (as soup) are served at table

¹**turf** \'tərf\ *n, pl* **turfs** \'tərfs\ *also* **turves** \'tərvz\ **1** : the upper layer of soil bound by grass and roots into a close mat; *also* : a piece of this **2** : an artificial substitute for turf (as on a playing field) **3** : a piece of peat dried for fuel **4** : a track or course for horse racing; *also* : horse racing as a sport or business

²**turf** *vb* : to cover with turf

tur·gid \'tər-jəd\ *adj* **1** : marked by distension : SWOLLEN **2** : excessively embellished in style or language : BOMBASTIC — **tur·gid·i·ty** \ˌtər-'jid-ət-ē\ *n*

¹**Turk** \'tərk\ *n* : a native or inhabitant of Turkey

²**Turk** *abbr* Turkey; Turkish

tur·key \'tər-kē\ *n, pl* **turkeys** [*Turkey*, country in western Asia and southeastern Europe; fr. confusion with the guinea fowl, supposed to be imported from Turkish territory] : a large American bird related to the domestic chicken and widely raised for food; *also* : its flesh

turkey buzzard *n* : TURKEY VULTURE

turkey vulture *n* : an American vulture common in South and Central America and in the U.S.

Turk·ish \'tər-kish\ *n* : the language of Turkey — **Turkish** *adj*

tur·mer·ic \'tər-mə-rik\ *n* : a spice or dyestuff obtained from the large aromatic deep-yellow rhizome of an East Indian perennial herb; *also* : this herb

tur·moil \'tər-ˌmȯil\ *n* : an extremely confused or agitated condition

¹**turn** \'tərn\ *vb* **1** : to move or cause to move around an axis or center : ROTATE, REVOLVE ⟨∼ a wheel⟩ **2** : to twist so as to effect a desired end ⟨∼ a key⟩ **3** : WRENCH ⟨∼ an ankle⟩ **4** : to change or cause to change position by moving through an arc of a circle ⟨∼ed his chair to the fire⟩ **5** : to cause to move around a center so as to show another side of ⟨∼ a page⟩ **6** : to revolve mentally : PONDER **7** : to become dizzy : REEL **8** : to reverse the sides or surfaces of ⟨∼ a pancake⟩ **9** : UPSET, DISORDER ⟨things ∼ed topsy-turvy⟩ ⟨∼ed his stomach⟩ **10** : to set in another esp. contrary direction **11** : to change one's course or direction **12** : TRANSFER ⟨∼ the task over to him⟩ **13** : to go around ⟨∼ a corner⟩ **14** : to reach or pass beyond ⟨∼ed twenty-one⟩ **15** : to direct toward or away from something; *also* : DEVOTE, APPLY **16** : to have recourse **17** : to become or make hostile **18** : to cause to become of a specified nature or appearance ⟨∼s the leaves yellow⟩ **19** : to make or become spoiled : SOUR **20** : to pass from one state to another ⟨water ∼s to ice⟩ **21** : CONVERT, TRANSFORM **22** : TRANSLATE, PARAPHRASE **23** : to give a rounded form to; *esp* : to shape by means of a lathe **24** : to gain by passing in trade ⟨∼ a quick profit⟩ — **turn color 1** : BLUSH **2** : to become pale — **turn loose** : to set free

²**turn** *n* **1** : a turning about a center or axis : REVOLUTION, ROTATION **2** : the action or an act of giving or taking a different direction ⟨make a left ∼⟩ **3** : a change of course or tendency ⟨a ∼ for the better⟩ **4** : a place at which something turns : BEND, CURVE **5** : a short walk or trip round about ⟨take a ∼ around the deck⟩ **6** : an act affecting another ⟨did him a good ∼⟩ **7** : a place, time, or opportunity accorded in a scheduled order ⟨waited his ∼ to be served⟩ **8** : a period of duty : SHIFT **9** : a short act esp. in a variety show **10** : a special purpose or requirement ⟨the job serves his ∼⟩ **11** : a skillful fashioning ⟨neat ∼ of phrase⟩ **12** : a single round (as of rope passed around an object) **13** : natural or special aptitude **14** : a usu. sudden and brief disorder of body or spirits; *esp* : a spell of nervous shock or faintness

turn·about \'tər-nə-ˌbau̇t\ *n* **1** : a reversal of direction, trend, or policy **2** : RETALIATION

turn·buck·le \'tərn-ˌbək-əl\ *n* : a link

with a screw thread at one or both ends for tightening a rod or stay

turn·coat \-ˌkōt\ *n* : one who forsakes his party or principles : RENEGADE

turn down \ˌtərn-ˈdau̇n, ˈtərn-\ *vb* : to decline to accept : REJECT — **turn-down** \ˈtərn-ˌdau̇n\ *n*

turn·er \ˈtər-nər\ *n* **1** : one that turns or is used for turning **2** : one that forms articles with a lathe

turn·ery \ˈtər-nə-rē\ *n, pl* **-er·ies** : the work, products, or shop of a turner

turn in *vb* **1** : to deliver up **2** : to inform on **3** : to acquit oneself of ⟨*turn in* a good job⟩ **4** : to go to bed

turn·ing \ˈtər-niŋ\ *n* **1** : the act or course of one that turns **2** : a place of a change of direction

tur·nip \ˈtər-nəp\ *n* **1** : a garden herb related to the cabbage with hairy leaves and an edible usu. white root **2** : RUTABAGA **3** : the root of a turnip

turn·key \ˈtərn-ˌkē\ *n, pl* **turnkeys** : one who has charge of a prison's keys

turn·off \ˈtərn-ˌȯf\ *n* : a place for turning off esp. from an expressway

turn off \ˌtərn-ˈȯf, ˈtərn-\ *vb* **1** : to deviate from a straight course or a main road **2** : to stop the functioning or flow of **3** : to cause to lose interest; *also* : to evoke a negative feeling in

turn on *vb* **1** : to get high or cause to get high as a result of using a drug (as marijuana) **2** : EXCITE, STIMULATE

turn·out \ˈtərn-ˌau̇t\ *n* **1** : an act of turning out **2** : a gathering of people for a special purpose **3** : a widened place in a highway for vehicles to pass or park **4** : manner of dress **5** : net yield : OUTPUT

turn out \ˌtərn-ˈau̇t, ˈtərn-\ *vb* **1** : EXPEL, EVICT **2** : PRODUCE **3** : to come forth and assemble **4** : to get out of bed **5** : to prove to be in the end

¹**turn·over** \ˈtərn-ˌō-vər\ *n* **1** : UPSET **2** : SHIFT, REVERSAL **3** : a filled pastry made by turning half of the crust over the other half **4** : the volume of business done **5** : movement (as of goods or people) into, through, and out of a place; *esp* : a cycle of purchase, sale, and replacement of a stock of goods **6** : the number of persons hired within a period to replace those leaving or dropped; *also* : the ratio of this num-

ber to that of the average force maintained

²**turn·over** \ˌtərn-ˌō-vər\ *adj* : capable of being turned over

turn·pike \ˈtərn-ˌpīk\ *n* [ME *turnepike* revolving frame bearing spikes and serving as a barrier, fr. *turnen* to turn + *pike*] **1** : TOLLGATE; *also* : an expressway on which tolls are charged **2** : a main road

turn·spit \-ˌspit\ *n* : a device for turning a spit

turn·stile \-ˌstīl\ *n* : a post with arms pivoted on the top set in a passageway so that persons can pass through only on foot one by one

turn·ta·ble \-ˌtā-bəl\ *n* : a circular platform that revolves (as for turning a locomotive or a phonograph record)

turn to *vb* : to apply oneself to work

turn up *vb* **1** : to come to light or bring to light : DISCOVER, APPEAR **2** : to arrive at an appointed time or place **3** : to happen unexpectedly

tur·pen·tine \ˈtər-pən-ˌtīn\ *n* **1** : a mixture of oil and resin obtained from various cone-bearing trees (as pines) **2** : an oil obtained from various turpentines by distillation and used as a solvent and paint thinner; *also* : a similar oil obtained from distillation of pine wood

tur·pi·tude \ˈtər-pə-ˌt(y)üd\ *n* : inherent baseness : DEPRAVITY

turps \ˈtərps\ *n* : TURPENTINE

tur·quoise *also* **tur·quois** \ˈtər-ˌk(w)ȯiz\ *n* [ME *turkeis, turcas,* fr. MF *turquoyse,* fr. fem. of *turquoys* Turkish, fr. OF, fr. *Turc* Turk] **1** : a blue, bluish green, or greenish gray mineral that contains a little copper and is valued as a gem **2** : a light greenish blue color

tur·ret \ˈtər-ət\ *n* **1** : a little tower often at an angle of a larger structure and merely ornamental **2** : a revolvable holder in a machine tool **3** : a low usu. revolving structure (as on a tank, warship, or airplane) in which one or more guns are mounted

¹**tur·tle** \ˈtərt-ᵊl\ *n, archaic* : TURTLEDOVE

²**turtle** *n, pl* **turtles** *also* **turtle** : any of an order of horny-beaked land, freshwater, or sea reptiles with the trunk enclosed in a bony shell

tur•tle•dove \'tərt-ᵊl-ˌdəv\ *n* : any of several small wild pigeons; *esp* : an Old World bird noted for plaintive cooing

tur•tle•neck \-ˌnek\ *n* : a high close-fitting turnover collar used esp. for sweaters; *also* : a sweater with a turtleneck

turves *pl of* TURF

Tus•ca•ro•ra \ˌtəs-kə-'rōr-ə\ *n, pl* **Tuscarora** *or* **Tuscaroras** : a member of an American Indian people of No. Carolina and later of New York and Ontario

tusk \'təsk\ *n* **1** : a long enlarged protruding tooth (as of an elephant, walrus, or boar) used to dig up food or as a weapon **2** : a long projecting tooth — **tusked** \'təskt\ *adj*

tusk•er \'təs-kər\ *n* : an animal with tusks; *esp* : a male elephant with two normally developed tusks

¹**tus•sle** \'təs-əl\ *n* **1** : a physical struggle : SCUFFLE **2** : an intense argument, controversy, or struggle

²**tussle** *vb* **tus•sled; tus•sling** \-(ə-)liŋ\ : to struggle roughly

tus•sock \'təs-ək\ *n* : a dense tuft esp. of grass or sedge; *also* : a hummock in marsh bound together by roots — **tussocky** *adj*

tussock moth *n* : any of numerous dull-colored moths that usu. have wingless females and larvae with long tufts of hair

tu•te•lage \'t(y)üt-ᵊl-ij\ *n* **1** : an act of guarding or protecting **2** : the state of being under a guardian or tutor **3** : instruction esp. of an individual

tu•te•lary \'t(y)üt-ᵊl-ˌer-ē\ *adj* : acting as a guardian ⟨∼ deity⟩ ⟨a ∼ power⟩

¹**tu•tor** \'t(y)üt-ər\ *n* **1** : a person charged with the instruction and guidance of another **2** : a private teacher

²**tutor** *vb* **1** : to have the guardianship of **2** : to teach or guide individually : COACH ⟨∼ed the boy in Latin⟩ **3** : to receive instruction esp. privately

tu•to•ri•al \t(y)ü-'tōr-ē-əl\ *n* : a class conducted by a tutor for one student or a small number of students

tut•ti–frut•ti \ˌtüt-i-'früt-ē, ˌtut-\ *n* [It, lit., all fruits] : a confection or ice cream containing chopped usu. candied fruits

tux•e•do \ˌtək-'sēd-ō\ *n, pl* **-dos** *or* **-does** [*Tuxedo* Park, N.Y.] **1** : a usu. black or blackish blue jacket **2** : semiformal evening clothes for men

TV \'tē-'vē\ *n* : TELEVISION

TVA *abbr* Tennessee Valley Authority

TV dinner \ˌtē-ˌvē-\ *n* : a frozen packaged dinner that needs only heating before serving

twad•dle \'twäd-ᵊl\ *n* : silly idle talk : DRIVEL — **twaddle** *vb*

twain \'twān\ *n* **1** : TWO **2** : PAIR

¹**twang** \'twaŋ\ *n* **1** : a harsh quick ringing sound like that of a plucked bowstring **2** : nasal speech or resonance **3** : the characteristic speech of a region

²**twang** *vb* **twanged; twang•ing** \'twaŋ-iŋ\ **1** : to sound or cause to sound with a twang **2** : to speak with a nasal twang

tweak \'twēk\ *vb* : to pinch and pull with a sudden jerk and twitch — **tweak** *n*

tweed \'twēd\ *n* [alter. of Sc *tweel* twill, fr. ME *twyll*] **1** : a rough woolen fabric made usu. in twill weaves **2** *pl* : tweed clothing; *esp* : a tweed suit

tweedy \'twēd-ē\ *adj* **tweed•i•er; -est** **1** : of or resembling tweed **2** : given to wearing tweeds **3** : suggestive of the outdoors in taste or habits

tween \(')twēn\ *prep* : BETWEEN

tweet \'twēt\ *n* : a chirping note — **tweet** *vb*

tweet•er \'twēt-ər\ *n* : a small loudspeaker that reproduces sounds of high pitch

twee•zers \'twē-zərz\ *n pl* [obs. E *tweeze*, n. (case for small implements) short for obs. E *etweese*, fr. pl. of obs. E *etwee*, fr. F *étui*] : a small pincerlike implement held between the thumb and forefinger for grasping something

twelve \'twelv\ *n* **1** : one more than 11 **2** : the 12th in a set or series **3** : something having 12 units — **twelfth** \'twelfth\ *adj or n* — **twelve** *adj or pron*

twelve•month \-ˌmənth\ *n* : YEAR

twen•ty \'twent-ē\ *n, pl* **twenties** : two times 10 — **twen•ti•eth** \-ē-əth\ *adj or n* — **twenty** *adj or pron*

twenty–twenty *or* **20/20** \ˌtwent-ē-'twent-ē\ *adj* : having a visual capacity to see detail that is normal for the human eye ⟨∼ vision⟩

twice \'twīs\ *adv* **1** : on two occasions **2** : two times ⟨∼ two is four⟩

¹twid·dle \'twid-ᵊl\ *vb* **twid·dled; twid·dling** \'twid-(ᵊ-)liŋ\ **1** : to be busy with trifles; *also* : to play idly with something **2** : to rotate lightly or idly

²twiddle *n* : TURN, TWIST

twig \'twig\ *n* : a small branch — **twig·gy** *adj*

twi·light \'twī-ˌlīt\ *n* **1** : the light from the sky between full night and sunrise or between sunset and full night **2** : a state of imperfect clarity; *also* : a period of decline — **twilight** *adj*

twill \'twil\ *n* [ME *twyll,* fr. OE *twilic* having a double thread, modif. of L *bilic-, bilix,* fr. *bi-* two + *licium* thread] **1** : a fabric with a twill weave **2** : a textile weave that gives an appearance of diagonal lines in the fabric

twilled \'twild\ *adj* : made with a twill weave

¹twin \'twin\ *adj* **1** : born with one another or as a pair at one birth ⟨∼ brother⟩ ⟨∼ girls⟩ **2** : made up of two similar or related members or parts **3** : being one of a pair ⟨∼ city⟩

²twin *vb* **twinned; twin·ning 1** : to bring forth twins **2** : to be coupled with another

³twin *n* **1** : either of two offspring produced at a birth **2** : one of two persons or things closely related to or resembling each other

¹twine \'twīn\ *n* **1** : a strong thread of two or three strands twisted together **2** : an act of entwining or interlacing — **twiny** *adj*

²twine *vb* **twined; twin·ing 1** : to twist together; *also* : to form by twisting **2** : INTERLACE, WEAVE **3** : to coil about a support **4** : to stretch or move in a sinuous manner — **twin·er** *n*

¹twinge \'twinj\ *vb* **twinged; twing·ing** \'twin-jiŋ\ *or* **twinge·ing** : to affect with or feel a sharp sudden pain

²twinge *n* : a sudden sharp stab (as of pain or distress)

¹twin·kle \'twiŋ-kəl\ *vb* **twin·kled; twin·kling** \-k(ə-)liŋ\ **1** : to shine or cause to shine with a flickering or sparkling light **2** : to appear bright with merriment **3** : to flutter or flit rapidly — **twin·kler** \-k(ə-)lər\ *n*

²twinkle *n* **1** : a wink of the eyelids; *also* : the duration of a wink **2** : an intermittent radiance **3** : a rapid flashing motion

twin·kling \'twiŋ-kliŋ\ *n* : the time occupied by a single wink : INSTANT **syn** instant, moment, minute, second, flash

¹twirl \'twərl\ *vb* **1** : to whirl round **2** : to pitch in a baseball game **syn** turn, revolve, rotate, circle, spin, swirl, pirouette — **twirl·er** \'twər-lər\ *n*

²twirl *n* **1** : an act of twirling **2** : COIL, WHORL

¹twist \'twist\ *vb* **1** : to unite by winding one thread or strand round another **2** : WREATHE, TWINE **3** : to turn so as to hurt ⟨∼ed her ankle⟩ **4** : to twirl into spiral shape **5** : to subject (as a shaft) to torsion **6** : to turn from the true form or meaning **7** : to pull off or break by torsion **8** : to follow a winding course **9** : to turn around

²twist *n* **1** : something formed by twisting or winding **2** : an act of twisting : the state of being twisted **3** : a spiral turn or curve; *also* : SPIN **4** : a turning aside **5** : ECCENTRICITY **6** : a distortion of meaning **7** : an unexpected turn or development **8** : DEVICE, TRICK **9** : a variant approach or method

twist·er \'twis-tər\ *n* **1** : one that twists; *esp* : a ball with a forward and spinning motion **2** : TORNADO; *also* : WATERSPOUT **2**

twit \'twit\ *vb* **twit·ted; twit·ting** : to reproach, taunt, or tease esp. by reminding of a fault or defect **syn** ridicule, deride, mock, razz

¹twitch \'twich\ *vb* **1** : to move or pull with a sudden motion : JERK **2** : to move jerkily : QUIVER

²twitch *n* **1** : an act or movement of twitching **2** : a short sharp contraction of muscle fibers

¹twit·ter \'twit-ər\ *vb* **1** : to make a succession of chirping noises **2** : to talk in a chattering fashion; *also* : TITTER **3** : to have a slight trembling of the nerves : FLUTTER

²twitter *n* **1** : a slight agitation of the nerves **2** : a small tremulous intermittent noise (as made by a swallow) **3** : a light chattering; *also* : TITTER

twixt \(')twikst\ *prep* : BETWEEN

two \'tü\ *n, pl* **twos 1** : one more than one **2** : the second in a set or series **3** : something having two units — **two** *adj or pron*

two cents *n* **1** : a sum or object of very

small value **2** *or* **two cents worth** : an opinion offered on a topic under discussion

two–faced \'tü-'fāst\ *adj* **1** : DOUBLE=DEALING, FALSE **2** : having two faces

two•fold \'tü-ˌfōld, -'fōld\ *adj* **1** : having two units or members **2** : being twice as much or as many — **twofold** \-'fōld\ *adv*

2,4–D \ˌtü-ˌfōr-'dē\ *n* : a white crystalline compound used as a weed killer

2,4,5–T \-ˌfīv-'tē\ *n* : an irritant compound used in brush and weed control

two•pence \'təp-əns, *US also* 'tü-ˌpens\ *n* : the sum of two pence

two•pen•ny \'təp-(ə-)nē, *US also* 'tü-ˌpen-ē\ *adj* : of the value of or costing twopence

two–ply \'tü-'plī\ *adj* **1** : woven as a double cloth **2** : consisting of two strands or thicknesses

two•some \'tü-səm\ *n* **1** : a group of two persons or things : COUPLE **2** : a golf match between two players

two–step \'tü-ˌstep\ *n* : a ballroom dance performed with a sliding step in march or polka time; *also* : a piece of music for this dance — **two–step** *vb*

two–time \'tü-ˌtīm\ *vb* : to betray (a spouse or lover) by secret lovemaking with another — **two–tim•er** *n*

two–way *adj* : involving two elements or allowing movement or use in two directions or manners

two–winged fly \ˌtü-ˌwiŋd-\ *n* : any of a large order of insects mostly with one pair of functional wings and another pair that if present are reduced to balancing organs and often with larvae without a head, eyes, or legs

twp *abbr* township

TWX *abbr* teletypewriter exchange

TX *abbr* Texas

-ty *n suffix* : quality : condition : degree ⟨real*ty*⟩

ty•coon \tī-'kün\ *n* [Jp *taikun*, fr. Chin *ta⁴* great + *chün¹* ruler] **1** : a masterful leader (as in politics) **2** : a powerful businessman or industrialist

tying *pres part of* TIE

tyke \'tīk\ *n* : a small child

tym•pan•ic membrane \tim-'pan-ik-\ *n* : EARDRUM

tym•pa•num \'tim-pə-nəm\ *n, pl* **-na** \-nə\ *also* **-nums** : EARDRUM; *also*

: MIDDLE EAR — **tym•pan•ic** \tim-'pan-ik\ *adj*

¹type \'tīp\ *n* [LL *typus*, fr. L & Gk; L *typus* image, fr. Gk *typos* blow, impression, model, fr. *typtein* to strike, beat] **1** : a person, thing, or event that foreshadows another to come : TOKEN, SYMBOL **2** : MODEL, EXAMPLE **3** : a distinctive stamp, mark, or sign : EMBLEM **4** : rectangular blocks usu. of metal each having a face so shaped as to produce a character when printed **5** : the letters or characters printed from or as if from type **6** : general character or form common to a number of individuals and setting them off as a distinguishable class ⟨horses of draft ∼⟩ **7** : a class, kind, or group set apart by common characteristics ⟨a seedless ∼ of orange⟩; *also* : something distinguishable as a variety ⟨reactions of this ∼⟩ **syn** sort, nature, character, description

²type *vb* **typed; typ•ing** **1** : to represent beforehand as a type **2** : to produce a copy of; *also* : REPRESENT, TYPIFY **3** : TYPEWRITE **4** : to identify as belonging to a type **5** : TYPECAST

type•cast \-ˌkast\ *vb* **-cast; -cast•ing** **1** : to cast (an actor) in a part calling for characteristics possessed by the actor himself **2** : to cast repeatedly in the same type of role

type•face \-ˌfās\ *n* : all type of a single design

type•found•er \-ˌfaun-dər\ *n* : one engaged in the design and production of metal printing type for hand composition — **type•found•ing** \-diŋ\ *n*

type•script \'tīp-ˌskript\ *n* : typewritten matter

type•set \-ˌset\ *vb* **-set; -set•ting** : to set in type : COMPOSE — **type•set•ter** \-ˌset-ər\ *n*

type•write \-ˌrīt\ *vb* **-wrote** \-ˌrōt\; **-writ•ten** \-ˌrit-ᵊn\ : to write with a typewriter

type•writ•er \-ˌrīt-ər\ *n* **1** : a machine for writing in characters similar to those produced by printers' types by means of types striking through an inked ribbon **2** : TYPIST

type•writ•ing \-ˌrīt-iŋ\ *n* : the use of a typewriter ⟨teach ∼⟩; *also* : the printing done with a typewriter

¹ty•phoid \'tī-ˌfoid, tī-'foid\ *adj* : of, relating to, or being a communicable bacterial disease (**typhoid fever**) marked by fever, diarrhea, prostration, and intestinal inflammation

²typhoid *n* : TYPHOID FEVER

ty·phoon \tī-'fün\ *n* : a tropical cyclone in the region of the Philippines or the China sea

ty·phus \'tī-fəs\ *n* : a severe infectious disease transmitted esp. by body lice, caused by a rickettsia, and marked by high fever, stupor and delirium, intense headache, and a dark red rash

typ·i·cal \'tip-i-kəl\ *adj* 1 : being or having the nature of a type 2 : exhibiting the essential characteristics of a group 3 : conforming to a type — **typ·i·cal·i·ty** \,tip-ə-'kal-ət-ē\ *n* — **typ·i·cal·ly** \-ē\ *adv* — **typ·i·cal·ness** *n*

typ·i·fy \'tip-ə-,fī\ *vb* **-fied; -fy·ing** 1 : to represent by an image, form, model, or resemblance 2 : to embody the essential or common characteristics of

typ·ist \'tī-pəst\ *n* : one who operates a typewriter

ty·po \'tī-pō\ *n, pl* **typos** : an error in typing or in setting type

ty·pog·ra·pher \tī-'päg-rə-fər\ *n* : one who designs or arranges printing

ty·pog·ra·phy \tī-'päg-rə-fē\ *n* : the art of printing with type; *also* : the style, arrangement, or appearance of matter printed from type — **ty·po·graph·ic**

\,tī-pə-'graf-ik\ *or* **ty·po·graph·i·cal** \-i-kəl\ *adj* — **ty·po·graph·i·cal·ly** \-ē\ *adv*

ty·ran·ni·cal \tə-'ran-i-kəl, tī-\ *also* **ty·ran·nic** \-ik\ *adj* : of or relating to a tyrant : DESPOTIC **syn** arbitrary, absolute, autocratic — **ty·ran·ni·cal·ly** \-i-k(ə-)lē\ *adv*

tyr·an·nize \'tir-ə-,nīz\ *vb* **-nized; -niz·ing** : to act as a tyrant : rule with unjust severity — **tyr·an·niz·er** *n*

ty·ran·no·saur \tə-'ran-ə-,sȯr\ *n* : TYRANNOSAURUS

ty·ran·no·sau·rus \tə-,ran-ə-'sȯr-əs\ *n* : a very large American flesh-eating dinosaur of the Cretaceous that had small forelegs and walked on its hind legs

tyr·an·nous \'tir-ə-nəs\ *adj* : TYRANNICAL — **tyr·an·nous·ly** *adv*

tyr·an·ny \'tir-ə-nē\ *n, pl* **-nies** 1 : oppressive power 2 : the rule or authority of a tyrant : government in which absolute power is vested in a single ruler 3 : a tyrannical act

ty·rant \'tī-rənt\ *n* 1 : an absolute ruler : DESPOT 2 : a ruler who governs oppressively or brutally 3 : one who uses authority or power harshly

ty·ro \'tī-rō\ *n, pl* **tyros** [ML, fr. L *tiro* young soldier, tyro] : a beginner in learning : NOVICE

tzar \'zär, '(t)sär\ var of CZAR

U

¹u \'yü\ *n, pl* **u's** *or* **us** \'yüz\ *often cap* : the 21st letter of the English alphabet

²u *abbr, often cap* unit

¹U \'yü\ *adj* : characteristic of the upper classes

²U *abbr* 1 [abbr. of *Union of Orthodox Hebrew Congregations*] kosher certification 2 university

³U *symbol* uranium

UAE *abbr* United Arab Emirates

UAR *abbr* United Arab Republic

UAW *abbr* United Automobile Workers

ubiq·ui·tous \yü-'bik-wət-əs\ *adj* : existing or being everywhere at the same time : OMNIPRESENT — **ubiq·ui·tous·ly** *adv* — **ubiq·ui·ty** \-wət-ē\ *n*

U–boat \'yü-,bōt\ *n* [trans. of G *u-boot,* short for *unterseeboot,* lit., undersea boat] : a German submarine

ud·der \'əd-ər\ *n* : an organ (as of a cow) consisting of two or more milk glands enclosed in a large hanging sac and each provided with a nipple

UFO \,yü-,ef-'ō\ *n, pl* **UFO's** *or* **UFOs** \-'ōz\ : an unidentified flying object; *esp* : FLYING SAUCER

ug·ly \'əg-lē\ *adj* **ug·li·er; -est** [ME, fr. ON *uggligr,* fr. *uggr* fear] 1 : FRIGHTFUL, DIRE 2 : offensive to the sight : HIDEOUS 3 : offensive or unpleasing to any sense 4 : morally objectionable : REPULSIVE 5 : likely to cause inconvenience or discomfort 6 : SURLY,

QUARRELSOME ⟨an ∼ disposition⟩ —
ug·li·ness \-lē-nəs\ *n*

UHF *abbr* ultrahigh frequency

UK *abbr* United Kingdom

ukase \yü-ˈkās, -ˈkāz\ *n* [F & Russ; F, fr. Russ *ukaz*, fr. *ukazat'* to show, order] : an edict esp. of a Russian emperor or government

Ukrai·ni·an \yü-ˈkrā-nē-ən\ *n* : a native or inhabitant of the Ukraine, U.S.S.R. — **Ukrainian** *adj*

uku·le·le \ˌyü-kə-ˈlā-lē\ *n* [Hawaiian ʻukulele, fr. ʻuku flea + lele jumping] : a small usu. 4-stringed guitar popularized in Hawaii

ul·cer \ˈəl-sər\ *n* 1 : an eroded sore often discharging pus 2 : something that festers and corrupts like an open sore — **ul·cer·ous** *adj*

ul·cer·ate \ˈəl-sə-ˌrāt\ *vb* **-at·ed; -at·ing** : to cause or become affected with an ulcer — **ul·cer·ative** \ˈəl-sə-ˌrāt-iv\ *adj*

ul·cer·ation \ˌəl-sə-ˈrā-shən\ *n* 1 : the process of forming or state of having an ulcer 2 : ULCER 1

ul·lage \ˈəl-ij\ *n* [ME *ulage*, fr. MF *eullage* act of filling a cask, fr. *eullier* to fill a cask, fr. OF *ouil* eye, bunghole, fr. L *oculus* eye] : the amount that a container (as a cask) lacks of being full

ul·na \ˈəl-nə\ *n* : the one of the two bones of the human forearm that is on the little-finger side; *also* : a corresponding bone of the forelimb of vertebrates above fishes

ul·ster \ˈəl-stər\ *n* : a long loose overcoat

ult *abbr* 1 ultimate 2 ultimo

ul·te·ri·or \ˌəl-ˈtir-ē-ər\ *adj* 1 : lying farther away : more remote 2 : situated beyond or on the farther side 3 : going beyond what is openly said or shown : HIDDEN ⟨∼ motives⟩

¹**ul·ti·mate** \ˈəl-tə-mət\ *adj* 1 : most remote in space or time : FARTHEST 2 : last in a progression : FINAL 3 : EXTREME, UTMOST 4 : finally reckoned 5 : FUNDAMENTAL, ABSOLUTE, SUPREME ⟨∼ reality⟩ 6 : incapable of further analysis or division : ELEMENTAL 7 : MAXIMUM — **ul·ti·mate·ly** *adv*

²**ultimate** *n* : something ultimate

ul·ti·ma·tum \ˌəl-tə-ˈmāt-əm, -ˈmät-\ *n*, *pl* **-tums** *or* **-ta** \-ə\ : a final condition or demand whose rejection will bring about a resort to forceful action

ul·ti·mo \ˈəl-tə-ˌmō\ *adj* [L *ultimo mense* in the last month] : of or occurring the month preceding the present

¹**ul·tra** \ˈəl-trə\ *adj* : going beyond others or beyond due limits : EXTREME

²**ultra** *n* : EXTREMIST

ul·tra·cen·tri·fuge \ˌəl-trə-ˈsen-trə-ˌfyüj\ *n* : a high-speed centrifuge able to separate small particles (as from colloidal suspension)

ul·tra·con·ser·va·tive \-kən-ˈsər-vət-iv\ *adj* : extremely conservative

ul·tra·fash·ion·able \-ˈfash-(ə-)nə-bəl\ *adj* : extremely fashionable

ul·tra·high \-ˈhī\ *adj* : very high : exceedingly high ⟨∼ vacuum⟩

ultrahigh frequency *n* : a radio frequency between 300 and 3000 megahertz

ul·tra·ma·rine \ˌəl-trə-mə-ˈrēn\ *n* 1 : a deep blue pigment 2 : a very bright deep blue color

ul·tra·mi·cro·scop·ic \-ˌmī-krə-ˈskäp-ik\ *adj* : too small to be seen with an ordinary microscope

ul·tra·mod·ern \-ˈmäd-ərn\ *adj* : extremely or excessively modern in idea, style, or tendency

ul·tra·mon·tane \-ˈmän-ˌtān, -ˌmän-ˈtān\ *adj* 1 : of or relating to countries or peoples beyond the mountains (as the Alps) 2 : favoring greater or absolute supremacy of papal over national or diocesan authority in the Roman Catholic Church — **ultramontane** *n*, *often cap* — **ul·tra·mon·tan·ism** \-ˈmänt-ᵊn-ˌiz-əm\ *n*

ul·tra·pure \-ˈpyu̇r\ *adj* : of the utmost purity

ul·tra·short \-ˈshȯrt\ *adj* 1 : very short in duration 2 : having a wavelength below 10 meters

ul·tra·son·ic \ˌəl-trə-ˈsän-ik\ *adj* : having a frequency too high to be heard by the human ear — **ul·tra·son·i·cal·ly** \-i-k(ə-)lē\ *adv*

ul·tra·son·ics \-ˈsän-iks\ *n* 1 : ultrasonic vibrations 2 : the science of ultrasonic phenomena

ul·tra·sound \-ˌsau̇nd\ *n* 1 : ultrasonic vibrations 2 : a diagnostic or therapeutic procedure or technique using ultrasound to form a two-dimensional image of internal body structures

ul·tra·vi·o·let \-ˈvī-ə-lət\ *adj* : having a

wavelength shorter than those of visible light and longer than those of X rays 〈~ radiation〉; *also* : producing or employing ultraviolet radiation — **ultraviolet** *n*

ul·tra vi·res \ˌəl-trə-ˈvī-rēz\ *adv or adj* [NL, lit., beyond power] : beyond the scope of legal power or authority

ul·u·late \ˈəl-yə-ˌlāt\ *vb* **-lat·ed; -lat·ing** : HOWL, WAIL

um·bel \ˈəm-bəl\ *n* : a flat-topped or ball-shaped flower cluster in which the individual flower stalks all arise at one point on the main stem

um·ber \ˈəm-bər\ *n* : a brown earthy substance valued as a pigment either in its raw state or burnt — **umber** *adj*

umbilical cord *n* : a cord arising from the navel that connects the fetus with the placenta

um·bi·li·cus \ˌəm-bə-ˈlī-kəs, ˌəm-ˈbil-i-\ *n, pl* **um·bi·li·ci** \ˌəm-bə-ˈlī-ˌkī, -ˌsī; ˌəm-ˈbil-ə-ˌkī\ *or* **um·bi·li·cus·es** : NAVEL — **um·bil·i·cal** \ˌəm-ˈbil-i-kəl\ *adj*

um·bra \ˈəm-brə\ *n, pl* **umbras** *or* **um·brae** \-(ˌ)brē, -ˌbrī\ **1** : SHADE, SHADOW **2** : the conical part of the shadow of a celestial body from which the sun's light is completely blocked

um·brage \ˈəm-brij\ *n* **1** : SHADE; *also* : FOLIAGE **2** : RESENTMENT, OFFENSE 〈take ~ at a remark〉

um·brel·la \ˌəm-ˈbrel-ə\ *n* **1** : a collapsible shade for protection against weather consisting of fabric stretched over hinged ribs radiating from a center pole **2** : something that resembles an umbrella in shape or purpose

umi·ak \ˈü-mē-ˌak\ *n* : an open Eskimo boat made of a wooden frame covered with skins

um·pire \ˈəm-ˌpī(ə)r\ *n* [ME *oumpere,* alter. of *noumpere* (the phrase *a noumpere* being understood as *an oumpere*), fr. MF *nomper* not equal, not paired, fr. *non* not + *per* equal, fr. L *par*] **1** : one having authority to decide finally a controversy or question between parties **2** : an official in a sport who rules on plays — **umpire** *vb*

ump·teen \ˈəmp-ˈtēn\ *adj* : very many : indefinitely numerous — **ump·teenth** \-ˈtēnth\ *adj*

UN *abbr* United Nations

un- \ˌən, ˈən\ *prefix* **1** : not : IN-, NON- **2** : opposite of : contrary to

unabashed	unavailable
unabated	unavenged
unabsorbed	unavowed
unabsorbent	unawakened
unacademic	unbaked
unaccented	unbaptized
unacceptable	unbeloved
unacclimatized	unblamed
unaccommodating	unbleached
unaccredited	unblemished
unacknowledged	unblinking
unacquainted	unbound
unadapted	unbranched
unadjusted	unbranded
unadorned	unbreakable
unadventurous	unbridgeable
unadvertised	unbrotherly
unaesthetic	unbruised
unaffiliated	unbrushed
unafraid	unbudging
unaggressive	unburied
unaided	unburned
unalike	unburnished
unallied	uncanceled
unalterable	uncanonical
unalterably	uncap
unaltered	uncapitalized
unambiguous	uncared-for
unambiguously	uncataloged
unambitious	uncaught
unanchored	uncensored
unanimated	uncensured
unannounced	unchallenged
unanswerable	unchangeable
unanswered	unchanged
unanticipated	unchanging
unapologetic	unchaperoned
unapparent	uncharacteristic
unappealing	unchecked
unappeased	unchivalrous
unappetizing	unchristened
unappreciated	unclad
unappreciative	unclaimed
unapproachable	unclassified
unappropriated	uncleaned
unapproved	unclear
unarmored	uncleared
unartistic	unclouded
unashamed	uncluttered
unasked	uncoated
unassertive	uncollected
unassisted	uncolored
unathletic	uncombed
unattainable	uncombined
unattempted	uncomely
unattended	uncomic
unattested	uncommercial
unattractive	uncompensated
unauthentic	uncomplaining
unauthenticated	uncompleted
unauthorized	uncomplicated

uncomplimentary	undeserving	unenviable	unhackneyed
uncompounded	undetected	unequipped	unhampered
uncomprehending	undetermined	unessential	unhardened
unconcealed	undeterred	unethical	unharmed
unconfined	undeveloped	unexaggerated	unharvested
unconfirmed	undifferentiated	unexcelled	unhatched
unconformable	undigested	unexceptional	unhealed
uncongenial	undignified	unexcited	unhealthful
unconnected	undiluted	unexciting	unheeded
unconquered	undiminished	unexperienced	unhelpful
unconsecrated	undimmed	unexpired	unheralded
unconsidered	undiplomatic	unexplained	unheroic
unconsolidated	undirected	unexploded	unhesitating
unconstrained	undiscerning	unexplored	unhindered
unconsumed	undisciplined	unexposed	unhonored
uncontaminated	undisclosed	unexpressed	unhoused
uncontested	undiscovered	unexpurgated	unhurried
uncontradicted	undiscriminating	unextinguished	unhurt
uncontrolled	undisguised	unfading	unhygienic
unconverted	undismayed	unfaltering	unidentified
unconvincing	undisputed	unfashionable	unidiomatic
uncooked	undissolved	unfashionably	unimaginable
uncooperative	undistinguished	unfathomable	unimaginative
uncoordinated	undistributed	unfeasible	unimpaired
uncordial	undisturbed	unfed	unimpassioned
uncorrected	undivided	unfeminine	unimpeded
uncorroborated	undogmatic	unfenced	unimportant
uncorrupted	undomesticated	unfermented	unimposing
uncountable	undone	unfertilized	unimpressive
uncreative	undoubled	unfilled	unimproved
uncredited	undramatic	unfiltered	unincorporated
uncropped	undraped	unfitted	uninfluenced
uncrowded	undrawn	unflagging	uninformative
uncrowned	undreamed	unflattering	uninformed
uncrystallized	undressed	unflavored	uninhabitable
uncultivated	undrinkable	unfocused	uninhabited
uncultured	undulled	unfolded	uninitiated
uncurbed	undutiful	unforced	uninjured
uncured	undyed	unforeseeable	uninspired
uncurious	uneager	unforeseen	uninstructed
uncurtained	uneatable	unforgivable	uninstructive
uncustomary	uneaten	unforgiving	uninsured
undamaged	uneconomic	unformulated	unintended
undamped	uneconomical	unfortified	uninteresting
undated	unedifying	unframed	uninvested
undazzled	uneducated	unfree	uninvited
undecided	unembarrassed	unfulfilled	uninviting
undecipherable	unemotional	unfunded	unjointed
undecked	unemphatic	unfunny	unjustifiable
undeclared	unenclosed	unfurnished	unjustified
undecorated	unencumbered	ungentle	unkept
undefeated	unendorsed	ungentlemanly	unknowable
undefended	unendurable	ungerminated	unknowledgeable
undefiled	unenforceable	unglazed	unlabeled
undefinable	unenforced	ungoverned	unladylike
undefined	unengaged	ungraceful	unlamented
undemanding	unenjoyable	ungraded	unleavened
undemocratic	unenlightened	ungrammatical	unlicensed
undenominational	unenterprising	ungrounded	unlighted
undependable	unentertaining	ungrudging	unlikable
undeserved	unenthusiastic	unguided	unlimited

unlined	unpalatable	unrefined	unsociable
unlisted	unpardonable	unreflecting	unsoiled
unlit	unpasteurized	unreflective	unsold
unliterary	unpatriotic	unregistered	unsoldierly
unlivable	unpaved	unregulated	unsolicited
unlobed	unperceived	unrehearsed	unsolvable
unlovable	unperceptive	unrelated	unsolved
unloved	unperformed	unreliable	unsorted
unloving	unperturbed	unrelieved	unspecified
unmade	unpitied	unreluctant	unspectacular
unmalicious	unplanned	unremarkable	unspent
unmanageable	unplanted	unremembered	unspiritual
unmanned	unpleasing	unremovable	unspoiled
unmanufactured	unplowed	unrepentant	unspoken
unmapped	unpoetic	unreported	unsportsmanlike
unmarked	unpolished	unrepresentative	unstained
unmarketable	unpolitical	unrepressed	unstated
unmarred	unpolluted	unrequited	unsterile
unmarried	unposed	unresistant	unstoppable
unmasculine	unpractical	unresisting	unstructured
unmatched	unpracticed	unresolved	unstylish
unmeant	unpredictable	unresponsive	unsubdued
unmeasured	unprejudiced	unrestful	unsubstantiated
unmeditated	unpremeditated	unrestricted	unsubtle
unmelodious	unprepared	unreturnable	unsuccessful
unmentioned	unpreparedness	unreturned	unsuccessfully
unmerited	unprepossessing	unrewarding	unsuitable
unmilitary	unpressed	unrhymed	unsuited
unmilled	unpretending	unrhythmic	unsullied
unmixed	unpretty	unripened	unsupervised
unmolested	unprivileged	unromantic	unsupportable
unmounted	unprocessed	unromantically	unsupported
unmovable	unproductive	unsafe	unsuppressed
unmoved	unprofessed	unsaid	unsure
unmusical	unprofessional	unsalable	unsurpassed
unnameable	unprogrammed	unsalted	unsuspected
unnamed	unprogressive	unsanitary	unsuspecting
unnecessary	unpromising	unsatisfactory	unsuspicious
unneighborly	unprompted	unsatisfied	unsweetened
unnewsworthy	unpronounceable	unscented	unsymmetrical
unnoticeable	unpropitious	unscheduled	unsympathetic
unnoticed	unprotected	unscholarly	unsystematic
unobjectionable	unproven	unsealed	untactful
unobliging	unprovided	unseasoned	untainted
unobservant	unprovoked	unseaworthy	untalented
unobserved	unpublished	unsegmented	untamed
unobserving	unpunished	unsensational	untanned
unobstructed	unquenchable	unsentimental	untapped
unobtainable	unquestioned	unserviceable	untarnished
unofficial	unraised	unsexual	untaxed
unofficially	unratified	unshaded	unteachable
unopened	unreachable	unshakable	untenable
unopposed	unreadable	unshaken	untenanted
unoriginal	unready	unshapely	untested
unorthodox	unrealistic	unshaven	unthankful
unostentatious	unrealized	unshed	unthoughtful
unowned	unrecognizable	unshorn	unthrifty
unpaged	unrecompensed	unsifted	untidy
unpaid	unrecorded	unsigned	untilled
unpainted	unrecoverable	unsinkable	untitled
unpaired	unredeemable	unsmiling	untouched

untraceable	unwarranted
untrained	unwary
untrammeled	unwashed
untranslatable	unwatched
untraveled	unwavering
untraversed	unweaned
untrimmed	unwearable
untrod	unwearied
untroubled	unweathered
untrustworthy	unwed
untruthful	unwelcome
unusable	unwished
unvaried	unwitnessed
unvarying	unwomanly
unventilated	unworkable
unverifiable	unworn
unverified	unworried
unversed	unwounded
unvisited	unwoven
unwanted	unwrinkled

un·able \ˌən-ˈā-bəl, ˈən-\ *adj* **1** : not able **2** : UNQUALIFIED, INCOMPETENT

un·abridged \ˌən-ə-ˈbrijd\ *adj* **1** : not abridged ⟨an ∼ edition of Shakespeare⟩ **2** : complete of its class : not based on one larger ⟨an ∼ dictionary⟩

un·ac·com·pa·nied \ˌən-ə-ˈkəmp-(ə-)nēd\ *adj* : not accompanied; *esp* : being without instrumental accompaniment

un·ac·count·able \ˌən-ə-ˈkaunt-ə-bəl\ *adj* **1** : not to be accounted for : INEXPLICABLE **2** : not responsible — **un·ac·count·ably** \-blē\ *adv*

un·ac·count·ed \-əd\ *adj* : not accounted ⟨the loss was ∼ for⟩

un·ac·cus·tomed \ˌən-ə-ˈkəs-təmd\ *adj* **1** : not customary : not usual or common **2** : not accustomed or habituated ⟨∼ to noise⟩

un·adul·ter·at·ed \ˌən-ə-ˈdəl-tə-ˌrāt-əd\ *adj* : PURE, UNMIXED

un·ad·vised \ˌən-əd-ˈvīzd\ *adj* **1** : done without due consideration : RASH **2** : not prudent — **un·ad·vis·ed·ly** \-ˈvī-zəd-lē\ *adv*

un·af·fect·ed \ˌən-ə-ˈfek-təd\ *adj* **1** : not influenced or changed mentally, physically, or chemically **2** : free from affectation : NATURAL, GENUINE — **un·af·fect·ed·ly** *adv*

un·alien·able \-ˈāl-yə-nə-bəl, -ˈā-lē-ə-\ *adj* : INALIENABLE

un·aligned \ˌən-ᵊl-ˈīnd\ *adj* : not associated with any one of competing international blocs ⟨∼ nations⟩

un·al·loyed \ˌən-ᵊl-ˈoid\ *adj* : UNMIXED, UNQUALIFIED, PURE ⟨∼ metals⟩

un–Amer·i·can \ˌən-ə-ˈmer-ə-kən\ *adj* : not characteristic of or consistent with American customs, principles, or traditions

unan·i·mous \yu̇-ˈnan-ə-məs\ *adj* [L *unanimus*, fr. *unus* one + *animus* mind] **1** : being of one mind : AGREEING **2** : formed with or indicating the agreement of all — **una·nim·i·ty** \yü-nə-ˈnim-ət-ē\ *n* — **unan·i·mous·ly** \yu̇-ˈnan-ə-məs-lē\ *adv*

un·arm \ˌən-ˈärm, ˈən-\ *vb* : DISARM

un·armed \-ˈärmd\ *adj* : not armed or armored

un·as·sail·able \ˌən-ə-ˈsā-lə-bəl\ *adj* : not assailable : not liable to doubt, attack, or question

un·as·sum·ing \ˌən-ə-ˈsü-miŋ\ *adj* : MODEST, RETIRING

un·at·tached \ˌən-ə-ˈtacht\ *adj* **1** : not married or engaged **2** : not joined or united

un·avail·ing \ˌən-ə-ˈvā-liŋ\ *adj* : being of no avail — **un·avail·ing·ly** *adv*

un·avoid·able \ˌən-ə-ˈvoid-ə-bəl\ *adj* : not avoidable : INEVITABLE — **un·avoid·ably** \-blē\ *adv*

¹un·aware \ˌən-ə-ˈwaər\ *adv* : UNAWARES

²unaware *adj* : not aware : IGNORANT — **un·aware·ness** *n*

un·awares \-ˈwaərz\ *adv* **1** : without knowing : UNINTENTIONALLY **2** : without warning : by surprise ⟨taken ∼⟩

un·bal·anced \ˌən-ˈbal-ənst\ *adj* **1** : not equally poised or balanced **2** : mentally disordered **3** : not adjusted so as to make credits equal to debits

un·bar \-ˈbär\ *vb* : UNBOLT, OPEN

un·bear·able \ˌən-ˈbar-ə-bəl\ *adj* : greater than can be borne ⟨∼ pain⟩ — **un·bear·ably** \-blē\ *adv*

un·beat·able \-ˈbēt-ə-bəl\ *adj* : not capable of being defeated

un·beat·en \-ˈbēt-ᵊn\ *adj* **1** : not pounded, beaten, or whipped **2** : UNTROD **3** : UNDEFEATED

un·be·com·ing \ˌən-bi-ˈkəm-iŋ\ *adj* : not becoming : UNSUITABLE, IMPROPER — **un·be·com·ing·ly** *adv*

un·be·knownst \ˌən-bi-ˈnōnst\ *also* **un·be·known** \-ˈnōn\ *adj* : happening without one's knowledge

un·be·lief \ˌən-bə-ˈlēf\ *n* : the withhold-

ing or absence of belief : DOUBT —
un·be·liev·ing \-'lē-viŋ\ adj
un·be·liev·able \-'lē-və-bəl\ adj : too
improbable for belief : INCREDIBLE —
un·be·liev·ably \-blē\ adv
un·be·liev·er \-'lē-vər\ n 1 : DOUBTER 2
: INFIDEL
un·bend \-'bend\ vb **-bent** \-'bent\;
-bend·ing 1 : to free from being bent
: make or become straight 2 : UNTIE 3
: to make or become less stiff or more
affable : RELAX
un·bend·ing \-'ben-diŋ\ adj : formal
and distant in manner : INFLEXIBLE
un·bi·ased \,ən-'bī-əst, 'ən-\ adj : free
from bias; esp : UNPREJUDICED
un·bid·den \-'bid-ªn\ also **un·bid** \-'bid\
adj : not bidden : UNASKED
un·bind \-'bīnd\ vb **-bound** \-'baúnd\;
-bind·ing 1 : to remove bindings from
: UNTIE 2 : RELEASE
un·blessed also **un·blest** \,ən-'blest,
'ən-\ adj 1 : not blessed 2 : EVIL
un·block \-'bläk\ vb : to free from being
blocked
un·blush·ing \-'bləsh-iŋ\ adj 1 : not
blushing 2 : SHAMELESS — **un·blush-**
ing·ly adv
un·bod·ied \-'bäd-ēd\ adj 1 : having no
body; also : DISEMBODIED 2 : FORMLESS
un·bolt \,ən-'bōlt, 'ən-\ vb : to open or
unfasten by withdrawing a bolt
un·bolt·ed \-'bōl-təd\ adj : not fastened
by bolts
un·born \-'bȯrn\ adj : not yet born
un·bo·som \-'búz-əm, -'büz-\ vb 1 : DIS-
CLOSE, REVEAL ⟨∼ed his secrets⟩ 2 : to
disclose the thoughts or feelings of
oneself
un·bound·ed \-'baún-dəd\ adj : having
no bounds or limits ⟨∼ enthusiasm⟩
un·bowed \,ən-'baúd, 'ən-\ adj 1 : not
bowed down 2 : UNSUBDUED
un·bri·dled \-'brīd-ªld\ adj 1 : UNRE-
STRAINED 2 : not confined by a bridle
un·bro·ken \-'brō-kən\ adj 1 : not damaged 2 : not subdued or tamed 3 : not
interrupted : CONTINUOUS
un·buck·le \-'bək-əl\ vb : to loose the
buckle of : UNFASTEN ⟨∼ a belt⟩
un·bur·den \-'bərd-ªn\ vb 1 : to free or
relieve from a burden 2 : to relieve
oneself of (as cares or worries) : cast
off
un·but·ton \-'bət-ªn\ vb : to unfasten
the buttons of ⟨∼ your coat⟩

un·called–for \,ən-'kȯld-,fȯr\ adj : not
called for, needed, or wanted
un·can·ny \-'kan-ē\ adj 1 : GHOSTLY,
MYSTERIOUS, EERIE 2 : suggesting
superhuman or supernatural powers
— **un·can·ni·ly** \-'kan-ªl-ē\ adv
un·ceas·ing \-'sē-siŋ\ adj : never ceasing — **un·ceas·ing·ly** adv
un·cer·e·mo·ni·ous \,ən-,ser-ə-'mō-nē-
əs\ adj : acting without or lacking ordinary courtesy : ABRUPT — **un·cer·e-**
mo·ni·ous·ly adv
un·cer·tain \,ən-'sərt-ªn, 'ən-\ adj 1
: not determined or fixed ⟨an ∼ quan-
tity⟩ 2 : subject to chance or change
: not dependable 3 : not definitely
known 4 : not sure ⟨∼ of the truth⟩ —
un·cer·tain·ly adv
un·cer·tain·ty \-ªn-tē\ n 1 : lack of certainty : DOUBT 2 : something that is
uncertain
un·chain \,ən-'chān, 'ən-\ vb : to free
by or as if by removing a chain
un·charged \,ən-'chärjd\ adj : having
no electrical charge
un·char·i·ta·ble \-'char-ət-ə-bəl\ adj
: not charitable; esp : severe in judging others — **un·char·i·ta·ble·ness** n —
un·char·i·ta·bly \-blē\ adv
un·chart·ed \-'chärt-əd\ adj 1 : not recorded on a map, chart, or plan 2
: UNKNOWN
un·chaste \-'chāst\ adj : not chaste —
un·chaste·ly adv — **un·chaste·ness**
\-'chās(t)-nəs\ n — **un·chas·ti·ty**
\-'chas-tət-ē\ n
un·chris·tian \-'kris-chən\ adj 1 : not of
the Christian faith 2 : contrary to the
Christian spirit
un·churched \-'chərcht\ adj : not belonging to or connected with a church
un·cial \'ən-shəl, -chəl; 'ən-sē-əl\ adj [L
uncialis inch-high, fr. uncia twelfth
part, ounce, inch] : relating to or written in a form of script with rounded
letters used esp. in early Greek and
Latin manuscripts — **uncial** n
un·cir·cu·lat·ed \,ən-'sər-kyə-,lāt-əd\
adj : issued for use as money but kept
out of circulation
un·cir·cum·cised \,ən-'sər-kəm-,sīzd,
'ən-\ adj : not circumcised; also
: HEATHEN
un·civ·il \,ən-'siv-əl, 'ən-\ adj 1 : not
civilized : BARBAROUS 2 : DISCOURTE-
OUS, ILL-MANNERED, IMPOLITE

un·civ·i·lized \-ˈsiv-ə-ˌlīzd\ *adj* **1** : not civilized : BARBAROUS **2** : remote from civilization : WILD

un·clasp \-ˈklasp\ *vb* : to open by or as if by loosing the clasp

un·cle \ˈəŋ-kəl\ *n* [ME, fr. OF, fr. L *avunculus* mother's brother] : the brother of one's father or mother; *also* : the husband of one's aunt

un·clean \ˌən-ˈklēn, ˈən-\ *adj* **1** : morally or spiritually impure **2** : prohibited by ritual law for use or contact **3** : DIRTY, FILTHY — **un·clean·ness** \-ˈklēn-nəs\ *n*

un·clean·ly \ˈklen-lē\ *adj* : morally or physically unclean — **un·clean·li·ness** \-lē-nəs\ *n*

un·clench \-ˈklench\ *vb* : to open from a clenched position : RELAX

Uncle Tom \ˌəŋ-kəl-ˈtäm\ *n* [fr. *Uncle Tom,* faithful Negro slave in Harriet Beecher Stowe's novel *Uncle Tom's Cabin* (1851-52)] : a black who is overeager to win the approval of whites

un·cloak \ˌən-ˈklōk, ˈən-\ *vb* **1** : to remove a cloak or cover from **2** : UNMASK, REVEAL

un·clog \-ˈkläg\ *vb* : to remove an obstruction from

un·close \-ˈklōz\ *vb* : OPEN — **un·closed** \-ˈklōzd\ *adj*

un·clothe \-ˈklōth\ *vb* : to strip of clothes or a covering — **un·clothed** \-ˈklōthd\ *adj*

un·coil \ˌən-ˈkȯil, ˈən-\ *vb* : to release or become released from a coiled state

un·com·fort·able \ˌən-ˈkəm(p)f-tə-bəl, ˈən-, -ˈkəm(p)-fərt-ə-\ *adj* **1** : causing discomfort **2** : feeling discomfort : UNEASY — **un·com·fort·ably** \-blē\ *adv*

un·com·mit·ted \ˌən-kə-ˈmit-əd\ *adj* : not committed; *esp* : not pledged to a particular belief, allegiance, or program

un·com·mon \ˌən-ˈkäm-ən, ˈən-\ *adj* **1** : not ordinarily encountered : UNUSUAL, RARE **2** : REMARKABLE, EXCEPTIONAL — **un·com·mon·ly** *adv*

un·com·mu·ni·ca·tive \ˌən-kə-ˈmyü-nə-ˌkāt-iv, -ni-kət-\ *adj* : not inclined to talk or impart information : RESERVED

un·com·pro·mis·ing \ˈən-ˈkäm-prə-ˌmī-

ziŋ\ *adj* : not making or accepting a compromise : UNYIELDING

un·con·cern \ˌən-kən-ˈsərn\ *n* **1** : lack of care or interest : INDIFFERENCE **2** : freedom from excessive concern or anxiety

un·con·cerned \-ˈsərnd\ *adj* **1** : not having any part or interest **2** : not anxious or upset : free of worry — **un·con·cern·ed·ly** \-ˈsər-nəd-lē\ *adv*

un·con·di·tion·al \ˌən-kən-ˈdish-(ə-)nəl\ *adj* : not limited in any way — **un·con·di·tion·al·ly** \-ē\ *adv*

un·con·di·tioned \-ˈdish-ənd\ *adj* **1** : not subject to conditions **2** : not acquired or learned : INHERENT, NATURAL **3** : producing an unconditioned response ⟨∼ stimuli⟩

un·con·quer·able \ˌən-ˈkäŋ-k(ə-)rə-bəl, ˈən-\ *adj* : incapable of being conquered or overcome : INDOMITABLE

un·con·scio·na·ble \-ˈkänch-(ə-)nə-bəl\ *adj* **1** : not guided or controlled by conscience **2** : not in accordance with what is right or just — **un·con·scio·na·bly** \-blē\ *adv*

¹un·con·scious \ˌən-ˈkän-chəs, ˈən-\ *adj* **1** : deprived of consciousness or awareness **2** : not realized by oneself : not consciously done **3** : of or relating to the unconscious — **un·con·scious·ly** *adv* — **un·con·scious·ness** *n*

²unconscious *n* : the part of one's mental life of which one is not ordinarily aware and which is revealed esp. in spontaneous behavior (as slips of the tongue) or in dreams

un·con·sti·tu·tion·al \ˌən-ˌkän-stə-ˈt(y)üsh-(ə-)nəl\ *adj* : not according to or consistent with the constitution of a state or society — **un·con·sti·tu·tion·al·i·ty** \-t(y)ü-shə-ˈnal-ət-ē\ *n* — **un·con·sti·tu·tion·al·ly** \-ˈt(y)üsh-(ə-)nə-lē\ *adv*

un·con·trol·la·ble \ˌən-kən-ˈtrō-lə-bəl\ *adj* : incapable of being controlled : UNGOVERNABLE — **un·con·trol·la·bly** \-blē\ *adv*

un·con·ven·tion·al \-ˈvench-(ə-)nəl\ *adj* : not conventional : being out of the ordinary — **un·con·ven·tion·al·i·ty** \-ˌven-chə-ˈnal-ət-ē\ *n* — **un·con·ven·tion·al·ly** \-ˈvench-(ə-)nə-lē\ *adv*

un·cork \ˌən-ˈkȯrk, ˈən-\ *vb* **1** : to draw a cork from **2** : to release from a sealed or pent-up state; *also* : to let go

un·count·ed \-'kaùnt-əd\ *adj* **1** : not counted **2** : INNUMERABLE

un·cou·ple \-'kəp-əl\ *vb* : DISCONNECT

un·couth \-'küth\ *adj* [OE *uncūth* unknown, unfamiliar, fr. *un-* + *cūth* known] **1** : strange, awkward, and clumsy in shape or appearance **2** : vulgar in conduct or speech : RUDE

un·cov·er \-'kəv-ər\ *vb* **1** : to make known : DISCLOSE, REVEAL **2** : to expose to view by removing some covering **3** : to take the cover from **4** : to remove the hat from; *also* : to take off the hat as a token of respect — **uncovered** \-ərd\ *adj*

un·crit·i·cal \,ən-'krit-i-kəl, 'ən-\ *adj* **1** : not critical : lacking in discrimination **2** : showing lack or improper use of critical standards or procedures

un·cross \-'kròs\ *vb* : to change from a crossed position ⟨~ed his legs⟩

unc·tion \'əŋk-shən\ *n* **1** : the act of anointing as a rite of consecration or healing **2** : exaggerated, assumed, or superficial earnestness of language or manner

unc·tu·ous \'əŋk-chə(-wə)s\ *adj* [ME, fr. MF or ML; MF *unctueux,* fr. ML *unctuosus,* fr. L *unctum* ointment, fr. *unguere* to anoint] **1** : FATTY, OILY **2** : full of unction in speech and manner; *esp* : insincerely smooth — **unc·tu·ous·ly** *adv*

un·curl \,ən-'kərl, 'ən-\ *vb* : to make or become straightened out from a curled or coiled position

un·cut \,ən-'kət, 'ən-\ *adj* **1** : not cut down or into **2** : not shaped by cutting ⟨an ~ diamond⟩ **3** : not having the folds of the leaves slit ⟨an ~ book⟩ **4** : not abridged or curtailed

un·daunt·ed \-'dònt-əd\ *adj* : not daunted : not discouraged or dismayed — **un·daunt·ed·ly** *adv*

un·de·ceive \,ən-di-'sēv\ *vb* : to free from deception, illusion, or error

un·de·mon·stra·tive \,ən-di-'män-strət-iv\ *adj* : restrained in expression of feeling : RESERVED

un·de·ni·able \,ən-di-'nī-ə-bəl\ *adj* **1** : plainly true : INCONTESTABLE **2** : unquestionably excellent or genuine — **un·de·ni·ably** \-blē\ *adv*

¹un·der \'ən-dər\ *adv* **1** : in or into a position below or beneath something **2** : below some quantity, level, or norm ⟨$10 or ~⟩ **3** : in or into a condition of subjection, subordination, or unconsciousness ⟨the ether put him ~⟩

²un·der \,ən-dər, 'ən-\ *prep* **1** : lower than and overhung, surmounted, or sheltered by ⟨~ a tree⟩ **2** : subject to the authority or guidance of ⟨served ~ him⟩ ⟨had the man ~ contract⟩ **3** : subject to the action or effect of ⟨~ an anesthetic⟩ **4** : within the division or grouping of ⟨items ~ this head⟩ **5** : less or lower than (as in size, amount, or rank) ⟨makes ~ $5000⟩

³under \'ən-dər\ *adj* **1** : lying below, beneath, or on the ventral side **2** : facing or protruding downward **3** : SUBORDINATE **4** : lower than usual, proper, or desired in amount, quality, or degree

un·der·achiev·er \,ən-dər-ə-'chē-vər\ *n* : one who performs below an expected level of proficiency

un·der·act \-'akt\ *vb* : to perform feebly or with restraint

un·der·ac·tive \-'ak-tiv\ *adj* : characterized by abnormally low activity ⟨~ glands⟩ — **un·der·ac·tiv·i·ty** \-,ak-'tiv-ət-ē\ *n*

un·der·age \-'āj\ *adj* : of less than mature or legal age

un·der·arm \-'ärm\ *adj* **1** : UNDERHAND **2** ⟨an ~ throw⟩ **2** : placed under or on the underside of the arms ⟨~ seams⟩ — **underarm** *adv or n*

un·der·bel·ly \'ən-dər-,bel-ē\ *n* **1** : the underside of a body or mass **2** : a vulnerable area

un·der·bid \,ən-dər-'bid\ *vb* **-bid; -bid·ding 1** : to bid less than another **2** : to bid too low

un·der·body \'ən-dər-,bäd-ē\ *n* : the lower parts of the body of a vehicle

un·der·bred \,ən-dər-'bred\ *adj* : marked by lack of good breeding

un·der·brush \'ən-dər-,brəsh\ *n* : shrubs and small trees growing beneath large trees

un·der·car·riage \-,kar-ij\ *n* **1** : a supporting framework (as of an automobile) **2** : the landing gear of an airplane

un·der·charge \,ən-dər-'chärj\ *vb* : to charge (as a person) too little — **undercharge** \'ən-dər-,chärj\ *n*

un·der·class·man \,ən-dər-'klas-mən\ *n* : a member of the freshman or sophomore class

un·der·clothes \'ən-dər-ˌklō(th)z\ *n pl* : UNDERWEAR

un·der·cloth·ing \-ˌklō-thiŋ\ *n* : UNDERWEAR

un·der·coat \-ˌkōt\ *n* **1** : a coat worn under another **2** : a growth of short hair or fur partly concealed by a longer growth ⟨a dog's ∼⟩ **3** : a coat of paint under another

un·der·coat·ing \-ˌkōt-iŋ\ *n* : a special waterproof coating applied to the underside of a vehicle

un·der·cov·er \ˌən-dər-'kəv-ər\ *adj* : acting or executed in secret; *esp* : employed or engaged in secret investigation ⟨∼ agent⟩

un·der·croft \'ən-dər-ˌkróft\ *n* [ME, fr. *under* + *crofte* crypt, fr. Middle Dutch, fr. ML *crupta*, fr. L *crypta*] : a vaulted chamber under a church

un·der·cur·rent \-ˌkər-ənt\ *n* **1** : a current below the surface **2** : a hidden tendency of feeling or opinion

un·der·cut \ˌən-dər-'kət\ *vb* **-cut; -cutting 1** : to cut away the underpart of **2** : to offer to sell or to work at a lower rate than **3** : to strike (the ball) obliquely downward so as to give a backward spin or elevation to the shot — **un·der·cut** \'ən-dər-ˌkət\ *n*

un·der·de·vel·oped \ˌən-dər-di-'vel-əpt\ *adj* **1** : not normally or adequately developed ⟨∼ muscles⟩ **2** : having a relatively low level of economic development ⟨the ∼ nations⟩

un·der·dog \'ən-dər-ˌdóg\ *n* **1** : the loser or predicted loser in a struggle **2** : a victim of injustice or persecution

un·der·done \ˌən-dər-'dən\ *adj* : not thoroughly done or cooked : RARE

un·der·draw·ers \'ən-dər-ˌdró(-ə)rz\ *n pl* : UNDERPANTS

un·der·em·pha·size \ˌən-dər-'em-fə-sīz\ *vb* : to emphasize inadequately — **un·der·em·pha·sis** \-səs\ *n*

un·der·em·ployed \-im-'plóid\ *adj* : having less than full-time or adequate employment

un·der·es·ti·mate \-'es-tə-ˌmāt\ *vb* : to set too low a value on

un·der·ex·pose \-ik-'spōz\ *vb* : to expose (a photographic plate or film) for less time than is needed — **un·der·ex·po·sure** \-'spō-zhər\ *n*

un·der·feed \ˌən-dər-'fēd\ *vb* **-fed** \-'fed\; **-feed·ing** : to feed inadequately

un·der·foot \-'fût\ *adv* **1** : under the feet ⟨flowers trampled ∼⟩ **2** : close about one's feet : in the way

un·der·fur \'ən-dər-ˌfər\ *n* : the thick soft undercoat of fur lying beneath the longer and coarser hair of a mammal

un·der·gar·ment \-ˌgär-mənt\ *n* : a garment to be worn under another

un·der·gird \ˌən-dər-'gərd\ *vb* **1** : to make secure underneath **2** : to brace up : STRENGTHEN

un·der·go \ˌən-dər-'gō\ *vb* **-went** \-'went\; **-gone** \-'gón, -'gän\; **-go·ing** \-'gō-iŋ, -'gó(-)iŋ\ **1** : to be subjected to : ENDURE **2** : to pass through : EXPERIENCE

un·der·grad·u·ate \ˌən-dər-'graj-(ə-)wət, -ə-ˌwāt\ *n* : a student at a university or college who has not taken a first degree

¹**un·der·ground** \ˌən-dər-'graúnd\ *adv* **1** : beneath the surface of the earth **2** : in secret

²**un·der·ground** \'ən-dər-ˌgraúnd\ *n* **1** : a space under the surface of the ground; *esp* : SUBWAY **2** : a secret political movement or group; *esp* : an organized body working in secret to overthrow a government or an occupying power **3** : an avant-garde group or movement that operates outside the establishment

³**underground** \'ən-dər-ˌgraúnd\ *adj* **1** : being or growing under the surface of the ground ⟨∼ stems⟩ **2** : conducted by secret means **3** : produced or published outside the establishment esp. by the avant-garde ⟨∼ movies⟩; *also* : of or relating to the avant-garde underground

un·der·growth \'ən-dər-ˌgrōth\ *n* : low growth (as of herbs and shrubs) on the floor of a forest

¹**un·der·hand** \'ən-dər-ˌhand\ *adv* **1** : in an underhanded or secret manner **2** : with an underhand motion

²**underhand** *adj* **1** : UNDERHANDED **2** : made with the hand kept below the level of the shoulder

¹**un·der·hand·ed** \ˌən-dər-'han-dəd\ *adv* : UNDERHAND

²**underhanded** *adj* : marked by secrecy and deception — **un·der·hand·ed·ly** *adv* — **un·der·hand·ed·ness** *n*

un·der·lie \-'lī\ *vb* **-lay** \-'lā\; **-lain** \-'lān\; **-ly·ing** \-'lī-iŋ\ **1** : to lie or be situated under **2** : to be at the basis of : form the foundation of : SUPPORT

un·der·line \'ən-dər-ˌlīn\ *vb* **1** : to draw a line under **2** : EMPHASIZE, STRESS — **underline** *n*

un·der·ling \'ən-dər-liŋ\ *n* : SUBORDINATE, INFERIOR

un·der·lip \ˌən-dər-'lip\ *n* : the lower lip

un·der·ly·ing \ˌən-dər-'lī-iŋ\ *adj* **1** : lying under or below **2** : FUNDAMENTAL, BASIC ⟨∼ principles⟩

un·der·mine \-'mīn\ *vb* **1** : to excavate beneath **2** : to weaken or wear away secretly or gradually

un·der·most \'ən-dər-ˌmōst\ *adj* : lowest in relative position — **undermost** *adv*

¹**un·der·neath** \ˌən-dər-'nēth\ *prep* **1** : directly under **2** : under subjection to

²**underneath** *adv* **1** : below a surface or object : BENEATH **2** : on the lower side

un·der·nour·ished \ˌən-dər-'nər-isht\ *adj* : supplied with insufficient nourishment — **un·der·nour·ish·ment** \-'nər-ish-mənt\ *n*

un·der·pants \'ən-dər-ˌpants\ *n pl* : short or long pants worn under an outer garment : DRAWERS

un·der·part \-ˌpärt\ *n* **1** : a part lying on the lower side esp. of a bird or mammal **2** : a subordinate or auxiliary part or role

un·der·pass \-ˌpas\ *n* : a passage underneath something ⟨a railroad ∼⟩

un·der·pay \ˌən-dər-'pā\ *vb* : to pay too little

un·der·pin·ning \'ən-dər-ˌpin-iŋ\ *n* : the material and construction (as a foundation) used for support of a structure — **un·der·pin** \ˌən-dər-'pin\ *vb*

un·der·play \ˌən-dər-'plā\ *vb* : to treat or handle with restraint; *esp* : to play a role with subdued force

un·der·pop·u·lat·ed \ˌən-dər-'päp-yə-ˌlāt-əd\ *adj* : having a lower than normal or desirable density of population

un·der·priv·i·leged \-'priv-(ə-)lijd\ *adj* : having fewer esp. economic and social privileges than others

un·der·pro·duc·tion \ˌən-dər-prə-'dək-shən\ *n* : the production of less than enough to satisfy the demand or of less than the usual supply

un·der·rate \ˌən-də(r)-'rāt\ *vb* : to rate or value too low

un·der·rep·re·sent·ed \-ˌrep-ri-'zent-əd\ *adj* : inadequately represented

un·der·score \'ən-dər-ˌskōr\ *vb* **1** : to draw a line under : UNDERLINE **2** : EMPHASIZE — **underscore** *n*

¹**un·der·sea** \ˌən-dər-ˌsē\ *adj* : being, carried on, or used beneath the surface of the sea

²**un·der·sea** \ˌən-dər-'sē\ *or* **un·der·seas** \-'sēz\ *adv* : beneath the surface of the sea

under secretary *n* : a secretary immediately subordinate to a principal secretary ⟨∼ of state⟩

un·der·sell \-'sel\ *vb* **-sold** \-'sōld\; **-sell·ing** : to sell articles cheaper than

un·der·sexed \-'sekst\ *adj* : deficient in sexual desire

un·der·shirt \'ən-dər-ˌshərt\ *n* : a collarless undergarment with or without sleeves

un·der·shoot \ˌən-dər-'shüt\ *vb* **-shot** \-'shät\; **-shoot·ing** **1** : to shoot short of or below (a target) **2** : to fall short of (a runway) in landing an airplane

un·der·shorts \'ən-dər-ˌshȯrts\ *n pl* : SHORT 2

un·der·shot \ˌən-dər-'shät\ *adj* **1** : having the lower front teeth projecting beyond the upper when the mouth is closed **2** : moved by water passing beneath ⟨an ∼ waterwheel⟩

un·der·side \'ən-dər-ˌsīd, ˌən-dər-'sīd\ *n* : the side or surface lying underneath

un·der·signed \'ən-dər-ˌsīnd\ *n, pl* **undersigned** : one who signs his name at the end of a document

un·der·sized \ˌən-dər-'sīzd\ *also* **un·der·size** \-'sīz\ *adj* : of a size less than is common, proper, or normal

un·der·skirt \'ən-dər-ˌskərt\ *n* : a skirt worn under an outer skirt; *esp* : PETTICOAT

un·der·slung \ˌən-dər-'sləŋ\ *adj* : suspended so as to extend below the axles ⟨an ∼ automobile frame⟩

un·der·stand \ˌən-dər-'stand\ *vb* **-stood** \-'stud\; **-stand·ing** **1** : to grasp the meaning of : COMPREHEND **2** : to have thorough or technical acquaintance with or expertness in ⟨∼ finance⟩ **3**

: GATHER, INFER ⟨I ∼ that you spread this rumor⟩ **4** : INTERPRET ⟨we ∼ this to be a refusal⟩ **5** : to have a sympathetic attitude **6** : to accept as settled ⟨it is *understood* that he will pay the expenses⟩ — **un·der·stand·able** \-ˈstan-də-bəl\ *adj* — **un·der·stand·ably** \-blē\ *adv*

¹**un·der·stand·ing** \ˌən-dər-ˈstan-diŋ\ *n* **1** : knowledge and ability to apply judgment : INTELLIGENCE **2** : ability to comprehend and judge ⟨a man of ∼⟩ **3** : agreement of opinion or feeling **4** : a mutual agreement informally or tacitly entered into

²**understanding** *adj* : endowed with understanding : TOLERANT, SYMPATHETIC

un·der·state \ˌən-dər-ˈstāt\ *vb* **1** : to represent as less than is the case **2** : to state with restraint esp. for greater effect — **un·der·state·ment** *n*

un·der·stood \ˌən-dər-ˈstud\ *adj* **1** : agreed upon **2** : IMPLICIT

un·der·sto·ry \ˈən-dər-ˌstōr-ē, -ˌstȯr-\ *n* : the plants of a forest undergrowth

un·der·study \ˈən-dər-ˌstəd-ē, ˌən-dər-ˈstəd-ē\ *vb* : to study another actor's part in order to be his substitute in an emergency — **understudy** \ˈən-dər-ˌstəd-ē\ *n*

un·der·sur·face \ˈən-dər-ˌsər-fəs\ *n* : UNDERSIDE

un·der·take \ˌən-dər-ˈtāk\ *vb* **-took** \-ˈtuk\; **-tak·en** \-ˈtā-kən\; **-tak·ing** **1** : to take upon oneself as a task : set about **2** : to put oneself under obligation **3** : GUARANTEE, PROMISE

un·der·tak·er \ˈən-dər-ˌtā-kər\ *n* : one whose business is to prepare the dead for burial and to take charge of funerals

un·der·tak·ing \ˈən-dər-ˌtā-kiŋ, ˌən-dər-ˈtā-kiŋ; *2 is* ˈən-dər-ˌtā-kiŋ *only*\ *n* **1** : the act of one who undertakes or engages in any project **2** : the business of an undertaker **3** : something undertaken **4** : PROMISE, GUARANTEE

under–the–counter *adj* : UNLAWFUL, ILLICIT ⟨∼ sale of drugs⟩

un·der·tone \ˈən-dər-ˌtōn\ *n* **1** : a low or subdued tone or utterance **2** : a subdued color (as seen through and modifying another color)

un·der·tow \-ˌtō\ *n* : the current beneath the surface that sets seaward when waves are breaking upon the shore

un·der·trick \-ˌtrik\ *n* : a trick by which a declarer in bridge falls short of making his contract

un·der·val·ue \ˌən-dər-ˈval-yü\ *vb* **1** : to value or estimate below the real worth **2** : to esteem lightly

un·der·wa·ter \ˌən-dər-ˌwȯt-ər, -ˌwät-\ *adj* : lying, growing, worn, or operating below the surface of the water — **un·der·wa·ter** \-ˈwȯt-, -ˈwät-\ *adv*

under way \-ˈwā\ *adv* **1** : into motion from a standstill **2** : in progress

un·der·wear \ˈən-dər-ˌwa(ə)r\ *n* : clothing or a garment worn next to the skin and under other clothing

un·der·weight \ˌən-dər-ˈwāt\ *n* : weight below what is normal, average, or necessary — **underweight** *adj*

un·der·wood \ˈən-dər-ˌwud\ *n* : UNDERBRUSH, UNDERGROWTH

un·der·world \-ˌwərld\ *n* **1** : the place of departed souls : HADES **2** : a social sphere below the level of ordinary life; *esp* : the world of organized crime

un·der·write \ˈən-də(r)-ˌrīt, ˌən-də(r)-ˈrīt\ *vb* **-wrote** \-ˌrōt, -ˈrōt\; **-writ·ten** \-ˌrit-ᵊn, -ˈrit-ᵊn\; **-writ·ing** \-ˌrīt-iŋ, -ˈrīt-\ **1** : to write under or at the end of something else **2** : to set one's name to an insurance policy and thereby become answerable for a designated loss or damage **3** : to subscribe to : agree to **4** : to agree to purchase (as bonds) usu. on a fixed date at a fixed price; *also* : to guarantee financial support of — **un·der·writ·er** *n*

un·de·sign·ing \ˌən-di-ˈzī-niŋ\ *adj* : having no artful, ulterior, or fraudulent purpose : SINCERE

un·de·sir·able \-ˈzī-rə-bəl\ *adj* : not desirable — **undesirable** *n*

un·de·vi·at·ing \ˌən-ˈdē-vē-ˌāt-iŋ, ˈən-\ *adj* : keeping a true course

un·dies \ˈən-dēz\ *n pl* : UNDERWEAR; *esp* : women's underwear

un·do \ˌən-ˈdü, ˈən-\ *vb* **-did** \-ˈdid\; **-done** \-ˈdən\; **-do·ing** \-ˈdü-iŋ\ **1** : to make or become unfastened or loosened : OPEN **2** : to make null or as if not done : REVERSE **3** : to bring to ruin; *also* : UPSET

un·do·ing \-ˈdü-iŋ\ *n* **1** : LOOSING, UN-

FASTENING **2** : RUIN; *also* : a cause of ruin **3** : REVERSAL

un·doubt·ed \-'daut-əd\ *adj* : not doubted or called into question : CERTAIN — **un·doubt·ed·ly** *adv*

¹**un·dress** \ˌən-'dres, 'ən-\ *vb* : to remove the clothes or covering of : STRIP, DISROBE

²**undress** *n* **1** : informal dress; *esp* : a loose robe or dressing gown **2** : ordinary dress **3** : NUDITY

un·due \-'d(y)ü\ *adj* **1** : not due **2** : exceeding or violating propriety or fitness

un·du·lant \'ən-jə-lənt, 'ən-d(y)ə-\ *adj* : UNDULATING

undulant fever *n* : a human disease caused by bacteria and marked by intermittent fever, pain and swelling in the joints, and great weakness

un·du·late \-ˌlāt\ *vb* **-lated; -lating** [LL *undula* small wave, fr. L *unda* wave] **1** : to have a wavelike motion or appearance **2** : to rise and fall in pitch or volume

un·du·la·tion \ˌən-jə-'lā-shən, ˌən-d(y)ə-\ *n* **1** : wavy or wavelike motion **2** : pulsation of sound **3** : a wavy appearance or outline — **un·du·la·to·ry** \'ən-jə-lə-ˌtōr-ē, 'ən-d(y)ə-\ *adj*

un·du·ly \ˌən-'d(y)ü-lē, 'ən-\ *adv* : in an undue manner; *esp* : EXCESSIVELY

un·dy·ing \-'dī-iŋ\ *adj* : not dying : IMMORTAL, PERPETUAL

un·earned \-'ərnd\ *adj* : not earned by labor, service, or skill ⟨~ income⟩

un·earth \ˌən-'ərth, 'ən-\ *vb* **1** : to draw from the earth : dig up ⟨~ buried treasure⟩ **2** : to bring to light : DISCOVER ⟨~ a secret⟩

un·earth·ly \-lē\ *adj* **1** : not of or belonging to the earth **2** : SUPERNATURAL, WEIRD, TERRIFYING

un·easy \'ən-'ē-zē\ *adj* **1** : AWKWARD, EMBARRASSED ⟨~ among strangers⟩ **2** : disturbed by pain or worry; *also* : RESTLESS — **un·eas·i·ly** \-'ē-zə-lē\ *adv* — **un·eas·i·ness** \-'ē-zē-nəs\ *n*

un·em·ployed \ˌən-im-'plóid\ *adj* : not employed; *esp* : not engaged in a gainful occupation

un·em·ploy·ment \-'plói-mənt\ *n* : lack of employment

un·end·ing \ˌən-'en-diŋ, 'ən-\ *adj* : having no ending : ENDLESS

un·equal \ˌən-'ē-kwəl, 'ən-\ *adj* **1** : not alike (as in size, amount, number, or value) **2** : not uniform : VARIABLE **3** : badly balanced or matched **4** : INADEQUATE, INSUFFICIENT — **un·equal·ly** \-ē\ *adv*

un·equaled *or* **un·equalled** \-kwəld\ *adj* : not equaled : UNPARALLELED

un·equiv·o·cal \ˌən-i-'kwiv-ə-kəl\ *adj* : leaving no doubt : CLEAR — **un·equiv·o·cal·ly** \-ē\ *adv*

un·err·ing \ˌən-'e(ə)r-iŋ, ˌən-'ər-\ *adj* : making no errors : CERTAIN, UNFAILING — **un·err·ing·ly** *adv*

UNES·CO \yü-'nes-kō\ *abbr* United Nations Educational, Scientific, and Cultural Organization

un·even \ˌən-'ē-vən, 'ən-\ *adj* **1** : ODD **3** **2** : not even : not level or smooth : RUGGED, RAGGED **3** : IRREGULAR; *also* : varying in quality — **un·even·ly** *adv* — **un·even·ness** \-vən-nəs\ *n*

un·event·ful \ˌən-i-'vent-fəl\ *adj* : not eventful : lacking interesting or noteworthy incidents

un·ex·am·pled \ˌən-ig-'zam-pəld\ *adj* : UNPRECEDENTED, UNPARALLELED

un·ex·cep·tion·able \ˌən-ik-'sep-sh(ə-)nə-bəl\ *adj* : not open to exception or objection : beyond reproach

un·ex·pect·ed \ˌən-ik-'spek-təd\ *adj* : not expected : UNFORESEEN — **un·ex·pect·ed·ly** *adv*

un·fail·ing \ˌən-'fā-liŋ, 'ən-\ *adj* **1** : not failing, flagging, or waning : CONSTANT **2** : INEXHAUSTIBLE **3** : INFALLIBLE, SURE — **un·fail·ing·ly** *adv*

un·fair \-'faər\ *adj* **1** : marked by injustice, partiality, or deception : UNJUST, DISHONEST **2** : not equitable in business dealings — **un·fair·ly** *adv* — **un·fair·ness** *n*

un·faith·ful \ˌən-'fāth-fəl, 'ən-\ *adj* **1** : not observant of vows, allegiance, or duty : DISLOYAL **2** : INACCURATE, UNTRUSTWORTHY — **un·faith·ful·ly** \-ē\ *adv* — **un·faith·ful·ness** *n*

un·fa·mil·iar \ˌən-fə-'mil-yər\ *adj* **1** : not well-known : STRANGE ⟨an ~ place⟩ **2** : not well acquainted ⟨~ with the subject⟩ — **un·fa·mil·iar·i·ty** \-ˌmil-'yar-ət-ē, -ˌmil-ē-'(y)ar-\ *n*

un·fas·ten \ˌən-'fas-ᵊn, 'ən-\ *vb* : to make or become loose : UNDO, DETACH

un·fa·vor·able \ˌən-'fāv-(ə-)rə-bəl, 'ən-\

adj : not favorable — **un·fa·vor·ably** \-blē\ *adv*

un·feel·ing \-'fē-liŋ\ *adj* **1** : lacking feeling : INSENSATE **2** : HARDHEARTED, CRUEL — **un·feel·ing·ly** *adv*

un·feigned \-'fānd\ *adj* : not feigned : not hypocritical : GENUINE

un·fet·ter \-'fet-ər\ *vb* **1** : to free from fetters **2** : LIBERATE

un·fil·ial \ˌən-'fil-ē-əl, 'ən-, -'fil-yəl\ *adj* : not observing the obligations of a child to a parent : UNDUTIFUL

un·fin·ished \ˌən-'fin-isht\ *adj* **1** : not brought to an end **2** : being in a rough or unpolished state

¹**un·fit** \-'fit\ *adj* : not fit or suitable; *esp* : physically or mentally unsound — **un·fit·ness** *n*

²**unfit** *vb* : DISABLE, DISQUALIFY

un·fix \-'fiks\ *vb* **1** : to loosen from a fastening : DETACH **2** : UNSETTLE

un·flap·pa·ble \-'flap-ə-bəl\ *adj* : not easily upset or panicked — **un·flap·pa·bly** *adv*

un·fledged \ˌən-'flejd\ *adj* : not feathered or ready for flight; *also* : IMMATURE, CALLOW

un·flinch·ing \-'flin-chiŋ\ *adj* : not flinching or shrinking : STEADFAST — **un·flinch·ing·ly** *adv*

un·fold \-'fōld\ *vb* **1** : to open the folds of : open up **2** : to lay open to view : DISCLOSE **3** : BLOSSOM, DEVELOP

un·for·get·ta·ble \ˌən-fər-'get-ə-bəl\ *adj* : not to be forgotten — **un·for·get·ta·bly** \-blē\ *adv*

un·formed \-'fōrmd\ *adj* : not regularly formed : SHAPELESS

un·for·tu·nate \-'fōrch-(ə-)nət\ *adj* **1** : not fortunate : UNLUCKY **2** : attended with misfortune **3** : UNSUITABLE — **unfortunate** *n* — **un·for·tu·nate·ly** *adv*

un·found·ed \ˌən-'faùn-dəd, 'ən-\ *adj* : lacking a sound basis : GROUNDLESS

un·freeze \-'frēz\ *vb* **-froze** \-'frōz\; **-fro·zen** \-'frōz-ᵊn\; **-freez·ing** **1** : to cause to thaw **2** : to remove from a freeze ⟨~ prices⟩

un·fre·quent·ed \ˌən-frē-'kwent-əd; ˌən-'frē-kwənt-, 'ən-\ *adj* : seldom visited or traveled over

un·friend·ly \ˌən-'fren-(d)lē, 'ən-\ *adj* **1** : not friendly or kind : HOSTILE **2** : UNFAVORABLE — **un·friend·li·ness** \-'fren-(d)lē-nəs\ *n*

un·frock \-'fräk\ *vb* : to deprive (as a priest) of the right to exercise the functions of his office

un·fruit·ful \-'früt-fəl\ *adj* **1** : not producing fruit or offspring : UNPRODUCTIVE **2** : yielding no desired or valuable result ⟨~ efforts⟩ — **un·fruit·ful·ness** *n*

un·furl \-'fərl\ *vb* : to loose from a furled state : UNFOLD

un·gain·ly \-'gān-lē\ *adj* [*un-* + *gainly* graceful, fr. *gain* direct, handy, fr. ME *geyn*, fr. OE *gēn*, fr. ON *gegn*] : CLUMSY, AWKWARD — **un·gain·li·ness** \-lē-nəs\ *n*

un·gen·er·ous \ˌən-'jen-(ə-)rəs, 'ən-\ *adj* : not generous or liberal : STINGY

un·gird \-'gərd\ *vb* : to divest of a restraining band or girdle : UNBIND

un·glued \ˌən-'glüd\ *adj* : UPSET, DISORDERED

un·god·ly \ˌən-'gäd-lē, -'gòd-; 'ən-\ *adj* **1** : IMPIOUS, IRRELIGIOUS **2** : SINFUL, WICKED **3** : OUTRAGEOUS — **un·god·li·ness** \-lē-nəs\ *n*

un·gov·ern·able \-'gəv-ər-nə-bəl\ *adj* : not capable of being governed, guided, or restrained : UNRULY

un·gra·cious \-'grā-shəs\ *adj* **1** : not courteous : RUDE **2** : not pleasing : DISAGREEABLE

un·grate·ful \ˌən-'grāt-fəl, 'ən-\ *adj* **1** : not thankful for favors **2** : not pleasing — **un·grate·ful·ly** \-ē\ *adv* — **un·grate·ful·ness** *n*

un·guard·ed \-'gärd-əd\ *adj* **1** : UNPROTECTED **2** : DIRECT, INCAUTIOUS

un·guent \'əŋ-gwənt, 'ən-\ *n* : a soothing or healing salve : OINTMENT

¹**un·gu·late** \'əŋ-gyə-lət, 'ən-, -ˌlāt\ *adj* [LL *ungulatus*, fr. L *ungula* hoof, fr. *unguis* nail, hoof] : having hoofs

²**ungulate** *n* : a hoofed mammal (as a cow, horse, or rhinoceros)

Unh *symbol* unnilhexium

un·hal·lowed \ˌən-'hal-ōd, 'ən-\ *adj* **1** : not consecrated : UNHOLY **2** : IMPIOUS, PROFANE **3** : contrary to accepted standards : IMMORAL

un·hand \ˌən-'hand\ *vb* : to remove the hand from : let go

un·hand·some \-'han-səm\ *adj* **1** : not beautiful or handsome : HOMELY **2** : UNBECOMING **3** : DISCOURTEOUS, RUDE

un·handy \-'han-dē\ *adj* : INCONVENIENT; *also* : AWKWARD

un·hap·py \-'hap-ē\ *adj* **1** : UNLUCKY,

UNFORTUNATE **2** : SAD, MISERABLE **3** : INAPPROPRIATE — **un·hap·pi·ly** \-'hap-ə-lē\ *adv* — **un·hap·pi·ness** \-ē-nəs\ *n*

un·har·ness \-'här-nəs\ *vb* : to remove the harness from (as a horse)

un·healthy \-'hel-thē\ *adj* **1** : not conducive to health : UNWHOLESOME **2** : SICKLY, DISEASED

un·heard \-'hərd\ *adj* **1** : not heard **2** : not granted a hearing

un·heard—of \-ˌəv, -ˌäv\ *adj* : previously unknown : UNPRECEDENTED

un·hinge \ˌən-'hinj, 'ən-\ *vb* **1** : to take from the hinges **2** : to make unstable (as one's mind)

un·hitch \-'hich\ *vb* : UNFASTEN, LOOSE

un·ho·ly \-'hō-lē\ *adj* : not holy : PROFANE, WICKED — **un·ho·li·ness** \-lē-nəs\ *n*

un·hook \-'hùk\ *vb* : to loose from a hook

un·horse \-'hòrs\ *vb* : to dislodge from or as if from a horse : UNSEAT

uni·ax·i·al \ˌyü-nē-'ak-sē-əl\ *adj* : having only one axis

uni·cam·er·al \ˌyü-ni-kam-(ə-)rəl\ *adj* : having a single legislative house or chamber

UNI·CEF \'yü-nə-ˌsef\ *abbr* [*United Nations International Children's Emergency Fund,* its former name] United Nations Children's Fund

uni·cel·lu·lar \ˌyü-ni-'sel-yə-lər\ *adj* : of or having a single cell

uni·corn \'yü-nə-ˌkòrn\ *n* [ME *unicorne,* fr. OF, fr. LL *unicornis,* fr. L, having one horn, fr. *unus* one + *cornu* horn] : a mythical animal with one horn in the middle of the forehead

uni·cy·cle \'yü-ni-ˌsī-kəl\ *n* : a vehicle that has a single wheel and is usu. propelled by pedals

uni·di·rec·tion·al \ˌyü-ni-də-'rek-sh(ə-)nəl, -dī-\ *adj* : having, moving in, or responsive in a single direction ⟨a ~ current⟩ ⟨a ~ microphone⟩

uni·fi·ca·tion \ˌyü-nə-fə-'kā-shən\ *n* : the act, process, or result of unifying : the state of being unified

¹**uni·form** \'yü-nə-ˌfòrm\ *adj* **1** : having always the same form, manner, or degree : not varying **2** : of the same form with others : conforming to one rule — **uni·form·ly** *adv*

²**uniform** *vb* : to clothe with a uniform

³**uniform** *n* : distinctive dress worn by members of a particular group (as an army or a police force)

uni·for·mi·ty \ˌyü-nə-'fòr-mət-ē\ *n, pl* **-ties** : the state of being uniform

uni·fy \'yü-nə-ˌfī\ *vb* **-fied; -fy·ing** : to make into a unit or a coherent whole : UNITE

uni·lat·er·al \ˌyü-nə-'lat-(ə-)rəl\ *adj* : of, having, affecting, or done by one side only — **uni·lat·er·al·ly** \-ē\ *adv*

un·im·peach·able \ˌən-im-'pē-chə-bəl\ *adj* : exempt from liability to accusation : BLAMELESS; *also* : not doubtable ⟨an ~ authority⟩

un·in·hib·it·ed \ˌən-in-'hib-ət-əd\ *adj* : free from inhibition; *also* : boisterously informal — **un·in·hib·it·ed·ly** *adv*

un·in·tel·li·gent \-'tel-ə-jənt\ *adj* : lacking intelligence

un·in·tel·li·gi·ble \-jə-bəl\ *adj* : not intelligible : OBSCURE — **un·in·tel·li·gi·bly** \-blē\ *adv*

un·in·ten·tion·al \ˌən-in-'tench-(ə-)nəl\ *adj* : not intentional — **un·in·ten·tion·al·ly** \-ē\ *adv*

un·in·ter·est·ed \ˌən-'in-t(ə-)rəs-təd, -tə-ˌres-; 'ən-\ *adj* : not interested : not having the mind or feelings engaged or aroused

un·in·ter·rupt·ed \ˌən-ˌint-ə-'rəp-təd\ *adj* : not interrupted : CONTINUOUS

union \'yü-nyən\ *n* **1** : an act or instance of uniting two or more things into one : the state of being so united : COMBINATION, JUNCTION **2** : a uniting in marriage **3** : something formed by a combining of parts or members; *esp* : a confederation of independent individuals (as nations or persons) for some common purpose **4** : an organization of workers (as a labor union or a trade union) formed to advance its members' interests esp. in respect to wages and working conditions **5** : a device emblematic of union used on or as a national flag; *also* : the upper inner corner of a flag **6** : a device for connecting parts (as of a machine); *esp* : a coupling for pipes

union·ism \'yü-nyə-ˌniz-əm\ *n* **1** : the principle or policy of forming or adhering to a union; *esp, cap* : adherence to the policy of a firm federal union prior to or during the U.S. Civil War **2** : the principles or system of trade unions — **union·ist** *n*

union•ize \\'yü-nyə-ˌnīz\ *vb* **-ized; -iz•ing** : to form into or cause to join a labor union — **union•iza•tion** \ˌyü-nyən-ə-'zā-shən\ *n*

union jack *n* **1** : a flag consisting of the part of a national flag that signifies union **2** *cap U&J* : the national flag of the United Kingdom

unique \yü-'nēk\ *adj* **1** : being the only one of its kind : SINGLE, SOLE **2** : very unusual : NOTABLE — **unique•ly** *adv* — **unique•ness** *n*

uni•sex \'yü-nə-ˌseks\ *adj* : not distinguishable as male or female; *also* : suitable or designed for both males or females — **unisex** *n*

uni•sex•u•al \ˌyü-nə-'sek-sh(ə-w)əl\ *adj* **1** : having only male or only female sex organs **2** : UNISEX

uni•son \'yü-nə-sən, -nə-zən\ *n* [MF, fr. ML *unisonus* having the same sound, fr. L *unus* one + *sonus* sound] **1** : sameness or identity in musical pitch **2** : the condition of being tuned or sounded at the same pitch or at an octave ⟨sing in ∼ rather than in harmony⟩ **3** : harmonious agreement or union : ACCORD

unit \'yü-nət\ *n* **1** : the least whole number : ONE **2** : a definite amount or quantity used as a standard of measurement **3** : a single thing or person or group that is a constituent of a whole; *also* : a part of a military establishment that has a prescribed organization — **unit** *adj*

Uni•tar•i•an \ˌyü-nə-'ter-ē-ən\ *n* : a member of a religious denomination stressing individual freedom of belief — **Uni•tar•i•an•ism** *n*

uni•tary \'yü-nə-ˌter-ē\ *adj* **1** : of or relating to a unit : characterized by unity **2** : not divided — **uni•tar•i•ly** \ˌyü-nə-'ter-ə-lē\ *adv*

unite \yü-'nīt\ *vb* **unit•ed; unit•ing** **1** : to put or join together so as to make one : COMBINE, COALESCE **2** : to join by a legal or moral bond (as nations by treaty); *also* : to join in interest or fellowship **3** : AMALGAMATE, CONSOLIDATE **4** : to join in an act

unit•ed \yü-'nīt-əd\ *adj* **1** : made one : COMBINED **2** : relating to or produced by joint action **3** : being in agreement : HARMONIOUS

unit•ize \'yü-nət-ˌīz\ *vb* **-ized; -iz•ing** **1**

: to form or convert into a unit **2** : to divide into units

uni•ty \'yü-nət-ē\ *n, pl* **-ties** **1** : the quality or state of being one : ONENESS, SINGLENESS **2** : a definite quantity or combination of quantities taken as one or for which 1 is made to stand in calculation **3** : CONCORD, ACCORD, HARMONY **4** : continuity without change ⟨∼ of purpose⟩ **5** : reference of all the parts of a literary or artistic composition to a single main idea **6** : totality of related parts **syn** solidarity, union, integrity

univ *abbr* **1** universal **2** university

uni•va•lent \ˌyü-ni-'vā-lənt\ *adj* : having a valence of one

uni•valve \'yü-ni-ˌvalv\ *n* : a mollusk (as a snail or whelk) having a shell with one valve — **univalve** *adj*

uni•ver•sal \ˌyü-nə-'vər-səl\ *adj* **1** : including, covering, or affecting the whole without limit or exception : UNLIMITED, GENERAL ⟨a ∼ rule⟩ **2** : present or occurring everywhere **3** : used or for use among all ⟨a ∼ language⟩ — **uni•ver•sal•ly** \-ē\ *adv*

Uni•ver•sal•ist \ˌyü-nə-'vər-s(ə-)ləst\ *n* : a member of a religious denomination now united with Unitarians that upholds the belief that all men will be saved

uni•ver•sal•i•ty \-vər-'sal-ət-ē\ *n* : the quality or state of being universal

uni•ver•sal•ize \-'vər-sə-ˌlīz\ *vb* **-ized; -iz•ing** : to make universal : GENERALIZE — **uni•ver•sal•iza•tion** \-ˌvər-sə-lə-'zā-shən\ *n*

universal joint *n* : a shaft coupling for transmitting rotation from one shaft to another not in a straight line with it

Universal Product Code *n* : a bar code that identifies a product's type and price for entry into a computer or cash register (as at a supermarket checkout)

uni•verse \'yü-nə-ˌvərs\ *n* [L *universum*, fr. neut. of *universus* entire, whole, fr. *unus* one + *versus* turned toward, fr. pp. of *vertere* to turn] : all created things and phenomena viewed as constituting one system or whole

uni•ver•si•ty \ˌyü-nə-'vər-s(ə-)tē\ *n, pl* **-ties** : an institution of higher learning authorized to confer degrees in various special fields (as theology, law, and medicine) as well as in the arts and sciences generally

un·just \ˌən-ˈjəst, ˈən-\ *adj* : characterized by injustice — **un·just·ly** *adv*

un·kempt \-ˈkempt\ *adj* **1** : ROUGH, UNPOLISHED **2** : not combed : DISHEVELED

un·kind \-ˈkīnd\ *adj* : wanting in kindness or sympathy : CRUEL, HARSH — **un·kind·ly** \-ˈkīn-(d)lē\ *adv* — **un·kind·ness** \-ˈkīn(d)-nəs\ *n*

un·kind·ly \-ˈkīn-(d)lē\ *adj* : UNKIND — **un·kind·li·ness** *n*

un·know·ing \ˌən-ˈnō-iŋ, ˈən-\ *adj* : not knowing : IGNORANT — **un·know·ing·ly** *adv*

un·known \-ˈnōn\ *adj* : not known : UNFAMILIAR; *also* : not ascertained — **unknown** *n*

un·lace \ˌən-ˈlās, ˈən-\ *vb* : to loose by undoing a lace

un·lade \-ˈlād\ *vb* **-lad·ed; -laded** *or* **-laden** \-ˈlād-ᵊn\; **-lad·ing** : to take the load or cargo from : UNLOAD

un·latch \-ˈlach\ *vb* **1** : to open or loose by lifting the latch **2** : to become loosed or opened

un·law·ful \ˌən-ˈlȯ-fəl, ˈən-\ *adj* **1** : not lawful : ILLEGAL **2** : ILLEGITIMATE — **un·law·ful·ly** \-ē\ *adv*

un·lead·ed \-ˈled-əd\ *adj* : not treated or mixed with lead or lead compounds

un·learn \-ˈlərn\ *vb* : to put out of one's knowledge or memory

un·learned \-ˈlər-nəd *for 1, 2;* -ˈlərnd *for 3*\ *adj* **1** : UNEDUCATED, ILLITERATE **2** : not learned by study : not known **3** : not learned by previous experience

un·leash \-ˈlēsh\ *vb* : to free from or as if from a leash

un·less \ən-ˌles, ˌən-\ *conj* : except on condition that ⟨won't go ∼ you do⟩

un·let·tered \ˌən-ˈlet-ərd, ˈən-\ *adj* : not educated : ILLITERATE

¹un·like \-ˈlīk\ *adj* **1** : not like : DISSIMILAR, DIFFERENT **2** : UNEQUAL — **un·like·ness** *n*

²unlike *prep* **1** : different from ⟨he's quite ∼ his brother⟩ **2** : unusual for ⟨it's ∼ him to be late⟩ **3** : differently from ⟨behaves ∼ his brother⟩

un·like·li·hood \ˌən-ˈlī-klē-ˌhu̇d, ˈən-\ *n* : IMPROBABILITY

un·like·ly \-ˈlī-klē\ *adj* **1** : not likely : IMPROBABLE **2** : likely to fail

un·lim·ber \ˌən-ˈlim-bər, ˈən-\ *vb* : to get ready for action

un·list·ed \ˌən-ˈlis-təd, ˈən-\ *adj* **1** : not appearing on a list; *esp* : not appearing in a telephone book **2** : being or involving a security not listed formally on an organized exchange

un·load \-ˈlōd\ *vb* **1** : to take away or off : REMOVE ⟨∼ cargo from a hold⟩; *also* : to get rid of **2** : to take a load from; *also* : to relieve or set free : UNBURDEN ⟨∼ one's mind of worries⟩ **3** : to get rid of or be relieved of a burden **4** : to sell in volume

un·lock \-ˈläk\ *vb* **1** : to unfasten through release of a lock **2** : RELEASE ⟨∼ed her emotions⟩ **3** : DISCLOSE, REVEAL

un·looked–for \-ˈlu̇kt-ˌfȯr\ *adj* : UNEXPECTED

un·loose \ˌən-ˈlüs\ *vb* : to relax the strain of : set free; *also* : UNTIE

un·loos·en \-ˈlüs-ᵊn\ *vb* : UNLOOSE

un·love·ly \-ˈləv-lē\ *adj* : having no charm or appeal : not amiable

un·lucky \-ˈlək-ē\ *adj* **1** : UNFORTUNATE, ILL-FATED **2** : likely to bring misfortune : INAUSPICIOUS **3** : REGRETTABLE — **un·luck·i·ly** \-ˈlək-ə-lē\ *adv*

un·man \ˌən-ˈman, ˈən-\ *vb* **1** : to deprive of manly courage **2** : CASTRATE

un·man·ly \-ˈman-lē\ *adj* : not manly : COWARDLY; *also* : EFFEMINATE

un·man·ner·ly \-ˈman-ər-lē\ *adj* : RUDE, IMPOLITE — **unmannerly** *adv*

un·mask \ˌən-ˈmask\ *vb* **1** : to strip of a mask or a disguise : EXPOSE **2** : to remove one's own disguise (as at a masquerade)

un·mean·ing \-ˈmē-niŋ\ *adj* : having no meaning : SENSELESS

un·meet \-ˈmēt\ *adj* : not meet or fit : UNSUITABLE, IMPROPER

un·men·tion·able \-ˈmench-(ə-)nə-bəl\ *adj* : not fit or proper to be talked about

un·mer·ci·ful \-ˈmər-si-fəl\ *adj* : not merciful : CRUEL, MERCILESS — **un·mer·ci·ful·ly** \-ē\ *adv*

un·mind·ful \-ˈmīnd-fəl\ *adj* : not mindful : CARELESS, UNAWARE

un·mis·tak·able \ˌən-mə-ˈstā-kə-bəl\ *adj* : not capable of being mistaken or misunderstood : CLEAR, OBVIOUS — **un·mis·tak·ably** \-blē\ *adv*

un·mit·i·gat·ed \ˌən-ˈmit-ə-ˌgāt-əd,

'-ən-** *adj* **1 : not softened or lessened **2** : ABSOLUTE, DOWNRIGHT ⟨an ∼ liar⟩

un·moor \-'mur\ *vb* **1** : to loose from or as if from moorings **2** : to cast off moorings

un·mor·al \-'mȯr-əl\ *adj* : having no moral perception or quality : being neither moral nor immoral — **un·mo·ral·i·ty** \ˌən-mə-'ral-ət-ē\ *n*

un·muz·zle \-'məz-əl\ *vb* : to remove a muzzle from

un·nat·u·ral \ˌən-'nach-(ə-)rəl, 'ən-\ *adj* : contrary to or acting contrary to nature or natural instincts : ARTIFICIAL, IRREGULAR; *also* : ABNORMAL — **un·nat·u·ral·ly** \-ē\ *adv* — **un·nat·u·ral·ness** *n*

un·nec·es·sar·i·ly \ˌən-ˌnes-ə-'ser-ə-lē\ *adv* **1** : not by necessity ⟨spent more money ∼⟩ **2** : to an unnecessary degree ⟨∼ harsh⟩

un·nerve \ˌən-'nərv, 'ən-\ *vb* : to deprive of nerve, courage, or self-control

un·nil·hex·i·um \ˌən-əl-'hek-sē-əm\ *n* [NL *unnil-* (fr. L *unus* one + *nil* zero) + Gk *hex* six + NL *-ium*] : the chemical element of atomic number 106

un·nil·pen·ti·um \-'pent-ē-əm\ *n* : the chemical element of atomic number 105

un·nil·qua·di·um \-'kwäd ē-əm\ *n* : the chemical element of atomic number 104

un·num·bered \-'nəm-bərd\ *adj* : not numbered or counted : INNUMERABLE

un·ob·tru·sive \ˌən-əb-'trü-siv\ *adj* : not obtrusive or forward : not bold : INCONSPICUOUS — **un·ob·tru·sive·ly** *adv*

un·oc·cu·pied \ˌən-'äk-yə-ˌpīd, 'ən-\ *adj* **1** : not busy : UNEMPLOYED **2** : not occupied : EMPTY, VACANT

un·or·ga·nized \-'ȯr-gə-ˌnīzd\ *adj* **1** : not formed or brought into an integrated or ordered whole **2** : not organized into unions ⟨∼ labor⟩

unp *abbr* unpaged

Unp *symbol* unnilpentium

un·pack \ˌən-'pak, 'ən-\ *vb* **1** : to separate and remove things packed **2** : to open and remove the contents of

un·par·al·leled \ˌən-'par-ə-ˌleld\ *adj* : having no parallel; *esp* : having no equal or match

un·par·lia·men·ta·ry \ˌən-ˌpär-lə-'ment-ə-rē, -ˌpärl-yə-, -'men-trē\ *adj* : contrary to parliamentary practice

un·peg \ˌən-'peg, 'ən-\ *vb* : to remove a peg from : UNFASTEN

un·per·son \'ən-'pərs-ᵊn, -ˌpərs-\ *n* : a person who usu. for political or ideological reasons is removed from recognition, consideration, or memory

un·pile \ˌən-'pīl, 'ən-\ *vb* : to take or disentangle from a pile

un·pin \-'pin\ *vb* : to remove a pin from : UNFASTEN

un·pleas·ant \-'plez-ᵊnt\ *adj* : not pleasant : DISAGREEABLE — **un·pleas·ant·ly** *adv* — **un·pleas·ant·ness** *n*

un·plug \ˌən-'pləg, 'ən-\ *vb* **1** : UNCLOG **2** : to remove (a plug) from a receptacle; *also* : to disconnect from an electric circuit by removing a plug

un·plumbed \-'pləmd\ *adj* **1** : not tested or measured with a plumb line **2** : not thoroughly explored

un·pop·u·lar \ˌən-'päp-yə-lər, 'ən-\ *adj* : not popular : looked upon or received unfavorably — **un·pop·u·lar·i·ty** \ˌən-ˌpäp-yə-'lar-ət-ē\ *n*

un·prec·e·dent·ed \ˌən-'pres-ə-ˌdent-əd, 'ən-\ *adj* : having no precedent : NOVEL, NEW

un·pre·ten·tious \ˌən-pri-'ten-chəs\ *adj* : not pretentious or pompous : MODEST ⟨∼ homes⟩

un·prin·ci·pled \ˌən-'prin-sə-pəld, 'ən-\ *adj* : lacking sound or honorable principles : UNSCRUPULOUS

un·print·able \-'print-ə-bəl\ *adj* : unfit to be printed

un·prof·it·able \ˌən-'präf-ət-ə-bəl, 'ən-, -'präf-tə-bəl\ *adj* : not profitable : USELESS, VAIN

Unq *symbol* unnilquadium

un·qual·i·fied \ˌən-'kwäl-ə-ˌfīd, 'ən-\ *adj* **1** : not having requisite qualifications **2** : not modified or restricted by reservations — **un·qual·i·fied·ly** \-ˌfī(-ə)d-lē\ *adv*

un·ques·tion·able \-'kwes-chə-nə-bəl\ *adj* **1** : acknowledged as beyond doubt **2** : INDISPUTABLE — **un·ques·tion·ably** \-blē\ *adv*

un·ques·tion·ing \-chə-niŋ\ *adj* : not questioning : accepting without examination or hesitation — **un·ques·tion·ing·ly** *adv*

un·qui·et \-'kwī-ət\ *adj* **1** : not quiet

unquote • unscramble

: AGITATED, DISTURBED **2** : physically, emotionally, or mentally restless : UNEASY

un·quote \'ən-ˌkwōt\ *n* — used orally to indicate the end of a direct quotation

un·rav·el \ˌən-'rav-əl, 'ən-\ *vb* **1** : to separate the threads of **2** : SOLVE ⟨~ a mystery⟩ **3** : to become unraveled

un·read \-'red\ *adj* **1** : not read **2** : not well informed through reading **3** : UNEDUCATED

un·re·al \-'rē(-ə)l\ *adj* : lacking in reality, substance, or genuineness — **un·re·al·i·ty** \ˌən-rē-'al-ət-ē\ *n*

un·rea·son·able \-'rēz-(ə-)nə-bəl\ *adj* **1** : not governed by or acting according to reason; *also* : not conformable to reason : ABSURD **2** : exceeding the bounds of reason or moderation — **un·rea·son·able·ness** *n* — **un·rea·son·ably** *adv*

un·rea·soned \-'rēz-ᵊnd\ *adj* : not based on reason or reasoning

un·rea·son·ing \-'rēz-(ə-)niŋ\ *adj* : not using or showing the use of reason as a guide or control

un·re·con·struct·ed \ˌən-ˌrē-kən-'strək-təd\ *adj* : not reconciled to some political, economic, or social change; *esp* : holding stubbornly to principles, beliefs, or views that are or are held to be outmoded

un·reel \ˌən-'rēl, 'ən-\ *vb* **1** : to unwind from or as if from a reel **2** : perform successfully

un·re·gen·er·ate \ˌən-ri-'jen-(ə-)rət\ *adj* : not regenerated or reformed

un·re·lent·ing \-'lent-iŋ\ *adj* **1** : not yielding in determination : STERN ⟨~ leader⟩ **2** : not letting up or weakening in vigor or pace : CONSTANT — **un·re·lent·ing·ly** *adv*

un·re·mit·ting \-'mit-iŋ\ *adj* : CONTINUOUS, INCESSANT, PERSEVERING — **un·re·mit·ting·ly** *adv*

un·re·served \-'zərvd\ *adj* **1** : not limited or partial : ENTIRE, UNQUALIFIED ⟨~ enthusiasm⟩ **2** : not cautious or reticent : FRANK, OPEN **3** : not set aside for special use — **un·re·serv·ed·ly** \-'zər-vəd-lē\ *adv*

un·rest \ˌən-'rest, 'ən-\ *n* : a disturbed or uneasy state : TURMOIL

un·re·strained \ˌən-ri-'strānd\ *adj* **1** : IMMODERATE, UNCONTROLLED **2** : SPONTANEOUS

un·re·straint \-ri-'strānt\ *n* : lack of restraint

un·rid·dle \ˌən-'rid-ᵊl, 'ən-\ *vb* : to read the riddle of : SOLVE

un·righ·teous \-'rī-chəs\ *adj* **1** : SINFUL, WICKED **2** : UNJUST — **un·righ·teous·ness** *n*

un·ripe \-'rīp\ *adj* : not ripe : IMMATURE

un·ri·valed *or* **un·ri·valled** \ˌən-'rī-vəld, 'ən-\ *adj* : having no rival : INCOMPARABLE

un·robe \-'rōb\ *vb* : DISROBE, UNDRESS

un·roll \-'rōl\ *vb* **1** : to unwind a roll of : open out **2** : DISPLAY, DISCLOSE **3** : to become unrolled or spread out

un·roof \-'rüf, -'rùf\ *vb* : to strip off the roof or covering of

un·ruf·fled \ˌən-'rəf-əld, 'ən-\ *adj* **1** : not agitated or upset **2** : not ruffled : SMOOTH ⟨~ water⟩

un·ruly \-'rü-lē\ *adj* [ME *unreuly*, fr. *un-* + *reuly* disciplined, fr. *reule* rule, fr. OF, fr. L *regula* straightedge, rule, fr. *regere* to lead straight] : not submissive to rule or restraint : TURBULENT ⟨~ passions⟩ — **un·rul·i·ness** \-'rü-lē-nəs\ *n*

UNRWA *abbr* United Nations Relief and Works Agency

un·sad·dle \ˌən-'sad-ᵊl, 'ən-\ *vb* **1** : to remove the saddle from a horse **2** : UNHORSE

un·sat·u·rat·ed \-'sach-ə-ˌrāt-əd\ *adj* **1** : capable of absorbing or dissolving more of something **2** : containing double or triple bonds between carbon atoms ⟨~ fats or oils⟩ — **un·sat·u·rate** \-rət\ *n*

un·saved \ˌən-'sāvd, 'ən-\ *adj* : not saved; *esp* : not rescued from eternal punishment

un·sa·vory \-'sāv-(ə-)rē\ *adj* **1** : TASTELESS **2** : unpleasant to taste or smell **3** : morally offensive

un·say \-'sā\ *vb* **-said** \-'sed\; **-say·ing** \-'sā-iŋ\ : to take back (something said) : RETRACT, WITHDRAW

un·scathed \-'skāt͟hd\ *adj* : wholly unharmed : not injured

un·schooled \-'sküld\ *adj* : not schooled : UNTAUGHT, UNTRAINED

un·sci·en·tif·ic \ˌən-ˌsī-ən-'tif-ik\ *adj* : not scientific : not in accord with the principles and methods of science

un·scram·ble \ˌən-'skram-bəl, 'ən-\ *vb* **1** : RESOLVE, CLARIFY **2** : to restore (as a radio message) to intelligible form

un•screw \-'skrü\ *vb* **1** : to draw the screws from **2** : to loosen by turning

un•scru•pu•lous \-'skrü-pyə-ləs\ *adj* : not scrupulous : UNPRINCIPLED — **un•scru•pu•lous•ly** *adv* — **un•scru•pu•lous•ness** *n*

un•seal \-'sēl\ *vb* : to break or remove the seal of : OPEN

un•search•able \-'sər-chə-bəl\ *adj* : not capable of being searched or explored

un•sea•son•able \-'sēz-(ə-)nə-bəl\ *adj* : not seasonable : happening or coming at the wrong time : UNTIMELY — **un•sea•son•ably** \-blē\ *adv*

un•seat \-'sēt\ *vb* **1** : to throw from one's seat esp. on horseback **2** : to remove from political office

un•seem•ly \-'sēm-lē\ *adj* : not according with established standards of good form or taste; *also* : not suitable — **un•seem•li•ness** *n*

un•seen \ˌən-'sēn, 'ən-\ *adj* : not seen : INVISIBLE

un•seg•re•gat•ed \-'seg-ri-ˌgāt-əd\ *adj* : not segregated; *esp* : free from racial segregation

un•self•ish \-'sel-fish\ *adj* : not selfish : GENEROUS — **un•self•ish•ly** *adv* — **un•self•ish•ness** *n*

un•set•tle \ˌən-'set-ᵊl, 'ən-\ *vb* : to move or loosen from a settled position : DISPLACE, DISTURB

un•set•tled \-'set-ᵊld\ *adj* **1** : not settled : not fixed (as in position or character) **2** : not calm : DISTURBED **3** : not decided in mind : UNDETERMINED **4** : not paid ⟨∼ accounts⟩ **5** : not occupied by settlers

un•shack•le \-'shak-əl\ *vb* : to free from shackles

un•shaped \-'shāpt\ *adj* : not shaped : RUDE ⟨∼ ideas⟩ ⟨∼ timber⟩

un•sheathe \ˌən-'shēth, 'ən-\ *vb* : to draw from or as if from a sheath

un•ship \-'ship\ *vb* **1** : to remove from a ship **2** : to remove or become removed from position ⟨∼ an oar⟩

un•shod \ˌən-'shäd, 'ən-\ *adj* : not shod : not wearing shoes

un•sight•ly \ˌən-'sīt-lē, 'ən-\ *adj* : unpleasant to the sight : UGLY

un•skilled \-'skild\ *adj* **1** : not skilled; *esp* : not skilled in a specified branch of work **2** : not requiring skill ⟨∼ labor⟩

un•skill•ful \-'skil-fəl\ *adj* : lacking in skill or proficiency — **un•skill•ful•ly** \-ē\ *adv*

un•sling \-'sliŋ\ *vb* **-slung** \-'sləŋ\; **-sling•ing** \-'sliŋ-iŋ\ **1** : to remove from being slung **2** : to take off the slings of esp. aboard ship

un•snap \-'snap\ *vb* : to loosen or free by or as if by undoing a snap

un•snarl \-'snärl\ *vb* : to remove snarls from : UNTANGLE

un•so•phis•ti•cat•ed \ˌən-sə-'fis-tə-ˌkāt-əd\ *adj* **1** : not worldly-wise : lacking sophistication **2** : SIMPLE

un•sought \ˌən-'sȯt, 'ən-\ *adj* : not sought : not searched for or asked for : not obtained by effort

un•sound \-'saund\ *adj* **1** : not healthy or whole; *also* : not mentally normal **2** : not valid **3** : not firmly made or fixed — **un•sound•ly** *adv* — **un•sound•ness** *n*

un•spar•ing \-'spa(ə)r-iŋ\ *adj* **1** : HARD, RUTHLESS **2** : not frugal : LIBERAL, PROFUSE

un•speak•able \-'spē-kə-bəl\ *adj* **1** : impossible to express in words **2** : extremely bad — **un•speak•ably** \-blē\ *adv*

un•spot•ted \-'spät-əd\ *adj* : free from spot or stain; *esp* : free from moral stain

un•sprung \-'sprəŋ\ *adj* : not sprung; *esp* : not equipped with springs

un•sta•ble \-'stā-bəl\ *adj* **1** : not stable **2** : FICKLE, VACILLATING; *also* : having defective emotional control **3** : readily changing (as by decomposing) in chemical or physical composition or in biological activity ⟨an ∼ atomic nucleus⟩

un•steady \ˌən-'sted-ē\ *adj* : not steady : UNSTABLE — **un•steadi•ly** \-'sted-ᵊl-ē\ *adv* — **un•steadi•ness** \-'sted-ē-nəs\ *n*

un•stint•ing \-'stint-iŋ\ *adj* : giving or being given freely or generously ⟨∼ praise⟩

un•stop \-'stäp\ *vb* **1** : UNCLOG **2** : to remove a stopper from

un•strap \-'strap\ *vb* : to remove or loose a strap from

un•stressed \ˌən-'strest, 'ən-\ *adj* : not stressed; *esp* : not bearing a stress or accent

un•strung \-'strəŋ\ *adj* **1** : having the

strings loose or detached **2** : nervously tired or anxious

un·stud·ied \-ˈstəd-ēd\ *adj* **1** : not acquired by study **2** : NATURAL, UNFORCED

un·sub·stan·tial \ˌən-səb-ˈstan-chəl\ *adj* : INSUBSTANTIAL

un·sung \ˌən-ˈsəŋ, ˈən-\ *adj* **1** : not sung **2** : not celebrated in song or verse ⟨∼ heroes⟩

un·swerv·ing \ˌən-ˈswer-viŋ, ˈən-\ *adj* **1** : not swerving or turning aside **2** : STEADY

un·tan·gle \-ˈtaŋ-gəl\ *vb* **1** : DISENTANGLE **2** : to straighten out : RESOLVE ⟨∼ a problem⟩

un·taught \-ˈtȯt\ *adj* **1** : not instructed or taught : IGNORANT **2** : NATURAL, SPONTANEOUS

un·think·able \-ˈthiŋ-kə-bəl\ *adj* : not to be thought of or considered as possible : INCREDIBLE

un·think·ing \ˌən-ˈthiŋ-kiŋ, ˈən-\ *adj* : not thinking; *esp* : THOUGHTLESS, HEEDLESS — **un·think·ing·ly** *adv*

un·thought \ˈən-ˈthȯt\ *adj* : not anticipated : UNEXPECTED ⟨*unthought*-of development⟩

un·tie \-ˈtī\ *vb* **-tied; -ty·ing** *or* **-tie·ing** **1** : to free from something that ties, fastens, or restrains : UNBIND **2** : DISENTANGLE, RESOLVE **3** : to become loosened or unbound

¹un·til \(ˌ)ən-ˌtil\ *prep* : up to the time of ⟨worked ∼ 5 o'clock⟩

²until *conj* **1** : up to the time that ⟨wait ∼ he calls⟩ **2** : to the point or degree that ⟨ran ∼ he was breathless⟩

¹un·time·ly \ˌən-ˈtīm-lē, ˈən-\ *adv* : at an inopportune time : UNSEASONABLY; *also* : PREMATURELY

²untimely *adj* : PREMATURE ⟨∼ death⟩; *also* : INOPPORTUNE, UNSEASONABLE

un·tir·ing \ˌən-ˈtī-riŋ\ *adj* : not becoming tired : INDEFATIGABLE — **un·tir·ing·ly** *adv*

un·to \ˌən-tə, ˈən-(ˌ)tü\ *prep* : TO

un·told \ˌən-ˈtōld, ˈən-\ *adj* **1** : not counted : VAST, NUMBERLESS **2** : not told : not revealed

¹un·touch·able \ˌən-ˈtəch-ə-bəl, ˈən-\ *adj* : forbidden to the touch

²untouchable *n* : a member of the lowest social class in India having in traditional Hindu belief the quality of defil-

ing by contact a member of a higher caste

un·tow·ard \ˈən-ˈtō(-ə)rd\ *adj* **1** : difficult to manage : STUBBORN, WILLFUL ⟨an ∼ child⟩ **2** : INCONVENIENT, TROUBLESOME ⟨an ∼ encounter⟩

un·tried \ˌən-ˈtrīd, ˈən-\ *adj* : not tested or proved by experience or trial; *also* : not tried in court

un·true \-ˈtrü\ *adj* **1** : not faithful : DISLOYAL **2** : not according with a standard of correctness **3** : FALSE

un·truth \ˌən-ˈtrüth, ˈən-\ *n* **1** : lack of truthfulness **2** : FALSEHOOD

un·tune \-ˈt(y)ün\ *vb* **1** : to put out of tune **2** : DISARRANGE, DISCOMPOSE

un·tu·tored \-ˈt(y)üt-ərd\ *adj* : UNTAUGHT, UNLEARNED, IGNORANT

un·twine \-ˈtwīn\ *vb* : UNWIND, DISENTANGLE

un·twist \ˌən-ˈtwist, ˈən-\ *vb* **1** : to separate the twisted parts of : UNTWINE **2** : to become untwined

un·used \-ˈyüst, -ˈyüzd *for 1;* -ˈyüzd *for 2*\ *adj* **1** : UNACCUSTOMED **2** : not used

un·usu·al \-ˈyü-zhə(-wə)l\ *adj* : not usual : UNCOMMON, RARE — **un·usu·al·ly** \-ē\ *adv*

un·ut·ter·able \ˌən-ˈət-ə-rə-bəl, ˈən-\ *adj* : being beyond the powers of description : INEXPRESSIBLE — **un·ut·ter·ably** \-blē\ *adv*

un·var·nished \-ˈvär-nisht\ *adj* **1** : not varnished **2** : not embellished : PLAIN ⟨the ∼ truth⟩

un·veil \ˌən-ˈvāl, ˈən-\ *vb* **1** : to remove a veil or covering from : DISCLOSE **2** : to remove a veil : reveal oneself

un·voiced \-ˈvȯist\ *adj* **1** : not verbally expressed : UNSPOKEN **2** : VOICELESS 2

un·war·rant·able \-ˈwȯr-ənt-ə-bəl\ *adj* : not justifiable : INEXCUSABLE — **un·war·rant·ably** \-blē\ *adv*

un·weave \-ˈwēv\ *vb* **-wove** \-ˈwōv\; **-wo·ven** \-ˈwō-vən\; **-weav·ing** : DISENTANGLE, RAVEL

un·well \ˌən-ˈwəl\ *adj* **1** : SICK, AILING **2** : MENSTRUATING

un·whole·some \-ˈhōl-səm\ *adj* **1** : harmful to physical, mental, or moral well-being **2** : CORRUPT, UNSOUND; *also* : offensive to the senses : LOATHSOME

un·wieldy \-ˈwēl-dē\ *adj* : not easily managed or handled because of size or weight : AWKWARD ⟨an ∼ tool⟩

un·will·ing \-'wil-iŋ\ *adj* : not willing — **un·will·ing·ly** *adv* — **un·will·ing·ness** *n*

un·wind \-'wīnd\ *vb* **-wound** \-'waúnd\; **-wind·ing 1** : to undo something that is wound : loose from coils **2** : to become unwound : be capable of being unwound **3** : RELAX

un·wise \ˌən-'wīz, 'ən-\ *adj* : not wise : FOOLISH — **un·wise·ly** *adv*

un·wit·ting \-'wit-iŋ\ *adj* **1** : not intended : INADVERTENT ⟨~ mistake⟩ **2** : not knowing : UNAWARE — **un·wit·ting·ly** *adv*

un·wont·ed \-'wȯnt-əd, -'wōnt-, -'wənt-\ *adj* **1** : RARE, UNUSUAL **2** : not accustomed by experience — **un·wont·ed·ly** *adv*

un·world·ly \-'wərl-(d)lē\ *adj* **1** : not of this world; *esp* : SPIRITUAL **2** : NAIVE **3** : not swayed by worldly considerations — **un·world·li·ness** \-'wərl-(d)lē-nəs\ *n*

un·wor·thy \ˌən-'wər-thē, 'ən-\ *adj* **1** : BASE, DISHONORABLE **2** : not meritorious : not worthy : UNDESERVING **3** : not deserved : UNMERITED ⟨~ treatment⟩ **un·wor·thi·ly** \-thə-lē\ *adv* — **un·wor·thi·ness** \-thē-nəs\ *n*

un·wrap \-'rap\ *vb* : to free from wrappings : DISCLOSE

un·writ·ten \-'rit-ᵊn\ *adj* **1** : not in writing : ORAL, TRADITIONAL ⟨an ~ law⟩ **2** : containing no writing : BLANK

un·yield·ing \ˌən-'yēl-diŋ, 'ən-\ *adj* **1** : characterized by lack of softness or flexibility **2** : characterized by firmness or obduracy

un·yoke \-'yōk\ *vb* : to free from a yoke; *also* : SEPARATE, DISCONNECT

un·zip \-'zip\ *vb* : to zip open : open by means of a zipper

¹up \'əp\ *adv* **1** : in or to a higher position or level; *esp* : away from the center of the earth **2** : from beneath a surface (as ground or water) **3** : from below the horizon **4** : in or into an upright position; *esp* : out of bed **5** : with greater intensity ⟨speak ~⟩ **6** : in or into a better or more advanced state or a state of greater intensity or activity ⟨stir ~ a fire⟩ **7** : into existence, evidence, or knowledge ⟨the missing book turned ~⟩ **8** : into consideration ⟨brought the matter ~⟩ **9** : to or at bat **10** : into possession or custody ⟨gave himself ~⟩ **11** : ENTIRE-

LY, COMPLETELY ⟨eat it ~⟩ **12** — used for emphasis ⟨clean ~ a room⟩ **13** : ASIDE, BY ⟨lay ~ supplies⟩ **14** : so as to arrive or approach ⟨ran ~ the path⟩ **15** : in a direction opposite to down **16** : in or into parts ⟨tear ~ paper⟩ **17** : to a stop ⟨pull ~ at the curb⟩ **18** : for each side ⟨the score was 15 ~⟩

²up *adj* **1** : risen above the horizon ⟨the sun is ~⟩ **2** : being out of bed ⟨~ by 6 o'clock⟩ **3** : relatively high ⟨prices are ~⟩ **4** : RAISED, LIFTED ⟨windows are ~⟩ **5** : BUILT, CONSTRUCTED ⟨the house is ~⟩ **6** : grown above a surface ⟨the corn is ~⟩ **7** : moving, inclining, or directed upward **8** : marked by agitation, excitement, or activity **9** : READY; *esp* : highly prepared **10** : going on : taking place ⟨find out what is ~⟩ **11** : EXPIRED, ENDED ⟨the time is ~⟩ **12** : well informed ⟨~ on the news⟩ **13** : being ahead or in advance of an opponent ⟨one hole ~ in a match⟩ **14** : presented for or being under consideration **15** : charged before a court ⟨~ for robbery⟩

³up *prep* **1** : to, toward, or at a higher point of ⟨~ a ladder⟩ **2** : to or toward the source of ⟨~ the river⟩ **3** : to or toward the northern part of ⟨~ the coast⟩ **4** : to or toward the interior of ⟨traveling ~ the country⟩ **5** : ALONG ⟨walk ~ the street⟩

⁴up *n* **1** : an upward course or slope **2** : a period or state of prosperity or success ⟨he had his ~s and downs⟩

⁵up *vb* **upped** *or in 2* **up**; **upped**; **up·ping**; **ups** *or in 2* **up 1** : to rise from a lying or sitting position **2** : to act abruptly or surprisingly ⟨she *upped* and left home⟩ **3** : to move or cause to move upward : ASCEND ⟨*upped* prices⟩

Upa·ni·shad \ü-'pän-i-ˌshäd\ *n* : one of a set of Vedic philosophical treatises

¹up·beat \'əp-ˌbēt\ *n* : an unaccented beat in a musical measure; *esp* : the last beat of the measure

²upbeat *adj* : OPTIMISTIC, CHEERFUL

up·braid \ˌəp-'brād\ *vb* : to criticize, reproach, or scold severely

up·bring·ing \'əp-ˌbriŋ-iŋ\ *n* : the process of bringing up and training

UPC *abbr* Universal Product Code

up·chuck \'ə-ˌchək\ *vb* : VOMIT

up·com·ing \ˌəp-ˌkəm-iŋ\ *adj* : FORTHCOMING, APPROACHING

up–coun·try \,əp-,kən-trē\ *adj* : of or relating to the interior of a country or a region — **up–country** \'əp-'kən-\ *adv*

up·date \,əp-'dāt\ *vb* : to bring up to date — **update** \'əp-,dāt\ *n*

up·draft \'əp-,draft, -,dráft\ *n* : an upward movement of gas (as air)

up·end \,əp-'end\ *vb* : to set, stand, or rise on end

up–front \'əp-'frənt\ *adj* **1** : HONEST, CANDID **2** : ADVANCE ⟨∼ payment⟩

up front *adv* : in advance ⟨paid *up front*⟩

¹**up·grade** \'əp-,grād\ *n* **1** : an upward grade or slope **2** : INCREASE, RISE

²**up·grade** \'əp-,grād, ,əp-'grād\ *vb* : to raise to a higher grade or position; *esp* : to advance to a job requiring a higher level of skill

up·growth \'əp-,grōth\ *n* : the process or result of growing up : upward growth : DEVELOPMENT

up·heav·al \,əp-'hē-vəl\ *n* **1** : the action or an instance of uplifting esp. of part of the earth's crust **2** : a violent agitation or change

¹**up·hill** \'əp-'hil\ *adv* : upward on a hill or incline; *also* : against difficulties

²**up·hill** \-,hil\ *adj* **1** : situated on elevated ground **2** : ASCENDING **3** : DIFFICULT, LABORIOUS

up·hold \,əp-'hōld\ *vb* **-held** \-'held\; **-hold·ing 1** : to give support to **2** : to support against an opponent **3** : to keep elevated — **up·hold·er** *n*

up·hol·ster \,əp-'hōl-stər\ *vb* **-stered; -ster·ing** \-st(ə-)riŋ\ : to furnish with or as if with upholstery — **up·hol·ster·er** *n*

up·hol·stery \-st(ə-)rē\ *n, pl* **-ster·ies** [ME *upholdester* upholsterer, fr. *upholden* to uphold, fr. *up + holden* to hold] : materials (as fabrics, padding, and springs) used to make a soft covering esp. for a seat

UPI *abbr* United Press International

up·keep \'əp-,kēp\ *n* : the act or cost of keeping up or maintaining; *also* : the state of being maintained

up·land \'əp-lənd, -,land\ *n* : high land esp. at some distance from the sea — **upland** *adj*

¹**up·lift** \,əp-'lift\ *vb* **1** : to lift or raise up : ELEVATE **2** : to improve the condition of esp. morally, socially, or intellectually

²**up·lift** \'əp-,lift\ *n* **1** : a lifting up; *esp* : an upheaval of the earth's surface **2** : moral or social improvement; *also* : a movement to make such improvement

up·mar·ket \,əp-'mär-kət\ *adj* : appealing to wealthy consumers

up·most \'ep-,mōst\ *adj* : UPPERMOST

up·on \ə-'pȯn, -'pän\ *prep* : ON

¹**up·per** \'əp-ər\ *adj* **1** : higher in physical position, rank, or order **2** : constituting the smaller and more restricted branch of a bicameral legislature **3** *cap* : being a later part or formation of a specific geological period **4** : being toward the interior ⟨the ∼ Amazon⟩ **5** : NORTHERN ⟨∼ New York State⟩

²**upper** *n* : one that is upper; *esp* : the parts of a shoe or boot above the sole

up·per·case \,əp-ər-'kās\ *adj* : CAPITAL 5 — **uppercase** *n*

upper class *n* : a social class occupying a position above the middle class and having the highest status in a society — **upper–class** *adj*

up·per·class·man \,əp-ər-'klas-mən\ *n* : a junior or senior in a college or high school

upper crust *n* : the highest social class or group; *esp* : the highest circle of the upper class

up·per·cut \'əp-ər-,kət\ *n* : a short swinging punch delivered (as in boxing) in an upward direction usu. with a bent arm

upper hand *n* : MASTERY, ADVANTAGE

up·per·most \'əp-ər-,mōst\ *adv* : in or into the highest or most prominent position — **uppermost** *adj*

up·pish \'əp-ish\ *adj* : UPPITY

up·pi·ty \'əp-ət-ē\ *adj* : ARROGANT, PRESUMPTUOUS

up·raise \,əp-'rāz\ *vb* : to lift up : ELEVATE

¹**up·right** \'əp-,rīt\ *adj* **1** : PERPENDICULAR, VERTICAL **2** : erect in carriage or posture **3** : morally correct : JUST — **upright** *adv* — **up·right·ly** *adv* — **up·right·ness** *n*

²**upright** *n* **1** : the state of being upright : a vertical position **2** : something that stands upright

upright piano *n* : a piano whose strings run vertically

up·ris·ing \'əp-,rī-ziŋ\ *n* : INSURRECTION, REVOLT, REBELLION

up·riv·er \'əp-'riv-ər\ *adv or adj* : toward or at a point nearer the source of a river

up·roar \'əp-ˌrȯr\ *n* [Dutch *oproer*, fr. Middle Dutch, fr. *op* up + *roer* motion] : a state of commotion, excitement, or violent disturbance

up·roar·i·ous \ˌəp-'rȯr-ē-əs\ *adj* **1** : marked by uproar **2** : extremely funny — **up·roar·i·ous·ly** *adv*

up·root \ˌəp-'rüt, -'ruṫ\ *vb* : to remove by or as if by pulling up by the roots

¹up·set \ˌəp-'set\ *vb* **-set; -set·ting 1** : to force or be forced out of the usual upright, level, or proper position **2** : to disturb emotionally : WORRY; *also* : to make somewhat ill **3** : UNSETTLE, DISARRANGE **4** : to defeat unexpectedly

²up·set \'əp-ˌset\ *n* **1** : an upsetting or being upset; *esp* : a minor physical disorder **2** : a derangement of plans or ideas

up·shot \'əp-ˌshät\ *n* : final result

up·side \'əp-ˌsīd\ *n* : the upper side

up·side down \ˌəp-ˌsīd-'dauṅ\ *adv* **1** : with the upper and the lower parts reversed in position **2** : in or into confusion or disorder — **upside-down** *adj*

up·si·lon particle \'yüp-sə-ˌlän-, 'əp-\ *n* : any of a group of unstable electrically neutral elementary particles that have a mass about 10 times that of a proton

¹up·stage \'əp-'stāj\ *adv or adj* : toward or at the rear of a theatrical stage

²up·stage \ˌəp-'stāj\ *vb* : to steal the show from

¹up·stairs \'əp-'staȧrz\ *adv* **1** : up the stairs : to or on a higher floor **2** : to or at a higher position

²up·stairs \ˌəp-ˌstaȧrz\ *adj* : situated above the stairs esp. on an upper floor ⟨~ bedroom⟩

³up·stairs \'əp-'staȧrz, 'əp-ˌstaȧrs\ *n sing or pl* : the part of a building above the ground floor

up·stand·ing \ˌəp-'stan-diŋ, 'əp-ˌstan-diŋ\ *adj* **1** : ERECT **2** : STRAIGHTFORWARD, HONEST

¹up·start \ˌəp-'stärt\ *vb* : to jump up suddenly

²up·start \'əp-ˌstärt\ *n* : one that has risen suddenly; *esp* : one that claims more personal importance than he warrants — **up·start** \ˌəp-\ *adj*

up·state \'əp-'stāt\ *adj* : of, relating to, or characteristic of a part of a state away from a large city and esp. to the north — **upstate** *adv* — **upstate** *n*

up·stream \'əp-'strēm\ *adv* : at or toward the source of a stream — **upstream** *adj*

up·stroke \'əp-ˌstrōk\ *n* : an upward stroke (as of a pen)

up·surge \-ˌsərj\ *n* : a rapid or sudden rise

up·swept \'əp-ˌswept\ *adj* : swept upward ⟨~ hairdo⟩

up·swing \'əp-ˌswiŋ\ *n* : an upward swing; *esp* : a marked increase or rise (as in activity)

up·take \'əp-ˌtāk\ *n* **1** : UNDERSTANDING, COMPREHENSION ⟨quick on the ~⟩ **2** : the process of absorbing and incorporating esp. into a living organism ⟨~ of iodine by the thyroid gland⟩

up·thrust \'əp-ˌthrəst\ *n* : an upward thrust; *esp* : an uplift of part of the earth's crust — **upthrust** *vb*

up·tight \'əp-'tīt\ *adj* **1** : TENSE, NERVOUS, UNEASY; *also* : ANGRY, INDIGNANT **2** : rigidly conventional

up–to–date *adj* **1** : extending up to the present time **2** : abreast of the times : MODERN — **up–to–date·ness** *n*

up·town \'əp-ˌtauṅ\ *n* : the upper part of a town or city; *esp* : the residential district — **up·town** \'əp-'tauṅ\ *adj or adv*

¹up·turn \'əp-ˌtərn, ˌəp-'tərn\ *vb* **1** : to turn (as earth) up or over **2** : to turn or direct upward

²up·turn \'əp-ˌtərn\ *n* : an upward turn esp. toward better conditions or higher prices

¹up·ward \'əp-wərd\ *or* **up·wards** \-wərdz\ *adv* **1** : in a direction from lower to higher **2** : toward a higher or better condition **3** : toward a greater amount or higher number, degree, or rate

²upward *adj* : directed or moving toward or situated in a higher place or level : ASCENDING

upwards of *also* **upward of** *adv* : more than : in excess of ⟨they cost *upwards of* $25 each⟩

up·well \ˌəp-'wel\ *vb* : to move or flow upward

up·well·ing \-'wel-iŋ\ *n* : a rising or an appearance of rising to the surface and flowing outward; *esp* : the movement of deep cold usu. nutrient-rich ocean water to the surface

up·wind \\'əp-'wind\ *adv or adj* : in the direction from which the wind is blowing

ura·cil \\'yùr-ə-ˌsil\ *n* : a pyrimidine base that is one of the four bases coding genetic information in the molecular chain of RNA

ura·ni·um \yù-'rā-nē-əm\ *n* : a silvery heavy radioactive metallic chemical element used as a source of atomic energy

Ura·nus \\'yùr-ə-nəs, yù-'rā-\ *n* [LL, heaven personified as a god, fr. Gk *Ouranos,* fr. *ouranos* sky, heaven] : the planet 7th in order from the sun

ur·ban \\'ər-bən\ *adj* : of, relating to, characteristic of, or constituting a city

ur·bane \ˌər-'bān\ *adj* [L *urbanus* urban, urbane, fr. *urbs* city] : very polite and polished in manner : SUAVE

ur·ban·ite \\'ər-bə-ˌnīt\ *n* : one living in a city

ur·ban·i·ty \ˌər-'ban-ət-ē\ *n, pl* **-ties** : the quality or state of being urbane

ur·ban·ize \\'ər-bə-ˌnīz\ *vb* **-ized; -iz·ing** : to cause to take on urban characteristics — **ur·ban·iza·tion** \ˌər-bə-nə-'zā-shən\ *n*

ur·chin \\'ər-chən\ *n* [ME, hedgehog, fr. MF *herichon,* fr. L *ericius*] : a pert or mischievous youngster

Ur·du \\'ùr-dü, 'ər-\ *n* [Hindi *urdū= zabān,* lit., camp language] : a language that is an official literary language of Pakistan and is widely used in India

urea \yù-'rē-ə\ *n* : a soluble nitrogenous compound that is the chief solid constituent of mammalian urine

ure·mia \yù-'rē-mē-ə\ *n* : accumulation in the blood of materials normally passed off in the urine resulting in a poisoned condition — **ure·mic** \-mik\ *adj*

ure·ter \\'yùr-ət-ər\ *n* : a duct that carries the urine from a kidney to the bladder

ure·thra \yù-'rē-thrə\ *n, pl* **-thras** or **-thrae** \-(ˌ)thrē\ : the canal that in most mammals carries off the urine from the bladder and in the male also serves as a genital duct — **ure·thral** \-thrəl\ *adj*

ure·thri·tis \ˌyùr-i-'thrīt-əs\ *n* : inflammation of the urethra

¹**urge** \\'ərj\ *vb* **urged; urging 1** : to present, advocate, or demand earnestly **2** : to try to persuade or sway ⟨~ a guest to stay⟩ **3** : to serve as a motive or reason for **4** : to impress or impel to some course or activity ⟨the dog *urged* the sheep onward⟩

²**urge** *n* **1** : the act or process of urging **2** : a force or impulse that urges or drives

ur·gent \\'ər-jənt\ *adj* **1** : calling for immediate attention : PRESSING **2** : urging insistently — **ur·gen·cy** \-jən-sē\ *n* — **ur·gent·ly** *adv*

uric \\'yùr-ik\ *adj* : of, relating to, or found in urine

uric acid *n* : a nearly insoluble acid that is the chief nitrogenous excretory product of birds but is present in only small amounts in mammalian urine

uri·nal \\'yùr-ən-ᵊl\ *n* **1** : a receptacle for urine **2** : a place for urinating

uri·nal·y·sis \ˌyùr-ə-'nal-ə-səs\ *n* : analysis of urine usu. for medical purposes

uri·nary \\'yùr-ə-ˌner-ē\ *adj* **1** : relating to, occurring in, or being organs for the formation and discharge of urine **2** : of, relating to, or found in urine

urinary bladder *n* : a membranous sac in many vertebrates that serves for the temporary retention of urine and discharges by the urethra

uri·nate \\'yùr-ə-ˌnāt\ *vb* **-nat·ed; -nat·ing** : to discharge urine — **uri·na·tion** \ˌyùr-ə-'nā-shən\ *n*

urine \\'yùr-ən\ *n* : a waste material from the kidneys that is usu. a yellowish watery liquid in mammals but is highly viscous in birds and reptiles

urn \\'ərn\ *n* **1** : a vessel that typically has the form of a vase on a pedestal and often is used to hold the ashes of the dead **2** : a closed vessel usu. with a spout for serving a hot beverage

uro·gen·i·tal \ˌyùr-ō-'jen-ə-tᵊl\ *adj* : of, relating to, or being the organs or functions of excretion and reproduction

urol·o·gy \yù-'räl-ə-jē\ *n* : a branch of medical science dealing with the urinary or urogenital tract and its disorders — **uro·log·ic** \ˌyùr-ə-'läj-ik\ *also*

uro·log·i·cal \-i-kəl\ *adj* — **urol·o·gist** \yu̇-'räl-ə-jəst\ *n*

Ur·sa Ma·jor \ͺər-sə-'mā-jər\ *n* [L, lit., greater bear] : the most conspicuous of the northern constellations that contains the stars which form the Big Dipper

Ursa Mi·nor \-'mī-nər\ *n* [L, lit., lesser bear] : the constellation including the north pole of the heavens and the stars that form the Little Dipper with the North Star at the tip of the handle

ur·sine \'ər-ͺsīn\ *adj* : of, relating to, or resembling a bear

ur·ti·car·ia \ͺərt-ə-'kar-ē-ə\ *n* [NL, fr. L *urtica* nettle] : HIVES

us \(')əs\ *pron, objective case of* WE

US *abbr* United States

USA *abbr* **1** United States Army **2** United States of America

us·able *also* **use·able** \'yü-zə-bəl\ *adj* : suitable or fit for use — **us·abil·i·ty** \ͺyü-zə-'bil-ət-ē\ *n*

USAF *abbr* United States Air Force

us·age \'yü-sij, -zij\ *n* **1** : habitual or customary practice or procedure **2** : the way in which words and phrases are actually used **3** : the action or mode of using **4** : manner of treating

USCG *abbr* United States Coast Guard

USDA *abbr* United States Department of Agriculture

¹**use** \'yüs\ *n* **1** : the act or practice of using or employing something : EMPLOYMENT, APPLICATION **2** : the fact or state of being used **3** : the way of using **4** : USAGE, CUSTOM **5** : the privilege or benefit of using something **6** : the ability or power to use something (as a limb) **7** : the legal enjoyment of property that consists in its employment, occupation, or exercise; *also* : the benefit or profit esp. from property held in trust **8** : USEFULNESS, UTILITY; *also* : the end served : OBJECT, FUNCTION **9** : the occasion or need to employ ⟨he had no more ∼ for it⟩ **10** : ESTEEM, LIKING ⟨had no ∼ for modern art⟩

²**use** \'yüz\ *vb* **used** \'yüzd; "*used to*" *usu* 'yüs-tə\; **us·ing** \'yü-ziŋ\ **1** : to put into action or service : EMPLOY **2** : to consume or take (as drugs) regularly **3** : UTILIZE ⟨∼ tact⟩; *also* : MANIPULATE ⟨*used* his friends to get ahead⟩ **4** : to expend or consume by putting to use

5 : to behave toward : TREAT ⟨*used* the horse cruelly⟩ **6** : to benefit from ⟨house could ∼ a coat of paint⟩ **7** — used in the past with *to* to indicate a former practice, fact, or state ⟨we *used* to work harder⟩ — **us·er** *n*

used \'yüzd\ *adj* **1** : having been used by another : SECONDHAND ⟨∼ cars⟩ **2** : ACCUSTOMED, HABITUATED ⟨∼ to the heat⟩

use·ful \'yüs-fəl\ *adj* : capable of being put to use : ADVANTAGEOUS; *esp* : serviceable for a beneficial end — **use·ful·ly** \-ē\ *adv* — **use·ful·ness** *n*

use·less \'yüs-ləs\ *adj* : having or being of no use : WORTHLESS — **use·less·ly** *adv* — **use·less·ness** *n*

USES *abbr* United States Employment Service

use up *vb* : to consume completely

¹**ush·er** \'əsh-ər\ *n* [ME *ussher,* fr. MF *ussier,* fr. (assumed) VL *ustiarius* doorkeeper, fr. L *ostium, ustium* door, mouth of a river] **1** : an officer who walks before a person of rank **2** : one who escorts people to their seats (as in a church or theater)

²**usher** *vb* **1** : to conduct to a place **2** : to precede as an usher, forerunner, or harbinger **3** : INAUGURATE, INTRODUCE ⟨∼ in a new era⟩

ush·er·ette \ͺəsh-ə-'ret\ *n* : a female usher (as in a theater)

USIA *abbr* United States Information Agency

USM *abbr* United States mail

USMC *abbr* United States Marine Corps

USN *abbr* United States Navy

USO *abbr* United Service Organizations

USP *abbr* United States Pharmacopeia

USPS *abbr* United States Postal Service

USS *abbr* United States ship

USSR *abbr* Union of Soviet Socialist Republics

usu *abbr* usual; usually

usu·al \'yü-zhə(-wə)l\ *adj* **1** : accordant with usage, custom, or habit : NORMAL **2** : commonly or ordinarily used **3** : ORDINARY **syn** customary, habitual, accustomed, routine — **usu·al·ly** \'yüzh-(ə-)wə-lē, 'yüzh-(ə-)lē\ *adv*

usu·fruct \'yü-zə-ͺfrəkt\ *n* [L *ususfructus,* fr. *usus et fructus* use and enjoyment] : the legal right to use and enjoy the benefits and profits of something belonging to another

usu•rer \\'yü-zhər-ər\ *n* : one that lends money esp. at an exorbitant rate

usu•ri•ous \yu̇-'zhu̇r-ē-əs\ *adj* : practicing, involving, or constituting usury ⟨a ~ rate of interest⟩

usurp \yu̇-'sərp, -'zərp\ *vb* [ME *usurpen*, fr. MF *usurper*, fr. L *usurpare*, lit., to take possession of by use, fr. *usu* (abl. of *usus* use) + *rapere* to seize] : to seize and hold by force or without right ⟨~ a throne⟩ — **usur•pa•tion** \ˌyü-sər-'pā-shən, -zər-\ *n* — **usurp•er** \yu̇-'sər-pər, -'zər-\ *n*

usu•ry \\'yüzh-(ə-)rē\ *n, pl* **-ries** [ME, fr. ML *usuria*, alter. of L *usura*, fr. *usus*, pp. of *uti* to use] **1** : the lending of money with an interest charge for its use **2** : an excessive rate or amount of interest charged; *esp* : interest above an established legal rate

UT *abbr* Utah

Ute \\'yüt\ *n, pl* **Ute** *or* **Utes** : a member of an American Indian people orig. ranging through Utah, Colorado, Arizona, and New Mexico

uten•sil \yu̇-'ten-səl\ *n* [ME, vessels for domestic use, fr. MF *utensile*, fr. L *utensilia*, fr. neut. pl. of *utensilis* useful, fr. *uti* to use] **1** : an instrument or vessel used in a household and esp. a kitchen **2** : an article serving a useful purpose

uter•us \\'yüt-ə-rəs\ *n, pl* **uteri** \\'yüt-ə-ˌrī\ *also* **uter•us•es** : the muscular organ of a female mammal in which the young develop before birth — **uter•ine** \-ˌrīn, -rən\ *adj*

utile \\'yüt-ᵊl, 'yü-ˌtīl\ *adj* : USEFUL

¹util•i•tar•i•an \yu̇-ˌtil-ə-'ter-ē-ən\ *n* : a person who believes in utilitarianism

²utilitarian *adj* **1** : of or relating to utilitarianism **2** : of or relating to utility : aiming at usefulness rather than beauty; *also* : serving a useful purpose

util•i•tar•i•an•ism \-ē-ə-ˌniz-əm\ *n* : a theory that the greatest good for the greatest number should be the main consideration in making a choice of actions

¹util•i•ty \yu̇-'til-ət-ē\ *n, pl* **-ties** **1** : USEFULNESS **2** : something useful or designed for use **3** : a business organiza-

tion performing a public service and subject to special governmental regulation **4** : a public service or a commodity (as electricity or water) provided by a public utility; *also* : equipment to provide such or a similar service

²utility *adj* **1** : capable of serving esp. as a substitute in various uses or positions ⟨a ~ outfielder⟩ ⟨a ~ knife⟩ **2** : being of a usable but inferior grade ⟨~ beef⟩

uti•lize \\'yüt-ᵊl-ˌīz\ *vb* **-lized; -liz•ing** : to make use of : turn to profitable account or use — **uti•li•za•tion** \ˌyüt-ᵊl-ə-'zā-shən\ *n*

ut•most \\'ət-ˌmōst\ *adj* **1** : situated at the farthest or most distant point : EXTREME **2** : of the greatest or highest degree, quantity, number, or amount — **utmost** *n*

uto•pia \yu̇-'tō-pē-ə\ *n* [fr. *Utopia*, imaginary island described in Sir Thomas More's *Utopia*, fr. Gk *ou* not, no + *topos* place] **1** *often cap* : a place of ideal perfection esp. in laws, government, and social conditions **2** : an impractical scheme for social improvement

¹uto•pi•an \-pē-ən\ *adj, often cap* **1** : of, relating to, or resembling a utopia **2** : proposing ideal social and political schemes that are impractical : VISIONARY

²utopian *n* **1** : a believer in the perfectibility of human society **2** : one that proposes or advocates utopian schemes

¹ut•ter \\'ət-ər\ *adj* [ME, remote, fr. OE *ūtera* outer, compar. adj. fr. *ūt* out, adv.] : ABSOLUTE, TOTAL ⟨~ ruin⟩ — **ut•ter•ly** *adv*

²utter *vb* [ME *uttren*, fr. *utter* outside, adv., fr. OE *ūtor*, compar. of *ūt* out] **1** : to send forth as a sound : express in usu. spoken words : PRONOUNCE, SPEAK **2** : to put (as currency) into circulation

ut•ter•ance \\'ət-ə-rəns, 'ə-trəns\ *n* **1** : something uttered; *esp* : an oral or written statement **2** : the action of uttering with the voice : SPEECH **3** : power, style, or manner of speaking

ut•ter•most \\'ət-ər-ˌmōst\ *adj* : EXTREME, UTMOST ⟨the ~ parts of the earth⟩ — **uttermost** *n*

U–turn \'yü-'tərn\ *n* : a turn resembling the letter U; *esp* : a 180-degree turn made by a vehicle in a road

UV *abbr* ultraviolet

U–val·ue \'yü-,val-yü\ *n* : a measure of the heat transmission through a building part (as a wall) or a given thickness of insulating material a low value of which indicates high insulating effectiveness

uvu·la \'yü-vyə-lə\ *n, pl* **-las** *or* **-lae** \-,lē, -,lī\ : the fleshy lobe hanging at the back of the palate — **uvu·lar** \-lər\ *adj*

UW *abbr* underwriter

ux·o·ri·ous \,ək-'sōr-ē-əs, ,əg-'zōr-\ *adj* : excessively devoted or submissive to a wife

V

¹v \'vē\ *n, pl* **v's** *or* **vs** \'vēz\ *often cap* : the 22d letter of the English alphabet

²v *abbr, often cap* **1** vector **2** velocity **3** verb **4** verse **5** versus **6** victory **7** vide **8** voice **9** volt; voltage **10** volume **11** vowel

V *symbol* vanadium

Va *abbr* Virginia

VA *abbr* **1** Veterans Administration **2** vice admiral **3** Virginia

va·can·cy \'vā-kən-sē\ *n, pl* **-cies** **1** : a vacating esp. of an office, position, or piece of property **2** : the state of being vacant **3** : a vacant office, position, or tenancy; *also* : the period during which it stands vacant **4** : empty space : VOID

va·cant \'vā-kənt\ *adj* **1** : not occupied ⟨~ seat⟩ ⟨~ room⟩ **2** : EMPTY ⟨~ space⟩ **3** : free from business or care ⟨a few ~ hours⟩ **4** : devoid of thought, reflection, or expression ⟨a ~ smile⟩ — **va·cant·ly** *adv*

va·cate \'vā-,kāt\ *vb* **va·cat·ed; va·cat·ing** **1** : to make void : ANNUL **2** : to make vacant (as an office or house); *also* : to give up the occupancy of

¹va·ca·tion \vā-'kā-shən, və-\ *n* : a period of rest from work : HOLIDAY

²vacation *vb* **-tioned; -tion·ing** \-sh(ə-)niŋ\ : to take or spend a vacation — **va·ca·tion·er** \-sh(ə-)nər\ *n*

va·ca·tion·ist \-sh(ə-)nəst\ *n* : a person taking a vacation

va·ca·tion·land \-shən-,land\ *n* : an area with recreational attractions and facilities for vacationists

vac·ci·nate \'vak-sə-,nāt\ *vb* **-nat·ed; -nat·ing** : to inoculate with a related harmless virus to produce immunity to smallpox; *also* : to administer a vaccine to usu. by injection

vac·ci·na·tion \,vak-sə-'nā-shən\ *n* **1** : the act of vaccinating **2** : the scar left by vaccinating

vac·cine \vak-'sēn, 'vak-,sēn\ *n* [L *vaccinus* of or from cows, fr. *vacca* cow; so called from the derivation of smallpox vaccine from cows] : material (as a preparation of killed or weakened virus or bacteria) used in vaccinating to induce immunity to a disease

vac·cin·ia \vak-'sin-ē-ə\ *n* : COWPOX

vac·il·late \'vas-ə-,lāt\ *vb* **-lat·ed; -lat·ing** **1** : SWAY, TOTTER; *also* : FLUCTUATE **2** : to incline first to one course or opinion and then to another : WAVER — **vac·il·la·tion** \,vas-ə-'lā-shən\ *n*

va·cu·ity \va-'kyü-ət-ē, və-\ *n, pl* **-ities** **1** : an empty space **2** : the state, fact, or quality of being vacuous **3** : something that is vacuous

vac·u·ole \'vak-yə-,wōl\ *n* : a usu. fluid-filled cavity in tissues or in the protoplasm of an individual cell — **vac·u·o·lar** \,vak-yə-'wō-lər, -,lär\ *adj*

vac·u·ous \'vak-yə-wəs\ *adj* **1** : EMPTY, VACANT, BLANK **2** : DULL, STUPID, INANE — **vac·u·ous·ly** *adv* — **vac·u·ous·ness** *n*

¹vac·u·um \'vak-yü-əm, -(,)yüm, -yəm\ *n, pl* **vacuums** *or* **vac·ua** \-yə-wə\ [L, fr. neut. of *vacuus* empty] **1** : a space entirely empty of matter **2** : a space from which most of the air has been removed (as by a pump) **3** : VOID, GAP **4** : VACUUM CLEANER — **vacuum** *adj*

²vacuum *vb* : to use a vacuum device (as a vacuum cleaner) on

vacuum bottle *n* : a cylindrical container with a vacuum between an inner and an outer wall used to keep liquids hot or cold

vacuum cleaner *n* : an electrical appliance for cleaning (as floors or rugs) by suction

vac·u·um–packed \ˌvak-yüm-ˈpakt, -yəm-\ *adj* : having much of the air removed before being hermetically sealed

vacuum tube *n* : an electron tube from which most of the air has been removed

va·de me·cum \ˌvād-ē-ˈmē-kəm\ *n, pl* **vade mecums** [L, go with me] : something (as a handbook or manual) carried as a constant companion

VADM *abbr* vice admiral

¹**vag·a·bond** \ˈvag-ə-ˌbänd\ *adj* **1** : WANDERING, HOMELESS **2** : of, characteristic of, or leading the life of a vagrant or tramp **3** : leading an unsettled or irresponsible life

²**vagabond** *n* : one leading a vagabond life; *esp* : TRAMP

va·gar·i·ous \vā-ˈger-ē-əs, və-\ *adj* : marked by vagaries : CAPRICIOUS — **va·gar·i·ous·ly** *adv*

va·ga·ry \ˈvā-gə-rē, və-ˈger-ē\ *n, pl* **-ries** : an odd or eccentric idea or action : WHIM, CAPRICE

va·gi·na \və-ˈjī-nə\ *n, pl* **-nae** \-(ˌ)nē\ *or* **-nas** [L, lit., sheath] : a canal that leads from the uterus to the external opening of the female sex organs — **vag·i·nal** \ˈvaj-ən-ᵊl\ *adj*

vag·i·ni·tis \ˌvaj-ə-ˈnīt-əs\ *n* : inflammation of the vagina

va·gran·cy \ˈvā-grən(t)-sē\ *n, pl* **-cies 1** : the quality or state of being vagrant; *also* : a vagrant act or notion **2** : the offense of being a vagrant

¹**va·grant** \ˈvā-grənt\ *n* : a person who has no job and wanders from place to place

²**vagrant** *adj* **1** : of, relating to, or characteristic of a vagrant **2** : following no fixed course : RANDOM, CAPRICIOUS ⟨∼ thoughts⟩ — **va·grant·ly** *adv*

vague \ˈvāg\ *adj* **vagu·er; vagu·est** [MF, fr. L *vagus*, lit., wandering] **1** : not clear, definite, or distinct **2** : not clearly felt or analyzed ⟨a ∼ unrest⟩ **syn** obscure, dark, enigmatic, ambiguous, equivocal — **vague·ly** *adv* — **vague·ness** *n*

vain \ˈvān\ *adj* [ME, fr. OF, fr. L *vanus* empty, vain] **1** : of no real value : IDLE, WORTHLESS **2** : FUTILE, UNSUCCESSFUL **3** : proud of one's looks or abilities **syn** conceited, narcissistic, vainglorious — **vain·ly** *adv*

vain·glo·ri·ous \(ˈ)vān-ˈglōr-ē-əs\ *adj* : marked by vainglory : BOASTFUL

vain·glo·ry \ˈvān-ˌglōr-ē\ *n* **1** : excessive or ostentatious pride esp. in one's own achievements **2** : vain display : VANITY

val *abbr* value; valued

va·lance \ˈval-əns, ˈvāl-\ *n* **1** : drapery hanging from an edge (as of an altar, table, or bed) **2** : a drapery or a decorative frame across the top of a window

vale \ˈvāl\ *n* : VALLEY, DALE

vale·dic·tion \ˌval-ə-ˈdik-shən\ *n* [L *valedictus,* pp. of *valedicere* to say farewell, fr. *vale* farewell + *dicere* to say] : an act or utterance of leave-taking : FAREWELL

vale·dic·to·ri·an \-ˌdik-ˈtōr-ē-ən\ *n* : the student usu. of the highest rank in a graduating class who pronounces the valedictory oration at commencement

vale·dic·to·ry \-ˈdik-t(ə-)rē\ *adj* : bidding farewell : delivered as a valediction ⟨a ∼ address⟩ — **valedictory** *n*

va·lence \ˈvā-ləns\ *n* [LL *valentia* power, capacity, fr. L *valēre* to be strong] : the combining power of an atom as shown by the number of electrons in its outermost energy level that are lost, gained, or shared in the formation of chemical bonds

valence electron *n* : an electron in the outer shell of an atom that determines the atom's chemical properties

Va·len·ci·ennes \və-ˌlen-sē-ˈen(z), ˌval-ən-sē-\ *n* : a fine handmade lace

val·en·tine \ˈval-ən-ˌtīn\ *n* : a sweetheart chosen or complimented on St. Valentine's Day; *also* : a greeting card sent on this day

Valentine Day *or* **Valentine's Day** *n* : SAINT VALENTINE'S DAY

¹**va·let** \ˈval-ət, ˈval-(ˌ)ā, va-ˈlā\ *n* **1** : a male servant who takes care of a man's clothes and performs personal services **2** : an attendant in a hotel who performs personal services for customers

²**valet** *vb* : to serve as a valet

val·e·tu·di·nar·i·an \ˌval-ə-ˌt(y)üd-ᵊn-

'er-ē-ən** *n* : a person of a weak or sickly constitution; *esp* : one whose chief concern is his invalidism — **val·e·tu·di·nar·i·an·ism \-ē-ə-ˌniz-əm\ *n*

val·iant \ˈval-yənt\ *adj* : having or showing valor : BRAVE, HEROIC **syn** valorous, doughty, courageous, bold, audacious, dauntless, undaunted, intrepid — **val·iant·ly** *adv*

val·id \ˈval-əd\ *adj* 1 : having legal force ⟨a ~ contract⟩ 2 : founded on truth or fact : capable of being justified or defended : SOUND ⟨a ~ argument⟩ ⟨~ reasons⟩ — **va·lid·i·ty** \və-ˈlid-ət-ē, va-\ *n* — **val·id·ly** \ˈval-əd-lē\ *adv*

val·i·date \ˈval-ə-ˌdāt\ *vb* -dat·ed; -dat·ing 1 : to make legally valid 2 : to confirm the validity of 3 : VERIFY — **val·i·da·tion** \ˌval-ə-ˈdā-shən\ *n*

va·lise \və-ˈlēs\ *n* [F] : TRAVELING BAG

val·ley \ˈval-ē\ *n, pl* **valleys** : a long depression between ranges of hills or mountains

val·or \ˈval-ər\ *n* [ME, fr. MF *valour*, fr. ML *valor* value, valor, fr. L *valēre* to be strong] : personal bravery **syn** heroism, prowess, gallantry — **val·or·ous** \ˈval-ə-rəs\ *adj*

val·o·ri·za·tion \ˌval-ə-rə-ˈzā-shən\ *n* : the support of commodity prices by any of various forms of government subsidy — **val·o·rize** \ˈval-ə-ˌrīz\ *vb*

valse \väls\ *n* [F] : WALTZ; *esp* : a concert waltz

'valu·able \ˈval-yə-(wə-)bəl\ *adj* 1 : having money value 2 : having great money value 3 : of great use or service **syn** invaluable, priceless, costly, expensive, dear, precious

²valuable *n* : a usu. personal possession of considerable value ⟨their ~s were stolen⟩

val·u·ate \ˈval-yə-ˌwāt\ *vb* -at·ed; -at·ing : to place a value on : APPRAISE — **val·u·a·tor** \-ˌwāt-ər\ *n*

val·u·a·tion \ˌval-yə-ˈwā-shən\ *n* 1 : the act or process of valuing; *esp* : appraisal of property 2 : the estimated or determined market value of a thing

'val·ue \ˈval-yü\ *n* 1 : a fair return or equivalent in money, goods, or services for something exchanged 2 : the worth of a thing : market price, purchasing power, or estimated worth 3 : an assigned or computed numerical quantity ⟨the ~ of x in an equation⟩ 4 : precise meaning ⟨~ of a word⟩ 5 : distinctive quality of sound in speech 6 : luminosity of a color : BRILLIANCE; *also* : the relation of one detail in a picture to another with respect to lightness or darkness 7 : the relative length of a tone or note 8 : something (as a principle or ideal) intrinsically valuable or desirable ⟨human rather than material ~s⟩ — **val·ue·less** *adj*

²value *vb* **val·ued; valu·ing** 1 : to estimate the monetary worth of : APPRAISE 2 : to rate in usefulness, importance, or general worth 3 : to consider or rate highly : PRIZE, ESTEEM — **val·u·er** *n*

val·ue–add·ed tax *n* : an incremental excise tax that is levied on the value added at each stage of the processing of a raw material or the production and distribution of a commodity

val·ued \ˈval-yüd\ *adj* : highly esteemed : PRIZED

valve \ˈvalv\ *n* 1 : a structure (as in a vein) that temporarily closes a passage or that permits movement in one direction only 2 : one of the pieces into which a ripe seed capsule or pod separates 3 : a device by which the flow of liquid, gas, or loose material in bulk may be regulated by a movable part; *also* : the movable part of such a device 4 : a device in a brass wind instrument for quickly varying the tube length in order to change the fundamental tone by some definite interval 5 : one of the separable usu. hinged pieces of which the shell of some animals and esp. bivalve mollusks consists — **valved** \ˈvalvd\ *adj* — **valve·less** *adj*

val·vu·lar \ˈval-vyə-lər\ *adj* 1 : resembling or functioning as a valve; *also* : opening by valves 2 : of or relating to a valve esp. of the heart

va·moose \və-ˈmüs, va-\ *vb* **va·moosed; va·moos·ing** [Sp *vamos* let us go] *slang* : to leave or go away quickly

'vamp \ˈvamp\ *vb* 1 : to provide with a new vamp 2 : to patch up with a new part 3 : INVENT, IMPROVISE ⟨~ up an excuse⟩

²vamp *n* 1 : the part of a boot or shoe

upper covering esp. the front part of the foot **2** : a short introductory musical passage often repeated

³**vamp** *n* : a woman who uses her charm and allurements to seduce and exploit men

⁴**vamp** *vb* : to practice seductive wiles on

vam·pire \ˈvam-ˌpī(ə)r\ *n* **1** : a night-wandering bloodsucking ghost **2** : a person who preys on other people; *esp* : a woman who exploits and ruins her lover **3** : any of various bats of Mexico and Central and South America that feed on the blood of animals including man; *also* : any of several bats believed to suck blood

¹**van** \ˈvan\ *n* : VANGUARD

²**van** *n* : a usu. enclosed wagon or motortruck for moving goods or animals; *also* : a versatile enclosed box-like motor vehicle with side or rear doors and side panels that often have windows

va·na·di·um \və-ˈnād-ē-əm\ *n* : a soft ductile metallic chemical element used to form alloys

Van Al·len belt \van-ˈal-ən-\ *n* : a belt of intense ionizing radiation in the earth's magnetosphere

van·dal \ˈvan-dᵊl\ *n* **1** *cap* : a member of a Germanic people who sacked Rome in A.D. 455 **2** : one who willfully mars or destroys property

van·dal·ism \-ˌiz-əm\ *n* : willful or malicious destruction or defacement of public or private property

van·dal·ize \-ˌīz\ *vb* **-ized; -iz·ing** : to subject to vandalism : DAMAGE

Van·dyke \van-ˈdīk\ *n* : a trim pointed beard

vane \ˈvān\ *n* [ME, fr. OE *fana* banner] **1** : a movable device attached to a high object to show the way the wind blows **2** : a thin flat or curved object that is rotated about an axis by a flow of fluid or that rotates to cause a fluid to flow or that redirects a flow of fluid ⟨the ∼s of a windmill⟩

van·guard \ˈvan-ˌgärd\ *n* **1** : the troops moving at the front of an army : VAN **2** : the forefront of an action or movement

va·nil·la \və-ˈnil-ə\ *n* [NL, genus name, fr. Sp *vainilla* vanilla (plant and fruit), dim. of *vaina* sheath, fr. L *vagina*

sheath, vagina] : a tropical American climbing orchid with beanlike pods; *also* : its pods or a flavoring extract made from these

van·ish \ˈvan-ish\ *vb* : to pass from sight or existence : disappear completely — **van·ish·er** *n*

van·i·ty \ˈvan-ət-ē\ *n, pl* **-ties 1** : something that is vain, empty, or useless **2** : the quality or fact of being useless or futile : FUTILITY **3** : undue pride in oneself or one's appearance : CONCEIT **4** : a small case for cosmetics : COMPACT

vanity plate *n* : an automobile license plate bearing distinctive letters or numbers designated by the owner

van·quish \ˈvaŋ-kwish, ˈvan-\ *vb* **1** : to overcome in battle or in a contest **2** : to gain mastery over (as an emotion)

van·tage \ˈvant-ij\ *n* **1** : superiority in a contest **2** : a position giving a strategic advantage or a commanding perspective

van·ward \ˈvan-wərd\ *adj* : being in or toward the vanguard : ADVANCED — **vanward** *adv*

va·pid \ˈvap-əd, ˈvā-pəd\ *adj* : lacking spirit, liveliness, or zest : FLAT, INSIPID — **va·pid·i·ty** \va-ˈpid-ət-ē\ *n* — **vap·id·ly** \ˈvap-əd-lē\ *adv* — **vap·id·ness** *n*

¹**va·por** \ˈvā-pər\ *n* **1** : fine separated particles (as fog or smoke) floating in the air and clouding it **2** : a substance in the gaseous state; *esp* : one that is liquid under ordinary conditions **3** : something insubstantial or fleeting **4** *pl* : a depressed or hysterical nervous condition

²**vapor** *vb* **1** : to rise or pass off in vapor **2** : to emit vapor

va·por·ing \ˈvā-p(ə-)riŋ\ *n* : an idle, boastful, or high-flown expression or speech — usu. used in pl.

va·por·ish \ˈvā-p(ə-)rish\ *adj* **1** : resembling or suggestive of vapor **2** : given to fits of depression or hysteria — **va·por·ish·ness** *n*

va·por·ize \ˈvā-pə-ˌrīz\ *vb* **-ized; -iz·ing** : to convert into vapor — **va·por·iza·tion** \ˌvā-pə-rə-ˈzā-shən\ *n*

va·por·iz·er \-ˌrī-zər\ *n* : a device that vaporizes something (as a medicated liquid)

vapor lock *n* : a partial or complete interruption of flow of a fluid (as fuel in an internal-combustion engine) caused by the formation of bubbles of vapor in the feeding system

va·por·ous \'vā-p(ə-)rəs\ *adj* 1 : consisting of or characteristic of vapor 2 : producing vapors : VOLATILE 3 : full of vapors : FOGGY, MISTY — **va·por·ous·ly** *adv* — **va·por·ous·ness** *n*

va·pory \'vā-p(ə-)rē\ *adj* : VAPOROUS, VAGUE

va·que·ro \vä-'ker-ō\ *n, pl* -ros [Sp, fr. *vaca* cow, fr. L *vacca*] : a ranch hand : COWBOY

var *abbr* 1 variable 2 variant; variation 3 variety 4 various

¹**vari·able** \'ver-ē-ə-bəl\ *adj* 1 : able or apt to vary : CHANGEABLE 2 : FICKLE 3 : not true to type : ABERRANT ⟨a ∼ wheat⟩ — **vari·abil·i·ty** \ˌver-ē-ə-'bil-ət-ē\ *n* — **vari·able·ness** \'ver-ē-ə-bəl-nəs\ *n* — **vari·ably** \-blē\ *adv*

²**variable** *n* 1 : something that is variable 2 : a quantity that may assume a succession of values; *also* : a symbol standing for any one of a class of things

vari·ance \'ver-ē-əns\ *n* 1 : variation or a degree of variation : DEVIATION 2 : DISAGREEMENT, DISPUTE 3 : a license to do something contrary to the usual rule ⟨a zoning ∼⟩ **syn** discord, contention, dissension, strife, conflict

¹**vari·ant** \'ver-ē-ənt\ *adj* 1 : differing from others of its kind or class 2 : varying usu. slightly from the standard or type

²**variant** *n* 1 : one that exhibits variation from a type or norm 2 : one of two or more different spellings or pronunciations of a word

vari·a·tion \ˌver-ē-'ā-shən\ *n* 1 : an act or instance of varying : a change in form, position, or condition : MODIFICATION, ALTERATION 2 : extent of change or difference 3 : divergence in qualities from those typical or usual to a group; *also* : one exhibiting such variation 4 : repetition of a musical theme with modifications in rhythm, tune, harmony, or key

vari·col·ored \'ver-i-ˌkəl-ərd\ *adj* : having various colors : VARIEGATED

var·i·cose \'var-ə-ˌkōs\ *adj* : abnormally and irregularly swollen ⟨∼ veins⟩

var·i·cos·i·ty \ˌvar-ə-'käs-ət-ē\ *n, pl* -ties 1 : the quality or state of being vari-

cose 2 : a varicose part or lesion (as of a vein)

var·ied \'ver-ēd\ *adj* 1 : having many forms or types : DIVERSE 2 : VARIEGATED — **var·ied·ly** *adv*

var·ie·gate \'ver-ē-ə-ˌgāt, 'ver-i-ˌgāt\ *vb* -gat·ed; -gat·ing 1 : to diversify in external appearance esp. with different colors 2 : to introduce variety into : DIVERSIFY — **var·ie·gat·ed** *adj* — **var·ie·ga·tion** \ˌver-ē-ə-'gā-shən, ˌver-i-'gā-\ *n*

va·ri·etal \və-'rī-ət-ᵊl\ *adj* : of or relating to a variety; *also* : being a variety rather than an individual or species

va·ri·ety \və-'rī-ət-ē\ *n, pl* -et·ies 1 : the state of being varied or various : DIVERSITY 2 : a collection of different things 3 : something varying from other things of the same general kind 4 : any of various groups of plants or animals within a species distinguished by characteristics not constant enough or too unimportant to separate species 5 : entertainment such as is given in a stage presentation comprising a series of performances (as songs, dances, or acrobatic acts)

var·i·o·rum \ˌver-ē-'ōr-əm\ *n* : an edition or text of a work containing notes by various persons or variant readings of the text

var·i·ous \'ver-ē-əs\ *adj* 1 : VARICOLORED 2 : of differing kinds : MULTIFARIOUS 3 : UNLIKE ⟨animals as ∼ as the jaguar and the sloth⟩ 4 : having a number of different aspects 5 : NUMEROUS, MANY 6 : INDIVIDUAL, SEPARATE **syn** divergent, disparate, different, dissimilar, diverse, unalike — **var·i·ous·ly** *adv*

va·ris·tor \va-'ris-tər\ *n* : a voltage-dependent electrical resistor

var·let \'vär-lət\ *n* [ME, fr. MF *vaslet, varlet* young nobleman, page] 1 : ATTENDANT 2 : SCOUNDREL, KNAVE

var·mint \'vär-mənt\ *n* [alter. of *vermin*] 1 : an animal considered a pest; *esp* : a mammal or bird classed as vermin and unprotected by game law 2 : a contemptible person : RASCAL

¹**var·nish** \'vär-nish\ *n* 1 : a liquid preparation that is spread on a surface and dries into a hard glossy coating; *also* : the glaze of this coating 2 : some-

thing suggesting varnish by its gloss **3** : outside show : GLOSS

²varnish *vb* **1** : to cover with varnish **2** : to cover or conceal with something that gives a fair appearance : gloss over

var·si·ty \\'vär-sət-ē, -stē\\ *n, pl* **-ties** [by shortening & alter. fr. *university*] **1** *Brit* : UNIVERSITY **2** : the principal team representing a college, school, or club

vary \\'ver-ē\\ *vb* **var·ied; vary·ing 1** : ALTER, CHANGE **2** : to make or be of different kinds : introduce or have variety : DIVERSIFY, DIFFER **3** : DEVIATE, SWERVE **4** : to diverge structurally or physiologically from typical members of a group

vas·cu·lar \\'vas-kyə-lər\\ *adj* [NL *vascularis,* fr. L *vasculum* small vessel, dim. of *vas* vase, vessel] : of or relating to a channel or system of channels for the conveyance of a body fluid (as blood or sap); *also* : supplied with or containing such vessels and esp. blood vessels

vascular plant *n* : a plant having a specialized conducting system that includes xylem and phloem

vase \\'vās, 'vāz\\ *n* : a usu. round vessel of greater depth than width used chiefly for ornament or for flowers

va·sec·to·my \\və-'sek-tə-mē, vā-'zek-\\ *n, pl* **-mies** : surgical excision of all or part of the sperm-carrying ducts of the testis usu. to induce permanent sterility

va·so·con·stric·tion \\,vas-ō-kən-'strik-shən, ,vāz-\\ *n* : narrowing of the interior diameter of blood vessels

va·so·con·stric·tor \\-tər\\ *n* : an agent (as a nerve fiber or a drug) that initiates or induces vasoconstriction

vas·sal \\'vas-əl\\ *n* **1** : a person under the protection of a feudal lord to whom he owes homage and loyalty : a feudal tenant **2** : one occupying a dependent or subordinate position — **vassal** *adj*

vas·sal·age \\-ə-lij\\ *n* **1** : the state of being a vassal **2** : the homage and loyalty due from a vassal **3** : SERVITUDE, SUBJECTION

¹vast \\'vast\\ *adj* : very great in size, amount, degree, intensity, or esp. extent **syn** enormous, huge, gigantic,

colossal, mammoth — **vast·ly** *adv* — **vast·ness** *n*

²vast *n* : a great expanse : IMMENSITY

vasty \\'vas-tē\\ *adj* : VAST, IMMENSE

vat \\'vat\\ *n* : a large vessel (as a tub or barrel) esp. for holding liquids in manufacturing processes

VAT *abbr* value-added tax

vat·ic \\'vat-ik\\ *adj* : PROPHETIC, ORACULAR

Vat·i·can \\'vat-i-kən\\ *n* **1** : the papal headquarters in Rome **2** : the papal government

va·tu \\'vä-,tü\\ *n, pl* **vatu** — see MONEY table

vaude·ville \\'vȯd-(ə-)vəl, 'väd-, 'vōd-, -(ə-),vil\\ *n* [F, fr. MF, popular satirical song, alter. of *vaudevire,* fr. *vau= de-Vire* valley of Vire, fr. *Vire,* town in northwest France where such songs were composed] : a stage entertainment consisting of unrelated acts (as of acrobats, comedians, dancers, or singers)

¹vault \\'vȯlt\\ *n* **1** : an arched masonry structure usu. forming a ceiling or roof; *also* : something (as the sky) resembling a vault **2** : a room or space covered by a vault esp. when underground and used for a special purpose (as for storage of valuables or wine supplies) **3** : a burial chamber; *also* : a usu. metal or concrete case in which a casket is enclosed at burial — **vaulty** *adj*

²vault *vb* : to form or cover with a vault

³vault *vb* : to leap vigorously esp. by aid of the hands or a pole — **vault·er** *n*

⁴vault *n* : an act of vaulting : LEAP

vault·ed \\'vȯl-təd\\ *adj* **1** : built in the form of a vault : ARCHED **2** : covered with a vault

vault·ing \\-tiŋ\\ *adj* : leaping upward : reaching for the heights ⟨~ ambition⟩

vaunt \\'vȯnt\\ *vb* [ME *vaunten,* fr. MF *vanter,* fr. LL *vanitare,* fr. L *vanitas* vanity] : BRAG, BOAST — **vaunt** *n*

vb *abbr* verb

VCR \\'vē-'sē-'är\\ *n* [*v*ideocassette *r*ecorder] : a videotape recorder that uses videocassettes

VD *abbr* venereal disease

veal \\'vēl\\ *n* : the flesh of a young calf

vec·tor \\'vek-tər\\ *n* **1** : a quantity that has magnitude and direction **2** : an organism (as a fly) that transmits disease germs

Ve·da \\ˈvād-ə\ *n* [Skt, lit., knowledge] : any of a class of Hindu sacred writings — **Ve·dic** \\ˈvād-ik\ *adj*

Ve·dan·ta \vā-ˈdänt-ə, və-, -ˈdant-\ *n* : an orthodox Hindu philosophy based on the Upanishads

veep \\ˈvēp\ *n* : VICE PRESIDENT

veer \\ˈviər\ *vb* : to shift from one direction or course to another **syn** turn, avert, deflect, divert — **veer** *n*

vee·ry \\ˈvi(ə)r-ē\ *n, pl* **veeries** : a tawny brown thrush of the woods of the eastern U.S.

veg·an \\ˈvej-ən, ˈvē-gən\ *n* : a strict vegetarian; *esp* : one who consumes no animal food or dairy products — **veg·an·ism** \\ˈvej-ə-ˌniz-əm, ˈvē-gə-\ *n*

¹**veg·e·ta·ble** \\ˈvej-(ə-)tə-bəl\ *adj* [ME, fr. ML *vegetabilis* vegetative, fr. *vegetare* to grow, fr. L, to animate, fr. *vegetus* lively, fr. *vegēre* to rouse, excite] **1** : of, relating to, or growing like plants **2** : made or obtained from plants ⟨∼ oils⟩ ⟨the ∼ kingdom⟩ **3** : suggesting that of a plant ⟨a ∼ existence⟩

²**vegetable** *n* **1** : PLANT 1 **2** : a usu. herbaceous plant grown for an edible part that is usu. eaten with the principal course of a meal; *also* : such an edible part

veg·e·tal \\ˈvej-ət-ᵊl\ *adj* **1** : VEGETABLE **2** : VEGETATIVE

veg·e·tar·i·an \ˌvej-ə-ˈter-ē-ən\ *n* : one that believes in or practices living solely on plant products — **vegetarian** *adj* — **veg·e·tar·i·an·ism** \-ē-ə-ˌniz-əm\ *n*

veg·e·tate \\ˈvej-ə-ˌtāt\ *vb* **-tat·ed; -tat·ing** : to grow in the manner of a plant; *esp* : to lead a dull inert life

veg·e·ta·tion \ˌvej-ə-ˈtā-shən\ *n* **1** : the act or process of vegetating; *also* : a dull inert existence **2** : plant life or cover (as of an area) — **veg·e·ta·tion·al** \-sh(ə-)nəl\ *adj*

veg·e·ta·tive \\ˈvej-ə-ˌtāt-iv\ *adj* **1** : of or relating to nutrition and growth esp. as contrasted with reproduction **2** : of, relating to, or composed of vegetation **3** : leading or marked by a passive, stupid, and dull existence

ve·he·mence \\ˈvē-ə-məns\ *n* : the quali-

ty or state of being vehement : INTENSITY, VIOLENCE

ve·he·ment \-mənt\ *adj* **1** : marked by great force or energy **2** : marked by strong feeling or expression : PASSIONATE **3** : strong in effect : INTENSE — **ve·he·ment·ly** *adv*

ve·hi·cle \\ˈvē-ˌ(h)ik-əl, ˈvē-ə-kəl\ *n* **1** : a medium by which a thing is applied or administered ⟨linseed oil is a ∼ for pigments⟩ **2** : a medium through or by means of which something is conveyed or expressed **3** : a means of carrying or transporting something : CONVEYANCE **syn** means, instrument, agent, agency, organ, channel — **ve·hic·u·lar** \vē-ˈhik-yə-lər\ *adj*

¹**veil** \\ˈvāl\ *n* **1** : a piece of often sheer or diaphanous material used to screen or curtain something or to cover the head or face **2** : the state accepted when a woman becomes a nun ⟨take the ∼⟩ **3** : something that hides or obscures like a veil

²**veil** *vb* : to cover with or as if with a veil : wear a veil

veil·ing \\ˈvā-liŋ\ *n* **1** : VEIL **2** : any of various sheer fabrics (as net or chiffon)

¹**vein** \\ˈvān\ *n* **1** : a fissure in rock filled with mineral matter; *also* : a bed of useful mineral matter **2** : one of the tubular branching vessels that carry blood from the capillaries toward the heart **3** : one of the vascular bundles forming the framework of a leaf **4** : one of the thickened ribs that stiffen the wings of an insect **5** : something (as a wavy variegation in marble) suggesting veins **6** : a distinctive mode of expression : STYLE **7** : something of distinctive character considered as running through something else : STRAIN **8** : MOOD, HUMOR — **veined** \\ˈvānd\ *adj*

²**vein** *vb* : to form or mark with or as if with veins — **vein·ing** *n*

vel *abbr* velocity

ve·lar \\ˈvē-lər\ *adj* : of or relating to a velum and esp. that of the soft palate

veld *or* **veldt** \\ˈvelt, ˈfelt\ *n* [Afrikaans *veld*, fr. Middle Dutch, field] : open grassland esp. in Africa usu. with scattered shrubs or trees

vel·lum \\ˈvel-əm\ *n* [ME *velim*, fr. MF *veelin*, fr. *veelin*, adj., of a calf, fr.

veel calf] **1** : a fine-grained lambskin, kidskin, or calfskin prepared for writing on or for binding books **2** : a paper manufactured to resemble vellum — **vellum** *adj*

ve·loc·i·pede \və-'läs-ə-ˌpēd\ *n* : an early bicycle

ve·loc·i·ty \və-'läs-(ə-)tē\ *n, pl* **-ties** : quickness of motion : SPEED ⟨the ∼ of light⟩

ve·lour *or* **ve·lours** \və-'lu̇r\ *n, pl* **velours** \-'lu̇rz\ : any of various textile fabrics with pile like that of velvet

ve·lum \'vē-ləm\ *n, pl* **ve·la** \-lə\ : a membranous partition (as the soft palate) resembling a veil

¹vel·vet \'vel-vət\ *n* [ME *veluet, velvet,* fr. MF *velu* shaggy, fr. L *villus* shaggy hair] **1** : a fabric characterized by a short soft dense warp pile **2** : something resembling or suggesting velvet (as in softness or luster) **3** : soft skin covering the growing antlers of deer **4** : the winnings of a player in a gambling game — **velvety** *adj*

²velvet *adj* **1** : made of or covered with velvet **2** : resembling or suggesting velvet : SMOOTH, SOFT, SLEEK

vel·ve·teen \ˌvel-və-'tēn\ *n* **1** : a fabric woven usu. of cotton in imitation of velvet **2** *pl* : clothes made of velveteen

Ven *abbr* venerable

ve·nal \'vēn-ᵊl\ *adj* : capable of being bought esp. by underhanded means : MERCENARY, CORRUPT — **ve·nal·i·ty** \vi-'nal-ət-ē\ *n* — **ve·nal·ly** \'vēn-ᵊl-ē\ *adv*

ve·na·tion \ve-'nā-shən, vē-\ *n* : an arrangement or system of veins ⟨the ∼ of the hand⟩ ⟨leaf ∼⟩

vend \'vend\ *vb* : SELL; *esp* : to sell as a hawker or peddler — **vend·ible** *adj*

vend·ee \ven-'dē\ *n* : one to whom a thing is sold : BUYER

vend·er \'ven-dər\ *n* : VENDOR

ven·det·ta \ven-'det-ə\ *n* : a feud between clans or families

vending machine *n* : a coin-operated machine for vending merchandise

ven·dor \'ven-dər, *for 1 also* ven-'do̩r\ *n* **1** : one that vends : SELLER **2** : VENDING MACHINE

¹ve·neer \və-'niər\ *n* [G *furnier,* fr. *furnieren* to veneer, fr. F *fournir* to furnish] **1** : a thin usu. superficial layer of material ⟨brick ∼⟩; *esp* : a thin layer of fine wood glued over a cheaper wood **2** : superficial display : GLOSS

²veneer *vb* : to overlay with a veneer

ven·er·a·ble \'ven-ər-(ə-)bəl, 'ven-rə-bəl\ *adj* **1** : deserving to be venerated — often used as a religious title **2** : made sacred by association

ven·er·ate \'ven-ə-ˌrāt\ *vb* **-at·ed; -at·ing** : to regard with reverential respect **syn** adore, revere, reverence, worship — **ven·er·a·tion** \ˌven-ə-'rā-shən\ *n*

ve·ne·re·al \və-'nir-ē-əl\ *adj* : of or relating to sexual intercourse or to diseases transmitted by it ⟨a ∼ infection⟩

venereal disease *n* : a contagious disease (as gonorrhea or syphilis) that is usu. acquired by having sexual intercourse with someone who already has it

ve·ne·tian blind \və-ˌnē-shən-\ *n* : a blind having thin horizontal parallel slats that can be adjusted to admit a desired amount of light

Ven·e·zue·lan \ˌven-əz-'wā-lən\ *n* : a native or inhabitant of Venezuela — **Venezuelan** *adj*

ven·geance \'ven-jəns\ *n* : punishment inflicted in retaliation for an injury or offense : RETRIBUTION

venge·ful \'venj-fəl\ *adj* : filled with a desire for revenge : VINDICTIVE — **venge·ful·ly** \-ē\ *adv*

ve·nial \'vē-nē-əl, -nyəl\ *adj* : capable of being forgiven : EXCUSABLE ⟨∼ sin⟩

ven·i·punc·ture \'vēn-ə-ˌpəŋk-chər, 'ven-ə-\ *n* : surgical puncture of a vein esp. for withdrawal of blood or for intravenous medication

ve·ni·re \və-'nī-rē\ *n* : a panel from which a jury is drawn

ve·ni·re fa·ci·as \-'fā-shē-əs\ *n* [ME, fr. ML, you should cause to come] : a writ summoning persons to appear in court to serve as jurors

ve·ni·re·man \və-'nī-rē-mən, -'nir-ē-\ *n* : a member of a venire

ven·i·son \'ven-ə-sən, -ə-zən\ *n, pl* **venisons** *also* **venison** [ME, fr. OF *veneison* hunting, game, fr. L *venatio,* fr. *venari* to hunt, pursue] : the edible flesh of a deer

ven·om \'ven-əm\ *n* [ME *venim, venom,* fr. OF *venim,* deriv. of L *venenum* magic charm, drug, poison] **1** : poisonous material secreted by some animals (as snakes, spiders, or bees) and transmitted usu. by biting or stinging **2** : something that poisons or embitters the mind or spirit : MALIGNITY, MALICE

ven·om·ous \\'ven-ə-məs\ *adj* **1** : full of venom : POISONOUS **2** : MALIGNANT, SPITEFUL, MALICIOUS **3** : secreting and using venom ⟨∼ snakes⟩ — **ven·om·ous·ly** *adv*

ve·nous \\'vē-nəs\ *adj* **1** : of, relating to, or full of veins **2** : being purplish red oxygen-deficient blood present in most veins

¹vent \\'vent\ *vb* **1** : to provide with a vent **2** : to serve as a vent for **3** : EXPEL, DISCHARGE **4** : to give expression to

²vent *n* **1** : an opportunity or way of escape or passage : OUTLET **2** : an opening for passage or escape (as of a fluid, gas, or smoke) or for relieving pressure

³vent *n* : a slit in a garment esp. in the lower part of a seam (as of a jacket or skirt)

ven·ti·late \\'vent-ᵊl-ˌāt\ *vb* **-lat·ed; -lat·ing** **1** : to discuss freely and openly ⟨∼ a question⟩ **2** : to give vent to ⟨∼ one's grievances⟩ **3** : to cause fresh air to circulate through (as a room or mine) so as to replace foul air **4** : to provide with a vent or outlet **syn** express, vent, air, utter, voice, broach — **ven·ti·la·tor** \-ᵊl-ˌāt-ər\ *n*

ven·ti·la·tion \ˌvent-ᵊl-'ā-shən\ *n* **1** : the act or process of ventilating **2** : circulation of air (as in a room) **3** : a system or means of providing fresh air

ven·tral \\'ven-trəl\ *adj* **1** : of or relating to the belly : ABDOMINAL **2** : of, relating to, or located on or near the surface of the body that in humans is the front but in most other animals is the lower surface — **ven·tral·ly** \-ē\ *adv*

ven·tri·cle \\'ven-tri-kəl\ *n* **1** : a chamber of the heart that receives blood from the atrium of the same side and pumps it into the arteries **2** : any of the communicating cavities of the brain that are continuous with the central canal of the spinal cord

ven·tril·o·quism \ven-'tril-ə-ˌkwiz-əm\ *n* [LL *ventriloquus* ventriloquist, fr. L *venter* belly + *loqui* to speak; fr. the belief that the voice is produced from

the ventriloquist's stomach] : the production of the voice in such a manner that the sound appears to come from a source other than the speaker — **ven·tril·o·quist** \-kwəst\ *n*

ven·tril·o·quy \-kwē\ *n* : VENTRILOQUISM

¹ven·ture \\'ven-chər\ *vb* **ven·tured; ven·tur·ing** \\'vench-(ə-)riŋ\ **1** : to expose to hazard : RISK **2** : to undertake the risks of : BRAVE **3** : to advance or put forward or expose to criticism or argument ⟨∼ an opinion⟩ **4** : to make a venure : run a risk : proceed despite danger : DARE

²venture *n* **1** : an undertaking involving chance or risk; *esp* : a speculative business enterprise **2** : something risked in a speculative venture : STAKE

ven·ture·some \\'ven-chər-səm\ *adj* **1** : involving risk : DANGEROUS, HAZARDOUS **2** : inclined to venture : BOLD, DARING **syn** adventurous, venturous, rash, reckless, foolhardy — **ven·ture·some·ly** *adv* — **ven·ture·some·ness** *n*

ven·tur·ous \\'vench-(ə-)rəs\ *adj* : VENTURESOME — **ven·tur·ous·ly** *adv* — **ven·tur·ous·ness** *n*

ven·ue \\'ven-yü\ *n* : the place in which the alleged events from which a legal action arises took place; *also* : the place from which the jury is taken and where the trial is held

Ve·nus \\'vē-nəs\ *n* : the planet second in order from the sun

Ve·nu·sian \vi-'n(y)ü-zhən\ *adj* : of or relating to the planet Venus

Ve·nus's–fly·trap \ˌvē-nəs(-əz)-'flī-ˌtrap\ *or* **Venus fly·trap** *n* : an insectivorous plant of the Carolina coast that has the leaf tip modified into an insect trap

ve·ra·cious \və-'rā-shəs\ *adj* **1** : TRUTHFUL, HONEST **2** : TRUE, ACCURATE — **ve·ra·cious·ly** *adv*

ve·rac·i·ty \və-'ras-ət-ē\ *n, pl* **-ties** **1** : devotion to truth : TRUTHFULNESS **2** : conformity with fact : ACCURACY **3** : something true

ve·ran·da *or* **ve·ran·dah** \və-'ran-də\ *n* : a long open usu. roofed porch

verb \\'vərb\ *n* : a word that is the grammatical center of a predicate and expresses an act, occurrence, or mode of being

¹ver·bal \\'vər-bəl\ *adj* **1** : of, relating to, or consisting of words; *esp* : having to do with words rather than with the ideas to be conveyed **2** : expressed in usu. spoken words : not written : ORAL ⟨a ∼ contract⟩ **3** : of, relating to, or formed from a verb **4** : LITERAL, VERBATIM — **ver·bal·ly** \-ē\ *adv*

²**verbal** *n* : a word that combines characteristics of a verb with those of a noun or adjective

verbal auxiliary *n* : an auxiliary verb

ver·bal·ize \ˈvər-bə-ˌlīz\ *vb* **-ized; -iz·ing 1** : to speak or write in wordy or empty fashion **2** : to express something in words : describe verbally **3** : to convert into a verb — **ver·bal·iza·tion** \ˌvər-bə-lə-ˈzā-shən\ *n*

verbal noun *n* : a noun derived directly from a verb or verb stem and in some uses having the sense and constructions of a verb

ver·ba·tim \(ˌ)vər-ˈbāt-əm\ *adv or adj* : in the same words : word for word

ver·be·na \(ˌ)vər-ˈbē-nə\ *n* : VERVAIN; *esp* : any of several garden plants with showy spikes of bright often fragrant flowers

ver·biage \ˈvər-bē-ij\ *n* **1** : superfluity of words or words with little meaning : WORDINESS **2** : DICTION, WORDING

ver·bose \(ˌ)vər-ˈbōs\ *adj* : using more words than are needed : WORDY **syn** prolix, diffuse, redundant, windy — **ver·bos·i·ty** \-ˈbäs-ət-ē\ *n*

ver·bo·ten \vər-ˈbōt-ᵊn\ *adj* [G] : forbidden usu. by authority and often unreasonably

ver·dant \ˈvərd-ᵊnt\ *adj* **1** : green with growing plants **2** : unripe in experience : GREEN — **ver·dant·ly** *adv*

ver·dict \ˈvər-(ˌ)dikt\ *n* [alter. of ME *verdit,* fr. Anglo-French (the French of medieval England), fr. OF *ver* true (fr. L *verus*) + *dit* saying, dictum, fr. L *dictum,* fr. *dicere* to say] **1** : the finding or decision of a jury on the matter submitted to it in trial **2** : DECISION, JUDGMENT

ver·di·gris \ˈvərd-ə-ˌgrēs, -ˌgris\ *n* : a green or bluish deposit that forms on copper, brass, or bronze surfaces when exposed to the weather

ver·dure \ˈvər-jər\ *n* : the greenness of growing vegetation; *also* : green vegetation

¹**verge** \ˈvərj\ *n* **1** : a staff carried as an emblem of authority or office **2**

: something that borders or bounds : EDGE, MARGIN **3** : BRINK, THRESHOLD

²**verge** *vb* **verged; verg·ing 1** : to be contiguous **2** : to be on the verge or border

³**verge** *vb* **verged; verg·ing 1** : to move or extend in some direction or toward some condition : INCLINE **2** : to be in transition or change

verg·er \ˈvər-jər\ *n* **1** *chiefly Brit* : an attendant who carries a verge (as before a bishop) **2** : SEXTON

ve·rid·i·cal \və-ˈrid-i-kəl\ *adj* **1** : TRUTHFUL **2** : not illusory : GENUINE

ver·i·fy \ˈver-ə-ˌfī\ *vb* **-fied; -fy·ing 1** : to confirm in law by oath **2** : to establish the truth, accuracy, or reality of **syn** authenticate, confirm, corroborate, substantiate, validate — **ver·i·fi·able** *adj* — **ver·i·fi·ca·tion** \ˌver-ə-fə-ˈkā-shən\ *n*

ver·i·ly \ˈver-ə-lē\ *adv* **1** : in very truth : CERTAINLY **2** : TRULY, CONFIDENTLY

veri·si·mil·i·tude \ˌver-ə-sə-ˈmil-ə-ˌt(y)üd\ *n* : the quality or state of appearing to be true : PROBABILITY; *also* : a statement that is apparently true **syn** plausibility

ver·i·ta·ble \ˈver-ət-ə-bəl\ *adj* : ACTUAL, GENUINE, TRUE — **ver·i·ta·bly** *adv*

ver·i·ty \ˈver-ət-ē\ *n, pl* **-ties 1** : the quality or state of being true or real : TRUTH, REALITY **2** : something (as a statement) that is true **3** : HONESTY, VERACITY

ver·meil *n* [MF] **1** \ˈvər-məl, -ˌmāl\ : VERMILION **2** \ver-ˈmā\ : gilded silver

ver·mi·cel·li \ˌvər-mə-ˈchel-ē, -ˈsel-\ *n* [It, lit., little worms] : a dough made in long solid strings smaller in diameter than spaghetti

ver·mic·u·lite \vər-ˈmik-yə-ˌlīt\ *n* : any of various minerals that result usu. from the expansion of mica granules at high temperatures to give a lightweight highly water-absorbent material

ver·mi·form appendix \ˈvər-mə-ˌform-\ *n* : APPENDIX 2

ver·mi·fuge \ˈvər-mə-ˌfyüj\ *n* : a medicine for destroying or expelling intestinal worms

ver·mil·ion *also* **ver·mil·lion** \vər-ˈmil-yən\ *n* : any of a number of very bright red colors not quite as bright as scarlet; *also* : a pigment yielding one of these colors

ver·min \\'vər-mən\ *n, pl* **vermin** [ME, fr. MF, deriv. of L *vermis* worm] : small common harmful or disgusting animals (as lice or mice) that are difficult to get rid of — **ver·min·ous** *adj*

ver·mouth \vər-'müth\ *n* [F *vermout,* fr. G *wermut* wormwood] : a white wine flavored with herbs and often used in combination with other beverages

¹**ver·nac·u·lar** \və(r)-'nak-yə-lər\ *adj* [L *vernaculus* native, fr. *verna* slave born in his master's house] **1** : of, relating to, or being a language or dialect native to a region or country rather than a literary, cultured, or foreign language **2** : of, relating to, or being the normal spoken form of a language **3** : applied to a plant or animal in common speech as distinguished from biological nomenclature ⟨~ names⟩

²**vernacular** *n* **1** : a vernacular language **2** : the mode of expression of a group or class **3** : a vernacular name of a plant or animal

ver·nal \\'vərn-ᵊl\ *adj* : of, relating to, or occurring in the spring

ver·nal·iza·tion \,vərn-ᵊl-ə-'zā-shən\ *n* : the act or process of hastening the flowering and fruiting of plants by treating seeds, bulbs, or seedlings so as to shorten the vegetative period — **ver·nal·ize** \\'vərn-ᵊl-,īz\ *vb*

ver·ni·er \\'vər-nē-ər\ *n* : a short scale made to slide along the divisions of a graduated instrument to indicate parts of divisions

ve·ron·i·ca \və-'rän-i-kə\ *n* : SPEEDWELL

ver·sa·tile \\'vər-sət-ᵊl\ *adj* : turning with ease from one thing or position to another; *esp* : having many aptitudes — **ver·sa·til·i·ty** \,vər-sə-'til-ət-ē\ *n*

verse \\'vərs\ *n* **1** : a line of poetry; *also* : STANZA **2** : metrical writing distinguished from poetry esp. by its lower level of intensity **3** : POETRY **4** : POEM **5** : one of the short divisions of a chapter in the Bible

versed \vərst\ *adj* : familiar from experience, study, or practice : SKILLED

ver·si·cle \\'vər-si-kəl\ *n* : a verse or sentence said or sung by a clergyman and followed by a response from the people

ver·si·fi·ca·tion \,vər-sə-fə-'kā-shən\ *n*

1 : the making of verses **2** : metrical structure

ver·si·fy \\'vər-sə-,fī\ *vb* **-fied; -fy·ing 1** : to write verse **2** : to turn into verse — **ver·si·fi·er** \-,fī(-ə)r\ *n*

ver·sion \\'vər-zhən\ *n* **1** : TRANSLATION; *esp* : a translation of the Bible **2** : an account or description from a particular point of view esp. as contrasted with another **3** : a form or variant of a type or original

vers li·bre \,ver-'lēbrᵉ\ *n, pl* **vers li·bres** *same*\ [F] : FREE VERSE

ver·so \\'vər-sō\ *n, pl* **versos** : a left-hand page

ver·sus \\'vər-səs\ *prep* **1** : AGAINST **2** ⟨the champion ~ the challenger⟩ **2** : in contrast or as an alternative to ⟨free trade ~ protection⟩

vert *abbr* vertical

ver·te·bra \\'vərt-ə-brə\ *n, pl* **-brae** \-,brā, -(,)brē\ *or* **-bras** [L] : one of the segments of bone or cartilage making up the backbone

ver·te·bral \(,)vər-'tē-brəl, 'vərt-ə-\ *adj* : of, relating to, or made up of vertebrae : SPINAL

vertebral column *n* : BACKBONE

¹**ver·te·brate** \\'vərt-ə-brət, -,brāt\ *adj* **1** : having a backbone **2** : of or relating to the vertebrates

²**vertebrate** *n* : any of a large group of animals (as mammals, birds, reptiles, amphibians, or fishes) that have a backbone or in some primitive forms a flexible rod of cells and that have a tubular nervous system arranged along the back and divided into a brain and spinal cord

ver·tex \\'vər-,teks\ *n, pl* **ver·ti·ces** \\'vərt-ə-,sēz\ *also* **ver·tex·es** [L *vertex, vortex* whirl, whirlpool, top of the head, summit, fr. *vertere* to turn] **1** : the point opposite to and farthest from the base of a geometrical figure **2** : the termination or intersection of lines or curves ⟨the ~ of an angle⟩ **3** : ZENITH 1 **4** : the highest point : TOP, SUMMIT

ver·ti·cal \\'vərt-i-kəl\ *adj* **1** : of, relating to, or located at the vertex : directly overhead **2** : rising perpendicularly from a level surface : UPRIGHT — **vertical** *n* — **ver·ti·cal·i·ty** \,vərt-ə-'kal-ət-ē\ *n* — **ver·ti·cal·ly** \-k(ə-)lē\ *adv*

ver·tig·i·nous \(ˌ)vər-ˈtij-ə-nəs\ *adj* : marked by, suffering from, or tending to cause dizziness

ver·ti·go \ˈvərt-i-ˌgō\ *n, pl* **-goes** *or* **-gos** : DIZZINESS, GIDDINESS

ver·vain \ˈvər-ˌvān\ *n* : any of a genus of herbs or low woody plants with often showy heads or spikes of tubular flowers

verve \ˈvərv\ *n* : liveliness of imagination; *also* : VIVACITY

¹**very** \ˈver-ē\ *adj* **veri·er; -est** [ME *verray, verry,* fr. OF *verai,* fr. L *verax* truthful, fr. *verus* true] **1** : EXACT, PRECISE ⟨the ∼ heart of the city⟩ **2** : exactly suitable ⟨the ∼ tool for the job⟩ **3** : ABSOLUTE, UTTER ⟨the *veriest* nonsense⟩ **4** — used as an intensive esp. to emphasize identity ⟨made the ∼ walls shake⟩ **5** : MERE, BARE ⟨the ∼ idea scared him⟩ **6** : SELFSAME, IDENTICAL ⟨the ∼ man I saw⟩

²**very** *adv* **1** : in actual fact : TRULY **2** : to a high degree : EXTREMELY

very high frequency *n* : a radio frequency of between 30 and 300 megahertz

ves·i·cant \ˈves-i-kənt\ *n* : an agent that causes blistering — **vesicant** *adj*

ves·i·cle \ˈves-i-kəl\ *n* : a membranous and usu. fluid-filled cavity in a plant or animal; *also* : BLISTER — **ve·sic·u·lar** \və-ˈsik-yə-lər\ *adj*

¹**ves·per** \ˈves-pər\ *n* **1** *cap* : EVENING STAR **2** : a vesper bell **3** *archaic* : EVENING, EVENTIDE

²**vesper** *adj* : of or relating to vespers or to the evening

ves·pers \-pərz\ *n pl, often cap* : a late afternoon or evening worship service

ves·per·tine \ˈves-pər-ˌtīn\ *adj* **1** : of, relating to, or taking place in the evening **2** : active, flowering, or flourishing in the evening

ves·sel \ˈves-əl\ *n* **1** : a hollow or concave utensil (as a barrel, bottle, bowl, or cup) for holding something **2** : a person held to be the recipient of a quality (as grace) **3** : a craft bigger than a rowboat for navigation of the water **4** : a tube in which a body fluid (as blood) is contained and circulated

¹**vest** \ˈvest\ *vb* **1** : to place or give into the possession or discretion of some person or authority **2** : to clothe with a particular authority, right, or property **3** : to become legally vested **4** : to clothe with or as if with a garment; *esp* : to garb in ecclesiastical vestments

²**vest** *n* **1** : a man's sleeveless garment for the upper body usu. worn under a suit coat; *also* : a similar garment for women **2** *chiefly Brit* : a man's sleeveless undershirt **3** : a front piece of a dress resembling the front of a vest

¹**ves·tal** \ˈves-t²l\ *adj* : CHASTE — **ves·tal·ly** \-ē\ *adv*

²**vestal** *n* : a chaste woman

vestal virgin *n* : a virgin consecrated to the Roman goddess Vesta and to the service of watching the sacred fire perpetually kept burning on her altar

vest·ed \ˈves-təd\ *adj* : fully and unconditionally guaranteed as a legal right, benefit, or privilege

vested interest *n* : an interest (as in an existing political, economic, or social arrangement) to which the holder has a strong commitment; *also* : one (as a corporation) having a vested interest

ves·ti·bule \ˈves-tə-ˌbyül\ *n* **1** : any of various bodily cavities forming or suggesting an entrance to some other part **2** : a passage or room between the outer door and the interior of a building — **ves·tib·u·lar** \ve-ˈstib-yə-lər\ *adj*

ves·tige \ˈves-tij\ *n* [F, fr. L *vestigium* footprint, track, vestige] : a trace or visible sign left by something lost or vanished; *also* : a minute remaining amount — **ves·ti·gial** \ve-ˈstij-(ē-)əl\ *adj* — **ves·ti·gial·ly** \-ē\ *adv*

vest·ing \ˈves-tiŋ\ *n* : the conveying to an employee of inalienable rights to share in a pension fund; *also* : the right so conveyed

vest·ment \ˈves(t)-mənt\ *n* **1** : an outer garment; *esp* : a ceremonial or official robe **2** *pl* : CLOTHING, GARB **3** : a garment or insignia worn by a clergyman when officiating or assisting at a religious service

vest–pocket *adj* : very small ⟨a ∼ park⟩

ves·try \ˈves-trē\ *n, pl* **vestries 1** : a room in a church for vestments, altar linens, and sacred vessels **2** : a room used for church meetings and classes **3** : a body administering the temporal affairs of an Episcopal parish

ves·try·man \-mən\ *n* : a member of a vestry

ves•ture \'ves-chər\ *n* **1** : a covering garment (as a robe) **2** : CLOTHING, APPAREL

¹vet \'vet\ *n* : VETERINARIAN, VETERINARY

²vet *adj or n* : VETERAN

vetch \'vech\ *n* : any of several herbs related to the pea including some valued for fodder

vet•er•an \'vet-(ə-)rən\ *n* [L *veteranus,* fr. *veteranus* old, of long experience, fr. *veter-, vetus* old] **1** : an old soldier of long service **2** : a former member of the armed forces **3** : a person of long experience in an occupation or skill — **veteran** *adj*

Veterans Day *n* : November 11 observed as a legal holiday in commemoration of the end of hostilities in 1918 and 1945

vet•er•i•nar•i•an \vet-(ə-)rən-'er-ē-ən, ˌvet-ᵊn-\ *n* : one qualified and authorized to treat injuries and diseases of animals

¹vet•er•i•nary \'vet-(ə-)rən-ˌer-ē, 'vet-ᵊn-\ *adj* : of, relating to, or being the medical care of animals and esp. domestic animals

²veterinary *n, pl* **-nar•ies** : VETERINARIAN

¹ve•to \'vēt-ō\ *n, pl* **vetoes** [L, I forbid] **1** : an authoritative prohibition **2** : a power of one part of a government to forbid the carrying out of projects attempted by another part; *esp* : a power vested in a chief executive to prevent the carrying out of measures adopted by a legislature **3** : the exercise of the power of veto; *also* : a document or message stating the reasons for a specific use of this power

²veto *vb* **1** : FORBID, PROHIBIT **2** : to refuse assent to (a legislative bill) so as to prevent enactment or cause reconsideration — **ve•to•er** *n*

vex \'veks\ *vb* **vexed** *also* **vext; vex•ing 1** : to bring trouble, distress, or agitation to **2** : to irritate or annoy by petty provocations **3** : to shake or toss about

vex•a•tion \vek-'sā-shən\ *n* **1** : the act of vexing **2** : the quality or state of being vexed : IRRITATION **3** : a cause of trouble or annoyance

vex•a•tious \-shəs\ *adj* **1** : causing vexation : ANNOYING, DISTRESSING **2** : full of distress or annoyance : TROUBLED

— **vex•a•tious•ly** *adv* — **vex•a•tious•ness** *n*

vexed \'vekst\ *adj* : fully debated or discussed ⟨a ∼ question⟩

VF *abbr* **1** video frequency **2** visual field

VFD *abbr* volunteer fire department

VFW *abbr* Veterans of Foreign Wars

VG *abbr* **1** very good **2** vicar-general

VHF *abbr* very high frequency

VI *abbr* Virgin Islands

via \ˌvī-ə, ˌvē-ə\ *prep* : by way of ⟨goods shipped ∼ the Panama Canal⟩

vi•a•ble \'vī-ə-bəl\ *adj* **1** : capable of living; *esp* : capable of surviving outside the mother's womb without artificial support ⟨a ∼ fetus⟩ **2** : capable of being put into practice : WORKABLE **3** : having a reasonable chance of succeeding ⟨a ∼ candidate⟩ — **vi•a•bil•i•ty** \ˌvī-ə-'bil-ət-ē\ *n* — **vi•a•bly** \'vī-ə-blē\ *adv*

via•duct \'vī-ə-ˌdəkt\ *n* : a bridge with high supporting towers or piers for carrying a road or railroad over something (as a valley, river, or road)

vi•al \'vī(-ə)l\ *n* : a small vessel for liquids

vi•and \'vī-ənd\ *n* : an article of food

vi•at•i•cum \vī-'at-i-kəm, vē-\ *n, pl* **-cums** *or* **-ca** \-kə\ **1** : the Christian Eucharist given to a person in danger of death **2** : an allowance esp. in money for traveling needs and expenses

vibes \'vībz\ *n pl* **1** : VIBRAPHONE **2** : VIBRATIONS

vi•brant \'vī-brənt\ *adj* **1** : VIBRATING, PULSATING **2** : pulsating with vigor or activity **3** : readily set in vibration : RESPONSIVE, SENSITIVE **4** : sounding from vibration — **vi•bran•cy** \-brən-sē\ *n*

vi•bra•phone \'vī-brə-ˌfōn\ *n* : a percussion instrument like the xylophone but with metal bars and motor-driven resonators

vi•brate \'vī-ˌbrāt\ *vb* **vi•brat•ed; vi•brat•ing 1** : OSCILLATE **2** : to set in vibration **3** : to be in vibration **4** : to respond sympathetically : THRILL **5** : WAVER, FLUCTUATE

vi•bra•tion \vī-'brā-shən\ *n* **1** : a rapid to-and-fro motion of the particles of an elastic body or medium (as a stretched cord) that produces sound **2** : an act of vibrating : a state of being vibrated : OSCILLATION **3** : a trembling motion **4** : VACILLATION **5** : a distinctive usu. emotional emanation or atmosphere that can be instinctively sensed — usu. used in pl. — **vi·bra·tion·al** \-sh(ə-)nəl\ *adj*

vi·bra·to \vi-'brät-ō\ *n, pl* **-tos** [It] : a slightly tremulous effect imparted to vocal or instrumental music

vi·bra·tor \'vī-ˌbrāt-ər\ *n* : one that vibrates or causes vibration; *esp* : a vibrating electrical device used in massage or for sexual stimulation

vi·bra·to·ry \'vī-brə-ˌtōr-ē\ *adj* : consisting in, capable of, or causing vibration

vi·bur·num \vī-'bər-nəm\ *n* : any of a genus of widely distributed shrubs or trees related to the honeysuckle and bearing small usu. white flowers in broad clusters

vic *abbr* vicinity

Vic *abbr* Victoria

vic·ar \'vik-ər\ *n* **1** : an administrative deputy **2** : an Anglican clergyman in charge of a dependent parish — **vi·car·i·ate** \vī-'ker-ē-ət\ *n*

vic·ar·age \'vik-ə-rij\ *n* : the benefice or house of a vicar

vicar–general *n, pl* **vicars–general** : an administrative deputy (as of a Roman Catholic or Anglican bishop)

vi·car·i·ous \vī-'ker-ē-əs, -'kar-\ *adj* **1** : acting for another **2** : done or suffered by one person on behalf of another or others ⟨a ~ sacrifice⟩ **3** : realized or experienced by one person through sympathetic sharing in the experience of another — **vi·car·i·ous·ly** *adv* — **vi·car·i·ous·ness** *n*

¹**vice** \'vīs\ *n* **1** : DEPRAVITY, WICKEDNESS **2** : a moral fault; *esp* : an immoral habit **3** : a physical imperfection : BLEMISH **4** : an undesirable behavior pattern in a domestic animal

²**vice** *chiefly Brit var of* VISE

³**vi·ce** \'vī-sē\ *prep* : in the place of : SUCCEEDING

vice admiral *n* : a commissioned officer in the navy or coast guard ranking above a rear admiral

vice·ge·rent \'vīs-'jir-ənt\ *n* : an administrative deputy of a king or magistrate — **vice·ge·ren·cy** \-ən-sē\ *n*

vi·cen·ni·al \vī-'sen-ē-əl\ *adj* : occurring once every 20 years

vice presidency *n* : the office of vice president

vice president *n* **1** : an officer ranking next to a president and usu. empowered to act for the president during an absence or disability **2** : a president's deputy in charge of a particular location or function

vice·re·gal \'vīs-'rē-gəl\ *adj* : of or relating to a viceroy

vice·roy \'vīs-ˌrȯi\ *n* : the governor of a country or province who rules as representative of the sovereign — **vice·roy·al·ty** \-əl-tē\ *n*

vice ver·sa \ˌvī-si-'vər-sə, (')vīs-'vər-\ *adv* : with the order reversed : CONVERSELY

vi·chys·soise \ˌvish-ē-'swäz, ˌvē-shē-\ *n* [F] : a thick soup made esp. from leeks or onions and potatoes, cream, and chicken stock and usu. served cold

Vi·chy water \'vish-ē-\ *n* : carbonated water

vic·i·nage \'vis-ᵊn-ij\ *n* : a neighboring or surrounding district : VICINITY

vi·cin·i·ty \və-'sin-ət-ē\ *n, pl* **-ties** [MF *vicinité,* fr. L *vicinitas,* fr. *vicinus* neighboring, fr. *vicus* row of houses, village] **1** : NEARNESS, PROXIMITY **2** : a surrounding area : NEIGHBORHOOD

vi·cious \'vish-əs\ *adj* **1** : addicted to vice : WICKED, DEPRAVED **2** : DEFECTIVE, FAULTY; *also* : INVALID **3** : IMPURE, FOUL **4** : having a savage disposition **5** : MALICIOUS, SPITEFUL **6** : worsened by internal causes that augment each other ⟨~ wage-price spiral⟩ — **vi·cious·ly** *adv* — **vi·cious·ness** *n*

vi·cis·si·tude \və-'sis-ə-ˌt(y)üd, vī-\ *n* **1** : the quality or state of being changeable **2** : a change or succession from one thing to another; *esp* : an irregular, unexpected, or surprising change

vic·tim \'vik-təm\ *n* **1** : a living being offered as a sacrifice in a religious rite **2** : an individual injured or killed (as by disease or accident) **3** : a person cheated, fooled, or injured ⟨a ~ of circumstances⟩

vic·tim·ize \'vik-tə-ˌmīz\ *vb* **-ized; -iz·ing** : to make a victim of — **vic·tim·iza·tion** \ˌvik-tə-mə-'zā-shən\ *n* — **vic·tim·iz·er** \'vik-tə-ˌmī-zər\ *n*

vic·tim·less *adj* : having no victim ⟨considered gambling to be a ~ crime⟩

vic·tor \ˈvik-tər\ *n* : WINNER, CONQUEROR

vic·to·ria \vik-ˈtōr-ē-ə\ *n* : a low 4-wheeled carriage with a folding top and a raised seat in front for the driver

¹Vic·to·ri·an \vik-ˈtōr-ē-ən\ *adj* **1** : of or relating to the reign of Queen Victoria of England or the art, letters, or tastes of her time **2** : typical of the standards, attitudes, or conduct of the age of Victoria esp. when considered prudish or narrow

²Victorian *n* : a person and esp. an author of the Victorian period

vic·to·ri·ous \vik-ˈtōr-ē-əs\ *adj* **1** : having won a victory : CONQUERING **2** : of, relating to, or characteristic of victory — **vic·to·ri·ous·ly** *adv*

vic·to·ry \ˈvik-t(ə-)rē\ *n, pl* **-ries 1** : the overcoming of an enemy or an antagonist **2** : achievement of mastery or success in a struggle or endeavor against odds

¹vict·ual \ˈvit-ᵊl\ *n* **1** : food usable by man **2** *pl* : food supplies : PROVISIONS

²victual *vb* **-ualed** *or* **-ualled; -ual·ing** *or* **-ual·ling 1** : to supply with food **2** : to store up provisions

vict·ual·ler *or* **vict·ual·er** \ˈvit-ᵊl-ər\ *n* : one that supplies provisions (as to an army or a ship)

vi·cu·ña *or* **vi·cu·na** \vi-ˈkün-yə, vī-; vī-ˈk(y)ü-nə\ *n* **1** : a So. American wild mammal related to the llama and alpaca; *also* : its wool **2** : a soft fabric woven from the wool of the vicuña; *also* : a sheep's wool imitation of this

vi·de \ˈvīd-ē, ˈvē-ˌdā\ *vb imper* [L] : SEE — used to direct a reader to another item

vi·de·li·cet \və-ˈdel-ə-ˌset, vī-; vi-ˈdā-li-ˌket\ *adv* [ME, fr. L, fr. *vidēre* to see + *licet* it is permitted] : that is to say : NAMELY

¹vid·eo \ˈvid-ē-ˌō\ *n* **1** : TELEVISION **2** : VIDEOTAPE

²video *adj* **1** : relating to or used in transmission or reception of the television image **2** : relating to or being images on a television screen or computer display ⟨a ~ terminal⟩

vid·eo·cas·sette \ˈvid-ē-ō-kə-ˌset\ *n* **1** : a case containing videotape for use with a VCR **2** : a recording (as of a movie) on a videocassette

videocassette recorder *n* : VCR

vid·eo·disc *or* **vid·eo·disk** \-ˌdisk\ *n* **1** : a disc similar in appearance and use to a phonograph record on which programs have been recorded for playback on a television set; *also* : OPTICAL DISC **2** : a recording (as of a movie) on a videodisc

video game *n* : an electronic game played on a video screen

vid·eo·phone \ˈvid-ē-ə-ˌfōn\ *n* : a telephone for transmitting both audio and video signals

¹vid·eo·tape \ˈvid-ē-ō-ˌtāp\ *n* : a recording of visual images and sound made on magnetic tape; *also* : the magnetic tape used for such a recording

²videotape *vb* : to make a videotape of ⟨~ a show⟩

videotape recorder *n* : a device for recording and playing back videotapes

vid·eo·tex \-ˌteks\ *also* **vid·eo·text** \-ˌtekst\ *n* : an interactive electronic communications system in which data transmitted by a computer appears on a subscriber's video display

vie \ˈvī\ *vb* **vied; vy·ing** \ˈvī-iŋ\ : to strive for superiority : CONTEND — **vi·er** \ˈvī(-ə)r\ *n*

Viet·cong \vē-ˈet-ˈkäŋ, ˌvē-ət-, -ˈkȯŋ\ *n, pl* **Vietcong** : an adherent of the Vietnamese communist movement

Viet·nam·ese \vē-ˌet-nə-ˈmēz, ˌvē-ət-, -ˈmēs\ *n, pl* **Vietnamese** : a native or inhabitant of Vietnam — **Vietnamese** *adj*

¹view \ˈvyü\ *n* **1** : the act of seeing or examining : INSPECTION; *also* : SURVEY **2** : a way of looking at or regarding something **3** : ESTIMATE, JUDGMENT ⟨stated his ~s⟩ **4** : a sight (as of a landscape) regarded for its pictorial quality **5** : extent or range of vision ⟨within ~⟩ **6** : OBJECT, PURPOSE ⟨done with a ~ to promotion⟩ **7** : a picture of a scene

²view *vb* **1** : to look at attentively : EXAMINE **2** : SEE, BEHOLD **3** : to examine mentally : CONSIDER — **view·er** *n*

view·er·ship \-ˌship\ *n* : a television audience esp. with respect to size or makeup

view·find·er \ˈvyü-ˌfīn-dər\ *n* : a device

on a camera for showing the view to be included in the picture

view·point \-ˌpȯint\ *n* : a position from which something is considered : POINT OF VIEW, STANDPOINT

vi·ges·i·mal \vī-ˈjes-ə-məl\ *adj* : based on the number 20

vig·il \ˈvij-əl\ *n* 1 : a religious observance formerly held on the night before a religious feast 2 : the day before a religious feast observed as a day of spiritual preparation 3 : evening or nocturnal devotions or prayers — usu. used in pl. 4 : an act or a time of keeping awake when sleep is customary; *esp* : WATCH 1

vig·i·lance \ˈvij-ə-ləns\ *n* : the quality or state of being vigilant

vigilance committee *n* : a committee of vigilantes

vig·i·lant \ˈvij-ə-lənt\ *adj* : alertly watchful esp. to avoid danger — **vig·i·lant·ly** *adv*

vig·i·lan·te \ˌvij-ə-ˈlant-ē\ *n* : a member of a volunteer committee organized to suppress and punish crime summarily (as when the processes of law appear inadequate)

¹vi·gnette \vin-ˈyet\ *n* [F, fr. MF *vignete,* fr. dim. of *vigne* vine] 1 : a small decorative design on or just before the title page of a book or at the beginning or end of a chapter 2 : a picture (as an engraving or a photograph) that shades off gradually into the surrounding ground 3 : a short descriptive literary sketch

²vignette *vb* **vi·gnett·ed; vi·gnett·ing** : to finish (as a photograph) in the manner of a vignette

vig·or \ˈvig-ər\ *n* 1 : active strength or energy of body or mind 2 : INTENSITY, FORCE

vig·or·ous \ˈvig-(ə-)rəs\ *adj* 1 : having vigor : ROBUST 2 : done with vigor : carried out forcefully and energetically — **vig·or·ous·ly** *adv* — **vig·or·ous·ness** *n*

Vi·king \ˈvī-kiŋ\ *n* [ON *vīkingr*] : one of the pirate Norsemen plundering the coasts of Europe in the 8th to 10th centuries

vil *abbr* village

vile \ˈvīl\ *adj* **vil·er; vil·est** 1 : morally despicable 2 : physically repulsive : FOUL 3 : of little worth 4 : DEGRAD-

ING, IGNOMINIOUS 5 : utterly bad or inferior ⟨∼ weather⟩ — **vile·ly** \ˈvīl-lē\ *adv* — **vile·ness** *n*

vil·i·fy \ˈvil-ə-ˌfī\ *vb* **-fied; -fy·ing** : to blacken the character of with abusive language : DEFAME **syn** malign, calumniate, slander, libel, traduce — **vil·i·fi·ca·tion** \ˌvil-ə-fə-ˈkā-shən\ *n* — **vil·i·fi·er** \ˈvil-ə-ˌfī(-ə)r\ *n*

vil·la \ˈvil-ə\ *n* 1 : a country estate 2 : the rural or suburban residence of a wealthy person

vil·lage \ˈvil-ij\ *n* 1 : a settlement usu. larger than a hamlet and smaller than a town 2 : an incorporated minor municipality 3 : the people of a village

vil·lag·er \ˈvil-ij-ər\ *n* : an inhabitant of a village

vil·lain \ˈvil-ən\ *n* 1 : VILLEIN 2 : a deliberate scoundrel or criminal

vil·lain·ess \-ə-nəs\ *n* : a woman who is a villain

vil·lain·ous \-ə-nəs\ *adj* 1 : befitting a villain : WICKED, EVIL 2 : highly objectionable : DETESTABLE **syn** vicious, iniquitous, nefarious, infamous, corrupt, degenerate — **vil·lain·ous·ly** *adv* — **vil·lain·ous·ness** *n*

vil·lainy \-ə-nē\ *n, pl* **-lain·ies** 1 : villainous conduct; *also* : a villainous act 2 : villainous character or nature : DEPRAVITY

vil·lein \ˈvil-ən, ˈvil-ˌān\ *n* 1 : a free villager of Anglo-Saxon times 2 : an unfree peasant having the status of a slave to a feudal lord

vil·len·age \ˈvil-ə-nij\ *n* 1 : the holding of land at the will of a feudal lord 2 : the status of a villein

vil·lous \ˈvil-əs\ *adj* : covered with fine hairs or villi

vil·lus \ˈvil-əs\ *n, pl* **vil·li** \ˈvil-ˌī, -(ˌ)ē\ : a slender usu. vascular process; *esp* : one of the tiny projections of the mucous membrane of the small intestine that function in the absorption of food

vim \ˈvim\ *n* : robust energy and enthusiasm : VITALITY

vin·ai·grette \ˌvin-i-ˈgret\ *n* [F] 1 : a sauce made typically of oil and vinegar, onions, parsley, and herbs 2 : a small box or bottle for holding aromatic preparations (as smelling salts)

vin·ci·ble \ˈvin-sə-bəl\ *adj* : capable of being overcome or subdued

vin·di·cate \ˈvin-də-ˌkāt\ *vb* **-cat·ed;**

-cat·ing **1** : AVENGE **2** : EXONERATE, ABSOLVE **3** : CONFIRM, SUBSTANTIATE **4** : to provide defense for : JUSTIFY **5** : to maintain a right to : ASSERT — **vin·di·ca·tor** \-ˌkāt-ər\ *n*

vin·di·ca·tion \ˌvin-də-ˈkā-shən\ *n* : a vindicating or being vindicated; *esp* : justification against denial or censure

vin·dic·tive \vin-ˈdik-tiv\ *adj* **1** : disposed to revenge **2** : intended for or involving revenge **3** : VICIOUS, SPITEFUL — **vin·dic·tive·ly** *adv* — **vin·dic·tive·ness** *n*

vine \ˈvīn\ *n* [ME, fr. OF *vigne*, fr. L *vinea* vine, vineyard, fr. fem. of *vineus* of wine, fr. *vinum* wine] **1** : GRAPE 2 **2** : a plant whose stem requires support and which climbs (as by tendrils) or trails along the ground; *also* : the the stem of such a plant

vin·e·gar \ˈvin-i-gər\ *n* [ME *vinegre*, fr. OF *vinaigre*, fr. *vin* wine + *aigre* keen, sour] : a sour liquid obtained by fermentation (as of cider, wine, or malt) and used in cookery and pickling

vin·e·gary \ˈvin-i-g(ə-)rē\ *adj* **1** : resembling vinegar : SOUR **2** : disagreeable in manner or disposition : CRABBED

vine·yard \ˈvin-yərd\ *n* **1** : a plantation of grapevines **2** : an area of physical or mental occupation

vi·nous \ˈvī-nəs\ *adj* **1** : of, relating to, or made with wine ⟨~ medications⟩ **2** : showing the effects of the use of wine

¹**vin·tage** \ˈvint-ij\ *n* **1** : a season's yield of grapes or wine **2** : WINE; *esp* : a usu. superior wine which comes from a single year **3** : the act or period of gathering grapes or making wine **4** : a period of origin ⟨clothes of 1890 ~⟩

²**vintage** *adj* **1** : of, relating to, or produced in a particular vintage **2** : of old, recognized, and enduring interest, importance, or quality : CLASSIC ⟨~ cars⟩ **3** : of the best and most characteristic — used with a proper noun

vint·ner \ˈvint-nər\ *n* : a dealer in wines

vi·nyl \ˈvīn-ᵊl\ *n* **1** : a chemical derived from ethylene by the removal of one hydrogen atom **2** : a polymer of a vinyl compound or a product (as a textile fiber) made from one

vinyl chloride *n* : a flammable gaseous carcinogenic compound used esp. to make vinyl resins

vi·ol \ˈvī(-ə)l\ *n* : a bowed stringed instrument chiefly of the 16th and 17th centuries having a fretted neck and usu. six strings

¹**vi·o·la** \vī-ˈō-lə, ˈvī-ə-lə\ *n* : VIOLET 1; *esp* : any of various hybrid garden plants with white, yellow, purple, or variously colored flowers that resemble but are smaller than the related pansies

²**vi·o·la** \vē-ˈō-lə\ *n* : an instrument of the violin family slightly larger and tuned lower than a violin — **vi·o·list** \-ləst\ *n*

vi·o·la·ble \ˈvī-ə-lə-bəl\ *adj* : capable of being violated

vi·o·late \ˈvī-ə-ˌlāt\ *vb* -lat·ed; -lat·ing **1** : BREAK, DISREGARD ⟨~ a law⟩ ⟨~ a frontier⟩ **2** : RAPE **3** : PROFANE, DESECRATE **4** : INTERRUPT, DISTURB ⟨*violated* his privacy⟩ — **vi·o·la·tor** \-ˌlāt-ər\ *n*

vi·o·la·tion \ˌvī-ə-ˈlā-shən\ *n* : an act or instance of violating : the state of being violated **syn** breach, infraction, trespass, infringement, transgression

vi·o·lence \ˈvī-ə-ləns\ *n* **1** : exertion of physical force so as to injure or abuse **2** : injury by or as if by infringement or profanation **3** : intense or furious often destructive action or force **4** : vehement feeling or expression : INTENSITY **5** : jarring quality : DISCORDANCE **syn** compulsion, coercion, duress, constraint

vi·o·lent \-lənt\ *adj* **1** : marked by extreme force or sudden intense activity; *esp* : marked by improper use of such force **2** : caused by or showing strong feeling ⟨~ words⟩ **3** : EXTREME, INTENSE **4** : caused by force : not natural ⟨~ death⟩ — **vi·o·lent·ly** *adv*

vi·o·let \ˈvī-ə-lət\ *n* **1** : any of a genus of herbs or woody-stemmed plants usu. with heart-shaped leaves and both aerial and underground flowers; *esp* : one with small solid-colored flowers **2** : a variable color averaging a reddish blue

vi·o·lin \ˌvī-ə-ˈlin\ *n* : a bowed stringed instrument with four strings that has a shallower body and a more curved bridge than a viol — **vi·o·lin·ist** \-əst\ *n*

vi·o·lon·cel·lo \ˌvī-ə-lən-'chel-ō\ *n* [It] : CELLO — **vi·o·lon·cel·list** \-əst\ *n*

VIP \ˌvē-ˌī-'pē\ *n, pl* **VIPs** \-'pēz\ [*very important person*] : a person of great influence or prestige; *esp* : a high official with special privileges

vi·per \'vī-pər\ *n* **1** : any of various sluggish heavy-bodied Old World venomous snakes **2** : PIT VIPER **3** : any venomous or reputedly venomous snake **4** : a vicious or treacherous person — **vi·per·ine** \-pə-ˌrīn\ *adj*

vi·ra·go \və-'räg-ō, -'rāg-\ *n, pl* **-goes** *or* **-gos** [L, manlike heroic woman, fr. *vir* man] : a scolding, quarrelsome, or loud overbearing woman **syn** amazon, termagant, scold, shrew, vixen

vi·ral \'vī-rəl\ *adj* : of, relating to, or caused by a virus

vir·eo \'vir-ē-ˌō\ *n, pl* **-e·os** [L, a small bird, fr. *virēre* to be green] : any of various small insect-eating American songbirds mostly olive green and grayish in color

¹**vir·gin** \'vər-jən\ *n* **1** : an unmarried woman devoted to religion **2** : an unmarried girl or woman **3** *cap* : the mother of Jesus **4** : a person who has not had sexual intercourse

²**virgin** *adj* **1** : free from stain : PURE, SPOTLESS **2** : CHASTE **3** : befitting a virgin : MODEST **4** : FRESH, UNSPOILED; *esp* : not altered by human activity ⟨∼ forest⟩ **5** : INITIAL, FIRST

¹**vir·gin·al** \'vər-jən-ᵊl\ *adj* : of, relating to, or characteristic of a virgin or virginity — **vir·gin·al·ly** \-ē\ *adv*

²**virginal** *n* : a small rectangular spinet without legs popular in the 16th and 17th centuries

Vir·gin·ia creeper \vər-ˌjin-yə-\ *n* : a No. American vine having leaves with five leaflets and bluish black berries

Virginia reel *n* : an American country-dance

vir·gin·i·ty \vər-'jin-ət-ē\ *n, pl* **-ties** **1** : the quality or state of being virgin; *esp* : MAIDENHOOD **2** : the unmarried life : CELIBACY

Vir·go \'vər-ˌgō\ *n* [L, lit., virgin] **1** : a zodiacal constellation between Leo and Libra usu. pictured as a young woman **2** : the 6th sign of the zodiac in astrology; *also* : one born under this sign

vir·gule \'vər-gyül\ *n* : a mark / used typically to denote "or" (as in *and/or*) or "per" (as in *feet/second*)

vir·i·des·cent \ˌvir-ə-'des-ᵊnt\ *adj* : slightly green : GREENISH

vir·ile \'vir-əl\ *adj* **1** : having the nature, powers, or qualities of a man **2** : MASCULINE, MALE **3** : MASTERFUL, FORCEFUL — **vi·ril·i·ty** \və-'ril-ət-ē\ *n*

vi·ri·on \'vī-rē-ˌän, 'vir-ē-\ *n* : a complete virus particle consisting of an RNA or DNA core with a protein coat

vi·rol·o·gy \vī-'räl-ə-jē\ *n* : a branch of science that deals with viruses — **vi·rol·o·gist** \-jəst\ *n*

vir·tu \ˌvər-'tü, vir-\ *n* **1** : a love of or taste for objects of art **2** : objects of art (as curios and antiques)

vir·tu·al \'vər-chə(-wə)l\ *adj* : being in essence or in effect though not formally recognized or admitted ⟨a ∼ dictator⟩ — **vir·tu·al·ly** \-ē\ *adv*

vir·tue \'vər-chü\ *n* [ME *virtu*, fr. OF, fr. L *virtus* strength, manliness, virtue, fr. *vir* man] **1** : conformity to a standard of right : MORALITY **2** : a particular moral excellence **3** : manly strength or courage : VALOR **4** : a commendable quality : MERIT **5** : active power to accomplish a given effect : POTENCY, EFFICACY **6** : chastity esp. in a woman

vir·tu·os·i·ty \ˌvər-chə-'wäs-ət-ē\ *n, pl* **-ties** : great technical skill in the practice of a fine art

vir·tu·o·so \ˌvər-chə-'wō-sō, -zō\ *n, pl* **-sos** *or* **-si** \-sē, -zē\ [It] **1** : one skilled in or having a taste for the fine arts **2** : one who excels in the technique of an art; *esp* : a highly skilled musical performer **syn** expert, adept, artist, doyen, master — **virtuoso** *adj*

vir·tu·ous \'vərch-(ə-)wəs\ *adj* **1** : having or showing virtue and esp. moral virtue **2** : CHASTE — **vir·tu·ous·ly** *adv*

vir·u·lent \'vir-(y)ə-lənt\ *adj* **1** : highly infectious ⟨a ∼ germ⟩; *also* : marked by a rapid and very severe course ⟨a ∼ disease⟩ **2** : extremely poisonous or venomous : NOXIOUS **3** : bitterly hostile : MALIGN — **vir·u·lence** \-ləns\ *n* — **vir·u·lent·ly** *adv*

vi·rus \'vī-rəs\ *n* [L, slimy liquid, poison, stench] **1** : any of a large group of submicroscopic infectious agents that have an outside coat of protein around a core of RNA or DNA, that can grow and multiply only in living cells, and that cause important diseases in human beings, lower animals, and plants; *also* : a disease caused by a virus **2** : something (as a corrupting influence) that poisons the mind or spirit

vis *abbr* **1** visibility **2** visual

¹**vi·sa** \'vē-zə, -sə\ *n* [F] **1** : an endorsement by the proper authorities on a passport to show that it has been examined and the bearer may proceed **2** : a signature by a superior official signifying approval of a document

²**visa** *vb* **vi·saed** \-zəd, -səd\; **vi·sa·ing** \-zə-iŋ, -sə-\ : to give a visa to (a passport)

vis·age \'viz-ij\ *n* : the face or countenance of a person or sometimes an animal; *also* : LOOK, APPEARANCE

¹**vis–à–vis** \ˌvēz-ə-'vē, ˌvēs-\ *prep* [F, lit., face-to-face] **1** : face-to-face with : OPPOSITE **2** : in relation to **3** : as compared with

²**vis–à–vis** *n, pl* **vis–à–vis** \-ə-'vē(z)\ **1** : one that is face-to-face with another **2** : ESCORT **3** : COUNTERPART **4** : TÊTE⸗À-TÊTE

³**vis–à–vis** *adv* : in company : TOGETHER

viscera pl of VISCUS

vis·cer·al \'vis-ə-rəl\ *adj* **1** : felt in or as if in the viscera **2** : of or relating to the viscera — **vis·cer·al·ly** \-ē\ *adv*

vis·cid \'vis-əd\ *adj* : VISCOUS — **vis·cid·i·ty** \vis-'id-ət-ē\ *n*

vis·cos·i·ty \vis-'käs-ət-ē\ *n, pl* **-ties** : the quality of being viscous; *esp* : the property of a fluid that causes it to resist flow

vis·count \'vī-ˌkaunt\ *n* : a member of the British peerage ranking below an earl and above a baron

vis·count·ess \-ˌkaunt-əs\ *n* **1** : the wife or widow of a viscount **2** : a woman who holds the rank of viscount in her own right

vis·cous \'vis-kəs\ *adj* [ME *viscouse,* fr. LL *viscosus* full of birdlime, viscous, fr. L *viscum* mistletoe, birdlime] **1** : having the sticky consistency of glue **2** : having or characterized by viscosity

vis·cus \'vis-kəs\ *n, pl* **vis·cera** \'vis-ə-rə\ : an internal organ of the body; *esp* : one (as the heart or liver) located in the cavity of the trunk

vise \'vīs\ *n* [MF *vis* something winding, fr. L *vitis* vine] : a tool with two jaws for holding or clamping work that typically close by a screw or lever

vis·i·bil·i·ty \ˌviz-ə-'bil-ət-ē\ *n, pl* **-ties 1** : the quality, condition, or degree of being visible **2** : the degree of clearness of the atmosphere

vis·i·ble \'viz-ə-bəl\ *adj* : capable of being seen ⟨∼ stars⟩; *also* : MANIFEST, APPARENT ⟨has no ∼ means of support⟩ — **vis·i·bly** *adv*

¹**vi·sion** \'vizh-ən\ *n* **1** : something seen otherwise than by ordinary sight (as in a dream or trance) **2** : a vivid picture created by the imagination **3** : the act or power of imagination **4** : unusual wisdom in foreseeing what is going to happen **5** : the act or power of seeing : SIGHT **6** : something seen; *esp* : a lovely sight

²**vision** *vb* **vi·sioned; vi·sion·ing** \'vizh-(ə-)niŋ\ : to see in or as if in a vision : IMAGINE, ENVISION

¹**vi·sion·ary** \'vizh-ə-ˌner-ē\ *adj* **1** : of the nature of a vision : ILLUSORY, UNREAL **2** : seeing or likely to see visions : given to dreaming or imagining **3** : not practical : UTOPIAN **syn** imaginary, fantastic, chimerical, quixotic

²**visionary** *n, pl* **-ar·ies 1** : one whose ideas or projects are impractical : DREAMER **2** : one who sees visions

¹**vis·it** \'viz-ət\ *vb* **1** : to go to see in order to comfort or help **2** : to call upon either as an act of courtesy or in a professional capacity **3** : to dwell with for a time as a guest **4** : to come to or upon as a reward, affliction, or punishment **5** : INFLICT **6** : to make a visit or regular or frequent visits **7** : CHAT, CONVERSE — **vis·it·able** *adj*

²**visit** *n* **1** : a short stay : CALL **2** : a brief residence as a guest **3** : a journey to and stay at a place **4** : a formal or professional call (as by a doctor)

vis·i·tant \'viz-ət-ənt\ *n* : VISITOR

vis·i·ta·tion \ˌviz-ə-'tā-shən\ *n* **1** : VISIT; *esp* : an official visit **2** : a special dispensation of divine favor or wrath; *also* : a severe trial

visiting nurse *n* : a nurse employed to visit sick persons or perform public⸗ health services in a community

vis·i·tor \'viz-ət-ər\ *n* : one that visits

vi·sor \'vī-zər\ *n* **1** : the front piece of a

helmet; *esp* : a movable upper piece **2** : VIZARD **3** : a projecting part (as on a cap) to shade the eyes — **vi·sored** \-zərd\ *adj*

vis·ta \'vis-tə\ *n* **1** : a distant view through or along an avenue or opening **2** : an extensive mental view over a series of years or events

VISTA *abbr* Volunteers in Service to America

¹vi·su·al \'vizh-(ə-w)əl\ *adj* **1** : of, relating to, or used in sight ⟨∼ organs⟩ **2** : perceived by vision ⟨a ∼ impression⟩ **3** : VISIBLE **4** : done by sight only ⟨∼ navigation⟩ **5** : of or relating to instruction by means of sight ⟨∼ aids⟩ — **vi·su·al·ly** \-ē\ *adv*

²visual *n* : something (as a picture, chart, or film) that appeals to the sight and is used for illustration, demonstration, or promotion — usu. used in pl.

vi·su·al·ize \'vizh-(ə-)wə-₁līz\ *vb* **-ized; -iz·ing** : to make visible; *esp* : to form a mental image of — **vi·su·al·iza·tion** \₁vizh-ə-(wə-)lə-'zā-shən\ *n* — **vi·su·al·iz·er** \'vizh-ə-(wə-)₁lī-zər\ *n*

vi·ta \'vēt-ə, 'vīt-ə\ *n, pl* **vi·tae** \'vē-₁tī, 'vīt-ē\ [L, lit., life] : a brief autobiographical sketch

vi·tal \'vīt-ᵊl\ *adj* **1** : concerned with or necessary to the maintenance of life **2** : full of life and vigor : ANIMATED **3** : of, relating to, or characteristic of life **4** : FATAL, MORTAL ⟨∼ wound⟩ **5** : FUNDAMENTAL, BASIC, INDISPENSABLE — **vi·tal·ly** \-ē\ *adv*

vi·tal·i·ty \vī-'tal-ət-ē\ *n, pl* **-ties 1** : the peculiarity distinguishing the living from the nonliving; *also* : capacity to live : mental and physical vigor **2** : enduring quality **3** : ANIMATION, LIVELINESS

vi·tal·ize \'vīt-ᵊl-₁īz\ *vb* **-ized; -iz·ing** : to impart life or vigor to : ANIMATE, ENERGIZE — **vi·tal·iza·tion** \₁vīt-ᵊl-ə-'zā-shən\ *n*

vi·tals \'vīt-ᵊlz\ *n pl* **1** : vital organs **2** : essential parts

vital signs *n pl* : the pulse rate, respiratory rate, body temperature, and sometimes blood pressure of a person

vital statistics *n pl* : statistics dealing with births, deaths, marriages, health, and disease

vi·ta·min \'vīt-ə-mən\ *n* : any of various organic substances that are essential in tiny amounts to most animals and some plants and are mostly obtained from foods

vitamin A *n* : any of several vitamins (as from egg yolk or fish-liver oils) required for healthy epithelium and sight

vitamin B *n* **1** : VITAMIN B COMPLEX **2** *or* **vitamin B₁** : THIAMINE

vitamin B complex *n* : a group of vitamins that are found widely in foods and are essential for normal function of certain enzymes and for growth

vitamin B₆ \-'bē-'siks\ *n* : any of several compounds that are considered essential to vertebrate nutrition

vitamin B₁₂ \-'bē-'twelv\ *n* : a complex cobalt-containing compound that occurs esp. in liver and is essential to normal blood formation, neural function, and growth; *also* : any of several compounds of similar action

vitamin C *n* : a vitamin found esp. in fruits and vegetables and needed by the body to prevent scurvy

vitamin D *n* : any or all of several vitamins that are needed for normal bone and tooth structure and are found esp. in fish-liver oils, egg yolk, and milk or are produced in response to ultraviolet light

vitamin E *n* : any of various oily fat-soluble liquid compounds that are found esp. in plants and are necessary in the body to prevent such ailments as infertility, the breakdown of muscles, and vascular problems

vitamin K *n* [Dan *k*oagulation coagulation] : any of several vitamins that are needed in order for blood to clot properly

vi·ti·ate \'vish-ē-₁āt\ *vb* **-at·ed; -at·ing 1** : CONTAMINATE, POLLUTE; *also* : DEBASE, PERVERT **2** : to make legally without force : INVALIDATE — **vi·ti·a·tion** \₁vish-ē-'ā-shən\ *n* — **vi·ti·a·tor** \'vish-ē-₁āt-ər\ *n*

vi·ti·cul·ture \'vit-ə-₁kəl-chər\ *n* : the growing of grapes — **vi·ti·cul·tur·al** \₁vit-ə-'kəlch-(ə-)rəl\ *adj* — **vi·ti·cul·tur·ist** \-rəst\ *n*

vit·re·ous \'vi-trē-əs\ *adj* **1** : of, relating to, or resembling glass **2** : GLASSY ⟨∼ rocks⟩ **3** : of, relating to, or being the clear colorless transparent jelly (vitreous humor) behind the lens in the eyeball

vit·ri·ol \ˈvi-trē-əl\ n : something resembling acid in being caustic, corrosive, or biting — **vit·ri·ol·ic** \ˌvi-trē-ˈäl-ik\ adj

vit·tles \ˈvit-ᵊlz\ n pl : VICTUALS

vi·tu·per·ate \vī-ˈt(y)ü-pə-ˌrāt, və-\ vb **-at·ed; -at·ing** : to abuse in words : SCOLD syn revile, berate, rate, upbraid, rail, lash — **vi·tu·per·a·tive** \-ˈt(y)ü-p(ə-)rət-iv, -pə-ˌrāt-\ adj — **vi·tu·per·a·tive·ly** adv

vi·tu·per·a·tion \(ˌ)vī-t(y)ü-pə-ˈrā-shən, və-\ n : lengthy harsh criticism or abuse

vi·va \ˈvē-və\ interj [It, long live, fr. vivere to live, fr. L] — used to express goodwill or approval

vi·va·ce \vē-ˈväch-ā\ adv or adj [It] : in a brisk spirited manner — used as a direction in music

vi·va·cious \və-ˈvā-shəs, vī-\ adj : lively in temper or conduct : ANIMATED, SPRIGHTLY — **vi·va·cious·ly** adv — **vi·va·cious·ness** n

vi·vac·i·ty \-ˈvas-ət-ē\ n : the quality or state of being vivacious

vi·var·i·um \vī-ˈvar-ē-əm, -ˈver-\ n, pl **-ia** \-ē-ə\ or **-iums** : an enclosure for keeping or raising and observing animals or plants indoors; esp : one for terrestrial animals

vi·va vo·ce \ˌvī-və-ˈvō-sē\ adj [ML, with the living voice] : expressed or conducted by word of mouth : ORAL ⟨viva voce examination⟩ ⟨viva voce voting⟩ — **viva voce** adv

viv·id \ˈviv-əd\ adj 1 : having the appearance of vigorous life or freshness : LIVELY 2 : BRILLIANT, INTENSE ⟨a ∼ red⟩ 3 : producing a strong impression on the senses : SHARP 4 : calling forth lifelike mental images — **viv·id·ly** adv — **viv·id·ness** n

viv·i·fy \ˈviv-ə-ˌfī\ vb **-fied; -fy·ing** 1 : to endue with life : ANIMATE 2 : to make vivid — **viv·i·fi·ca·tion** \ˌviv-ə-fə-ˈkā-shən\ n — **viv·i·fi·er** \ˈviv-ə-ˌfī(-ə)r\ n

vi·vip·a·rous \vī-ˈvip-(ə-)rəs, və-\ adj : producing living young from within the body rather than from eggs — **vi·vi·par·i·ty** \ˌvī-və-ˈpar-ət-ē, ˌviv-ə-\ n

vivi·sec·tion \ˌviv-ə-ˈsek-shən, ˈviv-ə-ˌsek-shən\ n : the cutting of or operation on a living animal; also : animal experimentation

vix·en \ˈvik-sən\ n 1 : a female fox 2 : an ill-tempered scolding woman syn shrew, scold, termagant, virago

viz \ˈnäm-lē, ˈviz, və-ˈdel-ə-ˌset\ abbr videlicet

viz·ard \ˈviz-ərd\ n : a mask for disguise or protection

vi·zier \və-ˈziər\ n : a high executive officer of many Muslim countries and esp. of the former Turkish empire

vi·zor var of VISOR

VOA abbr Voice of America

voc abbr 1 vocational 2 vocative

vocab abbr vocabulary

vo·ca·ble \ˈvō-kə-bəl\ n : TERM, NAME; esp : a word composed of various sounds or letters without regard to its meaning

vo·cab·u·lary \vō-ˈkab-yə-ˌler-ē\ n, pl **-lar·ies** 1 : a list or collection of words usu. alphabetically arranged and defined or explained : LEXICON 2 : a stock of words used in a language by a class or individual or in relation to a subject

vocabulary entry n : a word (as the noun book), hyphened or open compound (as the verb cross-refer or the noun boric acid), word element (as the affix -an), abbreviation (as agt), verbalized symbol (as Na), or term (as master of ceremonies) entered alphabetically in a dictionary for the purpose of definition or identification or expressly included as an inflected form (as the noun mice or the verb saw) or as a derived form (as the noun godlessness or the adverb globally) or related phrase (as in spite of) run on at its base word and usu. set in a type (as boldface) readily distinguishable from that of the lightface running text which defines, explains, or identifies the entry

¹**vo·cal** \ˈvō-kəl\ adj 1 : uttered by the voice : ORAL 2 : relating to, composed or arranged for, or sung by the human voice ⟨∼ music⟩ 3 : of, relating to, or having the power of producing voice 4 : full of voices : RESOUNDING 5 : given to expressing one's feelings or opinions in speech : TALKATIVE; also : OUTSPOKEN syn articulate, fluent, eloquent

²**vocal** *n* **1** : a vocal sound **2** : a vocal composition or its performance

vocal cords *n pl* : either of two pairs of elastic folds of mucous membrane that project into the cavity of the larynx and function in the production of vocal sounds

vo•cal•ic \vō-'kal-ik\ *adj* : of, relating to, or functioning as a vowel

vo•cal•ist \'vō-kə-ləst\ *n* : SINGER

vo•cal•ize \-ˌlīz\ *vb* **-ized; -iz•ing 1** : to give vocal expression to : UTTER; *esp* : SING **2** : to make voiced rather than voiceless — **vo•cal•iz•er** *n*

vo•ca•tion \vō-'kā-shən\ *n* **1** : a summons or strong inclination to a particular state or course of action ⟨religious ∼⟩ **2** : regular employment : OCCUPATION, PROFESSION — **vo•ca•tion•al** \-sh(ə-)nəl\ *adj*

vo•ca•tion•al•ism \-sh(ə-)nəl-ˌiz-əm\ *n* : emphasis on vocational training in education

voc•a•tive \'väk-ət-iv\ *adj* : of, relating to, or constituting a grammatical case marking the one addressed — **vocative** *n*

vo•cif•er•ate \vō-'sif-ə-ˌrāt\ *vb* **-at•ed; -at•ing** [L *vociferari*, fr. *voc-, vox* voice + *ferre* to bear] : to cry out loudly : CLAMOR, SHOUT — **vo•cif•er•a•tion** \-ˌsif-ə-'rā-shən\ *n*

vo•cif•er•ous \vō-'sif-(ə-)rəs\ *adj* : making or given to loud outcry : CLAMOROUS — **vo•cif•er•ous•ly** *adv* — **vo•cif•er•ous•ness** *n*

vod•ka \'väd-kə\ *n* [Russ, fr. *voda* water] : a colorless liquor of neutral spirits distilled from a mash (as of rye or wheat)

vogue \'vōg\ *n* [MF, action of rowing, course, fashion, fr. It *voga*, fr. *vogare* to row] **1** : popular acceptance or favor : POPULARITY **2** : a period of popularity **3** : something or someone in fashion at a particular time **syn** mode, fad, rage, craze, trend, fashion

vogu•ish \'vō-gish\ *adj* **1** : FASHIONABLE, SMART **2** : suddenly or temporarily popular

¹**voice** \'vȯis\ *n* **1** : sound produced through the mouth by vertebrates and esp. by human beings in speaking or shouting **2** : musical sound produced by the vocal cords : the power to produce such sound; *also* : one of the

melodic parts in a vocal or instrumental composition **3** : the vocal organs as a means of tone production ⟨train the ∼⟩ **4** : sound produced by vibration of the vocal cords as heard in vowels and some consonants **5** : the faculty of speech **6** : a sound suggesting vocal utterance ⟨the ∼ of the sea⟩ **7** : an instrument or medium of expression **8** : a choice, opinion, or wish openly expressed; *also* : right of expression **9** : distinction of form of a verb to indicate the relation of the subject to the action expressed by the verb

²**voice** *vb* **voiced; voic•ing 1** : to give voice or expression to : UTTER; *also* : ANNOUNCE **2** : to regulate the tone of ⟨∼ the pipes of an organ⟩ **syn** express, vent, air, ventilate

voice box *n* : LARYNX

voiced \'vȯist\ *adj* **1** : furnished with a voice ⟨soft-*voiced*⟩ **2** : uttered with voice — **voiced•ness** \'vȯis(t)-nəs, 'vȯi-səd-nəs\ *n*

voice•less \'vȯis-ləs\ *adj* **1** : having no voice **2** : not pronounced with voice — **voice•less•ly** *adv* — **voice•less•ness** *n*

voice•print \'vȯis-ˌprint\ *n* : an individually distinctive pattern of voice characteristics that is spectrographically produced

¹**void** \'vȯid\ *adj* **1** : containing nothing : EMPTY **2** : UNOCCUPIED, VACANT **3** : LACKING, DEVOID ⟨proposals ∼ of sense⟩ **4** : VAIN, USELESS **5** : of no legal force or effect : NULL

²**void** *n* **1** : empty space : EMPTINESS, VACUUM **2** : a feeling of want or hollowness

³**void** *vb* **1** : to make or leave empty; *also* : VACATE, LEAVE **2** : DISCHARGE, EMIT ⟨∼ urine⟩ **3** : to render void : ANNUL, NULLIFY — **void•able** *adj* — **void•er** *n*

voi•là \vwä-'lä\ *interj* [F] — used to call attention or to express satisfaction or approval

voile \'vȯil\ *n* : a sheer fabric from various fibers used for women's clothing and curtains

vol *abbr* **1** volume **2** volunteer

vol•a•tile \'väl-ət-ᵊl\ *adj* **1** : readily becoming a vapor at a relatively low temperature ⟨a ∼ liquid⟩ **2** : LIGHTHEARTED **3** : easily erupting into violent action **4** : CHANGEABLE — **vol·a·til·i·ty** \ˌväl-ə-'til-ət-ē\ *n* — **vol·a·til·ize** \'väl-ət-ᵊl-ˌīz\ *vb*

vol·ca·nic \väl-'kan-ik\ *adj* **1** : of or relating to a volcano **2** : explosively violent : VOLATILE ⟨∼ emotions⟩

volcanic glass *n* : natural glass produced by cooling of molten lava

vol·ca·nism \'väl-kə-ˌniz-əm\ *n* : volcanic power or action

vol·ca·no \väl-'kā-nō\ *n, pl* **-noes** *or* **-nos** [It *vulcano*, fr. L *Volcanus, Vulcanus* Roman god of fire and metalworking] : an opening in the earth's crust from which molten rock and steam issue; *also* : a hill or mountain composed of the ejected material

vol·ca·nol·o·gy \ˌväl-kə-'näl-ə-jē\ *n* : a branch of geology that deals with volcanic phenomena — **vol·ca·nol·o·gist** \-kə-'näl-ə-jəst\ *n*

vole \'vōl\ *n* : any of various mouselike or ratlike rodents that are closely related to the lemmings and muskrats

vo·li·tion \vō-'lish-ən\ *n* **1** : the act or the power of making a choice or decision : WILL **2** : a choice or decision made — **vo·li·tion·al** \-'lish-(ə-)nəl\ *adj*

¹**vol·ley** \'väl-ē\ *n, pl* **volleys 1** : a flight of missiles (as arrows or bullets) **2** : simultaneous discharge of a number of missile weapons **3** : a pouring forth of many things at the same instant ⟨a ∼ of oaths⟩

²**volley** *vb* **vol·leyed; vol·ley·ing 1** : to discharge or become discharged in or as if in a volley **2** : to hit an object of play in the air before it touches the ground

vol·ley·ball \-ˌbȯl\ *n* : a game played by volleying an inflated ball over a net; *also* : the ball used in this game

volt \'vōlt\ *n* : the mks unit of potential difference and electromotive force equal to the difference in potential between two points in a conducting wire carrying a constant current of one ampere when the power dissipated between the points is equal to one watt

volt·age \'vōl-tij\ *n* : potential difference measured in volts

vol·ta·ic \väl-'tā-ik, vōl-\ *adj* : of, relating to, or producing direct electric current by chemical action ⟨∼ current⟩

volte–face \ˌvȯlt-(ə-)'fäs\ *n* : a reversal in policy : ABOUT-FACE

volt·me·ter \'vōlt-ˌmēt-ər\ *n* : an instrument for measuring in volts the difference in potential between different points of an electrical circuit

vol·u·ble \'väl-yə-bəl\ *adj* : fluent and smooth in speech : GLIB **syn** garrulous, loquacious, talkative — **vol·u·bil·i·ty** \ˌväl-yə-'bil-ət-ē\ *n* — **vol·u·bly** \'väl-yə-blē\ *adv*

vol·ume \'väl-yəm\ *n* [ME, fr. MF, fr. L *volumen* roll, scroll, fr. *volvere* to roll] **1** : a series of printed sheets bound typically in book form; *also* : an arbitrary number of issues of a periodical **2** : space occupied as measured by cubic units ⟨the ∼ of a cylinder⟩ **3** : sufficient matter to fill a book ⟨her glance spoke ∼s⟩ **4** : AMOUNT ⟨increasing ∼ of business⟩ ; *also* : an aggregate forming a body or unit **5** : the degree of loudness of a sound **syn** body, bulk, mass

vo·lu·mi·nous \və-'lü-mə-nəs\ *adj* **1** : consisting of many folds or windings **2** : BULKY, LARGE **3** : filling or sufficient to fill a large volume or several volumes — **vo·lu·mi·nous·ly** \-'lü-mə-nəs-lē\ *adv* — **vo·lu·mi·nous·ness** *n*

¹**vol·un·tary** \'väl-ən-ˌter-ē\ *adj* **1** : done, made, or given freely and without compulsion ⟨a ∼ sacrifice⟩ **2** : not accidental : INTENTIONAL ⟨a ∼ slight⟩ **3** : of, relating to, or regulated by the will ⟨∼ behavior⟩ **4** : having power of free choice ⟨man is a ∼ agent⟩ **5** : provided or supported by voluntary action ⟨a ∼ hospital⟩ **syn** deliberate, willful, willing, witting — **vol·un·tari·ly** \ˌväl-ən-'ter-ə-lē\ *adv*

²**voluntary** *n, pl* **-tar·ies** : an organ solo played in a religious service

voluntary muscle *n* : muscle (as most striated muscle) under voluntary control

¹**vol·un·teer** \ˌväl-ən-'tiər\ *n* **1** : a person who of his own free will offers himself for a service or duty **2** : a plant growing spontaneously esp. from seeds lost from a previous crop

²**volunteer** *vb* **1** : to offer or give voluntarily **2** : to offer oneself as a volunteer

vo·lup·tu·ary \və-'ləp-chə-ˌwer-ē\ *n, pl* **-ar·ies** : one whose chief interest in life is the indulgence of sensual appetites

vo·lup·tuous \-chə(-wə)s\ *adj* **1** : giving sensual gratification ⟨~ furnishings⟩ **2** : given to or spent in enjoyment of luxury or pleasure **syn** luxurious, epicurean, sensuous, sensual — **vo·lup·tuous·ly** *adv* — **vo·lup·tuous·ness** *n*

vo·lute \və-ˈlüt\ *n* : a spiral or scroll= shaped decoration

¹**vom·it** \ˈväm-ət\ *n* : an act or instance of throwing up the contents of the stomach through the mouth; *also* : the matter discharged

²**vomit** *vb* **1** : to throw up the contents of the stomach as vomit **2** : to belch forth : GUSH

voo·doo \ˈvüd-ü\ *n, pl* **voodoos** [LaF *voudou*] **1** : VOODOOISM **2** : one who practices voodooism **3** : a charm or a fetish used in voodooism — **voodoo** *adj*

voo·doo·ism \-ˌiz-əm\ *n* **1** : a religion derived from African ancestor worship and consisting largely of sorcery **2** : the practice of sorcery

vo·ra·cious \vȯ-ˈrā-shəs, və-\ *adj* **1** : greedy in eating : RAVENOUS **2** : excessively eager : INSATIABLE ⟨a ~ reader⟩ **syn** gluttonous, ravening, rapacious — **vo·ra·cious·ly** *adv* — **vo·ra·cious·ness** *n* — **vo·rac·i·ty** \-ˈras-ət-ē\ *n*

vor·tex \ˈvȯr-ˌteks\ *n, pl* **vor·ti·ces** \ˈvȯrt-ə-ˌsēz\ *also* **vor·tex·es** \ˈvȯr-ˌtek-səz\ : a mass of whirling liquid forming a cavity in the center toward which things are drawn : WHIRLPOOL

vo·ta·ry \ˈvōt-ə-rē\ *n, pl* **-ries** **1** : ENTHUSIAST, DEVOTEE; *also* : a devoted adherent or admirer **2** : a devout or zealous worshiper

¹**vote** \ˈvōt\ *n* [ME, fr. L *votum* vow, wish, fr. *vovēre* to vow] **1** : a choice or opinion of a person or body of persons expressed usu. by a ballot, spoken word, or raised hand; *also* : the ballot, word, or gesture used to express a choice or opinion **2** : the decision reached by voting **3** : the right of suffrage **4** : a group of voters with some common characteristics ⟨the big city ~⟩ — **vote·less** *adj*

²**vote** *vb* **vot·ed; vot·ing** **1** : to cast a vote **2** : to choose, endorse, authorize, or defeat by vote **3** : to express an opinion **4** : to adjudge by general agreement : DECLARE **5** : to offer as a sug-

gestion : PROPOSE **6** : to cause to vote esp. in a given way — **vot·er** *n*

vo·tive \ˈvōt-iv\ *adj* : offered or performed in fulfillment of a vow or in petition, gratitude, or devotion

vou *abbr* voucher

vouch \ˈvau̇ch\ *vb* **1** : PROVE, SUBSTANTIATE **2** : to verify by examining documentary evidence **3** : to give a guarantee **4** : to supply supporting evidence or testimony; *also* : to give personal assurance

vouch·er \ˈvau̇-chər\ *n* **1** : an act of vouching **2** : one that vouches for another **3** : a documentary record of a business transaction **4** : a written affidavit or authorization **5** : a form indicating a credit against future purchases or expenditures

vouch·safe \vau̇ch-ˈsāf\ *vb* **vouch·safed; vouch·saf·ing** **1** : to grant or give often in a condescending manner **2** : to grant as a privilege or as a special favor — **vouch·safe·ment** *n*

¹**vow** \ˈvau̇\ *n* : a solemn promise or assertion; *esp* : one by which a person binds himself or herself to an act, service, or condition

²**vow** *vb* **1** : to make a vow or as a vow **2** : to bind or commit by a vow — **vow·er** \ˈvau̇(-ə)r\ *n*

vow·el \ˈvau̇(-ə)l\ *n* **1** : a speech sound produced without obstruction or friction in the mouth **2** : a letter representing such a sound

vox po·pu·li \ˈväks-ˈpäp-yə-ˌlī\ *n* [L, voice of the people] : popular sentiment

¹**voy·age** \ˈvȯi-ij\ *n* [ME, fr. OF *voiage*, fr. LL *viaticum*, fr. L, traveling money, fr. neut. of *viaticus* of a journey, fr. *via* way] : a journey esp. by water from one place or country to another

²**voyage** *vb* **voy·aged; voy·ag·ing** : to take or make a voyage — **voy·ag·er** *n*

voya·geur \ˌvȯi-ə-ˈzhər, ˌvwä-yä-\ *n* [CanF] : a person employed by a fur company to transport goods and men to and from remote stations esp. in the Canadian Northwest

voy·eur \vwä-ˈyər, vȯi-ˈər\ *n* : one who habitually seeks sexual stimulation by visual means — **voy·eur·ism** \-ˌiz-əm\ *n*

VP *abbr* **1** verb phrase **2** vice president

vs *abbr* **1** verse **2** versus

vss *abbr* **1** verses **2** versions

V/STOL *abbr* vertical short takeoff and landing

Vt *or* **VT** *abbr* Vermont

VTOL *abbr* vertical takeoff and landing

VTR *abbr* videotape recorder

vul·ca·nism \'vəl-kə-ˌniz-əm\ *n* : VOLCANISM

vul·ca·nize \'vəl-kə-ˌnīz\ *vb* **-nized; -niz-ing** : to treat rubber or rubberlike material chemically to give useful properties (as elasticity and strength) — **vul·ca·ni·za·tion** \ˌvəl-kə-nə-'zā-shən\ *n*

Vulg *abbr* Vulgate

vul·gar \'vəl-gər\ *adj* [ME, fr. L *vulgaris* of the mob, vulgar, fr. *vulgus* mob, common people] **1** : VERNACULAR ⟨the ∼ tongue⟩ **2** : of or relating to the common people : GENERAL, COMMON **3** : lacking cultivation or refinement : BOORISH; *also* : offensive to good taste or refined feelings **syn** gross, obscene, ribald, dirty, indecent, profane — **vul·gar·ly** *adv*

vul·gar·i·an \ˌvəl-'gar-ē-ən\ *n* : a vulgar person

vul·gar·ism \'vəl-gə-ˌriz-əm\ *n* **1** : a word or expression originated or used chiefly by illiterate persons **2** : a coarse expression : OBSCENITY **3** : VULGARITY

vul·gar·i·ty \ˌvəl-'gar-ət-ē\ *n, pl* **-ties 1** : an instance of coarseness of manners or language **2** : the quality or state of being vulgar

vul·gar·ize \'vəl-gə-ˌrīz\ *vb* **-ized; -iz-ing** : to make vulgar — **vul·gar·iza·tion** \ˌvəl-gə-rə-'zā-shən\ *n* — **vul·gar·iz·er** \'vəl-gə-ˌrī-zər\ *n*

Vul·gate \'vəl-ˌgāt\ *n* [ML *vulgata*, fr. LL *vulgata editio* edition in general circulation] : a Latin version of the Bible used by the Roman Catholic Church

vul·ner·a·ble \'vəln-(ə-)rə-bəl\ *adj* **1** : capable of being wounded : susceptible to wounds **2** : open to attack **3** : liable to increased penalties in contract bridge — **vul·ner·a·bil·i·ty** \ˌvəln-(ə-)rə-'bil-ət-ē\ *n* — **vul·ner·a·bly** \'vəln-(ə-)rə-blē\ *adv*

vul·pine \'vəl-ˌpīn\ *adj* : of, relating to, or resembling a fox esp. in cunning

vul·ture \'vəl-chər\ *n* **1** : any of various large birds (as a turkey vulture) related to hawks and eagles but having weaker claws and the head usu. naked and living chiefly on carrion **2** : a rapacious person

vul·va \'vəl-və\ *n, pl* **vul·vae** \-ˌvē\ [L] : the external parts of the female genital organs

vv *abbr* **1** verses **2** vice versa

vying *pres part of* VIE

W

¹**w** \'dəb-əl-(ˌ)yü\ *n, pl* **w's** *or* **ws** *often cap* : the 23d letter of the English alphabet

²**w** *abbr, often cap* **1** water **2** watt **3** week **4** weight **5** west **6** western **7** wide; width **8** wife **9** with

W *symbol* [G *Wolfram*] tungsten

WA *abbr* **1** Washington **2** Western Australia

Wac \'wak\ *n* [*Women's Army Corps*] : a member of the Women's Army Corps

wacky \'wak-ē\ *adj* **wacki·er; -est** : ECCENTRIC, CRAZY

¹**wad** \'wäd\ *n* **1** : a little mass, bundle, or tuft ⟨∼s of clay⟩ **2** : a soft mass of usu. light fibrous material **3** : a pliable plug (as of felt) used to retain a powder charge (as in a cartridge) **4** : a considerable amount (as of money) **5** : a roll of paper money

²**wad** *vb* **wad·ded; wad·ding 1** : to push a wad into ⟨∼ a gun⟩ **2** : to form into a wad **3** : to hold in by a wad ⟨∼ a bullet in a gun⟩ **4** : to stuff or line with a wad : PAD

wad·ding \'wäd-iŋ\ *n* **1** : WADS; *also* : material for making wads **2** : a soft mass or sheet of short loose fibers used for stuffing or padding

wad·dle \'wäd-ᵊl\ *vb* **wad·dled; wad·dling** \'wäd-(ᵊ-)liŋ\ : to walk with short steps swaying from side to side like a duck — **waddle** *n*

wade \'wād\ *vb* **wad·ed; wad·ing 1** : to step in or through a medium (as water) more resistant than air **2** : to move or go with difficulty or labor and often with determined vigor ⟨~ through a dull book⟩ — **wad·able** *or* **wade·able** \'wād-ə-bəl\ *adj* — **wade** *n*

wad·er \'wād-ər\ *n* **1** : one that wades **2** : WADING BIRD **3** *pl* : high waterproof rubber boots or trousers for wading

wa·di \'wäd-ē\ *n* [Ar] : a watercourse dry except in the rainy season esp. in southwestern Asia and northern Africa

wading bird *n* : any of many long≠legged birds (as sandpipers, cranes, or herons) that wade in water in search of food

Waf \'waf\ *n* [Women in the *Air Force*] : a member of the women's component of the Air Force

wa·fer \'wā-fər\ *n* **1** : a thin crisp cake or cracker **2** : a thin round piece of unleavened bread used in the Eucharist **3** : something (as a piece of candy or an adhesive seal) that resembles a wafer

waf·fle \'wäf-əl\ *n* : a soft but crisped cake of batter cooked in a special hinged metal utensil (**waffle iron**)

¹**waft** \'wäft, 'waft\ *vb* : to cause to move or go lightly by or as if by the impulse of wind or waves

²**waft** *n* **1** : a slight breeze : PUFF **2** : the act of waving

¹**wag** \'wag\ *vb* **wagged; wag·ging 1** : to sway or swing shortly from side to side or to-and-fro ⟨the dog *wagged* his tail⟩ **2** : to move in chatter or gossip ⟨scandal caused tongues to ~⟩

²**wag** *n* : an act of wagging : a wagging movement

³**wag** *n* : WIT, JOKER

¹**wage** \'wāj\ *vb* **waged; wag·ing 1** : to engage in : CARRY ON ⟨~ a war⟩ **2** : to be in process of being waged

²**wage** *n* **1** : payment for labor or services usu. according to contract **2** *pl* : RECOMPENSE, REWARD

¹**wa·ger** \'wā-jər\ *n* **1** : BET, STAKE **2** : something on which bets are laid : GAMBLE

²**wager** *vb* : BET — **wa·ger·er** *n*

wag·gery \'wag-ə-rē\ *n*, *pl* **-ger·ies 1** : mischievous merriment : PLEASAN-TRY **2** : JEST, TRICK

wag·gish \'wag-ish\ *adj* **1** : SPORTIVE, HUMOROUS **2** : resembling or characteristic of a wag : MISCHIEVOUS, ROGUISH, FROLICSOME

wag·gle \'wag-əl\ *vb* **wag·gled; wag·gling** \-(ə-)liŋ\ : to move backward and forward or from side to side : WAG — **waggle** *n*

wag·on \'wag-ən\ *n* **1** : a 4-wheeled vehicle; *esp* : one drawn by animals and used for freight or merchandise **2** : PA-TROL WAGON **3** : a child's 4-wheeled cart **4** : STATION WAGON

wag·on·er \'wag-ə-nər\ *n* : the driver of a wagon

wag·on·ette \ˌwag-ə-'net\ *n* : a light wagon with two facing seats along the sides behind a cross seat in front

wa·gon–lit \ˌvȧ-gōⁿ-'lē\ *n*, *pl* **wagons–lits** *or* **wagon–lits** \-gōⁿ-'lē(z)\ [F, fr. *wagon* railroad car + *lit* bed] : a railroad sleeping car

wagon train *n* : a group of wagons traveling overland

wag·tail \'wag-ˌtāl\ *n* : any of various slender-bodied mostly Old World birds with a long tail that jerks up and down

wa·hi·ne \wä-'hē-nä\ *n* **1** : a Polynesian woman **2** : a female surfer

wa·hoo \'wä-ˌhü\ *n*, *pl* **wahoos** : a large vigorous food and sport fish related to the mackerel and found in warm seas

waif \'wāf\ *n* **1** : something found without an owner and esp. by chance **2** : a stray person or animal; *esp* : a homeless child

wail \'wāl\ *vb* **1** : LAMENT, WEEP **2** : to make a sound suggestive of a mournful cry **3** : COMPLAIN — **wail** *n*

wail·ful \-fəl\ *adj* : SORROWFUL, MOURNFUL — **wail·ful·ly** \-ē\ *adv*

wain \'wān\ *n* : a usu. large heavy farm wagon

wain·scot \'wān-skət, -ˌskōt, -ˌskät\ *n* **1** : a usu. paneled wooden lining of an interior wall of a room **2** : the lower part of an interior wall when finished differently from the rest — **wainscot** *vb*

wain·scot·ing *or* **wain·scot·ting** \-ˌskōt-iŋ, -ˌskät-, -skət-\ *n* : material for a wainscot; *also* : WAINSCOT

wain·wright \'wān-ˌrīt\ *n* : a builder and repairer of wagons

waist \'wāst\ *n* **1** : the narrowed part of

the body between the chest and hips **2** : a part resembling the human waist esp. in narrowness or central position ⟨the ∼ of a ship⟩ **3** : a garment or part of a garment (as a blouse or bodice) for the upper part of the body

waist·band \'wās(t)-ˌband\ *n* : a band (as on trousers or a skirt) that fits around the waist

waist·coat \'wes-kət, 'wās(t)-ˌkōt\ *n, chiefly Brit* : VEST 1

waist·line \'wāst-ˌlīn\ *n* **1** : a line thought of as surrounding the waist at its narrowest part; *also* : the length of this **2** : the line at which the bodice and skirt of a dress meet

¹wait \'wāt\ *vb* **1** : to remain inactive in readiness or expectation : AWAIT ⟨∼ for orders⟩ **2** : POSTPONE, DELAY ⟨∼ dinner for late guests⟩ **3** : to act as attendant or servant ⟨∼ on customers⟩ **4** : to attend as a waiter : SERVE ⟨∼ tables⟩ ⟨∼ at a banquet⟩ **5** : to be ready

²wait *n* **1** : a position of concealment usu. with intent to attack or surprise ⟨lie in ∼⟩ **2** : an act or period of waiting

wait·er \'wāt-ər\ *n* **1** : one that waits upon another; *esp* : a man who waits on table **2** : TRAY

waiting game *n* : a strategy in which one or more participants withhold action in the hope of an opportunity for more effective action later

waiting room *n* : a room (as at a doctor's office) for the use of persons waiting

wait·ress \'wā-trəs\ *n* : a girl or woman who waits on table

waive \'wāv\ *vb* **waived; waiv·ing** [ME *weiven,* fr. OF *weyver,* fr. *waif* lost, unclaimed] **1** : to give up claim to ⟨*waived* his right to a trial⟩ **2** : POSTPONE

waiv·er \'wā-vər\ *n* : the act of waiving right, claim, or privilege; *also* : a document containing a declaration of such an act

¹wake \'wāk\ *vb* **woke** \'wōk\ *also* **waked** \'wākt\; **wo·ken** \'wō-kən\ *also* **waked** *or* **woke; wak·ing 1** : to be or remain awake; *esp* : to keep watch (as over a corpse) **2** : AWAKE, AWAKEN ⟨the baby *waked* up early⟩ ⟨the thunder *waked* him up⟩

²wake *n* **1** : the state of being awake **2** : a watch held over the body of a dead person prior to burial

³wake *n* : the track left by a ship in the water; *also* : a track left behind

wake·ful \'wāk-fəl\ *adj* : not sleeping or able to sleep : SLEEPLESS, ALERT — **wake·ful·ness** *n*

wak·en \'wā-kən\ *vb* **wak·ened; wak·en·ing** \'wāk-(ə-)niŋ\ : WAKE

wake–rob·in \'wāk-ˌräb-ən\ *n* : TRILLIUM

wak·ing \'wā-kiŋ\ *adj* : passed in a conscious or alert state ⟨every ∼ hour⟩

wale \'wāl\ *n* : a ridge esp. on cloth; *also* : the texture esp. of a fabric

¹walk \'wok\ *vb* [partly fr. ME *walken,* fr. OE *wealcan* to roll, toss and partly fr. ME *walkien,* fr. OE *wealcian* to roll up, muffle up] **1** : to move or cause to move on foot usu. at a natural unhurried gait ⟨∼ to town⟩ ⟨∼ a horse⟩ **2** : to pass over, through, or along by walking ⟨∼ the streets⟩ **3** : to perform or accomplish by walking ⟨∼ guard⟩ **4** : to follow a course of action or way of life ⟨∼ humbly in the sight of God⟩ **5** : to receive a base on balls; *also* : to give a base on balls to — **walk·er** *n*

²walk *n* **1** : a going on foot ⟨go for a ∼⟩ **2** : a place, path, or course for walking **3** : distance to be walked ⟨a 10-minute ∼ from here⟩ **4** : manner of living : CONDUCT, BEHAVIOR; *also* : social or economic status ⟨various ∼s of life⟩ **5** : manner of walking : GAIT; *esp* : a slow 4-beat gait of a horse **6** : BASE ON BALLS

walk·away \'wok-ə-ˌwā\ *n* : an easily won contest

walk·ie–talk·ie \'wo-kē-'to-kē\ *n* : a small portable radio transmitting and receiving set

¹walk–in \'wok-ˌin\ *adj* : large enough to be walked into ⟨a ∼ refrigerator⟩

²walk–in \'wok-ˌin\ *n* **1** : an easy election victory **2** : one that walks in

walking papers *n pl* : DISMISSAL, DISCHARGE

walking stick *n* **1** : a stick used in walking **2** *usu* **walk·ing·stick** : STICK INSECT; *esp* : one common in parts of the U.S.

walk–on \'wok-ˌon, -ˌän\ *n* : a small part or brief appearance in a dramatic production

walk·out \-ˌau̇t\ *n* **1** : a labor strike **2** : the action of leaving a meeting or organization as an expression of disapproval

walk·over \-ˌō-vər\ *n* : a one-sided contest : an easy victory

walk–up \ˈwȯk-ˌəp\ *n* : a building or apartment house without an elevator — **walk–up** *adj*

walk·way \-ˌwā\ *n* : a passage for walking

¹wall \ˈwȯl\ *n* [ME, fr. OE *weall*, fr. L *vallum* rampart, fr. *vallus* stake, palisade] **1** : a structure (as of stone or brick) intended for defense or security or for enclosing something **2** : one of the upright enclosing parts of a building or room **3** : the inside surface of a cavity or vessel ⟨the ∼ of a boiler⟩ **4** : something like a wall in appearance or function ⟨a tariff ∼⟩ — **walled** \ˈwȯld\ *adj*

²wall *vb* **1** : to provide, separate, or surround with or as if with a wall ⟨∼ in a garden⟩ **2** : to close (an opening) with or as if with a wall ⟨∼ up a door⟩

wal·la·by \ˈwäl-ə-bē\ *n, pl* **wallabies** *also* **wallaby** : any of various small or medium-sized kangaroos

wall·board \ˈwȯl-ˌbōrd\ *n* : a structural material (as of wood pulp or plaster) made in large sheets and used for sheathing interior walls and ceilings

wal·let \ˈwäl-ət\ *n* **1** : a bag or sack for carrying things on a journey **2** : a pocketbook with compartments (as for personal papers and usu. unfolded money) : BILLFOLD

wall·eye \ˈwȯl-ˌī\ *n* **1** : an eye with whitish iris or an opaque white cornea **2** : a large vigorous No. American food and sport fish related to the perches — **wall·eyed** \-ˌīd\ *adj*

wall·flow·er \ˈwȯl-ˌflau̇(-ə)r\ *n* **1** : any of several Old World plants related to the mustards; *esp* : one with showy fragrant flowers **2** : a person who usu. from shyness or unpopularity remains alone (as at a dance)

Wal·loon \wä-ˈlün\ *n* : a member of a chiefly Celtic people of southern and southeastern Belgium and adjacent parts of France — **Walloon** *adj*

¹wal·lop \ˈwäl-əp\ *vb* [ME, gallop, fr. Old Northern French *waloper* to gallop] **1** : to beat soundly : TROUNCE **2** : to hit hard : SOCK

²wallop *n* **1** : a powerful blow or impact **2** : the ability to hit hard **3** : emotional or psychological force : IMPACT

wal·lop·ing \ˈwäl-ə-piŋ\ *adj* **1** : LARGE, WHOPPING **2** : exceptionally fine or impressive

¹wal·low \ˈwäl-ō\ *vb* **1** : to roll oneself about in or as if in deep mud : FLOUNDER ⟨hogs ∼ing in the mire⟩ **2** : to live in or be filled with excessive pleasure ⟨∼ in luxury⟩

²wallow *n* : a muddy or dust-filled area where animals wallow

wall·pa·per \ˈwȯl-ˌpā-pər\ *n* : decorative paper for the walls of a room — **wallpaper** *vb*

wall–to–wall *adj* **1** : covering the entire floor ⟨*wall-to-wall* carpeting⟩ **2** : covering or filling one entire space or time ⟨crowds of *wall-to-wall* people⟩

wal·nut \ˈwȯl-(ˌ)nət\ *n* [ME *walnot*, fr. OE *wealhhnutu*, lit., foreign nut, fr. *Wealh* Welshman, foreigner + *hnutu* nut] **1** : an edible nut with a furrowed usu. rough shell and an adherent husk from any of a genus of trees related to the hickories; *esp* : the large edible nut of a Eurasian tree **2** : a tree that bears walnuts **3** : the usu. reddish to dark brown wood of a walnut used esp. in cabinetwork and veneers

wal·rus \ˈwȯl-rəs, ˈwäl-\ *n, pl* **walrus** *or* **wal·rus·es** : either of two large mammals of northern seas related to the seals and having ivory tusks

¹waltz \ˈwȯlts\ *vb* [G *walzer*, fr. *walzen* to roll, dance, fr. Old High German *walzan* to turn, roll] **1** : to dance a waltz **2** : to move or advance easily, successfully, or conspicuously ⟨he ∼ed through customs⟩

²waltz *n* **1** : a gliding dance done to music having three beats to the measure **2** : music for or suitable for waltzing

wam·ble \ˈwäm-bəl\ *vb* **wam·bled**; **wam·bling** \-b(ə-)liŋ\ : to progress unsteadily or with a lurching shambling gait

wam·pum \ˈwäm-pəm\ *n* [short for *wampumpeag*, fr. Narraganset (a North American Indian language) *wampompeag*, fr. *wampan* white + *api* string + *-ag* pl. suffix] **1** : beads made of shells strung in strands, belts, or sashes and used by No. American Indians as money and ornaments **2** *slang* : MONEY

wan \\'wän\ *adj* **wan•ner; wan•nest 1** : SICKLY, PALLID; *also* : FEEBLE **2** : DIM, FAINT **3** : LANGUID 〈a ∼ smile〉 — **wan•ly** *adv* — **wan•ness** \\'wän-nəs\ *n*

wand \\'wänd\ *n* **1** : a slender staff carried in a procession **2** : the staff of a fairy, diviner, or magician

wan•der \\'wän-dər\ *vb* **wan•dered; wan•der•ing** \-d(ə-)riŋ\ **1** : to move about aimlessly or without a fixed course or goal : RAMBLE **2** : STRAY **3** : to go astray in conduct or thought; *esp* : to become delirious — **wan•der•er** *n*

Wan•der•ing Jew *n* : any of several trailing or creeping plants some of which are often planted in hanging baskets

wan•der•lust \\'wän-dər-ˌləst\ *n* : strong longing for or impulse toward wandering

¹wane \\'wān\ *vb* **waned; wan•ing 1** : to grow gradually smaller or less 〈the moon ∼s〉 〈his strength *waned*〉 **2** : to lose power, prosperity, or influence **3** : to draw near an end 〈summer is *waning*〉

²wane *n* : a waning (as in size or power); *also* : a period in which something is waning

wan•gle \\'waŋ-gəl\ *vb* **wan•gled; wan•gling** \-g(ə-)liŋ\ **1** : to obtain by sly or roundabout means; *also* : to use trickery or questionable means to achieve an end **2** : MANIPULATE; *also* : FINAGLE

Wan•kel engine \\'väŋ-kəl-, 'waŋ-\ *n* : an internal-combustion rotary engine with a rounded triangular rotor functioning as a piston

¹want \\'wȯnt\ *vb* **1** : to fail to possess : LACK 〈they ∼ the necessities of life〉 **2** : to fall short by 〈it ∼s three minutes to six〉 **3** : to feel or suffer the need of **4** : NEED, REQUIRE 〈the house ∼s painting〉 **5** : to desire earnestly : WISH

²want *n* **1** : a lack of a required or usual amount : SHORTAGE **2** : dire need : DESTITUTION **3** : something wanted : DESIRE **4** : personal defect : FAULT

¹want•ing \-iŋ\ *adj* **1** : not present or in evidence : ABSENT **2** : falling below standards or expectations **3** : lacking in ability or capacity : DEFICIENT 〈∼ in common sense〉

²wanting *prep* **1** : WITHOUT 〈a book ∼ a cover〉 **2** : LESS, MINUS 〈a month ∼ two days〉

¹wan•ton \\'wȯnt-ᵊn\ *adj* [ME, undisciplined, fr. *wan*- deficient, wrong + *towen*, pp. of *teen* to draw, train, discipline] **1** : UNCHASTE, LEWD, LUSTFUL; *also* : SENSUAL **2** : having no regard for justice or for other persons' feelings, rights, or safety : MERCILESS, INHUMANE 〈∼ cruelty〉 **3** : having no just cause 〈a ∼ attack〉 — **wan•ton•ly** *adv* — **wan•ton•ness** *n*

²wanton *n* : a wanton individual; *esp* : a lewd or immoral person

³wanton *vb* **1** : to be wanton : act wantonly **2** : to pass or waste wantonly

wa•pi•ti \\'wäp-ət-ē\ *n, pl* **wapiti** *or* **wapitis** : ELK 2

¹war \\'wȯr\ *n* **1** : a state or period of usu. open and declared armed fighting between states or nations **2** : the art or science of warfare **3** : a state of hostility, conflict, or antagonism **4** : a struggle between opposing forces or for a particular end 〈∼ against disease〉 — **war•less** \-ləs\ *adj*

²war *vb* **warred; war•ring** : to engage in warfare : be in conflict

³war *abbr* warrant

¹war•ble \\'wȯr-bəl\ *n* **1** : a melodious succession of low pleasing sounds **2** : a musical trill

²warble *vb* **war•bled; war•bling** \-b(ə-)liŋ\ **1** : to sing or utter in a trilling manner or with variations **2** : to express by or as if by warbling

³warble *n* : a swelling under the hide esp. of the back of cattle, horses, and wild mammals caused by the maggot of a fly (**warble fly**); *also* : its maggot

war•bler \\'wȯr-blər\ *n* **1** : SONGSTER **2** : any of various small slender-billed Old World singing birds related to the thrushes and noted for their song **3** : any of various small bright-colored American insect-eating birds with a usu. weak and unmusical song

war•bon•net \\'wȯr-ˌbän-ət\ *n* : a feathered American Indian ceremonial headdress

war cry *n* **1** : a cry used by fighters in war **2** : a slogan used esp. to rally people to a cause

¹ward \\'wȯrd\ *n* **1** : a guarding or being under guard or guardianship; *esp*

: CUSTODY **2** : a body of guards **3** : a division of a prison **4** : a division in a hospital **5** : a division of a city for electoral or administrative purposes **6** : a person (as a child) under the protection of a guardian or a law court **7** : a person or body of persons under the protection or tutelage of a government **8** : a means of defense : PROTECTION

²ward *vb* : to turn aside : DEFLECT — usu. used with *off* ⟨~ off a blow⟩

¹-ward \wərd\ *also* **-wards** \wərdz\ *adj suffix* **1** : that moves, tends, faces, or is directed toward ⟨wind*ward*⟩ **2** : that occurs or is situated in the direction of ⟨sea*ward*⟩

²-ward *or* **-wards** *adv suffix* **1** : in a (specified) direction ⟨up*wards*⟩ ⟨after*ward*⟩ **2** : toward a (specified) point, position, or area ⟨sky*ward*⟩

war dance *n* : a dance performed by primitive peoples before going to war or in celebration of victory

war•den \'wȯrd-³n\ *n* **1** : GUARDIAN, KEEPER **2** : the governor of a town, district, or fortress **3** : an official charged with special supervisory or enforcement duties ⟨game ~⟩ ⟨air raid ~⟩ **4** : an official in charge of the operation of a prison **5** : one of two ranking lay officers of an Episcopal parish **6** : any of various British college officials

ward•er \'wȯrd-ər\ *n* : WATCHMAN, WARDEN

ward heeler \-ˌhē-lər\ *n* : a local worker for a political boss

ward•robe \'wȯrd-ˌrōb\ *n* [ME *warderobe,* fr. OF, fr. *warder* to guard + *robe* robe] **1** : a room or closet where clothes are kept; *also* : CLOTHESPRESS **2** : a collection of wearing apparel ⟨his summer ~⟩

ward•room \-ˌrüm, -ˌrum\ *n* : the quarters in a warship allotted to the commissioned officers except the captain; *esp* : the room allotted to these officers for meals

ward•ship \'wȯrd-ˌship\ *n* **1** : GUARDIANSHIP **2** : the state of being under care of a guardian

ware \'waər\ *n* **1** : manufactured articles or products of art or craft : GOODS **2** : an article of merchandise ⟨a ped-

dler hawking his ~s⟩ **3** : items (as dishes) of fired clay : POTTERY

ware•house \-ˌhaus\ *n* : a place for the storage of merchandise or commodities : STOREHOUSE — **warehouse** *vb* — **ware•house•man** \-mən\ *n* — **warehous•er** \-hau-zər, -sər\ *n*

ware•room \'waər-ˌrüm, -ˌrum\ *n* : a room in which goods are exhibited for sale

war•fare \'wȯr-ˌfaər\ *n* **1** : military operations between enemies : WAR; *also* : an activity undertaken by one country to weaken or destroy another ⟨economic ~⟩ **2** : STRUGGLE, CONFLICT

war•fa•rin \'wȯr-fə-rən\ *n* : an anticoagulant used as a rodent poison and in medicine

war•head \-ˌhed\ *n* : the section of a missile containing the charge

war–horse \-ˌhȯrs\ *n* **1** : a horse for use in war **2** : a veteran soldier or public person (as a politician)

war•like \-ˌlīk\ *adj* **1** : fond of war ⟨~ peoples⟩ **2** : of, relating to, or useful in war : MILITARY, MARTIAL ⟨~ supplies⟩ **3** : befitting or characteristic of war or of soldiers ⟨~ attitudes⟩

war•lock \-ˌläk\ *n* [ME *warloghe,* fr. OE *wǣrloga* one that breaks faith, the Devil, fr. *wǣr* faith, troth + *-loga* (fr. *lēogan* to lie)] : SORCERER, WIZARD

war•lord \-ˌlȯrd\ *n* **1** : a high military leader **2** : a military commander exercising local civil power by force ⟨former Chinese ~s⟩

¹warm \'wȯrm\ *adj* **1** : having or giving out heat to a moderate or adequate degree ⟨~ milk⟩ ⟨a ~ stove⟩ **2** : serving to retain heat ⟨~ clothes⟩ **3** : feeling or inducing sensations of heat ⟨~ from exercise⟩ ⟨a ~ climb⟩ **4** : showing or marked by strong feeling : ARDENT ⟨~ support⟩ **5** : marked by tense excitement or hot anger ⟨a ~ campaign⟩ **6** : giving a pleasant impression of warmth, cheerfulness, or friendliness ⟨~ colors⟩ ⟨a ~ tone of voice⟩ **7** : marked by or tending toward injury, distress, or pain ⟨made things ~ for the enemy⟩ **8** : newly made : FRESH ⟨a ~ scent⟩ **9** : near to a goal ⟨getting ~ in a search⟩ — **warm•ly** *adv*

²warm *vb* **1** : to make or become warm **2** : to give a feeling of warmth or vitality to **3** : to experience feelings of affection or pleasure ⟨she ~ed to her guest⟩ **4** : to reheat for eating ⟨~ed over the roast⟩ **5** : to make ready for operation or performance by preliminary exercise or operation ⟨~ up the motor⟩ **6** : to become increasingly ardent, interested, or competent ⟨the speaker ~ed to his topic⟩ — **warm·er** *n*

warm–blood·ed \-'bləd-əd\ *adj* : able to maintain a relatively high and constant body temperature essentially independent of that of the surroundings

warmed–over \'wȯrmd-'ō-vər\ *adj* **1** : REHEATED ⟨~ cabbage⟩ **2** : not fresh or new ⟨~ ideas⟩

warm·heart·ed \'wȯrm-'härt-əd\ *adj* : marked by warmth of feeling : CORDIAL — **warm·heart·ed·ness** *n*

warming pan *n* : a long-handled covered pan filled with live coals and formerly used to warm a bed

war·mon·ger \'wȯr-ˌməŋ-gər, -ˌmäŋ-\ *n* : one who urges or attempts to stir up war

warmth \'wȯrmth\ *n* **1** : the quality or state of being warm **2** : ZEAL, ARDOR, FERVOR

warm up \(')wȯrm-'əp\ *vb* : to engage in exercise or practice esp. before entering a game or contest — **warm–up** \'wȯrm-ˌəp\ *n*

warn \'wȯrn\ *vb* **1** : to put on guard : CAUTION; *also* : ADMONISH, COUNSEL **2** : to notify esp. in advance : INFORM **3** : to order to go or keep away

¹**warn·ing** \-iŋ\ *n* **1** : the act of warning : the state of being warned **2** : something that warns or serves to warn

²**warning** *adj* : serving as an alarm, signal, summons, or admonition ⟨~ bell⟩ — **warn·ing·ly** *adv*

¹**warp** \'wȯrp\ *n* **1** : the lengthwise threads on a loom or in a woven fabric **2** : a twist out of a true plane or straight line ⟨a ~ in a board⟩

²**warp** *vb* [ME *warpen*, fr. OE *weorpan* to throw] **1** : to turn or twist out of shape; *also* : to become so twisted **2** : to lead astray : PERVERT; *also* : FALSIFY, DISTORT

war paint *n* : paint put on the face and body by American Indians as a sign of going to war

war·path \'wȯr-ˌpath, -ˌpȧth\ *n* : the course taken by a party of American Indians going on a hostile expedition — **on the warpath** : ready to fight or argue

war·plane \-ˌplān\ *n* : a military airplane; *esp* : one armed for combat

¹**war·rant** \'wȯr-ənt, 'wär-\ *n* **1** : AUTHORIZATION; *also* : JUSTIFICATION, GROUND **2** : evidence (as a document) of authorization; *esp* : a legal writ authorizing an officer to take action (as in making an arrest, seizure, or search) **3** : a certificate of appointment issued to an officer of lower rank than a commissioned officer

²**warrant** *vb* **1** : to guarantee security or immunity to : SECURE **2** : to declare or maintain positively ⟨I ~ this is so⟩ **3** : to assure (a person) of the truth of what is said **4** : to guarantee to be as it appears or as it is represented ⟨~ goods as of the first quality⟩ **5** : SANCTION, AUTHORIZE **6** : to give proof of : ATTEST; *also* : GUARANTEE **7** : JUSTIFY ⟨his need ~s the expenditure⟩

warrant officer *n* **1** : an officer in the armed forces ranking next below a commissioned officer **2** : a commissioned officer ranking below an ensign in the navy or coast guard and below a second lieutenant in the marine corps

war·ran·ty \'wȯr-ənt-ē, 'wär-\ *n, pl* **-ties** : an expressed or implied statement that some situation or thing is as it appears to be or is represented to be; *esp* : a usu. written guarantee of the integrity of a product and of the maker's responsibility for the repair or replacement of defective parts

war·ren \'wȯr-ən, 'wär-\ *n* **1** : an area for the keeping of small game and esp. rabbits; *also* : an area where rabbits breed **2** : a crowded tenement or district

war·rior \'wȯr-yər, 'wȯr-ē-ər; 'wär-ē-, 'wär-yər\ *n* : a man engaged or experienced in warfare

war·ship \'wȯr-ˌship\ *n* : a military ship armed for combat

wart \'wȯrt\ *n* **1** : a small usu. horny projection on the skin; *esp* : one caused by a virus **2** : a protuberance resembling a wart (as on a plant) — **warty** *adj*

wart·hog \'wȯrt-ˌhȯg, -ˌhäg\ *n* : an African wild hog with large tusks and two pairs of rough warty protuberances below the eyes

war·time \'wȯr-ˌtīm\ *n* : a period during which a war is in progress

wary \'wa(ə)r-ē\ *adj* **wari·er; -est** : very cautious; *esp* : careful in guarding against danger or deception

was past 1st & 3d sing of BE

¹wash \'wȯsh, 'wäsh\ *vb* **1** : to cleanse with or as if with a liquid (as water) **2** : to wet thoroughly with water or other liquid **3** : to flow along the border of ⟨waves ∼ the shore⟩ **4** : to pass (a gas or gaseous mixture) through or over a liquid for purifying **5** : to pour or flow in a stream or current **6** : to move or remove by or as if by the action of water **7** : to cover or daub lightly with a liquid (as whitewash) **8** : to run water over (as gravel or ore) in order to separate valuable matter from refuse ⟨∼ sand for gold⟩ **9** : to undergo laundering ⟨a dress that doesn't ∼ well⟩ **10** : to stand a test ⟨that story will not ∼⟩ **11** : to be worn away by water

²wash *n* **1** : the act or process or an instance of washing or being washed **2** : articles to be washed or being washed **3** : the flow or action of a mass of water (as a wave) **4** : erosion by waves (as of the sea) **5** *West* : the dry bed of a stream **6** : worthless esp. liquid waste : REFUSE, SWILL **7** : a thin coat of paint (as watercolor) **8** : a disturbance in the air caused by the passage of a wing or propeller

³wash *adj* : WASHABLE

Wash *abbr* Washington

wash·able \-ə-bəl\ *adj* : capable of being washed without damage

wash–and–wear *adj* : of, relating to, or constituting a fabric or garment that needs little or no ironing after washing

wash·ba·sin \'wȯsh-ˌbās-ᵊn, 'wäsh-\ *n* : WASHBOWL

wash·board \-ˌbȯrd\ *n* : a grooved board to scrub clothes on

wash·bowl \-ˌbōl\ *n* : a large bowl for water for washing hands and face

wash·cloth \-ˌklȯth\ *n* : a cloth used for washing one's face and body

wash drawing *n* : watercolor painting in or chiefly in washes

washed–out \'wȯsht-ˈaut, 'wäsht-\ *adj* **1**

: faded in color **2** : EXHAUSTED ⟨felt ∼ after working all night⟩

washed–up \'wȯsht-ᵊp, 'wäsht-\ *adj* : no longer successful, popular, or needed

wash·er \'wȯsh-ər, 'wäsh-\ *n* **1** : a ring or perforated plate used around a bolt or screw to ensure tightness or relieve friction **2** : one that washes; *esp* : a machine for washing

wash·er·wom·an \-ˌwùm-ən\ *n* : a woman who works at washing clothes

wash·house \'wȯsh-ˌhaus, 'wäsh-\ *n* : a house or building used or equipped for washing and esp. for washing clothes

wash·ing \'wȯsh-iŋ, 'wäsh-\ *n* **1** : material obtained by washing **2** : a thin covering or coat ⟨a ∼ of silver⟩ **3** : articles washed or to be washed

washing soda *n* : SODIUM CARBONATE

Wash·ing·ton's Birthday \ˌwȯsh-iŋ-tənz-, ˌwäsh-\ *n* : the 3d Monday in February observed as a legal holiday

wash·out \'wȯsh-ˌaut, 'wäsh-\ *n* **1** : the washing away of earth (as from a road); *also* : a place where earth is washed away **2** : FAILURE; *esp* : one who fails in a course of training or study

wash·room \-ˌrüm, -ˌrùm\ *n* : a room equipped with washing and toilet facilities : LAVATORY

wash·stand \-ˌstand\ *n* **1** : a stand holding articles needed for washing face and hands **2** : a washbowl permanently set in place

wash·tub \-ˌtəb\ *n* : a tub for washing clothes or for soaking them before washing

wash·wom·an \'wȯsh-ˌwùm-ən, 'wäsh-\ *n* : WASHERWOMAN

washy \'wȯsh-ē, 'wäsh-\ *adj* **wash·i·er; -est** **1** : WEAK, WATERY **2** : PALLID **3** : lacking in vigor, individuality, or definiteness

wasp \'wäsp, 'wȯsp\ *n* : any of numerous social or solitary winged insects related to the bees and ants with biting mouthparts and in females and workers a formidable sting

WASP *or* **Wasp** *n* [*white Anglo-Saxon Protestant*] : an American of northern European and esp. British stock and of Protestant background

wasp·ish \'wäs-pish, 'wȯs-\ *adj* **1**

: SNAPPISH, IRRITABLE **2** : resembling a wasp in form; *esp* : slightly built

wasp waist *n* : a very slender waist

¹**was·sail** \'wäs-əl, wä-'sāl\ *n* [ME *wæs hæil,* fr. ON *ves heill* be well] **1** : an early English toast to someone's health **2** : a hot drink made with wine, beer, or cider, spices, sugar, and usu. baked apples and that is traditionally served at Christmas **3** : riotous drinking : REVELRY

²**wassail** *vb* **1** : CAROUSE **2** : to drink to the health or thriving of — **was·sail·er** *n*

Was·ser·mann test \ˌwäs-ər-mən-, ˌväs-\ *n* : a blood test for infection with syphilis

wast·age \'wā-stij\ *n* : loss by use, decay, erosion, or leakage or through wastefulness

¹**waste** \'wāst\ *n* **1** : a sparsely settled or barren region : DESERT; *also* : uncultivated land **2** : the act or an instance of wasting : the state of being wasted **3** : gradual loss or decrease by use, wear, or decay **4** : material left over, rejected, or thrown away; *also* : an unwanted product of a manufacturing or chemical process **5** : refuse (as garbage or rubbish) that accumulates about habitations; *also* : material (as feces) produced but not used by a living body — **waste·ful** \-fəl\ *adj* — **waste·ful·ly** \-ē\ *adv* — **waste·ful·ness** *n*

²**waste** *vb* **wast·ed; wast·ing 1** : DEVASTATE **2** : to wear away or diminish gradually : CONSUME **3** : to spend money or use property carelessly or uselessly : SQUANDER; *also* : to allow to be used inefficiently or become dissipated **4** : to lose or cause to lose weight, strength, or vitality ⟨*wasting* away from fever⟩ **5** : to become diminished in bulk or substance : DWINDLE — **wast·er** *n*

³**waste** *adj* **1** : being wild and uninhabited : BARREN, DESOLATE; *also* : UNCULTIVATED **2** : RUINED, DEVASTATED ⟨bombs laid ∼ the city⟩ **3** : discarded as worthless after being used ⟨∼ water⟩ **4** : excreted from or stored in inert form in a living body as a by-product of vital activity ⟨∼ matter from birds⟩ **5** : serving to conduct or hold refuse material; *esp* : carrying off superfluous water

waste·bas·ket \'wās(t)-ˌbas-kət\ *n* : a receptacle for refuse

waste·land \'wāst-ˌland, -lənd\ *n* : land that is barren or unfit for cultivation

waste·pa·per \'wās(t)-'pā-pər\ *n* : paper discarded as used, superfluous, or not fit for use

waste product *n* : material resulting from a process (as of metabolism or manufacture) that is of no further use to the system producing it

wast·rel \'wā-strəl\ *n* : one that wastes : SPENDTHRIFT

¹**watch** \'wäch, 'wȯch\ *vb* **1** : to be or stay awake intentionally : keep vigil ⟨∼*ed* by the patient's bedside⟩ ⟨∼ and pray⟩ **2** : to be on the lookout for danger : be on one's guard **3** : to keep guard ⟨∼ outside the door⟩ **4** : OBSERVE ⟨∼ a game⟩ **5** : to keep in view so as to prevent harm or warn of danger ⟨∼ a brush fire carefully⟩ **6** : to keep oneself informed about ⟨∼ his progress⟩ **7** : to lie in wait for esp. so as to take advantage of ⟨∼*ed* his opportunity⟩ — **watch·er** *n*

²**watch** *n* **1** : the act of keeping awake to guard, protect, or attend; *also* : a state of alert and continuous attention **2** : close observation **3** : one that watches : LOOKOUT, WATCHMAN, GUARD **4** : an allotted period for being on nautical duty; *also* : the members of a ship's company operating the vessel during such a period **5** : a portable timepiece carried on the person

watch·band \'wäch-ˌband, 'wȯch-\ *n* : the bracelet or strap of a wristwatch

watch·case \-ˌkās\ *n* : the outside metal covering of a watch

watch·dog \-ˌdȯg\ *n* **1** : a dog kept to guard property **2** : one that guards or protects

watch·ful \'wäch-fəl, 'wȯch-\ *adj* : steadily attentive and alert esp. to danger : VIGILANT — **watch·ful·ly** \-ē\ *adv* — **watch·ful·ness** *n*

watch·mak·er \-ˌmā-kər\ *n* : one that makes or repairs watches — **watch·mak·ing** \-ˌmā-kiŋ\ *n*

watch·man \-mən\ *n* : a person assigned to watch : GUARD

watch night *n* : a devotional service lasting until after midnight esp. on New Year's Eve

watch·tow·er \'wäch-ˌtaů(-ə)r, 'wŏch-\ *n* : a tower for a lookout

watch·word \-ˌwərd\ *n* **1** : a secret word used as a signal or sign of recognition **2** : a motto used as a slogan or rallying cry

¹wa·ter \'wȯt-ər, 'wät-\ *n* **1** : the liquid that descends as rain and forms rivers, lakes, and seas **2** : a natural mineral water — usu. used in pl. **3** *pl* : the water occupying or flowing in a particular bed; *also* : a band of seawater bordering on and under the control of a country ⟨sailing Canadian ∼s⟩ **4** : any of various liquids containing or resembling water; *esp* : a watery fluid (as tears, urine, or sap) formed or circulating in a living body **5** : a specified degree of thoroughness or completeness ⟨a scoundrel of the first ∼⟩ **6** : a wavy lustrous pattern (as of a textile)

²water *vb* **1** : to supply with or get or take water ⟨∼ horses⟩ ⟨the ship ∼ed at each port⟩ **2** : to treat (as cloth) so as to give a lustrous appearance in wavy lines **3** : to dilute by or as if by adding water to **4** : to form or secrete water or watery matter ⟨his eyes ∼ed⟩ ⟨my mouth ∼ed⟩

water ballet *n* : a synchronized sequence of movements performed by a group of swimmers

water bed *n* : a bed whose mattress is a plastic bag filled with water

wa·ter·borne \-ˌbŏrn\ *adj* : supported or carried by water

water buffalo *n* : a common oxlike often domesticated Asian bovine

water chestnut *n* : any of several aquatic plants (as a Chinese sedge) with edible underground parts or fruits; *also* : the edible part

water closet *n* : a compartment or room for defecation and urination into a toilet bowl : BATHROOM; *also* : a toilet bowl along with its accessories

wa·ter·col·or \'wȯt-ər-ˌkəl-ər, 'wät-\ *n* **1** : a paint whose liquid part is water **2** : the art of painting with watercolors **3** : a picture made with watercolors

wa·ter·course \-ˌkōrs\ *n* : a stream of water; *also* : the bed of a stream

wa·ter·craft \-ˌkraft\ *n* : a craft for water transport : SHIP, BOAT

wa·ter·cress \-ˌkres\ *n* : a perennial plant with white flowers related to the cabbage, found chiefly in clear running water, and used esp. in salads

wa·ter·fall \-ˌfŏl\ *n* : a very steep descent of the water of a stream

water flea *n* : any of various tiny active freshwater crustaceans

wa·ter·fowl \'wȯt-ər-ˌfaůl, 'wät-\ *n* **1** : a bird that frequents the water **2** **waterfowl** *pl* : wild ducks and geese hunted as game

wa·ter·front \-ˌfrənt\ *n* : land or a section of a town fronting or abutting on a body of water

water gap *n* : a pass in a mountain ridge through which a stream runs

water gas *n* : a poisonous flammable gaseous mixture of chiefly hydrogen and carbon monoxide made by forcing air and steam over red-hot coke or coal that is used as a fuel

water glass *n* : a drinking glass

watering place *n* : a resort that features mineral springs or bathing

water lily *n* : any of a family of aquatic plants with floating roundish leaves and showy solitary flowers

wa·ter·line \'wȯt-ər-ˌlīn, 'wät-\ *n* : any of several lines that are marked on the outside of a ship and correspond with the surface of the water when the ship is afloat on an even keel

wa·ter·logged \-ˌlȯgd, -ˌlägd\ *adj* : so filled or soaked with water as to be heavy or unmanageable ⟨a ∼ boat⟩

wa·ter·loo \ˌwȯt-ər-'lü, ˌwät-\ *n, pl* **-loos** [*Waterloo,* Belgium, scene of Napoleon's defeat in 1815] : a decisive defeat

¹wa·ter·mark \'wȯt-ər-ˌmärk, 'wät-\ *n* **1** : a mark indicating height to which water has risen **2** : a marking in paper visible when the paper is held up to the light

²watermark *vb* : to mark (paper) with a watermark

wa·ter·mel·on \-ˌmel-ən\ *n* : a large roundish or oblong fruit with sweet juicy usu. red pulp; *also* : an African vine related to the squashes that produces watermelons

water moccasin *n* : a venomous snake of the southern U.S. that is a pit viper related to the copperhead

water ouzel *n* : DIPPER 1

water pipe *n* : a tobacco-smoking device so arranged that the smoke is drawn through water

water polo *n* : a team game played in a swimming pool with a ball resembling a soccer ball

wa·ter·pow·er \\'wȯt-ər-ˌpau̇(-ə)r, 'wät-\\ *n* : the power of moving water used to run machinery

¹**wa·ter·proof** \\ˌwȯt-ər-'prüf, ˌwät-\\ *adj* : not letting water through; *esp* : covered or treated with a material to prevent permeation by water — **wa·ter·proof·ing** \\-iŋ\\ *n*

²**waterproof** \\'wȯt-ər-ˌprüf, 'wät-\\ *n* **1** : a waterproof fabric **2** *chiefly Brit* : RAINCOAT

³**waterproof** \\ˌwȯt-ər-'prüf, ˌwät-\\ *vb* : to make waterproof

wa·ter–re·pel·lent \\ˌwȯt-ə(r)-ri-'pel-ənt, ˌwät-\\ *adj* : treated with a finish that is resistant to penetration by water

wa·ter–re·sis·tant \\-ri-'zis-tənt\\ *adj* : WATER-REPELLENT

wa·ter·shed \\'wȯt-ər-ˌshed, 'wät-\\ *n* **1** : a dividing ridge between two drainage areas **2** : the region or area drained by a particular body of water

wa·ter·side \\-ˌsīd\\ *n* : the land bordering a body of water

water ski *n* : a ski used on water when the wearer is towed — **wa·ter–ski** *vb* — **wa·ter–ski·er** \\-ˌskē-ər\\ *n*

wa·ter·spout \\'wȯt-ər-ˌspau̇t, 'wät-\\ *n* **1** : a pipe for carrying off water from a roof **2** : a funnel-shaped cloud extending from a cumulus cloud down to a cloud of spray torn up by whirling winds from an ocean or lake

water strider *n* : any of various long-legged bugs that move about swiftly on the surface of the water

water table *n* : the upper limit of the portion of the ground wholly saturated with water

wa·ter·tight \\ˌwȯt-ər-'tīt, ˌwät-\\ *adj* **1** : constructed so as to keep water out **2** : so worded that its meaning cannot be misunderstood or its purpose defeated ⟨a ∼ contract⟩

wa·ter·way \\'wȯt-ər-ˌwā, 'wät-\\ *n* : a navigable body of water

wa·ter·wheel \\-ˌhwēl\\ *n* : a wheel rotated by direct action of water flowing against it

water wings *n pl* : an air-filled device to give support to a person's body when he is swimming or learning to swim

wa·ter·works \\'wȯt-ər-ˌwərks, 'wät-\\ *n pl* : a system of reservoirs, pipes, and machinery for supplying water (as to a city)

wa·tery \\'wȯt-ə-rē, 'wät-\\ *adj* **1** : containing, full of, or giving out water ⟨∼ clouds⟩ **2** : being like water : THIN, WEAK ⟨∼ lemonade⟩; *also* : being soft and soggy ⟨∼ turnips⟩

WATS \\'wäts\\ *abbr* Wide Area Telephone Service

watt \\'wät\\ *n* [after James *Watt* †1819 Scottish engineer and inventor] : the metric unit of power equal to the work done at the rate of one joule per second or to the power produced by a current of one ampere across a potential difference of one volt

watt·age \\'wät-ij\\ *n* : amount of power expressed in watts

wat·tle \\'wät-ᵊl\\ *n* **1** : a framework of rods with flexible branches or reeds interlaced used for fencing and esp. formerly in building; *also* : material for this framework **2** : a naked fleshy process hanging usu. from the head or neck (as of a bird) — **wat·tled** \\-ᵊld\\ *adj*

W Aust *abbr* Western Australia

¹**wave** \\'wāv\\ *vb* **waved; wav·ing** **1** : FLUTTER ⟨flags *waving* in the breeze⟩ **2** : to motion with the hands or with something held in them in signal or salute **3** : to become moved or brandished to-and-fro; *also* : BRANDISH, FLOURISH ⟨∼ a sword⟩ **4** : to move before the wind with a wavelike motion ⟨fields of *waving* grain⟩ **5** : to curve up and down like a wave : UNDULATE

²**wave** *n* **1** : a moving ridge or swell on the surface of water **2** : a wavelike formation or shape ⟨a ∼ in the hair⟩ **3** : the action or process of making wavy or curly **4** : a waving motion; *esp* : a signal made by waving something **5** : FLOW, GUSH ⟨a ∼ of color swept her face⟩ **6** : a rapid increase : SURGE ⟨a ∼ of buying⟩ ⟨a heat ∼⟩ **7** : a disturbance somewhat similar to a wave in water that transfers energy progressively from point to point ⟨a light ∼⟩ ⟨a sound ∼⟩ — **wave·like** *adj*

Wave \\'wāv\\ *n* [*W*omen *A*ccepted for *V*olunteer *E*mergency *S*ervice] : a woman serving in the navy

wave·length \\'wāv-ˌleŋth\\ *n* **1** : the distance in the line of advance of a wave from any one point (as a crest) to the next corresponding point **2** : a particular line of thought esp. as related to mutual understanding

wave·let \-lət\ *n* : a little wave : RIPPLE

wa·ver \'wā-vər\ *vb* **wa·vered; wa·ver·ing** \'wāv-(ə-)riŋ\ **1** : to vacillate between choices : fluctuate in opinion, allegiance, or direction **2** : REEL, TOTTER; *also* : QUIVER, FLICKER ⟨~*ing* flames⟩ **3** : FALTER **4** : to give an unsteady sound : QUAVER — **waver** *n* — **wa·ver·er** *n* — **wa·ver·ing·ly** *adv*

wavy \'wā-vē\ *adj* **wav·i·er; -est** : having waves : moving in waves

¹wax \'waks\ *n* **1** : a yellowish plastic substance secreted by bees for constructing the honeycomb **2** : any of various substances resembling beeswax

²wax *vb* : to treat or rub with wax

³wax *vb* **1** : to increase in size, numbers, strength, volume, or duration **2** : to increase in apparent size ⟨the moon ~*es* toward the full⟩ **3** : to pass from one state to another : BECOME ⟨~*ed* indignant⟩ ⟨the party ~*ed* merry⟩

wax bean *n* : a kidney bean with pods that turn creamy yellow to bright yellow when mature enough to use as a snap bean

wax·en \'wak-sən\ *adj* **1** : made of or covered with wax **2** : resembling wax (as in color or consistency)

wax myrtle *n* : any of various shrubs or trees with aromatic leaves; *esp* : an American evergreen shrub that produces small hard berries with a thick coating of white wax used for candles

wax·wing \'waks-ˌwiŋ\ *n* : any of a genus of singing birds that are mostly brown with a showy crest and velvety plumage

wax·work \-ˌwərk\ *n* **1** : an effigy usu. of a person in wax **2** *pl* : an exhibition of wax figures

waxy \'wak-sē\ *adj* **wax·i·er; -est 1** : made of or full of wax **2** : WAXEN **2**

way \'wā\ *n* **1** : a thoroughfare for travel or passage : ROAD, PATH, STREET **2** : ROUTE **3** : a course of action ⟨chose the easy ~⟩; *also* : opportunity, capability, or fact of doing as one pleases ⟨always had his own ~⟩ **4** : a possible course : POSSIBILITY ⟨no two ~s about

it⟩ **5** : METHOD, MODE ⟨this ~ of thinking⟩ ⟨a new ~ of painting⟩ **6** : FEATURE, RESPECT ⟨a good worker in many ~s⟩ **7** : the usual or characteristic state of affairs ⟨as is the ~ with old people⟩; *also* : individual characteristic or peculiarity ⟨used to his ~s⟩ **8** : DISTANCE ⟨a short ~ from here⟩ ⟨a long ~ from success⟩ **9** : progress along a course ⟨working his ~ through college⟩ **10** : something having direction : LOCALITY ⟨out our ~⟩ **11** : STATE, CONDITION ⟨that is the ~ things are⟩ **12** *pl* : an inclined structure upon which a ship is built or is supported in launching **13** : CATEGORY, KIND ⟨get what you need in the ~ of supplies⟩ **14** : motion or speed of a boat through the water — **by way of 1** : for the purpose of ⟨*by way of* illustration⟩ **2** : by the route through : VIA — **out of the way 1** : WRONG, IMPROPER **2** : SECLUDED, REMOTE — **under way 1** : in motion through the water **2** : in progress

way·bill \'wā-ˌbil\ *n* : a paper that accompanies a freight shipment and gives details of goods, route, and charges

way·far·er \'wā-ˌfar-ər\ *n* : a traveler esp. on foot — **way·far·ing** \-ˌfar-iŋ\ *adj*

way·lay \'wā-ˌlā\ *vb* **-laid** \-ˌlād\; **-lay·ing** : to lie in wait for often in order to seize, rob, or kill

way–out \'wā-'aut\ *adj* : FAR-OUT

-ways \ˌwāz\ *adv suffix* : in (such) a way, course, direction, or manner ⟨side*ways*⟩

ways and means *n pl* : methods and resources for accomplishing something and esp. for raising revenues needed by a state; *also* : a legislative committee concerned with this function

way·side \'wā-ˌsīd\ *n* : the side of or land adjacent to a road or path

way station *n* : an intermediate station on a line of travel (as a railroad)

way·ward \'wā-wərd\ *adj* [ME, short for *awayward* turned away, fr. *away*, adv. + *-ward* directed toward] **1** : taking one's own and usu. irregular or improper way : DISOBEDIENT ⟨~ children⟩ **2** : UNPREDICTABLE, IRREGULAR **3** : opposite to what is desired or expected ⟨~ fate⟩

WBC *abbr* white blood cells

WC *abbr* **1** water closet **2** without charge

WCTU *abbr* Women's Christian Temperance Union

we \(')wē\ *pron* **1** — used of a group that includes the speaker or writer **2** — used for the singular *I* by sovereigns and by writers (as of editorials)

weak \'wēk\ *adj* **1** : lacking strength or vigor : FEEBLE **2** : not able to sustain or resist much weight, pressure, or strain **3** : deficient in vigor of mind or character; *also* : resulting from or indicative of such deficiency ⟨a ∼ policy⟩ ⟨a ∼ will⟩ ⟨*weak*-minded⟩ **4** : not supported by truth or logic ⟨a ∼ argument⟩ **5** : not able to function properly **6** : lacking skill or proficiency; *also* : indicative of a lack of skill or aptitude **7** : wanting in vigor of expression or effect **8** : deficient in the usual or required ingredients : of less than usual strength ⟨∼ tea⟩ **9** : not having or exerting authority ⟨∼ government⟩; *also* : INEFFECTIVE, IMPOTENT **10** : of, relating to, or constituting a verb or verb conjugation that forms the past tense and past participle by adding *-ed* or *-d* or *-t* — **weak•ly** *adv*

weak•en \'wē-kən\ *vb* **weak•ened; weak•en•ing** \'wēk-(ə-)niŋ\ : to make or become weak **syn** enfeeble, debilitate, undermine, sap, cripple, disable

weak•fish \'wēk-,fish\ *n* [obs. Dutch *weekvis*, fr. D *week* soft + *vis* fish; fr. its tender flesh] : a common sport and market fish of the Atlantic coast of the U.S. related to the perches; *also* : any of several related food fishes

weak–kneed \'wēk-'nēd\ *adj* : lacking willpower or resolution

weak•ling \-liŋ\ *n* : a person who is physically, mentally, or morally weak

weak•ly \'wēk-lē\ *adj* : FEEBLE, WEAK

weak•ness \-nəs\ *n* **1** : the quality or state of being weak; *also* : an instance or period of being weak ⟨in a moment of ∼ he agreed to go⟩ **2** : FAULT, DEFECT **3** : an object of special desire or fondness ⟨coffee is her ∼⟩

¹weal \'wēl\ *n* : WELL-BEING, PROSPERITY

²weal *n* : WELT

weald \'wēld\ *n* [The *Weald*, wooded district in England, fr. ME *Weeld* the Weald, fr. OE *weald* wood, forest] **1** : FOREST **2** : a wild or uncultivated usu. upland region : WOLD

wealth \'welth\ *n* [ME *welthe*, welfare, prosperity, fr. *wele* weal] **1** : abundance of possessions or resources : AFFLUENCE, RICHES **2** : abundant supply : PROFUSION ⟨a ∼ of detail⟩ **3** : all property that has a money or an exchange value; *also* : all objects or resources that have economic value

wealthy \'wel-thē\ *adj* **wealth•i•er; -est** : having wealth : RICH, AFFLUENT, OPULENT

wean \'wēn\ *vb* **1** : to accustom (a young mammal) to take food otherwise than by nursing **2** : to free from a cause of dependence or preoccupation

weap•on \'wep-ən\ *n* **1** : something (as a gun, knife, or club) that may be used to fight with **2** : a means by which one contends against another

weap•on•less \'wep-ən-ləs\ *adj* : lacking weapons : UNARMED

weap•on•ry \-rē\ *n* **1** : WEAPONS **2** : the science of designing and making weapons

¹wear \'waər\ *vb* **wore** \'wōr\; **worn** \'wōrn\; **wear•ing** **1** : to bear on the person or use habitually for clothing or adornment ⟨∼ a coat⟩ ⟨∼ a wig⟩; *also* : to carry on the person ⟨∼ a gun⟩ **2** : to have or show an appearance of ⟨∼ a smile⟩ **3** : to impair, diminish, or decay by use or by scraping or rubbing ⟨clothes *worn* to shreds⟩ ⟨letters on the stone *worn* away by weathering⟩; *also* : to produce gradually by friction, rubbing, or wasting away ⟨∼ a hole in the rug⟩ **4** : to exhaust or lessen the strength of : WEARY, FATIGUE ⟨*worn* by care and toil⟩ **5** : to endure use : last under use or the passage of time ⟨this cloth ∼s well⟩ **6** : to diminish or fail with the passage of time ⟨the day ∼s on⟩ ⟨the effect of the drug *wore* off⟩ **7** : to grow or become by attrition, use, or age ⟨the coin was *worn* thin⟩ — **wear•able** \'war-ə-bəl\ *adj* — **wear•er** *n*

²wear *n* **1** : the act of wearing : the state of being worn ⟨clothes for everyday ∼⟩ **2** : clothing usu. of a particular kind or for a special occasion or use

⟨children's ~⟩ **3** : wearing or lasting quality ⟨the coat still has lots of ~ in it⟩ **4** : the result of wearing or use : impairment resulting from use ⟨her suit shows ~⟩

wear and tear \ˌwar-ən-ˈtaər\ *n* : the loss or injury to which something is subjected in the course of use; *esp* : normal depreciation

wear down *vb* : to weary and overcome by persistent resistance or pressure

wea·ri·some \ˈwir-ē-səm\ *adj* : causing weariness : TIRESOME — **wea·ri·some·ly** *adv* — **wea·ri·some·ness** *n*

wear out *vb* **1** : TIRE **2** : to make or become useless by wear

¹**wea·ry** \ˈwi(ə)r-ē\ *adj* **wea·ri·er; -est 1** : worn out in strength, endurance, vigor, or freshness **2** : expressing or characteristic of weariness ⟨a ~ sigh⟩ **3** : having one's patience, tolerance, or pleasure exhausted ⟨~ of war⟩ — **wea·ri·ly** \ˈwir-ə-lē\ *adv* — **wea·ri·ness** \-ē-nəs\ *n*

²**weary** *vb* **wea·ried; wea·ry·ing** : to become or make weary : TIRE

wea·sel \ˈwē-zəl\ *n, pl* **weasels** : any of various small slender flesh-eating mammals related to the minks

weasel word *n* [fr. the weasel's reputed habit of sucking the contents out of an egg while leaving the shell superficially intact] : a word used in order to evade or retreat from a direct or forthright statement or position

¹**weath·er** \ˈweth-ər\ *n* **1** : condition of the atmosphere with respect to heat or cold, wetness or dryness, calm or storm, clearness or cloudiness **2** : a particular and esp. a disagreeable atmospheric state : RAIN, STORM

²**weather** *vb* **1** : to expose to or endure the action of weather; *also* : to alter (as in color or texture) by such exposure **2** : to sail or pass to the windward of **3** : to bear up against successfully ⟨~ a storm⟩ ⟨~ troubles⟩

³**weather** *adj* : WINDWARD

weath·er–beat·en \ˈweth-ər-ˌbēt-ᵊn\ *adj* : altered by exposure to the weather; *also* : toughened or tanned by the weather ⟨~ face⟩

weath·er·board \-ˌbōrd\ *n* : CLAPBOARD

weath·er·board·ing \-ˌbōrd-iŋ\ *n* : CLAPBOARDS, SIDING

weath·er–bound \-ˌbaủnd\ *adj* : kept in port or at anchor or from travel or sport by bad weather

weath·er·cock \-ˌkäk\ *n* **1** : a weather vane shaped like a rooster **2** : a fickle person

weath·er·glass \ˈweth-ər-ˌglas\ *n* : BAROMETER

weath·er·ing \ˈweth-(ə-)riŋ\ *n* : the action of the weather in altering the color, texture, composition, or form of exposed objects; *also* : alteration thus effected

weath·er·ize \ˈweth-ə-ˌrīz\ *vb* **-ized; -iz·ing** : to make (as a house) better protected against winter weather esp. by adding insulation and by caulking joints — **weath·er·iza·tion** \ˌweth-ə-rə-ˈzā-shən\ *n*

weath·er·man \-ˌman\ *n* : one who reports and forecasts the weather : METEOROLOGIST

weath·er·proof \ˌweth-ər-ˈprüf\ *adj* : able to withstand exposure to weather without appreciable harm — **weatherproof** *vb*

weather strip *n* : a strip of material to make a seal where a door or window joins the sill or casing — **weath·er–strip** *vb*

weather vane *n* : VANE 1

weath·er·worn \ˈweth-ər-ˌwōrn\ *adj* : worn by exposure to the weather

¹**weave** \ˈwēv\ *vb* **wove** \ˈwōv\ *or* **weaved; wo·ven** \ˈwō-vən\ *or* **weaved; weav·ing 1** : to form by interlacing strands of material; *esp* : to make on a loom by interlacing warp and filling threads ⟨~ cloth⟩ **2** : to interlace (as threads) into a fabric and esp. cloth **3** : SPIN 2 **4** : CONTRIVE **5** : to unite in a coherent whole **6** : to work in ⟨*wove* the episodes into a story⟩ **7** : to direct or move in a winding or zigzag course esp. to avoid obstacles ⟨we *wove* our way through the crowd⟩ — **weav·er** *n*

²**weave** *n* : a pattern or method of weaving ⟨a coarse loose ~⟩

¹**web** \ˈweb\ *n* **1** : a fabric on a loom or coming from a loom **2** : COBWEB; *also* : SNARE, ENTANGLEMENT ⟨caught in a ~ of deceit⟩ **3** : an animal or plant membrane; *esp* : one uniting the toes (as in many birds) **4** : NETWORK ⟨a ~ of highways⟩ **5** : the series of barbs on each side of the shaft of a feather

²**web** *vb* **webbed; web·bing 1** : to cover

or provide with webs or a network **2** : ENTANGLE, ENSNARE **3** : to make a web

webbed \'webd\ *adj* : having or being toes or fingers united by a web ⟨the ∼ feet of ducks⟩

web·bing \'web-iŋ\ *n* : a strong closely woven tape designed for bearing weight and used esp. for straps, harness, or upholstery

web–foot·ed \'web-'fut-əd\ *adj* : having webbed feet

wed \'wed\ *vb* **wed·ded** *also* **wed; wed·ding 1** : to take, give, or join in marriage : enter into matrimony : MARRY **2** : to unite firmly

Wed *abbr* Wednesday

wed·ding \'wed-iŋ\ *n* **1** : a marriage ceremony usu. with accompanying festivities : NUPTIALS **2** : a joining in close association **3** : a wedding anniversary or its celebration

¹wedge \'wej\ *n* **1** : a solid triangular piece of wood or metal that tapers to a thin edge and is used to split logs or rocks or to raise heavy weights **2** : something (as an action or policy) that serves to open up a way for a breach, change, or intrusion **3** : a wedge-shaped object or part ⟨a ∼ of pie⟩

²wedge *vb* **wedged; wedg·ing 1** : to hold firm by or as if by driving in a wedge **2** : to force (something) into a narrow space **3** : to split apart with or as if with a wedge

wed·lock \'wed-ˌläk\ *n* [ME *wedlok,* fr. OE *wedlāc* marriage bond, fr. *wedd* pledge + *-lāc,* suffix denoting activity] : the state of being married : MARRIAGE, MATRIMONY

Wednes·day \'wenz-dē\ *n* [ME, fr. OE *wōdensdæg,* lit., day of Odin (supreme god of Norse mythology)] : the 4th day of the week

wee \'wē\ *adj* [ME *we,* fr. *we,* n., little bit, fr. OE *wǣge* weight] **1** : very small : TINY **2** : very early ⟨∼ hours of the morning⟩

¹weed \'wēd\ *n* : a plant that is not valued where it is growing and is usu. of rank growth; *esp* : one growing in cultivated ground to the damage of a crop

²weed *vb* **1** : to clear of or remove weeds or something harmful, inferior, or superfluous ⟨∼ a garden⟩ **2** : to get rid

of (unwanted items) ⟨∼ out the loafers from the crew⟩ — **weed·er** *n*

³weed *n* : GARMENT; *esp* : dress worn (as by a widow) as a sign of mourning — usu. used in pl.

weedy \'wēd-ē\ *adj* **1** : full of weeds **2** : resembling a weed esp. in vigor of growth or spread **3** : noticeably lean and scrawny : LANK

week \'wēk\ *n* **1** : seven successive days; *esp* : a calendar period of seven days beginning with Sunday and ending with Saturday **2** : the working or school days of the calendar week

week·day \'wēk-ˌdā\ *n* : a day of the week except Sunday or sometimes except Saturday and Sunday

¹week·end \-ˌend\ *n* : the period between the close of one working or business or school week and the beginning of the next

²weekend *vb* : to spend the weekend

¹week·ly \'wēk-lē\ *adj* **1** : occurring, done, produced, or issued every week **2** : computed in terms of one week — **weekly** *adv*

²weekly *n, pl* **weeklies** : a weekly publication

ween \'wēn\ *vb, archaic* : IMAGINE, SUPPOSE

wee·ny \'wē-nē\ *also* **ween·sy** \'wēn(t)-sē\ *adj* : exceptionally small

weep \'wēp\ *vb* **wept** \'wept\; **weep·ing 1** : to express emotion and esp. sorrow by shedding tears : BEWAIL, CRY **2** : to drip or exude (liquid) — **weep·er** *n*

weep·ing \'wē-piŋ\ *adj* **1** : TEARFUL **2** : having slender drooping branches

weeping willow *n* : an Asian willow with weeping branches

weepy \'wē-pē\ *adj* : inclined to weep : TEARFUL

wee·vil \'wē-vəl\ *n* : any of a suborder of mostly small beetles with a long head usu. curved into a snout and larvae that feed esp. in fruits or seeds — **wee·vily** *or* **wee·vil·ly** \'wēv-(ə-)lē\ *adj*

weft \'weft\ *n* **1** : WOOF 1 **2** : WEB, FABRIC; *also* : something woven

¹weigh \'wā\ *vb* [ME *weyen,* fr. OE *wegan* to move, carry, weigh] **1** : to ascertain the heaviness of by a balance **2** : to have weight or a specified weight **3** : to consider carefully : PONDER **4** : to merit consideration as important : COUNT ⟨evidence ∼*ing*

against him⟩ **5** : to heave up (an anchor) **6** : to press down with or as if with a heavy weight

²**weigh** *n* [alter. of *way*] : WAY — used in the phrase *under weigh*

weigh in *vb* : to have something weighed; *esp* : to have oneself weighed preliminary to participation in a sports event

¹**weight** \\'wāt\\ *n* **1** : the amount that something weighs; *also* : the standard amount that something should weigh **2** : a quantity or portion weighing usu. a certain amount **3** : a unit (as a pound or kilogram) of weight or mass; *also* : a system of such units **4** : a heavy object for holding or pressing something down; *also* : a heavy object for throwing or lifting in an athletic contest **5** : BURDEN ⟨a ~ of grief⟩ **6** : IMPORTANCE; *also* : INFLUENCE ⟨threw his ~ around⟩ **7** : overpowering force **8** : relative heaviness (as of a textile) **syn** significance, moment, consequence, import, authority, prestige, credit

²**weight** *vb* **1** : to load with or as if with a weight **2** : to oppress with a burden ⟨~ed down with cares⟩

weight·less \\'wāt-ləs\\ *adj* : having little weight : lacking apparent gravitational pull — **weight·less·ly** *adv* — **weight·less·ness** *n*

weighty \\'wāt-ē\\ *adj* **weight·i·er; -est** **1** : of much importance or consequence : MOMENTOUS, SERIOUS ⟨~ problems⟩ **2** : SOLEMN ⟨a ~ manner⟩ **3** : HEAVY **4** : exerting force, influence, or authority ⟨~ arguments⟩

weir \\'waər, 'wiər\\ *n* **1** : a fence set in a waterway for catching fish **2** : a dam in a river for the purpose of directing water to a mill or making a pond

weird \\'wiərd\\ *adj* [ME *wird, werd* fate, destiny, fr. OE *wyrd*] **1** : MAGICAL **2** : UNEARTHLY, MYSTERIOUS **3** : ODD, UNUSUAL, FANTASTIC **syn** eerie, uncanny, spooky — **weird·ly** *adv* — **weird·ness** *n*

Welch \\'welch\\ var of WELSH

¹**wel·come** \\'wel-kəm\\ *vb* **wel·comed; wel·com·ing** **1** : to greet cordially or courteously **2** : to accept, meet, or face with pleasure ⟨he ~s criticism⟩

²**welcome** *adj* **1** : received gladly into one's presence ⟨a ~ visitor⟩ **2** : giving pleasure : PLEASING ⟨~ news⟩ **3** : willingly permitted or admitted ⟨all are ~ to use the books⟩ **4** — used in the phrase "You're welcome" as a reply to an expression of thanks

³**welcome** *n* : a cordial greeting or reception

¹**weld** \\'weld\\ *vb* **1** : to unite (metal or plastic parts) either by heating and allowing the parts to flow together or by hammering or pressing together **2** : to unite closely or intimately ⟨~ed together in friendship⟩ — **weld·er** *n*

²**weld** *n* **1** : a welded joint **2** : union by welding

wel·fare \\'wel-ˌfa-ər\\ *n* **1** : the state of doing well esp. in respect to happiness, well-being, or prosperity ⟨the ~ of mankind⟩ **2** : organized efforts for the social betterment of a group in society **3** : RELIEF 2

welfare state *n* : a nation or state that assumes primary responsibility for the individual and social welfare of its citizens

wel·kin \\'wel-kən\\ *n* : SKY; *also* : AIR

¹**well** \\'wel\\ *n* **1** : a spring with its pool : FOUNTAIN; *also* : a source of supply ⟨a ~ of information⟩ **2** : a hole sunk in the earth to obtain a natural deposit (as of water, oil, or gas) **3** : an open space (as for a staircase) extending vertically through floors of a structure **4** : something suggesting a well

²**well** *vb* : to rise up and flow forth : RUN

³**well** *adv* **bet·ter** \\'bet-ər\\; **best** \\'best\\ **1** : in a good or proper manner : RIGHTLY; *also* : EXCELLENTLY, SKILLFULLY **2** : SATISFACTORILY, FORTUNATELY ⟨the party turned out ~⟩ **3** : ABUNDANTLY ⟨eat ~⟩ **4** : with reason or courtesy : PROPERLY ⟨I cannot ~ refuse⟩ **5** : COMPLETELY, FULLY, QUITE ⟨~ worth the price⟩ ⟨*well*-hidden⟩ **6** : INTIMATELY, CLOSELY ⟨I know him ~⟩ **7** : CONSIDERABLY, FAR ⟨~ over a million⟩ ⟨~ ahead⟩ **8** : without trouble or difficulty ⟨he could ~ have gone⟩ **9** : EXACTLY, DEFINITELY ⟨remember it ~⟩

⁴**well** *adj* **1** : PROSPEROUS; *also* : being in satisfactory condition or circumstances **2** : SATISFACTORY, PLEASING ⟨all is ~⟩ **3** : ADVISABLE, DESIRABLE ⟨it is not ~ to anger him⟩ **4** : free or recovered from infirmity or disease : HEALTHY **5** : FORTUNATE ⟨it is ~ that this has happened⟩

well–ad·vised \ˌwel-əd-ˈvīzd\ adj **1** : PRUDENT **2** : resulting from, based on, or showing careful deliberation or wise counsel ⟨∼ plans⟩

well–ap·point·ed \-ə-ˈpȯint-əd\ adj : having good and complete equipment

well–be·ing \ˈwel-ˈbē-iŋ\ n : the state of being happy, healthy, or prosperous

well·born \-ˈbȯrn\ adj : born of good stock either socially or physically

well–bred \-ˈbred\ adj : having or indicating good breeding : REFINED

well–con·di·tioned \ˌwel-kən-ˈdish-ənd\ adj **1** : characterized by proper disposition, morals, or behavior **2** : having a good physical condition : SOUND ⟨a ∼ animal⟩

well–de·fined \-di-ˈfīnd\ adj : having clearly distinguishable limits or boundaries ⟨a ∼ scar⟩

well–dis·posed \-dis-ˈpōzd\ adj : disposed to be friendly, favorable, or sympathetic

well–done \ˈwel-ˈdən\ adj **1** : rightly or properly performed **2** : cooked thoroughly

well–fa·vored \-ˈfā-vərd\ adj : GOODLOOKING, HANDSOME

well–fixed \-ˈfikst\ adj : financially well-off

well–found·ed \-ˈfaún-dəd\ adj : based on sound information, reasoning, judgment, or grounds ⟨∼ rumors⟩

well–groomed \-ˈgrümd, -ˈgrumd\ adj : well and neatly dressed or cared for ⟨∼ men⟩ ⟨a ∼ lawn⟩

well–ground·ed \-ˈgraún-dəd\ adj : having a firm foundation

well·head \-ˌhed\ n **1** : the source of a spring or a stream **2** : principal source **3** : the top of or a structure built over a well

well–heeled \-ˈhēld\ adj : financially well-off

well–knit \-ˈnit\ adj : well and firmly formed or framed ⟨a ∼ argument⟩

well–known \-ˈnōn\ adj : fully or widely known

well–mean·ing \-ˈmē-niŋ\ adj : having or based on excellent intentions

well–nigh \-ˈnī\ adv : ALMOST, NEARLY

well–off \-ˈȯf\ adj : being in good condition or circumstances; esp : WELLTO-DO

well–or·dered \-ˈȯrd-ərd\ adj : having an orderly procedure or arrangement

well–read \-ˈred\ adj : well informed through reading

well–round·ed \-ˈraún-dəd\ adj **1** : broadly trained, educated, and experienced **2** : COMPREHENSIVE ⟨a ∼ program of activities⟩

well–spo·ken \ˈwel-ˈspō-kən\ adj **1** : speaking well and esp. courteously **2** : spoken with propriety ⟨∼ words⟩

well·spring \-ˌspriŋ\ n : FOUNTAINHEAD, SPRING

well–timed \-ˈtīmd\ adj : coming or happening at an opportune moment : TIMELY

well–to–do \ˌwel-tə-ˈdü\ adj : having more than adequate material resources : PROSPEROUS

well–turned \ˈwel-ˈtərnd\ adj **1** : pleasingly rounded : SHAPELY ⟨a ∼ ankle⟩ **2** : pleasingly and appropriately expressed ⟨a ∼ phrase⟩

well–wish·er \ˈwel-ˌwish-ər, -ˈwish-\ n : one that wishes well to another — **well–wish·ing** \-iŋ\ adj or n

well–worn \-ˈwōrn\ adj **1** : worn by much use ⟨∼ shoes⟩ **2** : TRITE **3** archaic : worn well or properly ⟨∼ honors⟩

welsh \ˈwelsh, ˈwelch\ vb **1** : to cheat by avoiding payment of bets **2** : to break one's word ⟨∼ed on his promises⟩

Welsh \ˈwelsh\ n **1** Welsh pl : the people of Wales **2** : the Celtic language of Wales — **Welsh** adj — **Welsh·man** \-mən\ n

Welsh cor·gi \-ˈkȯr-gē\ n [W corgi, fr. cor dwarf + ci dog] : a short-legged long-backed dog with foxy head of either of two breeds of Welsh origin

Welsh rabbit n : melted often seasoned cheese poured over toast or crackers

Welsh rare·bit \-ˈraər-bət\ n : WELSH RABBIT

¹welt \ˈwelt\ n **1** : the narrow strip of leather between a shoe upper and sole to which other parts are stitched **2** : a doubled edge, strip, insert, or seam for ornament or reinforcement **3** : a ridge or lump raised on the skin usu. by a blow; also : a heavy blow

²welt vb **1** : to furnish with a welt **2** : to hit hard

¹wel·ter \ˈwel-tər\ vb **1** : WRITHE, TOSS; also : WALLOW **2** : to rise and fall or toss about in or with waves **3** : to become deeply sunk, soaked, or involved **4** : to be in turmoil

²welter *n* **1** : TURMOIL **2** : a chaotic mass or jumble

wel·ter·weight \'wel-tər-ˌwāt\ *n* : a boxer weighing more than 135 but not over 147 pounds

wen \'wen\ *n* : a cyst formed by blocking of a skin gland and filled with fatty material

wench \'wench\ *n* [ME *wenche,* short for *wenchel* child, fr. OE *wencel*] **1** : a young woman : GIRL **2** : a female servant

wend \'wend\ *vb* : to direct one's course : proceed on (one's way)

went past of GO

wept past and past part of WEEP

were past 2d sing, past pl, or past subjunctive of BE

were·wolf \'wer-ˌwu̇lf, 'wir-\ *n, pl* **were·wolves** \-ˌwu̇lvz\ [ME, fr. OE *werwulf,* fr. *wer* man + *wulf* wolf] : a person transformed into a wolf or capable of assuming a wolf's form

wes·kit \'wes-kət\ *n* : VEST 1

¹west \'west\ *adv* : to or toward the west

²west *n* **1** : the general direction of sunset **2** : the compass point directly opposite to east **3** *cap* : regions or countries west of a specified or implied point **4** *cap* : Europe and the Americas — **west·er·ly** \'wes-tər-lē\ *adv or adj* — **west·ward** *adv or adj* — **westwards** *adv*

³west *adj* **1** : situated toward or at the west **2** : coming from the west

¹west·ern \'wes-tərn\ *adj* **1** *cap* : of, relating to, or characteristic of a region conventionally designated West **2** : lying toward or coming from the west **3** *cap* : of or relating to the Roman Catholic or Protestant segment of Christianity — **West·ern·er** *n*

²western *n* **1** : one that is produced in or is characteristic of a western region and esp. the western U.S. **2** *often cap* : a novel, story, motion picture, or broadcast dealing with life in the western U.S. during the latter half of the 19th century

west·ern·ize \'wes-tər-ˌnīz\ *vb* **-ized; -izing** : to give western characteristics to

¹wet \'wet\ *adj* **wet·ter; wet·test 1** : consisting of or covered or soaked with liquid (as water) **2** : RAINY **3** : not dry

⟨~ paint⟩ **4** : permitting or advocating the manufacture and sale of intoxicating liquor ⟨a ~ town⟩ ⟨a ~ candidate⟩ **syn** damp, dank, moist, humid — **wetly** *adv* — **wet·ness** *n*

²wet *n* **1** : WATER; *also* : WETNESS, MOISTURE **2** : rainy weather : RAIN **3** : an advocate of a wet liquor policy

³wet *vb* **wet** *or* **wet·ted; wet·ting** : to make or become wet

wet blanket *n* : one that quenches or dampens enthusiasm or pleasure

weth·er \'weth-ər\ *n* : a male sheep castrated while immature

wet·land \'wet-ˌland, -lənd\ *n* : land or areas containing much soil moisture

wet nurse *n* : one who cares for and suckles young not her own

wet suit *n* : a rubber suit for swimmers that acts to retain body heat by keeping a layer of water against the body as insulation

wh *abbr* **1** which **2** white

WHA *abbr* World Hockey Association

¹whack \'hwak\ *vb* **1** : to strike with a smart or resounding blow **2** : to cut with or as if with a whack

²whack *n* **1** : a smart or resounding blow; *also* : the sound of such a blow **2** : PORTION, SHARE **3** : CONDITION, STATE ⟨the machine is out of ~⟩ **4** : an opportunity or attempt to do something : CHANCE **5** : a single action or occasion : TIME ⟨made three pies at a ~⟩

¹whale \'hwāl\ *n, pl* **whales 1** *or pl* **whale** : any of an order of marine mammals that lack hind limbs and have the front limbs modified into flippers; *esp* : one of the larger members of the order **2** : a person or thing impressive in size or quality ⟨a ~ of a story⟩

²whale *vb* **whaled; whal·ing** : to fish or hunt for whales

³whale *vb* **whaled; whal·ing 1** : THRASH **2** : to strike or hit vigorously

whale·boat \-ˌbōt\ *n* : a long narrow rowboat made with both ends sharp and sloping and formerly used by whalers

whale·bone \-ˌbōn\ *n* : a horny substance attached in plates to the upper jaw of some large whales (**whalebone** whales)

whal·er \'hwā-lər\ *n* **1** : a person or ship that hunts whales **2** : WHALEBOAT

wham·my \'hwam-ē\ *n, pl* **wham·mies** : JINX, HEX

wharf \'hworf\ *n, pl* **wharves** \'hworvz\ *also* **wharfs** : a structure alongside which ships lie to load and unload

wharf·age \'hwor-fij\ *n* : the provision or use of a wharf; *also* : the charge for using a wharf

wharf·in·ger \'hwor-fən-jər\ *n* : the operator or manager of a wharf

¹what \(')hwät, (')hwət\ *pron* **1** — used to inquire about the identity or nature of a being, an object, or some matter or situation ⟨∼ is he, a salesman⟩ ⟨∼'s that⟩ ⟨∼ happened⟩ **2** : that which ⟨I know ∼ you want⟩ **3** : WHATEVER 1 ⟨take ∼ you want⟩

²what *adv* **1** : in what respect : HOW ⟨∼ does he care⟩ **2** — used with *with* to introduce a prepositional phrase that expresses cause ⟨kept busy ∼ with school and work⟩

³what *adj* **1** — used to inquire about the identity or nature of a person, object, or matter ⟨∼ books does he read⟩ **2** : how remarkable or surprising ⟨∼ an idea⟩ **3** : WHATEVER

¹what·ev·er \hwät-'ev-ər\ *pron* **1** : anything or everything that ⟨does ∼ he wants to⟩ **2** : no matter what ⟨∼ you do, don't cheat⟩ **3** : WHAT 1 — used as an intensive ⟨∼ do you mean⟩

²whatever *adj* : of any kind at all ⟨no food ∼⟩

¹what·not \'hwät-ˌnät\ *pron* : any of various other things that might also be mentioned ⟨paper clips, pins, and ∼⟩

²whatnot *n* : a light open set of shelves for small ornaments

what·so·ev·er \ˌhwät-sə-'wev-ər\ *pron or adj* : WHATEVER

wheal \'hwēl\ *n* : a wale or welt on the skin; *also* : a suddenly-appearing itching or burning raised patch of skin

wheat \'hwēt\ *n* : a cereal grain that yields a fine white flour and is the chief breadstuff of temperate regions; *also* : any of several grasses whose white to dark red grains are wheat — **wheat·en** *adj*

wheat germ *n* : the vitamin-rich wheat embryo separated in milling

whee·dle \'hwēd-ᵊl\ *vb* **whee·dled; whee·dling** \'hwēd-(ᵊ-)liŋ\ **1** : to coax or entice by flattery **2** : to gain or get by wheedling

¹wheel \'hwēl\ *n* **1** : a disk or circular frame that turns on a central axis **2** : a device whose main part is a wheel **3** : something resembling a wheel (as in being round or turning) **4** : a curving or circular movement **5** : machinery that imparts motion : moving power ⟨the ∼s of government⟩ **6** : a person of importance **7** *pl, slang* : AUTOMOBILE — **wheeled** \'hwēld\ *adj* — **wheel·less** \'hwēl-ləs\ *adj*

²wheel *vb* **1** : ROTATE, REVOLVE **2** : to change direction as if turning on a pivot **3** : to convey or move on wheels or in a vehicle

wheel·bar·row \-ˌbar-ō\ *n* : a vehicle with handles and usu. one wheel for conveying small loads

wheel·base \-ˌbās\ *n* : the distance in inches between the front and rear axles of an automotive vehicle

wheel·chair \-ˌcheər\ *n* : a chair mounted on wheels esp. for the use of invalids

wheel·er \'hwē-lər\ *n* **1** : one that wheels **2** : something that has wheels — used in combination ⟨a side-*wheel·er*⟩ **3** : WHEELHORSE

wheel·er–deal·er \ˌhwē-lər-'dē-lər\ *n* : a shrewd operator esp. in business or politics

wheel·horse \'hwēl-ˌhors\ *n* **1** : a horse in a position nearest the wheels in a tandem or similar arrangement **2** : a steady and effective worker esp. in a political body

wheel·house \-ˌhaus\ *n* : PILOTHOUSE

wheel·wright \-ˌrīt\ *n* : a maker and repairer of wheels and wheeled vehicles

¹wheeze \'hwēz\ *vb* **wheezed; wheez·ing** : to breathe with difficulty usu. with a whistling sound

²wheeze *n* **1** : a sound of wheezing **2** : an often repeated and well-known joke **3** : a trite saying

wheezy \'hwē-zē\ *adj* **wheez·i·er; -est 1** : inclined to wheeze **2** : having a wheezing sound

whelk \'hwelk\ *n* : a large sea snail; *esp* : one much used as food in Europe

whelm \'hwelm\ *vb* : to overcome or engulf completely : OVERWHELM

¹whelp \'hwelp\ *n* **1** : one of the young of various carnivorous mammals (as a dog) **2** : a low contemptible fellow

²**whelp** *vb* : to give birth to (whelps) : bring forth whelps

¹**when** \(')hwen, hwən\ *adv* **1** : at what time ⟨~ will he return⟩ **2** : at or during which time ⟨a time ~ things were upset⟩

²**when** *conj* **1** : at or during the time that ⟨leave ~ I do⟩ **2** : every time that ⟨they all laughed ~ he sang⟩ **3** : in the event that : IF ⟨disqualified ~ he cheats⟩ **4** : ALTHOUGH ⟨quit politics ~ he might have had a great career in it⟩

³**when** \ˌhwen\ *pron* : what or which time ⟨since ~ have you been the boss⟩

⁴**when** \'hwen\ *n* : the time of a happening

whence \(')hwens\ *adv* **1** : from what place, source, or cause ⟨asked ~ the gifts came⟩ **2** : from or out of which ⟨the land ~ he came⟩

when·ev·er \hwen-'ev-ər, hwən-\ *conj or adv* : at whatever time

when·so·ev·er \'hwen-sə-ˌwev-ər\ *conj* : at whatever time

¹**where** \(')hwear\ *adv* **1** : at, in, or to what place ⟨~ is he⟩ ⟨~ did he go⟩ **2** : at, in, or to what situation, position, direction, circumstances, or respect ⟨~ does this road lead⟩

²**where** *conj* **1** : at, in, or to what place ⟨knows ~ the house is⟩ **2** : at, in, or to what situation, position, direction, circumstances, or respect ⟨shows ~ the road leads⟩ **3** : WHEREVER ⟨goes ~ he likes⟩ **4** : at, in, or to which place ⟨the town ~ she lives⟩ **5** : at, in, or to the place at, in, or to which ⟨stay ~ you are⟩ **6** : in a case, situation, or respect in which ⟨outstanding ~ endurance is called for⟩

³**where** \'hwear\ *n* **1** : PLACE, LOCATION ⟨the ~ and how of the accident⟩ **2** : what place ⟨~ is he from⟩

¹**where·abouts** \-ə-ˌbaůts\ *also* **where·about** \-ˌbaůt\ *adv* : about where ⟨~ does he live⟩

²**whereabouts** *n sing or pl* : the place where a person or thing is ⟨his present ~ are unknown⟩

where·as \hwer-'az\ *conj* **1** : when in fact : while on the contrary **2** : in view of the fact that : SINCE

where·at \-'at\ *conj* **1** : at or toward which **2** : in consequence of which : WHEREUPON

where·by \-'bī\ *conj* : by, through, or in accordance with which ⟨the means ~ he achieved his goal⟩

¹**where·fore** \'hwear-ˌfōr\ *adv* **1** : for what reason or purpose : WHY **2** : THEREFORE

²**wherefore** *n* : CAUSE, REASON

¹**where·in** \hwer-'in\ *adv* : in what : in what respect ⟨~ was he wrong⟩

²**wherein** *conj* **1** : in which : WHERE ⟨the city ~ he lives⟩ **2** : during which **3** : in what way : HOW ⟨showed him ~ he was wrong⟩

where·of \-'əv, -'äv\ *conj* **1** : of what ⟨knows ~ he speaks⟩ **2** : of which or whom ⟨books ~ the best are lost⟩

where·on \-'ȯn, -'än\ *conj* : on which ⟨the base ~ it rests⟩

where·so·ev·er \'hwer-sə-ˌwev-ər\ *conj* : WHEREVER

where·to \'hwear-ˌtü\ *conj* : to which

where·up·on \'hwer-ə-ˌpȯn, -ˌpän\ *conj* **1** : on which **2** : closely following and in consequence of which

¹**wher·ev·er** \hwer-'ev-ər\ *adv* : where in the world ⟨~ did she get that hat⟩

²**wherever** *conj* **1** : at, in, or to whatever place **2** : in any circumstance in which

where·with \'hwear-ˌwith, -ˌwith\ *conj* : with or by means of which

where·with·al \'hwer-with-ˌȯl, -with-\ *n* : MEANS, RESOURCES; *esp* : MONEY

wher·ry \'hwer-ē\ *n, pl* **wherries** : a light boat; *esp* : a long light rowboat sharp at both ends

whet \'hwet\ *vb* **whet·ted; whet·ting 1** : to sharpen by rubbing against or with a hard substance (as a whetstone) **2** : to make keen : STIMULATE ⟨~ the appetite⟩

wheth·er \'hweth-ər\ *conj* **1** : if it is or was true that ⟨ask ~ he is going⟩ **2** : if it is or was better ⟨uncertain ~ to go or stay⟩ **3** : whichever is or was the case, namely that ⟨~ we succeed or fail, we must try⟩ **4** : EITHER ⟨turned out well ~ by accident or design⟩

whet·stone \'hwet-ˌstōn\ *n* : a stone for sharpening blades

whey \'hwā\ *n* : the watery part of milk that separates after the milk sours and thickens

¹**which** \(')hwich\ *adj* **1** : being what one or ones out of a group ⟨~ tie should I wear⟩ **2** : WHICHEVER

²**which** *pron* **1** : which one or ones ⟨~ is

yours⟩ ⟨∼ are his⟩ ⟨he's a Swede or a Dane, I don't remember ∼⟩ **2** : WHICHEVER ⟨we have all kinds of them; take ∼ you like⟩ **3** — used to introduce a relative clause and to serve as a substitute therein for the substantive modified by the clause ⟨give me the money ∼ is coming to me⟩

¹**which•ev•er** \hwich-'ev-ər\ *adj* : no matter which ⟨∼ way you go⟩

²**whichever** *pron* : whatever one or ones

which•so•ev•er \‚hwich-sə-'wev-ər\ *pron or adj* : WHICHEVER

whick•er \'hwik-ər\ *vb* : NEIGH, WHINNY — **whicker** *n*

¹**whiff** \'hwif\ *n* **1** : a quick puff or slight gust esp. of air, gas, smoke, or spray **2** : an inhalation of odor, gas, or smoke **3** : a slight trace : HINT

²**whiff** *vb* **1** : to expel, puff out, or blow away in or as if in whiffs **2** : to inhale an odor

whif•fle•tree \'hwif-əl-(‚)trē\ *n* [alter. of *whippletree*] : the pivoted swinging bar to which the traces of a harness are fastened

Whig \'hwig\ *n* [short for *Whiggamore* (member of a Scottish group that marched to Edinburgh in 1648 to oppose the court party)] **1** : a member or supporter of a British political group of the 18th and early 19th centuries seeking to limit royal authority and increase parliamentary power **2** : an American favoring independence from Great Britain during the American Revolution **3** : a member or supporter of an American political party formed about 1834 to oppose the Democrats

¹**while** \'hwīl\ *n* **1** : a period of time ⟨stay a ∼⟩ **2** : the time and effort used : TROUBLE ⟨worth your ∼⟩

²**while** \(‚)hwīl\ *conj* **1** : during the time that ⟨she called ∼ you were out⟩ **2** : AS LONG AS ⟨∼ there's life there's hope⟩ **3** : ALTHOUGH ⟨∼ he's respected, he's not liked⟩

³**while** \'hwīl\ *vb* **whiled; whil•ing** : to cause to pass esp. pleasantly ⟨∼ away an hour⟩

¹**whi•lom** \'hwī-ləm\ *adv* [ME, lit., at times, fr. OE *hwīlum,* dat. pl. of *hwīl* time, while] *archaic* : FORMERLY

²**whilom** *adj* : FORMER ⟨his ∼ friends⟩

whilst \'hwīlst\ *conj, chiefly Brit* : WHILE

whim \'hwim\ *n* : a sudden wish, desire, or change of mind : NOTION, FANCY, CAPRICE

whim•per \'hwim-pər\ *vb* **whim•pered; whim•per•ing** \-p(ə-)riŋ\ : to make a low whining plaintive or broken sound — **whimper** *n*

whim•si•cal \'hwim-zi-kəl\ *adj* **1** : full of whims : CAPRICIOUS **2** : resulting from or characterized by whim or caprice : ERRATIC — **whim•si•cal•i•ty** \‚hwim-zə-'kal-ət-ē\ *n* — **whim•si•cal•ly** \'hwim-zi-k(ə-)lē\ *adv*

whim•sy *or* **whim•sey** \'hwim-zē\ *n, pl* **whimsies** *or* **whimseys** **1** : WHIM, CAPRICE **2** : a fanciful or fantastic device, object, or creation esp. in writing or art

whine \'hwīn\ *vb* **whined; whin•ing** [ME *whinen,* fr. OE *hwīnan* to whiz] **1** : to utter a usu. high-pitched plaintive or distressed cry; *also* : to make a sound similar to such a cry **2** : to utter a complaint with or as if with a whine — **whine** *n*

¹**whin•ny** \'hwin-ē\ *vb* **whin•nied; whin•ny•ing** : to neigh usu. in a low or gentle manner

²**whinny** *n, pl* **whinnies** : NEIGH

¹**whip** \'hwip\ *vb* **whipped; whip•ping** **1** : to move, snatch, or jerk quickly or forcefully ⟨∼ out a gun⟩ **2** : to strike with a slender lithe implement (as a lash) esp. as a punishment; *also* : SPANK **3** : to drive or urge on by or as if by using a whip **4** : to bind or wrap (as a rope or rod) with cord in order to protect and strengthen; *also* : to wind or wrap around something **5** : DEFEAT **6** : to stir up : INCITE ⟨∼ up enthusiasm⟩ **7** : to produce in a hurry ⟨∼ up a meal⟩ **8** : to beat (as eggs or cream) into a froth **9** : to gather together or hold together for united action **10** : to proceed nimbly or briskly; *also* : to thrash about like a whiplash — **whip•per** *n* — **whip into shape** : to bring forcefully to a desired state or condition

²**whip** *n* **1** : a flexible instrument used for whipping **2** : a stroke or cut with or as if with a whip **3** : a dessert made by whipping a portion of the ingredients ⟨prune ∼⟩ **4** : a person who han-

dles a whip; *esp* : a driver of horses **5** : a member of a legislative body appointed by his party to enforce party discipline and to secure the attendance of party members at important sessions **6** : a whipping or thrashing motion ⟨a ∼ of his tail⟩

whip·cord \-ˌkord\ *n* **1** : a thin tough cord made of braided or twisted hemp or catgut **2** : a cloth that is made of hard-twisted yarns and has fine diagonal cords or ribs

whip hand *n* : positive control : ADVANTAGE

whip·lash \ˈhwip-ˌlash\ *n* **1** : the lash of a whip **2** : WHIPLASH INJURY

whiplash injury *n* : injury resulting from a sudden sharp movement of the neck and head (as of a person in a vehicle that is struck from the front or rear)

whip·per·snap·per \ˈhwip-ər-ˌsnap-ər\ *n* : a small, insignificant, or presumptuous person

whip·pet \ˈhwip-ət\ *n* : any of a breed of small swift slender dogs that are widely used for racing

whipping boy *n* : SCAPEGOAT

whip·ple·tree \ˈhwip-əl-(ˌ)trē\ *n* : WHIFFLETREE

whip·poor·will \ˈhwip-ər-ˌwil\ *n* : an American bird with dull variegated plumage whose call is heard at nightfall and just before dawn

¹**whip·saw** \ˈhwip-ˌso\ *n* **1** : a narrow tapering saw that has hook teeth **2** : a 2-man crosscut saw

²**whipsaw** *vb* **1** : to saw with a whipsaw **2** : to worst in two opposite ways at once, by a 2-phase operation, or by the collusive action of two opponents

¹**whir** *also* **whirr** \ˈhwər\ *vb* **whirred; whir·ring** : to move, fly, or revolve with a whizzing sound : WHIZ

²**whir** *also* **whirr** *n* : a continuous fluttering or vibratory sound made by something in rapid motion

¹**whirl** \ˈhwərl\ *vb* **1** : to move or drive in a circle or similar curve esp. with force or speed **2** : to turn or cause to turn on or around an axis : SPIN **3** : to turn abruptly : WHEEL **4** : to pass, move, or go quickly **5** : to become dizzy or giddy : REEL

²**whirl** *n* **1** : a rapid rotating or circling movement; *also* : something under-

going such a movement **2** : COMMOTION, BUSTLE ⟨the social ∼⟩ **3** : a state of mental confusion

whirl·i·gig \ˈhwər-li-ˌgig\ *n* [ME *whirlegigg*, fr. *whirlen* to whirl + *gigg* top] **1** : a child's toy having a whirling motion **2** : MERRY-GO-ROUND **3** : something that continuously whirls or changes; *also* : a whirling course (as of events)

whirl·pool \ˈhwərl-ˌpül\ *n* : water moving rapidly in a circle so as to produce a depression in the center into which floating objects may be drawn

whirl·wind \-ˌwind\ *n* **1** : a small whirling windstorm **2** : a confused rush : WHIRL

whirly·bird \ˈhwər-lē-ˌbərd\ *n* : HELICOPTER

¹**whish** \ˈhwish\ *vb* : to move with a whizzing of swishing sound

²**whish** *n* : a rushing sound : SWISH

¹**whisk** \ˈhwisk\ *n* **1** : a quick light sweeping or brushing motion **2** : a small usu. wire kitchen implement for hand beating of food **3** : a flexible bunch (as of twigs, feathers, or straw) attached to a handle for use as a brush

²**whisk** *vb* **1** : to move nimbly and quickly **2** : to move or convey briskly ⟨∼ out a knife⟩ ⟨∼ed the children off to bed⟩ **3** : to beat or whip lightly ⟨∼ eggs⟩ **4** : to brush or wipe off lightly ⟨∼ a coat⟩

whisk broom *n* : a small broom with a short handle used esp. as a clothes brush

whis·ker \ˈhwis-kər\ *n* **1** *pl* : the part of the beard that grows on the sides of the face or on the chin **2** : one hair of the beard **3** : one of the long bristles or hairs growing near the mouth of an animal (as a cat or bird) — **whis·kered** \-kərd\ *adj*

whis·key *or* **whis·ky** \ˈhwis-kē\ *n, pl* **whiskeys** *or* **whiskies** [IrGael *uisce beathadh* & ScGael *uisge beatha*, lit., water of life] : a liquor distilled from the fermented mash of grain (as rye, corn, or barley)

¹**whis·per** \ˈhwis-pər\ *vb* **whis·pered; whis·per·ing** \-p(ə-)riŋ\ **1** : to speak very low or under the breath; *also* : to tell or utter by whispering ⟨∼ a secret⟩ **2** : to make a low rustling sound ⟨∼ing leaves⟩

²**whisper** *n* **1** : something communicated by or as if by whispering : HINT, RUMOR **2** : an act or instance of whispering; *esp* : speech without vibration of the vocal cords

whist \\'hwist\\ *n* : a card game played by four players in two partnerships with a deck of 52 cards

¹**whis•tle** \\'hwis-əl\\ *n* **1** : a device by which a shrill sound is produced ⟨steam ∼⟩ ⟨tin ∼⟩ **2** : a shrill clear sound made by forcing breath out or air in through the puckered lips **3** : the sound or signal produced by a whistle or as if by whistling **4** : the shrill clear note of an animal (as a bird)

²**whistle** *vb* **whis•tled; whis•tling** \\-(ə-)liŋ\\ **1** : to utter a shrill clear sound by blowing or drawing air through the puckered lips **2** : to utter a shrill note or call resembling a whistle **3** : to make a shrill clear sound esp. by rapid movements ⟨bullets *whistled* by him⟩ **4** : to blow or sound a whistle **5** : to signal or call by a whistle **6** : to produce, utter, or express by whistling ⟨∼ a tune⟩ — **whis•tler** \\-(ə-)lər\\ *n*

whis•tle–blow•er \\'hwis-əl-ˌblō-ər\\ *n* : INFORMER

whis•tle–stop \\'hwis-əl-ˌstäp\\ *n* **1** : a small station at which trains stop only on signal **2** : a small community **3** : a brief personal appearance by a political candidate orig. on the rear platform of a touring train

whit \\'hwit\\ *n* [prob. alter. of ME *wiht, wight* creature, thing, bit, fr. OE *wiht*] : the smallest part or particle imaginable : BIT

¹**white** \\'hwīt\\ *adj* **whit•er; whit•est 1** : free from color **2** : of the color of new snow or milk; *esp* : of the color white **3** : light or pallid in color ⟨lips ∼ with fear⟩ **4** : SILVERY; *also* : made of silver **5** : of, relating to, or being a member of a group or race characterized by light-colored skin **6** : free from spot or blemish : PURE, INNOCENT **7** : BLANK 3 ⟨∼ space in printed matter⟩ **8** : not intended to cause harm ⟨a ∼ lie⟩ **9** : wearing white ⟨∼ friars⟩ **10** : SNOWY ⟨∼ Christmas⟩ **11** : ARDENT, PASSIONATE ⟨∼ fury⟩ **12** : conservative or reactionary in politics

²**white** *n* **1** : the color of maximal lightness that characterizes objects which both reflect and transmit light : the opposite of black **2** : a white or light-colored part or thing ⟨the ∼ of an egg⟩; *also, pl* : white garments **3** : the light-colored pieces in a 2-player board game; *also* : the person by whom these are played **4** : one that is or approaches the color white **5** : a member of a light-skinned race **6** : a member of a conservative or reactionary political group

white ant *n* : TERMITE

white•bait \\'hwīt-ˌbāt\\ *n* : the young of a herring or a similar small fish used for food

white blood cell *n* : a blood cell that does not contain hemoglobin : LEUKOCYTE

white•cap \\'hwīt-ˌkap\\ *n* : a wave crest breaking into foam

white–col•lar \\'hwīt-ˈkäl-ər\\ *adj* : of, relating to, or constituting the class of salaried workers whose duties do not require the wearing of work clothes or protective clothing

white dwarf *n* : a small very dense whitish star of low luminosity

white elephant *n* [so called because white elephants were venerated in parts of Asia and maintained without being required to work] **1** : an Indian elephant of a pale color that is sometimes venerated in India, Sri Lanka, Thailand, and Burma **2** : something requiring much care and expense and yielding little profit **3** : an object no longer wanted by its owner though not without value to others

white–faced \\'hwīt-ˈfāst\\ *adj* **1** : having a wan pale face **2** : having the face white in whole or in part ⟨∼ cattle⟩

white feather *n* [fr. the superstition that a white feather in the plumage of a gamecock is a mark of a poor fighter] : a mark or symbol of cowardice

white•fish \\'hwīt-ˌfish\\ *n* : any of various freshwater food fishes related to the salmons and trouts

white flag *n* : a flag of plain white used as a flag of truce or as a token of surrender

white•fly \\'hwīt-ˌflī\\ *n* : any of numerous small insects that are injurious plant pests related to the scale insects

white gold *n* : a pale alloy of gold esp.

with nickel or palladium resembling platinum in appearance

white goods *n pl* : white fabrics or articles (as sheets or towels) typically made of cotton or linen

White·hall \'hwīt-ˌhȯl\ *n* : the British government

white·head \-ˌhed\ *n* : a small whitish lump in the skin due to retention of secretion in an oil gland duct

white heat *n* : a temperature higher than red heat at which a body becomes brightly incandescent so as to appear white

white–hot *adj* **1** : being at or radiating white heat **2** : FERVID

White House \-ˌhaůs\ *n* **1** : the executive department of the U.S. government **2** : a residence of the president of the U.S.

white lead *n* : a heavy white poisonous carbonate of lead used as a pigment in exterior paints

white matter *n* : the whitish part of nervous tissue consisting mostly of nerve-cell processes

whit·en \'hwīt-ᵊn\ *vb* **whit·ened; whit·en·ing** \'hwīt(-ᵊ-)niŋ\ : to make or become white **syn** blanch, bleach — **whit·en·er** \'hwīt-(ᵊ-)nǝr\ *n*

white·ness \'hwīt-nǝs\ *n* : the quality or state of being white

white pine *n* : a tall-growing pine of eastern No. America with leaves in clusters of five; *also* : its wood

white–pine blister rust *n* : a destructive disease of white pine caused by a rust fungus that passes part of its complex life cycle on currant or gooseberry bushes; *also* : this fungus

white sale *n* : a sale on white goods

white shark *n* : a large and dangerous shark of warm seas that is light colored below and darker above becoming dirty white in older and larger specimens

white slave *n* : a woman or girl held unwillingly for purposes of prostitution — **white slavery** *n*

white·tail \'hwīt-ˌtāl\ *n* : WHITE-TAILED DEER

white–tailed deer \ˌhwīt-ˌtāl-ˈdiǝr\ *n* : a No. American deer with a rather long tail white on the underside and with forward-arching antlers

white·wall \'hwīt-ˌwȯl\ *n* : an automo-bile tire having a white band on the sidewall

¹white·wash \-ˌwȯsh, -ˌwäsh\ *vb* **1** : to whiten with whitewash **2** : to clear of a charge of wrongdoing by offering excuses, hiding facts, or conducting a perfunctory investigation **3** : to prevent (an opponent) from scoring in a game or contest

²whitewash *n* **1** : a liquid mixture (as of lime and water) for whitening a surface **2** : a clearing of wrongdoing by whitewashing

white·wood \-ˌwůd\ *n* : any of various trees and esp. a tulip tree having light-colored wood; *also* : the wood of such a tree

¹whith·er \'hwith-ǝr\ *adv* **1** : to what place **2** : to what situation, position, degree, or end ⟨∼ will this drive him⟩

²whither *conj* **1** : to the place at, in, or to which; *also* : to which place **2** : to whatever place

whith·er·so·ev·er \ˌhwith-ǝr-sǝ-ˈwev-ǝr\ *conj* : to whatever place

¹whit·ing \'hwīt-iŋ\ *n* : any of several usu. light or silvery food fishes (as a hake) found mostly near seacoasts

²whiting *n* : calcium carbonate in the form of pulverized chalk or limestone used as a pigment and in putty

whit·ish \'hwīt-ish\ *adj* : somewhat white

whit·low \'hwit-ˌlō\ *n* : a deep inflammation of a finger or toe with pus formation

Whit·sun·day \'hwit-ˈsǝn-dē, -sǝn-ˌdā\ *n* [ME *Whitsonday,* fr. OE *hwīta sunnandaeg,* lit., white Sunday, prob. fr. the custom of wearing white robes by those newly baptized at this season] : PENTECOST

whit·tle \'hwit-ᵊl\ *vb* **whit·tled; whit·tling** \'hwit-(ᵊ-)liŋ\ **1** : to pare or cut off chips from the surface of (wood) with a knife; *also* : to cut or shape by such paring **2** : to reduce, remove, or destroy gradually as if by paring down : PARE ⟨∼ down expenses⟩

¹whiz *or* **whizz** \'hwiz\ *vb* **whizzed; whiz·zing** : to hum, whir, or hiss like a speeding object (as an arrow or ball) passing through air

²whiz *or* **whizz** *n, pl* **whiz·zes** : a hissing, buzzing, or whirring sound

³whiz *n, pl* **whiz·zes** : WIZARD 2

who \(')hü\ *pron* **1** : what or which person or persons ⟨∼ did it⟩ ⟨∼ is he⟩ ⟨∼ are they⟩ **2** : the person or persons that ⟨knows ∼ did it⟩ **3** \(͵)hü, ü\ — used to introduce a relative clause and to serve as a substitute therein for the substantive modified by the clause ⟨the man ∼ lives there is rich⟩ ⟨the people ∼ did it were caught⟩

WHO *abbr* World Health Organization

whoa \'wō, 'hwō, 'hō\ *vb imper* — a command (as to a draft animal) to stand still

who·dun·it *also* **who·dun·nit** \hü-'dən-ət\ *n* : a detective story or mystery story presented as a novel, play, or motion picture

who·ev·er \hü-'ev-ər\ *pron* : whatever person : no matter who

¹whole \'hōl\ *adj* [ME *hool* healthy, unhurt, entire, fr. OE *hāl*] **1** : being in healthy or sound condition : free from defect or damage : WELL, INTACT **2** : having all its proper parts or elements ⟨∼ milk⟩ **3** : constituting the total sum of : ENTIRE ⟨∼ continental landmasses⟩ **4** : each or all of the ⟨the ∼ family⟩ **5** : not scattered or divided : CONCENTRATED ⟨gave me his ∼ attention⟩ **6** : seemingly complete or total ⟨the ∼ idea is to help, not hinder⟩ **syn** entire, perfect, intact, sound — **whole·ness** *n*

²whole *n* **1** : a complete amount or sum : a number, aggregate, or totality lacking no part, member, or element **2** : something constituting a complex unity : a coherent system or organization of parts fitting or working together as one — **on the whole 1** : in view of all the circumstances or conditions **2** : in general

whole·heart·ed \'hōl-'härt-əd\ *adj* : undivided in purpose, enthusiasm, or will : HEARTY, ZESTFUL, SINCERE

whole note *n* : a musical note equal to one measure of four beats

whole number *n* : INTEGER

¹whole·sale \'hōl-͵sāl\ *n* : the sale of goods in quantity usu. for resale by a retail merchant

²wholesale *adj* **1** : performed on a large scale without discrimination ⟨∼ slaughter⟩ **2** : of, relating to, or engaged in wholesaling — **wholesale** *adv*

³wholesale *vb* **whole·saled**; **whole·sal·ing**

: to sell at wholesale — **whole·sal·er** *n*

whole·some \'hōl-səm\ *adj* **1** : promoting mental, spiritual, or bodily health or well-being ⟨∼ advice⟩ ⟨a ∼ environment⟩ **2** : sound in body, mind, or morals : HEALTHY **3** : PRUDENT ⟨∼ respect for the law⟩ — **whole·some·ness** *n*

whole step *n* : a musical interval comprising two half steps (as C–D or F♯–G♯)

whole wheat *adj* : made of ground entire wheat kernels

whol·ly \'hōl-(l)ē\ *adv* **1** : COMPLETELY, TOTALLY **2** : SOLELY, EXCLUSIVELY

whom \(')hüm\ *pron, objective case of* WHO

whom·ev·er \hüm-'ev-ər\ *pron, objective case of* WHOEVER

whom·so·ev·er \͵hüm-sə-'wev-ər\ *pron, objective case of* WHOSOEVER

¹whoop \'h(w)üp, 'h(w)ùp\ *vb* **1** : to shout or call loudly and vigorously **2** : to make the sound that follows a fit of coughing in whooping cough **3** : to go or pass with a loud noise **4** : to utter or express with a whoop; *also* : to urge, drive, or cheer with a whoop

²whoop *n* **1** : a whooping sound or utterance : SHOUT, HOOT **2** : a crowing sound accompanying the intake of breath after a fit of coughing in whooping cough

whooping cough *n* : an infectious disease esp. of children marked by convulsive coughing fits sometimes followed by a whoop

whooping crane *n* : a large white nearly extinct No. American crane noted for its loud whooping note

whoop·la \'h(w)üp-͵lä, 'h(w)ùp-\ *n* **1** : a noisy commotion **2** : boisterous merrymaking

whop·per \'hwäp-ər\ *n* : something unusually large or extreme of its kind; *esp* : a monstrous lie

whop·ping \'hwäp-iŋ\ *adj* : extremely large

whore \'hōr\ *n* : PROSTITUTE

whorl \'hwòrl, 'hwərl\ *n* **1** : a row of parts (as leaves or petals) encircling an axis and esp. a plant stem **2** : something that whirls or coils around a center : COIL, SPIRAL **3** : one of the turns of a snail shell

whorled \'hwòrld, 'hwərld\ *adj* : having or arranged in whorls

¹**whose** \('\)hüz\ *adj* : of or relating to whom or which esp. as possessor or possessors, agent or agents, or object or objects of an action ⟨asked ∼ bag it was⟩

²**whose** *pron* : whose one or ones ⟨∼ is this car⟩ ⟨∼ are those books⟩

who•so \'hü-‚sō\ *pron* : WHOEVER

who•so•ev•er \‚hü-sə-'wev-ər\ *pron* : WHOEVER

whs *or* **whse** *abbr* warehouse

whsle *abbr* wholesale

¹**why** \('\)hwī\ *adv* : for what reason, cause, or purpose ⟨∼ did you do it⟩

²**why** *conj* 1 : the cause, reason, or purpose for which ⟨that is ∼ you did it⟩ 2 : for which : on account of which ⟨knows the reason ∼ you did it⟩

³**why** \'hwī\ *n, pl* **whys** : REASON, CAUSE ⟨the ∼s of racial prejudice⟩

⁴**why** \(‚)wī, (‚)hwī\ *interj* — used to express surprise, hesitation, approval, disapproval, or impatience ⟨∼, here's what I was looking for⟩

WI *abbr* 1 West Indies 2 Wisconsin

WIA *abbr* wounded in action

wick \'wik\ *n* : a loosely bound bundle of soft fibers that draws up oil, tallow, or wax to be burned in a candle, oil lamp, or stove

wick•ed \'wik-əd\ *adj* 1 : morally bad : EVIL, SINFUL 2 : FIERCE, VICIOUS 3 : ROGUISH ⟨a ∼ glance⟩ 4 : REPUGNANT, VILE ⟨a ∼ odor⟩ 5 : HARMFUL, DANGEROUS ⟨a ∼ attack⟩ — **wick•ed•ly** *adv* — **wick•ed•ness** *n*

wick•er \'wik-ər\ *n* 1 : a small pliant branch (as an osier or a withe) 2 : WICKERWORK — **wicker** *adj*

wick•er•work \-‚wərk\ *n* : work made of osiers, twigs, or rods : BASKETRY

wick•et \'wik-ət\ *n* 1 : a small gate or door; *esp* : one forming a part of or placed near a larger one 2 : a window-like opening usu. with a grille or grate (as at a ticket office) 3 : a set of three upright rods topped by two crosspieces bowled at in cricket 4 : an arch through which the ball is driven in croquet

wick•i•up \'wik-ē-‚əp\ *n* : a hut used by nomadic Indians of the western and southwestern U.S. with a usu. oval base and a rough frame covered with reed mats, grass, or brushwood

wid *abbr* widow, widower

¹**wide** \'wīd\ *adj* **wider; wid•est** 1 : covering a vast area 2 : measured across or at right angles to the length 3 : not narrow : BROAD; *also* : ROOMY 4 : opened to full width ⟨eyes ∼ with wonder⟩ 5 : not limited : EXTENSIVE ⟨∼ experience⟩ 6 : far from the goal, mark, or truth ⟨a ∼ guess⟩ — **wide•ly** *adv*

²**wide** *adv* **wid•er; wid•est** 1 : over a great distance or extent : WIDELY ⟨searched far and ∼⟩ 2 : over a specified distance, area, or extent 3 : so as to leave a wide space between ⟨∼ apart⟩ 4 : so as to clear by a considerable distance ⟨ran ∼ around left end⟩ 5 : COMPLETELY, FULLY ⟨opened her eyes ∼⟩

wide–awake \‚wīd-ə-'wāk\ *adj* : fully awake; *also* : KNOWING, ALERT ⟨a group of ∼ young men⟩

wide–eyed \'wīd-'īd\ *adj* 1 : having the eyes wide open esp. with wonder or astonishment 2 : NAIVE

wide•mouthed \'wīd-'maủthd, -'maủtht\ *adj* 1 : having one's mouth opened wide (as in awe) 2 : having a wide mouth ⟨∼ jars⟩

wid•en \'wīd-ᵊn\ *vb* **wid•ened; wid•en•ing** \'wīd-(ᵊ-)niŋ\ : to make or become wide : BROADEN

wide•spread \'wīd-'spred\ *adj* 1 : widely scattered or prevalent ⟨∼ fear⟩ 2 : widely extended or spread out ⟨∼ wings⟩

¹**wid•ow** \'wid-ō\ *n* : a woman who has lost her husband by death and has not married again — **wid•ow•hood** *n*

²**widow** *vb* : to cause to become a widow

wid•ow•er \'wid-ə-wər\ *n* : a man who has lost his wife by death and has not married again

width \'width\ *n* 1 : a distance from side to side : the measurement taken at right angles to the length : BREADTH 2 : largeness of extent or scope; *also* : FULLNESS 3 : a measured and cut piece of material ⟨a ∼ of calico⟩ ⟨a ∼ of lumber⟩

wield \'wēld\ *vb* 1 : to use or handle esp. effectively ⟨∼ a broom⟩ ⟨∼ a pen⟩ 2 : to exert authority by means of : EMPLOY ⟨∼ influence⟩ — **wield•er** *n*

wie•ner \'wē-nər\ *n* [short for *wiener-*

wurst, fr. G, lit., Vienna sausage] : FRANKFURTER

wife \\'wīf\ *n, pl* **wives** \\'wīvz\ **1** *dial* : WOMAN **2** : a woman acting in a specified capacity — used in combination **3** : a married woman — **wife•hood** *n* — **wife•less** *adj* — **wife•ly** *adj*

wig \\'wig\ *n* [short for *periwig,* fr. MF *perruque,* fr. It *perrucca* hair, wig] : a manufactured covering of natural or synthetic hair for the head; *also* : TOUPEE

wi•geon *or* **wid•geon** \\'wij-ən\ *n, pl* **wigeon** *or* **wigeons** *or* **widgeon** *or* **widgeons** : any of several freshwater ducks between the teal and the mallard in size

wig•gle \\'wig-əl\ *vb* **wig•gled; wig•gling** \-(ə-)liŋ\ **1** : to move to and fro with quick jerky or shaking movements : JIGGLE **2** : WRIGGLE — **wiggle** *n*

wig•gler \\'wig-(ə-)lər\ *n* **1** : a larva or pupa of a mosquito **2** : one that wiggles

wig•gly \-(ə-)lē\ *adj* **1** : tending to wiggle ⟨a ∼ worm⟩ **2** : WAVY ⟨∼ lines⟩

wight \\'wīt\ *n* : a living being : CREATURE

wig•let \\'wig-lət\ *n* : a small wig used esp. to enhance a hairstyle

¹**wig•wag** \\'wig-,wag\ *vb* **1** : to signal by or as if by a flag or light waved according to a code **2** : to make or cause to make a signal (as with the hand or arm)

²**wigwag** *n* **1** : the art or practice of wigwagging **2** : the act of wigwagging

wig•wam \\'wig-,wäm\ *n* : a hut of the Indians of the eastern U.S. having typically an arched framework of poles overlaid with bark, rush mats, or hides

¹**wild** \\'wīld\ *adj* **1** : living in a state of nature and not ordinarily tamed ⟨∼ ducks⟩ **2** : growing or produced without human aid or care ⟨∼ honey⟩ ⟨∼ plants⟩ **3** : WASTE, DESOLATE ⟨∼ country⟩ **4** : UNCONTROLLED, UNRESTRAINED, UNRULY ⟨∼ passions⟩ ⟨a ∼ young stallion⟩ **5** : TURBULENT, STORMY ⟨a ∼ night⟩ **6** : EXTRAVAGANT, FANTASTIC, CRAZY ⟨∼ ideas⟩ **7** : indicative of strong passion, desire, or emotion ⟨a ∼ stare⟩ **8** : UNCIVILIZED, SAVAGE **9** : deviating from the natural or expected course : ERRATIC ⟨a ∼

throw⟩ **10** : having a denomination determined by the holder ⟨deuces ∼⟩ — **wild•ly** *adv* — **wild•ness** \\'wīl(d)-nəs\ *n*

²**wild** *adv* **1** : WILDLY **2** : without regulation or control ⟨running ∼⟩

³**wild** *n* **1** : WILDERNESS **2** : a natural or undomesticated state or existence

wild boar *n* : an Old World wild hog from which most domestic swine are descended

wild carrot *n* : a widely naturalized Eurasian weed that is probably the original of the cultivated carrot

¹**wild•cat** \\'wīl(d)-,kat\ *n, pl* **wildcats 1** : any of various small or medium≠sized cats (as a lynx or ocelot) **2** : a quick-tempered hard-fighting person

²**wildcat** *adj* **1** : not sound or safe ⟨∼ schemes⟩ **2** : initiated by a group of workers without formal union approval ⟨∼ strike⟩

³**wildcat** *vb* **wild•cat•ted; wild•cat•ting** : to drill an oil or gas well in a region not known to be productive

wil•de•beest \\'wil-də-,bēst\ *n, pl* **wildebeests** *also* **wildebeest** [Afrikaans *wildebees,* fr. *wilde* wild + *bees* ox] : GNU

wil•der•ness \\'wil-dər-nəs\ *n* [ME, fr. *wildern* wild, fr. OE *wilddēoren* of wild beasts] : an uncultivated and uninhabited region

wild•fire \\'wīl(d)-,fī(ə)r\ *n* : an uncontrollable fire — **like wildfire** : very rapidly

wild•fowl \-,faůl\ *n* : a bird and esp. a waterfowl (as a wild duck) hunted as game

wild–goose chase *n* : the pursuit of something unattainable

wild•life \\'wīl(d)-,līf\ *n* : nonhuman living things and esp. wild animals living in their natural environment

wild oat *n* **1** : any of several wild grasses **2** *pl* : offenses and indiscretions attributed to youthful exuberance ⟨was just sowing his *wild oats*⟩

wild rice *n* : a No. American aquatic grass; *also* : its edible seed

wild•wood \\'wīld-,wůd\ *n* : a wild or unfrequented wood

¹**wile** \\'wīl\ *n* **1** : a trick or stratagem intended to ensnare or deceive; *also* : a playful trick **2** : TRICKERY, GUILE

²**wile** *vb* **wiled; wil•ing** : LURE, ENTICE

¹**will** \wəl, (ə)l, (')wil\ *vb, past* **would**

\wəd, (ə)d, (')wu̇d\; *pres sing & pl* **will** **1** : WISH, DESIRE ⟨call it what you ∼⟩ **2** — used as an auxiliary verb to express (1) desire, willingness, or in negative constructions refusal ⟨∼ you have another⟩ ⟨he *won't* do it⟩, (2) customary or habitual action ⟨∼ get angry over nothing⟩, (3) simple futurity ⟨tomorrow we ∼ go shopping⟩, (4) capability or sufficiency ⟨the back seat ∼ hold three⟩, (5) determination or willfulness ⟨I ∼ go despite them⟩, (6) probability ⟨that ∼ be the mailman⟩, (7) inevitability ⟨accidents ∼ happen⟩, or (8) a command ⟨you ∼ do as I say⟩

²will \'wil\ *n* **1** : wish or desire often combined with determination ⟨the ∼ to win⟩ **2** : something desired; *esp* : a choice or determination of one having authority or power **3** : the act, process, or experience of willing : VOLITION **4** : the mental powers manifested as wishing, choosing, desiring, or intending **5** : a disposition to act according to principles or ends **6** : power of controlling one's own actions or emotions ⟨a man of iron ∼⟩ **7** : a legal document in which a person declares to whom his possessions are to go after his death

³will \'wil\ *vb* **1** : to dispose of by or as if by a will : BEQUEATH **2** : to determine by an act of choice; *also* : DECREE, ORDAIN **3** : INTEND, PURPOSE; *also* : CHOOSE

will·ful *or* **wil·ful** \'wil-fəl\ *adj* **1** : governed by will without regard to reason : OBSTINATE, STUBBORN **2** : INTENTIONAL ⟨∼ murder⟩ — **will·ful·ly** \-lē\ *adv*

wil·lies \'wil-ēz\ *n pl* : a fit of nervousness : JITTERS

will·ing \'wil-iŋ\ *adj* **1** : inclined or favorably disposed in mind : READY ⟨∼ to go⟩ **2** : prompt to act or respond ⟨∼ workers⟩ **3** : done, borne, or accepted voluntarily or without reluctance : VOLUNTARY **4** : of or relating to the will : VOLITIONAL — **will·ing·ly** *adv* — **will·ing·ness** *n*

wil·li·waw \'wil-ē-ˌwȯ\ *n* : a sudden violent gust of cold land air common along mountainous coasts of high latitudes

will-o'-the-wisp \ˌwil-ə-thə-'wisp\ *n* **1** : a light that appears at night over marshy grounds **2** : a misleading or elusive goal or hope

wil·low \'wil-ō\ *n* **1** : any of numerous quick-growing shrubs and trees with tough pliable shoots used in basketry **2** : an object made of willow wood

wil·low·ware \-ˌwaər\ *n* : dinnerware that is usu. blue and white and that is decorated with a story-telling design featuring a large willow tree by a little bridge

wil·lowy \'wil-ə-wē\ *adj* : PLIANT; *also* : gracefully tall and slender ⟨a ∼ young woman⟩

will·pow·er \'wil-ˌpau̇(-ə)r\ *n* : energetic determination : RESOLUTENESS

wil·ly-nil·ly \ˌwil-ē-'nil-ē\ *adv or adj* [alter. of *will I nill I* or *will ye nill ye* or *will he nill he*; *nill* fr. archaic *nill* to be unwilling, fr. ME *nilen*, fr. OE *nyllan*, fr. *ne* not + *wyllan* to wish] : without regard for one's choice : by compulsion ⟨they rushed us along ∼⟩

¹wilt \'wilt\ *vb* **1** : to lose or cause to lose freshness and become limp : DROOP **2** : to grow weak or faint : LANGUISH

²wilt *n* : any of various plant disorders marked by wilting and often shriveling

wily \'wī-lē\ *adj* **wil·i·er; -est** : full of guile : TRICKY — **wil·i·ness** \'wī-lē-nəs\ *n*

wimp \'wimp\ *n* : a weak or ineffectual person — **wimpy** \'wim-pē\ *adj*

¹wim·ple \'wim-pəl\ *n* : a cloth covering worn over the head and around the neck and chin by women esp. in the late medieval period and by some nuns

²wimple *vb* **wim·pled; wim·pling** \-p(ə-)liŋ\ **1** : to cover with or as if with a wimple **2** : to ripple or cause to ripple

¹win \'win\ *vb* **won** \'wən\; **win·ning** [ME *winnen*, fr. OE *winnan* to struggle] **1** : to gain the victory in or as if in a contest : SUCCEED **2** : to get possession of esp. by effort : GAIN **3** : to gain in or as if in battle or contest; *also* : to be the victor in ⟨*won* the war⟩ **4** : to obtain by work : EARN **5** : to solicit and gain the favor of; *esp* : to induce to accept oneself in marriage

²win *n* : VICTORY; *esp* : 1st place at the finish (as of a horse race)

wince \'wins\ *vb* **winced; winc•ing** : to shrink back involuntarily (as from pain) : FLINCH — **wince** *n*

winch \'winch\ *n* **1** : a machine that has a drum on which a rope or cable is wound for hauling or hoisting — **winch** *vb*

¹**wind** \'wind\ *n* **1** : a movement of the air **2** : a force or agency that carries along or influences : TENDENCY, TREND **3** : BREATH ⟨he had the ∼ knocked out of him⟩ **4** : gas generated in the stomach or intestines **5** : something insubstantial; *esp* : idle words **6** : air carrying a scent (as of game) **7** : INTIMATION ⟨they got ∼ of our plans⟩ **8** : WIND INSTRUMENTS; *also, pl* : players of wind instruments

²**wind** *vb* **1** : to get a scent of ⟨the dogs ∼*ed* the game⟩ **2** : to cause to be out of breath ⟨he was ∼*ed* from the climb⟩ **3** : to allow (as a horse) to rest so as to recover breath

³**wind** \'wīnd, 'wind\ *vb* **wind•ed** \'wīn-dəd, 'win-\ *or* **wound** \'waůnd\; **wind•ing** : to sound by blowing ⟨∼ a horn⟩

⁴**wind** \'wīnd\ *vb* **wound** \'waůnd\ *also* **wind•ed; wind•ing 1** : to have a curving course or shape ⟨a river ∼*ing* through the valley⟩ **2** : to move or lie so as to encircle **3** : ENTANGLE, INVOLVE **4** : to introduce stealthily : INSINUATE **5** : to encircle or cover with something pliable : WRAP, COIL, TWINE, TWIST ⟨∼ a bobbin⟩ **6** : to hoist or haul by a rope or chain and a winch ⟨∼ a ship to the wharf⟩ **7** : to tighten the spring of; *also* : CRANK **8** : to raise to a high level (as of excitement) **9** : to cause to move in a curving line or path **10** : to traverse on a curving course

⁵**wind** \'wīnd\ *n* : COIL, TURN

wind•age \'win-dij\ *n* : the influence of the wind in deflecting the course of a projectile through the air; *also* : the amount of such deflection

wind•bag \'win(d)-ˌbag\ *n* : an idly talkative person

wind•blown \-ˌblōn\ *adj* : blown by the wind; *also* : having the appearance of being blown by the wind

wind•break \-ˌbrāk\ *n* : something (as a growth of trees) serving as a shelter from the wind

wind–bro•ken \-ˌbrō-kən\ *adj, of a* horse : having the power of breathing impaired by disease

wind•burn \-ˌbərn\ *n* : skin irritation caused by wind

wind•chill \'win(d)-ˌchil\ *n* : a still-air temperature that would have the same cooling effect on exposed human flesh as a given combination of temperature and wind speed

windchill factor *n* : WINDCHILL

wind•er \'wīn-dər\ *n* : one that winds

wind•fall \'win(d)-ˌfȯl\ *n* **1** : something (as a tree or fruit) blown down by the wind **2** : an unexpected or sudden gift, gain, or advantage

wind•flow•er \-ˌflaů(-ə)r\ *n* : ANEMONE

¹**wind•ing** \'wīn-diŋ\ *n* : material (as wire) wound or coiled about an object

²**winding** *adj* **1** : having a pronounced curve; *esp* : SPIRAL ⟨∼ stairs⟩ **2** : having a course that winds ⟨a ∼ road⟩

wind•ing–sheet \-ˌshēt\ *n* : SHROUD

wind instrument *n* : a musical instrument (as a flute or horn) sounded by wind and esp. by the breath

wind•jam•mer \'win(d)-ˌjam-ər\ *n* : a sailing ship; *also* : one of its crew

wind•lass \'win-dləs\ *n* [ME *wyndlas*, alter. of *wyndas*, fr. ON *vindāss*, fr. *vinda* to wind + *āss* pole] : a winch used esp. on ships for hoisting or hauling

wind•mill \'win(d)-ˌmil\ *n* : a mill or machine worked by the wind turning sails or vanes that radiate from a central shaft

win•dow \'win-dō\ *n* [ME *windowe*, fr. ON *vindauga*, fr. *vindr* wind + *auga* eye] **1** : an opening in the wall of a building to let in light and air; *also* : the framework with fittings that closes such an opening **2** : WINDOWPANE **3** : an opening resembling or suggesting that of a window in a building — **win•dow•less** *adj*

window dressing *n* **1** : display of merchandise in a store window **2** : a showing made to create a good but sometimes false impression

win•dow•pane \'win-dō-ˌpān\ *n* : a pane in a window

win•dow–shop \-ˌshäp\ *vb* : to look at the displays in store windows without going inside the stores to make purchases — **win•dow–shop•per** *n*

win•dow•sill \-ˌsil\ *n* : the horizontal

member at the bottom of a window

wind·pipe \'win(d)-ˌpīp\ *n* : the passage for the breath from the larynx to the lungs

wind·proof \-'prüf\ *adj* : impervious to wind ⟨a ∼ jacket⟩

wind·row \'win-ˌ(d)rō\ *n* **1** : hay raked up into a row to dry **2** : a row of something (as dry leaves) swept up by or as if by the wind

wind shear *n* : a radical shift in wind speed and direction between slightly different altitudes

wind·shield \'win(d)-ˌshēld\ *n* : a transparent screen in front of the occupants of a vehicle

wind sock *n* : an open-ended truncated cloth cone mounted in an elevated position to indicate the direction of the wind

wind·storm \-ˌstȯrm\ *n* : a storm with high wind and little or no precipitation

wind·swept \'win(d)-ˌswept\ *adj* : swept by or as if by wind ⟨∼ plains⟩

wind tunnel *n* : an enclosed passage through which air is blown to determine the effects of wind pressure on an object

wind·up \'wīn-ˌdəp\ *n* **1** : CONCLUSION, FINISH **2** : a series of regular and distinctive motions made by a pitcher preliminary to delivering a pitch

wind up \(')wīn-'dəp\ *vb* **1** : to bring or come to a conclusion : END **2** : SETTLE **3** : to arrive in a place, situation, or condition at the end or as a result of a course of action ⟨*wound up* as paupers⟩ **4** : to give a preliminary swing to the arm

¹wind·ward \'win-(d)wərd\ *n* : the point or side from which the wind is blowing

²windward *adj* : being in or facing the direction from which the wind is blowing

windy \'win-dē\ *adj* **wind·i·er; -est 1** : having wind : exposed to winds ⟨a ∼ day⟩ ⟨a ∼ prairie⟩ **2** : STORMY **3** : FLATULENT **4** : indulging in or characterized by useless talk : VERBOSE

¹wine \'wīn\ *n* **1** : fermented grape juice used as a beverage **2** : the usu. fermented juice of a plant product (as fruit) used as a beverage ⟨rice ∼⟩

²wine *vb* **wined; win·ing** : to treat to or drink wine

wine cellar *n* : a room for storing wines; *also* : a stock of wines

wine·grow·er \-ˌgrō(-ə)r\ *n* : one that cultivates a vineyard and makes wine

wine·press \'wīn-ˌpres\ *n* : a vat in which juice is expressed from grapes by treading or by means of a plunger

¹wing \'wiŋ\ *n* **1** : one of the movable feathered or membranous paired appendages by means of which a bird, bat, or insect is able to fly **2** : something suggesting a wing in position, appearance, or function **3** : a plant or animal appendage or part likened to a wing; *esp* : one that is flat or broadly extended **4** : a turned-back or extended edge on an article of clothing **5** : a means of flight or rapid progress **6** : the act or manner of flying : FLIGHT **7** *pl* : the area at the side of the stage out of sight **8** : one of the positions or players on either side of a center position or line **9** : either of two opposing groups within an organization : FACTION **10** : a unit in military aviation consisting of two or more squadrons — **wing·less** *adj* — **on the wing** : in flight : FLYING — **under one's wing** : in one's charge or care

²wing *vb* **1** : to fit with wings; *also* : to enable to fly easily **2** : to pass through in flight : FLY ⟨∼ the air⟩ ⟨swallows ∼*ing* southward⟩ **3** : to achieve or accomplish by flying **4** : to let fly : DISPATCH ⟨∼ an arrow through the air⟩ **5** : to wound in the wing ⟨∼ a bird⟩; *also* : to wound without killing

wing·ding \'wiŋ-ˌdiŋ\ *n* : a wild, lively, or lavish party

winged \'wiŋd, *also except for* ''esp.'' *sense of 1* 'wiŋ-əd\ *adj* **1** : having wings esp. of a specified character **2** : soaring with or as if with wings : ELEVATED **3** : SWIFT, RAPID

wing·span \'wiŋ-ˌspan\ *n* : WINGSPREAD; *esp* : the distance between the tips of an airplane's wings

wing·spread \-ˌspred\ *n* : the spread of the wings; *esp* : the distance between the tips of the fully extended wings of a winged animal

¹wink \'wiŋk\ *vb* **1** : to close and open one eye quickly as a signal or hint **2** : to close and open the eyes quickly : BLINK **3** : to avoid seeing or noticing something ⟨∼ at a violation of the law⟩ **4** : TWINKLE, FLICKER **5** : to affect or influence by or as if by blinking the eyes ⟨he ~*ed* back his tears⟩ — **wink·er** \\'wiŋ-kər\\ *n*

²wink *n* **1** : a brief period of sleep : NAP **2** : an act of winking; *esp* : a hint or sign given by winking **3** : INSTANT ⟨dries in a ~⟩

win·ner \\'win-ər\\ *n* : one that wins

¹win·ning \\'win-iŋ\\ *n* **1** : VICTORY **2** : something won; *esp* : money won at gambling ⟨large ~*s*⟩

²winning *adj* **1** : successful esp. in competition **2** : ATTRACTIVE, CHARMING

win·now \\'win-ō\\ *vb* **1** : to remove (as chaff from grain) by a current of air; *also* : to free (as grain) from waste in this manner **2** : to get rid of (something unwanted) or to separate, sift, or sort (something) as if by winnowing

wino \\'wī-nō\\ *n, pl* **win·os** : one who is chronically addicted to drinking wine

win·some \\'win-səm\\ *adj* [ME *winsum*, fr. OE *wynsum*, fr. *wynn* joy] **1** : generally pleasing and engaging ⟨a ~ lass⟩ **2** : CHEERFUL, GAY — **win·some·ly** *adv* — **win·some·ness** *n*

¹win·ter \\'wint-ər\\ *n* **1** : the season of the year in any region in which the noonday sun shines most obliquely : the coldest period of the year **2** : YEAR ⟨a man of 70 ~*s*⟩ **3** : a time or season of inactivity or decay

²winter *adj* : occurring in or surviving winter; *esp* : sown in autumn for harvesting in the following spring or summer ⟨~ wheat⟩

³winter *vb* **win·tered; win·ter·ing** \\'wint-(ə-)riŋ\\ **1** : to pass or survive the winter **2** : to keep, feed, or manage through the winter ⟨~ cattle on silage⟩

win·ter·green \\'wint-ər-ˌgrēn\\ *n* **1** : a low evergreen plant of the heath family with white bell-shaped flowers and spicy red berries **2** : any of several plants related to the wintergreen **3** : an aromatic oil from the common wintergreen or its flavor or something flavored with it

win·ter·ize \\'wint-ə-ˌrīz\\ *vb* **-ized; -iz·ing** : to make ready for winter

win·ter–kill \\'wint-ər-ˌkil\\ *vb* : to kill or die by exposure to winter weather

winter squash *n* : any of various squashes or pumpkins that keep well in storage

win·ter·tide \\-ˌtīd\\ *n* : WINTER

win·ter·time \\-ˌtīm\\ *n* : WINTER

win·try \\'win-trē\\ *also* **win·tery** \\'win-t(ə-)rē\\ *adj* **win·tri·er; -est 1** : of, relating to, or characteristic of winter : coming in winter ⟨~ weather⟩ **2** : CHILLING, CHEERLESS ⟨a ~ welcome⟩

¹wipe \\'wīp\\ *vb* **wiped; wip·ing 1** : to clean or dry by rubbing ⟨~ dishes⟩ **2** : to remove by or as if by rubbing or cleaning ⟨~ away tears⟩ **3** : to erase completely : OBLITERATE **4** : DESTROY, ANNIHILATE ⟨the platoon was *wiped* out⟩ **5** : to pass or draw over a surface ⟨*wiped* his hand across his face⟩ — **wip·er** *n*

²wipe *n* **1** : an act or instance of wiping; *also* : BLOW, STRIKE, SWIPE **2** : something used for wiping

¹wire \\'wī(ə)r\\ *n* **1** : metal in the form of a thread or slender rod; *also* : a thread or rod of metal **2** *usu pl* : hidden or secret influences controlling the action of a person or body of persons ⟨pull ~*s* to get a nomination⟩ **3** : a line of wire for conducting electric current **4** : a telegraph or telephone wire or system; *esp* : WIRE SERVICE **5** : TELEGRAM, CABLEGRAM **6** : the finish line of a race

²wire *vb* **wired; wir·ing 1** : to provide or equip with wire ⟨~ a house⟩ **2** : to bind, string, or mount with wire **3** : to telegraph or telegraph to

wire·hair \\'wī(ə)r-ˌhaər\\ *n* : a wire-haired fox terrier

wire·haired \\-ˈhaərd\\ *adj* : having a stiff wiry outer coat of hair

¹wire·less \\-ləs\\ *adj* **1** : having no wire or wires **2** *chiefly Brit* : RADIO

²wireless *n* **1** : wireless telegraphy **2** *chiefly Brit* : RADIO

wire–pull·er \\'wī(ə)r-ˌpùl-ər\\ *n* : one who uses secret or underhanded means to influence the acts of a person or organization — **wire–pull·ing** \\-ˌpùl-iŋ\\ *n*

wire service *n* : a news agency that sends out syndicated news copy by wire to subscribers

wire·tap \\-ˌtap\\ *vb* : to tap a telephone or telegraph wire to get information — **wiretap** *n* — **wire·tap·per** \\-ˌtap-ər\\ *n*

wire·worm \\-ˌwərm\\ *n* : the slender hard-coated larva of certain beetles that is esp. destructive to plant roots

wir·ing \\'wī(ə)r-iŋ\\ *n* : a system of wires; *esp* : one for distributing electricity through a building

wiry \\'wī(ə)r-ē\\ *adj* **wir·i·er** \\'wī-rē-ər\\; **-est 1** : made of or resembling wire **2** : slender yet strong and sinewy — **wir·i·ness** \\'wī-rē-nəs\\ *n*

Wis *or* **Wisc** *abbr* Wisconsin

Wisd *abbr* Wisdom

wis·dom \\'wiz-dəm\\ *n* [ME, fr. OE *wīsdom*, fr. *wīs* wise] **1** : accumulated philosophic or scientific learning : KNOWLEDGE; *also* : INSIGHT **2** : good sense : JUDGMENT **3** : a wise attitude or course of action

Wisdom *n* — see BIBLE table

wisdom tooth *n* : the last tooth of the full set on each half of each jaw in man

¹wise \\'wīz\\ *n* : WAY, MANNER, FASHION ⟨in no ∼⟩ ⟨in this ∼⟩

²wise *adj* **wis·er; wis·est 1** : having wisdom : SAGE **2** : having or showing good sense or good judgment : SENSIBLE, SOUND, PRUDENT **3** : aware of what is going on : KNOWING; *also* : CRAFTY, SHREWD **4** : possessing inside information — **wise·ly** *adv*

wise·acre \\'wī-ˌzā-kər\\ *n* [Middle Dutch *wijssegger* soothsayer, fr. Old High German *wīzzago*] : SMART ALECK

¹wise·crack \\'wīz-ˌkrak\\ *n* : a clever, smart, or flippant remark

²wisecrack *vb* : to make a wisecrack

¹wish \\'wish\\ *vb* **1** : to have a desire : long for : CRAVE, WANT ⟨∼ you were here⟩ ⟨∼ for a puppy⟩ **2** : to form or express a wish concerning ⟨∼ed him a happy birthday⟩ **3** : BID ⟨he ∼ed me good morning⟩ **4** : to request by expressing a desire ⟨I ∼ you to go now⟩

²wish *n* **1** : an act or instance of wishing or desire : WANT; *also* : GOAL **2** : an expressed will or desire : MANDATE

wish·bone \\-ˌbōn\\ *n* : a forked bone in front of the breastbone in most birds

wish·ful \\'wish-fəl\\ *adj* **1** : expressive of a wish : HOPEFUL, LONGING; *also* : DESIROUS **2** : according with wishes rather than fact ⟨∼ thinking⟩

wishy–washy \\'wish-ē-ˌwȯsh-ē, -ˌwäsh-\\ *adj* : WEAK, INSIPID; *also* : morally feeble

wisp \\'wisp\\ *n* **1** : a small handful (as of hay or straw) **2** : a thin strand, strip, or fragment ⟨a ∼ of hair⟩; *also* : a thready streak ⟨a ∼ of smoke⟩ **3**

: something frail, slight, or fleeting ⟨a ∼ of a girl⟩ ⟨a ∼ of a smile⟩ — **wispy** *adj*

wis·te·ria \\wis-'tir-ē-ə\\ *or* **wis·ter·ia** \\-'tir-ē-ə *also* -'ter-\\ *n* : any of a genus of chiefly Asian mostly woody vines related to the peas and widely grown for their long showy clusters of blue, white, purple, or rose flowers

wist·ful \\'wist-fəl\\ *adj* : full of longing and unfulfilled desire : YEARNING ⟨a ∼ expression⟩ — **wist·ful·ly** \\-ē\\ *adv* — **wist·ful·ness** *n*

wit \\'wit\\ *n* **1** : reasoning power : INTELLIGENCE **2** : mental soundness : SANITY — usu. used in pl. **3** : RESOURCEFULNESS, INGENUITY; *esp* : quickness and cleverness in handling words and ideas **4** : a talent for making clever remarks; *also* : one noted for making witty remarks — **at one's wit's end** : at a loss for a means of solving a problem

¹witch \\'wich\\ *n* **1** : a person believed to have magic power; *esp* : SORCERESS **2** : an ugly old woman : HAG **3** : a charming or alluring girl or woman

²witch *vb* : BEWITCH

witch·craft \\'wich-ˌkraft\\ *n* : the power or practices of a witch : SORCERY

witch doctor *n* : a practitioner of magic in a primitive society

witch·ery \\'wich-(ə-)rē\\ *n, pl* **-er·ies 1** : SORCERY **2** : FASCINATION, CHARM

witch·grass \\'wich-ˌgras\\ *n* : any of several grasses that are weeds in cultivated areas

witch ha·zel \\'wich-ˌhā-zəl\\ *n* **1** : a No. American shrub bearing small yellow flowers in the fall **2** : an alcoholic solution of material from witch hazel bark used as a soothing astringent lotion

witch–hunt \\'wich-ˌhənt\\ *n* **1** : a searching out and persecution of persons accused of witchcraft **2** : the searching out and deliberate harassment of those (as political opponents) with unpopular views

witch·ing \\'wich-iŋ\\ *adj* : of, relating to, or suitable for sorcery or supernatural occurrences

wi·te·na·ge·mot *or* **wi·te·na·ge·mote** \\'wit-ᵊn-ə-gə-ˌmōt\\ *n* [OE *witena gemōt*, fr. *witena* (gen. pl. of *wita* sage, adviser) + *gemōt* assembly]

: an Anglo-Saxon council of nobles, prelates, and officials to advise the king on administrative and judicial matters

with \(ˈ)with, (ˈ)with\ *prep* **1** : AGAINST ⟨a fight ∼ his wife⟩ **2** : FROM ⟨parting ∼ friends⟩ **3** : in mutual relation to ⟨talk ∼ a friend⟩ **4** : in the company of ⟨a professor ∼ her students⟩ **5** : AS REGARDS, TOWARD ⟨is patient ∼ the children⟩ **6** : compared to ⟨on equal terms ∼ another⟩ **7** : in support of ⟨I'm ∼ you all the way⟩ **8** : in the presence of : CONTAINING ⟨tea ∼ sugar⟩ **9** : in the opinion of : as judged by ⟨their arguments had weight ∼ him⟩ **10** : BECAUSE OF, THROUGH ⟨pale ∼ anger⟩ **11** : in a manner indicating ⟨work ∼ a will⟩ **12** : GIVEN, GRANTED ⟨∼ your permission I'll leave⟩ **13** : HAVING ⟨came ∼ good news⟩ ⟨stood there ∼ his mouth open⟩ **14** : at the time of : right after ⟨∼ that he left⟩ **15** : DESPITE ⟨∼ all her cleverness, she failed⟩ **16** : so as not to cross or oppose ⟨swim ∼ the tide⟩

with·al \with-ˈȯl, with-\ *adv* **1** : together with this : BESIDES **2** *archaic* : THEREWITH **3** : on the other hand : NEVERTHELESS

with·draw \with-ˈdrȯ, with-\ *vb* **-drew** \-ˈdrü\; **-drawn** \-ˈdrȯn\; **-draw·ing** \-ˈdrȯ(-)iŋ\ **1** : to take back or away : draw away : REMOVE **2** : to call back (as from consideration) : RECALL, RESCIND; *also* : RETRACT ⟨∼ an accusation⟩ **3** : to go away : RETREAT, LEAVE **4** : to terminate one's participation in or use of something

with·draw·al \-ˈdrȯ(ə-)l\ *n* **1** : an act or instance of withdrawing **2** : the discontinuance of the use or administration of a drug and esp. a habit-forming drug; *also* : the often painful physiological and psychological symptoms produced by withdrawal **3** : a pathological retreat from the real world (as in some schizophrenic states)

with·drawn \with-ˈdrȯn\ *adj* **1** : ISOLATED, SECLUDED **2** : socially detached and unresponsive

withe \ˈwith\ *n* : a slender flexible twig or branch; *esp* : one used as a band or rope

with·er \ˈwith-ər\ *vb* **with·ered; with·er·ing** \-(ə-)riŋ\ **1** : to become dry and shrunken; *esp* : to shrivel from or as if from loss of bodily moisture **2** : to lose or cause to lose vitality, force, or freshness **3** : to cause to feel shriveled or blighted : STUN ⟨∼ed him with a glance⟩

with·ers \ˈwith-ərz\ *n pl* : the ridge between the shoulder bones of a horse; *also* : the corresponding part in other 4-footed animals

with·hold \with-ˈhōld, with-\ *vb* **-held** \-ˈheld\; **-hold·ing** **1** : to hold back : RESTRAIN; *also* : RETAIN **2** : to refrain from granting, giving, or allowing ⟨∼ permission⟩ ⟨∼ names⟩

withholding tax *n* : a tax on income withheld at the source

¹**with·in** \with-ˈin, with-\ *adv* **1** : in or into the interior : INSIDE **2** : inside oneself : INWARDLY ⟨calm without but furious ∼⟩

²**within** *prep* **1** : inside the limits or influence of ⟨∼ call⟩ **2** : in the limits or compass of ⟨∼ a mile⟩ **3** : in or to the inner part of ⟨∼ the room⟩

³**within** *n* : an inner place or area ⟨revolt from ∼⟩

with–it \ˈwith-ət\ *adj* : socially or culturally up-to-date

¹**with·out** \with-ˈaut, with-\ *prep* **1** : OUTSIDE **2** : LACKING ⟨she's ∼ hope⟩; *also* : not accompanied by or showing ⟨spoke ∼ thinking⟩ ⟨took his punishment ∼ flinching⟩

²**without** *adv* **1** : on the outside : EXTERNALLY **2** : with something lacking or absent ⟨has learned to do ∼⟩

with·stand \with-ˈstand, with-\ *vb* **-stood** \-ˈstud\; **-stand·ing** : to stand against : RESIST; *esp* : to oppose (as an attack) successfully

wit·less \ˈwit-ləs\ *adj* : lacking wit or understanding : mentally defective : FOOLISH — **wit·less·ly** *adv* — **wit·less·ness** *n*

¹**wit·ness** \ˈwit-nəs\ *n* [ME *witnesse*, fr. OE *witnes* knowledge, testimony, witness, fr. *wit* mind, intelligence] **1** : TESTIMONY ⟨bear ∼ to the fact⟩ **2** : one that gives evidence; *esp* : one who testifies in a cause or before a court **3** : one present at a transaction so as to be able to testify that it has taken place **4** : one who has personal knowledge or experience of some-

thing **5** : something serving as evidence or proof : SIGN

²witness *vb* **1** : to bear witness : TESTIFY **2** : to act as legal witness of **3** : to furnish proof of : BETOKEN **4** : to be a witness of **5** : to be the scene of ⟨this region has ∼*ed* many wars⟩

wit·ted \'wit-əd\ *adj* : having wit or understanding ⟨dull-*witted*⟩

wit·ti·cism \'wit-ə-ˌsiz-əm\ *n* : a witty saying or phrase

wit·ting \'wit-iŋ\ *adj* : done knowingly : INTENTIONAL — **wit·ting·ly** *adv*

wit·ty \'wit-ē\ *adj* **wit·ti·er; -est** : marked by or full of wit : AMUSING ⟨a ∼ writer⟩ ⟨a ∼ remark⟩ **syn** humorous, facetious, jocular, jocose — **wit·ti·ly** \'wit-ᵊl-ē\ *adv* — **wit·ti·ness** \-ē-nəs\ *n*

wive \'wīv\ *vb* **wived; wiv·ing** **1** : to marry a woman **2** : to take for a wife

wives pl of WIFE

wiz·ard \'wiz-ərd\ *n* [ME *wysard* wise man, fr. *wys* wise] **1** : MAGICIAN, SORCERER **2** : a very clever or skillful person ⟨a ∼ at chess⟩

wiz·ard·ry \'wiz-ə(r)-drē\ *n, pl* **-ries** **1** : magic skill : SORCERY, WITCHCRAFT **2** : great skill or cleverness in an activity

wiz·ened \'wiz-ᵊnd\ *adj* : dried up : SHRIVELED, WITHERED

wk *abbr* **1** week **2** work

WL *abbr* wavelength

wmk *abbr* watermark

WNW *abbr* west-northwest

WO *abbr* warrant officer

w/o *abbr* without

woad \'wōd\ *n* : a European herb related to the mustards; *also* : a blue dyestuff made from its leaves

wob·ble \'wäb-əl\ *vb* **wob·bled; wob·bling** \-(ə-)liŋ\ **1** : to move or cause to move with an irregular rocking or side-to-side motion **2** : TREMBLE, QUAVER **3** : WAVER, VACILLATE — **wobble** *n* — **wob·bly** \'wäb-(ə-)lē\ *adj*

woe \'wō\ *n* **1** : a condition of deep suffering from misfortune, affliction, or grief **2** : CALAMITY, MISFORTUNE ⟨economic ∼s⟩

woe·be·gone \'wō-bi-ˌgȯn\ *adj* : exhibiting woe, sorrow, or misery; *also* : DISMAL, DESOLATE

woe·ful *also* **wo·ful** \'wō-fəl\ *adj* **1** : full of woe : AFFLICTED **2** : involving,

bringing, or relating to woe **3** : PALTRY, DEPLORABLE — **woe·ful·ly** \-ē\ *adv*

wok \'wäk\ *n* : a bowl-shaped cooking utensil used esp. in the preparation of Chinese food

woke past of WAKE

woken past part of WAKE

wold \'wōld\ *n* : an upland plain or stretch of rolling land without woods

¹wolf \'wu̇lf\ *n, pl* **wolves** \'wu̇lvz\ **1** : any of several large erect-eared bushy-tailed doglike predatory mammals that often hunt in packs **2** : a fierce or destructive person **3** : a man forward, direct, and zealous in amatory attentions to women — **wolf·ish** *adj*

²wolf *vb* : to eat greedily : DEVOUR

wolf·hound \-ˌhau̇nd\ *n* : any of several large dogs orig. used in hunting wolves

wol·fram \'wu̇l-frəm\ *n* : TUNGSTEN

wol·ver·ine \ˌwu̇l-və-'rēn\ *n, pl* **wolverines** *also* **wolverine** : a dark shaggy-coated flesh-eating mammal of northern forests and associated tundra that is related to the weasels and sables

wom·an \'wu̇m-ən\ *n, pl* **wom·en** \'wim-ən\ [ME, fr. OE *wīfman*, fr. *wīf* woman, wife + *man* human being, man] **1** : an adult female person **2** : WOMANKIND **3** : feminine nature : WOMANLINESS **4** : a female servant or attendant

wom·an·hood \'wu̇m-ən-ˌhu̇d\ *n* **1** : the state of being a woman : the distinguishing qualities of a woman or of womankind **2** : WOMEN, WOMANKIND

wom·an·ish \'wu̇m-ə-nish\ *adj* **1** : of, relating to, or characteristic of a woman **2** : suitable to a woman rather than to a man : EFFEMINATE

wom·an·kind \'wu̇m-ən-ˌkīnd\ *n* : the females of the human race : WOMEN

wom·an·like \-ˌlīk\ *adj* : WOMANLY

wom·an·ly \-lē\ *adj* : having qualities characteristic of a woman — **wom·an·li·ness** \-lē-nəs\ *n*

woman suffrage *n* : possession and exercise of suffrage by women

womb \'wu̇m\ *n* **1** : UTERUS **2** : a place where something is generated or developed

wom·bat \'wäm-ˌbat\ *n* : any of several stocky burrowing Australian marsupials that resemble small bears

wom·en·folk \ˈwim-ən-ˌfōk\ *also* **wom·en·folks** \-ˌfōks\ *n pl* : WOMEN

¹**won** \ˈwən\ past and past part of WIN

²**won** \ˈwȯn\ *n, pl* **won** — see MONEY table

¹**won·der** \ˈwən-dər\ *n* **1** : a cause of astonishment or surprise : MARVEL; *also* : MIRACLE **2** : the quality of exciting wonder ⟨the charm and ∼ of the scene⟩ **3** : a feeling (as of awed astonishment or uncertainty) aroused by something extraordinary or affecting

²**won·der** *vb* **won·dered; won·der·ing** \-d(ə-)riŋ\ **1** : to feel surprise or amazement **2** : to feel curiosity or doubt

wonder drug *n* : MIRACLE DRUG

won·der·ful \ˈwən-dər-fəl\ *adj* **1** : exciting wonder : MARVELOUS, ASTONISHING **2** : unusually good : ADMIRABLE — **won·der·ful·ly** \-f(ə-)lē\ *adv* — **won·der·ful·ness** \-fəl-nəs\ *n*

won·der·land \-ˌland, -lənd\ *n* **1** : an imaginary place of delicate beauty or magical charm **2** : a place that excites admiration or wonder

won·der·ment \-mənt\ *n* **1** : ASTONISHMENT, SURPRISE **2** : a cause of or occasion for wonder **3** : curiosity about something

won·drous \ˈwən-drəs\ *adj* : WONDERFUL, MARVELOUS — **wondrous** *adv, archaic* — **won·drous·ly** *adv* — **won·drous·ness** *n*

¹**wont** \ˈwȯnt, ˈwōnt\ *adj* [ME *woned, wont,* fr. pp. of *wonen* to dwell, be used to, fr. OE *wunian*] **1** : ACCUSTOMED, USED ⟨as he was ∼ to do⟩ **2** : INCLINED, APT

²**wont** *n* : CUSTOM, USAGE, HABIT ⟨according to her ∼⟩

wont·ed \ˈwȯnt-əd, ˈwōnt-\ *adj* : ACCUSTOMED, CUSTOMARY ⟨his ∼ courtesy⟩

woo \ˈwü\ *vb* **1** : to try to gain the love of and usu. marriage with : COURT **2** : SOLICIT, ENTREAT **3** : to try to gain or bring about ⟨∼ public favor⟩ — **woo·er** *n*

¹**wood** \ˈwu̇d\ *n* **1** : a dense growth of trees usu. larger than a grove and smaller than a forest — often used in pl. **2** : a hard fibrous substance that is basically xylem and forms the bulk of trees and shrubs beneath the bark; *also* : this material fit or prepared for some use (as burning or building) **3** : something made of wood

²**wood** *adj* **1** : WOODEN **2** : suitable for holding, cutting, or working with wood **3** *or* **woods** \ˈwu̇dz\ : living or growing in woods

³**wood** *vb* **1** : to supply or load with wood esp. for fuel **2** : to cover with a growth of trees

wood alcohol *n* : METHANOL

wood·bine \ˈwu̇d-ˌbīn\ *n* : any of several climbing vines (as a honeysuckle or Virginia creeper)

wood·block \-ˌbläk\ *n* **1** : a block of wood **2** : WOODCUT

wood·chop·per \-ˌchäp-ər\ *n* : one engaged esp. in chopping down trees

wood·chuck \-ˌchək\ *n* : any of several No. American marmots; *esp* : a thickset grizzled marmot of the northeastern U.S. and Canada

wood·cock \ˈwu̇d-ˌkäk\ *n, pl* **woodcocks** : a brown No. American game bird with a short neck and long bill that is related to the snipe; *also* : a related and similar bird widespread in the Old World

wood·craft \-ˌkraft\ *n* **1** : skill and practice in matters relating to the woods esp. in maintaining oneself and making one's way or in hunting or trapping **2** : skill in shaping or constructing articles from wood

wood·cut \-ˌkət\ *n* **1** : a relief printing surface engraved on wood **2** : a print from a woodcut

wood·cut·ter \-ˌkət-ər\ *n* : a person who cuts wood esp. as an occupation

wood·ed \ˈwu̇d-əd\ *adj* : covered with woods or trees ⟨∼ slopes⟩

wood·en \ˈwu̇d-ᵊn\ *adj* **1** : made of wood **2** : lacking resilience : STIFF **3** : AWKWARD, CLUMSY — **wood·en·ly** *adv* — **wood·en·ness** \-ᵊn-(n)əs\ *n*

wood·en·ware \ˈwu̇d-ᵊn-ˌwaʀ\ *n* : articles made of wood for domestic use

wood·land \ˈwu̇d-lənd, -ˌland\ *n* : land covered with trees : FOREST

wood·lot \ˈwu̇d-ˌlät\ *n* : a relatively small area of trees kept usu. to meet fuel and timber needs ⟨a farm ∼⟩

wood louse *n* : a small flat grayish crustacean that lives esp. under stones and bark

wood·man \ˈwu̇d-mən\ *n* : WOODSMAN

wood·note \-ˌnōt\ *n* : verbal expression that is natural and artless

wood nymph *n* : a nymph living in the woods

wood·peck·er \ˈwu̇d-ˌpek-ər\ *n* : any of various usu. brightly marked climbing birds with stiff spiny tail feathers and a chisellike bill used to drill into trees for insects

wood·pile \-ˌpīl\ *n* : a pile of wood and esp. firewood

wood·shed \-ˌshed\ *n* : a shed for storing wood and esp. firewood

woods·man \ˈwu̇dz-mən\ *n* : a person who frequents or works in the woods; *esp* : one skilled in woodcraft

woodsy \ˈwu̇d-zē\ *adj* : relating to or suggestive of woods

wood·wind \ˈwu̇d-ˌwind\ *n* : one of a group of wind instruments including flutes, clarinets, oboes, bassoons, and sometimes saxophones

wood·work \-ˌwərk\ *n* 1 : work made of wood; *esp* : interior fittings (as moldings or stairways) of wood 2 : a place of hiding or seclusion ⟨came out of the ~ to claim the lost money⟩

woody \ˈwu̇d-ē\ *adj* **wood·i·er; -est** 1 : abounding or overgrown with woods 2 : of or containing wood or wood fibers 3 : resembling or characteristic of wood — **wood·i·ness** \ˈwu̇d-ē-nəs\ *n*

woof \ˈwu̇f\ *n* [alter. of ME *oof*, fr. OE *ōwef*, fr. *ō-* (fr. *on* on) + *wefan* to weave] 1 : the threads in a woven fabric that cross the warp 2 : a woven fabric; *also* : its texture

woof·er \ˈwu̇f-ər\ *n* : a loudspeaker that reproduces sounds of low pitch

wool \ˈwu̇l\ *n* 1 : the soft wavy or curly hair of some mammals and esp. the domestic sheep; *also* : something (as a textile or garment) made of wool 2 : material that resembles a mass of wool — **wooled** \ˈwu̇ld\ *adj*

¹**wool·en** *or* **wool·len** \ˈwu̇l-ən\ *adj* 1 : made of wool 2 : of or relating to the manufacture or sale of woolen products ⟨~ mills⟩

²**woolen** *or* **woollen** *n* 1 : a fabric made of wool 2 : garments of woolen fabric — usu. used in pl.

wool·gath·er·ing \-ˌgath-(ə-)riŋ\ *n* : the act of indulging in idle daydreaming

¹**wool·ly** *also* **wooly** \ˈwu̇l-ē\ *adj* **wool·li·er; -est** 1 : of, relating to, or bearing wool 2 : consisting of or resembling wool 3 : CONFUSED, BLURRY ⟨~ thinking⟩ 4 : marked by a lack of order or restraint ⟨the wild and ~ West of frontier times⟩

²**wool·ly** *also* **wool·ie** *or* **wooly** \ˈwu̇l-ē\ *n, pl* **wool·lies** : a garment made from wool; *esp* : underclothing of knitted wool

woolly aphid *n* : a plant louse covered with a dense coat of white filaments

woolly aphis *n* : WOOLLY APHID

woolly bear *n* : any of numerous very hairy caterpillars

wool·sack \ˈwu̇l-ˌsak\ *n* 1 *archaic* : a sack of or for wool 2 : the seat of the Lord Chancellor in the House of Lords

woo·zy \ˈwü-zē\ *adj* **woo·zi·er; -est** 1 : BEFUDDLED 2 : somewhat dizzy, nauseated, or weak — **woo·zi·ness** \ˈwü-zē-nəs\ *n*

¹**word** \ˈwərd\ *n* 1 : something that is said; *esp* : a brief remark 2 : a speech sound or series of speech sounds that communicates a meaning; *also* : a graphic representation of such a sound or series of sounds 3 : ORDER, COMMAND 4 *often cap* : the 2d person of the Trinity; *also* : GOSPEL 5 : NEWS, INFORMATION 6 : PROMISE 7 *pl* : QUARREL, DISPUTE 8 : a verbal signal : PASSWORD — **word·less** *adj*

²**word** *vb* : to express in words : PHRASE

word·age \ˈwərd-ij\ *n* 1 : WORDS 2 : number of words 3 : WORDING

word·book \ˈwərd-ˌbu̇k\ *n* : VOCABULARY, DICTIONARY

word·ing \ˈwərd-iŋ\ *n* : verbal expression : PHRASEOLOGY

word of mouth : oral communication

word·play \ˈwərd-ˌplā\ *n* : verbal wit

word processing *n* : the production of typewritten documents with automated and usu. computerized text-editing equipment

word processor *n* : a keyboard-operated terminal with a video display and a magnetic storage device for use in word processing; *also* : software to perform word processing

wordy \ˈwərd-ē\ *adj* **word·i·er; -est** : using many words : VERBOSE **syn** prolix, diffuse, redundant — **word·i·ness** \ˈwərd-ē-nəs\ *n*

wore past of WEAR

¹**work** \'wərk\ *n* **1** : TOIL, LABOR; *also* : EMPLOYMENT ⟨out of ∼⟩ **2** : TASK, JOB ⟨have ∼ to do⟩ **3** : the transference of energy when a force produces movement of a body **4** : DEED, ACHIEVEMENT **5** : a fortified structure of any kind **6** *pl* : engineering structures **7** *pl* : the buildings, grounds, and machinery of a factory **8** *pl* : the moving parts of a mechanism **9** : something produced by mental effort or physical labor; *esp* : an artistic production (as a book or needlework) **10** : WORKMANSHIP ⟨careless ∼⟩ **11** : material in the process of manufacture **12** *pl* : everything possessed, available, or belonging ⟨the whole ∼s went overboard⟩; *also* : subjection to drastic treatment ⟨gave him the ∼s⟩ **syn** occupation, employment, business, pursuit, calling — **in the works** : in process of preparation

²**work** *adj* **1** : used for work ⟨∼ elephants⟩ **2** : suitable or styled for wear while working ⟨∼ clothes⟩

³**work** *vb* **worked** \'wərkt\ *or* **wrought** \'ròt\; **work·ing** **1** : to bring to pass : EFFECT **2** : to fashion or create a useful or desired product through labor or exertion **3** : to prepare for use (as by kneading) **4** : to bring into a desired form by a process of cutting, hammering, scraping, pressing, or stretching ⟨∼ cold steel⟩ **5** : to set or keep in operation : OPERATE ⟨a pump ∼ed by hand⟩ **6** : to solve by reasoning or calculation ⟨∼ a problem⟩ **7** : to cause to toil or labor ⟨∼ed his men hard⟩; *also* : EXPLOIT **8** : to pay for with labor or service ⟨∼ off a debt⟩ **9** : to bring into some (specified) position or condition by stages ⟨the stream ∼ed itself clear⟩ **10** : CONTRIVE, ARRANGE ⟨we'll go if we can ∼ it⟩ **11** : to practice trickery or cajolery on for some end ⟨∼ed the management for a free ticket⟩ **12** : EXCITE, PROVOKE ⟨∼ed himself into a rage⟩ **13** : to exert oneself physically or mentally; *esp* : to perform work regularly for wages **14** : to function according to plan or design **15** : to produce a desired effect : SUCCEED **16** : to make way slowly and with difficulty ⟨he ∼ed forward through the crowd⟩ **17** : to permit of being worked ⟨this wood ∼s easily⟩ **18** : to be in restless motion; *also* : FERMENT 1 **19**

: to move slightly in relation to another part; *also* : to get into a specified condition slowly or imperceptibly ⟨the knot ∼ed loose⟩ — **work on 1** : AFFECT **2** : to try to influence or persuade — **work upon** : to have effect upon : operate on : PERSUADE, INFLUENCE

work·able \'wər-kə-bəl\ *adj* **1** : capable of being worked **2** : PRACTICABLE, FEASIBLE — **work·able·ness** *n*

work·a·day \'wərk-ə-ˌdā\ *adj* **1** : relating to or suited for working days **2** : PROSAIC, ORDINARY

work·a·hol·ic \ˌwərk-ə-'hòl-ik, -'häl-\ *n* : a compulsive worker

work·bag \'wərk-ˌbag\ *n* : a bag for holding implements or materials for work; *esp* : a bag for needlework

work·bas·ket \-ˌbas-kət\ *n* : a basket for needlework

work·bench \-ˌbench\ *n* : a bench on which work esp. of mechanics, machinists, and carpenters is performed

work·book \-ˌbùk\ *n* **1** : a booklet outlining a course of study **2** : a worker's manual **3** : a record of work done **4** : a student's book of problems to be answered directly on the pages

work·box \-ˌbäks\ *n* : a box for work instruments and materials

work·day \'wərk-ˌdā\ *n* **1** : a day on which work is done as distinguished from a day off **2** : the period of time in a day when work is performed

work·er \'wər-kər\ *n* **1** : one that works; *esp* : a person who works for wages **2** : one of the sexually undeveloped individuals of a colony of social insects (as bees, ants, or termites) that perform the work of the community

work ethic *n* : belief in work as a moral good

work farm *n* : a farm on which persons guilty of minor law violations are confined

work·horse \'wərk-ˌhòrs\ *n* **1** : a horse used chiefly for labor **2** : a person who undertakes arduous labor

work·house \-ˌhaùs\ *n* **1** *Brit* : POORHOUSE **2** : a house of correction where persons who have committed minor offenses are confined

¹**work·ing** \'wər-kiŋ\ *adj* **1** : adequate to allow work to be done ⟨a ∼ majority⟩

⟨a ～ knowledge of French⟩ **2** : adopted or assumed to help further work or activity ⟨a ～ draft of a treaty⟩ **3** : engaged in work ⟨a ～ journalist⟩ **4** : spent at work ⟨～ life⟩

²**working** n **1** : manner of functioning : OPERATION **2** pl : an excavation made in mining or tunneling

work·ing·man \'wər-kiŋ-ˌman\ n : one who works for wages usu. at manual labor

work·man \'wərk-mən\ n **1** : WORKING-MAN **2** : ARTISAN, CRAFTSMAN

work·man·like \-ˌlīk\ adj : worthy of a good workman : SKILLFUL

work·man·ship \-ˌship\ n : the art or skill of a workman : CRAFTSMANSHIP; also : the quality imparted to something in the process of making it ⟨a vase of exquisite ～⟩

work·out \'wərk-ˌaut\ n **1** : a practice or exercise to test or improve one's fitness esp. for athletic competition, ability, or performance **2** : a test or trial to determine ability or capacity or suitability

work out \ˌwərk-'aut, 'wərk-\ vb **1** : to bring about esp. by resolving difficulties **2** : DEVELOP, ELABORATE **3** : to prove effective, practicable, or suitable **4** : to amount to a total or calculated figure — used with at **5** : to engage in a workout

work·room \'wərk-ˌrüm, -ˌrum\ n : a room used esp. for manual work

work·shop \-ˌshäp\ n **1** : a small establishment where manufacturing or handicrafts are carried on **2** : a seminar emphasizing exchange of ideas and practical methods and given mainly for adults already employed in the field

work·sta·tion \-ˌstā-shən\ n : an area with equipment for a single worker; also : a usu. intelligent terminal connected to a computer network

work·ta·ble \-ˌtā-bəl\ n : a table for holding working materials and implements (as for needlework)

world \'wərld\ n [ME, fr. OE woruld human existence, this world, age, fr. a prehistoric compound whose first constituent is represented by OE wer man and whose second constituent is akin to OE eald old] **1** : the earth with its inhabitants and all things upon it **2**

: people in general : MANKIND **3** : the affairs of men ⟨withdraw from the ～⟩ **4** : UNIVERSE, CREATION **5** : a state of existence : scene of life and action ⟨the ～ of the future⟩ **6** : a distinctive class of persons or their sphere of interest ⟨the musical ～⟩ **7** : a part or section of the earth or its inhabitants by itself **8** : a great number or quantity ⟨a ～ of troubles⟩ **9** : a celestial body esp. if inhabited

world–beat·er \-ˌbēt-ər\ n : one that excels all others of its kind : CHAMPION

world·ling \-liŋ\ n : a person absorbed in the affairs and pleasures of the present world

world·ly \'wərld-lē\ adj **1** : of, relating to, or devoted to this world and its pursuits rather than to religion or spiritual affairs **2** : WORLDLY-WISE, SOPHISTICATED — **world·li·ness** \-lē-nəs\ n

world·ly–wise \-ˌwīz\ adj : possessing a practical and often shrewd understanding of human affairs

world·wide \'wərld-'wīd\ adj : extended throughout the entire world ⟨～ fame⟩

¹**worm** \'wərm\ n **1** : any of various small long usu. naked and soft-bodied round or flat invertebrate animals (as an earthworm, nematode, tapeworm, or maggot) **2** : a human being who is an object of contempt, loathing, or pity : WRETCH **3** : something that inwardly torments or devours **4** pl : infestation with or disease caused by parasitic worms **5** : a spiral or wormlike thing (as the thread of a screw) — **wormy** adj

²**worm** vb **1** : to free from worms ⟨～ a dog⟩ **2** : to move or cause to move or proceed slowly and deviously **3** : to obtain or extract by artful or insidious pleading, asking, or persuading ⟨～ed the truth out of him⟩ **4** : to insinuate or introduce (oneself) by devious or subtle means

worm–eat·en \'wərm-ˌēt-ᵊn\ adj **1** : eaten or burrowed by worms **2** : PITTED **3** : WORN-OUT, ANTIQUATED ⟨tried to update the ～ regulations⟩

worm gear n : a mechanical linkage consisting of a short rotating screw whose threads mesh with the teeth of a gear wheel

worm·hole \'wərm-ˌhōl\ *n* : a hole or passage burrowed by a worm

worm·wood \'wərm-ˌwůd\ *n* **1** : any of a genus of aromatic woody plants including the sagebrush and related plants; *esp* : one of Europe used in making absinthe **2** : something bitter or grievous : BITTERNESS

worn past part of WEAR

worn–out \'wōrn-'aůt\ *adj* : exhausted or used up by or as if by wear ⟨an old ∼ suit⟩ ⟨a ∼ automobile⟩

wor·ri·some \'wər-ē-səm\ *adj* **1** : causing distress or worry **2** : inclined to worry or fret

¹wor·ry \'wər-ē\ *vb* **wor·ried; wor·ry·ing 1** : to shake and mangle with the teeth ⟨a terrier ∼ing a rat⟩ **2** : to make anxious or upset ⟨his poor health *worries* his parents⟩ **3** : to feel or express great care or anxiety : FRET — **wor·ri·er** *n*

²worry *n, pl* **worries 1** : ANXIETY **2** : a cause of anxiety : TROUBLE

wor·ry·wart \'wər-ē-ˌwȯrt\ *n* : one who is inclined to worry unduly

¹worse \'wərs\ *adj, comparative of* BAD *or of* ILL **1** : bad or evil in a greater degree : less good; *esp* : more unwell **2** : more unfavorable, unpleasant, or painful

²worse *n* **1** : one that is worse **2** : a greater degree of ill or badness

³worse *adv, comparative of* BAD *or of* ILL : in a worse manner : to a worse extent or degree

wors·en \'wərs-ᵊn\ *vb* **wors·ened; wors·en·ing** \'wərs-(ᵊ-)niŋ\ : to make or become worse

¹wor·ship \'wər-shəp\ *n* [ME *worshipe* worthiness, repute, respect, reverence paid to a divine being, fr. OE *weorthscipe* worthiness, repute, respect, fr. *weorth* worthy, worth + -*scipe* -ship, suffix denoting quality or condition] **1** *chiefly Brit* : a person of importance — used as a title for officials (as magistrates and some mayors) **2** : reverence toward a divine being or supernatural power; *also* : the expression of such reverence **3** : extravagant respect or admiration for or devotion to an object of esteem ⟨∼ of the dollar⟩

²worship *vb* -shiped *or* -shipped; -ship-ing *or* -ship·ping **1** : to honor or reverence as a divine being or supernatural power **2** : IDOLIZE **3** : to perform or take part in worship — **wor·ship·er** *or* **wor·ship·per** *n*

wor·ship·ful \'wər-shəp-fəl\ *adj* **1** *archaic* : NOTABLE, DISTINGUISHED **2** *chiefly Brit* — used as a title for various persons or groups of rank or distinction **3** : VENERATING, WORSHIPING

¹worst \'wərst\ *adj, superlative of* BAD *or of* ILL **1** : most bad, evil, ill, or corrupt **2** : most unfavorable, unpleasant, or painful; *also* : most unsuitable, faulty, or unattractive **3** : least skillful or efficient **4** : most wanting in quality, value, or condition

²worst *adv, superlative of* ILL *or of* BAD *or* BADLY : to the extreme degree of badness or inferiority : in the worst manner

³worst *n* : one that is worst

⁴worst *vb* : DEFEAT

wor·sted \'wůs-təd, 'wər-stəd\ *n* [ME, fr. *Worsted* (now *Worstead*), England] : a smooth compact yarn from long wool fibers used esp. for firm napless fabrics, carpeting, or knitting; *also* : a fabric made from such yarn

wort \'wərt, 'wȯrt\ *n* : a solution obtained by infusion from malt and fermented to form beer

¹worth \'wərth\ *prep* **1** : equal in value to; *also* : having possessions or income equal to **2** : deserving of ⟨well ∼ the effort⟩

²worth *n* **1** : monetary value : the equivalent of a specified amount or figure **2** : the value of something measured by its qualities or by the esteem in which it is held **3** : moral or personal value : MERIT, EXCELLENCE **4** : WEALTH, RICHES

worth·less \'wərth-ləs\ *adj* **1** : lacking worth : VALUELESS; *also* : USELESS **2** : LOW, DESPICABLE — **worth·less·ness** *n*

worth·while \'wərth-'hwīl\ *adj* : being worth the time or effort spent

¹wor·thy \'wər-t͟hē\ *adj* **wor·thi·er; -est 1** : having worth or value : ESTIMABLE **2** : HONORABLE, MERITORIOUS **3** : having sufficient worth ⟨a man ∼ of the honor⟩ — **wor·thi·ly** \'wər-t͟hə-lē\ *adv* — **wor·thi·ness** \-t͟hē-nəs\ *n*

²worthy *n, pl* **worthies** : a worthy person

would \wəd, əd, d, (')wůd\ *past of* WILL **1** *archaic* : wish for : WANT **2** : strongly desire : WISH ⟨I ∼ I were young again⟩ **3** — used as an auxiliary to express (1) preference ⟨∼ rather run than fight⟩ , (2) wish, desire, or intent ⟨those who ∼ forbid gambling⟩ , (3) habitual action ⟨we ∼ meet often for lunch⟩ , (4) a contingency or possibility ⟨if he were coming, he ∼ be here by now⟩ , (5) probability ⟨∼ have won if he hadn't tripped⟩ , or (6) a request ⟨∼ you help us⟩ **4** : COULD **5** : SHOULD

would–be \ˌwu̇d-ˌbē\ *adj* : desiring, professing, or having the potential to be ⟨a ∼ artist⟩

¹wound \ˈwünd\ *n* **1** : an injury involving cutting or breaking of bodily tissue (as by violence, accident, or surgery) **2** : an injury or hurt to feelings or reputation

²wound *vb* : to inflict a wound to or in

³wound \ˈwau̇nd\ past and past part of WIND

wove past of WEAVE

woven past part of WEAVE

¹wow \ˈwau̇\ *n* : a striking success : HIT

²wow *vb* : to arouse enthusiastic approval

³wow *n* : a distortion in reproduced sound consisting of a slow rise and fall of pitch caused by speed variation in the reproducing system

WP *abbr* word processing; word processor

WPM *abbr* words per minute

wpn *abbr* weapon

¹wrack \ˈrak\ *n* **1** : a wrecked ship; *also* : WRECKAGE, WRECK **2** : sea vegetation (as kelp) esp. when cast up on the shore

²wrack *n* [ME, fr. OE *wræc* misery, punishment, something driven by the sea] **1** : RUIN, DESTRUCTION **2** : a remnant of something destroyed

wraith \ˈrāth\ *n, pl* **wraiths** \ˈrāths, ˈrāthz\ **1** : APPARITION; *also* : GHOST, SPECTER **2** : an insubstantial appearance : SHADOW

¹wran·gle \ˈraŋ-gəl\ *vb* **wran·gled; wran·gling** \-g(ə-)liŋ\ **1** : to quarrel angrily or peevishly : BICKER **2** : ARGUE **3** : to obtain by persistent arguing **4** : to herd and care for (livestock) on the range — **wran·gler** *n*

²wrangle *n* : an angry, noisy, or prolonged dispute or quarrel; *also* : CONTROVERSY

¹wrap \ˈrap\ *vb* **wrapped; wrap·ping 1** : to cover esp. by winding or folding **2** : to envelop and secure for transportation or storage : BUNDLE **3** : to enclose wholly : ENFOLD **4** : to coil, fold, draw, or twine about something **5** : SURROUND, ENVELOP; *also* : SUFFUSE **6** : INVOLVE, ENGROSS ⟨*wrapped* up in a hobby⟩ **7** : to conceal as if by enveloping or enfolding : HIDE **8** : to put on clothing : DRESS **9** : to be subject to covering or enclosing ⟨∼s up into a small package⟩

²wrap *n* **1** : WRAPPER, WRAPPING **2** : an article of clothing that may be wrapped around a person; *esp* : an outer garment (as a coat or shawl) **3** *pl* : SECRECY ⟨kept under ∼s⟩

wrap·around \ˈrap-ə-ˌrau̇nd\ *n* : a garment (as a dress) made with a full=length opening and adjusted to the figure by wrapping around

wrap·per \ˈrap-ər\ *n* **1** : that in which something is wrapped **2** : one that wraps **3** : an article of clothing worn wrapped around the body

wrap·ping \ˈrap-iŋ\ *n* : something used to wrap an object : WRAPPER

wrap–up \ˈrap-ˌəp\ *n* : a summarizing report

wrap up \(ˈ)rap-ˈəp\ *vb* **1** : SUMMARIZE, SUM UP **2** : to bring to a usu. successful conclusion

wrasse \ˈras\ *n* : any of various usu. brightly colored sea fishes including many food fishes

wrath \ˈrath\ *n* **1** : violent anger : RAGE **2** : retributory punishment for an offense or a crime : divine chastisement **syn** indignation, ire, fury, anger

wrath·ful \-fəl\ *adj* **1** : filled with wrath : very angry **2** : showing, marked by, or arising from anger — **wrath·ful·ly** \-ē\ *adv* — **wrath·ful·ness** *n*

wreak \ˈrēk\ *vb* **1** : to exact as a punishment : INFLICT ⟨∼ vengeance on an enemy⟩ **2** : to give free scope or rein to ⟨∼ed his wrath⟩ **3** : BRING ABOUT, CAUSE ⟨∼ havoc⟩

wreath \ˈrēth\ *n, pl* **wreaths** \ˈrēthz, ˈrēths\ : something (as boughs or flowers) intertwined into a circular shape

wreathe \ˈrēth\ *vb* **wreathed; wreath·ing 1** : to shape or take on the shape of a wreath : move or extend in circles or spirals **2** : to twist or become twisted esp. so as to show folds or creases ⟨a face *wreathed* in smiles⟩ **3** : to fold or coil around : ENTWINE

¹wreck \'rek\ *n* **1** : something (as goods) cast up on the land by the sea after a shipwreck **2** : SHIPWRECK **3** : the action of breaking up or destroying something : WRECKING **4** : broken remains (as of a ship or vehicle after heavy damage) **5** : something disabled or in a state of ruin; *also* : an individual broken in health or strength

²wreck *vb* **1** : SHIPWRECK **2** : to ruin or damage by breaking up : involve in disaster or ruin

wreck•age \'rek-ij\ *n* **1** : the act of wrecking : the state of being wrecked : RUIN **2** : the remains of a wreck

wreck•er \'rek-ər\ *n* **1** : one that searches for or works upon the wrecks of ships **2** : a truck equipped to remove disabled cars **3** : one that salvages junked automobile parts **4** : one that wrecks; *esp* : one that razes buildings

wren \'ren\ *n* : any of various small mostly brown singing birds with short wings and tail

¹wrench \'rench\ *vb* **1** : to move with a violent twist **2** : to pull, strain, or tighten with violent twisting or force **3** : to injure or disable by a violent twisting or straining **4** : to change (as the meaning of a word) violently : DISTORT **5** : to snatch forcibly : WREST **6** : to cause to suffer mental anguish

²wrench *n* **1** : a forcible twisting; *also* : an injury (as to one's ankle) by twisting **2** : a tool for holding, twisting, or turning an object (as a nut or bolt)

¹wrest \'rest\ *vb* **1** : to pull or move by a forcible twisting movement **2** : to gain with difficulty by or as if by force or violence ⟨∼ a living from the barren land⟩ ⟨∼ control of government from the dictator⟩

²wrest *n* : a forcible twist : WRENCH

¹wres•tle \'res-əl, 'ras-\ *vb* **wres•tled**; **wres•tling** \-(ə-)liŋ\ **1** : to scuffle with an opponent in an attempt to trip him or throw him down **2** : to contend against in wrestling **3** : to struggle for mastery (as with something difficult) ⟨∼ with a problem⟩ — **wres•tler** \'res-lər, 'ras-\ *n*

²wrestle *n* : the action or an instance of wrestling : STRUGGLE

wres•tling \'res-liŋ\ *n* : the sport of hand-to-hand combat between two opponents who seek to throw and pin each other

wretch \'rech\ *n* [ME *wrecche*, fr. OE *wrecca* outcast, exile] **1** : a miserable unhappy person **2** : a base, despicable, or vile person

wretch•ed \'rech-əd\ *adj* **1** : deeply afflicted, dejected, or distressed : MISERABLE **2** : WOEFUL, GRIEVOUS ⟨a ∼ accident⟩ **3** : DESPICABLE ⟨a ∼ trick⟩ **4** : poor in quality or ability : INFERIOR ⟨∼ workmanship⟩ — **wretch•ed•ness** *n*

wrig•gle \'rig-əl\ *vb* **wrig•gled**; **wrig•gling** \-(ə-)liŋ\ **1** : to twist and turn restlessly : SQUIRM ⟨*wriggled* in his chair⟩; *also* : to move or advance by twisting and turning ⟨a snake *wriggled* along the path⟩ **2** : to extricate oneself or bring into a state or place by maneuvering, twisting, or dodging ⟨∼ out of a difficulty⟩ — **wriggle** *n*

wrig•gler \'rig-(ə-)lər\ *n* **1** : one that wriggles **2** : WIGGLER 1

wring \'riŋ\ *vb* **wrung** \'rəŋ\; **wring•ing** \'riŋ-iŋ\ **1** : to squeeze or twist esp. so as to make dry or to extract moisture or liquid ⟨∼ clothes⟩ **2** : to get by or as if by forcible exertion or pressure : EXTORT ⟨∼ the truth out of him⟩ **3** : to twist so as to strain or sprain : CONTORT ⟨∼ his neck⟩ **4** : to twist together as a sign of anguish ⟨*wrung* her hands⟩ **5** : to affect painfully as if by wringing : TORMENT ⟨her plight *wrung* my heart⟩

wring•er \'riŋ-ər\ *n* : one that wrings; *esp* : a device for squeezing out liquid or moisture ⟨clothes ∼⟩

¹wrin•kle \'riŋ-kəl\ *n* **1** : a crease or small fold on a surface (as in the skin or in cloth) **2** : METHOD, TECHNIQUE **3** : INNOVATION, NOVELTY ⟨the latest ∼ in hairdos⟩ — **wrin•kly** \-k(ə-)lē\ *adj*

²wrinkle *vb* **wrin•kled**; **wrin•kling** \-k(ə-)liŋ\ : to develop or cause to develop wrinkles

wrist \'rist\ *n* : the joint or region between the hand and the arm; *also* : a corresponding part in a lower animal

wrist•band \'ris(t)-ˌband\ *n* **1** : the part of a sleeve covering the wrist **2** : a band encircling the wrist

wrist·let \'ris(t)-lət\ *n* : a band encircling the wrist; *esp* : a close-fitting knitted band attached to the top of a glove or the end of a sleeve

wrist·watch \-ˌwäch\ *n* : a small watch attached to a bracelet or strap to fasten about the wrist

writ \'rit\ *n* **1** : something written **2** : a legal order in writing issued in the name of the sovereign power or in the name of a court or judicial authority commanding the performance or nonperformance of a specified act **3** : a written order constituting a symbol of the power and authority of the issuer

write \'rīt\ *vb* **wrote** \'rōt\; **writ·ten** \'rit-ᵊn\ *also* **writ** \'rit\; **writ·ing** \'rīt-iŋ\ [ME *writen,* fr. OE *wrītan* to scratch, draw, inscribe] **1** : to form characters, letters, or words on a surface (as with a pen) ⟨learn to read and ~⟩ **2** : to form the letters or the words of (as on paper) : INSCRIBE ⟨*wrote* his name⟩ **3** : to put down on paper : give expression to in writing **4** : to make up and set down for others to read : COMPOSE ⟨~ music⟩ **5** : to pen, typewrite, or dictate a letter to **6** : to communicate by letter : CORRESPOND **7** : to be fitted for writing ⟨this pen ~s easily⟩

write–in \'rīt-ˌin\ *n* : a vote cast by writing in the name of a candidate; *also* : a candidate whose name is written in

write in \(ˈ)rīt-ˈin\ *vb* : to insert (a name not listed on a ballot) in an appropriate space; *also* : to cast (a vote) in this manner

write off *vb* **1** : to reduce the estimated value of : DEPRECIATE **2** : CANCEL ⟨*write off* a bad debt⟩

writ·er \'rīt-ər\ *n* : one that writes esp. as a business or occupation : AUTHOR

writer's cramp *n* : a painful spasmodic cramp of muscles of the hand or fingers brought on by excessive writing

write–up \'rīt-ˌəp\ *n* : a written account (as in a newspaper); *esp* : a flattering article

writhe \'rīth̲\ *vb* **writhed; writh·ing** **1** : to move or proceed with twists and turns ⟨~ in pain⟩ **2** : to suffer with shame or confusion : SQUIRM

writ·ing \'rīt-iŋ\ *n* **1** : the act of one that writes; *also* : HANDWRITING **2** : something (as a letter, book, or document) that is written or printed **3** : INSCRIPTION **4** : a style or form of composition **5** : the occupation of a writer

wrnt *abbr* warrant

¹wrong \'ròŋ\ *n* **1** : an injurious, unfair, or unjust act **2** : a violation of the legal rights of another person **3** : something that is contrary to justice, goodness, equity, or law ⟨know right from ~⟩ **4** : the state, position, or fact of being or doing wrong; *also* : the state of being guilty ⟨in the ~⟩

²wrong *adj* **wrong·er** \'ròŋ-ər\; **wrong·est** \'ròŋ-əst\ **1** : SINFUL, IMMORAL **2** : not right according to a standard or code : IMPROPER **3** : INCORRECT ⟨a ~ solution⟩ **4** : UNSATISFACTORY **5** : UNSUITABLE, INAPPROPRIATE **6** : constituting a surface that is considered the back, bottom, inside, or reverse of something ⟨iron only on the ~ side of the fabric⟩ **syn** false, erroneous, incorrect, inaccurate, untrue — **wrong·ly** *adv*

³wrong *adv* **1** : INCORRECTLY **2** : in a wrong direction, manner, position, or relation

⁴wrong *vb* **wronged; wrong·ing** \'ròŋ-iŋ\ **1** : to do wrong to : INJURE, HARM **2** : to treat unjustly : DISHONOR, MALIGN **syn** oppress, persecute, aggrieve

wrong·do·er \'ròŋ-ˈdü-ər\ *n* : a person who does wrong and esp. moral wrong — **wrong·do·ing** \-ˈdü-iŋ\ *n*

wrong·ful \'ròŋ-fəl\ *adj* **1** : WRONG, UNJUST **2** : UNLAWFUL — **wrong·ful·ly** \-ē\ *adv* — **wrong·ful·ness** *n*

wrong·head·ed \'ròŋ-ˈhed-əd\ *adj* : obstinately wrong : PERVERSE — **wrong·head·ed·ly** *adv* — **wrong·head·ed·ness** *n*

wrote past of WRITE

wroth \'ròth, 'rōth\ *adj* : filled with wrath : ANGRY

wrought \'ròt\ *adj* [ME, fr. pp. of *work·en* to work] **1** : FASHIONED, FORMED ⟨carefully ~ essays⟩ **2** : ORNAMENTED **3** : beaten into shape by tools : HAMMERED ⟨~ silver dishes⟩ **4** : deeply stirred : EXCITED ⟨gets easily ~ up over nothing⟩

wrought iron *n* : a commercial form of iron that contains less than 0.3 percent carbon and is tough, malleable, and relatively soft — **wrought–iron** *adj*

wrung past and past part of WRING

wry \'rī\ *adj* **wry•er** \'rī(-ə)r\; **wry•est** \'rī-əst\ **1** : having a bent or twisted shape ⟨a ∼ smile⟩; *esp* : turned abnormally to one side : CONTORTED ⟨a ∼ neck⟩ **2** : cleverly and often ironically humorous — **wry•ly** *adv* — **wry•ness** *n*

wry•neck \'rī-ˌnek\ *n* **1** : any of several birds related to the woodpeckers that

have a peculiar manner of twisting the head and neck **2** : a disorder marked by a twisting of the neck and head

WSW *abbr* west-southwest

wt *abbr* weight

wurst \'wərst, 'wu̇rst\ *n* : SAUSAGE

WV *or* **W Va** *abbr* West Virginia

WW *abbr* World War

w/w *abbr* wall-to-wall

WY *or* **Wyo** *abbr* Wyoming

X

¹x \'eks\ *n, pl* **x's** *or* **xs** \'ek-səz\ *often cap* **1** : the 24th letter of the English alphabet **2** : an unknown quantity

²x *vb* **x-ed** *also* **x'd** *or* **xed**; **x-ing** *or* **x'ing** : to cancel or obliterate with a series of *x*'s — usu. used with *out*

³x *abbr, often cap* experimental

⁴x *symbol* **1** times ⟨3 *x* 2 is 6⟩ **2** by ⟨a 3 *x* 5 index card⟩ **3** *often cap* power of magnification

Xan•thip•pe \zan-'t(h)ip-ē\ *or* **Xan•tip•pe** \-'tip-ē\ *n* [Gk *Xanthippē*, shrewish wife of Socrates] : an ill-tempered woman

x–ax•is \'eks-ˌak-səs\ *n* : the axis of a graph or a system of coordinates in a plane parallel to which abscissas are measured

X chromosome *n* : a sex chromosome that usually occurs paired in each female cell and single in each male cell in organisms (as human beings) in which the male normally has two unlike sex chromosomes

Xe *symbol* xenon

xe•bec \'zē-ˌbek\ *n* : a usu. 3-masted Mediterranean sailing ship with long overhanging bow and stern

xe•non \'zē-ˌnän, 'zen-ˌän\ *n* [Gk, neut. of *xenos* strange] : a heavy gaseous chemical element occurring in minute quantities in air

xe•no•pho•bia \ˌzen-ə-'fō-bē-ə, ˌzēn-\ *n* : fear and hatred of strangers or foreigners or of what is strange or foreign — **xe•no•phobe** \'zen-ə-ˌfōb, 'zēn-\ *n*

xe•ric \'zir-ik, 'zer-\ *adj* : low or deficient in moisture for the support of life

xe•rog•ra•phy \zə-'räg-rə-fē, zir-'äg-\ *n*

: a process for copying printed matter by the action of light on an electrically charged surface in which the latent image usu. is developed with powders — **xe•ro•graph•ic** \ˌzir-ə-'graf-ik\ *adj*

xe•ro•phyte \'zir-ə-ˌfīt\ *n* : a plant adapted for growth with a limited water supply — **xe•ro•phyt•ic** \ˌzir-ə-'fit-ik\ *adj*

XL *abbr* **1** extra large **2** extra long

Xmas \'kris-məs *also* 'eks-məs\ *n* [*X* (symbol for *Christ,* fr. the Gk letter chi (X), initial of *Christos* Christ) + *-mas* (in *Christmas*)] : CHRISTMAS

Xn *abbr* Christian

Xnty *abbr* Christianity

x–ra•di•a•tion \ˌeks-ˌrād-ē-'ā-shən\ *n, often cap* **1** : exposure to X rays **2** : radiation consisting of X rays

x–ray \'eks-ˌrā\ *vb, often cap* : to examine, treat, or photograph with X rays

X ray \'eks-ˌrā\ *n* **1** : a radiation of the same nature as light rays but of extremely short wavelength that is generated by the striking of a stream of electrons against a metal surface in a vacuum and that is able to penetrate through various thicknesses of solids **2** : a photograph taken with X rays — **X–ray** *adj*

XS *abbr* extra small

xu \'sü\ *n, pl* **xu** — see *dong* at MONEY table

xy•lem \'zī-ləm, -ˌlem\ *n* : woody tissue of higher plants that transports water and dissolved materials upward, functions also in support and storage, and lies central to the phloem

xy·lo·phone \\'zī-lə-ˌfōn\ *n* [Gk *xylon* wood + *phōnē* voice, sound] : a musical instrument consisting of a series of wooden bars graduated in length to produce the musical scale, supported on belts of straw or felt, and sounded by striking with two small wooden hammers — **xy·lo·phon·ist** \-ˌfō-nəst\ *n*

Y

¹y \\'wī\ *n, pl* **y's** *or* **ys** \\'wīz\ *often cap* : the 25th letter of the English alphabet

²y *abbr* **1** yard **2** year

¹Y \\'wī\ *n* : YMCA

²Y *symbol* yttrium

¹-y *also* **-ey** \ē\ *adj suffix* **1** : characterized by : full of ⟨dirt*y*⟩ ⟨clay*ey*⟩ **2** : having the character of : composed of ⟨ic*y*⟩ **3** : like : like that of ⟨hom*ey*⟩ ⟨wintr*y*⟩ ⟨stag*y*⟩ **4** : devoted to : addicted to : enthusiastic over ⟨hors*y*⟩ **5** : tending or inclined to ⟨sleep*y*⟩ ⟨chatt*y*⟩ **6** : giving occasion for (specified) action ⟨tear*y*⟩ **7** : performing (specified) action ⟨curl*y*⟩ **8** : somewhat : rather : -ISH ⟨chill*y*⟩ **9** : having (such) characteristics to a marked degree or in an affected or superficial way ⟨French*y*⟩

²-y \ē\ *n suffix, pl* **-ies** **1** : state : condition : quality ⟨beggar*y*⟩ **2** : activity, place of business, or goods dealt with ⟨laundr*y*⟩ **3** : whole body or group ⟨soldier*y*⟩

³-y *n suffix, pl* **-ies** : instance of a (specified) action ⟨entreat*y*⟩ ⟨inquir*y*⟩

YA *abbr* young adult

¹yacht \\'yät\ *n* [obs. D *jaght,* fr. Middle Low German *jacht,* short for *jachtschiff,* lit., hunting ship] : any of various relatively small ships used for pleasure cruising or racing

²yacht *vb* : to race or cruise in a yacht

yacht·ing \-iŋ\ *n* : the action, fact, or pastime of racing or cruising in a yacht

yachts·man \\'yäts-mən\ *n* : one who owns or sails a yacht

ya·hoo \\'yā-hü, 'yä-\ *n, pl* **yahoos** [fr. *Yahoo* one of a race of brutes having the form of men in Jonathan Swift's *Gulliver's Travels*] : a boorish, crass, or stupid person

Yah·weh \\'yä-ˌwä\ *also* **Yah·veh** \-ˌvä\ *n* : the God of the Hebrews

¹yak \\'yak\ *n, pl* **yaks** *also* **yak** : a large long-haired wild or domesticated ox of Tibet and adjacent Asian uplands

²yak *also* **yack** \\'yak\ *n* : persistent or voluble talk — **yak** *also* **yack** *vb*

yam \\'yam\ *n* **1** : the edible starchy root of a twining vine that largely replaces the potato as food in the tropics; *also* : a plant distantly related to the lilies that produces yams **2** : a usu. deep orange sweet potato

yam·mer \\'yam-ər\ *vb* **yam·mered**; **yam·mer·ing** \-(ə-)riŋ\ [alter. of ME *yomeren* to murmur, be sad, fr. OE *gēomrian*] **1** : WHIMPER **2** : CHATTER — **yammer** *n*

¹yank \\'yaŋk\ *n* : a strong sudden pull : JERK

²yank *vb* : to pull with a quick vigorous movement

Yank \\'yaŋk\ *n* : YANKEE

Yan·kee \\'yaŋ-kē\ *n* **1** : a native or inhabitant of New England; *also* : a native or inhabitant of the northern U.S. **2** : AMERICAN 2

yan·qui \\'yäŋ-kē\ *n, often cap* [Sp] : a citizen of the U.S. as distinguished from a Latin American

¹yap \\'yap\ *vb* **yapped**; **yap·ping** **1** : BARK, YELP **2** : GAB

²yap *n* **1** : a quick sharp bark **2** : CHATTER

¹yard \\'yärd\ *n* [ME, fr. OE *geard* enclosure, yard] **1** : a small enclosed area open to the sky and adjacent to a building **2** : the grounds of a building **3** : an enclosure for livestock **4** : an area set aside for a particular business or activity **5** : a system of railroad tracks for storing cars and making up trains

²yard *n* [ME *yarde,* fr. OE *gierd* twig, measure, yard] **1** — see WEIGHT table

2 : a long spar tapered toward the ends that supports and spreads the head of a sail

yard•age \-ij\ *n* : an aggregate number of yards; *also* : the length, extent, or volume of something as measured in yards

yard•arm \'yärd-,ärm\ *n* : either end of the yard of a square-rigged ship

yard•man \'yärd-mən, -,man\ *n* : a man employed in or about a yard

yard•mas•ter \-,mas-tər\ *n* : the person in charge of a railroad yard

yard•stick \'yärd-,stik\ *n* **1** : a graduated measuring stick three feet long **2** : a standard for making a critical judgment : CRITERION **syn** gauge, touchstone, benchmark, measure

yarn \'yärn\ *n* **1** : a continuous often plied strand composed of fibers or filaments and used in weaving and knitting to form cloth **2** : STORY; *esp* : a tall tale

yar•row \'yar-ō\ *n* : a strong-scented herb related to the daisies that has white or pink flowers in flat clusters

yaw \'yȯ\ *vb* : to deviate erratically from a course ⟨the ship ∼ed in the heavy seas⟩ — **yaw** *n*

yawl \'yȯl\ *n* : a 2-masted fore-and-aft rigged sailboat with the shorter mast aft of the rudder

¹yawn \'yȯn\ *vb* : to open wide; *esp* : to open the mouth wide usu. as an involuntary reaction to fatigue or boredom — **yawn•er** *n*

²yawn *n* : a deep usu. involuntary intake of breath through the wide-open mouth

yawp *or* **yaup** \'yȯp\ *vb* **1** : to make a raucous noise : SQUAWK **2** : CLAMOR, COMPLAIN — **yawp•er** *n*

yaws \'yȯz\ *n pl* : an infectious tropical disease caused by a spirochete closely resembling the causative agent of syphilis

y–ax•is \'wī-,ak-səs\ *n* : the axis of a graph or a system of coordinates in a plane parallel to which the ordinates are measured

Yb *symbol* ytterbium

YB *abbr* yearbook

Y chromosome *n* : a sex chromosome that is characteristic of male zygotes and cells in species in which the male

typically has two unlike sex chromosomes

yd *abbr* yard

¹ye \(')yē\ *pron* YOU 1

²ye \yē, yə, *or like* THE\ *definite article, archaic* : THE — used by early printers to represent the manuscript word þe (*the*)

¹yea \'yā\ *adv* **1** : YES — used in oral voting **2** : INDEED, TRULY

²yea *n* : an affirmative vote; *also* : a person casting such a vote

year \'yiər\ *n* **1** : the period of about 365¼ solar days required for one revolution of the earth around the sun **2** : a cycle of 365 or 366 days beginning with January 1; *also* : a calendar year specified usu. by a number **3** *pl* : a time of special significance ⟨∼s of plenty⟩ **4** *pl* : AGE ⟨advanced in ∼s⟩ **5** : a period of time other than a calendar year ⟨the school ∼⟩

year•book \-,bu̇k\ *n* **1** : a book published annually esp. as a report **2** : a school publication recording the history and activities of a graduating class

year•ling \'yiər-liŋ, 'yər-lən\ *n* : one that is or is rated as a year old

year•long \'yiər-'lȯŋ\ *adj* : lasting through a year

¹year•ly \'yiər-lē\ *adj* : ANNUAL

²yearly *adv* : every year

yearn \'yərn\ *vb* **1** : to feel a longing or craving **2** : to feel tenderness or compassion **syn** long, pine, hanker, hunger, thirst

yearn•ing \-iŋ\ *n* : a tender or urgent longing

year–round \'yiər-'rau̇nd\ *adj* : effective, employed, or operating for the full year : not seasonal ⟨a ∼ resort⟩

yeast \'yēst\ *n* **1** : a surface froth or a sediment in sugary liquids (as fruit juices) that consists largely of cells of a tiny fungus and is used in making alcoholic liquors and as a leaven in baking **2** : a commercial product containing yeast plants in a moist or dry medium **3** : any of various usu. one≠celled fungi that reproduce by budding and promote alcoholic fermentation **4** : the foam of waves : SPUME **5** : something that causes ferment or activity

yeasty \'yē-stē\ *adj* **yeast•i•er; -est** **1**

: of, relating to, or resembling yeast **2** : UNSETTLED **3** : full of vitality; *also* : FRIVOLOUS

yegg \\'yeg\\ *n* : one that breaks open safes to steal; *also* : ROBBER

¹yell \\'yel\\ *vb* : to utter a loud cry or scream : SHOUT

²yell *n* **1** : SHOUT **2** : a cheer used esp. to encourage an athletic team (as at a college)

¹yel·low \\'yel-ō\\ *adj* **1** : of the color yellow **2** : having a yellow complexion or skin **3** : SENSATIONAL ⟨~ journalism⟩ **4** : COWARDLY — **yel·low·ish** \\'yel-ə-wish\\ *adj*

²yellow *n* **1** : a color between green and orange in the spectrum : the color of ripe lemons or sunflowers **2** : something yellow; *esp* : the yolk of an egg **3** *pl* : any of several plant virus diseases marked by stunted growth and yellowing of foliage

³yellow *vb* : to make or turn yellow

yellow birch *n* : a No. American birch with thin lustrous gray or yellow bark; *also* : its strong hard pale wood

yellow fever *n* : an acute destructive virus disease marked by prostration, jaundice, fever, and often hemorrhage and transmitted by a mosquito

yellow jack *n* : YELLOW FEVER

yellow jacket *n* : any of various small social wasps having the body barred with bright yellow

yelp \\'yelp\\ *vb* [ME *yelpen* to boast, cry out, fr. OE *gielpan* to boast, exult] : to utter a sharp quick shrill cry — **yelp** *n*

¹yen \\'yen\\ *n, pl* **yen** — see MONEY table

²yen *n* [obs. E slang *yen-yen* craving for opium, fr. Chin *in-yan,* fr. *in* opium + *yan* craving] : a strong desire : LONGING

yeo·man \\'yō-mən\\ *n* **1** : an attendant or officer in a royal or noble household **2** : a naval petty officer who performs clerical duties **3** : a small farmer who cultivates his own land; *esp* : one of a class of English freeholders below the gentry

yeo·man·ry \\'yō-mən-rē\\ *n* : the body of yeomen and esp. of small landed proprietors

-yer — see -ER

yer·ba ma·té \\,yer-bə-'mä-,tā\\ *n* : MATÉ

¹yes \\'yes\\ *adv* — used as a function word esp. to express assent or agreement or to introduce a more emphatic or explicit phrase

²yes *n* : an affirmative reply

ye·shi·va *or* **ye·shi·vah** \\yə-'shē-və\\ *n, pl* **yeshivas** *or* **ye·shi·voth** \\-,shē-'vōt(h)\\ : a Jewish school esp. for religious instruction

yes–man \\'yes-,man\\ *n* : a person who endorses uncritically every opinion or proposal of a superior

¹yes·ter·day \\'yes-tərd-ē\\ *adv* **1** : on the day preceding today **2** : only a short time ago

²yesterday *n* **1** : the day last past **2** : time not long past

yes·ter·year \\'yes-tər-,yiər\\ *n* **1** : last year **2** : the recent past

¹yet \\(')yet\\ *adv* **1** : in addition : BESIDES; *also* : EVEN **5** **2** : up to now; *also* : STILL **3** : so soon as now ⟨not time to go ~⟩ **4** : EVENTUALLY **5** : NEVERTHELESS, HOWEVER

²yet *conj* : despite the fact that : BUT

ye·ti \\'yet-ē, 'yāt-\\ *n* [Tibetan] : ABOMINABLE SNOWMAN

yew \\'yü\\ *n* **1** : any of a genus of evergreen trees or shrubs with dark stiff poisonous needles and fleshy fruits **2** : the fine-grained wood of a yew; *esp* : that of an Old World yew

Yid·dish \\'yid-ish\\ *n* [Yiddish *yidish,* short for *yidish daytsh,* lit., Jewish German] : a language derived from German and spoken by Jews esp. of eastern Europe — **Yiddish** *adj*

¹yield \\'yēld\\ *vb* **1** : to give as fitting, owed, or required **2** : GIVE UP; *esp* : to give up possession of on claim or demand **3** : to bear as a natural product **4** : PRODUCE, SUPPLY **5** : to bring in : RETURN **6** : to give way (as to force or influence) **7** : to give place **syn** relinquish, cede, waive, surrender

²yield *n* : something yielded; *esp* : the amount or quantity produced or returned

yield·ing \\'yēl-diŋ\\ *adj* **1** : not rigid or stiff : FLEXIBLE **2** : SUBMISSIVE, COMPLIANT

YMCA \\,wī-,em-(,)sē-'ā\\ *n* : Young Men's Christian Association

YMHA \\,wī-,em-,ā-'chā\\ *n* : Young Men's Hebrew Association

YOB *abbr* year of birth

yo·del \\'yōd-ᵊl\\ *vb* **yo·deled** *or* **yo·delled;**

yo·del·ing *or* **yo·del·ling** \\ꞌyōd-(ə-)liŋ\ : to sing by suddenly changing from chest voice to falsetto and the reverse; *also* : to shout or call in this manner — **yodel** *n* — **yo·del·er** \\ꞌyōd-(ə-)lər\ *n*

yo·ga \\ꞌyō-gə\ *n* [Skt, lit., yoking, fr. *yunakti* he yokes] **1** *cap* : a Hindu theistic philosophy teaching the suppression of all activity of body, mind, and will in order that the self may realize its distinction from them and attain liberation **2** : a system of exercises for attaining bodily or mental control and well-being

yo·gi \\ꞌyō-gē\ *also* **yo·gin** \-gən, -ˌgin\ *n* **1** : a person who practices yoga **2** *cap* : an adherent of Yoga philosophy

yo·gurt *also* **yo·ghurt** \\ꞌyō-gərt\ *n* [Turk] : a soured slightly acid often flavored semisolid milk food made of skimmed cow's milk and milk solids to which cultures of bacteria have been added

¹yoke \\ꞌyōk\ *n, pl* **yokes 1** : a wooden bar or frame by which two draft animals (as oxen) are coupled at the heads or necks for working together; *also* : a frame fitted to a person's shoulders to carry a load in two equal portions **2** : a clamp that embraces two parts to hold or unite them in position **3** *pl usu* **yoke** : two animals yoked together **4** : SERVITUDE, BONDAGE **5** : TIE, LINK ⟨the ∼ of matrimony⟩ **6** : a fitted or shaped piece esp. at the shoulder of a garment **syn** couple, pair, brace

²yoke *vb* **yoked; yok·ing 1** : to put a yoke on : couple with a yoke **2** : to attach a draft animal to ⟨∼ a plow⟩ **3** : JOIN; *esp* : MARRY

yo·kel \\ꞌyō-kəl\ *n* : BUMPKIN

yolk \\ꞌyō(l)k\ *n* **1** : the yellow rounded inner mass of the egg of a bird or reptile **2** : the stored food material of an egg consisting chiefly of proteins, lecithin, and cholesterol — **yolked** \\ꞌyō(l)kt\ *adj*

Yom Kip·pur \ˌyōm-ki-ꞌpu̇r, ˌyäm-, -ꞌkip-ər\ *n* [Heb *yōm kippūr*, fr. *yōm* day + *kippūr* atonement] : a Jewish holiday observed in September or October with fasting and prayer as a day of atonement

¹yon \\ꞌyän\ *adj* : YONDER

²yon *adv* **1** : YONDER **2** : THITHER ⟨ran hither and ∼⟩

¹yon·der \\ꞌyän-dər\ *adv* : at or to that place

²yonder *adj* **1** : more distant ⟨the ∼ side of the river⟩ **2** : being at a distance within view ⟨∼ hills⟩

yore \\ꞌyōr\ *n* [ME, fr. *yore*, adv., long ago, fr. OE *geāra*, fr. *gēar* year] : time long past ⟨in days of ∼⟩

you \(ꞌ)yü, yə\ *pron* **1** : the person or persons addressed ⟨∼ are a nice person⟩ ⟨∼ are nice people⟩ **2** : ONE 2 ⟨∼ turn this knob to open it⟩

¹young \\ꞌyəŋ\ *adj* **youn·ger** \\ꞌyəŋ-gər\; **youn·gest** \\ꞌyəŋ-gəst\ **1** : being in the first or an early stage of life, growth, or development **2** : having little experience **3** : recently come into being **4** : YOUTHFUL **5** *cap* : belonging to or representing a new or revived usu. political group or movement — **young·ish** \\ꞌyəŋ-ish\ *adj*

²young *n, pl* **young** : young persons or lower animals

young·ling \\ꞌyəŋ-liŋ\ *n* : one that is young — **youngling** *adj*

young·ster \-stər\ *n* **1** : a young person **2** : CHILD

your \yər, (ꞌ)yu̇r, (ꞌ)yōr\ *adj* : of or relating to you or yourself

yours \\ꞌyu̇rz, ꞌyōrz\ *pron* : one or the ones belonging to you

your·self \yər-ꞌself\ *pron, pl* **yourselves** \-ꞌselvz\ : YOU — used reflexively, for emphasis, or in absolute constructions ⟨you'll hurt ∼⟩ ⟨do it ∼⟩ ⟨∼ a man, you should understand⟩

youth \\ꞌyüth\ *n, pl* **youths** \\ꞌyüthz, ꞌyüths\ **1** : the period of life between childhood and maturity **2** : a young man; *also* : young persons **3** : YOUTHFULNESS

youth·ful \\ꞌyüth-fəl\ *adj* **1** : of, relating to, or appropriate to youth **2** : being young and not yet mature **3** : FRESH, VIGOROUS — **youth·ful·ly** \-ē\ *adv* — **youth·ful·ness** *n*

youth hostel *n* : HOSTEL 2

yowl \\ꞌyau̇l\ *vb* : to utter a loud long mournful cry : WAIL — **yowl** *n*

yo–yo \\ꞌyō-(ˌ)yō\ *n, pl* **yo–yos** : a thick grooved double disk with a string attached to its center which is made to fall and rise to the hand by unwinding and rewinding on the string

yr *abbr* **1** year **2** your

yrbk *abbr* yearbook

YT *abbr* Yukon Territory

yt•ter•bi•um \i-'tər-bē-əm\ *n* : a rare metallic chemical element

yt•tri•um \'i-trē-əm\ *n* : a rare metallic chemical element

yu•an \'yü-ən, yu̇-'än\ *n, pl* **yuan 1** — see MONEY table **2** : the dollar of the Republic of China (Taiwan)

yuc•ca \'yək-ə\ *n* : any of a genus of plants related to the lilies that grow in dry regions and have white cup⸗ shaped flowers in erect clusters; *also* : the flower of this plant

yuck \'yək\ *interj* — used to express rejection or disgust

Yu•go•slav \ˌyü-gō-'släv, -'slav\ *n* : a native or inhabitant of Yugoslavia — **Yugoslav** *adj* — **Yu•go•sla•vi•an** \-'släv-ē-ən\ *adj or n*

yule \'yül\ *n, often cap* : CHRISTMAS

Yule log *n* : a large log formerly put on the hearth on Christmas Eve as the foundation of the fire

yule•tide \'yül-ˌtīd\ *n, often cap* : CHRISTMASTIDE

yum•my \'yəm-ē\ *adj* **yum•mi•er; -est** : highly attractive or pleasing

yup•pie \'yəp-ē\ *n* [*young urban professional* + *-ie* (as in hippie)] : a young college-educated adult employed in a well-paying profession and living and working in or near a large city

yurt \'yu̇rt\ *n* : a light round tent of skins or felt stretched over a lattice framework used by various nomadic tribes in Siberia, U.S.S.R.

YWCA \ˌwī-ˌdəb-əl-yu̇-(ˌ)sē-'ā\ *n* : Young Women's Christian Association

YWHA \-ˌā-'chā\ *n* : Young Women's Hebrew Association

Z

¹z \'zē\ *n, pl* **z's** *or* **zs** *often cap* : the 26th letter of the English alphabet

²z *abbr* **1** zero **2** zone

Z *symbol* atomic number

Zach *abbr* Zacharias

Zach•a•ri•as \ˌzak-ə-'rī-əs\ *n* — see BIBLE table

zaire \zä-'ir, 'zīr\ *n, pl* **zaires** *or* **zaire** — see MONEY table

Zair•ian \zä-'ir-ē-ən\ *n* : a native or inhabitant of Zaire — **Zairian** *adj*

Zam•bi•an \'zam-bē-ən\ *n* : a native or inhabitant of Zambia — **Zambian** *adj*

¹za•ny \'zā-nē\ *n, pl* **zanies** [It *zanni*, a traditional masked clown, fr. It (dial.) *Zanni*, nickname for *Giovanni* John] **1** : CLOWN, BUFFOON **2** : a silly or foolish person

²zany *adj* **za•ni•er; -est 1** : characteristic of a zany **2** : CRAZY, FOOLISH — **za•ni•ly** \'zā-nə-lē, 'zān-ᵊl-ē\ *adv* — **za•ni•ness** \'zā-nē-nəs\ *n*

zap \'zap\ *vb* **zapped; zap•ping** : DESTROY, KILL

zeal \'zēl\ *n* : eager and ardent interest in the pursuit of something : FERVOR **syn** enthusiasm, passion, ardor

zeal•ot \'zel-ət\ *n* : a zealous person; *esp* : a fanatical partisan **syn** enthusiast, bigot, fanatic

zeal•ous \'zel-əs\ *adj* : filled with, characterized by, or due to zeal — **zeal•ous•ly** *adv* — **zeal•ous•ness** *n*

ze•bra \'zē-brə\ *n, pl* **zebras** *also* **zebra** : any of several African mammals related to the horse but conspicuously striped with black or brown and white or buff

ze•bu \'zē-b(y)ü\ *n* : an Asian domesticated ox that differs from European cattle with which it crosses freely by a large fleshy hump over the shoulders and a loose skin with hanging folds

Zech *abbr* Zechariah

Zech•a•ri•ah \ˌzek-ə-'rī-ə\ *n* — see BIBLE table

zed \'zed\ *n, chiefly Brit* : the letter z

zeit•geist \'tsīt-ˌgīst, 'zīt-\ *n* [G, fr. *zeit* time + *geist* spirit] : the general intellectual, moral, and cultural state of an era

Zen \'zen\ *n* : a Japanese Buddhist sect that teaches self-discipline, meditation, and attainment of enlightenment through direct intuitive insight

ze•na•na \zə-'nän-ə\ *n* : HAREM, SERAGLIO

ze·nith \\'zē-nəth\ *n* **1** : the point in the heavens directly overhead **2** : the highest point : ACME **syn** culmination, pinnacle, apex

ze·o·lite \\'zē-ə-ˌlīt\ *n* : any of various feldsparlike silicates used as water softeners

Zeph *abbr* Zephaniah

Zeph·a·ni·ah \ˌzef-ə-'nī-ə\ *n* — see BI-BLE table

zeph·yr \\'zef-ər\ *n* **1** : a breeze from the west; *also* : a gentle breeze **2** : any of various lightweight fabrics and articles of clothing

zep·pe·lin \\'zep-(ə-)lən\ *n* [after Count Ferdinand von *Zeppelin* †1917 Ger. airship manufacturer] : a rigid airship consisting of a cylindrical trussed and covered frame

¹ze·ro \\'zē-rō\ *n, pl* **zeros** *also* **zeroes** [deriv. of Ar *ṣifr*] **1** : the numerical symbol 0 **2** : the number represented by the symbol 0 **3** : the point at which the graduated degrees or measurements on a scale (as of a thermometer) begin **4** : the lowest point

²zero *adj* **1** : of, relating to, or being a zero **2** : having no magnitude or quantity **3** : ABSENT, LACKING; *esp* : having no modified inflectional form

³zero *vb* : TRAIN ⟨∼ in artillery on the crossroads⟩

zero hour *n* : the time at which an event (as a military operation) is scheduled to begin

zest \\'zest\ *n* **1** : a quality of enhancing enjoyment : PIQUANCY **2** : keen enjoyment : RELISH, GUSTO — **zest·ful** \-fəl\ *adj* — **zest·ful·ly** \-ē\ *adv* — **zest·ful·ness** *n*

¹zig·zag \\'zig-ˌzag\ *n* : one of a series of short sharp turns, angles, or alterations in a course; *also* : something marked by such a series

²zigzag *adv* : in or by a zigzag path

³zigzag *adj* : having short sharp turns or angles

⁴zigzag *vb* **zig·zagged; zig·zag·ging** : to form into or proceed along a zigzag

zil·lion \\'zil-yən\ *n* : a large indeterminate number

Zim·ba·bwe·an \zim-'bäb-wē-ən\ *n* : a native or inhabitant of Zimbabwe — **Zimbabwean** *adj*

zinc \\'ziŋk\ *n* : a bluish white crystalline metallic chemical element that is commonly found in minerals and is used esp. as a protective coating for iron and steel

zinc ointment *n* : ZINC OXIDE OINTMENT

zinc oxide *n* : a white solid used as a pigment, in compounding rubber, and in ointments

zinc oxide ointment *n* : an ointment containing 20 percent of zinc oxide and used for skin disorders

zing \\'ziŋ\ *n* **1** : a shrill humming noise **2** : VITALITY — **zing** *vb*

zing·er \\'ziŋ-ər\ *n* **1** : a pointed witty remark or retort **2** : something causing or meant to cause interest, surprise, or shock

zin·nia \\'zin-ē-ə, 'zēn-yə\ *n* : any of a small genus of tropical American herbs related to the daisies and widely grown for their showy long-lasting flower heads

Zi·on \\'zī-ən\ *n* **1** : the Jewish people **2** : the Jewish homeland as a symbol of Judaism or of Jewish national aspiration **3** : HEAVEN **4** : UTOPIA

Zi·on·ism \\'zī-ə-ˌniz-əm\ *n* : an international movement orig. for the establishment of a Jewish national or religious community in Palestine and later for the support of modern Israel — **Zi·on·ist** \-nəst\ *adj or n*

¹zip \\'zip\ *vb* **zipped; zip·ping** : to move or act with speed or vigor

²zip *n* **1** : a sudden sharp hissing sound **2** : ENERGY, VIM

³zip *vb* **zipped; zip·ping** : to close or open with a zipper

zip code *n, often cap Z&I&P* [*zone improvement plan*] : a 5-digit number that identifies each postal delivery area in the U.S.

zip·per \\'zip-ər\ *n* : a fastener consisting of two rows of metal or plastic teeth on strips of tape and a sliding piece that closes an opening by drawing the teeth together

zip·py \\'zip-ē\ *adj* **zip·pi·er; -est** : BRISK, SNAPPY

zir·con \\'zər-ˌkän\ *n* : a zirconium-containing mineral several transparent varieties of which are used as gems

zir·co·ni·um \ˌzər-'kō-nē-əm\ *n* : a corrosion-resistant metallic element with a high melting point that occurs widely in combination and is used in alloys and ceramics

zith•er \'zi_th_-ər, 'zith-\ *n* : a musical instrument having 30 to 40 strings played with plectrum and fingers

zi•ti \'zēt-ē\ *n, pl* **ziti** [It] : tubular pasta of medium size

zlo•ty \'zlȯt-ē\ *n, pl* **zlo•tys** \-ēz\ *or* **zloty** — see MONEY table

Zn *symbol* zinc

zo•di•ac \'zōd-ē-ˌak\ *n* [ME, fr. MF *zodiaque,* fr. L *zodiacus,* fr. Gk *zōidiakos,* fr. *zōidion* carved figure, sign of the zodiac, fr. dim. of *zōion* living being, figure] **1** : an imaginary belt in the heavens that encompasses the paths of most of the planets and that is divided into 12 constellations or signs **2** : a figure representing the signs of the zodiac and their symbols — **zo•di•a•cal** \zō-'dī-ə-kəl\ *adj*

zom•bi *also* **zom•bie** \'zäm-bē\ *n* **1** : the voodoo snake deity **2** : the supernatural power held in voodoo belief to enter into and reanimate a dead body

zon•al \'zōn-ᵊl\ *adj* : of, relating to, or having the form of a zone — **zon•al•ly** \-ē\ *adv*

¹zone \'zōn\ *n* [L *zona* belt, zone, fr. Gk *zōnē*] **1** : any of five great divisions of the earth's surface made according to latitude and temperature and including the torrid zone about the equator, the two temperate zones lying between the torrid zone and the polar circles, and the two frigid zones lying between the polar circles and the poles **2** *archaic* : GIRDLE, BELT **3** : an encircling band or girdle ⟨a ∼ of trees⟩ **4** : an area or region set off or distinguished in some way from adjoining parts

²zone *vb* **zoned; zon•ing 1** : ENCIRCLE **2** : to arrange in or mark off into zones; *esp* : to divide (as a city) into sections reserved for different purposes — **zo•na•tion** \zō-'nā-shən\ *n*

zonked \'zäŋkt\ *adj* : being or acting as if under the influence of alcohol or a drug : HIGH

zoo \'zü\ *n, pl* **zoos** : a zoological garden or collection of living animals usu. for public display

zoo•ge•og•ra•phy \ˌzō-ə-jē-'äg-rə-fē\ *n* : a branch of biogeography concerned with the geographical distribution of animals — **zoo•ge•og•ra•pher** \-fər\ *n*

— **zoo•geo•graph•ic** \-ˌjē-ə-'graf-ik\ *also* **zoo•geo•graph•i•cal** \-i-kəl\ *adj*

zoo•keep•er \'zü-ˌkē-pər\ *n* : a person who keeps or cares for animals in a zoo

zool *abbr* zoological; zoology

zoological garden *n* : a garden or park where wild animals are kept for exhibition

zo•ol•o•gy \zō-'äl-ə-jē\ *n* : a branch of biology that deals with animals and the animal kingdom — **zo•o•log•i•cal** \ˌzō-ə-'läj-i-kəl\ *adj* — **zo•ol•o•gist** \zō-'äl-ə-jəst\ *n*

zoom \'züm\ *vb* **1** : to move with a loud hum or buzz **2** : to gain altitude quickly **3** : to focus a camera or microscope using a special lens that permits the apparent distance of the object to be varied — **zoom** *n*

zoom lens *n* : a camera lens in which the image size can be varied continuously while the image remains in focus

zoo•mor•phic \ˌzō-ə-'mȯr-fik\ *adj* **1** : having the form of an animal **2** : of, relating to, or being the representation of a deity in the form or with the attributes of an animal

zoo•plank•ton \ˌzō-ə-'plaŋk-tən, -ˌtän\ *n* : animal life of the plankton

zoo•spore \'zō-ə-ˌspōr\ *n* : a motile spore

zoot suit \'züt-\ *n* : a flashy suit of extreme cut typically consisting of a thigh-length jacket with wide padded shoulders and trousers that are wide at the top and narrow at the bottom — **zoot•suit•er** \-ˌsüt-ər\ *n*

Zo•ro•as•tri•an•ism \ˌzōr-ə-'was-trē-ə-ˌniz-əm\ *n* : a religion founded by the Persian prophet Zoroaster — **Zo•ro•as•tri•an** \-trē-ən\ *adj or n*

Zou•ave \zu̇-'äv\ *n* : a member of a French infantry unit orig. composed of Algerians wearing a brilliant uniform and conducting a quick spirited drill; *also* : a member of a military unit modeled on the Zouaves

zounds \'zau̇n(d)z\ *interj* [euphemism for *God's wounds*] — used as a mild oath

zoy•sia \'zȯi-shə, -zhə, -sē-ə, -zē-ə\ *n* : any of a genus of creeping perennial grasses having fine wiry leaves and including some used as lawn grasses

ZPG *abbr* zero population growth

Zr *symbol* zirconium

zuc•chet•to \zü-'ket-ō, tsü-\ *n, pl* **-tos** [It] : a small round skullcap worn by Roman Catholic ecclesiastics

zuc•chi•ni \zu̇-'kē-nē\ *n, pl* **-ni** *or* **-nis** [It] : a summer squash of bushy growth with smooth cylindrical dark green fruits; *also* : its fruit

Zu•lu \'zü-ˌlü\ *n, pl* **Zulu** *or* **Zulus** : a member of a Bantu-speaking people of South Africa; *also* : a Bantu language of the Zulus

Zu•ni \'zü-nē\ *or* **Zu•ñi** \-nyē\ *n, pl* **Zuni** *or* **Zunis** *or* **Zuñi** *or* **Zuñis** : a member of an American Indian people of northeastern Arizona; *also* : the language of the Zuni people

zwie•back \'swē-bak, 'swī-, 'zwē-, 'zwī-\ *n* [G, lit., twice baked, fr. *zwie*-twice + *backen* to bake] : a usu. sweetened bread that is baked and then sliced and toasted until dry and crisp

Zwing•li•an \'zwiŋ-(g)lē-ən, 'swiŋ-\ *adj* : of or relating to the Swiss religious reformer Ulrich Zwingli or his teachings — **Zwinglian** *n*

zy•gote \'zī-ˌgōt\ *n* : a cell formed by the union of two sexual cells; *also* : the developing individual produced from such a cell — **zy•got•ic** \zī-'gät-ik\ *adj*

Foreign Words and Phrases

ab·eunt stu·dia in mo·res \\'äb-e-ˌu̇nt-'stüd-ē-ˌä-ˌin-'mō-ˌräs\\ [L] : practices zealously pursued pass into habits

à bien·tôt \\à-byaⁿ-tō\\ [F] : so long : farewell

ab in·cu·na·bu·lis \\ˌäb-ˌiŋ-kə-'näb-ə-ˌlēs\\ [L] : from the cradle : from infancy

à bon chat, bon rat \\à-bōⁿ-'shà- bōⁿ-'rà\\ [F] : to a good cat, a good rat : retaliation in kind

à bouche ou·verte \\à-bü-shü-vert\\ [F] : with open mouth : eagerly : uncritically

ab ovo us·que ad ma·la \\äb-'ō-vō-ˌu̇s-kwe- ˌäd-'mäl-ä\\ [L] : from egg to apples : from soup to nuts : from beginning to end

à bras ou·verts \\à-brà-zü-ver\\ [F] : with open arms : cordially

ab·sit in·vi·dia \\'äb-ˌsit-in-'wid-ē-ˌä\\ [L] : let there be no envy or ill will

ab uno dis·ce om·nes \\äb-'ü-nō-ˌdis-ke-'òm-ˌnäs\\ [L] : from one learn to know all

ab ur·be con·di·ta \\äb-'u̇r-be-'kòn-də-ˌtä\\ [L] : from the founding of the city (Rome, founded 753 B.C.) — used by the Romans in reckoning dates

ab·usus non tol·lit usum \\'äb-ˌü-səs-ˌnōn-ˌtò-lət-'ü-səm\\ [L] : abuse does not take away use, i.e., is not an argument against proper use

à compte \\à-kōⁿt\\ [F] : on account

à coup sûr \\à-kü-su̇er\\ [F] : with sure stroke : surely

acte gra·tuit \\àk-tə-grà-twʸē\\ [F] : gratuitous impulsive act

ad ar·bi·tri·um \\ˌad-är-'bit-rē-əm\\ [L] : at will : arbitrarily

ad as·tra per as·pe·ra \\ad-'as-trə-ˌpər-'as-pə-rə\\ [L] : to the stars by hard ways — motto of Kansas

ad ex·tre·mum \\ˌad-ik-'strē-məm\\ [L] : to the extreme : at last

ad ka·len·das Grae·cas \\ˌäd-kə-'len-dəs-'grī-ˌkäs\\ [L] : at the Greek calends : never (since the Greeks had no calends)

ad ma·jo·rem Dei glo·ri·am \\äd-mä-'yōr-ˌem-'de-ˌē-'glōr-ē-ˌäm\\ [L] : to the greater glory of God — motto of the Society of Jesus

ad pa·tres \\äd-'pä-ˌträs\\ [L] : (gathered) to his fathers : deceased

à droite \\à-drwät\\ [F] : to or on the right hand

ad un·guem \\äd-'u̇ŋ-ˌgwem\\ [L] : to the fingernail : to a nicety : exactly (from the use of the fingernail to test the smoothness of marble)

ad utrum·que pa·ra·tus \\ˌäd-u̇-'tru̇m-kwe-pə-'rät-əs\\ [L] : prepared for either (event)

ad vi·vum \\äd-'wē-ˌwu̇m\\ [L] : to the life

ae·gri som·nia \\'ī-grē-'sòm-nē-ˌä\\ [L] : a sick man's dreams

ae·quam ser·va·re men·tem \\'ī-ˌkwäm-sər-ˌwä-rā-'men-ˌtem\\ [L] : to preserve a calm mind

ae·quo ani·mo \\'ī-ˌkwō-'än-ə-ˌmō\\ [L] : with even mind : calmly

ae·re per·en·ni·us \\'ī-rā-pə-'ren-ē-ˌu̇s\\ [L] : more lasting than bronze

à gauche \\à-gōsh\\ [F] : to or on the left hand

age quod agis \\'äg-e-ˌkwòd-'äg-is\\ [L] : do what you are doing : to the business at hand

à grands frais \\à-gräⁿ-fre\\ [F] : at great expense

à huis clos \\à-wʸē-klō\\ [F] : with closed doors

aide—toi, le ciel t'ai·dera \\ed-twà-lə-'syel-te-drà\\ [F] : help yourself (and) heaven will help you

ai·né \\e-nā\\ [F] : elder : senior (masc.)

ai·née \\e-nā\\ [F] : elder : senior (fem.)

à l'aban·don \\à-là-bäⁿ-dōᵐ\\ [F] : carelessly : in disorder

à la belle étoile \\à-là-bel-ā-twàl\\ [F] : under the beautiful star : in the open air at night

à la bonne heure \\à-là-bò-nœr\\ [F] : at a good time : well and good : all right

à la fran·çaise \\à-là-fräⁿ-sez\\ [F] : in the French style

à l'an·glaise \\à-läⁿ-glez\\ [F] : in the English style

alea jac·ta est \'äl-ē-,ä-,yäk-tə-'est\ [L] : the die is cast

à l'im·pro·viste \à-laⁿ-prȯ-vēst\ [F] : un-expectedly

ali·quan·do bo·nus dor·mi·tat Ho·me·rus \,äl-i-,kwän-dō-'bȯ-nəs-dȯr-'mē-tät-hō-'mer- əs\ [L] : sometimes (even) good Homer nods

alis vo·lat pro·pri·is \'äl-,ēs-'wȯ-,lät-'prō-prē-,ēs\ [L] : she flies with her own wings — motto of Oregon

al–ki \'al-,kī\ [Chinook Jargon] : by and by — motto of Washington

alo·ha oe \ä-,lō-hä-'ȯi, -'ō-ē\ [Hawaiian] : love to you : greetings : fare-well

al·ter idem \,ȯl-tər-'ī-,dem, ,äl-tər-'ē-\ [L] : second self

a max·i·mis ad mi·ni·ma \ä-'mäk-sə-,mēs-,äd-'min-ə-,mä\ [L] : from the greatest to the least

ami·cus hu·ma·ni ge·ne·ris \ä-'mē-kəs-hü-,män-ē-'gen-ə-rəs\ [L] : friend of the human race

ami·cus us·que ad aras \-,ùs-kwe-,äd-'är-,äs\ [L] : a friend as far as to the altars, i.e., except in what is con-trary to one's religion; *also* : a friend to the last extremity

ami de cour \à-,mēd-ə-'kùr\ [F] : court friend : insincere friend

amor pa·tri·ae \,äm-,ȯr-'pä-trē-,ī\ [L] : love of one's country

amor vin·cit om·nia \'ä-,mȯr-,wiŋ-kət-'ȯm-nē-ə\ [L] : love conquers all things

an·cienne no·blesse \äⁿ-syen-nȯ-bles\ [F] : old-time nobility : the French nobility before the Revolution of 1789

an·guis in her·ba \,äŋ-gwis-in-'her-,bä\ [L] : snake in the grass

ani·mal bi·pes im·plu·me \'än-i-,mäl-,bip-,äs-im-'plü-me\ [L] : two-legged animal without feathers (i.e., man)

ani·mis opi·bus·que pa·ra·ti \'än-ə-,mēs-,ȯ-pi-'bùs-kwe-pə-'rät-ē\ [L] : prepared in mind and resources — one of the mottoes of South Carolina

an·no ae·ta·tis su·ae \'än-ō-ī-,tät-is-'sü-,ī\ [L] : in the (specified) year of his (or her) age

an·no mun·di \,än-ō-'mùn-dē\ [L] : in the year of the world — used in reck-oning dates from the supposed period of the creation of the world, esp. as

fixed by James Ussher at 4004 B.C. or by the Jews at 3761 B.C.

an·no ur·bis con·di·tae \,än-ō-,ùr-bis-'kȯn-də-,tī\ [L] : in the year of the founded city (Rome, founded 753 B.C.)

an·nu·it coep·tis \,än-ə-,wit-'kȯip-,tēs\ [L] : He (God) has smiled on our un-dertakings — motto on the reverse of the Great Seal of the United States

à peu près \à-pœ-pre\ [F] : nearly : ap-proximately

à pied \à-pyā\ [F] : on foot

après moi le dé·luge \à-pre-mwà-lə-dā-lǖezh\ [F] : after me the deluge (at-tributed to Louis XV)

à pro·pos de bottes \à-prə-pōd-ə-bȯt\ [F] : apropos of boots — used to change the subject

à pro·pos de rien \-ryaⁿ\ [F] : apropos of nothing

aqua et ig·ni in·ter·dic·tus \,äk-wä-et-'ig-nē-,int-ər-'dik-təs\ [L] : forbidden to be furnished with water and fire : outlawed

Ar·ca·des am·bo \,är-kə-,des-'äm-bō\ [L] : both Arcadians : two persons of like occupations or tastes; *also* : two rascals

ar·rec·tis au·ri·bus \ä-'rek-,tēs-'aù-ri-,bùs\ [L] : with ears pricked up : at-tentively

ar·ri·ve·der·ci \ä-,rē-ve-'der chē\ [It] : till we meet again : farewell

ars est ce·la·re ar·tem \,ärs-,est-kā-,lär-ē-'är-,tem\ [L] : it is (true) art to con-ceal art

ars lon·ga, vi·ta bre·vis \ärs-'lȯŋ-,gä-,wē-,tä-'bre-wis\ [L] : art is long, life is short

a ter·go \ä-'ter-(,)gō\ [L] : from behind

à tort et à tra·vers \à-tȯr-ā-à-trà-ver\ [F] : wrong and crosswise : at random : without rhyme or reason

au bout de son la·tin \ō-büd-(ə)sōⁿ-là-taⁿ\ [F] : at the end of one's Latin : at the end of one's mental resources

au con·traire \ō-kōⁿ-trer\ [F] : on the contrary

au·de·mus ju·ra nos·tra de·fen·de·re \aù-'dā-məs-,yùr-ə-'nȯ-strə-dā-'fen-də-rā\ [L] : we dare defend our rights — motto of Alabama

au·den·tes for·tu·na ju·vat \aù-'den-,tās-fȯr-,tü-nə-'yù-,wät\ [L] : fortune favors the bold

au·di al·ter·am par·tem \ˈau̇-ˌdē-ˌäl-tə-ˌräm-ˈpär-ˌtem\ [L] : hear the other side

au fait \ō-fet, -fe\ [F] : to the point : fully competent : fully informed : socially correct

au fond \ō-fōⁿ\ [F] : at bottom : fundamentally

au grand sé·rieux \ō-gräⁿ-sā-ryœ\ [F] : in all seriousness

au pays des aveugles les borgnes sont rois \ō-pā-ē-dā-zȧ-vœglᵊ-lā-bȯrnʸ-ə-sōⁿ-rwä\ [F] : in the country of the blind the one-eyed men are kings

au pied de la lettre \ō-pyȧd-lȧ-letrᵊ\ [F] : literally

au·rea me·di·o·cri·tas \ˈau̇-rē-ə-ˌmed-ē-ˈȯ-krə-ˌtäs\ [L] : the golden mean

au reste \ō-rest\ [F] : for the rest : besides

aus·si·tôt dit, aus·si·tôt fait \ō-sē-tō-dē ō-sē-tō-fe\ [F] : no sooner said than done

aut Cae·sar aut ni·hil \au̇t-ˈkī-sär-ˌau̇t-ˈni-ˌhil\ [L] : either a Caesar or nothing

aut Caesar aut nul·lus \-ˈnu̇l-əs\ [L] : either a Caesar or a nobody

au·tres temps, au·tres mœurs \ō-trə-täⁿ ō-trə-mœrs\ [F] : other times, other customs

aut vin·ce·re aut mo·ri \au̇t-ˈwiŋ-kə-rē-ˌau̇t-ˈmȯ-ˌrē\ [L] : either to conquer or to die

aux armes \ō-zȧrm\ [F] : to arms

ave at·que va·le \ˈä-ˌwā-ˌät-kwe-ˈwä-ˌlā\ [L] : hail and farewell

à vo·tre san·té \ȧ-vȯt-säⁿ-tā, -vȯ-trə-\ [F] : to your health — used as a toast

beaux yeux \bō-zyœ\ [F] : beautiful eyes : beauty of face

bien en·ten·du \byaⁿ-näⁿ-täⁿ-dœ\ [F] : well understood : of course

bien–pen·sant \byaⁿ-päⁿ-säᵐ\ [F] : right-minded : one who holds orthodox views

bien·sé·ance \byaⁿ-sā-äⁿs\ [F] : propriety

bis dat qui ci·to dat \ˌbis-ˌdät-kwē-ˈki-tō-ˌdät\ [L] : he gives twice who gives promptly

bon ap·pé·tit \bȯ-nȧ-pā-tē\ [F] : good appetite : enjoy your meal

bon gré, mal gré \ˈbōⁿ-ˌgrā-ˈmȧl-ˌgrā\ [F] : whether with good grace or bad : willy-nilly

bo·nis avi·bus \ˌbȯ-ˌnēs-ˈä-wi-ˌbu̇s\ [L] : under good auspices

bon jour \bōⁿ-zhür\ [F] : good day : good morning

bonne foi \bȯn-fwä\ [F] : good faith

bon soir \bōⁿ-swȧr\ [F] : good evening

bru·tum ful·men \ˌbrüt-əm-ˈfu̇l-men\ [L] : insensible thunderbolt : a futile threat or display of force

buon gior·no \bwȯn-ˈjȯr-nō\ [It] : good day

ca·dit quae·stio \ˌkäd-ət-ˈkwī-stē-ˌō\ [L] : the question drops : the argument collapses

cau·sa si·ne qua non \ˈkau̇-ˌsä-ˌsin-ē-kwä-ˈnōn\ [L] : an indispensable cause or condition

ca·ve ca·nem \ˌkä-wā-ˈkän-ˌem\ [L] : beware the dog

ce·dant ar·ma to·gae \ˈkā-ˌdänt-ˌär-mə-ˈtō-ˌgī\ [L] : let arms yield to the toga : let military power give way to civil power — motto of Wyoming

ce n'est que le pre·mier pas qui coûte \snek-lə-prə-myā-pä-kē-küt\ [F] : it is only the first step that costs

c'est a dire \se-tȧ-dēr\ [F] : that is to say : namely

c'est au·tre chose \se-tōt-shōz, -tō-trə-\ [F] : that's a different thing

c'est la guerre \se-lȧ-ger\ [F] : that's war : it cannot be helped

c'est la vie \se-lȧ-vē\ [F] : that's life : that's how things happen

c'est plus qu'un crime, c'est une faute \se-plœ-kœⁿ-krēm se-tœn-fōt\ [F] : it is worse than a crime, it is a blunder

ce·te·ra de·sunt \ˌkāt-ə-ˌrä-ˈdā-ˌsu̇nt\ [L] : the rest is missing

cha·cun à son goût \shȧ-kœⁿ-nȧ-sōⁿ-gü\ [F] : everyone to his taste

châ·teau en Es·pagne \shä-tō-äⁿ-nes-pȧnʸ\ [F] : castle in Spain : a visionary project

cher·chez la femme \sher-shā-lȧ-fȧm\ [F] : look for the woman

che sa·rà, sa·rà \ˌkā-sä-ˌrä-sä-ˈrä\ [It] : what will be, will be

che·val de ba·taille \shə-vȧl-də-bȧ-täʸ\ [F] : war-horse : argument constantly relied on : favorite subject

co·gi·to, er·go sum \ˈkō-gi-ˌtō ˌer-gō-ˈsu̇m\ [L] : I think, therefore I exist

co·mé·die hu·maine \kȯ-mā-dē-ŭ̈e-men\ [F] : human comedy : the whole variety of human life

comme ci, comme ça \kȯm-sē-kȯm-sȧ\ [F] : so-so

com·pa·gnon de voy·age \kōⁿ-pȧ-nʸōⁿ-də-vwȧ-yȧzh\ [F] : traveling companion

compte ren·du \kōⁿt-räⁿ-dᵫ\ [F] : report (as of proceedings in an investigation)

con·cor·dia dis·cors \kän-kȯrd-ē-ä-ˈdis-ˌkȯrs\ [L] : discordant harmony

cor·rup·tio op·ti·mi pes·si·ma \kə-ˈrüp-tē-ˌō-ˈäp-tə-ˌmē-ˈpes-ə-ˌmä\ [L] : the corruption of the best is the worst of all

coup de maî·tre \küd-(ə-)metrᵃ\ [F] : masterstroke

coup d'es·sai \kü-dā-se\ [F] : experiment : trial

coûte que coûte \küt-kə-küt\ [F] : cost what it may

cre·do quia ab·sur·dum est \ˌkrād-ō-ˈkwē-ä- äp-ˌsùrd-əm-ˈest\ [L] : I believe it because it is absurd

cres·cit eun·do \ˌkres-kət-ˈeùn-dō\ [L] : it grows as it goes — motto of New Mexico

crise de nerfs *or* **crise des nerfs** \krēz-də-ner\ [F] : crisis of nerves : nervous collapse : hysterical fit

crux cri·ti·co·rum \ˈkrüks-ˌkrit-ə-ˈkōr-əm\ [L] : crux of critics

cum gra·no sa·lis \kùm-ˌgrän-ō-ˈsäl-is\ [L] : with a grain of salt

cus·tos mo·rum \ˌkùs-tōs-ˈmōr-əm\ [L] : guardian of manners or morals : censor

d'ac·cord \dȧ-kȯr\ [F] : in accord : agreed

dame d'hon·neur \dȧm-dȯ-nœr\ [F] : lady-in-waiting

dam·nant quod non in·tel·li·gunt \ˈdäm-ˌnänt-ˌkwȯd-ˌnōn-in-ˈtel-ə-ˌgùnt\ [L] : they condemn what they do not understand

de bonne grâce \də-bȯn-gräs\ [F] : with good grace : willingly

de gus·ti·bus non est dis·pu·tan·dum \dā-ˈgùs-tə-ˌbùs- ˌnōn-ˌest- ˌdis-pù-ˈtän-ˌdùm\ [L] : there is no disputing about tastes

Dei gra·tia \ˈde-ˌē-ˈgrät-ē-ˌä\ [L] : by the grace of God

de in·te·gro \dā-ˈint-ə-ˌgrō\ [L] : anew : afresh

de l'au·dace, en·core de l'au·dace, et tou·jours de l'au·dace \də-lō-ˈdȧs äⁿ-ˈkȯr-də-lō-dȧs ā-tü- ˈzhür-də-lō-dȧs\ [F] : audacity, more audacity, and ever more audacity

de·len·da est Car·tha·go \dā-ˈlen-dä-ˌest-kär-ˈtäg-ō\ [L] : Carthage must be destroyed

de·li·ne·a·vit \dā-ˌlē-nā-ˈä-wit\ [L] : he (or she) drew it

de mal en pis \də-mȧ-läⁿ-pē\ [F] : from bad to worse

de mi·ni·mis non cu·rat lex \dā-ˈmin-ə-ˌmēs-ˌnōn-ˌkü-ˌrät-ˈleks\ [L] : the law takes no account of trifles

de mor·tu·is nil ni·si bo·num \dā-ˈmȯrt-ə-ˌwēs-ˌnēl-ˌnis-ē-ˈbȯ-ˌnùm\ [L] : of the dead (say) nothing but good

de nos jours \də-nō-zhür\ [F] : of our time : contemporary — used postpositively esp. after a proper name

Deo fa·ven·te \ˌdā-ō-fä-ˈvent-ā\ [L] : with God's favor

Deo gra·ti·as \ˌdā-ō-ˈgrät-ē-ˌäs\ [L] : thanks (be) to God

de pro·fun·dis \ˌdā-prō-ˈfùn-dēs\ [L] : out of the depths

der Geist der stets ver·neint \dər-ˈgīst-dər-ˌshtāts-fer-ˈnīnt\ [G] : the spirit that ever denies — applied originally to Mephistopheles

de·si·pe·re in lo·co \dā-ˈsip-ə-rē-in-ˈlȯ-kō\ [L] : to indulge in trifling at the proper time

Deus vult \ˌdā-əs-ˈwùlt\ [L] : God wills it — rallying cry of the First Crusade

di·es fau·stus \ˌdē-ˌās-ˈfaù-stəs\ [L] : lucky day

dies in·fau·stus \-ˈin-ˌfaù-stəs\ [L] : unlucky day

dies irae \-ˈē-ˌrī\ [L] : day of wrath — used of the Judgment Day

Dieu et mon droit \dyᵫ-ā-mȯⁿ-drwä\ [F] : God and my right — motto on the British royal arms

Dieu vous garde \dyᵫ-vü-gȧrd\ [F] : God keep you

di·ri·go \ˈdē-ri-ˌgō\ [L] : I direct — motto of Maine

dis ali·ter vi·sum \ˌdēs-ˌäl-ə-ˌter-ˈwē-ˌsùm\ [L] : the Gods decreed otherwise

di·tat De·us \ˌdē-ˌtät-ˈdā-ˌùs\ [L] : God enriches — motto of Arizona

di·vi·de et im·pe·ra \ˈdē-wi-ˌde-ˌet-ˈim-pə-ˌrä\ [L] : divide and rule

do·cen·do dis·ci·mus \dȯ-ˌken-dō-ˈdis-ki-ˌmùs\ [L] : we learn by teaching

Foreign Words and Phrases

Do·mi·ne di·ri·ge nos \\'dȯ-mi-ˌne-ˌdē-ri-ge-'nōs\ [L] : Lord, direct us — motto of the City of London

Do·mi·nus vo·bis·cum \ˌdȯ-mi-ˌnu̇s-wō-'bēs-ˌku̇m\ [L] : the Lord be with you

dul·ce et de·co·rum est pro pa·tria mo·ri \ˌdu̇l-ˌket-de-'kȯr-ˌest-prō-ˌpä-trē-ˌä-'mȯ-ˌrē\ [L] : it is sweet and seemly to die for one's country

dum spi·ro, spe·ro \du̇m-'spē-rō-'spä-rō\ [L] : while I breathe I hope — one of the mottoes of South Carolina

dum vi·vi·mus vi·va·mus \du̇m-'wē-wē-ˌmu̇s-wē-'wäm-u̇s\ [L] : while we live, let us live

dux fe·mi·na fac·ti \ˌdu̇ks-ˌfā-mi-nä-'fäk-ˌtē\ [L] : a woman was leader of the exploit

ec·ce sig·num \ˌek-e-'sig-ˌnu̇m\ [L] : behold the sign : look at the proof

e con·tra·rio \ˌā-kȯn-'trär-ē-ˌō\ [L] : on the contrary

écra·sez l'in·fâme \ā-krä-zā-laⁿ-fäm\ [F] : crush the infamous thing

eheu fu·ga·ces la·bun·tur an·ni \ˌā-ˌheu̇-fu̇-'gä-ˌkäs-lä-ˌbu̇n-ˌtu̇r-'än-ˌē\ [L] : alas! the fleeting years glide on

ein' fes·te Burg ist un·ser Gott \īn-ˌfes-tə-'bu̇rk-ist-ˌu̇n-zər-'gȯt\ [G] : a mighty fortress is our God

em·bar·ras de ri·chesses \äⁿ-bȧ-räd-(ə-)rē-shes\ [F] : embarrassing surplus of riches : confusing abundance

em·bar·ras du choix \äⁿ-bȧ-rä-du̇e-shwȧ\ [F] : embarrassing variety of choice

en ami \äⁿ-nȧ-mē\ [F] : as a friend

en ef·fet \äⁿ-nā-fe\ [F] : in fact : indeed

en fa·mille \äⁿ-fä-mēy\ [F] : in or with one's family : at home : informally

en·fant gâ·té \äⁿ-fäⁿ-gä-tā\ [F] : spoiled child

en·fants per·dus \äⁿ-fäⁿ-per-du̇e\ [F] : lost children : soldiers sent to a dangerous post

en·fin \äⁿ-faⁿ\ [F] : in conclusion : in a word

en gar·çon \äⁿ-gȧr-sōᵐ\ [F] : as or like a bachelor

en pan·tou·fles \äⁿ-päⁿ-tüflᵃ\ [F] : in slippers : at ease : informally

en plein air \äⁿ-plen-er\ [F] : in the open air

en plein jour \äⁿ-plaⁿ-zhu̇r\ [F] : in broad day

en règle \äⁿ-reglᵃ\ [F] : in order : in due form

en re·tard \äⁿr-(ə-)tȧr\ [F] : behind time : late

en re·traite \äⁿ-rə-tret\ [F] : in retreat : in retirement

en re·vanche \äⁿr-(ə-)väⁿsh\ [F] : in return : in compensation

en se·condes noces \äⁿs-(ə-)gōⁿd-nȯs\ [F] : in a second marriage

en·se pe·tit pla·ci·dam sub li·ber·ta·te qui·e·tem \'en-se-ˌpet-ət-'pläk-i-ˌdäm-su̇b-ˌlē-ber-ˌtä-te-kwē-'ä-ˌtem\ [L] : with the sword she seeks calm repose under liberty — motto of Massachusetts

épa·ter les bour·geois \ā-pȧ-tā-lā-bür-zhwȧ\ [F] : to shock the middle classes

e plu·ri·bus unum \ˌē-ˌplu̇r-ə-bəs-'(y)ü-nəm, ˌā-ˌplu̇r-\ [L] : one out of many — used on the seal of the U.S. and on several U.S. coins

ep·pur si muo·ve \äp-ˌpür-sē-'mwȯ-vā\ [It] : and yet it does move — attributed to Galileo after recanting his assertion of the earth's motion

Erin go bragh \ˌer-ən-gə-'brȯ, -gō-'brä\ [IrGael *go brāth*, lit., till doomsday] : Ireland forever

er·ra·re hu·ma·num est \e-'rär-e-hü-ˌmän-əm-'est\ [L] : to err is human

es·prit de l'es·ca·lier \es-prēd-les-kȧ-lyā\ *or* **es·prit d'es·ca·lier** \-prē-des-\ [F] : staircase wit : repartee thought of only too late

es·se quam vi·de·ri \'es-ē-ˌkwäm-wi-'dā-rē\ [L] : to be rather than to seem — motto of North Carolina

est mo·dus in re·bus \est-'mȯ-du̇s-in-'rä-ˌbu̇s\ [L] : there is a proper measure in things, i.e., the golden mean should always be observed

es·to per·pe·tua \'es-ˌtō-pər-'pet-ə-ˌwä\ [L] : may she endure forever — motto of Idaho

et hoc ge·nus om·ne \et-ˌhōk-ˌgen-əs-'ȯm-ne\ *or* **et id genus omne** \et-ˌid-\ [L] : and everything of this kind

et in Ar·ca·dia ego \ˌet-in-är-ˌkäd-ē-ə-'eg-ō\ [L] : I too (lived) in Arcadia

et sic de si·mi·li·bus \et-ˌsēk-dā-si-'mil-ə-ˌbu̇s\ [L] : and so of like things

et tu Bru·te \et-'tü-'brü-te\ [L] : thou too, Brutus — exclamation attributed to Julius Caesar on seeing his friend Brutus among his assassins

eu·re·ka \yu̇-'rē-kə\ [Gk] : I have found it — motto of California

Ewig–Weib·li·che \ˌā-vik̲-'vīp-li-k̲ə\ [G] : eternal feminine

ex ani·mo \ek-'sän-ə-ˌmō\ [L] : from the heart : sincerely

ex·cel·si·or \ik-'sel-sē-ər, eks-'kel-sē-ˌȯr\ [L] : still higher — motto of New York

ex·cep·tio pro·bat re·gu·lam de re·bus non ex·cep·tis \eks-'kep-tē-ˌō-ˌprō-bät-'rā-gə-ˌläm-dā-'rā-ˌbu̇s-ˌnōn-eks-'kep-ˌtēs\ [L] : an exception establishes the rule as to things not excepted

ex·cep·tis ex·ci·pi·en·dis \eks-'kep-ˌtēs-eks-ˌkip-ē-'en-ˌdēs\ [L] : with the proper or necessary exceptions

ex·i·tus ac·ta pro·bat \'ek-sə-ˌtu̇s-ˌäk-tə-'prȯ-ˌbät\ [L] : the event justifies the deed

ex li·bris \eks-'lē-bris\ [L] : from the books of — used on bookplates

ex me·ro mo·tu \ˌeks-ˌmer-ō-'mō-tü\ [L] : out of mere impulse : of one's own accord

ex ne·ces·si·ta·te rei \ˌeks-ne-ˌkes-i-'tä-te-'rā(-ˌē)\ [L] : from the necessity of the case

ex ni·hi·lo ni·hil fit \eks-'ni-hi-ˌlō-ˌni-hil-'fit\ [L] : from nothing nothing is produced

ex pe·de Her·cu·lem \eks-ˌped-e-'her-kə-ˌlem\ [L] : from the foot (we may judge of the size of) Hercules : from a part we may judge of the whole

ex·per·to cre·di·te \eks-ˌpert-ō-'krād-ə-ˌte\ [L] : believe one who has had experience

ex un·gue le·o·nem \eks-'u̇ŋ-gwe-le-'ō-ˌnem\ [L] : from the claw (we may judge of) the lion : from a part we may judge of the whole

ex vi ter·mi·ni \eks-ˌwē-'ter-mə-ˌnē\ [L] : from the force of the term

fa·ci·le prin·ceps \ˌfäk-i-le-'priŋ-ˌkeps\ [L] : easily first

fa·ci·lis de·scen·sus Aver·no \'fäk-i-ˌlis-dā-ˌskän-ˌsu̇s-ä-'wer-nō\ *or* **facilis descensus Aver·ni** \-(ˌ)nē\ [L] : the descent to Avernus is easy : the road to evil is easy

fa·çon de par·ler \fȧ-sōⁿ-də-pȧr-lā\ [F] : manner of speaking : figurative or conventional expression

faire suivre \fer-swʸēvrᵃ\ [F] : have forwarded : please forward

fas est et ab ho·ste do·ce·ri \fäs-'est-et-äb-'hȯ-ste-dȯ-'kā-(ˌ)rē\ [L] : it is right to learn even from an enemy

Fa·ta vi·am in·ve·ni·ent \ˌfä-tä-'wē-ˌäm-in-'wen-ē-ˌent\ [L] : the Fates will find a way

fat·ti mas·chii, pa·ro·le fe·mi·ne \ˌfät-tē-'mäs-ˌkē pä-ˌrȯ-lā-'fä-mē-ˌnā\ [It] : deeds are males, words are females : deeds are more effective than words — motto of Maryland, where it is generally interpreted as meaning "manly deeds, womanly words"

faux bon·homme \fō-bȯ-nȯm\ [F] : pretended good fellow

faux–naïf \fō-nȧ-ēf\ [F] : pretending to be childlike

femme de cham·bre \fäm-də-shänbrᵃ\ [F] : chambermaid : lady's maid

fe·sti·na len·te \fe-ˌstē-nə-'len-ˌtā\ [L] : make haste slowly

feux d'ar·ti·fice \fœ-dȧr-tē-fēs\ [F] : fireworks : display of wit

fi·at ex·pe·ri·men·tum in cor·po·re vi·li \'fē-ˌät-ek-ˌsper-ē-'men-ˌtu̇m-in-ˌkȯr-pə-re-'wē-lē\ [L] : let experiment be made on a worthless body

fi·at ju·sti·tia, ru·at cae·lum \fe-ät-yu̇s-'tit-ē-ä ˌru̇-ät-'kī-ˌlu̇m\ [L] : let justice be done though the heavens fall

fi·at lux \ˌfē-ˌät-'lu̇ks\ [L] : let there be light

Fi·dei De·fen·sor \ˌfid-e-ˌē-dā-'fän-ˌsȯr\ [L] : Defender of the Faith — a title of the sovereigns of England

fi·dus Acha·tes \ˌfēd-əs-ä-'kä-ˌtās\ [L] : faithful Achates : trusty friend

fille de cham·bre \fēy-də-shänbrᵃ\ [F] : lady's maid

fille d'hon·neur \fēy-dȯ-nœr\ [F] : maid of honor

fils \fēs\ [F] : son — used after French proper names to distinguish a son from his father

fi·nem re·spi·ce \ˌfē-ˌnem-'rā-spi-ˌke\ [L] : consider the end

fi·nis co·ro·nat opus \ˌfē-nəs-kə-'rō-ˌnät-'ō-ˌpu̇s\ [L] : the end crowns the work

fluc·tu·at nec mer·gi·tur \'flu̇k-tə-ˌwät-ˌnek-'mer-gə-ˌtu̇r\ [L] : it is tossed by the waves but does not sink — motto of Paris

fo·lie de gran·deur *or* **fo·lie des gran·deurs** \fo-lē-də-gräⁿ-dœr\ [F] : delusion of greatness : megalomania

fors·an et haec olim me·mi·nis·se ju·va·bit \ˌfor-ˌsän-ˌet-'hīk-ˌō-lim-ˌmem-ə-'nis-e-yü-'wä-bit\ [L] : perhaps this too will be a pleasure to look back on one day

for·tes for·tu·na ju·vat \'for-ˌtās-for-ˌtü-nə-'yü-ˌwät\ [L] : fortune favors the brave

fron·ti nul·la fi·des \'fron-ˌtē-ˌnul-ə-'fid-ˌās\ [L] : no reliance can be placed on appearance

fu·it lli·um \'fü-ət-'il-ē-əm\ [L] : Troy has been (i.e., is no more)

fu·ror lo·quen·di \ˌfür-ˌor-lo-'kwen-(ˌ)dē\ [L] : rage for speaking

furor po·e·ti·cus \-po-'āt-i-kùs\ [L] : poetic frenzy

furor scri·ben·di \-skrē-'ben-(ˌ)dē\ [L] : rage for writing

Gal·li·ce \'gäl-ə-ˌke\ [L] : in French : after the French manner

gar·çon d'hon·neur \gar-sōⁿ-do-nœr\ [F] : bridegroom's attendant

garde du corps \gard-dŭe-kor\ [F] : bodyguard

gar·dez la foi \gar-dā-la-fwä\ [F] : keep faith

gau·de·a·mus igi·tur \ˌgaud-ē-'äm-əs-'ig-ə-ˌtur\ [L] : let us then be merry

gens d'é·glise \zhäⁿ-dā-glēz\ [F] : church people : clergy

gens de guerre \zhäⁿ-də-ger\ [F] : military people : soldiery

gens du monde \zhäⁿ-dŭe-mōⁿd\ [F] : people of the world : fashionable people

gno·thi se·au·ton \gə-'nō-thē-ˌse-au-'ton\ [Gk] : know thyself

grand monde \gräⁿ-mōⁿd\ [F] : great world : high society

guerre à ou·trance \ger-a-ü-träⁿs\ [F] : war to the uttermost

gu·ten Tag \ˌgüt-ᵊn-'täk\ [G] : good day

has·ta la vis·ta \ˌäs-tä-lä-'vēs-tä\ [Sp] : good-bye

haut goût \ō-gü\ [F] : high flavor : slight taint of decay

hic et ubi·que \ˌhēk-et-ù-'bē-kwe\ [L] : here and everywhere

hic ja·cet \hik-'jā-sət, hēk-'yäk-ət\ [L] : here lies — used preceding a name on a tombstone

hinc il·lae la·cri·mae \ˌhiŋk-ˌil-ˌī-'läk-ri-ˌmī\ [L] : hence those tears

hoc age \hōk-'äg-e\ [L] : do this : apply yourself to what you are about

hoc opus, hic la·bor est \hōk-'o-ˌpùs-ˌhēk-ˌlä-ˌbor-'est\ [L] : this is the hard work, this is the toil

homme d'af·faires \òm-da-fer\ [F] : man of business : business agent

homme d'es·prit \-des-prē\ [F] : man of wit

homme moyen sen·suel \òm-mwa-yaⁿ-säⁿ-sw^yel\ [F] : the average nonintellectual man

ho·mo sum: hu·ma·ni nil a me ali·e·num pu·to \'ho-mō-ˌsùm ˌhü-ˌmän-ē-'nēl-ä-ˌmā-ˌäl-ē-'ā-nəm-'pù-tō\ [L] : I am a man: I regard nothing that concerns man as foreign to my interests

ho·ni soit qui mal y pense \o-nē-swà-kē-màl-ē-päⁿs\ [F] : shamed be he who thinks evil of it — motto of the Order of the Garter

hu·ma·num est er·ra·re \hü-ˌmän-əm-ˌest-e-'rär-e\ [L] : to err is human

ich dien \ik-'dēn\ [G] : I serve — motto of the Prince of Wales

ici on parle fran·cais \ē-sē-ōⁿ-pàrl-(-ə)-fräⁿ-se\ [F] : French is spoken here

id est \id-'est\ [L] : that is

ig·no·ran·tia ju·ris ne·mi·nem ex·cu·sat \ˌig-nə-ˌränt-ē-ä-'yùr-əs-'nä-mə-ˌnem-eks-'kü-ˌsät\ [L] : ignorance of the law excuses no one

ig·no·tum per ig·no·ti·us \ig-'nōt-əm-ˌper-ig-'nōt-ē-ùs\ [L] : (explaining) the unknown by means of the more unknown

il faut cul·ti·ver no·tre jar·din \ēl-fō-kŭel-tē-vā-nòt-zhàr-daⁿ, -nò-trə-zhàr-\ [F] : we must cultivate our garden : we must tend to our own affairs

in ae·ter·num \ˌin-ī-'ter-ˌnùm\ [L] : forever

in du·bio \in-'dùb-ē-ˌō\ [L] : in doubt : undetermined

in fu·tu·ro \ˌin-fə-'tur-ō\ [L] : in the future

in hoc sig·no vin·ces \in-hōk-'sig-nō-'viŋ-ˌkās\ [L] : by this sign (the Cross) you will conquer

in li·mi·ne \in-'lē-mə-ˌne\ [L] : on the threshold : at the beginning

in om·nia pa·ra·tus \in-'ȯm-nē-ə-pə-'rä-ˌtủs\ [L] : ready for all things

in par·ti·bus in·fi·de·li·um \in-'pärt-ə-ˌbủs-ˌin-fə-'dā-lē-ˌủm\ [L] : in the regions of the infidels — used of a titular bishop having no diocesan jurisdiction, usu. in non-Christian countries

in prae·sen·ti \ˌin-prī-'sen-ˌtē\ [L] : at the present time

in sae·cu·la sae·cu·lo·rum \in-'sī-kủ-ˌlä-ˌsī-kə-'lōr-əm, -'sā-kủ-ˌlä-ˌsā-\ [L] : for ages of ages : forever and ever

insh·al·lah \ˌin-shä-'lä\ [Ar] : if Allah wills : God willing

in sta·tu quo an·te bel·lum \in-'stä-ˌtü-kwō-ˌänt-ē-'bel-əm\ [L] : in the same state as before the war

in·te·ger vi·tae sce·le·ris·que pu·rus \ˌin-tə-ˌger-'wē-ˌtī-ˌskel-ə-'ris-kwe-'pü-rəs\ [L] : upright of life and free from wickedness

in·ter nos \ˌint-ər-'nōs\ [L] : between ourselves

in·tra mu·ros \ˌin-trä-'mü-ˌrōs\ [L] : within the walls

in usum Del·phi·ni \in-'ü-səm-del-'fē-nē\ [L] : for the use of the Dauphin : expurgated

in utrum·que pa·ra·tus \ˌin-ü-'trủm-kwe-pə-'rä-ˌtủs\ [L] : prepared for either (event)

in·ve·nit \in-'wā-nit\ [L] : he (or she) devised it

in vi·no ve·ri·tas \in-'wē-nō-'wā-rə-ˌtäs\ [L] : there is truth in wine

in·vi·ta Mi·ner·va \in-'wē-ˌtä-mi-'ner-ˌwä\ [L] : Minerva being unwilling : without natural talent or inspiration

ip·sis·si·ma ver·ba \ip-ˌsis-ə-ˌmä-'wer-ˌbä\ [L] : the very words

ira fu·ror bre·vis est \ˌē-rä-'fủr-ˌȯr-'bre-wis-ˌest\ [L] : anger is a brief madness

j'ac·cuse \zhȧ-kǖez\ [F] : I accuse

jac·ta alea est \'yäk-ˌtä-ˌä-lē-ˌä-'est\ [L] : the die is cast

j'adoube \zhȧ-düb\ [F] : I adjust — used in chess when touching a piece without intending to move it

ja·nu·is clau·sis \ˌyän-ə-ˌwēs-'klaủ-ˌsēs\ [L] : behind closed doors

je main·tien·drai \zhə-maⁿ-tyaⁿ-drā\ [F] : I will maintain — motto of the Netherlands

jeu de mots \zhœd-(ə-)mō\ [F] : play on words : pun

Jo·an·nes est no·men eius \yō-'än-ās-est-ˌnō-men-'ā-yủs\ [L] : John is his name — motto of Puerto Rico

jo·lie laide \zhȯ-lē-led\ [F] : good-looking ugly woman : woman who is attractive though not conventionally pretty

jour·nal in·time \zhür-nȧl-aⁿ-tēm\ [F] : intimate journal : private diary

jus di·vi·num \ˌyủs-di-'wē-ˌnủm\ [L] : divine law

jus·ti·tia om·ni·bus \yủs-ˌtit-ē-ˌä-'ȯm-ni-ˌbủs\ [L] : justice for all — motto of the District of Columbia

j'y suis, j'y reste \zhē-swʸē-zhē-rest\ [F] : here I am, here I remain

la belle dame sans mer·ci \lȧ-bel-dȧm-säⁿ-mer-sē\ [F] : the beautiful lady without mercy

la·bo·ra·re est ora·re \'läb-ō-ˌrär-ā-ˌest-'ō-ˌrär-ā\ [L] : to work is to pray

la·bor om·nia vin·cit \'lä-ˌbȯr-ˌȯm-nē-ä-'wiŋ-kit\ [L] : labor conquers all things — motto of Oklahoma

la·cri·mae re·rum \ˌläk-ri-ˌmī-'rā-ˌrủm\ [L] : tears for things : pity for misfortune; *also* : tears in things : tragedy in life

lais·sez-al·ler *or* **lais·ser-al·ler** \le-sā-ȧ-lā\ [F] : letting go : lack of restraint

lap·sus ca·la·mi \ˌläp-sủs-'käl-ə-ˌmē\ [L] : slip of the pen

lap·sus lin·guae \-'liŋ-ˌgwī\ [L] : slip of the tongue

la reine le veut \lȧ-ren-lə-vœ\ [F] : the queen wills it

la·scia·te ogni spe·ran·za, voi ch'en·tra·te \läsh-'shä-tä-ˌō-nʸē-spä-'rän-tsä-ˌvō-ē-kän-'trä-tä\ [It] : abandon all hope, ye who enter

lau·da·tor tem·po·ris ac·ti \laủ-'dä-ˌtȯr-ˌtem-pə-ris-'äk-ˌtē\ [L] : one who praises past times

laus Deo \laủs-'dā-ō\ [L] : praise (be) to God

le cœur a ses rai·sons que la rai·son ne con·nait point \lə-kœr-ȧ-sā-re-zōⁿk-lȧ-re-zōⁿn-(ə-)kȯ-ne-pwaᵐ\ [F] : the heart has its reasons that reason knows nothing of

le roi est mort, vive le roi \lə-rwä-e-mȯr

vēv-lə-rwä\ [F] : the king is dead, long live the king

le roi le veut \-lə-vœ̆\ [F] : the king wills it

le roi s'avi•se•ra \-sȧ-vēz-rȧ\ [F] : the king will consider

le style, c'est l'homme \lə-stēl-se-lȯm\ [F] : the style is the man

l'état, c'est moi \lā-tȧ-se-mwȧ\ [F] : the state, it is I

l'étoile du nord \lā-twȧl-dü̆-nȯr\ [F] : the star of the north — motto of Minnesota

Lie•der•kranz \'lēd-ər-ˌkräns\ [G] : wreath of songs : German singing society

lit•tera scrip•ta ma•net \ˌlit-ə-ˌrä-ˌskrip-tə-'män-et\ [L] : the written letter abides

lo•cus in quo \ˌlȯ-kəs-in-'kwō\ [L] : place in which

l'union fait la force \lü̆-nyō̄ⁿ-fe-lȧ-fȯrs\ [F] : union makes strength — motto of Belgium

lu•sus na•tu•rae \ˌlü-səs-nə-'tu̇r-ē, -'tu̇r-ˌī\ [L] : freak of nature

ma foi \mȧ-fwä\ [F] : my faith! : indeed

mag•na est ve•ri•tas et prae•va•le•bit \ˌmäg-nä-ˌest-'wā-ri-ˌtäs-et-ˌprī-wä-'lā-bit\ [L] : truth is mighty and will prevail

mag•ni no•mi•nis um•bra \ˌmäg-nē-ˌnō-mə-nis-'ùm-brä\ [L] : the shadow of a great name

mai•son de san•té \mā-zō̄ⁿd-(ə-)sä̆ⁿ-tā\ [F] : private hospital : asylum

ma•lade ima•gi•naire \mȧ-lȧd-ē-mȧ-zhē-ner\ [F] : imaginary invalid : hypochondriac

ma•lis avi•bus \ˌmäl-ˌēs-'ä-wi-ˌbù̇s\ [L] : under evil auspices

ma•no a ma•no \ˌmän-ō-ä-'män-ō\ [Sp] : hand to hand : in direct competition or confrontation

man spricht Deutsch \män-shpriḳt-'dȯich\ [G] : German spoken

ma•riage de con•ve•nance \mȧ-ryȧzh-də-kō̄ⁿv-nä̆ⁿs\ [F] : marriage of convenience

mau•vaise honte \mȯ-vez-ō̄ⁿt\ [F] : bad shame : bashfulness

mau•vais quart d'heure \mȯ-ve-kȧr-dœr\ [F] : bad quarter hour : an uncomfortable though brief experience

me•dio tu•tis•si•mus ibis \'med-ē-ˌō-tü-

ˌtis-ə-mù̇s-'ē-bis\ [L] : you will go most safely by the middle course

me ju•di•ce \mā-'yüd-ə-ke\ [L] : I being judge : in my judgment

mens sa•na in cor•po•re sa•no \mäns-'sän-ə-in-ˌkȯr-pə-re-'sän-ō\ [L] : a sound mind in a sound body

me•um et tu•um \ˌmē-əm-ˌet-'tü-əm, ˌmā-əm-\ [L] : mine and thine : distinction of private property

mi•ra•bi•le vi•su \mi-ˌräb-ə-lā-'wē-sü\ [L] : wonderful to behold

mi•ra•bi•lia \ˌmir-ə-'bil-ē-ə\ [L] : wonders : miracles

mœurs \mœr(s)\ [F] : mores : attitudes, customs, and manners of a society

mo•le ru•it sua \'mō-le-ˌrù̇-it-'sù̇-ä\ [L] : it collapses from its own bigness

monde \mō̄ⁿd\ [F] : world : fashionable world : society

mon•ta•ni sem•per li•be•ri \mȯn-'tän-ē-ˌsem-pər-'lē-bə-ˌrē\ [L] : mountaineers are always free men — motto of West Virginia

mo•nu•men•tum ae•re per•en•ni•us \ˌmȯ-nə-'men-tù̇m-ˌī-re-pə-'ren-ē-ù̇s\ [L] : a monument more lasting than bronze — used of an immortal work of art or literature

mo•ri•tu•ri te sa•lu•ta•mus \ˌmȯr-ə-'tu̇r-ē-ˌtä-ˌsäl-ə-'täm-ù̇s\ *or* **morituri te sa•lu•tant** \-'säl-ə-ˌtänt\ [L] : we (or those) who are about to die salute thee

mul•tum in par•vo \ˌmù̇l-təm-in-'pär-vō\ [L] : much in little

mu•ta•to no•mi•ne de te fa•bu•la nar•ra•tur \mü-ˌtät-ō-'nō-mə-ne-dā-'tä-ˌfäb-ə-lä-nä-'rä-ˌtu̇r\ [L] : with the name changed the story applies to you

na•tu•ram ex•pel•las fur•ca, ta•men us•que re•cur•ret \nä-'tü-ˌräm-ek-ˌspel-äs-'fu̇r-ˌkä ˌtä-mən-'ù̇s-kwe-re-'ku̇r-et\ [L] : you may drive nature out with a pitchfork, but she will keep coming back

na•tu•ra non fa•cit sal•tum \nä-'tü-rä-ˌnōn-ˌfäk-ət-'säl-ˌtu̇m\ [L] : nature makes no leap

ne ce•de ma•lis \nā-ˌkā-de-'mäl-ˌēs\ [L] : yield not to misfortunes

ne•mo me im•pu•ne la•ces•sit \'nā-mō-'mā-im-ˌpü-nä-lä-'kes-ət\ [L] : no one attacks me with impunity — motto of Scotland and of the Order of the Thistle

ne quid ni·mis \ˌnā-ˌkwid-ˈnim-əs\ [L] : not anything in excess

n'est—ce pas? \nes-pä\ [F] : isn't it so?

nicht wahr? \niḵt-ˈvär\ [G] : not true? : isn't it so?

nil ad·mi·ra·ri \ˈnēl-ˌäd-mə-ˈrär-ē\ [L] : to be excited by nothing : equanimity

nil de·spe·ran·dum \ˈnēl-ˌdā-spā-ˈrän-dùm\ [L] : never despair

nil si·ne nu·mi·ne \ˈnēl-ˌsin-e-ˈnü-mə-ne\ [L] : nothing without the divine will — motto of Colorado

n'im·porte \naⁿ-pȯrt\ [F] : it's no matter

no·lens vo·lens \ˌnō-ˌlenz-ˈvō-ˌlenz\ [L] : unwilling (or) willing : willy-nilly

non om·nia pos·su·mus om·nes \nōn-ˈȯm-nē-ä-ˌpȯ-sə-mùs-ˈȯm-ˌnās\ [L] : we can't all (do) all things

non om·nis mo·ri·ar \nōn-ˈȯm-nis-ˈmȯr-ē-ˌär\ [L] : I shall not wholly die

non sans droict \nōⁿ-säⁿ-drwä\ [OF] : not without right — motto on Shakespeare's coat of arms

non sum qua·lis eram \ˌnōn-ˌsùm-ˌkwäl-əs-ˈer-ˌäm\ [L] : I am not what I used to be

nos·ce te ip·sum \ˌnȯs-ke-ˌtā-ˈip-ˌsùm\ [L] : know thyself

nos·tal·gie de la boue \nȯs-tȧl-zhēd-(ə-)lȧ-bü\ [F] : nostalgia for the mud : homesickness for the gutter

nous avons chan·gé tout ce·la \nü-zȧ-vōⁿ-shäⁿ-zhā-tü-slȧ\ [F] : we have changed all that

nous ver·rons ce que nous ver·rons \nü-ve-rōⁿs-(ə-)kə-nü-ve-rōᵐ\ [F] : we shall see what we shall see

no·vus ho·mo \ˌnȯ-wəs-ˈhȯ-mō\ [L] : new man : man newly ennobled : upstart

no·vus or·do se·clo·rum \-ˈȯr-ˌdō-sā-ˈklōr-əm\ [L] : a new cycle of the ages — motto on the reverse of the Great Seal of the United States

nu·gae \ˈnü-ˌgī\ [L] : trifles

nuit blanche \nwʸē-bläⁿsh\ [F] : white night : a sleepless night

nyet \ˈnyet\ [Russ] : no

ob·iit \ˈȯ-bē-ˌit\ [L] : he (or she) died

ob·scu·rum per ob·scu·ri·us \əb-ˈskyùr-əm-ˌper-əb-ˈskyùr-ē-əs\ [L] : (explaining) the obscure by means of the more obscure

ode·rint dum me·tu·ant \ˈōd-ə-ˌrint- ˌdùm-ˈmet-ə-ˌwänt\ [L] : let them hate, so long as they fear

odi et amo \ˈō-ˌdē-et-ˈäm-(ˌ)ō\ [L] : I hate and I love

om·ne ig·no·tum pro mag·ni·fi·co \ˌȯm-ne-ig-ˈnō-ˌtùm- prō-mäg-ˈnif-i-ˌkō\ [L] : everything unknown (is taken) as grand : the unknown tends to be exaggerated in importance or difficulty

om·nia mu·tan·tur, nos et mu·ta·mur in il·lis \ˌȯm-nē-ä-mü-ˈtän-ˌtùr ˌnōs-ˌet-mü-ˌtäm-ər-in-ˈil-ˌēs\ [L] : all things are changing, and we are changing with them

om·nia vin·cit amor \ˈȯm-nē-ä-ˈwiŋ-kət-ˈäm-ˌȯr\ [L] : love conquers all

onus pro·ban·di \ˌō-nəs-prō-ˈban-ˌdī, -dē\ [L] : burden of proof

ora pro no·bis \ˌō-rä-prō-ˈnō-ˌbēs\ [L] : pray for us

ore ro·tun·do \ˌōr-ä-rō-ˈtùn-dō\ [L] : with round mouth : eloquently

oro y pla·ta \ˌȯr-ō-ē-ˈplät-ə\ [Sp] : gold and silver — motto of Montana

o tem·pora! o mo·res! \ō-ˈtem-pə-rä-ō-ˈmō-ˌrās\ [L] : oh the times! oh the manners!

oti·um cum dig·ni·ta·te \ˈōt-ē-ˌùm-kùm-ˌdig-nə-ˈtä-te\ [L] : leisure with dignity

où sont les neiges d'an·tan? \ü-sōⁿ-lā-nezh-däⁿ-täᵐ\ [F] : where are the snows of yesteryear?

pal·li·da Mors \ˌpal-id-ə-ˈmȯrz\ [L] : pale Death

pa·nem et cir·cen·ses \ˈpän-ˌem-et-kir-ˈkän-ˌsās\ [L] : bread and circuses : provision of the means of life and recreation by government to appease discontent

pan·ta rhei \ˌpän-ˌtä-ˈ(h)rā\ [Gk] : all things are in flux

par avance \pȧr-ȧ-väⁿs\ [F] : in advance : by anticipation

par avion \pȧr-ȧ-vyōᵐ\ [F] : by airplane — used on airmail

par ex·em·ple \pȧr-āg-zäⁿplᵊ\ [F] : for example

par·tu·ri·unt mon·tes, nas·ce·tur ri·di·cu·lus mus \pär-ˌtùr-ē-ˌùnt-ˈmȯn-ˌtās näs-ˈkā-ˌtùr-ri-ˌdik-ə-lùs-ˈmüs\ [L] : the mountains are in labor, and a ridiculous mouse will be brought forth

pa·ter pa·tri·ae \ˈpä-ˌter-ˈpä-trē-ˌī\ [L] : father of his country

pau·cis ver·bis \ˌpau̇-ˌkēs-ˈwer-ˌbēs\ [L] : in a few words

pax vo·bis·cum \ˌpäks-vō-ˈbēs-ˌku̇m\ [L] : peace (be) with you

peine forte et dure \pen-fȯr-tā-du̇̇er\ [F] : strong and hard punishment : torture

per an·gus·ta ad au·gus·ta \per-ˈän-ˌgu̇s-tə-äd-ˈau̇-ˌgu̇s-tə\ [L] : through difficulties to honors

père \per\ [F] : father — used after French proper names to distinguish a father from his son

per·eant qui an·te nos nos·tra dix·e·runt \ˈper-e-ˌänt-kwē-ˌän-te-ˈnōs-ˈnȯs-trä-dēk-ˈsā-ˌru̇nt\ [L] : may they perish who have expressed our bright ideas before us

per·fide Al·bion \per-fēd-ál-byō̄ᵐ\ [F] : perfidious Albion (England)

peu a peu \pœ̆-á-pœ̆\ [F] : little by little

peu de chose \pœ̆d-(ə-)shōz\ [F] : a trifle

pièce d'oc·ca·sion \pyes-dȯ-kä-zyō̄ᵐ\ [F] : piece for a special occasion

pinx·it \ˈpiŋk-sət\ [L] : he (or she) painted it

place aux dames \plȧs-ō-dȧm\ [F] : (make) room for the ladies

ple·no ju·re \ˌplā-nō-ˈyu̇r-e\ [L] : with full right

plus ça change, plus c'est la même chose \plœ̆-sȧ-shäⁿzh plœ̆-se-lȧ-mem-shōz\ [F] : the more that changes, the more it's the same thing

plus roy·a·liste que le roi \plœ̆-rwȧ-yȧ-lēst-kəl-rwȧ\ [F] : more royalist than the king

po·cas pa·la·bras \ˌpō-käs-pä-ˈläb-räs\ [Sp] : few words

po·eta nas·ci·tur, non fit \pȯ-ˌā-tä-ˈnäs-kə-ˌtu̇r nōn-ˈfit\ [L] : a poet is born, not made

pol·li·ce ver·so \ˌpȯ-li-ke-ˈver-sō\ [L] : with thumb turned : with a gesture or expression of condemnation

post hoc, er·go prop·ter hoc \ˈpȯst-ˌhōk ˌer-gō-ˈprȯp-ter-ˌhōk\ [L] : after this, therefore on account of it (a fallacy of argument)

post ob·itum \pȯst-ˈȯ-bə-ˌtu̇m\ [L] : after death

pour ac·quit \pu̇r-ȧ-kē\ [F] : received payment

pour le mé·rite \pu̇r-lə-mā-rēt\ [F] : for merit

pro aris et fo·cis \prō-ˌä-ˌrēs-et-ˈfȯ-ˌkēs\ [L] : for altars and firesides

pro bo·no pu·bli·co \prō-ˌbȯ-nō-ˈpü-bli-ˌkō\ [L] : for the public good

pro hac vi·ce \prō-ˌhäk-ˈwik-e\ [L] : for this occasion

pro pa·tria \prō-ˈpä-trē-ˌä\ [L] : for one's country

pro re·ge, le·ge, et gre·ge \prō-ˈrā-ˌge-ˈlā-ˌge-et-ˈgreg-ˌe\ [L] : for the king, the law, and the people

pro re na·ta \ˌprō-ˌrā-ˈnät-ə\ [L] : for an occasion that has arisen : as needed — used in medical prescriptions

quand même \käⁿ-mem\ [F] : even though : whatever may happen

quan·tum mu·ta·tus ab il·lo \ˌkwänt-əm-mü-ˈtät-əs-äb-ˈil-ō\ [L] : how changed from what he once was

quan·tum suf·fi·cit \ˌkwänt-əm-ˈsəf-ə-ˌkit\ [L] : as much as suffices : a sufficient quantity — used in medical prescriptions

¿quién sa·be? \kyān-ˈsä-bā\ [Sp] : who knows?

qui fa·cit per ali·um fa·cit per se \kwē-ˌfäk-it-ˌper-ˈäl-ē-ˌu̇m-ˌfäk-it-ˌper-ˈsā\ [L] : he who does (anything) through another does it through himself

quis cus·to·di·et ip·sos cus·to·des? \ˌkwis-ku̇s-ˈtōd-ē-ˌet-ip-ˌsōs-ku̇s-ˈtō-ˌdās\ [L] : who will keep the keepers themselves?

qui s'ex·cuse s'ac·cuse \kē-ˈsek-ˌsku̇ez-ˈsȧ-ˌku̇ez\ [F] : he who excuses himself accuses himself

quis se·pa·ra·bit? \ˌkwis-ˌsä-pə-ˈräb-it\ [L] : who shall separate (us)? — motto of the Order of St. Patrick

qui trans·tu·lit sus·ti·net \kwē-ˈträns-tə-ˌlit-ˈsu̇s-tə-ˌnet\ [L] : He who transplanted sustains (us) — motto of Connecticut

qui va là? \kē-vȧ-lȧ\ [F] : who goes there?

quo·ad hoc \ˌkwȯ-ˌäd-ˈhōk\ [L] : as far as this : to this extent

quod erat de·mon·stran·dum \ˌkwȯd-ˈer-ˌät-ˌdem-ən-ˈsträn-dəm\ [L] : which was to be proved

quod erat fa·ci·en·dum \-ˌfäk-ē-ˈen-ˌdu̇m\ [L] : which was to be done

quod sem·per, quod ubi·que, quod ab om·ni·bus \kwȯd-ˈsem-ˌperkwȯd-ˈu̇b-i-ˌkwä ˌkwȯd-äb-ˈȯm-ni-ˌbu̇s\ [L]

: what (has been held) always, every-where, by everybody

quod vi·de \kwȯd-'wid-ˌe\ [L] : which see

quo·rum pars mag·na fui \'kwȯr-əm-ˌpärs-ˌmäg-nə-'fü-ē\ [L] : in which I played a great part

quos de·us vult per·de·re pri·us de·men·tat \kwōs-'de-ùs-ˌwùlt-'perd-ə-ˌre-ˌprē-ùs- dā-'men-ˌtät\ [L] : those whom a god wishes to destroy he first drives mad

quot ho·mi·nes, tot sen·ten·ti·ae \kwȯt-'hȯ-mə-ˌnās-ˌtȯt-sen-'ten-tē-ˌī\ [L] : there are as many opinions as there are men

quo va·dis? \kwō-'väd-is, -'wäd-\ [L] : whither are you going?

rai·son d'état \re-zōⁿ-dā-tà\ [F] : reason of state

re·cu·ler pour mieux sau·ter \rə-kṻ-lā-pür-myœ-sō-tā\ [F] : to draw back in order to make a better jump

reg·nat po·pu·lus \'reg-ˌnät-'pȯ-pə-ˌlùs\ [L] : the people rule — motto of Arkansas

re in·fec·ta \ˌrā-in-'fek-ˌtä\ [L] : the business being unfinished : without accomplishing one's purpose

re·li·gio lo·ci \re-ˌlig-ē-ˌō-'lȯ-ˌkē\ [L] : religious sanctity of a place

rem acu te·ti·gis·ti \rem-'ä-ˌkü-ˌtet-ə-'gis-tē\ [L] : you have touched the point with a needle : you have hit the nail on the head

ré·pon·dez s'il vous plait \rā-pōⁿ-dā-sēl-vü-ple\ [F] : reply, if you please

re·qui·es·cat in pa·ce \ˌrek-wē-'es-ˌkät-in-'päk-ˌe, ˌrā-kwē-'es-ˌkät-in-'päch-ˌā\ [L] : may he (or she) rest in peace — used on tombstones

re·spi·ce fi·nem \ˌrā-spi-ˌke-'fē-ˌnem\ [L] : look to the end : consider the outcome

re·sur·gam \re-'sùr-ˌgäm\ [L] : I shall rise again

re·te·nue \rət-nṻ\ [F] : self-restraint : reserve

re·ve·nons à nos mou·tons \rəv-nōⁿ-à-nō-mü-tōᵐ\ [F] : let us return to our sheep : let us get back to the subject

ruse de guerre \rṻz-də-ger\ [F] : war stratagem

rus in ur·be \ˌrüs-in-'ùr-ˌbe\ [L] : country in the city

sae·va in·dig·na·tio \ˌsī-wä-ˌin-dig-'nät-ē-ō\ [L] : fierce indignation

sal At·ti·cum \ˌsal-'at-i-kəm\ [L] : Attic salt : wit

salle à man·ger \sȧl-ȧ-mäⁿ-zhā\ [F] : dining room

sa·lus po·pu·li su·pre·ma lex es·to \ˌsäl-ˌüs-'pȯ-pə-ˌlē-sù-ˌprā-mə-ˌleks-'es-tō\ [L] : let the welfare of the people be the supreme law — motto of Missouri

sans doute \säⁿ-düt\ [F] : without doubt

sans gêne \säⁿ-zhen\ [F] : without embarrassment or constraint

sans peur et sans re·proche \säⁿ-pœr-ā-säⁿ-rə-'prȯsh\ [F] : without fear and without reproach

sans sou·ci \säⁿ-sü-sē\ [F] : without worry

sa·yo·na·ra \ˌsä-yə-'när-ə\ [Jp] : goodbye

sculp·sit \'skùlp-sit\ [L] : he (or she) carved it

scu·to bo·nae vo·lun·ta·tis tu·ae co·ro·nas·ti nos \'skü-ˌtō-'bȯ-ˌnī-ˌvȯ-lùn-ˌtät-əs-'tù-ˌī-ˌkȯr-ɔ-ˌnäs-tē-'nōs\ [L] : Thou hast crowned us with the shield of Thy good will — a motto on the Great Seal of Maryland

se·cun·dum ar·tem \se-ˌkùn-dəm-'är-ˌtem\ [L] : according to the art : according to the accepted practice of a profession or trade

secundum na·tu·ram \-nä-'tü-ˌräm\ [L] : according to nature : naturally

se de·fen·den·do \'sā-ˌdā-ˌfen-'den-dō\ [L] : in self-defense

se ha·bla es·pa·ñol \sā-ˌäb-lä-ˌäs-pä-'nʸȯl\ [Sp] : Spanish spoken

sem·per ea·dem \ˌsem-ˌper-'e-ä-ˌdem\ [L] : always the same (fem.) — motto of Queen Elizabeth I

sem·per fi·de·lis \ˌsem-pər-ᶠi-'dā-lis\ [L] : always faithful — motto of the U.S. Marine Corps

sem·per idem \ˌsem-ˌper-'ē-ˌdem\ [L] : always the same (masc.)

sem·per pa·ra·tus \ˌsem-pər-pä-'rät-əs\ [L] : always prepared — motto of the U.S. Coast Guard

se non è ve·ro, è ben tro·va·to \sā-ˌnōn-e-'vä-rō-e-ˌben-trō-'vä-tō\ [It] : even if it is not true, it is well conceived

sic itur ad as·tra \sēk-'i-ˌtùr-ˌäd-'äs-trə\ [L] : thus one goes to the stars : such is the way to immortality

sic sem·per ty·ran·nis \ˌsik-ˌsem-pər-ti-ˈran-is\ [L] : thus ever to tyrants — motto of Virginia

sic trans·it glo·ria mun·di \sēk-ˈträn-sət-ˌglȯr-ē-ä-ˈmȯn-dē\ [L] : so passes away the glory of the world

si jeu·nesse sa·vait, si vieil·lesse pou·vait! \sē-ˈzhœ-nes-ˈsȧ-ve sē-ˈvye-yes-ˈpü-ve\ [F] : if youth only knew, if age only could!

si·lent le·ges in·ter ar·ma \ˌsil-ˌent- ˈlā-ˌgās-ˌint-ər-ˈär-mä\ [L] : the laws are silent in the midst of arms

s'il vous plait \sēl-vü-ple\ [F] : if you please

si·mi·lia si·mi·li·bus cu·ran·tur \sim-ˈil-ē-ä-sim- ˈil-ə-bȯs-kü-ˈrän-ˌtȯr\ [L] : like is cured by like

si·mi·lis si·mi·li gau·det \ˈsim-ə-lis- ˈsim-ə-lē-ˈgau̇-ˌdet\ [L] : like takes pleasure in like

si mo·nu·men·tum re·qui·ris, cir·cum·spi·ce \ˌsē-ˌmȯ-nə-ˌment-əm-re-ˈkwē-rəs kir-ˈkȯm-spi-ke\ [L] : if you seek his monument, look around — epitaph of Sir Christopher Wren in St. Paul's, London, of which he was architect

si quae·ris pen·in·su·lam amoe·nam, cir·cum·spi·ce \sē-ˌkwī-rəs-pā-ˌnin-sə-ˌläm-ə-ˈmȯi-ˌnäm kir-ˈkȯm-spi-ke\ [L] : if you seek a beautiful peninsula, look around — motto of Michigan

sis·te vi·a·tor \ˌsis-te-wē-ˈä-ˌtȯr\ [L] : stop, traveler — used on Roman roadside tombs

si vis pa·cem, pa·ra bel·lum \sē-ˌwēs-ˈpä-ˌkem ˌpä-rä-ˈbel-ˌȯm\ [L] : if you wish peace, prepare for war

sol·vi·tur am·bu·lan·do \ˈsȯl-wi-ˌtȯr-ˌäm-bə-ˈlän-dō\ [L] : it is solved by walking : the problem is solved by a practical experiment

splen·di·de men·dax \ˈsplen-də-ˌdā-ˈmen-ˌdäks\ [L] : nobly untruthful

spo·lia opi·ma \ˈspȯ-lē-ə-ō-ˈpē-mə\ [L] : rich spoils : the arms taken by the victorious from the vanquished general

sta·tus in quo \ˈstät-əs-ˌin-ˈkwō\ [L] : state in which : the existing state

status quo an·te bel·lum \-kwō-ˌänt-ə-ˈbel-ȯm\ [L] : the state existing before the war

sua·vi·ter in mo·do, for·ti·ter in re \ˈswä-wə-ˌter- in-ˈmȯd-ō ˈfȯrt-ə-ˌter-in-ˈrā\ [L] : gently in manner, strongly in deed

sub ver·bo \sȯb-ˈwer-bō\ *or* **sub vo·ce** \sȯb-ˈwō-ke\ [L] : under the word — introducing a cross-reference in a dictionary or index

sunt la·cri·mae re·rum \sȯnt-ˌläk-ri-ˌmī-ˈrā-rȯm\ [L] : there are tears for things

suo ju·re \ˌsȯ-ō-ˈyȯr-e\ [L] : in his (or her) own right

suo lo·co \-ˈlȯ-kō\ [L] : in its proper place

suo Mar·te \-ˈmär-te\ [L] : by one's own exertions

su·um cui·que \ˌsȯ-əm-ˈkwik-we\ [L] : to each his own

tant mieux \täⁿ-myœ\ [F] : so much the better

tant pis \-pē\ [F] : so much the worse

tem·po·ra mu·tan·tur, nos et mu·ta·mur in il·lis \ˌtem-pə-rä-mü-ˈtän-ˌtȯr ˌnōs-ˌet-mü-ˌtäm-ər-in-ˈil-ˌēs\ [L] : the times are changing, and we are changing with them

tem·pus edax re·rum \ˈtem-pȯs-ˌed-ˌäks-ˈrā-rȯm\ [L] : time, that devours all things

tem·pus fu·git \ˌtem-pəs-ˈfyü-jət, -ˈfü-git\ [L] : time flies

ti·meo Da·na·os et do·na fe·ren·tes \ˌtim-ē-ˌō-ˈdän-ä-ˌōs-ˌet-ˌdō-nä-fe-ˈren-ˌtäs\ [L] : I fear the Greeks even when they bring gifts

to·ti·dem ver·bis \ˌtȯt-ə-ˌdem-ˈwer-bēs\ [L] : in so many words

to·tis vi·ri·bus \ˌtō-ˌtēs-ˈwē-ri-ˌbȯs\ [L] : with all one's might

to·to cae·lo \ˌtō-tō-ˈkī-lō\ *or* **toto coe·lo** \-ˈkȯi-lō\ [L] : by the whole extent of the heavens : diametrically

tou·jours per·drix \tü-zhür-per-drē\ [F] : always partridge : too much of a good thing

tour d'ho·ri·zon \tür-dȯ-rē-zōⁿ\ [F] : circuit of the horizon : general survey

tous frais faits \tü-fre-fe\ [F] : all expenses defrayed

tout à fait \tü-tȧ-fe\ [F] : altogether : quite

tout au con·traire \tü-tō-kōⁿ-trer\ [F] : quite the contrary

tout à vous \tü-tȧ-vü\ [F] : wholly yours : at your service

tout bien ou rien \tü-'bya\n- nü-'rya\m\ [F] : everything well (done) or nothing (attempted)

tout com·pren·dre c'est tout par·don·ner \'tü-kō\n-prä\n-drə se-'tü-pȧr-dȯ-nā\ [F] : to understand all is to forgive all

tout court \tü-kür\ [F] : quite short : simply; *also* : brusquely

tout de même \tüt-mem\ [F] : all the same : nevertheless

tout de suite \tüt-sw\ͬēt\ [F] : immediately; *also* : all at once : consecutively

tout en·sem·ble \tü-tä\n-sä\nbl\ᵃ\ [F] : all together : general effect

tout est per·du fors l'hon·neur \tü-te-per-dᵫ̄-fȯr-lȯ-nœr\ *or* **tout est perdu hors l'honneur** \-dᵫ̄-ȯr-\ [F] : all is lost save honor

tout le monde \tül-mō\nd\ [F] : all the world : everybody

tranche de vie \trä\nsh-də-'vē\ [F] : slice of life

trist·esse \trē-stes\ [F] : melancholy

tru·di·tur di·es die \'trüd-ə-ˌtür-ˌdi-ˌās-'di-ˌā\ [L] : day is pushed forth by day : one day hurries on another

tu·e·bor \tù-'ā-ˌbȯr\ [L] : I will defend — a motto on the Great Seal of Michigan

ua mau ke ea o ka ai·na i ka po·no \ù-ä-'mä-ù-ke-'e-ä- ō-kä-'ä-ē-nä- ˌē-kä-'pō-nō\ [Hawaiian] : the life of the land is established in righteousness — motto of Hawaii

ue·ber·mensch \'ᵫ̄-bər-ˌmensh\ [G] : superman

ul·ti·ma ra·tio re·gum \'ùl-ti-mä-ˌrät-ē-ō-'rā-gùm\ [L] : the final argument of kings, i.e., war

und so wei·ter \ùnt-zō-'vī-tər\ [G] : and so on

uno ani·mo \ˌü-nō-'än-ə-ˌmō\ [L] : with one mind : unanimously

ur·bi et or·bi \ˌùr-bē-ˌet-'ȯr-bē\ [L] : to the city (Rome) and the world

uti·le dul·ci \ˌüt-ᵊl-e-'dùl-ˌkē\ [L] : the useful with the agreeable

ut in·fra \ùt-'in-frä\ [L] : as below

ut su·pra \ùt-'sü-prä\ [L] : as above

va·de re·tro me, Sa·ta·na \ˌwä-de-'rā-trō-ˌmā-'sä-tə-ˌnä\ [L] : get thee behind me, Satan

vae vic·tis \wī-'wik-ˌtēs\ [L] : woe to the vanquished

va·ria lec·tio \ˌwär-ē-ä-'lek-tē-ˌō\ *pl* **va-**

ri·ae lec·ti·o·nes \'wär-ē-ˌī-ˌlek-tē-'ō-ˌnäs\ [L] : variant reading

va·ri·um et mu·ta·bi·le sem·per fe·mi·na \ˌwär-ē-ˌet-ˌmü-'tä-bə-le-ˌsem-ˌper-'fā-mə-nä\ [L] : woman is ever a fickle and changeable thing

ve·di Na·po·li e poi mo·ri \ˌvā-dē-'nä-pō-lē-ä-ˌpȯ-ē-'mȯ-rē\ [It] : see Naples, and then die

ve·ni, vi·di, vi·ci \ˌwā-nē-ˌwēd-ē-'wē-kē\ [L] : I came, I saw, I conquered

ven·tre à terre \vä\n-trȧ-ter\ [F] : belly to the ground : at very great speed

ver·ba·tim ac lit·te·ra·tim \wer-'bä-tim-ˌäk-ˌlit-ə-'rä-tim\ [L] : word for word and letter for letter

ver·bum sat sa·pi·en·ti est \ˌwer-bùm-'sät-ˌsäp-ē-'ent-ē-ˌest\ [L] : a word to the wise is sufficient

vin·cit om·nia ve·ri·tas \ˌwiŋ-ket- 'ȯm-nē-ä-'wā-rə-ˌtäs\ [L] : truth conquers all things

vin·cu·lum ma·tri·mo·nii \ˌwiŋ-kə-lùm-ˌmä-trə-'mō-nē-ˌē\ [L] : bond of marriage

vir·gi·ni·bus pu·e·ris·que \wir-'gin-ə-bùs-ˌpù-ə-'rēs-kwe\ [L] : for girls and boys

vir·tu·te et ar·mis \wir-'tü-te-ˌet-'är-mēs\ [L] : by valor and arms — motto of Mississippi

vis me·di·ca·trix na·tu·rae \'wēs ˌmed-i-'kä-triks-nä-'tü-ˌrī\ [L] : the healing power of nature

vive la dif·fé·rence \vēv(-ə)-lä-dē-fä-rä\ns\ [F] : long live the difference (between the sexes)

vive la reine \vēv-lȧ-ren\ [F] : long live the queen

vive le roi \vēv-lə-rwä\ [F] : long live the king

vix·e·re for·tes an·te Aga·mem·no·na \wik-ˌsā-re-'fȯr-ˌtäs-ˌänt-ˌäg-ə-'mem-nə-ˌnä\ [L] : brave men lived before Agamemnon

vogue la ga·lère \vȯg-lȧ-gȧ-ler\ [F] : let the galley be kept rowing : keep on, whatever may happen

voi·là \vwȧ-lȧ\ [F] : there you are : there you see (it)

voi·là tout \vwȧ-lȧ-tü\ [F] : that's all

vox et prae·te·rea ni·hil \'wōks-et-prī-ˌter-e-ä-'ni-ˌhil\ [L] : voice and nothing more

vox po·pu·li vox Dei \wōks-'pȯ-pə-ˌlē-

,wōks-'de-ē\ [L] : the voice of the people is the voice of God

Wan·der·jahr \'vän-dər-,yär\ [G] : year of wandering

wie geht's? \vē-'gāts\ [G] : how goes it?

Books of the Old Testament

ROMAN CATHOLIC CANON	PROTESTANT CANON	ROMAN CATHOLIC CANON	PROTESTANT CANON
Genesis	Genesis	Wisdom	
Exodus	Exodus	Ecclesiasticus	
Leviticus	Leviticus	Isaias	Isaiah
Numbers	Numbers	Jeremias	Jeremiah
Deuteronomy	Deuteronomy	Lamentations	Lamentations
Josue	Joshua	Baruch	
Judges	Judges	Ezechiel	Ezekiel
Ruth	Ruth	Daniel	Daniel
1 & 2 Kings	1 & 2 Samuel	Osee	Hosea
3 & 4 Kings	1 & 2 Kings	Joel	Joel
1 & 2 Paralipom- enon	1 & 2 Chronicles	Amos	Amos
		Abdias	Obadiah
1 Esdras	Ezra	Jonas	Jonah
2 Esdras	Nehemiah	Micheas	Micah
Tobias		Nahum	Nahum
Judith		Habacuc	Habakkuk
Esther	Esther	Sophonias	Zephaniah
Job	Job	Aggeus	Haggai
Psalms	Psalms	Zacharias	Zechariah
Proverbs	Proverbs	Malachias	Malachi
Ecclesiastes	Ecclesiastes	1 & 2 Machabees	
Canticle of Canticles	Song of Solomon		

JEWISH SCRIPTURE

Law	1 & 2 Kings	Nahum	Song of Songs
Genesis	Isaiah	Habakkuk	Ruth
Exodus	Jeremiah	Zephaniah	Lamentations
Leviticus	Ezekiel	Haggai	Ecclesiastes
Numbers	Hosea	Zechariah	Esther
Deuteronomy	Joel	Malachi	Daniel
Prophets	Amos	*Hagiographa*	Ezra
Joshua	Obadiah	Psalms	Nehemiah
Judges	Jonah	Proverbs	1 & 2 Chronicles
1 & 2 Samuel	Micah	Job	

PROTESTANT APOCRYPHA

1 & 2 Esdras	Wisdom of Solomon	Baruch	Susanna
Tobit	Ecclesiasticus or the Wisdom of Jesus Son of Sirach	Prayer of Azariah and the Song of the Three Holy Children	Bel and the Dragon
Judith			The Prayer of Manasses
Additions to Esther			1 & 2 Maccabees

Books of the New Testament

Matthew	Romans	1 & 2 Thess- alonians	1 & 2 Peter
Mark	1 & 2 Corinthians	1 & 2 Timothy	1, 2, 3 John
Luke	Galatians	Titus	Jude
John	Ephesians	Philemon	Revelation (Ro- man Catholic canon: Apocalypse)
Acts of the Apostles	Philippians	Hebrews	
	Colossians	James	

Metric System[1]

LENGTH

unit	number of meters	approximate U.S. equivalent
kilometer	1,000	0.62 mile
hectometer	100	109.36 yards
dekameter	10	32.81 feet
meter	1	39.37 inches
decimeter	0.1	3.94 inches
centimeter	0.01	0.39 inch
millimeter	0.001	0.039 inch

AREA

unit	number of square meters	approximate U.S. equivalent
square kilometer	1,000,000	0.3861 square mile
hectare	10,000	2.47 acres
are	100	119.60 square yards
square centimeter	0.0001	0.155 square inch

VOLUME

unit	number of cubic meters	approximate U.S. equivalent
cubic meter	1	1.307 cubic yards
cubic decimeter	0.10	61.023 cubic inches
cubic centimeter	0.000001	0.061 cubic inch

CAPACITY

unit	number of liters	*cubic*	*dry*	*liquid*
kiloliter	1,000	1.31 cubic yards		
hectoliter	100	3.53 cubic feet	2.84 bushels	
dekaliter	10	0.35 cubic foot	1.14 pecks	2.64 gallons
liter	1	61.02 cubic inches	0.908 quart	1.057 quarts
deciliter	0.1	6.1 cubic inches	0.18 pint	0.21 pint
centiliter	0.01	0.61 cubic inch		0.338 fluidounce
milliliter	0.001	0.061 cubic inch		0.27 fluidram

MASS AND WEIGHT

unit	number of grams	approximate U.S. equivalent
metric ton	1,000,000	1.102 short tons
kilogram	1,000	2.2046 pound
hectogram	100	3.527 ounces
dekagram	10	0.353 ounce
gram	1	0.035 ounce
decigram	0.10	1.543 grains
centigram	0.01	0.154 grain
milligram	0.001	0.015 grain

[1]For metric equivalents of U.S. units see Weights and Measures table

Money

NAME	SUBDIVISIONS	COUNTRY	NAME	SUBDIVISIONS	COUNTRY
afghani	100 puls	Afghanistan	dollar	100 cents	Singapore
austral		Argentina	dollar	100 cents	Trinidad and Tobago
baht *or* tical	100 satang	Thailand	dollar	100 cents	United States
balboa	100 centesimos	Panama			
birr	100 cents	Ethiopia	dollar	100 cents	Zimbabwe
bolivar	100 centimos	Venezuela	dong	100 xu	Vietnam
cedi	100 pesewas	Ghana	drachma	100 lepta	Greece
colon	100 centimos	Costa Rica	ekuele	100 centimos	Equatorial Guinea
colon	100 centavos	El Salvador			
cordoba	100 centavos	Nicaragua	escudo	100 centavos	Cape Verde
cruzado		Brazil	escudo	100 centavos	Portugal
dalasi	100 bututs	Gambia	escudo—see PESO, below		
deutsche mark	100 pfennigs	West Germany	florin—see GULDEN, below		
			forint	100 filler	Hungary
dinar	100 centimes	Algeria	franc	100 centimes	Belgium
dinar	1000 fils	Bahrain	franc	100 centimes	Benin
dinar	1000 fils	Iraq	franc	100 centimes	Burkina Faso
dinar	1000 fils	Jordan			
dinar	1000 fils	Kuwait	franc	100 centimes	Burundi
dinar	1000 dirhams	Libya	franc	100 centimes	Cameroon
dinar	1000 fils	Southern Yemen (People's Democratic Republic of Yemen)	franc	100 centimes	Central African Republic
			franc	100 centimes	Chad
			franc	100 centimes	Congo
			franc	100 centimes	Djibouti
			franc	100 centimes	France
dinar	1000 millimes	Tunisia	franc	100 centimes	Gabon
dinar	100 paras	Yugoslavia	franc	100 centimes	Ivory Coast
dirham	100 centimes	Morocco	franc	100 centimes	Luxembourg
dirham	1000 fils	United Arab Emirates	franc	100 centimes	Madagascar
			franc	100 centimes	Mali
dobra	100 centavos	Sao Tome and Principe	franc	100 centimes	Niger
			franc	100 centimes	Rwanda
			franc	100 centimes	Senegal
dollar	100 cents	Australia	franc	100 centimes *or* rappen	Switzerland
dollar	100 cents	Bahamas			
dollar	100 cents	Barbados	franc	100 centimes	Togo
dollar	100 cents	Belize	gourde	100 centimes	Haiti
dollar	100 cents	Bermuda	guarani	100 centimos	Paraguay
dollar	100 sen	Brunei	gulden *or* guilder *or* florin	100 cents	Netherlands
dollar	100 cents	Canada			
dollar *or* yuan	100 cents	China (Taiwan)	gulden *or* guilder *or* florin	100 cents	Suriname
dollar	100 cents	Ethiopia			
dollar	100 cents	Fiji	inti		Peru
dollar	100 cents	Grenada	kina	100 toea	Papua New Guinea
dollar	100 cents	Guyana			
dollar	100 cents	Hong Kong	kip	100 at	Laos
dollar	100 cents	Jamaica	koruna	100 halers	Czechoslovakia
dollar	100 cents	Liberia			
dollar	100 cents	New Zealand	krona	100 aurar (*sing* eyrir)	Iceland
dollar	100 cents	St. Vincent and the Grenadines	krona	100 ore	Sweden
			krone	100 ore	Denmark
			krone	100 ore	Norway

NAME	SUBDIVISIONS	COUNTRY
kwacha	100 tambala	Malawi
kwacha	100 ngwee	Zambia
kwanza	100 lwei	Angola
kyat	100 pyas	Burma
lek	100 qindarka	Albania
lempira	100 centavos	Honduras
leone	100 cents	Sierra Leone
leu	100 bani	Romania
lev	100 stotinki	Bulgaria
lilangeni (*pl* emalangeni)	100 cents	Swaziland
lira	100 centesimi	Italy
lira *or* pound	100 kurus *or* piasters	Turkey
lira—see POUND, below		
loti (*pl* maloti)	100 licente	Lesotho
mark *or* ostmark	100 pfennigs	East Germany
mark—see DEUTSCHE MARK, above		
markka	100 pennia	Finland
metical	100 centavos	Mozambique
naira	100 kobo	Nigeria
ngultrum	100 chetrums	Bhutan
ostmark—see MARK, above		
ouguiya	5 khoums	Mauritania
pa'anga	100 seniti	Tonga
pataca	100 avos	Macao
peseta	100 centimos	Spain
peso	100 centavos	Bolivia
peso	100 centavos	Chile
peso	100 centavos	Colombia
peso	100 centavos	Cuba
peso	100 centavos	Dominican Republic
peso	100 centavos	Guinea-Bissau
peso	100 centavos	Mexico
peso	100 sentimos *or* centavos	Philippines
peso	100 centesimos	Uruguay
pound	1000 mils	Cyprus
pound	100 piasters	Egypt
pound	100 pence	Ireland
pound	100 piasters	Lebanon
pound *or* lira	100 pence	Malta
pound	100 piasters	Sudan
pound	100 piasters	Syria
pound	100 pence	United Kingdom
pound—see LIRA, above		
pula	100 thebe	Botswana
quetzal	100 centavos	Guatemala
rand	100 cents	South Africa
rial	100 dinars	Iran
rial	1000 baizas	Oman
rial *or* riyal	100 fils	Yemen Arab Republic
riel	100 sen	Cambodia
ringgit	100 sen	Malaysia
riyal	100 dirhams	Qatar
riyal	20 qursh 100 halala	Saudi Arabia
riyal—see RIAL, above		
ruble	100 kopecks	U.S.S.R.
rupee	100 paise	India
rupee	100 cents	Mauritius
rupee	100 paisa	Nepal
rupee	100 paisa	Pakistan
rupee	100 cents	Seychelles
rupee	100 cents	Sri Lanka
rupiah	100 sen	Indonesia
schilling	100 groschen	Austria
shekel	100 agorot	Israel
shilingi—see SHILLING, below		
shilling	100 cents	Kenya
shilling	100 cents	Somalia
shilling *or* shilingi	100 senti *or* cents	Tanzania
shilling	100 cents	Uganda
sucre	100 centavos	Ecuador
syli	100 cauris	Guinea
taka	100 paisa	Bangladesh
tala	100 sene	Western Samoa
tical—see BAHT, above		
tugrik	100 mongo	Mongolia
vatu		Vanuatu
won	100 jun	North Korea
won	100 jeon	South Korea
yen	100 sen	Japan
yuan	100 fen	China (mainland)
yuan—see DOLLAR, above		
zaire	100 makuta (*sing*, likuta) 10,000 sengi	Zaire
zloty	100 groszy	Poland

Nations of the World

name and pronunciation	population
Afghanistan \af-'gan-ə-ıstan\	13,051,000
Albania \al-'bā-nē-ə\	2,841,000
Algeria \al-'jir-ē-ə\	16,948,000
Andorra \an-'dȯr-ə\	40,000
Angola \aŋ-'gō-lə, an-\	6,761,000
Antigua and Barbuda \an-'tē-gə-ən-bär-'büd-ə\	77,000
Argentina \ıär-jen 'tē-nə\	27,947,000
Australia \ȯ-'strāl-yə\	14,574,000
Austria \'ȯs-trē-ə\	7,555,000
Bahamas \bə-'häm-əz\	223,000
Bahrain \bä-'rān\	359,000
Bangladesh \ıbäŋ-glə-'desh, -'dash\	87,052,000
Barbados \bär-'bād-əs, -(ı)ōz, -(ı)äs\	249,000
Belgium \'bel-jəm\	9,849,000
Belize \bə-'lēz\	145,000
Benin \bə-'nin\	3,338,000
Bhutan \bü-'tan, -'tän\	1,333,000
Bolivia \bə-'liv-ē-ə\	4,613,000
Botswana \bät-'swän-ə\	937,000
Brazil \brə-'zil\	118,675,000
Brunei \brü-'nī\	193,000
Bulgaria \ıbəl-'gar-ē-ə, bùl-\	8,730,000
Burkina Faso \bùr-'kē-nə-'fä-sō\	5,638,000
Burma \'bər-mə\	35,314,000
Burundi \bù-'rün-dē\	3,638,000
Cambodia \kam-'bōd-ē-ə\	6,646,000
Cameroon \ıkam-ə-'rün\	7,090,000
Canada \'kan-əd-ə\	24,098,000
Cape Verde \-'vərd\	303,000
Central African Republic \-'af-ri-kən-\	2,055,000
Chad \'chad\	4,681,000
Chile \'chil-ē\	11,275,000
China, People's Republic of \-'chī-nə\	1,031,882,000
Colombia \kə-'ləm-bē-ə\	26,929,000
Comoro Islands \'käm-ə-ırō-\	421,000
Congo \'käŋ-go\	1,300,000
Costa Rica \ıkäs-tə-'rē-kə\	2,435,000
Cuba \'kyü-bə\	9,706,000
Cyprus \'sī-prəs\	613,000
Czechoslovakia \ıchek-ə-slō-'väk-ē-ə\	15,283,000

name and pronunciation	population
Denmark \'den-ımärk\	5,119,000
Djibouti \jə-'büt-ē\	323,000
Dominica \ıdäm-ə-'nē-kə\	74,000
Dominican Republic \də-ımin-i-kən-\	5,648,000
East Germany \-'jər-mən-ē\	16,706,000
Ecuador \'ek-wə-ıdȯr\	6,522,000
Egypt \'ē-jəpt\	36,626,000
El Salvador \el-'sal-və-ıdȯr\	4,813,000
Equatorial Guinea \-'gin-ē\	300,000
Ethiopia \ıe-thē-'ō-pē-ə\	32,775,000
Fiji \'fē-(ı)jē\	588,000
Finland \'fin-lənd\	4,718,000
France \'frans\	52,656,000
Gabon \ga-'bōn\	1,108,000
Gambia \'gam-bē-ə\	696,000
Ghana \'gän-ə\	12,244,000
Greece \'grēs\	9,707,000
Grenada \grə-'nād-ə\	110,000
Guatemala \ıgwät-ə-'mäl-ə\	6,044,000
Guinea \'gin-ē\	5,057,000
Guinea-Bissau \-bis-'aù\	768,000
Guyana \gī-'an-ə\	900,000
Haiti \'hāt-ē\	5,054,000
Honduras \hän-'d(y)ùr-əs\	3,955,000
Hungary \'həŋ-g(ə-)rē\	10,709,000
Iceland \'īs-lənd, -ıland\	235,000
India \'in-dē-ə\	685,185,000
Indonesia \ıin-də-'nē-zhə, -shə\	147,490,000
Iran \i-'ran, -'rän\	33,592,000
Iraq \i-'räk, -'rak\	12,000,000
Ireland (Irish Republic) \'ī(ə)r-lənd\	3,443,000
Israel \'iz-rē-əl\	4,112,000
Italy \'it-ə-lē\	56,244,000
Ivory Coast \'īv-(ə-)rē-\	6,710,000
Jamaica \jə-'mā-kə\	2,096,000
Japan \jə-'pan\	117,057,000
Jordan \'jȯrd-ən\	2,152,000
Kenya \'ken-yə, 'kēn-\	15,327,000
Kuwait \kə-'wāt\	1,356,000
Laos \'laùs, 'lä-ōs\	4,104,000
Lebanon \'leb-ə-nən\	3,161,000
Lesotho \lə-'sü-ıtü\	1,214,000
Liberia \lī-'bir-ē-ə\	1,503,000
Libya \'lib-ē-ə\	3,224,000

Nation	Population
Liechtenstein \ 'lik-tən-ıs(h)tīn \	26,000
Luxembourg \ 'lək-səm-ıbərg, 'lük-səm-ıbürg \	365,000
Madagascar \ ımad-ə-'gas-kər \	7,604,000
Malawi \mə-'lä-wē \	5,547,000
Malaysia \mə-'lā-zh(ē-)ə\ .	13,700,000
Maldives \ 'mȯl-ıdēvz, -ıdīvz\	143,000
Mali \ 'mäl-ē\	6,525,000
Malta \ 'mȯl-tə\	366,000
Mauritania \ ımȯr-ə-'tā-nē-ə\	1,420,000
Mauritius \mȯ-'rish-(ē-)əs\	993,000
Mexico \ 'mek-si-ıkō\	67,396,000
Monaco \ 'män-ə-ıkō\	27,000
Mongolia \män-'gōl-yə\ ..	1,595,000
Morocco \mə-'räk-ō\	21,392,000
Mozambique \ ımō-zəm-'bēk\	11,674,000
Nauru \nä-'ü-(ı)rü\	7,000
Nepal \nə-'pȯl\	15,020,000
Netherlands \ 'neth-ər-lən(d)z\	14,386,000
New Zealand \-'zē-lənd\ .	3,176,000
Nicaragua \ ınik-ə-'räg-wə\ ..	2,824,000
Niger \ 'nī-jər\	5,098,000
Nigeria \nī-'jir-ē-ə\	86,126,000
North Korea \-kə-'rē-ə\ ..	18,747,000
Norway \ 'nȯr-ıwā\	4,091,000
Oman \ō-'män\	1,079,000
Pakistan \ 'pak-i-ıstan, ıpäk-i-'stän\	83,782,000
Panama \ 'pan-ə-ımä\	1,825,000
Papua New Guinea \ 'päp-ə-wə-\	3,011,000
Paraguay \ 'par-ə-ıgwī, -ıgwä\	3,026,000
Peru \pə-'rü\	17,031,000
Philippines \ ıfil-ə-'pēnz, 'fil-ə-ıpēnz\	48,098,000
Poland \ 'pō-lənd\	35,061,000
Portugal \ 'pōr-chi-gəl\	9,784,000
Qatar \ 'kät-ər\	270,000
Romania \rü-'mā-nē-ə\ ...	21,560,000
Rwanda \rü-'än-də\	4,819,000
St. Christopher-Nevis \sänt-'kris-tə-fər-'nē-vəs\	44,000
St. Lucia \-'lü-shə\	122,000
St. Vincent and the Grenadines .... \-'vin-sənt ... ıgren-ə-'dēnz\	124,000
San Marino \ ısan-mə-'rē-nō\	19,000
Sao Tome and Principe \ ısaú-tə-'mä-ən-'prin-sə-pə\	89,000
Saudi Arabia \ ısaúd-ē-ə-'rä-bē-ə, sä-ıüd-ē-\	10,025,000
Senegal \ ısen-i-'gȯl\	5,811,000
Seychelles \sā-'chel(z)\ ...	62,000
Sierra Leone \sē-ıer-ə-lē-'ōn\	2,735,000
Singapore \ 'siŋ-(g)ə-ıpōr\	2,414,000
Solomon Islands \ 'säl-ə-mən-\	197,000
Somalia \sō-'mäl-ē-ə\	5,085,000
South Africa, Republic of ..	26,129,000
South Korea \-kə-'rē-ə\ ..	37,436,000
Spain \ 'spān\	37,746,000
Sri Lanka \(')srē-'läŋ-kə, (')shrē-\	14,850,000
Sudan \sü-'dan\	20,564,000
Suriname \ ısür-ə-'näm-ə\	352,000
Swaziland \ 'swäz-ē-ıland\	494,000
Sweden \ 'swēd-ən\	8,208,000
Switzerland \ 'swit-sər-lənd\	6,366,000
Syria \ 'sir-ē-ə\	9,172,000
Taiwan (Republic of China) \tī-'wän\	14,811,000
Tanzania \ ıtan-zə-'nē-ə\ ..	17,528,000
Thailand \ 'tī-ıland, -lənd\	44,278,000
Togo \ 'tō-gō\	2,703,000
Trinidad and Tobago \ 'trin-ə-ıdad-ən-tə-'bā-gō\	1,060,000
Tunisia \t(y)ü-'nē-zh(ē-)ə\	6,966,000
Turkey \ 'tər-kē\	44,737,000
Uganda \yü-'gan-də\	12,630,000
Union of Soviet Socialist Republics (U.S.S.R.) .... \-'sō-vē-ıet-, (ıyü-ıes-ıes-'är)\	262,436,000
United Arab Emirates \-'em-ə-rəts\	1,043,000
United Kingdom of Great Britain and Northern Ireland .... \-'brit-ən. .. 'ī(ə)r-lənd\ .... England \ 'iŋ-glənd\ .... Northern Ireland .... Scotland \ 'skät-lənd\ ... Wales \ 'wālz\ ...	55,671,000
United States of America \-ə-'mer-i-kə\	226,504,825
Uruguay \ '(y)ür-ə-ıgwī, 'yür-ə-ıgwä\	2,788,000
Vanuatu \ ıvan-ə-'wät-ü\ ..	112,000

Vatican City State
\ ˌvat-i-kən-\ 700
Venezuela
\ ˌven-əz(-ə)-ˈwā-lə\ 14,517,000
Vietnam \vē-ˈet-ˈnäm\ ... 52,742,000
Western Samoa
\-sə-ˈmō-ə\ 156,000
West Germany
\-ˈjər-mə-nē\ 61,371,000

Yemen, People's Democratic Republic of
\-ˈyem-ən\ 2,158,000
Yemen Arab Republic 5,238,000
Yugoslavia
\ ˌyü-gō-ˈsläv-ē-ə\ 22,839,000
Zaire \zä-ˈi(ə)r\ 30,261,000
Zambia \ ˈzam-bē-ə\ 5,680,000
Zimbabwe \zim-ˈbäb-wā\ . 7,550,000

Planets

SYMBOL	NAME	MEAN DISTANCE FROM THE SUN		PERIOD OF REVOLUTION IN DAYS OR YEARS	EQUA-TORIAL DIAMETER IN MILES
		astronomical units	million miles		
☿	Mercury	0.387	36.0	87.97 d.	3,031
♀	Venus	0.723	67.2	224.70 d.	7,521
⊕	Earth	1.000	92.9	365.26 d.	7,926
♂	Mars	1.524	141.5	686.98 d.	4.216
♃	Jupiter	5.203	483.4	11.86 y.	88,700
♄	Saturn	9.569	889.0	29.46 y.	74,500
♅	Uranus	19.309	1793.8	84.01 y.	31,600
♆	Neptune	30.284	2813.4	164.79 y.	30,200
♇	Pluto	39.781	3695.7	247.69 y.	1,900

Population of Places in the United States
Having 16,500 or More Inhabitants in 1980

A

Aberdeen, S. Dak.	25,956
Aberdeen, Wash.	18,739
Abilene, Tex.	98,315
Acton, Mass.	17,544
Addison, Ill.	29,759
Adrian, Mich.	21,186
Agawam, Mass.	26,271
Aiea, Hawaii	32,879
Akron, Ohio	237,177
Alameda, Calif.	63,852
Alamogordo, N. Mex.	24,024
Albany, Ga.	74,059
Albany, N.Y.	101,727
Albany, Oreg.	26,546
Albert Lea, Minn.	19,200
Albuquerque, N. Mex.	331,767
Alexandria, La.	51,565
Alexandria, Va.	103,217
Alhambra, Calif.	64,615
Alice, Tex.	20,961
Aliquippa, Pa.	17,094
Allen Park, Mich.	34,196
Allentown, Pa.	103,758
Alliance, Ohio	24,315
Alsip, Ill.	17,134
Altamonte Springs, Fla.	22,028
Alton, Ill.	34,171
Altoona, Pa.	57,078
Altus, Okla.	23,101
Alvin, Tex.	16,515
Amarillo, Tex.	149,230
Ames, Iowa	45,775
Amherst, Mass.	33,229
Amsterdam, N.Y.	21,872
Anaheim, Calif.	221,847
Anchorage, Alaska	174,431
Anderson, Ind.	64,695
Anderson, S.C.	27,313
Andover, Mass.	26,370
Annapolis, Md.	31,740
Ann Arbor, Mich.	107,966
Anniston, Ala.	29,523
Ansonia, Conn.	19,039
Antioch, Calif.	43,559
Appleton, Wis.	59,032
Apple Valley, Minn.	21,818
Arcadia, Calif.	45,994
Ardmore, Okla.	23,689
Arlington, Mass.	48,219
Arlington, Tex.	160,113
Arlington Heights, Ill.	66,116
Arnold, Mo.	19,141
Arvada, Colo.	84,576

Asbury Park, N.J.	17,015
Asheville, N.C.	53,583
Ashland, Ky.	27,064
Ashland, Ohio	20,326
Ashtabula, Ohio	23,449
Athens, Ga.	42,549
Athens, Ohio	19,743
Atlanta, Ga.	425,022
Atlantic City, N.J.	40,199
Attleboro, Mass.	34,196
Atwater, Calif.	17,530
Auburn, Ala.	28,471
Auburn, Me.	23,128
Auburn, N.Y.	32,548
Auburn, Wash.	26,417
Augusta, Ga.	47,532
Augusta, Me.	21,819
Aurora, Colo.	158,588
Aurora, Ill.	81,293
Austin, Minn.	23,020
Austin, Tex.	345,496
Azusa, Calif.	29,380

B

Bakersfield, Calif.	105,611
Baldwin, Pa.	24,598
Baldwin Park, Calif.	50,554
Baltimore, Md.	786,775
Bangor, Me.	31,643
Barberton, Ohio	29,751
Barnstable, Mass.	30,898
Barstow, Calif.	17,690
Bartlesville, Okla.	34,568
Bartlett, Tenn.	17,170
Batavia, N.Y.	16,703
Baton Rouge, La.	219,419
Battle Creek, Mich.	35,724
Bay City, Mich.	41,593
Bay City, Tex.	17,837
Bayonne, N.J.	65,047
Baytown, Tex.	56,923
Bay Village, Ohio	17,846
Beaumont, Tex.	118,102
Beavercreek, Ohio	31,589
Beaverton, Oreg.	30,582
Beckley, W. Va.	20,492
Bedford, Tex.	20,821
Bell, Calif.	25,450
Belle Glade, Fla.	16,535
Belleville, Ill.	41,580
Belleville, N.J.	35,367
Bellevue, Nebr.	21,813
Bellevue, Wash.	73,903
Bellflower, Calif.	53,441
Bell Gardens, Calif.	34,117

Bellingham, Wash.	45,794	Bristol, Tenn.	23,986
Bellwood, Ill.	19,811	Bristol, Va.	19,042
Belmont, Calif.	24,505	Brockton, Mass.	95,172
Belmont, Mass.	26,100	Broken Arrow, Okla.	35,761
Beloit, Wis.	35,207	Brookfield, Ill.	19,395
Bend, Oreg.	17,263	Brookfield, Wis.	34,035
Benton, Ark.	17,717	Brookline, Mass.	55,062
Berea, Ohio	19,567	Brooklyn Center, Minn.	31,230
Bergenfield, N.J.	25,568	Brooklyn Park, Minn.	43,332
Berkeley, Calif.	103,328	Brook Park, Ohio	26,195
Berkley, Mich.	18,637	Broomfield, Colo.	20,730
Berwyn, Ill.	46,849	Brownsville, Tex.	84,997
Bessemer, Ala.	31,729	Brownwood, Tex.	19,396
Bethany, Okla.	22,130	Brunswick, Ga.	17,605
Bethel Park, Pa.	34,755	Brunswick, Me.	17,366
Bethlehem, Pa.	70,419	Brunswick, Ohio	28,104
Bettendorf, Iowa	27,381	Bryan, Tex.	44,337
Beverly, Mass.	37,655	Buena Park, Calif.	64,165
Beverly Hills, Calif.	32,367	Buffalo, N.Y.	357,870
Biddeford, Me.	19,638	Burbank, Calif.	84,625
Big Spring, Tex.	24,804	Burbank, Ill.	28,462
Billerica, Mass.	36,727	Burlingame, Calif.	26,173
Billings, Mont.	66,798	Burlington, Iowa	29,529
Biloxi, Miss.	49,311	Burlington, Mass.	23,486
Binghamton, N.Y.	55,860	Burlington, N.C.	37,266
Birmingham, Ala.	284,413	Burlington, Vt.	37,712
Birmingham, Mich.	21,689	Burnsville, Minn.	35,674
Bismarck, N. Dak.	44,485	Burton, Mich.	29,976
Blacksburg, Va.	30,638	Butler, Pa.	17,026
Blaine, Minn.	28,558	Butte, Mont.	36,817
Bloomfield, Conn.	18,608		
Bloomfield, N.J.	47,792	**C**	
Bloomington, Ill.	44,189	Cahokia, Ill.	18,904
Bloomington, Ind.	52,044	Caldwell, Idaho	17,699
Bloomington, Minn.	81,831	Calumet City, Ill.	39,697
Blue Island, Ill.	21,853	Camarillo, Calif.	37,732
Blue Springs, Mo.	25,927	Cambridge, Mass.	95,322
Blytheville, Ark.	23,844	Camden, N.J.	84,910
Boca Raton, Fla.	49,505	Campbell, Calif.	27,067
Bogalusa, La.	16,976	Canton, Mass.	18,182
Boise, Idaho	102,451	Canton, Ohio	94,730
Bolingbrook, Ill.	37,261	Cape Coral, Fla.	32,103
Bossier City, La.	50,817	Cape Girardeau, Mo.	34,361
Boston, Mass.	562,994	Carbondale, Ill.	26,287
Boulder, Colo.	76,685	Carlisle, Pa.	18,314
Bountiful, Utah	32,877	Carlsbad, Calif.	35,490
Bowie, Md.	33,695	Carlsbad, N. Mex.	25,496
Bowling Green, Ky.	40,450	Carmel, Ind.	18,272
Bowling Green, Ohio	25,728	Carpentersville, Ill.	23,272
Boynton Beach, Fla.	35,624	Carrollton, Tex.	40,595
Bozeman, Mont.	21,645	Carson, Calif.	81,221
Bradenton, Fla.	30,170	Carson City, Nev.	32,022
Braintree, Mass.	36,337	Carteret, N.J.	20,598
Branford, Conn.	23,363	Cary, N.C.	21,763
Brea, Calif.	27,913	Casper, Wyo.	51,016
Bremerton, Wash.	36,208	Cedar Falls, Iowa	36,322
Bridgeport, Conn.	142,546	Cedar Rapids, Iowa	110,243
Bridgeton, Mo.	18,445	Centerville, Ohio	18,886
Bridgeton, N.J.	18,795	Central Falls, R.I.	16,995
Bristol, Conn.	57,370	Cerritos, Calif.	53,020
Bristol, R.I.	20,128	Champaign, Ill.	58,133

Chandler, Ariz.	29,673	Conroe, Tex.	18,034
Chapel Hill, N.C.	32,421	Conway, Ark.	20,375
Charleston, Ill.	19,355	Cookeville, Tenn.	20,535
Charleston, S.C.	69,510	Coon Rapids, Minn.	35,826
Charleston, W. Va.	63,968	Copperas Cove, Tex.	19,469
Charlotte, N.C.	314,447	Coral Gables, Fla.	43,241
Charlottesville, Va.	39,916	Coral Springs, Fla.	37,349
Chattanooga, Tenn.	169,565	Corona, Calif.	37,791
Chelmsford, Mass.	31,174	Coronado, Calif.	16,859
Chelsea, Mass.	25,431	Corpus Christi, Tex.	231,999
Chesapeake, Va.	114,486	Corsicana, Tex.	21,712
Cheshire, Conn.	21,788	Cortland, N.Y.	20,138
Chester, Pa.	45,794	Corvallis, Oreg.	40,960
Cheyenne, Wyo.	47,283	Costa Mesa, Calif.	82,562
Chicago, Ill.	3,005,072	Cottage Grove, Minn.	18,994
Chicago Heights, Ill.	37,026	Council Bluffs, Iowa	56,449
Chico, Calif.	26,601	Coventry, R.I.	27,065
Chicopee, Mass.	55,112	Covina, Calif.	33,751
Chillicothe, Ohio	23,420	Covington, Ky.	49,563
Chino, Calif.	40,165	Cranston, R.I.	71,992
Chula Vista, Calif.	83,927	Crystal, Minn.	25,543
Cicero, Ill.	61,232	Crystal Lake, Ill.	18,590
Cincinnati, Ohio	385,457	Cudahy, Calif.	17,984
Claremont, Calif.	30,950	Cudahy, Wis.	19,547
Clarksburg, W. Va.	22,371	Culver City, Calif.	38,139
Clarksdale, Miss.	21,137	Cumberland, Md.	25,933
Clarksville, Tenn.	54,777	Cumberland, R.I.	27,069
Clearfield, Utah	17,982	Cupertino, Calif.	34,015
Clearwater, Fla.	85,528	Cuyahoga Falls, Ohio	43,890
Cleburne, Tex.	19,218	Cypress, Calif.	40,391
Cleveland, Ohio	573,822		
Cleveland, Tenn.	26,415	**D**	
Cleveland Heights, Ohio	56,438	Dallas, Tex.	904,078
Cliffside Park, N.J.	21,464	Dalton, Ga.	20,939
Clifton, N.J.	74,388	Daly City, Calif.	78,519
Clinton, Iowa	32,828	Danbury, Conn.	60,470
Clovis, Calif.	33,021	Danvers, Mass.	24,100
Clovis, N. Mex.	31,194	Danville, Ill.	38,985
Coeur d'Alene, Idaho	20,054	Danville, Va.	45,642
Cohoes, N.Y.	18,144	Darien, Conn.	18,892
College Park, Ga.	24,632	Dartmouth, Mass.	23,966
College Park, Md.	23,614	Davenport, Iowa	103,264
College Station, Tex.	37,272	Davie, Fla.	20,877
Collinsville, Ill.	19,613	Davis, Calif.	36,640
Colonial Heights, Va.	16,509	Dayton, Ohio	203,371
Colorado Springs, Colo.	215,150	Daytona Beach, Fla.	54,176
Colton, Calif.	21,310	Dearborn, Mich.	90,660
Columbia, Mo.	62,061	Dearborn Heights, Mich.	67,706
Columbia, S.C.	99,296	Decatur, Ala.	42,002
Columbia, Tenn.	26,372	Decatur, Ga.	18,404
Columbia Heights, Minn.	20,029	Decatur, Ill.	94,081
Columbus, Ga.	169,441	Dedham, Mass.	25,298
Columbus, Ind.	30,614	Deerfield, Ill.	17,430
Columbus, Miss.	27,383	Deerfield Beach, Fla.	39,193
Columbus, Nebr.	17,328	Deer Park, Tex.	22,648
Columbus, Ohio	564,871	Defiance, Ohio	16,810
Compton, Calif.	81,286	De Kalb, Ill.	33,099
Concord, Calif.	103,255	Delaware, Ohio	18,780
Concord, N.H.	30,400	Del City, Okla.	28,424
Concord, N.C.	16,942	Delray Beach, Fla.	34,325
Connersville, Ind.	17,023	Del Rio, Tex.	30,034

Denison, Tex.	23,884	El Monte, Calif.	79,494
Denton, Tex.	48,063	Elmwood Park, Ill.	24,016
Denver, Colo.	492,365	Elmwood Park, N.J.	18,377
Depew, N.Y.	19,819	El Paso, Tex.	425,259
Derry, N.H.	18,875	Elyria, Ohio	57,538
Des Moines, Iowa	191,003	Emporia, Kans.	25,287
Des Plaines, Ill.	53,568	Enfield, Conn.	42,695
Detroit, Mich.	1,203,339	Englewood, Colo.	30,021
Dodge City, Kans.	18,001	Englewood, N.J.	23,701
Dolton, Ill.	24,766	Enid, Okla.	50,363
Dothan, Ala.	48,750	Enterprise, Ala.	18,033
Dover, Del.	23,512	Erie, Pa.	119,123
Dover, N.H.	22,377	Escondido, Calif.	64,355
Downers Grove, Ill.	42,572	Euclid, Ohio	59,999
Downey, Calif.	82,602	Eugene, Oreg.	105,624
Dracut, Mass.	21,249	Euless, Tex.	24,002
Duarte, Calif.	16,766	Eureka, Calif.	24,153
Dubuque, Iowa	62,321	Evanston, Ill.	73,706
Duluth, Minn.	92,811	Evansville, Ind.	130,496
Dumont, N.J.	18,334	Everett, Mass.	37,195
Duncan, Okla.	22,517	Everett, Wash.	54,413
Duncanville, Tex.	27,781	Evergreen Park, Ill.	22,260
Dunedin, Fla.	30,203		
Dunmore, Pa.	16,781	**F**	
Durham, N.C.	100,831		
		Fairbanks, Alaska	22,645
E		Fairborn, Ohio	29,702
		Fairfax, Va.	19,390
Eagan, Minn.	20,700	Fairfield, Calif.	58,099
Eagle Pass, Tex.	21,407	Fairfield, Conn.	54,849
East Chicago, Ind.	39,786	Fairfield, Ohio	30,777
East Cleveland, Ohio	36,957	Fair Lawn, N.J.	32,229
East Detroit, Mich.	38,280	Fairmont, W. Va.	23,863
East Hartford, Conn.	52,563	Fairview Park, Ohio	19,311
East Haven, Conn.	25,028	Fall River, Mass.	92,574
Eastlake, Ohio	22,104	Falmouth, Mass.	23,640
East Lansing, Mich.	51,392	Fargo, N. Dak.	61,383
East Liverpool, Ohio	16,687	Farmers Branch, Tex.	24,863
East Moline, Ill.	20,907	Farmington, N. Mex.	31,222
Easton, Mass.	16,623	Farmington Hills, Mich.	58,056
Easton, Pa.	26,027	Fayetteville, Ark.	36,608
East Orange, N.J.	77,690	Fayetteville, N.C.	59,507
East Peoria, Ill.	22,385	Ferguson, Mo.	24,740
East Point, Ga.	37,486	Ferndale, Mich.	26,227
East Providence, R.I.	50,980	Findlay, Ohio	35,594
East Ridge, Tenn.	21,236	Fitchburg, Mass.	39,580
East St. Louis, Ill.	55,200	Flagstaff, Ariz.	34,743
Eau Claire, Wis.	51,509	Flint, Mich.	159,611
Edina, Minn.	46,073	Floral Park, N.Y.	16,805
Edinburg, Tex.	24,075	Florence, Ala.	37,029
Edmond, Okla.	34,637	Florence, S.C.	30,062
Edmonds, Wash.	27,679	Florissant, Mo.	55,372
El Cajon, Calif.	73,892	Fond du Lac, Wis.	35,863
El Centro, Calif.	23,996	Fontana, Calif.	37,111
El Cerrito, Calif.	22,731	Forest Park, Ga.	18,782
El Dorado, Ark.	25,270	Forest Park, Ohio	18,675
Elgin, Ill.	63,798	Fort Collins, Colo.	65,092
Elizabeth, N.J.	106,201	Fort Dodge, Iowa	29,423
Elk Grove Village, Ill.	28,907	Fort Lauderdale, Fla.	153,279
Elkhart, Ind.	41,305	Fort Lee, N.J.	32,449
Elmhurst, Ill.	44,276	Fort Myers, Fla.	36,638
Elmira, N.Y.	35,327	Fort Pierce, Fla.	33,802

Fort Smith, Ark.	71,626	Grand Prairie, Tex.	71,462
Fort Walton Beach, Fla.	20,829	Grand Rapids, Mich.	181,843
Fort Wayne, Ind.	172,196	Grandview, Mo.	24,502
Fort Worth, Tex.	385,164	Granite City, Ill.	36,815
Foster City, Calif.	23,287	Great Bend, Kans.	16,608
Fountain Valley, Calif.	55,080	Great Falls, Mont.	56,725
Framingham, Mass.	65,113	Greeley, Colo.	53,006
Frankfort, Ky.	25,973	Green Bay, Wis.	87,899
Franklin, Mass.	18,217	Greenbelt, Md.	17,332
Franklin, Wis.	16,871	Greendale, Wis.	16,928
Franklin Park, Ill.	17,507	Greenfield, Mass.	18,436
Frederick, Md.	28,086	Greenfield, Wis.	31,467
Freeport, Ill.	26,266	Greensboro, N.C.	155,642
Freeport, N.Y.	38,272	Greensburg, Pa.	17,558
Fremont, Calif.	131,945	Greenville, Miss.	40,613
Fremont, Nebr.	23,979	Greenville, N.C.	35,740
Fremont, Ohio	17,834	Greenville, S.C.	58,242
Fresno, Calif.	218,202	Greenville, Tex.	22,161
Fridley, Minn.	30,228	Greenwich, Conn.	59,578
Fullerton, Calif.	102,034	Greenwood, Ind.	19,327
		Greenwood, Miss.	20,115
G		Greenwood, S.C.	21,613
Gadsden, Ala.	47,565	Gresham, Oreg.	33,005
Gahanna, Ohio	18,001	Gretna, La.	20,615
Gainesville, Fla.	81,371	Griffin, Ga.	20,728
Gaithersburg, Md.	26,424	Griffith, Ind.	17,026
Galesburg, Ill.	35,305	Grosse Pointe Woods, Mich.	18,886
Gallatin, Tenn.	17,191	Groton, Conn.	41,062
Gallup, N. Mex.	18,161	Grove City, Ohio	16,816
Galveston, Tex.	61,902	Groves, Tex.	17,090
Gardena, Calif.	45,165	Guilford, Conn.	17,375
Garden City, Kans.	18,256	Gulfport, Miss.	39,676
Garden City, Mich.	35,640		
Garden City, N.Y.	22,927	**H**	
Garden Grove, Calif.	123,351	Hackensack, N.J.	36,039
Gardner, Mass.	17,900	Hagerstown, Md.	34,132
Garfield, N.J.	26,803	Hallandale, Fla.	36,517
Garfield Heights, Ohio	34,938	Haltom City, Tex.	29,014
Garland, Tex.	138,857	Hamden, Conn.	51,071
Gary, Ind.	151,953	Hamilton, Ohio	63,189
Gastonia, N.C.	47,333	Hammond, Ind.	93,714
Germantown, Tenn.	20,459	Hampton, Va.	122,617
Gilroy, Calif.	21,641	Hamtramck, Mich.	21,300
Gladstone, Mo.	24,990	Hanford, Calif.	20,958
Glastonbury, Conn.	24,327	Hannibal, Mo.	18,811
Glen Cove, N.Y.	24,618	Hanover Park, Ill.	28,850
Glendale, Ariz.	97,172	Harlingen, Tex.	43,543
Glendale, Calif.	139,060	Harrisburg, Pa.	53,264
Glendale Heights, Ill.	23,163	Harrison, N.Y.	23,046
Glendora, Calif.	38,654	Harrisonburg, Va.	19,671
Glen Ellyn, Ill.	23,649	Hartford, Conn.	136,392
Glenview, Ill.	32,060	Harvey, Ill.	35,810
Gloucester, Mass.	27,768	Hastings, Nebr.	23,045
Gloversville, N.Y.	17,836	Hattiesburg, Miss.	40,829
Golden Valley, Minn.	22,775	Havelock, N.C.	17,718
Goldsboro, N.C.	31,871	Haverhill, Mass.	46,865
Goose Creek, S.C.	17,811	Hawthorne, Calif.	56,447
Goshen, Ind.	19,665	Hawthorne, N.J.	18,200
Grand Forks, N. Dak.	43,765	Hayward, Calif.	94,167
Grand Island, Nebr.	33,180	Hazel Park, Mich.	20,914
Grand Junction, Colo.	28,144	Hazleton, Pa.	27,318

Helena, Mont.	23,938
Hemet, Calif.	22,454
Hempstead, N.Y.	40,404
Henderson, Ky.	24,834
Henderson, Nev.	24,363
Hendersonville, Tenn.	26,561
Hermosa Beach, Calif.	18,070
Hialeah, Fla.	145,254
Hibbing, Minn.	21,193
Hickory, N.C.	20,757
Highland, Ind.	25,935
Highland Park, Ill.	30,611
Highland Park, Mich.	27,909
High Point, N.C.	63,380
Hillsboro, Oreg.	27,664
Hilo, Hawaii	35,269
Hingham, Mass.	20,339
Hinsdale, Ill.	16,726
Hobart, Ind.	22,987
Hobbs, N. Mex.	29,153
Hoboken, N.J.	42,460
Hoffman Estates, Ill.	37,272
Holland, Mich.	26,281
Hollywood, Fla.	121,323
Holyoke, Mass.	44,678
Homestead, Fla.	20,668
Homewood, Ala.	21,412
Homewood, Ill.	19,724
Honolulu, Hawaii	365,048
Hoover, Ala.	19,792
Hopewell, Va.	23,397
Hopkinsville, Ky.	27,318
Hot Springs, Ark.	35,781
Houma, La.	32,602
Houston, Tex.	1,595,138
Huber Heights, Ohio	35,480
Huntington, W. Va.	63,684
Huntington Beach, Calif.	170,505
Huntington Park, Calif.	46,223
Huntsville, Ala.	142,513
Huntsville, Tex.	23,936
Hurst, Tex.	31,420
Hutchinson, Kans.	40,284

I

Idaho Falls, Idaho	39,590
Imperial Beach, Calif.	22,689
Independence, Mo.	111,806
Indianapolis, Ind.	700,807
Indio, Calif.	21,611
Inglewood, Calif.	94,245
Inkster, Mich.	35,190
Inver Grove Heights, Minn.	17,171
Iowa City, Iowa	50,508
Irvine, Calif.	62,134
Irving, Tex.	109,943
Irvington, N.J.	61,493
Ithaca, N.Y.	28,732

J

Jackson, Mich.	39,739
Jackson, Miss.	202,895
Jackson, Tenn.	49,131
Jacksonville, Ark.	27,589
Jacksonville, Fla.	540,920
Jacksonville, Ill.	20,284
Jacksonville, N.C.	17,056
Jamestown, N.Y.	35,775
Janesville, Wis.	51,071
Jefferson City, Mo.	33,619
Jeffersonville, Ind.	21,220
Jennings, Mo.	17,026
Jersey City, N.J.	223,532
Johnson City, N.Y.	17,126
Johnson City, Tenn.	39,753
Johnston, R.I.	24,907
Johnstown, Pa.	35,496
Joliet, Ill.	77,956
Jonesboro, Ark.	31,530
Joplin, Mo.	38,893
Junction City, Kans.	19,305
Juneau, Alaska	19,528

K

Kailua, Hawaii	35,812
Kalamazoo, Mich.	79,722
Kaneohe, Hawaii	29,919
Kankakee, Ill.	30,141
Kansas City, Kans.	161,087
Kansas City, Mo.	448,159
Kearney, Nebr.	21,158
Kearny, N.J.	35,735
Keene, N.H.	21,449
Kenmore, N.Y.	18,474
Kenner, La.	66,382
Kennewick, Wash.	34,397
Kenosha, Wis.	77,685
Kent, Ohio	26,164
Kent, Wash.	23,152
Kentwood, Mich.	30,438
Kettering, Ohio	61,186
Key West, Fla.	24,382
Killeen, Tex.	46,296
Kingsport, Tenn.	32,027
Kingston, N.Y.	24,481
Kingsville, Tex.	28,808
Kinston, N.C.	25,234
Kirkland, Wash.	18,779
Kirksville, Mo.	17,167
Kirkwood, Mo.	27,987
Klamath Falls, Oreg.	16,661
Knoxville, Tenn.	175,030
Kokomo, Ind.	47,808

L

La Canada Flintridge, Calif.	20,153
Lackawanna, N.Y.	22,701
La Crosse, Wis.	48,347
Lafayette, Calif.	20,879
Lafayette, Ind.	43,011
Lafayette, La.	81,961
La Grange, Ga.	24,204

Laguna Beach, Calif.	17,901
La Habra, Calif.	45,232
Lake Charles, La.	75,226
Lake Jackson, Tex.	19,102
Lakeland, Fla.	47,406
Lake Oswego, Oreg.	22,868
Lakewood, Calif.	74,654
Lakewood, Colo.	112,860
Lakewood, Ohio	61,963
Lake Worth, Fla.	27,048
La Mesa, Calif.	50,308
La Mirada, Calif.	40,986
Lancaster, Calif.	48,027
Lancaster, Ohio	34,953
Lancaster, Pa.	54,725
Lansdale, Pa.	16,526
Lansing, Ill.	29,039
Lansing, Mich.	130,414
La Porte, Ind.	21,796
La Puente, Calif.	30,882
Laramie, Wyo.	24,410
Laredo, Tex.	91,449
Largo, Fla.	58,977
Las Cruces, N. Mex.	45,086
Las Vegas, Nev.	164,674
Lauderdale Lakes, Fla.	25,426
Lauderhill, Fla.	37,271
Laurel, Miss.	21,897
La Verne, Calif.	23,508
Lawndale, Calif.	23,460
Lawrence, Ind.	25,591
Lawrence, Kans.	52,738
Lawrence, Mass.	63,175
Lawton, Okla.	80,054
Layton, Utah	22,862
League City, Tex.	16,578
Leavenworth, Kans.	33,656
Lebanon, Pa.	25,711
Lee's Summit, Mo.	28,741
Lemon Grove, Calif.	20,780
Lenexa, Kans.	18,639
Leominster, Mass.	34,508
Lewiston, Idaho	27,986
Lewiston, Me.	40,481
Lewisville, Tex.	24,273
Lexington, Ky.	204,165
Lexington, Mass.	29,479
Libertyville, Ill.	16,520
Lima, Ohio	47,381
Lincoln, Nebr.	171,932
Lincoln, R.I.	16,949
Lincoln Park, Mich.	45,105
Linden, N.J.	37,836
Lindenhurst, N.Y.	26,919
Lindenwold, N.J.	18,196
Little Rock, Ark.	158,461
Littleton, Colo.	28,631
Livermore, Calif.	48,349
Livonia, Mich.	104,814
Lockport, N.Y.	24,844
Lodi, Calif.	35,221
Lodi, N.J.	23,956
Logan, Utah	26,844
Logansport, Ind.	17,899
Lombard, Ill.	37,295
Lomita, Calif.	18,807
Lompoc, Calif.	26,267
Long Beach, Calif.	361,334
Long Beach, N.Y.	34,073
Long Branch, N.J.	29,819
Longmont, Colo.	42,942
Longview, Tex.	62,762
Longview, Wash.	31,052
Lorain, Ohio	75,416
Los Altos, Calif.	25,769
Los Angeles, Calif.	2,966,763
Los Gatos, Calif.	26,593
Louisville, Ky.	298,451
Loveland, Colo.	30,244
Lowell, Mass.	92,418
Lubbock, Tex.	173,979
Ludlow, Mass.	18,150
Lufkin, Tex.	28,562
Lumberton, N.C.	18,241
Lynbrook, N.Y.	20,424
Lynchburg, Va.	66,743
Lyndhurst, Ohio	18,092
Lynn, Mass.	78,471
Lynnwood, Wash.	22,641
Lynwood, Calif.	48,548

M

McAlester, Okla.	17,255
McAllen, Tex.	66,281
McKeesport, Pa.	31,012
Macomb, Ill.	19,863
Macon, Ga.	116,896
Madera, Calif.	21,732
Madison, Wis.	170,616
Madison Heights, Mich.	35,375
Madisonville, Ky.	16,979
Malden, Mass.	53,386
Mamaroneck, N.Y.	17,616
Manchester, Conn.	49,761
Manchester, N.H.	90,936
Manhattan, Kans.	32,644
Manhattan Beach, Calif.	31,542
Manitowoc, Wis.	32,547
Mankato, Minn.	28,651
Mansfield, Conn.	20,634
Mansfield, Ohio	53,927
Manteca, Calif.	24,925
Maple Grove, Minn.	20,525
Maple Heights, Ohio	29,735
Maplewood, Minn.	26,990
Marblehead, Mass.	20,126
Margate, Fla.	36,044
Marietta, Ga.	30,829
Marina, Calif.	20,647
Marion, Ind.	35,874
Marion, Iowa	19,474
Marion, Ohio	37,040

Marlborough, Mass.	30,617	Missouri City, Tex.	24,533
Marquette, Mich.	23,288	Mobile, Ala.	200,452
Marshall, Tex.	24,921	Modesto, Calif.	106,105
Marshalltown, Iowa	26,938	Moline, Ill.	45,709
Marshfield, Mass.	20,916	Monroe, La.	57,597
Marshfield, Wis.	18,290	Monroe, Mich.	23,531
Martinez, Calif.	22,582	Monroeville, Pa.	30,977
Martinsville, Va.	18,149	Monrovia, Calif.	30,531
Maryville, Tenn.	17,480	Montclair, Calif.	22,628
Mason City, Iowa	30,144	Montclair, N.J.	38,321
Massapequa Park, N.Y.	19,779	Montebello, Calif.	52,929
Massillon, Ohio	30,557	Monterey, Calif.	27,558
Mattoon, Ill.	19,055	Monterey Park, Calif.	54,338
Mayfield Heights, Ohio	21,550	Montgomery, Ala.	177,857
Maywood, Calif.	21,810	Moore, Okla.	35,063
Maywood, Ill.	27,998	Moorhead, Minn.	29,998
Medford, Mass.	58,076	Morgan Hill, Calif.	17,060
Medford, Oreg.	39,603	Morgantown, W. Va.	27,605
Melbourne, Fla.	46,536	Morristown, N.J.	16,614
Melrose, Mass.	30,055	Morristown, Tenn.	19,683
Melrose Park, Ill.	20,735	Morton Grove, Ill.	23,747
Memphis, Tenn.	646,356	Moscow, Idaho	16,513
Menlo Park, Calif.	25,673	Moss Point, Miss.	18,998
Menomonee Falls, Wis.	27,845	Mountain Brook, Ala.	19,718
Mentor, Ohio	42,065	Mountain View, Calif.	58,655
Merced, Calif.	36,499	Mount Clemens, Mich.	18,806
Mercer Island, Wash.	21,522	Mountlake Terrace, Wash.	16,534
Meriden, Conn.	57,118	Mount Pleasant, Mich.	23,746
Meridian, Miss.	46,577	Mount Prospect, Ill.	52,634
Merrillville, Ind.	27,677	Mount Vernon, Ill.	17,193
Mesa, Ariz.	152,453	Mount Vernon, N.Y.	66,713
Mesquite, Tex.	67,053	Muncie, Ind.	77,216
Methuen, Mass.	36,701	Mundelein, Ill.	17,053
Miami, Fla.	346,865	Munster, Ind.	20,671
Miami Beach, Fla.	96,298	Murfreesboro, Tenn.	32,845
Michigan City, Ind.	36,850	Murray, Utah	25,750
Middletown, Conn.	39,040	Muscatine, Iowa	23,467
Middletown, N.Y.	21,454	Muskegon, Mich.	40,823
Middletown, Ohio	43,719	Muskogee, Okla.	40,011
Middletown, R.I.	17,216	Myrtle Beach, S.C.	18,446
Midland, Mich.	37,250		
Midland, Tex.	70,525	**N**	
Midwest City, Okla.	49,559	Nacogdoches, Tex.	27,149
Milford, Conn.	50,898	Nampa, Idaho	25,112
Milford, Mass.	23,390	Napa, Calif.	50,879
Mililani, Hawaii	21,365	Naperville, Ill.	42,330
Millbrae, Calif.	20,058	Naples, Fla.	17,581
Millington, Tenn.	20,236	Nashua, N.H.	67,865
Millville, N.J.	24,815	Nashville, Tenn.	446,027
Milpitas, Calif.	37,820	Natchez, Miss.	22,015
Milton, Mass.	25,860	Natchitoches, La.	16,664
Milwaukee, Wis.	636,212	Natick, Mass.	29,461
Milwaukie, Oreg.	17,931	National City, Calif.	48,772
Mineola, N.Y.	20,757	Naugatuck, Conn.	26,456
Minneapolis, Minn.	370,951	Nederland, Tex.	16,855
Minnetonka, Minn.	38,683	Needham, Mass.	27,901
Minot, N. Dak.	32,843	Neenah, Wis.	22,432
Miramar, Fla.	32,813	New Albany, Ind.	37,103
Mishawaka, Ind.	40,201	Newark, Calif.	32,126
Mission, Tex.	22,589	Newark, Del.	25,247
Missoula, Mont.	33,388	Newark, N.J.	329,248

Newark, Ohio	41,200
New Bedford, Mass.	98,478
New Berlin, Wis.	30,529
New Braunfels, Tex.	22,402
New Brighton, Minn.	23,269
New Britain, Conn.	73,840
New Brunswick, N.J.	41,442
Newburgh, N.Y.	23,438
New Canaan, Conn.	17,931
New Castle, Ind.	20,056
New Castle, Pa.	33,621
New Haven, Conn.	126,109
New Hope, Minn.	23,087
New Iberia, La.	32,766
Newington, Conn.	28,841
New Kensington, Pa.	17,660
New London, Conn.	28,842
New Milford, Conn.	19,420
New Milford, N.J.	16,876
New Orleans, La.	557,515
New Philadelphia, Ohio	16,883
Newport, Ky.	21,587
Newport, R.I.	29,259
Newport Beach, Calif.	62,556
Newport News, Va.	144,903
New Rochelle, N.Y.	70,794
Newton, Mass.	83,622
Newtown, Conn.	19,107
New York City, N.Y.	7,071,639
Bronx	1,168,972
Brooklyn	2,230,936
Manhattan	1,428,285
Queens	1,891,325
Richmond	352,121
Niagara Falls, N.Y.	71,384
Niles, Ill.	30,363
Niles, Ohio	23,088
Norco, Calif.	21,126
Norfolk, Nebr.	19,449
Norfolk, Va.	266,979
Normal, Ill.	35,672
Norman, Okla.	68,020
Norristown, Pa.	34,684
North Adams, Mass.	18,063
Northampton, Mass.	29,286
North Andover, Mass.	20,129
North Arlington, N.J.	16,587
North Attleboro, Mass.	21,095
Northbrook, Ill.	30,778
North Charleston, S.C.	62,534
North Chicago, Ill.	38,774
Northglenn, Colo.	29,847
North Haven, Conn.	22,080
North Kingstown, R.I.	21,938
North Las Vegas, Nev.	42,739
North Lauderdale, Fla.	18,479
North Little Rock, Ark.	64,288
North Miami, Fla.	42,566
North Miami Beach, Fla.	36,553
North Olmsted, Ohio	36,486
North Plainfield, N.J.	19,108

North Platte, Nebr.	24,479
North Providence, R.I.	29,188
North Richland Hills, Tex.	30,592
North Ridgeville, Ohio	21,522
North Royalton, Ohio	17,671
North Tonawanda, N.Y.	35,760
Norton Shores, Mich.	22,025
Norwalk, Calif.	85,286
Norwalk, Conn.	77,767
Norwich, Conn.	38,074
Norwood, Mass.	29,711
Norwood, Ohio	26,342
Novato, Calif.	43,916
Novi, Mich.	22,525
Nutley, N.J.	28,998

O

Oak Creek, Wis.	16,932
Oak Forest, Ill.	26,096
Oakland, Calif.	339,288
Oakland Park, Fla.	23,035
Oak Lawn, Ill.	60,590
Oak Park, Ill.	54,887
Oak Park, Mich.	31,537
Oak Ridge, Tenn.	27,662
Ocala, Fla.	37,170
Oceanside, Calif.	76,698
Odessa, Tex.	90,027
Ogden, Utah	64,407
Oklahoma City, Okla.	403,213
Olathe, Kans.	37,258
Olean, N.Y.	18,207
Olympia, Wash.	27,447
Omaha, Nebr.	314,255
Ontario, Calif.	88,820
Opelika, Ala.	21,896
Opelousas, La.	18,903
Orange, Calif.	91,788
Orange, N.J.	31,136
Orange, Tex.	23,628
Oregon, Ohio	18,675
Orem, Utah	52,399
Orlando, Fla.	128,291
Orland Park, Ill.	23,045
Ormond Beach, Fla.	21,378
Oshkosh, Wis.	49,620
Ossining, N.Y.	20,196
Oswego, N.Y.	19,793
Ottawa, Ill.	18,166
Ottumwa, Iowa	27,381
Overland, Mo.	19,620
Overland Park, Kans.	81,784
Owatonna, Minn.	18,632
Owensboro, Ky.	54,450
Oxford, Ohio	17,655
Oxnard, Calif.	108,195

P

Pacifica, Calif.	36,866
Paducah, Ky.	29,315
Palatine, Ill.	32,166

Palm Bay, Fla.	18,560
Palm Springs, Calif.	32,271
Palo Alto, Calif.	55,225
Palos Hills, Ill.	16,654
Pampa, Tex.	21,396
Panama City, Fla.	33,346
Paradise, Calif.	22,571
Paramount, Calif.	36,407
Paramus, N.J.	26,474
Paris, Tex.	25,498
Parkersburg, W. Va.	39,967
Park Forest, Ill.	26,222
Park Ridge, Ill.	38,704
Parma, Ohio	92,548
Parma Heights, Ohio	23,112
Pasadena, Calif.	119,374
Pasadena, Tex.	112,560
Pascagoula, Miss.	29,318
Pasco, Wash.	17,944
Passaic, N.J.	52,463
Paterson, N.J.	137,970
Pawtucket, R.I.	71,204
Peabody, Mass.	45,976
Pearl, Miss.	20,778
Pearl City, Hawaii	42,575
Peekskill, N.Y.	18,236
Pekin, Ill.	33,967
Pembroke Pines, Fla.	35,776
Pensacola, Fla.	57,619
Peoria, Ill.	124,160
Perth Amboy, N.J.	38,951
Petaluma, Calif.	33,834
Petersburg, Va.	41,055
Pharr, Tex.	21,381
Phenix City, Ala.	26,928
Philadelphia, Pa.	1,688,210
Phillipsburg, N.J.	16,647
Phoenix, Ariz.	789,704
Pico Rivera, Calif.	53,459
Pine Bluff, Ark.	56,636
Pinellas Park, Fla.	32,811
Piqua, Ohio	20,480
Pittsburg, Calif.	33,034
Pittsburg, Kans.	18,770
Pittsburgh, Pa.	423,938
Pittsfield, Mass.	51,974
Placentia, Calif.	35,041
Plainfield, N.J.	45,555
Plainview, Tex.	22,187
Plano, Tex.	72,331
Plantation, Fla.	48,501
Plant City, Fla.	19,270
Plattsburgh, N.Y.	21,057
Pleasant Hill, Calif.	25,124
Pleasanton, Calif	35,160
Plum, Pa.	25,390
Plymouth, Mass.	35,913
Plymouth, Minn.	31,615
Pocatello, Idaho	46,340
Point Pleasant, N.J.	17,747
Pomona, Calif.	92,742

Pompano Beach, Fla.	52,618
Ponca City, Okla.	26,238
Pontiac, Mich.	76,715
Poplar Bluff, Mo.	17,139
Portage, Ind.	27,409
Portage, Mich.	38,147
Port Angeles, Wash.	17,311
Port Arthur, Tex.	61,251
Port Chester, N.Y.	23,565
Porterville, Calif.	19,707
Port Hueneme, Calif.	17,803
Port Huron, Mich.	33,981
Portland, Me.	61,572
Portland, Oreg.	366,383
Port Orange, Fla.	18,756
Portsmouth, N.H.	26,254
Portsmouth, Ohio	25,943
Portsmouth, Va.	104,577
Pottstown, Pa.	22,729
Pottsville, Pa.	18,195
Poughkeepsie, N.Y.	29,757
Prairie Village, Kans.	24,657
Prattville, Ala.	18,647
Prescott, Ariz.	20,055
Prichard, Ala.	39,541
Providence, R.I.	156,804
Provo, Utah	73,907
Pueblo, Colo.	101,686
Pullman, Wash.	23,579
Puyallup, Wash.	18,251

Q

Quincy, Ill.	42,554
Quincy, Mass.	84,743

R

Racine, Wis.	85,725
Rahway, N.J.	26,723
Raleigh, N.C.	150,255
Rancho Cucamonga, Calif.	55,250
Rancho Palos Verdes, Calif.	36,577
Randolph, Mass.	28,218
Rantoul, Ill.	20,161
Rapid City, S. Dak.	46,492
Raytown, Mo.	31,759
Reading, Mass.	22,678
Reading, Pa.	78,686
Redding, Calif.	41,995
Redlands, Calif.	43,619
Redmond, Wash.	23,318
Redondo Beach, Calif.	57,102
Redwood City, Calif.	54,951
Reno, Nev.	100,756
Renton, Wash.	30,612
Revere, Mass.	42,423
Reynoldsburg, Ohio	20,661
Rialto, Calif.	37,474
Richardson, Tex.	72,496
Richfield, Minn.	37,851
Richland, Wash.	33,578
Richmond, Calif.	74,676

Richmond, Ind.	41,349	San Angelo, Tex.	73,240
Richmond, Ky.	21,705	San Antonio, Tex.	785,880
Richmond, Va.	219,214	San Benito, Tex.	17,988
Ridgefield, Conn.	20,120	San Bernardino, Calif.	117,490
Ridgewood, N.J.	25,208	San Bruno, Calif.	35,417
Riverside, Calif.	170,876	San Carlos, Calif.	24,710
Riviera Beach, Fla.	26,489	San Clemente, Calif.	27,325
Roanoke, Va.	100,220	San Diego, Calif.	875,538
Rochester, Minn.	57,890	San Dimas, Calif.	24,014
Rochester, N.H.	21,560	Sandusky, Ohio	31,360
Rochester, N.Y.	241,741	Sandy City, Utah	50,546
Rockford, Ill.	139,712	San Fernando, Calif.	17,731
Rock Hill, S.C.	35,344	Sanford, Fla.	23,176
Rock Island, Ill.	47,036	Sanford, Me.	18,020
Rock Springs, Wyo.	19,458	San Francisco, Calif.	678,974
Rockville, Md.	43,811	San Gabriel, Calif.	30,072
Rockville Centre, N.Y.	25,412	San Jose, Calif.	636,550
Rocky Mount, N.C.	41,283	San Juan Capistrano, Calif.	18,959
Rocky River, Ohio	21,084	San Leandro, Calif.	63,952
Rogers, Ark.	17,429	San Luis Obispo, Calif.	34,252
Rohnert Park, Calif.	22,965	San Marcos, Calif.	17,479
Rolling Meadows, Ill.	20,167	San Marcos, Tex.	23,420
Rome, Ga.	29,654	San Mateo, Calif.	77,561
Rome, N.Y.	43,826	San Pablo, Calif.	19,750
Romulus, Mich.	24,857	San Rafael, Calif.	44,700
Roseburg, Oreg.	16,644	Santa Ana, Calif.	203,713
Roselle, Ill.	16,948	Santa Barbara, Calif.	74,542
Roselle, N.J.	20,641	Santa Clara, Calif.	87,746
Rosemead, Calif.	42,604	Santa Cruz, Calif.	41,483
Rosenberg, Tex.	17,995	Santa Fe, N. Mex.	48,953
Roseville, Calif.	24,347	Santa Maria, Calif.	39,685
Roseville, Mich.	54,311	Santa Monica, Calif.	88,314
Roseville, Minn.	35,820	Santa Paula, Calif.	20,552
Roswell, Ga.	23,337	Santa Rosa, Calif.	83,205
Roswell, N. Mex.	39,676	Sarasota, Fla.	48,868
Roy, Utah	19,694	Saratoga, Calif.	29,261
Royal Oak, Mich.	70,893	Saratoga Springs, N.Y.	23,906
Ruston, La.	20,585	Saugus, Mass.	24,746
Rutherford, N.J.	19,068	Savannah, Ga.	141,390
Rutland, Vt.	18,436	Sayreville, N.J.	29,969
		Scarsdale, N.Y.	17,650
S		Schaumburg, Ill.	53,305
Sacramento, Calif.	275,741	Schenectady, N.Y.	67,972
Saginaw, Mich.	77,508	Schofield Barracks, Hawaii	18,851
St. Charles, Ill.	17,492	Scituate, Mass.	17,317
St. Charles, Mo.	37,379	Scottsdale, Ariz.	88,412
St. Clair Shores, Mich.	76,210	Scranton, Pa.	88,117
St. Cloud, Minn.	42,566	Seal Beach, Calif.	25,975
St. Joseph, Mo.	76,691	Seaside, Calif.	36,567
St. Louis, Mo.	453,085	Seattle, Wash.	493,846
St. Louis Park, Minn.	42,931	Sedalia, Mo.	20,927
St. Paul, Minn.	270,230	Seguin, Tex.	17,854
St. Petersburg, Fla.	238,647	Selma, Ala.	26,684
Salem, Mass.	38,220	Shaker Heights, Ohio	32,487
Salem, N.H.	24,124	Sharon, Pa.	19,057
Salem, Oreg.	89,233	Shawnee, Kans.	29,653
Salem, Va.	23,958	Shawnee, Okla.	26,506
Salina, Kans.	41,843	Sheboygan, Wis.	48,085
Salinas, Calif.	80,479	Shelton, Conn.	31,314
Salisbury, N.C.	22,677	Sherman, Tex.	30,413
Salt Lake City, Utah	163,033	Shively, Ky.	16,819

Shoreview, Minn.	17,300
Shreveport, La.	205,820
Shrewsbury, Mass.	22,674
Sidney, Ohio	17,657
Sierra Vista, Ariz.	24,937
Sikeston, Mo.	17,431
Simi Valley, Calif.	77,500
Simsbury, Conn.	21,161
Sioux City, Iowa	82,003
Sioux Falls, S. Dak.	81,343
Skokie, Ill.	60,278
Slidell, La.	26,718
Smithfield, R.I.	16,886
Smyrna, Ga.	20,312
Somerset, Mass.	18,813
Somerville, Mass.	77,372
South Bend, Ind.	109,727
Southbridge, Mass.	16,665
South El Monte, Calif.	16,623
South Euclid, Ohio	25,713
Southfield, Mich.	75,568
South Gate, Calif.	66,784
Southgate, Mich.	32,058
South Holland, Ill.	24,977
Southington, Conn.	36,879
South Kingstown, R.I.	20,414
South Lake Tahoe, Calif.	20,681
South Milwaukee, Wis.	21,069
South Pasadena, Calif.	22,681
South Plainfield, N.J.	20,521
South Portland, Me.	22,712
South St. Paul, Minn.	21,235
South San Francisco, Calif.	49,393
South Windsor, Conn.	17,198
Sparks, Nev.	40,780
Spartanburg, S.C.	43,968
Spokane, Wash.	171,300
Springdale, Ark.	23,458
Springfield, Ill.	99,637
Springfield, Mass.	152,319
Springfield, Mo.	133,116
Springfield, Ohio	72,563
Springfield, Oreg.	41,621
Spring Valley, N.Y.	20,537
Stamford, Conn.	102,453
Stanton, Calif.	23,723
State College, Pa.	36,130
Statesville, N.C.	18,622
Staunton, Va.	21,857
Sterling Heights, Mich.	108,999
Steubenville, Ohio	26,400
Stevens Point, Wis.	22,970
Stillwater, Okla.	38,268
Stockton, Calif.	149,779
Stoneham, Mass.	21,424
Stoughton, Mass.	26,710
Stow, Ohio	25,303
Stratford, Conn.	50,541
Streamwood, Ill.	23,456
Strongsville, Ohio	28,577
Suffolk, Va.	47,621

Sulphur, La.	19,709
Summit, N.J.	21,071
Sumter, S.C.	24,890
Sunnyvale, Calif.	106,618
Sunrise, Fla.	39,681
Superior, Wis.	29,571
Syracuse, N.Y.	170,105

T

Tacoma, Wash.	158,501
Talladega, Ala.	19,128
Tallahassee, Fla.	81,548
Tamarac, Fla.	29,376
Tampa, Fla.	271,523
Taunton, Mass.	45,001
Taylor, Mich.	77,568
Tempe, Ariz.	106,743
Temple, Tex.	42,483
Temple City, Calif.	28,972
Terre Haute, Ind.	61,125
Tewksbury, Mass.	24,635
Texarkana, Ark.	21,459
Texarkana, Tex.	31,271
Texas City, Tex.	41,403
Thomasville, Ga.	18,463
Thornton, Colo.	40,343
Thousand Oaks, Calif.	77,072
Tiffin, Ohio	19,549
Tinley Park, Ill.	26,171
Titusville, Fla.	31,910
Toledo, Ohio	354,635
Tonawanda, N.Y.	18,693
Topeka, Kans.	115,266
Torrance, Calif.	131,497
Torrington, Conn.	30,987
Tracy, Calif.	18,428
Trenton, Mich.	22,762
Trenton, N.J.	92,124
Troy, Mich.	67,102
Troy, N.Y.	56,638
Troy, Ohio	19,086
Trumbull, Conn.	32,989
Tucson, Ariz.	330,537
Tulare, Calif.	22,475
Tulsa, Okla.	360,919
Tupelo, Miss.	23,905
Turlock, Calif.	26,287
Tuscaloosa, Ala.	75,211
Tustin, Calif.	32,317
Twin Falls, Idaho	26,209
Tyler, Tex.	70,508

U

Union City, Calif.	39,406
Union City, N.J.	55,593
University City, Mo.	42,738
University Park, Tex.	22,254
Upland, Calif.	47,647
Upper Arlington, Ohio	35,648
Urbana, Ill.	35,978
Urbandale, Iowa	17,869

Utica, N.Y.	75,632	Westchester, Ill.	17,730
		West Chester, Pa.	17,435
V		West Covina, Calif.	80,291
Vacaville, Calif.	43,367	West Des Moines, Iowa	21,894
Valdosta, Ga.	37,596	Westerly, R.I.	18,580
Vallejo, Calif.	80,303	Westerville, Ohio	23,414
Valley Stream, N.Y.	35,769	Westfield, Mass.	36,465
Valparaiso, Ind.	22,247	Westfield, N.J.	30,447
Vancouver, Wash.	42,834	West Hartford, Conn.	61,301
Ventura (San Buenaventura),	74,474	West Haven, Conn.	53,184
Calif.		West Jordan, Utah	27,192
Vernon, Conn.	27,974	West Lafayette, Ind.	21,247
Vicksburg, Miss.	25,434	Westlake, Ohio	19,483
Victoria, Tex.	50,695	Westland, Mich.	84,603
Villa Park, Ill.	23,185	West Memphis, Ark.	28,138
Vincennes, Ind.	20,857	West Mifflin, Pa.	26,279
Vineland, N.J.	53,753	Westminster, Calif.	71,133
Virginia Beach, Va.	262,199	Westminster, Colo.	50,211
Visalia, Calif.	49,729	Westmont, Ill.	16,718
Vista, Calif.	35,834	West New York, N.J.	39,194
		West Orange, N.J.	39,510
W		West Palm Beach, Fla.	63,305
Waco, Tex.	101,261	Westport, Conn.	25,290
Wahiawa, Hawaii	16,911	West St. Paul, Minn.	18,527
Waipahu, Hawaii	29,139	West Springfield, Mass.	27,042
Wakefield, Mass.	24,895	West Warwick, R.I.	27,026
Walla Walla, Wash.	25,618	Wethersfield, Conn.	26,031
Wallingford, Conn.	37,274	Weymouth, Mass.	55,601
Walnut Creek, Calif.	53,643	Wheaton, Ill.	43,043
Walpole, Mass.	18,859	Wheat Ridge, Colo.	30,293
Waltham, Mass.	58,200	Wheeling, Ill.	23,266
Wareham, Mass.	18,457	Wheeling, W. Va.	43,070
Warner Robins, Ga.	39,893	White Bear Lake, Minn.	22,538
Warren, Mich.	161,134	Whitehall, Ohio	21,299
Warren, Ohio	56,629	White Plains, N.Y.	46,999
Warrensville Heights, Ohio	16,565	Whittier, Calif.	69,717
Warwick, R.I.	87,123	Wichita, Kans.	279,272
Washington, D.C.	637,651	Wichita Falls, Tex.	94,201
Washington, Pa.	18,363	Wickliffe, Ohio	16,790
Waterbury, Conn.	103,266	Wilkes-Barre, Pa.	51,551
Waterford, Conn.	17,843	Wilkinsburg, Pa.	23,669
Waterloo, Iowa	75,985	Williamsport, Pa.	33,401
Watertown, Conn.	19,489	Willoughby, Ohio	19,329
Watertown, Mass.	34,384	Willowick, Ohio	17,834
Watertown, N.Y.	27,861	Wilmette, Ill.	28,229
Watertown, Wis.	18,113	Wilmington, Del.	70,195
Waterville, Me.	17,779	Wilmington, Mass.	17,471
Watsonville, Calif.	23,543	Wilmington, N.C.	44,000
Waukegan, Ill.	67,653	Wilson, N.C.	34,424
Waukesha, Wis.	50,319	Winchester, Mass.	20,701
Wausau, Wis.	32,426	Winchester, Va.	20,217
Wauwatosa, Wis.	51,308	Windham, Conn.	21,062
Waycross, Ga.	19,371	Windsor, Conn.	25,204
Wayne, Mich.	21,159	Winona, Minn.	25,075
Webster Groves, Mo.	23,097	Winston-Salem, N.C.	131,885
Weirton, W. Va.	24,736	Winter Haven, Fla.	21,119
Wellesley, Mass.	27,209	Winter Park, Fla.	22,339
Wenatchee, Wash.	17,257	Winthrop, Mass.	19,294
Weslaco, Tex.	19,331	Wisconsin Rapids, Wis.	17,995
West Allis, Wis.	63,982	Woburn, Mass.	36,626
West Bend, Wis.	21,484	Woodland, Calif.	30,235

Woodridge, Ill. 22,322
Woonsocket, R.I. 45,914
Wooster, Ohio 19,289
Worcester, Mass. 161,799
Wyandotte, Mich. 34,006
Wyoming, Mich. 59,616

X

Xenia, Ohio 24,653

Y

Yakima, Wash. 49,826
Yarmouth, Mass. 18,449

Yonkers, N.Y. 195,351
Yorba Linda, Calif. 28,254
York, Pa. 44,619
Youngstown, Ohio 115,436
Ypsilanti, Mich. 24,031
Yuba City, Calif. 18,736
Yukon, Okla. 17,112
Yuma, Ariz. 42,433

Z

Zanesville, Ohio 28,655
Zion, Ill. 17,861

Population of the United States in 1980
SUMMARY BY STATES AND DEPENDENCIES
(Figures in parentheses give rank of states in population)

THE STATES AND THE DISTRICT OF COLUMBIA

Alabama	(22) . . .	3,893,888
Alaska	(50) . . .	586,412
Arizona	(29) . . .	2,718,215
Arkansas	(33) . . .	2,286,435
California	(1) . . .	23,667,902
Colorado	(28) . . .	2,889,964
Connecticut	(25) . . .	3,107,576
Delaware	(47) . . .	594,338
District of Columbia	. . . .	638,333
Florida	(7) . . .	9,746,324
Georgia	(13) . . .	5,463,105
Hawaii	(39) . . .	964,691
Idaho	(41) . . .	943,935
Illinois	(5) . . .	11,426,518
Indiana	(12) . . .	5,490,224
Iowa	(27) . . .	2,913,808
Kansas	(32) . . .	2,363,679
Kentucky	(23) . . .	3,660,777
Louisiana	(19) . . .	4,205,900
Maine	(38) . . .	1,124,660
Maryland	(18) . . .	4,216,975
Massachusetts	(11) . . .	5,737,037
Michigan	(8) . . .	9,262,078
Minnesota	(21) . . .	4,075,970
Mississippi	(31) . . .	2,520,638
Missouri	(15) . . .	4,916,686
Montana	(44) . . .	786,690
Nebraska	(35) . . .	1,569,825
Nevada	(43) . . .	800,493
New Hampshire	(42) . . .	920,610
New Jersey	(9) . . .	7,364,823
New Mexico	(37) . . .	1,302,894
New York	(2) . . .	17,558,072
North Carolina	(10) . . .	5,881,766
North Dakota	(46) . . .	652,717
Ohio	(6) . . .	10,797,630
Oklahoma	(26) . . .	3,025,290
Oregon	(30) . . .	2,633,105
Pennsylvania	(4) . . .	11,863,895
Rhode Island	(40) . . .	947,154
South Carolina	(24) . . .	3,121,820
South Dakota	(45) . . .	690,768
Tennessee	(17) . . .	4,591,120
Texas	(3) . . .	14,229,191
Utah	(36) . . .	1,461,037
Vermont	(48) . . .	511,456
Virginia	(14) . . .	5,356,818
Washington	(20) . . .	4,132,156
West Virginia	(34) . . .	1,949,644
Wisconsin	(16) . . .	4,705,767
Wyoming	(49) . . .	469,557
TOTAL		226,545,805

DEPENDENCIES

American Samoa	32,297
Guam	105,979
Puerto Rico	3,196,520
Virgin Islands of the U.S.	96,569
Other (Trust Territory of the Pacific Islands, etc.)	132,929
TOTAL	3,564,294
TOTAL U.S. & Dependencies	230,110,099

Population of Places in Canada
Having 16,500 or More Inhabitants in 1981

Ajax, Ont.	25,475	Beloeil, Que.	17,540
Alma, Que.	26,322	Boucherville, Que.	29,704
Anjou, Que.	37,346	Brampton, Ont.	149,030
Aylmer, Que.	26,695	Brandon, Man.	36,242
Barrie, Ont.	38,423	Brantford, Ont.	74,315
Beaconsfield, Que.	19,613	Brockville, Ont.	19,896
Beauport, Que.	60,447	Brossard, Que.	52,232
Belleville, Ont.	34,881	Burlington, Ont.	114,853

Burnaby, B.C.	136,494	Markham, Ont.	77,037
Caledon, Ont.	26,645	Mascouche, Que.	20,345
Calgary, Alta.	592,743	Medicine Hat, Alta.	40,380
Cambridge, Ont.	77,183	Milton, Ont.	28,067
Cap-de-la-Madeleine,		Mississauga, Ont.	315,056
Que.	32,626	Moncton, N.B.	54,743
Charlesbourg, Que.	68,326	Montreal, Que.	980,354
Châteauguay, Que.	36,928	Montreal-Nord, Que.	94,914
Chatham, Ont.	40,952	Mont-Royal, Que.	19,247
Chicoutimi, Que.	60,064	Moose Jaw, Sask.	33,941
Chilliwack, B.C.	40,642	Nanaimo, B.C.	47,069
Corner Brook, Nfld.	24,339	Nanticoke, Ont.	19,816
Cornwall, Ont.	46,144	Nepean, Ont.	84,361
Côte-St-Luc, Que.	27,531	Newcastle, Ont.	32,229
Dartmouth, N.S.	62,277	Newmarket, Ont.	29,753
Delta, B.C.	74,692	New Westminster,	
Dollard-des-Ormeaux,		B.C.	38,550
Que.	39,940	Niagara Falls, Ont.	70,960
Dorval, Que.	17,722	North Bay, Ont.	51,268
Drummondville, Que.	27,347	North Vancouver, B.C.	33,952
Dundas, Ont.	19,586	North York, Ont.	559,521
East York, Ont.	101,974	Oakville, Ont.	75,773
Edmonton, Alta.	532,246	Orillia, Ont.	23,955
Elliot Lake, Ont.	16,723	Oshawa, Ont.	117,519
Etobicoke, Ont.	298,713	Ottawa, Ont.	295,163
Fort Erie, Ont.	24,096	Outremont, Que.	24,338
Fort McMurray, Alta.	31,000	Owen Sound, Ont.	19,883
Fredericton, N.B.	43,723	Penticton, B.C.	23,181
Gaspé, Que.	17,261	Peterborough, Ont.	60,620
Gatineau, Que.	74,988	Pickering, Ont.	37,754
Glace Bay, N.S.	21,466	Pierrefonds, Que.	38,390
Gloucester, Ont.	72,859	Pointe-aux-Trembles,	
Granby, Que.	38,069	Que.	36,270
Grande Prairie, Alta.	24,263	Pointe-Claire, Que.	24,571
Greenfield Park, Que.	18,527	Port Alberni, B.C.	19,892
Guelph, Ont.	71,207	Port Colborne, Ont.	19,225
Haldimand, Ont.	16,866	Port Coquitlam, B.C.	27,535
Halifax, N.S.	114,594	Prince Albert, Sask.	31,380
Halton Hills, Ont.	35,190	Prince George, B.C.	67,559
Hamilton, Ont.	306,434	Quebec, Que.	166,474
Hull, Que.	56,225	Red Deer, Alta.	46,393
Joliette, Que.	16,987	Regina, Sask.	162,613
Jonquière, Que.	60,354	Repentigny, Que.	34,419
Kamloops, B.C.	64,048	Richmond Hill, Ont.	37,778
Kanata, Ont.	19,728	Rimouski, Que.	29,120
Kelowna, B.C.	59,196	Rouyn, Que.	17,224
Kingston, Ont.	52,616	St. Albert, Alta.	31,996
Kitchener, Ont.	139,734	St-Bruno-de-Montarville,	
La Baie, Que.	20,935	Que.	22,880
Lachine, Que.	37,521	St. Catharines, Ont.	124,018
LaSalle, Que.	76,299	Ste-Foy, Que.	68,883
Laval, Que.	268,335	Ste-Thérèse, Que.	18,750
Lethbridge, Alta.	54,072	St. Eustache, Que.	29,716
Lévis, Que.	17,895	St-Hubert, Que.	60,573
London, Ont.	254,280	St-Hyacinthe, Que.	38,246
Longueuil, Que.	124,320	St-Jean, Que.	35,640

St-Jerôme, Que.	25,123	Timmins, Ont.	46,114
Saint John, N.B.	80,521	Toronto, Ont.	599,217
St. John's, Nfld.	83,770	Trois-Rivières, Que.	50,466
St-Lambert, Que.	20,557	Val-d'Or, Que.	21,371
St-Laurent, Que.	65,900	Valley East, Ont.	20,433
St-Léonard, Que.	79,429	Valleyfield, Que.	29,574
St. Thomas, Ont.	28,165	Vancouver, B.C.	414,281
Sarnia, Ont.	50,892	Vanier, Ont.	18,792
Saskatoon, Sask.	154,210	Vaughan, Ont.	29,674
Sault Ste. Marie, Ont.	82,697	Verdun, Que.	61,287
Scarborough, Ont.	443,353	Vernon, B.C.	19,987
Sept-Iles, Que.	29,262	Victoria, B.C.	64,379
Shawinigan, Que.	23,011	Victoriaville, Que.	21,838
Sherbrooke, Que.	74,075	Waterloo, Ont.	49,428
Sorel, Que.	20,347	Welland, Ont.	45,448
Stoney Creek, Ont.	36,762	Westmount, Que.	20,480
Stratford, Ont.	26,262	Whitby, Ont.	36,698
Sudbury, Ont.	91,829	Windsor, Ont.	192,083
Sydney, N.S.	29,444	Winnipeg, Man.	564,473
Thetford Mines, Que.	19,965	Woodstock, Ont.	26,603
Thunder Bay, Ont.	112,486	York, Ont.	134,617

Population of Canada in 1981
Summary by Provinces and Territories

Alberta	2,237,724	Prince Edward Island	122,506
British Columbia	2,744,467	Quebec	6,438,403
Manitoba	1,026,241	Saskatchewan	948,313
New Brunswick	696,403	Yukon Territory	21,836
Newfoundland	567,681	Northwest Territories	45,741
Nova Scotia	847,442	TOTAL	24,098,473
Ontario	8,625,107		

Signs and Symbols

Astronomy

⊙ the sun; Sunday

◍, ☾, *or* ☽ the moon; Monday

● new moon

☽, ◍, ◗, ☾ first quarter

○ *or* ☺ full moon

☾, ◍, ☽, ☾ last quarter

☿ Mercury; Wednesday

♀ Venus; Friday

⊕, ⊖, *or* ♁ the earth

♂ Mars; Tuesday

♃ Jupiter; Thursday

♄ *or* ♄ Saturn; Saturday

♅, ♅, *or* ♅ Uranus

♆, ♆, *or* ♆ Neptune

♇ Pluto

☄ comet

* *or* ✳ fixed star

Business

a/c account ⟨in a/c with⟩

@ at; each ⟨4 apples @ 5¢ = 20¢⟩

℔ per

c/o care of

\# number if it precedes a numeral ⟨track #3⟩; pounds if it follows ⟨a 5# sack of sugar⟩

℔ pound; pounds

% percent

‰ per thousand

$ dollars

¢ cents

£ pounds

/ shillings

© copyrighted

® registered trademark

Mathematics

\+ plus; positive ⟨a + b = c⟩—used also to indicate omitted figures or an approximation

− minus; negative

± plus of minus ⟨the square root of $4a^2$ is ± 2a⟩

× multiplied by; times ⟨6 × 4 = 24⟩—also indicated by placing a dot between the factors ⟨6·4 = 24⟩ or by writing factors other than numerals without signs

÷ *or* :	divided by ⟨24÷6=4⟩—also indicated by writing the divisor under the dividend with a line between ⟨$\frac{24}{6}$=4⟩ or by writing the divisor after the dividend with an oblique line between ⟨3/8⟩
=	equals ⟨6+2=8⟩
≠ *or* ⧧	is not equal to
>	is greater than ⟨6>5⟩
>>	is much greater than
<	is less than ⟨3<4⟩
<<	is much less than
≧ *or* ≥	is greater than or equal to
≦ *or*	is less than or equal to
≯	is not greater than
≮	is not less than
≈	is approximately equal to
≡	is identical to
∽	equivalent; similar
≅	is congruent to
∝	varies directly as; is proportional to
:	is to; the ratio of
∴	therefore
∞	infinity
∠	angle; the angle ⟨∠ABC⟩
∟	right angle ⟨∟ABC⟩
⊥	the perpendicular; is perpendicular to ⟨AB⊥CD⟩
‖	parallel; is parallel to ⟨AB‖CD⟩
⊙ *or* ○	circle
⌒	arc of a circle
△	triangle
□	square
▭	rectangle
√ *or* √	radical—used without a figure to indicate a square root (as in √4=) or with an index above the sign to indicate the root to be taken (as √x) if the root is not a square root
( )	parentheses ⎫
[ ]	brackets ⎬ indicate that the quantities enclosed by them are to be taken together
{ }	braces ⎭
π	pi; the number 3.14159265+; the ration of the circumference of a circle to its diameter
°	degree ⟨60°⟩

′	minute; foot ⟨30′⟩
″	second; inch ⟨30″⟩
!	factorial—used to indicate the product of all the whole numbers up to and including a given preceding number
∪	union of two sets
∩	intersection of two sets
⊂	is included in, is a subset of
⊃	contains as a subset
∈ *or* ϵ	is an element of
∉	is not an element of
Λ *or* 0 *or* ϕ *or* {}	empty set, null set

Medicine

ĀĀ, Ā, *or* āā	of each
℞	take—used on prescriptions; prescription; treatment
☠	poison

APOTHECARIES' MEASURES

℥	ounce
f℥	fluidounce
f℈	fluidram
♍, ♏, ♏ *or* min	minim

APOTHECARIES' WEIGHTS

℔	pound
℥	ounce (as ℥ i or ℥ j, one ounce; ℥ ss, half an ounce; ℥ iss *or* ℥ jss, one ounce and a half; ℥ ij, two ounces)
℈	dram
Э	scruple

Miscellaneous

&	and
&c	et cetera; and so forth
" *or* "	ditto marks
/	virgule; used to mean "or" (as in *and/or*), "and/or" (as in *dead/wounded*), "per" (as in *feet/second*), indicates end of a line of verse; separates the figures of a date (4/8/74)

☞   index *or* fist
<   derived from
>   whence derived } used in
+   and   etymologies
*   assumed
†   died—used esp. in genealogies
✝   cross
☧   monogram from Greek XP signifying Christ
卐   swastika
✡   Judaism
☥   ankh
℣   versicle
℟   response
*   —used in Roman Catholic and Anglican service books to divide each verse of a psalm, indicating where the response begins
✠   *or* +—used in some service books to indicate where the sign of the cross is to be made; also used by certain Roman Catholic and Anglican prelates as a sign of the cross preceding their signatures
LXX   Septuagint
f/ or f: relative aperture of a photographic lens
🛡   civil defense
☮   peace

Reference marks

*	asterisk *or* star	§	section *or* numbered clause
†	dagger		
‡	double dagger	‖	parallels
		¶ *or* ℙ	paragraph

Stamps and stamp collecting

★	unused	⊞	block of four or more
○	used	⊠	entire cover or card

Weather

barometer, changes of
∧ Rising, then falling
⌐ Rising, then steady; or rising, then rising more slowly
╱ Rising steadily, or unsteadily
√ Falling or steady, then rising; or rising, then rising more quickly
— Steady, same as 3 hours ago
∨ Falling, then rising, same or lower than 3 hours ago
╲_ Falling, then steady; or falling then falling more slowly
╲ Falling steadily, or unsteadily
∧ Steady or rising, then falling; or falling, then falling more quickly
◎ calm
○ clear
◑ cloudy (partly)

● cloudy (completely overcast)
+ drifting or blowing snow
❯ drizzle
≡ fog
∞ freezing rain
▲▲▲▲ cold front
�ง⏝⏝ warm front
⏝⏝⏝ stationary front
)(funnel clouds
∞ haze
❧ hurricane
♀ tropical storm
• rain
⋮ rain and snow
✂ frost
♙ sandstorm or dust storm
▽ shower(s)
▾ shower of rain
⩒ shower of hail
△ sleet
∗ snow
↰ thunderstorm
⌇ visibility reduced by smoke

Weights and Measures[1]

UNIT	EQUIVALENT IN OTHER U.S. UNITS	METRIC EQUIVALENT
	WEIGHT	
	avoirdupois (ordinary commodities)	
ton		
short ton	200 short hundredweight, 2000 pounds	0.907 metric ton
long ton	200 long hundredweight, 2240 pounds	1.016 metric tons
hundredweight		
short hundred-weight	100 pounds, 0.05 short ton	45.359 kilograms
long hundredweight	112 pounds, 0.05 long ton	50.802 kilograms
pound	16 ounces, 7000 grains	0.454 kilograms
ounce	16 drams, 437.5 grains	28.350 grams
dram	27.344 grains, 0.0625 ounce	1.772 grams
grain	0.037 dram, 0.002286 ounce	0.0648 gram
	troy (precious metals, jewels)	
pound	12 ounces, 240 pennyweight, 5760 grains	0.0373 kilogram
ounce	20 pennyweight, 480 grains	31.103 grams
pennyweight	24 grains, 0.05 ounce	1.555 grams
grain	0.042 pennyweight, 0.002083 ounce	0.0648 gram
	apothecaries' (drugs)	
pound	12 ounces, 5760 grains	0.373 kilogram
ounce	8 drams, 480 grains	31.103 grams
dram	0.125 ounce, 60 grains	3.888 grams
grain	0.0166 dram, 0.002083 ounce	0.0648 gram
	comparison of weights	
avoirdupois pound	1.215 apothecaries' pound, 1.215 troy pound	0.454 kilogram
apothecaries' or troy pound	0.822 avoirdupois pound	0.373 kilogram
apothecaries' or troy ounce	1.097 avoirdupois ounce	31.103 grams
avoirdupois ounce	0.911 apothecaries' ounce, 0.911 troy ounce	28.350 grams
avoirdupois grain	1 apothecaries grain, 1 troy grain	0.0648 grain

[1]For U.S. equivalents of metric units see Metric System table

UNIT	EQUIVALENT IN OTHER U.S. UNITS	METRIC EQUIVALENT
CAPACITY		
U.S. liquid measure		
gallon	4 quarts (231 cubic inches)	3.785 liters
quart	2 pints (57.75 cubic inches)	0.946 liter
pint	4 gills (28.875 cubic inches)	0.473 liter
gill	4 fluidounces (7.219 cubic inches)	118.294 milliliters
fluidounce	8 fluidrams (1.805 cubic inches)	29.573 milliliters
fluidram	60 minims (0.226 cubic inch)	3.697 milliliters
minim	1/60 fluidram (0.003760 cubic inch)	0.061610 milliliter
U.S. dry measure		
bushel	4 pecks (2150.42 cubic inches)	35.239 liters
peck	8 quarts (537.605 cubic inches)	8.10 liters
quart	2 pints (67.201 cubic inches)	1.101 liters
pint	½ quart (33.600 cubic inches)	0.551 liter
LENGTH		
mile	5280 feet, 320 rods, 1760 yards	1.609 kilometers
rod	5.50 yards, 16.5 feet	5.029 meters
yard	3 feet, 36 inches	0.9144 meter
foot	12 inches, 0.333 yard	30.48 centimeters
inch	0.083 feet, 0.028 yard	2.54 centimeters
AREA		
square mile	640 acres, 102,400 square rods	2.590 square kilometers
acre	4840 square yards, 43,560 square feet	4047 square meters
square rod	30.25 square yards, 0.00625 acres	25.293 square meters
square yard	1296 square inches, 9 square feet	0.836 square meter
square foot	144 square inches, 0.111 square yard	0.093 square meter
square inch	0.0069 square foot, 0.00077 square yard	6.452 square centimeters
VOLUME		
cubic yard	27 cubic feet, 46,656 cubic inches	0.765 cubic meter
cubic foot	1728 cubic inches, 0.0370 cubic yard	0.028 cubic meter
cubic inch	0.00058 cubic foot, 0.0370 cubic yard	16.387 cubic centimeters